Standard & Poor's SmallCap 600 Guide

1996 Edition

Standard & Poor's

McGraw-Hill
New York San Francisco Washington, D.C. Auckland Bogotá
Caracas Lisbon London Madrid Mexico City Milan
Montreal New Delhi San Juan Singapore
Sydney Tokyo Toronto

FOR STANDARD & POOR'S
Vice President, Index Products & Services: Elliott Shurgin
Managing Editor: Shauna Morrison
Business Manager: Richard Albanese

McGraw-Hill

A Division of The **McGraw-Hill** *Companies*

1 2 3 4 5 6 7 8 9 0 AGM/AGM 9 0 0 9 8 7 6 5

ISBN 0-07-052155-7

The sponsoring editor for this book was David Conti, and the production supervisor was Thomas G. Kowalczyk. The front matter and introduction were set by North Market Street Graphics.

Printed and bound by Quebecor Printing.

This book is printed on acid-free paper.

The companies contained in this handbook represented the components of the S&P SmallCap 600 Index as of October 20, 1995. Additions to and deletions from the Index will cause its composition to change over time. Company additions and company deletions from the S&P equity indexes do not in any way reflect an opinion on the investment merits of the company.

ABOUT THE AUTHOR

Standard & Poor's, a division of The McGraw-Hill Companies, Inc., is the nation's leading securities information company. It provides a broad range of financial services, including the respected debt ratings and stock rankings, advisory services, data guides, and the most closely watched and widely reported gauges of stock market activity—the S&P 500, S&P MidCap 400, S&P SmallCap 600, and the S&P Super Composite 1500 stock price indexes. S&P products are marketed around the world and used extensively by financial professionals and individual investors.

Introduction

by James M. Nevler, C.F.A.

If you open any copy of *The Wall Street Journal* you will find numerous stock market indexes listed for your reading pleasure and investment research. On January 3, 1995, that list got a new addition, the Standard & Poor's SmallCap 600 Index. You will find it with its older siblings, the S&P 500 and S&P MidCap 400 Stock Indexes, and the S&P Super Composite 1500 Index, which was introduced in May 1995.

The S&P SmallCap 600 is a list of 600 companies which, on average, are considerably smaller than those in the S&P 500 or in the S&P MidCap 400 Index. Since there already were plenty of other stock indexes to follow, it would be logical to ask why the world needed another one. The answer: because institutional investors—the people who manage the funds in corporate retirement plans and mutual funds—asked S&P to develop a better way of monitoring the small-company sector of the stock market, as well as provide an index that could be used to build an investment portfolio of small but easily tradable companies.

Few individual investors can afford to build a personal portfolio of 600 common stocks. However, investors who do their own stock picking and understand why all stock portfolios should be diversified will find the SmallCap 600 to be a valuable tool. Research has shown that, over long investment horizons, stocks of smaller companies, as an investment class, will outperform stocks of larger companies. It was not that long ago that Microsoft, Wal-Mart, and COMPAQ Computer were all small companies. It only takes a reasonable number of such winners to turn a well-balanced portfolio of small-company stocks into a highly profitable investment.

However, those same studies of investment results have also shown that, over shorter time horizons, small companies can be much riskier to own than the far larger companies in the S&P 500. Many small companies—whether they are restaurant chains or technology firms—fail every year. Many others mature into solid companies that prosper for decades serving niche markets or loyal local customers. There are many such consistently profitable companies that provide hundreds of well-paying jobs and reliable dividends year in and year out. Yet their common stock prices may languish for years because they are in industries that are out of favor, because Wall Street analysts do not follow them, or because they may have once had financial problems. There is a crucial difference between a great company and a great stock; unfortunately, there is no sure-fire way to determine which is which. With literally thousands of small companies to choose from, the odds that any one of them, selected at random, will become the next Home Depot or Intel are about as long as the odds that any college basketball player, also chosen at random, will become the next Larry Bird or Michael Jordan.

If indeed the next Home Depot and Intel are hidden somewhere in the S&P SmallCap 600, it is not because S&P expects them to be superstars. On the contrary, as with all of the S&P Indexes, the stocks in the SmallCap 600 are there because they are expected to produce an index whose performance would be *typical* of the market segment from which they were selected. S&P's mission is not to beat the market, but to define it. Unlike the children in Lake Wobegon, all of the stocks in the S&P SmallCap 600 cannot be above average. As is the case in the S&P 500 and the MidCap 400, some stocks will beat their Index by a wide margin, others will be spectacularly worse, and most will perform somewhere in the middle of the pack. Ironically, however, over the long-term, the average performance of large, medium, and small capitalization stocks, as measured by their respective S&P Indices, has proven to be more than good enough to outperform most investment professionals.

Using the S&P Indexes to Measure the Market

While each day's trading on the stock market is often described in terms of bulls and bears, most individual common stocks could be described as members in a school of fish. That is because, more often than not, they tend to swim in the same direction as the overall market. Many studies of securities prices, including the theories for which Harry Markowitz and William Sharpe shared the 1990 Nobel Prize in Economic Science, have shown that one of the most important factors in the price performance of virtually any common stock is the overall performance of the stock market—the investment pool from which the school that the stock swims in is drawn.

Of course, some stocks move faster than others and lead the market—whether up or down—while most swim along unnoticed in the middle of the school. Others lag the market, both when prices head upstream and when they head for the bottom of the sea, and some stocks always go their own way. These volatility relationships to the overall market tend to be stable over relatively long periods of time and are measured with a statistic called beta. Betas are derived by running a statistical test called a regression on the performance of a stock against the performance of the overall stock market. However, before you can begin the test, you must first define the "market." The best way to do that is through a stock index. Thanks in large part to the work of Markowitz, Sharpe and their many disciples, the index universally used for that purpose is the Standard and Poor's 500 Index.

By definition, the S&P 500 has a beta of 1.0. A stock that moved in perfect correlation with the S&P 500 also would have a beta of 1.0. A stock with a beta of 1.5 would be expected to gain 1.5% for every 1% gain in the S&P 500, but would lose 1.5% for every 1% drop in the Index. However, as Markowitz pointed out, the performance of a properly diversified collection of smaller, more volatile stocks will not be much more risky than the overall market. Stocks with high betas in that portfolio will be canceled out by the performance of stocks with betas below 1.0 that lag the market, or by stocks with extremely low betas that have almost no response to the market. A stock with a negative beta, if you could find one, would move in the opposite direction to the S&P 500.

Using the S&P Indexes for Investment Management

One of the most important purposes of a stock index is to tell investors, in a way, where the fish are and which way the fish are running.

When the S&P 500 was introduced in 1957, all of the fish in its pool were listed on the New York Stock Exchange. The S&P 500 was designed as a sample drawn from that pool to represent the market performance of the leading companies in the leading industries in the U.S.

As both the U.S. economy and the equity markets grew, S&P expanded the selection pool for the S&P 500 to include stocks traded on the American Stock Exchange and over the counter on the Nasdaq quotation system. The S&P 500 remains broadly based, containing stocks in approximately 90 different industry groups ranging from aerospace/defense to trucking.

Because of the Index's mandate to select leading stocks in leading industries, the S&P 500 has evolved into a measure of large-capitalization stocks with a distinct, but modest, bias toward growth stocks. The average market capitalization of the companies in the S&P 500 at the end of 1995's third quarter was $8.6 billion, and the median valuation, the point at which the 500 stocks could be split into pools of the 250 largest and 250 smallest companies, was $4.5 billion.

The S&P MidCap 400 Index was created in 1991 to monitor the investment performance of midsized companies. When the MidCap 400 was created, it was drawn from a pool of companies not already in the S&P 500 Index with market capitalizations of between $5.2 billion and $300 million. The average market capitalization of a MidCap 400 stock at the end of the third quarter of 1995 was $1.5 billion.

Together, the S&P 500 and MidCap 400 account for 78% of the stock market's capitalization. However, they still do not track the performance of more than 4,800 other common stocks. That is the objective of the S&P SmallCap 600.

SmallCap Stocks

The first question to answer is the obvious one: What exactly is a small-cap stock? There is no obvious answer. Almost every expert has a unique definition. Some well-respected academic studies, for example, included stocks with market values of up to $2 billion. However, the consensus market value range at the end of 1993 appeared to run from $600 million down to $80 million, or from approximately the 50th percentile in market value down to about the 83rd percentile. This percentile range not only was used in developing and testing the SmallCap 600 Index, but it will also be used in screening future candidates for the Index. As overall market capitalizations rise or fall, so will the SmallCap's selection parameters.

As was noted above, potential investment performance is not one of the criteria for membership in any S&P equity index. Inclusion in any S&P Index—and this also goes for the decision not to select a stock—is not based on the investment merits of the company in question. A good company may pass all of our screens for inclusion but be passed over when a vacancy appears because its industry is already overrepresented in the appropriate index for that stock. Some of the screens are computer-generated, but unlike the Russell 1000 and Russell 2000 indexes, our mechanical market-capitalization screen is only the start of the selection process. The approximately 1,850 common stocks that met the SmallCap's capitalization parameters at the end of 1993 were subjected to the following additional requirements:

1. The company must be listed on either the New York Stock Exchange, American Stock Exchange, or Nasdaq Stock Market.
2. The company must have been trading for at least six months in order to be considered, whether it was an initial public offering or a spin-off by an established company.
3. Stocks that did not trade on any three business days during a 12-month period or, in the case of new issues, over the time period they have been public companies, are not considered.
4. Companies with stock prices below $1 are not considered.
5. The annualized share turnover rate must exceed 20% of the common shares outstanding. S&P defines share turnover as the trading volume over the previous 12 months divided by the average number of common shares outstanding during that time period.

6. Corporate ownership is reviewed. If 50% or more of the total common shares of a company are owned by another corporation, that company is not eligible because it is considered to be controlled by the other company. Companies in which 60% or more of the common shares are held by insiders, or by insiders in conjunction with another corporation's holdings, also are not eligible.
7. Companies in bankruptcy or in extreme financial distress are not selected for inclusion in the index. Except in rare instances, such as the Texaco bankruptcy, a filing for bankruptcy by a company in any S&P Index will result in its immediate removal. However, as long as it appears to be viable, a company is not removed from an Index just because it is in financial trouble.
8. Finally, the companies that survive the other screens are checked for their bid-ask spreads. The spread is calculated as the average of the percentage of the last sale for 30 consecutive trading days. Only those companies with spreads of 5% or less are considered. For example, if a stock has an average closing price of $5 a share, its closing spread can be no wider than 25 cents (5 bid—5 ¼ ask). Many Nasdaq stocks have spreads of more than 10%, and 20% to 25% is not unheard of.

The stocks in the candidate pool for the S&P SmallCap 600 were classified into 10 economic sectors: Basic Materials, Energy, Capital Goods, Consumer Cyclicals, Consumer Staples, Technology, Transportation, Services, Utilities and Financials. Stocks were then selected from each sector so that the total Index reflected the economic balance of the stocks in the S&P internal database. That diversity resulted in an Index that bears a strong family resemblance to its big brothers. As the following table shows, each of S&P's major industry sectors is well-represented within each Index and across all three Indexes.

Industry Group Representation as of 12/30/94

	S&P 500	MidCap 400	SmallCap 600
Industrials	77.6%	69.5%	76.7%
Utilities	10.0%	14.1%	4.3%
Financials	10.7%	14.6%	16.8%
Transportation	1.7%	1.8%	2.2%

Because the stocks in the SmallCap 600 were selected using the same general principles applied to the other S&P Indexes, they form a coherent package. In fact, S&P has developed a super-composite index that reflects the market-value-weighted performance of all 1,500 stocks in the three Indexes. The S&P Super Composite 1500 Index was introduced in May 1995. It consists of a market-value-weighted position in every stock in the S&P 500, S&P MidCap 400, and S&P SmallCap 600 Indexes. Yet, despite their strong family resemblances, the MidCap 400 and SmallCap 600 Indexes are not—like standard and toy poodles—simply scaled-down versions of the S&P 500 Index.

Using the SmallCap 600 for Investment Research

The total market value of the 600 companies in the SmallCap Index at the end of the third quarter of 1995 was $241 billion. That equaled about 4% of the market value of all the stocks in S&P's equity database, or just $29 billion more than the $212 billion combined capitalization of the two largest companies in the S&P 500, General Electric and AT&T. However, while they are dwarfed by the larger companies in the S&P 500, many of the stocks in the SmallCap 600 Index are large fish in their own small ponds. The Index includes such famous brand names as Chiquita Brands International and Toro Co., as well as companies such as Chemed Corp. (which owns 60% of Roto-Rooter) and the Forschner Group (the importer of Swiss Army knives and watches) whose products are household names. Many others have strong positions in important niche markets.

The average market value of a SmallCap company was about $401 million, less than 5% of the average in the S&P 500 and about 28% of the average market value in the MidCap 400. This difference was due both to a smaller number of shares outstanding at most SmallCap companies and to much lower per-share prices. The median share price of an S&P SmallCap stock was $19.50, compared with $27.25 for a MidCap stock and $39.625 for a company in the S&P 500.

The smaller number of shares outstanding and the lower prices at which many SmallCap 600 shares trade are two of the reasons why the stocks in the SmallCap tend to be more volatile than those in the S&P 500 or the MidCap 400. Another, as reflected in the Index's year-end 1994 average P/E ratio of 35.8, is their earnings patterns. High P/E ratios (calculated by dividing a company's per share price by its earnings per share) can be generated in two different ways, either by the market paying up for anticipated growth, or by a company's earnings falling short of expectations. Dividend yield is another significant difference between the average SmallCap stock and those in the MidCap 400 or S&P 500. Because many of the industrial companies in the SmallCap are in their expansion phase, they retain earnings to fund their growth and pay no dividends. As a result, the 1994 year-end dividend yield on the SmallCap 600 was 1.13%, compared with 2.87% on the S&P 500 and 2.10% on the MidCap 400.

Given their increased risk relative to the S&P 500 and the MidCap 400, why should investors own SmallCap stocks? Because, given a long-term time horizon, the SmallCap should outperform both of its larger siblings by a margin that will more than compensate for its higher short-term risks.

It is also possible for an individual investor to construct a well-diversified portfolio of small-cap stocks that will outperform the larger-cap indexes. Many of the 4,800 or more small companies to choose from are followed by very few brokerage firm analysts. There are hidden gems out there, not just neglected value stocks, but also classic growth stocks that have yet to develop a following. The problem is finding them, finding out enough about them, and finding their shares trading at a fair bid/ask spread.

Those three problems are minimized if the search begins with the stocks in the SmallCap 600. The stocks have been screened for liquidity, and each is covered by an unbiased Stock Report prepared by an analyst in the S&P Equity Research department. Those reports, which make up the remainder of this book, are an excellent place to begin researching a potential investment. Organize your search by first reading the names and the business summaries of each of the 600 companies, making a list as you go along of those that catch your fancy. Next, return to the reports, study those you've selected, and—using the information provided in the reports—pick the ones that you feel deserve serious additional investigation.

We have already prescreened the 600 companies in this book for several of the stock characteristics in which investors generally are most interested, including companies with consistently strong earnings growth, superior dividend payment histories, and those under-followed issues which could include some interesting "hidden values" for those investors willing to accept some degree of incremental risk. At the end of this introduction you will find charts listing companies which score highest on the basis of these criteria. So if you, like most investors, find these characteristics important in potential investments, you might want to turn first to the companies on these lists in your search for attractive investments.

Other Uses of this Book

Given this vast array of data, how might a business person seeking to find out about her competition, a marketing manager looking for clients, or a job seeker use it to best serve their respective purposes?

If you fall into one of these categories—a business person seeking to find out information about her competition, a marketing manager looking for clients, or a job seeker—your task will be arduous to be sure, but this book will provide you with an excellent starting point and your payoff can make it all worthwhile. You will have to go through this book page by page, looking for those companies that are in the industries in which you are interested, that are of the size and financial strength that appeal to you, that are located geographically in your territory or where you're willing to relocate, that have been profitable and growing, and so forth. And then you will have to read about just what's going on at those companies by referring to the appropriate "Business Summary," and "Important Developments" comments in these reports. But the companies you end up with can be those high-growth entities with the greatest potential.

Of course, this book won't do it all for you. It is, after all, just a starting point, not a conclusive summary of everything you might need to know. It is designed to educate, not to render advice or provide recommendations. But it will get you pointed in the right direction.

How to Read the Reports on the SmallCap 600

In the pages that follow, you will find a wealth of information on each of the 600 companies which comprise the S&P SmallCap 600 Index, information which will allow you to make reasoned investment, business, and personal judgments regarding these companies. But to get the most value from this book, you should take a few moments to familiarize yourself with just what you'll find on these pages.

Please note that during 1995, Standard & Poor's greatly improved the Stock Reports by adding a variety of new features to help you in making investment decisions. At the time this handbook was being prepared, some companies were not yet converted to the enhanced format and are presented in this book in their existing format.

Following is a glossary of terms and definitions used throughout this book. Please refer to this section as you encounter terms which need further clarification.

Enhanced Stock Report Terms

Quantitative Evaluations

S&P Opinion—Buy, hold or sell recommendations are provided using S&P's unique STARS (Stock Appreciation Ranking System), which measures short-term (six- to 12-month) appreciation potential of stocks. STARS performance is measured against the performance of the S&P 500 Index.

STARS Rankings are as follows:

- ***** Buy—Expected to be among the best performers over the next 12 months.
- **** Accumulate—Expected to be an above-average performer.
- *** Hold—Expected to be an average performer.
- ** Avoid—Likely to be a below-average performer.
- * Sell—Expected to be a well-below-average performer and fall in price.

Outlook—Using S&P's exclusive proprietary quantitative model, stocks are ranked in one of five Outlook Groups—ranging from Group 5, listing the most undervalued stocks, to Group 1, the most overvalued issues. Group 5 stocks are expected to generally outperform all others. To identify a stock that is in a strengthening or weakening position, a positive (+) or negative (–) Timing Index is placed next to the Outlook ranking. Using these rankings, here's what action should be taken:

5+ = Buy	2+ = Hold if in portfolio
5 = Hold if in portfolio	2– = Sell
4+ = Hold if in portfolio	1+ = Hold if in portfolio
4– = Sell	1– = Sell
3+ = Hold if in portfolio	
3– = Sell	

The Timing Index helps identify the right time to buy stocks, but its most important function is to indicate when it is time to sell. Because Group 5 stocks have historically produced the best results, S&P recommends buying only Group 5 stocks with a positive Timing Index. Then, hold onto each one for as long as it remains in a positive trend (positive Timing Index), even if the ranking falls as the stock appreciates toward overvalued status. This will reduce transaction costs and substantially raise your chances of outperforming the market in the long run. It will also raise the number of transactions which qualify as long-term capital gains for tax purposes.

Fair Value—The price at which a stock should sell today as calculated by S&P's computers using our quantitative model based on the company's earnings, growth potential, return on equity relative to the S&P 500 and its industry group, price to book ratio history, current yield relative to the S&P 500, and other factors. The current fair price is shown given today's S&P 500 level.

Risk—Rates the volatility of the stock's price over the past year.

Technical Evaluation—In researching the past market history of prices and trading volume for each company, S&P's computer models apply special technical methods and formulas to identify and project price trends for the stock. They analyze how the price of the stock is moving and evaluate the interrelationships between the moving averages to ultimately determine buy or sell signals—and to decide whether they're bullish, neutral or bearish for the stock. The date the signals were initiated is also provided so you can take advantage of a recent or ongoing uptrend in price, or see how a stock has performed over time since our last technical signal was generated.

Relative Strength Rank—Shows, on a scale of 1 to 99, how the stock has performed compared with all other companies in S&P's universe of companies on a rolling 13-week basis.

Insider Activity—Gives an insight as to insider sentiment by showing whether directors, officers and key employees—who may have proprietary information not available to the general public—are buying or selling the company's stock during the most recent six months.

Key Stock Statistics

Avg. Daily Vol.—The average daily trading volume of the stock for the past 20 days on a rolling basis, shown in millions.

Market Cap.—The price of the stock multiplied by the number of shares outstanding, shown in billions.

Insider Holdings—The percentage of outstanding shares held by directors, officers and key employees of the company, and others who hold a minimum of 10% of the outstanding shares.

Value of $10,000 Invested 5 years ago—The value today of a $10,000 investment in the stock made five years ago, assuming year-end reinvestment of dividends.

S&P Ranking

The investment process involves assessment of various factors—such as products and industry position, company resources and financial policy—with results that make some common stocks more highly esteemed than others. In this assessment, Standard & Poor's believes that earnings and dividend performance is the end result of the interplay of these factors and that, over the long run, the record of this performance has a considerable bearing on relative quality. The rankings, however, do not reflect all of the factors that may bear on stock quality.

Growth and stability of earnings and dividends are the key elements in Standard & Poor's earnings and dividend rankings for common stocks, which are designed to capsulize the nature of this record in a single symbol. It should be noted, however, that the process also takes into consideration certain adjustments and modifications deemed desirable in establishing such rankings.

These rankings are derived by means of a computerized scoring system based on per share earnings and dividend records of the most recent ten years. If a company does not have a ten-year public track record, S&P does not rank it. The lack of an S&P ranking in no way reflects upon the investment merits of a company. Basic scores are computed for earnings and dividends and then adjusted by a set of predetermined modifiers for growth, stability, and cyclicality. Adjusted scores for earnings and dividends are then combined to yield a final score.

The ranking system also makes allowance for the fact that, in general, corporate size imparts certain recognized advantages from an investment standpoint. Minimum size limits (in terms of corporate sales) are set for the various rankings, but exceptions may be made where a score reflects an outstanding earnings-dividend record.

The final score is then translated into one of the following rankings:

A+ Highest

A High

A−	Above Average
B+	Average
B	Below Average
B−	Lower
C	Lowest
D	In Reorganization
NR	No Ranking

In some instances, rankings may be modified by special considerations, such as natural disasters, massive strikes, or nonrecurring accounting adjustments.

It is important to note that a ranking is not a forecast of future market price performance, but is basically an appraisal of past performance of earnings and dividends and relative current standing. Consequently, rankings should not be used as market recommendations: a high-score stock may at times be so overpriced as to justify its sale while a low-score stock may be attractively priced for purchase. Rankings based upon earnings and dividend records are no substitute for complete analysis. They cannot take into account the potential effects of management changes, internal company policies not yet fully reflected in the earnings and dividend record, public relations standings, recent competitive shifts, and a host of other factors that may be relevant in investment decision making.

Beta

The beta coefficient is a measure of the volatility of a stock's price relative to the S&P 500 Index, which, as we have seen, is the proxy for the overall market. Because calculating a beta requires 60 months of performance data, S&P does not calculate betas of stocks that have been trading for less than five years.

Per Share Data ($) Tables

Tangible Book Value; Book Value (See also: "Common Equity" under Industrial)—Indicates the theoretical dollar amount per common share one might expect to receive from a company's tangible "book" assets should liquidation take place. Generally, book value is determined by adding the stated value of the common stock, paid-in capital and retained earnings and then subtracting intangible assets (excess cost over equity of acquired companies, goodwill, and patents), preferred stock at liquidating value and unamortized debt discount. Divide that amount by the outstanding shares to get book value per common share.

Cash Flow—Net income plus depreciation, depletion, and amortization, divided by shares used to calculate earnings per common share. (Also see: "Cash Flow" for Industrial Companies.)

Earnings—The amount a company reports as having been earned for the year on its common stock based on generally accepted accounting standards. Earnings may be indicated in terms of *primary* (common stock and common stock equivalents such as stock options and warrants) and *fully diluted* (reflecting dilution in earnings resulting if all contingent issuances of common stock materialized at the outset of the year), and are generally reported from continuing operations, before extraordinary items. INSURANCE companies report *operating earnings* before gains/losses on security transactions and *earnings* after such transactions.

Dividends—Generally total cash payments per share based on the ex-dividend dates over a twelve-month period. May also be reported on a declared basis where this has been established to be a company's payout policy.

Payout Ratio—Indicates the percentage of earnings paid out in dividends. It is calculated by dividing the annual dividend by the earnings. For INSURANCE companies *earnings* after gains/losses on security transactions are used.

Prices High/Low—Shows the calendar year high and low of a stock's market price.

P/E Ratio High/Low—The ratio of market price to earnings—essentially indicates the valuation investors place on a company's earnings. Obtained by dividing the annual earnings into the high and low market price for the year. For INSURANCE companies *operating earnings* before gains/losses on security transactions are used.

Net Asset Value—Appears on investment company reports and reflects the market value of stocks, bonds, and net cash divided by outstanding shares. The % DIFFERENCE indicates the percentage premium or discount of the market price over the net asset value.

Portfolio Turnover—Appears on investment company reports and indicates percentage of total security purchases and sales for the year to overall investment assets. Primarily mirrors trading aggressiveness.

Income/Balance Sheet Data Tables

Banks

Net Interest Income—Interest and dividend income, minus interest expense.

Loan Loss Provision—Amount charged to operating expenses to provide an adequate reserve to cover anticipated losses in the loan portfolio.

Taxable Equivalent Adjustment—Increase to render income from tax-exempt loans and securities comparable to fully taxed income.

Noninterest Income—Service fees, trading and other income, excluding gains/losses on securities transactions.

% Expenses/Op. Revenues—Noninterest expense as a percentage of taxable equivalent net interest income plus noninterest income (before securities gains/losses). A measure of cost control.

Commercial Loans—Commercial, industrial, financial, agricultural loans and leases, gross.

Other Loans—Gross consumer, real estate and foreign loans.

% Loan Loss Reserve—Contra-account to loan assets, built through provisions for loan losses, which serves as a cushion for possible future loan charge-offs.

% Loans/Deposits—Proportion of loans funded by deposits. A measure of liquidity and an indication of bank's ability to write more loans.

Earning Assets—Assets on which interest is earned.

Money Market Assets—Interest-bearing interbank deposits, federal funds sold, trading account securities.

Investment Securities—Federal, state, and local government bonds and other securities.

Gains/Losses on Securities Transactions—Realized losses on sales of securities, usually bonds.

Net Before Taxes—Amount remaining after operating expenses are deducted from income, including gains or losses on security transactions.

Effective Tax Rate—Actual income tax expense divided by net before taxes.

Net Income—The final profit before dividends (common/preferred) from all sources after deduction of expenses, taxes, and fixed charges, but before any discontinued operations or extraordinary items.

Net Interest Margin—A percentage computed by dividing net interest income, on a taxable equivalent basis, by average earning assets. Used as an analytical tool to measure profit margins from providing credit services.

% Return on Revenues—Net income divided by gross revenues.

% Return on Assets—Net income divided by average total assets. An analytical measure of asset-use efficiency and industry comparison.

% Return on Equity—Net income (minus preferred dividend requirements) divided by average common equity. Generally used to measure performance.

Total Assets—Includes interest-earning financial instruments—principally commercial, real estate, consumer loans and leases; investment securities/trading accounts; cash/money market investments; other owned assets.

Cash—Mainly vault cash, interest-bearing deposits placed with banks, reserves required by the Federal Reserve and items in the process of collection—generally referred to as float.

Government Securities—Includes United States Treasury securities and securities of other U.S. government agencies at book or carrying value. A bank's major "liquid asset."

State and Municipal Securities—State and municipal securities owned at book value.

Loans—All domestic and foreign loans (excluding leases), less unearned discount and reserve for possible losses. Generally considered a bank's principal asset.

Deposits—Primarily classified as either *demand* (payable at any time upon demand of depositor) or *time* (not payable within thirty days).

Deposits/Capital Funds—Average deposits divided by average capital funds. Capital funds include capital notes/debentures, other long-term debt, capital stock, surplus, and undivided profits. May be used as a "leverage" measure.

Long-Term Debt—Total borrowings for terms beyond one year including notes payable, mortgages, debentures, term loans, and capitalized lease obligations.

Common Equity—Includes common/capital surplus, undivided profits, reserve for contingencies and other capital reserves.

% Equity to Assets—Average common equity divided by average total assets. Used as a measure of capital adequacy.

% Equity to Loans—Average common equity divided by average loans. Reflects the degree of equity coverage to loans outstanding.

Industrial Companies

Following data is based on Form 10K Annual Report data as filed with SEC.

Revenues—Net sales and other operating revenues. Includes franchise/leased department income for retailers, and royalties for publishers and oil and mining companies. Excludes excise taxes for tobacco, liquor, and oil companies.

Operating Income—Net sales and operating revenues less cost of goods sold and operating expenses (including research and development, profit sharing, exploration and bad debt, but excluding depreciation and amortization).

% Operating Income of Revenues—Net sales and operating revenues divided into operating income. Used as a measure of operating profitability.

Capital Expenditures—The sum of additions at cost to property, plant and equipment and leaseholds, generally excluding amounts arising from acquisitions.

Depreciation—Includes noncash charges for obsolescence, wear on property, current portion of capitalized expenses (intangibles), and depletion charges.

Interest Expense—Includes all interest expense on short/long-term debt, amortization of debt discount/premium and deferred expenses (e.g., financing costs).

Net Before Taxes—Includes operating and nonoperating revenues (including extraordinary items not net of taxes), less all operating and nonoperating expenses, except income taxes and minority interest, but including equity in nonconsolidated subsidiaries.

Effective Tax Rate—Actual income tax charges divided by net before taxes.

Net Income—Profits derived from all sources after deduction of expenses, taxes, and fixed charges, but before any discontinued operations, extraordinary items, and dividends (preferred/common).

% Net Income of Revenues—Net income divided by sales/operating revenues.

Cash Flow—Net income (before extraordinary items and discontinued operations, and after preferred dividends) plus depreciation, depletion, and amortization.

Cash—Includes all cash and government and other marketable securities.

Current Assets—Those assets expected to be realized in cash or used up in the production of revenue within one year.

Current Liabilities—Generally includes all debts/obligations falling due within one year.

Current Ratio—Current assets divided by current liabilities. A measure of liquidity.

Total Assets—Current assets plus net plant and other noncurrent assets (intangibles and deferred items).

% Return on Assets—Net income divided by average total assets on a per common share basis. Used in industry analysis and as a measure of asset-use efficiency.

Long-Term Debt—Debts/obligations due after one year. Includes bonds, notes payable, mortgages, lease obligations, and industrial revenue bonds. Other Long-Term Debt, when reported as a separate account, is excluded. This account generally includes pension and retirement benefits.

Common Equity (See also: "Book Value" under Per Share Data Table)—Common stock plus capital surplus and retained earnings, less any difference between the carrying value and liquidating value of preferred stock.

Total Invested Capital—The sum of stockholders' equity plus long-term debt, capital lease obligations, deferred income taxes, investment credits, and minority interest.

% Long-Term Debt of Invested Capital—Long-term debt divided by total invested capital. Indicates how highly "leveraged" a business might be.

% Return on Equity—Net income less preferred dividend requirements divided by average common shareholders' equity on a per common share basis. Generally used to measure performance and industry comparisons.

Utilities

Operating Revenues—Represents the amount billed to customers by the utility.

Depreciation—Amounts charged to income to compensate for the decline in useful value of plant and equipment.

Maintenance—Amounts spent to keep plants in good operating condition.

Operating Ratio—Ratio of operating costs to operating revenues or the proportion of revenues absorbed by expenses. Obtained by dividing operating expenses including depreciation, maintenance, and taxes by revenues.

Fixed Charges Coverage—The number of times income before interest charges (operating income plus other income) after taxes covers total interest charges and preferred dividend requirements.

Construction Credits—Credits for interest charged to the cost of constructing new plant. A combination of allowance for equity funds used during construction and allowance for borrowed funds used during construction—credit.

Effective Tax Rate—Actual income tax expense divided by the total of net income and actual income tax expense.

Net Income—Amount of earnings for the year which is available for preferred and common dividend payments.

% Return on Revenues—Obtained by dividing net income for the year by revenues.

% Return on Invested Capital—Percentage obtained by dividing income available for fixed charges by average total invested capital.

% Return on Common Equity—Percentage obtained by dividing income available for common stock (net income less preferred dividend requirements) by average common equity.

Gross Property—Includes utility plant at cost, plant work in progress, and nuclear fuel.

Capital Expenditures Represents the amounts spent on capital improvements to plant and funds for construction programs.

Net Property—Includes items in gross property less provision for depreciation.

% Earned on Net Property—Percentage obtained by dividing operating income by average net property for the year. A measure of plant efficiency.

Total Invested Capital—Sum of total capitalization (common-preferred-debt), accumulated deferred income taxes, accumulated investment tax credits, minority interest, contingency reserves, and contributions in aid of construction.

Total Capitalization—Combined sum of total common equity, preferred stock, and long-term debt.

Long-Term Debt—Debt obligations due beyond one year from balance sheet date.

Capitalization Ratios—Reflect the percentage of each type of debt/equity issues outstanding to total capitalization. % DEBT is obtained by dividing total debt by the sum of debt, preferred, common, paid-in capital and retained earnings. % PREFERRED is obtained by dividing the preferred stocks outstanding by total capitalization. % COMMON, divide the sum of common stocks, paid-in capital and retained earnings by total capitalization.

Finally, at the very bottom of the right-hand page, you'll find general information about the company: its address and telephone number, the names of its senior executive officers and directors (usually including the name of the investor contact), the transfer agent and registrar for the stock, and the state in which the company is incorporated.

STOCKS OF COMPANIES WITH CONSISTENTLY STRONG EPS GROWTH

These issues have been selected for superior earnings growth. Each company has actual and estimated annual compounded earnings growth rates of 10% or higher. The list is sorted by estimated 1996 P/E.

Company (Ticker)	Business	Fiscal Year End	Earnings Per Share $ 1994 Actual	1995 Est.	1996 Est.	5-Year Proj. Growth Rate (%)	Recent Price	P/E on 1996 Est.
TNT Freightways(TNTF)	Trucking–gen'l commodities	Dec	1.45	1.69	2.10	13	18.50	8.8
Rollins Truck Leasing(RLC)	Truck, trailer leasing	Sep	0.86	0.94	1.08	12	10.00	9.3
Novellus Systems(NVLS)	Mfr of semiconductor equip	Dec	2.72	4.55	5.49	27	64.25	11.7
Zilog Inc(ZLG)	Mfr/mkt integrated circuits	Dec	1.80	2.19	2.76	21	34.13	12.4
Benchmark Electronics(BHE)	Mfrs circuit boards	Dec	1.41	1.72	2.13	23	26.88	12.6
Sunrise Medical(SMD)	Mfrs home health care prod	Jun	1.41	*1.63	1.87	16	24.50	13.1
Mutual Risk Management(MM)	Provides risk mgmt services	Dec	1.80	2.20	2.60	20	37.88	14.6
Digi International(DGII)	Data commun hardwr/softwr	Sep	1.15	1.39	1.69	20	26.13	15.5
Oakwood Homes(OH)	Mobile home mfr/retailer/prk	Sep	1.54	1.93	2.29	18	36.25	15.8
Vencor Inc(VC)	Acute/L–T care hospitals	Dec	1.20	1.44	1.87	23	29.88	16.0
St. John Knits(SJK)	Mfr women's clothing	Oct	1.82	2.33	2.86	17	46.13	16.1
Vivra Inc(V)	Dialysis/Health care ctrs	Nov	1.48	1.69	1.96	17	33.13	16.9
Amer Medical Response(EMT)	Provides ambulance services	Dec	1.05	1.31	1.64	22	28.63	17.5
Progress Software(PRGS)	Database mgmt sys/softwr	Nov	2.23	2.76	3.45	22	62.00	18.0
Books–A–Million(BAMM)	Book retailer so'eastern U.S.	Jan	0.47	0.60	0.74	27	13.88	18.8
Medicine Shoppe Intl(MSII)	Franchisor of pharmacies	Sep	1.84	2.12	2.38	15	44.63	18.8

*Actual 1995 EPS.

Chart based on October 20, 1995 prices and data.

Note: All earnings estimates are Wall Street consensus projections.

HIGH PROJECTED GROWTH AND TRADING BELOW $15

All the issues below meet the following criteria: market value and sales of under $400 million; a projected five-year growth rate of at least 12%; at least a 12% increase in 1995 and a 20% increase in1996 estimated earnings; a share price of between $5 and $15; and a P/E ratio of less than 20 based on projected 1996 earnings. The list is sorted by the five-year projected growth rate.

Company (Ticker)	Business	–1995– High	–1995– Low	Recent Price	Fiscal Year End	Earnings Per Share $ 1994 Actual	Earnings Per Share $ 1995 Est.	Earnings Per Share $ 1996 Est.	5-Year Proj. Growth Rate (%)	P/E on 1996 Est.
Books–A–Million(BAMM)	Book retailer so'eastern U.S.	18.62	12.37	13.88	Jan	0.47	0.60	0.74	27	18.8
Mariner Health Group(MRNR)	Subacute health care services	22.12	10.62	11.25	Dec	0.45	0.99	1.25	25	9.0
Republic Gypsum(RGC)	Mfr recycle paper board/gypsum	12.62	9.37	10.88	Jun	0.73	*1.10	1.25	25	8.7
Digital Microwave(DMIC)	Microwave radio/fiber optics	20.75	9.50	10.00	Mar	0.14	0.34	0.86	22	11.6
Westcott Communications(WCTV)	Prod train'g/educ'l programs	18.25	11.50	13.25	Dec	0.61	0.79	0.99	22	13.4
Chips/Technologies(CHPS)	Mkts microcomputer chips	15.87	6.25	12.00	Jun	0.16	*0.50	0.75	20	16.0
Flow International(FLOW)	Mfrs waterjet cutt'g systems	13.25	6.50	11.13	Apr	0.18	*0.53	0.64	20	17.4
TETRA Technologies(TTRA)	Waste recycl'g&treatm't svcs	15.75	10.25	13.13	Dec	0.48	0.68	0.94	20	14.0
Insituform Technol'A'(INSUA)	Mkts sewer/PL repair process	16.62	11.12	12.63	Dec	0.60	0.85	1.13	19	11.2
Kuhlman Corp(KUH)	Transformers,metal prod	13.50	10.37	11.38	Dec	0.73	1.05	1.20	19	9.5
Oceaneering Intl(OII)	Offshore oil/gas field serv	12.12	7.75	9.63	Mar	0.23	0.49	0.71	19	13.6
Pride Petroleum Svcs(PRDE)	Oil & gas well svcs in U.S.	10.50	4.75	9.88	Dec	0.30	0.56	0.68	19	14.5
Daniel Indus(DAN)	Measure, contr fluid devices	16.50	12.62	14.25	Sep	0.11	0.55	0.97	16	14.7
Simpson Indus(SMPS)	Machined metal auto parts	12.12	8.37	8.38	Dec	0.80	0.90	1.07	14	7.8
Oshkosh B'Gosh Cl'A'(GOSHA)	Clothing manufacturer	18.00	13.00	13.13	Dec	0.50	0.77	0.90	13	14.6
Syncor Int'l(SCOR)	Radiopharmaceuticals	12.12	6.37	10.00	Dec	0.11	0.45	0.60	13	16.7
Lechters Inc(LECH)	Sells housewrs/kitchen items	19.00	10.00	10.94	Jan	0.20	0.49	0.86	12	12.7
Plains Resources(PLX)	Oil & gas expl,devel,prod'n	11.00	5.50	7.44	Dec	0.04	0.20	0.54	12	13.8

*Actual 1995 EPS.

Chart based on October 20, 1995 prices and data.

Note: All earnings estimates are Wall Street consensus projections.

LOW ANALYTICAL COVERAGE, HIGH GROWTH RATE

The companies listed below are covered by three or fewer analysts out of the approximately 2,300 analysts that contribute earnings estimates to S&P's Analysts' Consensus Estimate (ACE) database. While broader coverage might result in stronger agreement on earnings projections, relative neglect by the financial community often gives purchasers of the stock an advantage. These issues show at least 10% compound annual growth in their actual or estimated earnings in each year from 1993 through 1996. The companies are sorted by their 1990 through 1995 earnings growth rate.

Company (Ticker)	Fiscal Year End	–1995– High	–1995– Low	Recent Price	Earnings Per Share $ 1993 Actual	1994 Actual	1995 Est.	1996 Est.	† 5-Yr. Proj. Growth Rate (%)	P/E on 1996 Est.
Primark Corp(PMK)	Dec	26.25	12.75	23.38	0.34	0.62	0.70	1.01	91.57	23.1
GoodMark Foods(GDMK)	May	18.75	13.25	18.50	0.56	0.88	*1.20	1.44	53.37	12.8
Firstbank Puerto Rico(FBP)	Dec	24.37	10.91	19.25	0.73	2.01	2.43	3.00	45.24	6.4
IDEXX Laboratories(IDXX)	Dec	44.75	16.87	41.25	0.29	0.40	0.61	0.83	43.78	49.7
Custom Chrome(CSTM)	Jan	25.12	15.75	23.50	1.10	1.27	1.55	1.82	35.92	12.9
Paxar Corp(PXR)	Dec	16.10	7.60	13.00	0.43	0.53	0.68	0.76	28.07	17.1
Gerber Scientific(GRB)	Apr	19.50	12.62	17.38	0.35	0.61	*0.76	1.00	28.00	17.4
Benchmark Electronics(BHE)	Dec	31.87	20.25	26.88	1.10	1.41	1.72	2.13	26.73	12.6
Nature's Sunshine Prod(NATR)	Dec	28.00	9.75	26.38	0.60	0.67	0.91	1.17	24.91	22.5
BMC Industries(BMC)	Dec	41.75	15.37	40.50	0.80	1.04	1.56	1.82	24.18	22.3
SEI Corp(SEIC)	Dec	24.50	16.75	20.50	0.78	0.96	1.11	1.42	22.25	14.4
Amer Mgmt Systems(AMSY)	Dec	28.00	16.50	27.25	0.69	0.90	1.07	1.29	20.10	21.1

†Five-year compound annual growth rate based on 1991 actual through 1996 estimated earnings. *Actual 1995 EPS.

Chart based on October 20, 1995 prices and data.

Note: All earnings estimates are Wall Street consensus projections

COMPANIES THAT HAVE STEADILY INCREASED THEIR DIVIDENDS OVER THE PAST FIVE YEARS

Each of the companies below carries a 5-year compound annual dividend growth rate of at least 5%, has increased its cash payment each year for at least 5 years, has at least a 10% five-year projected earnings growth rate and has a current indicated dividend rate greater than its actual 1994 payment. All of those listed, moreover, are expected to post 10% earnings increases in 1996 and have a dividend coverage ratio (1996 earnings estimate divided by dividends) of 1.4 or better.

Company (Ticker)	Fiscal Year End	Earnings Per Share $ 1994 Actual	1995 Est.	1996 Est.	5-Year Dividend Growth Rate (%)	Recent Price	Indicated Dividend Rate ($)	Yield (%)	P/E on 1996 Est.	5-Year Proj. Growth Rate (%)
Casey's Genl Stores(CASY)	Apr	0.73	*0.88	1.04	26.0	22.75	0.10	0.4	21.9	16
EatonVance(EAVN)	Oct	3.00	3.55	4.13	25.0	34.75	0.68	1.9	8.4	13
Arbor Drugs(ARBR)	Jul	0.57	*0.94	1.08	22.9	17.50	0.20	1.1	16.2	13
Medicine Shoppe Intl(MSII)	Sep	1.84	2.12	2.38	22.0	44.63	0.56	1.2	18.8	15
Owens & Minor(OMI)	Dec	0.15	0.28	0.64	20.4	12.25	0.18	1.4	19.1	26
Baldor Electric(BEZ)	Dec	0.93	1.10	1.27	15.4	25.00	0.36	1.4	19.7	12
Marcus Corp(MCS)	May	1.60	*1.84	2.07	14.8	35.38	0.40	1.1	17.1	17
Omnicare, Inc(OCR)	Dec	0.60	0.87	1.11	14.8	37.50	0.10	0.2	33.8	27
Rollins Truck Leasing(RLC)	Sep	0.86	0.94	1.08	13.0	10.00	0.16	1.6	9.3	12
Fluke Corp(FLK)	Apr	1.10	*1.86	2.34	12.5	36.88	0.60	1.6	15.8	12
Hilb,Rogal & Hamilton(HRH)	Dec	0.77	0.82	0.94	12.5	14.13	0.56	3.9	15.0	10
Gallagher(Arthur J.)(AJG)	Dec	2.17	2.49	2.84	11.1	34.75	1.00	2.8	12.2	13
Protective Life Corp(PL)	Dec	2.57	2.65	2.96	11.0	29.63	0.62	2.0	10.0	10
Fremont Genl(FMT)	Dec	3.25	3.41	3.77	10.4	29.75	0.80	2.6	7.9	11
Quaker Chemical(QCHM)	Dec	1.03	1.05	1.24	7.7	15.75	0.68	4.3	12.7	15
Apogee Enterprises(APOG)	Feb	0.97	1.32	1.73	7.6	14.25	0.34	2.3	8.2	20
KN Energy(KNE)	Dec	0.52	1.83	2.13	7.2	27.00	1.00	3.7	12.7	11

*Actual 1995 EPS.

Chart based on October 20, 1995 prices and data.

Note: All earnings estimates are Wall Street consensus projections.

SMALLCAP 600 - LOW 1996 P/E, HIGH PROJECTED GROWTH RATE

These issues are all members of the Standard & Poor's SmallCap 600 stock price index. Each is expected to show a 20% increase in its 1995 and 1996 earnings. All have a five-year projected earnings growth rate of at least 20% and are currently selling at less than 15 times estimated 1996 earnings. The list is sorted by their five-year projected growth rate.

Company (Ticker)	Business	Fisca Year End	Earnings Per Share $ 1993 Actual	1994 Actual	1995 Est.	1996 Est.	5-Year Proj. Growth Rate (%)	Recent Price	P/E on 1996 Est.
Texas Indus(TXI)	Cement,aggregate,concrete pd	May	0.11	2.29	*3.88	5.65	39	50.38	8.9
Novellus Systems(NVLS)	Mfr of semiconductor equip	Dec	1.10	2.72	4.55	5.49	27	64.25	11.7
Cobra Golf(CBRA)	Mfr,mkt golf clubs	Dec	0.50	1.21	1.78	2.21	25	25.25	11.4
Mariner Health Group(MRNR)	Subacute health care services	Dec	0.47	0.45	0.99	1.25	25	11.25	9.0
Wabash National(WNC)	Mfr/mkt truck trailers	Dec	0.90	1.32	1.76	2.37	25	28.25	11.9
Benchmark Electronics(BHE)	Mfrs circuit boards	Dec	1.10	1.41	1.72	2.13	23	26.88	12.6
Quanex Corp(NX)	Mfr specialty steel tubing	Oct	0.18	0.96	2.07	2.68	23	19.00	7.1
Integrated Device Tech(IDTI)	Mfrs integrated circuits	Mar	0.60	1.04	1.56	2.04	22	20.13	9.9
InterVoice(INTV)	Mfr phone voice response sys	Feb	0.64	0.15	1.13	1.46	22	19.44	13.3
Read–Rite Corp(RDRT)	Supply thinfilm record'g heads	Sep	0.02	0.43	2.41	3.45	22	38.13	11.1
Westcott Communications(WCTV)	Prod train'g/educ'l programs	Dec	0.47	0.61	0.79	0.99	22	13.25	13.4
Proffitts Inc(PRFT)	Oper specialty dept stores	Jan	0.62	1.46	1.89	2.41	21	28.75	11.9
VLSI Technology(VLSI)	Design/mfr integr'd circuits	Dec	0.45	0.85	1.35	1.97	21	25.50	12.9
Zilog Inc(ZLG)	Mfr/mkt integrated circuits	Dec	1.43	1.80	2.19	2.76	21	34.13	12.4
AMCOL Intl(ACOL)	World producer of bentonite	Dec	0.76	0.78	0.95	1.18	20	16.63	14.1
Apogee Enterprises(APOG)	Auto glass: alum window sys	Feb	0.25	0.97	1.32	1.73	20	14.25	8.2
Plexus Corp(PLXS)	Mfr electronic components	Sep	0.40	0.46	0.88	1.27	20	16.25	12.8
Rexel Inc(RXL)	Dstr elec mater'l for constr	Dec	0.40	0.38	0.75	0.91	20	11.00	12.1
TETRA Technologies(TTRA)	Waste recycl'g&treatm't svcs	Dec	0.07	0.48	0.68	0.94	20	13.13	14.0

*Actual 1995 EPS.

Chart based on October 20, 1995 prices and data.

Note: All earnings estimates are Wall Street consensus projections.

ALPHABETICAL INDEX TO THE S&P SMALLCAP 600

As of October 26, 1995, the following companies comprised the S&P SmallCap 600 Index. At that time, two-page Stock Reports were not available for all 600 companies. Where a Stock Report was not available, a ProFile has been substituted. ProFiles are noted by a **boldface** listing in the alphabetical index and can be found in a separate section in the back of this book. The lack of a Stock Report in no way reflects upon the investment merits of a company.

Control Data Systems
COR Therapeutics
Core Industries
Corrections Corp. of America
Coventry Corp.
Cross Timbers Oil
Cullen/Frost Bankers
Custom Chrome
Cygnus Inc.
Cyrix Corp.
Cyrk Inc.
Cytec Industries
CytRx Corp.

Dallas Semiconductor
Damark International
Dames & Moore
Daniel Industries
DEKALB Genetics
Delta Woodside Industries
Deposit Guaranty Corp.
Designs, Inc.
Devon Energy
Digi International
Digital Microwave
DiMon Inc.
Dionex Corp.
Dixie Yarns
Downey Financial Corp.
Dravo Corp.
Dress Barn
Dynatech Corp.

Eagle Hardware & Garden
Eastern Utilities Associates
Eaton Vance
Energen Corp.
Enhance Financial Services Group
Envoy Corp.
Enzo Biochem
Ethan Allen Interiors
Express Scripts

Fabri-Centers of America
Fastenal Company
Fay's Incorporated
Fedders Corp.
Fibreboard Corp.
Fidelity National Financial
Fieldcrest Cannon
Figgie International
Filene's Basement
FileNet Corp.
First American Financial
First Commercial Corp.
First Financial Corp. (Wis.)
First Michigan Bank Corp.
First Mississippi
FirstBank Puerto Rico
FirstFed Michigan
FirstMerit Corp.
Fisher Scientific International
Flagstar Companies
Flow International
Fluke Corp.
Foodmaker, Inc.
Forschner Group
Franklin Quest
Fremont General
Fresh Choice
Frontier Insurance Group
Frozen Food Express Industries

G & K Services
Galey & Lord
Gallagher (Arthur J.)
Genesis Health Ventures
Gentex Corp.
Geotek Communications
Gerber Scientific
Gerrity Oil & Gas
Glamis Gold Ltd.
GoodMark Foods
Gottschalks Inc.
GranCare, Inc.
Grand Casinos
Green Mountain Power
Greenfield Industries
Griffon Corporation
Groundwater Technology
Guilford Mills

HS Resources
Haggar Corp.
Handy & Harman
Harmon Industries
Hartmarx Corp.
Hauser Chemical Research
Hayes Wheels International
Heart Technology
Heartland Express
Hechinger Company
Hecla Mining
Helene Curtis Industries
Hi-LO Automotive
Hilb, Rogal and Hamilton
Hollywood Park
Hornbeck Offshore Services
Huffy Corp.
Hughes Supply
Hyperion Software

IHOP Corp.
IMCO Recycling
Ideon Group, Inc.
IDEXX Laboratories, Inc.
ImmuLogic Pharmaceutical
Immune Response Corporation
Imo Industries
INDRESCO Inc.
Input/Output, Inc.
Insituform Technologies
Insteel Industries
Insurance Auto Auctions
Integon Corp.
Integrated Circuit Systems
Integrated Health Services
Inter-Regional Financial Group
Interface, Inc.
Interim Services
Intermagnetics General
Intermet Corp.
International Family Entertainment
International Lottery & Totalizator Systems
International Rectifier
Interstate Bakeries
Interstate Power
InterVoice, Inc.
Invacare Corp.
Ionics, Inc.
Itron Inc.

J & J Snack Foods
JSB Financial
Jan Bell Marketing
Johnston Industries
Juno Lighting
Justin Industries

KCS Energy
KN Energy
K-Swiss Inc.
Kaman Corporation
Kasler Holding Co.
Kellwood Co.
KEMET Corp.
Kent Electronics
Keystone Financial
Kirby Corp.
Komag, Inc.
Kuhlman Corp.
Kysor Industrial

L.A. Gear
LSB Industries
La-Z-Boy Chair
Landmark Graphics
Landstar System
Lattice Semiconductor
Lechters, Inc.
Legg Mason

Levitz Furniture
Liberty Bancorp
Life Partners Group
Life Re Corp.
Lillian Vernon
Lilly Industries
Lincare Holdings
Lindsay Manufacturing
Liposome Co.
Living Centers of America
Loyola Capital
Lydall, Inc.

M.D.C. Holdings
M.S. Carriers
Magma Copper
Magna Group
Mail Boxes Etc.
Manitowoc Co.
Marcus Corporation
Mariner Health Group
Mark Twain Bancshares
Marshall Industries
Material Sciences
Maxim Integrated Products
Maxtor Corp.
McWhorter Technologies
Medaphis Corp.
Medicine Shoppe International
MedImmune, Inc.
Medusa Corp.
Merisel, Inc.
Merrill Corp.
Mesa Air Group
Mesa Inc.
Michaels Stores
MicroAge, Inc.
Microchip Technology
Mohawk Industries
Molecular Biosystems
Mosinee Paper
Mueller Industries
Musicland Stores
Mutual Risk Management
Mycogen Corporation
Myers Industries

N.S. Bancorp
NBTY, Inc.
NFO Research
NS Group
NTN Communications
Nash-Finch Co.
Nashua Corp.
National Auto Credit
National Data Corp.
National Re Corp.
Nature's Sunshine Products
Nautica Enterprises
Network Equipment Technologies
Network General Corp.
New England Business Service
New Jersey Resources
Newfield Exploration
Noble Drilling
Norand Corp.
North American Mortgage
North American Vaccine
Northwest Natural Gas
Northwestern Steel & Wire
Novellus Systems
Noven Pharmaceuticals

OHM Corp.
Oak Industries
Oakwood Homes
Oceaneering International
Offshore Logistics
Omega Environmental
Omnicare, Inc.
ONBANCorp
Orange & Rockland Utilities
Orbital Sciences Corp.
Orion Capital
Oshkosh B'Gosh
O'Sullivan Corp.
Owens & Minor
Oxford Industries

Pacific Scientific
Paragon Trade Brands
Patterson Dental
PAXAR Corp.
Payless Cashways
Pennsylvania Enterprises
PENWEST, LTD.
PerSeptive Biosystems
Pharmaceutical Marketing Service
Pharmaceutical Resources
Philadelphia Suburban
Phillips-Van Heusen
Phoenix Resource Cos.
PhyCor, Inc.
PictureTel Corp.
Piedmont National Gas
Pier 1 Imports
Pillowtex Corp.
Pioneer Group
Pioneer-Standard Electronics
Piper Jaffray
Plains Resources
Platinum Software
PLATINUM technology
Players International
Plenum Publishing
Plexus Corp.
Ply Gem Industries
Pogo Producing
Pool Energy Services Co.
Pope & Talbot
Premier Bancorp
Pride Petroleum Services
Primark Corp.
Prime Hospitality
Production Operators
Proffitt's Inc.
Progress Software
Protective Life Corp.
Protein Design Labs
Provident Bancorp
Public Service of North Carolina
Pure Tech International

Quaker Chemical
Quanex Corp.
Quantum Health Resources
Quick & Reilly

RCSB Financial Inc.
RailTex Inc.
Raymond James Financial
Read-Rite Corp.
Regal-Beloit Corp.
Regal Cinemas
Regeneron Pharmaceuticals
Republic Gypsum
Resound Corp.
Respironics, Inc.
Rexel, Inc.
Richfood Holdings Inc.
Riggs National Corp.
Roadmaster Industries
Roberts Pharmaceutical
Rollins Truck Leasing
Roosevelt Financial Group
Roper Industries
Ross Stores
Royal Appliance Mfg.
Russ Berrie
Rykoff-Sexton
Ryland Group

SCI Systems
SEI Corp.
SPS Technologies
SPX Corp.
S3 Incorporated
St. John Knits
St. Mary Land & Exploration
St. Paul Bancorp
Sanifill, Inc.

Sanmina Corp.
SciClone Pharmaceuticals
Score Board
Scotts Co.
Seitel, Inc.
Selective Insurance Group
SEQUUS Pharmaceuticals, Inc.
Shoe Carnival
ShopKo Stores
Shorewood Packaging
ShowBiz Pizza Time
Showboat, Inc.
Sierra Health Services
Sierra Pacific Resources
Simpson Industries
Skyline Corp.
SkyWest, Inc.
Smith (A.O.)
Smithfield Foods
Snyder Oil
Sonat Offshore Drilling
Sonic Corp.
Southern California Water
Southern Energy Homes
Southwest Gas
Southwestern Energy
Sovereign Bancorp
SpaceLabs Medical
Spartan Motors
Sports & Recreation
Standard Microsystems
Standard Motor Products
Standard Pacific
Standard Products
Standex International
Steel Technologies
Stein Mart
STERIS Corp.
Sterling Software
Stone & Webster
StrataCom, Inc.
Strawbridge & Clothier
Sturm, Ruger
Summit Bancorporation
Summit Technology
SunGard Data Systems
Sunrise Medical
Sunshine Mining & Refining
Super Food Services
Sybron International
Symmetricom
Syncor International
System Software Associates

TBC Corp.
TCBY Enterprises
TCF Financial
T J International
TNP Enterprises
TNT Freightways
TPI Enterprises
Taco Cabana
Tech Data Corp.
TECNOL Medical Products
Telxon Corp.
TETRA Technologies
Texas Industries
TheraTech, Inc.
Thomas Industries
Thomas Nelson, Inc.
Thor Industries
Three-Five Systems
Timberland Co.
Toll Brothers
Toro Co.
Tredegar Industries
Trenwick Group Inc.
Triarc Companies
Tricord Systems
True North Communications
Tseng Labs
Tuboscope Vetco International
Tultex Corp.
Tyco Toys

UNC Incorporated
USA Waste Services
Union Planters
United Cities Gas
United Illuminating
United Meridian
U.S. Bioscience
U.S. Filter
U.S. Trust Corp.
Universal Forest Products
Universal Health Services

VISX, Inc.
VLSI Technology
Valassis Communications
Valence Technology
Valmont Industries
Vencor, Inc.
Venture Stores
Vertex Pharmaceuticals
Vicor Corp.
Video Lottery Technologies
Viewlogic Systems
Vintage Petroleum
Vital Signs
Vivra Inc.

WD-40 Company
WHX Corp.
WICOR, Inc.
WMS Industries
Wabash National
Walbro Corporation
Wall Data
Washington Energy
Washington National
Waterhouse Investor Services
Watkins-Johnson
Watson Pharmaceuticals
Werner Enterprises
Westcott Communications
Western Waste Industries
Whitney Holding
Whittaker Corp.
Whole Foods Market
Williams-Sonoma Inc.
Winnebago Industries
Wiser Oil
Wolverine Tube
Wolverine World Wide
Wyle Electronics
Wynn's International

X-Rite, Inc.
Xircom, Inc.

Zebra Technologies Corp.
Zenith National Insurance
Zero Corp.
Zilog, Inc.
Zions Bancorporation
Zoll Medical

PART I

Stock Reports

In using the Stock Reports in this handbook, please pay particular attention to the dates attached to each evaluation, recommendation, or analysis section. Opinions rendered are as of that date and may change often. It is strongly suggested that before investing in any security you should obtain the current analysis on that issue.

To order the latest Standard & Poor's Stock Report on a company, for as little as $2.00 per report, please call:

S&P Reports On-Demand at 1-800-292-0808.

STANDARD & POOR'S

STOCK REPORTS

AAR Corp.

NYSE Symbol **AIR**
In S&P SmallCap 600

31-JUL-95

Industry: Aircraft manufacturing/ components

Summary: This leading supplier of products and services for the commercial and military aviation aftermarkets also makes containerization products and materials-handling equipment.

S&P Opinion: Hold (★★★)

Recent Price • 17
52 Wk Range • 18⅜-11⅞
Yield • 2.8%
12-Mo. P/E • 25.8

Quantitative Evaluations

Outlook (1 Lowest—5 Highest) • **5**
Fair Value • **20¼**
Risk • **Low**
Earn./Div. Rank • **B+**

Technical Eval. • **Bullish** since 4/95
Rel. Strength Rank (1 Lowest—99 Highest) • **65**
Insider Activity • **NA**

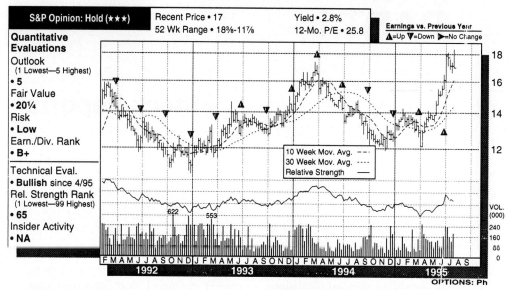

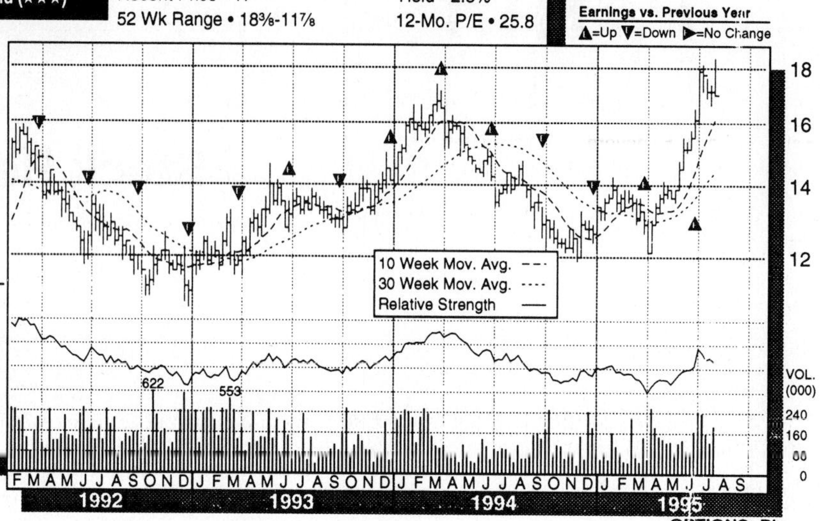

OPTIONS: Ph

Overview - 31-JUL-95

Sales for the fiscal year ended May 31, 1996, are expected to be about 10% above those recorded for 1994-5. Both manufacturing and overhaul activities are projected to benefit from the improving profitability in the airline industry. Department of defense work should also add to revenues. Trading sales are expected to advance from the increased buying and selling activities in the industry. Margins on manufacturing and overhaul operations are not anticipated to improve substantially, due to continued competitive pricing pressures. However, trading profitability should see some growth. Interest charges are expected to increase slightly with an additional promissory note.

Valuation - 31-JUL-95

AIR stock has rebound in recent months, primarily reflecting the improvement in the airline industry. Shares should stay strong while airline fundamentals are positive. They may also benefit from increased government work--military base closings have reduced Air Force capacity, requiring the government to outsource more work. However, AAR operates in extremely competitive industries, that have little barriers to entry. Thus margins cannot be raised significantly. Furthermore, the shares can fall quickly should conditions in the airline industry deteriorate. The company needs to develop a meaningful cost advantage over "mom and pop" shops and other small operations. At about 20 times our estimate of 1995-6 earnings, we view AAR shares as fully valued.

Key Stock Statistics

S&P EPS Est. 1996	0.85	Tang. Bk. Value/Share	11.52
P/E on S&P Est. 1996	20.0	Beta	1.38
Dividend Rate/Share	0.48	Shareholders	3,600
Shs. outstg. (M)	16.0	Market cap. (B)	$0.271
Avg. daily vol. (M)	0.039	Inst. holdings	81%
		Insider holdings	NA

Value of $10,000 invested 5 years ago: $ 5,794

Fiscal Year Ending May 31

	1995	% Change	1994	% Change	1993	% Change
Revenues (Million $)						
1Q	97.19	-1%	98.30	NM	98.10	-9%
2Q	99.4	7%	93.19	-9%	101.9	NM
3Q	125.2	30%	96.20	17%	82.34	-22%
4Q	129.6	8%	120.1	20%	100.4	-7%
Yr.	451.0	11%	407.8	7%	382.8	-9%
Income (Million $)						
1Q	2.00	-20%	2.49	—	—	—
2Q	2.07	-13%	2.38	52%	1.57	-42%
3Q	2.88	30%	2.21	NM	-5.71	NM
4Q	3.50	45%	2.41	84%	1.31	31%
Yr.	10.46	10%	9.48	NM	0.28	-97%
Earnings Per Share ($)						
1Q	0.13	-19%	0.16	-20%	0.20	-9%
2Q	0.13	-13%	0.15	50%	0.10	-41%
3Q	0.18	29%	0.14	NM	-0.36	NM
4Q	0.22	47%	0.15	88%	0.08	33%
Yr.	0.66	10%	0.60	NM	0.02	-97%

Next earnings report expected: mid September

Business Summary - 31-JUL-95

AAR Corp. is a leading supplier of products and services for the commercial and military aviation aftermarkets and for the industrial products market. Sales of similar products and services in recent years were:

	1993-4	1992-3	1991-2
Trading	49%	53%	50%
Overhaul	27%	28%	28%
Manufacturing	24%	19%	22%

Sales to the U. S. government accounted for 19% of total sales in 1993-4, 15% in 1992-3, and 13% in 1991-2.

Trading activities include sale, lease and exchange of equipment such as engines, avionics, accessories, airframe and engine parts and components. AAR also distributes new aviation hardware products and is engaged in lease financing of aircraft and engines.

Overhaul activities include aircraft maintenance, modification, special equipment installation and painting services, as well as terminal services for commercial and private aircraft.

AAR manufactures cargo-handling and restraint systems primarily for military aircraft. For non-aviation markets, it makes floor-cleaning and materials-handling equipment.

Important Developments

Jul. '95—AAR said that trading division sales climbed 14% in the fiscal year ended May 31, 1995. Sales from manufacturing rose 10%, and overhaul and repair revenues advanced 5.6%.

Jul. '95—The company announced that it was awarded government contracts valued at more than $9 million, including options. AAR will be providing overhaul of engine and airframe system components, as well as rapid deployment support products. In February, the company was awarded a government maintenance and overhaul contract valued at $16 million, including options.

Feb. '95—AAR signed a five-year inventory agreement with South African Airways to remarket 32,000 new line items with a manufacturer's list value of $41 million.

Capitalization

Long Term Debt: $120,149,000 (2/95).

Per Share Data ($)

(Year Ended May 31)

	1995	1994	1993	1992	1991	1990
Tangible Bk. Val.	NA	11.52	11.49	11.94	11.75	11.33
Cash Flow	NA	1.05	0.70	1.36	1.45	2.05
Earnings	0.66	0.60	0.02	0.63	0.93	1.60
Dividends	0.48	0.48	0.48	0.48	0.48	0.47
Payout Ratio	73%	80%	NM	76%	52%	29%
Cal. Yrs.	1994	1993	1992	1991	1990	1989
Prices - High	17 3/8	15	15 7/8	16 7/8	36 7/8	37 1/2
- Low	11 7/8	11 1/2	10 3/4	9 1/4	9 1/8	24
P/E Ratio - High	26	25	NM	27	40	23
- Low	18	19	NM	15	10	15

Income Statement Analysis (Million $)

	1994	%Chg	1993	%Chg	1992	%Chg	1991
Revs.	408	7%	383	-9%	423	-9%	467
Oper. Inc.	29.1	7%	27.2	-29%	38.2	-9%	42.0
Depr.	7.3	-33%	10.9	-6%	11.6	40%	8.3
Int. Exp.	9.6	19%	8.1	-4%	8.4	-17%	10.1
Pretax Inc.	13.7	NM	-1.9	NM	13.6	-36%	21.4
Eff. Tax Rate	31%	—	NM	—	26%	—	31%
Net Inc.	9.5	NM	0.3	-97%	10.0	-32%	14.8

Balance Sheet & Other Fin. Data (Million $)

	1994	1993	1992	1991	1990	1989
Cash	18.1	2.3	2.3	1.5	4.0	4.6
Curr. Assets	308	265	290	268	276	257
Total Assets	418	365	395	380	389	356
Curr. Liab.	68.0	72.0	92.0	79.0	91.0	128
LT Debt	116	66.3	67.3	69.0	72.3	25.7
Common Eqty.	189	189	197	194	190	172
Total Cap.	344	294	303	301	298	228
Cap. Exp.	6.4	8.9	8.2	8.9	10.4	11.0
Cash Flow	16.8	11.2	21.6	23.1	32.8	31.3

Ratio Analysis

	1994	1993	1992	1991	1990	1989
Curr. Ratio	4.5	3.7	3.1	3.4	3.0	2.0
% LT Debt of Cap.	33.6	22.6	22.2	22.9	24.3	11.3
% Net Inc.of Revs.	2.3	0.1	2.4	3.2	5.8	6.1
% Ret. on Assets	2.4	0.1	2.6	3.9	6.9	7.7
% Ret. on Equity	5.0	0.1	5.1	7.8	14.2	15.3

Dividend Data (Cash has been paid each year since 1973. A dividend reinvestment plan is available. A "poison pill" stock purchase rights plan was adopted in 1987 and amended in 1989.)

Amt. of Div. $	Date Decl.	Ex-Div. Date	Stock of Record	Payment Date
0.120	Oct. 12	Oct. 25	Oct. 31	Dec. 05 '94
0.120	Jan. 17	Jan. 31	Feb. 06	Mar. 03 '95
0.120	Apr. 11	Apr. 25	May. 01	Jun. 05 '95
0.120	Jul. 11	Jul. 27	Jul. 31	Sep. 03 '95

Data as orig. reptd.; bef. results of disc. opers. and/or spec. items. Per share data adj. for stk. divs. as of ex-div. date. E-Estimated. NA-Not Available. NM-Not Meaningful. NR-Not Ranked.

Office—1111 Nicholas Blvd., Elk Grove Village, IL 60007. **Tel**—(708) 439-3939. **Chrmn & CEO**—I. A. Eichner. **Pres & COO**—D. P. Storch. **VP, Secy & Investor Contact**—H. A. Pulsifer. **VP-Treas & CFO**—T. J. Romenesko. **Dirs**—A. R. Abboud, H. B. Bernick, I. A. Eichner, E. D. Jannotta, R. D. Judson, E. E. Schulze, J. D. Spungin, L. B. Stern, D. P. Storch, R. D. Tabery. **Transfer Agents & Registrars**—First National Bank of Chicago; First Chicago Trust Co. of New York, Jersey City, N.J. **Incorporated** in Delaware in 1966. **Empl**-1,860. **S&P Analyst:** Joe Victor Shammas

STANDARD & POOR'S

STOCK REPORTS

ABM Industries

NYSE Symbol **ABM**
In S&P SmallCap 600

11-AUG-95 **Industry:** Services

Summary: This company, the largest building services contractor on the NYSE, provides janitorial, air conditioning, elevator, engineering, lighting, parking and security services.

Quantitative Evaluations

Outlook (1 Lowest—5 Highest)
• **NA**
Fair Value
• **NA**
Risk
• **Low**
Earn./Div. Rank
• **A**

Technical Eval.
• **Bearish** since 6/94
Rel. Strength Rank (1 Lowest—99 Highest)
• **69**
Insider Activity
• **Neutral**

Recent Price • 25⅜
52 Wk Range • 25½-19⅞
Yield • 2.4%
12-Mo. P/E • 14.7

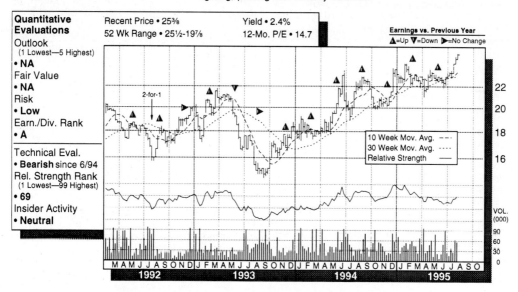

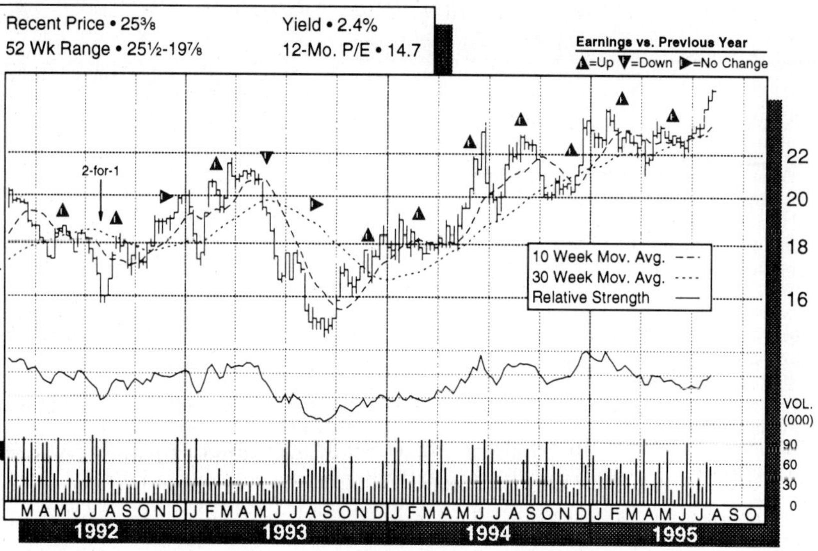

Business Profile - 11-AUG-95

This company (formerly American Building Maintenance Industries) provides a full range of services for building operations. ABM's janitorial services segment, which provides the bulk of revenues and earnings, has been fairly recession-resistant, evidenced by the long uptrend in earnings. ABM also provides HVAC, elevator, lighting and engineering services, along with parking and security operations. Recent revenue growth has been aided by acquisitions. Insiders hold 28% of the common stock.

Operational Review - 11-AUG-95

Total revenues in the six months ended April 30, 1995 rose 9%, year to year, reflecting volume and price increases, as well as sales generated from acquisitions in the janitorial and parking divisions. Margins widened on slower SG&A growth, which outweighed effects of increased competition and pricing pressure in certain divisions; operating income was up 21%. Following a 33% increase in interest expense due to higher bank borrowings for acquisitions, net income advanced 19%, to $0.75 a share.

Stock Performance - 04-AUG-95

In the past 30 trading days, ABM's shares have increased 10%, compared to a 2% rise in the S&P 500. Average trading volume for the past five days was 11,080 shares, compared with the 40-day moving average of 9,197 shares.

Key Stock Statistics

Dividend Rate/Share	0.60	Shareholders	3,600
Shs. outstg. (M)	9.2	Market cap. (B)	$0.234
Avg. daily vol. (M)	0.010	Inst. holdings	56%
Tang. Bk. Value/Share	7.12	Insider holdings	NA
Beta	0.34		

Value of $10,000 invested 5 years ago: $ 17,855

Fiscal Year Ending Oct. 31

	1995	% Change	1994	% Change	1993	% Change
Revenues (Million $)						
1Q	232.1	10%	210.8	13%	187.2	1%
2Q	234.4	9%	215.9	14%	188.7	-1%
3Q	—	—	225.0	17%	192.2	NM
4Q	—	—	233.0	14%	205.2	8%
Yr.	—	—	884.6	14%	773.3	2%
Income (Million $)						
1Q	3.39	20%	2.83	20%	2.36	12%
2Q	3.94	19%	3.32	24%	2.67	-6%
3Q	—	—	4.15	23%	3.38	4%
4Q	—	—	4.88	15%	4.23	12%
Yr.	—	—	15.17	20%	12.65	6%
Earnings Per Share ($)						
1Q	0.35	13%	0.31	11%	0.28	12%
2Q	0.40	11%	0.36	16%	0.31	-9%
3Q	—	—	0.45	15%	0.39	NM
4Q	—	—	0.53	13%	0.47	4%
Yr.	—	—	1.65	14%	1.45	1%

Next earnings report expected: mid September

ABM Industries

Business Summary - 11-AUG-95

ABM Industries Inc. (formerly American Building Maintenance Industries, Inc.) is the largest American-owned, NYSE-listed building services contractor. It provides elevator, engineering, janitorial, lighting, mechanical, parking and security services to thousands of commercial, industrial and institutional facilities across the U.S. and Canada.

Industry segment contributions in fiscal 1994 were:

	Revenues	Profits
Janitorial divisions	54%	56%
Amtech divisions	26%	27%
Other divisions	20%	17%

ABM Janitorial Services provides standard building cleaning services for office buildings, factories, stores, theaters, airport terminals and other institutions. Work is done under thousands of individually negotiated contracts, with the majority obtained through competitive bidding. Many contracts contain escalation clauses covering the full amount of any increases in wages, payroll taxes and insurance premiums. As of fiscal 1994 year-end, janitorial services were being provided in 84 offices in 29 states, the District of Columbia, and two Canadian provinces.

Easterday Janitorial Supply markets janitorial supplies and equipment, including several nationally advertised brands, through six sales offices. 32% of sales are to ABM Janitorial.

The Amtech services group consists of the following four divisions: CommAir Mechanical (servicing and installing air conditioning and heating equipment and providing energy management services), Amtech Elevator (installing and maintaining elevators and escalators), Amtech Lighting (providing relamping, fixture cleaning, and lighting maintenance services, and installing and repairing outdoor signage), and ABM Engineering (providing engineers to maintain and repair electrical, mechanical and plumbing systems).

Other divisions are: Ampco System Parking, which operates 1,321 parking lots and garages in 23 states; and ASI Security Services, which provides special investigative and security consulting services, and security guards.

Important Developments

Jun. '95—ABM announced record results for the second quarter of fiscal 1995, with net income up 19% from the year-ago quarter, on a 9% sales gain. The company also announced a $0.15 a share dividend for the third quarter, representing the 118th consecutive quarterly cash dividend.

Capitalization

Long Term Debt: $27,235,000 (4/95).

Per Share Data ($)

(Year Ended Oct. 31)

	1994	1993	1992	1991	1990	1989
Tangible Bk. Val.	6.96	5.97	8.02	7.11	5.90	5.13
Cash Flow	2.69	2.28	2.22	2.22	2.12	2.00
Earnings	1.65	1.45	1.43	1.36	1.24	1.13
Dividends	0.51	0.50	0.49	0.47	0.47	0.46
Payout Ratio	32%	34%	34%	35%	38%	42%
Prices - High	23⅞	21¾	20⅜	17⅞	20⅞	19⅞
- Low	17¼	14⅝	15¾	12⅜	12⅝	13¾
P/E Ratio - High	14	15	14	13	17	18
- Low	10	10	11	9	10	12

Income Statement Analysis (Million $)

	1994	%Chg	1993	%Chg	1992	%Chg	1991
Revs.	885	14%	773	2%	758	3%	739
Oper. Inc.	37.8	28%	29.6	11%	26.7	25%	21.4
Depr.	9.3	30%	7.2	8%	6.6	-5%	7.0
Int. Exp.	3.5	60%	2.2	5%	2.1	-34%	3.1
Pretax Inc.	25.1	24%	20.2	NM	20.4	10%	18.6
Eff. Tax Rate	40%	—	38%	—	41%	—	40%
Net Inc.	15.2	21%	12.6	5%	12.0	8%	11.1

Balance Sheet & Other Fin. Data (Million $)

	1994	1993	1992	1991	1990	1989
Cash	7.4	1.7	2.4	2.5	1.6	2.5
Curr. Assets	189	167	154	142	132	122
Total Assets	299	268	226	212	202	190
Curr. Liab.	99	90.3	78.5	80.1	66.5	63.6
LT Debt	25.3	20.9	15.4	9.5	20.0	20.0
Common Eqty.	124	110	101	90.0	79.6	69.4
Total Cap.	156	138	116	99	100	89.4
Cap. Exp.	8.5	6.2	5.2	5.7	6.1	6.0
Cash Flow	24.0	19.7	18.6	18.1	16.9	15.5

Ratio Analysis

	1994	1993	1992	1991	1990	1989
Curr. Ratio	1.9	1.8	2.0	1.8	2.0	1.9
% LT Debt of Cap.	16.2	15.2	13.3	9.6	20.1	22.4
% Net Inc.of Revs.	1.7	1.6	1.6	1.5	1.4	1.4
% Ret. on Assets	5.3	5.0	5.4	5.3	5.0	4.8
% Ret. on Equity	12.3	11.7	12.4	13.0	13.1	13.1

Dividend Data (Dividends have been paid since 1965. A "poison pill" stock purchase right was adopted in 1988.)

Amt. of Div. $	Date Decl.	Ex-Div. Date	Stock of Record	Payment Date
0.130	Sep. 20	Oct. 07	Oct. 14	Nov. 03 '94
0.150	Dec. 19	Jan. 09	Jan. 16	Feb. 03 '95
0.150	Mar. 21	Apr. 07	Apr. 13	May. 03 '95
0.150	Jun. 20	Jul. 12	Jul. 14	Aug. 03 '95

Data as orig. reptd.; bef. results of disc. opers. and/or spec. items. Per share data adj. for stk. divs. as of ex-div. date. E-Estimated. NA-Not Available. NM-Not Meaningful. NR-Not Ranked.

Office—50 Fremont St., 26th Floor, San Francisco, CA 94105. **Tel**—(415) 597-4500. **Chrmn**—S. J. Rosenberg. **Pres & CEO**—W. W. Steele. **EVP & Investor Contact**—Martinn Mandles. **VP & Secy**—H. H. Kahn. **VP & CFO**—D. H. Hebble. **Dirs**—M. B. Cattani, R. S. Dickerman, J. F. Egan, C. T. Horngren, H. L. Kotkins, M. H. Mandles, S. J. Rosenberg, T. Rosenberg, W. W. Steele, W. E. Walsh, B. A. Zaino. **Transfer Agent & Registrar**—Chemical Bank Trust Co. of California, SF. **Incorporated** in California in 1955; reincorporated in Delaware in 1985. **Empl**-42,000. **S&P Analyst:** Julie Santoriello

STANDARD & POOR'S

STOCK REPORTS

AGCO Corp.

NYSE Symbol **AG**
In S&P SmallCap 600

15-NOV-95 **Industry:** Machinery

Summary: AGCO is one of the world's largest makers and distributors of agricultural equipment.

Quantitative Evaluations
Outlook
(1 Lowest—5 Highest)
• **4**
Fair Value
• **52**
Risk
• **Average**
Earn./Div. Rank
• **NR**

Technical Eval.
• **Bullish** since 3/95
Rel. Strength Rank
(1 Lowest—99 Highest)
• **34**
Insider Activity
• **Favorable**

Recent Price • 45 1/8
52 Wk Range • 54 5/8-24 3/8
Yield • 0.1%
12-Mo. P/E • 6.7

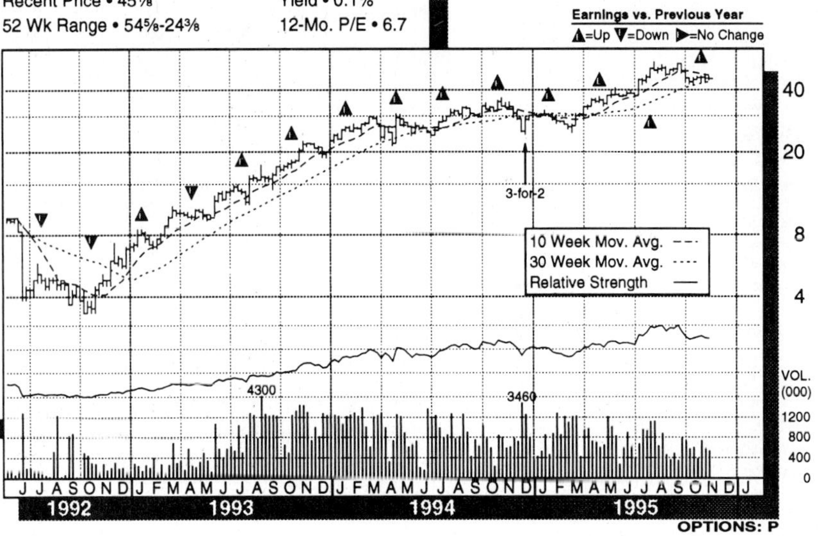

OPTIONS: P

Business Profile - 15-NOV-95

This leading maker and distributor of agricultural equipment has grown rapidly over the past two years through acquisitions. This helped AGCO increase its scale through added volume, as well as expanded sales of complementary products through multiple distribution channels. The company expects its strategy of adding new products, new dealers and new markets, with a focus on cost containment, to drive continued profitable growth.

Operational Review - 15-NOV-95

Net sales in the nine months ended September 30, 1995, increased 72%, paced by contributions from Massey Ferguson Group, Ltd. (acquired in June 1994). Margins widened, on the higher volume and successful cost reduction efforts in international operations. Excluding acquisition-related expenses, and treating 1994 results as fully taxes, net income advanced 93%, to $95.5 million ($3.52 a share), from $51 million ($2.17).

Stock Performance - 10-NOV-95

In the past 30 trading days, AG's shares have declined 0.82%, compared to a 1% rise in the S&P 500. Average trading volume for the past five days was 104,820 shares, compared with the 40-day moving average of 121,063 shares.

Key Stock Statistics

Dividend Rate/Share	0.04	Shareholders	200
Shs. outstg. (M)	22.6	Market cap. (B)	$0.995
Avg. daily vol. (M)	0.104	Inst. holdings	95%
Tang. Bk. Value/Share	15.97	Insider holdings	NA
Beta	NA		

Value of $10,000 invested 5 years ago: NA

Fiscal Year Ending Dec. 31

	1995	% Change	1994	% Change	1993	% Change
Revenues (Million $)						
1Q	443.5	148%	178.9	75%	102.1	56%
2Q	571.7	165%	215.7	42%	152.4	91%
3Q	484.2	NM	481.4	183%	170.1	102%
4Q	—	—	460.1	169%	171.1	101%
Yr.	—	—	1,359	128%	595.7	89%
Income (Million $)						
1Q	23.38	172%	8.59	NM	-9.66	NM
2Q	35.89	65%	21.77	61%	13.56	NM
3Q	36.20	14%	31.89	97%	16.21	NM
4Q	—	—	53.29	NM	13.98	NM
Yr.	—	—	115.5	NM	34.09	NM
Earnings Per Share ($)						
1Q	1.01	99%	0.51	NM	-0.72	NM
2Q	1.56	12%	1.39	49%	0.93	NM
3Q	1.54	7%	1.43	34%	1.07	NM
4Q	—	—	2.39	166%	0.90	NM
Yr.	—	—	6.13	176%	2.22	NM

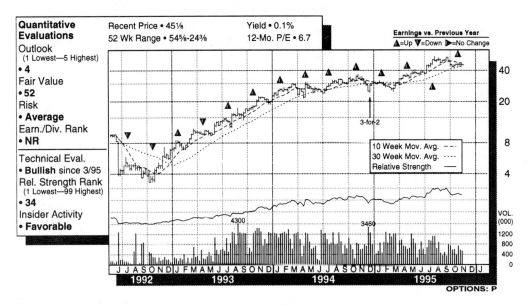

Next earnings report expected: early February

AGCO Corp.

Business Summary - 15-NOV-95

AGCO Corporation is a major manufacturer and distributor of farm equipment, machinery and replacement parts in the U.S. and Canada. Its products include tractors, combines, implements, hay tools and forage equipment. AGCO also distributes a full line of related replacement parts. Sales by product line in recent years were:

	1994	1993	1992
Replacement parts	20%	34%	37%
Combines	10%	16%	23%
Hay tools & forage equipment	10%	14%	21%
Tractors	57%	36%	19%
Other equipment	3%	---	---

AGCO participates in three segments of the North American tractor market: the compact category, which includes tractors in the under-40-hp range; the mid-range segment (40 to 100-hp); and the higher horsepower segment (in excess of 100-hp). Brand names include Massey Ferguson, AGCO, Allis, White and SAME.

The Gleaner combine product line consists of four models ranging from 170-bushel to 330-bushel bin capacity, while the Massey Ferguson line includes three models ranging from 180-bushel to 227-bushel bin capacity. Hay tools include self-propelled windowers and tractor-powered mowers, tedders and rakes, round balers, square balers, and forage harvesters.

The company also sells replacement parts for products sold under all of its brand names; many are proprietary. AGCO also recently expanded its replacement parts business with sales of a line of "all makes" parts in North America that are generic to the industry and are marketed under the Value Line brand name.

AGCO markets and distributes farm machinery, equipment and replacement parts to farmers through a network of more than 6,600 independent dealers around the world. Its replacement parts network consists of a 309,000 sq. ft. master warehouse in Batavia, IL. and regional distribution warehouses located throughout the U.S. and Canada.

Important Developments

Oct. '95—The company said fundamentals in the agricultural industry remained positive in North America, propelled by high net cash farm incomes, strong farmer balance sheets, record farm export demand, and strong commodity prices.

Capitalization

Long Term Debt: $754,391,000 (3/95); incl. $687,543,000 issued under revolving credit facilities.

Per Share Data ($) (Year Ended Dec. 31)

	1994	1993	1992	1991	1990	1989
Tangible Bk. Val.	12.93	8.35	7.01	3.51	NA	NA
Cash Flow	7.12	2.43	0.67	1.33	NA	NA
Earnings	6.13	2.22	0.54	1.38	NA	NA
Dividends	0.04	0.03	0.01	Nil	NA	NA
Payout Ratio	1%	1%	2%	Nil	NA	NA
Prices - High	36¾	22⅞	10⅜	NA	NA	NA
- Low	21½	6⅝	3⅜	NA	NA	NA
P/E Ratio - High	6	10	19	NA	NA	NA
- Low	4	3	6	NA	NA	NA

Income Statement Analysis (Million $)

	1994	%Chg	1993	%Chg	1992	%Chg	1991
Revs.	1,359	128%	596	89%	315	15%	275
Oper. Inc.	185	185%	64.8	NM	15.8	-5%	16.7
Depr.	17.8	NM	2.9	75%	1.7	NM	0.5
Int. Exp.	42.8	139%	17.9	44%	12.4	158%	4.8
Pretax Inc.	105	NM	34.1	NM	6.0	-31%	8.7
Eff. Tax Rate	NM	—	Nil	—	Nil	—	Nil
Net Inc.	116	NM	34.1	NM	6.0	-31%	8.7

Balance Sheet & Other Fin. Data (Million $)

	1994	1993	1992	1991	1990	1989
Cash	25.8	4.2	9.0	18.6	NA	NA
Curr. Assets	1,201	503	293	170	NA	NA
Total Assets	1,823	578	321	195	NA	NA
Curr. Liab.	703	160	67.0	75.9	NA	NA
LT Debt	594	174	121	41.0	NA	NA
Common Eqty.	401	120	93.7	18.2	NA	NA
Total Cap.	1,070	386	215	67.0	NA	NA
Cap. Exp.	20.7	6.7	4.4	7.2	NA	NA
Cash Flow	128	33.3	7.6	8.4	NA	NA

Ratio Analysis

	1994	1993	1992	1991	1990	1989
Curr. Ratio	1.7	3.1	4.4	2.2	NA	NA
% LT Debt of Cap.	55.5	45.0	56.4	61.2	NA	NA
% Net Inc.of Revs.	8.5	5.7	1.9	3.2	NA	NA
% Ret. on Assets	8.4	7.6	1.5	NA	NA	NA
% Ret. on Equity	37.0	28.3	8.4	NA	NA	NA

Dividend Data —Dividends were initiated in 1992. A poison pill stock purchase rights plan was adopted in January 1994.

Amt. of Div. $	Date Decl.	Ex-Div. Date	Stock of Record	Payment Date
3-for-2	Oct. 13	Dec. 16	Dec. 01	Dec. 15 '94
0.010	Feb. 08	Feb. 14	Feb. 21	Mar. 01 '95
0.010	Apr. 27	May. 10	May. 16	Jun. 01 '95
0.010	Jul. 28	Aug. 11	Aug. 15	Sep. 01 '95
0.010	Oct. 25	Nov. 13	Nov. 15	Dec. 01 '95

Data as orig. reptd.; bef. results of disc. opers. and/or spec. items. Per share data adj. for stk. divs. as of ex-div. date. Sum of 1994 qtrs. does not reconcile wi. full yr. due to change in shs. outst. E-Estimated. NA-Not Available. NM-Not Meaningful. NR-Not Ranked.

Office—4830 River Green Parkway, Duluth, GA 30136. **Tel**—(404) 813-9200. **Chrmn & CEO**—R. J. Ratliff. **Pres, CFO & Investor Contact**—Allen W. Ritchie (404-813-6110). **Dirs**—H. J. Claycamp, G. A. Hand, R. P. Johnston, J. P. Kaine, A. S. McDowell, C. S. Mechem, Jr., S. I. Oakford, R. J. Ratliff, J-P. Richard, A. W. Ritchie, H. Robinson, Jr., John Shumejda. **Transfer Agent & Registrar**—Trust Co. Bank, Atlanta. **Incorporated** in Delaware in 1991. **Empl**-5,789. **S&P Analyst:** G.A.S.

STANDARD & POOR'S

STOCK REPORTS

Acme Metals

NASDAQ Symbol **ACME**

In S&P SmallCap 600

02-OCT-95 **Industry:** Steel-Iron

Summary: This company (formerly Acme Steel) is an integrated producer of steel, steel strapping, welded steel pipe and tube, and automotive and truck jacks.

Quantitative Evaluations

Outlook (1 Lowest—5 Highest) • **NA**

Fair Value • **NA**

Risk • **Average**

Earn./Div. Rank • **B-**

Technical Eval. • **Bearish** since 7/95

Rel. Strength Rank (1 Lowest—99 Highest) • **43**

Insider Activity • **NA**

Recent Price • 17¼

52 Wk Range • 22¾-14½

Yield • Nil

12-Mo. P/E • 8.7

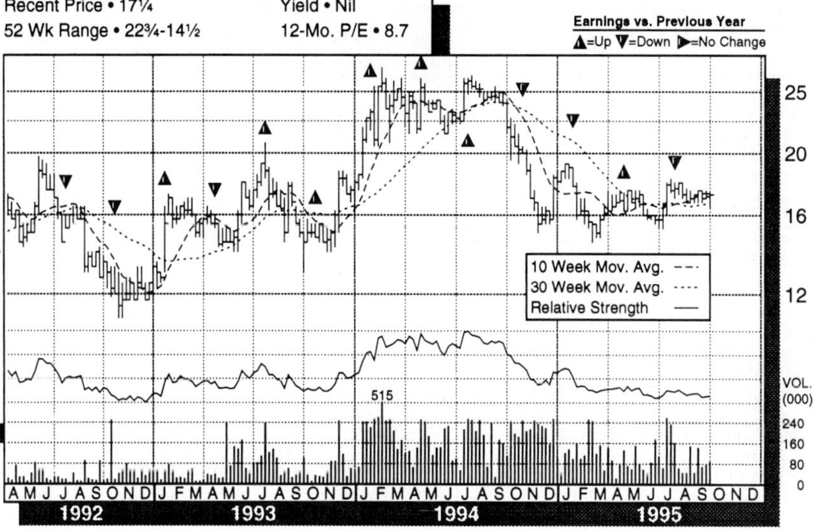

Business Profile - 02-OCT-95

In an effort to achieve long-term growth and profitability, Acme has been modernizing operations and acquiring downstream users of its steel products. In October 1994, construction started on a $372 million thin slab caster/hot strip mill complex, scheduled for startup in mid-1996. Acme expects the new process to cut processing time from 10 days to 90 minutes, and reduce manufacturing costs by more than $70 a ton. Acme is using $205 million from a 1994 debt offering to finance the project.

Operational Review - 02-OCT-95

Revenues in 1995's first half rose 4.4%, year to year, mostly due to higher average selling prices of finished steel, and increased shipments of pig iron and hot metal. Margins widened substantially, reflecting the higher prices, increased shipments and lower operating expenses; operating profit soared 72%. After a sharp rise in interest expense, which more than offset a large gain in interest income, net income advanced 61%, to $16,827,000, from $10,454,000.

Stock Performance - 29-SEP-95

In the past 30 trading days, ACME's shares have increased 3%, compared to a 5% rise in the S&P 500. Average trading volume for the past five days was 17,340 shares, compared with the 40-day moving average of 16,526 shares.

Key Stock Statistics

Dividend Rate/Share	Nil	Shareholders	7,500
Shs. outstg. (M)	11.6	Market cap. (B)	$0.200
Avg. daily vol. (M)	0.019	Inst. holdings	47%
Tang. Bk. Value/Share	20.77	Insider holdings	NA
Beta	0.05		

Value of $10,000 invested 5 years ago: $ 9,597

Fiscal Year Ending Dec. 31

	1995	% Change	1994	% Change	1993	% Change
Revenues (Million $)						
1Q	131.6	6%	123.6	15%	107.9	10%
2Q	136.2	2%	132.9	13%	117.2	17%
3Q	—	—	123.1	10%	111.9	18%
4Q	—	—	143.3	19%	120.5	23%
Yr.	—	—	522.9	14%	457.4	17%
Income (Million $)						
1Q	8.05	124%	3.60	NM	0.11	-50%
2Q	8.78	28%	6.86	NM	2.06	NM
3Q	—	—	0.77	NM	0.12	NM
4Q	—	—	7.54	90%	3.97	NM
Yr.	—	—	18.76	200%	6.26	NM
Earnings Per Share ($)						
1Q	0.69	8%	0.64	NM	0.02	-33%
2Q	0.75	-38%	1.20	NM	0.38	NM
3Q	—	—	-0.12	NM	0.02	NM
4Q	—	—	0.65	-11%	0.73	NM
Yr.	—	—	2.38	107%	1.15	NM

Next earnings report expected: early November

Acme Metals

02-OCT-95

Business Summary - 22-SEP-95

Acme Metals Incorporated (formerly Acme Steel Co.) is a fully integrated producer of steel, steel strapping, and strapping tools, welded steel tube and pipe, and automotive and light truck jacks. Contributions to sales in recent years were:

	1994	1993	1992
Sheet & strip steel	38%	37%	33%
Steel strapping	32%	33%	36%
Steel tubing	16%	16%	16%
Auto & truck jacks	8%	10%	11%
Semifinished steel	4%	2%	2%
Other	2%	2%	2%

Acme Steel Co. (44% of 1994 sales) produces sheet and strip steel, semi-finished steel and iron and other products. In the flat rolled steel strip market, it specializes in producing high carbon and alloy steels. Acme serves the industrial equipment, processor, automotive, agricultural, pipe and tube, tool manufacturer and industrial fastener markets. It is the smallest integrated U.S. steel producer.

The Steel Fabricating segment (56% of 1994 sales) consists of steel strapping and strapping tools, welded steel tube and auto and light truck jacks. The company is one of two major U.S. producers of steel strapping and strapping tools in North America, with sales to many markets, including forest products, paper, brick, agricultural, primary and fabricated metals and automotive. Alpha Tube (acquired 1989) is a leading producer of high quality welded carbon steel tubing used in furniture, recreation, contractors and automotive applications.

Universal Tool & Stamping Co. (acquired in 1987) produces automobile and light truck jacks and related accessories for the North American OEM market.

Acme's principal raw materials are iron ore and coal. Iron ore needs are satisfied through an equity interest in Wabush Mines in Newfoundland and Quebec, Canada, term contracts and open market purchases. Coal requirements are met through term contracts and open market purchases.

In March 1995, ACME signed an agreement with SMS Schloemann Siemag AG, its primary project equipment supplier, whereby ACME and SMS will share revenues from licensing improvement patents and process know-how developed.

Important Developments

Jul. '95—Commenting on third quarter 1995 prospects, ACME believes it will experience slowing demand and price pressure in both segments, as customers reduce their inventories, and as the economy weakens.

Capitalization

Long Term Debt: $270,730,000 (6/95).

Per Share Data ($)

(Year Ended Dec. 31)

	1994	1993	1992	1991	1990	1989
Tangible Bk. Val.	19.32	14.32	16.35	28.14	28.65	27.63
Cash Flow	4.35	3.95	2.20	2.22	3.48	5.23
Earnings	2.38	1.15	-0.53	-0.43	1.05	3.00
Dividends	Nil	Nil	0.02	Nil	Nil	Nil
Payout Ratio	Nil	Nil	NM	Nil	Nil	Nil
Prices - High	27¼	20¾	19¾	15¾	18½	26½
- Low	15	12¼	11	10¾	13	16½
P/E Ratio - High	11	18	NM	NM	18	9
- Low	6	11	NM	NM	12	6

Income Statement Analysis (Million $)

	1994	%Chg	1993	%Chg	1992	%Chg	1991
Revs.	523	14%	457	17%	391	4%	377
Oper. Inc.	58.6	97%	29.8	94%	15.4	17%	13.2
Depr.	15.5	2%	15.2	3%	14.7	4%	14.2
Int. Exp.	14.0	160%	5.4	-3%	5.6	32%	4.2
Pretax Inc.	28.7	176%	10.4	NM	-4.5	NM	-3.1
Eff. Tax Rate	35%	—	40%	—	NM	—	NM
Net Inc.	18.8	198%	6.3	NM	-2.8	NM	-2.3

Balance Sheet & Other Fin. Data (Million $)

	1994	1993	1992	1991	1990	1989
Cash	153	50.4	49.2	31.7	21.1	35.0
Curr. Assets	274	170	149	134	126	149
Total Assets	682	334	301	291	287	285
Curr. Liab.	81.4	77.2	59.4	50.0	56.7	61.1
LT Debt	265	49.3	56.0	59.5	59.5	59.5
Common Eqty.	223	83.0	89.0	151	153	147
Total Cap.	488	133	145	221	218	211
Cap. Exp.	56.3	11.7	7.6	10.6	28.6	15.0
Cash Flow	34.3	21.5	11.9	11.9	18.7	28.2

Ratio Analysis

	1994	1993	1992	1991	1990	1989
Curr. Ratio	3.4	2.2	2.5	2.7	2.2	2.4
% LT Debt of Cap.	59.3	37.2	38.5	26.9	27.3	28.2
% Net Inc.of Revs.	3.6	1.4	NM	NM	1.3	3.7
% Ret. on Assets	2.7	2.0	NM	NM	2.0	6.3
% Ret. on Equity	9.4	7.2	NM	NM	3.8	11.6

Dividend Data —Acme has never paid regular cash dividends. Special payments in 1988 and 1992 reflected redemption of stock purchase rights.

Data as orig. reptd.; bef. results of disc. opers. and/or spec. items. Per share data adj. for stk. divs. as of ex-div. date. E-Estimated. NA-Not Available. NM-Not Meaningful. NR-Not Ranked.

Office—13500 S. Perry Ave., Riverdale, IL 60627-1182. **Tel**—(708) 849-2500. **Chrmn & CEO**—B. W. H. Marsden. **Pres & COO**—S. D. Bennett. **VP-Fin & CFO**—J. F. Williams. **VP & Secy**—E. P. Weber, Jr. **Investor Contact**—Charles A. Nekvasil. **Dirs**—S. D. Bennet, C. J. Gauthier, E. G. Jordan, A. R. Laidlaw, F. A. LePage, R. C. MacDonald, B. W. H. Marsden, J. L. McCall, C. O'Cleireacain, W. P. Sovey, L. F. Sutherland, W. R. Wilson. **Transfer Agents & Registrars**—First Chicago Trust Co. of New York, Jersey City, NJ; Montreal Trust Co., Toronto. **Incorporated** in Delaware in 1969 under the name Interlake, Inc. **Empl**-2,748. **S&P Analyst:** Robert E. Friedman

STANDARD & POOR'S

STOCK REPORTS

ADAC Laboratories

NASDAQ Symbol **ADAC**

In S&P SmallCap 600

11-NOV-95 **Industry:** Medical equipment/ supply

Summary: This company designs, produces, markets and services medical imaging and information management products worldwide.

Quantitative Evaluations

Outlook (1 Lowest—5 Highest) • **3**

Fair Value • **12⅜**

Risk • **Average**

Earn./Div. Rank • **B**

Technical Eval. • **Bearish** since 9/95

Rel. Strength Rank (1 Lowest—99 Highest) • **44**

Insider Activity • **NA**

Recent Price • 11⅝

52 Wk Range • 13¾-7¼

Yield • 4.1%

12-Mo. P/E • 18.0

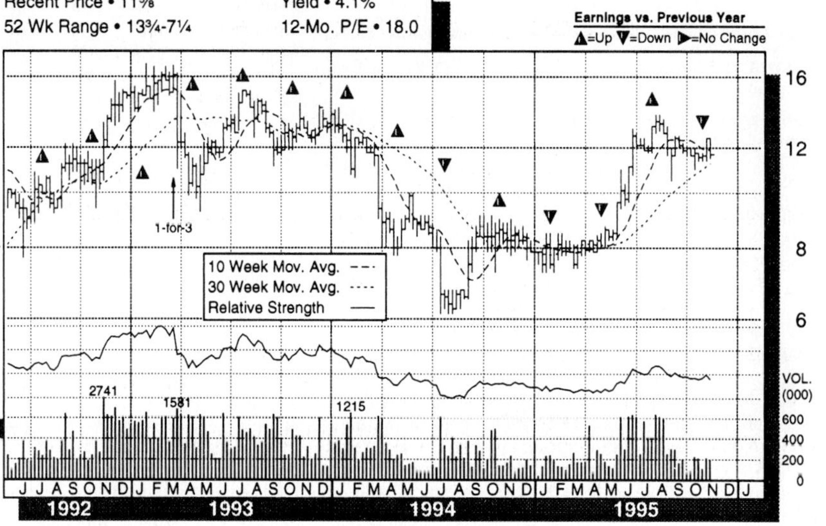

Business Profile - 06-NOV-95

This company is focusing on cost reduction programs and introducing new cost effective products as strategies to respond to a competitive nuclear medicine market. With significant international expansion in recent years, the company believes that it is well positioned to increase its share of the worldwide nuclear medicine market. Additionally, ADAC increased its presence in the healthcare information systems market with the recent acquisition of Community Health Computing.

Operational Review - 06-NOV-95

Revenues advanced in fiscal 1995, from those of the previous year, as a slight decline in net product sales was outweighed by an increase in field service revenues due to a larger installed base. Lower gross margins resulting from pricing pressures in the nuclear medicine market and a change in the product mix, were partly offset by lower SG&A and R&D expense. Results in fiscal 1994 were penalized by restructuring charges and litigation expenses offset by an income tax benefit.

Stock Performance - 10-NOV-95

In the past 30 trading days, ADAC's shares have declined 3%, compared to a 1% rise in the S&P 500. Average trading volume for the past five days was 39,320 shares, compared with the 40-day moving average of 32,010 shares.

Key Stock Statistics

Dividend Rate/Share	0.48	Shareholders	3,100
Shs. outstg. (M)	16.5	Market cap. (B)	$0.193
Avg. daily vol. (M)	0.036	Inst. holdings	51%
Tang. Bk. Value/Share	4.87	Insider holdings	NA
Beta	1.26		

Value of $10,000 invested 5 years ago: $ 7,695

Fiscal Year Ending Sep. 30

	1995	% Change	1994	% Change	1993	% Change
Revenues (Million $)						
1Q	44.23	-5%	46.55	28%	36.30	31%
2Q	44.73	-5%	47.30	26%	37.60	31%
3Q	45.62	14%	40.08	NM	39.72	28%
4Q	50.23	19%	42.36	-2%	43.34	29%
Yr.	184.8	5%	176.3	12%	156.9	29%
Income (Million $)						
1Q	2.43	-54%	5.31	29%	4.13	89%
2Q	2.75	-50%	5.50	25%	4.41	32%
3Q	3.05	NM	0.27	-94%	4.54	30%
4Q	2.84	-56%	6.43	29%	4.97	29%
Yr.	11.07	-37%	17.52	-3%	18.06	40%
Earnings Per Share ($)						
1Q	0.15	-55%	0.33	38%	0.24	60%
2Q	0.17	-48%	0.33	22%	0.27	29%
3Q	0.18	NM	0.02	-93%	0.28	33%
4Q	0.16	-59%	0.39	30%	0.30	25%
Yr.	0.65	-39%	1.06	-4%	1.10	36%

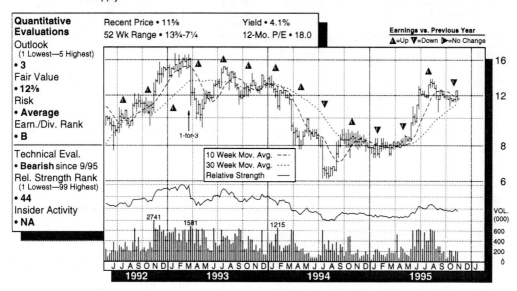

Next earnings report expected: late January

ADAC Laboratories

Business Summary - 08-AUG-95

ADAC Laboratories designs, manufactures, markets and services medical imaging and information systems used in hospitals and clinics in nuclear medicine, cardiology, radiology and oncology. Revenues in recent years were derived as follows:

	1993-1994	1992-1993	1991-1992
Product sales	78%	77%	76%
Field services	22%	23%	24%

International sales represented 16% of total revenues in fiscal 1994.

Nuclear medicine products accounted for about 67% of total revenues in fiscal 1994. ADAC's nuclear medicine products include a family of gamma cameras and image processing computer systems. The gamma cameras are designed to perform superior Single Photon Emission Computed Tomography (SPECT) imaging for cancer and cardiac disease screening. The market for nuclear medicine products and systems was depressed in 1994 as the spread of managed care in the U.S. hurt hospital capital budgets. ADAC estimated that the net effect was a decline in the North American market of about 27%. The decline was partially offset by a stable European market and growth in Asia and Latin America.

ADAC is a leader in both single-headed and multi-headed nuclear medcine cameras. Single-headed products are sold under the Argus, Cirrus and Genesys names, while multi-headed cameras are marketed under the Dual Genesys and Genesys Vertex names. About 70% of ADAC's nuclear medicine revenues in fiscal 1994 were derived from multi-headed cameras, with the balance from single-headed products. The Genesys Vertex accounts for over 50% of ADAC's nuclear medicine revenues.

Digital angiographic systems (3% of fiscal 1994 revenues) consist of X-ray imaging and digital angiography systems for both radiology and cardiology applications. Healthcare information systems (7%) include the QuadRIS computer-based patient record system used by radiology departments and hospitals; and the MARS II and IMAGES 3000 radiology information systems used in various patient record-keeping functions.

Important Developments

Jul. '95—The company completed the acquisition of Community Health Computing Corp. (CHCC) for $16.5 million plus expenses of about $1.9 million. CHCC is a Houston-based provider of clinical information systems with a large installed based of ancillary systems, especially in laboratory and radiology information systems. CHCC is also developing a new open-architecture laboratory information product called the LabStat.

Jun. '95—ADAC introduced two new dual-head camera systems: SOLUS EPIC and CARDIO EPIC.

Capitalization

Long Term Debt: None (4/95).

Per Share Data ($) (Year Ended Sep. 30)

	1995	1994	1993	1992	1991	1990
Tangible Bk. Val.	NA	4.65	3.60	2.76	2.58	2.55
Cash Flow	NA	1.41	1.40	0.99	0.27	0.39
Earnings	0.65	1.06	1.10	0.81	0.06	0.24
Dividends	0.60	0.48	0.40	0.36	Nil	0.24
Payout Ratio	92%	45%	40%	41%	Nil	102%
Prices - High	13¾	14⅛	16⅞	15¾	7⅞	18¾
- Low	7¼	6⅛	9¼	5⅛	3	2$^{1}/_{16}$
P/E Ratio - High	21	13	15	19	NM	7[illegible]
- Low	11	6	8	6	NM	9

Income Statement Analysis (Million $)

	1994	%Chg	1993	%Chg	1992	%Chg	1991
Revs.	176	12%	157	30%	121	20%	101
Oper. Inc.	25.9	4%	24.8	51%	16.4	108%	7.9
Depr.	5.8	15%	5.0	66%	3.0	-3%	3.1
Int. Exp.	NA	—	NA	—	NA	—	NA
Pretax Inc.	11.2	-43%	19.5	37%	14.2	NM	1.0
Eff. Tax Rate	NM	—	7.50%	—	9.40%	—	11%
Net Inc.	17.5	-3%	18.1	40%	12.9	NM	0.9

Balance Sheet & Other Fin. Data (Million $)

	1994	1993	1992	1991	1990	1989
Cash	7.2	6.7	11.9	5.7	10.6	7.6
Curr. Assets	92.1	69.5	54.2	47.7	48.2	52.3
Total Assets	122	95.1	77.2	60.1	59.0	60.4
Curr. Liab.	43.6	39.2	31.8	22.8	21.9	23.9
LT Debt	Nil	Nil	Nil	Nil	Nil	0.2
Common Eqty.	74.7	54.7	43.3	37.0	36.5	35.4
Total Cap.	74.7	54.7	43.3	37.0	36.5	35.6
Cap. Exp.	4.4	3.0	2.4	2.5	2.0	1.1
Cash Flow	23.3	23.1	15.9	4.0	5.8	18.6

Ratio Analysis

	1994	1993	1992	1991	1990	1989
Curr. Ratio	2.1	1.8	1.7	2.1	2.2	2.2
% LT Debt of Cap.	Nil	Nil	Nil	Nil	Nil	0.5
% Net Inc.of Revs.	9.9	11.5	10.6	0.9	4.4	17.4
% Ret. on Assets	15.8	20.6	18.5	1.5	5.6	29.9
% Ret. on Equity	26.5	36.3	31.6	2.4	9.2	59.0

Dividend Data —Dividends, suspended in 1990, were resumed in 1992.

Amt. of Div. $	Date Decl.	Ex-Div. Date	Stock of Record	Payment Date
0.120	Nov. 03	Dec. 23	Dec. 30	Jan. 09 '95
0.120	Mar. 22	Mar. 27	Mar. 31	Apr. 10 '95
0.120	Apr. 25	Jun. 28	Jun. 30	Jul. 10 '95
0.120	Jul. 19	Sep. 27	Sep. 29	Oct. 11 '95
0.120	Nov. 02	Dec. 27	Dec. 29	Jan. 08 '96

Data as orig. reptd.; bef. results of disc. opers. and/or spec. items. Per share data adj. for stk. divs. as of ex-div. date. E-Estimated. NA-Not Available. NM-Not Meaningful. NR-Not Ranked.

Office—540 Alder Dr., Milpitas, CA 95035. **Tel**—(408) 321-9100. **Chrmn**—S. D. Czerwinski. **Pres & CEO**—D. L. Lowe. **VP-Fin, CFO & Secy**—D. R. Mahoney. **Treas**—T. P. Sullivan. **Dirs**—S. D. Czerwinski, G. O. King, D. L. Lowe, T. A. McPherson, R. L. Miller, F. D. Rollo, E. H. Shea Jr. **Transfer Agent & Registrar**—Chemical Trust Co. of California, San Francisco. **Incorporated** in California in 1970. **Empl-** 594. **S&P Analyst:** Philip J. Birbara

Addington Resources

NASDAQ Symbol ADDR In S&P SmallCap 600 (Incl. in Nat'l Market)

Price	Range	P-E Ratio	Dividend	Yield	S&P Ranking	Beta
Oct. 12'95	1995					
14¼	15½–8	NM	None	None	C	0.52

Summary

This waste management, mine service, and mineral company intends to focus solely on environmental operations and sell all remaining businesses. Proceeds from these sales are to be used to expand environmental operations. The bulk of coal operations was sold in early 1994. In September 1995, ADDR agreed to sell its remaining coal mining operations, as well as its Belize citrus operations, to the Addington family. Following two years of net losses, profits were up sharply in the first half of 1995.

Business Summary

Addington Resources (as presently constituted) operates coal mines in Kentucky, provides contract mining and environmental services, and has interests in gold mining and agribusiness. In 1994, the bulk of the firm's coal assets were sold to Pittston Minerals Group for $157 million. Contributions by business segment to profits ($ million) in recent years:

	1994	1993	1992
Mining	$1.7	$7.3	$18.3
Environmental	5.4	–1.4	1.6
Other	1.3	0.3	1.4

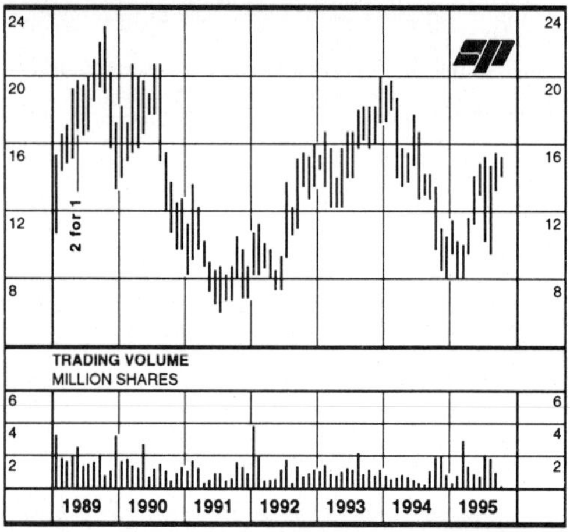

ADDR owns and operates four surface coal mines in eastern Kentucky which sold 3,883,000 tons of coal in 1994 at an average price of $26.29 a ton. Some 76% of coal sales, primarily to electric utilities, were made under long-term contracts. At 1994 year-end, demonstrated coal reserves were 38 million tons (51% low-sulfur).

At March 31, 1995 Addington Environmental, Inc. operated 10 solid waste landfills in Kentucky, North Carolina, Georgia and Florida. Total shipments to the landfills in 1994 were 1,134,000 tons. Some 29% of environmental services revenue in 1994 was generated from the collection of waste from residential and commercial customers in Kentucky, Florida and Georgia.

ADDR also performs contract coal mining services, worldwide employing conventional surface mining techniques and using a proprietary highwall mining machine. Royalties are collected from the lease of its highwall machine produced by Joy Technologies under a long-term license. Other activities include a gold mine in Arizona and interests in limestone and nepheline syenite and a citrus farm in Belize.

Important Developments

Sep. '95— Addington Resources agreed to sell its coal mining and Belize citrus operations to its largest shareholders—Larry, Bruce, and Robert Addington—for $30 million in cash, assumption of certain liabilities, one million ADDR common shares, plus additional considerations, subject to various factors including governmental and regulatory consents. ADDR was continuing to pursue the sale of its gold, limestone, and Wind Mountain operations.

Aug. '95— The company announced a series of moves that change the management and focus of the company, including election of a new chairman and addition of four new directors. The company changed its focus solely to environmental operations and planned to sell all remaining businesses. Proceeds from these sales are to be used to expand environmental operations. Separately, the Addington family agreed to sell to HPB Associates L.P. 2 million ADDR common shares. Of those, HPB had already bought 577,003 shares.

Next earnings report expected in mid-November.

Per Share Data ($)

Yr. End Dec. 31	[1]1994	[1]1993	1992	1991	1990	1989	[1]1988	1987	[1]1986	1985
Tangible Bk. Val.	[6]**7.58**	[6]7.97	8.98	8.25	8.89	7.95	5.56	4.42	2.64	0.90
Cash Flow	**0.10**	d0.05	1.54	0.37	1.52	1.25	1.78	1.86	1.28	NA
Earnings	[2]**d0.45**	[2]d1.04	0.72	[2]d0.41	[2]0.93	[2]0.67	[2,3]1.20	[2,4]1.06	[2,4]0.75	[2,4]0.66
Dividends	**Nil**	Nil	Nil	[5]Nil	[5]Nil	[5]Nil	[5]Nil	[5]Nil	[5]Nil	[5]Nil
Payout Ratio	**Nil**	Nil	Nil	Nil	Nil	Nil	Nil	Nil	Nil	Nil
Prices—High	**19¾**	20	16	13⅝	20¾	23	12⅝	15⅞	NA	NA
Low	**8**	12¼	7⅜	6	9¾	10¹¹⁄₁₆	9¼	7	NA	NA
P/E Ratio—	**NM**	NM	22–10	NM	22–10	34–16	11–8	15–7	NA	NA

Data as orig. reptd. Adj. for 100% stk. div. May 1989. **1.** Refl. merger or acq. **2.** Bef. spec. items of -0.23 in 1991, -0.06 in 1988, +0.16 in 1985. **3.** Ful. dil.: 1.18. **4.** Pro forma. **5.** To public. **6.** Includes intangibles. d-Deficit. NM-Not Meaningful. NA-Not Available.

Income Data (Million $)

Year Ended Dec. 31	Revs.	Oper. Inc.	% Oper. Inc. of Revs.	Cap. Exp.	Depr.	Int. Exp.	Net Bef. Taxes	Eff. Tax Rate	[3]Net Inc.	% Net Inc. of Revs.	Cash Flow
[1]**1994**	**151**	**24.6**	**16.3**	**63.2**	**8.8**	**2.1**	**d10.9**	**NM**	**d7.1**	**NM**	**1.6**
[1]1993	384	33.4	8.7	49.4	15.4	18.7	d21.6	NM	d16.2	NM	d0.8
1992	301	30.7	10.2	37.9	12.5	18.3	16.3	32.4%	11.0	3.7	23.5
1991	275	20.3	7.4	55.7	11.9	19.3	d10.3	NM	d6.2	NM	5.7
1990	269	24.0	8.9	58.9	8.9	19.0	20.0	29.5%	14.1	5.2	23.0
1989	247	31.0	12.5	34.8	7.4	21.3	12.3	23.6%	8.5	3.4	15.9
[1]1988	221	37.5	17.0	28.1	6.8	15.0	18.5	23.6%	14.0	6.3	20.8
1987	158	23.9	15.1	14.8	6.1	5.5	14.0	14.2%	12.0	7.6	18.1
[1]1986	93	16.3	17.6	16.5	5.1	3.0	8.8	[2]34.1%	[2]5.8	6.3	12.5
1985	58	10.2	17.6	10.9	2.5	2.0	6.9	[2]25.3%	[2]5.1	8.8	NA

Balance Sheet Data (Million $)

Dec. 31	Cash	Curr. Assets	Curr. Liab.	Curr. Ratio	Total Assets	% Ret. on Assets	Long Term Debt	Common Equity	Total Cap.	% LT Debt of Cap.	% Ret. on Equity
1994	**11.9**	**40**	**40.0**	**1.0**	**223**	**NM**	**41**	**120**	**164**	**25.1**	**NM**
1993	13.7	184	173.0	1.1	316	NM	12	125	140	8.5	NM
1992	33.0	99	65.8	1.5	339	3.3	128	137	273	46.9	8.4
1991	17.5	77	65.9	1.2	332	NM	135	126	266	50.7	NM
1990	34.8	97	54.6	1.8	337	4.3	144	135	283	50.9	11.0
1989	40.2	110	48.8	2.3	322	2.4	143	121	273	52.2	8.3
1988	47.3	99	27.9	3.5	289	6.7	188	65	262	71.8	23.9
1987	3.6	35	30.7	1.1	130	8.9	44	52	99	44.3	29.0
1986	1.0	20	17.9	1.1	60	12.2	29	13	42	68.6	59.6
1985	1.3	11	12.6	0.9	36	18.3	17	6	23	72.5	179.6

Data as orig. reptd. **1.** Refl. merger or acq. **2.** Pro forma. **3.** Bef. spec. items. d-Deficit. NM-Not Meaningful. NA-Not Available.

Operating Revenues (Million $)

Quarter:	1995	1994	1993	1992
Mar.	36.8	39.6	82.6	66.9
Jun.	52.9	35.5	92.1	74.6
Sep.		39.7	101.6	77.8
Dec.		36.3	107.9	82.2
		151.2	384.2	301.5

Revenues for the first half of 1995 advanced 19%, year to year, reflecting sales gains for landfill, waste collection, and total environmental operations. Profits more than doubled for total environmental and were up 62% for landfill, while the loss for waste collection services was down sharply. Overall income from operations was up 156%. After $6.0 million of other expenses (net), versus $118,000 of other income (net), and taxes at 33.0%, versus 32.0%, net income moved ahead 57%, to $0.43 a share from $0.27.

Common Share Earnings ($)

Quarter:	1995	1994	1993	1992
Mar.	0.12	0.18	d0.11	0.24
Jun.	0.31	0.10	Nil	0.13
Sep.		d0.75	0.16	0.23
Dec.		0.02	d1.08	0.12
		d0.45	d1.04	0.72

Dividend Data

No cash dividends have been declared since the initial public stock offering. A two-for-one stock split was effected in 1989.

Capitalization

Long Term Debt: $43,113,000 (6/95).

Common Stock: 15,293,651 shs. (8/13/95) ($1 par).
The Addington family owns 45.4%.
Shareholders: 258 of record (3/94).

d-Deficit.

Office—1500 North Big Run Rd., Ashland, KY 41102. **Tel**—(606) 928-3433. **Chrmn**—H. P. Berkowitz. **Pres**—K. J. Taylor. **VP, Treas & Secy**—Kathy Addington. **CFO & Investor Contact**—R. Douglas Striebel. **Dirs**—B. Addington, L. Addington, H. P. Berkowitz, H. Blumenstein, J. C. Fisher, J. Grosfield, R. Ravich, C. R. Whitehouse. **Transfer Agent**—Chemical Bank, NYC. **Incorporated** in Delaware in 1986. **Empl**—848.

 N.J. DeVita

ADVO, Inc.

NYSE Symbol **AD**
In S&P SmallCap 600

05-OCT-95

Industry: Advertising/Communications

Summary: ADVO is the largest direct-mail marketing company in the U.S. The company offers direct mail programs that pool advertisers and significantly reduce their postage costs.

Quantitative Evaluations
Outlook (1 Lowest—5 Highest) • **5⁻**
Fair Value • **32⅞**
Risk • **Average**
Earn./Div. Rank • **B**

Technical Eval. • **Bullish** since 7/95
Rel. Strength Rank (1 Lowest—99 Highest) • **96**
Insider Activity • **NA**

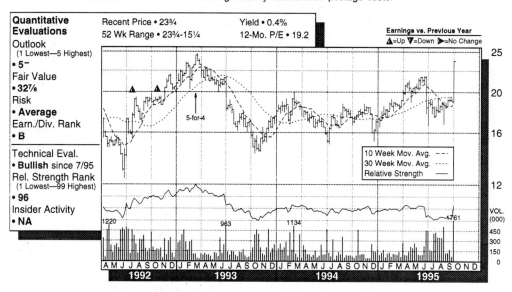

Recent Price • 23¾
52 Wk Range • 23¾-15¼
Yield • 0.4%
12-Mo. P/E • 19.2

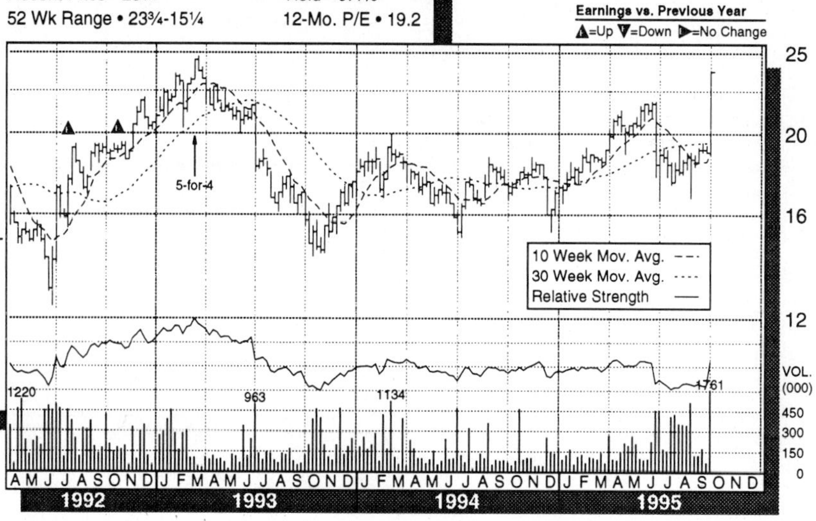

Business Profile - 05-OCT-95

The company has hired Goldman, Sachs & Co. to assist it in exploring alternatives to enhance shareholder value, including the potential sale of the entire company. ADVO is the nation's largest full-service direct marketing services company. The company reaches over 57 million households each week through its Mailbox Values shared mail program. ADVO also offers limited printing and transportation services. The company has 22 production facilities and 80 sales offices nationwide.

Operational Review - 28-SEP-95

Earnings growth slowed in the third quarter due to competitive pressures affecting the company's in-store marketing division. ADVO expects this division to continue to experience difficulties in the fourth quarter. The majority of revenue gains through the first nine months of the year reflect volume growth in shared mail pieces per package and an increase in packages mailed. ADVO has been able to offset increases in postal rates and paper prices with cost controls and productivity improvements.

Stock Performance - 29-SEP-95

In the past 30 trading days, AD's shares have increased 27%, compared to a 5% rise in the S&P 500. Average trading volume for the past five days was 352,100 shares, compared with the 40-day moving average of 102,585 shares.

Key Stock Statistics

Dividend Rate/Share	0.10	Shareholders	1,000
Shs. outstg. (M)	20.8	Market cap. (B)	$0.478
Avg. daily vol. (M)	0.120	Inst. holdings	61%
Tang. Bk. Value/Share	5.18	Insider holdings	NA
Beta	1.61		

Value of $10,000 invested 5 years ago: $ 32,960

Fiscal Year Ending Sep. 30

	1995	% Change	1994	% Change	1993	% Change
Revenues (Million $)						
1Q	263.1	7%	246.8	8%	228.0	22%
2Q	254.2	11%	229.7	8%	212.8	16%
3Q	273.2	7%	256.1	9%	235.4	13%
4Q	—	—	242.9	4%	234.6	12%
Yr.	—	—	975.5	7%	910.8	16%
Income (Million $)						
1Q	10.22	41%	7.25	26%	5.75	20%
2Q	2.80	15%	2.43	72%	1.41	131%
3Q	9.20	3%	8.91	16%	7.67	NM
4Q	—	—	6.58	NM	-11.65	NM
Yr.	—	—	25.17	NM	5.35	-74%
Earnings Per Share ($)						
1Q	0.44	52%	0.29	—	—	—
2Q	0.12	20%	0.10	—	—	—
3Q	0.39	3%	0.38	-49%	0.74	124%
4Q	—	—	0.28	NM	-0.53	NM
Yr.	—	—	1.05	NM	0.21	-76%

Next earnings report expected: late October

ADVO, Inc.

Business Summary - 05-OCT-95

Spun off from John Blair & Co. in 1986, ADVO, Inc. (formerly ADVO-System, Inc.) is the largest direct-mail marketing company in the U.S., reaching, on average, more than 57 million households every week through its Marriage Mail and Mailbox Values shared mail programs. ADVO believes that its proprietary mailing list is the largest in the U.S. It contains more than 108 million residential addresses, representing nearly all households in the continental U.S.

Approximately 94% of ADVO's revenues are derived from its shared mail programs through which advertisements of several different customers are included in a single mail package, which is targeted by ZIP Code. Under this system, ADVO pays the total postage expense, and advertisers are generally charged a selling price based upon, among other factors, the incremental weight of their promotional pieces. The use of ADVO's shared mail programs allows advertisers to reduce their postage costs to an average of about one-third that of conventional mailings.

As part of its shared mail programs, the company provides the addresses of the households receiving the mail package and sorts, processes and transports the advertising material for ultimate delivery through the U.S. Postal Service. Generally, larger businesses, such as food chains and mass merchandisers, provide ADVO with preprinted advertising materials in predetermined quantities.

In addition, the company provides solo mail services, which include addressing and processing of brochures and circulars for an individual customer. Each customer bears the full cost of postage and handling for each mailing, with ADVO charging a processing fee based on the services provided.

ADVO also rents portions of its mailing list; produces general commercial printing, as well as tabloids, for local customers; transports time-sensitive advertising material and general freight through the use of contract carriers; coordinates and produces custom promotional magazines, most of which are distributed by the company; and is involved in several joint ventures directed at enhancing its micromarketing service capabilities, such as proprietary databases and custom micromarketing.

Important Developments

Sep. '95—ADVO retained investment banker Goldman, Sachs & Co. to assist it in exploring strategic alternatives aimed at enhancing long-term sahreholder value. One alternative may include the sale of the entire company in one or a series of transactions.

Capitalization

Long Term Debt: None (6/95).

Per Share Data ($) (Year Ended Sep. 30)

	1994	1993	1992	1991	1990	1989
Tangible Bk. Val.	4.60	4.72	5.13	4.64	3.56	2.59
Cash Flow	1.51	0.57	1.21	1.18	1.05	0.52
Earnings	1.05	0.21	0.89	0.85	0.76	0.27
Dividends	0.09	0.06	Nil	Nil	Nil	Nil
Payout Ratio	9%	29%	Nil	Nil	Nil	Nil
Prices - High	20	24¾	22¼	18⅞	10	8⅞
- Low	15	14¼	12⅜	9	6¾	3¾
P/E Ratio - High	19	118	25	22	13	33
- Low	14	68	14	11	9	14

Income Statement Analysis (Million $)

	1994	%Chg	1993	%Chg	1992	%Chg	1991
Revs.	975	7%	911	16%	788	13%	697
Oper. Inc.	51.6	23%	41.8	15%	36.2	10%	33.0
Depr.	11.0	19%	9.2	22%	7.6	4%	7.3
Int. Exp.	NA	—	0.2	—	Nil	--	Nil
Pretax Inc.	41.3	NM	8.1	-73%	30.1	6%	28.3
Eff. Tax Rate	39%	—	34%	—	32%	—	32%
Net Inc.	25.2	NM	5.4	-74%	20.5	6%	19.3

Balance Sheet & Other Fin. Data (Million $)

	1994	1993	1992	1991	1990	1989
Cash	71.1	71.4	65.7	52.6	41.6	22.2
Curr. Assets	151	151	129	104	88.0	62.0
Total Assets	226	227	190	156	133	108
Curr. Liab.	104	91.3	72.7	56.6	55.7	49.2
LT Debt	Nil	Nil	Nil	Nil	Nil	Nil
Common Eqty.	108	118	95.7	78.1	56.3	40.5
Total Cap.	112	118	116	98.0	76.0	59.0
Cap. Exp.	13.3	14.2	11.2	7.8	6.8	5.3
Cash Flow	36.1	14.6	28.1	26.6	22.5	11.2

Ratio Analysis

	1994	1993	1992	1991	1990	1989
Curr. Ratio	1.4	1.7	1.8	1.8	1.6	1.3
% LT Debt of Cap.	Nil	Nil	Nil	Nil	Nil	Nil
% Net Inc.of Revs.	2.6	0.6	2.6	2.8	2.5	0.9
% Ret. on Assets	11.5	2.2	11.7	13.1	13.5	5.1
% Ret. on Equity	23.0	4.4	23.3	28.3	33.6	12.7

Dividend Data —Dividends were initiated in January 1993.

Amt. of Div. $	Date Decl.	Ex-Div. Date	Stock of Record	Payment Date
0.025	Sep. 14	Sep. 27	Oct. 03	Oct. 14 '94
0.025	Dec. 02	Dec. 23	Dec. 30	Jan. 13 '95
0.025	Mar. 14	Mar. 28	Apr. 03	Apr. 14 '95
0.025	Jun. 01	Jun. 28	Jun. 30	Jul. 14 '95
0.025	Sep. 12	Sep. 28	Oct. 02	Oct. 13 '95

Data as orig. reptd.; bef. results of disc. opers. and/or spec. items. Per share data adj. for stk. divs. as of ex-div. date. EPS for 3Q 1993 represent 9 mos. results. E-Estimated. NA-Not Available. NM-Not Meaningful. NR-Not Ranked.

Office—One Univac Lane, Windsor, CT 06095. **Tel**—(203) 285-6100. **Chrmn & CEO**—R. Kamerschen. **Pres**—J. P. Durrett. **Senior Exec VP**—L. G. Morris. **EVP-CFO**—L. W. Robinson. **SVP-Secy**—D. M. Stigler. **Dirs**—J. P. Durrett, J. W. Fritz, R. Kamerschen, L. Lachman, L. G. Morris, H. H. Newman, J. R. Rockwell, R. H. Stowe, J. L. Vogelstein. **Transfer Agent & Registrar**—Mellon Securities Transfer Services, East Hartford, Conn. **Incorporated** in Delaware in 1971. **Empl**-5,500. **S&P Analyst:** Stephen Madonna, CFA

STANDARD & POOR'S STOCK REPORTS

Air Express International

NASDAQ Symbol **AEIC**
In S&P SmallCap 600

15-AUG-95

Industry: Transportation

Summary: This worldwide air freight forwarder also provides ancillary transportation-related services. Foreign markets contribute a majority of revenues.

S&P Opinion: Hold (★★★)

Recent Price • 23¾
52 Wk Range • 26½-15⅛
Yield • 0.9%
12-Mo. P/E • 16.6

Quantitative Evaluations

Outlook
(1 Lowest—5 Highest)
• 1+

Fair Value
• 19¾

Risk
• **Average**

Earn./Div. Rank
• **B+**

Technical Eval.
• **Bullish** since 2/94

Rel. Strength Rank
(1 Lowest—99 Highest)
• **21**

Insider Activity
• **NA**

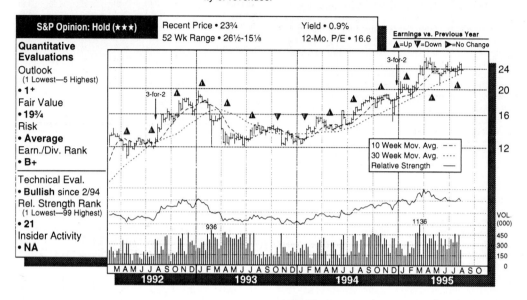

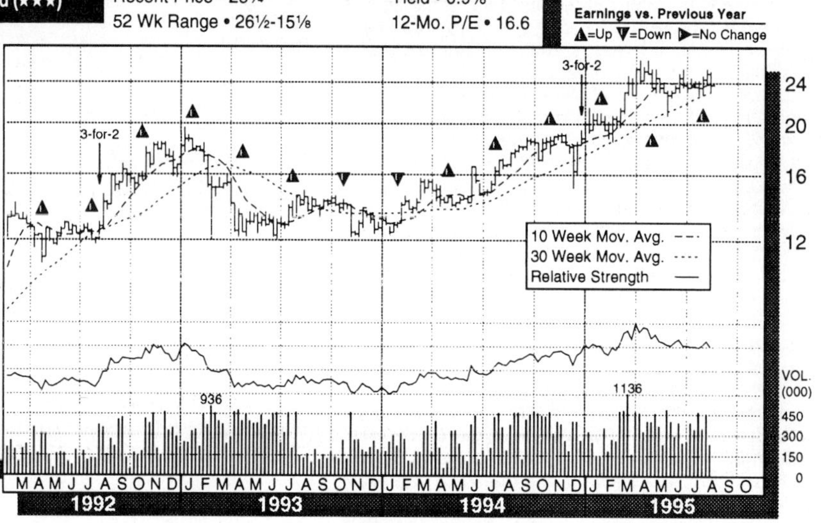

Overview - 15-AUG-95

Sales for 1995 are expected to rise significantly from those of 1994, aided by recent acquisitions. The worldwide economic recovery, as well as a trend toward greater international trade, should contribute to the growth. The average shipment weight is forecast to increase again in 1995, reflecting company efforts to secure higher-weight business. Pricing will remain competitive, but cost-cutting programs should minimize the margin erosion. Restraining profitability will be another disappointing year in Germany, where costs continue to outpace revenue growth.

Valuation - 15-AUG-95

As an air freight forwarder, Air Express is vulnerable to the pace of economic growth--customers generally attempt to reduce shipment sizes and identify alternative transportation modes during more difficult times. However, AEIC is somewhat insulated from the U.S. slowdown, due to its large proportion of international activity. In addition, the company is trying to realize more stable revenues and higher margins by increasing the services component in its shipments, thereby forging closer ties with its customers. The long-term outlook is positive, but domestic competitive pressures are expected to restrain near-term earnings. Accordingly, we view the shares are fairly valued.

Key Stock Statistics

S&P EPS Est. 1995	1.45	Tang. Bk. Value/Share	2.91
P/E on S&P Est. 1995	16.4	Beta	0.98
S&P EPS Est. 1996	1.75	Shareholders	1,000
Dividend Rate/Share	0.20	Market cap. (B)	$0.430
Shs. outstg. (M)	18.5	Inst. holdings	69%
Avg. daily vol. (M)	0.079	Insider holdings	NA

Value of $10,000 invested 5 years ago: $ 55,941

Fiscal Year Ending Dec. 31

	1995	% Change	1994	% Change	1993	% Change
Revenues ()						
1Q	284.1	39%	204.8	34%	153.0	-1%
2Q	304.4	28%	238.0	41%	168.5	NM
3Q	—	—	258.1	34%	192.1	12%
4Q	—	—	296.4	40%	211.8	21%
Yr.	—	—	997.4	37%	725.7	8%
Income ()						
1Q	5.11	47%	3.48	NM	3.45	7%
2Q	7.56	23%	6.15	15%	5.35	5%
3Q	—	—	6.31	68%	3.75	-29%
4Q	—	—	6.68	39%	4.79	-4%
Yr.	—	—	22.62	30%	17.34	-7%
Earnings Per Share ()						
1Q	0.29	45%	0.20	3%	0.19	4%
2Q	0.42	19%	0.35	15%	0.31	5%
3Q	E0.41	14%	0.36	69%	0.21	-29%
4Q	E0.33	-13%	0.38	39%	0.27	-5%
Yr.	E1.45	13%	1.28	29%	0.99	-8%

Next earnings report expected: late October

Air Express International

Business Summary - 15-AUG-95

Air Express International Corporation is a worldwide air freight forwarder. The company also offers freight forwarding by sea and various support services. Contributions by geographic region in 1994 were:

	Revs.	Profits
U.S.	37%	27%
Europe	32%	41%
Asia & other	31%	32%

An air freight forwarder obtains shipments from or for its customers, consolidates those bound for common destinations and delivers them in bulk to air carriers for transportation to various distribution points. Company employees or agents receive the shipments and distribute individual parcels to their final destinations. AEI neither owns nor operates any aircraft or ships.

At December 31, 1994, the company served 552 cities--230 in the U.S., 122 in Europe and 200 in Asia and other areas. Of the worldwide total, 188 cities were served by company-owned facilities and 364 by agents. In 1994, there were 1,630,000 shipments with an average weight of 483 pounds.

Air Express also provides ancillary services, such as door-to-door pickup and delivery of freight, warehousing and distribution, cargo assembly, protective packing, consolidation and customs clearance. Other transportation-related services include acting as a domestic surface freight forwarder, a customs broker and a warehouse operator.

The company's LOGIS logistics information system provides electronic interfacing with customers' computer systems, supplying shipment information, customs services and order entry and billing services.

In 1994, Air Express acquired Unimodal Australia Pty. Ltd., an ocean freight forwarder based in Australia; Banner International Ltd., an air freight forwarder located in New Zealand; and Pace Express Pty. Ltd., an air freight forwarder located in Australia. The company also purchased a 75% interest in Universal Airfreight AS, AEI's exclusive air freight agent in Norway.

Important Developments

Jun. '95—Air Express acquired Radix Group, Inc. for approximately 980,000 AEIC common shares and $0.5 million in cash. The U.S. customs broker, which also provides air freight and ocean freight forwarding services, had gross revenues of $65 million in 1994.

Capitalization

Long Term Debt: $86,278,000 (3/95), incl. $72.6 million of sub. debs. due 2003 & conv. into com. at $18.67 a sh.

Per Share Data () (Year Ended Dec. 31)

	1994	1993	1992	1991	1990	1989
Tangible Bk. Val.	2.72	2.35	2.31	2.19	1.36	0.52
Cash Flow	1.72	1.35	1.49	1.12	0.99	0.75
Earnings	1.28	0.99	1.08	0.80	0.67	0.51
Dividends	0.19	0.11	0.08	0.03	Nil	Nil
Payout Ratio	14%	11%	8%	4%	Nil	Nil
Prices - High	20	19⅝	18⅜	9⅝	5⅝	5¾
- Low	12¼	12	8¾	4¼	3⅛	4⅛
P/E Ratio - High	16	20	17	12	8	11
- Low	10	12	8	5	5	8

Income Statement Analysis ()

	1994	%Chg	1993	%Chg	1992	%Chg	1991
Revs.	997	37%	726	8%	672	12%	602
Oper. Inc.	45.9	22%	37.7	-3%	39.0	29%	30.2
Depr.	7.6	21%	6.3	-10%	7.1	28%	5.5
Int. Exp.	3.2	-14%	3.7	70%	2.2	-15%	2.6
Pretax Inc.	36.8	31%	28.0	-6%	29.9	30%	23.0
Eff. Tax Rate	39%	—	38%	—	38%	—	40%
Net Inc.	22.6	31%	17.3	-7%	18.6	35%	13.8

Balance Sheet & Other Fin. Data ()

	1994	1993	1992	1991	1990	1989
Cash	44.2	65.2	14.1	27.9	19.9	14.1
Curr. Assets	253	219	147	151	138	128
Total Assets	381	296	208	208	193	180
Curr. Liab.	194	139	136	118	112	107
LT Debt	84.0	78.5	7.1	24.9	28.4	32.3
Common Eqty.	99	78.1	65.4	65.3	52.4	40.5
Total Cap.	185	158	72.5	90.2	80.9	72.8
Cap. Exp.	12.1	4.9	15.2	6.8	6.4	3.0
Cash Flow	30.3	23.6	25.7	19.3	16.3	12.7

Ratio Analysis

	1994	1993	1992	1991	1990	1989
Curr. Ratio	1.3	1.6	1.1	1.3	1.2	1.2
% LT Debt of Cap.	45.4	49.8	9.8	27.6	35.2	44.4
% Net Inc.of Revs.	2.3	2.4	2.8	2.3	1.9	1.7
% Ret. on Assets	6.7	6.9	8.8	6.9	5.9	4.6
% Ret. on Equity	25.4	24.2	28.2	23.3	23.5	22.8

Dividend Data —Dividends, omitted in 1982, were resumed in 1991.

Amt. of Div. $	Date Decl.	Ex-Div. Date	Stock of Record	Payment Date
0.060	Sep. 09	Oct. 03	Oct. 07	Oct. 28 '94
3-for-2	Nov. 17	Dec. 22	Dec. 05	Dec. 21 '94
0.040	Nov. 17	Dec. 30	Jan. 06	Jan. 27 '95
0.040	Mar. 10	Apr. 03	Apr. 07	Apr. 28 '95
0.050	Jun. 23	Jul. 05	Jul. 07	Jul. 28 '95

Data as orig. reptd.; bef. results of disc. opers. and/or spec. items. Per share data adj. for stk. divs. as of ex-div. date. E-Estimated. NA-Not Available. NM-Not Meaningful. NR-Not Ranked.

Office—120 Tokeneke Road, Darien, CT 06820. **Tel**—(203) 655-7900. **Chrmn**—H. J. Hartong Jr. **Pres & CEO**—G. Rohrmann. **VP, CFO & Investor Contact**—Dennis M. Dolan (203) 655-5713. **VP & Secy**—D. J. McCauley. **Dirs**—J. M. Fowler, H. J. Hartong Jr., D. J. Keller, A. L. Lewis IV, R. T. Niner, G. Rohrmann. **Registrar & Transfer Agent**—Chemical Mellon Shareholder Services, NYC. **Incorporated** in Illinois in 1946; reincorporated in Delaware in 1982. **Empl**-4,783. **S&P Analyst:** Joe Victor Shammas

STANDARD & POOR'S

STOCK REPORTS

Alex. Brown Inc.

NYSE Symbol **AB**
In S&P SmallCap 600

23-AUG-95 **Industry:** Securities

Summary: Alex. Brown Inc. is a major investment banking and securities brokerage firm based in Baltimore, Md.

S&P Opinion: No Opinion

Recent Price • 59¾ | 52 Wk Range • 60¼-25 | Yield • 1.4% | 12-Mo. P/E • 12.4

Quantitative Evaluations

Outlook
(1 Lowest—5 Highest)
• **NA**

Fair Value
• **NA**

Risk
• **Average**

Earn./Div. Rank
• **B**

Technical Eval.
• **Bullish** since 8/95

Rel. Strength Rank
(1 Lowest—99 Highest)
• **93**

Insider Activity
• **Neutral**

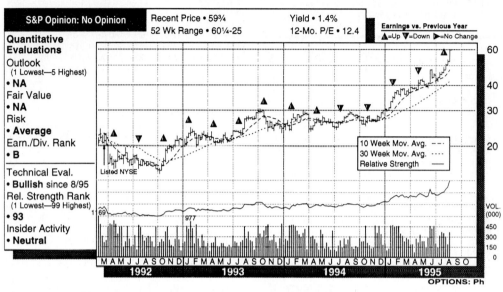

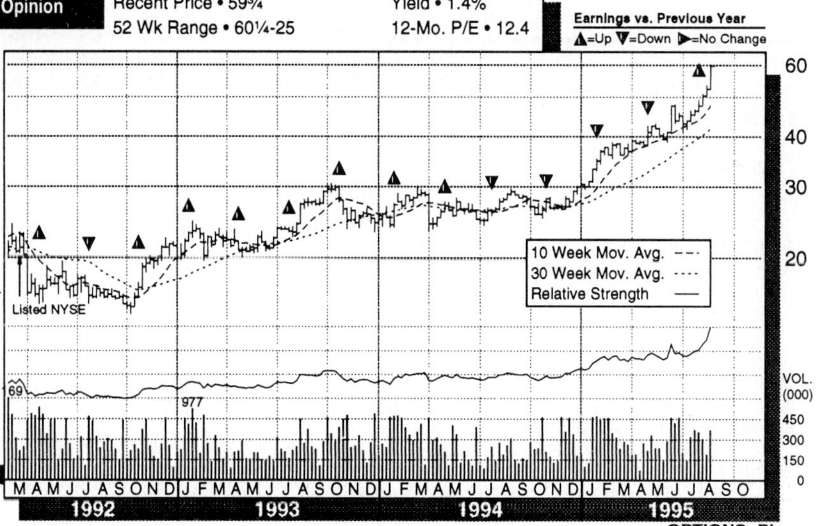

OPTIONS: Ph

Overview - 23-AUG-95

Profits are expected to improve further in 1996. AB obtains a large percentage of its profits from initial public offerings (IPOS) and mergers and acquisitions, two areas that are doing well and which carry high margins. IPOs are benefiting from the strong stock market and AB's strong presence in technology. Mergers and acquisitions has been aided by the trend toward consolidation in many industries. Commission income should benefit from the bull market and greater relative attractiveness of stocks compared with bonds. The strong market and lower rates should stimulate the company's investment banking business. Principal transactions should benefit from more active trading. Interest and dividends (net) will be aided by lower financing costs. Asset management fees are likely to increase.

Valuation - 23-AUG-95

The shares are up sharply from their 1994 low in response to the early 1995 drop in interest rates, solid earnings, and takeover speculation. Rumored buyers include a large commercial bank that wants to enter the investment banking business following the anticipated demise of Glass-Steagall or a foreign bank needing a U.S. partner to have a global presence. Price to book value is the preferred measure to use in valuing brokers because their highly liquid balance sheets can be readily marked to market. As of mid-August 1995, AB shares were trading at more than a 80% premium to book value, near a historical high.

Key Stock Statistics

S&P EPS Est. 1995	5.45	Tang. Bk. Value/Share	28.34
P/E on S&P Est. 1995	11.0	Beta	2.41
S&P EPS Est. 1996	6.00	Shareholders	600
Dividend Rate/Share	0.80	Market cap. (B)	$0.894
Shs. outstg. (M)	15.4	Inst. holdings	48%
Avg. daily vol. (M)	0.065	Insider holdings	NA

Value of $10,000 invested 5 years ago: $ 62,561

Fiscal Year Ending Dec. 31

	1995	% Change	1994	% Change	1993	% Change
Revenues (Million $)						
1Q	151.3	-7%	162.4	16%	139.7	13%
2Q	201.1	40%	143.9	11%	130.0	31%
3Q	—	—	145.4	4%	139.7	33%
4Q	—	—	153.8	-30%	218.8	71%
Yr.	—	—	605.5	-4%	628.2	38%
Income (Million $)						
1Q	16.40	-29%	23.02	15%	20.08	19%
2Q	22.99	59%	14.49	-3%	15.00	56%
3Q	—	—	13.28	-13%	15.23	37%
4Q	—	—	20.08	-48%	38.91	85%
Yr.	—	—	70.87	-21%	89.23	52%
Earnings Per Share ($)						
1Q	1.10	-25%	1.46	14%	1.28	22%
2Q	1.50	61%	0.93	-2%	0.95	58%
3Q	E1.35	55%	0.87	-8%	0.95	34%
4Q	E1.50	12%	1.34	-45%	2.42	77%
Yr.	E5.45	18%	4.60	-18%	5.61	51%

Next earnings report expected: mid October

Alex. Brown Inc.

Business Summary - 23-AUG-95

Alex. Brown Inc. is the parent of Alex. Brown & Sons, a major investment banking and securities brokerage firm that provides investment services to individuals and domestic and international institutional investors and provides investment banking services to corporate and municipal clients. Revenues in recent years:

	1994	1993	1992
Investment banking	33%	40%	37%
Principal transactions	20%	21%	20%
Interest & dividends	11%	8%	8%
Commissions	23%	21%	24%
Advisory & other	13%	10%	11%

At 1994 year-end, investment services to individual investors were provided through 434 investment representatives at 19 offices around the country. Average production of the investment representatives was $485,000.

Alex. Brown's mission is to be the leading investment bank in each of its seven core industries: consumer, environmental, financial services, health care, media/communications, technology and transportation.

The primary focus of AB's merchant banking business is the acquisition of companies with annual sales of $25 million to $250 million. As of December 31, 1994, merchant banking investments totaled $13.6 million, down from $16.6 million a year ago. AB also manages investment portfolios on behalf of retirement plans, foundations, endowments and high net worth individuals. At 1994 year-end, the firm was receiving fees as adviser, distributor or administrator for $7.3 billion in assets, down from $9.2 billion a year earlier.

At March 31, 1995 Alex. Brown had aggregate net capital of $225.8 million, which exceeded the minimum net capital requirements by $208.6 million.

Important Developments

Jul. '95—The company said that it filed a shelf registration statement covering the offering of up to $150 million of debt securities or convertible debt securities.

Capitalization

Long Term Debt: $64,491,000 (3/95), incl. $24.6 million of sub. debs. conv. into com. at $26.03 per sh.

Per Share Data ($)

(Year Ended Dec. 31)

	1994	1993	1992	1991	1990	1989
Tangible Bk. Val.	26.13	21.83	18.06	14.65	11.51	11.15
Cash Flow	NA	NA	NA	NA	NA	NA
Earnings	4.60	5.61	3.72	3.36	0.50	0.65
Dividends	0.65	0.55	0.43	0.31	0.25	0.17
Payout Ratio	14%	10%	11%	9%	50%	27%
Prices - High	30$^{3}/_{8}$	30$^{1}/_{2}$	27$^{3}/_{4}$	25$^{1}/_{2}$	15$^{7}/_{8}$	14$^{1}/_{2}$
- Low	23$^{1}/_{4}$	19$^{5}/_{8}$	14$^{1}/_{2}$	8$^{1}/_{4}$	6$^{3}/_{4}$	9$^{1}/_{2}$
P/E Ratio - High	7	5	7	8	32	22
- Low	5	3	4	2	14	15

Income Statement Analysis (Million $)

	1994	%Chg	1993	%Chg	1992	%Chg	1991
Commissions	140	6%	132	21%	109	16%	94.0
Int. Inc.	68.6	39%	49.3	34%	36.8	-7%	39.6
Total Revs.	605	-4%	628	38%	456	11%	411
Int. Exp.	21.9	47%	14.9	41%	10.6	-13%	12.2
Pretax Inc.	118	-20%	148	55%	95.4	14%	83.4
Eff. Tax Rate	40%	—	40%	—	39%	—	38%
Net Inc.	70.9	-21%	89.2	52%	58.6	13%	52.0

Balance Sheet & Other Fin. Data (Million $)

	1994	1993	1992	1991	1990	1989
Total Assets	1,346	1,283	1,085	866	787	944
Cash Items	24.0	57.0	87.1	82.1	57.9	8.9
Receivables	1,078	1,015	849	663	492	498
Secs. Owned	93.4	79.0	67.0	59.0	183	391
Sec. Borrowed	72.9	66.0	65.4	22.2	21.9	28.7
Due Brokers & Cust.	587	521	606	461	507	628
Other Liabs.	254	295	111	134	62.9	84.6
Capitalization:						
Debt	59.4	56.1	28.7	26.7	24.5	24.4
Equity	373	346	274	222	170	178
Total	433	402	303	248	194	202

Ratio Analysis

	1994	1993	1992	1991	1990	1989
% Ret. on Revs.	11.7	14.2	12.9	12.7	2.9	3.7
% Ret. on Assets	5.4	7.5	6.0	6.3	0.9	1.2
% Ret. on Equity	19.7	28.8	23.6	26.5	4.5	6.1

Dividend Data —Quarterly dividend payments began in 1986.

Amt. of Div. $	Date Decl.	Ex-Div. Date	Stock of Record	Payment Date
0.175	Oct. 18	Oct. 24	Oct. 28	Nov. 08 '94
0.175	Jan. 25	Jan. 31	Feb. 06	Feb. 15 '95
0.175	Apr. 24	Apr. 25	May. 01	May. 10 '95
0.200	Jul. 25	Aug. 03	Aug. 07	Aug. 16 '95

Data as orig. reptd.; bef. results of disc opers. and/or spec. items. Per share data adj. for stk. divs. as of ex-div. date. E-Estimated. NA-Not Available. NM-Not Meaningful. NR-Not Ranked.

Office—135 E. Baltimore St., Baltimore, MD 21202. **Tel**—(410) 727-1700. **Chrmn & CEO**—A. B. Krongard. **Pres & COO**—M. A. Shattuck. **Treas, CFO & Investor Contact**—Beverly L. Wright. **Secy**—R. F. Price. **Dirs**—L. A. Ault III, T. C. Barry, A. W. Brewster, B. H. Griswold IV, D. B. Hebb, Jr., A. B. Krongard, S. Muller, D. M. Norman, F. E. Richardson, M. A. Shattuck. **Transfer Agent & Registrar**—Chemical Bank, NYC. **Incorporated** in Maryland in 1986. **Empl**-2,300. **S&P Analyst:** Paul L. Huberman, CFA

STANDARD & POOR'S

STOCK REPORTS

Allen Group

NYSE Symbol **ALN**
In S&P SmallCap 600

14-NOV-95 **Industry:** Telecommunications

Summary: This company is primarily engaged in supplying equipment and services to the two-way wireless communications marketplace.

Quantitative Evaluations

Outlook
(1 Lowest—5 Highest)
• **2+**

Fair Value
• **25¼**

Risk
• **Average**

Earn./Div. Rank
• **B**

Technical Eval.
• **Bearish** since 10/95

Rel. Strength Rank
(1 Lowest—99 Highest)
• **14**

Insider Activity
• **Neutral**

Recent Price • 26¾
52 Wk Range • 39⅜-21¼
Yield • 0.8%
12-Mo. P/E • 20.6

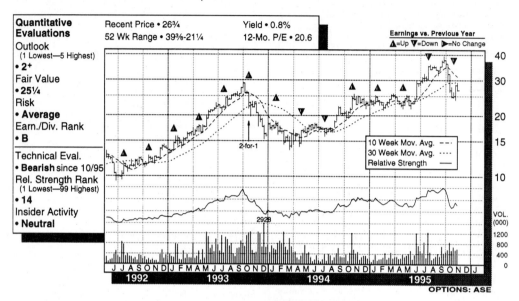

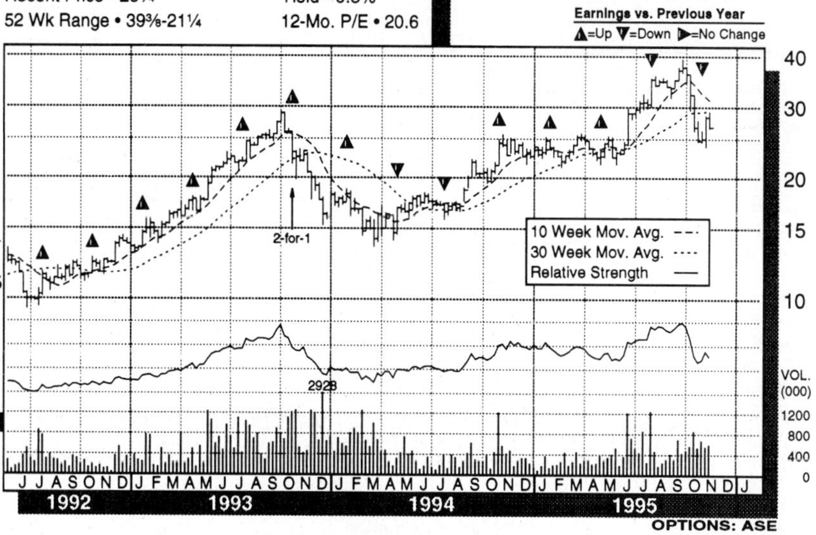

Business Profile - 14-NOV-95

Allen Group has evolved in recent years from a primary involvement in several segments of the automotive industry into a manufacturer of mobile telecommunications products. The company recently completed its evolution into a telecommunications company by spinning off most of its remaining automotive operations. ALN's growth in the next few years will be tied to the development of the next generation of cellular telecommunications systems employing PCS (Personal Communications Systems) standards.

Operational Review - 14-NOV-95

Year-to-date revenues (from continuing operations) were up nearly 50%, from the prior year period. This jump in sales was due to internal growth in the Mobile Communications businesses, the impact of the acquisition of 80% of FOR.E.M. S.p.A., and the geographic expansion of Marta's emissions testing program. The company noted that the strong order level in the Mobile Communications division resulted in record backlog levels at the end of the third quarter.

Stock Performance - 10-NOV-95

In the past 30 trading days, ALN's shares have declined 26%, compared to a 1% rise in the S&P 500. Average trading volume for the past five days was 116,820 shares, compared with the 40-day moving average of 115,545 shares.

Key Stock Statistics

Dividend Rate/Share	0.20	Shareholders	2,300
Shs. outstg. (M)	26.5	Market cap. (B)	$0.698
Avg. daily vol. (M)	0.112	Inst. holdings	81%
Tang. Bk. Value/Share	6.68	Insider holdings	NA
Beta	1.22		

Value of $10,000 invested 5 years ago: NA

Fiscal Year Ending Dec. 31

	1995	% Change	1994	% Change	1993	% Change
Revenues (Million $)						
1Q	92.08	20%	76.94	17%	66.00	5%
2Q	83.88	3%	81.77	18%	69.41	2%
3Q	88.30	5%	84.48	29%	65.60	-16%
4Q	—	—	88.16	12%	79.00	-9%
Yr.	—	—	331.4	18%	280.0	-5%
Income (Million $)						
1Q	7.06	31%	5.39	7%	5.02	45%
2Q	6.50	NM	6.47	-7%	6.95	48%
3Q	7.61	-11%	8.57	13%	7.56	37%
4Q	—	—	8.76	6%	8.25	32%
Yr.	—	—	29.19	-1%	29.52	48%
Earnings Per Share ($)						
1Q	0.27	29%	0.21	-26%	0.29	119%
2Q	0.24	-4%	0.25	-14%	0.29	53%
3Q	0.28	-15%	0.33	10%	0.30	30%
4Q	—	—	0.33	3%	0.32	23%
Yr.	—	—	1.12	-6%	1.19	47%

Next earnings report expected: late February

Allen Group

Business Summary - 14-NOV-95

Allen Group is a leading supplier to the worldwide two-way wireless communications marketplace of systems expansion, site management products and antennas; provides frequency planning, systems engineering services and design programs to current and emerging wireless markets; and operates centralized automotive emissions inspection programs. Sales and profit (in million of dollars) in 1994 were approximately:

	Sales	Profits
Mobile communications	98.8%	$39.3
Auto test & service	1.2%	-1.2

The mobile communications segment includes Allen Telecom and Comsearch. Allen Telecom produces telecommunications equipment, including Extend-A-Cell, paging repeaters, in-building repeaters and power amplifier systems, base station antennas, filters, combiners, isolators, duplexers, mobile antennas, and cellular phone accessories. Comsearch provides transmission planning services and software for microwave, satellite earth station, mobile and PCN communications markets. Extend-A-Cell systems, which have grown rapidly in recent years, provide inexpensive means to extend cellular telephone coverage into remote areas or areas with poor coverage within a cellular network. ALN expects to develop significant opportunities over the next few years to provide equipment and services in support of the telecommunications industry's expected rapid development of Personal Communications Systems (PCS), following government wide-band PCS frequency auctions during 1995.

Marta Technologies operates centralized auto emissions testing facilities in Maryland and Jacksonville, Florida. Marta was awarded contracts to operate programs in El Paso, Texas, Cincinnati, Ohio, and Northern Kentucky. Start-up of the El Paso program and bidding on additional programs in other states has been delayed by a change in the U.S. Environmental Protection Agency's position to one of allowing greater flexibility in designing state programs.

In September 1995, the company completed a planned spin-off the entire truck products segment into a new entity TransPro. This division accounted for approximately 35% of total (pre-spin-off) sales in 1994.

Important Developments

Sep. '95—ALN completed the spin-off its wholly owned subsidiary, TransPro, Inc. One share of common stock of TransPro (NYSE:TPR) was distributed for every four shares of ALN held. TransPro is comprised of three independent operating units: the Crown and G&O Manufacturing Co. units and GO/DAN Industries.

Capitalization

Long Term Debt: $31,900,000 (6/95).

Per Share Data ($)

(Year Ended Dec. 31)

	1994	1993	1992	1991	1990	1989
Tangible Bk. Val.	6.30	7.52	1.96	4.45	3.77	4.04
Cash Flow	1.47	1.56	1.18	1.01	0.08	0.82
Earnings	1.12	1.19	0.81	0.68	-0.29	0.34
Dividends	0.17	0.22	0.10	0.05	Nil	Nil
Payout Ratio	15%	18%	13%	7%	Nil	Nil
Prices - High	25⅝	29¼	15	10⅛	9⅛	7⅝
- Low	13½	13	9½	4½	4½	4⅛
P/E Ratio - High	23	25	19	15	NM	23
- Low	12	11	12	7	NM	12

Income Statement Analysis (Million $)

	1994	%Chg	1993	%Chg	1992	%Chg	1991
Revs.	331	18%	280	-5%	296	13%	262
Oper. Inc.	56.8	29%	44.1	6%	41.5	26%	33.0
Depr.	9.2	10%	8.4	13%	7.4	16%	6.3
Int. Exp.	4.4	38%	3.2	-53%	6.8	-3%	7.0
Pretax Inc.	46.9	42%	33.0	39%	23.7	29%	18.4
Eff. Tax Rate	38%	—	11%	—	16%	—	9.40%
Net Inc.	29.2	-1%	29.5	48%	19.9	20%	16.6

Balance Sheet & Other Fin. Data (Million $)

	1994	1993	1992	1991	1990	1989
Cash	55.2	11.2	4.4	7.5	0.8	22.7
Curr. Assets	178	131	164	159	179	186
Total Assets	358	325	388	308	330	318
Curr. Liab.	70.0	59.0	NA	NA	70.0	73.0
LT Debt	45.0	52.0	131	93.0	114	101
Common Eqty.	224	195	102	84.0	71.0	74.0
Total Cap.	271	247	291	236	242	233
Cap. Exp.	8.9	11.4	6.7	5.0	6.6	7.4
Cash Flow	38.4	35.7	23.3	18.9	1.4	14.9

Ratio Analysis

	1994	1993	1992	1991	1990	1989
Curr. Ratio	2.5	2.2	NA	NA	2.5	2.6
% LT Debt of Cap.	16.6	21.0	45.1	39.5	47.1	43.2
% Net Inc.of Revs.	8.8	10.5	6.7	6.3	NM	2.8
% Ret. on Assets	8.5	7.1	5.6	5.2	NM	3.1
% Ret. on Equity	13.9	16.7	16.6	16.2	NM	9.2

Dividend Data —Dividends were resumed in 1991 after omission in 1987. Prior to that, dividends had been paid since 1973. A "poison pill" stock purchase rights plan was adopted in 1988.

Amt. of Div. $	Date Decl.	Ex-Div. Date	Stock of Record	Payment Date
0.050	Dec. 08	Dec. 13	Dec. 19	Jan. 09 '95
0.050	Feb. 23	Mar. 02	Mar. 08	Apr. 06 '95
0.050	Apr. 28	Jun. 01	Jun. 07	Jul. 03 '95
Stk.	Sep. 08	Oct. 11	Sep. 29	Oct. 10 '95

Data as orig. reptd.; bef. results of disc. opers. and/or spec. items. Per share data adj. for stk. divs. as of ex-div. date. E-Estimated. NA-Not Available. NM-Not Meaningful. NR-Not Ranked.

Office—25101 Chagrin Boulevard, Beachwood, OH 44122. **Tel**—(216) 765-5800. **Chrmn**—P. W. Colburn. **Pres & CEO**—R. G. Paul. **Secy**—M. P. Folan III. **VP-Fin & Investor Contact**—R. A. Youdelman. **Dirs**—G. A. Chandler, P. W. Colburn, J. K. Conway, A. H. Gordon, W. O. Hunt, J. C. Lyons, R. G. Paul, C. W. Robinson, R. S. Vokey, W. M. Weaver Jr. **Transfer Agent & Registrar**—Harris Trust Co., NYC. **Incorporated** in Michigan in 1928; reincorporated in Delaware in 1969. **Empl- S&P Analyst:** Steven Jaworski

STANDARD & POOR'S

STOCK REPORTS

Alliance Pharmaceutical

NASDAQ Symbol **ALLP**

In S&P SmallCap 600

06-OCT-95

Industry: Drugs-Generic and OTC

Summary: This biotechnology firm is developing drugs based on its perfluorochemical technology, including a blood substitute and an intrapulmonary oxygen carrier.

Quantitative Evaluations

Outlook
(1 Lowest—5 Highest)
• **NA**

Fair Value
• **NA**

Risk
• **High**

Earn./Div. Rank
• **C**

Technical Eval.
• **Bullish** since 12/94

Rel. Strength Rank
(1 Lowest—99 Highest)
• **97**

Insider Activity
• **Neutral**

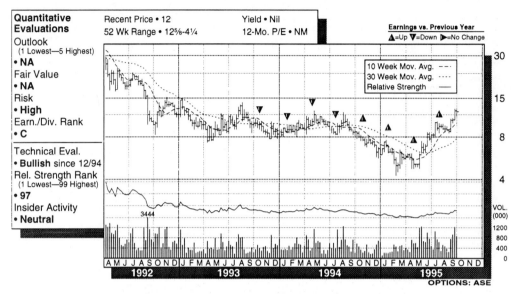

Recent Price • 12
52 Wk Range • 12⅝-4¼
Yield • Nil
12-Mo. P/E • NM

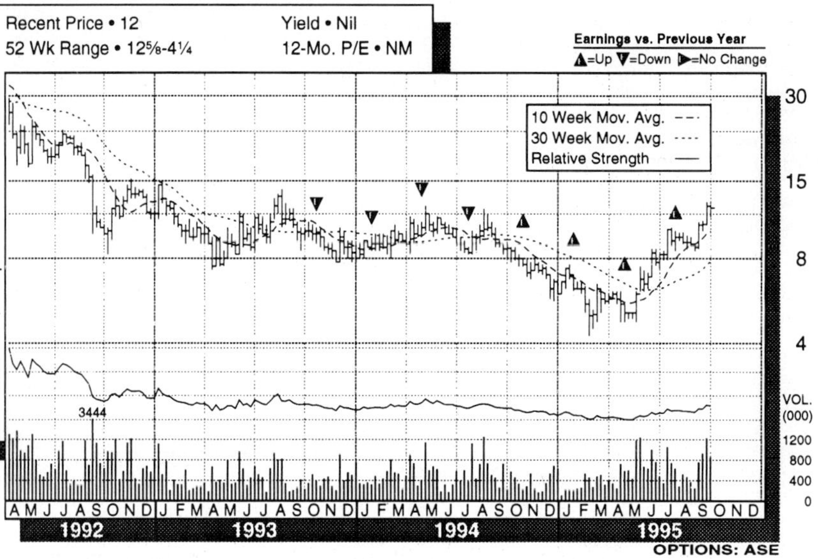

Business Profile - 06-OCT-95

Alliance is focusing on two lead drugs that use liquid perfluorochemical technology. Oxygent, a temporary intravascular oxygen carrier (blood substitute), is in clinical development, and LiquiVent, an oxygen carrier aiding in the treatment of respiratory distress syndrome, has recently begun Phase II trials. ALLP has collaborative research partnerships with Glaxo and Johnson & Johnson. The company derives most of its revenues from these partnerships as well as from equity offerings.

Operational Review - 06-OCT-95

Revenues (preliminary) in the fiscal year ended June 30, 1995, increased to $11.8 million, from $409,000 in the previous year, reflecting licensing payments from Johnson & Johnson affiliates for the development of Oxygent. Operating expenses rose to $42.1 million, versus $38.9 million, and the loss narrowed to $29,717,000 ($1.35 a share), from $36,946,000 ($1.83). ALLP expects to incur operating losses in the next several years.

Stock Performance - 29-SEP-95

In the past 30 trading days, ALLP's shares have increased 32%, compared to a 5% rise in the S&P 500. Average trading volume for the past five days was 167,600 shares, compared with the 40-day moving average of 142,259 shares.

Key Stock Statistics

Dividend Rate/Share	Nil	Shareholders	2,400
Shs. outstg. (M)	24.6	Market cap. (B)	$0.286
Avg. daily vol. (M)	0.221	Inst. holdings	32%
Tang. Bk. Value/Share	1.92	Insider holdings	NA
Beta	2.83		

Value of $10,000 invested 5 years ago: $ 10,265

Fiscal Year Ending Jun. 30

	1995	% Change	1994	% Change	1993	% Change
Revenues (Million $)						
1Q	5.18	NM	0.15	-80%	0.76	—
2Q	2.03	NM	0.10	-79%	0.48	—
3Q	2.48	NM	0.12	-79%	0.58	—
4Q	2.13	NM	0.04	-93%	0.55	—
Yr.	11.82	NM	0.41	-83%	2.37	—
Income (Million $)						
1Q	-8.13	NM	-7.84	—	—	—
2Q	-7.24	NM	-9.90	NM	-7.06	NM
3Q	-6.48	NM	-8.16	NM	-7.01	NM
4Q	-7.87	NM	-11.05	NM	-7.35	NM
Yr.	-29.72	NM	-36.95	NM	-26.38	NM
Earnings Per Share ($)						
1Q	-0.38	NM	-0.41	NM	-0.26	—
2Q	-0.34	NM	-0.52	NM	-0.37	—
3Q	-0.31	NM	-0.38	NM	-0.37	—
4Q	-0.32	NM	-0.52	NM	-0.39	—
Yr.	-1.35	NM	-1.83	NM	-1.39	—

Next earnings report expected: mid November

Alliance Pharmaceutical

Business Summary - 28-SEP-95

Alliance Pharmaceutical Corp. is developing medical therapeutic products based on perfluorochemical and emulsion technologies. These drug products include an intravascular oxygen carrier to prevent tissue hypoxia (oxygen deficiency); an intrapulmonary agent for use in the treatment of respiratory distress syndrome; and a diagnostic imaging agent for early detection of disease.

Alliance's therapeutic drug development efforts are based largely on a liquid perfluorochemical (PFC) known as perflubron. As a liquid PFC, perflubron is clear, colorless and nonflammable; however, it is twice as dense as water, will not conduct electricity, can dissolve gases in high concentrations and does not react with other chemicals. From a biological perspective, this means that perflubron does not generally affect bodily fluids and tissues.

Oxygent (perflubron emulsion) is in clinical development as a temporary intravascular oxygen carrier, or "blood substitute," for use in combination with autologous blood conservation methods to maintain tissue oxygenation during moderate- to high-blood-loss surgeries. Under an August 1994 agreement, Alliance is developing Oxygent with Ortho Biotech, Inc. and The R. W. Johnson Pharmaceutical Research Institute (both affiliates of Johnson & Johnson). Under the agreement, Alliance granted worldwide rights to the product in return for research funding, licensing and milestone fees and royalties.

LiquiVent (sterile perflubron) is being evaluated as an intrapulmonary oxygen carrier to treat respiratory distress syndrome, an acute disorder characterized by loss of normal lung function. Phase I/II trials to treat both infant and adult respiratory distress syndrome are near completion.

In November 1994, ALLP granted an exclusive license allowing Glaxo to use its fluorinated surfactants in certain metered-dose inhalers. The agreement provides for up-front payments of up to $2.5 million, plus future royalty payments.

Imagent US, a contrasting agent, is in preclinical development for use with ultrasound imaging. Sat Pad (approved in 1993) is a reusable product that improves the quality of images in certain magnetic resonance imaging techniques.

Important Developments

Jul. '95—The company commenced Phase II clinical trials for LiquiVent to treat adult patients suffering from acute respiratory failure. The FDA has granted Alliance Subpart E ("fast track") status in Liquivent tests due to the life threatening nature of the condition.
Apr. '95—The company completed a public offering of 3,175,000 common shares at $5 each. Net proceeds to the company approximated $14.5 million.

Capitalization

Long Term Debt: None (6/95).
Preferred Stock: 1,500,000 shs. ($0.01 par).

Per Share Data ($) (Year Ended Jun. 30)

	1995	1994	1993	1992	1991	1990
Tangible Bk. Val.	NA	2.33	2.68	3.99	0.91	1.93
Cash Flow	NA	-1.67	-1.24	-1.09	-1.02	-0.82
Earnings	-1.35	-1.83	-1.39	-1.25	-1.24	-0.94
Dividends	Nil	Nil	Nil	Nil	Nil	Nil
Payout Ratio	Nil	Nil	Nil	Nil	Nil	Nil
Prices - High	12⅝	12¼	15	44	32¼	12½
- Low	4¼	5⅝	7¼	8¼	9	5¼
P/E Ratio - High	NM	NM	NM	NM	NM	NM
- Low	NM	NM	NM	NM	NA	NA

Income Statement Analysis (Million $)

	1994	%Chg	1993	%Chg	1992	%Chg	1991
Revs.	0.4	-83%	2.4	31%	1.8	15%	1.6
Oper. Inc.	-35.4	NM	-25.8	NM	-19.8	NM	-15.4
Depr.	3.1	4%	3.0	6%	2.8	-10%	3.1
Int. Exp.	NM	—	0.0	-97%	0.3	-61%	0.9
Pretax Inc.	-36.9	NM	26.4	NM	-21.8	NM	-17.7
Eff. Tax Rate	NM	—	NM	—	Nil	—	Nil
Net Inc.	-36.9	NM	-26.4	NM	-21.8	NM	-17.7

Balance Sheet & Other Fin. Data (Million $)

	1994	1993	1992	1991	1990	1989
Cash	21.1	39.5	66.4	16.8	30.6	20.9
Curr. Assets	22.4	42.7	68.2	17.7	32.0	21.8
Total Assets	53.1	72.5	98.0	44.8	59.5	48.1
Curr. Liab.	3.0	3.0	2.7	2.0	2.1	1.9
LT Debt	Nil	Nil	0.2	8.3	8.5	8.6
Common Eqty.	49.8	69.1	94.6	33.9	48.8	37.5
Total Cap.	49.8	69.1	94.8	42.2	57.3	46.2
Cap. Exp.	1.9	2.5	3.6	1.3	3.0	0.9
Cash Flow	-33.9	-23.4	-19.0	-14.6	-10.9	-30.7

Ratio Analysis

	1994	1993	1992	1991	1990	1989
Curr. Ratio	7.6	14.5	25.6	8.7	15.0	11.3
% LT Debt of Cap.	Nil	Nil	0.2	19.8	14.8	18.7
% Net Inc.of Revs.	NM	NM	NM	NM	NM	NM
% Ret. on Assets	NM	NM	NM	NM	NM	NM
% Ret. on Equity	NM	NM	NM	NM	NM	NM

Dividend Data —No cash has been paid.

Data as orig. reptd.; bef. results of disc. opers. and/or spec. items. Per share data adj. for stk. divs. as of ex-div. date. E-Estimated. NA-Not Available. NM-Not Meaningful. NR-Not Ranked.

Office—3040 Science Park Rd., San Diego, CA 92121. **Tel**—(619) 558-4300. **Chrmn, Pres & CEO**—D. J. Roth. **Exec VP, CFO & Secy**—T. D. Roth. **Dirs**—C. O. Johnson, S. M. McGrath, D. E. O'Neill, H. M. Ranney, J. G. Riess, D. J. Roth, T. F. Zuck. **Transfer Agent & Registrar**—American Stock Transfer Co., NYC. **Incorporated** in New York in 1983. **Empl**-212. **S&P Analyst:** Thomas Tirney

STANDARD & POOR'S

STOCK REPORTS

Alliant Techsystems

NYSE Symbol **ATK**
In S&P SmallCap 600

08-AUG-95

Industry:
Arms/Ammunition

Summary: ATK, which conducts the former defense munitions and marine operations of Honeywell Inc., added the aerospace business of Hercules Inc. in March 1995.

S&P Opinion: Accumulate (★★★★)

Recent Price • 45½
52 Wk Range • 45⅝-27¼
Yield • Nil
12-Mo. P/E • NM

Quantitative Evaluations

Outlook
(1 Lowest—5 Highest)
• 1

Fair Value
• 39¼

Risk
• Average

Earn./Div. Rank
• NR

Technical Eval.
• Bearish since 7/95

Rel. Strength Rank
(1 Lowest—99 Highest)
• 83

Insider Activity
• Neutral

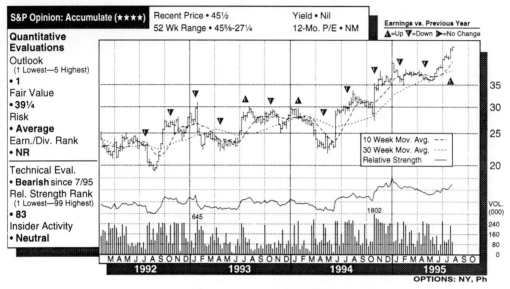

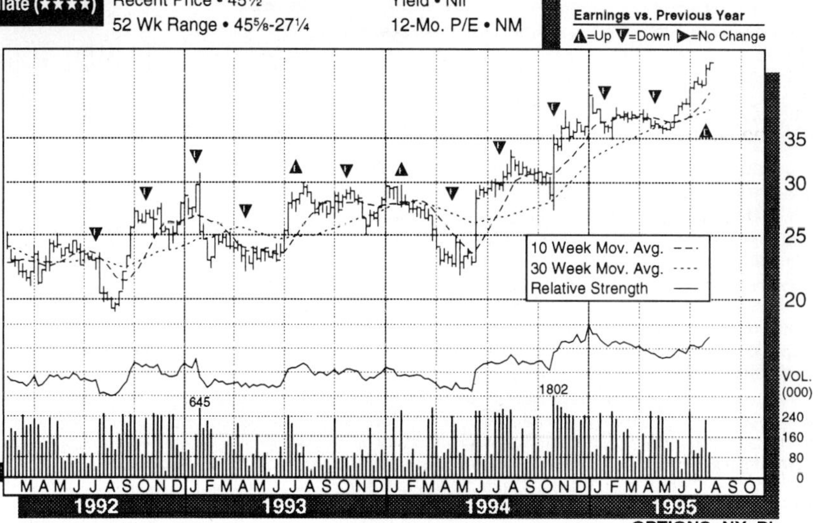

OPTIONS: NY, Ph

Overview - 08-AUG-95

Sales for 1995-6 are projected to climb substantially from those of 1994-5, reflecting the addition of Hercules' aerospace operations. On a pro forma basis, aerospace sales are expected to experience a 10% decline, reflecting the Titan and Trident programs. Marine systems revenues are expected to drop, due to the discontinuation of the Mk 50 Program. Defense systems revenues may edge up slightly. ATK's newly-formed emerging businesses unit is anticipated to achieve strong growth from demilitarization contracts. Earnings should improve from cost reduction efforts and the absence of certain large nonrecurring charges. However, higher interest charges, the resumption of taxes, and a greater number of outstanding shares will limit EPS improvement.

Valuation - 08-AUG-95

ATK shares have climbed in recent months following the purchase of the aerospace division and the election of R. K. Elliott as chairman. The stock has benefited from optimism that the larger company and new management will more effectively deal with the downtrend in government spending, and that recent restructuring efforts will improve weak margin performance. The new emerging business division should enable Alliant to expand its commercial operations. With Alliant better positioned for growth than it has been in years, and its shares trading at around 12 to 13 times estimated 1995-6 earnings, we view ATK stock as attractive.

Key Stock Statistics

S&P EPS Est. 1996	3.65	Tang. Bk. Value/Share	7.88
P/E on S&P Est. 1996	12.5	Beta	NA
Dividend Rate/Share	Nil	Shareholders	17,400
Shs. outstg. (M)	13.8	Market cap. (B)	$0.642
Avg. daily vol. (M)	0.029	Inst. holdings	59%
		Insider holdings	NA

Value of $10,000 invested 5 years ago: NA

Fiscal Year Ending Mar. 31

	1996	% Change	1995	% Change	1994	% Change
Revenues (Million $)						
1Q	292.9	73%	168.9	NM	168.5	-6%
2Q	—	—	137.2	NM	137.9	-52%
3Q	—	—	173.2	2%	169.7	-29%
4Q	—	—	309.7	3%	299.3	NM
Yr.	—	—	789.1	2%	775.3	-23%
Income (Million $)						
1Q	9.90	43%	6.92	-17%	8.38	84%
2Q	—	—	-14.19	NM	8.32	NM
3Q	—	—	3.75	-56%	8.57	NM
4Q	—	—	-69.08	NM	7.21	-18%
Yr.	—	—	-72.61	NM	32.47	NM
Earnings Per Share ($)						
1Q	0.73	7%	0.68	-18%	0.83	41%
2Q	E0.87	—	-1.44	NM	0.82	-20%
3Q	E1.00	—	0.37	-56%	0.84	NM
4Q	E1.05	—	-6.45	NM	0.71	-21%
Yr.	E3.65	—	-7.22	NM	3.21	NM

Next earnings report expected: mid November

Alliant Techsystems

Business Summary - 08-AUG-95

Alliant Techsystems, the former defense munitions and marine operations of Honeywell Inc., added the aerospace business of Hercules Inc. in March 1995. Hercules currently holds about a 30% stake in ATK. Contributions to sales in recent fiscal years were:

	1994-5	1993-4	1992-3
Aerospace	2%	---	---
Defense systems	60%	69%	73%
Marine systems	35%	29%	27%
Emerging business	3%	2%	---

In 1994-5, about 86% of sales were to the U.S. Government, versus 90% in 1993-4.

The Aerospace group produces solid propulsion systems, munitions propellants, defense electronics systems and composite structures. Major programs include strap-on boosters for the Titan IV and the Delta II rockets, the solid propulsion system for the Trident II missile, and rocket motors for the AMRAAM, TOW II, AGM-130, and Sparrow missiles.

The Defense Systems tank ammunition business comprises development and production of ammunition for the Army's M1A1 tank; and production of infantry weapons, artillery systems and air-delivered systems.

Marine Systems includes undersea weapons systems, mine countermeasure systems, acoustic sensors and signal processing systems, and undersea surveillance and range systems. It also provides engineering and testing services for information security. Major programs include the Mk 46 and MK 50 lightweight torpedoes, NT 37 heavyweight torpedo, and the AN/SQQ-89 anti-submarine warfare combat system.

The emerging business group provides demilitarization, environmental remediation, waste disposal, and safety management services. It also supplies batteries for military and commercial applications, and provides underseas acoustic processing/seismic equipment, secure data equipment, and simulation environments.

Important Developments

Jun. '95—ATK was awarded a $325 million contract by McDonnell Douglas to produce solid rocket propulsion systems for the Delta III space launch vehicle.
May '95—ATK noted that 1994-5 pretax results included $38 million in restructuring charges, $15 million in litigation settlement charges, and $25 million in charges related to a change of control and proxy contest.
Mar. '95—The company acquired Hercules Inc.'s aerospace division, which had annual revenues of about $640 million. The purchase price of $418 million consisted of $306 million in cash and 3.86 million new ATK shares. As planned, directors subsequently authorized a $50 million share repurchase program.

Capitalization

Long Term Debt: $383,751,000 (6/95).

Per Share Data ($) (Year Ended Mar. 31)

	1995	1994	1993	1992	1991	1990
Tangible Bk. Val.	7.88	6.44	5.21	16.92	NA	13.06
Cash Flow	-4.74	5.23	-2.03	7.50	NA	6.08
Earnings	-7.22	3.21	-4.68	4.57	NA	2.55
Dividends	Nil	Nil	Nil	Nil	NA	Nil
Payout Ratio	Nil	Nil	Nil	Nil	NA	Nil
Cal. Yrs.	1994	1993	1992	1991	1990	1989
Prices - High	40⅝	31	28⅝	29¼	15¼	NA
- Low	21¾	22	19⅛	13	8⅝	NA
P/E Ratio - High	NM	10	NM	6	6	NA
- Low	NM	7	NM	3	3	NA

Income Statement Analysis (Million $)

	1995	%Chg	1994	%Chg	1993	%Chg	1992
Revs.	789	2%	775	-23%	1,005	-15%	1,187
Oper. Inc.	42.6	-29%	60.0	-30%	86.0	-28%	120
Depr.	25.0	22%	20.5	-24%	26.9	-8%	29.2
Int. Exp.	11.4	39%	8.2	-64%	22.7	40%	16.2
Pretax Inc.	-72.6	NM	32.5	NM	-70.3	NM	74.2
Eff. Tax Rate	NM	—	Nil	—	NM	—	38%
Net Inc.	-72.6	NM	32.5	NM	-45.2	NM	45.7

Balance Sheet & Other Fin. Data (Million $)

	1995	1994	1993	1992	1991	1990
Cash	26.5	50.9	81.3	74.5	NA	13.9
Curr. Assets	464	287	350	345	NA	344
Total Assets	1,052	438	457	522	NA	507
Curr. Liab.	336	255	229	209	NA	225
LT Debt	395	Nil	65.0	108	NA	136
Common Eqty.	140	92.0	66.0	178	NA	132
Total Cap.	539	109	141	298	NA	271
Cap. Exp.	19.3	20.7	11.3	19.5	NA	31.6
Cash Flow	-47.6	53.0	-18.3	74.9	NA	58.1

Ratio Analysis

	1995	1994	1993	1992	1991	1990
Curr. Ratio	1.4	1.1	1.5	1.7	NA	1.5
% LT Debt of Cap.	73.3	Nil	46.5	36.0	NA	50.4
% Net Inc.of Revs.	NM	4.2	NM	3.9	NA	2.0
% Ret. on Assets	NM	7.2	NM	8.8	NA	NA
% Ret. on Equity	NM	41.1	NM	29.2	NA	NA

Dividend Data (No cash dividends have been paid on the common stock since its distribution in October 1990. A "poison pill" purchase right was distributed with the common stock.)

Data as orig. reptd.; bef. results of disc. opers. and/or spec. items. Per share data adj. for stk. divs. as of ex-div. date. Prior to 1992, yr. ended Dec. 31. Results in FY 1995, FY 1993 include substantial restructuring charges. E-Estimated. NA-Not Available. NM-Not Meaningful. NR-Not Ranked.

Office—600 Second St., N.E., Hopkins, MN 55343-8384. **Tel**—(612) 931-6000. **Fax**—(612) 931-5423. **Chrmn**—R. K. Elliott. **Pres & CEO**—R. Schwartz. **VP & CFO**—D. M. Fjelstul. **Secy**—C. H. Gauck. **Investor Contact**—Richard N. Jowett (612-931-6080). **Dirs**—R. K. Elliott, T. L. Gossage, J. M. Greenblatt, J. G. Guss, D. E. Jeremiah, G. N. Kelley, J. F. Mazzella, D. L. Nir, R. Schwartz. **Transfer Agent & Registrar**—Chemical Mellon Shareholder Services, NYC. **Incorporated** in Delaware in 1990. **Empl**-8,200. **S&P Analyst:** Joe Victor Shammas

STANDARD & POOR'S

STOCK REPORTS

ALLIED Group

NASDAQ Symbol **ALGR**

In S&P SmallCap 600

02-SEP-95 **Industry:** Insurance

Summary: This regional property-casualty insurance holding company specializes in personal lines, and markets its products throughout the central and western United States.

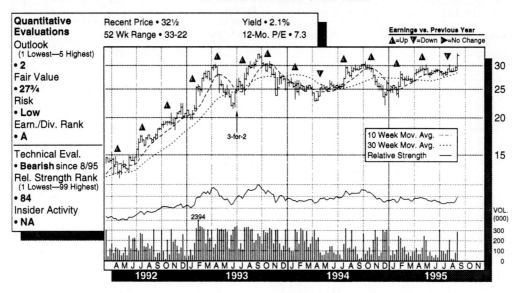

Quantitative Evaluations

Outlook (1 Lowest—5 Highest)
• **2**

Fair Value
• **27¾**

Risk
• **Low**

Earn./Div. Rank
• **A**

Technical Eval.
• **Bearish** since 8/95

Rel. Strength Rank (1 Lowest—99 Highest)
• **84**

Insider Activity
• **NA**

Recent Price • 32½ Yield • 2.1%
52 Wk Range • 33-22 12-Mo. P/E • 7.3

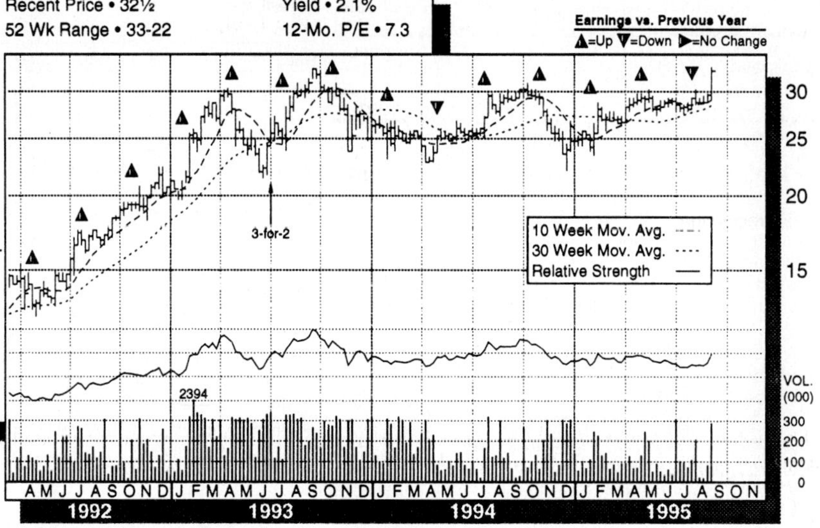

Business Profile - 01-SEP-95

ALGR has experienced steady improvement in its combined ratio and a 23.9% average return on equity over the recent four fiscal years. Management's stated goal is to maintain a 15% ROE by pursuing more transfer business, increasing its independent agency force, expanding its distribution system and building new territories. ALGR's debt to equity ratio at year-end 1994 was 36.73%, compared with 38.[illegible]5% for the property/casualty industry. Through an ESOP, employees control 29% of the voting shares.

Operational Review - 31-AUG-95

Revenues in the six months ended June 30, 1995, climbed 8.0%, year to year, reflecting a 10% increase in premiums earned, and a 14% rise in investment income. Total expenses were up 9.6%, paced by 12% higher losses and loss settlement costs related to adverse weather conditions in California and the Midwest. Pretax income was down 1.0%. After taxes at 28.5% versus 28.8%, net income slipped fractionally, to $25,140,492 ($2.36 a share; $1.69 fully diluted) from $25,307,149 ($2.40; $1.70).

Stock Performance - 01-SEP-95

In the past 30 trading days, ALGR's shares have increased 16%, compared to a 2% rise in the S&P 500. Average trading volume for the past five days was 56,780 shares, compared with the 40-day moving average of 21,690 shares.

Key Stock Statistics

Dividend Rate/Share	0.68	Shareholders	1,000
Shs. outstg. (M)	9.2	Market cap. (B)	$0.300
Avg. daily vol. (M)	0.020	Inst. holdings	73%
Tang. Bk. Value/Share	24.96	Insider holdings	NA
Beta	0.29		

Value of $10,000 invested 5 years ago: $ 41,875

Fiscal Year Ending Dec. 31

	1995	% Change	1994	% Change	1993	% Change
Revenues (Million $)						
1Q	132.3	10%	119.7	4%	114.8	8%
2Q	134.7	6%	127.3	6%	119.8	11%
3Q	—	—	127.1	NM	126.0	10%
4Q	—	—	133.2	9%	121.8	4%
Yr.	—	—	507.4	5%	482.4	8%
Income (Million $)						
1Q	12.38	8%	11.47	9%	10.48	35%
2Q	12.76	-8%	13.84	39%	9.99	51%
3Q	—	—	10.81	18%	9.14	33%
4Q	—	—	11.51	12%	10.32	39%
Yr.	—	—	47.62	19%	39.92	39%
Earnings Per Share ($)						
1Q	1.17	10%	1.06	NM	1.07	26%
2Q	1.19	-11%	1.34	47%	0.91	59%
3Q	—	—	1.00	25%	0.80	35%
4Q	—	—	1.07	16%	0.92	27%
Yr.	—	—	4.48	22%	3.68	36%

Next earnings report expected: late October

ALLIED Group

Business Summary - 01-SEP-95

ALLIED Group, Inc. is a regional holding company that writes, through subsidiaries, primarily personal automobile and homeowners lines of insurance. The company's subsidiaries also write commercial lines of insurance for small businesses, provide excess and surplus lines insurance, and offer investment and data processing services.

Contributions to pretax income by ongoing business segment in recent years:

	1994	1993
Property-casualty	81%	72%
Excess & surplus lines	7%	10%
Investment services	6%	10%
Data processing	6%	8%

Property-casualty insurance accounted for 85.0% of consolidated revenues in 1994. Products in this segment are marketed through three distribution systems: independent agencies, exclusive agencies, and direct mail and telemarketing. Effective January 1, 1993, the agreement was amended to increase the segment's participation in the pool to 64%, versus 60% previously.

The company's excess and surplus lines subsidiary, Western Heritage Insurance Co., primarily underwrites commercial property and casualty lines coverages that standard insurers are unable or unwilling to provide.

In 1994, the property-casualty segment had a statutory combined ratio of 97.1% (99.3% in 1993), which was divided by lines of business as follows: personal automobile 97.4% (98.3%), homeowners 107.4% (109.1%), and excess and surplus lines 99.9% (96.1%).

ALGR's investment services subsidiary originates, purchases and services single-family residential mortgages and acquires servicing rights from savings and loans, banks and other mortgage companies. Through its ALLIED Group Information Systems and The Freedom Group units, ALGR markets data processing services and a complete line of software products to affiliated and non-affiliated insurance companies.

Important Developments

Jul. '95—In reporting results for the second quarter, the company announced that for the 20th consecutive quarter, operating earnings exceeded those for the same period of the previous year. The combined and underwriting expense ratios improved, despite aftertax wind and hail losses of $0.76 per share for the six months, up from $0.42 in comparable 1994 period.

Capitalization

Notes Payable: $64,528,788 (6/95), incl. $3,460,000 payable to affiliates.
63/4% Series Pfd. Stk.: 1,827,222 shs. (no par). Owned by ALLIED Mutual; represents 15% ownership.
8% Conv. Pfd. Stk: 3,130,274 shs. (no par). Owned by ESOP; represents 29% ownership.

Per Share Data ($) (Year Ended Dec. 31)

	1994	1993	1992	1991	1990	1989
Tangible Bk. Val.	21.81	19.04	14.34	13.18	12.66	11.05
Oper. Earnings	3.05	3.41	2.55	1.71	1.07	0.97
Earnings	4.48	3.68	2.70	1.93	1.13	0.98
Dividends	0.60	0.51	0.44	0.37	0.32	0.29
Payout Ratio	13%	14%	16%	19%	28%	30%
Prices - High	31	32¾	22⅜	14⅜	9⅛	9
- Low	22	19⅝	11⅛	8⅛	8⅛	6⅜
P/E Ratio - High	7	9	8	7	8	9
- Low	5	5	4	4	7	7

Income Statement Analysis (Million $)

	1994	%Chg	1993	%Chg	1992	%Chg	1991
Premium Income	413	12%	368	15%	320	29%	248
Net Invest. Inc.	41.0	5%	39.0	19%	32.7	17%	28.0
Oth. Revs.	53.8	-28%	75.1	-20%	93.7	20%	78.2
Total Revs.	507	5%	482	8%	447	26%	354
Pretax Inc.	66.7	17%	56.8	46%	39.0	76%	22.1
Net Oper. Inc.	27.5	-25%	36.8	34%	27.4	76%	15.6
Net Inc.	47.6	19%	39.9	39%	28.7	69%	17.0

Balance Sheet & Other Fin. Data (Million $)

	1994	1993	1992	1991	1990	1989
Cash & Equiv.	11.9	12.2	10.2	8.8	7.3	7.4
Premiums Due	68.5	61.8	63.5	61.8	41.9	38.9
Inv Assets Bonds	645	589	452	351	299	204
Inv. Assets Stock	5.0	10.3	7.9	6.3	4.4	3.4
Inv. Assets Loans	Nil	Nil	Nil	Nil	Nil	Nil
Inv. Assets Total	656	607	460	357	303	207
Deferred Policy Cost	38.3	34.4	28.6	23.3	19.8	13.6
Total Assets	893	856	688	558	458	373
Debt	72.0	112	97.1	112	83.1	56.4
Common Eqty.	196	173	88.0	69.8	53.2	113

Ratio Analysis

	1994	1993	1992	1991	1990	1989
Prop&Cas Loss	69.6	59.4	59.8	64.7	63.2	76.2
Prop&Cas Expense	27.0	39.9	42.7	43.2	43.1	30.1
Prop&Cas Comb.	97.1	99.3	102.5	107.9	106.3	102.7
% Ret. on Revs.	9.4	8.3	6.4	4.8	3.5	4.7
% Return on Equity	21.9	25.0	27.4	21.3	11.2	9.2

Dividend Data —Cash payments were initiated in 1985. A dividend reinvestment plan is available.

Amt. of Div. $	Date Decl.	Ex-Div. Date	Stock of Record	Payment Date
0.150	Jul. 27	Sep. 12	Sep. 16	Sep. 30 '94
0.150	Oct. 20	Dec. 06	Dec. 12	Dec. 20 '94
0.170	Mar. 07	Mar. 16	Mar. 22	Mar. 31 '95
0.170	May. 09	Jun. 09	Jun. 13	Jun. 27 '95
0.170	Jul. 20	Sep. 08	Sep. 12	Sep. 26 '95

Data as orig. reptd.; bef. results of disc. opers. and/or spec. items. Per share data adj. for stk. divs. as of ex-div. date. E-Estimated. NA-Not Available. NM-Not Meaningful. NR-Not Ranked.

Office—701 Fifth Ave., Des Moines, IA 50391-2000. **Tel**—(515) 280-4617. **Chrmn**—J. E. Evans. **Pres (P-C)**—D. L. Andersen. **Pres (Fin)**—J. H. Shaffer. **Secy**—G. T. Oleson. **Dirs**—J. W. Callison, H. S. Carpenter, C. I. Colby, H. S. Evans, J. E. Evans, R. O. Jacobson, J. P. Taylor, W. E. Timmons, D. S. Willis. **Transfer Agent**—Harris Trust & Savings Bank, Chicago. **Incorporated** in Iowa in 1971. **Empl-** 2,067. **S&P Analyst:** Thomas C. Ferguson

Allwaste, Inc.

NYSE Symbol **ALW**
In S&P SmallCap 600

10-NOV-95 **Industry:** Pollution Control

Summary: This environmental services company provides industrial waste handling and container cleaning services, and recycles glass and other materials.

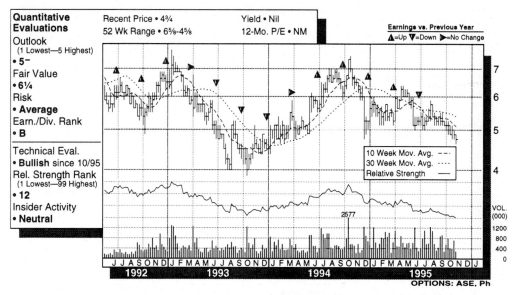

Quantitative Evaluations

Outlook
(1 Lowest—5 Highest)
• **5-**

Fair Value
• **6¼**

Risk
• **Average**

Earn./Div. Rank
• **B**

Technical Eval.
• **Bullish** since 10/95

Rel. Strength Rank
(1 Lowest—99 Highest)
• **12**

Insider Activity
• **Neutral**

Recent Price • 4¾
52 Wk Range • 6⅝-4⅝

Yield • Nil
12-Mo. P/E • NM

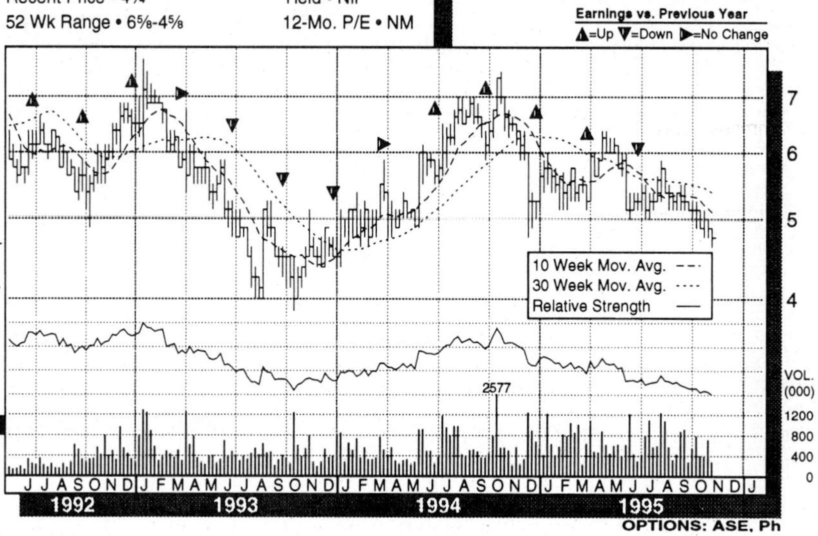

OPTIONS: ASE, Ph

Business Profile - 10-NOV-95

This environmental services company provides industrial waste handling, container cleaning, and other recycling. Although acquisitions have played a key role in the company's development, recently more of ALW's revenue growth has been internal. In September 1995, the company sold its glass recycling business and expects to recognize a $7 to $9 million gain in the first quarter of fiscal 1996. Following an earnings recovery in fiscal 1994, charges and reserves led to a loss in fiscal 1995.

Operational Review - 10-NOV-95

Revenues for the fiscal year ended August 31, 1995 (preliminary), declined 1.7%. Pretax charges totaling $11.9 million related to a wastewater treatment plant, investments in a previously owned asbestos abatement business, its Mexican operations and operating plant and equipment, led to a loss for the year. The company said it was enthusiastic about prospects in the coming year, based on sales in the first quarter of fiscal 1996.

Stock Performance - 03-NOV-95

In the past 30 trading days, ALW's shares have declined 7%, compared to a 2% rise in the S&P 500. Average trading volume for the past five days was 54,400 shares, compared with the 40-day moving average of 105,568 shares.

Key Stock Statistics

Dividend Rate/Share	Nil	Shareholders	3,400
Shs. outstg. (M)	39.2	Market cap. (B)	$0.171
Avg. daily vol. (M)	0.098	Inst. holdings	32%
Tang. Bk. Value/Share	1.08	Insider holdings	NA
Beta	0.89		

Value of $10,000 invested 5 years ago: $ 4,418

Fiscal Year Ending Aug. 31

	1995	% Change	1994	% Change	1993	% Change
Revenues (Million $)						
1Q	99.7	19%	83.43	15%	72.60	36%
2Q	93.70	16%	80.51	16%	69.53	39%
3Q	105.3	12%	94.17	21%	77.53	24%
4Q	96.58	5%	91.95	12%	82.08	21%
Yr.	344.3	-2%	350.1	16%	301.8	29%
Income (Million $)						
1Q	3.72	30%	2.87	-18%	3.49	10%
2Q	2.33	19%	1.96	3%	1.91	16%
3Q	3.04	-25%	4.04	66%	2.43	-31%
4Q	-10.48	NM	4.23	82%	2.33	-27%
Yr.	-3.88	NM	13.10	29%	10.17	-12%
Earnings Per Share ($)						
1Q	0.10	25%	0.08	-20%	0.10	11%
2Q	0.06	20%	0.05	NM	0.05	NM
3Q	0.08	-27%	0.11	57%	0.07	-30%
4Q	—	—	0.11	83%	0.06	-33%
Yr.	-0.10	NM	0.36	29%	0.28	-15%

Next earnings report expected: early January

Allwaste, Inc.

Business Summary - 09-NOV-95

Allwaste is an environmental services company that provides specialized waste handling, cleaning, processing and transportation services and container cleaning services. It is also a recycler of glass and other materials. The company has grown through an ambitious acquisition program, acquiring some 85 businesses since December 1986.

Business segment contributions in fiscal 1994 were:

	Revs.	Profits
Environmental services	69%	74%
Glass recycling	18%	12%
Container services	13%	14%

Within the environmental services segment, Allwaste provides air-moving and liquid vacuuming, hydroblasting and gritblasting, transportation, excavation and site remediation, dredging and dewatering, and other services from 70 locations in the U.S., Canada and Mexico. Customers are primarily in the petrochemical and refining, electric power, pulp and paper and automotive industries. Air-moving is an efficient method of removing and handling industrial wastes or salvageable materials contained in customers' tanks and containers by means of vacuuming with controlled-air velocity, while hydroblasting and gritblasting are effective methods of removing hard deposits from surfaces.

Recycling operations involve the collection and processing of "cullet" (broken or scrap glass) for sale to manufacturers of containers, fiberglass, reflective glass beads for highways and other glass-related products. With 23 plants and eight depots, the company believes it is the largest glass recycler and cullet processor in the U.S.

Container services, conducted from 25 locations in the U.S. and Canada, include the cleaning of over-the-highway tank-trailers, intermodal and railcar tanks and the cleaning, repair and maintenance of intermediate bulk containers. Wastewater pretreatment services are also provided.

Important Developments

Sep. '95—Allwaste finalized the sale of its glass recycling business to Equus II, Inc., for $57.1 million. ALW also owns warrants in the stock of the buyer, which can represent a significant future minority interest in the company. ALW expects to record a $7-$9 million gain on the transaction in the first quarter of fiscal 1996.

Jul. '95—The company announced that its board of directors authorized the repurchase of up to 5,000,000 shares between now and August 31, 1997.

Capitalization

Long Term Debt: $134,081,000 (5/95), incl. $38,867,000 of debs. conv. into com. at an avg. price of $6.93 a sh.

Per Share Data ($) (Year Ended Aug. 31)

	1995	1994	1993	1992	1991	1990
Tangible Bk. Val.	NA	0.99	1.05	1.13	1.06	1.60
Cash Flow	NA	1.00	0.84	0.77	0.61	0.77
Earnings	-0.10	0.36	0.28	0.33	0.28	0.42
Dividends	Nil	Nil	Nil	Nil	Nil	Nil
Payout Ratio	Nil	Nil	Nil	Nil	Nil	Nil
Prices - High	6 3/8	7 1/2	7 3/4	8 5/8	7	12 5/8
- Low	4 7/8	4 3/8	3 7/8	4 7/8	3 5/8	3 5/8
P/E Ratio - High	NM	21	28	26	25	30
- Low	NM	12	14	15	13	9

Income Statement Analysis (Million $)

	1994	%Chg	1993	%Chg	1992	%Chg	1991
Revs.	350	16%	302	29%	234	40%	167
Oper. Inc.	52.3	21%	43.2	11%	38.9	38%	28.2
Depr.	23.8	16%	20.5	30%	15.8	37%	11.5
Int. Exp.	6.9	21%	5.7	22%	4.7	54%	3.0
Pretax Inc.	21.0	24%	17.0	-10%	18.8	27%	14.8
Eff. Tax Rate	40%	—	40%	—	39%	—	35%
Net Inc.	13.1	28%	10.2	-11%	11.5	19%	9.7

Balance Sheet & Other Fin. Data (Million $)

	1994	1993	1992	1991	1990	1989
Cash	3.2	3.0	6.6	4.8	6.3	13.6
Curr. Assets	94.8	73.6	61.2	46.9	63.3	60.1
Total Assets	319	264	209	164	151	115
Curr. Liab.	62.2	61.3	41.5	31.6	27.0	21.5
LT Debt	123	91.5	71.7	53.9	48.1	37.8
Common Eqty.	121	105	90.0	75.6	72.4	52.4
Total Cap.	245	197	165	129	120	93.0
Cap. Exp.	37.8	39.6	33.6	17.9	20.5	15.3
Cash Flow	36.9	30.7	27.4	21.2	26.9	19.6

Ratio Analysis

	1994	1993	1992	1991	1990	1989
Curr. Ratio	1.5	1.2	1.5	1.5	2.3	2.8
% LT Debt of Cap.	50.2	46.4	43.4	41.6	39.9	40.5
% Net Inc.of Revs.	3.7	3.4	4.9	5.8	6.6	7.1
% Ret. on Assets	4.4	4.2	6.1	6.2	10.2	12.6
% Ret. on Equity	11.5	10.2	13.8	13.1	21.9	23.1

Dividend Data —No cash dividends have been paid.

Data as orig. reptd.; bef. results of disc. opers. and/or spec. items. Per share data adj. for stk. divs. as of ex-div. date. E-Estimated. NA-Not Available. NM-Not Meaningful. NR-Not Ranked.

Office—5151 San Felipe, Suite 1600, Houston, TX 77056. **Tel**—(713) 623-8777. **Chrmn**—R. L. Nelson Jr. **Pres & CEO**—R. M. Chiste. **SVP & COO**—D. E. Fanta. **SVP & Investor Contact**—F. Thorne-Thomsen, Jr. **VP-Secy**—W. L. Fielder. **Dirs**—M. A. Baker, D. H. Batchelder, R. J. Besquin, R. M. Chiste, J. U. Clarke, R. L. Knauss, R. L. Nelson Jr., R. L. Stanfa, T. J. Tierney, T. M. Young. **Transfer Agent & Registrar**—American Stock Transfer & Trust Co., NYC. **Incorporated** in Delaware in 1986. **Empl**-3,634. **S&P Analyst:** J. Santoriello

ALPHARMA INC.

NYSE Symbol ALO Options on Phila (Mar-Jun-Sep-Dec)

Price	Range	P–E Ratio	Dividend	Yield	S&P Ranking	Beta
Oct. 26'95	1995					
23⅜	24–17	NM	0.18	0.8%	B+	1.43

Summary

This company develops, makes and markets specialty generic and proprietary human pharmaceuticals and animal health products. The human pharmaceutical, fine chemical, animal health and aquatic animal health businesses of Apothekernes Laboratorium A.S. (A.L. Oslo—the company's largest shareholder) was acquired in October 1994, for $24 million in cash, plus warrants to buy 3.6 million Class A common shares. Charges associated with the transaction totaled $0.79 a share in the fourth quarter of 1994, and a loss of $0.08 a share was incurred for the full year.

Business Summary

ALPHARMA INC. (formerly A.L. Laboratories, then A.L. Pharma) is a U.S. multinational pharmaceutical concern that develops, manufactures and markets specialty generic and proprietary branded pharmaceuticals, animal drug products and bulk antibiotics. Operating through its Human Pharmaceuticals and Animal Health divisions, contributions (in 000's) in 1994 were:

	Revs.	Op. Profit
Pharmaceuticals (incl. bulk antibiotics)	70%	–$3,800
Animal health products	30%	28,500

The U.S. Pharmaceutical division conducts a specialty generic pharmaceutical business through four wholly owned subsidiaries. Barre-National Inc. is a leading U.S. producer (about 190 product presentations) of liquid generic pharmaceuticals sold to wholesalers and drug chains. NMC Laboratories Inc. produces and sells an extensive range of topical creams and ointments (about 90 product presentations), primarily prescription products. Able Laboratories Inc. makes and markets specialized prescription and over-the-counter (OTC) pharmaceuticals with an emphasis on suppositories, as well as dermatological creams and specialty tablets. ParMed Pharmaceuticals Inc. distributes over 1,800 generic prescription and OTC pharmaceuticals; drugs are contract manufactured and sold primarily to independent retail pharmacists via telemarketing throughout the U.S.

The International Pharmaceutical division makes and markets branded generic pharmaceuticals sold primarily in finished dosage form, in Europe and the Far East. The Fine Chemical division manufactures specialty bulk antibiotics for the pharmaceutical industry worldwide.

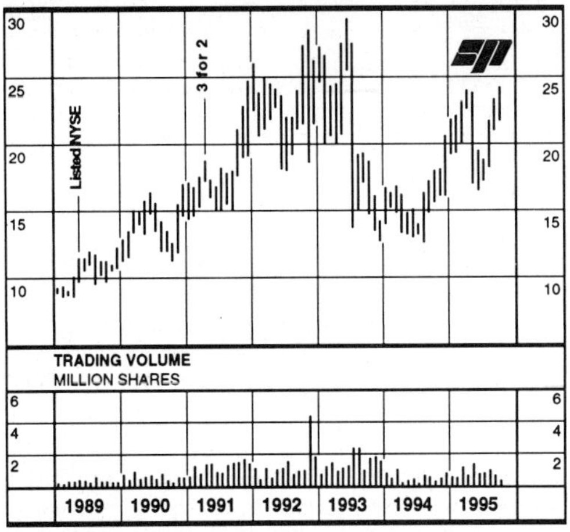

The Animal Health division manufactures and markets antibiotic feed additives for the poultry and swine industries. The Aquatic Animal Health division manufactures and markets vaccines for use in immunizing farmed fish against disease.

Important Developments

Oct. '95— The company received FDA approval to market branded and generic versions of Albuterol Sulfate Inhalation Solution. The market for the drug is approximately $120 million annually.

Sep. '95— ALPHARMA received FDA approval to manufacture and market Betamethasone Dipropionate Ointment. The drug has a branded market (Diprolene Ointment) of about $15 million. Other generics approved in 1995 include Fluocinonide Cream and Acetaminophen Suppositories.

Next earnings report expected in late October.

Per Share Data ($)

Yr. End Dec. 31	[1]1994	[1]1993	[1]1992	1991	[1]1990	1989	1988	[1]1987	[1]1986	1985
Tangible Bk. Val.	**2.43**	3.22	4.07	1.49	2.26	1.63	0.86	d1.13	2.01	2.15
Cash Flow	**0.77**	0.93	1.16	0.85	1.33	1.09	0.95	0.78	0.61	0.56
Earnings[2]	**d0.08**	0.40	0.62	0.30	0.84	0.71	0.58	0.49	0.41	0.40
Dividends	**0.180**	0.180	0.175	0.160	0.107	0.087	0.080	0.080	0.076	0.065
Payout Ratio	**NM**	45%	34%	54%	13%	12%	14%	16%	19%	16%
Prices—High	**20⅝**	29⅜	28½	24¾	17	12¼	10½	9¾	11½	8
Low	**12⅝**	12¾	18	14⅜	11¼	8⅝	5⅛	3⅞	6½	2¾
P/E Ratio—	**NM**	73–32	46–29	83–48	20–13	17–12	18–9	20–8	28–16	20–7

Data as orig. reptd. Adj. for stk. divs. of 50% Apr. 1991, 50% Jul. 1986, 50% Aug. 1985. **1.** Refl. merger or acq. **2.** Bef. results if disc. opers. of +0.26 in 1992 & bef. spec. item(s) of -0.03 in 1994. NM-Not Meaningful. d-Deficit.

Income Data (Million $)

Year Ended Dec. 31	[1]Revs.	Oper. Inc.	% Oper. Inc. of Revs.	Cap. Exp.	Depr.	Int. Exp.	Net Bef. Taxes	Eff. Tax Rate	[4]Net Inc.	% Net Inc. of Revs.	Cash Flow
[2]1994	**469**	**34.3**	**7.3**	**44.3**	**18.30**	**16.1**	**1.7**	**198.1%**	**d1.7**	**NM**	**16.6**
[2]1993	338	32.4	9.6	20.6	11.50	6.9	14.8	41.8%	8.6	2.5	20.1
[3]1992	295	38.3	13.0	16.9	9.76	10.3	17.6	35.3%	11.4	3.9	21.1
1991	291	24.3	8.4	10.5	9.22	12.3	7.7	33.6%	5.1	1.7	14.3
[2]1990	275	41.9	15.2	13.2	8.28	11.9	22.7	37.9%	14.1	5.1	22.4
1989	266	37.5	14.1	18.0	6.39	11.7	20.5	42.2%	11.8	4.4	18.2
1988	236	33.9	14.3	19.8	5.65	11.7	17.5	50.0%	8.8	3.7	14.4
[2]1987	157	19.6	12.5	29.9	4.02	4.7	13.7	51.7%	6.6	4.2	10.6
[2]1986	122	13.7	11.3	9.0	2.88	2.3	10.9	49.3%	5.5	4.5	8.4
1985	94	12.1	12.8	3.4	2.23	2.4	11.0	50.7%	5.5	5.8	7.7

Balance Sheet Data (Million $)

Dec. 31	Cash	Curr. Assets	Curr. Liab.	Curr. Ratio	Total Assets	% Ret. on Assets	Long Term Debt	Common Equity	Total Cap.	% LT Debt of Cap.	% Ret. on Equity
1994	**15.5**	**250**	**155**	**1.6**	**592**	**NM**	**220**	**181**	**429**	**51.3**	**NM**
1993	8.4	176	125	1.4	423	2.2	82	185	290	28.2	4.7
1992	5.6	155	87	1.8	372	2.8	74	184	281	26.2	6.9
1991	4.2	160	106	1.5	359	1.5	119	114	250	47.8	4.5
1990	8.5	148	96	1.5	328	4.6	101	111	230	44.1	13.8
1989	2.8	126	78	1.6	290	4.3	102	93	210	48.3	13.5
1988	6.0	114	77	1.5	267	3.0	94	82	189	49.8	11.7
1987	6.5	103	64	1.6	251	3.6	120	55	187	64.1	13.1
1986	5.1	65	52	1.3	119	5.2	15	45	68	22.2	13.2
1985	11.2	55	37	1.5	92	6.5	11	38	55	19.5	16.2

Data as orig. reptd. **1.** Incl. other inc. **2.** Refl. merger or acq. **3.** Excl. disc. opers. and reflects merger or acquis. **4.** Bef. results of disc. opers. d-Deficit. NM-Not Meaningful.

Total Revenues (Million $)

Quarter:	1995	1994	1993	1992
Mar.	126.1	107.4	77.8	71.2
Jun.	123.8	111.0	81.8	70.4
Sep.		117.4	83.0	70.1
Dec.		133.5	95.7	83.4
		469.3	338.2	295.1

Sales in the six months ended June 30, 1995, rose 15%, year to year (resta ted to reflect A.L. Oslo merger), due to improvements from international pharmaceuticals and contributions from the animal health segment. Margins widened, reflecting higher volumes and favorable currency exchange rates; operating profit was up 37%. After substantially higher interest expenses, and taxes at 38.7%, versus 37.9%, net income advanced 10%, to $6,979,000 ($0.32 a share), from $6,358,000 ($0.29).

Common Share Earnings ($)

Quarter:	1995	1994	1993	1992
Mar.	0.18	0.16	0.18	---
Jun.	0.14	0.13	0.12	---
Sep.		0.19	0.03	[1]0.52
Dec.		d0.56	0.07	0.10
		d0.08	0.40	0.62

Dividend Data

Dividends were initiated in 1984 on both Class A and Class B common stock.

Amt of Divd. $	Date Decl.	Ex-divd. Date	Stock of Record	Payment Date
0.04½	Dec. 16	Jan. 13	Jan. 20	Jan. 31'95
0.04½	Mar. 27	Apr. 4	Apr. 10	Apr. 24'95
0.04½	Jun. 08	Jul. 05	Jul. 07	Jul. 20'95
0.04½	Sep. 22	Oct. 04	Oct. 06	Oct. 20'95

Capitalization

Long Term Debt: $222,665,000 (6/95).

1. Nine mos. d-Deficit.

Office—One Executive Drive, Fort Lee, NJ 07024. **Tel**—(201) 947-7774. **Chrmn & CEO**—E. W. Sissener. **VP-Fin & CFO**—J. E. Smith. **Secy**—Beth P. Hecht. **Investor Contact**—Iris D. Daniels. **Dirs**—J. Balog, I. R. Cohen, T. G. Gibian, G. E. Hess, G.W. Munthe, E. W. Sissener, G.W. Sverdrup, E.G. Tandberg, P.G. Tombros. **Transfer Agent & Registrar**—First National Bank of Boston. **Reincorporated** in Delaware in 1983. **Empl**—2,700.

STANDARD & POOR'S

STOCK REPORTS

Amcast Industrial

NYSE Symbol **AIZ**
In S&P SmallCap 600

23-AUG-95 **Industry:** Machinery

Summary: Amcast manufactures metal products, specializing in flow control products and engineered components for the original equipment manufacturer market.

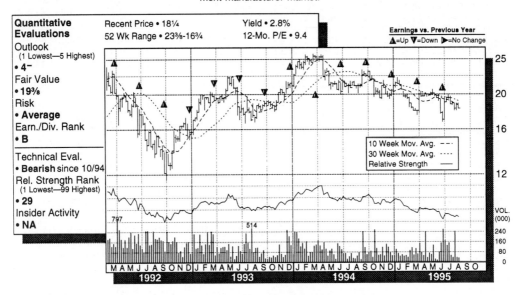

Quantitative Evaluations

Recent Price • 18¼ | Yield • 2.8%
52 Wk Range • 23⅜-16¾ | 12-Mo. P/E • 9.4

Outlook
(1 Lowest—5 Highest)
• **4-**

Fair Value
• **19⅜**

Risk
• **Average**

Earn./Div. Rank
• **B**

Technical Eval.
• **Bearish** since 10/94

Rel. Strength Rank
(1 Lowest—99 Highest)
• **29**

Insider Activity
• **NA**

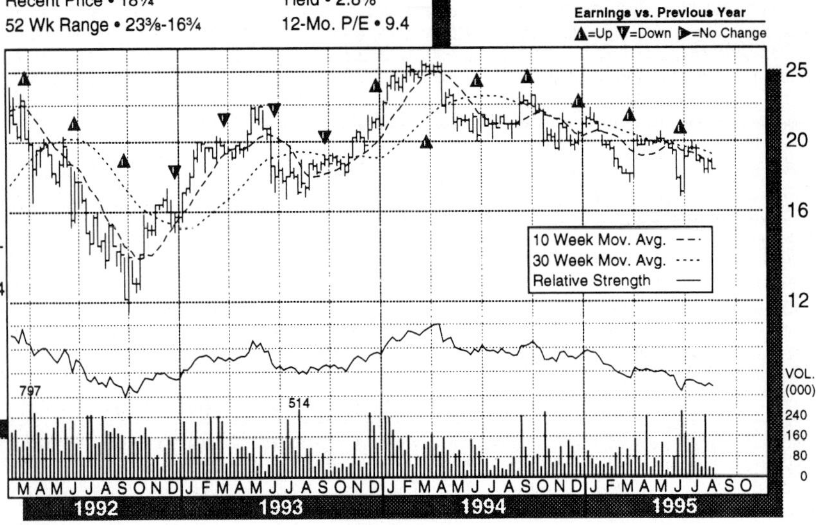

Business Profile - 23-AUG-95

The auto industry trend to replace components made of iron or steel with parts made of lighter-weight materials, such as aluminum, presents an opportunity to Amcast. The company predicts that over 50% of cars and trucks will have aluminum wheels by the year 2000. AIZ believes it is the largest domestic supplier of plumbing fittings; future trends in housing starts will determine Amcast's success in this area. Institutions hold more than 70% of the less than nine million shares outstanding.

Operational Review - 23-AUG-95

Sales for the nine months ended May 28, 1995, rose 23%, year to year, primarily reflecting price increases in the flow control products and engineered components segments designed to pass rising copper and aluminum costs on to customers. Margins narrowed, as product launch costs outweighed the benefits of higher prices; operating income was up 16%. After lower interest expense, and taxes at 35.5%, versus 34.5%, net income rose 20%, to $12.6 million ($1.48 a share), from $10.5 million ($1.25).

Stock Performance - 18-AUG-95

In the past 30 trading days, AIZ's shares have declined 6%, compared to a 0.51% rise in the S&P 500. Average trading volume for the past five days was 6,320 shares, compared with the 40-day moving average of 21,964 shares.

Key Stock Statistics

Dividend Rate/Share	0.52	Shareholders	6,400
Shs. outstg. (M)	8.5	Market cap. (B)	$0.160
Avg. daily vol. (M)	0.018	Inst. holdings	72%
Tang. Bk. Value/Share	14.09	Insider holdings	0%
Beta	0.72		

Value of $10,000 invested 5 years ago: $ 17,676

Fiscal Year Ending Aug. 31

	1995	% Change	1994	% Change	1993	% Change
Revenues (Million $)						
1Q	77.00	28%	60.33	14%	53.10	-12%
2Q	81.75	21%	67.70	20%	56.40	3%
3Q	86.40	22%	70.90	27%	55.77	-9%
4Q	—	—	72.93	27%	57.39	-6%
Yr.	—	—	271.9	22%	222.6	-6%
Income (Million $)						
1Q	3.62	35%	2.69	9%	2.46	-15%
2Q	4.28	22%	3.51	19%	2.95	24%
3Q	4.67	9%	4.29	26%	3.41	5%
4Q	—	—	3.97	23%	3.24	-7%
Yr.	—	—	14.45	20%	12.05	NM
Earnings Per Share ($)						
1Q	0.43	34%	0.32	7%	0.30	-33%
2Q	0.50	19%	0.42	20%	0.35	-3%
3Q	0.55	8%	0.51	24%	0.41	-5%
4Q	—	—	0.47	24%	0.38	-10%
Yr.	—	—	1.72	19%	1.44	-13%

Next earnings report expected: late October

Amcast Industrial

Business Summary - 23-AUG-95

Amcast Industrial Corporation is a leading manufacturer of metal products. Its principal business segments consist of brand-name flow control products marketed through national distribution channels and engineered components for original equipment manufacturers (OEMs). The company serves four major sectors of the economy: construction, automotive, industrial and aviation/defense. Business segment contributions in fiscal 1994 were:

	Sales	Profits
Flow control products	46%	66%
Engineered components	54%	34%

General Motors Corp. accounted for 33% of sales in fiscal 1994.

The flow control products segment includes the Superior Valve division, the Elkhart subsidiary and Amcast Industrial Ltd. Superior Valve produces valves and accessories used in air-conditioning and refrigeration systems and compressed gas cylinder valves for the welding, specialty, carbonic and medical gas industries. Elkhart produces wrot copper fittings for use in residential and commercial water systems, and it markets bronze pipe fittings and valves. Amcast Industrial Ltd. is the common Canadian marketing arm for Amcast's flow control units.

The engineered components division makes cast and fabricated metal products mainly for sale to OEMs in the transportation, construction, air-conditioning, refrigeration and aviation/defense industries. Products include castings for suspension, air-conditioning and anti-lock braking systems, master cylinders, differential carriers and cast aluminum wheels for use in autos and light trucks; and parts used in heating and air-conditioning systems. The company also designs and manufactures close-tolerance aluminum and specialty steel investment castings and related products for the aviation and aerospace industry.

Important Developments

May '95—Amcast announced plans to build a $25 million, 200,000-square-foot plant in Wapakoneta, Ohio, slated for startup in mid-1996, for production of aluminum automotive suspension components.

Capitalization

Long Term Debt: $19,545,000 (5/95).

Per Share Data ($) (Year Ended Aug. 31)

	1994	1993	1992	1991	1990	1989
Tangible Bk. Val.	12.70	11.46	11.01	10.33	8.93	10.88
Cash Flow	3.24	2.88	3.55	2.90	-0.20	2.58
Earnings	1.72	1.44	1.66	1.04	-1.97	1.12
Dividends	0.49	0.48	0.48	0.48	0.48	0.47
Payout Ratio	28%	33%	29%	46%	NM	42%
Prices - High	25⅞	22½	25	21¾	12½	13⅝
- Low	19⅜	15½	11⅝	6	6¼	10⅞
P/E Ratio - High	15	16	15	21	NM	12
- Low	11	11	7	6	NM	10

Income Statement Analysis (Million $)

	1994	%Chg	1993	%Chg	1992	%Chg	1991
Revs.	272	22%	223	-6%	237	-13%	271
Oper. Inc.	36.0	17%	30.9	-11%	34.9	28%	27.2
Depr.	12.8	7%	12.0	-12%	13.6	12%	12.1
Int. Exp.	1.6	-26%	2.1	-35%	3.3	-30%	4.7
Pretax Inc.	22.1	18%	18.8	NM	18.7	72%	10.9
Eff. Tax Rate	35%	—	36%	—	36%	—	38%
Net Inc.	14.5	20%	12.1	NM	12.0	79%	6.7

Balance Sheet & Other Fin. Data (Million $)

	1994	1993	1992	1991	1990	1989
Cash	15.4	2.3	3.1	1.6	1.7	1.0
Curr. Assets	97.0	75.0	74.0	91.0	94.0	101
Total Assets	194	177	174	179	185	195
Curr. Liab.	48.8	38.8	41.2	46.4	53.1	54.2
LT Debt	13.9	17.9	22.3	40.4	41.2	33.0
Common Eqty.	110	99	94.4	69.3	67.4	90.0
Total Cap.	128	119	117	116	113	134
Cap. Exp.	15.6	14.0	23.8	9.9	16.7	17.6
Cash Flow	27.3	24.1	25.6	18.8	-1.4	18.6

Ratio Analysis

	1994	1993	1992	1991	1990	1989
Curr. Ratio	2.0	1.9	1.8	2.0	1.8	1.9
% LT Debt of Cap.	10.9	15.1	19.0	34.9	36.5	24.7
% Net Inc.of Revs.	5.3	5.4	5.1	2.5	NM	2.4
% Ret. on Assets	7.8	6.9	5.9	3.8	NM	4.2
% Ret. on Equity	13.8	12.4	13.0	10.0	NM	9.0

Dividend Data —Dividends have been paid since 1936. A dividend reinvestment plan is available. A "poison pill" stock purchase right was adopted in 1988.

Amt. of Div. $	Date Decl.	Ex-Div. Date	Stock of Record	Payment Date
0.130	Aug. 17	Aug. 29	Sep. 05	Sep. 23 '94
0.130	Oct. 18	Nov. 28	Dec. 02	Dec. 23 '94
0.130	Feb. 23	Feb. 28	Mar. 06	Mar. 24 '95
0.130	May. 26	May. 31	Jun. 06	Jun. 23 '95

Data as orig. reptd.; bef. results of disc. opers. and/or spec. items. Per share data adj. for stk. divs. as of ex-div. date. E-Estimated. NA-Not Available. NM-Not Meaningful. NR-Not Ranked.

Office—7887 Washington Village Dr., Dayton, OH 45459. **Tel**—(513) 291-7000. **Chrmn**—L. W. Ladehoff. **Pres & CEO**—J. H. Shuey. **VP-Fin**—D. D. Watts. **VP-Secy**—D. G. Daly. **Dirs**—J. K. Baker, W. E. Blankley, P. H. Forster, I. W. Gorr, L. W. Ladehoff, E. T. O'Loughlin, W. G. Roth, J. H. Shuey, R. W. Van Sant. **Transfer Agent & Registrar**—Bank One, Indianapolis. **Incorporated** in Ohio in 1869. **Empl**-2,100. **S&P Analyst:** N. Rosenberg

AMCOL International

NASDAQ Symbol **ACOL**
In S&P SmallCap 600

25-SEP-95 **Industry:** Manufacturing/Distr

Summary: This leading producer of bentonite and bentonite specialty blends for industrial applications also makes superabsorbent polymers and has its own transportation operations.

Quantitative Evaluations
Outlook
(1 Lowest—5 Highest)
• 5+
Fair Value
• 22¾
Risk
• **Average**
Earn./Div. Rank
• A-

Technical Eval.
• **Bullish** since 6/95
Rel. Strength Rank
(1 Lowest—99 Highest)
• 69
Insider Activity
• **Neutral**

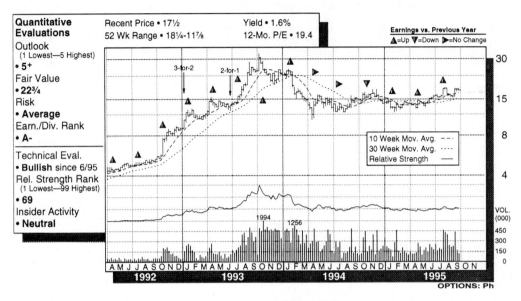

Recent Price • 17½
52 Wk Range • 18¼-11⅞
Yield • 1.6%
12-Mo. P/E • 19.4

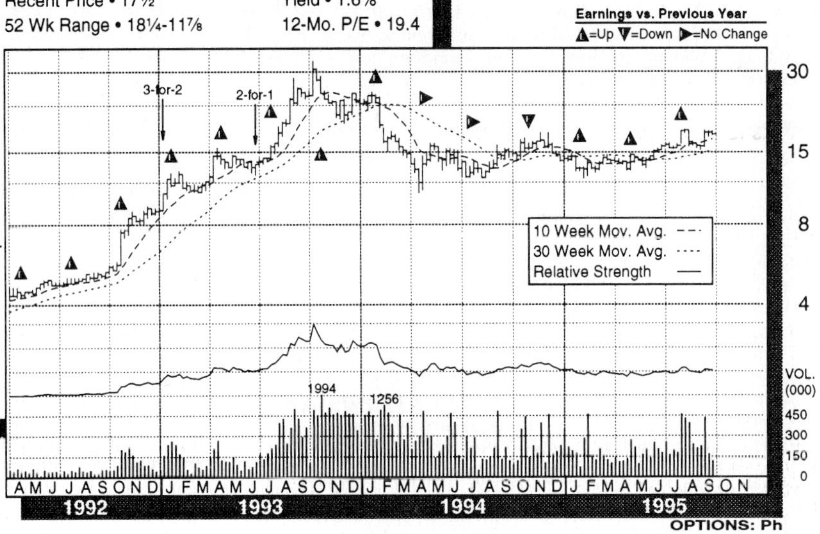

Business Profile - 25-SEP-95

The recent change in ACOL's name reflects not only its international presence, but also the transition from its traditional concentration on highly cyclical industrial markets to its growing diversification into consumable markets. While maintaining its former name (with its quality reputation) for the minerals segment, the new name should focus attention on its expansion into the markets for cat litter, agricultural carriers, environmental technologies, refining chemicals and transportation.

Operational Review - 25-SEP-95

Revenues grew 33% in the first half of 1995, reflecting acquisitions in environmental product lines and, aided by expansion in the U.K., exceptional strength in absorbent polymers. Despite a sharp rise in SG&A expenses (particularly in the environmental segment), margins widened and operating income surged 64%. Following a threefold increase in interest expense (on greater capital expenditure related debt) and a higher tax rate, net income advanced 42%.

Stock Performance - 22-SEP-95

In the past 30 trading days, ACOL's shares have increased 7%, compared to a 5% rise in the S&P 500. Average trading volume for the past five days was 22,240 shares, compared with the 40-day moving average of 56,077 shares.

Key Stock Statistics

Dividend Rate/Share	0.28	Shareholders	2,300
Shs. outstg. (M)	19.2	Market cap. (B)	$0.336
Avg. daily vol. (M)	0.049	Inst. holdings	25%
Tang. Bk. Value/Share	6.71	Insider holdings	NA
Beta	1.17		

Value of $10,000 invested 5 years ago: $ 46,367

Fiscal Year Ending Dec. 31

	1995	% Change	1994	% Change	1993	% Change
Revenues (Million $)						
1Q	78.75	36%	57.85	18%	48.90	23%
2Q	83.66	31%	64.01	16%	55.25	27%
3Q	—	—	71.98	26%	56.97	16%
4Q	—	—	71.61	23%	57.99	15%
Yr.	—	—	265.4	21%	219.1	20%
Income (Million $)						
1Q	3.63	46%	2.49	15%	2.16	157%
2Q	4.69	40%	3.35	17%	2.87	104%
3Q	—	—	4.24	10%	3.86	40%
4Q	—	—	5.20	23%	4.23	21%
Yr.	—	—	15.28	16%	13.12	54%
Earnings Per Share ($)						
1Q	0.19	46%	0.13	NM	0.13	143%
2Q	0.24	41%	0.17	NM	0.17	96%
3Q	—	—	0.22	-4%	0.23	35%
4Q	—	—	0.26	13%	0.23	10%
Yr.	—	—	0.78	3%	0.76	46%

Next earnings report expected: late October

AMCOL International

Business Summary - 18-SEP-95

AMCOL International (formerly American Colloid Company) is engaged in surface mining and processing of clays (principally bentonite) and the manufacture of absorbent polymers. The products are primarily used for their liquid-absorption properties. ACOL also operates a trucking and freight business, mainly for delivery of its own products. Business segment contributions in 1994 were:

	Sales	Profits
Minerals (primarily clays)	58%	65%
Absorbent polymers	22%	26%
Environmental	12%	6%
Transportation	8%	3%

Foreign sales represented 22% of 1994 revenues, with 14.7% derived from outside North America.

ACOL is a leading producer of bentonite, a nonmetallic clay composed primarily of a mineral called montmorillonite. The two basic types of bentonite produced--sodium bentonite and calcium bentonite--are used in hundreds of different products and processes in many different industries. A third type of clay, a less pure calcium montmorillonite called Fuller's earth, is used primarily as cat box filler and as a carrier for agri-chemicals.

The largest customers for bentonite are the metal-casting industry, which uses it as a bonding agent for molding sand, and the cat litter market. Through its wholly owned subsidiary, Colloid Environmental Technologies Company (CETCO), sodium bentonite and various other products and equipment are sold to the construction and environmental industries. Sodium and calcium bentonite proven reserves are estimated to be adequate for more than 30 years; Fuller's earth reserves are estimated to exceed 20 years.

Chemdal Corp. was formed in 1986 to make and market absorbent polymers, with emphasis on super-absorbent polymers (SAPs), which have extremely high water absorbency. The primary market for SAPs is personal care products, mostly baby diapers, with expansion expected in the agricultural market.

Transportation services include long-haul trucking and freight brokerage services and the lease of railroad cars to railroad lines for shipment of general commodities and company products (74% of the 1994 total).

Important Developments

Aug. '95—The company will form a new wholly owned subsidiary, Nanocur, to produced specialty, chemically modified clays as additives for plastics. Separately, its wholly owned American Colloid subsidiary plans to start-up at year-end 1995, a foundry compound blending plant near Lufkin, Texas. Earlier, in May, ACOL changed its name from American Colloid Company to AMCOL International Corporation.

Capitalization

Long Term Debt: $104,748,000 (6/95).

Per Share Data ($)

(Year Ended Dec. 31)

	1994	1993	1992	1991	1990	1989
Tangible Bk. Val.	6.71	6.47	3.19	3.13	2.94	2.78
Cash Flow	1.48	1.37	1.11	0.83	0.73	0.83
Earnings	0.78	0.76	0.51	0.25	0.15	0.32
Dividends	0.24	0.20	0.16	0.15	0.15	0.15
Payout Ratio	31%	26%	30%	57%	97%	45%
Prices - High	25¼	33	9⅜	4¼	4⅜	5⅛
- Low	10½	9⅛	3⅞	2 7/16	2⅞	3⅛
P/E Ratio - High	32	43	19	17	29	16
- Low	13	12	8	10	19	10

Income Statement Analysis (Million $)

	1994	%Chg	1993	%Chg	1992	%Chg	1991
Revs.	265	21%	219	20%	183	23%	149
Oper. Inc.	37.6	19%	31.6	20%	26.3	40%	18.8
Depr.	13.6	30%	10.5	8%	9.8	6%	9.2
Int. Exp.	3.0	NM	3.0	-13%	3.5	-20%	4.4
Pretax Inc.	22.2	18%	18.8	48%	12.7	131%	5.5
Eff. Tax Rate	31%	—	30%	—	32%	—	26%
Net Inc.	15.3	17%	13.1	54%	8.5	112%	4.0

Balance Sheet & Other Fin. Data (Million $)

	1994	1993	1992	1991	1990	1989
Cash	10.4	20.5	3.5	2.9	2.8	2.4
Curr. Assets	106	93.0	60.2	60.1	54.2	51.5
Total Assets	261	181	127	127	125	121
Curr. Liab.	36.6	27.4	21.1	20.8	14.2	16.0
LT Debt	71.5	16.7	38.3	43.8	47.8	43.7
Common Eqty.	141	125	55.6	54.4	52.7	51.2
Total Cap.	218	147	99	100	103	98.0
Cap. Exp.	81.0	32.1	11.3	7.9	8.5	14.4
Cash Flow	28.9	23.7	18.3	13.2	11.4	13.2

Ratio Analysis

	1994	1993	1992	1991	1990	1989
Curr. Ratio	2.9	3.4	2.9	2.9	3.8	3.2
% LT Debt of Cap.	32.8	11.3	38.6	43.9	46.4	44.7
% Net Inc.of Revs.	5.8	6.0	4.7	2.7	1.8	4.0
% Ret. on Assets	6.9	7.9	6.7	3.2	1.9	4.3
% Ret. on Equity	11.4	13.7	15.4	7.5	4.5	10.1

Dividend Data —Cash has been paid each year since 1937.

Amt. of Div. $	Date Decl.	Ex-Div. Date	Stock of Record	Payment Date
0.060	Nov. 08	Nov. 30	Dec. 06	Jan. 03 '95
0.060	Feb. 07	Feb. 14	Feb. 21	Mar. 10 '95
0.060	May. 09	May. 22	May. 27	Jun. 07 '95
0.070	Aug. 18	Aug. 30	Sep. 01	Sep. 09 '95

Data as orig. reptd.; bef. results of disc. opers. and/or spec. items. Per share data adj. for stk. divs. as of ex-div. date. E-Estimated. NA-Not Available. NM-Not Meaningful. NR-Not Ranked.

Office—One North Arlington, 1500 W. Shure Dr., Suite 500, Arlington Heights, IL 60004-7803. **Tel**—(708) 392-4600. **Chrmn**—C. E. Ray. **Pres & CEO**—J. Hughes. **SVP, CFO & Investor Contact**—Paul G. Shelton. **Secy**—C. O. Redman. **Dirs**—A. Brown, R. E. Driscoll III, R. A. Foos, R. H. Harris, J. Hughes, R. C. Humphrey, C. E. Ray, C. O. Redman, P. G. Shelton, E. P. Weaver, W. D. Weaver. **Transfer Agent**—Harris Trust & Savings Bank, Chicago. **Incorporated** in Delaware in 1959. **Empl**-1,328. **S&P Analyst:** Justin McCann

STANDARD & POOR'S

STOCK REPORTS

America Online

NASDAQ Symbol **AMER**

In S&P SmallCap 600

17-NOV-95

Industry: Data Processing

Summary: With more than 4 million subscribers, AMER is a leading provider of online services, including e-mail, conferencing, electronic magazines, online classes and Internet access.

S&P Opinion: Avoid (★★)

Recent Price • 81⅝
52 Wk Range • 88½-16½

Yield • Nil
12-Mo. P/E • NM

Quantitative Evaluations

Outlook
(1 Lowest—5 Highest)
• **1**

Fair Value
• **56⅜**

Risk
• **High**

Earn./Div. Rank
• **NR**

Technical Eval.
• **Bullish** since 8/94

Rel. Strength Rank
(1 Lowest—99 Highest)
• **94**

Insider Activity
• **NA**

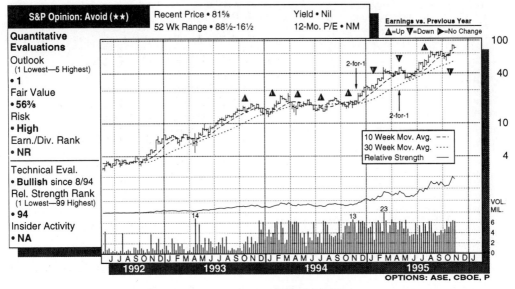

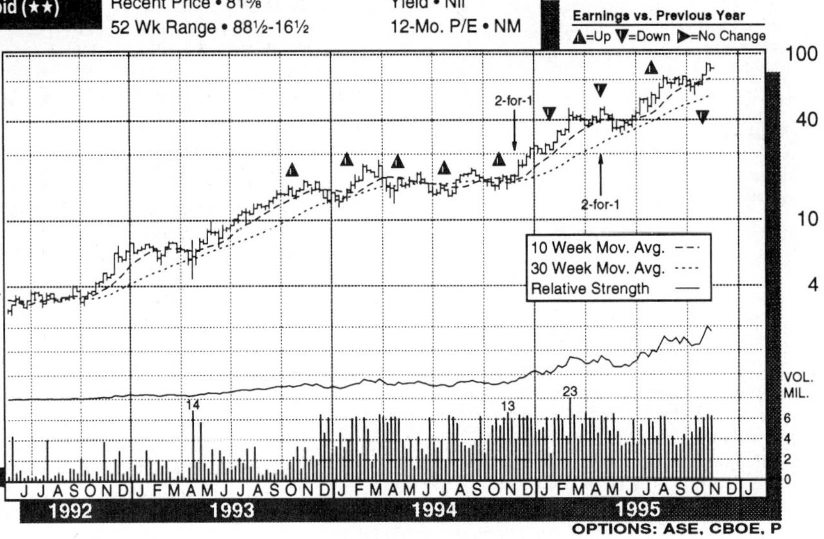

OPTIONS: ASE, CBOE, P

Overview - 17-NOV-95

Revenues through 1996 are expected to continue to rise sharply, reflecting the rapid growth of the online services market and benefits from AMER's strong marketing campaign. Margins are expected to be maintained, as volume efficiencies and other general cost savings offset lower pricing and continued high investments in sales, marketing and R&D. Operating earnings are expected to advance sharply on the increased volume and steady margins. Fiscal 1996 earnings will be hurt by a $0.43 a share charge related to the September 1995 acquisition of Ubique, Inc.; profits in fiscal 1995 were penalized by nonrecurring charges totaling $1.41 a share associated with recent Internet-related acquisitions, which should benefit future results.

Valuation - 17-NOV-95

The shares, which have risen sharply since late 1994, are currently trading near their all-time high. In addition, the stock has more than doubled since the beginning of the year. The company continues to execute well. It has reduced prices and continues to heavily market its services in order to build its installed base of users. Revenue and operating earnings have grown rapidly, and growth is expected to continue. Nevertheless, competitive threats are real, with major players Microsoft and AT&T developing their own online offerings. Given the competitive risks in the years to come, the shares are richly valued at about 100 times projected fiscal 1996 earnings.

Key Stock Statistics

S&P EPS Est. 1996	0.37	Tang. Bk. Value/Share	4.21
P/E on S&P Est. 1996	NM	Beta	NA
Dividend Rate/Share	Nil	Shareholders	1,100
Shs. outstg. (M)	40.0	Market cap. (B)	$ 3.2
Avg. daily vol. (M)	1.641	Inst. holdings	82%
		Insider holdings	NA

Value of $10,000 invested 5 years ago: NA

Fiscal Year Ending Jun. 30

	1996	% Change	1995	% Change	1994	% Change
Revenues (Million $)						
1Q	197.9	NM	56.94	NM	16.00	105%
2Q	—	—	76.40	NM	21.50	131%
3Q	—	—	109.1	NM	29.20	178%
4Q	—	—	151.9	NM	37.80	NM
Yr.	—	—	394.3	NM	104.4	161%
Income (Million $)						
1Q	-10.26	NM	1.48	44%	1.03	—
2Q	—	—	-38.73	NM	1.23	56%
3Q	—	—	-2.59	NM	1.82	109%
4Q	—	—	6.19	191%	2.13	196%
Yr.	—	—	-33.65	NM	6.21	102%
Earnings Per Share ($)						
1Q	-0.27	NM	0.04	14%	0.03	17%
2Q	E0.17	NM	-1.05	NM	0.04	33%
3Q	E0.23	NM	-0.07	NM	0.06	57%
4Q	E0.24	85%	0.13	100%	0.07	160%
Yr.	E0.37	NM	-0.99	NM	0.19	70%

Next earnings report expected: early February

America Online

Business Summary - 16-NOV-95

America Online, Inc. (AOL) is a leading provider of online services in the U.S., offering subscribers a wide variety of services including electronic mail, conferencing, software, computing support, electronic magazines and newspapers, online classes and Internet access.

Revenues are generated primarily from subscribers paying a monthly membership fee and hourly charges based on usage in excess of the number of hours provided as part of the monthly fee. The company's standard monthly membership fee, which includes five hours of service, is $9.95, with a $2.95 hourly fee for usage in excess of five hours. Other revenues consist principally of payments received from various third parties for certain product development activities conducted by the company.

Services offered on AOL are in the areas of Computing, Learning and Reference, News and Finance, Travel and Shopping, Games and Entertainment, Lifestyles and Interest, and People Connection.

The company also provides access to the Internet. AOL's goal is to "consumerize" the Internet by providing simple access to and use of the Internet for members fo the AOL service and for users seeking direct access to the Internet. The company introduced its Web browser in May 1995, which provides integrated World Wide Web access within the AOL service, and guides members to Web sites based on areas of consumer interest. The integrated approach allows the user to seamlessly use the full suite of AOL features, including chat and e-mail, while exploring the Internet, all under AOL's standard pricing structure.

Subscribers connect to the company's services using standard phone lines, and AOL has contracted with third-party data networks so that subscribers in more than 750 cities in the U.S. and Canada can dial a local number for connection. In April 1995, AOL entered into a joint venture with Bertelsmann to offer interactive services in Europe.

Important Developments

Nov. '95—AOL and Intuit, Inc. signed a strategic agreement to jointly provide electronic banking to AOL members starting in the first half of 1996. In addition, Intuit will revamp its online area on AOL and include links to its recently launched Internet Web site known as the Quicken Financial Network.

Oct. '95—America Online unveiled its new Internet service, GNN (Global Network Navigator), which is aimed at the segment of online consumers who seek a full-featured Internet-only solution, and the growing number of publishers interested in enhancing their presence on the World Wide Web.

Sep. '95—AOL acquired Ubique Ltd., an innovative Israeli company that offers real-time interaction and joint navigation for the Internet.

Capitalization

Long Term Debt: $19,496,000, incl. $2,127,000 of lease obligs. (6/95).

Per Share Data ($) (Year Ended Jun. 30)

	1995	1994	1993	1992	1991	1990
Tangible Bk. Val.	2.15	3.41	1.01	0.86	-1.29	NA
Cash Flow	1.13	0.23	0.14	0.13	0.07	NA
Earnings	-0.99	0.19	0.11	0.10	0.00	NA
Dividends	Nil	Nil	Nil	Nil	Nil	NA
Payout Ratio	Nil	Nil	Nil	Nil	Nil	NA
Prices - High	88½	29¼	17½	7⅜	NA	NA
- Low	24⅝	12	4½	2¾	NA	NA
P/E Ratio - High	NM	NM	NM	73	NA	NA
- Low	NM	NM	NM	27	NA	NA

Income Statement Analysis (Million $)

	1995	%Chg	1994	%Chg	1993	%Chg	1992
Revs.	394	NM	104	160%	40.0	48%	27.0
Oper. Inc.	103	NM	9.3	82%	5.1	33%	3.8
Depr.	72.1	NM	1.3	110%	0.6	22%	0.5
Int. Exp.	1.0	—	NA	—	NA	—	NA
Pretax Inc.	-18.5	NM	10.0	100%	5.0	39%	3.6
Eff. Tax Rate	NM	—	38%	—	38%	—	38%
Net Inc.	-33.6	NM	6.2	102%	3.1	39%	2.2

Balance Sheet & Other Fin. Data (Million $)

	1995	1994	1993	1992	1991	1990
Cash	64.1	67.7	14.3	14.0	1.0	NA
Curr. Assets	133	105	25.0	19.0	4.0	NA
Total Assets	406	148	32.0	24.0	8.0	NA
Curr. Liab.	133	40.4	8.6	4.4	3.8	NA
LT Debt	19.5	5.8	Nil	Nil	0.2	NA
Common Eqty.	218	99	23.8	18.9	-6.0	NA
Total Cap.	273	108	24.0	19.0	4.0	NA
Cap. Exp.	57.8	17.5	1.8	0.7	0.1	NA
Cash Flow	38.4	7.5	3.7	2.7	0.5	NA

Ratio Analysis

	1995	1994	1993	1992	1991	1990
Curr. Ratio	1.0	2.6	3.0	4.4	1.0	NA
% LT Debt of Cap.	7.1	5.4	Nil	Nil	4.8	NA
% Net Inc.of Revs.	NM	5.9	7.7	8.3	4.4	NA
% Ret. on Assets	NM	6.6	10.7	7.4	NA	NA
% Ret. on Equity	NM	9.7	13.9	NM	NA	NA

Dividend Data —No cash dividends have been paid. The company intends to retain its earnings to finance growth and does not expect to pay cash dividends in the foreseeable future.

Amt. of Div. $	Date Decl.	Ex-Div. Date	Stock of Record	Payment Date
2-for-1	Apr. 03	Apr. 28	Apr. 13	Apr. 27 '95
2-for-1	Oct. 31	Nov. 29	Nov. 14	Nov. 28 '95

Data as orig. reptd.; bef. results of disc. opers. and/or spec. items. Per share data adj. for stk. divs. as of ex-div. date. E-Estimated. NA-Not Available. NM-Not Meaningful. NR-Not Ranked.

Office—8619 Westwood Center Dr., Vienna, VA 22182-2285. **Tel**—(703) 448-8700. **Chrmn, Pres & CEO**—S. M. Case. **Sr VP, CFO & Treas**—L. J. Leader. **VP & Secy**—Ellen M. Kirsh. **Investor Contact**—Richard Hanlon (703) 556-3746. **Dirs**—J. G. Andress, S. M. Case, F. J. Caufield, R. Frankenburg, A. M. Haig Jr., J. V. Kimsey, W. N. Melton, T. J. Middlehoff, R. Pittman, S. C. Smith. **Transfer Agent & Registrar**—Chemical Bank, NYC. **Incorporated** in Delaware in 1985. **Empl**-2,481. **S&P Analyst:** Alan Aaron

American Bankers Ins. Group

NASDAQ Symbol ABIG (Incl. in Nat'l Market) In S&P SmallCap 600

Price	Range	P–E Ratio	Dividend	Yield	S&P Ranking	Beta
Aug. 30'95	1995					
33½	34⅝–23⅜	11	0.76	2.3%	B+	1.40

Summary

This holding company for American Bankers Life Assurance Co. of Florida and American Bankers Insurance Co. of Florida specializes in credit insurance. It also offers a broad range of other insurance products and services. Earnings rose 33%, year to year, in the first half of 1995, reflecting strong growth in net investment income.

Business Summary

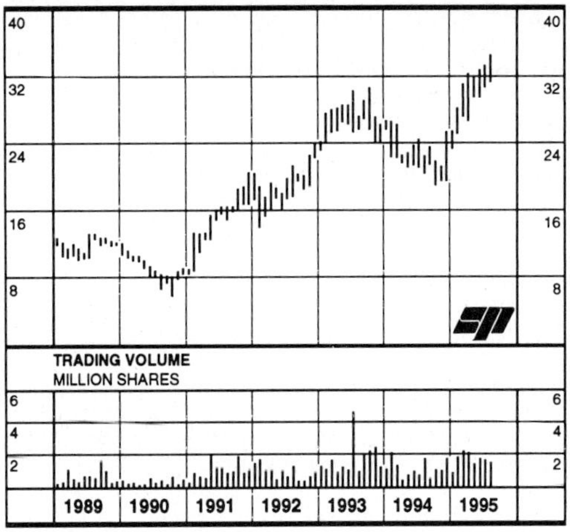

American Bankers Insurance Group, Inc. is the holding company for American Bankers Insurance Co. of Florida and American Bankers Life Assurance Co. of Florida. Its credit-related insurance products consist primarily of life, accidental death and dismemberment, unemployment, disability and property insurance issued in connection with the financing of consumer products.

Net premiums earned and pretax income in 1994 were derived as follows:

	Prems.	Income
Life	33%	32%
Property & casualty	67%	68%

Net premiums earned totaled $1.1 billion in 1994, up from $882.0 million in 1993, and were divided by product line as follows: credit property 16%, credit life 11%, credit A&H 13%, unemployment 17%, homeowners 4%, mobile home physical damage 7%, mortgage A&H 4%, group life 2%, livestock 3%, group A&H 3%, and other 20%.

Financial market products include a variety of property insurance such as homeowners' and coverages for comprehensive physical damage of mobile homes, autos, furniture, fixtures and other consumer goods; life and disability insurance primarily on consumer loans, mortgages and credit card balances; and unemployment insurance on credit card balances in connection with life, disability and property coverages.

Non-credit related insurance products and services include group life and disability sold through Blue Cross and Blue Shield and health maintenance organizations, individual life and disability products sold through employer-sponsored payroll deduction programs, flood insurance, livestock mortality insurance, individual lIfe insurance and annuity products sold primarily in Latin America and the Caribbean, and surety coverages.

Important Developments

Jul. '95— ABIG executed agreements to purchase about 90% of Consolidated International Group Inc.'s credit insurance business, which will enhance ABIG's client base in the U.S., Canada and Puerto Rico. The transaction results in the assumption of an existing block of unearned premiums totaling $61 million, and is expected to produce about $55 million annually in new premiums. The full positive impact on earnings is expected to occur in the beginning of the third quarter.

Apr. '95— ABIG agreed to market and administer Aventure Electronique Inc.'s extended service contracts. The extended service market is one of ABIG's targeted high-growth product lines.

Next earnings report expected in October.

Per Share Data ($)

Yr. End Dec. 31	1994	1993	1992	1991	1990	1989	1988	1987	1986	1985
Tangible Bk. Val.	**20.15**	[1]19.87	[1]16.38	[1]14.50	[1]12.31	[1]10.93	[1]9.89	[1]9.57	[1]12.39	[1]12.24
Oper. Earnings[3]	**NA**	NA	NA	2.55	1.92	1.23	1.31	d2.66	1.31	1.25
Earnings[2,3,4]	**2.74**	2.85	2.57	2.55	1.92	1.23	1.31	d2.53	2.03	1.45
Dividends	**0.71**	0.68	0.60	0.60	0.50	0.50	0.50	0.50	0.50	0.50
Relative Payout	**26%**	24%	23%	24%	26%	41%	38%	NM	25%	34%
Prices—High	**26¾**	30¾	24	20⅝	12⅛	13¼	13	16	17¼	14⅞
Low	**19**	23⅛	14	8⅜	5¾	10⅛	8⅜	7	11⅞	10⅜
P/E Ratio—	**10–7**	11–8	9–5	8–3	6–3	11–8	10–6	NM	13–9	12–8

Data as orig. reptd. **1.** As reptd. by co. **2.** Aft. gains/losses on security trans. **3.** Bef. spec. items of -0.05 in 1993, +0.17 in 1989, +1.09 in 1988. **4.** Ful. dil.: 2.78 in 1993, 2.39 in 1992, 2.22 in 1991, 1.69 in 1990, 1.17 in 1989. d-Deficit. NA-Not Available. NM-Not Meaningful.

Income Data (Million $)

Year Ended Dec. 31	Life Ins. In Force	Premium Income Life A & H	Premium Income Cas./ Prop.	Net Invest. Inc.	Oth. Revs.	Total Revs.	Comb. Loss-Exp. Ratio	Net Bef. Taxes	[1]Net Oper. Inc.	[1]Net Inc.	—% Return On— Revs.	—% Return On— Equity
1994	**32,129**	**360**	**734**	**74.4**	**18.0**	**1,187**	**96.0**	**79.8**	**NA**	**56.5**	**4.8**	**16.0**
1993	30,848	305	577	70.4	21.0	973	94.1	75.7	NA	53.3	5.5	15.7
1992	27,878	260	473	67.5	11.7	812	95.3	59.4	NA	42.3	5.2	17.4
1991	29,168	235	456	68.1	9.0	768	100.1	52.2	37.4	37.4	4.9	19.0
1990	31,098	233	428	72.3	11.4	746	101.8	40.0	27.8	27.8	3.7	16.6
1989	31,710	216	367	63.3	10.7	657	98.1	27.6	17.6	17.6	3.1	13.5
1988	30,949	252	373	65.0	41.0	731	107.5	42.8	16.8	16.8	2.3	12.7
1987	30,346	248	355	71.0	18.0	692	NA	d31.1	d34.0	d32.3	NM	NM
1986	26,938	239	308	78.3	d18.3	607	NA	22.3	16.7	26.0	2.7	11.4
1985	23,099	218	214	57.4	1.6	491	NA	15.9	13.9	16.1	2.8	11.7

Balance Sheet Data (Million $)

Dec. 31	Cash & Equiv.	[3]Premiums Due	Investment Assets Bonds	Investment Assets Stocks	Investment Assets Loans	Investment Assets Total	% Invest. Yield	Deferred Policy Costs	Total Assets	Debt	Common Equity
1994	**105.6**	**105.6**	**1,044**	**65.4**	**20.6**	**1,265**	**6.2**	**230**	**2,432**	**198**	**406**
1993	53.6	132.5	1,015	73.5	22.3	1,111	[2]6.7	199	2,160	159	399
1992	23.8	96.1	899	59.6	23.5	982	[2]7.1	175	1,404	140	268
1991	25.7	92.5	833	53.4	26.6	913	[2]7.6	156	1,277	177	216
1990	42.3	104.3	810	24.4	32.6	867	[2]8.5	172	1,260	197	178
1989	26.3	100.9	775	15.7	41.8	832	[2]8.8	170	1,197	148	158
1988	28.3	72.4	747	15.2	46.8	812	[2]7.6	172	1,145	136	143
1987	31.3	69.3	864	17.6	47.0	941	[2]7.5	210	1,339	129	122
1986	33.2	50.5	755	26.3	56.0	850	[2]7.0	193	1,200	115	158
1985	64.8	33.2	502	18.3	74.0	653	[2]7.7	154	986	106	136

Data as orig. reptd. **1.** Bef. spec. items. **2.** As reptd. by co. **3.** Incl. agents' bal. rec. d-Deficit. NA-Not Available. NM-Not Meaningful.

Review of Operations

Total premiums and other revenues rose 9.3%, year to year, in the six months ended June 30, 1995, paced by 42% growth in investment income, which is driven by advances in gross collected premiums. Following a 7.6% increase in total benefits and expenses, pretax income expanded 34%. After taxes, net income was up 33% to $30.9 million ($1.44 a share), from $23.3 million ($1.13).

Common Share Earnings ($)

Quarter:	1995	1994	1993	1992
Mar.	0.72	0.45	0.69	0.65
Jun.	0.77	0.68	0.64	0.60
Sep.		0.61	0.56	0.58
Dec.		1.00	0.96	0.74
		2.74	2.85	2.57

Finances

At December 31, 1994, total investments of $1.26 billion were divided: fixed maturities 83%, equity securities 5%, short-term and other investments 10%, and mortgage and policy loans and real estate 2%.

In a July 1993 public offering, 3,360,000 common shares (including 1,360,000 for selling stockholders) were sold at $27.25 each. Company net proceeds of $51.9 million were used to reduce debt incurred in connection with the acquisition of the Voyager Cos.

In May 1993, Voyager Life Insurance Co., Voyager Group, Inc. and their subsidiaries, which write credit-related insurance products, were acquired from Primerica Corp. for about $106 million in cash.

Dividend Data

Dividends have been paid by the company or its predecessors since 1950. A "poison pill" stock purchase rights plan was adopted in 1988.

Amt. of Divd. $	Date Decl.	Ex-divd. Date	Stock of Record	Payment Date
0.18	Nov. 14	Nov. 28	Dec. 2	Dec. 16'94
0.18	Feb. 21	Feb. 27	Mar. 3	Mar. 17'95
0.19	May 24	May 30	Jun. 5	Jun. 16'95
0.19	Aug. 21	Aug. 30	Sep. 1	Sep. 15'95

Capitalization

Debt: $232,727,000 (6/95).

Common Stock: 20,173,624 shs. ($1 par).
Officers and directors own 12%, incl. 9% controlled by R.K. Landon.
Institutions hold 73%.
Shareholders of record: 2,054 (12/94).

Office—11222 Quail Roost Drive, Miami, FL 33157-6596. **Tel**—(305) 253-2244. **Chrmn & CEO**—R. K. Landon. **Vice Chrmn, COO & Pres**—G. N. Gaston. **VP & Treas**—A. W. Heggen. **Secy**—L. Garcia. **Investor Contact**—P. Bruce Camacho (305-252-7060). **Dirs**—W. H. Allen, Jr., N. A. Buoniconti, A. M. Codina, P. Dolora, G. N. Gaston, D. L. Jones, J. F. Jorden, J. F. Kemp, R. K. Landon, M. G. MacNeill, E. M. Matalene Jr., A. H. Nahmad, N. J. St. George, R. C. Strauss, G. E. Williamson II. **Transfer Agent & Registrar**—Chemical Bank, NYC. **Incorporated** in Florida in 1978. **Empl**—2,206.

 Robert Schpoont

Amer. Management Systems

NASDAQ Symbol **AMSY**

In S&P SmallCap 600

12-OCT-95

Industry:
Data Processing

Summary: This company offers business and information technology consulting, reusable and customized software, and systems integration services for U.S. and multinational organizations.

Quantitative Evaluations

Outlook
(1 Lowest—5 Highest)
• **3+**

Fair Value
• **24⅝**

Risk
• **Average**

Earn./Div. Rank
• **B+**

Technical Eval.
• **Bullish** since 4/95

Rel. Strength Rank
(1 Lowest—99 Highest)
• **30**

Insider Activity
• **NA**

Recent Price • 25⅛
52 Wk Range • 28-15

Yield • Nil
12-Mo. P/E • 27.6

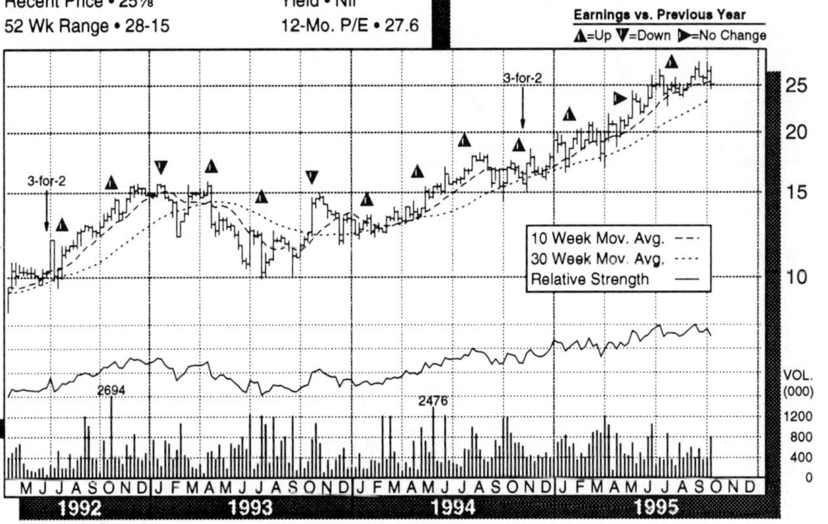

Business Profile - 12-OCT-95

Organizations in AMS's target markets --financial services, government agencies, educational groups and telecommunications firms-- have a crucial need to exploit the potential benefits of information and systems integration technology. This demand should persist as productivity gains are constantly sought. AMS's expansion into Europe should offer new opportunities for the company.

Operational Review - 12-OCT-95

All business units have been experiencing revenue growth, benefiting in part from AMS's expansion into Europe and strong demand from the telecommunications and financial services sectors. Greater increases in infrastructure costs, especially outside the U.S., caused the rise in operating expenses to outpace the growth rate of sales, resulting in a modest advance in earnings for 1995's first half.

Stock Performance - 06-OCT-95

In the past 30 trading days, AMSY's shares were unchanged, compared to a 4% rise in the S&P 500. Average trading volume for the past five days was 159,360 shares, compared with the 40-day moving average of 100,972 shares.

Key Stock Statistics

Dividend Rate/Share	Nil	Shareholders	1,000
Shs. outstg. (M)	26.5	Market cap. (B)	$0.643
Avg. daily vol. (M)	0.094	Inst. holdings	66%
Tang. Bk. Value/Share	5.54	Insider holdings	NA
Beta	1.38		

Value of $10,000 invested 5 years ago: $ 50,250

Fiscal Year Ending Dec. 31

	1995	% Change	1994	% Change	1993	% Change
Revenues (Million $)						
1Q	135.8	35%	100.3	16%	86.30	14%
2Q	157.5	43%	109.8	20%	91.80	13%
3Q	—	—	119.1	34%	88.98	4%
4Q	—	—	130.7	35%	96.97	7%
Yr.	—	—	459.9	26%	364.0	9%
Income (Million $)						
1Q	4.87	9%	4.48	18%	3.79	20%
2Q	6.58	13%	5.84	32%	4.43	3%
3Q	—	—	5.79	76%	3.29	-35%
4Q	—	—	7.02	12%	6.28	26%
Yr.	—	—	23.39	31%	17.79	2%
Earnings Per Share ($)						
1Q	0.18	NM	0.18	23%	0.15	22%
2Q	0.24	4%	0.23	33%	0.17	4%
3Q	—	—	0.22	74%	0.13	-34%
4Q	—	—	0.27	9%	0.25	28%
Yr.	—	—	0.90	30%	0.69	2%

Next earnings report expected: late October

Amer. Management Systems

Business Summary - 12-OCT-95

American Management Systems, Inc. (AMS) is engaged in helping large organizations solve complex management problems by applying information technology and systems engineering. Its marketing and development resources are targeted at large organizations that have a crucial need for these services. The company combines specific industry experience, business function expertise, proven systems development practices and technical competence to help clients achieve their business goals. Industries and markets served by AMS include: financial services institutions, federal agencies, state and local governments, educational institutions and telecommunications firms.

Another significant component of the company's business is the development of proprietary software products, either with its own funds or on a cost-shared basis with other organizations. These products are principally licensed as elements of custom tailored systems, and to a lesser extent, as stand-alone applications.

Services and products revenues by market in recent years were:

	1994	1993
Financial services institutions	22%	19%
Federal Government agencies	21%	29%
State & local government and education	20%	20%
Telecommunications firms	30%	24%
Other corporate clients	7%	8%

AMS's competition comes primarily from the management services units of large public accounting firms and consulting and system integration firms. Marketing is done principally by senior staff members (executive officers, vice presidents, senior principals, and principals) and by a relatively small number of full-time salespersons for each large market.

AMS has expanded internationally by establishing nine foreign subsidiaries or branches in Europe, Mexico and Canada.

Total revenues from the U.S. government were approximately $88.5 million (19% of total sales) in 1994, up from $80.1 million (22%) in 1993. Service and product revenues attributable to foreign operations of AMS and foreign subsidiaries totaled $92.1 million (20%) in 1994, up from $52.8 million (15%) in 1993. In 1994, approximately 85% of the company's business came from clients it worked with in the previous year.

Important Developments

Aug. '95—The company entered into an agreement with Lotus Development Corp. under which AMS will offer Lotus Notes products and related application design and development services to large enterprises.

Capitalization

Long Term Debt: $11,983,000 (3/95), incl. lease obligs.

Per Share Data ($)

(Year Ended Dec. 31)

	1994	1993	1992	1991	1990	1989
Tangible Bk. Val.	5.00	3.98	3.53	2.94	2.31	1.99
Cash Flow	1.70	1.03	1.00	0.80	0.73	0.48
Earnings	0.90	0.69	0.67	0.50	0.46	0.25
Dividends	Nil	Nil	Nil	Nil	Nil	Nil
Payout Ratio	Nil	Nil	Nil	Nil	Nil	Nil
Prices - High	$19\frac{1}{4}$	$15\frac{7}{8}$	$15\frac{5}{8}$	$12\frac{5}{8}$	$8\frac{3}{4}$	$8\frac{1}{4}$
- Low	12	$9\frac{7}{8}$	$8\frac{1}{8}$	$7\frac{1}{4}$	$4\frac{5}{8}$	$4\frac{5}{8}$
P/E Ratio - High	21	23	23	25	19	33
- Low	13	14	12	15	10	19

Income Statement Analysis (Million $)

	1994	%Chg	1993	%Chg	1992	%Chg	1991
Revs.	460	26%	364	9%	333	17%	285
Oper. Inc.	61.0	56%	39.0	5%	37.1	33%	28.0
Depr.	20.7	150%	8.3	7%	7.7	9%	7.1
Int. Exp.	1.4	103%	0.7	-32%	1.0	-35%	1.5
Pretax Inc.	39.5	29%	30.7	4%	29.4	40%	21.0
Eff. Tax Rate	41%	—	42%	—	41%	—	38%
Net Inc.	23.4	31%	17.8	2%	17.5	34%	13.1

Balance Sheet & Other Fin. Data (Million $)

	1994	1993	1992	1991	1990	1989
Cash	34.2	15.6	32.5	28.4	25.4	19.0
Curr. Assets	182	125	123	104	95.0	91.0
Total Assets	252	185	166	146	134	124
Curr. Liab.	92.5	57.9	50.3	47.9	47.3	41.6
LT Debt	12.9	11.0	4.4	10.0	12.3	14.0
Common Eqty.	138	99	85.5	68.9	53.5	47.5
Total Cap.	159	126	115	97.0	85.0	81.0
Cap. Exp.	17.0	13.3	7.6	9.4	6.8	7.4
Cash Flow	43.8	25.2	23.7	18.6	16.5	11.2

Ratio Analysis

	1994	1993	1992	1991	1990	1989
Curr. Ratio	2.0	2.2	2.4	2.2	2.0	2.2
% LT Debt of Cap.	8.1	8.7	3.8	10.3	14.5	17.4
% Net Inc.of Revs.	5.1	4.9	5.3	4.6	4.6	2.8
% Ret. on Assets	10.3	10.0	11.0	9.2	9.4	5.5
% Ret. on Equity	18.8	18.2	20.2	18.7	20.9	12.6

Dividend Data —No cash dividends have been paid. Three-for-two stock splits have been effected five times since 1985.

Amt. of Div. $	Date Decl.	Ex-Div. Date	Stock of Record	Payment Date
3-for-2	Sep. 23	Oct. 31	Oct. 07	Oct. 28 '94

Data as orig. reptd.; bef. results of disc. opers. and/or spec. items. Per share data adj. for stk. divs. as of ex-div. date. E-Estimated. NA-Not Available. NM-Not Meaningful. NR-Not Ranked.

Office—4050 Legato Rd., Fairfax, VA 22033. **Tel**—(703) 267-8000. **Chrmn**—C. O. Rossotti. **Vice Chrmn & CEO**—P. A. Brands. **Vice Chrmn**—P. W. Gross. **Pres**—P. M. Giuntini. **EVP, Treas & Secy**—F. A. Nicolai. **Dirs**—D. J. Altobello, P. A. Brands, S. R. Fenster, J. J. Forese, P. M. Giuntini, P. W. Gross, D. Leonard-Barton, F. L. Malek, F. A. Nicolai, C. O. Rossotti, G. R. Worley. **Transfer Agent & Registrar**—Mellon Securities Trust Co., New York, NY. **Incorporated** in Delaware in 1970. **Empl**-4,250. **S&P Analyst:** Steven A. Jaworski

STANDARD & POOR'S

American Medical Response

STOCK REPORTS

NYSE Symbol **EMT**

In S&P SmallCap 600

02-OCT-95 **Industry:** Health Care Centers

Summary: This company is a leading provider of emergency and non-emergency ambulance services in the U.S., with operations in 21 states.

Quantitative Evaluations

Outlook (1 Lowest—5 Highest)
• **NA**

Fair Value
• **NA**

Risk
• **Low**

Earn./Div. Rank
• **NR**

Technical Eval.
• **Neutral** since 9/95

Rel. Strength Rank (1 Lowest—99 Highest)
• **30**

Insider Activity
• **Unfavorable**

Recent Price • 28⅜
52 Wk Range • 31⅝-22¾
Yield • Nil
12-Mo. P/E • 23.3

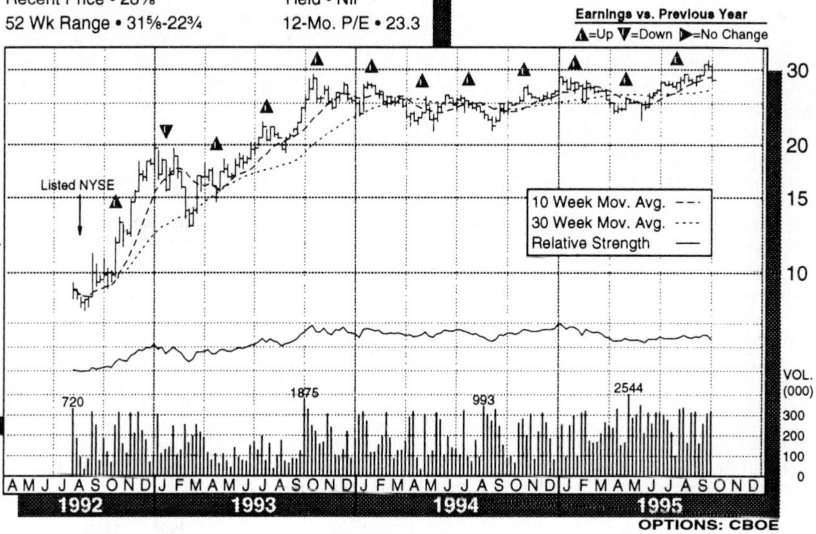

OPTIONS: CBOE

Business Profile - 02-OCT-95

EMT's future growth is dependent upon its ability to acquire additional service providers. The company has signed a letter of intent to acquire American Medical Response, Inc., the largest privately owned provider of ambulance services in the U.S., with annual revenues of over $100 million. EMT has made over 40 acquisitions since 1992. Expanding existing operations and improving the quality and efficiency of operations are also part of the company's growth strategy.

Operational Review - 02-OCT-95

The company has achieved rapid growth in revenues and earnings since its initial public offering in 1992, due primarily to acquisitions and the resulting improved operating efficiencies. Revenues for the first half of 1995 advanced 53% from the restated year-earlier level. Margins widened on the higher volume, but a higher effective tax rate and an increase in average shares stemming from a stock offering in May held down gains in net income and EPS.

Stock Performance - 29-SEP-95

In the past 30 trading days, EMT's shares were unchanged, compared to a 5% rise in the S&P 500. Average trading volume for the past five days was 97,740 shares, compared with the 40-day moving average of 82,041 shares.

Key Stock Statistics

Dividend Rate/Share	Nil	Shareholders	1,400
Shs. outstg. (M)	19.5	Market cap. (B)	$0.552
Avg. daily vol. (M)	0.069	Inst. holdings	70%
Tang. Bk. Value/Share	5.64	Insider holdings	NA
Beta	NA		

Value of $10,000 invested 5 years ago: NA

Fiscal Year Ending Dec. 31

	1995	% Change	1994	% Change	1993	% Change
Revenues (Million $)						
1Q	109.2	75%	62.24	50%	41.41	64%
2Q	111.4	50%	74.15	66%	44.80	70%
3Q	—	—	83.12	64%	50.62	89%
4Q	—	—	92.22	77%	52.20	86%
Yr.	—	—	311.7	65%	189.0	78%
Income (Million $)						
1Q	4.49	24%	3.63	112%	1.71	58%
2Q	5.84	59%	3.68	53%	2.40	61%
3Q	—	—	4.26	73%	2.46	66%
4Q	—	—	4.28	46%	2.93	81%
Yr.	—	—	15.25	-4%	15.85	180%
Earnings Per Share ($)						
1Q	0.32	52%	0.21	31%	0.16	14%
2Q	0.33	27%	0.26	18%	0.22	10%
3Q	—	—	0.29	32%	0.22	29%
4Q	—	—	0.29	32%	0.22	38%
Yr.	—	—	1.09	33%	0.82	22%

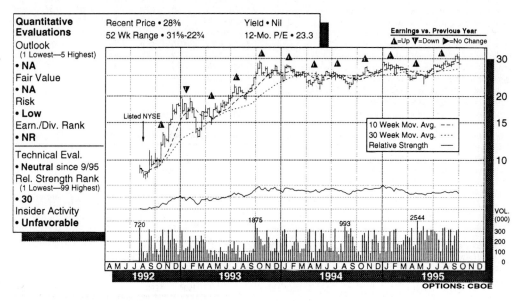

Next earnings report expected: early November

American Medical Response

Business Summary - 02-OCT-95

American Medical Response was formed in February 1992 with the strategic objective of becoming the leading national provider of ambulance services. Following the August 1992 acquisition of four ambulance service providers and several subsequent acquisitions, the company provides emergency pre-hospital medical care and ambulance services to patients in response to "911" emergency medical calls and provides non-emergency ambulance services to patients during transfer to and from health care facilities and residences. It also provides nonmedical transport services to the handicapped and elderly. As of August 1995, EMT provided services in 21 states.

American Medical generally provides emergency medical ambulance services pursuant to contracts with counties and municipalities. The company responds to "911" calls involving life-threatening emergencies with Advanced Life Support (ALS) ambulance units. ALS units, staffed by two paramedics or one paramedic and an emergency medical technician (EMT), are equipped with advanced life support equipment, such as cardiac monitors, defibrillators and oxygen delivery systems, and contain pharmaceuticals and medical supplies.

The company provides Basic Life Support (BLS) ambulance services in response to "911" calls when a patient's medical condition is not life-threatening, and to patients requiring a basic level of supervision during transfer to and from residences and health care facilities. A BLS ambulance unit is staffed by two EMTs and equipped with medical supplies and equipment necessary to administer first aid and basic medical treatment.

American Medical also provides critical care transport services to medically unstable patients, such as cardiac patients and neonatal patients, who require critical care while being transported between health care facilities. These services are typically provided pursuant to contracts with hospitals, HMOs and other health care facilities.

Approximately 10%, 8% and 6% of the company's total revenues in 1994 were derived from contracts with Alameda, Santa Clara and Contra Costa Counties, respectively, to provide 911 emergency ambulance services.

Important Developments

Aug. '95—The company entered into a definitive agreement to acquire Ambulance Service of America (ASA), headquartered in Massachusetts. ASA is the largest privately owned ambulance service in the U.S., with annual revenues of approximately $100 million.

Capitalization

Long Term Debt: $7,058,000 (6/95).

Per Share Data ($) (Year Ended Dec. 31)

	1994	1993	1992	1991	1990	1989
Tangible Bk. Val.	1.63	4.94	2.38	2.31	NA	NA
Cash Flow	1.97	1.43	1.10	1.06	0.79	0.63
Earnings	1.09	0.82	0.67	0.57	0.28	0.22
Dividends	Nil	Nil	Nil	NA	NA	NA
Payout Ratio	Nil	Nil	Nil	NA	NA	NA
Prices - High	28⅞	29¼	19⅞	NA	NA	NA
- Low	21½	12¾	8⅛	NA	NA	NA
P/E Ratio - High	26	36	30	NA	NA	NA
- Low	20	16	12	NA	NA	NA

Income Statement Analysis (Million $)

	1994	%Chg	1993	%Chg	1992	%Chg	1991
Revs.	312	65%	189	78%	106	13%	94.0
Oper. Inc.	41.8	68%	24.9	84%	13.5	7%	12.6
Depr.	12.8	81%	7.1	95%	3.6	-3%	3.8
Int. Exp.	1.4	70%	0.8	12%	0.8	-35%	1.2
Pretax Inc.	27.5	62%	17.0	87%	9.1	19%	7.7
Eff. Tax Rate	42%	—	44%	—	38%	—	44%
Net Inc.	15.9	67%	9.5	68%	5.7	32%	4.3

Balance Sheet & Other Fin. Data (Million $)

	1994	1993	1992	1991	1990	1989
Cash	6.5	31.4	14.4	14.8	NA	NA
Curr. Assets	87.8	74.7	42.6	38.3	NA	NA
Total Assets	233	132	66.5	49.1	NA	NA
Curr. Liab.	57.3	23.0	17.0	16.7	NA	NA
LT Debt	42.3	1.9	8.4	7.8	NA	NA
Common Eqty.	131	103	35.8	23.1	NA	NA
Total Cap.	176	109	48.4	30.9	NA	NA
Cap. Exp.	13.6	9.2	1.4	3.5	1.8	3.0
Cash Flow	28.6	16.6	9.3	8.1	5.9	4.8

Ratio Analysis

	1994	1993	1992	1991	1990	1989
Curr. Ratio	1.5	3.3	2.5	2.3	NA	NA
% LT Debt of Cap.	24.1	1.7	17.3	25.2	NA	NA
% Net Inc.of Revs.	5.1	5.0	5.3	4.6	2.9	2.9
% Ret. on Assets	8.4	8.7	7.8	NA	NA	NA
% Ret. on Equity	13.0	12.6	18.3	NA	NA	NA

Dividend Data —No dividends have been paid. The company intends to retain earnings to expand its business.

Data as orig. reptd.; bef. results of disc. opers. and/or spec. items. Per share data adj. for stk. divs. as of ex-div. date. E-Estimated. NA-Not Available. NM-Not Meaningful. NR-Not Ranked.

Office—67 Batterymarch St., Suite 300, Boston, MA 02110. **Tel**—(617) 261-1600. **Fax**—(617) 261-1610. **Chrmn** —P. M. Verrochi. **CEO & Pres**—P. T. Shirley. **EVP & Treas**—D. J. Puopolo. **SVP & Investor Contact**—Ronald M. Levenson. **Secy**—K. F. Higgins. **Dirs**—C. D. Baker, M. A. Baker, D. B. Hammond, J. E. McGrath, J. R. Paolella, D. J. Puopolo, W. E. Riggs, P. T. Shirley, J. L. Thompson, P. M. Verrochi. **Transfer Agent & Registrar**—Bank of Boston. **Incorporated** in Massachusetts in 1992; reincorporated in Delaware in 1992. **Empl**-7,002. **S&P Analyst:** Stephen Madonna, CFA

STANDARD & POOR'S

STOCK REPORTS

AMRESCO, INC.

NASDAQ Symbol **AMMB**
In S&P SmallCap 600

02-NOV-95 **Industry:** Services

Summary: This financial services company provides asset management and commercial real estate mortgage banking services to financial institutions, government agencies and private investors.

Quantitative Evaluations
Outlook
(1 Lowest—5 Highest)
• **NA**
Fair Value
• **NA**
Risk
• **Average**
Earn./Div. Rank
• **B-**

Technical Eval.
• **Bullish** since 5/95
Rel. Strength Rank
(1 Lowest—99 Highest)
• **17**
Insider Activity
• **Neutral**

Recent Price • 10⅞ Yield • 1.9%
52 Wk Range • 13½-5½ 12-Mo. P/E • 17.8

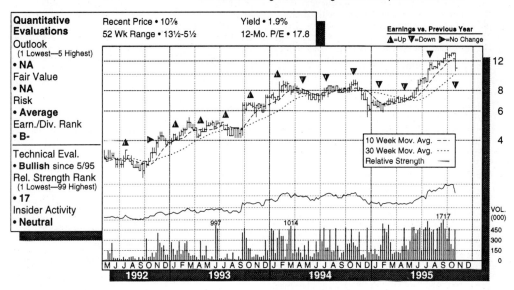

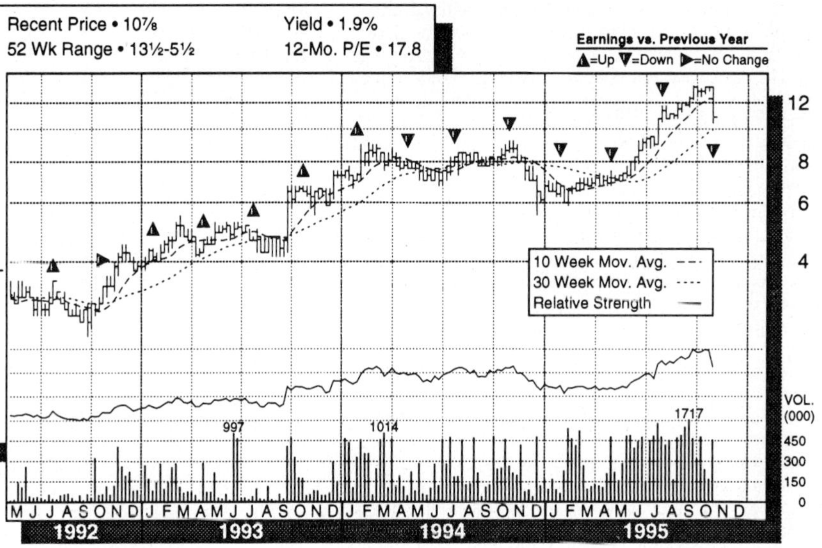

Business Profile - 02-NOV-95

AMRESCO's principal business--asset management and disposition services--expanded in the first nine months of 1995, as it entered into management contracts covering assets of approximately $1.45 billion. The company's strategic plans include the continued acquisition of asset portfolios, the generation of new asset management contracts and expansion of its commercial mortgage banking operations. AMMB is also looking to make the strategic acquisition of a pension real estate advisory firm.

Operational Review - 02-NOV-95

Revenues for the nine months ended September 30, 1995, fell 46%, year to year, due primarily to a 73% decline in asset management and resolution fees. Total expenses were down 47%, reflecting downsizing initiatives and the absence of expenses related to the conclusion of a management contract; pretax income dropped 40%. After taxes at 37.8%, versus 41.4%, income from continuing operations was off 37%, to $12,430,000 ($0.51 a share, based on 3.9% more shares), from $19,656,000 ($0.83).

Stock Performance - 27-OCT-95

In the past 30 trading days, AMMB's shares have declined 12%, compared to a 0.63% fall in the S&P 500. Average trading volume for the past five days was 94,380 shares, compared with the 40-day moving average of 144,433 shares.

Key Stock Statistics

Dividend Rate/Share	0.20	Shareholders	3,700
Shs. outstg. (M)	24.2	Market cap. (B)	$0.257
Avg. daily vol. (M)	0.076	Inst. holdings	29%
Tang. Bk. Value/Share	3.89	Insider holdings	NA
Beta	0.95		

Value of $10,000 invested 5 years ago: $ 42,037

Fiscal Year Ending Dec. 31

	1995	% Change	1994	% Change	1993	% Change
Revenues (Million $)						
1Q	20.84	-49%	40.56	-21%	51.61	NM
2Q	23.35	-42%	40.46	6%	38.00	192%
3Q	25.42	-46%	46.78	9%	42.86	NM
4Q	—	—	29.38	-33%	44.05	NM
Yr.	—	—	157.2	-11%	176.5	NM
Income (Million $)						
1Q	3.16	-41%	5.36	-22%	6.87	NM
2Q	4.08	-25%	5.43	-17%	6.52	NM
3Q	5.20	-41%	8.87	25%	7.09	NM
4Q	—	—	1.28	-66%	3.75	186%
Yr.	—	—	20.93	-14%	24.22	NM
Earnings Per Share ($)						
1Q	0.13	-43%	0.23	-62%	0.61	NM
2Q	0.17	-26%	0.23	-60%	0.58	NM
3Q	0.21	-43%	0.37	-41%	0.63	NM
4Q	—	—	0.05	-85%	0.33	175%
Yr.	—	—	0.88	-59%	2.15	NM

Next earnings report expected: late January

Business Summary - 02-NOV-95

AMRESCO, INC. (formed through the December 1993 merger of BEI Holdings, Ltd. and AMRESCO Holdings, Inc.) provides asset management and commercial real estate mortgage banking services to financial institutions, government agencies and private investors. Contributions to revenues in recent years were:

	1994	1993
Asset management & disposition	77%	98%
Earnings on asset portfolios	8%	2%
Mortgage banking	4%	---
Other	11%	Nil

Through its asset management business, AMRESCO purchases, manages and liquidates underperforming real estate and business loan portfolios and real estate properties. These troubled assets are acquired primarily from banks, insurance companies, the RTC and the FDIC. The company also provides asset management services for third parties.

Through the commercial mortgage banking business, AMRESCO provides a wide range of services, including loan origination, sale, placement, servicing and funding. AMRESCO entered the commercial mortgage banking business in 1994 through the acquisition of Holliday Fenoglio Dockerty & Gibson, Inc., a Houston-based commercial mortgage banker, and the formation of AMRESCO Capital Corp., a real estate capital market services company that commits and closes loans for sale to investors or placement in securitization offerings. The company has mortgage banking offices in Florida, Georgia, New York, Texas and Virginia.

AMMB also performs portfolio evaluations for clients seeking to invest capital in nonperforming and underperforming loans and associated real and personal property. Increasingly, such clients request that the adviser purchase a small equity stake in the purchased assets and then provide the asset management staff to perform management and disposition services for a fee. At December 31, 1994, the book value of such equity investments was $36 million.

Important Developments

Oct. '95—AMRESCO, Inc. signed a definitive agreement to acquire 16 pension fund advisory contracts from Acacia Realty Advisors, Inc.

Sep. '95—The company agreed to acquire 30 contracts to service approximately $6.2 billion in commercial real estate mortgages from EQ Services, Inc. and Equitable Real Estate Investment Management, Inc.

Capitalization

Debt: $140,520,000 (9/95).

Per Share Data ($) (Year Ended Dec. 31)

	1994	1993	1992	1991	1990	1989
Tangible Bk. Val.	4.81	3.65	2.41	3.05	3.10	2.24
Cash Flow	1.01	2.41	0.67	0.47	0.35	-0.59
Earnings	0.88	2.15	0.50	0.33	0.20	-0.75
Dividends	0.20	0.15	Nil	Nil	Nil	0.18
Payout Ratio	23%	7%	Nil	Nil	Nil	NM
Prices - High	9¼	7½	4½	5	3⅜	5½
- Low	5½	3¾	2⅜	2½	2	2⅛
P/E Ratio - High	11	3	9	15	17	NM
- Low	6	2	5	8	10	NM

Income Statement Analysis (Million $)

	1994	%Chg	1993	%Chg	1992	%Chg	1991
Revs.	140	-21%	177	NM	47.2	16%	40.7
Oper. Inc.	26.0	-41%	43.9	NM	8.8	151%	3.5
Depr.	3.0	2%	3.0	68%	1.8	28%	1.4
Int. Exp.	1.8	136%	0.8	NM	0.1	-29%	0.2
Pretax Inc.	35.7	-11%	40.2	NM	5.4	52%	3.6
Eff. Tax Rate	41%	—	40%	—	21%	—	6.20%
Net Inc.	20.9	-14%	24.2	NM	5.3	59%	3.3

Balance Sheet & Other Fin. Data (Million $)

	1994	1993	1992	1991	1990	1989
Cash	20.4	43.4	3.5	2.0	1.0	1.2
Curr. Assets	NA	NA	16.5	9.2	7.0	NA
Total Assets	172	164	44.3	50.6	49.6	57.7
Curr. Liab.	NA	NA	7.5	4.3	8.1	NA
LT Debt	16.5	28.1	0.3	0.2	1.6	9.2
Common Eqty.	114	91.7	35.7	43.8	38.5	33.5
Total Cap.	130	120	36.0	45.1	40.1	42.7
Cap. Exp.	2.1	0.9	0.8	1.5	0.9	2.5
Cash Flow	24.0	27.2	7.1	4.7	3.3	-5.5

Ratio Analysis

	1994	1993	1992	1991	1990	1989
Curr. Ratio	NA	NA	2.2	2.2	0.9	NA
% LT Debt of Cap.	12.7	23.5	0.7	0.3	4.1	21.5
% Net Inc.of Revs.	15.0	13.7	11.2	8.2	5.2	NM
% Ret. on Assets	12.1	23.3	13.0	6.7	3.6	NM
% Ret. on Equity	19.9	43.4	16.3	8.1	5.4	NM

Dividend Data —Dividends were omitted in 1989 and reinstated in 1993.

Amt. of Div. $	Date Decl.	Ex-Div. Date	Stock of Record	Payment Date
0.050	Aug. 10	Dec. 23	Dec. 31	Jan. 15 '95
0.050	Mar. 15	Mar. 27	Mar. 31	Apr. 15 '95
0.050	Jun. 07	Sep. 27	Sep. 30	Oct. 15 '95

Data as orig. reptd.; bef. results of disc. opers. and/or spec. items. Per share data adj. for stk. divs. as of ex-div. date. E-Estimated. NA-Not Available. NM-Not Meaningful. NR-Not Ranked.

Office—1845 Woodall Rogers Freeway, Suite 1400, Dallas, TX 75201. **Tel**—(214) 953-7700. **Chrmn & CEO**—R. H. Lutz Jr. **Pres & COO**—R. L. Adair. **Exec VP, CFO & Treas**—B. L. Edwards. **Secy**—L. K. Blackwell. **Investor Contact**—Thomas J. Andrus. **Dirs**—R. L. Adair III, J. P. Cotton Jr., R. L. Cravey, G. E. Eickhoff, W. S. Green, A. J. Jorgensen, R. H. Lutz Jr., J. J. McDonough, B. W. Schnitzer. **Transfer Agent & Registrar**—Trust Company Bank, Atlanta. **Incorporated** in Delaware in 1977. **Empl**-700. **S&P Analyst:** Brad Ohlmuller

AMSCO International

NYSE Symbol **ASZ**
In S&P SmallCap 600

19-SEP-95

Industry: Medical equipment/ supply

Summary: This company is a global provider of infection control and surgical equipment, services and disposable products to health care, scientific and industrial customers.

S&P Opinion: Accumulate (★★★★)

Recent Price • 21
52 Wk Range • 21⅝-7⅜
Yield • Nil
12-Mo. P/E • 25.3

Quantitative Evaluations

Outlook (1 Lowest—5 Highest)
• **4+**

Fair Value
• **21⅜**

Risk
• **High**

Earn./Div. Rank
• **NR**

Technical Eval.
• **Bullish** since 10/94

Rel. Strength Rank (1 Lowest—99 Highest)
• **87**

Insider Activity
• **Neutral**

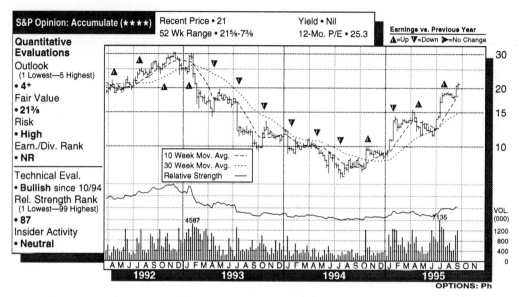

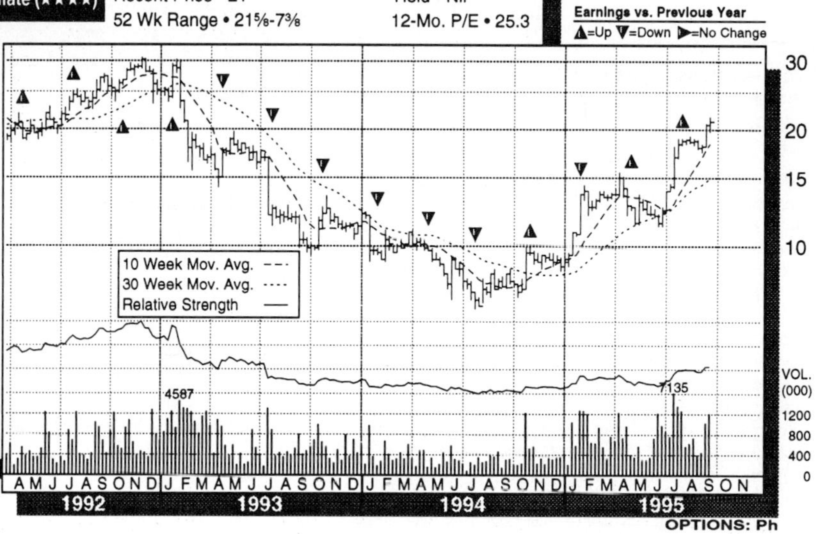

OPTIONS: Ph

Overview - 19-SEP-95

Sales in 1996 are likely to compare favorably with the $460 million indicated for 1995. Despite cautious buying patterns by key hospital and pharmaceutical customers and competitive conditions in medical equipment markets, volume should benefit from important new sole-source contracts with large hospital purchasing groups, such as those recently signed with AmeriNet, Inc. and Catholic Materials Management Association. Although scientific product orders were lower, a recent increase in domestic healthcare equipment orders bodes well for that sector. EPS should contine to benefit from cost streamlining measures, with a gain of about 14%, to $1.25, seen for 1996.

Valuation - 19-SEP-95

The shares have more than tripled from their mid-1994 low, buoyed by strength in the health care sector, improving earnings and takeover speculation. Profits have benefited from the divestiture of the deficit-ridden reusable hospital drapes and gowns business, and from a program initiated by new management to improve margins through rightsizing and cost streamlining measures. Despite a recent moratorium on new product submissions with the FDA (pending the completion of certain corrective actions), earnings should continue to grow in coming years, aided by eventual firming in key markets, anticipated new marketing alliances overseas, and continued close scrutiny of costs. AMSCO is also a potential takeover candidiate.

Key Stock Statistics

S&P EPS Est. 1995	1.10	Tang. Bk. Value/Share	3.37
P/E on S&P Est. 1995	19.1	Beta	NA
S&P EPS Est. 1996	1.25	Shareholders	1,700
Dividend Rate/Share	Nil	Market cap. (B)	$0.644
Shs. outstg. (M)	32.0	Inst. holdings	57%
Avg. daily vol. (M)	0.170	Insider holdings	NA

Value of $10,000 invested 5 years ago: NA

Fiscal Year Ending Dec. 31

	1995	% Change	1994	% Change	1993	% Change
Revenues (Million $)						
1Q	102.9	-2%	104.7	-6%	111.0	21%
2Q	101.1	-10%	112.1	-7%	120.2	-1%
3Q	—	—	116.5	-7%	124.8	4%
4Q	—	—	150.0	2%	146.8	-10%
Yr.	—	—	483.3	-4%	502.9	NM
Income (Million $)						
1Q	6.88	NM	0.68	-78%	3.14	-40%
2Q	6.70	NM	-1.55	NM	1.43	-82%
3Q	—	—	5.88	19%	4.95	-34%
4Q	—	—	-4.21	NM	6.15	-60%
Yr.	—	—	4.25	-73%	15.68	-57%
Earnings Per Share ($)						
1Q	0.21	NM	0.02	-80%	0.10	-38%
2Q	0.21	NM	-0.05	NM	0.05	-81%
3Q	E0.22	16%	0.19	19%	0.16	-30%
4Q	E0.46	NM	-0.14	NM	0.20	-57%
Yr.	E1.10	NM	0.13	-74%	0.50	-56%

Next earnings report expected: mid October

AMSCO International

Business Summary - 19-SEP-95

AMSCO manufactures, markets and services infection control, decontamination and surgical products. Its products are used primarily in the health care industry and by certain research, scientific and industrial customers. Sales by major product group in recent years were:

	1994	1993	1992
Infection control & decontamination products	47%	46%	47%
Surgical products	22%	32%	30%
Services	31%	22%	23%

Foreign operations accounted for 17% of total sales in 1994. R&D expenses represented 2.6% of total sales in 1994 (3.6% in 1993).

Infection control and decontamination products include sterilizers, washing equipment, accessories and related consumable items used by hospital, research, scientific and industrial professionals to prevent the spread of infectious diseases and biological contamination in the processing of pharmaceuticals, chemicals, research materials and food. AMSCO provides complete infection control and decontamination processing systems, including products used for cleaning, disinfecting, sterilizing, drying and aerating medical and scientific instruments, devices, chemicals and packaging.

Through Finn-Aqua (8% of 1994 sales), the company sells freeze-drying systems, water stills, GMP sterilizers, and pure-steam generators and condensers to the pharmaceutical and biotechnology industries.

The surgical product line of general surgical tables, lights and stainless steel cabinets is used by health care providers in both hospital and outpatient surgical settings. The surgical table product line consists primarily of general surgical tables, but AMSCO also offers specialty procedure tables for orthopedics, endoscopy and urology.

The field service staff provides OEM repair and maintenance for the company's infection control, decontamination and surgical equipment, as well as third-party repair, maintenance and management service for a wide variety of medical equipment.

Important Developments

Sep. '95—The company said recent discussions concerning a possible stock merger did not result in a mutually acceptable transaction and were therefore terminated.

Aug. '95—AMSCO signed a three-year, $80 million sole-source contract with AmeriNet, Inc., the largest U.S. healthcare group purchasing organization.

Capitalization

Long Term Debt: $102,793,000 (7/2/95).

Per Share Data ($) (Year Ended Dec. 31)

	1994	1993	1992	1991	1990	1989
Tangible Bk. Val.	2.68	4.09	3.29	3.95	0.53	-0.27
Cash Flow	0.70	1.22	1.72	1.46	1.26	0.98
Earnings	0.13	0.50	1.13	0.95	0.70	0.47
Dividends	Nil	Nil	Nil	Nil	Nil	Nil
Payout Ratio	Nil	Nil	Nil	Nil	Nil	Nil
Prices - High	12¼	30¼	30⅝	23½	NA	NA
- Low	6⅞	9½	18¼	14⅝	NA	NA
P/E Ratio - High	94	61	27	25	NA	NA
- Low	53	19	16	15	NA	NA

Income Statement Analysis (Million $)

	1994	%Chg	1993	%Chg	1992	%Chg	1991
Revs.	483	-3%	498	NM	498	23%	405
Oper. Inc.	66.4	9%	61.0	-28%	84.6	23%	68.7
Depr.	17.4	-23%	22.5	20%	18.8	24%	15.2
Int. Exp.	10.8	-6%	11.5	34%	8.6	46%	5.9
Pretax Inc.	12.0	-57%	27.6	-53%	58.4	24%	47.0
Eff. Tax Rate	65%	—	43%	—	38%	—	40%
Net Inc.	4.3	-73%	15.7	-57%	36.2	27%	28.4

Balance Sheet & Other Fin. Data (Million $)

	1994	1993	1992	1991	1990	1989
Cash	31.5	45.5	56.0	6.8	2.8	2.3
Curr. Assets	257	274	278	170	141	128
Total Assets	462	538	522	326	288	256
Curr. Liab.	121	104	94.0	88.9	82.6	66.6
LT Debt	103	153	167	28.7	97.1	102
Common Eqty.	180	226	210	198	96.0	72.0
Total Cap.	283	379	376	236	205	189
Cap. Exp.	14.0	33.0	53.0	13.3	18.5	7.2
Cash Flow	21.6	38.2	55.0	43.6	31.1	23.5

Ratio Analysis

	1994	1993	1992	1991	1990	1989
Curr. Ratio	2.1	2.6	3.0	1.9	1.7	1.9
% LT Debt of Cap.	36.3	40.4	44.3	12.2	47.4	53.9
% Net Inc.of Revs.	0.9	3.1	7.3	7.0	5.1	4.0
% Ret. on Assets	0.8	2.9	8.5	8.1	6.3	4.5
% Ret. on Equity	2.1	7.2	17.6	17.7	20.4	17.4

Dividend Data —Cash dividends have never been paid.

Data as orig. reptd.; bef. results of disc. opers. and/or spec. items. Per share data adj. for stk. divs. as of ex-div. date. E-Estimated. NA-Not Available. NM-Not Meaningful. NR-Not Ranked.

Office—Two Chatham Center, Suite 1100, 112 Washington Place, Pittsburgh, PA 15219. **Tel**—(412) 338-6500. **Chrmn**—F. DeFazio. **Pres & CEO**—R. A. Gilleland. **VP & CFO**—S. F. Kreger. **VP & Secy**—W. J. Rieflin. **VP & Treas**—J. R. Anke. **Investor Contact**—R. E. Butter (412-338-6542). **Dirs**—D. P. Barry, R. L. Carson, F. DeFazio, R. A. Gilleland, M. Feldberg, R. A. Ortenzio, P. M. Pohl. **Transfer Agent & Registrar**—Mellon Securities Trust Co., Pittsburgh. **Incorporated** in Delaware in 1987. **Empl**-3,100. **S&P Analyst:** Herman Saftlas

STANDARD & POOR'S

STOCK REPORTS

Amtech Corp.

NASDAQ Symbol **AMTC**

In S&P SmallCap 600

26-AUG-95 **Industry:** Electronics/Electric

Summary: Amtech designs, manufactures and supports a variety of software and hardware solutions based on radio frequency and wireless data communications technologies.

Quantitative Evaluations

Outlook
(1 Lowest—5 Highest)
• **NA**

Fair Value
• **NA**

Risk
• **High**

Earn./Div. Rank
• **B-**

Technical Eval.
• **Bullish** since 7/95

Rel. Strength Rank
(1 Lowest—99 Highest)
• **12**

Insider Activity
• **NA**

Recent Price • 6⅝ | Yield • Nil
52 Wk Range • 12¾-5¼ | 12-Mo. P/E • NM

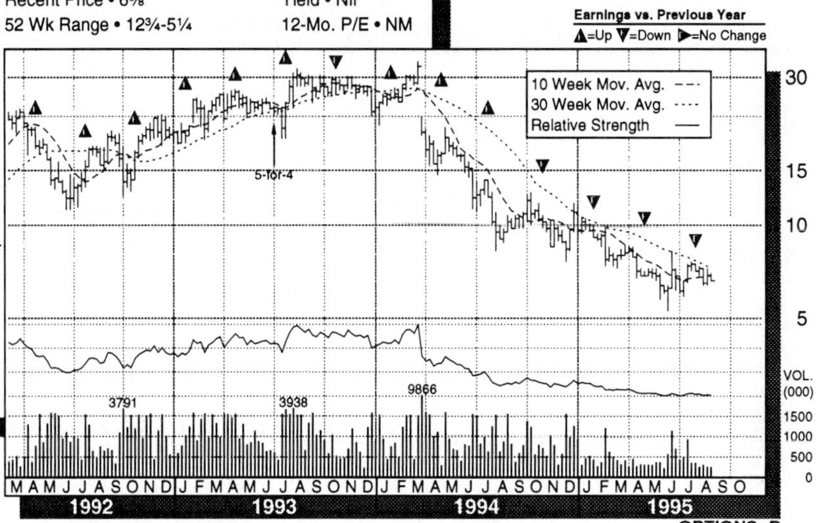

OPTIONS: P

Business Profile - 23-AUG-95

Amtech is pursuing growth opportunities by broadening its focus from transportation related solutions to include complementary products in the area of wireless communications. The acquisitions of Cardkey Systems and Cotag International, Ltd., along with its investment in WaveLink provide Amtech with expertise in this sector. Expansion opportunities for Amtech's traditional product lines exist in South America and the Far East where the transporation infrastructure requires modernization.

Operational Review - 23-AUG-95

Sales fell almost 30% in the first half of 1995, year to year, primarily attributable to the substantial completion of deliveries of automated equipment identification tags to North American railroads in mid-1994. Gross margins were negatively impacted by a shift in product mix away from AMTC's manufactured equipment toward lower margin software products. Near term results will be penalized by charges related to the Cardkey Systems acquistion. The quarterly dividend was omitted in May 1995.

Stock Performance - 25-AUG-95

In the past 30 trading days, AMTC's shares have declined 10%, compared to a 0.04% rise in the S&P 500. Average trading volume for the past five days was 47,180 shares, compared with the 40-day moving average of 78,926 shares.

Key Stock Statistics

Dividend Rate/Share	Nil	Shareholders	1,000
Shs. outstg. (M)	14.7	Market cap. (B)	$0.097
Avg. daily vol. (M)	0.051	Inst. holdings	29%
Tang. Bk. Value/Share	4.82	Insider holdings	NA
Beta	2.02		

Value of $10,000 invested 5 years ago: $ 9,329

Fiscal Year Ending Dec. 31

	1995	% Change	1994	% Change	1993	% Change
Revenues (Million $)						
1Q	13.94	-26%	18.96	62%	11.69	65%
2Q	13.00	-30%	18.51	39%	13.28	58%
3Q	—	—	12.21	-22%	15.66	25%
4Q	—	—	11.77	-37%	18.81	59%
Yr.	—	—	61.46	3%	59.42	49%
Income (Million $)						
1Q	-0.28	NM	3.68	123%	1.65	NM
2Q	-1.26	NM	3.40	41%	2.41	98%
3Q	—	—	0.50	-82%	2.72	-20%
4Q	—	—	0.08	-98%	3.59	50%
Yr.	—	—	7.66	-26%	10.37	43%
Earnings Per Share ($)						
1Q	-0.02	NM	0.25	123%	0.11	NM
2Q	-0.09	NM	0.23	44%	0.16	82%
3Q	—	—	0.03	-83%	0.18	-22%
4Q	—	—	0.01	-96%	0.24	50%
Yr.	—	—	0.52	-26%	0.70	37%

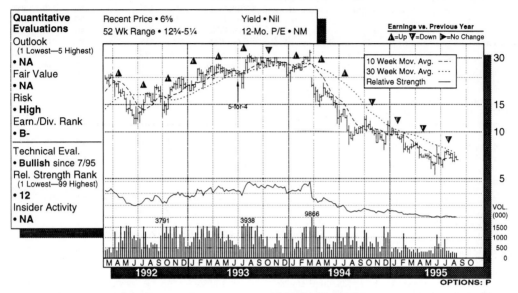

Next earnings report expected: early November

Amtech Corp.

Business Summary - 24-AUG-95

Amtech Corp. has primarily been engaged in the design and manufacture of a line of hardware and software products and providing related services involving radio frequency electronic identification (RFID) technology. Following the acquisitions during 1995 of Cotag International Ltd. (in January) and Cardkey Systems (in August), AMTC reorganized into three new market-oriented wireless data groups in an effort to broaden its focus beyond its traditional RFID products.

The company's Transportation Systems Group markets its high-frequency RFID technology, which permits remote identification of, and communication with, objects such as automobiles and railcars at higher speeds, at longer distances and in more difficult outdoor and industrial environments than technologies based on optical, magnetic or other techniques. Its targeted markets within the transportation and intelligent vehicle highway systems industries include electronic toll and traffic management, intermodal transportation, rail transportation, vehicle fleet management, and access control. It has developed products and services to address each of these markets, including identification hardware, such as tags, readers and field tag programmers, and software systems that range from simple reader control applications to large-scale electronic toll collection systems. In addition, the company provides various support services.

Amtech's Electronic Security Group comprises Cardkey Systems and Cotag International Ltd. Cardkey sells, installs and services electronic access control systems through an extensive international network of direct sales offices and resellers. Cotag manufactures low frequency RFID electronic security systems for hands-free personnel and vehicle access control, marketed to commercial, industrial, government and health care customers.

The company's Interactive Data Group consists of its investment (under which it may obtain up to a 75% equity interest) in WaveLink Technologies, a Canadian concern which has developed vehicle-mounted and hand-held terminals connected by wireless links to users' host computers in environments where mobile data collection is required. WaveLink's initial products are expected to be released to production in late 1995.

Important Developments

Aug. '95—Amtech anticipates recording a consolidated net loss of between $0.35 and $0.60 a share for 1995 on its August acquisition of Cardkey Systems, depending largely on the ultimate one-time charge to earnings to be determined for "purchased in-process R&D" being acquired. The one-time acquisition related charge will be recorded in the third quarter.

Capitalization

Long Term Debt: None (6/95).

Per Share Data ($)

(Year Ended Dec. 31)

	1994	1993	1992	1991	1990	1989
Tangible Bk. Val.	5.16	4.59	3.40	1.26	1.56	2.12
Cash Flow	0.72	0.84	0.63	-0.28	-0.48	-0.74
Earnings	0.52	0.70	0.51	-0.40	-0.57	-0.82
Dividends	0.08	0.06	Nil	Nil	Nil	Nil
Payout Ratio	15%	9%	Nil	Nil	Nil	Nil
Prices - High	33¾	32	23¾	15⅝	11¼	8
- Low	7⅝	18¼	11¼	4¾	4⅛	6
P/E Ratio - High	65	46	46	NM	NM	NM
- Low	15	26	22	NM	NM	NM

Income Statement Analysis (Million $)

	1994	%Chg	1993	%Chg	1992	%Chg	1991
Revs.	61.5	4%	59.4	49%	39.9	113%	18.7
Oper. Inc.	12.9	-11%	14.5	86%	7.8	NM	-3.9
Depr.	3.0	39%	2.1	28%	1.7	12%	1.5
Int. Exp.	Nil	—	Nil	—	Nil	—	Nil
Pretax Inc.	12.1	-14%	14.1	90%	7.4	NM	-5.0
Eff. Tax Rate	57%	—	27%	—	1.80%	—	Nil
Net Inc.	7.7	-26%	10.4	43%	7.3	NM	-5.0

Balance Sheet & Other Fin. Data (Million $)

	1994	1993	1992	1991	1990	1989
Cash	49.9	36.8	31.2	12.0	7.5	19.2
Curr. Assets	67.0	54.8	42.8	17.9	16.9	22.8
Total Assets	80.6	76.7	57.4	23.0	22.3	27.2
Curr. Liab.	3.5	7.1	4.7	4.3	3.3	1.7
LT Debt	Nil	Nil	Nil	Nil	Nil	Nil
Common Eqty.	75.3	66.8	48.8	16.0	18.9	25.5
Total Cap.	75.3	66.8	48.8	16.0	18.9	25.5
Cap. Exp.	2.3	7.3	1.1	1.1	1.9	2.5
Cash Flow	10.6	12.5	8.9	-3.5	-5.8	-6.6

Ratio Analysis

	1994	1993	1992	1991	1990	1989
Curr. Ratio	19.3	7.7	9.0	4.1	5.1	13.7
% LT Debt of Cap.	Nil	Nil	Nil	Nil	Nil	Nil
% Net Inc.of Revs.	12.5	17.4	18.2	NM	NM	NM
% Ret. on Assets	9.7	15.4	17.4	NM	NM	NM
% Ret. on Equity	10.8	17.8	21.7	NM	NM	NM

Dividend Data —Quarterly cash dividends were initiated in June 1993, and suspended in May 1995. A five-for-four stock split was effected in June 1993, and a three-for-two stock split was effected in February 1992.

Amt. of Div. $	Date Decl.	Ex-Div. Date	Stock of Record	Payment Date
0.020	Aug. 01	Aug. 30	Sep. 06	Sep. 26 '94
0.020	Nov. 03	Dec. 01	Dec. 07	Dec. 28 '94
0.020	Jan. 24	Mar. 01	Mar. 07	Mar. 28 '95

Data as orig. reptd.; bef. results of disc. opers. and/or spec. items. Per share data adj. for stk. divs. as of ex-div. date. E-Estimated. NA-Not Available. NM-Not Meaningful. NR-Not Ranked.

Office—17304 Preston Rd., Dallas, TX 75252. **Tel**—(214) 733-6600. **Pres & CEO**—G. R. Mortenson. **SVP, CFO & Treas**—S. M. York. **Secy**—R. A. Woessner. **Investor Contact**—Beverly Fuortes. **Dirs**—G. J. Fernandes, R. M. Gintel, E. W. Johnson, J. A. Landt, J. S. Marston, G. R. Mortenson, A. R. Sanchez, Jr. **Transfer Agent**—Society National Bank, Dallas. **Incorporated** in Texas in 1988. **Empl-** 685. **S&P Analyst:** Steven A. Jaworski

AMTROL Inc.

NASDAQ Symbol **AMTL**
In S&P SmallCap 600

10-OCT-95 **Industry:** Building

Summary: This company is a leading producer and marketer of water tanks and related products.

Quantitative Evaluations
Outlook
(1 Lowest—5 Highest)
• **NA**
Fair Value
• **NA**
Risk
• **Low**
Earn./Div. Rank
• **NR**

Technical Eval.
• **Bearish** since 7/95
Rel. Strength Rank
(1 Lowest—99 Highest)
• **25**
Insider Activity
• **NA**

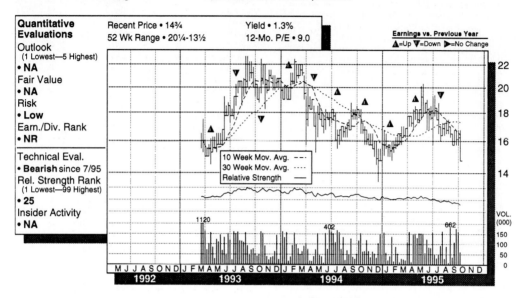

Recent Price • 14¾
52 Wk Range • 20¼-13½
Yield • 1.3%
12-Mo. P/E • 9.0

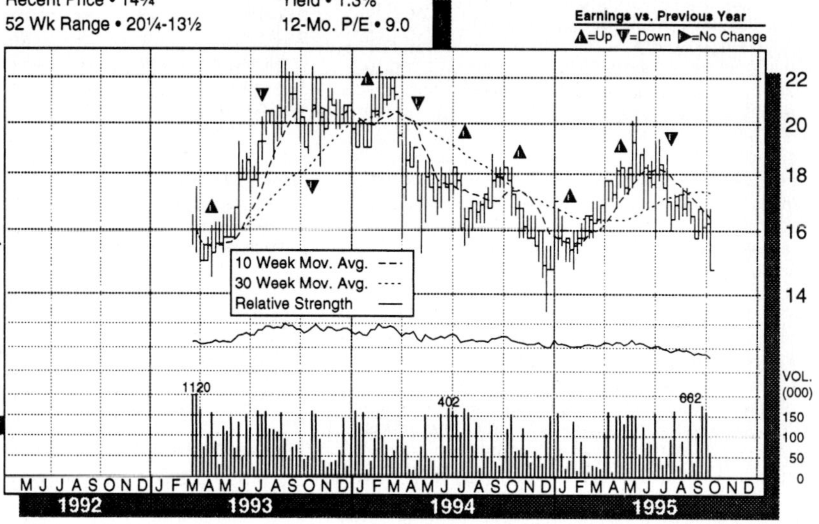

Business Profile - 10-OCT-95

In 1994, the company reorganized its structure into strategic business units to enhance its worldwide marketing and supply efforts and to better manage its global strategy. It also invested in capital projects to upgrade its systems and manufacturing capability, and broadened its distribution through OEM's as well as to do-it-yourself retailers. The company expects these actions to serve it well in 1995 and ensuing years as it grows and seeks out unique opportunities to broaden its business.

Operational Review - 10-OCT-95

Revenues in 1995's first six months rose 1.7%, year to year, reflecting moderating demand in the home sales and home improvement markets. Margins narrowed slightly, due to substantially higher raw material costs, which more than offset improved pricing and operating efficiencies; operating income slipped 1.2%. After a sharp increase in net other income, pretax income rose 1.3%. Net income increased to $0.86 a share, from $0.84.

Stock Performance - 06-OCT-95

In the past 30 trading days, AMTL's shares have declined 13%, compared to a 4% rise in the S&P 500. Average trading volume for the past five days was 11,920 shares, compared with the 40-day moving average of 45,067 shares.

Key Stock Statistics

Dividend Rate/Share	0.20	Shareholders	1,000
Shs. outstg. (M)	7.5	Market cap. (B)	$0.116
Avg. daily vol. (M)	0.046	Inst. holdings	48%
Tang. Bk. Value/Share	8.40	Insider holdings	NA
Beta	NA		

Value of $10,000 invested 5 years ago: NA

Fiscal Year Ending Dec. 31

	1995	% Change	1994	% Change	1993	% Change
Revenues (Million $)						
1Q	43.16	4%	41.70	6%	39.50	9%
2Q	47.63	NM	47.50	11%	42.70	6%
3Q	—	—	45.50	1%	44.90	15%
4Q	—	—	38.70	4%	37.20	13%
Yr.	—	—	173.5	6%	164.3	11%
Income (Million $)						
1Q	2.85	12%	2.54	5%	2.43	—
2Q	3.70	-4%	3.86	16%	3.34	—
3Q	—	—	3.87	2%	3.79	—
4Q	—	—	1.99	24%	1.61	—
Yr.	—	—	12.27	10%	11.18	—
Earnings Per Share ($)						
1Q	0.38	15%	0.33	-21%	0.42	62%
2Q	0.49	-4%	0.51	16%	0.44	-8%
3Q	—	—	0.51	2%	0.50	-11%
4Q	—	—	0.26	24%	0.21	11%
Yr.	—	—	1.61	3%	1.56	5%

Next earnings report expected: mid October

AMTROL Inc.

Business Summary - 10-OCT-95

AMTROL Inc. designs, manufactures and markets primarily well water tanks, hot water expansion tanks and non-returnable chemical containers used in flow control, storage, heating and other treatment of fluids in the water systems market and selected sectors of the heating, ventilating and air-conditioning (HVAC) market. Revenues in recent years were derived as follows:

	1994	1993	1992
Water systems products	57%	56%	57%
HVAC products	43%	44%	43%

The company's well water tanks, marketed under the Well-X-Trol and CHAMPION brand names for residential and commercial use, are pre-pressurized tanks that control pressure while maintaining the separation of air and water, thereby reducing wear on switches, pumps and other components caused by unnecessary on/off cycling. AMTROL also manufactures and markets a line of tanks and pump systems used to boost or maintain water pressure in remote or elevated areas served by local water systems and in high-rise office and apartment buildings, and specialized residential and commercial water treatment equipment such as water softeners, filters, reverse osmosis accumulators and other related systems used to purify or treat municipal and well water.

Other water systems products include portable watering systems used in landscaping, supermarket produce departments and plant nurseries; valves, fittings, accessories and safety devices for the swimming pool market; and automatic turf irrigation control systems.

HVAC products include expansion tanks, marketed under the Extrol and Therm-X-Trol brand names, which are used to control expanding water in a closed system and reduce corrosion caused by oxygen in the system. The company also produces commercial pressure boosting systems used to boost low pressure or to provide constant pressure, and shock suppressors used to eliminate water pipeline shock waves.

Other HVAC product lines include indirect-fired residential and commercial hot water heaters; pressure-rated containers used primarily to store, transport and dispense refrigerant gases for air-conditioning systems; air elimination equipment used to separate and vent air from system piping; and circulating and centrifugal pumps.

Important Developments

Aug. '95—In an effort to reduce operating costs and improve productivity, AMTL said it will close its Plano, Texas facility and take a $1.8 million pretax charge in the third quarter of 1995. This plant accounted for almost 25% of Amtrol's total chemical container capacity. AMTL said that the chemical container business is still part of its long-term strategy.

Capitalization

Long Term Debt: None (7/1/95).

Per Share Data ($)

(Year Ended Dec. 31)

	1994	1993	1992	1991	1990	1989
Tangible Bk. Val.	8.47	7.04	2.99	NA	NA	NA
Cash Flow	2.17	2.13	2.17	NA	NA	NA
Earnings	1.61	1.56	1.49	NA	NA	NA
Dividends	Nil	0.15	Nil	NA	NA	NA
Payout Ratio	Nil	10%	Nil	NA	NA	NA
Prices - High	22½	22¾	NA	NA	NA	NA
- Low	13½	14½	NA	NA	NA	NA
P/E Ratio - High	14	15	NA	NA	NA	NA
- Low	8	9	NA	NA	NA	NA

Income Statement Analysis (Million $)

	1994	%Chg	1993	%Chg	1992	%Chg	1991
Revs.	173	5%	164	11%	148	—	NA
Oper. Inc.	24.2	5%	23.1	12%	20.7	—	NA
Depr.	4.3	6%	4.1	9%	3.7	—	NA
Int. Exp.	0.3	-70%	0.9	-67%	2.8	—	NA
Pretax Inc.	20.0	9%	18.3	38%	13.3	—	NA
Eff. Tax Rate	39%	—	39%	—	38%	—	NA
Net Inc.	12.3	10%	11.2	37%	8.2	—	NA

Balance Sheet & Other Fin. Data (Million $)

	1994	1993	1992	1991	1990	1989
Cash	9.0	5.3	6.3	NA	NA	NA
Curr. Assets	55.9	47.6	41.9	NA	NA	NA
Total Assets	91.6	82.6	74.5	NA	NA	NA
Curr. Liab.	18.6	19.2	21.0	NA	NA	NA
LT Debt	2.4	3.3	29.7	NA	NA	NA
Common Eqty.	64.2	53.0	16.7	NA	NA	NA
Total Cap.	67.1	57.5	48.4	NA	NA	NA
Cap. Exp.	4.9	7.4	2.8	NA	NA	NA
Cash Flow	16.6	15.3	11.9	NA	NA	NA

Ratio Analysis

	1994	1993	1992	1991	1990	1989
Curr. Ratio	3.0	2.5	2.0	NA	NA	NA
% LT Debt of Cap.	3.5	5.8	61.3	NA	NA	NA
% Net Inc.of Revs.	7.1	6.8	5.5	NA	NA	NA
% Ret. on Assets	14.0	12.0	11.2	NA	NA	NA
% Ret. on Equity	20.9	29.4	63.4	NA	NA	NA

Dividend Data —Cash dividends were initiated in 1993.

Amt. of Div. $	Date Decl.	Ex-Div. Date	Stock of Record	Payment Date
0.050	Oct. 19	Oct. 31	Nov. 04	Nov. 15 '94
0.050	Feb. 02	Feb. 08	Feb. 14	Feb. 24 '95
0.050	Apr. 20	May. 01	May. 05	May. 15 '95
0.050	Jul. 17	Aug. 02	Aug. 04	Aug. 15 '95

Data as orig. reptd.; bef. results of disc. opers. and/or spec. items. Per share data adj. for stk. divs. as of ex-div. date. E-Estimated. NA-Not Available. NM-Not Meaningful. NR-Not Ranked.

Office—1400 Division Rd., West Warwick, RI 02893. **Tel**—(401) 884-6300. **Chrmn & CEO**—C. H. Kirk. **Pres & COO**—D. Beretta. **Sr VP & CFO**—E. J. Cooney. **VP & Secy**—M. J. Regan. **Dirs**—D. Beretta, H. H. Jacobi, C. H. Kirk, K. L. Kirk, A. W. Ondis, V. A. Sarni, L. R. Waxlax, H. H. Winkhaus. **Transfer Agent & Registrar**—Fleet National Bank, Providence, R.I. **Incorporated** in Rhode Island in 1973. **Empl**-1,000. **S&P Analyst:** Robert E. Friedman

STANDARD & POOR'S

STOCK REPORTS

Apogee Enterprises

NASDAQ Symbol **APOG**

In S&P SmallCap 600

21-OCT-95

Industry: Glass/products

Summary: This leading supplier of window and glass products and services derives the majority of its revenues from the automobile and construction industries.

Quantitative Evaluations

Outlook (1 Lowest—5 Highest) • **4-**

Fair Value • **15⅜**

Risk • **Low**

Earn./Div. Rank • **B**

Technical Eval. • **Bullish** since 9/95

Rel. Strength Rank (1 Lowest—99 Highest) • **18**

Insider Activity • **NA**

Recent Price • 14¼

52 Wk Range • 18½-14¼

Yield • 2.4%

12-Mo. P/E • 12.6

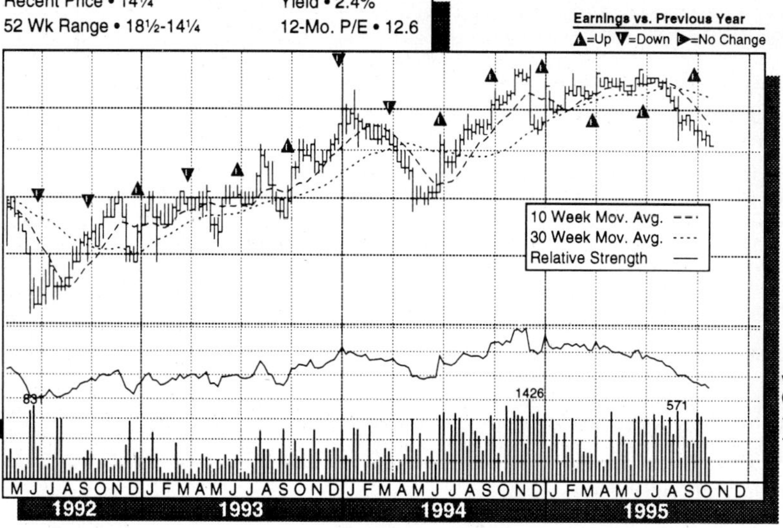

Business Profile - 19-OCT-95

APOG restructured its operating divisions into two business segments in late 1994-95 in order to focus on its primary markets. It recently completed the sale of its window coverings group, recording a $4.7 million gain in the second quarter. APOG noted that despite an improving building products and services segment, the company has a long way to go before it reaches its targeted level of earnings. The balance sheet is strong, and capital expenditures for 1995-96 are projected at $36 million.

Operational Review - 19-OCT-95

Net sales in the 27-week period ended September 2, 1995, advanced 21% from those of the 26-week year-earlier period, primarily reflecting higher building products and services volume and, to a lesser extent, increased automotive glass sales. Profitability benefited from the higher volume and well controlled operating costs and expenses, and net income rose 32%. The company expects continued progress in its building products and services segment to aid results for the balance of the fiscal year.

Stock Performance - 20-OCT-95

In the past 30 trading days, APOG's shares have declined 10%, compared to a 3% rise in the S&P 500. Average trading volume for the past five days was 12,100 shares, compared with the 40-day moving average of 33,305 shares.

Key Stock Statistics

Dividend Rate/Share	0.34	Shareholders	5,100
Shs. outstg. (M)	13.5	Market cap. (B)	$0.192
Avg. daily vol. (M)	0.045	Inst. holdings	45%
Tang. Bk. Value/Share	9.18	Insider holdings	NA
Beta	0.23		

Value of $10,000 invested 5 years ago: $ 10,315

Fiscal Year Ending Feb. 28

	1996	% Change	1995	% Change	1994	% Change
Revenues (Million $)						
1Q	219.0	22%	179.0	20%	148.8	14%
2Q	222.2	19%	186.0	6%	175.6	20%
3Q	—	—	186.3	NM	184.5	26%
4Q	—	—	205.4	15%	179.4	20%
Yr.	—	—	756.5	10%	688.2	20%
Income (Million $)						
1Q	3.48	34%	2.60	183%	0.92	188%
2Q	5.65	32%	4.29	76%	2.44	25%
3Q	—	—	3.76	30%	2.90	44%
4Q	—	—	2.39	NM	-2.95	NM
Yr.	—	—	13.05	NM	3.31	-27%
Earnings Per Share ($)						
1Q	0.26	37%	0.19	171%	0.07	NM
2Q	0.41	28%	0.32	78%	0.18	20%
3Q	—	—	0.28	NM	-0.22	NM
4Q	—	—	0.18	NM	-0.22	NM
Yr.	—	—	0.97	NM	0.25	-26%

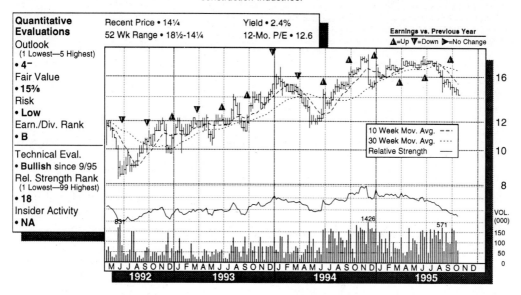

Next earnings report expected: late December

Apogee Enterprises

Business Summary - 20-OCT-95

Apogee Enterprises, Inc. makes custom aluminum window systems for nonresidential buildings, fabricates glass for architectural and automotive markets, and installs these products in buildings and automobiles. At the end of fiscal 1994-95, the company changed to two business segments from the previous four. Contributions in 1994-95 were:

	Revenues	Profits
Building products & services	67%	19%
Automotive glass	33%	81%

The company's building products and services segment's operating units consist of nonresidential construction, architectural metals, architectural glass and consumer. The segment's Harmon Contract unit is one of the world's largest designers and installers of curtainwall and window systems for nonresidential construction. The architectural metals unit operates under the name Wausau Metals, one of the largest U.S. fabricators of high-quality aluminum window and curtainwall systems. Other operations include Milco, a fabricator of high-performance, thermally efficient aluminum windows; and Linetec, which operates two metal coating plants. The glass unit (operating primarily under the Viracon and Marcon Coatings names) is a leading domestic producer of flat laminated safety glass, replacement foreign car windshields and non-glare picture framing glass.

The automotive glass segment is engaged in the automotive replacement glass business through its Harmon Glass service centers, Glass Depot distribution centers and Curvlite fabrication center. The Viratec Thin Films unit, a 50%-owned joint venture with Marvin Windows, was spun out of the former glass fabrication division. In 1994-95, this segment acquired or opened nine new distribution centers and 33 service centers, while closing one distribution and seven service centers, bringing its fiscal year end totals to 53 and 256, respectively.

In January 1995, the company acquired Cherrydale Glass Shops, Inc., a chain of 13 retail auto glass stores in the Washington, D.C. area, with sales of $15 million in 1994.

Important Developments

Aug. '95—Apogee completed the sale of its Nanik Window Coverings Group to Springs Industries, Inc. Nanik is one of the leading producers of custom venetian blinds and interior shutters for the designer and commercial markets in the U.S. Terms were not disclosed. Nanik accounted for less than 5% of the company's sales in 1994-95.

Capitalization

Long Term Debt: $79,591,000 (6/3/95).
Options: To buy 578,000 shs. at $8.95 to $18.91 ea. (2/95).

Per Share Data ($) (Year Ended Feb. 28)

	1995	1994	1993	1992	1991	1990
Tangible Bk. Val.	8.65	8.42	8.15	8.04	7.72	6.72
Cash Flow	2.09	1.43	1.48	1.84	2.22	1.93
Earnings	0.97	0.25	0.34	0.63	1.25	1.04
Dividends	0.31	0.29	0.27	0.26	0.24	0.20
Payout Ratio	32%	116%	79%	41%	19%	19%
Cal. Yrs.	1994	1993	1992	1991	1990	1989
Prices - High	18½	17¾	14	18	20⅛	18¾
- Low	11½	9¾	8¼	9½	13⅝	11⅞
P/E Ratio - High	19	71	41	29	16	18
- Low	12	39	24	15	11	11

Income Statement Analysis (Million $)

	1995	%Chg	1994	%Chg	1993	%Chg	1992
Revs.	757	10%	688	20%	572	-4%	596
Oper. Inc.	39.5	41%	28.0	30%	21.5	-48%	41.4
Depr.	15.2	-3%	15.7	4%	15.1	-7%	16.3
Int. Exp.	5.0	37%	3.6	21%	3.0	2%	2.9
Pretax Inc.	20.9	NM	6.6	2%	6.5	-59%	15.8
Eff. Tax Rate	39%	—	40%	—	30%	—	46%
Net Inc.	13.1	NM	3.3	-27%	4.5	-47%	8.5

Balance Sheet & Other Fin. Data (Million $)

	1995	1994	1993	1992	1991	1990
Cash	2.9	10.8	8.9	18.7	20.5	12.2
Curr. Assets	257	221	169	166	163	155
Total Assets	362	306	251	250	250	244
Curr. Liab.	136	141	100	101	102	95.0
LT Debt	80.6	35.7	28.4	25.3	29.4	41.4
Common Eqty.	125	114	112	114	109	96.0
Total Cap.	207	151	141	141	142	144
Cap. Exp.	25.0	15.2	9.3	15.9	17.2	18.1
Cash Flow	28.2	19.0	19.6	24.8	30.3	26.2

Ratio Analysis

	1995	1994	1993	1992	1991	1990
Curr. Ratio	1.9	1.6	1.7	1.6	1.6	1.6
% LT Debt of Cap.	39.0	23.6	20.2	17.9	20.7	28.8
% Net Inc.of Revs.	1.7	0.5	0.8	1.4	2.8	2.4
% Ret. on Assets	3.9	1.2	1.8	3.4	6.9	6.2
% Ret. on Equity	10.9	2.9	4.0	7.6	16.6	15.7

Dividend Data —Cash has been paid each year since 1974. A shareholder rights plan was adopted in 1990.

Amt. of Div. $	Date Decl.	Ex-Div. Date	Stock of Record	Payment Date
0.080	Oct. 20	Oct. 26	Nov. 01	Nov. 17 '94
0.080	Jan. 18	Jan. 25	Jan. 31	Feb. 16 '95
0.080	Apr. 24	May. 03	May. 09	May. 25 '95
0.080	Jul. 31	Aug. 11	Aug. 15	Aug. 31 '95
0.085	Oct. 17	Oct. 27	Oct. 31	Nov. 16 '95

Data as orig. reptd.; bef. results of disc. opers. and/or spec. items. Per share data adj. for stk. divs. as of ex-div. date. E-Estimated. NA-Not Available. NM-Not Meaningful. NR-Not Ranked.

Office—7900 Xerxes Ave. South, Minneapolis, MN 55431. **Tel**—(612) 835-1874. **Chrmn, Pres & CEO**—D. W. Goldfus. **VP-Fin, CFO & Investor Contact**—T. L. Hall. **Treas**—W. G. Gardner. **Dirs**—A. L. Andersen, G. K. Anderson, P. Burke, D. W. Goldfus, H. A. Hammerly, J. W. Levin, J. L. Martineau, L. J. Niederhofer, D. E. Nugent. **Transfer Agent & Registrar**—American Stock Transfer Co., NYC. **Incorporated** in Minnesota in 1949. **Empl-** 6,184. **S&P Analyst:** Stewart Scharf

STANDARD & POOR'S

STOCK REPORTS

Applebee's International

NASDAQ Symbol **APPB**

In S&P SmallCap 600

10-SEP-95 **Industry:** Food serving

Summary: This company develops, franchises and operates a growing chain of approximately 600 full-service Applebee's restaurants and 19 restaurants in the Rio Bravo group.

Quantitative Evaluations

Outlook (1 Lowest—5 Highest)
• **5**

Fair Value
• **43⅜**

Risk
• **High**

Earn./Div. Rank
• **NR**

Technical Eval.
• **Bullish** since 7/95

Rel. Strength Rank (1 Lowest—99 Highest)
• **79**

Insider Activity
• **NA**

Recent Price • 30⅞
52 Wk Range • 31¾-12¾

Yield • 0.2%
12-Mo. P/E • 41.7

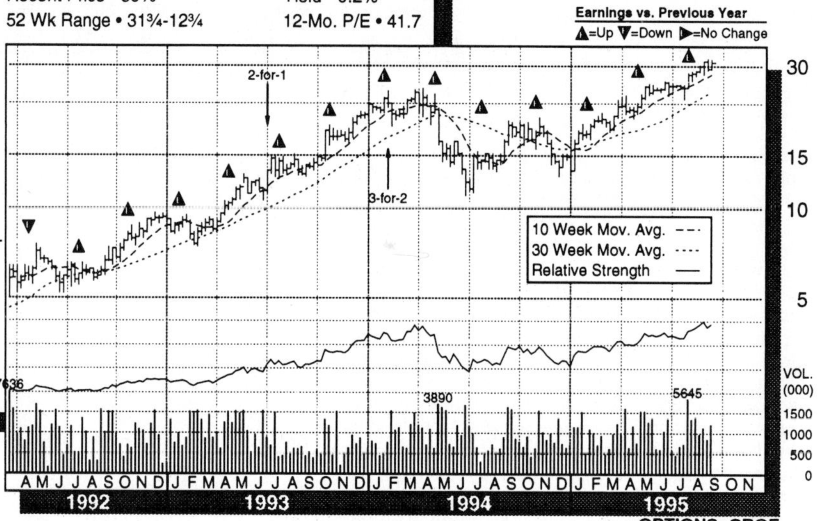

OPTIONS: CBOE

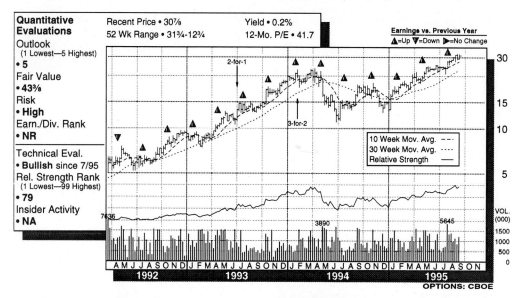

Business Profile - 07-SEP-95

This rapidly growing operator and franchisor of full-service restaurants believes it can continue to add more than 100 new Applebee's restaurants a year for several years, eventually reaching 1,200 - 1,500 restaurants. It also intends to open franchised Rio Bravo Cantina restaurants beginning in 1996. APPB plans to open at least 27 new company-owned Applebee's restaurants and four Rio Bravo Cantina restaurants in 1995. The consensus earnings estimate for 1995 is $0.88 a share.

Operational Review - 07-SEP-95

Operating revenues in the 26 weeks ended June 25, 1995, advanced 34%, year to year (as restated to include Innovative Restaurant Concepts on a pooling-of-interests basis), reflecting 33% higher company restaurant sales and a 43% increase in franchise income. Revenues benefited from additional units in operation and higher system-wide comparable-unit sales. Despite $1.8 million of merger-related expenses, and taxes at a higher rate, net income was up 35%.

Stock Performance - 08-SEP-95

In the past 30 trading days, APPB's shares have increased 10%, compared to a 2% rise in the S&P 500. Average trading volume for the past five days was 299,475 shares, compared with the 40-day moving average of 337,841 shares.

Key Stock Statistics

Dividend Rate/Share	0.05	Shareholders	800
Shs. outstg. (M)	30.5	Market cap. (B)	$0.940
Avg. daily vol. (M)	0.212	Inst. holdings	50%
Tang. Bk. Value/Share	3.08	Insider holdings	NA
Beta	1.81		

Value of $10,000 invested 5 years ago: $ 72,035

Fiscal Year Ending Dec. 31

	1995	% Change	1994	% Change	1993	% Change
Revenues (Million $)						
1Q	75.44	65%	45.63	108%	21.98	82%
2Q	83.80	69%	49.70	75%	28.43	111%
3Q	—	—	54.88	68%	32.75	121%
4Q	—	—	58.32	72%	33.92	111%
Yr.	—	—	208.5	78%	117.1	107%
Income (Million $)						
1Q	4.25	46%	2.92	69%	1.73	94%
2Q	6.81	93%	3.53	64%	2.15	68%
3Q	—	—	4.82	74%	2.77	81%
4Q	—	—	4.51	60%	2.82	97%
Yr.	—	—	15.78	66%	9.48	84%
Earnings Per Share ($)						
1Q	0.15	36%	0.11	27%	0.09	37%
2Q	0.24	71%	0.14	40%	0.10	58%
3Q	—	—	0.19	46%	0.13	69%
4Q	—	—	0.18	38%	0.13	86%
Yr.	—	—	0.62	41%	0.44	63%

Next earnings report expected: early November

Applebee's International

Business Summary - 07-SEP-95

Applebee's International, Inc. develops, franchises and operates a chain of full-service restaurants, principally under the name "Applebee's Neighborhood Grill & Bar." As of August 15, 1995, there were 598 Applebee's restaurants in operation in 43 states, one Canadian province and the island of Curacao, up from 505 at 1994 year end, with the greatest concentration in the Southeast. In addition, it operates 19 specialty restaurants as part of the Rio Bravo group. Revenues in recent years (restated for the acquisition of Pub Ventures of New England, Inc. and Innovative Restaurant Concepts Inc.):

	1994	1993	1992
Food & beverage sales	88%	88%	86%
Franchise income	12%	12%	14%

Organized in 1983, the company beginning in 1986 opened six restaurants as a franchisee of the Applebee's Neighborhood Grill & Bar division of Creative Food 'N Fun Co., an indirect subsidiary of W. R. Grace & Co. In March 1988, substantially all assets of the Applebee's division were purchased for about $21 million. At that time, the division operated 13 restaurants (excluding one not acquired) and there were 41 franchised units (including the company's six restaurants).

Each Applebee's restaurant offers an extensive selection of moderately priced high-quality food and beverage items appealing both to families and adult groups. Weighted average weekly sales per restaurant in 1994 were $41,376 for company-owned or operated units and $41,010 for franchised units.

Growth of the Applebee's chain since March 1988 has reflected active franchising efforts. The company intends to continue developing restaurants in current areas and certain new territories. APPB has also begun pursuing international franchising of the Applebee's concept, initially focusing on Canada, the Caribbean and Europe.

Important Developments

Aug. '95—Underwriters led by Piper Jaffray, Dillon Read and Montgomery Securities exercised their over-allotment option in connection with APPB's July 1995 public offering of 2.4 million common shares (including 300,000 shares sold by stockholders) at $26.50 per share. As a result, the underwriters received an additional 360,000 (45,000) shares at $26.50.

Mar. '95—The company acquired privately held Innovative Restaurant Concepts Inc. for approximately 2.8 million common shares (including stock options) and the assumption of about $13.7 million of Innovative debt.

Capitalization

Long Term Debt: $41,712,000 (6/95).
Minority Interest: $650,000.

Per Share Data ($)

(Year Ended Dec. 31)

	1994	1993	1992	1991	1990	1989
Tangible Bk. Val.	2.82	2.38	2.42	1.00	0.73	0.57
Cash Flow	1.01	0.67	0.41	0.39	0.29	0.19
Earnings	0.62	0.44	0.27	0.22	0.13	Nil
Dividends	0.05	0.04	0.03	0.02	0.01	Nil
Payout Ratio	8%	9%	12%	9%	10%	Nil
Prices - High	25¼	22½	9⅝	5⅛	7¼	5⅜
- Low	11	7⅜	4¾	2$^{5}/_{16}$	2	4¼
P/E Ratio - High	41	51	35	23	57	NM
- Low	18	17	17	10	16	NM

Income Statement Analysis (Million $)

	1994	%Chg	1993	%Chg	1992	%Chg	1991
Revs.	209	79%	117	107%	56.5	25%	45.1
Oper. Inc.	36.0	89%	19.0	103%	9.4	47%	6.3
Depr.	8.7	71%	5.1	95%	2.6	11%	2.4
Int. Exp.	1.2	NM	0.2	—	Nil	—	Nil
Pretax Inc.	25.6	66%	15.4	85%	8.3	66%	5.0
Eff. Tax Rate	34%	—	39%	—	39%	—	39%
Net Inc.	16.9	78%	9.5	84%	5.1	67%	3.1

Balance Sheet & Other Fin. Data (Million $)

	1994	1993	1992	1991	1990	1989
Cash	17.2	16.2	22.8	9.7	2.4	2.2
Curr. Assets	31.6	24.4	28.2	12.1	5.0	4.3
Total Assets	152	104	68.1	30.0	26.2	22.6
Curr. Liab.	27.9	19.2	8.0	6.2	5.4	2.8
LT Debt	23.7	2.2	0.1	Nil	Nil	Nil
Common Eqty.	96.7	79.2	58.6	23.2	20.4	19.3
Total Cap.	122	82.5	59.1	23.2	20.4	19.3
Cap. Exp.	40.4	37.8	9.2	1.3	4.7	1.6
Cash Flow	25.6	14.6	7.8	5.4	4.1	1.9

Ratio Analysis

	1994	1993	1992	1991	1990	1989
Curr. Ratio	1.1	1.3	3.5	1.9	0.9	1.5
% LT Debt of Cap.	19.4	2.6	0.1	Nil	Nil	Nil
% Net Inc.of Revs.	8.1	8.1	9.1	6.8	4.7	NM
% Ret. on Assets	12.4	10.7	9.1	11.0	7.4	NM
% Ret. on Equity	18.0	13.3	11.1	14.2	9.1	NM

Dividend Data —The company declared its initial annual cash dividend in 1990. A two-for-one stock split was effected in June 1993 and a three-for-two stock split was effected in January 1994.

Amt. of Div. $	Date Decl.	Ex-Div. Date	Stock of Record	Payment Date
0.050	Dec. 08	Dec. 14	Dec. 20	Jan. 27 '95

Data as orig. reptd.; bef. results of disc. opers. and/or spec. items. Per share data adj. for stk. divs. as of ex-div. date. E-Estimated. NA-Not Available. NM-Not Meaningful. NR-Not Ranked.

Office—4551 W. 107th Street, Suite 100, Overland Park, KS 66207. **Incorporated**—in Delaware in 1988. **Tel**—(913) 967-4000. **Chrmn & CEO**—A. J. Gustin, Jr. **Pres & COO**—L. L. Hill. **EVP & CFO**—G. D. Shadid. **VP-Fin & Treas**—T. M. O'Halloran. **VP-Secy**—R. T. Steinkamp. **Dirs**—D. P. Curran, A. J. Gustin, Jr., E. Hansen, J. P. Helms, K. D. Hill, L. L. Hill, R. A. Martin, J. H. Reck, B. Sack, R. D. Schoenbaum. **Transfer Agent & Registrar**—American Stock Transfer & Trust Co., NYC. **Empl**-12,600. **S&P Analyst:** Efraim Levy

STANDARD & POOR'S

STOCK REPORTS

Aquarion Co.

NYSE Symbol **WTR**

In S&P SmallCap 600

02-NOV-95 **Industry:** Utilities-Water

Summary: This holding company provides water service to 23 communities in three Connecticut counties, and operates six environmental testing laboratories and a utility consulting service.

Quantitative Evaluations

Outlook
(1 Lowest—5 Highest)
• **2+**

Fair Value
• **22⅛**

Risk
• **Low**

Earn./Div. Rank
• **B+**

Technical Eval.
• **Bullish** since 11/94

Rel. Strength Rank
(1 Lowest—99 Highest)
• **57**

Insider Activity
• **Favorable**

Recent Price • 23⅝
52 Wk Range • 24½-21½

Yield • 6.9%
12-Mo. P/E • 13.8

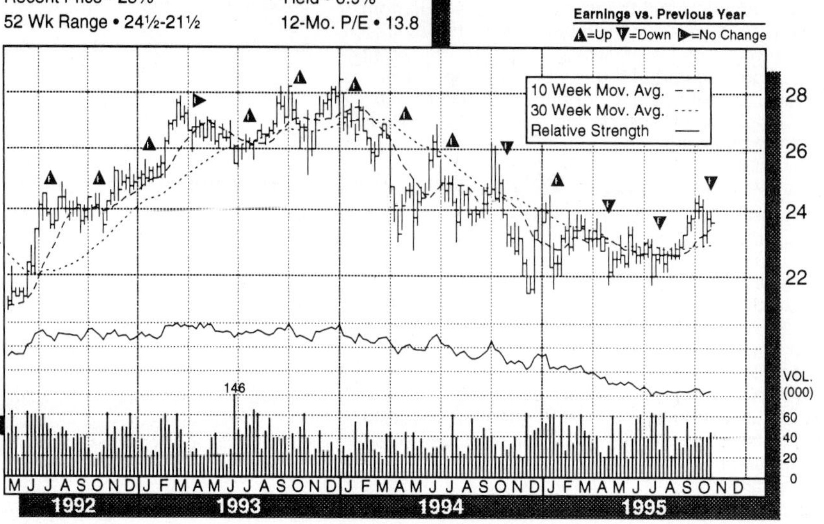

Business Profile - 02-NOV-95

WTR owns one of the 10 largest investor-owned water companies in the U.S., providing water service to 23 communities in Connecticut. It also conducts environmental testing, and in 1992 began offering various utility consulting services. Nonutility segments also include forest products and a small real estate operation. The Bridgeport Hydraulic Co. unit recently acquired the assets of The New Canaan Co., including New Canaan Water Co. and The Ridgefield Water Supply Co., in a tax free exchange.

Operational Review - 02-NOV-95

Operating revenues during the first nine months of 1995, fell 1.3%, year to year, although revenues rose in the third quarter. Operating results for the company's public water supply segment are ahead of 1994. However, gains from the sale of surplus water company land were lower; also there was a lack of cogeneration income from the forest products segment. After taxes at 43.5%, versus 39.2%, net income fell 8.6% to $8,740,000 ($1.31 a share), from $9,565,000 ($1.47).

Stock Performance - 27-OCT-95

In the past 30 trading days, WTR's shares were unchanged, compared to a 0.63% fall in the S&P 500. Average trading volume for the past five days was 8,800 shares, compared with the 40-day moving average of 7,859 shares.

Key Stock Statistics

Dividend Rate/Share	1.62	Shareholders	6,700
Shs. outstg. (M)	6.7	Market cap. (B)	$0.157
Avg. daily vol. (M)	0.009	Inst. holdings	24%
Tang. Bk. Value/Share	19.14	Insider holdings	NA
Beta	0.34		

Value of $10,000 invested 5 years ago: $ 14,122

Fiscal Year Ending Dec. 31

	1995	% Change	1994	% Change	1993	% Change
Revenues (Million $)						
1Q	25.60	NM	25.85	5%	24.69	NM
2Q	28.41	-4%	29.62	13%	26.19	NM
3Q	30.00	1%	29.65	3%	28.91	8%
4Q	—	—	36.86	34%	27.57	7%
Yr.	—	—	122.0	14%	107.4	4%
Income (Million $)						
1Q	2.39	-7%	2.57	19%	2.16	27%
2Q	3.11	-13%	3.57	33%	2.69	16%
3Q	3.24	-5%	3.42	-9%	3.77	28%
4Q	—	—	2.66	13%	2.36	43%
Yr.	—	—	12.22	11%	10.99	28%
Earnings Per Share ($)						
1Q	0.36	-10%	0.40	11%	0.36	NM
2Q	0.47	-15%	0.55	25%	0.44	13%
3Q	0.48	-8%	0.52	-10%	0.58	16%
4Q	—	—	0.40	11%	0.36	29%
Yr.	—	—	1.87	6%	1.76	17%

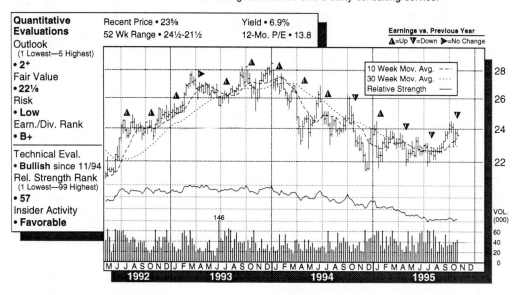

Next earnings report expected: late January

Aquarion Co.

Business Summary - 01-NOV-95

Aquarion Co. (formerly The Hydraulic Co.), through its utility subsidiaries, provides public water service to an area with an estimated population of 496,000 in three counties in Connecticut. Nonutility operations include six environmental testing laboratories, utility management services, forest products, and real estate. Contributions by industry segment in 1994 were:

	Revs.	Profits
Public water supply	60%	77%
Environmental laboratory & utility management	20%	3%
Forest products	18%	15%
Real estate	2%	5%

Bridgeport Hydraulic Co. (BHC) and its Stamford Water Co. unit collect, treat and distribute water for public and private use to residential, commercial, and industrial users, and for municipal and fire protection services in 23 communities in Fairfield, New Haven and Litchfield counties in Connecticut. In 1994, BHC derived 59% of its operating revenues from residential customers, 17% from commercial customers, 14% from fire protection customers, 5% from industrial customers, and 5% from other sources.

In 1994, 89% of BHC's water supply was provided by reservoirs, 10% by producing wells and 1% by purchases. At the end of 1994, its reservoirs, well fields and interconnections with other water utilities had an aggregate safe daily yield of 112.3 million gallons. The average daily demand for water from the utilities in 1994 was 68.5 million gallons/day. BHC's reservoirs have a storage capacity of 29.4 billion gallons.

The company invested $19,800,000 in property, plant and equipment in 1994 and anticipates capital expenditures of $41,000,000 in 1995.

Effective August 1993, the Connecticut Department of Public Utility Control awarded BHC a 20.7% water service rate increase, designed to provide $10.4 million in additional annual revenues and an 11.6% return on common equity.

In October 1994, BHC filed an application to implement a Construction-Work-in-Progress water rate surcharge to recover 90% of the carrying costs of capital used in the construction of a filtration plant at its Hemlocks Reservoir in Fairfield; estimated cost of the Safe Drinking Water Act-mandated facility is $50,000,000. A surcharge was approved in December 1994; BHC filed an application to increase the surcharge in January 1995.

Important Developments

Oct. '95—BHC acquired New Canaan Water Co. and The Ridgefield Water Supply Co. from The New Canaan Co. in a transaction valued at $2,829,000.

Capitalization

Long Term Debt: $121,542,000 (6/95).
Subsid. Red. Preferred Stock: $330,000.

Per Share Data ($) (Year Ended Dec. 31)

	1994	1993	1992	1991	1990	1989
Tangible Bk. Val.	19.14	18.64	17.71	16.87	17.34	22.29
Earnings	1.87	1.76	1.51	-1.75	1.48	2.10
Dividends	2.03	1.62	1.62	1.61	1.60	1.58
Payout Ratio	108%	92%	107%	NM	108%	75%
Prices - High	28	29¼	25½	27¼	25⅞	29⅝
- Low	21½	24⅝	20⅛	19⅞	19	24⅜
P/E Ratio - High	15	17	17	NM	17	14
- Low	11	14	13	NM	13	12

Income Statement Analysis (Million $)

	1994	%Chg	1993	%Chg	1992	%Chg	1991
Revs.	122	14%	107	4%	104	4%	100
Depr.	11.6	9%	10.6	12%	9.5	7%	8.9
Maint.	NA	—	NA	—	NA	—	NA
Fxd. Chgs. Cov.	3.7	30%	2.8	14%	2.5	NM	0.4
Constr. Credits	0.6	-8%	0.6	-9%	0.7	70%	0.4
Eff. Tax Rate	46%	—	38%	—	40%	—	NM
Net Inc.	12.2	11%	11.0	28%	8.6	NM	-8.5

Balance Sheet & Other Fin. Data (Million $)

	1994	1993	1992	1991	1990	1989
Gross Prop.	379	368	352	327	311	289
Cap. Exp.	19.8	17.9	25.4	17.9	19.1	20.1
Net Prop.	256	250	243	227	219	206
Capitalization:						
LT Debt	115	116	106	95.3	100	68.2
% LT Debt	51	51	52	55	52	42
Pfd.	0.3	0.4	0.4	2.2	2.5	3.2
% Pfd.	0.20	0.20	0.20	1.20	1.30	2.00
Common	112	111	97.2	75.5	90.5	90.3
% Common	49	49	48	44	47	56
Total Cap.	319	317	285	212	229	195

Ratio Analysis

	1994	1993	1992	1991	1990	1989
Oper. Ratio	83.6	81.7	83.2	84.1	81.1	78.0
% Earn. on Net Prop.	7.9	8.0	7.4	7.1	6.9	8.6
% Ret. on Revs.	10.0	10.2	8.3	NM	9.1	12.7
% Ret. On Invest.Cap	6.3	5.9	7.3	0.6	6.9	9.0
% Return On Com.Eqty	10.8	10.6	9.1	NM	7.8	11.3

Dividend Data —Dividends have been paid since 1890. A "poison pill" stock purchase rights plan was adopted in 1986. A dividend reinvestment plan is available.

Amt. of Div. $	Date Decl.	Ex-Div. Date	Stock of Record	Payment Date
0.405	Dec. 16	Dec. 30	Jan. 06	Jan. 30 '95
0.405	Mar. 24	Apr. 03	Apr. 07	Apr. 28 '95
0.405	Jun. 27	Jul. 06	Jul. 10	Jul. 28 '95
0.405	Sep. 27	Oct. 11	Oct. 13	Oct. 30 '95

Data as orig. reptd.; bef. results of disc opers. and/or spec. items. Per share data adj. for stk. divs. as of ex-div. date. E-Estimated. NA-Not Available. NM-Not Meaningful. NR-Not Ranked.

Office—835 Main St., Bridgeport, CT 06601. **Tel**—(203) 335-2333. **Chrmn**—J. E. McGregor. **Vice Chrmn**—W. S. Warner. **Pres & CEO**—R. K. Schmidt. **EVP-CFO & Treas**—Janet M. Hansen. **VP-Secy & Investor Contact**—Larry L. Bingaman (203-336-7626). **Dirs**—G. W. Edwards Jr., G. Etherington, J. D. Greenwood, D. M. Halsted, Jr., E. G. Hotard, E. D. Jones, J. E. McGregor, L. L. Pflieger, G. J. Ratcliffe, J. A. Urquhart, W. S. Warner. **Transfer Agent & Registrar**—Mellon Securities Trust Co., Ridgefield Park, N.J. **Incorporated** in Connecticut in 1857; reincorporated in Delaware in 1968. **Empl-679.** **S&P Analyst:** Michael C. Barr

STANDARD & POOR'S

STOCK REPORTS

Arbor Drugs

NASDAQ Symbol **ARBR**
In S&P SmallCap 600

18-OCT-95 **Industry:** Retail Stores

Summary: This company is the 15th largest drugstore chain in the U.S., with 168 full-service stores in operation, primarily in southeastern Michigan.

Quantitative Evaluations
Outlook (1 Lowest—5 Highest) • **2+**
Fair Value • **18⅛**
Risk • **Low**
Earn./Div. Rank • **B+**
Technical Eval. • **Bearish** since 4/95
Rel. Strength Rank (1 Lowest—99 Highest) • **70**
Insider Activity • **Neutral**

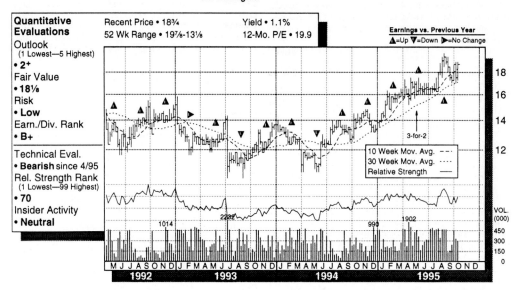

Recent Price • 18¾
52 Wk Range • 19⅞-13⅛
Yield • 1.1%
12-Mo. P/E • 19.9

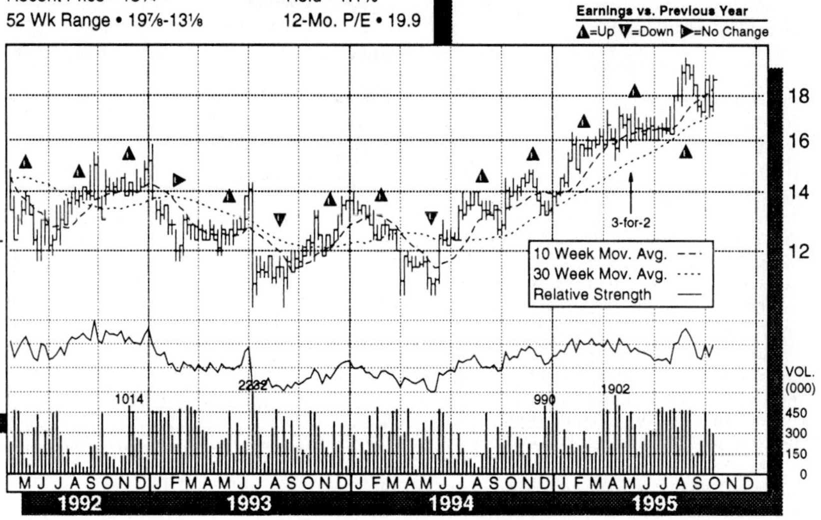

Business Profile - 18-OCT-95

One of the fastest growing and most successful drugstore chains, Arbor operates 168 full-service stores, primarily in southeastern Michigan. A high level of third-party pharmacy business (about 80% of pharmacy sales) has made Arbor less vulnerable to the typical gross margin erosion that has accompanied the increasing role of managed care in the health care industry. Future results should benefit from 12% annual growth of new stores, technological initiatives, and the "graying of America."

Operational Review - 18-OCT-95

Net sales for the fiscal year ended July 31, 1995, rose 14% over the prior year, aided by 13 additional stores in operation and a 9.0% gain in same-store sales. Pharmacy sales accounted for 49.8% of sales for the fiscal year. Gross margins narrowed, but SG&A expenses improved as a percentage of sales. In the absence of a $7.0 million charge resulting from the settlement of a third party provider's excess reimbursement claim, and after taxes at 34.0%, versus 41.2%, net income climbed 64%.

Stock Performance - 13-OCT-95

In the past 30 trading days, ARBR's shares have declined 1%, compared to a 4% rise in the S&P 500. Average trading volume for the past five days was 59,140 shares, compared with the 40-day moving average of 72,279 shares.

Key Stock Statistics

Dividend Rate/Share	0.20	Shareholders	6,800
Shs. outstg. (M)	24.7	Market cap. (B)	$0.458
Avg. daily vol. (M)	0.065	Inst. holdings	48%
Tang. Bk. Value/Share	5.02	Insider holdings	NA
Beta	1.17		

Value of $10,000 invested 5 years ago: $ 19,730

Fiscal Year Ending Jul. 31

	1995	% Change	1994	% Change	1993	% Change
Revenues (Million $)						
1Q	167.3	16%	143.8	16%	124.0	15%
2Q	185.1	16%	159.6	14%	140.4	13%
3Q	174.8	12%	155.6	17%	133.6	10%
4Q	179.9	13%	159.5	17%	136.7	10%
Yr.	707.2	14%	618.6	16%	535.0	12%
Income (Million $)						
1Q	4.71	17%	4.01	—	—	—
2Q	7.49	16%	6.47	24%	5.20	2%
3Q	5.23	NM	-1.62	NM	3.88	17%
4Q	5.64	8%	5.22	NM	-6.01	NM
Yr.	23.07	64%	14.08	104%	6.91	-56%
Earnings Per Share ($)						
1Q	0.19	16%	0.17	4%	0.16	14%
2Q	0.31	15%	0.27	25%	0.21	NM
3Q	0.21	NM	-0.07	NM	0.16	14%
4Q	0.23	8%	0.21	NM	-0.25	NM
Yr.	0.94	65%	0.57	99%	0.29	-56%

Next earnings report expected: mid November

Arbor Drugs

Business Summary - 18-OCT-95

Arbor Drugs, Inc. as of October 5, 1995, was operating 168 retail drugstores in Michigan (primarily in the southeastern part of the state) that offer a broad selection of nationally advertised and private-label goods, generally at discount prices. The company is the second largest drugstore chain in Michigan and the 15th largest in the U.S.

Contributions to net sales in recent fiscal years were:

	1994	1993
Prescription drugs	49%	47%
Health & beauty aids	22%	21%
Film & photo processing	5%	5%
Other merchandise	25%	27%

Arbor's drugstores range in gross size from about 5,000 to 20,000 sq. ft., averaging 11,000 sq. ft., and are either situated in strip shopping centers or are freestanding. The stores, generally open seven days and six evenings a week, each contain a computerized pharmacy featuring name-brand and generic prescription drugs. The company uses special promotions as well as extensive television, radio and direct-mail and newspaper circular advertising.

Each pharmacy department utilizes "Arbortech Plus," the company's advanced computerized pharmacy system. The system enables pharmacists to recall a customer's medical history and provide a complete record for tax or reimbursement purposes. Approximately 77% of Arbor's prescription sales are subject to third-party reimbursement programs.

A centralized point-of-sale system of purchasing, distribution, inventory control and marketing helps Arbor achieve consistency in merchandising and realize economies of scale. In 1988, the company opened a new 233,600-sq.-ft. distribution center in Novi, Mich. The center is nearly four times as large as the distribution center it replaced and can service up to 175 stores. About 80% of the merchandise purchased by the company for its drugstores is received at the distribution center for redistribution to units.

During fiscal 1994, the company opened eight new drugstores and acquired 11 additional locations. Additionally, the files of one underperforming store were sold and the store was closed. Arbor opened 15 drugstores in Michigan during fiscal 1995. A home delivery service was introduced in fiscal 1994.

Important Developments

May '95—According to a study conducted by Boston-based Metro Market Studies, ARBR has maintained its market share leadership position in the metropolitan Detroit area, and has increased its market share to 36.1% from 32.2% a year ago.

Capitalization

Notes Payable: $22,368,000 (4/95).
Minority Interest: $604,000.

Per Share Data ($) (Year Ended Jul. 31)

	1995	1994	1993	1992	1991	1990
Tangible Bk. Val.	NA	4.39	4.19	4.11	3.57	2.27
Cash Flow	NA	1.11	0.62	0.96	0.87	0.73
Earnings	0.94	0.57	0.29	0.65	0.59	0.51
Dividends	0.20	0.15	0.12	0.09	0.09	0.07
Payout Ratio	21%	27%	43%	14%	16%	14%
Prices - High	19 7/8	14 1/2	15 7/8	16 7/8	16 1/8	10 3/8
- Low	13 1/2	10 5/8	10 3/8	11 5/8	8 1/4	5 7/8
P/E Ratio - High	21	25	55	26	28	20
- Low	14	19	36	18	14	12

Income Statement Analysis (Million $)

	1994	%Chg	1993	%Chg	1992	%Chg	1991
Revs.	619	16%	535	12%	477	17%	406
Oper. Inc.	45.0	25%	36.0	11%	32.4	15%	28.1
Depr.	13.0	58%	8.2	10%	7.5	22%	6.2
Int. Exp.	1.9	-4%	2.0	-31%	2.9	-3%	3.0
Pretax Inc.	24.0	140%	10.0	-58%	23.6	19%	19.9
Eff. Tax Rate	41%	—	31%	—	33%	—	34%
Net Inc.	14.1	104%	6.9	-56%	15.8	21%	13.1

Balance Sheet & Other Fin. Data (Million $)

	1994	1993	1992	1991	1990	1989
Cash	37.7	44.9	48.2	37.1	14.9	23.0
Curr. Assets	141	134	126	108	73.0	71.0
Total Assets	234	216	200	176	132	119
Curr. Liab.	72.4	71.2	66.5	42.9	36.8	32.8
LT Debt	23.7	18.2	13.0	27.5	28.5	30.0
Common Eqty.	130	118	114	99	62.0	53.0
Total Cap.	161	144	134	133	95.0	86.0
Cap. Exp.	14.0	14.0	13.0	12.7	14.2	6.7
Cash Flow	27.0	15.1	23.3	19.2	15.5	13.1

Ratio Analysis

	1994	1993	1992	1991	1990	1989
Curr. Ratio	1.9	1.9	1.9	2.5	2.0	2.2
% LT Debt of Cap.	14.7	12.6	9.7	20.7	30.0	34.8
% Net Inc.of Revs.	2.3	1.3	3.3	3.2	3.2	3.1
% Ret. on Assets	6.3	3.3	8.4	8.1	8.8	8.4
% Ret. on Equity	11.3	5.9	14.8	15.5	19.2	18.9

Dividend Data —Cash dividends were initiated in late 1988.

Amt. of Div. $	Date Decl.	Ex-Div. Date	Stock of Record	Payment Date
0.075	Nov. 15	Nov. 30	Dec. 06	Jan. 03 '95
0.075	Feb. 22	Mar. 09	Mar. 15	Apr. 05 '95
3-for-2	Apr. 17	May. 16	May. 01	May. 15 '95
0.050	May. 23	Jun. 09	Jun. 13	Jul. 03 '95
0.050	Aug. 29	Sep. 08	Sep. 12	Oct. 03 '95

Data as orig. reptd.; bef. results of disc. opers. and/or spec. items. Per share data adj. for stk. divs. as of ex-div. date. E-Estimated. NA-Not Available. NM-Not Meaningful. NR-Not Ranked.

Office—3331 West Big Beaver, Troy, MI 48007. **Tel**—(810) 643-9420. **Chrmn, Pres & CEO**—E. Applebaum. **EVP & COO**—M. M. Ernst. **VP-Fin, Treas, Secy & Investor Contact**—Gilbert C. Gerhard. **Dirs**—E. Applebaum, M. M. Ernst, G. C. Gerhard, D. B. Hermelin, S. M. Partrich, L. M. Shahon, S. Valenti III. **Transfer Agent & Registrar**—Boston Financial Data Services, Inc., Boston **Incorporated** in Michigan in 1974. **Empl**-5,200. **S&P Analyst:** Maureen C. Carini

STANDARD & POOR'S

STOCK REPORTS

Ashworth Inc.

NASDAQ Symbol **ASHW**

In S&P SmallCap 600

24-OCT-95 **Industry:** Retail merchandiser

Summary: This company designs and manufactures Ashworth golf apparel and footwear and Ashworth Harry Logan men's sportwear.

Quantitative Evaluations

Outlook (1 Lowest—5 Highest)
• **NA**

Fair Value
• **NA**

Risk
• **High**

Earn./Div. Rank
• **NR**

Technical Eval.
• **Bearish** since 2/94

Rel. Strength Rank (1 Lowest—99 Highest)
• **11**

Insider Activity
• **NA**

Recent Price • 6⅞ | Yield • Nil
52 Wk Range • 11½-6⅜ | 12-Mo. P/E • 23.7

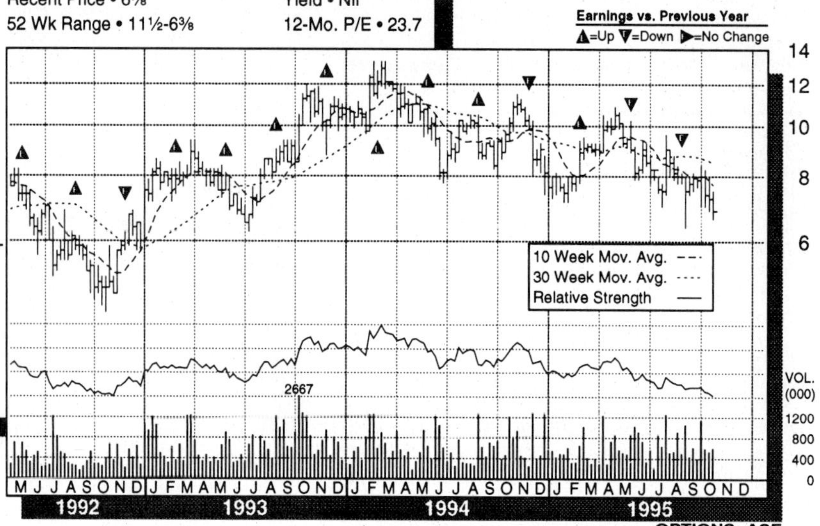

OPTIONS: ASE

Business Profile - 24-OCT-95

This maker of golf and other apparel has discontinued its women's and kids' product offerings, and will concentrate on men's products. Ashworth believes itself to be the top exclusive U.S. men's golf apparel company, and the fastest growing international brand. Sales of golf equipment and apparel have climbed in recent years, as new golfers take up the sport. However, the shares have fallen in recent periods, reflecting unfavorable earnings comparisons.

Operational Review - 24-OCT-95

Net sales in the nine months ended July 31, 1995, rose 25%, year to year, reflecting the continued expansion of distribution channels. Gross margins narrowed, reflecting an increased proportion of lower-margin international and outlet store sales, and results were hurt by an increase of $2.3 million in the inventory reserve; net income fell to $0.28 a share, from $0.39. Recent late deliveries, related to conversion to new inventory control software, should be eliminated in the next few months.

Stock Performance - 20-OCT-95

In the past 30 trading days, ASHW's shares have declined 11%, compared to a 3% rise in the S&P 500. Average trading volume for the past five days was 117,120 shares, compared with the 40-day moving average of 134,538 shares.

Key Stock Statistics

Dividend Rate/Share	Nil	Shareholders	1,100
Shs. outstg. (M)	11.9	Market cap. (B)	$0.080
Avg. daily vol. (M)	0.143	Inst. holdings	21%
Tang. Bk. Value/Share	3.10	Insider holdings	NA
Beta	0.97		

Value of $10,000 invested 5 years ago: NA

Fiscal Year Ending Oct. 31

	1995	% Change	1994	% Change	1993	% Change
Revenues (Million $)						
1Q	14.59	32%	11.04	49%	7.40	72%
2Q	26.44	24%	21.27	27%	16.69	65%
3Q	20.38	20%	16.96	32%	12.81	64%
4Q	—	—	11.57	30%	8.93	42%
Yr.	—	—	60.84	33%	45.82	60%
Income (Million $)						
1Q	0.81	13%	0.72	71%	0.42	121%
2Q	1.81	-27%	2.48	38%	1.80	53%
3Q	0.81	-47%	1.53	29%	1.19	125%
4Q	—	—	0.13	-76%	0.54	NM
Yr.	—	—	4.86	23%	3.95	96%
Earnings Per Share ($)						
1Q	0.07	17%	0.06	50%	0.04	100%
2Q	0.15	-25%	0.20	33%	0.15	36%
3Q	0.07	-46%	0.13	30%	0.10	100%
4Q	—	—	0.01	-80%	0.05	NM
Yr.	—	—	0.40	18%	0.34	79%

Next earnings report expected: early December

Ashworth Inc.

Business Summary - 24-OCT-95

Ashworth Inc. (formerly Charter Golf, Inc.) designs, markets and distributes a full line of quality golf and casual apparel under the Ashworth and Ashworth Harry Logan labels.

The Ashworth golf apparel line consists of men's and women's shirts, sweaters, shorts, vests, pants, pullovers, jackets, hats, weathergear and accessories. During 1994, the company began shipments of a line of golf hats, and shipments of a line of golf footwear were scheduled to begin in early 1995. Domestic sales of Ashworth golf apparel accounted for 72% of fiscal 1994 revenues.

Ashworth sells golf apparel in four lines: Spring, Summer, Graphics and Fall. The Spring and Summer lines, which constitute the major selling linos, together accounted for 75% of sales in fiscal 1994. The Fall and Graphics lines (primarily shirts with silkscreened designs) accounted for 23% and 2%, respectively, of the fiscal 1994 total. In fiscal 1994, shirts accounted for 71% of Ashworth golf apparel sales. About 94% of domestic Ashworth brand sales in fiscal 1994 were made to golf pro shops, country clubs and resorts through 40 independent sales representatives.

In April 1994, the company began shipments of a line of golf-inspired men's casual sportswear under the Ashworth Harry Logan trademark. The line is distributed to better department and specialty retail stores through nine sales representatives (five employed by ASHW).

In fiscal 1994, international sales accounted for 20% of the total, with the majority to Japan and the U.K. International markets also include other European nations, Canada, the Caribbean and certain counties in Asia.

As part of its inventory control measures, at the end of fiscal 1994 the company was operating seven factory outlet retail stores in California, Texas and Nebraska, and intended to open additional stores during fiscal 1995.

Important Developments

Aug. '95—Ashworth said narrower gross margins in the fiscal 1995 third quarter reflected an increased proportion of lower-margin international sales and a less favorable domestic product mix. The company also said it had boosted its inventory reserve by $500,000 to cover potential surges from late and missed deliveries.

Capitalization

Long Term Debt: $5,394,639 (7/95).
Options: To buy 2,680,761 com. shs. at $0.60 to $12.50 ea. (10/94).

Per Share Data ($) (Year Ended Oct. 31)

	1994	1993	1992	1991	1990	1989
Tangible Bk. Val.	2.84	2.31	1.87	0.73	0.50	0.03
Cash Flow	0.55	0.42	0.24	0.16	0.05	0.01
Earnings	0.40	0.34	0.19	0.13	0.04	-0.01
Dividends	Nil	Nil	Nil	Nil	Nil	Nil
Payout Ratio	Nil	Nil	Nil	Nil	Nil	Nil
Prices - High	13¼	12	9	7¼	4⅛	NA
- Low	7⅜	6¼	4⅜	2$\frac{3}{16}$	1	NA
P/E Ratio - High	33	35	47	56	NM	NA
- Low	18	18	23	17	NM	NA

Income Statement Analysis (Million $)

	1994	%Chg	1993	%Chg	1992	%Chg	1991
Revs.	60.8	33%	45.8	60%	28.6	68%	17.0
Oper. Inc.	10.2	33%	7.7	87%	4.1	61%	2.6
Depr.	1.9	78%	1.0	67%	0.6	125%	0.3
Int. Exp.	0.6	97%	0.3	24%	0.3	19%	0.2
Pretax Inc.	8.1	23%	6.5	93%	3.4	58%	2.1
Eff. Tax Rate	40%	—	40%	—	40%	—	42%
Net Inc.	4.9	23%	4.0	96%	2.0	63%	1.2

Balance Sheet & Other Fin. Data (Million $)

	1994	1993	1992	1991	1990	1989
Cash	5.3	7.7	5.8	0.6	1.4	0.0
Curr. Assets	34.6	26.5	21.2	8.4	4.9	1.3
Total Assets	47.3	33.5	25.7	10.1	5.4	1.6
Curr. Liab.	8.6	4.6	3.8	3.0	1.4	0.8
LT Debt	5.8	2.9	1.7	0.7	0.3	0.6
Common Eqty.	32.9	26.1	20.2	6.4	3.8	0.1
Total Cap.	38.7	28.9	21.9	7.2	4.1	0.7
Cap. Exp.	6.8	2.7	1.5	0.4	0.2	0.1
Cash Flow	6.7	5.0	2.7	1.5	0.4	0.0

Ratio Analysis

	1994	1993	1992	1991	1990	1989
Curr. Ratio	4.0	5.8	5.6	2.8	3.6	1.5
% LT Debt of Cap.	14.9	10.0	7.8	10.4	6.8	86.2
% Net Inc.of Revs.	8.0	8.6	7.1	7.3	3.4	NM
% Ret. on Assets	11.9	13.1	10.6	15.1	5.9	NM
% Ret. on Equity	16.3	16.7	14.4	22.9	12.8	NM

Dividend Data —No cash dividends have been paid.

Data as orig. reptd.; bef. results of disc. opers. and/or spec. items. Per share data adj. for stk. divs. as of ex-div. date. E-Estimated. NA-Not Available. NM-Not Meaningful. NR-Not Ranked.

Office—2791 Loker Avenue West, Carlsbad, CA 92008. **Tel**—(619) 438-6610. **Chrmn**—G. W. Montiel. **Pres & CEO**—R. H. Werschkul. **VP-Fin, CFO & Treas**—A. J. Newman. **Secy**—Monica M. McKenzie. **Dirs**—J. L. Ashworth, F. Couples, A. P. Gambucci, J. M. Hanson, Jr., G. W. Montiel. **Transfer Agent & Registrar**—American Securities Transfer, Inc., Denver. **Incorporated** in Delaware in 1987. **Empl**-356. **S&P Analyst:** Philip D. Wohl

STANDARD & POOR'S
Aspect Telecommunications
STOCK REPORTS

NASDAQ Symbol **ASPT**
In S&P SmallCap 600

02-OCT-95 **Industry:** Telecommunications

Summary: This company is a global provider of comprehensive business solutions for mission-critical call centers that exist to generate revenue, service customers, and handle inquiries.

Quantitative Evaluations
Outlook
(1 Lowest—5 Highest)
• **5**
Fair Value
• **37⅝**
Risk
• **Average**
Earn./Div. Rank
• **NR**

Technical Eval.
• **Bullish** since 1/95
Rel. Strength Rank
(1 Lowest—99 Highest)
• **86**
Insider Activity
• **Neutral**

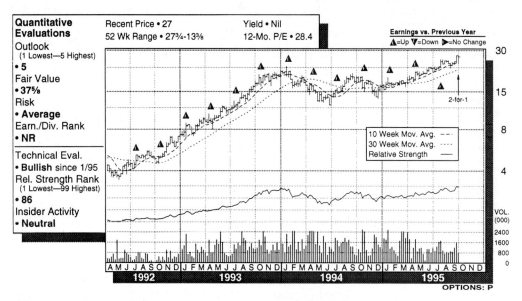

Recent Price • 27
52 Wk Range • 27¾-13⅜
Yield • Nil
12-Mo. P/E • 28.4

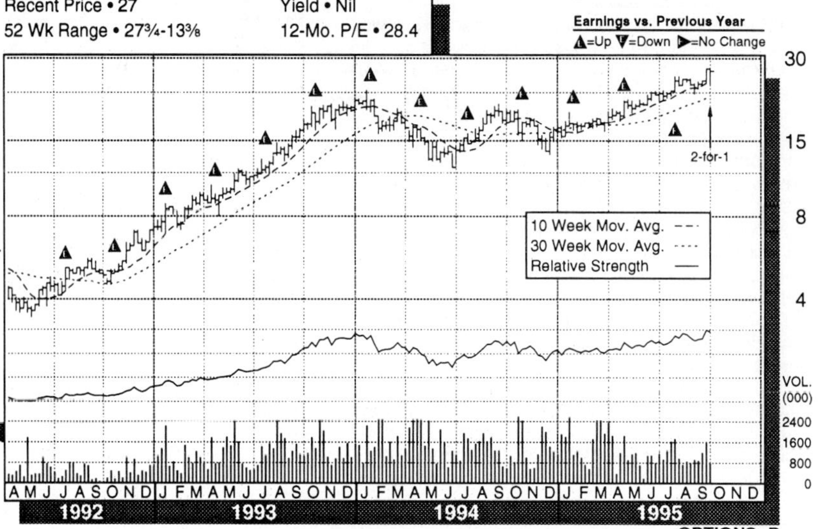

Business Profile - 02-OCT-95

Companies are increasingly recognizing that excellent customer service can be employed as a competitive advantage to differentiate their firms from competitors and gain market share. This increased emphasis on customer service by a wide variety of manufacturing and service companies has aided Aspect and led to a growing number of call transaction processing applications in such diverse industries as financial services, insurance and consumer products.

Operational Review - 02-OCT-95

Revenues have shown steady growth in recent periods, reflecting strong demand for the company's products and services. Gross margins have remained stable. R&D costs have been rising, as Aspect strives to keep its competitive edge, but other operating expenses have been well controlled, allowing earnings to display a strong upward trend. International expansion should aid future results.

Stock Performance - 29-SEP-95

In the past 30 trading days, ASPT's shares have increased 8%, compared to a 5% rise in the S&P 500. Average trading volume for the past five days was 151,160 shares, compared with the 40-day moving average of 194,436 shares.

Key Stock Statistics

Dividend Rate/Share	Nil	Shareholders	600
Shs. outstg. (M)	20.7	Market cap. (B)	$0.559
Avg. daily vol. (M)	0.223	Inst. holdings	80%
Tang. Bk. Value/Share	3.97	Insider holdings	NA
Beta	1.49		

Value of $10,000 invested 5 years ago: NA

Fiscal Year Ending Dec. 31

	1995	% Change	1994	% Change	1993	% Change
Revenues (Million $)						
1Q	42.73	30%	32.89	51%	21.80	40%
2Q	46.23	32%	35.12	52%	23.15	36%
3Q	—	—	38.17	37%	27.94	54%
4Q	—	—	41.06	22%	33.55	65%
Yr.	—	—	147.2	38%	106.5	50%
Income (Million $)						
1Q	5.15	29%	3.98	111%	1.89	NM
2Q	5.83	37%	4.25	96%	2.17	NM
3Q	—	—	4.51	41%	3.20	NM
4Q	—	—	4.83	14%	4.22	NM
Yr.	—	—	17.57	53%	11.48	180%
Earnings Per Share ($)						
1Q	0.24	30%	0.19	106%	0.09	NM
2Q	0.27	35%	0.20	90%	0.10	163%
3Q	—	—	0.21	40%	0.15	173%
4Q	—	—	0.22	15%	0.19	160%
Yr.	—	—	0.82	50%	0.54	173%

Next earnings report expected: mid October

Aspect Telecommunications

Business Summary - 02-OCT-95

Aspect Telecommunications Corporation develops, manufactures and supports call transaction processing systems--intelligent call control and management systems that can improve customer service and reduce operating costs for firms handling high volumes of telephone sales or inquiries.

Revenues in recent years were derived as follows:

	1994	1993	1992
Product sales	78%	78%	78%
Customer support	22%	22%	22%

The company's primary product, the Aspect CallCenter System, is an advanced architecture automatic call distributor (ACD) designed specifically for call transaction processing applications. The Aspect CallCenter fully integrates call processing, voice processing and data processing technologies. Product features enable firms to route and prioritize incoming calls flexibly, adapt to changing volumes of call traffic, instantaneously access caller data from connected computer systems, expand system capacity to meet growth in transaction volume, and take advantage of new public telephone network services. An important element in the company's delivery of call transaction processing is the optional Application Bridge which allows CallCenter to communicate directly with a company's data processing systems

During 1994, Aspect introduced Agility, a product that allows companies to expand the ways in which they interact with customers through call centers. Agility automates call center transactions and processes by complimenting call centers with software agent technology.

Other products include interface cards, the Aspect TeleSet (a telephone that allows an individual staff person to handle hundreds of calls per day), the Aspect TeleCaster (displays current performance information to telephone support staff), CustomView and Remote StaffCenter.

The company's products are marketed primarily through its direct sales organizations in North America and the U.K. Aspect also offers its products through independent distributors in certain states in the U.S., and in Canada, the Netherlands, and beginning in 1995, Germany. Sales outside North America accounted for 23% of total revenues in 1994, up from 21% in 1993, and provided 16% of operating income (7.4%).

Important Developments

Aug. '95—The company introduced Aspect WinSet for Windows, a PC application that delivers Anywhere Agent capabilities for call centers using Aspect CallCenter automatic call distribution systems.

Capitalization

Long Term Debt: $55,000,000 of sub. debs. conv. into 1,414,791 com. (6/95).

Per Share Data ($) (Year Ended Dec. 31)

	1994	1993	1992	1991	1990	1989
Tangible Bk. Val.	3.97	3.16	2.52	2.27	2.34	-2.54
Cash Flow	1.15	0.76	0.38	0.11	0.33	0.15
Earnings	0.82	0.54	0.20	-0.08	0.19	0.07
Dividends	Nil	Nil	Nil	Nil	Nil	Nil
Payout Ratio	Nil	Nil	Nil	NM	Nil	Nil
Prices - High	23	21⅝	7½	5⅜	11⅞	NA
- Low	12	7	3½	2⅞	3	NA
P/E Ratio - High	28	40	38	NM	64	NA
- Low	15	13	17	NM	16	NA

Income Statement Analysis (Million $)

	1994	%Chg	1993	%Chg	1992	%Chg	1991
Revs.	147	39%	106	49%	71.0	61%	44.2
Oper. Inc.	35.2	56%	22.6	157%	8.8	NM	0.5
Depr.	7.1	57%	4.5	27%	3.5	-9%	3.9
Int. Exp.	3.2	NM	0.9	NM	0.2	-28%	0.3
Pretax Inc.	28.3	51%	18.8	186%	6.6	NM	-1.7
Eff. Tax Rate	38%	—	39%	—	38%	—	Nil
Net Inc.	17.6	53%	11.5	180%	4.1	NM	-1.7

Balance Sheet & Other Fin. Data (Million $)

	1994	1993	1992	1991	1990	1989
Cash	103	93.1	36.2	32.8	32.3	8.7
Curr. Assets	143	123	55.5	48.2	44.9	15.7
Total Assets	166	138	64.6	57.0	54.5	20.8
Curr. Liab.	30.2	18.9	14.2	10.6	6.1	6.8
LT Debt	55.0	55.0	0.1	0.7	1.5	1.2
Common Eqty.	80.8	64.3	50.2	45.6	46.7	12.6
Total Cap.	136	119	50.2	46.3	48.2	13.8
Cap. Exp.	13.1	8.9	4.4	3.0	5.6	2.9
Cash Flow	24.6	16.0	7.6	2.2	6.3	2.5

Ratio Analysis

	1994	1993	1992	1991	1990	1989
Curr. Ratio	4.7	6.5	3.9	4.6	7.3	2.3
% LT Debt of Cap.	40.5	46.1	0.1	1.5	3.0	8.8
% Net Inc.of Revs.	11.9	10.8	5.8	NM	7.2	3.3
% Ret. on Assets	11.5	11.2	6.8	NM	4.3	6.6
% Ret. on Equity	24.2	19.9	8.6	NM	NM	11.8

Dividend Data —No cash dividends have been paid.

Amt. of Div. $	Date Decl.	Ex-Div. Date	Stock of Record	Payment Date
2-for-1	Aug. 21	Sep. 25	Sep. 01	Sep. 22 '95

Data as orig. reptd.; bef. results of disc. opers. and/or spec. items. Per share data adj. for stk. divs. as of ex-div. date. E-Estimated. NA-Not Available. NM-Not Meaningful. NR-Not Ranked.

Office—1730 Fox Dr., San Jose, CA 95131-2312. **Tel**—(408) 441-2200. **Pres, CEO & Investor Contact**—J. R. Carreker. **Secy**—C. W. Johnson. **Dirs**—J. R. Carreker, N. A. Fogelsong, J. L. Patterson, J. W. Peth. **Transfer Agent & Registrar**—First National Bank of Boston. **Incorporated** in California in 1985. **Empl**-640. **S&P Analyst:** Alan Aaron

STANDARD & POOR'S

STOCK REPORTS

Astec Industries

NASDAQ Symbol **ASTE**

In S&P SmallCap 600

10-OCT-95 **Industry:** Machinery

Summary: This company designs, engineers, manufactures and markets equipment and components used in the production and application of hot-mix asphalt and other construction aggregates.

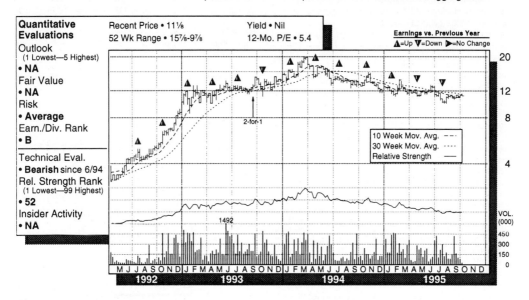

Quantitative Evaluations

Outlook (1 Lowest—5 Highest) • NA

Fair Value • NA

Risk • Average

Earn./Div. Rank • B

Technical Eval. • Bearish since 6/94

Rel. Strength Rank (1 Lowest—99 Highest) • 52

Insider Activity • NA

Recent Price • 11⅛ Yield • Nil

52 Wk Range • 15⅞-9⅞ 12-Mo. P/E • 5.4

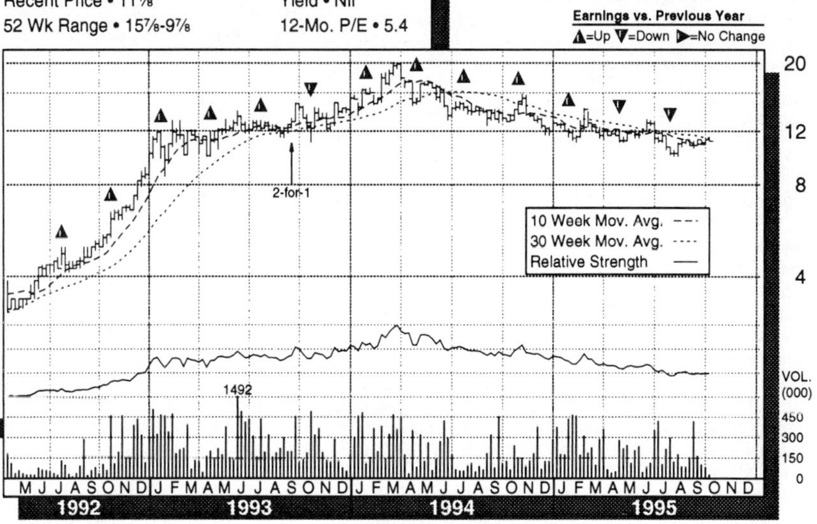

Business Profile - 10-OCT-95

As one of the leading manufacturers of road construction equipment, ASTE has been in the midst of a major expansion and modernization of its facilities. The program is scheduled to be completed in 1995 and should greatly enhance its operating efficiencies. International sales (24% of 1994 revenues) should benefit from the reorganization of the German operations and add to ASTE's strength in the domestic market.

Operational Review - 10-OCT-95

Revenues grew 17% in the first half of 1995, on higher domestic sales. However, operating income fell 18% (46% in the second quarter), hurt by a 29% increase (34% in the second quarter) in SG&A expenses. With a fivefold increase in interest expense outweighed by $2,946,000 in other income (in contrast to other expenses of $323,000 in the year-earlier period), pretax income rose 7.2%. After taxes at 44.9%, versus 5.0%, earnings plunged 40% to $0.50 a share (on 2.6% more shares).

Stock Performance - 06-OCT-95

In the past 30 trading days, ASTE's shares have declined 1%, compared to a 4% rise in the S&P 500. Average trading volume for the past five days was 4,840 shares, compared with the 40-day moving average of 27,708 shares.

Key Stock Statistics

Dividend Rate/Share	Nil	Shareholders	900
Shs. outstg. (M)	10.1	Market cap. (B)	$0.112
Avg. daily vol. (M)	0.018	Inst. holdings	30%
Tang. Bk. Value/Share	8.20	Insider holdings	NA
Beta	0.62		

Value of $10,000 invested 5 years ago: $ 25,428

Fiscal Year Ending Dec. 31

	1995	% Change	1994	% Change	1993	% Change
Revenues (Million $)						
1Q	57.54	24%	46.23	7%	43.40	27%
2Q	70.37	12%	62.69	20%	52.44	22%
3Q	—	—	49.02	26%	38.84	-2%
4Q	—	—	55.87	47%	38.13	18%
Yr.	—	—	213.8	24%	172.8	16%
Income (Million $)						
1Q	2.52	-13%	2.88	82%	1.58	NM
2Q	2.51	-52%	5.21	50%	3.48	28%
3Q	—	—	3.13	48%	2.12	6%
4Q	—	—	12.22	NM	2.16	66%
Yr.	—	—	23.44	151%	9.34	55%
Earnings Per Share ($)						
1Q	0.25	-14%	0.29	35%	0.22	—
2Q	0.25	-53%	0.53	18%	0.45	20%
3Q	—	—	0.32	45%	0.22	-20%
4Q	—	—	1.23	NM	0.22	26%
Yr.	—	—	2.38	122%	1.07	30%

Next earnings report expected: mid October

Astec Industries

Business Summary - 10-OCT-95

Astec Industries, Inc. designs, engineers, manufactures and markets equipment and components used in the production and application of hot-mix asphalt and for the production or processing of sand, gravel, crushed stone and other construction aggregates. Sales in recent years were derived as follows:

	1994	1993
Asphalt plants & components	47%	51%
Aggregates processing equipment	18%	23%
Mobile Construction equipment	14%	13%
Trenching & excavating equipment	12%	10%
Other	9%	3%

The Astec division markets a complete line of hot-mix asphalt plants, related components and soil remediation equipment. Asphalt plants typically consist of heating and storage equipment for liquid asphalt, cold-feed bins for storing aggregates, a drum mixer, air filters or other pollution control devices, hot storage bins for hot-mix asphalt, and a control house.

Telsmith designs, manufactures and sells equipment for the production and classification of sand, gravel and quarried stone for road and other construction applications. Products include jaw, cone and impact crushers, several types of feeders, vibrating screens, and washing and conveying equipment.

Heatec produces heaters and heat-transfer processing equpment for use in asphalt and other industries, such as food processing, asphalt roofing, leather processing, chemical and rubber, and agribusiness.

Roadtec manufactures asphalt paving equipment, material-transfer vehicles and milling machines. Trencor makes chain and wheel trenching equipment, canal excavators, rock saws and road miners.

In 1994, Astec acquired the remaining 50% of Wibau-Astec, a German based manufacturer of asphalt and stabilization plants, hot storage systems and soil remediation equipment. ASTE also acquired Gibat Ohl, a German manufacturer of batch asphalt plants, parts and controls.

The chairman and president, J.D. Brock, owns approximately 22% of the outstanding shares.

Important Developments

Jul. '95—Astec said the gain on the June 1995 sale of its German subsidiary, Wibau-Astec, to Wirtgen Gesellschaft mit beschrankter Haftung, approximately offset the subsidiary's losses in the second quarter.

Feb. '95—The company reported the collection of $14,947,000 in patent suit damages after a December 1994 ruling by the U.S. Supreme Court denied requests from Robert Mendenhall and CMI Corp. for a writ of certiorari, thus ending 14 years of litigation.

Capitalization

Long Term Debt: $29,900,000 (6/95).

Per Share Data ($) (Year Ended Dec. 31)

	1994	1993	1992	1991	1990	1989
Tangible Bk. Val.	8.20	6.34	3.54	2.70	2.20	4.41
Cash Flow	2.78	1.43	1.29	0.52	-1.30	-0.04
Earnings	2.38	1.07	0.82	0.08	-1.86	-0.54
Dividends	Nil	Nil	Nil	Nil	Nil	Nil
Payout Ratio	Nil	Nil	Nil	Nil	Nil	Nil
Prices - High	20⅛	15¾	10¼	3⅝	5¼	8¾
- Low	11⅝	8½	2¾	1 9/16	15/16	4⅛
P/E Ratio - High	8	15	13	48	NM	NM
- Low	5	8	3	21	NM	NM

Income Statement Analysis (Million $)

	1994	%Chg	1993	%Chg	1992	%Chg	1991
Revs.	214	24%	173	16%	149	10%	135
Oper. Inc.	17.7	31%	13.5	22%	11.1	16%	9.6
Depr.	3.9	27%	3.1	-10%	3.5	6%	3.3
Int. Exp.	0.7	-60%	1.8	-45%	3.2	-30%	4.6
Pretax Inc.	25.7	162%	9.8	53%	6.4	NM	0.6
Eff. Tax Rate	8.90%	—	4.40%	—	6.60%	—	10%
Net Inc.	23.4	152%	9.3	55%	6.0	NM	0.5

Balance Sheet & Other Fin. Data (Million $)

	1994	1993	1992	1991	1990	1989
Cash	10.5	15.8	13.8	13.7	8.6	0.8
Curr. Assets	102	76.5	67.8	68.0	90.3	96.2
Total Assets	156	103	88.0	91.0	112	128
Curr. Liab.	49.1	35.7	34.1	36.8	40.5	36.0
LT Debt	16.2	Nil	22.7	29.4	50.3	53.6
Common Eqty.	90.4	64.1	27.6	21.3	17.2	33.4
Total Cap.	107	64.1	50.3	50.7	67.5	87.0
Cap. Exp.	21.9	8.8	2.5	2.1	1.8	6.1
Cash Flow	27.4	12.4	9.5	3.8	-9.3	-0.3

Ratio Analysis

	1994	1993	1992	1991	1990	1989
Curr. Ratio	2.1	2.1	2.0	1.8	2.2	2.7
% LT Debt of Cap.	15.2	Nil	45.1	58.0	74.5	61.5
% Net Inc.of Revs.	11.0	5.4	4.0	0.4	NM	NM
% Ret. on Assets	18.0	8.5	6.7	0.5	NM	NM
% Ret. on Equity	30.1	18.5	24.4	2.7	NM	NM

Dividend Data —No cash dividends have been paid. A two-for-one stock split was effected in September 1993.

Data as orig. reptd.; bef. results of disc. opers. and/or spec. items. Per share data adj. for stk. divs. as of ex-div. date. E-Estimated. NA-Not Available. NM-Not Meaningful. NR-Not Ranked.

Incorporated—in Tennessee in 1972. **Office**—4101 Jerome Ave. (P.O. Box 72787), Chattanooga, TN 37407. **Tel**—(615) 867-4210. **Fax**—(615) 867-4127. **Chrmn, Pres & CEO**—J. D. Brock. **SVP-Treas, Secy & Investor Contact**—Albert E. Guth. **Dirs**—J. D. Brock, G. C. Dillon, D. K. Frierson, J. F. Gilbert, A. E. Guth, G. W. Jones, J. Martin, Jr., E. D. Sloan, Jr., W. N. Smith, J. R. Spear, R. G. Stafford. **Transfer Agent**—Chemical Bank, NYC. **Empl**-1,531. **S&P Analyst:** Justin McCann

STANDARD & POOR'S

STOCK REPORTS

Atmos Energy

NYSE Symbol **ATO**

In S&P SmallCap 600

23-SEP-95 **Industry:** Utilities-Gas

Summary: This company distributes natural gas to nearly 650,000 customers in Colorado, Kansas, Missouri, Kentucky, Louisiana and Texas.

Quantitative Evaluations

Outlook
(1 Lowest—5 Highest)
• **1+**

Fair Value
• **17⅞**

Risk
• **Low**

Earn./Div. Rank
• **B+**

Technical Eval.
• **Bullish** since 3/95

Rel. Strength Rank
(1 Lowest—99 Highest)
• **26**

Insider Activity
• **Neutral**

Recent Price • 19½
52 Wk Range • 20⅝-15⅞

Yield • 4.7%
12-Mo. P/E • 18.8

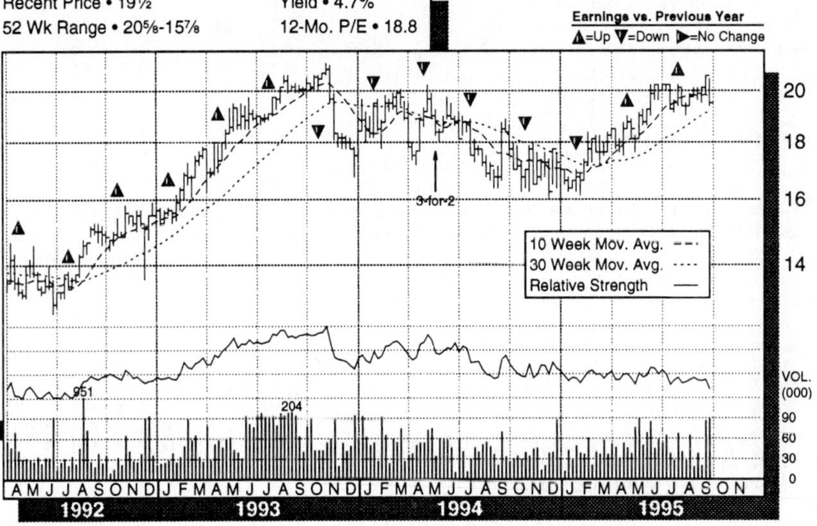

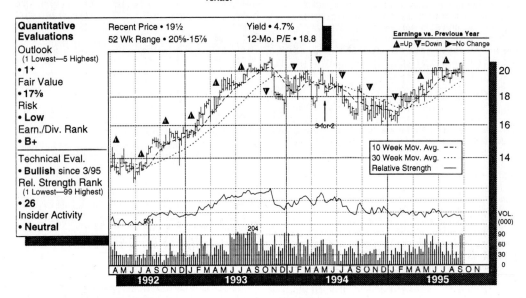

Business Profile - 30-AUG-95

Atmos distributes and sells natural gas to more than 650,000 customers in six states. It has been expanding its customer base through aggressive marketing programs, and is seeking further acquisitions of gas distribution properties. The company is subject to regulation in each state in which it operates. In addition, its business is affected by weather patterns, competition within the energy industry, and economic conditions in areas that it serves.

Operational Review - 30-AUG-95

Operating revenues in the first nine months of fiscal 1995 fell 15%, year to year, reflecting reduced gas sales and gas prices. Year to date in 1995, weather has been about 11% warmer than normal, and 10% warmer than the previous year. Purchased gas cost declined dramatically, and because of ongoing expense management programs, operating income actually climbed 8.5%. After higher interest charges, net income advanced 7.3%, to $20,503,000 ($1.33 a share), from $19,106,000 ($1.26).

Stock Performance - 22-SEP-95

In the past 30 trading days, ATO's shares have increased 0.65%, compared to a 5% rise in the S&P 500. Average trading volume for the past five days was 17,480 shares, compared with the 40-day moving average of 9,677 shares.

Key Stock Statistics

Dividend Rate/Share	0.92	Shareholders	18,000
Shs. outstg. (M)	15.5	Market cap. (B)	$0.302
Avg. daily vol. (M)	0.012	Inst. holdings	19%
Tang. Bk. Value/Share	10.50	Insider holdings	NA
Beta	0.47		

Value of $10,000 invested 5 years ago: $ 22,144

Fiscal Year Ending Sep. 30

	1995	% Change	1994	% Change	1993	% Change
Revenues (Million $)						
1Q	117.8	-19%	145.5	29%	112.4	5%
2Q	157.3	-16%	186.9	37%	136.2	17%
3Q	84.69	-6%	90.01	17%	77.18	32%
4Q	—	—	77.35	23%	62.75	7%
Yr.	—	—	499.8	29%	388.5	14%
Income (Million $)						
1Q	6.48	-9%	7.09	22%	5.82	23%
2Q	13.95	5%	13.24	21%	10.95	31%
3Q	0.08	NM	-1.22	NM	1.26	NM
4Q	—	—	-4.43	NM	-2.30	NM
Yr.	—	—	14.68	-7%	15.71	57%
Earnings Per Share ($)						
1Q	0.42	-11%	0.47	-14%	0.55	19%
2Q	0.91	5%	0.87	-15%	1.02	25%
3Q	0.01	NM	-0.08	NM	0.11	NM
4Q	—	—	-0.29	NM	-0.21	NM
Yr.	—	—	0.97	-33%	1.45	49%

Next earnings report expected: early November

Atmos Energy

Business Summary - 07-SEP-95

Atmos Energy Corp. (formerly Energas Co.) distributes and sells natural gas to more than 650,000 residential, commercial, industrial, agricultural and other customers in Colorado, Kansas, Missouri, Kentucky, Louisiana and Texas. Its service areas have economies based on oil and gas production, agriculture, food processing, and industry. The company also transports gas for others through parts of its distribution system and operates four public refueling facilities for vehicles powered by compressed natural gas in its service areas. The service area and customer base were expanded in late 1993 through the acquisition of Greeley Gas Co., which provides gas to nearly 105,000 customers. The Energas Co., which operates the Texas distribution system, has about 309,496 customers.

Gas revenues by customer type in recent fiscal years were as follows:

	1994	1993	1992	1991
Residential	49%	54%	55%	53%
Industrial (incl. agricultural)	24%	23%	22%	24%
Commercial	19%	18%	19%	19%
Other	8%	5%	4%	4%

A total of 649,319 meters were in service at the end of fiscal 1994, compared with 636,159 at the end of fiscal 1993, and 630,365 a year before that.

Record volumes of natural gas sold and transported in fiscal 1994 totaled about 151,395,000 Mcf, versus 149,187,000 Mcf in fiscal 1993.

In fiscal 1994, Atmos sold 116.1 million Mcf of gas, at an average sales price of $4.14 per Mcf and an average cost of $2.86 per Mcf sold, and transported 35.3 million Mcf of gas. This compared with 109.4 million Mcf sold in fiscal 1993 at an average sales price of $4.02 per Mcf and an average cost of $2.71 per Mcf, and 39.8 million Mcf of gas transported.

In November 1994, $40 million of debt was placed privately with two insurance companies; proceeds were used to pay down short-term debt.

The company intends to continue efforts to expand service and product usage within existing markets, but will also seek alternative growth opportunities. Atmos intends to consider and, when appropriate, pursue the acquisition of other natural gas distribution properties.

Important Developments

Jul. '95—A settlement agreement was filed with the Kentucky Public Service Commission for a total net operating income benefit of approximately $4.0 million, of which a portion becomes effective in August 1996. Separately, the Louisiana Public Service Commission approved a settlement of an investigation of the company's gas costs that exonerated the company; however, ATO will refund about $541,000, plus interest, to its Louisiana customers, over two years.

Capitalization

Long Term Debt: $131,303,000 (6/95).

Per Share Data ($) (Year Ended Sep. 30)

	1994	1993	1992	1991	1990	1989
Tangible Bk. Val.	9.78	10.39	9.17	8.88	8.71	8.51
Earnings	0.97	1.45	0.97	0.80	0.98	0.89
Dividends	0.88	0.85	0.83	0.80	0.77	0.75
Payout Ratio	91%	59%	85%	100%	79%	84%
Prices - High	20¼	21⅛	15⅞	15⅜	12½	12
- Low	15⅞	15⅛	12⅝	10½	10⅜	9¾
P/E Ratio - High	21	15	16	19	13	14
- Low	16	10	13	13	11	11

Income Statement Analysis (Million $)

	1994	%Chg	1993	%Chg	1992	%Chg	1991
Revs.	500	29%	388	14%	340	1%	336
Depr.	18.8	38%	13.6	NM	13.6	8%	12.6
Maint.	5.9	55%	3.8	17%	3.3	-16%	3.9
Fxd. Chgs. Cov.	2.8	-18%	3.5	44%	2.4	16%	2.1
Constr. Credits	NA	—	NA	—	NA	—	NA
Eff. Tax Rate	36%	—	37%	—	33%	—	28%
Net Inc.	14.7	-6%	15.7	57%	10.0	27%	7.9

Balance Sheet & Other Fin. Data (Million $)

	1994	1993	1992	1991	1990	1989
Gross Prop.	544	399	364	333	307	300
Cap. Exp.	50.4	38.4	33.3	30.2	25.3	21.6
Net Prop.	327	241	219	206	195	195
Capitalization:						
LT Debt	138	85.3	91.3	95.6	81.8	91.9
% LT Debt	48	42	49	51	51	54
Pfd.	Nil	Nil	Nil	Nil	Nil	Nil
% Pfd.	Nil	Nil	Nil	Nil	Nil	Nil
Common	150	118	96.0	90.3	79.8	77.7
% Common	52	58	51	49	49	46
Total Cap.	318	232	214	212	189	195

Ratio Analysis

	1994	1993	1992	1991	1990	1989
Oper. Ratio	94.7	93.3	94.0	94.6	94.5	94.9
% Earn. on Net Prop.	8.4	11.3	9.6	9.0	9.9	9.1
% Ret. on Revs.	2.9	4.0	2.9	2.4	2.5	2.4
% Ret. On Invest.Cap	9.1	11.6	9.7	9.0	10.4	9.6
% Return On Com.Eqty	10.2	14.7	10.8	9.3	11.4	10.5

Dividend Data —Dividends have been paid since 1984. Dividend reinvestment and direct stock purchase plans are available. A poison pill stock purchase rights plan was adopted in 1988. A three-for-two stock split was effected in May 1994.

Amt. of Div. $	Date Decl.	Ex-Div. Date	Stock of Record	Payment Date
0.230	Nov. 09	Nov. 18	Nov. 25	Dec. 12 '94
0.230	Feb. 08	Feb. 21	Feb. 27	Mar. 10 '95
0.230	May. 10	May. 19	May. 25	Jun. 12 '95
0.230	Aug. 09	Aug. 23	Aug. 25	Sep. 11 '95

Data as orig. reptd.; bef. results of disc opers. and/or spec. items. Per share data adj. for stk. divs. as of ex-div. date. E-Estimated. NA-Not Available. NM-Not Meaningful. NR-Not Ranked.

Office—1800 Three Lincoln Centre, 5430 LBJ Freeway, Dallas, TX 75240. **Tel**—(214) 934-9227. **Chrmn**—C. K. Vaughan. **Pres & COO**—R. F. Stephens. **EVP & CFO**—J. F. Purser. **Secy**—G. A. Blanscet. **VP & Investor Contact**—Jack W. Eversull. **Dirs**—T. W. Bain II, D. Busbee, P. E. Nichol, J. W. Norris, Jr., J. F. Purser, C. S. Quinn, L. Schlessman, R. F. Stephens, C. K. Vaughan, R. Ware II. **Transfer Agent & Registrar**—Bank of Boston. **Organized** in Texas in 1983. **Empl-** 1,698. **S&P Analyst:** Michael C. Barr

STANDARD & POOR'S

STOCK REPORTS

Augat Inc.

NYSE Symbol **AUG**
In S&P SmallCap 600

11-OCT-95 **Industry:** Electronics/Electric

Summary: This company is one of the world's largest manufacturers of electromechanical products used for the interconnection of circuits in electronic applications.

Quantitative Evaluations

Recent Price • 18½ | Yield • 0.9%
52 Wk Range • 24½-14½ | 12-Mo. P/E • 13.6

Outlook
(1 Lowest—5 Highest)
• **4-**

Fair Value
• **20¼**

Risk
• **Average**

Earn./Div. Rank
• **B-**

Technical Eval.
• **Bearish** since 7/95

Rel. Strength Rank
(1 Lowest—99 Highest)
• **11**

Insider Activity
• **Neutral**

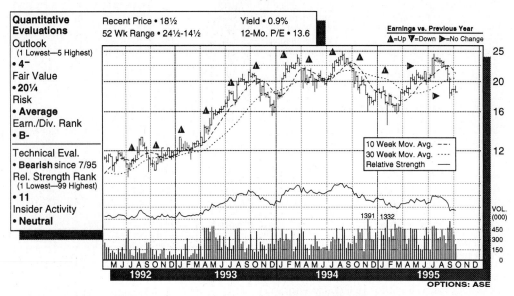

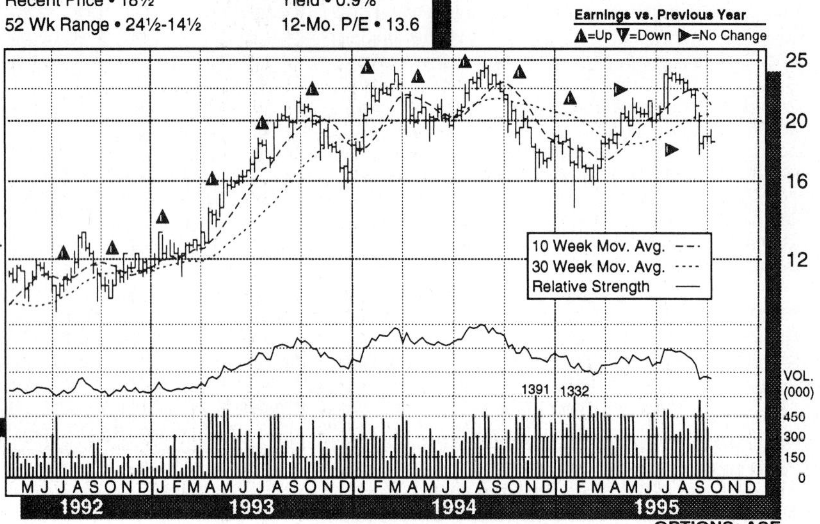

OPTIONS: ASE

Business Profile - 11-OCT-95

Augat's strategy is to grow within the communications, computer, automotive and industrial markets, mainly through customer partnerships, new-product introductions, acquisitions, and productivity improvements. Recent success has been driven by strength in the communications sector, which is expected to post 30%-35% higher sales in 1995, aided by two recent acquisitions. Weakness in the domestic automotive market will, however, be an offsetting factor, and is not expected to improve until 1996.

Operational Review - 11-OCT-95

Sales for the six months ended June 30, 1995, rose 1.3%, year to year, reflecting a sharp advance for communications products and strength for automotive components in Europe. These outweighed a drop in the interconnection business, and a weak domestic auto market. Margins widened slightly on the higher volume, improved manufacturing and cost controls, despite lower selling prices and higher input costs. EPS were unchanged at $0.66, as higher net income was offset by more shares outstanding.

Stock Performance - 06-OCT-95

In the past 30 trading days, AUG's shares have declined 17%, compared to a 4% rise in the S&P 500. Average trading volume for the past five days was 45,360 shares, compared with the 40-day moving average of 109,805 shares.

Key Stock Statistics

Dividend Rate/Share	0.16	Shareholders	1,600
Shs. outstg. (M)	19.6	Market cap. (B)	$0.349
Avg. daily vol. (M)	0.092	Inst. holdings	81%
Tang. Bk. Value/Share	11.41	Insider holdings	NA
Beta	0.77		

Value of $10,000 invested 5 years ago: $ 15,084

Fiscal Year Ending Dec. 31

	1995	% Change	1994	% Change	1993	% Change
Revenues (Million $)						
1Q	134.6	6%	127.4	26%	101.2	20%
2Q	130.6	-3%	134.4	26%	106.3	18%
3Q	—	—	127.7	28%	100.0	9%
4Q	—	—	141.2	25%	112.8	18%
Yr.	—	—	530.7	26%	420.3	16%
Income (Million $)						
1Q	5.80	2%	5.70	97%	2.90	107%
2Q	7.06	2%	6.95	93%	3.60	64%
3Q	—	—	6.40	56%	4.10	141%
4Q	—	—	7.15	43%	5.00	NM
Yr.	—	—	26.20	68%	15.60	137%
Earnings Per Share ($)						
1Q	0.30	NM	0.30	88%	0.16	100%
2Q	0.36	NM	0.36	89%	0.19	58%
3Q	—	—	0.33	50%	0.22	144%
4Q	—	—	0.37	42%	0.26	NM
Yr.	—	—	1.36	64%	0.83	131%

Next earnings report expected: late October

Augat Inc.

Business Summary - 10-OCT-95

Augat designs and produces a broad range of electromechanical products used for the interconnection of circuits in electronic applications. Sales contributions by major product area in recent years were:

	1994	1993	1992	1991
Interconnection products	25%	30%	35%	46%
Wiring sys. & components	55%	52%	50%	37%
Communications	20%	18%	15%	17%

In 1994, international operations accounted for 20% of total sales and 14% of operating income.

Augat manufactures interconnection hardware accessories, including high-performance sockets, switches, connectors and packaging panels for the computer, mobile communications, test and consumer electronics markets.

The company's wiring systems division manufactures products for the automotive and related industries, including automotive connectors, terminal blocks, power distribution centers, cables and specialty wiring harnesses, safety devices, audio systems and built-in cellular telephones. Augat emphasizes partnerships with customers and provides design capabilities to produce specific system solutions.

Augat's products for the telecommunications and cable television industries include main office distribution frame and operating office and PABX standard telephone application products, coaxial connectors, broadband amplification products and fiber-optic connectors. The company's strategy for these industries emphasizes developing new products, finding new applications for existing products and promoting products that serve both industries.

In May 1995, AUG acquired Photon Systems Corp., a leading designer and manufacturer of systems that enable telecommunications and cable companies to distribute signals over fiber-optic networks. The following month, the company acquired Elastomeric Technologies Inc., a manufacturer of customized interconnection technology, with annual revenues of approximately $5 million. Elastomeric provides packaging solutions for mobile electronics companies with applications in automobiles, cellular telephones, notebook computers, pagers and printers.

R&D costs totaled $20 million (3.8% of net sales) in 1994, versus $19 million (4.5%) the year before.

Important Developments

Sep. '95—The company said its earnings for the third quarter and full year 1995 will be lower than analysts' estimates, due solely to weakness in the automotive business. Augat expects third quarter earnings in the range of $0.20 and $0.25 a share, and full year earnings to be 4%-8% lower than in 1994.

Capitalization

Long Term Debt: $30,200,000 (6/95).
Options: To buy 1,383,525 shs. (12/94).

Per Share Data ($)

(Year Ended Dec. 31)

	1994	1993	1992	1991	1990	1989
Tangible Bk. Val.	10.90	9.20	8.34	8.18	11.48	10.24
Cash Flow	2.31	1.67	1.23	-0.34	1.84	1.75
Earnings	1.36	0.83	0.36	-1.21	0.95	0.83
Dividends	0.08	Nil	Nil	0.30	0.40	0.40
Payout Ratio	6%	Nil	Nil	NM	42%	48%
Prices - High	24⅞	21¾	13¼	14⅛	15¾	15⅜
- Low	16	11¼	8½	7⅞	8⅛	11½
P/E Ratio - High	18	26	37	NM	17	19
- Low	12	14	24	NM	9	14

Income Statement Analysis (Million $)

	1994	%Chg	1993	%Chg	1992	%Chg	1991
Revs.	531	26%	420	16%	362	28%	282
Oper. Inc.	60.3	38%	43.6	49%	29.3	85%	15.8
Depr.	18.4	16%	15.8	-1%	16.0	1%	15.8
Int. Exp.	4.2	-8%	4.6	-8%	5.0	105%	2.4
Pretax Inc.	39.7	68%	23.6	141%	9.8	NM	-21.6
Eff. Tax Rate	34%	—	34%	—	33%	—	NM
Net Inc.	26.2	68%	15.6	136%	6.6	NM	-22.1

Balance Sheet & Other Fin. Data (Million $)

	1994	1993	1992	1991	1990	1989
Cash	20.5	8.5	28.3	27.5	42.6	23.4
Curr. Assets	198	177	158	155	154	141
Total Assets	356	318	295	293	273	252
Curr. Liab.	71.7	57.6	50.8	60.9	37.3	40.6
LT Debt	35.0	45.8	56.9	50.2	12.9	16.1
Common Eqty.	238	202	181	177	209	186
Total Cap.	284	260	245	232	235	211
Cap. Exp.	31.5	20.4	14.5	14.2	17.9	18.0
Cash Flow	44.6	31.4	22.6	-6.2	33.1	31.5

Ratio Analysis

	1994	1993	1992	1991	1990	1989
Curr. Ratio	2.8	3.1	3.1	2.5	4.1	3.5
% LT Debt of Cap.	12.3	17.6	23.3	21.6	5.5	7.6
% Net Inc.of Revs.	4.9	3.7	1.8	NM	5.7	4.9
% Ret. on Assets	7.7	5.0	2.2	NM	6.5	5.6
% Ret. on Equity	11.8	8.0	3.7	NM	8.7	8.1

Dividend Data —Dividends, omitted since late 1991, were resumed in 1994. Prior to their suspension, dividends had been paid since 1970. A "poison pill" stock purchase rights plan was adopted in 1988.

Amt. of Div. $	Date Decl.	Ex-Div. Date	Stock of Record	Payment Date
0.040	Oct. 18	Nov. 04	Nov. 10	Nov. 30 '94
0.040	Jan. 31	Feb. 06	Feb. 10	Feb. 28 '95
0.040	Apr. 25	May. 04	May. 10	May. 31 '95
0.040	Jul. 20	Aug. 08	Aug. 10	Aug. 31 '95

Data as orig. reptd.; bef. results of disc. opers. and/or spec. items. Per share data adj. for stk. divs. as of ex-div. date. E-Estimated. NA-Not Available. NM-Not Meaningful. NR-Not Ranked.

Office—89 Forbes Blvd., P.O. Box 448, Mansfield, MA 02048. **Tel**—(508) 543-4300. **Fax**—(508) 543-7019. **Chrmn**—M. P. Joseph. **Pres & CEO**—W. R. Fenoglio. **VP, CFO & Investor Contact**—Ellen B. Richstone. **Treas**—L. M. Avallone. **Clerk**—T. E. Neely. **Dirs**—V. R. Alden, B. L. Crockett, J. D. Curtin Jr., S. S. Dennis III, W. R. Fenoglio, J. G. Fishman, M. P. Joseph, T. L. King, J. N. Lemasters, D. V. Ragone, A. J. Zakon. **Transfer Agent & Registrar**—First National Bank of Boston. **Incorporated** in Massachusetts in 1946. **Empl**-4,400. **S&P Analyst:** J. Santoriello

STANDARD & POOR'S

STOCK REPORTS

Auspex Systems

NASDAQ Symbol **ASPX**

In S&P SmallCap 600

10-OCT-95

Industry: Data Processing

Summary: This company develops, manufactures, distributes and supports a line of UNIX/NFS file servers that enhance the performance of large, multivendor client/server networks.

Quantitative Evaluations

Outlook (1 Lowest—5 Highest) • **NA**

Fair Value • **NA**

Risk • **High**

Earn./Div. Rank • **NR**

Technical Eval. • **Bullish** since 9/94

Rel. Strength Rank (1 Lowest—99 Highest) • **35**

Insider Activity • **Unfavorable**

Recent Price • 15

52 Wk Range • 18¾-5⅜

Yield • Nil

12-Mo. P/E • 29.4

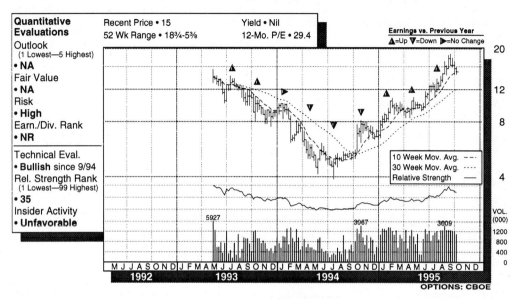

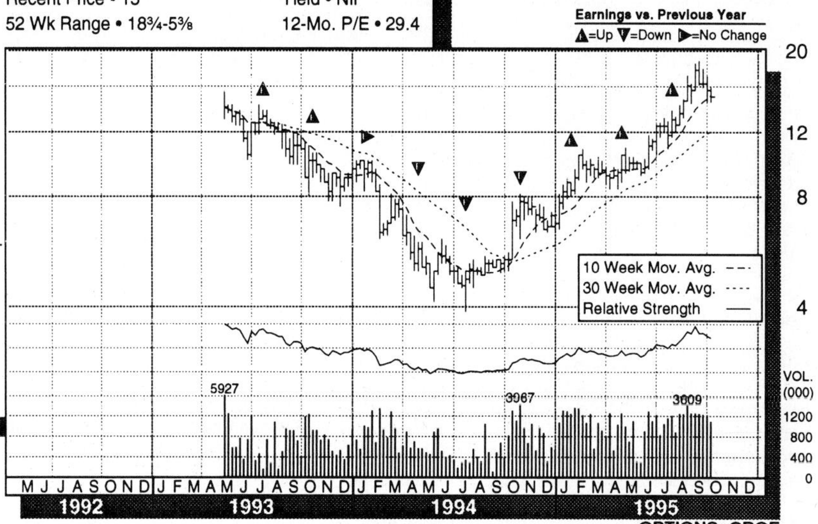

OPTIONS: CBOE

Business Profile - 10-OCT-95

Auspex is focused on penetrating new markets, such as the mechanical CAD market and the finance and banking markets, through the introduction of new products. Revenues increased 39% in fiscal 1995, reflecting strong demand for the company's new NetServer 7000 Series 500 line, and earnings were up 49%. The consensus estimate is for share earnings of $0.66 in fiscal 1996, up from $0.51 in fiscal 1995. Institutions hold approximately 50% of the roughly 24 million common shares outstanding.

Operational Review - 10-OCT-95

Based on a preliminary report, revenues for the fiscal year ended June 30, 1995, rose 39% from those of fiscal 1994, reflecting the successful introduction of several new products and growth of the company's North American sales force. Margins widened on the higher volume, and operating income increased 66%. After taxes at 22.0%, versus 15.0%, net income advanced 49%, to $12.4 million ($0.51 a share), from $8.3 million ($0.34).

Stock Performance - 06-OCT-95

In the past 30 trading days, ASPX's shares have declined 7%, compared to a 4% rise in the S&P 500. Average trading volume for the past five days was 217,540 shares, compared with the 40-day moving average of 359,400 shares.

Key Stock Statistics

Dividend Rate/Share	Nil	Shareholders	700
Shs. outstg. (M)	23.6	Market cap. (B)	$0.336
Avg. daily vol. (M)	0.259	Inst. holdings	50%
Tang. Bk. Value/Share	3.26	Insider holdings	NA
Beta	NA		

Value of $10,000 invested 5 years ago: NA

Fiscal Year Ending Jun. 30

	1995	% Change	1994	% Change	1993	% Change
Revenues (Million $)						
1Q	23.87	17%	20.40	30%	15.70	54%
2Q	26.44	30%	20.38	24%	16.40	23%
3Q	30.03	40%	21.44	9%	19.70	45%
4Q	35.28	67%	21.09	-3%	21.80	51%
Yr.	115.6	39%	83.28	13%	73.50	43%
Income (Million $)						
1Q	2.07	-15%	2.43	—	—	—
2Q	2.58	21%	2.14	—	—	—
3Q	3.37	56%	2.16	—	—	—
4Q	4.39	176%	1.59	—	—	—
Yr.	12.41	49%	8.32	2%	8.13	66%
Earnings Per Share ($)						
1Q	0.09	-10%	0.10	25%	0.08	100%
2Q	0.11	22%	0.09	NM	0.09	NM
3Q	0.14	56%	0.09	-10%	0.10	67%
4Q	0.18	157%	0.07	-22%	0.09	50%
Yr.	0.51	50%	0.34	-6%	0.36	44%

Next earnings report expected: late October

Auspex Systems

Business Summary - 28-SEP-95

Auspex Systems, Inc. develops, manufactures, distributes and supports a line of UNIX/NFS file servers, known as NetServers, that enhance the performance of large, multivendor client/server networks. The company's file servers use a proprietary Functional Multiprocessing (FMP) architecture that was designed specifically to overcome certain limitations inherent in file servers by optimizing most commonly executed tasks, namely file transfer and disk operation.

The FMP design offers an architectural solution to the input/output (I/O) performance gap (the imbalance between the processing power of workstation clients and the I/O rates of file servers) through distribution of all performance-limiting Network File Server (NFS) functions to a specialized I/O subsystem of dedicated file, network and disk processors. By isolating the host central processing unit and UNIX operating system from the file server's principal activity, the NetServer bypasses the internal bottleneck that slows the throughput of general-purpose computer architectures performing similar tasks.

Auspex's newest NetServer model, the NS 7000, introduced in June 1994, can simultaneously support applications such as database or high-speed, on-line system backup, as well as NFS input/output operations without one activity impairing the performance of the other. A base NetServer configuration includes a network processor, a file processor, a storage processor and a host processor, along with I/O cache memory and a rack for the first five SCSI disk drives, typically of 3.0 gigabytes capacity each. NetServer prices range from approximately $65,000 to more than $500,000, depending on the configuration.

Most of the company's sales are made to customers in the scientific, technical and engineering fields, where the need for high-performance file servers is the most critical. NetServers are most commonly used for applications such as software development, electronic computer-aided design and electronic computer-aided engineering, scientific and academic research, mechanical computer-aided design, technical publishing and financial and brokerage analysis.

Important Developments

Jun. '95—ASPX signed an agreement with Riverview Technology Partners (RTP) under which RTP would become an Auspex reseller in North America and the U.K. and would promote Auspex NetServers into the financial services market.

Capitalization

Long Term Debt: $159,000 of cap. lease obligs. (6/95).

Options: To purchase 2,962,948 shs. at $0.10 to $13.63 ea. (6/94).

Per Share Data ($) (Year Ended Jun. 30)

	1995	1994	1993	1992	1991	1990
Tangible Bk. Val.	NA	2.91	2.66	4.20	NA	NA
Cash Flow	NA	0.64	0.59	0.38	NA	NA
Earnings	0.51	0.34	0.36	0.25	NA	NA
Dividends	Nil	Nil	Nil	Nil	NA	NA
Payout Ratio	Nil	Nil	Nil	Nil	NA	NA
Prices - High	13¾	10	15½	NA	NA	NA
- Low	6½	3⅞	7½	NA	NA	NA
P/E Ratio - High	27	29	43	NA	NA	NA
- Low	13	11	22	NA	NA	NA

Income Statement Analysis (Million $)

	1994	%Chg	1993	%Chg	1992	%Chg	1991
Revs.	83.3	13%	73.5	43%	51.5	—	NA
Oper. Inc.	15.8	9%	14.5	81%	8.0	—	NA
Depr.	7.4	49%	5.0	92%	2.6	—	NA
Int. Exp.	0.1	-10%	0.1	NM	0.1	—	NA
Pretax Inc.	9.8	-2%	10.0	79%	5.6	—	NA
Eff. Tax Rate	15%	—	19%	—	12%	—	NA
Net Inc.	8.3	2%	8.1	66%	4.9	—	NA

Balance Sheet & Other Fin. Data (Million $)

	1994	1993	1992	1991	1990	1989
Cash	42.1	49.8	16.3	NA	NA	NA
Curr. Assets	75.8	68.2	27.4	NA	NA	NA
Total Assets	85.4	76.7	33.0	NA	NA	NA
Curr. Liab.	18.3	14.4	9.8	NA	NA	NA
LT Debt	0.4	0.8	0.7	NA	NA	NA
Common Eqty.	66.6	61.6	21.0	NA	NA	NA
Total Cap.	67.0	62.4	21.7	NA	NA	NA
Cap. Exp.	7.9	6.9	5.1	NA	NA	NA
Cash Flow	15.8	13.1	7.5	NA	NA	NA

Ratio Analysis

	1994	1993	1992	1991	1990	1989
Curr. Ratio	4.1	4.7	2.8	NA	NA	NA
% LT Debt of Cap.	0.6	1.3	3.1	NA	NA	NA
% Net Inc.of Revs.	10.0	11.1	9.5	NA	NA	NA
% Ret. on Assets	10.3	7.1	22.2	NA	NA	NA
% Ret. on Equity	13.0	10.2	39.8	NA	NA	NA

Dividend Data —No cash dividends have been paid. A "poison pill" stock purchase rights plan was adopted in April 1995.

Data as orig. reptd.; bef. results of disc. opers. and/or spec. items. Per share data adj. for stk. divs. as of ex-div. date. E-Estimated. NA-Not Available. NM-Not Meaningful. NR-Not Ranked.

Office—5200 Great America Pkwy., Santa Clara, CA 95054. **Tel**—(408) 986-2000. **Chrmn & CEO**—L. B. Boucher. **Pres & COO**—B. Moore **VP-Fin, CFO & Investor Contact**—Esther W. Lee. **Secy**—H. P. Massey Jr. **Dirs**—L. B. Boucher, R. S. Cheheyl, J. A. Downer, W. F. King, E. W. Lee, D. F. Marquardt, W. G. Van Auken. **Transfer Agent & Registrar**—First National Bank of Boston. **Incorporated** in California in 1987; reincorporated in Delaware in 1991. **Empl**-323. **S&P Analyst:** N. Rosenberg

STANDARD & POOR'S

STOCK REPORTS

Authentic Fitness

NYSE Symbol **ASM**
In S&P SmallCap 600

14-NOV-95 **Industry:** Textiles

Summary: This company makes swimwear, active fitness apparel and skiwear under various brand names including Speedo, Catalina and White Stag, and operates a growing chain of retail stores.

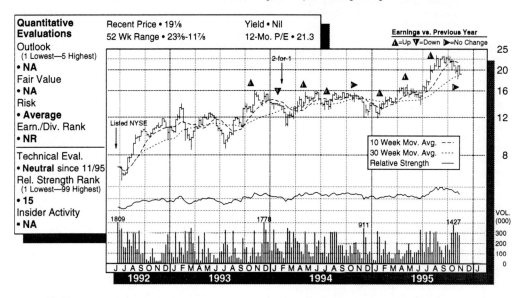

Quantitative Evaluations

Recent Price • 19⅛
52 Wk Range • 23⅜-11⅞
Yield • Nil
12-Mo. P/E • 21.3

Outlook
(1 Lowest—5 Highest)
• **NA**

Fair Value
• **NA**

Risk
• **Average**

Earn./Div. Rank
• **NR**

Technical Eval.
• **Neutral** since 11/95

Rel. Strength Rank
(1 Lowest—99 Highest)
• **15**

Insider Activity
• **NA**

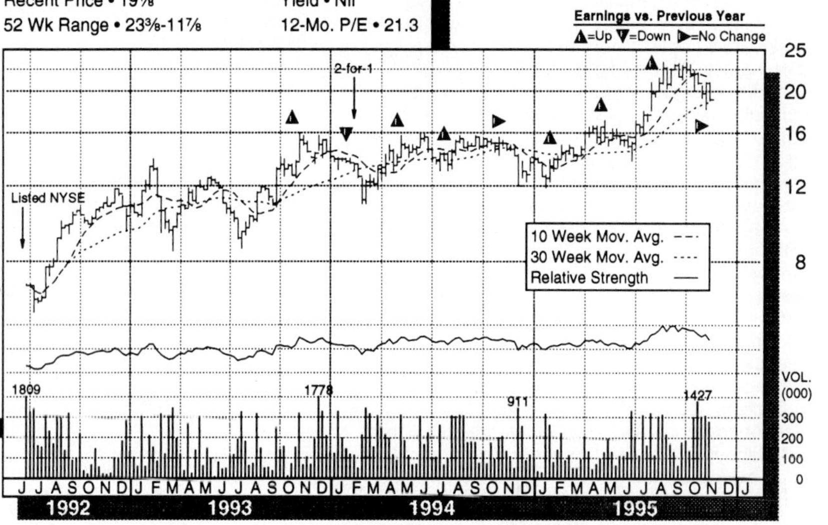

Business Profile - 13-NOV-95

Authentic Fitness is looking to grow in three major business areas: swimwear, activewear and retail. The company's strategy is to leverage its leading brand names by expanding its distribution channels and extending its product lines. Key elements of this include, opening new Speedo Authentic Fitness retail stores, expanding product offerings through mass merchandising, and entering international markets. ASM recently completed a public offering of 2.5 million common shares at $21.63 each.

Operational Review - 13-NOV-95

Revenues for the quarter ended September 30, 1995, advanced 14%, year to year, reflecting continued strength of the company's brands, and the expansion of the Speedo Authentic Fitness retail concept. However, profits were restricted by higher interest expenses related to the buyback of a warrant from GE Capital Corp., and costs to operate 52 new stores opened in fiscal 1995. Net income rose 5.3%, to $2.2 million ($0.10 per share), from $2.1 million ($0.10).

Stock Performance - 10-NOV-95

In the past 30 trading days, ASM's shares have declined 15%, compared to a 1% rise in the S&P 500. Average trading volume for the past five days was 55,680 shares, compared with the 40-day moving average of 79,822 shares.

Key Stock Statistics

Dividend Rate/Share	Nil	Shareholders	100
Shs. outstg. (M)	20.3	Market cap. (B)	$0.376
Avg. daily vol. (M)	0.125	Inst. holdings	57%
Tang. Bk. Value/Share	3.45	Insider holdings	NA
Beta	NA		

Value of $10,000 invested 5 years ago: NA

Fiscal Year Ending Jun. 30

	1996	% Change	1995	% Change	1994	% Change
Revenues (Million $)						
1Q	42.91	14%	37.60	31%	28.61	20%
2Q	—	—	56.32	53%	36.82	27%
3Q	—	—	74.85	40%	53.30	45%
4Q	—	—	97.37	63%	59.83	38%
Yr.	—	—	266.1	49%	178.6	34%
Income (Million $)						
1Q	2.18	5%	2.07	14%	1.81	—
2Q	—	—	4.45	NM	-0.81	NM
3Q	—	—	5.98	41%	4.23	42%
4Q	—	—	6.98	60%	4.35	71%
Yr.	—	—	19.47	103%	9.58	-2%
Earnings Per Share ($)						
1Q	0.10	NM	0.10	NM	0.10	18%
2Q	—	—	0.21	NM	-0.04	NM
3Q	—	—	0.28	40%	0.20	18%
4Q	—	—	0.32	60%	0.20	38%
Yr.	—	—	0.90	84%	0.49	-13%

Next earnings report expected: mid November

Authentic Fitness

Business Summary - 13-NOV-95

Authentic Fitness designs, contracts for the manufacture of, and markets swimwear, swim accessories, and active fitness apparel under the Speedo, Catalina, Anne Cole, Cole of California, Sandcastle, Sporting Life and Oscar de la Renta brand names; skiwear, activewear and swimwear under the White Stag brand name, and skiwear under the Edelweiss, Mountain Goat and Skiing Passport brand names. The company also operates Authentic Fitness retail stores which sell active fitness apparel under the Speedo and Speedo Authentic Fitness names. In fiscal 1995, 54% of ASM's revenues were derived from the Speedo division, 26% from the Designer Swimwear division, 12% from the White Stag/Skiwear division, and 8% from the Retail division.

The Speedo brand name is prominent in the competition swimwear market, and is the dominant brand in that market in the U.S. and Canada. The Speedo division's product lines consist of women's and men's competition swimwear; active fitness wear, consisting of women's fitness swimwear and the Speedo Authentic Fitness line of active fitness wear for women and men; men's swimwear and coordinating T-shirts; and accessories.

At October 31, 1995, ASM was operating a total of 76 Speedo Authentic Fitness retail stores (the first was opened in L.A. in late 1992), which offer a complete line of Speedo and Speedo Authentic Fitness products. If the units continue to perform to expectations, the company planned to have 200 in operation by the end of calendar 1996.

The Designer Swimwear division markets women's swimwear, activewear, sportswear and beachwear, and children's swimwear, under the Catalina, Cole of California, Anne Cole and Oscar de la Renta brand names. ASM owns the Catalina and Cole of California brands and licenses the Anne Cole and Oscar de la Renta trademarks.

The White Stag/Skiwear division designs, sources and markets a broad variety of skiwear, including parkas, ski suits, shells and ski pants. ASM hopes to capitalize on the potential mass appeal of the White Stag brand name by redirecting it to a line of activewear, outerwear, swimwear and accessories.

Important Developments

Oct. '95—The company sold publicly 2,500,000 ASM common shares at $21.63 each. Net proceeds were earmarked to pay a bridge loan that was used to finance the September 13, repurchase of 1,809,179 shares of the series A warrant held by General Electric Capital Corp.

Oct. '95—During the first quarter of fiscal 1996, ASM opened eight new retail stores. Twenty additional stores are under development.

Capitalization

Long Term Debt: $32,446,000 (7/1/95).

Per Share Data ($) (Year Ended Jun. 30)

	1995	1994	1993	1992	1991	1990
Tangible Bk. Val.	3.45	2.63	0.64	-0.13	-0.31	NA
Cash Flow	1.20	0.70	0.72	0.59	0.39	NA
Earnings	0.90	0.49	0.56	0.43	0.23	NA
Dividends	Nil	Nil	Nil	Nil	NA	NA
Payout Ratio	Nil	Nil	Nil	Nil	NA	NA
Prices - High	23 3/8	16	16	11 7/8	NA	NA
- Low	11 7/8	10 7/8	8 1/2	6 1/8	NA	NA
P/E Ratio - High	26	33	29	28	NA	NA
- Low	13	22	15	14	NA	NA

Income Statement Analysis (Million $)

	1995	%Chg	1994	%Chg	1993	%Chg	1992
Revs.	266	49%	179	35%	133	32%	101
Oper. Inc.	45.1	46%	30.8	38%	22.3	12%	19.9
Depr.	6.5	50%	4.3	56%	2.8	1%	2.7
Int. Exp.	7.0	59%	4.4	4%	4.3	12%	3.8
Pretax Inc.	31.6	93%	16.4	8%	15.2	14%	13.3
Eff. Tax Rate	38%	—	42%	—	36%	—	44%
Net Inc.	19.5	104%	9.6	-2%	9.8	32%	7.4

Balance Sheet & Other Fin. Data (Million $)

	1995	1994	1993	1992	1991	1990
Cash	0.8	1.1	0.1	0.4	0.1	NA
Curr. Assets	163	104	65.2	44.9	55.8	NA
Total Assets	278	198	118	98.0	109	NA
Curr. Liab.	96.5	49.8	37.9	24.2	35.5	NA
LT Debt	32.4	19.2	21.5	26.0	27.6	NA
Common Eqty.	142	122	57.0	47.8	44.2	NA
Total Cap.	182	148	80.2	73.8	73.7	NA
Cap. Exp.	19.3	13.9	1.8	0.8	NA	NA
Cash Flow	26.0	13.9	12.6	10.2	6.8	NA

Ratio Analysis

	1995	1994	1993	1992	1991	1990
Curr. Ratio	1.7	2.1	1.7	1.9	1.6	NA
% LT Debt of Cap.	17.8	12.9	26.8	35.2	37.4	NA
% Net Inc.of Revs.	7.3	5.3	7.4	6.3	4.6	NA
% Ret. on Assets	8.2	6.0	7.5	NA	NA	NA
% Ret. on Equity	14.8	10.7	18.4	NA	NA	NA

Dividend Data —The company declared an initial quarterly cash dividened in August 1995. A 2-for-1 stock split was effected in February 1994.

Amt. of Div. $	Date Decl.	Ex-Div. Date	Stock of Record	Payment Date
0.013	Aug. 17	Aug. 28	Aug. 30	Oct. 02 '95
0.013	Nov. 08	Nov. 29	Dec. 01	Jan. 03 '96

Data as orig. reptd.; bef. results of disc. opers. and/or spec. items. Per share data adj. for stk. divs. as of ex-div. date. E-Estimated. NA-Not Available. NM-Not Meaningful. NR-Not Ranked.

Office—7911 Haskell Ave., Van Nuys, CA 91410. **Tel**—(818) 376-0300. **Chrmn & CEO**—L. J. Wachner. **SVP & CFO**—N. Sohl. **VP-Fin & Secy**—W. W. Chan. **Dirs**—S. S. Arkin, S. D. Buchalter, J. A. Califano, Jr., W. S. Finkelstein, R. S. Rubin, L. J. Wachner, R. D. Walter. **Transfer Agent**—Bank of New York, NYC. **Incorporated** in Delaware in 1990. **Empl**-1,915. **S&P Analyst:** Maureen C. Carini

STANDARD & POOR'S

STOCK REPORTS

Aztar Corp.

NYSE Symbol **AZR**
In S&P SmallCap 600

26-JUL-95

Industry: Leisure/Amusement

Summary: Aztar operates three casino/hotels: one in Atlantic City and two in Nevada. AZR also operates a riverboat casino in Missouri; and has plans for another such facility in Indiana.

S&P Opinion: Accumulate (★★★★)

Recent Price • 8⅝ | Yield • Nil
52 Wk Range • 10-5⅜ | 12-Mo. P/E • 43.1

Quantitative Evaluations

Outlook (1 Lowest—5 Highest) • **5-**

Fair Value • **14⅜**

Risk • **Average**

Earn./Div. Rank • **NR**

Technical Eval. • **Bearish** since 3/95

Rel. Strength Rank (1 Lowest—99 Highest) • **55**

Insider Activity • **Neutral**

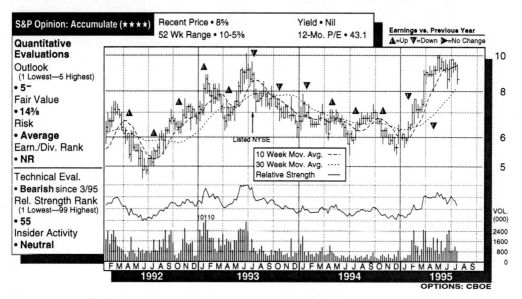

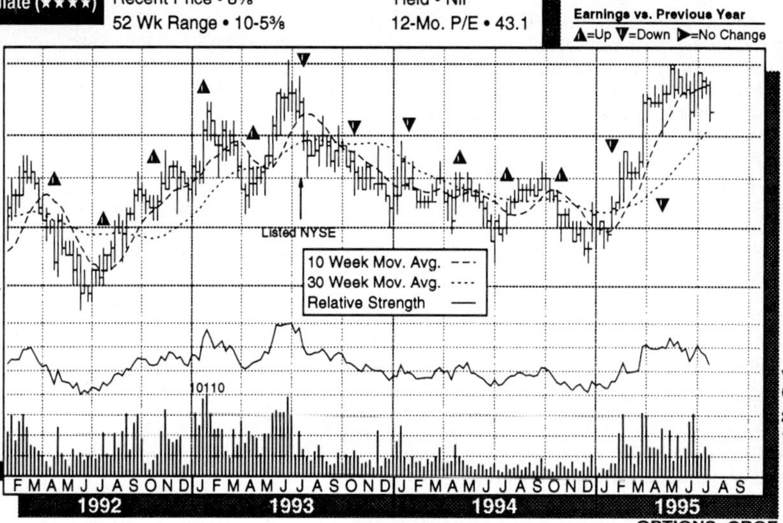

OPTIONS: CBOE

Overview - 26-JUL-95

In 1995, we expect double-digit profit growth from Atlantic City to be largely offset by lower earnings from AZR's two Nevada casino/hotels. We look for two new casino boats-- in Missouri and Indiana-- to make no more than a modest contribution to operating profit. The debut of the more significant Evansville, Ind., project is not likely to occur any earlier than late 1995. Our 1995 earnings estimate includes a preopening charge for the Missouri project, but excludes a propective charge related to the Indiana boat. Also, AZR's tax rate for 1995 is likely to be much higher than 1994's level, which was unsuaully low due to use of tax credits. In 1996, we expect the Evansville casino boat to be the primary contributor to AZR earnings growth.

Valuation - 26-JUL-95

The stock of this gaming company is up sharply from its 1994 low, but we continue to see appeal for capital gains. The shares are largely a bet on the prospective success of a new gaming project on the Ohio River in Evansville, Ind., and the possibility that AZR will be acquired by another company. In Evansville, we look for AZR to start operations with a strong local market position, with little competition nearby. However, several additional casino boats are planned for southeastern Indiana, and these facilities will likely compete with AZR's boat for customers in the Louisville, Ky., metropolitan market.

Key Stock Statistics

S&P EPS Est. 1995	0.30	Tang. Bk. Value/Share	9.46
P/E on S&P Est. 1995	28.7	Beta	1.75
S&P EPS Est. 1996	0.70	Shareholders	12,600
Dividend Rate/Share	Nil	Market cap. (B)	$0.357
Shs. outstg. (M)	38.1	Inst. holdings	56%
Avg. daily vol. (M)	0.201	Insider holdings	NA

Value of $10,000 invested 5 years ago: $ 10,454

Fiscal Year Ending Dec. 31

	1995	% Change	1994	% Change	1993	% Change
Revenues (Million $)						
1Q	135.6	4%	130.6	7%	122.3	4%
2Q	145.4	7%	135.8	4%	130.8	NM
3Q	—	—	146.9	2%	144.0	2%
4Q	—	—	128.3	5%	121.6	NM
Yr.	—	—	541.4	4%	518.8	1%
Income (Million $)						
1Q	1.96	-57%	4.55	188%	1.58	72%
2Q	0.53	-92%	6.58	68%	3.91	-35%
3Q	—	—	7.57	42%	5.33	-37%
4Q	—	—	-1.90	NM	0.56	-38%
Yr.	—	—	16.80	48%	11.38	-31%
Earnings Per Share ($)						
1Q	0.05	-55%	0.11	175%	0.04	100%
2Q	0.01	-94%	0.17	70%	0.10	-38%
3Q	E0.20	—	0.19	46%	0.13	-41%
4Q	E0.04	—	-0.05	NM	0.01	-50%
Yr.	E0.30	—	0.42	50%	0.28	-32%

Next earnings report expected: mid October

Business Summary - 22-JUL-95

Aztar Corp. was formed to own and operate the former gaming business of Ramada Inc. It operates one of 12 casino/hotels open in the Atlantic City market, and also has gaming facilities in Las Vegas and Laughlin, Nev. In April 1995, a new AZR casino boat opened in Carruthersville, Mo., and this may be followed by the debut of an Evansville, Ind., casino boat in late 1995. In 1994, 82% ($443 million) of AZR's total net revenues came from casino winnings.

AZR's TropWorld in Atlantic City includes 1,020 hotel rooms or suites, about 92,118 sq. ft. of casino space and about 80,000 sq. ft. of meeting space. One of the biggest casino/hotels in Atlantic City, it accounted for about 59% of AZR's net revenues in 1994. The casino contains about 2,797 slot machines and 99 gaming tables. TropWorld also has an indoor entertainment area known as Tivoli Pier. In February 1995, AZR started construction on a $75 million expansion of TropWorld. This project, to be completed in 1996, would add 628 hotel rooms.

In Las Vegas, AZR's Tropicana facility includes 1,906 hotel rooms and suites, 45,000 sq. ft. of casino space, about 100,000 sq. ft. of meeting space, and various other facilities. It has some 1,632 slot machines and 58 gaming tables. The Tropicana, which has a tropical island theme, is located on the Las Vegas Strip. In late 1993, Circus Circus Enterprises and MGM Grand opened new casino/hotels near the Tropicana.

AZR's third casino/hotel is the Ramada Express in Laughlin, Nev., a gaming area about 90 miles south of Las Vegas. The Ramada Express opened in June 1988, and has a Victorian-era railroad theme, including a train that runs on the property. The facility now includes about 1,500 guest rooms, and a 50,000 sq. ft. casino. A large expansion project, costing about $75 million, was completed in 1993.

Important Developments

Jul. '95—In 1995's second quarter, profit improvement from AZR's Atlantic City casino/hotel was more than offset by lower earnings from Nevada. Also, AZR incurred a preopening charge of $0.04 a share related to a new AZR casino boat in Carruthersville, Mo., which opened on April 28. Meanwhile, following regulatory approval in Indiana, AZR is looking to develop a large riverboat casino project on the Ohio River in Evansville. The casino boat may open by late 1995, with additional facilities completed about one year later. Also, in Atlantic City, a large expansion of AZR's TropWorld facility is underway. The $75 million project will consist primarily of a new 628-room tower, with completion expected in about mid-1996. TropWorld currently has about 1,020 rooms, and the room occupancy level in 1994 was 92%.

Capitalization

Long Term Debt: $420,183,000 (3/30/95).
Series B ESOP Conv. Pref. Stock: $4,923,000.

Per Share Data ($) (Year Ended Dec. 31)

	1994	1993	1992	1991	1990	1989
Tangible Bk. Val.	9.52	9.13	8.84	8.21	8.05	8.28
Cash Flow	1.39	1.10	1.14	0.76	0.24	0.05
Earnings	0.42	0.28	0.41	0.05	-0.42	-1.18
Dividends	Nil	Nil	Nil	Nil	Nil	Nil
Payout Ratio	Nil	Nil	Nil	Nil	Nil	Nil
Prices - High	7⅞	10⅛	7⅝	7⅝	8¼	9
- Low	5⅜	6	4⅝	2¾	2⅜	6½
P/E Ratio - High	19	36	19	NM	NM	NM
- Low	13	21	11	NM	NM	NM

Income Statement Analysis (Million $)

	1994	%Chg	1993	%Chg	1992	%Chg	1991
Revs.	541	4%	519	1%	512	6%	481
Oper. Inc.	106	60%	66.2	21%	54.7	54%	35.6
Depr.	37.0	17%	31.6	14%	27.6	2%	27.0
Int. Exp.	52.4	7%	48.9	52%	32.2	NM	32.4
Pretax Inc.	18.7	51%	12.4	-52%	26.0	NM	2.8
Eff. Tax Rate	10%	—	8.30%	—	37%	—	2.20%
Net Inc.	16.8	47%	11.4	-30%	16.4	NM	2.7

Balance Sheet & Other Fin. Data (Million $)

	1994	1993	1992	1991	1990	1989
Cash	52.0	40.0	100	82.2	74.1	99
Curr. Assets	94.0	82.0	158	121	116	149
Total Assets	915	877	850	638	642	678
Curr. Liab.	73.0	74.0	77.0	93.0	94.0	106
LT Debt	430	404	378	177	180	181
Common Eqty.	357	341	327	311	304	339
Total Cap.	821	781	749	520	521	545
Cap. Exp.	54.0	78.0	24.0	22.0	24.0	116
Cash Flow	53.2	42.3	43.4	28.9	9.7	2.1

Ratio Analysis

	1994	1993	1992	1991	1990	1989
Curr. Ratio	1.3	1.1	2.0	1.3	1.2	1.4
% LT Debt of Cap.	52.4	51.7	50.5	34.0	34.6	33.2
% Net Inc.of Revs.	3.1	2.2	3.2	0.6	NM	NM
% Ret. on Assets	1.9	1.3	2.2	0.4	NM	NM
% Ret. on Equity	4.6	3.2	5.0	0.6	NM	NM

Dividend Data (Initiation of common share dividends is not expected.)

Data as orig. reptd.; bef. results of disc. opers. and/or spec. items. Per share data adj. for stk. divs. as of ex-div. date. E-Estimated. NA-Not Available. NM-Not Meaningful. NR-Not Ranked.

Office—2390 East Camelback Rd., Suite 400, Phoenix, AZ 85016-3452. **Tel**—(602) 381-4100. **Chrmn, Pres & CEO**—P. E. Rubeli. **EVP & CFO**—R. M. Haddock. **Treas**—N. A. Ciarfalia. **VP-Secy**—N. W. Armstrong, Jr. **VP & Investor Contact**—Joe C. Cole. **Dirs**—J. B. Bohle, E. M. Carson, A. S. Gittlin, R. M. Haddock, J. R. Norton III, R. S. Rosow, P. E. Rubeli, R. Snell, V. V. Temen, T. W. Thomas, C. V. Willoughby. **Transfer Agent & Registrar**—First Interstate Bank, Encino, Calif. **Incorporated** in Delaware in 1989. **Empl**-8,200. **S&P Analyst:** Tom Graves, CFA

BE Aerospace

NASDAQ Symbol **BEAV**
In S&P SmallCap 600

14-NOV-95

Industry: Aircraft manufacturing/ components

Summary: BEAV makes cabin interior products for commercial aircraft, including seating, passenger entertainment and service systems, and galley structures and inserts.

Quantitative Evaluations

Outlook (1 Lowest—5 Highest)
• **2**

Fair Value
• **7⅞**

Risk
• **Average**

Earn./Div. Rank
• **NR**

Technical Eval.
• **Neutral** since 11/95

Rel. Strength Rank (1 Lowest—99 Highest)
• **73**

Insider Activity
• **NA**

Recent Price • 8½
52 Wk Range • 9¼-5¼
Yield • Nil
12-Mo. P/E • NM

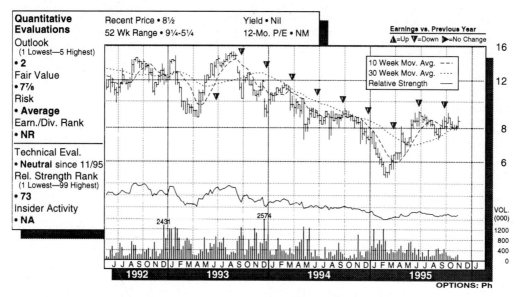

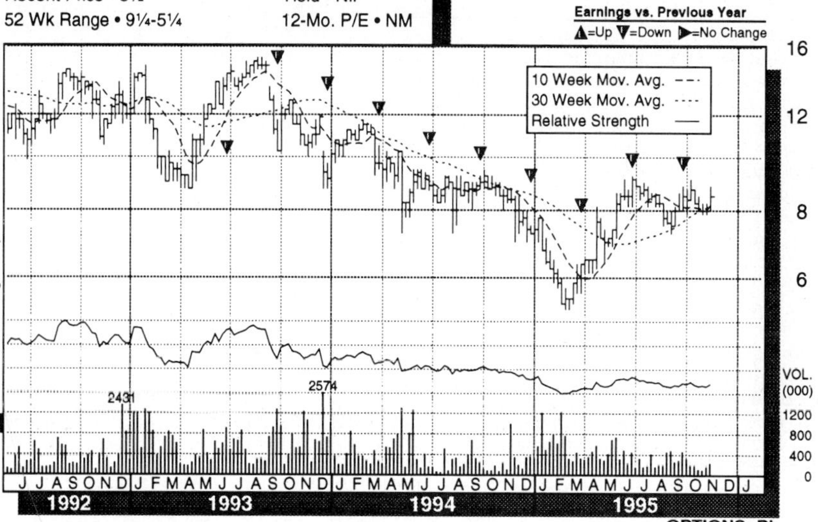

OPTIONS: Ph

Business Profile - 14-NOV-95

This manufacturer of cabin interior products for commercial aircraft has said it expected to benefit from the following: continued growth in world air traffic; a potential recovery in refurbishment and retrofit activity; and the recent receipt by Boeing and Airbus of a number of new aircraft orders. BE Aerospace has also said it believed that its MDDS interactive video system will provide the company with a significant competitive advantage over the next few years.

Operational Review - 14-NOV-95

Net sales for the first half of FY 96 (Feb.) rose only 0.2%. The nominal sales gain, a less favorable product mix, and more rapidly rising operating expenses led to a drop in operating profit of 28%. After 11% larger interest charges and a tax credit, versus taxes at 37.0%, the net loss was $375,000 ($0.02 a share), versus net income of $2.0 million ($0.13). The company expected third quarter revenues to surpass the second quarter and to return to profitability.

Stock Performance - 10-NOV-95

In the past 30 trading days, BEAV's shares have increased 1%, compared to a 1% rise in the S&P 500. Average trading volume for the past five days was 43,380 shares, compared with the 40-day moving average of 41,203 shares.

Key Stock Statistics

Dividend Rate/Share	Nil	Shareholders	300
Shs. outstg. (M)	16.2	Market cap. (B)	$0.138
Avg. daily vol. (M)	0.026	Inst. holdings	75%
Tang. Bk. Value/Share	NM	Insider holdings	NA
Beta	1.20		

Value of $10,000 invested 5 years ago: NA

Fiscal Year Ending Feb. 28

	1996	% Change	1995	% Change	1994	% Change
Revenues (Million $)						
1Q	55.59	-3%	57.57	20%	47.80	6%
2Q	57.45	4%	55.20	22%	45.10	-10%
3Q	—	—	57.28	13%	50.70	-1%
4Q	—	—	59.30	NM	59.76	16%
Yr.	—	—	229.4	13%	203.4	3%
Income (Million $)						
1Q	0.02	-98%	1.07	-32%	1.57	-35%
2Q	-0.40	NM	0.96	-43%	1.69	-43%
3Q	—	—	-14.57	NM	0.57	-83%
4Q	—	—	0.47	-69%	1.53	-56%
Yr.	—	—	-12.07	NM	5.36	-56%
Earnings Per Share ($)						
1Q	Nil	—	0.07	-36%	0.11	-50%
2Q	-0.02	NM	0.06	-45%	0.11	-58%
3Q	—	—	-0.90	NM	0.03	-90%
4Q	—	—	0.03	-70%	0.10	-62%
Yr.	—	—	-0.75	NM	0.35	-66%

Next earnings report expected: early January

BE Aerospace

Business Summary - 10-NOV-95

BE Aerospace, Inc. (formerly BE Avionics) is the leading manufacturer of commercial aircraft cabin interior products, including seating, passenger entertainment and service systems and galley structures and inserts. The company has built its leadership position through a number of acquisitions in recent years, including five in fiscal 1993-94. Export sales from the U.S. accounted for 27%, and sales to all customers in foreign countries accounted for 50%, of total sales in 1994-95.

The company's large base of installed equipment with airlines provides an important source of aftermarket business for spare parts, repairs and retrofits. Including acquisitions, the installed equipment base was valued at $1.7 billion at the end of 1994-95.

BEAV's tourist-class seats incorporate features not previously utilized in that class, such as top-mounted passenger control units, footrests and improved oxygen systems. First-class seats and some business class seats are equipped with an articulating bottom cushion suspension system, sophisticated hydraulic leg-rests and large tables. The company has also developed two types of seats that can be converted from a tourist-class, triple-row seat to a business-class, double-row seat, allowing airline customers to optimize the ratio of business-class to tourist-class seats for a given aircraft booking configuration.

The company has a leading share of the market for passenger control units, with more than 300 different designs, and related wiring and harness assemblies. It also makes an individual interactive seat video system, MDDS (multi-media digital distribution system), with such features as video games, pay-per-view, and shopping, advanced multiplexer systems, hard-wired distribution systems (also sold to rail and bus lines) and other passenger entertainment and service products.

Galley structures, which are among the most sophisticated and expensive of aircraft cabin interior products, are generally custom designed. BEAV is also the leading supplier of aircraft coffee makers and makes a broad line of specialized ovens.

Important Developments

Oct. '95—BEAV said it was still awaiting a substantial and sustained uptick in the airlines' level of cabin interior refurbishment and entertainment system upgrade activities. BEAV expected that anticipated higher earnings for the airlines and their minimal growth in capacity would soon translate into a higher level of cabin interior refurbishment and upgrade spending, as well as new aircraft purchases. Separately, in August, BEAV said that the U.S. government was investigating its 1992 and 1993 sales of passenger seats for installation on commercial aircraft owned by Iran Air. BEAV believes it operated in full compliance with the law.

Capitalization

Long Term Debt: $188,435,000 (8/95).

Per Share Data ($)

(Year Ended Feb. 28)

	1995	1994	1993	1992	1991	1990
Tangible Bk. Val.	7.79	8.38	7.39	5.42	3.18	2.36
Cash Flow	0.25	1.20	1.70	0.24	0.88	0.78
Earnings	-0.75	0.35	1.03	-0.18	0.65	0.43
Dividends	Nil	Nil	Nil	Nil	Nil	Nil
Payout Ratio	Nil	Nil	Nil	Nil	Nil	Nil
Cal. Yrs.	1994	1993	1992	1991	1990	1989
Prices - High	11¾	15¼	15¾	16¾	10¾	NA
- Low	7	8¾	9⅞	7½	4¾	NA
P/E Ratio - High	NM	44	15	NM	17	NA
- Low	NM	25	10	NM	7	NA

Income Statement Analysis (Million $)

	1995	%Chg	1994	%Chg	1993	%Chg	1992
Revs.	229	13%	203	3%	198	NM	12.0
Oper. Inc.	36.0	4%	34.5	12%	30.8	NM	0.7
Depr.	16.1	23%	13.1	64%	8.0	98%	4.0
Int. Exp.	15.0	6%	14.1	NM	4.0	—	NM
Pretax Inc.	-18.9	NM	8.8	-53%	18.8	NM	-2.6
Eff. Tax Rate	NM	—	39%	—	36%	—	NM
Net Inc.	-12.1	NM	5.4	-56%	12.2	NM	-1.7

Balance Sheet & Other Fin. Data (Million $)

	1995	1994	1993	1992	1991	1990
Cash	8.3	13.7	14.3	7.2	6.3	3.5
Curr. Assets	143	136	205	57.0	17.0	11.0
Total Assets	380	375	314	135	26.0	21.0
Curr. Liab.	66.0	59.5	71.0	30.0	3.4	3.5
LT Debt	173	159	128	41.0	Nil	2.0
Common Eqty.	125	134	108	57.0	22.0	16.0
Total Cap.	309	311	239	100	23.0	18.0
Cap. Exp.	12.2	11.0	7.3	1.1	0.4	0.4
Cash Flow	4.1	18.5	20.1	2.3	6.4	4.2

Ratio Analysis

	1995	1994	1993	1992	1991	1990
Curr. Ratio	2.2	2.3	2.9	1.9	5.0	3.1
% LT Debt of Cap.	55.8	51.2	53.6	40.6	Nil	9.1
% Net Inc.of Revs.	NM	2.6	6.1	NM	19.4	10.1
% Ret. on Assets	NM	1.5	6.6	NM	19.6	14.4
% Ret. on Equity	NM	4.2	15.7	NM	24.0	22.6

Dividend Data —The company has not paid any cash dividends. It has no present intention of doing so in the immediate future.

Data as orig. reptd.; bef. results of disc. opers. and/or spec. items. Per share data adj. for stk. divs. as of ex-div. date. E-Estimated. NA-Not Available. NM-Not Meaningful. NR-Not Ranked.

Office—1400 Corporate Center Way, Wellington, FL 33414. **Tel**—(407) 791-5000. **Fax**—(407) 791-7900. **Chrmn & CEO**—A. J. Khoury. **Pres & COO**—R. J. Khoury. **VP, CFO & Secy**—T. P. McCaffrey. **Treas**—J. P. Holtzman. **Investor Contact**—Jay Jacobson (212-889-6362). **Dirs**—J. C. Cowart, R. G. Hamermesh, A. J. Khoury, R. J. Khoury, P. W. Marshall, B. H. Rowe, H. Wyss. **Transfer Agent & Registrar**—First National Bank of Boston. **Incorporated** in Delaware in 1987. **Empl**-1,800. **S&P Analyst:** N.J. DeVita

STANDARD & POOR'S

STOCK REPORTS

BISYS Group

NASDAQ Symbol **BSYS**
In S&P SmallCap 600

16-SEP-95 **Industry:** Data Processing

Summary: This company is a leading national third-party provider of data processing and related services to financial institutions.

Quantitative Evaluations

Outlook (1 Lowest—5 Highest)
• **NA**

Fair Value
• **NA**

Risk
• **Average**

Earn./Div. Rank
• **NR**

Technical Eval.
• **Bullish** since 8/95

Rel. Strength Rank (1 Lowest—99 Highest)
• **86**

Insider Activity
• **NA**

Recent Price • 27⅞
52 Wk Range • 29-17½
Yield • Nil
12-Mo. P/E • NM

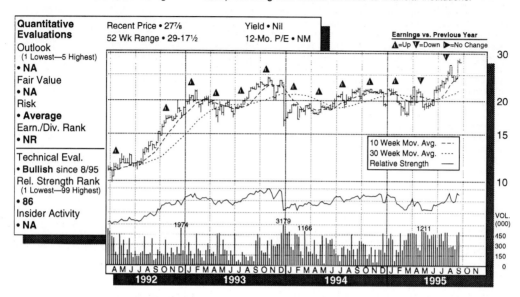

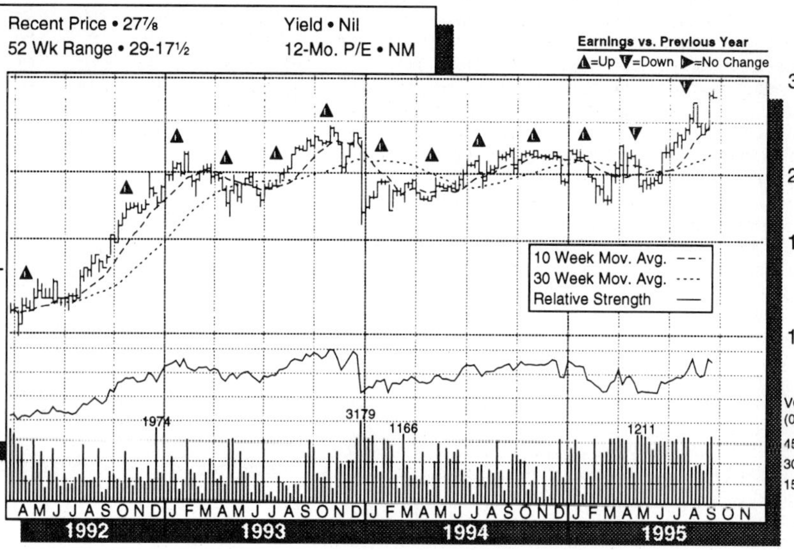

Business Profile - 15-SEP-95

The financial services industry is consistently challenged to compete more effectively, improving productivity while offering a broader array of products. Outsourcing services are a viable option for automating critical tasks and functions. Key to the success of outsourcing firms, like BISYS, is the ability to manage and automate functions that directly increase client revenues, integrate advanced technology to improve efficiency, and support customer demands.

Operational Review - 15-SEP-95

Revenue growth in recent periods has been derived primarily from acquisitions and sales to new clients. Higher operating costs, due in part to the integration of acquired companies and restructuring charges have hurt earnings. Results for the past two quarters were further penalized by one-time merger related charges, totaling $1.02 (net) per share. Near term prospects seem favorable as financial institutions continue to seek ways of cutting costs, including outsourcing of back office duties.

Stock Performance - 15-SEP-95

In the past 30 trading days, BSYS's shares have increased 9%, compared to a 4% rise in the S&P 500. Average trading volume for the past five days was 207,380 shares, compared with the 40-day moving average of 113,431 shares.

Key Stock Statistics

Dividend Rate/Share	Nil	Shareholders	1,200
Shs. outstg. (M)	22.9	Market cap. (B)	$0.639
Avg. daily vol. (M)	0.106	Inst. holdings	67%
Tang. Bk. Value/Share	NM	Insider holdings	NA
Beta	0.24		

Value of $10,000 invested 5 years ago: NA

Fiscal Year Ending Jun. 30

	1995	% Change	1994	% Change	1993	% Change
Revenues (Million $)						
1Q	37.46	49%	25.21	25%	20.20	25%
2Q	39.59	12%	35.33	70%	20.80	17%
3Q	49.06	34%	36.72	58%	23.27	18%
4Q	54.70	39%	39.40	64%	24.01	15%
Yr.	200.5	47%	136.7	55%	88.28	18%
Income (Million $)						
1Q	3.15	26%	2.50	—	—	—
2Q	3.81	15%	3.30	56%	2.11	NM
3Q	-15.47	NM	4.01	NM	-3.94	NM
4Q	0.63	-84%	3.94	19%	3.31	NM
Yr.	-6.48	NM	13.75	NM	3.38	NM
Earnings Per Share ($)						
1Q	0.20	25%	0.16	23%	0.13	NM
2Q	0.24	14%	0.21	40%	0.15	NM
3Q	-0.69	NM	0.25	NM	-0.25	NM
4Q	0.03	-88%	0.25	19%	0.21	NM
Yr.	-0.27	NM	0.86	NM	0.23	NM

Next earnings report expected: early November

BISYS Group

Business Summary - 15-SEP-95

The BISYS Group, Inc., organized in 1989 to acquire certain banking and thrift data processing operations of Automatic Data Processing, Inc., is a leading national third-party provider of information services and investment services to and through financial organizations. Services are offered through two major business units: Information Services and Investment Services. The majority of revenues come from services provided through a single integrated software product, TOTALPLUS, which includes comprehensive loan and deposit administration, branch automation and electronic banking services, operations and new business systems support, and accounting, financial management and regulatory reporting services.

The Information Services Group provides a full range of computing services using its single product family, TOTALPLUS. All TOTALPLUS host computer functions and client data reside on IBM mainframe (or compatible) computers located at four major data processing centers in the Philadelphia, Chicago, Cincinnati and Houston metropolitan areas. The centers are integrated with microcomputers or third-party proprietary terminals located on the client's premises.

TOTALPLUS supports virtually all aspects of a banking institution's automation requirements related to its operation, customer management and product distribution functions, proprietary central site and client site computing solutions. Capabilities include all deposit and loan requirements and general financial management of the institution, transaction and data management, electronic banking and customer information management.

Through its Investment Services Group, BISYS integrates its banking and mutual fund expertise to provide a wide array of specialized services. The group takes a consultative approach to its client relationships, offering innovative fee generated solutions. BISYS services over $25 billion in assets for mutual fund groups. Additionally, the group offers 401(k) marketing support, administration and recordkeeping through financial business partners to client companies.

Important Developments

Aug. '95—The company noted that during fiscal 1995's fourth quarter, it acquired Document Solutions, Inc, a leading imaging company, in exchange for about 1.8 million shares of its common stock. Additionally, BISYS sold off its Loan Services Division. The division, which had revenues of $5 million in fiscal 1995, was not profitable, and was not strategic to BISYS' long-term goals.

Mar. '95—BISYS acquired Concord Holding Corp., a leading provider of administrative and distribution services to bank-sponsored and other mutual funds, for about $120 million.

Capitalization

Long Term Debt: $3,853,000 (3/95).

Per Share Data ($) (Year Ended Jun. 30)

	1995	1994	1993	1992	1991	1990
Tangible Bk. Val.	NA	-0.30	3.99	1.09	-0.24	NA
Cash Flow	NA	1.28	0.53	-0.33	0.74	0.26
Earnings	-0.27	0.86	0.23	-2.64	-3.01	-4.32
Dividends	Nil	Nil	Nil	Nil	Nil	Nil
Payout Ratio	Nil	Nil	Nil	Nil	Nil	Nil
Prices - High	27¼	22⅜	24½	20	NA	NA
- Low	17½	17	16½	9⅞	NA	NA
P/E Ratio - High	NM	26	NM	NM	NM	NM
- Low	NM	20	NM	NA	NA	NA

Income Statement Analysis (Million $)

	1994	%Chg	1993	%Chg	1992	%Chg	1991
Revs.	137	55%	88.3	19%	74.5	18%	62.9
Oper. Inc.	26.0	29%	20.2	63%	12.4	-5%	13.1
Depr.	6.6	50%	4.4	-78%	20.2	-14%	23.4
Int. Exp.	1.0	NM	0.3	-94%	4.8	-31%	7.0
Pretax Inc.	18.4	149%	7.4	NM	-21.9	NM	-17.3
Eff. Tax Rate	25%	—	54%	—	Nil	—	Nil
Net Inc.	13.8	NM	3.4	NM	-21.9	NM	-17.3

Balance Sheet & Other Fin. Data (Million $)

	1994	1993	1992	1991	1990	1989
Cash	5.9	40.2	6.4	0.2	Nil	NA
Curr. Assets	28.8	55.3	17.7	11.6	9.3	NA
Total Assets	139	85.1	37.3	56.8	74.1	NA
Curr. Liab.	25.0	13.1	14.0	14.3	10.7	NA
LT Debt	27.4	0.1	6.2	50.6	54.4	NA
Common Eqty.	84.8	70.1	13.6	-28.7	-9.9	NA
Total Cap.	112	70.3	19.8	42.0	63.1	NA
Cap. Exp.	6.8	4.3	1.5	2.7	1.9	NA
Cash Flow	20.4	7.8	-2.9	4.6	1.3	NA

Ratio Analysis

	1994	1993	1992	1991	1990	1989
Curr. Ratio	1.2	4.2	1.3	0.8	0.9	NA
% LT Debt of Cap.	24.4	0.2	31.3	120.4	86.1	NA
% Net Inc.of Revs.	10.1	3.8	NM	NM	NM	NA
% Ret. on Assets	12.2	5.2	NM	NM	NM	NA
% Ret. on Equity	17.7	7.8	NM	NM	NM	NA

Dividend Data —No cash dividends have been paid on the common shares. The company does not intend to pay cash dividends in the foreseeable future.

Data as orig. reptd.; bef. results of disc. opers. and/or spec. items. Per share data adj. for stk. divs. as of ex-div. date. E-Estimated. NA-Not Available. NM-Not Meaningful. NR-Not Ranked.

Office—150 Clove Rd., Little Falls, NJ 07424. **Tel**—(201) 812-8600. **Chrmn & CEO**—L. J. Mangum. **Pres & COO**—P. H. Bourke. **SVP & CFO**—R. J. McMullan. **Secy**—C. T. Dwyer. **Dirs**—P. H. Bourke, J. W. DeDapper, J. J. Lyons, L. J. Mangum, N. P. Marcous, T. E. McInerney. **Transfer Agent & Registrar**—Bank of New York, NYC. **Incorporated** in Delaware in 1989. **Empl-** 1,250. **S&P Analyst:** Steven A. Jaworski

STANDARD & POOR'S

STOCK REPORTS

BMC Industries

NYSE Symbol **BMC**
In S&P SmallCap 600

02-OCT-95 **Industry:** Electronics/Electric

Summary: One of the world's largest makers of aperture masks for color TV tubes and computer monitors, this company is also a leading producer of polycarbonate, glass and plastic lenses.

Quantitative Evaluations

Recent Price • 38⅝
52 Wk Range • 39⅞-13⅛
Yield • 0.2%
12-Mo. P/E • 27.2

Outlook
(1 Lowest—5 Highest)
• NA

Fair Value
• NA

Risk
• Average

Earn./Div. Rank
• B

Technical Eval.
• Bullish since 12/92

Rel. Strength Rank
(1 Lowest—99 Highest)
• 88

Insider Activity
• NA

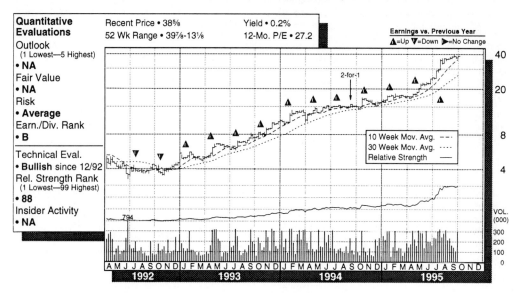

Earnings vs. Previous Year
▲=Up ▼=Down ▶=No Change

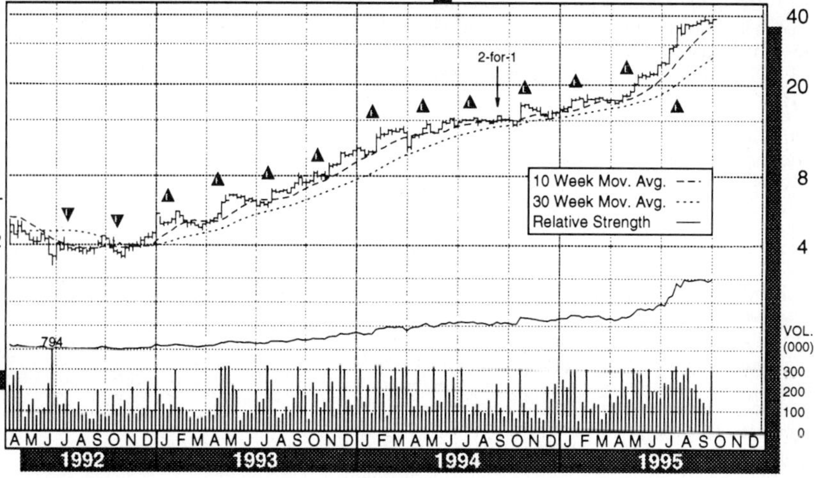

Business Profile - 02-OCT-95

BMC Industries is one of the world's largest manufacturers of aperture masks for color TV tubes and computer monitors. It also manufactures polycarbonate, glass and plastic eyeglass lenses; and precision etched metal and glass products. The company's long-term strategy for growth is based on continuous process improvement and the expansion of operations through internal capacity upgrades. The company intends to invest over $35 million in capital projects in 1995.

Operational Review - 02-OCT-95

Revenues in the first half of 1995 rose 19%, year to year, as the precision imaged products group enjoyed a 22% sales increase, driven by higher unit sales and an improved product mix. Margins benefited from the higher volume and better product mix, propelling net income to $0.87 a share from $0.55 in the first half of 1994. The company has a solid balance sheet, with a 2.0 current ratio and no long-term debt. The shares have risen sharply in recent years.

Stock Performance - 29-SEP-95

In the past 30 trading days, BMC's shares have increased 7%, compared to a 5% rise in the S&P 500. Average trading volume for the past five days was 59,320 shares, compared with the 40-day moving average of 48,218 shares.

Key Stock Statistics

Dividend Rate/Share	0.08	Shareholders	1,000
Shs. outstg. (M)	13.5	Market cap. (B)	$0.520
Avg. daily vol. (M)	0.036	Inst. holdings	58%
Tang. Bk. Value/Share	7.13	Insider holdings	NA
Beta	0.45		

Value of $10,000 invested 5 years ago: $ 101,586

Fiscal Year Ending Dec. 31

	1995	% Change	1994	% Change	1993	% Change
Revenues (Million $)						
1Q	61.33	17%	52.41	14%	46.02	-3%
2Q	69.65	22%	57.31	16%	49.28	6%
3Q	—	—	53.98	19%	45.21	6%
4Q	—	—	56.28	2%	54.93	24%
Yr.	—	—	220.0	13%	195.4	8%
Income (Million $)						
1Q	4.69	74%	2.70	90%	1.42	95%
2Q	7.48	60%	4.68	23%	3.81	30%
3Q	—	—	2.29	54%	1.49	66%
4Q	—	—	5.34	46%	3.67	48%
Yr.	—	—	15.00	45%	10.38	47%
Earnings Per Share ($)						
1Q	0.33	65%	0.20	67%	0.12	85%
2Q	0.53	56%	0.34	10%	0.31	19%
3Q	—	—	0.16	33%	0.12	50%
4Q	—	—	0.38	33%	0.29	36%
Yr.	—	—	1.10	31%	0.84	38%

Next earnings report expected: late October

BMC Industries

Business Summary - 02-OCT-95

BMC Industries manufactures precision imaged products and optical products. Business segment contributions in 1994 were:

	Sales	Profits
Precision imaged products	66%	73%
Optical products	34%	27%

International business accounted for 28% of sales in 1994 and Thomson, C.S.F. of France for 20%.

Precision imaged products include precision etched metal components, specialty printed circuits, precision electroformed components, and precision etched and filled glass products. The Peptech division makes and installs aperture mask production equipment, and also licenses BMC's related proprietary process technology.

Aperture masks are photochemically etched, fine grid screens that are a vital component of every color cathode ray tube used in color televisions and computer monitors. Aperture masks are sold directly to color TV tube manufacturers worldwide.

Optical Products (or Vision-Ease Lens) is a major U.S. producer of ophthalmic lenses, including semi-finished glass, hard resin plastic, and polycarbonate multifocal and single-vision lenses and finished polycarbonate single vision lenses for the personal eyewear market. These products are sold through a distribution network to over 1,000 optical wholesale or retail laboratories in the U.S. and to over 200 in international markets.

In April 1993, BMC agreed to provide $26 million of aperture mask production equipment to a manufacturing facility in China, with delivery scheduled for 1995.

In February 1994, the company initiated construction of a new production line at its Mullheim, Germany, facility. The line will produce computer monitor aperture masks, and is expected to be operational by the end of 1995. In January 1995, BCI announced plans to build a new television aperture mask line by 1997; site selection and groundbreaking is to begin by the end of 1995. The new line will add manufacturing for 7 to 9 million television aperture masks, focused primarily on the market for large masks.

Important Developments

Jul. '95—The company said that its two core operations enjoyed improved profit margins in the first half of 1995. Management said that this was due to improved operating efficiencies and the company's focus on high-margin growth opportunities in its primary markets.

Capitalization

Long Term Debt: None (6/95).

Per Share Data ($) (Year Ended Dec. 31)

	1994	1993	1992	1991	1990	1989
Tangible Bk. Val.	6.11	5.15	3.40	2.84	2.05	1.64
Cash Flow	1.70	1.46	1.29	1.42	0.79	0.98
Earnings	1.10	0.84	0.61	0.74	0.17	0.48
Dividends	0.04	Nil	Nil	Nil	Nil	Nil
Payout Ratio	4%	Nil	Nil	Nil	Nil	Nil
Prices - High	16¾	10¾	6⅛	4¾	5¾	5¼
- Low	9¾	4⅝	3¼	1 9/16	1 9/16	3⅜
P/E Ratio - High	15	13	10	6	33	11
- Low	9	6	5	2	9	7

Income Statement Analysis (Million $)

	1994	%Chg	1993	%Chg	1992	%Chg	1991
Revs.	220	13%	195	8%	181	-11%	203
Oper. Inc.	35.0	26%	27.7	29%	21.5	-19%	26.5
Depr.	8.3	6%	7.8	-3%	8.0	6%	7.6
Int. Exp.	3.1	-39%	5.1	-24%	6.7	-18%	8.2
Pretax Inc.	24.3	60%	15.2	97%	7.7	-23%	10.0
Eff. Tax Rate	38%	—	32%	—	9.20%	—	18%
Net Inc.	15.0	44%	10.4	48%	7.0	-15%	8.2

Balance Sheet & Other Fin. Data (Million $)

	1994	1993	1992	1991	1990	1989
Cash	14.3	10.9	9.4	12.2	1.9	10.9
Curr. Assets	78.8	72.0	68.0	70.0	74.0	68.0
Total Assets	139	130	119	125	128	116
Curr. Liab.	40.0	37.0	33.0	35.0	39.0	29.0
LT Debt	Nil	18.3	35.4	46.4	56.4	61.7
Common Eqty.	81.8	58.9	37.5	30.9	22.4	17.9
Total Cap.	82.8	78.0	74.0	79.0	81.0	81.0
Cap. Exp.	13.5	7.9	6.8	6.3	10.1	15.6
Cash Flow	23.3	18.2	15.1	15.8	8.7	11.0

Ratio Analysis

	1994	1993	1992	1991	1990	1989
Curr. Ratio	2.0	1.9	2.1	2.0	1.9	2.4
% LT Debt of Cap.	0.1	23.5	47.8	58.8	70.0	76.2
% Net Inc.of Revs.	6.8	5.3	3.9	4.1	1.1	3.3
% Ret. on Assets	10.3	8.2	5.7	6.5	1.5	4.7
% Ret. on Equity	19.8	21.2	20.4	30.8	9.1	34.5

Dividend Data —Cash dividends were resumed in 1994 after a nine-year hiatus.

Amt. of Div. $	Date Decl.	Ex-Div. Date	Stock of Record	Payment Date
0.020	Sep. 01	Sep. 15	Sep. 21	Oct. 05 '94
0.020	Dec. 09	Dec. 15	Dec. 21	Jan. 04 '95
0.020	Mar. 10	Mar. 16	Mar. 22	Apr. 05 '95
0.020	Jun. 09	Jun. 19	Jun. 21	Jul. 05 '95
0.020	Sep. 08	Sep. 18	Sep. 20	Oct. 04 '95

Data as orig. reptd.; bef. results of disc. opers. and/or spec. items. Per share data adj. for stk. divs. as of ex-div. date. E-Estimated. NA-Not Available. NM-Not Meaningful. NR-Not Ranked.

Office—Two Appletree Square, Minneapolis, MN 55425. **Tel**—(612) 851-6000. **Chrmn, Pres & CEO**—P. B. Burke. **VP-Fin & CFO**—M. D. Kerr. **Secy & Treas**—M. P. Hawks. **Investor Contact**—Michael P. Hawks. **Dirs**—L. D. Altman, P. B. Burke, J. W. Castro, J. E. Davis, N. C. Mears, S. W. Richey, R. A. Swalin. **Transfer Agent & Registrar**—Norwest Bank Minnesota, St. Paul. **Incorporated** in Minnesota in 1907. **Empl**-1,853. **S&P Analyst:** M.T.C.

STANDARD & POOR'S

STOCK REPORTS

BMC West Corp.

NASDAQ Symbol **BMCW**
In S&P SmallCap 600

05-SEP-95

Industry: Retail Stores

Summary: This regional distributor and retailer of building materials operates more than 50 centers in 14 distinct regional markets in 10 western states.

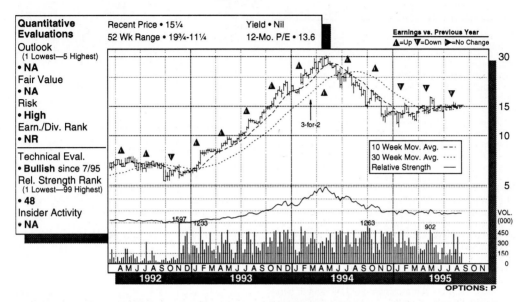

Quantitative Evaluations

Outlook
(1 Lowest—5 Highest)
• **NA**

Fair Value
• **NA**

Risk
• **High**

Earn./Div. Rank
• **NR**

Technical Eval.
• **Bullish** since 7/95

Rel. Strength Rank
(1 Lowest—99 Highest)
• **48**

Insider Activity
• **NA**

Recent Price • 15¼
52 Wk Range • 19¾-11¼
Yield • Nil
12-Mo. P/E • 13.6

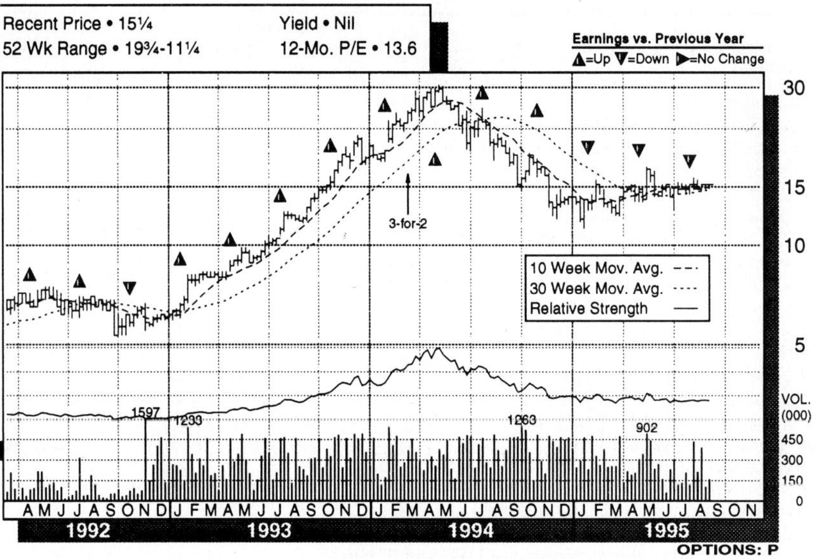

OPTIONS: P

Business Profile - 05-SEP-95

This company operates 53 building materials centers in 14 distinct regional markets in the western U.S. It believes that its geographical diversification lessens the effect of a downturn in any individual market. Aiming to grow through acquisitions, BMCW expects to average five per year over the next several years. Its goal is to double sales over a five-year period. Its typical targeted acquisition is situated in a growing medium-size city with a population of 50,000 to 250,000.

Operational Review - 05-SEP-95

Higher sales in the first half of 1995-96, primarily reflected contributions from recent acquisitions. Same-store sales fell 14%, hurt by a soft housing market, lower commodity wood prices and less favorable weather in most markets. The lower volume, combined with short-term expenses and higher interest costs related to the acquisitions, led to a sharp decline in net income. Earnings per share were further impacted by an 18% increase in outstanding shares.

Stock Performance - 01-SEP-95

In the past 30 trading days, BMCW's shares have increased 3%, compared to a 2% rise in the S&P 500. Average trading volume for the past five days was 30,520 shares, compared with the 40-day moving average of 42,845 shares.

Key Stock Statistics

Dividend Rate/Share	Nil	Shareholders	7,500
Shs. outstg. (M)	9.5	Market cap. (B)	$0.144
Avg. daily vol. (M)	0.042	Inst. holdings	62%
Tang. Bk. Value/Share	7.42	Insider holdings	NA
Beta	NA		

Value of $10,000 invested 5 years ago: NA

Fiscal Year Ending Dec. 31

	1995	% Change	1994	% Change	1993	% Change
Revenues (Million $)						
1Q	120.5	8%	112.1	52%	73.90	31%
2Q	166.2	17%	141.8	37%	103.3	35%
3Q	—	—	157.8	43%	110.2	32%
4Q	—	—	135.4	21%	112.2	50%
Yr.	—	—	547.1	37%	399.6	37%
Income (Million $)						
1Q	0.50	-76%	2.09	NM	0.43	NM
2Q	2.47	-45%	4.53	61%	2.81	92%
3Q	—	—	5.02	51%	3.33	47%
4Q	—	—	2.62	18%	2.22	NM
Yr.	—	—	14.26	62%	8.79	146%
Earnings Per Share ($)						
1Q	0.05	-81%	0.26	NM	0.05	NM
2Q	0.25	-54%	0.54	46%	0.37	42%
3Q	—	—	0.55	28%	0.43	7%
4Q	—	—	0.27	-4%	0.28	NM
Yr.	—	—	1.62	43%	1.13	82%

Next earnings report expected: early November

BMC West Corp.

Business Summary - 05-SEP-95

BMC West Corporation is a leading distributor and retailer of building materials in the western U.S. Products are sold primarily to professional contractors, as well as to advanced, service-oriented consumers. In addition to distributing products, the company conducts value-added conversion activities that include pre-hanging doors, fabricating roof trusses, pre-assembling windows and pre-cutting lumber to meet customer specifications.

As of August 1, 1995, the company was operating 53 building materials centers in Colorado, Idaho, Washington, California, Utah, Texas, Oregon, Nevada, Montana and Arizona. BMC believes that most of these centers hold first or second place in local market share and that the company has the largest sales volume in each region of any distributor and retailer of building materials serving the professional contractor.

Company products, including lumber, oriented strand board, plywood, roofing materials, wallboard, pre-hung doors, roof trusses, pre-assembled windows, cabinets, hardware, paint and tools, are used primarily for new residential construction, light commercial construction and repair and remodeling projects. Each BMC store carries about 13,000 stock-keeping units (SKUs). Although product mix varies by location, a core group of about 9,000 SKUs is typically stocked in each center. Wood products accounted for 51% of 1994 sales.

BMC offers customers assistance with project designs and material specifications, coordination of order delivery to job sites, provision of credit and referral of retail customers to pre-qualified contractors.

In 1994, professional contractors accounted for 77% of net sales (79% in 1993), advanced, service-oriented consumers 22% (19%) and wholesale customers 1% (2%). No one customer accounted for over 2% of 1994 net sales.

During 1994, the company acquired a total of 10 locations for an aggregate cost of approximately $55 million in cash and common stock.

Products sold by BMC are purchased from more than 2,800 suppliers. No single supplier accounted for over 13% of total purchases in 1994. Boise Cascade is the largest supplier.

Important Developments

Aug. '95—The company said that value-added products gained an increasing share of sales in the second quarter of 1995-96. This trend was expected to continue with a new truss plant put into service in Boise, Idaho in June 1995, and another one under construction in Fresno, California.

Capitalization

Long Term Debt: $95,160,000 (3/95).
Red. Preferred Stock: $1,931,000.

Per Share Data ($)

(Year Ended Dec. 31)

	1994	1993	1992	1991	1990	1989
Tangible Bk. Val.	9.43	6.17	4.57	3.71	2.81	1.93
Cash Flow	2.25	1.53	1.09	0.78	1.62	1.09
Earnings	1.62	1.13	0.62	0.21	0.82	0.39
Dividends	Nil	Nil	Nil	Nil	Nil	Nil
Payout Ratio	Nil	Nil	Nil	Nil	Nil	Nil
Prices - High	30½	21½	7½	6⅞	NA	NA
- Low	12	5⅞	5⅜	3⅞	NA	NA
P/E Ratio - High	19	19	12	33	NA	NA
- Low	7	5	9	19	NA	NA

Income Statement Analysis (Million $)

	1994	%Chg	1993	%Chg	1992	%Chg	1991
Revs.	547	37%	400	37%	291	33%	219
Oper. Inc.	33.5	57%	21.3	76%	12.1	61%	7.5
Depr.	5.6	83%	3.0	14%	2.7	20%	2.2
Int. Exp.	6.5	43%	4.6	-8%	4.9	-7%	5.3
Pretax Inc.	23.0	56%	14.7	199%	4.9	NM	0.9
Eff. Tax Rate	38%	—	40%	—	27%	—	12%
Net Inc.	14.3	63%	8.8	146%	3.6	NM	0.8

Balance Sheet & Other Fin. Data (Million $)

	1994	1993	1992	1991	1990	1989
Cash	5.2	1.6	0.7	0.6	0.4	0.8
Curr. Assets	128	94.0	59.8	46.1	43.8	40.1
Total Assets	222	142	92.0	73.5	68.1	57.8
Curr. Liab.	51.4	33.7	20.9	16.2	15.0	14.1
LT Debt	76.4	53.3	32.3	32.9	40.2	33.2
Common Eqty.	85.9	48.4	33.8	19.4	8.2	5.7
Total Cap.	170	108	71.1	57.3	53.2	43.7
Cap. Exp.	15.1	15.5	7.6	4.8	6.3	1.9
Cash Flow	19.8	11.8	6.2	3.0	4.9	3.3

Ratio Analysis

	1994	1993	1992	1991	1990	1989
Curr. Ratio	2.5	2.8	2.9	2.8	2.9	2.8
% LT Debt of Cap.	45.0	49.5	45.5	57.4	75.6	76.0
% Net Inc.of Revs.	2.6	2.2	1.2	0.4	1.1	0.6
% Ret. on Assets	7.4	7.3	3.7	0.8	4.0	2.2
% Ret. on Equity	20.0	20.8	11.6	4.7	35.5	22.9

Dividend Data —No cash dividends have been paid on the common stock. A three-for-two stock split was effected March 4, 1994. A shareholder rights plan was adopted in July 1993.

Data as orig. reptd.; bef. results of disc. opers. and/or spec. items. Per share data adj. for stk. divs. as of ex-div. date. E-Estimated. NA-Not Available. NM-Not Meaningful. NR-Not Ranked.

Office—1475 Tyrell Lane, Boise, ID 83707-2008. **Tel**—(208) 331-4300. **Chrmn**—G. E. McCown. **Pres & CEO**—D. S. Hendrickson. **VP, Treas & Investor Contact**—Ellis C. Goebel. **Dirs**—H. J. Brown, W. J. Fix, R. V. Hansberger, R. B. Hellman Jr., D. S. Hendrickson, G. O. Mabry, G. E. McCown, R. E. Mellor, P. S. O'Neill. **Transfer Agent & Registrar**—American Stock Transfer & Trust Co., NYC. **Incorporated** in Delaware in 1987. **Empl**-2,473. **S&P Analyst:** Maureen C. Carini

STANDARD & POOR'S
STOCK REPORTS

BW/IP, Inc.

NASDAQ Symbol **BWIP**
In S&P SmallCap 600

16-NOV-95 **Industry:** Machinery

Summary: This company is a worldwide supplier of advanced technology fluid transfer and control equipment, systems and services, including highly engineered pumps and precision seals.

S&P Opinion: Accumulate (★★★★)

Recent Price • 16½
52 Wk Range • 20¼-14
Yield • 2.7%
12-Mo. P/E • 16.2

Quantitative Evaluations

Outlook (1 Lowest—5 Highest) • **5**
Fair Value • **20⅞**
Risk • **Low**
Earn./Div. Rank • **NR**

Technical Eval. • **Bullish** since 10/95
Rel. Strength Rank (1 Lowest—99 Highest) • **21**
Insider Activity • **NA**

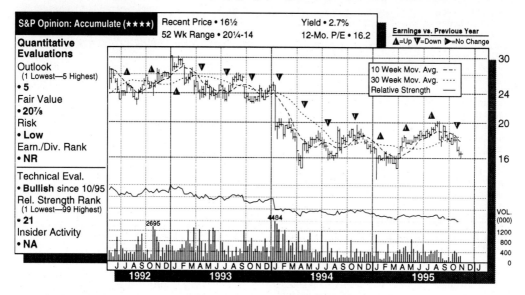

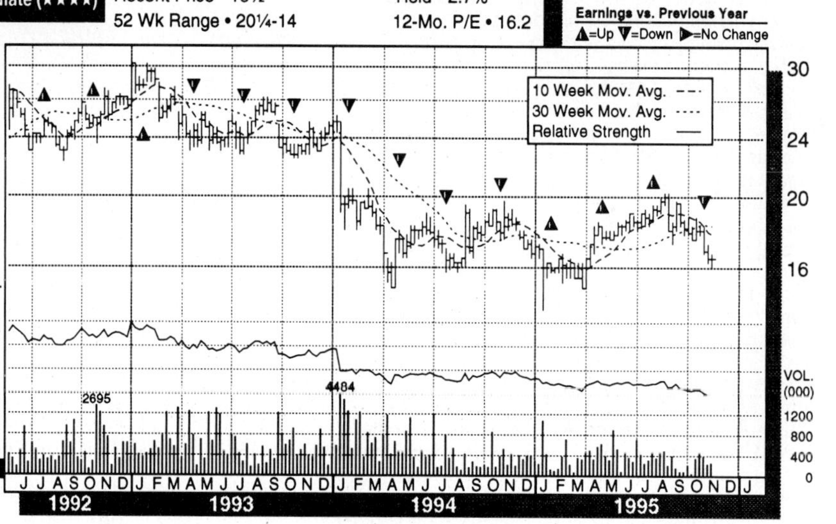

Overview - 16-NOV-95

BWIP's primary objective is to increase original equipment manufacturer (OEM) sales to expand its customer base, which generally leads to repeat sales of higher-margin aftermarket products. To this end, the company began a multi-year cost reduction program in 1994 to improve its market position in the fiercely competitive OEM segment. BWIP's expected improved competitive position from cost reduction intiatives and anticipated receipt of previously deferred Asian power-related orders should increase OEM sales and earnings in 1996. Aftermarket sales and earnings should also advance in 1996, due to acquisitions in the seal division, and BWIP's high-margin nuclear parts backlog.

Valuation - 16-NOV-95

The company's shares have declined in recent years, mostly due to disappointing earnings results. However, BWIP's expected improved OEM market position, anticipated receipt of previously deferred Asian OEM power orders and increased aftermarket business from acquisitions should improve revenue and earnings results in 1996. BWIP's continuing focus on expanding its overseas markets (especially Asia) and increasing the proportion of higher margin aftermarket sales should boost revenue and earnings longer term. With shares trading at 11 times 1996 estimated earnings, we believe BWIP shares are attractively priced for accumulation as a long-term investment.

Key Stock Statistics

S&P EPS Est. 1995	1.16	Tang. Bk. Value/Share	5.22
P/E on S&P Est. 1995	14.2	Beta	NA
S&P EPS Est. 1996	1.50	Shareholders	5,800
Dividend Rate/Share	0.44	Market cap. (B)	$0.391
Shs. outstg. (M)	24.3	Inst. holdings	79%
Avg. daily vol. (M)	0.053	Insider holdings	NA

Value of $10,000 invested 5 years ago: NA

Fiscal Year Ending Dec. 31

	1995	% Change	1994	% Change	1993	% Change
Revenues (Million $)						
1Q	107.0	11%	96.71	-3%	100.0	-12%
2Q	110.3	5%	105.5	NM	105.0	-5%
3Q	110.1	-7%	117.9	6%	111.0	8%
4Q	—	—	128.5	15%	112.0	6%
Yr.	—	—	448.7	5%	427.2	-1%
Income (Million $)						
1Q	5.54	4%	5.31	-23%	6.93	-41%
2Q	6.53	9%	6.00	-29%	8.51	-34%
3Q	6.27	-11%	7.07	-15%	8.34	-8%
4Q	—	—	8.46	NM	-5.00	NM
Yr.	—	—	26.84	50%	17.85	-58%
Earnings Per Share ($)						
1Q	0.23	5%	0.22	-24%	0.29	-41%
2Q	0.27	8%	0.25	-29%	0.35	-33%
3Q	0.26	-10%	0.29	-15%	0.34	-8%
4Q	E0.40	14%	0.35	NM	-0.20	NM
Yr.	E1.16	5%	1.11	50%	0.74	-58%

Next earnings report expected: mid February

Business Summary - 16-NOV-95

BW/IP, Inc., through its pump and seal divisions, is a worldwide supplier of industrial pumps, and seal products and services. BWIP's offerings are sold to the petroleum (56% of 1994 net revenues), power (21%), chemical (11%) and other (12%) markets.

Industrial pumps accounted for 71% of net sales in 1994 (77% in 1993) and seal products and services for 29% (23%). Original equipment manufacturer (OEM) pump and seal sales accounted for 42% of net revenues in 1994 (43% in 1993); the higher margin aftermarket sales accounted for 58% (57%). The aftermarket business includes supplying parts, making repairs, and providing technical services.

About 30% of sales and 29% of operating income were derived from Western Europe in 1994, while other international regions accounted for 18% of sales and 28% of operating income.

BWIP's pump division designs, makes, distributes and services industrial pumps mainly for use in the petroleum and power (fossil fuel and nuclear utilities) industries. In early 1994, BWIP reorganized its pump sales force and created a new territory for the Asian region. BWIP intends to focus on increasing sales to those engineering and construction firms that build most of the largest power and petroleum projects in Asia. In May 1995, BWIP acquired a centrifugal pump and coker switch valve maker ($12 million in annual sales) that marketed its products mostly to the petroleum, petrochemical and steel industries.

BWIP's seal division makes mechanical seals for industrial pumps used by the oil refining and chemical processing industries. The company believes it is the world's second largest mechanical seal manufacturer. BWIP also makes a dry gas seal used in gas transmission and oil and gas production markets and markets mechanical seals of an Australian company, pursuant to a licensing agreement entered into in 1993. In 1994, the Seal division acquired two seal companies, U.S.-based Five Star Seal Corp. (1994 sales of $6 million) and German-based Pacific Wietz.

Important Developments

Oct. '95—Commenting on 1995's third quarter results, BWIP noted that petroleum industry orders for mechanical seals, aftermarket pump parts and service and original equipment are ahead of order levels in 1994. BWIP also noted that although it believes much growth opportunity exists in Asia for power-related business, current bookings have been sluggish due to order deferrals. BWIP anticipates, however, that pent-up demand for power in Asia will accelerate future bookings.

Capitalization

Long Term Debt: $64,350,000 (9/95).

Per Share Data ($) (Year Ended Dec. 31)

	1994	1993	1992	1991	1990	1989
Tangible Bk. Val.	4.97	5.15	4.92	4.31	-0.25	-1.55
Cash Flow	1.69	1.27	2.25	1.88	1.38	0.89
Earnings	1.11	0.74	1.75	1.38	0.89	0.49
Dividends	0.38	0.30	0.22	0.08	Nil	Nil
Payout Ratio	34%	41%	12%	6%	Nil	Nil
Prices - High	25¾	30¼	30¾	23¼	NA	NA
- Low	15	22½	19¾	13⅜	NA	NA
P/E Ratio - High	23	41	18	17	NA	NA
- Low	14	30	11	10	NA	NA

Income Statement Analysis (Million $)

	1994	%Chg	1993	%Chg	1992	%Chg	1991
Revs.	449	5%	427	-1%	433	NM	430
Oper. Inc.	63.4	-8%	68.9	-20%	86.4	2%	85.1
Depr.	14.2	10%	12.9	7%	12.1	6%	11.4
Int. Exp.	6.3	3%	6.1	-32%	9.0	-45%	16.3
Pretax Inc.	42.3	60%	26.4	-59%	64.1	32%	48.4
Eff. Tax Rate	37%	—	32%	—	34%	—	36%
Net Inc.	26.8	50%	17.9	-58%	42.5	36%	31.2

Balance Sheet & Other Fin. Data (Million $)

	1994	1993	1992	1991	1990	1989
Cash	9.2	7.7	10.2	20.5	18.1	7.4
Curr. Assets	214	214	175	179	162	141
Total Assets	368	341	328	332	314	299
Curr. Liab.	105	90.8	68.6	69.4	87.1	81.2
LT Debt	53.0	54.0	66.0	100	145	171
Common Eqty.	166	146	153	140	32.0	11.0
Total Cap.	221	201	222	244	207	199
Cap. Exp.	12.1	17.1	13.7	14.5	8.8	7.3
Cash Flow	41.0	30.7	54.6	42.6	27.9	18.2

Ratio Analysis

	1994	1993	1992	1991	1990	1989
Curr. Ratio	2.0	2.4	2.6	2.6	1.9	1.7
% LT Debt of Cap.	23.9	27.1	29.8	41.0	70.3	86.0
% Net Inc.of Revs.	6.0	4.2	9.8	7.3	7.0	4.9
% Ret. on Assets	7.6	5.3	12.9	7.8	8.6	6.0
% Ret. on Equity	17.2	11.9	29.1	33.1	83.9	111.2

Dividend Data —Cash dividends were initiated in 1991.

Amt. of Div. $	Date Decl.	Ex-Div. Date	Stock of Record	Payment Date
0.100	Oct. 28	Dec. 09	Dec. 15	Jan. 04 '95
0.100	Feb. 28	Mar. 08	Mar. 14	Apr. 04 '95
0.110	May. 16	Jun. 09	Jun. 13	Jul. 05 '95
0.110	Jul. 25	Sep. 11	Sep. 13	Oct. 05 '95
0.110	Oct. 20	Dec. 11	Dec. 13	Jan. 03 '96

Data as orig. reptd.; bef. results of disc. opers. and/or spec. items. Per share data adj. for stk. divs. as of ex-div. date. E-Estimated. NA-Not Available. NM-Not Meaningful. NR-Not Ranked.

Office—200 Oceangate Blvd., Suite 900, Long Beach, CA 90802. **Tel**—(310) 435-3700. **Fax**—(310) 436-7203. **Chrmn**—P. C. Valli. **Pres & CEO**—B. G. Rethore. **EVP-Fin & CFO**—E. P. Cross. **VP & Secy**—J. D. Hannesson. **Investor Contact**—Dan Peoples. **Dirs**—E. P. Cross, J. J. Gavin Jr., G. D. Leal, H. J. Meany, J. S. Pignatelli, B. G. Rethore, W. C. Rusnack, P. C. Valli. **Transfer Agent & Registrar**—Bank One, Indianapolis. **Incorporated** in Delaware in 1987. **Empl**-2,967. **S&P Analyst:** Robert E. Friedman

STANDARD & POOR'S

STOCK REPORTS

Baker (J.) Inc.

NASDAQ Symbol **JBAK**

In S&P SmallCap 600

28-SEP-95

Industry: Retail Stores

Summary: This diversified retailer of footwear and apparel operates licensed and wholesale footwear departments in other stores, specialty apparel stores and shoe stores.

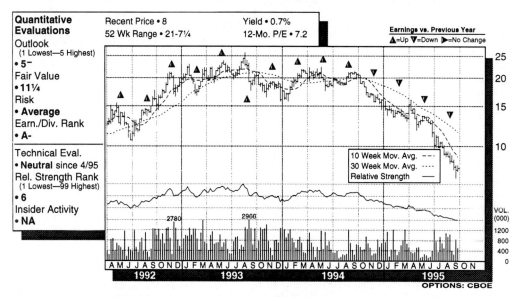

Quantitative Evaluations

Outlook (1 Lowest—5 Highest)
• **5-**

Fair Value
• **11¼**

Risk
• **Average**

Earn./Div. Rank
• **A-**

Technical Eval.
• **Neutral** since 4/95

Rel. Strength Rank (1 Lowest—99 Highest)
• **6**

Insider Activity
• **NA**

Recent Price • 8
52 Wk Range • 21-7¼
Yield • 0.7%
12-Mo. P/E • 7.2

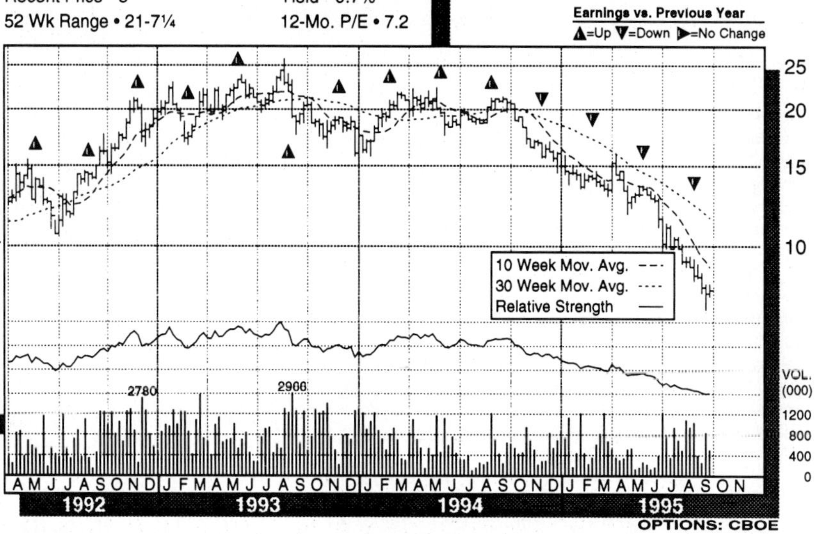

OPTIONS: CBOE

Business Profile - 28-SEP-95

This company, primarily an operator of licensed shoe departments in department stores, significantly expanded its footwear operations via the 1993 acquisitions of Morse Shoe and Tishkoff Enterprises (renamed Shoe Corp. of America--SCOA). It also sells apparel through two growing retail chains. Due to the continuing poor performance of the Fayva footwear division, the company said that it intends to dispose of the chain by the end of fiscal 1996.

Operational Review - 28-SEP-95

A modest gain in total sales for the six months ended July 21, 1995, reflected SCOA's addition of new licensed departments, and contributions from new specialty apparel stores, partly offset by the absence of wholesale footwear departments closed in the 1994-95 second quarter, and by same-store sales declines of 4.2% and 1.8% for footwear and apparel, respectively. Gross margins narrowed, and SG&A costs rose more rapidly. With higher interest and taxes, net income plunged 80%.

Stock Performance - 22-SEP-95

In the past 30 trading days, JBAK's shares have declined 14%, compared to a 5% rise in the S&P 500. Average trading volume for the past five days was 97,960 shares, compared with the 40-day moving average of 139,972 shares.

Key Stock Statistics

Dividend Rate/Share	0.06	Shareholders	500
Shs. outstg. (M)	13.9	Market cap. (B)	$0.112
Avg. daily vol. (M)	0.091	Inst. holdings	87%
Tang. Bk. Value/Share	16.24	Insider holdings	NA
Beta	1.22		

Value of $10,000 invested 5 years ago: $ 4,032

Fiscal Year Ending Jan. 31

	1996	% Change	1995	% Change	1994	% Change
Revenues (Million $)						
1Q	231.4	5%	221.0	15%	193.0	77%
2Q	272.5	6%	256.3	10%	232.5	75%
3Q	—	—	262.0	17%	224.4	64%
4Q	—	—	303.3	13%	268.5	77%
Yr.	—	—	1,043	14%	918.9	73%
Income (Million $)						
1Q	0.64	-80%	3.20	29%	2.48	60%
2Q	1.40	-80%	7.13	12%	6.39	100%
3Q	—	—	6.59	2%	6.49	79%
4Q	—	—	6.69	-16%	7.96	62%
Yr.	—	—	23.62	1%	23.31	76%
Earnings Per Share ($)						
1Q	0.05	-78%	0.23	28%	0.18	20%
2Q	0.10	-81%	0.52	11%	0.47	57%
3Q	—	—	0.47	-2%	0.48	41%
4Q	—	—	0.49	-14%	0.57	24%
Yr.	—	—	1.71	NM	1.70	36%

Next earnings report expected: late November

Baker (J.) Inc.

Business Summary - 28-SEP-95

J. Baker, Inc. is engaged primarily in the retail sale of footwear and, to a lesser extent, sells apparel through two retail chains.

Sales and profit contributions by business segment in 1994-95 were:

	Sales	Profits
Footwear	78%	63%
Apparel	22%	37%

In its licensed shoe department operations, the company sells a wide variety of family footwear, mostly under its own trademarks or on an unbranded basis, although it also sells name brand merchandise at discounted prices. At January 28, 1995, the SCOA division (acquired in December 1993) operated 448 licensed shoe departments in 14 chains, predominantly in conventional, full-service department stores. Merchandise includes mainly national brands, as well as private label footwear.

At the end of 1994-95, Baker operated a total of 1,690 licensed shoe departments under license agreements with 44 different department store operators in 42 states and the District of Columbia. About 18% (306) of the departments were operated under license with Ames Department Stores, which accounted for 9.5% of 1994-95 revenues. In addition, there were 113 licensed departments in the Rose's Stores, Inc. chain in the Southeast, and 92 in Jamesway discount department stores in the Mid-Atlantic.

At January 28, 1995, Morse operated 154 licensed departments in Hill's Department stores, 136 in the Bradlees chain, and 126 in ShopKo stores. Operations under agreements with these three chains accounted for 16% of net sales in 1994-95.

Wholesale customers are mass merchandising department store chains comparable to those in which the company operates licensed departments.

The Parade of Shoes chain (191 stores in 12 states at 1994-95 year end) emphasizes the retail sale of women's shoes on a one-price basis. The Fayva shoe chain (368 stores in 16 states) operates self-selection retail stores offering footwear for the entire family.

Baker is also engaged in the retail sale of apparel through Casual Male Big & Tall men's stores (319, including 65 opened in 1994-95) and Work 'n Gear work clothing stores (61).

Important Developments

Sep. '95—J. Baker said that it intends to dispose of its 357-store Fayva footwear division by the end of fiscal 1996. The company expects to take a one-time restructuring charge in the third quarter to reflect the disposal.

Capitalization

Long Term Debt: $243,441,772 (7/95), incl. $70,353,000 of 7% sub. debs. due 2002, conv. into com. at $16.125 a sh.

Per Share Data ($)

(Year Ended Jan. 31)

	1995	1994	1993	1992	1991	1990
Tangible Bk. Val.	16.13	14.51	12.81	9.88	9.05	8.40
Cash Flow	3.08	2.74	2.13	1.63	1.45	2.00
Earnings	1.71	1.70	1.25	0.78	0.73	1.46
Dividends	0.06	0.06	0.06	0.06	0.06	0.06
Payout Ratio	4%	4%	6%	8%	8%	5%
Cal. Yrs.	1994	1993	1992	1991	1990	1989
Prices - High	22 3/8	25 7/8	21 1/4	14 1/8	22 1/8	22 3/8
- Low	14 1/2	15 3/8	9 1/8	3	3 1/4	9 7/8
P/E Ratio - High	13	15	17	18	30	15
- Low	8	9	7	4	4	7

Income Statement Analysis (Million $)

	1995	%Chg	1994	%Chg	1993	%Chg	1992
Revs.	1,043	13%	919	73%	532	8%	494
Oper. Inc.	65.0	12%	58.0	50%	38.6	21%	32.0
Depr.	19.0	34%	14.2	52%	9.4	6%	8.8
Int. Exp.	9.7	20%	8.1	-1%	8.2	-21%	10.4
Pretax Inc.	36.9	1%	36.4	73%	21.1	64%	12.9
Eff. Tax Rate	36%	—	36%	—	37%	—	38%
Net Inc.	23.6	1%	23.3	75%	13.3	66%	8.0

Balance Sheet & Other Fin. Data (Million $)

	1995	1994	1993	1992	1991	1990
Cash	4.9	3.6	6.4	2.5	4.5	4.6
Curr. Assets	374	322	279	198	191	161
Total Assets	579	502	432	297	283	237
Curr. Liab.	138	135	140	99	81.0	88.0
LT Debt	205	155	95.9	79.5	97.5	58.4
Common Eqty.	223	200	173	105	92.0	85.0
Total Cap.	434	355	271	193	196	149
Cap. Exp.	44.5	24.1	11.2	5.5	15.0	16.9
Cash Flow	42.6	37.5	22.6	16.8	14.8	18.1

Ratio Analysis

	1995	1994	1993	1992	1991	1990
Curr. Ratio	2.7	2.4	2.0	2.0	2.4	1.8
% LT Debt of Cap.	47.1	43.6	35.4	41.1	49.7	39.3
% Net Inc.of Revs.	2.3	2.5	2.5	1.6	1.8	3.3
% Ret. on Assets	4.4	4.9	3.3	2.7	2.8	7.0
% Ret. on Equity	11.1	12.4	8.7	8.0	8.3	20.0

Dividend Data —Quarterly cash dividends were initiated in 1987. Payments are limited by a credit agreement.

Amt. of Div. $	Date Decl.	Ex-Div. Date	Stock of Record	Payment Date
0.015	Sep. 20	Oct. 12	Oct. 18	Oct. 28 '94
0.015	Dec. 15	Jan. 13	Jan. 20	Jan. 27 '95
0.015	Mar. 29	Apr. 11	Apr. 18	Apr. 28 '95
0.015	Jun. 06	Jul. 14	Jul. 18	Jul. 28 '95
0.015	Sep. 19	Oct. 13	Oct. 17	Oct. 27 '95

Data as orig. reptd.; bef. results of disc. opers. and/or spec. items. Per share data adj. for stk. divs. as of ex-div. date. E-Estimated. NA-Not Available. NM-Not Meaningful. NR-Not Ranked.

Office—555 Turnpike St., Canton, MA 02021. **Tel**—(617) 828-9300. **Chrmn**—S. N. Baker. **Pres & CEO**—J. M. Socol. **SEVP, CFO & Secy**—A. J. Weinstein. **Dirs**—S. N. Baker, J. C. Clifford, E. D. Cruce, N. R. Greenberg, D. Kahn, T. H. Lee, D. Pulver, M. M. Rosenblatt, S. Simon, J. M. Socol. **Transfer Agent & Registrar**—Fleet National Bank, Providence, RI. **Incorporated** in Massachusetts in 1985. **Empl**-14,654. **S&P Analyst:** Maureen C. Carini

STANDARD & POOR'S

STOCK REPORTS

Baldor Electric

NYSE Symbol **BEZ**
In S&P SmallCap 600

18-SEP-95 **Industry:** Electronics/Electric

Summary: This company is a leading manufacturer of industrial electric motors and drives for a wide variety of markets.

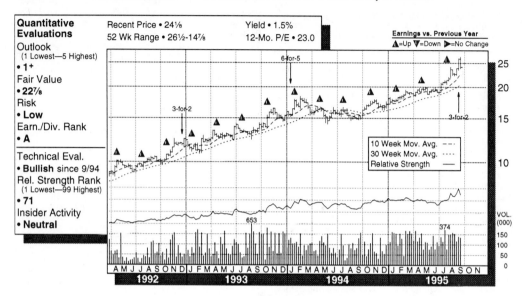

Quantitative Evaluations
Outlook
(1 Lowest—5 Highest)
• **1+**
Fair Value
• **22⅞**
Risk
• **Low**
Earn./Div. Rank
• **A**

Technical Eval.
• **Bullish** since 9/94
Rel. Strength Rank
(1 Lowest—99 Highest)
• **71**
Insider Activity
• **Neutral**

Recent Price • 24⅛
52 Wk Range • 26½-14⅞
Yield • 1.5%
12-Mo. P/E • 23.0

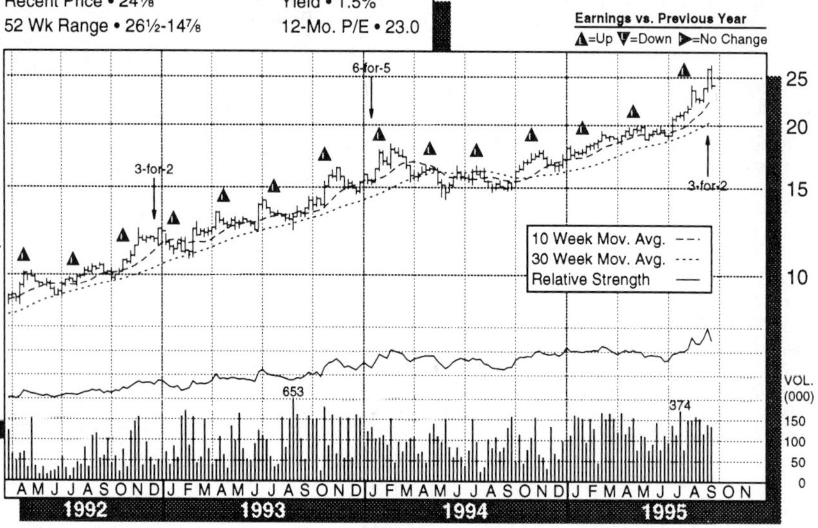

Business Profile - 18-SEP-95

This leading manufacturer of industrial electric motors for a wide variety of markets also makes advanced technology control systems such as servo products and brushless DC controls. Motors accounted for 84% of the company's revenues in 1994. The company's strategy is based on continuously expanding its line of electric motors, while at the same time increasing the drive product line to complement the motor line. Baldor has also been improving its factories and manufacturing capacity.

Operational Review - 18-SEP-95

Net sales for the first half of 1995 rose 17%, year to year, reflecting strong, broad-based growth across product lines and geographical areas. Distributor and OEM business was good, and sales of drives (motors coupled with controls) continued to increase faster than motor sales. Margins benefited from the higher sales volume, and productivity and cost improvements. Net income rose 30%, to $0.55 a share from $0.43 (both adjusted for the September 1995 3-for-2 split).

Stock Performance - 15-SEP-95

In the past 30 trading days, BEZ's shares have increased 11%, compared to a 4% rise in the S&P 500. Average trading volume for the past five days was 26,660 shares, compared with the 40-day moving average of 29,553 shares.

Key Stock Statistics

Dividend Rate/Share	0.36	Shareholders	3,700
Shs. outstg. (M)	27.6	Market cap. (B)	$0.666
Avg. daily vol. (M)	0.030	Inst. holdings	39%
Tang. Bk. Value/Share	7.15	Insider holdings	NA
Beta	0.65		

Value of $10,000 invested 5 years ago: $ 34,265

Fiscal Year Ending Dec. 31

	1995	% Change	1994	% Change	1993	% Change
Revenues (Million $)						
1Q	114.6	18%	97.48	13%	86.55	17%
2Q	121.8	16%	104.8	16%	90.67	13%
3Q	—	—	105.4	16%	90.70	14%
4Q	—	—	110.4	25%	88.67	4%
Yr.	—	—	418.1	17%	356.6	12%
Income (Million $)						
1Q	7.67	35%	5.68	24%	4.59	35%
2Q	8.26	25%	6.60	28%	5.15	28%
3Q	—	—	6.82	41%	4.85	31%
4Q	—	—	7.26	50%	4.84	17%
Yr.	—	—	26.36	36%	19.43	27%
Earnings Per Share ($)						
1Q	0.27	33%	0.20	20%	0.17	36%
2Q	0.29	23%	0.23	30%	0.18	20%
3Q	—	—	0.24	38%	0.17	30%
4Q	—	—	0.25	46%	0.17	16%
Yr.	—	—	0.93	34%	0.69	25%

Next earnings report expected: mid October

Baldor Electric

Business Summary - 18-SEP-95

Baldor Electric manufactures electric motors and drives, as well as speed reducers, industrial grinders, buffers, polishing lathes, stampings, casting and repair parts. The company has made a number of acquisitions; however, the majority of its growth has been derived internally from broadening its markets and product lines.

Industrial electric motors represent about 84% of the company's business. The AC (alternating current) motor product line ranges in size from 1/50 through 600 horsepower and the DC (direct current) motor product line ranges from 1/50 through 700 horsepower.

Industrial control products, which include servo products, brushless DC and SCR controls, and inverter and vector drives, account for some 13% of the company's business. With these products, Baldor provides its customers with the ability to purchase an integrated industrial motor and drives system.

Motors and drives are manufactured for general purpose uses (stock products) and for individual customer requirements and specifications (custom products). Stock product sales represent approximately 63% of the company's business, with most going to customers who place orders for immediate shipment.

Marketing of products is conducted throughout the U.S. and in over 55 foreign countries. The field sales organization consists of over 50 independent manufacturers' representative groups, including 25 in the U.S., with the remainder in Canada, Europe, Latin America, Australia and the Far East.

Custom products are sold directly to OEMs (original equipment manufacturers). Stock products are sold to independent distributors for resale, often as replacement components in industrial machinery that is being modernized or upgraded for improved performance.

Many of the components used in its products are manufactured by Baldor itself, including laminations, motor hardware, and aluminum die castings. Manufacturing its own components permits the company to achieve a high degree of control over cost, quality and availability. Baldor's motor manufacturing operations also include machining, stamping, welding, winding, assembling, and finishing operations.

Important Developments

Aug. '95—The company said that its directors recently approved a stock repurchase plan. Under the plan, the company may purchase up to 1.5 million shares (adjusted for the subsequent 3-for-2 split) to be used for stock options, the employee benefit plan, and other corporate uses.

Capitalization

Long Term Debt: $25,420,000 (7/95).

Per Share Data ($)

(Year Ended Dec. 31)

	1994	1993	1992	1991	1990	1989
Tangible Bk. Val.	6.71	5.95	5.44	5.06	4.76	4.41
Cash Flow	1.39	1.07	0.95	0.85	0.96	0.86
Earnings	0.93	0.69	0.56	0.44	0.54	0.50
Dividends	0.28	0.22	0.19	0.18	0.18	0.16
Payout Ratio	30%	31%	34%	39%	33%	31%
Prices - High	18 3/8	16 1/2	12 1/2	9 1/4	8 1/8	9 1/8
- Low	14 1/8	10 3/4	8 1/4	5 3/4	6	5 3/4
P/E Ratio - High	20	24	23	21	15	18
- Low	15	16	15	13	11	11

Income Statement Analysis (Million $)

	1994	%Chg	1993	%Chg	1992	%Chg	1991
Revs.	418	17%	357	12%	319	12%	286
Oper. Inc.	55.9	31%	42.6	19%	35.9	16%	30.9
Depr.	13.1	22%	10.7	NM	10.8	NM	10.9
Int. Exp.	1.3	31%	1.0	8%	0.9	-29%	1.3
Pretax Inc.	43.2	33%	32.4	30%	25.0	29%	19.4
Eff. Tax Rate	39%	—	40%	—	39%	—	39%
Net Inc.	26.4	36%	19.4	27%	15.3	29%	11.9

Balance Sheet & Other Fin. Data (Million $)

	1994	1993	1992	1991	1990	1989
Cash	34.8	30.2	22.7	12.0	7.7	6.8
Curr. Assets	181	152	129	117	113	104
Total Assets	283	238	212	203	201	186
Curr. Liab.	62.6	43.4	32.0	32.4	38.0	33.9
LT Debt	26.3	22.5	23.2	24.4	25.3	22.5
Common Eqty.	184	161	145	134	124	115
Total Cap.	221	195	180	171	163	152
Cap. Exp.	22.1	15.0	11.6	9.8	13.7	14.9
Cash Flow	39.5	30.1	26.0	22.8	24.6	22.4

Ratio Analysis

	1994	1993	1992	1991	1990	1989
Curr. Ratio	2.9	3.5	4.0	3.6	3.0	3.1
% LT Debt of Cap.	11.9	11.6	12.9	14.3	15.5	14.8
% Net Inc.of Revs.	6.3	5.4	4.8	4.2	4.8	4.7
% Ret. on Assets	10.0	8.6	7.3	5.9	7.3	7.4
% Ret. on Equity	15.2	12.6	10.9	9.2	11.8	11.9

Dividend Data —Dividends have been paid since 1938. A "poison pill" stock purchase rights plan was adopted in 1988. A 6-for-5 stock split was paid in January 1994.

Amt. of Div. $	Date Decl.	Ex-Div. Date	Stock of Record	Payment Date
0.120	Nov. 08	Dec. 05	Dec. 09	Jan. 03 '95
0.120	Feb. 06	Mar. 06	Mar. 10	Mar. 31 '95
0.120	May. 08	Jun. 06	Jun. 09	Jun. 30 '95
3-for-2	Aug. 07	Sep. 07	Aug. 18	Sep. 06 '95
0.090	Aug. 07	Sep. 14	Sep. 18	Sep. 29 '95

Data as orig. reptd.; bef. results of disc. opers. and/or spec. items. Per share data adj. for stk. divs. as of ex-div. date. E-Estimated. NA-Not Available. NM-Not Meaningful. NR-Not Ranked.

Office—5711 R.S. Boreham, Jr. St., Fort Smith, AR 72902. **Tel**—(501) 646-4711. **Chrmn**—R. S. Boreham Jr. **Pres & CEO**—R. L. Qualls. **VP-Fin, CFO, Secy, Treas, & Investor Contact**—Lloyd G. Davis. **Dirs**—J. W. Asher, Jr., F. C. Ballman, O. A. Baumann, R. S. Boreham, Jr., R. J. Messey, R. L. Proost, R. L. Qualls, G. A. Schock, W. J. Wheat. **Transfer Agent & Registrar**—Wachovia Bank of North Carolina, N.A., Winston-Salem. **Incorporated** in Missouri in 1920. **Empl**-3,404. **S&P Analyst:** M.T.C.

STANDARD & POOR'S

Ballard Medical Products

STOCK REPORTS

NYSE Symbol **BMP**
In S&P SmallCap 600

25-JUL-95 **Industry:** Medical equipment/ supply

Summary: This company manufactures and markets specialized, niche medical products that are used in many areas within the hospital.

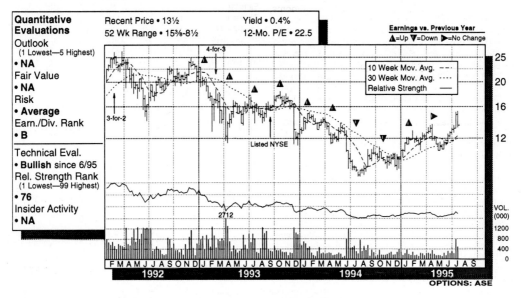

Quantitative Evaluations
Outlook
(1 Lowest—5 Highest)
• **NA**
Fair Value
• **NA**
Risk
• **Average**
Earn./Div. Rank
• **B**

Technical Eval.
• **Bullish** since 6/95
Rel. Strength Rank
(1 Lowest—99 Highest)
• **76**
Insider Activity
• **NA**

Recent Price • 13½
52 Wk Range • 15⅜-8½
Yield • 0.4%
12-Mo. P/E • 22.5

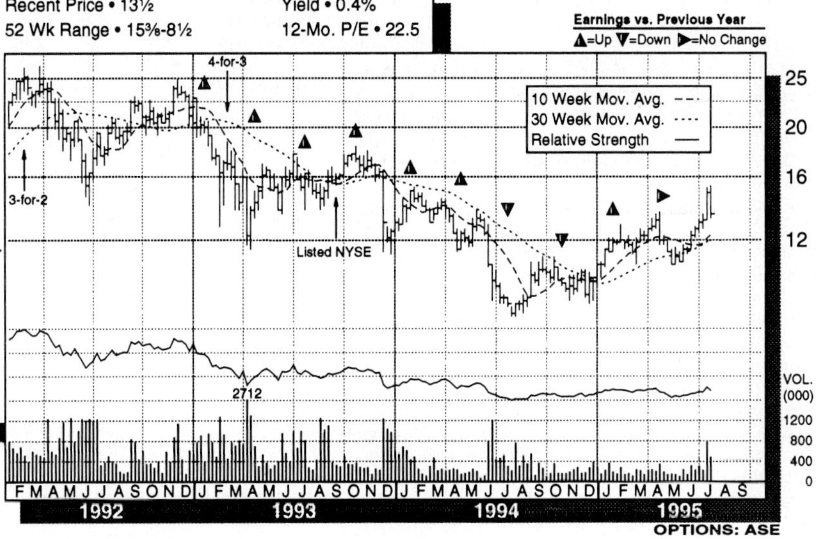

OPTIONS: ASE

Business Profile - 25-JUL-95

Ballard's strategy will continue to be to focus on specialized critical care, operating room and alternate care sites, since it believes that these areas will be least affected by changes in the healthcare industry. In 1994, the company restructured its distribution system to adjust to changes occurring in the industry, with the size of the sales force stabilized and the sales management team enlarged. This has begun to generate new business in many hospitals and other accounts.

Operational Review - 25-JUL-95

Sales for the first nine months of fiscal 1995 rose 14%, year to year, aided by higher Trach Care and MIC product sales, especially MIC enteral feeding catheters. Despite a strong gain in third-quarter earnings, profitability was limited by new product costs, a less favorable product mix and higher raw material and labor costs. Net income for the nine months was up 9.8% (excluding a credit from an accounting change in the fiscal 1994 period).

Stock Performance - 21-JUL-95

In the past 30 trading days, BMP's shares have increased 17%, compared to a 5% rise in the S&P 500. Average trading volume for the past five days was 93,780 shares, compared with the 40-day moving average of 67,929 shares.

Key Stock Statistics

Dividend Rate/Share	0.06	Shareholders	14,600
Shs. outstg. (M)	26.5	Market cap. (B)	$0.364
Avg. daily vol. (M)	0.087	Inst. holdings	35%
Tang. Bk. Value/Share	3.23	Insider holdings	NA
Beta	1.36		

Value of $10,000 invested 5 years ago: $ 30,936

Fiscal Year Ending Sep. 30

	1995	% Change	1994	% Change	1993	% Change
Revenues (Million $)						
1Q	18.51	15%	16.04	9%	14.69	30%
2Q	20.03	11%	18.05	11%	16.29	30%
3Q	21.25	15%	18.45	11%	16.68	30%
4Q	—	—	12.54	-27%	17.08	30%
Yr.	—	—	65.06	NM	64.80	30%
Income (Million $)						
1Q	4.57	6%	4.30	5%	4.11	6%
2Q	4.98	2%	4.86	5%	4.62	35%
3Q	5.27	21%	4.34	-10%	4.80	29%
4Q	—	—	1.29	-74%	5.01	25%
Yr.	—	—	14.78	-20%	18.54	38%
Earnings Per Share ($)						
1Q	0.17	6%	0.16	7%	0.15	50%
2Q	0.18	NM	0.18	6%	0.17	42%
3Q	0.19	19%	0.16	-11%	0.18	29%
4Q	—	—	0.05	-72%	0.18	20%
Yr.	—	—	0.55	-19%	0.68	39%

Next earnings report expected: mid October

Ballard Medical Products

Business Summary - 25-JUL-95

Ballard Medical Products manufactures and markets specialized, niche medical products. Sales are generated in many areas within the hospital, such as intensive-care units, emergency services, gastrointestinal and radiology procedure rooms, main operating rooms, burn units and outpatient/satellite surgicenters. In 1993, BMP acquired Medical Innovations Corp. (MIC).

BMP's flagship product in intensive care/critical care is Trach Care, a closed endotracheal suctioning catheter system that enables patients with endotracheal tubes, on ventilators, to have their airways suctioned clean while maintaining ventilator support, thus improving patient care. Trach Care is available in sizes from adult to neonatal. The Bal Cath catheter product is designed to obtain broncho alveolar lavage samples for use in the diagnosis of nosocomial and opportunistic infections without using a bronchoscope. The Safety Drain provides clinicians with a way to empty the ventilator circuit of condensate without opening it; users are thereby able to complete the closed system started with Trach Care, thus providing additional safety for both clinician and patient.

Other products produced by BMP include Safety Shield (surgical mask), Easi-Lav (closed gastric lavage system) and Char Flo (a unique charcoal delivery system designed for use in overdose patients). Foam Care foamers and solutions are designed for use throughout the hospital but are the company's principal product in the operating room.

MIC's principal products include the MIC Gastrostomy Tube (which has a unique design that eliminates inadvertent tube displacement and controls gastric leakage), the MIC-KEY Skin Level Gastrostomy Feeding Kit (a device with an intra-stomach balloon, thus allowing for easy replacement), and the MIC Gastro-Enteric Tube and MIC Jejunal Tube (which are each surgically placed in the operating room and provide access to both the stomach and jejunum).

Important Developments

Jul. '95—BMP signed an agreement to purchase a 19.5% preferred equity interest in Neuro Navigational Corp. (NNC) for $2 million, with an option to acquire all of NNC's assets. NNC develops, makes and markets fiberoptic imaging technology and disposable microtools designed for minimally invasive brain surgery.

May '95—Ballard acquired Cox Medical Enterprises, Inc., a manufacturer of disposable endoscopic devices, for $4 million.

Capitalization

Long Term Debt: None (3/95).

Per Share Data ($)

(Year Ended Sep. 30)

	1994	1993	1992	1991	1990	1989
Tangible Bk. Val.	2.98	2.33	2.10	1.27	0.85	0.59
Cash Flow	0.64	0.74	0.52	0.38	0.26	0.18
Earnings	0.54	0.68	0.49	0.36	0.24	0.17
Dividends	Nil	0.04	0.03	0.02	0.02	Nil
Payout Ratio	Nil	6%	6%	6%	9%	Nil
Prices - High	15¼	22⅞	26½	23¼	7⅞	4⅝
- Low	8½	11¼	14	6⅞	4¼	3
P/E Ratio - High	28	34	54	65	32	28
- Low	16	17	29	19	18	18

Income Statement Analysis (Million $)

	1994	%Chg	1993	%Chg	1992	%Chg	1991
Revs.	67.3	1%	66.5	34%	49.8	31%	38.0
Oper. Inc.	24.4	-14%	28.4	43%	19.8	41%	14.0
Depr.	2.5	53%	1.6	95%	0.8	30%	0.6
Int. Exp.	Nil	—	Nil	—	Nil	—	Nil
Pretax Inc.	23.2	-19%	28.8	34%	21.5	45%	14.8
Eff. Tax Rate	36%	—	36%	—	37%	—	37%
Net Inc.	14.8	-20%	18.5	37%	13.5	45%	9.3

Balance Sheet & Other Fin. Data (Million $)

	1994	1993	1992	1991	1990	1989
Cash	31.4	23.2	27.9	20.1	13.9	8.4
Curr. Assets	59.8	52.2	45.5	28.0	21.0	14.2
Total Assets	92.6	80.3	58.8	36.7	24.9	15.9
Curr. Liab.	2.2	7.5	4.3	4.4	4.3	2.2
LT Debt	Nil	Nil	Nil	Nil	Nil	Nil
Common Eqty.	90.4	72.5	54.2	31.9	20.4	13.6
Total Cap.	90.4	72.8	54.5	32.4	20.5	13.8
Cap. Exp.	6.3	4.0	5.3	5.5	2.6	0.6
Cash Flow	17.3	20.2	14.3	9.9	6.5	4.4

Ratio Analysis

	1994	1993	1992	1991	1990	1989
Curr. Ratio	27.1	7.0	10.6	6.4	4.8	6.5
% LT Debt of Cap.	Nil	Nil	Nil	Nil	Nil	Nil
% Net Inc.of Revs.	22.0	27.9	27.0	24.4	20.7	19.3
% Ret. on Assets	17.0	26.5	27.9	29.6	29.1	28.4
% Ret. on Equity	18.0	29.1	30.9	34.8	34.8	34.8

Dividend Data (Cash dividends are paid annually. A four-for-three stock split was effected in 1993.)

Amt. of Div. $	Date Decl.	Ex-Div. Date	Stock of Record	Payment Date
0.060	Nov. 30	Dec. 06	Dec. 12	Dec. 28 '94

Data as orig. reptd.; bef. results of disc. opers. and/or spec. items. Per share data adj. for stk. divs. as of ex-div. date. E-Estimated. NA-Not Available. NM-Not Meaningful. NR-Not Ranked.

Office—12050 Lone Peak Parkway, Draper, UT 84020. **Tel**—(801) 572-6800. **Chrmn, CEO & Pres**—D. H. Ballard. **VP & Secy**—E. M. Chamberlain. **Treas & Investor Contact**—Kenneth R. Sorenson. **Dirs**—D. H. Ballard, D. H. Ballard Jr., J. I. Bloomberg, E. M. Chamberlain, P. W. Hess, R. V. Petersen, J. D. VanWagoner. **Transfer Agents**—First Security Bank of Utah, Salt Lake City; Registrar & Transfer Co., Cranford, N.J. **Incorporated** in Utah in 1978. **Empl**-692. **S&P Analyst:** A.M.A.

STANDARD & POOR'S

STOCK REPORTS

BancTec, Inc.

NASDAQ Symbol **BTEC**

In S&P SmallCap 600

12-OCT-95

Industry: Data Processing

Summary: BancTec is a leading provider of electronic and document-based financial transaction processing systems, application software and support services.

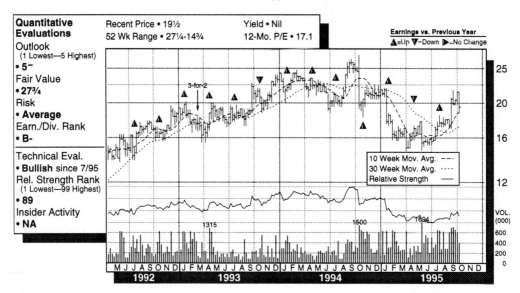

Quantitative Evaluations

Outlook
(1 Lowest—5 Highest)
• **5-**

Fair Value
• **27¾**

Risk
• **Average**

Earn./Div. Rank
• **B-**

Technical Eval.
• **Bullish** since 7/95

Rel. Strength Rank
(1 Lowest—99 Highest)
• **89**

Insider Activity
• **NA**

Recent Price • 19½
52 Wk Range • 27¼-14¾

Yield • Nil
12-Mo. P/E • 17.1

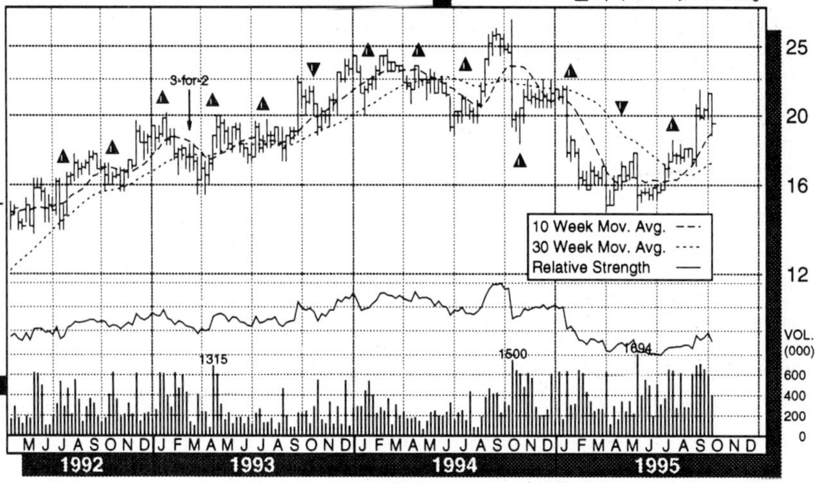

Business Profile - 12-OCT-95

This leading provider of electronic and document-based financial transaction processing systems, application software and support services has been growing rapidly both internally and through acquisitions. The pending acquisition of Recognition International will significantly increase BTEC's revenue base (to about $500 million) but results will be penalized by a related restructuring charge of about $65 million incurred upon closing of the transaction.

Operational Review - 12-OCT-95

Net income for the first quarter of fiscal 1995-96 advanced 3.3%, year to year, on a 5.3% gain in revenues, despite a decrease in revenues from traditional financial document processing products. Network services revenues rose 25%, year to year, and gains were also recorded in community banking products, electronic payment software products and the supplies business. BTEC believes that it is beginning to realize the benefits of the restructuring implemented during 1994-95's second half.

Stock Performance - 06-OCT-95

In the past 30 trading days, BTEC's shares have increased 8%, compared to a 4% rise in the S&P 500. Average trading volume for the past five days was 79,780 shares, compared with the 40-day moving average of 157,359 shares.

Key Stock Statistics

Dividend Rate/Share	Nil	Shareholders	1,500
Shs. outstg. (M)	11.0	Market cap. (B)	$0.222
Avg. daily vol. (M)	0.152	Inst. holdings	69%
Tang. Bk. Value/Share	5.10	Insider holdings	NA
Beta	0.46		

Value of $10,000 invested 5 years ago: $ 18,871

Fiscal Year Ending Mar. 31

	1996	% Change	1995	% Change	1994	% Change
Revenues (Million $)						
1Q	73.15	5%	69.47	27%	54.88	12%
2Q	—	—	73.23	37%	53.34	-21%
3Q	—	—	77.76	31%	59.54	6%
4Q	—	—	77.09	-3%	79.80	32%
Yr.	—	—	297.5	20%	247.5	6%
Income (Million $)						
1Q	3.82	3%	3.70	13%	3.28	17%
2Q	—	—	4.07	21%	3.36	-10%
3Q	—	—	4.43	4%	4.26	18%
4Q	—	—	0.31	-94%	5.45	30%
Yr.	—	—	12.51	-23%	16.34	14%
Earnings Per Share ($)						
1Q	0.35	6%	0.33	10%	0.30	11%
2Q	—	—	0.36	20%	0.30	-12%
3Q	—	—	0.40	5%	0.38	15%
4Q	—	—	0.03	-94%	0.48	26%
Yr.	—	—	1.12	-23%	1.45	10%

Next earnings report expected: mid October

BancTec, Inc.

Business Summary - 11-OCT-95

BancTec is a leading provider of electronic and document-based financial transaction processing systems, application software and support services. The company develops products for banking, financial services, insurance, government, utility, telecommunications, retail and other industries. It also designs and manufactures document processing hardware and scanners for value added resellers (VARs) and original equipment manufacturer (OEM) customers and provides network support services to users of local area networks (LANs) and personal computers (PCs).

Revenue contributions in recent years:

	1994-95	1993-94
Equipment and software	56%	54%
Maintenance and other services	44%	46%

Equipment and software products include the ImageFIRST family of high-speed image systems for use in a variety of document processing applications; the 9400 Document Processing System for remittance and/or sales draft applications by organizations that require automation but do not require high-speed image-based systems; the 4300 Document Processing System for use by financial institutions to re-encode and re-introduce repaired documents into the check processing cycle; and low, medium and high-speed readers/sorters and document processing-related components that read magnetic character recognition (MICR) and optical character recognition (OCR) data from financial documents and sort them.

In fiscal 1994-95, the company introduced ImageFIRST OpenArchive, which is designed specifically for high speed archiving of financial document images and related transaction data.

Maintenance and other service products include installation and maintenance of BTEC equipment and software, third party LAN and PC maintenance services, and third party service for reader/sorters.

Important Developments

May '95—BTEC agreed to acquire Recognition International Inc. (REC) in a pooling-of-interests transaction. Terms call for BTEC to exchange 0.59 of a common share for each of the 15.4 million REC common shares outstanding (about 9.1 million BTEC shares will be issued). At the time of closing, which is subject to approval by shareholders at meetings set for mid-October, BTEC would incur a $65 million restructuring charge for anticipated costs of consolidating operations. REC, which sustained a $27 million net loss on revenues of $219 million in fiscal 1994, markets hardware designed to input data from documents for processing and software products used for image processing and workflow automation.

Capitalization

Long Term Debt: $42,577,000 (6/95).

Per Share Data ($) (Year Ended Mar. 31)

	1995	1994	1993	1992	1991	1990
Tangible Bk. Val.	4.65	3.41	6.41	5.42	8.57	7.45
Cash Flow	3.29	3.14	2.65	2.49	2.01	2.09
Earnings	1.12	1.45	1.32	1.18	1.08	1.06
Dividends	Nil	Nil	Nil	Nil	Nil	Nil
Payout Ratio	Nil	Nil	Nil	Nil	Nil	Nil
Cal. Yrs.	1994	1993	1992	1991	1990	1989
Prices - High	26½	24¼	19⅞	11⅜	16	13⅛
- Low	18¼	15½	11⅛	5	6½	6¾
P/E Ratio - High	24	17	15	10	15	12
- Low	16	11	8	4	6	6

Income Statement Analysis (Million $)

	1995	%Chg	1994	%Chg	1993	%Chg	1992
Revs.	298	20%	248	6%	234	23%	191
Oper. Inc.	52.1	18%	44.3	9%	40.6	14%	35.6
Depr.	24.2	29%	18.8	30%	14.5	12%	13.0
Int. Exp.	5.7	NM	1.9	-17%	2.2	-40%	3.7
Pretax Inc.	19.8	-14%	22.9	9%	21.1	13%	18.7
Eff. Tax Rate	43%	—	40%	—	40%	—	38%
Net Inc.	12.5	-23%	16.3	13%	14.4	23%	11.7

Balance Sheet & Other Fin. Data (Million $)

	1995	1994	1993	1992	1991	1990
Cash	11.1	12.6	25.3	7.8	6.3	16.7
Curr. Assets	156	137	117	97.5	87.0	91.8
Total Assets	307	276	195	173	153	157
Curr. Liab.	124	90.6	66.9	54.4	45.2	49.9
LT Debt	42.5	50.6	12.2	19.6	27.4	34.4
Common Eqty.	137	128	110	92.3	78.9	70.0
Total Cap.	180	180	126	117	106	104
Cap. Exp.	26.7	24.8	15.2	16.1	13.7	10.9
Cash Flow	36.7	35.2	28.8	24.7	19.9	20.6

Ratio Analysis

	1995	1994	1993	1992	1991	1990
Curr. Ratio	1.3	1.5	1.7	1.8	1.9	1.8
% LT Debt of Cap.	23.6	28.1	9.7	16.8	25.8	33.0
% Net Inc.of Revs.	4.2	6.6	6.1	6.1	5.8	5.6
% Ret. on Assets	4.3	6.9	7.5	7.1	7.0	6.7
% Ret. on Equity	9.5	13.5	13.6	13.5	14.5	16.1

Dividend Data —No cash has been paid. The company intends to continue a policy of retaining earnings for operations and planned expansion of its business or to repurchase its common stock. A three-for-two stock split was effected in March 1993.

Data as orig. reptd.; bef. results of disc. opers. and/or spec. items. Per share data adj. for stk. divs. as of ex-div. date. E-Estimated. NA-Not Available. NM-Not Meaningful. NR-Not Ranked.

Office—4435 Spring Valley Rd., Dallas, TX 75244. **Tel**—(214) 450-7700. **Chrmn & CEO**—G. N. Clark, Jr. **Pres**—N. A. Stuart, Jr. **SVP-CFO**—R. Rajaji. **Investor Contact**—Gary T. Robinson. **SVP & Secy**—T. V. Mongan. **Treas**—M. N. Lavey. **Dirs**—G. N. Clark, Jr., M. E. Faherty, P. J. Ferri, R. Fulgham, T. G. Kamp, M. A. Stone, N. A. Stuart, Jr., M. J. Volding. **Transfer Agent & Registrar**—Chemical Bank, NYC. **Reincorporated** in Delaware in 1987. **Empl**-2,274. **S&P Analyst:** JJS

Bangor Hydro-Electric

NYSE Symbol BGR

Price	Range	P-E Ratio	Dividend	Yield	S&P Ranking	Beta
Aug. 10'95	1995					
11⅛	12⅞–9⅛	19	0.72	6.5%	B	0.50

Summary

This company, the second largest electric utility in Maine, serves 97,000 customers in the eastern and east coastal parts of the state. Results have deteriorated significantly since mid-1993, and the quarterly dividend was reduced by about 45% in June 1995, reflecting the weak earnings and concerns about ongoing competition within the electric utility industry.

Business Summary

Bangor Hydro-Electric is an electric utility serving some 97,000 customers in a 4,900-square-mile area in eastern and east coastal Maine. Counties served include Penobscot, Hancock, Washington, Waldo, Piscataquis and Aroostook. BGR also sells energy to other utilities for resale. Contributions to electric revenues by class of customer in recent years were:

	1994	1993	1992
Residential	31%	31%	38%
Commercial	31%	30%	31%
Industrial	37%	37%	22%
Other	1%	2%	9%

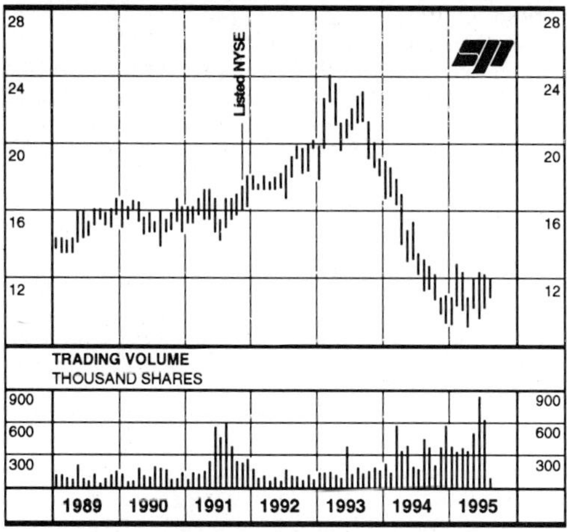

Kwh sales in 1994 amounted to 1,775,919 (1,801,604 in 1993). Total generated and purchased power was 1,912,827 kwh (1,937,165), of which 24% was nuclear-generated, 14% was hydro-generated, 2% was oil-generated, 10% was biomass/refuse-generated, and 50% was NEPOOL and other. Average residential rates in 1994 were 12.39¢ per kwh, and annual usage was 6,073 kwh per residential customer, compared with 12.47¢ and 6,118 kwh in 1993.

BGR owns seven hydroelectric generating stations, 11 internal combustion stations, two oil-fired units and more than 600 miles of transmission lines and 3,400 miles of distribution lines. In addition, it owns a 7% interest in Maine Yankee Atomic Power Co. and has power purchase agreements with other New England energy companies.

The company's construction program consists of extensions and improvements of its transmission and distribution facilities, capital improvements to existing generating stations, development of new information systems, costs associated with the licensing of new and existing hydroelectric projects and other general projects within the company's service area. BGR projects that capital expenditures will aggregate about $55 million in the period from 1995 through 1997.

Important Developments

Jun. '95— Bangor announced a reduction in its quarterly common dividend to $0.18 per share, from the $0.33 per share paid since early 1992. The company noted in March that a reduction in the payment was likely because of continued pressure on earnings and the necessity to avoid further rate increases in a more competitive environment. In addition, Bangor said that the financing of pending agreements to repurchase two high-cost power contracts with non-utility generators is, in addition to raising the company's debt level, expected to contain covenants that may restrict Bangor's ability to maintain the high payout ratio of recent years.

Next earnings report expected in late October.

Per Share Data ($)

Yr. End Dec. 31	1994	1993	1992	1991	1990	1989	1988	1987	1986	1985
Tangible Bk. Val.	**14.50**	15.09	15.17	14.86	15.16	14.89	14.21	13.63	12.93	12.13
Cash Flow	**1.61**	1.44	2.37	2.10	2.45	2.87	2.67	2.56	2.52	d0.41
Earnings	**0.84**	0.63	1.60	1.33	1.52	1.91	1.69	1.67	1.70	d1.22
Dividends	**1.32**	1.32	1.32	1.29	1.25	1.18	1.10	1.02	0.85	0.80
Payout Ratio	**163%**	223%	83%	105%	82%	62%	65%	61%	50%	NM
Prices—High	**19**	24⅛	20¼	18⅛	16¾	16¾	15¾	16½	15⅝	10⅞
Low	**9⅝**	17⅞	16¾	14¼	13⅞	13½	12½	11¼	10	6⅝
P/E Ratio—	**23–11**	38–28	13–10	14–11	11–9	9–7	9–7	10–7	9–6	NM

Data as orig. reptd. NM-Not Meaningful. d-Deficit.

Income Data (Million $)

Year Ended Dec. 31	Revs.	Oper. Inc.	% Oper. Inc. of Revs.	Cap. Exp.	Depr.	Int. Exp.	Net Bef. Taxes	Eff. Tax Rate	Net Inc.	% Net Inc. of Revs.	Cash Flow
1994	**174**	**26.3**	**15.1**	**24.1**	**5.40**	**12.5**	**11.1**	**33.1%**	**7.5**	**4.3**	**11.2**
1993	178	26.3	14.8	27.6	4.75	4.8	7.4	28.1%	5.3	3.0	8.4
1992	177	28.2	16.0	26.5	4.12	11.0	16.1	36.5%	10.3	5.8	12.8
1991	147	23.1	15.8	20.2	3.79	11.5	12.0	31.6%	8.2	5.6	10.4
1990	134	25.7	19.2	23.4	4.16	11.6	13.1	36.1%	8.4	6.2	10.9
1989	121	25.2	20.9	27.1	4.26	10.5	13.7	35.9%	8.8	7.3	12.8
1988	114	24.8	21.7	18.5	4.39	8.6	12.2	36.5%	7.8	6.8	11.9
1987	97	28.6	29.4	11.8	3.94	9.5	16.7	52.8%	7.9	8.1	11.4
1986	102	32.0	31.4	19.4	3.68	11.3	18.6	52.2%	8.9	8.7	11.2
1985	98	20.3	20.7	23.6	3.59	12.2	d12.0	NM	d4.1	NM	d1.8

Balance Sheet Data (Million $)

Dec. 31	Cash	Curr. Assets	Curr. Liab.	Curr. Ratio	Total Assets	% Ret. on Assets	Long Term Debt	Common Equity	Total Cap.	% LT Debt of Cap.	% Ret. on Equity
1994	**2.0**	**36.1**	**55.3**	**0.7**	**381**	**1.8**	**116**	**104**	**311**	**37.4**	**5.5**
1993	2.4	37.9	59.9	0.6	374	1.5	119	94	301	39.5	3.9
1992	1.5	39.8	41.8	1.0	289	3.6	101	82	245	41.1	10.6
1991	2.4	48.8	52.9	0.9	279	2.7	82	80	225	36.2	8.2
1990	7.0	40.9	51.5	0.8	270	3.3	99	68	216	41.4	10.1
1989	1.0	32.9	45.7	0.7	234	4.1	67	66	187	35.6	13.1
1988	1.6	29.9	35.4	0.8	195	4.4	61	63	158	38.8	12.1
1987	2.6	24.2	19.6	1.2	177	4.6	66	61	156	42.3	12.6
1986	8.7	30.1	9.8	3.1	164	4.6	80	58	153	51.9	13.5
1985	5.5	23.1	26.4	0.9	181	NM	82	54	154	53.2	NM
1984	13.9	32.1	29.7	1.1	200	6.8	82	63	170	48.5	18.9

Data as orig. reptd. d-Deficit. NM-Not Meaningful.

Operating Revenues (Million $)

Quarter:	1995	1994	1993	1992
Mar.	48.3	46.4	49.7	48.0
Jun.	43.7	39.7	40.5	39.7
Sep.		42.6	43.5	41.9
Dec.		45.5	45.0	47.2
		174.1	178.0	176.8

Revenues in the six months ended June 30, 1995, rose 6.9%, year to year, aided by a 15.9% base rate increase effective March 1, 1994, and the elimination of seasonal rates for certain customers. Results in the second quarter were hurt by costs related to the repair of steam generators at the Maine Yankee nuclear plant (and costs related to the purchase of alternate power), and net income fell 49%, to $1,596,927 ($0.11 a share, on 7.6% more shares), from $3,102,543 ($0.34).

Common Share Earnings ($)

Quarter:	1995	1994	1993	1992
Mar.	0.40	0.11	0.46	0.40
Jun.	d0.29	0.22	0.42	0.34
Sep.		0.37	0.46	0.46
Dec.		0.12	d0.71	0.40
		0.84	0.63	1.60

Finances

In March 1994, Bangor raised $14.1 million through the public sale of 867,500 common shares. Proceeds were used to reduce outstanding short term debt.

Dividend Data

Common dividends have been paid since 1925. A dividend reinvestment plan is available. Payments in the past 12 months:

Amt of Divd. $	Date Decl.	Ex-divd. Date	Stock of Record	Payment Date
0.33	Sep. 21	Sep. 27	Oct. 3	Oct. 20'95
0.33	Dec. 21	Dec. 23	Jan. 2	Jan. 20'95
0.33	Mar. 15	Mar. 26	Mar. 31	Apr. 20'95
0.18	Jun. 14	Jun. 24	Jun. 30	Jul. 20'95

Capitalization

Long Term Debt: $114,922,000 (3/95).

Red. Preferred Stock: $13,758,000.

Cum. Preferred Stock: $4,734,000.

Common Stock: 7,229,344 shs. ($5 par).
Institutions hold about 27%.
Shareholders of record: 7,705 (12/94).

d-Deficit.

Office—33 State St. (P.O. Box 932), Bangor, ME 04402-0932. **Tel**—(207) 990-6936. **Chrmn, Pres & CEO**—R. S. Briggs. **CFO & Treas**—R. C. Weiser. **Investor Contact**—Donna Guiggey. **Contr**—D. R. Black. **Dirs**—R. S. Briggs, W. C. Bullock, Jr., J. J. Bush, D. M. Carlisle, A. E. Cianchette, H. S. Dudman, G. C. Eames, R. H. Foster, C. R. Lee. **Transfer Agent**—Chemical Bank, NYC. **Registrars**—Chemical Bank, NYC; Mellon Securities Trust Co., Fort Lee, N.J. **Incorporated** in Maine in 1924. **Empl**—475.

STANDARD & POOR'S
STOCK REPORTS

Barrett Resources

NYSE Symbol **BRR**
In S&P SmallCap 600

13-OCT-95 **Industry:** Oil and Gas

Summary: This Denver-based independent natural gas and oil exploration and production company is also involved in gas gathering, marketing and trading activities.

Quantitative Evaluations

Outlook (1 Lowest—5 Highest) • **NA**

Fair Value • **NA**

Risk • **Average**

Earn./Div. Rank • **B-**

Technical Eval. • **Bullish** since 7/95

Rel. Strength Rank (1 Lowest—99 Highest) • **39**

Insider Activity • **NA**

Recent Price • 21⅝ | 52 Wk Range • 25⅞-16⅞ | Yield • Nil | 12-Mo. P/E • 80.1

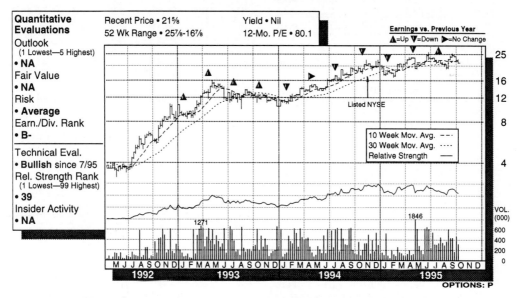

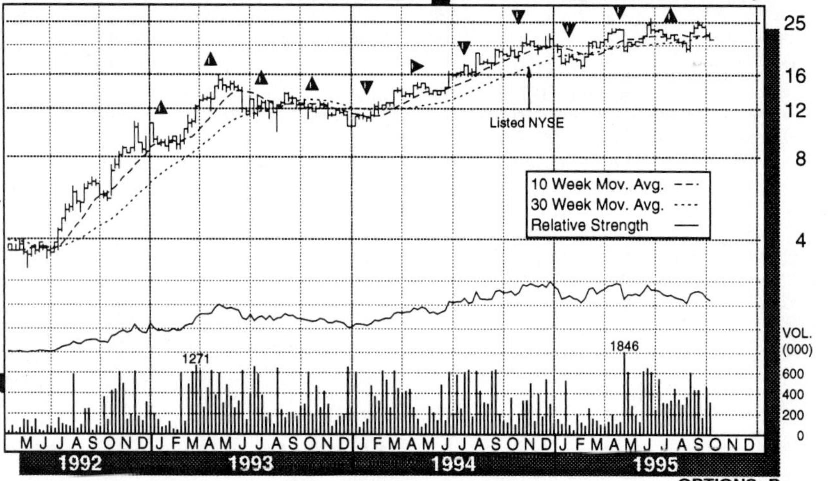

OPTIONS: P

Business Profile - 13-OCT-95

Barrett is an independent natural gas and oil exploration and production company, with major emphasis in the Rocky Mountain region and Oklahoma. Over 96% of total production in fiscal 1994 was natural gas. The company is also involved in marketing and trading activities and gas gathering. The July 1995 acquisition of Plains Petroleum Co. for about 13.4 million common shares on a pooling-of-interests basis has significantly increased Barrett's oil and gas production.

Operational Review - 13-OCT-95

Based on a brief report, total revenues for the nine months ended June 30, 1995, advanced 51%, year to year, primarily reflecting higher revenues from natural gas trading activities and increases in oil and gas production. Although average oil sales prices rose 26%, profitability was penalized by a 25% drop in average gas sales prices, to $1.46 per Mcf from $1.94 per Mcf in the year-earlier period. Net income fell 33%. Earnings per share declined to $0.20 from $0.30.

Stock Performance - 06-OCT-95

In the past 30 trading days, BRR's shares have increased 9%, compared to a 4% rise in the S&P 500. Average trading volume for the past five days was 61,920 shares, compared with the 40-day moving average of 78,100 shares.

Key Stock Statistics

Dividend Rate/Share	Nil	Shareholders	1,800
Shs. outstg. (M)	24.8	Market cap. (B)	$0.545
Avg. daily vol. (M)	0.061	Inst. holdings	31%
Tang. Bk. Value/Share	6.34	Insider holdings	NA
Beta	0.05		

Value of $10,000 invested 5 years ago: $ 35,306

Fiscal Year Ending Sep. 30

	1995	% Change	1994	% Change	1993	% Change
Revenues (Million $)						
1Q	14.88	55%	9.58	-16%	11.39	100%
2Q	14.55	55%	9.37	-28%	13.04	78%
3Q	14.70	51%	9.72	NM	9.67	108%
4Q	—	—	11.61	55%	7.51	26%
Yr.	—	—	40.27	-3%	41.61	76%
Income (Million $)						
1Q	0.21	-81%	1.12	-16%	1.33	NM
2Q	0.90	-47%	1.69	22%	1.39	132%
3Q	1.30	62%	0.80	-28%	1.11	NM
4Q	—	—	0.84	-56%	1.92	NM
Yr.	—	—	4.44	-23%	5.76	NM
Earnings Per Share ($)						
1Q	0.02	-78%	0.09	-36%	0.14	NM
2Q	0.07	-50%	0.14	NM	0.14	133%
3Q	0.11	57%	0.07	-22%	0.09	NM
4Q	—	—	0.07	-56%	0.16	NM
Yr.	—	—	0.37	-30%	0.53	NM

Next earnings report expected: late December

Barrett Resources

Business Summary - 13-OCT-95

Barrett Resources is a Denver-based independent natural gas and oil exploration and production company that is also involved in marketing, trading, and gas gathering. Net revenues in recent years were derived as follows:

	1994	1993
Oil & gas production	44%	36%
Trading revenues	56%	63%
Gas gathering	NM	1%

In its oil and gas exploration and development, the company's primary emphasis is in the Rocky Mountain region and Oklahoma. It is currently operating major projects in the Piceance Basin in Colorado, the Anadarko and Arkoma Basins in Oklahoma, and the Wind River Basin in Wyoming. BRR acts as the operator, when possible, of the exploration or development drilling program. As of September 30, 1994, the company was serving as operator for about 221 producing wells, 32 shut-in wells, two wells that were drilling, six wells that were being completed, and six wells that were waiting on completion.

In fiscal 1994, the company produced and sold 9,069,000 Mcf of gas at an average price of $1.85 per Mcf (versus 7,214,300 Mcf at $1.89 per Mcf in fiscal 1993) and 53,700 bbls. of oil at $14.34 per bbl. (74,890 bbls. at $17.59 the year before). Over 96% of BRR's total production in fiscal 1994 was natural gas. As of September 30, 1994, Barrett owned working interests in 89,289 gross (25,711 net) developed acres and 168,510 gross (49,135 net) undeveloped acres. It held interests in 400 gross (113.82 net) productive gas wells and 77 gross (4.03 net) productive oil wells. Estimated proved reserves totaled 149,206,000 Mcf of gas and 484,380 bbls. of oil, compared with 62,470,000 Mcf and 270,915 bbls. a year before.

Gas marketing and trading activities consist of marketing Barrett's own production, marketing the production of others from wells operated by the company, and trading that consist of the purchase and resale of natural gas. Barrett has entered into a number of gas sales agreements on behalf of itself and its industry partners. As of September 30, 1994, about 5% of Barrett's production was committed to gas sales contracts that bid fixed prices.

Important Developments

Jul. '95—BRR acquired Plains Petroleum Corp. for some 13.4 million common shares. PLP had estimated proved reserves of 313 billion cubic feet of natural gas and 11 million barrels of oil at December 31, 1994, located primarily in Kansas, Texas, New Mexico, and Wyoming. Its production in 1994 was 23.9 Bcf of gas and 1,236,000 bbls. of oil.

Capitalization

Long Term Debt: $36,000,000 (6/95).

Per Share Data ($) (Year Ended Sep. 30)

	1994	1993	1992	1991	1990	1989
Tangible Bk. Val.	6.15	5.82	4.49	4.25	4.09	2.89
Cash Flow	0.95	1.08	0.43	0.42	0.43	0.43
Earnings	0.37	0.53	0.09	0.17	0.19	0.14
Dividends	Nil	Nil	Nil	Nil	Nil	Nil
Payout Ratio	Nil	Nil	Nil	Nil	Nil	Nil
Prices - High	22¾	16	10¾	6½	8¾	7
- Low	10⅜	8⅜	3⅛	3¼	5⅛	2⅞
P/E Ratio - High	61	30	NM	38	46	50
- Low	28	16	NM	19	27	21

Income Statement Analysis (Million $)

	1994	%Chg	1993	%Chg	1992	%Chg	1991
Revs.	40.3	-3%	41.6	76%	23.6	70%	13.9
Oper. Inc.	10.4	-5%	10.9	NM	3.6	20%	3.0
Depr. Depl. & Amort.	6.9	14%	6.1	86%	3.3	35%	2.4
Int. Exp.	0.0	NM	0.0	-67%	0.0	-25%	0.0
Pretax Inc.	4.5	-24%	5.9	NM	0.9	-49%	1.9
Eff. Tax Rate	1.50%	—	2.60%	—	1.90%	—	7.80%
Net Inc.	4.4	-23%	5.8	NM	0.9	-46%	1.7

Balance Sheet & Other Fin. Data (Million $)

	1994	1993	1992	1991	1990	1989
Cash	9.7	35.2	11.3	18.9	19.9	5.3
Curr. Assets	28.8	53.3	19.9	24.4	28.6	8.6
Total Assets	106	91.0	57.0	55.0	51.0	26.0
Curr. Liab.	33.0	22.5	13.3	12.9	10.9	8.1
LT Debt	Nil	Nil	Nil	Nil	Nil	0.1
Common Eqty.	72.9	68.2	43.3	42.0	40.4	17.6
Total Cap.	72.9	68.2	43.3	42.6	40.4	17.7
Cap. Exp.	47.8	21.4	9.9	10.9	8.1	4.6
Cash Flow	11.3	11.8	4.2	4.1	3.4	2.6

Ratio Analysis

	1994	1993	1992	1991	1990	1989
Curr. Ratio	0.9	2.4	1.5	1.9	2.6	1.1
% LT Debt of Cap.	Nil	Nil	Nil	Nil	Nil	0.5
% Ret. on Assets	4.5	7.2	1.7	3.2	3.1	3.7
% Ret. on Equity	6.3	9.5	2.2	4.2	4.3	5.2

Dividend Data —No cash dividends have been paid. Barrett anticipates that all earnings will be retained for the development of its business and that no cash dividends will be declared for the foreseeable future.

Data as orig. reptd.; bef. results of disc opers. and/or spec. items. Per share data adj. for stk. divs. as of ex-div. date. E-Estimated. NA-Not Available. NM-Not Meaningful. NR-Not Ranked.

Office—1125 Seventeenth St., Denver, CO 80202. **Tel**—(303) 297-3900. **Chrmn & CEO**—W. J. Barrett. **Pres & COO**—P. M. Rady. **VP-Fin & Treas**—R. W. Howard. **EVP-Secy**—J. F. Keller. **Dirs**—W. J. Barrett, C. R. Buford, J. M. Fitzgibbons, H. L. J. M. Gieskes, J. F. Keller, P. M. Rady, A. R. Reed, J. T. Rodgers, P. S. E. Schreiber. **Transfer Agent & Registrar**—Bank of Boston. **Incorporated** in Delaware in 1987. **Empl-78. S&P Analyst:** JJS

STANDARD & POOR'S

STOCK REPORTS

Bell Industries

NYSE Symbol **BI**
In S&P SmallCap 600

17-OCT-95 **Industry:** Electronics/Electric

Summary: Bell Industries distributes products for the electronics, computer, graphics and other industrial markets.

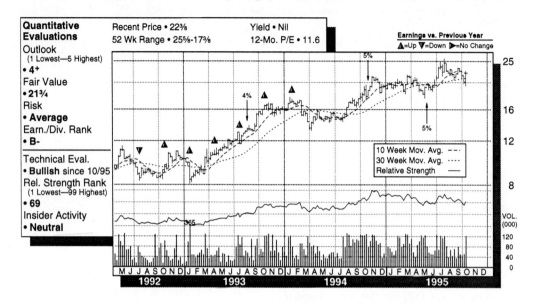

Quantitative Evaluations

Outlook
(1 Lowest—5 Highest)
• **4+**

Fair Value
• **21¾**

Risk
• **Average**

Earn./Div. Rank
• **B-**

Technical Eval.
• **Bullish** since 10/95

Rel. Strength Rank
(1 Lowest—99 Highest)
• **69**

Insider Activity
• **Neutral**

Recent Price • 22⅜
52 Wk Range • 25⅝-17⅜

Yield • Nil
12-Mo. P/E • 11.6

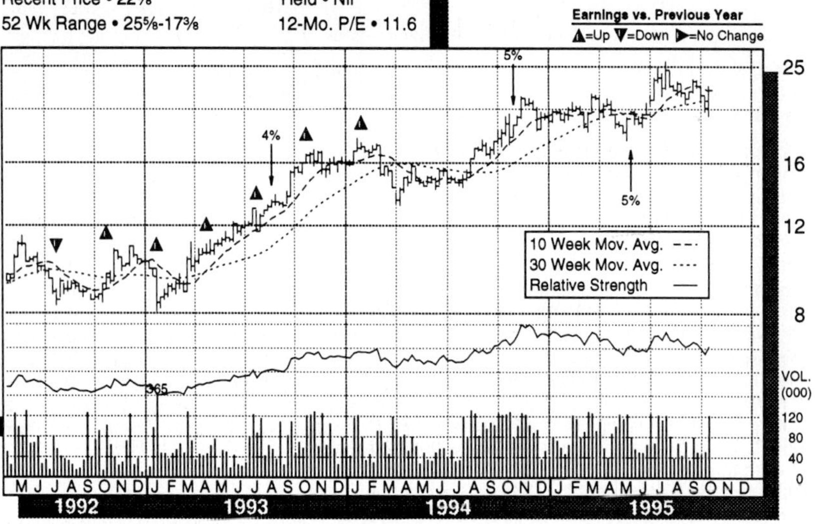

Business Profile - 13-OCT-95

Bell is primarily a distributor of electronic components. It also distributes graphic arts and recreation-related products, and manufactures computer and electronic components. Earnings have been in an uptrend in recent periods, led by the core electronics distribution business which recorded a 17% gain in sales for the third quarter. The company's order bookings and backlog continue to be very strong.

Operational Review - 13-OCT-95

Sales for the nine months ended September 30, 1995, advanced 13%, year to year, reflecting gains in all three business segments. Despite reduced profits from the graphic arts and recreational products segments, overall profitability improved on the strong performance by the electronics business. With interest expense down 17%, the gain in pretax income was extended to 30%. After taxes at 42.0%, versus 42.1%, net income also was up 30%. Earnings per share rose to $1.56 from $1.22.

Stock Performance - 13-OCT-95

In the past 30 trading days, BI's shares have increased 4%, compared to a 4% rise in the S&P 500. Average trading volume for the past five days was 25,940 shares, compared with the 40-day moving average of 12,705 shares.

Key Stock Statistics

Dividend Rate/Share	Nil	Shareholders	1,500
Shs. outstg. (M)	6.8	Market cap. (B)	$0.155
Avg. daily vol. (M)	0.014	Inst. holdings	53%
Tang. Bk. Value/Share	13.97	Insider holdings	NA
Beta	1.10		

Value of $10,000 invested 5 years ago: $ 25,261

Fiscal Year Ending Dec. 31

	1995	% Change	1994	% Change	1993	% Change
Revenues (Million $)						
1Q	126.9	—	--	—	106.7	15%
2Q	141.6	—	--	—	102.2	19%
3Q	148.6	17%	127.1	12%	113.5	25%
4Q	—	—	128.3	NM	128.7	34%
Yr.	—	—	255.4	-43%	451.2	24%
Income (Million $)						
1Q	2.56	—	—	—	0.31	-47%
2Q	4.22	—	—	—	-1.26	NM
3Q	4.28	51%	2.84	106%	1.38	NM
4Q	—	—	2.47	20%	2.06	39%
Yr.	—	—	5.31	6%	5.01	NM
Earnings Per Share ($)						
1Q	0.36	—	--	—	0.30	72%
2Q	0.60	—	--	—	0.20	NM
3Q	0.60	47%	0.41	39%	0.30	48%
4Q	—	—	0.35	-31%	0.51	74%
Yr.	—	—	0.76	-42%	1.31	89%

Next earnings report expected: late October

Bell Industries

Business Summary - 16-OCT-95

Bell Industries is primarily a distributor of electronic components. It also distributes graphic arts and recreation-related products, and manufactures computer and electronic components. Business segment contributions in 1994 (calendar year ended December 31):

	Sales	Profits
Electronics	80%	83%
Graphic arts	12%	6%
Recreational products	8%	11%

Electronic components distribution involves the sale of semiconductors, passive components, connectors, power supplies and board level products from more than 30 sales facilities located nationwide. Major lines include National Semiconductor, Analog Devices, SGS-Thomson, IBM Microelectronics, Microchip, Maxim, Aromat, and Kemet.

Bell's microcomputer systems and services business, based in Indiana, is an authorized reseller of personal computers and related products made by IBM, Apple, Compaq, and Hewlett-Packard.

Electronics manufacturing involves the production of high-precision, close tolerance products for the computer and aerospace markets. Products include switches, push buttons, and electro-luminescent panels used in commercial aircraft; precision stampings used in personal computers; and electronic components, including coils, filters, and chokes marketed under the J. W. Miller name.

The graphic arts group distributes electronic imaging equipment, film, plates, chemicals, printing supplies, sophisticated cameras, and lithographic plates throughout Arizona, California and southern Nevada to the advertising and printing industries.

Recreational products include marine equipment and motorcycle helmets, and replacement parts for motorcycles, mobile homes, snowmobiles and recreational vehicles. Sales are made to dealers and wholesalers in the Midwest.

Important Developments

Sep. '95—Bell announced that Sterling Electronics Corp., the 10th largest publicly-owned electronics distributor, had rejected its proposed merger offer made in August. Bell had proposed a merger of the two companies, offering to exchange 1 Bell common share for each of Sterling's 6.5 million common shares outstanding.

Capitalization

Long Term Debt: $25,381,000 (6/95); incl. $1.7 million of cap. lease obligs.

Per Share Data ($)

(Year Ended Dec. 31)

	1994	1993	1992	1991	1990	1989
Tangible Bk. Val.	13.97	13.10	11.94	12.48	12.65	12.81
Cash Flow	1.17	2.12	1.41	0.67	0.81	1.92
Earnings	0.76	1.31	0.73	0.06	0.10	1.22
Dividends	Nil	Nil	0.35	0.35	2.09	2.04
Payout Ratio	Nil	Nil	48%	NM	NM	165%
Prices - High	$21\frac{3}{4}$	$17\frac{7}{8}$	17	$11\frac{1}{2}$	$11\frac{7}{8}$	$16\frac{3}{8}$
- Low	$12\frac{1}{2}$	$13\frac{1}{8}$	$8\frac{1}{8}$	$8\frac{1}{4}$	$7\frac{7}{8}$	$10\frac{1}{2}$
P/E Ratio - High	NM	14	23	NM	NM	13
- Low	NM	10	11	NM	NM	9

Income Statement Analysis (Million $)

	1994	%Chg	1993	%Chg	1992	%Chg	1991
Revs.	255	-43%	451	24%	365	-12%	414
Oper. Inc.	13.9	-46%	25.8	37%	18.8	26%	14.9
Depr.	2.9	-48%	5.6	22%	4.6	12%	4.1
Int. Exp.	1.9	-58%	4.5	-19%	5.5	2%	5.4
Pretax Inc.	9.2	-41%	15.7	80%	8.7	NM	1.0
Eff. Tax Rate	42%	—	42%	—	42%	—	58%
Net Inc.	5.3	-42%	9.1	82%	5.0	NM	0.4

Balance Sheet & Other Fin. Data (Million $)

	1994	1993	1992	1991	1990	1989
Cash	3.6	4.4	10.7	14.6	6.1	3.3
Curr. Assets	174	157	139	161	157	142
Total Assets	200	185	175	192	189	176
Curr. Liab.	57.7	49.2	41.4	46.6	38.0	51.5
LT Debt	36.3	36.1	44.4	49.6	53.3	24.0
Common Eqty.	102	96.0	86.0	92.0	94.0	95.0
Total Cap.	138	132	131	142	148	121
Cap. Exp.	1.4	2.6	5.7	8.7	5.7	5.4
Cash Flow	8.2	14.6	9.6	4.5	5.5	12.9

Ratio Analysis

	1994	1993	1992	1991	1990	1989
Curr. Ratio	3.0	3.2	3.4	3.5	4.1	2.8
% LT Debt of Cap.	26.3	27.4	34.0	34.9	36.0	19.9
% Net Inc.of Revs.	2.1	2.0	1.4	0.1	0.2	2.1
% Ret. on Assets	NM	5.0	2.7	0.2	0.4	4.6
% Ret. on Equity	NM	10.0	5.6	0.4	0.7	7.9

Dividend Data —Cash dividends, been paid since 1973, were suspended in February 1993. A 4% stock dividend paid in September 1993, and 5% stock dividends were paid in November 1994 and June 1995.

Data as orig. reptd.; bef. results of disc. opers. and/or spec. items. Per share data adj. for stk. divs. as of ex-div. date. Yrs. ended Jun. 30 of fol. cal. yr. prior to 1994. Data for 1994 is for six mos. ended Jun. 30. E-Estimated. NA-Not Available. NM-Not Meaningful. NR-Not Ranked.

Office—11812 San Vincente Blvd., Los Angeles, CA 90049-5069. **Tel**—(310) 826-2355. **Chrmn & CEO**—T. Williams. **Pres & COO**—B. M. Jaffe. **VP-CFO & Investor Contact**—Tracy A. Edwards. **Secy**—J. J. Cost. **Dirs**—J. J. Cost, A. L. Craig, G. M. Graham, B. M. Jaffe, M. Rosenberg, C. S. Troy, T. Williams. **Transfer Agent & Registrar**—Harris Trust Co., Los Angeles, CA. **Incorporated** in California in 1959; reincorporated in Delaware in 1979; reincorporated in California in 1995. **Empl**-1,400. **S&P Analyst:** JJS

Benchmark Electronics

ASE Symbol **BHE**
In S&P SmallCap 600

08-SEP-95 **Industry:** Electronics/Electric

Summary: This company provides manufacturing services to original equipment manufacturers in the electronics industry.

Quantitative Evaluations

Outlook
(1 Lowest—5 Highest)
• **NA**

Fair Value
• **NA**

Risk
• **Average**

Earn./Div. Rank
• **NR**

Technical Eval.
• **Bullish** since 7/95

Rel. Strength Rank
(1 Lowest—99 Highest)
• **50**

Insider Activity
• **NA**

Recent Price • 28⅛
52 Wk Range • 30¼-20¼
Yield • Nil
12-Mo. P/E • 18.5

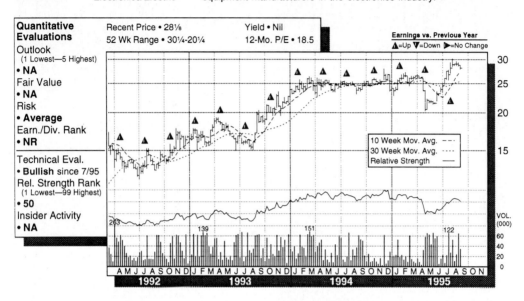

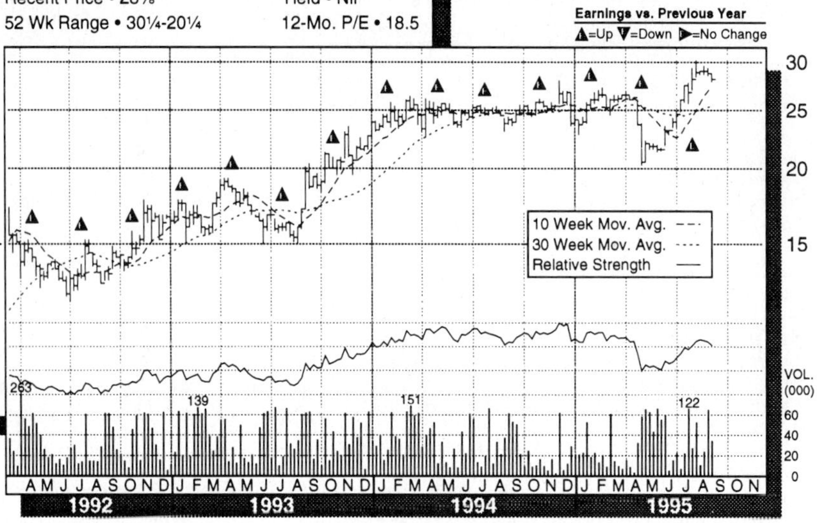

Business Profile - 08-SEP-95

This company provides manufacturing services to original equipment manufacturers (OEMs) in the electronics industry. Continued outsourcing of products by OEMs has kept bookings, revenues and earnings strong. The company's business strategy is to maintain existing and establish new long-term manufacturing relationships with OEMs in a diverse group of industries.

Operational Review - 08-SEP-95

Revenues in the first half of 1995 fell 5.1%, year to year, primarily reflecting delayed shipments of finished products caused by shortages of certain components. Margins improved, and net income increased to $0.77 a share from $0.66 in the first half of 1994.

Stock Performance - 01-SEP-95

In the past 30 trading days, BHE's shares have increased 5%, compared to a 2% rise in the S&P 500. Average trading volume for the past five days was 6,800 shares, compared with the 40-day moving average of 10,018 shares.

Key Stock Statistics

Dividend Rate/Share	Nil	Shareholders	100
Shs. outstg. (M)	4.0	Market cap. (B)	$0.113
Avg. daily vol. (M)	0.009	Inst. holdings	62%
Tang. Bk. Value/Share	10.40	Insider holdings	NA
Beta	0.98		

Value of $10,000 invested 5 years ago: NA

Fiscal Year Ending Dec. 31

	1995	% Change	1994	% Change	1993	% Change
Revenues (Million $)						
1Q	23.12	-5%	24.28	60%	15.20	52%
2Q	23.65	-6%	25.05	47%	17.06	47%
3Q	—	—	25.10	28%	19.57	30%
4Q	—	—	23.75	-1%	24.03	72%
Yr.	—	—	98.17	29%	75.86	50%
Income (Million $)						
1Q	1.57	17%	1.34	60%	0.84	35%
2Q	1.59	15%	1.38	37%	1.01	40%
3Q	—	—	1.47	20%	1.23	43%
4Q	—	—	1.59	15%	1.38	50%
Yr.	—	—	5.77	29%	4.47	43%
Earnings Per Share ($)						
1Q	0.38	15%	0.33	57%	0.21	5%
2Q	0.39	15%	0.34	36%	0.25	32%
3Q	—	—	0.36	20%	0.30	36%
4Q	—	—	0.39	15%	0.34	55%
Yr.	—	—	1.41	28%	1.10	33%

Next earnings report expected: late October

Benchmark Electronics

Business Summary - 08-SEP-95

Benchmark Electronics, Inc. provides contract manufacturing services to original equipment manufacturers (OEMs) in the electronics industry. The company specializes in assembling printed circuit boards for customers requiring low to medium volume of high quality, technologically complex boards for industrial and business applications.

Substantially all services are provided on a turnkey basis, i.e., Benchmark buys components from suppliers, assembles these components into finished printed circuit boards and performs post-assembly testing. This method of contract manufacturing provides the company with both materials and labor income. The consignment method, which uses customer provided components, provides the company with manufacturing income only.

The company specializes in assembling printed circuit boards using surface mount and pin-through-hole technologies. Surface mount technology, which is becoming the leading interconnection technology, is a largely automated process that allows for the placement of a higher density of components directly on both sides of a printed circuit board. It has been adopted for many major electronics products including communications equipment, business computers, testing equipment, medical devices and industrial equipment. The company also provides pin-through-hole assembly services for customers that have not shifted or do not have the economies of scale to justify the change to surface mount technology.

Manufacturing operations are conducted at a new facility in Angleton, Tex., which became fully operational in November 1994. In late 1990, a second facility was established in Beaverton, Ore., to provide prompt, turnkey printed circuit board assembly services to customers with operations in the West. Benchmark has been actively examining opportunities for the establishment or acquisition of a third regional manufacturing facility, but has been unable to identify a location that meets its criteria for expansion.

Benchmark markets its services through its executive officers and sales personnel. The company has been historically reliant on a few customers for the majority of its revenues. Its largest customer in 1994, Sequent Computer Systems, Inc., accounted for about 49% of total revenues.

Important Developments

Aug. '94—The company said it had a backlog of approximately $72,210,000 at June 30, 1995, up from $59,500,000 at December 31, 1994. Management said that the high level of backlog was due to an intensive marketing effort, and represented a more diversified mix of customers.

Capitalization

Long Term Debt: None (3/95).

Per Share Data ($) (Year Ended Dec. 31)

	1994	1993	1992	1991	1990	1989
Tangible Bk. Val.	10.01	8.59	7.42	5.10	4.44	1.69
Cash Flow	1.87	1.45	1.14	0.92	0.92	0.73
Earnings	1.41	1.10	0.83	0.66	0.76	0.65
Dividends	Nil	Nil	Nil	Nil	Nil	Nil
Payout Ratio	Nil	Nil	Nil	Nil	Nil	Nil
Prices - High	28	23⅞	17¾	12¼	8¾	NA
- Low	22½	15	10⅜	4⅝	3⅝	NA
P/E Ratio - High	20	22	21	19	12	NA
- Low	16	14	13	7	5	NA

Income Statement Analysis (Million $)

	1994	%Chg	1993	%Chg	1992	%Chg	1991
Revs.	98.2	29%	75.9	50%	50.6	52%	33.3
Oper. Inc.	10.7	35%	7.9	47%	5.4	45%	3.8
Depr.	1.9	33%	1.4	23%	1.1	39%	0.8
Int. Exp.	Nil	—	Nil	—	Nil	—	Nil
Pretax Inc.	9.0	30%	6.9	46%	4.8	45%	3.3
Eff. Tax Rate	36%	—	36%	—	34%	—	36%
Net Inc.	5.8	29%	4.5	43%	3.1	49%	2.1

Balance Sheet & Other Fin. Data (Million $)

	1994	1993	1992	1991	1990	1989
Cash	8.4	10.1	13.3	3.1	7.1	0.1
Curr. Assets	38.5	42.0	30.3	15.6	15.7	5.1
Total Assets	48.2	47.4	34.4	20.0	17.4	6.6
Curr. Liab.	7.6	12.9	4.5	3.3	2.8	2.3
LT Debt	Nil	Nil	Nil	Nil	Nil	0.1
Common Eqty.	40.1	34.2	29.6	16.3	14.2	3.5
Total Cap.	40.7	34.6	29.8	16.5	14.3	3.7
Cap. Exp.	6.3	2.8	0.9	7.2	0.5	1.3
Cash Flow	7.7	5.9	4.3	2.9	2.4	1.5

Ratio Analysis

	1994	1993	1992	1991	1990	1989
Curr. Ratio	5.1	3.3	6.8	4.7	5.6	2.2
% LT Debt of Cap.	Nil	Nil	Nil	Nil	Nil	2.4
% Net Inc.of Revs.	5.9	5.9	6.2	6.3	9.4	7.6
% Ret. on Assets	12.0	10.9	10.6	11.3	14.6	26.1
% Ret. on Equity	15.5	14.0	12.5	13.8	20.6	50.3

Dividend Data —No cash dividends have been paid. Benchmark expects to retain earnings for operation and expansion of its business.

Data as orig. reptd.; bef. results of disc. opers. and/or spec. items. Per share data adj. for stk. divs. as of ex-div. date. E-Estimated. NA-Not Available. NM-Not Meaningful. NR-Not Ranked.

Office—3000 Technology Drive, Angleton, TX 77515. **Tel**—(409) 849-6550. **Chrmn**—J. C. Custer. **Pres & CEO**—D. E. Nigbor. **EVP-Fin, Secy, Treas & Investor Contact**—Cary T. Fu. **Dirs**—S. A. Barton, G. W. Bodzy, J. C. Custer, P. G. Dorflinger, C. T. Fu, D. E. Nigbor. **Transfer Agent & Registrar**—Society National Bank, Houston. **Incorporated** in Texas in 1981. **Empl**-439. **S&P Analyst:** M.T.C.

STANDARD & POOR'S

STOCK REPORTS

Benton Oil & Gas

NASDAQ Symbol **BNTN**

In S&P SmallCap 600

10-OCT-95 **Industry:** Oil and Gas

Summary: This independent oil and gas exploration and production company has domestic operations in the Gulf Coast region of Louisiana, and international operations in Russia and Venezuela.

Quantitative Evaluations
Outlook
(1 Lowest—5 Highest)
• **NA**
Fair Value
• **NA**
Risk
• **Average**
Earn./Div. Rank
• **NR**

Technical Eval.
• **Bearish** since 8/95
Rel. Strength Rank
(1 Lowest—99 Highest)
• **10**
Insider Activity
• **NA**

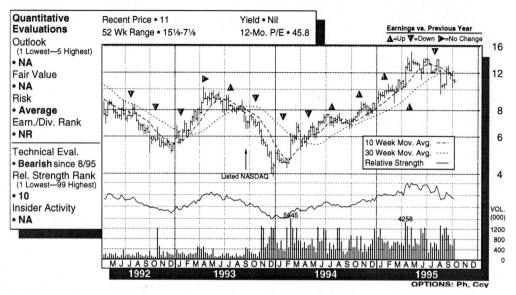

Recent Price • 11 Yield • Nil
52 Wk Range • 15⅛-7⅛ 12-Mo. P/E • 45.8

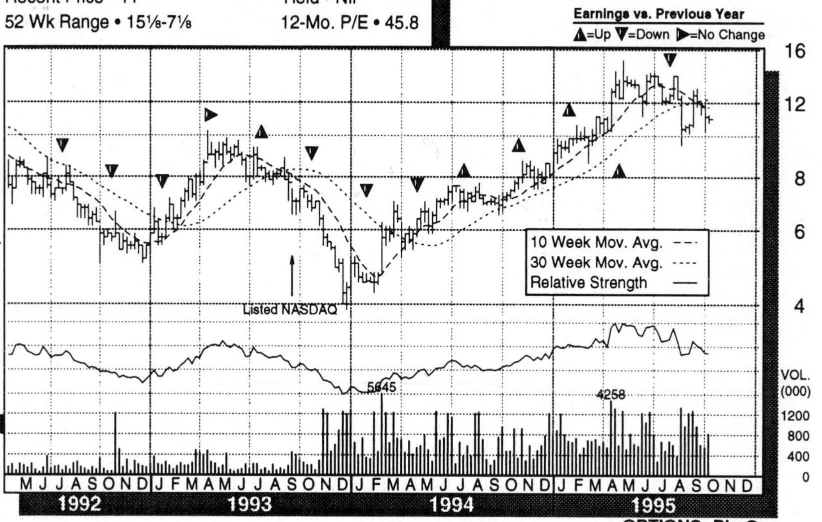

OPTIONS: Ph, Ccv

Business Profile - 10-OCT-95

BNTN seeks to exploit underdeveloped existing oil and gas fields through in-house design and interpretation of 3-D seismic surveys, workovers, recompletions, redrilling, and exploration and development drilling. Benton also forms joint ventures with industry participants under which it performs a seismic study and/or development program in exchange for an interest in the project area. In 1995, the company plans to drill 36 wells in Russia, 22 wells in Venezuela and eight wells in the U.S. Gulf.

Operational Review - 10-OCT-95

Total revenues for the six months ended June 30, 1995, advanced 113%, year to year, reflecting increased crude oil production and prices in Venezuela and Russia, as well as higher domestic natural gas production levels. Despite sharply higher interest expense, due to increased borrowings used to fund Venezuelan and Russian operations, and minority interest, resulting from the company's increased interest in Benton-Vinccler, and net income rose to $3,151,601 ($0.12 a share) from $1,663 ($0.00).

Stock Performance - 06-OCT-95

In the past 30 trading days, BNTN's shares have increased 5%, compared to a 4% rise in the S&P 500. Average trading volume for the past five days was 163,400 shares, compared with the 40-day moving average of 257,487 shares.

Key Stock Statistics

Dividend Rate/Share	Nil	Shareholders	1,200
Shs. outstg. (M)	25.1	Market cap. (B)	$0.257
Avg. daily vol. (M)	0.145	Inst. holdings	49%
Tang. Bk. Value/Share	3.69	Insider holdings	NA
Beta	1.14		

Value of $10,000 invested 5 years ago: $ 45,118

Fiscal Year Ending Dec. 31

	1995	% Change	1994	% Change	1993	% Change
Revenues (Million $)						
1Q	12.66	NM	3.76	116%	1.74	-21%
2Q	13.21	56%	8.48	NM	1.63	-33%
3Q	—	—	9.57	NM	1.36	-32%
4Q	—	—	12.90	NM	3.08	54%
Yr.	—	—	34.70	NM	7.81	-10%
Income (Million $)						
1Q	2.04	NM	-1.14	NM	-0.75	NM
2Q	1.11	-3%	1.14	NM	-0.73	NM
3Q	—	—	1.83	NM	-1.21	NM
4Q	—	—	1.13	NM	-2.14	NM
Yr.	—	—	2.95	NM	-4.83	NM
Earnings Per Share ($)						
1Q	0.08	NM	-0.05	NM	-0.04	NM
2Q	0.04	-20%	0.05	NM	-0.04	NM
3Q	—	—	0.07	NM	-0.07	NM
4Q	—	—	0.05	NM	-0.10	NM
Yr.	—	—	0.12	NM	-0.26	NM

Next earnings report expected: mid November

Benton Oil & Gas

Business Summary - 10-OCT-95

Benton Oil and Gas Co. explores, develops and manages oil and gas properties primarily in the Gulf Coast region of Louisiana, the West Siberia region of Russia, and the eastern region of Venezuela. It also has operations in Texas, Mississippi and California.

At December 31, 1994, net proved crude oil and condensate reserves were 78,480,000 bbl.; natural gas reserves were 16,077,000 Mcf.

One of Benton's major assets is the West Cote Blanche Bay Field in southern Louisiana (operated by Texaco), where it has a 32.5% working interest. The company is involved in a five-phase project, in conjunction with Texaco, to enhance development of the field. In November 1994, Benton sold 25% of its working interest in the field to Tenneco for $5.8 million and future consideration of up to $3.7 million.

In December 1991, Benton entered a joint venture with two Russian partners to explore, produce and market oil and natural gas from the North Gubkinskoye and nearby fields in the West Siberia region in Russia. Benton has a 34% interest in the venture, GEOILBENT. The field has over 60 wells delineated, of which GEOILBENT has identified nine wells which are capable of being placed on production. At December 31, 1994, net proved reserves of BNTN attributable to the North Gubkinskoye field represented 22% of Benton's total reserves. In mid-1993, a 37-mile oil pipeline was completed, and production from the first three wells began.

In July 1992, the company formed Benton-Vinccler to reactivate and further develop three Venezuelan oil fields. At December 31, 1994, Benton's net proved reserves at the fields represented 75% of its total reserves. In January 1994, BNTN boosted its interest in Benton-Vinccler from 50% to 80% for $13 million and 200,000 BNTN common shares.

Important Developments

Jul. '95—Benton announced that oil production from the Uracoa oil field located in Monagas, Venezuela, has continued to increase to its current level of 17,000 barrels of oil per day (BOPD), compared with 6,700 BOPD a year ago. Production from the field is currently from 36 wells, and an additional 65 wells are expected to be drilled over the next several years in order to fully develop the field.

Capitalization

Long Term Debt: $53,268,253 (6/95).
Minority Interest: $3,486,233.
Options and Warrants: To buy 3,708,811 shs. (12/94).

Per Share Data ($)

(Year Ended Dec. 31)

	1994	1993	1992	1991	1990	1989
Tangible Bk. Val.	3.54	3.40	2.89	1.96	1.17	0.57
Cash Flow	0.53	-0.12	0.01	0.28	0.12	-0.10
Earnings	0.12	-0.26	-0.22	0.03	0.01	-0.13
Dividends	Nil	Nil	Nil	Nil	Nil	Nil
Payout Ratio	Nil	NM	NM	Nil	Nil	Nil
Prices - High	$9\frac{1}{8}$	$10\frac{1}{4}$	$11\frac{1}{8}$	$18\frac{3}{4}$	$8\frac{3}{8}$	$2\frac{5}{8}$
- Low	$4\frac{1}{4}$	$3\frac{7}{8}$	5	$6\frac{1}{8}$	2	$1\frac{1}{4}$
P/E Ratio - High	76	NM	NM	NM	NM	NM
- Low	35	NM	NM	NA	NA	NA

Income Statement Analysis (Million $)

	1994	%Chg	1993	%Chg	1992	%Chg	1991
Revs.	32.1	NM	7.4	-12%	8.4	-25%	11.2
Oper. Inc.	17.3	NM	-0.5	NM	1.7	-64%	4.9
Depr. Depl. & Amort.	10.3	NM	2.6	-14%	3.0	NM	3.0
Int. Exp.	3.9	98%	2.0	7%	1.8	10%	1.7
Pretax Inc.	5.8	NM	-4.8	NM	-2.9	NM	0.5
Eff. Tax Rate	12%	—	NM	—	NM	—	34%
Net Inc.	3.0	NM	-4.8	NM	-2.9	NM	0.3

Balance Sheet & Other Fin. Data (Million $)

	1994	1993	1992	1991	1990	1989
Cash	33.7	36.3	13.7	3.7	5.1	1.5
Curr. Assets	62.4	39.5	14.8	7.0	8.1	2.2
Total Assets	163	109	68.2	49.4	27.3	4.5
Curr. Liab.	40.6	12.8	4.3	21.8	9.9	1.5
LT Debt	31.9	11.8	11.3	7.4	7.3	0.4
Common Eqty.	88.3	84.0	50.5	20.2	10.1	2.6
Total Cap.	122	95.8	63.9	27.6	17.3	3.0
Cap. Exp.	38.4	26.1	17.0	25.4	22.6	4.8
Cash Flow	13.3	-2.2	0.1	3.4	1.0	-0.4

Ratio Analysis

	1994	1993	1992	1991	1990	1989
Curr. Ratio	1.5	3.1	3.4	0.3	0.8	1.5
% LT Debt of Cap.	26.2	12.3	17.7	26.9	41.9	13.9
% Ret. on Assets	2.2	NM	NM	0.8	0.7	NM
% Ret. on Equity	3.4	NM	NM	2.1	1.6	NM

Dividend Data —No cash dividends have been paid. A "poison pill" stockholder rights plan was adopted in 1995. Stock dividends of 100% each were paid in July 1990 and February 1991.

Data as orig. reptd.; bef. results of disc opers. and/or spec. items. Per share data adj. for stk. divs. as of ex-div. date. E-Estimated. NA-Not Available. NM-Not Meaningful. NR-Not Ranked.

Office—1145 Eugenia Place, Suite 200, Carpinteria, CA 93013. **Tel**—(805) 566-5600. **Chrmn, Pres & CEO**—A. E. Benton. **VP-Fin, CFO & Investor Contact**—D. H. Pratt. **Dirs**—A. E. Benton, R. W. Fetzner, W. H. Gumma, B. M. McIntyre, M. B. Wray. **Transfer Agent & Registrar**—First Interstate Bank, Los Angeles. **Incorporated** in Delaware in 1988. **Empl**-38. **S&P Analyst:** N. Rosenberg

STANDARD & POOR'S

STOCK REPORTS

Birmingham Steel

NYSE Symbol **BIR**
In S&P SmallCap 600

16-AUG-95

Industry: Steel-Iron

Summary: This company operates mini-mills that produce rebar and merchant products and also specializes in making high quality rod and wire at its American Steel & Wire subsidiary.

S&P Opinion: Accumulate (★★★★)

Recent Price • 19¾
52 Wk Range • 27⅝-17½
Yield • 2.0%
12-Mo. P/E • 11.4

Quantitative Evaluations

Outlook
(1 Lowest—5 Highest)
• **5-**

Fair Value
• **22⅜**

Risk
• **Average**

Earn./Div. Rank
• **NR**

Technical Eval.
• **Bearish** since 8/95

Rel. Strength Rank
(1 Lowest—99 Highest)
• **50**

Insider Activity
• **NA**

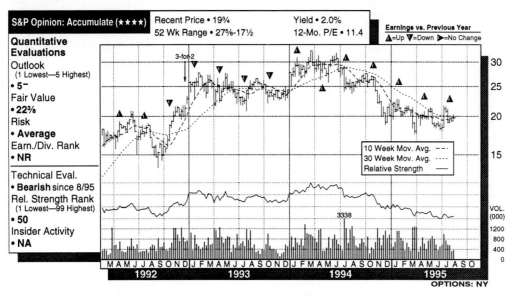

Earnings vs. Previous Year
▲=Up ▼=Down ▶=No Change

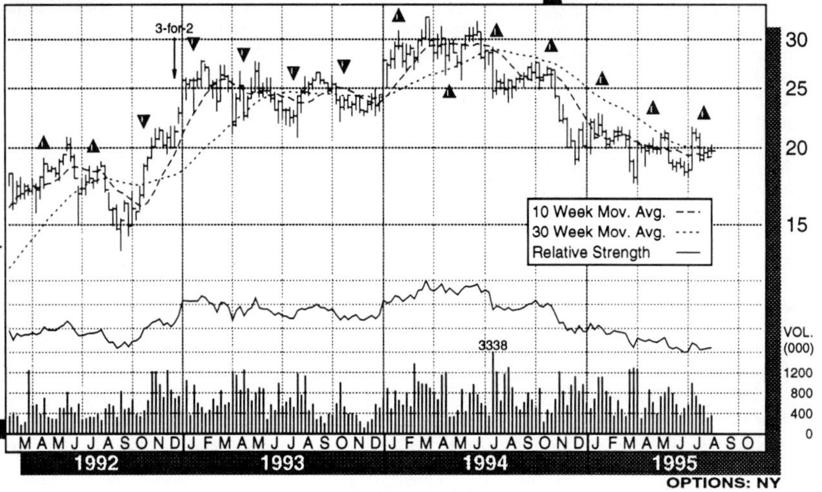

OPTIONS: NY

Overview - 10-AUG-95

We expect BIR to post a 10% sales gain in fiscal 1996, on increased volume and pricing for rebar, merchant products, and rod and wire. The rate of advance will trail fiscal 1995's strong pace, reflecting less vibrant demand for durable goods. We project shipments totaling 2.5 million tons, versus fiscal 1995's 2.4 million, and anticipate lower unit costs as a result of higher capacity utilization, greater operating efficiencies and only modest increases in scrap costs. Margin improvement will lead to higher earnings in fiscal 1996. Long-term sales and earnings will be boosted by plans to double shipping capacity to 4.2 million tons by 1999, construction of a melt shop to decrease outside billet purchases, a greater portion of higher margin products, industry consodidation and acquisitions.

Valuation - 16-AUG-95

We are maintaining our accumulate rating on BIR based on the stock's valuation relative to fiscal 1996's estimated earnings and our very positive long-term view of the company. BIR has underperformed the market through mid-August 1995; the shares were virtually unchanged from 1994's year end versus a gain of some 22% in the S&P 500. Quarterly earnings in fiscal 1996 could be erratic due to the impact of the capital program and this may cause some volatility in the shares. However, we believe the trend in the share price will be up in 1996. Also, the stock repurchase program will provide a cushion for the price.

Key Stock Statistics

S&P EPS Est. 1996	2.10	Tang. Bk. Value/Share	13.84
P/E on S&P Est. 1996	9.4	Beta	1.36
Dividend Rate/Share	0.40	Shareholders	700
Shs. outstg. (M)	28.5	Market cap. (B)	$0.574
Avg. daily vol. (M)	0.089	Inst. holdings	68%
		Insider holdings	NA

Value of $10,000 invested 5 years ago: $ 11,949

Fiscal Year Ending Jun. 30

	1995	% Change	1994	% Change	1993	% Change
Revenues (Million $)						
1Q	220.6	73%	127.6	14%	112.0	NM
2Q	203.2	38%	146.8	50%	98.10	10%
3Q	236.9	16%	204.2	77%	115.1	11%
4Q	224.8	NM	224.3	91%	117.2	3%
Yr.	885.5	26%	702.9	59%	442.3	6%
Income (Million $)						
1Q	12.21	NM	3.31	—	—	—
2Q	12.37	NM	3.76	12%	3.36	-27%
3Q	13.26	159%	5.12	NM	0.36	-90%
4Q	12.81	41%	9.06	NM	2.41	-62%
Yr.	50.65	138%	21.25	66%	12.79	-36%
Earnings Per Share ($)						
1Q	0.42	180%	0.15	-52%	0.31	-3%
2Q	0.42	147%	0.17	6%	0.16	-41%
3Q	0.45	125%	0.20	NM	0.02	-90%
4Q	0.45	45%	0.31	182%	0.11	-63%
Yr.	1.74	102%	0.86	43%	0.60	-46%

Next earnings report expected: mid October

Birmingham Steel

Business Summary - 16-AUG-95

As of June 30, 1994 Birmingham operated four nonunion mini-mills across the U. S., producing steel reinforcing bar (rebar) used in the construction industry, and rounds, bars, flats and strips that are sold to fabricators and other merchants. Following the November 1993 acquisition of American Steel & Wire, it makes steel rod and wire primarily for the automotive, fastener, welding, appliance and aerospace industries.

Melting operations are conducted in Birmingham, Ala., Jackson, Miss., Kankakee, Ill., and Seattle, Wash. BIR's mini-mills use ferrous scrap in electric arc furnaces to produce a limited range of products. In fiscal 1994, scrap costs accounted for 49% of total manufacturing costs, up from 42% in fiscal 1993. The average cost of scrap was $127 a ton in fiscal 1994, $99 a ton in fiscal 1993 and $92 ton in fiscal 1992.

During fiscal 1994, melt shop output and rolling mill production totaled 1,864,000 and 1,615,000 tons, respectively. Melting capacity at the end of fiscal 1994 was 2.2 million tons, while rolling capacity was 1.9 million tons.

BIR shipped 2,100,000 tons in fiscal 1994, versus 1,616,000 tons in fiscal 1993 and 1,448,000 tons in fiscal 1992. Of total tonnage shipped in fiscal 1994, 53% was rebar, 18% merchant products, 16% rod and wire, 5% was for roof support system products produced at company plants, and 8% was semi-finished billet.

In fiscal 1994, reinforcing bar, merchant products, rod and wire, semifinished steel billets and mine roof products, accounted respectively for 53%, 18%, 16%, 8% and 5% of shipments. BIR's average combined steel and mine roof support selling price per ton was $330 in fiscal 1994, versus $274 in fiscal 1993.

In calendar 1993, the company shipped 23.4% of the rebar and 4.7% of the merchant products consumed that year in the U. S.

Important Developments

Aug. '95—BIR reported share earnings of $0.45 on flat sales for fiscal 1995's fourth quarter, versus $0.31 a year earlier. Shipments for fiscal 1995's fourth quarter totaled 620,000 tons, versus 633,000 tons a year earlier. The company attributed the decline to equipment problems and decreased demand from service centers. Shipments for the full fiscal year totaled 2,375,000 tons, up from 2,130,000 tons. BIR said that it expected fiscal 1996's results to exceed fiscal 1995 but noted that earnings for the first and fourth quarters of the fiscal year would be affected by start-up of new equipment and equipment modifications.

Jan. '95—BIR announced plans to repurchase up to 2,950,000 common shares (about 10% of the shares outstanding) over a three year-period, at prices not to exceed $30 a share.

Capitalization

Long Term Debt: $142,500,000 (3/95).

Per Share Data ($)

(Year Ended Jun. 30)

	1995	1994	1993	1992	1991	1990
Tangible Bk. Val.	NA	14.21	10.36	10.03	7.80	8.13
Cash Flow	NA	1.99	1.41	2.04	0.83	1.62
Earnings	1.74	0.86	0.60	1.11	NM	0.89
Dividends	0.40	0.40	0.37	0.33	0.33	0.33
Payout Ratio	23%	47%	61%	35%	NM	37%
Prices - High	22¾	32⅝	20¾	25¾	15⅝	18¾
- Low	17½	18¾	15¾	13⅝	8⅜	7
P/E Ratio - High	13	38	46	23	NM	21
- Low	10	22	30	12	NM	8

Income Statement Analysis (Million $)

	1994	%Chg	1993	%Chg	1992	%Chg	1991
Revs.	703	59%	442	6%	418	2%	408
Oper. Inc.	69.9	64%	42.7	-22%	55.0	51%	36.5
Depr.	27.7	60%	17.3	3%	16.8	20%	14.0
Int. Exp.	11.1	28%	8.7	-12%	9.9	9%	9.1
Pretax Inc.	35.8	68%	21.3	-34%	32.2	NM	1.0
Eff. Tax Rate	41%	—	40%	—	38%	—	98%
Net Inc.	21.2	66%	12.8	-36%	19.9	—	NM

Balance Sheet & Other Fin. Data (Million $)

	1994	1993	1992	1991	1990	1989
Cash	28.9	0.3	0.5	0.5	0.1	1.0
Curr. Assets	276	147	128	127	136	141
Total Assets	690	456	388	345	314	301
Curr. Liab.	62.7	114	54.0	92.0	114	108
LT Debt	143	90.1	93.7	98.4	27.2	31.0
Common Eqty.	439	223	215	134	151	145
Total Cap.	623	339	331	250	197	191
Cap. Exp.	40.4	76.0	56.1	69.8	35.4	24.8
Cash Flow	48.9	30.1	36.7	14.5	29.7	50.5

Ratio Analysis

	1994	1993	1992	1991	1990	1989
Curr. Ratio	4.4	1.3	2.4	1.4	1.2	1.3
% LT Debt of Cap.	22.9	26.6	28.3	39.3	13.8	16.2
% Net Inc.of Revs.	3.0	2.9	4.8	NM	3.7	8.8
% Ret. on Assets	3.7	3.0	4.8	NM	5.3	14.0
% Ret. on Equity	6.4	5.8	10.4	NM	11.1	30.7

Dividend Data —Dividends were initiated in early 1988.

Amt. of Div. $	Date Decl.	Ex-Div. Date	Stock of Record	Payment Date
0.100	Jul. 21	Aug. 08	Aug. 12	Aug. 23 '94
0.100	Oct. 18	Oct. 24	Oct. 28	Nov. 08 '94
0.100	Jan. 24	Jan. 30	Feb. 03	Feb. 14 '95
0.100	Apr. 17	Apr. 21	Apr. 27	May. 09 '95
0.100	Aug. 02	Aug. 10	Aug. 14	Aug. 25 '95

Data as orig. reptd.; bef. results of disc. opers. and/or spec. items. Per share data adj. for stk. divs. as of ex-div. date. E-Estimated. NA-Not Available. NM-Not Meaningful. NR-Not Ranked.

Office—1000 Urban Center Parkway, Suite 300, Birmingham, AL 35242-2516. **Tel**—(205) 970-1200. **Chrmn & CEO**—J. A. Todd, Jr. **Vice Chrmn**—P. H. Ekberg. **EVP & CFO**—J. M. Casey. **VP & Investor Contact**—J. Daniel Garrett. **Secy**—C. W. Pecher. **Dirs**—W. J. Cabaniss, Jr., C. S. Clegg, E. M. de Windt, P. E. Ekberg, J. M. Harbert III, H. Holiday Jr., E. B. Jones, R. H. Jones, G. A. Stinson, J. A. Todd, Jr., T. N. Tyrrell, T. E. Wyckoff. **Transfer Agent & Registrar**—First Union National Bank, Charlotte, NC. **Incorporated** in Delaware in 1983. **Empl**-1,855. **S&P Analyst:** Leo Larkin

Bolt Beranek and Newman

NYSE Symbol **BBN**
In S&P SmallCap 600

10-OCT-95 **Industry:** Electronics/Electric

Summary: Bolt Beranek and Newman provides products and services in the areas of internetworking, data analysis, and collaborative and acoustic systems.

Quantitative Evaluations

Outlook
(1 Lowest—5 Highest)
• **NA**
Fair Value
• **NA**
Risk
• **High**
Earn./Div. Rank
• **B-**

Technical Eval.
• **Bearish** since 8/95
Rel. Strength Rank
(1 Lowest—99 Highest)
• **51**
Insider Activity
• **Neutral**

Recent Price • 36¼
52 Wk Range • 39⅜-12⅝
Yield • Nil
12-Mo. P/E • 10.0

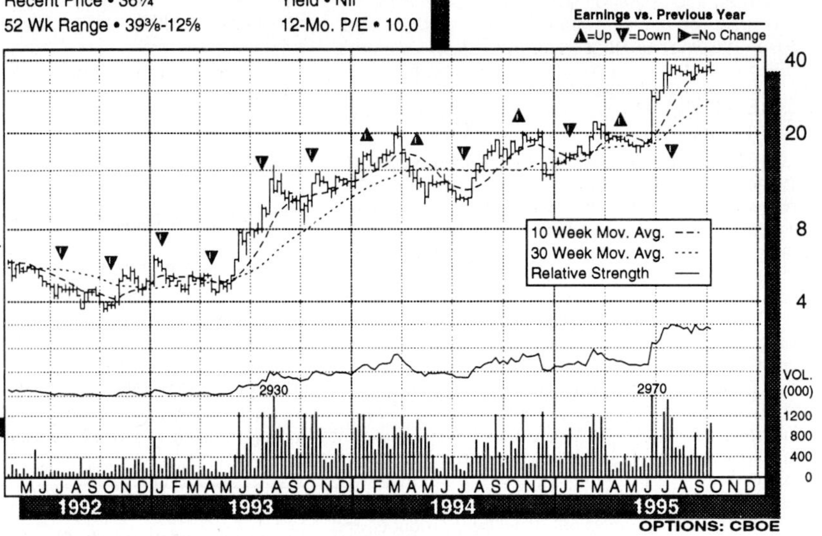

Business Profile - 10-OCT-95

This provider of products and services in internetworking, data analysis, and collaborative and acoustic systems has been making substantial investments in its BBN Planet Internet services subsidiary. In the fiscal 1995 third quarter, BBN Planet expanded its managed Internet access and value-added service businesses from regional to nationwide. In June 1995, AT&T agreed to sell BBN's Internet-access services to businesses, guaranteeing BBN a minimum of $120 million over the next three years.

Operational Review - 10-OCT-95

Revenues for the fiscal year ended June 30, 1995 (preliminary), rose 9.7%, year to year. The loss from operations increased to $18.8 million, from $8.4 million, reflecting increased spending on sales, marketing and new product development (particularly internetworking capabilities, software, and collaborative technologies for business users). However, a $105 million gain on the January 1995 LightStream sale led to net income of $64.8 million, in contrast to a net loss of $7.8 million.

Stock Performance - 06-OCT-95

In the past 30 trading days, BBN's shares have increased 2%, compared to a 4% rise in the S&P 500. Average trading volume for the past five days was 208,660 shares, compared with the 40-day moving average of 128,449 shares.

Key Stock Statistics

Dividend Rate/Share	Nil	Shareholders	2,700
Shs. outstg. (M)	17.3	Market cap. (B)	$0.592
Avg. daily vol. (M)	0.138	Inst. holdings	53%
Tang. Bk. Value/Share	0.44	Insider holdings	NA
Beta	1.68		

Value of $10,000 invested 5 years ago: $ 53,752

Fiscal Year Ending Jun. 30

	1995	% Change	1994	% Change	1993	% Change
Revenues (Million $)						
1Q	51.74	4%	49.93	-23%	64.50	8%
2Q	51.17	6%	48.41	-19%	59.80	-8%
3Q	51.96	7%	48.53	-11%	54.80	-13%
4Q	60.16	22%	49.24	-9%	54.37	-23%
Yr.	215.0	10%	196.1	-16%	233.4	-10%
Income (Million $)						
1Q	-1.81	NM	-1.95	NM	0.13	-89%
2Q	-1.93	NM	-1.67	NM	-25.14	NM
3Q	74.47	NM	-2.26	NM	-6.64	NM
4Q	-5.89	NM	-1.95	NM	-0.62	NM
Yr.	64.84	NM	-7.82	NM	-32.26	NM
Earnings Per Share ($)						
1Q	-0.11	NM	-0.12	NM	0.01	-83%
2Q	-0.11	NM	-0.10	NM	-1.61	NM
3Q	4.11	NM	-0.14	NM	-0.42	NM
4Q	-0.34	NM	-0.12	NM	-0.04	NM
Yr.	3.61	NM	-0.48	NM	-2.05	NM

Next earnings report expected: late October

Bolt Beranek and Newman

Business Summary - 10-OCT-95

Bolt Beranek and Newman provides products and services in the internetworking, data analysis, and collaborative and acoustic systems areas. The company has five business units, including one operating division and four operating subsidiaries. Sales and profits (in millions) were derived as follows in fiscal 1994:

	Sales	Profits
Internetworking	39%	-$11.3
Data analysis software	18%	0.3
Collaborative systems & acoustic technologies	43%	3.5

The U.S. government accounted for about 67% of sales in fiscal 1994.

BBN Systems and Technologies (BBNST), an operating division, provides a range of advanced systems and technologies to government and commercial organizations, and conducts virtually all of BBN's government contract activities. BBNST's activities include network services, defense communications and network systems.

BBN Software Products, a wholly owned subsidiary, develops and markets data analysis and visualization software products, designed primarily for manufacturing, engineering and health industry applications.

BBN Planet (a majority owned subsidiary; formerly BBN Internet Services) provides Internet services on a worldwide basis. Services include around-the-clock network operations, comprehensive problem tracking and resolution, network security, electronic publishing, and on-site field support.

HARK Systems Corp. develops, markets and supports a continuous speech recognition software product.

In January 1995, BBN sold the assets of Lightstream Corp. to Cisco Systems at a gain of $105 million.

Important Developments

Sep. '95—AT&T said its AT&T WorldNet Managed Internet Service is now available. This service, which is being offered in conjunction with BBN's BBN Planet subsidiary, allows businesses to access, operate, and maintain leased-line connections to the Internet. AT&T's first three customers for the new service are Promus Hotel Corp., Associated Group Inc., and McCann-Erickson Worldwide. In July 1995, AT&T acquired an $8 million equity position in BBN Planet. In June 1995, AT&T had agreed to sell BBN's Internet-access services to businesses, guaranteeing BBN a minimum of $120 million of additional revenues over the next three years.

Aug. '95—BBN said Eli Lilly & Co. will use BBN's clinical research software to help implement speed-to-market initiatives for new medicines.

Capitalization

Long Term Debt: $73,510,000 (6/95) of 6% debs. due 2012, conv. into 2,823,000 com.

Options: To purchase 2,450,000 shs. at $4.63 to $15.25 ea. (6/94).

Per Share Data ($) (Year Ended Jun. 30)

	1995	1994	1993	1992	1991	1990
Tangible Bk. Val.	NA	0.44	0.63	2.66	2.53	2.33
Cash Flow	NA	0.08	-1.31	1.13	1.42	-0.70
Earnings	3.61	-0.48	-2.05	0.24	0.49	-1.91
Dividends	Nil	Nil	0.03	0.06	0.06	0.06
Payout Ratio	Nil	Nil	NM	23%	12%	NM
Prices - High	39⅜	21½	14¾	6¾	9⅜	7⅝
- Low	14⅝	10	3⅝	3⅝	4⅜	3⅞
P/E Ratio - High	11	NM	NM	28	19	NM
- Low	4	NM	NM	15	9	NM

Income Statement Analysis (Million $)

	1994	%Chg	1993	%Chg	1992	%Chg	1991
Revs.	196	-16%	233	-10%	258	-5%	271
Oper. Inc.	0.7	NM	-0.2	NM	21.3	-4%	22.1
Depr.	9.1	-22%	11.7	-19%	14.4	-15%	17.0
Int. Exp.	4.6	2%	4.5	-7%	4.8	-16%	5.8
Pretax Inc.	-9.9	NM	-32.3	NM	4.2	-54%	9.2
Eff. Tax Rate	NM	—	NM	—	Nil	—	1.60%
Net Inc.	-7.8	NM	-32.3	NM	4.2	-54%	9.1

Balance Sheet & Other Fin. Data (Million $)

	1994	1993	1992	1991	1990	1989
Cash	67.1	56.8	45.8	66.9	61.8	56.5
Curr. Assets	113	115	125	142	137	160
Total Assets	136	141	163	183	186	231
Curr. Liab.	53.0	56.8	46.8	53.7	56.0	65.6
LT Debt	73.5	73.8	73.7	84.1	86.5	85.9
Common Eqty.	7.3	10.0	42.0	44.0	43.0	78.0
Total Cap.	83.0	84.0	116	129	130	166
Cap. Exp.	6.9	7.9	11.7	10.8	11.2	27.7
Cash Flow	1.3	-20.6	18.6	26.0	-12.8	-6.7

Ratio Analysis

	1994	1993	1992	1991	1990	1989
Curr. Ratio	2.1	2.0	2.7	2.7	2.4	2.4
% LT Debt of Cap.	88.6	88.0	63.6	65.3	66.5	51.9
% Net Inc.of Revs.	NM	NM	1.6	3.3	NM	NM
% Ret. on Assets	NM	NM	2.5	5.0	NM	NM
% Ret. on Equity	NM	NM	10.1	21.2	NM	NM

Dividend Data —Dividends had been paid since 1974 prior to omission in December 1992. A "poison pill" stock purchase rights plan was adopted in 1988.

Data as orig. reptd.; bef. results of disc. opers. and/or spec. items. Per share data adj. for stk. divs. as of ex-div. date. E-Estimated. NA-Not Available. NM-Not Meaningful. NR-Not Ranked.

Office—150 CambridgePark Drive, Cambridge, MA 02140. **Tel**—(617) 873-2000. **Pres & CEO**—G. H. Conrades, **SVP & CFO**—R. A. Goldwasser. **Dirs**—J. M. Albertine, G. H. Conrades, L. J. Fjeldstad, G. N. Hatsopoulos, S. R. Levy, R. McKenna, A. L. Nichols, R. D. Wellington. **Transfer Agent & Registrar**—First National Bank of Boston. **Incorporated** in Massachusetts in 1953. **Empl**-1,700. **S&P Analyst:** N.J. DeVita

STANDARD & POOR'S

STOCK REPORTS

Bombay Co.

NYSE Symbol **BBA**
In S&P SmallCap 600

25-SEP-95

Industry:
Retail Stores

Summary: This specialty retailer markets traditionally styled furniture, prints and accessories through a chain of more than 430 Bombay Company stores in the U.S. and Canada.

Quantitative Evaluations

Outlook
(1 Lowest—5 Highest)
• **5**
Fair Value
• **10¾**
Risk
• **High**
Earn./Div. Rank
• **B-**

Technical Eval.
• **Bullish** since 9/95
Rel. Strength Rank
(1 Lowest—99 Highest)
• **25**
Insider Activity
• **Neutral**

Recent Price • 8¼
52 Wk Range • 13¼-7⅛
Yield • Nil
12-Mo. P/E • NM

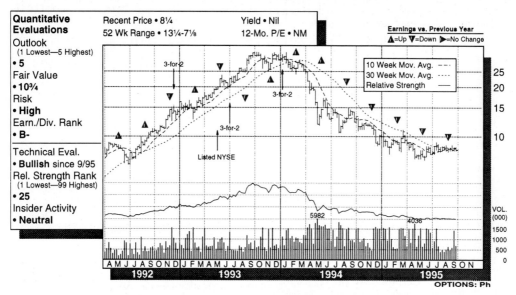

Earnings vs. Previous Year
▲=Up ▼=Down ▶=No Change

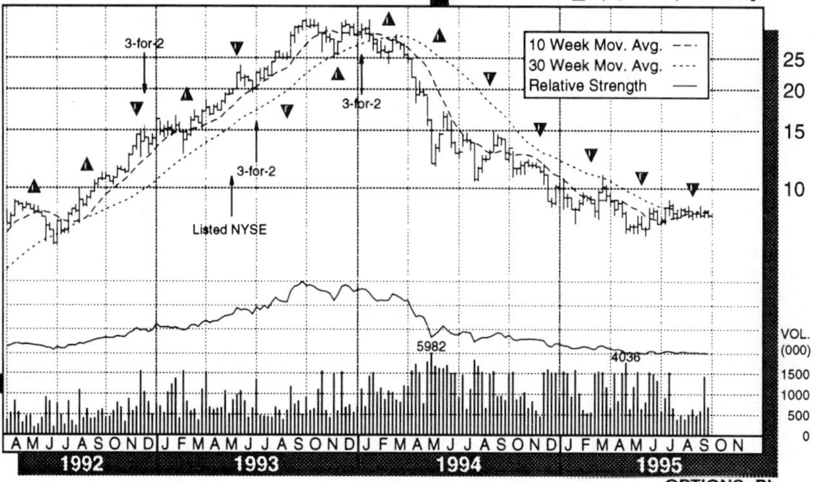

OPTIONS: Ph

Business Profile - 22-SEP-95

This company sells ready-to-assemble furniture, prints and accessories through 432 Bombay stores in the U.S. and Canada, offering traditionally styled products. The company plans to convert almost all Bombay units into much larger format stores. In May 1995, Bombay closed its 58-store Alex & Ivy home furnishing chain. BBA's immediate focus is on marketing and to deliver a constantly changing assortment of attractively priced, fashionable home furnishings.

Operational Review - 22-SEP-95

Net sales for the six months ended July 29, 1995, advanced 3.2%, year to year. Same-store sales for Bombay Company stores decreased 7% and included 38 stores that were converted to a large store format (over 12 months). Margins narrowed on the lower volume and a more promotional sales environment. Despite a $6.0 million credit for the adjustment of a store closing reserve for the Alex & Ivy chain, net earnings dropped 55%, to $0.06 per share (based on 1.5% fewer shares), from $0.12.

Stock Performance - 22-SEP-95

In the past 30 trading days, BBA's shares have declined 3%, compared to a 5% rise in the S&P 500. Average trading volume for the past five days was 134,180 shares, compared with the 40-day moving average of 130,538 shares.

Key Stock Statistics

Dividend Rate/Share	Nil	Shareholders	4,000
Shs. outstg. (M)	37.1	Market cap. (B)	$0.306
Avg. daily vol. (M)	0.159	Inst. holdings	42%
Tang. Bk. Value/Share	3.76	Insider holdings	NA
Beta	1.33		

Value of $10,000 invested 5 years ago: NA

Fiscal Year Ending Jan. 31

	1996	% Change	1995	% Change	1994	% Change
Revenues (Million $)						
1Q	77.94	21%	64.34	31%	49.08	17%
2Q	69.67	-11%	78.20	24%	63.00	-19%
3Q	—	—	77.47	23%	62.85	20%
4Q	—	—	142.9	23%	115.7	93%
Yr.	—	—	362.9	25%	290.7	25%
Income (Million $)						
1Q	1.78	-25%	2.36	NM	-6.54	NM
2Q	0.32	-86%	2.27	-36%	3.55	-48%
3Q	—	—	0.36	-86%	2.60	163%
4Q	—	—	-14.33	NM	14.69	NM
Yr.	—	—	-9.34	NM	14.30	49%
Earnings Per Share ($)						
1Q	0.05	-17%	0.06	NM	-0.18	NM
2Q	0.01	-83%	0.06	-33%	0.09	-69%
3Q	—	—	0.01	-86%	0.07	NM
4Q	—	—	-0.38	NM	0.38	NM
Yr.	—	—	-0.25	NM	0.36	57%

Next earnings report expected: mid October

Bombay Co.

Business Summary - 22-SEP-95

The Bombay Company, Inc. is a leading specialty retailer of home furnishings, prints and accessories. As of late August 1995, it was operating 432 Bombay stores throughout the U.S. and Canada, up from 428 at the end of 1994-5. The Bombay stores offer traditionally styled furnishings; furniture sold is ready-to-assemble. In January 1995, the company announced that it was closing its 58-store Alex & Ivy chain, which offered home decor products influenced by European and American country styles. The geographic breakdown of sales and operating profits (before store conversion costs) in the seven months ended January 28, 1995 (not including store closing costs) was:

	Sales	Profits
U.S.	90%	81%
Canada	10%	19%

Bombay stores sell 18th and 19th century English-style reproduction furniture, prints and accessories, with over 90% of the stores located in upscale malls. The stores formerly had averaged 1,700 sq. ft. in size, but in 1992 the company began to convert the stores to a larger format of about 4,000 sq. ft. In February 1993, the company said it would convert nearly all existing stores to a larger format over a five-year period. As of January 28, 1995, a total of 198 larger-format stores were in operation, with 230 remaining in the regular format. The sales mix for the seven months ended January 28, 1995, consisted of: 45% furniture, 22% wood and metal accessories, 16% wall decor (principally prints, mirrors and sconces) and 17% lamps, decorative accessories and other categories.

Merchandise is manufactured to company specifications through a network of manufacturers located principally in Asia, the U.S., Canada, Mexico and South America. About 65% of production needs are provided from overseas sources.

Important Developments

Aug. '95—Total sales for the four weeks ended August 26, 1995, advanced 5.2%, year to year. Same-store sales rose 1%. For the 30 weeks ended August 26, total sales edged up 0.3%, despite a 6% decline in same-store sales.

Aug. '95—Bombay noted that the closing of all Alex & Ivy stores was completed in early May and that final costs were less than expected. Accordingly, BBA recorded a credit of approximately $6.0 million during the first half of 1995-6 to reflect the adjustment.

Capitalization

Long Term Debt: None (7/95).

Per Share Data ($)

(Year Ended Jan. 31)

	1995	1994	1993	1992	1991	1990
Tangible Bk. Val.	3.66	4.02	3.21	1.81	1.48	1.69
Cash Flow	-0.21	0.83	0.42	0.46	0.35	0.33
Earnings	-0.39	0.60	0.23	0.29	0.18	0.21
Dividends	Nil	Nil	Nil	Nil	Nil	Nil
Payout Ratio	Nil	Nil	Nil	Nil	Nil	Nil
Cal. Yrs.	1994	1993	1992	1991	1990	1989
Prices - High	32¾	32⅞	16¼	5¼	5½	5½
- Low	8¾	12⅝	4½	1$^{15}/_{16}$	1⅞	2$^{3}/_{16}$
P/E Ratio - High	55	NM	56	29	27	22
- Low	15	NM	15	10	9	9

Income Statement Analysis (Million $)

	1995	%Chg	1994	%Chg	1993	%Chg	1992
Revs.	241	-24%	317	37%	232	32%	176
Oper. Inc.	23.7	-48%	45.7	40%	32.7	52%	21.5
Depr.	6.8	-24%	8.9	33%	6.7	19%	5.7
Int. Exp.	0.4	NM	0.1	-53%	0.2	-64%	0.5
Pretax Inc.	-24.3	NM	37.6	181%	13.4	-15%	15.7
Eff. Tax Rate	NM	—	39%	—	39%	—	39%
Net Inc.	-14.7	NM	22.9	179%	8.2	-15%	9.6

Balance Sheet & Other Fin. Data (Million $)

	1995	1994	1993	1992	1991	1990
Cash	30.7	20.4	42.8	10.1	1.0	3.3
Curr. Assets	128	119	111	45.0	34.2	27.7
Total Assets	190	181	143	79.2	66.2	69.2
Curr. Liab.	50.1	29.3	24.1	17.4	14.5	11.8
LT Debt	Nil	Nil	Nil	Nil	2.5	2.5
Common Eqty.	135	147	116	59.1	47.3	53.6
Total Cap.	135	147	116	59.1	49.7	56.1
Cap. Exp.	22.1	35.3	15.0	7.5	8.9	11.6
Cash Flow	-7.9	31.8	14.9	15.3	11.0	9.5

Ratio Analysis

	1995	1994	1993	1992	1991	1990
Curr. Ratio	2.5	4.1	4.6	2.6	2.4	2.4
% LT Debt of Cap.	Nil	Nil	Nil	Nil	5.0	4.4
% Net Inc.of Revs.	NM	7.2	3.5	5.5	4.2	5.3
% Ret. on Assets	NM	14.0	7.1	13.1	8.6	8.1
% Ret. on Equity	NM	17.3	9.0	17.9	11.6	12.0

Dividend Data —A three-for-two stock was split effected in December 1993, following similar splits in July 1993, December 1992, March 1992 and October 1987. The most recent cash payment was in 1983. Tandy Brands Accessories Inc. was spun off in December 1990.

Data as orig. reptd.; bef. results of disc. opers. and/or spec. items. Per share data adj. for stk. divs. as of ex-div. date. Yrs. ended Jun. 30 prior to 1995. Pro forma data for FY 1995 & FY 1994 (ended Jan.) in Revs., Income & EPS tbls.; data for FY 1995 in Per Share Data & Income Statement Analysis tbls. is for seven mos. ended Jan. E-Estimated. NA-Not Available. NM-Not Meaningful. NR-Not Ranked.

Office—550 Bailey Ave., Suite 700, Fort Worth, TX 76107. **Tel**—(817) 347-8200. **Chrmn**—C. R. Thompson. **Pres & CEO**—R. E. M. Nourse. **Exec VP & CFO**—J. E. Herlihy. **VP & Secy**—M. J. Veitenheimer. **Treas**—G. W. Wehlitz Jr. **Dirs**—B. Bass, E. H. Damon, R. S. Jackson, A. R. Megarry, C. E. Niles, R. E. M. Nourse, R. E. Runice, C. R. Thompson, S. Young. **Transfer Agent & Registrar**—First National Bank of Boston. **Incorporated** in Delaware in 1975. **Empl**-5,000. **S&P Analyst:** Maureen C. Carini

STANDARD & POOR'S

STOCK REPORTS

Boomtown, Inc.

NASDAQ Symbol **BMTN**

In S&P SmallCap 600

23-SEP-95

Industry: Leisure/Amusement

Summary: This company operates western-themed casinos in Nevada, Mississippi and Louisiana.

S&P Opinion: Hold (★★★)

Recent Price • 10¼
52 Wk Range • 17¾-9

Yield • Nil
12-Mo. P/E • NM

Quantitative Evaluations

Outlook
(1 Lowest—5 Highest)
• NA

Fair Value
• NA

Risk
• High

Earn./Div. Rank
• NR

Technical Eval.
• Bearish since 8/95

Rel. Strength Rank
(1 Lowest—99 Highest)
• 13

Insider Activity
• NA

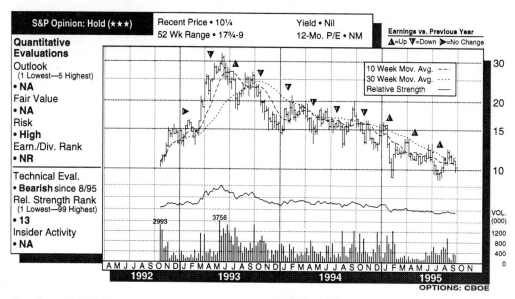

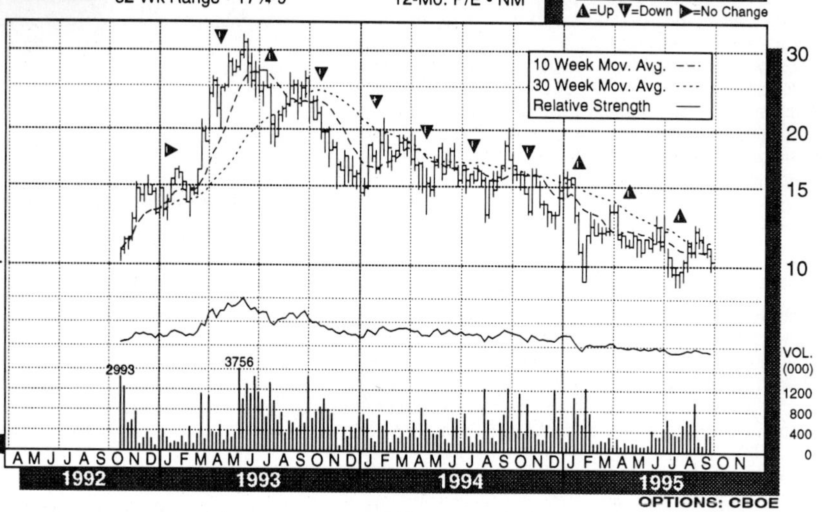

Overview - 21-SEP-95

We expect that BMTN's fiscal 1995 profit will be helped by the presence of a casino boat in Louisiana. Also, thus far in fiscal 1995, one-time charges have reduced BMTN's overall earnings by about $0.40 a share, but this is less than the full-year impact of pre-opening charges in fiscal 1994, when three new BMTN gaming projects opened. From Reno, we expect BMTN's fiscal 1995 profit to decline, including an adverse impact from weather in the first half of the year. We look for no more than modest earnings from Biloxi, Miss., and a loss from Las Vegas. BMTN's future earnings would be helped if some high-cost operating leases could be retired. Also, profits could benefit from the addition of hotel rooms at several properties. However, BMTN's financial flexibility has been limited by conditions related to a 1993 issuance of 11.5% first mortgage notes.

Valuation - 21-SEP-95

After disappointing operating results, and a failure to win approval for additional projects in new gaming markets, we have lowered our opinion on the stock to "hold." However, we look for the prospect of earnings improvement in fiscal 1996 to provide some support for the stock. Also, BMTN may have opportunities to become part of joint ventures in which its Western theme is applied to additional gaming facilities. A new CFO at the company could boost BMTN's visibility with both investors and other gaming companies. The stock has some appeal as a speculative holding.

Key Stock Statistics

S&P EPS Est. 1995	0.13	Tang. Bk. Value/Share	10.85
P/E on S&P Est. 1995	78.8	Beta	1.33
S&P EPS Est. 1996	0.70	Shareholders	400
Dividend Rate/Share	Nil	Market cap. (B)	$0.095
Shs. outstg. (M)	9.2	Inst. holdings	36%
Avg. daily vol. (M)	0.058	Insider holdings	NA

Value of $10,000 invested 5 years ago: NA

Fiscal Year Ending Sep. 30

	1995	% Change	1994	% Change	1993	% Change
Revenues (Million $)						
1Q	54.16	NM	14.79	17%	12.60	3%
2Q	55.59	NM	13.46	26%	10.70	-6%
3Q	59.95	164%	22.68	45%	15.60	3%
4Q	—	—	52.44	166%	19.74	17%
Yr.	—	—	103.4	76%	58.65	5%
Income (Million $)						
1Q	0.24	100%	0.12	-76%	0.51	—
2Q	0.40	NM	-0.38	NM	0.05	—
3Q	-1.85	NM	-2.36	NM	1.55	—
4Q	—	—	-4.21	NM	2.84	—
Yr.	—	—	-7.82	NM	4.95	101%
Earnings Per Share ($)						
1Q	0.03	NM	-0.01	NM	0.06	NM
2Q	0.04	NM	-0.04	NM	0.01	-86%
3Q	-0.20	NM	-0.25	NM	0.21	NM
4Q	E0.26	NM	-0.46	NM	0.35	-29%
Yr.	E0.13	NM	-0.90	NM	0.65	7%

Next earnings report expected: late November

Boomtown, Inc.

Business Summary - 21-SEP-95

Boomtown, Inc. operates four western-themed casinos in the Reno (Nev.) and Las Vegas areas; in Biloxi, Miss.; and in Harvey, La., near New Orleans. In total, the four BMTN properties have about 422 hotel rooms, 130,000 sq. ft. of casino space, 4,380 slot machines, and 156 table games. Three of BMTN's casinos have opened since May 1994.

In the Reno area, BMTN's facility is located seven miles west of the city, on I-80, which connects Reno with Northern California population centers. Boomtown Reno, which resembles an old west town, includes a 40,000 sq. ft. casino, a 122-room hotel, a 35,000 sq. ft. family entertainment center, an indoor 18 hole western-themed miniature golf course, a 16-acre truck stop with about 200 parking spaces, a 203-space, and a full-service recreational vehicle park.

Boomtown Las Vegas opened in May 1994, and is located on I-15, which links Southern California with Las Vegas. The casino resort features an old west mining theme, and 30,000 sq. ft. of casino space. Also, there are 300 hotel rooms, a 460-space recreational vehicle resort, and restaurants.

In July 1994, Boomtown Biloxi opened on Mississippi's Gulf Coast. The facility includes about 30,000 sq. ft. of gaming space. The casino is built on a floating, 400-foot barge extending into the Back Bay, and the project also includes a land-based building. Other features include restaurants and a 20,000 sq. ft. family entertainment center, which has a dynamic motion theater.

In August 1994, Boomtown New Orleans opened in Harvey, La., just outside New Orleans. The 30,000 sq. ft. casino is located on a replica of a paddlewheel riverboat. Also, a large land-based building includes a restaurant and a family entertainment center.

Important Developments

Aug. '95—BMTN's fiscal 1995 third quarter results included about $5.7 million (pretax) of unusual or one-time charges. This largely related to unsuccessful efforts to win approval for new casino projects, and a terminated merger and financing proposal which involved BMTN, National Gaming Corp., and Hospitality Franchise Systems. In particular, BMTN's development efforts included losing a competition to be chosen for a new gaming project in Lawrenceburg, Ind., which is close to Cincinnati, Ohio. If the $5.7 million of one-time charges are excluded from BMTN's third quarter, the company's after-tax earnings would have been about $0.16 a share. Also, BMTN was looking to finalize plans for expanding existing facilities, and said that it would continue to explore joint ventures and other quality opportunities.

Capitalization

Long Term Debt: $107,185,000 (6/95).
Warrants: To buy 472,500 shs.

Per Share Data ($) (Year Ended Sep. 30)

	1994	1993	1992	1991	1990	1989
Tangible Bk. Val.	10.95	11.01	3.94	2.35	NA	NA
Cash Flow	-0.26	1.10	1.51	1.66	NA	NA
Earnings	-0.90	0.65	0.61	0.71	NA	NA
Dividends	Nil	Nil	Nil	Nil	NA	NA
Payout Ratio	Nil	Nil	Nil	Nil	NA	NA
Prices - High	21¼	32½	15¾	NA	NA	NA
- Low	12⅛	12½	10	NA	NA	NA
P/E Ratio - High	NM	50	26	NA	NA	NA
- Low	NM	19	16	NA	NA	NA

Income Statement Analysis (Million $)

	1994	%Chg	1993	%Chg	1992	%Chg	1991
Revs.	102	78%	57.4	5%	54.9	5%	52.1
Oper. Inc.	-1.8	NM	10.7	-15%	12.6	5%	12.0
Depr.	5.6	67%	3.3	NM	3.3	-5%	3.5
Int. Exp.	11.5	NM	1.0	-69%	3.4	-21%	4.2
Pretax Inc.	-11.0	NM	8.0	93%	4.1	-16%	4.9
Eff. Tax Rate	NM	—	38%	—	40%	—	42%
Net Inc.	-7.8	NM	4.9	101%	2.5	-13%	2.8

Balance Sheet & Other Fin. Data (Million $)

	1994	1993	1992	1991	1990	1989
Cash	11.4	17.6	5.0	5.7	NA	NA
Curr. Assets	23.5	20.6	7.4	7.5	NA	NA
Total Assets	238	109	55.9	52.6	NA	NA
Curr. Liab.	25.3	4.3	5.7	9.3	NA	NA
LT Debt	105	Nil	32.0	29.1	NA	NA
Common Eqty.	108	101	13.3	7.9	NA	NA
Total Cap.	213	104	50.2	43.0	NA	NA
Cap. Exp.	121	23.8	6.5	2.2	NA	NA
Cash Flow	-2.2	8.3	5.6	6.2	NA	NA

Ratio Analysis

	1994	1993	1992	1991	1990	1989
Curr. Ratio	0.9	4.8	1.3	0.8	NA	NA
% LT Debt of Cap.	49.3	Nil	63.7	67.7	NA	NA
% Net Inc.of Revs.	NM	8.6	4.5	5.4	NA	NA
% Ret. on Assets	NM	4.0	4.5	5.3	NA	NA
% Ret. on Equity	NM	7.3	21.3	39.9	NA	NA

Dividend Data —No cash dividends have been paid on the common stock, and the company intends to retain earnings for the development of its business.

Data as orig. reptd.; bef. results of disc. opers. and/or spec. items. Per share data adj. for stk. divs. as of ex-div. date. E-Estimated. NA-Not Available. NM-Not Meaningful. NR-Not Ranked.

Office—P.O. Box 399, Verdi, NV 89439-0399. **Tel**—(702) 345-8680. **Chrmn & CEO**—T. J. Parrott. **Pres & COO**—R. N. Scott. **SVP, CFO & Investor Contact**—G. Thomas Baker. **Dirs**—R. J. Goeglein, P. Harris, R. F. List, T. J. Parrott, E. P. Roski, Jr., R. N. Scott. **Transfer Agent & Registrar**—First Interstate Bank of California, SF. **Incorporated** in Delaware in 1987. **Empl-** 3,880. **S&P Analyst:** Tom Graves, CFA

STANDARD & POOR'S

STOCK REPORTS

Bowne & Co.

ASE Symbol **BNE**
In S&P SmallCap 600

30-AUG-95 **Industry:** Graphic Arts

Summary: This company specializes in financial documentation and communications services for corporate compliance and public financing worldwide.

Quantitative Evaluations

Outlook (1 Lowest—5 Highest)
• **NA**

Fair Value
• **NA**

Risk
• **Average**

Earn./Div. Rank
• **B+**

Technical Eval.
• **Bearish** since 5/95

Rel. Strength Rank (1 Lowest—99 Highest)
• **42**

Insider Activity
• **NA**

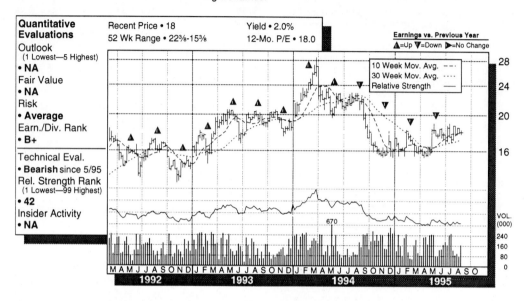

Recent Price • 18
52 Wk Range • 22⅜-15⅝
Yield • 2.0%
12-Mo. P/E • 18.0

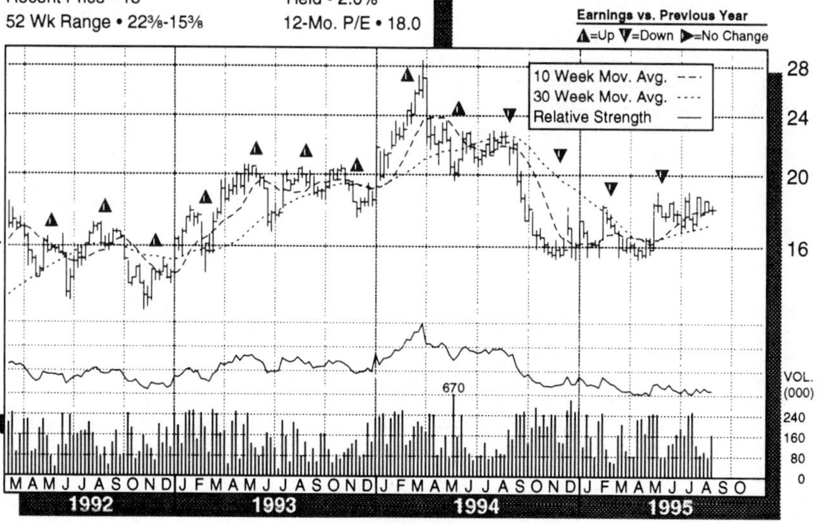

Business Profile - 30-AUG-95

Revenues and earnings are being hurt by a cyclical slowdown in higher-margined transactional-related financial market business. BNE's longer-term success should depend, in part, on continuing to adapt to an environment in which documents are increasingly made available in electronic formats. Meanwhile, the stock, which is selling far below its 1994 high, may be helped if interest rates move lower, since this would encourage refinancings-- and financial printing-- by customers.

Operational Review - 30-AUG-95

Net sales for the six months ended April 30, 1995, fell 11%, year to year, relecting lower levels of public financing activity. However, BNE's nontransactional revenue sources continued to grow, and if this trend continues, it should help to make BNE's overall business less cyclical. BNE's net income for fiscal 1995's first six months was down 64%, and per-share earnings fell to $0.44, from $1.24.

Stock Performance - 25-AUG-95

In the past 30 trading days, BNE's shares have increased 3%, compared to a 0.04% rise in the S&P 500. Average trading volume for the past five days was 32,740 shares, compared with the 40-day moving average of 34,690 shares.

Key Stock Statistics

Dividend Rate/Share	0.36	Shareholders	1,500
Shs. outstg. (M)	17.4	Market cap. (B)	$0.311
Avg. daily vol. (M)	0.024	Inst. holdings	51%
Tang. Bk. Value/Share	11.23	Insider holdings	NA
Beta	2.11		

Value of $10,000 invested 5 years ago: $ 17,749

Fiscal Year Ending Oct. 31

	1995	% Change	1994	% Change	1993	% Change
Revenues (Million $)						
1Q	76.81	-6%	82.08	35%	61.00	10%
2Q	102.5	-14%	119.2	33%	89.60	6%
3Q	—	—	95.59	16%	82.48	9%
4Q	—	—	83.80	-16%	100.1	50%
Yr.	—	—	380.6	14%	333.3	18%
Income (Million $)						
1Q	2.03	-70%	6.66	72%	3.87	12%
2Q	5.71	-62%	14.87	28%	11.60	12%
3Q	—	—	6.02	-17%	7.29	12%
4Q	—	—	3.69	-71%	12.56	58%
Yr.	—	—	31.24	-12%	35.32	25%
Earnings Per Share ($)						
1Q	0.12	-68%	0.38	65%	0.23	15%
2Q	0.33	-62%	0.86	28%	0.67	10%
3Q	—	—	0.35	-17%	0.42	11%
4Q	—	—	0.21	-71%	0.73	59%
Yr.	—	—	1.80	-12%	2.05	24%

Next earnings report expected: early September

Bowne & Co.

Business Summary - 30-AUG-95

Bowne & Co., founded in 1775, is the world's largest financial printer. Revenues in recent fiscal years were derived as follows:

	1994	1993
Financial & corporate printing	82%	87%
Commercial & legal printing	18%	13%

Financial printing includes registration statements, prospectuses, loan agreements and similar documents. Financial activities requiring disclosure-type printing include mergers, tender offers, acquisitions, money market and bond funds, unit investment trusts, and public debt financings. Through its 43 facilities around the world, Bowne serves the financial and legal communities by meeting their global document-building and communications needs. Utilizing state-of-the-art computer and telecommunications technology, Bowne is able to distribute documents anywhere in the world. By emphasising personalized service, confidentiality, accuracy, and fast turnaround, Bowne has been successful in gaining market share.

Corporate printing encompasses the production of annual and interim reports to shareholders, annual proxy statements and applications for listing on stock exchanges. This type of work is seasonal, with the greatest number of proxy statements and annual reports printed during the company's second fiscal quarter. During the second quarter of 1993, the SEC began to require that filings by public companies be made electronically on the new EDGAR. Bowne, which helped to develop the system over a 10-year period, expects to generate new revenues from services related to EDGAR.

Bowne of Canada, the largest financial printer in Canada, with plants in Toronto and Montreal, accounted for 15% of total corporate sales and 10% of net income in fiscal 1994. The company also conducts overseas operations at locations in Europe, Latin America and the Pacific Rim.

Important Developments

Jun. '95—Bowne said that indicators of increased activity in the capital markets included the strength of stock prices, interest rates moving lower, and higher levels of merger-and-acquisition and initial public offering activity. BNE said that its offices were busier than they had been in some time. Also, BNE said that it has developed software programs to convert traditional compliance documents, such as prospectuses and shareholder reports, into electronic formats.

Capitalization

Long Term Debt: $3,031,000 (4/95).

Per Share Data ($)

(Year Ended Oct. 31)

	1994	1993	1992	1991	1990	1989
Tangible Bk. Val.	12.82	11.37	9.71	8.46	7.80	6.58
Cash Flow	2.67	2.71	2.29	1.48	1.12	1.04
Earnings	1.80	2.05	1.65	0.84	0.49	0.46
Dividends	0.32	0.30	0.26	0.25	0.25	0.25
Payout Ratio	18%	12%	16%	30%	51%	53%
Prices - High	28½	21¾	18⅜	16½	15	14½
- Low	15⅜	14¾	13⅛	9⅝	8	10½
P/E Ratio - High	16	11	11	20	31	32
- Low	9	7	8	11	16	23

Income Statement Analysis (Million $)

	1994	%Chg	1993	%Chg	1992	%Chg	1991
Revs.	381	14%	333	18%	282	19%	236
Oper. Inc.	65.3	-5%	68.4	20%	57.0	60%	35.7
Depr.	15.2	33%	11.4	5%	10.9	NM	10.8
Int. Exp.	1.1	-52%	2.3	-19%	2.9	-19%	3.5
Pretax Inc.	54.2	-8%	59.0	26%	47.0	87%	25.1
Eff. Tax Rate	42%	—	40%	—	40%	—	43%
Net Inc.	31.2	-12%	35.3	25%	28.3	98%	14.3

Balance Sheet & Other Fin. Data (Million $)

	1994	1993	1992	1991	1990	1989
Cash	38.5	33.1	55.7	30.8	29.7	37.8
Curr. Assets	158	153	131	113	93.0	100
Total Assets	292	284	244	226	204	205
Curr. Liab.	51.3	64.7	42.7	38.7	26.6	28.5
LT Debt	3.2	8.8	22.3	30.8	34.2	34.4
Common Eqty.	223	197	167	144	132	131
Total Cap.	226	206	189	175	167	166
Cap. Exp.	27.2	24.5	17.5	9.3	13.8	12.0
Cash Flow	46.4	46.7	39.2	25.1	19.2	18.3

Ratio Analysis

	1994	1993	1992	1991	1990	1989
Curr. Ratio	3.1	2.4	3.1	2.9	3.5	3.5
% LT Debt of Cap.	1.4	4.3	11.8	17.6	20.6	20.7
% Net Inc.of Revs.	8.2	10.6	10.0	6.1	4.2	4.3
% Ret. on Assets	10.8	13.3	12.0	6.6	4.1	4.0
% Ret. on Equity	14.9	19.4	18.1	10.3	6.4	6.2

Dividend Data —Cash has been paid each year since 1941.

Amt. of Div. $	Date Decl.	Ex-Div. Date	Stock of Record	Payment Date
0.090	Aug. 24	Sep. 02	Sep. 09	Sep. 21 '94
0.090	Nov. 23	Dec. 23	Dec. 30	Jan. 11 '95
0.090	Mar. 01	Mar. 13	Mar. 17	Mar. 29 '95
0.090	May. 31	Jun. 14	Jun. 16	Jun. 28 '95

Data as orig. reptd.; bef. results of disc. opers. and/or spec. items. Per share data adj. for stk. divs. as of ex-div. date. E-Estimated. NA-Not Available. NM-Not Meaningful. NR-Not Ranked.

Office—345 Hudson St., New York, NY 10014. **Tel**—(212) 924-5500. **Chrmn, Pres & CEO**—R. H. Koontz. **VP-Fin & CFO**—J. P. O'Neil. **VP, Secy & Shareholder Contact**—D. F. Bauer. **Dirs**—R. M. Conway, R. H. Koontz, E. H. Meyer, H. M. Schwarz, W. M. Smith, T. O. Stanley, B. B. Wadsworth, R. R. West. **Transfer Agent & Registrar**—Bank of New York, NYC. **Incorporated** in New York in 1968. **Empl**-2,700. **S&P Analyst:** Tom Graves, CFA

STANDARD & POOR'S

Box Energy Corp.

STOCK REPORTS

NASDAQ Symbol **BOXXB**

In S&P SmallCap 600

25-SEP-95 **Industry:** Oil and Gas

Summary: This independent energy company explores for, develops and produces oil and natural gas. It has interests offshore the Gulf of Mexico and in Texas and Louisiana.

Quantitative Evaluations

Outlook (1 Lowest—5 Highest)
• **NA**

Fair Value
• **NA**

Risk
• **Average**

Earn./Div. Rank
• **NR**

Technical Eval.
• **Bullish** since 7/95

Rel. Strength Rank (1 Lowest—99 Highest)
• **33**

Insider Activity
• **NA**

Recent Price • 10 | Yield • Nil
52 Wk Range • 11¼-7⅝ | 12-Mo. P/E • 38.5

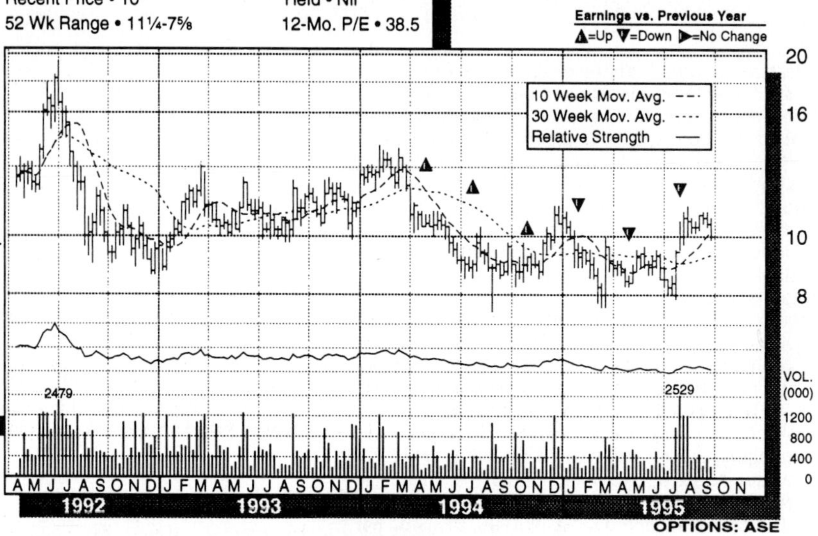

Business Profile - 25-SEP-95

This independent energy company owns interests in oil and gas properties in the South Pass area of the Gulf of Mexico and other drilling prospects in Texas and Louisiana. Revenues and earnings rebounded in 1994, aided by increased natural gas production and favorable long-term natural gas contracts. Although Box Brothers Holding Co., which owns 57% of the voting Class A shares, filed for bankruptcy protection in August 1994, the company does not expect this to affect day-to-day operations.

Operational Review - 25-SEP-95

Revenues for the six months ended June 30, 1995%, declined 11%, year to year, reflecting decreases in oil and natural gas production and a drop in the price of natural gas, which were partially offset by increased prices for oil. Margins narrowed, as exploration expenses soared and because of reorganization costs undertaken as part of long-term planning efforts. After taxes at 27.5%, versus 35.2%, net income fell 71%, to $1,577,000 ($0.08 a share), from $5,415,000 ($0.26).

Stock Performance - 22-SEP-95

In the past 30 trading days, BOXXB's shares have declined 6%, compared to a 5% rise in the S&P 500. Average trading volume for the past five days was 42,180 shares, compared with the 40-day moving average of 117,823 shares.

Key Stock Statistics

Dividend Rate/Share	Nil	Shareholders	2,100
Shs. outstg. (M)	20.8	Market cap. (B)	$0.208
Avg. daily vol. (M)	0.069	Inst. holdings	15%
Tang. Bk. Value/Share	3.75	Insider holdings	NA
Beta	0.10		

Value of $10,000 invested 5 years ago: NA

Fiscal Year Ending Dec. 31

	1995	% Change	1994	% Change	1993	% Change
Revenues (Million $)						
1Q	14.51	11%	13.10	52%	8.60	NM
2Q	12.56	-27%	17.30	99%	8.70	144%
3Q	—	—	16.03	64%	9.80	51%
4Q	—	—	12.85	29%	10.00	41%
Yr.	—	—	59.24	60%	37.10	88%
Income (Million $)						
1Q	0.74	-66%	2.15	187%	0.75	NM
2Q	0.84	-74%	3.27	NM	1.02	-85%
3Q	—	—	3.25	NM	-0.44	NM
4Q	—	—	0.49	-42%	0.84	-94%
Yr.	—	—	9.16	NM	2.16	-89%
Earnings Per Share ($)						
1Q	0.04	-60%	0.10	NM	0.03	—
2Q	0.04	-75%	0.16	NM	0.05	—
3Q	—	—	0.16	NM	-0.02	—
4Q	—	—	0.02	-50%	0.04	—
Yr.	—	—	0.44	NM	0.10	-89%

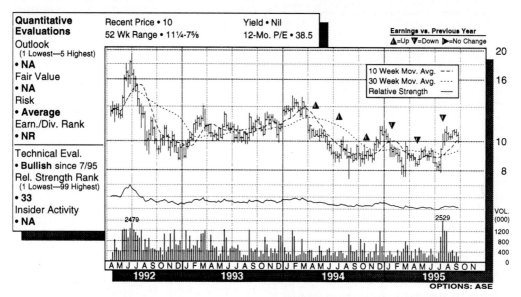

Next earnings report expected: early November

Box Energy Corp.

Business Summary - 25-SEP-95

Box Energy Corporation is an independent energy company engaged in the exploration for and development and production of oil and natural gas. Its most significant interests are in oil and gas leases covering three contiguous offshore blocks in the Gulf of Mexico, known as the South Pass Blocks 86, 87 and 89, and an oil well in West Delta Block 128.

The three South Pass blocks are operated by Marathon Oil Co., an affiliate of USX Corp. The company, Marathon, Amerada Hess Corp. and Louisiana Land & Exploration Co. each own a 25% working interest in South Pass Blocks 86 and 89, while the company, Marathon and Amerada each own 33.3% working interests in South Pass Block 87. In December 1993, Box Energy acquired a 20% working interest in the West Delta well. Marathon, which also serves as the operator, and Amerada own the remaining working interests in West Delta Block 128. Oil and gas acreage in which the company held an interest at 1994 year-end consisted of 10,000 gross (2,500 net) developed acres and 9,196 (3,295) undeveloped acres.

At December 31, 1994, Box Energy had interests in 23 gross (5.75 net) producing oil wells and two (0.50) producing gas wells, with estimated net proved reserves of 3,298,000 bbl. of oil and 50.3 Bcf of natural gas. The aftertax present value of the estimated future net cash flows (discounted at 10%) of proved reserves was $124.5 million.

Production in 1994 amounted to 1,796 bbl. of oil per day and 17.2 MMcf of natural gas per day. The average sales price received in 1994 was $15.51 per bbl. of oil and $7.46 per Mcf of natural gas.

During 1994, the company participated in drilling six gross (2.22 net) exploratory wells, of which one (0.20) was productive and five (2.02) were dry, and two (0.5) development wells, both of which were productive.

Box Energy sells its oil production from South Pass Blocks 86 and 89 to Marathon and its natural gas production from South Pass Block 89 to Texas Eastern, a subsidiary of Panhandle Eastern Corp. Marathon and Texas Eastern accounted for 18% and 63%, respectively, of total oil and gas revenues in 1994.

In addition to acreage in Texas, Louisiana and New Mexico, the company owns about 10,300 non-oil and gas acres in several noncontiguous tracts of land in southern Louisiana and southern Mississippi, several of which are leased to third parties for farming, grazing, sand and gravel, hunting and other purposes.

Important Developments

Sep. '95—Two gas wells were recently brought into production in South Pass Block 89.

Capitalization

Long Term Debt: $55,077,000 (6/95).
Class A Common Stock: 3,250,110 shs. ($1 par).
Class B Common Stock: 17,553,010 shs. ($1 par); nonvoting.

Per Share Data ($)

(Year Ended Dec. 31)

	1994	1993	1992	1991	1990	1989
Tangible Bk. Val.	3.63	3.25	3.15	2.27	2.74	0.67
Cash Flow	0.97	0.59	1.11	0.29	3.31	0.25
Earnings	0.44	0.10	0.92	0.13	3.05	-0.12
Dividends	Nil	Nil	Nil	0.60	1.00	0.40
Payout Ratio	Nil	Nil	Nil	446%	32%	NM
Prices - High	14⅛	13¼	19½	6¾	4⅝	4½
- Low	7½	8¾	5⅞	3¼	1¾	2⅛
P/E Ratio - High	32	NM	21	52	2	NM
- Low	17	NM	6	25	1	NM

Income Statement Analysis (Million $)

	1994	%Chg	1993	%Chg	1992	%Chg	1991
Revs.	57.0	70%	33.5	79%	18.7	-9%	20.6
Oper. Inc.	28.1	91%	14.7	NM	4.3	-35%	6.6
Depr. Depl. & Amort.	11.1	10%	10.1	159%	3.9	22%	3.2
Int. Exp.	5.1	2%	5.0	NM	1.1	NM	0.2
Pretax Inc.	14.2	NM	2.1	NM	-0.5	NM	2.7
Eff. Tax Rate	36%	—	NM	—	NM	—	Nil
Net Inc.	9.2	NM	2.2	-89%	19.2	NM	2.7

Balance Sheet & Other Fin. Data (Million $)

	1994	1993	1992	1991	1990	1989
Cash	40.5	30.6	38.2	1.1	28.3	0.2
Curr. Assets	46.2	36.0	41.5	2.3	34.5	4.8
Total Assets	135	129	129	53.0	64.0	35.0
Curr. Liab.	4.5	4.5	3.9	4.3	5.7	2.9
LT Debt	55.1	56.7	57.0	Nil	Nil	15.4
Common Eqty.	75.5	67.7	65.5	46.3	55.9	13.6
Total Cap.	131	124	123	46.0	56.0	29.0
Cap. Exp.	16.6	18.9	19.1	25.9	9.7	10.6
Cash Flow	20.2	12.3	23.1	5.9	67.5	5.2

Ratio Analysis

	1994	1993	1992	1991	1990	1989
Curr. Ratio	10.4	8.0	10.5	0.5	6.0	1.7
% LT Debt of Cap.	42.2	45.6	46.6	NM	NM	53.1
% Ret. on Assets	6.9	1.7	21.0	4.7	126.5	NM
% Ret. on Equity	12.8	3.2	34.1	5.4	180.9	NM

Dividend Data —No cash dividends have been paid since 1991.

Data as orig. reptd.; bef. results of disc opers. and/or spec. items. Per share data adj. for stk. divs. as of ex-div. date. E-Estimated. NA-Not Available. NM-Not Meaningful. NR-Not Ranked.

Office—8201 Preston Rd., Suite 600, Dallas, TX 75225-6211. **Tel**—(214) 890-8000. **Chrmn**—D. D. Box. **Pres & CEO**—T. D. Box. **VP & CFO**—Jill M. Killam. **Secy**—W. J. Burnett. **Investor Contact**—Patty Dickerson (214) 890-8010. **Dirs**—J. F. Arning, D. D. Box, T. D. Box, K. R. Hance Sr., J. L. Kelsey, A. C. Shapiro, N. W. Smith, E. D. Walker Jr., R. S. Whitesell Jr. **Transfer Agent & Registrar**—American Stock Transfer & Trust Co., NYC. **Incorporated** in Delaware in 1991. **Empl**-54. **S&P Analyst:** Michael C. Barr

STANDARD & POOR'S

STOCK REPORTS

Broderbund Software

NASDAQ Symbol **BROD**

In S&P SmallCap 600

15-NOV-95 **Industry:** Data Processing

Summary: This company develops and markets personal computer software for the home, school and small business markets.

S&P Opinion: Hold (★★★)

Recent Price • 66¾ | 52 Wk Range • 78¾-31¼ | Yield • Nil | 12-Mo. P/E • 38.8

Quantitative Evaluations

Outlook (1 Lowest—5 Highest) **• 5**

Fair Value **• 85½**

Risk **• High**

Earn./Div. Rank **• NR**

Technical Eval. **• Bullish** since 10/95

Rel. Strength Rank (1 Lowest—99 Highest) **• 18**

Insider Activity **• Neutral**

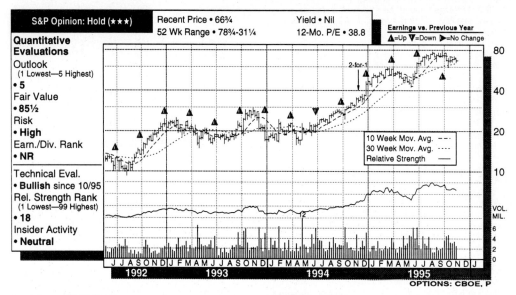

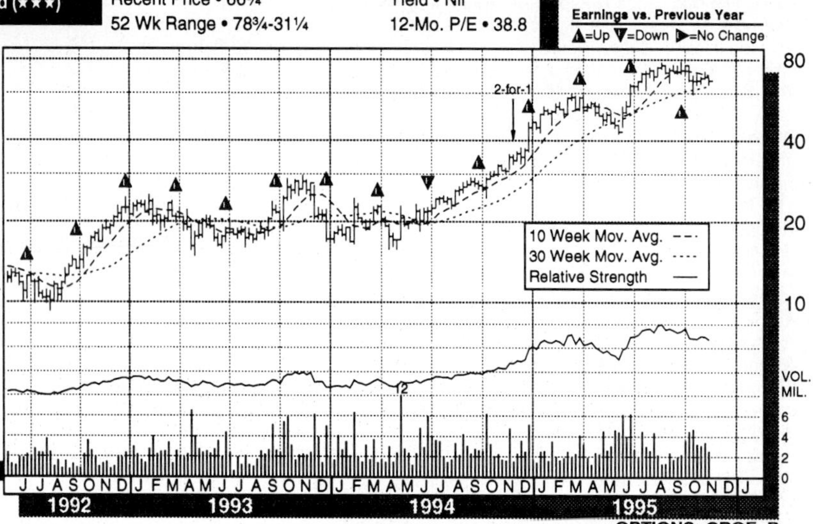

OPTIONS: CBOE, P

Overview - 15-NOV-95

Revenues should advance sharply in fiscal 1996, aided by continued strength in personal productivity, education and entertainment software categories, spurred by further increases in sales of home PCs. The successful acquisition of The Learning Company, as well as smaller software vendors, would further spur revenues. Margins should widen on the higher volume, a more favorable product mix of CD-ROM based programs and well controlled expenses. Earnings are expected to benefit from the higher revenues and wider margins.

Valuation - 15-NOV-95

The shares of this leading vendor of education, entertainment and personal productivity software products have outperformed the market thus far in 1995, aided by strong sales and earnings growth. The consumer software market, in which the company competes, continues to benefit from the growth of PCs in the home. As an established vendor, Broderbund has secured shelf space with retailers, and is growing at least as fast as the market. The stock trades at a premium valuation, which is deserved in light of the sales and earnings growth we project. However, uncertainties related to the pending acquisition of The Learning Company raises risk. We expect the shares to trade in line with the market in the coming months.

Key Stock Statistics

S&P EPS Est. 1996	2.15	Tang. Bk. Value/Share	5.77
P/E on S&P Est. 1996	31.0	Beta	NA
Dividend Rate/Share	Nil	Shareholders	300
Shs. outstg. (M)	20.5	Market cap. (B)	$ 1.3
Avg. daily vol. (M)	0.563	Inst. holdings	91%
		Insider holdings	NA

Value of $10,000 invested 5 years ago: NA

Fiscal Year Ending Aug. 31

	1995	% Change	1994	% Change	1993	% Change
Revenues (Million $)						
1Q	53.09	62%	32.80	NM	32.60	52%
2Q	45.21	78%	25.35	4%	24.36	22%
3Q	36.11	40%	25.72	56%	16.44	10%
4Q	37.18	33%	27.91	26%	22.22	19%
Yr.	171.6	54%	111.8	17%	95.58	27%
Income (Million $)						
1Q	11.59	86%	6.24	28%	4.88	45%
2Q	10.37	133%	4.46	21%	3.69	34%
3Q	7.03	NM	-4.11	NM	2.11	31%
4Q	7.19	61%	4.47	52%	2.94	52%
Yr.	36.19	NM	11.06	-19%	13.63	41%
Earnings Per Share ($)						
1Q	0.57	84%	0.31	27%	0.24	40%
2Q	0.50	127%	0.22	19%	0.19	32%
3Q	0.33	NM	-0.21	NM	0.10	31%
4Q	0.33	50%	0.22	52%	0.15	45%
Yr.	1.72	NM	0.55	-19%	0.68	37%

Next earnings report expected: late December

Broderbund Software

Business Summary - 14-NOV-95

Broderbund Software, Inc. develops, publishes and markets personal computer software for the home, school and small business markets. Products are offered primarily in three consumer software categories: personal productivity, education and entertainment. Since its founding in 1980, the company has sold more than 23 million units of consumer software. Broderbund seeks to develop products that may be expanded into families of related sequel or complementary products.

Personal productivity products include the Print Shop Family (33% of fiscal 1994 revenues), which enables users to produce, manipulate and create printed output, such as personalized signs, posters, banners, calendars, stationery, greeting cards and other personal documents.

Educational products include the Carmen Sandiego Family (14% of revenues), a series of games designed to stimulate the player's interest in and knowledge of geography, history and astronomy; and the Early Learning Family (10% of revenues), which includes The Playroom, The Treehouse, The Backyard and the Kid Pix software titles and assists children between the ages of three and 10 in acquiring basic skills and developing creativity. Living Books (13% of revenues), a joint venture with Random House, is a series of CD-ROM-based, interactive, animated storybooks, that let children learn, listen and explore via the multimedia capabilities of personal computers.

Entertainment products (15% of revenues) include Myst, a highly animated adventure, and Prince of Persia and its sequel, Prince of Persia 2: The Shadow and the Flame, both arcade-style adventure games.

Affiliated-label products (9% of revenues) are software titles developed by third parties, but distributed and marketed by Broderbund.

Other products (7% of revenues) include assorted reference and education software products and a variety of printing, graphics and other personal productivity products.

Products are sold through distributors and directly to software specialty retail chains, computer superstores, mass merchandisers, discount warehouse stores and educational dealers, as well as directly to schools. In fiscal 1994, the company's largest distributor, Ingram Micro, accounted for 21% of net revenues.

Important Developments

Nov. '95—Broderbund raised its acquisition offer for The Learning Company (LRNG), a maker of educational software products, following a rival bid from a third company for LRNG. Broderbund's offer for LRNG, which is valued at about $515 million, calls for 0.92 BROD common shares to be exchanged for each LRNG common share.

Capitalization

Long Term Debt: None (8/95).

Per Share Data ($) (Year Ended Aug. 31)

	1995	1994	1993	1992	1991	1990
Tangible Bk. Val.	NA	4.09	3.27	2.38	1.77	NA
Cash Flow	NA	0.70	0.82	0.54	0.40	0.38
Earnings	1.72	0.55	0.68	0.50	0.38	0.33
Dividends	Nil	Nil	Nil	Nil	Nil	Nil
Payout Ratio	Nil	Nil	Nil	Nil	Nil	Nil
Prices - High	78¾	29⅛	29⅝	24⅝	13¼	NA
- Low	42¼	15¾	14⅞	9¼	5½	NA
P/E Ratio - High	46	53	44	50	35	NA
- Low	25	29	22	19	15	NA

Income Statement Analysis (Million $)

	1994	%Chg	1993	%Chg	1992	%Chg	1991
Revs.	112	17%	95.6	27%	75.1	35%	55.8
Oper. Inc.	32.1	37%	23.4	54%	15.2	30%	11.7
Depr.	3.0	10%	2.8	153%	1.1	79%	0.6
Int. Exp.	Nil	—	Nil	—	Nil	—	0.1
Pretax Inc.	19.8	-10%	21.9	41%	15.5	34%	11.6
Eff. Tax Rate	44%	—	38%	—	38%	—	39%
Net Inc.	11.1	-18%	13.6	41%	9.7	37%	7.1

Balance Sheet & Other Fin. Data (Million $)

	1994	1993	1992	1991	1990	1989
Cash	75.0	54.3	31.4	29.6	18.3	NA
Curr. Assets	90.3	69.0	47.9	39.6	30.9	NA
Total Assets	97.7	77.2	56.2	42.7	32.9	30.1
Curr. Liab.	17.3	14.2	10.5	10.3	7.6	NA
LT Debt	Nil	Nil	Nil	Nil	Nil	Nil
Common Eqty.	80.2	62.0	44.2	32.4	25.3	22.4
Total Cap.	80.2	62.7	45.3	32.4	25.3	22.4
Cap. Exp.	1.0	2.4	2.9	1.8	0.8	0.6
Cash Flow	14.1	16.4	10.7	7.5	7.0	3.3

Ratio Analysis

	1994	1993	1992	1991	1990	1989
Curr. Ratio	5.2	4.9	4.6	3.8	4.1	NA
% LT Debt of Cap.	Nil	Nil	Nil	Nil	Nil	Nil
% Net Inc.of Revs.	9.9	14.3	12.9	12.7	12.3	7.2
% Ret. on Assets	12.5	20.2	16.5	18.7	19.8	9.6
% Ret. on Equity	15.3	25.4	22.5	24.5	26.1	12.8

Dividend Data —No cash dividends have been paid. A two-for-one stock split was paid November 21, 1994.

Amt. of Div. $	Date Decl.	Ex-Div. Date	Stock of Record	Payment Date
2-for-1	Oct. 06	Nov. 22	Oct. 25	Nov. 21 '94

Data as orig. reptd.; bef. results of disc. opers. and/or spec. items. Per share data adj. for stk. divs. as of ex-div. date. E-Estimated. NA-Not Available. NM-Not Meaningful. NR-Not Ranked.

Office—500 Redwood Blvd., Novato, CA 94948-6121. **Tel**—(415) 382-4400. **Chrmn & CEO**—D. G. Carlston. **Pres & COO**—W. M. McDonagh. **VP & CFO**—M. Shannahan. **VP & Secy**—T. L. Marcus. **Investor Contact**—Robin E. Linstrom (415) 382-4449. **Dirs**—E. R. Auer, G. L. Buckmiller, D. G. Carlston, S. Cook, W. P. Egan, D. Liddle, W. M. McDonagh, L. Wilkinson. **Transfer Agent & Registrar**—Chemical Trust Co. of California, San Francisco. **Incorporated** in California in 1981. **Empl**-402. **S&P Analyst:** Peter C. Wood, CFA

CCB Financial

NASDAQ Symbol **CCBF**
In S&P SmallCap 600

31-OCT-95 **Industry:** Banking

Summary: This bank holding company, through its subsidiaries, operates 153 branch offices in central North Carolina.

Quantitative Evaluations
Outlook
(1 Lowest—5 Highest)
• **2+**
Fair Value
• **45⅛**
Risk
• **Low**
Earn./Div. Rank
• **A**

Technical Eval.
• **Bearish** since 9/95
Rel. Strength Rank
(1 Lowest—99 Highest)
• **57**
Insider Activity
• **Unfavorable**

Recent Price • 48½
52 Wk Range • 51¾-32¾
Yield • 3.1%
12-Mo. P/E • 10.2

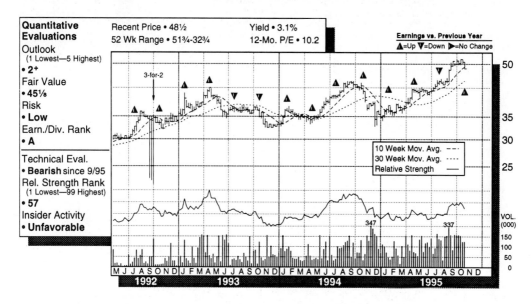

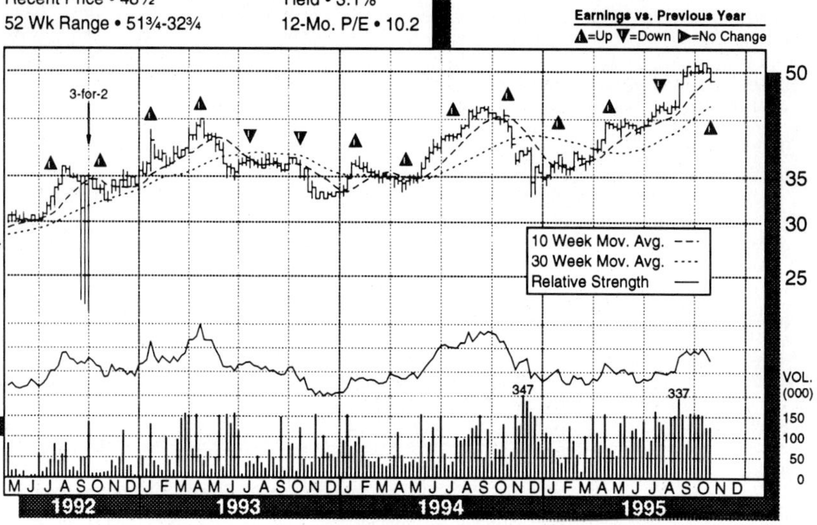

Business Profile - 31-OCT-95

This bank holding company operates 153 offices in central North Carolina. It is continuing an aggressive program of acquiring North Carolina savings banks. In May 1995, Security Capital Bancorp (SCBC) was purchased in exchange for stock valued at about $244 million. The acquisition boosted the asset base 35%, to $4.6 billion, making CCB the seventh largest bank in North Carolina.

Operational Review - 31-OCT-95

Net interest income in the nine months ended September 30, 1995, advanced 14% year to year, reflecting a 15% increase in average earning assets, partly offset by narrower net interest margins. The loan loss provision declined 4.8%, to $5.8 million. Noninterest income rose 7.3%, and with 14% higher noninterest expenses (including a $10.3 million merger-related charge), and lower taxes, net income was up 31%, to $40,797,000 ($2.73 a share), from $31,226,000 ($2.03, as adjusted).

Stock Performance - 27-OCT-95

In the past 30 trading days, CCBF's shares have declined 5%, compared to a 0.63% fall in the S&P 500. Average trading volume for the past five days was 24,620 shares, compared with the 40-day moving average of 34,436 shares.

Key Stock Statistics

Dividend Rate/Share	1.52	Shareholders	4,000
Shs. outstg. (M)	14.9	Market cap. (B)	$0.722
Avg. daily vol. (M)	0.030	Inst. holdings	27%
Tang. Bk. Value/Share	29.35	Insider holdings	NA
Beta	0.74		

Value of $10,000 invested 5 years ago: $ 23,114

Fiscal Year Ending Dec. 31

	1995	% Change	1994	% Change	1993	% Change
Revenues (Million $)						
1Q	107.5	67%	64.21	33%	48.39	-3%
2Q	111.8	63%	68.51	28%	53.34	2%
3Q	111.2	55%	71.93	20%	60.11	20%
4Q	—	—	77.62	14%	67.91	33%
Yr.	—	—	282.3	23%	229.8	13%
Income (Million $)						
1Q	14.90	76%	8.45	33%	6.35	27%
2Q	9.19	-6%	9.75	47%	6.64	-12%
3Q	16.71	65%	10.15	45%	6.98	9%
4Q	—	—	10.14	10%	9.25	45%
Yr.	—	—	38.48	32%	29.22	15%
Earnings Per Share ($)						
1Q	0.99	11%	0.89	10%	0.81	25%
2Q	0.62	-39%	1.02	23%	0.83	-16%
3Q	1.12	5%	1.07	29%	0.83	-1%
4Q	—	—	1.08	5%	1.03	26%
Yr.	—	—	4.06	16%	3.50	6%

Next earnings report expected: mid January

CCB Financial

Business Summary - 31-OCT-95

CCB Financial Corporation is the holding company for Central Carolina Bank & Trust Co. and Graham Savings Bank, Inc. Following the May 1995 acquisition of Security Capital Bancorp, CCB operated 157 offices in the Piedmont (central) section of North Carolina. It also owns Central Carolina Bank-Georgia, a special purpose credit card bank.

As of December 31, 1994, gross loans and leases outstanding totaled $2.51 billion and were divided:

Real estate--mortgage	50%
Commercial, financial & agricultural	18%
Consumer	9%
Real estate--construction	14%
Credit card	8%
Leases	1%

The reserve for loan and lease losses at December 31, 1994, was $31,283,000 ($26,963,000 a year earlier), equal to 1.25% (1.25%) of loans and leases outstanding. Net chargeoffs amounted to $4,600,000 in 1994 ($4,289,000 in 1993), or 0.20% (0.24%) of average loans and leases. Nonaccrual, past-due and restructured loans and other real estate acquired through foreclosure totaled $13,983,000 at 1994 year end ($23,252,000 a year earlier), amounting to 0.39% (0.71%) of total assets.

Average deposits totaling $2.83 billion in 1994 were divided: 14% demand, 14% savings and NOW accounts, 30% money market, and 42% time.

Total income in 1994 was derived as follows: 70% interest and fees on loans and lease financing, 13% interest and dividends on investment securities, 2% other interest income, 7% service charges on deposit accounts, and 8% other noninterest income.

On a taxable-equivalent basis, the average yield on total interest-earning assets in 1994 was 8.02% (7.83% in 1993), while the average rate paid on total interest-bearing liabilities was 3.75% (3.52%), for a net spread of 4.27% (4.31%).

Nonbanking subsidiaries are engaged in real estate development, the issuance of collateralized mortgage obligations, and the sale of various annuity and mutual fund products.

In 1993, the company acquired Citizens Savings Bank, Lenoir, NC (deposits of $112.8 million), and Graham Savings Bank ($93.3 million).

Important Developments

May '95—The company purchased Security Capital Bancorp (SCBC) in exchange for stock valued at about $244 million. The acquisition boosted the asset base from $3.4 billion to $4.7 billion, making CCB the seventh largest bank in North Carolina, with the fourth largest market share in the Charlotte region.

Capitalization

Long Term Debt: $87,301,000 (6/95).

Per Share Data ($)

(Year Ended Dec. 31)

	1994	1993	1992	1991	1990	1989
Tangible Bk. Val.	27.60	26.37	24.40	22.23	20.38	18.67
Earnings	4.06	3.50	3.30	2.81	2.70	2.78
Dividends	1.32	1.24	1.14	1.05	0.99	0.93
Payout Ratio	33%	35%	35%	37%	37%	34%
Prices - High	44½	42½	36⅛	29⅞	26⅞	29⅛
- Low	32¾	32½	22⅛	16⅝	16⅛	22⅛
P/E Ratio - High	11	12	11	11	10	10
- Low	8	9	7	6	6	8

Income Statement Analysis (Million $)

	1994	%Chg	1993	%Chg	1992	%Chg	1991
Net Int. Inc.	145	24%	117	18%	99	8%	92.1
Tax Equiv. Adj.	5.2	12%	4.7	6%	4.4	-12%	5.0
Non Int. Inc.	39.7	9%	36.4	19%	30.6	-6%	32.6
Loan Loss Prov.	892	NM	6.4	8%	6.0	-19%	7.4
% Exp/Op Revs.	63%	—	67%	—	66%	—	67%
Pretax Inc.	57.4	31%	43.9	18%	37.2	23%	30.3
Eff. Tax Rate	33%	—	33%	—	32%	—	29%
Net Inc.	38.5	32%	29.2	15%	25.3	18%	21.5
% Net Int. Marg.	4.90%	—	4.90%	—	5.20%	—	5.10%

Balance Sheet & Other Fin. Data (Million $)

	1994	1993	1992	1991	1990	1989
Earning Assets:						
Money Mkt.	174	205	106	NA	117	NA
Inv. Securities	592	617	498	419	394	371
Com'l Loans	544	411	346	373	313	296
Other Loans	1,964	1,751	1,179	1,077	1,072	1,012
Total Assets	3,548	3,258	2,312	2,158	2,102	1,984
Demand Deposits	430	421	344	298	298	305
Time Deposits	2,602	2,395	1,684	1,587	1,547	1,431
LT Debt	77.0	78.0	27.7	25.6	25.7	29.3
Common Eqty.	251	251	190	170	155	142

Ratio Analysis

	1994	1993	1992	1991	1990	1989
% Ret. on Assets	1.2	1.1	1.2	1.0	1.0	1.1
% Ret. on Equity	14.9	13.9	14.3	13.3	14.0	15.8
% Loan Loss Resv.	1.3	1.3	1.3	1.2	1.2	1.1
% Loans/Deposits	82.7	76.7	75.0	76.6	74.8	75.1
% Equity to Assets	7.8	7.8	8.1	7.8	7.3	7.2

Dividend Data —Cash payments have been made each year since 1934. A dividend reinvestment plan is available.

Amt. of Div. $	Date Decl.	Ex-Div. Date	Stock of Record	Payment Date
0.340	Oct. 18	Dec. 09	Dec. 15	Jan. 03 '95
0.340	Jan. 18	Mar. 09	Mar. 15	Apr. 03 '95
0.340	Apr. 18	Jun. 13	Jun. 15	Jul. 03 '95
0.380	Jul. 18	Sep. 13	Sep. 15	Oct. 02 '95
0.380	Oct. 17	Dec. 13	Dec. 15	Jan. 02 '96

Data as orig. reptd.; bef. results of disc opers. and/or spec. items. Per share data adj. for stk. divs. as of ex-div. date. E-Estimated. NA-Not Available. NM-Not Meaningful. NR-Not Ranked.

Office—111 Corcoran St., P.O. Box 931, Durham, NC 27702. **Tel**—(919) 683-7777. **Chrmn**—W. L. Burns, Jr. **Pres & CEO**—E. C. Roessler. **SVP & Investor Contact**—W. Harold Parker, Jr. **Dirs**—J. H. Beall III, J. B. Brame, Jr., T. B. Burnett, W. L. Burns, Jr., E. S. Holmes, O. G. Kenan, E. J. McDonald, H. W. McKay, Jr., E. B. Munson, E. C. Roessler, H. A. Tate, Jr., P. Wynn, Jr. **Transfer Agent**—First Union National Bank of North Carolina, Charlotte. **Incorporated** in North Carolina in 1903. **Empl**-1,937. **S&P Analyst:** Robert Schpoont

CDI Corp.

NYSE Symbol **CDI**
In S&P SmallCap 600

02-OCT-95 **Industry:** Services

Summary: This company is a leading provider of technical and engineering services for both industry and government. It also provides temporary office support and recruits executives.

Quantitative Evaluations

Recent Price • 20⅜ — Yield • Nil
52 Wk Range • 26⅝-12⅞ — 12-Mo. P/E • 14.1

Outlook
(1 Lowest—5 Highest)
• **4**

Fair Value
• **21¼**

Risk
• **Average**

Earn./Div. Rank
• **B**

Technical Eval.
• **Bearish** since 11/94

Rel. Strength Rank
(1 Lowest—99 Highest)
• **48**

Insider Activity
• **NA**

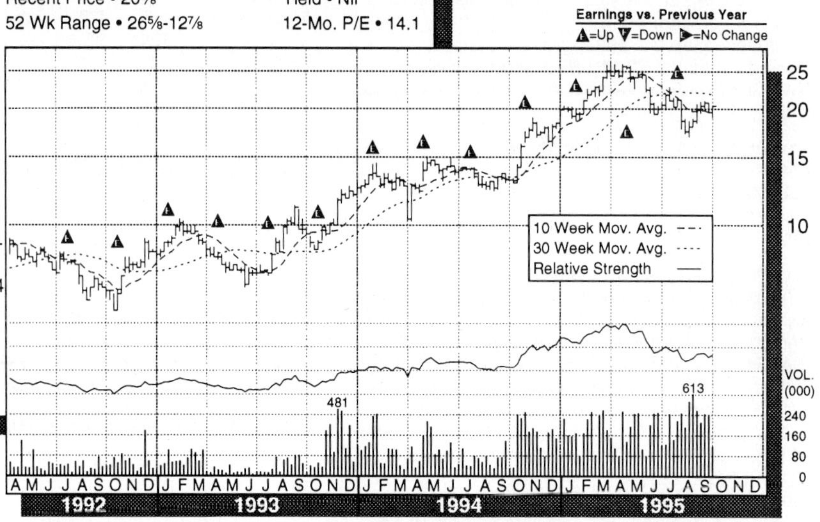

Business Profile - 29-SEP-95

CDI primarily provides technical and engineering services for both industry and government. It also provides temporary office and clerical support and recruits management, technical and sales personnel for permanent employment. The company believes that the demand for its services should remain healthy as the trend toward outsourcing continues. In addition, management feels that new international opportunities will arise as foreign companies increasingly turn toward outsourcing.

Operational Review - 02-OCT-95

Revenues in the first half of 1995 rose 27%, year to year, as all three business segments enjoyed higher sales. Technical Services' revenues increased 27%, driven by strong telecommunications and chemicals growth. Temporary Services' revenues were up 14%, while those for Management Recruiters rose 40%; net income surged to $0.75 a share from $0.43. The company has a solid balance sheet, with a 2.4 current ratio and long-term debt at about 33% of total capitalization.

Stock Performance - 29-SEP-95

In the past 30 trading days, CDI's shares have increased 13%, compared to a 5% rise in the S&P 500. Average trading volume for the past five days was 22,880 shares, compared with the 40-day moving average of 66,946 shares.

Key Stock Statistics

Dividend Rate/Share	Nil	Shareholders	700
Shs. outstg. (M)	19.7	Market cap. (B)	$0.402
Avg. daily vol. (M)	0.043	Inst. holdings	33%
Tang. Bk. Value/Share	6.73	Insider holdings	NA
Beta	0.67		

Value of $10,000 invested 5 years ago: $ 14,051

Fiscal Year Ending Dec. 31

	1995	% Change	1994	% Change	1993	% Change
Revenues (Million $)						
1Q	319.0	28%	249.2	15%	217.5	7%
2Q	332.1	25%	264.9	13%	233.5	9%
3Q	—	—	288.7	24%	232.7	7%
4Q	—	—	294.8	24%	237.6	9%
Yr.	—	—	1,098	19%	921.3	8%
Income (Million $)						
1Q	7.14	81%	3.94	NM	0.90	38%
2Q	7.76	74%	4.46	184%	1.57	96%
3Q	—	—	6.63	126%	2.94	126%
4Q	—	—	7.33	NM	2.42	NM
Yr.	—	—	22.37	186%	7.83	127%
Earnings Per Share ($)						
1Q	0.36	80%	0.20	NM	0.05	67%
2Q	0.39	67%	0.23	191%	0.08	100%
3Q	—	—	0.34	127%	0.15	114%
4Q	—	—	0.37	NM	0.12	NM
Yr.	—	—	1.13	183%	0.40	135%

Next earnings report expected: late October

CDI Corp.

Business Summary - 02-OCT-95

CDI Corp. provides engineering, scientific and technical contract services to other companies on a project basis; furnishes, on a temporary basis, people to work in offices; and finds and recruits middle-level executives. Business segment contributions in 1994 were:

	Revs.	Profits
Technical services	84%	74%
Temporary services	11%	11%
Management recruitment	5%	15%

The Technical Services division hires technical personnel and provides their services to customers on a temporary basis to work on expansion and development programs, to staff special projects, to meet peak-period manpower needs and to provide skills that may not otherwise be available to the customer. Engineering, drafting and designing services are provided for large industrial corporations in the aircraft/aerospace, automotive, chemicals, electronics, industrial equipment, information processing, marine, petroleum/petrochemicals, power/energy, telecommunications and other fields. Technical Services provides work both in customers' facilities (in-customer) and in its own facilities; approximately 70% of business is provided through in-customer work. During 1994, approximately 12% of the segment's revenues were from various divisions of General Motors, compared to 12% in 1993, 15% in 1992, and 21% in 1991.

The Temporary Services division provides clerical, secretarial, office support, new product demonstration and survey, and semi-skilled light industrial personnel to customers on a temporary basis. Customers use temporary services to meet peak-period manpower needs, to temporarily replace employees on vacation, and to staff special projects.

The Management Recruiters division recruits management, technical and sales personnel for permanent employment positions in such capacities as accounting, administrative, data processing, managerial, personnel, production, research and development, sales, supervision and technical.

Important Developments

Jul. '95—Management noted some softening of demand in the automotive industry, although the company expects the manufacturers to maintain a steady level of design activity. CDI has reduced its concentration in the automotive industry in recent years.

Capitalization

Long Term Debt: $74,306,000 (6/95).

Per Share Data ($)

(Year Ended Dec. 31)

	1994	1993	1992	1991	1990	1989
Tangible Bk. Val.	5.93	4.70	4.17	4.08	4.85	4.38
Cash Flow	1.85	1.17	0.95	0.45	1.36	1.66
Earnings	1.13	0.40	0.17	-0.39	0.61	1.05
Dividends	Nil	Nil	Nil	Nil	Nil	Nil
Payout Ratio	Nil	Nil	Nil	Nil	Nil	Nil
Prices - High	19 7/8	13 1/8	10 3/8	9 3/4	15 5/8	18 1/2
- Low	10 1/4	6 7/8	6	5 3/4	5 5/8	9 7/8
P/E Ratio - High	18	33	61	NM	26	18
- Low	9	17	35	NM	9	9

Income Statement Analysis (Million $)

	1994	%Chg	1993	%Chg	1992	%Chg	1991
Revs.	1,098	19%	921	8%	855	11%	768
Oper. Inc.	55.1	74%	31.7	26%	25.2	52%	16.6
Depr.	14.2	-7%	15.3	NM	15.2	-8%	16.6
Int. Exp.	4.1	10%	3.7	-9%	4.1	-13%	4.7
Pretax Inc.	36.8	192%	12.6	114%	5.9	NM	-9.2
Eff. Tax Rate	39%	—	38%	—	43%	—	NM
Net Inc.	22.4	187%	7.8	129%	3.4	NM	-7.6

Balance Sheet & Other Fin. Data (Million $)

	1994	1993	1992	1991	1990	1989
Cash	5.2	20.4	2.5	3.3	4.3	4.0
Curr. Assets	224	193	172	157	174	195
Total Assets	298	267	244	228	255	274
Curr. Liab.	96.2	85.1	56.8	49.5	73.0	71.7
LT Debt	58.8	62.0	72.2	67.1	61.2	90.9
Common Eqty.	139	117	109	105	113	102
Total Cap.	198	179	185	176	179	199
Cap. Exp.	14.0	11.2	8.8	4.1	17.3	24.6
Cash Flow	36.5	23.2	18.7	8.9	26.8	32.7

Ratio Analysis

	1994	1993	1992	1991	1990	1989
Curr. Ratio	2.3	2.3	3.0	3.2	2.4	2.7
% LT Debt of Cap.	29.7	34.7	39.0	38.1	34.1	45.6
% Net Inc.of Revs.	2.0	0.8	0.4	NM	1.3	2.3
% Ret. on Assets	7.9	3.1	1.5	NM	4.6	8.7
% Ret. on Equity	17.5	7.0	3.2	NM	11.2	22.5

Dividend Data —No cash dividends have been paid since 1970.

Data as orig. reptd.; bef. results of disc. opers. and/or spec. items. Per share data adj. for stk. divs. as of ex-div. date. E-Estimated. NA-Not Available. NM-Not Meaningful. NR-Not Ranked.

Office—1717 Arch St., Philadelphia, PA 19103-2768. **Tel**—(215) 569-2200. **Chrmn & Pres**—W. R. Garrison. **VP-Secy**—J. R. Seiders. **Exec VP-Finance & Investor Contact**—Edgar D. Landis. **Dirs**—W. E. Blankley, W. R. Garrison, C. M. Hoechst, L. C. Karlson, E. D. Landis, A. M. Levantin, A. B. Miller, J. W. Pope, A. I. Rosenberg, B. J. Winokur. **Transfer Agent & Registrar**—Mellon Bank N.A., Ridgefield Park, NJ. **Incorporated** in Pennsylvania in 1950. **Empl**-1,500. **S&P Analyst:** M.T.C.

STANDARD & POOR'S

STOCK REPORTS

CMAC Investment

NYSE Symbol **CMT**
In S&P SmallCap 600

07-SEP-95 **Industry:** Insurance

Summary: This company provides private mortgage insurance to residential mortgage lenders, including mortgage bankers, mortgage brokers, commercial banks and savings institutions.

Quantitative Evaluations
Outlook
(1 Lowest—5 Highest)
• **NA**
Fair Value
• **NA**
Risk
• **Average**
Earn./Div. Rank
• **NR**

Technical Eval.
• **Bullish** since 5/95
Rel. Strength Rank
(1 Lowest—99 Highest)
• **76**
Insider Activity
• **Neutral**

Recent Price • 50½
52 Wk Range • 50½-24⅞
Yield • 0.4%
12-Mo. P/E • 13.4

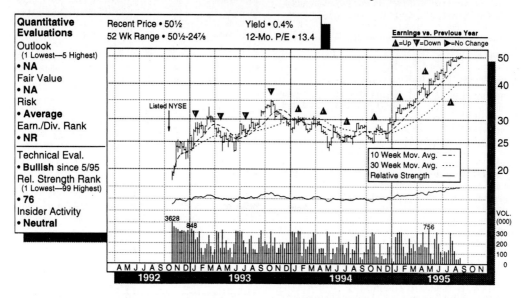

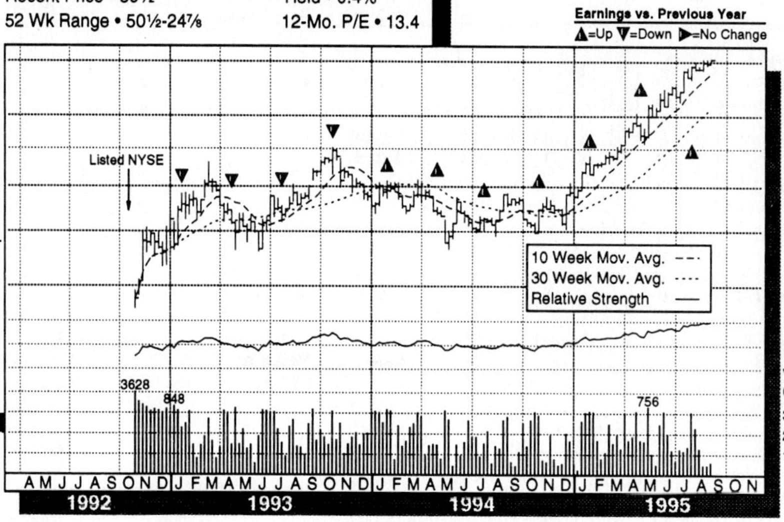

Business Profile - 07-SEP-95

CMAC is the sixth largest private mortgage insurer in the U.S., with a 7.0% share of the new primary private mortgage insurance (PMI) market at year-end 1994. At June 30, 1995, direct primary insurance in force totaled $29.3 billion, up 23% from the level a year earlier. The company anticipates further growth in insurance in force, as government initiatives on affordable housing boost lending to low- and moderate-income borrowers, expanding the PMI market.

Operational Review - 07-SEP-95

Total revenues in the six months ended June 30, 1995, climbed 23%, year to year, spurred by a 26% jump in premiums earned, and by greater net investment income. Total expenses advanced 24%, reflecting a higher provision for losses; pretax income was up 21%. After taxes at 26.3%, versus 27.8%, net income rose 23%, to $23,843,000 ($1.96 a share), from $19,375,000 ($1.60).

Stock Performance - 01-SEP-95

In the past 30 trading days, CMT's shares have increased 7%, compared to a 2% rise in the S&P 500. Average trading volume for the past five days was 11,700 shares, compared with the 40-day moving average of 26,828 shares.

Key Stock Statistics

Dividend Rate/Share	0.20	Shareholders	2,600
Shs. outstg. (M)	11.1	Market cap. (B)	$0.572
Avg. daily vol. (M)	0.013	Inst. holdings	86%
Tang. Bk. Value/Share	24.35	Insider holdings	NA
Beta	NA		

Value of $10,000 invested 5 years ago: NA

Fiscal Year Ending Dec. 31

	1995	% Change	1994	% Change	1993	% Change
Revenues (Million $)						
1Q	36.93	23%	30.10	26%	23.83	39%
2Q	39.69	23%	32.33	16%	27.94	25%
3Q	—	—	33.24	19%	27.94	26%
4Q	—	—	34.87	16%	30.18	39%
Yr.	—	—	130.5	22%	107.2	28%
Income (Million $)						
1Q	11.30	22%	9.25	34%	6.92	47%
2Q	12.54	24%	10.13	25%	8.13	36%
3Q	—	—	10.60	18%	9.02	70%
4Q	—	—	11.16	11%	10.05	74%
Yr.	—	—	41.13	21%	34.12	57%
Earnings Per Share ($)						
1Q	0.93	22%	0.76	38%	0.55	-18%
2Q	1.03	23%	0.84	27%	0.66	-22%
3Q	—	—	0.88	19%	0.74	-3%
4Q	—	—	0.93	12%	0.83	48%
Yr.	—	—	3.41	23%	2.78	NM

Next earnings report expected: late October

CMAC Investment

Business Summary - 07-SEP-95

CMAC Investment Corp. offers private mortgage insurance to residential mortgage lenders, including mortgage bankers, mortgage brokers, commercial banks and savings institutions. Private mortgage insurance (also called mortgage guarantee insurance) provides credit risk protection to lenders making residential first mortgage loans on which the down payment is less than 20% of the purchase price.

CMAC increased its share of the new primary private mortgage insurance market to 7.0% in 1994, from 6.4% in 1993. Refinancing represented 19.6% of new insurance written and 15.8% of new premiums written in 1994. At the end of 1994, the company had $25.8 billion of direct primary insurance in force, representing $5.0 billion of direct primary risk.

The company generates a substantial portion of income from earnings on its investment portfolio, at least 95% of which, according to its investment policy, must consist of cash, cash equivalents and investment grade securities. At December 31, 1994, the entire investment portfolio was rated investment grade, and contained no real estate, mortgage loans or private placements.

CMAC also offers to primary lenders pool insurance that serves as a credit enhancement for certain mortgage backed securities, in addition to primary insurance. Primary insurance covers defaults and certain expenses related to defaults and subsequent foreclosure on individual loans, which sum to the "claim amount". At December 31, 1994, primary insurance accounted for 97.6% of net risk in force, and pool insurance for 2.4%.

The company generally covers 7% to 30% of the claim amount, which is itself typically about 114% of the outstanding principal on the mortgage insured. The lender selects the amount of coverage based on the level needed to bring the loan into compliance with requirements for sale to FHLMC and FNMA. At December 31, 1994, the average coverage on primary insurance in force was 19.5%, down from 19.3% at December 31, 1993.

CMAC has a field sales force of 70 people, organized into regions, providing local sales representation throughout the U.S.

Important Developments

Jul. '95—CMAC attributed growth in insurance in force in the 1995 second quarter to improvement in its persistency level (the percentage of policies that stay in force to the end of the period of coverage), which reached 87%, versus 80% at the end of 1994 and 75% at June 30, 1994.

Capitalization

Long Term Debt: None (6/95).
$4.125 Preferred Stock: $40,000,000 (800,000 shs. at $50 liquid. pref. per sh.). Held by Reliance Group Holdings.

Per Share Data ($) (Year Ended Dec. 31)

	1994	1993	1992	1991	1990	1989
Tangible Bk. Val.	21.82	19.41	16.50	15.52	NA	NA
Oper. Earnings	NA	NA	NA	NA	NA	NA
Earnings	3.41	2.78	2.79	1.81	1.30	-0.32
Dividends	0.20	0.20	Nil	NA	NA	NA
Payout Ratio	6%	7%	Nil	NA	NA	NA
Prices - High	30⅞	35⅛	26½	NA	NA	NA
- Low	23¼	23	18	NA	NA	NA
P/E Ratio - High	9	13	9	NA	NA	NA
- Low	7	8	6	NA	NA	NA

Income Statement Analysis (Million $)

	1994	%Chg	1993	%Chg	1992	%Chg	1991
Premium Income	106	30%	81.6	22%	67.1	9%	61.7
Net Invest. Inc.	22.6	8%	20.9	50%	13.9	13%	12.3
Oth. Revs.	1.8	-61%	4.6	82%	2.5	NM	-2.6
Total Revs.	131	22%	107	28%	83.5	17%	71.4
Pretax Inc.	56.4	17%	48.2	49%	32.4	82%	17.8
Net Oper. Inc.	NA	—	NA	—	20.8	50%	13.9
Net Inc.	41.1	21%	34.1	56%	21.8	72%	12.7

Balance Sheet & Other Fin. Data (Million $)

	1994	1993	1992	1991	1990	1989
Cash & Equiv.	3.9	7.6	2.3	NA	NA	NA
Premiums Due	NA	NA	NA	NA	NA	NA
Inv Assets Bonds	359	327	304	NA	NA	NA
Inv. Assets Stock	Nil	Nil	Nil	NA	NA	NA
Inv. Assets Loans	Nil	Nil	Nil	NA	NA	NA
Inv. Assets Total	359	327	304	NA	NA	NA
Deferred Policy Cost	16.9	16.2	NA	NA	NA	NA
Total Assets	410	375	335	NA	NA	NA
Debt	Nil	Nil	Nil	Nil	NA	NA
Common Eqty.	240	213	181	170	NA	NA

Ratio Analysis

	1994	1993	1992	1991	1990	1989
Prop&Cas Loss	37.7	38.6	47.0	59.8	65.3	NA
Prop&Cas Expense	27.6	27.6	27.6	30.6	32.8	NA
Prop&Cas Comb.	65.3	66.2	74.6	90.4	98.1	NA
% Ret. on Revs.	31.5	31.8	26.0	17.8	14.0	NM
% Return on Equity	18.2	15.7	15.9	NM	NM	NM

Dividend Data —Payments were initiated in early 1993.

Amt. of Div. $	Date Decl.	Ex-Div. Date	Stock of Record	Payment Date
0.050	Oct. 19	Nov. 01	Nov. 07	Dec. 01 '94
0.050	Jan. 25	Jan. 31	Feb. 06	Mar. 01 '95
0.050	Apr. 19	May. 09	May. 15	Jun. 01 '95
0.050	Jul. 19	Aug. 02	Aug. 04	Sep. 01 '95

Data as orig. reptd.; bef. results of disc. opers. and/or spec. items. Per share data adj. for stk. divs. as of ex-div. date. E-Estimated. NA-Not Available. NM-Not Meaningful. NR-Not Ranked.

Office—1601 Market St., Philadelphia, PA 19103. **Tel**—(215) 564-6600. **Chrmn**—H. Wender. **Pres**—F. P. Filipps. **VP & Secy**—T. J. Shelley, Jr. **VP-Fin**—C. R. Quint. **Dirs**—D. C. Carney, C. M. Fagin, J. W. Jennings, J. C. Miller, R. W. Moore, R. W. Richards, A. W. Schweiger, H. Wender. **Transfer Agent & Registrar**—Bank of New York, NYC. **Incorporated** in Delaware in 1991. **Empl**-311. **S&P Analyst:** Brad Ohlmuller

Cabot Oil & Gas

NYSE Symbol **COG**
In S&P SmallCap 600

12-OCT-95 **Industry:** Oil and Gas

Summary: This company explores for, produces, purchases and markets natural gas and, to a lesser extent, produces and sells crude oil.

Quantitative Evaluations
Outlook
(1 Lowest—5 Highest)
• **NA**
Fair Value
• **NA**
Risk
• **Average**
Earn./Div. Rank
• **NR**

Technical Eval.
• **Bearish** since 11/93
Rel. Strength Rank
(1 Lowest—99 Highest)
• **49**
Insider Activity
• **NA**

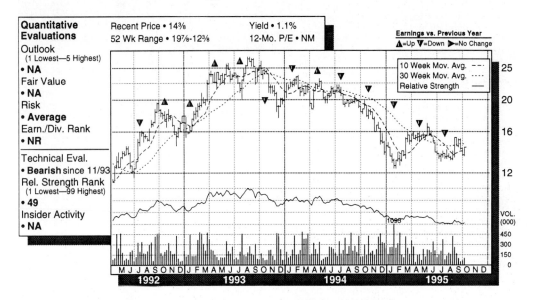

Recent Price • 14 3/8
52 Wk Range • 19 7/8-12 3/8
Yield • 1.1%
12-Mo. P/E • NM

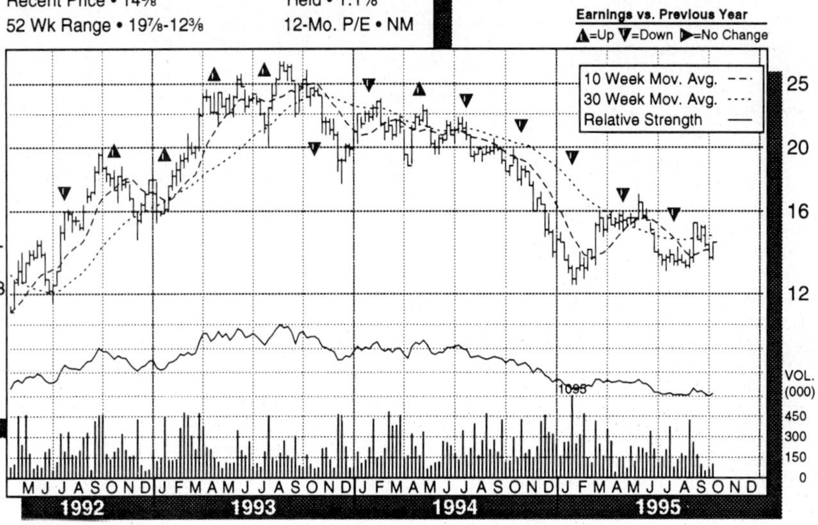

Business Profile - 20-JUL-95

Cabot Oil & Gas explores for, develops, produces, stores, transports, purchases and markets natural gas and, to a lesser extent, produces and sells crude oil. In early 1994, Washington Energy Resources Co. (WERCO) was acquired for cash and stock valued at $169 million. In January 1995, COG announced a cost reduction program that included a voluntary early retirement program, a 15% targeted work force reduction, and a management consolidation.

Operational Review - 12-OCT-95

Revenues in the six months ended June 30, 1995, declined 10% year to year, as increased natural gas production was outweighed by lower natural gas prices. After $6.8 million in charges related to a cost reduction program, significantly higher interest expense, and despite a tax benefit of $6.9 million versus taxes at 40.0%, a net loss of $10.7 million ($0.59 a share) contrasted with net income of $3.9 million ($0.10).

Stock Performance - 06-OCT-95

In the past 30 trading days, COG's shares have increased 6%, compared to a 4% rise in the S&P 500. Average trading volume for the past five days was 19,180 shares, compared with the 40-day moving average of 33,108 shares.

Key Stock Statistics

Dividend Rate/Share	0.16	Shareholders	1,400
Shs. outstg. (M)	22.8	Market cap. (B)	$0.322
Avg. daily vol. (M)	0.014	Inst. holdings	61%
Tang. Bk. Value/Share	10.00	Insider holdings	NA
Beta	0.85		

Value of $10,000 invested 5 years ago: NA

Fiscal Year Ending Dec. 31

	1995	% Change	1994	% Change	1993	% Change
Revenues (Million $)						
1Q	58.12	-12%	65.84	51%	43.48	13%
2Q	51.35	-9%	56.45	47%	38.38	25%
3Q	—	—	55.76	66%	33.50	2%
4Q	—	—	59.02	21%	48.96	7%
Yr.	—	—	237.1	44%	164.3	11%
Income (Million $)						
1Q	-6.82	NM	5.23	34%	3.90	61%
2Q	-3.90	NM	-1.38	NM	1.13	NM
3Q	—	—	-3.03	NM	-2.80	NM
4Q	—	—	-1.82	NM	1.32	-54%
Yr.	—	—	-1.00	NM	3.52	58%
Earnings Per Share ($)						
1Q	-0.36	NM	0.23	21%	0.19	58%
2Q	-0.23	NM	-0.11	NM	0.04	NM
3Q	—	—	-0.20	NM	-0.16	NM
4Q	—	—	-0.14	NM	0.04	-71%
Yr.	—	—	-0.25	NM	0.10	-9%

Next earnings report expected: late October

Cabot Oil & Gas

Business Summary - 11-OCT-95

Cabot Oil & Gas explores for, develops, produces, stores, transports, purchases and markets natural gas and, to a lesser extent, produces and sells crude oil. The company's core areas are concentrated in two regions: the Appalachian Region of West Virginia, Pennsylvania and New York, and the Western Region, with operations in the Rocky Mountains, Anadarko area of Oklahoma, and onshore Gulf Coast.

At December 31, 1994, estimated proved reserves aggregated 953,083,000 Mcf of natural gas (84.6% developed) and 8,036,000 bbl. of crude oil and condensate (95.9%), versus 808,280,000 Mcf of natural gas (82.9% developed) and 2,826,000 bbl. of crude oil and condensate (83.0%) a year earlier.

Properties at December 31, 1994, consisted of 1,199,226 gross (999,946 net) developed acres and 776,566 gross (604,095 net) undeveloped acres. Interests were held in 5,227 gross (4,309.6 net) productive gas wells and 648 gross (204.0 net) productive oil wells. During 1994, COG completed 203 gross (167.8 net) development wells, of which 188 (156.0) were productive. The company drilled five exploratory wells in 1994. During 1994, COG acquired 422 gross (136.8 net) gas wells and 104 gross (52.3) oil wells. At December 31, 1994, nine wells were in progress.

Natural gas sales volumes rose to 105,300,000 Mcf in 1994, from 64,500,000 Mcf in 1993. The weighted average natural gas sales price decreased to $2.14 per Mcf in 1994, from $2.40 in 1993. Crude oil and condensate sales soared to 824,000 bbl., from 345,000 bbl., while the average price increased to $16.66 per bbl., from $16.58.

The company also operates several gas gathering and transmission systems made up of 3,600 miles of pipeline, enabling COG to connect new wells quickly and to transport natural gas from the wellhead directly to interstate pipelines, local distribution companies and industrial users, or to two gas storage fields in West Virginia.

Important Developments

Aug. '95—COG announced that it had sold various non-core oil and gas properties in the Western region during the second quarter of 1995. Total proceeds of about $7.7 million were used primarily to reduce debt. The company said that other properties are presently being reviewed for possible sale in the second half of 1995.

Capitalization

Long Term Debt: $250,307,000 (6/95).
$3.125 Preferred Stock: 692,439 shs. ($50 stated value). Conv. into com. at $21 a sh.
6% Conv. Red. Pfd. Stock: 1,134,000 shs. ($50 stated value). Conv. into com. at $28.75 a sh.

Per Share Data ($) (Year Ended Dec. 31)

	1994	1993	1992	1991	1990	1989
Tangible Bk. Val.	10.67	5.61	5.78	5.83	5.62	4.67
Cash Flow	2.23	1.78	1.65	1.34	1.84	1.82
Earnings	-0.25	0.10	0.11	0.01	0.57	0.02
Dividends	0.16	0.16	0.16	0.16	0.12	NA
Payout Ratio	NM	160%	147%	430%	21%	NA
Prices - High	23¾	27	20	18⅛	18½	NA
- Low	13⅜	15⅜	10¼	11¼	14	NA
P/E Ratio - High	NM	NM	NM	NM	32	NA
- Low	NM	NM	NM	NM	25	NA

Income Statement Analysis (Million $)

	1994	%Chg	1993	%Chg	1992	%Chg	1991
Revs.	237	45%	164	11%	148	6%	140
Oper. Inc.	69.5	29%	54.0	10%	48.9	9%	44.8
Depr. Depl. & Amort.	54.6	58%	34.5	10%	31.5	16%	27.2
Int. Exp.	16.7	62%	10.3	5%	9.8	4%	9.4
Pretax Inc.	-1.6	NM	9.7	18%	8.2	34%	6.1
Eff. Tax Rate	NM	—	64%	—	73%	—	79%
Net Inc.	-1.0	NM	3.5	59%	2.2	69%	1.3

Balance Sheet & Other Fin. Data (Million $)

	1994	1993	1992	1991	1990	1989
Cash	3.8	2.9	1.1	2.2	2.0	0.6
Curr. Assets	52.0	44.6	41.7	32.9	25.2	25.3
Total Assets	688	445	349	334	302	289
Curr. Liab.	53.7	37.3	32.8	35.9	33.6	38.5
LT Debt	268	169	120	105	80.0	92.0
Common Eqty.	243	115	118	119	115	93.0
Total Cap.	629	401	310	296	260	247
Cap. Exp.	73.0	129	37.0	46.1	39.5	NA
Cash Flow	49.2	36.5	33.8	27.4	37.7	36.4

Ratio Analysis

	1994	1993	1992	1991	1990	1989
Curr. Ratio	1.0	1.2	1.3	0.9	0.8	0.7
% LT Debt of Cap.	42.6	42.1	38.7	35.5	30.8	37.1
% Ret. on Assets	NM	0.9	0.7	0.4	4.9	NA
% Ret. on Equity	NM	1.8	1.9	0.2	9.7	NA

Dividend Data —Quarterly dividends were initiated in mid-1990. In connection with an exchange offer by Cabot Corp. in March 1991, COG implemented a shareholder rights plan.

Amt. of Div. $	Date Decl.	Ex-Div. Date	Stock of Record	Payment Date
0.040	Oct. 28	Nov. 09	Nov. 16	Nov. 30 '94
0.040	Jan. 26	Feb. 08	Feb. 14	Feb. 28 '95
0.040	Apr. 27	May. 12	May. 18	May. 31 '95
0.040	Aug. 03	Aug. 15	Aug. 17	Aug. 31 '95

Data as orig. reptd.; bef. results of disc opers. and/or spec. items. Per share data adj. for stk. divs. as of ex-div. date. E-Estimated. NA-Not Available. NM-Not Meaningful. NR-Not Ranked.

Office—15375 Memorial Dr., Houston, TX 77079. **Tel**—(713) 589-4600. **Chrmn, CEO & Pres**—C. P. Siess Jr. . **VP, CFO & Investor Contact**—R. R. Seegmiller. **Secy**—Lisa A. Machesney. **Dirs**—R. F. Bailey, S. W. Bodman, H. O. Boswell, J. G. L. Cabot, W. E. Esler, W. H. Knoell, C. M. Mueller, C. W. Nance, C. P. Siess, Jr., W. P. Vititoe. **Transfer Agent & Registrar**—First National Bank of Boston. **Incorporated** in Delaware in 1989. **Empl**-495. **S&P Analyst:** N. Rosenberg

STANDARD & POOR'S
STOCK REPORTS

Calgene, Inc.

NASDAQ Symbol **CGNE**
In S&P SmallCap 600

04-OCT-95 **Industry:** Chemicals

Summary: Calgene develops genetically engineered plants and plant products, mainly tomatoes, cotton and rapeseed (canola). Monsanto (MTC) plans to acquire a 49.9% stake in the company.

Quantitative Evaluations

Outlook
(1 Lowest—5 Highest)
• **NA**

Fair Value
• **NA**

Risk
• **High**

Earn./Div. Rank
• **C**

Technical Eval.
• **Bearish** since 7/95

Rel. Strength Rank
(1 Lowest—99 Highest)
• **16**

Insider Activity
• **NA**

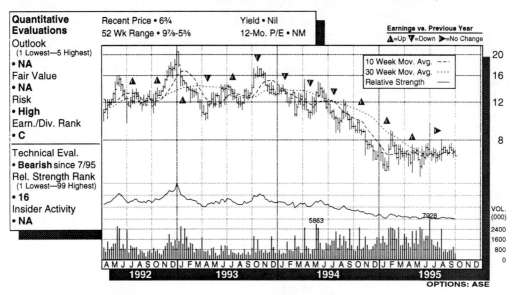

Recent Price • 6¾   Yield • Nil
52 Wk Range • 9⅞-5⅝   12-Mo. P/E • NM

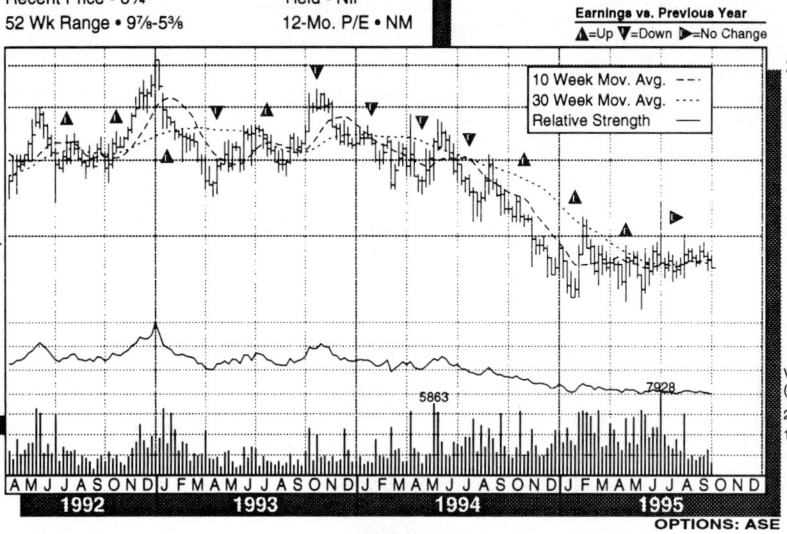

Business Profile - 04-OCT-95

CGNE is a leader in the application of recombinant DNA technology to plants. In 1991, it discontinued certain operations to concentrate on tomatoes, cotton and canola. In May 1994, CGNE's tomatoes were approved for commercial sale by the FDA. In June 1995, Monsanto Co. agreed to acquire a 49.9% stake in CGNE, in exchange for a $30 million equity contribution, certain patent rights, and its Garguilo tomato business. CGNE expects to cut SG&A and R&D expenses in fiscal 1996 by about $2 million.

Operational Review - 04-OCT-95

Based on a preliminary report, revenues advanced 44% in the fiscal year ended June 30, 1995, reflecting higher cotton seed and vine-ripened tomato sales and a $3.75 million technology license sale. Despite higher costs, the operating loss was substantially reduced, aided by a 24% drop in SG&A expenses. With reduced equity in net loss of affiliates, and despite $1,098,000 in losses on the disposition of assets, the net loss narrowed to $1.04 a share, on 18% more shares, from $1.71.

Stock Performance - 29-SEP-95

In the past 30 trading days, CGNE's shares have declined 8%, compared to a 5% rise in the S&P 500. Average trading volume for the past five days was 93,920 shares, compared with the 40-day moving average of 191,259 shares.

Key Stock Statistics

Dividend Rate/Share	Nil	Shareholders	3,600
Shs. outstg. (M)	30.2	Market cap. (B)	$0.198
Avg. daily vol. (M)	0.152	Inst. holdings	20%
Tang. Bk. Value/Share	1.05	Insider holdings	NA
Beta	1.13		

Value of $10,000 invested 5 years ago: $ 7,714

Fiscal Year Ending Jun. 30

	1995	% Change	1994	% Change	1993	% Change
Revenues (Million $)						
1Q	6.85	10%	6.25	16%	5.40	26%
2Q	13.29	111%	6.30	43%	4.40	19%
3Q	19.52	47%	13.32	22%	10.90	7%
4Q	17.00	26%	13.53	55%	8.73	46%
Yr.	56.66	44%	39.40	34%	29.33	21%
Income (Million $)						
1Q	-9.54	NM	-10.42	NM	-4.85	NM
2Q	-5.65	NM	-10.77	NM	-6.25	NM
3Q	-4.46	NM	-9.79	NM	-5.78	NM
4Q	-10.95	NM	-11.82	NM	-8.34	NM
Yr.	-30.60	NM	-42.80	NM	-25.22	NM
Earnings Per Share ($)						
1Q	-0.35	NM	-0.43	NM	-0.23	NM
2Q	-0.19	NM	-0.44	NM	-0.28	NM
3Q	-0.15	NM	-0.39	NM	-0.25	NM
4Q	-0.35	NM	-0.35	NM	-0.34	NM
Yr.	-1.04	NM	-1.71	NM	-1.11	NM

Next earnings report expected: early November

Calgene, Inc.

Business Summary - 21-SEP-95

Calgene, Inc. is developing a portfolio of genetically engineered plants and plant products for the seed, food and oleochemical industries. Products include tomatoes, cotton and rapeseed (canola).

Tomotoes with extended shelf life and better taste have been developed. The research has resulted in the patented gene FLAVR SAVR, licensed to Calgene by Campbell Soup Co. In October 1992, the USDA deregulated FLAVR SAVR tomatoes, allowing the company to grow and ship them commercially without USDA permits. In May 1994, the FDA approved their commercial sale. The tomatoes are marketed under the MacGregor's brand.

The company is engineering cotton that is herbicide and insect resistant. BXN cotton, currently under development, is resistant to the herbicide bromoxynil. Engineered plants have shown no adverse effects from the herbicide in field trials. In February 1994, the USDA approved commercial production of BXN cotton; commercial introduction is expected in 1995. Calgene has also developed a cotton variety (Bt cotton) that has demonstrated a significant level of control of heliothis, the principal cotton insect pest. Company scientists are also in the early stages of developing cotton varieties that produce colored fiber and varieties that exhibit improved fiber quality. The cotton seed unit, Stoneville Pedigreed Seed, is the second largest U.S. cotton seed company.

Calgene is also developing a family of genetically modified rapeseed oils. Products under development include a high-stearate oil (for margarine that requires no hydrogenation); a high-laurate oil (for soaps and detergents); a high-myristate oil (for milder soaps and personal care products); a medium chain fatty acid/ triglyceride (for lubricants and high-energy foods); and a low-saturate oil (as a healthier cooking oil). Although most products are several years from introduction, the company plans 1995 commercial sales of oil produced from its high-laurate rapeseed varieties, subject to USDA deregulation. Calgene currently makes and distributes plant oil-based chemicals.

The company has established research and/or business relationships with major international corporations, including Campbell Soup, Rhone-Poulenc, P&G, Unilever, Mobil and Rousell-Uclaf. In addition, through a 65%-owned joint venture with Kirin Brewery Co. Ltd., Calgene is developing insect- and disease-resistant potato varieties.

Important Developments

Jun. '95— Calgene signed a letter of intent with Monsanto Co., which would acquire a 49.9% equity interest in CGNE in exchange for its Gargiulo tomato packing and shipping business, certain patent rights, and an equity contribution of $30 million, including a $10 million advance in exchange for a convertible note.

Capitalization

Long Term Debt: $3,955,000 (3/95).

Per Share Data ($) (Year Ended Jun. 30)

	1995	1994	1993	1992	1991	1990
Tangible Bk. Val.	NA	0.78	1.99	1.15	0.79	0.73
Cash Flow	NA	-1.55	-0.97	-1.13	-1.08	-0.70
Earnings	-1.04	-1.71	-1.11	-1.34	-1.43	-0.95
Dividends	Nil	Nil	Nil	Nil	Nil	Nil
Payout Ratio	Nil	Nil	Nil	Nil	Nil	Nil
Prices - High	9⅝	15⅜	20⅝	20⅝	11¾	10⅜
- Low	5⅜	8⅝	9⅞	9⅝	5⅛	4½
P/E Ratio - High	NM	NM	NM	NM	NM	NM
- Low	NM	NM	NM	NM	NA	NA

Income Statement Analysis (Million $)

	1994	%Chg	1993	%Chg	1992	%Chg	1991
Revs.	37.7	39%	27.2	24%	21.9	-16%	26.1
Oper. Inc.	-39.0	NM	-23.1	NM	-17.7	NM	-10.9
Depr.	4.1	33%	3.1	-8%	3.3	-16%	4.0
Int. Exp.	0.7	9%	0.7	-18%	0.8	-9%	0.9
Pretax Inc.	-42.8	NM	-25.2	NM	-19.5	NM	-14.9
Eff. Tax Rate	NM	—	NM	—	NM	—	NM
Net Inc.	-42.8	NM	-25.2	NM	-18.6	NM	-14.4

Balance Sheet & Other Fin. Data (Million $)

	1994	1993	1992	1991	1990	1989
Cash	20.7	39.8	41.3	36.2	23.8	32.6
Curr. Assets	32.9	53.2	56.6	52.2	35.4	47.4
Total Assets	78.3	88.4	85.2	83.1	79.6	79.4
Curr. Liab.	28.2	18.9	18.3	19.4	13.4	8.6
LT Debt	4.2	3.7	4.4	5.1	5.1	2.7
Common Eqty.	44.4	65.8	33.0	26.0	30.4	39.4
Total Cap.	48.6	69.5	66.9	63.8	66.2	70.8
Cap. Exp.	4.4	4.6	1.5	1.5	5.1	4.0
Cash Flow	-38.7	-22.1	-18.1	-12.4	-7.4	-5.0

Ratio Analysis

	1994	1993	1992	1991	1990	1989
Curr. Ratio	1.2	2.8	3.1	2.7	2.6	5.5
% LT Debt of Cap.	8.6	5.3	6.5	7.9	7.7	3.8
% Net Inc.of Revs.	NM	NM	NM	NM	NM	NM
% Ret. on Assets	NM	NM	NM	NM	NM	NM
% Ret. on Equity	NM	NM	NM	NM	NM	NM

Dividend Data —No cash has been paid on the common shares.

Data as orig. reptd.; bef. results of disc. opers. and/or spec. items. Per share data adj. for stk. divs. as of ex-div. date. E-Estimated. NA-Not Available. NM-Not Meaningful. NR-Not Ranked.

Office—1920 Fifth St., Davis, CA 95616. **Tel**—(916) 753-6313. **Chrmn & CEO**—R. H. Salquist. **Pres & COO**—R. N. Stacey. **VP-Fin & Secy**—M. J. Motroni. **Investor Contact**—Carolyn Hayworth. **Dirs**—D. L. Baeder, R. E. Baker, W. Haug, D. Helinski, H. D. Palefsky, R. H. Salquist, R. N. Stacey, C. V. Stinnett, A. J. Vangelos, A. M. Veneman, J. L. Vohs. **Transfer Agent & Registrar**—First National Bank of Boston. **Incorporated** in California in 1980; reincorporated in Delaware in 1987. **Empl**-338. **S&P Analyst:** Justin McCann

STANDARD & POOR'S

STOCK REPORTS

California Federal Bank

NYSE Symbol **CAL**
In S&P SmallCap 600

24-AUG-95 **Industry:** Banking

Summary: This company is one of the largest thrifts in the U.S., based on assets of $14.3 billion at June 30, 1995. The bank is well capitalized under regulatory capital standards.

S&P Opinion: Hold (★★★)

Recent Price • 13⅞
52 Wk Range • 14¼-9¼
Yield • Nil
12-Mo. P/E • 2.8

Quantitative Evaluations
Outlook (1 Lowest—5 Highest) • **3**
Fair Value • **13¾**
Risk • **Average**
Earn./Div. Rank • **C**

Technical Eval. • **Bullish** since 12/94
Rel. Strength Rank (1 Lowest—99 Highest) • **57**
Insider Activity • **NA**

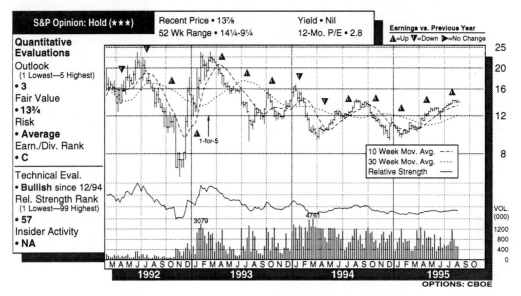

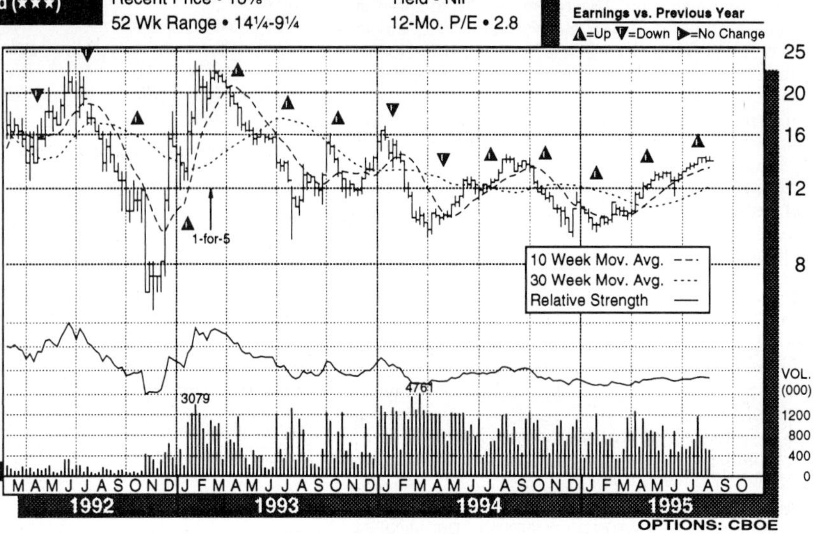

Overview - 24-AUG-95

Profits are expected to improve in 1996, mainly due to expansion of the interest rate spread, the difference between the rate earned on loans and other assets and the rate paid out on deposits. Under S&P's scenario of declining interest rates through mid-1996, deposit costs would reprice downwards and thus interest expense would also decline. CAL receives an extra spread benefit in a declining rate environment in that, for administrative reasons, its loan rates tend to fall slower than its deposit costs. Another contributor to the estimated 1996 earnings gains are cost reductions at all levels of the company. Asset quality is very good and modest improvement is expected.

Valuation - 24-AUG-95

Signs point to CAL being a consolidation candidate. Most importantly, the board is controlled by representatives of former bondholder groups, who are interested in recouping their earlier investment. However, the stock is trading at a 20% plus premium to book value, higher than the industry average and possibly close to the premium CAL would realize in a takeover situation. As an earnings play, the company has made impressive strides in improving its core profitability, but its return on assets in the June 1995 quarter of 0.51% was well below what the typical thrift earns. Future earnings should improve further. Weighing all these factors, we rate the stock an average performer.

Key Stock Statistics

S&P EPS Est. 1995	1.05	Tang. Bk. Value/Share	11.82
P/E on S&P Est. 1995	13.2	Beta	2.76
S&P EPS Est. 1996	1.50	Shareholders	6,100
Dividend Rate/Share	Nil	Market cap. (B)	$0.683
Shs. outstg. (M)	49.2	Inst. holdings	66%
Avg. daily vol. (M)	0.126	Insider holdings	NA

Value of $10,000 invested 5 years ago: $ 1,743

Fiscal Year Ending Dec. 31

	1995	% Change	1994	% Change	1993	% Change
Revenues (Million $)						
1Q	260.1	8%	241.5	-19%	299.9	-19%
2Q	266.4	8%	247.1	-11%	278.6	-15%
3Q	—	—	373.7	44%	258.9	-23%
4Q	—	—	246.0	NM	246.7	-24%
Yr.	—	—	1,109	2%	1,084	-23%
Income (Million $)						
1Q	14.70	NM	-322.4	NM	10.50	-20%
2Q	21.70	107%	10.50	NM	-45.50	NM
3Q	—	—	149.5	NM	-56.80	NM
4Q	—	—	13.00	NM	-53.70	NM
Yr.	—	—	-149.4	NM	-145.5	NM
Earnings Per Share ($)						
1Q	0.17	NM	-11.39	NM	0.40	NM
2Q	0.31	82%	0.17	NM	-1.83	NM
3Q	0.25	-91%	2.87	NM	-2.35	NM
4Q	0.32	146%	0.13	NM	-2.22	NM
Yr.	1.05	NM	-3.82	NM	-5.98	NM

Next earnings report expected: late October

California Federal Bank

Business Summary - 24-AUG-95

California Federal Bank is one of the largest thrifts in the U.S., based on assets of $14.2 billion at year-end 1994. After sale of the Southeast division in August 1994, it has 131 savings and lending offices in California and Nevada. Following a debt-for-equity swap in 1993, former bondholders gained control of the board and retained an investment adviser to explore ways to maximize shareholder value. Loans receivable of $9.0 billion at 1994 year end, versus $9.9 billion a year earlier, were divided:

	1994	1993
1-4 Residential fixed-rate	8%	9%
1-4 Residential adjust.-rate	65%	52%
Income-property	23%	33%
Consumer	2%	2%
Equity & other	2%	4%

At December 31, 1994, 88.9% of the bank's portfolio of loans and mortgage-backed securities consisted of adjustable-rate instruments. The one-year gap (difference between assets and liabilities repricing/maturing within one year as a percentage of interest-earning assets) was -0.74% at 1994 year end. Loans originated in 1994 were $2.8 billion, down from $2.9 bilion in 1993. Nonperforming assets (including restructured loans) were $223.1 million (1.57% of assets) at 1994 year end, versus $805.7 million (5.26%) a year ago. Net chargeoffs in 1994 were $117.6 million (0.83% of assets), down from $226.1 million (1.48%) in 1993. The allowance for losses at 1994 year end was $211.6 million (1.49% of assets), against $254.3 million (1.66%).

Of total deposits of $8.4 billion at year-end 1994, 12% were checking, 22% passbook and money market accounts, 7% certificate accounts of three to six months, 31% certificates of seven to twelve months, 19% certificates of 13 to 24 months, and 9% other.

In 1994, the bank sold $1.3 billion of problem assets and 44 branches located in Florida and Georgia.

Important Developments

Aug. '95—CAL announced a plan under which it would reorganize as a holding company, to be named Cal Fed Bancorp Inc. Under the proposal, which is subject to the requisite approvals, each share of CAL common stock would be exchanged for one share of Cal Fed Bancorp Inc. common.

Jul. '95—The company said that, assuming a stabilization of the interest rate environment, it would expect the spread to widen further in coming quarters.

Capitalization

FHLB Advances: $2,376,000,000 (6/95).
Other Borrowings: $58,800,000.
Preferred Stock: $266 million, incl. 3,400,000 shs. of 7.75% noncum pfd. conv. into com. at $26.25 a sh.

Per Share Data ($)

(Year Ended Dec. 31)

	1994	1993	1992	1991	1990	1989
Tangible Bk. Val.	10.82	20.96	26.14	101.15	122.60	173.15
Earnings	-3.82	-5.98	-10.45	-25.75	-43.85	16.40
Dividends	Nil	Nil	Nil	0.30	5.40	7.00
Payout Ratio	Nil	NM	NM	NM	NM	43%
Prices - High	16¾	23¾	23¾	43⅛	108¾	142½
- Low	9¼	9⅛	6¼	5	10⅝	90
P/E Ratio - High	NM	NM	NM	NM	NM	9
- Low	NM	NM	NM	NM	NM	5

Income Statement Analysis (Million $)

	1994	%Chg	1993	%Chg	1992	%Chg	1991
Net Int. Inc.	341	-15%	402	-8%	439	2%	430
Loan Loss Prov.	75.0	-54%	164	30%	126	-26%	171
Non Int. Inc.	201	187%	70.0	-35%	108	NM	-43.0
Non Int. Exp.	611	34%	457	-4%	474	20%	395
Pretax Inc.	-142	NM	-147	NM	-54.0	NM	-178
Eff. Tax Rate	NM	—	NM	—	NM	—	NM
Net Inc.	-148	NM	-145	NM	-62.0	NM	-131
% Net Int. Marg.	2.34%	—	2.59%	—	2.61%	—	2.28%

Balance Sheet & Other Fin. Data (Million $)

	1994	1993	1992	1991	1990	1989
Total Assets	14,182	15,326	17,236	18,395	24,509	26,191
Loans	11,261	12,194	13,350	14,975	16,961	19,961
Deposits	8,361	12,601	13,847	14,828	17,210	15,668
Capitalization:						
Debt	3,068	1,397	2,204	2,150	3,311	3,912
Equity	532	797	942	1,006	1,143	1,425
Total	3,866	2,288	3,146	3,157	4,454	5,337

Ratio Analysis

	1994	1993	1992	1991	1990	1989
% Ret. on Assets	NM	NM	NM	NM	NM	0.3
% Ret. on Equity	NM	NM	NM	NM	NM	5.9
% Loan Loss Resv.	1.9	2.1	2.3	2.1	1.4	0.7
% Risk Based Capital	12.5	9.7	9.2	7.3	7.4	7.1
Price Times Book Value:						
High	1.5	1.1	0.9	0.4	0.9	0.8
Low	0.9	0.4	0.2	0.1	0.1	0.5

Dividend Data —Common dividends were omitted in July 1991. A stock dividend of a Goodwill Participation Security was distributed July 28,1995, for each 10 common shares held.

Amt. of Div. $	Date Decl.	Ex-Div. Date	Stock of Record	Payment Date
Stk.	—	Jul. 31	Jul. 14	Jul. 28 '95

Data as orig. reptd.; bef. results of disc opers. and/or spec. items. Per share data adj. for stk. divs. as of ex-div. date. E-Estimated. NA-Not Available. NM-Not Meaningful. NR-Not Ranked.

Office—5700 Wilshire Blvd., Los Angeles, CA 90036. **Tel**—(213) 932-4200. **Chrmn**—D. Gilbert. **Pres & CEO**—E. G. Harshfield. **Secy**—D. J. Wallis. **VP-Investor Contact**—James F. Hurley (213-930-9750). **Dirs**— M. Arthur, J. F. Davis, J. J. Gaffney, D. Gilbert, E. G. Harshfield, C. A. LoBue, T. F. Michels. **Transfer Agent & Registrar**—Chemical Trust Co., LA & NYC. **Chartered** —as a Federal Savings Bank. **Empl**-2,300. **S&P Analyst:** Paul L. Huberman, CFA

California Microwave

NASDAQ Symbol **CMIC**
In S&P SmallCap 600

04-NOV-95

Industry:
Telecommunications

Summary: This company is the leading U.S. supplier of telecommunications satellite earth stations and microwave radios used in wireless communications.

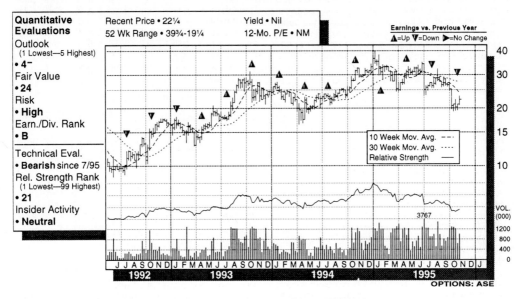

Quantitative Evaluations

Outlook
(1 Lowest—5 Highest)
• **4⁻**

Fair Value
• **24**

Risk
• **High**

Earn./Div. Rank
• **B**

Technical Eval.
• **Bearish** since 7/95

Rel. Strength Rank
(1 Lowest—99 Highest)
• **21**

Insider Activity
• **Neutral**

Recent Price • 22¼
52 Wk Range • 39¾-19¼

Yield • Nil
12-Mo. P/E • NM

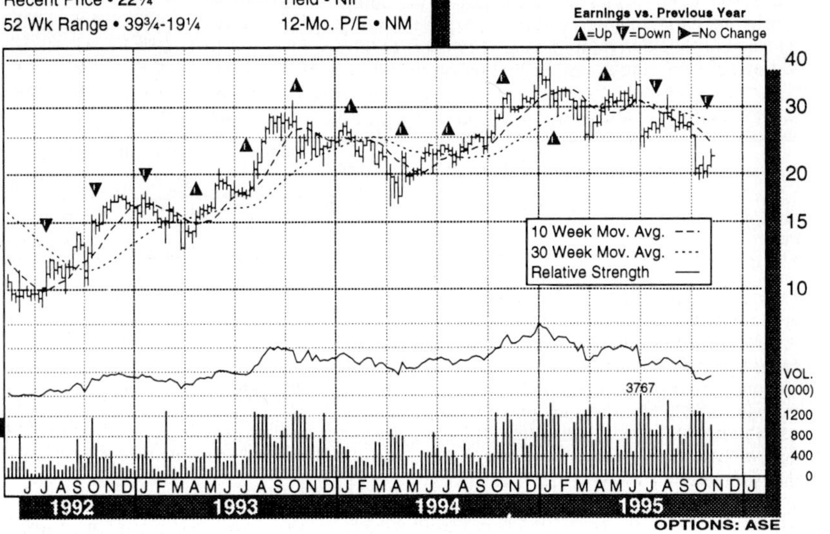

OPTIONS: ASE

Business Profile - 02-NOV-95

CMIC is one of the world's three leading providers of terrestrial radio and communication satellite earth station systems and products, and the U.S. industry leader. It anticipates significant revenues for its microwave radios for the PCS market, starting in 1996. the company recently acquired Microwave Networks Inc., a maker of digital microwave transmission products and systems.

Operational Review - 03-NOV-95

Revenues in the first quarter of fiscal 1996 (Jun.), rose fractionally, year to year, restricted by delays in orders from satellite communications and PCS markets. Gross margins widened slightly, on sales growth for higher margin wireless products relative to intelligence and satellite system sales, but with higher operating expenses, net income declined slightly, to $5,177,000 ($0.31), from $5,107,000 ($0.32 a share).

Stock Performance - 03-NOV-95

In the past 30 trading days, CMIC's shares have declined 16%, compared to a 2% rise in the S&P 500. Average trading volume for the past five days was 200,580 shares, compared with the 40-day moving average of 252,568 shares.

Key Stock Statistics

Dividend Rate/Share	Nil	Shareholders	1,800
Shs. outstg. (M)	15.7	Market cap. (B)	$0.350
Avg. daily vol. (M)	0.250	Inst. holdings	70%
Tang. Bk. Value/Share	6.47	Insider holdings	NA
Beta	1.02		

Value of $10,000 invested 5 years ago: $ 28,709

Fiscal Year Ending Jun. 30

	1996	% Change	1995	% Change	1994	% Change
Revenues (Million $)						
1Q	115.8	NM	115.1	84%	62.52	4%
2Q	—	—	119.1	44%	82.60	32%
3Q	—	—	121.9	16%	104.7	45%
4Q	—	—	111.8	-6%	119.2	65%
Yr.	—	—	467.9	27%	369.0	38%
Income (Million $)						
1Q	5.11	-1%	5.18	56%	3.32	—
2Q	—	—	5.94	68%	3.53	58%
3Q	—	—	6.04	56%	3.87	51%
4Q	—	—	-25.05	NM	4.35	40%
Yr.	—	—	-7.90	NM	15.06	51%
Earnings Per Share ($)						
1Q	0.31	-3%	0.32	19%	0.27	17%
2Q	—	—	0.37	32%	0.28	17%
3Q	—	—	0.37	23%	0.30	20%
4Q	—	—	-1.60	NM	0.35	35%
Yr.	—	—	-0.51	NM	1.20	22%

Next earnings report expected: mid January

California Microwave

Business Summary - 03-NOV-95

California Microwave, Inc. (CMIC) manufactures systems and products used worldwide in satellite and wireless communications for the transmission of voice, data, facsimile and video.

In 1992, as part of plans to significantly expand its presence in the wireless area, the company acquired Microwave Radio Corp. (MRC), a manufacturer of digital and analog fixed-link and portable microwave radios. TeleSciences Transmission Systems, Inc. (TTS), a maker of digital and analog microwave radios for the cellular, personal communications network and private network markets, was purchased in 1993. CMIC expects wireless sales to continue to grow as a percentage of sales.

Wireless products, which provided 49% of sales in fiscal 1995 (Jun.), include analog and digital microwave radios and other equipment used in land-based point-to-point and point-to-multipoint communications. CMIC is a leading manufacturer of microwave radios for cellular and other personal communications networks, for private voice and data communications networks, and for portable electronic news gathering and studio-to-transmitter links. Through MRC and TTS, the company makes short-distance and long-distance microwave radio systems for worldwide applications in cellular and portable personal communications networks and systems. Through TTS, CMIC manufactures and sells digital and analog microwave radio systems for the interconnection of statewide public safety mobile networks.

The company is a leader in design, assembly, integration and installation of satellite earth stations, from the largest international gateway earth stations, through mid-size earth stations, to very small portable earth stations. It also manufactures certain electronic equipment, such as modems and frequency converters, that is incorporated into earth stations. Satellite communications represented 37% of fiscal 1995 sales.

CMIC integrates electronic and electro-optical intelligence systems (14% of fiscal 1995 sales) for both airborne and ground-based applications for the U.S. government. Sales to the government accounted for 23% of revenues in fiscal 1995.

In May 1995, the company acquired Microwave Networks, Inc. (MNI), a maker of digital microwave transmission products with $60 million in revenues anticipated for 1995.

Important Developments

Oct. '95—CMIC said that although new orders booked in the fiscal 1996 first quarter rose substantially from the fiscal 1995 fourth quarter's bookings of $73 million, orders were down 10% because of continued delays in satellite communications and PCS markets.

Capitalization

Long Term Debt: $75,526,000 (9/95).

Per Share Data ($) (Year Ended Jun. 30)

	1995	1994	1993	1992	1991	1990
Tangible Bk. Val.	6.47	6.34	7.26	4.57	6.79	5.84
Cash Flow	0.41	1.96	1.65	0.97	1.32	1.26
Earnings	-0.51	1.20	0.98	0.56	0.93	0.80
Dividends	Nil	Nil	Nil	Nil	Nil	Nil
Payout Ratio	Nil	Nil	Nil	Nil	Nil	Nil
Prices - High	39¾	38¼	31¼	19½	25	10
- Low	23½	16½	12¾	8¾	6⅜	5⅝
P/E Ratio - High	NM	32	32	35	27	13
- Low	NM	14	13	16	7	7

Income Statement Analysis (Million $)

	1995	%Chg	1994	%Chg	1993	%Chg	1992
Revs.	468	27%	369	38%	267	34%	199
Oper. Inc.	31.9	-11%	35.8	45%	24.7	78%	13.9
Depr.	14.2	47%	9.6	43%	6.7	78%	3.8
Int. Exp.	4.8	71%	2.8	21%	2.3	156%	0.9
Pretax Inc.	-11.3	NM	23.9	50%	15.9	99%	8.0
Eff. Tax Rate	NM	—	37%	—	37%	—	36%
Net Inc.	-7.9	NM	15.1	51%	10.0	96%	5.1

Balance Sheet & Other Fin. Data (Million $)

	1995	1994	1993	1992	1991	1990
Cash	2.6	13.7	5.4	4.7	4.2	1.7
Curr. Assets	223	193	108	88.3	74.7	67.4
Total Assets	327	294	170	147	98.0	90.0
Curr. Liab.	97.2	81.3	45.1	31.6	28.8	29.0
LT Debt	67.8	70.1	5.3	40.3	2.2	5.2
Common Eqty.	154	141	119	75.3	67.5	55.7
Total Cap.	222	211	124	116	70.0	61.0
Cap. Exp.	26.8	16.4	10.8	9.6	3.6	3.9
Cash Flow	6.3	24.7	16.7	8.9	11.4	10.6

Ratio Analysis

	1995	1994	1993	1992	1991	1990
Curr. Ratio	2.3	2.4	2.4	2.8	2.6	2.3
% LT Debt of Cap.	30.5	33.2	4.2	34.9	3.2	8.6
% Net Inc.of Revs.	NM	4.1	3.7	2.6	4.5	4.6
% Ret. on Assets	NM	6.4	5.5	4.1	8.3	7.5
% Ret. on Equity	NM	11.4	9.2	7.0	12.7	12.7

Dividend Data —No cash dividends have been paid. A poison pill stock purchase rights plan was adopted in 1989.

Data as orig. reptd.; bef. results of disc. opers. and/or spec. items. Per share data adj. for stk. divs. as of ex-div. date. E-Estimated. NA-Not Available. NM-Not Meaningful. NR-Not Ranked.

Office—985 Almanor Ave., Sunnyvale, CA 94086. **Tel**—(408) 732-4000. **Chrmn, Pres & CEO**—P. F. Otto. **EVP & CFO**—G. E. Pierce. **VP & Secy**—G. L. Spillane. **VP & Investor Contact**—Stephanie M. Day. **Dirs**—J. J. Adorjan, E. E. David, Jr., A. M. Gray, A. H. Hausman, R. A. Helliwell, G. F. Johnson, D. B. Leeson, P. F. Otto. **Transfer Agent & Registrar**—First National Bank of Boston. **Incorporated** in California in 1968; reincorporated in Delaware in 1987. **Empl-** 2,382. **S&P Analyst:** Alan Aaron

STANDARD & POOR'S

STOCK REPORTS

Camco International

NYSE Symbol **CAM**
In S&P SmallCap 600

29-AUG-95 **Industry:** Oil and Gas

Summary: Camco provides oilfield equipment and services for numerous specialty applications in key phases of oil and gas drilling, completion and production maintenance and improvement.

Quantitative Evaluations

Outlook
(1 Lowest—5 Highest)
• **NA**

Fair Value
• **NA**

Risk
• **Average**

Earn./Div. Rank
• **NR**

Technical Eval.
• **Bearish** since 8/95

Rel. Strength Rank
(1 Lowest—99 Highest)
• **44**

Insider Activity
• **NA**

Recent Price • 22¾ | Yield • 0.9%
52 Wk Range • 24¾-16⅝ | 12-Mo. P/E • 17.4

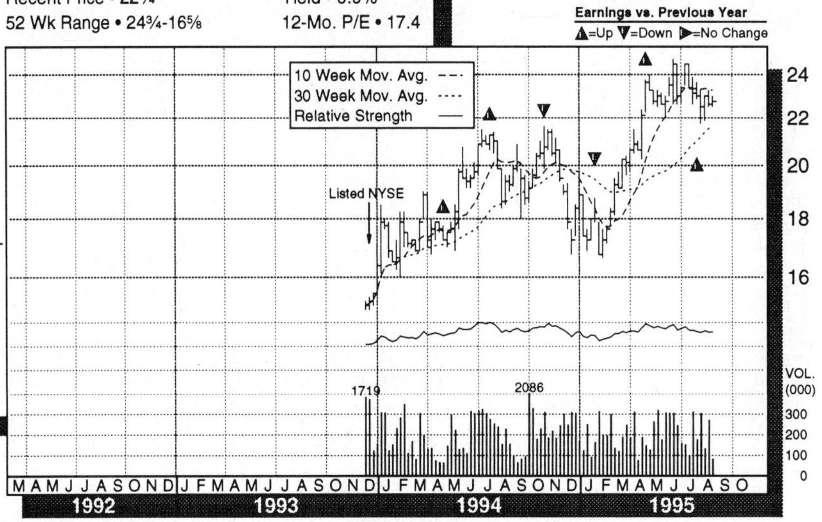

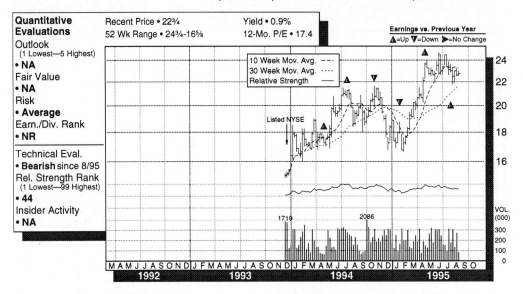

Business Profile - 29-AUG-95

The company's business strategy is to serve markets where its technology and services make it possible for customers to produce oil and gas in increasingly remote and technically demanding environments. It also provides its customers with technical innovations in products and services that lower finding and production costs. Internally, CAM seeks to minimize the effects of oil and gas price volatility and maximize profitability under varying market conditions by managing costs.

Operational Review - 29-AUG-95

Revenues declined 3.5%, year to year, in the first half of 1995, as electrical submersible pump sales were reduced in the former Soviet Union, which is experiencing a shortage of hard currency, and completion equipment sales fell in the Far East. Gross margin widened, primarily as a result of reduced manufacturing costs and improved product pricing in selected markets. After taxes at 27.8%, versus 29.0%, net income advanced 31% to $16,845,000 ($0.69 a share), from $12,826,000 ($0.51).

Stock Performance - 25-AUG-95

In the past 30 trading days, CAM's shares have declined 3%, compared to a 0.04% rise in the S&P 500. Average trading volume for the past five days was 15,960 shares, compared with the 40-day moving average of 41,644 shares.

Key Stock Statistics

Dividend Rate/Share	0.20	Shareholders	100
Shs. outstg. (M)	24.1	Market cap. (B)	$0.557
Avg. daily vol. (M)	0.040	Inst. holdings	86%
Tang. Bk. Value/Share	7.82	Insider holdings	NA
Beta	NA		

Value of $10,000 invested 5 years ago: NA

Fiscal Year Ending Dec. 31

	1995	% Change	1994	% Change	1993	% Change
Revenues (Million $)						
1Q	139.8	NM	139.9	9%	128.6	—
2Q	134.8	-7%	144.5	NM	145.6	—
3Q	—	—	155.7	6%	146.6	—
4Q	—	—	150.0	-9%	165.5	—
Yr.	—	—	590.1	NM	586.3	17%
Income (Million $)						
1Q	10.09	42%	7.11	NM	1.14	—
2Q	6.76	18%	5.71	44%	3.96	—
3Q	—	—	8.75	-34%	13.29	—
4Q	—	—	6.90	-28%	9.59	—
Yr.	—	—	28.47	43%	19.87	NM
Earnings Per Share ($)						
1Q	0.41	46%	0.28	180%	0.10	—
2Q	0.28	22%	0.23	NM	-0.01	—
3Q	—	—	0.34	-17%	0.41	—
4Q	—	—	0.28	-3%	0.29	—
Yr.	—	—	1.13	43%	0.79	NM

Next earnings report expected: mid November

Camco International

Business Summary - 29-AUG-95

Camco International Inc. is one of the world's leading providers of oilfield equipment and services for numerous specialty applications in key phases of oil and gas drilling, completion and production maintenance and improvement. The company is the world's leading producer of electric submersible pump systems and gas lift systems and is one of the world's two leading providers of synthetic diamond drill bits. Camco also operates the largest fleet of coiled tubing units in the U.S., is one of the world's two leading providers of subsurface safety valve systems and is the world's third largest provider of roller cone drill bits.

The company has two core segments: equipment and services. Profit contributions (in millions) by segment in recent years were:

	1994	1993	1992	1991
Oilfield equipment	$53.7	$45.1	-$29.7	$28.3
Oilfield services	3.3	6.1	9.7	16.4

The oilfield equipment business (81% of 1994 revenues) is conducted principally under the names Reda, Lawrence Technology, Hycalog, Reed and Camco Products. Reda manufactures electric submersible pumps used to lift large volumes of fluids from producing wells. Lawrence Technology makes electric cables and wire used with electric submersible pumps. Hycalog manufactures synthetic diamond drill bits. Reed makes roller cone drill bits. Camco Products makes gas lift systems to increase the volume of production from oil wells, subsurface safety valves used as fail-safe devices to shut in oil and gas wells in emergencies, and packers used in the completion and production phases of oil and gas development.

The oilfield services bsiness (19% of 1994 revenues) is conducted principally under the names Camco Coiled Tubing and Camco Wireline. Camco Coiled Tubing provides coiled tubing services and nitrogen services and performs other downhole operations used in initial completion of wells and in maintenance and treatment during the productive life of a well. Camco Wireline provides mechanical wireline services to install or retrieve downhole flow control devices and obtain reservoir data using specialized instruments.

Important Developments

Jul. '95—CAM reported that cash provided by operating activities was $3.4 million during the first six months of 1995, a decrease of $25.6 million from the first half of 1994, reflecting increasing working capital requirements. Net proceeds from the disposal of assets increased cash flow by $7.6 million. Cash was used to fund capital expenditures of $7.7 million, reduce debt by $2.4 million and to purchase Site Oil Tools. Cash stood at $29.6 million at June 30, 1995.

Capitalization

Long Term Debt: $86,744,000 (6/95).

Per Share Data ($)

(Year Ended Dec. 31)

	1994	1993	1992	1991	1990	1989
Tangible Bk. Val.	7.35	6.54	6.32	NA	NA	NA
Cash Flow	2.44	2.08	-0.31	NA	NA	NA
Earnings	1.13	0.79	-1.75	NA	NA	NA
Dividends	0.20	Nil	NA	NA	NA	NA
Payout Ratio	18%	Nil	NA	NA	NA	NA
Prices - High	21⅝	17⅞	NA	NA	NA	NA
- Low	16	15	NA	NA	NA	NA
P/E Ratio - High	19	22	NA	NA	NA	NA
- Low	14	19	NA	NA	NA	NA

Income Statement Analysis (Million $)

	1994	%Chg	1993	%Chg	1992	%Chg	1991
Revs.	590	NM	586	17%	500	—	NA
Oper. Inc.	76.8	6%	72.7	163%	27.6	—	NA
Depr.	32.8	5%	31.3	-13%	35.9	—	NA
Int. Exp.	5.9	-67%	18.1	133%	7.8	—	NA
Pretax Inc.	40.1	43%	28.0	NM	-34.8	—	NA
Eff. Tax Rate	29%	—	29%	—	NM	—	NA
Net Inc.	28.5	43%	19.9	NM	-43.6	—	NA

Balance Sheet & Other Fin. Data (Million $)

	1994	1993	1992	1991	1990	1989
Cash	36.0	30.7	8.0	NA	NA	NA
Curr. Assets	306	323	307	NA	NA	NA
Total Assets	635	661	647	NA	NA	NA
Curr. Liab.	140	155	147	NA	NA	NA
LT Debt	86.0	106	107	NA	NA	NA
Common Eqty.	364	356	353	NA	NA	NA
Total Cap.	461	475	478	NA	NA	NA
Cap. Exp.	24.5	16.8	23.4	NA	NA	NA
Cash Flow	61.2	52.2	-7.8	NA	NA	NA

Ratio Analysis

	1994	1993	1992	1991	1990	1989
Curr. Ratio	2.2	2.1	2.1	NA	NA	NA
% LT Debt of Cap.	18.7	22.4	22.3	NA	NA	NA
% Net Inc.of Revs.	4.8	3.4	NM	NA	NA	NA
% Ret. on Assets	4.5	Nil	NA	NA	NA	NA
% Ret. on Equity	8.1	Nil	NA	NA	NA	NA

Dividend Data —Quarterly dividends on the common stock were initiated in 1994.

Amt. of Div. $	Date Decl.	Ex-Div. Date	Stock of Record	Payment Date
0.050	Aug. 12	Aug. 17	Aug. 23	Sep. 06 '94
0.050	Oct. 28	Nov. 08	Nov. 15	Dec. 06 '94
0.050	Feb. 23	Mar. 01	Mar. 07	Mar. 28 '95
0.050	May. 10	May. 17	May. 23	Jun. 13 '95
0.050	Jul. 20	Jul. 28	Aug. 01	Aug. 22 '95

Data as orig. reptd.; bef. results of disc. opers. and/or spec. items. Per share data adj. for stk. divs. as of ex-div. date. E-Estimated. NA-Not Available. NM-Not Meaningful. NR-Not Ranked.

Office—7030 Ardmore, Houston, TX 77054. **Tel**—(713) 747-4000. **Chrmn, Pres & CEO**— G. D. Nicholson. **Sr VP-Fin & CFO**—H. S. Yates. **VP & Secy**—R. R. Randall. **Dirs**—H. H. Goerner, R. L. Howard, W. J. Johnson, W. A. Krause, G. D. Nicholson, C. P. Siess Jr., G. H. Tausch. **Transfer Agent & Registrar**—First Chicago Trust Co. of New York, NYC. **Incorporated** in Delaware. **Empl**-4,264. **S&P Analyst:** Michael C. Barr

Capital Re

NYSE Symbol **KRE**
In S&P SmallCap 600

28-SEP-95

Industry: Insurance

Summary: Through subsidiaries, KRE provides specialty reinsurance, particularly financial guaranty for investment grade municipal bonds, mortgage guaranty and credit reinsurance.

Quantitative Evaluations

Outlook
(1 Lowest—5 Highest)
• **NA**

Fair Value
• **NA**

Risk
• **Average**

Earn./Div. Rank
• **NR**

Technical Eval.
• **Bullish** since 7/95

Rel. Strength Rank
(1 Lowest—99 Highest)
• **79**

Insider Activity
• **Neutral**

Recent Price • 29¾
52 Wk Range • 30-20½
Yield • 0.7%
12-Mo. P/E • 10.7

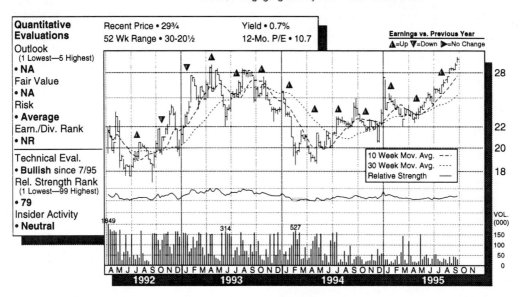

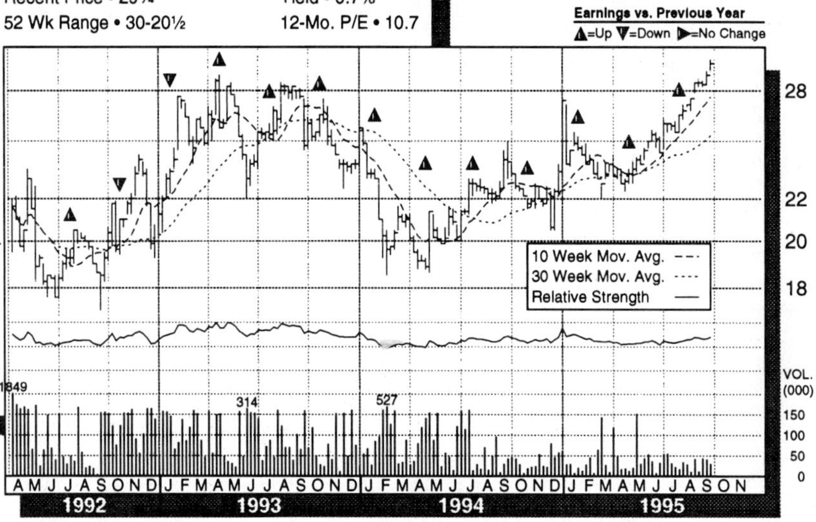

Business Profile - 19-SEP-95

The majority of KRE's gross premiums written derive from municipal bond reinsurance. Despite weakness in this sector during the first half of 1995, the company continued to grow as a result of its 1994 diversification into mortgage guaranty reinsurance, which contributed in excess of 28% of the company's total earned premiums that year. With an industry combined ratio of 78%, mortgage reinsurance is highly profitable and should enhance KRE's profitability.

Operational Review - 10-SEP-95

In the six months ended June 30, 1995, total revenues slipped 1.5%, year to year, as a 10% decline in net premiums earned was offset by a 22% increase in net investment income. Total expenses fell 6.6%, paced by 29% lower acquisition costs. Pretax income gained 3.3%. After taxes at 23.9%, versus 26.2%, net income climbed 6.6% to $22,338,000 ($1.51 a share) from $20,958,000 ($1.41).

Stock Performance - 22-SEP-95

In the past 30 trading days, KRE's shares have increased 10%, compared to a 5% rise in the S&P 500. Average trading volume for the past five days was 5,580 shares, compared with the 40-day moving average of 5,792 shares.

Key Stock Statistics

Dividend Rate/Share	0.20	Shareholders	NA
Shs. outstg. (M)	14.8	Market cap. (B)	$0.438
Avg. daily vol. (M)	0.007	Inst. holdings	37%
Tang. Bk. Value/Share	25.07	Insider holdings	NA
Beta	NA		

Value of $10,000 invested 5 years ago: NA

Fiscal Year Ending Dec. 31

	1995	% Change	1994	% Change	1993	% Change
Revenues (Million $)						
1Q	25.57	-7%	27.46	65%	16.67	—
2Q	28.10	4%	27.00	44%	18.80	—
3Q	—	—	23.02	-10%	25.60	44%
4Q	—	—	23.97	30%	18.41	43%
Yr.	—	—	101.5	28%	79.48	36%
Income (Million $)						
1Q	11.08	6%	10.41	16%	8.99	37%
2Q	11.26	7%	10.55	15%	9.16	6%
3Q	—	—	9.58	NM	9.59	49%
4Q	—	—	9.27	8%	8.61	1%
Yr.	—	—	39.81	10%	36.35	21%
Earnings Per Share ($)						
1Q	0.75	7%	0.70	17%	0.60	5%
2Q	0.76	7%	0.71	16%	0.61	2%
3Q	—	—	0.65	2%	0.64	49%
4Q	—	—	0.63	9%	0.58	2%
Yr.	—	—	2.69	11%	2.43	13%

Next earnings report expected: late October

Capital Re

Business Summary - 20-SEP-95

Capital Re Corp. is a holding company with two principal subsidiaries: Capital Reinsurance Co., which reinsures financial guarantees of investment grade debt, primarily municipal bond insurance; and Capital Mortgage Reinsurance Co., dedicated exclusively to serving the mortgage guaranty insurance industry. Financial guaranty insurers guarantee to holders of debt obligations the full and timely payment of principal and interest. The distribution of the reinsurance portfolio by type of obligation (% of net par in force):

	12/94
Municipal:	
Tax-backed	35.4%
Utility	22.8%
Health care	11.3%
Special revenue	11.7%
Housing	2.8%
Total municipal	84.0%
Total non-municipal	16.0%

At December 31, 1994, the net par amount of outstanding obligations was $28.4 billion, of which 12.8% had been issued in California, 12.4% in New York, 7.4% in Florida, 6.4% in Pennsylvania, and 5.7% in Texas.

The reinsurance of financial guarantees of municipal bonds in the U.S. market has given the company a predictable source of revenues in the form of unearned premium reserve, and thus a foundation for diversification into the reinsurance of mortgage guarantees and related risk product lines, such as export credit and surety reinsurance.

In August 1993, KRE purchased the remaining 51.5% of Credit Reinsurance Co. it did not already own. Credit Re is a holding company which, through its principal subsidiary, Bermuda-based KRE Ltd., is engaged in the business of reinsurance of financial guaranty, mortgage guaranty and other related special risk product lines.

KRE has expanded its reinsurance business, emphasizing mortgage guaranty reinsurance and, to a lesser extent, credit reinsurance.

Important Developments

Jul. '95—KRE reported that the decline in net premiums written in the second quarter and first half of 1995 was primarily the result of decreased volume in the municipal market and the high degree of selectivity with which it has assumed municipal bond reinsurance business. The company's expense ratio, for those respective periods, improved to 51.6% and 54.8%, from 55.6% and 58.4% in the comparable periods of 1994.

Capitalization

Long Term Debt: $90,725,000 (6/95).
Subsidiary Preferred Stock: $75,000,000.

Per Share Data ($)

(Year Ended Dec. 31)

	1994	1993	1992	1991	1990	1989
Tangible Bk. Val.	22.02	21.66	18.71	16.38	14.22	NA
Oper. Earnings	2.61	2.39	1.90	2.00	NA	NA
Earnings	2.69	2.43	2.16	2.14	1.95	NA
Dividends	0.20	0.20	0.15	NA	NA	NA
Payout Ratio	7%	8%	7%	NA	NA	NA
Prices - High	27⅞	29	24¼	NA	NA	NA
- Low	18½	20⅜	17⅛	NA	NA	NA
P/E Ratio - High	10	12	11	NA	NA	NA
- Low	7	8	8	NA	NA	NA

Income Statement Analysis (Million $)

	1994	%Chg	1993	%Chg	1992	%Chg	1991
Premium Income	58.9	31%	44.9	62%	27.8	41%	19.7
Net Invest. Inc.	40.1	25%	32.1	35%	23.8	44%	16.5
Oth. Revs.	2.5	4%	2.4	-65%	6.9	36%	5.1
Total Revs.	102	28%	79.5	36%	58.4	41%	41.3
Pretax Inc.	53.1	6%	49.9	26%	39.6	38%	28.6
Net Oper. Inc.	38.7	8%	35.8	35%	26.6	29%	20.7
Net Inc.	39.8	9%	36.4	21%	30.2	36%	22.2

Balance Sheet & Other Fin. Data (Million $)

	1994	1993	1992	1991	1990	1989
Cash & Equiv.	13.5	10.0	8.3	5.5	4.3	6.0
Premiums Due	4.0	3.1	13.2	9.8	9.6	4.3
Inv Assets Bonds	574	514	416	238	180	NA
Inv. Assets Stock	Nil	Nil	Nil	Nil	Nil	NA
Inv. Assets Loans	Nil	Nil	Nil	Nil	Nil	NA
Inv. Assets Total	637	552	444	273	203	181
Deferred Policy Cost	90.6	75.5	53.9	40.9	28.2	19.7
Total Assets	810	712	538	339	254	212
Debt	90.7	90.7	74.6	2.3	Nil	NA
Common Eqty.	326	324	280	190	145	122

Ratio Analysis

	1994	1993	1992	1991	1990	1989
Prop&Cas Loss	NA	NA	NA	NA	NA	NA
Prop&Cas Expense	NA	NA	NA	NA	NA	NA
Prop&Cas Comb.	NA	NA	NA	NA	NA	NA
% Ret. on Revs.	39.2	45.7	51.6	53.6	54.4	51.7
% Return on Equity	12.2	12.3	12.8	14.3	12.7	11.7

Dividend Data —Payments were initiated in June 1992.

Amt. of Div. $	Date Decl.	Ex-Div. Date	Stock of Record	Payment Date
0.050	Jul. 28	Sep. 16	Sep. 22	Sep. 29 '94
0.050	Dec. 15	Dec. 19	Dec. 23	Dec. 28 '94
0.050	Feb. 23	Mar. 16	Mar. 22	Mar. 29 '95
0.050	Jun. 02	Jun. 20	Jun. 22	Jun. 29 '95
0.050	Aug. 24	Sep. 19	Sep. 21	Sep. 28 '95

Data as orig. reptd.; bef. results of disc. opers. and/or spec. items. Per share data adj. for stk. divs. as of ex-div. date. E-Estimated. NA-Not Available. NM-Not Meaningful. NR-Not Ranked.

Office—1325 Ave. of the Americas, New York, NY 10019. **Tel**—(212) 974-0100. **Chrmn, CEO & Pres**—M. E. Satz. **SVP & CFO**—D. A. Buzen. **SVP & Secy**—A. S. Roseman. **Investor Contact**—Cathy C. Bailey. **Dirs**—D. L. Hollingsworth, R. L. Huber, S. D. Kesler, H. Menhard, S. H. Newman, P. H. Robinson, T. D. Ruane, M. E. Satz, D. R. Skowronski, J. F. Stuermer. **Transfer Agent & Registrar**—Mellon Securities Trust Co., NYC. **Incorporated** in Delaware in 1991. **Empl-** 52. **S&P Analyst:** Thomas C. Ferguson

STANDARD & POOR'S

Capitol American Financial

STOCK REPORTS

NYSE Symbol **CAF**

In S&P SmallCap 600

24-AUG-95 **Industry:** Insurance

Summary: This company underwrites, markets and distributes individual supplemental health and accident insurance in the U.S.

Quantitative Evaluations

Outlook
(1 Lowest—5 Highest)
• **NA**

Fair Value
• **NA**

Risk
• **Low**

Earn./Div. Rank
• **NR**

Technical Eval.
• **Bearish** since 6/95

Rel. Strength Rank
(1 Lowest—99 Highest)
• **48**

Insider Activity
• **Neutral**

Recent Price • 22 3/8
52 Wk Range • 24 3/8-19 3/4
Yield • 1.6%
12-Mo. P/E • 9.0

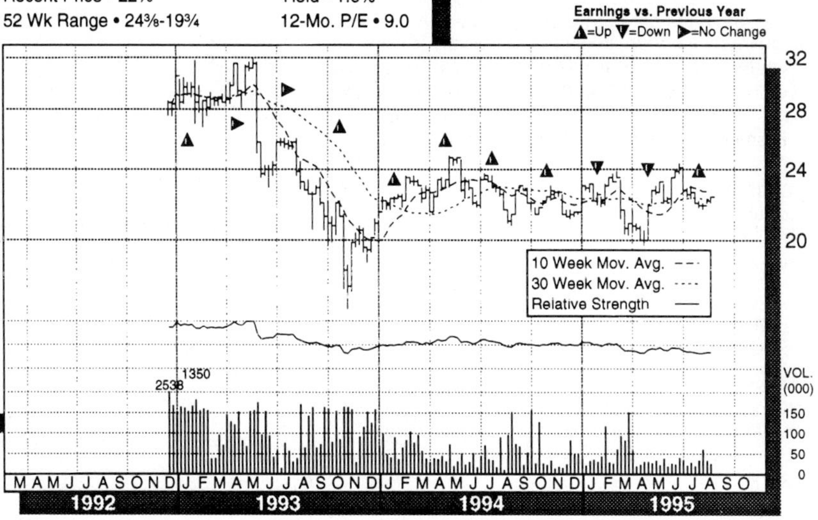

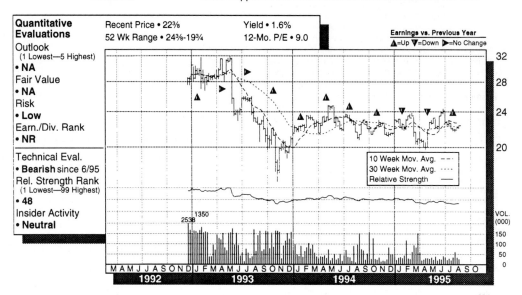

Business Profile - 24-AUG-95

CAF is a niche marketer of supplemental accident and health insurance, purchased by individuals and families to offset the non-medical costs associated with specific injuries and illnesses. Over the last decade, revenues and earnings have compounded annually at 26% and 30%, respectively. CAF's growth strategy calls for expanding relationships with contracted sales organizations, adding complementary products to its current offerings, and broadening its reach beyond a predominantly rural market.

Operational Review - 24-AUG-95

Revenues for the six months ended June 30, 1995, advanced 9.3%, year to year, primarily reflecting 7.6% growth in premiums earned and a 21% rise in income from investments. Total benefits and expenses were up 13%, driven by a 25% increase in general and administrative expenses, and 15% higher policyholders' benefits costs. Pretax income fell 2.3%. After taxes at 36.5%, versus 35.0%, net income declined 4.5% to $22,960,000 ($1.31 a share) from $24,053,000 ($1.33).

Stock Performance - 18-AUG-95

In the past 30 trading days, CAF's shares have declined 0.56%, compared to a 0.51% rise in the S&P 500. Average trading volume for the past five days was 4,720 shares, compared with the 40-day moving average of 6,208 shares.

Key Stock Statistics

Dividend Rate/Share	0.36	Shareholders	2,000
Shs. outstg. (M)	17.5	Market cap. (B)	$0.399
Avg. daily vol. (M)	0.008	Inst. holdings	21%
Tang. Bk. Value/Share	14.48	Insider holdings	NA
Beta	NA		

Value of $10,000 invested 5 years ago: NA

Fiscal Year Ending Dec. 31

	1995	% Change	1994	% Change	1993	% Change
Revenues (Million $)						
1Q	80.48	9%	73.57	9%	67.45	18%
2Q	81.87	9%	74.90	10%	68.36	15%
3Q	—	—	76.79	8%	70.97	15%
4Q	—	—	79.10	9%	72.61	13%
Yr.	—	—	304.4	9%	279.4	15%
Income (Million $)						
1Q	10.62	-12%	12.07	20%	10.04	21%
2Q	12.34	3%	11.98	11%	10.78	25%
3Q	—	—	11.04	1%	10.92	24%
4Q	—	—	9.69	-18%	11.82	27%
Yr.	—	—	44.78	3%	43.55	24%
Earnings Per Share ($)						
1Q	0.60	-9%	0.66	22%	0.54	NM
2Q	0.71	6%	0.67	16%	0.58	NM
3Q	—	—	0.62	5%	0.59	7%
4Q	—	—	0.55	-14%	0.64	10%
Yr.	—	—	2.50	6%	2.36	8%

Next earnings report expected: late October

Capitol American Financial

Business Summary - 24-AUG-95

Through its primary subsidiary, Capitol American Life Insurance Co., this holding company underwrites, markets and distributes individual supplemental health and accident insurance via a network of independent agents, agent organizations and brokers. Capitol America's primary product is cancer insurance, which accounted for 69% of premiums earned in the three years through 1994. Other products include accident insurance, intensive care insurance, and to a lesser extent, heart care and hospital indemnity insurance.

Premiums earned by product line in recent years:

	1994	1993
Cancer insurance	67.3%	69.1%
Accident policies	15.8%	15.8%
Intensive care insurance	10.8%	10.9%
Other	6.1%	4.2%

The company's policies provide lifestyle protection through payments made directly to the policyholder following diagnosis of or treatment for a covered illness or injury. Payments are designed to be used at the policyholder's discretion for any purpose. Benefits have historically been consistent with expectations. CAF has a large base of renewal premiums, which provide a stable and predictable source of revenue.

Approximately 92% of CAF's policies over the last three years have been sold with an optional return of premium rider. The rider generally provides that, after a policy has been in force for a specified time or upon the policyholder reaching a certain age, CAF will pay to the policyholder or beneficiary under the policy, the aggregate amount of all premiums paid to CAF under the policy, without interest, less all claims paid by CAF under the policy.

Capitol American is licensed in 47 states and the District of Columbia. The sales force is organized into a consumer marketing group (which produced 63% of earned premiums in 1994), and a business marketing group (37%).

Important Developments

Mar. '95—CAF settled proceedings with the insurance regulatory authorities of five states (North Dakota, South Dakota, Missouri, Wisconsin, and Iowa) involving the sales practices of its agents in those states. The settlement, which included a payment of approximately $320,000 in each state, does not affect CAF's ability to sell in those states, but it does impose costs. In releasing second quarter results, management indicated that while sales for the period were adversely impacted by the proceedings, they should not materially affect CAF's financial position.

Capitalization

Notes Payable: $28,000,000 (6/95).

Per Share Data ($)

(Year Ended Dec. 31)

	1994	1993	1992	1991	1990	1989
Tangible Bk. Val.	13.34	11.58	9.61	-0.64	NA	NA
Oper. Earnings	NA	NA	2.19	1.77	NA	0.97
Earnings	2.50	2.36	2.19	1.77	1.37	0.97
Dividends	0.32	0.28	Nil	NA	NA	NA
Payout Ratio	13%	12%	Nil	NA	NA	NA
Prices - High	24⅞	32	31	NA	NA	NA
- Low	20¾	16¾	24	NA	NA	NA
P/E Ratio - High	10	14	14	NA	NA	NA
- Low	8	7	11	NA	NA	NA

Income Statement Analysis (Million $)

	1994	%Chg	1993	%Chg	1992	%Chg	1991
Life Ins. In Force	705	4%	677	—	NA	—	NA
Premium Income Life	263	7%	245	—	NA	—	NA
Prem.Inc A & H	NA	—	NA	—	NA	—	NA
Premium Income Other	NA	—	NA	—	NA	—	NA
Net Invest. Inc.	41.0	22%	33.5	47%	22.8	30%	17.5
Total Revs.	304	9%	279	15%	243	18%	206
Pretax Inc.	68.7	NM	68.6	29%	53.0	20%	44.2
Net Oper. Inc.	NA	—	NA	—	NA	—	28.9
Net Inc.	44.8	3%	43.5	24%	35.0	21%	28.9

Balance Sheet & Other Fin. Data (Million $)

	1994	1993	1992	1991	1990	1989
Cash & Equiv.	8.0	7.7	7.7	62.2	NA	NA
Premiums Due	14.4	12.6	NA	NA	NA	NA
Inv Assets Bonds	512	413	326	244	NA	NA
Inv. Assets Stock	7.3	6.8	8.3	8.2	NA	NA
Inv. Assets Loans	Nil	Nil	Nil	Nil	NA	NA
Inv. Assets Total	519	420	334	252	NA	NA
Deferred Policy Cost	236	213	NA	NA	NA	NA
Total Assets	793	668	548	515	NA	NA
Debt	24.0	22.0	20.0	21.0	NA	NA
Common Eqty.	234	211	178	162	NA	NA

Ratio Analysis

	1994	1993	1992	1991	1990	1989
% Ret. on Revs.	14.7	15.6	14.4	14.0	14.0	12.7
% Ret. on Assets	6.1	7.2	NA	NA	NA	NA
% Ret. on Equity	20.1	22.4	26.1	NA	NA	NA
% Invest. Yield	8.7	8.9	8.4	NA	NA	NA

Dividend Data —Dividends were initiated early in 1993.

Amt. of Div. $	Date Decl.	Ex-Div. Date	Stock of Record	Payment Date
0.080	Sep. 20	Oct. 28	Nov. 03	Nov. 17 '94
0.090	Jan. 24	Jan. 27	Feb. 02	Feb. 16 '95
0.090	Mar. 21	Apr. 28	May. 04	May. 18 '95
0.090	Jul. 18	Aug. 01	Aug. 03	Aug. 17 '95

Data as orig. reptd.; bef. results of disc. opers. and/or spec. items. Per share data adj. for stk. divs. as of ex-div. date. E-Estimated. NA-Not Available. NM-Not Meaningful. NR-Not Ranked.

Office—1001 Lakeside Ave., Cleveland OH 44114. **Tel**—(216) 696-6400. **Chrmn, Pres & CEO**—D. H. Gunning. **SVP-CFO**—D. B. Kelly. **SVP-Secy**—R. T. Nelson. **Investor Contact**—Douglas B. Kelly. **Dirs**—R. H. Andrews Jr., R. A. Garda, D. H. Gunning, W. H. Heller, B. J. Hershey, M. T. Moore, R. T. Moriarty, R. L. Osborne, J. H. Outcalt, W. R. Robertson. **Transfer Agent**—National City Bank, Cleveland, Ohio. **Organized** in Ohio in 1970. **Empl**-276. **S&P Analyst:** Thomas C. Ferguson

STANDARD & POOR'S

STOCK REPORTS

Caraustar Industries

NASDAQ Symbol **CSAR**

In S&P SmallCap 600

10-SEP-95

Industry: Paper/Products

Summary: This major manufacturer of recycled paperboard and converted paperboard products operates 42 converting facilities and 25 recycling and waste collection facilities.

Quantitative Evaluations

Outlook
(1 Lowest—5 Highest)
• **NA**

Fair Value
• **NA**

Risk
• **Average**

Earn./Div. Rank
• **NR**

Technical Eval.
• **Bearish** since 8/95

Rel. Strength Rank
(1 Lowest—99 Highest)
• **63**

Insider Activity
• **NA**

Recent Price • 21¼ | Yield • 2.0%

52 Wk Range • 23-15¾ | 12-Mo. P/E • 13.9

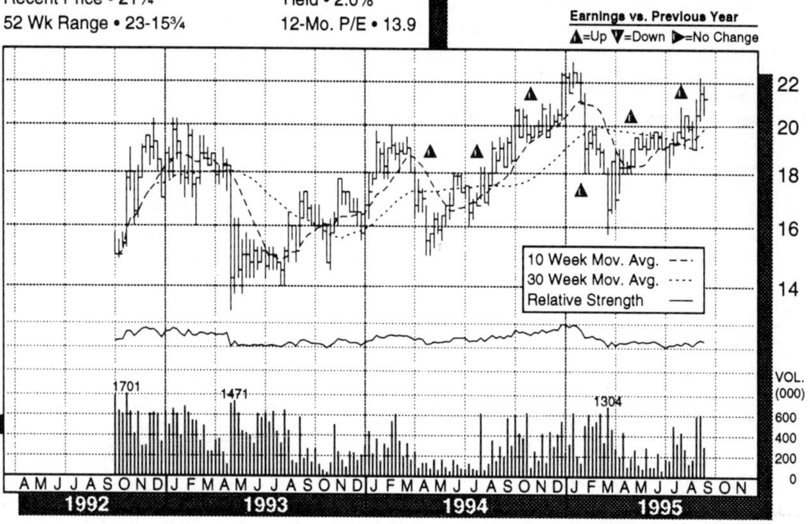

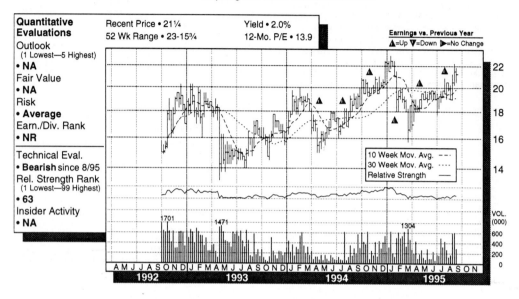

Business Profile - 24-AUG-95

CSAR has spent an average of $14.9 million annually for capital expenditures during the past five years, primarily to expand and upgrade its paperboard production and converting capacity. The company intends to continue to upgrade its existing facilities, and expects to spend $28 million annually for the next four years. In April 1995, CSAR adopted a shareholder rights plan as a defense against possible takeover attempts. Earnings for the next five years are projected to grow 13% annually.

Operational Review - 07-SEP-95

Net sales climbed 35%, year to year, in the first half of 1995, primarily reflecting increased selling prices for paperboard and converted products. Margins were hurt by increased waste paper prices, which forced the company to raise prices for its paper mill and converted products; the gain in net income was held to 28%. Management expects waste paper costs to decline by $30 per ton in the third quarter, while product selling prices remain flat.

Stock Performance - 08-SEP-95

In the past 30 trading days, CSAR's shares have increased 9%, compared to a 2% rise in the S&P 500. Average trading volume for the past five days was 71,850 shares, compared with the 40-day moving average of 71,644 shares.

Key Stock Statistics

Dividend Rate/Share	0.42	Shareholders	700
Shs. outstg. (M)	25.6	Market cap. (B)	$0.543
Avg. daily vol. (M)	0.083	Inst. holdings	51%
Tang. Bk. Value/Share	4.30	Insider holdings	NA
Beta	NA		

Value of $10,000 invested 5 years ago: NA

Fiscal Year Ending Dec. 31

	1995	% Change	1994	% Change	1993	% Change
Revenues (Million $)						
1Q	130.4	34%	97.00	21%	80.40	7%
2Q	139.7	36%	102.7	22%	84.20	11%
3Q	—	—	112.4	32%	85.30	—
4Q	—	—	119.1	29%	92.50	18%
Yr.	—	—	431.2	26%	342.4	11%
Income (Million $)						
1Q	9.02	23%	7.34	12%	6.57	-9%
2Q	10.41	32%	7.90	11%	7.14	25%
3Q	—	—	9.31	43%	6.50	23%
4Q	—	—	10.93	69%	6.48	33%
Yr.	—	—	35.48	30%	27.31	10%
Earnings Per Share ($)						
1Q	0.35	21%	0.29	12%	0.26	—
2Q	0.40	29%	0.31	11%	0.28	—
3Q	—	—	0.36	24%	0.29	—
4Q	—	—	0.42	68%	0.25	—
Yr.	—	—	1.38	28%	1.08	-14%

Next earnings report expected: late October

Caraustar Industries

Business Summary - 07-SEP-95

Caraustar Industries, Inc. manufactures recycled paperboard and converted paperboard products. Operating 63 facilities in the U.S. and Mexico, it manufactures its products primarily from recycled wastepaper.

The company's primary manufacturing activity is the production of uncoated recycled paperboard. In this process, wastepaper is reduced to pulp, cleaned and refined and then processed into various grades of paperboard for internal consumption or sale in four principal markets: tubes, cores and composite containers; folding cartons; gypsum wallboard facing paper; and miscellaneous other specialty and converted products. Caraustar operates 12 paperboard mills in 10 states. In 1994, about 41% of the recycled paperboard sold by its paperboard mills was consumed internally by the company's converting facilities; the remaining 59% was sold to manufacturers in various industries. External sales of unconverted paperboard accounted for 32% of 1994 net sales.

Caraustar derived 38% of net sales in both 1994 and 1993 from sales of tubes, cores and composite containers, together with sales of unconverted paperboard to independent manufacturers of tubes, cores and composite containers; 14% from folding cartons and related products, together with external sales of boxboard grades of unconverted paperboard; 24% from sales of gypsum wallboard and gypsum facing paper; 16% (18% in 1993) from other specialty, converted and laminated products; 4% (3%) from sales of injection-molded and extruded plastic products; and 4% (3%) from external sales of waste paper.

As of July 1995, the company had 42 converting facilities that produced tubes, cores and composite containers, folding cartons and set-up boxes and specialty converted products.

Caraustar's tube and core converting plants obtain most of their recycled paperboard from its paperboard mills. Because of the relatively high cost of shipping tubes and cores, these facilities generally serve customers within a relatively small geographic area.

The company purchases 60% of its wastepaper requirements from independent waste paper sources.

Important Developments

Aug. '95—Gibraltar Packaging Group, Inc., terminated its merger pact with Caraustar, after an investigation at Gibraltar's G. B. Labels site revealed groundwater contamination. The estimated remediation costs are between $750,000 and $1.1 million. In March, CSAR definitively agreed to acquire Gibraltar for about $35 million and assumption of about $38 million of existing debt. Gibraltar manufactures folding cartons and other packaging products.

Capitalization

Long Term Debt: $83,439,000 (6/95).
Minority Interest: $248,000.

Per Share Data ($) (Year Ended Dec. 31)

	1994	1993	1992	1991	1990	1989
Tangible Bk. Val.	3.76	2.86	1.93	-3.89	NA	NA
Cash Flow	1.95	1.57	1.74	1.68	NA	NA
Earnings	1.38	1.08	1.26	1.19	NA	NA
Dividends	0.38	0.33	0.08	Nil	NA	NA
Payout Ratio	27%	30%	8%	Nil	NA	NA
Prices - High	22½	20¼	20¼	NA	NA	NA
- Low	15	13¼	14⅞	NA	NA	NA
P/E Ratio - High	16	19	16	NA	NA	NA
- Low	11	12	12	NA	NA	NA

Income Statement Analysis (Million $)

	1994	%Chg	1993	%Chg	1992	%Chg	1991
Revs.	456	25%	365	18%	309	12%	276
Oper. Inc.	78.9	29%	61.0	-1%	61.7	4%	59.1
Depr.	14.5	16%	12.5	32%	9.5	12%	8.5
Int. Exp.	6.9	1%	6.8	-45%	12.3	-25%	16.4
Pretax Inc.	57.6	36%	42.5	7%	39.9	17%	34.2
Eff. Tax Rate	38%	—	36%	—	38%	—	38%
Net Inc.	35.5	30%	27.3	10%	24.9	17%	21.2

Balance Sheet & Other Fin. Data (Million $)

	1994	1993	1992	1991	1990	1989
Cash	12.5	14.4	23.7	3.1	NA	NA
Curr. Assets	101	82.6	75.1	48.8	NA	NA
Total Assets	267	221	184	134	NA	NA
Curr. Liab.	52.3	39.6	28.6	47.4	NA	NA
LT Debt	83.0	84.0	83.0	126	NA	NA
Common Eqty.	102	74.4	47.6	-68.7	NA	NA
Total Cap.	204	171	146	71.0	NA	NA
Cap. Exp.	29.3	21.3	16.6	10.6	NA	NA
Cash Flow	50.0	39.8	34.4	29.8	NA	NA

Ratio Analysis

	1994	1993	1992	1991	1990	1989
Curr. Ratio	1.9	2.1	2.6	1.0	NA	NA
% LT Debt of Cap.	41.0	48.9	57.3	176.7	NA	NA
% Net Inc.of Revs.	7.8	7.5	8.1	7.7	NA	NA
% Ret. on Assets	14.5	13.4	13.5	NA	NA	NA
% Ret. on Equity	39.9	44.6	NM	NA	NA	NA

Dividend Data —Cash dividends were initiated in late 1992. A "poison pill" shareholder rights plan was adopted in 1995.

Amt. of Div. $	Date Decl.	Ex-Div. Date	Stock of Record	Payment Date
0.090	Aug. 23	Sep. 16	Sep. 22	Oct. 10 '94
0.105	Nov. 03	Dec. 16	Dec. 22	Jan. 09 '95
0.105	Mar. 08	Mar. 16	Mar. 22	Apr. 10 '95
0.105	Apr. 26	Jun. 19	Jun. 21	Jul. 10 '95
0.105	Aug. 24	Sep. 20	Sep. 22	Oct. 09 '95

Data as orig. reptd.; bef. results of disc. opers. and/or spec. items. Per share data adj. for stk. divs. as of ex-div. date. E-Estimated. NA-Not Available. NM-Not Meaningful. NR-Not Ranked.

Office—3100 Washington St., Austell, GA 30001. **Tel**—(404) 948-3101. **Chrmn**—J. G. Dalton. **Pres & CEO**—T. V. Brown. **VP, CFO & Investor Contact**—H. Lee Thrash III. **VP & Secy**—Ann F. Strickland. **Dirs**—T. V. Brown, J. G. Dalton, M. F. Forrest, R. M. Holt Jr., J. D. Munford, B. M. Prillaman, R. M. Robinson, J. E. Rogers, H. L. Thrash III. **Transfer Agent & Registrar**—First Union National Bank of North Carolina, Charlotte. **Incorporated** in North Carolina in 1980. **Empl**-3,386. **S&P Analyst:** Stewart Scharf

STANDARD & POOR'S

STOCK REPORTS

Carmike Cinemas

NYSE Symbol **CKE**
In S&P SmallCap 600

31-JUL-95

Industry: Filmed Entertainment

Summary: In terms of total theaters and screens operated, Carmike is the second largest motion picture exhibitor in the U.S. Operations have grown through acquisitions and new construction.

Quantitative Evaluations

Outlook (1 Lowest—5 Highest)
• **NA**
Fair Value
• **NA**
Risk
• **Average**
Earn./Div. Rank
• **B**

Technical Eval.
• **Bearish** since 7/95
Rel. Strength Rank (1 Lowest—99 Highest)
• **14**
Insider Activity
• **NA**

Recent Price • 22½
52 Wk Range • 25½-17¾
Yield • Nil
12-Mo. P/E • 12.6

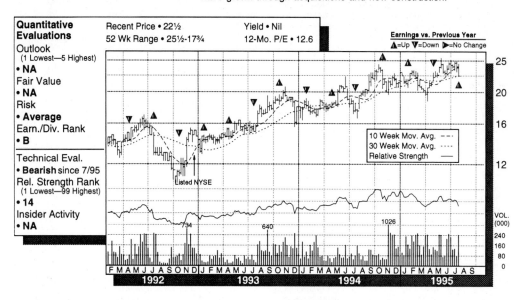

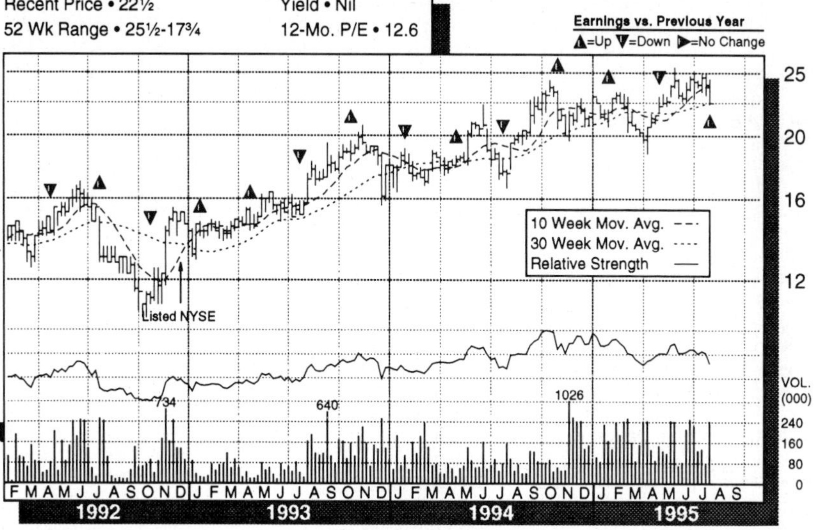

Business Profile - 31-JUL-95

In terms of the number of theaters and screens operated, Carmike is the second largest U.S. motion picture exhibitor, and the leading exhibitor in the southern portion of the country. The company added 241 screens in 1994, and continues to expand through theater acquisitions and construction. Following a sharp decline in attendance in the 1995 first quarter, gross theater revenues in the second quarter resumed their long uptrend.

Operational Review - 31-JUL-95

Acquisitions, new theater openings and blockbuster summer films contributed to higher total revenues in the first half of 1995. Operating expenses rose more rapidly, and operating income declined. Despite reduced interest expense, net income was sharply lower, reflecting a first quarter loss. However, a recent increase in ticket prices, together with screen acquisitions and the addition of new theaters, should boost future results.

Stock Performance - 28-JUL-95

In the past 30 trading days, CKE's shares have declined 5%, compared to a 4% rise in the S&P 500. Average trading volume for the past five days was 50,740 shares, compared with the 40-day moving average of 36,754 shares.

Key Stock Statistics

Dividend Rate/Share	Nil	Shareholders	800
Shs. outstg. (M)	11.2	Market cap. (B)	$0.251
Avg. daily vol. (M)	0.031	Inst. holdings	67%
Tang. Bk. Value/Share	11.27	Insider holdings	NA
Beta	1.19		

Value of $10,000 invested 5 years ago: $ 16,216

Fiscal Year Ending Dec. 31

	1995	% Change	1994	% Change	1993	% Change
Revenues (Million $)						
1Q	63.90	-5%	67.43	57%	43.00	21%
2Q	91.23	34%	68.09	34%	50.98	22%
3Q	—	—	109.0	32%	82.40	84%
4Q	—	—	83.10	27%	65.40	30%
Yr.	—	—	327.6	35%	241.8	41%
Income (Million $)						
1Q	-2.06	NM	1.66	91%	0.87	18%
2Q	4.16	158%	1.61	-15%	1.90	-17%
3Q	—	—	10.28	41%	7.29	NM
4Q	—	—	3.40	88%	1.81	-8%
Yr.	—	—	16.95	43%	11.86	94%
Earnings Per Share ($)						
1Q	-0.18	NM	0.20	82%	0.11	10%
2Q	0.37	85%	0.20	-17%	0.24	-20%
3Q	—	—	1.25	39%	0.90	NM
4Q	—	—	0.36	64%	0.22	-12%
Yr.	—	—	2.00	33%	1.50	88%

Next earnings report expected: late October

Carmike Cinemas

Business Summary - 31-JUL-95

Carmike Cinemas, Inc. is the second largest motion picture exhibitor in the U.S., in terms of the number of theaters and screens operated, and is the leading exhibitor in the southern portion of the U.S. The company has expanded primarily by acquiring theater chains.

As of mid-May 1995, the company was operating 471 theaters in 31 states, with a total of 2,046 screens. Theaters are principally in smaller communities, with populations of 40,000 to 200,000, where Carmike is the sole or leading exhibitor.

Total revenues in recent years were derived as follows:

	1994	1993	1992	1991
Admissions	71%	69%	69%	68%
Concessions & other	29%	31%	31%	32%

Of 445 theaters operated at December 31, 1994, nearly all were multi-screen. Of the screens owned by Carmike, over 99% were located in multi-screen theaters, with over 89% in theaters with three or more screens. Most of the theaters principally exhibit first-run films, but the company also converts marginally profitable theaters to Discount Theatres that exhibit films previously shown on a first-run basis. At 1994 year-end, there were 71 Discount Theatres.

During 1994, the company finalized the acquisition of 178 screens from Cinema World and 48 screens from General Cinema. In addition, it built five new theater complexes, with 43 screens, and added 15 screens to existing complexes.

Important Developments

Jul. '95—Carmike announced the acquisition from NYSE-listed Cineplex Odeon of 28 theaters (with 145 screens) in Florida and Georgia, for $22 million in cash.

May '95—The company said its first quarter loss reflected an industry-wide decline in ticket sales.

Nov. '94—The public sale of 2,875,000 Class A common shares produced net proceeds of $58.2 million. Proceeds were earmarked for acquisition and construction of theaters, debt reduction, and general corporate purposes.

Capitalization

Long Term Debt: $155,110,000 (3/95), incl. $19,087,000 of lease obligs.

Class A Common Stock: 9,740,101 shs. ($0.03 par); one vote per sh.

Class B Common Stock: 1,420,700 shs. ($0.03 par); 10 votes per sh. (72% of voting power); conv. sh.-for-sh. into Cl. A; divs. equal to 85% of Cl. A. Closely held, primarily by the Patrick family.

Per Share Data ($) (Year Ended Dec. 31)

	1994	1993	1992	1991	1990	1989
Tangible Bk. Val.	11.54	7.94	8.51	8.63	7.85	5.60
Cash Flow	4.66	3.55	2.25	1.95	1.83	2.23
Earnings	2.00	1.50	0.80	0.75	0.84	1.22
Dividends	Nil	Nil	Nil	Nil	Nil	Nil
Payout Ratio	Nil	Nil	Nil	Nil	Nil	Nil
Prices - High	24⅜	20¾	17	17¼	16⅜	13⅞
- Low	16⅜	12⅞	10½	9	7¼	7¾
P/E Ratio - High	12	14	21	23	19	11
- Low	8	9	13	12	9	6

Income Statement Analysis (Million $)

	1994	%Chg	1993	%Chg	1992	%Chg	1991
Revs.	328	36%	242	41%	172	18%	146
Oper. Inc.	67.8	35%	50.3	53%	32.9	14%	28.8
Depr.	22.5	38%	16.3	47%	11.1	20%	9.2
Int. Exp.	17.4	18%	14.8	25%	11.8	16%	10.2
Pretax Inc.	28.2	42%	19.8	96%	10.1	5%	9.6
Eff. Tax Rate	40%	—	40%	—	40%	—	41%
Net Inc.	17.0	43%	11.9	95%	6.1	7%	5.7

Balance Sheet & Other Fin. Data (Million $)

	1994	1993	1992	1991	1990	1989
Cash	22.7	32.7	32.1	24.0	30.4	15.2
Curr. Assets	33.5	42.2	39.0	32.7	40.2	20.1
Total Assets	378	327	230	184	179	135
Curr. Liab.	44.2	37.2	27.3	17.0	15.8	12.5
LT Debt	144	181	120	91.6	94.0	85.1
Common Eqty.	172	93.9	75.7	69.2	63.3	32.8
Total Cap.	333	290	203	167	163	122
Cap. Exp.	29.1	33.5	13.3	22.7	34.1	31.0
Cash Flow	39.5	28.1	17.2	14.9	13.7	11.4

Ratio Analysis

	1994	1993	1992	1991	1990	1989
Curr. Ratio	0.8	1.1	1.4	1.9	2.5	1.6
% LT Debt of Cap.	43.2	62.3	59.2	54.8	57.7	69.5
% Net Inc.of Revs.	5.2	4.9	3.6	3.9	4.9	6.3
% Ret. on Assets	4.1	4.2	2.9	3.1	3.3	5.0
% Ret. on Equity	11.2	13.6	8.4	8.6	11.3	21.2

Dividend Data (No dividends have been paid since the company's initial public stock offering. Carmike's loan agreement prohibits the payment of cash dividends.)

Data as orig. reptd.; bef. results of disc. opers. and/or spec. items. Per share data adj. for stk. divs. as of ex-div. date. E-Estimated. NA-Not Available. NM-Not Meaningful. NR-Not Ranked.

Office—1301 First Ave., Columbus, GA 31901. **Tel**—(706) 576-3400. **Chrmn**—C. L. Patrick. **Pres & CEO**—M. W. Patrick. **VP-Fin, Treas, CFO & Investor Contact**—John O. Barwick III. **VP & Secy**—L. M. Adams. **Dirs**—J. W. Jordan II, C. L. Patrick, C. L. Patrick, Jr., M. W. Patrick, C. E. Sanders, D. W. Zalaznick. **Transfer Agent & Registrar**—Synovus Trust Co., Columbus. **Incorporated** in Delaware in 1982. **Empl**-8,060. **S&P Analyst:** Efraim Levy

STANDARD & POOR'S

STOCK REPORTS

Cascade Natural Gas

NYSE Symbol **CGC**
In S&P SmallCap 600

11-OCT-95 **Industry:** Utilities-Gas

Summary: This natural gas distributor serves more than 90 communities in Washington and Oregon.

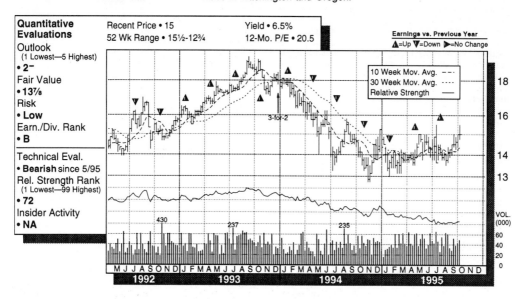

Quantitative Evaluations
Outlook
(1 Lowest—5 Highest)
• **2-**
Fair Value
• **13⅞**
Risk
• **Low**
Earn./Div. Rank
• **B**

Technical Eval.
• **Bearish** since 5/95
Rel. Strength Rank
(1 Lowest—99 Highest)
• **72**
Insider Activity
• **NA**

Recent Price • 15
52 Wk Range • 15½-12¾
Yield • 6.5%
12-Mo. P/E • 20.5

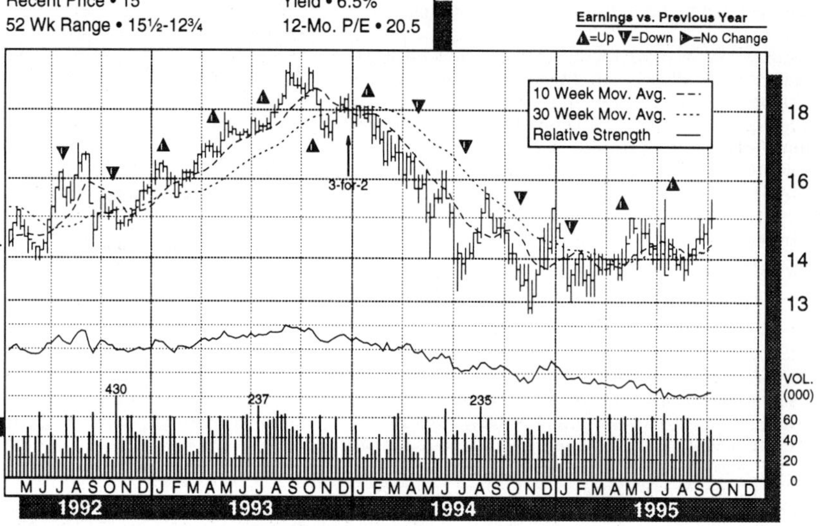

Business Profile - 11-OCT-95

This natural gas distributor serves over 144,000 customers in 90 communities in Washington and Oregon, with a total population of 724,000. Over the 12 months ended June 30, 1995, CGC's customer base increased 6.8%, compared to 8.1% for the 1994 period. This growth rate is high compared to the national average of 2%, and Cascade expects this to continue, given the demand for converting existing buildings to gas. Management is considering a preferred stock issue to provide long term capital.

Operational Review - 11-OCT-95

Operating margin in the first half of 1995 was up 12% over the 1994 period. Of the total margin, core margin rose 12% due to an increase in the number and consumption rate of residential and commercial customers, as well as higher Oregon rates to cover costs associated with additional transmission capacity needed to meet growth. Deliveries to a cogeneration customer added in April 1994 led to a 12% advance in non-core margin as well. Net earnings available to common shareholders jumped 41%.

Stock Performance - 06-OCT-95

In the past 30 trading days, CGC's shares have increased 6%, compared to a 4% rise in the S&P 500. Average trading volume for the past five days was 9,800 shares, compared with the 40-day moving average of 10,177 shares.

Key Stock Statistics

Dividend Rate/Share	0.96	Shareholders	9,200
Shs. outstg. (M)	9.1	Market cap. (B)	$0.135
Avg. daily vol. (M)	0.009	Inst. holdings	19%
Tang. Bk. Value/Share	9.93	Insider holdings	NA
Beta	0.29		

Value of $10,000 invested 5 years ago: $ 17,457

Fiscal Year Ending Dec. 31

	1995	% Change	1994	% Change	1993	% Change
Revenues (Million $)						
1Q	64.61	NM	64.75	5%	61.73	31%
2Q	34.71	-4%	36.26	-2%	37.14	34%
3Q	—	—	28.87	-2%	29.44	17%
4Q	—	—	62.53	6%	59.15	13%
Yr.	—	—	192.4	3%	187.4	23%
Income (Million $)						
1Q	5.73	19%	4.81	-27%	6.56	75%
2Q	-0.88	NM	-1.28	NM	-0.84	NM
3Q	—	—	-2.33	NM	-1.97	NM
4Q	—	—	4.55	-12%	5.15	25%
Yr.	—	—	5.76	-35%	8.89	84%
Earnings Per Share ($)						
1Q	0.63	17%	0.54	-36%	0.84	56%
2Q	-0.11	NM	-0.16	NM	-0.13	NM
3Q	—	—	-0.28	NM	-0.25	NM
4Q	—	—	0.50	-15%	0.59	4%
Yr.	—	—	0.60	-43%	1.05	67%

Next earnings report expected: late October

Cascade Natural Gas

Business Summary - 11-OCT-95

Cascade Natural Gas distributes natural gas in 90 communities in Washington and Oregon, with a population of about 724,000. The principal industrial activities in the company's service area include the production of pulp, paper and converted paper products, plywood, chemical fertilizers, industrial chemicals, cement, clay and ceramic products and textiles, refining of crude oil, smelting and forming of aluminum, food processing and canning, and the drying and curing of wood and agricultural products. Revenues by customer class in recent years were:

	1994	1993	1992
Residential	27%	25%	25%
Industrial (firm)	6%	6%	6%
Industrial (interruptible)	1%	1%	1%
Commercial (firm)	26%	25%	25%
Non-core (interruptible)	35%	38%	37%
Commercial (interruptible)	2%	1%	2%
Transportation	4%	4%	4%

Therm sales in 1994 came to 528,284,000, up from 498,414,000 in 1993. About 81% of the company's business is in Washington. Customers served at year-end 1994 totaled 142,839, up from 132,668 a year earlier. Residential customers totaled 113,398, firm commercial customers 22,035, firm industrial 327, and interruptible 32, all classified as core customers. In addition, there were 91 noncore customers using nontraditional unbundled gas supplies and services initially made available during 1989.

The majority of Cascade's natural gas supply is transported via Northwest Pipeline Corp. Baseload supply is provided by six major Canadian long-term gas supply contracts. During 1994, the company purchased 59.3% of its total gas supplies under firm gas supply contracts, 39.3% on the spot market, and 1.4% from customer assigned contracts.

Cascade has four non-utility subsidiaries that are engaged in financing CGC's customers' purchases of energy-efficient appliances, exploration of natural gas, and ownership of certain real property in Oregon. The subsidiaries, which account for less than 5% of the consolidated assets of the company, do not have a significant impact on Cascade's financial condition or results of operations.

Important Developments

Jul. '95—Cascade reported that temperatures based on estimated degree days for the second quarter of 1995 were 10% warmer than normal, but 22% colder than the prior year period. Separately, the company said that June 30, 1995, year-to-date capital expenditures were $15,320,000. The remainder of the $39.5 million total capital budget will be funded with operating cash flow and short term lines of credit.

Capitalization

Long Term Debt: $100,000,000 (6/95).
Red. Preferred Stock: $7,200,000.

Per Share Data ($) (Year Ended Dec. 31)

	1994	1993	1992	1991	1990	1989
Tangible Bk. Val.	9.84	10.00	9.05	8.59	8.33	7.91
Earnings	0.60	1.05	0.63	1.14	1.26	1.29
Dividends	0.96	0.94	0.93	0.90	0.87	0.85
Payout Ratio	160%	90%	146%	79%	69%	66%
Prices - High	18⅛	19½	17	16⅞	12⅝	13¾
- Low	12¾	15½	13⅝	11⅛	10⅛	9⅜
P/E Ratio - High	30	18	27	15	10	11
- Low	21	14	21	10	8	7

Income Statement Analysis (Million $)

	1994	%Chg	1993	%Chg	1992	%Chg	1991
Revs.	192	3%	187	23%	152	-1%	154
Depr.	10.1	10%	9.1	9%	8.4	9%	7.7
Maint.	NA	—	NA	—	NA	—	NA
Fxd. Chgs. Cov.	2.0	-23%	2.5	37%	1.9	-24%	2.4
Constr. Credits	0.2	-38%	0.3	45%	0.2	38%	0.2
Eff. Tax Rate	35%	—	37%	—	37%	—	36%
Net Inc.	5.8	-35%	8.9	84%	4.8	-37%	7.7

Balance Sheet & Other Fin. Data (Million $)

	1994	1993	1992	1991	1990	1989
Gross Prop.	342	315	284	249	231	217
Cap. Exp.	27.0	33.0	35.3	19.7	16.4	12.9
Net Prop.	214	197	175	148	137	129
Capitalization:						
LT Debt	100	87.0	74.7	57.1	60.8	60.1
% LT Debt	45	48	49	47	51	52
Pfd.	7.2	7.5	8.0	8.3	2.4	2.9
% Pfd.	3.70	4.20	5.20	6.70	2.10	2.50
Common	87.7	85.7	69.2	57.2	54.9	51.7
% Common	45	48	46	47	47	45
Total Cap.	214	198	168	137	132	129

Ratio Analysis

	1994	1993	1992	1991	1990	1989
Oper. Ratio	92.6	91.4	92.0	90.8	89.8	90.2
% Earn. on Net Prop.	7.0	8.7	7.5	9.9	12.2	13.5
% Ret. on Revs.	3.0	4.7	3.2	5.0	5.2	4.9
% Ret. On Invest.Cap	6.9	8.8	8.2	11.6	13.0	13.0
% Return On Com.Eqty	6.0	11.0	6.7	13.4	15.4	16.6

Dividend Data —Dividends have been paid since 1964. A dividend reinvestment plan is available. A "poison pill" stock purchase right was adopted in 1993.

Amt. of Div. $	Date Decl.	Ex-Div. Date	Stock of Record	Payment Date
0.240	Sep. 30	Oct. 07	Oct. 14	Nov. 15 '94
0.240	Dec. 13	Jan. 09	Jan. 13	Feb. 15 '95
0.240	Mar. 17	Apr. 07	Apr. 14	May. 15 '95
0.240	Jun. 21	Jul. 12	Jul. 14	Aug. 15 '95
0.240	Sep. 25	Oct. 11	Oct. 13	Nov. 15 '95

Data as orig. reptd.; bef. results of disc opers. and/or spec. items. Per share data adj. for stk. divs. as of ex-div. date. E-Estimated. NA-Not Available. NM-Not Meaningful. NR-Not Ranked.

Office—222 Fairview Ave. North, Seattle, WA 98109. **Tel**—(206) 624-3900. **Chrmn & CEO**—W. B. Matsuyama. **Pres & COO**—R. E. Boyd. **EVP, CFO & Secy**—D. E. Bennett. **Treas**—J. E. Haug. **Investor Contact**—F. Frank Mansell. **Dirs**—D. E. Bennett, C. Burnham, Jr., M. C. Clapp, D. A. Ederer, H. L. Hubbard, W. B. Matsuyama, B. G. Ragen, A. V. Smith, M. A. Williams. **Transfer Agent & Registrar**—Bank of New York, NYC. **Incorporated** in Washington in 1953. **Empl**-476. **S&P Analyst:** J. Santoriello

STANDARD & POOR'S STOCK REPORTS

Casey's General Stores

NASDAQ Symbol **CASY**
In S&P SmallCap 600

24-SEP-95

Industry: Retail Stores

Summary: This company operates over 940 convenience stores in nine midwestern states, selling a broad selection of food, beverage, health and automotive products.

Quantitative Evaluations

Outlook
(1 Lowest—5 Highest)
• **3+**

Fair Value
• **20⅞**

Risk
• **Average**

Earn./Div. Rank
• **B+**

Technical Eval.
• **Bullish** since 9/94

Rel. Strength Rank
(1 Lowest—99 Highest)
• **90**

Insider Activity
• **Neutral**

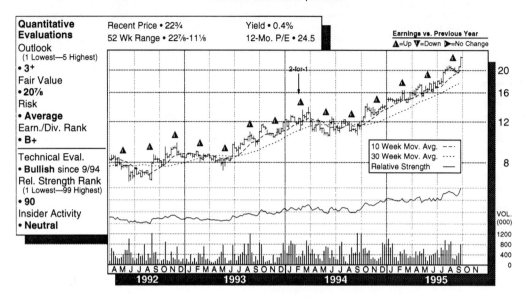

Recent Price • 22¾
52 Wk Range • 22⅞-11⅛
Yield • 0.4%
12-Mo. P/E • 24.5

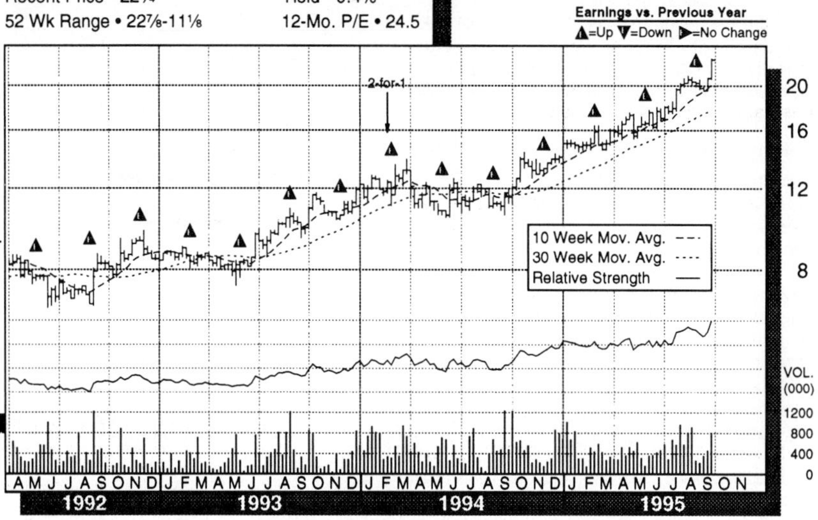

Business Profile - 19-SEP-95

Casey's operates more than 940 Midwest convenience stores that sell a broad selection of food, beverage, health and automotive products. Gasoline sales account for over 50% of retail sales, but a much smaller portion of profits. Results in recent periods benefited from an aggressive store opening program, combined with strict cost controls. The company expects to achieve $1 billion in annual sales from about 1,000 stores by December 1996.

Operational Review - 24-SEP-95

A 14% gain in net sales in the quarter ended July 31, 1995, was fueled by the addition of 54 new stores and a greater volume of gasoline sold. Wider gross margins per gallon of gasoline more than offset weaker gross margins on grocery and general merchandise, and pretax income climbed 21%. After taxes at 37.7%, versus 38.7%, net income grew 23%, and the company turned in its 19th consecutive quarter of increased earnings.

Stock Performance - 22-SEP-95

In the past 30 trading days, CASY's shares have increased 10%, compared to a 5% rise in the S&P 500. Average trading volume for the past five days was 158,840 shares, compared with the 40-day moving average of 110,538 shares.

Key Stock Statistics

Dividend Rate/Share	0.10	Shareholders	2,600
Shs. outstg. (M)	26.1	Market cap. (B)	$0.593
Avg. daily vol. (M)	0.091	Inst. holdings	64%
Tang. Bk. Value/Share	6.92	Insider holdings	NA
Beta	0.42		

Value of $10,000 invested 5 years ago: $ 42,543

Fiscal Year Ending Apr. 30

	1996	% Change	1995	% Change	1994	% Change
Revenues (Million $)						
1Q	253.0	14%	221.3	14%	193.7	9%
2Q	—	—	223.7	20%	187.0	6%
3Q	—	—	199.4	15%	172.6	9%
4Q	—	—	204.5	15%	177.9	10%
Yr.	—	—	848.8	16%	731.2	9%
Income (Million $)						
1Q	7.90	23%	6.43	35%	4.75	16%
2Q	—	—	7.53	40%	5.38	21%
3Q	—	—	5.72	42%	4.04	28%
4Q	—	—	3.19	34%	2.38	49%
Yr.	—	—	22.88	38%	16.56	25%
Earnings Per Share ($)						
1Q	0.30	20%	0.25	16%	0.22	16%
2Q	—	—	0.29	21%	0.24	20%
3Q	—	—	0.22	22%	0.18	29%
4Q	—	—	0.12	20%	0.10	33%
Yr.	—	—	0.88	21%	0.73	22%

Next earnings report expected: early December

Casey's General Stores

Business Summary - 24-SEP-95

Casey's General Stores, Inc. operates convenience stores in nine midwestern states. The stores sell a wide range of food, beverages, tobacco products, health and beauty aids, automotive products and other nonfood items. They also offer gasoline for sale on a self-service basis. In 1994-95, 54% of retail sales and 9.4% of gross profits came from the sale of gasoline. As of April 30, 1995, there were 927 stores, including 186 franchised units, mostly in Iowa (308), Missouri (217) and Illinois (208), with the remainder in Kansas, Minnesota, Nebraska, South Dakota, Wisconsin and Indiana.

The company has traditionally located its stores in small towns not served by national-chain convenience stores. About 74% of all Casey's stores operate in areas with populations under 5,000; 6% are located in communities with populations exceeding 20,000.

Each store typically carries more than 2,500 food and nonfood items. The products offered are those normally found in a supermarket, except that the stores do not sell produce or fresh meats, and selection generally is limited to one or two well known brands. Most staple foodstuffs are of nationally advertised brands.

Casey's stores sell regional brands of dairy and bakery products. About 93% of all stores offer beer. Nonfood items include tobacco products, health and beauty aids, school supplies, housewares, pet and photo supplies, ammunition and automotive products.

Snack centers, which sell sandwiches, fountain drinks and other items, are in 99% of the stores, while pizza was available in 95% of the stores at the end of 1994-95. In addition, take-out fried chicken was available at 4% of the stores. Donuts, prepared on store premises, are available in 99% of the stores. Cinnamon rolls and cookies have also been introduced.

Casey's intends to continue to increase the number of company-owned stores, as well as the proportion of company-owned stores to franchised units, because of the greater profitability of such outlets and the company's greater operating control. Casey's believes that small towns located in its eight-state market area offer substantial opportunities for growth. A total of 60 new company stores were opened in 1994-95, 56 in 1993-94, 36 in 1992-93, and 23 in 1991-92. Casey's plans to open 65 stores in 1995-96, substantially all of which will be located in Iowa, Illinois and Minnesota.

Important Developments

Aug. '95—Casey's said it had opened 16 new stores during the first quarter of 1995-96. At July 31, 1995, the company was operating 941 stores, comprised of 756 corporate-owned and 185 franchise outlets.

Capitalization

Long Term Debt: $58,053,203 (7/95); incl. $8.1 million of lease obligs.

Per Share Data ($) (Year Ended Apr. 30)

	1995	1994	1993	1992	1991	1990
Tangible Bk. Val.	6.92	6.11	4.87	4.32	3.85	3.47
Cash Flow	1.73	1.54	1.30	1.12	0.95	0.80
Earnings	0.88	0.73	0.60	0.52	0.40	0.36
Dividends	0.10	0.08	0.06	0.06	0.05	Nil
Payout Ratio	11%	10%	10%	12%	12%	Nil
Cal. Yrs.	1994	1993	1992	1991	1990	1989
Prices - High	15⅝	12⅜	9¾	8⅝	5⅝	7⅛
- Low	10⅜	7⅜	6⅜	2⅝	2½	3⅞
P/E Ratio - High	17	17	16	16	14	20
- Low	12	10	11	6	6	11

Income Statement Analysis (Million $)

	1995	%Chg	1994	%Chg	1993	%Chg	1992
Revs.	854	39%	615	6%	578	10%	525
Oper. Inc.	65.2	26%	51.9	23%	42.2	15%	36.6
Depr.	22.2	21%	18.4	19%	15.5	17%	13.3
Int. Exp.	6.4	-20%	8.0	28%	6.2	16%	5.4
Pretax Inc.	37.4	39%	27.0	26%	21.5	16%	18.5
Eff. Tax Rate	39%	—	39%	—	38%	—	38%
Net Inc.	22.9	38%	16.6	25%	13.3	16%	11.5

Balance Sheet & Other Fin. Data (Million $)

	1995	1994	1993	1992	1991	1990
Cash	6.8	11.9	18.1	8.8	8.9	7.7
Curr. Assets	43.2	41.4	46.5	33.0	31.6	30.5
Total Assets	345	318	281	219	198	185
Curr. Liab.	77.0	75.5	55.5	46.6	35.8	29.9
LT Debt	60.0	61.4	99	61.4	63.8	64.5
Common Eqty.	180	158	108	95.9	84.8	79.5
Total Cap.	267	242	224	172	161	155
Cap. Exp.	52.6	67.1	51.4	35.4	22.7	35.2
Cash Flow	45.1	35.0	28.8	24.8	21.3	18.5

Ratio Analysis

	1995	1994	1993	1992	1991	1990
Curr. Ratio	0.5	0.5	0.8	0.7	0.9	1.0
% LT Debt of Cap.	22.5	25.4	44.1	35.7	39.5	41.6
% Net Inc.of Revs.	2.7	2.7	2.3	2.2	1.7	1.8
% Ret. on Assets	6.9	5.1	5.3	5.5	4.8	4.8
% Ret. on Equity	13.5	11.6	13.1	12.7	11.2	11.1

Dividend Data —A poison pill stock purchase rights plan was adopted in 1989. Cash dividends were initiated in 1990. A two-for-one stock split was effected in February 1994.

Amt. of Div. $	Date Decl.	Ex-Div. Date	Stock of Record	Payment Date
0.020	Aug. 29	Oct. 26	Nov. 01	Nov. 15 '94
0.020	Dec. 05	Jan. 26	Feb. 01	Feb. 15 '95
0.020	Feb. 27	Apr. 25	May. 01	May. 15 '95
0.025	Jun. 20	Jul. 28	Aug. 01	Aug. 15 '95
0.025	Aug. 29	Oct. 30	Nov. 01	Nov. 15 '95

Data as orig. reptd.; bef. results of disc. opers. and/or spec. items. Per share data adj. for stk. divs. as of ex-div. date. E-Estimated. NA-Not Available. NM-Not Meaningful. NR-Not Ranked.

Office—One Convenience Blvd., Ankeny, IA 50021. **Tel**—(515) 965-6100. **Chrmn & CEO**—D. F. Lamberti. **Pres & COO**—R. M. Lamb. **Secy**—J. G. Harmon. **CFO, Treas & Investor Contact**—Douglas K. Shull. **Dirs**—G. A. Doerner, J. R. Fitzgibbon, J. G. Harmon, K. H. Haynie, R. M. Lamb, D. F. Lamberti, D. K. Shull, J. P. Taylor. **Transfer Agent & Registrar**—United Missouri Bank of Kansas City. **Incorporated** in Iowa in 1967. **Empl**-8,035. **S&P Analyst:** Maureen C. Carini

STANDARD & POOR'S

Cash America International

STOCK REPORTS

NYSE Symbol **PWN**

In S&P SmallCap 600

13-SEP-95 **Industry:** Finance

Summary: This company is operates the largest chain of pawnshops in the world, with some 366 locations in the U.S., the U.K. and Sweden.

Quantitative Evaluations

Outlook (1 Lowest—5 Highest) • **5-**

Fair Value • **8**

Risk • **Average**

Earn./Div. Rank • **B+**

Technical Eval. • **Bullish** since 8/95

Rel. Strength Rank (1 Lowest—99 Highest) • **31**

Insider Activity • **NA**

Recent Price • 6⅞

52 Wk Range • 9⅞-6¼

Yield • 0.7%

12-Mo. P/E • 12.5

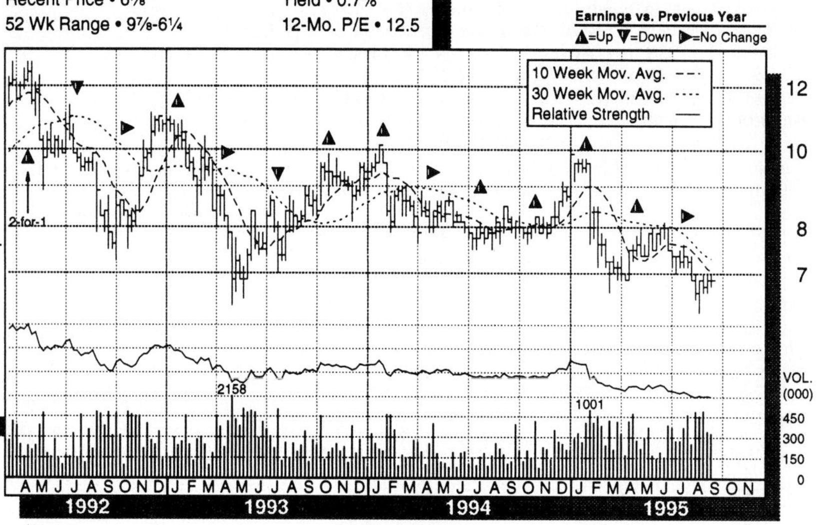

Business Profile - 08-SEP-95

This leading pawnshop operator has conducted an aggessive expansion program in the U.S.; in 1994, it opened 41 new units and acquired 11 stores. This continues its stategy of increasing its share of consumer loan business, and expanding its penetration in regional and local markets. PWN's recent alliance with check cashing concern Mr. Payroll Corp. is intended to boost store traffic by bringing check-cashing customers into its pawnshops and to enhance service to its existing customers.

Operational Review - 08-SEP-95

Total revenues for the six months ended June 30, 1995, rose 26%, year to year, reflecting increases of 28% and 33% in pawn service charges on loans and pawn shop sales, respectively. Loans outstanding at June 30, 1995, grew to $78,941,000, from $59,878,000 a year earlier. Total operating expenses climbed 23%, and operating income advanced 29%. After net interest expense more than doubled, net income was up 7.9%, to $6,457,000 ($0.22 a share), from $5,987,000 ($0.21).

Stock Performance - 08-SEP-95

In the past 30 trading days, PWN's shares have declined 5%, compared to a 2% rise in the S&P 500. Average trading volume for the past five days was 81,475 shares, compared with the 40-day moving average of 106,315 shares.

Key Stock Statistics

Dividend Rate/Share	0.05	Shareholders	900
Shs. outstg. (M)	28.6	Market cap. (B)	$0.204
Avg. daily vol. (M)	0.109	Inst. holdings	70%
Tang. Bk. Value/Share	4.27	Insider holdings	NA
Beta	0.73		

Value of $10,000 invested 5 years ago: $ 9,371

Fiscal Year Ending Dec. 31

	1995	% Change	1994	% Change	1993	% Change
Revenues (Million $)						
1Q	71.20	29%	55.31	6%	52.10	27%
2Q	70.20	23%	57.20	9%	52.45	25%
3Q	—	—	63.26	15%	55.08	23%
4Q	—	—	86.33	32%	65.34	13%
Yr.	—	—	262.1	17%	225.0	21%
Income (Million $)						
1Q	3.35	14%	2.93	5%	2.80	NM
2Q	3.10	1%	3.06	20%	2.54	-10%
3Q	—	—	4.21	15%	3.67	18%
4Q	—	—	5.30	10%	4.83	13%
Yr.	—	—	15.50	12%	13.84	6%
Earnings Per Share ($)						
1Q	0.12	20%	0.10	NM	0.10	NM
2Q	0.11	NM	0.11	22%	0.09	-10%
3Q	—	—	0.15	15%	0.13	18%
4Q	—	—	0.18	6%	0.17	13%
Yr.	—	—	0.54	12%	0.48	7%

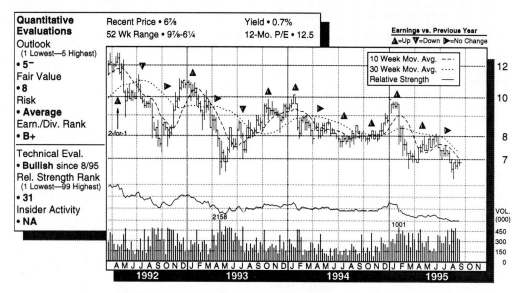

Next earnings report expected: late October

Cash America International

Business Summary - 13-SEP-95

Cash America International (formerly Cash America Investments) operates pawnshops that lend money on the security of pledged tangible personal property. As of December 31, 1994, the company was operating 300 pawnshops in the U.S., with by far the greatest concentration in Texas. Other locations were in Louisiana, Oklahoma, Tennessee, Florida, Georgia, Kentucky, Ohio, Colorado, Indiana, Missouri, North Carolina, South Carolina and Alabama. The company expanded into Europe in early 1992 through the acquisition of 26 pawnshops in the U.K. As of December 31, 1994, the company was operating 30 pawnshops in the U.K. and 10 in Sweden.

Contributions to revenues in recent years:

	1994	1993	1992
Sales	59.6%	62.2%	61.9%
Pawn service charges	40.4%	37.7%	37.9%
Other	0.0%	0.1%	0.2%

The number of pawnshops in operation at the end of recent years:

1994	340
1993	280
1992	249

To compensate for their loans, pawnshops contract for what PWN refers to as a pawn service charge, based on a percentage of the loan amount and on the size and duration of the loan. Service charges (or loan rates) generally range from 12% to 240% annually. Pledged property is held through the term of the loan, which is generally one month, with an automatic 60-day extension unless paid earlier or renewed.

In a majority of cases, loans are paid in full with accrued service charges or are renewed through payment of the accrued service charges. In the event that the borrower does not pay the loan, the unredeemed collateral is forfeited and is sold in the resale operation of the pawnshop.

Customers generally are individuals who do not have checking accounts and who conduct most or all of their transactions on a cash basis.

PWN acquires existing pawnshops and establishes new stores that can benefit from centralized management and operations. It intends to continue to concentrate on multiple shops in regional and local markets, in order to expand market penetration.

Important Developments

Jul. '95—The company reported that it added 22 stores in the U.S. and four stores in the U.K. during the first six months of 1995, bringing the total number of pawnshops in operation to 366 at June 30, 1995.

Capitalization

Long Term Debt: $119,796,000 (12/94).

Per Share Data ($) (Year Ended Dec. 31)

	1994	1993	1992	1991	1990	1989
Tangible Bk. Val.	4.17	3.77	3.58	2.74	2.50	2.22
Cash Flow	0.34	0.71	0.70	0.63	0.52	0.42
Earnings	0.54	0.48	0.45	0.43	0.37	0.30
Dividends	0.05	0.05	0.05	0.04	0.03	0.02
Payout Ratio	9%	10%	10%	9%	7%	7%
Prices - High	$10\frac{1}{8}$	11	$12\frac{7}{8}$	$9\frac{3}{4}$	$10\frac{1}{4}$	$7\frac{5}{8}$
- Low	$7\frac{1}{2}$	$6\frac{3}{8}$	$7\frac{1}{4}$	6	$5\frac{3}{4}$	$3\frac{1}{4}$
P/E Ratio - High	19	23	29	23	28	26
- Low	14	13	16	14	16	11

Income Statement Analysis (Million $)

	1994	%Chg	1993	%Chg	1992	%Chg	1991
Revs.	262	16%	225	21%	186	35%	138
Oper. Inc.	40.2	26%	31.9	11%	28.7	30%	22.0
Depr.	8.8	32%	6.7	-5%	7.0	48%	4.7
Int. Exp.	6.3	67%	3.8	128%	1.6	-8%	1.8
Pretax Inc.	25.0	15%	21.8	7%	20.3	16%	17.5
Eff. Tax Rate	38%	—	36%	—	36%	—	40%
Net Inc.	15.5	12%	13.8	6%	13.0	24%	10.5

Balance Sheet & Other Fin. Data (Million $)

	1994	1993	1992	1991	1990	1989
Cash	4.8	2.2	4.2	1.4	3.0	3.8
Curr. Assets	189	132	122	77.8	66.5	53.0
Total Assets	324	245	216	138	117	98.0
Curr. Liab.	21.0	14.2	12.5	7.1	6.9	6.7
LT Debt	120	64.0	50.0	30.5	20.1	9.6
Common Eqty.	183	167	154	100	89.9	81.6
Total Cap.	303	231	204	131	110	91.0
Cap. Exp.	22.8	16.7	19.6	7.7	5.8	5.2
Cash Flow	24.3	20.5	20.0	15.3	12.6	10.1

Ratio Analysis

	1994	1993	1992	1991	1990	1989
Curr. Ratio	9.0	9.3	9.8	11.0	9.6	7.9
% LT Debt of Cap.	39.5	27.7	24.5	23.4	18.2	10.5
% Net Inc.of Revs.	5.9	6.2	7.0	7.6	7.5	8.0
% Ret. on Assets	5.4	6.0	6.8	8.3	8.0	7.7
% Ret. on Equity	8.8	8.6	9.5	11.1	10.1	8.9

Dividend Data —Special cash dividends were paid in January of 1988 and 1989. Quarterly dividends were initiated in April 1989.

Amt. of Div. $	Date Decl.	Ex-Div. Date	Stock of Record	Payment Date
0.013	Oct. 31	Nov. 03	Nov. 09	Nov. 23 '94
0.013	Feb. 01	Feb. 06	Feb. 10	Feb. 24 '95
0.013	May. 01	May. 04	May. 10	May. 24 '95
0.013	Aug. 02	Aug. 07	Aug. 09	Aug. 23 '95

Data as orig. reptd.; bef. results of disc. opers. and/or spec. items. Per share data adj. for stk. divs. as of ex-div. date. E-Estimated. NA-Not Available. NM-Not Meaningful. NR-Not Ranked.

Office—1600 West 7th St., Fort Worth, TX 76102-2599. **Tel**—(817) 335-1100. **Chrmn & CEO**—J. R. Daugherty. **Pres & COO**—D. R. Feehan. **VP & CFO**—D. R. Westerfeld. **VP & Secy**—H. Simpson. **Investor Contacts**—Michele L. Rosenblum; Thomas Bessant, Jr. **Dirs**—M. A. Cohn, J. R. Daugherty, A. R. Dike, D. R. Feehan, J. H. Greer, B. D. Hunter, C. H. Morris, Jr., C. P. Motheral, S. W. Rizzo, R. L. Waltrip. **Transfer Agent & Registrar**—First Interstate Bank of Texas. **Incorporated** in Texas in 1984. **Empl**-2,475. **S&P Analyst:** Brad Ohlmuller

Casino Magic

NASDAQ Symbol **CMAG**
In S&P SmallCap 600

03-OCT-95 **Industry:** Leisure/Amusement

Summary: This company owns and operates gaming casinos in Mississippi, South Dakota, Argentina and Greece.

Quantitative Evaluations

Outlook
(1 Lowest—5 Highest)
• **NA**

Fair Value
• **NA**

Risk
• **High**

Earn./Div. Rank
• **NR**

Technical Eval.
• **Bullish** since 9/95

Rel. Strength Rank
(1 Lowest—99 Highest)
• **21**

Insider Activity
• **Neutral**

Recent Price • 5 3/8
52 Wk Range • 7 3/4-4 5/8
Yield • Nil
12-Mo. P/E • NM

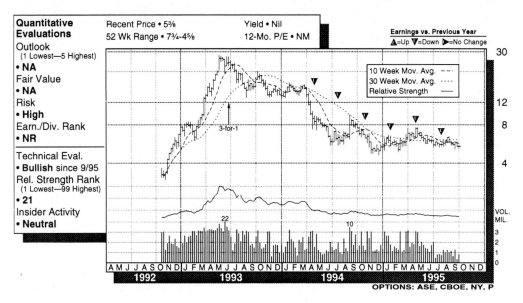

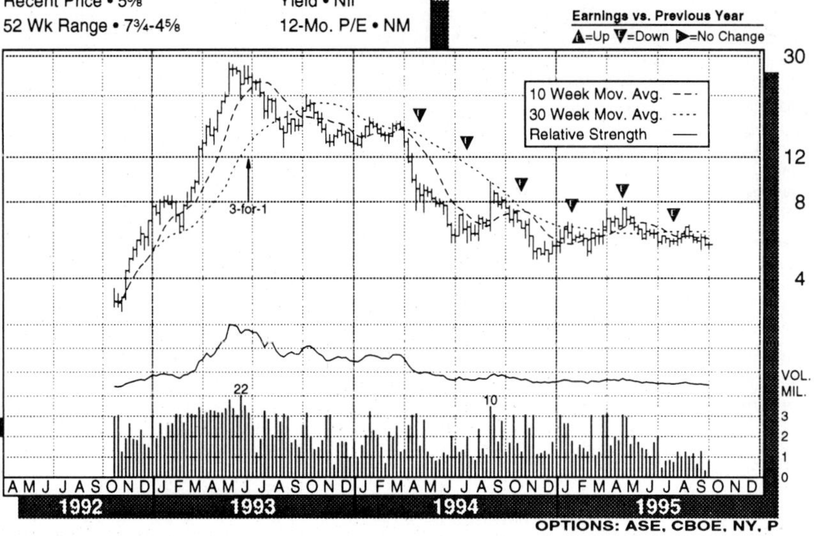

OPTIONS: ASE, CBOE, NY, P

Business Profile - 03-OCT-95

To offset lower revenues from Mississippi Gulf Coast Casinos, this casino operator plans to cut its annual budget by $15 million and to launch new operations to diversify its business. CMAG expects its two casinos in South America and American-style casino in Greece to contribute a meaningful portion of sales and earnings improvement in the second half of 1995. The company plans to open a casino on the border of North Dakota and South Dakota in late 1995.

Operational Review - 03-OCT-95

Revenues in the first half of 1995 declined 13%, year to year, as lower casino revenues at the Bay St. Louis facility outweighed initial contributions from three new foreign casinos. After $2.4 million of preopening costs and higher advertising and marketing expenses, operating income dropped 51%. Results were further penalized by initial operating losses from an unconsoliated subsidiary managing a casino in Greece, and a net loss replaced net income.

Stock Performance - 29-SEP-95

In the past 30 trading days, CMAG's shares have declined 15%, compared to a 5% rise in the S&P 500. Average trading volume for the past five days was 153,060 shares, compared with the 40-day moving average of 188,474 shares.

Key Stock Statistics

Dividend Rate/Share	Nil	Shareholders	1,400
Shs. outstg. (M)	34.1	Market cap. (B)	$0.188
Avg. daily vol. (M)	0.150	Inst. holdings	10%
Tang. Bk. Value/Share	2.74	Insider holdings	NA
Beta	NA		

Value of $10,000 invested 5 years ago: NA

Fiscal Year Ending Dec. 31

	1995	% Change	1994	% Change	1993	% Change
Revenues (Million $)						
1Q	43.17	-17%	51.94	34%	38.72	—
2Q	45.19	-9%	49.87	6%	46.98	—
3Q	—	—	45.56	-26%	61.44	—
4Q	—	—	37.65	-32%	55.28	—
Yr.	—	—	185.0	-9%	202.4	NM
Income (Million $)						
1Q	0.32	-89%	2.97	-78%	13.49	—
2Q	-1.60	NM	1.86	-81%	9.79	—
3Q	—	—	-0.22	NM	8.61	—
4Q	—	—	-7.64	NM	6.61	—
Yr.	—	—	-3.03	NM	38.51	NM
Earnings Per Share ($)						
1Q	0.01	-90%	0.10	-78%	0.45	—
2Q	-0.05	NM	0.07	-78%	0.32	—
3Q	—	—	-0.01	NM	0.28	—
4Q	—	—	-0.26	NM	0.22	—
Yr.	—	—	-0.10	NM	1.32	NM

Next earnings report expected: mid November

Casino Magic

Business Summary - 03-OCT-95

Casino Magic Corp. owns and operates gaming casinos in Bay St. Louis and Biloxi, Miss., Deadwood, S.D., Neuquen City and San Martin de los Andes in Argentina and Porto Carras, Greece (49% owned). It also has joint agreements to develop, own or manage several other casino projects. Revenues and operating income (in 000s) in 1994 were derived as follows:

	Revs.	Oper. Inc.
Bay St. Louis casino	58%	$27,186
Biloxi casino	41%	-9,624
Other	1%	-25,578

The Bay St. Louis facility is a two-level dockside gaming casino with 39,500 sq. ft. of gaming space containing 1,110 slot machines, 64 table games and a 35-seat keno parlor. An adjacent three-story land-based casino support building contains a 150-seat buffet restaurant, snack bar, 200-seat steak restaurant, gift shop and lounge area for live entertainment. Expansion plans may include a hotel with several specialty restaurants, swimming pools, a convention center and a championship golf and putting course.

The Biloxi facility is a three-level dockside gaming casino with 47,200 sq. ft. of gaming space containing 1,188 slot machines, 50 table games and a 35-seat keno parlor. It also has a 300-seat buffet restaurant, McDonald's restaurant and 100-seat table-service specialty restaurant, bar and lounge.

Important Developments

Aug. '95—CMAG agreed to sell its Goldiggers Casino in Deadwood, S.D., to Royal Casino Group. The price will consist of a new class of Royal Casino redeemable, non-dividend paying convertible preferred stock valued at $3 million, plus warrants to purchase 500,000 Royal Casino common shares at $4 a share.
Jun. '95—The company said it had agreed to acquire from Touristiki Georgiki Exagogiki S.A. the 51% interest in Porto Carras Casino S.A. that it does not already own, as well as three hotels and related assets in Porto Carras, Greece, where it opened a casino in May 1995. Total consideration is expected to be about $75 million.
May '95—CMAG acquired Casino One Corp., a unit of Gaming Corp. of America, in exchange for 2,125,000 common shares. Earlier, in March, the company said that in order to offset lower revenues from Mississippi Gulf Coast casinos, it would cut its annual budget by $15 million and launch new operations to diversify its business.

Capitalization

Long Term Debt: $136,974,734 (6/95).

Per Share Data ($) (Year Ended Dec. 31)

	1994	1993	1992	1991	1990	1989
Tangible Bk. Val.	2.66	2.65	0.99	-0.07	NA	NA
Cash Flow	0.26	1.54	0.34	-0.07	NA	NA
Earnings	-0.10	1.32	0.31	-0.07	NA	NA
Dividends	Nil	Nil	Nil	Nil	NA	NA
Payout Ratio	Nil	Nil	Nil	Nil	NA	NA
Prices - High	17¼	28⅜	8	NA	NA	NA
- Low	4⅝	6	1⅝	NA	NA	NA
P/E Ratio - High	NM	21	26	NA	NA	NA
- Low	NM	5	5	NA	NA	NA

Income Statement Analysis (Million $)

	1994	%Chg	1993	%Chg	1992	%Chg	1991
Revs.	185	-8%	202	NM	27.0	NM	2.0
Oper. Inc.	37.6	-49%	73.9	NM	12.7	NM	-0.2
Depr.	10.7	74%	6.1	NM	0.7	NM	0.2
Int. Exp.	16.6	114%	7.8	NM	2.1	NM	0.3
Pretax Inc.	-3.2	NM	59.7	NM	8.0	NM	-1.1
Eff. Tax Rate	NM	—	36%	—	37%	—	NM
Net Inc.	-3.0	NM	38.5	NM	5.0	NM	-1.1

Balance Sheet & Other Fin. Data (Million $)

	1994	1993	1992	1991	1990	1989
Cash	30.7	61.8	8.5	0.1	NA	NA
Curr. Assets	46.0	71.6	9.8	0.2	NA	NA
Total Assets	253	223	61.0	4.0	NA	NA
Curr. Liab.	1.8	21.6	23.8	4.1	NA	NA
LT Debt	136	132	13.0	NM	NA	NA
Common Eqty.	79.6	66.9	24.9	-0.7	NA	NA
Total Cap.	220	201	38.0	-1.0	NA	NA
Cap. Exp.	29.8	86.7	46.6	2.1	NA	NA
Cash Flow	7.6	44.6	5.7	-1.0	NA	NA

Ratio Analysis

	1994	1993	1992	1991	1990	1989
Curr. Ratio	3.3	0.4	0.1	NA	NA	NA
% LT Debt of Cap.	65.6	33.6	NM	NA	NA	NA
% Net Inc.of Revs.	19.0	18.6	NM	NA	NA	NA
% Ret. on Assets	27.1	14.6	NM	NA	NA	NA
% Ret. on Equity	83.9	NM	NM	NA	NA	NA

Dividend Data —No cash dividends have been paid. CMAG intends to retain earnings to fund operations and expand its business, and does not expect to pay cash dividends in the foreseeable future. A three-for-one stock split was effected in June 1993.

Data as orig. reptd.; bef. results of disc. opers. and/or spec. items. Per share data adj. for stk. divs. as of ex-div. date. E-Estimated. NA-Not Available. NM-Not Meaningful. NR-Not Ranked.

Office—711 Casino Magic Dr., Bay St. Louis, MS 39520. **Tel**—(601) 467-9257. **Chrmn**—M. F. Torguson. **Pres & COO**—D. B. Cooper. **EVP, CFO & Treas**—J. S. Osman. **Dirs**—W. W. Bednarczyk, R. H. Frommelt, A. J. Kokesch, W. K. Lund, P. M. Sidders, M. F. Torguson, E. T. Welch. **Transfer Agent & Registrar**—Norwest Bank Minnesota, South St. Paul. **Incorporated** in Minnesota in 1992. **Empl**-2,510. **S&P Analyst:** Efraim Levy

STANDARD & POOR'S

STOCK REPORTS

Catalina Marketing

NYSE Symbol **POS**
In S&P SmallCap 600

23-OCT-95

Industry: Advertising/Communications

Summary: Catalina is a leader in point-of-scan electronic marketing, delivering customized checkout coupons for manufacturers' products to targeted customers based on their purchases.

Quantitative Evaluations

Recent Price • 50
52 Wk Range • 62-40
Yield • Nil
12-Mo. P/E • 26.5

Outlook
(1 Lowest—5 Highest)
• **NA**
Fair Value
• **NA**
Risk
• **Average**
Earn./Div. Rank
• **NR**

Technical Eval.
• **Bearish** since 8/95
Rel. Strength Rank
(1 Lowest—99 Highest)
• **13**
Insider Activity
• **Unfavorable**

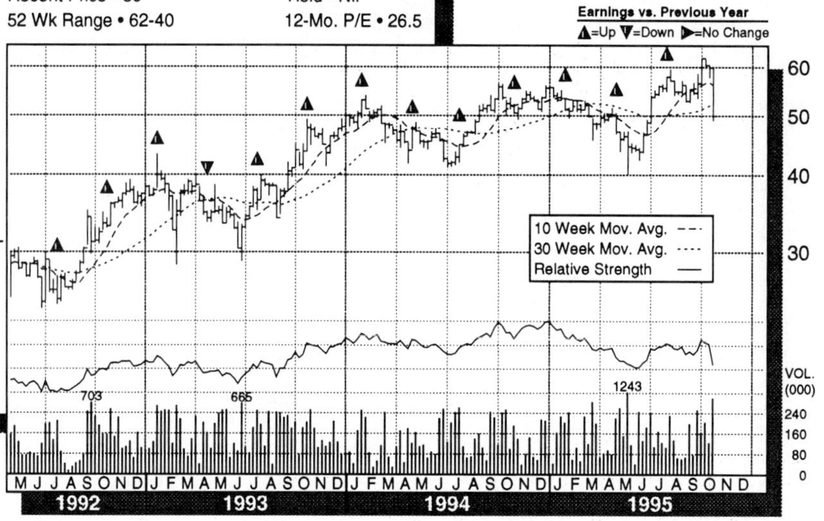

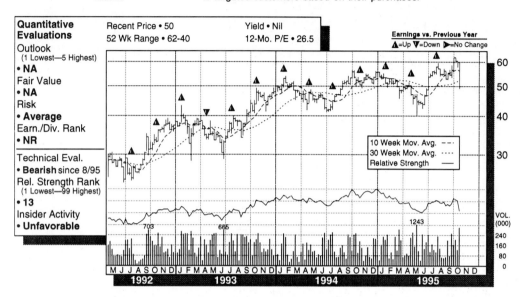

Business Profile - 20-OCT-95

Catalina provides packaged goods manufacturers and retailers with cost-effective promotions delivered to consumers at the checkout. Its technology enables it to customize products to individual shopper buying behavior. The company will deliver advertising and promotional services via the Internet, beginning in California in January 1996. Catalina has repuchased 472,400 common shares, and has announced plans to spend up to $10 million for additional purchases.

Operational Review - 20-OCT-95

Sales in the first half of 1995-6 rose 18%, year to year, as the number of stores using the company's network increased from about 8,000 to more than 9,000. Margins were hurt by greater spending for new business ventures, but EPS gained 20%, aided by higher other income. Catalina has stated that sales growth will be below its goals for the remainder of 1995-6. The balance sheet is strong, with no long term debt and over $28 million in cash.

Stock Performance - 20-OCT-95

In the past 30 trading days, POS's shares have declined 9%, compared to a 3% rise in the S&P 500. Average trading volume for the past five days was 192,000 shares, compared with the 40-day moving average of 54,854 shares.

Key Stock Statistics

Dividend Rate/Share	Nil	Shareholders	400
Shs. outstg. (M)	9.6	Market cap. (B)	$0.479
Avg. daily vol. (M)	0.072	Inst. holdings	76%
Tang. Bk. Value/Share	5.28	Insider holdings	NA
Beta	NA		

Value of $10,000 invested 5 years ago: NA

Fiscal Year Ending Mar. 31

	1996	% Change	1995	% Change	1994	% Change
Revenues (Million $)						
1Q	30.61	12%	27.45	52%	18.08	10%
2Q	30.94	25%	24.75	17%	21.23	24%
3Q	—	—	30.27	20%	25.19	29%
4Q	—	—	30.78	14%	26.96	44%
Yr.	—	—	113.3	24%	91.45	27%
Income (Million $)						
1Q	5.14	9%	4.70	78%	2.64	19%
2Q	5.33	26%	4.22	11%	3.80	63%
3Q	—	—	4.76	39%	3.42	37%
4Q	—	—	3.54	26%	2.80	137%
Yr.	—	—	17.23	36%	12.67	54%
Earnings Per Share ($)						
1Q	0.52	16%	0.45	73%	0.26	18%
2Q	0.54	29%	0.42	14%	0.37	61%
3Q	—	—	0.47	42%	0.33	32%
4Q	—	—	0.36	33%	0.27	125%
Yr.	—	—	1.71	38%	1.24	53%

Next earnings report expected: mid January

Catalina Marketing

Business Summary - 20-OCT-95

Catalina Marketing Corporation provides consumer product manufacturers and supermarket retailers a cost-effective method of implementing a targeted consumer marketing strategy. Its point-of-scan electronic marketing network delivers checkout coupons directly to targeted consumers at supermarket checkouts based on their purchases.

At the end of 1994-5, the company's network was installed in more than 9,000 stores nationwide, reaching more than 120 million households weekly. Catalina distributed over 1,750 million checkout coupons and other promotions in 1994-5. Manufacturers controlled by RJR/Nabisco Corp. accounted for 11% of revenues in 1994-5.

The principal service provided by Catalina is the checkout coupon, a manufacturer's coupon or other promotion delivered directly to targeted shoppers based on their purchases of the same, competitive or complementary products. The company offers manufacturers 13 four-week cycles during the year, for more than 500 product categories. The purchaser of a particular category is given the exclusive right to have coupons printed for that category for each cycle purchased. Catalina receives a fee from manufacturers for each promotion distributed, in addition to a minimum category fee determined by the estimated number of shoppers reached. Checkout coupons generated more than 95% of revenues in each of the past three fiscal years.

The Catalina Marketing network links the company's software, personal computers, central databases and specially designed thermal printers to checkout scanning equipment. Catalina's system evaluates scanner data, matches it with a programmed promotion, and directs the thermal printer, located near the cash register, to print the appropriate promotion.

Catalina enters into agreements with supermarket chains to install its network in all or selected stores. Upon installation, the retailer pays a one-time charge for each store, and generally agrees to use the Catalina Marketing network in its stores for five years. The company currently owns and supports the network equipment and pays distribution fees to retailers based on the number of promotions printed in the stores.

Important Developments

Oct. '95—The shares fell over 10% on October 17, following the release of Catalina's second quarter earnings. The company said it expects revenue growth of 15% to 20% for the remainder of 1995-6. It believes that it can meet an earlier goal of annual revenue growth of 20% to 30% in the 1996-7.

Capitalization

Long Term Debt: None (6/95).

Per Share Data ($)

(Year Ended Mar. 31)

	1995	1994	1993	1992	1991	1990
Tangible Bk. Val.	5.66	4.55	3.08	2.04	1.85	NA
Cash Flow	3.21	2.36	1.73	1.34	0.69	NA
Earnings	1.71	1.24	0.81	0.51	0.16	NA
Dividends	Nil	Nil	Nil	Nil	NA	NA
Payout Ratio	Nil	Nil	Nil	Nil	NA	NA
Cal. Yrs.	1994	1993	1992	1991	1990	1989
Prices - High	56¼	50¼	39¼	NA	NA	NA
- Low	41¼	28½	20	NA	NA	NA
P/E Ratio - High	33	41	49	NA	NA	NA
- Low	24	23	25	NA	NA	NA

Income Statement Analysis (Million $)

	1995	%Chg	1994	%Chg	1993	%Chg	1992
Revs.	113	24%	91.4	27%	71.9	39%	51.7
Oper. Inc.	42.9	44%	29.8	17%	25.5	81%	14.1
Depr.	15.1	32%	11.4	23%	9.3	18%	7.8
Int. Exp.	Nil	—	Nil	—	0.1	-80%	0.3
Pretax Inc.	27.9	45%	19.2	44%	13.3	99%	6.7
Eff. Tax Rate	40%	—	40%	—	38%	—	29%
Net Inc.	17.2	35%	12.7	54%	8.2	73%	4.8

Balance Sheet & Other Fin. Data (Million $)

	1995	1994	1993	1992	1991	1990
Cash	30.7	26.9	25.6	6.5	4.2	NA
Curr. Assets	60.2	51.2	39.9	25.8	12.5	NA
Total Assets	99	85.5	61.2	44.5	31.1	NA
Curr. Liab.	42.7	40.2	31.9	23.3	18.1	NA
LT Debt	Nil	Nil	Nil	2.4	2.5	NA
Common Eqty.	55.5	44.9	29.3	18.8	10.5	NA
Total Cap.	56.6	45.3	29.3	21.2	13.0	NA
Cap. Exp.	20.3	25.2	12.2	11.6	9.8	3.7
Cash Flow	32.3	24.1	17.5	12.6	6.3	3.0

Ratio Analysis

	1995	1994	1993	1992	1991	1990
Curr. Ratio	1.4	1.3	1.3	1.1	0.7	NA
% LT Debt of Cap.	Nil	Nil	Nil	11.2	19.3	NA
% Net Inc.of Revs.	15.2	13.9	11.4	9.2	4.3	2.3
% Ret. on Assets	18.7	17.0	15.4	13.2	NA	NA
% Ret. on Equity	34.4	33.7	33.8	36.9	NA	NA

Dividend Data —Catalina does not expect to pay cash dividends in the foreseeable future.

Data as orig. reptd.; bef. results of disc. opers. and/or spec. items. Per share data adj. for stk. divs. as of ex-div. date. E-Estimated. NA-Not Available. NM-Not Meaningful. NR-Not Ranked.

Office—11300 Ninth St. North, St. Petersburg, FL 33716. **Tel**—(813) 579-5000. **Chrmn**—T. D. Greer. **Pres & CEO**—G. W. Off. **SVP & CFO**—P.B. Livingston. **Dirs**—F. W. Beinecke, P. Collins, S. I. D'Agostino, T. D. Greer, T. G. Mendell, H. Monat, G. W. Off, T. Smith, D. C. Walker, M. B. Wilson. **Transfer Agent & Registrar**—Chemical Trust Co. of California, LA. **Incorporated** in Delaware in 1992. **Empl**-450. **S&P Analyst:** Stephen Madonna, CFA

STANDARD & POOR'S

STOCK REPORTS

Cato Corp.

NASDAQ Symbol **CACOA**

In S&P SmallCap 600

28-AUG-95

Industry: Retail Stores

Summary: This long-established retailer operates more than 655 stores in 22 states, offering women's popular-priced apparel for fashion-conscious junior, missy and large-size customers.

Quantitative Evaluations

Outlook
(1 Lowest—5 Highest)
• **NA**

Fair Value
• **NA**

Risk
• **High**

Earn./Div. Rank
• **B-**

Technical Eval.
• **Bearish** since 8/95

Rel. Strength Rank
(1 Lowest—99 Highest)
• **6**

Insider Activity
• **NA**

Recent Price • 7
52 Wk Range • 12¼-5

Yield • 2.3%
12-Mo. P/E • 12.5

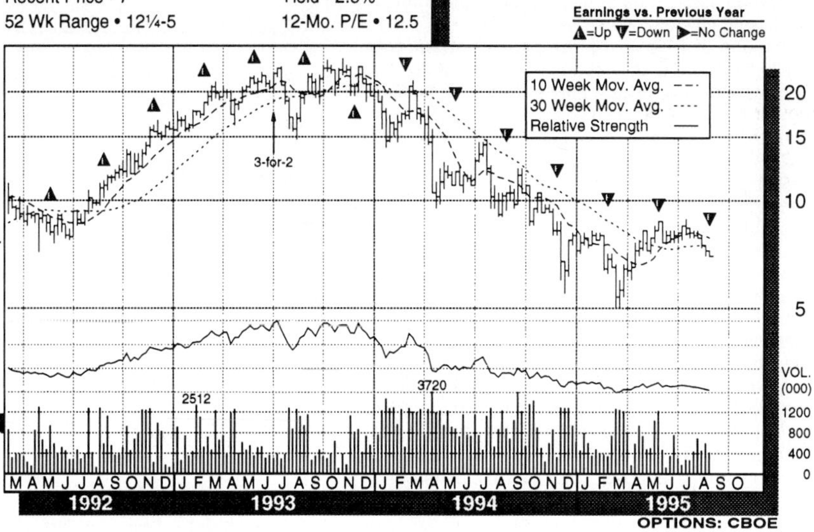

OPTIONS: CBOE

Business Profile - 28-AUG-95

This long-established retailer operates some 659 stores in 22 states, principally in non-metropolitan areas. Stores feature women's first-quality, value-priced apparel for the fashion-conscious junior, missy and large-size customer. Earnings in recent periods have been hurt by the ongoing sluggishness in the ladies' apparel environment. In light of the poor sales, Cato said that it would slow its store growth in 1995-96, and would concentrate on improving productivity.

Operational Review - 28-AUG-95

A modest year-to-year gain in revenues for the first half of 1995-96 primarily reflected contributions from 41 additional stores in operation. Same-store sales declined 4%. Gross margins narrowed, as increased markdowns were taken to combat the ongoing weakness in the apparel sales environment. After taxes at 33.5%, versus 36.5%, net income was down 17%, to $10.5 million from $12.5 million. Earnings per share were based on 2.7% fewer shares outstanding.

Stock Performance - 25-AUG-95

In the past 30 trading days, CACOA's shares have declined 16%, compared to a 0.04% rise in the S&P 500. Average trading volume for the past five days was 79,800 shares, compared with the 40-day moving average of 81,795 shares.

Key Stock Statistics

Dividend Rate/Share	0.16	Shareholders	8,000
Shs. outstg. (M)	28.4	Market cap. (B)	$0.199
Avg. daily vol. (M)	0.105	Inst. holdings	46%
Tang. Bk. Value/Share	5.21	Insider holdings	NA
Beta	1.97		

Value of $10,000 invested 5 years ago: $ 31,165

Fiscal Year Ending Jan. 31

	1996	% Change	1995	% Change	1994	% Change
Revenues (Million $)						
1Q	117.8	4%	113.1	17%	96.71	23%
2Q	114.7	1%	113.3	15%	98.36	25%
3Q	—	—	112.2	15%	97.52	22%
4Q	—	—	137.6	8%	127.3	23%
Yr.	—	—	476.2	13%	419.9	23%
Income (Million $)						
1Q	7.50	-9%	8.21	-13%	9.40	44%
2Q	2.96	-32%	4.33	-26%	5.84	49%
3Q	—	—	2.80	-37%	4.44	28%
4Q	—	—	2.77	-46%	5.13	-1%
Yr.	—	—	18.11	-27%	24.80	30%
Earnings Per Share ($)						
1Q	0.26	-7%	0.28	-13%	0.32	9%
2Q	0.10	-33%	0.15	-25%	0.20	36%
3Q	—	—	0.10	-33%	0.15	18%
4Q	—	—	0.10	-41%	0.17	-9%
Yr.	—	—	0.62	-26%	0.84	14%

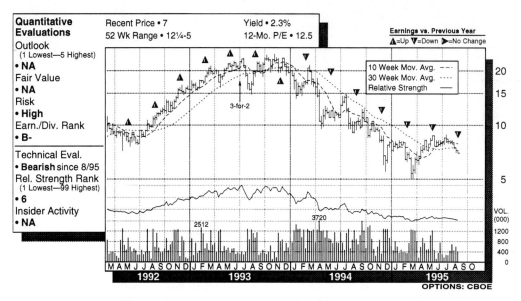

Next earnings report expected: mid November

Cato Corp.

Business Summary - 28-AUG-95

The Cato Corporation has operated retail specialty stores for more than 44 years. At July 29, 1995, it had 659 stores in 22 states, principally in the South and Southeast. The stores operate under the "Cato," "Cato Fashions" or "Cato Plus" names, featuring women's popular-priced apparel for the fashion-conscious junior, missy and large-size customer. The company also has an off-price division (108 stores), which operates stores under the "It's Fashion!" name, featuring primarily sportswear and accessories at 20% to 80% off regular retail prices.

The total number of stores at the end of recent fiscal years was:

1995	538
1994	575
1993	505
1992	487
1991	528

Cato stores feature head-to-toe dressing for its customers, including a broad assortment of apparel and accessories for ages 18 to 45, including casual and dressy sportwear, dresses careerwear, coats, hosiery, shoes, costume jewelry, handbags and millinery. A substantial portion of the company's merchandise is sold under its private labels. About 29% of 1994-95 retail sales represented merchandise for large size customers. Most stores range in size from 4,800 to 8,000 sq. ft. and are located primarily in strip shopping centers anchored by major discount stores such as Kmart and Wal-Mart.

The "It's Fashion!" stores average only 3,000 sq. ft., and offer limited selections of first-quality women's apparel and accessories. Most of the merchandise for these stores is purchased at closeout prices from manufacturers with excessive inventories due to overruns or order cancellations.

In 1994-95, CACOA opened 80 new stores and closed nine locations, versus 86 new stores opened and 16 closed during 1993-94. In addition, 30 stores were relocated and 20 expanded. During 1995-96, it expects to open an additional 35 new stores, relocate 18 stores and expand 10 stores. The company will also close about 10 to 15 stores.

Important Developments

Aug. '95—Cato said total sales in the four weeks ended July 29, 1995, rose 5%, year to year; same-store sales were down 2%.

Capitalization

Long Term Debt: None (7/95).
Class A Common Stock: 23,172,796 shs. ($0.03 1/3 par); one vote per sh.
Class B Common Stock: 5,264,317 shs. ($0.03 1/3 par); 10 votes per sh.

Per Share Data ($)

(Year Ended Jan. 31)

	1995	1994	1993	1992	1991	1990
Tangible Bk. Val.	4.98	4.50	2.94	1.37	0.91	1.37
Cash Flow	0.86	1.02	0.89	0.63	-0.23	-0.04
Earnings	0.62	0.84	0.74	0.43	-0.45	-0.24
Dividends	0.15	0.09	0.04	Nil	0.01	0.05
Payout Ratio	23%	10%	5%	Nil	Nil	NM
Cal. Yrs.	1994	1993	1992	1991	1990	1989
Prices - High	21 1/2	24 3/4	16 5/8	10 1/8	2 7/16	3 1/2
- Low	5 1/2	14 3/4	7 1/8	3/8	3/8	2 3/16
P/E Ratio - High	35	29	23	23	NM	NM
- Low	9	18	10	1	NM	NM

Income Statement Analysis (Million $)

	1995	%Chg	1994	%Chg	1993	%Chg	1992
Revs.	476	13%	420	23%	341	24%	274
Oper. Inc.	35.7	-19%	44.0	25%	35.1	55%	22.7
Depr.	6.8	25%	5.5	32%	4.2	-4%	4.3
Int. Exp.	0.4	52%	0.3	-79%	1.2	-63%	3.3
Pretax Inc.	28.5	-26%	38.3	29%	29.7	97%	15.1
Eff. Tax Rate	37%	—	35%	—	36%	—	37%
Net Inc.	18.1	-27%	24.8	30%	19.1	101%	9.5

Balance Sheet & Other Fin. Data (Million $)

	1995	1994	1993	1992	1991	1990
Cash	46.2	42.6	29.7	16.6	3.0	5.1
Curr. Assets	143	139	94.2	69.5	55.3	60.2
Total Assets	201	179	122	95.0	83.0	97.0
Curr. Liab.	48.9	47.2	40.4	36.3	29.9	26.6
LT Debt	Nil	Nil	Nil	24.9	29.4	34.0
Common Eqty.	142	128	78.2	30.5	20.0	30.3
Total Cap.	146	131	80.9	56.2	49.4	69.3
Cap. Exp.	25.5	17.2	7.6	1.7	1.8	4.3
Cash Flow	24.9	30.3	23.3	13.9	-5.1	-0.9

Ratio Analysis

	1995	1994	1993	1992	1991	1990
Curr. Ratio	2.9	2.9	2.3	1.9	1.8	2.3
% LT Debt of Cap.	Nil	Nil	Nil	44.3	59.6	49.0
% Net Inc.of Revs.	3.8	5.9	5.6	3.5	NM	NM
% Ret. on Assets	9.5	16.1	16.2	10.6	NM	NM
% Ret. on Equity	13.4	23.5	33.3	37.6	NM	NM

Dividend Data—Cash dividends on the Class A common, omitted in May 1990, were resumed in May 1992. No cash dividends have been paid on the Class B stock.

Amt. of Div. $	Date Decl.	Ex-Div. Date	Stock of Record	Payment Date
0.040	Aug. 25	Sep. 06	Sep. 12	Sep. 26 '94
0.040	Dec. 01	Dec. 13	Dec. 19	Jan. 02 '95
0.040	Feb. 23	Mar. 07	Mar. 13	Mar. 27 '95
0.040	May. 25	Jun. 15	Jun. 12	Jul. 03 '95
0.040	Aug. 24	Sep. 07	Sep. 11	Sep. 25 '95

Data as orig. reptd.; bef. results of disc. opers. and/or spec. items. Per share data adj. for stk. divs. as of ex-div. date. E-Estimated. NA-Not Available. NM-Not Meaningful. NR-Not Ranked.

Office—8100 Denmark Rd., Charlotte, NC 28273-5975. **Tel**—(704) 554-8510. **Chrmn & CEO**—W. H. Cato. Jr. **Vice Chrmn**—E. T. Cato. **Pres**—L. McFarland Jenkins. **EVP, CFO & Secy**—A. E. Wiley. **SVP, Treas & Investor Contact**—V. Hollis Scott. **Dirs**—R. W. Bradshaw, Jr., E. T. Cato, J. P. D. Cato, T. E. Cato, W. H. Cato, Jr., G. S. Currin, P. Fulton, C. C. Goodyear, G. Hamrick, R. L. Kirby, L. McFarland Jenkins, H. A. Severson, J. H. Shaw, A. F. Sloan, A. E. Wiley. **Transfer Agent & Registrar**—First Union National Bank, Charlotte. **Incorporated** in Delaware in 1946. **Empl**-6,600. **S&P Analyst:** Maureen C. Carini

STANDARD & POOR'S

STOCK REPORTS

CellPro, Inc.

NASDAQ Symbol **CPRO**
In S&P SmallCap 600

19-SEP-95

Industry: Drugs-Generic and OTC

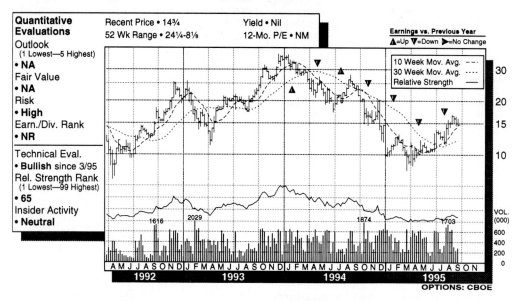

Summary: This company develops, manufactures and markets continuous-flow, cell selection systems used for therapeutic, diagnostic and research applications.

Quantitative Evaluations

Outlook (1 Lowest—5 Highest)
• **NA**
Fair Value
• **NA**
Risk
• **High**
Earn./Div. Rank
• **NR**

Technical Eval.
• **Bullish** since 3/95
Rel. Strength Rank (1 Lowest—99 Highest)
• **65**
Insider Activity
• **Neutral**

Recent Price • 14¾
52 Wk Range • 24¼-8⅛
Yield • Nil
12-Mo. P/E • NM

OPTIONS: CBOE

Business Profile - 14-SEP-95

CellPro initiated a Phase III trial in January 1995 to demonstrate the CEPRATE SC system's ability to deplete tumor cells from peripheral blood. In July 1995, CellPro received European marketing approval to sell CEPRATE SC in the 18-nation European Economic Area. CEPRATE SC is also sold in Canada and Israel. The CEPRATE LC system is sold for laboratory purposes only. Phase I/II trials for dose intensified, multicycle chemotherapy are currently underway.

Operational Review - 19-SEP-95

Total revenues in the three months ended June 30, 1995, advanced 26%, year to year, based on higher product sales ($1.2 million vs. $803,718). Interest income was marginally higher. Costs rose substantially in all areas led by increases in R&D expenditures from ongoing clinical studies. The net loss widened to $5,948,367 ($0.45 a share) from $3,246,400 ($0.25). The company had cash and equivalents totaling $58 million at the end of June.

Stock Performance - 15-SEP-95

In the past 30 trading days, CPRO's shares have increased 4%, compared to a 4% rise in the S&P 500. Average trading volume for the past five days was 55,400 shares, compared with the 40-day moving average of 151,956 shares.

Key Stock Statistics

Dividend Rate/Share	Nil	Shareholders	NA
Shs. outstg. (M)	14.1	Market cap. (B)	$0.211
Avg. daily vol. (M)	0.095	Inst. holdings	45%
Tang. Bk. Value/Share	6.17	Insider holdings	NA
Beta	NA		

Value of $10,000 invested 5 years ago: NA

Fiscal Year Ending Mar. 31

	1996	% Change	1995	% Change	1994	% Change
Revenues (Million $)						
1Q	2.20	26%	1.75	197%	0.59	—
2Q	—	—	1.84	179%	0.66	—
3Q	—	—	2.22	164%	0.84	155%
4Q	—	—	2.39	68%	1.42	149%
Yr.	—	—	8.20	134%	3.51	103%
Income (Million $)						
1Q	-5.95	NM	-3.25	NM	-3.01	NM
2Q	—	—	-4.20	NM	-3.34	NM
3Q	—	—	-4.82	NM	-3.36	NM
4Q	—	—	-6.71	NM	-5.40	NM
Yr.	—	—	-18.99	NM	-15.12	NM
Earnings Per Share ($)						
1Q	-0.45	NM	-0.25	NM	-0.26	—
2Q	—	—	-0.32	NM	-0.29	—
3Q	—	—	-0.37	NM	-0.29	NM
4Q	—	—	-0.51	NM	-0.44	NM
Yr.	—	—	-1.45	NM	-1.27	NM

Next earnings report expected: late October

CellPro, Inc.

Business Summary - 19-SEP-95

CellPro, Inc. is engaged in developing, manufacturing and marketing proprietary cell selection systems that can be used for a variety of therapeutic, diagnostic and research applications. The company is preparing an amendment to a premarket approval application filed with the FDA in December 1993 for its CEPRATE Stem Cell (SC) system for use in autologous bone marrow transplantation. Additional applications for the system, including use as an adjunct to dose-intensified multicycle cancer chemotherapy and gene therapy, are being developed.

The company's technology selects cells by using a patented high-affinity avidin-biotin binding process. The process takes advantage of monoclonal antibodies for selectivity and the strong affinity between avidin (a protein) and biotin (a vitamin) to allow cell selection to be performed in a high-volumes. Cellular therapy, in which purified cell populations obtained from tissues such as bone marrow or blood are used to treat a variety of diseases, depends on the collection of specific target cells, or the removal of particular cellular contaminants, from a mixture of cells. Bone marrow transplantation, a significant application of cellular therapy, is increasingly being used to treat patients with certain forms of cancer.

The company's CEPRATE SC system is designed to provide a supply of purified stem cells that can be used in cellular therapies without causing the problems frequently experienced with current transplantation techniques. The administration of purified stem cells may allow cancer patients to receive intensified doses of chemotherapy, thereby extending disease-free survival rates. CEPRATE SC is currently being used for autologous bone marrow transplantation in over 150 clinics in 19 countries, including Canada, Israel, and the European Economic Area.

A new Phase III trial to test CEPRATE SC's effectiveness to deplete cells in peripheral blood was initiated in January 1995. The two-year trial is powered for 134 myeloma patients. Several Phase I/II trials for applications in dose-intensified chemotherapy to treat solid tissue tumors are currently underway.

CellPro's first commercial product, the CEPRATE LC Laboratory Cell Separator, introduced in October 1991, allows selection of various types of hematopoietic cells for research purposes.

Important Developments

Jul. '95—CellPro concluded its collaboration with Corange International, modifying their 1993 agreement. The settlement calls for Corange to pay CellPro $30 million in exchange for 1,000,000 newly issued CellPro common shares and certain supply rights. In the original agreement, Corange was to purchase a 15% stake in CellPro for $110 million.

Capitalization

Long Term Debt: $365,250 (6/95).

Per Share Data ($) (Year Ended Mar. 31)

	1995	1994	1993	1992	1991	1990
Tangible Bk. Val.	6.17	7.63	4.95	3.41	-8.26	NA
Cash Flow	-1.22	-1.13	-1.10	-1.21	-5.34	NA
Earnings	-1.45	-1.27	-1.23	-1.25	-5.59	NA
Dividends	Nil	Nil	Nil	Nil	Nil	NA
Payout Ratio	Nil	Nil	Nil	Nil	Nil	NA
Cal. Yrs.	1994	1993	1992	1991	1990	1989
Prices - High	36¼	36½	25½	19¼	NA	NA
- Low	9⅝	11¼	7¼	9¾	NA	NA
P/E Ratio - High	NM	NM	NM	NM	NA	NA
- Low	NM	NA	NA	NA	NA	NA

Income Statement Analysis (Million $)

	1995	%Chg	1994	%Chg	1993	%Chg	1992
Revs.	4.2	NM	1.4	NM	0.3	NM	0.1
Oper. Inc.	-19.8	NM	-14.4	NM	-11.4	NM	-6.6
Depr.	3.1	87%	1.6	35%	1.2	NM	0.3
Int. Exp.	0.2	-24%	0.2	NM	0.2	31%	0.2
Pretax Inc.	-19.0	NM	-15.1	NM	-11.4	NM	-9.1
Eff. Tax Rate	Nil	—	Nil	—	Nil	—	Nil
Net Inc.	-19.0	NM	-15.1	NM	-11.4	NM	-9.1

Balance Sheet & Other Fin. Data (Million $)

	1995	1994	1993	1992	1991	1990
Cash	64.7	95.5	55.9	30.3	4.0	NA
Curr. Assets	69.5	98.4	56.8	31.1	4.0	NA
Total Assets	90.0	111	62.0	35.0	5.0	NA
Curr. Liab.	8.3	10.5	3.9	4.6	0.5	NA
LT Debt	0.5	0.8	0.9	0.5	0.5	NA
Common Eqty.	80.8	99	57.4	30.0	-5.4	NA
Total Cap.	81.0	100	58.0	30.0	5.0	NA
Cap. Exp.	11.1	8.6	2.9	2.4	0.5	NA
Cash Flow	-15.9	-13.5	-10.2	-8.7	-3.5	NA

Ratio Analysis

	1995	1994	1993	1992	1991	1990
Curr. Ratio	8.4	9.4	14.5	6.8	8.7	NA
% LT Debt of Cap.	0.6	0.8	1.5	1.5	9.8	NA
% Net Inc.of Revs.	NM	NM	NM	NM	NM	NA
% Ret. on Assets	NM	NM	NM	NM	NM	NA
% Ret. on Equity	NM	NM	NM	NM	NM	NA

Dividend Data —No cash dividends have been paid. The company does not expect to pay cash dividends in the foreseeable future.

Data as orig. reptd.; bef. results of disc. opers. and/or spec. items. Per share data adj. for stk. divs. as of ex-div. date. E-Estimated. NA-Not Available. NM-Not Meaningful. NR-Not Ranked.

Office—22215 - 26th Ave., S.E., Bothell, WA 98021. **Tel**—(206) 485-7644. **Chrmn**—J. S. Lacob. **Pres & CEO**—R. D. Murdock. **Sr VP-Fin & CFO**—L. G. Culver. **Investor Contact**—Lee M. Parker. **Dirs**—L. G. Culver, J. L. Green, T. D. Kiley, J. S. Lacob, R. D. Murdock, C. P. Waite Jr. **Transfer Agent & Registrar**—First National Bank of Boston. **Incorporated** in Delaware in 1987. **Empl**-180. **S&P Analyst:** Thomas Tirney

STANDARD & POOR'S

STOCK REPORTS

Central Hudson Gas & Electric

NYSE Symbol **CNH**

In S&P SmallCap 600

07-AUG-95

Industry: Util.-Diversified

Summary: This medium-sized utility provides electric and, to a lesser extent, gas service to a large area of New York's mid-Hudson River Valley.

Quantitative Evaluations

Outlook (1 Lowest—5 Highest)
• 3^{+}

Fair Value
• 26⅜

Risk
• Low

Earn./Div. Rank
• B

Technical Eval.
• **Bullish** since 6/95

Rel. Strength Rank (1 Lowest—99 Highest)
• 32

Insider Activity
• Neutral

Recent Price • 26⅝
52 Wk Range • 27¾-22⅞

Yield • 7.9%
12-Mo. P/E • 10.6

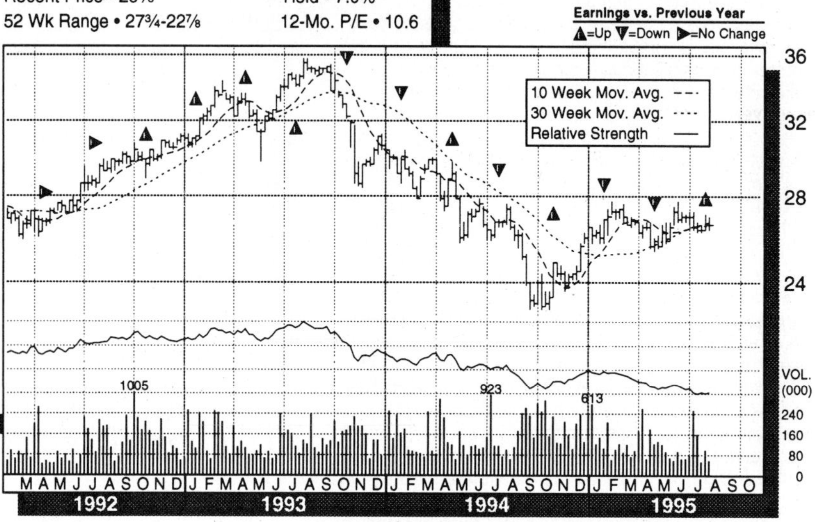

Business Profile - 04-AUG-95

CNH's Hudson River Valley territory in New York reflects a diversified economy, but one that has been negatively impacted by the downsizing of its largest electricity customer, IBM. Electric power is mainly supplied by oil and coal and, to a lesser extent, nuclear (approximately 14%), gas and hydro facilities and through purchases. The company plans $296 million in construction expenditures over the next five years to improve its generating facilities and expand distribution capabilities.

Operational Review - 04-AUG-95

Earnings during the first half of 1995 decreased 1.9% to $30.42 million ($1.21 a share), from $31.0 million ($1.67) in the same period one year ago. However, earnings improved in the second quarter, as a result of reduced operation and maintenance costs at the company's electric generating plant, decreased interest expenses, and an after-tax gain of $600,000 from the sale of long-term stock investments.

Stock Performance - 04-AUG-95

In the past 30 trading days, CNH's shares have declined 1%, compared to a 2% rise in the S&P 500. Average trading volume for the past five days was 11,020 shares, compared with the 40-day moving average of 24,015 shares.

Key Stock Statistics

Dividend Rate/Share	2.10	Shareholders	26,400
Shs. outstg. (M)	17.3	Market cap. (B)	$0.461
Avg. daily vol. (M)	0.018	Inst. holdings	39%
Tang. Bk. Value/Share	22.46	Insider holdings	NA
Beta	0.44		

Value of $10,000 invested 5 years ago: $ 16,765

Fiscal Year Ending Dec. 31

	1995	% Change	1994	% Change	1993	% Change
Revenues (Million $)						
1Q	144.7	-11%	162.8	6%	153.4	4%
2Q	118.6	1%	117.2	NM	117.7	-7%
3Q	—	—	116.1	-3%	120.1	NM
4Q	—	—	119.5	-5%	126.2	-4%
Yr.	—	—	515.7	NM	517.4	-1%
Income (Million $)						
1Q	19.56	-11%	22.07	10%	20.09	26%
2Q	10.86	22%	8.93	-20%	11.21	11%
3Q	—	—	12.43	17%	10.59	-8%
4Q	—	—	7.50	-15%	8.81	-13%
Yr.	—	—	50.93	1%	50.39	6%
Earnings Per Share ($)						
1Q	1.06	-13%	1.22	6%	1.15	25%
2Q	0.55	22%	0.45	-24%	0.59	7%
3Q	—	—	0.65	18%	0.55	-13%
4Q	—	—	0.36	-12%	0.41	-25%
Yr.	—	—	2.68	NM	2.68	1%

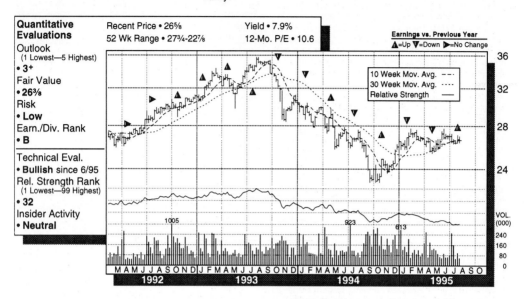

Next earnings report expected: late November

Central Hudson Gas & Electric

Business Summary - 04-AUG-95

Central Hudson Gas & Electric supplies electricity to 259,765 customers and natural gas to 59,424 customers in a 2,600 sq. mi. area in the Hudson River Valley of New York. The company's territory has a diversified economy, including manufacturing industries, research firms, farms, governmental agencies, public and private institutions, resorts, and wholesale and retail trade operations. Electric sales accounted for 80% of revenues and 89% of operating earnings in 1994. Contributions to electric revenues by customer class in recent years were:

	1994	1993	1992	1991
Residential	44%	42%	39%	37%
Commercial	32%	30%	28%	28%
Industrial	20%	22%	25%	25%
Other	4%	6%	8%	10%

The fuel mix in 1994 was oil 10%, coal 36%, gas 8%, purchased power 30%, nuclear 14% and hydro 2%. In 1994, electric sales were down 2.9%, reflecting the slowdown in the regional economy. During 1994, IBM accounted for 12% of total electric revenues and 6% of total gas revenues.

The company's gas system consists of 159 miles of transmission pipelines and 939 miles of distribution pipelines. CNH has in place five firm contracts for the supply of 10,241,383 Mcf of natural gas, all of which are with third party suppliers. Firm sales of natural gas increased 3.7% from those of 1993, reflecting an increase in the number of customers.

During 1987, CNH completed a major construction program with the conversion of two oil-burning units to coal and completion of the Nine Mile 2 nuclear plant (9%-owned). The construction program amounted to \$57.2 million in 1994, a \$4.1 million increase from \$53.1 million expended in 1993. Construction expenditures for 1995 through 1999 are projected at \$296 million, including \$56.6 million for 1995. The company expected 100% of 1995 capital spending to be financed internally.

Important Developments

Jun. '95—Niagara Mohawk announced that its Nine Mile 2 nuclear plant, which is located in Lycoming, N.Y., returned to service after upgrades were performed during a refueling outage. Generating capacity will increase 7% to 9%, with an upgraded capacity of 1,130 Mw. CNH is one of five co-owners of the facility. Separately, at March 31, 1995, CNH had no short term debt outstanding, \$16 million in short term securities, and \$52 million of committed short term credit available.

Capitalization

Long Term Debt: \$389,625,000 (3/95).
Red. Preferred Stock: \$35,000,000.
Cum. Preferred Stock: \$46,030,000.

Per Share Data (\$)

(Year Ended Dec. 31)

	1994	1993	1992	1991	1990	1989
Tangible Bk. Val.	22.46	21.91	22.69	21.96	21.76	21.11
Earnings	2.68	2.68	2.65	2.40	2.38	2.28
Dividends	2.07	2.03	1.96	1.88	1.80	1.76
Payout Ratio	77%	77%	74%	78%	76%	77%
Prices - High	30 3/8	35 3/4	31 1/4	29	24 7/8	24 1/8
- Low	22 7/8	28 3/8	25 7/8	22 5/8	20	20 3/8
P/E Ratio - High	11	13	12	12	10	11
- Low	9	11	10	9	8	9

Income Statement Analysis (Million \$)

	1994	%Chg	1993	%Chg	1992	%Chg	1991
Revs.	516	NM	517	-1%	524	6%	495
Depr.	40.4	2%	39.7	NM	39.6	6%	37.2
Maint.	32.7	-5%	34.5	NM	34.2	9%	31.5
Fxd. Chgs. Cov.	3.6	7%	3.3	22%	2.7	13%	2.4
Constr. Credits	1.4	-7%	1.5	NM	1.5	-32%	2.2
Eff. Tax Rate	35%	—	35%	—	34%	—	33%
Net Inc.	50.9	NM	50.4	6%	47.7	11%	42.9

Balance Sheet & Other Fin. Data (Million \$)

	1994	1993	1992	1991	1990	1989
Gross Prop.	1,359	1,329	1,302	1,272	1,212	1,173
Cap. Exp.	58.0	54.0	62.0	71.0	51.0	42.0
Net Prop.	931	915	905	885	855	848
Capitalization:						
LT Debt	389	392	441	416	408	447
% LT Debt	43	44	49	49	50	53
Pfd.	81.0	81.0	80.2	81.0	81.0	81.0
% Pfd.	8.90	7.20	8.90	9.50	9.90	9.50
Common	437	418	378	360	334	321
% Common	48	37	42	42	41	38
Total Cap.	1,146	1,122	1,012	962	913	931

Ratio Analysis

	1994	1993	1992	1991	1990	1989
Oper. Ratio	85.8	85.6	85.8	84.7	84.5	83.7
% Earn. on Net Prop.	7.9	8.2	8.3	8.7	9.1	9.0
% Ret. on Revs.	9.9	9.7	9.1	8.7	8.1	8.3
% Ret. On Invest.Cap	7.2	7.5	8.1	8.4	8.9	8.8
% Return On Com.Eqty	10.7	11.3	10.8	10.6	10.8	10.1

Dividend Data (Dividends have been paid since 1903. A dividend reinvestment plan is available.)

Amt. of Div. \$	Date Decl.	Ex-Div. Date	Stock of Record	Payment Date
0.520	Sep. 23	Oct. 04	Oct. 11	Nov. 01 '94
0.520	Dec. 16	Jan. 04	Jan. 10	Feb. 01 '95
0.520	Mar. 24	Apr. 04	Apr. 10	May. 01 '95
0.525	Jun. 26	Jul. 06	Jul. 10	Aug. 01 '95

Data as orig. reptd.; bef. results of disc opers. and/or spec. items. Per share data adj. for stk. divs. as of ex-div. date. E-Estimated. NA-Not Available. NM-Not Meaningful. NR-Not Ranked.

Office—284 South Ave. Poughkeepsie, NY 12601-4879. **Tel**—(914) 452-2000. **Chrmn & CEO**—J. E. Mack III. **Pres & COO**—P. J. Ganci. **VP-Fin & Contr**—J. F. Drain. **Treas & Investor Contact**—Steven V. Lant (914-486-5254). **Dirs**— L. W. Cross, J. Effron, R. H. Eyman, F. D. Fergusson, H. K. Fridrich, E. F. X. Gallagher, P. J. Ganci, C. LaForge, J. E. Mack III, H. C. St. John, E. P. Swyer. **Transfer Agent & Registrar**—First Chicago Trust Co. of New York, Jersey City, NJ. **Incorporated** in New York in 1926. **Empl**-1,327. **S&P Analyst:** Michael C. Barr

Central Vermont Public Service

NYSE Symbol **CV**
In S&P SmallCap 600

13-OCT-95 **Industry:** Utilities-Electric

Summary: This small electric utility serves a large portion of Vermont and parts of New Hampshire.

Quantitative Evaluations
Outlook (1 Lowest—5 Highest) • **3-**
Fair Value • **13⅝**
Risk • **Low**
Earn./Div. Rank • **B**
Technical Eval. • **Bearish** since 10/93
Rel. Strength Rank (1 Lowest—99 Highest) • **46**
Insider Activity • **Neutral**

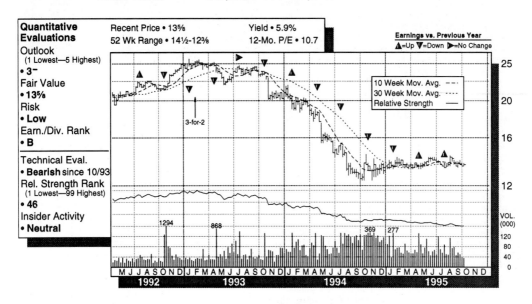

Recent Price • 13⅝ Yield • 5.9%
52 Wk Range • 14½-12⅜ 12-Mo. P/E • 10.7

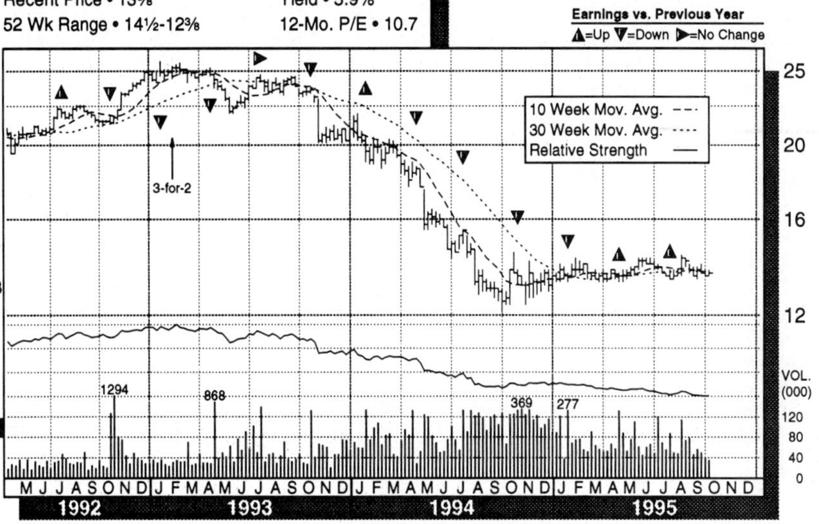

Business Profile - 13-OCT-95

This company is the largest electric utility in Vermont, serving half of the state's 567,000 residents. Through a subsidiary, it also serves about 10,000 customers in parts of New Hampshire. As part of a new corporate strategy, in November 1994, CV changed its dividend payout target to 60% of earnings and cut its dividend 44%. The company also authorized the repurchase of up to two million common shares; 154,000 shares had been repurchased as of July 31, 1995.

Operational Review - 13-OCT-95

Net income for 1995's first half advanced 20%, year to year, reflecting the 5.07% increase in Vermont retail rates that went into effect in late 1994. However, residential sales were down 4%, due partly to unusually warm winter weather. Commercial and industrial sales both increased, reflecting slow growth in the regional economy. The near-term outlook is enhanced by the improving economy, the warm summer weather and expansions at several customers' businesses.

Stock Performance - 06-OCT-95

In the past 30 trading days, CV's shares have declined 4%, compared to a 4% rise in the S&P 500. Average trading volume for the past five days was 6,760 shares, compared with the 40-day moving average of 12,379 shares.

Key Stock Statistics

Dividend Rate/Share	0.80	Shareholders	17,000
Shs. outstg. (M)	11.6	Market cap. (B)	$0.158
Avg. daily vol. (M)	0.010	Inst. holdings	19%
Tang. Bk. Value/Share	14.56	Insider holdings	NA
Beta	0.35		

Value of $10,000 invested 5 years ago: $ 10,805

Fiscal Year Ending Dec. 31

	1995	% Change	1994	% Change	1993	% Change
Revenues (Million $)						
1Q	86.86	4%	83.89	-2%	85.32	2%
2Q	62.85	9%	57.68	1%	57.00	2%
3Q	—	—	59.03	-3%	60.99	7%
4Q	—	—	76.56	NM	76.10	-4%
Yr.	—	—	277.2	NM	279.4	1%
Income (Million $)						
1Q	13.80	9%	12.61	-15%	14.83	-4%
2Q	-1.06	NM	-2.00	NM	-0.92	NM
3Q	—	—	-0.79	NM	-0.35	NM
4Q	—	—	4.99	-36%	7.74	25%
Yr.	—	—	14.80	-30%	21.29	NM
Earnings Per Share ($)						
1Q	1.13	9%	1.04	-17%	1.26	-7%
2Q	-0.13	NM	-0.22	NM	-0.14	NM
3Q	—	—	-0.11	NM	-0.09	NM
4Q	—	—	0.38	-38%	0.61	22%
Yr.	—	—	1.08	-34%	1.64	-4%

Next earnings report expected: early November

Central Vermont Public Service

Business Summary - 13-OCT-95

Central Vermont Public Service Corporation and its Connecticut Valley Electric unit supply electricity to customers in nearly three-quarters of Vermont's towns, villages and cities and to parts of New Hampshire bordering the Connecticut River. About half of Vermont's 567,000 residents receive service from the company, as do 10,000 customers in 13 New Hampshire towns. Contributions to revenues by customer class in recent years were:

	1994	1993	1992	1991
Residential	36%	35%	36%	39%
Commercial & industrial	43%	42%	43%	47%
Other electric utilities	19%	19%	19%	14%
Other	2%	4%	2%	NM

Power sources in 1994 were 47% nuclear, 26% hydro, 7% coal, 13% oil and 7% wood and other; 20% of the power supply was imported from Canada. Peak load in 1994 was 415 mw, and system capability at time of peak was 547 mw, for a reserve margin of 32%. Average residential usage in 1994 was 7,442 kwh, and the average residential rate was $0.1048 per kwh, versus 7,512 kwh and $0.1034, respectively, in 1993.

CV's nuclear power is derived primarily from its 31.3% (156-mw entitlement) interest in the Vermont Yankee plant. The company also has interests in the Maine Yankee nuclear plant (2.0%, 16.9 mw), Connecticut Yankee (2.0%, 11.6 mw) and Yankee Atomic (3.5%). In early 1992, Yankee Atomic decided to permanently discontinue operation of its plant. CV's share of the shutdown cost is about $12.4 million.

In October 1994, the Vermont Public Service Board approved an increase in CV's retail rates of $10.2 million, or 5.07%, effective November 1994. The rate case also lowered the company's allowed return on common equity from 12% to 10%.

CV's wholly owned Catamount Energy Corp. subsidiary invests in nonregulated energy-related projects. Currently, Catamount has interests in four operating independent power projects. CV's nonutility subsidiary, SmartEnergy Services, Inc., provides reliable energy-efficient products and services, including the rental of electric water heaters.

Important Developments

Jul. '95—Catamount Energy Corp. sold a 24.75% limited partnership interest in Appomattox Cogeneration Limited Partnership (ACLP) to a subsidiary of CIPSCO Investment Co. Catamount will retain a 25.25% partnership interest in ACLP as both a general and limited partner.

Capitalization

Long Term Debt: $140,076,000 (6/95).
Cum. Preferred & Preference Stock: $28,054,000.

Per Share Data ($) (Year Ended Dec. 31)

	1994	1993	1992	1991	1990	1989
Tangible Bk. Val.	14.56	15.03	14.21	14.03	13.68	13.36
Earnings	1.08	1.64	1.71	1.65	1.62	1.73
Dividends	1.42	1.42	1.39	1.39	1.37	1.34
Payout Ratio	131%	87%	81%	84%	85%	78%
Prices - High	22	25¾	25	22⅞	19⅝	19⅜
- Low	12⅛	20⅛	19½	17	14⅝	14¾
P/E Ratio - High	20	16	15	14	12	11
- Low	11	12	11	10	9	9

Income Statement Analysis (Million $)

	1994	%Chg	1993	%Chg	1992	%Chg	1991
Revs.	277	NM	279	1%	275	18%	233
Depr.	16.5	7%	15.4	7%	14.4	16%	12.4
Maint.	12.2	4%	11.7	-2%	11.9	6%	11.2
Fxd. Chgs. Cov.	3.6	-2%	3.7	23%	3.0	14%	2.7
Constr. Credits	0.4	NM	0.1	-73%	0.4	-43%	0.7
Eff. Tax Rate	45%	—	38%	—	37%	—	25%
Net Inc.	14.8	-31%	21.3	NM	21.4	15%	18.6

Balance Sheet & Other Fin. Data (Million $)

	1994	1993	1992	1991	1990	1989
Gross Prop.	450	432	419	401	386	339
Cap. Exp.	22.6	20.5	20.5	19.0	21.2	28.0
Net Prop.	325	319	316	312	306	268
Capitalization:						
LT Debt	141	144	131	154	154	115
% LT Debt	41	41	40	45	50	43
Pfd.	28.1	35.1	35.1	35.1	15.1	15.1
% Pfd.	8.30	9.90	11	10	4.90	5.70
Common	171	174	159	152	142	135
% Common	50	49	49	45	46	51
Total Cap.	401	414	361	374	346	301

Ratio Analysis

	1994	1993	1992	1991	1990	1989
Oper. Ratio	92.4	90.7	89.5	88.4	88.9	87.7
% Earn. on Net Prop.	6.6	8.2	9.2	8.8	8.9	10.7
% Ret. on Revs.	5.3	7.6	7.8	8.0	7.6	8.0
% Ret. On Invest.Cap	6.1	7.8	9.3	8.8	9.7	10.6
% Return On Com.Eqty	7.2	11.0	11.8	11.8	12.0	13.0

Dividend Data —Dividends have been paid since 1944. A dividend reinvestment plan is available.

Amt. of Div. $	Date Decl.	Ex-Div. Date	Stock of Record	Payment Date
0.355	Oct. 03	Oct. 25	Oct. 31	Nov. 15 '94
0.200	Dec. 05	Jan. 25	Jan. 31	Feb. 15 '95
0.200	Apr. 03	Apr. 24	Apr. 28	May. 15 '95
0.200	Jul. 10	Jul. 27	Jul. 31	Aug. 15 '95
0.200	Oct. 02	Oct. 27	Oct. 31	Nov. 15 '95

Data as orig. reptd.; bef. results of disc opers. and/or spec. items. Per share data adj. for stk. divs. as of ex-div. date. E-Estimated. NA-Not Available. NM-Not Meaningful. NR-Not Ranked.

Office—77 Grove St., Rutland, VT 05701. **Tel**—(802) 773-2711. **Chrmn**—F. R. Keyser Jr. **Pres & CEO**—R. H. Young Jr. **Secy**—J. M. Kraus. **Treas & Investor Contact**—Jonathan W. Booraem (802-747-5223). **Dirs**—F. H. Bertrand, R. P. Bliss Jr., E. Coleman, L. F. Hackett, F. R. Keyser Jr., M. A. McKenzie, G. P. Mills, P. L. Smith, R. D. Stout, T. C. Webb. **Transfer Agents & Registrars**—Co.'s office; First National Bank of Boston. **Incorporated** in Vermont in 1929. **Empl**-696. **S&P Analyst:** JJS

Centura Banks

NYSE Symbol **CBC**
In S&P SmallCap 600

11-OCT-95 **Industry:** Banking

Summary: This bank holding company, with approximately $5.1 billion in assets, provides a full range of personal, business and trust banking services in North Carolina.

Quantitative Evaluations
Outlook
(1 Lowest—5 Highest)
• **NA**
Fair Value
• **NA**
Risk
• **Low**
Earn./Div. Rank
• **A**

Technical Eval.
• **Bullish** since 6/95
Rel. Strength Rank
(1 Lowest—99 Highest)
• **84**
Insider Activity
• **Neutral**

Recent Price • 33⅜
52 Wk Range • 33⅜-20⅞
Yield • 2.8%
12-Mo. P/E • 12.8

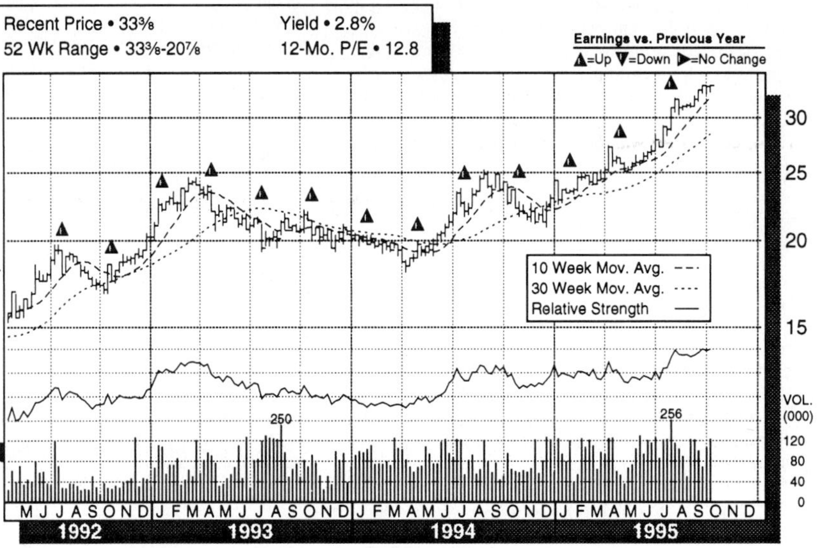

Business Profile - 05-OCT-95

In the face of increasing competition from traditional and non-traditional providers of financial services, Centura has set out to become the primary provider of all financial services to each of its customers. So far in 1995, Centura has invested over $10 million to enhance its product mix, expand its delivery systems, automate the branch system, and implement new employee incentive programs. Acquisitions will continue to play a major role in the bank's future growth.

Operational Review - 11-OCT-95

Net interest income for the nine months ended September 30, 1995, rose 13% year to year, mainly due to strong loan demand. The provision for loan losses increased 6.7% to $5,600,000 from $5,250,000. Noninterest income advanced 14% on higher brokerage commissions and an increase in other service charges. Following 10% higher noninterest expense, pretax income climbed 20%. After taxes at 36.4% versus 36.1% net income was also up 20%, to $42,864,000 ($1.96 a share) from $35,861,000 ($1.70).

Stock Performance - 06-OCT-95

In the past 30 trading days, CBC's shares have increased 7%, compared to a 4% rise in the S&P 500. Average trading volume for the past five days was 30,560 shares, compared with the 40-day moving average of 21,444 shares.

Key Stock Statistics

Dividend Rate/Share	0.92	Shareholders	10,200
Shs. outstg. (M)	22.4	Market cap. (B)	$0.742
Avg. daily vol. (M)	0.020	Inst. holdings	23%
Tang. Bk. Value/Share	18.12	Insider holdings	NA
Beta	0.07		

Value of $10,000 invested 5 years ago: NA

Fiscal Year Ending Dec. 31

	1995	% Change	1994	% Change	1993	% Change
Revenues (Million $)						
1Q	96.25	20%	80.34	15%	69.61	11%
2Q	105.9	28%	82.52	13%	73.29	16%
3Q	116.8	33%	87.79	13%	77.83	24%
4Q	—	—	91.06	10%	83.14	11%
Yr.	—	—	341.7	12%	303.9	15%
Income (Million $)						
1Q	13.87	32%	10.50	-11%	11.77	86%
2Q	13.79	15%	12.00	4%	11.52	75%
3Q	15.20	14%	13.36	42%	9.43	32%
4Q	—	—	13.70	64%	8.35	21%
Yr.	—	—	49.56	21%	41.07	53%
Earnings Per Share ($)						
1Q	0.67	34%	0.50	6%	0.47	17%
2Q	0.63	11%	0.57	12%	0.51	21%
3Q	0.66	5%	0.63	7%	0.59	31%
4Q	—	—	0.65	14%	0.57	33%
Yr.	—	—	2.35	10%	2.14	26%

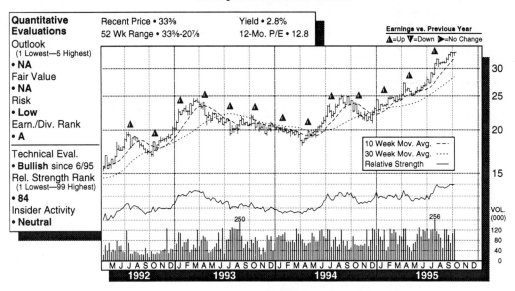

Next earnings report expected: early January

Centura Banks

Business Summary - 11-OCT-95

Centura Banks is a bank holding company that owns Centura Bank, a state-chartered bank that provides full-service commercial and consumer banking and trust services from its headquarters in Rocky Mount, N.C. It also provides various other financial services and engages in mortgage banking activities. As of year-end 1994, the bank was operating 147 offices in 88 communities in the Piedmont, Coastal Plains, Outer Banks, Sandhill and Mountain areas of North Carolina.

Total loans outstanding were $2.95 billion at year-end 1994, compared with $2.58 billion a year before. Loans were divided as follows:

	1994	1993
Commercial, financial & agricultural	16.8%	15.8%
Consumer	7.4%	7.5%
Real estate--mortgage	60.5%	64.4%
Real estate--construction	10.2%	8.3%
Leases & other	5.1%	4.0%

Consolidated deposits of $3.47 billion at 1994 year-end were apportioned: 77% interest-bearing, 15% noninterest-bearing demand, and 8% time deposits over $100,000.

Total income for 1994 was derived: 69% from interest and fees on loans, 17% from investment securities, 7% from deposit fees and charges, and 7% from other noninterest income.

Loans accounted for 72% of gross interest earning assets (taxable equivalent basis) at December 31, 1994, taxable securities for 26%, and tax exempt securities and short-term investments for 2%. The average yield on interest-earning assets in 1994 was 7.88% (7.82% in 1993), while the average rate paid on interest-earning liabilities was 3.43% (3.49%), for a net spread of 4.45% (4.33%).

The allowance for loan losses at December 31, 1994, totaled $44.9 million (1.52% of loans outstanding), compared with $40.5 million (1.57%) a year earlier. Net chargeoffs in 1994 amounted to $2.5 million ($5.6 million in 1993), equal to 0.09% (0.23%) of average loans. At December 31, 1994, nonperforming assets amounted to $21.3 million (0.50% of total assets), down from $26.2 million (0.63%) a year earlier.

Important Developments

Aug. '95—Centura announced that it has entered into a marketing agreement with Jefferson-Pilot in which annuities and investment products of Jefferson-Pilot Life and Jefferson-Pilot Investor Services will be sold through Centura Securities Inc. and Centura Insurance Services Inc.

Capitalization

Long Term Debt: $186,862,000 (3/95).

Per Share Data ($) (Year Ended Dec. 31)

	1994	1993	1992	1991	1990	1989
Tangible Bk. Val.	15.79	14.98	13.36	12.29	12.45	11.78
Earnings	2.35	2.14	1.70	0.62	1.27	1.70
Dividends	0.74	0.69	0.63	0.60	0.15	NA
Payout Ratio	31%	32%	37%	98%	NM	NA
Prices - High	25¼	24⅝	20½	16	13¾	NA
- Low	18	19¼	12½	11⅝	12⅜	NA
P/E Ratio - High	11	12	12	26	11	NA
- Low	8	9	7	19	10	NA

Income Statement Analysis (Million $)

	1994	%Chg	1993	%Chg	1992	%Chg	1991
Net Int. Inc.	182	19%	153	22%	125	19%	105
Tax Equiv. Adj.	5.7	-7%	6.1	NM	6.1	-8%	6.7
Non Int. Inc.	48.6	-5%	51.1	41%	36.3	25%	29.1
Loan Loss Prov.	6.7	-21%	8.5	-44%	15.1	-28%	20.8
% Exp/Op Revs.	62%	—	64%	—	65%	—	72%
Pretax Inc.	77.4	24%	62.2	56%	39.9	NM	11.5
Eff. Tax Rate	36%	—	34%	—	33%	—	24%
Net Inc.	49.6	21%	41.1	53%	26.9	NM	8.8
% Net Int. Marg.	4.96%	—	4.81%	—	4.87%	—	4.80%

Balance Sheet & Other Fin. Data (Million $)

	1994	1993	1992	1991	1990	1989
Earning Assets:						
Money Mkt.	376	521	63.1	28.2	20.2	38.0
Inv. Securities	539	668	566	530	504	465
Com'l Loans	2,950	2,579	441	413	636	1,684
Other Loans	NA	NA	1,675	1,386	1,168	NA
Total Assets	4,240	4,139	3,029	2,612	2,605	2,434
Demand Deposits	536	507	397	324	344	361
Time Deposits	2,934	3,103	2,259	1,993	1,960	1,766
LT Debt	109	44.9	45.9	16.4	22.4	17.4
Common Eqty.	324	311	211	182	174	164

Ratio Analysis

	1994	1993	1992	1991	1990	1989
% Ret. on Assets	1.2	1.1	0.9	0.3	0.7	1.0
% Ret. on Equity	15.6	15.6	13.3	5.0	10.5	15.2
% Loan Loss Resv.	1.5	1.6	1.5	1.5	1.1	1.1
% Loans/Deposits	85.0	71.5	79.7	77.6	78.3	79.2
% Equity to Assets	7.8	7.3	7.0	7.0	6.7	6.7

Dividend Data —Dividends were initiated in 1990. A dividend reinvestment plan is available.

Amt. of Div. $	Date Decl.	Ex-Div. Date	Stock of Record	Payment Date
0.190	Nov. 16	Nov. 23	Nov. 30	Dec. 15 '94
0.190	Feb. 15	Feb. 22	Feb. 28	Mar. 15 '95
0.200	Apr. 19	May. 24	May. 31	Jun. 15 '95
0.230	Jul. 20	Aug. 29	Aug. 31	Sep. 15 '95

Data as orig. reptd.; bef. results of disc opers. and/or spec. items. Per share data adj. for stk. divs. as of ex-div. date. E-Estimated. NA-Not Available. NM-Not Meaningful. NR-Not Ranked.

Office—134 North Church St., Rocky Mount, NC 27804. **Tel**—(919) 977-4400. **Chrmn & CEO**—R. R. Mauldin. **Pres & COO**—C. W. Sewell Jr. **CFO & Investor Contact**—Frank L. Pattillo. **Dirs**—R. H. Barnhardt, T. B. Battle, C. W. Beasley, T. A. Betts Jr., J. R. Futrell Jr., J. H. High, R. L. Hubbard, W. H. Kincheloe, C. T. Lane, R. R. Mauldin, O. T. Parks III, F. L. Pattillo, M. B. Pearsall, C. M. Reeves III, C. W. Sewell Jr., A. P. Thorpe III, W. H. Wilkerson, J. G. Wood. **Transfer Agent & Registrar**—Registrar & Transfer Co., Cranford, N.J. **Incorporated** in North Carolina in 1990. **Empl**-1,869. **S&P Analyst:** Brad Ohlmuller

STANDARD & POOR'S

STOCK REPORTS

Cephalon, Inc.

NASDAQ Symbol **CEPH**

In S&P SmallCap 600

10-AUG-95

Industry: Drugs-Generic and OTC

Summary: This neuroscience company is developing therapeutic products to treat neurodegenerative diseases, such as ALS (Lou Gehrig's disease), Alzheimer's, and head and spinal injuries.

Quantitative Evaluations

Recent Price • 23⅜ | Yield • Nil
52 Wk Range • 24-5¾ | 12-Mo. P/E • NM

Outlook
(1 Lowest—5 Highest)
• **NA**

Fair Value
• **NA**

Risk
• **High**

Earn./Div. Rank
• **NR**

Technical Eval.
• **Bullish** since 11/94

Rel. Strength Rank
(1 Lowest—99 Highest)
• **99**

Insider Activity
• **Neutral**

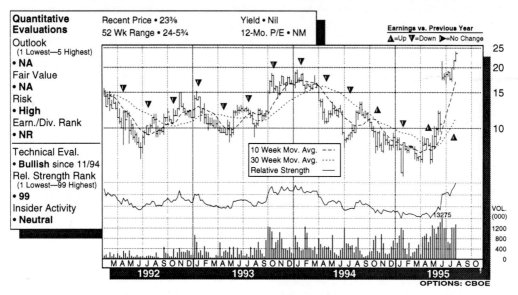

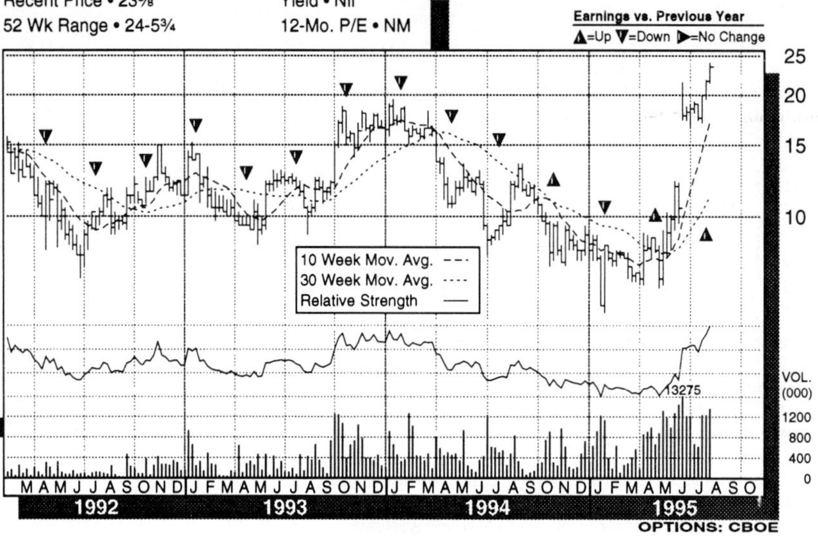

OPTIONS: CBOE

Business Profile - 10-AUG-95

In June 1995, the company released Phase III data indicating that Myotrophin was successful in slowing the progression of ALS. Shares of the stock have since more than doubled in value. Cephalon is currently working on filing a New Drug Application for Myotrophin by early 1996. A stock offering that raised $84.4 million for the company was completed in August 1995. Major collaborative arrangements include those with Chiron, TAP Pharmaceuticals, SmithKline Beecham and Bristol-Myers.

Operational Review - 10-AUG-95

Contract revenues in the first half of 1995 ballooned 66% ($17.5 million vs. $10.5 million), year to year, chiefly reflecting a reimbursement payment from Chiron. Higher R&D expenditures resulted from an expansion of the modafinil research program and SG&A costs were up due to increased marketing activities. The net loss narrowed to $16,563,000 ($0.90 a share, on 16% more average shares), from $18,510,000 ($1.17).

Stock Performance - 04-AUG-95

In the past 30 trading days, CEPH's shares have increased 29%, compared to a 2% rise in the S&P 500. Average trading volume for the past five days was 817,760 shares, compared with the 40-day moving average of 618,520 shares.

Key Stock Statistics

Dividend Rate/Share	Nil	Shareholders	400
Shs. outstg. (M)	22.1	Market cap. (B)	$0.648
Avg. daily vol. (M)	0.600	Inst. holdings	49%
Tang. Bk. Value/Share	5.50	Insider holdings	NA
Beta	NA		

Value of $10,000 invested 5 years ago: NA

Fiscal Year Ending Dec. 31

	1995	% Change	1994	% Change	1993	% Change
Revenues (Million $)						
1Q	2.63	-16%	3.14	59%	1.98	—
2Q	14.91	101%	7.41	7%	6.91	73%
3Q	—	—	5.21	18%	4.40	128%
4Q	—	—	5.92	63%	3.64	16%
Yr.	—	—	21.68	28%	16.92	87%
Income (Million $)						
1Q	-12.58	NM	-11.78	NM	-5.83	NM
2Q	-3.98	NM	-6.73	NM	-1.98	NM
3Q	—	—	-7.64	NM	-5.16	192%
4Q	—	—	-9.92	NM	-6.27	109%
Yr.	—	—	-36.07	NM	-19.24	NM
Earnings Per Share ($)						
1Q	-0.69	NM	-0.81	NM	-0.64	NM
2Q	-0.22	NM	-0.39	NM	-0.18	NM
3Q	—	—	-0.42	NM	-0.44	NM
4Q	—	—	-0.54	NM	-0.53	NM
Yr.	—	—	-2.13	NM	-1.77	NM

Next earnings report expected: early November

Cephalon, Inc.

Business Summary - 10-AUG-95

Since its inception in 1987, Cephalon, Inc. has been engaged primarily in R&D related to the discovery of therapeutic drugs for neurodegenerative disorders, including ALS, Alzheimer's disease, head and spinal injuries, stroke and other diseases of the nervous system.

Product development programs are directed toward promoting neuronal survival using neurotrophic factors and various classes of small molecules (neurons are the specialized conducting cells of the nervous system). Neurotrophic factor-based products are being developed for disorders such as ALS and peripheral neuropathy.

Cephalon is developing Myotrophin to treat ALS (Lou Gehrig's disease), which affects 25,000 persons in the U.S. Phase III trial results were released in June 1995, showing statistically significant, dose-related success in slowing the progression of the disease. Cephalon is currently in the process of filing a New Drug Application for Myotrophin.

In January 1994, the company began a collaboration with Chiron Corp. for the global (except for Japan) development and commercialization of Myotrophin and certain other technologies in the neurological field.

In the area of peripheral neuropathy, the company plans to focus on development of Myotrophin for chemotherapy-induced neuropathies, post-polio syndrome, diabetic neuropathy and Charcot-Marie-Tooth (CMT) Syndrome, disorders believed to affect about one million persons in the U.S. Separately, in August 1994, the company began Phase III clinical trials of modafinil for the treatment of narcolepsy.

In July 1994, the company and Bristol-Myers Squibb entered into an agreement to copromote Stadol nasal spray to neurologists in the U.S. Also in 1994, an additional collaboration was formed with TAP Pharmaceuticals Inc. to develop compounds for the treatment of prostate disease in the U.S.

Important Developments

Aug. '95—Cephalon completed a common stock offering of 3,988,310 shares, including the exercise of an underwriter's option to cover over-allotments. Total proceeds to the company were approximately $84.4 million. Earlier, in July, the company offered to purchase up to 400 limited partnerships in Cephalon Clinical Partners for $50,000 in cash, expiring August 1, 1995.

Jun. '95—The company announced successful results for its Phase III study of Myotrophin in the treatment of ALS. Patients with ALS who received Myotrophin experienced less disease severity, slower progression of disease, and better functional ability than patients who received a placebo.

Capitalization

Long Term Debt: $36,914,000 (6/95).
Options & Warrants: To buy about 2,474,635 shs. at $0.10 to $18.00 ea. (12/94).

Per Share Data ($) (Year Ended Dec. 31)

	1994	1993	1992	1991	1990	1989
Tangible Bk. Val.	6.17	5.28	6.25	6.91	1.90	1.12
Cash Flow	-1.74	-1.28	-0.55	-0.18	-0.54	-0.35
Earnings	-2.13	-1.77	-0.80	-0.26	-0.59	-0.39
Dividends	Nil	Nil	Nil	Nil	Nil	Nil
Payout Ratio	Nil	Nil	Nil	Nil	Nil	Nil
Prices - High	19½	18¾	16¾	19½	NA	NA
- Low	7½	8½	7	11	NA	NA
P/E Ratio - High	NM	NM	NM	NM	NM	NM
- Low	NM	NM	NM	NA	NA	NA

Income Statement Analysis (Million $)

	1994	%Chg	1993	%Chg	1992	%Chg	1991
Revs.	21.7	28%	16.9	87%	9.1	80%	5.0
Oper. Inc.	-28.3	NM	-14.6	NM	-8.0	NM	-4.0
Depr.	6.7	25%	5.3	141%	2.2	NM	0.6
Int. Exp.	1.4	72%	0.8	NM	0.2	NM	0.0
Pretax Inc.	-36.1	NM	-19.2	NM	-7.2	NM	-2.0
Eff. Tax Rate	NM	—	NM	—	NM	—	Nil
Net Inc.	-36.1	NM	-19.2	NM	-7.2	NM	-2.0

Balance Sheet & Other Fin. Data (Million $)

	1994	1993	1992	1991	1990	1989
Cash	105	49.4	33.8	24.4	9.7	4.7
Curr. Assets	113	51.7	37.3	25.0	10.0	4.9
Total Assets	140	78.1	71.1	61.7	10.9	5.6
Curr. Liab.	10.8	3.4	2.3	0.8	0.7	0.4
LT Debt	16.1	11.6	12.0	Nil	0.4	0.4
Common Eqty.	113	63.1	56.7	60.9	9.7	4.8
Total Cap.	129	74.7	68.7	60.9	10.2	5.2
Cap. Exp.	10.5	6.8	4.7	1.2	0.1	0.1
Cash Flow	-29.4	-13.9	-4.9	-1.4	-2.8	-1.5

Ratio Analysis

	1994	1993	1992	1991	1990	1989
Curr. Ratio	10.4	15.1	16.1	30.0	14.2	12.4
% LT Debt of Cap.	12.5	15.5	17.5	Nil	4.3	7.8
% Net Inc.of Revs.	NM	NM	NM	NM	NM	NM
% Ret. on Assets	NM	NM	NM	NM	NM	NM
% Ret. on Equity	NM	NM	NM	NM	NM	NM

Dividend Data (Cash dividends have never been paid. Cephalon intends to retain any earnings to finance growth. A "poison pill" stock purchase rights plan was adopted in November 1993.)

Data as orig. reptd.; bef. results of disc. opers. and/or spec. items. Per share data adj. for stk. divs. as of ex-div. date. E-Estimated. NA-Not Available. NM-Not Meaningful. NR-Not Ranked.

Office—145 Brandywine Pkwy., West Chester, PA 19380. **Tel**—(610) 344-0200. **Pres & CEO**—F. Baldino Jr. **Exec VP, COO & Secy**—B. A. Peacock. **Dirs**—F. Baldino Jr., W. P. Egan, R. J. Feeney, M. D. Greenacre, K. E. Moley, B. A. Peacock, H. Witzel. **Transfer Agent & Registrar**—American Stock Transfer & Trust Co., NYC. **Incorporated** in Delaware in 1987. **Empl**-312. **S&P Analyst:** Thomas Timey

Cerner Corp.

NASDAQ Symbol **CERN**
In S&P SmallCap 600

02-NOV-95 **Industry:** Electronics/Electric

Summary: CERN provides health information systems for use in healthcare organizations that allow information to be shared among clinical disciplines and across multiple facilities.

Quantitative Evaluations
Outlook
(1 Lowest—5 Highest)
• 4
Fair Value
• 30¼
Risk
• Average
Earn./Div. Rank
• B

Technical Eval.
• Bearish since 10/95
Rel. Strength Rank
(1 Lowest—99 Highest)
• 11
Insider Activity
• Neutral

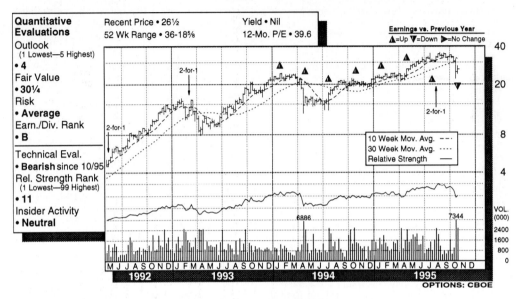

Recent Price • 26½
52 Wk Range • 36-18⅝
Yield • Nil
12-Mo. P/E • 39.6

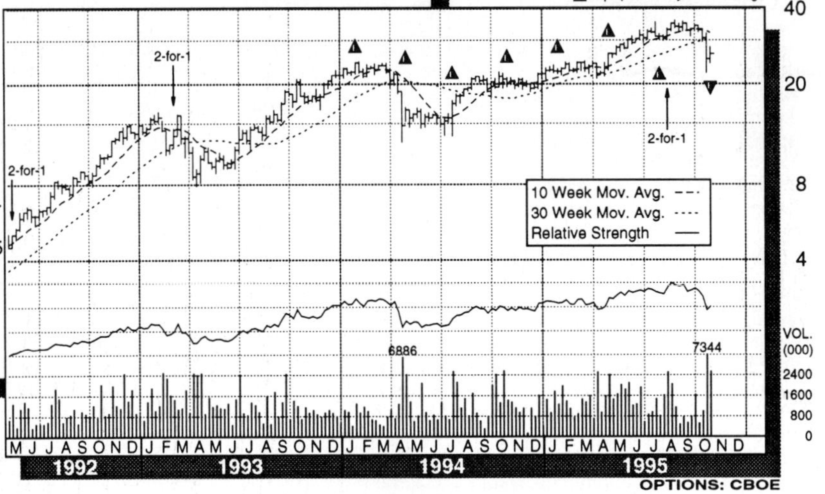

OPTIONS: CBOE

Business Profile - 02-NOV-95

Cerner Corp. hopes to benefit from the increasing consolidation of healthcare institutions. It believes larger provider networks will require a major investment in information technology that automates the process of healthcare across a network of providers and facilities. CERN recently acquired Virtus Technology, a developer of products that enable clinicians to capture laboratory results by automation.

Operational Review - 20-OCT-95

After several periods of rapid growth, Cerner Corp. reported sharply lower earnings in the third quarter of 1995. Sales rose just 2% and net income fell 31% for the quarter. The company attributed the declining earnings to difficulties in completing several agreements that were expected to be signed in the quarter. Also, international business was responsible for a meaningful loss, due to extended contract cycles involving various government initiatives.

Stock Performance - 27-OCT-95

In the past 30 trading days, CERN's shares have declined 19%, compared to a 0.63% fall in the S&P 500. Average trading volume for the past five days was 761,500 shares, compared with the 40-day moving average of 417,759 shares.

Key Stock Statistics

Dividend Rate/Share	Nil	Shareholders	1,000
Shs. outstg. (M)	31.6	Market cap. (B)	$0.822
Avg. daily vol. (M)	0.709	Inst. holdings	50%
Tang. Bk. Value/Share	3.21	Insider holdings	NA
Beta	1.63		

Value of $10,000 invested 5 years ago: $ 169,600

Fiscal Year Ending Dec. 31

	1995	% Change	1994	% Change	1993	% Change
Revenues (Million $)						
1Q	43.20	42%	30.50	27%	24.10	—
2Q	49.00	23%	39.80	34%	29.80	—
3Q	41.72	2%	40.90	27%	32.30	—
4Q	—	—	44.70	30%	34.30	28%
Yr.	—	—	155.9	29%	120.6	19%
Income (Million $)						
1Q	4.54	51%	3.00	17%	2.56	75%
2Q	6.18	26%	4.90	48%	3.31	52%
3Q	3.49	-31%	5.07	25%	4.07	37%
4Q	—	—	6.53	42%	4.61	38%
Yr.	—	—	19.50	34%	14.56	47%
Earnings Per Share ($)						
1Q	0.15	50%	0.10	11%	0.09	—
2Q	0.21	24%	0.17	42%	0.12	—
3Q	0.11	-35%	0.17	21%	0.14	—
4Q	—	—	0.22	38%	0.16	39%
Yr.	—	—	0.66	32%	0.50	45%

Next earnings report expected: early February

Cerner Corp.

Business Summary - 02-NOV-95

Cerner Corp. designs, develops, markets, installs and supports health information systems for use in healthcare organizations, including hospitals, clinics, physicians offices, reference laboratories, health maintenance organizations, large integrated delivery systems and integrated health organizations. Its systems are designed around a Health Network Architecture (HNA) and are intrarelated to share patient information.

Cerner's PathNet Laboratory Information System addresses the information management needs of five clinical areas: general laboratory, microbiology, blood bank transfusion services, blood bank donor services and anatomic pathology. PathNet automates the ordering and reporting of procedures, the production of accurate and timely reports and the maintenance of accessible clinical records.

The MedNet Internal Medicine Information System addresses the clinical information needs of various internal medicine areas such as cardiology, neuro-diagnostics, rehabilitation services, nutritional services and many ancillary areas. MedNet automates procedure requests, patient and therapist scheduling and the processing, validation and presentation of results, and provides reports on clinical activity, workload and billing charges.

The RadNet Radiology Information System addresses the operational and management requirements of diagnostic radiation and radiation oncology departments, providing such tasks as scheduling patients, modifying orders and tracking patients.

The PharmNet Pharmacy Information System provides intrarelation in an HNA environment for rapid pharmacy order entry and support of clinical pharmacy in either an inpatient or outpatient setting. PharmNet streamlines order entry; produces medication, intravenous fill lists and medication administration records; and screens for drug-drug interactions, drug-food and drug-lab interferences.

The ProNet Orders Management Information System addresses the needs of care providers and medical staff in the areas of order entry, order review and/or validation, interdepartmental/interfacility communication and order result inquiry and reporting.

The MSmeds Pharmacy Information System focuses on meeting the specialized and individual needs of the pharmacy department by providing fast order entry capabilities and safeguards that ensure the integrity of patient therapy.

Important Developments

Oct. '95—Cerner shares fell nearly 17% over a two day period following the release of lower third quarter earnings. CERN attributed the declining earnings to difficulty in completing agreements that were expected to be signed in the quarter.

Capitalization

Long Term Debt: $32,781,000 (7/95).

Per Share Data ($) (Year Ended Dec. 31)

	1994	1993	1992	1991	1990	1989
Tangible Bk. Val.	2.84	2.05	1.51	1.09	0.96	0.97
Cash Flow	0.86	0.63	0.44	0.25	0.12	0.17
Earnings	0.66	0.50	0.35	0.18	0.06	0.12
Dividends	Nil	Nil	Nil	Nil	Nil	Nil
Payout Ratio	Nil	Nil	Nil	Nil	Nil	Nil
Prices - High	24¾	22⅞	14⅛	3¼	1¾	2
- Low	11¾	7⅞	2⅞	1⅛	⅝	1³⁄₁₆
P/E Ratio - High	38	46	41	18	31	17
- Low	18	16	8	7	14	10

Income Statement Analysis (Million $)

	1994	%Chg	1993	%Chg	1992	%Chg	1991
Revs.	156	29%	121	20%	101	31%	77.0
Oper. Inc.	39.9	42%	28.1	46%	19.3	93%	10.0
Depr.	6.1	62%	3.8	37%	2.8	42%	1.9
Int. Exp.	1.9	188%	0.6	-7%	0.7	-23%	0.9
Pretax Inc.	32.5	35%	24.1	48%	16.3	114%	7.6
Eff. Tax Rate	40%	—	40%	—	39%	—	38%
Net Inc.	19.5	34%	14.6	47%	9.9	111%	4.7

Balance Sheet & Other Fin. Data (Million $)

	1994	1993	1992	1991	1990	1989
Cash	15.3	16.8	13.7	8.7	7.1	7.4
Curr. Assets	83.7	67.2	45.9	39.7	38.6	45.2
Total Assets	156	105	67.0	56.0	52.0	55.0
Curr. Liab.	31.3	24.6	15.4	17.1	17.8	23.3
LT Debt	30.2	10.4	8.3	8.0	7.7	1.6
Common Eqty.	85.8	64.2	38.6	27.5	24.1	28.1
Total Cap.	125	80.0	51.0	39.0	35.0	32.0
Cap. Exp.	32.2	7.1	4.7	1.8	3.2	1.3
Cash Flow	25.6	18.3	12.7	6.6	3.2	5.0

Ratio Analysis

	1994	1993	1992	1991	1990	1989
Curr. Ratio	2.7	2.7	3.0	2.3	2.2	1.9
% LT Debt of Cap.	24.2	12.9	16.2	20.5	22.4	5.1
% Net Inc.of Revs.	12.5	12.1	9.8	6.1	3.0	6.3
% Ret. on Assets	14.8	16.6	16.1	8.6	3.1	7.0
% Ret. on Equity	25.7	27.7	29.8	18.1	6.4	13.6

Dividend Data —No cash dividends have been paid. The company intends to retain its earnings for use in its business and does not anticipate paying cash dividends in the foreseeable future. The common stock was split 2-for-1 in May 1992, March 1993, and August 1995.

Data as orig. reptd.; bef. results of disc. opers. and/or spec. items. Per share data adj. for stk. divs. as of ex-div. date. E-Estimated. NA-Not Available. NM-Not Meaningful. NR-Not Ranked.

Office—2800 Rockcreek Pky., Suite 601, Kansas City, MO 64117. **Tel**—(816) 221-1024. **Chrmn & CEO**—N. L. Patterson. **Pres & COO**—C. W. Illig. **Treas**—M. M. Evans. **Dirs**—G. E. Bisbee, Jr., D. J. Hart, M. E. Herman, D. M. Margulies, N. L. Patterson, C. S. Runnion, III, T. C. Tinstman. **Transfer Agent & Registrar**—First Chicago Trust Co. of New York, Jersey City, N.J. **Incorporated** in Missouri in 1980. **Empl**-1,200. **S&P Analyst:** Stephen Madonna, CFA

Champion Enterprises

NYSE Symbol **CHB**
In S&P SmallCap 600

11-OCT-95

Industry:
Mobile/Modular Homes

Summary: The holding company for Champion Home Builders, other manufactured housing units and a mid-size bus company, CHB is the second largest manufactured housing supplier in the U.S.

Quantitative Evaluations

Outlook
(1 Lowest—5 Highest)
• **5**

Fair Value
• **22½**

Risk
• **Average**

Earn./Div. Rank
• **B-**

Technical Eval.
• **Bullish** since 7/95

Rel. Strength Rank
(1 Lowest—99 Highest)
• **86**

Insider Activity
• **NA**

Recent Price • 19⅜
52 Wk Range • 20⅝-13⅜
Yield • Nil
12-Mo. P/E • 11.3

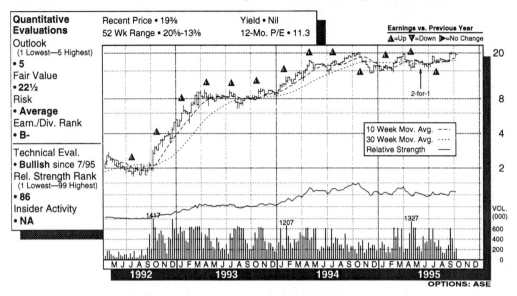

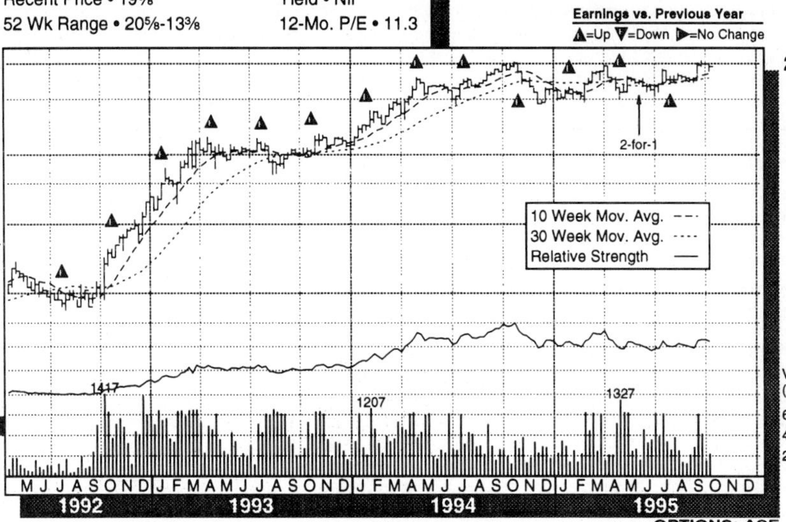

OPTIONS: ASE

Business Profile - 11-OCT-95

This company has grown rapidly through acquisitions and is currently the second largest U.S. supplier of manufactured housing. CHB said in September 1995 that its unit shipments in July and August were continuing the strong trend of the second quarter. It also expected earnings to grow 20% annually over the next three years and it was comfortable with analysts' estimates of $1.85 to $1.90 a share for 1995. In May 1995, the company announced a $10 million stock repurchase program.

Operational Review - 11-OCT-95

For the first half of 1995, revenues from continuing operations rose 41%, year to year, aided by continued strength in the manufactured housing market and acquisitions. Margins widened, reflecting improved manufacturing efficiencies in the bus segment. However, following increased interest expense and a higher tax rate, income was limited to a 14% gain to $14,504,000 ($0.92 a share) from $12,713,000 ($0.84). Results in the 1994 period exclude income from discontinued operations of $0.12 a share.

Stock Performance - 06-OCT-95

In the past 30 trading days, CHB's shares have increased 12%, compared to a 4% rise in the S&P 500. Average trading volume for the past five days was 42,740 shares, compared with the 40-day moving average of 54,979 shares.

Key Stock Statistics

Dividend Rate/Share	Nil	Shareholders	18,000
Shs. outstg. (M)	15.3	Market cap. (B)	$0.296
Avg. daily vol. (M)	0.072	Inst. holdings	51%
Tang. Bk. Value/Share	0.84	Insider holdings	NA
Beta	1.02		

Value of $10,000 invested 5 years ago: $ 155,000

Fiscal Year Ending Dec. 31

	1995	% Change	1994	% Change	1993	% Change
Revenues (Million $)						
1Q	179.1	43%	125.0	67%	75.00	34%
2Q	218.0	39%	157.1	85%	84.71	20%
3Q	—	—	168.8	83%	91.99	24%
4Q	—	—	164.8	83%	90.26	29%
Yr.	—	—	615.7	80%	341.9	—
Income (Million $)						
1Q	5.76	20%	4.79	149%	1.92	54%
2Q	8.74	10%	7.93	162%	3.03	63%
3Q	—	—	8.15	112%	3.85	129%
4Q	—	—	4.33	82%	2.38	NM
Yr.	—	—	25.19	125%	11.18	133%
Earnings Per Share ($)						
1Q	0.36	12%	0.32	141%	0.13	170%
2Q	0.55	8%	0.51	143%	0.21	68%
3Q	—	—	0.52	96%	0.26	96%
4Q	—	—	0.28	72%	0.16	113%
Yr.	—	—	1.63	112%	0.77	126%

Next earnings report expected: early November

Champion Enterprises

Business Summary - 03-OCT-95

Champion Enterprises, Inc., formed in June 1987 as the holding company for Champion Home Builders Co. and its subsidiaries, is primarily engaged in the production and sale of manufactured homes and medium-size buses. In 1992, the company sold its recreational vehicle business, and also changed to a calendar-year reporting basis, from a fiscal year ending February 28. Contributions by segment in 1994 were:

	Sales	Profits
Housing	93%	96%
Commercial vehicles	7%	4%

Through Champion Home Builders Co. and Moduline International, Inc., the company produces manufactured homes in one or more sections, in sizes ranging from 650 sq. ft. to over 2,000 sq. ft. More than 600 floor plans are available nationally, under about 40 different trade names. In 1994, 20,986 manufactured homes were shipped, up 68% from the level of 1993. Champion's total market share rose to 7.7%, from 6.2%, while the number of dealer locations increased 59%, to about 1,550 retail locations. Dutch Housing, Inc., acquired in March 1994, added $165 million in sales and $13 million in earnings.

Through Champion Motor Coach, Inc., the company produces mid-size buses under the brand names Challenger, CTS, Centurion, Champ, Crusader and Commander. Champion's total market share is 15%. Buses are sold to municipalities and private businesses such as shuttle fleets, nursing homes, hotels, and airports. There are about 75 independent distributors of mid-size buses in the U.S. and Canada.

As of early 1995, the company operated 23 manufacturing facilities (22 manufactured housing plants and one mid-size bus plant) in 14 states and one Canadian province.

Important Developments

Sep. '95—The company announced plans for two new manufactured housing plants to open in 1996 in Alabama and Texas. CHB also said it would continue to search for acquisitions, and that it had at least $100 million in investment capacity to make other acquisitions and expansions.

Aug. '95—CHB's Champion Motor Coach division received a contract to make 74 to 86 mid-sized buses for the Suburban Mobility Authority for Regional Transportation, headquartered in Detroit, Mich., totaling $5.2 million. Separately, the division announced it was awarded a multi-million dollar contract to build 71 cutaway buses under a contract with Laidlaw Transit Ltd.

Capitalization

Long Term Debt: $1,386,000 (7/95).

Per Share Data ($)

(Year Ended Dec. 31)

	1994	1993	1992	1991	1990	1989
Tangible Bk. Val.	2.79	3.18	2.43	2.31	1.78	1.77
Cash Flow	1.88	0.92	0.46	0.11	0.19	-0.82
Earnings	1.63	0.77	0.34	-0.05	0.03	-0.99
Dividends	Nil	Nil	Nil	Nil	Nil	Nil
Payout Ratio	Nil	Nil	Nil	Nil	Nil	Nil
Prices - High	20⅜	9⅞	5½	3	2	2 7/16
- Low	8¾	4⅝	1 7/16	1 3/16	15/16	1⅛
P/E Ratio - High	12	13	16	NM	80	NM
- Low	5	6	4	NM	38	NM

Income Statement Analysis (Million $)

	1994	%Chg	1993	%Chg	1992	%Chg	1991
Revs.	616	80%	342	46%	235	-13%	270
Oper. Inc.	40.6	194%	13.8	92%	7.2	NM	1.4
Depr.	3.9	75%	2.2	36%	1.6	-24%	2.2
Int. Exp.	0.8	67%	0.5	-34%	0.7	-36%	1.1
Pretax Inc.	34.1	171%	12.6	110%	6.0	NM	0.1
Eff. Tax Rate	26%	—	11%	—	19%	—	NM
Net Inc.	25.2	125%	11.2	133%	4.8	NM	-0.6

Balance Sheet & Other Fin. Data (Million $)

	1994	1993	1992	1991	1990	1989
Cash	73.0	34.4	20.7	15.1	10.9	7.8
Curr. Assets	97.8	74.4	58.5	56.7	48.0	51.9
Total Assets	171	98.0	81.0	81.0	77.0	83.0
Curr. Liab.	79.1	42.5	36.6	39.2	40.5	45.1
LT Debt	Nil	2.8	3.8	4.5	5.4	6.5
Common Eqty.	79.3	45.9	34.0	31.4	24.1	23.3
Total Cap.	79.3	48.7	37.8	35.8	29.5	30.0
Cap. Exp.	10.6	6.6	2.8	2.3	1.7	5.1
Cash Flow	29.1	13.4	6.5	1.5	2.6	-11.5

Ratio Analysis

	1994	1993	1992	1991	1990	1989
Curr. Ratio	1.2	1.8	1.6	1.4	1.2	1.2
% LT Debt of Cap.	Nil	5.8	10.1	12.5	18.4	21.8
% Net Inc.of Revs.	4.1	3.3	2.0	NM	0.1	NM
% Ret. on Assets	18.4	12.3	5.9	NM	0.4	NM
% Ret. on Equity	39.5	27.6	14.5	NM	1.4	NM

Dividend Data —No cash dividends have been paid since July 1974.

Amt. of Div. $	Date Decl.	Ex-Div. Date	Stock of Record	Payment Date
2-for-1	May. 01	May. 31	May. 15	May. 30 '95

Data as orig. reptd.; bef. results of disc. opers. and/or spec. items. Per share data adj. for stk. divs. as of ex-div. date. Prior to 1992 yrs. ended Feb. of fol. cal. yr. E-Estimated. NA-Not Available. NM-Not Meaningful. NR-Not Ranked.

Office—2701 University Dr., Suite 320, Auburn Hills, MI 48326. **Tel**—(313) 340-9090. **Chrmn, Pres & CEO**—W. R. Young, Jr. **EVP & CFO**—A. Jacqueline Dout. **VP & Secy**—L. M. Balius. **Dirs**—R. W. Anestis, S. Isakow, G. R. Mrkonic, J. S. Savary, C. S. Valdiserri, W. R. Young, Jr. **Transfer Agent & Registrar**—Harris Trust and Savings Bank, Chicago. **Incorporated** in Michigan in 1953. Reincorporated in Delaware in 1987. **Empl**-4,500. **S&P Analyst:** J.C.

STANDARD & POOR'S

STOCK REPORTS

Charter Medical

ASE Symbol **CMD**
In S&P SmallCap 600

20-NOV-95 **Industry:** Health Care Centers

Summary: Charter Medical operates 102 psychiatric hospitals in 33 states and two foreign countries.

S&P Opinion: Accumulate (★★★★)

Recent Price • 18⅜
52 Wk Range • 23⅜-13⅞
Yield • Nil
12-Mo. P/E • NM

Quantitative Evaluations

Outlook
(1 Lowest—5 Highest)
• NA

Fair Value
• NA

Risk
• Average

Earn./Div. Rank
• NR

Technical Eval.
• Neutral since 11/95

Rel. Strength Rank
(1 Lowest—99 Highest)
• 34

Insider Activity
• NA

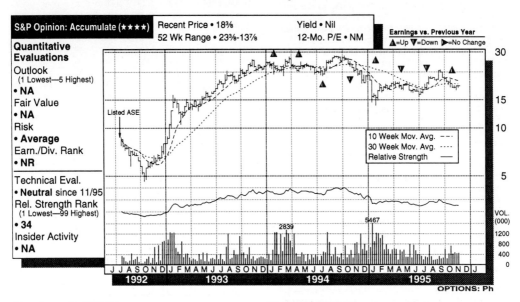

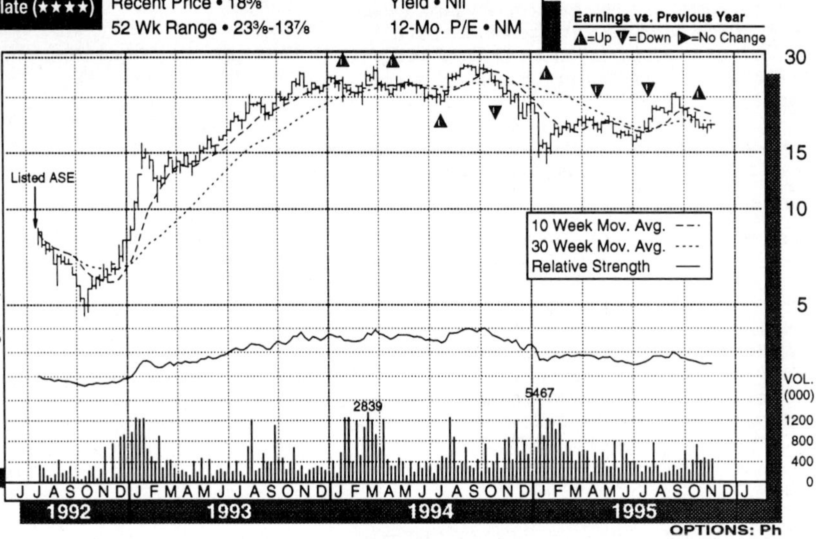

OPTIONS: Ph

Overview - 20-NOV-95

Market conditions in the psychiatric hospital sector are expected to remain challenging, but Charter is pursuing a strategy designed to generate steady revenue and earnings gains in FY 1996 and beyond. With pricing and utilization likely to remain under pressure from payers, CMD has taken steps to assure that its services are cost-effective (an increased emphasis on outpatient and other alternative services) and cover a wide range of patient needs. In addition, the recently-announced transaction with Green Spring will further Charter's goal of becoming the first truly integrated provider of behavioral healthcare. Networking through joint ventures with other hospitals and physician group practices should also boost results going forward.

Valuation - 20-NOV-95

Charter Medical is creating an fully integrated behavioral care network, a characteristic which will attract managed care payers seeking to streamline their provider relationships. Although fundamental conditions in the psychiatric care sector are not expected to improve dramatically in the near future, Charter's ability to capture market share from smaller regional competitors, along with improved operating efficiencies, should allow for strong revenue and profit gains going forward. The company reported somewhat disappointing operating earnings of $2.15 a share in FY 1995 (Sep.), but we see FY 1996 EPS rising to $2.40, and would accumulate the shares on weakness.

Key Stock Statistics

S&P EPS Est. 1996	2.40	Tang. Bk. Value/Share	0.51
P/E on S&P Est. 1996	7.7	Beta	NA
Dividend Rate/Share	Nil	Shareholders	1,200
Shs. outstg. (M)	28.4	Market cap. (B)	$0.522
Avg. daily vol. (M)	0.087	Inst. holdings	69%
		Insider holdings	NA

Value of $10,000 invested 5 years ago: NA

Fiscal Year Ending Sep. 30

	1996	% Change	1995	% Change	1994	% Change
Revenues (Million $)						
1Q	—	—	263.8	26%	208.8	-8%
2Q	—	—	304.8	43%	212.6	-9%
3Q	—	—	304.8	38%	220.9	-5%
4Q	—	—	283.3	8%	262.4	27%
Yr.	—	—	1,152	27%	904.7	NM
Income (Million $)						
1Q	—	—	0.35	NM	-3.87	NM
2Q	—	—	-15.10	NM	1.12	NM
3Q	—	—	1.68	-20%	2.11	NM
4Q	—	—	-29.89	NM	-46.37	NM
Yr.	—	—	-42.96	NM	-47.00	NM
Earnings Per Share ($)						
1Q	E0.49	NM	0.01	NM	-0.15	NM
2Q	E0.70	NM	-0.53	NM	0.04	NM
3Q	E0.69	NM	0.06	-25%	0.08	NM
4Q	E0.52	NM	-1.07	NM	-1.72	NM
Yr.	E2.40	NM	-1.54	NM	-1.78	NM

Next earnings report expected: early February

Charter Medical

Business Summary - 20-NOV-95

Charter Medical Corp. is an international behavioral healthcare provider. At June 30, 1995, it was operating 108 behavioral health systems in the U.S. and Europe.

The psychiatric hospitals operated by the company provide structured and intensive treatment programs for mental health and alcohol and drug dependency disorders in children, adolescents and adults. The specialization of programs enables the clinical staff to provide care that is specific to the patient's needs and facilitates monitoring the patient's progress. A typical treatment program integrates physicians and other patient-care professionals with structured activities, providing patients with testing, adjunctive therapies (occupational, recreational and other), group therapy, individual therapy and educational programs. Charter's residential treatment centers offer less intensive and longer stay services than do acute care psychiatric hospitals. At June 30, 1995, the company's psychiatric hospitals had an aggregate capacity of 9,585 licensed beds.

In fiscal 1994, Medicare provided 27% of hospital gross patient revenues, Medicaid 16%, HMOs and PPOs 14%, the government's CHAMPUS program 5%, and other (primarily Blue Cross and commercial insurance) 38%.

The company's hospitals have been impacted by negative factors influencing the entire psychiatric hospital industry, including reduced inpatient length of stays and lower average reimbursement. In response, the company has strengthened its cost controls, reviewed its hospital portfolio and sold, closed or leased hospitals or consolidated certain operations, and developed strategies to increase outpatient services and partial hospitalization programs to meet the demands of the marketplace.

Important Developments

Oct. '95—Charter agreed to acquire a 51% interest in Green Spring Health Services, Inc., the largest managed behavioral health care firm for Blue Cross/Blue Shield organizations in the U.S., and the second largest publicly-held manager of behavioral health care benefits, for $73.2 million in cash and common stock. Following the transaction, which will create the largest integrated behavioral health care company in the U.S., Charter will become a new holding company named Magellan Health Services Inc. (combined projected 1996 revenues of $1.4 billion), which will be comprised of three primary operating companies: Charter Behavioral Health Systems, Green Spring Health Services, and Magellan Public Solutions. Closing of the transaction is expected in January 1996.

Capitalization

Long Term Debt: $540,000,000 (6/95).

Per Share Data ($) (Year Ended Sep. 30)

	1995	1994	1993	1992	1991	1990
Tangible Bk. Val.	NA	1.06	2.29	0.42	3.09	NA
Cash Flow	NA	-0.75	-0.53	0.05	2.08	NA
Earnings	-1.54	-1.78	-1.59	-1.50	-1.43	NA
Dividends	Nil	Nil	Nil	Nil	Nil	NA
Payout Ratio	Nil	Nil	Nil	Nil	Nil	NA
Prices - High	23¼	28½	27	8¾	NA	NA
- Low	13⅞	21¼	8	4⅝	NA	NA
P/E Ratio - High	NM	NM	NM	NM	NA	NA
- Low	NM	NM	NM	NM	NA	NA

Income Statement Analysis (Million $)

	1994	%Chg	1993	%Chg	1992	%Chg	1991
Revs.	905	NM	898	-30%	1,275	7%	1,195
Oper. Inc.	111	3%	108	-56%	246	13%	218
Depr.	27.2	3%	26.4	-32%	38.6	-56%	87.2
Int. Exp.	44.0	-44%	78.0	-12%	88.5	-10%	98.3
Pretax Inc.	-58.0	NM	-38.0	NM	-9.6	NM	-27.0
Eff. Tax Rate	NM	—	NM	—	NM	—	NM
Net Inc.	-47.0	NM	-40.0	NM	-37.7	NM	-35.4

Balance Sheet & Other Fin. Data (Million $)

	1994	1993	1992	1991	1990	1989
Cash	130	86.0	144	117	NA	NA
Curr. Assets	325	232	355	345	NA	NA
Total Assets	961	838	1,306	1,428	NA	NA
Curr. Liab.	215	273	315	227	NA	NA
LT Debt	533	350	846	991	NA	NA
Common Eqty.	56.0	57.0	10.4	76.7	NA	NA
Total Cap.	602	446	877	1,068	NA	NA
Cap. Exp.	105	11.0	28.0	NA	NA	NA
Cash Flow	-20.0	-13.0	1.3	51.8	NA	NA

Ratio Analysis

	1994	1993	1992	1991	1990	1989
Curr. Ratio	1.5	0.9	1.1	1.5	NA	NA
% LT Debt of Cap.	88.6	78.5	96.5	92.8	NA	NA
% Net Inc.of Revs.	NM	NM	NM	NM	NA	NA
% Ret. on Assets	NM	NM	NM	NM	NA	NA
% Ret. on Equity	NM	NM	NM	NM	NA	NA

Dividend Data —Cash dividend payments, suspended since September 1988, are currently prohibited under terms of certain debt agreements.

Data as orig. reptd.; bef. results of disc. opers. and/or spec. items. Per share data adj. for stk. divs. as of ex-div. date. E-Estimated. NA-Not Available. NM-Not Meaningful. NR-Not Ranked.

Office—3414 Peachtree Rd., Suite 1400, Atlanta, GA 30326. **Tel**—(404) 841-9200. **Chrmn & CEO**—E. M. Crawford. **EVP & CFO**—L. W. Drinkard. **Treas**—J. R. Bedenbaugh. **Secy**—L. C. Newlin. **Investor Contact**—Nancy Gore. **Dirs**—E.M. Banks, E.M. Crawford, A.C. Dimitriadis, L.W. Drinkard, A.D. Frazier Jr., R.H. Kiefer, G.L. McManis. **Transfer Agent & Registrar**—First Union National Bank of North Carolina, Charlotte. **Incorporated** in Delaware in 1969. **Empl**-9,500. **S&P Analyst:** Robert M. Gold

STANDARD & POOR'S

STOCK REPORTS

Charter One Financial

NASDAQ Symbol **COFI**

In S&P SmallCap 600

30-AUG-95 **Industry:** Banking

Summary: This holding company owns Charter One Bank F.S.B., Ohio's largest thrift institution, with assets of $6.3 billion at June 30, 1995.

S&P Opinion: Accumulate (★★★★)

Recent Price • 28
52 Wk Range • 28⅞-17¾
Yield • 2.6%
12-Mo. P/E • 9.2

Quantitative Evaluations

Outlook
(1 Lowest—5 Highest)
• NA

Fair Value
• NA

Risk
• Low

Earn./Div. Rank
• NR

Technical Eval.
• Bullish since 2/95

Rel. Strength Rank
(1 Lowest—99 Highest)
• 83

Insider Activity
• NA

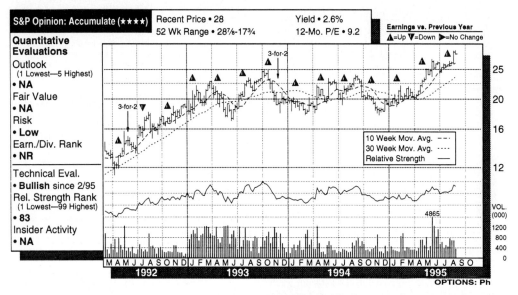

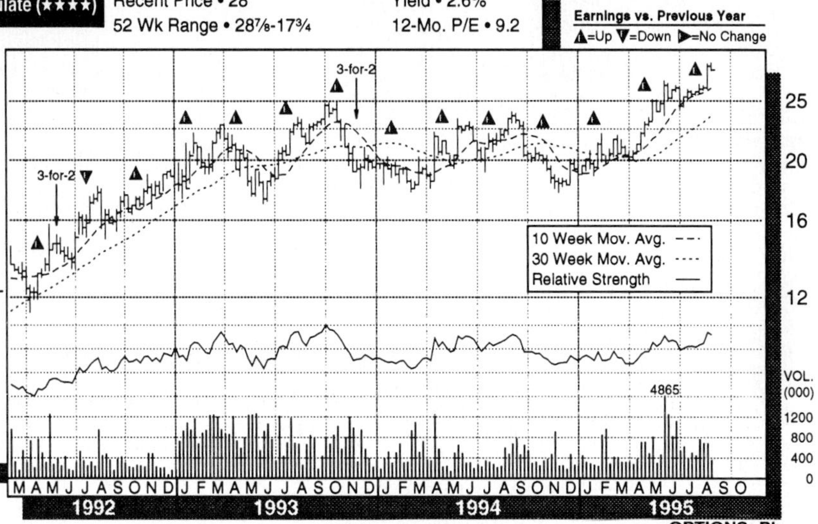

OPTIONS: Ph

Overview - 16-AUG-95

Assuming the FirstFed Michigan merger is completed in late 1995, profits for 1996 should increase modestly. The merger is expected to contribute to cost efficiencies and slight growth in loans and fee income. COFI is expanding its home equity and consumer loan portfolio. Second, the interest rate spread is anticipated to widen, primarily reflecting the effect of lower interest rates on COFI's funding costs, a major expense item. Asset quality is excellent, and the company is well-reserved; thus, a lower credit provision is possible. General and administrative cost ratios should decline, resulting from the previously mentioned merger-related efficiencies.

Valuation - 16-AUG-95

Recent strength in the stock reflects lower interest rates and a favorable response to the pending FirstFed Michigan merger, which presents opportunities for revenue enhancement and efficiency gains. The shares have appeal at about eight times projected 1996 earnings per share, well below the P/E on the S & P 500. The company's return on equity of 18.2% in the second quarter places it in the top 15% of publicly-traded thrifts. Charter One unlike most other thrifts has a consistent growth record; earnings per share have increased each year for the past five years. When the FirstFed deal is completed Charter One shares may benefit from a wider institutional following.

Key Stock Statistics

S&P EPS Est. 1995	3.10	Tang. Bk. Value/Share	18.27
P/E on S&P Est. 1995	9.1	Beta	1.96
S&P EPS Est. 1996	3.25	Shareholders	4,500
Dividend Rate/Share	0.76	Market cap. (B)	$0.648
Shs. outstg. (M)	22.4	Inst. holdings	68%
Avg. daily vol. (M)	0.127	Insider holdings	NA

Value of $10,000 invested 5 years ago: $ 41,271

Fiscal Year Ending Dec. 31

	1995	% Change	1994	% Change	1993	% Change
Revenues (Million $)						
1Q	123.4	29%	95.34	NM	95.28	-1%
2Q	127.3	23%	103.6	7%	96.78	4%
3Q	—	—	109.1	13%	96.55	4%
4Q	—	—	115.7	21%	95.99	7%
Yr.	—	—	423.7	10%	384.6	3%
Income (Million $)						
1Q	17.80	12%	15.90	24%	12.79	42%
2Q	18.22	6%	17.20	7%	16.10	58%
3Q	—	—	17.33	7%	16.16	37%
4Q	—	—	17.18	5%	16.39	34%
Yr.	—	—	67.61	10%	61.44	42%
Earnings Per Share ($)						
1Q	0.77	12%	0.69	21%	0.57	24%
2Q	0.79	7%	0.74	7%	0.69	31%
3Q	E0.76	1%	0.75	7%	0.70	17%
4Q	E0.78	5%	0.74	4%	0.71	15%
Yr.	E3.10	6%	2.92	9%	2.67	21%

Next earnings report expected: mid October

Charter One Financial

Business Summary - 16-AUG-95

Charter One Financial, Inc. owns Charter One Bank F.S.B. a federally chartered savings bank based in Cleveland, Ohio. At December 31, 1994, Charter One operated 96 full service banking offices and four loan production offices in Ohio's major markets. Since 1980, the company has significantly expanded its asset base through a number of acquisitions. Loans receivable of $3.6 billion at December 31, 1994 and $3.3 billion a year earlier were divided as follows:

	1994	1993
One-to-four family	76%	76%
Consumer	11%	8%
Commercial real estate	7%	8%
Other	6%	8%

The loan portfolio at 1994 year-end was split 46% to 54% between adjustable and fixed rate instruments.

At December 31, 1994, nonperforming assets (nonperforming loans and repossessed assets) were $38.2 million (0.62% of assets), versus $46.4 million (0.89%) a year earlier. The allowance for loan losses at 1994 year-end was $36.9 million (0.60% of assets), up from $35.1 million (0.67%) a year earlier. Net loans charged off totaled $1.0 million (0.03% of average loans) in 1994, versus $884,000 (0.03%) in 1993.

Deposits at 1994 year-end of $4.36 billion were divided as follows: 63% certificates, 14% savings, 14% money market, and 9% checking accounts. The average yield on interest-earning assets was 7.17% in 1994 (7.44% in 1993), and the average rate paid on interest-bearing liabilities was 4.11% (4.08%), for a spread of 3.06% (3.36%).

Important Developments

May '95—Charter One said that it had reached a definitive agreement to merge with FirstFed Michigan Corp. in a merger of equals to form one of the strongest thrifts in the region. The stock deal is valued at about $600 million based on the closing price of COFI shares at August 15, 1995. The combined company will have a total of 157 branches in Ohio and Michigan, about $13 billion in total assets and a leverage capital ratio in excess of 6%. Completion was anticipated during the fourth quarter, subject to various approvals.

Capitalization

Long Term Debt: $1,420,716,000 (6/95).

Per Share Data ($)

(Year Ended Dec. 31)

	1994	1993	1992	1991	1990	1989
Tangible Bk. Val.	16.35	16.42	13.35	11.92	10.09	9.06
Earnings	2.92	2.67	2.21	2.06	1.12	1.09
Dividends	0.59	0.41	0.31	0.28	0.25	0.21
Payout Ratio	20%	15%	14%	14%	22%	20%
Prices - High	24	25	20	14¼	8⅜	9⅞
- Low	17¾	17	11⅜	5⅝	4¼	4⅜
P/E Ratio - High	8	9	9	7	8	9
- Low	6	6	5	3	4	4

Income Statement Analysis (Million $)

	1994	%Chg	1993	%Chg	1992	%Chg	1991
Net Int. Inc.	178	5%	170	25%	136	55%	88.0
Loan Loss Prov.	2.8	-46%	5.2	-21%	6.5	2%	6.4
Non Int. Inc.	28.1	7%	26.2	2%	25.7	-19%	31.9
Non Int. Exp.	102	4%	97.9	10%	88.7	45%	61.2
Pretax Inc.	101	8%	93.4	40%	66.5	27%	52.5
Eff. Tax Rate	33%	—	34%	—	35%	—	36%
Net Inc.	67.6	10%	61.4	42%	43.3	29%	33.5
% Net Int. Marg.	3.23%	—	3.53%	—	3.32%	—	2.83%

Balance Sheet & Other Fin. Data (Million $)

	1994	1993	1992	1991	1990	1989
Total Assets	6,130	5,215	4,262	3,666	3,069	2,127
Loans	5,581	4,715	3,772	3,239	2,627	1,775
Deposits	4,368	4,179	3,643	3,187	2,505	1,778
Capitalization:						
Debt	1,319	604	305	221	350	131
Equity	369	370	253	188	157	170
Total	1,688	974	558	409	507	301

Ratio Analysis

	1994	1993	1992	1991	1990	1989
% Ret. on Assets	1.2	1.3	1.0	1.0	0.7	0.8
% Ret. on Equity	17.9	18.1	18.7	19.4	11.9	10.8
% Loan Loss Resv.	0.7	0.7	0.8	0.7	0.5	0.3
% Risk Based Capital	13.4	14.4	12.1	9.5	8.7	NA
Price Times Book Value:						
High	1.5	1.5	1.5	1.2	0.8	1.1
Low	1.1	1.0	0.8	0.5	0.4	0.5

Dividend Data —Cash dividends were initiated in 1989. A dividend reinvestment plan is available.

Amt. of Div. $	Date Decl.	Ex-Div. Date	Stock of Record	Payment Date
0.170	Oct. 20	Oct. 28	Nov. 03	Nov. 18 '94
0.170	Jan. 17	Jan. 25	Jan. 31	Feb. 14 '95
0.090	Apr. 19	May. 02	May. 08	May. 23 '95
0.190	Jul. 19	Aug. 03	Aug. 07	Aug. 22 '95

Data as orig. reptd.; bef. results of disc opers. and/or spec. items. Per share data adj. for stk. divs. as of ex-div. date. E-Estimated. NA-Not Available. NM-Not Meaningful. NR-Not Ranked.

Office—1215 Superior Ave., Cleveland, OH 44114. **Tel**—(216) 566-5300. **Chrmn, Pres, CEO & Investor Contact**—Charles John Koch. **Secy**—R. J. Vana. **Sr VP & Treas**—L. A. Krysinski. **Dirs**—N. P. Auburn, E. B. Carroll, O. J. Cerny, D. M. Fugo, C. F. Ipavec, G. M. Jones, C. J. Koch, J. D. Koch, R. L. Moore, A. H. Poll, V. A. Ptak, C. A. Shirk. **Transfer Agent & Registrar**—Bank of Boston. **Incorporated** in Delaware in 1987. **Empl**-1,403. **S&P Analyst:** Paul Huberman, CFA

STANDARD & POOR'S

Checkers Drive-In Restaurants

STOCK REPORTS

NASDAQ Symbol **CHKR**
In S&P SmallCap 600

09-SEP-95 **Industry:** Food serving

Summary: This company operates and franchises quick-service "double drive-thru" restaurants operating under the Checkers name.

Quantitative Evaluations

Outlook
(1 Lowest—5 Highest)
• **NA**

Fair Value
• **NA**

Risk
• **High**

Earn./Div. Rank
• **NR**

Technical Eval.
• **Bearish** since 12/93

Rel. Strength Rank
(1 Lowest—99 Highest)
• **7**

Insider Activity
• **NA**

Recent Price • 2
52 Wk Range • $5\frac{1}{8}$-$1\frac{13}{16}$

Yield • Nil
12-Mo. P/E • NM

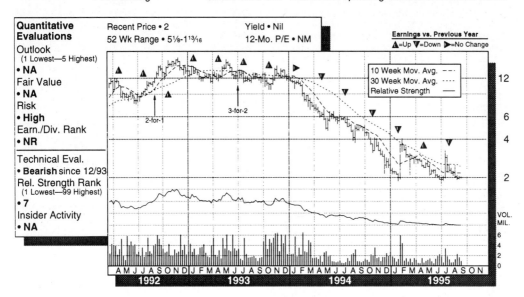

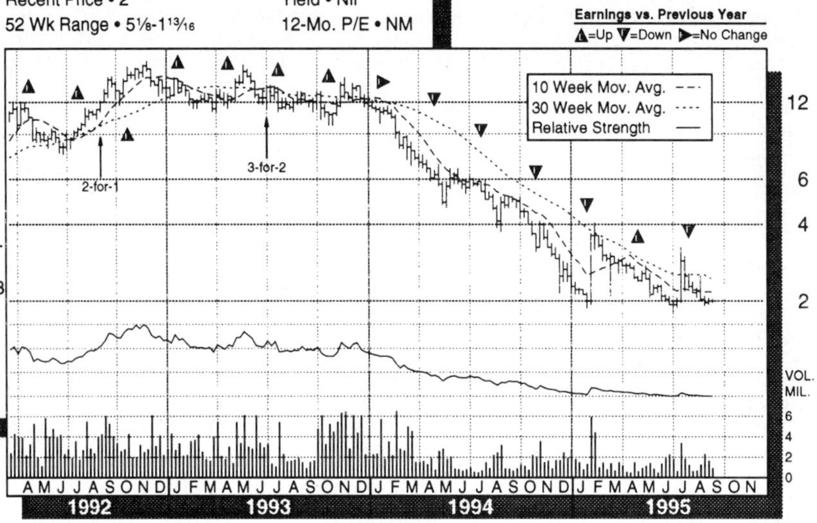

Business Profile - 31-AUG-95

This growing operator and franchisor of quick-service "double drive-thru" restaurants posted a loss in 1994, reflecting price discounting by competitors and dilution of sales of existing units by the opening of additional units in certain markets. For 1995, Checkers plans to focus on core markets to improve marketing and operating efficiencies, and to stress expansion through less expensive franchised development. Its goal is for franchisees to represent 65% of stores in operation.

Operational Review - 31-AUG-95

Revenues in the 24 weeks ended June 19, 1995, declined, year to year, reflecting a decrease of $3.6 million in modular restaurant revenues and lower franchise fees. Restaurant margins narrowed, and the modular manufacturing division recorded an operating loss. With higher advertising and interest expense, and greater depreciation charges, despite the absence of a $4.5 million provision for divested units, the net loss widened.

Stock Performance - 08-SEP-95

In the past 30 trading days, CHKR's shares have declined 12%, compared to a 2% rise in the S&P 500. Average trading volume for the past five days was 210,050 shares, compared with the 40-day moving average of 253,310 shares.

Key Stock Statistics

Dividend Rate/Share	Nil	Shareholders	6,200
Shs. outstg. (M)	51.5	Market cap. (B)	$0.103
Avg. daily vol. (M)	0.297	Inst. holdings	5%
Tang. Bk. Value/Share	1.67	Insider holdings	NA
Beta	0.03		

Value of $10,000 invested 5 years ago: NA

Fiscal Year Ending Dec. 31

	1995	% Change	1994	% Change	1993	% Change
Revenues (Million $)						
1Q	47.46	-11%	53.35	36%	39.10	137%
2Q	49.95	3%	48.53	6%	45.60	127%
3Q	—	—	52.20	7%	49.01	112%
4Q	—	—	66.92	20%	55.79	93%
Yr.	—	—	221.1	17%	189.5	114%
Income (Million $)						
1Q	-1.69	NM	-1.76	NM	3.62	83%
2Q	-1.23	NM	1.27	-66%	3.76	46%
3Q	—	—	0.39	-91%	4.12	39%
4Q	—	—	-6.65	NM	3.21	NM
Yr.	—	—	-6.75	NM	14.70	38%
Earnings Per Share ($)						
1Q	-0.03	NM	-0.04	NM	0.07	40%
2Q	-0.02	NM	0.03	-63%	0.08	33%
3Q	—	—	0.01	-89%	0.09	29%
4Q	—	—	-0.13	NM	0.07	NM
Yr.	—	—	-0.14	NM	0.31	24%

Next earnings report expected: early November

Checkers Drive-In Restaurants

09-SEP-95

Business Summary - 08-SEP-95

Checkers Drive-In Restaurants, Inc. develops, owns, operates and franchises quick-service "double drive-thru" restaurants under the Checkers name. The restaurants are designed to provide fast and efficient automobile-oriented service incorporating a 1950s diner and art deco theme with a highly visible, distinctive and uniform look intended to appeal to customers of all ages.

At Aug 2, 1995, there were 501 restaurants (up from 473 at September 30, 1994), of which 250 were company-operated (including joint ventures) and 251 franchised, operating in 23 states and Washington D.C., with the heaviest concentrations in Florida, Georgia and Alabama.

The restaurants feature quarter-pound hamburgers, cheeseburgers and bacon cheeseburgers, specially seasoned french fries, hot dogs and deluxe chili dogs, chicken and fish sandwiches, specially seasoned french fries as well as soft drinks and old fashioned premium milk shakes, at everyday low prices. The restaurants are targeted to benefit from substantial growth in off-premises consumption of food products and a trend to spend less money when dining out. The typical cost of a meal of a hamburger, french fries and small soft drink is generally $2.57.

Checkers restaurants are less than one-fourth the size of the typical restaurants of the four largest fast-food hamburger chains (670 to 760 sq. ft.). and require about one-third to one half the land area. Substantially all restaurants opened after May 1990 consist of a fully equipped, manufactured modular building (a Modular Restaurant Package) produced and installed by the company.

The company expects to open 40 to 70 additional restaurants in 1995-96, including 5 to 15 company-owned and 35 to 55 franchised, as it plans to rebalance its restaurant portfolio to achieve 65% franchise/35% company-owned distribution. Substantially all new restaurants will include the lower cost Modular Restaurant Packages.

Important Developments

Mar. '95—Checkers recorded a provision of $9.1 million in 1994 for site improvements, settlement of leases and relocation of building and equipment packages for the closure of underperforming restaurants. In addition, it incurred a $5.3 million charge, primarily related to a slowdown of new restaurant development and associated writeoffs. It also announced a four-point plan for 1995, including positioning its product around taste, value and speed; improving customer-related operations performance; restructuring processes and reducing costs; and rebalancing new restaurant growth in favor of franchised units.

Capitalization

Long Term Liabilities: $51,294,000 (3/95).
Minority Interest: $698,542.

Per Share Data ($)

(Year Ended Dec. 31)

	1994	1993	1992	1991	1990	1989
Tangible Bk. Val.	1.77	1.96	1.62	0.79	0.03	NA
Cash Flow	0.17	0.43	0.29	0.13	0.05	NA
Earnings	-0.14	0.31	0.25	0.11	0.04	NA
Dividends	Nil	Nil	Nil	Nil	Nil	NA
Payout Ratio	Nil	Nil	Nil	Nil	Nil	NA
Prices - High	$12\frac{1}{4}$	$16\frac{7}{8}$	$17\frac{3}{8}$	$6\frac{5}{8}$	NA	NA
- Low	$2\frac{1}{8}$	$9\frac{3}{4}$	$5\frac{3}{4}$	$3\frac{1}{2}$	NA	NA
P/E Ratio - High	NM	54	70	60	NA	NA
- Low	NM	31	23	33	NA	NA

Income Statement Analysis (Million $)

	1994	%Chg	1993	%Chg	1992	%Chg	1991
Revs.	221	16%	190	114%	88.6	110%	42.2
Oper. Inc.	23.1	-22%	29.7	68%	17.7	157%	6.9
Depr.	15.1	169%	5.6	183%	2.0	133%	0.9
Int. Exp.	3.9	NM	0.5	—	NA	—	0.6
Pretax Inc.	-11.1	NM	23.8	41%	16.9	196%	5.7
Eff. Tax Rate	NM	—	35%	—	34%	—	30%
Net Inc.	-6.8	NM	15.1	41%	10.7	189%	3.7

Balance Sheet & Other Fin. Data (Million $)

	1994	1993	1992	1991	1990	1989
Cash	3.5	3.4	21.1	16.0	0.6	NA
Curr. Assets	16.2	16.9	26.2	17.9	1.4	NA
Total Assets	197	180	91.9	43.5	11.5	NA
Curr. Liab.	48.8	25.5	9.3	8.0	5.1	NA
LT Debt	31.7	36.6	0.5	1.8	4.3	NA
Common Eqty.	109	110	78.4	31.9	1.1	NA
Total Cap.	144	154	82.3	35.1	6.1	NA
Cap. Exp.	34.8	90.9	39.9	10.0	5.3	NA
Cash Flow	8.4	20.7	12.7	4.5	1.7	NA

Ratio Analysis

	1994	1993	1992	1991	1990	1989
Curr. Ratio	0.3	0.7	2.8	2.2	2.2	NA
% LT Debt of Cap.	22.0	23.8	0.6	5.0	71.6	NA
% Net Inc.of Revs.	NM	8.0	12.1	8.7	5.3	NA
% Ret. on Assets	NM	10.9	15.2	12.7	NA	NA
% Ret. on Equity	NM	15.6	18.8	22.1	NA	NA

Dividend Data —No cash dividends have been paid, and the company does not intend to pay any in the foreseeable future. The shares were split three for two in mid-1993, two for one in September 1992, and three for two in February 1992.

Data as orig. reptd.; bef. results of disc. opers. and/or spec. items. Per share data adj. for stk. divs. as of ex-div. date. E-Estimated. NA-Not Available. NM-Not Meaningful. NR-Not Ranked.

Office—Barnett Bank Building, 600 Cleveland St., Clearwater, FL 34615. **Tel**—(813) 441-3500. **Chrmn**—H. G. Brown. **Vice Chrmn & CEO**—J. F. White, Jr. **Pres & COO**—R. C. Postle. **EVP, Treas & Secy**—J. D. Brown. **VP & Acting CFO**—R. R. Castaneda. **Dirs**—H. G. Brown, J. D. Brown, H. S. Cline, G. W. Cook, F. E. Fisher, La-Van Hawkins, A. H. Hines, Jr., R. C. Postle, J. F. White, Jr. **Transfer Agent & Registrar**—Mellon Financial Services, Pittsburgh. **Reincorporated** in Delaware in 1991. **Empl-** 8,046. **S&P Analyst:** Efraim Levy

STANDARD & POOR'S

STOCK REPORTS

Chemed Corp.

NYSE Symbol **CHE**
In S&P SmallCap 600

12-OCT-95 **Industry:** Chemicals

Summary: This company has positions in medical and dental supplies, home healthcare services and hospice care, sanitary maintenance products and services, and cleaning and appliance repair.

Quantitative Evaluations
Outlook
(1 Lowest—5 Highest)
• **NA**
Fair Value
• **NA**
Risk
• **Low**
Earn./Div. Rank
• **B+**

Technical Eval.
• **Bearish** since 6/95
Rel. Strength Rank
(1 Lowest—99 Highest)
• **45**
Insider Activity
• **Neutral**

Recent Price • 35½
52 Wk Range • 36½-30⅜
Yield • 6.0%
12-Mo. P/E • 8.4

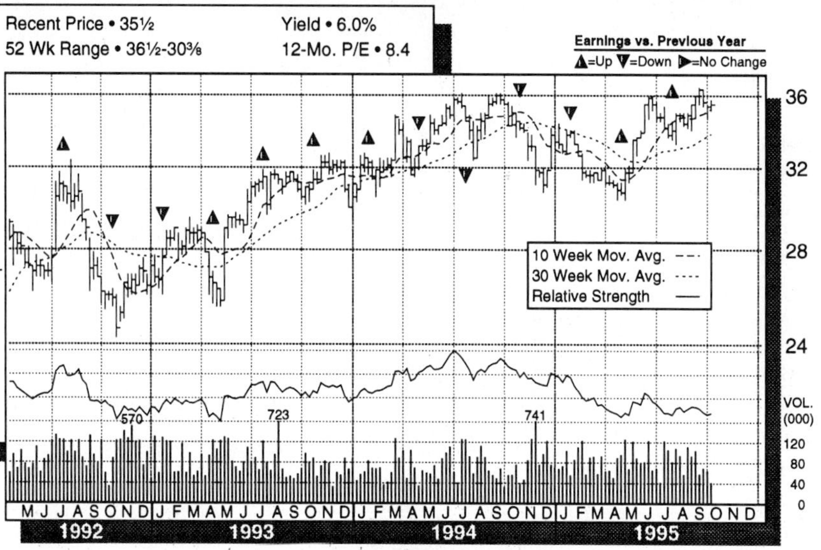

Business Profile - 11-OCT-95

Chemed has operations in medical and dental supply manufacturing and distribution; home healthcare services and hospice care; plumbing, drain cleaning, and appliance repair and maintenance; and sanitation supplies. Performance in the first half of 1995 represents a marked improvement over prior year results, reflecting huge growth in the home healthcare services business, as well as steady growth, effective cost management, and strategic acquisitions and divestitures in other business segments.

Operational Review - 12-OCT-95

Sales for the first half of 1995 rose 11% year to year, reflecting higher revenues at all four operating units, especially Patient Care, which benefited from branch openings. Growth in Roto Rooter's basic cleaning and plumbing service outweighed the fall-off in service contract revenues. Margins improved for all divisions except Veratex, which should recover following the recent sale of its retail division. Income from continuing operations advanced 39%, strengthened by gains from investments.

Stock Performance - 06-OCT-95

In the past 30 trading days, CHE's shares have increased 2%, compared to a 4% rise in the S&P 500. Average trading volume for the past five days was 8,000 shares, compared with the 40-day moving average of 15,113 shares.

Key Stock Statistics

Dividend Rate/Share	2.08	Shareholders	6,700
Shs. outstg. (M)	9.9	Market cap. (B)	$0.342
Avg. daily vol. (M)	0.012	Inst. holdings	32%
Tang. Bk. Value/Share	5.67	Insider holdings	NA
Beta	0.87		

Value of $10,000 invested 5 years ago: $ 15,014

Fiscal Year Ending Dec. 31

	1995	% Change	1994	% Change	1993	% Change
Revenues (Million $)						
1Q	169.9	12%	152.1	26%	120.5	30%
2Q	177.3	10%	161.4	27%	127.2	29%
3Q	—	—	166.1	19%	139.8	36%
4Q	—	—	165.5	20%	137.5	28%
Yr.	—	—	645.0	23%	525.1	31%
Income (Million $)						
1Q	5.39	66%	3.24	-21%	4.08	30%
2Q	5.30	20%	4.43	-9%	4.86	12%
3Q	—	—	3.21	-23%	4.16	16%
4Q	—	—	3.66	-9%	4.04	27%
Yr.	—	—	14.53	-15%	17.14	20%
Earnings Per Share ($)						
1Q	0.55	67%	0.33	-21%	0.42	31%
2Q	0.54	20%	0.45	-10%	0.50	14%
3Q	—	—	0.33	-23%	0.43	16%
4Q	—	—	0.37	-10%	0.41	24%
Yr.	—	—	1.47	-16%	1.75	21%

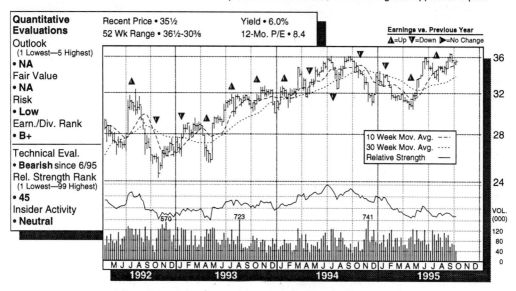

Next earnings report expected: late October

Chemed Corp.

Business Summary - 11-OCT-95

Chemed Corp. manufactures and distributes medical and dental supplies, provides home healthcare services and hospice care, performs plumbing, drain cleaning and residential appliance and air conditioning repair, and provides sanitary maintenance products and services. Segment contributions in 1994:

	Sales	Profits
National Sanitary Supply	48%	30%
Roto-Rooter	26%	46%
Veratex	15%	16%
Patient Care	11%	8%

National Sanitary Supply Co. (85%-owned) is the largest distributor of sanitary maintenance products in the U.S., offering more than 10,000 items through 67 operations in 17 states. The company provides a broad line of janitorial products such as cleaning chemicals, paper goods, plastic products, waste handling products and other janitorial supplies to customers that include hotels/motels, schools, hospitals/nursing homes, food service companies, industrial/commercial and government agencies located primarily in the western, southwestern and midwestern U.S.

Roto-Rooter, Inc. (59%-owned) provides sewer, drain and pipe cleaning services and appliance and plumbing repair and maintenance services and consumer products to residential, commercial, industrial and municipal clients. It serves 88% of the U.S. population through both independent franchisees and company-owned operations.

The Veratex Group manufactures and distributes disposable medical and dental supplies to the non-hospital alternate care market through its Tidi Products, Inc. subsidiary.

Patient Care (acquired in January 1994) provides complete home healthcare services for patients in the New York--New Jersey--Connecticut area.

Chemed also has interests in Omnicare, Inc., a publicly traded health care company that provides pharmacy management services to nursing homes and other long-term-care facilities; privately-held Vitas Healthcare Corp. (formerly Hospice Care Inc.), an operator of comprehensive inpatient and home care hospices; and NYSE-listed EXEL Ltd. (XL), a provider of excess liability insurance.

Important Developments

Jul. '95—The company completed the sale of its Veratex retail operations for an undisclosed amount. Chemed said that it prefers to concentrate on its stronger wholesale operation, Tidi Products, Inc., which recently acquired a manufacturer and distributor of economically priced disposable paper products with annual sales of $12 million.

Capitalization

Long Term Debt: $89,496,000 (6/95).
Minority Interest: $38,436,000.

Per Share Data ($) (Year Ended Dec. 31)

	1994	1993	1992	1991	1990	1989
Tangible Bk. Val.	5.24	2.05	5.65	7.58	11.04	11.77
Cash Flow	2.56	2.65	2.10	1.68	2.51	3.45
Earnings	1.47	1.75	1.45	1.10	1.60	2.61
Dividends	2.04	2.01	2.00	1.97	1.96	1.84
Payout Ratio	139%	115%	137%	177%	121%	72%
Prices - High	36⅛	32¾	32⅜	28¼	36¾	38¾
- Low	30¼	25½	24¼	17¼	18	32½
P/E Ratio - High	25	19	22	26	23	15
- Low	21	15	17	16	11	12

Income Statement Analysis (Million $)

	1994	%Chg	1993	%Chg	1992	%Chg	1991
Revs.	645	23%	525	31%	401	14%	352
Oper. Inc.	39.8	24%	32.0	49%	21.5	31%	16.4
Depr.	10.7	21%	8.8	39%	6.3	8%	5.9
Int. Exp.	8.8	-1%	8.9	56%	5.7	NM	5.7
Pretax Inc.	29.8	-1%	30.2	26%	23.9	24%	19.2
Eff. Tax Rate	37%	—	31%	—	27%	—	28%
Net Inc.	14.5	-15%	17.1	20%	14.3	30%	11.0

Balance Sheet & Other Fin. Data (Million $)

	1994	1993	1992	1991	1990	1989
Cash	24.2	15.8	47.7	83.0	1.4	6.5
Curr. Assets	183	145	162	163	144	150
Total Assets	505	430	405	364	328	335
Curr. Liab.	143	128	104	85.0	94.0	88.0
LT Debt	92.0	98.0	104	78.0	82.0	86.0
Common Eqty.	186	137	134	139	113	121
Total Cap.	322	267	266	245	227	242
Cap. Exp.	18.4	13.9	8.2	11.4	13.0	14.1
Cash Flow	25.2	26.0	20.6	16.9	26.0	34.6

Ratio Analysis

	1994	1993	1992	1991	1990	1989
Curr. Ratio	1.3	1.1	1.6	1.9	1.5	1.7
% LT Debt of Cap.	28.6	36.7	39.0	31.8	36.2	35.5
% Net Inc.of Revs.	2.3	3.3	3.6	3.1	2.8	4.4
% Ret. on Assets	3.1	4.1	3.7	3.5	5.0	7.6
% Ret. on Equity	9.0	12.6	10.5	9.0	14.2	21.6

Dividend Data —Dividends have been paid since 1971. A dividend reinvestment plan is available.

Amt. of Div. $	Date Decl.	Ex-Div. Date	Stock of Record	Payment Date
0.510	Nov. 03	Nov. 17	Nov. 23	Dec. 09 '94
0.510	Feb. 02	Feb. 15	Feb. 22	Mar. 10 '95
0.510	May. 15	May. 22	May. 26	Jun. 09 '95
0.520	Aug. 02	Aug. 16	Aug. 18	Sep. 08 '95

Data as orig. reptd.; bef. results of disc. opers. and/or spec. items. Per share data adj. for stk. divs. as of ex-div. date. E-Estimated. NA-Not Available. NM-Not Meaningful. NR-Not Ranked.

Office—2600 Chemed Center, 255 E. Fifth St, Cincinnati, OH 45202. **Tel**—(513) 762-6900. **Chrmn & CEO**—E. L. Hutton. **Pres**—K. J. McNamara. **EVP-Treas & Investor Contact**—Timothy S. O'Toole. **Secy**—Naomi C. Dallob. **Dirs**—J. A. Cunningham, J. H. Devlin, C. H. Erhart Jr., J. F. Gemunder, W. R. Griffin, E. L. Hutton, T. C. Hutton, W. L. Krebs, S. E. Laney, K. J. McNamara, J. M. Mount, T. S. O'Toole, D. W. Robbins Jr., P. C. Voet. **Transfer Agent & Registrar**—Mellon Bank, Pittsburgh, Pa. **Incorporated** in Delaware in 1970. **Empl**-6,602. **S&P Analyst:** J. Santoriello

STANDARD & POOR'S STOCK REPORTS

Chips and Technologies

NASDAQ Symbol **CHPS**
In S&P SmallCap 600

04-NOV-95

Industry:
Electronics/Electric

Summary: This company derives nearly two-thirds of its revenues from graphic controller products for personal computers. It also produces core logic and input/output products.

S&P Opinion: Hold (★★★)

Recent Price • 10
52 Wk Range • 15⅞-5¾
Yield • Nil
12-Mo. P/E • 15.9

Quantitative Evaluations
Outlook
(1 Lowest—5 Highest)
• **1+**
Fair Value
• **6**
Risk
• **High**
Earn./Div. Rank
• **B-**

Technical Eval.
• **Bearish** since 8/95
Rel. Strength Rank
(1 Lowest—99 Highest)
• **6**
Insider Activity
• **Unfavorable**

Overview - 02-NOV-95

Sales in FY 96 (Jun.) are expected to climb 35%-40%, reflecting new product introductions and design-wins. CHPS has established a major position in the market for flat panel controllers, and will be ramping up production of those products. It will also be shipping a new generation chip set for 486 microprocessors and introducing a chip set for Intel's Pentium microprocessor. The company is expected to introduce a new 64-bit multi-media family of products in fiscal 1996. These innovative products should help CHPS maintain its leading position in the graphics controller market. Additionally, the decision by Compaq Computers to disband its internal design division could allow CHPS to become a major supplier to that company.

Valuation - 02-NOV-95

We continue to recommend holding CHPS. Sales and earnings are expected to grow, albeit at a slower pace than in recent periods, in the next several quarters fueled by the company's leading position as a supplier of graphics chips to the portable computer industry. Investors should remember that results are highly dependent on the portable computer sector. The recent postponement of a secondary offering, due to a potential delay in production at a supplier, caused the shares to tumble. We believe that the sell-off was excessive. However, lingering concerns over this action could restrict near-term share appreciation. On the strength of stronger than expected sales and operating margins in recent periods we are raising our fiscal 1996 EPS estimate to $0.86.

Key Stock Statistics

S&P EPS Est. 1996	0.86	Tang. Bk. Value/Share	3.33
P/E on S&P Est. 1996	11.6	Beta	1.61
Dividend Rate/Share	Nil	Shareholders	1,200
Shs. outstg. (M)	20.3	Market cap. (B)	$0.203
Avg. daily vol. (M)	0.619	Inst. holdings	41%
		Insider holdings	NA

Value of $10,000 invested 5 years ago: $ 5,555

Fiscal Year Ending Jun. 30

	1996	% Change	1995	% Change	1994	% Change
Revenues (Million $)						
1Q	37.22	83%	20.37	-4%	21.17	-20%
2Q	—	—	23.28	4%	22.44	-21%
3Q	—	—	27.23	89%	14.44	-33%
4Q	—	—	33.85	120%	15.39	-29%
Yr.	—	—	104.7	43%	73.44	-25%
Income (Million $)						
1Q	4.43	NM	1.26	NM	0.32	
2Q	—	—	2.37	NM	0.72	NM
3Q	—	—	2.11	NM	0.15	NM
4Q	—	—	3.65	139%	1.53	NM
Yr.	—	—	9.39	NM	2.71	NM
Earnings Per Share ($)						
1Q	0.20	186%	0.07	NM	0.02	NM
2Q	E0.21	62%	0.13	NM	0.04	NM
3Q	E0.23	109%	0.11	NM	0.01	NM
4Q	E0.22	22%	0.18	100%	0.09	NM
Yr.	E0.86	72%	0.50	NM	0.16	NM

Next earnings report expected: mid January

Chips and Technologies

Business Summary - 02-NOV-95

Chips and Technologies, Inc., designs, develops and markets very large scale integrated (VLSI) circuits for the personal computing industry.

Media products consist of VLSI circuit products that provide video display capabilities for cathode ray tube (CRT) and flat panel displays. The company's video display controllers are compatible with the IBM VGA graphics standard and support advanced modes such as SVGA that allow a greater number of colors to be displayed at higher levels of resolution. The company further segments its business into portable families focused on portable display applications. The company is a leading supplier of graphic accelerators to the rapidly growing portable computer industry. The most common portable computing devices are the notebook and sub-notebook computers. Media products also consist of CRT display controllers.

The company's core logic products provide the circuitry that implements the digital pathways of a personal computer and support industry standard bus and processor architectures. As part of its core logic portfolio, the company also provides complementary devices that implement standard communications protocols through serial and parallel ports to allow the interface to the personal computer of peripheral devices such as disk drives, printers and modems.

All products are designed using CHPS's modular TechBlock design library. This methodology captures designs at the functional software level rather than at the hardware circuit level. These design modules enable CHPS to reduce product development time. The ability to re-use design modules allows products to be easily modified to meet specific customer and market needs.

Primary customers are manufacturers of a broad range of IBM-compatible and other standard microcomputer systems, subsystems and add-in circuit boards. Export sales represented 47% of revenues in fiscal 1995, versus 56% in fiscal 1994.

The company does not own its own manufacturing plants but subcontracts to independent suppliers for the manufacture of its products.

Important Developments

Oct. '95—CHPS postponed indefinitely a previously announced stock offering (3.35 million common shares) due to uncertainities concerning a potential delay in production at a foundry supplying the company. Management said that in a "worst-case scenerio", the delay could cause revenues to come in 5%-10% below expectations in the second half of fiscal 1996. CHPS added that it is entirely possible that the delay would be resolved and revenues would not be affected, but believed that it would not be "prudent" to hold a stock offering given the current situation.

Capitalization

Long Term Obligations: $1,977,000 (9/95).

Per Share Data ($)

(Year Ended Jun. 30)

	1995	1994	1993	1992	1991	1990
Tangible Bk. Val.	3.33	1.56	1.19	4.62	8.51	9.31
Cash Flow	0.60	0.37	-2.59	-3.15	0.18	2.49
Earnings	0.50	0.16	-3.13	-4.00	-0.71	1.88
Dividends	Nil	Nil	Nil	Nil	Nil	Nil
Payout Ratio	Nil	Nil	Nil	Nil	Nil	Nil
Prices - High	14 7/8	7 5/8	6 7/8	14 1/8	13 1/2	23 1/2
- Low	6 1/4	3 5/8	2 3/4	3 1/4	6 1/2	5 1/4
P/E Ratio - High	30	47	NM	NM	NM	13
- Low	12	23	NM	NM	NM	3

Income Statement Analysis (Million $)

	1995	%Chg	1994	%Chg	1993	%Chg	1992
Revs.	105	43%	73.0	-26%	98.0	-30%	141
Oper. Inc.	11.0	NM	2.0	NM	-20.8	NM	-43.7
Depr.	2.7	-21%	3.4	-60%	8.6	-30%	12.2
Int. Exp.	NA	—	NA	—	1.6	9%	1.5
Pretax Inc.	10.3	NM	0.7	NM	-49.1	NM	-83.8
Eff. Tax Rate	9.30%	—	NM	—	NM	—	NM
Net Inc.	9.4	NM	2.7	NM	-49.1	NM	-57.4

Balance Sheet & Other Fin. Data (Million $)

	1995	1994	1993	1992	1991	1990
Cash	22.4	22.5	30.3	14.2	37.6	72.3
Curr. Assets	74.9	43.0	50.0	88.0	116	163
Total Assets	85.8	55.0	65.0	121	159	202
Curr. Liab.	18.3	19.4	36.2	42.7	37.2	59.0
LT Debt	NM	8.0	8.9	3.8	6.8	8.6
Common Eqty.	65.7	26.0	19.0	72.0	114	134
Total Cap.	65.7	34.0	29.0	76.0	121	143
Cap. Exp.	3.4	1.7	0.7	2.5	8.6	13.5
Cash Flow	12.1	6.1	-40.5	-45.2	2.4	38.7

Ratio Analysis

	1995	1994	1993	1992	1991	1990
Curr. Ratio	4.1	2.2	1.4	2.1	3.1	2.8
% LT Debt of Cap.	NM	23.6	31.2	5.1	5.6	6.0
% Net Inc.of Revs.	9.0	3.7	NM	NM	NM	10.0
% Ret. on Assets	11.0	4.5	NM	NM	NM	17.1
% Ret. on Equity	20.4	11.8	NM	NM	NM	24.5

Dividend Data —No cash dividends have been paid.

Data as orig. reptd.; bef. results of disc. opers. and/or spec. items. Per share data adj. for stk. divs. as of ex-div. date. E-Estimated. NA-Not Available. NM-Not Meaningful. NR-Not Ranked.

Office—3050 Zanker Rd., San Jose, CA 95134. **Tel**—(408) 434-0600. **Pres & CEO**—J. F. Stafford. **CFO & Investor Contact**—T. R. Christoffersen. **Dirs**—G. P. Carter, H. A. Jarrat, J. F. Stafford, B. V. Vonderschmitt. **Transfer Agent & Registrar**—Bank of Boston, Palo Alto, CA. **Incorporated** in California in 1984; reincorporated in Delaware in 1986. **Empl-** 185. **S&P Analyst:** Steven A. Jaworski

STANDARD & POOR'S

Chiquita Brands International

STOCK REPORTS

NYSE Symbol **CQB**

In S&P SmallCap 600

14-AUG-95 **Industry:** Food

Summary: This company is a leading producer, processor and distributor of fresh fruits and vegetables and prepared food products marketed under the Chiquita and other brand names.

Quantitative Evaluations

Recent Price • 16⅛ Yield • 1.2%

52 Wk Range • 17½-12⅛ 12-Mo. P/E • NM

Outlook (1 Lowest—5 Highest)
• **1+**

Fair Value
• **14**

Risk
• **Average**

Earn./Div. Rank
• **B-**

Technical Eval.
• **Bullish** since 6/95

Rel. Strength Rank (1 Lowest—99 Highest)
• **85**

Insider Activity
• **Neutral**

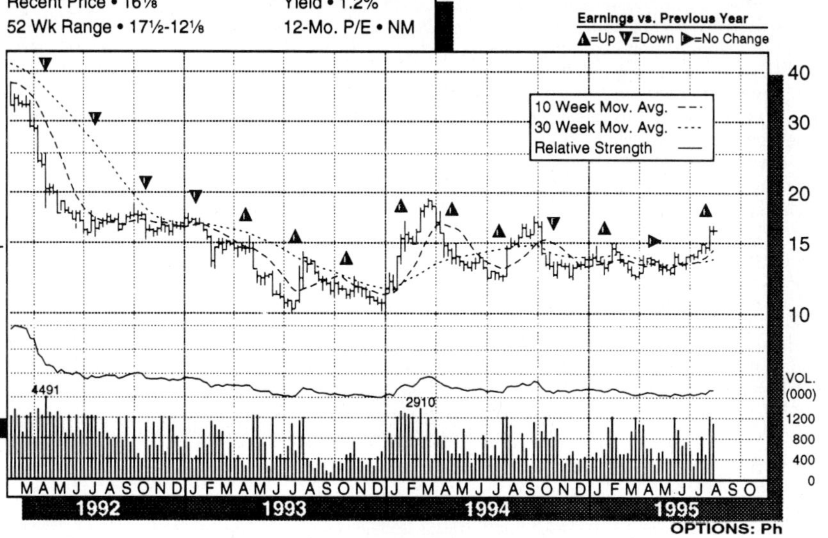

OPTIONS: Ph

Business Profile - 14-AUG-95

The primary cause of losses in recent years was the increasingly restrictive and discriminatory trade policy imposed by the European Union on the Latin American banana industry. The U.S. government has threatened retaliation against the European Union if the policy continues. CQB will benefit significantly when non-EU banana prices recover from depressed levels. The company's financial strategy is to deleverage the balance sheet and lower the overall cost of capital.

Operational Review - 14-AUG-95

Sales in the six months ended June 30, 1995, increased, year to year. A slight decline in profits from the sale of bananas was offset by improvement in other food product lines; operating income was flat. After lower net interest expense resulting from debt refinancing and reduction, net income advanced. Results in the respective periods exclude extraordinary losses of $0.08 and $0.39, from the prepayment of debt.

Stock Performance - 11-AUG-95

In the past 30 trading days, CQB's shares have increased 15%, compared to a 2% rise in the S&P 500. Average trading volume for the past five days was 216,560 shares, compared with the 40-day moving average of 152,556 shares.

Key Stock Statistics

Dividend Rate/Share	0.20	Shareholders	7,700
Shs. outstg. (M)	50.2	Market cap. (B)	$0.810
Avg. daily vol. (M)	0.195	Inst. holdings	73%
Tang. Bk. Value/Share	6.55	Insider holdings	NA
Beta	0.44		

Value of $10,000 invested 5 years ago: $ 10,500

Fiscal Year Ending Dec. 31

	1995	% Change	1994	% Change	1993	% Change
Revenues (Million $)						
1Q	1,028	-3%	1,056	44%	731.1	3%
2Q	1,086	8%	1,007	48%	682.3	-13%
3Q	—	—	900.9	63%	552.3	-10%
4Q	—	—	997.4	76%	567.1	-9%
Yr.	—	—	3,962	56%	2,533	-7%
Income (Million $)						
1Q	37.63	6%	35.53	29%	27.53	195%
2Q	29.42	-5%	30.95	NM	7.67	NM
3Q	—	—	-80.65	NM	-25.87	-64%
4Q	—	—	-34.53	NM	-60.42	-60%
Yr.	—	—	-48.70	NM	-51.08	NM
Earnings Per Share ($)						
1Q	0.62	NM	0.62	17%	0.53	NM
2Q	0.55	8%	0.51	NM	0.15	NM
3Q	—	—	-1.59	NM	-0.50	NM
4Q	—	—	-0.70	NM	-1.17	NM
Yr.	—	—	-1.07	NM	-0.99	NM

Next earnings report expected: early November

Chiquita Brands International

Business Summary - 03-AUG-95

Chiquita Brands International is a leading producer, processor and distributor of fresh and prepared food products marketed under the Chiquita and other brand names. Principal production and processing operations are conducted in the U.S. and Central and South America. Geographic contributions in 1994:

	Sales	Profits
North America	68%	25%
Central & South America	5%	15%
Europe & other	28%	60%

The fresh foods segment features a full line of fresh fruits and vegetables, including bananas, the company's principal product. In recent years, the product base has been widened to include additional fresh fruits sold under the Chiquita name (including avocadoes, citrus, grapes, kiwi, nectarines and mangos) and apples, peaches, grapes, strawberries, cherries, pears, tomatoes and plums sold under other brand names. Fresh vegetables include lettuce, celery, onions, broccoli, carrots, beans, potatoes and asparagus. As a result of the more diverse product line, banana sales made up 60% of total sales in 1994, down from 72% in 1990. Bananas are grown by subsidiaries or purchased from suppliers in areas including Panama, Colombia, Costa Rica, Ecuador, Guatemala, Honduras, Mexico and the Philippines.

Prepared foods include fruit- and vegetable-based juices sold primarily in the United States; processed fruit and vegetables, including processed bananas, sold worldwide under the Chiquita, Friday and other brand names; wet, fresh-cut and ready-to-eat salads sold under the Club Chef and Naked Foods brands; and other consumer packaged foods (primarily margarine and shortening) sold in Latin America by the Numar division.

In the first quarter of 1994, CQB's John Morrel & Co. subsidiary sold its Specialty Meat Group for $53 million to SMG, Inc. The company plans to discontinue all meat division operations.

Important Developments

May '95—E.U. and U.S. officials reported no progress in recently ended talks on the dispute between the E.U. and U.S. over current E.U. restrictions on banana imports from Latin America. In January 1995, the U.S. threatened $1 billion of trade sanctions if the dispute was not solved. The two sides hope to reach agreement by June 1995.

Capitalization

Long Term Debt: $1,355,936,000 (3/95).
Series A Cum. Pfd. Stk: 2,875,000 shs. ($1 par).
Series C Pfd. Stk: 648,310 shs. (no par).
Options: To buy 5,213,758 shs. at $5.75 to $34.44 ea. (12/94).

Per Share Data ($) (Year Ended Dec. 31)

	1994	1993	1992	1991	1990	1989
Tangible Bk. Val.	5.63	7.77	9.01	15.38	11.53	8.84
Cash Flow	1.07	0.92	-2.73	3.87	3.43	2.81
Earnings	-1.07	-0.99	-4.28	2.55	2.23	1.70
Dividends	0.20	0.44	0.66	0.55	0.35	0.20
Payout Ratio	NM	NM	NM	21%	17%	11%
Prices - High	19³/₈	17³/₄	40¹/₈	50³/₄	32¹/₈	17⁵/₈
- Low	11¹/₄	10	15¹/₄	29³/₈	16	12⁷/₈
P/E Ratio - High	NM	NM	NM	20	14	10
- Low	NM	NM	NM	12	7	8

Income Statement Analysis (Million $)

	1994	%Chg	1993	%Chg	1992	%Chg	1991
Revs.	3,962	56%	2,533	-7%	2,723	-41%	4,627
Oper. Inc.	283	37%	206	NM	45.1	-85%	293
Depr.	116	13%	103	28%	80.4	21%	66.7
Int. Exp.	174	-2%	178	1%	176	50%	117
Pretax Inc.	-35.0	NM	-39.0	NM	-216	NM	183
Eff. Tax Rate	NM	—	NM	—	NM	—	30%
Net Inc.	-49.0	NM	-51.0	NM	-221	NM	128

Balance Sheet & Other Fin. Data (Million $)

	1994	1993	1992	1991	1990	1989
Cash	179	151	413	830	349	289
Curr. Assets	918	770	1,071	1,682	1,136	918
Total Assets	2,902	2,741	2,881	3,143	2,174	1,613
Curr. Liab.	651	504	588	698	698	499
LT Debt	1,365	1,438	1,411	1,227	522	417
Common Eqty.	443	544	617	968	688	464
Total Cap.	2,010	2,040	2,086	2,195	1,210	881
Cap. Exp.	149	197	410	411	323	131
Cash Flow	56.0	47.0	-140	195	144	112

Ratio Analysis

	1994	1993	1992	1991	1990	1989
Curr. Ratio	1.4	1.5	1.8	2.4	1.6	1.8
% LT Debt of Cap.	67.9	70.5	67.7	55.9	43.1	47.3
% Net Inc.of Revs.	NM	NM	NM	2.8	2.2	1.8
% Ret. on Assets	NM	NM	NM	4.6	4.6	4.4
% Ret. on Equity	NM	NM	NM	14.9	15.3	15.6

Dividend Data (Dividends on the capital shares were resumed in 1985 after having been omitted since late 1982. A dividend reinvestment plan is available.)

Amt. of Div. $	Date Decl.	Ex-Div. Date	Stock of Record	Payment Date
0.050	Aug. 01	Aug. 15	Aug. 21	Sep. 07 '94
0.050	Oct. 31	Nov. 15	Nov. 21	Dec. 07 '94
0.050	Feb. 02	Feb. 14	Feb. 21	Mar. 07 '95
0.050	Apr. 27	May. 15	May. 21	Jun. 07 '95
0.050	Jul. 27	Aug. 17	Aug. 21	Sep. 07 '95

Data as orig. reptd.; bef. results of disc. opers. and/or spec. items. Per share data adj. for stk. divs. as of ex-div. date. E-Estimated. NA-Not Available. NM-Not Meaningful. NR-Not Ranked.

Office—250 East Fifth St., Cincinnati, OH 45202. **Tel**—(513) 784-8011. **Chrmn & CEO**—C. H. Lindner. **Pres & COO**—K. E. Lindner. **Exec VP & CFO**—S. G. Warshaw. **VP & Secy**—C. R. Morgan. **Investor Contact**—Sandra W. Heimann. **Dirs**—H. F. Culverhouse, C. H. Lindner, K. E. Lindner, S. C. Lindner, F. J. Runk, J. H. Sisco, W. W. Verity, O. W. Waddell, R. F. Walker. **Transfer Agent & Registrar**—Securities Transfer Co., Cincinnati. **Incorporated** in New Jersey in 1899 as United Fruit Co. **Empl**-40,000. **S&P Analyst:** Efraim Levy

STANDARD & POOR'S

STOCK REPORTS

Cineplex Odeon

NYSE Symbol **CPX**

In S&P SmallCap 600

11-OCT-95

Industry: Filmed Entertainment

Summary: This Canadian company is one of the largest theatre operators in North America, owning and operating 1,482 screens in 322 locations in the U.S. and Canada.

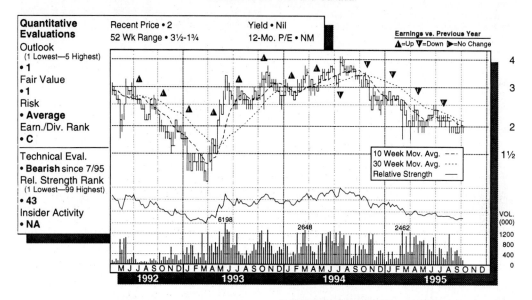

Quantitative Evaluations

Outlook
(1 Lowest—5 Highest)
• **1**

Fair Value
• **1**

Risk
• **Average**

Earn./Div. Rank
• **C**

Technical Eval.
• **Bearish** since 7/95

Rel. Strength Rank
(1 Lowest—99 Highest)
• **43**

Insider Activity
• **NA**

Recent Price • 2
52 Wk Range • 3½-1¾

Yield • Nil
12-Mo. P/E • NM

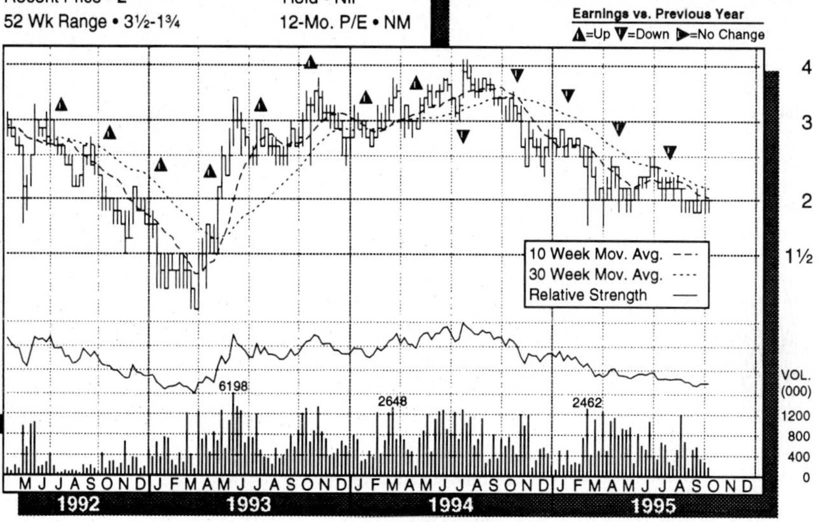

Business Profile - 11-OCT-95

Cineplex Odeon is primarily engaged in the operation of motion picture theatres in the U.S. and Canada, controlling 1,482 screens in 322 locations. Approximately 30% of total revenues in 1994 were derived from Canadian operations. In June 1995, the company sold 28 theatres in Georgia and Florida to Carmike Cinemas Inc., generating proceeds of $22 million which CPX will use to pay down debt and to fund a building program.

Operational Review - 11-OCT-95

Revenues for the first half of 1995 fell 6.1%, year to year, as theaters experienced reduced attendance, which resulted in lower admissions and concessions revenues. The lower attendance was primarily due to the lack of commercially successful film products. Margins were squeezed by the lower sales volume, and the net loss widened to $0.26 a share from $0.12 in the first half of 1994. In the second quarter of 1995, CPX's planned merger with theater operator Cinemark USA was aborted.

Stock Performance - 06-OCT-95

In the past 30 trading days, CPX's shares were unchanged, compared to a 4% rise in the S&P 500. Average trading volume for the past five days was 32,200 shares, compared with the 40-day moving average of 98,538 shares.

Key Stock Statistics

Dividend Rate/Share	Nil	Shareholders	1,900
Shs. outstg. (M)	114.8	Market cap. (B)	$0.230
Avg. daily vol. (M)	0.051	Inst. holdings	5%
Tang. Bk. Value/Share	1.16	Insider holdings	NA
Beta	0.33		

Value of $10,000 invested 5 years ago: $ 2,962

Fiscal Year Ending Dec. 31

	1995	% Change	1994	% Change	1993	% Change
Revenues (Million $)						
1Q	110.0	-16%	130.8	12%	116.7	-10%
2Q	122.5	5%	116.4	-13%	133.3	2%
3Q	—	—	163.8	-2%	166.9	26%
4Q	—	—	128.4	NM	129.4	3%
Yr.	—	—	539.4	-1%	546.2	5%
Income (Million $)						
1Q	-15.11	NM	-0.39	NM	-10.20	NM
2Q	-15.15	NM	-12.49	NM	1.03	NM
3Q	—	—	5.88	-42%	10.08	NM
4Q	—	—	-7.17	NM	0.06	NM
Yr.	—	—	-14.17	NM	0.97	NM
Earnings Per Share ($)						
1Q	-0.13	—	Nil	—	-0.10	NM
2Q	-0.13	NM	-0.11	NM	0.01	NM
3Q	—	—	0.05	-44%	0.09	NM
4Q	—	—	-0.07	—	Nil	—
Yr.	—	—	-0.13	NM	0.01	NM

Next earnings report expected: early November

Cineplex Odeon

Business Summary - 11-OCT-95

Cineplex Odeon is engaged primarily in the operation of motion picture theatres in the U.S. and Canada. As of August, 1995, the company was one of the largest film exhibitors in North America, with 1,482 screens in 322 locations in 6 Canadian provinces and 14 U.S. states. In 1989, Cineplex began a restructuring program to concentrate on its core theatre exhibition business in major markets, selling its live-theatre division in 1989 and its interest in Universal City Cinemas in 1990. In 1991, the company discontinued its participation in New Visions, a film production and distribution joint venture. Contributions to revenues in recent years were as follows:

	1994	1993	1992
Admissions	71%	71%	72%
Concessions	25%	25%	24%
Other	4%	4%	4%

Canada accounted for 30% of revenues in 1994 and 1993, with the U.S. accounting for the balance in both years.

Most of CPX's theatres are multiscreen units that display first-run movies and offer concession stands. During 1994, CPX opened 2 new theaters with 15 screens, acquired 5 theaters with 17 screens and refurbished 3 existing theaters, adding 2 new screens. Also during 1994, the company sold or closed 12 theaters with a total of 33 screens.

CPX obtains licenses to exhibit films by negotiating with, or submitting bids to, the film's distributors. Licenses typically specify rental fees based upon the higher of a gross receipts formula or a theatre admissions revenue-sharing formula. CPX predominantly obtains licenses for "first-run" films.

Cineplex Odeon Films distributes films in Canada for exhibitions in theatres, for broadcast by network, syndicated and pay television and for sale on videocassettes. In 1994, CPX's distribution activity in Canada included theatrical distribution services for Columbia, Tri-Star, Savoy and Gramercy. The company has substantially discontinued its direct film releasing activities in the U.S. and, in 1990, had wound down its international distribution activities.

Important Developments

Jun. '95—The company sold 28 theaters (with a total of 145 screens) in Georgia and Florida to Carmike Cinemas Inc., generating proceeds of $22 million. CPX intends to use $13.9 million of the funds to reduce debt, and the balance to fund a new building program.

Capitalization

Long Term Debt: US$386,337,000 (6/95), incl. $11.2 million of capital lease obligations.

Per Share Data ($)

(Year Ended Dec. 31)

	1994	1993	1992	1991	1990	1989
Tangible Bk. Val.	1.38	1.48	1.57	2.06	2.63	6.30
Cash Flow	0.24	0.36	-0.03	-0.46	-2.43	-0.89
Earnings	-0.13	0.01	-0.48	-1.14	-3.27	-1.65
Dividends	Nil	Nil	Nil	Nil	Nil	Nil
Payout Ratio	Nil	Nil	Nil	Nil	Nil	Nil
Prices - High	$4\frac{1}{8}$	$3\frac{3}{4}$	$3\frac{3}{4}$	$6\frac{1}{8}$	$7\frac{1}{2}$	$16\frac{3}{8}$
- Low	$2\frac{1}{4}$	$1\frac{1}{8}$	$1\frac{1}{2}$	$1\frac{3}{4}$	$1\frac{7}{8}$	$6\frac{3}{8}$
P/E Ratio - High	NM	NM	NM	NM	NM	NM
- Low	NM	NM	NM	NM	NM	NM

Income Statement Analysis (Million $)

	1994	%Chg	1993	%Chg	1992	%Chg	1991
Revs.	539	-1%	546	5%	519	-4%	538
Oper. Inc.	65.0	-3%	67.0	97%	34.0	10%	31.0
Depr.	40.7	9%	37.4	-3%	38.5	NM	38.2
Int. Exp.	33.4	19%	28.1	-20%	35.1	-34%	53.5
Pretax Inc.	-12.0	NM	3.0	NM	-40.0	NM	-65.0
Eff. Tax Rate	NM	—	63%	—	NM	—	NM
Net Inc.	-14.0	NM	1.0	NM	-41.0	NM	-64.0

Balance Sheet & Other Fin. Data (Million $)

	1994	1993	1992	1991	1990	1989
Cash	1.2	1.3	1.4	1.1	Nil	37.5
Curr. Assets	21.0	29.0	31.0	40.0	64.0	137
Total Assets	686	697	742	805	856	1,107
Curr. Liab.	91.0	140	120	169	150	172
LT Debt	387	343	420	420	535	592
Common Eqty.	196	200	199	214	168	301
Total Cap.	583	544	619	634	703	929
Cap. Exp.	33.0	11.0	26.0	20.0	68.0	127
Cash Flow	27.0	38.0	-3.0	-26.0	-115	-43.0

Ratio Analysis

	1994	1993	1992	1991	1990	1989
Curr. Ratio	0.2	0.2	0.3	0.2	0.4	0.8
% LT Debt of Cap.	66.3	63.2	67.9	66.3	76.1	63.7
% Net Inc.of Revs.	NM	0.2	NM	NM	NM	NM
% Ret. on Assets	NM	0.1	NM	NM	NM	NM
% Ret. on Equity	NM	0.5	NM	NM	NM	NM

Dividend Data —CPX has not paid any dividends on its common or subordinated restricted voting shares.

Data as orig. reptd.; bef. results of disc. opers. and/or spec. items. Per share data adj. for stk. divs. as of ex-div. date. E-Estimated. NA-Not Available. NM-Not Meaningful. NR-Not Ranked.

Office—1303 Yonge St., Toronto, Ontario M4T 2Y9 Canada. **Tel**—(416) 323-6600. **Chrmn**—E. L. Kolber. **Pres & CEO**—A. Karp. **EVP & CFO**—E. Jacob. **EVP & Secy**—M. Herman. **Investor Contact**—Howard Lichtman. **Dirs**—R. P. Bratty, J. H. Daniels, B. Hack, E. Jacob, A. Karp, E. L. Kolber, A. J. Parsons, C. S. Paul, E. W. Pertsch, T. P. Pollock, R. Rabinovitch, J. D. Raymond. **Transfer Agents & Registrars**—Montreal Trust Co. of Canada, Toronto; Chemical Bank, NYC. **Incorporated** in Ontario in 1977. **Empl**-1,814. **S&P Analyst:** M.T.C.

STANDARD & POOR'S

STOCK REPORTS

Circon Corp.

NASDAQ Symbol **CCON**

In S&P SmallCap 600

11-SEP-95

Industry: Medical equipment/ supply

Summary: This company manufactures and markets medical endoscope and electrosurgery systems for diagnosis and minimally invasive surgery.

Quantitative Evaluations

Outlook (1 Lowest—5 Highest) • **NA**

Fair Value • **NA**

Risk • **High**

Earn./Div. Rank • **B-**

Technical Eval. • **Bearish** since 8/95

Rel. Strength Rank (1 Lowest—99 Highest) • **82**

Insider Activity • **Neutral**

Recent Price • 21

52 Wk Range • 24¼-10¾

Yield • Nil

12-Mo. P/E • 34.4

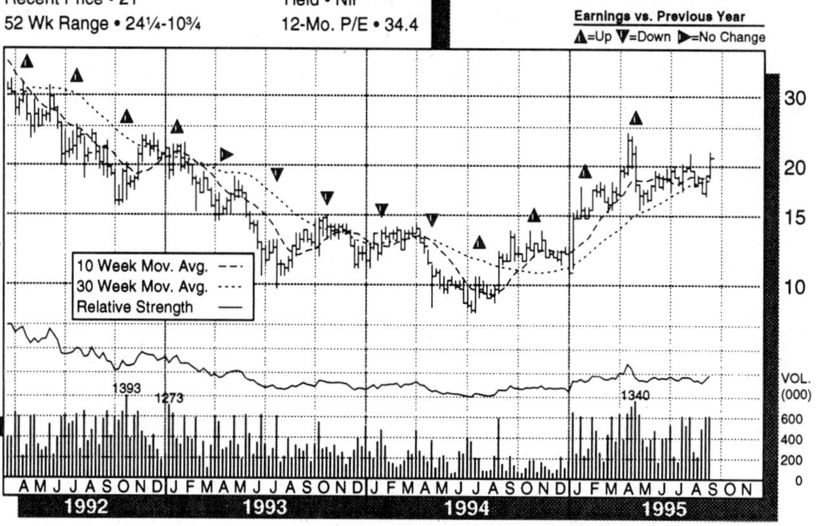

Business Profile - 07-SEP-95

With the August 1995 aquisition of Cabot Medical, Circon became the largest producer of minimally invasive surgery products specializing in urology and gynecology. Significant synergies should be realized, as the companies' products are highly complementary, and are often used by the same doctors. Also, demand for medical products should increase due to improving trends in hospital purchases as well as cost and patient benefits associated with minimally invasive surgery.

Operational Review - 07-SEP-95

Revenue growth in recent periods reflects higher sales from both domestic and international medical sectors due to improvements in the health care equipment market, as well as the introduction of new products. Margins widened due to manufacturing efficiencies from higher production volumes, and net income continued its upward trend.

Stock Performance - 08-SEP-95

In the past 30 trading days, CCON's shares have increased 6%, compared to a 2% rise in the S&P 500. Average trading volume for the past five days was 188,675 shares, compared with the 40-day moving average of 111,231 shares.

Key Stock Statistics

Dividend Rate/Share	Nil	Shareholders	1,000
Shs. outstg. (M)	12.3	Market cap. (B)	$0.258
Avg. daily vol. (M)	0.108	Inst. holdings	26%
Tang. Bk. Value/Share	9.61	Insider holdings	NA
Beta	2.47		

Value of $10,000 invested 5 years ago: $ 40,000

Fiscal Year Ending Dec. 31

	1995	% Change	1994	% Change	1993	% Change
Revenues (Million $)						
1Q	22.47	8%	20.83	-4%	21.70	6%
2Q	25.94	18%	21.93	5%	20.93	-2%
3Q	—	—	22.47	NM	22.45	16%
4Q	—	—	23.71	6%	22.30	NM
Yr.	—	—	88.94	2%	87.30	5%
Income (Million $)						
1Q	1.11	41%	0.79	-47%	1.48	1%
2Q	1.83	106%	0.89	NM	0.15	-90%
3Q	—	—	1.12	13%	0.99	-28%
4Q	—	—	1.01	NM	-0.60	NM
Yr.	—	—	3.81	86%	2.05	-68%
Earnings Per Share ($)						
1Q	0.22	120%	0.10	-44%	0.18	NM
2Q	—	—	0.11	NM	0.02	-89%
3Q	—	—	0.14	17%	0.12	-29%
4Q	—	—	0.12	NM	-0.07	NM
Yr.	—	—	0.47	88%	0.25	-68%

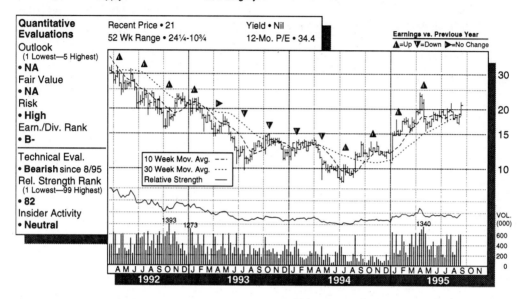

Next earnings report expected: late October

Circon Corp.

Business Summary - 11-SEP-95

Circon Corporation manufactures and markets endoscope and electrosurgery systems for diagnosis and minimally invasive surgery. The company also designs, assembles and markets miniature color video systems used in endoscope systems.

Minimally invasive surgery refers to surgical procedures that can be accomplished without a major incision or other traumatization of the patient. One of the most important minimally invasive surgical techniques is endoscopy, a procedure that utilizes optical instruments inserted into the body either through a natural orifice or through a small incision. In addition to decreasing patient trauma and frequently avoiding general anesthesia, endoscopy can reduce or eliminate postoperative hospitalization. Resulting cost savings and patient benefits have caused government reimbursement programs, as well as private insurance and prepaid health plans, to encourage the use of endoscopic procedures over traditional open surgery.

Circon offers the complete optical-video chain, which combines the use of a medical endoscope system with a medical video system and consists of an endoscope, a miniature color video camera, adapter optics, a high-intensity light source, a fiber-optic light cable, one or more video monitors and a videocassette recorder. The system allows the surgeon to perform procedures viewing a magnified image of the subject organ or tissue on a video monitor, rather than directly through the endoscope eyepiece, thereby reducing surgeon fatigue by alleviating eye and back strain caused by prolonged viewing through the eyepiece of the endoscope and increasing operating room coordination, staff efficiency and motivation by allowing the entire operating room to view the medical procedure.

The company's endoscope and video systems are used in hospitals, ambulatory surgical centers and physicians' offices for a growing number of medical specialties, including urology, arthroscopy, laparoscopy, gynecology and thoracoscopy.

Circon also offers customers all the separate components constituting the optical-video chain, and it manufactures and distributes borescopes, video systems, specialty glass and other products for nonmedical applications. The company's products are sold through direct sales forces in the U.S. and Germany and through dealers in 40 other countries. International sales accounted for 16% of the total in 1994.

Important Developments

Aug. '95—CCON acquired Cabot Medical Corp., a producer of gynecology sterilization and gynecology-laparoscopy suction/irrigation devices, for approximately 4.3 million Circon common shares.

Capitalization

Long Term Debt: None (6/95).
Options: To buy 920,033 shs. at $3 to $19.125 ea. (12/94).

Per Share Data ($) (Year Ended Dec. 31)

	1994	1993	1992	1991	1990	1989
Tangible Bk. Val.	9.58	9.11	8.94	8.05	2.90	2.55
Cash Flow	0.73	0.52	1.00	0.71	0.34	0.25
Earnings	0.47	0.25	0.77	0.45	0.06	-0.02
Dividends	Nil	Nil	Nil	Nil	Nil	Nil
Payout Ratio	Nil	Nil	Nil	Nil	Nil	Nil
Prices - High	14¼	22¾	50	33½	11¼	6⅝
- Low	8½	9¾	15¾	10½	4⅜	3½
P/E Ratio - High	30	91	65	74	NM	NM
- Low	18	39	20	23	NM	NM

Income Statement Analysis (Million $)

	1994	%Chg	1993	%Chg	1992	%Chg	1991
Revs.	88.9	2%	87.3	5%	83.5	21%	68.9
Oper. Inc.	7.7	7%	7.2	-31%	10.4	41%	7.4
Depr.	2.1	-2%	2.2	15%	1.9	11%	1.7
Int. Exp.	0.3	NM	0.0	—	Nil	—	0.8
Pretax Inc.	5.9	95%	3.0	-68%	9.3	92%	4.9
Eff. Tax Rate	35%	—	32%	—	32%	—	38%
Net Inc.	3.8	86%	2.0	-68%	6.3	111%	3.0

Balance Sheet & Other Fin. Data (Million $)

	1994	1993	1992	1991	1990	1989
Cash	20.8	22.3	24.0	25.5	0.3	0.1
Curr. Assets	59.4	58.4	61.4	56.2	24.8	22.9
Total Assets	95.0	87.5	83.5	75.0	41.9	39.8
Curr. Liab.	10.8	8.5	8.7	9.1	7.8	10.8
LT Debt	0.1	Nil	0.3	Nil	14.8	11.7
Common Eqty.	78.6	74.6	72.2	65.2	19.3	17.2
Total Cap.	84.0	78.4	74.7	66.0	34.1	28.9
Cap. Exp.	8.3	8.3	5.1	3.1	1.9	1.1
Cash Flow	5.9	4.2	8.2	4.7	1.9	1.4

Ratio Analysis

	1994	1993	1992	1991	1990	1989
Curr. Ratio	5.5	6.8	7.1	6.2	3.2	2.1
% LT Debt of Cap.	0.2	Nil	0.4	Nil	43.5	40.6
% Net Inc.of Revs.	4.3	2.4	7.6	4.4	0.6	NM
% Ret. on Assets	4.1	2.4	8.0	4.5	0.8	NM
% Ret. on Equity	4.9	2.8	9.2	6.5	1.8	NM

Dividend Data —No cash has been paid, and Circon's intention is to continue to retain all of its earnings for use in the business.

Data as orig. reptd.; bef. results of disc. opers. and/or spec. items. Per share data adj. for stk. divs. as of ex-div. date. E-Estimated. NA-Not Available. NM-Not Meaningful. NR-Not Ranked.

Office—460 Ward Dr., Santa Barbara, CA 93111. **Tel**—(805) 685-5100. **Chrmn, Pres & CEO**—R. A. Auhll. **EVP, CFO & Investor Contact**—R. Bruce Thompson. **VP & Secy**—D. J. Meaney Jr. **Dirs**—R. A. Auhll, J. F. Blokker, H. R. Frank, P. W. Hartloff Jr., R. R. Schulte. **Transfer Agent & Registrar**—First Interstate Bank, Los Angeles. **Incorporated** in California in 1977; reincorporated in Delaware in 1987. **Empl**-762. **S&P Analyst:** Philip J. Birbara

CLARCOR Inc.

NYSE Symbol **CLC**
In S&P SmallCap 600

31-AUG-95 **Industry:** Machinery

Summary: CLC produces various kinds of filters and also manufactures containers and packaging used primarily for consumer products.

Quantitative Evaluations

Recent Price • 22⅞ | Yield • 2.7%
52 Wk Range • 23¾-18⅛ | 12-Mo. P/E • 15.5

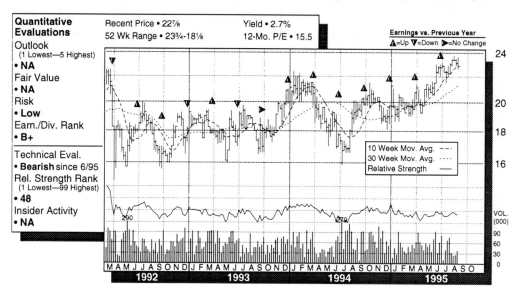

Outlook
(1 Lowest—5 Highest)
• **NA**

Fair Value
• **NA**

Risk
• **Low**

Earn./Div. Rank
• **B+**

Technical Eval.
• **Bearish** since 6/95

Rel. Strength Rank
(1 Lowest—99 Highest)
• **48**

Insider Activity
• **NA**

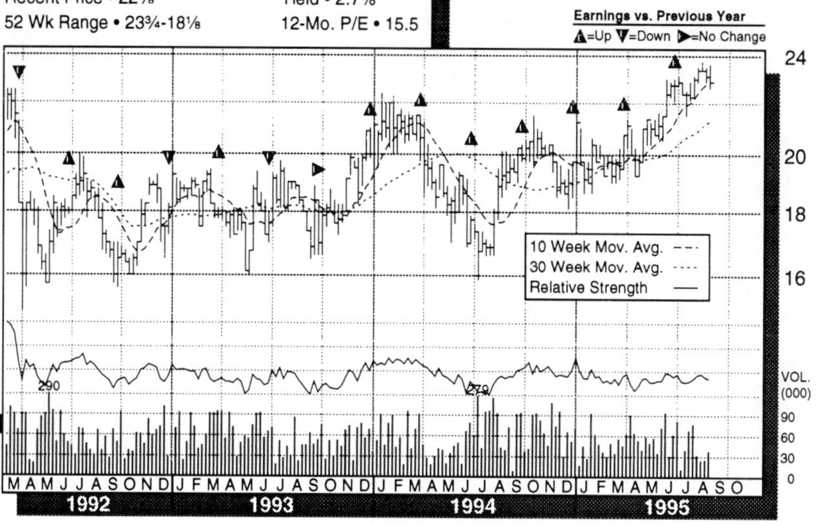

Business Profile - 30-AUG-95

After bottoming in 1992, earnings for this manufacturer of filters and containers have been in an uptrend. CLC's strategy includes growth through acquisitions and internal expansion, with emphasis placed on entry into new markets and new product development. Gross margins should continue to improve as acquisitions and start-ups are integrated into existing operations. Operating margins are likely to benefit from further implementation of productivity improvements.

Operational Review - 30-AUG-95

For the six months ended June 3, 1995, profits were up 13% for filtration products (on strong sales gains for heavy duty and railroad locomotive products) and 58% for consumer products. Overall operating profit increased 17%. Although other expenses were much lower, a higher tax rate held the gain in net income before special items to 17%. Assuming continuing strength in both segments, overall operating profits could increase by 10% to 15% for fiscal 1995. CLC has a strong balance sheet.

Stock Performance - 25-AUG-95

In the past 30 trading days, CLC's shares have increased 2%, compared to a 0.04% rise in the S&P 500. Average trading volume for the past five days was 7,460 shares, compared with the 40-day moving average of 7,892 shares.

Key Stock Statistics

Dividend Rate/Share	0.63	Shareholders	1,900
Shs. outstg. (M)	14.8	Market cap. (B)	$0.340
Avg. daily vol. (M)	0.007	Inst. holdings	58%
Tang. Bk. Value/Share	7.21	Insider holdings	NA
Beta	0.59		

Value of $10,000 invested 5 years ago: $ 18,958

Fiscal Year Ending Nov. 30

	1995	% Change	1994	% Change	1993	% Change
Revenues (Million $)						
1Q	62.14	11%	55.89	33%	41.91	3%
2Q	70.48	8%	65.13	31%	49.73	10%
3Q	—	—	67.72	5%	64.63	27%
4Q	—	—	81.38	18%	69.04	33%
Yr.	—	—	270.1	20%	225.3	19%
Income (Million $)						
1Q	3.97	16%	3.42	11%	3.09	5%
2Q	4.91	17%	4.18	50%	2.78	-37%
3Q	—	—	5.88	16%	5.06	NM
4Q	—	—	7.16	17%	6.14	48%
Yr.	—	—	20.63	20%	17.25	4%
Earnings Per Share ($)						
1Q	0.27	17%	0.23	10%	0.21	5%
2Q	0.33	18%	0.28	47%	0.19	-34%
3Q	—	—	0.40	18%	0.34	NM
4Q	—	—	0.48	14%	0.42	56%
Yr.	—	—	1.39	20%	1.16	5%

Next earnings report expected: mid October

CLARCOR Inc.

Business Summary - 30-AUG-95

CLARCOR manufactures filtration and consumer products for domestic and international markets. Business segment contributions from continuing operations in fiscal 1994 were:

	Sales	Profits
Filtration products	74%	82%
Consumer products	26%	18%

The Filtration Products Group consists primarily of the following subsidiaries: Baldwin Filters, Airguard Industries, Clark Filter, MicroPure Filtration, Baldwin Filters N.V., and Baldwin Filters Ltd. In addition, CLC owns 5% of G.U.D., 50% of Baldwin Filters (Aust.) Pty. Ltd, and 90% of FIBAMEX.

CLC markets a line of over 18,200 oil, air, fuel, coolant, and hydraulic fluid filters which are used in a wide variety of applications, including engines, equipment, environmentally controlled areas and processes whose effectiveness, reliability, and durability are essential.

Filters are sold throughout the U.S. and Canada and world-wide, primarily in the replacement market for truck, auto, marine, construction, industrial and farm equipment and food and beverage processing. In addition, some filters are sold to the original equipment market.

Consumer products operations are conducted through the J. L. Clark subsidiary which produces more than 1,500 different types and sizes of containers and metal packaging specialties.

Flat sheet decorating is produced by use of state-of-the-art lithography equipment. Metal, plastic, and paper containers and plastic closures manufactured by the company are used in marketing a wide variety of dry and paste form products, such as food specialties (tea, spices, dry bakery prducts, potato chips, pretzels, and candy); cosmetics and toiletries; drugs and pharmaceuticals; chemical specialties (hand cleaners, soaps and special cleaning compounds); and tobacco products. Metal packaging specialties include shells for dry batteries, dispensers for razor blades, and spools for insulated and fine wire.

Important Developments

Jun. '95—CLC said it was exploring a significant number of potential acquisitions and joint venture opportunities--primarily in filtration--with the potential to expand product lines, leverage distribution capabilities, and improve the operating performance of acquired companies.

Jun. '95—CLC said that it plans to expand plastic manufacturing capacity to meet increased demand for its combiTop closure. The company expected to significantly increase its plastic sales in fiscal 1995 and 1996 as production is gradually stepped up to meet demand.

Capitalization

Long Term Debt: $13,300,000 (6/95).

Per Share Data ($) (Year Ended Nov. 30)

	1994	1993	1992	1991	1990	1989
Tangible Bk. Val.	6.93	6.00	5.79	5.03	4.13	3.33
Cash Flow	1.88	1.59	1.46	1.74	1.90	0.89
Earnings	1.39	1.16	1.10	1.24	1.37	0.47
Dividends	0.62	0.61	0.60	0.55	0.52	0.48
Payout Ratio	45%	52%	55%	44%	38%	91%
Prices - High	$22\frac{3}{8}$	$21\frac{1}{8}$	$22\frac{1}{2}$	$22\frac{5}{8}$	$17\frac{7}{8}$	19
- Low	$15\frac{7}{8}$	16	15	14	$11\frac{7}{8}$	$11\frac{3}{4}$
P/E Ratio - High	16	18	20	18	13	40
- Low	11	14	14	11	9	25

Income Statement Analysis (Million $)

	1994	%Chg	1993	%Chg	1992	%Chg	1991
Revs.	270	20%	225	25%	180	NM	180
Oper. Inc.	39.7	12%	35.4	11%	32.0	-16%	38.2
Depr.	7.3	16%	6.3	17%	5.4	-27%	7.3
Int. Exp.	2.8	-21%	3.5	-7%	3.8	3%	3.7
Pretax Inc.	32.6	20%	27.1	7%	25.3	-11%	28.5
Eff. Tax Rate	37%	—	36%	—	35%	—	35%
Net Inc.	20.6	19%	17.3	5%	16.5	-11%	18.5

Balance Sheet & Other Fin. Data (Million $)

	1994	1993	1992	1991	1990	1989
Cash	19.6	13.8	15.1	9.6	14.8	4.8
Curr. Assets	99	86.2	93.6	75.2	72.6	58.0
Total Assets	188	170	161	158	144	131
Curr. Liab.	39.5	23.3	25.3	20.6	20.8	21.4
LT Debt	17.0	24.6	29.3	35.8	35.8	32.6
Common Eqty.	117	105	100	96.0	83.0	73.0
Total Cap.	140	133	132	137	123	110
Cap. Exp.	11.4	17.9	6.6	8.1	8.6	8.3
Cash Flow	27.9	23.5	21.9	25.8	28.2	15.1

Ratio Analysis

	1994	1993	1992	1991	1990	1989
Curr. Ratio	2.5	2.6	3.7	3.7	3.5	2.7
% LT Debt of Cap.	12.1	18.4	22.1	26.1	29.0	29.8
% Net Inc.of Revs.	7.6	7.7	8.8	10.3	9.5	3.9
% Ret. on Assets	11.5	10.5	10.3	12.2	14.9	6.3
% Ret. on Equity	18.6	17.0	16.9	20.7	26.4	8.9

Dividend Data —Cash has been paid each year since 1921. A dividend reinvestment plan is available. A "poison pill" stock purchase right was adopted in 1986.

Amt. of Div. $	Date Decl.	Ex-Div. Date	Stock of Record	Payment Date
0.158	Aug. 03	Oct. 07	Oct. 14	Oct. 28 '94
0.158	Dec. 13	Jan. 09	Jan. 13	Jan. 27 '95
0.158	Mar. 31	Apr. 07	Apr. 14	Apr. 28 '95
0.158	Jun. 15	Jul. 12	Jul. 14	Jul. 28 '95

Data as orig. reptd.; bef. results of disc. opers. and/or spec. items. Per share data adj. for stk. divs. as of ex-div. date. E-Estimated. NA-Not Available. NM-Not Meaningful. NR-Not Ranked.

Office—2323 Sixth St., P.O. Box 7007, Rockford, IL 61125. **Tel**—(815) 962-8867. **Chrmn, CEO & Investor Contact**—Lawrence E. Gloyd. **Pres**—N. E. Johnson. **VP-CFO**—B. A. Klein. **VP-Treas**—W. F. Knese. **VP-Secy**—M. C. Arne. **Dirs**—J. M. Adam, M. R. Brown, C. J. Dargene, F. A. Fiorenza, L. E. Gloyd, D. J. Godfrey Jr., S. K. Smith Jr., R. A. Snell, D. A. Wolf. **Transfer Agent & Registrar**—First Chicago Trust Co. of New York, Jersey City, NJ. **Incorporated** in Delaware in 1969. **Empl**-2,211. **S&P Analyst:** N.J. DeVita

STANDARD & POOR'S

STOCK REPORTS

Coast Savings Financial

NYSE Symbol **CSA**

In S&P SmallCap 600

01-SEP-95

Industry: Banking

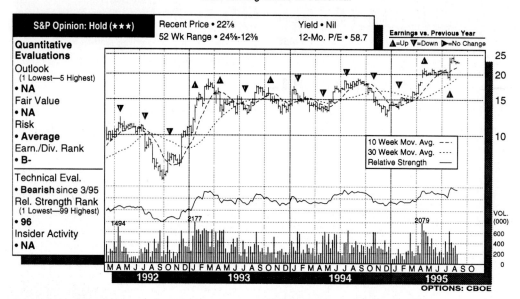

Summary: Coast Savings Financial is the holding company for Coast Federal Bank, one of the largest thrifts in the U.S., with some 92 retail banking offices in California.

S&P Opinion: Hold (★★★)

Recent Price • 22⅞

52 Wk Range • 24⅝-12⅜

Yield • Nil

12-Mo. P/E • 58.7

Quantitative Evaluations

Outlook
(1 Lowest—5 Highest)
• **NA**

Fair Value
• **NA**

Risk
• **Average**

Earn./Div. Rank
• **B-**

Technical Eval.
• **Bearish** since 3/95

Rel. Strength Rank
(1 Lowest—99 Highest)
• **96**

Insider Activity
• **NA**

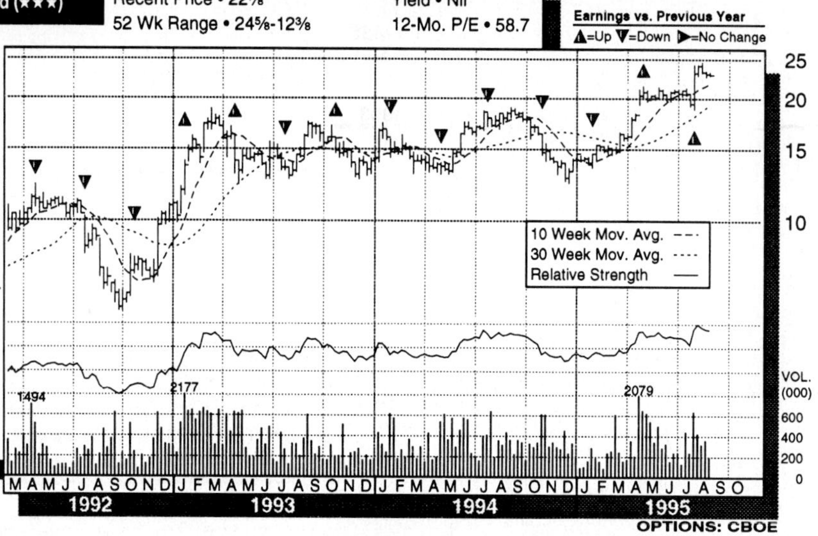

OPTIONS: CBOE

Overview - 01-SEP-95

Profits are expected to post a solid advance in 1996. The main positive is an anticipated widening of the interest rate spread. Based on a projected decline in market interest rates, Coast's deposit costs are expected to reprice downwards. At the same time funding costs are moving down, loan yields should remain relatively inflated because of administrative lags inherent in the process of recalculating the monthly interest rate. Loan volume, however, will remain sluggish as consumers will probably prefer fixed rate mortgages offered by competitors. Asset quality is quite good, and reserves are ample; thus, a lower loan loss provision is likely. Good cost control is anticipated. Gains on loan sales are possible.

Valuation - 01-SEP-95

Coast shares have rallied with the recent drop in interest rates and expectations for consolidation among California-based S&Ls. The shares are trading at about a 15% premium to tangible book value per share, modestly higher than the industry average. Over the years, Coast has consistently lost money or produced subpar returns on equity. Some evidence of a turnaround is present: a lower level of problem assets, a reduced cost structure, and balance sheet growth. The chairman is near retirement age and owns a large block of stock, suggesting that CSA is a long-term takeover target.

Key Stock Statistics

S&P EPS Est. 1995	1.15	Tang. Bk. Value/Share	20.64
P/E on S&P Est. 1995	19.9	Beta	2.13
S&P EPS Est. 1996	1.65	Shareholders	4,400
Dividend Rate/Share	Nil	Market cap. (B)	$0.516
Shs. outstg. (M)	18.5	Inst. holdings	67%
Avg. daily vol. (M)	0.142	Insider holdings	NA

Value of $10,000 invested 5 years ago: $ 21,927

Fiscal Year Ending Dec. 31

	1995	% Change	1994	% Change	1993	% Change
Revenues (Million $)						
1Q	156.6	19%	132.1	-6%	141.0	-18%
2Q	167.2	27%	132.1	NM	131.8	-18%
3Q	—	—	139.2	-2%	142.0	-5%
4Q	—	—	134.1	-17%	161.1	8%
Yr.	—	—	537.5	-7%	575.9	-9%
Income (Million $)						
1Q	3.48	NM	-6.72	NM	4.14	41%
2Q	5.63	199%	1.88	-63%	5.13	-23%
3Q	—	—	2.29	-47%	4.30	23%
4Q	—	—	-3.99	NM	3.67	-85%
Yr.	—	—	-6.54	NM	17.24	-54%
Earnings Per Share ($)						
1Q	0.18	NM	-0.36	NM	0.25	39%
2Q	0.30	NM	0.10	-63%	0.27	-34%
3Q	E0.32	167%	0.12	-48%	0.23	10%
4Q	E0.35	NM	-0.22	NM	0.20	-86%
Yr.	E1.15	NM	-0.35	NM	0.94	-59%

Next earnings report expected: late October

Coast Savings Financial

Business Summary - 30-AUG-95

Coast Savings Financial owns Coast Federal Bank, a thrift operating 92 retail banking offices in California. CSA also owns an insurance agency. Following a period of diversification in the early-and mid-1980s, Coast refocused on traditional thrift activities. Gross loans receivable totaled $5.8 billion at 1994 year end, up from $5.0 billion at year-end 1993 (excluding MBS of $1.7 billion and $2.0 billion as of the respective dates), and were divided:

	1994	1993
Real Estate:		
One to four units	57%	49%
More than four units	24%	28%
Commercial	15%	19%
Second mortgage	1%	1%
Other	3%	3%

At year-end 1994, Coast had about 95% of its portfolio in adjustable rate loans. Real estate loan originations in 1994 totaled $1.9 billion, up from $1.2 billion in 1993. The one-year gap (difference between assets and liabilities repricing/maturing within one year as a percentage of assets) was +6% at 1994 year-end. Problem assets (excluding assets covered from loss by regulators) were $141.9 million at year-end 1994 (1.73% of assets), down from $220 million at 1993 year end (2.72% of assets). Reserves were $85 million (1.02% of assets) at December 31, 1994, down from $120 million (1.48%) a year earlier. Net charge-offs in 1994 amounted to $100 million (1.2% of assets), compared with $81 million (1.0%) in 1993.

Deposits of $5.9 billion at 1994 year end were divided: 8% checking, 15% money market saving, 23% seven-month time deposits, 18% one-year and 14-month time deposits, 12% 18-month and two-year time deposits, and 24% other. The yield on interest-earning assets in 1994 was about 6.53% (6.83% in 1993), and the cost of funds was 4.06% (4.15%), for a net spread of 2.48% (2.67%).

Important Developments

Jul. '95—Coast Savings said that loan originations for the second quarter of 1995 totaled $261 million, essentially all of which were single-family adjustable rate mortgages tied to the Eleventh District cost of funds index.

Capitalization

FHLB Advances: $634,450,000 (6/95).
Other Borrowings: $1,314,720,000.

Per Share Data ($) (Year Ended Dec. 31)

	1994	1993	1992	1991	1990	1989
Tangible Bk. Val.	19.71	20.62	19.38	16.43	13.58	15.60
Earnings	-0.35	0.94	2.27	2.68	-4.14	-4.87
Dividends	Nil	Nil	Nil	Nil	0.30	0.40
Payout Ratio	Nil	Nil	Nil	Nil	NM	NM
Prices - High	19	18⅞	12¼	9⅝	12⅛	20⅜
- Low	12⅜	9⅞	6	2¼	1⅝	9⅜
P/E Ratio - High	NM	20	5	4	NM	NM
- Low	NM	11	3	1	NM	NM

Income Statement Analysis (Million $)

	1994	%Chg	1993	%Chg	1992	%Chg	1991
Net Int. Inc.	188	-7%	202	NM	202	-2%	207
Loan Loss Prov.	75.0	23%	61.0	33%	46.0	-44%	82.0
Non Int. Inc.	42.9	-29%	60.3	NM	11.9	-87%	94.4
Non Int. Exp.	172	-13%	197	27%	155	-10%	172
Pretax Inc.	-16.0	NM	4.0	-80%	20.0	-57%	47.0
Eff. Tax Rate	NM	—	NM	—	NM	—	11%
Net Inc.	-6.5	NM	17.2	-54%	37.1	-11%	41.7
% Net Int. Marg.	2.19%	—	2.49%	—	2.48%	—	3.15%

Balance Sheet & Other Fin. Data (Million $)

	1994	1993	1992	1991	1990	1989
Total Assets	8,197	8,095	8,352	8,596	10,217	11,244
Loans	7,527	6,980	7,286	7,469	9,102	9,981
Deposits	5,880	5,909	6,135	7,100	8,708	8,903
Capitalization:						
Debt	1,820	1,657	1,704	1,064	1,128	1,876
Equity	375	394	326	279	224	226
Total	2,195	2,051	2,030	1,343	1,352	2,102

Ratio Analysis

	1994	1993	1992	1991	1990	1989
% Ret. on Assets	NM	0.2	0.4	0.4	NM	NM
% Ret. on Equity	NM	4.8	12.3	16.6	NM	NM
% Loan Loss Resv.	1.1	1.7	1.5	1.8	1.0	0.5
% Risk Based Capital	10.5	11.5	10.5	8.2	6.6	7.1
Price Times Book Value:						
High	1.0	0.9	0.6	0.6	0.9	1.3
Low	0.6	0.5	0.3	0.1	0.1	0.6

Dividend Data —Dividends were omitted in 1990 after having been paid since 1987. A "poison pill" stock purchase rights plan was adopted in 1989.

Data as orig. reptd.; bef. results of disc opers. and/or spec. items. Per share data adj. for stk. divs. as of ex-div. date. E-Estimated. NA-Not Available. NM-Not Meaningful. NR-Not Ranked.

Office—1000 Wilshire Blvd., Los Angeles, CA 90017. **Tel**—(213) 362-2000. **Chrmn & CEO**—R. Martin. **Pres & COO**—R. L. Hunt II. **Secy**—P. Finch. **Investor Contact**—Mark Neal (213-362-2134). **Dirs**—L. S. Angvire, G. D. Barrone, R. M. Blakely, W. R. Holly Jr., R. L. Hunt II, J. P. Libby, R. Martin, J. P. Miscoll, K. W. Renken, H. B. Starkey Jr. **Transfer Agent & Registrar**—Chemical Bank, SF. **Organized** in California in 1935; incorporated in Delaware in 1989. **Empl**-1,731. **S&P Analyst:** Paul L. Huberman, CFA

Coca-Cola Bottling Co. Consol.

STOCK REPORTS

NASDAQ Symbol **COKE**
In S&P SmallCap 600

24-SEP-95

Industry: Beverages

Summary: This company is engaged in bottling, canning and marketing carbonated soft drinks, primarily products of the Coca-Cola Co., in the Southeast.

Quantitative Evaluations

Outlook (1 Lowest—5 Highest) • **2+**
Fair Value • **30¾**
Risk • **Low**
Earn./Div. Rank • **B-**

Technical Eval. • **Bullish** since 1/95
Rel. Strength Rank (1 Lowest—99 Highest) • **62**
Insider Activity • **NA**

Recent Price • 35
52 Wk Range • 35⅞-24
Yield • 2.9%
12-Mo. P/E • 20.3

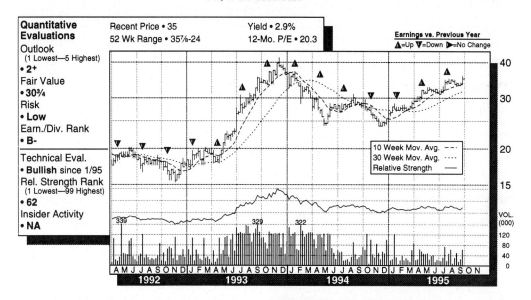

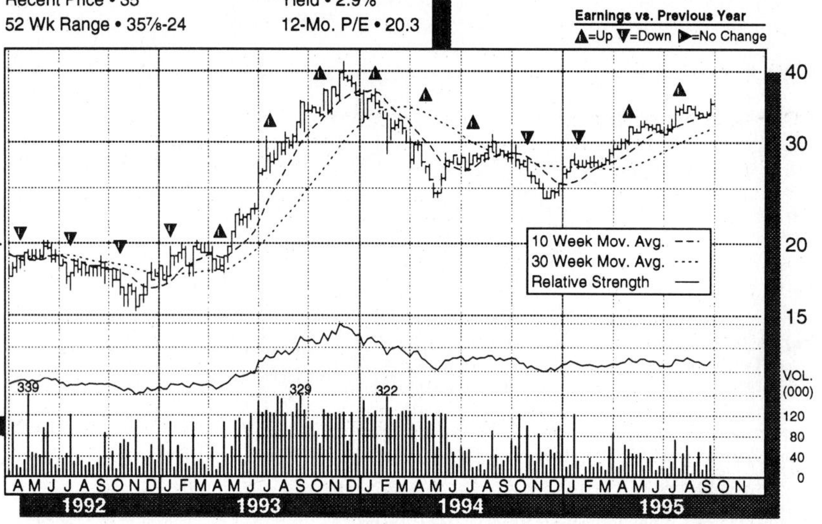

Business Profile - 15-SEP-95

In comparing the first half of 1995 to the first half of 1990, net sales, operating cash flow and operating income grew at average annual rates of 12%, 12% and 17%, respectively. Gross margins in the first half of 1995 widened as the company passed on major increases in packaging costs to consumers. Future results should benefit from increased per capita consumption of the company's products. Analysts expect the company to earn $1.79 per share in 1995.

Operational Review - 22-SEP-95

Revenues in the first half of 1995 rose 4%, year to year, primarily reflecting higher average selling prices for franchise sales. Margins benefited as higher selling prices outweighed increased packaging costs. Income from operations was up 17%, and after taxes at 39.7%, versus 43.0%, income climbed 22%. Results in the 1994 period exclude a $0.24 a share charge from an accounting change.

Stock Performance - 22-SEP-95

In the past 30 trading days, COKE's shares have increased 0.72%, compared to a 5% rise in the S&P 500. Average trading volume for the past five days was 12,340 shares, compared with the 40-day moving average of 7,433 shares.

Key Stock Statistics

Dividend Rate/Share	1.00	Shareholders	1,200
Shs. outstg. (M)	9.3	Market cap. (B)	$0.325
Avg. daily vol. (M)	0.007	Inst. holdings	31%
Tang. Bk. Value/Share	NM	Insider holdings	NA
Beta	1.25		

Value of $10,000 invested 5 years ago: $ 18,701

Fiscal Year Ending Dec. 31

	1995	% Change	1994	% Change	1993	% Change
Revenues (Million $)						
1Q	171.0	4%	163.8	6%	154.3	4%
2Q	207.9	4%	200.7	3%	194.5	12%
3Q	—	—	188.4	3%	182.1	7%
4Q	—	—	171.0	10%	156.0	-4%
Yr.	—	—	723.9	5%	687.0	5%
Income (Million $)						
1Q	1.96	30%	1.51	12%	1.35	NM
2Q	8.05	20%	6.70	11%	6.03	NM
3Q	—	—	4.90	-14%	5.72	NM
4Q	—	—	1.04	-40%	1.73	78%
Yr.	—	—	14.15	-5%	14.83	NM
Earnings Per Share ($)						
1Q	0.21	31%	0.16	7%	0.15	NM
2Q	0.87	21%	0.72	11%	0.65	NM
3Q	—	—	0.53	-15%	0.62	NM
4Q	—	—	0.11	-39%	0.18	NM
Yr.	—	—	1.52	-5%	1.60	NM

Next earnings report expected: late October

Coca-Cola Bottling Co. Consol.

Business Summary - 22-SEP-95

Coca-Cola Bottling Co. Consolidated bottles, cans and markets carbonated soft drinks, primarily products of the Coca-Cola Co. Prior to 1984, the company's business was concentrated in North Carolina, but, through a major expansion program, its operating territory has been extended to an 11-state area in the Southeast. Major markets include North Carolina, Mobile, Ala., Columbus, Ga., Nashville, Tenn., Charleston, W. Va., and Roanoke, Va. The population within the franchise area approximates 11.7 million. In addition, South Carolina is covered through a joint venture.

COKE holds exclusive territorial franchises to bottle and market Coca-Cola classic, diet Coke, Cherry Coke, Minute Maid, Sprite and other Coca-Cola soft drink products. It has similar rights to produce and sell other soft drink brands, including Dr Pepper, Welch's flavors, Seagrams' products, Barq's Root Beer and Sundrop, but it is prohibited from dealing in any product that is an imitation of or substitute for any Coca-Cola product.

In 1994, products of the Coca-Cola Co. accounted for 88% of soft drink sales. During 1994, 74% of total sales were through the "take-home market" (supermarkets, convenience stores and other retail outlets); the remaining sales were made in the "cold drink market" (primarily vending machines).

Piedmont Coca-Cola Bottling Partnership (formed in July 1993) is an equally owned joint venture with Coca-Cola Co. It produces and markets soft drink products in certain North and South Carolina bottling territorries. COKE provides a majority of the soft drink products to Piedmont and receives a fee for managing the business.

During the past several years, COKE has attempted to concentrate its soft drink production into fewer facilities for efficiency and to meet changing market conditions. Since May 1984, four major production centers have been closed, one each in the Carolinas and Roanoke market areas and two in the Columbus market area. At the end of 1994, COKE had four production facilities and 54 distribution centers.

In November 1994, COKE signed a five-year agreement with Vermont Pure Natural Spring Water for distribution in southeastern New England.

Important Developments

Jul. '95—Management attributed the advance in its fiscal first half net income to higher prices and volume growth, which outweighed a sharp increase in packaging costs.

Capitalization

Long Term Debt: $429,670,000 (6/95).
Class B Common Stock: 1,336,362 shs. ($1 par); ea. conv. into one com. sh.; 20 votes per sh.
J.F. Harrison and family control 86% of the voting power (incl. 31% of the com. and 20% of the Cl. B shs. owned by the Coca-Cola Co.).

Per Share Data ($) (Year Ended Dec. 31)

	1994	1993	1992	1991	1990	1989
Tangible Bk. Val.	-31.61	-33.39	-56.60	-40.28	-12.94	-10.26
Cash Flow	5.45	5.71	4.19	3.47	3.19	2.70
Earnings	1.52	1.60	-0.23	0.24	-0.02	-0.32
Dividends	1.00	0.88	0.88	0.88	0.88	0.88
Payout Ratio	66%	55%	NM	366%	NM	NM
Prices - High	37¼	41½	20¾	26½	25	32½
- Low	24	17	15¼	16¼	15	22
P/E Ratio - High	25	26	NM	NM	NM	NM
- Low	16	11	NM	NM	NM	NM

Income Statement Analysis (Million $)

	1994	%Chg	1993	%Chg	1992	%Chg	1991
Revs.	724	5%	687	5%	656	41%	465
Oper. Inc.	92.2	-3%	95.3	13%	84.4	49%	56.6
Depr.	36.5	-4%	38.1	-6%	40.5	36%	29.7
Int. Exp.	31.4	1%	31.0	-16%	36.9	71%	21.6
Pretax Inc.	24.4	2%	24.0	NM	4.9	63%	3.0
Eff. Tax Rate	42%	—	38%	—	57%	—	0.70%
Net Inc.	14.1	-5%	14.8	NM	2.1	-28%	2.9

Balance Sheet & Other Fin. Data (Million $)

	1994	1993	1992	1991	1990	1989
Cash	1.8	1.3	1.4	1.0	3.2	3.4
Curr. Assets	59.6	58.4	49.2	59.5	35.5	36.9
Total Assets	664	648	786	785	468	449
Curr. Liab.	78.2	81.9	66.1	72.6	46.8	39.6
LT Debt	433	434	555	479	238	230
Common Eqty.	34.0	30.0	26.0	155	161	167
Total Cap.	556	544	691	696	409	400
Cap. Exp.	49.0	29.0	33.0	24.0	16.0	26.0
Cash Flow	50.6	52.9	38.4	31.9	29.3	24.6

Ratio Analysis

	1994	1993	1992	1991	1990	1989
Curr. Ratio	0.8	0.7	0.7	0.8	0.8	0.9
% LT Debt of Cap.	77.8	79.8	80.4	68.9	58.0	57.5
% Net Inc.of Revs.	2.0	2.2	0.3	0.6	0.1	NM
% Ret. on Assets	2.2	2.1	0.3	0.5	0.1	NM
% Ret. on Equity	44.5	53.2	NM	1.4	NM	NM

Dividend Data —Cash has been paid each year since 1967. A dividend reinvestment plan is available.

Amt. of Div. $	Date Decl.	Ex-Div. Date	Stock of Record	Payment Date
0.250	Nov. 09	Nov. 18	Nov. 25	Dec. 09 '94
0.250	Feb. 09	Feb. 16	Feb. 23	Mar. 09 '95
0.250	May. 08	May. 19	May. 25	Jun. 08 '95
0.250	Aug. 08	Aug. 23	Aug. 25	Sep. 08 '95

Data as orig. reptd.; bef. results of disc. opers. and/or spec. items. Per share data adj. for stk. divs. as of ex-div. date. E-Estimated. NA-Not Available. NM-Not Meaningful. NR-Not Ranked.

Office—1900 Rexford Rd., Charlotte, NC 28211. **Tel**—(704) 551-4400. **Chrmn**—J. F. Harrison, Jr. **Co-Vice-Chrmn & CEO**—J. F. Harrison III. **Co-Vice-Chrmn**—R. M. Henson. **Pres & COO**—J. L. Moore, Jr. **VP-CFO & Investor Contact**—D. V. Singer. **VP & Treas**—B. B. Jackson. **Secy**—J. F. Henry, Jr. **Dirs**—J. M. Belk, J. F. Harrison, Jr., J. F. Harrison III, R. M. Henson, H. R. Jones, D. L. Kennedy, Jr., H. W. McKay Belk, N. McWherter, J. L. Moore, J. W. Murrey III. **Transfer Agent**—First Union National Bank, Charlotte. **Reincorporated** in Delaware in 1980. **Empl**-4,700. **S&P Analyst:** Efraim Levy

Coeur d'Alene Mines

NYSE Symbol **CDE**
In S&P SmallCap 600

15-NOV-95 **Industry:** Mining/Diversified

Summary: Based in Coeur d'Alene, Idaho, this company is a leading producer of silver and gold with controlling interests in mines in Nevada, Chile and New Zealand.

S&P Opinion: Hold (★★★)

Recent Price • 19¼
52 Wk Range • 21⅝-14⅜
Yield • 0.8%
12-Mo. P/E • NM

Quantitative Evaluations
Outlook
(1 Lowest—5 Highest)
• **NA**
Fair Value
• **NA**
Risk
• **Average**
Earn./Div. Rank
• **B-**

Technical Eval.
• **Neutral** since 11/95
Rel. Strength Rank
(1 Lowest—99 Highest)
• **40**
Insider Activity
• **NA**

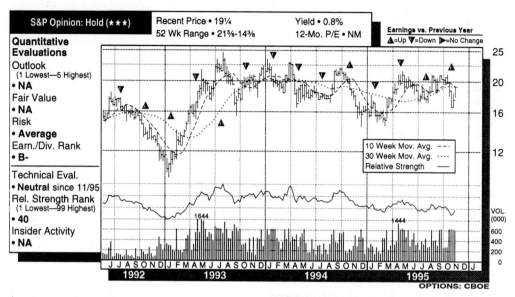

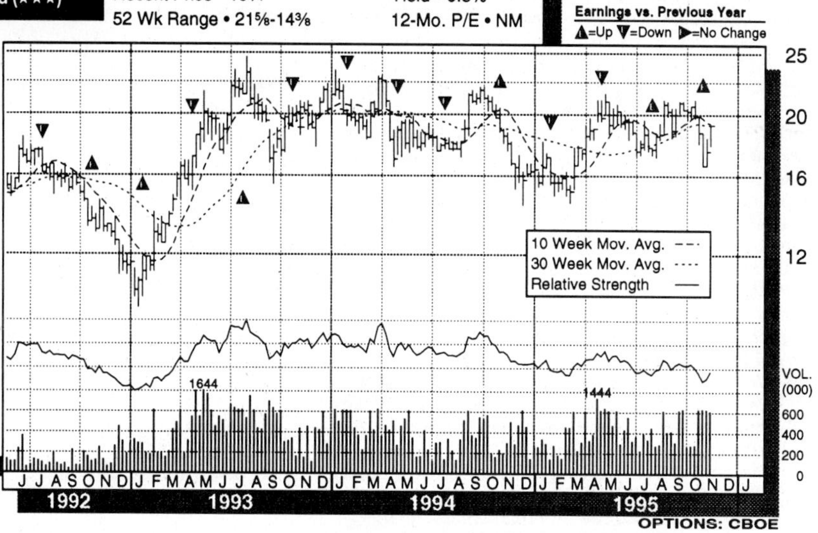

Overview - 15-NOV-95

Revenues in 1996 should increase sharply, mostly from expected higher silver and gold production from CDE's Fachinal Mine, and to a lesser extent, from a slight rise in gold and silver prices. Gross margins should increase, reflecting the expected greater production, higher gold and silver prices, and lower production costs at the Rochester Mine (CDE's largest operation). Interest expense should decrease about $5.2 million in 1996 following conversion of CDE's 7% subordinated debentures in December 1995. The conversion will increase CDE's common stock outstanding from 15.6 million to approximately 20.5 million shares.

Valuation - 15-NOV-95

In general, the stock performance of precious metal companies is highly sensitive to volatile external forces such as inflation expectations, interest rate movements, currency fluctuations, domestic and international political climates, and industrial demand. Stock prices seem to bear little relation to company-specific performance. Although CDE should report favorable earnings results for 1996, continued controlled inflation, a slowing economy, high short-term interest rates and a stronger dollar should keep CDE shares trading in a narrow range. Accordingly, we believe CDE shares are fairly valued.

Key Stock Statistics

S&P EPS Est. 1995	0.12	Tang. Bk. Value/Share	10.11
P/E on S&P Est. 1995	NM	Beta	-0.21
S&P EPS Est. 1996	0.66	Shareholders	8,900
Dividend Rate/Share	0.15	Market cap. (B)	$0.289
Shs. outstg. (M)	15.6	Inst. holdings	56%
Avg. daily vol. (M)	0.163	Insider holdings	NA

Value of $10,000 invested 5 years ago: $ 9,413

Fiscal Year Ending Dec. 31

	1995	% Change	1994	% Change	1993	% Change
Revenues (Million $)						
1Q	20.28	-11%	22.90	91%	11.98	-2%
2Q	25.68	15%	22.29	19%	18.66	37%
3Q	29.02	23%	23.53	4%	22.60	86%
4Q	—	—	22.31	-16%	26.56	97%
Yr.	—	—	91.02	9%	83.72	63%
Income (Million $)						
1Q	-3.37	NM	-2.60	NM	-1.98	NM
2Q	1.24	NM	-1.33	NM	-1.01	NM
3Q	2.04	24%	1.64	NM	-10.39	NM
4Q	—	—	-1.65	NM	0.09	-93%
Yr.	—	—	-3.94	NM	-13.29	NM
Earnings Per Share ($)						
1Q	-0.20	NM	-0.17	NM	-0.13	NM
2Q	0.08	NM	-0.09	NM	-0.07	NM
3Q	0.13	18%	0.11	NM	-0.68	NM
4Q	E0.11	NM	-0.11	NM	0.01	-89%
Yr.	E0.12	NM	-0.26	NM	-0.87	NM

Next earnings report expected: late February

Coeur d'Alene Mines

Business Summary - 15-NOV-95

CDE's 100%-owned Rochester silver-gold mine in Nevada is one of the largest and lowest cost primary silver producing mines in North America. Some 7.85 million tons of ore were mined in 1994, yielding 5,937,770 oz. of silver and 56,886 oz. of gold at cash costs of $3.57 per oz. of silver equivalent. At year-end 1994, proven and probable reserves stood at 101.6 million oz. of silver and 872,000 oz. of gold.

CDE's 80%-owned Golden Cross mine (New Zealand) produced 67,400 oz. of gold and 222,246 oz. of silver for CDE's account. Cash costs rose to an average $277 per oz. of gold equivalent in 1994, from an average $220 per oz. in eight months of CDE ownership in 1993, reflecting a decrease in underground ore grade, an unusually rainy 1994 first quarter and harder open-pit grinding ore. Exploration drilling in 1994 identified an additional 259,000 oz. of gold reserves principally in the open-pit area. Proven and probable reserves (100% basis) were estimated in 1994 at 601,000 oz. of gold and 2.6 million oz. of silver.

In September 1994, CDE gained operating control of the El Bronce (Chile) gold mine, in which it has a 51% interest in any profits, with an option to gain a 51% equity interest. CDE initiated a program to boost annual output to over 60,000 oz. from 40,000 oz.

In January 1995, CDE and ASARCO Inc. formed Silver Valley Resources, which consists of the fully developed Galena and Coeur silver properties (Idaho), and the adjoining Caladay, an advanced stage silver exploration property. Galena and Coeur were placed on standby in 1992 and 1991, respectively, awaiting higher silver prices.

CDE's Fachinal mine (Chile) became operational in November 1995. Fachinal is expected to produce about 2.7 million oz. of silver and 44,000 oz. of gold in its first full year of operaton. Proved and probable reserves are estimated at 14.6 million oz. of silver and 320,000 oz. of gold.

Important Developments

Oct. '95—CDE said it expects to obtain final development permits for its Kensington gold property in Alaska in the 1996 second quarter. In June 1995, CDE acquired the remaining 50% interest in Kensington for $32.5 million, plus a scaled royalty on one million oz. of future gold production. CDE estimates two years of development, output of 200,000 oz./year of gold and reserves of 1.95 million oz. Production is contingent upon a $400/oz. gold price.

Capitalization

Long Term Debt: $226,103,092 (6/95), incl. $100 million of 6 3/8% sub. debs. conv. into com. at $26.20 a sh.; $75 million of 7% sub. debs. conv. into com. at $15.68 a sh.; and $50 million of 6% sub. debs. conv. into com. at $26 a sh.

Per Share Data ($)

(Year Ended Dec. 31)

	1994	1993	1992	1991	1990	1989
Tangible Bk. Val.	10.29	11.14	11.81	12.01	13.86	12.04
Cash Flow	0.90	-0.03	0.30	-0.48	0.50	1.94
Earnings	-0.26	-0.87	-0.05	-0.94	-0.17	0.94
Dividends	0.15	0.15	0.15	0.15	0.15	0.15
Payout Ratio	NM	NM	NM	NM	NM	16%
Prices - High	23½	24⅝	18⅜	23	31	24⅛
- Low	14⅜	9⅞	10⅞	13⅜	13⅜	15½
P/E Ratio - High	NM	NM	NM	NM	NM	26
- Low	NM	NM	NM	NM	NM	16

Income Statement Analysis (Million $)

	1994	%Chg	1993	%Chg	1992	%Chg	1991
Revs.	91.0	16%	78.2	52%	51.5	-13%	59.2
Oper. Inc.	13.5	150%	5.4	NM	-2.9	NM	-1.3
Depr.	17.8	38%	12.9	138%	5.4	-22%	7.0
Int. Exp.	15.6	68%	9.3	126%	4.1	5%	3.9
Pretax Inc.	-3.7	NM	-16.7	NM	-4.5	NM	-15.0
Eff. Tax Rate	NM	—	NM	—	NM	—	NM
Net Inc.	-3.9	NM	-13.3	NM	-0.8	NM	-14.4

Balance Sheet & Other Fin. Data (Million $)

	1994	1993	1992	1991	1990	1989
Cash	143	85.0	156	111	105	80.0
Curr. Assets	192	129	192	145	138	102
Total Assets	413	326	325	262	239	196
Curr. Liab.	18.5	21.6	9.8	14.2	9.9	9.5
LT Debt	227	129	131	58.0	60.0	61.0
Common Eqty.	160	171	181	184	166	120
Total Cap.	389	302	315	246	229	186
Cap. Exp.	33.3	68.6	21.5	16.7	17.9	12.7
Cash Flow	13.9	-0.4	4.7	-7.4	5.2	19.4

Ratio Analysis

	1994	1993	1992	1991	1990	1989
Curr. Ratio	10.4	6.0	19.5	10.3	13.9	10.8
% LT Debt of Cap.	58.4	42.8	41.6	23.5	26.0	33.0
% Net Inc.of Revs.	NM	NM	NM	NM	NM	13.6
% Ret. on Assets	NM	NM	NM	NM	NM	4.9
% Ret. on Equity	NM	NM	NM	NM	NM	8.1

Dividend Data —Annual cash dividends were initiated in 1988. A "poison pill" stock purchase rights plan was adopted in 1989.

Amt. of Div. $	Date Decl.	Ex-Div. Date	Stock of Record	Payment Date
0.150	Mar. 21	Apr. 04	Apr. 10	Apr. 21 '95

Data as orig. reptd.; bef. results of disc. opers. and/or spec. items. Per share data adj. for stk. divs. as of ex-div. date. E-Estimated. NA-Not Available. NM-Not Meaningful. NR-Not Ranked.

Office—P.O. Box I, Coeur d'Alene, ID 83816-0316. **Tel**—(208) 667-3511. **Chrmn, Pres & CEO**—D. E. Wheeler. **SVP & COO**—M. L. Clark. **SVP, CFO & Treas**—J. A. Sabala. **Secy**—W. F. Boyd. **Investor Contact**—Anthony R. Ebersole. **Dirs**—C. D. Andrus, J. C. Bennett, J. J. Curran, J. T. Grade, D. B. Hagadone, J. A. McClure, J. A. Sabala, D. E. Wheeler. **Transfer Agent & Registrar**—First Interstate Bank, Encino, CA. **Incorporated** in Idaho in 1928. **Empl**-925. **S&P Analyst:** Robert E. Friedman

STANDARD & POOR'S

STOCK REPORTS

Collagen Corp.

NASDAQ Symbol **CGEN**

In S&P SmallCap 600

18-SEP-95

Industry: Medical equipment/ supply

Summary: This company develops, makes and markets biomedical devices for the treatment of defective, diseased, traumatized or aging human tissues.

Quantitative Evaluations

Outlook (1 Lowest—5 Highest)
• **1-**

Fair Value
• **16⅛**

Risk
• **Average**

Earn./Div. Rank
• **B**

Technical Eval.
• **Bearish** since 7/95

Rel. Strength Rank (1 Lowest—99 Highest)
• **57**

Insider Activity
• **NA**

Recent Price • 19
52 Wk Range • 28½-15
Yield • 0.8%
12-Mo. P/E • 20.4

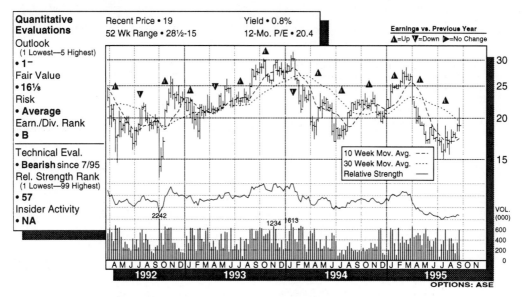

Earnings vs. Previous Year
▲=Up ▼=Down ▶=No Change

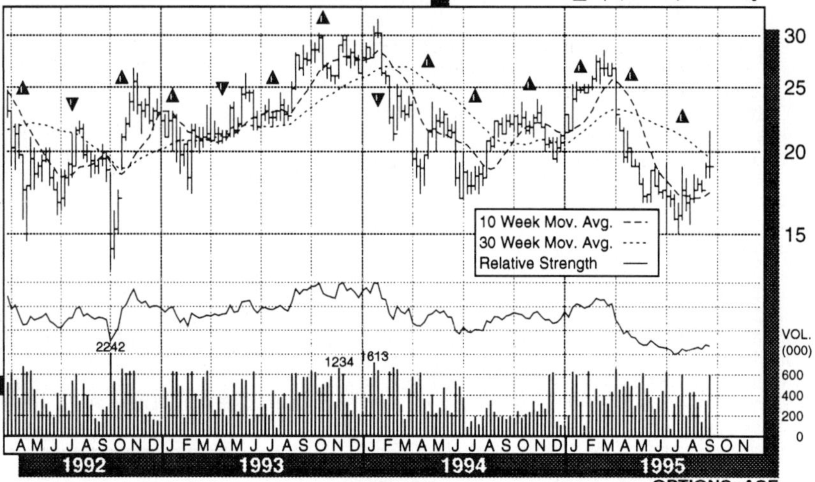

OPTIONS: ASE

Business Profile - 18-SEP-95

Collagen recently increased its stake in Lipomatrix, Inc., manufacturer of the Trilucent breast implant, to 90%. The triglyceride-filled implant has a better safety profile than current products on the market. Although Trilucent should give a boost to sales going forward, the company expects to have lower sales of other products, most notably the Contigen implant, in fiscal 1996. Consequently, Collagen said fiscal 1996 results will be similar to those of fiscal 1995.

Operational Review - 18-SEP-95

Revenues (preliminary) in the fiscal year ended June 30, 1995, increased 11%, from those of 1994, boosted by international sales in dermatology and plastic surgery products. Gross margins widened (74% vs. 71%), and after decreased R&D expenditures and moderately higher SG&A expenses, operating income surged 38%. After a $5.1 million gain on the sale of Target Therapeutics stock, and taxes at 45.9%, versus 44.4%, net earnings soared 78%, to $8.8 million, ($0.93 a share) from $4.9 million ($0.50).

Stock Performance - 15-SEP-95

In the past 30 trading days, CGEN's shares have increased 13%, compared to a 4% rise in the S&P 500. Average trading volume for the past five days was 119,140 shares, compared with the 40-day moving average of 77,946 shares.

Key Stock Statistics

Dividend Rate/Share	0.15	Shareholders	1,200
Shs. outstg. (M)	9.3	Market cap. (B)	$0.177
Avg. daily vol. (M)	0.072	Inst. holdings	59%
Tang. Bk. Value/Share	5.25	Insider holdings	NA
Beta	1.38		

Value of $10,000 invested 5 years ago: NA

Fiscal Year Ending Jun. 30

	1995	% Change	1994	% Change	1993	% Change
Revenues (Million $)						
1Q	16.43	15%	14.31	40%	10.22	-29%
2Q	18.87	11%	16.93	39%	12.15	-26%
3Q	17.03	9%	15.59	56%	10.01	-42%
4Q	20.23	8%	18.73	8%	17.36	-8%
Yr.	72.56	11%	65.55	32%	49.74	-26%
Income (Million $)						
1Q	1.31	70%	0.77	—	—	—
2Q	2.25	77%	1.27	-88%	11.00	NM
3Q	2.51	101%	1.25	NM	-0.83	NM
4Q	2.70	66%	1.63	37%	1.19	NM
Yr.	8.76	78%	4.92	-49%	9.73	NM
Earnings Per Share ($)						
1Q	0.14	75%	0.08	NM	-0.15	NM
2Q	0.24	85%	0.13	-88%	1.06	NM
3Q	0.26	100%	0.13	NM	-0.08	NM
4Q	0.29	71%	0.17	42%	0.12	NM
Yr.	0.93	86%	0.50	-47%	0.95	NM

Next earnings report expected: late October

Collagen Corp.

Business Summary - 18-SEP-95

Collagen Corporation develops, manufactures and markets on a worldwide basis high quality biocompatible products used in the repair or replacement of aged or damaged human tissue. The company also holds equity positions in other companies which use its technology.

Collagen has developed a proprietary process for the commercial manufacture of collagen and "tissue-like" implants. The company's collagen products are derived from calf-hide collagen, which is processed into a highly purified form. The company pioneered the development of collagen in injectible non-surgical augmentation and repair of aged or damaged tissue. Its core products are primarily used in the treatment of facial wrinkles, scars and incontinence, and in bone repair.

CGEN's cosmetic and reconstructive surgery line consists of three injectable collagen products. Zyderm I and II Collagen Implants are intended for superficial intradermal correction of small soft-tissue contour deficiencies, mainly facial lines and acne scars.

CGEN's Collagraft Implant is used in combination with the patient's own bone marrow to form an implant that enhances bone repair. Sales of Collagraft Implant amounted to $3.0 million in fiscal 1995 (up from $2.7 million in fiscal 1994).

The company's Contigen Bard Collagen Implant, a product developed in conjunction with C.R. Bard Inc. (which holds global marketing rights), was approved for U.S. marketing in September 1993. The product is used to treat a form of stress urinary incontinence called intrinsic sphincter deficiency.

CGEN's Collagraft Bone Graft Matrix (developed in collaboration with Zimmer), is a bone graft alternative for the treatment of bone fractures.

LipoMatrix Inc. (90% owned) has developed a proprietary breast implant for use in breast reconstruction and augmentation. Target Therapeutics Inc. (29% owned) develops, produces and markets micro-catheters and micro-coils for use in minimally invasive procedures to treat vascular diseases. Otogen Corp. (40% owned) is developing PEG-collagen-based tympanostomy tubes and tympanic membrane prostheses for use as substitutes for cranial bone and dura in the ear.

Important Developments

Aug. '95—Collagen agreed to purchase 50% of breast implant affiliate, LipoMatrix, bringing its stake to 90%. Collagen plans to pay approximately $18 million for the stake and the transaction is expected to close in early January 1996. Lipomatrix manufactures the Trilucent breast implant, a triglyceride-filled implant.

Capitalization

Long Term Debt: $1,494,000 (6/95).

Per Share Data ($)

(Year Ended Jun. 30)

	1995	1994	1993	1992	1991	1990
Tangible Bk. Val.	NA	4.97	5.38	5.28	3.28	4.48
Cash Flow	NA	0.89	1.32	0.59	0.82	0.79
Earnings	0.93	0.50	0.95	0.14	0.53	0.46
Dividends	0.25	0.10	Nil	Nil	Nil	Nil
Payout Ratio	27%	20%	Nil	Nil	Nil	Nil
Prices - High	28½	31¾	30	31	34	24⅝
- Low	15	17	15	13¼	13	14¾
P/E Ratio - High	31	63	32	NM	64	54
- Low	16	34	16	NM	25	32

Income Statement Analysis (Million $)

	1994	%Chg	1993	%Chg	1992	%Chg	1991
Revs.	65.6	32%	49.7	-26%	67.2	9%	61.4
Oper. Inc.	12.5	—	Nil	—	-1.5	NM	11.4
Depr.	3.9	1%	3.9	-17%	4.7	65%	2.8
Int. Exp.	Nil	—	Nil	—	0.9	-32%	1.4
Pretax Inc.	8.8	-52%	18.3	NM	3.9	-55%	8.6
Eff. Tax Rate	44%	—	47%	—	32%	—	41%
Net Inc.	4.9	-49%	9.7	NM	1.4	-72%	5.1

Balance Sheet & Other Fin. Data (Million $)

	1994	1993	1992	1991	1990	1989
Cash	12.7	19.6	44.7	16.5	24.2	21.5
Curr. Assets	32.1	37.0	68.8	39.0	40.7	35.5
Total Assets	74.5	76.0	95.5	67.6	70.8	65.1
Curr. Liab.	15.9	12.5	18.0	18.8	12.2	10.9
LT Debt	Nil	Nil	Nil	9.4	12.9	15.8
Common Eqty.	49.1	54.9	57.2	37.8	44.2	37.5
Total Cap.	57.3	62.8	76.7	48.3	58.4	53.9
Cap. Exp.	4.0	2.5	4.5	5.5	13.3	13.7
Cash Flow	8.8	13.6	6.1	7.9	7.0	5.1

Ratio Analysis

	1994	1993	1992	1991	1990	1989
Curr. Ratio	2.0	3.0	3.8	2.1	3.3	3.3
% LT Debt of Cap.	Nil	Nil	Nil	19.5	22.0	29.4
% Net Inc.of Revs.	7.5	19.6	2.1	8.3	7.5	6.6
% Ret. on Assets	6.5	11.5	1.7	6.8	5.9	4.5
% Ret. on Equity	9.5	17.6	2.9	11.4	9.9	7.9

Dividend Data —Cash dividends were initiated in June 1994. A shareholder rights plan was adopted in November 1994.

Amt. of Div. $	Date Decl.	Ex-Div. Date	Stock of Record	Payment Date
0.075	Nov. 14	Dec. 09	Dec. 15	Jan. 10 '95
0.075	Jun. 05	Jun. 13	Jun. 15	Jul. 15 '95

Data as orig. reptd.; bef. results of disc. opers. and/or spec. items. Per share data adj. for stk. divs. as of ex-div. date. E-Estimated. NA-Not Available. NM-Not Meaningful. NR-Not Ranked.

Office—2500 Faber Place, Palo Alto, CA 94303. **Tel**—(415) 856-0200. **Chrmn & CEO**—H. D. Palefsky. **Pres & COO**—G. S. Petersmeyer. **VP-Fin & CFO**—D. Foster. **Secy**—C. W. Johnson. **Investor Contact**—Lisa Morgensai (415-354-4612). **Dirs**—A. L. Bakar, J. R. Daniels, W. G. Davis, R. W. Dennis, C. W. Johnson, T. R. Knapp, M. F. Mee, H. D. Palefsky, R. Perkins, G. S. Petersmeyer, C. W. Pettinga, R. H. Salquist. **Transfer Agent & Registrar**—Bank of New York, NYC. **Incorporated** in California in 1975; reincorporated in Delaware in 1987. **Empl**-336. **S&P Analyst:** Thomas Tirney

STANDARD & POOR'S

STOCK REPORTS

Collective Bancorp

NASDAQ Symbol **COFD**

In S&P SmallCap 600

22-OCT-95

Industry: Banking

Summary: COFD is the holding company for Collective Bank, which operates 79 banking offices providing depositary and lending services to individuals and businesses throughout New Jersey.

Quantitative Evaluations

Outlook
(1 Lowest—5 Highest)
• **NA**

Fair Value
• **NA**

Risk
• **Average**

Earn./Div. Rank
• **B**

Technical Eval.
• **Bullish** since 5/95

Rel. Strength Rank
(1 Lowest—99 Highest)
• **62**

Insider Activity
• **NA**

Recent Price • 25⅛
52 Wk Range • 26¼-15½
Yield • 3.2%
12-Mo. P/E • 9.4

Earnings vs. Previous Year
▲=Up ▼=Down ▶=No Change

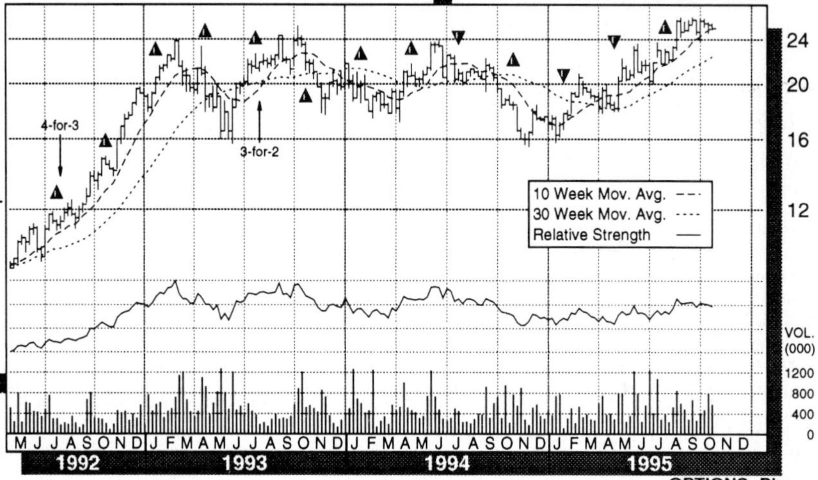

OPTIONS: Ph

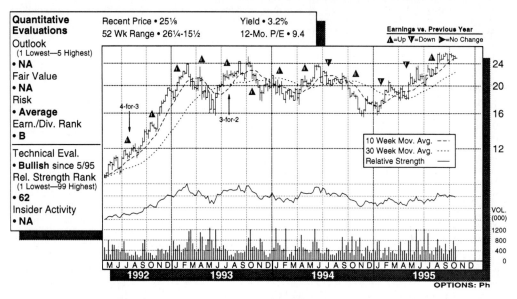

Business Profile - 22-OCT-95

Collective Bancorp is the largest publicly traded thrift institution in New Jersey, operating 79 full-service banking offices throughout a 13-county region of the state. Reflecting the company's growth strategy, in the three years ended June 30, 1995, it acquired $1.1 billion of deposits. In fiscal 1995, rising interest rates and a flattening yield curve had a significant negative impact on Collective's net interest income.

Operational Review - 13-OCT-95

In the three months ended September 30, 1995, net interest income fell 12%, year to year, principally reflecting a 32% increase in total interest expense. Noninterest income was up 65%, due to a gain on the sale of loans and securities, which contrasted with a loss in the earlier period, and 48% higher financial service fees and other income. Noninterest expense was up 8.9%. After taxes at 35.7%, versus 35.6%, net income declined 18%, to $13,197,000 ($0.65 a share), from $15,989,000 ($0.78).

Stock Performance - 20-OCT-95

In the past 30 trading days, COFD's shares have declined 1%, compared to a 3% rise in the S&P 500. Average trading volume for the past five days was 113,260 shares, compared with the 40-day moving average of 98,421 shares.

Key Stock Statistics

Dividend Rate/Share	0.80	Shareholders	1,400
Shs. outstg. (M)	20.4	Market cap. (B)	$0.511
Avg. daily vol. (M)	0.110	Inst. holdings	46%
Tang. Bk. Value/Share	15.21	Insider holdings	NA
Beta	1.31		

Value of $10,000 invested 5 years ago: $ 76,648

Fiscal Year Ending Jun. 30

	1996	% Change	1995	% Change	1994	% Change
Revenues (Million $)						
1Q	92.92	13%	82.34	27%	64.68	20%
2Q	—	—	85.29	29%	65.95	23%
3Q	—	—	89.00	24%	71.78	30%
4Q	—	—	93.13	20%	77.71	—
Yr.	—	—	349.8	26%	277.2	22%
Income (Million $)						
1Q	13.20	-17%	15.99	7%	14.96	—
2Q	—	—	14.98	-3%	15.47	48%
3Q	—	—	12.95	-19%	16.05	34%
4Q	—	—	13.63	-17%	16.47	12%
Yr.	—	—	57.54	-3%	59.37	27%
Earnings Per Share ($)						
1Q	0.65	-17%	0.78	7%	0.73	52%
2Q	—	—	0.73	-3%	0.75	46%
3Q	—	—	0.63	-19%	0.78	34%
4Q	—	—	0.66	5%	0.63	-13%
Yr.	—	—	2.80	-3%	2.89	26%

Next earnings report expected: early January

Collective Bancorp

Business Summary - 22-OCT-95

Collective Bancorp, Inc. is the holding company for Collective Bank, which operates 79 full-service banking offices throughout New Jersey. Collective Bank also originates residential mortgage loans throughout the middle Atlantic region through its subsidiary, Collective Mortgage Services, Inc. Based on total assets of $5.1 billion at June 30, 1995, Collective was the largest publicly traded thrift institution in New Jersey.

Collective currently emphasizes the origination of shorter-term, adjustable-rate mortgage loans, consumer loans and the purchase of adjustable-rate mortgage loans secured by single-family residences.

Gross loans receivable totaling $2.40 billion as of June 30, 1995, were divided:

Conventional--existing property	81%
Commercial	8%
FHA & VA	4%
Home equity	3%
Other loans	4%

At June 30, 1995, the allowance for loan losses was $14.1 million (0.59% of gross loans receivable), against $18.0 million (0.75%) a year earlier. Net chargeoffs in fiscal 1995 totaled $4,120,000, versus $6,637,000 in fiscal 1994. Classified assets amounted to $19.9 million (0.39% of total assets) at fiscal 1995 year end, down from $31.7 million (0.69%) a year earlier.

Interest on mortgages provided 42% of total income in fiscal 1995, interest on other loans 5%, interest on mortgage-backed securities 42%, interest and dividends on investments 7%, service charges 1%, and other financial service fees and noninterest income 3%.

Deposits totaled $3.3 billion at June 30, 1995, and were divided: 59% certificates, 22% savings and investment accounts, 14% NOW accounts, 3% money market, and 2% noninterest-bearing demand.

The average yield on interest-earning assets in fiscal 1995 was 7.18% (7.14% in fiscal 1994), while the cost of average interest-bearing liabilities was 3.18% (3.28%), for a net interest margin of 3.00% (3.86%).

Important Developments

Oct. '95—Management noted that expanding the level of normally recurring fee income generated from core banking operations is one of its top priorities. In the quarter ended September 30, 1995, fee income grew 27%, year to year.

Capitalization

FHLB Advances: $395,000,000 (6/95).
Other Borrowed Funds: $1,052,920,000.

Per Share Data ($) (Year Ended Jun. 30)

	1995	1994	1993	1992	1991	1990
Tangible Bk. Val.	15.21	13.10	11.64	9.51	8.04	7.09
Earnings	2.80	2.89	2.29	1.67	1.02	0.52
Dividends	0.60	0.54	0.32	0.16	0.12	0.10
Payout Ratio	21%	19%	14%	10%	11%	19%
Prices - High	23¾	23⅞	25⅜	19¾	10⅛	4
- Low	15¾	15½	15⅝	8¾	3⅜	2⅛
P/E Ratio - High	8	8	1	12	10	40
- Low	6	5	7	5	3	21

Income Statement Analysis (Million $)

	1995	%Chg	1994	%Chg	1993	%Chg	1992
Net Int. Inc.	141	-4%	146	28%	114	33%	85.5
Loan Loss Prov.	0.2	-86%	1.7	-39%	2.8	90%	1.5
Non Int. Inc.	13.4	74%	7.7	-32%	11.4	-36%	17.8
Non Int. Exp.	65.5	10%	59.4	20%	49.7	1%	49.1
Pretax Inc.	88.2	-5%	92.4	27%	72.8	38%	52.6
Eff. Tax Rate	35%	—	36%	—	36%	—	38%
Net Inc.	51.5	-13%	59.4	27%	46.9	45%	32.4
% Net Int. Marg.	3.00%	—	3.86%	—	4.23%	—	3.61%

Balance Sheet & Other Fin. Data (Million $)

	1995	1994	1993	1992	1991	1990
Total Assets	5,111	4,589	3,466	2,500	2,505	2,326
Loans	4,486	4,048	3,138	2,219	2,272	2,079
Deposits	3,278	3,004	2,792	2,114	1,976	1,608
Capitalization:						
Debt	395	250	20.0	20.0	115	160
Equity	328	280	235	192	144	128
Total	723	530	255	212	259	288

Ratio Analysis

	1995	1994	1993	1992	1991	1990
% Ret. on Assets	1.2	1.5	1.8	1.3	0.7	0.4
% Ret. on Equity	18.9	23.2	23.4	19.0	13.2	7.3
% Loan Loss Resv.	0.3	0.3	0.5	0.1	0.2	0.1
% Risk Based Capital	16.5	16.5	17.5	14.9	12.9	NA
Price Times Book Value:						
High	1.6	1.8	2.2	1.5	1.3	0.6
Low	1.0	1.3	1.3	0.9	0.4	0.3

Dividend Data —Cash payments were initiated in 1987.

Amt. of Div. $	Date Decl.	Ex-Div. Date	Stock of Record	Payment Date
0.150	Oct. 03	Oct. 07	Oct. 14	Oct. 26 '94
0.150	Jan. 04	Jan. 10	Jan. 17	Jan. 31 '95
0.150	Apr. 04	Apr. 10	Apr. 17	Apr. 27 '95
0.200	Jul. 06	Jul. 14	Jul. 18	Jul. 27 '95
0.200	Oct. 03	Oct. 12	Oct. 16	Oct. 26 '95

Data as orig. reptd.; bef. results of disc opers. and/or spec. items. Per share data adj. for stk. divs. as of ex-div. date. E-Estimated. NA-Not Available. NM-Not Meaningful. NR-Not Ranked.

Office—158 Philadelphia Ave., Egg Harbor, NJ 08215. **Tel**—(609) 625-1110. **Chrmn & CEO**—T. H. Hamilton. **Vice-Chrmn**—E. J. McColgan. **Sr Exec VP, Secy & Investor Contact**—Scott Page. **Dirs**—W. J. Bahr, G. W. French, T. H. Hamilton, M. Lerman, D. S. MacAllaster, E. J. McColgan, W. R. Miller, R. F. Mutschler Jr., H. O. Wunsch. **Transfer Agent & Registrar**—Midlantic National Bank, Edison, N.J. **Incorporated** in Delaware in 1988; bank chartered in New Jersey in 1927. **Empl**-905. **S&P Analyst:** Thomas C. Ferguson

STANDARD & POOR'S

STOCK REPORTS

Comair Holdings

NASDAQ Symbol **COMR**

In S&P SmallCap 600

31-OCT-95

Industry:
Air Transport

Summary: This Cincinnati-based holding company owns COMAIR, Inc., a regional airline and Delta Connection carrier that serves about 80 cities in the U.S., Canada and the Bahamas.

S&P Opinion: Accumulate (★★★★)

Recent Price • 27
52 Wk Range • 29⅝-9⅛

Yield • 1.0%
12-Mo. P/E • 18.6

Quantitative Evaluations

Outlook
(1 Lowest—5 Highest)
• **4+**

Fair Value
• **27⅞**

Risk
• **High**

Earn./Div. Rank
• **A-**

Technical Eval.
• **Bullish** since 10/95

Rel. Strength Rank
(1 Lowest—99 Highest)
• **94**

Insider Activity
• **Unfavorable**

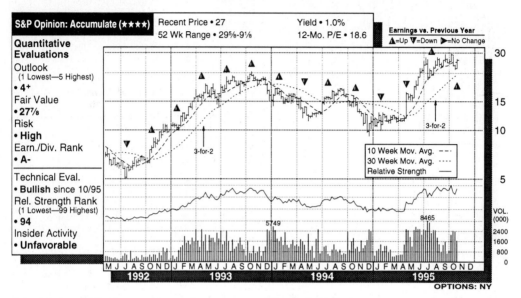

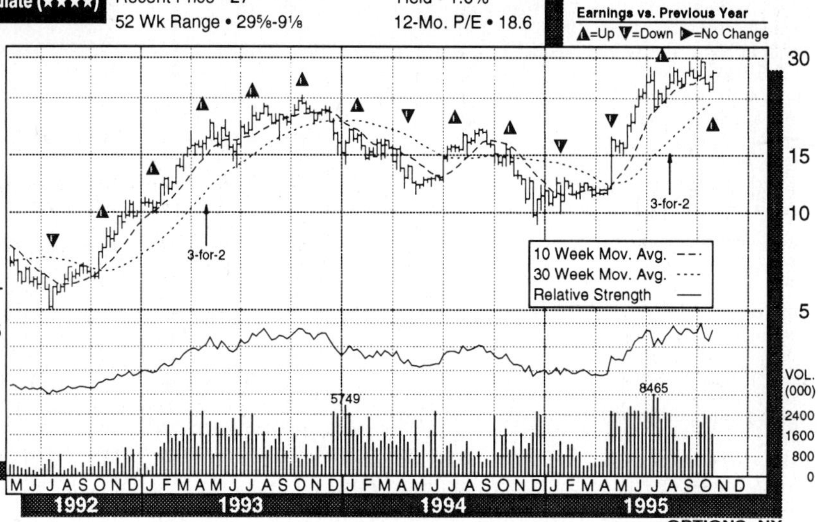

OPTIONS: NY

Overview - 31-OCT-95

Revenues are expected to rise substantially in fiscal 1996 (Mar.), spurred by increased capacity from the addition of 10 new 50-seat Canadair jets. Improved industry conditions, with robust traffic growth and higher average fares, should also boost revenues. Unit costs are projected at the same to slightly higher than year-earlier levels, reflecting Delta Connection fees and jet aircraft operating costs. Margins should widen, on higher load factor (plane occupancy) and yield (average fare). Interest costs are expected to increase, reflecting higher debt levels to finance aircraft purchases.

Valuation - 31-OCT-95

The shares have outperformed the market since the beginning of 1995, reflecting aggressive route expansion and better industry conditions. Although there are concerns about the impact of the planned 1996 entry of Southwest Airlines into Florida, COMAIR's exposure will be relatively small. Results should benefit as the company, together with Delta, builds the Cincinnati airport into a major hub. A shift to small, extremely efficient Canadair jets will also aid earnings. Cash flow is strong, and the dividend was recently boosted 31%. We view the stock as attractive for long-term capital appreciation.

Key Stock Statistics

S&P EPS Est. 1996	1.85	Tang. Bk. Value/Share	5.85
P/E on S&P Est. 1996	14.6	Beta	1.50
S&P EPS Est. 1997	1.85	Shareholders	2,400
Dividend Rate/Share	0.28	Market cap. (B)	$0.845
Shs. outstg. (M)	29.5	Inst. holdings	55%
Avg. daily vol. (M)	0.442	Insider holdings	NA

Value of $10,000 invested 5 years ago: $ 74,493

Fiscal Year Ending Mar. 31

	1996	% Change	1995	% Change	1994	% Change
Revenues (Million $)						
1Q	115.4	31%	87.87	25%	70.50	26%
2Q	111.3	24%	89.98	24%	72.71	26%
3Q	—	—	90.06	18%	76.17	15%
4Q	—	—	92.80	20%	77.26	13%
Yr.	—	—	360.7	22%	296.6	20%
Income (Million $)						
1Q	16.56	76%	9.41	17%	8.03	NM
2Q	14.09	74%	8.09	27%	6.37	121%
3Q	—	—	6.79	-16%	8.11	32%
4Q	—	—	5.02	-17%	6.02	-23%
Yr.	—	—	29.30	3%	28.53	48%
Earnings Per Share ($)						
1Q	0.57	94%	0.29	19%	0.25	185%
2Q	0.48	80%	0.27	33%	0.20	100%
3Q	E0.40	76%	0.23	-11%	0.25	15%
4Q	E0.40	131%	0.17	-7%	0.19	-30%
Yr.	E1.85	91%	0.97	9%	0.89	29%

Next earnings report expected: late January

Comair Holdings

Business Summary - 31-OCT-95

Comair Holdings, Inc. is the holding company for COMAIR, Inc., a Cincinnati-based regional air carrier that became a Delta Connection carrier in 1984. As of August 1995, the company served 81 cities in the U.S., Canada and the Bahamas. Operating data (passenger- and seat-miles in millions) in recent years:

	1994-5	1993-4	1992-3
Rev. passenger-miles	1,015	696	545
Available seat-miles	2,042	1,477	1,182
Load factor	49.7%	47.1%	46.1%
Breakeven load factor	42.9%	39.1%	39.7%
Rev. per RPM (cents)	34.0	40.6	42.9
Cost per ASM (cents)	14.8	16.1	17.3

About 44% of the company's business in fiscal 1995 (Mar.) was provided through interlining arrangements with Delta Air Lines under the Delta Connection program, versus 49% in fiscal 1995. Under these arrangements, COMAIR generally provides the short-haul portions of a longer multi-carrier trip.

Since initiation of the Delta Connection program, COMAIR has sought to accommodate leisure and business travelers seeking connections through Delta's hubs in Cincinnati and Orlando. Under its agreement with Delta, the company can offer passengers lower joint fares, coordinated schedules for timely connections and Delta Frequent Flyer Mileage.

At March 31, 1995, the company operated 64 turboprop aircraft: 17 Saab SF-340s (seating capacity of 33 each), 40 Embraer Brasilias (30) and seven Fairchild Metro IIIs (19); and 11 Canadair Jet aircraft (50). In addition, 10 Canadair aircraft were on order, and COMAIR also had a conditional order for 15 aircraft, subject to financing arrangements, and options for 25 more.

COMAIR operates a fixed-based facility at the Cincinnati/Northern Kentucky International Airport, providing a full range of refueling, maintenance and avionics services for aircraft. It also owns and operates six aircraft in charter service and operates a flight training center near Orlando, FL.

Important Developments

Oct. '95—COMAIR said passenger traffic in the first half of fiscal 1996 (Mar.) advanced 23%, year to year, while capacity was up 18%. Load factor rose to 53.4%, from 51.1%.

Aug. '95—The company announced expansion plans for its Cincinnatti hub. Beginning in December 1995, COMAIR intends to increase operations to 233 weekday departures from 222. The company also said Delta would grow to 219 Cincinnatti departures, from 203.

Capitalization

Long Term Debt: $77,707,901 (6/95).

Per Share Data ($) (Year Ended Mar. 31)

	1995	1994	1993	1992	1991	1990
Tangible Bk. Val.	5.35	5.25	4.51	2.87	2.54	2.19
Cash Flow	1.95	1.63	1.43	1.21	1.17	0.99
Earnings	0.97	0.89	0.69	0.45	0.47	0.47
Dividends	0.19	0.16	0.12	0.12	0.12	0.10
Payout Ratio	19%	18%	21%	27%	25%	21%
Cal. Yrs.	1994	1993	1992	1991	1990	1989
Prices - High	18⅛	23	10⅞	7⅛	6	4⅜
- Low	9⅛	9⅞	5	3⅝	3⅛	2½
P/E Ratio - High	19	26	16	16	13	9
- Low	9	11	7	8	7	5

Income Statement Analysis (Million $)

	1995	%Chg	1994	%Chg	1993	%Chg	1992
Revs.	361	22%	297	20%	248	14%	217
Oper. Inc.	77.0	8%	71.4	35%	53.0	26%	41.9
Depr.	30.0	24%	24.1	16%	20.7	NM	20.7
Int. Exp.	3.8	36%	2.8	-19%	3.5	-5%	3.7
Pretax Inc.	47.7	-3%	49.2	53%	32.1	55%	20.7
Eff. Tax Rate	39%	—	42%	—	40%	—	40%
Net Inc.	29.3	3%	28.5	48%	19.3	56%	12.4

Balance Sheet & Other Fin. Data (Million $)

	1995	1994	1993	1992	1991	1990
Cash	84.0	111	110	45.7	38.7	32.2
Curr. Assets	120	141	130	59.8	58.3	46.8
Total Assets	347	285	256	181	167	128
Curr. Liab.	78.8	63.9	60.2	45.1	37.8	27.0
LT Debt	79.9	27.1	34.6	41.6	48.7	33.0
Common Eqty.	157	169	145	79.5	69.4	60.0
Total Cap.	265	218	192	133	128	101
Cap. Exp.	112	40.4	27.9	44.7	54.8	53.4
Cash Flow	59.3	52.7	40.0	33.1	32.0	27.2

Ratio Analysis

	1995	1994	1993	1992	1991	1990
Curr. Ratio	1.5	2.2	2.2	1.3	1.5	1.7
% LT Debt of Cap.	30.2	12.4	18.0	31.4	38.0	32.8
% Net Inc.of Revs.	8.1	9.6	7.8	5.7	6.5	8.3
% Ret. on Assets	9.7	10.5	8.3	7.1	8.9	12.3
% Ret. on Equity	18.9	18.1	16.2	16.6	20.2	23.7

Dividend Data —Cash dividends were initiated in 1987.

Amt. of Div. $	Date Decl.	Ex-Div. Date	Stock of Record	Payment Date
0.080	Jan. 24	Jan. 31	Feb. 06	Feb. 15 '95
0.080	Apr. 26	May. 02	May. 08	May. 17 '95
0.080	Jul. 18	Jul. 26	Jul. 28	Aug. 10 '95
3-for-2	Jul. 18	Aug. 11	Jul. 28	Aug. 10 '95
0.070	Oct. 20	Oct. 30	Nov. 01	Nov. 10 '95

Data as orig. reptd.; bef. results of disc. opers. and/or spec. items. Per share data adj. for stk. divs. as of ex-div. date. E-Estimated. NA-Not Available. NM-Not Meaningful. NR-Not Ranked.

Office—P.O. Box 75021, Cincinnati/Northern Kentucky International Airport, Cincinnati, OH 45275. **Tel**—(606) 767-2550. **Chrmn & CEO**—D. R. Mueller. **Pres & COO**—D. A. Siebenburgen. **SVP, CFO & Investor Contact**—Randy D. Rademacher. **Secy**—R. D. Siegel. **Dirs**—R. H. Castellini, P. H. Forster, J. A. Haas, D. R. Mueller, R. A. Mueller, C. J. Murphy III, D. A. Siebenburgen, G. L. Wolken, M. W. Worth. **Transfer Agent & Registrar**—Mellon Bank, Pittsburgh. **Incorporated** in Ohio in 1981. **Empl**-2,292. **S&P Analyst:** Joe Victor Shammas

Commercial Federal Corp.

NYSE Symbol CFB In S&P SmallCap 600

Price	Range	P–E Ratio	Dividend	Yield	S&P Ranking	Beta
Sep. 11'95	1995					
35⅝	37¾–20⅜	17	None	None	B–	1.02

Summary

The principal subsidiary of this financial services holding company is Commercial Federal Bank, the largest depository institution in Nebraska. CFB has expanded through a number of recent acquisitions. Results in fiscal 1995 were hurt by a $21.4 million goodwill writeoff. In August 1995, trading in the company's shares shifted to the NYSE from the NASDAQ system.

Business Summary

Commercial Federal Corporation is a financial holding company whose principal subsidiary is Commercial Federal Bank, Nebraska's largest depository institution and a federal savings and loan association until its charter was changed in August 1990. As of June 30, 1994, the company was operating 65 branches—27 in Nebraska, 20 in Colorado, five in Kansas and 13 in Oklahoma. Operations were significantly expanded in October 1993 through the acquisition of Heartland Federal Savings and Loan Association of Ponca City, Okla.

At June 30, 1994, gross loans receivable totaled $4.93 billion, and were divided:

Conventional mortgage	58.1%
Mortgage–backed securities	26.2%
FHA & VA loans	8.0%
Commercial real estate	3.8%
Consumer & other loans	3.9%

The allowance for loan losses was $42,926,000 at June 30, 1994 ($45,106,000 a year earlier), equal to 1.18% (1.32%) of loans outstanding. Net chargeoffs in fiscal 1994 totaled $3,263,000 (0.13% of average loans), up from $2,133,000 (0.13%) in fiscal 1993. Nonperforming assets amounted to $64.0 million (1.16% of total assets) at June 30, 1994, down from $93.4 million (1.92%) a year earlier.

Total deposits of $3.36 billion at June 30, 1994, were apportioned: certificates 72%, market-rate savings 6%, passbook 14%, and NOW 8%.

Interest on loans receivable provided 71% of total income in fiscal 1994, interest on mortgage-backed securities 14%, interest on investment securities 6%, loan servicing fees 5%, and other noninterest income 4%.

The average yield on interest-earning assets was 7.41% in fiscal 1994 (8.37% in fiscal 1993), while the average rate paid on interest-bearing liabilities was 5.02% (5.84%), for an interest rate spread of 2.39% (2.53%).

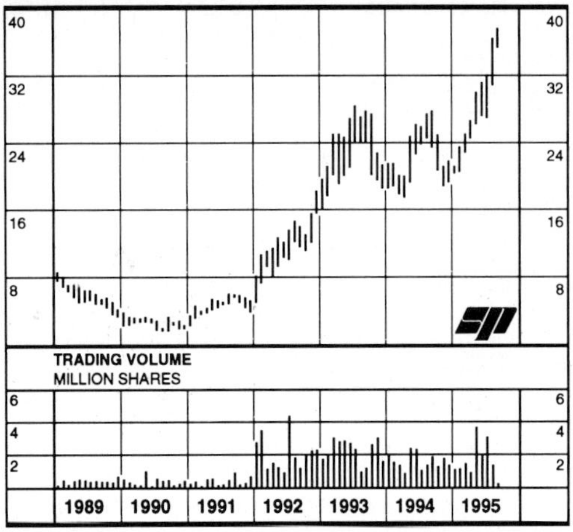

Important Developments

Aug. '95— CFB agreed to acquire Conservative Savings Corp. (CSC), parent of Omaha, Neb.-based Conservative Savings Bank, FSB (nine offices with deposits of $198.1 million), for cash and stock valued at about $41.5 million. The transaction is expected to close no later than March 31, 1996. Also in August, the company's common stock began trading on the New York Stock Exchange. CFB shifted its listing from NASDAQ to the NYSE to increase the shares' visibility.

Apr. '95— The company acquired Provident Federal Savings Bank (five branches in Lincoln, Neb. with about $60 million in deposits), for $7.5 million.

Next earnings report expected in early November.

Per Share Data ($)

Yr. End Jun. 30	1995	1994	1993	1992	1991	1990	1989	1988	1987	1986
Tangible Bk. Val.	**NA**	16.60	15.02	12.89	7.77	2.75	d1.88	NA	NA	NA
Earnings[1,2]	**2.11**	d0.44	2.43	5.03	1.19	d4.61	0.04	0.19	2.99	3.16
Dividends	**Nil**	Nil	Nil	Nil	Nil	Nil	Nil	Nil	Nil	Nil
Payout Ratio	**Nil**	Nil	Nil	Nil	Nil	Nil	Nil	Nil	Nil	Nil
Prices[3]—High	**37¾**	27⅞	28½	18⅜	6⅛	3⅞	8⅝	13¾	19⅜	19⅜
Low	**20⅜**	17½	16¼	5	2¼	1⅝	3⅜	7⅜	8⅜	11⅝
P/E Ratio—	**18–10**	NM	12–7	4–1	5–2	NM	NM	72–39	6–3	6–4

Data as orig. reptd. Adj. for 50% stk. div. May 1986. **1.** Ful. dil. **2.** Bef. spec. items of +0.45 in 1994, -2.95 in 1993, -0.60 in 1992, +1.52 in 1991, +0.28 in 1989, -0.30 in 1987. **3.** Cal. yr. NM-Not Meaningful. NA-Not Available. d-Deficit.

Income Data (Million $)

Year Ended June 30	Int. Inc.	Int. Exp.	Net Int. Inc.	Loan Loss Prov.	Non Int. Inc.	Non Int. Exp.	Net Bef. Taxes	Eff. Tax Rate	[1]Net Inc.	% Net Int. Margin	% Return On Assets	% Return On Equity
1994	**365**	**240**	**125.5**	**6.03**	**32.3**	**143.2**	**8.6**	**165.7%**	**d5.6**	**2.30**	**NM**	**NM**
1993	373	256	116.3	5.70	23.3	83.2	50.6	39.2%	30.8	2.53	0.7	12.0
1992	412	327	85.0	7.38	68.5	78.8	67.4	37.3%	42.3	1.98	0.9	21.0
1991	483	427	55.1	9.14	52.8	74.4	24.4	62.5%	9.1	1.42	0.2	6.0
1990	536	475	61.0	27.57	20.2	83.2	d29.6	NM	d31.9	1.50	NM	NM
1989	595	506	89.1	9.81	43.9	119.1	4.1	93.1%	0.3	1.52	NM	0.2
1988	528	431	97.4	9.53	42.4	124.8	5.5	78.3%	1.2	1.88	NM	1.0
1987	NA	266	NA	NA	NA	NA	36.4	45.9%	19.7	NA	0.5	16.1
1986	NA	254	NA	NA	NA	NA	27.6	37.2%	17.3	NA	0.6	20.8
1985	NA	249	NA	NA	NA	NA	12.3	32.3%	8.1	NA	0.3	15.7

Balance Sheet Data (Million $)

June 30	Total Assets	Loans	Deposits	Cash & Secs.	% Loan Loss Resv.	Capitalization [2]Debt	Capitalization Equity	Capitalization Total	% Equity To Assets	% Risk Based Capital	Price Times Book Value HI–LO
1994	**5,521**	**4,898**	**3,356**	**302**	**1.2**	**1,584**	**279**	**1,863**	**5.4**	**13.1**	**1.7–1.1**
1993	4,871	4,231	2,391	281	1.3	1,924	278	2,202	5.4	12.8	1.9–1.1
1992	4,641	3,860	2,301	351	1.2	1,509	237	1,746	4.1	8.9	1.2–0.4
1991	5,078	4,074	2,249	451	1.3	1,414	166	1,580	2.9	6.6	0.8–0.3
1990	5,619	4,630	2,405	384	0.5	1,317	141	1,457	2.3	6.3	1.4–0.6
1989	6,064	5,153	2,852	301	0.6	1,430	130	1,560	2.0	NA	0.5–0.3
1988	6,655	5,565	3,207	495	0.6	1,769	129	1,898	20.0	NA	0.7–0.5
1987	5,764	4,736	3,113	372	NA	1,348	118	1,467	2.5	NA	1.0–0.7
1986	3,068	2,685	1,666	234	NA	799	99	898	2.9	NA	1.2–0.7
1985	2,626	2,331	1,359	183	NA	741	65	811	2.0	NA	0.7–0.3

Data as orig. reptd. **1.** Bef. spec. items. **2.** Incl. FHLB advances. NA-Not Available. d-Deficit. NM-Not Meaningful.

Review of Operations

Based on a preliminary report, income in the fiscal year ended June 30, 1995, surged to $27.5 million ($2.11 a share), from a loss of $5.6 million ($0.44) in the previous year. The fiscal 1995 reported net income reflected the accelerated write-off of approximately $21.4 million ($1.64) of goodwill acquired prior to 1994. Results for fiscal 1994 exclude a $0.45 a share credit from the cumulative effect of accounting changes.

At June 30, 1995, nonperforming assets were down 9.0%, to $58.1 million.

[1]Common Share Earnings ($)

Quarter:	1994–95	1993–94	1992–93	1991–92
Sep.	0.04	0.65	0.48	0.51
Dec.	0.10	0.70	0.58	2.99
Mar.	1.04	0.75	0.66	1.20
Jun.	0.94	d2.54	0.72	0.53
	2.11	d0.44	2.43	[2]5.03

Dividend Data

No cash dividends have been paid on the public shares.

Finances

Effective June 30, 1994, CFB changed its method of valuation of intangible assets, relating to acquisitions made during 1986 through 1988 of five troubled savings institutions, incorporating a fair value concept. A third-party appraisal in fiscal 1994 of intangible assets found a fair value estimate of $41.0 million, classifying $19.6 million as core value of deposits, and $21.4 million as goodwill; and resulted in an impairment of intangible assets of $52.7 million ($43.9 million aftertax) recorded in fiscal 1994's fourth quarter. The $21.4 million of goodwill was amortized over the first six months of fiscal 1995, and the $19.6 million of core deposits is being amortized on a straight line basis over the next 34 months.

In July 1994, the company acquired for about $9 million in cash Home Federal Savings & Loan, wihc operated two branches in Ada, Okla., and had deposits of about $87 million.

Capitalization

FHLB Advances: $1,691,215,000 (3/95).

Other Borrowings: $56,223,000.

Common Stock: 12,877,754 shs. ($0.01 par).
Institutions hold 65%.
Shareholders: About 2,139 (9/94).

1. Ful. dil. **2.** Sum of quarters does not equal full-year amount bec. of change in shs. d-Deficit.

Office—2120 S. 72nd St., Omaha, NE 68124. **Tel**—(402) 554-9200. **Chrmn & CEO**—W. A. Fitzgerald. **Pres, COO & CFO**—J. A. Laphen. **SVP & Secy**—G. L. Matter. **VP & Investor Contact**—Stan R. Blakey (402-390-6553). **Dirs**—T. K. Anderson, W. A. Fitzgerald, R. F. Krohn, C. M. Lillis, C. G. Mammel, S. G. Marvin, R. S. Milligan, J. P. O'Donnell, M. T. O'Neil. **Transfer Agent**—Chemical Bank, NYC. **Organized** in Nebraska in 1983. **Empl**—1,150.

STANDARD & POOR'S

STOCK REPORTS

Commercial Metals

NYSE Symbol **CMC**
In S&P SmallCap 600

24-AUG-95 **Industry:** Metal

Summary: This company manufactures, recycles and markets steel, metal products and other materials, and provides related services.

Quantitative Evaluations

Outlook (1 Lowest—5 Highest)
• **3+**

Fair Value
• **28**

Risk
• **Low**

Earn./Div. Rank
• **B+**

Technical Eval.
• **Bullish** since 12/94

Rel. Strength Rank (1 Lowest—99 Highest)
• **56**

Insider Activity
• **NA**

Recent Price • 29
52 Wk Range • 29⅛-23⅜
Yield • 1.7%
12-Mo. P/E • 11.7

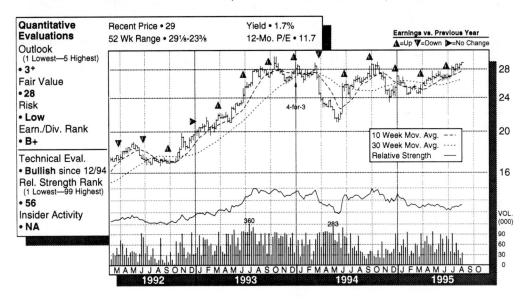

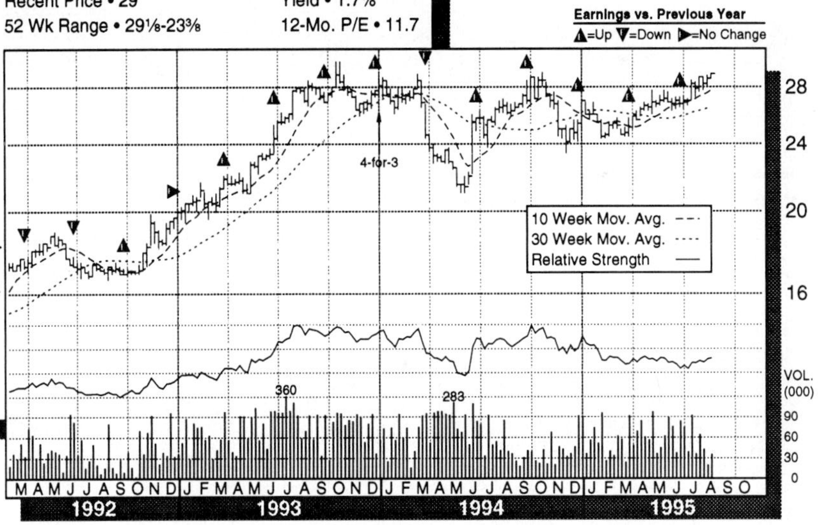

Business Profile - 22-AUG-95

CMC is focused on growing and modernizing its higher return manufacturing and related businesses. Steel and steel related products, representing 75% of CMC's business in fiscal 1994, have become increasingly important to the company's operations. CMC expects conditions to continue to improve in most of its markets, aided primarily by increased business and government spending, partially offset by an expected slowdown in residential construction in the U.S.

Operational Review - 22-AUG-95

Revenues in the nine months ended May 31, 1995, rose 25%, reflecting sales increases in the recycling and manufacturing segments of 56% and 55%, respectively; marketing/trading revenues fell 9%. Margins widened on the higher sales volume, and operating income advanced 57%. Despite a non-recurring, $6.7 million litigation accrual charge, and after taxes at 34.7%, versus 36.9%, net income surged 63%, to $28.0 million ($1.85 a share) from $17.1 million ($1.13).

Stock Performance - 18-AUG-95

In the past 30 trading days, CMC's shares have increased 7%, compared to a 0.51% rise in the S&P 500. Average trading volume for the past five days was 6,840 shares, compared with the 40-day moving average of 10,656 shares.

Key Stock Statistics

Dividend Rate/Share	0.48	Shareholders	2,200
Shs. outstg. (M)	15.3	Market cap. (B)	$0.442
Avg. daily vol. (M)	0.009	Inst. holdings	48%
Tang. Bk. Value/Share	19.19	Insider holdings	NA
Beta	0.76		

Value of $10,000 invested 5 years ago: $ 19,893

Fiscal Year Ending Aug. 31

	1995	% Change	1994	% Change	1993	% Change
Revenues (Million $)						
1Q	413.7	9%	380.0	17%	324.4	26%
2Q	533.0	37%	389.9	-5%	411.7	57%
3Q	572.5	30%	440.6	NM	438.0	52%
4Q	—	—	447.2	15%	387.2	12%
Yr.	—	—	1,658	6%	1,558	35%
Income (Million $)						
1Q	6.37	11%	5.72	101%	2.85	1%
2Q	10.28	141%	4.27	-12%	4.85	NM
3Q	11.37	59%	7.15	11%	6.45	134%
4Q	—	—	9.03	20%	7.51	16%
Yr.	—	—	26.17	21%	21.66	73%
Earnings Per Share ($)						
1Q	0.44	15%	0.38	96%	0.19	NM
2Q	0.67	139%	0.28	-15%	0.33	NM
3Q	0.73	52%	0.48	10%	0.43	132%
4Q	—	—	0.63	27%	0.50	10%
Yr.	—	—	1.75	20%	1.46	68%

Next earnings report expected: mid October

Commercial Metals

Business Summary - 24-AUG-95

Commercial Metals operates in raw material and industrial product-related activities, including worldwide marketing and trading, manufacturing and fabrication of steel, copper tube production, and metals recycling. Business segment contributions in fiscal 1994 were:

	Sales	Profits
Marketing and trading	45%	23%
Manufacturing	35%	65%
Recycling	20%	9%
Financial services	Nil	3%

International sales, including exports from the U.S., accounted for 47% of total revenues in fiscal 1994, up from 42% in fiscal 1993.

Through a network of trading offices around the world, CMC markets and trades primary and secondary metals, steel, ores and concentrates, industrial minerals, ferroalloys, chemicals, and other materials used by a variety of industries. The marketing and trading segment also provides services including market and technical information, financing, transportation and shipping, storage, insurance and hedging.

The manufacturing group, which is growing rapidly, includes a copper tube minimill, three steel minimills, 12 steel fabricating plants, a steel joist manufacturing facility, three metals recycling yards, three fence post manufacturing plants, six warehouse stores which sell supplies and equipment to the concrete installation trade, and two railcar rebuilding facilities. In fiscal 1994, the company's three minimills shipped a total of about 1.2 million tons of steel products.

Recycling operations include 27 metals processing plants across the Sunbelt, and a railroad salvage company that dismantles and recovers steel rail, track components and other materials from obsolete or abandoned railroads. In fiscal 1994, CMC's recycling plants collected, processed and recycled about 1.2 million tons of scrap metal. With the exception of precious metals, practically all recycleable metals capable of being recycled are processed by these plants.

CMC Finanz AG, a bank-like institution established under Swiss law in 1984, conducts business as an international finance company with emphasis on commercial banking services related to financing international transactions. Net interest income in fiscal 1994 came to $1.5 million, down from $1.7 million in fiscal 1993.

Important Developments

Jul. '95—CMC announced the sale of $100 million of unsecured 7.20% notes due 2005, underwritten by Goldman, Sachs & Co., Lehman Brothers and Morgan Stanley & Co. Proceeds will be used to refinance long term debt, reduce short term borrowings and for general corporate purposes.

Capitalization

Long Term Debt: $118,069,000 (5/95).

Per Share Data ($) (Year Ended Aug. 31)

	1994	1993	1992	1991	1990	1989
Tangible Bk. Val.	17.01	15.96	14.92	14.43	13.97	12.68
Cash Flow	3.77	3.31	2.64	2.49	3.16	3.15
Earnings	1.75	1.46	0.87	0.84	1.70	1.85
Dividends	0.46	0.39	0.39	0.39	0.38	0.31
Payout Ratio	26%	27%	44%	46%	21%	17%
Prices - High	29⅛	30	20⅛	16¾	16¾	17⅞
- Low	21	19⅜	14⅛	12¼	12⅛	14⅞
P/E Ratio - High	17	21	23	20	10	10
- Low	12	13	16	15	7	8

Income Statement Analysis (Million $)

	1994	%Chg	1993	%Chg	1992	%Chg	1991
Revs.	1,666	6%	1,569	35%	1,166	NM	1,161
Oper. Inc.	80.3	12%	71.8	28%	55.9	11%	50.5
Depr.	30.1	10%	27.4	7%	25.6	8%	23.6
Int. Exp.	10.4	6%	9.8	-3%	10.1	5%	9.6
Pretax Inc.	40.9	17%	35.1	73%	20.3	11%	18.3
Eff. Tax Rate	36%	—	38%	—	38%	—	35%
Net Inc.	26.2	21%	21.7	74%	12.5	4%	12.0

Balance Sheet & Other Fin. Data (Million $)

	1994	1993	1992	1991	1990	1989
Cash	38.3	47.4	47.4	33.2	38.6	65.6
Curr. Assets	446	398	378	319	289	315
Total Assets	605	542	516	461	416	419
Curr. Liab.	271	215	204	199	149	155
LT Debt	72.1	76.7	87.2	45.5	54.4	60.5
Common Eqty.	243	235	212	204	200	191
Total Cap.	334	327	312	262	267	264
Cap. Exp.	48.2	37.6	24.5	42.7	43.7	26.4
Cash Flow	56.3	49.0	38.1	35.6	48.1	48.6

Ratio Analysis

	1994	1993	1992	1991	1990	1989
Curr. Ratio	1.6	1.9	1.9	1.6	1.9	2.0
% LT Debt of Cap.	21.6	23.5	28.0	17.4	20.4	23.0
% Net Inc.of Revs.	1.6	1.4	1.1	1.0	2.3	2.2
% Ret. on Assets	4.6	4.0	2.6	2.8	6.4	7.5
% Ret. on Equity	11.1	9.5	6.0	6.0	13.6	15.9

Dividend Data —Dividends have been paid since 1964.

Amt. of Div. $	Date Decl.	Ex-Div. Date	Stock of Record	Payment Date
0.120	Sep. 20	Oct. 07	Oct. 14	Oct. 28 '94
0.120	Dec. 09	Jan. 09	Jan. 13	Jan. 26 '95
0.120	Mar. 15	Apr. 07	Apr. 14	Apr. 28 '95
0.120	Jun. 19	Jul. 12	Jul. 14	Jul. 28 '95

Data as orig. reptd.; bef. results of disc. opers. and/or spec. items. Per share data adj. for stk. divs. as of ex-div. date. E-Estimated. NA-Not Available. NM-Not Meaningful. NR-Not Ranked.

Office—7800 Stemmons Freeway, P.O. Box 1046, Dallas, TX 75221. **Tel**—(214) 689-4300. **Pres & CEO**—S. A. Rabin. **VP & Secy**—D. M. Sudbury. **VP, Treas & CFO**—L. A. Engels. **Investor Contact**—Bob Davis (214-689-4354). **Dirs**—A. A. Eisenstat, M. Feldman, L. E. Hirsch, A. L. Howell, W. F. Kammann, R. E. Loewenberg, C. B. Peterson, S. A. Rabin, M. Selig. **Transfer Agent & Registrar**—Chemical Bank, NYC. **Incorporated** in Delaware in 1946. **Empl**-5,553. **S&P Analyst:** N. Rosenberg

STANDARD & POOR'S

STOCK REPORTS

CommNet Cellular, Inc.

NASDAQ Symbol **CELS**

In S&P SmallCap 600

01-NOV-95

Industry: Telecommunications

Summary: This company operates, manages and finances cellular telephone systems in which its subsidiaries and affiliates hold ownership interest.

Quantitative Evaluations

Outlook
(1 Lowest—5 Highest)
• **NA**

Fair Value
• **NA**

Risk
• **Average**

Earn./Div. Rank
• **C**

Technical Eval.
• **Bullish** since 10/95

Rel. Strength Rank
(1 Lowest—99 Highest)
• **19**

Insider Activity
• **Neutral**

Recent Price • 25¾

52 Wk Range • 30¾-21¼

Yield • Nil

12-Mo. P/E • NM

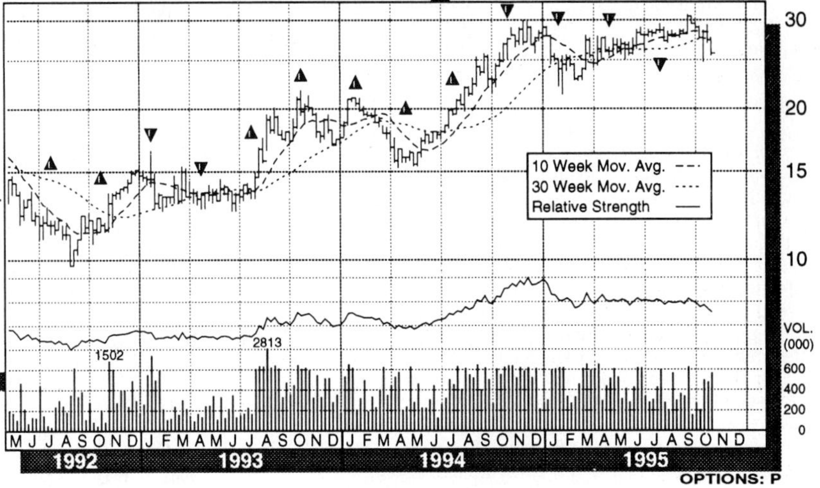

OPTIONS: P

Business Profile - 01-NOV-95

Cellular telephone systems in which CELS holds interests constitute the largest geographic collection of contiguous cellular markets in the U.S. In fiscal 1994 (Sep.), subscribers in managed markets increased 64%, and the company doubled its network, constructing and activating 101 new cell sites. For fiscal 1995, CELS planned to add another 100 cell sites and invest $70 million in its network.

Operational Review - 01-NOV-95

Net revenues in the nine months ended June 30, 1995, rose 50%, year to year, reflecting subscriber growth in consolidated markets, an increase in the number of markets consolidated, and greater coverage in cellular markets. The operating loss narrowed to $1.9 million, from $5.6 million. However, with greater equity in net loss of affiliates, and in the absence of $3.2 million in net gains from the sale of affiliates, the loss per share grew to $1.33, from $1.06.

Stock Performance - 27-OCT-95

In the past 30 trading days, CELS's shares have declined 16%, compared to a 0.63% fall in the S&P 500. Average trading volume for the past five days was 111,560 shares, compared with the 40-day moving average of 84,241 shares.

Key Stock Statistics

Dividend Rate/Share	Nil	Shareholders	500
Shs. outstg. (M)	13.3	Market cap. (B)	$0.334
Avg. daily vol. (M)	0.093	Inst. holdings	69%
Tang. Bk. Value/Share	NM	Insider holdings	NA
Beta	1.47		

Value of $10,000 invested 5 years ago: $ 10,957

Fiscal Year Ending Sep. 30

	1995	% Change	1994	% Change	1993	% Change
Revenues (Million $)						
1Q	19.28	51%	12.77	110%	6.07	192%
2Q	19.06	39%	13.69	115%	6.38	NM
3Q	24.18	58%	15.31	58%	9.67	99%
4Q	—	—	19.60	70%	11.56	97%
Yr.	—	—	61.36	82%	33.69	126%
Income (Million $)						
1Q	-6.44	NM	-4.71	NM	-7.18	NM
2Q	-5.84	NM	-4.57	NM	-5.27	NM
3Q	-3.55	NM	-2.97	NM	-6.64	NM
4Q	—	—	-4.50	NM	-0.59	NM
Yr.	—	—	-16.75	NM	-19.67	NM
Earnings Per Share ($)						
1Q	-0.55	NM	-0.42	NM	-0.86	NM
2Q	-0.49	NM	-0.39	NM	-0.62	NM
3Q	-0.29	NM	-0.25	NM	-0.77	NM
4Q	—	—	-0.38	NM	-0.07	NM
Yr.	—	—	-1.45	NM	-2.30	NM

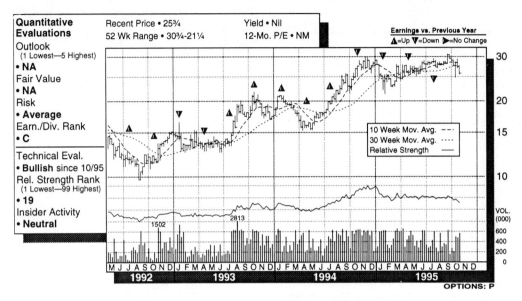

Next earnings report expected: early December

CommNet Cellular, Inc.

Business Summary - 01-NOV-95

CommNet Cellular, Inc. (formerly Cellular Inc.), formed in 1983 by six independent telephone companies, operates, manages and finances cellular telephone systems, primarily in the mountain and plains regions of the U.S.

Revenues in recent fiscal years were derived as follows:

	1994	1993	1992
Cellular service	86%	86%	83%
Equipment sales	14%	14%	17%

CELS has concentrated on creating an integrated network of contiguous cellular systems comprised of markets that it manages. To date, the network has evolved from the company's participation in the MSA (metropolitan statistical area) and RSA (rural statistical area) licensing process conducted by the FCC. Within this network, CELS provides substantially all services typically offered by landline telephones, including custom calling features such as call forwarding, call waiting, three-way conference calling, and, in most cases, voice mail services. Its network consists of 55 markets (spanning eight states), comprised of 48 RSA markets and 7 MSA markets. At September 30, 1994, RSA and MSA markets managed by the company had 68,291 and 30,711 subscribers, respectively (for a total of 99,002).

At September 30, 1994, the company's cellular interests represented about 3.2 million net population equivalents (pops) in 94 markets located in 16 states. These markets consist of 84 RSA markets having a total of 6.3 million pops, and 10 MSAs having a total of 1.3 million pops, of which CELS's interests represent 2.6 million net company pops and 610,000 net pops, respectively.

Important Developments

Sep. '95—The company obtained a new $165 million credit facility, increases its bank commitment by $35 million.

Jul. '95—CELS sold $80 million of 11 1/4% subordinated notes due 2005. Net proceeds of $77.4 million were used to call the company's 6 3/4% convertible subordinated debentures. Of the $74,747,000 principal amount outstanding, $41,852,000 was redeemed and the balance of $32,895,000 was converted into common stock.

Capitalization

Long Term Debt: $273,530,979 (6/95)
Minority Interest: $4,349,967.

Per Share Data ($) (Year Ended Sep. 30)

	1994	1993	1992	1991	1990	1989
Tangible Bk. Val.	-5.50	-8.71	-6.55	-15.46	-7.64	2.57
Cash Flow	-0.35	0.03	-0.42	-4.21	-1.27	-1.32
Earnings	-1.45	-2.30	-2.44	-6.00	-1.68	-1.45
Dividends	Nil	Nil	Nil	Nil	Nil	Nil
Payout Ratio	Nil	Nil	Nil	Nil	Nil	Nil
Prices - High	29 7/8	21 3/4	18 1/4	17 1/2	25	30
- Low	15 1/4	12 1/2	9 3/4	7 1/4	6 1/4	14
P/E Ratio - High	NM	NM	NM	NM	NM	NM
- Low	NM	NM	NM	NA	NA	NA

Income Statement Analysis (Million $)

	1994	%Chg	1993	%Chg	1992	%Chg	1991
Revs.	61.4	82%	33.7	126%	14.9	NM	4.9
Oper. Inc.	10.1	123%	4.5	NM	-4.2	NM	-6.4
Depr.	12.7	-37%	20.0	42%	14.1	64%	8.6
Int. Exp.	21.3	30%	16.4	11%	14.8	32%	11.2
Pretax Inc.	-16.2	NM	-19.7	NM	-17.0	NM	-28.7
Eff. Tax Rate	NM	—	NM	—	Nil	—	Nil
Net Inc.	-16.8	NM	-19.7	NM	-17.0	NM	-28.7

Balance Sheet & Other Fin. Data (Million $)

	1994	1993	1992	1991	1990	1989
Cash	23.3	66.8	38.3	31.4	41.8	79.3
Curr. Assets	43.3	79.1	44.2	36.2	44.0	79.9
Total Assets	282	269	208	182	150	112
Curr. Liab.	17.8	15.5	14.7	20.9	11.9	12.9
LT Debt	244	258	188	183	131	86.0
Common Eqty.	15.9	-9.4	4.2	-22.1	6.3	13.0
Total Cap.	264	252	193	161	138	99
Cap. Exp.	31.5	7.6	7.5	6.4	7.1	1.1
Cash Flow	-4.1	0.3	-2.9	-20.1	-5.9	-5.6

Ratio Analysis

	1994	1993	1992	1991	1990	1989
Curr. Ratio	2.4	5.1	3.0	1.7	3.7	6.2
% LT Debt of Cap.	92.4	102.3	97.8	113.7	95.4	86.8
% Net Inc.of Revs.	NM	NM	NM	NM	NM	NM
% Ret. on Assets	NM	NM	NM	NM	NM	NM
% Ret. on Equity	NM	NM	NM	NM	NM	NM

Dividend Data —No dividends have been paid. Terms of the company's financing agreements restrict payments.

Data as orig. reptd.; bef. results of disc. opers. and/or spec. items. Per share data adj. for stk. divs. as of ex-div. date. E-Estimated. NA-Not Available. NM-Not Meaningful. NR-Not Ranked.

Office—5990 Greenwood Plaza Blvd., Englewood, CO 80111. **Tel**—(303) 694-3234. **Chrmn, Pres & CEO**—A. C. Pohs. **EVP, CFO, Treas & Investor Contact**—Daniel P. Dwyer. **Secy**—Amy M. Shapiro. **Dirs**—D. P. Dwyer, J. E. Hayes, Jr., R. J. Paden, A. C. Pohs, D. E. Simmons. **Transfer Agent**—State Street Bank and Trust Co., Boston. **Incorporated** in Colorado in 1983. **Empl**-404. **S&P Analyst:** M.C.C.

Commonwealth Energy System

NYSE Symbol **CES**
In S&P SmallCap 600

17-OCT-95

Industry: Utilities-Electric

Summary: CES is an exempt public utility holding company with investments in four operating public utility companies in central and eastern Massachusetts.

Quantitative Evaluations

Outlook
(1 Lowest—5 Highest)
• **NA**
Fair Value
• **NA**
Risk
• **Low**
Earn./Div. Rank
• **B+**

Technical Eval.
• **Bullish** since 9/95
Rel. Strength Rank
(1 Lowest—99 Highest)
• **67**
Insider Activity
• **NA**

Recent Price • 41¼
52 Wk Range • 43⅜-35⅝
Yield • 7.2%
12-Mo. P/E • 10.0

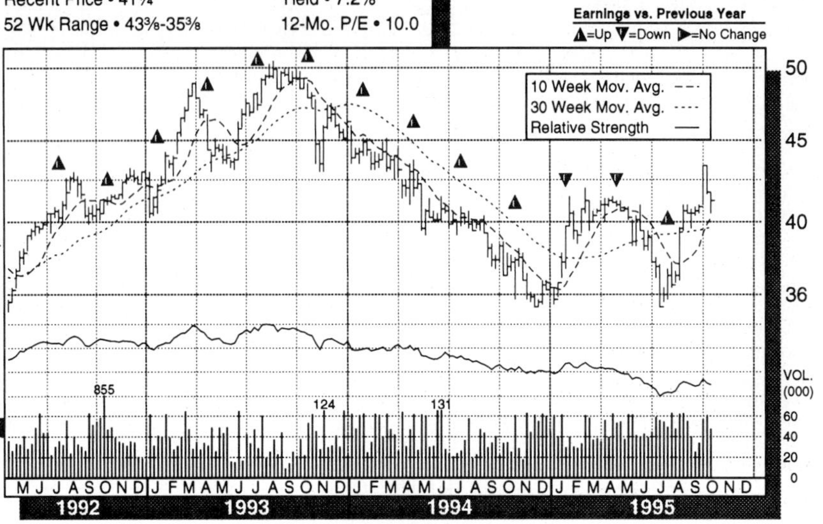

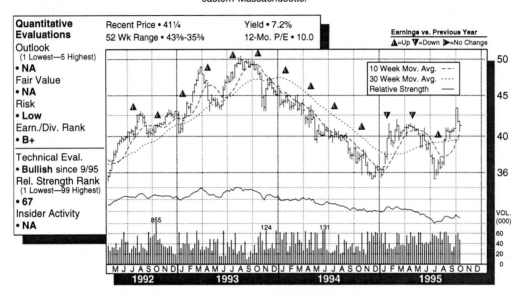

Business Profile - 25-JUN-95

In an effort to remain competitive, CES has moved to eliminate or defer electric power purchases from non-utility generators. Also, the company has enhanced service to customers by introducing a new quasi-firm rate alternative for high-volume, dual-fuel users of natural gas. CES recently launched a new marketing initiative to further pursue the emerging steam market. The company is continuing to emphasize cost controls by reducing payroll expenses and introducing new technology.

Operational Review - 13-OCT-95

Earnings fell, year to year, in the first half of 1995, primarily reflecting a significant decrease in operating revenues. Electric operating revenues were down 9.4% as a result of lower fuel and purchased power costs and lower unit sales due to extremely mild weather conditions compared to the record cold experienced in early 1994. Gas operating revenues decreased 12% due to lower firm unit sales and lower gas costs, somewhat offset by higher off-system and quasi-firm sales that began in 1994.

Stock Performance - 13-OCT-95

In the past 30 trading days, CES's shares have increased 2%, compared to a 4% rise in the S&P 500. Average trading volume for the past five days was 9,400 shares, compared with the 40-day moving average of 10,467 shares.

Key Stock Statistics

Dividend Rate/Share	3.00	Shareholders	15,000
Shs. outstg. (M)	10.7	Market cap. (B)	$0.446
Avg. daily vol. (M)	0.010	Inst. holdings	21%
Tang. Bk. Value/Share	35.57	Insider holdings	NA
Beta	0.50		

Value of $10,000 invested 5 years ago: $ 16,549

Fiscal Year Ending Dec. 31

	1995	% Change	1994	% Change	1993	% Change
Revenues (Million $)						
1Q	265.2	-15%	312.9	13%	276.9	7%
2Q	208.1	-3%	213.6	5%	203.4	5%
3Q	—	—	223.3	2%	217.9	9%
4Q	—	—	228.7	-6%	244.6	-4%
Yr.	—	—	978.6	4%	940.7	4%
Income (Million $)						
1Q	20.93	-25%	27.95	16%	24.10	18%
2Q	6.43	71%	3.76	73%	2.17	144%
3Q	—	—	6.22	9%	5.70	12%
4Q	—	—	11.04	-21%	13.90	3%
Yr.	—	—	48.97	7%	45.83	15%
Earnings Per Share ($)						
1Q	1.95	-27%	2.68	15%	2.34	17%
2Q	0.58	81%	0.32	78%	0.18	NM
3Q	—	—	0.57	10%	0.52	11%
4Q	—	—	1.02	-23%	1.33	2%
Yr.	—	—	4.59	5%	4.37	14%

Next earnings report expected: late October

Commonwealth Energy System

Business Summary - 13-OCT-95

Commonwealth Energy System is a holding company with investments in four operating public utilities that operate entirely within central and eastern Massachusetts. Subsidiaries include Cambridge Electric Light, Canal Electric (wholesale sales only), Commonwealth Electric, Commonwealth Gas, COM/Energy Steam and Hopkinton LNG Corp. CES also has five real estate trusts. In addition, the system has a 1.4% interest in a jointly owned oil-fired generating unit and also owns from 2.5% to 4.5% interests in five nuclear power plants. Segment contributions in 1994 were:

	Revs.	Profits
Electric	65%	69%
Gas	33%	26%
Steam & other	2%	5%

Cambridge Electric and Commonwealth Electric serve approximately 308,000 year-round retail customers (plus 49,000 seasonal) in 41 communities in eastern Massachusetts covering 1,112 square miles with a population of 645,000. Cambridge Electric also sells power at wholesale to the Town of Belmont, Mass. Commonwealth Gas serves about 232,000 customers in a 1,067-square-mile area encompassing 49 communities with a population of 1,128,000. Steam, which is produced by Cambridge Electric in connection with the generation of electricity, is purchased by COM/Energy Steam and, together with its own production, is distributed to 20 customers in Cambridge and one customer in Boston.

During 1994, CES sold 8,425 million kwh of electricity, versus 8,245 million in 1993, of which 55% was sold to retail customers and 45% to wholesale customers. Peak demand in 1994 was 962 mw, and system net capability totaled 1,188 mw, for a capacity margin of 23%.

Gas sales in 1994 totaled 47,354 billion British thermal units (BBTU), up 15% from 1993.

Important Developments

May '95—Commonwealth Electric, Cambridge Electric and the Attorney General of Massachusetts entered into rate settlement agreements which call for, among other things, a $2.7 million retail base rate decrease and a moratorium on retail rate filings until October 1998 for Commonwealth, a $1.5 million refund to Cambridge's customers, the full expensing of Commonwealth's postretirement benefit costs, the allowance of deferrals of certain long term purchased power and transmission capacity costs allowed for both companies, and the prohibition of both companies from seeking to recover restructuring costs.

Capitalization

Long Term Debt: $396,732,000 (6/95), not incl. $13.8 million of capital lease obligs.
Red. Cum. Preferred Stock: $14,410,000.

Per Share Data ($) (Year Ended Dec. 31)

	1994	1993	1992	1991	1990	1989
Tangible Bk. Val.	34.41	32.74	31.08	30.06	31.13	31.87
Earnings	4.59	4.37	3.83	1.82	2.16	4.14
Dividends	2.98	2.92	2.92	2.92	2.89	2.80
Payout Ratio	65%	67%	76%	160%	134%	68%
Prices - High	46	50½	43¼	40	39	38½
- Low	35⅜	40¼	34⅞	30	29⅛	29⅝
P/E Ratio - High	10	12	11	22	18	9
- Low	8	9	9	16	13	7

Income Statement Analysis (Million $)

	1994	%Chg	1993	%Chg	1992	%Chg	1991
Revs.	979	4%	941	4%	906	7%	850
Depr.	50.1	3%	48.5	-5%	50.9	21%	42.0
Maint.	36.5	-10%	40.6	2%	39.8	-10%	44.3
Fxd. Chgs. Cov.	3.3	4%	3.2	7%	3.0	33%	2.2
Constr. Credits	0.1	-50%	0.2	-95%	4.1	NM	0.8
Eff. Tax Rate	53%	—	54%	—	53%	—	49%
Net Inc.	49.0	7%	45.8	15%	39.9	105%	19.5

Balance Sheet & Other Fin. Data (Million $)

	1994	1993	1992	1991	1990	1989
Gross Prop.	1,460	1,410	1,385	1,336	1,304	1,232
Cap. Exp.	58.0	54.0	51.0	61.0	87.0	106
Net Prop.	999	985	979	963	966	916
Capitalization:						
LT Debt	432	463	377	384	430	348
% LT Debt	53	57	53	55	57	51
Pfd.	14.7	15.5	16.3	17.1	17.9	18.8
% Pfd.	1.80	1.90	2.30	2.40	2.40	2.80
Common	363	337	315	301	307	311
% Common	45	41	45	43	41	46
Total Cap.	1,094	1,090	967	931	971	884

Ratio Analysis

	1994	1993	1992	1991	1990	1989
Oper. Ratio	90.5	90.9	91.2	90.6	92.2	91.2
% Earn. on Net Prop.	9.4	8.8	8.2	8.2	6.7	8.1
% Ret. on Revs.	5.0	4.9	4.4	2.3	2.8	5.2
% Ret. On Invest.Cap	8.5	8.8	8.6	6.9	7.1	9.4
% Return On Com.Eqty	13.7	13.7	12.5	6.0	6.9	13.3

Dividend Data —Dividends have been paid since 1947. A dividend reinvestment plan is available.

Amt. of Div. $	Date Decl.	Ex-Div. Date	Stock of Record	Payment Date
0.750	Sep. 22	Oct. 04	Oct. 11	Nov. 01 '94
0.750	Dec. 15	Jan. 04	Jan. 10	Feb. 01 '95
0.750	Mar. 23	Apr. 03	Apr. 07	May. 01 '95
0.750	Jun. 22	Jul. 06	Jul. 10	Aug. 01 '95
0.750	Sep. 28	Oct. 05	Oct. 10	Nov. 01 '95

Data as orig. reptd.; bef. results of disc opers. and/or spec. items. Per share data adj. for stk. divs. as of ex-div. date. E-Estimated. NA-Not Available. NM-Not Meaningful. NR-Not Ranked.

Office—One Main St., Cambridge, MA 02142-9150. **Tel**—(617) 225-4000. **Chrmn**—S. A. Buckler. **Chrmn & CEO**—W. G. Poist. **VP-Secy**—M. P. Sullivan. **VP-Fin, Treas & Investor Contact**—James D. Rappoli. **Trustees**—S. A. Buckler, P. H. Cressy, H. Dormitzer, B. L. Francis, F. M. Hundley, W. J. O'Brien, W. G. Poist, M. C. Ruettgers, G. L. Wilson. **Transfer Agent & Registrar**—First National Bank of Boston. **Organized** in Massachusetts in 1926. **Empl**-2,169. **S&P Analyst:** J. Santoriello

STANDARD & POOR'S

Community Health Systems

STOCK REPORTS

NYSE Symbol **CYH**
In S&P SmallCap 600

29-SEP-95 **Industry:** Health Care Centers

Summary: This company owns and operates hospitals in growing communities outside major urban areas in the southeastern and southwestern U.S.

Quantitative Evaluations

Outlook (1 Lowest—5 Highest)
• **NA**

Fair Value
• **NA**

Risk
• **Average**

Earn./Div. Rank
• **NR**

Technical Eval.
• **Bullish** since 4/93

Rel. Strength Rank (1 Lowest—99 Highest)
• **69**

Insider Activity
• **NA**

Recent Price • 40¾
52 Wk Range • 42¾-22⅛
Yield • Nil
12-Mo. P/E • 36.4

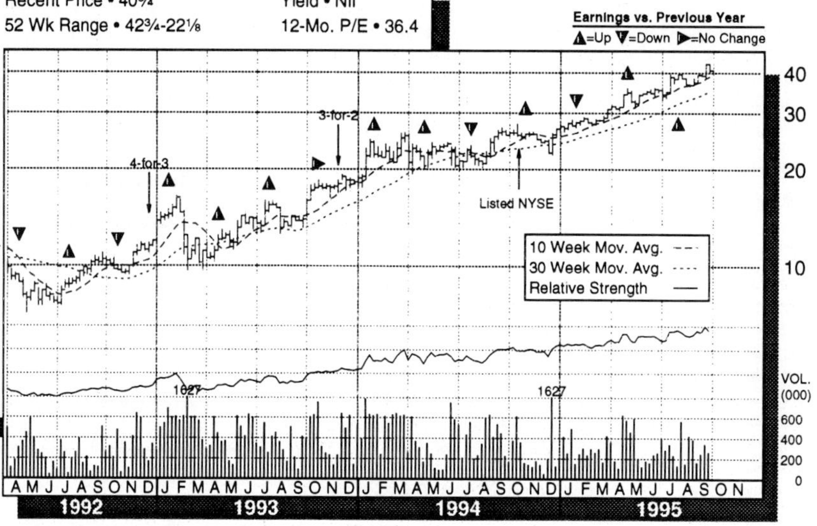

Business Profile - 29-SEP-95

Although acute-care hospitals continue to face increasing competition from lower-cost alternate-site providers, this company's results should continue to improve, aided by its focus on less competitive geographic markets and by an ongoing acquisition program. The company targets hospitals which lack resources to operate at maximum efficiency. Upon acquisition of a hospital, the company implements financial and operating policies which improve efficiency and achieve the company's financial goals.

Operational Review - 29-SEP-95

Net operating revenues continued to climb in the first half of 1995, reflecting the acquisition of new hospitals, an improved payor mix, and gains in inpatient and outpatient admissions. Operating margins widened with improvements in staffing ratios and the implementation of purchasing contracts for the recently acquired Hallmark hospitals. Net income advanced sharply. The company recorded a nonrecurring charge of $0.79 a share for the Hallmark acquisition in the fourth quarter of 1994.

Stock Performance - 22-SEP-95

In the past 30 trading days, CYH's shares have increased 11%, compared to a 5% rise in the S&P 500. Average trading volume for the past five days was 51,720 shares, compared with the 40-day moving average of 64,110 shares.

Key Stock Statistics

Dividend Rate/Share	Nil	Shareholders	6,000
Shs. outstg. (M)	19.5	Market cap. (B)	$0.787
Avg. daily vol. (M)	0.055	Inst. holdings	88%
Tang. Bk. Value/Share	11.89	Insider holdings	NA
Beta	NA		

Value of $10,000 invested 5 years ago: NA

Fiscal Year Ending Dec. 31

	1995	% Change	1994	% Change	1993	% Change
Revenues (Million $)						
1Q	142.1	21%	117.5	112%	55.40	35%
2Q	137.4	21%	113.8	102%	56.23	28%
3Q	—	—	113.7	93%	58.97	38%
4Q	—	—	122.2	87%	65.30	33%
Yr.	—	—	467.2	98%	235.9	33%
Income (Million $)						
1Q	12.07	94%	6.21	58%	3.93	21%
2Q	9.29	115%	4.33	30%	3.34	25%
3Q	—	—	4.01	98%	2.03	NM
4Q	—	—	-3.16	NM	3.30	24%
Yr.	—	—	11.39	-10%	12.59	19%
Earnings Per Share ($)						
1Q	0.61	53%	0.40	18%	0.34	19%
2Q	0.47	68%	0.28	-3%	0.29	21%
3Q	—	—	0.26	44%	0.18	NM
4Q	—	—	-0.19	NM	0.28	17%
Yr.	—	—	0.73	-34%	1.10	16%

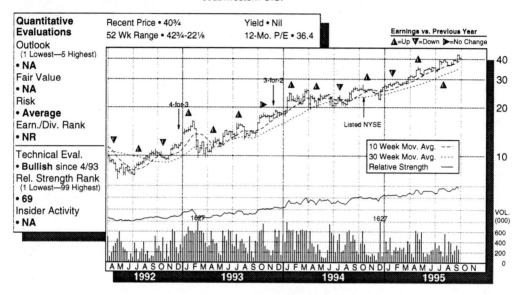

Next earnings report expected: late October

Community Health Systems

Business Summary - 25-SEP-95

Community Health Systems, Inc. was organized in 1985 and, following its October 1994 merger with Hallmark Healthcare Corp., now owns and operates 40 hospitals with an aggregate of 3,791 licensed beds in 17 states, primarily in growing communities outside major urban areas in the southeastern and southwestern regions of the U.S.

The company focuses on a less-competitive segment of the hospital market. Hospitals in growing communities outside major urban areas generally do not face pricing pressures from nearby hospitals, health maintenance organizations (HMOs) and preferred provider organizations (PPOs) as in urban areas. Although residents of these communities often seek hospital services in larger urban areas, a small reduction in this out-migration can significantly increase revenues and operating profits.

General acute-care hospitals offer inpatient care, intensive and cardiac care, diagnostic services, CT scanning and emergency services, most of which are physician-staffed 24 hours a day, seven days a week. Outpatient services include same-day surgery, laboratory, X-ray, respiratory therapy, cardiology and physical therapy. Some of CYH's hospitals also provide such specialty services as full-service obstetrics, orthopedic surgery and psychiatric and chemical dependency units.

Consistent with industry trends, the company's hospitals have experienced a significant shift from inpatient to outpatient care, beginning with the phase-in of the Medicare prospective payment system in 1983 and other measures that encourage outpatient utilization. Inpatient services provided 64.9% of net revenues in 1994, outpatient services 30.5%, home health care services 2.4% and nonpatient services 2.2%.

Private payors (primarily private insurance) accounted for 41.9% of hospital revenues in 1994, Medicare for 42.4%, Medicaid 12.0% and managed care (primarily HMOs and PPOs) and nonpatient revenue 3.7%.

In December 1994, CYH sold 3.6 million common shares in a public offering at $22.00 a share. Net proceeds were used to repay outstanding indebtedness.

Important Developments

Aug. '95—CYH acquired the operations of Middle Kentucky River Medical Center through assumption of a long-term lease. Middle Kentucky, a 55-bed facility, had 1994 revenues of $20 million.

Capitalization

Long Term Debt: $187,298,000 (6/95).
Options: To purchase 1,697,000 shs. at $0.92 to $27.25 ea. (12/94).

Per Share Data ($) (Year Ended Dec. 31)

	1994	1993	1992	1991	1990	1989
Tangible Bk. Val.	10.72	6.82	5.62	5.52	2.47	1.15
Cash Flow	2.49	2.01	1.55	1.37	1.41	1.15
Earnings	0.73	1.10	0.95	0.85	0.59	0.15
Dividends	Nil	Nil	Nil	Nil	Nil	Nil
Payout Ratio	Nil	Nil	Nil	Nil	Nil	Nil
Prices - High	27¾	19¼	13⅞	11⅝	NA	NA
- Low	17½	9⅝	7⅛	8	NA	NA
P/E Ratio - High	38	18	15	14	NA	NA
- Low	24	9	7	9	NA	NA

Income Statement Analysis (Million $)

	1994	%Chg	1993	%Chg	1992	%Chg	1991
Revs.	467	98%	236	33%	177	28%	138
Oper. Inc.	84.9	102%	42.0	44%	29.2	25%	23.4
Depr.	27.6	163%	10.5	57%	6.7	28%	5.2
Int. Exp.	24.0	142%	9.9	74%	5.7	-15%	6.7
Pretax Inc.	21.4	NM	21.6	26%	17.2	15%	14.9
Eff. Tax Rate	47%	—	42%	—	38%	—	42%
Net Inc.	11.4	-10%	12.6	19%	10.6	23%	8.6

Balance Sheet & Other Fin. Data (Million $)

	1994	1993	1992	1991	1990	1989
Cash	32.1	31.7	4.2	9.7	0.6	2.8
Curr. Assets	139	91.8	46.2	40.8	31.2	35.6
Total Assets	535	302	193	157	130	137
Curr. Liab.	78.1	34.5	28.0	21.9	24.0	27.2
LT Debt	202	166	79.8	65.7	83.0	93.2
Common Eqty.	205	76.0	61.9	59.5	13.8	10.2
Total Cap.	439	261	160	130	101	107
Cap. Exp.	20.5	69.1	59.3	7.1	2.6	4.6
Cash Flow	39.0	23.1	17.3	13.8	8.8	7.0

Ratio Analysis

	1994	1993	1992	1991	1990	1989
Curr. Ratio	1.8	2.7	1.6	1.9	1.3	1.3
% LT Debt of Cap.	46.1	63.8	49.9	50.4	82.0	87.5
% Net Inc.of Revs.	2.4	5.3	6.0	6.2	2.8	0.9
% Ret. on Assets	2.2	5.1	6.0	4.2	2.7	0.7
% Ret. on Equity	6.8	18.2	17.3	20.0	30.3	9.5

Dividend Data —No cash dividends have been paid. The company intends to retain earnings for use in its business and, therefore, does not expect to pay cash dividends in the foreseeable future. A four-for-three stock split was effected in December 1992 and a three-for-two split in November 1993. A "poison pill" stock purchase rights plan was adopted in September 1995.

Data as orig. reptd.; bef. results of disc. opers. and/or spec. items. Per share data adj. for stk. divs. as of ex-div. date. E-Estimated. NA-Not Available. NM-Not Meaningful. NR-Not Ranked.

Office—3707 FM 1960 West, Suite 500, Houston, TX 77068-5704. **Tel**—(713) 537-5230. **Fax**—(713) 537-9265. **Chrmn**—R. E. Ragsdale. **Pres & CEO**—E. T. Chaney. **EVP & COO**—M. S. Rash. **SVP, CFO-Fin & Investor Contact**—Deborah G. Moffett. **Dirs**—E. T. Chaney, T. P. Cooper, M. R. Ferguson, G. O. Johnson, J. T. McAfee Jr., R. E. Ragsdale, K. W. Slayden, D. L. Steffy. **Transfer Agent & Registrar**—Society National Bank, Houston. **Incorporated** in Delaware in 1985. **Empl**-7,000. **S&P Analyst:** Philip J. Birbara

Compression Labs

NASDAQ Symbol **CLIX**
In S&P SmallCap 600

06-OCT-95

Industry:
Electronics/Electric

Summary: This company is a leader in videoconferencing and video broadcast systems utilizing Compressed Digital Video technology.

Quantitative Evaluations

Outlook
(1 Lowest—5 Highest)
• **NA**

Fair Value
• **NA**

Risk
• **High**

Earn./Div. Rank
• **C**

Technical Eval.
• **Bullish** since 9/95

Rel. Strength Rank
(1 Lowest—99 Highest)
• **14**

Insider Activity
• **NA**

Recent Price • 7⅞
52 Wk Range • 11⅜-6⅛

Yield • Nil
12-Mo. P/E • NM

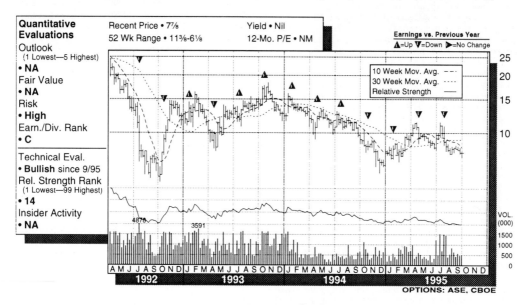

Earnings vs. Previous Year
▲=Up ▼=Down ▶=No Change

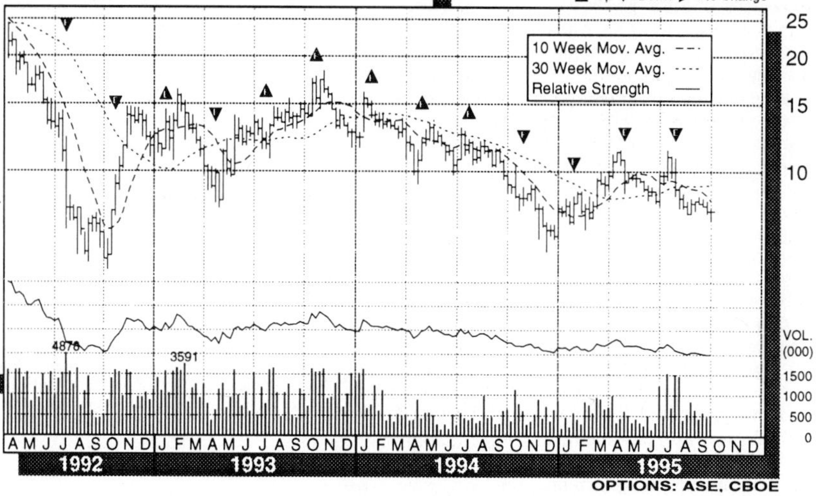

OPTIONS: ASE, CBOE

Business Profile - 06-OCT-95

CLIX is a recognized leader in the manufacture of video communications systems based on CDV technology, which compresses the data required to transmit digital video signals, reducing the cost and the time of transmitting these signals. In order to maintain and expand its market position, the company focuses on maintaining leadership in CDV technology, developing products compatible with industry standards, and expanding product offerings.

Operational Review - 06-OCT-95

Revenues in the first half of 1995 decreased 1.5%, year to year, as a decline in sales of broadcast products outweighed increased sales of videoconferencing products. Results were hurt by a less favorable product mix in the broadcast market, and by lower selling prices in the videoconferencing market in the first quarter. A net loss of $0.14 a share replaced net income of $0.04.

Stock Performance - 29-SEP-95

In the past 30 trading days, CLIX's shares have increased 2%, compared to a 5% rise in the S&P 500. Average trading volume for the past five days was 97,600 shares, compared with the 40-day moving average of 108,969 shares.

Key Stock Statistics

Dividend Rate/Share	Nil	Shareholders	1,100
Shs. outstg. (M)	15.3	Market cap. (B)	$0.117
Avg. daily vol. (M)	0.105	Inst. holdings	37%
Tang. Bk. Value/Share	5.84	Insider holdings	NA
Beta	1.92		

Value of $10,000 invested 5 years ago: $ 8,289

Fiscal Year Ending Dec. 31

	1995	% Change	1994	% Change	1993	% Change
Revenues (Million $)						
1Q	40.05	6%	37.79	51%	25.02	18%
2Q	38.40	-8%	41.84	18%	35.60	32%
3Q	—	—	38.92	1%	38.47	35%
4Q	—	—	38.43	-9%	42.24	35%
Yr.	—	—	157.0	11%	141.3	31%
Income (Million $)						
1Q	-2.09	NM	0.03	NM	-3.29	NM
2Q	0.10	-82%	0.57	NM	-0.99	NM
3Q	—	—	-0.99	NM	0.25	NM
4Q	—	—	0.50	-7%	0.54	NM
Yr.	—	—	0.11	NM	-3.48	NM
Earnings Per Share ($)						
1Q	-0.14	—	Nil	—	-0.29	NM
2Q	0.01	-75%	0.04	NM	-0.09	NM
3Q	—	—	-0.07	NM	0.02	—
4Q	—	—	0.03	-25%	0.04	NM
Yr.	—	—	0.01	NM	-0.30	NM

Next earnings report expected: early November

Compression Labs

Business Summary - 06-OCT-95

Compression Labs, Inc., is a leader in the design and manufacture of visual communication products based on Compressed Digital Video (CDV) technology. The company uses proprietary and industry standard algorithms to compress the data required to transmit digital video and audio signals, thereby reducing the time and cost of data transmission. Its technology is used for signals transmitted by microwave, terrestrial, satellite, and cable systems.

The company operates in two major business segments: interactive videoconferencing products and broadcast products. Its line of videoconferencing systems offer two-way, full color, motion videoconferencing using a range of different bandwidths. Major products are the Rembrandt II/VP large group video codec product line, the Radiance family of prepackaged large group videoconferencing systems, and the eclipse small and mid range group videoconference systems; broadcast products include the SpectrumSaver digital broadcast television systems and the Magnitude family of broadcast video products. Videoconferencing and broadcast products accounted for 72% and 20% of revenues in 1994, respectively.

The Rembrandt product, introduced in 1991, uses CLIX's proprietary CDV technology. It was the first codec to provide a full range of functions (a codec is required at each site of a videoconference to perform both coding and decoding functions). In additon to Rembrandt's range of features, the company believes that its proprietary algorithms enable its products to provide superior picture quality. Prices range from $34,000 to $47,500.

The company has formed strategic relationships with American Telephone and Telegraph, Bell Atlantic, Norstan, Pacific Bell and Sprint/North Supply to offer domestic customers turnkey videoconferencing services. Internationally, CLIX has distribution arrangements with Internet Video Communications (UK), Keytech S.A. (South America), J S TELECOM (France), and Deutsch Telekom (Germany).

Multimedia and personal video products, which accounted for less than 8% of revenues in 1994, include the Videophone and the Cameo Personal Video System, a computer-based video telephone product.

Important Developments

Sep. '95—CLIX signed an agreement with Northamber PLC, the largest U.K.-owned distributor of computing, office equipment, networking, and communications products, to distribute the company's eclipse videoconferencing products. Separately, CLIX announced the opening of offices in Melbourne, Australia, and Tokyo, Japan, to market videoconferencing products in the Asia/Pacific market.

Capitalization

Long Term Debt: $1,519,000 incl. capital lease obligs. (6/95).

Per Share Data ($)

(Year Ended Dec. 31)

	1994	1993	1992	1991	1990	1989
Tangible Bk. Val.	5.93	5.21	4.99	5.21	4.16	3.87
Cash Flow	0.80	0.51	0.30	-1.14	0.63	0.36
Earnings	0.01	-0.30	-0.29	-1.55	0.27	0.10
Dividends	Nil	Nil	Nil	Nil	Nil	Nil
Payout Ratio	Nil	Nil	Nil	Nil	Nil	Nil
Prices - High	16 1/8	18 3/8	35 1/4	29 1/4	16 3/8	11 1/4
- Low	6 1/8	8	5 1/2	8 1/4	9 1/4	3 1/8
P/E Ratio - High	NM	NM	NM	NM	61	NM
- Low	NM	NM	NM	NM	34	NM

Income Statement Analysis (Million $)

	1994	%Chg	1993	%Chg	1992	%Chg	1991
Revs.	157	11%	141	31%	108	49%	72.6
Oper. Inc.	12.7	105%	6.2	85%	3.4	-43%	5.9
Depr.	12.0	27%	9.5	42%	6.7	65%	4.0
Int. Exp.	0.8	-4%	0.8	43%	0.6	41%	0.4
Pretax Inc.	0.1	NM	-3.5	NM	-3.3	NM	-15.1
Eff. Tax Rate	NM	—	NM	—	NM	—	NM
Net Inc.	0.1	NM	-3.5	NM	-3.3	NM	-15.1

Balance Sheet & Other Fin. Data (Million $)

	1994	1993	1992	1991	1990	1989
Cash	11.3	20.5	13.4	14.4	4.7	10.5
Curr. Assets	98.0	94.6	69.8	67.3	40.7	29.2
Total Assets	132	125	94.7	82.5	55.9	39.8
Curr. Liab.	44.2	42.6	37.9	24.6	16.7	8.5
LT Debt	0.5	1.0	Nil	Nil	4.4	0.3
Common Eqty.	87.0	66.4	56.9	57.9	34.8	31.0
Total Cap.	87.5	82.4	56.9	57.9	39.1	31.2
Cap. Exp.	9.4	8.3	10.2	3.9	5.1	3.9
Cash Flow	12.1	6.0	3.4	-11.1	6.1	3.3

Ratio Analysis

	1994	1993	1992	1991	1990	1989
Curr. Ratio	2.2	2.2	1.8	2.7	2.4	3.4
% LT Debt of Cap.	0.6	1.2	Nil	Nil	11.2	0.8
% Net Inc.of Revs.	0.1	NM	NM	NM	5.0	3.1
% Ret. on Assets	0.1	NM	NM	NM	5.3	2.4
% Ret. on Equity	0.1	NM	NM	NM	7.7	3.0

Dividend Data —No cash has been paid.

Data as orig. reptd.; bef. results of disc. opers. and/or spec. items. Per share data adj. for stk. divs. as of ex-div. date. E-Estimated. NA-Not Available. NM-Not Meaningful. NR-Not Ranked.

Office—2860 Junction Ave., San Jose, CA 95134. **Tel**—(408) 435-3000. **Chrmn, Pres & CEO**—J. E. Tyson. **SVP, CFO, Secy & Investor Contact**—W. A. Berry. **Dirs**—A. G. Anderson, R. J. Casale, E. E. David, Jr., R. B. Liepold, J. E. Tyson, D. A. Wegmann. **Registrar & Transfer Agent**—First National Bank of Boston. **Incorporated** in California in 1976; reincorporated in Delaware in 1987. **Empl**-549. **S&P Analyst:** Mike Cavanaugh

STANDARD & POOR'S
STOCK REPORTS

CompUSA

NYSE Symbol **CPU**
In S&P SmallCap 600

24-AUG-95 **Industry:** Retail Stores

Summary: This company is the leading operator of large format computer superstores, with 86 stores open as of August 1995, in 41 major metropolitan areas of the U.S.

Quantitative Evaluations
Outlook (1 Lowest—5 Highest) • **5**
Fair Value • **40⅞**
Risk • **High**
Earn./Div. Rank • **NR**
Technical Eval. • **Neutral** since 12/94
Rel. Strength Rank (1 Lowest—99 Highest) • **88**
Insider Activity • **NA**

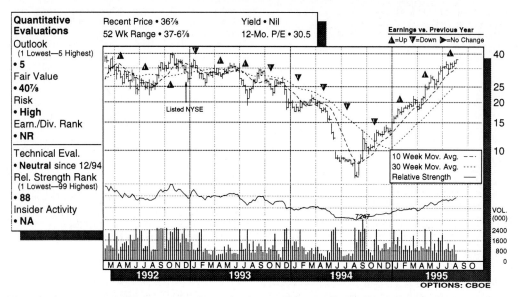

Recent Price • 36⅞
52 Wk Range • 37-6⅞
Yield • Nil
12-Mo. P/E • 30.5

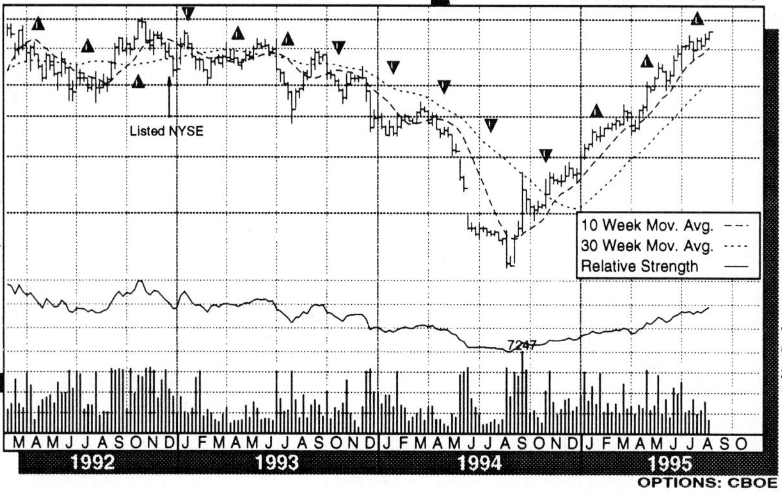

OPTIONS: CBOE

Business Profile - 24-AUG-95

This leading operator of computer superstores combines a high level of customer service and technical support with aggressive pricing. CompUSA is seeking to capitalize on its advantage as a low-cost supplier of computer products by opening new superstores in most major markets; it now has 86 stores in operation. Future results should continue to benefit from a long-term strengthening in demand for computer products, with an added boost from the August 1995 launch of Windows 95.

Operational Review - 24-AUG-95

Revenues for fiscal 1994-95 (preliminary) advanced 31% from those of the prior year, reflecting new stores in operation and a 10% gain in same-store sales. Gross margins widened. A 66% drop in pre-opening expenses, combined with a 3.8% decline in net interest and other expense, led to a pretax profit, versus a pretax loss (which partly reflected a $9.9 million restructuring charge). Earnings of $1.21 a share based on 4.5% more shares, contrasted with a loss of $0.92.

Stock Performance - 18-AUG-95

In the past 30 trading days, CPU's shares have increased 10%, compared to a 0.51% rise in the S&P 500. Average trading volume for the past five days was 106,960 shares, compared with the 40-day moving average of 219,418 shares.

Key Stock Statistics

Dividend Rate/Share	Nil	Shareholders	2,700
Shs. outstg. (M)	18.6	Market cap. (B)	$0.690
Avg. daily vol. (M)	0.182	Inst. holdings	61%
Tang. Bk. Value/Share	7.71	Insider holdings	NA
Beta	NA		

Value of $10,000 invested 5 years ago: NA

Fiscal Year Ending Jun. 30

	1995	% Change	1994	% Change	1993	% Change
Revenues (Million $)						
1Q	585.7	34%	436.6	66%	263.4	53%
2Q	761.8	42%	536.9	65%	324.5	61%
3Q	776.1	30%	599.1	63%	366.5	70%
4Q	689.5	20%	573.2	48%	387.5	63%
Yr.	2,813	31%	2,146	60%	1,342	62%
Income (Million $)						
1Q	-3.15	NM	-0.99	—	—	—
2Q	12.10	NM	-5.52	NM	2.96	-19%
3Q	12.10	NM	3.35	-22%	4.28	35%
4Q	4.29	NM	-13.61	NM	3.79	67%
Yr.	22.96	NM	-16.76	NM	12.31	20%
Earnings Per Share ($)						
1Q	-0.17	NM	-0.05	NM	0.08	60%
2Q	0.51	NM	-0.30	NM	0.16	-53%
3Q	0.63	NM	0.18	-22%	0.23	21%
4Q	0.22	NM	-0.74	NM	0.20	43%
Yr.	1.21	NM	-0.92	NM	0.67	-6%

Next earnings report expected: late October

Business Summary - 24-AUG-95

CompUSA is the leading operator of large format computer superstores in the U.S. The company opened its first retail store in April 1985 and its first superstore in April 1988. At August 9, 1995, the company was operating 86 superstores in 41 metropolitan areas in 26 states. The number of stores at fiscal year end in recent years:

1994	76
1993	48
1992	28
1991	20
1990	10

The company offers thousands of microcomputer hardware, software and related products in its 18,000 to 36,500 square foot superstores at prices substantially below manufacturers' suggested retail prices. The company combines its large computer superstore format with a high level of customer service, technical support amd classroom training.

Hardware products, which constitute the majority of the company's sales, include desktop and portable microcomputers, peripherals such as printers, modems, monitors and data storage devices, add-on circuit boards, connectivity products and certain business machines. Primary brands sold in this category include Apple, Compaq, Dell, Epson, Hewlett-Packard, Maxtor, Packard Bell, Sony, Texas Instruments and Toshiba. The company also sells its own brand of hardware products under the name Compudyne. During fiscal 1993's third quarter, CPU outsourced the majority of the assembly of its Compudyne brand computers to a third party manufacturer, but still performs limited assembly operations in its stores on some of them to configure them to customer requirements.

CPU also sells approximately 2,000 different software packages, including both IBM-compatible and Apple software packages. Primary brands include Borland, Lotus, Microsoft, Software Publishing and WordPerfect.

Accessories sold by CPU include a broad range of computer-related items and supplies such as diskettes, printer products, mice and other input devices, connectors and furniture.

CPU also focuses on sales to business, government and institutions.

Important Developments

Aug. '95—CompUSA filed a registration statement with the SEC for a proposed public offering of 1.75 million common shares. The company intends to use the net proceeds to finance new store openings, for working capital requirements and for general corporate purposes.

Capitalization

Long Term Debt: $117,500,000 (6/24/95), incl. capital lease obligations.

Per Share Data ($) (Year Ended Jun. 30)

	1995	1994	1993	1992	1991	1990
Tangible Bk. Val.	NA	7.71	8.58	5.31	-3.61	NA
Cash Flow	NA	-0.10	1.14	1.07	-1.17	0.26
Earnings	1.21	-0.92	0.67	0.71	-1.58	0.16
Dividends	Nil	Nil	Nil	Nil	Nil	Nil
Payout Ratio	Nil	Nil	Nil	Nil	Nil	Nil
Prices - High	38¼	22¼	37	40½	23¾	NA
- Low	14¾	6¾	19	19¼	15	NA
P/E Ratio - High	32	NM	55	57	NM	NA
- Low	12	NM	28	27	NM	NA

Income Statement Analysis (Million $)

	1994	%Chg	1993	%Chg	1992	%Chg	1991
Revs.	2,146	60%	1,342	62%	827	52%	544
Oper. Inc.	15.8	-48%	30.2	71%	17.7	NM	-3.9
Depr.	14.9	72%	8.7	87%	4.6	87%	2.5
Int. Exp.	12.0	NM	2.2	-17%	2.7	-30%	3.8
Pretax Inc.	-19.1	NM	19.8	82%	10.9	NM	-10.2
Eff. Tax Rate	NM	—	38%	—	5.60%	—	NM
Net Inc.	-16.8	NM	12.3	19%	10.3	NM	-9.7

Balance Sheet & Other Fin. Data (Million $)

	1994	1993	1992	1991	1990	1989
Cash	22.5	97.5	12.8	1.6	3.6	NA
Curr. Assets	392	375	178	100	52.0	NA
Total Assets	495	438	208	121	64.0	NA
Curr. Liab.	196	163	121	78.0	40.0	NA
LT Debt	153	115	3.4	29.8	20.7	NA
Common Eqty.	146	159	83.5	-16.9	1.5	NA
Total Cap.	299	275	87.0	42.0	22.2	NA
Cap. Exp.	46.2	32.4	10.3	7.9	6.3	NA
Cash Flow	-1.9	21.0	13.6	-8.5	2.4	NA

Ratio Analysis

	1994	1993	1992	1991	1990	1989
Curr. Ratio	2.0	2.3	1.5	1.3	1.3	NA
% LT Debt of Cap.	51.2	41.9	3.9	70.9	93.2	NA
% Net Inc.of Revs.	NM	0.9	1.2	NM	0.5	NA
% Ret. on Assets	NM	3.6	4.0	NA	NA	NA
% Ret. on Equity	NM	9.5	NM	NA	NA	NA

Dividend Data —The company has not paid dividends. A "poison pill" stock purchase rights plan was adopted in April 1994.

Data as orig. reptd.; bef. results of disc. opers. and/or spec. items. Per share data adj. for stk. divs. as of ex-div. date. E-Estimated. NA-Not Available. NM-Not Meaningful. NR-Not Ranked.

Office—14951 N. Dallas Parkway, Dallas, TX 75240. **Tel**—(214) 383-4000. **Chrmn**—G. Bateman. **Pres & CEO**—J. Halpin. **EVP, CFO & Treas**—J. Skinner. **EVP & COO**—H. Compton. **Investor Contact**—N. Greene-Hunt. **Dirs**—G. H. Bateman, L. J. Berry, W. D. Feldberg, D. Groussman, J. Halpin, L. Mittman, K. J. Roche, E. Weiner. **Transfer Agent & Registrar**—Bank One, Indianapolis. **Incorporated** in Deleware in 1988. **Empl**-7,819. **S&P Analyst:** Maureen C. Carini

STANDARD & POOR'S
STOCK REPORTS

Cone Mills

NYSE Symbol **COE**
In S&P SmallCap 600

01-NOV-95 **Industry:** Textiles

Summary: The world's largest producer of denim fabrics, Cone also makes a variety of other apparel fabrics and sells decorative fabrics and polyurethane foam to home furnishings markets.

Quantitative Evaluations

Outlook
(1 Lowest—5 Highest)
• **3**

Fair Value
• **11⅝**

Risk
• **Low**

Earn./Div. Rank
• **NR**

Technical Eval.
• **Bullish** since 7/95

Rel. Strength Rank
(1 Lowest—99 Highest)
• **10**

Insider Activity
• **Unfavorable**

Recent Price • 11½
52 Wk Range • 14⅜-10⅝
Yield • Nil
12-Mo. P/E • 24.0

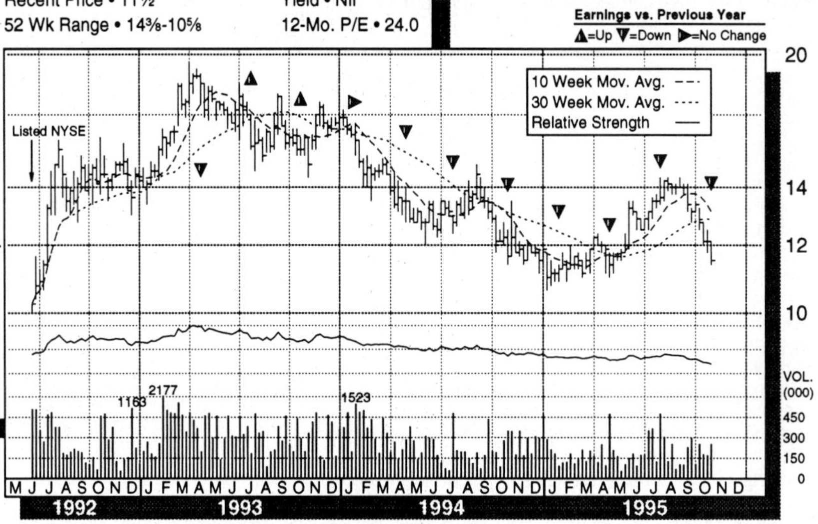

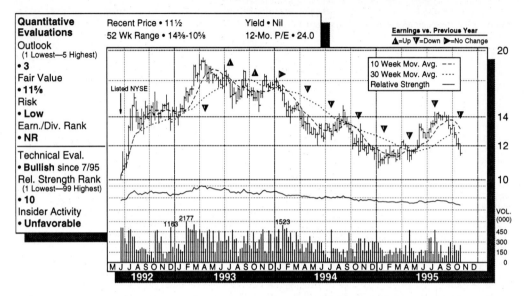

Business Profile - 01-NOV-95

Founded in 1891, this company is the world's largest producer of denim fabrics and the largest commission printer of home furnishings fabrics in North America. It is also the largest domestic exporter of apparel fabrics and a major exporter of printed home furnishings products. Earnings are expected to remain under pressure through the end of 1995, reflecting weak sportswear and decorative print fabrics markets.

Operational Review - 01-NOV-95

Net sales in the first nine months of 1995 advanced 15%, year to year. Declining earnings reflected sharply higher cotton costs, weak home decorative print fabric markets and noncash charges of Mexican affiliates related primarily to the peso devaluation. The lower profits in the decorative print home furnishings market reflected weak furniture markets and customer preferences for fabrics other than prints.

Stock Performance - 27-OCT-95

In the past 30 trading days, COE's shares have declined 14%, compared to a 0.63% fall in the S&P 500. Average trading volume for the past five days was 49,460 shares, compared with the 40-day moving average of 39,790 shares.

Key Stock Statistics

Dividend Rate/Share	Nil	Shareholders	600
Shs. outstg. (M)	27.4	Market cap. (B)	$0.298
Avg. daily vol. (M)	0.042	Inst. holdings	54%
Tang. Bk. Value/Share	5.84	Insider holdings	NA
Beta	NA		

Value of $10,000 invested 5 years ago: NA

Fiscal Year Ending Dec. 31

	1995	% Change	1994	% Change	1993	% Change
Revenues (Million $)						
1Q	226.2	15%	195.9	NM	195.0	12%
2Q	232.9	16%	201.7	NM	202.5	11%
3Q	231.7	14%	203.5	6%	192.6	13%
4Q	—	—	205.1	15%	179.0	NM
Yr.	—	—	806.2	5%	769.2	9%
Income (Million $)						
1Q	3.64	-64%	10.03	-21%	12.62	5%
2Q	-1.59	NM	9.85	-28%	13.67	26%
3Q	5.87	-31%	8.56	-28%	11.81	8%
4Q	—	—	7.32	-36%	11.51	NM
Yr.	—	—	35.75	-28%	49.60	9%
Earnings Per Share ($)						
1Q	0.11	-68%	0.34	-19%	0.42	-21%
2Q	-0.06	NM	0.33	-30%	0.47	4%
3Q	0.19	-32%	0.28	-30%	0.40	14%
4Q	—	—	0.24	-38%	0.39	NM
Yr.	—	—	1.19	-29%	1.68	NM

Next earnings report expected: early February

Cone Mills

Business Summary - 30-OCT-95

Cone Mills is the largest producer of denim fabrics in the world and the largest commission printer of home furnishings fabrics in North America. Industry segment contributions in 1994:

	Sales	Profits
Apparel fabrics	74%	71%
Home furnishings fabrics	26%	29%

The company manufactures a wide variety of denim apparel fabrics (some 500 different styles in 1994), and believes it produces a broader range of fashion denim than any of its competitors. Cone is the largest supplier to Levi Strauss and the sole supplier of denims for Levi's 501 jeans. In 1994, Levi Strauss accounted for 34% of COE's revenues (35% in the preceding year).

COE is also a leading producer of selected specialty fabrics, including plaid and chamois flannel shirting fabrics, specialty print fabrics and two-ply, polyester/rayon uniform and sportswear fabrics.

The company serves the home furnishings market through its Carlisle Finishing Co., John Wolf Decorative Fabrics and Olympic Products Co. divisions. Olympic manufactures polyurethane foam and related products used in upholstered furniture, mattresses, carpet padding and specialty patient care applications. The Raytex division is a leading commission printer of wide fabrics used primarily in home furnishings products. Carlisle is the largest commission printer of home furnishings fabrics in the U.S. John Wolf is a leading designer and marketer of printed and woven fabrics for use in upholstery, draperies and bedspreads. The company completed its screen printing addition in 1994 and expects to add the fourth of five new screen printing machines in 1995.

All manufacturing is performed in the U.S., with sales and marketing activities conducted through a worldwide distribution network. About 30% of Cone's current denim production is exported, with the company's denim products currently sold in over 35 countries. In 1994, sales to unaffiliated foreign customers (primarily in Europe) accounted for 18% of revenues (17% in 1993); export sales represented 18% of sales in 1994.

Important Developments

Oct. '95—The company said it has encountered strong domestic and export denim markets, but has seen weakness in the specialty sportswear and decorative print fabrics markets.

Capitalization

Long Term Debt: $161,822,000 (10/1/95).
Class A Preferred Stock: 383,948 shs. ($100 par); nonvoting. Almost all held by Cone Mills ESOP.

Per Share Data ($) (Year Ended Dec. 31)

	1994	1993	1992	1991	1990	1989
Tangible Bk. Val.	5.84	6.19	4.52	3.35	NA	NA
Cash Flow	2.02	2.43	2.50	1.07	NA	NA
Earnings	1.19	1.68	1.67	0.29	NA	NA
Dividends	Nil	Nil	Nil	NA	NA	NA
Payout Ratio	Nil	Nil	Nil	NA	NA	NA
Prices - High	17¼	19⅝	16	NA	NA	NA
- Low	11⅛	13⅜	10	NA	NA	NA
P/E Ratio - High	14	12	10	NA	NA	NA
- Low	9	8	6	NA	NA	NA

Income Statement Analysis (Million $)

	1994	%Chg	1993	%Chg	1992	%Chg	1991
Revs.	806	5%	769	9%	705	11%	633
Oper. Inc.	86.0	-20%	107	9%	98.0	75%	56.0
Depr.	23.3	11%	21.0	5%	20.0	-2%	20.4
Int. Exp.	7.9	13%	7.0	-36%	10.9	-43%	19.0
Pretax Inc.	55.5	-30%	79.5	13%	70.2	NM	19.8
Eff. Tax Rate	36%	—	38%	—	35%	—	38%
Net Inc.	35.8	-28%	49.6	9%	45.4	NM	12.2

Balance Sheet & Other Fin. Data (Million $)

	1994	1993	1992	1991	1990	1989
Cash	1.2	0.5	7.3	6.4	NA	NA
Curr. Assets	213	202	216	259	NA	NA
Total Assets	524	432	402	443	NA	NA
Curr. Liab.	118	104	121	127	NA	NA
LT Debt	126	77.0	77.0	138	NA	NA
Common Eqty.	198	172	125	135	NA	NA
Total Cap.	400	324	277	312	NA	NA
Cap. Exp.	37.5	38.7	25.4	NA	NA	NA
Cash Flow	56.3	67.8	60.8	28.0	NA	NA

Ratio Analysis

	1994	1993	1992	1991	1990	1989
Curr. Ratio	1.8	1.9	1.8	2.0	NA	NA
% LT Debt of Cap.	31.5	23.8	27.6	44.1	NA	NA
% Net Inc.of Revs.	4.4	6.4	6.4	1.9	NA	NA
% Ret. on Assets	7.5	11.9	6.3	NA	NA	NA
% Ret. on Equity	18.0	31.5	49.3	NA	NA	NA

Dividend Data —No cash has been paid.

Data as orig. reptd.; bef. results of disc. opers. and/or spec. items. Per share data adj. for stk. divs. as of ex-div. date. E-Estimated. NA-Not Available. NM-Not Meaningful. NR-Not Ranked.

Office—1201 Maple St., Greensboro, NC 27405. **Tel**—(910) 379-6220. **Chrmn**—D. L. Trogdon. **Pres & CEO**—J. P. Danahy. **VP-CFO**—J. L. Bakane. **Treas & Investor Contact**—David E. Bray. **Secy**—T. L. Weatherford. **Dirs**—J. L. Bakane, D. R. Bray, J. P. Danahy, L. W. Gaulden, J. C. Kimmel, C. M. Reid, J. W. Rosenblum, D. L. Trogdon, R. S. Vetack, B. W. Willis III. **Transfer Agent & Registrar**—First Union National Bank of North Carolina, Charlotte, N.C. **Incorporated** in North Carolina. **Empl**-8,100. **S&P Analyst:** Philip D. Wohl

Connecticut Energy

NYSE Symbol **CNE**
In S&P SmallCap 600

12-OCT-95 **Industry:** Utilities-Gas

Summary: This holding company's principal subsidiary, Southern Connecticut Gas Co., provides natural gas to 155,000 customers in Fairfield, New Haven, and Middlesex counties.

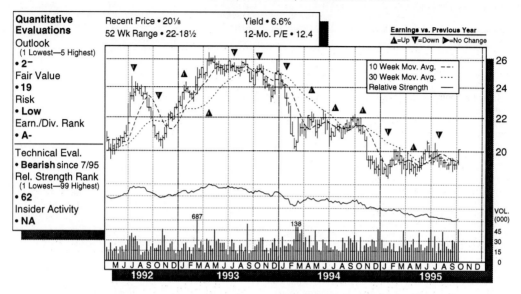

Quantitative Evaluations

Outlook
(1 Lowest—5 Highest)
• **2-**

Fair Value
• **19**

Risk
• **Low**

Earn./Div. Rank
• **A-**

Technical Eval.
• **Bearish** since 7/95

Rel. Strength Rank
(1 Lowest—99 Highest)
• **62**

Insider Activity
• **NA**

Recent Price • 20⅛
52 Wk Range • 22-18½
Yield • 6.6%
12-Mo. P/E • 12.4

Earnings vs. Previous Year
▲=Up ▼=Down ▶=No Change

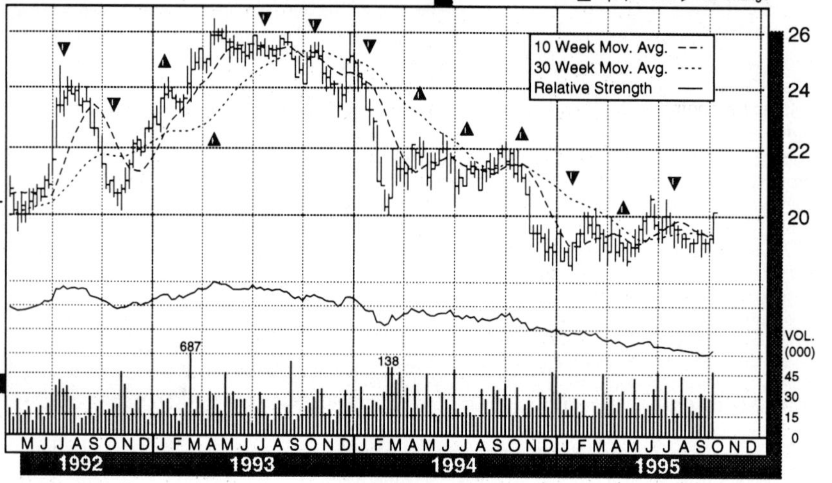

Business Profile - 12-OCT-95

CNE's Southern Connecticut service territory has experienced slow economic growth in recent years, but has benefited from a 6.6% rate increase since December 1993. The company has been able to increase load growth primarily through the conversion of homes to gas heat. The Weather Normalization Adjustment supported margins during the first nine months of 1995 and should enhance long term stability by adjusting the amounts billed to customers to offset the effects of abnormal weather on volume.

Operational Review - 12-OCT-95

Net income for the nine months ended June 30, 1995, rose 7.2% year to year, primarily reflecting improved margins due to higher interruptible sales volumes, made possible by competitive gas prices and excess supply caused by warmer weather, plus added transportation volumes. The warm weather led to a 12% decrease in firm sales volume but translated into upward adjustments in cash collections under the Weather Normalization clause, which outweighed the downward adjustments for lower gas costs.

Stock Performance - 06-OCT-95

In the past 30 trading days, CNE's shares have increased 5%, compared to a 4% rise in the S&P 500. Average trading volume for the past five days was 13,320 shares, compared with the 40-day moving average of 6,138 shares.

Key Stock Statistics

Dividend Rate/Share	1.30	Shareholders	12,100
Shs. outstg. (M)	8.8	Market cap. (B)	$0.174
Avg. daily vol. (M)	0.008	Inst. holdings	21%
Tang. Bk. Value/Share	14.97	Insider holdings	NA
Beta	0.22		

Value of $10,000 invested 5 years ago: $ 16,193

Fiscal Year Ending Sep. 30

	1995	% Change	1994	% Change	1993	% Change
Revenues (Million $)						
1Q	65.52	-2%	66.71	4%	64.20	15%
2Q	103.3	-8%	111.8	22%	91.61	2%
3Q	39.76	8%	36.84	9%	33.78	-4%
4Q	—	—	25.49	10%	23.21	4%
Yr.	—	—	240.9	13%	212.8	5%
Income (Million $)						
1Q	4.94	-1%	5.00	-14%	5.84	43%
2Q	15.72	14%	13.75	17%	11.71	10%
3Q	-1.99	NM	-1.34	NM	-2.27	NM
4Q	—	—	-4.57	NM	-4.23	NM
Yr.	—	—	12.84	16%	11.05	8%
Earnings Per Share ($)						
1Q	0.57	-15%	0.67	-16%	0.80	40%
2Q	1.79	1%	1.77	11%	1.59	6%
3Q	-0.23	NM	-0.16	NM	-0.31	NM
4Q	—	—	-0.53	NM	-0.57	NM
Yr.	—	—	1.58	5%	1.50	5%

Next earnings report expected: early November

Connecticut Energy

12-OCT-95

Business Summary - 11-OCT-95

Connecticut Energy Corporation is a holding company whose main subsidiary, Southern Connecticut Gas (SG), is engaged in the retail distribution of natural gas for residential, commercial and industrial uses. About 155,000 customers are served, primarily in 22 towns, including the urban communities of Bridgeport and New Haven, in an area along the Southern Connecticut coast from Westport to Old Saybrook. SG is also authorized to lay mains and sell gas in an additional ten towns in the service area. In December 1993, CNE was granted a $13.4 million rate increase.

Revenue contributions by class of customer in recent fiscal years were as follows:

	1994	1993	1992
Residential	61%	62%	63%
Commercial	21%	22%	22%
Firm industrial	9%	9%	9%
Interruptible	9%	7%	5%
Other (incl. subsidiaries)	1%	---	1%

Gas sales volume (including gas delivered but not yet billed at year end) in MMcf. (million cu. ft.) and average cost of gas per Mcf. (thousand cu. ft.) sold in recent fiscal years:

	1994	1993	1992
Gas sold	34.3	29.1	29.8
Cost of gas	$4.22	$4.30	$4.02

In fiscal 1994, firm sales represented approximately 91% of operating revenues and about 66% of total gas throughput. Firm sales to industrial customers are likely to continue at a smaller percentage of future sales because of the changing character of the local economy and continuing regulatory developments affecting the natural gas industry.

In recent years, new construction in the service area has slowed dramatically, and focus has been placed on adding load along existing mains, which genrally requires a lower capital outlay. Less than 50% of the residences along SG's mains heat with natural gas, and the conversion of these homes to natural gas heat has been a major factor in increased load growth during recent years. In the residential heating market, during fiscal 1994, heating conversions accounted for 61% of new customer additions.

Important Developments

Jul. '95—SG said that total volumes of gas sold in the third quarter and first nine months of fiscal 1995 grew 141% and 55%, respectively, primarily from sales to interruptible customers and transportation volumes under a July 1994 contract with Connecticut Power and Light Co.

Capitalization

Long Term Debt: $119,776,000 (6/95).

Per Share Data ($) (Year Ended Sep. 30)

	1994	1993	1992	1991	1990	1989
Tangible Bk. Val.	13.72	12.47	11.91	12.36	11.74	11.98
Earnings	1.58	1.50	1.43	1.38	1.12	1.28
Dividends	1.29	1.28	1.27	1.24	1.23	1.20
Payout Ratio	82%	85%	88%	90%	110%	94%
Prices - High	25	26½	24¾	20⅜	18	18⅞
- Low	18⅝	22½	18⅞	14¼	14½	14
P/E Ratio - High	16	18	17	15	16	15
- Low	12	15	13	10	13	11

Income Statement Analysis (Million $)

	1994	%Chg	1993	%Chg	1992	%Chg	1991
Revs.	241	13%	213	5%	203	13%	179
Depr.	13.0	7%	12.1	7%	11.3	8%	10.5
Maint.	4.0	9%	3.7	1%	3.7	1%	3.6
Fxd. Chgs. Cov.	2.6	13%	2.3	6%	2.2	-10%	2.4
Constr. Credits	Nil	—	Nil	—	Nil	—	Nil
Eff. Tax Rate	30%	—	26%	—	24%	—	39%
Net Inc.	12.8	15%	11.1	9%	10.2	13%	9.0

Balance Sheet & Other Fin. Data (Million $)

	1994	1993	1992	1991	1990	1989
Gross Prop.	332	314	294	274	255	242
Cap. Exp.	26.7	26.1	22.8	20.4	23.4	23.7
Net Prop.	234	222	210	199	189	181
Capitalization:						
LT Debt	120	121	94.1	87.4	91.5	79.7
% LT Debt	49	55	50	49	55	51
Pfd.	NA	0.6	0.7	0.7	0.8	0.8
% Pfd.	NA	0.30	0.40	0.40	0.50	0.60
Common	126	100	92.6	88.6	74.4	75.0
% Common	51	45	49	50	45	48
Total Cap.	301	239	205	194	182	170

Ratio Analysis

	1994	1993	1992	1991	1990	1989
Oper. Ratio	89.6	89.1	89.0	88.9	90.3	80.8
% Earn. on Net Prop.	11.0	10.7	10.9	10.2	9.1	9.9
% Ret. on Revs.	5.3	5.2	5.0	5.0	4.0	4.6
% Ret. On Invest.Cap	9.1	10.2	10.9	10.4	9.7	10.1
% Return On Com.Eqty	11.4	11.5	11.3	11.0	9.3	10.6

Dividend Data —Dividends have been paid by CNE and its predecessors since 1850. A dividend reinvestment plan is available.

Amt. of Div. $	Date Decl.	Ex-Div. Date	Stock of Record	Payment Date
0.325	Nov. 29	Dec. 05	Dec. 09	Dec. 30 '94
0.325	Jan. 31	Mar. 13	Mar. 17	Mar. 31 '95
0.325	May. 23	Jun. 14	Jun. 16	Jun. 30 '95
0.325	Jul. 25	Sep. 13	Sep. 15	Sep. 29 '95

Data as orig. reptd.; bef. results of disc opers. and/or spec. items. Per share data adj. for stk. divs. as of ex-div. date. E-Estimated. NA-Not Available. NM-Not Meaningful. NR-Not Ranked.

Office—855 Main St., Bridgeport, CT 06604. **Tel**—(203) 579-1732. **Chrmn, Pres & CEO**—J. R. Crespo. **VP-Fin, CFO & Treas**—C. A. Forest. **VP-Secy**—J. R. Tiano. **Investor Contact**—Judith E. Falango. **Dirs**—H. Chauncey Jr., J. P. Comer, J. R. Crespo, R. M. Hoyt, R. F. Freeman, P. H. Johnson, N. M. Marsilius III, S. M. Sugden, C. D. Turner, H. B. Wasserman. **Transfer Agent & Registrar**—First National Bank of Boston. **Incorporated** in Connecticut in 1967; reincorporated in Connecticut in 1979. **Empl**-572. **S&P Analyst:** J. Santoriello

Consumers Water

NASDAQ Symbol **CONW**
In S&P SmallCap 600

16-OCT-95

Industry:
Utilities-Water

Summary: This utility holding company owns nine water utilities with 27 separate systems providing water services to over 221,000 customers in Ohio, Illinois and four northeastern states.

Quantitative Evaluations

Outlook
(1 Lowest—5 Highest)
• **NA**
Fair Value
• **NA**
Risk
• **Low**
Earn./Div. Rank
• **B+**

Technical Eval.
• **Bearish** since 10/93
Rel. Strength Rank
(1 Lowest—99 Highest)
• **47**
Insider Activity
• **NA**

Recent Price • 16½
52 Wk Range • 18½-14½
Yield • 7.3%
12-Mo. P/E • 12.6

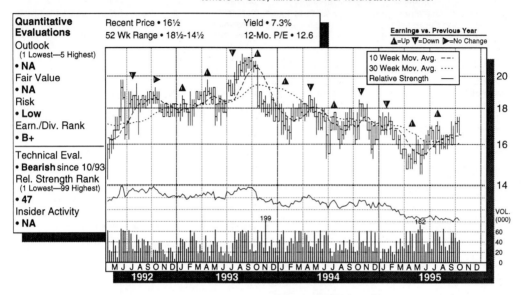

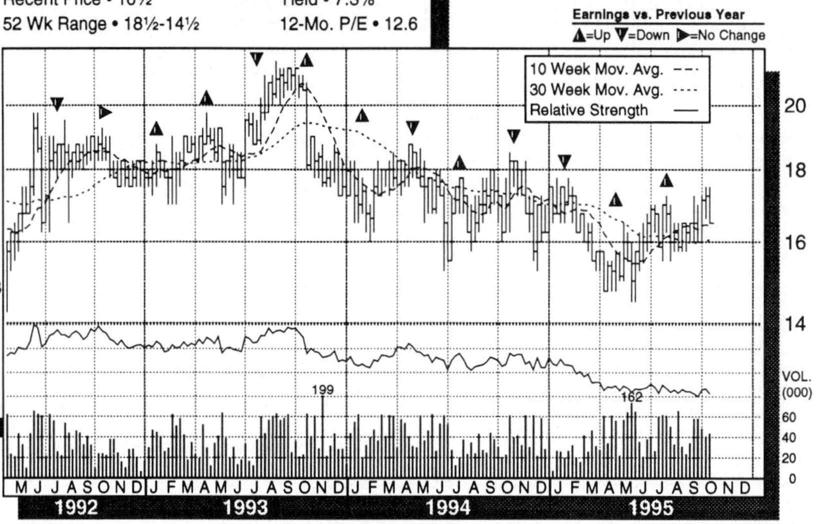

Business Profile - 13-OCT-95

Consumers Water is a utility holding company with nine water utilities in Ohio, Illinois, and four northeastern states. CONW has acquired seven water systems over the past five years. Gains on the sale of property pushed otherwise negative earnings to the plus side in the first half of 1995. Unsuccessful bidding and low margin contracts for the Consumers Applied Technologies subsidiary hurt operating earnings, and led to a shift in focus toward higher margin technical and engineering work.

Operational Review - 16-OCT-95

Operating revenues for the first half of 1995 rose 8.6% year to year, primarily due to a 7.5% rise in water utility operations due to rate increases. Utility operating margins improved, but overall margins narrowed as Consumers Applied Technologies completed its meter installation work for the City of New York but bid unsuccessfully for additional New York City meter projects. Following higher interest expense on increased debt balances, earnings before gains on property sales fell 7.8%.

Stock Performance - 13-OCT-95

In the past 30 trading days, CONW's shares have increased 2%, compared to a 4% rise in the S&P 500. Average trading volume for the past five days was 8,580 shares, compared with the 40-day moving average of 8,531 shares.

Key Stock Statistics

Dividend Rate/Share	1.20	Shareholders	6,000
Shs. outstg. (M)	8.4	Market cap. (B)	$0.139
Avg. daily vol. (M)	0.009	Inst. holdings	18%
Tang. Bk. Value/Share	12.22	Insider holdings	NA
Beta	0.47		

Value of $10,000 invested 5 years ago: $ 13,414

Fiscal Year Ending Dec. 31

	1995	% Change	1994	% Change	1993	% Change
Revenues (Million $)						
1Q	22.53	8%	20.82	NM	20.94	4%
2Q	25.52	9%	23.45	4%	22.50	-1%
3Q	—	—	25.17	3%	24.50	1%
4Q	—	—	23.90	13%	21.12	-6%
Yr.	—	—	93.34	5%	89.08	NM
Income (Million $)						
1Q	1.60	42%	1.13	-46%	2.11	92%
2Q	2.89	13%	2.56	47%	1.74	-23%
3Q	—	—	3.29	-9%	3.61	31%
4Q	—	—	3.02	-33%	4.54	139%
Yr.	—	—	10.00	-17%	12.00	50%
Earnings Per Share ($)						
1Q	0.19	36%	0.14	-52%	0.29	81%
2Q	0.35	13%	0.31	29%	0.24	-25%
3Q	—	—	0.40	-20%	0.50	28%
4Q	—	—	0.37	-38%	0.60	122%
Yr.	—	—	1.22	-25%	1.63	43%

Next earnings report expected: early November

Consumers Water

Business Summary - 16-OCT-95

Consumers Water Company supplies water from 27 separate systems to 221,000 industrial, commercial and residential customers in six states. The company also owns 100% of Consumers Applied Technologies, Inc., formerly C/P Utility Services, a provider of technical services to utilities.

Contributions to water revenues by class of customer in recent years were as follows:

	1994	1993
Residential	65%	65%
Commercial	13%	13%
Fire protection	13%	13%
Industrial	9%	9%

The company owned 3,204 miles of mains at year-end 1994. Consumers owns directly or indirectly at least 90% of the voting stock of nine water companies, the largest of which, Ohio Water Service Co., accounted for 33% of water utility revenues in 1993. Other subsidiaries operate in Illinois, Pennsylvania, New Jersey, New Hampshire and Maine.

Of the 27 primary water systems, 14 have surface supplies (lakes, ponds and streams) as their source of supply; 11 obtain water principally or entirely from wells; two obtain their water supplies from adjacent systems, one of which is an affiliated utility. Less than 5% of CONW subsidiaries' water usage is purchased from other systems. In general, the company considers the surface and well supplies at its subsidiaries to be adequate for anticipating average daily demand and normal peak demand.

During 1994, Maine Water Co. and Wanakah Water Co. merged into Camden & Rockland Water Co. The name of the surviving corporation was then changed to Consumers Maine Water Co. In October 1994, the Damariscotta & Newcastle division of its Consumer Maine Water Co. subsidiary was taken by local communities by eminent domain for $600,000.

Consumers Applied Technologies, Inc. offers utility services, primarily in the areas of corrosion control, meter services, contract operations, water conservation, and environmental engineering services.

Important Developments

Jul. '95—The company reported that during the first six months of 1995, it had settled five rate cases for $6.0 million in annualized revenue increases. There are four cases pending that seek $5.1 million in additional revenue, and the company plans to file for two additional cases, timed to seek recovery of and return on funds used to finance its capital expenditure programs. Also during this time, $2.0 million was spent to complete the new $16 million water treatment plant in Pennsylvania.

Capitalization

Long Term Debt: $138,398,000 (6/95).
Minority Interest: $2,348,000.
$5.25 Cum. Pfd. Stk.: 10,690 shs. ($100 par).

Per Share Data ($) (Year Ended Dec. 31)

	1994	1993	1992	1991	1990	1989
Tangible Bk. Val.	19.67	12.05	11.82	11.62	10.56	11.95
Earnings	1.22	1.63	1.14	1.46	1.21	1.15
Dividends	1.17	1.14	1.13	1.11	1.09	1.05
Payout Ratio	96%	70%	99%	76%	90%	91%
Prices - High	18¾	21½	19¾	18½	18¼	20½
- Low	15¼	17	14¼	13¾	10	14¾
P/E Ratio - High	15	13	17	13	15	18
- Low	12	10	13	9	6	13

Income Statement Analysis (Million $)

	1994	%Chg	1993	%Chg	1992	%Chg	1991
Revs.	93.3	5%	89.1	NM	89.6	5%	85.2
Depr.	9.0	13%	8.0	4%	7.7	21%	6.4
Maint.	NA	—	NA	—	5.3	-7%	5.7
Fxd. Chgs. Cov.	2.1	5%	2.0	20%	1.7	13%	1.5
Constr. Credits	1.4	82%	0.8	111%	0.4	-66%	1.1
Eff. Tax Rate	34%	—	33%	—	34%	—	34%
Net Inc.	10.0	-17%	12.0	50%	8.0	-15%	9.4

Balance Sheet & Other Fin. Data (Million $)

	1994	1993	1992	1991	1990	1989
Gross Prop.	396	360	349	313	303	287
Cap. Exp.	39.3	34.7	26.3	30.7	24.3	26.1
Net Prop.	327	297	289	258	251	237
Capitalization:						
LT Debt	130	124	120	101	105	100
% LT Debt	56	55	58	55	61	57
Pfd.	3.3	3.3	3.3	3.3	3.3	3.4
% Pfd.	1.40	1.50	1.60	1.80	1.90	1.90
Common	101	96.9	84.2	80.1	64.0	71.5
% Common	43	43	41	43	37	41
Total Cap.	322	303	276	244	228	226

Ratio Analysis

	1994	1993	1992	1991	1990	1989
Oper. Ratio	78.8	79.0	78.8	79.5	78.9	79.4
% Earn. on Net Prop.	6.3	6.4	6.9	6.9	7.0	7.9
% Ret. on Revs.	10.7	13.5	9.0	11.1	9.0	7.9
% Ret. On Invest.Cap	7.1	6.7	7.6	8.0	8.8	8.7
% Return On Com.Eqty	10.1	13.2	9.8	13.1	10.8	9.7

Dividend Data —Cash has been paid in each year since 1951. A dividend reinvestment plan is available.

Amt. of Div. $	Date Decl.	Ex-Div. Date	Stock of Record	Payment Date
0.295	Sep. 12	Nov. 04	Nov. 10	Nov. 25 '94
0.295	Dec. 07	Feb. 06	Feb. 10	Feb. 24 '95
0.295	Apr. 05	May. 04	May. 10	May. 25 '95
0.295	Jun. 30	Aug. 08	Aug. 10	Aug. 25 '95
0.300	Sep. 11	Nov. 08	Nov. 10	Nov. 24 '95

Data as orig. reptd.; bef. results of disc opers. and/or spec. items. Per share data adj. for stk. divs. as of ex-div. date. E-Estimated. NA-Not Available. NM-Not Meaningful. NR-Not Ranked.

Office—Three Canal Plaza, Portland, ME 04101. **Tel**—(207) 773-6438. **Chrmn**—D. R. Hastings II. **Vice Chrmn**—J. W. L. White. **Pres & CEO**—P. L. Haynes. **VP & Secy**—B. R. Mullany. **SVP-CFO**—J. F. Isacke. **VP & Treas**—R. E. Ervin. **Dirs**—C. Elia, D. R. Hastings II, P. L. Haynes, J. S. Ketchum, J. E. Menario, J. E. Newman, J. E. Palmer Jr., E. D. Rosen, W. B. Russell, J. H. Schiavi, J. W. L. White. **Transfer Agent**—Continental Stock Transfer & Trust Company, NYC. **Incorporated** in Maine in 1926. **Empl**-640. **S&P Analyst:** J. Santoriello

STANDARD & POOR'S

STOCK REPORTS

Continental Homes Holding

NYSE Symbol **CON**
In S&P SmallCap 600

23-SEP-95 **Industry:** Building

Summary: Continental Homes Holding constructs and finances single-family homes in Phoenix, Ariz.; Austin and San Antonio, Tex.; Denver, Colo.; Miami, Fla.; and Southern California.

Quantitative Evaluations
Outlook
(1 Lowest—5 Highest)
• **NA**
Fair Value
• **NA**
Risk
• **Average**
Earn./Div. Rank
• **B**

Technical Eval.
• **Bullish** since 5/95
Rel. Strength Rank
(1 Lowest—99 Highest)
• **75**
Insider Activity
• **Neutral**

Recent Price • 21
52 Wk Range • 22⅝-11
Yield • 1.0%
12-Mo. P/E • 10.0

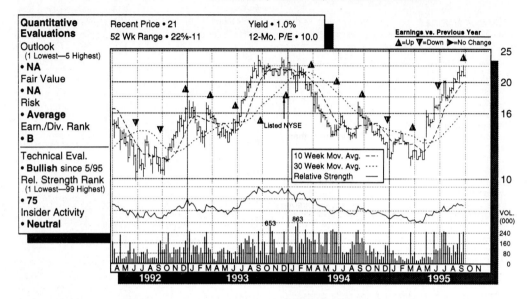

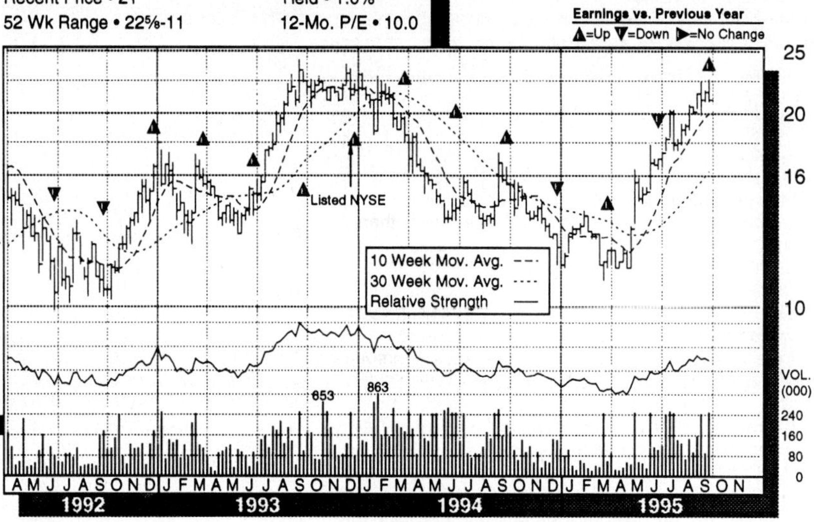

Business Profile - 30-AUG-95

With the acquisition of Miami-based Heftler Realty Co. in November, 1994, Continental Homes now operates in six markets. The Miami, Fla. market was ranked first in single-family housing starts in 1994, and the Phoenix, Ariz. market, where CON was the leading non-retirement homebuilder for the tenth consecutive year, ranked third. Despite a 5.6% rise in net income in fiscal 1995, per share earnings declined, due to a 12% increase in average shares outstanding.

Operational Review - 30-AUG-95

Revenues in the fiscal year ended May 31, 1995, advanced 24% from those of the previous year, reflecting a 13% increase in home sales, aided by new operations in Texas and Florida, and an 8% rise in average selling price resulting from higher prices in the Phoenix and Denver markets. After higher costs associated with the opening of new subdivisions, and taxes at 45.7%, versus 43.5%, net income was up 5.6%, to $13.8 million ($1.99 a share, $1.82 fully diluted) from $13.1 million ($2.11, $1.88).

Stock Performance - 22-SEP-95

In the past 30 trading days, CON's shares have increased 10%, compared to a 5% rise in the S&P 500. Average trading volume for the past five days was 64,400 shares, compared with the 40-day moving average of 31,833 shares.

Key Stock Statistics

Dividend Rate/Share	0.20	Shareholders	100
Shs. outstg. (M)	6.9	Market cap. (B)	$0.145
Avg. daily vol. (M)	0.042	Inst. holdings	60%
Tang. Bk. Value/Share	13.89	Insider holdings	NA
Beta	2.54		

Value of $10,000 invested 5 years ago: $ 27,846

Fiscal Year Ending May 31

	1996	% Change	1995	% Change	1994	% Change
Revenues (Million $)						
1Q	146.4	37%	107.0	37%	78.39	52%
2Q	—	—	97.94	9%	90.10	74%
3Q	—	—	114.1	53%	74.64	63%
4Q	—	—	113.4	8%	105.5	83%
Yr.	—	—	432.5	24%	348.7	68%
Income (Million $)						
1Q	5.22	15%	4.52	40%	3.24	65%
2Q	—	—	3.09	-4%	3.23	99%
3Q	—	—	3.07	12%	2.73	84%
4Q	—	—	3.14	-19%	3.89	91%
Yr.	—	—	13.82	6%	13.08	84%
Earnings Per Share ($)						
1Q	0.75	15%	0.65	5%	0.62	59%
2Q	—	—	0.44	-21%	0.56	75%
3Q	—	—	0.44	13%	0.39	34%
4Q	—	—	0.45	-20%	0.56	44%
Yr.	—	—	1.99	-6%	2.11	53%

Next earnings report expected: late September

Continental Homes Holding

Business Summary - 07-SEP-95

Continental Homes Holding Corp. designs, constructs and sells single-family homes for the entry-level and move-up buyer in Phoenix, Ariz; Austin and San Antonio, Tex.; Denver, Colo.; Miami, Fla.; and Southern California.

Contributions to total homes delivered by area during fiscal 1995 (ended May 31) were:

Phoenix	50%
Austin and San Antonio	37%
Denver	6%
Miami	4%
Southern California	3%

In recent years, the company has built and delivered more single-family homes in the Phoenix area than any other homebuilder.

Continental has 20 subdivisions in Phoenix, 16 in Austin, six in Denver, six in San Antonio, three in Miami and three in Southern California. The company acquires both undeveloped land and improved lots ready for home construction. Its supervisory personnel deal directly with independent engineers and contractors in the development process, including land and site planning and constructing site facilities.

Continental's mortgage banking subsidiaries, American Western Mortgage Co. (AWMC) and Miltex Management, Inc. (MMI), provided financing to some 51% and 61% of Continental's customers in Phoenix and Austin, respectively, in 1994-95. AWMC and MMI complete the process of loan applications, perform credit checks, submit applications to mortgage lenders for approval, and originate and sell mortgage loans.

In July 1993, the company acquired Milburn Investments, the leading volume builder of single family homes in the Austin, Tex., metropolitan area, for about $26.2 million in cash and stock. In January 1994, CON acquired Aspen Homes, a builder of single-family homes in San Antonio, Tex., with annual revenues of $15 million. In November 1994, Continental Homes entered the Miami, Fla., market through the acquisition of Heftler Realty Co., a local homebuilder, for approximately $28.5 million in cash.

Important Developments

May '95—The company announced that net new orders for fiscal 1995 were 3,427 units, up 20% from 2,844 units in fiscal 1994. The backlog at fiscal year end 1995 consisted of 1,493 homes (with an aggregate sales value of $198 million), versus 1,136 ($147 million) at the end of fiscal 1994.

Capitalization

Total Debt: $232,825,000 (5/95), including $32.7 million of 6.88% subordinated notes, convertible into common at $23.50 a share.
Options: To purchase 244,635 shares at $4.00 to $21.38 ea. (5/95).

Per Share Data ($) (Year Ended May 31)

	1995	1994	1993	1992	1991	1990
Tangible Bk. Val.	13.89	13.19	9.50	8.23	7.39	7.50
Cash Flow	2.43	2.32	1.48	0.44	0.21	1.27
Earnings	1.99	2.11	1.38	0.27	0.03	0.97
Dividends	0.20	0.20	0.20	0.20	0.20	Nil
Payout Ratio	10%	11%	15%	79%	606%	Nil
Cal. Yrs.	1994	1993	1992	1991	1990	1989
Prices - High	23⅛	24¼	18¾	14	8½	9½
- Low	11½	12½	9⅞	2¼	1½	3½
P/E Ratio - High	12	11	14	52	NM	10
- Low	6	6	7	8	NM	4

Income Statement Analysis (Million $)

	1995	%Chg	1994	%Chg	1993	%Chg	1992
Revs.	432	23%	351	69%	208	22%	170
Oper. Inc.	33.3	7%	31.1	61%	19.3	65%	11.7
Depr.	3.1	133%	1.3	156%	0.5	-35%	0.8
Int. Exp.	21.9	36%	16.1	22%	13.2	29%	10.2
Pretax Inc.	25.5	10%	23.1	91%	12.1	NM	2.2
Eff. Tax Rate	46%	—	44%	—	41%	—	40%
Net Inc.	13.8	5%	13.1	85%	7.1	NM	1.3

Balance Sheet & Other Fin. Data (Million $)

	1995	1994	1993	1992	1991	1990
Cash	12.8	28.8	11.6	5.1	2.7	2.2
Curr. Assets	NA	NA	NA	NA	NA	NA
Total Assets	387	305	188	163	143	147
Curr. Liab.	NA	NA	NA	NA	NA	NA
LT Debt	234	165	111	102	104	107
Common Eqty.	110	99	51.6	44.4	28.6	29.2
Total Cap.	344	266	163	146	131	136
Cap. Exp.	1.0	0.5	0.2	0.5	0.3	0.3
Cash Flow	16.9	14.4	7.6	2.1	0.8	4.3

Ratio Analysis

	1995	1994	1993	1992	1991	1990
Curr. Ratio	NA	NA	NA	NA	NA	NA
% LT Debt of Cap.	67.4	62.1	68.4	69.9	79.7	78.6
% Net Inc.of Revs.	3.2	3.7	3.4	0.8	0.1	2.5
% Ret. on Assets	4.0	4.7	4.0	0.7	0.1	2.5
% Ret. on Equity	13.2	15.6	14.7	3.0	0.4	12.4

Dividend Data —Dividends were initiated in August 1990.

Amt. of Div. $	Date Decl.	Ex-Div. Date	Stock of Record	Payment Date
0.050	Sep. 19	Sep. 26	Sep. 30	Oct. 14 '94
0.050	Dec. 21	Dec. 23	Dec. 30	Jan. 13 '95
0.050	Mar. 21	Mar. 27	Mar. 31	Apr. 14 '95
0.050	Jun. 20	Jun. 30	Jul. 05	Jul. 14 '95
0.050	Sep. 18	Oct. 02	Oct. 04	Oct. 13 '95

Data as orig. reptd.; bef. results of disc. opers. and/or spec. items. Per share data adj. for stk. divs. as of ex-div. date. E-Estimated. NA-Not Available. NM-Not Meaningful. NR-Not Ranked.

Office—7001 North Scottsdale Rd., Suite 2050, Scottsdale, AZ 85253. **Tel**—(602) 483-0006. **Co-CEOs**—D. R. Loback, K. R. Wade. **Pres**—R. J. Wade. **CFO, Treas & Secy**—Kenda B. Gonzales. **Dirs**—B. S. Anderson, W. T. Hickcox, D. R. Loback, J. A. Rudd, W. Steinberg, K. R. Wade, R. J. Wade. **Transfer Agent & Registrar**—Bank One, Phoenix. **Incorporated** in Delaware in 1986. **Empl-** 441. **S&P Analyst:** N. Rosenberg

Continuum Co.

NYSE Symbol **CNU**
In S&P SmallCap 600

22-JUL-95

Industry:
Data Processing

Summary: Continuum provides computer software and services for life, property and casualty insurance and other financial services companies.

Quantitative Evaluations

Outlook
(1 Lowest—5 Highest)
• **NA**

Fair Value
• **NA**

Risk
• **Average**

Earn./Div. Rank
• **B**

Technical Eval.
• **Bullish** since 4/95

Rel. Strength Rank
(1 Lowest—99 Highest)
• **81**

Insider Activity
• **Neutral**

Recent Price • 36½ | Yield • Nil
52 Wk Range • 36½-19¾ | 12-Mo. P/E • 24.7

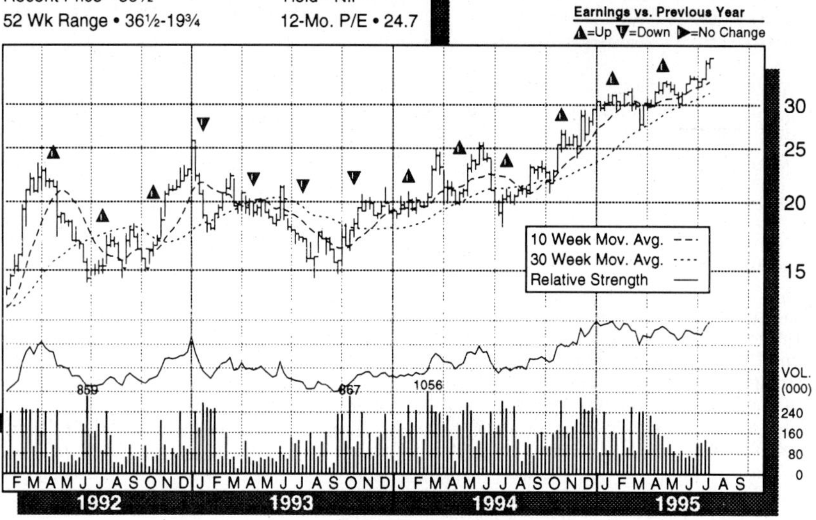

Business Profile - 28-JUN-95

This leading international provider of computer software and consulting services to insurance companies returned to profitability in 1994-5 with record earnings, aided by a growing outsourcing business and a restructuring. CNU's strategy includes providing the European insurance industry with computer systems for all distribution channels. The company should continue to benefit from the trend in the insurance industry to seek new technologies and software to improve efficiency.

Operational Review - 28-JUN-95

Total revenues (preliminary) soared 33% in the fiscal year ended March 31, 1995. Results benefited from increases in license and service revenue and gross profit; lower marketing and administration expenses as a percent of revenues; and the absence of $48.6 million of restructuring and other charges. Net income of $26.2 million ($1.38 a share, on 15% more shares) replaced a net loss of $29.8 million ($1.79).

Stock Performance - 21-JUL-95

In the past 30 trading days, CNU's shares have increased 11%, compared to a 5% rise in the S&P 500. Average trading volume for the past five days was 20,880 shares, compared with the 40-day moving average of 19,861 shares.

Key Stock Statistics

Dividend Rate/Share	Nil	Shareholders	2,000
Shs. outstg. (M)	19.1	Market cap. (B)	$0.698
Avg. daily vol. (M)	0.024	Inst. holdings	47%
Tang. Bk. Value/Share	3.47	Insider holdings	NA
Beta	0.97		

Value of $10,000 invested 5 years ago: $ 31,566

Fiscal Year Ending Mar. 31

	1996	% Change	1995	% Change	1994	% Change
Revenues (Million $)						
1Q	94.57	29%	73.32	32%	55.51	86%
2Q	—	—	76.89	48%	51.89	67%
3Q	—	—	82.54	28%	64.71	115%
4Q	—	—	90.79	28%	70.85	116%
Yr.	—	—	323.5	33%	242.9	96%
Income (Million $)						
1Q	7.83	40%	5.60	NM	-0.78	NM
2Q	—	—	6.28	NM	-38.61	NM
3Q	—	—	6.85	62%	4.23	160%
4Q	—	—	7.48	38%	5.41	NM
Yr.	—	—	26.20	NM	-29.75	NM
Earnings Per Share ($)						
1Q	0.40	33%	0.30	NM	-0.05	NM
2Q	—	—	0.33	NM	-2.61	NM
3Q	—	—	0.36	50%	0.24	60%
4Q	—	—	0.39	34%	0.29	93%
Yr.	—	—	1.38	NM	-1.79	NM

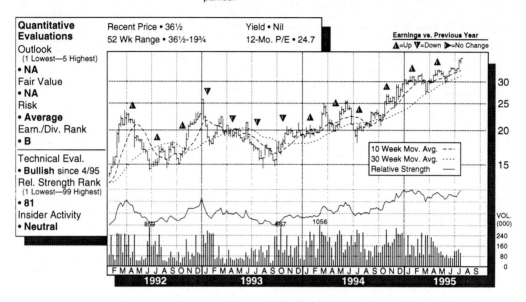

Next earnings report expected: mid October

Continuum Co.

Business Summary - 06-JUL-95

Continuum is a leading international provider of data processing services, computer software and associated services for the insurance industry. The company's revenues are primarily derived from providing outsourcing services to the insurance industry, licensing sophisticated software systems, and providing related development, installation, customization, enhancement and maintenance services. Continuum's software products are designed for use on IBM and IBM compatible mainframe computers and workstations, and are used primarily by life and property and casualty insurance companies. Revenue sources in recent fiscal years (ended March 31) were as follows:

	1995	1994	1993
Service	93%	94%	89%
Software system licensing	7%	6%	11%
Interest income	Nil	Nil	1%

Foreign operations accounted for 67% of revenues in 1993-4.

Important software products include the CCA (Client/Contract Administration) software system and COGEN. CCA is an administrative and marketing computer software system for life insurance firms divided into four modules covering four management areas: client, product, contract, and distribution. COGEN provides property and casualty insurance companies with client handling, underwriting, claims management, reinsurance, payables, and receivables management, regulatory reporting, and productivity tools.

In October 1993, CNU acquired Vantage Computer Systems Inc. (provides the insurance industry with data processing and other services) for 4 million common shares. In August 1993, CNU acquired Paxus Corp. (consulting and computer services) for 3.8 million common shares.

Important Developments

May '95—Continuum agreed to acquire Ra Group Ltd. from Sun Alliance Group Plc for about $9 million. Ra Group, with annual revenues of about $15 million, provides computer systems to insurance brokers in the UK, predominantly in the property and casualty sector. **Apr. '95**—CNU said that Royal Indemnity Co. and Allied Group had purchased licenses to use COLOSSUS, CNU's artificial intelligence software system that assists insurance adjusters in evaluating bodily injury claims. CNU will begin recognizing revenues under these contracts in the first quarter of 1995-6. Separately, CNU agreed to provide outsourcing services (administration and data processing) for Allianz Life Insurance Co. of North America. The six-year contract is worth about $45 million.

Capitalization

Long Term Debt: $25,379,000 (3/95).

Per Share Data ($)

(Year Ended Mar. 31)

	1995	1994	1993	1992	1991	1990
Tangible Bk. Val.	NA	1.82	5.43	4.86	4.11	2.53
Cash Flow	NA	-1.38	0.96	1.12	1.11	0.84
Earnings	1.38	-1.79	0.60	0.81	0.93	0.64
Dividends	Nil	Nil	Nil	Nil	Nil	Nil
Payout Ratio	Nil	Nil	Nil	Nil	Nil	Nil
Cal. Yrs.	1994	1993	1992	1991	1990	1989
Prices - High	30½	25¾	25¾	19⅞	21½	12½
- Low	18	14½	12¼	10⅛	9⅛	6⅛
P/E Ratio - High	22	NM	43	25	23	20
- Low	13	NM	20	13	10	10

Income Statement Analysis (Million $)

	1994	%Chg	1993	%Chg	1992	%Chg	1991
Revs.	242	97%	123	-2%	126	12%	113
Oper. Inc.	23.6	84%	12.8	-26%	17.3	-2%	17.6
Depr.	6.8	68%	4.0	19%	3.4	90%	1.8
Int. Exp.	3.8	NM	0.4	-26%	0.5	26%	0.4
Pretax Inc.	34.7	NM	9.4	-37%	14.9	-3%	15.4
Eff. Tax Rate	NM	—	32%	—	42%	—	42%
Net Inc.	-29.8	NM	6.4	-26%	8.6	-3%	8.9

Balance Sheet & Other Fin. Data (Million $)

	1994	1993	1992	1991	1990	1989
Cash	10.7	46.4	69.8	42.1	15.2	3.8
Curr. Assets	89.3	73.4	99	64.4	31.8	19.4
Total Assets	174	117	122	121	43.0	34.0
Curr. Liab.	69.0	34.3	63.6	32.3	16.6	13.3
LT Debt	19.1	21.2	1.0	2.2	Nil	Nil
Common Eqty.	50.8	59.1	52.2	43.7	22.2	16.3
Total Cap.	74.6	81.7	54.8	48.3	24.1	18.4
Cap. Exp.	8.5	1.2	3.7	3.4	0.7	0.4
Cash Flow	-23.0	10.4	12.0	10.7	7.4	4.8

Ratio Analysis

	1994	1993	1992	1991	1990	1989
Curr. Ratio	1.3	2.1	1.6	2.0	1.9	1.5
% LT Debt of Cap.	25.7	26.0	1.8	4.6	Nil	Nil
% Net Inc.of Revs.	NM	5.2	6.9	7.9	6.9	1.8
% Ret. on Assets	NM	5.3	7.1	10.3	14.3	3.4
% Ret. on Equity	NM	11.5	17.9	25.3	28.7	7.6

Dividend Data (Dividends were omitted in 1986. The shares were split two for one in July 1990.)

Data as orig. reptd.; bef. results of disc. opers. and/or spec. items. Per share data adj. for stk. divs. as of ex-div. date. E-Estimated. NA-Not Available. NM-Not Meaningful. NR-Not Ranked.

Office—9500 Arboretum Blvd., Austin, TX 78759-6399. **Tel**—(512) 345-5700. **Fax**—(512) 338-7041. **Chrmn**—R. C. Carroll. **Pres & CEO**—W. M. Long. **VP-Secy, Treas & CFO**—J. L. Westermann III. **Dirs**—L. C. Anderson, T. G. Brown, R. C. Carroll, W. M. Long, T. A. McDonnell, C. S. Quinn, E. C. Stanton III, E. L. Walker. **Transfer Agent & Registrar**—American Stock Transfer & Trust, NYC. **Incorporated** in Texas in 1968; reincorporated in Delaware in 1987. **Empl**- 2,700. **S&P Analyst:** N.J. DeVita

STANDARD & POOR'S

Control Data Systems

STOCK REPORTS

NASDAQ Symbol **CDAT**

In S&P SmallCap 600

12-SEP-95 **Industry:** Data Processing

Summary: This global systems integrator develops and implements open systems solutions for operational problems in manufacturing design, network communications and database management.

Quantitative Evaluations

Outlook (1 Lowest—5 Highest) • **NA**

Fair Value • **NA**

Risk • **Average**

Earn./Div. Rank • **NR**

Technical Eval. • **Bearish** since 5/95

Rel. Strength Rank (1 Lowest—99 Highest) • **80**

Insider Activity • **NA**

Recent Price • 10⅜

52 Wk Range • 10¾-5⅞

Yield • Nil

12-Mo. P/E • NM

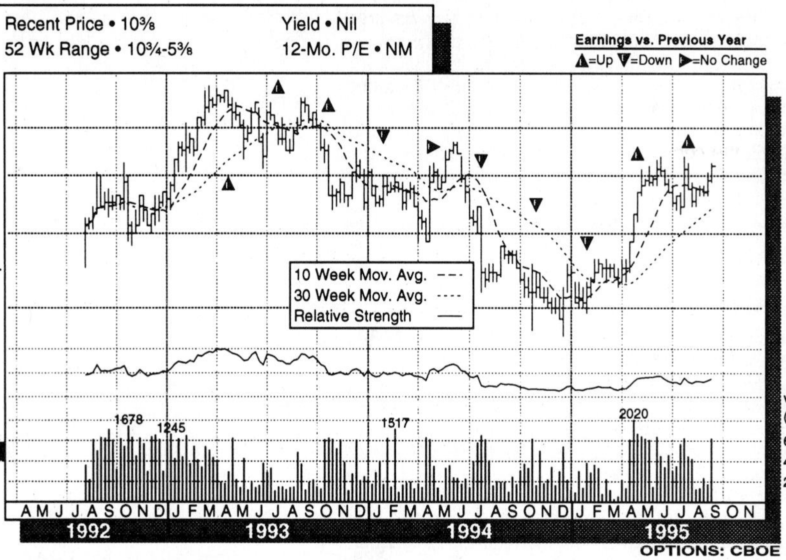

OPTIONS: CBOE

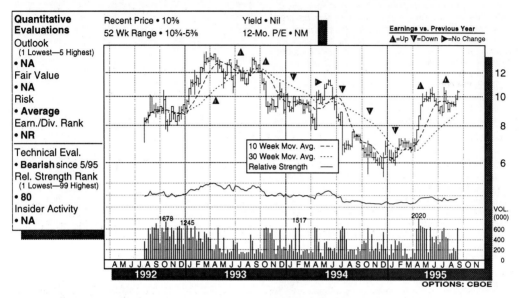

Business Profile - 12-SEP-95

In response to the computer industry's shift from a central mainframe environment to a distributed client-server environment, CDAT stopped the development of new proprietary hardware products and refocused its efforts on billable customer projects, hardware and software remarketing, restructured its sales and service and organization, and acquired small systems integration companies.

Operational Review - 12-SEP-95

Revenues have fallen in recent periods as a drop in hardware and maintenance support sales outweighed higher demand for software and service sales. Going forward, year to year revenues are expected to decline due to the recent sale of five international divisions. Gross margins, which have been narrowing, are expected to improve as the divested operations produced lower margin products. Future earnings should also be helped by the company's restructuring efforts.

Stock Performance - 08-SEP-95

In the past 30 trading days, CDAT's shares have increased 9%, compared to a 2% rise in the S&P 500. Average trading volume for the past five days was 207,150 shares, compared with the 40-day moving average of 81,790 shares.

Key Stock Statistics

Dividend Rate/Share	Nil	Shareholders	19,200
Shs. outstg. (M)	12.8	Market cap. (B)	$0.136
Avg. daily vol. (M)	0.087	Inst. holdings	67%
Tang. Bk. Value/Share	5.41	Insider holdings	NA
Beta	NA		

Value of $10,000 invested 5 years ago: NA

Fiscal Year Ending Dec. 31

	1995	% Change	1994	% Change	1993	% Change
Revenues (Million $)						
1Q	130.1	-11%	145.6	41%	103.0	-13%
2Q	129.1	-2%	131.3	14%	115.0	-13%
3Q	—	—	113.7	17%	97.00	-16%
4Q	—	—	133.7	-2%	137.0	-10%
Yr.	—	—	524.2	16%	452.0	-13%
Income (Million $)						
1Q	2.20	62%	1.36	1%	1.34	NM
2Q	2.26	NM	0.68	-84%	4.32	NM
3Q	—	—	-4.98	NM	0.98	NM
4Q	—	—	-91.47	NM	2.48	-75%
Yr.	—	—	-94.40	NM	9.12	NM
Earnings Per Share ($)						
1Q	0.17	70%	0.10	NM	0.10	NM
2Q	0.18	NM	0.05	-84%	0.32	NM
3Q	—	—	-0.36	NM	0.07	NM
4Q	—	—	-6.63	NM	0.17	-79%
Yr.	—	—	-6.87	NM	0.66	NM

Next earnings report expected: late October

Control Data Systems

Business Summary - 12-SEP-95

Control Data Systems, Inc. is a systems integrator that develops and implements open systems solutions for the operational problems of customers in technical, government and commercial markets worldwide. The company develops custom solutions based on hardware, software and peripherals available from its growing group of open systems technology partners and suppliers. CDAT focuses on integrating computer solutions to business-specific problems in manufacturing design, network communications and database management.

In 1989, the company developed a strategy to capitalize on the shift in the computer industry from proprietary nonstandard hardware and operating system software to distributed open systems consisting of hardware and operating system software from one or multiple vendors based on industry standards. CDAT is changing its business focus to the marketing and integration of open systems and the development, marketing and integration of application software. Additionally, the company provides hardware and software maintenance services for proprietary and open systems hardware through engineers located throughout the world. International sales accounted for 72% of total revenues in 1994, versus 65% the year before.

Revenue contributions by product and service in recent years were:

	1994	1993	1992
Hardware products	53%	44%	46%
Software and services	29%	31%	28%
Maintenance and support	18%	25%	26%

The company is differentiated from other integrators because it is not capitive to a particular product set or technology. This objectivity allows it to work in a multi-vendor environment without bias. Initially, CDAT began integrating UNIX based open systems products into its customer solutions. During 1993, the company signed remarketing agreements with Sun Microsystems, Hewlett-Packard and Acer America. As a Sun Microsystems integrator, Control Data remarkets Sun's complete line of workstations, servers and software.

CDAT offers computer-aided design, manufacturing and engineering (CAD/CAM/CAE) software that provides simultaneous engineering or automated merging of engineering analysis, design, drafting and manufacturing functions.

Important Developments

Sep. '95—CDAT sold five international subsidiaries to Ameridata Technologies. Inc. The company is expected to receive approximately $25 to $30 million for the operations.

Capitalization

Long Term Debt: None (6/95).

Per Share Data ($) (Year Ended Dec. 31)

	1994	1993	1992	1991	1990	1989
Tangible Bk. Val.	5.22	10.83	12.76	NA	NA	NA
Cash Flow	-5.83	1.96	-9.04	-0.47	6.43	-9.75
Earnings	-6.87	0.66	-12.03	-4.14	1.76	-15.12
Dividends	Nil	Nil	Nil	Nil	Nil	Nil
Payout Ratio	Nil	Nil	Nil	Nil	Nil	Nil
Prices - High	11⅜	14⅛	10½	NA	NA	NA
- Low	5⅜	8¾	7	NA	NA	NA
P/E Ratio - High	NM	21	NM	NA	NA	NA
- Low	NM	13	NM	NA	NA	NA

Income Statement Analysis (Million $)

	1994	%Chg	1993	%Chg	1992	%Chg	1991
Revs.	524	16%	452	-13%	517	-10%	574
Oper. Inc.	12.3	-41%	21.0	-17%	25.3	22%	20.8
Depr.	14.3	-20%	17.8	-47%	33.4	-14%	39.0
Int. Exp.	1.3	-34%	2.0	-8%	2.1	-49%	4.2
Pretax Inc.	-93.0	NM	11.0	NM	-131	NM	-39.0
Eff. Tax Rate	NM	—	17%	—	NM	—	NM
Net Inc.	-94.0	NM	9.0	NM	-133	NM	-44.0

Balance Sheet & Other Fin. Data (Million $)

	1994	1993	1992	1991	1990	1989
Cash	85.0	82.0	134	14.0	25.0	41.0
Curr. Assets	252	271	303	277	NA	NA
Total Assets	301	353	374	373	424	536
Curr. Liab.	159	137	142	150	NA	NA
LT Debt	Nil	Nil	7.1	0.5	NA	NA
Common Eqty.	82.0	175	159	192	237	308
Total Cap.	83.0	176	167	194	NA	NA
Cap. Exp.	9.0	11.4	17.0	25.5	29.2	NA
Cash Flow	-80.0	27.0	-100	-5.0	68.0	-102

Ratio Analysis

	1994	1993	1992	1991	1990	1989
Curr. Ratio	1.6	2.0	2.1	1.8	NA	NA
% LT Debt of Cap.	Nil	Nil	4.3	0.3	NA	NA
% Net Inc.of Revs.	NM	2.0	NM	NM	3.2	NM
% Ret. on Assets	NM	2.4	NM	NM	3.9	NM
% Ret. on Equity	NM	5.2	NM	NM	6.9	NM

Dividend Data —No dividends have been paid. The company intends to retain earnings for use in its business and does not expect to pay cash dividends for the foreseeable future.

Data as orig. reptd.; bef. results of disc. opers. and/or spec. items. Per share data adj. for stk. divs. as of ex-div. date. EPS in 1994 4Q incl. nonrecurring charges of 6.89. E-Estimated. NA-Not Available. NM-Not Meaningful. NR-Not Ranked.

Office—4201 Lexington Ave. North, Arden Hills, MN 55126-6198. **Tel**—(612) 482-2401. **Pres & CEO**—J. E. Ousley. **Secy**—R. W. Beha. **CFO & Investor Contact**—Joseph F. Killoran. **Dirs**—W. D. Bell, G. A. Dove, M. A. Gumucio, W. D. Hajjar, K. A. Libbey, J. E. Ousley. **Transfer Agent & Registrar**—Bank of New York, NYC. **Incorporated** in Delaware in 1992. **Empl**-2,000. **S&P Analyst:** Steven A. Jaworski

COR Therapeutics

NASDAQ Symbol **CORR**
In S&P SmallCap 600

04-OCT-95

Industry: Drugs-Generic and OTC

Summary: This company is engaged in the discovery, development and commercialization of biopharmaceutical products to treat and prevent severe cardiovascular diseases.

Quantitative Evaluations

Outlook
(1 Lowest—5 Highest)
• **NA**
Fair Value
• **NA**
Risk
• **High**
Earn./Div. Rank
• **NR**

Technical Eval.
• **Bullish** since 7/95
Rel. Strength Rank
(1 Lowest—99 Highest)
• **13**
Insider Activity
• **Neutral**

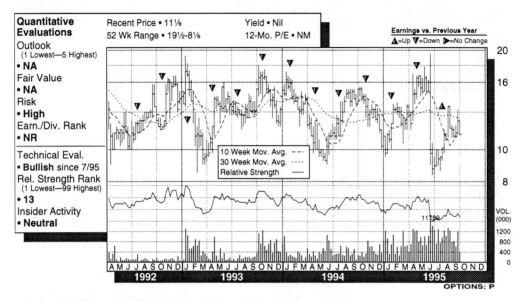

Recent Price • 11⅛
52 Wk Range • 19½-8⅛
Yield • Nil
12-Mo. P/E • NM

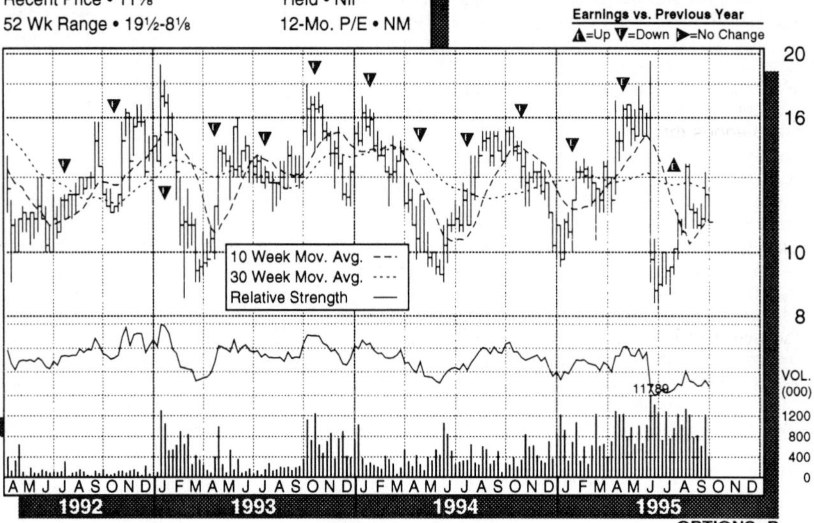

OPTIONS: P

Business Profile - 04-OCT-95

CORR reported disappointing preliminary results in its much anticipated Phase III Integrelin trial for the prevention of abrupt closure following angioplasty. The drug's performance did not meet the endpoints required for regulatory approval and CORR's stock price suffered as a result. The company is evaluating alternatives, including another Phase III trial. A $20 million licensing fee was recorded in the second quarter of 1995, from a collaboration agreement with Schering-Plough.

Operational Review - 04-OCT-95

Revenues in the six months ended June 30, 1995, were $21,050,000 compared to $22,000, year to year, reflecting payments under the April 1995 collaboration agreement with Schering-Plough. R&D expenditures and administrative costs increased slightly and net income of $3.0 million ($0.15 a share, based on 6.8% more average shares) replaced a loss of $16.1 million ($0.85).

Stock Performance - 29-SEP-95

In the past 30 trading days, CORR's shares have declined 18%, compared to a 5% rise in the S&P 500. Average trading volume for the past five days was 77,140 shares, compared with the 40-day moving average of 239,290 shares.

Key Stock Statistics

Dividend Rate/Share	Nil	Shareholders	300
Shs. outstg. (M)	19.2	Market cap. (B)	$0.204
Avg. daily vol. (M)	0.152	Inst. holdings	44%
Tang. Bk. Value/Share	4.51	Insider holdings	NA
Beta	NA		

Value of $10,000 invested 5 years ago: NA

Fiscal Year Ending Dec. 31

	1995	% Change	1994	% Change	1993	% Change
Revenues (Million $)						
1Q	0.00	-95%	0.02	-96%	0.50	32%
2Q	21.05	—	Nil	—	0.59	18%
3Q	—	—	Nil	—	0.10	-77%
4Q	—	—	0.50	-63%	1.36	NM
Yr.	—	—	0.52	-80%	2.55	53%
Income (Million $)						
1Q	-8.66	NM	-5.32	NM	-3.35	NM
2Q	11.62	NM	-10.83	NM	-4.28	NM
3Q	—	—	-13.13	NM	-5.41	NM
4Q	—	—	-10.26	NM	-6.63	NM
Yr.	—	—	-39.54	NM	-19.67	NM
Earnings Per Share ($)						
1Q	-0.45	NM	-0.28	NM	-0.23	NM
2Q	0.57	NM	-0.57	NM	-0.29	NM
3Q	—	—	-0.68	NM	-0.36	NM
4Q	—	—	-0.53	NM	-0.38	NM
Yr.	—	—	-2.07	NM	-1.27	NM

Next earnings report expected: late October

COR Therapeutics

Business Summary - 04-OCT-95

COR Therapeutics, Inc. is involved in the discovery, development and commercialization of novel biopharmaceutical products to treat and prevent severe cardiovascular diseases. The company combines its knowledge of molecular and cellular biology of cardiovascular diseases with advanced drug discovery techniques. COR plans to market products for which it obtains approval either directly or through licensing arrangements with large pharmaceutical firms.

Efforts are focused primarily on the development of inhibitors that address the treatment of arterial thrombosis, venous thrombosis and restenosis (a renarrowing of blood vessels following angioplasty). COR's most advanced product, Integrelin, completed Phase III clinical trials in May 1995 for the prevention of abrupt closure following coronary angioplasty, with disappointing results. In other indications, the company has completed a Phase II trial of Integrelin in the treatment of unstable angina and plans to enter Phase III trials sometime in 1995. A Phase II trial of the product with thrombolytics for the prevention and treatment of acute myocardial infarction (heart attack) is underway.

In April 1995, COR signed a worldwide collaboration agreement with Schering-Plough to develop and commercialize Integrelin. Schering paid COR a $20 million licensing fee and would make additional milestone payments (up to $100 million) upon reaching certain performance goals.

In May 1993, COR modified and expanded a collaborative relationship (begun in 1991) with Eli Lilly & Co. for the development of cardiovascular products (excluding Integrelin). The agreement provides for joint research, development and commercialization in North America, Europe and Japan of all intravenous and oral products resulting from the collaboration. Lilly made a $1.3 million milestone payment to COR in connection with the modified agreement and also paid $2.8 million under an earlier agreement over a two-year period through May 1993.

COR entered into a collaborative agreement with the Ortho unit of Johnson & Johnson (J&J) in 1993 for the development and commercialization of novel pharmaceuticals. J&J purchased $8 million of COR common stock and made a $500,000 milestone payment to COR in 1994.

The company also has an agreement with Kyowa Hakko Kogyo Co. Ltd of Japan, focusing on the discovery and development of small-molecule pharmaceuticals.

Important Developments

Jul. '95—The company reported that it had cash and short-term equivalents of $93.3 million at the end of the second quarter ended June 30, 1995.

Capitalization

Long Term Debt: $5,107,000 (6/95).

Per Share Data ($) (Year Ended Dec. 31)

	1994	1993	1992	1991	1990	1989
Tangible Bk. Val.	4.51	6.44	4.09	4.99	-9.10	NM
Cash Flow	-1.96	-1.16	-0.79	-0.52	-0.81	-0.45
Earnings	-2.07	-1.27	-0.86	-0.62	-0.93	-0.51
Dividends	Nil	Nil	Nil	Nil	Nil	Nil
Payout Ratio	Nil	Nil	Nil	Nil	Nil	Nil
Prices - High	17¼	19¼	18	22	NA	NA
- Low	9	8½	9	7½	NA	NA
P/E Ratio - High	NM	NM	NM	NM	NM	NM
- Low	NM	NM	NM	NA	NA	NA

Income Statement Analysis (Million $)

	1994	%Chg	1993	%Chg	1992	%Chg	1991
Revs.	0.5	-80%	2.5	53%	1.7	-31%	2.4
Oper. Inc.	-42.1	NM	-21.2	NM	-11.6	NM	-5.0
Depr.	2.1	27%	1.7	86%	0.9	5%	0.9
Int. Exp.	0.2	-43%	0.3	58%	0.2	-30%	0.3
Pretax Inc.	-39.5	NM	-19.7	NM	-10.2	NM	-5.1
Eff. Tax Rate	NM	—	NM	—	NM	—	Nil
Net Inc.	-39.5	NM	-19.7	NM	-10.2	NM	-5.1

Balance Sheet & Other Fin. Data (Million $)

	1994	1993	1992	1991	1990	1989
Cash	94.0	122	49.1	58.7	4.3	5.6
Curr. Assets	97.0	124	50.1	59.2	4.4	6.1
Total Assets	106	130	53.8	61.0	6.7	8.2
Curr. Liab.	15.0	8.1	4.4	1.7	0.9	0.8
LT Debt	4.7	3.1	0.8	0.9	1.3	1.1
Common Eqty.	87.0	119	48.6	58.4	-9.4	-3.7
Total Cap.	91.0	122	49.4	59.2	5.7	7.5
Cap. Exp.	6.7	4.4	2.8	0.3	0.9	1.4
Cash Flow	-37.4	-18.0	-9.3	-4.3	-5.0	-2.4

Ratio Analysis

	1994	1993	1992	1991	1990	1989
Curr. Ratio	6.5	15.3	11.3	34.4	4.7	7.8
% LT Debt of Cap.	5.1	2.5	1.7	1.4	23.0	15.3
% Net Inc.of Revs.	NM	NM	NM	NM	NM	NM
% Ret. on Assets	NM	NM	NM	NM	NM	NM
% Ret. on Equity	NM	NM	NM	NM	NM	NM

Dividend Data —No cash dividends have been paid. In January 1995, the company adopted a preferred stock purchase rights plan.

Data as orig. reptd.; bef. results of disc. opers. and/or spec. items. Per share data adj. for stk. divs. as of ex-div. date. E-Estimated. NA-Not Available. NM-Not Meaningful. NR-Not Ranked.

Office—256 East Grand Ave., South San Francisco, CA 94080. **Tel**—(415) 244-6800. **Pres & CEO**—V. M. Kailian. **VP & Secy**—R. L. Douglas Jr. **VP-Fin & CFO**—Laura A. Brege. **Contr**—P. S. Roddy. **Dirs**—S. R. Coughlin, J. T. Doluisio, J. T. Jackson, V. M. Kailian, E. Mario, R. R. Momsen, L. H. Smith Jr., W. H. Younger Jr. **Transfer Agent & Registrar**—Chemical Trust Co. of California, San Francisco. **Incorporated** in Delaware in 1988. **Empl**-129. **S&P Analyst:** Thomas Tirney

STANDARD & POOR'S

STOCK REPORTS

Core Industries

NYSE Symbol **CRI**
In S&P SmallCap 600

16-OCT-95

Industry: Manufacturing/Distr

Summary: This company is a diversified manufacturer of specialty products used in test, measurement and control devices, fluid control and construction and farm equipment.

Quantitative Evaluations

Outlook
(1 Lowest—5 Highest)
• NA

Fair Value
• NA

Risk
• Average

Earn./Div. Rank
• B-

Technical Eval.
• **Bullish** since 7/95

Rel. Strength Rank
(1 Lowest—99 Highest)
• 53

Insider Activity
• NA

Recent Price • 11¾
52 Wk Range • 12⅝-8⅝

Yield • 2.0%
12-Mo. P/E • 30.1

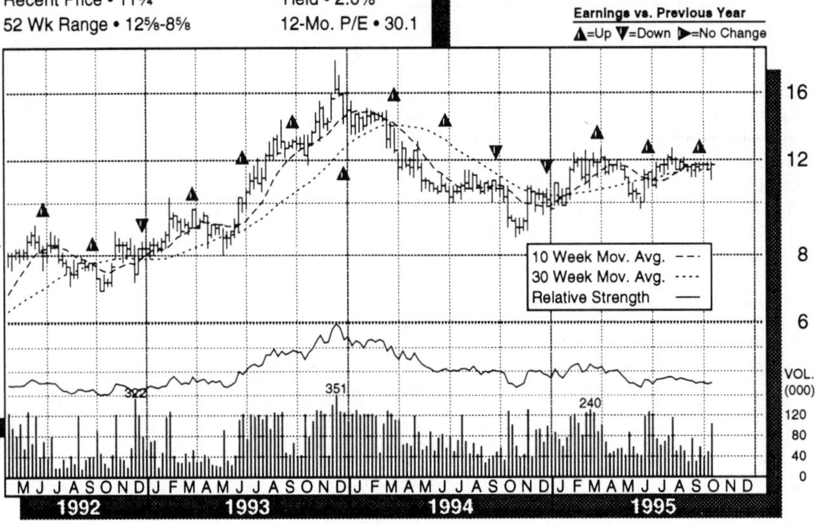

Business Profile - 16-OCT-95

Core Industries is a manufacturer of specialized products serving niches in three markets--fluid controls and construction products; test, measurement and control products (formerly electronics); and farm equipment--each with complete capability for engineering, manufacturing and marketing innovative, high-quality products. CRI recently announced that it will divest its Cherokee division, citing an inconsistent fit with the rest of the company's products, customer profiles and industry traits.

Operational Review - 16-OCT-95

Based on a preliminary report, sales from continuing operations for the fiscal year ended August 31, 1995, rose 13% from those of fiscal 1994. Earnings were $1.09 a share, up from $0.85 in fiscal 1994, excluding a one-time gain of $0.09. These figures also exclude results from the discontinued operations of the Cherokee division, which amounted to a net loss of $0.70 a share in fiscal 1995 and income of $0.08 a share in fiscal 1994.

Stock Performance - 13-OCT-95

In the past 30 trading days, CRI's shares have increased 1%, compared to a 4% rise in the S&P 500. Average trading volume for the past five days was 20,500 shares, compared with the 40-day moving average of 10,887 shares.

Key Stock Statistics

Dividend Rate/Share	0.24	Shareholders	2,400
Shs. outstg. (M)	9.8	Market cap. (B)	$0.115
Avg. daily vol. (M)	0.012	Inst. holdings	41%
Tang. Bk. Value/Share	7.69	Insider holdings	NA
Beta	0.70		

Value of $10,000 invested 5 years ago: $ 13,368

Fiscal Year Ending Aug. 31

	1995	% Change	1994	% Change	1993	% Change
Revenues (Million $)						
1Q	54.10	NM	54.01	17%	46.10	1%
2Q	55.65	12%	49.59	6%	46.90	9%
3Q	63.50	5%	60.58	7%	56.48	19%
4Q	47.46	-14%	55.27	-4%	57.60	22%
Yr.	—	—	219.4	6%	207.1	13%
Income (Million $)						
1Q	2.02	-31%	2.91	79%	1.63	NM
2Q	2.36	10%	2.14	22%	1.76	NM
3Q	3.13	28%	2.45	9%	2.25	34%
4Q	3.10	24%	2.51	-14%	2.93	79%
Yr.	10.69	7%	10.01	17%	8.57	NM
Earnings Per Share ($)						
1Q	0.21	-30%	0.30	76%	0.17	-15%
2Q	0.24	9%	0.22	22%	0.18	NM
3Q	0.32	28%	0.25	9%	0.23	35%
4Q	0.32	28%	0.25	-17%	0.30	76%
Yr.	1.09	7%	1.02	16%	0.88	NM

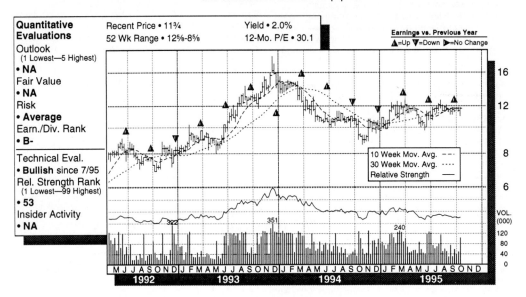

Next earnings report expected: late October

Core Industries

Business Summary - 16-OCT-95

Core Industries Inc is a diversified manufacturing concern involved in the production of specialty products for commercial and industrial use. Contributions by industry segment in fiscal 1995 were:

	Sales	Profits
Fluid control & construction	43%	45%
Test, measurement & control	34%	29%
Farm equipment	23%	26%

Fluid control and construction products include valves and pipeline strainers for various fluid control purposes, molded plastic parts, metal stampings and hinges. This segment also includes mechanical contracting for the construction industry. Most of the products are sold through dealers and manufacturers' representatives throughout the U.S. and in certain other countries. In fiscal 1994's third quarter, CRI purchased a fabricator of strainers and other specialty flow control products and sold a division that manufactured metal doors and frames for the construction industry. In January 1995, CRI purchased a designer and fabricator of skid-mounted pipeline metering systems and fabricated strainers.

Test, measurement and control devices and systems are made for industrial use and power supplies and components for the computer industry. Products include volt/amp/ohmmeters, multimeters and recorders, harmonic analyzers, torque measurement and control systems, electronic fasteners, power supplies and precision carbide components. In January 1995, the Amprobe Instrument division acquired a producer of refrigerant recycling and recovery products.

Farm equipment includes plows, grain drills, cultivators and other soil tillage equipment, grain augers and cleaners, feeders and forage and harvesting dump wagons. Products are sold principally through separate dealers and distributors throughout the U.S. and contiguous Canadian provinces. In December 1993, CRI purchased the grain drill business of Best Manufacturing. In September 1993, the company sold its Du-Al Manufacturing Co. farm division.

Important Developments

Oct. '95—CRI announced that it will divest its Cherokee division, whose power supply products, customers and industry characteristics it believes are not compatible with its focus businesses. Proceeds will be diverted into the fluid control and test, measurement and control operations.

Capitalization

Long Term Debt: $32,609,000 (8/95).

Per Share Data ($)

(Year Ended Aug. 31)

	1995	1994	1993	1992	1991	1990
Tangible Bk. Val.	NA	7.34	6.50	5.83	7.67	7.89
Cash Flow	NA	1.55	1.40	0.59	0.98	1.19
Earnings	1.09	1.02	0.88	0.02	0.17	0.40
Dividends	0.36	0.24	0.18	0.30	0.48	0.72
Payout Ratio	33%	24%	23%	NM	289%	182%
Prices - High	$12\frac{5}{8}$	$15\frac{1}{2}$	$15\frac{1}{2}$	$9\frac{1}{8}$	$8\frac{1}{4}$	$12\frac{3}{4}$
- Low	$9\frac{3}{4}$	$8\frac{5}{8}$	$7\frac{7}{8}$	$5\frac{3}{8}$	5	4
P/E Ratio - High	12	15	18	NM	49	32
- Low	9	8	9	NM	29	10

Income Statement Analysis (Million $)

	1994	%Chg	1993	%Chg	1992	%Chg	1991
Revs.	219	6%	207	13%	184	-25%	244
Oper. Inc.	23.6	7%	22.0	43%	15.4	-3%	15.8
Depr.	5.2	NM	5.2	-7%	5.6	-31%	8.0
Int. Exp.	4.6	-10%	5.1	-18%	6.2	-9%	6.8
Pretax Inc.	16.1	21%	13.3	NM	1.4	-42%	2.4
Eff. Tax Rate	38%	—	35%	—	87%	—	32%
Net Inc.	10.0	16%	8.6	NM	0.2	-88%	1.6

Balance Sheet & Other Fin. Data (Million $)

	1994	1993	1992	1991	1990	1989
Cash	14.6	0.7	1.9	1.0	1.2	1.1
Curr. Assets	114	109	115	134	143	142
Total Assets	156	151	157	188	198	198
Curr. Liab.	31.1	28.4	37.2	40.9	50.7	45.9
LT Debt	41.6	47.1	50.1	52.3	48.0	49.1
Common Eqty.	79.0	71.0	64.4	92.3	96.5	100
Total Cap.	122	120	116	147	148	152
Cap. Exp.	5.0	4.9	6.4	4.5	7.0	8.1
Cash Flow	15.2	13.7	5.7	9.6	11.7	14.3

Ratio Analysis

	1994	1993	1992	1991	1990	1989
Curr. Ratio	3.7	3.9	3.1	3.3	2.8	3.1
% LT Debt of Cap.	34.0	39.4	43.1	35.5	32.5	32.3
% Net Inc.of Revs.	4.6	4.1	0.1	0.7	1.6	3.0
% Ret. on Assets	6.5	5.6	0.1	0.8	2.0	3.7
% Ret. on Equity	13.3	12.6	0.2	1.7	3.9	7.1

Dividend Data —Dividends have been paid since 1943. A "poison pill" stock purchase rights plan was adopted in 1987.

Amt. of Div. $	Date Decl.	Ex-Div. Date	Stock of Record	Payment Date
0.060	Oct. 19	Dec. 05	Dec. 09	Dec. 31 '94
0.060	Oct. 19	Dec. 06	Dec. 12	Jan. 02 '95
0.060	Jan. 10	Feb. 28	Mar. 06	Mar. 27 '95
0.060	Apr. 19	May. 30	Jun. 05	Jun. 26 '95
0.060	Jul. 31	Aug. 30	Sep. 01	Sep. 25 '95

Data as orig. reptd.; bef. results of disc. opers. and/or spec. items. Per share data adj. for stk. divs. as of ex-div. date. E-Estimated. NA-Not Available. NM-Not Meaningful. NR-Not Ranked.

Office—500 North Woodward Ave., P.O. Box 2000, Bloomfield Hills, MI 48303-2000. **Tel**—(810) 642-3400. **Fax**—(810) 642-6816. **Pres & CEO**—D. R. Zimmer. **Exec VP & Secy**—L. J. Murphy. **VP-Fin, CFO & Investor Contact**—Raymond H. Steben Jr. (810) 901-1575. **Treas**—T. G. Hooper. **Dirs**—J. Alix, R. P. Kughn, H. M. Marko, L. J. Murphy, A. E. Schwartz, R. G. Stone Jr., D. R. Zimmer. **Transfer Agent & Registrar**—Harris Trust & Savings Bank, Chicago. **Incorporated** in Nevada in 1964. **Empl**-2,428. **S&P Analyst:** J. Santoriello

Corrections Corp. of America

NYSE Symbol **CXC**
In S&P SmallCap 600

29-SEP-95 **Industry:** Services

Summary: This company, which designs, builds and manages prisons and other correctional institutions for governmental agencies, is the leader in the private-sector corrections industry.

Quantitative Evaluations

Recent Price • 47⅛
52 Wk Range • 49⅝-11½
Yield • Nil
12-Mo. P/E • 79.9

Outlook
(1 Lowest—5 Highest)
• **5**
Fair Value
• **84**
Risk
• **Average**
Earn./Div. Rank
• **B-**

Technical Eval.
• **Bullish** since 7/95
Rel. Strength Rank
(1 Lowest—99 Highest)
• **84**
Insider Activity
• **Neutral**

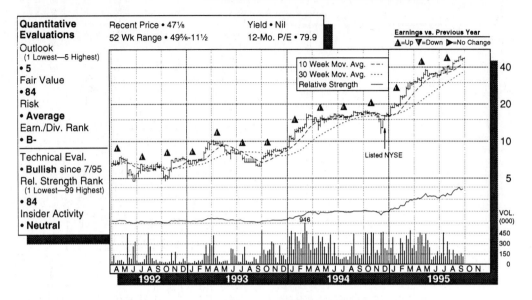

Earnings vs. Previous Year
▲=Up ▼=Down ▶=No Change

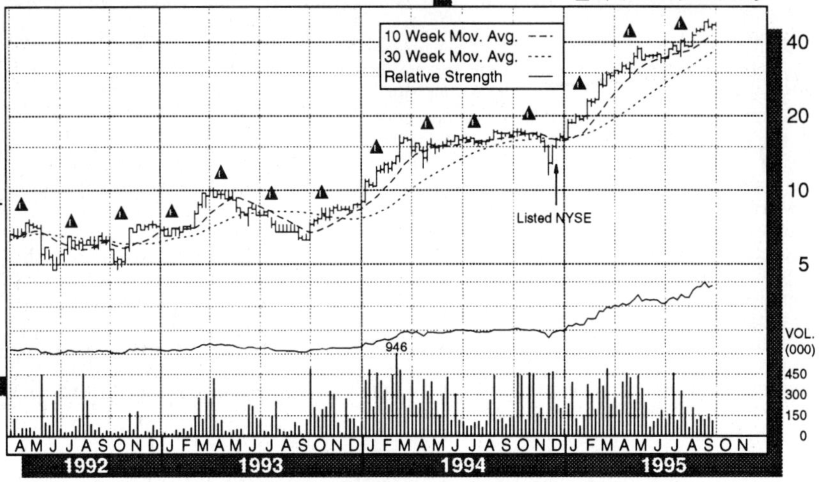

Business Profile - 29-SEP-95

The number of CXC prison beds under contract has grown from 9,331 at the beginning of 1994 to 21,675 at mid-1995. The company achieved this growth by obtaining contracts to build additional facilities as well as through acquisitions. Additional growth may result from various political and social trends, including public sentiment in favor of longer jail sentences and privatizing government services.

Operational Review - 29-SEP-95

Revenue growth accelerated in the second quarter, aided by strong demand for the company's services and acquisitions. Margins improved on the higher volume. As the company brings additional beds on-line, general and administrative expenses should continue to decrease as a percentage of sales. Gains in earnings per share were limited by the company incurring a full tax rate for the first time, and a non-recurring charge of $0.02 a share related to the Concept Inc. acquisition in April.

Stock Performance - 22-SEP-95

In the past 30 trading days, CXC's shares have increased 23%, compared to a 5% rise in the S&P 500. Average trading volume for the past five days was 21,440 shares, compared with the 40-day moving average of 28,292 shares.

Key Stock Statistics

Dividend Rate/Share	Nil	Shareholders	700
Shs. outstg. (M)	15.1	Market cap. (B)	$0.704
Avg. daily vol. (M)	0.038	Inst. holdings	35%
Tang. Bk. Value/Share	4.58	Insider holdings	NA
Beta	1.35		

Value of $10,000 invested 5 years ago: $ 31,949

Fiscal Year Ending Dec. 31

	1995	% Change	1994	% Change	1993	% Change
Revenues (Million $)						
1Q	34.61	26%	27.40	6%	25.78	42%
2Q	47.87	63%	29.33	12%	26.29	18%
3Q	—	—	30.84	15%	26.78	11%
4Q	—	—	33.14	21%	27.36	6%
Yr.	—	—	120.7	14%	106.2	18%
Income (Million $)						
1Q	2.67	110%	1.27	44%	0.88	115%
2Q	2.91	126%	1.29	30%	0.99	36%
3Q	—	—	2.20	116%	1.02	34%
4Q	—	—	2.41	143%	0.99	62%
Yr.	—	—	7.18	85%	3.89	54%
Earnings Per Share ($)						
1Q	0.17	70%	0.10	25%	0.08	100%
2Q	0.16	60%	0.10	11%	0.09	13%
3Q	—	—	0.16	78%	0.09	13%
4Q	—	—	0.17	89%	0.09	50%
Yr.	—	—	0.53	51%	0.35	35%

Next earnings report expected: early November

Corrections Corp. of America

Business Summary - 29-SEP-95

Corrections Corporation of America manages prisons and other correctional and detention facilities for governmental agencies. Since beginning operations in 1983, it has been the leader in privatizing such facilities. As of June 1995, 21,675 beds in 36 facilities were under contract in nine U.S. states, Puerto Rico, Australia and the U.K.

The company assumes complete responsibility for operating and maintaining correctional facilities. Services include facility administration, security, inmate supervision, facility maintenance, foodservice and health care. Certain facilities also offer rehabilitation programs. CXC also provides financing, design and construction of new facilities and redesign and renovation of existing facilities.

Facilities include county, state and federal adult correction and detention units, as well as several juvenile facilities. The facilities range in capacity from 63 to 1,336 inmates. The company also has a 50% stake in Corrections Corp. of Australia, formed in 1989, and holds a contract to manage a 244-bed prison for the State of Queensland, Australia. CXC also has a 33% interest in UK Detention Services, a U.K. venture that manages a 649-bed prison for the British government.

Compensation to CXC is based on the number of inmates held in each facility. Contracts may provide fixed per diem or monthly rates; some also provide for minimum guarantees. In 1994, the average occupancy rate was 96.0%, up from 92.1% in 1993.

In 1994, the U.S. Marshal Service and the State of Texas each accounted for about 15% of revenues, and the State of Tennessee 13%.

At March 1995, the company had eight facilities under construction. In addition, the company was pursuing 17 facility prospects with a total of 11,700 beds for which it had not submitted proposals and three prospects for a total of 1,300 beds for which proposals had been submitted.

Important Developments

Sep. '95—The company reach agreement with Citrus County Fla. to operate 300 adult male and female jail beds in an existing county-owned facility. The contract carries an initial three year term and is expected to produce annual revenues in excess of $4 million.

Aug. '95—CXC acquired Corrections Partners, Inc. (CPI) by granting 700,000 shares of restricted stock to the owners of privately-held CPI. CPI currently operates four facilities totaling 1,060 beds, with contracts to manage, when built, another three facilities with 1,886 beds. Separately, CXC signed an agreement to manage the 1,000 bed facility in Eden, Tex. The agreements will add $24 million in annual revenues.

Capitalization

Long Term Debt: $42,956,000 (6/95).
Options & Warrants: To purchase about 4,446,495 shs. (12/94).

Per Share Data ($) (Year Ended Dec. 31)

	1994	1993	1992	1991	1990	1989
Tangible Bk. Val.	4.56	3.34	3.05	2.75	2.80	2.85
Cash Flow	0.83	0.64	0.56	0.06	0.19	0.31
Earnings	0.53	0.36	0.26	-0.20	0.02	0.17
Dividends	Nil	Nil	Nil	Nil	Nil	Nil
Payout Ratio	Nil	Nil	Nil	Nil	Nil	Nil
Prices - High	17¾	10¼	8	10½	16½	15¼
- Low	8⅞	6¼	4¾	4⅜	7	7⅜
P/E Ratio - High	33	28	31	NM	NM	90
- Low	17	17	18	NM	NM	43

Income Statement Analysis (Million $)

	1994	%Chg	1993	%Chg	1992	%Chg	1991
Revs.	121	21%	100	11%	90.2	33%	67.9
Oper. Inc.	16.6	51%	11.0	14%	9.7	57%	6.2
Depr.	4.1	45%	2.8	-3%	2.9	19%	2.4
Int. Exp.	5.0	-10%	5.6	-9%	6.1	-4%	6.4
Pretax Inc.	9.3	129%	4.0	58%	2.6	NM	-1.9
Eff. Tax Rate	20%	—	2.00%	—	1.60%	—	NM
Net Inc.	7.4	87%	4.0	57%	2.5	NM	-1.9

Balance Sheet & Other Fin. Data (Million $)

	1994	1993	1992	1991	1990	1989
Cash	4.1	6.3	5.2	5.2	5.7	1.5
Curr. Assets	32.0	24.7	24.3	16.8	18.1	12.5
Total Assets	130	100	102	96.7	94.1	67.6
Curr. Liab.	17.9	12.5	13.4	8.8	7.3	5.0
LT Debt	46.5	48.7	55.4	57.8	61.8	37.0
Common Eqty.	58.3	32.0	28.5	25.2	25.0	25.6
Total Cap.	108	87.3	88.9	88.0	86.9	62.6
Cap. Exp.	23.2	1.9	11.2	8.3	25.7	18.0
Cash Flow	11.3	6.3	5.4	0.6	1.8	2.8

Ratio Analysis

	1994	1993	1992	1991	1990	1989
Curr. Ratio	1.8	2.0	1.8	1.9	2.5	2.5
% LT Debt of Cap.	42.9	55.8	62.3	65.7	71.2	59.1
% Net Inc.of Revs.	6.1	3.9	2.8	NM	0.4	4.4
% Ret. on Assets	5.6	3.9	2.5	NM	0.2	2.8
% Ret. on Equity	14.2	11.5	9.0	NM	0.8	6.6

Dividend Data —No cash dividends have been paid.

Data as orig. reptd.; bef. results of disc. opers. and/or spec. items. Per share data adj. for stk. divs. as of ex-div. date. E-Estimated. NA-Not Available. NM-Not Meaningful. NR-Not Ranked.

Office—102 Woodmont Blvd., Nashville, TN 37205. **Tel**—(615) 292-3100. **Chrmn & CEO**—D. R. Crants. **Pres**—D. L Myers. **VP-Fin, Secy & Treas**—D. K. Massengale. **VP & Investor Contact**—Peggy W. Lawrence. **Dirs**—W. F. Andrews, S. W. Bartholomew Jr., T. W. Beasley, D. R. Crants, J. P. Cuny, R. H. Fulton, T. D. Hutto. **Registrar & Transfer Agent**—First Union National Bank, Charlotte, N.C. **Incorporated** in Delaware in 1986. **Empl**-2,771. **S&P Analyst:** Stephen Madonna, CFA

Coventry Corp.

NASDAQ Symbol CVTY (Incl. in Nat'l Market) Options on Phila In S&P SmallCap 600

Price	Range	P-E Ratio	Dividend	Yield	S&P Ranking	Beta
Aug. 25'95	1995					
17⅝	31–11	19	None	None	NR	NA

Summary

This company provides a wide range of health care benefit options through five regional HMOs, including a Florida-based Medicaid HMO acquired in April 1995. Long-term prospects are enhanced by strong enrollment gains, but medical cost inflation is expected to restrict profits in 1995.

Current Outlook

Share earnings for 1995 should be $0.95 (before charges of $0.04), versus 1994's $0.96. A gain to $1.20 is projected for 1996.

The initiation of cash dividends is not expected.

Despite the likelihood of enrollment growth of 10% to 15%, the profit outlook for the second half of 1995 is clouded by rising medical costs in certain markets, particularly Pittsburgh and St. Louis. However, we expect earnings to rebound significantly in 1996, as the cost structure benefits from cost-cutting and reorganization efforts. Coventry could potentially lure a suitor, based on its attractive markets and current low valuation per enrollee.

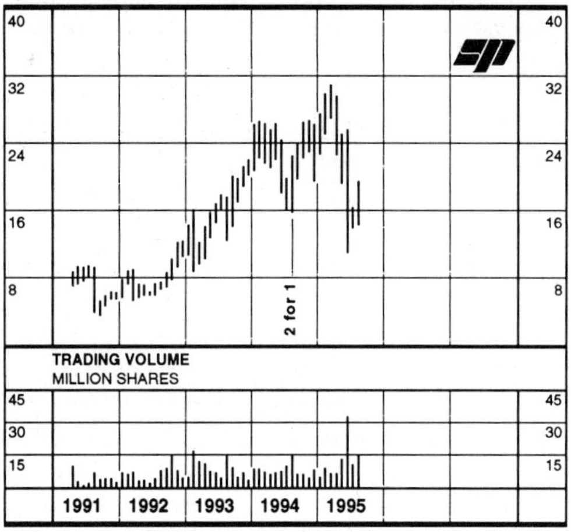

Revenues (Million $)

Quarter:	1995	1994	1993	1992
Mar.	199	185	139	103
Jun.	198	186	142	104
Sep.		189	149	109
Dec.		188	153	113
		747	583	430

Revenues in the six months ended June 30, 1995, advanced 7.4%, year to year, boosted by a 12% enrollment gain. Results were hurt by rising medical costs in certain markets, and after charges of $0.11 a share related to staff restructuring in Pittsburgh and St. Louis, share earnings declined to $0.45 (before merger-related charges of $0.04), from $0.50.

Common Share Earnings ($)

Quarter:	1995	1994	1993	1992
Mar.	0.32	0.24	0.19	0.12
Jun.	0.13	0.27	0.20	0.14
Sep.	E0.20	0.27	0.21	0.15
Dec.	E0.30	0.20	0.21	0.17
	E0.95	0.96	0.80	0.57

Important Developments

Aug. '95— Coventry said that although higher medical utilization hurt second quarter results, it believes that appropriate corrective actions have been taken. The company is restructuring its provider contracts and implementing stricter utilization controls for outpatient services in an effort to control its medical costs. These actions should begin to aid earnings in the fourth quarter.

Aug. '95— The company acquired Jacksonville, Fla.-based HealthCare USA, a Medicaid HMO serving about 27,000 members, in exchange for common stock valued at $45 million. The acquisition was expected to be neutral to modestly additive to 1995 earnings. Earlier, in May, Coventry was selected to provide Medicaid services to over 150,000 recipients in St. Louis, Mo., and in four surrounding counties. Services will be provided through HealthCare USA.

Next earnings report expected in early November.

Per Share Data ($)

Yr. End Dec. 31	1994	1993	1992	1991	1990	1989	1988	1987
Tangible Bk. Val.	**0.60**	0.53	d0.17	d0.78	d1.39	NA	NA	NA
Cash Flow	**1.28**	1.07	0.78	0.65	0.96	0.94	0.71	0.14
Earnings[1]	**0.96**	0.80	0.57	0.40	0.59	0.59	0.42	0.06
Dividends	**Nil**	Nil	Nil	Nil	Nil	Nil	Nil	Nil
Payout Ratio	**Nil**	Nil	Nil	Nil	Nil	Nil	Nil	Nil
Prices—High	**26¾**	22⅛	12⅜	9½	NA	NA	NA	NA
Low	**15¾**	8¾	5¼	3½	NA	NA	NA	NA
P/E Ratio—	**28–16**	28–11	22–9	24–9	NA	NA	NA	NA

Data as orig. reptd. Adj. for stk. div. of 100% Aug. 1994. **1.** Bef. results of disc. ops. of -0.15 in 1992, -3.56 in 1991 & spec. items of +0.17 in 1992, +0.17 in 1991. E-Estimated. d-Deficit. NA-Not Available.

Income Data (Million $)

Year Ended Dec. 31	Revs.	Oper. Inc.	% Oper. Inc. of Revs.	Cap. Exp.	Depr.	Int. Exp.	Net Bef. Taxes	Eff. Tax Rate	[2]Net Inc.	% Net Inc. of Revs.	Cash Flow
1994	**747**	**66.5**	**8.9**	**21.30**	**9.24**	**2.66**	**56.0**	**43.5%**	**28.1**	**3.8**	**37.3**
1993	583	48.2	8.3	12.80	7.12	2.72	40.3	40.2%	20.3	3.5	27.4
1992	430	33.5	7.8	4.42	5.29	3.67	25.9	41.0%	13.8	3.2	19.1
[1]1991	340	24.1	7.1	3.15	5.70	5.63	16.0	38.0%	8.7	2.6	14.4
1990	394	28.0	7.1	3.95	6.27	9.88	15.9	36.9%	10.0	2.5	16.3
1989	218	21.1	9.7	3.27	3.61	7.56	13.7	33.0%	9.1	4.2	12.7
1988	84	11.8	14.1	0.40	1.50	4.31	7.5	27.1%	5.5	6.5	7.0
1987	10	1.4	13.4	NA	0.21	0.72	0.8	17.0%	0.7	6.5	0.9

Balance Sheet Data (Million $)

Dec. 31	Cash	Curr. Assets	Curr. Liab.	Curr. Ratio	Total Assets	% Ret. on Assets	Long Term Debt	Common Equity	Total Cap.	% LT Debt of Cap.	% Ret. on Equity
1994	**75.4**	**114.0**	**132.0**	**0.9**	**332**	**9.4**	**65.1**	**130.8**	**196**	**33.2**	**24.5**
1993	71.3	100.0	107.0	0.9	243	9.1	37.3	87.9	134	27.9	26.6
1992	55.3	78.2	75.9	1.0	193	7.8	47.4	62.4	114	41.5	25.2
1991	23.3	43.4	53.6	0.8	164	0.8	54.2	47.3	105	51.8	3.4
1990	43.5	90.0	97.5	0.9	269	4.5	80.0	64.4	157	51.1	17.3
1989	31.6	56.3	51.0	1.1	180	5.0	60.5	51.5	119	51.0	21.6

Data as orig. reptd. **1.** Excl. disc. ops. **2.** Bef. spec. items. NA-Not Available.

Business Summary

Coventry Corporation is a managed health care company that provides comprehensive health care services through regional HMOs located in Pittsburgh and Harrisburg, Pennsylvania, St. Louis, Missouri, Richmond, Virginia, and Jacksonville, Florida.

The company's HMOs furnish comprehensive health care services to their enrollees, including ambulatory and inpatient physician care, hospital care, pharmacy, dental, eye care, mental health, ancillary diagnostic and therapeutic services. In general, a fixed monthly enrollment fee covers all required services, although some benefit plans require co-payments or deductibles in addition to the basic enrollment premium. Coventry's HMOs also offer enrollees fully-insured flexible provider products, including preferred provider organization (PPO) and point of service (POS) products, for additional deductibles and co-payments. At June 30, 1995, HMO enrollment totaled 626,092 members, up from 557,858 members a year earlier.

HMO enrollees have historically been primarily employees of relatively large commercial entities. The company has recently increased its marketing efforts to mid- to small-size employer groups. Coventry emphasizes the staff-model HMO, which it believes provides the most efficient managed health care delivery system. The company also uses the open-panel structure to provide service in areas where enrollees are more geographically dispersed or in conjuction with staff-model HMO operations as additional primary-care locations.

The company's Pittsburgh and St. Louis HMOs operate primarily under the staff model, delivering health care services through physicians employed exclusively by the HMO. The exclusive full-time employment of physicians enables the HMO to predict costs effectively, maintain quality and respond quickly to consumer issues. Coventry's central Pennsylvania HMO is an open-panel HMO. Under the open-panel structure, individual physicians or physician groups provide services to enrollees through contractual arrangements with the HMO but also maintain independent practices in which they provide services to patients who are not HMO enrollees. The company normally compensates these open-panel physicians with a fixed monthly fee per HMO enrollee assigned to the physician.

Dividend Data

No cash dividends have been paid.

Finances

In December 1994, Coventry acquired Southern Health Management Corp., the parent company of a physician-owned HMO with 45,000 members located in Richmond and central Virginia, for common stock valued at about $75 million.

In October 1994, the company acquired the remaining 20% interest in HealthAmerica Pennsylvania, Coventry's largest health plan with about 370,000 members in Pittsburgh and Central Pennsylvania, for $50 million in cash.

Capitalization

Long Term Debt: $65,090,000 (12/94).

Common Stock: 32,150,000 shs. ($0.01 par).
Institutions hold 77%.
Shareholders: About 440 of record (3/95).

Office—53 Century Blvd., Nashville, TN 37214. **Tel**—(615) 391-2440. **Chrmn, Pres & CEO**—P. Hertik. **SVP, CFO, Treas & Investor Contact**—Richard H. Jones. **VP & Secy**—S. R. Smith. **Dirs**—J. H. Austin, L. DeFrance, E. D. Farley, Jr., P. Hertik, W. T. Hjorth, L. Kugelman. **Transfer Agent**—Mellon Securities Trust Co., Ridgefield Park, NJ. **Incorporated** in Delaware in 1986. **Empl**—2,400.

 Robert M. Gold

STANDARD & POOR'S

STOCK REPORTS

Cross Timbers Oil

NYSE Symbol **XTO**
In S&P SmallCap 600

13-OCT-95 **Industry:** Oil and Gas

Summary: This oil and gas production and transportation company has properties in Oklahoma, Texas, New Mexico and Kansas.

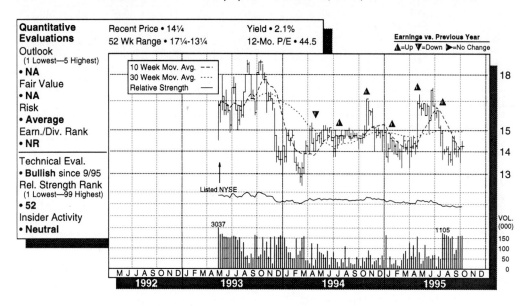

Quantitative Evaluations
Outlook
(1 Lowest—5 Highest)
• **NA**
Fair Value
• **NA**
Risk
• **Average**
Earn./Div. Rank
• **NR**

Technical Eval.
• **Bullish** since 9/95
Rel. Strength Rank
(1 Lowest—99 Highest)
• **52**
Insider Activity
• **Neutral**

Recent Price • 14¼
52 Wk Range • 17¼-13¼
Yield • 2.1%
12-Mo. P/E • 44.5

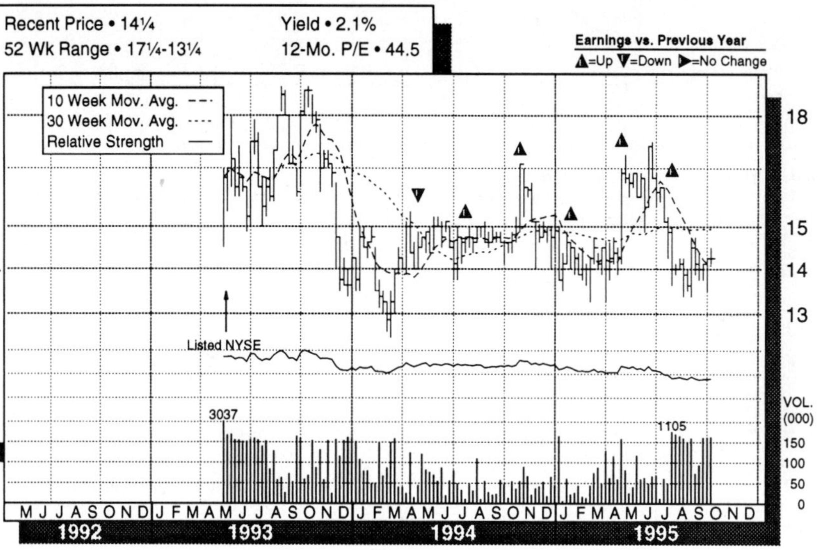

Business Profile - 13-OCT-95

Cross Timbers is engaged in acquiring, exploiting and developing oil and gas properties. It operates 80% of its properties. In 1993, XTO announced a goal of acquiring $250 million in properties over the next five years. In August 1995, XTO purchased gas producing properties and a gathering system and processing plant for about $121 million. XTO seeks to acquire a balance of oil and gas properties with established, long-lived production, strong operating margins, and development potential.

Operational Review - 13-OCT-95

Revenues for the six months ended June 30, 1995, advanced 12%, year to year. Profitability benefited from lower production expenses and higher oil prices, but lower natural gas prices were restrictive. Aided by gains totaling $2.4 million from the sale of equity securities and the sale of properties, net income increased to $2,406,000 ($0.15 a share) from $329,000 ($0.02) in the year-earlier period.

Stock Performance - 06-OCT-95

In the past 30 trading days, XTO's shares have increased 5%, compared to a 4% rise in the S&P 500. Average trading volume for the past five days was 56,040 shares, compared with the 40-day moving average of 41,718 shares.

Key Stock Statistics

Dividend Rate/Share	0.30	Shareholders	200
Shs. outstg. (M)	18.2	Market cap. (B)	$0.262
Avg. daily vol. (M)	0.050	Inst. holdings	53%
Tang. Bk. Value/Share	7.13	Insider holdings	NA
Beta	NA		

Value of $10,000 invested 5 years ago: NA

Fiscal Year Ending Dec. 31

	1995	% Change	1994	% Change	1993	% Change
Revenues (Million $)						
1Q	24.22	7%	22.61	46%	15.47	—
2Q	27.94	16%	24.02	26%	19.09	—
3Q	—	—	25.29	13%	22.47	—
4Q	—	—	24.36	15%	21.15	—
Yr.	—	—	96.28	23%	78.18	-27%
Income (Million $)						
1Q	1.46	NM	-0.44	NM	0.01	—
2Q	0.94	22%	0.77	NM	-0.84	—
3Q	—	—	1.52	NM	-0.19	—
4Q	—	—	1.20	54%	0.78	—
Yr.	—	—	3.05	NM	-0.25	NM
Earnings Per Share ($)						
1Q	0.09	NM	-0.03	—	Nil	—
2Q	0.06	20%	0.05	NM	-0.06	—
3Q	—	—	0.10	NM	-0.01	—
4Q	—	—	0.08	60%	0.05	—
Yr.	—	—	0.19	NM	-0.02	NM

Next earnings report expected: late October

Cross Timbers Oil

Business Summary - 13-OCT-95

Cross Timbers Oil is engaged in the acquisition, exploitation and development of producing oil and gas properties and the marketing and transportation of oil and natural gas. XTO's oil and gas properties are concentrated mainly in major producing basins in Oklahoma and East Texas, and in the Permian Basin of West Texas and New Mexico. The company owns and operates a gas gathering system in Major County, Oklahoma, where a significant portion of its gas is produced. XTO also markets natural gas and trades crude oil. Most of the company's gas production is sold to purchasers at the wellhead at market prices.

The company's strategy is to acquire producing properties with established production histories and strong operating margins, long reserve lives, and the potential for exploitation, development and product price escalation. XTO focuses primarily on acquisitions from major oil companies of operated properties valued in excess of $5 million that it believes provide opportunities to increase production and reserves through operational enhancements, geologic evaluation and reservoir engineering. The company also seeks to acquire facilites related to the production, processing, marketing and transportation of oil and gas.

XTO's oil and gas reserves are primarily in long-lived fields with well established production histories. As of December 31, 1994, estimated proved oil and gas reserves totaled 33.6 million bbl. of oil and 177.1 million Mcf of natural gas, or a total of 63.1 million NEB (net equivalent barrels of oil). Also at that date, XTO owned interests in 5,230 gross (1,108.4 net) wells. The discounted present value of the company's estimated proved reserves (before income taxes) was $247.9 million at December 31, 1994.

In 1993, Cross Timbers announced a goal to acquire $250 million in properties over the ensuing five years.

Important Developments

Aug. '95—XTO acquired gas producing properties and a related gathering system and processing plant for about $121 million from Santa Fe Minerals, Inc. The properties acquired consist primarily of operated interests in the Hugoton Field of Kansas and Oklahoma. The purchase was funded by bank borrowings.

Aug. '95—The company completed a public offering of 2,250,000 common shares, including 500,000 sold through exercise of underwriters' overallotment options. Certain shareholders sold an additional approximate 2,100,000 as part of the offering.

Capitalization

Long Term Debt: $160,000,000 (6/95).

Per Share Data ($)

(Year Ended Dec. 31)

	1994	1993	1992	1991	1990	1989
Tangible Bk. Val.	7.12	7.23	7.32	NA	NA	NA
Cash Flow	2.18	1.42	1.92	NA	NA	NA
Earnings	0.19	-0.28	0.45	NA	NA	NA
Dividends	0.30	0.22	NA	NA	NA	NA
Payout Ratio	158%	NM	NA	NA	NA	NA
Prices - High	16⅝	18⅞	NA	NA	NA	NA
- Low	12½	12⅞	NA	NA	NA	NA
P/E Ratio - High	87	NM	NA	NA	NA	NA
- Low	66	NM	NA	NA	NA	NA

Income Statement Analysis (Million $)

	1994	%Chg	1993	%Chg	1992	%Chg	1991
Revs.	96.0	23%	78.1	-27%	107	—	NA
Oper. Inc.	44.2	49%	29.7	-25%	39.4	—	NA
Depr. Depl. & Amort.	31.7	29%	24.6	4%	23.7	—	NA
Int. Exp.	8.3	48%	5.6	18%	4.7	—	NA
Pretax Inc.	4.8	NM	-0.4	NM	11.0	—	NA
Eff. Tax Rate	36%	—	NM	—	34%	—	NA
Net Inc.	3.0	NM	-4.0	NM	7.2	—	NA

Balance Sheet & Other Fin. Data (Million $)

	1994	1993	1992	1991	1990	1989
Cash	7.8	2.1	4.3	NA	NA	NA
Curr. Assets	26.9	22.8	21.8	NA	NA	NA
Total Assets	292	258	220	NA	NA	NA
Curr. Liab.	28.5	25.3	15.9	NA	NA	NA
LT Debt	143	112	79.9	NA	NA	NA
Common Eqty.	113	115	120	NA	NA	NA
Total Cap.	264	233	204	NA	NA	NA
Cap. Exp.	30.0	105	NA	NA	NA	NA
Cash Flow	34.8	20.6	31.0	NA	NA	NA

Ratio Analysis

	1994	1993	1992	1991	1990	1989
Curr. Ratio	0.9	0.9	1.4	NA	NA	NA
% LT Debt of Cap.	54.1	48.1	39.1	NA	NA	NA
% Ret. on Assets	1.1	NM	NA	NA	NA	NA
% Ret. on Equity	2.7	NM	NA	NA	NA	NA

Dividend Data —Quarterly dividends were initiated with the July 1993 payment.

Amt. of Div. $	Date Decl.	Ex-Div. Date	Stock of Record	Payment Date
0.075	Aug. 16	Sep. 26	Sep. 30	Oct. 14 '94
0.075	Nov. 15	Dec. 23	Dec. 30	Jan. 13 '95
0.075	Feb. 21	Mar. 27	Mar. 31	Apr. 14 '95
0.075	May. 16	Jun. 28	Jun. 30	Jul. 14 '95
0.075	Aug. 15	Sep. 27	Sep. 29	Oct. 13 '95

Data as orig. reptd.; bef. results of disc opers. and/or spec. items. Per share data adj. for stk. divs. as of ex-div. date. E-Estimated. NA-Not Available. NM-Not Meaningful. NR-Not Ranked.

Office—810 Houston St., Fort Worth, TX 76102. **Tel**—(817) 870-2800. **Chrmn**—J. Brumley. **Vice Chrmn & CEO**—B. R. Simpson. **Vice Chrmn & Pres**—S. E. Palko. **SVP-CFO & Investor Contact**—Louis G. Baldwin. **Dirs**—J. Brumley, C. B. Chitty, J. L. King Jr., S. E. Palko, S. G. Sherman, B. R. Simpson, G. U. Wyper. **Transfer Agent & Registrar**—Chemical Shareholder Services, Dallas. **Organized** in Delaware in 1990. **Empl**-225. **S&P Analyst:** JJS

STANDARD & POOR'S

STOCK REPORTS

Cullen/Frost Bankers

NASDAQ Symbol **CFBI**
In S&P SmallCap 600

07-OCT-95 **Industry:** Banking

Summary: The largest multibank holding company in Texas, Cullen/Frost owns two subsidiary banks with 33 offices in five major markets in the state.

Quantitative Evaluations
Outlook
(1 Lowest—5 Highest)
• NA
Fair Value
• NA
Risk
• Low
Earn./Div. Rank
• B

Technical Eval.
• Bullish since 2/95
Rel. Strength Rank
(1 Lowest—99 Highest)
• 75
Insider Activity
• NA

Recent Price • 47⅜
52 Wk Range • 48¼-28½
Yield • 3.0%
12-Mo. P/E • 13.1

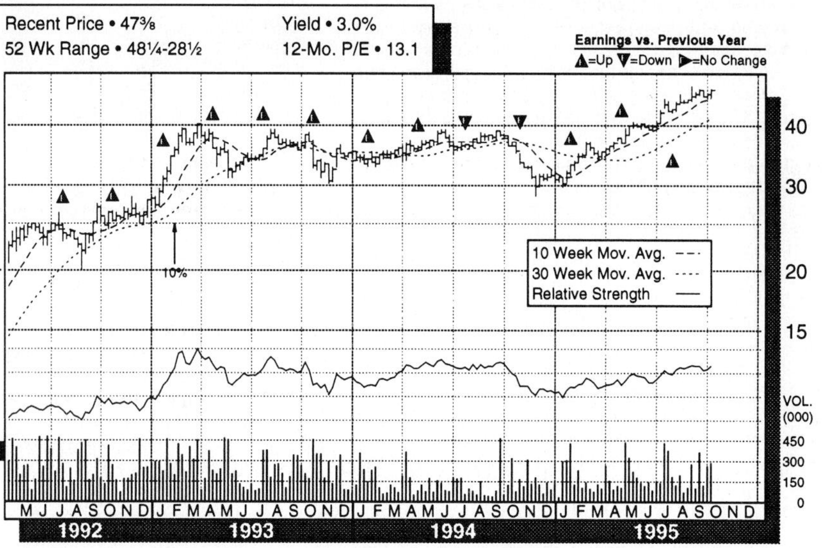

Business Profile - 23-JUL-95

This multibank holding company, the largest in Texas with $4.0 billion in assets, provides commercial, correspondent, consumer and asset-based banking services, as well as trust and discount brokerage services. Cullen/Frost continues to expand through acquisitions, focusing on five major markets in southern Texas: San Antonio, Austin, Houston/Galveston, Corpus Christi and McAllen (on the Texas-Mexico border). Despite acquisition-related loan growth, credit quality remains strong.

Operational Review - 23-JUL-95

Net interest income in the six months ended June 30, 1995, increased 10%, year to year, aided by strong loan growth. There was a $3.8 million provision for loan losses, versus no provision. Noninterest income was up 13%, and following well controlled noninterest expenses, pretax income climbed 20%. After taxes at 35.2%, versus 34.7%, net income advanced 19%, to $21,862,000 ($1.94 a share), from $18,340,000 ($1.64).

Stock Performance - 06-OCT-95

In the past 30 trading days, CFBI's shares have increased 5%, compared to a 4% rise in the S&P 500. Average trading volume for the past five days was 56,480 shares, compared with the 40-day moving average of 40,028 shares.

Key Stock Statistics

Dividend Rate/Share	1.40	Shareholders	2,600
Shs. outstg. (M)	11.2	Market cap. (B)	$0.528
Avg. daily vol. (M)	0.051	Inst. holdings	57%
Tang. Bk. Value/Share	28.85	Insider holdings	NA
Beta	1.06		

Value of $10,000 invested 5 years ago: $ 49,419

Fiscal Year Ending Dec. 31

	1995	% Change	1994	% Change	1993	% Change
Revenues (Million $)						
1Q	79.41	18%	67.08	5%	63.84	NM
2Q	86.66	26%	68.99	2%	67.81	6%
3Q	—	—	74.12	12%	65.94	5%
4Q	—	—	72.14	6%	68.26	11%
Yr.	—	—	282.3	6%	265.9	6%
Income (Million $)						
1Q	10.64	17%	9.10	17%	7.79	NM
2Q	11.22	21%	9.24	-14%	10.73	199%
3Q	—	—	9.49	-21%	11.98	130%
4Q	—	—	9.59	15%	8.31	3%
Yr.	—	—	37.42	-4%	38.80	120%
Earnings Per Share ($)						
1Q	0.94	16%	0.81	14%	0.71	184%
2Q	0.99	21%	0.82	-15%	0.96	182%
3Q	—	—	0.84	-21%	1.07	118%
4Q	—	—	0.85	15%	0.74	28%
Yr.	—	—	3.33	-4%	3.48	110%

Next earnings report expected: mid October

Cullen/Frost Bankers

Business Summary - 06-OCT-95

Cullen/Frost Bankers, Inc., as of December 31, 1994, owned two banks with a total of 28 offices in four major Texas banking markets: San Antonio, Austin, Corpus Christi, and Houston/Galveston. In April 1994, it exchanged its Cullen/Frost Bank in Dallas for Texas Commerce Bank in Corpus Christi. The main subsidiary, Frost National Bank of San Antonio, had assets of $3.68 billion at December 31, 1994. Based on FRB data at that date, Cullen/Frost was the sixth largest banking organization and the largest multibank holding company in Texas.

Loans at December 31, 1994, totaled $1.48 billion and were divided:

Real estate	48%
Commercial & industrial	25%
Consumer	22%
International	3%
Other	2%

The reserve for loan losses at 1994 year end was $25,741,000 ($26,298,000 a year earlier), or 1.74% (2.11%) of loans outstanding (net of unearned discount). There was a net recovery of loans in 1994 of $2,127,000 (0.16% of average loans), versus $486,000 (0.04%) in 1993. Real estate net recoveries in 1994 were $0.6 million, against net chargeoffs of $1.1 million in 1993. As of December 31, 1994, nonperforming assets totaled $19.9 million (1.34% of total loans plus foreclosed assets), down from $31.1 million (2.47%) a year earlier.

Deposits averaged $3.12 billion in 1994 and were apportioned: 27% time, 26% demand, 25% savings and interest-on-checking, 18% money market, and 4% public funds. International deposits, principally from Mexico, averaged $521 million, or 17% of total average deposits.

Interest income on loans, including fees, accounted for 38% of total income in 1994, interest on investment securities 34%, other interest income 1%, trust department income 10%, service charges on deposit accounts 9%, and other noninterest income 8%.

On a tax-equivalent basis, the average yield on interest-earning assets was 6.62% in 1994 (6.35% in 1993), while the average rate paid on interest-bearing liabilities was 2.79% (2.57%), for a net spread of 3.83% (3.78%).

Important Developments

Jul. '95—In the first seven months of 1995, Cullen/Frost acquired three banks: Valley Bancshares Inc. (deposits of $50 million), McAllen; National Commerce Bank ($115 million), Houston; and two San Antonio branches of Comerica Bank Texas ($37 million). Terms were not disclosed.

Capitalization

Long Term Debt: None (6/95).

Per Share Data ($)

(Year Ended Dec. 31)

	1994	1993	1992	1991	1990	1989
Tangible Bk. Val.	26.56	24.85	19.80	17.55	17.79	18.92
Earnings	3.33	3.48	1.66	0.02	-0.85	0.28
Dividends	0.67	0.15	Nil	Nil	Nil	Nil
Payout Ratio	20%	4%	Nil	Nil	Nil	Nil
Prices - High	39¼	40¼	28⅝	13⅞	10⅝	16¾
- Low	28½	26⅞	12¼	5⅝	4¾	9¼
P/E Ratio - High	12	12	17	NM	NM	59
- Low	9	8	7	NM	NM	33

Income Statement Analysis (Million $)

	1994	%Chg	1993	%Chg	1992	%Chg	1991
Net Int. Inc.	136	6%	128	9%	117	7%	109
Tax Equiv. Adj.	0.6	-27%	0.9	-22%	1.1	-46%	2.1
Non Int. Inc.	80.9	8%	74.8	20%	62.1	12%	55.5
Loan Loss Prov.	Nil	—	-6.1	—	NM	—	10.0
% Exp/Op Revs.	71%	—	85%	—	85%	—	93%
Pretax Inc.	57.6	51%	38.1	48%	25.8	NM	0.8
Eff. Tax Rate	35%	—	NM	—	32%	—	76%
Net Inc.	37.4	-4%	38.8	120%	17.6	NM	0.2
% Net Int. Marg.	4.40%	—	4.29%	—	4.47%	—	4.13%

Balance Sheet & Other Fin. Data (Million $)

	1994	1993	1992	1991	1990	1989
Earning Assets:						
Money Mkt.	168	250	283	99	276	449
Inv. Securities	1,594	1,612	1,414	1,439	1,237	1,257
Com'l Loans	383	312	268	301	377	462
Other Loans	1,099	944	756	787	908	922
Total Assets	3,794	3,639	3,151	3,079	3,255	3,505
Demand Deposits	832	881	766	669	656	647
Time Deposits	2,256	2,268	2,003	2,097	2,222	2,333
LT Debt	Nil	Nil	13.4	14.7	16.3	17.5
Common Eqty.	293	274	206	176	173	179

Ratio Analysis

	1994	1993	1992	1991	1990	1989
% Ret. on Assets	1.0	1.1	0.6	0.0	NM	0.1
% Ret. on Equity	13.0	15.6	9.2	0.1	NM	1.5
% Loan Loss Resv.	1.7	2.1	3.2	4.0	3.6	3.1
% Loans/Deposits	47.7	39.6	36.5	38.8	44.1	46.0
% Equity to Assets	7.8	7.1	6.3	5.7	5.4	5.1

Dividend Data —Cash dividends, paid since 1899, were omitted in 1987 and resumed in October 1993.

Amt. of Div. $	Date Decl.	Ex-Div. Date	Stock of Record	Payment Date
0.220	Oct. 25	Nov. 25	Dec. 01	Dec. 15 '94
0.220	Feb. 07	Feb. 23	Mar. 01	Mar. 15 '95
0.220	Apr. 25	May. 25	Jun. 01	Jun. 15 '95
0.350	Jul. 25	Aug. 30	Sep. 01	Sep. 15 '95

Data as orig. reptd.; bef. results of disc opers. and/or spec. items. Per share data adj. for stk. divs. as of ex-div. date. E-Estimated. NA-Not Available. NM-Not Meaningful. NR-Not Ranked.

Office—P.O. Box 1600, 100 W. Houston St., San Antonio, TX 78205. **Tel**—(210) 220-4011. **Chrmn & CEO**—T. C. Frost. **Pres**—R. S. McClane. **EVP & Treas**—P. D. Green. **Secy**—Diane M. Jack. **Investor Contact**—Bart Vincent (210-220-4878). **Dirs**—I. Arnold Jr., R. S. Caldwell, R. R. Cardenas, H. E. Catto, H. H. Cullen, R. H. Cullen, R. W. Evans, Jr., W. N. Finnegan III, J. H. Frost, T. C. Frost, J. W. Gorman, Jr., J. L. Hayne, H. L. Kempner, Jr., R. M. Kleberg III, Q. Lee, R. S. — McClane, J. G. Muir, Jr., W. B. Osborn, Jr., R. G. Pope, H. J. Richter, C. Vaughan, Jr. **Transfer Agent & Registrar**—Frost National Bank, San Antonio. **Organized** in 1966. **Empl-** 1,862. **S&P Analyst:** Robert Schpoont

Custom Chrome

NASDAQ Symbol **CSTM**
In S&P SmallCap 600

19-OCT-95

Industry:
Auto parts/equipment

Summary: This company, which offers over 11,000 products, is the world's largest independent wholesale supplier of aftermarket parts and accessories for Harley-Davidson motorcycles.

Quantitative Evaluations
Outlook
(1 Lowest—5 Highest)
• **NA**
Fair Value
• **NA**
Risk
• **Average**
Earn./Div. Rank
• **NR**

Technical Eval.
• **Bullish** since 2/95
Rel. Strength Rank
(1 Lowest—99 Highest)
• **61**
Insider Activity
• **NA**

Recent Price • 22¾
52 Wk Range • 25⅛-15¾
Yield • Nil
12-Mo. P/E • 15.6

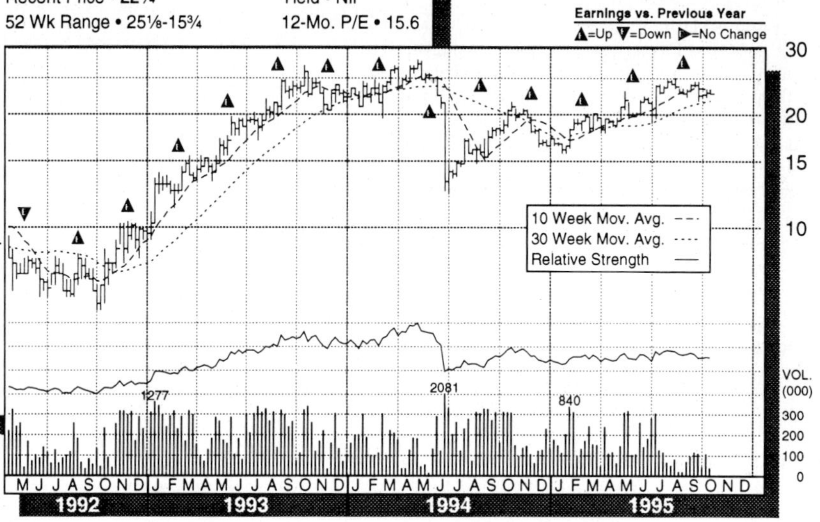

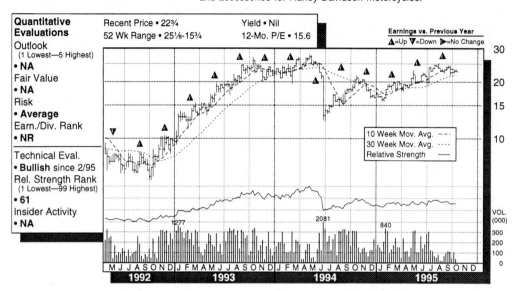

Business Profile - 05-OCT-95

CSTM's new marketing initiative has begun to boost sales, and results are expected to continue to improve for the balance of 1995-96. The company seeks to increase the penetration of its existing markets by providing a wider selection of products supported by strategically located warehouses. Sales in the first two quarters of the fiscal year are generally greater than sales in the second half, due to more orders placed by dealers in anticipation of and during the warm-weather months.

Operational Review - 19-OCT-95

Net sales in the six months ended July 31, 1995, advanced 23%, year to year, reflecting new products, increased European demand and improved sales in Southern California following the opening of a new distribution center. Profitability benefited from the higher volume and, although SG&A and interest expense rose more rapidly, net income was up 25%. CSTM expects future earnings to benefit from new products introduced during the past 12 months and an aggressive R&D program.

Stock Performance - 13-OCT-95

In the past 30 trading days, CSTM's shares have declined 2%, compared to a 4% rise in the S&P 500. Average trading volume for the past five days was 7,080 shares, compared with the 40-day moving average of 14,836 shares.

Key Stock Statistics

Dividend Rate/Share	Nil	Shareholders	300
Shs. outstg. (M)	5.1	Market cap. (B)	$0.119
Avg. daily vol. (M)	0.015	Inst. holdings	85%
Tang. Bk. Value/Share	8.78	Insider holdings	NA
Beta	NA		

Value of $10,000 invested 5 years ago: NA

Fiscal Year Ending Jan. 31

	1996	% Change	1995	% Change	1994	% Change
Revenues (Million $)						
1Q	24.49	16%	21.10	16%	18.23	33%
2Q	25.95	30%	20.00	5%	19.04	33%
3Q	—	—	17.55	11%	15.79	25%
4Q	—	—	16.27	15%	14.19	20%
Yr.	—	—	74.90	11%	67.25	28%
Income (Million $)						
1Q	2.55	21%	2.11	26%	1.68	41%
2Q	2.63	29%	2.04	1%	2.01	35%
3Q	—	—	1.25	23%	1.02	55%
4Q	—	—	1.03	27%	0.81	50%
Yr.	—	—	6.42	17%	5.51	42%
Earnings Per Share ($)						
1Q	0.50	19%	0.42	27%	0.33	38%
2Q	0.51	24%	0.41	3%	0.40	33%
3Q	—	—	0.25	25%	0.20	54%
4Q	—	—	0.20	25%	0.16	45%
Yr.	—	—	1.27	15%	1.10	41%

Next earnings report expected: early December

Custom Chrome

Business Summary - 19-OCT-95

Custom Chrome, Inc. is the world's largest independent wholesale supplier of aftermarket parts and accessories for motorcycles manufactured by Harley-Davidson, Inc. The company distributes its own products as well as products made by other manufacturers. It offers over 11,000 products to more than 4,600 dealers.

The company distributes thousands of aftermarket parts and accessories, including replacement parts, custom parts, accessories and apparel. It offers products in 16 different categories, ranging from apparel and leather to engine products. Custom Chrome offers a large number of proprietary products, which it designs and engineers and for which it typically owns the manufacturing tooling. The proprietary products are not widely available from any other source, allowing the company to obtain higher margins than may be available on products for which it acts only as a distributor.

Custom Chrome has created several brand names, including C.C. Rider, RevTech, Premium, Dyno Power, Tour Ease and Bullskins, under which it markets both proprietary and nonproprietary products supplied by third parties. In addition, the company markets and sells a number of products, such as fenders, gas tanks and ignition parts, under the Custom Chrome name. It also distributes a number of products from selected aftermarket manufacturers, such as Champion spark plugs, Dunlop tires, Crane cams, Accel electrical parts and Russell braided lines and tubing under the manufacturer's brand name.

The company distributes products from its 101,000-sq.-ft. distribution facility in Visalia, Calif., or from one of its other distribution facilities in Louisville, Ky. (90,000 sq. ft.; opened in August 1988), and Harrisburg, Pa. (66,000 sq. ft.; March 1992).

Custom Chrome's North American customer market consists of about 600 Harley-Davidson franchise dealers and about 5,000 independent motorcycle dealers. It also sells to about 600 overseas motorcycle dealers.

During 1994-95, about 325 new proprietary products and more than 775 non-proprietary products were added to the company's product line.

Important Developments

Sep. '95—The company believes its investment in new distribution and marketing facilities, products and personnel has allowed it to increase market share and strengthen its leadership position in the Harley-Davidson aftermarket for parts and accessories.

Capitalization

Long Term Debt: $19,669,000 (7/95), incl. lease obligs.
Options: To buy 546,435 shs. at $7.00 to $23.75 ea. (1/95).

Per Share Data ($) (Year Ended Jan. 31)

	1995	1994	1993	1992	1991	1990
Tangible Bk. Val.	7.71	6.54	5.08	2.31	-2.75	NA
Cash Flow	1.58	1.40	1.00	0.68	0.06	NA
Earnings	1.27	1.10	0.78	0.33	-1.03	NA
Dividends	Nil	Nil	Nil	Nil	Nil	NA
Payout Ratio	Nil	Nil	Nil	Nil	Nil	NA
Cal. Yrs.	1994	1993	1992	1991	1990	1989
Prices - High	28	27	11¾	10½	NA	NA
- Low	12¼	9¼	6	6	NA	NA
P/E Ratio - High	22	25	15	32	NA	NA
- Low	10	8	8	18	NA	NA

Income Statement Analysis (Million $)

	1995	%Chg	1994	%Chg	1993	%Chg	1992
Revs.	74.9	11%	67.3	28%	52.4	20%	43.6
Oper. Inc.	12.9	12%	11.5	38%	8.3	-3%	8.6
Depr.	1.6	3%	1.5	36%	1.1	4%	1.1
Int. Exp.	0.7	-16%	0.8	5%	0.8	-76%	3.3
Pretax Inc.	10.6	15%	9.2	43%	6.4	NM	1.4
Eff. Tax Rate	40%	—	40%	—	40%	—	27%
Net Inc.	6.4	17%	5.5	42%	3.9	NM	1.0

Balance Sheet & Other Fin. Data (Million $)

	1995	1994	1993	1992	1991	1990
Cash	9.0	Nil	Nil	Nil	Nil	NA
Curr. Assets	45.1	29.6	23.3	16.4	16.2	NA
Total Assets	64.3	47.3	40.5	32.8	34.4	NA
Curr. Liab.	5.8	10.8	11.6	9.0	13.5	NA
LT Debt	19.5	4.8	4.7	4.6	26.9	NA
Common Eqty.	38.6	31.7	24.1	19.2	-6.0	NA
Total Cap.	58.6	36.5	28.8	23.8	20.9	NA
Cap. Exp.	3.3	1.5	1.6	0.5	0.2	NA
Cash Flow	8.0	7.0	5.0	2.1	0.1	NA

Ratio Analysis

	1995	1994	1993	1992	1991	1990
Curr. Ratio	7.8	2.7	2.0	1.8	1.2	NA
% LT Debt of Cap.	33.3	13.0	16.3	19.4	128.9	NA
% Net Inc.of Revs.	8.6	8.2	7.4	2.4	NM	NA
% Ret. on Assets	11.4	12.4	10.6	1.9	NM	NA
% Ret. on Equity	18.0	19.5	17.9	NM	NM	NA

Dividend Data —No dividends have been paid. Custom Chrome intends to retain all earnings for use in the expansion of its business and, therefore, does not expect to pay any dividends in the foreseeable future.

Data as orig. reptd.; bef. results of disc. opers. and/or spec. items. Per share data adj. for stk. divs. as of ex-div. date. E-Estimated. NA-Not Available. NM-Not Meaningful. NR-Not Ranked.

Office—16100 Jacqueline Court, Morgan Hill, CA 95037. **Tel**—(408) 778-0500. **Chrmn, Pres & CEO**—I. J. Panzica. **Vice Chrmn**—T. Cruze, Sr. **VP-Fin, CFO, Secy & Investor Contact**—James J. Kelly Jr. **Dirs**—L. M. Allan, T. Cruze, Sr., J. F. Keenan, J. J. Kelly Jr., I. J. Panzica. **Transfer Agent & Registrar**—Bank of Boston, NYC. **Incorporated** in California in 1970; reincorporated in Delaware in 1990. **Empl**-301. **S&P Analyst:** Stewart Scharf

Cyrix Corp.

NASDAQ Symbol CYRX (Incl. in Nat'l Market) Options on ASE, CBOE & Pacific In S&P SmallCap 600

Price	Range	P-E Ratio	Dividend	Yield	S&P Ranking	Beta
Oct. 3'95	1995					
38⅜	49¾–16¾	16	None	None	NR	NA

Summary

Cyrix designs, develops and markets high-performance processors for the personal computer industry. CYRX is exiting the entry-level 486 microprocessor marketplace in favor of its Pentium-class 5x86 and M1 chips.

Business Summary

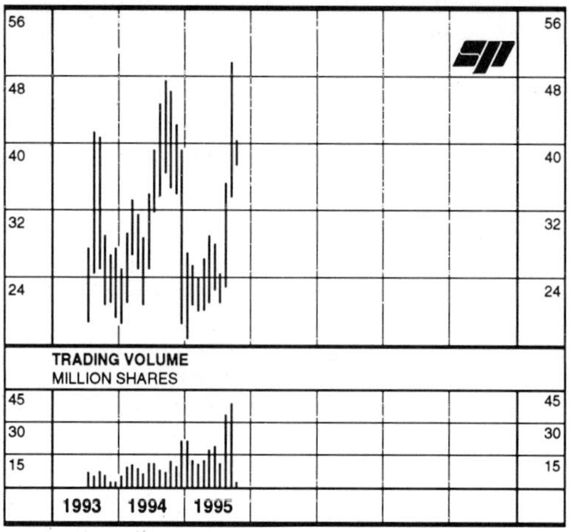

Cyrix Corp. designs, develops and markets IBM-compatible microprocessors and math coprocessors for the personal computer industry. The company utilizes a design system consisting of industry standard and Cyrix proprietary hardware and software design components, continued refinement of product specifications, simulations and testing for IBM compatibility.

In 1994, Cyrix's dominant product category was 486 instruction-set compatible microprocessors; revenues from its Cx486DX and Cx486DX2 chips accounted for about 75% of the company's product revenue in 1994. Cyrix is developing new microprocessor products targeted at the high performance segment of the personal computer market. Its new processors include the M1 product family, based on superscalar and superpipelined architectures; and the 5x86, a full-featured Pentium-class microprocessor to compete with Intel's offerings in the fifth-generation x86 marketplace. As computer makers have shifted from the 486 to the next generation of microprocessors, CYRX has decided to exit the 486 market and concentrate on the M1 and 5x86. Shipments of the M1 and the 5x86 began in mid-1995.

CYRX does not manufacture its own products but instead utilizes the services of qualified semiconductor manufacturers that offer leading CMOS process technologies. Cyrix currently has an agreement with SGS-Thomson Microelectronics pursuant to which SGS-Thomson manufactures products for sale to the company through December 1997. SGS-Thomson also has the right to manufacture and sell certain current and future Cyrix products under its own name. In April 1994, CYRX signed an agreement whereby IBM Corp.'s Microelectronics division will manufacture specified quantities of Cyrix-designed products for sale to the company through December 1999 at defined prices. Cyrix also committed to make a capital equipment investment of about $88 million in an IBM facility by June 1995.

Cyrix sells most of its products to original equipment manufacturers. In 1994 and 1993, sales to international customers accounted for 52% and 48%, respectively, of the company's revenues.

Research and development activities are focused on the design of competitive microprocessors and designing microprocessors that use advanced process technologies; cost production and performance improvements in existing and future products; and enhancing the company's design system and procedures. Research and development expenditures amounted to $24.8 million (10% of net sales) in 1994 and $15.7 million (13%) in 1993.

Important Developments

Sep. '95— CYRX said it was on target to ship larger quantities of M1 chips in the fourth quarter, following the shipment of several thousand M1 chips in the third quarter. Cyrix expected to cease shipping 486 chips by the end of the third quarter or early in the fourth quarter; the 5x86 processor was expected to produce substantial revenues in the third quarter, with higher production volumes planned for the fourth quarter.

Next earnings report expected in mid-October.

Per Share Data ($)

Yr. End Dec. 31	1994	1993	1992
Tangible Bk. Val.	**6.70**	4.58	5.94
Cash Flow	**2.36**	1.35	0.63
Earnings	**1.88**	1.06	0.49
Dividends	**Nil**	Nil	Nil
Payout Ratio	**Nil**	Nil	Nil
Prices—High	**47½**	41⅜	NA
Low	**18½**	18¾	NA
P/E Ratio—	**25–10**	39–18	NA

Data as orig. reptd. NA-Not Available.

Income Data (Million $)

Year Ended Dec. 31	Revs.	Oper. Inc.	% Oper. Inc. of Revs.	Cap. Exp.	Depr.	Int. Exp.	Net Bef. Taxes	Eff. Tax Rate	Net Inc.	% Net Inc. of Revs.	Cash Flow
1994	**246**	**65.4**	**26.6**	**24.0**	**9.64**	**0.72**	**57.4**	**34.5%**	**37.6**	**15.3**	**47.2**
1993	125	35.2	28.1	14.8	5.36	0.63	30.4	35.4%	19.6	15.7	25.0
1992	73	15.7	21.5	6.6	2.49	0.30	13.6	38.0%	8.4	11.5	10.9

Balance Sheet Data (Million $)

Dec. 31	Cash	Curr. Assets	Curr. Liab.	Curr. Ratio	Total Assets	% Ret. on Assets	Long Term Debt	Common Equity	Total Cap.	% LT Debt of Cap.	% Ret. on Equity
1994	**59.2**	**132.2**	**52.1**	**2.5**	**196**	**24.1**	**18.3**	**125.7**	**144.0**	**12.7**	**35.8**
1993	50.1	93.0	23.9	3.9	115	12.4	6.8	84.0	90.8	7.5	20.3
1992	27.2	38.5	14.0	2.7	50	NA	4.8	27.2	36.2	13.2	NA

Data as orig. reptd. NA-Not Available.

Revenues (Million $)

Quarter:	1995	1994	1993	1992
Mar.	85.1	46.3	29.0	14.5
Jun.	50.2	58.7	32.1	15.0
Sep.		68.1	31.1	16.4
Dec.		73.0	32.8	27.0
		246.1	125.1	72.9

Net revenues in the first half of 1995 advanced 29%, year to year, reflecting a 15% gain in product sales and receipt of $15 million in royalty revenue in settlement of a dispute with Texas Instruments; in the 1995 second quarter, however, product sales declined 14% on aggressive pricing in the 486 chip marketplace, which CYRX is exiting in favor of its 5x86 product. Gross margins narrowed, but with well-controlled operating expenses, operating income gained 41%. With $10 million of income from a litigation settlement, versus $500,000 a year earlier, and interest expense, against interest income, pretax income expanded 76%. After taxes at 35.2%, versus 34.2%, net income was up 73%, to $24,979,000 ($1.26 a share), from $14,399,000 ($0.72).

Common Share Earnings ($)

Quarter:	1995	1994	1993	1992
Mar.	0.88	0.26	0.37	0.10
Jun.	0.38	0.46	0.42	0.10
Sep.		0.52	0.25	0.06
Dec.		0.63	0.06	0.23
		1.88	[1]1.06	0.49

Dividend Data

No cash dividends have been paid. The company intends to retain its earnings for reinvestment in its business.

Finances

In the second quarter of 1995, CYRX recorded settlement income of $10 million from Intel Corp., which decided not to further appeal a January 1994 court decision concerning certain of CYRX's microprocessor products. In 1994's first quarter, Cyrix recorded a one-time settlement payment of $500,000 from Intel related to litigation concerning the company's math coprocessor products.

In 1995's first quarter, Cyrix received $15 million in royalty revenue in settlement of a dispute with Texas Instruments.

In July 1993, Cyrix completed its initial public offering of 2,300,000 common shares (2,200,000 new financing) at $16 a share. Net proceeds of about $32.1 million were used for general corporate purposes, working capital and the potential investment in or acquisition of a semiconductor manufacturing facility.

Capitalization

Long Term Debt: $58,783,000 (6/95).

Common Stock: Apx. 19,100,000 shs. ($0.004 par).
Institutions hold about 25%.
Shareholders of record: 522 (2/95).

1. Does not add due to change in shs. outstanding.

Office—2703 North Central Expressway, Richardson, TX 75080. **Tel**—(214) 994-8387. **Pres & CEO**—G. D. Rogers. **VP-Fin**—T. W. Kinnear. **Dirs**—H. B. Cash, J. Kemp, G. D. Rogers, L. J. Sevin, M. Sharp. **Transfer Agent & Registrar**—Bank One Texas, Dallas. **Incorporated** in Delaware in 1988. **Empl**—309.

 Stephen R. Biggar

Cytec Industries

NYSE Symbol **CYT**
In S&P SmallCap 600

16-OCT-95 **Industry:** Chemicals

Summary: This company manufactures specialty chemicals and specialty materials sold worldwide to a broad range of industries.

Quantitative Evaluations
Outlook (1 Lowest—5 Highest) • **NA**
Fair Value • **NA**
Risk • **Average**
Earn./Div. Rank • **NR**

Technical Eval. • **Bullish** since 5/95
Rel. Strength Rank (1 Lowest—99 Highest) • **83**
Insider Activity • **NA**

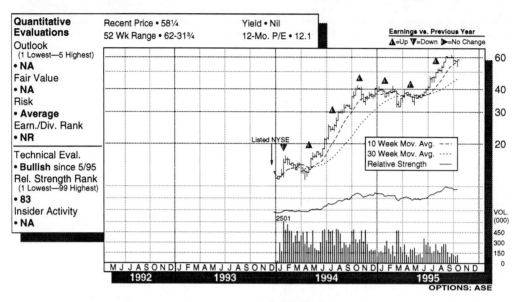

Recent Price • 58¼
52 Wk Range • 62-31¾
Yield • Nil
12-Mo. P/E • 12.1

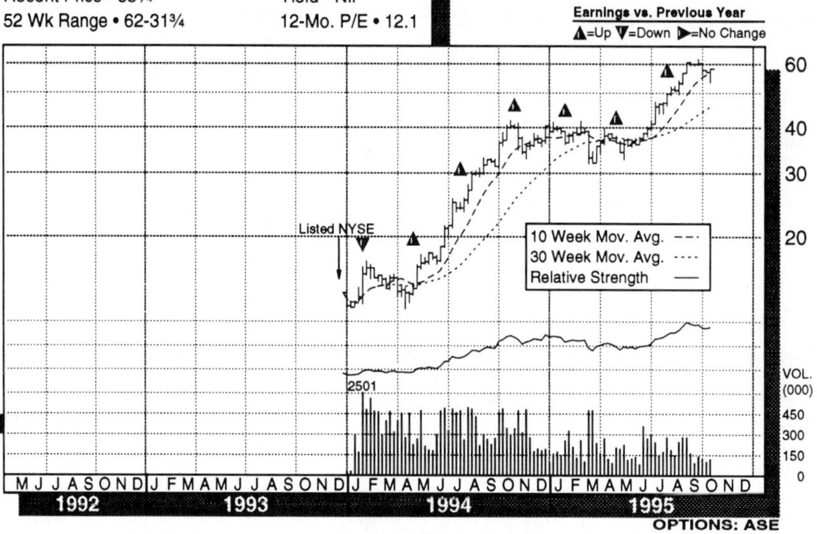

OPTIONS: ASE

Business Profile - 12-OCT-95

CYT, which has been growing internationally, sees further market share gains in 1995 in water treating, paper and mineral processing chemicals and other areas. It plans to gradually reduce capital expenditures over the next few years as it shifts from investing in building block chemicals to specialty chemicals. The company expects expenditures to total $100 million to $110 million in 1995. The Fortier plant upgrade should add 125 million pounds per year of capacity for acrylonitrile.

Operational Review - 12-OCT-95

Sales advanced 20%, year to year, in the first half of 1995, reflecting increased volume in both domestic and international markets, especially in specialty chemicals internationally. Profitability benefited from the increased volume and well controlled costs and expenses, and net income more than doubled. The company expects its 30% joint venture with Methanex Corp. to yield at least $1.00 a share (fully diluted) in additional earnings in 1995.

Stock Performance - 13-OCT-95

In the past 30 trading days, CYT's shares have declined 4%, compared to a 4% rise in the S&P 500. Average trading volume for the past five days was 23,600 shares, compared with the 40-day moving average of 32,521 shares.

Key Stock Statistics

Dividend Rate/Share	Nil	Shareholders	38,600
Shs. outstg. (M)	13.2	Market cap. (B)	$0.768
Avg. daily vol. (M)	0.024	Inst. holdings	46%
Tang. Bk. Value/Share	4.93	Insider holdings	NA
Beta	NA		

Value of $10,000 invested 5 years ago: NA

Fiscal Year Ending Dec. 31

	1995	% Change	1994	% Change	1993	% Change
Revenues (Million $)						
1Q	310.7	20%	258.1	10%	235.4	1%
2Q	333.1	20%	278.4	13%	246.6	NM
3Q	—	—	276.8	11%	248.5	4%
4Q	—	—	288.0	20%	240.2	2%
Yr.	—	—	1,101	13%	970.7	2%
Income (Million $)						
1Q	22.12	169%	8.21	90%	4.31	-47%
2Q	22.58	69%	13.35	NM	1.90	-82%
3Q	—	—	15.42	NM	-100.0	NM
4Q	—	—	19.09	148%	7.69	-39%
Yr.	—	—	56.07	NM	-86.08	NM
Earnings Per Share ($)						
1Q	1.37	NM	0.35	NM	0.05	-86%
2Q	1.40	87%	0.75	NM	-0.14	NM
3Q	—	—	0.88	NM	-8.06	NM
4Q	—	—	1.15	NM	0.31	-56%
Yr.	—	—	3.15	NM	-7.83	NM

Next earnings report expected: early November

Cytec Industries

Business Summary - 16-OCT-95

Cytec Industries Inc. manufacturers and markets chemical products worldwide for a wide range of industries, including water treatment, paper, chemical and polymer processing, coatings, plastics, mining, aerospace and automotive. A significant portion of CYT's specialty chemicals and specialty materials use building block chemicals manufactured by the company. Contributions by geographic area in 1994 were:

	Sales	Profits
United States	77%	72%
Other Western Hemisphere	5%	8%
Eastern Hemisphere	18%	20%

Specialty chemicals (about 62% of 1994 sales) include water treating, paper and mining chemicals (acrylamide-based organic flocculants and aluminum sulfate inorganic flocculants) used to enhance the separation of water from solid waste or particulate matter; coatings and resins (melamine cross-linking resins) used for automotive, marine, wood and metal finishings and appliance, container and industrial maintenance coatings; and polymer additives.

Specialty materials (25% of sales) include acrylic fibers used in sweaters, fleecewear, athletic, crew and dress socks, hats, scarves, gloves, blankets, home furnishings and industrial products; adhesives for aerospace and high-performance industrial applications; and advanced composites (resin-impregnated fabrics and tapes) for the aerospace, automotive, sporting goods, military and marine industries.

Building block chemicals (13% of sales) consist of ammonia, acrylonitrile and sulfuric acid, which is used in many industrial chemical processes. During 1994, the company expanded acrylamide capacity at its Fortier plant by about 30%.

In July 1994, CYT received $13.3 million from LaRoche Industries Inc. for a 50% joint-venture interest to own and operate Cytec's existing ammonia production facility in Fortier, La. About 15% of the company's ammonia production is sold to LaRoche.

Important Developments

Sep. '95—Under terms of a revised agreement the company said that it would use the proceeds of a planned public offering of 3.2 million common shares and internally generated funds to repurchase its Series B preferred stock aggregating $114 million. The shares, held by American Cyanamid Co., a unit of American Home Products Corp., are convertible into 5.55 million common shares. Pursuant to this agreement with Cyanamid, in August, Cytec repurchased its Series A preferred stock for about $90 million.

Capitalization

Long Term Debt: $1,000,000 (6/95)
Preferred Stock: $114,000,000.
Held by American Cyanamid Co. (a unit of American Home Products Corp.).

Per Share Data ($) (Year Ended Dec. 31)

	1994	1993	1992	1991	1990	1989
Tangible Bk. Val.	4.93	0.87	NA	NA	NA	NA
Cash Flow	9.09	-1.66	8.64	NA	NA	NA
Earnings	3.15	-7.83	2.14	NA	NA	NA
Dividends	Nil	Nil	NA	NA	NA	NA
Payout Ratio	Nil	Nil	NA	NA	NA	NA
Prices - High	41⅞	14	NA	NA	NA	NA
- Low	12⅝	13⅛	NA	NA	NA	NA
P/E Ratio - High	13	NM	NA	NA	NA	NA
- Low	4	NM	NA	NA	NA	NA

Income Statement Analysis (Million $)

	1994	%Chg	1993	%Chg	1992	%Chg	1991
Revs.	1,101	13%	971	2%	951	—	NA
Oper. Inc.	147	NM	-10.0	NM	128	—	NA
Depr.	78.1	-2%	79.3	-5%	83.6	—	NA
Int. Exp.	0.2	-93%	2.2	91%	1.1	—	NA
Pretax Inc.	91.0	NM	-82.4	NM	66.1	—	NA
Eff. Tax Rate	38%	—	NM	—	36%	—	NA
Net Inc.	56.0	NM	-86.1	NM	42.1	—	NA

Balance Sheet & Other Fin. Data (Million $)

	1994	1993	1992	1991	1990	1989
Cash	97.7	43.5	72.0	NA	NA	NA
Curr. Assets	439	323	326	NA	NA	NA
Total Assets	1,199	1,082	1,067	NA	NA	NA
Curr. Liab.	320	262	264	NA	NA	NA
LT Debt	Nil	Nil	Nil	NA	NA	NA
Common Eqty.	83.2	31.3	32.3	NA	NA	NA
Total Cap.	304	238	232	NA	NA	NA
Cap. Exp.	116	NA	NA	NA	NA	NA
Cash Flow	120	-21.4	111	NA	NA	NA

Ratio Analysis

	1994	1993	1992	1991	1990	1989
Curr. Ratio	1.4	1.2	1.2	NA	NA	NA
% LT Debt of Cap.	Nil	Nil	Nil	NA	NA	NA
% Net Inc.of Revs.	5.1	NM	4.4	NA	NA	NA
% Ret. on Assets	4.9	NA	NA	NA	NA	NA
% Ret. on Equity	72.0	NA	NA	NA	NA	NA

Dividend Data —The company indicated in its information statement dated December 1993 that it does not expect to pay cash dividends on its common stock in the foreseeable future. The preferred stock held by American Cyanamid has annual dividend requirements of $14.64 million.

Data as orig. reptd.; bef. results of disc. opers. and/or spec. items. Per share data adj. for stk. divs. as of ex-div. date. E-Estimated. NA-Not Available. NM-Not Meaningful. NR-Not Ranked.

Office—Five Garret Mountain Plaza, West Paterson, NJ 07424. **Tel**—(201) 357-3100. **Chrmn, Pres & CEO**—D. D. Fry. **VP-CFO**—J. P. Cronin. **VP-Secy**—E. F. Jackman. **Investor Contact**—Kumar Shah. **Dirs**—J. G. Affleck, F. W. Armstrong, G. A. Burns, D. D. Fry, L. L. Hoynes Jr., W. P. Powell. **Transfer Agent & Registrar**—Mellon Securities Trust Co., Ridgefield Park, N.J. **Incorporated** in Delaware in 1993. **Empl**-5,000. **S&P Analyst:** S.S.

STANDARD & POOR'S

STOCK REPORTS

CytRx Corp.

NASDAQ Symbol **CYTR**

In S&P SmallCap 600

30-OCT-95

Industry: Drugs-Generic and OTC

Summary: This company is developing human critical-care therapies. Through subsidiaries, it also researches vaccine adjuvants and sells feed additives for animals.

Quantitative Evaluations

Recent Price • 1⅟₁₆ | Yield • Nil

52 Wk Range • 3⅜-⅞ | 12-Mo. P/E • NM

Outlook
(1 Lowest—5 Highest)
• NA

Fair Value
• NA

Risk
• High

Earn./Div. Rank
• NR

Technical Eval.
• Bullish since 7/95

Rel. Strength Rank
(1 Lowest—99 Highest)
• NA

Insider Activity
• NA

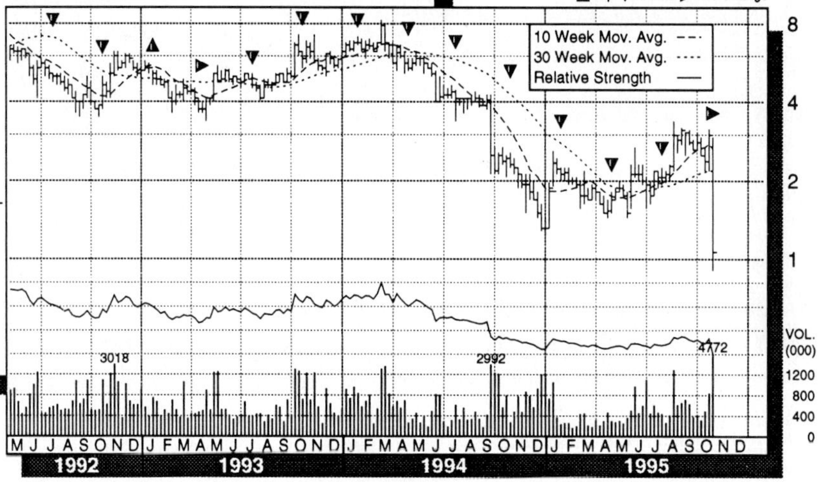

Business Profile - 29-OCT-95

In Phase II/III trials, the company's lead drug candidate, RheothRx, only showed efficacy to treat acute vascular diseases at dosage levels associated with unacceptable kidney side effects. Licensing partner Glaxo-Wellcome notified CytRx that it will cease development of RheothRx and return the licensing rights. CytRx said it would have to evaluate the clinical data before it decided on further or alternative development of RheothRx.

Operational Review - 29-OCT-95

Revenues in the nine months ended September 30, 1995, were flat, year to year, based on roughly the same amount of interest and research income. Higher R&D spending ($5.2 million vs. $4.7 million) coupled with a $2.5 million one-time charge due to an accounting change and realized investment losses further widened the deficit; the net loss totaled $8,670,000 ($0.27 a share) compared to $5,436,000 ($0.17).

Stock Performance - 27-OCT-95

In the past 30 trading days, CYTR's shares have declined 62%, compared to a 0.63% fall in the S&P 500. Average trading volume for the past five days was 954,480 shares, compared with the 40-day moving average of 216,533 shares.

Key Stock Statistics

Dividend Rate/Share	Nil	Shareholders	1,500
Shs. outstg. (M)	31.6	Market cap. (B)	$0.034
Avg. daily vol. (M)	0.319	Inst. holdings	6%
Tang. Bk. Value/Share	1.07	Insider holdings	NA
Beta	2.41		

Value of $10,000 invested 5 years ago: $ 6,178

Fiscal Year Ending Dec. 31

	1995	% Change	1994	% Change	1993	% Change
Revenues (Million $)						
1Q	0.55	-10%	0.61	-62%	1.61	101%
2Q	0.58	-8%	0.63	-54%	1.36	5%
3Q	0.62	-2%	0.63	-46%	1.16	-24%
4Q	—	—	0.61	45%	0.42	-69%
Yr.	—	—	2.49	-45%	4.54	-9%
Income (Million $)						
1Q	-3.37	NM	-1.66	NM	0.02	NM
2Q	-3.35	NM	-1.97	NM	-0.22	NM
3Q	-1.95	NM	-1.94	NM	-0.98	NM
4Q	—	—	-2.26	NM	-2.04	NM
Yr.	—	—	-7.70	NM	-3.23	NM
Earnings Per Share ($)						
1Q	-0.11	NM	-0.05	—	Nil	—
2Q	-0.11	NM	-0.06	NM	-0.01	NM
3Q	-0.06	NM	-0.06	NM	-0.03	—
4Q	—	—	-0.07	NM	-0.06	NM
Yr.	—	—	-0.24	NM	-0.10	—

Next earnings report expected: early February

CytRx Corp.

Business Summary - 29-OCT-95

CytRx Corporation is involved in research to develop a series of copolymers to manipulate and affect certain biologic processes. Product development efforts are focused on therapeutics for the treatment of vascular and infectious diseases and cancer. In addition, the company is developing a vaccine adjuvant system through its Vaxcel subsidiary, and feed additives through its Vetlife unit. Net sales to date have consisted of sales of TiterMax vaccine adjunct for use in research laboratories. Revenues in recent years were derived as follows:

	1994	1993	1992
Net sales	20%	11%	11%
License fees	--	33%	40%
Investment & other	80%	56%	49%

In April 1990, CytRx entered into an exclusive worldwide license agreement with Glaxo-Wellcome (GW) with respect to its lead agent, RheothRx, a blood flow enhancing, anti-clotting, cell protectant agent used to treat damaged tissue. Glaxo-Wellcome agreed to conduct R&D on the drug on a worldwide basis and has invested over $60 million on RheothRx (not including $9 million in license and milestone payments). Phase II/III clinical trials have been focused primarily on the use of RheothRx to treat heart attacks. Disappointing trial results were released in October 1995 and subsequently, Glaxo-Wellcome notified CytRx that it would cease RheothRx development and return its licensing rights.

In February 1995, CytRx filed an Investigational New Drug (IND) application with the FDA for its Protox drug to treat serious infectious diseases. ProTox, which has already received Orphan Drug status, is a broad spectrum anti-infective agent for the treatment of certain AIDS-related opportunistic infections.

Other products in development include Optivax, a patented system to enhance the effectiveness of vaccines and CRL-1336, a compound used to reverse the resistance of tumors to chemotherapeutic drugs. CRL-1336 is currently in Phase I trials.

In May 1995, CytRx formed a subsidiary, Proceutics, Inc. to provide high quality preclinical development and analysis services to drug and drug research companies.

Important Developments

Oct. '95—Results of a Phase II/III study of RheothRx to treat heart attack indicated benefit only in certain clinical evaluations and were limited to high dose levels associated with unacceptable toxicity. Lower dosages were not associated with any clinical benefit. After the results were disclosed, research partner Glaxo-Wellcome decided to cease development of RheothRx and terminate its license for the product.

Capitalization

Long Term Debt: None (9/95).

Per Share Data ($) (Year Ended Dec. 31)

	1994	1993	1992	1991	1990	1989
Tangible Bk. Val.	1.20	1.51	1.63	0.89	0.04	-0.04
Cash Flow	-0.24	-0.10	Nil	0.12	-0.04	-0.26
Earnings	-0.24	-0.10	Nil	0.12	-0.05	-0.28
Dividends	Nil	Nil	Nil	Nil	Nil	Nil
Payout Ratio	Nil	Nil	Nil	Nil	Nil	Nil
Prices - High	8¼	7¼	11¾	6⅝	3¾	2$^{1}/_{16}$
- Low	1¼	3⅜	3½	¾	$^{13}/_{16}$	$^{7}/_{16}$
P/E Ratio - High	NM	NM	NM	56	NM	NM
- Low	NM	NM	NM	7	NM	NM

Income Statement Analysis (Million $)

	1994	%Chg	1993	%Chg	1992	%Chg	1991
Revs.	0.5	-75%	2.0	-21%	2.5	-47%	4.8
Oper. Inc.	-9.4	NM	-5.6	NM	-2.4	NM	2.4
Depr.	0.4	86%	0.2	110%	0.1	NM	0.1
Int. Exp.	0.0	—	Nil	—	NA	—	0.0
Pretax Inc.	-7.8	NM	-3.2	NM	-0.1	NM	2.6
Eff. Tax Rate	NM	—	NM	—	NM	—	1.40%
Net Inc.	-7.8	NM	-3.2	NM	-0.1	NM	2.5

Balance Sheet & Other Fin. Data (Million $)

	1994	1993	1992	1991	1990	1989
Cash	30.8	44.3	50.9	22.7	1.1	0.2
Curr. Assets	31.4	44.9	51.3	22.8	1.1	0.2
Total Assets	38.7	49.8	52.8	23.8	1.7	1.0
Curr. Liab.	0.6	2.1	1.5	1.1	0.7	1.5
LT Debt	Nil	Nil	Nil	Nil	0.2	0.2
Common Eqty.	38.0	47.7	51.2	22.7	0.8	-0.7
Total Cap.	38.0	47.7	51.2	22.7	1.0	-0.5
Cap. Exp.	2.8	3.1	0.3	0.1	0.0	0.1
Cash Flow	-7.4	-3.0	0.0	2.6	-0.8	-4.4

Ratio Analysis

	1994	1993	1992	1991	1990	1989
Curr. Ratio	49.4	21.6	33.0	20.9	1.5	0.2
% LT Debt of Cap.	Nil	Nil	NA	Nil	19.7	NM
% Net Inc.of Revs.	NM	NM	NM	52.6	NM	NM
% Ret. on Assets	NM	NM	NM	19.3	NM	NM
% Ret. on Equity	NM	NM	NM	21.2	NM	NM

Dividend Data —No cash dividends have been paid.

Data as orig. reptd.; bef. results of disc. opers. and/or spec. items. Per share data adj. for stk. divs. as of ex-div. date. E-Estimated. NA-Not Available. NM-Not Meaningful. NR-Not Ranked.

Office—154 Technology Pkwy., Technology Park/Atlanta, Norcross, GA 30092. **Tel**—(404) 368-9500. **Chrmn**—H. H. McDade, Jr. **Pres & CEO**—J. J. Luchese. **VP-Fin, Secy & Investor Contact**—James M. Yahres (ext. 102). **Dirs**—J. Bowman, R. C. Carnahan, Jr., J. J. Luchese, H. H. McDade, Jr., S. Vescovi. **Transfer Agent & Registrar**—American Stock Transfer & Trust Co., NYC. **Incorporated** in Delaware in 1985. **Empl**-55. **S&P Analyst:** Thomas Tirney

STANDARD & POOR'S

STOCK REPORTS

Dallas Semiconductor

NYSE Symbol **DS**
In S&P SmallCap 600

16-OCT-95

Industry: Electronics/Electric

Summary: Dallas Semiconductor makes high-performance CMOS integrated circuits and semiconductor-based subsystems for numerous specialized applications.

Quantitative Evaluations

Outlook
(1 Lowest—5 Highest)
• **5**

Fair Value
• **23**

Risk
• **Average**

Earn./Div. Rank
• **B**

Technical Eval.
• **Bearish** since 9/95

Rel. Strength Rank
(1 Lowest—99 Highest)
• **59**

Insider Activity
• **Neutral**

Recent Price • 21⅝
52 Wk Range • 24⅞-13⅜
Yield • 0.5%
12-Mo. P/E • 17.4

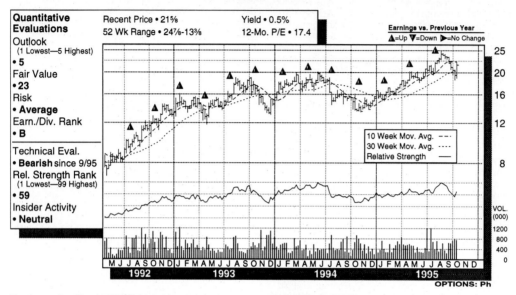

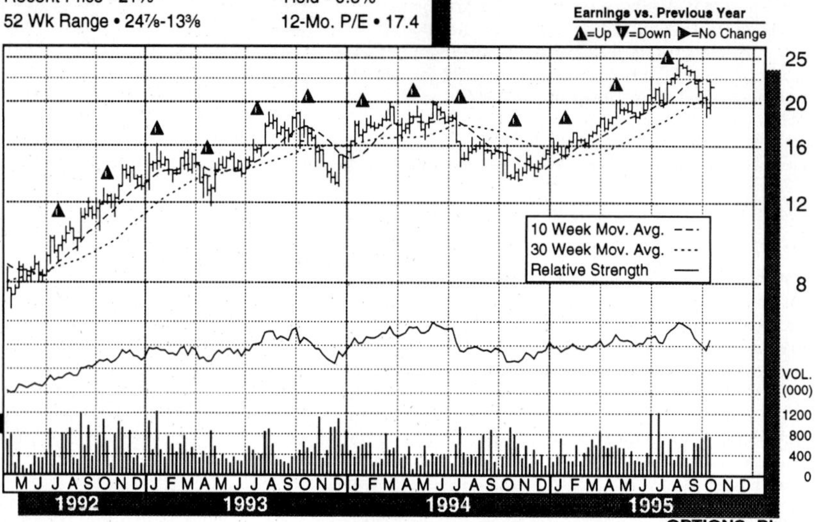

OPTIONS: Ph

Business Profile - 13-OCT-95

This company develops integrated circuits and semiconductor systems for innovative and cost effective solutions to electronic design problems. DS continuously invests in non-commodity products to serve multiple markets and customers, trying to avoid products and markets prone to volatile pricing and sudden obsolescence. It achieved its eleventh consecutive year of record sales and eighth straight year of record earnings in 1994. Based on the first nine months of 1995, this trend should continue.

Operational Review - 13-OCT-95

Record sales and earnings were reported for the nine months ended October 2, 1995, as the Telecommunications, System Extension, Microcontroller, Timekeeping, NVSRAMs, and Automatic Identification product families contributed to 27% higher revenues and a 20% rise in net income. Margins narrowed slightly on higher sales commissions and increased personnel and advertising costs; operating income was up 20%. The dividend payout was 7.8%, compared to nil for the prior year period.

Stock Performance - 13-OCT-95

In the past 30 trading days, DS's shares have declined 8%, compared to a 4% rise in the S&P 500. Average trading volume for the past five days was 149,780 shares, compared with the 40-day moving average of 120,721 shares.

Key Stock Statistics

Dividend Rate/Share	0.10	Shareholders	700
Shs. outstg. (M)	26.3	Market cap. (B)	$0.568
Avg. daily vol. (M)	0.144	Inst. holdings	68%
Tang. Bk. Value/Share	8.21	Insider holdings	NA
Beta	1.07		

Value of $10,000 invested 5 years ago: $ 34,039

Fiscal Year Ending Dec. 31

	1995	% Change	1994	% Change	1993	% Change
Revenues (Million $)						
1Q	52.04	21%	43.18	22%	35.50	40%
2Q	57.04	27%	45.04	17%	38.35	28%
3Q	60.51	34%	45.20	10%	41.00	30%
4Q	—	—	48.01	14%	42.00	26%
Yr.	—	—	181.4	16%	156.9	31%
Income (Million $)						
1Q	8.17	11%	7.33	31%	5.60	55%
2Q	8.85	18%	7.50	22%	6.15	32%
3Q	9.55	30%	7.37	8%	6.82	37%
4Q	—	—	7.55	8%	7.02	32%
Yr.	—	—	29.75	16%	25.59	38%
Earnings Per Share ($)						
1Q	0.30	11%	0.27	29%	0.21	50%
2Q	0.32	19%	0.27	17%	0.23	28%
3Q	0.34	26%	0.27	8%	0.25	32%
4Q	—	—	0.28	8%	0.26	30%
Yr.	—	—	1.09	15%	0.95	34%

Next earnings report expected: early February

Dallas Semiconductor

Business Summary - 16-OCT-95

Dallas Semiconductor manufactures high-performance CMOS (complementary metal oxide silicon) integrated circuits and semiconductor-based subsystems. DS uses advanced technologies, including powering CMOS chips with lithium energy cells, direct laser writing to enhance chip capabilities, and special packaging to improve functionality. Customers include OEMs in personal computers and workstations, scientific and medical equipment, industrial controls, automatic identification, and telecommunications markets.

Export business (mainly to Europe and the Far East) accounted for 38% of net sales in 1994.

As of December 31, 1994, the company had developed 215 base products, with more than 1,000 product variations. During 1994, 25 new base products were developed, versus 21 in 1993. DS has a policy of generally not selling or licensing manufacturing or marketing rights to its products or the underlying proprietary technologies.

Products are organized into 14 groups sharing common technologies, markets or applications. The Timekeeping and NVRAM (nonvolatile RAM) groups are the company's largest product families. Other product families include Intelligent Sockets, Microcontrollers, Telecommunications, Silicon Timed Circuits, Software Authorization, User Insertable Memory, Multiport Memory, Battery Backup and Battery Charges, System Extension, SIP Stik Prefabs, Teleservicing and Automatic Identification.

NVRAM products integrate a lithium power source and intelligent control circuitry to retain data even in the absence of system power. Timekeeping products include a clock/calendar within a single component, powered for more than 10 years, which employs a self-contained lithium energy source in conjunction with a silicon chip and quartz. Other manufactured products enhance system functionality; control a wide variety of electronic systems; increase capacity of voice communication links; control the transmission of data between component parts; provide security for software and data; facilitate user configuration of standard products; aid in transporting data among different systems; protect data when power fails; extend the usefulness of systems without encumbering design; improve system assembly; monitor equipment performance; and provide links between portable units and bases.

Important Developments

Jul. '95—The company reported that as of July 2, 1995, a total of 180,000 shares had been repurchased as part of a program initiated in 1994 that authorized the repurchase of up to 500,000 shares.

Capitalization

Long Term Debt: None (10/95).

Per Share Data ($) (Year Ended Dec. 31)

	1994	1993	1992	1991	1990	1989
Tangible Bk. Val.	7.66	6.53	5.47	4.69	4.08	3.53
Cash Flow	1.65	1.47	1.21	1.08	0.99	0.79
Earnings	1.09	0.95	0.71	0.58	0.56	0.45
Dividends	Nil	Nil	Nil	Nil	Nil	Nil
Payout Ratio	Nil	Nil	Nil	Nil	Nil	Nil
Prices - High	20⅛	19	14½	12⅜	9⅝	8⅝
- Low	13⅜	11¾	7	5⅜	4⅛	5¾
P/E Ratio - High	18	20	20	21	17	19
- Low	12	12	10	9	7	13

Income Statement Analysis (Million $)

	1994	%Chg	1993	%Chg	1992	%Chg	1991
Revs.	181	15%	157	31%	120	15%	104
Oper. Inc.	57.2	13%	50.8	29%	39.5	18%	33.4
Depr.	15.3	10%	13.9	6%	13.1	2%	12.9
Int. Exp.	0.0	-69%	0.1	-59%	0.3	-66%	0.9
Pretax Inc.	45.1	14%	39.7	37%	29.0	26%	23.0
Eff. Tax Rate	34%	—	36%	—	36%	—	36%
Net Inc.	29.7	16%	25.6	38%	18.6	27%	14.7

Balance Sheet & Other Fin. Data (Million $)

	1994	1993	1992	1991	1990	1989
Cash	17.5	32.3	21.8	45.8	45.9	38.8
Curr. Assets	92.6	91.2	68.0	80.4	78.8	69.3
Total Assets	221	187	156	129	120	106
Curr. Liab.	26.5	21.0	20.6	11.5	15.2	14.0
LT Debt	Nil	Nil	Nil	4.3	7.7	8.8
Common Eqty.	195	166	136	113	97.0	83.0
Total Cap.	195	166	136	118	105	92.0
Cap. Exp.	44.7	21.1	15.8	13.1	15.7	16.9
Cash Flow	45.0	39.5	31.7	27.6	24.8	19.6

Ratio Analysis

	1994	1993	1992	1991	1990	1989
Curr. Ratio	3.5	4.3	3.3	7.0	5.2	4.9
% LT Debt of Cap.	Nil	Nil	Nil	3.6	7.3	9.6
% Net Inc.of Revs.	16.4	16.3	15.4	14.2	13.8	13.5
% Ret. on Assets	14.6	14.8	12.8	11.7	12.2	11.2
% Ret. on Equity	16.5	16.8	14.7	13.9	15.3	14.3

Dividend Data —Quarterly dividends were initiated with the March 1995 payment. A "poison pill" stock purchase right was adopted in 1988.

Amt. of Div. $	Date Decl.	Ex-Div. Date	Stock of Record	Payment Date
0.025	Feb. 02	Feb. 09	Feb. 15	Mar. 01 '95
0.025	Apr. 27	May. 09	May. 15	Jun. 01 '95
0.025	Aug. 02	Aug. 11	Aug. 15	Sep. 01 '95

Data as orig. reptd.; bef. results of disc. opers. and/or spec. items. Per share data adj. for stk. divs. as of ex-div. date. E-Estimated. NA-Not Available. NM-Not Meaningful. NR-Not Ranked.

Office—4401 South Beltwood Parkway, Dallas, TX 75244-3292. **Tel**—(214) 450-0400. **Chrmn, CEO & Pres**—C. V. Prothro. **VP-Fin & Investor Contact**—Alan P. Hale. **Secy**—T. A. Mack. **Dirs**—M. L. Bolan, R. L. King, C. C. Mai, C. V. Prothro, M. D. Sampels, C. J. Santoro, E. R. Zumwalt. **Transfer Agent & Registrar**—Chemical Shareholder Services Group, Inc., Dallas. **Incorporated** in Delaware in 1984. **Empl**-821. **S&P Analyst:** J. Santoriello

STANDARD & POOR'S

STOCK REPORTS

Dames & Moore

NYSE Symbol **DM**
In S&P SmallCap 600

16-OCT-95

Industry: Pollution Control

Summary: DM provides environmental, engineering, and construction management services worldwide.

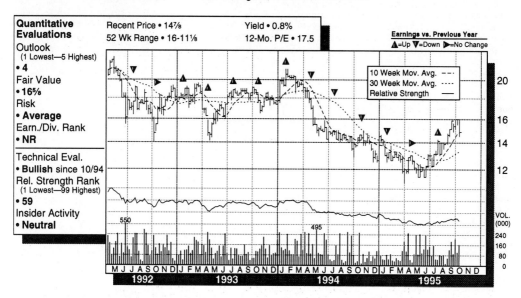

Quantitative Evaluations

Recent Price • 14⅞
52 Wk Range • 16-11⅛
Yield • 0.8%
12-Mo. P/E • 17.5

Outlook
(1 Lowest—5 Highest)
• 4

Fair Value
• 16⅝

Risk
• Average

Earn./Div. Rank
• NR

Technical Eval.
• Bullish since 10/94

Rel. Strength Rank
(1 Lowest—99 Highest)
• 59

Insider Activity
• Neutral

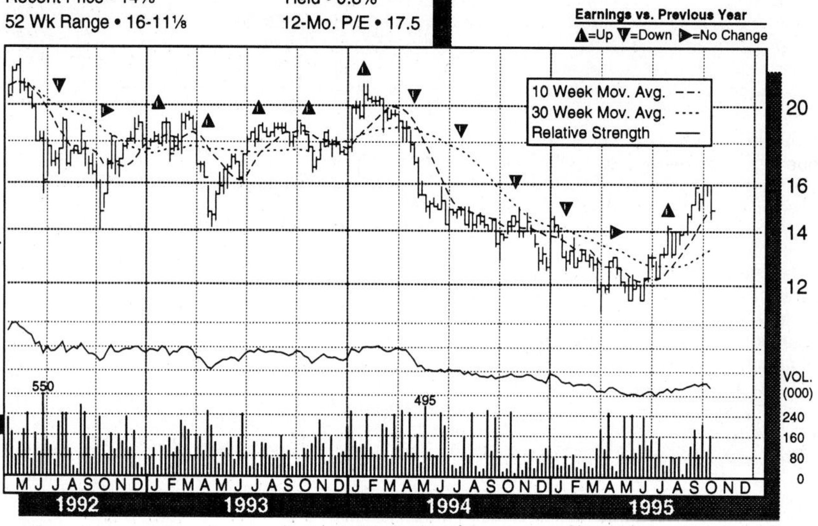

Business Profile - 16-OCT-95

This worldwide provider of environmental and engineering services has recently undergone a transition to becoming a full-service engineering and construction management firm. A strategically important factor in that transition was the April 1995 acquisition of O'Brien-Kreitzberg & Associates, a project and construction management firm. This acquisition and others in April 1995 increased DM's sales base by over $155 million. DM sees long term growth potential in international operations.

Operational Review - 16-OCT-95

Net revenues for the three months ended June 30, 1995, advanced 43%, year to year, reflecting three acquisitions made in March and April 1995. Expenses rose more rapidly, however, and the gain in operating profit was cut to 16%. After lower other income (net) and a lower tax rate, net income was up 12%. Share earnings amounted to $0.25, versus $0.23 (before a $0.04 special charge from the cumulative effect of an accounting change).

Stock Performance - 13-OCT-95

In the past 30 trading days, DM's shares have increased 2%, compared to a 4% rise in the S&P 500. Average trading volume for the past five days was 32,360 shares, compared with the 40-day moving average of 23,682 shares.

Key Stock Statistics

Dividend Rate/Share	0.12	Shareholders	400
Shs. outstg. (M)	22.7	Market cap. (B)	$0.338
Avg. daily vol. (M)	0.028	Inst. holdings	37%
Tang. Bk. Value/Share	3.68	Insider holdings	NA
Beta	NA		

Value of $10,000 invested 5 years ago: NA

Fiscal Year Ending Mar. 31

	1996	% Change	1995	% Change	1994	% Change
Revenues (Million $)						
1Q	100.7	43%	70.19	8%	64.97	NM
2Q	—	—	64.66	1%	63.84	NM
3Q	—	—	66.25	2%	65.18	4%
4Q	—	—	67.87	13%	59.83	NM
Yr.	—	—	269.0	6%	253.8	NM
Income (Million $)						
1Q	5.73	33%	4.31	-29%	6.06	16%
2Q	—	—	5.59	-11%	6.27	4%
3Q	—	—	4.92	-26%	6.62	5%
4Q	—	—	3.05	4%	2.93	-47%
Yr.	—	—	18.67	-15%	21.88	-5%
Earnings Per Share ($)						
1Q	0.25	9%	0.23	-15%	0.27	17%
2Q	—	—	0.25	-11%	0.28	4%
3Q	—	—	0.22	-24%	0.29	4%
4Q	—	—	0.13	NM	0.13	-48%
Yr.	—	—	0.83	-14%	0.97	-6%

Next earnings report expected: early November

Dames & Moore

Business Summary - 13-OCT-95

Dames & Moore provides environmental, engineering, and construction management services to its clients on a global basis. The company specializes in value-added services designed to enhance its clients' business, financial, regulatory compliance and technological decisions, as well as the public's acceptance of those decisions. DM serves a broad range of clients in both the private and public sectors.

Until the close of fiscal 1994-5, the company's services generally fell within two broad categories: environmental services which accounted for 70% of revenues and engineering and other specialized consulting services which accounted for the remaining 30%. The acquisition of O'Brien-Kreitzberg on March 31, 1995 made construction management a significant new line of business for the company. If O'Brien-Kreitzberg had been acquired at the beginning of fiscal 1994-5, construction management would have comprised about 20% of net revenues.

International activities accounted for 13% of total net revenues in fiscal 1994-5.

Environmental services are provided in three key areas: hazardous waste management and remediation; environmental assessment, facility permitting and regulatory compliance; and other specialized environmental services.

Engineering and other specialized consulting services consists primarily of civil and geotechnical engineering; seismic risk analysis and structural/earthquake engineering; water supply; transportation design; planning; and process chemical engineering.

Construction management consists primarily of oversight for project schedule, cost control, and qualtiy throughout design and engineering, construction, and occupant move-in.

Important Developments

Aug. '95—Dames & Moore said that it utilized about $39 million of multi-year lines of credit from a number of banks, primarily to fund the acquisitions of Walk, Haydel & Associates (WH) and Hardcastle & Richards Consulting Engineers (HR). DM acquired WH and HR, as well as O'Brien-Kreitzberg & Associates (OK), in March and April 1995. In each case terms were not disclosed. WH is a New Orleans-based firm specializing in project management, design engineering, environmental design, architecture and construction management, with fiscal 1994-5 revenues of about $44 million. HR, an Australian engineering design firm, serving Australia and Southeast Asia, generated revenues of about A$8.6 million (US$6 million) in fiscal 1994. OK, a San Francisco-based project and construction management company, had gross revenues of about $107 million in 1994.

Capitalization

Long Term Debt: $27,011,000 (6/95).

Per Share Data ($) (Year Ended Mar. 31)

	1995	1994	1993	1992	1991	1990
Tangible Bk. Val.	4.72	5.79	5.57	4.65	3.64	2.68
Cash Flow	1.10	1.23	1.30	1.25	1.08	0.82
Earnings	0.83	0.97	1.03	0.97	0.87	0.67
Dividends	0.15	0.12	0.12	Nil	Nil	Nil
Payout Ratio	18%	12%	12%	Nil	Nil	Nil
Cal. Yrs.	1994	1993	1992	1991	1990	1989
Prices - High	21¼	19⅝	22¾	NA	NA	NA
- Low	12½	14⅛	14	NA	NA	NA
P/E Ratio - High	26	20	22	NA	NA	NA
- Low	15	15	14	NA	NA	NA

Income Statement Analysis (Million $)

	1995	%Chg	1994	%Chg	1993	%Chg	1992
Revs.	269	6%	254	NM	252	-3%	260
Oper. Inc.	38.2	-4%	39.9	-6%	42.5	17%	36.4
Depr.	6.2	4%	5.9	-1%	6.0	5%	5.8
Int. Exp.	0.2	50%	0.1	-72%	0.4	-73%	1.3
Pretax Inc.	31.8	-12%	36.0	-5%	37.9	17%	32.4
Eff. Tax Rate	41%	—	39%	—	39%	—	40%
Net Inc.	18.7	-15%	21.9	-5%	23.1	19%	19.4

Balance Sheet & Other Fin. Data (Million $)

	1995	1994	1993	1992	1991	1990
Cash	25.3	59.2	55.1	47.7	21.4	14.0
Curr. Assets	155	155	146	126	102	90.0
Total Assets	225	180	161	143	116	102
Curr. Liab.	59.1	35.5	35.7	37.6	43.2	48.8
LT Debt	2.3	Nil	Nil	Nil	Nil	Nil
Common Eqty.	162	145	125	105	72.9	53.7
Total Cap.	164	145	126	105	72.9	53.7
Cap. Exp.	4.9	3.7	4.3	6.1	6.0	4.0
Cash Flow	24.9	27.8	29.2	25.2	18.7	16.5

Ratio Analysis

	1995	1994	1993	1992	1991	1990
Curr. Ratio	2.6	4.4	4.1	3.4	2.4	1.8
% LT Debt of Cap.	1.4	Nil	Nil	Nil	Nil	Nil
% Net Inc.of Revs.	6.9	8.6	9.2	7.5	6.2	7.5
% Ret. on Assets	9.2	12.8	15.2	NA	16.0	15.3
% Ret. on Equity	12.2	16.2	20.1	NA	27.6	27.2

Dividend Data —Dividends were initiated in June 1992.

Amt. of Div. $	Date Decl.	Ex-Div. Date	Stock of Record	Payment Date
0.030	Nov. 08	Dec. 13	Dec. 19	Jan. 03 '95
0.030	Mar. 08	Mar. 14	Mar. 20	Apr. 03 '95
0.030	May. 23	Jun. 15	Jun. 19	Jul. 03 '95
0.030	Aug. 16	Sep. 14	Sep. 18	Oct. 02 '95

Data as orig. reptd.; bef. results of disc. opers. and/or spec. items. Per share data adj. for stk. divs. as of ex-div. date. E-Estimated. NA-Not Available. NM-Not Meaningful. NR-Not Ranked.

Office—911 Wilshire Blvd., Suite 700, Los Angeles, CA 90017. **Tel**—(213) 683-1560. **Chrmn**—G. D. Leal. **Pres & CEO**—A. C. Darrow. **VP-CFO & Investor Contact**—Luke F. Botica. **Secy**—M. Yellen. **Dirs**—N. A. Barkeley, A. C. Darrow, G. D. Leal, R. J. Lynch, Jr., A. R. Moore, M. R. Peevey, H. Peipers, R. M. Perry, J. E. Seitz, J. P. Trudinger, R. C. Tucker. **Transfer Agent & Registrar**—Chemical Trust Co. of California, LA. **Incorporated** in Delaware in 1992. **Empl**-4,100. **S&P Analyst:** N.J. DeVita

STANDARD & POOR'S

STOCK REPORTS

Daniel Industries

NYSE Symbol **DAN**

In S&P SmallCap 600

16-OCT-95

Industry: Machinery

Summary: Daniel makes fluid measurement products for oil and natural gas producers, transporters and refiners. It also supplies pipeline valves, fasteners and energy recovery products.

Quantitative Evaluations

Recent Price • 14⅝

52 Wk Range • 16½-12

Yield • 1.2%

12-Mo. P/E • NM

Outlook (1 Lowest—5 Highest)
• **2+**

Fair Value
• **13¼**

Risk
• **Average**

Earn./Div. Rank
• **B-**

Technical Eval.
• **Bullish** since 9/94

Rel. Strength Rank (1 Lowest—99 Highest)
• **30**

Insider Activity
• **NA**

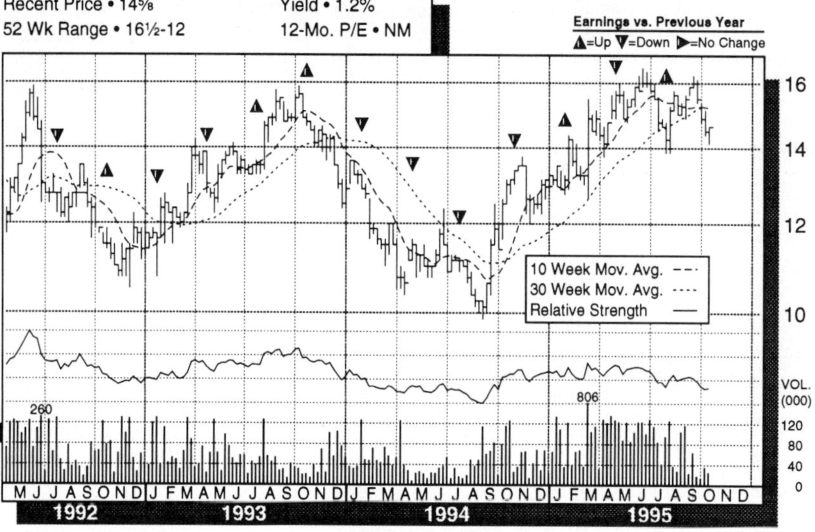

Business Profile - 16-OCT-95

To improve profitability, Daniel adopted a restructuring plan in February 1995 that entailed divesting low margin, non-core business lines; investing the proceeds from the divestitures as well as future capital funds in activities directly related to its core natural gas related businesses; and reducing S,G&A expenses of the ongoing businesses by more than $10 million. Benefits of the restructuring began to be realized in the third quarter of fiscal 1995, as net earnings reached $0.11 a share.

Operational Review - 13-OCT-95

Revenues for the nine months ended June 30, 1995, fell 15%, year to year, as a decline in flow measurement systems sales outweighed a slight increase in energy products revenues, which mostly reflected greater demand for fasteners. Margins improved on changes in flow product mix, higher fastener prices, and benefits of the restructuring, which were partially offset by an inventory write-down. Following a $16.1 million restructuring charge, the net loss widened substantially.

Stock Performance - 13-OCT-95

In the past 30 trading days, DAN's shares have declined 6%, compared to a 4% rise in the S&P 500. Average trading volume for the past five days was 4,800 shares, compared with the 40-day moving average of 10,064 shares.

Key Stock Statistics

Dividend Rate/Share	0.18	Shareholders	1,500
Shs. outstg. (M)	12.1	Market cap. (B)	$0.177
Avg. daily vol. (M)	0.004	Inst. holdings	57%
Tang. Bk. Value/Share	9.51	Insider holdings	NA
Beta	2.02		

Value of $10,000 invested 5 years ago: $ 10,132

Fiscal Year Ending Sep. 30

	1995	% Change	1994	% Change	1993	% Change
Revenues (Million $)						
1Q	42.30	4%	40.58	13%	35.90	-36%
2Q	38.74	-20%	48.63	13%	43.11	-18%
3Q	42.03	-25%	56.24	12%	50.01	10%
4Q	—	—	58.32	14%	51.26	-9%
Yr.	—	—	203.8	13%	180.3	-14%
Income (Million $)						
1Q	0.60	NM	-0.84	NM	-0.34	NM
2Q	-9.71	NM	0.12	-90%	1.19	-55%
3Q	1.28	167%	0.48	-73%	1.81	50%
4Q	—	—	1.57	-33%	2.36	64%
Yr.	—	—	1.32	-74%	5.03	-40%
Earnings Per Share ($)						
1Q	0.05	NM	-0.07	NM	-0.03	NM
2Q	-0.81	NM	0.01	-90%	0.10	-55%
3Q	0.11	175%	0.04	-73%	0.15	50%
4Q	—	—	0.13	-35%	0.20	67%
Yr.	—	—	0.11	-74%	0.42	-40%

Next earnings report expected: mid November

Daniel Industries

Business Summary - 16-OCT-95

Daniel Industries, Inc. manufactures products and systems used to measure rates of flow and accumulated volumes of fluids, primarily oil and natural gas. Other important products are pipeline valves, fasteners and energy recovery products. Contributions by industry segment in fiscal 1994 were (profits in 000s):

	Sales	Profits
Flow measurement	72%	$13,454
Energy products	28%	-1,501

International business (including exports) accounted for about 60% of revenues in fiscal 1994.

Flow measurement products include orifice measurement products, which measure pressure declines to determine rates of flow and accumulated volumes, primarily of natural gas; fluid measurement products, which use turbines whose frequency of rotation indicates rates of flow and accumulated volumes of fluid, primarily of crude oil; and positive displacement and oval gear meters for the measurement of liquid flows.

Other flow measurement products are electronic instruments used in conjunction with the company's flow measurement products that instantaneously compute and display the rate of flow and accumulated volumes of fluid; and large flow measurement systems, which include specialized electronic and control systems for the automation of liquid petroleum product loading systems. The company has developed several related software programs and has an in-house programming capability to meet specific customer needs.

Energy products consist primarily of pipeline valves, fasteners and energy recovery products. Fabricated gate valves are used in metering systems and other applications that require precise cutoff or control of pipeline flows. Fasteners include stud bolts, nuts, ring joint gaskets and industrial flanges. Energy recovery products include large steam generators (used for enhanced oil recovery operations), fabricated equipment items (for pipeline and production facilities), pipeline blow-down skids (to remove certain toxic materials from major gas pipelines), LACT units, separators, strainers, heater-treater units and small liquid meter provers. On June 30, 1995, Daniel sold its energy fabrication company, En-Fab Systems, to the management of the unit, as part of its restructuring plan .

Important Developments

Aug. '95—The company said earnings for the third quarter of fiscal 1995 were $0.19 a share, excluding an $0.08 loss on the sale of an airplane, compared to $0.11 a year ago. DAN attributes this renewed performance to strength in the domestic natural gas industry and expects it to continue throughout 1995 based on the high level of orders it has received.

Capitalization

Long Term Debt: $8,571,000 (6/95).

Per Share Data ($) (Year Ended Sep. 30)

	1994	1993	1992	1991	1990	1989
Tangible Bk. Val.	10.13	9.67	9.86	9.31	8.64	7.81
Cash Flow	0.70	0.93	1.22	0.35	1.31	1.22
Earnings	0.11	0.42	0.70	-0.18	0.78	0.60
Dividends	0.18	0.18	0.18	0.18	0.18	0.18
Payout Ratio	164%	43%	26%	NM	23%	30%
Prices - High	13¾	15⅞	15⅞	24½	17¾	16½
- Low	9⅞	10¾	10½	9⅛	13⅜	8⅝
P/E Ratio - High	NM	38	23	NM	23	28
- Low	NM	26	15	NM	17	14

Income Statement Analysis (Million $)

	1994	%Chg	1993	%Chg	1992	%Chg	1991
Revs.	204	13%	180	-14%	210	4%	202
Oper. Inc.	11.2	-24%	14.8	-31%	21.6	-8%	23.4
Depr.	7.1	17%	6.1	-2%	6.3	8%	5.8
Int. Exp.	1.9	-8%	2.1	-13%	2.4	-13%	2.8
Pretax Inc.	2.1	-74%	8.1	-38%	13.0	NM	-2.8
Eff. Tax Rate	38%	—	38%	—	35%	—	NM
Net Inc.	1.3	-74%	5.0	-40%	8.4	NM	-2.0

Balance Sheet & Other Fin. Data (Million $)

	1994	1993	1992	1991	1990	1989
Cash	2.5	23.2	29.2	31.2	12.7	10.8
Curr. Assets	112	105	112	132	98.0	89.0
Total Assets	187	178	177	192	156	144
Curr. Liab.	45.7	38.0	34.1	53.1	34.0	28.3
LT Debt	11.4	14.3	17.1	20.0	23.6	26.4
Common Eqty.	122	121	120	113	94.0	85.0
Total Cap.	142	140	143	139	122	115
Cap. Exp.	13.6	11.8	8.8	11.5	9.5	3.6
Cash Flow	8.5	11.1	14.6	3.8	13.6	12.5

Ratio Analysis

	1994	1993	1992	1991	1990	1989
Curr. Ratio	2.4	2.8	3.3	2.5	2.9	3.1
% LT Debt of Cap.	8.1	10.2	12.0	14.4	19.4	22.9
% Net Inc.of Revs.	0.6	2.8	4.0	NM	4.8	3.6
% Ret. on Assets	0.7	2.8	4.5	NM	5.4	4.3
% Ret. on Equity	1.1	4.2	7.1	NM	9.1	7.5

Dividend Data —Dividends have been paid since 1948. A "poison pill" stock purchase right was adopted in 1990.

Amt. of Div. $	Date Decl.	Ex-Div. Date	Stock of Record	Payment Date
0.045	Feb. 03	Feb. 27	Mar. 03	Mar. 24 '95
0.045	Apr. 07	Jun. 13	Jun. 15	Jun. 29 '95
0.045	Aug. 25	Sep. 12	Sep. 14	Sep. 29 '95
0.045	Sep. 18	Nov. 29	Dec. 01	Dec. 18 '95

Data as orig. reptd.; bef. results of disc. opers. and/or spec. items. Per share data adj. for stk. divs. as of ex-div. date. E-Estimated. NA-Not Available. NM-Not Meaningful. NR-Not Ranked.

Office—9753 Pine Lake Dr., Houston, TX 77055. **Tel**—(713) 467-6000. **Chrmn**—R. L. O'Shields **Pres & CEO**—W. A. Griffin III. **VP-Secy & Treas**—M. R. Yellin. **VP-Fin, CFO & Investor Contact**—Henry G. Schopfer III. **Dirs**—R. H. Clemons Jr., G. Gayle Jr., W. A. Griffin, W. A. Griffin III, R. C. Lassiter, L. E. Linbeck Jr., W. C. Morris, R. L. O'Shields, B. E. O'Neill. **Transfer Agent & Registrar**—Wachovia Bank of North Carolina. **Incorporated** in Texas in 1965; reincorporated in Delaware in 1988. **Empl**-1,450. **S&P Analyst:** J. Santoriello

DEKALB Genetics

NASDAQ Symbol **SEEDB**
In S&P SmallCap 600

16-AUG-95 **Industry:** Food

Summary: This company is engaged in the research, production and marketing of agricultural seed, hybrid swine, and egg-laying hen breeding stock.

Quantitative Evaluations

Outlook (1 Lowest—5 Highest)
• **3+**
Fair Value
• **39¾**
Risk
• **Average**
Earn./Div. Rank
• **NR**

Technical Eval.
• **Bullish** since 7/95
Rel. Strength Rank (1 Lowest—99 Highest)
• **29**
Insider Activity
• **NA**

Recent Price • 41
52 Wk Range • 45-24½
Yield • 2.0%
12-Mo. P/E • 16.5

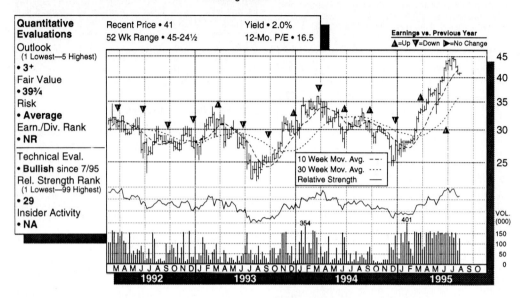

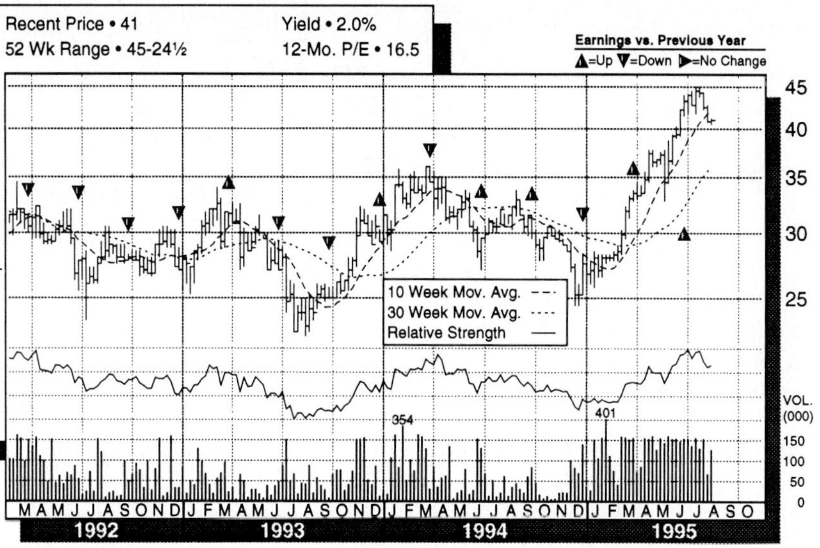

Business Profile - 16-AUG-95

The company expects fiscal 1995 to be another year of increased seed corn market share. After lower U.S. seed corn acreage in fiscal 1995, it anticipates a large increase in U.S. seed corn acreage. Seed operations' profitability in recent periods has benefited from improved margins. Depressed hog prices contributed to losses from swine operations; however, DEKALB said that recent hog price improvement should return swine operations to profitability in the fiscal fourth quarter.

Operational Review - 16-AUG-95

Revenues for the nine months ended May 31, 1995, advanced, year to year, reflecting increased seed sales. Despite the absence of an after-tax credit of $2,100,000 from the suspension of the defined benefit portion of the company's pension plan, earnings from continuing operations advanced. Results exclude income of $1,200,000 from discontinued operations, versus a loss of $500,000, and a $0.09 a share special charge for the cumulative effect of an accounting change in the fiscal 1994 interim.

Stock Performance - 11-AUG-95

In the past 30 trading days, SEEDB's shares have declined 7%, compared to a 2% rise in the S&P 500. Average trading volume for the past five days was 25,120 shares, compared with the 40-day moving average of 30,851 shares.

Key Stock Statistics

Dividend Rate/Share	0.80	Shareholders	2,100
Shs. outstg. (M)	5.2	Market cap. (B)	$0.208
Avg. daily vol. (M)	0.023	Inst. holdings	70%
Tang. Bk. Value/Share	16.85	Insider holdings	NA
Beta	0.94		

Value of $10,000 invested 5 years ago: $ 12,095

Fiscal Year Ending Aug. 31

	1995	% Change	1994	% Change	1993	% Change
Revenues (Million $)						
1Q	49.20	21%	40.80	-14%	47.20	6%
2Q	148.4	4%	143.0	11%	129.2	-4%
3Q	104.9	-2%	107.3	16%	92.40	-5%
4Q	—	—	28.90	27%	22.70	-5%
Yr.	—	—	320.0	10%	291.5	-3%
Income (Million $)						
1Q	-1.20	NM	0.80	NM	0.80	-69%
2Q	7.70	20%	6.40	-10%	7.10	27%
3Q	3.60	64%	2.20	NM	-1.80	NM
4Q	—	—	1.20	NM	-3.00	NM
Yr.	—	—	11.00	NM	3.10	-69%
Earnings Per Share ($)						
1Q	-0.23	NM	0.24	60%	0.15	-71%
2Q	1.48	20%	1.23	-11%	1.38	28%
3Q	0.68	58%	0.43	NM	-0.36	NM
4Q	—	—	0.22	NM	-0.58	NM
Yr.	—	—	2.11	NM	0.59	-70%

Next earnings report expected: late October

DEKALB Genetics

Business Summary - 16-AUG-95

DEKALB Genetics Corporation is engaged in the development and continual improvement of products of major importance to three segments of modern agriculture: seed (primarily corn, soybeans, sorghum and sunflower), hybrid swine breeding stock, and egg-laying poultry breeding stock. The company conducts major research and development programs of those genetically determined characteristics that are of primary importance to efficient and economical production in its business areas. Contributions in fiscal 1994 were derived as follows (profits in millions):

	Revs.	Profit
Seed	77%	$19.5
Swine	17%	5.7
Poultry	6%	-0.3

Seed operations include the research of hybrid corn, hybrid sorghum, sorghum-sudangrass, hybrid sunflower, and varietal soybean seeds. The company contracts with growers to produce the seeds of such plants, and markets them under the DEKALB name. It also markets varietal alfalfa and other forage mixtures. Sales of hybrid corn accounted for about 75% of worldwide seed revenues in fiscal 1994. The international division operates in most areas of the world where corn, sorghum, soybean, alfalfa and sunflower seed are grown. Wholly owned subsidiaries are located in Argentina, Canada and Italy.

DEKALB Swine Breeders Inc. is involved in the research and development of hybrid swine breeding stock, and sells hybrid breeding swine and related services to hog producers in domestic and international markets. The company believes it is the largest such producer in the U.S.

DEKALB Poultry Research is the largest producer of egg-laying breeding stock in North America, with about one-third of the market. It conducts a genetic research and development program to improve the performance of egg-laying hens. The unit sells its products to hatchery distributors and to customers in the egg-producing business in the North American market, as well as to distributors and customers in more than 30 countries outside of North America.

Important Developments

Jul. '95—DEKALB said that it expected higher sales volume and market share for its hybrid seed corn in the fiscal year ending August 31, 1995. However, revenues and earnings from continuing operations will be lower than anticipated, reflecting weather induced reductions in U.S. corn acreage. For 1996, it expects a big increase in U.S. corn acreage.

Capitalization

Long Term Debt: $85,000,000 (5/95).
Cl. A Common Stock: 792,376 shs. (no par); voting. Members of the Roberts family own 40%.
Cl. B Common Stock: 4,371,332 shs. (no par); non-voting.

Per Share Data ($)

(Year Ended Aug. 31)

	1994	1993	1992	1991	1990	1989
Tangible Bk. Val.	15.55	13.84	14.18	12.57	12.99	18.81
Cash Flow	4.31	2.78	3.94	4.56	4.35	3.68
Earnings	2.11	0.59	1.94	2.84	2.72	2.14
Dividends	0.80	0.80	0.80	0.80	0.70	0.30
Payout Ratio	38%	133%	40%	26%	26%	14%
Prices - High	36	34	34½	43¼	44¾	41
- Low	24½	22½	23½	26¾	30	24½
P/E Ratio - High	17	58	18	15	16	19
- Low	12	38	12	9	11	11

Income Statement Analysis (Million $)

	1994	%Chg	1993	%Chg	1992	%Chg	1991
Revs.	320	10%	292	-3%	300	9%	276
Oper. Inc.	32.5	96%	16.6	-27%	22.7	-29%	32.1
Depr.	11.5	2%	11.3	9%	10.4	9%	9.5
Int. Exp.	8.2	-6%	8.7	9%	8.0	11%	7.2
Pretax Inc.	14.9	NM	0.6	-96%	14.4	-40%	24.0
Eff. Tax Rate	26%	—	NM	—	31%	—	35%
Net Inc.	11.0	NM	3.1	-69%	10.0	-36%	15.7

Balance Sheet & Other Fin. Data (Million $)

	1994	1993	1992	1991	1990	1989
Cash	6.2	3.5	9.4	1.3	0.8	17.8
Curr. Assets	164	167	156	126	103	112
Total Assets	319	316	303	264	238	199
Curr. Liab.	95.0	100	72.4	49.7	47.9	35.9
LT Debt	85.0	85.2	90.1	84.1	56.4	0.5
Common Eqty.	121	114	116	107	116	105
Total Cap.	219	211	223	208	185	159
Cap. Exp.	18.2	15.9	21.3	15.5	15.7	15.4
Cash Flow	22.5	14.4	20.4	25.2	24.6	20.7

Ratio Analysis

	1994	1993	1992	1991	1990	1989
Curr. Ratio	1.7	1.7	2.2	2.5	2.2	3.1
% LT Debt of Cap.	38.9	40.5	40.3	40.5	30.4	0.3
% Net Inc.of Revs.	3.4	1.1	3.3	5.7	5.6	4.7
% Ret. on Assets	3.5	1.0	3.5	6.5	7.0	6.0
% Ret. on Equity	9.3	2.7	9.0	14.7	13.9	12.2

Dividend Data —Class A and Class B shares receive equal dividend payments.

Amt. of Div. $	Date Decl.	Ex-Div. Date	Stock of Record	Payment Date
0.200	Aug. 12	Aug. 22	Aug. 26	Sep. 09 '94
0.200	Nov. 14	Nov. 18	Nov. 25	Dec. 09 '94
0.200	Feb. 10	Feb. 17	Feb. 24	Mar. 10 '95
0.200	May. 12	May. 22	May. 26	Jun. 09 '95
0.200	Aug. 11	Aug. 23	Aug. 25	Sep. 08 '95

Data as orig. reptd.; bef. results of disc. opers. and/or spec. items. Per share data adj. for stk. divs. as of ex-div. date. E-Estimated. NA-Not Available. NM-Not Meaningful. NR-Not Ranked.

Office—3100 Sycamore Rd., DeKalb, IL 60115-9600. **Tel**—(815) 758-3461. **Chrmn & CEO**—B. P. Bickner. **Pres & COO**—R. O. Ryan. **VP-Fin & CFO**—T. R. Rauman. **Treas**—D. R. Wagley. **SVP & Secy**—J. H. Witmer, Jr. **Dirs**—C. J. Arntzen, A. Aves, B. P. Bickner, T. R. Hamachek, P. H. Hatfield, D. C. Roberts, R. O. Ryan, H. B. White. **Transfer Agent**—American Stock and Transfer, NYC. **Incorporated** in Delaware in 1988. **Empl**-2,131. **S&P Analyst:** Efraim Levy

STANDARD & POOR'S

STOCK REPORTS

Delta Woodside Industries

NYSE Symbol **DLW**

In S&P SmallCap 600

30-AUG-95 **Industry:** Textiles

Summary: This company derives the major portion of its revenues from the production of textile fabrics and apparel. It also makes Nautilus fitness equipment.

Quantitative Evaluations

Recent Price • 8¾ | Yield • 4.8%

52 Wk Range • 11⅞-7½ | 12-Mo. P/E • 20.8

Outlook (1 Lowest—5 Highest)
• **3⁻**

Fair Value
• **8⅝**

Risk
• **Average**

Earn./Div. Rank
• **NR**

Technical Eval.
• **Bearish** since 8/95

Rel. Strength Rank (1 Lowest—99 Highest)
• **20**

Insider Activity
• **NA**

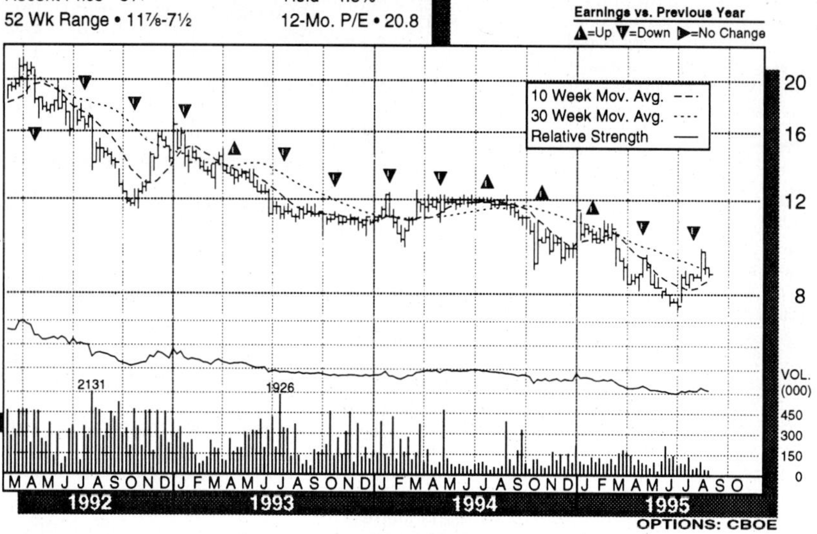

OPTIONS: CBOE

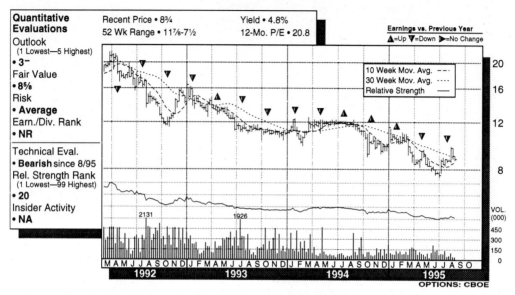

Business Profile - 30-AUG-95

This company derives the majority of its revenues from the production of textile fabrics and apparel; it also makes Nautilus fitness equipment. A large loss in fiscal 1994 reflected the establishment of over $35 million of reserves and a sluggish apparel market. Although sales remained sluggish in fiscal 1995, a modest profit was recorded. The shares, which are down some 30% from their 1994 high, were recently trading at around 19 to 20 times the consensus EPS estimate of $0.45 for fiscal 1996.

Operational Review - 30-AUG-95

Sales for fiscal 1995 declined 2.6% from those of fiscal 1994, reflecting the absence of the Harper Brothers operation sold in June 1994 and sluggish apparel sales. Fiscal 1995 earnings included a pre-tax gain of $7.0 million from a reversal of litigation reserves due to a lawsuit reward reduction. The fiscal 1994 loss included pre-tax charges of $27.1 million and $6.3 million, to establish the litigation expense reserve and for net restructuring expenses, respectively.

Stock Performance - 25-AUG-95

In the past 30 trading days, DLW's shares have increased 4%, compared to a 0.04% rise in the S&P 500. Average trading volume for the past five days was 7,080 shares, compared with the 40-day moving average of 14,338 shares.

Key Stock Statistics

Dividend Rate/Share	0.40	Shareholders	2,300
Shs. outstg. (M)	24.4	Market cap. (B)	$0.204
Avg. daily vol. (M)	0.040	Inst. holdings	54%
Tang. Bk. Value/Share	10.53	Insider holdings	NA
Beta	1.04		

Value of $10,000 invested 5 years ago: $ 9,618

Fiscal Year Ending Jun. 30

	1995	% Change	1994	% Change	1993	% Change
Revenues (Million $)						
1Q	141.3	-4%	146.4	-4%	153.0	-10%
2Q	142.5	-5%	149.3	-8%	163.0	-1%
3Q	150.9	-3%	155.2	-12%	176.4	5%
4Q	162.9	NM	162.8	-16%	194.2	-3%
Yr.	597.5	-3%	613.8	-11%	686.2	-3%
Income (Million $)						
1Q	4.16	132%	1.79	—	—	—
2Q	0.37	NM	-32.00	NM	6.04	-25%
3Q	0.94	-86%	6.58	-26%	8.92	NM
4Q	4.62	-27%	6.32	16%	5.46	-60%
Yr.	10.10	NM	-17.30	NM	28.20	-30%
Earnings Per Share ($)						
1Q	0.17	143%	0.07	-75%	0.28	-42%
2Q	0.02	NM	-1.31	NM	0.23	-23%
3Q	0.04	-85%	0.27	-23%	0.35	3%
4Q	0.19	-27%	0.26	24%	0.21	-58%
Yr.	0.42	NM	-0.70	NM	1.07	-34%

Next earnings report expected: mid November

Delta Woodside Industries

Business Summary - 30-AUG-95

Delta Woodside Industries makes a variety of textile fabrics and apparel. The fabric divisions produce woven and knit fabrics, ultimately used for apparel, home furnishings and other products, while the apparel division produces woven and knit apparel, primarily casualwear. Delta also operates a fitness equipment division. The office products division was sold in 1994. Segment contributions in fiscal 1994 (operating profits in millions) were:

	Sales	Profits
Textile fabrics	65%	$19.6
Apparel, incl. retail stores	28%	-31.3
Fitness equipment, office products & other	7%	-3.0

The textile fabrics division conducts woven fabrics operations through the Delta Mills Marketing unit, which produces finished and unfinished fabrics. Finished woven fabrics are sold for use in the production of men's and women's apparel and professional uniforms. Unfinished products (greige goods), which are produced in a variety of lightweight woven fabrics, are sold primarily to converters who arrange for the dyeing, printing and finishing of the fabric, for ultimate use by manufacturers of apparel, home furnishings and other products. Knitted fabrics are produced through the Stevcoknit subsidiary, which knits and finishes a wide range of circular knit fabrics for use in the manufacture of knit apparel. It also spins yarn for the apparel division.

The apparel division produces and markets both woven and knit apparel. Products include the Duck Head line of men's and boys' casualwear, which consists of pants, shorts and shirts. The knit apparel business includes T-shirts and sweatshirts, which are sold under the Duck Head and Delta Apparel labels and various private labels. The company also has 36 outlet stores located throughout the Southeast (as of the end of the fiscal 1994 second quarter), which principally sell closeout and irregular Duck Head products, as well as apparel items manufactured by others.

The fitness equipment division (established through the early 1993 acquisition of Nautilus International) produces weight resistance and aerobic equipment for the institutional, medical and home markets.

Important Developments

Jun. '95—DLW reached a settlement in the commissions lawsuit involving its Duck Head Apparel unit. As a result, the company reduced its litigation reserve, which led to a pretax gain of $7 million in the fiscal 1995 fourth quarter.

Capitalization

Long Term Debt: $199,099,000 (4/95).

Per Share Data ($) (Year Ended Jun. 30)

	1995	1994	1993	1992	1991	1990
Tangible Bk. Val.	NA	11.75	12.72	12.08	8.17	6.76
Cash Flow	NA	0.16	1.71	2.18	1.99	0.97
Earnings	0.42	-0.70	1.07	1.62	1.27	0.32
Dividends	0.40	0.40	0.40	0.35	0.30	0.30
Payout Ratio	95%	NM	37%	23%	26%	95%
Prices - High	11 3/8	12 1/2	16 1/4	22	25 1/4	11 1/2
- Low	7 1/2	9 3/4	10 1/4	11 1/2	5	3 5/8
P/E Ratio - High	27	NM	15	14	20	36
- Low	18	NM	10	7	4	11

Income Statement Analysis (Million $)

	1994	%Chg	1993	%Chg	1992	%Chg	1991
Revs.	614	-10%	686	-3%	705	19%	590
Oper. Inc.	38.1	-42%	65.6	-28%	90.7	25%	72.6
Depr.	21.3	25%	17.1	25%	13.7	NM	13.6
Int. Exp.	8.6	8%	8.0	-32%	11.8	-47%	22.2
Pretax Inc.	-25.9	NM	45.2	-31%	65.8	75%	37.6
Eff. Tax Rate	NM	—	38%	—	39%	—	36%
Net Inc.	-17.3	NM	28.2	-30%	40.0	67%	24.0

Balance Sheet & Other Fin. Data (Million $)

	1994	1993	1992	1991	1990	1989
Cash	2.1	3.7	0.9	0.4	1.6	1.9
Curr. Assets	337	346	344	282	258	183
Total Assets	567	574	525	434	414	331
Curr. Liab.	95.0	84.0	78.0	176	191	109
LT Debt	162	130	110	71.2	85.7	88.8
Common Eqty.	285	336	319	173	127	127
Total Cap.	466	484	443	255	222	221
Cap. Exp.	29.9	55.7	42.9	15.9	21.7	60.3
Cash Flow	4.0	45.3	53.7	37.5	18.2	38.8

Ratio Analysis

	1994	1993	1992	1991	1990	1989
Curr. Ratio	3.5	4.1	4.4	1.6	1.4	1.7
% LT Debt of Cap.	34.8	26.9	24.9	27.9	38.6	40.2
% Net Inc.of Revs.	NM	4.1	5.7	4.1	1.2	5.3
% Ret. on Assets	NM	5.1	7.5	5.3	1.6	11.6
% Ret. on Equity	NM	8.6	15.0	15.2	4.7	27.6

Dividend Data —Dividends were initiated in 1988.

Amt. of Div. $	Date Decl.	Ex-Div. Date	Stock of Record	Payment Date
0.100	Aug. 24	Aug. 26	Sep. 01	Sep. 07 '94
0.100	Nov. 10	Nov. 18	Nov. 25	Dec. 06 '94
0.100	Feb. 02	Feb. 13	Feb. 17	Mar. 06 '95
0.100	May. 12	May. 16	May. 22	Jun. 06 '95
0.100	Aug. 17	Aug. 24	Aug. 28	Sep. 06 '95

Data as orig. reptd.; bef. results of disc. opers. and/or spec. items. Per share data adj. for stk. divs. as of ex-div. date. E-Estimated. NA-Not Available. NM-Not Meaningful. NR-Not Ranked.

Office—233 North Main St., Hammond Square, Suite 200, Greenville, SC 29601. **Tel**—(803) 232-8301. **Pres & CEO**—E. E. Maddrey II. **EVP, Treas & CFO**—B. C. Rainsford. **VP, Secy & Investor Contact**—Jane H. Greer. **Dirs**—C. C. Guy, J. F. Kane, M. Lennon, E. E. Maddrey II, B. Mickel, B. A. Mickel, B. C. Rainsford. **Transfer Agent**—First Union National Bank of North Carolina, Charlotte. **Incorporated** in South Carolina in 1972. **Empl**-8,100. **S&P Analyst:** Philip D. Wohl

STANDARD & POOR'S STOCK REPORTS

Deposit Guaranty Corp.

NASDAQ Symbol **DEPS**
In S&P SmallCap 600

30-OCT-95 **Industry:** Banking

Summary: Deposit Guaranty owns banks in Mississippi and Louisiana, with total assets exceeding $5.93 billion at September 30, 1995.

Quantitative Evaluations

Outlook (1 Lowest—5 Highest)
• **NA**
Fair Value
• **NA**
Risk
• **Low**
Earn./Div. Rank
• **A-**

Technical Eval.
• **Bullish** since 12/94
Rel. Strength Rank (1 Lowest—99 Highest)
• **85**
Insider Activity
• **Neutral**

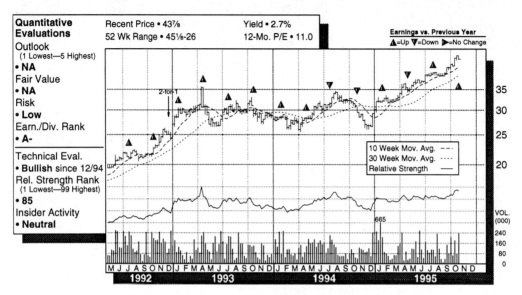

Recent Price • 43⅞
52 Wk Range • 45⅛-26
Yield • 2.7%
12-Mo. P/E • 11.0

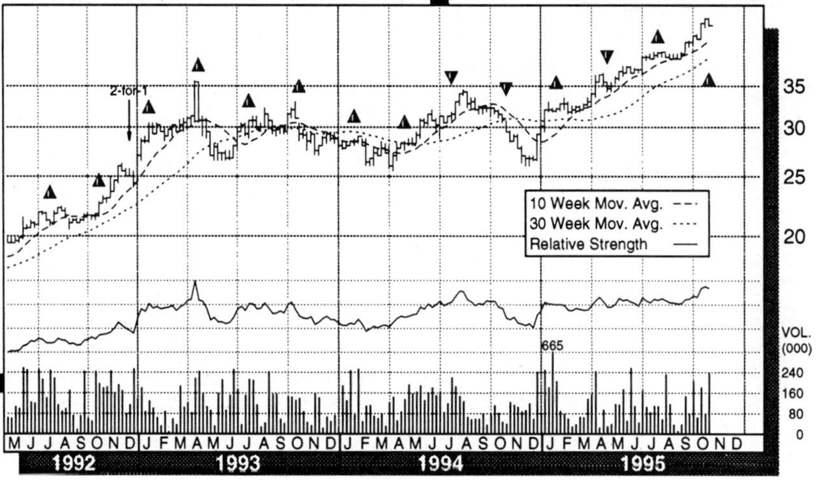

Business Profile - 17-JUL-95

Total loans increased 18% in 1994, the result of acquisitions and growth in the company's market area. At year-end, there was no loan concentration of 10% or more in any single industry. A strategy of increasing consumer lending entails expanding credit to moderate-income borrowers. Credit quality has improved, and the provision for loan losses is not expected to be a drag on earnings. In 1994, local economies grew at a greater pace than the national economy.

Operational Review - 30-OCT-95

Based on a preliminary report, net income rose 15%, year to year, in the nine months ended September 30, 1995, to $56,057,000 ($2.93 a share), from $48,579,000 ($2.75), principally reflecting wider net interest margins. Results in 1995 were adversely affected by an after-tax provision for loan losses of $1.3 million, which contrasted with a negative provision of $1.8 million in 1994. Earnings in the 1994 period also benefited from a net gain of $6.0 million from the sale of securities.

Stock Performance - 27-OCT-95

In the past 30 trading days, DEPS's shares have increased 6%, compared to a 0.63% fall in the S&P 500. Average trading volume for the past five days was 46,640 shares, compared with the 40-day moving average of 25,987 shares.

Key Stock Statistics

Dividend Rate/Share	1.20	Shareholders	6,000
Shs. outstg. (M)	18.9	Market cap. (B)	$0.827
Avg. daily vol. (M)	0.028	Inst. holdings	25%
Tang. Bk. Value/Share	25.57	Insider holdings	NA
Beta	0.73		

Value of $10,000 invested 5 years ago: $ 41,324

Fiscal Year Ending Dec. 31

	1995	% Change	1994	% Change	1993	% Change
Revenues (Million $)						
1Q	113.4	14%	99.9	8%	92.47	-10%
2Q	119.8	27%	94.47	NM	94.16	-4%
3Q	—	—	97.66	3%	94.43	-2%
4Q	—	—	108.8	17%	93.05	-3%
Yr.	—	—	400.8	7%	374.1	-5%
Income (Million $)						
1Q	17.97	-4%	18.67	34%	13.92	80%
2Q	17.37	11%	15.71	-26%	21.18	90%
3Q	20.71	46%	14.20	-6%	15.03	19%
4Q	—	—	18.55	13%	16.43	17%
Yr.	—	—	67.13	NM	66.55	46%
Earnings Per Share ($)						
1Q	0.93	-12%	1.06	34%	0.79	61%
2Q	0.91	2%	0.89	-26%	1.20	85%
3Q	1.09	36%	0.80	-6%	0.85	16%
4Q	—	—	1.05	13%	0.93	15%
Yr.	—	—	3.80	NM	3.77	41%

Next earnings report expected: late January

Deposit Guaranty Corp.

Business Summary - 30-OCT-95

Deposit Guaranty Corp. is a multibank holding company offering complete banking and trust services to commercial, industrial and agricultural customers through its two banking subsidiaries: 98%-owned Deposit Guaranty National Bank, the second largest bank in Mississippi, with 139 locations; and Commercial National Bank, the fifth largest bank in Louisiana, with 24 locations in the Shreveport market. At December 31, 1994, gross loans outstanding amounted to $2.88 billion, up from $2.44 billion a year earlier, divided as follows:

	1994	1993
Commercial, financial & agricultural	32%	29%
Real estate--construction	3%	3%
Real estate--mortgage	40%	43%
Consumer	25%	25%

The allowance for possible loan losses at the end of 1994 totaled $55.9 million (1.95% of gross loans), compared with $62.0 million (2.56%) a year earlier. Net chargeoffs during 1994 were $2.6 million (0.10% of average loans), versus net recoveries of $3.2 million in 1993. As of December 31, 1994, nonperforming assets aggregated $32.2 million (0.63% of total assets), compared with $43.7 million (0.89%) a year earlier.

Average deposits of $4.0 billion in 1994 were apportioned: demand 21%, savings 40% and time 39%. On a tax-equivalent basis, the average yield on total interest-earning assets in 1994 was 7.09% (7.04% in 1993), while the average rate paid on interest-bearing liabilities was 3.52% (3.47%), for a net interest rate spread of 3.57% in each year.

Important Developments

Oct. '95—The Deposit Guaranty Mortgage Co. subsidiary completed its acquisition of First Mortgage Corp., which operates six offices in Nebraska and Oklahoma and services a portfolio of $1.1 billion. First Mortgage will operate as a wholly owned subsidiary of Deposit Guaranty Mortgage Co., retaining its name and management. The loan servicing and corporate offices will remain in Omaha. Separately, Deposit Guaranty acquired Merchants National Bank in Fort Smith, Arkansas, with approximately $280 million in total assets.

Capitalization

Long Term Debt: None (6/95).

Per Share Data ($) (Year Ended Dec. 31)

	1994	1993	1992	1991	1990	1989
Tangible Bk. Val.	25.23	22.41	19.56	18.08	16.82	16.05
Earnings	3.80	3.77	2.67	2.04	1.55	1.99
Dividends	1.06	0.93	0.80	0.78	0.78	0.76
Payout Ratio	28%	25%	30%	38%	50%	38%
Prices - High	34½	35¾	27	17⅞	14⅛	16¾
- Low	25½	26½	16⅝	9⅞	8⅞	12⅝
P/E Ratio - High	9	9	10	9	9	8
- Low	7	7	6	5	6	6

Income Statement Analysis (Million $)

	1994	%Chg	1993	%Chg	1992	%Chg	1991
Net Int. Inc.	181	4%	175	5%	167	11%	151
Tax Equiv. Adj.	5.5	-5%	5.8	-31%	8.4	-27%	11.5
Non Int. Inc.	79.9	7%	74.9	5%	71.0	13%	62.8
Loan Loss Prov.	-4.8	NM	16.0	54%	10.4	-40%	17.3
% Exp/Op Revs.	68%	—	67%	—	68%	—	69%
Pretax Inc.	100	6%	93.9	57%	59.8	41%	42.3
Eff. Tax Rate	33%	—	29%	—	24%	—	24%
Net Inc.	67.1	NM	66.6	46%	45.5	41%	32.2
% Net Int. Marg.	4.23%	—	4.16%	—	4.12%	—	3.78%

Balance Sheet & Other Fin. Data (Million $)

	1994	1993	1992	1991	1990	1989
Earning Assets:						
Money Mkt.	364	279	632	501	491	313
Inv. Securities	1,339	1,683	1,558	1,667	1,262	733
Com'l Loans	928	713	750	880	1,020	800
Other Loans	1,950	1,727	1,519	1,484	1,580	1,522
Total Assets	5,131	4,898	4,994	5,059	4,923	3,745
Demand Deposits	948	875	916	722	712	567
Time Deposits	3,091	3,046	3,086	3,354	3,298	2,377
LT Debt	Nil	Nil	Nil	24.0	24.0	24.5
Common Eqty.	444	396	344	286	266	254

Ratio Analysis

	1994	1993	1992	1991	1990	1989
% Ret. on Assets	1.4	1.4	0.9	0.7	0.5	0.9
% Ret. on Equity	15.6	18.1	14.4	11.7	9.5	12.8
% Loan Loss Resv.	2.0	2.6	3.3	3.8	3.5	1.4
% Loans/Deposits	70.8	61.7	56.0	56.7	63.1	76.8
% Equity to Assets	8.7	7.6	6.6	5.7	5.7	6.9

Dividend Data —Dividends have been paid by the company or its predecessor in each year since 1938. A dividend reinvestment plan is available.

Amt. of Div. $	Date Decl.	Ex-Div. Date	Stock of Record	Payment Date
0.280	Nov. 15	Dec. 12	Dec. 16	Jan. 03 '95
0.280	Feb. 21	Mar. 10	Mar. 16	Apr. 03 '95
0.300	May. 16	Jun. 14	Jun. 16	Jul. 03 '95
0.300	Aug. 15	Sep. 13	Sep. 16	Oct. 02 '95

Data as orig. reptd.; bef. results of disc opers. and/or spec. items. Per share data adj. for stk. divs. as of ex-div. date. E-Estimated. NA-Not Available. NM-Not Meaningful. NR-Not Ranked.

Office—210 East Capitol St., Jackson, MS 39201. **Tel**—(601) 354-8564. **Chrmn & CEO**—E. B. Robinson Jr. **Pres & COO**—H. L. McMillan Jr. **Exec VP & CFO**—A. L. McDonald. **Secy**—R. G. Barnett. **Investor Contact**—Pam Kloha (601-968-4759). **Dirs**—M. B. Bemis, R. H. Bremer, W. H. Holman Jr., W. A. Hood Jr., C. L. Irby, H. L. McMillan Jr., R. D. McRae Jr., W. R. Newman III, J. N. Palmer, E. B. Robinson Jr., S. C. Walker, J. K. Williams. **Transfer Agent & Registrar**—Deposit Guaranty National Bank. **Incorporated** in Mississippi in 1968. **Empl-**2,613. **S&P Analyst:** Thomas C. Ferguson

STANDARD & POOR'S

STOCK REPORTS

Designs, Inc.

NASDAQ Symbol **DESI**
In S&P SmallCap 600

21-SEP-95 **Industry:** Retail Stores

Summary: This specialty retailer offers quality casual apparel and accessories, featuring a broad selection of Levi Strauss & Co., Timberland and private-label merchandise.

Quantitative Evaluations
Outlook (1 Lowest—5 Highest) • **NA**
Fair Value • **NA**
Risk • **High**
Earn./Div. Rank • **NR**
Technical Eval. • **Bearish** since 9/95
Rel. Strength Rank (1 Lowest—99 Highest) • **8**
Insider Activity • **NA**

Recent Price • 8
52 Wk Range • 11¼-6⅝
Yield • Nil
12-Mo. P/E • 7.0

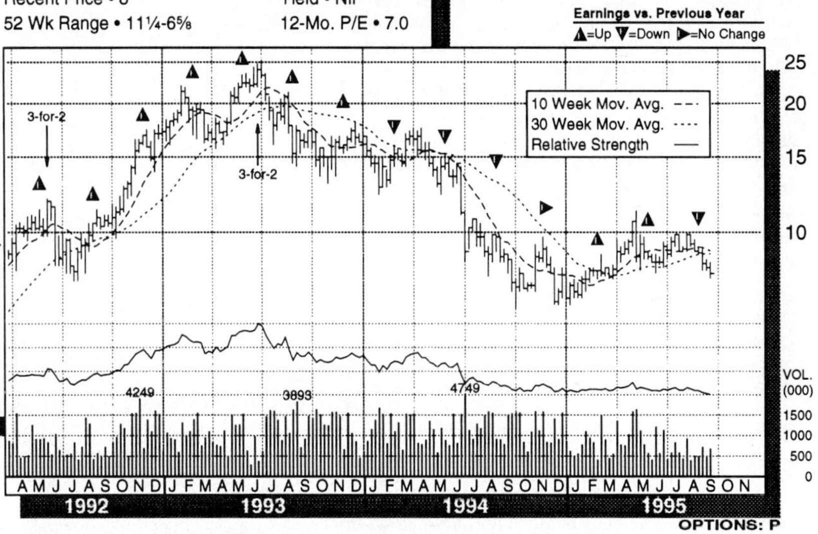

OPTIONS: P

Business Profile - 21-SEP-95

The recent acquisition of Boston Traders has provided DESI with an exclusive branded private-label to complement the Levi's, Dockers, and Timberland products in its "Designs" stores. Short-term earnings are likely to be restricted by planned investments in marketing and advertising, merchandise design and product development, sourcing, distribution, and the development of updated store formats. However, the synergies that exist between Boston Traders and DESI should benefit long term results.

Operational Review - 21-SEP-95

Higher sales in 1995-96's first half reflected more stores in operation and 5.0% higher same-store sales. Gross margins were essentially unchanged, but SG&A expenses were higher to support the development of the Boston Traders product line and increased healthcare costs. With a $2.2 million gain from better-than-anticipated terms for the closing of underperforming stores, operating income soared 53%. After minority interest, per share comparisons were enhanced by 1.4% fewer shares outstanding.

Stock Performance - 15-SEP-95

In the past 30 trading days, DESI's shares have declined 19%, compared to a 4% rise in the S&P 500. Average trading volume for the past five days was 131,640 shares, compared with the 40-day moving average of 115,195 shares.

Key Stock Statistics

Dividend Rate/Share	Nil	Shareholders	400
Shs. outstg. (M)	15.8	Market cap. (B)	$0.128
Avg. daily vol. (M)	0.115	Inst. holdings	22%
Tang. Bk. Value/Share	6.19	Insider holdings	NA
Beta	-0.16		

Value of $10,000 invested 5 years ago: $ 47,990

Fiscal Year Ending Jan. 31

	1996	% Change	1995	% Change	1994	% Change
Revenues (Million $)						
1Q	57.34	17%	49.00	12%	43.94	22%
2Q	66.99	19%	56.39	10%	51.34	26%
3Q	—	—	80.76	10%	73.53	15%
4Q	—	—	79.80	11%	72.12	13%
Yr.	—	—	265.9	10%	240.9	18%
Income (Million $)						
1Q	1.60	NM	0.10	-82%	0.55	NM
2Q	1.19	-27%	1.62	-16%	1.93	35%
3Q	—	—	6.66	-2%	6.77	17%
4Q	—	—	8.52	NM	-3.58	NM
Yr.	—	—	16.90	198%	5.67	-54%
Earnings Per Share ($)						
1Q	0.10	NM	0.01	-67%	0.03	NM
2Q	0.08	-20%	0.10	-17%	0.12	20%
3Q	—	—	0.42	NM	0.42	5%
4Q	—	—	0.54	NM	-0.22	NM
Yr.	—	—	1.06	194%	0.36	-57%

Next earnings report expected: mid November

Designs, Inc.

Business Summary - 21-SEP-95

As of late August 1995, Designs, Inc. was operating 124 specialty retail stores offering clothing and accessories manufactured or licensed by Levi Strauss & Co.; certain of the stores also featured Timberland brand apparel and private-label merchandise. Of the total, 51 were mall-based units operated under the name "Designs" and 61 were off-price outlet stores operating under the "Levi's Outlet by Designs" name. Also included were 11 "Original Levi's" stores, and one "Levi's Outlet" store, categorized as "concept" stores and operated by a joint venture between subsidiaries of the company and Levi's Only Stores, Inc. (LOS), a wholly owned subsidiary of Levi Strauss. The stores are located throughout the eastern half of the U.S. Following the April 1995 acquisition of Boston Trading Ltd., Inc., the company began operating 33 "Boston Traders Outlet" store locations, featuring the Boston Traders product line.

Sales by store type in recent fiscal years were:

	1994-95	1993-94	1992-93
Designs	26%	32%	38%
Outlet	64%	60%	59%
Concept	10%	8%	3%

The company's "Designs" and "Outlet" stores are merchandised to capitalize on the strength of the Levi's and Dockers brand names. Designs believes that the Levi's label is one of the most recognized apparel trademarks in the world and that the Dockers brand name is one of the most recognized product names in the U.S.

"Designs" stores are located in enclosed shopping malls and offer the broadest selection of Levi Strauss merchandise available from a single retailer. Select stores also carry Timberland brand apparel as well as a line of private-label merchandise. The stores generally average 6,000 sq. ft. in size.

"Outlet" stores are located in manufacturers' outlet parks and destination shopping centers and sell manufacturing overruns, discontinued lines and irregulars purchased by the company directly from Levi Strauss & Co. and end-of-season merchandise transferred from "Designs" stores. Stores range in size from 8,000 to 17,000 sq. ft.

"Original Levi's" stores, located in upscale malls and urban locations, offer the most fashion-forward jeanswear products in the Levi's brand clothing lines. Stores range from 3,500 to 9,000 sq. ft.

Important Developments

Aug. '95—DESI said that total sales for the four weeks ended August 26, 1995, slid 1.3%, year to year; same-store sales fell 12%. Year-to-date, total sales grew 14%, on 1% lower same-store sales.

Capitalization

Long Term Debt: None (7/95).

Per Share Data ($) (Year Ended Jan. 31)

	1995	1994	1993	1992	1991	1990
Tangible Bk. Val.	6.07	5.09	4.69	2.56	1.74	1.55
Cash Flow	1.49	0.68	1.15	0.77	0.55	0.15
Earnings	1.06	0.36	0.84	0.40	0.19	-0.15
Dividends	Nil	Nil	Nil	Nil	Nil	Nil
Payout Ratio	Nil	Nil	Nil	Nil	Nil	Nil
Cal. Yrs.	1994	1993	1992	1991	1990	1989
Prices - High	17½	25¼	19⅛	6⅝	3¼	3
- Low	6⅝	13	5⅜	2⅝	1³⁄₁₆	1⁹⁄₁₆
P/E Ratio - High	17	70	21	17	18	NM
- Low	6	36	6	6	6	NM

Income Statement Analysis (Million $)

	1995	%Chg	1994	%Chg	1993	%Chg	1992
Revs.	266	10%	241	18%	204	35%	151
Oper. Inc.	31.2	4%	29.9	10%	27.3	82%	15.0
Depr.	6.9	32%	5.2	15%	4.6	5%	4.3
Int. Exp.	0.6	-60%	1.5	-47%	2.9	5%	2.8
Pretax Inc.	28.4	199%	9.5	-54%	20.6	152%	8.2
Eff. Tax Rate	41%	—	40%	—	40%	—	41%
Net Inc.	16.9	196%	5.7	-54%	12.3	157%	4.8

Balance Sheet & Other Fin. Data (Million $)

	1995	1994	1993	1992	1991	1990
Cash	22.4	13.6	30.2	16.6	3.3	0.6
Curr. Assets	82.1	68.0	74.0	48.5	27.3	23.7
Total Assets	127	120	102	69.4	50.5	47.9
Curr. Liab.	26.8	32.4	18.1	15.6	9.4	8.3
LT Debt	Nil	6.0	10.0	18.0	21.5	21.5
Common Eqty.	95.7	81.2	74.4	35.5	19.6	17.5
Total Cap.	100	87.2	84.4	53.8	41.1	39.6
Cap. Exp.	12.6	8.1	5.8	3.3	3.4	8.0
Cash Flow	23.8	10.9	16.9	9.1	6.2	1.7

Ratio Analysis

	1995	1994	1993	1992	1991	1990
Curr. Ratio	3.1	2.1	4.1	3.1	2.9	2.8
% LT Debt of Cap.	Nil	6.9	11.9	33.5	52.3	54.4
% Net Inc.of Revs.	6.4	2.4	6.0	3.2	1.7	NM
% Ret. on Assets	13.8	5.1	13.6	7.3	4.3	NM
% Ret. on Equity	19.2	7.3	21.4	16.0	11.3	NM

Dividend Data —No cash dividends have been paid since the initial public offering. The common stock was split three for two in June 1992 and June 1993. A shareholder rights plan was adopted in May 1995.

Data as orig. reptd.; bef. results of disc. opers. and/or spec. items. Per share data adj. for stk. divs. as of ex-div. date. E-Estimated. NA-Not Available. NM-Not Meaningful. NR-Not Ranked.

Office—1244 Boylston St., Chestnut Hill, MA 02167. **Tel**—(617) 739-6722. **Chrmn**—S. I. Berger. **Pres & CEO**—J. H. Reichman. **CFO**—W. D. Richins. **Sr VP & Secy**—S. N. Semel. **Dirs**—S. I. Berger, J. G. Groninger, B. M. Manuel, J. H. Reichman, M. Shapiro, P. L. Thigpen. **Transfer Agent & Registrar**—First National Bank of Boston. **Incorporated** in Delaware in 1976. **Empl**-2,500. **S&P Analyst:** Maureen C. Carini

STANDARD & POOR'S

STOCK REPORTS

Devon Energy

ASE Symbol **DVN**
In S&P SmallCap 600

24-AUG-95 **Industry:** Oil and Gas

Summary: This independent oil and gas exploration, production and development company has grown rapidly through acquisitions in recent years.

Quantitative Evaluations

Outlook (1 Lowest—5 Highest) • **2**

Fair Value • **19½**

Risk • **Average**

Earn./Div. Rank • **NR**

Technical Eval. • **Bullish** since 7/95

Rel. Strength Rank (1 Lowest—99 Highest) • **29**

Insider Activity • **Neutral**

Recent Price • 20⅜
52 Wk Range • 23¼-16
Yield • 0.6%
12-Mo. P/E • 44.3

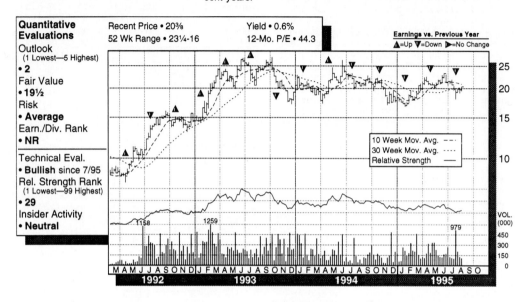

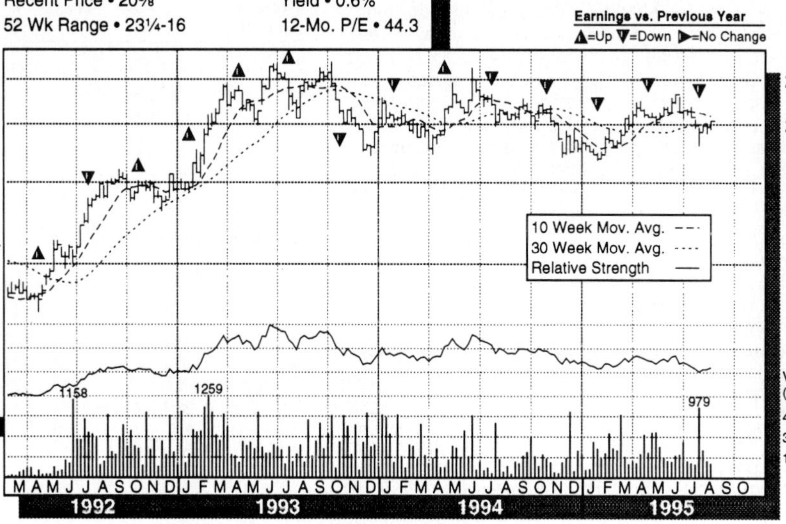

Business Profile - 24-AUG-95

This company balances oil and gas reserves and production in order to insulate earnings and cash flow from the volatility of prices for oil and gas, which trade in different markets. it also maintains access to differing markets to offset demand variations. Economies of scale are achieved by geographic concentration of assets; non-strategic and high cost properties are sold. Properties acquired are long-lived and economical at low energy prices. Devon also strives to keep debt low.

Operational Review - 24-AUG-95

Revenues fell 4.4% in the first half of 1995, as a sharp decline in natural gas prices and lower production outweighed higher oil and NGL production and prices. Expenses climbed, with the largest contributor being the Alta properties added in 1994. Increased well workover expenses are expected to continue into the second half of 1995. Interest expense and DD&A also rose; net income plummeted 61%, to $3,471,224 ($0.16 a share), from $8,930,827 ($0.42).

Stock Performance - 18-AUG-95

In the past 30 trading days, DVN's shares have declined 5%, compared to a 0.51% rise in the S&P 500. Average trading volume for the past five days was 20,080 shares, compared with the 40-day moving average of 50,677 shares.

Key Stock Statistics

Dividend Rate/Share	0.12	Shareholders	1,400
Shs. outstg. (M)	22.1	Market cap. (B)	$0.447
Avg. daily vol. (M)	0.040	Inst. holdings	81%
Tang. Bk. Value/Share	9.38	Insider holdings	NA
Beta	0.29		

Value of $10,000 invested 5 years ago: $ 15,303

Fiscal Year Ending Dec. 31

	1995	% Change	1994	% Change	1993	% Change
Revenues (Million $)						
1Q	23.76	-9%	26.14	9%	23.88	189%
2Q	25.65	NM	25.52	3%	24.87	165%
3Q	—	—	25.30	8%	23.53	-9%
4Q	—	—	23.81	-10%	26.48	-6%
Yr.	—	—	100.8	2%	98.76	38%
Income (Million $)						
1Q	1.03	-79%	4.88	25%	3.90	NM
2Q	2.44	-40%	4.05	-23%	5.24	NM
3Q	—	—	3.06	-20%	3.81	-27%
4Q	—	—	1.76	-72%	6.23	-15%
Yr.	—	—	13.74	-32%	20.19	38%
Earnings Per Share ($)						
1Q	0.05	-78%	0.23	21%	0.19	NM
2Q	0.11	-42%	0.19	-24%	0.25	NM
3Q	—	—	0.14	-22%	0.18	-31%
4Q	—	—	0.08	-73%	0.30	-19%
Yr.	—	—	0.64	-30%	0.92	-2%

Next earnings report expected: early November

Devon Energy

Business Summary - 24-AUG-95

Devon Energy Corporation engages in oil and gas property acquisition, production, remarketing and exploration and development activities, primarily in the mid-continent, Gulf Coast and Rocky Mountain areas of the U.S. The company's single largest reserve position relates to interests in two federal units in northwest New Mexico: the Northeast Blanco Unit and the San Juan 32-9 Unit Fruitland Coal Participating Area. Its second largest reserve position is related to the Grayburg-Jackson Field in the southeast New Mexico portion of the Permian Basin. Devon also owns other significant interests in the Permian Basin of western Texas and southeastern New Mexico. The company was privately held prior to September 1988.

At December 31, 1994, proved reserves consisted of 347,560,000 Mcf of gas (369,254,000 at 1993 year-end) and 47,607,000 bbl. of oil and natural gas liquids (16,751,000). The present value of estimated future net cash flows before taxes at December 31, 1994, was $398,206,000, discounted at 10%.

Production in 1994 totaled 39,335,000 Mcf of natural gas (35,598,000 in 1993) and 2,968,000 bbl. of oil and natural gas liquids (2,748,000). As of December 31, 1994, the company owned interests in 4,221 producing wells, of which 2,996 gross (745 net) were oil wells and 1,225 gross (419 net) were natural gas wells. Acreage amounted to 408,138 gross (190,936 net) developed acres and 269,860 gross (163,918 net) undeveloped acres.

The acquisition of ASE-listed Alta Energy Corp., Devon's 14th major acquisition in seven years, was completed in May 1994, for about $65 million in cash, stock and assumption of debt. The Alta properties, with estimated proved reserves of 24.7 million bbl. of oil and 13.0 Bcf of natural gas, increased the company's proved reserves by about one-third. By year-end 1994, Devon had sold or otherwise disposed of most of Alta's minor properties. Alta's most significant property, the Grayburg-Jackson Field in southeast New Mexico, complemented the company's existing Permian Basin properties.

In early 1995, the company announced a transaction with an unrelated industrial and transportation concern covering substantially all of Devon's San Juan Basin properties. Although the financial impact of the agreement would be significant, it is subject to a material unresolved contingency. The company had received $17.9 million in funding through June 30, 1995, subject to refund and recorded as a liability on the June 30, 1995, balance sheet. The contingency could be resolved by the end of 1995.

Important Developments

Jul. '95—Devon had $92 million of borrowings available under its credit lines. Separately, under a swap agreement, it had hedged $75 million of debt.

Capitalization

Long Term Debt: $95,000,000 (6/95).

Per Share Data ($) (Year Ended Dec. 31)

	1994	1993	1992	1991	1990	1989
Tangible Bk. Val.	9.36	8.30	7.39	5.96	8.02	8.01
Cash Flow	2.20	2.28	2.38	1.79	0.95	0.86
Earnings	0.64	0.92	0.94	-1.99	0.03	0.01
Dividends	0.12	0.09	Nil	Nil	Nil	Nil
Payout Ratio	19%	10%	Nil	Nil	Nil	Nil
Prices - High	26½	27¼	16	12½	15¼	14¾
- Low	16	14⅜	7⅝	8⅝	9¾	4⅝
P/E Ratio - High	41	30	17	NM	NM	NM
- Low	25	16	8	NM	NM	NM

Income Statement Analysis (Million $)

	1994	%Chg	1993	%Chg	1992	%Chg	1991
Revs.	101	2%	99	40%	70.6	139%	29.6
Oper. Inc.	60.5	5%	57.6	40%	41.0	NM	-11.8
Depr. Depl. & Amort.	33.7	20%	28.2	42%	19.9	155%	7.8
Int. Exp.	5.4	59%	3.4	30%	2.6	19%	2.2
Pretax Inc.	21.4	-18%	26.0	33%	19.5	NM	-21.1
Eff. Tax Rate	36%	—	26%	—	25%	—	NM
Net Inc.	13.7	-29%	19.2	32%	14.6	NM	-15.0

Balance Sheet & Other Fin. Data (Million $)

	1994	1993	1992	1991	1990	1989
Cash	8.3	19.6	5.6	7.7	7.3	4.6
Curr. Assets	25.3	36.4	24.1	17.2	18.1	11.1
Total Assets	351	286	226	102	124	98.0
Curr. Liab.	17.0	21.3	11.5	13.0	13.8	7.3
LT Debt	98.0	80.0	54.5	32.0	28.0	9.5
Common Eqty.	206	173	153	51.8	69.6	69.0
Total Cap.	332	262	212	86.0	106	86.0
Cap. Exp.	36.0	87.0	135	14.1	31.3	15.4
Cash Flow	47.5	47.4	32.8	15.6	8.2	7.4

Ratio Analysis

	1994	1993	1992	1991	1990	1989
Curr. Ratio	1.5	1.7	2.1	1.3	1.3	1.5
% LT Debt of Cap.	29.5	30.6	25.7	37.2	26.5	11.1
% Ret. on Assets	4.2	7.5	6.2	NM	2.3	0.9
% Ret. on Equity	7.1	11.7	9.3	NM	0.3	0.1

Dividend Data —Quarterly dividends were initiated in 1993.

Amt. of Div. $	Date Decl.	Ex-Div. Date	Stock of Record	Payment Date
0.030	Sep. 02	Sep. 09	Sep. 15	Sep. 30 '94
0.030	Dec. 01	Dec. 09	Dec. 15	Dec. 30 '94
0.030	Mar. 01	Mar. 09	Mar. 15	Mar. 31 '95
0.030	Jun. 01	Jun. 13	Jun. 15	Jun. 30 '95

Data as orig. reptd.; bef. results of disc opers. and/or spec. items. Per share data adj. for stk. divs. as of ex-div. date. E-Estimated. NA-Not Available. NM-Not Meaningful. NR-Not Ranked.

Office—20 North Broadway, Suite 1500, Oklahoma City, OK 73102-8260. **Tel**—(405) 235-3611. **Fax**—(405) 552-4550. **Chrmn**—J. W. Nichols. **Pres & CEO**—J. L. Nichols. **VP-Fin**—W. T. Vaughn. **Secy**—M. J. Moon. **Treas**—G. L. McGee. **Investor Contact**—Vince White (405-552-4505). **Dirs**—T. F. Ferguson, D. M. Gavrin, M. E. Gellert, J. L. Nichols, J. W. Nichols, H. R. Sanders Jr. **Transfer Agent & Registrar**—First National Bank of Boston. **Organized** in Oklahoma in 1971. **Empl**-192. **S&P Analyst:** Michael C. Barr

Digi International

NASDAQ Symbol **DGII**
In S&P SmallCap 600

23-SEP-95 **Industry:** Data Processing

Summary: Digi is a leading producer of data communications hardware and software products that permit microcomputers to function as multiuser and networked computer systems.

Quantitative Evaluations

Outlook (1 Lowest—5 Highest)
• **NA**

Fair Value
• **NA**

Risk
• **Average**

Earn./Div. Rank
• **NR**

Technical Eval.
• **Bullish** since 7/95

Rel. Strength Rank (1 Lowest—99 Highest)
• **77**

Insider Activity
• **Unfavorable**

Recent Price • 28⅝
52 Wk Range • 30¼-13¼
Yield • Nil
12-Mo. P/E • 22.2

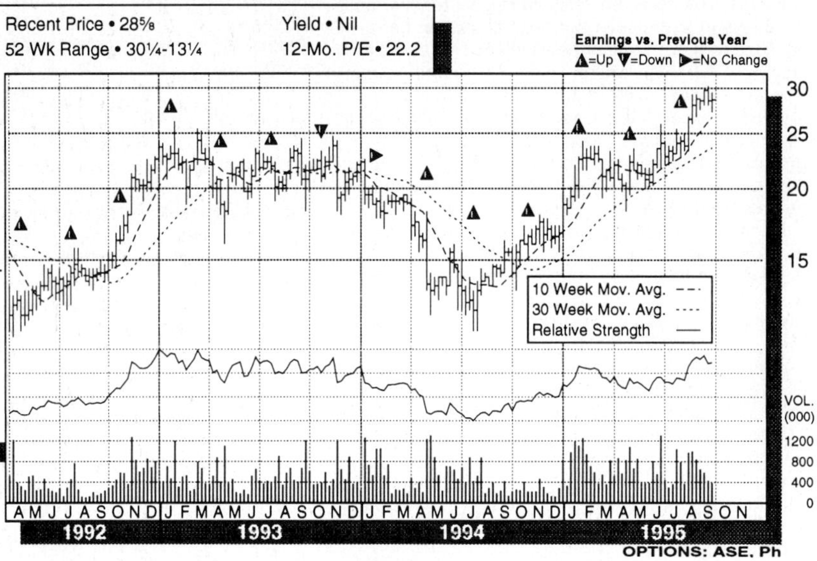

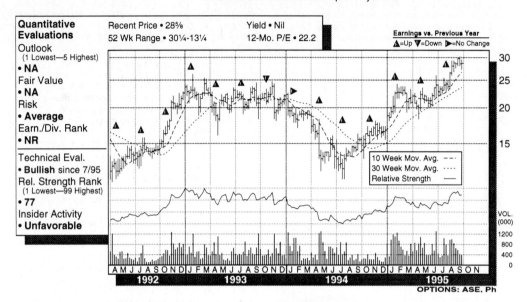

OPTIONS: ASE, Ph

Business Profile - 22-SEP-95

Digi's earnings power has been driven by its leadership role in providing enabling technology for the multi-user arena. The company has also been able to enter into strategic alliances, at the technical and marketing levels, with major platform and operating system vendors such as Microsoft, IBM, Novell and Compaq. Growth should continue as the company capitalizes on the growing demand for cost-effective, high-performance networking products. Digi has no long term debt and a strong cash flow.

Operational Review - 22-SEP-95

The company has been experiencing strong sales growth, reflecting increased demand in all market segments. Sales in the remote access and local area network (LAN) markets have been particularly strong. Digi expects that these two sectors will continue to experience rapid growth into the foreseeable future. Growth in the multi-user sector, which makes up approximately two-thirds of total revenues, is expected to stabilize in future periods.

Stock Performance - 22-SEP-95

In the past 30 trading days, DGII's shares have increased 8%, compared to a 5% rise in the S&P 500. Average trading volume for the past five days was 73,400 shares, compared with the 40-day moving average of 131,200 shares.

Key Stock Statistics

Dividend Rate/Share	Nil	Shareholders	400
Shs. outstg. (M)	13.5	Market cap. (B)	$0.386
Avg. daily vol. (M)	0.108	Inst. holdings	57%
Tang. Bk. Value/Share	6.80	Insider holdings	NA
Beta	2.36		

Value of $10,000 invested 5 years ago: $ 88,076

Fiscal Year Ending Sep. 30

	1995	% Change	1994	% Change	1993	% Change
Revenues (Million $)						
1Q	37.88	46%	25.99	15%	22.63	80%
2Q	40.08	27%	31.65	39%	22.74	62%
3Q	41.18	17%	35.19	49%	23.56	67%
4Q	—	—	38.12	56%	24.45	43%
Yr.	—	—	130.9	40%	93.39	62%
Income (Million $)						
1Q	4.49	11%	4.04	NM	4.03	68%
2Q	4.60	12%	4.12	8%	3.81	36%
3Q	4.85	15%	4.22	12%	3.77	31%
4Q	—	—	4.33	31%	3.30	-2%
Yr.	—	—	16.70	13%	14.78	29%
Earnings Per Share ($)						
1Q	0.32	14%	0.28	NM	0.28	65%
2Q	0.33	18%	0.28	8%	0.26	30%
3Q	0.35	21%	0.29	12%	0.26	24%
4Q	—	—	0.31	35%	0.23	-4%
Yr.	—	—	1.15	13%	1.02	24%

Next earnings report expected: mid November

Digi International

Business Summary - 22-SEP-95

Digi International Inc. is a leading producer of data communications hardware and software products that deliver solutions for multiuser environments, remote access, local area and wide area networks. The company's principal products control the input and output (I/O) of data between the central processing unit (CPU) of a microcomputer or workstation and terminals and other serial devices.

International customers, mainly in Europe, accounted for 21% of net sales in fiscal 1994 (22% in fiscal 1993).

The company's business was founded in July 1985, and operations began in September 1985, after certain assets were acquired from Digigraphic Systems Corp. Commercial sales of data communications products began in January 1986, and the business has been profitable in each interim reporting period since the September 1986 quarter.

Digi produces a wide range of multichannel communications products, many of which have built-in intelligence and data storage capabilities that can be used to offload from the host CPU the time-consuming data control functions associated with serial I/O. The ability to offload the host CPU is due primarily to the on-board operating system found on all of Digi's intelligent communications products. This synergy between Digi's hardware and its software is a key factor that sets the company apart from its competition.

The company's communications controllers are compatible with most major UNIX operating systems, as well as the OS/2, DOS, Windows and NetWare environments. Digi's other products contribute to providing connectivity solutions in multiuser and networked systems environments.

Digi's products are designed to work together within multiuser systems, thereby enabling the company's customers to provide high-performance, cost-effective, integrated solutions to end-users. Products are sold through a network of more than 89 distributors in the U.S., Canada and 54 other countries.

In April 1993, the company acquired Star Gate Technologies, Inc., in exchange for 431,000 common shares. Star Gate is a provider of data communications hardware and software products, specializing in factory automation, and derives a majority of its sales through the OEM channel.

Important Developments

Jul. '95—The company signed a definitive purchase agreement with privately held LAN Access Corp. Terms were not disclosed. The acquisition would strengthen Digi's position in the remote access market by significantly expanding its product line to a full spectrum of solutions.

Capitalization

Long Term Debt: None (6/95).

Per Share Data ($) (Year Ended Sep. 30)

	1994	1993	1992	1991	1990	1989
Tangible Bk. Val.	6.64	5.68	4.62	3.77	1.72	0.70
Cash Flow	1.25	1.14	0.94	0.75	0.44	0.33
Earnings	1.15	1.02	0.82	0.65	0.41	0.31
Dividends	Nil	Nil	Nil	Nil	Nil	Nil
Payout Ratio	Nil	Nil	Nil	Nil	Nil	Nil
Prices - High	22½	26¼	24¼	20½	7⅜	3⅞
- Low	11¼	16	11	5⅞	2⅞	3
P/E Ratio - High	20	26	30	32	18	13
- Low	10	16	13	9	7	9

Income Statement Analysis (Million $)

	1994	%Chg	1993	%Chg	1992	%Chg	1991
Revs.	131	40%	93.4	62%	57.8	42%	40.8
Oper. Inc.	25.8	12%	23.1	38%	16.7	36%	12.3
Depr.	1.5	-20%	1.9	9%	1.7	35%	1.3
Int. Exp.	Nil	—	Nil	—	Nil	—	Nil
Pretax Inc.	25.4	13%	22.5	36%	16.6	39%	11.9
Eff. Tax Rate	34%	—	34%	—	31%	—	33%
Net Inc.	16.7	13%	14.8	30%	11.4	43%	8.0

Balance Sheet & Other Fin. Data (Million $)

	1994	1993	1992	1991	1990	1989
Cash	37.3	51.5	40.3	34.6	12.7	2.5
Curr. Assets	84.3	78.0	59.4	45.9	18.9	6.5
Total Assets	103	88.9	66.5	53.2	21.4	7.5
Curr. Liab.	11.6	8.4	4.0	2.3	1.0	1.6
LT Debt	Nil	Nil	Nil	Nil	Nil	Nil
Common Eqty.	91.1	80.5	62.5	50.9	20.4	5.8
Total Cap.	91.1	80.5	62.5	50.9	20.4	5.8
Cap. Exp.	3.9	4.2	1.2	2.2	0.7	0.4
Cash Flow	18.2	16.6	13.2	9.3	5.4	3.0

Ratio Analysis

	1994	1993	1992	1991	1990	1989
Curr. Ratio	7.2	9.3	15.0	19.5	18.5	4.0
% LT Debt of Cap.	Nil	Nil	Nil	Nil	Nil	Nil
% Net Inc.of Revs.	12.8	15.8	19.8	19.5	21.7	19.3
% Ret. on Assets	17.7	18.7	19.1	20.6	31.5	47.6
% Ret. on Equity	19.8	20.3	20.2	21.5	35.2	64.5

Dividend Data —No cash dividends have been paid. A two-for-one stock split was effected in March 1991, and a three-for-two split was effected in March 1992.

Data as orig. reptd.; bef. results of disc. opers. and/or spec. items. Per share data adj. for stk. divs. as of ex-div. date. E-Estimated. NA-Not Available. NM-Not Meaningful. NR-Not Ranked.

Office—6400 Flying Cloud Dr., Eden Prairie, MN 55344. **Tel**—(612) 943-9020. **Chrmn**—J. P. Schinas. **Pres & CEO**—E. F. Kamm, Jr. **VP, CFO, Treas & Investor Contact**—Gerald A. Wall. **Secy**—J. E. Nicholson. **Dirs**—W. K. Drake, R. E. Eichhorn, E. F. Kamm, Jr., M. Moroz, R. E. Offerdahl, J. P. Schinas, D. Stanley. **Transfer Agent & Registrar**—Norwest Bank Minnesota, South St. Paul. **Incorporated** in Delaware in 1989. **Empl-** 430. **S&P Analyst:** Steven A. Jaworski

STANDARD & POOR'S

STOCK REPORTS

Digital Microwave

NASDAQ Symbol **DMIC**
In S&P SmallCap 600

16-OCT-95 **Industry:** Telecommunications

Summary: DMIC makes advanced, high-performance, short-haul digital microwave radio communication products.

Quantitative Evaluations

Outlook (1 Lowest—5 Highest) • **2-**
Fair Value • **10⅝**
Risk • **High**
Earn./Div. Rank • **C**

Technical Eval. • **Bullish** since 9/95
Rel. Strength Rank (1 Lowest—99 Highest) • **72**
Insider Activity • **Neutral**

Recent Price • 12⅝
52 Wk Range • 20¾-9½
Yield • Nil
12-Mo. P/E • NM

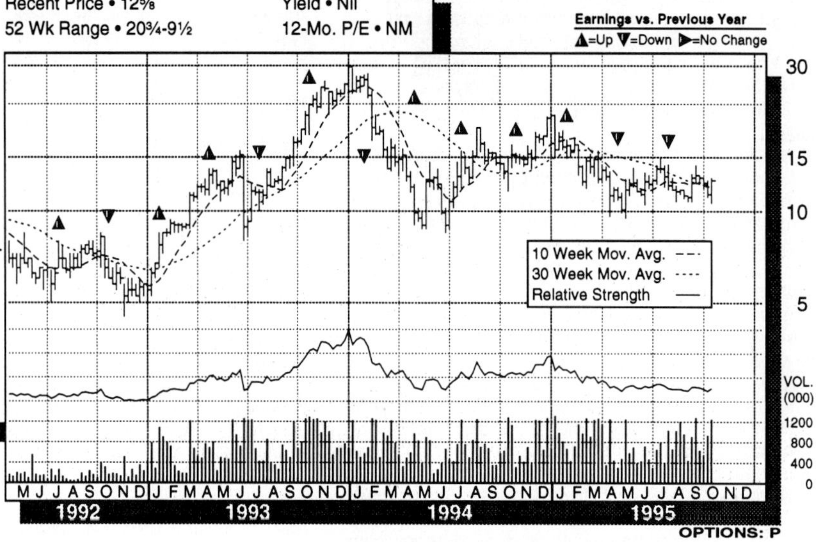

Business Profile - 16-OCT-95

This manufacturer of digital microwave products used in cellular telephone systems, private networks, and other applications returned to profitability in fiscal 1994-95 following three years of losses. DMIC has been focusing on improving its order process functions to reduce overall inventory levels and provide faster delivery to customers. In addition, an inventory of standard products is being created to provide faster response to customer needs.

Operational Review - 16-OCT-95

Sales for the three months ended June 30, 1995, advanced 16%, year to year, reflecting increased product shipments. However, pricing pressure, shipments of interim product at no margin due to delays in acceptance of Spectrum II equipment, provisions for excess and obsolete inventory, and startup costs related to Specturm II led to a drop in operating profit of 74%. After higher other expenses, net income fell 87%, to $0.02 a share, from $0.14.

Stock Performance - 13-OCT-95

In the past 30 trading days, DMIC's shares have increased 13%, compared to a 4% rise in the S&P 500. Average trading volume for the past five days was 319,140 shares, compared with the 40-day moving average of 202,159 shares.

Key Stock Statistics

Dividend Rate/Share	Nil	Shareholders	300
Shs. outstg. (M)	15.6	Market cap. (B)	$0.198
Avg. daily vol. (M)	0.184	Inst. holdings	47%
Tang. Bk. Value/Share	2.60	Insider holdings	NA
Beta	0.82		

Value of $10,000 invested 5 years ago: $ 4,208

Fiscal Year Ending Mar. 31

	1996	% Change	1995	% Change	1994	% Change
Revenues (Million $)						
1Q	39.69	16%	34.28	46%	23.52	-19%
2Q	—	—	37.09	22%	30.31	31%
3Q	—	—	48.92	60%	30.64	10%
4Q	—	—	33.36	6%	31.54	13%
Yr.	—	—	153.6	32%	116.0	7%
Income (Million $)						
1Q	0.24	-87%	1.87	NM	0.10	-92%
2Q	—	—	2.32	76%	1.32	NM
3Q	—	—	2.76	NM	-22.45	NM
4Q	—	—	-4.97	NM	-1.47	NM
Yr.	—	—	1.98	NM	-22.50	NM
Earnings Per Share ($)						
1Q	0.02	-86%	0.14	NM	0.01	-90%
2Q	—	—	0.17	70%	0.10	NM
3Q	—	—	0.20	NM	-2.03	NM
4Q	—	—	-0.37	NM	0.11	10%
Yr.	—	—	0.14	NM	-1.81	NM

Next earnings report expected: late October

Digital Microwave

Business Summary - 16-OCT-95

Digital Microwave designs, manufactures and markets advanced, high-performance digital microwave equipment for a wide variety of short- and medium-haul communication applications worldwide. Products are designed for use by telecommunication operators providing personal communication services (PCS)/personal communication networks (PCN), mobile telephone services, and local access, as well as for use in private networks worldwide.

International business accounted for 87% of total net sales in fiscal 1994-5.

Products are offered to wireless service providers such as Panafon in Greece, Piltel in the Philippines, Airtouch Cellular, E-Plus in Germany and U.S. West New Vector; telephone companies and common carriers such as British Telecom and Mercury Cummunications Ltd.; and private networks such as the State of California and the U.S. Forestry Service.

The company's digital microwave radios consist of three basic components: a digital modem for interfacing with digital terminal equipment, a radio frequency (RF) unit for converting a low frequency carrier signal from the modem to a high frequency microwave signal, and an antenna to radiate transmitting signals and capture receiving signals.

DMIC manufactures digital microwave products that operate within the 2, 6, 7, 8, 10, 11, 13, 15, 18, 23 and 38 GHz frequency bands. These radios are used in point-to-point applications by cellular phone companies, telephone operating companies, utilities, Fortune 1000 companies, utilities, and government and military agencies.

Important Developments

Oct. '95—Digital Microwave introduced a 2XE3 option for its Quantum digital microwave radio product line.
Aug. '95—The company sold 2,063,982 of its common shares in an offering to investors outside the U.S. Net proceeds of $19.1 million were earmarked to reduce debt, provide working capital, and be used for general corporate purposes.
Jul. '95—DMIC said that in the fiscal 1995-96 first quarter it received $36 million in bookings shippable over the next 12 months. Backlog on June 30, 1995, was $87 million, down from $93 million on March 31, 1995.
Jul. '95—Digital Microwave said it reached agreement with E-Plus Mobilfunk GmbH regarding the immediate delivery of DMIC's Spectrum II digital microwave radio equipment. Field trials and acceptance testing of Spectrum II had been recently completed.

Capitalization

Long Term Debt: $5,056,000, incl. $612,000 of capital lease obligs. (6/95).
Options: To purchase 1,463,705 shs. at $0.50 to $26.00 ea. (3/95).

Per Share Data ($)

(Year Ended Mar. 31)

	1995	1994	1993	1992	1991	1990
Tangible Bk. Val.	2.57	2.23	3.82	4.42	6.09	5.71
Cash Flow	0.60	-1.29	0.08	-1.04	0.77	1.32
Earnings	0.14	-1.81	-0.55	-1.64	0.30	1.07
Dividends	Nil	Nil	Nil	Nil	Nil	Nil
Payout Ratio	Nil	Nil	Nil	Nil	Nil	Nil
Cal. Yrs.	1994	1993	1992	1991	1990	1989
Prices - High	29⅜	30	12½	20¼	34½	34¼
- Low	8½	5¼	4½	6½	11	19⅝
P/E Ratio - High	NM	NM	NM	NM	NM	32
- Low	NM	NM	NM	NM	NM	18

Income Statement Analysis (Million $)

	1995	%Chg	1994	%Chg	1993	%Chg	1992
Revs.	154	33%	116	7%	108	20%	90.0
Oper. Inc.	9.1	-17%	10.9	NM	0.3	NM	-11.2
Depr.	6.4	-1%	6.4	-16%	7.7	7%	7.2
Int. Exp.	0.5	-12%	0.6	-43%	1.1	-20%	1.3
Pretax Inc.	2.2	NM	-21.4	NM	-6.7	NM	-23.9
Eff. Tax Rate	10%	—	NM	—	NM	—	NM
Net Inc.	2.0	NM	-22.5	NM	-6.7	NM	-19.7

Balance Sheet & Other Fin. Data (Million $)

	1995	1994	1993	1992	1991	1990
Cash	3.0	4.7	5.4	2.3	3.7	0.1
Curr. Assets	88.6	72.6	61.9	72.8	90.8	81.8
Total Assets	103	84.0	73.0	87.0	108	94.0
Curr. Liab.	61.6	54.6	26.5	33.6	35.0	26.5
LT Debt	6.4	0.5	0.2	0.6	0.9	0.1
Common Eqty.	34.6	28.6	46.3	53.0	72.6	67.7
Total Cap.	41.0	29.1	46.5	53.6	73.5	67.7
Cap. Exp.	8.1	5.9	4.5	3.7	9.6	8.1
Cash Flow	8.3	-16.0	1.0	-12.4	9.5	16.3

Ratio Analysis

	1995	1994	1993	1992	1991	1990
Curr. Ratio	1.4	1.3	2.3	2.2	2.6	3.1
% LT Debt of Cap.	15.5	1.6	0.4	1.2	1.3	0.1
% Net Inc.of Revs.	1.3	NM	NM	NM	2.8	11.9
% Ret. on Assets	2.1	NM	NM	NM	3.7	16.0
% Ret. on Equity	6.1	NM	NM	NM	5.4	21.9

Dividend Data —No cash has been paid.

Data as orig. reptd.; bef. results of disc. opers. and/or spec. items. Per share data adj. for stk. divs. as of ex-div. date. E-Estimated. NA-Not Available. NM-Not Meaningful. NR-Not Ranked.

Office—170 Rose Orchard Way, San Jose, CA 95134. **Tel**—(408) 943-0777. **Co-Chrmn**—R. C. Alberding & C. H. Higgerson. **Pres & CEO**—C. D. Kissner. **VP-CFO**—C. A. Thomsen. **Investor Contact**—Rebecca Wallo. **Dirs**—R. C. Alberding, W. E. Gibson, J. M. Gill, C. H. Higgerson, C. D. Kissner, B. B. Oliver. **Transfer Agent**—Chemical Mellon Shareholder Services, San Francisco, CA. **Reincorporated** in Delaware in 1987. **Empl**-606. **S&P Analyst:** N.J. DeVita

DiMon Inc.

NYSE Symbol DMN In S&P SmallCap 600

Price	Range	P–E Ratio	Dividend	Yield	S&P Ranking	Beta
Sep. 19'95	1995					
16	18⅝–14	NM	0.54	3.4%	NR	1.22

Summary

This company was formed via the 1995 merger of two leaf tobacco processors, Dibrell Brothers, Inc. and Monk-Austin, Inc. It is the world's second largest leaf tobacco dealer, and the largest importer and exporter of fresh cut flowers. The recent elimination of the U.S. domestic content law is expected to contribute to a return to profitability in fiscal 1996.

Business Summary

DiMon Inc., formed through the April 1995 merger of Dibrell Brothers, Inc. and Monk-Austin, Inc., is an international company engaged in two businesses. It purchases, processes, stores and sells leaf tobacco; and it imports and distributes fresh cut flowers. The company is the world's second largest leaf tobacco dealer, and the largest importer and exporter of fresh cut flowers.

About 60% of Dibrell's revenues come from purchasing and processing leaf tobacco in the U.S. and foreign countries, and then selling that tobacco to manufacturers of cigarettes and other tobacco products. It selects, finances, purchases, transports, processes and packs leaf tobacco in 11 countries. The remaining 40% of revenues come from purchasing and selling fresh cut flowers. These operations are conducted through a German subsidiary with operations in 19 countries and a unit in The Netherlands, the largest source of cut flowers in the world.

Monk-Austin is engaged exclusively in purchasing and processing leaf tobacco on a worldwide basis. It provides flue-cured and burley tobaccos, the two major ingredients of "American blend" cigarettes, to large multinational cigarette manufacturers and to government entities that manufacture cigarettes in certain foreign countries.

Depending on the local market, the company either buys tobacco at auction or contracts in advance to buy tobacco directly from farmers or from local entities that have arranged for purchases from farmers. Under contracts where it agrees to buy the grower's entire crop, it also provides agronomic and other technical and financial assistance to improve the quality of the crop.

Over the last decade, two trends have emerged in the tobacco industry: greater market share for American blend cigarettes in foreign markets, and increased consumer demand for discount or value priced cigarettes. These trends have led to growing demand for flue-cured and burley tobaccos, especially foreign grown tobaccos, which are typically less expensive than those grown in the U.S.

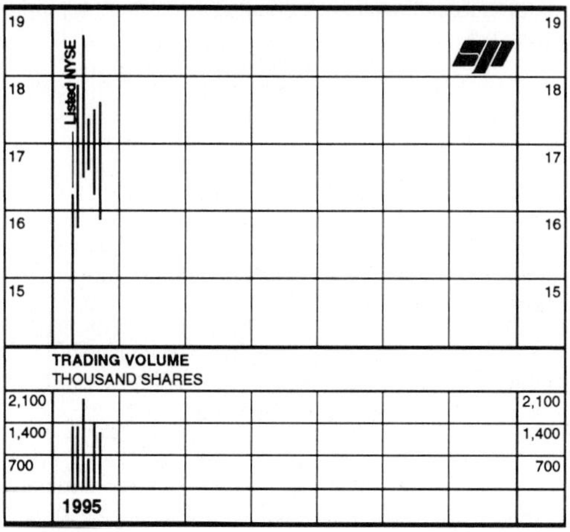

Important Developments

Sep. '95— The company said that the recent elimination of the U.S. domestic content law restricting the amount of foreign tobacco in American cigarettes is expected to contribute to a return to profitability in fiscal 1996. Separately, DiMon attributed its loss in fiscal 1995 primarily to a pretax charge of $26.0 million for restructuring and merger related costs, a $9.2 million valuation charge on tobacco inventories, and higher interest expense.

Apr. '95— Dibrell Brothers, Inc. and Monk-Austin, Inc. merged to form a new company, DiMon Inc. Dibrell and Monk-Austin shareholders received 1.5 and 1.0 DiMon shares, respectively, for each share held. Following the merger, Dibrell shareholders held about 52% of DiMon's shares.

Next earnings report expected in mid-November.

Per Share Data ($)

Yr. End Jun. 30	1995	[3]1994	[3]1993	[3]1992
Tangible Bk. Val.	**NA**	[5]5.85	NA	NA
Cash Flow	**NA**	0.58	2.47	2.25
Earnings[1,4]	**[3]d0.79**	d0.17	1.81	1.57
Dividends	**Nil**	NA	NA	NA
Payout Ratio	**Nil**	NA	NA	NA
Prices[2]—High	**18⅝**	NA	NA	NA
Low	**14**	NA	NA	NA
P/E Ratio—	**NM**	NA	NA	NA

Data as reptd. in joint proxy statement/prospectus date Mar. 2, 1995. **1.** Bef. spec. items. **2.** Cal. yr. **3.** Pro forma. **4.** Ful. dil.: 1.62 in 1993, 1.40 in 1992. **5.** As of Dec. 31, 1994. d-Deficit. NM-Not Meaningful. NA-Not Available.

Income Data (Million $)

Year Ended Jun. 30	Revs.	Oper. Inc.	% Oper. Inc. of Revs.	Cap. Exp.	Depr.	Int. Exp.	Net Bef. Taxes	Eff. Tax Rate	[1]Net Inc.	% Net Inc. of Revs.	Cash Flow
[2]1994	**1,447**	**49**	**3.4**	**NA**	**28.8**	**35.1**	**d1.4**	**NM**	**d6.6**	**NM**	**22.3**
[2]1993	1,677	138	8.3	NA	24.5	38.1	94.5	28.6%	67.0	4.0	91.5
[2]1992	1,698	135	7.9	NA	24.0	42.8	79.3	29.8%	54.1	3.2	79.5

Balance Sheet Data (Million $)

Jun. 30	Cash	Curr. Assets	Curr. Liab.	Curr. Ratio	Total Assets	% Ret. on Assets	Long Term Debt	Common Equity	Total Cap.	% LT Debt of Cap.	% Ret. on Equity
[3]1994	**22.7**	**938**	**741**	**1.3**	**1,307**	**NA**	**245**	**277**	**566**	**43.3**	**NA**

Data as reptd. in joint proxy statement/prospectus dated Mar. 2, 1995. **1.** Bef. spec. items. **2.** Pro forma. **3.** As of Dec. 31, 1994, pro forma. d-Deficit. NA-Not Available. NM-Not Meaningful.

Revenues (Million $)

Quarter:	[1]1994–95	[1]1994	[1]1993	[1]1992
Sep.	---	---	---	---
Dec.	[2]903	[2]722	---	---
Mar.	644	403	---	---
Jun.	380	322	---	---
	1,928	1,447	1,677	1,698

Sales (pro forma, to reflect the merger of Dibrell Brothers and Monk-Austin) in the fiscal year ended June 30, 1995, increased 33%, to $1.93 billion, reflecting a turnaround in the world tobacco market and Monk-Austin's sale of U.S. burley to R.J. Reynolds Tobacco Co. A writedown of year-end inventory following the worldwide oversupply of tobacco, and the R.J. Reynolds sales contributed to lower tobacco margins. A small operating loss in the flower division, reflecting poor results in the U.S., contrasted with an operating profit. After pretax charges of $26.0 million for restructuring and merger related costs, and $9.2 million for the inventory writedown, operating income totaled $11.5 million. After nonoperating items, including interest charges, taxes and minority interest, there was a loss of $30.2 million ($0.79 a share).

Common Share Earnings ($)

Quarter:	[1]1994–95	[1]1994	[1]1993	[1]1992
Sep.	---	---	---	---
Dec.	[2]d0.05	[2]0.50	---	---
Mar.	0.18	0.17	---	---
Jun.	d1.05	d0.84	---	---
	d0.79	d0.17	1.81	1.57

Finances

In May 1995, DiMon sold its stake in Intabex Dibrell (Malawi) Ltd. and related interests to its former partner, Intabex Holdings Worlwide SA.

In April 1995, the company acquired Austria Tabakwerke AG and Austria Tabak Einkaufs-und Handelsorganisation Gesellschaft mbH's tobacco operations in Greece, Turkey and Bulgaria. In addition, it was to purchase certain operating assets of Austro-Hellenique in Salonica, Greece, the shares of Austro Turk, in Izmir, Turkey, and sales operations in Bulgaria. The operations in Greece, Turkey and Bulgaria have combined annual revenues of about $60 million.

DiMon has lines of credit totaling $250 million. There was no outstanding balance at June 30, 1995.

In March 1994, Monk-Austin agreed to buy R. J. Reynolds Tobacco Co.'s U.S. tobacco needs from the auction market beginning with the 1994 crop. The agreement was expected to add $200 to $300 million to annual net revenues.

DiMon recorded $26 million in pretax charges in fiscal 1995, in connection with its April 1995 merger, and expects additional charges in fiscal 1996, most likely totaling $5 to $10 million. The costs include those related to closing duplicative facilities; consolidating operations and systems; severance pay for terminations, early retirement, and related employee benefits; and expenses incurred in connection with the merger.

Dividend Data

Quarterly dividends were initiated in September 1995. A poison pill stock purchase rights plan was adopted at the time of the company's formation.

Amt. of Divd. $	Date Decl.	Ex–divd. Date	Stock of Record	Payment Date
0.13½	Aug. 25	Aug. 31	Sep. 5	Sep. 15'95

Capitalization

Long Term Debt: $348,900,000 (6/95), incl. $56.4 million of 7.75% debs. conv. into com. at $13.44 a sh.

Minority Interest: $945,000

Common Stock: 38,068,047 shs. (no par). The Monk family owns nearly 35%. Institutions hold 32%.

1. Pro forma. **2.** Six mos. d-Deficit.

Office—512 Bridge St., P.O. Box 681, Danville, VA 24543-0681. **Tel**—(804) 792-7511. **Chrmn & CEO**—C. B. Owen, Jr. **Pres**—A. C. Monk III. **SVP & CFO**—T. H. Faucett. **Dirs**—W. G. Barker, Jr., L. N. Dibrell III, H. F. Frigon, J. M. Hines, J. E. Johnson, Jr., T. F. Keller, J. L. Lanier, Jr., A. C. Monk III, R. T. Monk, Jr., W. C. Monk, C. B. Owen, Jr, N. A. Scher. **Transfer Agent & Registrar**—First Union National Bank, Charlotte, NC. **Incorporated** Virginia in 1995. **Empl**—6,000.

 Efraim Levy

STANDARD & POOR'S

STOCK REPORTS

Dionex Corp.

NASDAQ Symbol **DNEX**
In S&P SmallCap 600

22-AUG-95 **Industry:** Specialty instruments

Summary: DNEX makes chromatography systems and related products that isolate and identify the components of chemical mixtures.

Quantitative Evaluations

Outlook (1 Lowest—5 Highest)
• **1+**

Fair Value
• **44¾**

Risk
• **Low**

Earn./Div. Rank
• **B+**

Technical Eval.
• **Bullish** since 9/94

Rel. Strength Rank (1 Lowest—99 Highest)
• **75**

Insider Activity
• **NA**

Recent Price • 50¼
52 Wk Range • 51¾-33½
Yield • Nil
12-Mo. P/E • 18.7

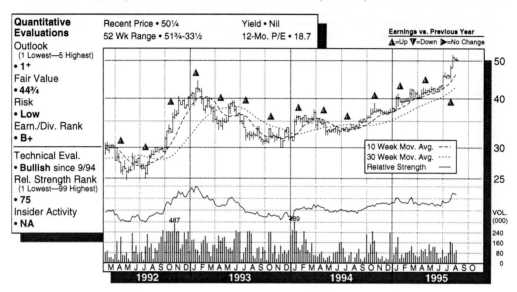

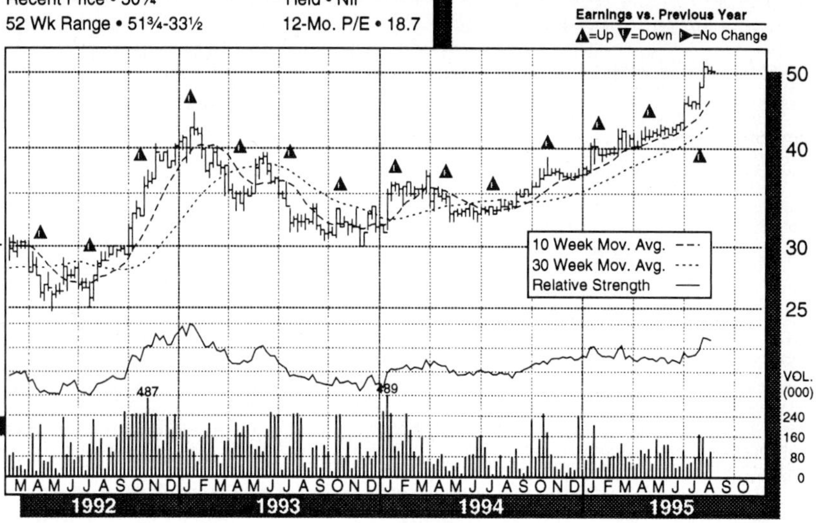

Business Profile - 22-AUG-95

This manufacturer of chromatography systems and related products used to isolate and identify the components of chemical mixtures has experienced more than 10 consecutive years of rising earnings. Assuming the success of a new solvent extraction system initially shipped in the fiscal 1995 fourth quarter, earnings should continue to advance in fiscal 1996. An ongoing program has resulted in the repurchase of 817,000 common shares in fiscal 1995. DNEX has a strong balance sheet.

Operational Review - 22-AUG-95

Net sales for the fiscal year ended June 30, 1995 (preliminary), advanced 9.6%, year to year, reflecting growth in all major geographic markets. However, a $2.2 million goodwill writeoff led to a cut in the gain in operating profit to 2.5%. Despite a higher tax rate, other income of $4.1 million and higher interest income (net) enabled net income to move ahead 16%. Share earnings were $2.69 on 4.6% fewer shares--reflecting a stock repurchase program--versus $2.21.

Stock Performance - 18-AUG-95

In the past 30 trading days, DNEX's shares have increased 10%, compared to a 0.51% rise in the S&P 500. Average trading volume for the past five days was 19,740 shares, compared with the 40-day moving average of 19,846 shares.

Key Stock Statistics

Dividend Rate/Share	Nil	Shareholders	2,100
Shs. outstg. (M)	7.0	Market cap. (B)	$0.353
Avg. daily vol. (M)	0.027	Inst. holdings	74%
Tang. Bk. Value/Share	15.04	Insider holdings	0%
Beta	1.26		

Value of $10,000 invested 5 years ago: $ 18,785

Fiscal Year Ending Jun. 30

	1995	% Change	1994	% Change	1993	% Change
Revenues (Million $)						
1Q	27.04	6%	25.46	1%	25.10	17%
2Q	30.62	9%	28.13	5%	26.90	12%
3Q	30.58	10%	27.72	4%	26.65	6%
4Q	31.78	13%	28.22	5%	26.98	5%
Yr.	120.0	10%	109.5	4%	105.6	10%
Income (Million $)						
1Q	4.20	24%	3.38	—	—	—
2Q	5.04	12%	4.49	5%	4.27	16%
3Q	5.15	13%	4.54	6%	4.28	10%
4Q	5.38	16%	4.63	9%	4.24	7%
Yr.	19.77	16%	17.04	5%	16.30	11%
Earnings Per Share ($)						
1Q	0.55	25%	0.44	2%	0.43	13%
2Q	0.68	17%	0.58	9%	0.53	18%
3Q	0.71	20%	0.59	11%	0.53	13%
4Q	0.75	25%	0.60	13%	0.53	10%
Yr.	2.69	22%	2.21	9%	2.02	13%

Next earnings report expected: mid October

Dionex Corp.

Business Summary - 16-AUG-95

Dionex Corporation develops, manufactures, markets and services chromatography systems used to identify the components of chemical mixtures. The company's systems are focused on three product areas: ion chromatography, bioseparations and supercritical fluid chromatography, and are used in a wide variety of industries.

In fiscal 1994, 57% of revenues was derived from business outside of North America.

The commercialization of ion chromatography, the company's core business, is a technology that separates ionic (charged) molecules, usually found in water-based solutions, and typically identifies them based on their electrical conductivity. The sale of these systems and related columns, suppressors, detectors and automation and other products accounts for a majority of revenues.

The DX-300 series product is used to analyze biological molecules such as proteins, carbohydrates and amino acids. A capillary electrophoresis system, the CES-I, is an emerging analytical technique that separates molecules based on their charge-to-mass ratios, size or other characteristics. The CarboPac MAI column is used for HPLC separation of reduced carbohydrates. In fiscal 1994, the DX500 series of chromatography systems for ion chromatography and HPLC was introduced, which will gradually replace the DX300 series.

Product lines in the area of supercritical fluid use the techniques of supercritical fluid chromatography, a form of chromatography that separates compounds dissolved in a supercritical fluid and identifies them with a variety of detection techniques; and supercritical fluid extraction, a sample preparation technique that passes a supercritical fluid through a solid or liquid sample to extract the compounds of interest for subsequent analysis. A supercritical fluid is one that has been put under pressure and heated until it has characteristics of both a liquid and a gas.

Other products include automation devices, chromatography columns, detectors, data analysis systems, and other products for chemical analysis.

Marketing is carried out by DNEX's own sales force in Belgium, Canada, France, Germany, Italy, Japan, the Netherlands, Switzerland, the U.K. and the U.S. At international locations where it does not have a sales force, the company has developed a network of distributors and sales agents.

Important Developments

Jul. '95—DNEX said it was pleased with the initial market response to its Accelerated Solvent Extraction system. This fully automated system, first shipped to customers in the fiscal 1995 fourth quarter, is designed to significantly reduce extraction times, solvent usage, and cost per extraction.

Capitalization

Long Term Debt: None (6/95).

Per Share Data ($)

(Year Ended Jun. 30)

	1995	1994	1993	1992	1991	1990
Tangible Bk. Val.	NA	14.68	12.49	11.83	9.66	8.75
Cash Flow	NA	2.53	2.27	2.01	1.90	1.64
Earnings	2.69	2.21	2.02	1.78	1.69	1.44
Dividends	Nil	Nil	Nil	Nil	Nil	Nil
Payout Ratio	Nil	Nil	Nil	Nil	Nil	Nil
Prices - High	46¾	37½	44½	41	34	27¾
- Low	37	31¼	31	24¾	18½	14½
P/E Ratio - High	17	17	22	23	20	19
- Low	14	14	15	14	11	10

Income Statement Analysis (Million $)

	1994	%Chg	1993	%Chg	1992	%Chg	1991
Revs.	110	4%	106	10%	96.4	8%	89.3
Oper. Inc.	27.4	6%	25.8	15%	22.4	8%	20.7
Depr.	2.5	26%	2.0	3%	1.9	9%	1.8
Int. Exp.	0.3	-46%	0.5	-32%	0.7	8%	0.6
Pretax Inc.	26.1	5%	24.9	11%	22.5	3%	21.8
Eff. Tax Rate	35%	—	35%	—	35%	—	35%
Net Inc.	17.0	4%	16.3	11%	14.7	4%	14.2

Balance Sheet & Other Fin. Data (Million $)

	1994	1993	1992	1991	1990	1989
Cash	51.3	42.5	49.5	48.3	50.8	54.1
Curr. Assets	92.5	82.9	84.7	80.6	80.4	78.8
Total Assets	133	118	120	109	106	99
Curr. Liab.	21.1	22.1	23.8	23.2	21.8	16.9
LT Debt	0.1	0.1	0.1	0.2	0.2	0.2
Common Eqty.	111	94.9	94.9	85.3	83.7	81.1
Total Cap.	112	96.0	96.2	86.2	84.5	81.3
Cap. Exp.	7.8	1.2	8.5	4.5	3.8	2.8
Cash Flow	19.5	18.3	16.7	15.9	14.8	14.6

Ratio Analysis

	1994	1993	1992	1991	1990	1989
Curr. Ratio	4.4	3.8	3.6	3.5	3.7	4.7
% LT Debt of Cap.	0.1	0.1	0.1	0.2	0.2	0.2
% Net Inc.of Revs.	15.6	15.4	15.3	15.9	16.1	17.0
% Ret. on Assets	13.6	14.1	13.0	13.1	13.0	14.0
% Ret. on Equity	16.6	17.6	16.6	16.8	16.1	17.1

Dividend Data —No cash has been paid. A two-for-one stock split was effected in 1986.

Data as orig. reptd.; bef. results of disc. opers. and/or spec. items. Per share data adj. for stk. divs. as of ex-div. date. E-Estimated. NA-Not Available. NM-Not Meaningful. NR-Not Ranked.

Office—1228 Titan Way, Sunnyvale, CA 94086. **Tel**—(408) 737-0700. **Pres & CEO**—A. B. Bowman. **Secy**—J. C. Gaither **VP-CFO & Investor Contact**—Michael W. Pope. **Dirs**—D. L. Anderson, J. F. Battey, A. B. Bowman, B. J. Moore. **Transfer Agent & Registrar**—First National Bank of Boston. **Incorporated** in California in 1980; reincorporated in Delaware in 1986. **Empl**-637. **S&P Analyst:** N.J. DeVita

STANDARD & POOR'S

STOCK REPORTS

Dixie Yarns

NASDAQ Symbol **DXYN**

In S&P SmallCap 600

23-OCT-95

Industry: Textiles

Summary: This company, which makes value-added textile and floorcovering products for specialty markets, has been concentrating on expansion in the floorcovering area.

Quantitative Evaluations

Outlook (1 Lowest—5 Highest)
• **5-**

Fair Value
• **7**

Risk
• **Average**

Earn./Div. Rank
• **B-**

Technical Eval.
• **Bullish** since 7/95

Rel. Strength Rank (1 Lowest—99 Highest)
• **14**

Insider Activity
• **Neutral**

Recent Price • 5⅝
52 Wk Range • 8-4⅞

Yield • Nil
12-Mo. P/E • 31.6

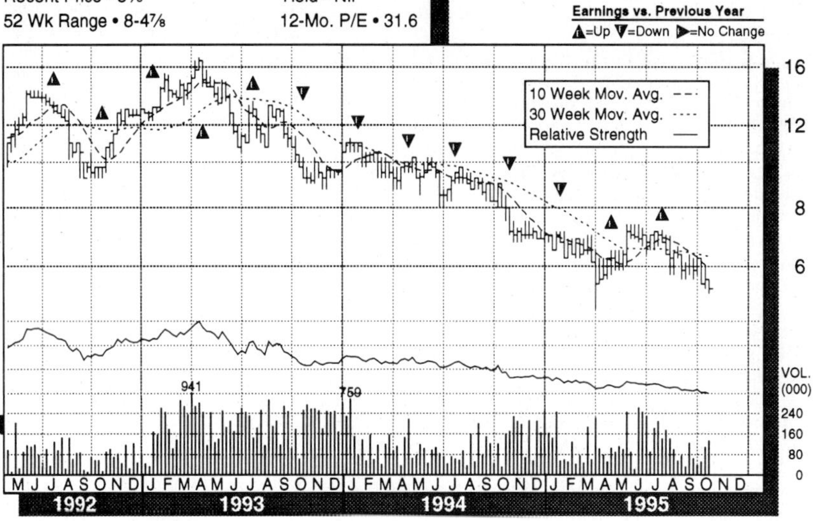

Business Profile - 23-OCT-95

This maker of textile and floorcovering products has made several acquisitions in the carpet industry, and now derives more than 50% of its revenues from floorcovering. In August 1995, DXYN agreed to sell its Newton, N.C., open-end cotton yarn spinning facility for approximately $6.0 million. Dixie anticipated that proceeds from the sale would be used to reduce indebtedness. In July 1995, Dixie repurchased 1,029,446 of its common shares for $18.3 million.

Operational Review - 12-OCT-95

Despite increased year-over-year comparisons in the first half of 1995, Dixie said that results fell short of anticipated levels due primarily to weak demand from softness in retail sales of textile and floorcovering products. The company noted that it does not expect results to improve significantly during the remainder of 1995 unless demand for textile and floorcovering products increases. DXYN its continuing to reduce costs as well as dispose of underperforming assets.

Stock Performance - 20-OCT-95

In the past 30 trading days, DXYN's shares have declined 10%, compared to a 3% rise in the S&P 500. Average trading volume for the past five days was 26,380 shares, compared with the 40-day moving average of 15,615 shares.

Key Stock Statistics

Dividend Rate/Share	Nil	Shareholders	5,400
Shs. outstg. (M)	10.5	Market cap. (B)	$0.056
Avg. daily vol. (M)	0.016	Inst. holdings	48%
Tang. Bk. Value/Share	9.64	Insider holdings	NA
Beta	1.27		

Value of $10,000 invested 5 years ago: $ 4,167

Fiscal Year Ending Dec. 31

	1995	% Change	1994	% Change	1993	% Change
Revenues (Million $)						
1Q	181.6	10%	164.8	36%	120.8	1%
2Q	177.8	NM	178.3	10%	161.4	31%
3Q	—	—	173.9	14%	152.5	34%
4Q	—	—	171.5	7%	159.9	41%
Yr.	—	—	688.5	16%	594.6	27%
Income (Million $)						
1Q	0.88	NM	-4.34	NM	0.91	NM
2Q	0.43	NM	0.12	-94%	2.06	57%
3Q	—	—	0.50	-40%	0.84	-60%
4Q	—	—	0.50	-43%	0.87	-56%
Yr.	—	—	-3.23	NM	4.68	-17%
Earnings Per Share ($)						
1Q	0.06	NM	-0.33	NM	0.10	NM
2Q	0.03	NM	0.01	-94%	0.18	20%
3Q	—	—	0.04	-43%	0.07	-71%
4Q	—	—	0.04	-43%	0.07	-70%
Yr.	—	—	-0.24	NM	0.41	-37%

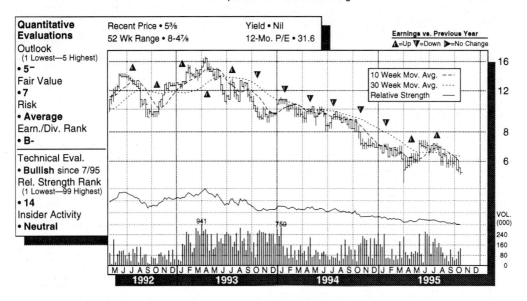

Next earnings report expected: early November

Dixie Yarns

Business Summary - 23-OCT-95

Dixie Yarns, Inc. manufactures value-added textile and floorcovering products for specialty markets. In recent years is has restructured its textile operations and expanded into floorcoverings (three acquisitions have been made since 1993). Segment sales and operating income in 1994 were:

	Sales	Profits
Floorcoverings	52%	44%
Textile products	48%	56%

The company's floorcovering business makes and markets carpet yarns and floorcovering products for specialty markets through Candlewick Yarns, Carriage Industries (acquired in March 1993), Masland Carpets (July 1993) and Patrick Carpet Mills (June 1994). Candlewick is one of the world's largest independent carpet yarn manufacturers. Its customers include end-use product manufacturers in the bath rug, automotive and broadloom carpet markets. Carriage is a vertically integrated carpet manufacturer serving the manufactured housing, recreational vehicle, small boat, exposition/trade show, contract/residential and home center/needlebond markets. Masland markets broadloom products for specification by the architectural and design communiities, and residential carpet and designer rugs to a select group in interior design showrooms and high-end specialty retailers.

During 1995, Patrick Carpet's manufacturing operations will be consolidated into Masland Carpet's Atmore, Ala., facility. The majority of 1995 spending is expected to be directed toward the floorcovering business. The largest projects include the completion of a new distribution center at Carriage Industries and a major expansion of the Atmore tufting and finishing facility.

In the textile area, Dixie makes yarns, industrial sewing threads and knit fabrics from natural and man-made fibers, focusing on high-end value added products. It concentrates on narrow groups of products, related by manufacturing processes, performance qualities and end uses, with no single group accounting for as much as 10% of revenues over the past three years. Textile products are sold primarily to manufacturers in the apparel, domestics, drapery and upholstery, hosiery, industrial fabrics, transportation and other industries.

Important Developments

Aug. '95—Dixie said it is continuing its efforts to reduce costs and dispose of undesirable assets.

Capitalization

Long Term Debt: $194,540,000 (7/1/95); incl. $44,782,000 of 7% sub. debs. due 2012, conv. into com. at $32.20 a sh.
Class B Common Stock: 735,228 shs. ($3 par); 20 votes per sh., conv. sh.-for-sh. into com.

Per Share Data ($) (Year Ended Dec. 31)

	1994	1993	1992	1991	1990	1989
Tangible Bk. Val.	9.53	10.06	12.46	11.91	15.20	14.70
Cash Flow	2.41	2.96	3.26	-0.43	2.71	2.71
Earnings	-0.24	0.41	0.65	-2.88	0.71	1.13
Dividends	0.20	0.20	0.20	0.42	0.68	0.68
Payout Ratio	NM	49%	31%	NM	96%	57%
Prices - High	11¼	16¾	14¼	15¼	16¼	22½
- Low	6¾	8¾	8¾	7½	7⅞	14
P/E Ratio - High	NM	41	22	NM	23	20
- Low	NM	21	13	NM	11	12

Income Statement Analysis (Million $)

	1994	%Chg	1993	%Chg	1992	%Chg	1991
Revs.	689	16%	595	27%	470	-4%	492
Oper. Inc.	41.3	12%	36.8	-17%	44.5	55%	28.7
Depr.	35.2	21%	29.2	28%	22.9	6%	21.6
Int. Exp.	13.7	7%	12.8	19%	10.8	-11%	12.2
Pretax Inc.	-11.9	NM	9.0	-20%	11.3	NM	-31.6
Eff. Tax Rate	NM	—	48%	—	50%	—	NM
Net Inc.	-3.2	NM	4.7	-18%	5.7	NM	-25.4

Balance Sheet & Other Fin. Data (Million $)

	1994	1993	1992	1991	1990	1989
Cash	1.9	4.0	1.4	2.3	2.0	3.4
Curr. Assets	153	148	128	136	141	139
Total Assets	488	497	372	347	359	347
Curr. Liab.	63.8	59.2	45.0	37.0	43.8	37.8
LT Debt	182	182	165	154	126	111
Common Eqty.	171	176	145	141	174	185
Total Cap.	413	424	324	306	314	307
Cap. Exp.	36.0	116	26.0	38.0	31.0	33.0
Cash Flow	32.0	33.9	28.5	-3.8	26.0	28.1

Ratio Analysis

	1994	1993	1992	1991	1990	1989
Curr. Ratio	2.4	2.5	2.9	3.7	3.2	3.7
% LT Debt of Cap.	44.0	43.0	50.9	50.3	40.1	36.1
% Net Inc.of Revs.	NM	0.8	1.2	NM	1.2	2.1
% Ret. on Assets	NM	1.0	1.6	NM	2.0	3.6
% Ret. on Equity	NM	2.6	3.9	NM	4.0	6.4

Dividend Data —Cash dividends, which had been paid in each year since 1954, were omitted on February 24, 1995. The most recent quarterly payment of $0.05 a share was made on December 9, 1994.

Amt. of Div. $	Date Decl.	Ex-Div. Date	Stock of Record	Payment Date
0.050	Nov. 18	Nov. 21	Nov. 28	Dec. 09 '94

Data as orig. reptd.; bef. results of disc. opers. and/or spec. items. Per share data adj. for stk. divs. as of ex-div. date. E-Estimated. NA-Not Available. NM-Not Meaningful. NR-Not Ranked.

Office—1100 S. Watkins St., Chattanooga, TN 37404. **Tel**—(615) 698-2501. **Chrmn, Pres, CEO**—D. K. Frierson. **SVP, CFO & Investor Contact**—Glenn M. Grandin (615-493-7279). **Treas**—G. A. Harmon. **Secy**—S. T. Klein. **Dirs**—P. K. Brock, L. A. Brooks, Jr., D. K. Frierson, P. K. Frierson, J. F. Harrison, Jr., J. H. Martin, Jr., P. L. Smith, J. T. Spence, Jr., R. J. Sudderth, Jr. **Transfer Agent**—Trust Co. Bank, Atlanta. **Incorporated** in Tennessee in 1920. **Empl**-6,900. **S&P Analyst:** Philip D. Wohl

STANDARD & POOR'S

Downey Financial Corp.

STOCK REPORTS

NYSE Symbol **DSL**

In S&P SmallCap 600

30-OCT-95 **Industry:** Banking

Summary: This company, through its Downey Savings and Loan subsidiary, provides diversified savings and loan services and operates 52 offices in Northern and Southern California.

Quantitative Evaluations

Outlook
(1 Lowest—5 Highest)
• **3-**

Fair Value
• **20⅞**

Risk
• **Average**

Earn./Div. Rank
• **B-**

Technical Eval.
• **Bearish** since 5/95

Rel. Strength Rank
(1 Lowest—99 Highest)
• **63**

Insider Activity
• **NA**

Recent Price • 20⅜
52 Wk Range • 22-14

Yield • 2.4%
12-Mo. P/E • 17.9

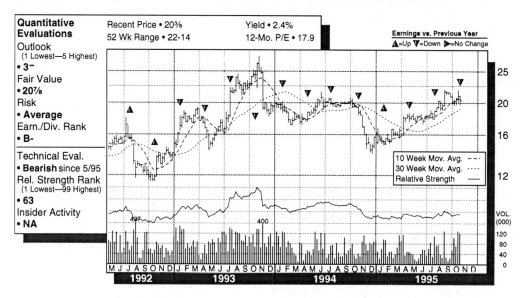

Earnings vs. Previous Year
▲=Up ▼=Down ▶=No Change

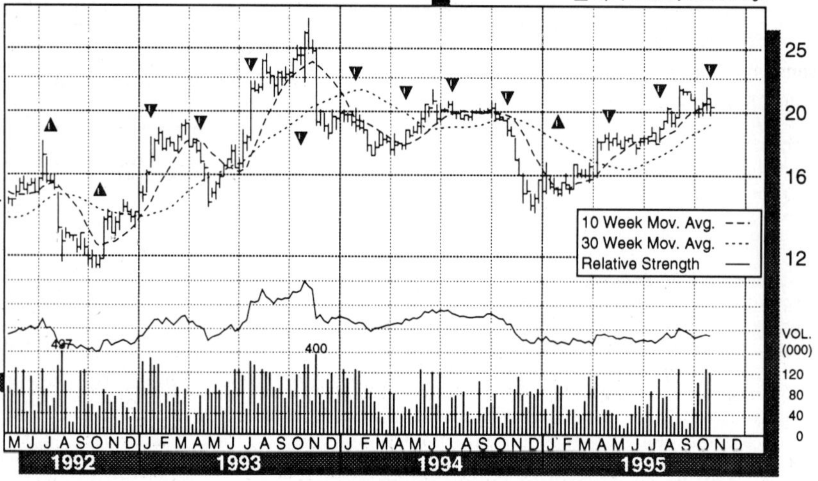

Business Profile - 27-OCT-95

The company took a number of steps to improve its financial performance in 1994 that included a leadership transition and a recommitment to growing the fundamental business. As a result, Downey achieved record residential mortgage loan volume, significantly expanded its retail deposit base, improved credit quality and increased operating efficiency. The company believes it has the necessary product base and delivery systems in place for the future.

Operational Review - 27-OCT-95

Net interest income in the first nine months of 1995 declined 6.1%, year to year, as growth in average earning assets was offset by a lower effective interest spread. The provision for loan losses was 83% higher, at $7.7 million. Noninterest income was down 4.2%, hurt by lower other income, and despite a 1.0% drop in noninterest expense, net income fell 29%, to $12,768,000 ($0.79 a share), from $17,911,000 ($1.11).

Stock Performance - 27-OCT-95

In the past 30 trading days, DSL's shares have declined 5%, compared to a 0.63% fall in the S&P 500. Average trading volume for the past five days was 25,960 shares, compared with the 40-day moving average of 16,087 shares.

Key Stock Statistics

Dividend Rate/Share	0.48	Shareholders	1,000
Shs. outstg. (M)	16.2	Market cap. (B)	$0.329
Avg. daily vol. (M)	0.026	Inst. holdings	29%
Tang. Bk. Value/Share	22.91	Insider holdings	NA
Beta	1.09		

Value of $10,000 invested 5 years ago: $ 13,208

Fiscal Year Ending Dec. 31

	1995	% Change	1994	% Change	1993	% Change
Revenues (Million $)						
1Q	79.91	46%	54.71	-7%	58.90	-20%
2Q	84.24	43%	58.76	-7%	62.85	-13%
3Q	85.67	38%	62.24	4%	60.06	-11%
4Q	—	—	70.99	32%	53.97	-12%
Yr.	—	—	246.7	5%	235.8	-14%
Income (Million $)						
1Q	3.21	-44%	5.76	-19%	7.14	-37%
2Q	4.18	-36%	6.49	-31%	9.47	-17%
3Q	5.38	-5%	5.67	-26%	7.71	-27%
4Q	—	—	5.62	33%	4.24	-51%
Yr.	—	—	23.53	-18%	28.55	-32%
Earnings Per Share ($)						
1Q	0.20	-44%	0.36	-18%	0.44	-37%
2Q	0.26	-35%	0.40	-31%	0.58	-17%
3Q	0.33	-6%	0.35	-27%	0.48	-26%
4Q	—	—	0.35	35%	0.26	-52%
Yr.	—	—	1.46	-17%	1.76	-32%

Next earnings report expected: mid January

Downey Financial Corp.

Business Summary - 30-OCT-95

Downey Financial Corp. is a bank holding company that owns Downey Savings and Loan Association, a federally-licensed savings association that operates 52 offices in California. Downey offers primarily retail banking and residential real estate lending services in key Northern and Southern California markets.

Gross loans outstanding increased sharply to $4.1 billion at year-end 1994, compared with $2.9 billion a year before. Almost all of the new loan volume consists of single family adjustable rate loans. Gross loans outstanding at year end 1994 and 1993 were divided as follows:

	1994	1993
Real estate-residential	91%	84%
Real estate-commercial	7%	12%
Real estate-construction	---	2%
Consumer and other	2%	2%

The effective interest rate spread in 1994 was 2.99%, down from 3.44% the previous year. The average yield on loans, investment securities and other interest bearing assets in 1994 was 6.43%, and the average rate paid on deposits and borrowings was 3.63%. In 1993, the yield on loans was 6.82% and the average rate paid on deposits and borrowings was 3.54%.

Nonperforming assets at 1994 year-end were $65.6 million (1.41% of total assets), versus $69.6 million (2.01%) a year earlier. The allowance for estimated losses at December 31, 1994, was $25.7 million (0.62% of gross loans), versus $26.8 million (0.92%) at December 31, 1993. Net chargeoffs during 1994 came to $5.4 million, up from $2.7 million in 1993.

At year-end 1994, deposits totaled $3.6 billion, up 16% from $3.1 billion at year-end 1993. The company recorded a $320 million increase in deposits in the fourth quarter, of which 45% was from retail deposits acquired through Wall Street activities.

Important Developments

Aug. '95—The company noted that operations of its Downey Affiliated Insurance Agency commenced in the second quarter of 1995, at which time representatives were available in Downey's branches to offer annuity products to current customers and potential new customers. Downey Affiliated was incorporated as a wholly owned subsidiary in January 1995 and subsequently capitalized with $400,000.

Capitalization

FHLB Advances: $212,995,000 (9/95).
Borrowings: $207,696,000 (9/95), incl. $196,917,000 in commercial paper.

Per Share Data ($)

(Year Ended Dec. 31)

	1994	1993	1992	1991	1990	1989
Tangible Bk. Val.	22.24	21.21	18.91	16.55	15.29	12.95
Earnings	1.46	1.76	2.59	1.54	2.60	0.17
Dividends	0.48	0.35	0.32	0.31	0.28	0.27
Payout Ratio	33%	20%	12%	20%	11%	159%
Prices - High	21⅝	27¾	18	18⅜	19¾	24⅛
- Low	14	14¼	11¼	10⅝	10⅛	10¼
P/E Ratio - High	15	16	7	12	8	NM
- Low	10	8	4	7	4	NM

Income Statement Analysis (Million $)

	1994	%Chg	1993	%Chg	1992	%Chg	1991
Net Int. Inc.	106	-5%	112	-3%	116	NM	115
Loan Loss Prov.	4.2	NM	1.1	-88%	9.0	59%	5.7
Non Int. Inc.	17.6	25%	14.1	-8%	15.3	NM	-11.4
Non Int. Exp.	79.7	4%	76.4	4%	73.2	9%	67.3
Pretax Inc.	40.2	-17%	48.4	-2%	49.5	61%	30.8
Eff. Tax Rate	42%	—	41%	—	16%	—	19%
Net Inc.	23.5	-18%	28.6	-32%	41.9	68%	24.9
% Net Int. Marg.	2.99%	—	3.44%	—	3.53%	—	3.11%

Balance Sheet & Other Fin. Data (Million $)

	1994	1993	1992	1991	1990	1989
Total Assets	4,651	3,467	3,478	3,778	4,168	4,099
Loans	4,189	2,917	2,766	3,254	3,002	2,713
Deposits	3,557	3,069	3,108	3,355	3,361	3,511
Capitalization:						
Debt	477	13.7	15.0	97.0	262	22.0
Equity	366	351	313	277	257	219
Total	843	365	328	373	519	241

Ratio Analysis

	1994	1993	1992	1991	1990	1989
% Ret. on Assets	0.6	0.8	1.2	0.6	1.0	0.1
% Ret. on Equity	6.6	8.6	14.2	9.3	17.6	1.3
% Loan Loss Resv.	0.6	0.9	1.0	0.6	0.6	0.6
% Risk Based Capital	14.2	16.9	14.4	12.1	11.1	9.4
Price Times Book Value:						
High	1.0	1.3	1.0	1.1	1.3	1.9
Low	0.6	0.7	0.6	0.6	0.7	0.8

Dividend Data —Following a special dividend in late 1985, quarterly cash dividends were resumed in 1986 after a five-year hiatus.

Amt. of Div. $	Date Decl.	Ex-Div. Date	Stock of Record	Payment Date
0.120	Oct. 26	Nov. 02	Nov. 08	Nov. 23 '94
0.120	Jan. 25	Feb. 03	Feb. 09	Feb. 24 '95
0.120	Apr. 26	May. 04	May. 10	May. 26 '95
0.120	Jul. 26	Aug. 08	Aug. 10	Aug. 25 '95
0.120	Oct. 26	Nov. 03	Nov. 07	Nov. 22 '95

Data as orig. reptd.; bef. results of disc opers. and/or spec. items. Per share data adj. for stk. divs. as of ex-div. date. E-Estimated. NA-Not Available. NM-Not Meaningful. NR-Not Ranked.

Office—3501 Jamboree Rd., Newport Beach, CA 92660. **Tel**—(714) 854-0300. **Chrmn**—M. L. McAlister. **Pres & CEO**—S. W. Prough. **EVP-Secy**—D. E. Royer. **SVP & Controller**—R. D. Silver. **EVP, CFO & Investor Contact**—Thomas E. Prince. **Dirs**—D. J. Aigner, C. E. Jones, P. Kouri, M. L. McAlister, G. McQuarrie, S. W. Prough, L. Smull, S. Yellen. **Transfer Agent & Registrar**—American Stock Transfer & Trust Co. **Incorporated** in California in 1957; reincorporated in Delaware in 1994. **Empl-** 1,065. **S&P Analyst:** S.R.B.

Dravo Corp.

NYSE Symbol **DRV**
In S&P SmallCap 600

28-AUG-95 **Industry:** Building

Summary: Following the recent sale of its construction aggregates subsidiary, Dravo is now primarily a lime producer.

Quantitative Evaluations

Outlook
(1 Lowest—5 Highest)
• **5+**

Fair Value
• **17⅜**

Risk
• **Average**

Earn./Div. Rank
• **C**

Technical Eval.
• **Bearish** since 5/95

Rel. Strength Rank
(1 Lowest—99 Highest)
• **47**

Insider Activity
• **NA**

Recent Price • 14
52 Wk Range • 14¾-9¾
Yield • Nil
12-Mo. P/E • NM

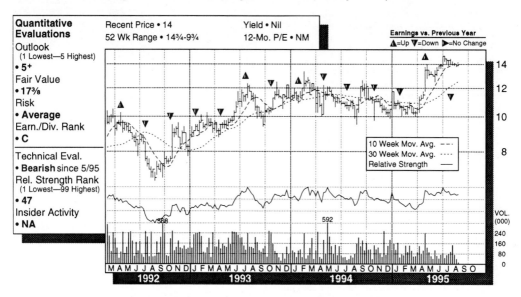

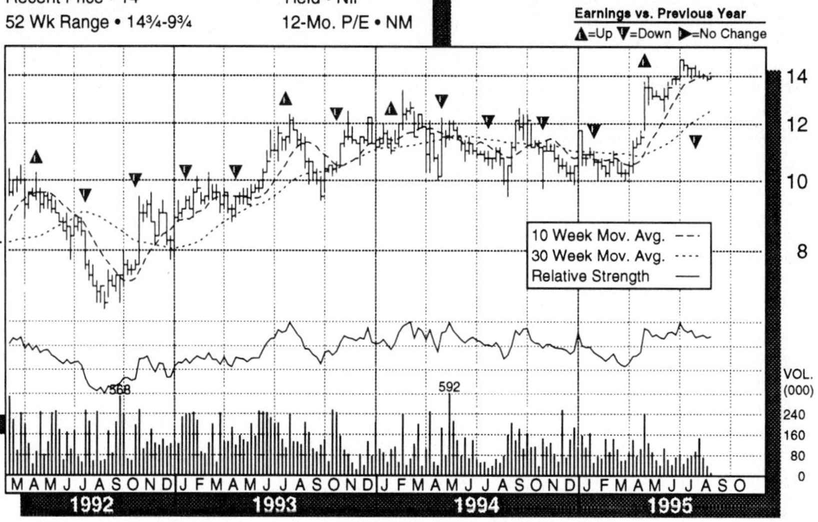

Business Profile - 28-AUG-95

Currently increasing installed lime production capacity to three million tons per year, Dravo supplies material for use in a variety of industrial applications to customers in the Ohio River and lower Mississippi River Valley regions, as well as the southeastern United States. Technical support provided to lime customers as part of an extensive research and development program is aimed at finding additional uses for Dravo's lime products and new markets for its lime-related technologies.

Operational Review - 28-AUG-95

Revenues for the six months ended June 30, 1995, rose 14% from the year-earlier period's pro forma amount (which reflects the sale of the Basic Materials subsidiary). Gross margins widened, but SG&A expenses climbed 22%. Following a nearly threefold increase in net other expense, income was down 5.4%, to $5,253,000 ($0.04 a share), from a pro forma $5,553,000 ($0.29). Results for the 1994 period exclude a $1,361,000 ($0.09) charge from the cumulative effect of an accounting change.

Stock Performance - 25-AUG-95

In the past 30 trading days, DRV's shares have declined 3%, compared to a 0.04% rise in the S&P 500. Average trading volume for the past five days was 1,960 shares, compared with the 40-day moving average of 13,826 shares.

Key Stock Statistics

Dividend Rate/Share	Nil	Shareholders	3,200
Shs. outstg. (M)	14.8	Market cap. (B)	$0.207
Avg. daily vol. (M)	0.013	Inst. holdings	69%
Tang. Bk. Value/Share	5.16	Insider holdings	NA
Beta	0.19		

Value of $10,000 invested 5 years ago: $ 8,615

Fiscal Year Ending Dec. 31

	1995	% Change	1994	% Change	1993	% Change
Revenues (Million $)						
1Q	33.91	-41%	57.68	-7%	61.81	1%
2Q	35.70	-51%	72.63	3%	70.19	-1%
3Q	—	—	75.31	-1%	76.13	4%
4Q	—	—	72.50	4%	69.46	2%
Yr.	—	—	278.0	NM	277.6	2%
Income (Million $)						
1Q	2.54	NM	-1.27	NM	0.39	-49%
2Q	2.72	-14%	3.15	-15%	3.70	6%
3Q	—	—	3.87	-9%	4.23	-6%
4Q	—	—	-0.82	NM	26.70	NM
Yr.	—	—	4.93	-86%	35.13	NM
Earnings Per Share ($)						
1Q	0.13	NM	-0.13	NM	-0.02	NM
2Q	0.14	-18%	0.17	-19%	0.21	11%
3Q	—	—	0.22	-8%	0.24	-8%
4Q	—	—	-0.10	NM	1.77	NM
Yr.	—	—	0.16	-93%	2.20	NM

Next earnings report expected: early November

Dravo Corp.

Business Summary - 28-AUG-95

In late 1994, Dravo Corporation sold substantially all the assets and certain liabilities of Dravo Basic Materials Company, its construction aggregates subsidiary, to Martin Marietta Materials, Inc. As a result, Dravo is now primarily a lime company operating principally in the United States. Activities include the production of lime for utility, metallurgical, pulp and paper, municipal, construction and miscellaneous chemical and industrial applications. Operations are carried on principally by a wholly owned subsidiary, Dravo Lime Company. All of the properties on which the company's reserves are located are physically accessible for purposes of mining and processing limestone into lime.

Dravo Lime, one of the largest U.S. lime producers, owns and operates three integrated lime production facilities, two in Kentucky and one in Alabama. The Black River plant in Butler, Ky., is nearing completion of a two-kiln expansion. When that expansion is on line, Dravo Lime's annual quicklime capacity will total approximately three million tons.

The Maysville facility, a 1,050,000-ton-per-year plant near Maysville, Ky., produces material, marketed under the tradename Thiosorbic Lime, that has a product chemistry ideally suited for removing sulphur dioxide from power plant stack gases. All of Maysville's output is committed under long-term contracts with utility companies in the Ohio Valley region. All contracts contain provisions for price escalation. Owned reserves at the Maysville site are recovered from a mine 950 feet underground and are considered adequate to sustain the current three-kiln production in excess of 30 years. Dravo Lime also holds options on additional limestone reserves to sustain production for an addditional 30-year period.

In conjunction with the sale of Dravo Basic Materials' assets, Dravo Lime entered into agreements appointing Martin Marietta Materials the exclusive distributor of aggregate by-products produced by Dravo Lime in the lime production process. As part of the agreement covering Dravo Lime's Longview facility in Alabama, an aggregates processing facility is being constructed that will make available between 500,000 and 1,000,000 tons of aggregates annually for purchase by Martin Marietta.

Important Developments

Jan. '95—Martin Marietta Materials acquired substantially all of the assets of Dravo's construction aggregates business for $120.5 million.

Capitalization

Long Term Debt: $36,293,000 (3/95).
$12.35 Series D Conv. Exch. Pref. Stk.: 200,000 shs. ($100 liquid. pref.); ea. conv. into 8 com. shs.
$2.475 Series B Conv. Pref. Stk.: 27,386 shs. ($1 par); ea. conv. into 3.216 com. shs.

Per Share Data ($)

(Year Ended Dec. 31)

	1994	1993	1992	1991	1990	1989
Tangible Bk. Val.	5.06	5.91	6.27	5.63	7.57	6.41
Cash Flow	1.35	3.41	1.78	1.85	1.99	1.86
Earnings	0.16	2.20	0.52	0.65	0.90	0.82
Dividends	Nil	Nil	Nil	Nil	Nil	Nil
Payout Ratio	Nil	Nil	Nil	Nil	Nil	Nil
Prices - High	13⅜	12½	10½	13¾	17¼	22¾
- Low	9½	8¾	6⅝	5¾	9¾	13
P/E Ratio - High	84	6	20	21	19	28
- Low	59	4	13	9	11	16

Income Statement Analysis (Million $)

	1994	%Chg	1993	%Chg	1992	%Chg	1991
Revs.	278	NM	278	2%	273	-8%	296
Oper. Inc.	32.0	-10%	35.6	-7%	38.2	-11%	42.7
Depr.	17.6	-2%	18.0	-3%	18.6	5%	17.7
Int. Exp.	12.4	35%	9.2	-12%	10.5	-6%	11.2
Pretax Inc.	5.5	-48%	10.5	-17%	12.7	-21%	16.1
Eff. Tax Rate	11%	—	NM	—	19%	—	24%
Net Inc.	4.9	-86%	35.1	NM	10.3	-16%	12.3

Balance Sheet & Other Fin. Data (Million $)

	1994	1993	1992	1991	1990	1989
Cash	2.0	0.8	1.0	1.7	1.6	1.5
Curr. Assets	160	108	113	110	109	115
Total Assets	307	272	269	272	300	283
Curr. Liab.	154	49.0	53.0	64.0	99	80.0
LT Debt	42.4	88.5	88.0	90.0	55.0	62.0
Common Eqty.	75.0	88.0	93.0	83.0	112	95.0
Total Cap.	139	198	203	195	189	179
Cap. Exp.	44.8	13.6	8.5	19.7	29.1	12.4
Cash Flow	20.0	50.6	26.4	27.4	29.5	27.7

Ratio Analysis

	1994	1993	1992	1991	1990	1989
Curr. Ratio	1.0	2.2	2.1	1.7	1.1	1.4
% LT Debt of Cap.	30.5	44.7	43.4	46.0	28.9	34.5
% Net Inc.of Revs.	1.8	12.7	3.8	4.1	5.4	5.3
% Ret. on Assets	1.7	13.0	3.8	4.3	5.4	5.2
% Ret. on Equity	2.9	36.0	8.8	9.9	12.8	14.0

Dividend Data —Common dividends were omitted in 1987, after having been paid since 1939. A "poison pill" stock purchase right was adopted in 1986.

Data as orig. reptd.; bef. results of disc. opers. and/or spec. items. Per share data adj. for stk. divs. as of ex-div. date. E-Estimated. NA-Not Available. NM-Not Meaningful. NR-Not Ranked.

Office—3600 One Oliver Plaza, Pittsburgh, PA 15222. **Tel**—(412) 566-3000. **Pres & CEO**—C. A. Gilbert. **Exec VP & CFO**—E. F. Ladd III. **VP & Secy**—J. J. Puhala. **Investor Contact**—Ron W. Sommer (412) 566-5597. **Dirs**—A. E. Byrnes, C. A. Gilbert, J. C. Huntington Jr., W. E. Kassling, W. G. Roth, K. M. Weis. **Transfer Agent & Registrar**—Continental Stock Transfer & Trust Co., NYC. **Incorporated** in Pennsylvania in 1936. **Empl**-768. **S&P Analyst:** K.J.G.

STANDARD & POOR'S

STOCK REPORTS

Dress Barn

NASDAQ Symbol **DBRN**

In S&P SmallCap 600

10-OCT-95 **Industry:** Retail Stores

Summary: This retailer operates a growing chain of women's apparel stores, mainly in the eastern U.S., offering moderate- to better-quality brandname merchandise at discount prices.

Quantitative Evaluations

Outlook (1 Lowest—5 Highest) • **3+**

Fair Value • **9¾**

Risk • **Average**

Earn./Div. Rank • **B+**

Technical Eval. • **Bearish** since 7/95

Rel. Strength Rank (1 Lowest—99 Highest) • **36**

Insider Activity • **NA**

Recent Price • 9⅝ | Yield • Nil

52 Wk Range • 11⅛-8¾ | 12-Mo. P/E • 11.7

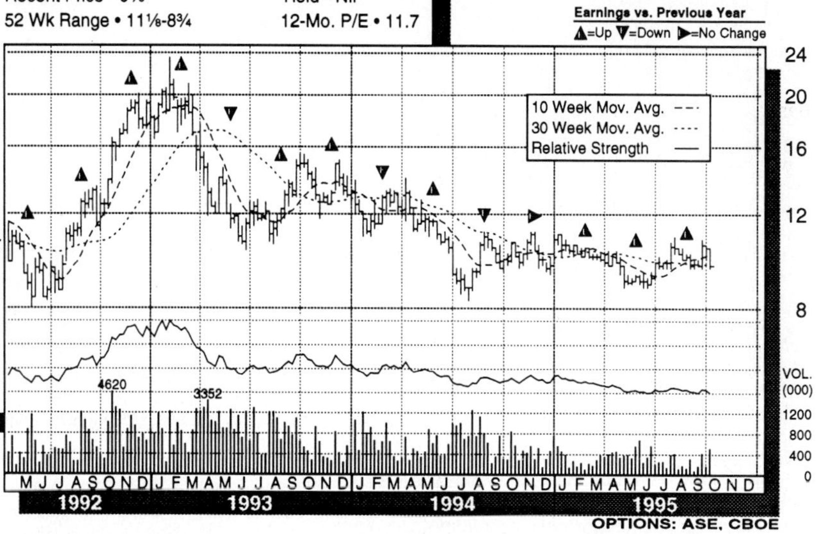

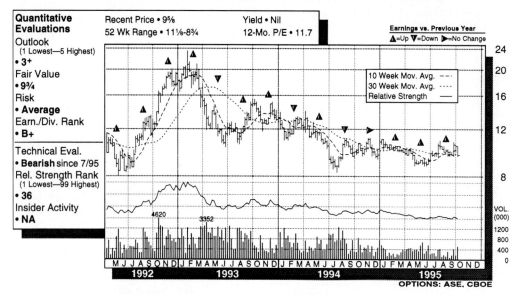

OPTIONS: ASE, CBOE

Business Profile - 10-OCT-95

This retailer operates a chain of women's apparel stores in 43 states, emphasizing fashion and value, offering in-season, moderate- to better-quality brand name merchandise at a discount. DBRN opened 108 new stores and closed 30 underperforming stores in fiscal 1995, ending the year with 766 stores in operation. To support its rapid growth, DBRN recently consolidated five separate distribution facilities and moved its corporate headquarters to a new 510,000 sq. ft. facility in Suffern, N.Y.

Operational Review - 05-OCT-95

Net sales for the 52 weeks ended July 29, 1995, advanced 9.5% from those of the prior year, reflecting contributions from 78 additional stores, partially offset by a 1.0% decline in same-store sales. Profitability benefited from higher initial margins, which offset increased markdowns, and well-controlled operating costs. After taxes at 37.0% in each period, net income rose 13%, to $18,285,000 ($0.82 per share), from $16,153,000 ($0.73).

Stock Performance - 06-OCT-95

In the past 30 trading days, DBRN's shares have declined 4%, compared to a 4% rise in the S&P 500. Average trading volume for the past five days was 100,220 shares, compared with the 40-day moving average of 47,626 shares.

Key Stock Statistics

Dividend Rate/Share	Nil	Shareholders	1,800
Shs. outstg. (M)	22.3	Market cap. (B)	$0.215
Avg. daily vol. (M)	0.060	Inst. holdings	41%
Tang. Bk. Value/Share	7.79	Insider holdings	NA
Beta	0.30		

Value of $10,000 invested 5 years ago: $ 8,555

Fiscal Year Ending Jul. 31

	1995	% Change	1994	% Change	1993	% Change
Revenues (Million $)						
1Q	130.1	9%	119.7	14%	104.9	19%
2Q	116.7	9%	106.6	8%	98.58	18%
3Q	123.5	9%	112.9	19%	95.22	5%
4Q	130.6	10%	118.2	-2%	120.8	20%
Yr.	500.8	10%	457.3	9%	419.6	16%
Income (Million $)						
1Q	6.39	NM	6.41	15%	5.55	41%
2Q	2.42	14%	2.13	-36%	3.31	94%
3Q	5.00	16%	4.31	23%	3.50	-26%
4Q	4.47	35%	3.31	-50%	6.68	16%
Yr.	18.28	13%	16.15	-15%	19.04	18%
Earnings Per Share ($)						
1Q	0.29	NM	0.29	16%	0.25	39%
2Q	0.11	10%	0.10	-33%	0.15	88%
3Q	0.22	16%	0.19	19%	0.16	-27%
4Q	0.20	33%	0.15	-50%	0.30	15%
Yr.	0.82	12%	0.73	-15%	0.86	16%

Next earnings report expected: late November

Dress Barn

Business Summary - 10-OCT-95

The Dress Barn, Inc. operates women's apparel stores that feature in-season, moderate- to better-quality merchandise at "off" prices. At July 30, 1994, it was operating 688 units (up from 100 stores at the end of fiscal 1984), mostly located in the East and operated under the Dress Barn (567 stores) and Dress Barn Woman (98) names. Included in the Dress Barn division are 23 SBX stores, a test concept in outlet malls, featuring casual apparel.

Dress Barn stores emphasize merchandise with nationally recognized brandnames, bearing the manufacturers' labels, at substantial discounts from regular department store prices and selected to appeal mainly to price-conscious and fashion-minded women in middle- to upper-income brackets and primarily in the 18- to 40-year age range. Sportswear accounts for more than half of sales volume, and dresses, suits, blazers and accessories for the balance. The clothing is stocked in junior, misses' and petite sizes and styles in the Dress Barn units and larger sizes of similar styles in the Dress Barn Woman units. About 60% of merchandise is sold under nationally recognized brand names, with the remainder consisting of private labels and non-nationally advertised brands.

Most Dress Barn stores are located in strip shopping centers or enclosed malls, and each store has between 3,500 and 5,000 sq. ft. of selling space. Virtually all units are open seven days a week. About 50% of sales are made for cash, with the balance consisting of credit card sales (using VISA, MasterCard, American Express and Discover).

The company uses a computerized merchandise control system to track buyers' orders, warehouse receiving, price marking, shipments to stores, inventories, markdowns, store sales and individual merchandise item performance. To keep merchandise seasonal and in current fashion, Dress Barn management receives weekly computer reports on sales and inventory levels (utilizing markdowns to expedite selling), which are organized by department, class, vendor, style, color and store.

In fiscal 1995, Dress Barn opened 108 stores and closed 30 underperforming stores, compared to 82 stores opened and 35 closed in fiscal 1994. The company's goal is to be operating 1,000 stores within the next five years.

Important Developments

Oct. '95—Dress Barn reported that sales for the five weeks ended September 30, 1995, totaled $55.8 million, a 12% increase, year to year. Same-store sales were up 2%.

Capitalization

Long Term Debt: $3,500,000 (4/95).
Options: To buy 1,257,342 shs. at $3.00 to $12.50 ea. (7/94).

Per Share Data ($) (Year Ended Jul. 31)

	1995	1994	1993	1992	1991	1990
Tangible Bk. Val.	NA	7.15	6.42	5.51	4.74	4.11
Cash Flow	NA	1.27	1.31	1.12	0.99	0.87
Earnings	0.82	0.73	0.86	0.74	0.68	0.64
Dividends	Nil	Nil	Nil	Nil	Nil	Nil
Payout Ratio	Nil	Nil	Nil	Nil	Nil	Nil
Prices - High	11	14	23½	20⅛	15½	12¾
- Low	8¾	8¼	10¼	7¾	6	4¾
P/E Ratio - High	13	19	27	27	23	20
- Low	11	11	12	10	9	7

Income Statement Analysis (Million $)

	1994	%Chg	1993	%Chg	1992	%Chg	1991
Revs.	457	9%	420	16%	363	12%	325
Oper. Inc.	35.9	-4%	37.3	24%	30.1	9%	27.5
Depr.	12.0	22%	9.8	21%	8.1	20%	6.8
Int. Exp.	Nil	—	Nil	—	Nil	—	Nil
Pretax Inc.	25.6	-14%	29.7	19%	25.0	5%	23.7
Eff. Tax Rate	37%	—	36%	—	35%	—	37%
Net Inc.	16.2	-15%	19.0	17%	16.2	8%	15.0

Balance Sheet & Other Fin. Data (Million $)

	1994	1993	1992	1991	1990	1989
Cash	62.0	61.1	50.7	39.1	35.2	31.9
Curr. Assets	146	143	125	95.0	86.0	71.0
Total Assets	218	202	173	138	125	101
Curr. Liab.	56.8	59.1	51.0	32.6	30.2	23.4
LT Debt	Nil	Nil	Nil	Nil	Nil	Nil
Common Eqty.	159	142	120	103	93.0	76.0
Total Cap.	161	143	122	105	95.0	78.0
Cap. Exp.	25.5	21.9	14.9	10.1	14.5	11.8
Cash Flow	28.1	28.9	24.3	21.7	19.6	22.6

Ratio Analysis

	1994	1993	1992	1991	1990	1989
Curr. Ratio	2.6	2.4	2.4	2.9	2.8	3.0
% LT Debt of Cap.	Nil	Nil	Nil	Nil	Nil	Nil
% Net Inc.of Revs.	3.5	4.5	4.5	4.6	5.1	7.6
% Ret. on Assets	7.7	10.1	10.4	11.6	12.6	20.9
% Ret. on Equity	10.7	14.4	14.5	15.6	16.9	28.6

Dividend Data —No cash has been paid.

Data as orig. reptd.; bef. results of disc. opers. and/or spec. items. Per share data adj. for stk. divs. as of ex-div. date. E-Estimated. NA-Not Available. NM-Not Meaningful. NR-Not Ranked.

Office—30 Dunnigan Drive, Suffern, NY 10901. **Tel**—(914) 369-4500. **Chrmn & CEO**—E. S. Jaffe. **Pres & COO**—B. Steinberg. **SVP, CFO & Investor Contact**—Armand Correia. **Treas & Secy**—Roslyn S. Jaffe. **Dirs**—K. Eppler, E. S. Jaffe, R. S. Jaffe, D. Jonas, E. D. Solomon, B. Steinberg. **Transfer Agent & Registrar**—Midlantic National Bank, Edison, N.J. **Incorporated** in Connecticut in 1966. **Empl**-6,400. **S&P Analyst:** Maureen C. Carini

STANDARD & POOR'S

STOCK REPORTS

Dynatech Corp.

NASDAQ Symbol **DYTC**

In S&P SmallCap 600

07-AUG-95 **Industry:** Telecommunications

Summary: This diversified maker of high-technology products has restructured operations to focus on core markets supporting voice, data and video communications.

S&P Opinion: Buy (★★★★★)

Recent Price • 19¼ | Yield • Nil

52 Wk Range • 22¾-10⅜ | 12-Mo. P/E • 16.2

Quantitative Evaluations

Outlook
(1 Lowest—5 Highest)
• 4+

Fair Value
• 20⅞

Risk
• Average

Earn./Div. Rank
• B

Technical Eval.
• Bullish since 4/95

Rel. Strength Rank
(1 Lowest—99 Highest)
• 22

Insider Activity
• Neutral

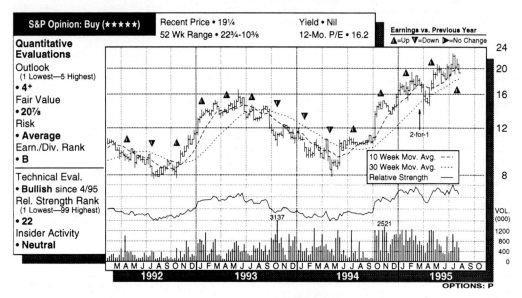

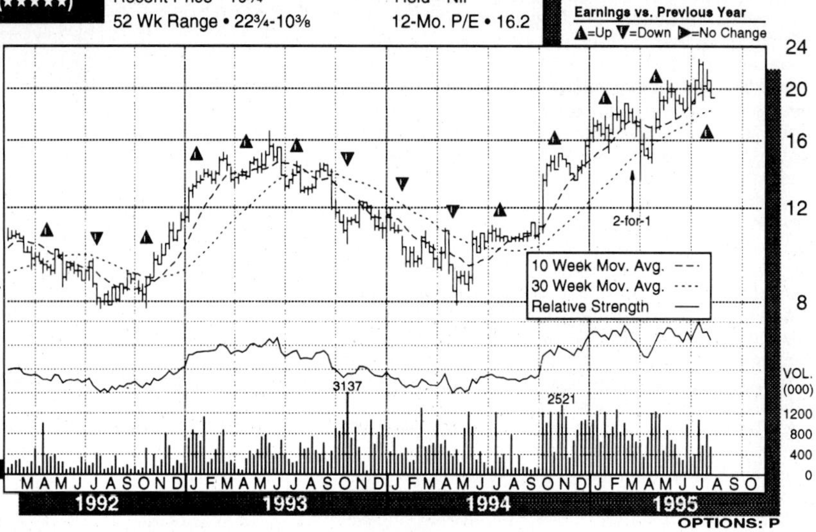

Overview - 07-AUG-95

Revenues from the information support products group should see continued strong growth in fiscal 1995-96. As telecommunications service providers upgrade and expand to meet customer demands, the need for Dynatech's communications test equipment will grow. Diversified instrumentation group revenues will benefit from the recent U.S. Food and Drug Administration approval of a diagnostic radiation product, which was already selling well overseas. However, year-to-year comparisons will be hurt by the expected sale of the final product lines marked for divestiture. Operating margins should benefit from the recent restructuring, and results will further benefit from lower interest expense.

Valuation - 07-AUG-95

The shares have risen sharply in 1995 on continued strong earnings growth. Despite this appreciation, we believe strong upside potential still exists. The rapidly changing landscape of the telecommunications services markets will result in new competitors, thus expanding Dynatech's customer base beyond the traditional telephone companies. This trend is happening on a global basis, not just in the United States. As a result of a growing presence in Europe, Asia and South America, the company's international business is growing even faster than its strong domestic operations. We recommend the shares for long-term capital appreciation.

Key Stock Statistics

S&P EPS Est. 1996	1.35	Tang. Bk. Value/Share	7.13
P/E on S&P Est. 1996	14.3	Beta	0.80
Dividend Rate/Share	Nil	Shareholders	1,100
Shs. outstg. (M)	17.6	Market cap. (B)	$0.338
Avg. daily vol. (M)	0.147	Inst. holdings	60%
		Insider holdings	NA

Value of $10,000 invested 5 years ago: $ 22,985

Fiscal Year Ending Mar. 31

	1996	% Change	1995	% Change	1994	% Change
Revenues (Million $)						
1Q	118.3	NM	117.8	NM	117.8	-3%
2Q	—	—	121.4	9%	111.4	-16%
3Q	—	—	127.2	12%	113.4	-15%
4Q	—	—	122.4	6%	116.0	-17%
Yr.	—	—	488.8	7%	458.5	-13%
Income (Million $)						
1Q	4.63	27%	3.66	6%	3.45	150%
2Q	—	—	5.08	54%	3.29	-22%
3Q	—	—	5.61	NM	1.43	-73%
4Q	—	—	5.84	NM	-34.39	NM
Yr.	—	—	20.19	NM	-26.22	NM
Earnings Per Share ($)						
1Q	0.26	33%	0.19	5%	0.19	147%
2Q	E0.33	—	0.29	63%	0.17	-24%
3Q	E0.37	—	0.32	NM	0.08	-74%
4Q	E0.39	—	0.33	NM	-1.85	NM
Yr.	E1.35	—	1.13	NM	-1.41	NM

Next earnings report expected: late October

Dynatech Corp.

Business Summary - 07-AUG-95

Dynatech Corporation operates in two business segments: Information Support Products and Diversified Instrumentation. Contributions to sales in recent fiscal years were:

	1994-95	1993-94
Information Support Products	75%	72%
Diversified Instrumentation	25%	28%

In April 1994, DYTC announced a major restructuring that would focus its resources on core markets supporting voice, data and video communications. Operations were reorganized into two new segments, and 13 nonstrategic businesses were identified for divestiture. As of June 30, 1995, all but one business had been sold. The final sale is expected to be completed in August 1995.

The primary business segment is the Information Support Products group, which includes the communications test, data transmission, industrial connectivity and display product lines. Communications test products encompass various portable instruments and test systems which are sold to service providers, such as the regional Bell operating companies, long-distance carriers and cable television operators, and to service users such as large corporate and government network operators. These products are also sold to manufacturers of communications equipment and systems.

The data transmission product line, along with communications test equipment, is one of the company's two fastest growing areas. These products provide users of information networks with management tools to ensure reliable network operation and products to condition the data for transmission via public or private networks. The company's DynaStar product family addresses the growing demand to link local area networks (LANs) to wide area networks (WANs).

Industrial connectivity products include personal computers designed to operate in adverse environments. Display products consist primarily of professional video equipment and interactive graphics hardware and software.

The Diversified Instrumentation segment sells medical and diagnostic products which do not relate to information support. This segment's newest product, FOCUS, is a three dimensional radiation therapy treatment planning system.

Important Developments

Feb. '95—The company's FOCUS radiation therapy treatment planning system was approved for sale in the United States by the Food and Drug Administration.

Capitalization

Long Term Debt: $7,915,000 (3/95).

Per Share Data ($) (Year Ended Mar. 31)

	1995	1994	1993	1992	1991	1990
Tangible Bk. Val.	7.13	7.67	9.29	8.61	7.99	7.04
Cash Flow	1.92	-0.67	1.70	1.49	1.54	1.34
Earnings	1.13	-1.41	0.90	0.71	0.82	0.71
Dividends	Nil	Nil	Nil	Nil	Nil	Nil
Payout Ratio	Nil	Nil	Nil	Nil	Nil	Nil
Cal. Yrs.	1994	1993	1992	1991	1990	1989
Prices - High	16¾	16⅝	11¾	12⅝	10¼	10¼
- Low	7⅞	10¼	7¾	7	6⅛	8¼
P/E Ratio - High	15	NM	13	18	13	14
- Low	7	NM	9	10	7	11

Income Statement Analysis (Million $)

	1995	%Chg	1994	%Chg	1993	%Chg	1992
Revs.	489	7%	458	-13%	528	9%	486
Oper. Inc.	49.7	130%	21.6	-56%	48.9	10%	44.4
Depr.	14.1	2%	13.8	-7%	14.8	2%	14.5
Int. Exp.	3.9	3%	3.8	-47%	7.2	25%	5.8
Pretax Inc.	34.8	NM	-32.7	NM	29.3	25%	23.5
Eff. Tax Rate	42%	—	NM	—	44%	—	43%
Net Inc.	20.2	NM	-26.2	NM	16.4	22%	13.4

Balance Sheet & Other Fin. Data (Million $)

	1995	1994	1993	1992	1991	1990
Cash	27.8	23.1	23.7	35.0	32.8	26.6
Curr. Assets	185	195	199	200	194	187
Total Assets	256	281	305	316	296	274
Curr. Liab.	93.0	104	80.0	74.1	67.1	59.8
LT Debt	7.9	33.0	51.3	81.5	75.9	76.9
Common Eqty.	154	143	172	159	150	137
Total Cap.	163	176	225	242	229	215
Cap. Exp.	16.4	17.8	14.3	16.3	16.8	15.0
Cash Flow	34.3	-12.5	31.2	27.9	29.1	27.6

Ratio Analysis

	1995	1994	1993	1992	1991	1990
Curr. Ratio	2.0	1.9	2.5	2.7	2.9	3.1
% LT Debt of Cap.	4.8	18.7	22.8	33.6	33.2	35.8
% Net Inc.of Revs.	4.1	NM	3.1	2.8	3.2	3.4
% Ret. on Assets	7.7	NM	5.3	4.4	5.5	5.8
% Ret. on Equity	14.0	NM	9.9	8.8	11.0	11.1

Dividend Data (No cash has been paid. A 2-for-1 stock split was effected in March 1995.)

Amt. of Div. $	Date Decl.	Ex-Div. Date	Stock of Record	Payment Date
2-for-1	Jan. 27	Feb. 16	Feb. 15	Mar. 15 '95

Data as orig. reptd.; bef. results of disc. opers. and/or spec. items. Per share data adj. for stk. divs. as of ex-div. date. E-Estimated. NA-Not Available. NM-Not Meaningful. NR-Not Ranked.

Office—3 New England Executive Park, Burlington, MA 01803-5087. **Tel**—(617) 272-6100. **Chrmn**—R. K. Lochridge. **Pres & CEO**—J. F. Reno. **CFO & Treas**—Robert H. Hertz. **Secy**—E. T. O'Dell. **Investor Contact**—Steve Cantor. **Dirs**—R. M. Bittner, T. Cohn, W. R. Cook, O. G. Gabbard, J. B. Hangstefer, R. K. Lochridge, R. G. Paul, J. F. Reno, P. Stern. **Transfer Agent & Registrar**—First National Bank of Boston. **Incorporated** in Massachusetts in 1959. **Empl**-2,600. **S&P Analyst:** Kevin J. Gooley

STANDARD & POOR'S

Eagle Hardware & Garden

STOCK REPORTS

NASDAQ Symbol **EAGL**
In S&P SmallCap 600

11-SEP-95 **Industry:** Retail Stores

Summary: This home improvement retailer operates 24 warehouse centers, primarily in the Western U.S., serving a wide range of do-it-yourself customers and professional contractors.

Quantitative Evaluations

Outlook (1 Lowest—5 Highest)
• **5**
Fair Value
• **9⅜**
Risk
• **High**
Earn./Div. Rank
• **NR**

Technical Eval.
• **Bearish** since 8/95
Rel. Strength Rank (1 Lowest—99 Highest)
• **56**
Insider Activity
• **Neutral**

Recent Price • 7¾
52 Wk Range • 13¾-6
Yield • Nil
12-Mo. P/E • NM

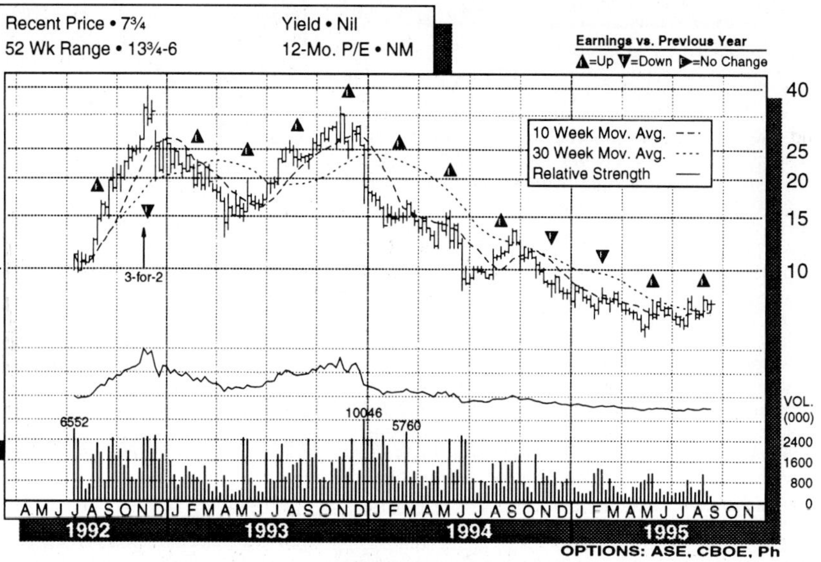

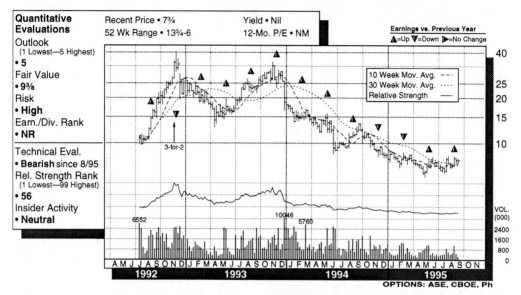

OPTIONS: ASE, CBOE, Ph

Business Profile - 07-SEP-95

This company operates 24 warehouse home improvement centers in Washington, Utah, Alaska, Hawaii, Montana, Oregon and Colorado, serving a wide range of do-it-yourself customers and professional contractors. Growth in the number of Eagle stores led to sharply higher sales in 1994-95, but narrower gross margins, greater interest expense and a loss on the sale of the company's Canadian subsidiary resulted in a net loss for the year.

Operational Review - 11-SEP-95

Net sales in the 26 weeks ended July 28, 1995, climbed 20%, year to year, primarily benefiting from more stores in operation. Same-store sales were lower, reflecting continued store cannibalization, slow economic growth in most of the company's markets, and increased competition. Results in the 1995 period include $0.03 per share from reimbursement by Eagle's insurance carrier of previously expensed legal fees following the settlement of shareholder litigation against the company.

Stock Performance - 08-SEP-95

In the past 30 trading days, EAGL's shares have declined 2%, compared to a 2% rise in the S&P 500. Average trading volume for the past five days was 58,400 shares, compared with the 40-day moving average of 115,015 shares.

Key Stock Statistics

Dividend Rate/Share	Nil	Shareholders	1,600
Shs. outstg. (M)	22.8	Market cap. (B)	$0.177
Avg. daily vol. (M)	0.115	Inst. holdings	7%
Tang. Bk. Value/Share	6.42	Insider holdings	NA
Beta	NA		

Value of $10,000 invested 5 years ago: NA

Fiscal Year Ending Jan. 31

	1996	% Change	1995	% Change	1994	% Change
Revenues (Million $)						
1Q	130.1	25%	104.0	94%	53.60	99%
2Q	167.8	16%	144.8	70%	85.30	183%
3Q	—	—	148.2	62%	91.60	129%
4Q	—	—	121.8	32%	92.40	84%
Yr.	—	—	518.8	61%	322.9	119%
Income (Million $)						
1Q	2.68	20%	2.24	35%	1.66	84%
2Q	4.55	34%	3.39	28%	2.65	182%
3Q	—	—	2.04	-44%	3.65	NM
4Q	—	—	-13.95	NM	2.79	43%
Yr.	—	—	-6.28	NM	10.76	159%
Earnings Per Share ($)						
1Q	0.12	20%	0.10	11%	0.09	29%
2Q	0.20	33%	0.15	25%	0.12	71%
3Q	—	—	0.09	-44%	0.16	NM
4Q	—	—	-0.61	NM	0.12	9%
Yr.	—	—	-0.28	NM	0.50	92%

Next earnings report expected: late November

Eagle Hardware & Garden

Business Summary - 11-SEP-95

Eagle Hardware & Garden, Inc. operates 24 warehouse home improvement centers in Washington, Utah, Alaska, Hawaii, Montana, Oregon and Colorado that serve a wide range of do-it-yourself customers and professional contractors. Operations in western Canada were sold in late 1994.

The company's home centers average 128,000 square feet and feature some 57,000 stock keeping units. A focal point of each center is an innovative, centrally located Design Center that features a kitchen and bath display area of about 8,000 sq. ft. with 27 different styles of kitchen cabinets, brand name appliances and a large selection of bathroom fixtures. The Design Center also features a wide variety of countertops, wallpaper, floor coverings and window treatments, as well as a design coordinator who works with customers to plan home decorating projects.

Eagle's merchandise selection is broad enough to allow a customer to purchase virtually every item needed to build an entire house. Net sales by product category in 1994-95 were: plumbing, electrical and lighting 27%; lumber and building materials 24%; paint and decor 19%; tools and hardware 16%; and lawn and garden supplies 14%.

The company's centers also offer such specialized services as a cut shop, where customers can have window screen, fencing, glass, netting, chain, hose, rope and other materials custom cut; a licensed locksmith for assistance with locks, keys and home and commercial security systems; an idea center that features over 290 titles of do-it-yourself books, plans and video tapes; free or low-cost delivery service; personnel to assist in designing and planning projects and selecting appropriate materials; and a separate lumber and building materials cashier and loading area. In addition, most centers also offer professional product installation services.

Eagle's expansion strategy is to increase market share in existing markets and to open home centers in selected new markets. Two new stores were opened in the fourth quarter of 1994-95. The company expects to open five additional stores in 1995-96.

In December 1994, EAGL sold most of the assets of its Canadian subsidiary to West Fraser Timber Co. Ltd. for about $20 million. Results for the fourth quarter of 1994-95 reflected a $12,715,000 loss on the sale, as well as a $1,616,000 writeoff of a previously recognized Canadian deferred tax benefit.

Important Developments

Aug. '95—Eagle opened its first two stores in the Denver, Colo., market. In May, the company opened three new stores -- in Lynnwood and Issaquah, Wash., and Orem, Utah.

Capitalization

Long Term Debt: $98,386,0000 (7/95).

Per Share Data ($) (Year Ended Jan. 31)

	1995	1994	1993	1992	1991	1990
Tangible Bk. Val.	6.30	6.56	4.07	0.65	NA	NA
Cash Flow	0.02	0.65	0.36	0.12	NA	NA
Earnings	-0.28	0.50	0.26	0.09	NA	NA
Dividends	Nil	Nil	Nil	Nil	NA	NA
Payout Ratio	Nil	Nil	Nil	Nil	NA	NA
Cal. Yrs.	1994	1993	1992	1991	1990	1989
Prices - High	18¼	34¾	40½	NA	NA	NA
- Low	7⅝	12¾	9⅜	NA	NA	NA
P/E Ratio - High	NM	70	NM	NA	NA	NA
- Low	NM	26	NM	NA	NA	NA

Income Statement Analysis (Million $)

	1995	%Chg	1994	%Chg	1993	%Chg	1992
Revs.	519	61%	323	120%	147	188%	51.0
Oper. Inc.	24.4	26%	19.4	149%	7.8	NM	1.2
Depr.	6.8	102%	3.3	122%	1.5	NM	0.4
Int. Exp.	6.5	NM	0.4	20%	0.3	NM	0.0
Pretax Inc.	0.5	-97%	16.8	162%	6.4	NM	1.1
Eff. Tax Rate	NM	—	36%	—	35%	—	Nil
Net Inc.	-6.3	NM	10.8	157%	4.2	NM	1.1

Balance Sheet & Other Fin. Data (Million $)

	1995	1994	1993	1992	1991	1990
Cash	5.4	2.5	1.3	0.2	NA	NA
Curr. Assets	148	111	52.0	26.0	NA	NA
Total Assets	322	212	103	37.0	NA	NA
Curr. Liab.	68.9	54.7	29.8	14.1	NA	NA
LT Debt	104	4.9	Nil	Nil	NA	NA
Common Eqty.	144	149	72.0	4.0	NA	NA
Total Cap.	252	156	72.0	23.0	NA	NA
Cap. Exp.	101	58.0	36.3	10.4	NA	NA
Cash Flow	0.5	14.1	5.7	1.5	NA	NA

Ratio Analysis

	1995	1994	1993	1992	1991	1990
Curr. Ratio	2.1	2.0	1.7	1.8	NA	NA
% LT Debt of Cap.	41.3	3.1	Nil	Nil	NA	NA
% Net Inc.of Revs.	NM	3.3	2.8	2.2	NA	NA
% Ret. on Assets	NM	6.2	3.8	NA	NA	NA
% Ret. on Equity	NM	8.9	10.0	NA	NA	NA

Dividend Data —No cash dividends have been paid. The company intends to retain earnings for use in the expansion of its business and does not expect to pay cash dividends in the foreseeable future.

Data as orig. reptd.; bef. results of disc. opers. and/or spec. items. Per share data adj. for stk. divs. as of ex-div. date. E-Estimated. NA-Not Available. NM-Not Meaningful. NR-Not Ranked.

Office—981 Powell Ave. S.W., Renton, WA 98055. **Tel**—(206) 227-5740. **Fax**—(206) 204-5169. **Chrmn & CEO**—D. J. Heerensperger. **Pres & COO**—R. T. Takata. **EVP-Fin & CFO**—R. P. Maccarone. **Asst Treas & Investor Contact**—Steve Stenberg. **Dirs**—R. D. Crockett, H. D. Douglas, D. J. Heerensperger, H. Sarkowsky, R. T. Takata, T. M. Wight. **Transfer Agent & Registrar**—First Interstate Bank of Washington, Encino, Calif. **Incorporated** in Washington in 1989. **Empl**-2,600. **S&P Analyst:** Maureen C. Carini

STANDARD & POOR'S

STOCK REPORTS

Energen Corp.

NYSE Symbol **EGN**
In S&P SmallCap 600

12-OCT-95 **Industry:** Utilities-Gas

Summary: Through its Alabama Gas unit, this company is the largest natural gas distributor in Alabama, serving about 445,000 customers.

Quantitative Evaluations

Outlook
(1 Lowest—5 Highest)
• **3-**

Fair Value
• **21⅛**

Risk
• **Low**

Earn./Div. Rank
• **A**

Technical Eval.
• **Bearish** since 3/95

Rel. Strength Rank
(1 Lowest—99 Highest)
• **67**

Insider Activity
• **Neutral**

Recent Price • 21⅝
52 Wk Range • 23½-19¾
Yield • 5.2%
12-Mo. P/E • 11.3

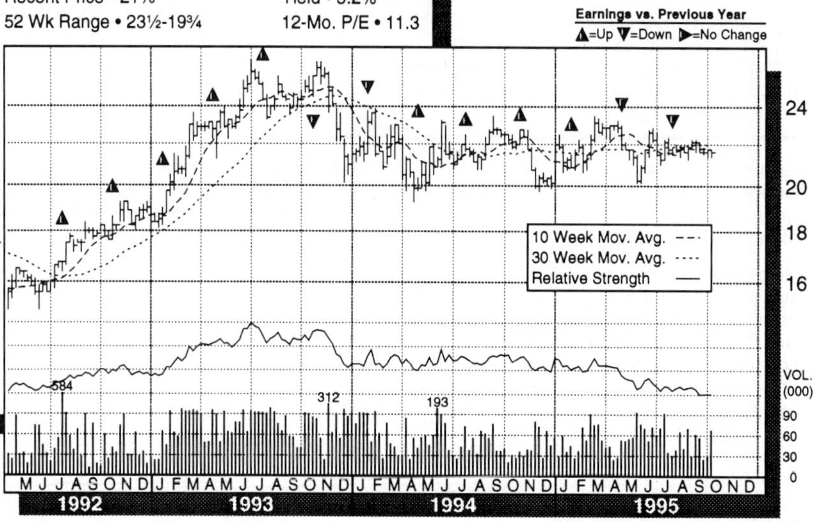

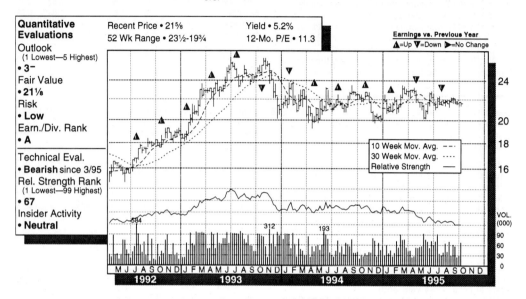

Business Profile - 19-JUL-95

In response to the adoption of FERC Order 636, Alagasco, EGN's natural gas utility, recently invested in underground storage working gas and increased its equity base. In fiscal 1995, Alagasco is facing the potential renegotiation of its rate-setting mechanism. The Taurus Exploration unit is continuing to focus on its strategy of balancing producing property acquisitions with targeted offshore exploration and development, while enhancing its coal-bed methane operations.

Operational Review - 12-OCT-95

Earnings fell in the first nine months of fiscal 1995, reflecting lower natural gas production volumes and coalbed methane operating fees at Taurus due to lower natural gas prices, which were partially offset by a $500,000 gain from a gas sales contract buyout. Results benefited from Alagasco earning its allowed rate of return on a higher level of equity. 1994's third quarter results include an $0.18 a share gain from the sale of propane assets and a reduced investment of combustion technology.

Stock Performance - 06-OCT-95

In the past 30 trading days, EGN's shares have declined 1%, compared to a 4% rise in the S&P 500. Average trading volume for the past five days was 13,320 shares, compared with the 40-day moving average of 9,600 shares.

Key Stock Statistics

Dividend Rate/Share	1.16	Shareholders	6,000
Shs. outstg. (M)	10.9	Market cap. (B)	$0.243
Avg. daily vol. (M)	0.009	Inst. holdings	38%
Tang. Bk. Value/Share	16.79	Insider holdings	NA
Beta	0.54		

Value of $10,000 invested 5 years ago: $ 14,372

Fiscal Year Ending Sep. 30

	1995	% Change	1994	% Change	1993	% Change
Revenues (Million $)						
1Q	73.48	-16%	87.92	5%	84.10	6%
2Q	140.8	-16%	168.1	12%	149.6	7%
3Q	61.53	-16%	73.13	-3%	75.32	11%
4Q	—	—	47.94	NM	48.04	8%
Yr.	—	—	377.1	6%	357.1	8%
Income (Million $)						
1Q	2.74	19%	2.30	-14%	2.67	NM
2Q	21.71	-2%	22.19	11%	19.95	8%
3Q	1.13	-71%	3.95	NM	1.08	145%
4Q	—	—	-4.69	NM	-5.62	NM
Yr.	—	—	23.75	31%	18.08	15%
Earnings Per Share ($)						
1Q	0.25	14%	0.22	-15%	0.26	NM
2Q	1.99	-2%	2.03	4%	1.95	8%
3Q	0.10	-72%	0.36	NM	0.11	175%
4Q	—	—	-0.43	NM	-0.55	NM
Yr.	—	—	2.19	24%	1.77	15%

Next earnings report expected: late October

Energen Corp.

Business Summary - 12-OCT-95

Energen Corp. (formerly Alagasco, Inc.) is a diversified energy holding company whose Alabama Gas Co. (Alagasco) subsidiary distributes natural gas in central and northern Alabama. Nonutility operations include coalbed methane projects, oil and gas exploration and production and other complementary diversified businesses. Segment contributions in fiscal 1994 were:

	Revs.	Profits
Gas distribution	91%	81%
Oil & gas production	6%	15%
Other	3%	4%

Gas sold and transported amounted to 97,531,000 Mcf in fiscal 1994, up from 94,438,000 Mcf in fiscal 1993. The average number of customers served in fiscal 1994 was 435,137 (427,372).

The Alagasco distribution system is connected to two major interstate pipeline systems, Southern Natural Gas Co. and Transcontinental Gas Pipe Line Corp. The company also has firm supply contracts with intrastate suppliers. Alagasco uses spot-market gas to supplement its system supply and serve its transportation customers when it is economical to do so.

As part of Alagasco's plans for customer growth and service area expansion, Alagasco has acquired 19 municipal systems since October 1985, adding about 42,000 customers to the distribution system.

Taurus Exploration, Inc. is involved in the exploration and production of natural gas and oil in the Gulf of Mexico and through coalbed methane projects in Alabama's Black Warrior Coal Basin. Proved oil and gas reserves at fiscal 1994 year-end totaled 69.0 Bcf (oil expressed in natural gas equivalents), of which 39% was coalbed methane. Total oil and gas production rose to 10.3 Bcf in 1994, from 7.5 Bcf in 1993.

EGN operates an intrastate gas pipeline and gathering system and has an 8% interest in an industrial combustion systems company. In June 1994, EGN sold its assets in its propane distribution business.

Excluding municipal gas system acquisitions, capital and exploration spending for fiscal 1995 is estimated at $66 million.

Important Developments

Oct. '95—Taurus Exploration invested $11.5 million with United Meridian Corp. for the purchase of working interests in 30 Permian Basin fields and four Gulf Coast region fields from Pennzoil Exploration and Production Co.

Aug. '95—Energen offered an early retirement option to 7.0% of its 820 salaried, non-officer Alagasco employees. Retirement, for those electing to take the option, becomes effective October 1, 1995, and the cost of the program will be reflected as a one-time charge in fiscal 1995.

Capitalization

Long Term Debt: $115,000,000 (3/95).

Per Share Data ($) (Year Ended Sep. 30)

	1994	1993	1992	1991	1990	1989
Tangible Bk. Val.	15.30	13.60	12.75	12.07	12.21	11.68
Earnings	2.19	1.77	1.54	1.42	1.35	1.19
Dividends	1.09	1.05	1.01	0.96	0.90	0.86
Payout Ratio	50%	59%	66%	67%	66%	72%
Prices - High	23⅞	26¾	19¼	18⅞	20½	24⅜
- Low	19¼	18⅛	15	16	16	15⅜
P/E Ratio - High	11	15	13	13	15	20
- Low	9	10	10	11	12	13

Income Statement Analysis (Million $)

	1994	%Chg	1993	%Chg	1992	%Chg	1991
Revs.	377	6%	357	8%	332	2%	326
Depr.	28.0	11%	25.3	-4%	26.3	9%	24.1
Maint.	9.5	2%	9.2	2%	9.1	11%	8.2
Fxd. Chgs. Cov.	3.5	16%	3.0	19%	2.5	3%	2.5
Constr. Credits	NA	—	NA	—	NA	—	NA
Eff. Tax Rate	22%	—	16%	—	2.40%	—	2.50%
Net Inc.	23.8	31%	18.1	15%	15.7	11%	14.1

Balance Sheet & Other Fin. Data (Million $)

	1994	1993	1992	1991	1990	1989
Gross Prop.	465	429	411	393	377	357
Cap. Exp.	45.5	43.7	22.5	46.9	41.9	59.5
Net Prop.	233	213	208	206	205	203
Capitalization:						
LT Debt	118	85.9	90.6	77.7	82.8	86.2
% LT Debt	41	38	41	39	40	43
Pfd.	Nil	Nil	1.8	1.8	1.8	2.5
% Pfd.	Nil	Nil	0.80	0.90	0.90	1.20
Common	167	140	130	122	121	113
% Common	59	62	58	61	59	56
Total Cap.	292	232	230	225	236	236

Ratio Analysis

	1994	1993	1992	1991	1990	1989
Oper. Ratio	92.2	92.5	93.2	92.9	93.0	94.1
% Earn. on Net Prop.	13.1	12.7	10.8	11.2	11.9	9.6
% Ret. on Revs.	6.3	5.1	4.7	4.3	4.1	3.6
% Ret. On Invest.Cap	13.4	12.5	11.5	10.7	10.3	8.9
% Return On Com.Eqty	15.5	13.4	12.5	12.0	11.3	11.0

Dividend Data —Dividends have been paid since 1943. A dividend reinvestment plan is available.

Amt. of Div. $	Date Decl.	Ex-Div. Date	Stock of Record	Payment Date
0.280	Oct. 26	Nov. 08	Nov. 15	Dec. 01 '94
0.280	Jan. 27	Feb. 09	Feb. 15	Mar. 01 '95
0.280	Apr. 26	May. 09	May. 15	Jun. 01 '95
0.290	Jul. 27	Aug. 11	Aug. 15	Sep. 01 '95

Data as orig. reptd.; bef. results of disc opers. and/or spec. items. Per share data adj. for stk. divs. as of ex-div. date. E-Estimated. NA-Not Available. NM-Not Meaningful. NR-Not Ranked.

Office—2101 Sixth Ave. North, Birmingham, AL 35203. **Tel**—(205) 326-2700. **Chrmn & CEO**—R. J. Lysinger. **Pres**—W. M. Warren, Jr. **EVP-Fin, Treas & CFO**—G. C. Ketcham. **Secy**—D. C. Reynolds. **Investor Contact**—Julie S. Ryland (205-326-8421). **Dirs**—S. D. Ban, J. M. Davis, Jr., J. S. M. French, R. J. Lysinger, J. M. Merritt, D. Nabers Jr., H. Saunders, Jr., G. S. Shirley, W. R. Taylor, W. M. Warren, Jr. **Transfer Agent & Registrar**—Harris Trust Co. of New York, NYC. **Incorporated** in Alabama in 1929. **Empl**-1,488. **S&P Analyst:** Ronald J. Gross

STANDARD & POOR'S

STOCK REPORTS

Enhance Financial Services

NYSE Symbol **EFS**

In S&P SmallCap 600

07-OCT-95

Industry: Insurance

Summary: This company engages primarily in the reinsurance of financial guaranties of municipal and asset-backed debt obligations issued by monoline financial guaranty insurers.

Quantitative Evaluations

Outlook (1 Lowest—5 Highest)
• **NA**

Fair Value
• **NA**

Risk
• **Low**

Earn./Div. Rank
• **NR**

Technical Eval.
• **Bearish** since 6/95

Rel. Strength Rank (1 Lowest—99 Highest)
• **69**

Insider Activity
• **NA**

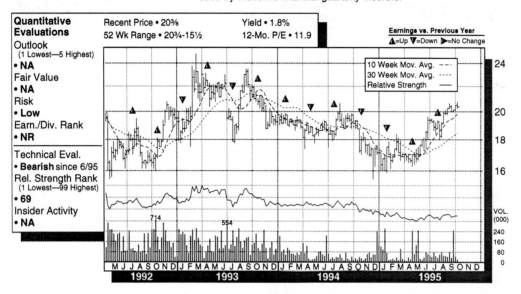

Recent Price • 20⅜
52 Wk Range • 20¾-15½
Yield • 1.8%
12-Mo. P/E • 11.9

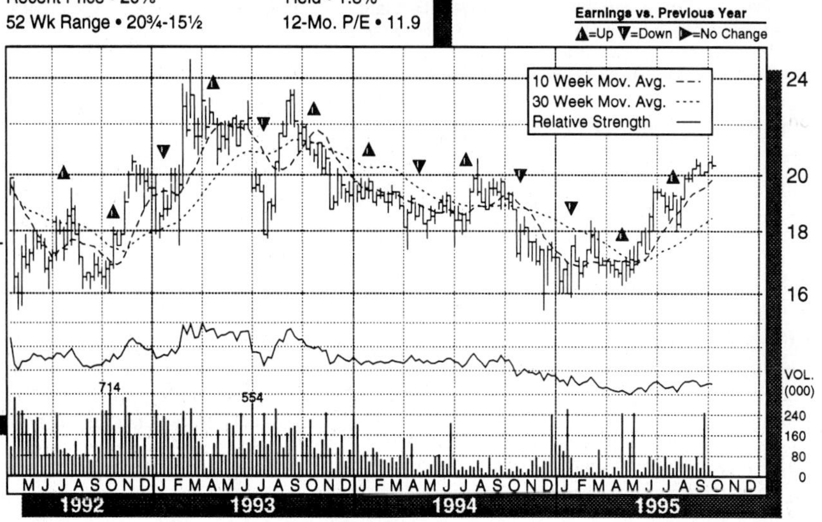

Business Profile - 04-OCT-95

Results of this financial guaranty reinsurance provider are heavily influenced by interest rates and their effect on new-issue municipal bond and refunding volume. Although gross premiums written declined 20% in the first half of 1995, the current low interest rate environment could provide a boost to municipal bond underwriting. To reduce the earnings volatility inherent in its business, EFS has begun to diversify into specialty insurance, such as direct insurance for multifamily housing bonds.

Operational Review - 02-OCT-95

Total revenues for the six months ended June 30, 1995, rose 10%, year to year, as an increase in net premiums earned and higher net investment income outweighed lower realized gains on the sale of investments. Total expenses advanced 3.9%, and operating income was up 15%. With a 5.9% decline in interest expense, pretax income rose 20%. After taxes at 23.8%, versus 21.7%, net income was up 17%, to $21,574,000 ($1.24 a share, based on 3.4% fewer shares), from $18,445,000 ($1.02).

Stock Performance - 06-OCT-95

In the past 30 trading days, EFS's shares have increased 3%, compared to a 4% rise in the S&P 500. Average trading volume for the past five days was 3,700 shares, compared with the 40-day moving average of 15,654 shares.

Key Stock Statistics

Dividend Rate/Share	0.36	Shareholders	100
Shs. outstg. (M)	17.3	Market cap. (B)	$0.352
Avg. daily vol. (M)	0.020	Inst. holdings	42%
Tang. Bk. Value/Share	22.81	Insider holdings	NA
Beta	0.18		

Value of $10,000 invested 5 years ago: NA

Fiscal Year Ending Dec. 31

	1995	% Change	1994	% Change	1993	% Change
Revenues (Million $)						
1Q	25.54	5%	24.21	-9%	26.60	38%
2Q	26.30	15%	22.81	-18%	27.95	35%
3Q	—	—	26.04	-17%	31.51	29%
4Q	—	—	23.38	-4%	24.28	17%
Yr.	—	—	96.44	-13%	110.3	29%
Income (Million $)						
1Q	10.45	NM	10.44	-16%	12.46	53%
2Q	11.12	39%	8.00	118%	3.67	-63%
3Q	—	—	8.59	-29%	12.13	3%
4Q	—	—	-0.46	NM	9.72	24%
Yr.	—	—	26.56	-30%	37.97	NM
Earnings Per Share ($)						
1Q	0.60	3%	0.58	-16%	0.69	53%
2Q	0.64	42%	0.45	125%	0.20	-63%
3Q	—	—	0.48	-28%	0.67	3%
4Q	—	—	-0.03	NM	0.54	26%
Yr.	—	—	1.49	-29%	2.09	NM

Next earnings report expected: early November

Enhance Financial Services

Business Summary - 01-AUG-95

Enhance Financial Services Group Inc. engages primarily in the reinsurance of financial guaranties of municipal and asset-backed debt obligations issued by monoline financial guaranty insurers. The company conducts substantially all of its business through wholly owned Enhance Reinsurance Co. and Asset Guaranty Reinsurance Co. Monoline financial guaranty insurers guaranty to holders of debt obligations the full and timely payment of principal and interest. In conducting its reinsurance business, EFS assumes a portion of the risk insured by primary insurers and receives a portion of the premiums collected by them. At December 31, 1994, the composition of its insurance portfolio by bond type (% of total insurance in force) was:

Municipal:	
General obligation/tax supported	31.2%
Utilities	20.3%
Healthcare	12.0%
Airport/transportation	9.9%
Housing revenue	2.9%
Other	4.8%
Total municipal	81.1%
Asset-backed:	
Consumer obligations	8.2%
Investor-owned utilities	7.1%
Commercial mortgage	0.8%
Other	2.8%
Total asset-backed	18.9%

Total insurance in force at December 31, 1994, was $48.4 billion, of which 12.8% had been issued in California, 9.9% in New York, 8.3% in Florida, 6.2% in Texas, 6.2% in Pennsylvania and 5.0% in Illinois.

Enhance Reinsurance Co. received AAA claims-paying ability ratings from Standard & Poor's, Moody's and Duff & Phelps, and Asset Guaranty Insurance Co. was rated AAA by Duff & Phelps and AA by Standard & Poor's.

In addition to the reinsurance of monoline financial guaranty insurers, EFS uses its expertise in underwriting financial and credit risks to engage in certain specialty activities. In the past few years, it has expanded its business to include issuing limited amounts of primary insurance of smaller municipals and real estate-backed debt obligations and reinsuring other specialty lines.

Important Developments

May '95—EFS reported that it purchased 204,300 shares of its common stock at an average price of $16.19 per share in 1995's first quarter. As of May 12, 1995, EFS had purchased a total of 974,500 shares under the previously announced buyback program.

Capitalization

Long Term Debt: $79,800,000 (3/95).

Per Share Data ($) (Year Ended Dec. 31)

	1994	1993	1992	1991	1990	1989
Tangible Bk. Val.	20.45	20.14	18.29	16.46	14.46	12.65
Oper. Earnings	NA	NA	NA	NA	NA	NA
Earnings	1.49	2.09	2.07	1.85	1.60	1.55
Dividends	0.32	0.28	0.24	NA	NA	NA
Payout Ratio	21%	13%	12%	NA	NA	NA
Prices - High	20⅝	24⅞	21¼	NA	NA	NA
- Low	15½	17½	15½	NA	NA	NA
P/E Ratio - High	14	12	10	NA	NA	NA
- Low	10	8	7	NA	NA	NA

Income Statement Analysis (Million $)

	1994	%Chg	1993	%Chg	1992	%Chg	1991
Premium Income	61.8	4%	59.6	31%	45.6	27%	35.9
Net Invest. Inc.	39.0	19%	32.8	8%	30.3	11%	27.2
Oth. Revs.	-4.3	NM	17.9	91%	9.3	39%	6.7
Total Revs.	96.4	-13%	110	29%	85.2	22%	69.8
Pretax Inc.	32.7	-35%	50.3	2%	49.4	21%	40.9
Net Oper. Inc.	NA	—	NA	—	NA	—	NA
Net Inc.	26.6	-30%	38.0	1%	37.6	16%	32.4

Balance Sheet & Other Fin. Data (Million $)

	1994	1993	1992	1991	1990	1989
Cash & Equiv.	39.1	20.4	21.5	13.3	10.5	9.0
Premiums Due	9.8	10.5	8.0	9.7	8.4	3.6
Inv Assets Bonds	620	622	487	428	352	258
Inv. Assets Stock	0.7	0.5	0.5	0.4	1.6	2.1
Inv. Assets Loans	Nil	Nil	Nil	Nil	Nil	Nil
Inv. Assets Total	651	624	488	429	360	279
Deferred Policy Cost	74.0	66.2	54.6	48.4	41.4	34.5
Total Assets	765	735	584	509	430	330
Debt	79.8	81.2	7.6	9.0	Nil	Nil
Common Eqty.	360	364	332	288	253	189

Ratio Analysis

	1994	1993	1992	1991	1990	1989
Prop&Cas Loss	37.0	37.0	20.4	14.2	9.1	0.1
Prop&Cas Expense	56.7	54.9	57.6	65.8	55.6	57.2
Prop&Cas Comb.	93.7	91.9	78.0	80.0	64.7	57.3
% Ret. on Revs.	27.5	34.4	44.2	46.4	52.5	60.9
% Return on Equity	7.3	10.9	12.1	12.0	11.3	13.0

Dividend Data —Dividends were initiated in 1992.

Amt. of Div. $	Date Decl.	Ex-Div. Date	Stock of Record	Payment Date
0.080	Dec. 12	Dec. 13	Dec. 19	Dec. 23 '94
0.090	Mar. 16	Mar. 21	Mar. 27	Mar. 31 '95
0.090	Jun. 01	Jun. 08	Jun. 12	Jun. 16 '95
0.090	Sep. 07	Sep. 14	Sep. 18	Sep. 22 '95

Data as orig. reptd.; bef. results of disc. opers. and/or spec. items. Per share data adj. for stk. divs. as of ex-div. date. E-Estimated. NA-Not Available. NM-Not Meaningful. NR-Not Ranked.

Office—335 Madison Ave., New York, NY 10017. **Tel**—(212) 983-3100. **Chrmn**—A. R. Tessler. **Vice Chrmn**—W. O. Sellers. **Pres & CEO**—D. J. Gross. **Exec VP & CFO**—R. M. Rosenberg. **Exec VP & Secy**—S. Bergman. **Sr VP & Investor Contact**—Sheila Brody. **Dirs**—J. T. Anderson, A. Dubroff, D. J. Gross, B. W. Harries, D. R. Markin, C. J. Marsico, B. D. Monus, W. O. Sellers, R. J. Shima, Z. Stait-Gardner, S. R. Stuart, A. R. Tessler, F. K. Wallison. **Transfer Agent & Registrar**—Chemical Bank, NYC. **Incorporated** in New York in 1985. **Empl-** 79. **S&P Analyst:** Brad Ohlmuller

STANDARD & POOR'S

STOCK REPORTS

Enzo Biochem

ASE Symbol **ENZ**
In S&P SmallCap 600

27-SEP-95

Industry:
Drugs-Generic and OTC

Summary: This biotechnology company is engaged in research, manufacturing and marketing of diagnostic and research products based on molecular biology and genetic engineering.

Quantitative Evaluations

Outlook
(1 Lowest—5 Highest)
• **NA**

Fair Value
• **NA**

Risk
• **Average**

Earn./Div. Rank
• **C**

Technical Eval.
• **Bullish** since 6/95

Rel. Strength Rank
(1 Lowest—99 Highest)
• **95**

Insider Activity
• **NA**

Recent Price • 21¼
52 Wk Range • 23-9

Yield • Nil
12-Mo. P/E • 18.6

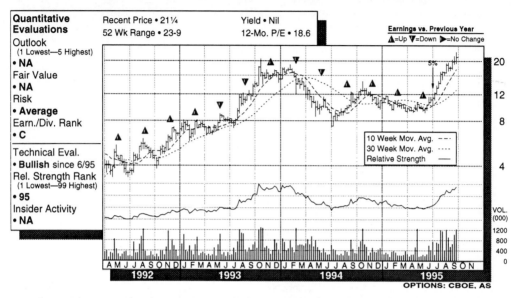

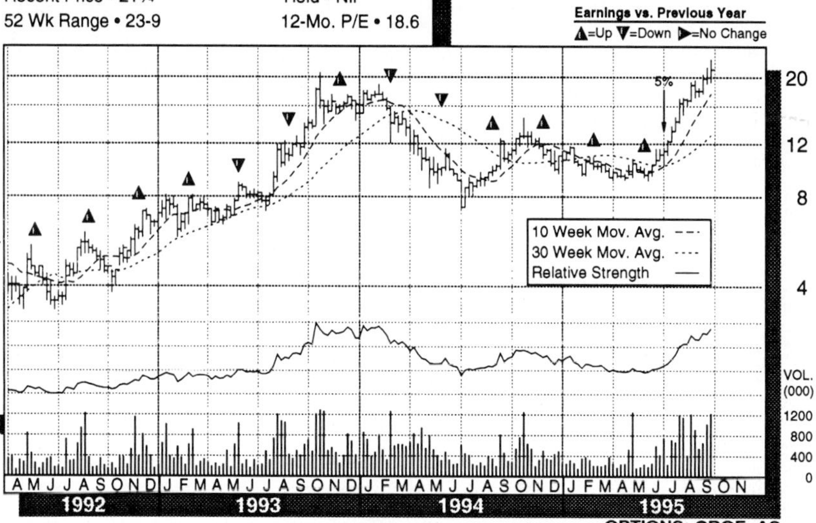

OPTIONS: CBOE, AS

Business Profile - 26-SEP-95

Enzo returned to profitability in fiscal 1994, with the aid of a legal settlement received from Johnson & Johnson (J&J) in the last quarter. Although the company is operating on a break-even level, profitability has increased in fiscal 1995 due to legal payments in connection with the J&J settlement. Enzo is currently engaged in identifying strategic partners to aid in bringing new products to market.

Operational Review - 15-SEP-95

Revenues in the nine months ended April 30, 1995, soared 60%, year to year, reflecting a greater volume of tests performed and increased product sales. Margins narrowed slightly, but following a $21 million litigation settlement, pretax income advanced to $22.6 million from a loss of $79,000. After taxes, net income totaled $19.5 million ($0.93 a share), compared with a loss of $119,000 ($0.01). Results in the fiscal 1994 period exclude an extraordinary gain of $150,000 ($0.01).

Stock Performance - 22-SEP-95

In the past 30 trading days, ENZ's shares have increased 27%, compared to a 5% rise in the S&P 500. Average trading volume for the past five days was 274,580 shares, compared with the 40-day moving average of 186,708 shares.

Key Stock Statistics

Dividend Rate/Share	Nil	Shareholders	1,800
Shs. outstg. (M)	20.8	Market cap. (B)	$0.432
Avg. daily vol. (M)	0.182	Inst. holdings	7%
Tang. Bk. Value/Share	1.72	Insider holdings	NA
Beta	NM		

Value of $10,000 invested 5 years ago: $ 61,551

Fiscal Year Ending Jul. 31

	1995	% Change	1994	% Change	1993	% Change
Revenues (Million $)						
1Q	8.03	55%	5.18	-6%	5.50	4%
2Q	7.04	57%	4.48	-10%	4.96	-2%
3Q	8.22	68%	4.88	2%	4.80	-12%
4Q	—	—	8.27	73%	4.77	-8%
Yr.	—	—	22.80	14%	20.03	-4%
Income (Million $)						
1Q	18.74	NM	0.52	30%	0.40	NM
2Q	0.55	NM	-0.51	NM	0.07	NM
3Q	0.24	NM	-0.14	NM	-0.07	NM
4Q	—	—	5.22	NM	-6.78	NM
Yr.	—	—	5.10	NM	-6.38	NM
Earnings Per Share ($)						
1Q	0.86	NM	0.03	51%	0.02	NM
2Q	0.03	NM	-0.03	NM	0.01	NM
3Q	0.01	NM	-0.01	—	Nil	—
4Q	—	—	0.25	NM	-0.37	NM
Yr.	—	—	0.24	NM	-0.34	NM

Next earnings report expected: late September

Enzo Biochem

Business Summary - 27-SEP-95

Enzo Biochem Inc. is a biotechnology company that researches, develops, manufactures and markets innovative health care products. It has proprietary technologies and expertise in manipulating and modifying genetic material and other biological molecules. It also provides diagnostic services to the medical community.

In fiscal 1994, 23% of revenues came from product sales (11% in fiscal 1993), and 77% from clinical reference laboratory services (89%).

Enzo Diagnostics Inc. develops and markets biomedical products used largely to detect viral infections using DNA probes that have been non-radioactively labeled with the company's proprietary BioProbe technology. Its product development programs are focused on the Bioprobe nucleic acid probes that can detect sexually transmitted and other infectious diseases such as AIDS, herpes, chlamydia, tuberculosis, hepatitis and cytomegalovirus.

Enzo markets two BioProbe products: PathoGene DNA probe kits to detect a variety of specific viruses, and BioPape DNA probe kits to detect certain types of human papillomavirus (HPV) in pap smear samples. ENZ also markets two Microplate Hybridization Assays (MHAs) to detect HIV-1 virus causing AIDS and a bacteria that causes tuberculosis. In fiscal 1993, it added three more MHAs, including tests to detect HIV-2 and hepatitis B and C viruses.

EnzoLabs operates a clinical reference laboratory offering diagnostic services to the greater New York medical community. The services include a variety of tests to detect precancerous conditions, cervical cancers and sexually transmitted diseases.

Enzo Therapeutics is applying its technological capabilities for manipulating genetic material to the development of therapeutic treatments for a variety of cancers and infections.

ENZ has a non-exclusive supply agreement with Boehringer Mannheim Biochemicals to distribute to the global medical research market biochemical products manufactured and supplied by Enzo.

In October 1994, Johnson & Johnson and two of its subsidiaries settled litigation with Enzo and paid the company $35 million in connection with an agreement to develop and market products using DNA probes and other technologies.

Important Developments

Jun. '95—Unilever PLC withdrew its opposition to ENZ's genetic antisense technology patent. The European Patent Office issued a preliminary opinion in February upholding Enzo's patent against Unilever and another challenger, Calgene.

Capitalization

Long Term Debt: $4,450,000 (4/95) incl. $4,336,000 of capital lease obligs.
Options & warrants: to buy 1,536,509 shs. at $1.50 to $16.00 ea.

Per Share Data ($) (Year Ended Jul. 31)

	1994	1993	1992	1991	1990	1989
Tangible Bk. Val.	1.96	1.10	1.16	-0.90	0.04	0.21
Cash Flow	0.29	-0.29	-0.01	-0.83	-0.28	-0.30
Earnings	0.24	-0.34	-0.09	-0.90	-0.34	-0.35
Dividends	Nil	Nil	Nil	Nil	Nil	Nil
Payout Ratio	Nil	Nil	Nil	Nil	Nil	Nil
Prices - High	18⅞	20¾	7¼	8⅛	4⅜	4¾
- Low	7¼	5⅞	3⅛	9/16	1 11/16	2½
P/E Ratio - High	79	NM	NM	NM	NM	NM
- Low	30	NM	NA	NA	NA	NA

Income Statement Analysis (Million $)

	1994	%Chg	1993	%Chg	1992	%Chg	1991
Revs.	22.8	14%	20.0	-2%	20.5	4%	19.8
Oper. Inc.	-2.7	NM	-1.7	NM	1.8	NM	-1.6
Depr.	1.1	-4%	1.2	10%	1.0	13%	0.9
Int. Exp.	0.1	-58%	0.3	-89%	2.3	-56%	5.2
Pretax Inc.	2.2	NM	-6.3	NM	-1.1	NM	-10.8
Eff. Tax Rate	NM	—	NM	—	NM	—	NM
Net Inc.	5.1	NM	-6.4	NM	-1.2	NM	-10.8

Balance Sheet & Other Fin. Data (Million $)

	1994	1993	1992	1991	1990	1989
Cash	4.2	0.7	0.8	0.6	7.9	30.4
Curr. Assets	25.7	7.9	9.4	9.7	16.2	36.7
Total Assets	65.0	47.6	49.8	49.3	66.5	74.6
Curr. Liab.	8.6	10.3	12.1	43.4	5.6	5.5
LT Debt	4.4	4.2	4.2	4.5	48.1	53.9
Common Eqty.	51.2	32.4	33.0	1.1	12.7	15.1
Total Cap.	55.8	36.8	37.4	5.8	60.9	69.1
Cap. Exp.	1.8	3.5	2.4	9.0	8.2	4.2
Cash Flow	6.2	-5.2	-0.2	-9.9	-3.3	-3.7

Ratio Analysis

	1994	1993	1992	1991	1990	1989
Curr. Ratio	3.0	0.8	0.8	0.2	2.9	6.7
% LT Debt of Cap.	7.8	11.3	11.2	78.6	78.9	78.0
% Net Inc.of Revs.	22.4	NM	NM	NM	NM	NM
% Ret. on Assets	8.7	NM	NM	NM	NM	NM
% Ret. on Equity	11.8	NM	NM	NM	NM	NM

Dividend Data —No cash has been paid.

Amt. of Div. $	Date Decl.	Ex-Div. Date	Stock of Record	Payment Date
5%	Jun. 14	Jun. 29	Jul. 03	Jul. 31 '95

Data as orig. reptd.; bef. results of disc. opers. and/or spec. items. Per share data adj. for stk. divs. as of ex-div. date. E-Estimated. NA-Not Available. NM-Not Meaningful. NR-Not Ranked.

Office—60 Executive Blvd., Farmingdale, NY 11735. **Tel**—(516) 755-5500. **Chrmn, Pres & CEO**—E. Rabbani. **EVP & Secy**—B. W. Weiner. **EVP & Treas**—S. K. Rabbani. **Dirs**—J. J. Delucca, E. Rabbani, S. K. Rabbani, J. B. Sias, B. W. Weiner. **Transfer Agent**—Continental Stock Transfer & Trust Co., NYC. **Incorporated** in New York in 1976. **Empl**-190. **S&P Analyst:** Thomas Tirney

STANDARD & POOR'S

STOCK REPORTS

Ethan Allen Interiors

NYSE Symbol **ETH**
In S&P SmallCap 600

10-OCT-95 **Industry:** Home Furnishings

Summary: Ethan Allen Interiors manufactures home furnishings which are retailed through Ethan Allen Galleries (most of which are owned by independent dealers).

Quantitative Evaluations

Recent Price • 20½ Yield • Nil
52 Wk Range • 25⅜-17¼ 12-Mo. P/E • 13.1

Outlook
(1 Lowest—5 Highest)
• **NA**
Fair Value
• **NA**
Risk
• **Average**
Earn./Div. Rank
• **NR**

Technical Eval.
• **Bullish** since 9/95
Rel. Strength Rank
(1 Lowest—99 Highest)
• **33**
Insider Activity
• **NA**

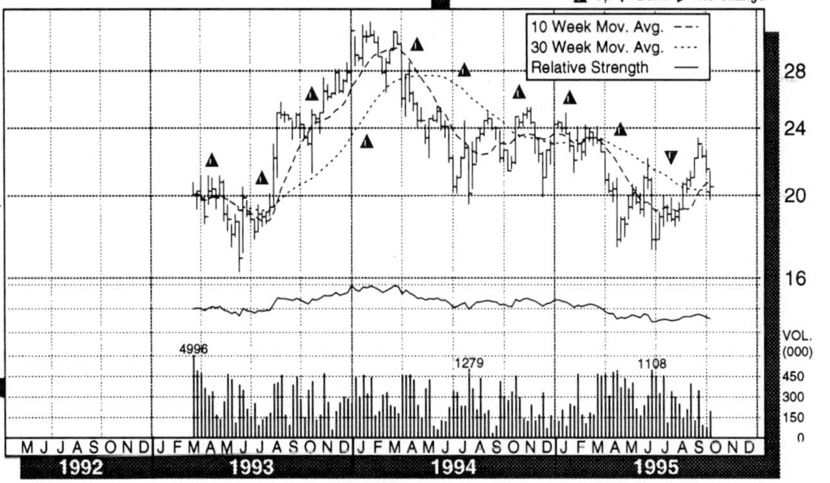

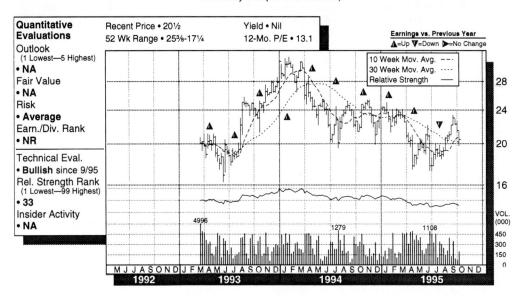

Business Profile - 10-OCT-95

This company is a leading manufacturer and retailer of home furnishings. Ethan Allen has taken steps to control inventories, including implementing selective shutdowns in manufacturing. The company has said it also planned to aggressively pursue its growth strategy--including investing in technology, employee training, and new stores--to be better positioned for the future.

Operational Review - 10-OCT-95

Net sales for the fiscal year ended June 30, 1995 (preliminary), advanced 8.9%, year to year. Fourth quarter fiscal 1995 factors--a weak retail environmnet, lower sales volumes, and higher manufacturing and other costs--led to only a nominal rise in net income for the full year. Share earnings were $1.56 (before special items), versus $1.53. Due to uncertainty in the economy, ETH was cautious about the first half of fiscal 1996, but anticipated a better second half.

Stock Performance - 06-OCT-95

In the past 30 trading days, ETH's shares have declined 2%, compared to a 4% rise in the S&P 500. Average trading volume for the past five days was 38,320 shares, compared with the 40-day moving average of 39,803 shares.

Key Stock Statistics

Dividend Rate/Share	Nil	Shareholders	400
Shs. outstg. (M)	14.3	Market cap. (B)	$0.289
Avg. daily vol. (M)	0.036	Inst. holdings	76%
Tang. Bk. Value/Share	7.95	Insider holdings	NA
Beta	NA		

Value of $10,000 invested 5 years ago: NA

Fiscal Year Ending Jun. 30

	1995	% Change	1994	% Change	1993	% Change
Revenues (Million $)						
1Q	113.5	17%	96.77	13%	85.60	—
2Q	125.7	16%	108.3	12%	96.80	—
3Q	123.6	7%	115.9	17%	99.2	—
4Q	113.2	-3%	116.3	13%	102.6	—
Yr.	476.1	9%	437.3	14%	384.2	9%
Income (Million $)						
1Q	5.84	35%	4.32	—	—	—
2Q	7.14	23%	5.82	—	—	—
3Q	6.89	12%	6.17	—	—	—
4Q	2.86	-54%	6.27	—	—	—
Yr.	22.73	NM	22.57	35%	16.73	NM
Earnings Per Share ($)						
1Q	0.40	38%	0.29	53%	0.19	58%
2Q	0.49	26%	0.39	34%	0.29	NM
3Q	0.47	12%	0.42	31%	0.32	100%
4Q	0.20	-53%	0.43	34%	0.32	NM
Yr.	1.56	2%	1.53	37%	1.12	NM

Next earnings report expected: mid October

Ethan Allen Interiors

Business Summary - 06-OCT-95

Ethan Allen Interiors, through its wholly owned subsidiary, Ethan Allen Inc., is a leading manufacturer and retailer of home furnishings. As of June 30, 1994, ETH's products were sold through a network of 285 Ethan Allen Galleries (up from 276 at fiscal 1993 year-end), which exclusively sell Ethan Allen products. Of that total, the company owned and operated 55 North American galleries, while independent dealers owned and operated 211 North American galleries and 19 galleries located abroad. Sales to independent dealer-owned stores accounted for about 71% of net sales in fiscal 1994.

Ethan Allen's products are positioned in terms of selection, quality and value within what management feels are the four most important style categories in home furnishings today: Formal, American Country, Casual Contemporary and Classic Elegance. The company has grouped its products into collections within these categories. Sales breakdown by collection: Each collection includes case goods (61% of fiscal 1994 sales), consisting primarily of bedroom and dining room furniture, wall units and tables; upholstered products (28%), consisting largely of sofas, loveseats, chairs, recliners and swivel rockers; and home furnishing accessories (11%), including carpeting and area rugs, lighting products, clocks, wall decor, bedding ensembles, draperies and decorative accessories.

The company employs a "showcase gallery" concept wherein products are displayed in complete room ensembles, which include furnishings, wall decor, window treatments, floor coverings, accents and accessories. Management believes that the gallery concept results in higher sales of Ethan Allen products by encouraging the customer to purchase a complete home collection, including case goods, upholstery and accessories, and by providing for a high level of service. The average size of an Ethan Allen gallery is 15,000 square feet.

Ethan Allen is one of the 10 largest manufacturers of household furniture in the U.S. It produces or assembles about 91% of its products at 20 manufacturing facilities. During fiscal 1993, the company completed a program of rationalizing its manufacturing operations, and has closed seven of its less efficient, high cost manufacturing locations in recent years.

Important Developments

Aug. '95—ETH said that fourth quarter fiscal 1995 results were hurt by a weak retail environment. Net income was adversely affected by lower sales volume, plus higher manufacturing costs. There was some improvement in year-to-year written order trends in July. However, due to the uncertainty in the economy, ETH was cautious about the fiscal 1996 first half, but anticipated a better second half.

Capitalization

Long Term Debt: $114,244,000 (12/94), incl. $2.6 million of capital lease obligations.

Per Share Data ($) (Year Ended Jun. 30)

	1995	1994	1993	1992	1991	1990
Tangible Bk. Val.	NA	11.98	8.99	3.61	NA	NA
Cash Flow	NA	2.49	0.83	1.42	NA	NA
Earnings	1.56	1.53	-0.21	-0.23	NA	NA
Dividends	Nil	Nil	Nil	NA	NA	NA
Payout Ratio	Nil	Nil	Nil	NA	NA	NA
Prices - High	25	32	31½	NA	NA	NA
- Low	17¼	19½	16¼	NA	NA	NA
P/E Ratio - High	16	21	NM	NA	NA	NA
- Low	11	13	NM	NA	NA	NA

Income Statement Analysis (Million $)

	1994	%Chg	1993	%Chg	1992	%Chg	1991
Revs.	437	14%	384	9%	351	—	NA
Oper. Inc.	62.8	24%	50.7	56%	32.5	—	NA
Depr.	13.3	-4%	13.8	-30%	19.6	—	NA
Int. Exp.	13.3	-68%	41.8	NM	13.2	—	NA
Pretax Inc.	38.6	NM	-3.4	NM	1.1	—	NA
Eff. Tax Rate	42%	—	NM	—	69%	—	NA
Net Inc.	22.6	NM	-2.3	NM	0.3	—	NA

Balance Sheet & Other Fin. Data (Million $)

	1994	1993	1992	1991	1990	1989
Cash	6.7	4.8	4.6	NA	NA	NA
Curr. Assets	167	148	142	NA	NA	NA
Total Assets	413	396	391	NA	NA	NA
Curr. Liab.	64.4	57.4	48.5	NA	NA	NA
LT Debt	139	154	161	NA	NA	NA
Common Eqty.	171	116	95.2	NA	NA	NA
Total Cap.	347	337	340	NA	NA	NA
Cap. Exp.	12.2	7.7	NA	NA	NA	NA
Cash Flow	35.2	11.0	16.8	NA	NA	NA

Ratio Analysis

	1994	1993	1992	1991	1990	1989
Curr. Ratio	2.6	2.6	2.9	NA	NA	NA
% LT Debt of Cap.	40.1	45.6	47.6	NA	NA	NA
% Net Inc.of Revs.	5.2	NM	0.1	NA	NA	NA
% Ret. on Assets	5.3	NM	NA	NA	NA	NA
% Ret. on Equity	14.6	NM	NA	NA	NA	NA

Dividend Data —The company intends to retain earnings for working capital, capital expenditures, general corporate purposes and the reduction of outstanding debt, and does not expect to pay any cash dividends in the foreseeable future.

Data as orig. reptd.; bef. results of disc. opers. and/or spec. items. Per share data adj. for stk. divs. as of ex-div. date. Pro forma data in 1993 (Income & EPS tbls. only) & 1992. E-Estimated. NA-Not Available. NM-Not Meaningful. NR-Not Ranked.

Office—Ethan Allen Drive, Danbury, CT 06813. **Tel**—(203) 743-8000. **Chrmn, Pres & CEO**—M. F. Kathwari. **VP-Treas, Secy & Investor Contact**—E. P. Schade. (203-743-8217). **Dirs**—D. H. Chow, C. A. Clark, K. Gamble, M. F. Kathwari, D. K. Kelsey, H. G. McDonell, E. H. Meyer, W. W. Sprague. **Transfer Agent & Registrar**—Harris Trust Co. of New York, NYC. **Empl**-5,884. **S&P Analyst:** N.J. DeVita

Express Scripts

NASDAQ Symbol **ESRX**
In S&P SmallCap 600

14-NOV-95

Industry:
Health Care Centers

Summary: This pharmacy benefit manager provides services designed to contain the cost of prescription drugs and monitor the cost and quality of pharmacy services.

Quantitative Evaluations

Outlook
(1 Lowest—5 Highest)
• **NA**

Fair Value
• **NA**

Risk
• **High**

Earn./Div. Rank
• **NR**

Technical Eval.
• **Bullish** since 6/95

Rel. Strength Rank
(1 Lowest—99 Highest)
• **76**

Insider Activity
• **Neutral**

Recent Price • 40¼
52 Wk Range • 44¾-25
Yield • Nil
12-Mo. P/E • 35.6

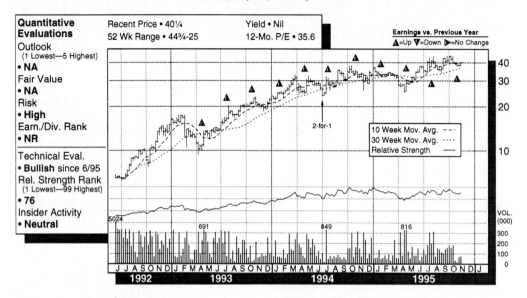

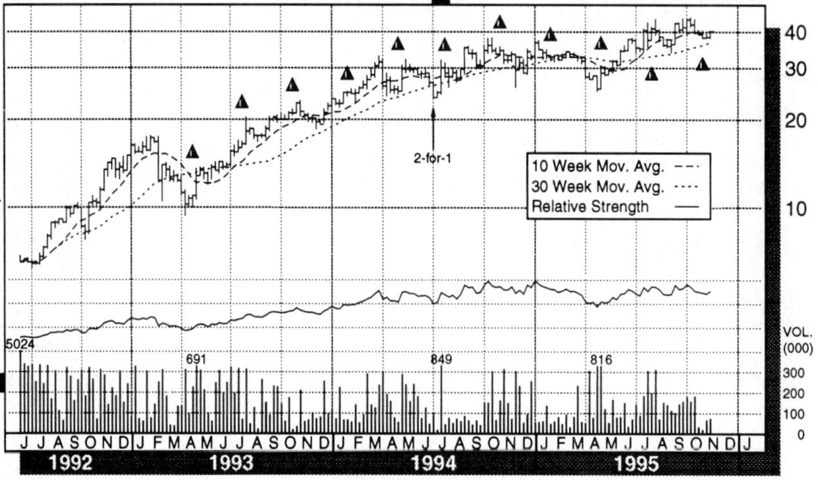

Business Profile - 14-NOV-95

ESRX originally developed its services for HMOs owned or managed by Sanus Corp. Health Systems. NYLIFE HealthCare owns Sanus, as well as 100% of the Class B stock of Express Scripts. ESRX recently formed an alliance with Amercian Healthcare Systems (AHS) and became AHS's preferred provider of pharmacy benefit management services to its shareholder hospital systems. The company also signed agreements with three insurance companies to provide pharmacy benefit management services in Canada.

Operational Review - 14-NOV-95

Express Scripts has experienced rapid growth in sales and earnings since its 1992 IPO. Further gains were made in the first nine months of 1995; sales climbed 43%, and net income gained 50%. Sales growth reflected a continued increase in the number of plan participants. Margins widened on economies of scale from the higher volume, despite a 48% jump in SG&A expense. Results also benefited from an increase in net interest income.

Stock Performance - 10-NOV-95

In the past 30 trading days, ESRX's shares have declined 9%, compared to a 1% rise in the S&P 500. Average trading volume for the past five days was 14,460 shares, compared with the 40-day moving average of 21,283 shares.

Key Stock Statistics

Dividend Rate/Share	Nil	Shareholders	100
Shs. outstg. (M)	14.8	Market cap. (B)	$0.606
Avg. daily vol. (M)	0.010	Inst. holdings	31%
Tang. Bk. Value/Share	4.22	Insider holdings	NA
Beta	NA		

Value of $10,000 invested 5 years ago: NA

Fiscal Year Ending Dec. 31

	1995	% Change	1994	% Change	1993	% Change
Revenues (Million $)						
1Q	118.0	42%	83.08	NM	26.70	79%
2Q	135.1	50%	89.97	NM	29.50	75%
3Q	138.5	38%	100.7	NM	30.70	64%
4Q	—	—	110.8	NM	33.40	64%
Yr.	—	—	384.5	NM	120.3	70%
Income (Million $)						
1Q	4.27	59%	2.68	65%	1.62	102%
2Q	4.53	55%	2.92	53%	1.91	68%
3Q	4.83	38%	3.51	57%	2.24	71%
4Q	—	—	3.61	55%	2.33	70%
Yr.	—	—	12.72	57%	8.10	75%
Earnings Per Share ($)						
1Q	0.28	56%	0.18	64%	0.11	38%
2Q	0.30	50%	0.20	54%	0.13	30%
3Q	0.31	41%	0.22	47%	0.15	67%
4Q	—	—	0.24	50%	0.16	60%
Yr.	—	—	0.84	53%	0.55	53%

Next earnings report expected: early January

Express Scripts

Business Summary - 14-NOV-95

Express Scripts, Inc. provides healthcare management services designed to contain the cost of prescription drugs and monitor the cost and quality of pharmacy services provided to those enrolled in or entitled to benefits under a health plan (plan participants). It also provides vision care services and home infusion therapy services and supplies in selected markets.

Pharmacy benefit management services include mail pharmacy, pharmacy network and claims administration, drug utilization review and benefit plan design services. The company dispenses prescription drugs to plan participants through mail pharmacies in St. Louis, Mo., and Tempe, Ariz. Medications dispensed through the mail pharmacies are primarily maintenance medications prescribed for chronic disorders. During 1994, Express Scripts dispensed 1,594,000 prescriptions through the mail. It believes that mail pharmacy services provide cost savings, as a result of its ability to buy pharmaceuticals in bulk, negotiate favorable pricing arrangements and dispense a longer-term supply than is generally available from retail pharmacies, thereby reducing dispensing fees. Mail pharmacy services accounted for 32% of net revenues in 1994.

Pharmacy network and claims administration services (65% of net revenues in 1994) include processing claims for prescription drugs purchased at local retail pharmacies. At December 31, 1994, Express Scripts had contracts with more than 37,000 pharmacies throughout the U.S. and in Puerto Rico, to dispense prescriptions to plan participants.

Vision care services are provided through a network of providers, consisting primarily of optometrists and ophthalmologists, in the metropolitan areas of Houston, Dallas, St. Louis, Washington, D.C., Chicago and New York City. They offer discount services to vision plan participants. Home infusion services, designed to limit the length of hospital stays by permiting certain therapies to be administered at home, include administration of prescription drugs by catheter, feeding tube or intravenously. Vision care and home infusion services accounted for 1% and 2%, respectively, of net revenues in 1994.

Important Developments

Sep. '95—Express Scripts and an affiliate of American Healthcare Systems (AHS) signed a letter of intent for a broad corporate alliance. Under terms of the agreement, ESRX will become AHS's preferred vendor of pharmacy benefit management services to AHS's shareholder hospital systems and their managed care affiliates. Express Scripts will issue up to 500,000 shares of its Class A common stock to AHS based on achievement by AHS of certain benchmarks and joint purchasing goals.

Capitalization

Long Term Debt: None (6/95).

Per Share Data ($)

(Year Ended Dec. 31)

	1994	1993	1992	1991	1990	1989
Tangible Bk. Val.	3.56	2.60	2.05	0.33	NA	NA
Cash Flow	1.06	0.68	0.44	0.34	NA	NA
Earnings	0.84	0.55	0.36	0.28	NA	NA
Dividends	Nil	Nil	Nil	Nil	NA	NA
Payout Ratio	Nil	Nil	Nil	Nil	NA	NA
Prices - High	38¼	23½	16½	NA	NA	NA
- Low	22	9⅜	6¼	NA	NA	NA
P/E Ratio - High	46	43	46	NA	NA	NA
- Low	26	17	17	NA	NA	NA

Income Statement Analysis (Million $)

	1994	%Chg	1993	%Chg	1992	%Chg	1991
Revs.	385	NM	120	69%	71.0	51%	47.0
Oper. Inc.	23.8	61%	14.8	78%	8.3	57%	5.3
Depr.	3.3	70%	2.0	93%	1.0	38%	0.7
Int. Exp.	0.1	17%	0.1	NM	0.1	-60%	0.2
Pretax Inc.	20.8	60%	13.0	76%	7.4	57%	4.7
Eff. Tax Rate	39%	—	38%	—	37%	—	38%
Net Inc.	12.7	57%	8.1	75%	4.6	61%	2.9

Balance Sheet & Other Fin. Data (Million $)

	1994	1993	1992	1991	1990	1989
Cash	5.7	2.0	11.8	3.5	NA	NA
Curr. Assets	92.8	63.3	40.1	16.6	NA	NA
Total Assets	108	75.4	45.4	20.2	NA	NA
Curr. Liab.	55.9	37.1	15.7	16.8	NA	NA
LT Debt	Nil	Nil	Nil	Nil	NA	NA
Common Eqty.	52.5	38.3	29.7	3.4	NA	NA
Total Cap.	52.5	38.3	29.7	3.4	NA	NA
Cap. Exp.	6.3	7.1	2.5	1.8	NA	NA
Cash Flow	16.0	10.0	5.6	3.6	NA	NA

Ratio Analysis

	1994	1993	1992	1991	1990	1989
Curr. Ratio	1.7	1.7	2.6	1.0	NA	NA
% LT Debt of Cap.	Nil	Nil	Nil	Nil	NA	NA
% Net Inc.of Revs.	3.3	6.7	6.5	6.1	NA	NA
% Ret. on Assets	13.8	13.3	12.6	NA	NA	NA
% Ret. on Equity	28.0	23.7	26.9	NA	NA	NA

Dividend Data —No cash dividends have been paid. A two-for-one stock split was effected in June 1994.

Data as orig. reptd.; bef. results of disc. opers. and/or spec. items. Per share data adj. for stk. divs. as of ex-div. date. E-Estimated. NA-Not Available. NM-Not Meaningful. NR-Not Ranked.

Office—14000 Riverport Dr., Maryland Heights, MO 63043. **Tel**—(314) 770-1666. **Chrmn**—H. L. Waltman. **Pres & CEO**—B. A. Toan. **Exec VP, CFO, Treas & Investor Contact**—Stuart L. Bascomb. **Secy**—T. M. Boudreau **Dirs**—B. N. Del Bello, L. M. Gammill Jr., R. M. Kerman Jr., R. A. Norling, S. N. Steinig, S. Sternberg, B. A. Toan, H. L. Waltman, N. Zachary. **Transfer Agent & Registrar**—Boatmen's Trust Co., St. Louis. **Incorporated** in Missouri in 1986; reincorporated in Delaware in 1992. **Empl**-860. **S&P Analyst:** Stephen Madonna, CFA

STANDARD & POOR'S

STOCK REPORTS

Fabri-Centers of America

NYSE Symbol **FCA.A**

In S&P SmallCap 600

23-OCT-95

Industry: Retail Stores

Summary: FCA is the leading U.S. fabric and craft retailer, currently operating 939 stores, primarily under the names Jo-Ann Fabrics and Crafts, and Cloth World.

Quantitative Evaluations

Outlook (1 Lowest—5 Highest)
• **NA**

Fair Value
• **NA**

Risk
• **Average**

Earn./Div. Rank
• **B-**

Technical Eval.
• **NA**

Rel. Strength Rank (1 Lowest—99 Highest)
• **74**

Insider Activity
• **NA**

Recent Price • 14½ | 52 Wk Range • 16⅛-7¼ | Yield • Nil | 12-Mo. P/E • 20.1

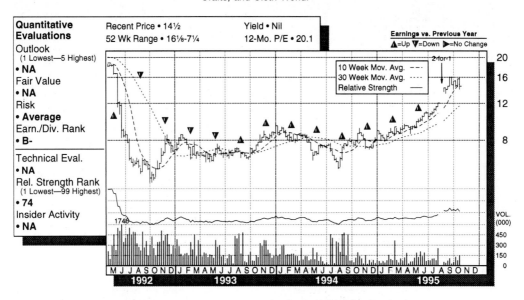

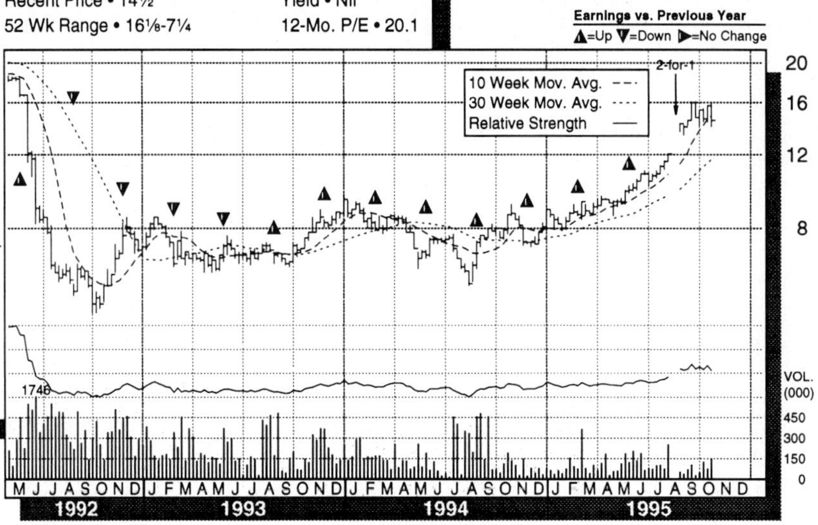

Business Profile - 23-OCT-95

The conversion of approximately 300 of FCA's Cloth World stores to the Jo-Ann Fabrics and Crafts format, which provides an expanded assortment of craft and seasonal merchandise, is progressing rapidly. During the first half of 1995-96, over 180 of the stores were remodeled and remerchandised. The remaining stores are expected to be completed before Thanksgiving, in time to aid the seasonally strong fourth quarter. The company also expects to open 50 to 70 new superstores during the year.

Operational Review - 23-OCT-95

Net sales in the 26 weeks ended July 29, 1995, climbed 43%, year to year, primarily reflecting the inclusion of Cloth World, which contributed 28% of net sales. Same-store sales at Jo-Ann's Fabrics grew 3.7%. Results benefited from the higher volume and improvements in inventory management, which resulted in fewer markdowns. The net loss narrowed to $3,056,000 ($0.16 per share, based on 2.3% more shares outstanding), from $6,455,000 ($0.35).

Stock Performance - 20-OCT-95

In the past 30 trading days, FCA.A's shares were unchanged, compared to a 3% rise in the S&P 500. Average trading volume for the past five days was 29,360 shares, compared with the 40-day moving average of 15,744 shares.

Key Stock Statistics

Dividend Rate/Share	Nil	Shareholders	1,000
Shs. outstg. (M)	18.4	Market cap. (B)	$0.267
Avg. daily vol. (M)	0.019	Inst. holdings	27%
Tang. Bk. Value/Share	8.66	Insider holdings	NA
Beta	1.54		

Value of $10,000 invested 5 years ago: $ 31,635

Fiscal Year Ending Jan. 31

	1996	% Change	1995	% Change	1994	% Change
Revenues (Million $)						
1Q	183.3	38%	132.7	-5%	139.8	6%
2Q	168.5	49%	112.8	NM	113.2	-3%
3Q	—	—	175.4	19%	147.1	-8%
4Q	—	—	256.3	41%	182.1	-2%
Yr.	—	—	677.3	16%	582.1	1%
Income (Million $)						
1Q	0.28	NM	-1.26	NM	-1.68	NM
2Q	-3.33	NM	-5.20	NM	-5.43	NM
3Q	—	—	4.08	15%	3.54	109%
4Q	—	—	14.11	34%	10.54	19%
Yr.	—	—	11.73	69%	6.96	35%
Earnings Per Share ($)						
1Q	0.02	NM	-0.07	NM	-0.09	NM
2Q	-0.17	NM	-0.28	NM	-0.29	NM
3Q	—	—	0.22	16%	0.19	124%
4Q	—	—	0.75	33%	0.57	22%
Yr.	—	—	0.63	68%	0.38	39%

Next earnings report expected: mid November

Fabri-Centers of America

Business Summary - 23-OCT-95

Fabri-Centers of America, Inc. operates retail fabric stores that sell a wide variety of fashion and decorator fabrics, plus notions, crafts, patterns, and sewing accessories. At August 14, 1995, it operated 939 stores in 48 states. During 1994-95, the company opened 38 superstores, acquired 342 Cloth World stores and closed 71 stores. It expects all remaining Cloth World stores to be remodeled or remerchandised by the end of 1995-96. The majority of stores operate under the Jo-Ann Fabrics and Cloth World names. At the end of 1994-95, 83% of stores were superstores. In 1995-96, FCA expects to open about 50 to 70 superstores, while closing 80 to 90 smaller locations. Sales from continuing operations in recent years were derived as follows:

	1994-95	1993-94	1992-93
Fabric	49%	47%	46%
Notions/crafts	47%	49%	49%
Other	4%	4%	5%

As a result of competitive industry conditions and the need to offer a greater merchandise selection, since 1987-88 FCA has been replacing smaller fabric stores, generally averaging 5,000 sq. ft., with superstores of over 9,000 sq. ft. Reflecting a need to conserve capital, the pace of conversion slowed in recent years. The distribution of stores in operation at January 31 of recent years was:

	1995	1994	1993	1992	1991
Super	804	502	486	342	218
Conventional	160	153	207	322	399
Total	964	655	693	664	617

The company's fabric stores sell a wide variety of merchandise, primarily for customers who make their own clothing and complete home decorating projects. Fabrics include woolens, rayons, cottons, laces, synthetics, drapery and home furnishings fabrics and are customarily sold by the yard. Notions include cutting instruments, trimmings, buttons, threads and zippers, while crafts consist of seasonal merchandise, craft supplies, fabric paints, florals and stitchery.

Important Developments

Aug. '95—During the first half of 1995-96, the company opened 17 new superstores and closed 42 smaller stores. Separately, in a recapitalization, each existing FCA common share was exchanged for one new voting Class A common share and one nonvoting Class B common share.

Capitalization

Long Term Debt: $177,977,000 (7/95), incl. $56,983,000 of debs. conv. into com. at $24.38 a sh.
Class A Common Stock: 9,185,752 shs. (no par).
Class B Common Stock: 9,185,752 shs. (no par). Nonvoting.

Per Share Data ($) (Year Ended Jan. 31)

	1995	1994	1993	1992	1991	1990
Tangible Bk. Val.	8.53	8.19	8.00	7.67	5.16	4.51
Cash Flow	1.31	0.96	0.74	1.27	1.03	0.86
Earnings	0.63	0.38	0.27	0.95	0.71	0.57
Dividends	Nil	Nil	Nil	Nil	Nil	Nil
Payout Ratio	Nil	Nil	Nil	Nil	Nil	Nil
Cal. Yrs.	1994	1993	1992	1991	1990	1989
Prices - High	9 3/8	9 5/8	23 5/8	23	8 5/8	4 7/8
- Low	5 7/8	6 1/4	5	7 1/2	4 5/8	3 5/8
P/E Ratio - High	15	26	88	24	12	9
- Low	9	17	19	8	6	6

Income Statement Analysis (Million $)

	1995	%Chg	1994	%Chg	1993	%Chg	1992
Revs.	677	16%	582	1%	574	22%	469
Oper. Inc.	40.3	46%	27.6	21%	22.8	-38%	36.7
Depr.	12.8	17%	10.9	22%	9.0	50%	6.0
Int. Exp.	8.4	52%	5.6	NM	5.5	62%	3.4
Pretax Inc.	19.1	72%	11.1	34%	8.3	-70%	27.4
Eff. Tax Rate	39%	—	38%	—	38%	—	36%
Net Inc.	11.7	67%	7.0	35%	5.2	-70%	17.5

Balance Sheet & Other Fin. Data (Million $)

	1995	1994	1993	1992	1991	1990
Cash	21.9	7.7	6.6	8.6	5.2	5.1
Curr. Assets	326	246	242	221	166	129
Total Assets	427	337	352	286	205	158
Curr. Liab.	127	76.6	93.6	99	72.2	58.3
LT Debt	127	103	104	40.1	52.1	28.6
Common Eqty.	162	149	148	143	77.0	68.2
Total Cap.	299	260	258	186	132	99
Cap. Exp.	11.7	8.5	32.3	19.7	15.9	9.8
Cash Flow	24.5	17.9	14.1	23.5	16.3	13.3

Ratio Analysis

	1995	1994	1993	1992	1991	1990
Curr. Ratio	2.6	3.2	2.6	2.2	2.3	2.2
% LT Debt of Cap.	42.5	39.4	40.4	21.5	39.3	28.8
% Net Inc.of Revs.	1.7	1.2	0.9	3.7	2.9	2.6
% Ret. on Assets	3.1	2.0	1.6	6.5	6.2	6.0
% Ret. on Equity	7.5	4.7	3.6	14.7	15.6	13.7

Dividend Data —Cash dividends were omitted in 1987, after having been paid since 1969. A "poison pill" stock purchase rights plan was adopted in 1990. A two-for-one stock split was effected in August 1995.

Amt. of Div. $	Date Decl.	Ex-Div. Date	Stock of Record	Payment Date
2-for-1	Jul. 28	Aug. 17	Aug. 02	Aug. 16 '95

Data as orig. reptd.; bef. results of disc. opers. and/or spec. items. Per share data adj. for stk. divs. as of ex-div. date. E-Estimated. NA-Not Available. NM-Not Meaningful. NR-Not Ranked.

Office—5555 Darrow Rd., Hudson, OH 44236. **Tel**—(216) 656-2600. **Chrmn, Pres & CEO**—A. Rosskamm. **Vice Chrmn, CFO & Investor Contact**—Robert Norton. **SVP & Secy**—Betty Rosskamm. **VP-Fin & Treas**—F. Piccirillo. **Dirs**—S. S. Cowen, I. Gumberg, S. J. Krasney, F. A. Newman, R. Norton, A. Rosskamm, B. Rosskamm, A. Zimmerman. **Transfer Agent & Registrar**—Society National Bank, Cleveland. **Incorporated** in Ohio in 1951. **Empl**-17,600. **S&P Analyst:** Maureen C. Carini

Fay's Incorporated

NYSE Symbol **FAY**
In S&P SmallCap 600

31-AUG-95 **Industry:** Retail Stores

Summary: This company operates a chain of 276 discount drug stores, located mainly in upstate New York, and also operates smaller chains of office supply and auto supply stores.

Quantitative Evaluations
Recent Price • 7¾
52 Wk Range • 9⅜-6
Yield • 2.5%
12-Mo. P/E • 16.1

Outlook (1 Lowest—5 Highest)
• **NA**
Fair Value
• **NA**
Risk
• **Average**
Earn./Div. Rank
• **B+**

Technical Eval.
• **Bearish** since 6/95
Rel. Strength Rank (1 Lowest—99 Highest)
• **49**
Insider Activity
• **NA**

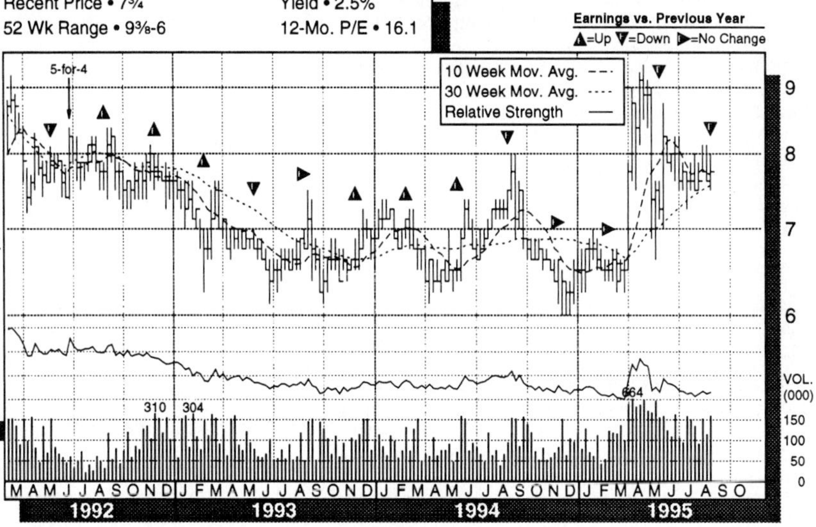

Business Profile - 31-AUG-95

This company operates the 13th largest drug store chain in the United States, with stores located in New York, Pennsylvania, Vermont and New Hampshire. Following weaker than expected first quarter results from all three of its retail divisions, Fay's said that it would refocus its attention and financial resources on its core drug store and other health care related businesses. The company has begun exploring the possible divestiture of its Wheels Discount and Paper Cutter stores.

Operational Review - 31-AUG-95

Year-to-year net sales growth for the 26 weeks ended July 29, 1995, benefited from 13 additional stores in operation and a 0.9% gain in same-store sales. However, gross margins declined sharply in the drugstore division on a higher percentage of sales made through third party prescription plans. Profitability was further impacted by weakened demand for seasonal and general merchandise. Earnings per share were further reduced by 2.2% more shares outstanding.

Stock Performance - 25-AUG-95

In the past 30 trading days, FAY's shares have increased 2%, compared to a 0.04% rise in the S&P 500. Average trading volume for the past five days was 50,380 shares, compared with the 40-day moving average of 31,646 shares.

Key Stock Statistics

Dividend Rate/Share	0.20	Shareholders	9,300
Shs. outstg. (M)	20.6	Market cap. (B)	$0.162
Avg. daily vol. (M)	0.035	Inst. holdings	23%
Tang. Bk. Value/Share	3.86	Insider holdings	NA
Beta	1.14		

Value of $10,000 invested 5 years ago: $ 10,629

Fiscal Year Ending Jan. 31

	1996	% Change	1995	% Change	1994	% Change
Revenues (Million $)						
1Q	266.4	11%	239.0	10%	216.7	2%
2Q	269.9	7%	252.4	14%	221.9	3%
3Q	—	—	260.6	15%	226.0	5%
4Q	—	—	286.1	12%	255.1	-1%
Yr.	—	—	1,038	13%	919.7	2%
Income (Million $)						
1Q	0.77	-61%	1.97	NM	-1.10	NM
2Q	0.97	-62%	2.58	-16%	3.07	4%
3Q	—	—	2.21	NM	2.19	45%
4Q	—	—	5.88	NM	5.87	12%
Yr.	—	—	12.64	26%	10.03	-11%
Earnings Per Share ($)						
1Q	0.04	-60%	0.10	NM	-0.05	NM
2Q	0.05	-62%	0.13	-13%	0.15	NM
3Q	—	—	0.11	NM	0.11	38%
4Q	—	—	0.29	NM	0.29	12%
Yr.	—	—	0.62	24%	0.50	-11%

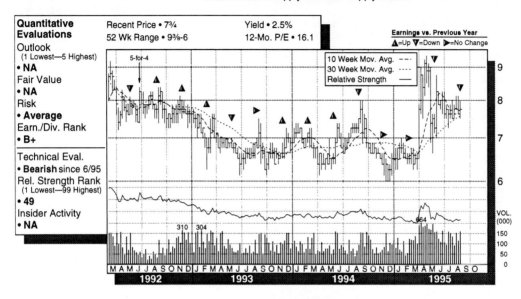

Next earnings report expected: early November

Fay's Incorporated

Business Summary - 31-AUG-95

Fay's is a diversified retailer primarily operating discount drug stores under the name Fay's Drugs, mainly in upstate New York. At July 1995, it was operating 381 stores, consisting of 276 drug stores (214 Fay's drug stores and 62 traditional drug stores), 75 Wheels Discount Auto Supply stores, and 30 Paper Cutter discount office supply, book and greeting card stores (one liquor store, also operated, is not included in the store count). The total number of stores in operation at the end of recent fiscal years was:

1995	376
1994	331
1993	308
1992	313
1991	249

All Fay's Drug stores are leased. Most range in size from 12,000 to 16,000 sq. ft., and are located in suburban shopping centers with adjacent paved and lighted parking facilities. Major classifications of products sold, and percentage of revenues attributable to each in 1994-95: prescription and proprietary drugs 52%, health and beauty aids 10%, tobacco 6%, consumer hard goods 6%, and miscellaneous merchandise 26%.

Each prescription department has a computerized pharmacy system called AccuFays designed to reduce paperwork involved in governmental and private health plans and to reduce the time it takes to receive payment from these programs. The mail-order pharmacy services division markets mail-order prescription services to prescription benefit programs.

The Paper Cutter stores offer office supplies, books, party supplies and greeting cards at everyday discount prices. The Wheels Discount stores feature replacement parts, tools and accessories at discount prices for the serious do-it-yourself customer.

During 1994-95, the company added three Fay's drug stores, two traditional drug stores, eight Wheels Discount Auto Supply stores and three Paper Cutter stores. In August 1994, Fay's acquired Peterson Drug Co., which operates 12 drug stores in western New York. In addition, two traditional drug stores were converted into Fay's Drug Stores, and one Fay's and one traditional drug store were closed.

Important Developments

May '95—Fay's said that it has begun exploring the possible divestiture of some or all of its two non-drugstore retail businesses: Wheels Discount Auto Supply and The Paper Cutter.

Capitalization

Long Term Debt: $82,973,000 (4/95), incl. $1.5 million of lease obligs.

Per Share Data ($) (Year Ended Jan. 31)

	1995	1994	1993	1992	1991	1990
Tangible Bk. Val.	3.86	4.78	4.70	4.30	4.00	3.55
Cash Flow	1.42	1.16	1.23	1.06	1.22	1.01
Earnings	0.62	0.50	0.56	0.44	0.64	0.54
Dividends	0.20	0.20	0.19	0.16	0.16	0.16
Payout Ratio	32%	40%	34%	36%	25%	29%
Cal. Yrs.	1994	1993	1992	1991	1990	1989
Prices - High	8	$7\frac{3}{4}$	$9\frac{1}{4}$	$12\frac{5}{8}$	$12\frac{3}{8}$	12
- Low	6	$6\frac{1}{8}$	7	$6\frac{1}{4}$	$6\frac{1}{4}$	$6\frac{7}{8}$
P/E Ratio - High	13	16	16	29	14	22
- Low	10	12	13	14	9	13

Income Statement Analysis (Million $)

	1995	%Chg	1994	%Chg	1993	%Chg	1992
Revs.	1,038	13%	920	2%	903	8%	836
Oper. Inc.	46.8	12%	41.9	1%	41.3	15%	35.8
Depr.	16.3	23%	13.3	NM	13.3	7%	12.4
Int. Exp.	8.5	8%	7.9	-7%	8.5	6%	8.0
Pretax Inc.	22.1	28%	17.3	-12%	19.7	35%	14.6
Eff. Tax Rate	43%	—	42%	—	43%	—	41%
Net Inc.	12.6	26%	10.0	-11%	11.2	29%	8.7

Balance Sheet & Other Fin. Data (Million $)

	1995	1994	1993	1992	1991	1990
Cash	1.9	1.0	0.9	8.9	4.5	20.2
Curr. Assets	213	195	174	174	139	123
Total Assets	314	208	256	264	209	191
Curr. Liab.	112	104	82.5	83.9	75.0	61.3
LT Debt	83.2	67.4	76.5	91.2	51.9	56.1
Common Eqty.	107	96.8	94.0	84.9	77.2	67.8
Total Cap.	190	164	171	176	130	125
Cap. Exp.	15.7	10.3	7.5	26.4	11.5	15.8
Cash Flow	28.9	23.3	24.5	21.0	22.3	19.3

Ratio Analysis

	1995	1994	1993	1992	1991	1990
Curr. Ratio	1.9	1.9	2.1	2.1	1.8	2.0
% LT Debt of Cap.	43.8	41.0	44.9	51.8	39.8	44.8
% Net Inc.of Revs.	1.2	1.1	1.2	1.0	1.8	1.8
% Ret. on Assets	4.2	3.7	4.3	3.6	6.1	5.8
% Ret. on Equity	12.3	10.4	12.5	10.6	16.9	16.3

Dividend Data —Dividends were initiated in 1975. A dividend reinvestment plan is available. A "poison pill" stock purchase right was adopted in 1995.

Amt. of Div. $	Date Decl.	Ex-Div. Date	Stock of Record	Payment Date
0.050	Jul. 23	Sep. 19	Sep. 23	Oct. 07 '94
0.050	Dec. 05	Dec. 19	Dec. 23	Jan. 06 '95
0.050	Jan. 30	Mar. 20	Mar. 24	Apr. 07 '95
0.050	May. 25	Jun. 21	Jun. 23	Jul. 07 '95
0.050	Jul. 28	Sep. 20	Sep. 22	Oct. 06 '95

Data as orig. reptd.; bef. results of disc. opers. and/or spec. items. Per share data adj. for stk. divs. as of ex-div. date. E-Estimated. NA-Not Available. NM-Not Meaningful. NR-Not Ranked.

Office—7245 Henry Clay Blvd., Liverpool, NY 13088. **Tel**—(315) 451-8000. **Chrmn & CEO**—H. A. Panasci, Jr. **Pres**—D. H. Panasci. **SVP & Secy**—W. D. Wolfson. **VP-Fin, CFO & Investor Contact**—James F. Poole, Jr. **Treas**—P. T. Anderson. **Dirs**—R. H. Altman, R. J. Bennett, L. H. Flanagan, T. Lombardi, Jr., H. M. Miller, G. L. Moreau, D. H. Panasci, H. A. Panasci, Jr., A. A. Townsend, W. D. Wolfson. **Transfer Agent & Registrar**—American Stock Transfer & Trust Co., NYC. **Incorporated** in New York in 1966. **Empl**-9,000. **S&P Analyst:** Maureen C. Carini

STANDARD & POOR'S

STOCK REPORTS

Fedders Corp.

NYSE Symbol **FJC**

26-SEP-95 **Industry:** Building

Summary: This manufacturer of room air conditioners has the largest share of the U.S. room air conditioner market.

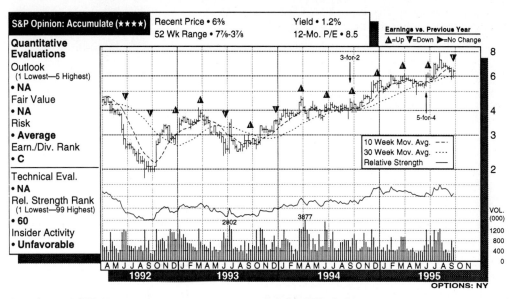

S&P Opinion: Accumulate (★★★★)

Recent Price • 6⅜ | 52 Wk Range • 7⅞-3⅞ | Yield • 1.2% | 12-Mo. P/E • 8.5

Quantitative Evaluations

Outlook (1 Lowest—5 Highest) • **NA**

Fair Value • **NA**

Risk • **Average**

Earn./Div. Rank • **C**

Technical Eval. • **NA**

Rel. Strength Rank (1 Lowest—99 Highest) • **60**

Insider Activity • **Unfavorable**

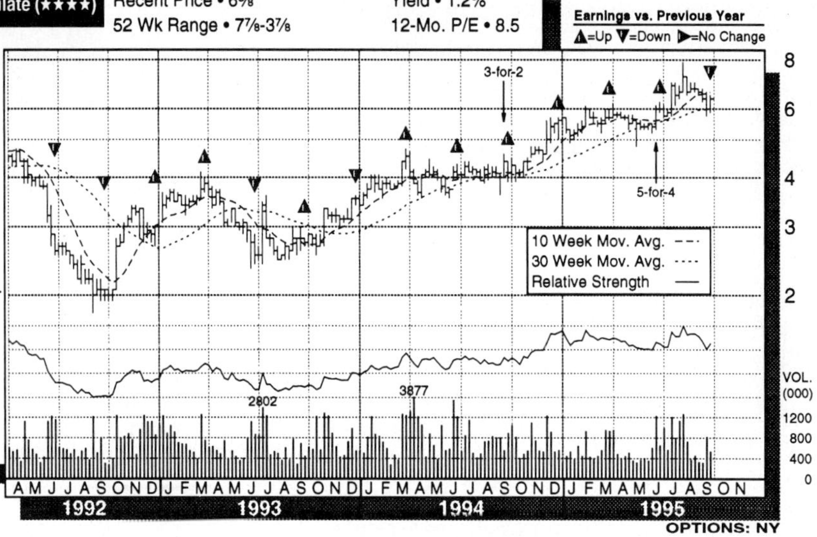

Overview - 26-SEP-95

Sales are expected to continue in a strong uptrend in fiscal 1996, reflecting 1995's hot summer, empty pipelines, increased market share due new accounts and larger orders from existing customers. A recently arranged joint venture in China should boost international sales. Domestically, FJC will increase peak season capacity for 1996, while keeping capital expenditures low and manufacturing for just-in-time delivery. Air conditioner shipments will be concentrated in the April through July period. Profitability will benefit from the increased volume, a global sourcing program and lower interest charges. Net income growth, however, will be hurt by a tax rate of 40%, up from 18% in fiscal 1995.

Valuation - 26-SEP-95

Profitability was restored at Fedders in fiscal 1994 (after four years of losses due to unfavorable weather and excess industrywide inventories), as a result of restructuring efforts. Fedders has now become the sole domestic room air conditioner producer that manufacturers for just-in-time delivery. The shares climbed nicely in 1994 from an adjusted low of nearly 3 3/8, which we attribute to the renewed earnings growth. The stock has traded in a fairly narrow range so far in 1995. Although earnings growth will be flat in fiscal 1996 (but only due to a substantially higher tax bracket), we believe the shares, trading at about 11 times their estimated fiscal 1996 earnings, should be accumulated.

Key Stock Statistics

S&P EPS Est. 1995	0.60	Tang. Bk. Value/Share	0.94
P/E on S&P Est. 1995	10.6	Beta	1.47
S&P EPS Est. 1996	0.60	Shareholders	5,500
Dividend Rate/Share	0.08	Market cap. (B)	$0.264
Shs. outstg. (M)	39.9	Inst. holdings	13%
Avg. daily vol. (M)	0.104	Insider holdings	NA

Value of $10,000 invested 5 years ago: $ 9,923

Fiscal Year Ending Aug. 31

	1995	% Change	1994	% Change	1993	% Change
Revenues (Million $)						
1Q	20.13	91%	10.53	-21%	13.30	-4%
2Q	72.36	96%	36.96	NM	36.60	-27%
3Q	145.9	52%	95.81	90%	50.46	-46%
4Q	—	—	88.27	52%	58.24	67%
Yr.	—	—	231.6	46%	158.6	-18%
Income (Million $)						
1Q	-1.22	NM	-3.89	NM	-2.56	NM
2Q	5.57	NM	1.13	NM	-0.89	NM
3Q	17.81	53%	11.64	NM	0.48	-83%
4Q	—	—	10.33	NM	1.19	NM
Yr.	—	—	19.21	NM	-1.78	NM
Earnings Per Share ($)						
1Q	-0.03	NM	-0.10	NM	-0.07	NM
2Q	0.14	NM	0.03	NM	-0.02	NM
3Q	0.35	18%	0.30	NM	0.01	-88%
4Q	E0.14	-45%	0.26	NM	0.03	NM
Yr.	E0.60	22%	0.49	NM	-0.05	NM

Next earnings report expected: late September

Fedders Corp.

Business Summary - 26-SEP-95

Fedders Corporation is the largest U.S. manufacturer of room air conditioners, principally for the residential market. In 1992, the company underwent a restructuring and sold its Rotorex compressor plant to NYCOR, Inc. for about $72.8 million and closed two plants in New Jersey.

Air conditioners are manufactured in models ranging in capacity from 5,000 BTU per hour to 32,000 BTU. Products are sold under the brand names Fedders, Airtemp and Emerson Quiet Kool, as well as under private label. While each brand provides similar capacity, the differences are due to special features and appearance. The company sells primarily to retail chains and buying groups.

Since 1988, FJC has made a series of acquisitions, including a plant manufacturing air conditioners and plastic components, a Canadian marketer of room air conditioners, a manufacturer of rotary compressors (subsequently sold) and, in 1991, Emerson Quiet Kool, a manufacturer of room air conditioners and dehumidifiers.

In 1994, the company created the Fedders Asia subsidiary to coordinate the manufacture of Fedders products in the Far East, to develop products specifically for the Asian market and to maximize the effectiveness of the company's global sourcing of components. The company continues to seek strategic alliances in key global markets through joint ventures.

Important Developments

Jul. '95—FJC entered into a joint-venture agreement with Ningbo General Air Conditioner Factory to manufacture room air conditioners in China. FJC will have a 60% interest and Ningbo a 40% interest in the joint venture, called Fedders Xinle Co. Ltd., which will be initially capitalized with $24 million.

Jun. '95—FJC attributed the 52% year-to-year surge in sales and the 53% increase in net income in the third quarter to its ability to meet customers' just-in-time requirements and its accurate-response production program.

Capitalization

Long Term Debt: $5,390,000 (5/95).

Class A Common Stock: 18,678,000 shs. ($1 par); nonvoting to the extent provided under Delaware law.

Class B Common Stock: 2,268,000 shs. ($1 par); 10 votes per sh. in certain circumstances in election of directors; div. 10% below com. div.; conv. sh.-for-sh. into com.; about 97% owned by Giordano family.

Per Share Data ($)

(Year Ended Aug. 31)

	1994	1993	1992	1991	1990	1989
Tangible Bk. Val.	1.08	0.45	-0.44	0.14	0.77	0.93
Cash Flow	0.61	0.09	-0.32	-0.02	-0.02	0.92
Earnings	0.49	-0.05	-0.70	-0.32	-0.45	0.64
Dividends	Nil	Nil	Nil	0.19	0.26	0.21
Payout Ratio	Nil	Nil	Nil	NM	NM	34%
Prices - High	$4\frac{3}{4}$	$4\frac{1}{8}$	$5\frac{3}{8}$	$5\frac{3}{4}$	$9\frac{1}{4}$	$9\frac{3}{4}$
- Low	$3\frac{3}{8}$	$2\frac{5}{16}$	$1\frac{13}{16}$	$3\frac{3}{8}$	$2\frac{5}{8}$	$6\frac{3}{8}$
P/E Ratio - High	10	NM	NM	NM	NM	15
- Low	7	NM	NM	NM	NM	10

Income Statement Analysis (Million $)

	1994	%Chg	1993	%Chg	1992	%Chg	1991
Revs.	232	46%	159	-17%	192	NM	191
Oper. Inc.	28.7	NM	6.9	-8%	7.5	-14%	8.7
Depr.	4.8	-4%	5.0	-63%	13.6	28%	10.6
Int. Exp.	4.1	-2%	4.2	-73%	15.6	32%	11.8
Pretax Inc.	19.8	NM	-2.3	NM	-25.0	NM	13.7
Eff. Tax Rate	3.00%	—	NM	—	NM	—	NM
Net Inc.	19.2	NM	-1.8	NM	-24.9	NM	-11.2

Balance Sheet & Other Fin. Data (Million $)

	1994	1993	1992	1991	1990	1989
Cash	34.9	8.6	8.7	2.9	Nil	Nil
Curr. Assets	66.0	42.0	78.0	88.0	114	163
Total Assets	101	81.0	179	197	215	281
Curr. Liab.	28.0	25.0	106	95.0	56.0	108
LT Debt	17.3	23.4	45.0	49.0	88.4	81.6
Common Eqty.	49.3	24.2	19.0	44.2	61.5	82.6
Total Cap.	68.0	54.0	70.0	98.0	156	168
Cap. Exp.	3.6	2.7	3.7	3.6	7.1	8.9
Cash Flow	24.0	3.2	-11.3	-0.6	-0.5	30.6

Ratio Analysis

	1994	1993	1992	1991	1990	1989
Curr. Ratio	2.4	1.7	0.7	0.9	2.1	1.5
% LT Debt of Cap.	25.5	43.6	64.4	50.2	56.8	48.5
% Net Inc.of Revs.	8.3	NM	NM	NM	NM	6.0
% Ret. on Assets	20.6	NM	NM	NM	NM	9.3
% Ret. on Equity	51.4	NM	NM	NM	NM	34.3

Dividend Data —Cash dividends, omitted in 1991, were resumed in mid-1995. In April 1995, FJC declared a dividend of one Class A share for every four shares of common, Class A or Class B stock held.

Amt. of Div. $	Date Decl.	Ex-Div. Date	Stock of Record	Payment Date
Stk.	Apr. 25	Jun. 15	May. 31	Jun. 14 '95
0.020	Jun. 27	Aug. 23	Aug. 25	Sep. 05 '95

Data as orig. reptd.; bef. results of disc. opers. and/or spec. items. Per share data adj. for stk. divs. as of ex-div. date. E-Estimated. NA-Not Available. NM-Not Meaningful. NR-Not Ranked.

Office—Westgate Corporate Center, 505 Martinsville Rd., P.O. Box 813, Liberty Corner, NJ 07938. **Tel**—(908) 604-8686. **Chrmn**—S. Giordano. **Vice Chrmn, Pres & CEO**—S. Giordano Jr. **Exec VP, CFO & Investor Contact**—Robert L. Laurent Jr. **Secy**—S. A. Muscarnera. **Dirs**—W. J. Brennan, J. Giordano, S. Giordano, S. Giordano Jr., H. S. Modlin, C. R. Moll, S. A. Muscarnera, A. E. Puleo. **Transfer Agent & Registrar**—Bank of Boston. **Incorporated** in New York in 1913; reincorporated in Delaware in 1984. **Empl**-1,800. **S&P Analyst:** Elizabeth Vandeventer

STANDARD & POOR'S

STOCK REPORTS

Fibreboard Corp.

ASE Symbol **FBD**
In S&P SmallCap 600

03-OCT-95 **Industry:** Building

Summary: This leading building products company manufactures vinyl products and industrial insulation, and also operates two resorts in California.

Quantitative Evaluations

Outlook
(1 Lowest—5 Highest)
• NA

Fair Value
• NA

Risk
• Average

Earn./Div. Rank
• B-

Technical Eval.
• Bearish since 9/95

Rel. Strength Rank
(1 Lowest—99 Highest)
• 81

Insider Activity
• Unfavorable

Recent Price • 25⅞
52 Wk Range • 27-13⅛

Yield • Nil
12-Mo. P/E • 8.5

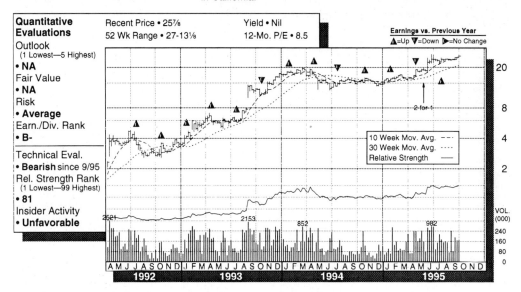

Earnings vs. Previous Year
▲=Up ▼=Down ▶=No Change

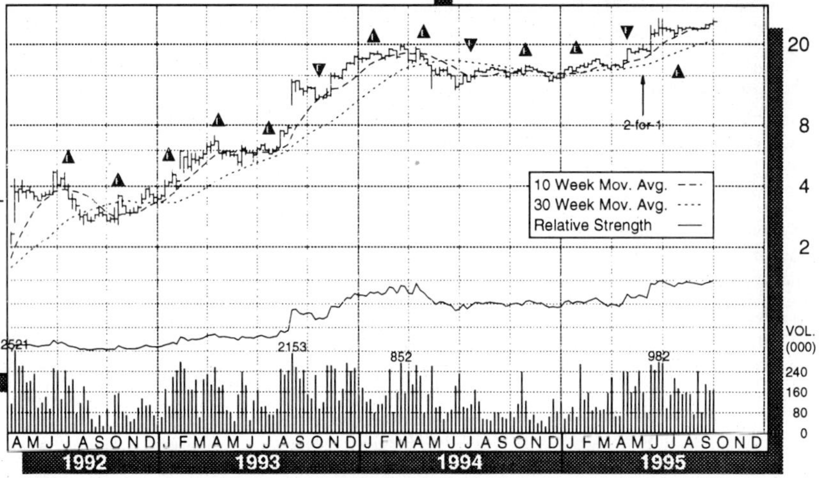

Business Profile - 03-OCT-95

In 1994, FBD began an acquisition program, with the purchase of a vinyl siding maker. FBD expects to use $200 million of credit facilities to finance expansion plans; proceeds from the recent sale of its wood products segment will also be used. In July 1995, FBD obtained a lower court approval (subject to appeal), which resolves earlier asbestos-related personal injury settlement disputes. A recently-announced program to repurchase up to $20 million of FBD stock should help boost share earnings.

Operational Review - 03-OCT-95

Revenues in 1995's first six months soared 74%, year to year, due to the August 1994 Norandex acquisition, and higher industrial insulation and resort operation sales. Margins eroded, mostly reflecting a sharp rise in SG&A expenses from FBD stock-based incentive compensation contributions; the gain in operating income was held to 36%. After a sharp increase in interest expense due to debt incurred from the Norandex acquisition, the aftertax gain in net income was further limited to 4.5%.

Stock Performance - 29-SEP-95

In the past 30 trading days, FBD's shares have increased 7%, compared to a 5% rise in the S&P 500. Average trading volume for the past five days was 33,060 shares, compared with the 40-day moving average of 31,095 shares.

Key Stock Statistics

Dividend Rate/Share	Nil	Shareholders	12,400
Shs. outstg. (M)	8.5	Market cap. (B)	$0.220
Avg. daily vol. (M)	0.030	Inst. holdings	27%
Tang. Bk. Value/Share	10.38	Insider holdings	NA
Beta	1.34		

Value of $10,000 invested 5 years ago: $ 39,056

Fiscal Year Ending Dec. 31

	1995	% Change	1994	% Change	1993	% Change
Revenues (Million $)						
1Q	129.0	50%	86.30	15%	74.89	6%
2Q	124.2	108%	59.61	-8%	65.02	9%
3Q	—	—	80.39	36%	59.14	9%
4Q	—	—	137.4	108%	66.16	22%
Yr.	—	—	363.7	37%	265.2	11%
Income (Million $)						
1Q	5.65	-24%	7.46	15%	6.48	18%
2Q	4.35	106%	2.11	-37%	3.37	25%
3Q	—	—	13.02	NM	1.19	2%
4Q	—	—	4.46	NM	0.74	NM
Yr.	—	—	27.04	131%	11.71	24%
Earnings Per Share ($)						
1Q	0.63	-25%	0.83	11%	0.74	10%
2Q	0.48	104%	0.24	-40%	0.39	18%
3Q	—	—	1.45	NM	0.13	-4%
4Q	—	—	0.50	NM	0.08	NM
Yr.	—	—	3.01	126%	1.33	16%

Next earnings report expected: late October

Fibreboard Corp.

Business Summary - 03-OCT-95

Fibreboard Corporation makes vinyl siding and insulation products, and operates two resorts. FBD sold its wood products segment in September 1995. About 39,600 asbestos-related personal injury claims are pending against the company. Segment contributions in 1994:

	Sales	Profits
Wood products	50%	36%
Norandex	24%	23%
Industrial insulation	15%	18%
Resort operations	11%	23%

Building Products consists of Norandex Inc., and the Industrial Insulation Products Group.

Norandex Inc. (acquired in August 1994) manufactures vinyl siding for exterior residential applications. Siding is distributed, together with a variety of other exterior building products, through a company-owned network of 71 branches.

The Industrial Insulation Products Group (Pabco) makes molded industrial insulation (CalSil), fireproofing board, metal jacketing and panel industrial fireproofing board (Super Firetemp) under an exclusive North American license.

FBD also owns, develops and operates Northstar-at-Tahoe, a 6,800 acre year-round destination resort in Northern California, and Sierra-at-Tahoe, a day ski area (acquired in July 1993 for $13 million).

Important Developments

Sep. '95—FBD said it completed the sale of its Wood Products Group to Sierra Pacific Industries for about $245 million. The proceeds will be used to reduce debt and fund future expansion. FBD will recognize an after-tax gain of $75 million ($8.34 a share), which will be reported in the third quarter.
Sep. '95—FBD agreed to acquire Vytec Corp. for about $35 million-$40 million in cash. FBD believes the transaction will be completed by October 30, 1995. FBD expects Vytec to contribute to fourth quarter 1995 results. Vytec, with 1994 revenues of $50 million, is a leading Canadian vinyl-siding producer, with plants in London, Ont. and Vancouver, B.C. FBD believes that Vytec will expand its vinyl siding capacity by 70%.
Aug. '95—FBD agreed to buy the ski and golf assets of Bear Mountain Ltd., a California-based day ski resort, for about $20 million. FBD noted it will become the largest ski operator in California, with expected revenues of $50 million-$60 million annually.

Capitalization

Long Term Debt: $99,988,000 (6/95); excl. $23,041,000 of asbestos-related debt.

Per Share Data ($) (Year Ended Dec. 31)

	1994	1993	1992	1991	1990	1989
Tangible Bk. Val.	17.21	13.66	13.02	12.20	18.08	18.06
Cash Flow	4.25	2.53	2.61	-1.01	1.68	1.77
Earnings	3.01	1.33	1.15	-3.42	0.32	0.49
Dividends	Nil	Nil	Nil	Nil	Nil	Nil
Payout Ratio	Nil	Nil	Nil	Nil	Nil	Nil
Prices - High	19¾	17⅞	4⅞	3⅜	7⅜	9⅝
- Low	11⅞	3½	1$^{1}/_{16}$	$^{13}/_{16}$	⅞	6
P/E Ratio - High	7	13	4	NM	23	20
- Low	4	3	1	NM	3	12

Income Statement Analysis (Million $)

	1994	%Chg	1993	%Chg	1992	%Chg	1991
Revs.	364	37%	265	10%	240	3%	234
Oper. Inc.	38.9	37%	28.4	13%	25.2	NM	3.1
Depr.	11.1	6%	10.5	-13%	12.0	-38%	19.3
Int. Exp.	4.9	31%	3.8	-14%	4.4	-18%	5.3
Pretax Inc.	45.4	128%	19.9	19%	16.7	NM	-32.2
Eff. Tax Rate	41%	—	41%	—	44%	—	NM
Net Inc.	27.0	131%	11.7	24%	9.4	NM	-27.3

Balance Sheet & Other Fin. Data (Million $)

	1994	1993	1992	1991	1990	1989
Cash	8.8	5.3	16.0	16.3	7.1	38.8
Curr. Assets	138	115	91.0	93.0	109	104
Total Assets	1,186	1,230	1,050	589	353	298
Curr. Liab.	70.3	66.0	74.9	86.9	94.5	71.7
LT Debt	124	44.9	33.9	37.0	27.9	27.7
Common Eqty.	145	120	108	99	142	140
Total Cap.	288	187	155	145	198	184
Cap. Exp.	9.4	13.1	5.4	27.1	31.2	24.0
Cash Flow	38.2	22.2	21.4	-8.1	13.1	13.7

Ratio Analysis

	1994	1993	1992	1991	1990	1989
Curr. Ratio	2.0	1.7	1.2	1.1	1.2	1.5
% LT Debt of Cap.	42.9	24.0	21.8	25.6	14.1	15.0
% Net Inc.of Revs.	7.4	4.4	3.9	NM	1.0	1.7
% Ret. on Assets	2.2	1.0	1.1	NM	0.8	1.3
% Ret. on Equity	20.3	10.2	9.0	NM	1.8	2.7

Dividend Data —No cash dividends have been paid. A shareholder rights plan, adopted in 1988, was amended in 1994.

Amt. of Div. $	Date Decl.	Ex-Div. Date	Stock of Record	Payment Date
2-for-1	Apr. 17	May. 22	Apr. 27	May. 19 '95

Data as orig. reptd.; bef. results of disc. opers. and/or spec. items. Per share data adj. for stk. divs. as of ex-div. date. E-Estimated. NA-Not Available. NM-Not Meaningful. NR-Not Ranked.

Office—2121 N. California Blvd., Suite 560, Walnut Creek, CA 94596. **Tel**—(510) 274-0700. **Chrmn, Pres & CEO**—J. D. Roach. **SVP-Fin & CFO**—J. P. Donohue. **SVP & Secy**—M. R. Douglas. **Investor Contact**—Stephen L. DeMaria. **Dirs**—P. R. Bogue, W. D. Eberle, G. R. Evans, G. B. James, J. W. Koeberer, J. F. Miller, J. D. Roach. **Transfer Agent**—First National Bank of Boston. **Incorporated** in Delaware in 1917. **Empl**-3,500. **S&P Analyst:** Robert E. Friedman

STANDARD & POOR'S

STOCK REPORTS

Fidelity National Financial

NYSE Symbol **FNF**
In S&P SmallCap 600

10-OCT-95 **Industry:** Insurance

Summary: FNF, through subsidiaries, is one of the largest U.S. title insurance underwriters engaged in the business of issuing title insurance and other title-related services.

Quantitative Evaluations
Outlook (1 Lowest—5 Highest)
• **NA**
Fair Value
• **NA**
Risk
• **Average**
Earn./Div. Rank
• **B+**

Technical Eval.
• **Bullish** since 5/95
Rel. Strength Rank (1 Lowest—99 Highest)
• **43**
Insider Activity
• **Neutral**

Recent Price • 13½
52 Wk Range • 15⅛-9¾
Yield • 2.1%
12-Mo. P/E • NM

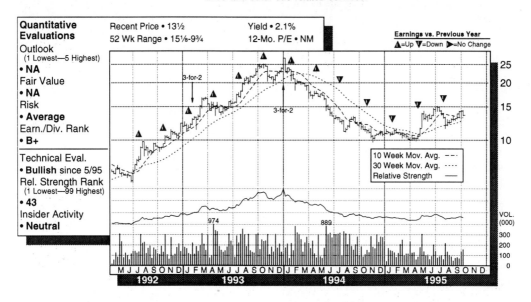

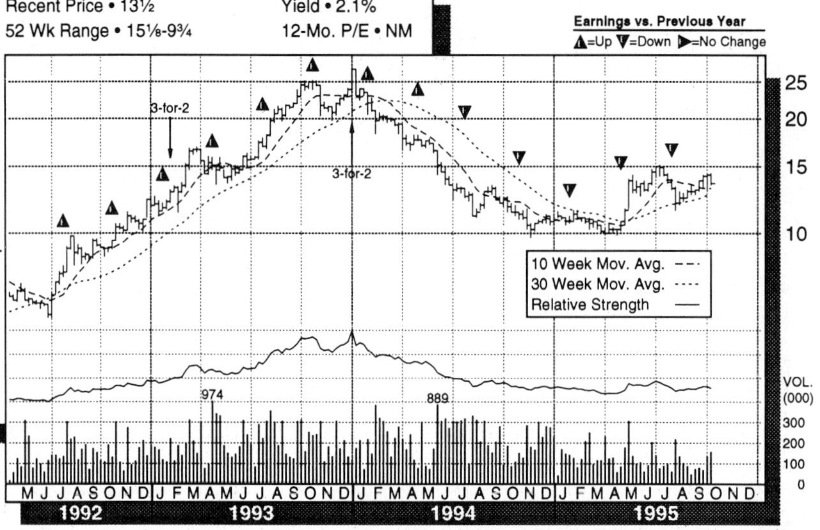

Business Profile - 10-OCT-95

The higher interest rates seen in recent periods, coupled with consumer uncertainty regarding employment and overall economic conditions, have penalized the resale and new home markets. The Fed's rate cut earlier in the year may brighten prospects for home sales, and thus aid firms like FNF which provide related services. The company has implemented aggressive cost-cutting measures to better withstand market cyclicality.

Operational Review - 10-OCT-95

Revenues in the six months ended June 30, 1995, fell 35%, year to year, reflecting a decline in refinancing activity and the stagnation of the residential resale and new home sale markets. Cost cutting efforts have helped reduce expenses. A net loss of $1.4 million ($0.12 a share, on 26% fewer average shares outstanding) contrasted with net income of $11.0 million ($0.69). Results for 1995 exclude an extraordinary loss of $0.07 from the early retirement of debt.

Stock Performance - 06-OCT-95

In the past 30 trading days, FNF's shares have increased 5%, compared to a 4% rise in the S&P 500. Average trading volume for the past five days was 30,660 shares, compared with the 40-day moving average of 18,436 shares.

Key Stock Statistics

Dividend Rate/Share	0.28	Shareholders	1,100
Shs. outstg. (M)	11.1	Market cap. (B)	$0.145
Avg. daily vol. (M)	0.021	Inst. holdings	25%
Tang. Bk. Value/Share	6.07	Insider holdings	NA
Beta	1.87		

Value of $10,000 invested 5 years ago: $ 55,389

Fiscal Year Ending Dec. 31

	1995	% Change	1994	% Change	1993	% Change
Revenues (Million $)						
1Q	83.06	-42%	143.6	30%	110.3	53%
2Q	95.49	-26%	129.4	-12%	147.3	81%
3Q	—	—	113.3	-27%	154.3	43%
4Q	—	—	106.4	-35%	163.5	35%
Yr.	—	—	492.8	-14%	575.4	51%
Income (Million $)						
1Q	-2.45	NM	6.81	58%	4.30	99%
2Q	1.02	-72%	3.58	-62%	9.45	93%
3Q	—	—	2.31	-78%	10.46	NM
4Q	—	—	-2.96	NM	12.08	159%
Yr.	—	—	9.75	-73%	36.30	140%
Earnings Per Share ($)						
1Q	-0.20	NM	0.43	39%	0.31	66%
2Q	0.09	-61%	0.23	-63%	0.63	60%
3Q	—	—	0.16	-76%	0.67	172%
4Q	—	—	-0.22	NM	0.76	124%
Yr.	—	—	0.65	-73%	2.37	103%

Next earnings report expected: early November

Fidelity National Financial

10-OCT-95

Business Summary - 06-OCT-95

Fidelity National Financial, through subsidiaries, writes title insurance policies and performs other title-related services such as escrow, collection and trust activities in connection with real estate transactions. Revenue sources in recent years:

	1994	1993	1992
Title insurance	75%	75%	72%
Escrow fees	11%	12%	16%
Other fees	12%	11%	11%
Other income	2%	2%	1%

Title insurance policies state the terms and conditions upon which a title underwriter will insure title to real estate. The policies are issued on the basis of a preliminary report or commitment prepared after a search of public records, maps or other relevant documents to ascertain title ownership and the existence of easements, restrictions, rights of way, conditions, encumbrances or other matters affecting the title to, or use of, real property.

FNF's title insurance services are provided through its branch operations and through independent title insurance agents who issue policies on behalf of the company. FNF's principal subsidiaries--Fidelity National Title Insurance Co., Fidelity National Title Insurance Co. of Pennsylvania, Fidelity National Title Insurance Co. of California, Fidelity National Title Insurance Co. of New York, Fidelity National Title Insurance Co. of Tennessee and American Title Insurance Co.--are licensed to issue title insurance policies in 49 states, Washington D.C., the Bahamas, British West Indies, the Virgin Islands and Puerto Rico.

In connection with its issuance of title insurance, Fidelity holds funds and documents in escrow for delivery in real estate transactions upon closing. FNF also conducts a general real estate trust business, and derives revenue from other ancillary services.

Important Developments

Sep. '95—FNF executed a definitive agreement to acquire Nations Title, Inc., a wholly owned subsidiary of Nations Holding Group, for $21 per share in cash and 160,000 FNF common shares. Together with its wholly owned subsidiaries, Nations Title is the nation's eighth largest title insurance underwriter, with 1994 revenues of $297 million.

Aug. '95—The company acquired Los Angeles-based Southern Title Company for an undisclosed amount of cash. The acquired company, whose name will be changed to Fidelity National Title Company of California, will operate as an underwritten title company of Fidelity National Financial.

Capitalization

Notes Payable: $131,200,000 (6/95).
Minority Interest: $358,000.

Per Share Data ($)

(Year Ended Dec. 31)

	1994	1993	1992	1991	1990	1989
Tangible Bk. Val.	7.72	7.26	4.39	3.03	2.44	2.15
Oper. Earnings	NA	NA	NA	NA	NA	0.42
Earnings	0.65	2.37	1.17	0.58	0.49	0.43
Dividends	0.28	0.23	0.17	0.15	0.13	0.09
Payout Ratio	43%	10%	15%	26%	27%	21%
Prices - High	26⅞	27¼	12⅜	6	3¾	3⅛
- Low	9¾	11⅛	5⅞	2½	2 7/16	1 13/16
P/E Ratio - High	41	11	11	10	8	7
- Low	15	5	5	4	5	4

Income Statement Analysis (Million $)

	1994	%Chg	1993	%Chg	1992	%Chg	1991
Premium Income	369	-14%	430	49%	289	77%	163
Net Invest. Inc.	3.3	-73%	12.1	181%	4.3	91%	2.3
Oth. Revs.	112	-15%	131	47%	89.1	61%	55.5
Total Revs.	493	-14%	575	51%	382	73%	221
Pretax Inc.	12.3	-77%	52.5	NM	8.0	-20%	10.0
Net Oper. Inc.	NA	—	NA	—	NA	—	NA
Net Inc.	9.7	-73%	36.3	NM	5.2	-16%	6.2

Balance Sheet & Other Fin. Data (Million $)

	1994	1993	1992	1991	1990	1989
Cash & Equiv.	34.7	42.7	48.5	21.0	11.3	10.1
Premiums Due	41.6	28.5	15.7	15.2	11.9	13.1
Inv Assets Bonds	176	212	84.1	3.6	5.2	4.0
Inv. Assets Stock	15.5	6.3	2.8	7.0	0.7	1.9
Inv. Assets Loans	Nil	Nil	Nil	Nil	Nil	Nil
Inv. Assets Total	218	226	94.1	10.9	5.9	5.9
Deferred Policy Cost	Nil	Nil	Nil	Nil	Nil	Nil
Total Assets	418	396	249	125	106	90.1
Debt	142	52.8	26.1	30.3	24.5	14.7
Common Eqty.	74.0	115	62.4	38.2	28.7	27.8

Ratio Analysis

	1994	1993	1992	1991	1990	1989
Prop&Cas Loss	6.3	4.2	7.2	6.0	5.2	4.5
Prop&Cas Expense	NA	NA	NA	NA	NA	NA
Prop&Cas Comb.	NA	NA	NA	NA	NA	NA
% Ret. on Revs.	2.0	6.3	4.0	2.8	2.8	3.1
% Return on Equity	10.3	40.3	30.0	18.6	18.5	18.5

Dividend Data —Dividends were initiated in 1987.

Amt. of Div. $	Date Decl.	Ex-Div. Date	Stock of Record	Payment Date
0.070	Sep. 20	Oct. 04	Oct. 11	Nov. 04 '94
0.070	Dec. 12	Jan. 09	Jan. 16	Feb. 03 '95
0.070	Mar. 28	Apr. 07	Apr. 13	May. 04 '95
0.070	Jun. 20	Jul. 07	Jul. 11	Jul. 21 '95
0.070	Sep. 14	Oct. 04	Oct. 06	Oct. 17 '95

Data as orig. reptd.; bef. results of disc. opers. and/or spec. items. Per share data adj. for stk. divs. as of ex-div. date. E-Estimated. NA-Not Available. NM-Not Meaningful. NR-Not Ranked.

Office—17911 Von Karman Ave., Irvine, CA 92714. **Tel**—(714) 622-5000. **Chrmn & CEO**—W.P. Foley II. **Pres**—F. P. Willey. **EVP-CFO & Treas**—C.A. Strunk. **VP-Secy**—M. Jones Kane. **VP-Investor Contact**—Jo Etta Bandy. **Dirs**—W. P. Foley II, W. A. Imparato, D. M. Koll, D. D. Lane, S. C. Mahood, J. T. Talbot, C. H. Thompson, F. P. Willey. **Transfer Agent & Registrar**—Continental Stock Transfer & Trust Co., NYC. **Reincorporated** in Delaware in 1986. **Empl**-3,500. **S&P Analyst:** N. Rosenberg

STANDARD & POOR'S

STOCK REPORTS

Fieldcrest Cannon

NYSE Symbol **FLD**

In S&P SmallCap 600

24-AUG-95 **Industry:** Textiles

Summary: Fieldcrest Cannon produces bedding and bath home textiles. Major brand names include Charisma, Royal Velvet, Touch of Class, Cannon Royal Family, St. Marys and Cannon Monticello.

S&P Opinion: Hold (★★★)

Recent Price • 23⅝

52 Wk Range • 29⅛-19¾

Yield • Nil

12-Mo. P/E • 12.8

Quantitative Evaluations

Outlook (1 Lowest—5 Highest) • **4-**

Fair Value • **24**

Risk • **Average**

Earn./Div. Rank • **B**

Technical Eval. • **Bullish** since 12/94

Rel. Strength Rank (1 Lowest—99 Highest) • **48**

Insider Activity • **Neutral**

Earnings vs. Previous Year

▲=Up ▼=Down ▶=No Change

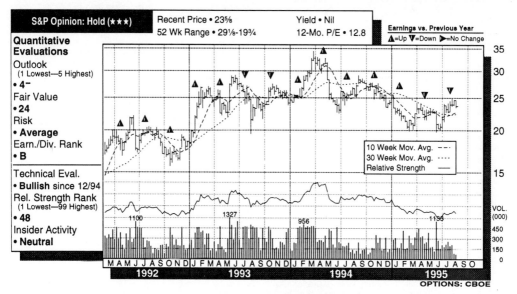

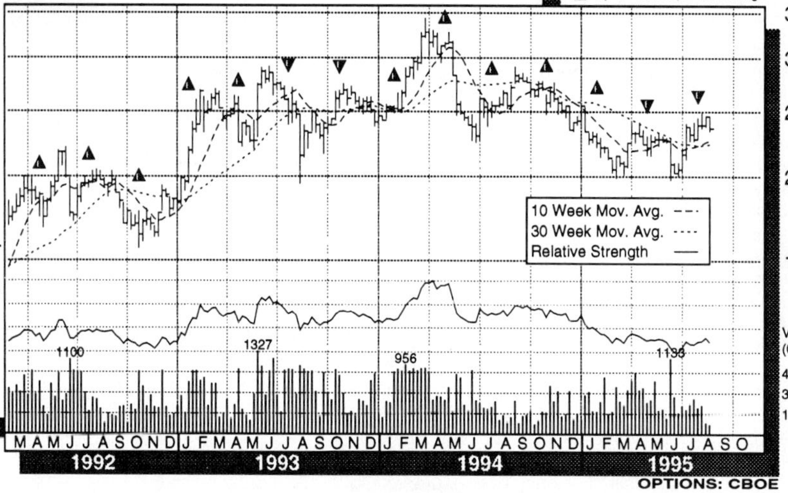

OPTIONS: CBOE

Overview - 24-AUG-95

Sales for 1995 should continue to advance, reflecting higher volume of bath and bedding textile products, as well as increased market penetration and efforts to expand overseas. Sales will also be boosted by acquisitions, including the purchase of Sure Fit, a slipcover manufacturer whose 1994 sales were estimated at $55 million. Margins are expected to narrow on reduced mill activity in the first half of the year, slower than expected volume during the spring season, higher raw material prices, and the inability to fully offset higher cotton and polyester price increases by raising prices. Interest charges could be higher. Earnings comparisons will be further hurt by one-time reorganization charges of about $0.78 a share, and the absence of a one-time gain of $0.20.

Valuation - 24-AUG-95

We are retaining a neutral opinion on this stock for now, mainly reflecting an uncertain earnings outlook. Following restructuring efforts to improve the company's cost structure in the early 1990s, FLD's shares climbed from a low of 5 3/4 in 1990 to a high of 34 3/8 in 1994. Since mid-1994, however, these shares have trended downward, and have been trading in a fairly narrow range for most of 1995. We believe this mainly reflects concerns that margins would suffer from FLD's inability to fully pass on higher cotton and polyester costs, as well as softening demand for home textile products.

Key Stock Statistics

S&P EPS Est. 1995	1.15	Tang. Bk. Value/Share	17.85
P/E on S&P Est. 1995	20.5	Beta	0.82
S&P EPS Est. 1996	2.60	Shareholders	2,700
Dividend Rate/Share	Nil	Market cap. (B)	$0.210
Shs. outstg. (M)	8.9	Inst. holdings	89%
Avg. daily vol. (M)	0.022	Insider holdings	NA

Value of $10,000 invested 5 years ago: $ 11,292

Fiscal Year Ending Dec. 31

	1995	% Change	1994	% Change	1993	% Change
Revenues (Million $)						
1Q	257.1	11%	232.3	-12%	263.0	-3%
2Q	273.0	7%	254.8	NM	256.5	-19%
3Q	—	—	279.3	9%	256.7	-15%
4Q	—	—	297.4	5%	282.9	-14%
Yr.	—	—	1,064	6%	1,000	-18%
Income (Million $)						
1Q	3.56	-35%	5.50	47%	3.73	NM
2Q	-1.54	NM	6.68	62%	4.12	-24%
3Q	—	—	8.48	NM	-0.51	NM
4Q	—	—	10.10	16%	8.67	11%
Yr.	—	—	30.75	105%	14.97	-27%
Earnings Per Share ($)						
1Q	0.28	-45%	0.51	65%	0.31	NM
2Q	-0.30	NM	0.64	88%	0.34	-33%
3Q	E0.56	-33%	0.84	NM	-0.04	NM
4Q	E0.61	-41%	1.03	34%	0.77	18%
Yr.	E1.15	-62%	3.02	144%	1.24	-31%

Next earnings report expected: mid October

Fieldcrest Cannon

Business Summary - 24-AUG-95

Fieldcrest Cannon (formerly Fieldcrest Mills) manufactures a broad range of home furnishing textile products. In August 1993, the company sold its Karastan Bigelow rug and carpet division to Mohawk Carpets for about $148 million, and realized an after-tax gain of $9.2 million. Following the sale of the rug and carpet division, nearly all of FLD's sales were derived from home furnishings products. In addition, nearly 90% of the company's sales were derived from products carrying FLD's principal brand names, which include Fieldcrest, Royal Velvet, Touch of Class, Charisma, St. Marys, Cannon, Monticello and Royal Family. The remainder of sales were derived from private label products.

The bath division produces bath towel ensembles, bath rugs, accent rugs and kitchen products. The bed division makes sheets, decorative bedding and window treatments. The blanket division provides bed blankets and decorative throws.

All products carrying the Royal Velvet, Touch of Class and Cannon Royal Family brands are distributed to department stores, specialty home furnishings stores and catalog merchandisers. St. Marys and Cannon Monticello brands are distributed through mass retailers. Private brand labels are distributed through large chain stores. Additional channels of distribution include institutional, government and premium accounts. Products are also distributed internationally.

Important Developments

Jul. '95—FLD attributed its second quarter 1995 loss of $0.02 a share to a one-time $0.32 charge related to reorganizing the company, lower mill activity, and higher raw material prices. The company said that certain price increases implemented to recover higher cotton and other raw material price hikes were expected to occur in the third quarter.

Capitalization

Long Term Debt: $362,846,000 (6/95), incl. $125 million of 6% debs. due 1997 to 2001 & conv. into com. at $44.25 a share.
$3.00 Series A Conv. Preferred Stock: 1,500,000 shs. ($.01 par); conv. into common shares. Privately held.

Per Share Data ($) (Year Ended Dec. 31)

	1994	1993	1992	1991	1990	1989
Tangible Bk. Val.	26.40	22.10	23.76	23.33	23.01	27.24
Cash Flow	6.45	4.14	5.10	3.77	0.47	5.31
Earnings	3.02	1.24	1.81	0.30	-3.64	2.28
Dividends	Nil	Nil	Nil	Nil	0.50	0.77
Payout Ratio	Nil	Nil	Nil	Nil	NM	34%
Prices - High	34⅜	29⅛	22⅛	18	23¾	30¼
- Low	22½	18⅛	11⅞	5⅞	5¾	18⅝
P/E Ratio - High	11	23	12	60	NM	13
- Low	7	15	7	20	NM	8

Income Statement Analysis (Million $)

	1994	%Chg	1993	%Chg	1992	%Chg	1991
Revs.	1,064	6%	1,000	-18%	1,217	NM	1,212
Oper. Inc.	100	2%	98.0	-17%	118	34%	88.0
Depr.	29.8	-12%	34.0	-8%	37.0	2%	36.2
Int. Exp.	23.3	-16%	27.7	-33%	41.3	-9%	45.5
Pretax Inc.	46.3	72%	26.9	-24%	35.6	NM	7.8
Eff. Tax Rate	34%	—	44%	—	43%	—	59%
Net Inc.	30.7	105%	15.0	-26%	20.4	NM	3.2

Balance Sheet & Other Fin. Data (Million $)

	1994	1993	1992	1991	1990	1989
Cash	5.9	3.9	4.7	9.3	13.1	6.5
Curr. Assets	418	413	461	468	443	505
Total Assets	783	740	864	883	856	861
Curr. Liab.	135	151	164	330	157	177
LT Debt	318	295	353	253	404	342
Common Eqty.	231	193	284	243	239	281
Total Cap.	592	523	679	533	676	670
Cap. Exp.	52.0	25.0	25.0	44.0	95.0	47.0
Cash Flow	56.1	48.5	57.4	39.3	4.9	54.7

Ratio Analysis

	1994	1993	1992	1991	1990	1989
Curr. Ratio	3.1	2.7	2.8	1.4	2.8	2.8
% LT Debt of Cap.	53.7	56.3	52.0	47.5	59.7	51.0
% Net Inc.of Revs.	2.9	1.5	1.7	0.3	NM	1.7
% Ret. on Assets	4.0	2.2	2.2	0.4	NM	2.8
% Ret. on Equity	12.3	7.3	7.2	1.3	NM	8.6

Dividend Data —Dividends were omitted in December 1990, after having been paid since 1960. A "poison pill" stock purchase rights plan was adopted in 1993.

Data as orig. reptd.; bef. results of disc. opers. and/or spec. items. Per share data adj. for stk. divs. as of ex-div. date. E-Estimated. NA-Not Available. NM-Not Meaningful. NR-Not Ranked.

Office—326 East Stadium Drive, Eden, NC 27288. **Tel**—(910) 627-3000. **Chrmn & CEO**—J. M. Fitzgibbons. **Pres**—C. G. Horn. **VP-Secy**—M. K. Doss. **VP-CFO & Investor Contact**—T. R. Staab. **Dirs**—T. H. Barrett, J. M. Fitzgibbons, W. E. Ford, J. C. Harned, N. T. Herndon, R. Horchow, W. D. Kimbrell, C. J. Kjorlien. **Transfer Agent & Registrar**—The First National Bank of Boston, Boston, MA. **Incorporated** in Delaware in 1953. **Empl**-13,926. **S&P Analyst:** Elizabeth Vandeventer

STANDARD & POOR'S

STOCK REPORTS

Figgie International

NASDAQ Symbol **FIGIA**
In S&P SmallCap 600

16-OCT-95 **Industry:** Manufacturing/Distr

Summary: Figgie International is a diversified manufacturer of electronic systems, protective breathing and oxygen equipment and instruments, and aerial work platforms.

Quantitative Evaluations

Outlook (1 Lowest—5 Highest)
• **NA**

Fair Value
• **NA**

Risk
• **High**

Earn./Div. Rank
• **C**

Technical Eval.
• **Bearish** since 7/95

Rel. Strength Rank (1 Lowest—99 Highest)
• **69**

Insider Activity
• **NA**

Recent Price • 12⅜
52 Wk Range • 14⅛-4⅝

Yield • Nil
12-Mo. P/E • NM

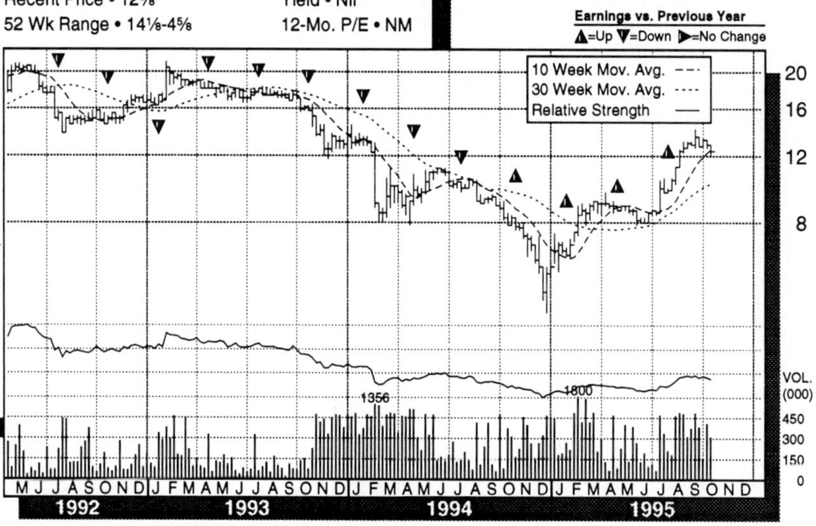

Business Profile - 16-OCT-95

Since early 1994, this company has classified numerous business units as discontinued and has been selling them to shore up its finances. Ongoing operations comprise the manufacture of electronic systems, protective breathing and oxygen equipment and instruments, and aerial work platforms. A February 1995 business plan calls for focusing on technology-driven operations and divesting certain businesses (accounting for about half of company sales) to reduce debt and restore profitability.

Operational Review - 16-OCT-95

Net sales from continuing operations for the first half of 1995 advanced 14%, year to year. Despite the absence of a tax credit, better gross margins, well controlled operating expenses, and lower other expenses enabled the net loss to drop to $13.9 million ($0.77 a share), from $26.3 million ($1.47, before a $0.67 loss from discontinued operations). FIGIA continued to expect to return to profitability in the 1995 third quarter, despite higher than anticipated interest costs.

Stock Performance - 13-OCT-95

In the past 30 trading days, FIGIA's shares have declined 5%, compared to a 4% rise in the S&P 500. Average trading volume for the past five days was 61,160 shares, compared with the 40-day moving average of 90,692 shares.

Key Stock Statistics

Dividend Rate/Share	Nil	Shareholders	12,600
Shs. outstg. (M)	18.4	Market cap. (B)	$0.228
Avg. daily vol. (M)	0.062	Inst. holdings	51%
Tang. Bk. Value/Share	2.83	Insider holdings	NA
Beta	0.27		

Value of $10,000 invested 5 years ago: $ 6,527

Fiscal Year Ending Dec. 31

	1995	% Change	1994	% Change	1993	% Change
Revenues (Million $)						
1Q	85.27	17%	73.11	-60%	181.1	-39%
2Q	88.69	11%	80.03	-61%	204.0	-29%
3Q	—	—	79.79	-58%	189.4	-32%
4Q	—	—	86.49	-55%	194.3	-37%
Yr.	—	—	319.4	-58%	768.6	-34%
Income (Million $)						
1Q	-8.04	NM	-16.25	NM	-0.37	NM
2Q	-5.83	NM	-10.07	NM	-0.28	NM
3Q	—	—	-10.85	NM	-16.46	NM
4Q	—	—	-48.08	NM	-162.2	NM
Yr.	—	—	-85.25	NM	-179.3	NM
Earnings Per Share ($)						
1Q	-0.44	NM	-0.91	NM	-0.02	NM
2Q	-0.32	NM	-0.56	NM	-0.01	NM
3Q	—	—	-0.61	NM	-0.92	NM
4Q	—	—	-2.74	NM	-9.03	NM
Yr.	—	—	-4.81	NM	-10.09	NM

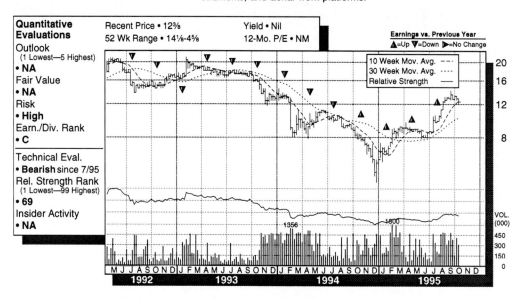

Next earnings report expected: mid November

Figgie International

Business Summary - 11-OCT-95

Figgie International Inc.'s ongoing operations comprise three manufacturing segments: sophisticated electronic systems; protective breathing and oxygen equipment and instruments; and aerial work platforms. Since early 1994, FIGIA has classified numerous business units as discontinued and has been selling them to satisfy lenders and refinance and reduce debt and lease obligations. Business segment contributions in 1994:

Interstate Electronics	36%
Scott/Taylor Environmental Instruments	37%
Snorkel	27%

Interstate Electronics products include sophisticated telemetry, instrumentation and data recording systems and position measuring systems, Global Positioning Systems (GPS) for the U.S. Navy's Polaris/Poseidon, TRIDENT, and TRIDENT II ships; precise GPS for aircraft and turnkey test ranges; and GPS for commercial and business aircraft and landing systems.

Scott division products consist primarily of the Scott Air Pak and other life support products for fire fighting and personal protection against industrial contaminants; air purifying products that provide protection against environmental and safety hazards; and protective breathing equipment and oxygen masks.

Taylor Environmental Instruments products include consumer thermometers, barometers, and hygrometers; and temperature and environmental measuring and testing devices. These products are used in laboratories, hospitals and other areas.

Snorkel division products consist mainly of self-propelled aerial work platforms and scissorlifts used in construction and maintenance activities; and self-propelled telescopic and articulating booms.

FIGIA sold its leasing business in June 1995 and its Ohio-based packaging operations March 1995.

Important Developments

Sep. '95—FIGIA sold its Automatic Sprinkler business in North America and its UK and French material handling businesses. In August, FIGIA sold its SP/Sheffer Division. In July, FIGIA sold its Fire Protection Systems divison for $48 million and assumption of $15 million of liabilities. Also in July, FIGIA sold its Safway Steel Products subsidiary. From June 30, 1994 to June 30, 1995, FIGIA's total debt was reduced to $314 million, from $570 million. Plans called for cutting total debt to $220 million by year-end 1995.

Sep. '95—According to an SEC filing, the Figgie family intends to explore alternatives for both maximizing the value of FIGIA shares for all shareholders and providing liquidity for the family's investment in the company.

Capitalization

Long Term Debt: $226,147,000 (6/95).

Per Share Data ($) (Year Ended Dec. 31)

	1994	1993	1992	1991	1990	1989
Tangible Bk. Val.	2.44	7.30	16.15	15.44	14.23	12.34
Cash Flow	-2.46	-8.74	3.53	3.95	4.08	4.32
Earnings	-4.81	-10.09	1.61	1.72	2.28	3.04
Dividends	Nil	0.43	0.50	0.50	0.50	0.40
Payout Ratio	Nil	NM	33%	31%	24%	13%
Prices - High	14½	22	26½	25	35½	32
- Low	4⅝	12½	17	16½	15	25⅛
P/E Ratio - High	NM	NM	16	15	16	11
- Low	NM	NM	11	10	7	8

Income Statement Analysis (Million $)

	1994	%Chg	1993	%Chg	1992	%Chg	1991
Revs.	319	-59%	769	-34%	1,173	-6%	1,243
Oper. Inc.	27.0	NM	-47.0	NM	109	-13%	126
Depr.	41.6	73%	24.0	-29%	33.6	2%	32.8
Int. Exp.	42.9	21%	35.6	-7%	38.3	-10%	42.7
Pretax Inc.	-107	NM	-250	NM	41.2	-5%	43.2
Eff. Tax Rate	NM	—	NM	—	31%	—	31%
Net Inc.	-85.0	NM	-178	NM	28.3	-6%	30.1

Balance Sheet & Other Fin. Data (Million $)

	1994	1993	1992	1991	1990	1989
Cash	47.0	34.0	117	110	98.0	83.0
Curr. Assets	460	534	516	NA	NA	NA
Total Assets	644	998	1,113	1,109	1,066	1,027
Curr. Liab.	316	677	282	NA	NA	NA
LT Debt	234	65.0	353	373	375	367
Common Eqty.	65.0	203	395	378	352	317
Total Cap.	300	289	798	804	760	714
Cap. Exp.	60.0	96.0	112	98.0	81.0	78.0
Cash Flow	-44.0	-154	61.9	62.9	71.1	89.5

Ratio Analysis

	1994	1993	1992	1991	1990	1989
Curr. Ratio	1.5	0.8	1.8	NA	NA	NA
% LT Debt of Cap.	78.2	22.4	44.3	46.3	49.4	51.4
% Net Inc.of Revs.	NM	NM	2.4	2.4	2.9	4.8
% Ret. on Assets	NM	NM	2.6	2.8	3.8	6.6
% Ret. on Equity	NM	NM	7.3	8.2	11.9	20.1

Dividend Data —Cash was paid by the company and its predecessor in each year since 1965. Payments were suspended in early 1994.

Data as orig. reptd.; bef. results of disc. opers. and/or spec. items. Per share data adj. for stk. divs. as of ex-div. date. E-Estimated. NA-Not Available. NM-Not Meaningful. NR-Not Ranked.

Office—4420 Sherwin Road, Willoughby, OH 44094. **Tel**—(216) 953-2700. **Chrmn & Pres**—J. P. Reilly. **VP-CFO**—S. L. Siemborski. **VP-Secy**—L. A. Harthun. **Treas**—J. M. Schulte. **Investor Contact**—Ira Gamm. **Dirs**—F. J. Brinkman, V. A. Chiarucci, D. S. Coenen, A. V. Gangnes, J. S. Lanahan, F. R. McKnight, H. Nesbitt II, J. P. Reilly, C. B. Robertson III, H. B. Scott, S. L. Siemborski, A. A. Sommer, Jr., W. M. Vannoy. **Transfer Agent & Registrar**—First National Bank of Boston. **Incorporated** in Ohio in 1963; reincorporated in Delaware in 1983. **Empl**-6,000. **S&P Analyst:** N.J. DeVita

STANDARD & POOR'S

STOCK REPORTS

Filene's Basement

NASDAQ Symbol **BSMT**

In S&P SmallCap 600

22-OCT-95 **Industry:** Retail Stores

Summary: This company operates 50 off-price specialty stores offering focused assortments of fashionable, nationally recognized branded and private-label family apparel and accessories.

Quantitative Evaluations

Outlook (1 Lowest—5 Highest)
• NA

Fair Value
• NA

Risk
• High

Earn./Div. Rank
• NR

Technical Eval.
• Bearish since 8/95

Rel. Strength Rank (1 Lowest—99 Highest)
• 4

Insider Activity
• NA

Recent Price • 3¾ | 52 Wk Range • 7⅞-3

Yield • Nil | 12-Mo. P/E • NM

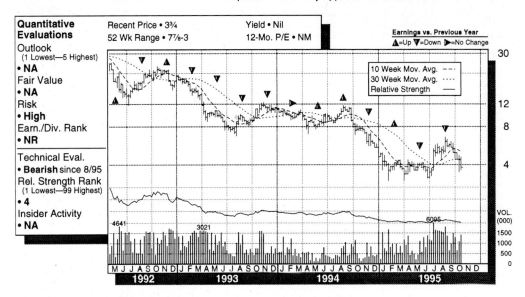

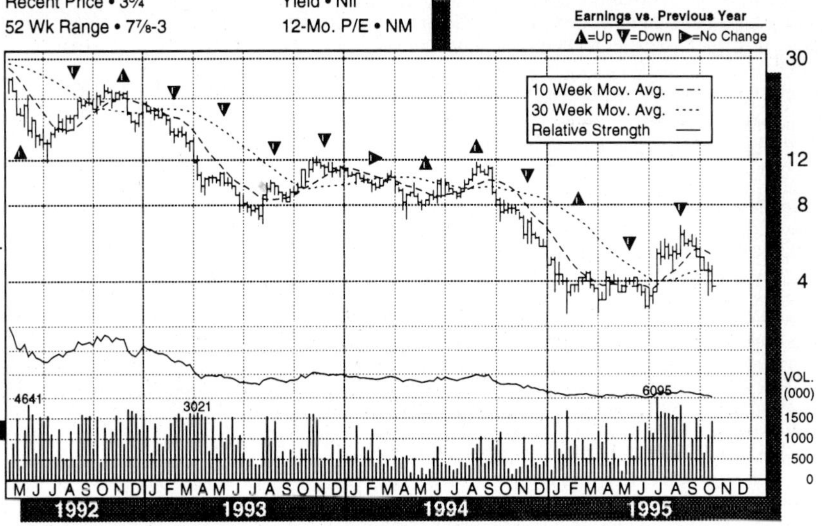

Business Profile - 22-OCT-95

Filene's operates 50 off-price specialty stores serving quality value-oriented customers with nationally recognized branded and private-label family apparel and accessories. Most of the stores are located in the Northeast, including the flagship store in Boston. An extremely competitive and promotional retail environment and general softness in the apparel industry have depressed BSMT's sales in recent periods. Earnings have also been penalized by store opening costs and store closing reserves.

Operational Review - 22-OCT-95

Net sales in the 26 weeks ended July 29, 1995, slid 2.3%, year to year, restricted by a 6.0% decline in same-store sales. Gross margins narrowed on the lower volume and increasingly competitive pricing conditions. Profitability was further restricted by costs associated with new store openings, and a loss of $0.11 per share contrasted with income of $0.01. Results in the 1994 period exclude a $0.10 per share charge for the repurchase of debt.

Stock Performance - 20-OCT-95

In the past 30 trading days, BSMT's shares have declined 34%, compared to a 3% rise in the S&P 500. Average trading volume for the past five days was 281,220 shares, compared with the 40-day moving average of 225,659 shares.

Key Stock Statistics

Dividend Rate/Share	Nil	Shareholders	1,700
Shs. outstg. (M)	20.5	Market cap. (B)	$0.078
Avg. daily vol. (M)	0.219	Inst. holdings	43%
Tang. Bk. Value/Share	5.07	Insider holdings	NA
Beta	NA		

Value of $10,000 invested 5 years ago: NA

Fiscal Year Ending Jan. 31

	1996	% Change	1995	% Change	1994	% Change
Revenues (Million $)						
1Q	127.7	-4%	133.1	11%	120.1	8%
2Q	130.3	NM	130.9	9%	119.6	11%
3Q	—	—	165.8	3%	161.0	6%
4Q	—	—	178.5	NM	178.1	12%
Yr.	—	—	608.3	5%	578.8	9%
Income (Million $)						
1Q	-1.91	NM	0.18	NM	-1.37	NM
2Q	-0.36	NM	0.01	NM	-1.36	NM
3Q	—	—	4.06	-29%	5.72	-33%
4Q	—	—	-3.16	NM	-7.15	NM
Yr.	—	—	1.09	NM	-4.16	NM
Earnings Per Share ($)						
1Q	-0.09	NM	0.01	NM	-0.06	NM
2Q	-0.02	—	Nil	—	-0.06	NM
3Q	—	—	0.19	-30%	0.27	-33%
4Q	—	—	-0.16	NM	-0.35	NM
Yr.	—	—	0.05	NM	-0.20	NM

Next earnings report expected: mid November

Filene's Basement

Business Summary - 22-OCT-95

Filene's Basement Corp. is the holding company for Filene's Basement, Inc., a leading off-price specialty store chain offering focused assortments of fashionable, nationally recognized branded and private-label family apparel and accessories. Prices are typically 20% to 60% below those of traditional department stores. As of August 14, 1995, the company operated 50 stores, principally in the Northeast and Midwest, including the flagship store in Boston.

The Boston store operates under a unique marketing concept (the Automatic Markdown Plan) whereby merchandise on hand after 14 selling days is marked down 25% and an additional 25% for each of two successive seven-selling-day periods. Merchandise remaining after 35 days is given to charity. The company's 51 branch stores, which do not operate under the Plan but do take aggressive markdowns, have an average of about 21,900 sq. ft. of selling space. Stores open throughout 1994-95 averaged $9.6 million in sales volume and $438 in sales per sq. ft. of selling space outside the Boston area. The downtown Boston store generated more than $1,553 in sales per sq. ft. of selling space in 1994-95.

Filene's Basement is able to offer discounts because of its strategy of buying pre-season programmed merchandise, including overruns and end-of-season surpluses at advantageous prices. In addition, the company keeps cost of merchandise low because its vendors do not need to build into their pricing structure any anticipation of returns, markdown allowances or advertising allowances.

The company's branded offerings are complemented by "retail stocks"- family apparel and accessories purchased directly from major upscale retailers like Barney's, Bloomingdale's, Lord & Taylor and Neiman Marcus. Filene's Basement also has an assortment of private label products manufactured in the Far East.

Filene's seeks to open stores in existing markets where it can leverage advertising, purchasing, transportation and other regional expenses. The company opened two new stores in 1994-95--one in Manchester, Conn., and one in Fairfield, Va. Additionally, one underperforming store in Buffalo, N.Y., was closed, and three other stores were relocated.

Important Developments

Oct. '95—Total sales in the five weeks ended September 30, 1995, declined 2%, year to year; same-store sales slid 5%. Separately, Filene's reached an agreement in principle for a new $95 million secured loan facility, replacing an existing $50 million revolving credit agreement and a $35 million term loan agreement.

Capitalization

Long Term Debt: $38,878,000 (7/95), incl. lease obligs.

Per Share Data ($) (Year Ended Jan. 31)

	1995	1994	1993	1992	1991	1990
Tangible Bk. Val.	4.40	4.36	4.42	3.53	1.61	NA
Cash Flow	0.69	0.39	1.40	1.34	1.16	1.00
Earnings	0.05	-0.20	0.87	0.82	0.52	0.14
Dividends	Nil	Nil	Nil	Nil	Nil	Nil
Payout Ratio	Nil	Nil	Nil	Nil	Nil	Nil
Cal. Yrs.	1994	1993	1992	1991	1990	1989
Prices - High	11¾	20½	37	30	NA	NA
- Low	4½	6¾	11¾	14½	NA	NA
P/E Ratio - High	NM	NM	43	37	NA	NA
- Low	NM	NM	14	18	NA	NA

Income Statement Analysis (Million $)

	1995	%Chg	1994	%Chg	1993	%Chg	1992
Revs.	608	5%	579	9%	529	14%	465
Oper. Inc.	19.1	-23%	24.7	-46%	45.4	5%	43.2
Depr.	13.4	8%	12.4	8%	11.5	12%	10.3
Int. Exp.	4.1	5%	3.9	NM	3.9	-42%	6.7
Pretax Inc.	2.1	NM	-5.5	NM	30.4	12%	27.1
Eff. Tax Rate	47%	—	NM	—	39%	—	40%
Net Inc.	1.1	NM	-4.2	NM	18.7	15%	16.3

Balance Sheet & Other Fin. Data (Million $)

	1995	1994	1993	1992	1991	1990
Cash	4.6	0.3	4.5	7.6	5.5	1.7
Curr. Assets	142	141	133	120	84.0	66.0
Total Assets	239	237	216	189	148	132
Curr. Liab.	83.9	87.9	75.0	64.3	57.1	49.1
LT Debt	39.1	25.7	25.9	30.9	77.0	82.0
Common Eqty.	112	113	115	94.0	14.0	1.0
Total Cap.	151	138	141	124	91.0	83.0
Cap. Exp.	NA	22.9	21.3	14.3	7.6	4.8
Cash Flow	14.5	8.3	30.1	26.4	19.2	16.7

Ratio Analysis

	1995	1994	1993	1992	1991	1990
Curr. Ratio	1.7	1.6	1.8	1.9	1.5	1.3
% LT Debt of Cap.	25.9	18.6	18.4	24.9	85.7	98.8
% Net Inc.of Revs.	0.2	NM	3.5	3.5	2.3	0.8
% Ret. on Assets	0.5	NM	9.2	NM	6.5	2.2
% Ret. on Equity	1.0	NM	17.8	NM	31.5	NM

Dividend Data —No cash has been paid. Filene's intends to retain earnings for use in its business.

Data as orig. reptd.; bef. results of disc. opers. and/or spec. items. Per share data adj. for stk. divs. as of ex-div. date. E-Estimated. NA-Not Available. NM-Not Meaningful. NR-Not Ranked.

Office—40 Walnut St., Wellesley, MA 02181. **Tel**—(617) 348-7000. **Chrmn & CEO**—S. J. Gerson. **Pres, COO & Treas**—M. Anathan III. **SVP & CFO**—G. L. Crittenden. **Dirs**—M. Anathan III, J. Eyler, S. J. Gerson, W. W. Helman IV, R. P. Henderson, H. Leppo, P. D. Paganucci. **Transfer Agent & Registrar**—State Street Bank & Trust Co., Boston. **Incorporated** in Massachusetts in 1988. **Empl**-3,000. **S&P Analyst:** Maureen C. Carini

FileNet Corp.

NASDAQ Symbol **FILE**
In S&P SmallCap 600

06-NOV-95 **Industry:** Data Processing

Summary: This company specializes in imaging and business process automation solutions that electronically capture, store, retrieve, transmit and manage document images, data and text.

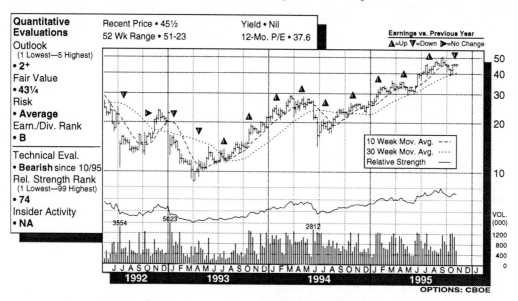

Quantitative Evaluations
Outlook
(1 Lowest—5 Highest)
• 2+
Fair Value
• 43¼
Risk
• Average
Earn./Div. Rank
• B

Technical Eval.
• Bearish since 10/95
Rel. Strength Rank
(1 Lowest—99 Highest)
• 74
Insider Activity
• NA

Recent Price • 45½
52 Wk Range • 51-23
Yield • Nil
12-Mo. P/E • 37.6

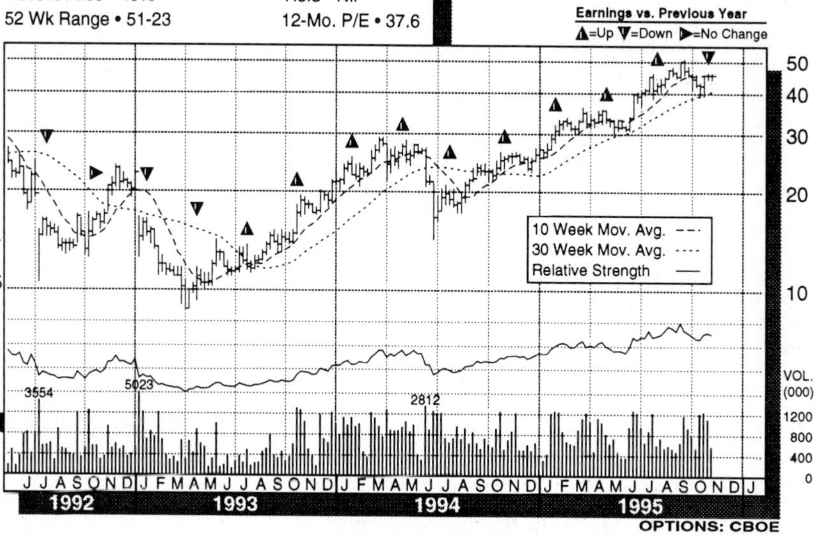

OPTIONS: CBOE

Business Profile - 06-NOV-95

FileNet provides imaging and business process automation solutions for paper-intensive organizations. The company has been changing its strategic focus to software and services from hardware; the higher margins resulting from such a change led to record results in 1994. FileNet's plans for 1995 include expanding its direct sales force in North America, Europe and Australia, penetrating new market segments, and selling its products through new distribution partners.

Operational Review - 06-NOV-95

Total revenues rose 22% in the first nine months of 1995, reflecting a 58% increase in software revenue and a 9% increase in service revenue, partially offset by an 8% decrease in hardware revenue. Gross margins widened as a result of a more favorable product mix, but results were penalized by an aftertax charge of $5 million related to the August 1995 acquisition of Watermark Software, Inc. Net income fell 20% to $6,500,000 ($0.47 a share) from $8,100,000 ($0.63).

Stock Performance - 03-NOV-95

In the past 30 trading days, FILE's shares have declined 0.27%, compared to a 2% rise in the S&P 500. Average trading volume for the past five days was 113,420 shares, compared with the 40-day moving average of 198,050 shares.

Key Stock Statistics

Dividend Rate/Share	Nil	Shareholders	700
Shs. outstg. (M)	12.9	Market cap. (B)	$0.585
Avg. daily vol. (M)	0.227	Inst. holdings	59%
Tang. Bk. Value/Share	10.36	Insider holdings	NA
Beta	1.94		

Value of $10,000 invested 5 years ago: $ 41,363

Fiscal Year Ending Dec. 31

	1995	% Change	1994	% Change	1993	% Change
Revenues (Million $)						
1Q	46.62	20%	38.75	12%	34.70	NM
2Q	53.81	20%	44.90	17%	38.26	11%
3Q	53.50	26%	42.59	7%	39.96	8%
4Q	—	—	53.45	17%	45.85	44%
Yr.	—	—	179.7	13%	158.8	15%
Income (Million $)						
1Q	3.95	66%	2.38	NM	0.24	-88%
2Q	4.72	15%	4.12	NM	1.33	122%
3Q	0.30	-92%	3.87	75%	2.21	101%
4Q	—	—	5.69	43%	3.99	NM
Yr.	—	—	16.06	107%	7.77	NM
Earnings Per Share ($)						
1Q	0.33	65%	0.20	NM	0.02	-89%
2Q	0.38	9%	0.35	192%	0.12	140%
3Q	0.02	-94%	0.34	70%	0.20	100%
4Q	—	—	0.48	37%	0.35	NM
Yr.	—	—	1.37	93%	0.71	NM

Next earnings report expected: early February

FileNet Corp.

Business Summary - 01-NOV-95

FileNet Corporation develops, markets and services document image processing systems and WorkFlo computer systems designed to improve the productivity and customer service capabilities of organizations that process, file and retrieve substantial volumes of paper documents.

FileNet's family of systems provides a number of advantages over traditional document processing methods, including rapid access to any single document image contained in a multimillion-page filing system, the ability to simultaneously view and process document images, data and text at the same workstation, and concurrent access by multiple users to the same files. The company's WorkFlo software offers further productivity benefits by allowing users to develop applications programs that automate their particular document processing procedures, and enables the FileNet system to be easily customized to address a wide variety of document processing applications.

The company's software products are used in a client/server environment. The Image Management Services (IMS) software is used to organize, store, and access multiple types of information such as document images, data, text, graphics, voice and photographs. IMS software supports the IBM AIX/6000, Hewlett-Packard HP-UX, and Sun Microsystems Solaris Unix operating systems. The company's proprietary WorkFlo application development software enables the user to develop business process automation programs. Revise software is used for revision and redlining in document management, while the company's Computer Output to Laser Disk (COLD) reads computer output from magnetic tape or disk files generated on another computer system, and stores the information on optical disks. The company also offers hardware in its Series 6000 product line. These products run on standard hardware utilizing IBM's RISC technology, and consist mainly of servers and optical storage and retreival units.

The company's systems are used for a variety of applications, including mortgage loan servicing, credit card customer service, insurance claims processing, retirement account management, technical document management and change control, and the management of personnel and other records.

Important Developments

Aug. '95—FILE completed its acquisition of Watermark Software Inc., a leading supplier of client/server-based workflow and document-imaging software for production-level applications, for 1.42 million shares of FILE common stock, valued at about $64 million, in exchange for all of the privately held stock and options of Watermark. FILE incurred a $5.0 million after-tax charge, in 1995's third quarter, related to the acquisition.

Capitalization

Long Term Debt: None (7/95).

Per Share Data ($) (Year Ended Dec. 31)

	1994	1993	1992	1991	1990	1989
Tangible Bk. Val.	9.42	7.71	6.87	7.59	6.77	6.43
Cash Flow	2.07	1.31	-0.14	1.29	1.00	0.75
Earnings	1.37	0.71	-0.76	0.75	0.37	0.29
Dividends	Nil	Nil	Nil	Nil	Nil	Nil
Payout Ratio	Nil	Nil	Nil	Nil	Nil	Nil
Prices - High	29¼	23	37½	25	21½	13¾
- Low	14¼	8¾	10½	6¾	5	7½
P/E Ratio - High	21	32	NM	33	58	47
- Low	10	12	NM	9	14	26

Income Statement Analysis (Million $)

	1994	%Chg	1993	%Chg	1992	%Chg	1991
Revs.	180	13%	159	15%	138	13%	122
Oper. Inc.	27.7	48%	18.7	197%	6.3	-64%	17.5
Depr.	8.1	23%	6.6	2%	6.5	12%	5.8
Int. Exp.	0.1	-73%	0.4	-36%	0.6	32%	0.4
Pretax Inc.	21.4	71%	12.5	NM	-9.8	NM	12.5
Eff. Tax Rate	25%	—	38%	—	NM	—	35%
Net Inc.	16.1	107%	7.8	NM	-8.0	NM	8.1

Balance Sheet & Other Fin. Data (Million $)

	1994	1993	1992	1991	1990	1989
Cash	41.0	43.5	29.3	32.8	22.3	19.7
Curr. Assets	95.1	96.3	77.2	76.3	66.7	62.5
Total Assets	142	123	102	104	91.0	82.0
Curr. Liab.	34.7	37.6	28.9	23.6	22.8	18.6
LT Debt	Nil	0.2	0.1	0.2	0.3	0.6
Common Eqty.	104	82.8	72.7	78.2	67.5	63.1
Total Cap.	107	85.1	73.5	80.2	67.8	63.7
Cap. Exp.	10.7	6.7	10.6	6.3	8.2	7.5
Cash Flow	24.2	14.4	-1.5	13.9	10.3	7.7

Ratio Analysis

	1994	1993	1992	1991	1990	1989
Curr. Ratio	2.7	2.6	2.7	3.2	2.9	3.4
% LT Debt of Cap.	Nil	0.2	0.1	0.3	0.4	0.9
% Net Inc.of Revs.	8.9	4.9	NM	6.6	3.7	3.6
% Ret. on Assets	12.0	6.9	NM	8.2	4.3	3.9
% Ret. on Equity	16.9	9.9	NM	11.0	5.7	4.8

Dividend Data —The company has never paid a dividend on its common stock and does not expect to pay any cash dividends in the foreseeable future. A "poison pill" stock purchase rights plan was adopted in 1988.

Data as orig. reptd.; bef. results of disc. opers. and/or spec. items. Per share data adj. for stk. divs. as of ex-div. date. E-Estimated. NA-Not Available. NM-Not Meaningful. NR-Not Ranked.

Office—3565 Harbor Blvd., Costa Mesa, CA 92626. **Tel**—(714) 966-3400. **Chrmn, Pres, CEO**—T. J. Smith. **SVP-Fin, CFO & Investor Contact**—Mark S. St. Clare. **Dirs**—F. K. Fluegel, J. B. Jamieson, W. P. Lyons, J. C. Savage, T. J. Smith. **Transfer Agent & Registrar**—First National Bank of Boston. **Incorporated** in California in 1982; reincorporated in Delaware in 1987. **Empl**-940. **S&P Analyst:** Ronald J. Gross

STANDARD & POOR'S

STOCK REPORTS

First American Financial

NYSE Symbol **FAF**
In S&P SmallCap 600

05-OCT-95 **Industry:** Insurance

Summary: Through subsidiaries, this California-based holding company provides real estate financial services, including title insurance, home warranty, tax monitoring, and trust services.

Quantitative Evaluations

Outlook (1 Lowest—5 Highest)
• **3+**
Fair Value
• **24**
Risk
• **Average**
Earn./Div. Rank
• **B**

Technical Eval.
• **Bullish** since 5/95
Rel. Strength Rank (1 Lowest—99 Highest)
• **33**
Insider Activity
• **NA**

Recent Price • 24⅛
52 Wk Range • 25½-16
Yield • 2.6%
12-Mo. P/E • NM

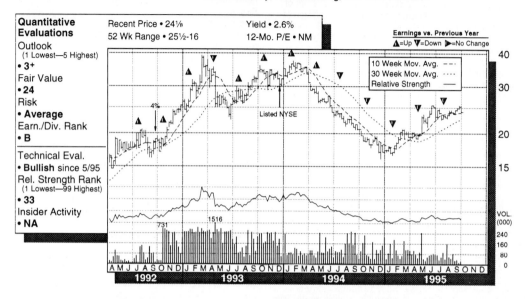

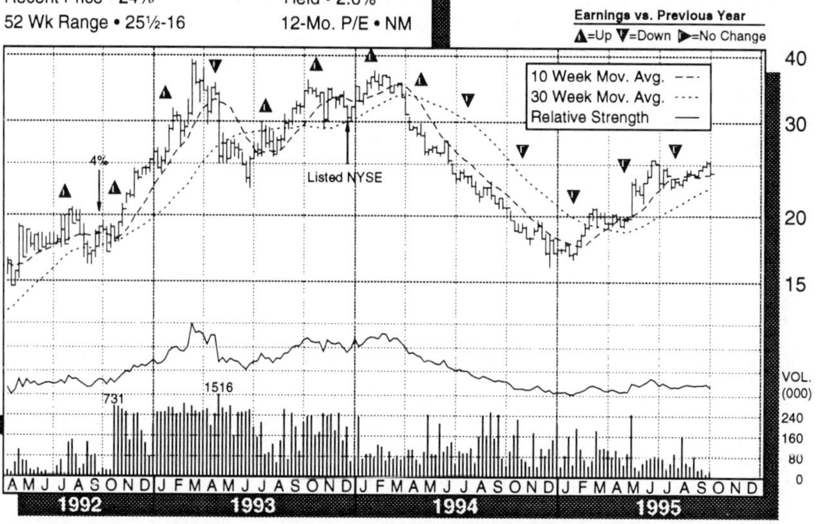

Business Profile - 28-SEP-95

Investors recently bid up the shares of First American Financial to a 52-week high, due to a decline in mortgage interest rates. Despite the agonizingly slow recovery in the California economy, FAF began to see an improvement in its title insurance business in the second quarter of 1995. In early 1995, the real estate information services subsidiary made two acquisitions that will allow the company to provide a full line of real estate-related financial services to the mortgage industry.

Operational Review - 28-SEP-95

Revenues for the six months ended June 30, 1995, fell 25%, year to year, primarily reflecting lower operating revenues due to increased mortgage interest rates. Total expenses and premium taxes dropped 19% and 26%, respectively, and a pretax loss of $19,672,000 contrasted with income of $29,932,000. After an income tax benefit of $8,100,000, versus taxes at 43.1%, the net loss was $11,572,000 ($1.01 a share), against income of $17,032,000 ($1.49).

Stock Performance - 29-SEP-95

In the past 30 trading days, FAF's shares were unchanged, compared to a 5% rise in the S&P 500. Average trading volume for the past five days was 4,020 shares, compared with the 40-day moving average of 10,951 shares.

Key Stock Statistics

Dividend Rate/Share	0.60	Shareholders	3,300
Shs. outstg. (M)	11.4	Market cap. (B)	$0.265
Avg. daily vol. (M)	0.005	Inst. holdings	56%
Tang. Bk. Value/Share	18.86	Insider holdings	NA
Beta	0.89		

Value of $10,000 invested 5 years ago: $ 23,853

Fiscal Year Ending Dec. 31

	1995	% Change	1994	% Change	1993	% Change
Revenues (Million $)						
1Q	261.1	-30%	372.4	34%	279.0	22%
2Q	293.2	-21%	369.0	11%	333.5	19%
3Q	—	—	334.9	-11%	376.8	35%
4Q	—	—	300.1	-27%	409.1	26%
Yr.	—	—	1,376	-2%	1,398	25%
Income (Million $)						
1Q	-12.71	NM	9.40	110%	4.48	-28%
2Q	1.14	-85%	7.63	-56%	17.52	31%
3Q	—	—	4.79	-76%	19.58	73%
4Q	—	—	-2.88	NM	20.51	67%
Yr.	—	—	18.95	-69%	62.09	44%
Earnings Per Share ($)						
1Q	-1.11	NM	0.82	105%	0.40	-43%
2Q	0.10	-85%	0.67	-57%	1.55	3%
3Q	—	—	0.42	-76%	1.72	38%
4Q	—	—	-0.25	NM	1.80	64%
Yr.	—	—	1.66	-70%	5.47	20%

Next earnings report expected: late October

First American Financial

Business Summary - 28-SEP-95

The First American Financial Corporation conducts title insurance and related operations through First American Title Insurance Co. and its affiliates. Business is conducted in all states (except Iowa), the District of Columbia, Puerto Rico, Guam, Mexico, the Virgin Islands, the Bahamas, Canada and the U.K. Based on American Land Title Association statistics, FAF's national title insurance market share rose to 19.5% in 1994, from 19.2% in 1993. The company has the largest or second largest market share in title insurance in each of 33 states and in the District of Columbia.

Pretax profit contributions by segment in 1994 were:

Title insurance	58%
Real estate information	27%
Home warranty	10%
Trust & banking	5%

The title insurance business involves the issuance of policies that guarantee ownership of real property and provide protection from liens, encumbrances and other title defects not specified in the contract. The company markets its title insurance services through a salesforce of about 1,000 people. In 1994, 46% of title insurance revenues were generated from the company's direct sales operations. The company emphasizes direct sales, as opposed to agency operations, to be able to control operations more easily, realize greater profits and reduce title claims risk.

With the acquisition of TRTS Data Services, Inc., in 1991, FAF believes that its First American Real Estate Information Services, Inc. subsidiary is the second largest provider of tax monitoring services in the U.S. In general, providers of tax monitoring services indemnify mortgage lenders against losses stemming from a failure to monitor delinquent taxes. During 1994, the company acquired all of its minority interests in Metropolitan Credit Reporting Services, Inc. and Metropolitan Property Reporting Services, Inc., a provider of credit information reports for mortgage lenders.

The company also conducts a general trust business, as well as banking, records management and home warranty services.

Important Developments

Sep. '95—First American Financial Corp. announced that it has purchased the property inspection and preservation operations of Lomas Field Services, Inc., from Lomas Mortgage USA. The newly formed company, First American Field Services, will operate as a subsidiary of First American Real Estate Information Services, Inc.

Capitalization

Notes & Contracts Payable: $87,381,000 (6/95).
Minority Interest: $21,811,000.

Per Share Data ($) (Year Ended Dec. 31)

	1994	1993	1992	1991	1990	1989
Tangible Bk. Val.	20.25	20.21	14.38	9.31	12.30	12.33
Oper. Earnings	1.69	5.43	NA	NA	NA	NA
Earnings	1.66	5.47	4.55	0.32	0.33	1.30
Dividends	0.60	0.51	0.41	0.39	0.39	0.35
Payout Ratio	36%	9%	9%	120%	117%	27%
Prices - High	37½	39¼	26¾	12¾	14¼	16⅞
- Low	16	22½	11¾	6¼	6½	11⅛
P/E Ratio - High	23	7	6	40	43	13
- Low	10	4	3	20	20	9

Income Statement Analysis (Million $)

	1994	%Chg	1993	%Chg	1992	%Chg	1991
Premium Income	1,222	-2%	1,249	25%	998	35%	738
Net Invest. Inc.	19.4	-3%	19.9	52%	13.1	-32%	19.2
Oth. Revs.	135	5%	129	NM	0.1	—	Nil
Total Revs.	1,376	-2%	1,398	25%	1,115	47%	757
Pretax Inc.	32.0	-69%	104	45%	71.5	NM	6.1
Net Oper. Inc.	19.3	-69%	61.8	—	NA	—	NA
Net Inc.	18.9	-70%	62.1	43%	43.3	NM	3.0

Balance Sheet & Other Fin. Data (Million $)

	1994	1993	1992	1991	1990	1989
Cash & Equiv.	154	130	120	77.4	67.2	72.8
Premiums Due	47.1	64.6	48.2	38.5	27.1	35.8
Inv Assets Bonds	149	166	138	68.1	81.6	72.8
Inv. Assets Stock	21.8	21.1	7.6	2.7	8.0	10.1
Inv. Assets Loans	40.5	33.3	30.8	26.8	15.0	NA
Inv. Assets Total	255	262	219	136	138	144
Deferred Policy Cost	26.6	23.5	18.4	Nil	Nil	Nil
Total Assets	829	786	691	520	465	451
Debt	89.6	85.0	82.0	93.0	102	97.0
Common Eqty.	292	284	217	138	146	147

Ratio Analysis

	1994	1993	1992	1991	1990	1989
Prop&Cas Loss	9.0	10.1	9.8	10.3	11.3	9.4
Prop&Cas Expense	99.7	92.2	93.4	90.2	91.1	89.0
Prop&Cas Comb.	108.7	102.3	103.2	100.5	102.4	98.4
% Ret. on Revs.	1.4	4.4	3.9	0.4	0.5	1.9
% Return on Equity	6.6	24.8	24.4	2.1	2.3	9.7

Dividend Data —Cash has been paid each year since 1909.

Amt. of Div. $	Date Decl.	Ex-Div. Date	Stock of Record	Payment Date
0.150	Aug. 29	Sep. 26	Sep. 30	Oct. 14 '94
0.150	Dec. 08	Dec. 23	Dec. 30	Jan. 13 '95
0.150	Feb. 23	Mar. 27	Mar. 31	Apr. 14 '95
0.150	Jun. 22	Jun. 30	Jul. 05	Jul. 14 '95
0.150	Aug. 28	Sep. 27	Sep. 29	Oct. 13 '95

Data as orig. reptd.; bef. results of disc. opers. and/or spec. items. Per share data adj. for stk. divs. as of ex-div. date. E-Estimated. NA-Not Available. NM-Not Meaningful. NR-Not Ranked.

Office—114 East 5th St., Santa Ana, CA 92701-4642. **Tel**—(714) 558-3211. **Chrmn**—D. P. Kennedy. **Pres**—P. S. Kennedy. **VP, CFO & Investor Contact**—Thomas A. Klemens. **VP & Secy**—M. R. Arnesen. **Dirs**—G. L. Argyros, J. D. Chatham, W. G. Davis, J. L. Doti, L. W. Douglas Jr., P. B. Fay Jr., F. C. Harrington, D. P. Kennedy, P. S. Kennedy, R. B. McLain, A. R. Moiso, R. J. Munzer, F. E. O'Bryan, R. B. Payne, V. M. Ueberroth. **Transfer Agent & Registrar**—First American Trust Co., Santa Ana. **Incorporated** in California in 1894. **Empl**-9,033. **S&P Analyst:** Brad Ohlmuller

STANDARD & POOR'S

STOCK REPORTS

First Commercial Corp.

NASDAQ Symbol **FCLR**
In S&P SmallCap 600

30-OCT-95 **Industry:** Banking

Summary: This multi-bank holding company owns 12 banks in Arkansas, including the largest in the state, eight banks in Texas, one in Tennessee and a 50% interest in an Oklahoma bank.

Quantitative Evaluations

Outlook (1 Lowest—5 Highest) • **3-**

Fair Value • **29¼**

Risk • **Low**

Earn./Div. Rank • **A**

Technical Eval. • **Bullish** since 12/94

Rel. Strength Rank (1 Lowest—99 Highest) • **85**

Insider Activity • **Neutral**

Recent Price • 29½ | Yield • 2.7%

52 Wk Range • 30⅝-19½ | 12-Mo. P/E • 13.2

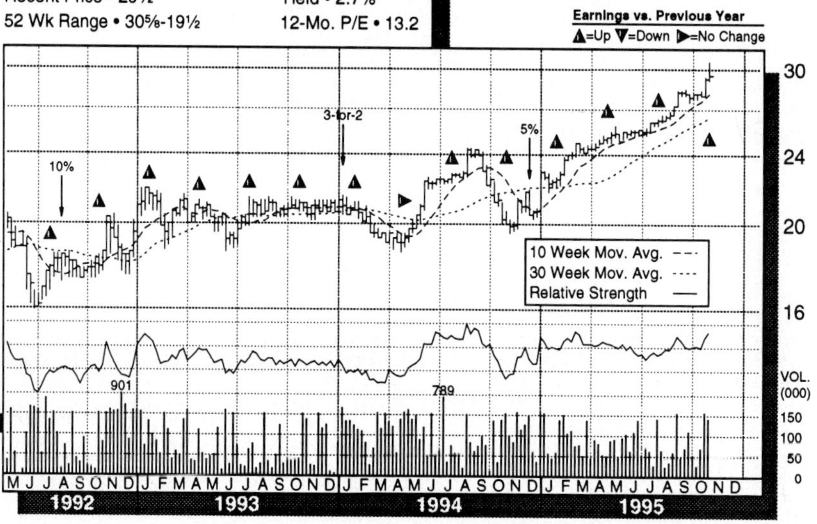

Business Profile - 30-OCT-95

Over the past two years this super community banking company has grown considerably through a number of acquisitions, adding 12 banks and approximately $1.8 billion in assets. First Commercial plans to continue to expand in its existing markets and enter additional markets by adding new affiliates. Investments in technology, made in 1994, are expected to be implemented throughout 1995, increasing efficiency, speed and customer service at the company's affiliate banks.

Operational Review - 30-OCT-95

Net interest income for the nine months ended September 30, 1995, rose 12%, year to year, primarily due to the 1994 third quarter acquisitions of banks in Palestine and Kilgore, TX. The loan loss provision increased 49%, to $1,565,000, from $1,049,000. Following a 6.2% decline in noninterest income and 4.5% higher noninterest expense, pretax income advanced 8.8%. After taxes at 34.0%, versus 32.9%, net income was up 7.0%, to $40,021,000 ($1.68 a share), from $37,391,000 ($1.55).

Stock Performance - 27-OCT-95

In the past 30 trading days, FCLR's shares have increased 5%, compared to a 0.63% fall in the S&P 500. Average trading volume for the past five days was 28,240 shares, compared with the 40-day moving average of 18,697 shares.

Key Stock Statistics

Dividend Rate/Share	0.80	Shareholders	3,300
Shs. outstg. (M)	23.7	Market cap. (B)	$0.700
Avg. daily vol. (M)	0.023	Inst. holdings	21%
Tang. Bk. Value/Share	15.38	Insider holdings	NA
Beta	0.80		

Value of $10,000 invested 5 years ago: $ 32,989

Fiscal Year Ending Dec. 31

	1995	% Change	1994	% Change	1993	% Change
Revenues (Million $)						
1Q	86.39	10%	78.35	42%	54.99	-6%
2Q	91.54	15%	79.63	34%	59.62	3%
3Q	96.44	18%	81.87	36%	59.98	7%
4Q	—	—	86.55	38%	62.77	17%
Yr.	—	—	326.4	38%	237.4	4%
Income (Million $)						
1Q	12.33	3%	11.97	29%	9.26	17%
2Q	13.36	5%	12.71	40%	9.10	10%
3Q	14.33	13%	12.72	35%	9.45	10%
4Q	—	—	12.92	33%	9.68	13%
Yr.	—	—	50.31	34%	37.49	12%
Earnings Per Share ($)						
1Q	0.52	5%	0.50	NM	0.50	16%
2Q	0.56	6%	0.53	11%	0.48	7%
3Q	0.60	13%	0.53	8%	0.50	8%
4Q	—	—	0.55	9%	0.50	9%
Yr.	—	—	2.10	7%	1.97	10%

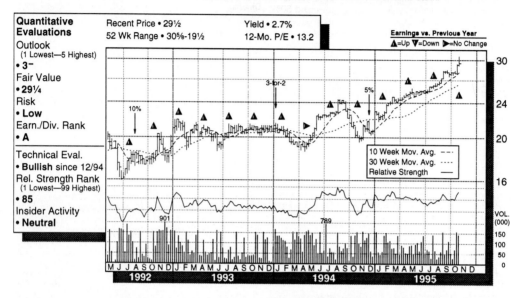

Next earnings report expected: mid January

First Commercial Corp.

Business Summary - 19-OCT-95

First Commercial Corporation is a multibank holding company headquartered in Little Rock, Ark. It owns 12 Arkansas banks, including First Commercial Bank, Little Rock (the largest bank in Arkansas). It also owns one bank in Tennessee, eight banks in Texas and 50% of Security National Bank & Trust Co. of Norman, Okla. In addition, the company provides mortgage financing and servicing and investment advisory and personal trust services through three affiliated companies.

Gross loans and leases outstanding totaled $2.58 billion at December 31, 1994, and were divided:

Commercial, financial & agricultural	19%
Real estate--construction	4%
Real estate--mortgage	48%
Consumer	27%
Direct lease financing	1%
Other	1%

The allowance for possible loan and lease losses at the end of 1994 was $45,325,000 ($48,080,000 a year earlier), or 1.79% (2.19%) of outstanding loans and leases. Net loans and leases charged off totaled $983,000 in 1994 ($3,161,000 in 1993), equal to 0.14% (0.54%) of average loans and leases outstanding. As of December 31, 1994, nonperforming loans amounted to $13,299,000 ($15,699,000 a year earlier), or 0.52% (0.72%) of total loans and leases outstanding, net of unearned income.

Deposits of $3.83 billion at 1994 year-end consisted of 20% noninterest-bearing transaction accounts, 40% interest-bearing transaction and savings accounts, 9% certificates of deposit of $100,000 or more and 31% other time deposits.

On a tax-equivalent basis, the average yield on interest-earning assets was 6.82% in 1994 (6.89% in 1993), while the average rate paid on interest-bearing liabilities was 3.18% (3.23%), for a net spread of 3.64% (3.66%).

Important Developments

Oct. '95—First Commercial Mortgage Company (FCMC), a wholly owned subsidiary of First Commercial Corp, completed its acquisition of servicing rights and other assets from the former National Home Mortgage Company. The transaction adds approximately $5 billion in loan servicing rights and brings FCMC's total servicing portfolio to over $7.5 billion and 128,000 loans.

Oct. '95—Total assets at September 30, 1995, were $4.6 billion, up 5% from a year ago. Total loans and leases increased 14%, to $2.8 billion, while total deposits remained unchanged at $3.9 billion.

Capitalization

Long Term Debt: $11,471,000 (9/95).

Per Share Data ($) (Year Ended Dec. 31)

	1994	1993	1992	1991	1990	1989
Tangible Bk. Val.	13.44	13.48	12.04	10.73	9.16	8.19
Earnings	2.10	1.97	1.79	1.59	1.36	1.18
Dividends	0.74	0.61	0.49	0.42	0.37	0.32
Payout Ratio	35%	31%	28%	26%	27%	27%
Prices - High	24⅜	21⅞	21	19⅝	10¾	11⅜
- Low	18⅝	18⅝	16	8½	8⅜	8⅜
P/E Ratio - High	12	11	12	12	8	10
- Low	9	9	9	5	6	7

Income Statement Analysis (Million $)

	1994	%Chg	1993	%Chg	1992	%Chg	1991
Net Int. Inc.	159	38%	115	9%	106	13%	93.3
Tax Equiv. Adj.	3.6	93%	1.9	-20%	2.4	-29%	3.3
Non Int. Inc.	68.5	29%	53.1	14%	46.5	13%	41.3
Loan Loss Prov.	3.1	-6%	3.3	-51%	6.6	-16%	7.9
% Exp/Op Revs.	68%	—	66%	—	63%	—	64%
Pretax Inc.	74.3	40%	53.2	10%	48.4	25%	38.8
Eff. Tax Rate	32%	—	30%	—	31%	—	28%
Net Inc.	50.3	34%	37.5	12%	33.4	20%	27.9
% Net Int. Marg.	4.30%	—	4.30%	—	4.60%	—	4.70%

Balance Sheet & Other Fin. Data (Million $)

	1994	1993	1992	1991	1990	1989
Earning Assets:						
Money Mkt.	72.0	126	40.5	80.0	71.1	86.3
Inv. Securities	1,309	1,147	823	856	565	385
Com'l Loans	519	337	264	274	302	384
Other Loans	2,062	1,469	1,206	1,150	964	594
Total Assets	4,374	3,401	2,619	2,615	2,122	1,583
Demand Deposits	768	644	504	472	353	371
Time Deposits	3,058	2,398	1,821	1,866	1,539	1,024
LT Debt	8.2	19.2	32.3	37.3	30.2	31.8
Common Eqty.	343	249	217	192	150	119

Ratio Analysis

	1994	1993	1992	1991	1990	1989
% Ret. on Assets	1.2	1.2	1.3	1.2	1.1	1.2
% Ret. on Equity	15.0	15.4	15.7	16.0	15.6	15.2
% Loan Loss Resv.	1.8	2.2	2.2	2.4	2.2	2.3
% Loans/Deposits	66.3	59.4	62.0	59.7	65.7	62.0
% Equity to Assets	7.8	7.8	7.9	7.2	7.1	7.6

Dividend Data —Cash has been paid since 1981. A dividend reinvestment plan allows shareholders to purchase additional common shares at 95% of market value.

Amt. of Div. $	Date Decl.	Ex-Div. Date	Stock of Record	Payment Date
5%	Nov. 15	Dec. 09	Dec. 15	Jan. 03 '95
0.200	Nov. 15	Dec. 12	Dec. 16	Jan. 03 '95
0.200	Feb. 22	Mar. 09	Mar. 15	Apr. 03 '95
0.200	May. 16	Jun. 13	Jun. 15	Jul. 03 '95
0.200	Aug. 15	Sep. 13	Sep. 15	Oct. 02 '95

Data as orig. reptd.; bef. results of disc opers. and/or spec. items. Per share data adj. for stk. divs. as of ex-div. date. E-Estimated. NA-Not Available. NM-Not Meaningful. NR-Not Ranked.

Office—400 W. Capitol Ave., Little Rock, AR 72201. **Tel**—(501) 371-7000. **Chrmn, Pres & CEO**—B. Grace. **Vice Chrmn**—J. R. Cobb. **CFO, Treas & Investor Contact**—J. Lynn Wright. **Secy**—D. B. Rogers. **Dirs**—J. W. Allison, T. Arnold, W. H. Bowen, P. Clark, J. R. Cobb, R. G. Cress, C. W. Cupp Jr., B. Grace, W. E. Hussman Jr., F. E. Joyce, J. G. Justus, W. M. Lemley, C. H. Murphy Jr., M. W. Murphy, W. C. Nolan Jr., S. C. Sowell, P. D. Tilley. **Transfer Agent & Registrar**—First Commercial Bank, Little Rock. **Incorporated** in Arkansas in 1980. **Empl**-2,525. **S&P Analyst:** Brad Ohlmuller

First Financial Corp. (Wis.)

NASDAQ Symbol **FFHC**
In S&P SmallCap 600

19-SEP-95 **Industry:** Banking

Summary: This thrift holding company owns First Financial Bank, FSB, which operates 129 banking offices throughout Wisconsin and Illinois.

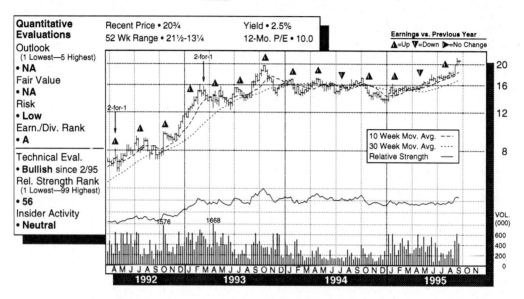

Quantitative Evaluations
Outlook (1 Lowest—5 Highest)
• **NA**
Fair Value
• **NA**
Risk
• **Low**
Earn./Div. Rank
• **A**
Technical Eval.
• **Bullish** since 2/95
Rel. Strength Rank (1 Lowest—99 Highest)
• **56**
Insider Activity
• **Neutral**

Recent Price • 20¾ Yield • 2.5%
52 Wk Range • 21½-13¼ 12-Mo. P/E • 10.0

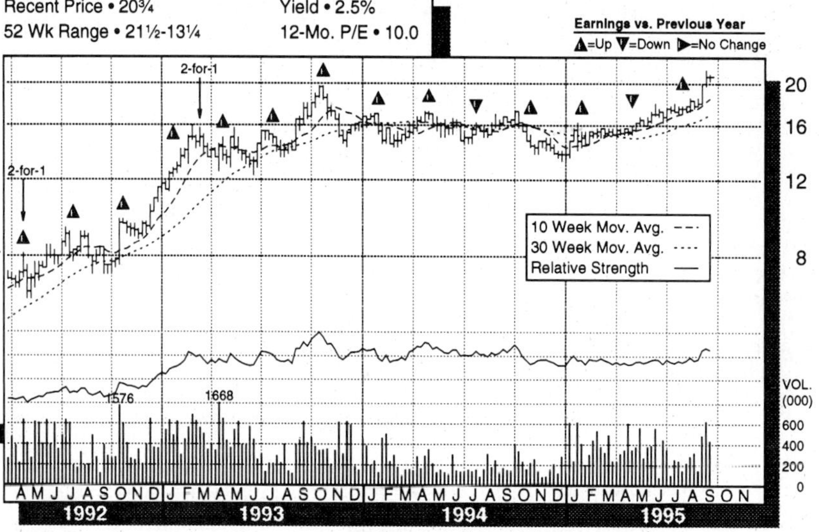

Business Profile - 12-SEP-95

This thrift holding company, with assets of approximately $5.5 billion, is the parent of First Financial Bank, Wisconsin's largest thrift institution. The February 1995 aquisition of FirstRock Bancorp, Inc., which had six offices and $376.5 million in assets, is expected to result in significant cost savings through the consolidation of duplicative back-office operations. With an efficiency ratio below 49% in 1995's second quarter, FFHC continues to have one of the best ratios in the industry.

Operational Review - 12-SEP-95

Net interest income in the six months ended June 30, 1995, rose 6.2%, year to year, as restated for the February 1995 acquisition of FirstRock Bancorp. The provision for loan losses climbed 25%, to $4,192,000, from $3,362,000. With 53% higher non-interest income and a 7.9% increase in non-interest expense, pretax income climbed 18%. After taxes at 36.4%, versus 38.0%, net income was up 22%, to $27,132,000 ($0.90 a share), from $22,230,000 ($0.74).

Stock Performance - 15-SEP-95

In the past 30 trading days, FFHC's shares have increased 17%, compared to a 4% rise in the S&P 500. Average trading volume for the past five days was 86,060 shares, compared with the 40-day moving average of 73,521 shares.

Key Stock Statistics

Dividend Rate/Share	0.48	Shareholders	4,000
Shs. outstg. (M)	29.5	Market cap. (B)	$0.569
Avg. daily vol. (M)	0.101	Inst. holdings	35%
Tang. Bk. Value/Share	11.22	Insider holdings	NA
Beta	0.54		

Value of $10,000 invested 5 years ago: $ 61,414

Fiscal Year Ending Dec. 31

	1995	% Change	1994	% Change	1993	% Change
Revenues (Million $)						
1Q	113.1	21%	93.11	NM	93.05	18%
2Q	115.1	21%	95.27	1%	93.99	15%
3Q	—	—	97.79	3%	95.19	15%
4Q	—	—	101.5	6%	95.61	12%
Yr.	—	—	387.2	2%	377.8	15%
Income (Million $)						
1Q	10.83	-12%	12.28	29%	9.55	69%
2Q	16.31	117%	7.53	-33%	11.17	83%
3Q	—	—	13.75	21%	11.33	50%
4Q	—	—	14.77	12%	13.17	44%
Yr.	—	—	48.33	7%	45.22	59%
Earnings Per Share ($)						
1Q	0.36	-27%	0.49	22%	0.40	63%
2Q	0.54	80%	0.30	-36%	0.47	81%
3Q	—	—	0.54	12%	0.48	45%
4Q	—	—	0.58	7%	0.54	42%
Yr.	—	—	1.91	2%	1.88	55%

Next earnings report expected: mid October

First Financial Corp. (Wis.)

Business Summary - 12-SEP-95

First Financial Corporation (formerly First Financial S&L) is the holding company for First Financial Bank, FSB, Wisconsin's largest thrift institution. The First Financial-Port Savings Bank, SA unit was merged into First Financial Bank in October 1994. The southern Illinois market was entered through the 1990 acquisition of Illini Federal Savings and Loan Association of Fairview Heights, and NorthLand Bank of Wisconsin (assets of $127.4 million) was acquired in February 1994. First Financial currently has 130 locations throughout Wisconsin and southern Illinois.

Total loans receivable (before unearned discount and allowance for losses) of $3.28 billion at year-end 1994 and $2.90 billion at December 31, 1993, were divided:

	1994	1993
Real estate mortgage loans:		
Residential	62.3%	64.1%
Commercial and other	3.5%	3.2%
Construction	1.9%	2.0%
Credit card loans	6.1%	7.2%
Home equity loans	7.2%	6.7%
Education loans	5.8%	5.8%
Manufactured housing loans	4.7%	5.7%
Consumer loans	7.9%	5.3%
Business loans	0.6%	---

The allowance for loan losses totaled $22,457,000 (0.70% of loans outstanding) at the end of 1994, versus $23,226,000 (0.80%) a year earlier. Net charge-offs in 1994 amounted to $8,067,000 (0.26% of average loans outstanding), versus $8,905,000 (0.32%) in 1993. At December 31, 1994, nonperforming assets came to $29,721,000 (0.58% of total assets), versus $15,057,000 (0.32%) a year earlier.

Consolidated deposits at the end of 1994 were divided: passbook 18.1%, interest-bearing checking 7.1%, non-interest-bearing checking 2.7%, variable-rate insured money-market accounts 7.1%, certificates maturing in one year or less 8.0%, and long-term certificates 57.1%.

The average yield on interest earning assets was 7.46% in 1994 (7.70% in 1993), and the average rate paid on interest bearing liabilities was 4.13% (4.37%), resulting in a net interest spread of 3.33% (3.33%).

Important Developments

Jul. '95—FFHC reported that earnings for the first six months of 1995 (before acquisition-related charges) advanced 40%, to $31,161,000 ($1.04 a share), from $22,230,000 ($0.74) in the 1994 period. In connection with the February 1995 acquisition of FirstRock Bancorp, Inc., the company recorded a pretax charge of $6.5 million ($4 million, after taxes) in the 1995 period.

Capitalization

Borrowings: $520,606,000 (6/95).

Per Share Data ($) (Year Ended Dec. 31)

	1994	1993	1992	1991	1990	1989
Tangible Bk. Val.	10.13	8.62	7.34	6.26	5.47	5.74
Earnings	1.91	1.88	1.21	0.80	0.70	0.63
Dividends	0.40	0.35	0.22	0.16	0.16	0.16
Payout Ratio	21%	19%	18%	20%	23%	25%
Prices - High	17¼	19¾	11¾	5⅞	4¼	5⅛
- Low	13¼	11¼	5⅝	2¾	2$^{7}/_{16}$	3¼
P/E Ratio - High	9	11	10	7	6	8
- Low	7	6	5	3	3	5

Income Statement Analysis (Million $)

	1994	%Chg	1993	%Chg	1992	%Chg	1991
Net Int. Inc.	164	9%	150	30%	115	20%	96.0
Loan Loss Prov.	6.5	-36%	10.2	-27%	13.9	-24%	18.3
Non Int. Inc.	25.8	-32%	37.7	17%	32.2	-6%	34.3
Non Int. Exp.	107	NM	106	19%	88.7	9%	81.4
Pretax Inc.	76.1	6%	72.1	62%	44.6	44%	30.9
Eff. Tax Rate	37%	—	37%	—	36%	—	40%
Net Inc.	48.3	7%	45.2	59%	28.4	54%	18.5
% Net Int. Marg.	3.34%	—	3.36%	—	3.32%	—	3.28%

Balance Sheet & Other Fin. Data (Million $)

	1994	1993	1992	1991	1990	1989
Total Assets	5,104	4,775	3,908	3,220	3,142	2,457
Loans	3,225	2,923	2,211	1,991	2,169	1,989
Deposits	4,064	4,051	3,206	2,936	2,883	2,098
Capitalization:						
Debt	682	439	462	65.0	45.0	131
Equity	278	235	194	165	150	137
Total	960	673	656	230	195	268

Ratio Analysis

	1994	1993	1992	1991	1990	1989
% Ret. on Assets	1.0	1.0	0.8	0.6	0.5	0.6
% Ret. on Equity	18.6	21.2	15.8	11.9	11.2	10.8
% Loan Loss Resv.	0.7	0.8	0.8	0.8	NA	NA
% Risk Based Capital	13.5	12.3	11.7	NA	NA	NA
Price Times Book Value:						
High	1.7	2.3	1.6	0.9	0.8	0.8
Low	1.3	1.3	0.8	0.4	0.4	0.5

Dividend Data —Cash has been paid since 1981.

Amt. of Div. $	Date Decl.	Ex-Div. Date	Stock of Record	Payment Date
0.100	Aug. 18	Sep. 09	Sep. 15	Sep. 30 '94
0.100	Nov. 16	Dec. 09	Dec. 15	Dec. 31 '94
0.120	Feb. 15	Mar. 09	Mar. 15	Mar. 31 '95
0.120	May. 17	Jun. 13	Jun. 15	Jun. 30 '95
0.120	Aug. 16	Sep. 13	Sep. 15	Sep. 30 '95

Data as orig. reptd.; bef. results of disc opers. and/or spec. items. Per share data adj. for stk. divs. as of ex-div. date. E-Estimated. NA-Not Available. NM-Not Meaningful. NR-Not Ranked.

Offices—1305 Main St., Stevens Point, WI 54481. **Tel**—(715) 341-0400. **Chrmn**—R. S. Gaiswinkler . **Pres & CEO**—J. C. Seramur. **VP, Treas & CFO**—T. Neuschaefer. **Secy**—R. Salinger. **Investor Contact**—Ken Csinicsek. **Dirs**—R. S. Gaiswinkler, G. M. Haferbecker, J. O. Heinecke, R. T. Kehr, P. C. Kehrer, R. P. Konopacky, G. R. Leach, I. H. Robers, J. C. Seramur, J. H. Sproule, R. R. Staven, N. L. Wanta, A. G. West. **Transfer Agent & Registrar**—Norwest Bank-Minnesota, South St. Paul. **Chartered** in 1965 (First State in 1981). **Empl**-1,283. **S&P Analyst:** Brad Ohlmuller

STANDARD & POOR'S

First Michigan Bank Corp.

STOCK REPORTS

NASDAQ Symbol **FMBC**

In S&P SmallCap 600

28-SEP-95 **Industry:** Banking

Summary: FMBC is a $2.9 billion diversified financial services company with 14 affiliates and 83 offices throughout the state of Michigan.

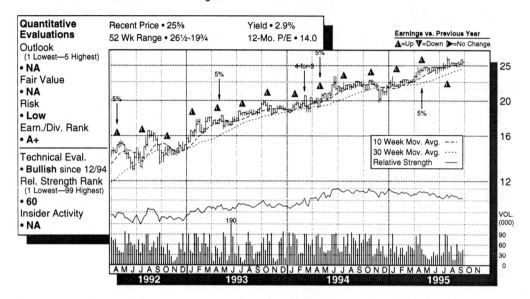

Quantitative Evaluations

Outlook (1 Lowest—5 Highest)
• **NA**

Fair Value
• **NA**

Risk
• **Low**

Earn./Div. Rank
• **A+**

Technical Eval.
• **Bullish** since 12/94

Rel. Strength Rank (1 Lowest—99 Highest)
• **60**

Insider Activity
• **NA**

Recent Price • 25⅝
52 Wk Range • 26½-19¾
Yield • 2.9%
12-Mo. P/E • 14.0

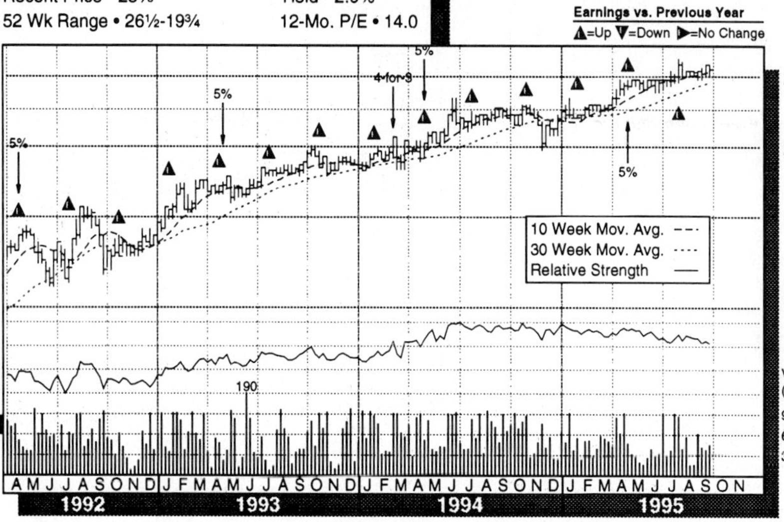

Business Profile - 28-SEP-95

FMBC has shown consistent earnings and dividend growth. Profitability indicators have been favorable, with ROA and ROE at 1.23% and 15.19%, respectively, in 1994. Capital adequacy ratios far exceeded regulatory minimums. Asset quality remains strong, but liquidity may be limited, with loans equal to 67% of total assets. A share repurchase program is continuing.

Operational Review - 28-SEP-95

Total income in the six months ended June 30, 1995, rose 25%, year to year, principally reflecting a 34% increase in interest and fees on loans. The provision for loan losses advanced 17%. Noninterest expenses were up 8.2%, driven by 9.3% higher salaries and employee benefits costs. After taxes at 24.8%, versus 23.0%, net income was up 8.6%, to $16,709,000 ($0.91 a share), from 15,387,000 ($0.83, as adjusted).

Stock Performance - 22-SEP-95

In the past 30 trading days, FMBC's shares have increased 0.49%, compared to a 5% rise in the S&P 500. Average trading volume for the past five days was 9,000 shares, compared with the 40-day moving average of 7,972 shares.

Key Stock Statistics

Dividend Rate/Share	0.76	Shareholders	5,000
Shs. outstg. (M)	18.2	Market cap. (B)	$0.472
Avg. daily vol. (M)	0.010	Inst. holdings	12%
Tang. Bk. Value/Share	12.79	Insider holdings	NA
Beta	0.26		

Value of $10,000 invested 5 years ago: $ 28,814

Fiscal Year Ending Dec. 31

	1995	% Change	1994	% Change	1993	% Change
Revenues (Million $)						
1Q	63.23	24%	50.95	14%	44.83	-4%
2Q	66.94	25%	53.53	15%	46.73	NM
3Q	—	—	54.83	15%	47.62	3%
4Q	—	—	57.36	20%	47.70	3%
Yr.	—	—	211.0	13%	186.9	NM
Income (Million $)						
1Q	8.10	9%	7.44	20%	6.19	11%
2Q	8.60	8%	7.95	15%	6.91	19%
3Q	—	—	8.20	16%	7.05	18%
4Q	—	—	8.27	15%	7.20	14%
Yr.	—	—	31.18	14%	27.35	15%
Earnings Per Share ($)						
1Q	0.44	10%	0.40	13%	0.35	11%
2Q	0.47	10%	0.43	7%	0.40	17%
3Q	—	—	0.46	15%	0.40	17%
4Q	—	—	0.47	12%	0.42	14%
Yr.	—	—	1.75	11%	1.57	15%

Next earnings report expected: mid October

First Michigan Bank Corp.

Business Summary - 28-SEP-95

FMBC owns 13 subsidiary community banks engaged in commercial and retail banking and one primarily engaged in trust services. The banks operate 83 branch offices throughout Michigan. The company has two non-bank subsidiaries, providing credit life, health and accident insurance to customers of the banks, and also offering brokerage services. The three largest subsidiary banks, FMB-First Michigan Bank, FMB-Lumberman's Bank and FMB-First Michigan Bank--Grand Rapids, accounted for 69% of consolidated total assets at year-end 1994. Since the end of 1987, FMBC has acquired FMB-Reed City Bank, FMB-Commercial Bank, FMB-Security Bank, FMB-Maynard Allen Bank, FMB-Trust, FMB-Northwestern Bank, FMB-Old State Bank and Superior Financial Corp.

Gross loans outstanding totaled $1.79 billion at December 31, 1994, and were divided:

	1994	1993
Commercial, financial & agricultural	28%	28%
Real estate--residential	25%	25%
Real estate--commercial	21%	21%
Consumer	20%	20%
Real estate--construction	6%	6%

The allowance for loan losses amounted to $22,564,000 at 1994 year-end (equal to 1.26% of gross loans outstanding), versus $19,484,000 (1.28%) a year earlier. Net chargeoffs during 1994 totaled $3,229,000 (0.20% of average loans), down from $3,373,000 (0.24%) in 1993. As of December 31, 1994, nonperforming assets (including real estate acquired through foreclosure) amounted to $10,322,000 (0.58% of total assets), compared with $11,354,000 (0.75%) a year earlier.

Average deposits of $2.17 billion in 1994 were apportioned: 49% time, 39% savings and NOW accounts, and 12% noninterest-bearing.

Interest and fees on loans provided 68% of total income for 1994, interest on investment securities 19%, service charges 5.5%, trust department income 2.5% and other noninterest income 5%.

On a tax-equivalent basis, the average yield on interest-earning assets was 8.12% in 1994 (7.93% in 1993), while the average rate paid on interest-bearing liabilities was 3.67% (3.63%), for a net spread of 4.45% (4.30%).

Important Developments

Jul. '95—In quarter ended June 30, loans grew 16% over those of the previous year, and credit quality remained high, with nonperforming assets at 0.50% of total loans outstanding.

Capitalization

Long Term Debt: $6,609,000 (6/95).

Per Share Data ($)

(Year Ended Dec. 31)

	1994	1993	1992	1991	1990	1989
Tangible Bk. Val.	11.98	11.21	10.14	9.15	8.22	7.41
Earnings	1.75	1.57	1.37	1.20	1.13	1.05
Dividends	0.67	0.49	0.40	0.37	0.33	0.29
Payout Ratio	38%	31%	29%	31%	29%	28%
Prices - High	23 3/8	20 1/8	16 1/2	12 5/8	10 1/2	11
- Low	18 1/2	15 1/4	10 3/4	8 1/8	6 1/2	8
P/E Ratio - High	13	13	12	11	9	11
- Low	11	10	8	7	6	8

Income Statement Analysis (Million $)

	1994	%Chg	1993	%Chg	1992	%Chg	1991
Net Int. Inc.	108	18%	91.6	6%	86.3	13%	76.4
Tax Equiv. Adj.	7.2	4%	6.9	9%	6.3	8%	5.9
Non Int. Inc.	27.6	-6%	29.4	15%	25.6	34%	19.1
Loan Loss Prov.	6.3	26%	5.0	-19%	6.2	14%	5.4
% Exp/Op Revs.	62%	—	63%	—	64%	—	65%
Pretax Inc.	41.0	16%	35.4	18%	29.9	21%	24.8
Eff. Tax Rate	24%	—	23%	—	21%	—	19%
Net Inc.	31.2	14%	27.3	15%	23.7	19%	20.0
% Net Int. Marg.	4.91%	—	4.80%	—	4.80%	—	4.70%

Balance Sheet & Other Fin. Data (Million $)

	1994	1993	1992	1991	1990	1989
Earning Assets:						
Money Mkt.	4.3	12.3	38.3	15.9	42.9	37.5
Inv. Securities	684	677	623	566	451	380
Com'l Loans	503	411	401	503	451	398
Other Loans	1,289	1,071	914	732	677	620
Total Assets	2,689	2,327	2,161	1,966	1,748	1,558
Demand Deposits	289	231	234	188	176	172
Time Deposits	1,995	1,764	1,619	1,505	1,330	1,164
LT Debt	4.9	7.0	7.7	9.0	5.1	5.9
Common Eqty.	209	192	175	156	131	114

Ratio Analysis

	1994	1993	1992	1991	1990	1989
% Ret. on Assets	1.2	1.2	1.2	1.1	1.1	1.1
% Ret. on Equity	15.2	14.9	14.2	13.8	14.5	15.0
% Loan Loss Resv.	1.3	1.3	1.3	1.3	1.3	1.3
% Loans/Deposits	78.4	74.3	70.9	72.8	74.9	76.3
% Equity to Assets	8.1	8.2	8.1	7.8	7.5	7.3

Dividend Data —Cash has been paid each year since 1977. A dividend reinvestment and stock purchase plan is available.

Amt. of Div. $	Date Decl.	Ex-Div. Date	Stock of Record	Payment Date
0.190	Dec. 08	Dec. 23	Dec. 30	Jan. 27 '95
0.190	Mar. 09	Mar. 27	Mar. 31	Apr. 28 '95
5%	Mar. 09	Apr. 24	Apr. 28	May. 31 '95
0.190	Jun. 08	Jun. 28	Jun. 30	Jul. 28 '95
0.190	Aug. 10	Sep. 27	Sep. 29	Oct. 27 '95

Data as orig. reptd.; bef. results of disc opers. and/or spec. items. Per share data adj. for stk. divs. as of ex-div. date. E-Estimated. NA-Not Available. NM-Not Meaningful. NR-Not Ranked.

Office—One Financial Plaza, 10717 Adams Street, Holland, MI 49423. **Tel**—(616) 396-9200. **Chrmn & CEO**—D. M. Ondersma. **Pres, COO & Secy**—S. A. Stream. **EVP, CFO & Investor Contact**—Larry D. Fredricks (616-396-9389). **Dirs**—R. A. Andersen, J. H. Bloem, D. M. Cassard, D. A. Hayes, R. J. Kapenga, M. B. Leeke, D. W. Maine, J. H. Miller, D. M. Ondersma, M. J. Prins, J. W. Spoelhof, S. A. Stream. **Transfer Agent & Registrar**—FMB Shareholder Services. **Incorporated** in Michigan in 1973. **Empl**-1,700. **S&P Analyst:** Thomas C. Ferguson

First Mississippi

NYSE Symbol **FRM**
In S&P 500

07-OCT-95

Industry:
Chemicals

Summary: This company has interests in industrial and specialty chemicals, nitrogen fertilizer, and technology-based ventures. FRM plans to spin off 81%-owned FirstMiss Gold.

S&P Opinion: Accumulate (★★★★)

Recent Price • 37½
52 Wk Range • 40⅛-19½
Yield • 1.1%
12-Mo. P/E • 13.4

Quantitative Evaluations

Outlook
(1 Lowest—5 Highest)
• **2+**
Fair Value
• **38¼**
Risk
• **Average**
Earn./Div. Rank
• **B**

Technical Eval.
• **Bullish** since 8/94
Rel. Strength Rank
(1 Lowest—99 Highest)
• **83**
Insider Activity
• **Unfavorable**

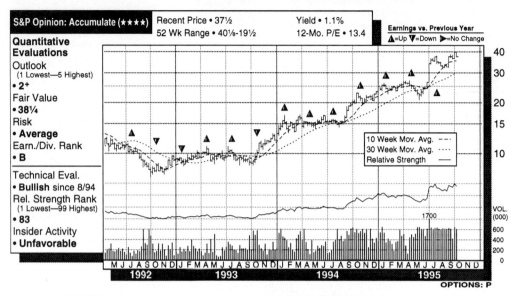

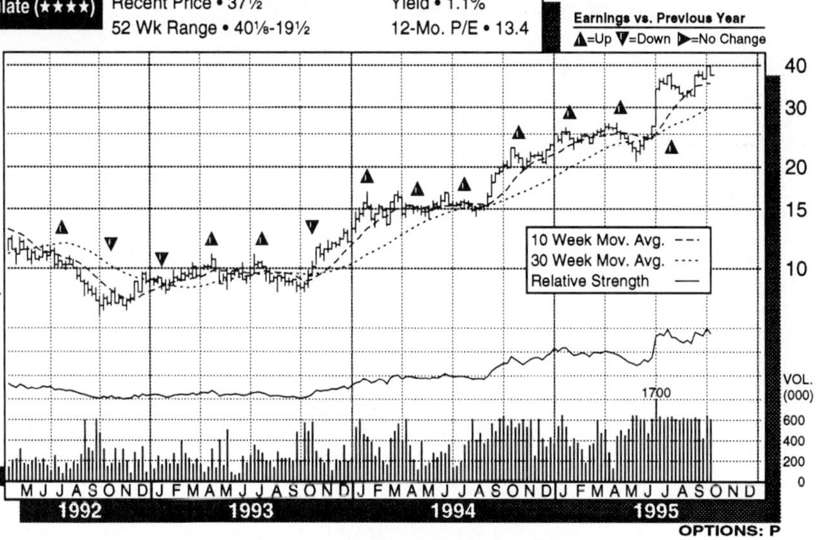

Overview - 06-OCT-95

We see chemical profits in fiscal 1996 continuing to advance on growing contributions from specialties and custom manufacturing, while aniline will be helped by a recent capacity expansion and expected pickups in the housing and durable goods markets. Fertilizer profits should remain very strong with prices remaining at current high levels and favorable feedstock costs. The combustion and plasma segment may turn profitable, reflecting a high order backlog and lower development costs. Results at 81%-owned FirstMiss Gold should improve as output from the new high-grade underground mine reaches 1,200 tons per day by January 1996. The spin-off of the gold unit to shareholders will occur in late October 1995.

Valuation - 27-SEP-95

The stock has been a strong performer since mid-1994, due to increased results of the fertilizer and chemicals segments and improved prospects for FirstMiss Gold (currently valued at about $16 per FRM share). We recommend purchase of the stock, in view of the potentially higher value of the gold unit resulting from the development of the high grade Turquoise Ridge deposit. The rest of FRM is selling at only about 7 times estimated EPS for fiscal 1996. We expect that the specialty chemicals business will continue to grow in fiscal 1996, while the combustion and plasma segment may finally turn profitable. The fertilizer cycle could continue to be strong in 1996 on higher crop acreage and application rates.

Key Stock Statistics

S&P EPS Est. 1996	3.25	Tang. Bk. Value/Share	11.37
P/E on S&P Est. 1996	11.5	Beta	0.24
Dividend Rate/Share	0.40	Shareholders	6,100
Shs. outstg. (M)	20.6	Market cap. (B)	$0.772
Avg. daily vol. (M)	0.139	Inst. holdings	64%
		Insider holdings	NA

Value of $10,000 invested 5 years ago: NA

Fiscal Year Ending Jun. 30

	1995	% Change	1994	% Change	1993	% Change
Revenues (Million $)						
1Q	156.9	38%	113.3	10%	102.7	-27%
2Q	144.0	24%	115.9	11%	104.6	-21%
3Q	176.3	36%	129.6	25%	103.6	-16%
4Q	165.6	11%	149.4	25%	119.1	-8%
Yr.	642.8	26%	508.2	18%	429.9	-18%
Income (Million $)						
1Q	15.02	NM	0.80	-54%	1.74	-67%
2Q	12.94	NM	3.07	NM	-0.65	NM
3Q	19.65	NM	4.85	NM	-0.07	NM
4Q	10.17	14%	8.94	NM	1.65	45%
Yr.	57.79	NM	17.66	NM	2.68	-37%
Earnings Per Share ($)						
1Q	0.74	NM	0.04	-56%	0.09	-67%
2Q	0.63	NM	0.15	NM	0.04	-60%
3Q	0.95	NM	0.24	—	Nil	—
4Q	0.49	11%	0.44	NM	0.08	33%
Yr.	2.80	NM	0.88	NM	0.13	-38%

Next earnings report expected: late October

First Mississippi

Business Summary - 06-OCT-95

This diversified company has interests in chemicals, fertilizer, and technology-based ventures, and plans to spin-off its gold unit. Segment contributions in fiscal 1995 (profits in million $) were:

	Sales	Profits
Chemicals	33%	$40.0
Fertilizer	37%	86.3
Gold	11%	-16.3
Other	19%	-6.2

About 7% of fiscal 1995 sales were exports.

First Chemical produces aniline, nitrated aromatics, aromatic amines, and specialty intermediate and electronic chemicals. A 23% interest is held in Melamine Chemicals, Inc.

Triad Chemical (50% owned) operates at Donaldsonville, La., an ammonia plant (annual capacity of 420,000 tons) and a urea plant (520,000). Wholly owned AMPRO operates an ammonia plant (446,000 tons) at Donaldsonville.

FirstMiss Gold Inc. (81% owned) has a gold mine and mill and heap-leach operations at Getchell, Nev. Underground ore production began in mid-fiscal 1995. Proved reserves were 1,434,900 oz. at June 30, 1995.

Other operations include thermal plasma energy systems and equipment for aluminum recovery, waste treatment and steel production; industrial burners, flares and incinerators; and steel melting and casting operations. In fiscal 1993, FRM discontinued operations in oil and gas, coal and several technology businesses.

Important Developments

Sep. '95—Directors approved the spin-off of 81%-owned FirstMiss Gold Inc. (FRMG). Each FRM shareholder of record October 10, 1995 will receive 0.7 of a share of FRMG for each FRM share held. The action followed the pre-feasibility study of FRMG's Turquoise Ridge gold deposit, which brings FRMG's reserves to 2.7 million ounces. FRMG estimated that the capital required to bring the initial phase of the Turquoise Ridge underground mine into commercial production of 2,000 tons per day would be about $85 million. Initial production would commence in mid-1998.

Jul. '95—FRM achieved record earnings in fiscal 1995 on record fertilizer and chemical profits, despite write-downs and operating losses in the gold business. Combustion and thermal plasma losses were less than half those of fiscal 1994.

Capitalization

Long Term Debt: $84,406,000 (6/95).
Minority Interests: $6,001,000.

Per Share Data ($)

(Year Ended Jun. 30)

	1995	1994	1993	1992	1991	1990
Tangible Bk. Val.	11.40	8.85	8.05	9.50	9.56	9.65
Cash Flow	4.48	2.28	1.53	2.88	2.20	2.00
Earnings	2.80	0.88	0.13	0.21	0.27	0.22
Dividends	0.43	0.30	0.30	0.30	0.30	0.30
Payout Ratio	15%	34%	223%	141%	111%	135%
Prices - High	38	25	13¼	14⅞	12⅜	17⅜
- Low	20¾	12¾	8⅜	7¼	7¾	7⅞
P/E Ratio - High	14	28	NM	71	46	79
- Low	7	14	NM	35	29	36

Income Statement Analysis (Million $)

	1995	%Chg	1994	%Chg	1993	%Chg	1992
Revs.	643	27%	508	18%	430	-18%	525
Oper. Inc.	127	87%	67.8	56%	43.4	-35%	66.5
Depr.	34.6	22%	28.3	1%	27.9	-47%	53.0
Int. Exp.	9.7	-4%	10.1	-22%	13.0	31%	9.9
Pretax Inc.	87.2	182%	30.9	NM	3.9	-51%	7.9
Eff. Tax Rate	38%	—	39%	—	44%	—	37%
Net Inc.	57.8	NM	17.7	NM	2.7	-36%	4.2

Balance Sheet & Other Fin. Data (Million $)

	1995	1994	1993	1992	1991	1990
Cash	41.1	5.0	15.9	19.1	8.2	9.1
Curr. Assets	200	139	131	136	125	150
Total Assets	452	378	384	468	476	512
Curr. Liab.	90.3	60.0	80.7	76.0	93.0	96.0
LT Debt	84.4	104	114	154	143	166
Common Eqty.	233	178	161	188	188	190
Total Cap.	347	296	289	382	374	410
Cap. Exp.	54.9	20.0	41.0	36.0	47.0	65.0
Cash Flow	92.4	45.9	30.5	57.2	43.4	39.8

Ratio Analysis

	1995	1994	1993	1992	1991	1990
Curr. Ratio	2.2	2.3	1.6	1.8	1.3	1.6
% LT Debt of Cap.	24.3	35.1	39.3	40.4	38.1	40.5
% Net Inc.of Revs.	9.0	3.5	0.6	0.8	1.0	0.9
% Ret. on Assets	13.9	4.6	0.6	0.9	1.1	0.9
% Ret. on Equity	28.1	10.4	1.5	2.2	2.8	2.3

Dividend Data —Dividends have been paid since 1973. A dividend reinvestment plan is available. A "poison pill" stock purchase rights plan was adopted in 1989.

Amt. of Div. $	Date Decl.	Ex-Div. Date	Stock of Record	Payment Date
0.087	Nov. 11	Nov. 23	Nov. 30	Dec. 15 '94
0.087	Feb. 28	Mar. 09	Mar. 15	Mar. 30 '95
0.100	May. 23	Jun. 02	Jun. 08	Jun. 23 '95
0.100	Aug. 23	Aug. 31	Sep. 05	Sep. 20 '95
Stk.	Sep. 28	Oct. 23	Oct. 10	Oct. 20 '95

Data as orig. reptd.; bef. results of disc. opers. and/or spec. items. Per share data adj. for stk. divs. as of ex-div. date. E-Estimated. NA-Not Available. NM-Not Meaningful. NR-Not Ranked.

Office—700 North St., P.O. Box 1249, Jackson, MS 39215-1249. **Tel**—(601) 948-7550. **Chrmn & CEO**—J. K. Williams. **Pres**—T. G. Tepas. **VP & CFO**—R. M. Summerford. **Secy & Investor Contact**—James L. McArthur. **Dirs**—R. P. Anderson, P. A. Becker, J. W. Crook, J. E. Fligg, R. P. Guyton, C. P. Moreton, P. W. Murrill, W. A. Percy II, M. T. Reed, Jr., L. R. Speed, R. G. Turner, J. K. Williams. **Transfer Agents**—KeyCorp Shareholder Srvices, Cleveland, Ohio; Co. offices. **Registrars**—KeyCorp Shareholder Services, Cleveland; Deposit Guaranty National Bank, Jackson, Miss. **Incorporated** in Mississippi in 1957. **Empl-** 1,215. **S&P Analyst:** Richard O'Reilly, CFA

FirstBank Puerto Rico

NYSE Symbol FBP In S&P SmallCap 600

Price	Range	P-E Ratio	Dividend	Yield	S&P Ranking	Beta
Feb. 6'95	1995					
17⅜	17⅜–16⅝	6	None	None	NR	–0.09

Summary

This Puerto Rico state-chartered commercial bank (formerly First Federal Savings Bank) operates 30 branches. In October 1994, it converted to a commercial bank charter, from a savings bank charter, and agreed to sell its First Florida Savings Bank subsidiary to First Union National Bank of Florida. Earnings rose sharply in 1994.

Business Summary

FirstBank Puerto Rico (formerly First Federal Savings Bank) is the second largest commercial bank of Puerto Rican ownership, based on $2.2 billion of assets at 1994 year-end. The bank offers a variety of financial services, including deposit and checking accounts and a wide selection of consumer loans, through a main office and 28 full-service branch offices in Puerto Rico and two in the U.S. Virgin Islands, with the branch network particularly strong in the San Juan metropolitan area. Wholly owned First Florida Savings Bank operates three branches in the Miami, Fla., area.

Net loans totaled $1.3 billion as of June 30, 1994, and were divided as follows:

Real estate loans:	
Residential mortgage	24%
Commercial mortgage	12%
Gov't insured	5%
Other	2%
Commercial	9%
Consumer & other:	
Auto	23%
Personal	18%
Other	10%
Allowance for possible losses	(3%)

Loans originated in 1993 totaled $608.2 million, compared with $380.7 million the year before; loan purchases amounted to $20.0 million, versus $18.6 million. Loan sales in 1993 amounted to $35.8 million.

A substantial part of the bank's loan portfolio consists of loans made to home buyers secured by single-family dwellings. FBP originates FHA/VA loans, FHLMC and FNMA conventional conforming loans (which qualify for sale in the secondary market) and nonconforming loans. The bank also holds substantial amounts of commercial and consumer loans. Commercial loans and auto loans are especially important within the bank's portfolio.

During 1993, FBP converted part of its conventional mortgage loans into a $37 million CMO.

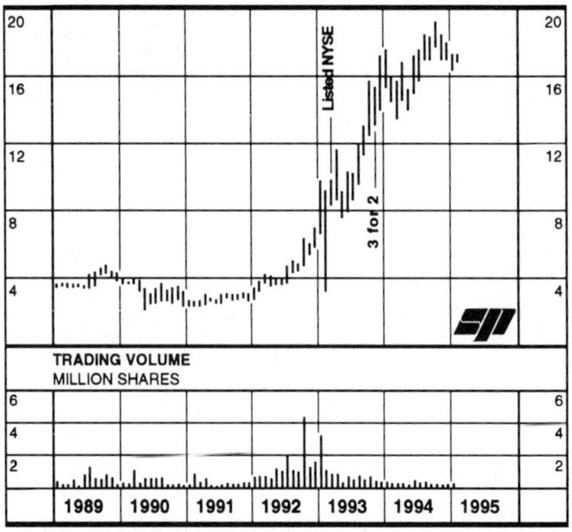

These securitized loans have lower risk-based capital requirements, can be used as collateral and can be sold easily. FBP retains the servicing on these securities, which provides a fee of ⅜ of 1%.

The allowance for loan losses totaled $35.0 million (2.57% of total loans and loans held for sale) at June 30, 1994, versus $30.5 million (2.46%) at 1993 year-end. Net loan chargeoffs totaled $3.8 million (0.28% of average loans outstanding) in the six months ended June 30, 1994.

Important Developments

Oct. '94— Effective as of the close of business on October 31, FBP converted its federal savings bank charter to that of a Puerto Rico state-chartered commercial bank known as FirstBank Puerto Rico. Separately, FBP agreed to sell its First Florida Savings Bank subsidiary to First Union National Bank of Florida for approximately $9.5 million. Based in Miami, First Florida has three branch offices, assets of about $97 million and deposits of approximately $80 million.

Next earnings report expected in mid-January.

Per Share Data ($)

Yr. End Dec. 31	1994	1993	1992	1991	1990	1989	1988
Tangible Bk. Val.	**NA**	9.05	5.40	3.79	2.68	4.57	4.03
Earnings[1]	**3.01**	1.89	1.11	0.84	d2.17	0.91	0.98
Dividends	**Nil**	Nil	Nil	Nil	0.053	0.210	NA
Payout Ratio	**Nil**	Nil	Nil	Nil	NM	23%	NA
Prices—High	**19¼**	17¼	7	3³⁄₃₂	4³⁄₃₂	4¾	NA
Low	**13½**	6¾	2¾	2¹¹⁄₃₂	2³⁄₃₂	3¹³⁄₃₂	NA
P/E Ratio—	**6–4**	9–4	6–2	4–3	NM	5–4	NA

Data as orig. reptd. Adj. for stk. div(s). of 50% Nov. 1993, 50% Mar. 1993, 10% Dec. 1992. **1.** Bef. spec. items of +0.62 in 1993, -0.09 in 1992, -0.14 in 1991. d-Deficit. NM-Not Meaningful. NA-Not Available.

Income Data (Million $)

Year Ended Dec. 31	Int. Inc.	Int. Exp.	Net Int. Inc.	Loan Loss Prov.	Non Int. Inc.	Non Int. Exp.	Net Bef. Taxes	Eff. Tax Rate	[1]Net Inc.	% Net Int. Margin	% Return On Assets	% Return On Equity
1993	**159**	**72.0**	**87.0**	**18.7**	**17.1**	**57.0**	**28.5**	**22.9%**	**22.0**	**4.81**	**1.1**	**29.8**
1992	159	86.0	73.0	13.6	13.6	54.7	18.3	15.8%	15.3	4.04	0.8	26.9
1991	172	109.9	61.8	16.4	18.9	51.4	12.9	11.0%	11.5	3.39	0.6	24.6
1990	189	129.3	59.5	32.0	12.6	57.8	d17.6	NM	d17.7	3.20	NM	NM
1989	192	133.6	58.8	11.3	13.2	48.1	12.5	6.4%	11.7	3.20	0.6	19.1
1988	162	106.5	55.5	8.5	8.9	42.8	13.0	4.2%	12.5	3.46	0.7	[1]NA

Balance Sheet Data (Million $)

Dec. 31	Total Assets	[2]Loans	Deposits	Cash & Secs.	% Loan Loss Resv.	Capitalization [3]Debt	Capitalization Equity	Capitalization Total	% Equity To Assets	% Risk Based Capital	Price Times Book Value HI–LO
1993	**1,914**	**1,207**	**1,371**	**626**	**2.5**	**131**	**92.8**	**224**	**5.1**	**9.05**	**1.9–0.3**
1992	1,889	1,152	1,337	644	2.7	141	54.3	230	2.5	9.20	1.3–0.5
1991	1,898	1,235	1,374	569	2.3	196	39.9	271	1.8	7.10	0.8–0.6
1990	1,908	1,299	1,309	511	2.0	247	30.1	312	2.1	4.30	1.5–0.8
1989	1,928	1,316	1,301	523	0.5	264	48.8	347	2.4	NA	1.0–0.7
1988	1,819	1,206	1,105	539	0.4	309	41.9	385	NA	NA	NA

Data as orig. reptd. **1.** Bef. spec. items. **2.** Net. **3.** Total debt incl. current portion. d-Deficit. NM-Not Meaningful. NA-Not Available.

Review of Operations

Based on a brief report, net interest income increased to $103.6 million in 1994 from $87.0 million in 1993, resulting in higher operational profits as the bank positioned itself to serve the needs of consumers and commercial entities in Puerto Rico. Net income totaled $31.0 million ($3.01 a share) versus $22.0 million ($1.89). Results exclude an extraordinary charge of $0.04 a share in 1994 and a $0.62-a-share credit from an accounting change in 1993.

Common Share Earnings ($)

Quarter:	1994	1993	1992
Mar.	0.70	0.31	0.23
Jun.	0.74	0.37	0.26
Sep.	0.77	0.55	0.29
Dec.	0.80	0.66	0.33
	3.01	1.89	1.11

Dividend Data

The most recent cash dividend on the common shares was paid in March 1990. Three-for-two stock splits were effected in November 1993 and March 1993. A 10% stock dividend was paid in December 1992.

Finances

The conversion to a state-chartered bank has important tax advantages and will allow FBP to avoid limits placed on thrifts regarding the amount they can invest in commercial and consumer loans.

As of June 30, 1994, total deposits aggregated $1.41 billion and were divided: certificate accounts 44%, passbooks 35%, interest-bearing checking 14% and noninterest bearing 7%.

At June 30, 1994, nonperforming assets (consisting of nonaccruing loans, real estate owned, past-due loans and repossessed property) aggregated $63.8 million (3.24% of total assets), down from $72.1 million (3.77%) at 1993 year end.

The average yield on earning assets was 9.20% for the six months ended June 30, 1994 (8.73% in the year-earlier period), while the average rate paid on interest-bearing liabilities was 4.25% (4.46%), for an interest rate spread of 4.95% (4.27%).

The bank was in full regulatory capital compliance as of June 30, 1994. Its regulatory capital position was as follows: tangible capital was 5.15% of tangible assets, core capital was 5.18% of total adjusted assets and total capital was 9.30% of risk-weighted assets. All of these percentages were above required levels.

On June 29, 1994, the bank repurchased, at a net premium of $428,871, its $50 million real rate bonds. The real rate bonds had a maturity date of June 1, 1998, with an estimate cost higher than the alternative sources of funds available to the bank. Therefore, the bank will receive the benefit of the reduction in the cost on the $50 million funding in coming periods.

In August 1993, the bank repurchased from the FDIC's FSLIC Resolution Fund 685,876 shares of preferred stock and warrants to purchase 1,627,016 (adjusted) of its common shares for a total cash payment of $29.5 million.

Capitalization

FHLB Advances: $58,000,000 (6/94).

Term Notes: $52,850,000.

Common Stock: 10,022,570 shs. ($0.01 par).
Officers & directors own about 22%.
Institutions hold some 14%.
Shareholders of record: 733 (12/93).

Office—1519 Ponce de Leon Ave., Stop 23-1/2, Santurce, PR 00908. **Tel**—(809) 729-8200. **Chrmn**—G. E. Malaret. **Pres & CEO**—A. Alvarez-Perez. **Exec VP, CFO & Investor Contact**—Annie Astor de Carbonell (809) 724-1715. **VP-Secy**—A. Escriba Oliver. **Dirs**—A. Alvarez-Perez, J. M. Calderon-Bartolomei, F. D. Fernandez, A. Lopez-Ortiz, G. E. Malaret, H. M. Nevares, A. Pavia-Villamil, J. Teixidor. **Transfer Agent & Registrar**—Bank of New York, NYC. **Organized** in Puerto Rico in 1948. **Empl**—1,024.

STANDARD & POOR'S

STOCK REPORTS

FirstFed Michigan

NASDAQ Symbol **FFOM**

In S&P SmallCap 600

11-SEP-95 **Industry:** Banking

Summary: This Detroit-based savings and loan holding company has agreed to merge into Charter One Financial in a stock transaction that is expected to close by year end.

Quantitative Evaluations

Outlook
(1 Lowest—5 Highest)
• **NA**

Fair Value
• **NA**

Risk
• **Average**

Earn./Div. Rank
• **B-**

Technical Eval.
• **Bullish** since 7/95

Rel. Strength Rank
(1 Lowest—99 Highest)
• **83**

Insider Activity
• **NA**

Recent Price • 35¼

52 Wk Range • 35½-17⅜

Yield • 1.8%

12-Mo. P/E • 12.6

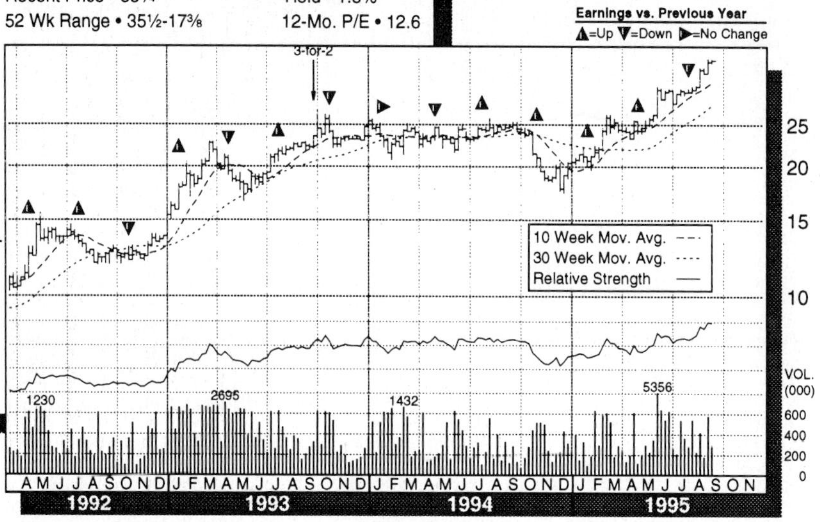

Business Profile - 11-SEP-95

FFOM is a holding company whose principal subsidiary, First Federal of Michigan, is one of the largest savings and loan associations in the state. The company plans to merge with Charter One Financial, Inc., in a stock transaction that is expected to close by year-end 1995. After the merger, FFOM shareholders will own about 50% of the new entity, which will have $13 billion in total assets and 150 retail offices.

Operational Review - 10-SEP-95

In the six months ended June 30, 1995, net interest income fell 11%, year to year. In the absence of a prior-year financial restructuring charge of $155,364,000, and after 9.2% lower operating costs, pretax income of $37,274,000 replaced a loss of $115,432,000. After taxes at 34.7%, versus a $35,240,000 credit, earnings of $24,339,000 ($1.28 a share) contrasted with a loss of $80,192,000 ($4.30). Results in the 1994 period exclude extraordinary charges totaling $41,095,000 ($2.20).

Stock Performance - 08-SEP-95

In the past 30 trading days, FFOM's shares have increased 18%, compared to a 2% rise in the S&P 500. Average trading volume for the past five days was 69,075 shares, compared with the 40-day moving average of 71,915 shares.

Key Stock Statistics

Dividend Rate/Share	0.64	Shareholders	3,900
Shs. outstg. (M)	18.7	Market cap. (B)	$0.660
Avg. daily vol. (M)	0.072	Inst. holdings	57%
Tang. Bk. Value/Share	25.68	Insider holdings	NA
Beta	0.83		

Value of $10,000 invested 5 years ago: $ 43,195

Fiscal Year Ending Dec. 31

	1995	% Change	1994	% Change	1993	% Change
Revenues (Million $)						
1Q	162.1	NM	160.6	-14%	187.6	-11%
2Q	161.1	8%	149.6	-21%	189.6	-8%
3Q	—	—	157.9	-13%	181.9	-9%
4Q	—	—	152.5	-13%	175.6	-9%
Yr.	—	—	625.7	-15%	734.7	-9%
Income (Million $)						
1Q	11.51	NM	-94.97	NM	9.17	-2%
2Q	12.83	-13%	14.77	15%	12.86	76%
3Q	—	—	13.69	49%	9.18	9%
4Q	—	—	14.51	42%	10.20	11%
Yr.	—	—	-51.99	NM	41.40	21%
Earnings Per Share ($)						
1Q	0.61	NM	-5.08	NM	0.50	-10%
2Q	0.67	-14%	0.78	15%	0.68	57%
3Q	—	—	0.72	47%	0.49	-2%
4Q	—	—	0.77	43%	0.54	NM
Yr.	—	—	-2.79	NM	2.21	9%

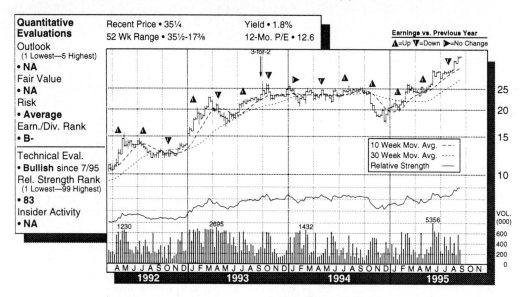

Next earnings report expected: mid October

FirstFed Michigan

Business Summary - 10-SEP-95

FFOM's principal operations are conducted by First Federal of Michigan. FirstFed historically has concentrated its business in Michigan, and currently has 63 offices in the state's lower peninsula. FFOM is primarily engaged in the business of obtaining funds in the form of deposits and borrowings and investing such funds in secured loans on residential properties, mortgage-backed securities and investment-grade securities.

Gross loans receivable at December 31, 1994, totaled $3.12 billion, versus $3.41 billion a year earlier, divided as follows:

Real estate loans:	
Existing property	92%
Construction	1%
Commercial	4%
Other loans	3%

As of December 31, 1994, total assets were $8.40 billion, versus $9.26 billion a year earlier; cash-equivalent assets and mortgage-backed securities had a book value of $5.06 billion, against $5.58 billion at year-end 1993.

The allowance for loan losses amounted to $28.0 million (0.89% of total loans) at December 31, 1994, versus $29.6 million (0.87%) at the end of 1993. Net loan chargeoffs in 1994 were $1.8 million (0.06% of average loans), compared with $3.0 million (0.08%) the year before. At year-end 1994, nonperforming and restructured real estate assets totaled $26.3 million (0.31% of total assets), against $47.9 million (0.52%) a year earlier.

Interest on loans contributed 44% of total interest income in 1994, interest on mortgage-backed securities 51%, and interest on other investments 5%.

Deposits of $2.72 billion at the end of 1994 were divided: 35% retail CDs, 14% brokered CDs, 10% jumbo CDs, 19% regular accounts, 12% money market, and 10% checking accounts.

The net interest rate spread widened to 1.32% in 1994, from 1.12% the year before.

Important Developments

May '95—FFOM signed a definitive agreement, subject to approvals, to merge with Charter One Financial, Inc. The transaction is expected to close in the fourth quarter of 1995, and the surviving entity will be called Charter One Financial, Inc. Terms of the agreement call for FFOM shareholders to receive 1.2 shares of COFI for each FFOM common share in a tax-free exchange. Following the transaction, FFOM shareholders will own approximately 50% of the combined company.

Capitalization

FHLB Advances: $1,502,200,000 (6/95).

Per Share Data ($) (Year Ended Dec. 31)

	1994	1993	1992	1991	1990	1989
Tangible Bk. Val.	24.33	28.39	30.25	28.29	26.39	26.36
Earnings	-2.79	2.21	2.03	2.03	0.66	0.63
Dividends	0.54	0.47	0.41	0.20	0.40	0.40
Payout Ratio	NM	21%	20%	10%	61%	63%
Prices - High	25⅞	27	15¾	11⅝	10⅜	14⅝
- Low	17⅜	15⅛	8¾	6⅝	5⅞	8⅞
P/E Ratio - High	NM	12	8	6	16	23
- Low	NM	7	4	3	9	14

Income Statement Analysis (Million $)

	1994	%Chg	1993	%Chg	1992	%Chg	1991
Net Int. Inc.	134	-2%	137	23%	111	9%	102
Loan Loss Prov.	0.2	-92%	2.4	-60%	6.0	-17%	7.2
Non Int. Inc.	-139	NM	11.0	-56%	25.0	-49%	48.6
Non Int. Exp.	72.1	-10%	79.8	3%	77.3	-13%	88.9
Pretax Inc.	-79.0	NM	66.0	25%	53.0	-4%	55.0
Eff. Tax Rate	NM	—	37%	—	35%	—	38%
Net Inc.	-52.0	NM	41.0	21%	34.0	NM	34.0
% Net Int. Marg.	1.46%	—	1.40%	—	1.50%	—	1.28%

Balance Sheet & Other Fin. Data (Million $)

	1994	1993	1992	1991	1990	1989
Total Assets	8,399	9,264	9,399	9,415	10,676	11,490
Loans	7,640	8,543	8,410	7,676	7,770	9,005
Deposits	2,721	3,101	3,445	3,778	3,659	4,347
Capitalization:						
Debt	5,064	5,405	5,174	4,831	6,127	6,332
Equity	455	565	508	473	440	437
Total	5,519	5,970	5,682	5,303	6,567	6,714

Ratio Analysis

	1994	1993	1992	1991	1990	1989
% Ret. on Assets	NM	0.4	0.4	0.3	0.1	0.2
% Ret. on Equity	NM	7.6	8.4	7.5	2.1	5.2
% Loan Loss Resv.	0.4	0.1	0.4	0.3	0.3	0.2
% Risk Based Capital	15.9	17.5	14.8	13.2	10.4	10.0
Price Times Book Value:						
High	1.1	1.0	0.5	0.4	0.4	0.6
Low	0.7	0.5	0.3	0.2	0.2	0.3

Dividend Data —Cash payments, omitted in June 1991, were reinstated in February 1992.

Amt. of Div. $	Date Decl.	Ex-Div. Date	Stock of Record	Payment Date
0.140	Aug. 17	Aug. 25	Aug. 31	Sep. 12 '94
0.140	Nov. 16	Nov. 23	Nov. 30	Dec. 12 '94
0.150	Feb. 22	Feb. 27	Mar. 03	Mar. 15 '95
0.150	May. 17	May. 24	May. 31	Jun. 12 '95
0.160	Aug. 16	Aug. 24	Aug. 28	Sep. 11 '95

Data as orig. reptd.; bef. results of disc opers. and/or spec. items. Per share data adj. for stk. divs. as of ex-div. date. E-Estimated. NA-Not Available. NM-Not Meaningful. NR-Not Ranked.

Office—1001 Woodward Ave., Detroit, MI 48226-1904. **Federally chartered**—in 1983; originally chartered in 1933. **Tel**—(313) 965-1400. **Chrmn, CEO & Pres**—C. G. Harling. **Treas**—R. W. Neu. **Secy**—W. S. Fambrough. **Investor Contact**—Ellen Batkie. **Dirs**—C. G. Harling, C. M. Heidel, R. J. Jacob, P. J. Meathe, R. W. Neu, H. R. Nolte Jr., F. C. Reynolds, J. L. Schostak, M. Shaevsky, E. R. Williams. **Transfer Agent & Registrar**—Bank of Boston, Boston. **Empl**-1,133. **S&P Analyst:** Thomas C. Ferguson

FirstMerit Corp.

NASDAQ Symbol FMER (Incl. in Nat'l Market) In S&P SmallCap 600

Price	Range	P–E Ratio	Dividend	Yield	S&P Ranking	Beta
Aug. 31'95	1995					
26¾	27¼–21⁷⁄₁₆	19	1.00	3.8%	A	0.61

Summary

This holding company (formerly First Bancorporation of Ohio) owns eight banks that operate more than 160 offices, primarily in northeastern Ohio. Earnings fell 68% in the first half of 1995, hurt by a lower net interest margin, a higher loan loss provision, and charges related to the acquisition of CIVISTA Corp. and an early retirement program.

Business Summary

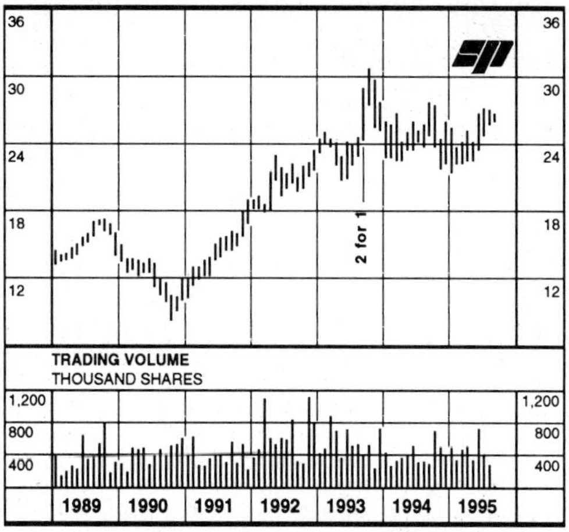

FirstMerit Corporation (formerly First Bancorporation of Ohio) is a holding company for eight banks, operating primarily in northeastern Ohio. Its principal subsidiary is First National Bank of Ohio, which had 70 offices at February 1, 1995. Other units are Old Phoenix National Bank of Medina (16 offices), EST National Bank (formerly Elyria Savings & Trust National Bank) (24), Peoples National Bank (13), Citizens National Bank (formed after the January 1995 acquisition of Citizens Savings Bank of Canton, and subsequent merger with The First National Bank in Massillon) (20), Bancorp Trust Co., NA, of Collier and Lee, Fla. (2), Peoples Bank, NA (16), and Life Savings Bank, FSB (5). During 1994, FMER converted two of its former savings association subsidiaries, Peoples Federal Savings Bank and Peoples Savings Bank, into national banks.

Total loans of $3.18 billion at 1994 year end were divided:

Commercial, financial & agricultural..	15%
Real estate	56%
Instalment (net of unearned income)	24%
Lease financing..................................	5%

As of December 31, 1994, the allowance for possible loan losses was $33,108,000 ($32,338,000 a year earlier), or 1.16% (1.25%) of loans outstanding. Net chargeoffs in 1994 were $3,691,000 ($4,596,000 in 1993), equal to 0.13% (0.18%) of average loans. At 1994 year end, total nonperforming assets, including nonaccrual loans, restructured loans and other real estate owned, were $15,445,000 (0.49% of total loans), versus $21,973,000 (0.84%) a year earlier.

Total deposits of $3.86 billion at December 31, 1994, were divided: noninterest-bearing demand 19%, interest-bearing demand 9%, savings 34%, and certificates and other time deposits 38%.

Interest and fees on loans contributed 63% of total income in 1994, interest and dividends on investment securities 22% (taxable 20% and nontaxable 2%), trust department 4%, service charges on deposits 5%, and other noninterest income 6%.

On a tax-equivalent basis, the average yield on interest-earning assets in 1994 was 7.58% (7.81% in 1993), while the average rate paid on interest-bearing liabilities was 3.36% (3.37%), for a net interest rate spread of 4.22% (4.44%).

FMER Credit Life Insurance Co. is engaged in the underwriting of credit life and credit accident and health insurance directly related to the extension of credit by the banks to their customers.

Important Developments

Mar. '95— The company changed its name to FirstMerit Corporation, reflecting the broader geographic scope of its operations.

Next earnings report expected in mid-October.

Per Share Data ($)

Yr. End Dec. 31	1994	1993	1992	1991	[1]1990	[1]1989	[1]1988	[1]1987	1986	[1]1985
Tangible Bk. Val.	**15.89**	15.51	13.34	12.02	12.27	12.27	11.88	10.96	10.02	9.10
Earnings[2]	**2.22**	2.19	2.02	1.58	1.39	1.60	1.56	1.56	1.45	1.28
Dividends	**0.985**	0.900	0.823	0.803	0.763	0.732	0.688	0.619	0.513	0.475
Payout Ratio	**44%**	41%	41%	51%	55%	46%	44%	40%	35%	37%
Prices—High	**27¾**	30¾	23½	19	15	17⁵⁄₁₆	16⅝	16¾	19¼	13
Low	**21¾**	20¾	17⅞	10¼	8¼	13¼	12⅜	11¾	12⅜	8¼
P/E Ratio—	**13–10**	14–9	12–9	12–7	11–6	11–8	11–8	11–8	13–9	10–6

Data as orig. reptd. Adj. for stk. divs. of 100% Sep. 1993, 50% Dec. 1986, 100% Dec. 1985. **1.** Refl. merger or acq. **2.** Bef. spec. item(s) of +0.06 in 1988.

Income Data (Million $)

Year Ended Dec. 31	Net Int. Inc.	Tax Equiv. Adj.	Non Int. Inc.	Loan Loss Prov.	% Exp./ Op. Revs.	Net Bef. Taxes	Eff. Tax Rate	[2]Net Inc.	% Net Int. Margin	—% Return On— Assets	Equity
1994	**201**	**4.59**	**56.9**	**4.5**	**63.6**	**86.4**	**30.2%**	**60.3**	**4.85**	**1.32**	**14.1**
1993	184	5.25	54.3	6.6	62.1	80.7	31.6%	55.2	5.28	1.39	14.7
1992	180	5.60	49.2	17.4	59.7	73.1	30.6%	50.7	5.37	1.34	14.8
1991	152	6.90	44.1	11.4	64.1	55.0	28.0%	39.6	4.68	1.07	12.5
[1]1990	141	9.10	37.9	11.7	64.6	46.1	24.2%	34.9	4.53	0.97	11.7
[1]1989	129	10.20	34.2	7.1	61.6	50.0	22.8%	38.6	4.71	1.19	13.6
[1]1988	108	10.70	30.2	5.0	61.1	42.1	19.4%	33.9	4.85	1.26	14.2
[1]1987	103	15.70	27.9	6.0	57.0	41.6	18.4%	33.9	5.30	1.37	14.9
1986	94	22.40	26.3	5.1	56.5	35.6	11.9%	31.4	5.38	1.31	15.3
[1]1985	84	22.50	19.4	4.9	56.3	27.9	1.5%	27.5	5.57	1.31	14.5

Balance Sheet Data (Million $)

Dec. 31	Total Assets	—Earning Assets— Mon. Mkt. Assets	Inv. Secs.	Com'l Loans	Other Loans	% Loan Loss Resv.	—Deposits— Demand	Time	% Loans/ Deposits	Long Term Debt	Common Equity	% Equity To Assets
1994	**4,924**	**4**	**1,378**	**626**	**2,554**	**1.20**	**1,080**	**2,783**	**82.3**	**Nil**	**432**	**9.3**
1993	3,997	59	1,210	487	1,909	1.30	688	2,739	69.9	Nil	392	9.5
1992	3,916	95	1,167	442	1,881	1.26	639	2,745	68.6	Nil	358	9.1
1991	3,766	82	1,119	419	1,832	1.14	531	2,737	68.8	Nil	327	8.6
1990	3,722	NA	1,046	422	1,739	1.09	529	2,700	66.7	Nil	308	8.3
1989	3,334	NA	914	546	1,406	1.00	500	2,344	68.4	16.9	297	8.8
1988	3,049	NA	876	481	1,251	0.98	464	2,184	65.4	21.2	258	9.2
1987	2,638	NA	873	494	893	1.11	444	1,820	61.1	Nil	238	9.2
1986	2,477	NA	963	455	706	1.16	452	1,713	53.4	Nil	217	8.6
1985	2,404	NA	1,003	432	660	1.16	408	1,661	52.4	Nil	197	9.0

Data as orig. reptd. **1.** Refl. merger or acq. **2.** Bef. spec. item(s). NA-Not Available.

Review of Operations

Net interest income rose 3.4%, year to year, in the six months ended June 30, 1995, as growth in interest earning assets outweighed a narrower net interest margin (4.50% versus 4.81%). After a $0.48 a share charge related to an acquisition in the first quarter and a $0.06 a share charge for an early retirement program in the second quarter, net income was down 68%, to $11,480,000 ($0.34 a share), from $35,728,000 ($1.07).

Common Share Earnings ($)

Quarter:	1995	1994	1993	1992
Mar.	d0.04	0.56	0.53	0.49
Jun.	0.38	0.55	0.57	0.48
Sep.		0.55	0.56	0.51
Dec.		0.57	0.54	0.54
		2.22	2.19	2.02

Dividend Data

Cash dividends have been paid each year by the company or a predecessor since 1939. A dividend reinvestment plan is available. A "poison pill" stock purchase rights plan was adopted in October 1993.

Amt. of Divd. $	Date Decl.	Ex-divd. Date	Stock of Record	Payment Date
0.25	Nov. 17	Nov. 21	Nov. 28	Dec. 12'94
0.25	Feb. 16	Feb. 21	Feb. 27	Mar. 13'95
0.25	May 18	May 23	May 30	Jun. 12'95
0.25	Aug. 17	Aug. 24	Aug. 28	Sep. 11'95

Finances

In January 1995, Citizens Savings Bank of Canton, the main unit of CIVISTA Corp., was acquired in exchange for stock valued at $162 million. A charge of $0.48 a share was incurred, primarily related to the recapture of tax credits.

In April 1994, the company acquired Great Northern Financial Corp. (GNFC), parent of Great Northern Savings (assets of $384 million), in exchange for stock. In March 1994, it acquired Life Federal Savings Bank, Clearwater, Fla. (deposits of $25 million), from the Resolution Trust Corp., for $2.3 million.

In September 1990, Peoples Savings Bank (Ashtabula, Ohio) was acquired in exchange for stock.

Capitalization

Long Term Debt: None (6/95).

Common Stock: 33,484,365 shs. (no par).
Shareholders: 7,322 of record (2/95).

d-Deficit.

Office—III Cascade Plaza, 7th Floor, Akron, OH 44308. **Tel**—(216) 384-8000. **Chrmn**—H. L. Flood. **Pres & CEO**—J. R. Cochran. **SVP, Treas & Investor Contact**—G. J. Elek. **SVP & Secy**—T. E. Patton. **Dirs**—J. C. Blickle, R. M. Carter, R. A. Chenoweth, E. A. Dalton, H. L. Flood, R. G. Gilbert, T. L. Haines, R. L. Hardgrove, C. J. Isroff, P. A. Lloyd II, R. G. Merzweiler, S. E. Myers, G. H. Neal, R. T. Read, J. T. Rogers, Jr., D. Spitzer. **Transfer Agent**—First National Bank of Ohio. **Incorporated** in Ohio in 1962. **Empl**—3,359.

 Robert Schpoont

STANDARD & POOR'S

STOCK REPORTS

Fisher Scientific Int'l

NYSE Symbol **FSH**
In S&P SmallCap 600

07-OCT-95 **Industry:** Medical equipment/ supply

Summary: This company is the oldest and largest supplier of scientific instruments, supplies and equipment to the scientific community.

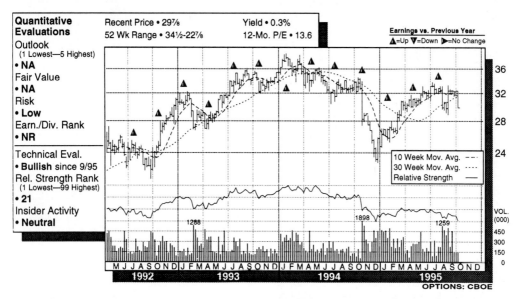

Quantitative Evaluations
Outlook
(1 Lowest—5 Highest)
• **NA**
Fair Value
• **NA**
Risk
• **Low**
Earn./Div. Rank
• **NR**

Technical Eval.
• **Bullish** since 9/95
Rel. Strength Rank
(1 Lowest—99 Highest)
• **21**
Insider Activity
• **Neutral**

Recent Price • 29⅞
52 Wk Range • 34½-22⅞
Yield • 0.3%
12-Mo. P/E • 13.6

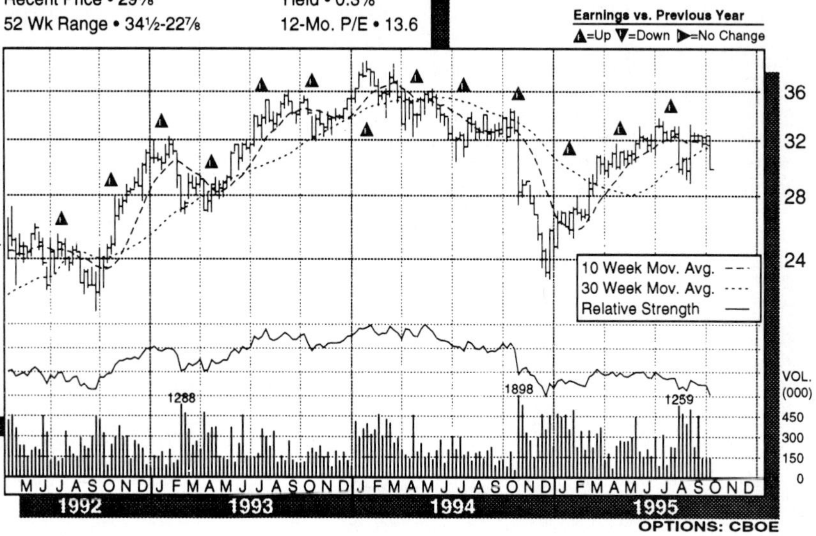

Business Profile - 03-OCT-95

This company's strong revenue growth is the result of an aggressive acquisition program in both domestic and international businesses. FSH is now working to integrate these businesses and investing in information technology to realize productivity improvements. Fisher expects that once implemented, these changes will uplift its competitive position on a global basis across a broad range of products and services, with a concomitant improvement in profitability.

Operational Review - 03-OCT-95

Sales continued to trend upward in the first half of 1995, reflecting acquisitions and growth in the company's principal markets. Margins narrowed, due to a less favorable product mix and costs incurred in the development of an integrated worldwide supply capability. Pretax income declined, but net income rose slightly on a lower effective tax rate. The company expects to incur one-time charges of $40 to $45 million in the second half of 1995 and $20 to $25 million in 1996 to improve efficiency.

Stock Performance - 06-OCT-95

In the past 30 trading days, FSH's shares have increased 0.42%, compared to a 4% rise in the S&P 500. Average trading volume for the past five days was 27,460 shares, compared with the 40-day moving average of 81,213 shares.

Key Stock Statistics

Dividend Rate/Share	0.08	Shareholders	300
Shs. outstg. (M)	16.2	Market cap. (B)	$0.484
Avg. daily vol. (M)	0.045	Inst. holdings	71%
Tang. Bk. Value/Share	4.36	Insider holdings	NA
Beta	1.85		

Value of $10,000 invested 5 years ago: NA

Fiscal Year Ending Dec. 31

	1995	% Change	1994	% Change	1993	% Change
Revenues (Million $)						
1Q	303.1	26%	240.4	5%	228.2	17%
2Q	314.9	17%	269.7	12%	240.9	19%
3Q	—	—	307.4	18%	260.2	23%
4Q	—	—	309.2	24%	249.1	21%
Yr.	—	—	1,127	15%	978.4	20%
Income (Million $)						
1Q	6.80	3%	6.60	10%	6.00	22%
2Q	10.20	NM	10.10	17%	8.60	32%
3Q	—	—	10.10	4%	9.70	17%
4Q	—	—	8.90	7%	8.30	17%
Yr.	—	—	35.70	10%	32.60	22%
Earnings Per Share ($)						
1Q	0.42	2%	0.41	11%	0.37	16%
2Q	0.62	2%	0.61	17%	0.52	27%
3Q	—	—	0.61	3%	0.59	13%
4Q	—	—	0.55	8%	0.51	19%
Yr.	—	—	2.18	9%	2.00	20%

Next earnings report expected: late October

Fisher Scientific Int'l

Business Summary - 01-AUG-95

Fisher Scientific International is the oldest and largest supplier of instruments, supplies and equipment to the scientific community in North America. FSH provides a selection of more than 150,000 products. The company's products fall into two basic categories: laboratory consumables and supplies (such as test tubes, rubber gloves, chemicals, filters and other staples); and essential laboratory instruments and equipment (such as balances, centrifuges, microscopes, spectrophotometers and safety equipment). Consumable supplies and research chemicals represent approximately 70% of sales, while instruments, supplies and equipment represent approximately 30%.

Fisher's market consists of four principal sectors: (i) scientific research and development activities conducted by chemical, environmental, biotechnology, pharmaceutical and other businesses; (ii) educational activities in research institutes, medical schools, universities, colleges, and elementary and high schools; (iii) medical research and testing in hospitals, clinics, independent reference facilities and physicians' offices; and (iv) users of occupational health and safety products.

Over one million copies of The Fisher Catalog are published biannually, with supplements tailored to various growth markets such as biotechnology, research chemicals and occupational health and safety. The Fisher Catalog is designed both as a buying guide to Fisher's products and as a reference providing product specifications and technical information to assist the scientist. Information on all products offered by Fisher can be obtained through Fisher RIMS, an electronic order entry system that provides paperless purchasing, receiving, billing and product distribution to the company's larger customers. Medium- and smaller-size customers are served by the Lightning system, which permits direct access to Fisher's on-line order-entry and information system.

In addition to supplying leading brands of instruments, supplies and equipment, Fisher offers research chemicals, instruments, apparatus and laboratory workstations of its own manufacture. Approximately one-quarter of Fisher's sales are of products it manufactures.

In 1994, Fisher acquired Figgie International Inc.'s Safety Supply America division, a leading provider of industrial health and safety products to industrial, electronic and pharmaceutical markets.

Important Developments

Feb. '95—FSH said that it expected moderation of profit growth seen in 1994 to continue through much of 1995, due to further outlays to integrate manufacturing units and recently acquired distribution firms.

Capitalization

Long Term Debt: $129,700,000 (3/95), incl. $125,000,000 of notes conv. into com. at $35.125 a sh.

Per Share Data ($) (Year Ended Dec. 31)

	1994	1993	1992	1991	1990	1989
Tangible Bk. Val.	3.48	3.20	2.46	5.03	NA	NA
Cash Flow	3.36	3.23	2.46	1.26	1.51	NA
Earnings	2.18	2.00	1.66	0.51	0.82	NA
Dividends	0.08	0.08	0.08	Nil	NA	NA
Payout Ratio	4%	4%	5%	Nil	NA	NA
Prices - High	38¾	36⅛	31¼	15½	NA	NA
- Low	22⅞	26¾	15½	13¾	NA	NA
P/E Ratio - High	18	18	19	30	NA	NA
- Low	10	13	9	27	NA	NA

Income Statement Analysis (Million $)

	1994	%Chg	1993	%Chg	1992	%Chg	1991
Revs.	1,127	15%	978	20%	814	7%	758
Oper. Inc.	83.3	3%	80.7	37%	59.0	20%	49.2
Depr.	19.4	-3%	20.0	56%	12.8	14%	11.2
Int. Exp.	9.0	14%	7.9	NM	1.9	-44%	3.4
Pretax Inc.	63.0	9%	58.0	23%	47.0	194%	16.0
Eff. Tax Rate	43%	—	44%	—	44%	—	51%
Net Inc.	36.0	9%	33.0	22%	27.0	NM	8.0

Balance Sheet & Other Fin. Data (Million $)

	1994	1993	1992	1991	1990	1989
Cash	45.0	104	14.4	28.5	Nil	NA
Curr. Assets	358	335	215	206	182	NA
Total Assets	723	674	534	420	363	NA
Curr. Liab.	195	173	142	115	103	NA
LT Debt	128	128	43.3	26.3	33.4	NA
Common Eqty.	219	181	151	105	120	NA
Total Cap.	347	309	195	131	154	NA
Cap. Exp.	17.7	12.9	4.1	3.0	2.9	NA
Cash Flow	55.0	53.0	40.0	19.0	20.0	NA

Ratio Analysis

	1994	1993	1992	1991	1990	1989
Curr. Ratio	1.8	1.9	1.5	1.8	1.8	NA
% LT Debt of Cap.	37.0	41.4	22.3	20.0	21.7	NA
% Net Inc.of Revs.	3.2	3.3	3.3	1.0	1.6	NA
% Ret. on Assets	5.1	5.4	5.5	1.9	2.9	NA
% Ret. on Equity	17.9	19.6	20.4	6.4	7.7	NA

Dividend Data —Payments were initiated in 1992.

Amt. of Div. $	Date Decl.	Ex-Div. Date	Stock of Record	Payment Date
0.020	Sep. 20	Sep. 29	Oct. 05	Oct. 19 '94
0.020	Dec. 05	Dec. 14	Dec. 20	Jan. 04 '95
0.020	Mar. 16	Mar. 27	Mar. 31	Apr. 15 '95
0.020	Jun. 13	Jun. 26	Jun. 28	Jul. 13 '95
0.020	Sep. 20	Oct. 03	Oct. 05	Oct. 20 '95

Data as orig. reptd.; bef. results of disc. opers. and/or spec. items. Per share data adj. for stk. divs. as of ex-div. date. E-Estimated. NA-Not Available. NM-Not Meaningful. NR-Not Ranked.

Office—Liberty Lane, Hampton, NH 03842. **Tel**—(603) 929-2650. **Chrmn**—M. D. Dingman. **Pres & CEO**—P. M. Montrone. **Sr VP & CFO**—P. M. Meister. **VP & Secy**—M. A. Underberg. **Investor Contact**—John Dionne (603) 929-2322. **Dirs**—P. E. Beekman, M. D. Dingman, G. J. Lewis, E. A. Montgomery Jr., P. M. Montrone, T. P. Stafford. **Transfer Agent & Registrar**—Mellon Bank, Pittsburgh. **Incorporated** in Delaware in 1991. **Empl**-4,800. **S&P Analyst:** Philip J. Birbara

STANDARD & POOR'S

STOCK REPORTS

Flagstar Companies

NASDAQ Symbol **FLST**

In S&P SmallCap 600

05-SEP-95 **Industry:** Food serving

Summary: This holding company owns one of the largest foodservice businesses in the U.S., primarily consisting of Hardee's, Quincy's, Denny's and El Pollo Loco restaurants.

Quantitative Evaluations

Outlook (1 Lowest—5 Highest) • **NA**

Fair Value • **NA**

Risk • **High**

Earn./Div. Rank • **NR**

Technical Eval. • **Bearish** since 8/95

Rel. Strength Rank (1 Lowest—99 Highest) • **5**

Insider Activity • **NA**

Recent Price • 5 | 52 Wk Range • 9¾-4¼ | Yield • Nil | 12-Mo. P/E • NM

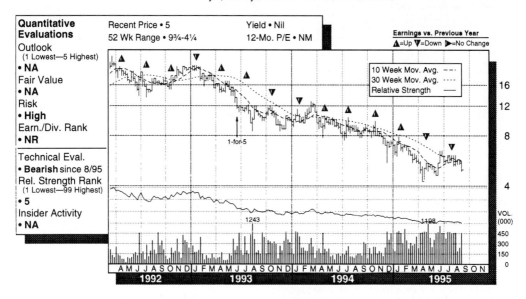

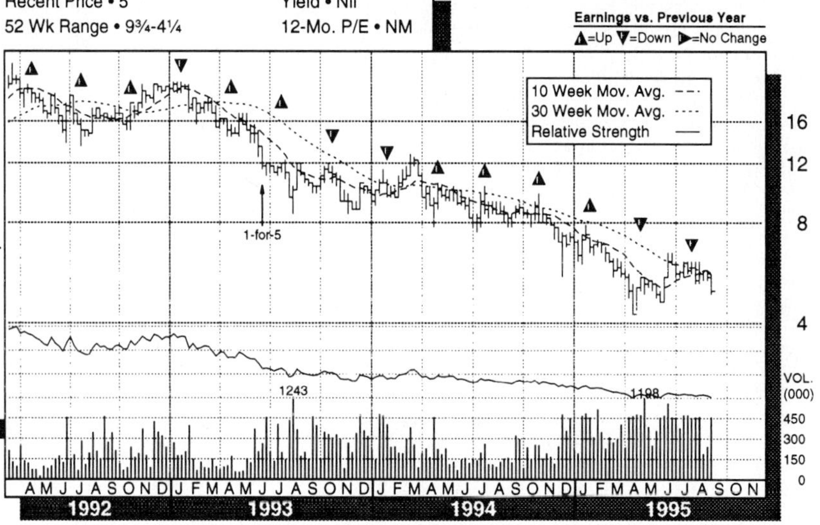

Business Profile - 05-SEP-95

The company's financial structure is very highly leveraged. While cash flows have been, and management expects them to continue to be, sufficient to cover interest costs, operations in recent years have fallen short of expectations. Results have reflected negative operating trends, including consistently low annual growth in average unit sales at three of the company's chains, increased competitive pressure, lower customer traffic, and limited resources to respond to changes.

Operational Review - 05-SEP-95

Revenues in the first half of 1995, edged up slightly, year to year, as three of the company's four chains had positive comparable-store sales. Expenses rose less rapidly; operating income advanced. After higher interest and debt costs, the loss from continuing operations widened to $28,737,000, from $25,539,000. Results exclude a loss from discontinued operations in the 1995 period and a profit from the sale of the Canteen food and vending subsidiary in the 1994 period.

Stock Performance - 01-SEP-95

In the past 30 trading days, FLST's shares have declined 13%, compared to a 2% rise in the S&P 500. Average trading volume for the past five days was 97,420 shares, compared with the 40-day moving average of 93,378 shares.

Key Stock Statistics

Dividend Rate/Share	Nil	Shareholders	10,500
Shs. outstg. (M)	42.4	Market cap. (B)	$0.212
Avg. daily vol. (M)	0.072	Inst. holdings	20%
Tang. Bk. Value/Share	NM	Insider holdings	NA
Beta	1.03		

Value of $10,000 invested 5 years ago: $ 2,222

Fiscal Year Ending Dec. 31

	1995	% Change	1994	% Change	1993	% Change
Revenues (Million $)						
1Q	636.5	2%	626.3	-29%	879.0	2%
2Q	681.5	NM	679.6	-32%	1,001	7%
3Q	—	—	700.6	-35%	1,075	8%
4Q	—	—	659.5	-35%	1,015	10%
Yr.	—	—	2,666	-33%	3,970	7%
Income (Million $)						
1Q	-22.40	NM	-12.65	NM	-30.07	NM
2Q	-6.33	NM	-12.89	NM	-11.85	NM
3Q	—	—	4.25	NM	-6.71	NM
4Q	—	—	4.47	NM	-1,599	NM
Yr.	—	—	-16.82	NM	-1,647	NM
Earnings Per Share ($)						
1Q	-0.61	NM	-0.38	NM	-0.80	NM
2Q	-0.23	NM	-0.21	NM	-0.36	NM
3Q	—	—	0.02	NM	-0.24	NM
4Q	—	—	0.02	NM	-37.83	NM
Yr.	—	—	-0.14	NM	-39.23	NM

Next earnings report expected: late October

Flagstar Companies

Business Summary - 29-AUG-95

Flagstar Companies, Inc. (formerly TW Holdings), through its Flagstar Corp. subsidiary, is one of the largest foodservice companies in the U.S., with operations primarily in the restaurant business.

Restaurant operations, concentrated in the western and southern U.S., include: Hardee's, a fast-food hamburger chain; Quincy's, a steakhouse chain designed to provide limited dining service at moderate prices; Denny's, the largest full-service family restaurant chain in the U.S.; and El Pollo Loco, a fast-food chain specializing in char-broiled chicken.

At June 30, 1995, there were 1,562 Denny's units (956 company operated, 547 franchised and 59 foreign joint ventures) and 212 El Pollo Loco restaurants (114 company operated, 96 franchised and two foreign joint ventures) in operation. At that date, the company was also operating 204 Quincy's restaurants and was the franchisee of 600 Hardee's units.

The average check in 1994 at company-owned units was $4.75 at the Denny's units, $6.59 at El Pollo Loco, $5.79 at Quincy's and $3.11 at Hardee's. Of Flagstar's owned and operated restaurants, average unit sales in 1994 were $1.25 million for Denny's, $1.35 million for Quincy's, $1.21 million for Hardee's and $931,900 for El Pollo Loco.

Important Developments

Jul. '95—The company announced an agreement to sell its Proficient Food Company subsidiary to MBM Corp. for $130 million. The sale of Proficient, a food products and supplies distribution company, is expected to be completed at the end of the third quarter of 1995. Separately, FLST said it will sell TW Recreational Services ($144 million in sales in 1994) to Northbrook Corp. for $110 million. The divestiture of TW, which operates its recreation services business, is expected to close in the fourth quarter. Flagstar is still looking for a buyer for its Volume Services Inc. ($182 million) subsidiary. Proceeds from the sales were earmarked to repay short-term borrowings or long-term debt, or to fund the company's remodeling and capital expenditure programs.

Nov. '94—NDI, a black-owned company, agreed to purchase, operate and develop up to 47 Denny's restaurants over the next six years in New York and New Jersey.

Capitalization

Long Term Debt: $2,053,578,000 (6/95).
Preferred Stock: 6,300,000 shs.
Warrants: To buy 15,000,000 com. shs. at $17.50 (held by KKR).

Per Share Data ($) (Year Ended Dec. 31)

	1994	1993	1992	1991	1990	1989
Tangible Bk. Val.	-25.67	-35.16	-33.95	-68.25	-68.40	-67.75
Cash Flow	1.89	-33.41	6.80	6.80	6.45	NA
Earnings	-0.14	-39.23	-2.35	-3.05	-3.05	-10.75
Dividends	Nil	Nil	Nil	Nil	Nil	Nil
Payout Ratio	Nil	Nil	Nil	Nil	Nil	Nil
Prices - High	12¾	20⅞	23¾	23⅛	29¾	22½
- Low	5½	8½	13⅜	10⅝	12¼	17½
P/E Ratio - High	NM	NM	NM	NM	NM	NM
- Low	NM	NM	NM	NA	NA	NA

Income Statement Analysis (Million $)

	1994	%Chg	1993	%Chg	1992	%Chg	1991
Revs.	2,666	-33%	3,970	7%	3,720	3%	3,618
Oper. Inc.	334	-26%	453	-4%	471	7%	442
Depr.	130	-47%	247	9%	227	4%	218
Int. Exp.	227	-15%	266	-13%	304	-2%	309
Pretax Inc.	-19.0	NM	-1,728	NM	-58.4	NM	-86.0
Eff. Tax Rate	NM	—	NM	—	NM	—	NM
Net Inc.	-17.0	NM	-1,627	NM	-51.8	NM	-67.6

Balance Sheet & Other Fin. Data (Million $)

	1994	1993	1992	1991	1990	1989
Cash	66.7	45.0	39.3	19.2	23.3	7.8
Curr. Assets	258	251	207	190	210	252
Total Assets	1,582	1,797	3,390	3,385	3,496	3,632
Curr. Liab.	386	556	491	547	531	881
LT Debt	2,068	2,352	2,179	2,261	2,306	1,948
Common Eqty.	-1,062	-1,422	132	77.0	139	207
Total Cap.	1,027	953	2,600	2,566	2,800	2,642
Cap. Exp.	154	225	178	109	149	72.0
Cash Flow	99	-1,414	169	151	142	NA

Ratio Analysis

	1994	1993	1992	1991	1990	1989
Curr. Ratio	0.7	0.5	0.4	0.3	0.4	0.3
% LT Debt of Cap.	201.4	247.0	83.8	88.1	82.3	73.7
% Net Inc.of Revs.	NM	NM	NM	NM	NM	NM
% Ret. on Assets	NM	NM	NM	NM	NM	NM
% Ret. on Equity	NM	NM	NM	NM	NM	NM

Dividend Data —No common dividends have been paid.

Data as orig. reptd.; bef. results of disc. opers. and/or spec. items. Per share data adj. for stk. divs. as of ex-div. date. E-Estimated. NA-Not Available. NM-Not Meaningful. NR-Not Ranked.

Office—203 E. Main St., Spartanburg, SC 29319-9722. **Tel**—(803) 597-8000. **Chrmn, Pres & CEO**—J. B. Adamson. **EVP & CFO**—C. R. Campbell. **VP & Secy**—R. J. Parish. **Investor Contact**—L. Gosnell. **Dirs**—J. B. Adamson, M. Chu, V. K. Farris, H. R. Kravis, A. A. Levison, P. E. Raether, J. J. Richardson, C. S. Robbins, G. R. Roberts, L. E. Smart, M. T. Tokarz. **Transfer Agent & Registrar**—Continental Stock Transfer & Trust Co., NYC. **Incorporated** in Delaware in 1988. **Empl**-100,000. **S&P Analyst:** Efraim Levy

STANDARD & POOR'S

STOCK REPORTS

Flow International

NASDAQ Symbol **FLOW**

In S&P SmallCap 600

01-NOV-95

Industry: Manufacturing/Distr

Summary: This company is a leading producer of ultrahigh-pressure waterjet cutting and cleaning systems, and a provider of access systems, robotics, and factory automation equipment.

Quantitative Evaluations

Outlook (1 Lowest—5 Highest) • **4**

Fair Value • **13½**

Risk • **Average**

Earn./Div. Rank • **B**

Technical Eval. • **Bullish** since 12/94

Rel. Strength Rank (1 Lowest—99 Highest) • **45**

Insider Activity • **NA**

Recent Price • 11⅝ | 52 Wk Range • 13¼-6⅛ | Yield • Nil | 12-Mo. P/E • 21.1

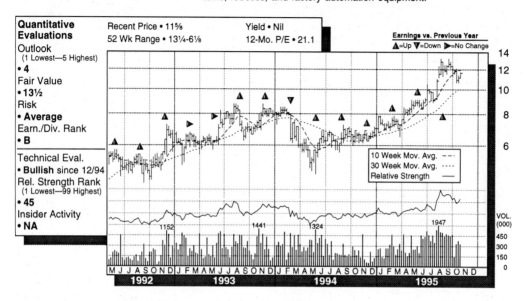

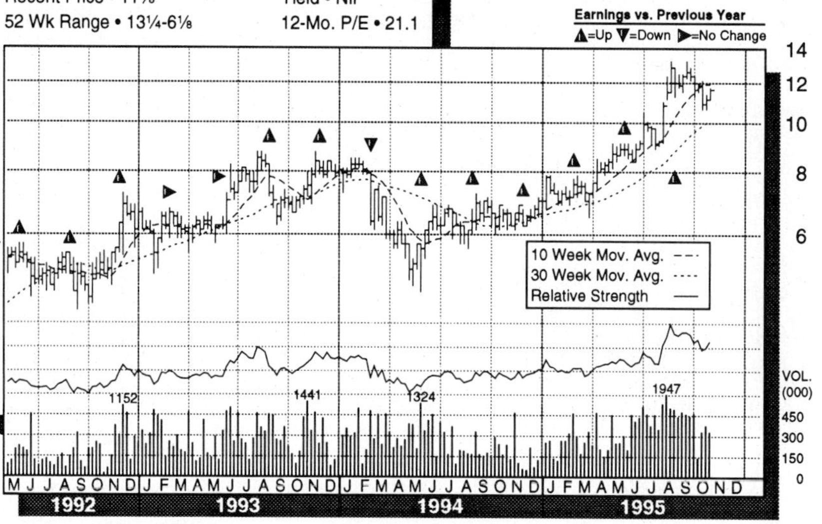

Business Profile - 01-NOV-95

Revenues surpassed $100 million in fiscal 1995 (Apr.), and Flow aims to pass $200 million by 1998. It hopes to achieve this through international expansion, with sales outside the U.S. (which accounted for 32% of fiscal 1995 revenues) providing about 50% of the total. To accelerate growth in Asia, the company recently formed a 51%-owned joint venture in Japan. The recent acquisition of two robotics manufacturers allows Flow to provide enhanced control and operation of its waterjet systems.

Operational Review - 01-NOV-95

Revenues grew 35% in the first quarter of fiscal 1996, paced by robotics acquisitions and UHP strength in European markets. Margins narrowed, restricted by costs related to integration of new businesses; operating income increased 27%. Net interest and other expense rose less rapidly, and pretax income climbed 29%. Net income was up 25%; EPS, on 5.6% more shares, rose 17%.

Stock Performance - 27-OCT-95

In the past 30 trading days, FLOW's shares have declined 8%, compared to a 0.63% fall in the S&P 500. Average trading volume for the past five days was 65,480 shares, compared with the 40-day moving average of 88,364 shares.

Key Stock Statistics

Dividend Rate/Share	Nil	Shareholders	1,600
Shs. outstg. (M)	14.7	Market cap. (B)	$0.163
Avg. daily vol. (M)	0.062	Inst. holdings	40%
Tang. Bk. Value/Share	2.54	Insider holdings	NA
Beta	-0.19		

Value of $10,000 invested 5 years ago: $ 32,068

Fiscal Year Ending Apr. 30

	1996	% Change	1995	% Change	1994	% Change
Revenues (Million $)						
1Q	33.01	35%	24.51	27%	19.36	NM
2Q	—	—	26.76	9%	24.59	18%
3Q	—	—	27.19	32%	20.56	9%
4Q	—	—	31.56	31%	24.13	20%
Yr.	—	—	110.0	24%	88.63	12%
Income (Million $)						
1Q	2.06	25%	1.65	49%	1.11	—
2Q	—	—	2.16	20%	1.80	—
3Q	—	—	1.62	NM	-1.79	NM
4Q	—	—	2.30	60%	1.44	29%
Yr.	—	—	7.73	NM	2.55	-39%
Earnings Per Share ($)						
1Q	0.14	17%	0.12	50%	0.08	14%
2Q	—	—	0.15	15%	0.13	44%
3Q	—	—	0.11	NM	-0.13	NM
4Q	—	—	0.15	50%	0.10	25%
Yr.	—	—	0.53	194%	0.18	-40%

Next earnings report expected: late November

Flow International

Business Summary - 01-NOV-95

Flow International Corporation (formerly Flow Systems, Inc.) designs, develops, makes, markets and services ultrahigh-pressure (over 30,000 lbs. per sq. in., or psi) waterjets and related products and services. Revenues by product line in recent years were:

	1994-95	1993-94
UHP waterjet systems	33%	23%
UHP spare parts	26%	30%
Access systems	31%	33%
Hydro services	10%	14%

Ultrahigh-pressure waterjet systems can be used to cut metallic and nonmetallic materials. Intensifier and direct-drive pumps are the core component of the products, propelling ultrahigh-pressured water through a narrow nozzle, and generating a high-velocity waterjet or abrasivejet. In the latter case, abrasives are added to the waterjet stream. The products can make a narrow precision cut effectively and cleanly, without disadvantages associated with mechanical cutting technologies. Flow sells systems worldwide to the aerospace, automotive, disposable products, food processing, glass, metal cutting, marble and stonecutting, oil field services and paper industries. Its systems are also used for industrial cleaning applications. The large proportion of waterjet replacement parts sold helps to insulate the company from the effects of economic downturns.

The company also manufactures robotic articulation equipment used in the cutting process, as well as other automation systems such as pick and place, and load/unload operations. In December 1994, Flow acquired Dynovation Machine Systems Inc., which produces robotic waterjet cutting cells and automated assembly systems. In January 1995, it purchased ASI Robotics Systems, which makes high accuracy gantry robots and related systems.

Flow makes, rents, sells and services scaffolding products for use in structural maintenance and construction applications. It sells both mobile and permanently installed access systems for use in structural maintenance and construction applications.

The company also offers HydroMilling and HydroCleaning services on a subcontract basis for the removal of deteriorated concrete from highway bridges and other reinforced concrete surfaces, as well as for the removal of rubber and paint from airport runways.

Important Developments

Aug. '95—Flow said UHP sales were up 57% in the fiscal 1996 (Apr.) first quarter, aided by two robotic acquisitions. For comparable UHP units, European operations advanced 52%, while domestic sales increased 3%.

Capitalization

Long Term Obligations: $34,103,000 (7/95).
Minority Interest: $1,154,000.

Per Share Data ($) (Year Ended Apr. 30)

	1995	1994	1993	1992	1991	1990
Tangible Bk. Val.	2.54	2.58	2.43	2.30	2.11	2.20
Cash Flow	0.89	0.45	0.54	0.47	0.14	0.44
Earnings	0.53	0.18	0.30	0.23	-0.08	0.20
Dividends	Nil	Nil	Nil	Nil	Nil	Nil
Payout Ratio	Nil	Nil	Nil	Nil	Nil	Nil
Cal. Yrs.	1994	1993	1992	1991	1990	1989
Prices - High	8½	8¾	7¼	4⅛	5	4⅜
- Low	4⅝	5	3	1⅜	1⅛	2¾
P/E Ratio - High	16	49	24	18	NM	22
- Low	9	28	10	6	NM	14

Income Statement Analysis (Million $)

	1995	%Chg	1994	%Chg	1993	%Chg	1992
Revs.	110	24%	88.6	12%	79.1	63%	48.4
Oper. Inc.	16.9	114%	7.9	-23%	10.3	38%	7.5
Depr.	5.2	33%	3.9	17%	3.3	25%	2.7
Int. Exp.	2.4	32%	1.8	25%	1.4	42%	1.0
Pretax Inc.	9.3	198%	3.1	-46%	5.8	42%	4.1
Eff. Tax Rate	17%	—	18%	—	28%	—	25%
Net Inc.	7.7	NM	2.5	-39%	4.2	36%	3.1

Balance Sheet & Other Fin. Data (Million $)

	1995	1994	1993	1992	1991	1990
Cash	1.1	1.4	0.1	0.8	1.5	0.7
Curr. Assets	66.0	55.1	47.4	28.2	28.5	33.8
Total Assets	106	78.2	69.3	43.7	41.0	48.4
Curr. Liab.	21.4	29.7	22.3	12.5	13.2	13.2
LT Debt	33.4	10.6	12.5	4.4	4.6	10.4
Common Eqty.	49.8	35.4	31.7	26.6	22.7	23.8
Total Cap.	84.1	48.5	46.9	31.2	27.7	35.2
Cap. Exp.	5.6	6.2	7.8	3.9	2.3	4.0
Cash Flow	12.9	6.4	7.3	5.4	1.6	5.4

Ratio Analysis

	1995	1994	1993	1992	1991	1990
Curr. Ratio	3.1	1.9	2.1	2.3	2.2	2.6
% LT Debt of Cap.	39.7	21.8	26.7	14.1	16.7	29.6
% Net Inc.of Revs.	7.0	2.9	5.3	6.4	NM	5.4
% Ret. on Assets	8.4	3.4	7.1	7.0	NM	6.0
% Ret. on Equity	17.6	7.3	13.6	10.5	NM	10.9

Dividend Data —No cash dividends have been paid. A poison pill stock purchase rights plan was adopted in 1990.

Data as orig. reptd.; bef. results of disc. opers. and/or spec. items. Per share data adj. for stk. divs. as of ex-div. date. E-Estimated. NA-Not Available. NM-Not Meaningful. NR-Not Ranked.

Office—23500-64th Ave. S, Kent, WA 98032. **Tel**—(206) 850-3500. **Chrmn, Pres & CEO**—R. W. Tarrant. **EVP & COO**—T. A. Cross. **CFO**—Elaine P. Scherba. **Secy**—J. S. Leness. **Dirs**—L. J. Alpinieri, L. J. Andrews, J. S. Cargill, D. J. Evans, R. A. O'Brien, A. I. Prentice, K. M. Roberts, R. W. Tarrant, D. D. Thornton. **Transfer Agent & Registrar**—First Interstate Bank of Washington, Seattle. **Incorporated** in Washington in 1980; reincorporated in Delaware in 1983. **Empl**-792. **S&P Analyst:** Justin McCann

Fluke Corp.

NYSE Symbol FLK In S&P SmallCap 600

Price	Range	P-E Ratio	Dividend	Yield	S&P Ranking	Beta
Sep. 28'95	1995					
38	42½–27¾	18	0.60	1.6%	B–	0.97

Summary

This company makes precision electronic test equipment for scientific, educational, industrial and government applications. Earnings have been rebounding strongly, aided by contributions from new products. Trading in the shares shifted to the NYSE from the ASE on April 10, 1995.

Business Summary

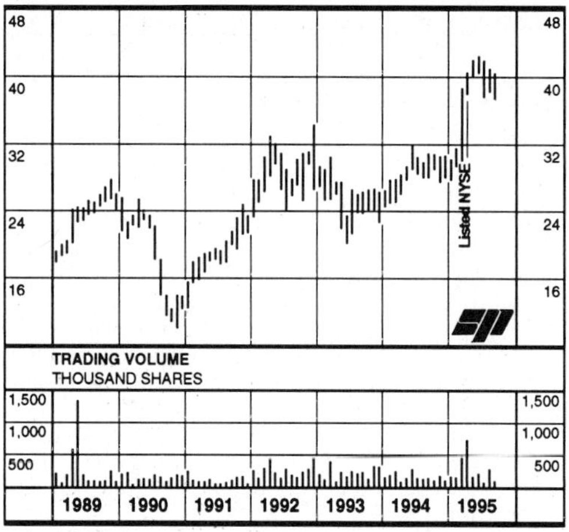

Fluke Corporation (formerly John Fluke Mfg. Co.) is engaged in the design, development, manufacture and sale of commercial electronic test and measurement instruments for scientific, educational, industrial and government applications. International revenues contributed 56% of the total in fiscal 1994-95, up from 53% in 1993-94.

Fluke manufactures a broad range of products utilized in test and measurement instrument applications. The product line includes digital voltmeters and multimeters used in laboratories, research and production testing; electronic counters, which measure specific electrical events in the domains of time and frequency; digital thermometers; digital board testers; function generators; data loggers; calibrators and standards; automatic test systems used in calibration laboratories, industry and aerospace facilities; PC-based data acquisition systems and software; logic analyzers; oscilloscopes; test tools for local area networks; and systems elements.

In 1992-93, the company introduced an automotive meter instrument and an automotive ScopeMeter test tool. In 1993-94, Fluke introduced 13 new products, including five new products in its line of LAN troubleshooting tools. The company also expanded into the electrical power quality market with its Fluke 40/41 family of Power Harmonics Analyzers. New product introductions totaled 10 in 1994-95, including a new family of documenting process calibrators for the process industries.

In May 1993, the company completed the acquisition of the test and measurement business of Philips Electronics N.V. for $42.5 million, consisting of $23.1 million in cash and one million Fluke common shares. The acquisition added about $125 million to annual revenues, and some 900 employees in Europe. As part of the transaction, the Series A convertible preferred stock that Philips owned was converted into 538,144 common shares, giving Philips ownership of 19.5% of the common shares.

Important Developments

May '95— Fluke signed an agreement with the Automotive division of Robert Bosch Corp. that will make Bosch the sole European distributor for the Fluke 98 Automotive ScopeMeter, a new tool specifically designed for the automotive service industry that combines the capabilities of a multimeter, oscilloscope, ignition analyzer and data recorder.

Next earnings report expected in late November.

Per Share Data ($)

Yr. End Apr. 30[1]	1995	[2]1994	[3]1993	1992	1991	1990	1989	1988	1987	1986
Tangible Bk. Val.	**19.27**	16.82	[4]21.31	[4]20.44	[4]18.46	[4]18.12	[4]17.00	[4]15.92	12.63	13.24
Cash Flow	**3.87**	5.02	1.33	3.67	1.98	3.14	4.48	[5]2.46	1.43	2.31
Earnings	**1.86**	1.10	0.40	2.16	0.46	1.72	2.80	[5]1.35	0.23	1.30
Dividends	**0.56**	0.52	0.26	0.48	0.40	[6]0.37	0.15	Nil	Nil	Nil
Payout Ratio	**30%**	47%	65%	20%	84%	20%	4%	Nil	Nil	Nil
Calendar Years	**1994**	1993	1992	1991	1990	1989	1988	1987	1986	1985
Prices—High	**32**	30½	34⅜	24⅞	25⅝	27¾	19⅜	28⅝	26⅝	26⅛
Low	**24⅝**	20¼	23⅜	12½	10⅛	17⅞	14⅛	13⅜	18	18⅛
P/E Ratio—	**17–13**	28–18	NA	54–27	15–6	10–6	14–10	NM	21–14	16–11

Data as orig. reptd. Adj. for stk. divs. of 5% Mar. 1988, 5% Feb. 1987, 5% Feb. 1986, 5% Feb. 1985. **1.** Yrs. ended Sep. 30 prior to 1993. **2.** Refl. merger or acq. **3.** Seven mos. **4.** Incl. intangibles. **5.** 53 wks. **6.** Five payments. NA-Not Available. NM-Not Meaningful.

Income Data (Million $)

Year Ended Apr. 30[1]	Revs.	Oper. Inc.	% Oper. Inc. of Revs.	Cap. Exp.	Depr.	Int. Exp.	Net Bef. Taxes	Eff. Tax Rate	Net Inc.	% Net Inc. of Revs.	Cash Flow
1995	**382**	**40.2**	**10.5**	**14.1**	**16.0**	**1.44**	**24.0**	**38.0%**	**14.9**	**3.9**	**30.9**
[2]1994	358	48.4	13.5	13.1	31.6	1.53	14.1	37.5%	8.8	2.5	40.4
[3]1993	132	9.9	7.5	6.2	6.6	0.02	4.0	28.2%	2.8	2.2	9.4
1992	272	31.2	11.5	10.1	10.9	0.25	21.2	28.2%	15.2	5.6	25.8
1991	240	24.0	10.0	10.9	10.8	0.06	3.4	6.9%	3.2	1.3	13.7
1990	234	25.6	10.9	11.4	10.2	0.55	[4]14.7	17.1%	12.2	5.2	22.2
1989	248	37.2	15.0	10.5	14.1	0.59	[4]36.2	36.0%	23.5	9.3	37.1
1988	225	24.2	10.8	15.7	10.3	0.45	[4]17.8	30.2%	[5]12.4	5.5	22.7
1987	206	24.2	11.7	8.3	10.4	1.83	6.2	67.5%	2.0	1.0	12.4
1986	209	26.8	12.8	9.0	9.5	2.41	16.9	28.1%	12.2	5.8	21.6

Balance Sheet Data (Million $)

Apr. 30[1]	Cash	Curr. Assets	Curr. Liab.	Curr. Ratio	Total Assets	% Ret. on Assets	Long Term Debt	Common Equity	Total Cap.	% LT Debt of Cap.	% Ret. on Equity
1995	**28.9**	**183**	**59.4**	**3.1**	**276**	**5.7**	**21.6**	**175**	**206**	**10.5**	**8.9**
1994	6.5	154	56.4	2.7	246	3.8	14.7	158	182	8.1	5.5
1993	24.4	111	26.6	4.2	172	NA	Nil	135	142	Nil	NA
1992	16.4	114	34.1	3.3	176	8.9	0.4	129	138	0.3	12.1
1991	5.7	102	38.1	2.7	166	2.1	0.2	116	124	0.1	2.6
1990	1.3	91	21.7	4.2	152	7.9	0.1	118	125	0.1	10.5
1989	2.6	97	33.6	2.9	157	15.7	2.3	110	119	1.9	21.6
1988	12.4	106	31.5	3.4	176	7.3	0.7	132	140	0.5	10.5
1987	12.2	106	47.4	2.2	167	1.2	0.8	107	116	0.7	1.8
1986	31.3	113	25.6	4.4	178	7.1	16.7	124	148	11.3	10.3

Data as orig. reptd. **1.** Yrs. ended Sep. 30 prior to 1993. **2.** Refl. merger or acq. **3.** Seven mos. **4.** Incl. equity in earns. of nonconsol. subs. **5.** Refl. acctg. change. NA-Not Available.

Revenues (Million $)

Quarter:	1995–96	1994–95	1993–94	1992–93
Jul.	98.7	86.0	84.7	---
Oct.		91.6	89.6	---
Jan.		99.1	87.6	[1]74.0
Apr.		105.4	96.1	58.1
		382.1	357.9	32.1

Revenues for the quarter ended July 28, 1995, rose 15%, year to year, aided by contributions from new products. Net income was up 72%, reflecting the higher margins associated with newer mission-centric products, and well controlled costs. Earnings increased to $0.50 a share from $0.30 in the year-earlier period.

Total orders for the 1995-96 first quarter were $98.6 million, up 23% from the depressed year-earlier level, paced by strength overseas.

Common Share Earnings ($)

Quarter:	1995–96	1994–95	1993–94	1992–93
Jul.	0.50	0.30	0.18	---
Oct.		0.40	0.24	---
Jan.		0.53	0.30	[1]0.01
Apr.		0.63	0.38	0.39
		1.86	1.10	0.40

1. Four mos. ended Jan. 31, 1993

Dividend Data

Stock distributions were made annually from 1968 to 1988; cash dividends were initiated in 1989 and have been boosted each year since. A "poison pill" shareholder rights plan has been adopted.

Amt of Divd. $	Date Decl.	Ex-divd. Date	Stock of Record	Payment Date
0.14	Dec. 19	Jan. 23	Jan. 27	Feb. 17'95
0.14	Mar. 13	Apr. 24	Apr. 28	May 19'95
0.15	Jun. 26	Jul. 26	Jul. 28	Aug. 18'95
0.15	Sep. 14	Oct. 25	Oct. 27	Nov. 17'95

Capitalization

Long Term Obligations: $17,279,000 (7/95).

Common Stock: 7,981,926 shs. ($0.25 par).
The Fluke family owns or controls 19%.
Philips Electronics N.V. owns 14%.
Institutions hold nearly 50%.
Shareholders: 1,882 of record (4/95).

Options: To buy 1,046,120 shs. at $11.88 to $40.38 a sh. (4/95).

Office—6920 Seaway Blvd., Everett, WA 98203 (P.O. Box 9090, Everett, WA 98206-9090). **Tel**—(206) 347-6100. **Chrmn & CEO**—W. G. Parzybok, Jr. **Pres & COO**—G. M. Winn. **VP & CFO**—B. L. Rowan. **VP & Treas**—J. R. Smith. **VP & Secy**—D. G. McKnight. **Investor Contact**—Gary V. Ball (206-356-5262). **Dirs**—J. P. Bingham, P. M. Condit, J. D. Durbin, D. L. Fluke, J. M. Fluke, Jr., R. S. Miller, Jr., W. H. Neukon, W. G. Parzybok, Jr., N. S. Rogers, S. C. Tumminello, J. E. Warjone, G. M. Winn. **Transfer Agent & Registrars**—First National Bank of Boston. **Incorporated** in Washington in 1953. **Empl**—2,495.

STANDARD & POOR'S

STOCK REPORTS

Foodmaker, Inc.

NYSE Symbol **FM**
In S&P SmallCap 600

12-SEP-95 **Industry:** Food serving

Summary: This company operates and franchises Jack In The Box, a leading regional fast-food chain. It also owns a 39% interest in full service restaurant operator Family Restaurants Inc.

Quantitative Evaluations
Outlook (1 Lowest—5 Highest) • **NA**
Fair Value • **NA**
Risk • **High**
Earn./Div. Rank • **NR**

Technical Eval. • **Bearish** since 8/95
Rel. Strength Rank (1 Lowest—99 Highest) • **71**
Insider Activity • **NA**

Recent Price • 6⅝
52 Wk Range • 7¼-3¼
Yield • Nil
12-Mo. P/E • NM

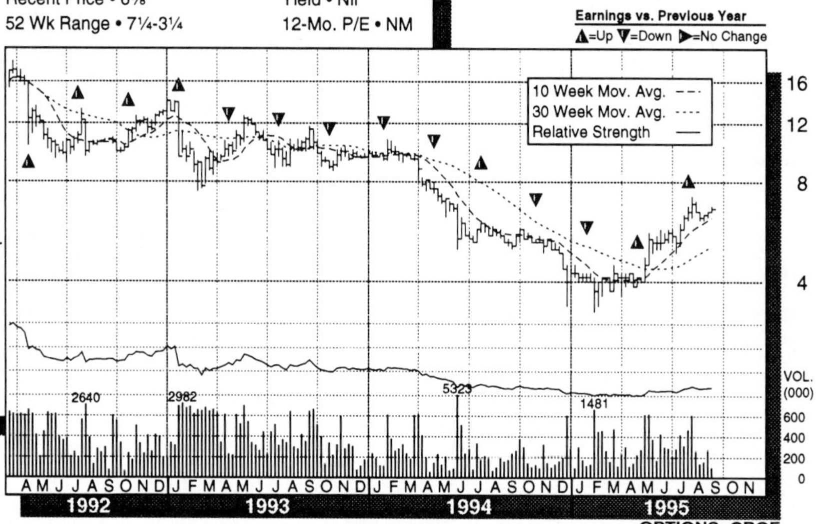

OPTIONS: CBOE

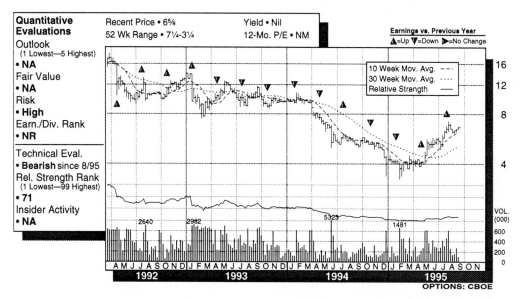

Business Profile - 12-SEP-95

This company operates and franchise Jack In The Box fast-food restaurants. It is seeking to strengthen its brand identity, and to introduce new products, promotions and advertising in order to boost sales. It also intends to expand in Asia, the Middle East and Latin America. The shares have rebounded from a record low, as sales rose in recent periods. Revenues have been depressed since a 1993 outbreak of food-borne illness at certain Jack In The Box restaurants.

Operational Review - 12-SEP-95

Revenues in the 40 weeks ended July 9, 1995, declined 10%, year to year. However, comparable company-owned restaurant sales were higher in the second and third quarters, and a profit in the third quarter was the first quarterly profit since December 1992. After charges of $57.2 million to writedown the company's interest in Family Restaurants Inc. and $8 million to settle stockholder class action litigation, the net loss widened substantially.

Stock Performance - 08-SEP-95

In the past 30 trading days, FM's shares have increased 2%, compared to a 2% rise in the S&P 500. Average trading volume for the past five days was 23,875 shares, compared with the 40-day moving average of 59,559 shares.

Key Stock Statistics

Dividend Rate/Share	Nil	Shareholders	700
Shs. outstg. (M)	38.7	Market cap. (B)	$0.257
Avg. daily vol. (M)	0.033	Inst. holdings	30%
Tang. Bk. Value/Share	0.70	Insider holdings	NA
Beta	NA		

Value of $10,000 invested 5 years ago: NA

Fiscal Year Ending Sep. 30

	1995	% Change	1994	% Change	1993	% Change
Revenues (Million $)						
1Q	293.7	-23%	381.6	-5%	403.0	10%
2Q	229.7	5%	218.7	-11%	244.9	-12%
3Q	244.1	8%	225.8	-19%	280.2	NM
4Q	—	—	227.2	-27%	312.2	7%
Yr.	—	—	1,053	-15%	1,241	2%
Income (Million $)						
1Q	-72.30	NM	-4.40	NM	11.50	NM
2Q	-3.15	NM	-22.91	NM	-22.18	NM
3Q	2.62	NM	-3.43	NM	-30.78	NM
4Q	—	—	-5.52	NM	-2.67	NM
Yr.	—	—	-36.27	NM	-44.13	NM
Earnings Per Share ($)						
1Q	-1.87	NM	-0.11	NM	0.29	142%
2Q	-0.08	NM	-0.59	NM	-0.58	NM
3Q	0.07	NM	-0.09	NM	-0.81	NM
4Q	—	—	-0.14	NM	-0.07	NM
Yr.	—	—	-0.94	NM	-1.15	NM

Next earnings report expected: early November

Foodmaker, Inc.

Business Summary - 12-SEP-95

Foodmaker owns, operates and franchises Jack In The Box restaurants, and owns a 39% interest in Family Restaurants Inc. (formerly The Restaurant Enterprise Group). As of August 2, 1995, it was operating and franchising a total of 1,243 Jack In The Box restaurant units (859 company-operated and 384 franchised). The number of restaurants in operation at the end of recent fiscal years was:

	1994	1993	1992	1991
Jack In The Box	1,224	1,172	1,155	1,089

Jack In The Box, a chain of restaurants located principally in the West and Southwest, directs its menu and marketing strategy primarily toward adult fast-food customers. The restaurants offer Chicken Fajita Pita and sourdough sandwiches not commonly offered in the fast-food hamburger segment, as well as traditional fast-foods such as hamburgers and french fries. The menu features 45 to 50 items, including hamburgers, specialty sandwiches, salads, Mexican foods, finger foods, breakfast foods, side dishes and desserts.

Family Restaurants (FRI; 39% owned) operates 694 restaurants in 34 states, and licenses or franchises 251 restaurants, primarily in Japan, South Korea and Europe. As part of prepackaged bankruptcy proceedings, FRI acquired Foodmaker's Chi-Chi's division, the largest chain of full-service Mexican restaurants in the U.S. Chi-Chi's serve moderately priced Mexican food and alcoholic beverages in a festive atmosphere designed to appeal to a families. The menu features primarily Sonoran-style Mexican food, including several types of chimichangas, tacos, burritos, enchiladas and Mexican desserts. Apollo Adivsors L.P. and Leonard Green & Partners L.P. own 57% of FRI, and its management owns the balance.

FM's plans for Jack In The Box call for opening 300 to 350 new company-operated restaurants and 40 new franchised outlets over five years.

Important Developments

Aug. '95—FM's profit in 12 weeks ended July 9, 1995, was its first quarterly profit since the January 1993 outbreak of food-borne illness at certain Jack In The Box outlets.

Mar. '95—The company restated results for the period ended January 22, 1995, reflecting the writedown of its investment in Family Restaurants Inc. (FRI). The loss for the period rose to $72.3 million ($1.87 a share), from $20.5 million ($0.53) reported earlier. As a result of adverse publicity regarding the nutritional value of Mexican food and subsequent sales declines, FM felt it would be unlikely to recover certain long-lived intangible assets of Chi-Chi's Mexican Restaurantes.

Capitalization

Long Term Debt: $455,238,000 (4/16/95).

Per Share Data ($)

(Year Ended Sep. 30)

	1994	1993	1992	1991	1990	1989
Tangible Bk. Val.	0.18	-1.49	1.24	0.83	NA	NA
Cash Flow	-0.12	-0.05	1.83	1.87	NA	NA
Earnings	-0.94	-1.15	0.67	0.57	NA	NA
Dividends	Nil	Nil	Nil	NA	NA	NA
Payout Ratio	Nil	NM	Nil	NA	NA	NA
Prices - High	10¾	14	18½	NA	NA	NA
- Low	3⅜	7½	9⅛	NA	NA	NA
P/E Ratio - High	NM	NM	28	NA	NA	NA
- Low	NM	NM	14	NA	NA	NA

Income Statement Analysis (Million $)

	1994	%Chg	1993	%Chg	1992	%Chg	1991
Revs.	1,053	-15%	1,241	2%	1,219	5%	1,157
Oper. Inc.	57.0	-34%	86.0	-42%	149	NM	150
Depr.	31.6	-25%	42.4	12%	37.8	-25%	50.3
Int. Exp.	55.9	-3%	57.8	-21%	73.2	23%	59.3
Pretax Inc.	-33.3	NM	-66.2	NM	38.7	-5%	40.6
Eff. Tax Rate	NM	—	NM	—	43%	—	46%
Net Inc.	-36.3	NM	-44.1	NM	21.9	NM	22.0

Balance Sheet & Other Fin. Data (Million $)

	1994	1993	1992	1991	1990	1989
Cash	36.0	4.5	20.0	1.4	NA	NA
Curr. Assets	107	94.0	106	67.0	NA	NA
Total Assets	740	890	915	845	NA	NA
Curr. Liab.	148	203	167	159	NA	NA
LT Debt	448	500	501	505	NA	NA
Common Eqty.	100	139	247	182	NA	NA
Total Cap.	553	657	748	687	NA	NA
Cap. Exp.	92.0	59.0	77.0	NA	NA	NA
Cash Flow	-4.6	-1.7	59.7	72.3	NA	NA

Ratio Analysis

	1994	1993	1992	1991	1990	1989
Curr. Ratio	0.7	0.5	0.6	0.4	NA	NA
% LT Debt of Cap.	81.0	76.2	67.0	73.5	NA	NA
% Net Inc.of Revs.	NM	NM	1.8	1.9	NA	NA
% Ret. on Assets	NM	NM	1.1	NA	NA	NA
% Ret. on Equity	NM	NM	NM	NA	NA	NA

Dividend Data —Foodmaker does not intend to pay cash dividends.

Data as orig. reptd.; bef. results of disc. opers. and/or spec. items. Per share data adj. for stk. divs. as of ex-div. date. E-Estimated. NA-Not Available. NM-Not Meaningful. NR-Not Ranked.

Office—9330 Balboa Ave., San Diego, CA 92123. **Tel**—(619) 571-2121. **Chrmn CEO & Pres**—J. W. Goodall, Jr. **EVP, CFO & Investor Contact**—Charles W. Duddles. **VP & Secy**—W. E. Rulon. **VP & Contr**—R. L. Suttie. **Dirs**—M. E. Alpert, P. T. Carter, C. W. Duddles, E. Gibbons, J. W. Goodall, Jr., L. I. Green, R. J. Nugent, Jr., L. R. Payne, C. V. Walker. **Transfer Agent & Registrar**—First Interstate Bank of California, LA. **Incorporated** in Delaware in 1971. **Empl**-22,000. **S&P Analyst:** Efraim Levy

STANDARD & POOR'S

STOCK REPORTS

Forschner Group

NASDAQ Symbol **FSNR**

In S&P SmallCap 600

05-SEP-95

Industry:
Retail merchandiser

Summary: This company, the exclusive U.S., Canadian and Caribbean distributor of the Victorinox Original Swiss Army Knife, also sells Swiss Army Brand watches and cutlery.

Quantitative Evaluations

Outlook
(1 Lowest—5 Highest)
• **NA**

Fair Value
• **NA**

Risk
• **Average**

Earn./Div. Rank
• **B**

Technical Eval.
• **Bullish** since 7/95

Rel. Strength Rank
(1 Lowest—99 Highest)
• **55**

Insider Activity
• **Favorable**

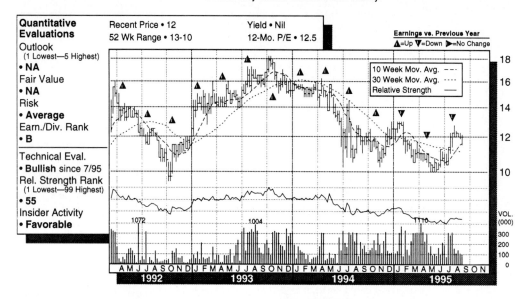

Recent Price • 12
52 Wk Range • 13-10

Yield • Nil
12-Mo. P/E • 12.5

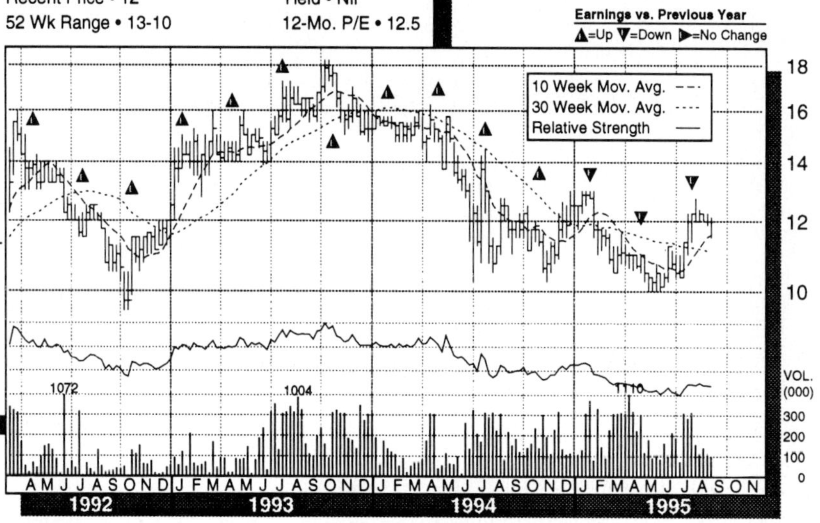

Business Profile - 05-SEP-95

This company is the exclusive U.S., Canadian and Caribbean distributor of the Victorinox Original Swiss Army knife. It also sells watches and other products carrying the Swiss Army Brand name, and cutlery. Swiss Army knife maker Victorinox owns a 9.7% interest in Forschner. The company holds a minority interest in Forschner Enterprises, an investment vehicle formed in 1994, and also owns a 20% interest in Simmons Outdoor Corp. and a 37% interest in SweetWater Inc.

Operational Review - 05-SEP-95

The significant decline in sales and earnings in the second quarter of 1995 reflect the conclusion of a promotional campaign for a single customer, which accounted for 41.5% of second quarter 1994 sales. Also negatively impacting second quarter results was the weakness of the dollar against the Swiss franc. Excluding the promotional campaign, sales of company's major products were higher in the second quarter and the first half of the year.

Stock Performance - 01-SEP-95

In the past 30 trading days, FSNR's shares were unchanged, compared to a 2% rise in the S&P 500. Average trading volume for the past five days was 19,600 shares, compared with the 40-day moving average of 42,253 shares.

Key Stock Statistics

Dividend Rate/Share	Nil	Shareholders	400
Shs. outstg. (M)	8.2	Market cap. (B)	$0.098
Avg. daily vol. (M)	0.022	Inst. holdings	50%
Tang. Bk. Value/Share	9.39	Insider holdings	NA
Beta	1.00		

Value of $10,000 invested 5 years ago: $ 10,666

Fiscal Year Ending Dec. 31

	1995	% Change	1994	% Change	1993	% Change
Revenues (Million $)						
1Q	29.37	9%	27.05	54%	17.60	29%
2Q	25.92	-35%	39.94	88%	21.20	44%
3Q	—	—	37.26	35%	27.69	38%
4Q	—	—	40.19	12%	36.03	39%
Yr.	—	—	144.4	41%	102.5	38%
Income (Million $)						
1Q	1.27	-18%	1.54	88%	0.82	78%
2Q	0.22	-84%	1.38	45%	0.95	70%
3Q	—	—	3.43	22%	2.81	54%
4Q	—	—	3.01	11%	2.72	31%
Yr.	—	—	9.36	28%	7.30	48%
Earnings Per Share ($)						
1Q	0.15	-29%	0.21	75%	0.12	20%
2Q	0.03	-82%	0.17	21%	0.14	56%
3Q	—	—	0.42	5%	0.40	43%
4Q	—	—	0.37	-3%	0.38	23%
Yr.	—	—	1.16	12%	1.04	30%

Next earnings report expected: late October

Forschner Group

Business Summary - 25-AUG-95

The Forschner Group, Inc. is the exclusive U.S., Canadian and Caribbean distributor of the Victorinox Original Swiss Army Knife, Victorinox cutlery and Victorinox watches. The company also sells its own line of watches and other high-quality Swiss-made products under its Swiss Army Brand.

Victorinox Swiss Army Knives are multi-blade pocket knives containing implements capable of more functions than standard pocket knives. For example, the most popular Classic knife, with a suggested retail price of $20, features a knife, scissors, nail file with screwdriver tip, toothpick and tweezers. Forschner markets more than 40 different models of Victorinox Original Swiss Army Knives, containing up to 22 different implements, and ranging from a basic knife with a suggested retail price of $10 to the highest-priced model at about $145. Swiss Army Knives accounted for 36% of 1994 sales.

Forschner's line of Swiss Army Brand products includes seven models of watches ranging from the Renegade, at a suggested retail price of $75, to a chronograph with a suggested retail price of $495. The company also sells Swiss Army Brand sunglasses and compasses. Watches and other Swiss Army Brand products produced 51% of 1994 sales. Sales of Swiss Army Brand products are seasonal, with demand typically strongest from July through December.

The majority of Forschner's professional cutlery products, made of stainless steel, are manufactured by Victorinox and other makers in Germany, England and Brazil. Customers for cutlery include distributors of hotel, restaurant, butcher and slaughterhouse supplies and retail cutlery stores throughout the U.S. and Canada. The company also sells the Victorinox line of floral knives to wholesale florists. In 1994, sales of these products represented 13% of the total.

In April 1994, the company formed Forschner Enterprises, an investment entity, to acquire interests in businesses that offer the opportunity for significant equity growth. Forschner received Series A preferred shares in return for an investment of $7 million (a 33% interest). Upon completion of a private placement of 3,000,000 Forschner Enterprises Series B preferred shares, the company's stake would be cut to 13%.

Important Developments

Jul. '95—The company won a preliminary injunction which banned three Manhattan retailers from using the Swiss Army trade name, trademark, or logo.

Capitalization

Long Term Debt: None (6/95).

Per Share Data ($) (Year Ended Dec. 31)

	1994	1993	1992	1991	1990	1989
Tangible Bk. Val.	10.07	8.65	6.70	3.22	2.71	1.95
Cash Flow	1.56	1.39	0.94	0.62	0.58	0.80
Earnings	1.16	1.04	0.80	0.45	0.51	0.75
Dividends	Nil	Nil	Nil	Nil	Nil	Nil
Payout Ratio	Nil	Nil	Nil	Nil	Nil	Nil
Prices - High	16¼	18¼	16	12¾	12½	14½
- Low	10¼	12	9½	5¾	4½	5
P/E Ratio - High	14	18	20	28	25	19
- Low	9	12	12	13	9	7

Income Statement Analysis (Million $)

	1994	%Chg	1993	%Chg	1992	%Chg	1991
Revs.	144	40%	103	39%	74.1	23%	60.1
Oper. Inc.	20.2	46%	13.8	43%	9.6	86%	5.2
Depr.	3.2	27%	2.5	188%	0.9	19%	0.7
Int. Exp.	0.0	NM	0.0	-88%	0.3	-38%	0.4
Pretax Inc.	16.0	39%	11.5	29%	8.9	151%	3.5
Eff. Tax Rate	42%	—	37%	—	45%	—	45%
Net Inc.	9.4	28%	7.3	48%	4.9	152%	2.0

Balance Sheet & Other Fin. Data (Million $)

	1994	1993	1992	1991	1990	1989
Cash	18.0	7.8	6.6	0.1	2.3	0.8
Curr. Assets	78.6	57.6	43.7	25.2	21.4	17.1
Total Assets	106	78.0	54.3	29.0	24.7	20.0
Curr. Liab.	23.9	17.7	10.8	6.8	8.3	4.6
LT Debt	Nil	Nil	Nil	8.1	4.7	7.3
Common Eqty.	82.4	60.4	43.0	13.3	11.0	7.4
Total Cap.	82.4	60.4	43.5	21.9	16.2	15.2
Cap. Exp.	1.7	2.8	1.1	0.7	0.7	0.2
Cash Flow	12.6	9.8	5.8	2.7	2.4	3.3

Ratio Analysis

	1994	1993	1992	1991	1990	1989
Curr. Ratio	3.3	3.3	4.1	3.7	2.6	3.7
% LT Debt of Cap.	Nil	Nil	Nil	37.2	29.3	48.3
% Net Inc.of Revs.	6.5	7.1	6.7	3.3	4.2	7.0
% Ret. on Assets	9.5	10.7	9.9	7.2	9.1	15.8
% Ret. on Equity	12.2	13.6	15.5	16.0	22.2	46.8

Dividend Data —Cash dividends have never been paid.

Data as orig. reptd.; bef. results of disc. opers. and/or spec. items. Per share data adj. for stk. divs. as of ex-div. date. E-Estimated. NA-Not Available. NM-Not Meaningful. NR-Not Ranked.

Office—One Research Drive, Shelton, CT 06484. **Tel**—(203) 929-6391. **Co-Chrmn & Co-CEO**—J. W. Kennedy, M. L. Hart. **EVP & CFO**—T. D. Cunningham. **SVP, Secy & Treas**—T. M. Lupinski. **Dirs**—A. C. Allen, T. A. Barron, T. D. Cunningham, V. D. Farrell, Jr., H. M. Friedman, P. Gilson, M. L. Hart, J. W. Kennedy, K. R. Lively, L. Marx, L. Marx, Jr., S. G. Mortimer III, S. R. Rawn, Jr., E. M. Reynolds, J. Spencer, J. V. Tunney. **Transfer Agent & Registrar**—Registrar & Transfer Co., Cranford, NJ. **Incorporated** in Delaware in 1974. **Empl**-193. **S&P Analyst:** Stephen Madonna, CFA

STANDARD & POOR'S

STOCK REPORTS

Franklin Quest

NYSE Symbol **FNQ**
In S&P SmallCap 600

02-AUG-95 **Industry:** Education

Summary: This company provides time management products and training seminars to corporations, government agencies and the general public, which are designed to improve productivity.

Quantitative Evaluations

Outlook (1 Lowest—5 Highest)
• **5**

Fair Value
• **34⅞**

Risk
• **Average**

Earn./Div. Rank
• **NR**

Technical Eval.
• **Bearish** since 3/95

Rel. Strength Rank (1 Lowest—99 Highest)
• **5**

Insider Activity
• **NA**

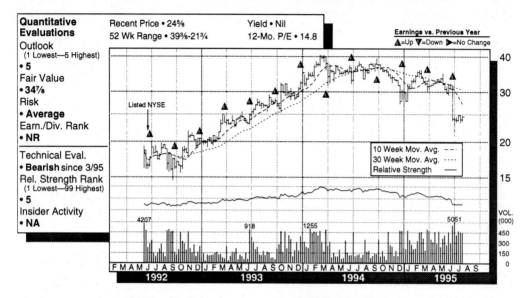

Recent Price • 24⅝
52 Wk Range • 39⅜-21¾

Yield • Nil
12-Mo. P/E • 14.8

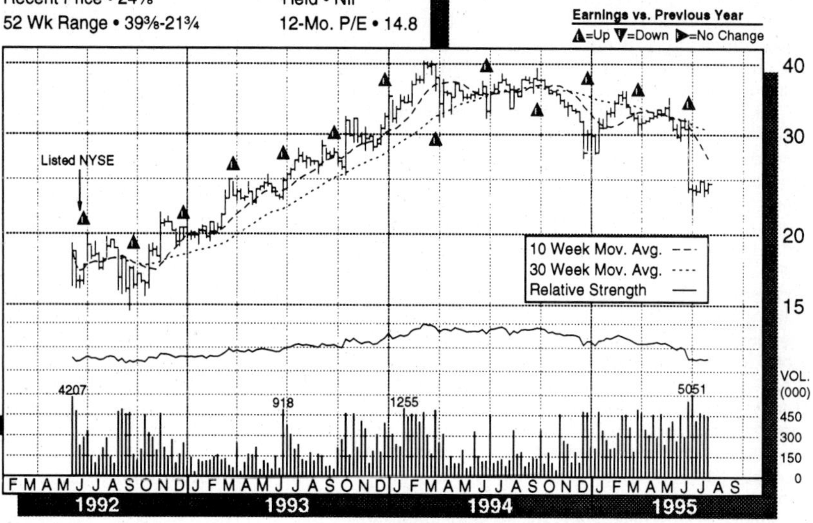

Business Profile - 02-AUG-95

Franklin Quest's products are primarily marketed through catalogs and over 50 retail stores. Seminars are marketed by a direct sales force to more than 2,000 institutional clients. The company plans to open 20 additional retail stores in fiscal 1995. In June 1995, FNQ began to repurchase up to one million of its common shares under a previously announced board authorization.

Operational Review - 02-AUG-95

Franklin Quest's sales and earnings have risen rapidly over the past several years, and this trend continued through the first nine months of fiscal 1994-95. Sales and earnings for the third quarter increased 21%, while sales and earnings for the first nine months of the fiscal year rose 27%. However, the company stock fell sharply as a result of slowed seminar revenue growth. Some analysts reasoned that lower growth in seminar sales may portend a slower growth rate for the entire company.

Stock Performance - 28-JUL-95

In the past 30 trading days, FNQ's shares have declined 20%, compared to a 4% rise in the S&P 500. Average trading volume for the past five days was 88,280 shares, compared with the 40-day moving average of 287,120 shares.

Key Stock Statistics

Dividend Rate/Share	Nil	Shareholders	NA
Shs. outstg. (M)	21.7	Market cap. (B)	$0.518
Avg. daily vol. (M)	0.111	Inst. holdings	53%
Tang. Bk. Value/Share	7.82	Insider holdings	NA
Beta	NA		

Value of $10,000 invested 5 years ago: NA

Fiscal Year Ending Aug. 31

	1995	% Change	1994	% Change	1993	% Change
Revenues (Million $)						
1Q	71.06	26%	56.44	28%	44.00	35%
2Q	74.67	33%	56.17	26%	44.48	38%
3Q	59.38	21%	48.91	34%	36.62	37%
4Q	—	—	54.42	35%	40.43	38%
Yr.	—	—	215.9	30%	165.5	37%
Income (Million $)						
1Q	12.43	25%	9.93	30%	7.62	39%
2Q	12.01	33%	9.03	34%	6.74	39%
3Q	6.37	21%	5.27	33%	3.97	47%
4Q	—	—	6.69	31%	5.09	44%
Yr.	—	—	30.92	32%	23.42	41%
Earnings Per Share ($)						
1Q	0.56	22%	0.46	28%	0.36	13%
2Q	0.53	29%	0.41	28%	0.32	10%
3Q	0.28	17%	0.24	26%	0.19	19%
4Q	—	—	0.30	25%	0.24	41%
Yr.	—	—	1.40	27%	1.10	18%

Next earnings report expected: late September

Franklin Quest

Business Summary - 02-AUG-95

Franklin Quest is a provider of training seminars and products such as notebooks and software, designed to improve individual productivity through effective time management. The seminars and products are based upon the company's time management system, which enables individuals to better manage their time by identifying goals and prioritizing the tasks necessary to achieve them through the use of the company's primary product, the Franklin Day Planner. In fiscal 1994, time management products accounted for 77% of the company's total revenues, with seminars contributing the remaining 23%.

The Franklin Planner consists of a paper-based, refillable binder with various planning aids, monthly and annual calendars, and personal management sections. Products are marketed through a catalog, 52 company-operated retail stores located in 22 states and, to a lesser degree, a direct sales force. Retail store sales were $54.5 million in fiscal 1993-94, up from $34.4 million in fiscal 1992-93.

Seminars are marketed by the direct sales force to more than 2,000 institutional clients such as corporations, government agencies and other organizations, as well as to the general public. Franklin also offers a program in which employees of institutional clients are trained and certified to conduct seminars for in-house employees. Since 1987, about 1.1 million persons have been trained to use the Franklin system.

In February 1994, the company acquired Shipley Associates and two related entities for $23 million. The Shipley Division provides training, consulting services and products designed to improve written and oral business communication skills for clients in the U.S. and Europe.

In July 1994, Franklin acquired the operations of the National Institute of Fitness, a total fitness, exercise and nutritional training center located near St. George, Utah. Franklin offers a weekly training program, as well as a special health and fitness module to be a part of the Franklin Planner.

Important Developments

Jun. '95—Third quarter sales and earnings rose 21% from the previous year's third quarter. Retail sales increased 25% in part due to additional stores in operation; training sales rose 21%, partially due to acquisitions; and catalog sales grew 9%.

Capitalization

Long Term Debt: $12,299,000 (2/95), incl. capital lease obligations.
Options: To purchase 3,094,550 com. shs. at $1.11 to $34.50 ea. (8/94).

Per Share Data ($) (Year Ended Aug. 31)

	1994	1993	1992	1991	1990	1989
Tangible Bk. Val.	6.61	5.55	4.15	3.64	NA	NA
Cash Flow	1.64	1.30	1.08	0.70	0.25	0.12
Earnings	1.40	1.10	0.93	0.61	0.18	0.09
Dividends	Nil	Nil	Nil	NA	NA	NA
Payout Ratio	Nil	Nil	Nil	NA	NA	NA
Prices - High	40½	35¼	21⅞	NA	NA	NA
- Low	27¼	19⅛	14⅝	NA	NA	NA
P/E Ratio - High	29	32	24	NA	NA	NA
- Low	19	17	16	NA	NA	NA

Income Statement Analysis (Million $)

	1994	%Chg	1993	%Chg	1992	%Chg	1991
Revs.	216	31%	165	36%	121	48%	82.0
Oper. Inc.	54.9	31%	41.9	37%	30.5	63%	18.7
Depr.	5.3	23%	4.3	58%	2.7	76%	1.5
Int. Exp.	0.9	-16%	1.1	-18%	1.3	6%	1.2
Pretax Inc.	51.0	32%	38.7	41%	27.4	65%	16.6
Eff. Tax Rate	39%	—	40%	—	39%	—	35%
Net Inc.	30.9	32%	23.4	41%	16.6	54%	10.8

Balance Sheet & Other Fin. Data (Million $)

	1994	1993	1992	1991	1990	1989
Cash	49.7	63.5	58.2	53.0	NA	NA
Curr. Assets	113	108	89.4	NA	NA	NA
Total Assets	198	145	114	102	NA	NA
Curr. Liab.	28.0	23.5	20.6	NA	NA	NA
LT Debt	7.6	8.2	10.6	8.0	NA	NA
Common Eqty.	162	113	82.4	71.1	NA	NA
Total Cap.	170	121	93.1	79.1	NA	NA
Cap. Exp.	24.6	13.0	16.3	4.4	4.0	4.9
Cash Flow	36.2	27.7	19.3	12.4	4.8	2.3

Ratio Analysis

	1994	1993	1992	1991	1990	1989
Curr. Ratio	4.0	4.6	4.3	NA	NA	NA
% LT Debt of Cap.	4.5	6.8	11.4	10.1	NA	NA
% Net Inc.of Revs.	14.3	14.2	13.7	13.2	6.6	5.7
% Ret. on Assets	17.9	17.9	20.1	NA	NA	NA
% Ret. on Equity	22.3	23.7	32.3	NA	NA	NA

Dividend Data (In its initial offering prospectus dated June 1992, the company stated that it did not intend to pay cash dividends.)

Data as orig. reptd.; bef. results of disc. opers. and/or spec. items. Per share data adj. for stk. divs. as of ex-div. date. E-Estimated. NA-Not Available. NM-Not Meaningful. NR-Not Ranked.

Office—2200 West Parkway Blvd., Salt Lake City, UT 84119-2331. **Tel**—(801) 975-1776. **Chrmn & CEO**—H. W. Smith. **Pres**—A. B. Crouch. **SVP-CFO & Treas**—J. L. Atwood. **SVP-Secy**—V. J. Christensen. **Dirs**—J. L. Atwood, J. M. Beggs, R. F. Bennett, B. B. Campbell, V. J. Christensen, A. B. Crouch, R. H. Daines, E. J. Garn, D. P. Howells, T. H. Lenagh, H. W. Smith. **Transfer Agent & Registrar**—Zions First National Bank, Salt Lake City, Utah. **Incorporated** In Utah in 1983. **Empl**-2,018. **S&P Analyst:** Stephen Madonna, CFA

Fremont General

NYSE Symbol FMT In S&P SmallCap 600

Price	Range	P-E Ratio	Dividend	Yield	S&P Ranking	Beta
Aug. 30'95	1995					
27	28 3/4–17 5/32	8	0.80	3.0%	B	0.48

Summary

Through its subsidiaries, this company provides insurance and financial services, including workers' compensation, malpractice and life insurance and asset-based lending. Recent results have been bolstered by the early 1995 acquisition of Casualty Insurance Co.

Business Summary

Fremont General Corporation is engaged, through subsidiaries, in insurance and financial services. Its principal product lines are California workers' compensation, medical malpractice, life insurance and varied financial services for commercial and individual customers.

In 1994, operating revenues and pretax income (in 000) by business segment were derived as follows:

	Revs.	Profits
Workers' compensation	70.2%	$62,199
Medical malpractice	5.1%	6,583
Property and casualty corporate & other	0.6%	-7,517
Financial services	23.6%	28,014
Corporate	0.5%	-7,708

Through its Fremont Compensation unit, the company offers workers' compensation insurance almost exclusively in California. In 1994, net premiums earned from the workers' compensation line amounted to $401.5 million ($426.8 million the year before), with a combined ratio of 97.6% (101.6%). The medical malpractice insurance operation writes standard professional liability insurance for physicians, primarily in California. Net premiums earned from the medical malpractice line were $28.6 million in 1994 ($25.1 million in 1993), with a combined ratio of 93.4% (77.8%).

The company's financial services operations offer life insurance products, provide commercial finance/asset-based lending and have thrift and loan activities. Life insurance products, including annuities, credit life and disability insurance and term life insurance for consumers, are offered through intermediaries such as insurance brokers, lending institutions, automobile dealers and credit associations.

FMT's commercial finance business consists of asset-based loans to small and medium-size businesses. Loans are secured primarily by accounts receivable and inventory, and range in size from

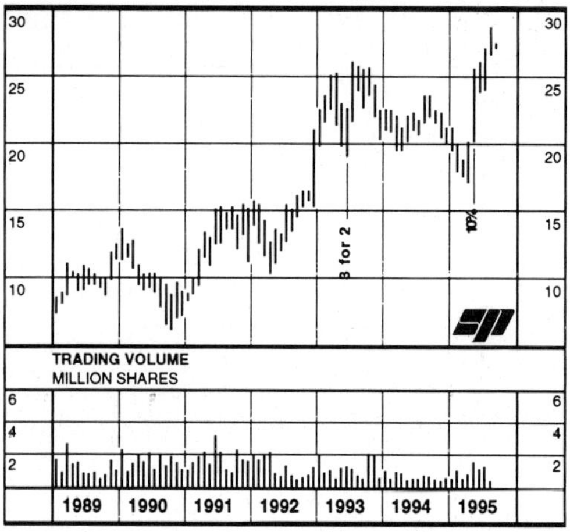

$500,000 to $10 million. At December 31, 1994, the loan portfolio amounted to $557 million.

In 1990, FMT acquired the holding company for Investors Thrift, a California thrift and loan that serves customers through its 11-branch network. The thrift and loan portfolio totaled $827.0 million at 1994 year end and was divided: 83% commercial real estate, 13% consumer real estate, and 4% contract loans.

Important Developments

Feb. '95— FMT completed the acquisition of Casualty Insurance Co. (assets of about $1 billion), the Illinois-based workers' compensation insurance unit of Continental Corp., for $250 million. Fremont said the acquisition would significantly affect its financial statements, and make FMT the nation's largest private mono-line underwriter of workers' compensation, with combined premiums of approximately $800 million.

Next earnings report expected in late October.

Per Share Data ($)

Yr. End Dec. 31	1994	1993	[2]1992	[2]1991	[2]1990	[2]1989	[2]1988	[3]1987	[3]1986	[2]1985
Tangible Bk. Val.	**19.04**	20.02	[1]20.75	[1]15.53	[1]13.70	[1]12.32	[1]11.57	[1]10.08	[1]10.79	[1]12.48
Oper. Earnings[4]	**NA**	NA	NA	NA	[5]NA	[5]NA	1.1909	0.1545	0.9636	d1.6000
Earnings[4,6]	**[5]3.25**	[5]2.78	[5]2.58	[5]2.35	[5]1.92	[5]1.32	0.97	0.15	0.99	d1.53
Dividends[7]	**0.682**	0.655	0.588	0.509	0.485	0.424	0.364	0.364	0.291	0.291
Payout Ratio	**21%**	24%	23%	22%	25%	32%	38%	250%	29%	NM
Prices—High	**23 5/8**	26 1/8	21 1/16	15 15/32	13 5/8	12 1/2	8 3/16	12 7/16	20 19/32	18 1/32
Low	**19 17/32**	19 3/32	10 5/16	8 11/32	6 1/8	7 11/32	5 5/16	4 25/32	9 1/4	9 27/32
P/E Ratio—	**7–6**	9–7	8–4	7–4	7–3	9–6	7–4	82–35	21–10	NM

Data as orig. reptd. Adj. for stk. divs. of 10% May 1995, 50% Jun. 1993. **1.** As reptd. by co. **2.** Refl. merger or acq. **3.** Refl. sale or disposal. **4.** Bef. spec. items of +3.18 in 1992, +0.06 in 1990, +0.13 in 1988, +0.15 in 1987, -0.06 in 1985 & results of disc. opers. of +0.16 in 1991, -0.02 in 1990, -0.24 in 1988, -0.74 in 1987, -2.32 in 1986, +6.62 in 1985. **5.** Ful. dil.: 2.73 in 1994, 2.48 in 1993, 2.30 in 1992, 2.15 in 1991, 1.80 in 1990, 1.28 in 1989. **6.** Aft. gains/losses on security trans. **7.** Declared. d-Deficit. NA-Not Available. NM-Not Meaningful.

Income Data (Million $)

Year Ended Dec. 31	Premium Income	Net Invest. Inc.	Oth. Revs.	Total Revs.	Property & Casualty Underwriting Ratios Loss	Expense	Comb.	Net Bef. Taxes	[3]Net Oper. Inc.	[3]Net Inc.	—% Return On— Revs.	Equity
1994	**448**	**77**	**128.0**	**653**	**63.1**	**23.4**	**86.5**	**81.6**	**NA**	**55.8**	**8.5**	**15.5**
1993	470	77	104.2	651	70.0	21.3	91.3	64.3	NA	42.7	6.6	13.3
1992	429	71	98.8	599	80.4	22.5	102.9	48.6	NA	35.2	5.9	14.3
1991	434	74	73.3	581	72.7	24.5	97.2	41.0	NA	32.1	5.5	16.2
[1]1990	430	83	60.7	573	73.7	24.4	98.1	39.0	NA	26.1	4.6	14.8
[1]1989	350	80	40.5	467	64.6	24.4	89.0	22.2	NA	17.7	3.8	11.0
[1]1988	305	69	37.8	408	75.6	23.6	99.2	23.2	20.1	16.4	4.0	9.9
[2]1987	47	20	33.0	100	76.9	23.4	100.3	3.3	2.6	2.5	2.6	1.4
[2]1986	41	24	28.0	93	82.3	27.7	110.7	18.0	16.9	17.4	18.1	8.2
[1]1985	477	106	20.0	597	88.3	39.0	119.3	d52.4	d28.5	d27.2	NM	NM

Balance Sheet Data (Million $)

Dec. 31	Cash & Equiv.	Premiums Due	——Investment Assets—— [4]Bonds	Stocks	Loans	Total	% Invest. Yield	Deferred Policy Costs	Total Assets	[6]Debt	Common Equity
1994	**44.7**	**48.6**	**697**	**190**	**1,441**	**2,330**	**3.6**	**59.3**	**3,067**	**645**	**351**
1993	48.6	76.7	996	57	846	1,902	4.6	55.2	2,601	530	369
1992	62.6	64.8	780	Nil	689	1,472	[5]8.5	57.5	2,080	309	281
1991	41.8	62.0	770	Nil	520	1,293	[5]9.1	60.7	1,964	249	210
1990	47.7	64.0	761	Nil	432	1,205	[5]10.3	59.6	1,982	187	187
1989	64.6	71.0	994	Nil	188	1,195	[5]9.3	54.9	1,489	214	165
1988	84.3	49.0	754	Nil	253	1,022	[5]8.7	37.4	1,240	289	155
1987	12.4	3.0	241	Nil	216	464	[5]7.9	30.0	581	308	170
1986	10.5	4.0	231	Nil	170	410	[5]10.1	27.0	561	249	188
1985	75.8	102.0	1,015	Nil	134	1,149	[5]11.3	39.8	1,484	167	222

Data as orig. reptd. **1.** Refl. merger or acq. **2.** Refl. sale or disposal. **3.** Bef. spec. items & results of disc. ops. **4.** Incl. short-term invest. **5.** As reptd. by co. **6.** Incl. curr. portion. d-Deficit. NA-Not Available. NM-Not Meaningful.

Review of Operations

Total revenues advanced 44%, year to year, in the six months ended June 30, 1995, benefiting from the Casualty Insurance Company acquisition and strong increases in net investment and loan interest income; net premiums earned expanded 39%. Following higher property and casualty and medical malpractice combined ratios, an 18% rise in financial services income, and lower interest and corporate expenses, pretax income rose 12%. After taxes at 32.4%, against 32.7%, net income was up 13%, to $31.1 million ($1.80 a share; $1.51 fully diluted) from $27.6 million ($1.60; $1.35, as adjusted).

Common Share Earnings ($)

Quarter:	1995	1994	1993	1992
Mar.	0.83	0.78	0.67	0.61
Jun.	0.97	0.82	0.70	0.61
Sep.		0.82	0.71	0.64
Dec.		0.83	0.74	0.73
		3.25	2.78	2.57

Finances

In August 1994, FMT obtained a revolving line of credit, expiring August 1995, that permits borrowings of up to $180 million, of which $171 million was outstanding at March 31, 1995.

In October 1993, Fremont sold in a public offering an aggregate of $373.8 million principal amount of liquid yield option notes, due 2013, convertible into FMT common stock at $31.86 a share. Net proceeds approximated $135 million.

Dividend Data

Cash has been paid in each year since 1976.

Amt. of Divd. $	Date Decl.	Ex-divd. Date	Stock of Record	Payment Date
0.19	Nov. 11	Dec. 23	Dec. 30	Jan. 31'95
0.19	Feb. 9	Mar. 27	Mar. 31	Apr. 28'95
10%	May 11	May 23	May 30	Jun. 15'95
0.20	May 11	Jun. 28	Jun. 30	Jul. 31'95
0.20	Aug. 11	Sep. 27	Sep. 29	Oct. 31'95

Capitalization

Long Term Debt: $542,462,000 (3/95).

Common Stock: 16,926,000 shs. ($1 par).
Institutions hold about 72%.
Shareholders: 1,311 of record (12/94).

Office—2020 Santa Monica Blvd., Suite 600, Santa Monica, CA 90404. **Tel**—(310) 315-5500. **Chrmn & CEO**—J. A. McIntyre. **Pres & COO**—L. J. Rampino. **SVP, Treas, CFO & Investor Contact**—Wayne R. Bailey. **Secy**—E. J. Lieber. **Dirs**—H. I. Flournoy, C. D. Kranwinkle, J. A. McIntyre, D. W. Morrisroe, L. J. Rampino, D. C. Ross, K. L. Trefftzs. **Transfer Agent & Registrar**—Chemical Trust Co. of California. **Incorporated** in Nevada in 1972. **Empl**—1,463.

 Robert Schpoont

STANDARD & POOR'S

STOCK REPORTS

Fresh Choice

NASDAQ Symbol **SALD**

In S&P SmallCap 600

17-AUG-95 **Industry:** Food serving

Summary: This chain of 58 casual restaurants features specialty and traditional salads, hot pasta dishes, soups, bakery goods and desserts in a self-service format.

Quantitative Evaluations

Outlook (1 Lowest—5 Highest) • **NA**

Fair Value • **NA**

Risk • **High**

Earn./Div. Rank • **NR**

Technical Eval. • **Neutral** since 8/95

Rel. Strength Rank (1 Lowest—99 Highest) • **3**

Insider Activity • **NA**

Recent Price • 8⅜

52 Wk Range • 23½-5⅛

Yield • Nil

12-Mo. P/E • NM

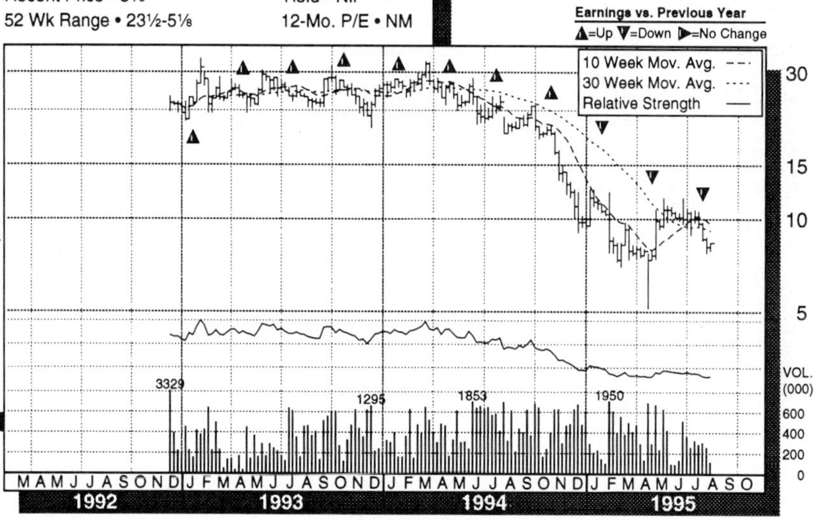

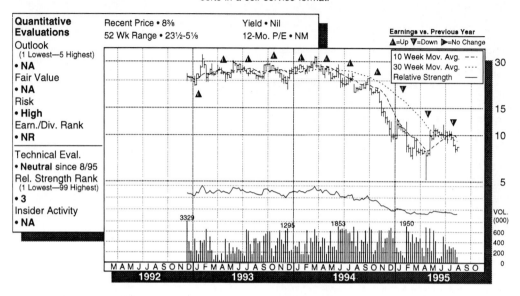

Business Profile - 10-AUG-95

Fresh Choice has grown by adding new restaurants. However, same-store sales have been declining in recent periods, and the company has put expansion plans on hold. To improve comparable-store sales, SALD increased marketing, reinstated its two-tiered price structure to enhance the price/value of its offerings, expanded its menu operations to give customers the option of a more filling meal, and is investing more in training to improve the overall restaurant experience at its units.

Operational Review - 10-AUG-95

Revenues in the 24 weeks ended June 11, 1995, rose, year to year, reflecting additional locations in operation; comparable-restaurant sales slid 17%. Expenses rose more rapidly than sales, reflecting severance and remodeling costs and increased food costs. After a tax credit of $1,636,000, versus taxes at 37.3%, a net loss contrasted with income. In an effort to focus on improving current operations, the company has increased marketing efforts and suspended expansion plans.

Stock Performance - 11-AUG-95

In the past 30 trading days, SALD's shares have declined 20%, compared to a 2% rise in the S&P 500. Average trading volume for the past five days was 21,920 shares, compared with the 40-day moving average of 60,862 shares.

Key Stock Statistics

Dividend Rate/Share	Nil	Shareholders	400
Shs. outstg. (M)	5.5	Market cap. (B)	$0.044
Avg. daily vol. (M)	0.042	Inst. holdings	37%
Tang. Bk. Value/Share	8.77	Insider holdings	NA
Beta	NA		

Value of $10,000 invested 5 years ago: NA

Fiscal Year Ending Dec. 31

	1995	% Change	1994	% Change	1993	% Change
Revenues (Million $)						
1Q	16.93	5%	16.13	50%	10.72	54%
2Q	19.17	6%	18.01	47%	12.27	48%
3Q	—	—	18.88	45%	13.00	38%
4Q	—	—	23.94	36%	17.64	41%
Yr.	—	—	76.97	44%	53.63	44%
Income (Million $)						
1Q	-1.28	NM	0.66	53%	0.43	169%
2Q	-1.56	NM	1.15	58%	0.73	78%
3Q	—	—	1.33	23%	1.08	108%
4Q	—	—	0.07	-91%	0.82	128%
Yr.	—	—	3.20	5%	3.05	112%
Earnings Per Share ($)						
1Q	-0.23	NM	0.12	33%	0.09	125%
2Q	-0.28	NM	0.21	31%	0.16	33%
3Q	—	—	0.24	14%	0.21	40%
4Q	—	—	0.01	-93%	0.15	67%
Yr.	—	—	0.58	-5%	0.61	53%

Next earnings report expected: late September

Fresh Choice

Business Summary - 17-AUG-95

Fresh Choice, Inc. was operating 58 casual, upscale restaurants as of early July 1995. The restaurants, which operate under the Fresh Choice name, are located primarily in Northern and Central California, with additional units in the Dallas, Seattle and Arlington, Va., areas. They feature an extensive selection of high quality, freshly made specialty and traditional salads, hot pasta dishes, soups, bakery goods and desserts, offered in a self-service format. The company seeks to create a distinctive dining experience that combines the selection, quality and ambiance of full-service, casual restaurants with the convenience and low price appeal of traditional buffet restaurants.

The company believes it provides its customers with excellent price/value by offering a two-tier pricing system. Customers can select either a salad/bakery/dessert option for one low price of $4.95 for lunch and $6.25 for dinner, or include soup, pizza and pasta products for $5.95 for lunch and $7.25 for dinner. It uses only fresh produce and high quality ingredients in its menu offerings. To reinforce the company's commitment to freshness, many of Fresh Choice's food offerings are prepared in exhibition-style cooking areas throughout the day. Its wide variety of food and attractive prices are designed to appeal to a wide range of customers, including families, business professionals, students and senior citizens. The company also believes the Fresh Choice concept appeals to health conscious diners who are focused on the nutritional content of their meals.

Each Fresh Choice restaurant is configured with a 60-ft. single or double-sided salad bar featuring specialty tossed and prepared salads and an extensive choice of salad ingredients and dressings. At the end of the salad bar, separate exhibition-style cooking areas offer fresh soups, hot pasta dishes, hot potatoes, hot muffins and other warm bakery goods. A variety of fresh fruits and desserts is offered at a separate serving area. A typical single-sided salad bar restaurant averages 5,500 sq. ft. and seats about 160 people.

The company's strategy is to open restaurants in high-profile sites in each of its target markets. It has located its restaurants in regional malls, strip centers and freestanding locations. The company opened 15 restaurants in 1994 and 14 restaurants in 1993.

Important Developments

Jul. '95—Fresh Choice said it opened four restaurants in the second quarter. In April, SALD said it put expansion plans on hold, reflecting weak same-store sales in recent quarters.

Capitalization

Long Term Debt: $286,000 of cap. lease obligs. (6/11/95).
Options: To buy 371,653 shs. at $0.17 to $27.50 each.

Per Share Data ($) (Year Ended Dec. 31)

	1994	1993	1992	1991	1990	1989
Tangible Bk. Val.	8.85	8.23	4.74	0.26	-0.50	NA
Cash Flow	1.42	1.02	0.77	0.59	0.40	0.19
Earnings	0.58	0.61	0.40	0.23	0.14	-0.08
Dividends	Nil	Nil	Nil	Nil	Nil	Nil
Payout Ratio	Nil	Nil	Nil	Nil	Nil	Nil
Prices - High	32½	33¼	25	NA	NA	NA
- Low	9	19¾	13	NA	NA	NA
P/E Ratio - High	56	55	63	NA	NA	NA
- Low	16	32	33	NA	NA	NA

Income Statement Analysis (Million $)

	1994	%Chg	1993	%Chg	1992	%Chg	1991
Revs.	77.0	44%	53.6	44%	37.1	57%	23.6
Oper. Inc.	9.3	38%	6.8	63%	4.1	49%	2.8
Depr.	4.7	120%	2.1	57%	1.3	11%	1.2
Int. Exp.	0.2	-5%	0.2	-51%	0.4	37%	0.3
Pretax Inc.	4.9	NM	4.8	98%	2.5	86%	1.3
Eff. Tax Rate	35%	—	37%	—	41%	—	40%
Net Inc.	3.2	5%	3.0	112%	1.4	82%	0.8

Balance Sheet & Other Fin. Data (Million $)

	1994	1993	1992	1991	1990	1989
Cash	6.2	18.2	11.6	1.7	1.5	NA
Curr. Assets	9.6	21.8	13.0	3.0	2.1	NA
Total Assets	58.5	52.7	28.2	13.9	9.3	5.5
Curr. Liab.	6.6	4.6	4.1	3.0	1.7	NA
LT Debt	0.5	0.9	1.3	2.9	1.5	1.1
Common Eqty.	49.3	45.2	21.8	1.2	0.5	0.1
Total Cap.	50.6	47.0	23.1	10.4	7.3	4.5
Cap. Exp.	23.7	19.7	5.8	3.9	2.8	2.6
Cash Flow	7.8	5.2	2.8	2.0	1.3	0.2

Ratio Analysis

	1994	1993	1992	1991	1990	1989
Curr. Ratio	1.5	4.7	3.2	1.0	1.2	NA
% LT Debt of Cap.	1.0	1.9	5.6	28.0	20.2	24.8
% Net Inc.of Revs.	4.2	5.7	3.9	3.4	3.1	NM
% Ret. on Assets	5.7	7.0	3.1	6.8	6.2	NM
% Ret. on Equity	6.7	8.5	10.7	11.9	10.0	NM

Dividend Data —No cash dividends have been paid, and the company does not anticipate paying any in the foreseeable future.

Data as orig. reptd.; bef. results of disc. opers. and/or spec. items. Per share data adj. for stk. divs. as of ex-div. date. E-Estimated. NA-Not Available. NM-Not Meaningful. NR-Not Ranked.

Incorporated—in California in 1986; reincorporated in Delaware in 1992. **Office**—2901 Tasman Dr., Suite 109, Santa Clara, CA 95054. **Tel**—(408) 986-8661. **Chrmn & CEO**—C. A. Lynch. **VP & CFO**—D. A. Anderson. **VP & Secy**—J. B. Wells. **Dirs**—B. K. Adams, Jr., W. R. Hawley, C. R. Hays, C. A. Lynch. **Transfer Agent & Registrar**—Chemical Trust Co. of California, SF. **Empl**-2,200. **S&P Analyst:** Efraim Levy

STANDARD & POOR'S

Frontier Insurance Group

STOCK REPORTS

NYSE Symbol **FTR**
In S&P SmallCap 600

12-SEP-95 **Industry:** Insurance

Summary: Through subsidiaries, this holding company conducts business as a specialty property and casualty insurer and reinsurer. Principal lines include medical and dental malpractice.

Quantitative Evaluations
Outlook
(1 Lowest—5 Highest)
• **5**
Fair Value
• **34¼**
Risk
• **Average**
Earn./Div. Rank
• **B+**

Technical Eval.
• **Bullish** since 4/95
Rel. Strength Rank
(1 Lowest—99 Highest)
• **56**
Insider Activity
• **Neutral**

Recent Price • 29¼
52 Wk Range • 32-16¾
Yield • 1.7%
12-Mo. P/E • 21.5

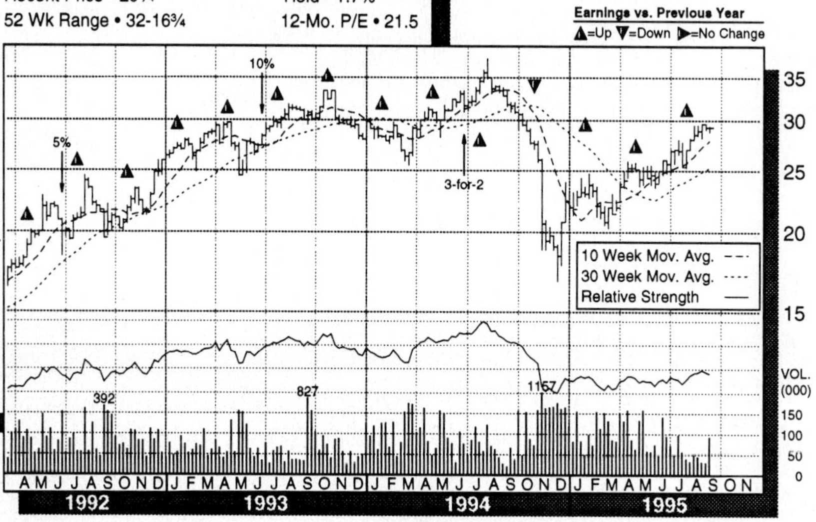

Business Profile - 12-SEP-95

This well diversified specialty insurer and reinsurer's results were severely penalized in 1994 by adverse developments in its malpractice operations in Florida. However, Wall Street estimates point to recovery in 1995, with per share earnings projections at $2.42, compared with 1994's actual of $1.31. Longer term, the company should continue to benefit from anticipated premium hikes, and improvements in its underwriting results.

Operational Review - 12-SEP-95

In the six months ended June 30, 1995, net premiums written rose 26% and total revenues were up 34%, year to year. The primary factors driving this growth were strength in most of FTR's core and new business programs and an increase in investment funds. Expenses advanced 45%, primarily reflecting 49% higher losses and a 70% rise in policy acquisition costs. After taxes at 24.8%, versus 29.1%, net income was up 4.3% to $14,671,000 ($1.13 a share) from $14,067,000 ($1.08).

Stock Performance - 08-SEP-95

In the past 30 trading days, FTR's shares have increased 8%, compared to a 2% rise in the S&P 500. Average trading volume for the past five days was 22,850 shares, compared with the 40-day moving average of 9,356 shares.

Key Stock Statistics

Dividend Rate/Share	0.48	Shareholders	900
Shs. outstg. (M)	13.1	Market cap. (B)	$0.379
Avg. daily vol. (M)	0.010	Inst. holdings	48%
Tang. Bk. Value/Share	16.05	Insider holdings	NA
Beta	1.00		

Value of $10,000 invested 5 years ago: $ 35,624

Fiscal Year Ending Dec. 31

	1995	% Change	1994	% Change	1993	% Change
Revenues (Million $)						
1Q	51.77	26%	41.16	12%	36.78	33%
2Q	53.91	42%	37.95	9%	34.80	16%
3Q	—	—	46.44	29%	36.14	11%
4Q	—	—	54.43	73%	31.44	-14%
Yr.	—	—	180.0	29%	139.2	10%
Income (Million $)						
1Q	6.89	2%	6.74	22%	5.54	18%
2Q	7.78	6%	7.33	21%	6.07	24%
3Q	—	—	-5.08	NM	5.15	23%
4Q	—	—	7.99	25%	6.40	24%
Yr.	—	—	16.98	-27%	23.16	22%
Earnings Per Share ($)						
1Q	0.53	2%	0.52	1%	0.51	18%
2Q	0.60	5%	0.57	2%	0.56	22%
3Q	—	—	-0.39	NM	0.47	20%
4Q	—	—	0.61	24%	0.49	3%
Yr.	—	—	1.31	-35%	2.03	15%

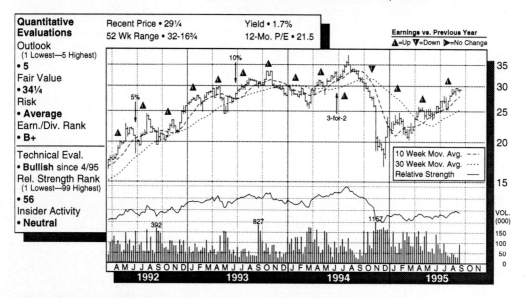

Next earnings report expected: early November

Frontier Insurance Group

Business Summary - 12-SEP-95

Frontier Insurance Group, an insurance holding company, operates through five wholly owned subsidiaries: Frontier Insurance Co., Frontier Pacific Insurance Co., Medical Professional Liability Agency, Inc., Pioneer Claim Management Inc. and Spencer Douglass Insurance Associates. The company, a specialty property and casualty insurer and reinsurer, performs claims adjusting and management services, and acts as an insurance agent and broker. At December 31, 1994, it was licensed in 49 states, the District of Columbia and Puerto Rico.

Net premiums written in 1994 totaled $187.3 million, compared with $118.8 million the year before, and were divided as follows:

	1994	1993
Medical malpractice (including dental)	47.8%	45.4%
Workers' compensation	10.6%	18.6%
General liability	18.3%	14.1%
Surety	19.4%	18.4%
Other	3.9%	3.5%

The company seeks to identify niche markets where competition is limited and it believes appropriate premium rates are available to realize an underwriting profit. FTR directly underwrites specialty niche-market programs including preferred-risk malpractice for physicians, chiropractors and dentists. At 1994 year-end, about 16,255 physicians and 2,435 dentists were insured under the company's medical malpractice insurance program. FTR also directly underwrites workers' compensation, general liability, surety bonds for small contractors, product liability and custom bonds.

FTR no longer assumes reinsurance from unaffiliated companies other than that derived from its required participation in residual market pools.

The company directly underwrites general liability coverage for day care centers, small commercial businesses and contractors, and for a variety of farm and agricultural risks. FTR also underwrites pest control operators, fire protection equipment dealers and installers, and security guards. The company underwrites umbrella coverage up to $5 million over underlying $1 million general liability coverage.

Important Developments

Aug. '95—FTR finalized arrangements with Associated International Insurance Co. to jointly underwrite a commercial earthquake insurance program in California. This program is heavily reinsured to minimize the exposure. The company expects the program to generate $18 million of direct premium on an annual basis to FTR. Separately, in June, FTR added $45 million to the capital and surplus of Frontier Insurance Company, its primary subsidiary.

Capitalization

Long Term Debt: $25,000,000 (6/95).

Per Share Data ($)

(Year Ended Dec. 31)

	1994	1993	1992	1991	1990	1989
Tangible Bk. Val.	14.65	14.34	9.89	8.52	5.86	4.60
Oper. Earnings	1.38	2.03	1.75	1.47	1.27	1.05
Earnings	1.31	2.03	1.76	1.52	1.27	1.11
Dividends	0.46	0.38	0.36	Nil	Nil	Nil
Payout Ratio	35%	19%	20%	Nil	Nil	Nil
Prices - High	37½	33⅜	26½	16	17¼	10¼
- Low	16¾	24½	14⅞	9¼	7⅜	5¼
P/E Ratio - High	29	16	15	11	14	9
- Low	13	12	8	6	6	5

Income Statement Analysis (Million $)

	1994	%Chg	1993	%Chg	1992	%Chg	1991
Premium Income	157	35%	116	10%	105	35%	78.0
Net Invest. Inc.	24.5	9%	22.5	13%	19.9	25%	15.9
Oth. Revs.	-1.2	NM	0.3	-84%	1.7	-28%	2.3
Total Revs.	180	29%	139	9%	127	32%	96.3
Pretax Inc.	21.3	-30%	30.3	20%	25.2	25%	20.1
Net Oper. Inc.	17.9	-22%	23.0	—	NA	—	NA
Net Inc.	17.0	-27%	23.2	22%	19.0	27%	15.0

Balance Sheet & Other Fin. Data (Million $)

	1994	1993	1992	1991	1990	1989
Cash & Equiv.	11.4	17.8	5.0	14.4	4.1	3.8
Premiums Due	41.1	28.4	28.2	24.7	26.6	18.0
Inv Assets Bonds	346	276	242	208	153	114
Inv. Assets Stock	48.7	7.5	9.9	1.1	3.8	4.9
Inv. Assets Loans	Nil	Nil	Nil	Nil	Nil	Nil
Inv. Assets Total	408	344	262	235	165	131
Deferred Policy Cost	13.2	6.8	5.9	3.2	2.2	Nil
Total Assets	599	522	341	300	215	170
Debt	Nil	Nil	Nil	Nil	Nil	Nil
Common Eqty.	190	186	107	91.2	49.7	39.0

Ratio Analysis

	1994	1993	1992	1991	1990	1989
Prop&Cas Loss	70.8	66.7	71.2	69.7	73.7	75.1
Prop&Cas Expense	27.0	26.5	25.6	26.3	24.0	23.7
Prop&Cas Comb.	97.8	93.3	96.8	96.0	97.7	98.8
% Ret. on Revs.	9.4	16.7	15.0	15.6	12.5	14.8
% Return on Equity	9.1	15.8	19.2	21.3	24.3	27.5

Dividend Data —Cash dividends on the common stock were initiated in 1992.

Amt. of Div. $	Date Decl.	Ex-Div. Date	Stock of Record	Payment Date
0.120	Aug. 12	Sep. 26	Sep. 30	Oct. 20 '94
0.120	Nov. 22	Dec. 23	Dec. 30	Jan. 19 '95
0.120	Mar. 17	Mar. 27	Mar. 31	Apr. 20 '95
0.120	May. 22	Jun. 28	Jun. 30	Jul. 20 '95
0.120	Aug. 21	Sep. 27	Sep. 29	Oct. 19 '95

Data as orig. reptd.; bef. results of disc. opers. and/or spec. items. Per share data adj. for stk. divs. as of ex-div. date. E-Estimated. NA-Not Available. NM-Not Meaningful. NR-Not Ranked.

Office—195 Lake Louise Marie Rd., Rock Hill, NY 12775-8000. **Tel**—(914) 796-2100. **Chrmn & Pres**—W. A. Rhulen. **SVP-Fin & Treas**—D. F. Plante. **Secy**—J. P. Loughlin. **Investor Contact**—Linda Markovits. **Dirs**—J. M. Farrow, D. C. Moat, L. E. O'Brien, P. L. Rhulen, W. A. Rhulen. **Transfer Agent & Registrar**—American Stock Transfer & Trust Co., NYC. **Incorporated** in Delaware in 1986. **Empl**-455. **S&P Analyst:** Thomas C. Ferguson

STANDARD & POOR'S

STOCK REPORTS

Frozen Food Express

NASDAQ Symbol **FFEX**
In S&P SmallCap 600

15-NOV-95 **Industry:** Trucking

Summary: This company is the largest publicly owned, full-service motor carrier of perishable commodities in North America.

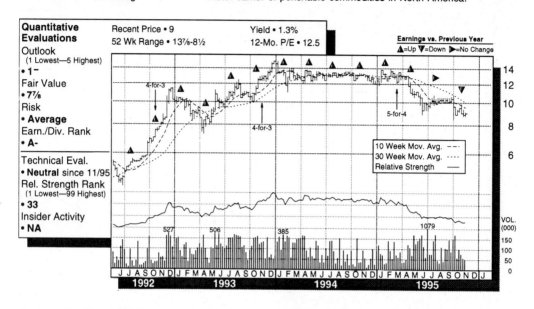

Quantitative Evaluations
Outlook
(1 Lowest—5 Highest)
• **1-**
Fair Value
• **7⅞**
Risk
• **Average**
Earn./Div. Rank
• **A-**

Technical Eval.
• **Neutral** since 11/95
Rel. Strength Rank
(1 Lowest—99 Highest)
• **33**
Insider Activity
• **NA**

Recent Price • 9
52 Wk Range • 13⅞-8½
Yield • 1.3%
12-Mo. P/E • 12.5

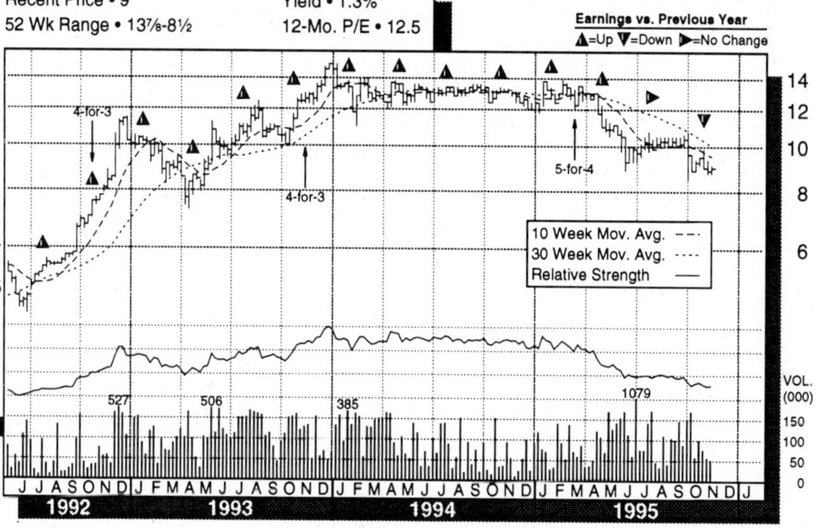

Business Profile - 15-NOV-95

FFEX provides full-truckload, less-than-truckload and distribution services, as well as the ability to handle freight, throughout most of North America. In the first nine months of 1995, 100 company-operated and 130 owner-operator full-truckload tractors were added to the fleet. The motor carrier industry has experienced declines in productivity and equipment utilization in 1995, mainly because of an increase in the number of trucks in proportion to the amount of freight available for transport.

Operational Review - 15-NOV-95

Revenues for the first nine months of 1995 rose 6.6%, year to year. However, an imbalance of trucks and freight caused per-truck utilization and freight rates to decline, resulting in a narrowing of margins. Pretax income fell 18%. After taxes at 30.1%, versus 32.9%, net income was down 14%. Earnings per share were equal to $0.47, compared with $0.55 in the year-earlier period.

Stock Performance - 10-NOV-95

In the past 30 trading days, FFEX's shares have declined 6%, compared to a 1% rise in the S&P 500. Average trading volume for the past five days was 10,080 shares, compared with the 40-day moving average of 24,533 shares.

Key Stock Statistics

Dividend Rate/Share	0.12	Shareholders	6,000
Shs. outstg. (M)	16.1	Market cap. (B)	$0.147
Avg. daily vol. (M)	0.012	Inst. holdings	23%
Tang. Bk. Value/Share	4.34	Insider holdings	NA
Beta	1.29		

Value of $10,000 invested 5 years ago: $ 45,675

Fiscal Year Ending Dec. 31

	1995	% Change	1994	% Change	1993	% Change
Revenues (Million $)						
1Q	66.98	11%	60.30	23%	48.96	10%
2Q	73.84	5%	70.30	23%	57.03	17%
3Q	75.78	4%	72.54	20%	60.56	20%
4Q	—	—	71.48	17%	60.85	19%
Yr.	—	—	274.6	21%	227.4	17%
Income (Million $)						
1Q	1.79	2%	1.75	30%	1.35	23%
2Q	3.81	NM	3.79	28%	2.96	27%
3Q	2.10	-39%	3.43	24%	2.77	33%
4Q	—	—	2.91	23%	2.37	45%
Yr.	—	—	11.87	26%	9.44	32%
Earnings Per Share ($)						
1Q	0.11	10%	0.10	25%	0.08	11%
2Q	0.23	NM	0.23	25%	0.18	23%
3Q	0.13	-38%	0.21	25%	0.17	27%
4Q	—	—	0.18	25%	0.14	41%
Yr.	—	—	0.72	24%	0.58	29%

Next earnings report expected: early January

Frozen Food Express

Business Summary - 15-NOV-95

Frozen Food Express Industries, Inc. is the largest refrigerated trucking company in North America, with operations that extend from Montreal throughout the continental U.S. to Mexico City. Its primary cargo is processed foods and meats, but it also carries confectionery goods, dairy products, pharmaceuticals, medical supplies, fruits and vegetables, cosmetics and heat-sensitive aerospace manufacturing materials. Both truckload and less-than-truckload (LTL) service is provided.

Freight revenues in recent years were derived as follows:

	1994	1993	1992
Truckload	65%	62%	60%
LTL	35%	38%	40%

The company's truckload service is nonscheduled and operates over irregular routes within the route authority. Prior to 1987, truckload operations were conducted mostly through the use of equipment and drivers under agreements with independent contractors. In 1987, FFEX began to introduce a new fleet of company-owned truckload equipment operated by company drivers.

FFEX is the largest LTL motor carrier of perishables in the U.S., and the only North American continent-wide refrigerated LTL trucker that uses multiple-compartment, multi-temperature trailers to ensure the integrity of the perishable products it transports. It is also the only continent-wide LTL trucking system that provides regularly scheduled service. Scheduling, billing and climate control information is provided through an on-line computer system.

At the end of 1994, the company's equipment in service included 1,099 company-operated tractors, plus 505 owner-operator tractors, and 2,406 company-provided trailers, plus 21 trailers provided by owner-operators. FFEX's fleet serves 7,000 customers and makes pickups and deliveries in 6,500 cities and towns. Its trucks also take Mexico-bound shipments to its terminal in Laredo, TX, where they are picked up by a Mexican trucking company for delivery in Mexico. Tractors return from Laredo with full-truckload shipments of Mexico-produced frozen vegetables for delivery to U.S. processing and packaging plants.

Important Developments

Nov. '95—FFEX said an earnings decline in the first nine months of 1995 primarily reflected a decrease in per-truck utilization, weak freight rates and an increase in insurance costs.

Capitalization

Long Term Debt: $6,000,000 (9/95).
Options: To buy 1,001,318 shs. at $1.00 to $12.40 ea. (12/94).

Per Share Data ($) (Year Ended Dec. 31)

	1994	1993	1992	1991	1990	1989
Tangible Bk. Val.	4.03	3.31	2.72	2.03	2.06	1.88
Cash Flow	1.31	1.19	0.95	0.89	0.82	0.69
Earnings	0.72	0.58	0.45	0.34	0.25	0.26
Dividends	Nil	0.10	0.08	0.06	0.06	0.05
Payout Ratio	Nil	16%	17%	20%	24%	18%
Prices - High	15	15	$11\frac{1}{2}$	$4\frac{1}{8}$	$2\frac{3}{4}$	$3\frac{1}{2}$
- Low	11	$7\frac{1}{4}$	4	$1\frac{13}{16}$	$1\frac{13}{16}$	$2\frac{1}{8}$
P/E Ratio - High	21	26	26	12	11	13
- Low	15	12	9	5	7	8

Income Statement Analysis (Million $)

	1994	%Chg	1993	%Chg	1992	%Chg	1991
Revs.	275	21%	227	16%	195	10%	177
Oper. Inc.	28.5	15%	24.7	26%	19.6	11%	17.6
Depr.	9.8	-1%	9.9	24%	8.0	-3%	8.3
Int. Exp.	NA	—	0.8	70%	0.4	-67%	1.3
Pretax Inc.	17.8	24%	14.4	29%	11.2	31%	8.6
Eff. Tax Rate	33%	—	35%	—	36%	—	39%
Net Inc.	11.9	26%	9.4	32%	7.1	37%	5.2

Balance Sheet & Other Fin. Data (Million $)

	1994	1993	1992	1991	1990	1989
Cash	4.4	3.8	3.7	3.2	0.5	1.6
Curr. Assets	57.1	48.1	37.4	29.9	26.9	18.9
Total Assets	117	109	86.0	66.9	74.3	58.8
Curr. Liab.	31.4	27.2	20.4	14.3	13.8	9.3
LT Debt	9.0	17.0	12.0	7.1	21.3	14.0
Common Eqty.	64.3	52.0	41.8	35.1	30.0	27.3
Total Cap.	77.8	72.5	58.2	47.4	56.5	46.5
Cap. Exp.	13.6	23.6	20.3	2.2	17.7	13.5
Cash Flow	21.6	19.4	15.2	13.5	11.9	10.0

Ratio Analysis

	1994	1993	1992	1991	1990	1989
Curr. Ratio	1.8	1.8	1.8	2.1	1.9	2.0
% LT Debt of Cap.	11.6	23.4	20.6	15.0	37.8	30.2
% Net Inc.of Revs.	4.3	4.2	3.7	2.9	2.3	3.1
% Ret. on Assets	10.5	9.6	9.8	6.6	5.4	7.0
% Ret. on Equity	20.3	19.9	19.6	14.5	12.5	14.5

Dividend Data —Cash has been paid each year since 1971. The company's target is to pay out 15% to 20% of the preceding year's profits.

Amt. of Div. $	Date Decl.	Ex-Div. Date	Stock of Record	Payment Date
0.030	Feb. 08	Feb. 16	Feb. 23	Mar. 03 '95
5-for-4	Feb. 08	Mar. 06	Feb. 23	Mar. 03 '95
0.030	May. 10	May. 18	May. 24	Jun. 01 '95
0.030	Aug. 09	Aug. 21	Aug. 23	Aug. 31 '95
0.030	Nov. 08	Nov. 20	Nov. 22	Dec. 01 '95

Data as orig. reptd.; bef. results of disc. opers. and/or spec. items. Per share data adj. for stk. divs. as of ex-div. date. E-Estimated. NA-Not Available. NM-Not Meaningful. NR-Not Ranked.

Office—1145 Empire Central Place, Dallas, TX 75247-4309; P.O. Box 655888, Dallas 75265-5888. **Tel**—(214) 630-8090. **Chrmn, Pres & CEO**—S. M. Stubbs, Jr. **Vice Chrmn**—E. O. Weller. **EVP & COO**—C. G. Robertson. **SVP & CFO**—B. G. Cott. **Secy**—L. W. Bartholomew. **Treas**—T. G. Yetter. **Dirs**—B. R. Blackmarr, B. G. Cott, L. Hallman, W. G. Lord, T. M. O'Connor, C. G. Robertson, S. M. Stubbs, Jr., E. O. Weller. **Transfer Agent**—First National Bank of Boston. **Incorporated** in Texas in 1969. **Empl**-2,288. **S&P Analyst:** JJS

STANDARD & POOR'S

STOCK REPORTS

G & K Services

NASDAQ Symbol **GKSRA**

In S&P SmallCap 600

03-OCT-95 **Industry:** Services

Summary: This company is one of the leading U.S. suppliers of uniforms and related textile products used in a wide range of businesses and institutions.

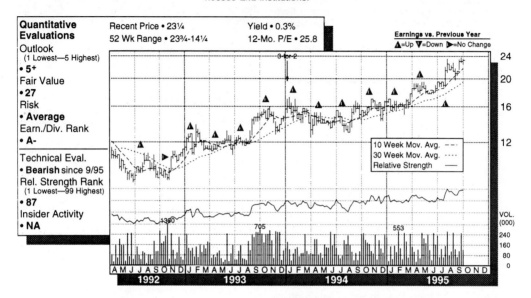

Quantitative Evaluations

Outlook (1 Lowest—5 Highest) • **5+**

Fair Value • **27**

Risk • **Average**

Earn./Div. Rank • **A-**

Technical Eval. • **Bearish** since 9/95

Rel. Strength Rank (1 Lowest—99 Highest) • **87**

Insider Activity • **NA**

Recent Price • 23¼ Yield • 0.3%

52 Wk Range • 23¾-14¼ 12-Mo. P/E • 25.8

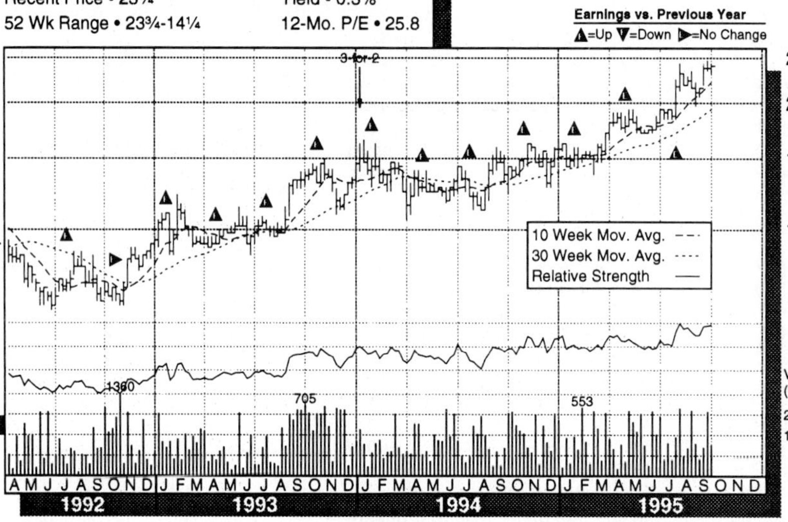

Business Profile - 03-OCT-95

G & K operates in 27 states and two Canadian provinces from 30 processing plants and 47 sales and service centers. The company opened a new plant in Kansas City during the third quarter, and will soon be opening plants in San Jose, Seattle, near Ft. Lauderdale and Cambridge, Ontario. G & K is also making investments in various areas to allow for future expansion. In September 1994, the company acquired the assets of uniform manufacturer BCP Corp. for an estimated $7.5 million to $8.0 million.

Operational Review - 03-OCT-95

Revenue growth in fiscal 1995 was paced by increases in new account sales in the U.S (25%) and Canada (17%). Furthermore, customer retention rates in both countries rose for the third consecutive year. In addition, the direct purchase group, operating independently of the rental division for the first time, almost doubled itssales. Earnings were aided by cost reductions in plant processing, merchandise expense, and administrative overhead.

Stock Performance - 29-SEP-95

In the past 30 trading days, GKSRA's shares have increased 6%, compared to a 5% rise in the S&P 500. Average trading volume for the past five days was 23,720 shares, compared with the 40-day moving average of 34,695 shares.

Key Stock Statistics

Dividend Rate/Share	0.07	Shareholders	700
Shs. outstg. (M)	20.4	Market cap. (B)	$0.485
Avg. daily vol. (M)	0.037	Inst. holdings	53%
Tang. Bk. Value/Share	3.33	Insider holdings	NA
Beta	0.74		

Value of $10,000 invested 5 years ago: $ 26,679

Fiscal Year Ending Jun. 30

	1995	% Change	1994	% Change	1993	% Change
Revenues (Million $)						
1Q	60.53	13%	53.35	8%	49.40	3%
2Q	65.55	18%	55.53	10%	50.70	3%
3Q	66.72	17%	57.13	12%	51.00	5%
4Q	69.67	18%	59.22	4%	56.75	16%
Yr.	262.5	17%	225.2	8%	207.9	7%
Income (Million $)						
1Q	4.36	29%	3.38	—	—	—
2Q	4.65	26%	3.69	46%	2.52	11%
3Q	4.42	21%	3.66	44%	2.54	45%
4Q	4.86	20%	4.06	12%	3.63	68%
Yr.	18.29	24%	14.79	33%	11.12	30%
Earnings Per Share ($)						
1Q	0.21	24%	0.17	42%	0.12	NM
2Q	0.23	28%	0.18	42%	0.13	12%
3Q	0.22	22%	0.18	42%	0.13	46%
4Q	0.24	20%	0.20	11%	0.18	69%
Yr.	0.90	23%	0.73	33%	0.55	29%

Next earnings report expected: late October

G & K Services

Business Summary - 03-OCT-95

G & K Services, Inc. leases and maintains uniforms and related textile products. It serves customers in 27 states through a total of 29 plants and 56 sales and service centers. Operations in Canada were expanded with the October 1990 acquisition of Work Wear Corp. of Canada, Ltd., which consisted of 22 locations, including eight processing plants.

G & K supplies a standard line of work garments, specialized uniforms for corporate identity programs, anti-static garments, ultra-clean particle-free garments and dress clothing for supervisors, sales personnel and others needing upgraded work apparel. Uniform rentals accounted for 60% of total revenues in fiscal 1994. Non-uniform rental items, including floor mats, dust mops and cloths, wiping towels and linens, accounted for 40%.

The company's products are used in a wide range of businesses and institutions, including pharmaceutical and electronics manufacturers, transportation and distribution firms, healthcare and foodservice operations, auto dealerships, equipment repair companies, schools and office buildings. Customers are offered a wide array of services, including advice and assistance in choosing fabrics, styles and colors, as well as professional cleaning, finishing, repair and replacement of uniforms. Soiled uniforms are picked up at the customer's location and returned clean on a weekly cycle.

G & K intends to continue to invest in technology and capacity to support growth. In fiscal 1994, it began work on a new plant in Kansas City, and acquired land for future plants in Florida, Seattle, and Cambridge, Ontario. In 1993, G & K opened a new processing plant in Albuquerque, N.M. It has also entered new markets around Charlotte, N.C., and in the Tampa/Orlando areas of central Florida since 1992. It plans to spend more than $30 million to add capacity in fiscal 1995.

Important Developments

Aug. '95—In reporting fourth quarter and fiscal 1995 results, the company said that it expects continued strong revenue growth and some further margin improvement in fiscal 1996.

Capitalization

Long Term Debt: $69,900,000 (4/1/95).

Per Share Data ($)

(Year Ended Jun. 30)

	1995	1994	1993	1992	1991	1990
Tangible Bk. Val.	NA	2.76	1.97	1.29	0.75	3.04
Cash Flow	NA	1.50	1.26	1.12	0.91	0.83
Earnings	0.90	0.73	0.55	0.43	0.35	0.51
Dividends	0.09	0.07	0.07	0.07	0.07	0.07
Payout Ratio	10%	10%	12%	16%	19%	13%
Prices - High	23½	17¼	16	13⅜	12⅜	11
- Low	15	12½	10⅞	8⅝	7⅛	5⅞
P/E Ratio - High	26	24	29	31	35	22
- Low	17	17	20	20	20	12

Income Statement Analysis (Million $)

	1994	%Chg	1993	%Chg	1992	%Chg	1991
Revs.	225	8%	208	7%	195	11%	176
Oper. Inc.	45.5	15%	39.5	11%	35.6	27%	28.0
Depr.	15.8	9%	14.5	4%	14.0	24%	11.3
Int. Exp.	5.8	-20%	7.3	-14%	8.5	2%	8.3
Pretax Inc.	25.3	32%	19.1	35%	14.1	15%	12.3
Eff. Tax Rate	42%	—	42%	—	39%	—	43%
Net Inc.	14.8	33%	11.1	29%	8.6	21%	7.1

Balance Sheet & Other Fin. Data (Million $)

	1994	1993	1992	1991	1990	1989
Cash	5.1	4.6	2.1	2.2	0.6	2.6
Curr. Assets	63.5	59.0	52.3	56.7	32.5	30.2
Total Assets	205	202	200	206	101	83.0
Curr. Liab.	34.2	36.4	33.9	28.7	16.1	13.8
LT Debt	54.7	59.8	68.4	85.9	9.1	3.8
Common Eqty.	101	90.2	82.4	76.8	69.9	61.0
Total Cap.	167	162	164	175	84.0	70.0
Cap. Exp.	17.6	14.4	16.3	18.4	21.8	14.2
Cash Flow	30.6	25.6	22.6	18.4	18.0	15.3

Ratio Analysis

	1994	1993	1992	1991	1990	1989
Curr. Ratio	1.9	1.6	1.5	2.0	2.0	2.2
% LT Debt of Cap.	32.8	36.9	41.8	49.1	10.8	5.4
% Net Inc.of Revs.	6.6	5.4	4.4	4.0	8.6	7.6
% Ret. on Assets	7.3	5.5	4.2	4.6	11.1	10.4
% Ret. on Equity	15.5	12.9	10.8	9.6	15.6	14.5

Dividend Data —Cash has been paid each year since 1968.

Amt. of Div. $	Date Decl.	Ex-Div. Date	Stock of Record	Payment Date
0.017	Sep. 01	Sep. 16	Sep. 22	Oct. 07 '94
0.017	Oct. 28	Nov. 29	Dec. 05	Jan. 03 '95
0.017	Feb. 22	Mar. 15	Mar. 17	Mar. 31 '95
0.017	May. 18	Jun. 02	Jun. 08	Jun. 22 '95
0.017	Aug. 31	Sep. 20	Sep. 22	Oct. 06 '95

Data as orig. reptd.; bef. results of disc. opers. and/or spec. items. Per share data adj. for stk. divs. as of ex-div. date. E-Estimated. NA-Not Available. NM-Not Meaningful. NR-Not Ranked.

Office—505 Waterford Park, Minneapolis, MN 55441. **Tel**—(612) 546-7440. **Chrmn & CEO**—R. Fink. **Pres & COO**—W. Hope. **CFO, Secy, Treas & Investor Contact**—Stephen F. LaBelle. **Dirs**—B. G. Allbright, P. Baszucki, R. Fink, W. Fortun, D. Goldfus, W. Hope, B. Sweet. **Transfer Agent & Registrar**—Norwest Bank, Minneapolis. **Incorporated** in Minnesota in 1934. **Empl**-3,966. **S&P Analyst:** Stephen Madonna

Galey & Lord

NYSE Symbol **GNL**
In S&P SmallCap 600

12-SEP-95 **Industry:** Textiles

Summary: This company is a leading manufacturer of high-quality woven cotton and cotton-blended apparel fabrics sold principally to manufacturers of sportswear and commercial uniforms.

Quantitative Evaluations

Outlook
(1 Lowest—5 Highest)
• **4**

Fair Value
• **13⅞**

Risk
• **Average**

Earn./Div. Rank
• **NR**

Technical Eval.
• **Bearish** since 7/95

Rel. Strength Rank
(1 Lowest—99 Highest)
• **12**

Insider Activity
• **NA**

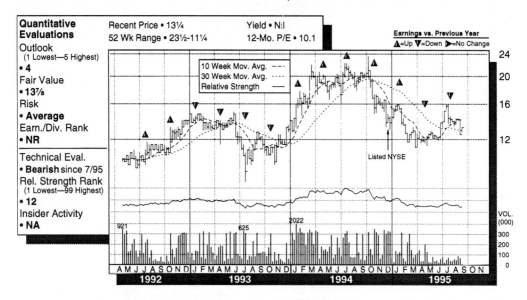

Recent Price • 13¼
52 Wk Range • 23½-11¼
Yield • Nil
12-Mo. P/E • 10.1

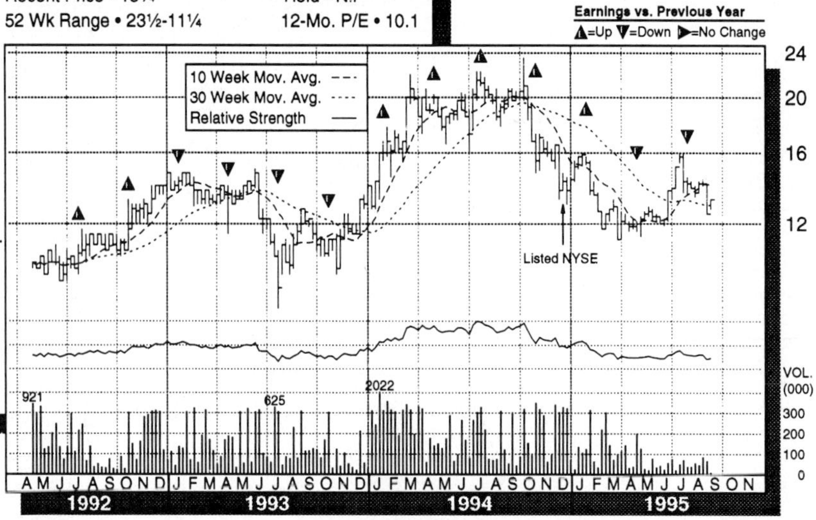

Business Profile - 12-SEP-95

This leading manufacturer of high-quality woven apparel fabrics expanded into the home furnishings fabrics market via an acquisition in April 1994. In July 1995, GNL said it is closing its apparel print businesses, and expects to take up to a $15 million ($0.75 a share) business closing charge and will also incur related losses from the apparel print operations in the fiscal 1995 fourth quarter.

Operational Review - 12-SEP-95

Net sales in the nine months ended July 1, 1995, advanced 17%, year to year, primarily reflecting the April 1994 acquisition of the Home Fashion Fabrics unit. Greater losses in the apparel print operation led to a slight decline in operating income. The order backlog dropped 29%, reflecting a poor retail environment for apparel and rapid customer inventory adjustments, and, in home furnishings, the company's reluctance to be sold too far ahead in a period of rising raw material costs.

Stock Performance - 08-SEP-95

In the past 30 trading days, GNL's shares have declined 6%, compared to a 2% rise in the S&P 500. Average trading volume for the past five days was 1,750 shares, compared with the 40-day moving average of 9,736 shares.

Key Stock Statistics

Dividend Rate/Share	Nil	Shareholders	1,200
Shs. outstg. (M)	11.8	Market cap. (B)	$0.153
Avg. daily vol. (M)	0.010	Inst. holdings	81%
Tang. Bk. Value/Share	4.91	Insider holdings	NA
Beta	NA		

Value of $10,000 invested 5 years ago: NA

Fiscal Year Ending Sep. 30

	1995	% Change	1994	% Change	1993	% Change
Revenues (Million $)						
1Q	127.2	28%	99.1	17%	84.70	-5%
2Q	133.3	20%	111.5	9%	102.4	18%
3Q	127.2	5%	120.8	18%	102.4	17%
4Q	—	—	119.8	24%	96.27	8%
Yr.	—	—	451.1	17%	385.8	9%
Income (Million $)						
1Q	4.78	12%	4.28	6%	4.03	10%
2Q	4.06	-12%	4.59	32%	3.48	17%
3Q	2.01	-60%	5.04	64%	3.08	4%
4Q	—	—	4.98	77%	2.82	-20%
Yr.	—	—	18.89	41%	13.41	2%
Earnings Per Share ($)						
1Q	0.40	11%	0.36	6%	0.34	-19%
2Q	0.34	-11%	0.38	31%	0.29	-15%
3Q	0.17	-60%	0.42	62%	0.26	-4%
4Q	—	—	0.41	71%	0.24	-20%
Yr.	—	—	1.56	39%	1.12	-14%

Next earnings report expected: early November

Galey & Lord

Business Summary - 12-SEP-95

Galey & Lord, Inc. is a leading manufacturer of fabrics, which it sells to apparel manufacturers for use in the production of various lines of clothing. The April 1994 acquisition of the Decorative Prints business of Burlington Industries marked Galey's entry into the home furnishings fabrics industry. Net sales by product line in recent fiscal years:

	1994	1993	1992
Woven fabrics:			
Sportswear	62%	60%	57%
Uniforms	13%	18%	19%
Corduroy	9%	9%	10%
Printed fabrics	7%	10%	14%
Synthetic fabrics	3%	3%	---
Home furnishings fabrics	6%	---	---

The company's principal products are spun woven medium-weight cotton and cotton blended fabrics. Galey manufactures a relatively limited number of basic fabric styles and enhances the value of fabrics to its customers through a wide variety of mechanical and chemical finishing processes, including dyeing, napping, sueding and prewashing. During fiscal 1993, the company began shipping woven 100% cotton "Wrinkle-Free" fabrics to meet industry demand for easy-care fabrics. Woven fabrics are sold primarily to manufacturers of menswear, uniforms, and branded and private-label womenswear.

In its uniform fabric product line, Galey stresses durability, fitness for use, continuity of color and customer service. The company also sells chemically treated fabrics, including a fire-retardant finish and an antibacterial finish. Uniform fabrics are distributed to the industrial laundry, hospitality and health care markets.

Galey makes corduroy to customer order in various wales and widths, for sale to manufacturers of menswear, womenswear and childrenswear. GNL's synthetic fabrics division provides coordinated fabrics to the marketplace for two-piece dress ensembles. The company plans to close its apparel print businesses.

Through its Home Fashion Fabrics unit (formerly the Decorative Prints business of Burlington Industries; acquired in April 1994), the company sells greige, dyed and printed fabrics to the home furnishings trade for use in bedspreads, comforters and curtains.

Important Developments

Jul. '95—GNL's order backlog at July 1, 1995, was $99.0 million, versus $139.0 million at July 2, 1994, reflecting declines in all businesses.

Capitalization

Long Term Debt: $164,736,000 (7/95).

Per Share Data ($)

(Year Ended Sep. 30)

	1994	1993	1992	1991	1990	1989
Tangible Bk. Val.	4.02	4.98	3.80	0.26	NA	NA
Cash Flow	2.27	1.69	2.01	1.08	NA	NA
Earnings	1.56	1.12	1.30	0.26	NA	NA
Dividends	Nil	Nil	Nil	Nil	NA	NA
Payout Ratio	Nil	Nil	Nil	Nil	NA	NA
Prices - High	23½	15	14¾	NA	NA	NA
- Low	12¾	8½	9½	NA	NA	NA
P/E Ratio - High	15	13	11	NA	NA	NA
- Low	8	8	7	NA	NA	NA

Income Statement Analysis (Million $)

	1994	%Chg	1993	%Chg	1992	%Chg	1991
Revs.	451	17%	386	9%	353	7%	329
Oper. Inc.	47.5	37%	34.7	-4%	36.3	42%	25.5
Depr.	8.5	25%	6.8	NM	6.8	5%	6.4
Int. Exp.	8.4	29%	6.5	-33%	9.7	-32%	14.3
Pretax Inc.	30.7	43%	21.4	8%	19.9	NM	4.7
Eff. Tax Rate	39%	—	37%	—	34%	—	36%
Net Inc.	18.9	41%	13.4	2%	13.1	NM	3.0

Balance Sheet & Other Fin. Data (Million $)

	1994	1993	1992	1991	1990	1989
Cash	6.1	2.7	3.5	5.2	NA	NA
Curr. Assets	173	141	116	105	NA	NA
Total Assets	299	202	173	164	NA	NA
Curr. Liab.	58.3	42.2	45.0	42.7	NA	NA
LT Debt	150	95.0	80.0	106	NA	NA
Common Eqty.	77.7	59.1	45.2	4.4	NA	NA
Total Cap.	24.0	160	127	121	NA	NA
Cap. Exp.	22.4	11.7	7.3	4.3	NA	NA
Cash Flow	27.4	20.2	19.2	8.4	NA	NA

Ratio Analysis

	1994	1993	1992	1991	1990	1989
Curr. Ratio	3.0	3.3	2.6	2.5	NA	NA
% LT Debt of Cap.	62.4	59.6	63.0	88.1	NA	NA
% Net Inc.of Revs.	4.2	3.5	3.7	0.9	NA	NA
% Ret. on Assets	7.5	7.1	6.4	NA	NA	NA
% Ret. on Equity	27.3	25.6	48.2	NA	NA	NA

Dividend Data —The company has never paid dividends on its common stock and intends to retain earnings for operation and expansion of its business.

Data as orig. reptd.; bef. results of disc. opers. and/or spec. items. Per share data adj. for stk. divs. as of ex-div. date. E-Estimated. NA-Not Available. NM-Not Meaningful. NR-Not Ranked.

Office—980 Avenue of the Americas, New York, NY 10018. **Tel**—(212) 465-3000. **Chrmn, Pres & CEO**—A. C. Wiener. **EVP, CFO, Secy, Treas & Investor Contact**—Michael R. Harmon. **Dirs**—L. Abraham, P. G. Gillease, W. deR. Holt, H. S. Jacobs, W. M. R. Mapel, S. C. Sherrill, A. C. Wiener. **Transfer Agent & Registrar**—First Union National Bank of North Carolina, Charlotte. **Incorporated** in Delaware in 1987. **Empl**-4,237. **S&P Analyst:** Philip D. Wohl

Gallagher (Arthur J.)

NYSE Symbol **AJG**
In S&P SmallCap 600

05-OCT-95 **Industry:** Insurance

Summary: This company provides insurance brokerage, risk management and other insurance-related services for commercial, industrial, individual and other clients.

Quantitative Evaluations
Outlook (1 Lowest—5 Highest) • **4-**
Fair Value • **$38\frac{7}{8}$**
Risk • **Low**
Earn./Div. Rank • **A-**

Technical Eval. • **Bullish** since 9/95
Rel. Strength Rank (1 Lowest—99 Highest) • **28**
Insider Activity • **Neutral**

Recent Price • $35\frac{1}{2}$
52 Wk Range • $38-29\frac{5}{8}$
Yield • 2.9%
12-Mo. P/E • 15.3

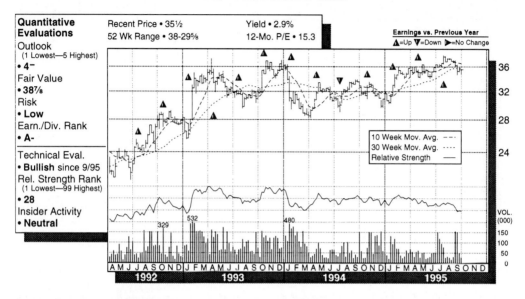

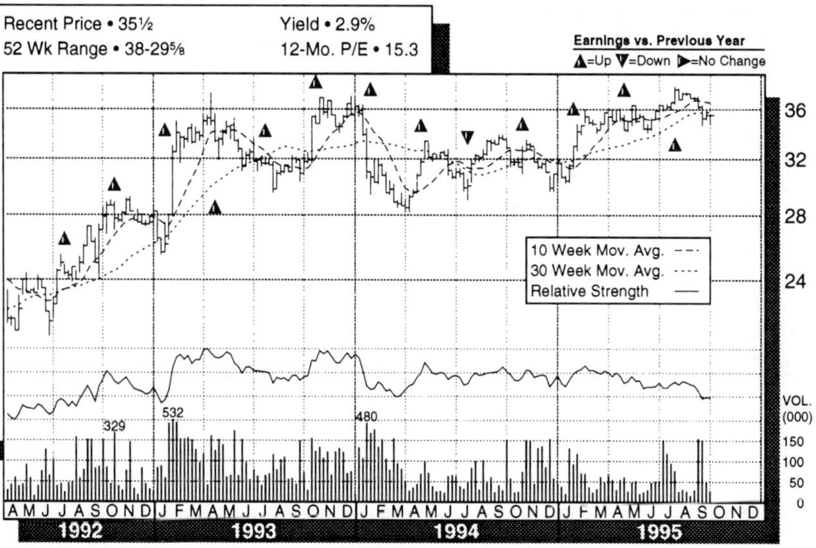

Business Profile - 28-JUN-95

Operations continue to expand under an aggressive acquisition program that began in 1986. Falling interest rates and weak economic conditions have put pressure on investment income, and a soft insurance pricing environment has somewhat restricted earnings gains. However, earnings should benefit from expected sales growth in the risk management, benefits, and self-insurance service areas, and from acquisition and share repurchase programs.

Operational Review - 05-OCT-95

Revenues in the first half of 1995 advanced 12%, year to year, despite soft pricing in the insurance marketplace, as commissions and fees rose on internal growth and acquisitions; investment income increased 81%. Total expenses were up 11%, reflecting business expansion costs, including additional employees, benefits and other operating expenses. After taxes at 35.0%, versus 36.6%, net earnings climbed 22%, to $12.0 million ($0.76 a share), from $9.8 million ($0.61).

Stock Performance - 29-SEP-95

In the past 30 trading days, AJG's shares have declined 5%, compared to a 5% rise in the S&P 500. Average trading volume for the past five days was 5,360 shares, compared with the 40-day moving average of 13,421 shares.

Key Stock Statistics

Dividend Rate/Share	1.00	Shareholders	600
Shs. outstg. (M)	15.1	Market cap. (B)	$0.524
Avg. daily vol. (M)	0.019	Inst. holdings	48%
Tang. Bk. Value/Share	6.38	Insider holdings	NA
Beta	0.32		

Value of $10,000 invested 5 years ago: $ 16,695

Fiscal Year Ending Dec. 31

	1995	% Change	1994	% Change	1993	% Change
Revenues (Million $)						
1Q	90.52	9%	82.95	16%	71.44	15%
2Q	91.16	13%	80.94	10%	73.64	15%
3Q	—	—	97.65	10%	89.07	20%
4Q	—	—	94.83	14%	83.52	16%
Yr.	—	—	356.4	12%	317.7	16%
Income (Million $)						
1Q	6.28	20%	5.23	33%	3.94	23%
2Q	5.72	27%	4.52	-37%	7.19	115%
3Q	—	—	12.81	8%	11.85	32%
4Q	—	—	11.98	33%	9.04	13%
Yr.	—	—	34.54	7%	32.27	37%
Earnings Per Share ($)						
1Q	0.40	25%	0.32	19%	0.27	29%
2Q	0.36	29%	0.28	-38%	0.45	96%
3Q	—	—	0.81	9%	0.74	23%
4Q	—	—	0.77	38%	0.56	6%
Yr.	—	—	2.17	7%	2.02	29%

Next earnings report expected: mid October

Gallagher (Arthur J.)

Business Summary - 05-OCT-95

Arthur J. Gallagher & Co. provides insurance brokerage, risk management and related services in the U.S. and abroad. Its two major sources of operating revenues are commissions from brokerage and risk management operations, and service fees from risk management operations.

Total revenues in recent years were derived from:

	1994	1993	1992	1991
Commissions	58%	55%	57%	60%
Fees	39%	40%	39%	36%
Investment	3%	5%	4%	4%

The company's principal activity is the negotiation and placement of insurance for its clients. Gallagher places insurance for and services commercial, industrial, institutional, governmental, religious and personal accounts throughout the U.S. and abroad. It acts as an agent in soliciting, negotiating and effecting contracts of insurance through insurance companies worldwide, and also as a broker in procuring contracts of insurance on behalf of insureds. Specific coverages include property and casualty, marine, employee benefits, pension and life insurance products. AJG also places surplus lines coverage (coverage not available from insurance companies licensed by the states in which the risks are located) for various specialized risks, and provides reinsurance services to its clients.

The company provides professional consulting services to assist clients in analyzing risks and determining whether proper protection is best obtained through the purchase of insurance or through retention of all or a portion of those risks and the adoption of risk management policies and cost-effective loss control and prevention programs. Services are provided by Gallagher Bassett Services, Inc. through a network of more than 100 offices throughout the U.S.

In connection with its risk management services, Gallagher provides self-insurance programs for large institutions, risk sharing pools and associations, and large commercial and industrial customers. The Gallagher Benefits Services division specializes in risk management of human resources through fully insured and self-insured programs.

International operations include a joint venture with American Re Corp. that markets insurance products in the U.K., and facilities in Bermuda. Gallagher Bassett International, Ltd. provides brokerage services to and arranges overseas risk management and loss control services for multinational organizations.

Important Developments

Sep. '95—AJG acquired IMC Risk Management Group, Inc., of Kansas City, Mo., a property casualty insurance company. Terms were not disclosed.

Capitalization

Long Term Debt: $2,760,000 (3/95).

Per Share Data ($)

(Year Ended Dec. 31)

	1994	1993	1992	1991	1990	1989
Tangible Bk. Val.	6.01	7.49	5.88	5.72	6.35	5.88
Cash Flow	2.63	2.42	1.99	1.72	1.86	1.70
Earnings	2.17	2.02	1.57	1.31	1.42	1.42
Dividends	0.88	0.72	0.64	0.64	0.60	0.52
Payout Ratio	41%	36%	39%	46%	40%	35%
Prices - High	36$^{3}/_{8}$	37$^{3}/_{8}$	29$^{1}/_{4}$	28$^{3}/_{8}$	25	26$^{1}/_{2}$
- Low	28$^{1}/_{8}$	25$^{1}/_{2}$	21	19	19$^{3}/_{4}$	16$^{1}/_{8}$
P/E Ratio - High	17	19	19	22	18	19
- Low	13	13	13	15	14	11

Income Statement Analysis (Million $)

	1994	%Chg	1993	%Chg	1992	%Chg	1991
Revs.	356	12%	318	17%	272	17%	232
Oper. Inc.	62.3	5%	59.2	35%	43.7	23%	35.6
Depr.	7.4	15%	6.4	3%	6.2	6%	5.9
Int. Exp.	1.7	-7%	1.9	-23%	2.4	8%	2.3
Pretax Inc.	53.2	4%	51.2	42%	36.1	36%	26.5
Eff. Tax Rate	35%	—	37%	—	35%	—	29%
Net Inc.	34.5	7%	32.3	37%	23.5	25%	18.8

Balance Sheet & Other Fin. Data (Million $)

	1994	1993	1992	1991	1990	1989
Cash	151	130	112	116	112	69.0
Curr. Assets	351	364	274	257	227	195
Total Assets	451	464	401	376	320	294
Curr. Liab.	342	306	275	256	206	190
LT Debt	3.4	24.5	20.0	20.0	20.0	20.0
Common Eqty.	97.0	121	91.2	85.8	81.9	74.2
Total Cap.	100	146	111	106	102	94.0
Cap. Exp.	7.4	7.0	5.8	7.7	7.2	4.7
Cash Flow	41.9	38.7	29.7	24.7	23.2	20.7

Ratio Analysis

	1994	1993	1992	1991	1990	1989
Curr. Ratio	1.0	1.2	1.0	1.0	1.1	1.0
% LT Debt of Cap.	3.4	16.8	18.0	18.9	19.6	21.2
% Net Inc.of Revs.	9.7	10.2	8.6	8.1	8.9	10.0
% Ret. on Assets	7.7	7.4	5.9	5.1	5.7	6.0
% Ret. on Equity	32.1	30.1	26.1	20.9	22.3	24.3

Dividend Data —Dividends have been paid since 1972. A poison pill stock purchase rights plan was adopted in 1987.

Amt. of Div. $	Date Decl.	Ex-Div. Date	Stock of Record	Payment Date
0.220	Sep. 21	Sep. 26	Sep. 30	Oct. 14 '94
0.220	Nov. 17	Dec. 23	Dec. 30	Jan. 13 '95
0.250	Jan. 23	Mar. 27	Mar. 31	Apr. 14 '95
0.250	May. 09	Jun. 28	Jun. 30	Jul. 14 '95
0.250	Jul. 18	Sep. 27	Sep. 29	Oct. 13 '95

Data as orig. reptd.; bef. results of disc. opers. and/or spec. items. Per share data adj. for stk. divs. as of ex-div. date. E-Estimated. NA-Not Available. NM-Not Meaningful. NR-Not Ranked.

Office—Two Pierce Place, Itasca, IL 60143-3141. **Founded**—in 1927; reincorporated in Delaware in 1972. **Tel**—(708) 773-3800. **Chrmn**—R. E. Gallagher. **Vice Chrmn**—J. P. Gallagher. **Pres & CEO**—J. P. Gallagher, Jr. **VP-Fin, CFO & Investor Contact**—Michael J. Cloherty. **Secy**—C. E. Fasig. **Dirs**—T. K. Brooker, J. G. Campbell, M. J. Cloherty, J. P. Gallagher, J. P. Gallagher, Jr., R. E. Gallagher, J. M. Greenberg, P. A. Marineau, W. F. McClure, J. R. Wimmer. **Transfer Agent & Registrar**—Harris Trust & Savings Bank, Chicago. **Empl**-3,308. **S&P Analyst:** Robert Schpoont

STANDARD & POOR'S

STOCK REPORTS

Genesis Health Ventures

NYSE Symbol **GHV**

In S&P SmallCap 600

04-OCT-95

Industry:
Health Care Centers

Summary: This company provides basic and specialty health care services to the elderly through health care networks serving five eastern U.S. markets.

Quantitative Evaluations

Outlook
(1 Lowest—5 Highest)
• **NA**

Fair Value
• **NA**

Risk
• **Average**

Earn./Div. Rank
• **NR**

Technical Eval.
• **Bullish** since 9/92

Rel. Strength Rank
(1 Lowest—99 Highest)
• **46**

Insider Activity
• **NA**

Recent Price • 35¾ | Yield • Nil

52 Wk Range • 37¼-25⅜ | 12-Mo. P/E • 22.2

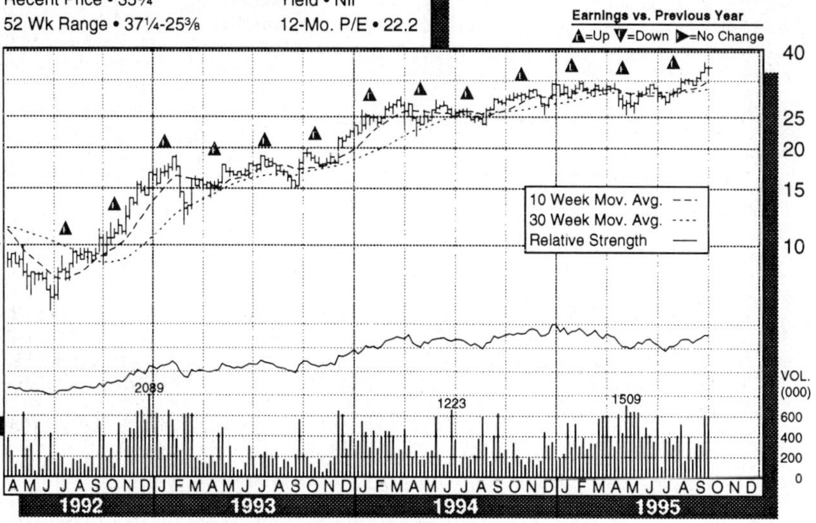

Business Profile - 04-OCT-95

Genesis Health Ventures plans to grow with an expanding elderly population and by concentrating on meeting the needs of managed care organizations. Profitability is expected to improve with increased utilization and a greater array of services. Working with third-party payors, the company's goal is to create and market pre-paid, all inclusive healthcare plans that will help older adults stay healthy, as well as take care of them when they are sick.

Operational Review - 04-OCT-95

Revenues soared in recent periods, reflecting continued strong growth in specialty services and higher management fees and other revenues. Margins widened, and net income advanced sharply. Earnings per share advanced to a lesser extent due to more shares outstanding. Results in 1994-95 exclude a $0.10 a share charge for the restructuring of indebtedness.

Stock Performance - 29-SEP-95

In the past 30 trading days, GHV's shares have increased 9%, compared to a 5% rise in the S&P 500. Average trading volume for the past five days was 125,020 shares, compared with the 40-day moving average of 81,900 shares.

Key Stock Statistics

Dividend Rate/Share	Nil	Shareholders	400
Shs. outstg. (M)	14.7	Market cap. (B)	$0.480
Avg. daily vol. (M)	0.120	Inst. holdings	78%
Tang. Bk. Value/Share	6.61	Insider holdings	NA
Beta	NA		

Value of $10,000 invested 5 years ago: NA

Fiscal Year Ending Sep. 30

	1995	% Change	1994	% Change	1993	% Change
Revenues (Million $)						
1Q	111.6	55%	71.91	37%	52.30	10%
2Q	116.9	19%	98.64	85%	53.25	13%
3Q	126.0	20%	105.4	90%	55.59	13%
4Q	—	—	112.7	92%	58.62	12%
Yr.	—	—	388.6	77%	219.8	12%
Income (Million $)						
1Q	4.81	65%	2.92	45%	2.02	62%
2Q	5.81	62%	3.58	33%	2.70	70%
3Q	4.96	5%	4.71	44%	3.28	66%
4Q	—	—	6.48	65%	3.92	36%
Yr.	—	—	17.69	49%	11.91	54%
Earnings Per Share ($)						
1Q	0.31	35%	0.23	21%	0.19	27%
2Q	0.38	36%	0.28	22%	0.23	35%
3Q	0.42	24%	0.34	31%	0.26	37%
4Q	—	—	0.40	29%	0.31	7%
Yr.	—	—	1.33	33%	1.00	25%

Next earnings report expected: late November

Genesis Health Ventures

04-OCT-95

Business Summary - 26-SEP-95

Genesis Health Ventures provides a broad range of basic and specialty health care services to meet the medical and physical needs of the elderly through healthcare networks located in five geographic markets in the eastern U.S. As of September 1994, the company's networks included 96 geriatric care facilities, five institutional pharmacies, six medical supply distribution centers, four certified rehabilitation agencies, four home healthcare agencies, 16 managed retirement communities, and four primary care physician clinics.

Revenue contributions in recent fiscal years:

	1994	1993	1992
Basic health care	62%	61%	69%
Specialty medical	32%	34%	26%
Management services & other	6%	5%	5%

The payor mix of basic and specialty medical services revenue in fiscal 1994 was 41% private pay and other, 16% Medicare, and 43% Medicaid.

Of the 96 geriatric care facilities operated by GHV, 44 were owned, 14 were leased, and 31 were managed. Owned and leased facilities at September 30, 1994, contained 7,583 licensed beds and had an average occupancy rate of 92% in fiscal 1994. The five geographic markets served by the company are: Hartford, Conn./Springfield, Mass.; Delaware Valley (Greater Philadelphia and Wilmington, Del.); Southern Delaware/Eastern Shore of Maryland; Baltimore, Md./Washington, D.C.; and Central Florida.

The company's goal is to provide cost-effective healthcare services and improved patient outcomes. In treating its patients, GHV endeavors to increase patients' medical well-being and functional capacity while reducing dependency on others. The services it offers are focused on six clinical initiatives which it believes are the central medical and physical issues facing the elderly. These initiatives are rehabilitation, nutrition management, intravenous therapy, bowel/bladder care, respiratory therapy, and wound management.

Specialty medical services provided by the company include pharmacy and medical supply, rehabilitation, subacute care, physician services, and home health care services. GHV also provides management, development and marketing services to 15 life care communities with a total of approximately 6,000 residents.

Important Developments

Sep. '95—GHV entered into a 20-year license agreement with Health Data Sciences, to develop a clinical administration and healthcare management system.

Aug. '95—The company agreed to acquire McKerley Health Care Centers, which owns or leases 15 geriatric care facilities in N.H. and Vt., for $82.5 million.

Capitalization

Long Term Debt: $273,000,000 (3/95), including $86,250,000 of 6% conv. sub. debs.

Per Share Data ($)

(Year Ended Sep. 30)

	1994	1993	1992	1991	1990	1989
Tangible Bk. Val.	6.23	8.67	6.28	3.86	-0.92	NA
Cash Flow	2.15	1.49	1.55	1.43	1.29	NA
Earnings	1.33	1.00	0.80	0.56	0.12	NA
Dividends	Nil	Nil	Nil	Nil	Nil	NA
Payout Ratio	Nil	Nil	Nil	Nil	Nil	NA
Prices - High	32	24 1/8	17	12 3/4	NA	NA
- Low	21 3/4	11 1/2	6 1/4	6 3/4	NA	NA
P/E Ratio - High	24	24	21	23	NA	NA
- Low	16	12	8	12	NA	NA

Income Statement Analysis (Million $)

	1994	%Chg	1993	%Chg	1992	%Chg	1991
Revs.	389	77%	220	12%	196	15%	171
Oper. Inc.	53.9	81%	29.7	5%	28.4	30%	21.8
Depr.	10.9	90%	5.8	-21%	7.2	48%	4.9
Int. Exp.	15.7	NM	5.1	-42%	8.8	-21%	11.1
Pretax Inc.	27.7	47%	18.9	52%	12.4	114%	5.8
Eff. Tax Rate	36%	—	37%	—	38%	—	38%
Net Inc.	17.7	49%	11.9	54%	7.7	114%	3.6

Balance Sheet & Other Fin. Data (Million $)

	1994	1993	1992	1991	1990	1989
Cash	4.3	4.0	1.3	1.3	1.1	NA
Curr. Assets	120	69.7	51.9	40.7	32.8	NA
Total Assets	512	237	189	173	150	NA
Curr. Liab.	53.3	19.6	19.9	26.0	25.6	NA
LT Debt	251	83.8	80.2	89.8	97.7	NA
Common Eqty.	195	125	82.7	37.7	12.1	NA
Total Cap.	456	216	167	145	122	NA
Cap. Exp.	26.6	23.5	7.3	18.2	16.9	NA
Cash Flow	28.6	17.7	14.9	8.0	4.9	NA

Ratio Analysis

	1994	1993	1992	1991	1990	1989
Curr. Ratio	2.3	3.6	2.6	1.6	1.3	NA
% LT Debt of Cap.	55.1	38.9	48.1	61.8	80.1	NA
% Net Inc.of Revs.	4.6	5.4	3.9	2.1	0.5	NA
% Ret. on Assets	4.5	5.1	3.3	1.1	NA	NA
% Ret. on Equity	10.3	10.6	10.8	8.5	NA	NA

Dividend Data —No cash dividends have been paid. A "poison pill" stock purchase rights plan was adopted in April 1995.

Data as orig. reptd.; bef. results of disc. opers. and/or spec. items. Per share data adj. for stk. divs. as of ex-div. date. E-Estimated. NA-Not Available. NM-Not Meaningful. NR-Not Ranked.

Office—148 West State St., Kennett Square, PA 19348. **Tel**—(610) 444-6350. **Chrmn & CEO**—M. R. Walker. **Pres & COO**—R. R. Howard. **VP-CFO**—G. V. Hager Jr. **VP-Secy**—L. J. Hoch. **Dirs**—R. R. Howard, S. H. Howard, R. C. Lipitz, S. E. Luongo, A. B. Miller, F. F. Nazem, M. R. Walker. **Transfer Agent**—Mellon Financial Services, Ridgefield Park, NJ. **Incorporated** in Pennsylvania in 1985. **Empl**-14,500. **S&P Analyst:** Philip J. Birbara

STANDARD & POOR'S

STOCK REPORTS

Gentex Corp.

NASDAQ Symbol **GNTX**

In S&P SmallCap 600

25-JUL-95

Industry: Electronics/Electric

Summary: Gentex manufactures automatic-dimming rearview mirrors for the automotive industry and fire protection products for commercial applications.

Quantitative Evaluations

Outlook (1 Lowest—5 Highest)
• **NA**

Fair Value
• **NA**

Risk
• **Average**

Earn./Div. Rank
• **B**

Technical Eval.
• **Bullish** since 7/95

Rel. Strength Rank (1 Lowest—99 Highest)
• **77**

Insider Activity
• **NA**

Recent Price • 21½
52 Wk Range • 27½-15¾

Yield • Nil
12-Mo. P/E • 21.7

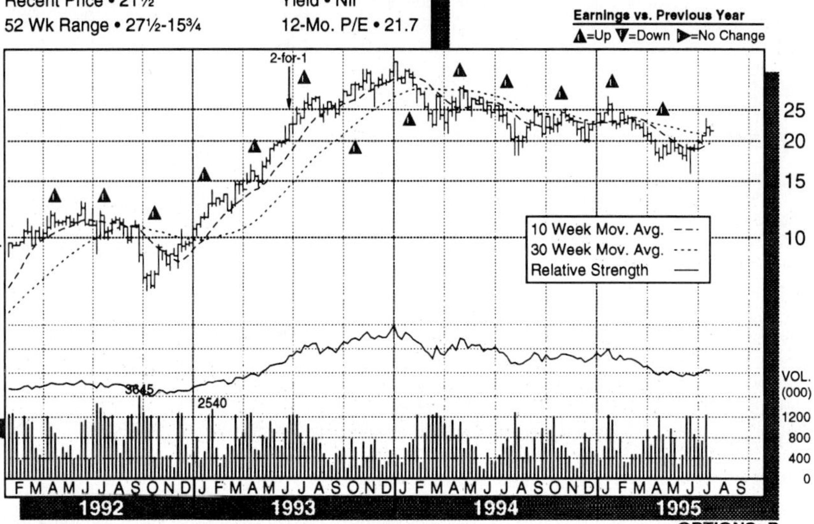

OPTIONS: P

Business Profile - 25-JUL-95

Revenue growth has been led by non-U.S. sales, which have been up substantially this year. With the majority of its revenues tied to the automotive sector, Gentex is vulnerable to a slowdown in that cyclical industry. While its international exposure helps to reduce the company's overall dependence on the U.S. market, advances in sales and earnings could begin to slow as world economies downshift to slower, more stable growth.

Operational Review - 21-JUL-95

Sales continue to exhibit impressive growth led by the European and Asian automotive markets. Margins, however, narrowed due to the reduced production schedule of many light vehicles in North America, price reductions associated with recently awarded long-term contracts, and increased patent litigation expense accruals. These factors caused the company to report only a modest growth in earnings for the first half of the year.

Stock Performance - 21-JUL-95

In the past 30 trading days, GNTX's shares have increased 13%, compared to a 5% rise in the S&P 500. Average trading volume for the past five days was 81,940 shares, compared with the 40-day moving average of 190,889 shares.

Key Stock Statistics

Dividend Rate/Share	Nil	Shareholders	1,800
Shs. outstg. (M)	16.6	Market cap. (B)	$0.366
Avg. daily vol. (M)	0.175	Inst. holdings	48%
Tang. Bk. Value/Share	4.32	Insider holdings	NA
Beta	0.73		

Value of $10,000 invested 5 years ago: $ 33,725

Fiscal Year Ending Dec. 31

	1995	% Change	1994	% Change	1993	% Change
Revenues (Million $)						
1Q	26.04	23%	21.16	39%	15.27	82%
2Q	26.02	26%	20.71	51%	13.74	33%
3Q	—	—	23.09	49%	15.47	36%
4Q	—	—	24.80	29%	19.19	27%
Yr.	—	—	89.76	41%	63.66	41%
Income (Million $)						
1Q	4.59	12%	4.10	105%	2.00	156%
2Q	4.00	NM	3.99	104%	1.96	56%
3Q	—	—	3.98	78%	2.24	95%
4Q	—	—	4.40	21%	3.65	95%
Yr.	—	—	16.47	67%	9.84	94%
Earnings Per Share ($)						
1Q	0.27	12%	0.24	100%	0.12	140%
2Q	0.23	NM	0.23	92%	0.12	60%
3Q	—	—	0.23	77%	0.13	86%
4Q	—	—	0.26	24%	0.21	83%
Yr.	—	—	0.97	64%	0.59	90%

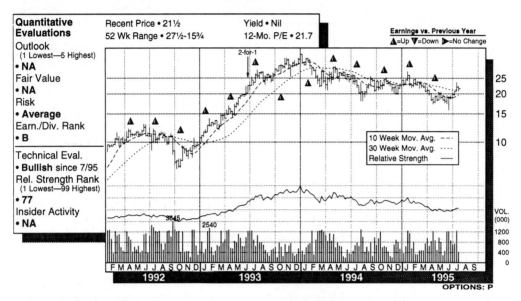

Next earnings report expected: mid October

Gentex Corp.

Business Summary - 25-JUL-95

Gentex Corporation designs, develops, manufactures and markets proprietary products employing electro-optical technology. The company has two primary product lines: automatic rearview mirrors for automobiles and fire protection products for commercial applications. Gentex phased out its Glass Products Group during 1994. Contributions to net sales in recent years were:

	1994	1993	1992
Automatic mirrors	79%	72%	76%
Fire protection products	22%	27%	22%
Other	--	1%	2%

The automotive products line consists of Interior Night Vision Safety (NVS) Mirrors and Exterior NVS Mirror subassemblies. NVS mirrors gradually darken to the degree necessary to eliminate rearview glare from approaching headlights. Interior NVS Mirrors are factory-installed options on nearly 80 domestic and foreign 1995 car and light truck models. Gentex sold about 1,395,000 Interior NVS Mirrors in 1994, 958,000 the year before and 703,000 in 1992. During 1991, Gentex introduced the Exterior NVS Mirror, which utilizes the company's electrochromic technology to permit its use in outside rearview mirrors. The systen is a factory-installed option on nine car models and standard equipment on four other models in the 1995 car year. Gentex sold 365,000 Exterior NVS Mirror subassemblies in 1994, up from 191,000 in 1993.

In North America, mirrors are sold to Ford Motor Co., General Motors Corp. and Chrysler Corp. Overseas, Gentex supplies mirrors to BMW, Fiat, Opel, Rolls Royce, Mercedes-Benz, Bentley, Hyundai, Daewoo, Toyota and Nissan. R&D efforts are directed toward development of electrochromic technology for use in complete mirror systems and in windows for the automotive and architectural markets, sunroofs and sunglasses.

The fire protection products line consists of more than 40 different models of smoke detectors and 50 different models of signaling devices. Gentex's fire protection products provide the flexibility to be wired as part of multiple-function systems and consequently are generally used in large office buildings, hotels, military bases, colleges and other commercial establishments. Products are sold directly to fire protection and security product distributors and original equipment manufacturers.

Important Developments

Jul. '95—In announcing record results for the first half of 1995, Gentex noted that its Night Vision Safety mirror shipments to customers outside North America were up 180% during the period.

Capitalization

Long Term Debt: None (6/95).

Per Share Data ($) (Year Ended Dec. 31)

	1994	1993	1992	1991	1990	1989
Tangible Bk. Val.	4.32	3.03	2.09	1.82	1.70	1.61
Cash Flow	1.14	0.71	0.42	0.20	0.14	0.21
Earnings	0.97	0.59	0.32	0.12	0.08	0.15
Dividends	Nil	Nil	Nil	Nil	Nil	Nil
Payout Ratio	Nil	Nil	Nil	Nil	Nil	Nil
Prices - High	35¼	35¼	13	6¾	7⅛	7⅜
- Low	18	10⅛	6⅝	2⁷⁄₁₆	2⅝	2¼
P/E Ratio - High	36	60	41	56	95	47
- Low	19	17	21	20	34	15

Income Statement Analysis (Million $)

	1994	%Chg	1993	%Chg	1992	%Chg	1991
Revs.	89.8	41%	63.7	41%	45.1	68%	26.9
Oper. Inc.	26.0	63%	16.0	88%	8.5	170%	3.2
Depr.	3.0	41%	2.1	28%	1.6	29%	1.3
Int. Exp.	Nil	—	0.0	-94%	0.2	-67%	0.5
Pretax Inc.	24.7	68%	14.7	94%	7.6	184%	2.7
Eff. Tax Rate	33%	—	33%	—	33%	—	30%
Net Inc.	16.5	68%	9.9	94%	5.1	171%	1.9

Balance Sheet & Other Fin. Data (Million $)

	1994	1993	1992	1991	1990	1989
Cash	19.3	13.3	7.8	14.3	10.9	14.1
Curr. Assets	36.4	27.1	17.8	20.8	15.6	20.1
Total Assets	80.5	55.2	40.3	37.2	33.9	32.5
Curr. Liab.	8.7	5.5	4.0	8.6	1.7	1.9
LT Debt	Nil	Nil	Nil	0.1	6.1	6.1
Common Eqty.	71.4	49.5	35.5	28.2	25.9	24.2
Total Cap.	71.8	49.7	36.2	28.6	32.2	30.7
Cap. Exp.	6.2	3.4	4.2	2.2	2.4	4.1
Cash Flow	19.5	12.0	6.7	3.1	2.2	2.9

Ratio Analysis

	1994	1993	1992	1991	1990	1989
Curr. Ratio	4.2	4.9	4.4	2.4	9.3	10.9
% LT Debt of Cap.	Nil	Nil	Nil	0.3	18.9	19.9
% Net Inc.of Revs.	18.3	15.5	11.2	6.9	5.3	8.8
% Ret. on Assets	24.1	20.4	12.9	5.2	3.3	9.1
% Ret. on Equity	27.0	23.0	15.8	6.8	4.5	12.2

Dividend Data (The company has never paid cash dividends. A two-for-one stock split was effected in June 1993.)

Data as orig. reptd.; bef. results of disc. opers. and/or spec. items. Per share data adj. for stk. divs. as of ex-div. date. E-Estimated. NA-Not Available. NM-Not Meaningful. NR-Not Ranked.

Office—600 N. Centennial, Zeeland, MI 49464. **Tel**—(616) 772-1800. **Chrmn & CEO**—F. Bauer. **Exec VP**—K. LaGrand. **VP-Fin & Treas**—E. Jen. **Secy & Investor Contact**—Connie Hamblin. **Dirs**—F. Bauer, H. J. Byker, M. E. Fouts, K. LaGrand, A. Lanting, J. Mulder, T. Thompson, L. L. Weber. **Transfer Agent**—American Stock Transfer & Trust Co., NYC **Incorporated** in Michigan in 1974. **Empl**-714. **S&P Analyst:** Steven A. Jaworski

STANDARD & POOR'S

STOCK REPORTS

Geotek Communications

NASDAQ Symbol **GOTK**

In S&P SmallCap 600

13-SEP-95

Industry: Telecommunications

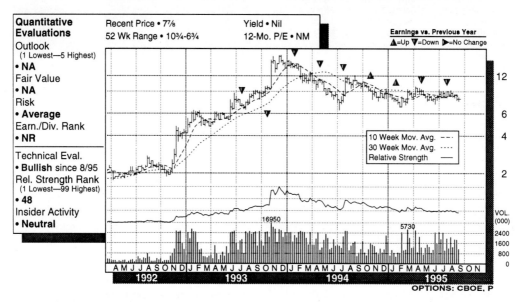

Summary: This company is an international provider of wireless mobile telcommunications services to commercial businesses.

Quantitative Evaluations

Outlook
(1 Lowest—5 Highest)
• **NA**

Fair Value
• **NA**

Risk
• **Average**

Earn./Div. Rank
• **NR**

Technical Eval.
• **Bullish** since 8/95

Rel. Strength Rank
(1 Lowest—99 Highest)
• **48**

Insider Activity
• **Neutral**

Recent Price • 7⅞

52 Wk Range • 10¾-6¾

Yield • Nil

12-Mo. P/E • NM

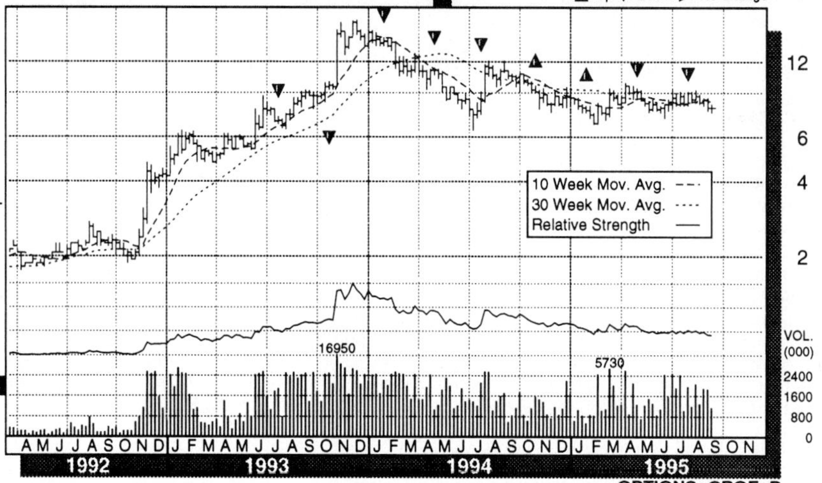

OPTIONS: CBOE, P

Business Profile - 13-SEP-95

This provider of mobile wireless communications systems targets companies that rely on this type of communication to coordinate fleets of vehicles or mobile personnel. Geotek recently introduced a new digital wireless communications system that utilizes GOTK's proprietary FHMA technology. Earlier this year, GOTK expanded its European presence by acquiring equity stakes in two German mobile radio networks.

Operational Review - 13-SEP-95

Revenues for the six months ended June 30, 1995 rose 24%, year to year, reflecting growth in both equipment and service sales. Margins narrowed, and the net loss widened to $0.54 a share from $0.35 in the first half of 1994. Future results should benefit from the recent introduction of the products and services of its new digital communications network.

Stock Performance - 08-SEP-95

In the past 30 trading days, GOTK's shares have declined 13%, compared to a 2% rise in the S&P 500. Average trading volume for the past five days was 280,250 shares, compared with the 40-day moving average of 314,477 shares.

Key Stock Statistics

Dividend Rate/Share	Nil	Shareholders	1,300
Shs. outstg. (M)	51.5	Market cap. (B)	$0.444
Avg. daily vol. (M)	0.346	Inst. holdings	17%
Tang. Bk. Value/Share	0.63	Insider holdings	NA
Beta	0.43		

Value of $10,000 invested 5 years ago: $ 39,375

Fiscal Year Ending Dec. 31

	1995	% Change	1994	% Change	1993	% Change
Revenues (Million $)						
1Q	19.20	23%	15.60	111%	7.40	—
2Q	20.31	25%	16.20	72%	9.40	-27%
3Q	—	—	17.63	18%	14.90	80%
4Q	—	—	23.60	50%	15.70	162%
Yr.	—	—	72.99	54%	47.40	74%
Income (Million $)						
1Q	-13.72	NM	-7.17	NM	-3.02	NM
2Q	-12.39	NM	-9.16	NM	-2.75	NM
3Q	—	—	-12.10	NM	-37.89	NM
4Q	—	—	-13.98	NM	-6.73	NM
Yr.	—	—	-42.41	NM	-50.39	NM
Earnings Per Share ($)						
1Q	-0.28	NM	-0.16	NM	-0.13	—
2Q	-0.26	NM	-0.20	NM	-0.11	NM
3Q	—	—	-0.26	NM	-0.99	NM
4Q	—	—	-0.28	NM	-0.33	NM
Yr.	—	—	-0.90	NM	-1.56	NM

Next earnings report expected: mid November

Geotek Communications

Business Summary - 13-SEP-95

Geotek Communications, Inc. (formerly Geotek Industries) is an international provider of wireless communication services to commercial companies and business organizations, and manufactures telecommunication products. The company intends to become a leading international provider of integrated multi-function, digital wireless communication services with the introduction of GeoNet, a national wireless telecommunications network to begin commercial operations in Philadelphia in mid-1995. Geotek disposed of its defense electronics interests in 1992 and now focuses on its wireless activities. The Wireless Communication Group owns interests in a joint venture that holds commercial rights to digital wireless telecommunications technology developed by an Israeli government agency. The Communications Products Group develops, makes and markets telephone and telecommuncations peripherals, commercial audio, paging, data dispatch and power supply products.

In 1992, the company entered into a joint venture to develop and commercialize digital wireless telecommunications technology developed by Israel's Rafael Armament Development Authority. The technology, based on narrowband spread spectrum frequency hopping techniques, allows greater call capacity per frequency channel, better communications quality and call security, and more cost-effective systems and services.

Geotek holds a 56% interest in the Rafael joint venture through wholly owned PowerSpectrum Inc. (PSI), which has non-Israel worldwide rights to systems using technology developed by the joint venture. GOTK acquired National Band Three (NBTL), a British data communications company; a 25% interest in Cumulous, a California SMR service company; and a 76% interest in GMSI, a Canadian mobile data company. It has also acquired specialized mobile radio licenses in the 900 mhz frequency spectrum in cities throughout the U.S. Using these licenses and systems to be developed with Rafael technology, GOTK aims to establish GeoNet service to 35 cities by the end of 1997.

Important Developments

Aug. '95—Geotek completed the sale of its shareholdings in Speech Design Gmbh and Bogen Corp. to European Gateway Acquisition Corp. In exchange for its holdings in these companies, Geotek received $7 million in cash, a convertible promissory note for $3 million, 3,701,919 shares of European Gateway common stock, and warrants to purchase 200,000 additional shares of European Gateway.

Capitalization

Long Term Debt: $39,689,000 (6/95).

Per Share Data ($)

(Year Ended Dec. 31)

	1994	1993	1992	1991	1990	1989
Tangible Bk. Val.	0.62	1.60	0.56	-0.97	0.26	NA
Cash Flow	-0.80	-1.50	-0.21	0.06	-0.96	NA
Earnings	-0.90	-1.56	-0.29	-0.24	-1.32	NA
Dividends	Nil	Nil	Nil	Nil	Nil	NA
Payout Ratio	Nil	Nil	Nil	Nil	Nil	NA
Prices - High	16	17⅝	4¾	2⅛	2⅛	NA
- Low	6⅜	4¼	1⅝	1	1	NA
P/E Ratio - High	NM	NM	NM	NM	NM	NA
- Low	NM	NM	NM	NM	NA	NA

Income Statement Analysis (Million $)

	1994	%Chg	1993	%Chg	1992	%Chg	1991
Revs.	73.0	54%	47.4	74%	27.2	-26%	36.8
Oper. Inc.	-30.5	NM	-15.6	NM	-2.0	NM	2.5
Depr.	4.7	145%	1.9	133%	0.8	-47%	1.6
Int. Exp.	3.1	20%	2.6	135%	1.1	-39%	1.8
Pretax Inc.	-41.6	NM	-51.8	NM	-2.4	NM	-0.1
Eff. Tax Rate	NM	—	NM	—	NM	—	NM
Net Inc.	-42.4	NM	-50.4	NM	-2.4	NM	-0.1

Balance Sheet & Other Fin. Data (Million $)

	1994	1993	1992	1991	1990	1989
Cash	52.0	59.5	3.0	3.6	8.2	NA
Curr. Assets	79.6	79.9	18.5	18.4	18.2	NA
Total Assets	180	135	39.3	46.6	39.8	NA
Curr. Liab.	32.5	21.4	11.1	17.2	15.5	NA
LT Debt	29.4	4.0	2.6	7.3	6.5	NA
Common Eqty.	77.4	68.3	22.3	15.3	11.5	NA
Total Cap.	147	113	27.0	23.1	18.0	NA
Cap. Exp.	10.5	2.3	0.9	0.7	0.8	0.8
Cash Flow	-39.8	-48.7	-2.3	0.3	-3.1	-1.7

Ratio Analysis

	1994	1993	1992	1991	1990	1989
Curr. Ratio	2.4	3.7	1.7	1.1	1.2	NA
% LT Debt of Cap.	20.0	3.5	9.6	31.5	36.1	NA
% Net Inc.of Revs.	NM	NM	NM	NM	NM	NM
% Ret. on Assets	NM	NM	NM	NM	NM	NA
% Ret. on Equity	NM	NM	NM	NM	NM	NA

Dividend Data —No dividends have been paid on the common shares, and no payments are expected in the foreseeable future.

Data as orig. reptd.; bef. results of disc. opers. and/or spec. items. Per share data adj. for stk. divs. as of ex-div. date. E-Estimated. NA-Not Available. NM-Not Meaningful. NR-Not Ranked.

Office—20 Craig Rd., Montvale, NJ 07645. **Tel**—(201) 930-9305. **Chrmn**—W. J. Churchill. **Pres & CEO**—Y. I. Eitan. **EVP, COO & CFO**—Y. Bibring. **Secy**—A. Siegel. **Investor Contact**—Randy Miller. **Dirs**—W. E. Auch, G. Calhoun, P. Chatterjee, W. J. Churchill, Y. I. Eitan, H. Griffin, R. Krants, R. Liebhaber, H. Rosen, K. W. Sharer, W. Spier. **Transfer Agent & Registrar**—Registrar & Transfer Co., Cranford, N.J. **Incorporated** in Delaware in 1988. **Empl**-400. **S&P Analyst:** Mike Cavanaugh

STANDARD & POOR'S

STOCK REPORTS

Gerber Scientific

NYSE Symbol **GRB**
In S&P SmallCap 600

13-OCT-95 **Industry:** Electronics/Electric

Summary: This company manufactures and services computer-aided design and computer-aided manufacturing systems that automate design and production processes in a broad range of industries.

Quantitative Evaluations

Outlook
(1 Lowest—5 Highest)
• **3**
Fair Value
• **17¼**
Risk
• **Low**
Earn./Div. Rank
• **B**

Technical Eval.
• **Bearish** since 5/95
Rel. Strength Rank
(1 Lowest—99 Highest)
• **45**
Insider Activity
• **NA**

Recent Price • 17⅛
52 Wk Range • 19½-11⅞
Yield • 1.9%
12-Mo. P/E • 20.9

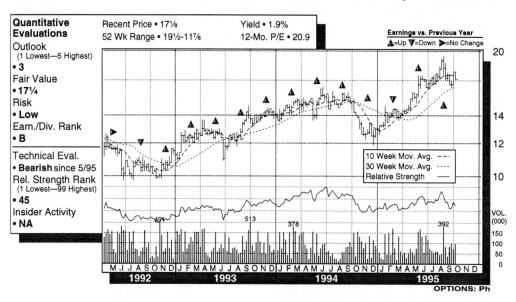

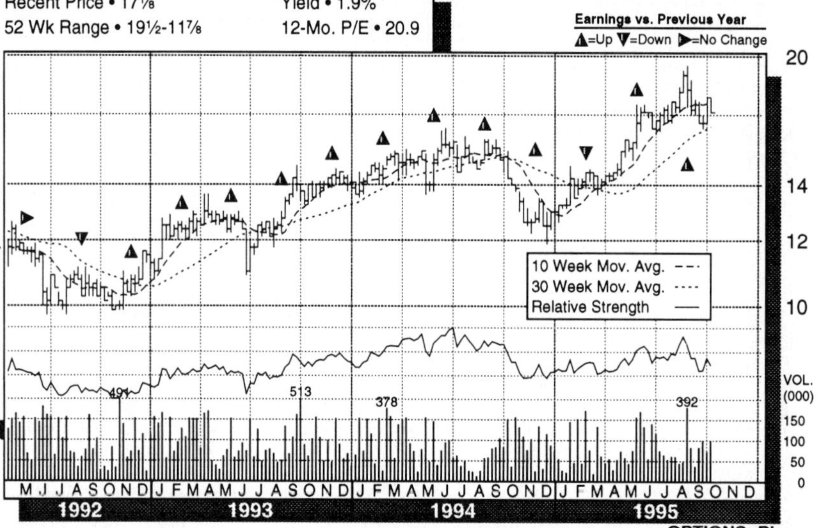

OPTIONS: Ph

Business Profile - 13-OCT-95

Gerber is a manufacturer and servicer of computer-aided design and computer-aided manufacturing systems to automate design and production processes in various industries. The company recorded higher earnings for each of the past three fiscal years. Prospects for fiscal 1995-96 are enhanced by newer products which are increasing Gerber's marketing positions, ongoing cost controls and a heavy commitment to research and development.

Operational Review - 13-OCT-95

Revenues for the three months ended July 31, 1995, advanced 26%, year to year, with product sales up 27% and service revenues rising 21%. Profitability benefited from the higher volume as well as the September 1994 acquisition of Microdynamics. The gain in pretax income was extended to 39%. After taxes at 29.7%, versus 32.6%, net income was up 45%. Earnings rose to $0.19 a share from $0.13 in the year-earlier period.

Stock Performance - 06-OCT-95

In the past 30 trading days, GRB's shares have declined 6%, compared to a 4% rise in the S&P 500. Average trading volume for the past five days was 19,780 shares, compared with the 40-day moving average of 23,200 shares.

Key Stock Statistics

Dividend Rate/Share	0.32	Shareholders	1,900
Shs. outstg. (M)	23.8	Market cap. (B)	$0.407
Avg. daily vol. (M)	0.018	Inst. holdings	69%
Tang. Bk. Value/Share	8.32	Insider holdings	NA
Beta	0.90		

Value of $10,000 invested 5 years ago: $ 11,849

Fiscal Year Ending Apr. 30

	1996	% Change	1995	% Change	1994	% Change
Revenues (Million $)						
1Q	88.19	26%	70.03	8%	64.93	4%
2Q	—	—	72.94	15%	63.31	-2%
3Q	—	—	82.81	30%	63.78	3%
4Q	—	—	96.92	41%	68.72	5%
Yr.	—	—	322.7	24%	260.7	3%
Income (Million $)						
1Q	4.49	45%	3.10	64%	1.89	—
2Q	—	—	4.05	55%	2.62	26%
3Q	—	—	4.78	-20%	5.98	150%
4Q	—	—	6.18	53%	4.04	69%
Yr.	—	—	18.11	25%	14.53	74%
Earnings Per Share ($)						
1Q	0.19	46%	0.13	63%	0.08	33%
2Q	—	—	0.17	55%	0.11	22%
3Q	—	—	0.20	-20%	0.25	150%
4Q	—	—	0.26	53%	0.17	70%
Yr.	—	—	0.76	25%	0.61	74%

Next earnings report expected: late November

Gerber Scientific

Business Summary - 13-OCT-95

Gerber Scientific and its subsidiaries manufacture and service computer-aided design and computer-aided manufacturing (CAD/CAM) systems to automate design and production processes in a broad range of industries. Contributions to sales by product classes in recent fiscal years were:

	1994-95	1993-94
Cutting, nesting & material handling	57%	51%
Microprocessor & PC-controlled production	29%	33%
Interactive imaging & inspection systems	8%	11%
Optical lens manufacturing	6%	5%

International business accounted for 48% of total revenues in fiscal 1994-95.

The company conducts its business primarily through four wholly owned operating subsidiaries.

Gerber Garment Technology produces computer-controlled systems for materials handling, marker-making (nesting), cutting and spreading of flexible materials, such as fabrics and composites, in the apparel, aerospace, automotive, furniture and other industries. In March 1994, the subsidiary acquired Niebuhr Maskinfabrik A/S, a Danish manufacturer of computer-automated fabric spreading and cutting room equipment, for about $1 million. In September 1994, GGT purchased Microdynamics, Inc., a leading supplier of computer-aided design (CAD), graphic design, and product management systems for the apparel, footwear and other sewn goods industries. GGT is continuing to develop, manufacture, market and support the Microdynamics' product lines.

Gerber Scientific Products makes microprocessor- and PC-controlled production systems for the signmaking, graphic arts and screenprinting industries.

Gerber Systems' products include turnkey interactive imaging and inspection systems for the aerospace, automotive, electronics, and printing industries.

Gerber Optical's products consist primarily of computer-controlled production systems for the ophthalmic lens manufacturing industry.

Research and development expenses equaled 8.1% of total revenues in fiscal 1994-95.

Important Developments

Aug. '95—During the three months ended July 31, 1995, Gerber received new orders totaling $84.3 million, up 15% from $73.5 million in the year-earlier period. At July 31, backlog was $49.9 million, versus $52.0 million a year earlier.

Capitalization

Long Term Debt: $7,483,000 (7/95).

Per Share Data ($)

(Year Ended Apr. 30)

	1995	1994	1993	1992	1991	1990
Tangible Bk. Val.	8.32	8.38	8.33	8.35	8.26	8.24
Cash Flow	1.23	1.01	0.77	0.69	0.69	1.71
Earnings	0.76	0.61	0.35	0.31	0.34	1.36
Dividends	0.30	0.23	0.20	0.20	0.20	0.16
Payout Ratio	39%	38%	57%	64%	59%	12%
Cal. Yrs.	1994	1993	1992	1991	1990	1989
Prices - High	16⅜	14¾	15¼	14¾	15⅞	21
- Low	11⅞	10¾	9¾	8	7	14⅛
P/E Ratio - High	22	24	44	48	47	15
- Low	16	18	28	26	21	10

Income Statement Analysis (Million $)

	1995	%Chg	1994	%Chg	1993	%Chg	1992
Revs.	323	24%	261	3%	254	2%	250
Oper. Inc.	31.0	50%	20.6	14%	18.0	11%	16.2
Depr.	11.4	18%	9.7	-4%	10.1	11%	9.1
Int. Exp.	0.5	31%	0.3	-31%	0.5	-72%	1.8
Pretax Inc.	25.1	17%	21.4	75%	12.2	8%	11.3
Eff. Tax Rate	28%	—	32%	—	32%	—	34%
Net Inc.	18.1	25%	14.5	75%	8.3	12%	7.4

Balance Sheet & Other Fin. Data (Million $)

	1995	1994	1993	1992	1991	1990
Cash	10.2	15.6	17.3	50.6	48.8	29.7
Curr. Assets	147	130	121	186	197	197
Total Assets	324	286	270	277	288	277
Curr. Liab.	68.4	41.9	38.1	42.9	55.0	51.5
LT Debt	7.5	7.7	7.9	8.1	9.2	9.5
Common Eqty.	237	225	215	214	210	205
Total Cap.	254	244	232	231	228	224
Cap. Exp.	12.5	4.6	6.5	8.8	6.3	6.9
Cash Flow	29.5	24.2	18.4	16.5	16.2	40.8

Ratio Analysis

	1995	1994	1993	1992	1991	1990
Curr. Ratio	2.1	3.1	3.2	4.3	3.6	3.8
% LT Debt of Cap.	3.0	3.2	3.4	3.5	4.0	4.2
% Net Inc.of Revs.	5.6	5.6	3.3	3.0	3.0	10.6
% Ret. on Assets	5.9	5.2	3.0	2.6	2.8	12.3
% Ret. on Equity	7.8	6.6	3.9	3.5	3.8	16.9

Dividend Data —Dividends were initiated in 1978.

Amt. of Div. $	Date Decl.	Ex-Div. Date	Stock of Record	Payment Date
0.080	Nov. 04	Nov. 09	Nov. 16	Nov. 30 '94
0.080	Feb. 02	Feb. 08	Feb. 14	Feb. 28 '95
0.080	May. 05	May. 11	May. 17	May. 31 '95
0.080	Aug. 01	Aug. 16	Aug. 18	Aug. 31 '95

Data as orig. reptd.; bef. results of disc. opers. and/or spec. items. Per share data adj. for stk. divs. as of ex-div. date. E-Estimated. NA-Not Available. NM-Not Meaningful. NR-Not Ranked.

Office—83 Gerber Rd. West, South Windsor, CT 06074. **Tel**—(203) 644-1551. **Fax**—(203) 643-7039. **Chrmn & Pres**—H. J. Gerber. **Sr VP-Fin & CFO**—G. M. Gentile. **Treas**—G. K. Bennett. **Secy**—D. J. Gerber. **Dirs**—G. M. Gentile, D. J. Gerber, H. J. Gerber, E. E. Hood, S. Simon, A. R. Towbin, W. J. Vereen. **Transfer Agent & Registrar**—Chemical Mellon Shareholder Services Co., East Hartford, Conn. **Incorporated** in Connecticut in 1948. **Empl**-1,700. **S&P Analyst:** JJS

STANDARD & POOR'S

STOCK REPORTS

Gerrity Oil & Gas

NYSE Symbol **GOG**
In S&P SmallCap 600

12-SEP-95

Industry:
Oil and Gas

Summary: Gerrity is an independent energy company primarily engaged in the drilling of low risk oil and gas development wells.

Quantitative Evaluations

Outlook
(1 Lowest—5 Highest)
• **NA**

Fair Value
• **NA**

Risk
• **High**

Earn./Div. Rank
• **NR**

Technical Eval.
• **Bearish** since 12/93

Rel. Strength Rank
(1 Lowest—99 Highest)
• **7**

Insider Activity
• **NA**

Recent Price • 3½
52 Wk Range • 7¾-2⅝

Yield • Nil
12-Mo. P/E • NM

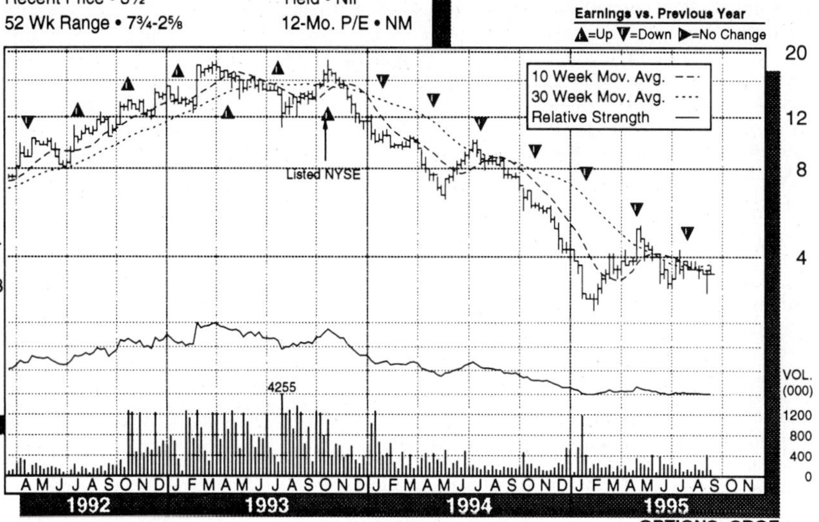

OPTIONS: CBOE

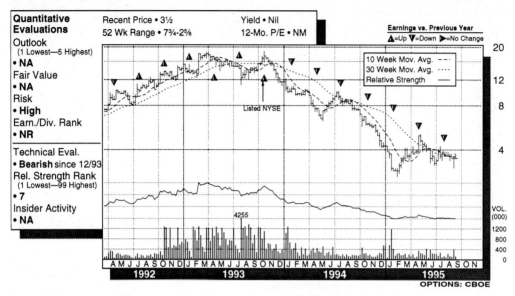

Business Profile - 12-SEP-95

Gerrity was formed in 1990 to consolidate certain oil and gas assets, mainly in the Wattenberg Field of Colorado's Denver-Julesburg Basin. The company's focus on low-cost, low-risk activities in a single basin has contributed to its successful development. GOG should benefit from continued acquisition efforts and increased production. It issued $100 million of debentures in June 1994 to prepay bank debt. In January 1995, GOG announced plans to reduce corporate overhead by approximately 30%.

Operational Review - 12-SEP-95

Revenues during the six months ended June 30, 1995, declined 14%, year to year, reflecting both lower production of oil and prices for gas. Higher depletion, depreciation and amortization costs resulted from greater capitalized expenses and depressed gas prices. Interest expense also rose, due to the increase in the average interest rate on the company's borrowings. A net loss of $2,881,000 ($0.37 a share, after preferred dividends), contrasted with net income of $3,999,000 ($0.13).

Stock Performance - 08-SEP-95

In the past 30 trading days, GOG's shares have declined 3%, compared to a 2% rise in the S&P 500. Average trading volume for the past five days was 29,200 shares, compared with the 40-day moving average of 31,772 shares.

Key Stock Statistics

Dividend Rate/Share	Nil	Shareholders	200
Shs. outstg. (M)	13.8	Market cap. (B)	$0.047
Avg. daily vol. (M)	0.038	Inst. holdings	66%
Tang. Bk. Value/Share	6.80	Insider holdings	NA
Beta	0.34		

Value of $10,000 invested 5 years ago: NA

Fiscal Year Ending Dec. 31

	1995	% Change	1994	% Change	1993	% Change
Revenues (Million $)						
1Q	14.79	-4%	15.34	14%	13.51	188%
2Q	14.59	-22%	18.81	NM	18.75	NM
3Q	—	—	15.97	-11%	17.88	142%
4Q	—	—	15.47	-12%	17.66	94%
Yr.	—	—	65.59	-3%	67.79	155%
Income (Million $)						
1Q	-1.63	NM	1.76	21%	1.45	169%
2Q	-1.25	NM	2.24	-54%	4.92	NM
3Q	—	—	-1.34	NM	4.78	NM
4Q	—	—	-1.92	NM	2.44	-9%
Yr.	—	—	0.74	-95%	13.60	168%
Earnings Per Share ($)						
1Q	-0.20	NM	0.05	-55%	0.11	83%
2Q	-0.17	NM	0.08	-74%	0.31	NM
3Q	—	—	-0.18	NM	0.27	93%
4Q	—	—	-0.22	NM	0.10	-55%
Yr.	—	—	-0.27	NM	0.78	56%

Next earnings report expected: early November

Gerrity Oil & Gas

Business Summary - 11-SEP-95

Gerrity Oil & Gas was formed in 1990 for the principal purpose of combining and operating oil and gas properties that were owned by two firms controlled by Robert W. Gerrity (the Gerrity Corps.) and properties held by Aeneas Venture Corp. and Okabena E-2 Corp. The consolidation occurred simultaneously with the closing of GOG's initial public offering in August 1990.

The company, which is involved mainly in drilling low-risk oil and gas development wells, has concentrated its activities in the Wattenberg Field of the Denver-Julesburg Basin in Colorado and Wyoming. As of December 31, 1994, the company operated 1,829 wells in which it had an interest in the Wattenberg Field. GOG also had an inventory of approximately 1,447 drillsites. In addition, GOG has identified approximately 560 recompletion opportunities. The company's estimated average cost for recompleting existing wells is approximately $55,000 per recompletion, resulting in average per well addition to gross producing revenues of approximately 27,000 boe.

Proved reserves at December 31, 1994, totaled 237,028,000 Mcf of natural gas (181,392,000 developed; 55,636,000 undeveloped) and 21,297,000 bbl. of oil and condensate (13,717,000 developed; 7,580,000 undeveloped). Net 1994 production was 2,040,000 bbl. of oil and condensate and 19,587,000 Mcf of gas, and average sales prices were $15.19 per bbl. and $1.71 per Mcf. GOG owned 234 gross (197 net) producing gas wells and 1,698 gross (1,614 net) producing oil wells as of December 31, 1994. During 1994, the company drilled and completed 114.0 gross (112.6 net) development wells, all but one of which were commercially successful, and no exploratory wells.

Gerrity Well Services, Inc., a wholly-owned subsidiary formed in March 1993, provides GOG and other entities with well site development, water hauling and related services for which the company previously paid outside contractors. GTT, Inc., another subsidiary, was formed in September 1994 to facilitate the purchase and sale, aggregation, quality control and marketing of petroleum products.

In January 1995, GOG announced plans to implement a program to reduce corporate overhead by approximately 30% through a combination of staff reductions and other cost cutting measures.

Important Developments

Aug. '95—During the six months ended June 30, 1995, GOG drillled 30 oil and gas wells and performed 14 recompletions. Net cash used in investing was $16,693,000, financed by operating activities of $12,151,000 and borrowings totaling $8,000,000.

Capitalization

Long Term Debt: $137,000,000 (6/95).
$12 Conv. Preferred Stock: 379,500 shs. ($200 liq. pref.); conv. into 10.392 com. shs.

Per Share Data ($) (Year Ended Dec. 31)

	1994	1993	1992	1991	1990	1989
Tangible Bk. Val.	7.17	7.62	7.14	4.39	3.41	NA
Cash Flow	2.09	2.63	1.53	1.38	1.33	1.46
Earnings	-0.27	0.78	0.50	0.30	0.20	0.35
Dividends	Nil	Nil	Nil	Nil	Nil	Nil
Payout Ratio	Nil	Nil	Nil	Nil	Nil	Nil
Prices - High	12¼	18⅝	15¼	8⅛	8½	NA
- Low	3⅞	10¾	6⅜	3⅛	4⅜	NA
P/E Ratio - High	NM	24	31	27	43	NA
- Low	NM	14	13	10	22	NA

Income Statement Analysis (Million $)

	1994	%Chg	1993	%Chg	1992	%Chg	1991
Revs.	64.6	NM	65.1	149%	26.1	67%	15.6
Oper. Inc.	43.0	-10%	47.8	167%	17.9	69%	10.6
Depr. Depl. & Amort.	32.7	29%	25.4	142%	10.5	46%	7.2
Int. Exp.	11.5	32%	8.7	NM	1.7	76%	1.0
Pretax Inc.	0.8	-95%	16.9	168%	6.3	134%	2.7
Eff. Tax Rate	5.30%	—	20%	—	20%	—	27%
Net Inc.	0.7	-95%	13.6	167%	5.1	159%	2.0

Balance Sheet & Other Fin. Data (Million $)

	1994	1993	1992	1991	1990	1989
Cash	0.1	0.9	6.1	10.5	0.7	0.3
Curr. Assets	15.8	18.1	15.5	13.6	3.7	2.7
Total Assets	338	328	239	58.9	34.2	28.1
Curr. Liab.	25.7	45.2	27.8	6.7	5.9	3.1
LT Debt	129	92.0	107	8.3	5.8	0.9
Common Eqty.	99	105	97.4	41.5	20.5	22.6
Total Cap.	304	273	205	50.7	26.7	23.5
Cap. Exp.	48.0	110	190	21.9	10.8	7.3
Cash Flow	28.9	36.0	15.6	9.2	6.3	8.8

Ratio Analysis

	1994	1993	1992	1991	1990	1989
Curr. Ratio	0.6	0.4	0.6	2.0	0.6	0.9
% LT Debt of Cap.	42.5	33.8	52.3	16.3	21.8	3.9
% Ret. on Assets	0.2	4.8	3.1	3.5	NM	4.4
% Ret. on Equity	NM	10.4	6.5	5.3	NM	5.4

Dividend Data —No dividends have been paid on the common stock. The company does not plan to do so for the foreseeable future.

Data as orig. reptd.; bef. results of disc opers. and/or spec. items. Per share data adj. for stk. divs. as of ex-div. date. E-Estimated. NA-Not Available. NM-Not Meaningful. NR-Not Ranked.

Office—4100 E. Mississippi Ave., Suite 1200, Denver, CO 80222. **Tel**—(303) 757-1110. **Chrmn, Pres & CEO**—R. W. Gerrity. **Sr VP & COO**—B. J. Cree. **VP-Cont**—J. A. Tuell. **Investor Contact**—K. Wonstolen. **Dirs**—B. J. Cree, K. Crouch, R. W. Gerrity, T. J. Kane, K. R. Van Horn, D. Waggaman. **Transfer Agent & Registrar**—Chemical Bank, New York. **Incorporated** in Delaware in 1990. **Empl**-219. **S&P Analyst:** Michael C. Barr

Glamis Gold

NYSE Symbol GLG Options on CBOE In S&P SmallCap 600

Price	Range	P–E Ratio	Dividend	Yield	S&P Ranking	Beta
Aug. 8'95	1995					
7⅜	9⅜–7¼	41	[2]0.06	[1]0.6%	B–	–0.37

Summary

This Canadian mining company operates three gold mines in California and is pursuing new mining opportunities. After rising sharply in fiscal 1994, earnings declined in the first nine months of fiscal 1995, despite increased gold production.

Business Summary

Glamis Gold Ltd. is engaged in the mining and extraction of precious metals by the heap leach method and in the exploration for and development of precious metals properties. Its operations are mainly in the U.S. and are conducted through its Glamis Gold Inc. subsidiary, which has three wholly owned subsidiaries: Chemgold, Rand Mining Co. and Glamis Gold Exploration.

GLG's three principal mines currently are the Picacho, Yellow Aster and Baltic (which began production in early fiscal 1994) mines, which process ore using the heap leach method. Mining at Alto was discontinued in 1992. Gold production (in ounces) at the various mines in recent fiscal years:

	1994	1993
Picacho	23,333	27,578
Yellow Aster	41,297	49,888
Baltic	39,837	---
Alto	---	416
Total	104,467	77,882

The Picacho Mine, located in Imperial County, Calif., was leased in 1979 for 20 years with a renewal right for an additional 20 years. The lease provides for a royalty payment of 10% of net smelter returns. At fiscal 1994 year-end, ore reserves totaled 4.7 million tons of proven/probable ore grading 0.034 ounces per ton.

The lease on the Yellow Aster Mine, located in Kern County, Calif., continues for as long as a royalty of 6% of net returns is paid. At fiscal 1994 year-end, mineable proven/probable reserves at Yellow Aster were 32.6 million tons, with a grading of 0.024 ounces of gold per ton.

The Baltic Mine is located about one mile northeast of the Yellow Aster Mine. Production began early in fiscal 1994, and the mine is expected to produce 40,000 ounces of gold per year. At the end of fiscal 1994, total reserves amounted to 21.7 million tons, with a grading of 0.022 ounces of gold per ton.

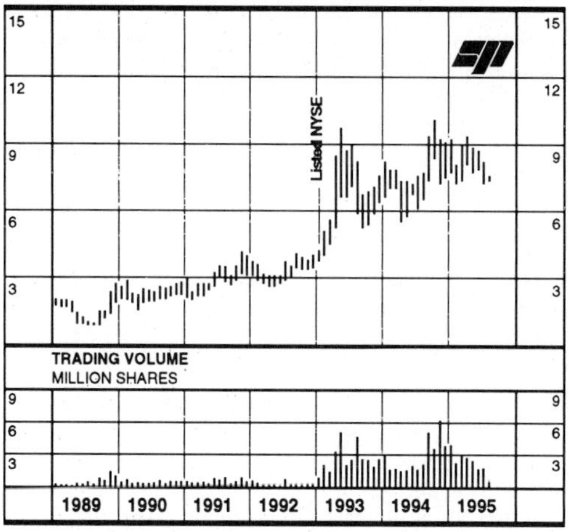

The company holds a 100% interest in a property located in Imperial County, Calif. (the Imperial Project), which is currently being explored, and has entered into a letter agreement pursuant to which it may earn a 60% interest in the Cieneguita property located in the State of Chihuahua, Mexico.

The average price received per ounce of gold in fiscal 1994 was U.S.$375, up from U.S.$338 in fiscal 1993. Cash cost of production was U.S.$192 in fiscal 1994, up from U.S.$186 the year before.

Important Developments

Jun. '95— Glamis Gold announced its intention to make an offer to acquire Eldorado Corporation Ltd., a Bermuda corporation that produces gold from a mine in Mexico, for a combination of cash and Glamis common stock with a total value of approximately $134 million. Calling the proposed bid "inadequate," Eldorado's board recommended that its securityholders reject the offer.

Per Share Data (U.S. $)

Yr. End Jun. 30	1994	1993	1992	1991	1990	1989	1988
Tangible Bk. Val.	**2.41**	2.30	1.55	1.55	1.32	1.04	1.28
Cash Flow	**0.61**	0.39	0.46	0.58	0.42	0.11	0.18
Earnings	**0.24**	0.04	0.09	0.24	0.26	d0.27	0.05
Dividends	**0.060**	0.047	0.052	0.034	Nil	Nil	Nil
Payout Ratio[3]	**25%**	118%	58%	14%	Nil	Nil	Nil
Prices[4]—High	**10⅛**	9¾	4⅛	4⅛	2⅞	2¾	4¾
Low	**5½**	3¾	2⅝	2	1⅝	⅞	1¾
P/E Ratio—	**42–23**	NM	46–29	17–8	11–6	NM	95–35

Data as orig. reptd. Based on Canadian GAAP. Book values conv. to U.S.$ at fiscal yr.-end exchange rates (see Balance Sheet Data); earnings conv. to U.S.$ at fiscal yr.'s avg. exchange rates (see Income Data). According to U.S. GAAP, approx. earnings were: 1994—0.21, 1993—0.03, 1992—0.09, 1991—0.24, 1990—0.26, 1989—d0.31, 1988—0.06. **1.** Based on current rate of exchange. **2.** In Canadian funds, bef. 15% Canadian tax to U.S. residents. **3.** Ratio varies from com. sh. payout due to taxes & exchange rates. **4.** Cal. yr. d-Deficit. NM-Not Meaningful.

Income Data (Million Can. $)

Year Ended Jun. 30	[1]($) Per Can. $	Revs.	Oper. Inc.	% Oper. Inc. of Revs.	Cap. Exp.	Depr.	Int. Exp.	Net Bef. Taxes	Eff. Tax Rate	Net Inc.	% Net Inc. of Revs.	Cash Flow
1994	**0.748**	**52.4**	**18.4**	**35.1**	**17.7**	**12.28**	**Nil**	**9.56**	**17.2%**	**7.91**	**15.1**	**20.2**
1993	0.782	32.8	9.3	28.4	[2]16.8	7.83	Nil	1.83	52.7%	0.86	2.6	8.7
1992	0.863	32.8	10.3	31.5	[2]10.5	7.41	1.1	2.02	18.3%	1.65	5.0	9.1
1991	0.869	29.0	12.5	43.1	[2]18.8	6.50	1.1	5.74	18.7%	4.67	16.1	11.2
1990	0.854	19.4	9.0	46.4	[2]10.2	3.00	0.7	6.58	24.2%	4.99	25.8	8.0
1989	0.835	14.1	d0.2	NM	[2]11.2	7.35	0.7	d7.38	NM	d5.21	NM	2.1
1988	0.783	13.6	4.3	31.2	[2]7.6	2.96	NM	1.45	28.6%	1.04	7.6	4.0

Balance Sheet Data (Million Can. $)

Jun. 30	[1]($) Per Can. $	Cash	Curr. Assets	Curr. Liab.	Curr. Ratio	Total Assets	% Ret. on Assets	Long Term Debt	Common Equity	Total Cap.	% LT Debt of Cap.	% Ret. on Equity
1994	**0.723**	**17.71**	**31.7**	**3.64**	**8.7**	**92.1**	**9.1**	**Nil**	**86.7**	**87.2**	**Nil**	**10.3**
1993	0.801	22.44	29.8	3.91	7.6	81.8	1.3	9.7	66.4	77.0	12.6	1.8
1992	0.835	6.14	15.8	2.54	6.2	55.5	3.4	19.0	32.2	52.1	36.5	5.3
1991	0.875	0.07	5.1	3.01	1.7	41.8	12.2	8.4	29.8	38.2	21.9	16.9
1990	0.858	5.61	10.1	8.00	1.3	34.5	14.7	0.6	25.3	26.1	2.2	22.0
1989	0.837	2.94	9.2	6.99	1.3	33.5	NM	NM	20.1	20.3	NM	NM
1988	0.824	3.97	8.4	2.88	2.9	30.1	3.5	Nil	25.4	27.0	Nil	4.2

Data as orig. reptd. Based on Canadian GAAP. **1.** Fiscal yr's. avg. exchange rates for Income Data, fiscal yr.-end exchange rates for Balance Sheet. **2.** Net. d-Deficit. NM-Not Meaningful.

[1]Revenues (Million $)

Quarter:	1994–95	1993–94	1992–93	1991–92
Sep.	10.85	7.98	8.93	7.85
Dec.	8.99	13.75	8.58	7.42
Mar.	9.97	13.94	7.53	7.84
Jun.		16.77	7.81	7.82
		52.44	32.85	32.80

Revenues (in U.S. dollars) for the nine months ended March 31, 1995, advanced 11%, year to year, primarily reflecting increased gold production due to the Baltic Mine being placed into production in August 1993. Most major categories of expense rose more rapidly, interest costs increased and net other income declined. Pretax income fell 67%. After taxes at 15.5%, versus 36.6%, net income was $1,159,000 ($0.04 a share, on 5.3% more shares), down 56% from $2,627,000 ($0.11).

Effective July 1, 1994, the company adopted the U.S. dollar as its reporting currency.

[1]Common Share Earnings ($)

Quarter:	1994–95	1993–94	1992–93	1991–92
Sep.	0.04	0.05	0.07	0.04
Dec.	Nil	0.08	0.05	0.03
Mar.	Nil	0.12	0.01	d0.02
Jun.		0.07	d0.08	0.05
		0.32	0.05	0.10

Finances

In May 1995, the company said it received an independent report indicating proven and probable reserves for the Imperial Project of 1.5 million ounces of gold, which would increase the company's total reserves to about 2.9 million ounces. The Imperial Project is expected to produce 84,000 ounces of gold per year over a life of 13 years. A final feasibility report on the project is expected in April 1996. Total capital expenditures are estimated to be $39.4 million by the year ending June 30, 1998, when the project is expected to reach full production status.

The company expected to invest in fiscal 1995 approximately U.S.$11.4 million in its United States operations for fixed-asset additions and U.S.$6.4 million for mine development costs. Total cash requirements for capital outlays during fiscal 1995 were estimated at U.S.$18.5 million. Management expected that cash on hand, operating cash flow and a bank line of credit would provide sufficient funds.

In fiscal 1994, the company called for redemption the remaining C$4,804,000 of its 8% convertible debentures due 1996. A total of 2,615,100 common shares were converted at C$3.35 each.

Dividend Data

Dividends are paid annually. The company paid $0.06 (in Canadian funds, before 15% Canadian tax to U.S. residents) in the fiscal years 1994, 1993 and 1992.

Capitalization

Long Term Liabilities: $1,890,000 (3/95).

Common Stock: 26,047,707 shs. (no par). Shareholders of record: 1,935.

1. In Canadian $ prior to 1994-95. d-Deficit.

Office—3324 Four Bentall Centre, 1055 Dunsmuir St., Vancouver, BC, Canada V7X 1L3. **Tel**—(604) 681-3541. **Fax**—(604) 681-9306. **Chrmn**—C. F. Millar. **Pres & CEO**—A. D. Rovig. **CFO & Treas**—L. B. Anderson. **Secy**—G. B. Finlayson. **VP & Investor Contact**—James R. Billingsley. **Dirs**—J. Barbeau, J. R. Billingsley, I. S. Davidson, C. F. Millar, F. S. O'Kelly, A. D. Rovig. **Transfer Agents & Registrars**—Montreal Trust, Vancouver; United Missouri Trust Co., NYC. **Incorporated** in British Columbia in 1972. **Empl**—222.

STANDARD & POOR'S

STOCK REPORTS

GoodMark Foods

NASDAQ Symbol **GDMK**

In S&P SmallCap 600

02-OCT-95 **Industry:** Food

Summary: This company, the leading U.S. producer and marketer of meat snack products, also makes nonmeat snack items and distributes meat products on a regional basis.

Quantitative Evaluations

Outlook (1 Lowest—5 Highest)
• **3+**

Fair Value
• **16¾**

Risk
• **Average**

Earn./Div. Rank
• **B**

Technical Eval.
• **Bearish** since 8/95

Rel. Strength Rank (1 Lowest—99 Highest)
• **85**

Insider Activity
• **Neutral**

Recent Price • 18½
52 Wk Range • 18½-13¼
Yield • 0.9%
12-Mo. P/E • 15.8

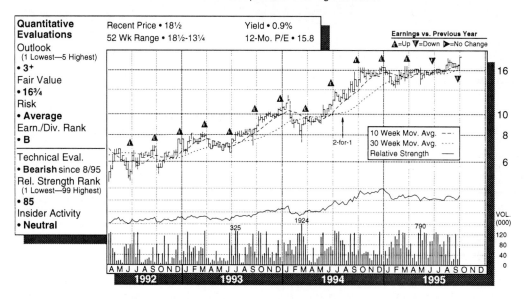

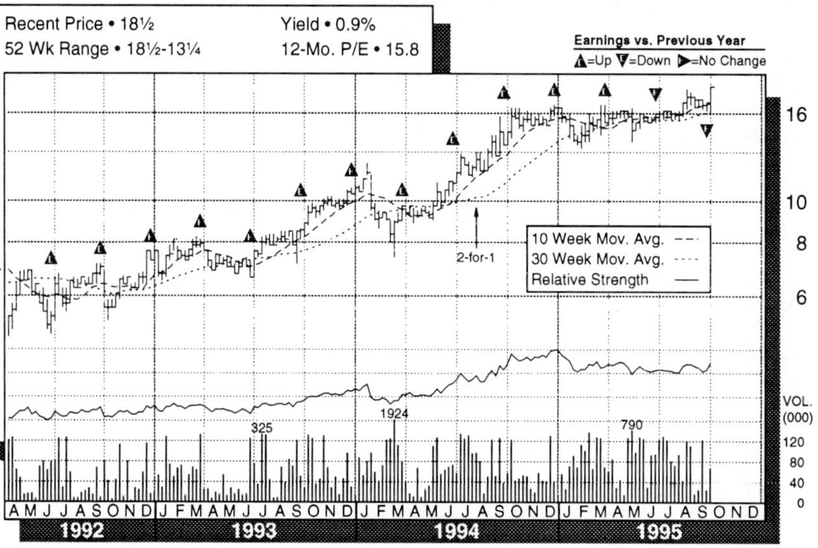

Business Profile - 02-OCT-95

The 1995-96 first quarter was the second consecutive quarter in which earnings declined from a year earlier; earnings had previously been in a strong uptrend. Increased marketing expense is expected to negatively affect second quarter results as well; however, a particularly strong second half of the fiscal year should result in another record year for sales and earnings. Cash dividends, initiated in mid-1993, were boosted 33% with the August 1995 payment.

Operational Review - 18-SEP-95

Net sales in the 13 weeks ended August 27, 1995, rose modestly, year to year, led by gains in snack sales and a successful new product launch. Margins narrowed on stiff price competition in the packaged meat category and increased marketing expense. After taxes at 36.2%, versus 37.6%, net income declined. Management expects near-term results to benefit from continued low meat prices, good volume growth and improving efficiencies.

Stock Performance - 29-SEP-95

In the past 30 trading days, GDMK's shares have increased 6%, compared to a 5% rise in the S&P 500. Average trading volume for the past five days was 13,120 shares, compared with the 40-day moving average of 13,705 shares.

Key Stock Statistics

Dividend Rate/Share	0.16	Shareholders	2,000
Shs. outstg. (M)	7.7	Market cap. (B)	$0.143
Avg. daily vol. (M)	0.013	Inst. holdings	46%
Tang. Bk. Value/Share	5.97	Insider holdings	NA
Beta	0.87		

Value of $10,000 invested 5 years ago: $ 23,201

Fiscal Year Ending May 31

	1996	% Change	1995	% Change	1994	% Change
Revenues (Million $)						
1Q	46.27	7%	43.41	11%	39.27	17%
2Q	—	—	44.49	8%	41.15	16%
3Q	—	—	41.15	17%	35.07	9%
4Q	—	—	48.38	9%	44.20	11%
Yr.	—	—	177.4	11%	159.7	13%
Income (Million $)						
1Q	2.72	-5%	2.85	71%	1.67	—
2Q	—	—	3.08	69%	1.82	9%
3Q	—	—	1.95	59%	1.23	12%
4Q	—	—	1.72	-28%	2.39	119%
Yr.	—	—	9.60	35%	7.11	46%
Earnings Per Share ($)						
1Q	0.34	-8%	0.37	95%	0.19	65%
2Q	—	—	0.38	73%	0.22	13%
3Q	—	—	0.24	50%	0.16	28%
4Q	—	—	0.21	-32%	0.31	148%
Yr.	—	—	1.20	36%	0.88	57%

Next earnings report expected: mid December

GoodMark Foods

Business Summary - 02-OCT-95

GoodMark Foods, Inc. is the leading producer of meat snacks in the U.S., and also manufactures and distributes nonmeat snack foods and is a regional supplier of packaged meat products.

GoodMark's principal meat snack products are meat sticks, beef jerky and pickled meats sold under the Slim Jim, Pemmican, Penrose and Smokey Mountain brand names. The widely recognized line of Slim Jim meat sticks consists of 30 varieties of ready-to-eat dry sausage made of meat, spices and seasonings. Flavors include spicy, Tabasco, Summer Sausage, Beef 'n Cheese, Mild flavors, Beef Steak and Pepperoni. Beef jerky includes both Pemmican natural style jerky, made from thinly sliced beef that has been seasoned and dried, as well as Slim Jim jerky, made from beef that has been chopped, seasoned, formed, thinly sliced and dried, and Smokey Mountain premium quality chopped and formed jerky. Penrose beef and pork products are sausages that are seasoned, cooked, pickled, and packed in a variety of sizes. These brands account for more than a 40% share of the meat snack market.

Andy Capp's extruded products are french fry shaped snacks that are baked rather than fried from a grain and vegetable base. Flavors include hot, pub, cheddar and ranch.

Rachel's Brownies are double-chocolate, peanut butter chocolate and butterscotch brownies offered in several size packages for sale to supermarkets, convenience stores and leading airlines. The line also includes a variety of cookies and fruit bars.

Packaged meats, such as sausage, frankfurters, bologna and luncheon meats, are sold regionally under the Jesse Jones brand name; the primary markets are North and South Carolina and Virginia.

The company also makes meat snacks, extruded snacks and hot dogs for sale by others under private label and co-packing agreements.

Over the past several years, strong demand in duty-free stores has led to expanded distribution in Japan, Taiwan, Singapore, Hong Kong, the Caribbean and Canada.

Important Developments

Sep. '95—Management reiterated its expectation that higher marketing costs will reduce earnings in 1995-96's second quarter to below those of the year-earlier level. However, strong sales and earnings gains in the remaining two quarters are expected to result in another year of record results.
Jun. '95—Directors authorized the repurchase of an additional 250,000 company shares.

Capitalization

Long Term Debt: $21,650,000 (8/95).
Options: To buy 994,870 shs. at $2.75 to $9.25 ea.

Per Share Data ($)

(Year Ended May 31)

	1995	1994	1993	1992	1991	1990
Tangible Bk. Val.	5.97	4.54	4.14	3.89	3.51	3.34
Cash Flow	1.79	1.36	0.90	0.74	0.59	0.73
Earnings	1.20	0.88	0.56	0.38	0.17	0.42
Dividends	0.12	0.10	Nil	Nil	Nil	Nil
Payout Ratio	10%	11%	Nil	Nil	Nil	Nil
Cal. Yrs.	1994	1993	1992	1991	1990	1989
Prices - High	16¾	10¾	7⅞	7¼	8⅜	10
- Low	7⅜	6½	4¾	3½	4	6⅛
P/E Ratio - High	14	12	14	19	51	24
- Low	6	7	9	9	24	15

Income Statement Analysis (Million $)

	1995	%Chg	1994	%Chg	1993	%Chg	1992
Revs.	177	11%	160	13%	141	-2%	144
Oper. Inc.	20.1	30%	15.5	36%	11.4	9%	10.5
Depr.	4.7	24%	3.8	31%	2.9	-9%	3.2
Int. Exp.	0.1	-13%	0.2	-64%	0.4	-68%	1.3
Pretax Inc.	15.4	35%	11.4	43%	8.0	53%	5.2
Eff. Tax Rate	38%	—	38%	—	39%	—	38%
Net Inc.	9.6	35%	7.1	47%	4.9	51%	3.2

Balance Sheet & Other Fin. Data (Million $)

	1995	1994	1993	1992	1991	1990
Cash	0.4	0.5	3.3	6.3	5.4	5.2
Curr. Assets	31.3	25.3	25.3	31.0	30.3	27.3
Total Assets	86.8	59.6	57.7	63.3	68.0	57.4
Curr. Liab.	16.7	13.4	11.4	13.3	15.3	13.0
LT Debt	20.2	5.5	4.5	13.7	19.9	13.6
Common Eqty.	46.2	37.4	38.6	33.5	30.2	28.8
Total Cap.	70.1	46.1	46.3	49.9	52.7	44.4
Cap. Exp.	26.3	6.2	4.0	3.3	6.1	5.9
Cash Flow	14.3	10.9	7.8	6.4	5.1	6.4

Ratio Analysis

	1995	1994	1993	1992	1991	1990
Curr. Ratio	1.9	1.9	2.2	2.3	2.0	2.1
% LT Debt of Cap.	28.8	11.9	9.8	27.5	37.7	30.7
% Net Inc.of Revs.	5.4	4.5	3.4	2.2	1.0	2.6
% Ret. on Assets	13.2	12.8	8.0	4.9	2.3	6.7
% Ret. on Equity	23.0	19.8	13.4	10.1	4.8	13.3

Dividend Data —Cash dividends were initiated in mid-1993.

Amt. of Div. $	Date Decl.	Ex-Div. Date	Stock of Record	Payment Date
0.030	Sep. 23	Oct. 07	Oct. 14	Nov. 01 '94
0.030	Dec. 19	Jan. 09	Jan. 13	Feb. 01 '95
0.030	Mar. 21	Apr. 07	Apr. 14	May. 01 '95
0.040	Jun. 23	Jul. 12	Jul. 14	Aug. 01 '95
0.040	Sep. 29	Oct. 11	Oct. 13	Nov. 01 '95

Data as orig. reptd.; bef. results of disc. opers. and/or spec. items. Per share data adj. for stk. divs. as of ex-div. date. E-Estimated. NA-Not Available. NM-Not Meaningful. NR-Not Ranked.

Office—6131 Falls of Neuse Rd., Raleigh, NC 27609. **Tel**—(919) 790-9940. **Chrmn & CEO**—R. E. Doggett. **Pres & COO**—R. C. Miller. **VP, CFO, Treas & Investor Contact**—P. L. Brunswick. **VP & Secy**—A. C. Blalock. **Dirs**—H. H. Bradley, T. W. D'Alonzo, R. E. Doggett, D. H. Grubb, R. C. Miller, R. B. Seidensticker, R. Tillman, Jr. **Transfer Agent & Registrar**—First Union National Bank, Charlotte. **Incorporated** in North Carolina in 1982. **Empl**-947. **S&P Analyst:** Efraim Levy

STANDARD & POOR'S

STOCK REPORTS

Gottschalks Inc.

NYSE Symbol **GOT**
In S&P SmallCap 600

16-OCT-95 **Industry:** Retail Stores

Summary: This regional department store chain operates 32 department stores and 25 specialty stores in smaller cities in California, Washington, Oregon and Nevada.

Quantitative Evaluations

Outlook (1 Lowest—5 Highest) • 3

Fair Value • 6⅞

Risk • **Average**

Earn./Div. Rank • **B-**

Technical Eval. • **Bearish** since 8/95

Rel. Strength Rank (1 Lowest—99 Highest) • 31

Insider Activity • **NA**

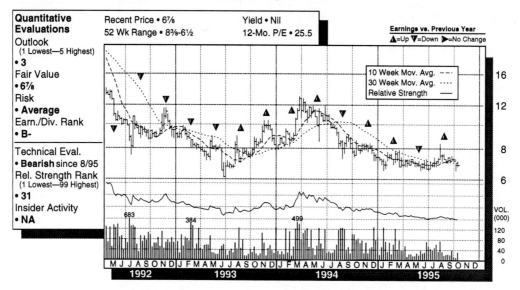

Recent Price • 6⅞ Yield • Nil
52 Wk Range • 8⅜-6½ 12-Mo. P/E • 25.5

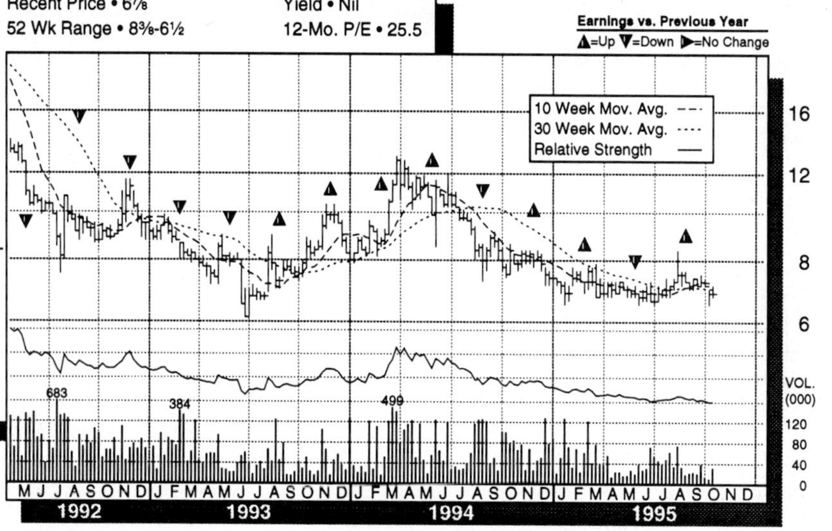

Business Profile - 13-OCT-95

This regional department store chain derives most of its revenues from Gottschalks department stores, which are located mainly in smaller California cities. A weak retail environment, increased competition and poor weather have hurt recent same-store sales. GOT has fought back by aggressively soliciting credit sales, and by spreading overhead costs over a larger sales base by adding new stores. It has also re-formulated its merchandising strategy, increased promotions, and refinanced its debt.

Operational Review - 16-OCT-95

Sales gains in the 1995-96 first half reflected five new store openings. Same-store sales slid 2.1% year to year, restricted by unusually cold and rainy weather and price competition from two financially troubled local retailers. Gross margins narrowed on store pre-opening costs and discounting necessitated by the lower volume, heightened competition, and merchandise changes. Excluding an unusual charge in the prior year period related to a legal settlement, the net loss widened.

Stock Performance - 13-OCT-95

In the past 30 trading days, GOT's shares have declined 4%, compared to a 4% rise in the S&P 500. Average trading volume for the past five days was 6,060 shares, compared with the 40-day moving average of 4,254 shares.

Key Stock Statistics

Dividend Rate/Share	Nil	Shareholders	1,200
Shs. outstg. (M)	10.4	Market cap. (B)	$0.072
Avg. daily vol. (M)	0.004	Inst. holdings	19%
Tang. Bk. Value/Share	7.53	Insider holdings	NA
Beta	-0.06		

Value of $10,000 invested 5 years ago: $ 7,857

Fiscal Year Ending Jan. 31

	1996	% Change	1995	% Change	1994	% Change
Revenues (Million $)						
1Q	80.98	12%	72.50	10%	65.83	-2%
2Q	94.61	17%	80.52	6%	76.22	2%
3Q	—	—	78.84	4%	75.75	5%
4Q	—	—	134.0	8%	124.6	6%
Yr.	—	—	363.6	6%	342.4	3%
Income (Million $)						
1Q	-3.16	NM	-2.34	NM	-3.61	NM
2Q	-1.96	NM	-3.98	NM	-2.43	NM
3Q	—	—	-0.57	NM	-1.77	NM
4Q	—	—	8.41	64%	5.13	NM
Yr.	—	—	1.52	NM	-2.67	NM
Earnings Per Share ($)						
1Q	-0.30	NM	-0.22	NM	-0.35	NM
2Q	-0.19	NM	-0.38	NM	-0.23	NM
3Q	—	—	-0.05	NM	-0.17	NM
4Q	—	—	0.81	65%	0.49	NM
Yr.	—	—	0.15	NM	-0.26	NM

Next earnings report expected: mid November

Gottschalks Inc.

Business Summary - 16-OCT-95

Gottschalks operates 32 Gottschalks department stores (including three junior satellite stores) and 25 Village East specialty stores. The stores are located primarily in smaller cities in California, with a small number of stores in Tacoma, Wash., and Klamath Falls, Ore. The vast majority of sales are derived from the Gottschalks department stores.

The number of Gottschalks department stores in operation at the end of recent fiscal years was:

1995	32
1994	27
1993	25
1992	24
1991	22
1990	20

Gottschalks department stores typically offer brand-name fashion apparel, shoes and accessories for men, women and children, cosmetics, jewelry, china, housewares, home appliances and furnishings, electronics and other goods. Village East specialty stores offer apparel for larger women. The company's stores carry primarily moderately priced merchandise, complemented with a mix of higher and budget priced merchandise. The vast majority of the stores are located in regional shopping malls, and nearly all stores are leased.

The company leases the fine jewelry, shoe, maternity wear and custom drapery departments and the restaurants and beauty salons in its department stores. Independent operators supply their own merchandise, sales personnel and advertising, and pay Gottschalks a percentage of gross sales as rent.

In 1994, two Gotttschalks stores were opened, in Oakhurst and Sacramento, Calif., and a Village East store opened in Sacramento. In the first half of fiscal 1995-96, five new Gottschalks stores were opened, in Auburn, San Bernardino, Visalia, and Watsonville, Calif., and Carson City, Nev. In October 1995, Gottschalks expects to open a new 113,000 sq. ft. department store in Tracy, Calif.

Important Developments

Oct. '95—Sales in the five weeks ended September 30, 1995, totaled $33.1 million, up 9.5% year to year. Same-store sales declined 8.0%. Year to date figures are up 12% and down 3.2%, respectively.

Aug. '95—The company said it increased its revolving credit facility with Shawmut Capital and Wells Fargo Bank to $66 million from $50 million to support expanding inventory needs.

Capitalization

Long Term Debt: $44,741,000 (7/95), incl. $9.6 million of capitalized lease obligs.

Per Share Data ($) (Year Ended Jan. 31)

	1995	1994	1993	1992	1991	1990
Tangible Bk. Val.	7.90	7.73	7.98	9.02	7.01	6.29
Cash Flow	0.71	0.33	-0.19	0.94	1.34	0.88
Earnings	0.15	-0.26	-0.77	0.44	0.80	0.46
Dividends	Nil	Nil	Nil	Nil	Nil	Nil
Payout Ratio	Nil	Nil	Nil	Nil	Nil	Nil
Cal. Yrs.	1994	1993	1992	1991	1990	1989
Prices - High	13	10⅜	22½	26⅜	15	13⅜
- Low	7	6⅛	7½	11⅝	8⅝	8
P/E Ratio - High	87	NM	NM	60	19	29
- Low	47	NM	NM	26	11	17

Income Statement Analysis (Million $)

	1995	%Chg	1994	%Chg	1993	%Chg	1992
Revs.	373	6%	351	3%	340	5%	324
Oper. Inc.	21.5	62%	13.3	68%	7.9	-53%	16.9
Depr.	5.9	-3%	6.1	NM	6.0	24%	4.9
Int. Exp.	10.3	20%	8.6	22%	7.0	NM	7.0
Pretax Inc.	2.3	NM	-3.9	NM	-12.0	NM	7.0
Eff. Tax Rate	35%	—	NM	—	NM	—	39%
Net Inc.	1.5	NM	-2.7	NM	-8.0	NM	4.3

Balance Sheet & Other Fin. Data (Million $)

	1995	1994	1993	1992	1991	1990
Cash	5.5	1.2	1.1	3.3	1.4	2.8
Curr. Assets	127	140	131	131	121	99
Total Assets	253	248	240	234	208	166
Curr. Liab.	89.0	108	114	62.6	84.9	60.8
LT Debt	33.7	31.5	15.0	50.3	41.6	44.8
Common Eqty.	83.6	82.1	84.5	95.7	58.7	51.8
Total Cap.	123	120	106	152	106	99
Cap. Exp.	4.5	6.5	12.1	15.0	25.8	38.0
Cash Flow	7.4	3.4	-2.0	9.2	10.8	7.1

Ratio Analysis

	1995	1994	1993	1992	1991	1990
Curr. Ratio	1.4	1.3	1.1	2.1	1.4	1.6
% LT Debt of Cap.	27.3	26.3	14.2	33.2	39.3	45.3
% Net Inc.of Revs.	0.4	NM	NM	1.3	2.2	1.5
% Ret. on Assets	0.6	NM	NM	1.7	3.4	2.4
% Ret. on Equity	1.8	NM	NM	5.0	11.6	7.3

Dividend Data —No cash dividends have been paid. A two-for-one stock split was effected in April 1987.

Data as orig. reptd.; bef. results of disc. opers. and/or spec. items. Per share data adj. for stk. divs. as of ex-div. date. E-Estimated. NA-Not Available. NM-Not Meaningful. NR-Not Ranked.

Office—7 River Park Place East, Fresno, CA 93720. **Tel**—(209) 434-8000. **Chrmn & CEO**—J. W. Levy. **Vice Chrmn**—G. H. Blum. **Pres & COO**—S. J. Furst. **SVP & CFO**—A. A. Weinstein. **Dirs**—G. H. Blum, S. J. Furst, M. Gutmann, B. W. Levy, J. W. Levy, S. Levy, J. J. Penbera, F. R. Ruiz, O. J. Woodward III. **Registrar & Transfer Agent**—Chemical Mellon Shareholder Services, SF. **Incorporated** in California in 1912; reincorporated in Delaware in 1986. **Empl**-5,377. **S&P Analyst:** J. Santoriello

STANDARD & POOR'S

STOCK REPORTS

GranCare, Inc.

NYSE Symbol **GC**
In S&P SmallCap 600

03-NOV-95

Industry:
Health Care Centers

Summary: This company operates long-term health care facilities and provides pharmacy services.

Quantitative Evaluations

Recent Price • 13 | Yield • Nil
52 Wk Range • 19⅛-12¾ | 12-Mo. P/E • 14.8

Outlook
(1 Lowest—5 Highest)
• NA

Fair Value
• NA

Risk
• Average

Earn./Div. Rank
• NR

Technical Eval.
• Bullish since 10/95

Rel. Strength Rank
(1 Lowest—99 Highest)
• 24

Insider Activity
• Neutral

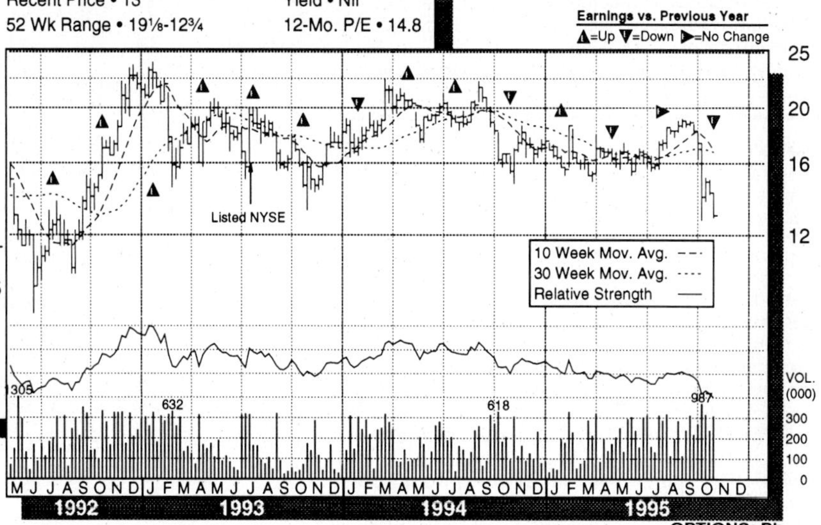

OPTIONS: Ph

Business Profile - 03-NOV-95

GranCare has expanded rapidly through acquisitions of pharmacies and long-term care facilities, which it integrates into existing operations to realize cost savings and synergies. GranCare's marketing strategy is to develop strategic relationships with large acute care hospitals. By providing a broad range of health care services in various settings, including subacute facilities and patients' homes, GranCare avoids duplication and provides a smooth transition between each phase of care.

Operational Review - 03-NOV-95

Revenues in the nine months ended September 30, 1995 advanced 14%, year to year, reflecting the acquisition of long term health care facilities and specialty medical businesses. Results in the third quarter include one-time charges of $11.8 million related to the acquisition of Evergreen Healthcare, as compared with a restructuring charge of $8.2 million in the third quarter of 1994. Net income declined 20%, and EPS decreased to $0.55 from $0.75.

Stock Performance - 27-OCT-95

In the past 30 trading days, GC's shares have declined 31%, compared to a 0.63% fall in the S&P 500. Average trading volume for the past five days was 75,480 shares, compared with the 40-day moving average of 81,544 shares.

Key Stock Statistics

Dividend Rate/Share	Nil	Shareholders	300
Shs. outstg. (M)	23.8	Market cap. (B)	$0.354
Avg. daily vol. (M)	0.086	Inst. holdings	32%
Tang. Bk. Value/Share	0.44	Insider holdings	NA
Beta	NA		

Value of $10,000 invested 5 years ago: NA

Fiscal Year Ending Dec. 31

	1995	% Change	1994	% Change	1993	% Change
Revenues (Million $)						
1Q	144.1	10%	130.9	8%	121.3	96%
2Q	158.6	19%	133.6	6%	126.5	99%
3Q	208.5	46%	143.3	10%	130.6	73%
4Q	—	—	141.4	9%	129.5	29%
Yr.	—	—	549.2	8%	508.0	68%
Income (Million $)						
1Q	3.71	-19%	4.56	52%	3.00	66%
2Q	5.22	5%	4.96	56%	3.17	63%
3Q	-0.52	NM	1.27	-64%	3.49	22%
4Q	—	—	4.39	NM	-0.32	NM
Yr.	—	—	15.18	25%	12.17	23%
Earnings Per Share ($)						
1Q	0.26	-24%	0.34	3%	0.33	50%
2Q	0.36	NM	0.36	3%	0.35	52%
3Q	-0.02	NM	0.09	-75%	0.36	20%
4Q	—	—	0.30	NM	-0.03	NM
Yr.	—	—	1.08	8%	1.00	-7%

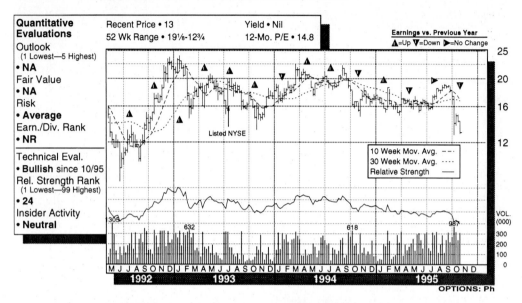

Next earnings report expected: early November

GranCare, Inc.

Business Summary - 01-NOV-95

GranCare, Inc. operates 79 long-term health care facilities with about 10,600 licensed beds in California, Michigan, Wisconsin, Arizona, Colorado and South Dakota. The company also provides pharmacy services through 23 institutional pharmacies to patients in certain of its own facilities, in facilities operated by others, and to patients receiving home health care. Net revenues in recent years were derived as follows:

	1994	1993
Skilled nursing services	50%	57%
Specialty medical		
Therapy, subacute & other	19%	20%
Pharmacy	31%	23%

Skilled nursing services consist of the operation of skilled nursing facilities, which focus on the care of medically dependent patients with multiple medical or behavioral problems requiring special care and treatment, and retirement living centers, which provide furnished rooms and suites designed for patients who are able to live independently within a sheltered community or who require minimal nursing attention.

Therapy services are provided to residents at the company's facilities, and include physical, occupational, speech, respiratory, ventilator and psychological therapies.

GranCare's institutional pharmacies provide long term health care facilities, acute care hospitals and other institutions with a variety of products and services, including prescription drugs, pharmacy consulting, computerized medical record administration, enteral, urological, total parenteral nutrition and intravenous therapies, and wound care management.

In 1992, the company established a home health care operation to provide skilled nursing services, therapy and home health aides. It also is developing a variety of laboratory services at several of its facilities, and operates specialized units to provide subacute and other care to medically complex patients.

Important Developments

Jul. '95—GranCare completed the acquisition of Evergreen Healthcare Inc. (EHI) in a transaction whereby each of the 12.6 million shares of EHI was converted into 0.775 shares of GranCare. In addition to cost savings and efficiencies in administrative and operations, the merger will allow GC's Compupharm operation to service Evergreen's 3,000 Indiana beds and 4,000 beds in other markets.

Apr. '95—GC acquired Cornerstone Health Management, a subsidiary of Healthtrust, for $49 million. Cornerstone, which had revenues of $37 million in fiscal 1994, implements and manages geriatric specialty programs.

Capitalization

Long Term Debt: $320,347,000 (9/95).

Per Share Data ($) (Year Ended Dec. 31)

	1994	1993	1992	1991	1990	1989
Tangible Bk. Val.	3.34	3.33	4.37	1.80	-1.79	NA
Cash Flow	1.95	1.72	1.55	1.08	NA	NA
Earnings	1.08	1.00	1.08	0.69	-0.49	NA
Dividends	Nil	Nil	Nil	Nil	Nil	NA
Payout Ratio	Nil	Nil	Nil	Nil	Nil	NA
Prices - High	22½	24	23¾	13½	NA	NA
- Low	14¾	13¼	8¾	9¾	NA	NA
P/E Ratio - High	21	24	22	20	NA	NA
- Low	14	13	8	14	NA	NA

Income Statement Analysis (Million $)

	1994	%Chg	1993	%Chg	1992	%Chg	1991
Revs.	536	6%	506	69%	300	73%	173
Oper. Inc.	51.9	4%	50.1	106%	24.3	111%	11.5
Depr.	12.2	41%	8.6	97%	4.4	78%	2.5
Int. Exp.	20.1	6%	18.9	NM	5.3	21%	4.3
Pretax Inc.	24.1	19%	20.3	25%	16.3	157%	6.3
Eff. Tax Rate	37%	—	40%	—	39%	—	40%
Net Inc.	15.2	25%	12.2	23%	9.9	160%	3.8

Balance Sheet & Other Fin. Data (Million $)

	1994	1993	1992	1991	1990	1989
Cash	25.7	21.6	4.0	12.6	2.9	NA
Curr. Assets	156	131	65.6	45.3	24.8	NA
Total Assets	409	336	201	80.5	65.9	NA
Curr. Liab.	71.5	68.4	51.4	33.4	21.0	NA
LT Debt	205	177	74.0	25.2	49.3	NA
Common Eqty.	107	70.8	51.1	12.6	-12.1	NA
Total Cap.	329	263	144	45.6	37.8	NA
Cap. Exp.	10.6	14.2	90.6	10.3	NA	NA
Cash Flow	27.4	20.8	14.3	5.9	-1.5	NA

Ratio Analysis

	1994	1993	1992	1991	1990	1989
Curr. Ratio	2.2	1.9	1.3	1.4	1.2	NA
% LT Debt of Cap.	62.4	67.2	51.5	55.4	130.3	NA
% Net Inc.of Revs.	2.8	2.4	3.3	2.2	NM	NA
% Ret. on Assets	3.9	4.1	6.4	3.3	NM	NA
% Ret. on Equity	16.4	17.8	28.8	NM	NM	NA

Dividend Data —No dividends have been paid. The company intends to retain earnings to provide funds for the operation and expansion of its business.

Data as orig. reptd.; bef. results of disc. opers. and/or spec. items. Per share data adj. for stk. divs. as of ex-div. date. E-Estimated. NA-Not Available. NM-Not Meaningful. NR-Not Ranked.

Office—1 Ravinia Dr., Atlanta, GA 30346. **Tel**—(404) 393-0199. **Chrmn & CEO**—G. E. Burleson. **EVP & CFO**—J. A. Schneider. **EVP & Secy**—E. W. Benton. **SVP & Investor Contact**—Kay Brown. **Dirs**—C. M. Blalack, G. E. Burleson, A. Hubenette, J. S. Kanter, W. G. Petty Jr., E. V. Regan, G. U. Rolle. **Transfer Agent**—American Stock Transfer and Trust Co., New York, NY. **Incorporated** in California in 1990. **Empl**-11,400. **S&P Analyst:** Philip J. Birbara

STANDARD & POOR'S

STOCK REPORTS

Grand Casinos

NYSE Symbol **GND**
In S&P SmallCap 600

06-SEP-95 **Industry:** Leisure/Amusement

Summary: This casino entertainment company develops, constructs and manages land-based and dockside casinos in emerging gaming markets.

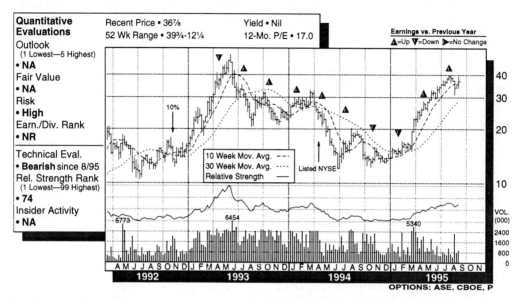

Quantitative Evaluations

Outlook
(1 Lowest—5 Highest)
• **NA**
Fair Value
• **NA**
Risk
• **High**
Earn./Div. Rank
• **NR**

Technical Eval.
• **Bearish** since 8/95
Rel. Strength Rank
(1 Lowest—99 Highest)
• **74**
Insider Activity
• **NA**

Recent Price • 36⅞
52 Wk Range • 39¾-12¼
Yield • Nil
12-Mo. P/E • 17.0

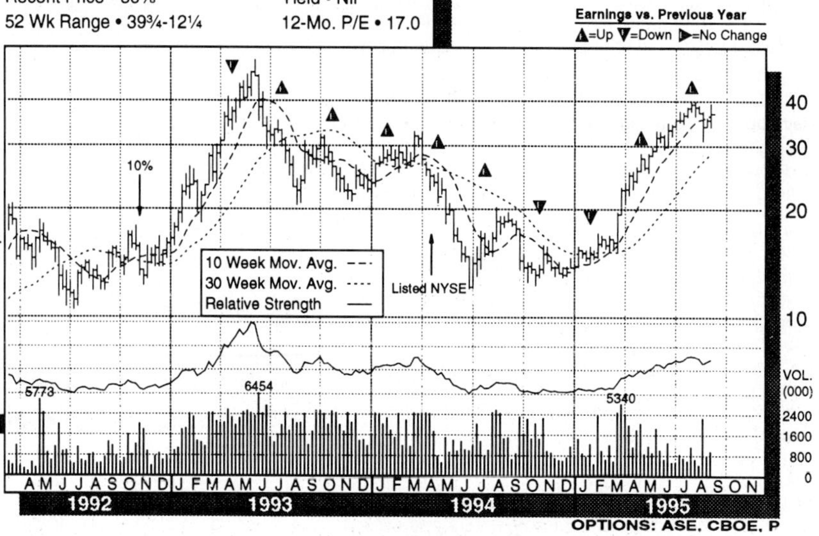

OPTIONS: ASE, CBOE, P

Business Profile - 05-SEP-95

This casino entertainment company develops, constructs and manages land-based and dockside casinos in emerging gaming markets. GND currently operates six casinos, including two floating casinos, which it owns, located on the Gulf Coast in Mississippi, and four land-based, Indian-owned casinos in Minnesota and Louisiana. The floating casinos have accounted for the bulk of revenues in recent periods. Several additional properties are under construction or in development.

Operational Review - 01-SEP-95

Net revenues for the six months ended July 2, 1995, climbed 23%, year to year, primarily reflecting the startup of the company's Grand Casino Coushatta in January 1995. Profitability benefited from efficiency measures initiated during 1994, and pretax income more than doubled. After taxes at 39.1% versus 34.1%, and minority interest, net income rose to $33,342,000 ($1.47 a share, based on 2.1% more shares), from $13,337,000 ($0.60).

Stock Performance - 01-SEP-95

In the past 30 trading days, GND's shares have declined 4%, compared to a 2% rise in the S&P 500. Average trading volume for the past five days was 187,660 shares, compared with the 40-day moving average of 184,925 shares.

Key Stock Statistics

Dividend Rate/Share	Nil	Shareholders	800
Shs. outstg. (M)	22.4	Market cap. (B)	$0.843
Avg. daily vol. (M)	0.217	Inst. holdings	43%
Tang. Bk. Value/Share	12.14	Insider holdings	NA
Beta	NA		

Value of $10,000 invested 5 years ago: NA

Fiscal Year Ending Dec. 31

	1995	% Change	1994	% Change	1993	% Change
Revenues (Million $)						
1Q	81.56	22%	66.80	NM	0.70	-53%
2Q	94.70	24%	76.18	NM	24.40	NM
3Q	—	—	76.39	55%	49.30	NM
4Q	—	—	66.42	56%	42.60	NM
Yr.	—	—	285.8	144%	117.0	NM
Income (Million $)						
1Q	15.08	168%	5.62	NM	-1.49	NM
2Q	18.27	137%	7.71	84%	4.19	NM
3Q	—	—	9.72	16%	8.39	NM
4Q	—	—	5.93	-23%	7.66	NM
Yr.	—	—	28.98	55%	18.75	NM
Earnings Per Share ($)						
1Q	0.68	172%	0.25	NM	-0.10	NM
2Q	0.79	126%	0.35	35%	0.26	NM
3Q	—	—	0.44	-8%	0.48	NM
4Q	—	—	0.27	-21%	0.34	NM
Yr.	—	—	1.30	23%	1.06	NM

Next earnings report expected: late October

Grand Casinos

Business Summary - 06-SEP-95

Grand Casinos is a casino entertainment company that develops, constructs and manages land-based and dockside casinos in emerging gaming markets on both Indian and company-owned sites. It seeks to distinguish itself within its markets by offering facilities with extensive non-gaming amenities, such as hotels, theaters, and recreational vehicle parks.

GND owns and operates Grand Casino Biloxi and Grand Casino Gulfport, the largest and second largest casinos on the Mississippi Gulf Coast. The company developed and currently manages Grand Casino Mille Lacs and Grand Casino Hinckley, two land-based, Indian-owned casinos in Minnesota, as well as Grand Casino Avoyelles in Marksville, La. (opened June 1994) and Grand Casino Coushatta in Kinder, La. (January 1995). In April 1995, construction began on a 200-room hotel adjacent to the Avoyelles casino, scheduled for completion in December 1995.

Grand Casino Gulfport is located in the Gulfport harbor. It is a three-story building set upon moored steel linked barges. It opened May 14, 1993. Grand Casino Biloxi, opened on January 17, 1994, is located 15 miles east of Gulfport, and is the largest dockside casino on the Mississippi Gulf Coast. GND is currently developing two hotels with 400 and 500 rooms, respectively, next to the Gulfport and Biloxi casinos.

Grand Casino Mille Lacs, the first casino developed and managed by the company, is located 90 miles northwest of Minneapolis, Minn.; it opened in 1991. Grand Casino Hinckley is located near Hinckley, Minn. A 150-room hotel was opened next to the Hinckley casino in May 1994.

The company owns a 61% interest in Stratosphere Corp., which is constructing the Stratosphere Tower, Casino & Hotel complex, which will be centered around a planned 1,149 ft. observation tower on the Las Vegas Strip. The new complex will be integrated with the adjoining Vegas World casino property, which GND purchsed in November 1994 for about $51 million.

GND owns about 39% of Grand Gaming Corp., which owns a potential gaming site and about 2,000 acres of adjoining property 18 miles south of Memphis, Tenn. Grand Gaming plans to develop a destination resort, featuring a dockside gaming casino with up to 150,000 sq. ft. of gaming space.

Important Developments

Aug. '95—The company agreed to acquire Grand Gaming Corp. and Gaming Corporation of America., in exchange for GND common stock. As part of the agreement, GND will own 100% of Grand Gaming Corp.'s Diamond Lakes Resort project in Tunica County, Miss.

Capitalization

Long Term Debt: $323,769,000 (7/2/95).
Minority Interest: $29,169,000

Per Share Data ($) (Year Ended Dec. 31)

	1994	1993	1992	1991	1990	1989
Tangible Bk. Val.	11.85	11.13	3.71	0.52	NA	NA
Cash Flow	2.08	1.31	0.29	0.21	NA	NA
Earnings	1.30	1.06	0.28	0.22	NA	NA
Dividends	Nil	Nil	Nil	Nil	NA	NA
Payout Ratio	Nil	Nil	Nil	Nil	NA	NA
Prices - High	32 7/8	52	22	8 3/4	NA	NA
- Low	12	15 3/4	7 1/8	4 1/2	NA	NA
P/E Ratio - High	25	49	78	40	NA	NA
- Low	9	15	25	20	NA	NA

Income Statement Analysis (Million $)

	1994	%Chg	1993	%Chg	1992	%Chg	1991
Revs.	286	144%	117	NM	7.0	NM	2.0
Oper. Inc.	69.3	106%	33.7	NM	3.9	95%	2.0
Depr.	17.5	NM	4.4	NM	0.1	—	Nil
Int. Exp.	14.1	33%	10.6	NM	0.1	—	Nil
Pretax Inc.	44.5	57%	28.3	NM	4.7	124%	2.1
Eff. Tax Rate	35%	—	34%	—	28%	—	Nil
Net Inc.	29.0	54%	18.8	NM	3.3	57%	2.1

Balance Sheet & Other Fin. Data (Million $)

	1994	1993	1992	1991	1990	1989
Cash	30.0	158	30.0	1.0	NA	NA
Curr. Assets	66.0	183	39.0	2.0	NA	NA
Total Assets	484	427	58.0	5.0	NA	NA
Curr. Liab.	56.3	47.3	3.2	0.5	NA	NA
LT Debt	123	119	Nil	Nil	NA	NA
Common Eqty.	277	248	54.0	4.0	NA	NA
Total Cap.	428	367	55.0	4.0	NA	NA
Cap. Exp.	89.0	210	10.0	Nil	NA	NA
Cash Flow	46.5	23.2	3.5	2.1	NA	NA

Ratio Analysis

	1994	1993	1992	1991	1990	1989
Curr. Ratio	1.2	3.9	12.2	4.4	NA	NA
% LT Debt of Cap.	28.8	32.3	0.5	Nil	NA	NA
% Net Inc.of Revs.	10.1	16.0	47.1	85.8	NA	NA
% Ret. on Assets	6.4	7.3	10.0	NA	NA	NA
% Ret. on Equity	11.0	11.3	10.8	NA	NA	NA

Dividend Data —No cash dividends have been paid. A 10% stock dividend was paid in November 1992.

Data as orig. reptd.; bef. results of disc. opers. and/or spec. items. Per share data adj. for stk. divs. as of ex-div. date. E-Estimated. NA-Not Available. NM-Not Meaningful. NR-Not Ranked.

Office—13705 First Ave. North, Minneapolis, MN 55441-5444. **Tel**—(612) 449-9092. **Chrmn & CEO**—L. Berman. **Pres**—P. Cruzen. **CFO**—T. J. Cope. **EVP-Secy & Investor Contact**—T. J. Brosig. **Dirs**—D. W. Anderson, L. Berman, T. J. Brosig, P.R. Cruzen, M. Goldfarb, D. L. Rogers, N. I. Sell, S. M. Taube, J. Waller. **Transfer Agent & Registrar**—Norwest Bank Minnesota, South St. Paul. **Incorporated** in Minnesota in 1991. **Empl**-3,800. **S&P Analyst:** M.C.C.

STANDARD & POOR'S

STOCK REPORTS

Green Mountain Power

NYSE Symbol **GMP**
In S&P SmallCap 600

02-NOV-95 **Industry:** Utilities-Electric

Summary: This small electric utility provides service to about one-third of the population of Vermont. Electric generation is primarily hydropower and nuclear.

Quantitative Evaluations
Outlook (1 Lowest—5 Highest) • 1-
Fair Value • 20
Risk • Low
Earn./Div. Rank • A-

Technical Eval. • Bearish since 9/95
Rel. Strength Rank (1 Lowest—99 Highest) • 76
Insider Activity • NA

Recent Price • 27⅜
52 Wk Range • 28¼-23⅞
Yield • 7.7%
12-Mo. P/E • 12.2

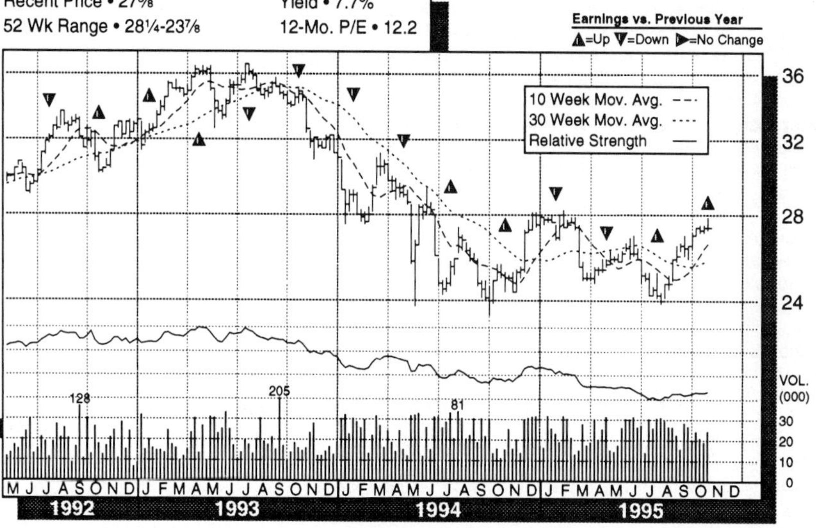

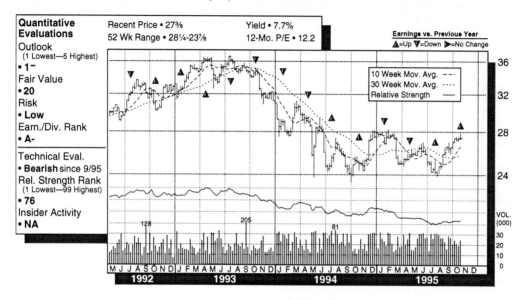

Business Profile - 30-OCT-95

This small electric utility recently began implementing a redesign of the company in order to meet anticipated increased competition in its markets. The dividend, which increased steadily through 1993 despite stagnant earnings, currently provides an above-average yield in excess of 7.5%. Going forward, GMP intends to grow earnings to a level that will reduce the dividend payout from 1994's 95%, to a level (about 75%) that can be sustained through market cycles and significant industry change.

Operational Review - 30-OCT-95

Operating revenues for the nine months ended September 30, 1995, advanced 5.4%, year to year, aided by a general retail rate increase, increased usage, and growth in the number of small business customers. Net income was up 5.1%, to $7,707,000 ($1.63 per share, based on 3.4% more shares outstanding), from $7,333,000 ($1.61).

Stock Performance - 27-OCT-95

In the past 30 trading days, GMP's shares have increased 4%, compared to a 0.63% fall in the S&P 500. Average trading volume for the past five days was 4,800 shares, compared with the 40-day moving average of 4,531 shares.

Key Stock Statistics

Dividend Rate/Share	2.12	Shareholders	6,500
Shs. outstg. (M)	4.7	Market cap. (B)	$0.131
Avg. daily vol. (M)	0.004	Inst. holdings	20%
Tang. Bk. Value/Share	21.01	Insider holdings	NA
Beta	0.38		

Value of $10,000 invested 5 years ago: $ 15,843

Fiscal Year Ending Dec. 31

	1995	% Change	1994	% Change	1993	% Change
Revenues (Million $)						
1Q	40.02	-1%	40.61	NM	40.75	3%
2Q	37.13	11%	33.60	NM	33.43	NM
3Q	39.78	8%	36.68	3%	35.65	5%
4Q	—	—	37.30	NM	37.43	-3%
Yr.	—	—	148.2	NM	147.3	1%
Income (Million $)						
1Q	3.23	-20%	4.04	-6%	4.30	6%
2Q	1.99	60%	1.24	28%	0.97	-39%
3Q	3.07	16%	2.65	29%	2.05	-26%
4Q	—	—	3.07	-7%	3.31	-4%
Yr.	—	—	11.00	3%	10.63	-10%
Earnings Per Share ($)						
1Q	0.65	-24%	0.85	-9%	0.93	4%
2Q	0.38	65%	0.23	35%	0.17	-47%
3Q	0.60	11%	0.54	32%	0.41	-31%
4Q	—	—	0.62	-10%	0.69	-7%
Yr.	—	—	2.23	1%	2.20	-13%

Next earnings report expected: late January

Green Mountain Power

Business Summary - 30-OCT-95

Green Mountain Power Corporation supplies electricity to approximately 80,500 customers in five areas of Vermont with an estimated population of 195,000. In addition, the company supplies firm wholesale customers, including four municipal and two cooperative utilities in Vermont and two utilities in other states. Important industries in the service territory are electronics (including computer assembly and components manufacturing), granite fabrication, service enterprises such as government, insurance and tourism (particularly winter recreation) and dairy and general farming. Contributions to revenues by customer class in recent years were:

	1994	1993	1992	1991
Residential & lease	34%	33%	32%	30%
Commercial & industrial (small)	32%	32%	31%	29%
Commercial & industrial (large)	21%	21%	22%	20%
Other	14%	14%	15%	21%

Electric energy sales to IBM accounted for about 14% of GMP's operating revenues in 1994.

Electric energy sources in 1994 were hydroelectric (39%), nuclear (36%), coal (11%), oil, natural gas and other sources (5%) and purchased (10%). Net system capability in 1994 was 438.2 mw, and peak demand was 308.3 mw, for a capacity margin of 30%. The company has committed itself to the development and implementation of demand-side management programs as part of its long-term resource strategy.

GMP has a 17.9% equity interest in the 520-mw Vermont Yankee nuclear plant, placed in operation in 1972, which supplied about 35% of the company's 1994 energy requirements. Hydro-Quebec, which provided about 30% of the company's energy requirements in 1994, will continue to be GMP's largest single source of power as a result of a new 20-year arrangement negotiated in 1994.

GMP holds a 30% interest in Vermont Electric Power Co. (VELCO), which owns nearly all the transmission network that serves Vermont and that interconnects with the transmission system serving New England. It also has two wholly owned unregulated energy-related subsidiaries: Green Mountain Propane Gas Co. and Mountain Energy Inc. and an unregulated water heater leasing operation.

The company projects capital expenditures for 1995-1999 totaling $92 million, including $22 million for 1995. Approximately 90% of these capital requirements are expected to be funded internally.

Important Developments

Sep. '95—GMP requested a 12.7% retail rate increase from the Vermont Public Service Board. The increase would raise an additional $18.3 million in annual revenue for the company.

Capitalization

Long Term Debt: $71,467,000 (6/95).
Cum. Preferred Stock: $9,135,000.

Per Share Data ($)

(Year Ended Dec. 31)

	1994	1993	1992	1991	1990	1989
Tangible Bk. Val.	21.01	20.65	20.15	19.38	19.10	18.79
Earnings	2.23	2.20	2.54	2.45	2.29	2.36
Dividends	2.12	2.11	2.08	2.04	2.00	1.95
Payout Ratio	95%	96%	82%	83%	87%	83%
Prices - High	31¼	36⅝	33⅝	30¼	27⅛	27⅞
- Low	23⅜	30¾	29	22	21¼	22⅛
P/E Ratio - High	14	17	13	12	12	12
- Low	10	14	11	9	9	9

Income Statement Analysis (Million $)

	1994	%Chg	1993	%Chg	1992	%Chg	1991
Revs.	148	NM	147	1%	145	NM	144
Depr.	10.7	25%	8.6	6%	8.1	14%	7.1
Maint.	4.5	3%	4.3	-7%	4.7	8%	4.3
Fxd. Chgs. Cov.	3.0	-5%	3.1	-7%	3.3	11%	3.0
Constr. Credits	0.8	27%	0.6	62%	0.4	8%	0.4
Eff. Tax Rate	33%	—	29%	—	29%	—	29%
Net Inc.	11.0	3%	10.6	-10%	11.9	13%	10.5

Balance Sheet & Other Fin. Data (Million $)

	1994	1993	1992	1991	1990	1989
Gross Prop.	245	236	223	215	204	179
Cap. Exp.	13.5	15.9	15.3	14.8	14.3	20.2
Net Prop.	176	171	165	160	152	132
Capitalization:						
LT Debt	85.2	90.8	79.6	68.9	73.4	57.0
% LT Debt	44	46	44	42	47	44
Pfd.	9.1	9.4	9.6	9.8	10.1	3.4
% Pfd.	4.70	4.80	5.30	5.90	6.50	2.60
Common	101	97.1	92.6	87.5	71.9	69.5
% Common	52	49	51	53	46	54
Total Cap.	223	224	203	185	173	145

Ratio Analysis

	1994	1993	1992	1991	1990	1989
Oper. Ratio	90.2	89.9	88.7	89.9	90.7	91.5
% Earn. on Net Prop.	8.4	8.8	10.1	9.3	9.6	9.8
% Ret. on Revs.	7.4	7.2	8.2	7.3	6.1	6.3
% Ret. On Invest.Cap	8.1	8.2	9.6	9.7	9.9	10.6
% Return On Com.Eqty	10.3	10.3	12.2	12.5	12.0	12.5

Dividend Data —Dividends have been paid since 1951. A dividend reinvestment plan is available. A "poison pill" stock purchase rights plan was adopted in 1987.

Amt. of Div. $	Date Decl.	Ex-Div. Date	Stock of Record	Payment Date
0.530	Nov. 14	Dec. 09	Dec. 15	Dec. 30 '94
0.530	Feb. 15	Mar. 09	Mar. 15	Mar. 31 '95
0.530	May. 18	Jun. 14	Jun. 16	Jun. 30 '95
0.530	Aug. 08	Sep. 12	Sep. 14	Sep. 29 '95

Data as orig. reptd.; bef. results of disc opers. and/or spec. items. Per share data adj. for stk. divs. as of ex-div. date. E-Estimated. NA-Not Available. NM-Not Meaningful. NR-Not Ranked.

Office—25 Green Mountain Drive, P.O. Box 850, South Burlington, VT 05402. **Tel**—(802) 864-5731. **Pres & CEO**—D. G. Hyde. **EVP & COO**—A. N. Terreri. **Secy**—Donna S. Laffan. **VP, CFO, Treas & Investor Contact**—C. L. Dutton. **Dirs**—T. P. Salmon (Chrmn), R. E. Boardman, N. L. Brue, W. B. Bruett, M. O. Burns, L. E. Chickering, J. V. Cleary, R. I. Fricke, D. G. Hyde, E. A. Irving, M. L. Johnson, R. W. Page. **Transfer Agent & Registrar**—Chemical Bank, NYC. **Incorporated** in Vermont in 1928. **Empl**-373. **S&P Analyst:** M.C.C.

STANDARD & POOR'S

STOCK REPORTS

Griffon Corporation

NYSE Symbol **GFF**
In S&P SmallCap 600

11-SEP-95

Industry:
Conglomerate/diversified

Summary: Griffon Corp. (formerly Instrument Systems) is a diversified manufacturer of home and commercial products, electronic communication systems and specialty plastic films.

Quantitative Evaluations

Outlook
(1 Lowest—5 Highest)
• 3−

Fair Value
• 8⅛

Risk
• Low

Earn./Div. Rank
• B-

Technical Eval.
• **Bearish** since 7/95

Rel. Strength Rank
(1 Lowest—99 Highest)
• 46

Insider Activity
• NA

Recent Price • 8¼
52 Wk Range • 9½-7⅜

Yield • Nil
12-Mo. P/E • 10.9

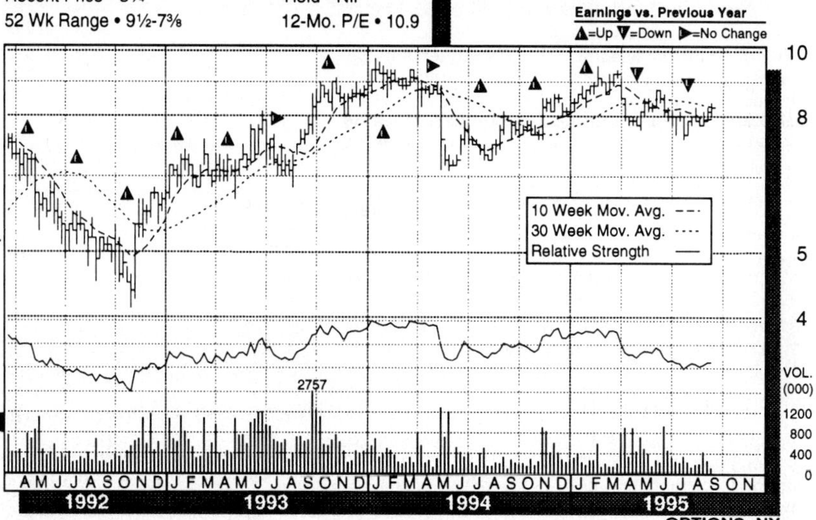

OPTIONS: NY

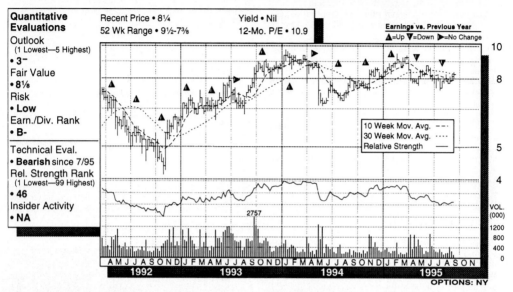

Business Profile - 11-SEP-95

Griffon Corp. is a diversified manufacturer of home and commercial products, electronic communication systems, and specialty plastic films. The company changed its name from Instrument Systems in March 1995 to better reflect its expanded operations. In December 1994, it repurchased about 3 million of its common shares through a Dutch auction. The company acquired Residential Construction Specialties, Inc., a building products concern with annual revenues of $30 million, in November 1994.

Operational Review - 11-SEP-95

The increase in revenues through the first nine months of 1995 reflects higher sales in the building products segment due to acquisitions and higher unit sales of garage doors. Operating income from this segment rose in the nine month period, but unfavorable results in specialty plastic films led to lower overall operating profits. Net income declined 16% in the first nine months and 31% in the third quarter. EPS comparisons were helped by the December 1994 Dutch auction.

Stock Performance - 08-SEP-95

In the past 30 trading days, GFF's shares have increased 5%, compared to a 2% rise in the S&P 500. Average trading volume for the past five days was 27,600 shares, compared with the 40-day moving average of 46,300 shares.

Key Stock Statistics

Dividend Rate/Share	Nil	Shareholders	16,000
Shs. outstg. (M)	30.9	Market cap. (B)	$0.255
Avg. daily vol. (M)	0.049	Inst. holdings	73%
Tang. Bk. Value/Share	4.17	Insider holdings	NA
Beta	1.78		

Value of $10,000 invested 5 years ago: $ 47,142

Fiscal Year Ending Sep. 30

	1995	% Change	1994	% Change	1993	% Change
Revenues (Million $)						
1Q	133.6	15%	116.2	12%	104.0	-20%
2Q	120.2	13%	105.9	12%	94.73	-30%
3Q	135.2	8%	125.3	16%	108.2	-6%
4Q	—	—	141.7	9%	130.5	11%
Yr.	—	—	489.0	12%	437.0	-13%
Income (Million $)						
1Q	7.72	13%	6.81	21%	5.61	38%
2Q	3.25	-34%	4.93	6%	4.63	1%
3Q	5.05	-31%	7.37	9%	6.76	1%
4Q	—	—	10.60	11%	9.56	10%
Yr.	—	—	29.71	12%	26.56	10%
Earnings Per Share ($)						
1Q	0.22	22%	0.18	20%	0.15	15%
2Q	0.10	-23%	0.13	NM	0.13	8%
3Q	0.15	-25%	0.20	11%	0.18	NM
4Q	—	—	0.29	16%	0.25	9%
Yr.	—	—	0.80	14%	0.70	6%

Next earnings report expected: early November

Griffon Corporation

Business Summary - 08-SEP-95

Griffon Corp. (formerly Instrument Systems) manufactures home and commercial products, specialty plastic films and electronic information and communication systems. Contributions in fiscal 1994:

	Sales	Profits
Home & commercial products	57%	45%
Specialty plastic films	24%	38%
Electronic communication systems	19%	17%

Sales to agencies of the U.S. government, either as prime contractor or subcontractor, were 13% of sales in fiscal 1994 (14% the year before).

The home and commercial products segment includes Clopay, one of the largest U.S. manufacturers of residential garage doors. Clopay sells a broad line of steel and wood garage doors and other building products for distribution throughout North America to retail, professional installer and wholesale channels. Significant retail customers include Home Depot and Lowe's. The company also manufactures a broad line of specialty hardware primarily for the foodservice industry under the name Standard-Keil, components for beverage dispensing equipment under the name Tap-Rite, and synthetic batting -- a material used in layers or sheeting for lining, as a furniture filling, for packaging and as filters.

Specialty plastic films and laminated products (also made by Clopay) are sold to various consumer and health care markets. Products include moisture barriers used in disposable diapers, adult incontinence products and sanitary napkins, surgical drapes and medical garments.

Through its Telephonics subsidiary, the company manufactures advanced information and communication systems for government, aerospace, industrial and commercial markets. It designs, manufactures and logistically supports advanced military communication systems, avionics for commercial airlines, command and control systems, strategic communications systems, VLSI/LSI circuits, microwave components, test instrumentation, microwave landing systems, maritime surveillance radars and air traffic control systems.

Important Developments

Jul. '95—The company reported that operating income declined in its plastic films segment in the third quarter because of increased costs of raw materials, the phaseout of a laminated product for a major customer, and delays in receipt of anticipated orders. Operating income for the building products and the electronic information and communications systems segment were approximately the same as the prior year period.

Capitalization

Long Term Debt: $15,966,000 (3/95).

Per Share Data ($) (Year Ended Sep. 30)

	1994	1993	1992	1991	1990	1989
Tangible Bk. Val.	4.17	3.56	3.06	1.52	0.90	0.31
Cash Flow	1.06	0.95	0.97	0.88	0.65	0.38
Earnings	0.80	0.70	0.66	0.51	0.32	0.13
Dividends	Nil	Nil	Nil	Nil	Nil	Nil
Payout Ratio	Nil	Nil	Nil	Nil	Nil	Nil
Prices - High	9¾	9⅛	8¼	6⅞	2⅜	2
- Low	6⅝	6	4⅛	1⅜	1¼	1
P/E Ratio - High	12	13	13	13	7	15
- Low	8	9	6	3	4	8

Income Statement Analysis (Million $)

	1994	%Chg	1993	%Chg	1992	%Chg	1991
Revs.	489	12%	437	-13%	500	1%	494
Oper. Inc.	59.7	11%	53.7	-8%	58.1	16%	50.1
Depr.	9.8	3%	9.5	-14%	11.1	NM	11.2
Int. Exp.	1.8	-5%	1.9	-73%	7.0	-48%	13.5
Pretax Inc.	50.3	14%	44.3	3%	42.9	49%	28.8
Eff. Tax Rate	41%	—	40%	—	40%	—	40%
Net Inc.	29.7	12%	26.6	10%	24.1	56%	15.4

Balance Sheet & Other Fin. Data (Million $)

	1994	1993	1992	1991	1990	1989
Cash	58.4	37.6	24.4	23.5	27.5	33.4
Curr. Assets	223	200	152	202	193	185
Total Assets	293	270	247	304	295	271
Curr. Liab.	102	82.8	74.0	78.1	79.4	71.6
LT Debt	16.0	25.0	25.0	105	119	123
Common Eqty.	159	145	128	66.0	49.0	33.0
Total Cap.	192	186	170	224	214	198
Cap. Exp.	9.2	8.4	13.4	15.2	19.5	25.4
Cash Flow	39.5	36.0	35.1	26.6	19.3	11.2

Ratio Analysis

	1994	1993	1992	1991	1990	1989
Curr. Ratio	2.2	2.4	2.1	2.6	2.4	2.6
% LT Debt of Cap.	8.1	13.2	14.9	47.1	55.6	62.3
% Net Inc.of Revs.	6.1	6.1	4.8	3.1	2.1	1.2
% Ret. on Assets	10.8	10.3	7.7	5.1	3.3	1.9
% Ret. on Equity	20.0	19.5	22.9	26.7	23.2	9.7

Dividend Data —No dividends have been paid on the common stock. A "poison pill" stock purchase rights plan was adopted in 1986.

Data as orig. reptd.; bef. results of disc. opers. and/or spec. items. Per share data adj. for stk. divs. as of ex-div. date. E-Estimated. NA-Not Available. NM-Not Meaningful. NR-Not Ranked.

Office—100 Jericho Quadrangle, Jericho, NY 11753. **Tel**—(516) 938-5544. **Chrmn & CEO**—H. R. Blau. **Pres**—R. Balemian. **Secy**—S. E. Rowland. **VP-Treas & Investor Contact**—Patrick L. Alesia. **Dirs**—H.A. Alpert, R. Balemian, B. M. Bell, H. R. Blau, R. Bradley, A. M. Buchman, C. A. Hill Jr., R. J. Kramer, M. Paulson, J. W. Stansberry, M. S. Sussman, W. H. Waldorf, L. L. Wolff. **Transfer Agent & Registrar**—American Stock Transfer & Trust Co., NYC. **Reincorporated** in Delaware in 1970. **Empl**-2,900. **S&P Analyst:** Stephen Madonna, CFA

STANDARD & POOR'S

Groundwater Technology

STOCK REPORTS

NASDAQ Symbol **GWTI**

In S&P SmallCap 600

14-NOV-95 **Industry:** Pollution Control

Summary: Groundwater Technology provides a wide range of environmental consulting and remediation services primarily for the petroleum industry.

Quantitative Evaluations

Outlook (1 Lowest—5 Highest)
• **3-**

Fair Value
• **14¾**

Risk
• **Average**

Earn./Div. Rank
• **B**

Technical Eval.
• **Bearish** since 12/94

Rel. Strength Rank (1 Lowest—99 Highest)
• **88**

Insider Activity
• **NA**

Recent Price • 14¾

52 Wk Range • 15½-11½

Yield • Nil

12-Mo. P/E • 21.1

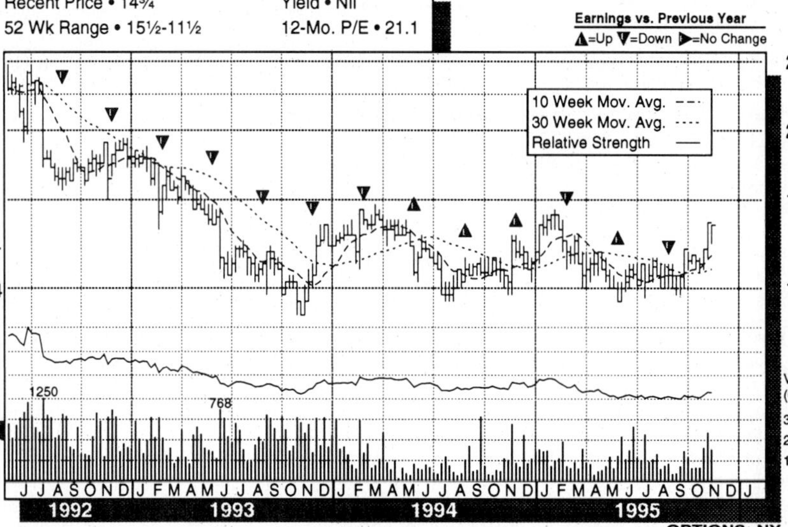

OPTIONS: NY

Business Profile - 14-NOV-95

Groundwater Technology provides a wide range of environmental consulting and remediation services. The company has been following a dual strategy of enhancing geographic presence and increasing its technical capabilities through both internal growth and acquisitions. In November 1995, GWTI signed a letter of intent to sell the assets of its GTEL Environmental Laboratories subsidiary. The company has a strong balance sheet, with no long-term debt at 1994-5 year-end.

Operational Review - 14-NOV-95

Net revenues for the 13 weeks ended July 29, 1995, rose 1.7%, year to year. Gross margins narrowed, reflecting increased labor and benefit expenses (related to acquisitions in 1994-5) and losses at GTEL Environmental Laboratories. Pretax income fell 64%. After taxes at 39.6%, versus 39.5%, net income also was down 64%, to $412,000 ($0.06 a share, based on 3.4% fewer shares), from $1,139,000 ($0.16).

Stock Performance - 10-NOV-95

In the past 30 trading days, GWTI's shares have increased 12%, compared to a 1% rise in the S&P 500. Average trading volume for the past five days was 30,100 shares, compared with the 40-day moving average of 24,503 shares.

Key Stock Statistics

Dividend Rate/Share	Nil	Shareholders	1,300
Shs. outstg. (M)	6.9	Market cap. (B)	$0.100
Avg. daily vol. (M)	0.030	Inst. holdings	52%
Tang. Bk. Value/Share	14.05	Insider holdings	NA
Beta	0.24		

Value of $10,000 invested 5 years ago: $ 7,375

Fiscal Year Ending Apr. 30

	1996	% Change	1995	% Change	1994	% Change
Revenues (Million $)						
1Q	31.05	2%	30.50	5%	29.00	-18%
2Q	—	—	49.02	62%	30.20	-10%
3Q	—	—	30.10	NM	30.30	-2%
4Q	—	—	47.79	64%	29.10	-6%
Yr.	—	—	190.1	60%	118.6	-9%
Income (Million $)						
1Q	0.41	-64%	1.14	NM	-2.69	NM
2Q	—	—	1.75	119%	0.80	-57%
3Q	—	—	1.19	-15%	1.40	-11%
4Q	—	—	1.54	14%	1.35	NM
Yr.	—	—	5.62	NM	0.85	-86%
Earnings Per Share ($)						
1Q	0.06	-63%	0.16	NM	-0.35	NM
2Q	—	—	0.25	127%	0.11	-54%
3Q	—	—	0.17	-11%	0.19	-10%
4Q	—	—	0.22	16%	0.19	NM
Yr.	—	—	0.80	NM	0.11	-86%

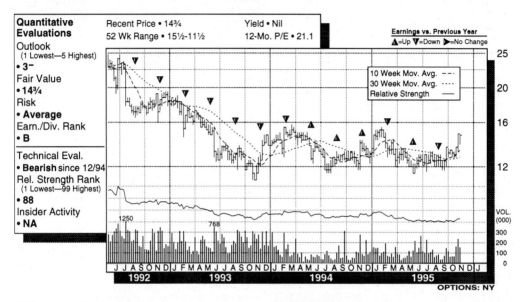

Next earnings report expected: mid November

Groundwater Technology

Business Summary - 14-NOV-95

Groundwater Technology, Inc. and its subsidiaries provide a full range of environmental, consulting, engineering and remediation services to a variety of commercial and industrial customers and federal, state and local government agencies. As of 1994-5 year-end, the company was operating from 47 consulting offices and four laboratories throughout the U.S. and 13 offices in six other countries. Also, GWTI's joint venture with a German company had offices at six locations in Germany, Austria and Hungary. Gross revenue breakdown by customer category in 1994-5:

Petroleum	44%
Industrial/commercial	35%
Federal, state & local government	12%
International	9%

The three largest petroleum customers accounted for about 14% of gross revenues in 1994-5.

Principal services are detailed, scientific environmental assessment and remediation programs, which combine elements of hydrogeology, geochemistry, chemistry, biochemestry and engineering.

A typical program generally includes interaction with the appropriate governmental regulatory agencies, detailed site assessment that may include installation of a series of monitoring wells, design and implementation of a cost-effective remediation system, construction management services and ongoing monitoring and maintenance of the system for the duration of the program.

These assessments and remediation programs are generally in response to regulatory programs adopted by state agencies as well as U.S. Environmental Protection Agency (EPA) programs.

The Groundwater Technology Government Services subsidiary provides environmental services to the Department of Defense and other federal and state agencies. The GTEL Environmental Laboratories subsidiary operates analytical laboratories in New Hampshire, California, Kansas and Florida for the analysis of inorganic and organic contaminants present in soil, water and air.

Important Developments

Nov. '95—GWTI signed a letter of intent to sell the assets of its GTEL Environmental Laboratories Inc. subsidiary to Nytest Environmental Inc. The transaction was expected to be completed before year-end 1995, subject to certain conditions. Terms were not disclosed.

Capitalization

Long Term Debt: None (7/95).
Options: To buy 899,746 shs. at $11.13 to $25 ea. (4/95).

Per Share Data ($)

(Year Ended Apr. 30)

	1995	1994	1993	1992	1991	1990
Tangible Bk. Val.	13.96	13.16	13.24	12.77	11.41	10.51
Cash Flow	1.94	1.21	1.77	2.20	1.76	1.57
Earnings	0.80	0.11	0.76	1.30	1.10	1.10
Dividends	Nil	Nil	Nil	Nil	Nil	Nil
Payout Ratio	Nil	Nil	Nil	Nil	Nil	Nil
Cal. Yrs.	1994	1993	1992	1991	1990	1989
Prices - High	15¾	19	26¾	31½	27¾	30¼
- Low	11½	11	16	17¾	15¾	18¼
P/E Ratio - High	20	NM	35	24	25	28
- Low	14	NM	21	14	14	17

Income Statement Analysis (Million $)

	1995	%Chg	1994	%Chg	1993	%Chg	1992
Revs.	190	60%	119	-9%	131	-32%	194
Oper. Inc.	15.5	38%	11.2	-25%	15.0	-31%	21.7
Depr.	8.0	-2%	8.2	4%	7.9	11%	7.1
Int. Exp.	Nil	—	Nil	—	Nil	—	Nil
Pretax Inc.	9.3	NM	1.3	-86%	9.6	-42%	16.6
Eff. Tax Rate	40%	—	33%	—	38%	—	38%
Net Inc.	5.6	NM	0.9	-85%	5.9	-43%	10.3

Balance Sheet & Other Fin. Data (Million $)

	1995	1994	1993	1992	1991	1990
Cash	25.9	30.5	50.4	49.3	40.7	40.0
Curr. Assets	100	92.1	96.3	99	85.3	74.7
Total Assets	121	113	121	124	108	93.0
Curr. Liab.	24.0	19.3	20.0	23.2	18.8	9.6
LT Debt	Nil	Nil	Nil	Nil	Nil	Nil
Common Eqty.	97.0	94.0	101	101	90.0	84.0
Total Cap.	97.0	94.0	101	101	90.0	84.0
Cap. Exp.	4.2	7.0	5.6	9.6	9.1	8.8
Cash Flow	13.6	9.1	13.8	17.4	14.1	12.7

Ratio Analysis

	1995	1994	1993	1992	1991	1990
Curr. Ratio	4.2	4.8	4.8	4.3	4.5	7.8
% LT Debt of Cap.	Nil	Nil	Nil	Nil	Nil	Nil
% Net Inc.of Revs.	2.9	0.7	4.5	5.3	5.5	7.1
% Ret. on Assets	4.8	0.8	4.9	8.8	8.8	10.1
% Ret. on Equity	5.9	0.9	6.0	10.8	10.2	11.2

Dividend Data —No cash dividends have been paid.

Data as orig. reptd.; bef. results of disc. opers. and/or spec. items. Per share data adj. for stk. divs. as of ex-div. date. E-Estimated. NA-Not Available. NM-Not Meaningful. NR-Not Ranked.

Office—100 River Ridge Dr., Norwood, MA 02062. **Tel**—(617) 769-7600. **Fax**—(617) 769-7992. **Chrmn & Pres**—W. C. Barber. **VP, CFO, Treas & Investor Contact**—Robert E. Sliney Jr.. **VP & Secy**—Catherine L. Farrell. **Dirs**—W. C. Barber, A. S. Bufferd, B. Henry, R. P. Schechter. **Transfer Agent & Registrar**—State Street Bank & Trust Co., Boston. **Incorporated** in Delaware in 1975. **Empl**-1,568. **S&P Analyst:** N. J. DeVita

STANDARD & POOR'S

STOCK REPORTS

Guilford Mills

NYSE Symbol **GFD**
In S&P SmallCap 600

26-SEP-95 **Industry:** Textiles

Summary: Guilford Mills is a leading producer of warp knit fabrics used to manufacture apparel, automobile interiors and home furnishings.

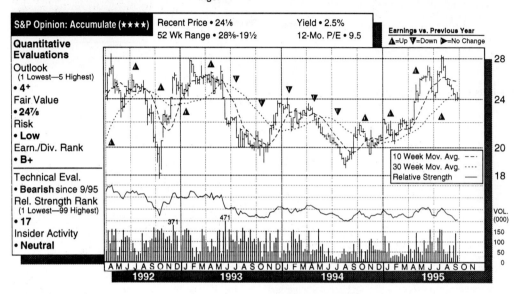

S&P Opinion: Accumulate (★★★★)
Recent Price • 24⅛
52 Wk Range • 28⅜-19½
Yield • 2.5%
12-Mo. P/E • 9.5

Quantitative Evaluations
Outlook (1 Lowest—5 Highest) • **4+**
Fair Value • **24⅞**
Risk • **Low**
Earn./Div. Rank • **B+**
Technical Eval. • **Bearish** since 9/95
Rel. Strength Rank (1 Lowest—99 Highest) • **17**
Insider Activity • **Neutral**

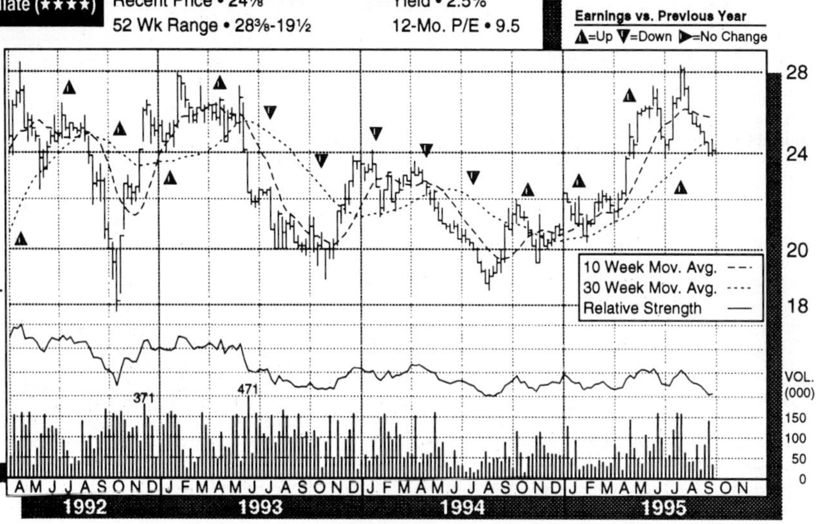

Overview - 26-SEP-95

Sales for the fiscal year ending September 1996 should continue in an uptrend. Demand for automotive body cloth fabrics should continue to be strong, on share gains in the U.S. and Europe. Demand for apparel stretch fabrics and various other specialty fabrics should continue to be on the rise. Industrial fabrics could show some growth as a result of new fabric introductions. Overseas sales should continue their strong momentum on improved economies there. New fabric introductions in all areas of the business will aid growth. Approximately 50% of GFD's sales are generated by products that were created in the past five years. Profit growth should far outpace sales increases as margins widen on more efficient manufacturing.

Valuation - 26-SEP-95

The shares are off more than 10% from their 1995 high. We feel this decline mainly reflects concern by investors about the weak apparel sector. However, GFD, known as a major innovator in the textile industry, mainly produces highly specialized apparel fabrics, which tend to serve growing markets (e.g., activewear) and are typically competitive with imports. In addition, GFD's automotive fabric division is the market leader and continues to see its share increase. Based on our earnings projection for the fiscal year ending September 1996, the stock is currently selling at the low end of its historical yearly price/earnings multiple range and should be accumulated.

Key Stock Statistics

S&P EPS Est. 1995	2.60	Tang. Bk. Value/Share	18.45
P/E on S&P Est. 1995	9.3	Beta	0.83
S&P EPS Est. 1996	2.80	Shareholders	600
Dividend Rate/Share	0.60	Market cap. (B)	$0.340
Shs. outstg. (M)	14.1	Inst. holdings	57%
Avg. daily vol. (M)	0.015	Insider holdings	NA

Value of $10,000 invested 5 years ago: $ 18,141

Fiscal Year Ending Sep. 30

	1995	% Change	1994	% Change	1993	% Change
Revenues (Million $)						
1Q	182.0	15%	158.0	NM	157.0	12%
2Q	202.0	29%	156.0	2%	153.0	3%
3Q	210.8	15%	183.0	-5%	192.0	5%
4Q	--	—	207.0	47%	141.0	-7%
Yr.	--	—	704.0	9%	643.0	3%
Income (Million $)						
1Q	6.10	58%	3.85	—	—	—
2Q	9.38	139%	3.93	-25%	5.21	24%
3Q	11.25	26%	8.94	46%	6.14	29%
4Q	—	—	8.41	-21%	10.69	-3%
Yr.	—	—	25.12	20%	20.95	-16%
Earnings Per Share ($)						
1Q	0.44	57%	0.28	-26%	0.38	23%
2Q	0.67	139%	0.28	-38%	0.45	29%
3Q	0.80	23%	0.65	-17%	0.78	-4%
4Q	E0.69	13%	0.61	NM	-0.08	NM
Yr.	E2.60	43%	1.82	—	--	—

Next earnings report expected: mid November

Guilford Mills

Business Summary - 26-SEP-95

Guilford Mills, Inc. primarily produces, processes and sells warp knit fabrics. GFD knits synthetic yarn, primarily nylon, acetate and polyester, on warp knitting machinery into warp knit fabrics, which it then dyes and finishes. Finished fabrics are sold to customers for use in a broad range of apparel, automotive and home furnishings products. The company also designs, knits, dyes, prints and finishes elastomeric and circular knit fabrics for sale primarily to swimwear, dress and sportswear manufacturers. Additionally, the company has introduced woven velour fabric capabilities in its expanding automotive business. Contributions to sales in recent fiscal years were:

	9/94	6/93	6/92
Apparel	51%	54%	64%
Automotive	38%	33%	22%
Home furnishings	8%	10%	14%
Other	3%	3%	---

International sales accounted for 14% of sales in both fiscal 1994 and fiscal 1993.

The research and development department works closely with customers to develop patterns and create new fabrics and styles. Direct expenditures for research and development totaled $14.7 million in fiscal 1994 and $15.8 million in fiscal 1993.

The company operates 16 manufacturing and warehousing operations in the U.S. and two facilities in the U.K., two facilities in Mexico and four stores in Mexico.

In August 1994, the company acquired 55% of the outstanding stock of Grupo Ambar, S.A. de C.V. and subsidiaries, increasing its ownership in this leading manufacturer of knit textile fabrics in Mexico to 75%.

Important Developments

Jul. '95—GFD attributed the 15% year-to-year increase in sales for the third quarter of fiscal 1995 mainly to stronger sales of automotive fabrics. Despite higher raw material prices, net income advanced 26% on operating efficiencies. Separately, the company announced a new president and chief operating officer, Mr. John Emrich, who has been employed at GFD since 1985.

Capitalization

Long Term Debt: $165,754,000 (4/2/95), incl. $66.2 million of 6% debs. due 1999-2012 & conv. into com. at $29.50 a sh.

Per Share Data ($)

(Year Ended Sep. 30)

	1994	1993	1992	1991	1990	1989
Tangible Bk. Val.	17.45	15.89	15.08	13.28	13.12	14.12
Cash Flow	4.68	4.11	3.84	2.99	1.33	3.32
Earnings	1.82	2.11	1.85	1.02	-0.57	1.78
Dividends	0.60	0.60	0.57	0.53	0.53	0.53
Payout Ratio	33%	28%	31%	53%	NM	30%
Prices - High	24 1/8	28	28 1/2	22 3/8	16 7/8	22 7/8
- Low	18 1/2	18 7/8	17 3/4	11 3/8	9 1/4	15 1/2
P/E Ratio - High	13	13	15	22	NM	13
- Low	10	9	10	11	NM	9

Income Statement Analysis (Million $)

	1994	%Chg	1993	%Chg	1992	%Chg	1991
Revs.	704	8%	654	6%	615	16%	529
Oper. Inc.	91.2	14%	79.8	5%	76.2	34%	56.8
Depr.	39.3	43%	27.4	2%	26.8	2%	26.4
Int. Exp.	12.4	52%	8.2	17%	7.0	-17%	8.4
Pretax Inc.	38.9	-11%	43.9	29%	34.1	70%	20.1
Eff. Tax Rate	35%	—	34%	—	27%	—	32%
Net Inc.	25.1	-13%	28.9	16%	24.9	83%	13.6

Balance Sheet & Other Fin. Data (Million $)

	1994	1993	1992	1991	1990	1989
Cash	6.1	17.9	15.9	14.3	25.4	40.2
Curr. Assets	264	249	227	204	227	255
Total Assets	565	507	414	375	390	410
Curr. Liab.	111	96.6	87.5	80.0	88.9	76.8
LT Debt	165	147	77.0	80.0	92.0	96.0
Common Eqty.	244	220	206	178	176	208
Total Cap.	429	386	301	278	287	319
Cap. Exp.	48.0	102	35.8	26.6	31.3	46.6
Cash Flow	64.5	56.2	51.7	39.9	18.9	49.1

Ratio Analysis

	1994	1993	1992	1991	1990	1989
Curr. Ratio	2.4	2.6	2.6	2.6	2.6	3.3
% LT Debt of Cap.	38.4	38.2	25.5	28.8	32.1	30.1
% Net Inc.of Revs.	3.6	4.4	4.0	2.6	NM	4.2
% Ret. on Assets	4.7	6.2	6.2	3.5	NM	6.7
% Ret. on Equity	10.8	13.5	12.8	7.7	NM	13.2

Dividend Data —Dividends have been paid since 1973. A "poison pill" stock purchase right was adopted in 1990.

Amt. of Div. $	Date Decl.	Ex-Div. Date	Stock of Record	Payment Date
0.150	Nov. 17	Nov. 21	Nov. 28	Dec. 09 '94
0.150	Jan. 24	Jan. 27	Feb. 02	Feb. 14 '95
0.150	Apr. 24	Apr. 28	May. 04	May. 16 '95
0.150	Jul. 25	Aug. 01	Aug. 03	Aug. 15 '95

Data as orig. reptd.; bef. results of disc. opers. and/or spec. items. Per share data adj. for stk. divs. as of ex-div. date. E-Estimated. NA-Not Available. NM-Not Meaningful. NR-Not Ranked.

Office—4925 West Market St., Greensboro, NC 27407. **Tel**—(910) 316-4000. **Chrmn & CEO**—C. A. Hayes. **Pres & COO**—J. Emrich. **VP-CFO**—T. E. Geremski. **VP-Secy**—S. Jacobs. **Investor Contact**—Jaime Vasquez. **Dirs**—T. Adachi, D. B. Dixon, M. Fishman, T. E. Geremski, P. G. Gillease, G. Greenberg, S. C. Hassenfelt, C. A. Hayes, S. R. Jacobs, S. R. Kry, P. R. McGarr. **Transfer Agent & Registrar**—Wachovia Bank of North Carolina, Winston-Salem. **Reincorporated** in Delaware in 1971. **Empl**-5,410. **S&P Analyst:** Elizabeth Vandeventer

HS Resources

NYSE Symbol **HSE**
In S&P SmallCap 600

22-SEP-95 **Industry:** Oil and Gas

Summary: This independent oil and gas exploration and production company focuses its efforts in the Rocky Mountain area of the U.S.

Quantitative Evaluations

Outlook
(1 Lowest—5 Highest)
• **NA**
Fair Value
• **NA**
Risk
• **Average**
Earn./Div. Rank
• **NR**

Technical Eval.
• **Bearish** since 11/94
Rel. Strength Rank
(1 Lowest—99 Highest)
• **27**
Insider Activity
• **NA**

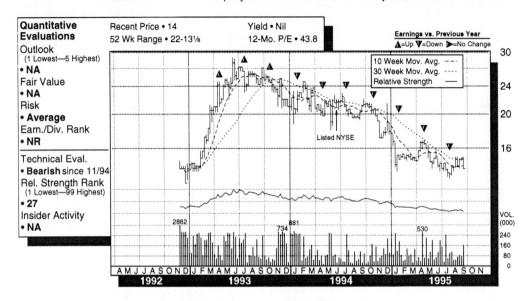

Recent Price • 14
52 Wk Range • 22-13⅛
Yield • Nil
12-Mo. P/E • 43.8

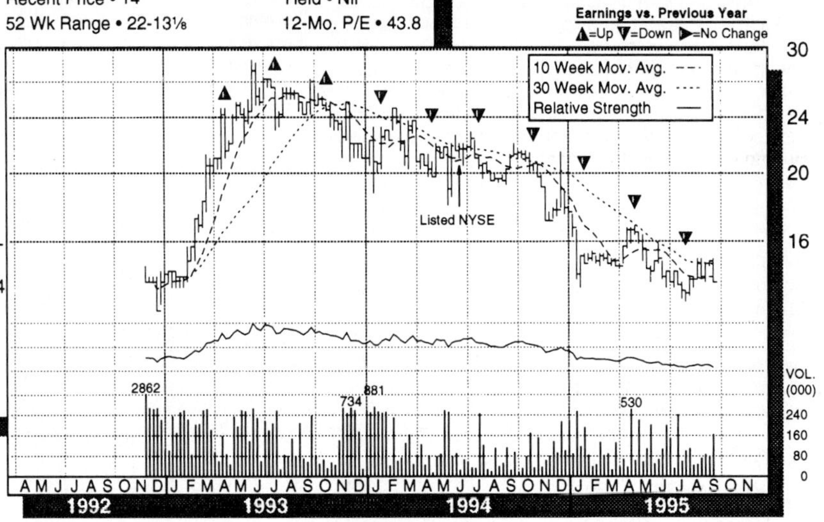

Business Profile - 19-SEP-95

This independent oil and gas exploration and production firm's drilling program is concentrated in the Wattenberg Field area of the Denver-Julesberg Basin in Colorado, where it has a significant acreage position. While prices per BOE are still depressed, increased production from Wattenberg has allowed HSE to maintain strong cash flow, with which it intends to invest in growth opportunities. Capital expenditures in 1995 are to be reduced to $45 million from $50-$60 million due to low gas prices.

Operational Review - 19-SEP-95

Revenues during the six months ended June 30, 1995, rose 5.2%, year to year, reflecting a 16% production gain that was partially offset by a 27% drop in natural gas prices. Margins narrowed on higher lease operating, depletion, depreciation and amortization costs associated with the increased production, and greater interest expense. After taxes at 38.4%, versus 38.1%, net income plunged 75% to $820,000 ($0.07 a share), from $3,322,000 ($0.28).

Stock Performance - 15-SEP-95

In the past 30 trading days, HSE's shares have declined 0.88%, compared to a 4% rise in the S&P 500. Average trading volume for the past five days was 32,360 shares, compared with the 40-day moving average of 17,433 shares.

Key Stock Statistics

Dividend Rate/Share	Nil	Shareholders	300
Shs. outstg. (M)	10.9	Market cap. (B)	$0.157
Avg. daily vol. (M)	0.023	Inst. holdings	65%
Tang. Bk. Value/Share	11.02	Insider holdings	NA
Beta	NA		

Value of $10,000 invested 5 years ago: NA

Fiscal Year Ending Dec. 31

	1995	% Change	1994	% Change	1993	% Change
Revenues (Million $)						
1Q	15.76	12%	14.09	39%	10.14	132%
2Q	14.85	-1%	15.01	21%	12.41	82%
3Q	—	—	15.79	15%	13.75	86%
4Q	—	—	15.51	39%	11.19	24%
Yr.	—	—	60.40	27%	47.48	72%
Income (Million $)						
1Q	0.64	-63%	1.73	-36%	2.72	—
2Q	0.18	-89%	1.59	-46%	2.94	—
3Q	—	—	1.68	-42%	2.88	—
4Q	—	—	1.26	-17%	1.52	—
Yr.	—	—	6.26	-38%	10.06	114%
Earnings Per Share ($)						
1Q	0.06	-60%	0.15	-44%	0.27	NM
2Q	0.02	-86%	0.14	-50%	0.28	75%
3Q	—	—	0.14	-48%	0.27	50%
4Q	—	—	0.11	-8%	0.12	-64%
Yr.	—	—	0.53	-43%	0.93	35%

Next earnings report expected: early November

HS Resources

Business Summary - 22-SEP-95

HS Resources explores for, develops and produces crude oil and natural gas primarily in the Rocky Mountain region of the U.S. Its major drilling is concentrated in the Wattenberg Field area of the Denver-Julesberg Basin (D-J Basin) in Colorado, where the company is one of the largest operators and has a significant acreage position. Additional drilling is conducted in the other areas where the company has large acreage positions -- the Denver-Julesberg Basin outside the Wattenberg Field area, the Williston Basin in Montana, the Sand Wash Basin in Colorado and Wyoming, and the Hugoton Embayment in Kansas.

At December 31, 1994, estimated proved reserves totaled 18,301,000 bbl. of crude oil (59% developed) and 265.3 Bcf of natural gas (71% developed), compared with 16,300,000 bbl. of oil (36%) and 252.4 Bcf of gas (45%) a year before. The standardized measure of future net cash flows, discounted at 10%, was $230.3 million at December 31, 1994, compared with $165.8 million a year earlier. Production in 1994 totaled 1,664,000 bbl. of oil and 20,108,000 Mcf of natural gas, versus 967,000 bbl. and 14,684,000 Mcf the year before. Average prices were $14.83 per barrel and $1.70 per Mcf in 1994, against $16.09 per barrel and $2.03 per Mcf in 1993.

The company held interests in 966 gross (823.1 net) productive oil wells and 150 gross (125.0 net) gas wells at the end of 1994, the majority of which were located in the D-J Basin. Approximately 79% of the Wattenberg area wells were operated by the company, and HSE generally held 100% of the working interest in the wells it operated. The company held 111,000 gross (78,000 net) developed and 973,000 gross (680,000 net) undeveloped acres at the end of 1994.

During 1994, the company drilled 163 wells in the Wattenberg Field and also recompleted 89 producing wells. Reflecting both a less aggressive capital expenditure program and increasing allocations to other projects, it is anticipated that the company will spend approximately $12 million in the Wattenberg Field to drill 50 wells and recomplete 50 wells in 1995.

In 1994, HSE sold the vast majority of its produced gas to Amoco, pursuant to a contract under which Amoco accounted for 78%, 85% and 88% of respective 1994, 1993 and 1992 gas revenues. It sold 81% of its oil production to Amoco Production Co. in 1994.

Important Developments

Aug. '95—HSE announced that it had signed a Term Sheet with the Trust Co. of the West covering a proposed $90 million non-recourse, off-balance sheet financing facility. It complements HSE's $60 million bank credit facility, and may be used for a variety of purposes. Also, the company is reducing its 1995 capital expenditure program to $45 million from $50-$60 million due to low gas prices.

Capitalization

Long Term Debt: $123,508,000 (6/95).

Per Share Data ($) (Year Ended Dec. 31)

	1994	1993	1992	1991	1990	1989
Tangible Bk. Val.	10.94	10.38	8.31	10.30	NA	NA
Cash Flow	2.68	2.34	2.00	1.35	NA	NA
Earnings	0.53	0.93	0.69	0.16	NA	NA
Dividends	Nil	Nil	Nil	Nil	NA	NA
Payout Ratio	Nil	Nil	Nil	Nil	NA	NA
Prices - High	24¾	29	14¾	NA	NA	NA
- Low	17⅛	13¾	12¾	NA	NA	NA
P/E Ratio - High	47	31	21	NA	NA	NA
- Low	32	15	18	NA	NA	NA

Income Statement Analysis (Million $)

	1994	%Chg	1993	%Chg	1992	%Chg	1991
Revs.	60.2	27%	47.3	73%	27.4	114%	12.8
Oper. Inc.	42.5	23%	34.5	71%	20.2	153%	8.0
Depr. Depl. & Amort.	25.1	64%	15.3	74%	8.8	100%	4.4
Int. Exp.	9.4	152%	3.7	-32%	5.4	17%	4.7
Pretax Inc.	10.1	-38%	16.2	113%	7.6	NM	1.0
Eff. Tax Rate	38%	—	38%	—	38%	—	40%
Net Inc.	6.3	-38%	10.1	115%	4.7	NM	0.6

Balance Sheet & Other Fin. Data (Million $)

	1994	1993	1992	1991	1990	1989
Cash	0.7	21.1	7.1	7.4	NA	NA
Curr. Assets	13.4	32.4	12.3	11.3	NA	NA
Total Assets	269	228	120	83.0	NA	NA
Curr. Liab.	15.8	16.2	8.7	9.0	NA	NA
LT Debt	103	74.4	20.6	36.3	NA	NA
Common Eqty.	119	113	79.0	28.0	NA	NA
Total Cap.	246	207	109	73.0	NA	NA
Cap. Exp.	86.0	100	45.0	19.0	NA	NA
Cash Flow	31.3	25.4	13.5	5.0	NA	NA

Ratio Analysis

	1994	1993	1992	1991	1990	1989
Curr. Ratio	0.8	2.0	1.4	1.3	NA	NA
% LT Debt of Cap.	42.0	35.9	18.9	50.0	NA	NA
% Ret. on Assets	2.5	5.5	2.3	NA	NA	NA
% Ret. on Equity	5.4	9.9	5.3	NA	NA	NA

Dividend Data —Dividends have never been paid on the common stock. The company said in its 1994 Form 10-K that it did not intend to declare cash dividends on its common stock in the foreseeable future, but would retain its earnings to support the growth of the business.

Data as orig. reptd.; bef. results of disc opers. and/or spec. items. Per share data adj. for stk. divs. as of ex-div. date. E-Estimated. NA-Not Available. NM-Not Meaningful. NR-Not Ranked.

Office—One Maritime Plaza, San Francisco CA 94111. **Tel**—(415) 433-5795. **Chrmn & CEO**—N. J. Sutton. **Pres**—P. M. Highum. **VP-Fin & CFO**—J. E. Duffy. **VP-Secy**—R. B. Jacobs. **Investor Contact**—Susan Gonsalves (303-296-3600-X416). **Dirs**—J. E. Duffy, K. A. Hersh, P. M. Highum, N. J. Sutton. **Transfer Agent & Registrar**—Harris Trust Co. of California, Los Angeles. **Incorporated** in Delaware in 1987. **Empl**-181. **S&P Analyst:** Michael C. Barr

Haggar Corp.

NASDAQ Symbol **HGGR**
In S&P SmallCap 600

19-SEP-95

Industry:
Textiles

Summary: This company designs, manufactures, imports and markets men's casual and dress apparel products primarily under the Haggar and Reed St. James brand names.

Quantitative Evaluations

Recent Price • 19
52 Wk Range • 28½-17¾
Yield • 1.1%
12-Mo. P/E • NM

Outlook
(1 Lowest—5 Highest)
• **NA**

Fair Value
• **NA**

Risk
• **Average**

Earn./Div. Rank
• **NR**

Technical Eval.
• **Bullish** since 12/94

Rel. Strength Rank
(1 Lowest—99 Highest)
• **21**

Insider Activity
• **NA**

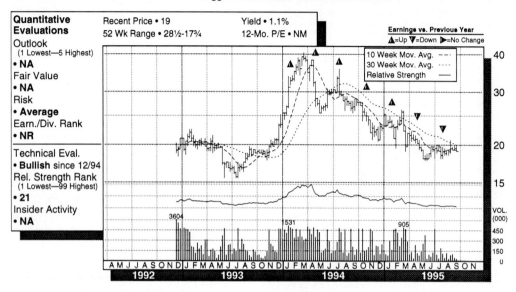

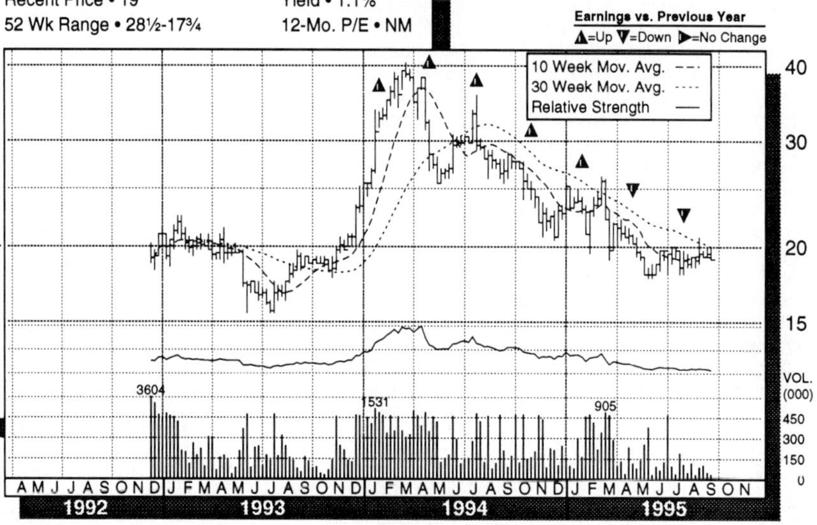

Business Profile - 19-SEP-95

This leading men's apparel concern recently moved to align its domestic and offshore manufacturing mix and bring inventory levels in line with corporate goals by closing its Robstown, Tex., plant, reducing the schedules of other domestic plants, and booking additional markdown reserves against its Spring 1995 shirt line. HGGR has opened three new outlet stores, through which it intends to establish a new distribution channel for its products, showcase its apparel, and try new marketing concepts.

Operational Review - 19-SEP-95

Sales in the nine months ended June 30, 1995, slid 6.1%, year to year, hurt by the collapse of the roof at the main distribution center in Dallas, which not only destroyed inventory, but hindered HGGR's ability to ship product during the third quarter. HGGR relocated its distribution function to satellite buildings, resulting in inefficiencies and additional costs. Haggar recorded a $24 million related charge in the third quarter, and is currently in the process of preparing an insurance claim.

Stock Performance - 15-SEP-95

In the past 30 trading days, HGGR's shares have increased 2%, compared to a 4% rise in the S&P 500. Average trading volume for the past five days was 6,200 shares, compared with the 40-day moving average of 14,123 shares.

Key Stock Statistics

Dividend Rate/Share	0.20	Shareholders	300
Shs. outstg. (M)	8.5	Market cap. (B)	$0.162
Avg. daily vol. (M)	0.013	Inst. holdings	66%
Tang. Bk. Value/Share	16.92	Insider holdings	NA
Beta	NA		

Value of $10,000 invested 5 years ago: NA

Fiscal Year Ending Sep. 30

	1995	% Change	1994	% Change	1993	% Change
Revenues (Million $)						
1Q	121.0	10%	110.2	34%	82.00	—
2Q	121.1	2%	118.3	13%	104.9	—
3Q	85.18	-29%	120.2	44%	83.40	—
4Q	—	—	142.5	15%	123.8	—
Yr.	—	—	491.2	25%	394.1	4%
Income (Million $)						
1Q	5.34	20%	4.45	NM	0.53	—
2Q	2.17	-73%	8.04	26%	6.37	—
3Q	-19.74	NM	5.69	160%	2.19	—
4Q	—	—	7.50	27%	5.92	—
Yr.	—	—	25.68	71%	15.01	21%
Earnings Per Share ($)						
1Q	0.62	22%	0.51	183%	0.18	—
2Q	0.25	-73%	0.92	23%	0.75	—
3Q	-2.30	NM	0.65	150%	0.26	—
4Q	—	—	0.86	23%	0.70	—
Yr.	—	—	2.95	57%	1.88	—

Next earnings report expected: early November

Haggar Corp.

Business Summary - 19-SEP-95

Haggar Corp. designs, manufactures, imports and markets men's and boys' casual and dress apparel products, including slacks, shorts, suits, sportcoats and shirts. Products are marketed directly to retailers throughout the U.S. primarily under the Haggar and Reed St. James brand names, as well as under retailers' own labels.

A significant portion of the company's apparel lines consists of basic, recurring styles that are less susceptible to fashion obsolescence. Haggar-brand products accounted for about 83% of apparel sales in fiscal 1994, and are divided into four distinct apparel lines: Haggar Imperial offers top-quality, classic dress and casual styling in slacks, sportcoats and custom-fit suits; Haggar City Casuals consists of casual styles and fits in clothes that are appropriate for the office or a night on the town; Haggar Casuals include a contemporary line of casual slacks and shorts that are generously cut for a relaxed fit, and a collection of cotton knit and woven shirts; and Haggar offers dress and casual apparel with quality features at popular prices for slacks, shorts, sportcoats and custom-fit suits. Haggar-brand products are sold nationwide primarily to major department stores.

Through its Horizon Group mass retailer division, HGGR markets Reed St. James branded products, including dress slacks, casual slacks, shorts, custom-fit suits, sportcoats and shirts. Reed St. James products are offered at lower prices than the Haggar line, and are generally sold to mass-market retailers. Horizon Group also markets Mustang brand jeans and shorts; Reed Stretch jeans; and the Taos Country Western Collection, a line of sportcoats, pants and suit separates marketed to better western specialty stores. The division also manages the licensing of products bearing the Reed St. James brand, and signed a licensing agreement in 1994 to sell men's pants and shorts under the John Weitz brand.

The company also manufactures specialty-label men's apparel, mainly for major department stores and mass merchandisers.

Major introductions in the past few years have included a line of Haggar wrinkle-free casual cotton pants; new lines of shirts, including Haggar wrinkle-free cotton shirts, to complement its casual product lines; and its line of boys' apparel. The company operates four retail outlet stores located in Dallas and Hillsboro, Tex., Branson, Mo. and Lancaster, Pa.

Important Developments

May '95—A portion of the roof of the company's main distribution center in Dallas, Texas, collapsed as a result of severe weather. Although HGGR maintains insurance, it could not fully assess the impact of this event on its business, operations, finances and future plans.

Capitalization

Long Term Debt: $68,787,000 (6/95).

Per Share Data ($)

(Year Ended Sep. 30)

	1994	1993	1992	1991	1990	1989
Tangible Bk. Val.	18.51	15.70	11.15	NA	NA	NA
Cash Flow	3.31	2.28	2.26	NA	NA	NA
Earnings	2.95	1.88	1.70	NA	NA	NA
Dividends	0.20	0.10	Nil	NA	NA	NA
Payout Ratio	7%	6%	Nil	NA	NA	NA
Prices - High	40½	25½	21½	NA	NA	NA
- Low	20½	15½	16½	NA	NA	NA
P/E Ratio - High	14	14	13	NA	NA	NA
- Low	7	8	10	NA	NA	NA

Income Statement Analysis (Million $)

	1994	%Chg	1993	%Chg	1992	%Chg	1991
Revs.	491	25%	394	3%	381	—	NA
Oper. Inc.	42.3	75%	24.2	NM	24.1	—	NA
Depr.	3.2	2%	3.1	-17%	3.7	—	NA
Int. Exp.	1.3	-16%	1.5	-62%	4.0	—	NA
Pretax Inc.	42.0	80%	23.3	19%	19.5	—	NA
Eff. Tax Rate	39%	—	36%	—	36%	—	NA
Net Inc.	25.7	71%	15.0	21%	12.4	—	NA

Balance Sheet & Other Fin. Data (Million $)

	1994	1993	1992	1991	1990	1989
Cash	2.6	17.9	0.4	NA	NA	NA
Curr. Assets	215	179	146	NA	NA	NA
Total Assets	257	206	170	NA	NA	NA
Curr. Liab.	84.3	67.4	49.3	NA	NA	NA
LT Debt	15.0	5.5	28.2	NA	NA	NA
Common Eqty.	158	133	93.0	NA	NA	NA
Total Cap.	173	139	121	NA	NA	NA
Cap. Exp.	15.4	6.5	NA	NA	NA	NA
Cash Flow	28.8	18.1	15.1	NA	NA	NA

Ratio Analysis

	1994	1993	1992	1991	1990	1989
Curr. Ratio	2.6	2.7	3.0	NA	NA	NA
% LT Debt of Cap.	8.7	3.9	23.2	NA	NA	NA
% Net Inc.of Revs.	5.2	3.8	3.3	NA	NA	NA
% Ret. on Assets	11.1	7.9	NA	NA	NA	NA
% Ret. on Equity	17.6	13.2	NA	NA	NA	NA

Dividend Data —Cash dividends have been paid since 1993.

Amt. of Div. $	Date Decl.	Ex-Div. Date	Stock of Record	Payment Date
0.050	Oct. 19	Oct. 25	Oct. 31	Nov. 14 '94
0.050	Jan. 18	Jan. 24	Jan. 30	Feb. 13 '95
0.050	Apr. 20	Apr. 26	May. 02	May. 16 '95
0.050	Jul. 19	Jul. 27	Jul. 31	Aug. 14 '95

Data as orig. reptd.; bef. results of disc. opers. and/or spec. items. Per share data adj. for stk. divs. as of ex-div. date. E-Estimated. NA-Not Available. NM-Not Meaningful. NR-Not Ranked.

Office—6113 Lemmon Ave., Dallas, TX 75209. **Tel**—(214) 352-8481. **Chrmn & CEO**—J. M. Haggar III. **Pres & COO**—F. D. Bracken. **Exec VP-Fin, CFO, Treas & Secy**—R. A. Beattie. **Investor Contact**—Carla Morgan (214) 956-4611. **Dirs**—R. A. Beattie, F. D. Bracken, N. E. Brinker, C. H. Cantu, R. F. Evans, E. R. Haggar, J. M. Haggar III, R. Heath, W. E. Vaughan III. **Tarnsfer Agent & Registrar**—Chemical Bank, NYC. **Incorporated** in Nevada in 1989. **Empl**-6,400. **S&P Analyst:** Maureen C. Carini

STANDARD & POOR'S

Handy & Harman

STOCK REPORTS

NYSE Symbol **HNH**
In S&P SmallCap 600

10-OCT-95 **Industry:** Metal

Summary: This company engages in the manufacture of precious metals products, automotive original equipment, and specialty wire and tubing.

Quantitative Evaluations

Outlook (1 Lowest—5 Highest)
• **NA**

Fair Value
• **NA**

Risk
• **Average**

Earn./Div. Rank
• **B-**

Technical Eval.
• **Bearish** since 7/95

Rel. Strength Rank (1 Lowest—99 Highest)
• **40**

Insider Activity
• **NA**

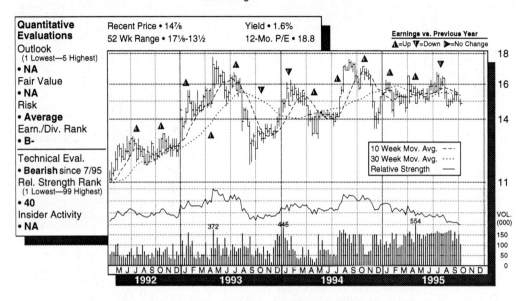

Recent Price • 14⅞ Yield • 1.6%
52 Wk Range • 17⅛-13½ 12-Mo. P/E • 18.8

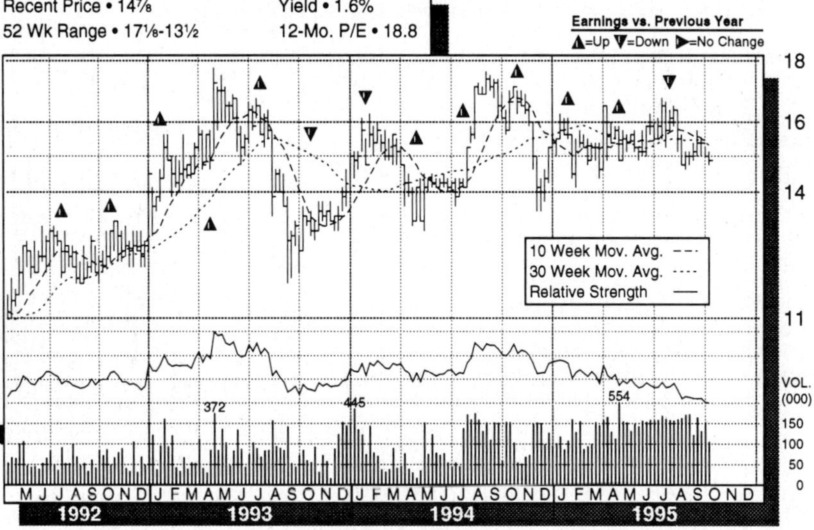

Business Profile - 10-OCT-95

HNH intends to continue to expand its profit base through acquisitions, as well as through selective investments in existing businesses. The company plans to widen its Sumco Inc. unit's involvement in precious metals plating for a variety of industries. Additionally, prospects for its new Denmark tubing facility are encouraging. In June 1995, the company said it planned to exit the karat gold fabricated product line in its East Providence, Rhode Island facility.

Operational Review - 10-OCT-95

Revenues in the first half of 1995 advanced modestly, year to year, as higher wire/tubing sales were offset by a weak precious metals segment and lower OEM volume. Profitability was hurt by a $6.0 million restructuring charge in the second quarter for the planned discontinuance of the karat gold fabricated product line and, following higher interest expense, net income dropped 57%.

Stock Performance - 06-OCT-95

In the past 30 trading days, HNH's shares have declined 0.83%, compared to a 4% rise in the S&P 500. Average trading volume for the past five days was 20,720 shares, compared with the 40-day moving average of 46,477 shares.

Key Stock Statistics

Dividend Rate/Share	0.24	Shareholders	2,300
Shs. outstg. (M)	14.1	Market cap. (B)	$0.212
Avg. daily vol. (M)	0.035	Inst. holdings	56%
Tang. Bk. Value/Share	6.06	Insider holdings	NA
Beta	1.34		

Value of $10,000 invested 5 years ago: $ 10,572

Fiscal Year Ending Dec. 31

	1995	% Change	1994	% Change	1993	% Change
Revenues (Million $)						
1Q	198.3	5%	188.7	20%	157.8	14%
2Q	196.0	-2%	199.7	23%	162.0	10%
3Q	—	—	194.7	20%	162.0	15%
4Q	—	—	198.2	12%	176.4	22%
Yr.	—	—	781.5	19%	658.3	15%
Income (Million $)						
1Q	5.19	17%	4.45	42%	3.13	11%
2Q	-1.12	NM	5.07	52%	3.33	4%
3Q	—	—	3.48	NM	0.21	-92%
4Q	—	—	3.51	57%	2.23	-23%
Yr.	—	—	16.51	86%	8.90	-24%
Earnings Per Share ($)						
1Q	0.37	16%	0.32	45%	0.22	10%
2Q	-0.08	NM	0.36	50%	0.24	4%
3Q	—	—	0.25	NM	0.02	-90%
4Q	—	—	0.25	56%	0.16	-24%
Yr.	—	—	1.18	84%	0.64	-24%

Next earnings report expected: early November

Handy & Harman

Business Summary - 10-OCT-95

Handy & Harman manufactures precious metals products and provides refining services; manufactures automotive original equipment (OEM); manufactures specialty wire and tubing; and manufactures other non-precious metal products. Contributions by industry segment in 1994:

	Revs.	Profits
Precious metals	56%	32%
Automotive (OEM)	23%	30%
Wire/tubing	19%	33%
Other metal businesses	2%	4%

Precious metals operations consist of products and refining activities. Products include wire (sterling and other alloys of silver used in the aerospace, electronics and appliance industries), rolled products (sterling and alloys of other precious metals used in the electrical, electronics, nuclear power, defense and aerospace industries) and powder products (precious metal powders and flakes used in electronic parts and powder metal contacts, batteries and conductive coatings). Refining operations involve recovering precious metals from waste and scrap, metal-bearing objects and high-grade mining concentrates and bullion.

Automotive OEM products--made from steel, stainless steel and other metals--include tubular products (air pipes, brake and fuel lines and components of fuel delivery systems) and control assemblies for automotive applications.

The company produces silver/tin alloy powders for use in dental applications, and silver/copper alloy powders for use in industrial brazing applications.

Wire and tubing products, made from nonprecious metals (stainless steel, nickel alloy and carbon and alloy steel), are used by the aircraft, petrochemical, automotive, appliance, refrigeration and instrumentation industries.

Other nonprecious metal products include plastic and steel fittings and connections, plastic pipe and nonferrous thermite welding powders.

In September 1994, the company acquired Sumco, Inc., a precision electroplating firm focusing on plating electronic connectors and connector stock for the automotive, telecommunications and computer industries. Sumco had sales of $22.5 million.

Important Developments

Jun. '95—The company recorded a $6.0 million restructuring charge in the second quarter of 1995, reflecting its planned exiting of the karat gold fabricated product line. Additionally, HNH incurred other charges of $3.5 million related to the continuing operation in its Fairfiled, Conn. facility, and $600,000 for the sale of its two automotive cable business units.

Capitalization

Long Term Debt: $112,000,000 (6/95).

Per Share Data ($) (Year Ended Dec. 31)

	1994	1993	1992	1991	1990	1989
Tangible Bk. Val.	5.90	6.45	5.94	5.41	8.14	7.99
Cash Flow	2.22	1.68	1.85	0.49	2.02	1.86
Earnings	1.18	0.64	0.84	-0.62	0.70	0.56
Dividends	0.20	0.20	0.20	0.43	0.66	0.66
Payout Ratio	17%	32%	24%	NM	95%	119%
Prices - High	$17\frac{5}{8}$	$17\frac{3}{4}$	$14\frac{5}{8}$	$15\frac{1}{4}$	$18\frac{7}{8}$	$21\frac{1}{2}$
- Low	13	$11\frac{3}{4}$	10	$9\frac{1}{4}$	$10\frac{3}{8}$	15
P/E Ratio - High	15	28	17	NM	27	38
- Low	11	18	12	NM	15	27

Income Statement Analysis (Million $)

	1994	%Chg	1993	%Chg	1992	%Chg	1991
Revs.	781	19%	658	15%	572	24%	462
Oper. Inc.	61.6	29%	47.6	-6%	50.7	26%	40.3
Depr.	14.6	NM	14.7	4%	14.2	-8%	15.5
Int. Exp.	16.0	3%	15.5	-5%	16.3	-27%	22.2
Pretax Inc.	28.3	86%	15.2	-20%	19.1	NM	-11.2
Eff. Tax Rate	42%	—	42%	—	39%	—	NM
Net Inc.	16.5	85%	8.9	-24%	11.7	NM	-8.7

Balance Sheet & Other Fin. Data (Million $)

	1994	1993	1992	1991	1990	1989
Cash	2.6	3.3	2.8	1.6	3.2	3.7
Curr. Assets	187	233	201	191	274	272
Total Assets	405	413	371	359	472	456
Curr. Liab.	154	121	92.0	96.0	222	209
LT Debt	132	189	186	181	114	115
Common Eqty.	106	92.0	85.0	77.0	118	116
Total Cap.	251	292	279	263	250	247
Cap. Exp.	18.6	15.0	14.4	12.7	16.0	24.0
Cash Flow	31.1	23.6	25.9	6.9	28.2	25.9

Ratio Analysis

	1994	1993	1992	1991	1990	1989
Curr. Ratio	1.2	1.9	2.2	2.0	1.2	1.3
% LT Debt of Cap.	52.4	64.7	66.8	69.0	45.6	46.6
% Net Inc.of Revs.	2.1	1.4	2.0	NM	1.7	1.2
% Ret. on Assets	4.0	2.3	3.2	NM	2.1	1.7
% Ret. on Equity	16.7	10.1	14.4	NM	8.3	6.6

Dividend Data —Dividends have been paid since 1905. A dividend reinvestment plan is available. A "poison pill" stock purchase rights plan was adopted in 1989.

Amt. of Div. $	Date Decl.	Ex-Div. Date	Stock of Record	Payment Date
0.050	Oct. 27	Nov. 08	Nov. 15	Dec. 01 '94
0.060	Jan. 26	Feb. 09	Feb. 15	Mar. 01 '95
0.060	Apr. 27	May. 09	May. 15	Jun. 01 '95
0.060	Jun. 28	Aug. 11	Aug. 15	Sep. 01 '95

Data as orig. reptd.; bef. results of disc. opers. and/or spec. items. Per share data adj. for stk. divs. as of ex-div. date. E-Estimated. NA-Not Available. NM-Not Meaningful. NR-Not Ranked.

Office—250 Park Ave., New York, NY 10177. **Tel**—(212) 661-2400. **Chrmn & CEO**—R. N. Daniel. **Pres & COO**—F. E. Grzelecki. **VP-Secy**—P. E. Dixon. **VP-Treas**—S. B. Mudd. **Dirs**—C. A. Abramson, R. E. Cornelia, R. N. Daniel, G. G. Garbacz, F. E. Grzelecki, G. M. Nichols, H. P. Sotos, E. J. Sussman. **Transfer Agent & Registrar**—Chemical Bank, NYC. **Incorporated** in New York in 1905 as successor to business founded in 1867. **Empl**-4,826. **S&P Analyst:** S.S.

STANDARD & POOR'S

STOCK REPORTS

Harmon Industries

NASDAQ Symbol **HRMN**

In S&P SmallCap 600

18-OCT-95 **Industry:** Rail Equipment

Summary: Harmon makes railroad crossing protection systems, signal control track circuits, centralized traffic control systems, and locomotive control and radio communication equipment.

Quantitative Evaluations

Outlook (1 Lowest—5 Highest) • **5-**

Fair Value • **19½**

Risk • **Average**

Earn./Div. Rank • **B**

Technical Eval. • **Bearish** since 9/95

Rel. Strength Rank (1 Lowest—99 Highest) • **15**

Insider Activity • **Neutral**

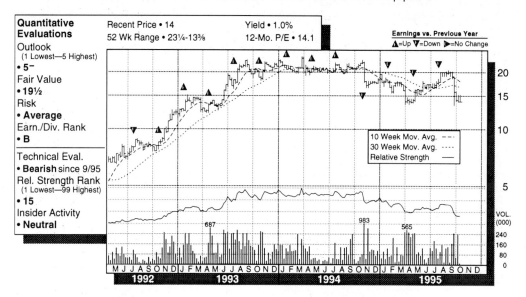

Recent Price • 14 | Yield • 1.0%

52 Wk Range • 23¼-13⅜ | 12-Mo. P/E • 14.1

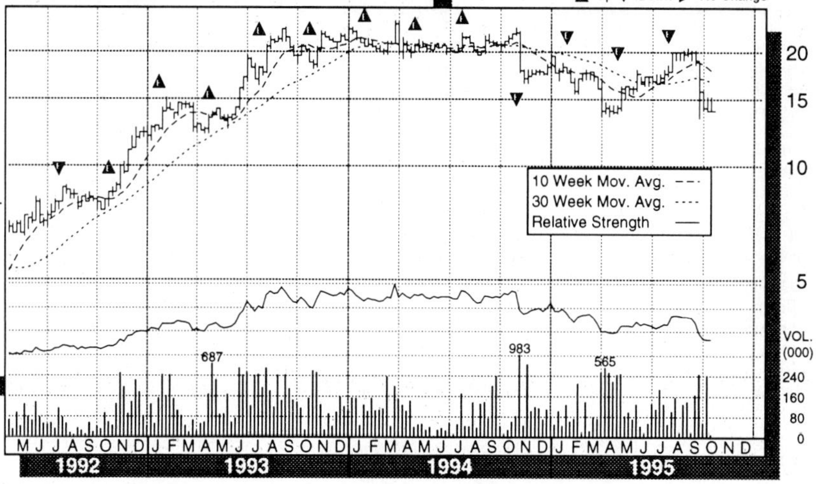

Business Profile - 18-OCT-95

This railroad equipment maker has expanded into the rail transit market since 1991. Through the end of 1994, it had received rail transit contracts in excess of $50 million. The acquisition of the transportation business of Servo Corp. is expected to considerably strengthen its position in train inspection systems. Serrmi Services Inc., acquired in early 1995, will help Harmon become an efficient supplier of highway crossing installation services.

Operational Review - 18-OCT-95

Revenues in the 1995 first half rose 7.2%, year to year, aided by acquisitions and gains for most product and service lines, with the exception of asset management services. However, operating income fell 37%, as results were restricted by acquisition-related costs, higher R&D and marketing expense, and computer system startup costs. Despite greater interest expense, the decline in net income was held to 28%. At June 30, 1995, backlog totaled $55.0 million, up from $36.5 million a year earlier.

Stock Performance - 13-OCT-95

In the past 30 trading days, HRMN's shares have declined 30%, compared to a 4% rise in the S&P 500. Average trading volume for the past five days was 1,720 shares, compared with the 40-day moving average of 27,615 shares.

Key Stock Statistics

Dividend Rate/Share	0.15	Shareholders	700
Shs. outstg. (M)	6.8	Market cap. (B)	$0.104
Avg. daily vol. (M)	0.026	Inst. holdings	48%
Tang. Bk. Value/Share	5.55	Insider holdings	NA
Beta	1.25		

Value of $10,000 invested 5 years ago: $ 20,985

Fiscal Year Ending Dec. 31

	1995	% Change	1994	% Change	1993	% Change
Revenues (Million $)						
1Q	29.42	14%	25.90	26%	20.62	24%
2Q	32.90	2%	32.17	41%	22.85	24%
3Q	—	—	29.45	9%	27.13	17%
4Q	—	—	32.19	12%	28.69	20%
Yr.	—	—	119.7	21%	99.3	21%
Income (Million $)						
1Q	0.71	-53%	1.50	53%	0.98	151%
2Q	2.10	-10%	2.33	35%	1.73	38%
3Q	—	—	2.15	-2%	2.20	28%
4Q	—	—	1.66	-16%	1.98	41%
Yr.	—	—	7.64	11%	6.88	50%
Earnings Per Share ($)						
1Q	0.10	-57%	0.23	35%	0.17	NM
2Q	0.30	-17%	0.36	29%	0.28	17%
3Q	—	—	0.33	-3%	0.34	3%
4Q	—	—	0.25	-17%	0.30	15%
Yr.	—	—	1.16	5%	1.11	28%

Next earnings report expected: early November

Harmon Industries

Business Summary - 18-OCT-95

Harmon Industries, Inc. is a leading global supplier of signal and control products to Class I, short line freight and mass transit railroads. It also provides customized asset management services through a warehousing and distribution business.

Class I and short line railroads are the company's core customers. Short lines carry freight to and from small cities and factory sidings to Class I railroads, which in turn carry freight across the U.S. and Canada. Harmon supplies freight haulers with a wide variety of patented signal and train control products, which, in many cases, have become the industry standard. As railroad purchasing trends favor control systems, the company plans to benefit from this growth area.

Harmon has been servicing a portion of the rail transit market for many years, supplying relatively mature systems with compatible components. It is a relative newcomer to rail transit systems. In 1991, it entered the new construction market with a $4.7 million award for control systems for St. Louis Metro Link. The transit market offers strong growth potential, as concerns over air quality and relief of urban traffic congestion grow.

In 1987, Consolidated Asset Management Co. (CAMCO) was formed to provide services to the railroad industry, including assembly and storage of materials for track repair projects. CAMCO provides railroads with a single source and a wide variety of commonly used parts, reducing the long lead times required by many manufacturers. It allows railroads to reduce operating costs, as they are able to eliminate certain parts warehouses and downsize repair and maintenance facilties, since materials and repairs can often be provided more quickly and at a lower cost by outside vendors.

In December 1994, the company acquired Servo Corp.'s transportation division, which makes hot box detector systems and monitoring components. In February 1995, it purchased the assets of Serrmi Services Inc., which provides signal design engineering, wiring and highway crossing installation services to Short Line and Class I freight railroads.

Important Developments

Oct. '95—The company said it had received orders totaling $2.7 million for railroad products and services.
Sep. '95—Harmon announced that it will not meet earnings expectations for the 1995 third quarter full year. It said problems integrating the transportation product line from the Servo acquisition, together with decreased orders, reflecting railroad industry consolidation, were the primary reasons for expected disappointing results.

Capitalization

Long Term Debt: $6,689,000 (6/95).

Per Share Data ($) (Year Ended Dec. 31)

	1994	1993	1992	1991	1990	1989
Tangible Bk. Val.	5.22	5.22	2.78	1.41	1.09	2.71
Cash Flow	1.56	1.45	1.23	0.97	1.40	0.94
Earnings	1.16	1.11	0.87	0.57	0.65	0.25
Dividends	0.15	Nil	Nil	Nil	0.06	0.13
Payout Ratio	13%	Nil	Nil	Nil	10%	50%
Prices - High	24¼	23¼	12⅝	7¼	7⅜	8⅞
- Low	16½	11⅝	3⅜	3½	3½	5¾
P/E Ratio - High	21	21	15	13	11	36
- Low	14	10	4	6	5	23

Income Statement Analysis (Million $)

	1994	%Chg	1993	%Chg	1992	%Chg	1991
Revs.	120	21%	99	21%	81.9	16%	70.9
Oper. Inc.	15.5	14%	13.6	33%	10.2	5%	9.7
Depr.	2.6	24%	2.1	10%	1.9	-2%	2.0
Int. Exp.	0.3	-40%	0.4	-67%	1.3	-39%	2.2
Pretax Inc.	12.7	14%	11.1	57%	7.1	54%	4.6
Eff. Tax Rate	40%	—	38%	—	35%	—	37%
Net Inc.	7.6	11%	6.9	50%	4.6	57%	2.9

Balance Sheet & Other Fin. Data (Million $)

	1994	1993	1992	1991	1990	1989
Cash	0.3	3.1	0.4	0.4	0.5	0.4
Curr. Assets	42.7	37.0	25.6	23.3	24.3	27.9
Total Assets	68.4	53.0	38.5	36.6	41.4	50.4
Curr. Liab.	21.1	16.2	14.8	13.7	16.4	13.4
LT Debt	0.7	0.4	4.9	11.9	17.2	19.9
Common Eqty.	43.1	33.1	15.2	7.4	5.7	14.8
Total Cap.	43.8	33.5	20.1	19.3	23.0	35.3
Cap. Exp.	3.2	3.6	2.2	1.1	2.2	5.9
Cash Flow	10.3	9.0	6.5	4.9	6.6	4.3

Ratio Analysis

	1994	1993	1992	1991	1990	1989
Curr. Ratio	2.0	2.3	1.7	1.7	1.5	2.1
% LT Debt of Cap.	1.7	1.3	24.4	61.8	75.0	56.4
% Net Inc.of Revs.	6.4	6.9	5.6	4.1	4.3	1.6
% Ret. on Assets	12.2	14.0	11.8	7.3	6.6	2.4
% Ret. on Equity	19.5	27.0	39.6	43.7	29.5	8.1

Dividend Data —Dividends, omitted in August 1990, were reintated in May 1994.

Amt. of Div. $	Date Decl.	Ex-Div. Date	Stock of Record	Payment Date
0.075	Nov. 23	Nov. 28	Nov. 30	Dec. 15 '94
0.075	May. 09	May. 24	May. 31	Jun. 15 '95

Data as orig. reptd.; bef. results of disc. opers. and/or spec. items. Per share data adj. for stk. divs. as of ex-div. date. E-Estimated. NA-Not Available. NM-Not Meaningful. NR-Not Ranked.

Office—1300 Jefferson Ct., Blue Springs, MO 64015. **Tel**—(816) 229-3345. **Chrmn**—R. E. Harmon. **Pres & CEO**—B. E. Olsson. **EVP-Fin, CFO, Treas, Secy & Investor Contact**—Charles M. Foudree. **Dirs**—T. F. Eagleton, B. M. Flohr, C. M. Foudree, R. L. Gray, R. E. Harmon, H. M. Kohn, D. W. List, G. E. Myers, B. E. Olsson, D. V. Rentz, J. C. Whittaker. **Transfer Agent & Registrar**—United Missouri Bank, Kansas City. **Incorporated** in Missouri in 1961. **Empl**-985. **S&P Analyst:** Robert E. Friedman

STANDARD & POOR'S

STOCK REPORTS

Hartmarx Corp.

NYSE Symbol **HMX**
In S&P SmallCap 600

27-SEP-95 **Industry:** Textiles

Summary: This company manufactures and markets men's and women's business, casual and golfing apparel under a number of leading brand names.

S&P Opinion: Accumulate (★★★★) Recent Price • 6¼ Yield • Nil
52 Wk Range • 6⅞-4¼ 12-Mo. P/E • 69.4

Quantitative Evaluations
Outlook (1 Lowest—5 Highest) • **1+**
Fair Value • **5⅜**
Risk • **Average**
Earn./Div. Rank • **B-**

Technical Eval. • **Bearish** since 9/95
Rel. Strength Rank (1 Lowest—99 Highest) • **49**
Insider Activity • **NA**

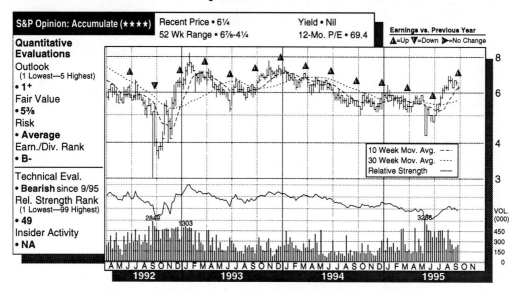

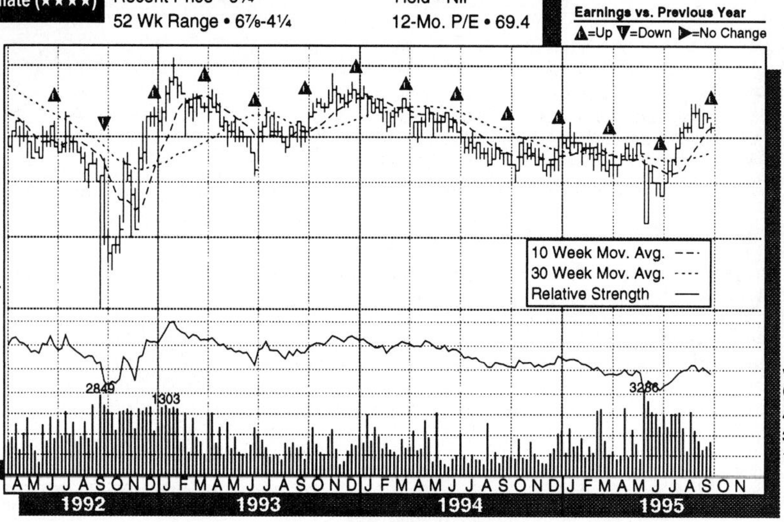

Overview - 27-SEP-95

Sales from ongoing businesses for fiscal 1995 should improve moderately from fiscal 1994's depressed level, as a result of stronger demand for men's formal and informal business clothing; the introduction of new apparel lines including suits carrying the Tommy Hilfiger, Perry Ellis, and Daniel Hechter names; increased share of golf clothes; higher sales at the Barrie Pace Ltd. catalog; and expansion overseas. Margins will benefit from expense reduction efforts at the manufacturing businesses, including factory consolidations, reduced overhead costs, and sourcing in Latin America. Profitability will be boosted by the absence of losses at the IWA division, due to the discontinuance of two unprofitable lines there. Earnings will benefit from lower interest costs.

Valuation - 27-SEP-95

After trending downward for most of 1995, these shares have rebounded somewhat. We attribute this stronger performance to favorable reactions to the divestiture of money-losing Kuppenheimers. We now feel this company is currently poised for growth. Through its restructuring efforts, HMX has gotten out of all of its money-losing businesses, and can now focus on strengthening its profitable, well-known branded apparel manufacturing businesses. The company has sizeable share in the markets it serves, and is particularly well-positioned in the fast-growing men's casual and golf apparel businesses. We recommend that investors accumulate this stock.

Key Stock Statistics

S&P EPS Est. 1995	0.50	Tang. Bk. Value/Share	3.33
P/E on S&P Est. 1995	12.5	Beta	1.52
S&P EPS Est. 1996	0.60	Shareholders	6,900
Dividend Rate/Share	Nil	Market cap. (B)	$0.204
Shs. outstg. (M)	32.7	Inst. holdings	45%
Avg. daily vol. (M)	0.049	Insider holdings	NA

Value of $10,000 invested 5 years ago: $ 3,751

Fiscal Year Ending Nov. 30

	1995	% Change	1994	% Change	1993	% Change
Revenues (Million $)						
1Q	171.5	-4%	177.9	-5%	187.0	-39%
2Q	135.0	-18%	164.0	-5%	171.9	-37%
3Q	—	—	196.1	4%	189.0	-28%
4Q	—	—	179.7	-2%	184.1	-13%
Yr.	—	—	717.7	-2%	732.0	-31%
Income (Million $)						
1Q	0.14	NM	-0.72	NM	-1.24	NM
2Q	-2.99	NM	-3.12	NM	-3.48	NM
3Q	—	—	3.52	84%	1.91	NM
4Q	—	—	20.34	125%	9.03	60%
Yr.	—	—	20.01	NM	6.22	NM
Earnings Per Share ($)						
1Q	Nil	—	-0.02	NM	-0.04	NM
2Q	-0.09	NM	-0.10	NM	-0.11	NM
3Q	E0.25	127%	0.11	83%	0.06	NM
4Q	E0.34	-46%	0.63	117%	0.29	32%
Yr.	E0.50	-19%	0.62	NM	0.20	NM

Next earnings report expected: late September

Hartmarx Corp.

Business Summary - 20-SEP-95

Hartmarx is a leading manufacturer of men's and women's apparel. In late 1992, HMX took steps to significantly downsize its money-losing retail operations (44% of fiscal 1992 sales), by selling its principal retail division, Hartmarx Specialty Stores Inc., which operated 200 stores. HMX also closed its Old Mill stores and 80 Kuppenheimer stores. In July 1995, Hartmarx sold its remaining Kuppenheimer stores. These transactions have enabled HMX to focus on its profitable apparel manufacturing businesses.

In fiscal 1994, Hartmarx's business consisted of three groups. The largest, the Men's Apparel group manufactures well-known, prestigious brands of men's tailored clothing, sportswear and slacks. Tailored clothing is produced through the Hart Schaffner & Marx, Hickey-Freeman and Intercontinental Branded Apparel businesses. Slacks and sportswear are produced mainly through the Trans-Apparel Group, Biltwell and Bobby Jones business units. This group also operates nine Sansabelt stores. The Womens Apparel group consists of Barrie Pace, a direct mail company that offers a wide range of apparel and accessories to the business and professional woman, and IWA, which designs and sources women's career apparel and sportswear for sale to department and specialty stores under owned and licensed brand names. The third group, Kuppenheimers, was sold in July 1995.

The company's merchandising strategy is to market a wide selection of men's tailored clothing and sportswear and women's career apparel and sportswear across a wide variety of fashion directions, price points and distribution channels. In fiscal 1994, tailored clothing represented approximately 61% of HMX's total sales, men's sportswear and slacks 31%, and women's apparel 8%.

Important Developments

Jul. '95—HMX sold its Kuppenheimer stores to Kupp Acquisition Corp. as part of its strategy to focus on its profitable apparel manufacturing business, reduce debt and increase equity. HMX received $12 million, plus a promissory note in the amount of $2.5 million. HMX will also be paid an additional $2.0 million over the next four years.

Jun. '95—HMX attributed its second quarter decline in sales from continuing operations to lower sales of moderately-priced private label tailored clothing which is being de-emphasized in favor of higher-margin branded products. Included in the net loss was a $3.7 million charge related to a settlement of licensing program disputes, which was partially offset by a $2.8 million gain on the sale of a plant.

Capitalization

Long Term Debt: $150,870,000 (5/95).

Per Share Data ($)

(Year Ended Nov. 30)

	1994	1993	1992	1991	1990	1989
Tangible Bk. Val.	3.95	3.41	2.72	11.32	14.60	18.37
Cash Flow	1.05	0.65	-7.54	-0.21	-1.33	2.48
Earnings	0.62	0.20	-8.59	-1.74	-3.11	0.89
Dividends	Nil	Nil	Nil	0.60	0.90	1.17
Payout Ratio	Nil	Nil	Nil	NM	NM	132%
Prices - High	7⅜	8¼	8⅝	13¼	19⅞	28⅛
- Low	5	5⅛	3	6⅞	5½	18¾
P/E Ratio - High	12	41	NM	NM	NM	32
- Low	8	26	NM	NM	NM	21

Income Statement Analysis (Million $)

	1994	%Chg	1993	%Chg	1992	%Chg	1991
Revs.	718	-2%	732	-31%	1,054	-13%	1,215
Oper. Inc.	38.1	2%	37.4	NM	2.5	NM	0.3
Depr.	13.8	-2%	14.1	-48%	26.9	-20%	33.8
Int. Exp.	21.2	-7%	22.9	9%	21.1	-11%	23.8
Pretax Inc.	11.0	83%	6.0	NM	-226	NM	-60.0
Eff. Tax Rate	NM	—	3.00%	—	NM	—	NM
Net Inc.	20.0	NM	6.0	NM	-219	NM	-38.0

Balance Sheet & Other Fin. Data (Million $)

	1994	1993	1992	1991	1990	1989
Cash	2.8	1.5	22.4	6.6	2.7	2.9
Curr. Assets	312	338	430	579	578	698
Total Assets	392	405	512	740	762	908
Curr. Liab.	97.0	89.0	193	347	243	277
LT Debt	167	207	249	105	227	271
Common Eqty.	128	109	70.0	287	293	360
Total Cap.	295	316	319	393	519	631
Cap. Exp.	7.1	6.0	9.5	15.2	16.1	52.3
Cash Flow	34.0	20.0	-192	-5.0	-26.0	48.0

Ratio Analysis

	1994	1993	1992	1991	1990	1989
Curr. Ratio	3.2	3.8	2.2	1.7	2.4	2.5
% LT Debt of Cap.	56.6	65.6	77.9	26.9	43.7	42.9
% Net Inc.of Revs.	2.8	0.8	NM	NM	NM	1.3
% Ret. on Assets	5.0	1.2	NM	NM	NM	2.1
% Ret. on Equity	16.7	6.4	NM	NM	NM	4.7

Dividend Data —The quarterly dividend was omitted on January 23, 1992. Prior to omission, dividends had been paid since 1939. A "poison pill" stock purchase rights plan was adopted in 1986.

Data as orig. reptd.; bef. results of disc. opers. and/or spec. items. Per share data adj. for stk. divs. as of ex-div. date. E-Estimated. NA-Not Available. NM-Not Meaningful. NR-Not Ranked.

Office—101 North Wacker Drive, Chicago, IL 60606. **Tel**—(312) 372-6300. **Chrmn & CEO**—E. O. Hand. **Pres**—H. B. Patel. **EVP-CFO**—G. R. Morgan. **EVP-Secy**—M. D. Allen. **VP-Treas & Investor Contact**—James E. Condon. **Dirs**—A. R. Abboud, L. Baldrige, J. A. Cole, R. F. Farley, E. O. Hand, D. P. Jacobs, M. L. Marsh, C. Marshall, C. K. Olson, T. M. Othman, H. B. Patel, S. L. Scott, S. F. Segnar. **Transfer Agents & Registrars**—The First National Bank of Chicago, Chicago, Ill.; First Chicago Trust Co. of New York, NYC. **Incorporated** in New York in 1911; reincorporated in Delaware in 1983. **Empl**-11,000. **S&P Analyst:** Elizabeth Vandeventer

STANDARD & POOR'S
STOCK REPORTS

Hauser Chemical Research

NASDAQ Symbol **HAUS**
In S&P SmallCap 600

24-SEP-95 **Industry:** Chemicals

Summary: This company produces natural flavor extracts for the food and beverage industry, natural compounds for pharmaceutical, cosmetic and veterinary uses, and secondary forest products.

Quantitative Evaluations
Outlook (1 Lowest—5 Highest) • **NA**
Fair Value • **NA**
Risk • **Average**
Earn./Div. Rank • **B**

Technical Eval. • **Bullish** since 6/95
Rel. Strength Rank (1 Lowest—99 Highest) • **48**
Insider Activity • **NA**

Recent Price • 5½
52 Wk Range • 6⅝-4¼
Yield • Nil
12-Mo. P/E • NM

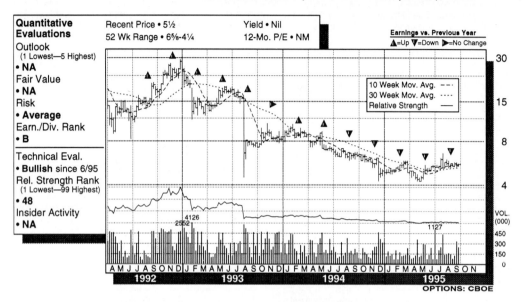

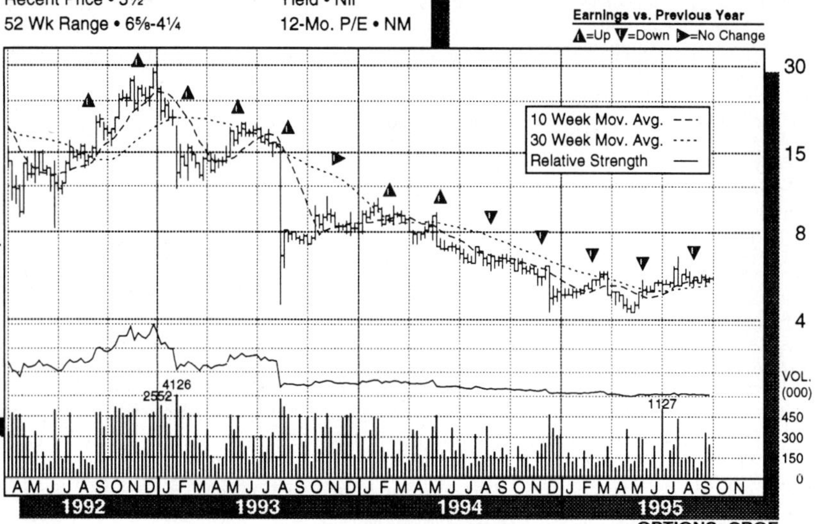

Business Profile - 24-SEP-95

Hauser has had to refocus operations after the paclitaxel supply contract with Bristol-Myers Squibb was terminated. The contract had provided Hauser with most of its revenues in the three years prior to fiscal 1995. To offset lost revenues, the company began supplying bulk paclitaxel to American Home Products. Hauser has shifted its efforts to other business areas, including its natural flavors unit and the sale of secondary forest products.

Operational Review - 24-SEP-95

Revenues in the three months ended July 31, 1995, dropped 22%, year to year, reflecting expiration of a supply contract with Bristol-Myers Squibb and lower sales of flavoring ingredients. Results were penalized by the lower volume, as well as by higher marketing and administration costs. A net loss of $1.8 million ($0.17 a share) contrasted with income of $70,042 ($0.01).

Stock Performance - 22-SEP-95

In the past 30 trading days, HAUS's shares have declined 1%, compared to a 5% rise in the S&P 500. Average trading volume for the past five days was 49,060 shares, compared with the 40-day moving average of 34,056 shares.

Key Stock Statistics

Dividend Rate/Share	Nil	Shareholders	900
Shs. outstg. (M)	10.5	Market cap. (B)	$0.059
Avg. daily vol. (M)	0.041	Inst. holdings	31%
Tang. Bk. Value/Share	7.34	Insider holdings	NA
Beta	2.52		

Value of $10,000 invested 5 years ago: NA

Fiscal Year Ending Apr. 30

	1996	% Change	1995	% Change	1994	% Change
Revenues (Million $)						
1Q	4.03	-22%	5.18	-77%	22.80	25%
2Q	—	—	6.72	-54%	14.46	-4%
3Q	—	—	5.61	-57%	13.04	NM
4Q	—	—	5.39	-47%	10.14	-22%
Yr.	—	—	22.90	-62%	60.38	2%
Income (Million $)						
1Q	-1.76	NM	0.07	-98%	3.15	—
2Q	—	—	0.90	-57%	2.07	6%
3Q	—	—	-1.96	NM	2.43	20%
4Q	—	—	-1.71	NM	2.67	38%
Yr.	—	—	-2.70	NM	10.32	27%
Earnings Per Share ($)						
1Q	-0.17	NM	0.01	-97%	0.30	43%
2Q	—	—	0.09	-55%	0.20	NM
3Q	—	—	-0.19	NM	0.23	21%
4Q	—	—	-0.16	NM	0.25	25%
Yr.	—	—	-0.26	NM	0.98	22%

Next earnings report expected: early November

STANDARD & POOR'S

Hauser Chemical Research

STOCK REPORTS

24-SEP-95

Business Summary - 24-SEP-95

Hauser Chemical Research, Inc. is a leader in the extraction and purification of specialty products from natural sources. Its proprietary technologies enable it to produce natural products, often at higher quality, yield and concentration and at lower cost than conventional procedures. These products are made for several major companies addressing a broad spectrum of markets, including pharmaceuticals, flavors, veterinary medicine and cosmetics.

Hauser began its transition to become a multi-product, multi-customer manufacturer of special products from natural resources in the fiscal year ended April 30, 1995. In the three years prior to fiscal 1995, susbstantially all of the company's revenues were derived from the sale of paclitaxel to Bristol-Myers Squibb Co.

In an effort to replace the business represented by the Bristol-Myers contract, a strategic alliance was consummated with American Home Products (AHP) in May 1994 to supply AHP with bulk paclitaxel. Separately, the company and AHP entered into a two-year R&D agreement to develop new products derived from naturally or semi-synthetically produced taxanes.

The company's Food Ingredients unit produces flavoring ingredients for Tastemaker, the world's fifth largest flavor producer. Hauser commercially produces herbal extracts such as hibiscus, rosehips, chicory and others for use in ready-to-drink beverages, yogurts, ethnic foods, teas and other natural food products.

Hauser's Food Additives business was established in fiscal 1995 to capitalize on the increasing number of non-flavor food ingredients emerging from the company's pipeline. Food additives such as preservatives, stabilizers and colorants are currently being formulated into products.

The Technical Services division provides interdisciplinary laboratory testing services, chemical engineering services and contract R&D.

Wholly owned Hauser Northwest Inc. collects yew bark in the Pacific Northwest. To expand this business into the collection and sale of secondary forest products, Ironwood Evergreens Inc. of Olympia, Wash., was acquired in May 1994.

Important Developments

Jul. '95—Hauser acquired the business of Herbert Shuster, Inc., an independent consumer products R&D firm and contract laboratory. Quincy, Mass.-based Shuster had gross revenues in 1994 of about $6.6 million. The purchase involved approximately $4 million in cash and has a performance-based earnout.

Capitalization

Long Term Debt: $204,490 (6/95), incl. $163,396 of cap. lease oblgs.

Per Share Data ($) (Year Ended Apr. 30)

	1995	1994	1993	1992	1991	1990
Tangible Bk. Val.	7.34	7.69	6.68	5.73	0.58	0.25
Cash Flow	0.07	1.42	1.17	0.38	0.15	0.02
Earnings	-0.26	0.98	0.80	0.31	0.08	-0.04
Dividends	Nil	Nil	Nil	Nil	Nil	Nil
Payout Ratio	Nil	Nil	Nil	Nil	Nil	Nil
Cal. Yrs.	1994	1993	1992	1991	1990	1989
Prices - High	10½	25¼	31	23½	2⅞	NA
- Low	4¼	4½	8¼	2⅛	1⅜	NA
P/E Ratio - High	NM	26	39	76	36	NM
- Low	NM	5	10	7	17	NM

Income Statement Analysis (Million $)

	1995	%Chg	1994	%Chg	1993	%Chg	1992
Revs.	22.9	-62%	60.4	2%	59.3	132%	25.6
Oper. Inc.	-2.8	NM	19.5	23%	15.9	NM	5.1
Depr.	3.4	-26%	4.6	23%	3.7	NM	0.7
Int. Exp.	0.0	—	Nil	—	0.0	-75%	0.0
Pretax Inc.	-4.4	NM	16.1	23%	13.1	162%	5.0
Eff. Tax Rate	NM	—	36%	—	38%	—	40%
Net Inc.	-2.7	NM	10.3	26%	8.1	169%	3.0

Balance Sheet & Other Fin. Data (Million $)

	1995	1994	1993	1992	1991	1990
Cash	24.7	23.2	12.6	18.8	0.8	Nil
Curr. Assets	39.4	39.6	27.7	29.1	5.6	2.1
Total Assets	82.6	84.6	73.4	45.6	8.1	3.4
Curr. Liab.	2.3	1.9	2.5	2.2	2.2	1.3
LT Debt	0.1	Nil	Nil	0.1	0.3	1.1
Common Eqty.	77.4	80.8	69.7	39.8	2.6	1.0
Total Cap.	80.3	82.6	70.9	43.4	5.9	2.1
Cap. Exp.	4.0	9.4	11.5	12.5	0.8	0.7
Cash Flow	0.7	14.9	11.9	3.8	0.8	0.1

Ratio Analysis

	1995	1994	1993	1992	1991	1990
Curr. Ratio	17.3	20.5	11.1	13.1	2.6	1.6
% LT Debt of Cap.	0.1	Nil	Nil	0.2	5.0	51.0
% Net Inc.of Revs.	NM	17.1	13.7	11.8	5.9	NM
% Ret. on Assets	NM	13.1	11.5	10.3	7.0	NM
% Ret. on Equity	NM	13.7	12.6	13.7	21.9	NM

Dividend Data —No cash dividends have been paid.

Data as orig. reptd.; bef. results of disc. opers. and/or spec. items. Per share data adj. for stk. divs. as of ex-div. date. E-Estimated. NA-Not Available. NM-Not Meaningful. NR-Not Ranked.

Office—5555 Airport Blvd., Boulder, CO 80301. **Tel**—(303) 443-4662. **Chrmn, Pres & CEO**—D. P. Stull. **CFO & Treas**—W. E. Paukert. **Secy**—G. L. Huckabee. **Dirs**—W. E. Coleman, S. J. Cristol, R. J. Daughenbaugh, R. L. Hauser, C. W. Roser, R. F. Saydah, H. V. Shuster, D. P. Stull, B. M. Tolbert. **Transfer Agent & Registrar**—American Securities Transfer Inc., Denver. **Incorporated** in Delaware in 1985. **Empl**-273. **S&P Analyst:** Thomas Tirney

STANDARD & POOR'S

STOCK REPORTS

Hayes Wheels International

NYSE Symbol **HAY**

In S&P SmallCap 600

06-SEP-95

Industry: Auto parts/equipment

Summary: Hayes manufactures original equipment automotive wheels, including cast and fabricated aluminum and fabricated steel wheels in the U.S. and Europe.

Quantitative Evaluations

Outlook
(1 Lowest—5 Highest)
• **NA**

Fair Value
• **NA**

Risk
• **Average**

Earn./Div. Rank
• **NR**

Technical Eval.
• **Bullish** since 6/95

Rel. Strength Rank
(1 Lowest—99 Highest)
• **73**

Insider Activity
• **NA**

Recent Price • 22 | Yield • 0.3%

52 Wk Range • 27¼-15¼ | 12-Mo. P/E • 12.8

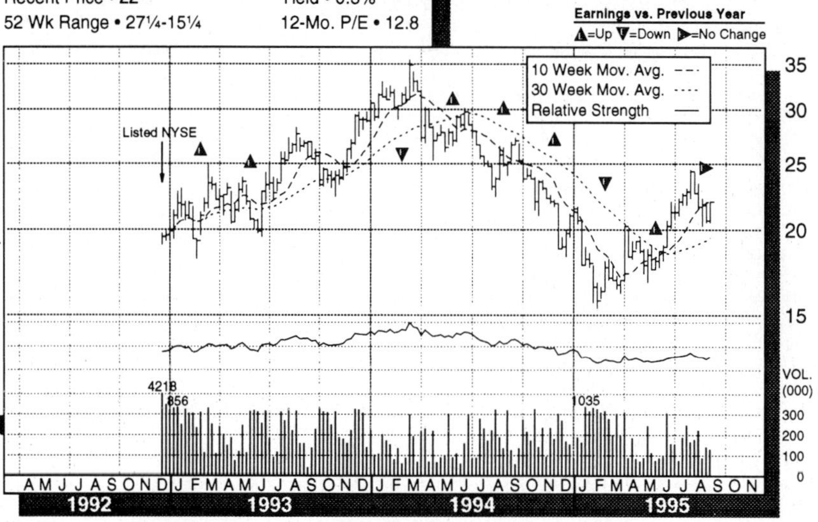

Business Profile - 06-SEP-95

HAY's growth continues to be driven by a shift in demand to more highly styled and expensive cast and fabricated aluminum wheels from traditional fabricated steel wheels. The company also seeks to expand its market position by introducing new designs and styles, as well as new manufacturing processes which permit greater creativity while lowering cost and lightening weight of the wheels.

Operational Review - 06-SEP-95

Sales for the six months ended July 31, 1995, advanced 21%, year to year, on a more favorable product mix, price increases in North America to pass through higher aluminum prices, and a jump in European volume. Hurt by soft unit sales in North America and higher interest expense, pretax income was flat. Aided by lower taxes, net income rose modestly. Despite the soft first half, HAY remains optimistic about the rest of 1995-96, due to important product launches over the next few quarters.

Stock Performance - 01-SEP-95

In the past 30 trading days, HAY's shares have declined 3%, compared to a 2% rise in the S&P 500. Average trading volume for the past five days was 25,380 shares, compared with the 40-day moving average of 33,408 shares.

Key Stock Statistics

Dividend Rate/Share	0.06	Shareholders	200
Shs. outstg. (M)	17.6	Market cap. (B)	$0.406
Avg. daily vol. (M)	0.027	Inst. holdings	48%
Tang. Bk. Value/Share	4.62	Insider holdings	NA
Beta	NA		

Value of $10,000 invested 5 years ago: NA

Fiscal Year Ending Jan. 31

	1996	% Change	1995	% Change	1994	% Change
Revenues (Million $)						
1Q	159.7	20%	133.0	19%	111.7	4%
2Q	151.4	21%	125.1	27%	98.80	-9%
3Q	—	—	140.3	31%	107.4	10%
4Q	—	—	139.2	26%	110.3	15%
Yr.	—	—	537.6	26%	428.2	5%
Income (Million $)						
1Q	8.30	5%	7.90	32%	6.00	—
2Q	7.20	NM	7.20	29%	5.60	—
3Q	—	—	7.90	49%	5.30	—
4Q	—	—	6.90	-10%	7.70	—
Yr.	—	—	29.90	22%	24.60	46%
Earnings Per Share ($)						
1Q	0.47	4%	0.45	32%	0.34	36%
2Q	0.41	NM	0.41	28%	0.32	—
3Q	—	—	0.39	30%	0.30	—
4Q	—	—	0.39	-11%	0.44	-38%
Yr.	—	—	1.70	21%	1.40	46%

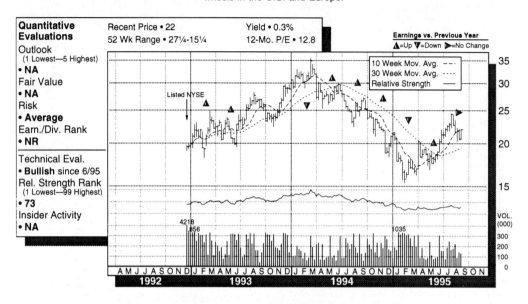

Next earnings report expected: late November

Hayes Wheels International

Business Summary - 06-SEP-95

Hayes Wheels International designs and manufactures wheels for the original equipment passenger car and light truck market. It is the largest cast aluminum wheel producer in Europe with a 15% market share and the second largest in North America with 23% of the market. HAY also has 23% of the North American fabricated steel wheel market.

Sales by geographic region in recent years were:

	1994-95	1993-94	1992-93
U.S.	88%	87%	80%
Europe	12%	13%	20%

Cast aluminum wheels (Western Wheel) accounted for 63% of sales in 1994-95, and fabricated steel and aluminum wheels for 37%. About 82% of the company's aluminum wheels were produced in the U.S., with the balance produced in Europe; all steel wheels were produced in the U.S. About 85% of Western Wheel's 1994-95 production was sold to General Motors, Ford and Chrysler, 4% to Mazda, Nissan, Honda and Isuzu in Japan, and 9% to Japanese transplants in the U.S. HAY owns 60% of Nippon Western Pacific, a Japanese company that provides sales and service support in the Japanese aluminum wheel market.

Fabricated wheel offerings were recently revamped with the addition of ultra-light weight fabricated aluminum wheels, new full-face steel wheel designs, clad cover technology including chrome skin wheels, and full-face modular wheels which combine a highly styled cast aluminum center with a fabricated aluminum rim. The new ultra-light fabricated aluminum wheels, which are 20% lighter than cast aluminum ones, are expected to account for $150 million in revenues by the 1998 model year. In 1994-95, General Motors, Ford and Chrysler accounted for 93% of fabricated steel wheel revenues.

HAY operates six major U.S. manufacturing plants, with a total of more than 2.0 million square feet of space. Three foreign plants with an aggregate of 500,000 square feet operate in Europe. HAY has a 45% interest in a Czech Republic joint venture and smaller joint venture interests in wheel producers in Venezuela, Italy and Kentucky.

Important Developments

Aug. '95—HAY said that the lower margins in the second quarter were due to extended summer shutdowns at automaker plants and delay in the ramp-up of production of the new Chrysler minivan. With production stabilizing, inventories now reduced, and key investments in place to break bottlenecks and improve efficiencies, HAY expected margins to improve in the second half.

Capitalization

Long Term Debt: $121,900,000 (7/95).

Per Share Data ($)

(Year Ended Jan. 31)

	1995	1994	1993	1992	1991	1990
Tangible Bk. Val.	5.37	3.85	NA	2.42	NA	NA
Cash Flow	3.07	2.45	NA	1.94	NA	NA
Earnings	1.70	1.40	0.96	0.56	NA	NA
Dividends	0.06	0.06	Nil	NA	NA	NA
Payout Ratio	4%	4%	Nil	NA	NA	NA
Cal. Yrs.	1994	1993	1992	1991	1990	1989
Prices - High	35½	30⅞	NA	NA	NA	NA
- Low	18¼	18⅛	NA	NA	NA	NA
P/E Ratio - High	21	22	NA	NA	NA	NA
- Low	11	13	NA	NA	NA	NA

Income Statement Analysis (Million $)

	1995	%Chg	1994	%Chg	1993	%Chg	1992
Revs.	538	26%	428	5%	409	3%	399
Oper. Inc.	86.5	20%	72.0	—	NA	—	55.1
Depr.	24.0	30%	18.5	—	NA	—	21.7
Int. Exp.	13.4	-1%	13.6	—	NA	—	14.4
Pretax Inc.	49.9	18%	42.2	—	NA	—	20.2
Eff. Tax Rate	40%	—	42%	—	NA	—	48%
Net Inc.	29.9	22%	24.6	46%	16.9	71%	9.9

Balance Sheet & Other Fin. Data (Million $)

	1995	1994	1993	1992	1991	1990
Cash	0.5	5.3	NA	Nil	NA	NA
Curr. Assets	158	114	NA	99	NA	NA
Total Assets	590	528	NA	489	NA	NA
Curr. Liab.	131	108	NA	119	NA	NA
LT Debt	111	103	NA	104	NA	NA
Common Eqty.	216	185	NA	172	NA	NA
Total Cap.	367	324	NA	324	NA	NA
Cap. Exp.	39.9	38.4	NA	NA	NA	NA
Cash Flow	53.9	43.1	NA	31.6	NA	NA

Ratio Analysis

	1995	1994	1993	1992	1991	1990
Curr. Ratio	1.2	1.1	NA	0.8	NA	NA
% LT Debt of Cap.	30.4	31.7	NA	32.1	NA	NA
% Net Inc.of Revs.	5.6	5.7	4.1	2.5	NA	NA
% Ret. on Assets	54.0	4.8	NA	NA	NA	NA
% Ret. on Equity	14.9	13.1	NA	NA	NA	NA

Dividend Data —Quarterly cash dividends were initiated in 1993.

Amt. of Div. $	Date Decl.	Ex-Div. Date	Stock of Record	Payment Date
0.015	Sep. 08	Sep. 12	Sep. 16	Oct. 03 '94
0.015	Dec. 09	Dec. 12	Dec. 16	Jan. 05 '95
0.015	Mar. 09	Mar. 13	Mar. 17	Apr. 03 '95
0.015	Jun. 09	Jun. 15	Jun. 19	Jul. 03 '95

Data as orig. reptd.; bef. results of disc. opers. and/or spec. items. Per share data adj. for stk. divs. as of ex-div. date. E-Estimated. NA-Not Available. NM-Not Meaningful. NR-Not Ranked.

Office—38481 Huron River Drive, Romulus, MI 48174. **Tel**—(313) 941-2000. **Chrmn**—J. E. Utley. **Pres & CEO**—R. Cucuz. **VP-Fin & CFO**—W. D. Showers. **VP & Secy**—D. M. Sandberg. **Investor Contact**—Dale Vermilya. **Dirs**—R. Cucuz, J. A. Gilroy, J. S. Rodewig, J. E. Utley, K. L. Way. **Transfer Agent & Registrar**—Chemical Mellon Shareholder Services, NYC. **Incorporated** in Delaware in 1987. **Empl**-3,070. **S&P Analyst:** Joshua M. Harari, CFA.

Heart Technology

NASDAQ Symbol **HRTT**
In S&P SmallCap 600

31-AUG-95

Industry: Medical equipment/ supply

Summary: This manufacturer of the Rotablator system, a device to remove plaque from blocked arteries, has agreed to be acquired by NYSE-listed Boston Scientific Corp.

Quantitative Evaluations

Outlook
(1 Lowest—5 Highest)
• **NA**
Fair Value
• **NA**
Risk
• **High**
Earn./Div. Rank
• **NR**

Technical Eval.
• **Bullish** since 12/94
Rel. Strength Rank
(1 Lowest—99 Highest)
• **95**
Insider Activity
• **Neutral**

Recent Price • 25⅞
52 Wk Range • 27⅜-15½
Yield • Nil
12-Mo. P/E • 26.7

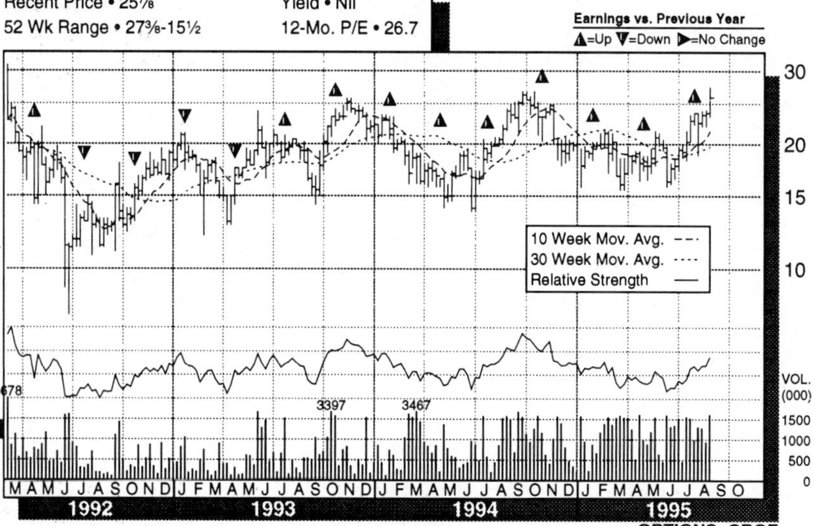

OPTIONS: CBOE

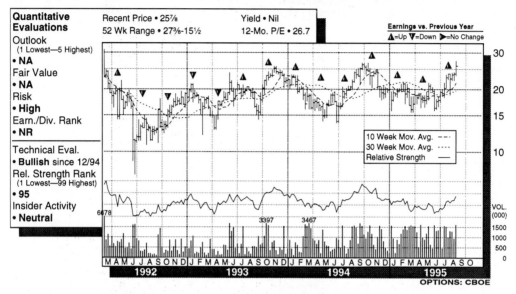

Business Profile - 31-AUG-95

This company has experienced rapid growth, spurred by strong demand for its Rotoblator system, which is used in coronary applications. Production capacity has been significantly increased to meet sales expectations, while ensuring adequate inventory. HRTT has also added sales staff and increased its physician training program. In August 1995, the company agreed to be acquired by NYSE-listedc Boston Scientific Corp. (BSX), with each HRTT common share to be exchanged for $27 in BSX common stock.

Operational Review - 31-AUG-95

Revenues soared in recent periods, spurred by strong demand for the Rotablator in the U.S. and abroad. Results also benefited from increased production capacity. Margins widened on the greater volume; operating income has surged. Results were somewhat restricted by higher taxes, in the absence of tax credits.

Stock Performance - 25-AUG-95

In the past 30 trading days, HRTT's shares have increased 28%, compared to a 0.04% rise in the S&P 500. Average trading volume for the past five days was 537,800 shares, compared with the 40-day moving average of 285,728 shares.

Key Stock Statistics

Dividend Rate/Share	Nil	Shareholders	600
Shs. outstg. (M)	17.6	Market cap. (B)	$0.474
Avg. daily vol. (M)	0.287	Inst. holdings	70%
Tang. Bk. Value/Share	5.31	Insider holdings	NA
Beta	NA		

Value of $10,000 invested 5 years ago: NA

Fiscal Year Ending Dec. 31

	1995	% Change	1994	% Change	1993	% Change
Revenues (Million $)						
1Q	17.52	60%	10.93	NM	1.32	-45%
2Q	19.43	38%	14.05	NM	3.75	40%
3Q	—	—	16.24	138%	6.81	NM
4Q	—	—	17.19	85%	9.28	NM
Yr.	—	—	58.39	176%	21.16	NM
Income (Million $)						
1Q	2.12	NM	0.66	NM	-1.68	NM
2Q	2.13	NM	-0.15	NM	-1.13	NM
3Q	—	—	3.25	NM	0.17	NM
4Q	—	—	10.25	NM	0.66	NM
Yr.	—	—	14.02	NM	-1.98	NM
Earnings Per Share ($)						
1Q	0.12	NM	0.04	NM	-0.12	NM
2Q	0.12	NM	-0.01	NM	-0.08	NM
3Q	—	—	0.18	NM	0.01	NM
4Q	—	—	0.56	NM	0.04	NM
Yr.	—	—	0.77	NM	-0.13	NM

Next earnings report expected: mid October

Heart Technology

Business Summary - 31-AUG-95

Heart Technology makes and markets devices to treat atherosclerosis, a progressive and degenerative disease in which cholesterol and other fatty materials are deposited on the walls of arterial blood vessels, forming diseased, inelastic tissue called plaque. The company's Rotablator system treats atherosclerosis through a patented rotational ablation method that mechanically removes arterial plaque and opens clogged arterial passages.

The Rotablator system consists of a disposable guide wire, a disposable catheter-advancer, a control console and a disposable wireClip guide wire gripping device. In rotational ablation, the slender, flexible disposable catheter is inserted into an artery and guided to the narrowed or blocked diseased area. At the end of the catheter is a football-shaped burr, the front half of which is coated with small diamond crystals. A drive mechanism, located outside the patient's body, rotates the burr at up to 190,000 rpm, removing microscopic particles of plaque that are eliminated through the body's circulatory system.

On the market in Canada, Europe and Australia since 1991, the Rotablator system was approved by the FDA in June 1993 for U.S. sale to remove plaque in blocked coronary arteries. As of December 1994, the company had agreements with distributors in 30 countries, and foreign sales equaled 16% of total sales in 1994.

As of December 1994, HRTT had trained over 700 physicians in 260 hospitals throughout the U.S. in the use of the Rotablator. As of December 1994, it was producing Rotablator systems at an annualized rate of 75,000 per year. The company is also developing a patented thrombectomy device designed to remove certain types of blood clots.

Important Developments

Aug. '95—The company agreed to be acquired by NYSE-listed Boston Scientific Corp. (BSX), with each HRTT common share to be exchanged for $27 of BSX common stock. The transaction is expected to be completed in the 1995 fourth quarter.

Jul. '95—HRTT received formal FDA approval of its new production facility. The facility allows the company to increase annual production capacity for the Rotoblator system from 75,000 to 200,000 units.

Capitalization

Long Term Debt: $11,038,000 (6/95).

Options: To purchase 1,098,031 shs. at $0.01 to $25.25 ea. (12/94).

Per Share Data ($) (Year Ended Dec. 31)

	1994	1993	1992	1991	1990	1989
Tangible Bk. Val.	5.06	4.20	4.60	4.94	NA	NA
Cash Flow	0.98	-0.01	-0.79	-0.25	-0.27	-0.41
Earnings	0.77	-0.13	-0.88	-0.34	-0.35	-0.50
Dividends	Nil	Nil	Nil	Nil	Nil	Nil
Payout Ratio	Nil	Nil	Nil	Nil	Nil	Nil
Prices - High	26¾	25¾	31	NA	NA	NA
- Low	13¾	12	7¾	NA	NA	NA
P/E Ratio - High	35	NM	NM	NA	NA	NA
- Low	18	NM	NM	NA	NA	NA

Income Statement Analysis (Million $)

	1994	%Chg	1993	%Chg	1992	%Chg	1991
Revs.	58.4	175%	21.2	NM	5.3	-15%	6.2
Oper. Inc.	12.0	NM	-2.4	NM	-6.2	NM	-2.7
Depr.	3.8	114%	1.8	50%	1.2	33%	0.9
Int. Exp.	0.1	—	Nil	—	0.1	-55%	0.1
Pretax Inc.	7.4	NM	-2.0	NM	-12.0	NM	-3.4
Eff. Tax Rate	NM	—	NM	—	NM	—	Nil
Net Inc.	14.0	NM	-2.0	NM	-12.0	NM	-3.4

Balance Sheet & Other Fin. Data (Million $)

	1994	1993	1992	1991	1990	1989
Cash	42.8	46.0	60.6	2.5	0.7	NA
Curr. Assets	68.5	56.4	66.2	10.9	3.2	NA
Total Assets	109	73.6	72.5	16.1	9.0	NA
Curr. Liab.	7.3	4.3	2.7	1.9	0.3	NA
LT Debt	13.0	Nil	Nil	0.6	Nil	NA
Common Eqty.	88.6	69.3	69.8	13.7	8.8	NA
Total Cap.	102	69.3	69.8	14.3	8.8	NA
Cap. Exp.	22.5	13.0	2.1	0.4	0.2	1.4
Cash Flow	17.8	-0.2	-10.8	-2.5	-2.5	-3.5

Ratio Analysis

	1994	1993	1992	1991	1990	1989
Curr. Ratio	9.4	13.1	24.3	5.8	11.3	NA
% LT Debt of Cap.	12.8	Nil	Nil	4.0	Nil	NA
% Net Inc.of Revs.	24.0	NM	NM	NM	NM	NM
% Ret. on Assets	14.9	NM	NM	NM	NM	NA
% Ret. on Equity	17.2	NM	NM	NM	NM	NA

Dividend Data —No cash dividends have been paid, and none is expected in the foreseeable future.

Data as orig. reptd.; bef. results of disc. opers. and/or spec. items. Per share data adj. for stk. divs. as of ex-div. date. E-Estimated. NA-Not Available. NM-Not Meaningful. NR-Not Ranked.

Office—17425 Northeast Union Hill Road, Redmond, WA 98052. **Tel**—(206) 869-6160. **Chrmn, Pres & CEO**—D. C. Auth. **VP-Fin, CFO, Treas & Investor Contact**—William L. Scott. **Dirs**—D. C. Auth, M. Buchbinder, D. J. Evans, C. R. Larkin, Jr., L. C. Pell, J. E. Warjone, G. M. Winn. **Transfer Agent & Registrar**—Chemical Trust Co. of California, SF. **Incorporated** in Delaware in 1989. **Empl**-430. **S&P Analyst:** Philip J. Birbara

Hecla Mining

NYSE Symbol **HL**
In S&P SmallCap 600

14-SEP-95 **Industry:** Mining/Diversified

Summary: This company produces gold, silver lead and zinc from properties in the U.S. and Mexico. HL also produces kaolin, ball clay and other industrial minerals.

S&P Opinion: Hold (★★★)

Recent Price • 12¼
52 Wk Range • 13½-8⅝
Yield • Nil
12-Mo. P/E • NM

Quantitative Evaluations

Outlook
(1 Lowest—5 Highest)
• NA

Fair Value
• NA

Risk
• Average

Earn./Div. Rank
• C

Technical Eval.
• Bearish since 5/93

Rel. Strength Rank
(1 Lowest—99 Highest)
• 73

Insider Activity
• NA

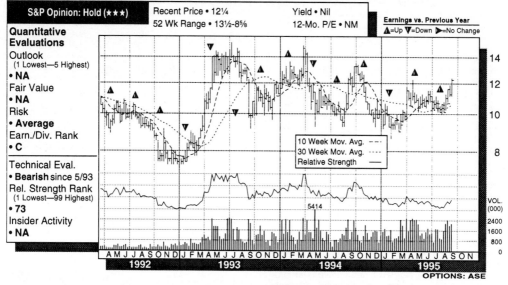

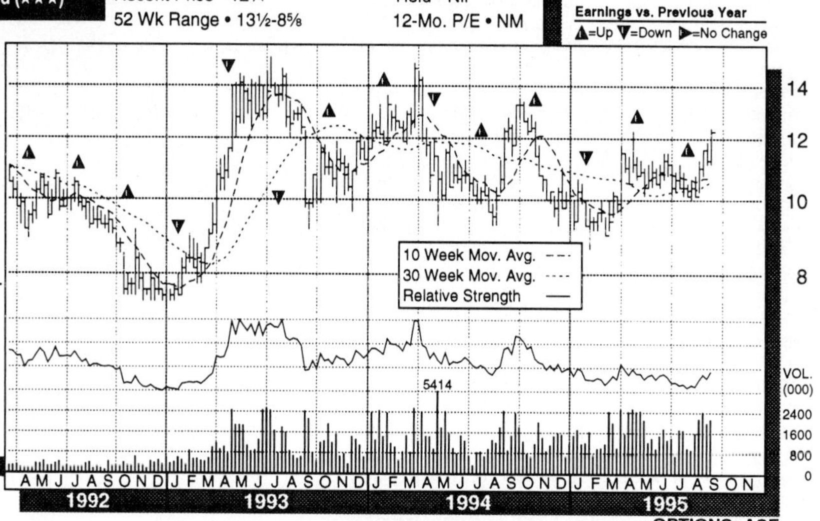

OPTIONS: ASE

Overview - 14-SEP-95

Gold volumes should increase sharply in 1995, primarily reflecting the full-year production from the new Grouse Creek and La Choya mines and the acquisition of the American Girl mine in March 1994. Offsetting will be reduced contributions from the Republic mine, which closed in February. Silver production should increase sharply, reflecting the start up of Grouse Creek and resumption of production at the Lucky Friday mine which was shut for three months in late 1994 following an ore-conveyance mishap. While silver production costs will fall, gold production costs are expected to increase, primarily reflecting startup costs associated with Grouse Creek. While prices for gold and silver may be flat, lead and zinc prices should advance, year to year. The loss will narrow, reflecting the absence of 1994's charge.

Valuation - 14-SEP-95

Shares of this diversified mining concern staged a partial recovery in 1995, largely tracking the movement in silver prices. Though HL derives less than 10% of its revenues from silver, it has significant silver reserves, reflecting a 30% stake in the idle Greens Creek property in Alaska. That mine is expected to be redeveloped and resume production in 1997. HL also has a development agreement with War Eagle Mining on a significant silver deposit in Mexico. Nevertheless, with inflation subdued, we see little significant upside for precious metals and anticipate continued small losses for HL into 1996.

Key Stock Statistics

S&P EPS Est. 1995	-0.10	Tang. Bk. Value/Share	3.34
P/E on S&P Est. 1995	NM	Beta	0.06
Dividend Rate/Share	Nil	Shareholders	13,200
Shs. outstg. (M)	48.2	Market cap. (B)	$0.585
Avg. daily vol. (M)	0.479	Inst. holdings	41%
		Insider holdings	NA

Value of $10,000 invested 5 years ago: $ 8,801

Fiscal Year Ending Dec. 31

	1995	% Change	1994	% Change	1993	% Change
Revenues (Million $)						
1Q	35.71	36%	26.34	26%	20.87	-29%
2Q	42.24	11%	38.00	65%	23.09	-14%
3Q	—	—	35.28	81%	19.54	-25%
4Q	—	—	29.08	58%	18.35	NM
Yr.	—	—	128.8	57%	81.85	-19%
Income (Million $)						
1Q	-2.46	NM	-5.65	NM	-4.77	NM
2Q	2.24	NM	0.70	NM	-2.01	NM
3Q	—	—	0.82	NM	-1.13	NM
4Q	—	—	-20.47	NM	-3.82	NM
Yr.	—	—	-23.78	NM	-11.74	NM
Earnings Per Share ($)						
1Q	-0.09	NM	-0.19	NM	-0.15	NM
2Q	0.01	NM	-0.03	NM	-0.06	NM
3Q	E0.01	NM	-0.03	NM	-0.09	NM
4Q	E-0.03	NM	-0.47	NM	-0.17	NM
Yr.	E-0.10	NM	-0.74	NM	-0.48	NM

Next earnings report expected: early November

Hecla Mining

Business Summary - 14-SEP-95

Hecla produces gold, silver lead and zinc from properties in the U.S. and Mexico and kaolin clay and other industrial minerals. Contributions to gross profits (in millions $) by business line::

	1994	1993
Gold	$7.1	$4.0
Silver	-4.6	-9.3
Industrial minerals	7.3	5.0
Specialty metals	Nil	0.5

The La Choya mine (100%-owned) in Mexico, which commenced operations in February 1994, produced 47,861 oz. of gold and 6,019 oz. of silver in 1994. Grouse Creek (80%-owned), located in Idaho, commenced production in December 1994. It produced 2,093 oz. of gold and 8,763 oz. of silver in 1994. The Republic mine, located in Washington was closed in February 1995. In 1994 Republic produced 39,085 oz. of gold and 283,326 oz. of silver. The American Girl mine (47%-owned), located in California was acquired in March 1994. American Girl produced 30,624 oz. of gold and 18,366 oz. of silver in 1994. The Cactus mine (75%-owned), located in California, will wind down operations in 1995. In 1994 Cactus produced 7,610 oz. of gold and 19,555 oz. of silver. The Lucky Friday mine in Idaho produced 1,306,884 oz. of gold, 13,214 tons of lead, 2,431 tons of zinc and nominal amounts of gold and copper in 1994.

Total gold production in 1994 was 127,878 oz. at an average cash cost of $273/oz., compared with 95,907 oz. in 1993 at $229/oz. Silver production in 1994 was 1,642,913 oz. at an average cash cost of $5.81/oz., compared with 2,992,499 oz. in 1993 at $5.45/oz. Proven and probable reserves at 1994 year-end aggregated 2.1 million oz. of gold, 75.9 million oz. of silver, 185,558 tons of lead and 351,124 tons of zinc.

HL produces ball clay, kaolin and sodium feldspar, three of the four ingredients needed to produce ceramic products. HL also processes bark and scoria used for landscaping.

Important Developments

Aug. '95—HL entered into an agreement with Santa Fe Pacific Gold Corp. (GLD) to explore and develop HL's Golden Eagle deposit in Washington. GLD can earn a 70% share in the property, which contains an estimated 1.1 million oz. of gold, by investing $7.5 million over a three-year period. In June HL and War Eagle Mining agreed to a joint venture whereby HL would earn 60% in War's La Fortuna silver/gold property (Mexico) by spending $5 million over four years. La Fortuna is reported to contain 1.6 million oz. of gold and 376 million oz. of silver.

Capitalization

Long Term Debt: $23,057,000 (6/95).
$3.50 Cum. Preferred Stock: 2,300,000 shs. ($0.25 par); ea. conv. into 3.2154 com. shs.

Per Share Data ($)

(Year Ended Dec. 31)

	1994	1993	1992	1991	1990	1989
Tangible Bk. Val.	3.34	3.56	3.60	4.95	4.95	4.79
Cash Flow	-0.39	-0.11	-1.14	0.17	0.84	-0.17
Earnings	-0.74	-0.48	-1.59	-0.51	0.19	-0.83
Dividends	Nil	Nil	Nil	Nil	0.05	0.05
Payout Ratio	Nil	Nil	Nil	Nil	26%	NM
Prices - High	15	15¼	12¼	12⅝	16⅜	16⅛
- Low	9¼	7⅜	7¼	6⅝	6⅝	11½
P/E Ratio - High	NM	NM	NM	NM	86	NM
- Low	NM	NM	NM	NM	35	NM

Income Statement Analysis (Million $)

	1994	%Chg	1993	%Chg	1992	%Chg	1991
Revs.	129	57%	82.0	-19%	101	-14%	118
Oper. Inc.	-3.3	NM	0.4	NM	-28.5	NM	10.1
Depr.	14.8	21%	12.2	-12%	13.9	-32%	20.5
Int. Exp.	2.6	-48%	5.0	-27%	6.9	-1%	7.0
Pretax Inc.	-24.2	NM	-12.7	NM	-49.6	NM	-18.5
Eff. Tax Rate	NM	—	NM	—	NM	—	NM
Net Inc.	-23.8	NM	-11.7	NM	-49.2	NM	-15.4

Balance Sheet & Other Fin. Data (Million $)

	1994	1993	1992	1991	1990	1989
Cash	7.3	65.4	3.3	5.6	16.4	15.5
Curr. Assets	51.3	97.2	33.0	46.9	48.4	49.2
Total Assets	335	333	222	258	232	222
Curr. Liab.	23.5	19.6	12.7	12.6	11.7	14.4
LT Debt	2.0	49.5	70.4	76.9	70.2	65.0
Common Eqty.	161	123	114	150	134	129
Total Cap.	280	290	186	232	210	198
Cap. Exp.	66.6	58.7	23.2	19.5	29.9	40.6
Cash Flow	-17.1	-3.6	-35.3	5.1	22.7	-4.5

Ratio Analysis

	1994	1993	1992	1991	1990	1989
Curr. Ratio	2.2	5.0	2.6	3.7	4.1	3.4
% LT Debt of Cap.	0.7	17.1	37.9	33.2	33.4	32.8
% Net Inc.of Revs.	NM	NM	NM	NM	3.9	NM
% Ret. on Assets	NM	NM	NM	NM	2.3	NM
% Ret. on Equity	NM	NM	NM	NM	3.9	NM

Dividend Data —Dividends were omitted in November 1991.

Data as orig. reptd.; bef. results of disc. opers. and/or spec. items. Per share data adj. for stk. divs. as of ex-div. date. E-Estimated. NA-Not Available. NM-Not Meaningful. NR-Not Ranked.

Office—6500 Mineral Drive, Coeur d'Alene, ID 83814-8788. **Tel**—(208) 769-4100. **Chrmn, Pres & CEO**—A. Brown. **VP & Secy**—M. B. White. **VP-Fin & Treas**—J. P. Stilwell. **VP-Investor Contact**—W. Bill Booth. **Dirs**—A. Brown, J. E. Clute, J. Coors, Jr., L. O. Erdahl, W. A. Griffith, C. L. McAlpine, J. E. Ordonez, R. J. Stoehr. **Transfer Agent & Registrar**—American Stock Transfer & Trust, NYC. **Incorporated** in Wash. in 1898; reincorporated in Delaware in 1983. **Empl**-1,204. **S&P Analyst:** Stephen R. Klein

Helene Curtis Industries

STANDARD & POOR'S

STOCK REPORTS

NYSE Symbol **HC**

In S&P SmallCap 600

27-AUG-95

Industry: Cosmetics/Toiletries

Summary: This company is a leading maker of hair and skin care products and antiperspirants, marketed under the Suave, Salon Selectives, Finesse, Vibrance and Degree brand names.

Quantitative Evaluations

Outlook (1 Lowest—5 Highest)
• **4-**

Fair Value
• **30**

Risk
• **Average**

Earn./Div. Rank
• **B+**

Technical Eval.
• **Bullish** since 7/95

Rel. Strength Rank (1 Lowest—99 Highest)
• **27**

Insider Activity
• **Neutral**

Recent Price • 29¾ | Yield • 1.1%

52 Wk Range • 36⅜-27¾ | 12-Mo. P/E • 15.7

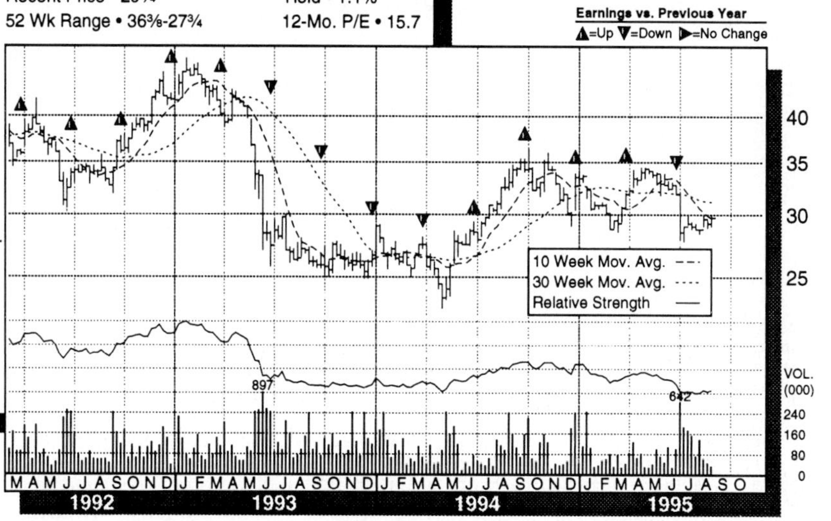

Business Profile - 24-AUG-95

HC's growth strategy involves the continued support of its brands worldwide through the creation of new and innovative products and by leveraging the equity in its existing brands. The Suave Baby Care line, introduced in June 1994, has been progressing steadily toward its goal of 5% market share in its first full year. The company's Degree antiperspirant/deodorant brand continues to see solid growth in international markets including Canada, Australia, New Zealand and Scandinavia.

Operational Review - 27-AUG-95

Domestic net sales edged up 4.0%, year to year, in the first quarter of 1995-96, reflecting contributions from the Suave Baby Care line, as well as continued growth in the antiperspirant/deodorant and skin care categories. Hair care sales were flat. International net sales slid 2.0%, primarily reflecting lower sales in Japan and the U.K. Net income fell sharply as a less profitable sales mix was only partially offset by higher sales and lower advertising and promotion expenses.

Stock Performance - 25-AUG-95

In the past 30 trading days, HC's shares have increased 2%, compared to a 0.04% rise in the S&P 500. Average trading volume for the past five days was 6,200 shares, compared with the 40-day moving average of 21,756 shares.

Key Stock Statistics

Dividend Rate/Share	0.32	Shareholders	1,500
Shs. outstg. (M)	9.9	Market cap. (B)	$0.294
Avg. daily vol. (M)	0.014	Inst. holdings	41%
Tang. Bk. Value/Share	22.33	Insider holdings	NA
Beta	0.75		

Value of $10,000 invested 5 years ago: $ 12,460

Fiscal Year Ending Feb. 28

	1996	% Change	1995	% Change	1994	% Change
Revenues (Million $)						
1Q	270.9	2%	265.7	9%	243.4	NM
2Q	—	—	352.5	4%	338.1	5%
3Q	—	—	282.4	6%	266.9	NM
4Q	—	—	365.0	8%	338.7	1%
Yr.	—	—	1,266	7%	1,187	2%
Income (Million $)						
1Q	191.0	NM	1.44	73%	0.83	-67%
2Q	—	—	6.60	56%	4.24	-48%
3Q	—	—	3.36	21%	2.78	-33%
4Q	—	—	7.77	20%	6.45	-11%
Yr.	—	—	19.17	34%	14.29	-35%
Earnings Per Share ($)						
1Q	0.02	-87%	0.15	67%	0.09	-65%
2Q	—	—	0.70	59%	0.44	-49%
3Q	—	—	0.35	17%	0.30	-32%
4Q	—	—	0.82	21%	0.68	-11%
Yr.	—	—	2.02	34%	1.51	-35%

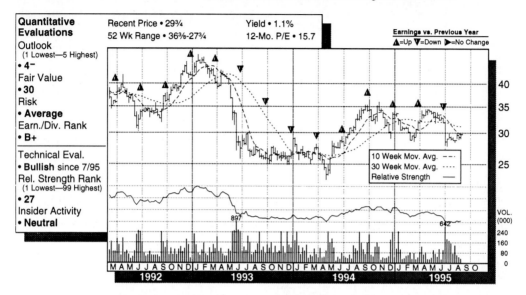

Next earnings report expected: late September

Helene Curtis Industries

Business Summary - 27-AUG-95

Helene Curtis Industries, Inc. develops, manufactures and markets personal care products consisting primarily of consumer brandname hair and skin care products, antiperspirants and deodorants. The company is one of the leading sellers of hair care products in the U.S. it also makes professional hair care products and salon appliances.

The Consumer Products division markets a wide variety of hair care products to consumers under the Suave, Finesse, Salon Selectives and Vibrance brand names. It also markets skin care products and antiperspirants under the Suave name and the Degree line of antiperspirants.

Suave products are targeted to consumers who desire a quality product priced below premium-priced lines. The company sells Suave shampoo, conditioner, styling aids, skin care, facial care and antiperspirant products for this price-value segment of the market. In terms of units sold, Suave is both the best-selling shampoo and best-selling conditioner in the U.S. In August 1994, HC initiated shipments of the Suave Baby Care line, which includes baby shampoos, powders, wipes, a baby oil, lotion and baby bath.

Salon Selectives shampoos, conditioners and styling aids (the third largest brand of hair care products in the U.S.) are marketed to consumers interested in purchasing items that were traditionally available only in beauty salons and that can be customized to their hair and lifestyle needs. Finesse is marketed as a premium-priced line of hair care products and includes shampoo, conditioner, hair spray, gel and mousse. The Vibrance line is targeted toward consumers who desire healthy-looking hair.

The Professional division develops and markets a wide range of permanent-wave and other hair care products for use in beauty salons and for resale to consumers through salons. Brand names include: Quantum, Naturelle and Hair Specifics hair care products, and ISO, Catio Therm, Post Impressions, One Better, Impact, Even Heat, Fine Solutions and Luxuriance permanent waves.

HC sells its products in more than 100 countries through wholly owned subsidiaries, licensees and distributors. Operations in Japan accounted for 22% of sales and 18% of operating profits in 1994-95, while other international areas accounted for 14% of sales, but incurred operating losses of $5.8 million.

Important Developments

Jul. '95—HC said it will reintroduce its Vibrance brand in the U.S. and launch a Helene Curtis Organic Care line in Canada. These product lines contain organic ingredients and are designed to meet emerging consumer demand for organic, healthy hair care products.

Capitalization

Long Term Debt: $141,751,000 (5/95).
Class B Common Stock: 3,048,029 shs. ($0.50 par).

Per Share Data ($) (Year Ended Feb. 28)

	1995	1994	1993	1992	1991	1990
Tangible Bk. Val.	22.33	20.19	18.95	17.01	15.36	15.22
Cash Flow	5.29	3.73	4.67	3.73	2.02	2.82
Earnings	2.02	1.51	2.33	2.04	0.70	1.81
Dividends	0.24	0.24	0.24	0.20	0.20	0.17
Payout Ratio	12%	16%	10%	10%	30%	10%
Cal. Yrs.	1994	1993	1992	1991	1990	1989
Prices - High	36⅜	47⅜	45½	43¾	28	35⅛
- Low	22¾	24⅞	30¼	23⅞	17½	19¼
P/E Ratio - High	18	31	20	21	40	19
- Low	11	16	13	12	25	11

Income Statement Analysis (Million $)

	1995	%Chg	1994	%Chg	1993	%Chg	1992
Revs.	1,266	7%	1,187	2%	1,168	15%	1,020
Oper. Inc.	76.1	35%	56.2	-20%	70.5	14%	61.9
Depr.	31.0	48%	21.0	-6%	22.3	39%	16.0
Int. Exp.	8.9	17%	7.6	-3%	7.8	-24%	10.3
Pretax Inc.	36.2	32%	27.5	-32%	40.5	14%	35.6
Eff. Tax Rate	47%	—	48%	—	45%	—	46%
Net Inc.	19.2	34%	14.3	-35%	22.1	15%	19.2

Balance Sheet & Other Fin. Data (Million $)

	1995	1994	1993	1992	1991	1990
Cash	5.1	2.8	7.6	9.5	2.3	6.1
Curr. Assets	406	368	378	331	290	246
Total Assets	647	612	600	526	467	398
Curr. Liab.	254	217	226	193	174	124
LT Debt	137	161	154	146	126	109
Common Eqty.	220	199	186	166	149	147
Total Cap.	369	376	356	319	281	264
Cap. Exp.	27.0	45.0	35.4	35.6	32.3	49.3
Cash Flow	50.2	35.3	44.4	35.2	18.9	26.3

Ratio Analysis

	1995	1994	1993	1992	1991	1990
Curr. Ratio	1.6	1.7	1.7	1.7	1.7	2.0
% LT Debt of Cap.	37.2	42.9	43.3	45.9	44.9	41.2
% Net Inc.of Revs.	1.5	1.2	1.9	1.9	0.7	2.3
% Ret. on Assets	3.0	2.4	3.9	3.9	1.5	4.6
% Ret. on Equity	9.1	7.4	12.5	12.2	4.4	12.1

Dividend Data —Dividends were placed on a quarterly basis in 1989.

Amt. of Div. $	Date Decl.	Ex-Div. Date	Stock of Record	Payment Date
0.060	Jul. 12	Aug. 08	Aug. 12	Aug. 26 '94
0.060	Oct. 17	Nov. 04	Nov. 10	Nov. 25 '94
0.060	Jan. 10	Jan. 31	Feb. 06	Feb. 20 '95
0.080	Apr. 25	May. 08	May. 12	May. 26 '95
0.080	Jul. 11	Aug. 09	Aug. 11	Aug. 25 '95

Data as orig. reptd.; bef. results of disc. opers. and/or spec. items. Per share data adj. for stk. divs. as of ex-div. date. E-Estimated. NA-Not Available. NM-Not Meaningful. NR-Not Ranked.

Office—325 North Wells St., Chicago, IL 60610. **Tel**—(312) 661-0222. **Chrmn**—G. S. Gidwitz. **Vice Chrmn**—J. L. Gidwitz. **Pres & CEO**—R. J. Gidwitz. **EVP & COO**—M. Goldman. **VP & CFO**—L. A. Gyenes. **Treas**—A. A. Schneider. **VP & Secy**—R. A. Wentz. **Investor Contact**—Diane Falanga. **Dirs**—M. L. Burman, F. W. Considine, C. G. Cooper, G. S. Gidwitz, J. L. Gidwitz, R. J. Gidwitz, M. Goldman, A. J. Smith, G. P. Smith, J. C. Stetson. **Transfer Agent & Registrar**—Harris Trust & Savings Bank, Chicago. **Incorporated** in Illinois in 1928; reincorporated in Delaware in 1984. **Empl**-3,400. **S&P Analyst:** Maureen C. Carini

Hi-LO Automotive

NYSE Symbol **HLO**
In S&P SmallCap 600

02-NOV-95 **Industry:** Retail Stores

Summary: This company operates more than 190 automotive aftermarket parts stores in Texas, Louisiana and California that sell to retail and commercial customers.

S&P Opinion: Avoid (★★)

Recent Price • 5½
52 Wk Range • 11¾-5⅝
Yield • Nil
12-Mo. P/E • 12.8

Quantitative Evaluations
Outlook
(1 Lowest—5 Highest)
• 5
Fair Value
• 7¾
Risk
• Average
Earn./Div. Rank
• NR

Technical Eval.
• Bullish since 8/95
Rel. Strength Rank
(1 Lowest—99 Highest)
• 5
Insider Activity
• Neutral

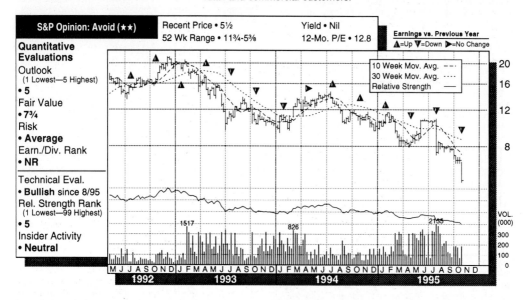

Overview - 31-OCT-95

The failure of the acquisition bid by Chief Auto Parts in July 1995 poses a problem for HLO unless it is purchased by another suitor in the near future. Same-store sales should be down for the year due to lack of interest from do-it-yourself customers who would rather shop at larger and more aggressive competitors such as AutoZone and Pep Boys. Despite the company's efforts to lower distribution costs by upgrading and expanding its Houston distribution center in 1994, we expect intense competitive pricing to take a toll on operating margins over the course of 1995. Together with continued high levels of start-up and remodeling costs, the pricing pressures will result in lower net income in 1995.

Valuation - 02-NOV-95

Our avoid recommendation on HLO reflects concern over the company's gloomy earnings outlook for 1995 and the longer term outlook for increased competition from larger and stronger participants in the automotive aftermarket. The increased focus on HLO's traditional do-it-yourself and commercial customers by larger players like AutoZone and Pep Boys will result in intense competitive pricing pressures that will offset efforts to materially boost earnings. In this environment, we think the stock will continue to underperform.

Key Stock Statistics

S&P EPS Est. 1995	0.40	Tang. Bk. Value/Share	10.57
P/E on S&P Est. 1995	13.8	Beta	NA
S&P EPS Est. 1996	0.50	Shareholders	NA
Dividend Rate/Share	Nil	Market cap. (B)	$0.063
Shs. outstg. (M)	10.7	Inst. holdings	57%
Avg. daily vol. (M)	0.039	Insider holdings	NA

Value of $10,000 invested 5 years ago: NA

Fiscal Year Ending Dec. 31

	1995	% Change	1994	% Change	1993	% Change
Revenues (Million $)						
1Q	60.20	15%	52.37	16%	45.23	11%
2Q	71.00	16%	61.12	18%	51.80	3%
3Q	72.20	15%	62.68	7%	58.50	14%
4Q	—	—	59.20	19%	49.72	11%
Yr.	—	—	235.4	15%	205.2	10%
Income (Million $)						
1Q	0.70	-59%	1.70	6%	1.61	12%
2Q	1.56	-48%	3.00	58%	1.90	-30%
3Q	0.64	-77%	2.77	26%	2.20	-17%
4Q	—	—	1.68	58%	1.06	-43%
Yr.	—	—	9.13	36%	6.71	-23%
Earnings Per Share ($)						
1Q	0.06	-63%	0.16	NM	0.16	7%
2Q	0.15	-46%	0.28	56%	0.18	-36%
3Q	0.06	-77%	0.26	30%	0.20	-26%
4Q	E0.13	-19%	0.16	60%	0.10	-47%
Yr.	E0.40	-53%	0.85	33%	0.64	-28%

Next earnings report expected: late January

Hi-LO Automotive

Business Summary - 02-NOV-95

Hi-LO Automotive sells automotive aftermarket parts and accessories for domestic and imported cars and light trucks to "do-it-yourself" (DIY) consumers and commercial auto repair shops. At 1994 year end, HLO had 178 stores, with 72 in the Houston metropolitan area, 31 in the Dallas/Fort Worth area, 67 in other parts of Texas and Louisiana, and eight in Southern California.

Products sold include "hard parts" such as engine and transmission parts, chassis parts, brake parts, batteries, shock absorbers and struts, mufflers and other exhaust system parts, filters, and high performance parts; and accessories such as tools and hardware, seat covers, floor mats, gauges, mirrors and car radios and speakers. It also sells maintenance products such as motor oil, antifreeze, polish, paints and cleaners, and oil and fuel additives. HLO's stores stock between 19,000 and 30,000 stock keeping units (SKUs). The stores are supplied by a Houston distribution center, which stocks approximately 75,000 SKUs.

HLO aggressively prices merchandise with discounts from manufacturers' suggested list prices, volume discounts to commercial customers and promotions. HLO has a "meet or beat any price" policy.

About 67% of sales were to the DIY segment and 33% to commercial customers in 1994. Since 1989, HLO has focused on expanding commercial sales. The program includes a commercial manager at each store and a commercial sales force. Stores generally deliver commercial orders within 60 minutes.

HLO's business is seasonal, primarily due to the impact of weather on sales. Weather extremes tend to enhance sales by causing a higher incidence of parts failure and higher sales of seasonal items. Rain, however, tends to cause deferral of elective service. Sales and profits are normally highest in the second and third quarters of the year.

Important Developments

Oct. '95—Same-store sales in the first nine months of 1995 declined 2.5%, year to year. During the period, HLO opened eight new stores -- one in Austin, one in Fort Worth, one in Dallas, two in San Antonio, and three elsewhere in Texas. HLO had 194 stores at the end of October 1995.

Jul. '95—Chief Auto Parts Inc. advised Hi-LO that it would not proceed with the acquisition of the company because it did not believe it could meet the conditions of its acquisition finance facility.

Capitalization

Long Term Debt: $44,017,000 (9/95).

Per Share Data ($) (Year Ended Dec. 31)

	1994	1993	1992	1991	1990	1989
Tangible Bk. Val.	10.36	9.51	7.96	7.04	-5.65	-10.80
Cash Flow	1.43	1.11	1.40	1.29	1.44	1.21
Earnings	0.85	0.64	0.89	0.80	0.77	0.62
Dividends	Nil	Nil	Nil	Nil	NA	NA
Payout Ratio	Nil	Nil	Nil	Nil	NA	NA
Prices - High	$14\frac{5}{8}$	$20\frac{3}{4}$	$21\frac{1}{2}$	$15\frac{1}{4}$	NA	NA
- Low	$9\frac{1}{4}$	$9\frac{1}{2}$	13	$9\frac{3}{8}$	NA	NA
P/E Ratio - High	17	32	24	19	NA	NA
- Low	11	15	15	12	NA	NA

Income Statement Analysis (Million $)

	1994	%Chg	1993	%Chg	1992	%Chg	1991
Revs.	235	15%	205	10%	187	20%	156
Oper. Inc.	23.8	30%	18.3	-19%	22.7	10%	20.7
Depr.	6.3	26%	5.0	-2%	5.1	21%	4.2
Int. Exp.	2.2	22%	1.8	-40%	3.0	-36%	4.7
Pretax Inc.	14.4	35%	10.7	-21%	13.6	25%	10.9
Eff. Tax Rate	36%	—	37%	—	37%	—	37%
Net Inc.	9.1	36%	6.7	-23%	8.7	26%	6.9

Balance Sheet & Other Fin. Data (Million $)

	1994	1993	1992	1991	1990	1989
Cash	1.0	1.7	1.3	3.2	2.2	2.0
Curr. Assets	97.1	74.9	71.1	60.8	54.1	53.1
Total Assets	186	155	140	123	116	114
Curr. Liab.	24.9	20.7	19.7	19.6	25.9	25.1
LT Debt	43.4	28.4	39.7	30.5	56.4	63.9
Common Eqty.	111	102	77.1	67.8	27.1	21.0
Total Cap.	155	134	120	102	88.0	88.0
Cap. Exp.	22.0	19.2	12.9	5.6	5.4	5.0
Cash Flow	15.4	11.7	13.7	11.1	9.5	7.7

Ratio Analysis

	1994	1993	1992	1991	1990	1989
Curr. Ratio	3.9	3.6	3.6	3.1	2.1	2.1
% LT Debt of Cap.	28.1	21.2	33.1	29.9	64.0	72.5
% Net Inc.of Revs.	3.9	3.3	4.6	4.4	3.5	3.6
% Ret. on Assets	5.4	4.3	6.6	2.1	4.4	3.9
% Ret. on Equity	8.6	7.2	11.9	10.3	20.8	20.9

Dividend Data —No cash dividends have been paid. HLO is retaining its earnings for operation and expansion of its business.

Data as orig. reptd.; bef. results of disc. opers. and/or spec. items. Per share data adj. for stk. divs. as of ex-div. date. E-Estimated. NA-Not Available. NM-Not Meaningful. NR-Not Ranked.

Office—2575 West Bellfort, Houston, TX 77054. **Tel**—(713) 663-6700. **Chrmn & Pres**—T. M. Young. **VP-CFO & Investor Contact**—Gary D. Walther. **VP-Secy**—K. G. Hutchins. **Dirs**—R. C. Adkerson, R. Q. Armstrong, C. P. Durkin Jr., E. J. Lowrey, E. T. Story Jr., T. M. Young. **Transfer Agent & Registrar**—Chemical Shareholder Services Group, Dallas. **Incorporated** in Delaware in 1987. **Empl**-3,246. **S&P Analyst:** Philip D. Wohl

STANDARD & POOR'S

Hilb, Rogal and Hamilton

STOCK REPORTS

NYSE Symbol **HRH**
In S&P SmallCap 600

14-NOV-95 **Industry:** Insurance

Summary: This company places insurance (principally property and casualty insurance) with insurance carriers and underwriters on behalf of its clients.

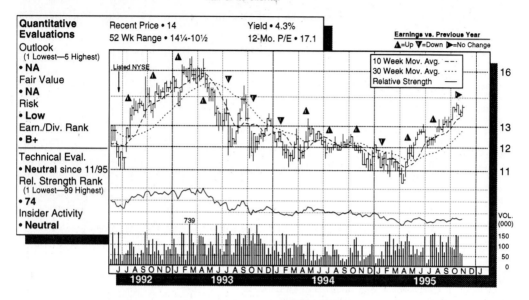

Quantitative Evaluations
Outlook
(1 Lowest—5 Highest)
• **NA**
Fair Value
• **NA**
Risk
• **Low**
Earn./Div. Rank
• **B+**

Technical Eval.
• **Neutral** since 11/95
Rel. Strength Rank
(1 Lowest—99 Highest)
• **74**
Insider Activity
• **Neutral**

Recent Price • 14
52 Wk Range • 14¼-10½
Yield • 4.3%
12-Mo. P/E • 17.1

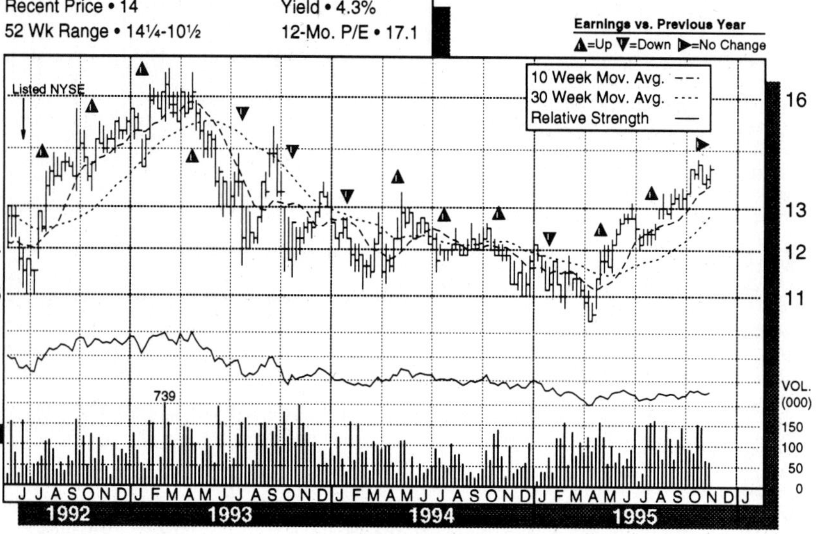

Business Profile - 14-NOV-95

HRH has grown rapidly by acquiring independent agencies, and plans further aggressive expansion. The 1994 sale of two third-party administrators, as well as agency offices in Hartford, Memphis and San Diego, allowed the company to pursue acquisitions in the first nine months of 1995. HRH, which is facing fierce price competition in its markets, has focused on selling unprofitable businesses, providing broader support and more specialized services, and improving operational efficiency.

Operational Review - 14-NOV-95

Commissions and fees in the nine months ended September 30, 1995, rose 14% from those of the year-earlier period, as restated, reflecting higher commissions from acquisitions of new insurance agencies. Operating expenses increased, and with higher compensation costs, despite reduced interest expense and a lower effective tax rate, the gain in net income was held to 5.0%, to $10,627,237 ($0.73 a share, on fewer shares), from $10,123,698 ($0.68).

Stock Performance - 10-NOV-95

In the past 30 trading days, HRH's shares have increased 5%, compared to a 1% rise in the S&P 500. Average trading volume for the past five days was 12,000 shares, compared with the 40-day moving average of 20,995 shares.

Key Stock Statistics

Dividend Rate/Share	0.60	Shareholders	800
Shs. outstg. (M)	14.4	Market cap. (B)	$0.201
Avg. daily vol. (M)	0.021	Inst. holdings	38%
Tang. Bk. Value/Share	1.18	Insider holdings	NA
Beta	0.51		

Value of $10,000 invested 5 years ago: $ 9,190

Fiscal Year Ending Dec. 31

	1995	% Change	1994	% Change	1993	% Change
Revenues (Million $)						
1Q	39.36	NM	39.33	6%	37.02	9%
2Q	36.57	4%	35.19	7%	32.82	7%
3Q	36.39	7%	34.13	5%	32.39	7%
4Q	—	—	32.16	-2%	32.73	7%
Yr.	—	—	140.8	4%	134.9	7%
Income (Million $)						
1Q	4.95	5%	4.73	27%	3.73	24%
2Q	3.31	13%	2.92	75%	1.67	-10%
3Q	2.39	-3%	2.47	50%	1.65	-17%
4Q	—	—	1.27	-8%	1.38	-10%
Yr.	—	—	11.39	35%	8.42	NM
Earnings Per Share ($)						
1Q	0.34	6%	0.32	10%	0.29	16%
2Q	0.23	15%	0.20	67%	0.12	-25%
3Q	0.17	NM	0.17	42%	0.12	-29%
4Q	—	—	0.09	-10%	0.10	-23%
Yr.	—	—	0.77	26%	0.61	-14%

Next earnings report expected: mid February

Hilb, Rogal and Hamilton

Business Summary - 14-NOV-95

Hilb, Rogal and Hamilton, through a rapidly growing network of wholly owned insurance agencies, places insurance, including property, casualty, marine, aviation and employee benefits, with insurance carriers and underwriters on behalf of its clients. Its agencies operate 55 offices in 17 states and the District of Columbia. The company was formed in 1982 to acquire the existing business of Insurance Management Corp., which had been in business for 13 years. Revenues in recent years were derived as follows:

	1994	1993	1992
Commissions & fees	94%	97%	98%
Investment income & other	6%	3%	2%

HRH derives income primarily from the sale of insurance products to clients, generally in the form of commissions paid by insurance carriers with which clients' insurance is placed. The company acts as an agent in soliciting, negotiating and effecting contracts of insurance through insurance companies and occasionally as a broker in procuring contracts of insurance through insurance on behalf of insureds.

The company has grown principally by acquiring independent agencies with significant local market share in small to medium-size metropolitan areas. Since 1984, it has acquired more than 131 independent agencies. Its growth strategy emphasizes acquisitions of established independent agencies staffed by local professionals, and centralization of certain administrative functions. HRH emphasizes local customer service by experienced personnel with established community relationships. It expects to continue to add qualified agencies in new and existing markets.

HRH has also established direct access to certain foreign insurance markets without the need to share commissions with excess and surplus lines brokers. This allows the company to enhance revenues from insurance products written by foreign insurers, and to provide a broader array of insurance products to clients.

Important Developments

Nov. '95—The company said that thus far in 1995, it had acquired 12 insurance agencies and other books of business for $13.44 million in purchase accounting transactions. Pro forma EPS for the nine months ended September 30, 1995, were $0.70.

Capitalization

Long Term Debt: $8,843,045 (9/95).

Per Share Data ($)

(Year Ended Dec. 31)

	1994	1993	1992	1991	1990	1989
Tangible Bk. Val.	1.21	1.05	-0.72	-0.71	-1.10	-1.17
Cash Flow	1.40	1.29	1.48	1.37	1.40	1.55
Earnings	0.77	0.61	0.71	0.57	0.65	0.76
Dividends	0.50	0.45	0.41	0.37	0.30	0.19
Payout Ratio	65%	74%	58%	65%	47%	25%
Prices - High	13⅜	16⅞	15⅝	17½	19	20⅝
- Low	11	11⅜	11	11¼	11¼	10¾
P/E Ratio - High	17	28	22	31	29	27
- Low	14	19	15	20	17	14

Income Statement Analysis (Million $)

	1994	%Chg	1993	%Chg	1992	%Chg	1991
Revs.	141	4%	135	7%	126	10%	115
Oper. Inc.	29.4	20%	24.4	NM	24.5	16%	21.2
Depr.	9.3	-2%	9.5	3%	9.2	5%	8.8
Int. Exp.	0.8	-34%	1.2	-26%	1.7	-20%	2.1
Pretax Inc.	18.8	42%	13.2	NM	13.1	37%	9.6
Eff. Tax Rate	39%	—	36%	—	36%	—	35%
Net Inc.	11.4	36%	8.4	NM	8.4	35%	6.2

Balance Sheet & Other Fin. Data (Million $)

	1994	1993	1992	1991	1990	1989
Cash	35.7	12.1	26.6	23.2	23.7	24.4
Curr. Assets	84.9	81.1	76.9	72.2	73.5	66.0
Total Assets	1.6	156	139	132	133	113
Curr. Liab.	87.1	81.9	85.2	77.5	79.0	63.8
LT Debt	3.2	7.0	13.0	14.7	18.1	22.3
Common Eqty.	66.4	64.3	38.8	37.1	33.7	25.6
Total Cap.	69.6	71.3	53.8	51.8	51.8	48.5
Cap. Exp.	2.2	3.0	2.4	2.2	2.9	6.7
Cash Flow	20.7	17.9	17.6	15.0	13.3	11.8

Ratio Analysis

	1994	1993	1992	1991	1990	1989
Curr. Ratio	1.0	1.0	0.9	0.9	0.9	1.0
% LT Debt of Cap.	4.6	9.9	24.2	28.4	34.9	46.1
% Net Inc.of Revs.	8.1	6.2	6.7	5.4	6.3	7.4
% Ret. on Assets	7.1	5.5	5.9	4.4	4.4	4.9
% Ret. on Equity	17.4	16.5	21.2	16.5	18.5	21.8

Dividend Data —Dividends were initiated in 1987. Recent payments were:

Amt. of Div. $	Date Decl.	Ex-Div. Date	Stock of Record	Payment Date
0.140	Nov. 02	Dec. 09	Dec. 15	Dec. 30 '94
0.140	Feb. 08	Mar. 13	Mar. 17	Mar. 31 '95
0.140	May. 03	Jun. 13	Jun. 15	Jun. 30 '95
0.140	Aug. 01	Sep. 13	Sep. 16	Sep. 30 '95
0.150	Nov. 08	Dec. 13	Dec. 15	Dec. 29 '95

Data as orig. reptd.; bef. results of disc. opers. and/or spec. items. Per share data adj. for stk. divs. as of ex-div. date. E-Estimated. NA-Not Available. NM-Not Meaningful. NR-Not Ranked.

Office—4235 Innslake Drive, P. O. Box 1220, Glen Allen, VA 23060-1220. **Tel**—(804) 747-6500. **Fax**—(804) 747-6046. **Chrmn & CEO**—R. H. Hilb. **Pres. & COO**—A. L. Rogal. **SVP-Fin & CFO**—T. J. Korman. **SVP, Secy & Investor Contact**—Diane F. Fox. **Dirs**—J. C. Adams, Jr., T. L. Chandler, Jr., N. H. Davis, Jr., P. J. Faccenda, J. S. M. French, R. H. Hilb, T. H. O'Brien, A. L. Rogal, R. S. Ukrop. **Transfer Agent & Registrar**—Mellon Securities Trust Co., Ridgefield Park, NJ. **Incorporated** in Virginia in 1982. **Empl**-1,700. **S&P Analyst:** RJD

STANDARD & POOR'S

STOCK REPORTS

Huffy Corp.

NYSE Symbol **HUF**
In S&P SmallCap 600

25-OCT-95 **Industry:** Leisure/Amusement

Summary: This leading manufacturer of bicycles also makes basketball backboards, lawn and garden tools and juvenile products, and provides inventory, assembly and supplier services.

Quantitative Evaluations

Outlook (1 Lowest—5 Highest)
• **2⁻**

Fair Value
• **9⅞**

Risk
• **Low**

Earn./Div. Rank
• **B+**

Technical Eval.
• **Bullish** since 7/95

Rel. Strength Rank (1 Lowest—99 Highest)
• **10**

Insider Activity
• **NA**

Recent Price • 10¼
52 Wk Range • 15⅞-10⅛
Yield • 3.4%
12-Mo. P/E • 60.3

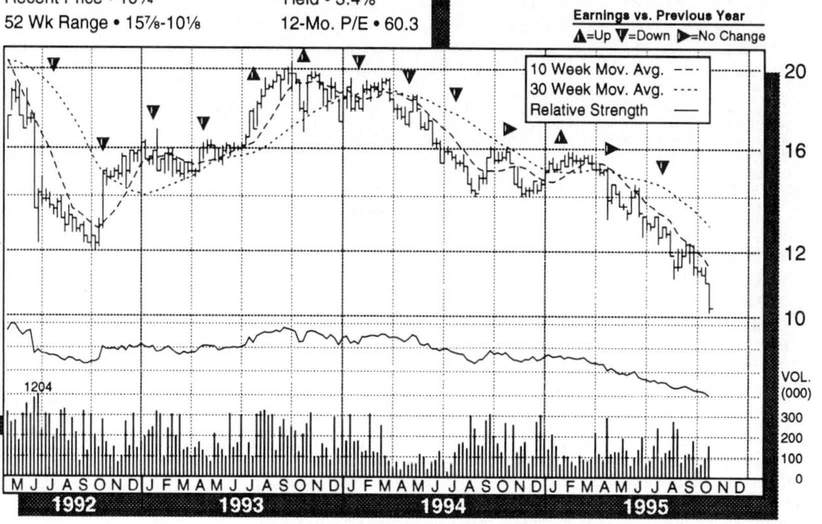

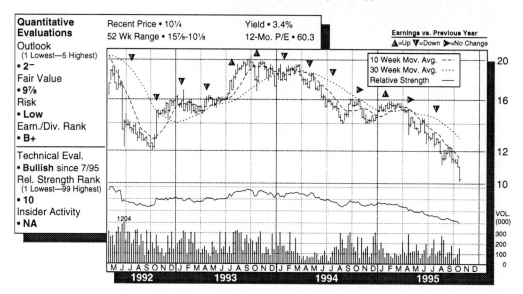

Business Profile - 25-OCT-95

This company, the largest producer of bicycles in the U.S., also makes a line of nonpowered lawn and garden tools, sells juvenile products and sporting goods, and provides a variety of retail services. Huffy believes that all of its product companies enjoy strong brand recognition, maintain solid market share positions, and are positioned for recovery at retail with innovative products being introduced. A share repurchase program is continuing.

Operational Review - 25-OCT-95

Net sales in the nine months ended September 30, 1995, declined 1.3%, year to year. A soft retail environment and a shift in mix toward promotionally priced products penalized by results; net income plunged 99%. The shares have dropped over 30% in 1995, reflecting stiff competition and slower consumer spending. Huffy expects to report a loss in 1995, but hopes to return to profitability in 1996, on the strength of new product offerings.

Stock Performance - 20-OCT-95

In the past 30 trading days, HUF's shares have declined 16%, compared to a 3% rise in the S&P 500. Average trading volume for the past five days was 30,620 shares, compared with the 40-day moving average of 21,290 shares.

Key Stock Statistics

Dividend Rate/Share	0.34	Shareholders	8,500
Shs. outstg. (M)	13.4	Market cap. (B)	$0.134
Avg. daily vol. (M)	0.019	Inst. holdings	67%
Tang. Bk. Value/Share	8.08	Insider holdings	NA
Beta	1.34		

Value of $10,000 invested 5 years ago: $ 9,197

Fiscal Year Ending Dec. 31

	1995	% Change	1994	% Change	1993	% Change
Revenues (Million $)						
1Q	200.6	6%	189.2	-12%	215.0	20%
2Q	200.4	-7%	214.9	-2%	220.1	22%
3Q	148.9	-3%	153.3	-8%	167.2	7%
4Q	—	—	162.0	4%	155.5	-17%
Yr.	—	—	719.5	-5%	757.9	8%
Income (Million $)						
1Q	4.42	-9%	4.85	-1%	4.91	-16%
2Q	0.35	-96%	7.96	16%	6.87	41%
3Q	-4.49	NM	2.60	13%	2.31	31%
4Q	—	—	2.02	NM	-17.92	NM
Yr.	—	—	17.42	NM	-3.83	NM
Earnings Per Share ($)						
1Q	0.33	NM	0.33	-13%	0.38	-14%
2Q	0.03	-94%	0.53	-2%	0.54	46%
3Q	-0.33	NM	0.18	NM	0.18	29%
4Q	—	—	0.14	NM	-1.26	NM
Yr.	—	—	1.20	NM	-0.30	NM

Next earnings report expected: late January

Huffy Corp.

Business Summary - 25-OCT-95

Huffy Corp. is a leading maker of bicycles, and has expanded its product line to include the design, manufacture and marketing of other recreational and leisure products, and juvenile products. It also operates a national in-store assembly and warranty service business, and provides inventory services to retailers. Business segment contributions in 1994 were:

	Revs.	Profits
Recreational & leisure products	64%	60%
Juvenile products	17%	17%
Retail services	19%	23%

Recreational and leisure products include the Huffy brand of bicycles, which is distributed primarily through national and regional high volume retailers and is the largest selling brand of bicycles in the U.S. Bicycles accounted for 41% of revenues in 1994. The division also manufactures a line of basketball products (11% of revenues), including goals, backboards and accessories for use at home. In November 1990, Huffy acquired True Temper Hardware Co. (12%), one of the three leading suppliers of nonpowered lawn and garden tools, snow tools and cutting tools.

Juvenile products are sold under the prominent brand names Gerry and Snugli. Gerry baby products consist of car seats, infant carriers, frame carriers, safety gates, toilet trainers, electronic baby monitors, and a broad line of wood juvenile products previously sold under the Nu-Line name. Snugli baby products consist of infant carriers.

In the retail services area, the Huffy Service First unit provides in-store assembly, repair and display services to major retailers in all 50 states, Puerto Rico and the Virgin Islands for a variety of products including bicycles, gas grills, physical fitness equipment, lawn mowers and furniture. It also offers merchandising services, consisting of the installation and periodic maintenance of displays and merchandise replenishment to vendors who supply high volume retailers. The Washington Inventory Service unit provides physical inventory services on a nationwide basis to meet the financial reporting and inventory control requirements of retailers.

Important Developments

Oct. '95—Huffy said it had implemented price hikes to offset material cost increases it experienced. The company added that Huffy Bicycle Co. would continue to reduce production costs in an effort to regain its position as the lowest cost supplier in the bicycle industry.

Capitalization

Long Term Debt: $56,763,000 (9/95).

Per Share Data ($) (Year Ended Dec. 31)

	1994	1993	1992	1991	1990	1989
Tangible Bk. Val.	7.94	7.46	6.78	7.17	5.89	5.23
Cash Flow	2.59	1.26	2.31	2.76	2.26	1.96
Earnings	1.20	-0.30	0.92	1.52	1.37	1.17
Dividends	0.34	0.30	0.30	0.28	0.27	0.23
Payout Ratio	28%	NM	32%	18%	19%	19%
Prices - High	19½	20⅜	24⅜	22¼	17⅛	15⅜
- Low	14	14⅝	12	9⅞	8½	8¾
P/E Ratio - High	16	NM	26	15	13	13
- Low	12	NM	13	7	6	7

Income Statement Analysis (Million $)

	1994	%Chg	1993	%Chg	1992	%Chg	1991
Revs.	719	-5%	758	8%	703	4%	679
Oper. Inc.	52.1	-7%	56.1	24%	45.4	-19%	56.2
Depr.	20.2	NM	20.3	13%	18.0	11%	16.2
Int. Exp.	6.4	-26%	8.7	-9%	9.6	7%	9.0
Pretax Inc.	27.6	NM	-3.1	NM	18.6	-41%	31.5
Eff. Tax Rate	37%	—	NM	—	36%	—	37%
Net Inc.	17.4	NM	-3.8	NM	11.8	-40%	19.8

Balance Sheet & Other Fin. Data (Million $)

	1994	1993	1992	1991	1990	1989
Cash	1.6	4.1	3.5	8.5	21.9	51.9
Curr. Assets	189	197	207	197	177	153
Total Assets	322	319	335	317	292	235
Curr. Liab.	99	104	116	98.0	90.0	73.0
LT Debt	58.6	43.2	74.9	80.2	84.3	57.5
Common Eqty.	133	136	118	125	107	96.0
Total Cap.	192	179	193	205	191	153
Cap. Exp.	35.7	21.3	23.9	21.1	9.5	13.8
Cash Flow	37.6	16.4	29.8	36.0	29.8	25.2

Ratio Analysis

	1994	1993	1992	1991	1990	1989
Curr. Ratio	1.9	1.9	1.8	2.0	2.0	2.1
% LT Debt of Cap.	30.5	24.1	38.9	39.1	44.1	37.6
% Net Inc.of Revs.	2.4	NM	1.7	2.9	3.5	3.3
% Ret. on Assets	5.7	NM	3.7	6.5	6.9	7.1
% Ret. on Equity	13.5	NM	9.9	17.0	17.9	16.7

Dividend Data —Dividends have been paid since 1966. A dividend reinvestment plan is available. A new poison pill stock purchase rights plan was adopted in 1989.

Amt. of Div. $	Date Decl.	Ex-Div. Date	Stock of Record	Payment Date
0.085	Aug. 22	Oct. 11	Oct. 17	Nov. 01 '94
0.085	Dec. 09	Jan. 09	Jan. 16	Feb. 01 '95
0.085	Feb. 17	Apr. 10	Apr. 17	May. 01 '95
0.085	Jun. 12	Jul. 13	Jul. 17	Aug. 01 '95
0.085	Sep. 20	Oct. 12	Oct. 16	Nov. 01 '95

Data as orig. reptd.; bef. results of disc. opers. and/or spec. items. Per share data adj. for stk. divs. as of ex-div. date. E-Estimated. NA-Not Available. NM-Not Meaningful. NR-Not Ranked.

Office—225 Byers Rd., Miamisburg, OH 45342. **Tel**—(513) 866-6251. **Chrmn, Pres & CEO**—R. L. Molen. **EVP & COO**—G. E. Morin. **VP & Secy**—N. A. Michaud. **VP-Fin & CFO**—T. A. Frederick. **VP, Treas & Investor Contact**—Pamela J. Whipps (513-865-5457). **Dirs**—T. D. Gleason, W. K. Hall, S. P. Huffman, L. B. Keene, J. D. Michaels, D. K. Miller, R. L. Molen, J. F. Robeson, P. W. Rooney, G. W. Smith, T. C. Sullivan, F. G. Wall. **Transfer Agent & Registrar**—Bank One, Indianapolis. **Incorporated** in Ohio in 1928. **Empl**-6,955. **S&P Analyst:** Philip D. Wohl

STANDARD & POOR'S

STOCK REPORTS

Hughes Supply

NYSE Symbol **HUG**

In S&P SmallCap 600

05-OCT-95 **Industry:** Building

Summary: This company is an important wholesale distributor of materials, equipment and supplies to the construction industry, with sales outlets in 13 states.

Quantitative Evaluations

Outlook (1 Lowest—5 Highest)
• **3**

Fair Value
• **24**

Risk
• **Average**

Earn./Div. Rank
• **B**

Technical Eval.
• **Bearish** since 7/95

Rel. Strength Rank (1 Lowest—99 Highest)
• **76**

Insider Activity
• **NA**

Recent Price • 24
52 Wk Range • 27¼-15⅞

Yield • 1.1%
12-Mo. P/E • 12.0

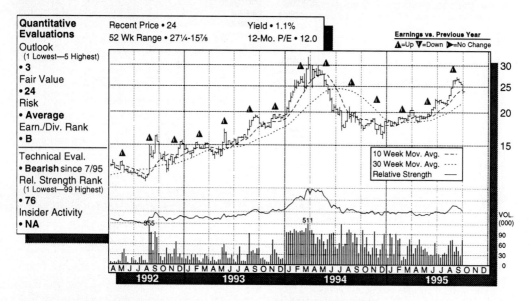

Earnings vs. Previous Year
▲=Up ▼=Down ▶=No Change

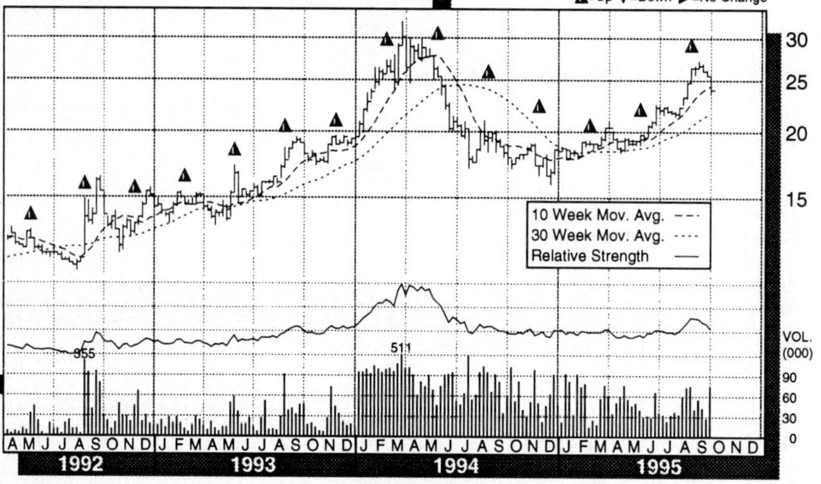

Business Profile - 04-OCT-95

Hughes Supply is a wholesale distributor of a broad range of materials, equipment and supplies to the construction industry and mechanical trades, with over 180 sales outlets in 13 states, mostly in the Southeast. The company's strategy to increase its market share has led to numerous acquisitions in the past two years. Hughes believes it will benefit from increased multi-family housing starts and a rebound in industrial and commercial construction during 1995.

Operational Review - 04-OCT-95

Revenues for the first half of 1995-96 rose 28%, year to year, primarily due to newly acquired and opened wholesale outlets, and to a lesser extent, increased construction volume in the Southeast. Gross margins benefited from the higher sales volume, and with well-controlled operating expenses, net income advanced 43% to $1.06 a share (on 13% more shares) from $0.84. The shares have risen over 30% from their 1995 low of 17 3/4.

Stock Performance - 29-SEP-95

In the past 30 trading days, HUG's shares have declined 3%, compared to a 5% rise in the S&P 500. Average trading volume for the past five days was 14,540 shares, compared with the 40-day moving average of 11,236 shares.

Key Stock Statistics

Dividend Rate/Share	0.28	Shareholders	1,100
Shs. outstg. (M)	6.6	Market cap. (B)	$0.166
Avg. daily vol. (M)	0.010	Inst. holdings	45%
Tang. Bk. Value/Share	22.60	Insider holdings	NA
Beta	0.16		

Value of $10,000 invested 5 years ago: $ 14,273

Fiscal Year Ending Jan. 31

	1996	% Change	1995	% Change	1994	% Change
Revenues (Million $)						
1Q	233.8	27%	184.0	30%	141.6	15%
2Q	260.5	29%	202.6	24%	163.9	21%
3Q	—	—	210.6	18%	179.0	29%
4Q	—	—	205.3	21%	169.5	29%
Yr.	—	—	802.5	21%	660.9	25%
Income (Million $)						
1Q	2.45	47%	1.67	157%	0.65	NM
2Q	4.23	41%	3.01	75%	1.72	NM
3Q	—	—	2.78	51%	1.84	192%
4Q	—	—	2.87	41%	2.03	101%
Yr.	—	—	10.33	64%	6.29	178%
Earnings Per Share ($)						
1Q	0.39	22%	0.32	113%	0.15	NM
2Q	0.66	29%	0.51	38%	0.37	NM
3Q	—	—	0.47	17%	0.40	167%
4Q	—	—	0.48	23%	0.39	63%
Yr.	—	—	1.79	33%	1.35	150%

Next earnings report expected: mid November

Hughes Supply

Business Summary - 04-OCT-95

Hughes Supply is a leading wholesale distributor of a broad range of materials, equipment, and supplies for use in the construction industry. The company has nine major product lines: electrical, plumbing, electric utility, building materials, pool equipment and supplies, water and sewer, air conditioning and heating, water systems, and industrial pipe, valves and fittings.

As of 1994-95 year end, Hughes operated 62 sales outlets in Florida, 29 in Georgia, 21 in North Carolina, and smaller numbers in Ohio, South Carolina, Mississippi, Tennessee, Alabama, Indiana, Pennsylvania, Virginia, Kentucky and Maryland.

Each of the company's outlets handles one or more of HUG's product lines. Sales are made primarily to contractors, electric utilities, municipalities and industrial accounts. The company employs approximately 350 outside sales representatives who call on customers and who also work with architects, engineers and manufacturers' representatives when major construction projects are involved.

Products sold by the company are purchased from over 5,000 manufacturers and suppliers, no single one of which accounted for more than 7% of HUG's total purchases during 1994-95. HUG serves more than 45,000 wholesale customers, with no customer accounting for over 1% of annual sales.

The company's marketing strategy has led to the expansion of its geographic markets served through numerous acquisitions over the past two years. In September 1995, the company completed the acquisition of Atlantic Pump & Equipment Co., a distributor of pool products and irrigation systems, for an undisclosed amount of cash. In August, HUG acquired Moore Electric Supply, an electrical supplies distributor with $55 million in annual sales, for an undisclosed amount of common stock.

Important Developments

Oct. '95—Hughes Supply said it had acquired ESET, Inc., a Hixson, Tenn., electric utility supplies and equipment distributor with $5 million in annual sales; and Cascade Pools Co., a distributor of pool supplies with branches in Kentucky, Tennessee, South Carolina, Alabama, and New Jersey, with annual sales of about $25 million. Terms of both transactions were not disclosed.

Capitalization

Long Term Debt: $111,779,000 (7/95), incl. $2,583,000 of capital lease obligations.

Per Share Data ($)

(Year Ended Jan. 31)

	1995	1994	1993	1992	1991	1990
Tangible Bk. Val.	21.75	20.28	19.94	19.51	20.72	19.89
Cash Flow	3.31	2.96	2.10	0.73	2.60	3.22
Earnings	1.79	1.25	0.54	-0.97	0.49	1.33
Dividends	0.21	0.14	0.12	0.30	0.36	0.34
Payout Ratio	12%	11%	22%	NM	70%	25%
Cal. Yrs.	1994	1993	1992	1991	1990	1989
Prices - High	32¼	19⅝	16⅜	13⅞	18⅜	21⅞
- Low	15⅞	13¼	10½	10⅛	9¾	17½
P/E Ratio - High	18	16	30	NM	38	16
- Low	9	11	19	NM	20	13

Income Statement Analysis (Million $)

	1995	%Chg	1994	%Chg	1993	%Chg	1992
Revs.	802	21%	661	25%	528	10%	481
Oper. Inc.	28.2	42%	19.8	74%	11.4	78%	6.4
Depr.	8.8	17%	7.5	14%	6.6	-8%	7.1
Int. Exp.	4.9	6%	4.6	-1%	4.7	-21%	5.9
Pretax Inc.	17.4	64%	10.6	186%	3.7	NM	-6.1
Eff. Tax Rate	41%	—	41%	—	39%	—	NM
Net Inc.	10.3	64%	6.3	178%	2.3	NM	-4.0

Balance Sheet & Other Fin. Data (Million $)

	1995	1994	1993	1992	1991	1990
Cash	3.2	1.1	2.3	5.6	3.2	2.1
Curr. Assets	260	204	170	165	164	176
Total Assets	329	263	225	216	220	236
Curr. Liab.	95.1	68.6	60.3	56.9	46.1	58.5
LT Debt	101	99	79.9	76.3	85.6	82.8
Common Eqty.	131	94.4	83.3	81.5	86.5	92.7
Total Cap.	232	194	163	159	173	177
Cap. Exp.	11.8	8.3	8.5	4.9	7.2	10.7
Cash Flow	19.1	13.8	8.8	3.1	11.3	15.5

Ratio Analysis

	1995	1994	1993	1992	1991	1990
Curr. Ratio	2.7	3.0	2.8	2.9	3.6	3.0
% LT Debt of Cap.	43.5	51.2	49.0	48.1	49.4	46.8
% Net Inc.of Revs.	1.3	1.0	0.4	NM	0.4	1.2
% Ret. on Assets	3.5	2.4	1.0	NM	1.0	2.8
% Ret. on Equity	9.2	6.7	2.7	NM	2.5	7.1

Dividend Data —Dividends have been paid since 1976. A "poison pill" stock purchase right was adopted in 1988.

Amt. of Div. $	Date Decl.	Ex-Div. Date	Stock of Record	Payment Date
0.060	Oct. 11	Oct. 26	Nov. 01	Nov. 14 '94
0.060	Jan. 26	Feb. 07	Feb. 13	Feb. 24 '95
0.070	Mar. 15	May. 01	May. 05	May. 19 '95
0.070	Jul. 07	Aug. 02	Aug. 04	Aug. 18 '95

Data as orig. reptd.; bef. results of disc. opers. and/or spec. items. Per share data adj. for stk. divs. as of ex-div. date. E-Estimated. NA-Not Available. NM-Not Meaningful. NR-Not Ranked.

Office—20 North Orange Ave., Suite 200, Orlando, FL 32802. **Tel**—(407) 841-4755. **Chrmn, CEO & Investor Contact**—David H. Hughes. **Pres & COO**—A. S. Hall Jr. **CFO & Treas**—J. S. Zepf. **Secy**—R. N. Blackford. **Dirs**—J. D. Baker II, R. N. Blackford, J. B. Ellis, A. S. Hall Jr., C. M. Hames, D. H. Hughes, R. V. Hughes, V. S. Hughes, D. C. Martin, H. B. McManaway. **Transfer Agent & Registrar**—American Stock Transfer & Trust Co., NYC. **Incorporated** in Florida in 1947. **Empl**-2,800. **S&P Analyst:** M.T.C.

STANDARD & POOR'S

STOCK REPORTS

Hyperion Software

NASDAQ Symbol **HYSW**

In S&P SmallCap 600

25-SEP-95

Industry: Data Processing

Summary: This company (formerly IMRS Inc.) develops, markets and supports network-based business information software products for multi-division or multi-location companies worldwide.

Quantitative Evaluations

Outlook (1 Lowest—5 Highest)
• **NA**

Fair Value
• **NA**

Risk
• **High**

Earn./Div. Rank
• **NR**

Technical Eval.
• **Bearish** since 7/95

Rel. Strength Rank (1 Lowest—99 Highest)
• **87**

Insider Activity
• **Neutral**

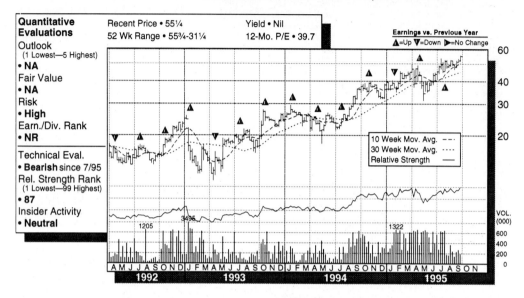

Recent Price • 55¼
52 Wk Range • 55¾-31¼

Yield • Nil
12-Mo. P/E • 39.7

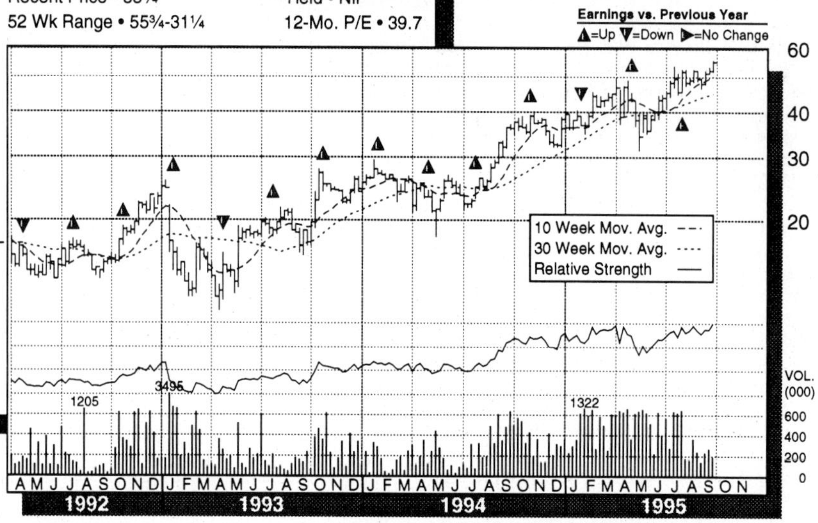

Business Profile - 25-SEP-95

Fundamentals in the computer industry have improved in recent periods, aided by growing demand for technology products that increase productivity. Hyperion has capitalized on demand for information software products by focusing on financial-related software. The growing popularity of Microsoft Windows in the business environment should aid future sales of the company's Windows-compatible products. International expansion should play a big role in sales growth for the foreseeable future.

Operational Review - 25-SEP-95

Revenues rose strongly in fiscal 1995, reflecting an increased number of licenses sold, growth in the installed customer base and gains internationally. Greater operating efficiencies helped offset a 64% jump in R&D spending and approximately $1 million net ($0.11 per share) of acquisition-related costs. Continued international expansion should boost future results. Non-U.S. sales soared 71% during fiscal 1995 from those of the prior year.

Stock Performance - 22-SEP-95

In the past 30 trading days, HYSW's shares have increased 13%, compared to a 5% rise in the S&P 500. Average trading volume for the past five days was 36,320 shares, compared with the 40-day moving average of 44,385 shares.

Key Stock Statistics

Dividend Rate/Share	Nil	Shareholders	1,800
Shs. outstg. (M)	7.8	Market cap. (B)	$0.433
Avg. daily vol. (M)	0.042	Inst. holdings	93%
Tang. Bk. Value/Share	6.95	Insider holdings	NA
Beta	NA		

Value of $10,000 invested 5 years ago: NA

Fiscal Year Ending Jun. 30

	1995	% Change	1994	% Change	1993	% Change
Revenues (Million $)						
1Q	26.30	71%	15.35	37%	11.20	32%
2Q	30.06	56%	19.24	37%	14.00	28%
3Q	30.08	67%	18.04	35%	13.32	37%
4Q	50.68	60%	31.76	41%	22.51	33%
Yr.	137.1	63%	84.38	38%	61.03	33%
Income (Million $)						
1Q	1.23	52%	0.81	—	—	—
2Q	2.01	-1%	2.04	48%	1.38	25%
3Q	1.40	17%	1.20	NM	-0.82	NM
4Q	6.86	56%	4.41	42%	3.10	35%
Yr.	12.14	43%	8.47	98%	4.28	2%
Earnings Per Share ($)						
1Q	0.22	100%	0.11	38%	0.08	33%
2Q	0.23	-12%	0.26	44%	0.18	13%
3Q	0.16	7%	0.15	NM	-0.12	NM
4Q	0.78	37%	0.57	39%	0.41	28%
Yr.	1.39	28%	1.09	91%	0.57	-8%

Next earnings report expected: late October

Hyperion Software

Business Summary - 25-SEP-95

Hyperion Software Corporation (formerly IMRS Inc.) develops, markets and supports enterprise-level financial applications for client/server environments. Its software addresses the accounting, financial consolidation, management reporting and information access needs of large corporations worldwide. The company designs products specifically for network implementation, providing fast, multi-user acess to centrally controlled and secure corporate data. Revenues in recent fiscal years were derived as follows:

	1994	1993	1992
Software licenses	55%	54%	59%
License renewals & services	45%	46%	41%

The company's products include Hyperion, Micro Control and FASTAR, which consolidate and report financial and other business data; OnTrack, a complete executive information product; and FinalForm, for controlled data collection.

Hyperion software is an advanced business information consolidation and reporting product designed to use the capabilities of the Microsoft Windows graphical operating environment. Software sales have grown from 70 corporate headquarters clients in the fiscal 1993 third quarter to nearly 900 at March 31, 1995. A headquarters site license is priced at $125,000, with reporting site licenses priced at $4,500 or less, depending on the number of sites.

Micro Control consolidates, reports and maintains, in a single integrated database, a company's financial and statistical reporting information, including actual, budget, forecast, plan and prior year data. Micro Control enables a financial staff to independently manage the collection, consolidation, analysis and reporting of financial data without the need for technical training. The company also offers complementary Micro Control modules that allow users to link directly to Lotus 1-2-3 and Microsoft Excel.

FASTAR is a spreadsheet-based financial consolidation and reporting system targeted at organizations oriented to spreadsheet-based solutions. OnTrack is a Microsoft Windows-based information access product designed to operate on local area networks. FinalForm is used to design, implement and control forms for detailed and consistent data collection.

Important Developments

Jul. '95—In reporting fiscal 1995 results, Hyperion noted that its 64%, year over year, increase in R&D costs reflected the company's stepped-up investment in its suite of client/server accounting products. Additionally, the company said post merger results for Pillar Corp., acquired in December 1994, exceeded expectations.

Capitalization

Mortgage Payable: $8,910,000 (6/95).

Per Share Data ($) (Year Ended Jun. 30)

	1995	1994	1993	1992	1991	1990
Tangible Bk. Val.	NA	7.33	5.86	5.13	1.77	NA
Cash Flow	NA	1.47	0.93	0.86	0.82	NA
Earnings	1.39	1.09	0.57	0.62	0.47	NA
Dividends	Nil	Nil	Nil	Nil	Nil	NA
Payout Ratio	Nil	Nil	Nil	Nil	Nil	NA
Prices - High	53¾	40¼	27¾	25	22	NA
- Low	31¼	18	11¼	13¾	12	NA
P/E Ratio - High	39	37	49	40	47	NA
- Low	22	17	20	22	26	NA

Income Statement Analysis (Million $)

	1994	%Chg	1993	%Chg	1992	%Chg	1991
Revs.	84.4	38%	61.0	33%	46.0	34%	34.3
Oper. Inc.	16.8	82%	9.2	9%	8.4	16%	7.3
Depr.	2.9	14%	2.5	56%	1.6	-19%	2.0
Int. Exp.	0.1	-33%	0.1	-68%	0.4	-21%	0.5
Pretax Inc.	14.6	104%	7.1	3%	6.9	55%	4.5
Eff. Tax Rate	42%	—	40%	—	40%	—	41%
Net Inc.	8.5	98%	4.3	2%	4.2	58%	2.7

Balance Sheet & Other Fin. Data (Million $)

	1994	1993	1992	1991	1990	1989
Cash	35.4	22.9	22.9	4.8	NA	NA
Curr. Assets	69.6	49.3	41.8	17.6	NA	NA
Total Assets	89.4	64.6	51.2	23.9	NA	NA
Curr. Liab.	35.4	23.1	16.8	12.1	NA	NA
LT Debt	Nil	Nil	Nil	2.7	NA	NA
Common Eqty.	52.3	40.5	33.3	8.7	NA	NA
Total Cap.	54.0	41.5	34.4	11.8	NA	NA
Cap. Exp.	5.3	4.7	3.0	1.1	NA	NA
Cash Flow	11.4	6.8	5.8	4.7	NA	NA

Ratio Analysis

	1994	1993	1992	1991	1990	1989
Curr. Ratio	2.0	2.1	2.5	1.5	NA	NA
% LT Debt of Cap.	Nil	Nil	Nil	23.2	NA	NA
% Net Inc.of Revs.	10.0	7.0	9.1	7.7	NA	NA
% Ret. on Assets	10.9	7.2	10.2	NA	NA	NA
% Ret. on Equity	18.0	11.3	18.7	NA	NA	NA

Dividend Data —No cash dividends have been paid. Hyperion intends to retain earnings to finance growth and does not expect to pay cash dividends in the foreseeable future.

Data as orig. reptd.; bef. results of disc. opers. and/or spec. items. Per share data adj. for stk. divs. as of ex-div. date. E-Estimated. NA-Not Available. NM-Not Meaningful. NR-Not Ranked.

Office—777 Long Ridge Rd., Stamford, CT 06902. **Tel**—(203) 321-3500. **Chrmn, Pres & CEO**—J. A. Perakis. **VP-Fin, CFO & Investor Contact**—Lucy R. Ricciardi. **VP & Secy**—C. M. Schiff. **Dirs**—G. G. Greenfield, H. S. Gruner, W. W. Helman IV, M. A. Lucini, A. Papone, J. A. Perakis, R. W. Thompson. **Transfer Agent & Registrar**—American Stock Transfer & Trust Co., NYC. **Incorporated** in Delaware in 1981. **Empl**-900. **S&P Analyst:** Steven A. Jaworski

IHOP Corp.

NASDAQ Symbol IHOP (Incl. in Nat'l Market) Options on Phila In S&P SmallCap 600

Price	Range	P–E Ratio	Dividend	Yield	S&P Ranking	Beta
Oct. 9'95	1995					
23⅜	30½–21½	15	None	None	NR	NA

Summary

This company develops, franchises and operates International House of Pancakes restaurants, one of the best-known national family restaurant chains in the U.S.

Business Summary

IHOP Corp. develops, franchises and operates the International House of Pancakes chain of restaurants. The restaurants are known for the quality and variety of their pancakes, waffles and other breakfast specialties, as well as a wide selection of moderately priced lunch and dinner items. Revenues in recent years were derived:

	1994	1993
Franchise operations:		
Rent	17%	16%
Service fees and other	39%	34%
Company restaurants	27%	33%
Other	17%	17%

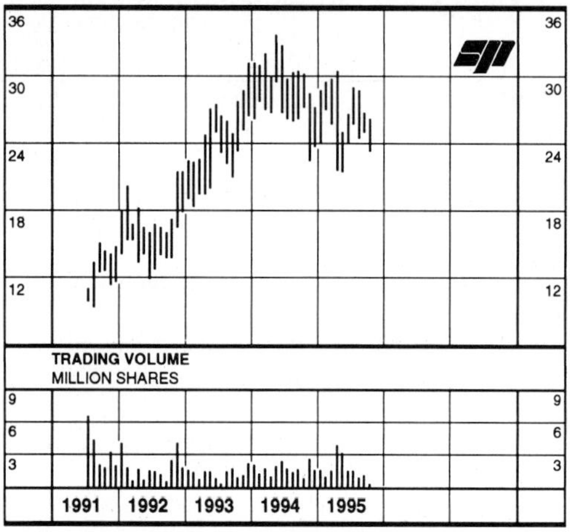

At December 31, 1994, there were 620 restaurants in operation (572 a year earlier), including 451 operated by franchisees, 123 by area licensees and 46 by the company, located in 36 states, Canada and Japan, with the largest concentration in California (126), Florida (94) and Texas (60). IHOP opened 54 new restaurants in 1994 and closed six restaurants. In 1995, IHOP plans to open about 67 restaurants, including 45 by the company and 22 by franchisees and area licensees.

The IHOP menu offers a broad selection of breakfast, lunch and dinner entrees priced to represent good value and to appeal to the general population. Marketing programs include discounts and specials to increase customer traffic and encourage repeat visits. IHOP also actively participates in the establishment of purchasing cooperatives among franchisees to ensure food quality and consistency and to achieve cost savings.

IHOP's approach to franchising is founded on the franchisees' active involvement in the day-to-day operation of their respective restaurants, a concept that the company views as providing a quality of management and dedication generally unmatched by salaried employees or passive investors. In addition, IHOP typically develops, equips and operates the restaurant prior to franchising and remains the franchisee's landlord, providing the company with enhanced profits and increased control over the franchise system.

The company intends to add restaurants to the IHOP system primarily through the development of new restaurants in major markets where it has a core customer base. The company may also acquire non-IHOP restaurants for conversion. New restaurants average about 4,500 sq. ft. with 160 seats, compared to older restaurants that average 3,000 sq. ft. with 100 seats. In the past five years, the company has remodeled and updated about 85 then company-operated restaurants at an average cost per unit of $84,000. All franchise agreements executed since 1982 contain a provision that requires IHOP's franchisees to periodically remodel their restaurants.

Important Developments

Jul. '95— During the first half of 1995, IHOP opened 22 new restaurants, bringing the total number of IHOP units open to 639 as of June 30. In April, the company acquired 10 Chicago-area Shoney's restaurants; four of those units have been convereted to IHOP restaurants, with the remainder to be converted by the end of 1995.

Next earnings report expected in late October.

Per Share Data ($)

Yr. End Dec. 31	1994	1993	1992	1991	1990
Tangible Bk. Val.	**8.12**	6.26	4.81	3.76	d0.44
Cash Flow	**2.28**	1.77	1.54	1.43	1.44
Earnings[1]	**1.60**	1.15	0.98	0.73	0.53
Dividends	**Nil**	Nil	Nil	Nil	Nil
Payout Ratio	**Nil**	Nil	Nil	Nil	Nil
Prices—High	**33¾**	31¼	21½	15⅛	NA
Low	**22½**	18⅜	11⅞	9⅜	NA
P/E Ratio—	**21–14**	27–16	22–12	21–13	NA

Data as orig. reptd. Adj. for stk. div. of 1000% Jul. 1991. **1.** Bef. spec. items of -0.09 in 1992, -0.09 in 1991. NA-Not Available. d-Deficit.

Income Data (Million $)

Year Ended Dec. 31	Revs.	Oper. Inc.	% Oper. Inc. of Revs.	Cap. Exp.	Depr.	Int. Exp.	Net Bef. Taxes	Eff. Tax Rate	[1]Net Inc.	% Net Inc. of Revs.	Cash Flow
1994	**145**	**33.6**	**23.1**	**30.5**	**6.38**	**6.81**	**25.0**	**39.5%**	**15.1**	**10.4**	**21.5**
1993	139	29.0	20.9	40.9	5.74	5.64	18.6	42.3%	10.7	7.7	16.5
1992	112	22.2	19.9	29.3	5.01	4.76	14.8	40.8%	8.8	7.9	13.8
1991	103	17.6	17.1	20.3	4.94	5.66	9.0	40.8%	5.3	5.1	10.1
1990	95	14.7	15.4	13.9	4.91	6.29	5.5	43.4%	3.1	3.3	7.8

Balance Sheet Data (Million $)

Dec. 31	Cash	Curr. Assets	Curr. Liab.	Curr. Ratio	Total Assets	% Ret. on Assets	Long Term Debt	Common Equity	Total Cap.	% LT Debt of Cap.	% Ret. on Equity
1994	**2.04**	**21.2**	**17.2**	**1.2**	**203**	**7.9**	**78.0**	**88.3**	**184**	**42.4**	**18.9**
1993	1.18	19.9	16.6	1.2	180	6.5	66.4	71.2	162	41.0	16.5
1992	5.66	21.7	18.1	1.2	150	6.6	53.8	58.0	130	41.3	16.4
1991	2.67	15.9	15.1	1.0	113	4.0	38.8	48.7	97	39.9	14.7
1990	1.65	13.0	19.7	0.7	94	NA	50.5	13.3	74	68.5	NA

Data as orig. reptd. **1.** Bef. spec. items.

Revenues (Million $)

Quarter:	1995	1994	1993
Mar.	33.2	32.8	30.2
Jun.	40.1	37.2	35.5
Sep.		37.3	38.2
Dec.		42.8	38.6
		150.0	142.5

Revenues for the six months ended June 30, 1995, rose 4.8%, year to year; system-wide comparable sales per restaurant increased 1.5%. Results were penalized by severance costs of $800,000 ($0.05 a share, after tax) associated with a realignment of responsibilities in restaurant operations, restaurant development and purchasing functions, and net income declined 1.8%, to $5,845,000 ($0.62 a share), from $5,954,000 ($0.63).

Common Share Earnings ($)

Qaurter:	1995	1994	1993
Mar.	0.19	0.24	0.16
Jun.	0.43	0.39	0.15
Sep.		0.40	0.37
Dec.		0.57	0.48
		1.60	1.15

Dividend Data

No cash dividends have been paid.

Finances

At March 31, 1995, the company had $7.5 million available under a $10 million unsecured bank revolving credit agreement.

Franchise agreements generally require the payment of an initial franchise and development fee of $200,000 to $350,000 (depending on the location), of which 20% is paid in cash. The balance is financed by the company over five to eight years. IHOP also receives continuing revenues from the franchisee, including a royalty fee equal to 4.5% of sales, rental income from the leasing of the restaurant and related equipment, revenue from the sale of certain proprietary products, a local advertising fee usually paid to a cooperative, and a national advertising fee equal to 1% of sales.

Capitalization

Long Term Debt: $80,758,000 (3/95), incl. $45.7 million of cap. lease obligs.

Common Stock: 9,318,483 shs. ($0.01 par). Institutions hold about 88%

Office—525 N. Brand Blvd., Glendale, CA 91203-1903. **Tel**—(818) 240-6055. **Chrmn, Pres & CEO**—R. K. Herzer. **VP-Fin, CFO & Treas**—F. G. Silny. **VP & Secy**—M. D. Weisberger. **Dirs**—H. F. Christie, F. Edelstein, M. S. Gordon, R. K. Herzer, N. C. Hulsey, L. A. Kay, C. W. Nahas, P. W. Rose. **Transfer Agent**—Chemical Trust Co. of California, Los Angeles. **Incorporated** in Delaware in 1976. **Empl**—2,175.

 Stephen R. Biggar

STANDARD & POOR'S

STOCK REPORTS

IMCO Recycling

NYSE Symbol **IMR**
In S&P SmallCap 600

16-OCT-95 **Industry:** Pollution Control

Summary: This company is the largest independent recycler of aluminum, recycling beverage cans, can scrap and dross, and by-products of aluminum manufacturing.

Quantitative Evaluations

Outlook (1 Lowest—5 Highest)
• **5**

Fair Value
• **28¼**

Risk
• **Average**

Earn./Div. Rank
• **NR**

Technical Eval.
• **Bearish** since 8/94

Rel. Strength Rank (1 Lowest—99 Highest)
• **69**

Insider Activity
• **Neutral**

Recent Price • 21¾
52 Wk Range • 23¾-12½
Yield • 0.6%
12-Mo. P/E • 22.9

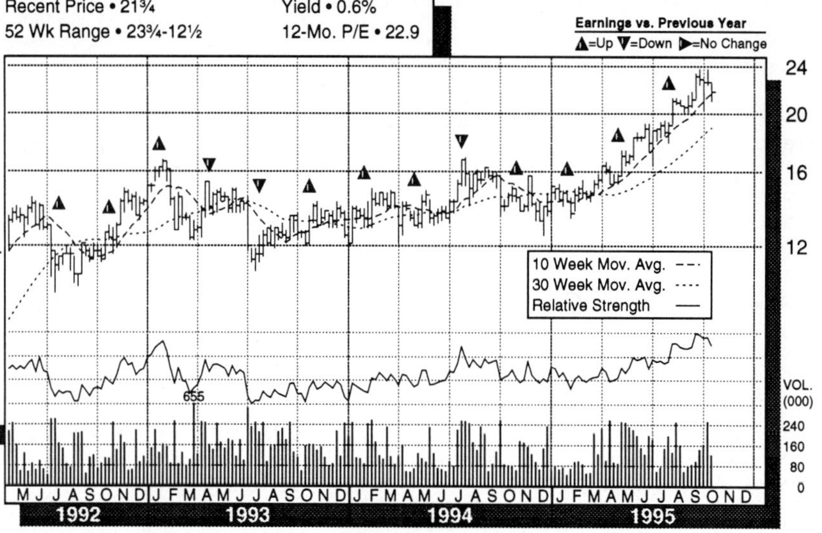

Business Profile - 16-OCT-95

IMR has been increasing its processing capacity through acquisitions of recycling facilities and the expansion of existing plants. The company expects to have 70% more capacity in 1996, versus the 1994 level, as it recently completed its plans to acquire five aluminum recycling plants with total annual capacity of 390 million pounds. IMR also formed a joint venture with a German-based aluminum company, which is expected to generate annual revenues of $250 million.

Operational Review - 16-OCT-95

Revenues for the first half of 1995 rose 35%, year to year, reflecting higher processing volume, primarily due to the acquisition of the Loudon, Tenn. plant and the expansion of the Uhrichsville, Ohio aluminum recycling facility. Profitability benefited from the higher volume and cost control efforts, which helped lower unit manufacturing costs, and in the absence of a litigation charge, net income was up 91%. The company expects continued increased customer demand and positive results.

Stock Performance - 13-OCT-95

In the past 30 trading days, IMR's shares have increased 5%, compared to a 4% rise in the S&P 500. Average trading volume for the past five days was 24,420 shares, compared with the 40-day moving average of 28,238 shares.

Key Stock Statistics

Dividend Rate/Share	0.14	Shareholders	600
Shs. outstg. (M)	11.8	Market cap. (B)	$0.256
Avg. daily vol. (M)	0.040	Inst. holdings	51%
Tang. Bk. Value/Share	5.88	Insider holdings	NA
Beta	0.63		

Value of $10,000 invested 5 years ago: $ 34,439

Fiscal Year Ending Dec. 31

	1995	% Change	1994	% Change	1993	% Change
Revenues (Million $)						
1Q	30.75	42%	21.68	38%	15.74	-4%
2Q	29.72	29%	23.07	24%	18.64	27%
3Q	—	—	26.21	38%	19.04	24%
4Q	—	—	30.16	45%	20.80	50%
Yr.	—	—	101.1	36%	74.22	23%
Income (Million $)						
1Q	2.89	42%	2.03	19%	1.71	-9%
2Q	2.96	185%	1.04	-47%	1.96	2%
3Q	—	—	2.59	20%	2.16	11%
4Q	—	—	2.81	28%	2.19	27%
Yr.	—	—	8.47	6%	8.02	7%
Earnings Per Share ($)						
1Q	0.24	33%	0.18	20%	0.15	-12%
2Q	0.25	178%	0.09	-47%	0.17	-6%
3Q	—	—	0.22	16%	0.19	12%
4Q	—	—	0.24	26%	0.19	27%
Yr.	—	—	0.73	4%	0.70	4%

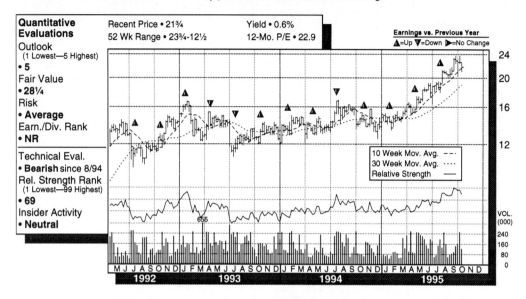

Next earnings report expected: early November

Business Summary - 12-OCT-95

IMCO Recyling recycles aluminum and magnesium from used aluminum beverage cans, aluminum and magnesium scrap, and aluminum and magnesium dross (by-products of aluminum and magnesium production). It entered the zinc recycling business in January 1992 via an acquisition. Approximately 96% of the company's capacity in 1994 was used to recycle for a fee metal owned by customers (a service called tolling).

Contributions from each of IMCO's products and services (percent of total pounds processed) in recent years:

	1994	1993	1992
Tolled aluminum	93%	92%	91%
Purchased aluminum	3%	4%	4%
Magnesium	1%	1%	1%
Zinc	3%	3%	4%

In its recycling process, the company uses its rotary furnaces to convert used beverage cans, aluminum dross and aluminum scrap into molten metal, which is then delivered to customers in molten form or ingots.

As of October 1995, IMCO was operating 11 recycling plants with a total annual processing capacity of 1.3 billion pounds of aluminum and 50 pounds of other metals. Aluminum plants were located in California (100 million pounds), Kentucky (200 million pounds), Ohio (285 million pounds), Oklahoma (135 million pounds), Indiana (150 million pounds), Tennessee (230 million pounds) and several other states.

Principal customers for metal recycled by the company are U.S. primary aluminum producers; Alcoa accounted for 30% of 1994 revenues, while Barmet Aluminum accounted for 12%.

During 1995, the company upgraded and expanded its Loudon, Tenn. aluminum recycling facility, Phoenix Smelting Corp., increasing Loudon's annual production capacity by 50% to 180 million pounds. The company wil also spend about $6.3 million to build a plant adjacent to its Morgantown, Ky. facility that will process salt cake. Completion is seen by early 1996.

Important Developments

Oct. '95—IMCO completed its plans to acquire five aluminum recycling plants with a total capacity of 390 million pounds. The company purchased Illinois-based Alumar Associates, Inc., for $8.5 million in cash and stock, and a Bedford, Indiana plant for $8.5 million. IMR said the five facilities, along with other acquisitions and expansions within the IMCO system, and its planned European joint venture with VAW aluminum AG, would increase the company's capacity to 1.7 billion pounds in 1996, a 70% increase from 1994.

Capitalization

Long Term Debt: $11,250,000 (6/95).

Per Share Data ($) (Year Ended Dec. 31)

	1994	1993	1992	1991	1990	1989
Tangible Bk. Val.	5.38	4.50	3.83	2.92	2.34	1.84
Cash Flow	1.36	1.23	1.01	0.84	0.80	0.69
Earnings	0.73	0.70	0.67	0.52	0.53	0.54
Dividends	0.10	Nil	Nil	Nil	Nil	Nil
Payout Ratio	14%	Nil	Nil	Nil	Nil	Nil
Prices - High	16⅞	16¾	15⅛	11⅜	6⅞	8½
- Low	12⅛	10⅞	6½	5⅜	4	4¾
P/E Ratio - High	23	24	23	22	13	16
- Low	17	16	10	10	8	9

Income Statement Analysis (Million $)

	1994	%Chg	1993	%Chg	1992	%Chg	1991
Revs.	101	36%	74.2	23%	60.2	22%	49.2
Oper. Inc.	23.6	32%	17.9	26%	14.2	33%	10.7
Depr.	7.4	19%	6.2	62%	3.8	10%	3.5
Int. Exp.	1.3	-7%	1.4	NM	1.4	NM	1.4
Pretax Inc.	13.7	23%	11.1	14%	9.8	49%	6.5
Eff. Tax Rate	38%	—	28%	—	23%	—	15%
Net Inc.	8.5	6%	8.0	7%	7.5	34%	5.6

Balance Sheet & Other Fin. Data (Million $)

	1994	1993	1992	1991	1990	1989
Cash	2.9	1.7	12.0	9.2	6.1	6.3
Curr. Assets	27.9	19.8	19.9	18.1	17.1	15.9
Total Assets	96.8	79.4	68.9	53.0	47.7	45.1
Curr. Liab.	10.6	10.7	8.6	3.3	3.8	5.9
LT Debt	11.9	8.0	10.5	13.0	13.0	13.0
Common Eqty.	68.3	57.1	48.9	35.8	29.9	25.3
Total Cap.	85.0	68.1	60.3	49.6	44.0	39.3
Cap. Exp.	6.6	11.9	16.9	7.1	4.8	8.9
Cash Flow	15.8	14.2	11.3	9.1	8.8	6.9

Ratio Analysis

	1994	1993	1992	1991	1990	1989
Curr. Ratio	2.6	1.9	2.3	5.4	4.5	2.7
% LT Debt of Cap.	14.0	11.8	17.4	26.2	29.6	33.1
% Net Inc.of Revs.	8.4	10.8	12.4	11.4	10.5	14.5
% Ret. on Assets	9.5	10.9	12.0	11.0	12.4	12.2
% Ret. on Equity	13.3	15.1	17.2	17.0	20.8	30.9

Dividend Data —A special dividend of $0.10 was paid on January 26, 1995, and directors declared an initial quarterly dividend of $0.035 on May 15, 1995.

Amt. of Div. $	Date Decl.	Ex-Div. Date	Stock of Record	Payment Date
0.100	Dec. 16	Dec. 22	Dec. 29	Jan. 26 '95
0.035	May. 15	May. 24	May. 31	Jun. 16 '95
0.035	Jul. 28	Aug. 29	Aug. 31	Sep. 15 '95
0.035	Oct. 13	Nov. 28	Nov. 30	Dec. 15 '95

Data as orig. reptd.; bef. results of disc. opers. and/or spec. items. Per share data adj. for stk. divs. as of ex-div. date. E-Estimated. NA-Not Available. NM-Not Meaningful. NR-Not Ranked.

Office—5215 North O'Connor Blvd., Suite 940, Irving, TX 75039. **Tel**—(214) 869-6575. **Chrmn**—D. V. Ingram. **Pres & CEO**—F. H. Romanelli. **COO**—R. L. Kerr. **EVP, CFO, Secy & Investor Contact**—Paul V. Dufour. **VP & Treas**—J. B. Walburg. **Dirs**—J. M. Brundrett, R. L. Cheek, J. J. Fleming, R. W. Hanselman, D. V. Ingram, T. A. James, D. Navarro, J. C. Page, F. H. Romanelli. **Transfer Agent & Registrar**—Mellon Securities Trust Co., Pittsburgh. **Incorporated** in 1985 in Delaware. **Empl**-740. **S&P Analyst:** Stewart Scharf

STANDARD & POOR'S

STOCK REPORTS

Ideon Group, Inc.

NYSE Symbol **IQ**
In S&P SmallCap 600

29-AUG-95 **Industry:** Services

Summary: This company (formerly SafeCard Services) is the world's largest provider of credit card registry services, and also offers other services through its credit card issuer clients.

Quantitative Evaluations

Outlook
(1 Lowest—5 Highest)
• 5

Fair Value
• 15⅝

Risk
• High

Earn./Div. Rank
• B+

Technical Eval.
• NA

Rel. Strength Rank
(1 Lowest—99 Highest)
• 15

Insider Activity
• Favorable

Recent Price • 10⅜
52 Wk Range • 21⅜-8⅜
Yield • 1.9%
12-Mo. P/E • 10.4

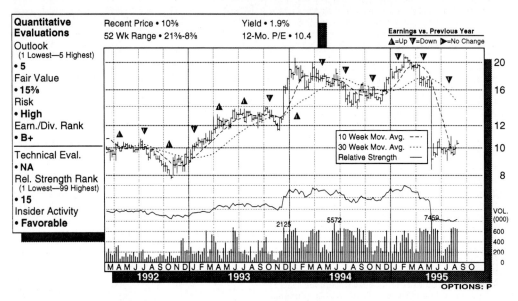

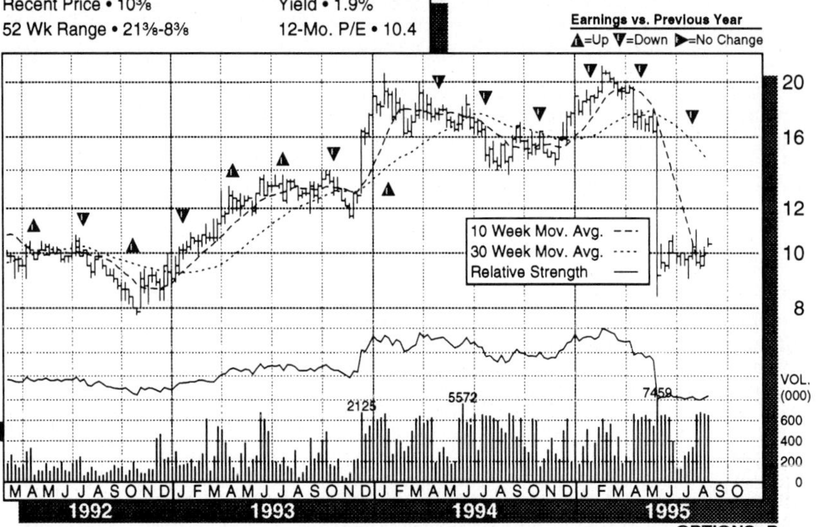

OPTIONS: P

Business Profile - 29-AUG-95

Plans for a major restructuring were announced in July 1995, after two new product introductions faltered. In February 1995, the company acquired National Leisure Group, Inc., a provider of vaction travel packages, for $15 million in cash and up to $4 million in stock. IQ is engaged in 10 lawsuits, nine of which involve its former chairman, Peter Hamlos. In May, directors authorized the repurchase of up to 2.5 million common shares.

Operational Review - 29-AUG-95

In December 1994, Ideon changed its fiscal year end from October 31 to December 31. A loss in the 1995 second quarter reflected a $73 million pretax charge for restructuring costs and product abandonment. The charge resulted from a lack of consumer repsonse to the company's expanded PGA TOUR Partners and Family Protection Network programs, both launched in April 1995. Excluding the charge, IQ would have shown breakeven results on a pretax basis.

Stock Performance - 25-AUG-95

In the past 30 trading days, IQ's shares have increased 6%, compared to a 0.04% rise in the S&P 500. Average trading volume for the past five days was 228,560 shares, compared with the 40-day moving average of 184,644 shares.

Key Stock Statistics

Dividend Rate/Share	0.20	Shareholders	900
Shs. outstg. (M)	28.9	Market cap. (B)	$0.304
Avg. daily vol. (M)	0.301	Inst. holdings	68%
Tang. Bk. Value/Share	4.15	Insider holdings	NA
Beta	0.36		

Value of $10,000 invested 5 years ago: $ 19,627

Fiscal Year Ending Dec. 31

	1995	% Change	1994	% Change	1993	% Change
Revenues (Million $)						
1Q	59.73	44%	41.39	10%	37.57	-4%
2Q	57.73	36%	42.56	9%	39.12	NM
3Q	—	—	44.17	11%	39.72	NM
4Q	—	—	47.43	18%	40.20	2%
Yr.	—	—	175.6	12%	156.6	NM
Income (Million $)						
1Q	0.30	-95%	6.44	-28%	8.90	9%
2Q	-46.67	NM	3.80	-55%	8.53	NM
3Q	—	—	6.64	-11%	7.49	-17%
4Q	—	—	1.14	-83%	6.56	54%
Yr.	—	—	18.02	-43%	31.48	40%
Earnings Per Share ($)						
1Q	0.01	-96%	0.24	-20%	0.30	11%
2Q	-1.62	NM	0.14	-52%	0.29	NM
3Q	—	—	0.23	-15%	0.27	-10%
4Q	—	—	0.04	-83%	0.24	71%
Yr.	—	—	0.63	-43%	1.10	47%

Next earnings report expected: late October

Ideon Group, Inc.

Business Summary - 29-AUG-95

Ideon Group, Inc. (formerly Safecard Services, Inc.) provides a variety of services to credit card customers of its credit card issuer clients. Subscribers are acquired through direct mail and telephone sales.

The company's primary service is a credit card loss notification system called Hot-Line, through which IQ notifies card issuers upon being informed that a subscriber's credit cards have been lost or stolen; there are also various ancillary service features. Annual fees are $15. The company also sells multi-year subscriptions, generally for a three-year period, at prices ranging from $39 to $45, providing for advance payment of the full subscription price. Hot-Line provided 70% and 73% of subscription revenues in fiscal 1994 and 1993, respectively.

Through arrangements with credit card issuers, IQ markets fee-based credit cards, generally to the issuer's existing no fee cardholders. For an annual fee of $15 to $25, cardholders who subscribe to fee-based credit cards typically receive a new credit card (from the card issuer), as well as services such as credit card registration, discounts on travel, insurance and other services provided or obtained by the company. Fees from card programs provided 15% and 13% of subscription revenues in fiscal 1994 and 1993, respectively.

Other services offered include Date Reminder, which provides subscribers by mail a monthly computer-generated reminder, listing personal dates and events registered by the subscriber in addition to standard holidays; CreditLine Services, under which subscribers receive a comprehensive personal credit report biography either annually or upon request, and other services such as a date reminder and a social security update; and a discount travel service.

The National Leisure Group, acquired in January 1995, provides vacation travel packages to credit card companies, retailers and wholesale clubs.

Contracts with Citicorp (South Dakota) N.A. and related entities contributed 30% and 34% of consolidated subscription revenue in fiscal 1994 and 1993, respectively.

Important Developments

Jul. '95—IQ said it plans to discontinue its child registration and missing child search services; cut back on its SafeCard Services unit; redesign its PGA Tour Partners program; and reduce corporate headquarters staff by 60%. A related charge of $73 million was recorded in the 1995 second quarter.

Capitalization

Bank Notes: None (3/95).

Per Share Data ($)

(Year Ended Dec. 31)

	1994	1993	1992	1991	1990	1989
Tangible Bk. Val.	6.53	6.54	6.21	5.50	4.53	3.65
Cash Flow	0.68	1.13	0.77	1.04	0.95	0.85
Earnings	0.63	1.10	0.75	1.02	0.93	0.82
Dividends	0.20	0.20	0.15	0.15	0.13	0.10
Payout Ratio	32%	18%	18%	13%	12%	11%
Prices - High	$20\frac{3}{4}$	$16\frac{5}{8}$	12	$11\frac{3}{8}$	$11\frac{3}{4}$	7
- Low	$13\frac{3}{4}$	$8\frac{7}{8}$	$7\frac{3}{4}$	$5\frac{7}{8}$	$5\frac{3}{8}$	$4\frac{1}{4}$
P/E Ratio - High	33	15	16	11	13	9
- Low	22	8	10	6	6	5

Income Statement Analysis (Million $)

	1994	%Chg	1993	%Chg	1992	%Chg	1991
Revs.	176	12%	157	8%	146	4%	141
Oper. Inc.	19.9	-39%	32.8	-7%	35.3	7%	33.1
Depr.	1.4	57%	0.9	12%	0.8	-11%	0.9
Int. Exp.	NA	—	Nil	—	NA	—	NA
Pretax Inc.	24.2	-43%	42.4	47%	28.9	-30%	41.5
Eff. Tax Rate	26%	—	26%	—	22%	—	29%
Net Inc.	18.0	-43%	31.5	40%	22.5	-24%	29.7

Balance Sheet & Other Fin. Data (Million $)

	1994	1993	1992	1991	1990	1989
Cash	5.7	3.0	31.0	61.0	73.0	40.0
Curr. Assets	NA	98.0	115	140	146	104
Total Assets	472	378	377	352	325	281
Curr. Liab.	NA	145	139	125	118	108
LT Debt	Nil	Nil	Nil	3.3	3.5	3.6
Common Eqty.	218	158	165	145	119	97.0
Total Cap.	238	185	196	191	167	139
Cap. Exp.	8.0	1.0	6.4	1.8	0.9	0.3
Cash Flow	19.4	32.3	23.3	30.6	27.8	25.6

Ratio Analysis

	1994	1993	1992	1991	1990	1989
Curr. Ratio	NA	0.7	0.8	1.1	1.2	1.0
% LT Debt of Cap.	Nil	Nil	Nil	1.7	2.1	2.6
% Net Inc.of Revs.	10.3	20.1	15.4	21.1	21.6	23.1
% Ret. on Assets	3.9	8.7	6.1	8.8	8.9	9.5
% Ret. on Equity	8.9	20.5	14.4	22.5	24.9	26.3

Dividend Data —Dividends returned to a quarterly basis in December 1992.

Amt. of Div. $	Date Decl.	Ex-Div. Date	Stock of Record	Payment Date
0.050	Sep. 09	Sep. 15	Sep. 21	Sep. 30 '94
0.050	Dec. 09	Dec. 15	Dec. 21	Dec. 29 '94
0.050	Feb. 24	Mar. 15	Mar. 21	Mar. 29 '95
0.050	Apr. 28	Jun. 19	Jun. 21	Jun. 29 '95

Data as orig. reptd.; bef. results of disc. opers. and/or spec. items. Per share data adj. for stk. divs. as of ex-div. date. Prior to 1995, fisc. yr. ended Oct. 31. E-Estimated. NA-Not Available. NM-Not Meaningful. NR-Not Ranked.

Office—3001 E. Pershing Blvd., Cheyenne, WY 82001. **Tel**—(307) 771-2700. **Chrmn & CEO**—P. G. Kahn. **Vice Chrmn & CFO**—G.T. Frankland. **Pres & COO**—J. R. Birk. **VP & Investor Contact**—William Lackey (904-928-1836). **Dirs**—W. T. Bacon, Jr., M. L. Burman, J. E. Bush, R. L. Dilenschneider, A. W. Herbert, Jr., P. G. Kahn, E. Miller, T. F. Petway III. **Transfer Agent & Registrar**—American Stock Transfer & Trust Co., NYC. **Incorporated** in Delaware in 1969. **Empl**-779. **S&P Analyst:** Stephen Madonna, CFA

Immune Response

STANDARD & POOR'S
STOCK REPORTS

NASDAQ Symbol **IMNR**
In S&P SmallCap 600

04-OCT-95 **Industry:** Drugs-Generic and OTC

Summary: This company is developing products to treat HIV infection and autoimmune disease. Its TargeTech unit is developing technology to correct gene defects and treat hepatitis.

Quantitative Evaluations
Outlook (1 Lowest—5 Highest) • **NA**
Fair Value • **NA**
Risk • **High**
Earn./Div. Rank • **NR**
Technical Eval. • **Bullish** since 8/95
Rel. Strength Rank (1 Lowest—99 Highest) • **95**
Insider Activity • **Unfavorable**

Recent Price • 7½ Yield • Nil
52 Wk Range • 8¾-2⅝ 12-Mo. P/E • NM

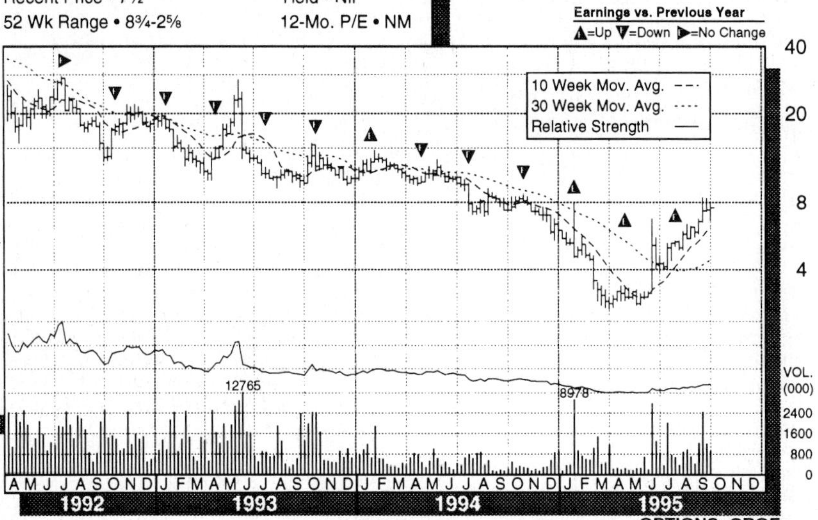

OPTIONS: CBOE

Business Profile - 04-OCT-95

Arbitration concerning the joint venture with Rhone-Poulenc Rorer was settled in March 1995, with IMNR retaining control of all R&D of the HIV immunotherapeutic. Immune Response's costs are expected to increase significantly. The company has yet to obtain FDA approval to proceed with Phase III trials. Two Phase II trials for psoriasis and rheumatoid arthritis commenced during the second quarter of 1995.

Operational Review - 04-OCT-95

Revenues for the six months ended June 30, 1995, were down 45%, year to year, reflecting a much lower amount of contract research revenue. R&D spending increased to $8.5 million, from $6.8 million, due to the assumption of all development responsibilities for the HIV immunotherapeutic. After lower administrative costs, higher investment income, and equity in reduced losses of a joint venture with Rhone-Poulenc Rorer, the net loss was $8.8 million ($0.53 a share), versus $9.9 million ($0.60).

Stock Performance - 29-SEP-95

In the past 30 trading days, IMNR's shares have increased 37%, compared to a 5% rise in the S&P 500. Average trading volume for the past five days was 179,940 shares, compared with the 40-day moving average of 227,138 shares.

Key Stock Statistics

Dividend Rate/Share	Nil	Shareholders	1,100
Shs. outstg. (M)	16.7	Market cap. (B)	$0.119
Avg. daily vol. (M)	0.300	Inst. holdings	20%
Tang. Bk. Value/Share	3.54	Insider holdings	NA
Beta	NM		

Value of $10,000 invested 5 years ago: NA

Fiscal Year Ending Dec. 31

	1995	% Change	1994	% Change	1993	% Change
Revenues (Million $)						
1Q	1.31	6%	1.24	11%	1.12	6%
2Q	0.13	-91%	1.40	20%	1.17	46%
3Q	—	—	2.59	119%	1.18	15%
4Q	—	—	1.81	39%	1.30	13%
Yr.	—	—	7.03	47%	4.77	18%
Income (Million $)						
1Q	-4.50	NM	-4.63	NM	-3.87	NM
2Q	-4.35	NM	-5.30	NM	-4.35	NM
3Q	—	—	-3.26	NM	-3.11	NM
4Q	—	—	-4.21	NM	-4.41	NM
Yr.	—	—	-17.40	NM	-15.74	NM
Earnings Per Share ($)						
1Q	-0.27	NM	-0.28	NM	-0.23	NM
2Q	-0.26	NM	-0.32	NM	-0.26	NM
3Q	—	—	-0.20	NM	-0.19	NM
4Q	—	—	-0.25	NM	-0.27	NM
Yr.	—	—	-1.05	NM	-0.95	NM

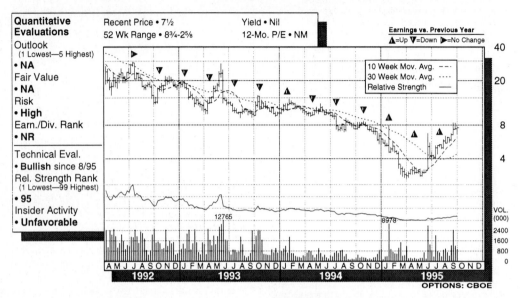

Next earnings report expected: late October

Immune Response

Business Summary - 04-OCT-95

The Immune Response Corporation is a biopharmaceutical company focused on developing, manufacturing and marketing proprietary products to treat human immunodeficiency virus (HIV) infection, which is believed to lead to acquired immune deficiency syndrome (AIDS), and for the treatment of certain major autoimmune diseases (particularly rheumatoid arthritis, multiple sclerosis and psoriasis). Wholly owned TargeTech, Inc. is developing a core technology intended for treatment of human diseases through gene therapy.

IMNR's first product under development is an HIV therapeutic vaccine that uses inactivated HIV depleted of its outer coat (envelope protein gp120). IMNR believes that this approach may produce a more potent therapeutic product than those based on the viral envelope or other virus subunits.

Immunization Products Ltd., a joint venture with Rhone-Poulenc Rorer Inc., presented results of a Phase II/III clinical trial of its HIV immunotherapeutic in July 1993. In January 1995, an FDA advisory committee recommended that the agency allow the company to conduct a Phase III human clinical trial of its HIV immunotherapeutic involving more than 3,000 patients. FDA approval for Phase III trials is still pending. In March 1995, the company regained all product rights for the HIV immunotherapeutic from Rhone-Poulenc Rorer

In the area of autoimmune diseases, the company is developing products that induce an immune response to inhibit or destroy specific autoreactive T cells by targeting the cells via unique markers on their T cell receptors. IMNR has identified specific T cells from joints of rheumatoid arthritis patients that it believes are causing damage to the joint tissue. Phase II trials of an arthritis therapeutic began in July 1995. Additionally, the company is researching treatments for psoriasis, a skin disease, using the same techniques as those to fight arthritis. A Phase II trial commenced in September 1995.

Wholly owned TargeTech Inc. is developing a technology designed to enable direct intravenous injection of gene drugs, DNA/RNA fragments (antisense) and drugs targeted specifically to a receptor on liver cells.

Important Developments

Sep. '95—The company agreed to supply its HIV immunotherapeutic to Trinity Medical Group of Thailand in a planned study of up to 10,000 HIV-infected individuals. Earlier, during the second quarter, Immune Response began a Phase II trial to treat rheumatoid arthritis and another Phase II trial for psoriasis.

Capitalization

Long Term Debt: None (6/95).

Per Share Data ($)

(Year Ended Dec. 31)

	1994	1993	1992	1991	1990	1989
Tangible Bk. Val.	4.01	5.13	6.09	7.10	2.90	-1.24
Cash Flow	-0.97	-0.88	-2.15	-0.20	-0.12	-0.62
Earnings	-1.05	-0.95	-2.19	-0.23	-0.12	-0.63
Dividends	Nil	Nil	Nil	Nil	Nil	Nil
Payout Ratio	Nil	Nil	Nil	Nil	Nil	Nil
Prices - High	13¾	28½	47¼	62¾	7⅞	NA
- Low	5⅝	9¼	12¼	2⅞	2¾	NA
P/E Ratio - High	NM	NM	NM	NM	NM	NM
- Low	NM	NM	NM	NA	NA	NA

Income Statement Analysis (Million $)

	1994	%Chg	1993	%Chg	1992	%Chg	1991
Revs.	7.0	48%	4.8	18%	4.0	-5%	4.3
Oper. Inc.	-10.8	NM	-10.0	NM	-6.6	NM	-4.1
Depr.	1.3	7%	1.2	95%	0.6	61%	0.4
Int. Exp.	NA	—	NA	—	Nil	—	Nil
Pretax Inc.	-17.4	NM	-15.7	NM	-33.8	NM	-3.0
Eff. Tax Rate	NM	—	NM	—	NM	—	Nil
Net Inc.	-17.4	NM	-15.7	NM	-33.8	NM	-3.0

Balance Sheet & Other Fin. Data (Million $)

	1994	1993	1992	1991	1990	1989
Cash	59.0	75.0	90.0	104	25.0	7.0
Curr. Assets	61.0	77.0	93.0	106	28.0	9.0
Total Assets	68.0	87.0	103	110	33.0	10.0
Curr. Liab.	1.4	1.5	2.0	1.4	0.7	0.4
LT Debt	Nil	0.3	0.5	Nil	Nil	Nil
Common Eqty.	67.0	85.0	101	108	32.0	-6.0
Total Cap.	67.0	85.0	101	108	32.0	10.0
Cap. Exp.	0.8	0.9	4.2	0.6	2.9	0.0
Cash Flow	-16.1	-14.6	-33.1	-2.6	-1.2	-4.6

Ratio Analysis

	1994	1993	1992	1991	1990	1989
Curr. Ratio	43.4	50.8	45.9	74.1	40.8	23.7
% LT Debt of Cap.	Nil	0.3	0.5	Nil	Nil	Nil
% Net Inc.of Revs.	NM	NM	NM	NM	NM	NM
% Ret. on Assets	NM	NM	NM	NM	NM	NM
% Ret. on Equity	NM	NM	NM	NM	NM	NM

Dividend Data —Cash dividends have never been paid. The company does not expect to pay any cash dividends for the foreseeable future.

Data as orig. reptd.; bef. results of disc. opers. and/or spec. items. Per share data adj. for stk. divs. as of ex-div. date. E-Estimated. NA-Not Available. NM-Not Meaningful. NR-Not Ranked.

Office—5935 Darwin Ct., Carlsbad, CA 92008. **Tel**—(619) 431-7080. **Chrmn**—J. B. Glavin. **Pres & CEO**—D. J. Carlo. **VP-Fin, CFO, Secy & Treas**—C. J. Cashion. **Investor Contact**—Debra L. Altman. **Dirs**—D. J. Carlo, J. B. Glavin, K. B. Kimberlin, G. S. Omenn, J. Simon, W. M. Sullivan, P. M. Young. **Transfer Agent & Registrar**—First Interstate Bank, Los Angeles. **Incorporated** in Delaware in 1986. **Empl**-111. **S&P Analyst:** Thomas Tirney

STANDARD & POOR'S

STOCK REPORTS

Imo Industries

NYSE Symbol **IMD**

In S&P SmallCap 600

02-SEP-95

Industry: Electronics/Electric

Summary: This company is a leading international supplier of mechanical and electronic controls, engineered power products, and related support services.

Quantitative Evaluations

Outlook (1 Lowest—5 Highest)
• **1**

Fair Value
• **6⅝**

Risk
• **High**

Earn./Div. Rank
• **C**

Technical Eval.
• **Bullish** since 3/95

Rel. Strength Rank (1 Lowest—99 Highest)
• **61**

Insider Activity
• **Neutral**

Recent Price • 9⅜

52 Wk Range • 12½-6⅛

Yield • Nil

12-Mo. P/E • 3.0

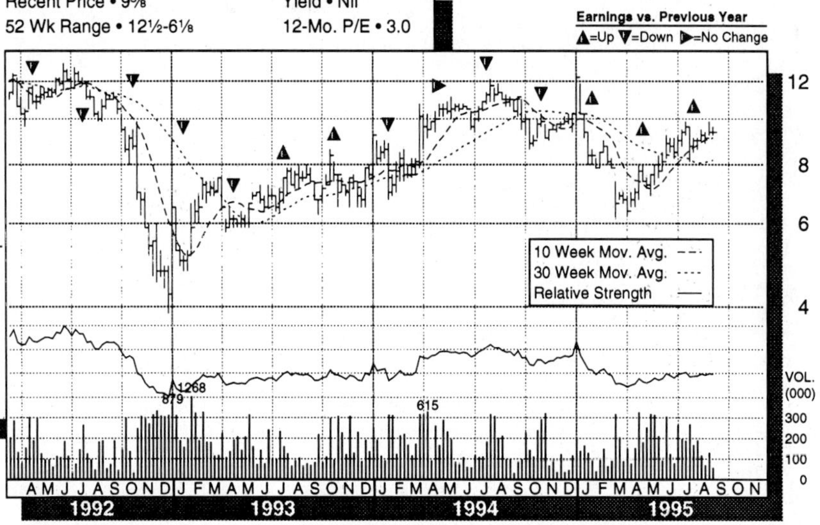

Business Profile - 18-AUG-95

Imo Industries has undergone a major restructuring, selling off divisions in an attempt to reduce debt. Through the first six months of 1995, the company had shed over $100 million in long-term debt. In March, 1995, shareholders' equity was restored to a positive value as a result of the gain on the sale of the Turbomachinery operations. At June 30, 1995, shareholder equity was approximately $18 million, versus a deficit of $28 million at year end 1994.

Operational Review - 18-AUG-95

Revenues in the six months ended June 30, 1995, rose 7.5%, year to year, as sales in the Morse Controls and Pumps, Power Transmission & Instrumentation divisions increased by 11% and 9%, respectively. Margins widened, due to higher sales volume, as well as cost savings resulting from restructuring efforts. Net income from continuing operations advanced to $6,960,000 ($0.41 a share) from $499,000 ($0.03). Results for 1995 exclude an extraordinary loss of $0.24 from the extinguishment of debt.

Stock Performance - 01-SEP-95

In the past 30 trading days, IMD's shares have increased 7%, compared to a 2% rise in the S&P 500. Average trading volume for the past five days was 10,760 shares, compared with the 40-day moving average of 29,005 shares.

Key Stock Statistics

Dividend Rate/Share	Nil	Shareholders	24,300
Shs. outstg. (M)	17.1	Market cap. (B)	$0.160
Avg. daily vol. (M)	0.018	Inst. holdings	63%
Tang. Bk. Value/Share	NM	Insider holdings	NA
Beta	0.82		

Value of $10,000 invested 5 years ago: $ 6,936

Fiscal Year Ending Dec. 31

	1995	% Change	1994	% Change	1993	% Change
Revenues (Million $)						
1Q	124.4	12%	110.7	-34%	167.0	-27%
2Q	127.2	3%	123.2	-26%	167.0	-32%
3Q	—	—	113.4	-26%	154.0	-24%
4Q	—	—	116.5	-24%	153.1	-39%
Yr.	—	—	463.9	-28%	641.1	-31%
Income (Million $)						
1Q	3.55	NM	0.51	24%	0.41	-69%
2Q	3.41	NM	-0.01	NM	3.47	NM
3Q	—	—	2.05	-57%	4.74	NM
4Q	—	—	1.11	NM	-47.76	NM
Yr.	—	—	3.67	NM	-39.14	NM
Earnings Per Share ($)						
1Q	0.21	NM	0.03	NM	0.03	-63%
2Q	0.20	—	Nil	—	0.20	NM
3Q	—	—	0.12	-57%	0.28	NM
4Q	—	—	0.07	NM	-2.82	NM
Yr.	—	—	0.22	NM	-2.31	NM

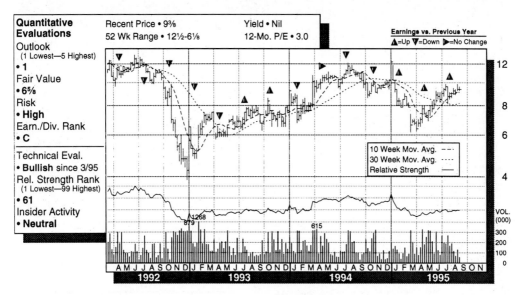

Next earnings report expected: early November

Imo Industries

Business Summary - 01-SEP-95

Imo Industries Inc. is an integrated international manufacturer of proprietary products focused on controls and engineered power products and their support services. Segment contributions in 1994 (operating profits in million $):

	Sales	Profits
Pumps, Power Transmission	55%	$29.1
Morse Controls	42%	$14.7
Other	2%	Nil

The company markets its products primarily through its own direct sales force, which accounted for 75% of total sales in 1994; the remaining sales were made through agents and distributors. Fiat S.p.A. was the company's largest customer in 1994, comprising 50% of Morse Control's sales and 21% of consolidated sales. Sales to the Department of Defense totaled 7% in 1994, down from a high of 22% in 1992.

The Pump, Power Transmission and Instrumentation segment produces a wide range of products that control the speed, force and direction of motion in processes and products. Major products include a wide range of pumps, including a proprietary line of three screw pumps; gears and speed reducers; and adjustable-speed motor drives. Other instruments include liquid level indicators and switches, and vibration and pressure transducers.

The Morse Controls segment manufactures precision mechanical and electronic control products and systems used primarily for aviation, marine, automotive and industrial applications. Products include cable and control systems (used in steering, throttle control and valve adjustment), a manual gear shift system (used in Fiat and Lotus autos), actuators, window controls, latches, and door panels and assemblies.

In January 1995, IMD sold its Delaval Turbine and Turbocare divisions and its 50% interest in Delaval-Stork, a Dutch joint venture, to Mannesmann Demag of Germany for $124 million. Also in January, the company sold its Baird Analytical Instruments unit to Thermo Instrument Systems, Inc. for about $12.3 million in cash. In June 1995, the company sold most of the assets of its Electro-Optical Systems to Litton Industries.

Important Developments

Jun. '95—Imo announced that it completed the sale of most of its Electro-Optical Systems business to Litton Industries, including all the assets of Varo Inc. and Baird Optical Systems, other than real estate and the Varo Electronic Systems division. Proceeds from the sale were used to pay off domestic bank debt and to redeem $40 million of subordinated debentures.

Capitalization

Long Term Debt: $271,425,000 (6/95).
Minority Interest: $2,270,000.

Per Share Data ($) (Year Ended Dec. 31)

	1994	1993	1992	1991	1990	1989
Tangible Bk. Val.	-6.49	-7.52	1.48	6.87	6.88	7.25
Cash Flow	1.14	-0.94	-1.26	2.63	2.81	3.21
Earnings	0.22	-2.32	-3.26	0.68	1.20	1.88
Dividends	Nil	Nil	0.38	0.50	0.49	0.41
Payout Ratio	Nil	Nil	NM	74%	38%	22%
Prices - High	12½	9¼	13¾	17¾	18⅜	22¾
- Low	6¾	4¾	3⅞	9⅜	6⅝	13⅞
P/E Ratio - High	57	NM	NM	26	15	12
- Low	31	NM	NM	14	6	7

Income Statement Analysis (Million $)

	1994	%Chg	1993	%Chg	1992	%Chg	1991
Revs.	464	-30%	662	-29%	928	-9%	1,024
Oper. Inc.	54.0	-10%	60.0	7%	56.0	-47%	106
Depr.	15.7	-32%	23.2	-31%	33.7	3%	32.8
Int. Exp.	33.8	-27%	46.3	-23%	60.4	-2%	61.9
Pretax Inc.	6.5	NM	-24.0	NM	-80.6	NM	20.2
Eff. Tax Rate	38%	—	NM	—	NM	—	38%
Net Inc.	3.7	NM	-39.1	NM	-55.0	NM	11.4

Balance Sheet & Other Fin. Data (Million $)

	1994	1993	1992	1991	1990	1989
Cash	26.9	19.9	19.4	13.7	8.2	64.8
Curr. Assets	278	307	446	464	503	508
Total Assets	575	638	995	1,046	1,093	1,019
Curr. Liab.	143	200	335	237	264	205
LT Debt	377	354	320	410	423	422
Common Eqty.	-28.0	-34.0	241	337	334	333
Total Cap.	359	335	588	779	797	790
Cap. Exp.	9.2	13.9	23.0	28.8	34.0	84.5
Cash Flow	19.3	-15.9	-21.3	44.2	49.7	58.0

Ratio Analysis

	1994	1993	1992	1991	1990	1989
Curr. Ratio	1.9	1.5	1.3	2.0	1.9	2.5
% LT Debt of Cap.	105.1	105.4	54.4	52.6	53.1	53.4
% Net Inc.of Revs.	0.8	NM	NM	1.1	2.1	4.0
% Ret. on Assets	0.6	NM	NM	1.1	2.1	3.8
% Ret. on Equity	NM	NM	NM	3.4	6.6	10.6

Dividend Data —Dividends were omitted in October 1992 after having been initiated in 1987. Due to provisions of its long term debt agreements, IMD is prohibited from declaring or paying cash dividends until July 31, 1997.

Data as orig. reptd.; bef. results of disc. opers. and/or spec. items. Per share data adj. for stk. divs. as of ex-div. date. E-Estimated. NA-Not Available. NM-Not Meaningful. NR-Not Ranked.

Office—1009 Lenox Drive, Lawrenceville, NJ 08648. **Tel**—(609) 896-7600. **Chrmn, Pres & CEO**—D. K. Farrar. **EVP-CFO**—W. M. Brown. **EVP-Secy**—T. J. Bird. **Investor Contact**—Paul B. Lazovick. **Dirs**—J. B. Edwards, D. K. Farrar, J. S. Gould, R. J. Grosh, C. P. Thacher, D. C. Trauscht, A. E. Van Leuven. **Transfer Agent & Registrar**—First Chicago Trust Company of New York, Jersey City, NJ. **Incorporated** in Delaware in 1901. **Empl-** 3,900. **S&P Analyst:** N. Rosenberg

INDRESCO Inc.

NYSE Symbol **ID**
In S&P SmallCap 600

12-SEP-95 **Industry:** Mining/Diversified

Summary: This company manufactures refractory products, recycling/processing equipment, mining equipment, flanges and specialized industrial tools used by a wide range of industries.

Quantitative Evaluations
Outlook (1 Lowest—5 Highest)
• **NA**
Fair Value
• **NA**
Risk
• **Average**
Earn./Div. Rank
• **NR**

Technical Eval.
• **Bearish** since 5/95
Rel. Strength Rank (1 Lowest—99 Highest)
• **75**
Insider Activity
• **NA**

Recent Price • 17⅜
52 Wk Range • 17⅜-10⅞
Yield • Nil
12-Mo. P/E • 11.7

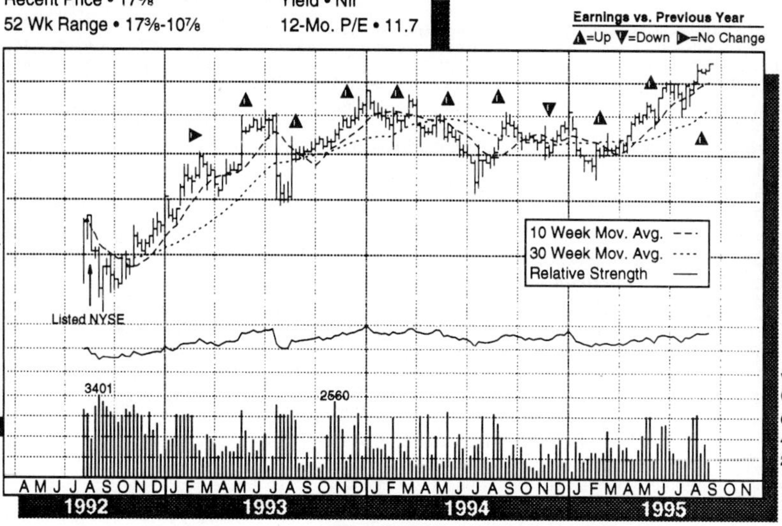

Business Profile - 12-SEP-95

INDRESCO, which was spun off from Dresser Industries in August 1992, operates Dresser's former products and equipment businesses. These include the manufacture of refractory products, walking draglines and power shovels, underground mining machines, pneumatic tools and hydraulic drilling equipment, and screw air compressors. Results in recent periods have been aided by contributions from three new businesses, REFMEX, Shred Pax and Ameri-Forge, and from an internal restructuring program.

Operational Review - 07-SEP-95

Revenues for the nine months ended July 31, 1995, climbed 35%, year to year, reflecting contributions from recent acqusitions. The new REFMEX and RECSA, Mexican and Chilean refractory operations added substantial profitability to solid results at Harbison-Walker. The surface mining equipment business is also returning to profitability from its first-half loss position. Earnings per share comparisons were further enhanced by 6.1% fewer shares outstanding.

Stock Performance - 08-SEP-95

In the past 30 trading days, ID's shares have increased 9%, compared to a 2% rise in the S&P 500. Average trading volume for the past five days was 43,225 shares, compared with the 40-day moving average of 80,928 shares.

Key Stock Statistics

Dividend Rate/Share	Nil	Shareholders	9,900
Shs. outstg. (M)	22.7	Market cap. (B)	$0.397
Avg. daily vol. (M)	0.089	Inst. holdings	71%
Tang. Bk. Value/Share	11.81	Insider holdings	NA
Beta	NA		

Value of $10,000 invested 5 years ago: NA

Fiscal Year Ending Oct. 31

	1995	% Change	1994	% Change	1993	% Change
Revenues (Million $)						
1Q	126.3	26%	99.9	-19%	123.1	-7%
2Q	142.0	34%	106.3	-21%	134.0	-2%
3Q	155.0	43%	108.4	-15%	127.5	-9%
4Q	—	—	126.2	-19%	155.4	4%
Yr.	—	—	440.8	-18%	540.0	-3%
Income (Million $)						
1Q	3.20	NM	0.90	NM	-4.50	NM
2Q	9.90	94%	5.10	42%	3.60	NM
3Q	11.40	33%	8.60	56%	5.50	NM
4Q	—	—	10.00	-40%	16.80	NM
Yr.	—	—	24.60	15%	21.40	NM
Earnings Per Share ($)						
1Q	0.14	NM	0.04	NM	-0.16	NM
2Q	0.43	105%	0.21	62%	0.13	NM
3Q	0.50	43%	0.35	75%	0.20	NM
4Q	—	—	0.42	-31%	0.61	NM
Yr.	—	—	1.02	31%	0.78	NM

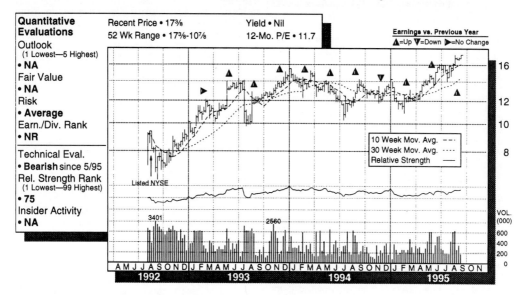

Next earnings report expected: mid December

INDRESCO Inc.

Business Summary - 12-SEP-95

INDRESCO is involved in three lines of business: mining and specialty equipment, minerals and refractory products, and industrial tool. Business segment contributions (excluding Komatsu Dresser and Komdresco) in fiscal 1994:

	Sales	Profits
Mining & Specialty Equipment	29%	0.5%
Minerals & Refractory Products	55%	76.9%
Industrial Tool	16%	22.6%

Foreign business accounted for 25% of total revenues in fiscal 1994.

The Marion division is a leading producer of walking and crawler draglines, electric mining shovels, rotary blast-hole drills and related equipment used in surface mining sold in the U.S. and abroad. Coal producers accounted for about 70% of the division's revenues in recent years. The Jeffrey operations produce underground continuous mining machines, haulage systems and related equipment (used in underground bituminous coal mines), as well as shearers (used in longwall underground coal mining). In 1994 Jeffrey continued to improve its mining equipment to better enable it to capitalize on the growing market for low seam continuous miners.

The Harbison-Walker Refractories (HWR) division is a leading supplier of refractory products and an overseas licensor of technology. HWR mines and processes certain minerals, and manufactures over 200 refractory products. Refractories are used in virtually every industrial process requiring heating or containment of a solid, liquid or gas at a high temperature. Iron and steel producers account for a substantial portion of refractory sales. Refmex and RefGreen, acquired in September 1994, are the largest producer in Mexico of high quality refractories serving the Mexican, U.S., Central and South American markets.

Industrial Tool includes Cleco pneumatic tools (such as assembly tools used in electronic, aircraft, and automotive markets) and maintenance and fabrication tools (supplied to petroleum refineries, chemical plants, foundries and steel mills); and Quackenbush pneumatic and hydraulic precision drilling equipment (used in aircraft and aerospace industries and in mobile machining applications), and airtool cleaners and expanders (used in heat exchangers and boilers).

Important Developments

Aug. '95—With continuing strength in major product areas, improving surface mining equipment bookings and backlog, and a strong financial position, ID expects further profit improvements in fiscal 1996.

Capitalization

Long Term Debt: $3,900,000 (4/95).

Per Share Data ($) (Year Ended Oct. 31)

	1994	1993	1992	1991	1990	1989
Tangible Bk. Val.	11.81	11.15	12.70	NA	NA	NA
Cash Flow	1.41	1.29	-1.40	0.24	NA	NA
Earnings	1.02	0.78	-1.84	-0.18	NA	NA
Dividends	Nil	Nil	Nil	NA	NA	NA
Payout Ratio	Nil	Nil	Nil	NA	NA	NA
Prices - High	15½	15½	10⅛	NA	NA	NA
- Low	10¼	9	6⅜	NA	NA	NA
P/E Ratio - High	15	20	NM	NA	NA	NA
- Low	10	12	NA	NA	NA	NA

Income Statement Analysis (Million $)

	1994	%Chg	1993	%Chg	1992	%Chg	1991
Revs.	437	-19%	538	-4%	559	-10%	618
Oper. Inc.	27.7	-14%	32.3	52%	21.2	NM	-2.3
Depr.	9.3	-32%	13.7	12%	12.2	11%	11.0
Int. Exp.	NM	—	Nil	—	Nil	—	NA
Pretax Inc.	24.6	122%	11.1	NM	-50.8	NM	3.5
Eff. Tax Rate	Nil	—	NM	—	NM	—	234%
Net Inc.	24.6	15%	21.4	NM	-50.1	NM	-4.7

Balance Sheet & Other Fin. Data (Million $)

	1994	1993	1992	1991	1990	1989
Cash	27.0	116	32.4	8.0	NA	NA
Curr. Assets	277	307	249	234	NA	NA
Total Assets	478	461	491	516	NA	NA
Curr. Liab.	130	110	131	115	NA	NA
LT Debt	2.0	Nil	1.9	2.7	NA	NA
Common Eqty.	274	288	352	396	NA	NA
Total Cap.	289	288	355	401	NA	NA
Cap. Exp.	13.0	10.4	15.3	NA	NA	NA
Cash Flow	33.9	35.1	-37.9	6.3	NA	NA

Ratio Analysis

	1994	1993	1992	1991	1990	1989
Curr. Ratio	2.1	2.8	1.9	2.0	NA	NA
% LT Debt of Cap.	0.7	Nil	0.5	0.7	NA	NA
% Net Inc.of Revs.	5.6	4.0	NM	NM	NA	NA
% Ret. on Assets	5.6	4.7	NM	NA	NA	NA
% Ret. on Equity	9.4	6.9	NM	NA	NA	NA

Dividend Data —No dividends have been paid. A "poison pill" stock purchase right was distributed with ID's common stock in the August 1992 spin-off.

Data as orig. reptd.; bef. results of disc. opers. and/or spec. items. Per share data adj. for stk. divs. as of ex-div. date. E-Estimated. NA-Not Available. NM-Not Meaningful. NR-Not Ranked.

Office—2121 San Jacinto St., Suite 2500, Dallas, TX 75201. **Tel**—(214) 953-4500. **Chrmn, Pres & CEO**—J. L. Jackson. **VP-Fin Treas & CFO**—G. G. Garrison. **VP-Secy**—S. G. Barnett. **Dirs**—D. H. Blake, S. B. Casey Jr., R. Fulgham, J. L. Jackson, R. W. Vieser. **Transfer Agent & Registrar**—Bank of New York, NYC. **Incorporated** in Delaware in 1972. **Empl**-4,045. **S&P Analyst:** M.C.C.

STANDARD & POOR'S

STOCK REPORTS

Input/Output, Inc.

NYSE Symbol **IO**
In S&P SmallCap 600

26-OCT-95 **Industry:** Oil and Gas

Summary: This company designs, makes and markets seismic data acquisition systems. Most revenues come from outside the U.S.

S&P Opinion: Accumulate (★★★★) Recent Price • 40⅛ | 52 Wk Range • 41¾-19 | Yield • Nil | 12-Mo. P/E • 28.9

Quantitative Evaluations
Outlook (1 Lowest—5 Highest) • **5**
Fair Value • **47¼**
Risk • **Average**
Earn./Div. Rank • **NR**

Technical Eval. • **Bearish** since 8/95
Rel. Strength Rank (1 Lowest—99 Highest) • **71**
Insider Activity • **Neutral**

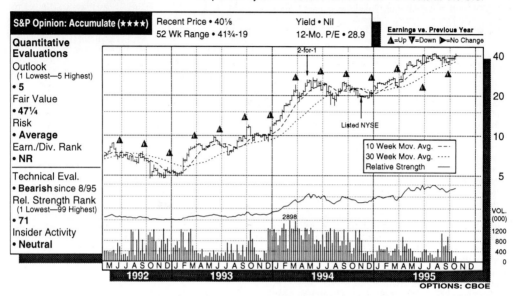

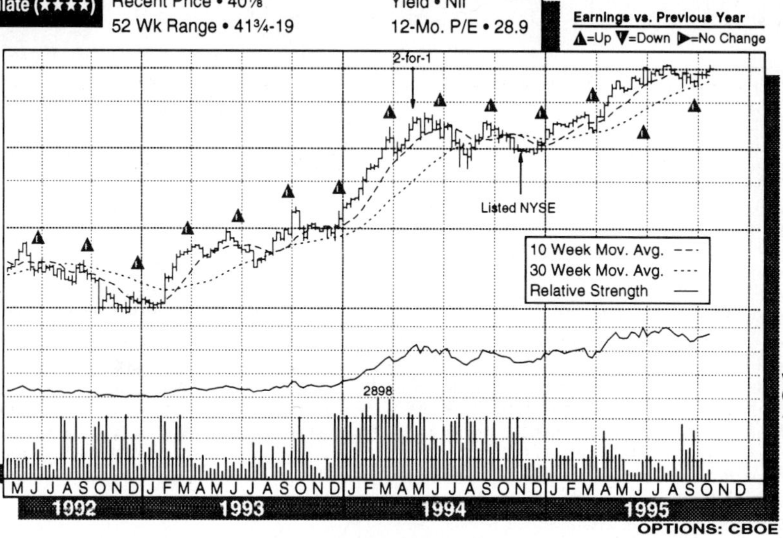

OPTIONS: CBOE

Overview - 26-OCT-95

IO designs, makes and markets seismic data acquisition systems and instruments crucial to the exploration activities of the oil and gas industry. Sales are to contractors, who collect customer-specified data, and to major, independent and foreign government-owned oil and gas companies. Most sales are made either overseas or to domestic customers who deploy company systems internationally. IO has sold a number of systems to Russia, and anticipates further sales to this market as experience with 3-D seismic grows. Its products are designed to provide superior perfomance across a wide range of operating environments. Investment in R&D, design and manufacturing leads developement of high performance products. The company also seeks strategic acquisitions, like its recent purchase of Western Geophysical.

Valuation - 26-OCT-95

The shares have been boosted by the recent acquisition of Western Geophysical, and by record earnings in 1994-95. Further earnings growth can be expected, as the oil and gas industry increasingly relies upon the type of products that IO provides. Western Geophysical product lines, including marine capabilities, are complementary, and can be expected to add to revenues and profits. IO has established a pattern of sensible acquisitions; benefits from Western Geophysical should be seen within six months, at which time the shares should see more appreciation. Based on their growth potential and current price, the shares are capable of further gains.

Key Stock Statistics

S&P EPS Est. 1996	1.52	Tang. Bk. Value/Share	7.54
P/E on S&P Est. 1996	26.4	Beta	NA
S&P EPS Est. 1997	1.75	Shareholders	200
Dividend Rate/Share	Nil	Market cap. (B)	$0.713
Shs. outstg. (M)	18.3	Inst. holdings	104%
Avg. daily vol. (M)	0.051	Insider holdings	NA

Value of $10,000 invested 5 years ago: NA

Fiscal Year Ending May 31

	1996	% Change	1995	% Change	1994	% Change
Revenues (Million $)						
1Q	54.76	100%	27.32	63%	16.78	48%
2Q	—	—	34.22	65%	20.80	46%
3Q	—	—	34.51	29%	26.70	87%
4Q	—	—	38.65	23%	31.47	118%
Yr.	—	—	134.7	41%	95.75	77%
Income (Million $)						
1Q	6.40	32%	4.84	104%	2.37	—
2Q	—	—	6.04	59%	3.81	—
3Q	—	—	6.71	28%	5.25	89%
4Q	—	—	6.91	34%	5.14	112%
Yr.	—	—	24.50	48%	16.56	81%
Earnings Per Share ($)						
1Q	0.34	31%	0.26	68%	0.15	63%
2Q	E0.37	16%	0.32	31%	0.24	44%
3Q	E0.40	11%	0.36	7%	0.33	76%
4Q	E0.41	11%	0.37	19%	0.31	94%
Yr.	E1.52	16%	1.31	25%	1.05	71%

Next earnings report expected: mid December

Business Summary - 26-OCT-95

Input/Output, Inc. is a leading designer and manufacturer of land-based seismic data acquisition systems and seismic instruments. IO markets its systems and instruments to the oil and gas exploration and production industry worldwide. Revenues by geographic area in recent years were as follows:

	1994-95	1993-94	1992-93
U.S.	31%	30%	20%
China	2%	5%	25%
Canada & Mexico	21%	43%	26%
Former Soviet Union	19%	5%	11%
Pakistan & India	1%	1%	6%
South America	8%	9%	5%
Europe	12%	4%	1%
Other	6%	3%	6%

IO believes that its principal product, the I/O SYSTEM product line, is the most technologically advanced land-based seismic data acquisition system. The system's multichannel capacity and flexible configuration capabilities allow for efficient and precise collection of seismic data, and make it ideally suited for multichannel 3-D seismic surveys, used increasingly in exploration and development activities. The price of a fully-equipped I/O SYSTEM typically averages $2.0 million, but can range from $800,000 to $4.5 million. Additionally, during fiscal 1994-95, the company introduced its new ocean bottom cable system for use in shallow marine and transition zone environments.

On June 30, 1995, a company subsidiary acquired the assets of the Exploration Products Group of the Western Geophysical Division of Western Atlas International, Inc., for $121.3 million. The business includes the manufacture, sale and marketing of marine and land seismic data acquisition systems; marine streamers; marine streamer navigation, positioning and quality control systems and related software products and certain other products and equipment related to seismic data.

Products are marketed through a direct sales force and several international manufacturers' representatives. Principal customers are seismic contractors who operate seismic crews using land-based seismic data acquisition systems to collect data in accordance with customer specifications or for their own seismic data liabraries. Other customers include major independent and foreign government-owned oil and gas companies that may require their contractors to use IO equipment.

Important Developments

Oct. '95—The company registered a planned public offering of 2,500,000 common shares.

Capitalization

Long Term Debt: None (5/95).

Per Share Data ($) (Year Ended May 31)

	1995	1994	1993	1992	1991	1990
Tangible Bk. Val.	8.09	6.03	3.20	2.58	2.02	1.03
Cash Flow	1.50	1.17	0.71	0.61	0.57	0.39
Earnings	1.31	1.05	0.62	0.54	0.50	0.33
Dividends	Nil	Nil	Nil	Nil	Nil	Nil
Payout Ratio	Nil	Nil	Nil	Nil	Nil	Nil
Cal. Yrs.	1994	1993	1992	1991	1990	1989
Prices - High	27¼	12¼	8⅞	6⅞	NA	NA
- Low	11⅞	4⅞	4¾	2¾	NA	NA
P/E Ratio - High	21	12	14	13	NA	NA
- Low	9	5	8	5	NA	NA

Income Statement Analysis (Million $)

	1995	%Chg	1994	%Chg	1993	%Chg	1992
Revs.	135	41%	95.8	77%	54.2	19%	45.5
Oper. Inc.	35.1	43%	24.6	78%	13.8	14%	12.1
Depr.	3.6	90%	1.9	30%	1.5	33%	1.1
Int. Exp.	0.0	-81%	0.2	-20%	0.2	-33%	0.3
Pretax Inc.	35.4	48%	24.0	80%	13.3	12%	11.9
Eff. Tax Rate	31%	—	31%	—	32%	—	34%
Net Inc.	24.5	48%	16.6	82%	9.1	17%	7.8

Balance Sheet & Other Fin. Data (Million $)

	1995	1994	1993	1992	1991	1990
Cash	57.4	58.4	4.5	9.0	6.3	1.3
Curr. Assets	121	101	40.1	29.2	26.1	16.7
Total Assets	105	132	61.5	46.3	40.8	30.9
Curr. Liab.	15.9	13.5	10.4	7.4	8.0	12.7
LT Debt	Nil	Nil	0.4	0.6	2.1	5.9
Common Eqty.	147	116	47.9	37.4	29.3	11.2
Total Cap.	147	117	49.5	38.9	32.9	18.2
Cap. Exp.	6.0	4.0	3.7	1.8	4.7	2.1
Cash Flow	28.1	18.4	10.6	8.9	6.6	4.3

Ratio Analysis

	1995	1994	1993	1992	1991	1990
Curr. Ratio	7.6	7.5	3.8	3.9	3.3	1.3
% LT Debt of Cap.	Nil	Nil	0.9	1.4	6.3	32.3
% Net Inc.of Revs.	18.2	17.3	16.9	17.2	15.9	12.7
% Ret. on Assets	16.3	16.2	16.7	18.0	14.0	12.0
% Ret. on Equity	18.5	19.2	21.1	23.5	25.9	37.9

Dividend Data —No cash has been paid, and no payments are expected in the foreseeable future. A two-for-one stock split was effected in May 1994.

Data as orig. reptd.; bef. results of disc. opers. and/or spec. items. Per share data adj. for stk. divs. as of ex-div. date. E-Estimated. NA-Not Available. NM-Not Meaningful. NR-Not Ranked.

Office—12300 Parc Crest Dr., Stafford, TX 77477. **Tel**—(713) 933-3339. **Fax**—(713) 879-9826. **Chrmn**—C. E. Selecman. **Pres & CEO**—G. D. Owens. **SVP, CFO & Secy**—R. P. Brindley. **VP & Investor Contact**—Christine R. Eilert. **Dirs**—R. P. Brindley, S. H. Carter, Jr., E. E. Cook, G. H. Denison, T. H. Elliott, Jr., P. T. Flawn, G. T. Graves III, G. D. Owens, C. E. Selecman, M. J. Sheen. **Transfer Agent**—KeyCorp Shareholder Services, Inc., Houston. **Incorporated** in Delaware in 1979. **Empl**-1,239. **S&P Analyst:** Michael C. Barr

Insituform Technologies

NASDAQ Symbol **INSUA**
In S&P SmallCap 600

07-AUG-95 **Industry:** Services

Summary: This company (formerly Insituform of North America) provides patented methods of reconstructing deteriorated pipelines and manholes with little or no excavation.

Quantitative Evaluations
Outlook (1 Lowest—5 Highest) • **NA**
Fair Value • **NA**
Risk • **Low**
Earn./Div. Rank • **B-**
Technical Eval. • **Bearish** since 5/95
Rel. Strength Rank (1 Lowest—99 Highest) • **76**
Insider Activity • **Neutral**

Recent Price • 15
52 Wk Range • 15⅛-10¾
Yield • Nil
12-Mo. P/E • 26.8

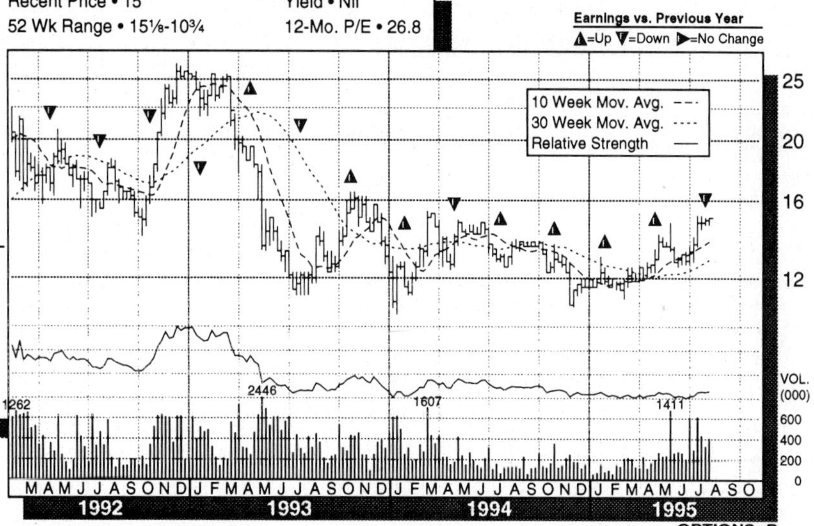

OPTIONS: P

Business Profile - 07-AUG-95

INSUA plans to continue to develop and acquire new technologies, significantly increase its rate of penetration of the industrial market and exploit its broad international presence and the worldwide rights to the Insituform process and other technologies. The company expects to focus on the Far East, Japan and India. Additionally, the company will establish economies of scale and greater operations flexibility through its proposed merger with Insituform Mid-America.

Operational Review - 07-AUG-95

Total revenues climbed in the first half of 1995, as increased construction contract revenues from acquired operations offset lower net sales. Profitability was hurt by increased construction costs and, following a $2.2 million after-tax litigation settlement charge, which outweighed a gain on the disposal of the company's investment in Enviroq Corp., net income declined. Near-term results should benefit from higher construction volume and controlled costs.

Stock Performance - 04-AUG-95

In the past 30 trading days, INSUA's shares have increased 17%, compared to a 2% rise in the S&P 500. Average trading volume for the past five days was 80,060 shares, compared with the 40-day moving average of 83,697 shares.

Key Stock Statistics

Dividend Rate/Share	Nil	Shareholders	2,100
Shs. outstg. (M)	14.4	Market cap. (B)	$0.215
Avg. daily vol. (M)	0.093	Inst. holdings	33%
Tang. Bk. Value/Share	1.37	Insider holdings	NA
Beta	1.91		

Value of $10,000 invested 5 years ago: $ 18,461

Fiscal Year Ending Dec. 31

	1995	% Change	1994	% Change	1993	% Change
Revenues (Million $)						
1Q	39.83	31%	30.48	90%	16.08	-23%
2Q	43.61	37%	31.80	53%	20.78	-22%
3Q	—	—	40.95	27%	32.20	15%
4Q	—	—	45.02	43%	31.45	56%
Yr.	—	—	148.3	47%	100.5	5%
Income (Million $)						
1Q	1.92	31%	1.47	-44%	2.61	18%
2Q	1.08	-50%	2.17	54%	1.41	-45%
3Q	—	—	3.62	23%	2.95	117%
4Q	—	—	2.53	NM	0.28	NM
Yr.	—	—	9.79	35%	7.26	NM
Earnings Per Share ($)						
1Q	0.13	30%	0.10	-44%	0.18	13%
2Q	0.07	-53%	0.15	50%	0.10	-44%
3Q	—	—	0.25	19%	0.21	110%
4Q	—	—	0.18	NM	0.02	NM
Yr.	—	—	0.68	33%	0.51	NM

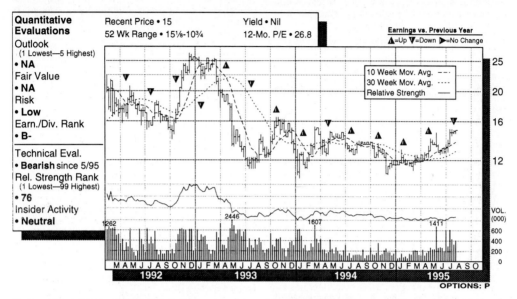

Next earnings report expected: early November

Insituform Technologies

Business Summary - 07-AUG-95

Insituform Technologies (formerly Insituform of North America) provides a trenchless means of rehabilitating sewers, tunnels and pipelines. The company also offers the NuPipe Process in the U.S. and overseas, and had been engaged in the rehabilitation of downhole tubulars for the oil industry under the UltraPipe name from April 1992 until December 1993, when it discontinued the tubular business. Business segment contributions in 1994 (profits in millions) were:

	Revs.	Profits
Pipeline technology	26%	$25.6
Construction	74%	1.3

Pipeline technology primarily involves licensing, selling and servicing trenchless pipeline reconstruction technology and products. Construction consists mainly of the installation of trenchless pipeline reconstruction materials.

The Insituform technology utilizes the INSUA manufactured Insitutube that serves as a carrier for liquid thermosetting plastic resins. At the job site, this tube is positioned in the pipe to be reconstructed through a manhole. Once the tube is in place and positioned tightly against the inner walls of the old pipe, heated water is used to cure the resin, forming a jointless, structural, corrosion-resistant new pipe--the Insitupipe--within the old pipe.

The NuPipe subsidiary repairs pipe by first heating material which is then pulled into the pipe to be repaired. Once in place, the NuPipe is expanded tightly against the walls of the old pipe, forming a jointless, corrosion resistant pipe-within-a-pipe.

INSUA receives royalties from a network of sublicensees that distribute and install Insituform and NuPipe in the U.S. The NuPipe Ltd. subsidiary markets and installs NuPipe in the U.K., while NuPipe International is responsible for worldwide licensing outside the U.S. The Insituform Southwest subsidiary installs Insituform and NuPipe in the southwestern U.S.

Important Developments

May '95—Insituform definitively agreed to acquire Insituform Mid-America (Nasdaq; INSMA) for an exchange of stock. Holders of INSMA's Class A shares will receive 1.15 shares of INSUA's Class A common stock. Holders of INSMA's Class B common stock will convert their shares into Class A stock. Closing is expected late in the third quarter of 1995.

Capitalization

Long Term Debt: $47,925,000 (3/95).

Per Share Data ($) (Year Ended Dec. 31)

	1994	1993	1992	1991	1990	1989
Tangible Bk. Val.	5.15	4.45	3.91	5.74	3.77	3.58
Cash Flow	1.20	0.95	-0.15	1.97	0.35	0.55
Earnings	0.68	0.51	-0.45	1.77	0.22	0.46
Dividends	Nil	Nil	Nil	Nil	Nil	Nil
Payout Ratio	Nil	Nil	Nil	Nil	Nil	Nil
Prices - High	15⅜	25¾	26½	20⅝	8⅝	11½
- Low	10½	11¼	14	3¼	2 7/16	6⅞
P/E Ratio - High	23	50	NM	12	39	25
- Low	15	22	NM	2	11	15

Income Statement Analysis (Million $)

	1994	%Chg	1993	%Chg	1992	%Chg	1991
Revs.	148	47%	101	5%	95.8	NM	30.4
Oper. Inc.	26.1	59%	16.4	28%	12.8	126%	5.7
Depr.	7.5	19%	6.3	52%	4.2	159%	1.6
Int. Exp.	3.2	133%	1.4	NM	0.2	—	NA
Pretax Inc.	16.5	50%	11.0	NM	-2.0	NM	24.4
Eff. Tax Rate	37%	—	30%	—	NM	—	42%
Net Inc.	9.8	34%	7.3	NM	-6.2	NM	14.3

Balance Sheet & Other Fin. Data (Million $)

	1994	1993	1992	1991	1990	1989
Cash	17.7	16.1	14.3	25.9	13.9	13.0
Curr. Assets	71.7	56.3	43.7	37.8	20.7	19.5
Total Assets	162	129	87.4	58.1	41.9	40.2
Curr. Liab.	38.9	28.0	24.0	5.8	5.4	4.3
LT Debt	47.3	36.3	7.3	6.4	6.7	7.3
Common Eqty.	73.9	63.4	54.5	45.6	29.4	27.9
Total Cap.	124	101	63.4	52.2	36.5	35.6
Cap. Exp.	9.0	5.3	6.1	1.5	1.7	2.8
Cash Flow	17.3	13.6	-2.1	15.9	2.7	4.3

Ratio Analysis

	1994	1993	1992	1991	1990	1989
Curr. Ratio	1.8	2.0	1.8	6.5	3.8	4.5
% LT Debt of Cap.	38.3	35.9	11.6	12.3	18.3	20.5
% Net Inc.of Revs.	6.6	7.2	NM	46.9	7.7	17.0
% Ret. on Assets	6.7	6.6	NM	28.3	4.1	9.4
% Ret. on Equity	14.2	12.2	NM	37.8	5.9	13.9

Dividend Data (No cash has been paid.)

Data as orig. reptd.; bef. results of disc. opers. and/or spec. items. Per share data adj. for stk. divs. as of ex-div. date. E-Estimated. NA-Not Available. NM-Not Meaningful. NR-Not Ranked.

Office—1770 Kirby Parkway, Suite 300, Memphis, TN 38138. **Tel**—(901) 759-7473. **Chrmn**—J. D. Krugman. **Pres & CEO**—J-P. Richard. **SVP & CFO**—W. A. Martin. **Secy**—H. Kailes. **Dirs**—P. A. Biddelman, B. Chandler, D. K. Chick, W. Gorham, J. D. Krugman, J-P. Richard, S. Roth, S. Spengler, S. Weinig, R. B. Wight, Jr. **Transfer Agent & Registrar**—American Stock Transfer Co., NYC. **Incorporated** in Delaware in 1980. **Empl**-800. **S&P Analyst:** Stewart Scharf

Insteel Industries

NYSE Symbol **III**
In S&P SmallCap 600

07-SEP-95 **Industry:** Metal

Summary: This company produces concrete wire reinforcing products, industrial wire, galvanized fencing products, nails, specialty wire fabrics, and building panels.

Quantitative Evaluations
Outlook
(1 Lowest—5 Highest)
• **4-**
Fair Value
• **8⅝**
Risk
• **Average**
Earn./Div. Rank
• **B**

Technical Eval.
• **Bearish** since 7/95
Rel. Strength Rank
(1 Lowest—99 Highest)
• **60**
Insider Activity
• **Neutral**

Recent Price • 7¾
52 Wk Range • 9-6⅞
Yield • 3.0%
12-Mo. P/E • 8.4

Earnings vs. Previous Year
▲=Up ▼=Down ▶=No Change

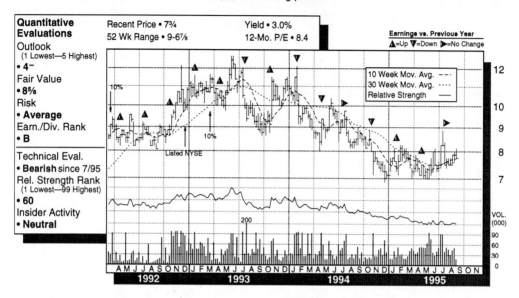

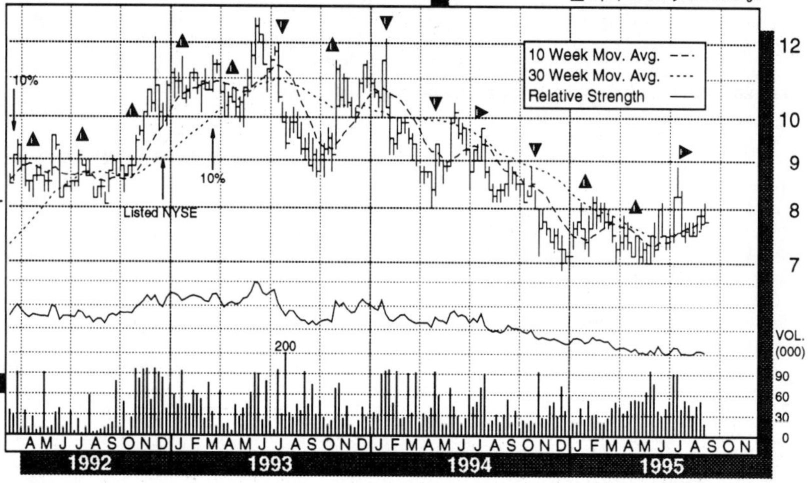

Business Profile - 01-SEP-95

Earnings soared in fiscal 1995's first half, due to an improvement in sales of wire products. However, because III anticipated greater demand for wire products, fiscal 1995's third quarter ended with excessive inventory levels. Margins could erode if market softness forces III to discount prices. The ICS division continues to incur losses as volumes remain well below breakeven levels. III said the Panel/Mex Mexican joint venture should operate close to breakeven through the balance of 1995.

Operational Review - 06-SEP-95

Revenues in fiscal 1995's first nine months rose 9.1%, year to year, mostly due to modest volume and price increases of Insteel's wire and wire products. Margins widened, due to improved production efficiencies from the PC strand plant, which more than offset a rise in SG&A expenses from higher profit-sharing costs; operating income climbed 34%. After a tax benefit, versus taxes at 38.6%, net income soared to $0.75 a share, from $0.28 (before a $0.16 accounting credit).

Stock Performance - 01-SEP-95

In the past 30 trading days, III's shares have increased 3%, compared to a 2% rise in the S&P 500. Average trading volume for the past five days was 3,440 shares, compared with the 40-day moving average of 9,403 shares.

Key Stock Statistics

Dividend Rate/Share	0.24	Shareholders	600
Shs. outstg. (M)	8.4	Market cap. (B)	$0.068
Avg. daily vol. (M)	0.007	Inst. holdings	29%
Tang. Bk. Value/Share	8.54	Insider holdings	NA
Beta	1.58		

Value of $10,000 invested 5 years ago: $ 12,228

Fiscal Year Ending Sep. 30

	1995	% Change	1994	% Change	1993	% Change
Revenues (Million $)						
1Q	503.3	NM	50.56	-6%	53.92	NM
2Q	66.00	17%	56.27	-14%	65.43	4%
3Q	69.36	-3%	71.54	13%	63.15	5%
4Q	—	—	69.30	10%	63.25	NM
Yr.	—	—	247.7	NM	245.8	2%
Income (Million $)						
1Q	0.68	NM	0.02	-95%	0.44	2%
2Q	4.03	NM	0.71	-50%	1.41	107%
3Q	1.60	1%	1.58	-1%	1.60	16%
4Q	0.26	—	—	—	2.85	54%
Yr.	—	—	3.77	-40%	6.29	45%
Earnings Per Share ($)						
1Q	0.08	—	Nil	—	0.07	10%
2Q	0.48	NM	0.09	-47%	0.17	56%
3Q	0.19	NM	0.19	NM	0.19	-13%
4Q	—	—	0.18	-47%	0.34	17%
Yr.	—	—	0.45	-44%	0.80	18%

Next earnings report expected: early November

Insteel Industries

Business Summary - 06-SEP-95

Insteel Industries, through its wholly-owned subsidiary, Insteel Wire Products Co. (IWP), makes wire and wire products. IWP, through its Insteel Construction Systems division (ICS), also manufactures the Insteel 3-D building panel.

Welded wire fabric is used for reinforcement of roadways and bridges, concrete pipe, airport construction and precast concrete. III produces both commodity reinforcing products and specially engineered reinforcing products. Prestressed concrete strand (PC strand) is a sophisticated reinforcing product used in construction of structural members, bridges, buildings, parking decks, pilings, railroad ties and utility poles. A new PC strand plant commenced operations in January 1994. Wire Rope Corp. of America's PC strand business was acquired in April 1994.

High and low carbon industrial wire is sold to manufacturers of springs used in the furniture, bedding and automobile industries, as well as to manufacturers of mechanical springs, display racks, grocery carts, concrete accessories, and numerous other products. Galvanized wire is sold to manufacturers of fencing and strapping where corrosion resistance qualities are important. IWP also makes nails for the construction and industrial markets.

Insteel fabricates agricultural fencing products, using its galvanized wire, for use on farms, and in commercal and residential applications.

Wholly-owned Insteel Construction Systems (ICS) makes a wire reinforced building panel known as the Insteel 3-D system, which is a three-dimensional welded wire space frame integrated with an expanded polystyrene insulating core that is used in wall construction. During the second quarter of fiscal 1995, III purchased the remaining 30% of ICS. ICS merged into IWP, where it operates as a separate division. Insteel Panel/Mex, a 3-D joint venture, began operations in Mexico in November 1992.

Important Developments

Aug. '95—Directors authorized the repurchase of up to one million Insteel common shares.

Jul. '95—III began building a technologically advanced facility next to an existing plant in Andrews, S.C. This facility will produce nails for the construction and industrial markets. Production is expected to begin in the first quarter of fiscal 1996. Insteel previously announced plans to expand capacity of its PC strand plant, with purchase commitments expected to be made in fiscal 1995's fourth quarter. III expects both projects to cost a total of $9 million.

Capitalization

Long Term Debt: $24,966,000 (6/95).

Per Share Data ($)

(Year Ended Sep. 30)

	1994	1993	1992	1991	1990	1989
Tangible Bk. Val.	7.98	7.61	7.04	6.56	6.47	6.15
Cash Flow	1.22	1.52	1.73	1.32	1.55	1.59
Earnings	0.45	0.80	0.68	0.26	0.55	1.07
Dividends	0.24	0.23	0.21	0.19	0.17	0.15
Payout Ratio	53%	29%	31%	72%	31%	14%
Prices - High	12⅛	12¾	12⅛	8⅛	8½	9⅛
- Low	7⅜	8⅝	7⅝	5¼	4	5⅝
P/E Ratio - High	27	16	18	31	15	8
- Low	16	11	11	20	7	5

Income Statement Analysis (Million $)

	1994	%Chg	1993	%Chg	1992	%Chg	1991
Revs.	247	NM	245	2%	240	NM	240
Oper. Inc.	13.3	NM	13.4	2%	13.1	22%	10.7
Depr.	6.3	12%	5.7	-17%	6.8	2%	6.7
Int. Exp.	2.4	58%	1.5	-38%	2.5	-16%	3.0
Pretax Inc.	5.3	-25%	7.1	49%	4.8	195%	1.6
Eff. Tax Rate	41%	—	19%	—	19%	—	30%
Net Inc.	3.8	-40%	6.3	45%	4.3	162%	1.7

Balance Sheet & Other Fin. Data (Million $)

	1994	1993	1992	1991	1990	1989
Cash	1.2	9.3	0.4	3.8	Nil	10.2
Curr. Assets	64.5	64.3	57.2	55.6	62.5	54.2
Total Assets	139	133	113	109	119	90.0
Curr. Liab.	39.3	33.9	30.0	27.1	35.6	18.9
LT Debt	26.8	29.2	30.4	32.1	33.7	27.3
Common Eqty.	66.5	62.9	44.9	41.7	41.1	38.4
Total Cap.	100	99	82.8	81.8	83.1	70.9
Cap. Exp.	10.7	19.7	9.8	3.4	10.9	4.5
Cash Flow	10.1	12.0	11.2	8.3	9.7	10.0

Ratio Analysis

	1994	1993	1992	1991	1990	1989
Curr. Ratio	1.6	1.9	1.9	2.1	1.8	2.9
% LT Debt of Cap.	26.9	29.5	36.8	39.3	40.5	38.5
% Net Inc.of Revs.	1.5	2.6	1.8	0.7	1.4	3.4
% Ret. on Assets	2.8	4.5	3.9	1.5	3.4	8.0
% Ret. on Equity	5.8	10.4	10.0	4.0	8.8	18.9

Dividend Data —Cash payments were initiated in 1986. A dividend reinvestment plan is available.

Amt. of Div. $	Date Decl.	Ex-Div. Date	Stock of Record	Payment Date
0.060	Aug. 01	Sep. 12	Sep. 16	Oct. 01 '94
0.060	Nov. 10	Dec. 12	Dec. 16	Jan. 02 '95
0.060	Feb. 08	Mar. 13	Mar. 17	Apr. 03 '95
0.060	May. 02	Jun. 14	Jun. 16	Jul. 03 '95
0.060	Aug. 16	Sep. 13	Sep. 15	Oct. 02 '95

Data as orig. reptd.; bef. results of disc. opers. and/or spec. items. Per share data adj. for stk. divs. as of ex-div. date. E-Estimated. NA-Not Available. NM-Not Meaningful. NR-Not Ranked.

Office—1373 Boggs Drive, Mount Airy, NC 27030. **Tel**—(919) 786-2141. **Chrmn**—H. O. Woltz, Jr. **Pres & CEO**—H. O. Woltz III. **CFO & Treas**—M. C. Gazmarian. **VP & Secy**—G. D. Kniskern. **Dirs**—T. J. Cumby, L. E. Hannen, F. H. Johnson, C. B. Newsome, J. D. Noell III, W. A. Rogers II, C. R. Vaughn, H. O. Woltz, Jr., H. O. Woltz III, J. E. Woltz. **Transfer Agent**—First Union National Bank of North Carolina, Charlotte, NC. **Incorporated** in North Carolina in 1953. **Empl**-1,013. **S&P Analyst:** Robert E. Friedman

Insurance Auto Auctions

STANDARD & POOR'S
STOCK REPORTS

NASDAQ Symbol **IAAI**
In S&P SmallCap 600

18-SEP-95 **Industry:** Services

Summary: A leading seller of automobile salvage in the U.S., this company provides insurance companies a cost-effective means to process and sell total-loss and recovered theft vehicles.

S&P Opinion: Avoid (★★)

Recent Price • 11¼
52 Wk Range • 37½-10⅝
Yield • Nil
12-Mo. P/E • 12.0

Quantitative Evaluations

Outlook
(1 Lowest—5 Highest)
• NA

Fair Value
• NA

Risk
• High

Earn./Div. Rank
• NR

Technical Eval.
• Bearish since 7/95

Rel. Strength Rank
(1 Lowest—99 Highest)
• NA

Insider Activity
• Neutral

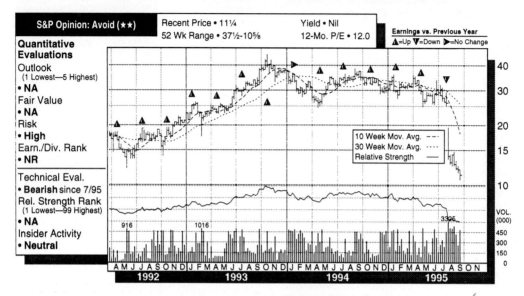

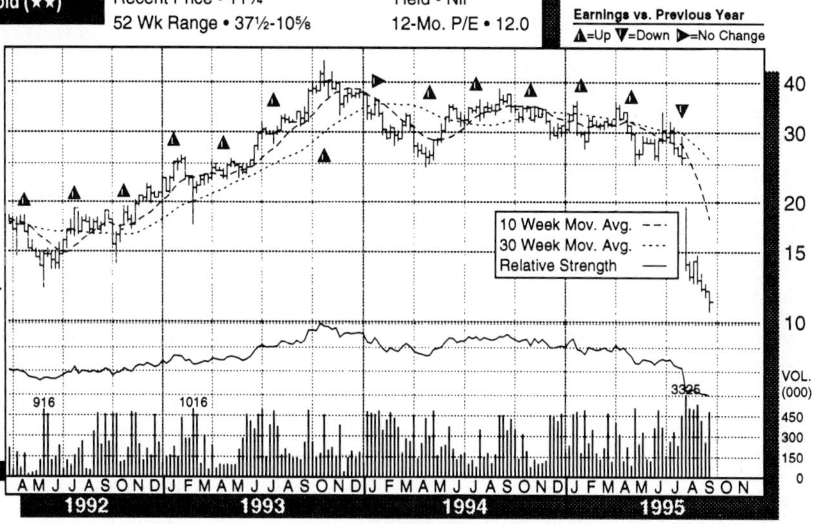

Overview - 15-SEP-95

Although revenues are expected to continue to advance for the balance of 1995, primarily reflecting additional acquisitions of salvage pools, profitability will be penalized by weak margins on certain purchase agreements and softer volumes in the Northeast and Midwest combined with increased infrastructure investments. Results are seen recovering in 1996, as the company has begun taking actions to reduce per unit operating expenses while selectively raising certain fees. Additionally, IAAI is expected to try to reduce its cost of sales by tightening administration of its purchase agreements and working to better manage vehicle processing expenses.

Valuation - 15-SEP-95

The shares have lost some 70% of their value during 1995, as the company experienced slower volume growth of incoming vehicles at certain of its Midwest and Northeast operations during the first half of the year. The weak volume reflected unusually mild winter weather, which led to fewer accidents and lower insurance claims activity in those regions. Although the company has begun cost-cutting efforts, which should lead to an improvement in earnings in 1996, we suggest avoiding purchase of the stock at this time. The shares are trading at 14 times our reduced $0.80 EPS estimate for 1995, and 12 times our $0.95 projection for 1996.

Key Stock Statistics

S&P EPS Est. 1995	0.80	Tang. Bk. Value/Share	0.88
P/E on S&P Est. 1995	14.1	Beta	NA
S&P EPS Est. 1996	0.95	Shareholders	200
Dividend Rate/Share	Nil	Market cap. (B)	$0.127
Shs. outstg. (M)	11.3	Inst. holdings	74%
Avg. daily vol. (M)	0.187	Insider holdings	NA

Value of $10,000 invested 5 years ago: NA

Fiscal Year Ending Dec. 31

	1995	% Change	1994	% Change	1993	% Change
Revenues (Million $)						
1Q	60.24	60%	37.63	77%	21.32	64%
2Q	65.19	54%	42.37	61%	26.32	82%
3Q	—	—	41.38	45%	28.54	79%
4Q	—	—	50.75	82%	27.91	62%
Yr.	—	—	172.1	65%	104.1	72%
Income (Million $)						
1Q	2.68	33%	2.01	66%	1.21	78%
2Q	1.92	-37%	3.05	74%	1.75	51%
3Q	—	—	3.05	55%	1.97	64%
4Q	—	—	2.87	70%	1.69	27%
Yr.	—	—	10.99	66%	6.62	51%
Earnings Per Share ($)						
1Q	0.24	33%	0.18	20%	0.15	36%
2Q	0.17	-37%	0.27	29%	0.21	17%
3Q	E0.18	-33%	0.27	23%	0.22	38%
4Q	E0.21	-19%	0.26	63%	0.16	NM
Yr.	E0.80	-18%	0.98	32%	0.74	21%

Next earnings report expected: early November

Insurance Auto Auctions

Business Summary - 15-SEP-95

Insurance Auto Auctions, Inc. (formerly Los Angeles Auto Salvage, Inc.) is the third largest and only publicly traded automotive salvage company in the U.S., providing insurance companies a cost-effective, turnkey means to process and sell total-loss and recovered theft vehicles. It buys such vehicles from insurance companies for resale and also sells vehicles on consignment for insurers.

As of August 1995, the company had more than 40 auction sites in the U.S., including California (10), Oregon (3) and Arizona (2), as well as Hawaii, Texas, New York, Maryland, Massachusetts, Illinois, Michigan, New Jersey, Missouri, Georgia and the state of Washington.

As a result of the acquisition of 14 auto salvage pool operations since 1992, 12 of which operated on the consignment method, 73% of the vehicles processed by the company in 1994 were sold under the consignment method. As the company integrates these acquired salvage operations into the IAA system, it will seek to convert these accounts to the purchase agreement method wherever possible. On the consignment sales method, vehicles are not owned by the company and costs associated with consignment vehicle processing and sales are proportionally lower. In 1994, the purchase method accounted for 85,700 vehicles, up 45% from 1993.

In 1994, vehicles from IAAI's three largest suppliers--Allstate Insurance Co. State Farm Insurance Co. and Farmers Insurance Group--accounted for about 52% of the company's unit sales.

In December 1994, the company signed an agreement with The Hertz Corp. to be the preferred provider of automotive salvage services.

Important Developments

Aug. '95—Insurance Auto Auctions entered into an agreement with ITT Hartford Insurance Co. under which ITT Hartford consolidated its salvage function with two vendors. IAAI is expected to process 50% of ITT Hartford's paid total losses nationally under the agreement, which should represent more than 13,000 cars per year.

Jun. '95—The company acquired ADB Auction Systems, Inc., and ASC Auctions, Inc. ADB operates six salvage facilities servicing Maryland, Washington, D.C., Virginia and parts of Pennsylvania and Delaware. In 1994, ADB processed 55,000 vehicles.

Mar. '95—IAAI acquired Sadisco Richmond, Inc., a processor of 10,000 vehicles annually in the Richmond, Va., area.

Capitalization

Long Term Debt: $28,819,000 (6/95).

Per Share Data ($) (Year Ended Dec. 31)

	1994	1993	1992	1991	1990	1989
Tangible Bk. Val.	12.43	11.18	5.38	2.24	-0.29	0.76
Cash Flow	1.47	0.97	0.71	0.44	0.83	0.33
Earnings	0.98	0.74	0.61	-3.13	-0.19	0.21
Dividends	Nil	Nil	Nil	Nil	Nil	Nil
Payout Ratio	Nil	Nil	Nil	Nil	Nil	Nil
Prices - High	38⅝	45½	23	20	NA	NA
- Low	24½	17½	12⅛	11	NA	NA
P/E Ratio - High	39	61	38	NM	NA	NA
- Low	25	24	20	NA	NA	NA

Income Statement Analysis (Million $)

	1994	%Chg	1993	%Chg	1992	%Chg	1991
Revs.	172	65%	104	72%	60.5	45%	41.8
Oper. Inc.	24.6	94%	12.7	99%	6.4	65%	3.9
Depr.	5.5	167%	2.0	193%	0.7	-41%	1.2
Int. Exp.	0.4	NM	0.1	44%	0.1	-94%	1.5
Pretax Inc.	19.1	74%	11.0	75%	6.3	NM	-11.7
Eff. Tax Rate	43%	—	40%	—	31%	—	NM
Net Inc.	11.0	67%	6.6	50%	4.4	NM	-11.5

Balance Sheet & Other Fin. Data (Million $)

	1994	1993	1992	1991	1990	1989
Cash	10.4	30.4	17.3	10.7	3.0	0.3
Curr. Assets	41.4	48.0	26.1	15.8	6.6	3.6
Total Assets	174	144	51.9	18.6	12.3	4.7
Curr. Liab.	29.3	19.2	6.5	4.9	4.7	2.5
LT Debt	0.2	1.1	0.9	Nil	6.9	0.3
Common Eqty.	140	124	44.4	13.7	-0.7	1.9
Total Cap.	140	125	45.4	13.7	6.2	2.2
Cap. Exp.	5.5	4.1	0.9	0.6	0.7	0.6
Cash Flow	16.5	8.7	5.1	1.8	3.1	1.2

Ratio Analysis

	1994	1993	1992	1991	1990	1989
Curr. Ratio	1.4	2.5	4.0	3.2	1.4	1.4
% LT Debt of Cap.	0.2	0.8	2.0	Nil	111.5	13.3
% Net Inc.of Revs.	6.4	6.4	7.2	NM	0.7	2.4
% Ret. on Assets	6.9	6.2	11.4	NM	7.9	17.0
% Ret. on Equity	8.3	7.2	13.9	NM	NA	42.3

Dividend Data —No dividends have been paid, and the company currently plans to retain all earnings to support the development and expansion of its business.

Data as orig. reptd.; bef. results of disc. opers. and/or spec. items. Per share data adj. for stk. divs. as of ex-div. date. E-Estimated. NA-Not Available. NM-Not Meaningful. NR-Not Ranked.

Office—7245 Laurel Canyon Blvd., North Hollywood, CA 91605. **Tel**—(818) 764-3200. **Chrmn & CEO**—B. S. Scott. **Pres & COO**—C. Knowles. **SVP-Fin & CFO**—W. L. Overell. **EVP, Secy & Investor Contact**—W. W. Liebeck (415-233-1952). **Dirs**—S. B. Gould, C. G. Knowles, W. W. Liebeck, M. R. Martin, T. J. O'Malia, R. A. Rosenthal, B. S. Scott, G. E. Tullman. **Transfer Agent**—Bank of Boston. **Incorporated** in California in 1982. **Empl**-540. **S&P Analyst:** Stewart Scharf

STANDARD & POOR'S

STOCK REPORTS

Integon Corp.

NYSE Symbol **IN**
In S&P SmallCap 600

07-NOV-95 **Industry:** Insurance

Summary: Through subsidiaries, this company underwrites and markets nonstandard automobile insurance to individuals in 22 states, primarily in the Southeast and Northeast.

Quantitative Evaluations
Outlook
(1 Lowest—5 Highest)
• **NA**
Fair Value
• **NA**
Risk
• **Average**
Earn./Div. Rank
• **NR**

Technical Eval.
• **Bullish** since 5/95
Rel. Strength Rank
(1 Lowest—99 Highest)
• **43**
Insider Activity
• **Neutral**

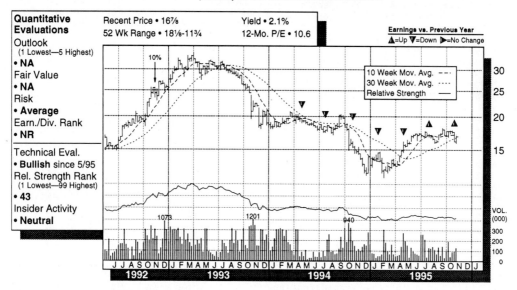

Recent Price • 16⅞
52 Wk Range • 18⅛-11¾
Yield • 2.1%
12-Mo. P/E • 10.6

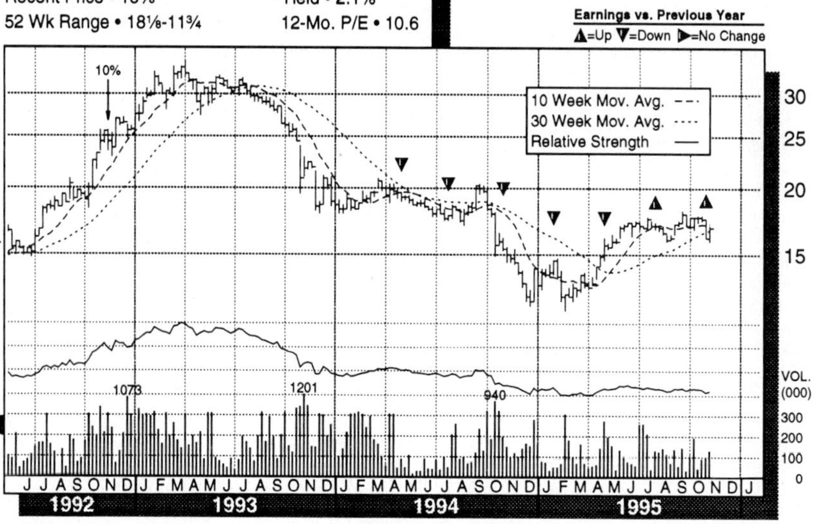

Business Profile - 07-NOV-95

Integon expects the nonstandard auto insurance market to grow 8% to 10% annually. The company entered Louisiana and Rhode Island in early 1995, and plans to write insurance in 30 to 35 states by year-end 1996, representing 90% of the nonstandard auto insurance market. Operating earnings continue to be affected by a higher loss ratio, which increased to 73.1% in the first nine months of 1995, up from 68.0% a year ago. IN plans to improve operating earnings through rate increases in key markets.

Operational Review - 07-NOV-95

Revenues in the nine months ended September 30, 1995, rose 96%, year to year, reflecting higher premiums earned due to the acquisition of Bankers and Shippers. However, expenses more than doubled, led by an increase in loss expenses and policy acquisition costs. Earnings per share were $1.40 (including $0.26 in investment gains), compared to $1.19 (after a $0.02 investment loss). Per share results exclude a $0.17 extraordinary loss and a $0.04 extraordinary gain in the respective periods.

Stock Performance - 03-NOV-95

In the past 30 trading days, IN's shares have declined 0.74%, compared to a 2% rise in the S&P 500. Average trading volume for the past five days was 25,460 shares, compared with the 40-day moving average of 20,200 shares.

Key Stock Statistics

Dividend Rate/Share	0.36	Shareholders	200
Shs. outstg. (M)	15.7	Market cap. (B)	$0.263
Avg. daily vol. (M)	0.018	Inst. holdings	54%
Tang. Bk. Value/Share	6.53	Insider holdings	NA
Beta	NA		

Value of $10,000 invested 5 years ago: NA

Fiscal Year Ending Dec. 31

	1995	% Change	1994	% Change	1993	% Change
Revenues (Million $)						
1Q	142.7	94%	73.53	17%	62.76	—
2Q	152.2	95%	78.14	19%	65.58	—
3Q	162.6	98%	82.30	20%	68.80	—
4Q	—	—	135.6	93%	70.37	—
Yr.	—	—	369.6	38%	267.5	24%
Income (Million $)						
1Q	7.04	-12%	7.97	-39%	13.05	—
2Q	9.12	26%	7.21	-31%	10.51	—
3Q	9.91	176%	3.59	-63%	9.69	—
4Q	—	—	3.77	-62%	10.03	—
Yr.	—	—	22.54	-48%	43.29	36%
Earnings Per Share ($)						
1Q	0.36	-28%	0.50	-33%	0.75	—
2Q	0.49	7%	0.46	-23%	0.60	—
3Q	0.55	139%	0.23	-59%	0.56	—
4Q	—	—	0.19	-69%	0.62	—
Yr.	—	—	1.38	-45%	2.53	38%

Next earnings report expected: late January

Integon Corp.

Business Summary - 03-NOV-95

Integon Corporation, through its wholly owned property and casualty insurance subsidiaries, specializes in underwriting and marketing nonstandard automobile insurance to individuals. Operations were expanded significantly through the October 1994 acquisition of Bankers and Shippers Insurance Co. IN currently markets its products through more than 11,000 independent agencies in 22 states; principally in North Carolina, with expansion in recent years in Virginia, Tennessee, Georgia, Florida, Ohio, Alabama and Indiana. Contributions to net premiums written by line of business in recent years:

	1994	1993
Nonstandard automobile	92%	90%
Preferred automobile	7%	10%
Other	1%	Nil

Integon's nonstandard automobile insurance products are designed for drivers who are unable to obtain coverage from standard market carriers due to prior driving records, other underwriting criteria or market conditions. IN expects the market for nonstandard automobile insurance to continue to grow, as some large multi-line insurance companies continue to tighten their underwriting standards, pushing more clients into the nonstandard market. In addition, more vigorous enforcement of state motor vehicle laws, resulting in more drivers with points or forced to purchase insurance, should aid the nonstandard market.

Integon has pursued a strategy of establishing itself as a low-cost provider of nonstandard automobile insurance, while maintaining a commitment to provide superior service to both agents and insureds. This has been accomplished primarily through the automation of certain marketing, underwriting and administrative functions. The company believes that significant competitive advantages exist as a result of this strategy of automation. Integon has produced expense ratios well below the industry average. The company also has the administrative capacity to write a greater volume of nonstandard automobile insurance while maintaining its position as a low-cost provider.

Important Developments

Sep. '95—The North Carolina Department of Insurance announced that it has granted the insurance industry's request for a continuance of auto insurance rate hearings, due to concerns over the quality and accuracy of data underlying the industry's rate hike request. The granting of the continuance will delay a rate increase request, in which insurers were asking for an increase of 4.5%, that was originally submitted to the Department in May.

Capitalization

Notes Payable: $150,814,000 (9/95).
$3.875 Conv. Pfd. Stk.: 1,437,500 shs. ($0.01 par); liq. val. $50 a sh.; conv. into com. at $19.05 a sh.

Per Share Data ($) (Year Ended Dec. 31)

	1994	1993	1992	1991	1990	1989
Tangible Bk. Val.	5.01	4.41	3.21	2.15	NA	NA
Oper. Earnings	1.42	2.16	1.69	1.05	0.71	NA
Earnings	1.38	2.53	1.84	1.09	0.71	NA
Dividends	0.36	0.32	0.16	Nil	NA	NA
Payout Ratio	26%	13%	9%	Nil	NA	NA
Prices - High	20⅞	34⅞	27½	Nil	NA	NA
- Low	12	17⅞	13½	NA	NA	NA
P/E Ratio - High	15	14	15	NA	NA	NA
- Low	9	7	7	NA	NA	NA

Income Statement Analysis (Million $)

	1994	%Chg	1993	%Chg	1992	%Chg	1991
Premium Income	334	48%	226	24%	182	13%	161
Net Invest. Inc.	17.9	-6%	19.0	12%	17.0	33%	12.8
Oth. Revs.	17.2	-25%	22.9	39%	16.5	—	NA
Total Revs.	370	38%	268	25%	215	16%	186
Pretax Inc.	32.2	-49%	63.5	36%	46.8	59%	29.4
Net Oper. Inc.	23.3	-37%	37.0	26%	29.3	—	NA
Net Inc.	22.5	-48%	43.3	36%	31.9	67%	19.1

Balance Sheet & Other Fin. Data (Million $)

	1994	1993	1992	1991	1990	1989
Cash & Equiv.	39.2	18.7	20.0	17.3	NA	NA
Premiums Due	150	58.7	37.3	24.1	NA	NA
Inv Assets Bonds	389	230	227	150	NA	NA
Inv. Assets Stock	Nil	Nil	Nil	Nil	NA	NA
Inv. Assets Loans	Nil	Nil	Nil	Nil	NA	NA
Inv. Assets Total	389	230	227	150	NA	NA
Deferred Policy Cost	36.5	18.0	14.0	11.7	NA	NA
Total Assets	1,152	657	403	333	NA	NA
Debt	172	92.0	75.0	57.0	NA	NA
Common Eqty.	195	127	116	84.0	NA	NA

Ratio Analysis

	1994	1993	1992	1991	1990	1989
Prop&Cas Loss	70.8	63.0	57.0	63.3	65.5	NA
Prop&Cas Expense	21.7	22.0	20.9	24.3	24.0	NA
Prop&Cas Comb.	92.5	85.0	77.9	87.6	89.5	NA
% Ret. on Revs.	6.1	16.2	14.8	10.3	7.2	NA
% Return on Equity	14.0	35.6	32.1	NA	NA	NA

Dividend Data —Payments were initiated in 1992.

Amt. of Div. $	Date Decl.	Ex-Div. Date	Stock of Record	Payment Date
0.090	Nov. 10	Nov. 25	Dec. 01	Dec. 15 '94
0.090	Feb. 16	Feb. 23	Mar. 01	Mar. 15 '95
0.090	May. 11	May. 25	Jun. 01	Jun. 15 '95
0.090	Aug. 08	Aug. 30	Sep. 01	Sep. 15 '95
0.090	Nov. 06	Nov. 29	Dec. 01	Dec. 15 '95

Data as orig. reptd.; bef. results of disc. opers. and/or spec. items. Per share data adj. for stk. divs. as of ex-div. date. E-Estimated. NA-Not Available. NM-Not Meaningful. NR-Not Ranked.

Office—500 West Fifth St., Winston-Salem, NC 27152. **Tel**—(910) 770-2000. **Chrmn**—J. C. Head III. **Pres**—J. T. Lambie. **VP & CFO**—B. M. Emerson II. **VP & Secy**—J. J. Johnson. **Investor Contact**—Gay Huntsman. **Dirs**—J. C. Head III, C. H. Jamison, J. T. Lambie, J. B. McKinnon, F. B. Whittemore. **Transfer Agent & Registrar**—First Chicago Trust Co. of New York, Jersey City, N.J. **Incorporated** in Delaware in 1989. **Empl**-1,760. **S&P Analyst:** Brad Ohlmuller

STANDARD & POOR'S
Integrated Circuit Systems

STOCK REPORTS

NASDAQ Symbol **ICST**

In S&P SmallCap 600

05-AUG-95 **Industry:** Electronics/Electric

Summary: This company makes and sells mixed-signal integrated circuits for frequency timing, multimedia, and data communications applications.

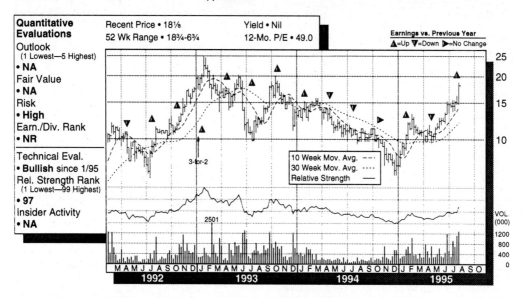

Quantitative Evaluations

Outlook (1 Lowest—5 Highest) • **NA**

Fair Value • **NA**

Risk • **High**

Earn./Div. Rank • **NR**

Technical Eval. • **Bullish** since 1/95

Rel. Strength Rank (1 Lowest—99 Highest) • **97**

Insider Activity • **NA**

Recent Price • 18⅛

52 Wk Range • 18¾-6¾

Yield • Nil

12-Mo. P/E • 49.0

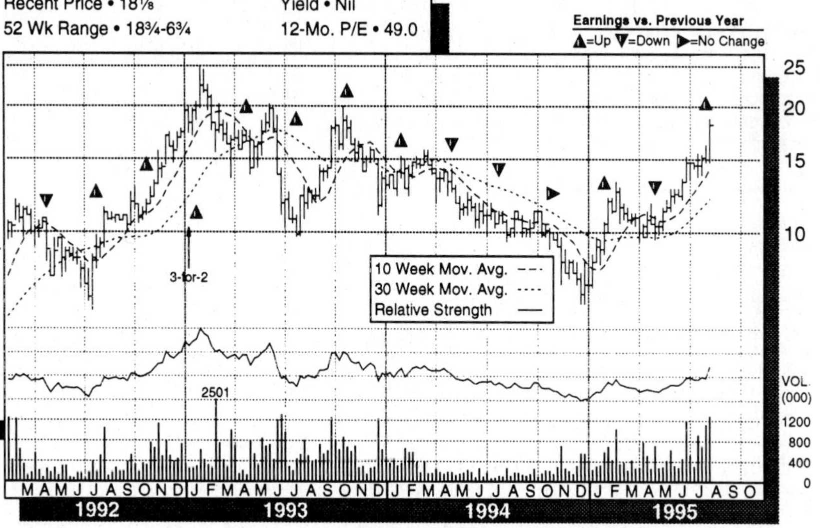

Business Profile - 04-AUG-95

ICST is the world's leading supplier of frequency timing generator (FTG) products, having shipped over 80 million devices since 1989. The company believes that its FTG products are included in over 50% of newly shipped computers. ICST's strategy is to expand its FTG business in existing and new advanced high-performance timing applications. Also, the company is redirecting its multimedia business to emphasize graphics and video applications, and downsizing its Turtle Beach subsidiary.

Operational Review - 04-AUG-95

Revenues for the first nine months of fiscal 1995 rose 14%, year to year, reflecting growth in frequency timing products and multimedia chipsets, including the newly acquired ARK Logic, Inc. Gross margins widened but earnings were hurt by a $7.4 million pretax charge related to the downsizing and redirection of the multimedia business and a $4.1 million charge related to the ARK acquisition. Losses continued at the Turtle Beach subsidiary.

Stock Performance - 04-AUG-95

In the past 30 trading days, ICST's shares have increased 23%, compared to a 2% rise in the S&P 500. Average trading volume for the past five days was 433,180 shares, compared with the 40-day moving average of 187,528 shares.

Key Stock Statistics

Dividend Rate/Share	Nil	Shareholders	300
Shs. outstg. (M)	11.1	Market cap. (B)	$0.200
Avg. daily vol. (M)	0.244	Inst. holdings	21%
Tang. Bk. Value/Share	5.24	Insider holdings	NA
Beta	2.19		

Value of $10,000 invested 5 years ago: NA

Fiscal Year Ending Jun. 30

	1995	% Change	1994	% Change	1993	% Change
Revenues (Million $)						
1Q	22.55	17%	19.29	28%	15.10	NM
2Q	25.88	14%	22.61	18%	19.24	NM
3Q	27.79	11%	25.04	19%	21.10	NM
4Q	—	—	26.89	38%	19.52	130%
Yr.	—	—	93.82	25%	74.91	NM
Income (Million $)						
1Q	2.86	-1%	2.90	—	—	—
2Q	3.34	17%	2.86	22%	2.35	NM
3Q	-5.18	NM	3.48	-1%	3.52	NM
4Q	—	—	2.99	-7%	3.22	171%
Yr.	—	—	12.22	8%	11.28	NM
Earnings Per Share ($)						
1Q	0.26	NM	0.26	13%	0.23	NM
2Q	0.30	15%	0.26	4%	0.25	NM
3Q	-0.47	NM	0.31	-11%	0.35	192%
4Q	—	—	0.27	-13%	0.31	94%
Yr.	—	—	1.11	-3%	1.15	167%

Next earnings report expected: mid October

Integrated Circuit Systems

Business Summary - 04-AUG-95

Integrated Circuit Systems, Inc. designs, manufactures and markets innovative very-large-scale integrated (VLSI) circuits, including standard and custom application-specific integrated circuit (ASIC) products using mixed analog/digital technology. Products are marketed to OEMs for use in video graphics display products, central processing unit (CPU) systems, PC multimedia and portable device battery charging applications. In July 1993, ICST acquired Turtle Beach Systems, Inc., a provider of PC-based sound generation and editing hardware and software. Revenues in recent fiscal years were derived as follows:

	1994	1993	1992
Standard products	83%	77%	64%
ASIC products	17%	23%	36%

ICST's video frequency timing generator (FTG) products are mixed analog/digital integrated circuits that produce the high-frequency video dot timing function required by the video graphics array (VGA) display adaptors of IBM-compatible computers. FTG products replace multiple crystal oscillators and certain peripheral circuitry, providing savings of board space, power consumption and cost. ICST has also modified the design of its FTGs for applications in high resolution computer aided design workstation display systems.

PC multimedia applications allow the PC user to input, create, manipulate and combine sound, images, text, graphics and animation. Products provide the capability to overlay graphic images on live and recorded television video, and to duplicate actual sound through storage and retrieval of digitized wave patterns that imitate sound by approximating wave patterns.

ICST also markets power management IC controllers for the efficient recharging of NiCd batteries used n portable computers.

In fiscal 1994, international sales, primarily to the Pacific Rim area, accounted for 41% of revenues (43% in fiscal 1993).

Important Developments

Apr. '95—ICST announced a redirection of its multimedia business strategy, which will emphasize graphics and video applications. Also, the company said that it will record a one-time charge of $4.4 million in fiscal 1995's third quarter, related to cost reduction measures, redirection of the multimedia strategy and the downsizing of its Turtle Beach subsidiary. Separately, ICST purchased 51% of ARK Logic, Inc., a developer of graphical user interface compatible display adapter chips for personal computers, for about $7.3 million.

Capitalization

Long Term Debt: $3,574,000 (3/95).
Options: To buy 1,830,000 shs. at $0.85 to $15.83 ea. (6/94)

Per Share Data ($)

(Year Ended Jun. 30)

	1994	1993	1992	1991	1990	1989
Tangible Bk. Val.	5.15	4.19	2.09	1.61	0.37	NA
Cash Flow	1.28	1.33	0.52	0.42	0.15	NA
Earnings	1.11	1.15	0.43	0.33	0.07	NA
Dividends	Nil	Nil	Nil	Nil	Nil	NA
Payout Ratio	Nil	Nil	Nil	Nil	Nil	NA
Prices - High	15¾	25	20⅜	7	NA	NA
- Low	9½	9¾	6⅞	4⅜	NA	NA
P/E Ratio - High	14	22	47	21	NA	NA
- Low	9	8	15	13	NA	NA

Income Statement Analysis (Million $)

	1994	%Chg	1993	%Chg	1992	%Chg	1991
Revs.	93.8	25%	74.9	NM	22.6	81%	12.5
Oper. Inc.	20.3	-3%	21.0	NM	5.4	66%	3.2
Depr.	1.9	8%	1.8	177%	0.6	45%	0.4
Int. Exp.	0.5	55%	0.3	NM	0.0	-75%	0.1
Pretax Inc.	18.5	2%	18.2	NM	5.0	88%	2.7
Eff. Tax Rate	34%	—	38%	—	37%	—	37%
Net Inc.	12.2	8%	11.3	NM	3.2	88%	1.7

Balance Sheet & Other Fin. Data (Million $)

	1994	1993	1992	1991	1990	1989
Cash	9.6	17.6	6.1	7.6	0.0	NA
Curr. Assets	48.3	41.3	15.0	12.3	2.8	NA
Total Assets	73.5	54.8	18.4	13.9	4.2	NA
Curr. Liab.	13.0	8.2	3.5	2.6	1.3	NA
LT Debt	3.8	3.3	0.1	0.2	1.1	NA
Common Eqty.	55.7	42.7	14.6	10.9	1.7	NA
Total Cap.	60.4	46.6	14.9	11.3	2.9	NA
Cap. Exp.	4.6	7.6	2.5	0.9	0.5	NA
Cash Flow	14.1	13.0	3.8	2.1	0.7	NA

Ratio Analysis

	1994	1993	1992	1991	1990	1989
Curr. Ratio	3.7	5.1	4.3	4.7	2.2	NA
% LT Debt of Cap.	6.2	7.1	0.8	1.6	40.1	NA
% Net Inc.of Revs.	13.0	15.1	14.1	13.7	4.7	NA
% Ret. on Assets	18.6	27.6	19.5	16.8	NA	NA
% Ret. on Equity	24.2	35.2	24.7	25.3	NA	NA

Dividend Data (Under the terms of a credit agreement, the company is restricted from paying cash dividends without prior lender approval. A three-for-two stock split was effected December 31, 1992.)

Data as orig. reptd.; bef. results of disc. opers. and/or spec. items. Per share data adj. for stk. divs. as of ex-div. date. E-Estimated. NA-Not Available. NM-Not Meaningful. NR-Not Ranked.

Office—2435 Boulevard of the Generals, Norristown, PA 19403. **Tel**—(610) 630-5300. **Chrmn**—H. I. Boreen. **Pres, CEO & COO**—D. W. Sear. **Sr VP & CFO**—H. E. Tan. **Dirs**—E. H. Arnold, H. I. Boreen, R. Gassner, H. Morgan, J. L. Pickitt, S. E. Prodromou, D. W. Sear. **Transfer Agent & Registrar**—StockTrans, Inc., Ardmore, Pa. **Incorporated** in Pennsylvania in 1976. **Empl**- 279. **S&P Analyst:** Ronald J. Gross

Integrated Health Services

NYSE Symbol **IHS**
In S&P SmallCap 600

13-SEP-95

Industry:
Health Care Centers

Summary: This diversified health services company provides a full range of subacute and post-acute medical services through its integrated healthcare system.

S&P Opinion: Accumulate (★★★★)

Recent Price • 31¾
52 Wk Range • 42½-25¼
Yield • 0.1%
12-Mo. P/E • 13.6

Quantitative Evaluations

Outlook
(1 Lowest—5 Highest)
• **NA**

Fair Value
• **NA**

Risk
• **Average**

Earn./Div. Rank
• **NR**

Technical Eval.
• **Bullish** since 8/95

Rel. Strength Rank
(1 Lowest—99 Highest)
• **38**

Insider Activity
• **NA**

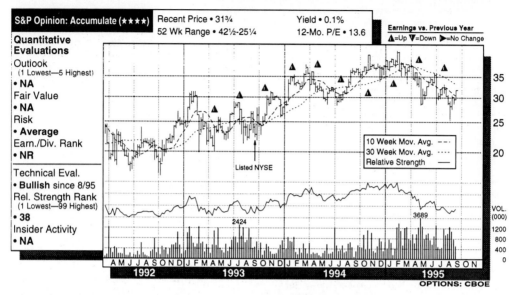

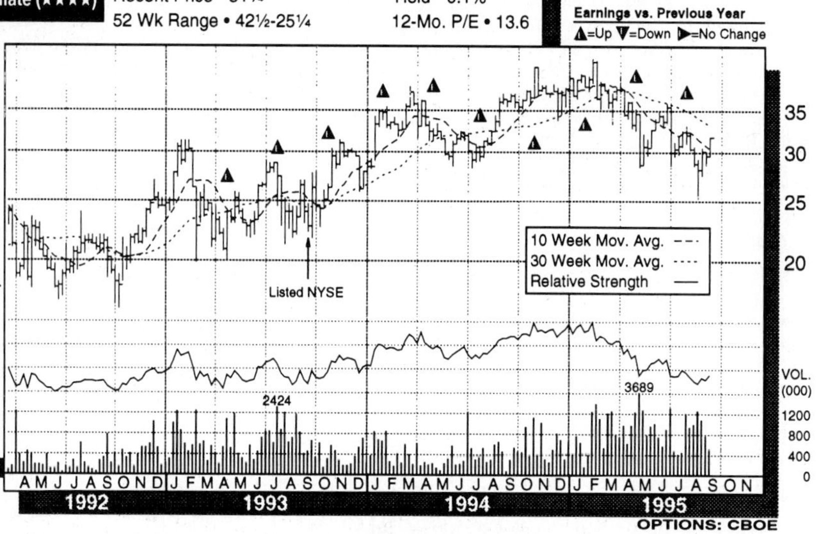

Overview - 13-SEP-95

Integrated Health Services is a leading participant in the rapidly-growing subacute care segment of the domestic health care industry. The company's network is designed to provide a full array of services required by patients needing additional care following their release from a general acute care hospital. As a provider of such care, which is typically 30% to 60% below the cost of similar care at a general hospital, IHS is well-positioned to obtain business from a growing field of managed care entities seeking to lower their medical costs. The company's explosive growth in recent years reflected the conversion of nursing home beds to subacute beds, and strategic acquisitions.

Valuation - 13-SEP-95

Expectations for sharp revenue and earnings gains through 1996 reflect solid industry fundamentals and IHS' ability to successfully implement its operating strategies. The company should benefit from several trends in the healthcare sector, including the early discharge of patients from acute care hospitals (as a result of payer pressures) and favorable demographics (the rising proportion of individuals over the age of 65). Subacute operating margins have been in the 25% to 30% range, and although increased competition could reduce these margins, we believe the overall market potential should limit this compression. The shares, selling at a recent multiple well below our projected growth rate, are an attractive long term holding.

Key Stock Statistics

S&P EPS Est. 1995	2.63	Tang. Bk. Value/Share	9.02
P/E on S&P Est. 1995	12.1	Beta	NA
S&P EPS Est. 1996	3.40	Shareholders	500
Dividend Rate/Share	0.02	Market cap. (B)	$0.667
Shs. outstg. (M)	21.3	Inst. holdings	96%
Avg. daily vol. (M)	0.169	Insider holdings	NA

Value of $10,000 invested 5 years ago: NA

Fiscal Year Ending Dec. 31

	1995	% Change	1994	% Change	1993	% Change
Revenues (Million $)						
1Q	265.4	101%	132.3	130%	57.60	34%
2Q	278.1	100%	138.7	120%	63.00	41%
3Q	—	—	177.2	145%	72.20	39%
4Q	—	—	235.4	163%	89.47	61%
Yr.	—	—	683.6	142%	282.2	44%
Income (Million $)						
1Q	13.65	114%	6.39	73%	3.70	80%
2Q	13.93	106%	6.77	65%	4.11	44%
3Q	—	—	9.86	114%	4.60	44%
4Q	—	—	12.19	128%	5.35	51%
Yr.	—	—	35.21	98%	17.75	52%
Earnings Per Share ($)						
1Q	0.61	49%	0.41	37%	0.30	36%
2Q	0.62	41%	0.44	33%	0.33	32%
3Q	E0.68	31%	0.52	49%	0.35	30%
4Q	E0.72	22%	0.59	55%	0.38	27%
Yr.	E2.63	34%	1.96	44%	1.36	31%

Next earnings report expected: late October

Integrated Health Services

Business Summary - 13-SEP-95

Integrated Health Services Inc. is a leading provider of subacute healthcare services, using nursing facilities as platforms to provide various medical and rehabilitative services more typically delivered in the acute care hospital setting. Recently, IHS expanded its services beyond subacute care to create a post-acute healthcare system in each of its service regions. At the end of 1994, Integrated was operating 167 geriatric care facilities (113 owned or leased and 54 managed) and 107 located within 60 of these facilities, as well as nine retirement facilities, six geriatric care facilities (currently held for sale) and nine psychiatric care facilities.

Revenue contributions in recent years were:

	1994	1993	1992
Basic medical services	40%	40%	51%
Specialty medical services	55%	52%	42%
Management services & other	5%	8%	7%

IHS provides subacute care through medical specialty units (MSUs), which are typically 20 to 75 bed specialty units with physical identities, specialized medical technology and staffs separate from the geriatric care facilities in which they are located. MSUs are designed to provide levels and quality of care similar to those provided in the hospital, but at per diem treatment costs which the company believes are generally 30% to 60% below the cost of such care in acute care hospitals.

Specialty medical services include a complex care program (post-surgical, cancer and other patients requiring long recovery periods); a program for those requiring ventilator assistance for breathing; a wound management program; a cardiac care program; rehabilitative services; home healthcare services; institutional pharmacy services; a specialized treatment program for Alzheimer's disease; and hospice services.

During 1994, the company derived about 42% of its patient revenues from private pay sources, 35% from Medicare, and 23% from Medicaid.

Important Developments

Aug. '95—IHS completed its acquisition of IntegraCare Inc. in a transaction under which each IntegraCare share will be exchanged for 0.2167 of a share of IHS common. IntegraCare provides physical, occupational and speech therapy to skilled nursing facilities, outpatient rehabilitation clinics, home health agencies, hospitals and schools in Florida, and is developing an integrated network of primary care and specialty physician practices throughout the state of Florida.

Capitalization

Long Term Debt: $541,786,000 (12/94), incl. $258,750,000 of 5.75%- 6% sub. debs. due 2001-2003 & conv. into com. at $32.125-$32.60 a sh.

Per Share Data ($)

(Year Ended Dec. 31)

	1994	1993	1992	1991	1990	1989
Tangible Bk. Val.	22.24	12.28	12.38	9.75	-149.48	NA
Cash Flow	3.41	1.71	1.28	1.13	0.94	NA
Earnings	1.96	1.36	1.04	0.82	0.42	NA
Dividends	0.02	Nil	Nil	Nil	Nil	NA
Payout Ratio	1%	Nil	Nil	Nil	Nil	NA
Prices - High	41⅛	31⅜	29¼	22½	NA	NA
- Low	28⅛	19⅞	16¾	13¾	NA	NA
P/E Ratio - High	21	23	28	27	NA	NA
- Low	14	15	16	17	NA	NA

Income Statement Analysis (Million $)

	1994	%Chg	1993	%Chg	1992	%Chg	1991
Revs.	682	143%	281	44%	195	35%	144
Oper. Inc.	102	167%	38.2	63%	23.4	60%	14.6
Depr.	26.0	NM	4.6	68%	2.8	24%	2.2
Int. Exp.	24.7	153%	9.8	169%	3.6	-40%	6.1
Pretax Inc.	56.3	93%	29.1	55%	18.8	135%	8.0
Eff. Tax Rate	38%	—	39%	—	38%	—	26%
Net Inc.	35.2	101%	17.5	50%	11.7	98%	5.9

Balance Sheet & Other Fin. Data (Million $)

	1994	1993	1992	1991	1990	1989
Cash	60.0	60.0	104	16.0	2.0	NA
Curr. Assets	240	161	168	61.0	22.0	NA
Total Assets	1,238	768	312	156	102	NA
Curr. Liab.	170	100	22.7	19.1	19.7	NA
LT Debt	542	388	140	47.0	56.0	NA
Common Eqty.	443	209	146	87.0	-162	NA
Total Cap.	1,060	667	288	135	81.0	NA
Cap. Exp.	91.0	343	41.0	8.3	14.7	NA
Cash Flow	61.2	22.4	14.4	8.1	3.1	NA

Ratio Analysis

	1994	1993	1992	1991	1990	1989
Curr. Ratio	1.4	1.6	7.4	3.2	1.1	NA
% LT Debt of Cap.	51.1	58.2	48.8	35.0	68.9	NA
% Net Inc.of Revs.	5.2	6.3	6.0	4.1	1.7	NA
% Ret. on Assets	3.0	3.1	4.5	1.3	NA	NA
% Ret. on Equity	9.4	9.3	8.9	NM	NA	NA

Dividend Data —An initial annual dividend of $0.02 a share was paid January 10, 1995.

Amt. of Div. $	Date Decl.	Ex-Div. Date	Stock of Record	Payment Date
0.020	Dec. 15	Dec. 23	Dec. 30	Jan. 10 '95

Data as orig. reptd.; bef. results of disc. opers. and/or spec. items. Per share data adj. for stk. divs. as of ex-div. date. E-Estimated. NA-Not Available. NM-Not Meaningful. NR-Not Ranked.

Office—10065 Red Run Blvd., Owings Mills, MD 21117. **Tel**—(410) 998-8400. **Chrmn & CEO**—R. N. Elkins. **Pres & COO**—L. P. Cirka. **SVP-Fin**—D. N. Chichester. **SVP & Investor Contact**—Marc B. Levin. **Dirs**—L. P. Cirka, R. N. Elkins, C. N. Newhall III, T. F. Nicholson, R. M. Scrushy, J. L. Silverman, G. H. Strong, R. Walkingshaw. **Transfer Agent & Registrar**—American Stock Transfer & Trust Co., NYC. **Incorporated** in Delaware in 1986. **Empl**-21,200. **S&P Analyst:** R.M.G.

STANDARD & POOR'S **Inter-Regional Financial Group**

STOCK REPORTS

NYSE Symbol **IFG**
In S&P SmallCap 600

05-OCT-95 **Industry:** Securities

Summary: This holding company, through Dain Bosworth Inc. and Rauscher Pierce Refsnes, Inc., is one of the largest U.S. regional full-service brokers and investment bankers.

Quantitative Evaluations

Outlook (1 Lowest—5 Highest)
• **NA**

Fair Value
• **NA**

Risk
• **Low**

Earn./Div. Rank
• **B-**

Technical Eval.
• **Bullish** since 1/95

Rel. Strength Rank (1 Lowest—99 Highest)
• **87**

Insider Activity
• **NA**

Recent Price • 36
52 Wk Range • 36¼-22
Yield • 1.8%
12-Mo. P/E • 12.6

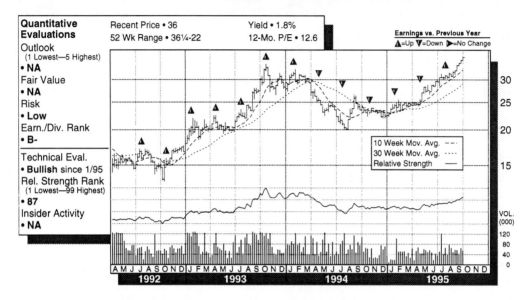

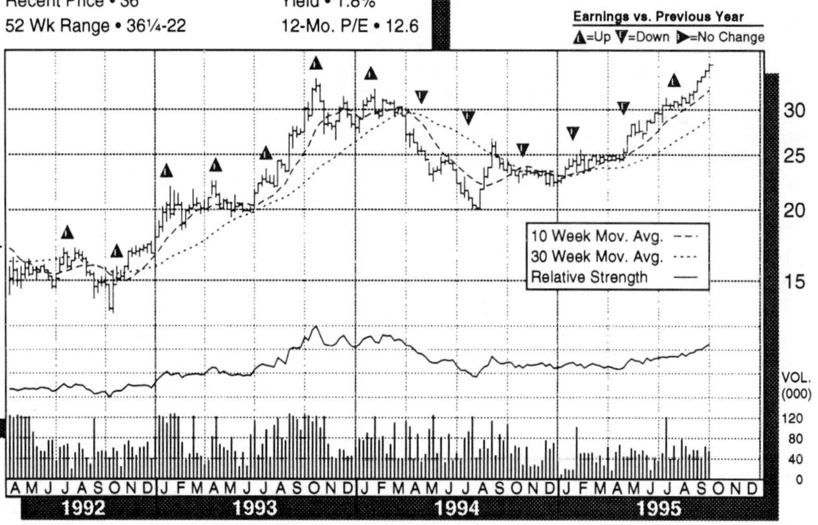

Business Profile - 05-OCT-95

This holding company, through its subsidiaries, is one of the largest U.S. regional full-service brokers and investment bankers. IFG, which invested in growth during the downturn in 1994 (when 14 new offices and 176 investment executives (net) were added), is benefiting from resurgent financial markets. In October 1994, it acquired the privately held parent of fixed-income securities firm Clayton Brown & Associates, for about $24 million.

Operational Review - 05-OCT-95

Revenues in the first half of 1995 rose 13%, year to year, as improved stock and bond markets aided fixed-income, institutional equity sales and OTC trading. Dain Bosworth's net revenues advanced 9.9%, and Rauscher Pierce Refsnes was up 2.0%. Interest expense more than doubled, and with 9.4% higher other expenses, reflecting business expansion, net income declined 12%, to $14.2 million ($1.71 a share), from $16.1 million ($1.90).

Stock Performance - 29-SEP-95

In the past 30 trading days, IFG's shares have increased 17%, compared to a 5% rise in the S&P 500. Average trading volume for the past five days was 10,640 shares, compared with the 40-day moving average of 11,582 shares.

Key Stock Statistics

Dividend Rate/Share	0.64	Shareholders	5,700
Shs. outstg. (M)	8.1	Market cap. (B)	$0.285
Avg. daily vol. (M)	0.017	Inst. holdings	19%
Tang. Bk. Value/Share	25.55	Insider holdings	NA
Beta	1.61		

Value of $10,000 invested 5 years ago: $ 45,123

Fiscal Year Ending Dec. 31

	1995	% Change	1994	% Change	1993	% Change
Revenues (Million $)						
1Q	134.0	2%	131.1	10%	118.8	8%
2Q	147.2	25%	117.6	-4%	122.5	16%
3Q	—	—	118.2	-13%	136.0	32%
4Q	—	—	129.4	-4%	134.3	12%
Yr.	—	—	496.3	-3%	511.6	17%
Income (Million $)						
1Q	5.56	-45%	10.17	NM	10.14	17%
2Q	8.64	46%	5.91	-42%	10.26	21%
3Q	—	—	5.85	-60%	14.46	84%
4Q	—	—	3.52	-73%	12.80	34%
Yr.	—	—	25.45	-47%	47.65	38%
Earnings Per Share ($)						
1Q	0.67	-44%	1.20	-2%	1.22	22%
2Q	1.04	49%	0.70	-43%	1.23	26%
3Q	—	—	0.71	-59%	1.72	87%
4Q	—	—	0.43	-72%	1.51	36%
Yr.	—	—	3.04	-46%	5.67	41%

Next earnings report expected: mid October

Inter-Regional Financial Group

Business Summary - 05-OCT-95

Through its two primary subsidiaries, Dain Bosworth Inc. and Rauscher Pierce Refsnes, Inc., Inter-Regional Financial Group offers investment banking and securities services throughout the western half of the U.S. Other units manage a series of money-market funds, provide fixed-income portfolio management services, engage in real estate services and provide securities and settlement activities. In October 1994, Dain Bosworth acquired Chicago-based Clayton Brown Holding Co., which specializes in fixed-income securities brokerage. Revenues and pretax income (in millions) in 1994 were derived as follows:

	Revs.	Pretax Inc.
Dain Bosworth	63%	$28.0
Rauscher Pierce Refsnes	36%	14.6
Other	1%	-2.7

Dain Bosworth Inc. and Rauscher Pierce Refsnes, Inc. provide broker-dealer and investment banking services through 95 offices in the Midwest, Southwest, Pacific Northwest and Rocky Mountain states. At year-end 1994, Dain Bosworth had 854 sales representatives and Rauscher Pierce Refsnes employed 324 sales representatives.

Both firms are dealers in corporate, tax-exempt and government fixed-income securities and corporate equity securities, act as agents in the purchase and sale of securities, options, commodities and futures contracts traded on various exchanges, assist clients in planning to meet their financial needs and advise them on means of raising capital, and act as principals in the purchase and sale to their customers of securities of the U.S. Government and its agencies, including repurchase agreements and certain other money-market instruments. Dain Bosworth and Rauscher Pierce Refsnes also have research departments that provide analysis, investment recommendations and market information, with an emphasis on companies located in their respective regions.

Subsidiaries also include IFG Asset Management Services, Inc. (formerly Insight Investment Management, Inc.), which manages a series of mutual funds, Great Hall Investment Funds, and provides private fixed-income portfolio management services to individuals and institutions; Regional Operations Group, Inc., a registered broker-dealer formed in April 1993 to perform the securities operations and settlement activities of Dain Bosworth and Rauscher Pierce Refsnes; and Dain Corp., which provides real estate investment services.

Important Developments

Jul. '95—IFG said it opened 14 new offices and added 176 (net) investment executives in 1994.

Capitalization

Long Term Debt: $43,983,000 (6/95).

Per Share Data ($)

(Year Ended Dec. 31)

	1994	1993	1992	1991	1990	1989
Tangible Bk. Val.	24.30	21.86	16.33	12.56	9.19	7.52
Cash Flow	NA	NA	NA	NA	NA	NA
Earnings	3.04	5.67	4.03	2.50	0.16	0.34
Dividends	0.56	0.28	0.12	Nil	Nil	Nil
Payout Ratio	18%	5%	3%	Nil	Nil	Nil
Prices - High	32⅝	34	19½	17¾	8½	10⅝
- Low	20	17⅞	13⅛	5	4⅞	7
P/E Ratio - High	11	6	5	7	53	31
- Low	7	3	3	2	30	21

Income Statement Analysis (Million $)

	1994	%Chg	1993	%Chg	1992	%Chg	1991
Commissions	131	-6%	139	17%	119	21%	98.0
Int. Inc.	75.2	37%	54.9	-1%	55.5	-26%	74.7
Total Revs.	496	-3%	512	17%	438	16%	378
Int. Exp.	38.9	36%	28.7	-11%	32.4	-42%	55.7
Pretax Inc.	39.8	-49%	77.4	44%	53.7	63%	33.0
Eff. Tax Rate	36%	—	38%	—	36%	—	36%
Net Inc.	25.5	-46%	47.6	38%	34.5	64%	21.1

Balance Sheet & Other Fin. Data (Million $)

	1994	1993	1992	1991	1990	1989
Total Assets	1,953	1,786	1,271	1,461	1,368	1,520
Cash Items	361	595	536	625	649	724
Receivables	917	710	479	502	304	363
Secs. Owned	319	271	141	214	204	218
Sec. Borrowed	150	124	19.0	62.0	96.0	117
Due Brokers & Cust.	1,117	1,149	923	1,047	883	997
Other Liabs.	444	314	181	221	268	282
Capitalization:						
Debt	47.0	22.0	16.0	27.0	45.0	62.0
Equity	195	178	132	103	74.0	59.0
Total	242	200	148	131	121	124

Ratio Analysis

	1994	1993	1992	1991	1990	1989
% Ret. on Revs.	5.1	9.3	7.9	5.6	0.4	0.9
% Ret. on Assets	1.3	3.1	2.5	1.5	0.1	0.2
% Ret. on Equity	13.6	30.7	29.4	23.7	1.7	4.9

Dividend Data —Quarterly cash payments, omitted in 1983, were resumed in April 1992.

Amt. of Div. $	Date Decl.	Ex-Div. Date	Stock of Record	Payment Date
0.160	Oct. 27	Nov. 04	Nov. 10	Nov. 23 '94
0.160	Feb. 01	Feb. 17	Feb. 24	Mar. 10 '95
0.160	May. 02	May. 10	May. 16	May. 30 '95
0.160	Aug. 09	Aug. 21	Aug. 23	Sep. 05 '95

Data as orig. reptd.; bef. results of disc opers. and/or spec. items. Per share data adj. for stk. divs. as of ex-div. date. E-Estimated. NA-Not Available. NM-Not Meaningful. NR-Not Ranked.

Office—Dain Bosworth Plaza, 60 S. Sixth St., Minneapolis, MN 55402-4422. **Tel**—(612) 371-7750. **Chrmn, Pres & CEO**—I. Weiser. **Secy**—Carla J. Smith. **EVP, CFO & Treas**—L. C. Fornetti. **Investor Contact**—B. J. French. **Dirs**—J. C. Appel, S. S. Boren, F. G. Fitz-Gerald, L. Perlman, C. A. Rundell Jr., R. L. Ryan, A. R. Schulze, Jr., I. Weiser. **Transfer Agent & Registrar**—Norwest Bank Minnesota, Minneapolis. **Incorporated** in Delaware in 1973. **Empl**-3,340. **S&P Analyst:** Robert Schpoont

STANDARD & POOR'S

STOCK REPORTS

Interface, Inc.

NASDAQ Symbol **IFSIA**
In S&P SmallCap 600

02-NOV-95

Industry:
Home Furnishings

Summary: The company is a leader in the worldwide commercial interiors market, offering floorcoverings, fabrics, specialty chemicals, and interior architectural products.

Quantitative Evaluations

Outlook
(1 Lowest—5 Highest)
• **3+**

Fair Value
• **16**

Risk
• **Average**

Earn./Div. Rank
• **A-**

Technical Eval.
• **Bearish** since 10/95

Rel. Strength Rank
(1 Lowest—99 Highest)
• **53**

Insider Activity
• **NA**

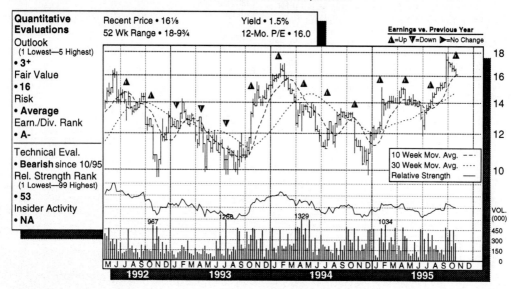

Recent Price • 16⅛
52 Wk Range • 18-9¾

Yield • 1.5%
12-Mo. P/E • 16.0

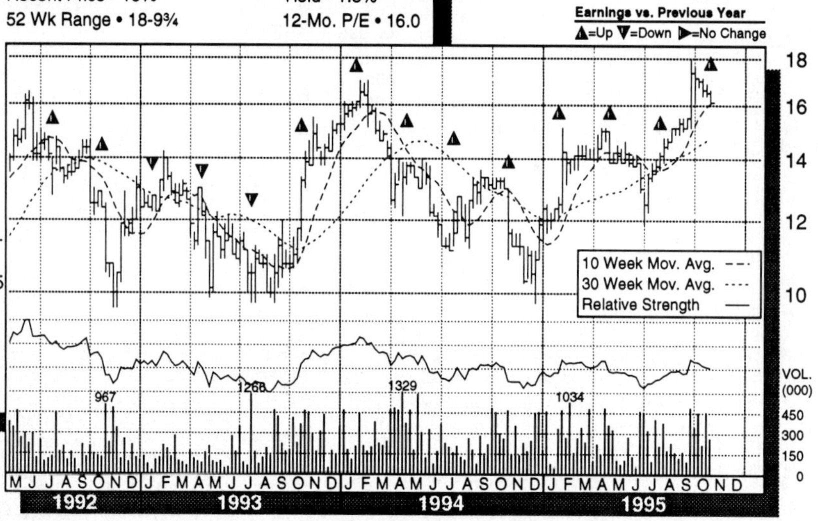

Business Profile - 27-OCT-95

This company, which is the world's largest manufacturer of modular carpet, also makes designer-oriented broadloom carpeting for commercial and institutional applications, interior fabrics for use in open-plan office furniture systems, and certain specialty chemicals. Interface is attempting to replicate the turnaround of its Americas carpet tile business to other geographic regions and businesses. IFSIA plans to meet cost savings objectives in 1995, designed to eliminate wasteful production.

Operational Review - 02-NOV-95

Net sales in the first nine months of 1995 advanced 13%, year to year. Net income improved 33%, to $0.72 a share, aided by reduced manufacturing costs in the carpet tile operations, particularly in the U.S. as Interface implemented a make-to-order production strategy. This strategy had led to increased manufacturing efficiencies and a shift to higher-margin products. The company plans to implement a similar strategy to increase European profits during the fourth quarter of 1995.

Stock Performance - 27-OCT-95

In the past 30 trading days, IFSIA's shares have increased 4%, compared to a 0.63% fall in the S&P 500. Average trading volume for the past five days was 52,180 shares, compared with the 40-day moving average of 73,528 shares.

Key Stock Statistics

Dividend Rate/Share	0.24	Shareholders	700
Shs. outstg. (M)	18.3	Market cap. (B)	$0.287
Avg. daily vol. (M)	0.061	Inst. holdings	64%
Tang. Bk. Value/Share	1.06	Insider holdings	NA
Beta	1.89		

Value of $10,000 invested 5 years ago: $ 10,172

Fiscal Year Ending Dec. 31

	1995	% Change	1994	% Change	1993	% Change
Revenues (Million $)						
1Q	191.3	19%	160.7	19%	135.0	-13%
2Q	202.8	12%	181.7	21%	150.1	NM
3Q	203.3	10%	185.0	10%	167.6	16%
4Q	—	—	196.9	14%	172.4	18%
Yr.	—	—	725.3	16%	625.1	5%
Income (Million $)						
1Q	4.02	43%	2.81	28%	2.20	-42%
2Q	5.08	37%	3.71	35%	2.75	-19%
3Q	5.33	25%	4.25	23%	3.45	82%
4Q	—	—	5.69	25%	4.54	44%
Yr.	—	—	16.46	19%	13.85	13%
Earnings Per Share ($)						
1Q	0.20	43%	0.14	8%	0.13	-41%
2Q	0.25	39%	0.18	13%	0.16	-20%
3Q	0.27	29%	0.21	5%	0.20	82%
4Q	—	—	0.28	8%	0.26	44%
Yr.	—	—	0.82	9%	0.75	6%

Next earnings report expected: late January

Interface, Inc.

Business Summary - 02-NOV-95

Interface, Inc. (formerly Interface Flooring Systems) is the world's largest manufacturer and marketer of modular carpet for commercial, institutional and residential use. It also makes and sells broadloom carpeting for commercial and institutional applications, interior fabrics for use in open-plan office furniture systems, and antimicrobial and stain-resistant chemicals for use in a variety of interior finishes.

The company's traditional core business has been the development, manufacture, marketing and servicing of modular carpet (carpet tile and six-foot roll goods), which offers advantages over broadloom carpet and other soft surface flooring, such as easy access to under-floor telephone, electrical and computer wiring, rotation of carpet between high- and low-wear areas, redesign of office work areas and easy installation and replacement. Principal modular carpet subsidiaries are U.S.-based Interface Flooring Systems and Netherlands-based Interface Europe B.V.

Through the acquisitions of Bentley Mills in June 1993 and Prince Street Technologies in March 1994, Interface has established a significant presence in the broadloom carpet market. Bentley makes high-quality, designer-oriented broadloom carpeting used primarily for commercial and institutional applications. Prince Street manufactures innovative and technically advanced tufted broadloom carpeting used mainly in the U.S. commercial market.

IFSIA's Guilford of Maine unit is the leading U.S. producer of interior fabrics for use in open-plan office furniture systems. It also designs, makes and markets fabrics for use as upholstery, window treatments and wall and ceiling coverings.

Through its Interface Research Corp. and Rockland React-Rite subsidiaries, the company manufactures specialty chemicals, including antimicrobial, soil-resistant and stain-inhibiting additives for use in a wide variety of interior finishes. Another U.S. subsidiary, Pandel, makes vinyl carpet tile backing, specialty mats and foam products.

In June 1995, Interface acquired Toltec Fabrics, Inc. (with 1994 sales of $20 million), a maker of fabrics for the contract and home furnishings upholstery market.

Important Developments

Oct. '95—Interface signed a letter of intent to acquire the assets of the Intek office panel fabric business of Springs Industries, Inc.

Capitalization

Long Term Debt: $338,389,000 (7/2/95), incl. $103,925,000 of 8% sub. debs. due 2013 & conv. into Cl. A com. at $16.92 a sh.
7% Pfd. Stock: $25,000,000, conv. into com. at $14.7875 a sh.; nonvoting.
Cl. A Common Stock: 15,238,355 shs.
Cl. B Common Stock: 3,011,998 shs.
Elects majority of directors.

Per Share Data ($) (Year Ended Dec. 31)

	1994	1993	1992	1991	1990	1989
Tangible Bk. Val.	0.62	-0.42	3.07	3.27	2.96	1.08
Cash Flow	2.38	1.93	1.50	1.79	2.38	2.28
Earnings	0.82	0.75	0.71	0.52	1.37	1.43
Dividends	0.24	0.24	0.24	0.24	0.24	0.21
Payout Ratio	29%	32%	34%	46%	18%	15%
Prices - High	17	15½	16½	14¼	19¾	19⅜
- Low	9¾	9¾	9⅝	7⅞	6¾	14⅝
P/E Ratio - High	21	21	23	27	14	14
- Low	12	13	14	15	5	10

Income Statement Analysis (Million $)

	1994	%Chg	1993	%Chg	1992	%Chg	1991
Revs.	725	16%	625	5%	594	2%	582
Oper. Inc.	79.0	19%	66.6	23%	54.1	-10%	59.9
Depr.	28.2	38%	20.5	51%	13.6	-38%	22.0
Int. Exp.	24.1	6%	22.8	4%	21.9	-6%	23.3
Pretax Inc.	25.7	21%	21.3	15%	18.6	30%	14.3
Eff. Tax Rate	36%	—	35%	—	34%	—	38%
Net Inc.	16.5	20%	13.8	12%	12.3	38%	8.9

Balance Sheet & Other Fin. Data (Million $)

	1994	1993	1992	1991	1990	1989
Cash	7.1	8.7	10.2	10.4	10.1	18.7
Curr. Assets	292	267	232	263	271	244
Total Assets	688	642	534	569	582	526
Curr. Liab.	117	126	94.0	112	114	112
LT Debt	314	292	235	240	255	244
Common Eqty.	214	182	186	199	198	157
Total Cap.	570	516	441	457	468	414
Cap. Exp.	21.3	28.7	13.7	15.9	32.8	23.0
Cash Flow	42.9	33.4	25.9	30.9	40.9	39.1

Ratio Analysis

	1994	1993	1992	1991	1990	1989
Curr. Ratio	2.5	2.1	2.5	2.3	2.4	2.2
% LT Debt of Cap.	55.0	56.5	53.5	52.5	54.4	59.0
% Net Inc.of Revs.	2.3	2.2	2.1	1.5	3.8	4.2
% Ret. on Assets	2.4	2.3	2.2	1.5	4.3	4.8
% Ret. on Equity	7.3	7.0	6.4	4.5	13.3	16.7

Dividend Data —Any dividend paid on the Class A stock must be paid on the Class B.

Amt. of Div. $	Date Decl.	Ex-Div. Date	Stock of Record	Payment Date
0.060	Oct. 26	Nov. 04	Nov. 11	Nov. 25 '94
0.060	Mar. 02	Mar. 13	Mar. 17	Mar. 31 '95
0.060	Apr. 25	May. 08	May. 12	May. 26 '95
0.060	Jul. 28	Aug. 09	Aug. 11	Aug. 25 '95
0.060	Oct. 25	Nov. 08	Nov. 10	Nov. 24 '95

Data as orig. reptd.; bef. results of disc. opers. and/or spec. items. Per share data adj. for stk. divs. as of ex-div. date. E-Estimated. NA-Not Available. NM-Not Meaningful. NR-Not Ranked.

Office—2859 Paces Ferry Rd., Suite 2000, Atlanta, GA 30339. **Tel**—(404) 437-6800. **Chrmn, Pres & CEO**—R. C. Anderson. **VP-Fin, CFO, Treas & Investor Contact**—Daniel T. Hendrix. **VP & Secy**—D. W. Porter. **Dirs**—R. C. Anderson, B. L. DeMoura, C. R. Eitel, C. I. Gable, J. M. Henton, J. S. Lanier II, D. Milton, R. R. Renfroe, D. E. Russell, L. G. Saulter, C. E. Terry, D. G. Thomas, C. C. van Andel. **Transfer Agent**—Wachovia Bank and Trust Co., Winston-Salem, N.C. **Incorporated** in Georgia in 1981. **Empl**-4,660. **S&P Analyst:** Philip D. Wohl

Intermagnetics General

ASE Symbol **IMG**
In S&P SmallCap 600

13-SEP-95 **Industry:** Electronics/Electric

Summary: IMG manufactures superconducting magnet systems and superconducting wire for use primarily in MRI medical diagnostic imaging systems and produces cryogenic refrigeration equipment.

Quantitative Evaluations

Outlook (1 Lowest—5 Highest)
• **NA**

Fair Value
• **NA**

Risk
• **High**

Earn./Div. Rank
• **B**

Technical Eval.
• **Bullish** since 5/95

Rel. Strength Rank (1 Lowest—99 Highest)
• **78**

Insider Activity
• **Neutral**

Recent Price • 17¾
52 Wk Range • 19¾-10
Yield • Nil
12-Mo. P/E • 50.7

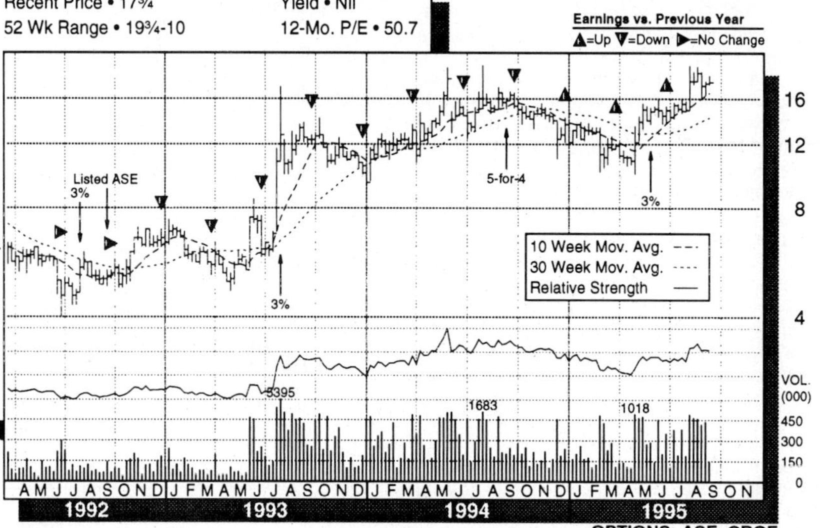

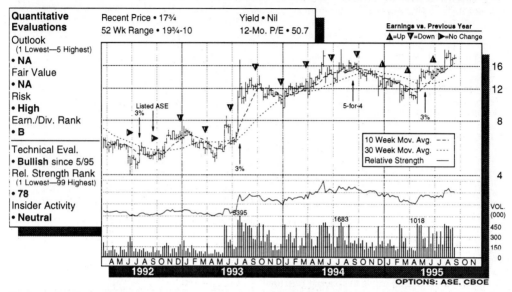

OPTIONS: ASE, CBOE

Business Profile - 05-SEP-95

The bulk of IMG's revenues are provided by its magnetic products segment, with the majority of sales consisting of MRI related products. Sales to the company's two largest customers, N.V. Philips and General Electric, combined for 73% of total revenues in fiscal 1995. Revenues and earnings rose sharply in fiscal 1995, led by a substantial increase in magnetic products sales. The company is seeking commercial applications for its family of environmentally acceptable refrigerants.

Operational Review - 08-SEP-95

Revenues in the fiscal year ended May 28, 1995, advanced 64% from those of the prior year, reflecting a 79% revenue increase in the magnetic products segment due to increased sales of a new family of magnet systems for MRI. Margins widened on the higher volume, and operating income surged 75%. After taxes at 38.5%, versus 40.0%, net income tripled, to $4.0 million ($0.35 a share) from $1.3 million ($0.11). Results for 1994 exclude a gain of $0.08 a share from the effect of an accounting change.

Stock Performance - 08-SEP-95

In the past 30 trading days, IMG's shares have increased 19%, compared to a 2% rise in the S&P 500. Average trading volume for the past five days was 35,725 shares, compared with the 40-day moving average of 92,231 shares.

Key Stock Statistics

Dividend Rate/Share	Nil	Shareholders	2,000
Shs. outstg. (M)	11.2	Market cap. (B)	$0.205
Avg. daily vol. (M)	0.077	Inst. holdings	12%
Tang. Bk. Value/Share	4.87	Insider holdings	NA
Beta	1.11		

Value of $10,000 invested 5 years ago: $ 43,430

Fiscal Year Ending May 31

	1995	% Change	1994	% Change	1993	% Change
Revenues (Million $)						
1Q	14.90	35%	11.01	-18%	13.50	-5%
2Q	19.79	65%	12.01	-20%	15.10	6%
3Q	21.65	76%	12.28	-12%	13.90	-2%
4Q	27.54	73%	15.95	15%	13.81	-11%
Yr.	83.88	64%	51.24	-9%	56.31	-3%
Income (Million $)						
1Q	0.25	14%	0.22	—	—	—
2Q	0.83	NM	0.18	-80%	0.91	-13%
3Q	1.10	NM	0.33	-41%	0.56	-45%
4Q	1.84	NM	0.53	-10%	0.59	-46%
Yr.	4.01	NM	1.26	-60%	3.14	-26%
Earnings Per Share ($)						
1Q	0.02	-17%	0.02	-79%	0.11	NM
2Q	0.07	NM	0.02	-83%	0.09	-14%
3Q	0.10	NM	0.03	-41%	0.05	-46%
4Q	0.16	NM	0.04	-38%	0.06	-45%
Yr.	0.35	192%	0.12	-63%	0.32	-25%

Next earnings report expected: mid September

Intermagnetics General

Business Summary - 08-SEP-95

Intermagnetics General Corporation primarily designs and manufactures superconductive magnets and materials and other magnetic products. It also produces cryogenic refrigeration equipment. Net export sales (primarily to Europe) accounted for 62% of total sales in 1994-5 (43% in 1993-4).

The company produces the two principal low-temperature superconductive materials that are commercially available for the construction of superconductive magnets: niobium-titanium wire and niobium-tin wire. Sales of superconductive wire accounted for 24%, 26% and 23% of net sales in 1994-5, 1993-4 and 1992-3, respectively.

Intermagnetics sells superconductive magnet systems used in mobile and stationary magnetic resonance imaging (MRI) systems. Systems include the superconductive magnet, electronic systems required to energize, monitor, control and protect the magnet, and the cryostat that maintains the extremely low-temperature environment necessary for operation. MRI magnet systems accounted for 46% of sales in 1994-5, up from 31% in 1993-4.

Through its APD Cryogenic Inc. unit, IMG is a supplier of specialty cryogenic refrigeration equipment for use in medical diagnostics, laboratory research, missile guidance systems, and semiconductor manufacturing.

Pursuant to a five-year contract for certain magnets, which expires in June 1997, a unit of N.V. Philips accounted for 52%, 32% and 46% of net sales in 1994-5, 1993-4 and 1992-3, respectively. In addition, GE, under a long-term arrangement for superconducting wire, accounted for 21%, 26% and 16% of net sales in 1994-5, 1993-4 and 1992-3, respectively. Also, the U.S. government accounted for 9%, 16% and 17% of net sales in each of the three most recent fiscal years.

The company has developed a family of environmentally acceptable refrigerants, known as FRIGC, as a replacement for ozone-depleting chlorofluorocarbons (CFCs) currently being used as refrigerants for a variety of applications. IMG's FR-12 refrigerant, developed for use as a replacement for Freon R-12 in the automobile air conditioning refrigerant aftermarket, is the first commercial product from this family of refrigerants.

Important Developments

Jul. '95—The company successfuly obtained final EPA listing of FRIGC FR-12 refrigerant as an acceptable substitute for R-12 in mobile air conditioning applications.

Capitalization

Long Term Debt: $39,807,000 (5/95).
Options: To buy 1,463,576 shs. at $2.67 to $14.93 ea. (5/95).

Per Share Data ($) (Year Ended May 31)

	1995	1994	1993	1992	1991	1990
Tangible Bk. Val.	4.87	4.32	3.98	3.81	3.25	2.95
Cash Flow	0.63	0.40	0.57	0.68	0.52	0.29
Earnings	0.35	0.12	0.32	0.43	0.29	0.10
Dividends	Nil	Nil	Nil	Nil	Nil	Nil
Payout Ratio	Nil	Nil	Nil	Nil	Nil	Nil
Cal. Yrs.	1994	1993	1992	1991	1990	1989
Prices - High	19¾	17¼	7⅞	10⅛	5⅜	6
- Low	9½	4¾	4	3⅞	3¼	3⅞
P/E Ratio - High	57	NM	23	23	18	65
- Low	27	NM	13	9	11	41

Income Statement Analysis (Million $)

	1995	%Chg	1994	%Chg	1993	%Chg	1992
Revs.	83.9	64%	51.2	-9%	56.3	-3%	58.2
Oper. Inc.	10.7	74%	6.2	-11%	6.9	-9%	7.6
Depr.	3.3	NM	3.3	19%	2.7	10%	2.5
Int. Exp.	2.8	—	NA	—	NA	—	NA
Pretax Inc.	6.5	NM	2.1	-46%	3.9	-18%	4.8
Eff. Tax Rate	39%	—	40%	—	20%	—	11%
Net Inc.	4.0	NM	1.3	-60%	3.1	-26%	4.3

Balance Sheet & Other Fin. Data (Million $)

	1995	1994	1993	1992	1991	1990
Cash	13.0	13.2	1.6	1.0	0.5	0.8
Curr. Assets	62.1	56.3	31.2	32.4	32.4	35.5
Total Assets	104	93.8	58.4	53.2	49.3	50.8
Curr. Liab.	9.4	7.0	11.6	7.5	9.5	13.6
LT Debt	39.8	39.9	5.0	10.7	9.7	10.4
Common Eqty.	53.3	46.9	41.8	35.1	30.1	26.7
Total Cap.	94.3	86.8	46.8	45.7	39.8	37.2
Cap. Exp.	3.9	9.4	3.1	4.9	3.9	4.3
Cash Flow	7.3	4.5	5.9	6.8	5.0	2.7

Ratio Analysis

	1995	1994	1993	1992	1991	1990
Curr. Ratio	6.6	8.1	2.7	4.3	3.4	2.6
% LT Debt of Cap.	42.3	45.9	10.7	23.3	24.4	28.1
% Net Inc.of Revs.	4.8	2.5	5.6	7.3	4.6	1.8
% Ret. on Assets	4.1	1.7	5.4	8.2	5.6	1.8
% Ret. on Equity	8.0	2.8	7.8	12.9	9.8	3.2

Dividend Data —No cash dividends have been paid. A five-for-four stock split was effected in September 1994.

Amt. of Div. $	Date Decl.	Ex-Div. Date	Stock of Record	Payment Date
3%	Mar. 22	May. 24	May. 31	Jun. 15 '95

Data as orig. reptd.; bef. results of disc. opers. and/or spec. items. Per share data adj. for stk. divs. as of ex-div. date. E-Estimated. NA-Not Available. NM-Not Meaningful. NR-Not Ranked.

Office—450 Old Niskayuna Rd., Latham, NY 12110. **Tel**—(518) 782-1122. **Chrmn, Pres & CEO**—C. H. Rosner. **SVP-Fin & CFO**—M. C. Zeigler. **Secy**—A. L. Goldberger. **Dirs**—J. C. Abeles, E. E. David, Jr., J. E. Goldman, T. L. Kempner, C. H. Rosner, S. Weinig. **Transfer Agent & Registrar**—American Stock Transfer & Trust Co., NYC. **Incorporated** in New York in 1971. **Empl**-494. **S&P Analyst:** N. Rosenberg

STANDARD & POOR'S

STOCK REPORTS

Intermet Corp.

NASDAQ Symbol **INMT**

In S&P SmallCap 600

04-NOV-95 **Industry:** Auto parts/equipment

Summary: This company provides precision iron parts to automotive and industrial customers primarily in North America and Europe.

Quantitative Evaluations

Outlook (1 Lowest—5 Highest) • **1+**

Fair Value • **10**

Risk • **Average**

Earn./Div. Rank • **C**

Technical Eval. • **Bullish** since 10/95

Rel. Strength Rank (1 Lowest—99 Highest) • **65**

Insider Activity • **Unfavorable**

Recent Price • 12¼ | Yield • Nil

52 Wk Range • 14⅛-4¾ | 12-Mo. P/E • 81.7

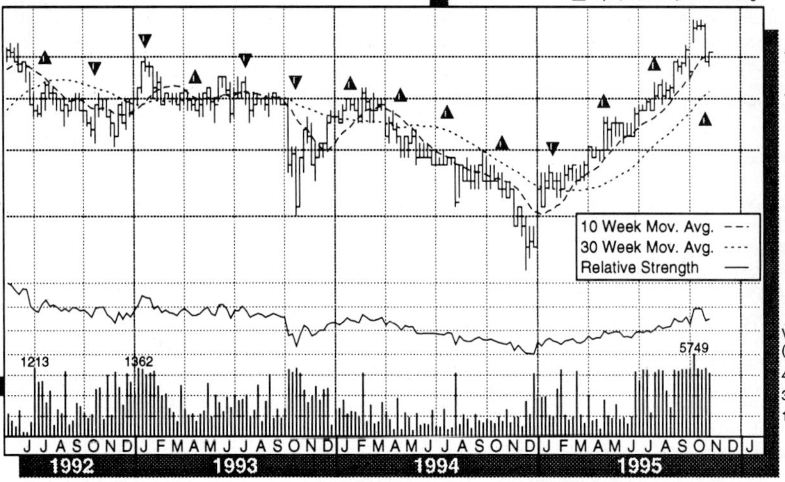

Business Profile - 02-NOV-95

INMT recently rejected an unsolicited $13.50-a-share buyout offer from GWM, Inc. and Kelso & Co. L.P. INMT has been improving its results through cost-cutting programs and manufacturing efficiencies, and moved its headquarters from Atlanta to near Detroit during the 1995 third quarter. The company also sold two businesses not aligned with its casting operations. Through the first nine months of 1995, INMT improved its debt-to-capital ratio to 42%, from 61%.

Operational Review - 02-NOV-95

Net sales advanced 15% in the first nine months of 1995, reflecting increased volume in all operating units, in part due to a new production line at the New River Castings plant. Gross margins widened on the strong sales, and with improved operating efficiencies, cost-cutting efforts and favorable exchange rates, which outweighed higher other expense, net income rose more than 300%. The company expects orders to be strong for the balance of the year.

Stock Performance - 03-NOV-95

In the past 30 trading days, INMT's shares have declined 1%, compared to a 2% rise in the S&P 500. Average trading volume for the past five days was 118,380 shares, compared with the 40-day moving average of 313,945 shares.

Key Stock Statistics

Dividend Rate/Share	Nil	Shareholders	800
Shs. outstg. (M)	24.7	Market cap. (B)	$0.303
Avg. daily vol. (M)	0.199	Inst. holdings	44%
Tang. Bk. Value/Share	3.23	Insider holdings	NA
Beta	1.81		

Value of $10,000 invested 5 years ago: $ 16,210

Fiscal Year Ending Dec. 31

	1995	% Change	1994	% Change	1993	% Change
Revenues (Million $)						
1Q	153.3	29%	118.9	-3%	122.8	41%
2Q	149.0	20%	124.6	2%	122.7	13%
3Q	117.3	-3%	121.0	31%	92.69	-8%
4Q	—	—	136.8	29%	106.1	2%
Yr.	—	—	501.3	13%	444.2	11%
Income (Million $)						
1Q	6.52	NM	1.71	138%	0.72	NM
2Q	9.54	NM	2.44	102%	1.21	-43%
3Q	3.38	NM	0.37	NM	-21.27	NM
4Q	—	—	-15.51	NM	-1.17	NM
Yr.	—	—	-10.99	NM	-20.50	NM
Earnings Per Share ($)						
1Q	0.26	NM	0.07	133%	0.03	NM
2Q	0.39	NM	0.10	100%	0.05	-50%
3Q	0.14	NM	0.02	NM	-0.87	NM
4Q	—	—	-0.63	NM	-0.05	NM
Yr.	—	—	-0.45	NM	-0.83	NM

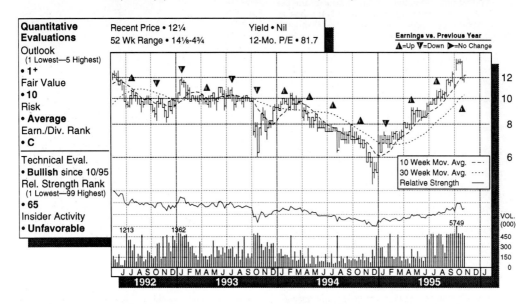

Next earnings report expected: early February

Intermet Corp.

Business Summary - 03-NOV-95

Intermet Corporation is a world leader in the manufacture of precision iron castings for automotive and industrial equipment producers. The company manufactures a wide array of ductile and gray iron castings at nine foundries in Georgia, Minnesota, Ohio, Pennsylvania, Virginia and Germany. Sales by market in recent years were:

	1994	1993
U.S. passenger cars and light trucks	76%	74%
U.S. industrial	9%	10%
Foreign	15%	16%

Products manufactured for the automotive, light-truck and heavy-truck industries include brake parts, steering system components, differential cases, camshafts and crankshafts. Intermet also makes products for construction equipment manufacturers, valve and air-conditioning equipment producers and farm equipment makers. The company is seeking to expand its products to include aluminum castings.

Intermet's marketing strategy emphasizes complex castings requiring precise metallurgical and dimensional standards. The six largest customers contributed 79% of 1994 sales, with Chrysler, Ford and General Motors accounting for 23%, 23% and 14%, respectively.

In 1994, shipments of castings totaled 419,000 tons, or 84% of average foundry capacity. Sales of ductile iron castings in 1994 represented 89% of total castings sales.

In April 1993, Intermet sold its Kockums foundry operations in Sweden. In August 1992, Intermet purchased the remaining 40% interest in New River Castings Co. from Ford Motor Co. for $4 million in cash and $500,000 in New River preferred stock.

Important Developments

Oct. '95—Intermet said it has rejected a $13.50-a-share buyout offer from Atlanta-based GWM, Inc., and New-York-based Kelso & Co., L.P. The company noted that it plans to pursue its strategic business plan, and that costs associated with handling the offer will have some impact on fourth quarter earnings.
Sep. '95—INMT agreed to purchase the Bodine-Robinson aluminum foundry in Alexander City, Ala. Separately, INMT sold its Chesterfield, Mich., machining facility.

Capitalization

Long Term Debt: $61,098,000 (10/1/95).
Minority Interest: $2,837,000.

Per Share Data ($)

(Year Ended Dec. 31)

	1994	1993	1992	1991	1990	1989
Tangible Bk. Val.	2.24	2.84	3.91	4.93	4.84	6.31
Cash Flow	0.73	0.18	0.90	1.36	0.65	1.52
Earnings	-0.45	-0.83	-0.06	0.42	-0.49	0.68
Dividends	Nil	0.12	0.16	0.14	0.20	0.20
Payout Ratio	Nil	NM	NM	33%	NM	29%
Prices - High	10½	12	13¼	9	9⅝	13¼
- Low	4¾	6	7¼	4½	3⅝	6⅞
P/E Ratio - High	NM	NM	NM	21	NM	19
- Low	NM	NM	NM	11	NM	10

Income Statement Analysis (Million $)

	1994	%Chg	1993	%Chg	1992	%Chg	1991
Revs.	501	13%	444	10%	402	26%	320
Oper. Inc.	41.7	64%	25.4	-9%	27.8	1%	27.4
Depr.	29.0	16%	24.9	13%	22.0	11%	19.8
Int. Exp.	7.6	14%	6.7	53%	4.3	2%	4.3
Pretax Inc.	-5.1	NM	-29.1	NM	2.3	-81%	11.9
Eff. Tax Rate	NM	—	NM	—	187%	—	26%
Net Inc.	-11.0	NM	-20.5	NM	-1.5	NM	8.8

Balance Sheet & Other Fin. Data (Million $)

	1994	1993	1992	1991	1990	1989
Cash	13.7	11.2	6.1	8.5	7.3	6.4
Curr. Assets	123	109	89.3	76.1	81.1	96.8
Total Assets	306	307	274	214	215	277
Curr. Liab.	93.5	69.0	58.9	58.9	48.3	60.4
LT Debt	88.0	102	69.5	32.9	45.1	74.8
Common Eqty.	68.0	76.0	101	105	104	114
Total Cap.	159	185	174	153	165	214
Cap. Exp.	24.9	43.6	59.7	25.9	25.0	69.9
Cash Flow	18.1	4.4	20.5	28.6	13.7	32.2

Ratio Analysis

	1994	1993	1992	1991	1990	1989
Curr. Ratio	1.3	1.6	1.5	1.3	1.7	1.6
% LT Debt of Cap.	55.3	55.1	39.8	21.5	27.3	35.0
% Net Inc.of Revs.	NM	NM	NM	2.8	NM	3.7
% Ret. on Assets	NM	NM	NM	4.2	NM	5.8
% Ret. on Equity	NM	NM	NM	8.5	NM	13.3

Dividend Data —Dividends were initiated in 1985, and omitted in October 1993. The last payment was $0.04 a share in August 1993.

Data as orig. reptd.; bef. results of disc. opers. and/or spec. items. Per share data adj. for stk. divs. as of ex-div. date. E-Estimated. NA-Not Available. NM-Not Meaningful. NR-Not Ranked.

Office—1450 W. Long Lake Rd., Suite 150, Troy, MI 48098. **Tel**—(810) 952-1503. **Chrmn & CEO**—J. Doddridge. **VP-Fin, CFO & Investor Contact**—Doratha Christoph. **VP & Secy**—J. W. Rydel. **Dirs**—V. R. Alden, J. F. Broyles, J. P. Crecine, J. Doddridge, A. Dorfmueller, Jr., J. B. Ellis, W. E. Gross, Jr., A. W. Hardy, G. W. Matthews, Jr., H. C. McKenzie, Jr., J. M. Reynolds, C. W. Tarr. **Transfer Agent & Registrar**—Trust Co. Bank, Atlanta. **Incorporated** in Georgia in 1984. **Empl-** 4,415. **S&P Analyst:** Stewart Scharf

International Rectifier

NYSE Symbol **IRF**
In S&P SmallCap 600

11-SEP-95 **Industry:** Electronics/Electric

Summary: A major worldwide supplier of power semiconductors, this company is the leading producer in the fast-growing power MOSFET (metal oxide silicon field effect transistor) market.

Quantitative Evaluations

Outlook
(1 Lowest—5 Highest)
• **2+**

Fair Value
• **38¼**

Risk
• **Average**

Earn./Div. Rank
• **B-**

Technical Eval.
• **Bullish** since 7/95

Rel. Strength Rank
(1 Lowest—99 Highest)
• **85**

Insider Activity
• **NA**

Recent Price • 42¼
52 Wk Range • 44½-18¼
Yield • Nil
12-Mo. P/E • 25.1

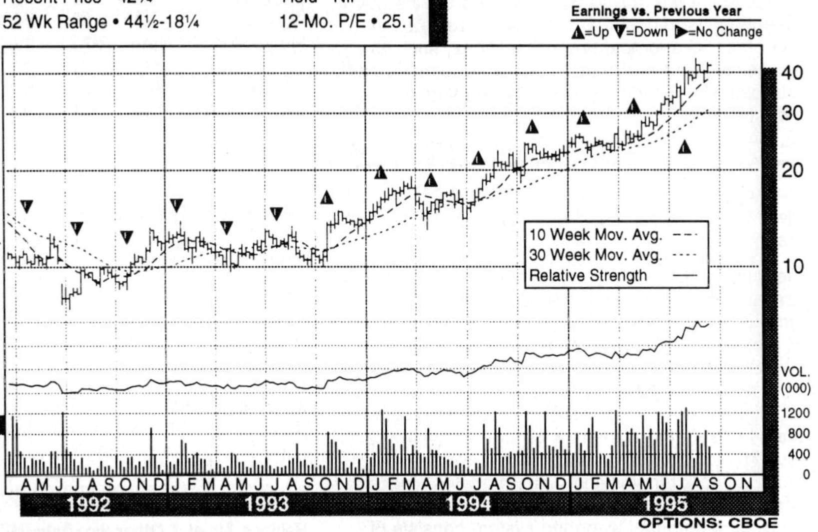

OPTIONS: CBOE

Business Profile - 11-SEP-95

International Rectifier is the leader in the fast-growing power MOSFET (metal oxide silicon field effect transistor) market and is a major worldwide supplier of other power semiconductors. Earnings have grown rapidly in recent quarters, aided by strong industry conditions, broadening applications for MOSFETs and manufacturing efficiencies. In a November 1994 public offering, more than 4.5 million common shares were sold at $22.50 each; proceeds were earmarked for financing plant expansion.

Operational Review - 11-SEP-95

Revenues for the fiscal year ended June 30, 1995, climbed 30% from those of fiscal 1994, reflecting growing demand for MOSFET products and positive industry conditions for thyristor and rectifier sales. Greater manufacturing efficiencies and a more favorable product mix led to wider margins, while net interest expense improved on funds received from a common stock offering in November 1994. Net income rose 151%. Average shares outstanding increased 15%.

Stock Performance - 08-SEP-95

In the past 30 trading days, IRF's shares have increased 6%, compared to a 2% rise in the S&P 500. Average trading volume for the past five days was 132,100 shares, compared with the 40-day moving average of 192,805 shares.

Key Stock Statistics

Dividend Rate/Share	Nil	Shareholders	1,800
Shs. outstg. (M)	25.2	Market cap. (B)	$ 1.1
Avg. daily vol. (M)	0.141	Inst. holdings	71%
Tang. Bk. Value/Share	13.71	Insider holdings	NA
Beta	NM		

Value of $10,000 invested 5 years ago: $ 73,478

Fiscal Year Ending Jun. 30

	1995	% Change	1994	% Change	1993	% Change
Revenues (Million $)						
1Q	92.25	26%	73.09	12%	65.00	10%
2Q	102.8	30%	79.10	12%	70.50	8%
3Q	111.9	33%	84.25	19%	70.60	NM
4Q	122.1	32%	92.43	22%	75.73	7%
Yr.	429.0	30%	328.9	17%	281.7	6%
Income (Million $)						
1Q	6.50	NM	1.98	—	—	—
2Q	8.37	173%	3.07	NM	-1.99	NM
3Q	10.75	155%	4.21	NM	0.13	-94%
4Q	13.78	113%	6.46	NM	0.71	-35%
Yr.	39.40	151%	15.71	NM	-3.03	NM
Earnings Per Share ($)						
1Q	0.32	NM	0.10	NM	-0.09	NM
2Q	0.37	147%	0.15	NM	-0.10	NM
3Q	0.43	105%	0.21	NM	0.01	-90%
4Q	0.54	69%	0.32	NM	0.04	-20%
Yr.	1.68	115%	0.78	NM	-0.15	NM

Next earnings report expected: mid October

International Rectifier

Business Summary - 11-SEP-95

International Rectifier Corporation is a major worldwide supplier of power semiconductor components used in a broad range of industrial, commercial and defense applications. Sales contributions by product category in recent fiscal years were:

	1995	1994	1993
Growth products	84%	82%	78%
Mature products	16%	18%	22%

Growth products are primarily power MOSFETs (metal oxide silicon field effect transistors). The company is the worldwide market leader in these products, which switch or condition electricity at relatively high voltage and current levels. IRF believes that the market for power MOSFETs will continue to grow rapidly, following 28% average annual growth from 1991 through 1995.

Other growth products include Schottky diodes, Fast Recovery diodes, insulated gate bipolar transistors (IGBTs) and Control integrated circuits. Most of these products are still in the early stages of development.

Mature products are power diodes and thyristors that employ traditional silicon processing technology. The market for these products is expected to continue to reflect demand for capital goods.

Sales by region were as follows: 46% from North America, 28% from Europe and 26% from Asia. Foreign operations accounted for 48% of sales and 20% of operating profit in fiscal 1995.

The company's products serve all major market sectors, including automobile, computer/peripheral, office equipment, consumer electronics, communications and industrial applications. Future growth is expected from increased demand for applications in portable electronics, automotive electronics, electronic lighting ballasts and variable-speed motors. Research and development spending averaged 5% of annual sales for the past three years.

The company used the majority of funds raised from a public offering in November 1994 to expand its wafer fabrication plant, in order to meet the growing demand for power MOSFETs. With an estimated cost of $75 million, IRF expects to increase capacity by 75%, allowing for $185 million in additional product shipments at full utilization.

Important Developments

Jul. '95—The company said its ratio of bookings to billings was 1.33 in the fiscal 1995 fourth quarter.

Capitalization

Long Term Debt: $23,881,000 (6/95).
Options: To purchase 802,200 shs. at $5.87 to $31.87 ea. (6/95).

Per Share Data ($) (Year Ended Jun. 30)

	1995	1994	1993	1992	1991	1990
Tangible Bk. Val.	13.71	9.97	9.20	9.62	9.06	1.88
Cash Flow	2.67	1.55	0.55	1.22	2.16	1.16
Earnings	1.68	0.78	-0.15	0.46	1.30	0.18
Dividends	Nil	Nil	Nil	Nil	Nil	Nil
Payout Ratio	Nil	Nil	Nil	Nil	Nil	Nil
Prices - High	38⅝	24⅜	15	16⅛	25¼	12⅛
- Low	22⅛	13	9⅝	7⅜	9⅛	4¼
P/E Ratio - High	23	31	NM	35	19	67
- Low	13	17	NM	16	7	24

Income Statement Analysis (Million $)

	1995	%Chg	1994	%Chg	1993	%Chg	1992
Revs.	429	30%	329	17%	282	6%	265
Oper. Inc.	71.8	82%	39.4	139%	16.5	-37%	26.2
Depr.	23.4	47%	15.9	12%	14.2	-8%	15.4
Int. Exp.	0.4	-89%	3.6	NM	3.6	157%	1.4
Pretax Inc.	47.5	151%	18.9	NM	-2.6	NM	10.5
Eff. Tax Rate	17%	—	17%	—	NM	—	12%
Net Inc.	39.4	151%	15.7	NM	-3.0	NM	9.2

Balance Sheet & Other Fin. Data (Million $)

	1995	1994	1993	1992	1991	1990
Cash	53.8	13.1	8.5	8.5	24.3	2.4
Curr. Assets	234	157	128	136	125	92.0
Total Assets	496	331	278	286	250	218
Curr. Liab.	106	89.7	69.8	68.4	49.8	66.3
LT Debt	23.9	27.0	12.0	12.0	12.0	120
Common Eqty.	345	203	186	192	180	22.0
Total Cap.	379	230	198	204	192	143
Cap. Exp.	107	37.1	21.8	33.0	14.2	5.6
Cash Flow	62.8	31.6	11.1	24.6	28.6	13.6

Ratio Analysis

	1995	1994	1993	1992	1991	1990
Curr. Ratio	2.2	1.7	1.8	2.0	2.5	1.4
% LT Debt of Cap.	6.3	11.6	6.0	5.7	6.2	84.2
% Net Inc.of Revs.	9.2	4.8	NM	3.5	6.8	0.9
% Ret. on Assets	9.5	5.2	NM	3.4	5.5	1.0
% Ret. on Equity	14.4	8.1	NM	5.0	15.8	11.2

Dividend Data —Annual dividends, paid since 1973, were omitted in 1982. The shares were split three for two in 1984 and two for one in 1983.

Data as orig. reptd.; bef. results of disc. opers. and/or spec. items. Per share data adj. for stk. divs. as of ex-div. date. E-Estimated. NA-Not Available. NM-Not Meaningful. NR-Not Ranked.

Office—233 Kansas St., El Segundo, CA 90245. **Tel**—(310) 322-3331. **Fax**—(310) 322-3332. **Chrmn & Pres**—E. Lidow. **VP & CFO**—M. P. McGee. **Secy**—G. A. Koris. **Investor Contact**—Shelley Wagers (310) 607-8848. **Dirs**—D. S. Burns, G. Krsek, A. Lidow, D. B. Lidow, E. Lidow, R. J. Mueller, J. D. Plummer, J. O. Vance, R. E. Vogt. **Transfer Agent & Registrar**—Chemical Trust Co. of California, Los Angeles. **Incorporated** in California in 1947; reincorporated in Delaware in 1979. **Empl**-3,310. **S&P Analyst:** Julie Santoriello

STANDARD & POOR'S

Interstate Bakeries

STOCK REPORTS

NYSE Symbol **IBC**
In S&P SmallCap 600

16-OCT-95 **Industry:** Food

Summary: This company is the largest independent baker and distributor of fresh bakery products in the U.S., operating 66 bakeries throughout the United States.

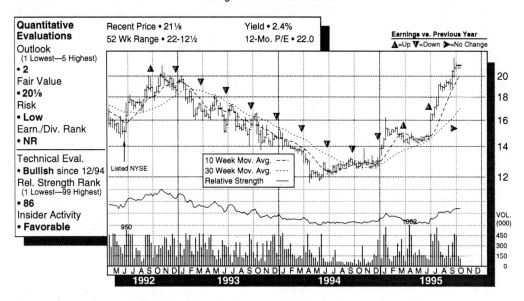

Quantitative Evaluations
Outlook
(1 Lowest—5 Highest)
• **2**
Fair Value
• **20⅛**
Risk
• **Low**
Earn./Div. Rank
• **NR**

Technical Eval.
• **Bullish** since 12/94
Rel. Strength Rank
(1 Lowest—99 Highest)
• **86**
Insider Activity
• **Favorable**

Recent Price • 21⅛
52 Wk Range • 22-12½

Yield • 2.4%
12-Mo. P/E • 22.0

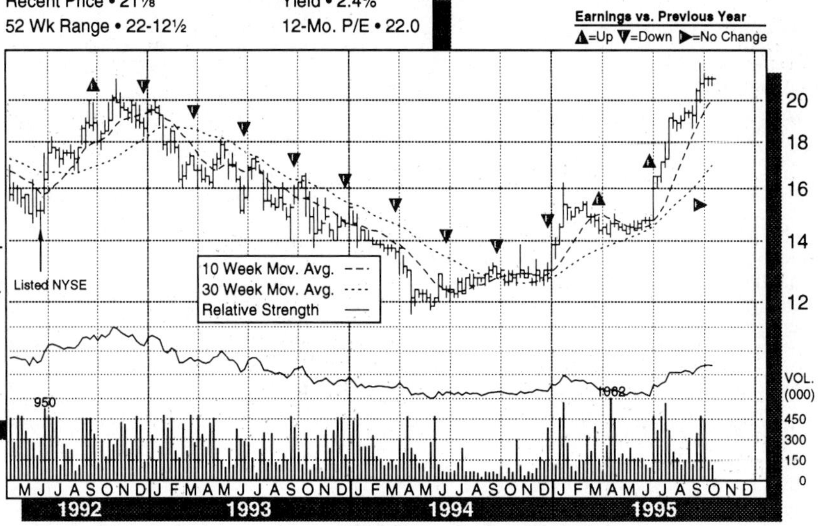

Business Profile - 16-OCT-95

With the July 1995 acquisition of Continental Baking, IBC is now the largest U.S. baker and distributor of fresh bakery products. IBC expects to benefit from leveraging the combined strengths of both companies including the market clout of having a stronger presence in branded products throughout the U.S. The stock is up sharply from its 1994 low of less than $12 a share. VCS Holding Co. owns 46% of the shares.

Operational Review - 16-OCT-95

Sales for the 12 weeks ended August 26, 1995, advanced 72%, year to year, reflecting the July 1995 Continental Baking Company (CBC) acquisition. However, higher selling and delivery expenses at the new bakeries, increased depreciation/amortization, 47% higher interest charges, and 36% more common shares (due to the CBC acquisition) led to a 30% drop in share earnings. IBC expected a tough, challenging year in fiscal 1995-96 that will impact near term quarterly performance.

Stock Performance - 13-OCT-95

In the past 30 trading days, IBC's shares have increased 9%, compared to a 4% rise in the S&P 500. Average trading volume for the past five days was 21,680 shares, compared with the 40-day moving average of 58,274 shares.

Key Stock Statistics

Dividend Rate/Share	0.50	Shareholders	3,400
Shs. outstg. (M)	36.6	Market cap. (B)	$0.772
Avg. daily vol. (M)	0.068	Inst. holdings	37%
Tang. Bk. Value/Share	NM	Insider holdings	NA
Beta	NA		

Value of $10,000 invested 5 years ago: NA

Fiscal Year Ending May 31

	1996	% Change	1995	% Change	1994	% Change
Revenues (Million $)						
1Q	471.4	91%	247.0	-8%	269.7	-2%
2Q	—	—	280.7	4%	268.9	-1%
3Q	—	—	358.2	7%	336.3	-2%
4Q	—	—	309.7	16%	267.8	-3%
Yr.	—	—	1,223	7%	1,143	-2%
Income (Million $)						
1Q	5.73	-3%	5.89	-16%	6.99	—
2Q	—	—	6.06	-17%	7.29	-23%
3Q	—	—	3.10	NM	-2.47	NM
4Q	—	—	5.65	43%	3.94	-48%
Yr.	—	—	20.70	31%	15.75	-49%
Earnings Per Share ($)						
1Q	0.21	NM	0.21	-36%	0.33	-25%
2Q	—	—	0.31	-14%	0.36	-20%
3Q	—	—	0.16	NM	-0.12	NM
4Q	—	—	0.29	45%	0.20	-44%
Yr.	—	—	1.05	35%	0.78	-47%

Next earnings report expected: early December

Interstate Bakeries

Business Summary - 12-OCT-95

Interstate Bakeries, through its wholly-owned operating subsidiary, Interstate Brands Corp., is now the largest baker and distributor of fresh baked products in the U.S. With the July 1995 acquisition of Continental Baking Co. from Ralston Purina Co., IBC was operating 66 bakeries throughout the U.S. and delivering baked products to more than 250,000 food outlets on more than 10,000 delivery routes. The company's products are distributed through its direct route system, through its approximately 1,400 company-operated thrift stores and, to some extent, through distributors.

Sales breakdown in recent fiscal years (ending May 31):

	1995	1994	1993
Bread division	72%	68%	66%
Cake division	26%	30%	33%
Other	2%	1%	1%

The principal products of the bread division are white breads, variety breads, lite breads, rolls, buns, and English muffins, marketed under brand names, including Butternut, Cotton's Holsum, Eddy's, Holsum, Merita, Millbrook, Mrs. Karl's, Sweetheart and Weber's. The majority of this division's sales is generated by white breads and variety breads (whole wheat, rye, and other whole grain breads). The Bread Division is the largest licensed baker and distributor of Roman Meal and Sun Maid breads.

The cake division produces fresh baked sweet goods, including snack cakes, donuts, sweet rolls, snack pies, breakfast pastries, variety cakes, large cakes, and shortcakes, approximately 90% of which is sold under the Dolly Madison Bakery brand name.

Dry products consist of branded, dry, bread-based products, including traditional stuffing and salad croutons, sold mostly under the Mrs. Cubbison's brand name.

Continental Baking Co. (CBC) bread products are marketed under the brand names Wonder, HomePride, Bread Du Jour, and Beefsteak.

CBC cake products are sold under the Hostess brand name and include the following product names: Twinkies, Ding Dongs, Ho Ho's, and Suzy Q's.

Important Developments

Jul. '95—Interstate Bakeries acquired Continental Baking Co. from Ralston Purina Co. for approximately $220 million in cash and 16,923,000 common shares. Continental Baking makes Wonder bread and Hostess snack cakes and has annual sales of $1.95 billion. The addition of Continental was expected to boost IBC's market share to nearly 20%.

Capitalization

Long Term Debt: $425,213,000 (8/95).

Per Share Data ($)

(Year Ended May 31)

	1995	1994	1993	1992	1991	1990
Tangible Bk. Val.	-2.55	-2.69	-1.91	-2.62	-4.42	NA
Cash Flow	2.76	2.33	2.95	3.17	2.82	NA
Earnings	1.05	0.78	1.46	1.49	1.19	NA
Dividends	0.50	0.50	0.47	0.33	NA	NA
Payout Ratio	48%	63%	32%	25%	NA	NA
Cal. Yrs.	1994	1993	1992	1991	1990	1989
Prices - High	$15\frac{1}{8}$	20	$21\frac{1}{8}$	$19\frac{3}{8}$	NA	NA
- Low	$11\frac{5}{8}$	$13\frac{3}{4}$	$14\frac{3}{8}$	$15\frac{1}{4}$	NA	NA
P/E Ratio - High	14	26	14	13	NA	NA
- Low	11	18	10	10	NA	NA

Income Statement Analysis (Million $)

	1995	%Chg	1994	%Chg	1993	%Chg	1992
Revs.	1,223	7%	1,143	-2%	1,166	2%	1,146
Oper. Inc.	90.9	3%	87.9	-15%	103	-2%	105
Depr.	33.6	6%	31.6	NM	31.6	NM	31.6
Int. Exp.	17.7	20%	14.7	-17%	17.7	-29%	25.0
Pretax Inc.	39.7	23%	32.3	-40%	54.0	10%	49.1
Eff. Tax Rate	48%	—	51%	—	43%	—	38%
Net Inc.	20.7	31%	15.8	-49%	30.8	10%	27.9

Balance Sheet & Other Fin. Data (Million $)

	1995	1994	1993	1992	1991	1990
Cash	3.7	5.0	4.6	2.2	1.8	NA
Curr. Assets	120	115	119	103	95.0	NA
Total Assets	598	575	587	574	572	NA
Curr. Liab.	109	107	118	125	136	NA
LT Debt	212	201	189	211	229	NA
Common Eqty.	198	187	202	195	167	NA
Total Cap.	444	424	432	429	414	NA
Cap. Exp.	34.3	31.2	30.6	23.5	21.4	NA
Cash Flow	54.3	47.3	62.4	59.4	58.4	NA

Ratio Analysis

	1995	1994	1993	1992	1991	1990
Curr. Ratio	1.1	1.1	1.0	0.8	0.7	NA
% LT Debt of Cap.	47.7	47.5	43.8	49.3	55.4	NA
% Net Inc.of Revs.	1.7	1.4	2.6	2.4	2.2	NA
% Ret. on Assets	3.5	2.7	5.3	1.8	NA	NA
% Ret. on Equity	10.7	8.1	15.5	NM	NA	NA

Dividend Data —Dividends were initiated in late 1991.

Amt. of Div. $	Date Decl.	Ex-Div. Date	Stock of Record	Payment Date
0.125	Sep. 21	Oct. 07	Oct. 14	Nov. 01 '94
0.125	Dec. 08	Jan. 09	Jan. 16	Feb. 01 '95
0.125	Mar. 30	Apr. 07	Apr. 13	May. 01 '95
0.125	Jun. 29	Jul. 12	Jul. 14	Aug. 01 '95
0.125	Sep. 20	Oct. 12	Oct. 16	Nov. 01 '95

Data as orig. reptd.; bef. results of disc. opers. and/or spec. items. Per share data adj. for stk. divs. as of ex-div. date. E-Estimated. NA-Not Available. NM-Not Meaningful. NR-Not Ranked.

Office—12 East Armour Blvd., Kansas City, MO 64111. **Tel**—(816) 561-6600. **Chrmn & CEO**—C. A. Sullivan. **Pres**—M. D. Kafoure. **VP-Treas**—P. E. Yarick. **VP-Secy**—R. S. Sutton. **Dirs**—G. K. Baum, L. Benatar, E. G. Bewkes, Jr., P. Briggs, R. B. Calhoun, Jr., J. R. Elsesser, F. E. Horton, W. P. Stiritz, C. A. Sullivan. **Transfer Agent & Registrar**—United Missouri Bank, Kansas City; Interstate Bakeries, Kansas City. **Incorporated** In Delaware in 1987. **Empl**-35,000. **S&P Analyst:** N.J. DeVita

Interstate Power

NYSE Symbol **IPW**
In S&P SmallCap 600

13-SEP-95 **Industry:** Util.-Diversified

Summary: This moderate-sized utility provides electricity and natural gas in small communities in Iowa, Minnesota and Illinois.

Quantitative Evaluations

Outlook (1 Lowest—5 Highest)
• 1

Fair Value
• 19⅝

Risk
• Low

Earn./Div. Rank
• B+

Technical Eval.
• Bullish since 8/95

Rel. Strength Rank (1 Lowest—99 Highest)
• 57

Insider Activity
• Neutral

Recent Price • 25¼
52 Wk Range • 25⅝-20⅞
Yield • 8.1%
12-Mo. P/E • 12.6

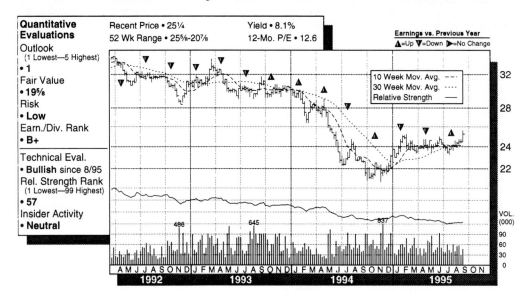

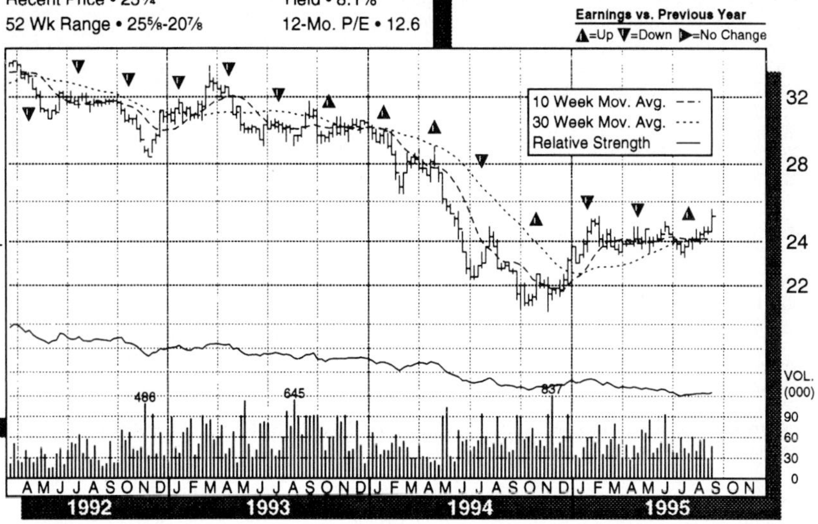

Business Profile - 13-SEP-95

Interstate Power is engaged in the generation, purchase, transmission, distribution and sale of electricity. IPW also engages in the distribution and sale of natural gas. The electric retail service territory is a residential, agricultural and widely diversified industrial area with an estimated population of 338,000. Operating income in 1994 was 99% derived from electricity operations. IPW currently has applications pending for increases in electric and gas rates in Iowa and Minnesota.

Operational Review - 13-SEP-95

Earnings rose in 1995's first half, as improved electric margins offset a decrease in gas margins. Electric margins benefited from increased residential and industrial sales during 1995's second quarter. Gas margins were hurt, however, by lower residential and commercial sales during 1995's first quarter. Despite the recording of other expense, versus income, and higher interest expense on short-term borrowings, share earnings were up 9.1%.

Stock Performance - 08-SEP-95

In the past 30 trading days, IPW's shares have increased 5%, compared to a 2% rise in the S&P 500. Average trading volume for the past five days was 11,525 shares, compared with the 40-day moving average of 9,315 shares.

Key Stock Statistics

Dividend Rate/Share	2.08	Shareholders	16,300
Shs. outstg. (M)	9.6	Market cap. (B)	$0.245
Avg. daily vol. (M)	0.010	Inst. holdings	14%
Tang. Bk. Value/Share	19.15	Insider holdings	NA
Beta	0.24		

Value of $10,000 invested 5 years ago: $ 15,085

Fiscal Year Ending Dec. 31

	1995	% Change	1994	% Change	1993	% Change
Revenues (Million $)						
1Q	82.77	-3%	85.58	NM	84.99	11%
2Q	72.05	NM	71.86	2%	70.11	2%
3Q	—	—	79.81	3%	77.25	23%
4Q	—	—	70.40	-9%	77.12	NM
Yr.	—	—	307.6	NM	309.5	8%
Income (Million $)						
1Q	7.78	-16%	9.25	10%	8.39	-8%
2Q	3.87	187%	1.35	-32%	1.98	-52%
3Q	—	—	6.87	95%	3.52	88%
4Q	—	—	3.20	-37%	5.10	25%
Yr.	—	—	20.67	9%	18.99	-1%
Earnings Per Share ($)						
1Q	0.74	-19%	0.91	11%	0.82	-8%
2Q	0.34	NM	0.07	-36%	0.11	-69%
3Q	—	—	0.65	110%	0.31	158%
4Q	—	—	0.27	-43%	0.47	31%
Yr.	—	—	1.92	11%	1.73	NM

Next earnings report expected: mid October

Interstate Power

Business Summary - 11-SEP-95

Interstate Power provides electric and gas service in a 10,000 square mile area of northeast Iowa (74% of revenues), southern Minnesota (19%) and Illinois (7%). The largest city served is Dubuque, Iowa.

Electric sales accounted for 85% of revenues and 99% of operating income in 1994. Contributions to electric revenues by customer class:

	1994	1993	1992
Residential	28%	28%	28%
General service & farm	19%	20%	21%
Large power & light	45%	44%	44%
Other	8%	8%	7%

Electricity is distributed to 161,983 customers in 234 communities and surrounding rural areas, and wholesale to 19 communities. In 1994, 93% of electricity was coal generated, principally by six plants (two partially owned) with a net capability of 901 mw. The company also has 124.8 mw of internal combustion and gas turbine units.

In 1994, IPW sold 5,374,734 mwh of electricity, up 5.6% from 1993. Peak demand in 1994 was 932 mw and net capability at time of peak (including 283 mw of purchased power) was 1,309 mw. Average residential rates were $0.0739 per kwh ($0.0724 in 1993), on average annual usage of 7,799 kwh (7,816).

IPW is a member of the Mid-Continent Area Power Pool (MAPP), a group of 47 interconnected electric power suppliers. In 1992, IPW entered into three long-term power purchase contracts with area electric utilities to provide 230 to 255 mw of capacity over the period from May 1992 through April 2001.

Natural gas is distributed to 48,584 customers in 39 communities. IPW sold or transported 33,654 MMcf of gas in 1994, down from 34,009 in 1993. Residential customers accounted for 55% of gas revenues in 1994, commercial customers for 28%, transportation for 5% and industrial for 12%.

Important Developments

Aug. '95—IPW filed an application for a $2.2 million annual increase in Iowa gas rates, with a request for increased interim rates of $2.1 million annually, to be effective August 31, 1995. A decision on the interim rate increase is expected by October 29, 1995, and a final decision is anticipated by June 1996.

Jun. '95—IPW increased interim electric rates in Iowa by $7.1 million annually, and interim gas rates in Minnesota by $1.5 million annually, subject to refund. Final decisions on the Iowa and Minnesota applications are expected in February 1996 and March 1996, respectively. Separately, IPW filed for a $4.6 million annual increase in Minnesota electric rates. A decision is expected by the second quarter of 1996.

Capitalization

Long Term Debt: $189,068,000 (6/95).
Preferred Stock: $34,802,000.

Per Share Data ($)

(Year Ended Dec. 31)

	1994	1993	1992	1991	1990	1989
Tangible Bk. Val.	19.15	19.22	20.01	20.51	19.72	19.00
Earnings	1.92	1.73	1.74	2.84	2.56	2.73
Dividends	2.08	2.08	2.08	2.04	2.00	2.00
Payout Ratio	108%	120%	120%	72%	78%	73%
Prices - High	30¼	34⅛	35¼	34¼	26¾	25¾
- Low	20⅞	29	28⅜	24⅞	22⅞	21¼
P/E Ratio - High	16	20	20	12	10	9
- Low	11	17	16	9	9	8

Income Statement Analysis (Million $)

	1994	%Chg	1993	%Chg	1992	%Chg	1991
Revs.	308	NM	309	8%	285	-2%	290
Depr.	28.2	4%	27.0	4%	25.9	2%	25.3
Maint.	17.2	1%	17.0	NM	17.0	-3%	17.6
Fxd. Chgs. Cov.	2.3	3%	2.3	NM	2.3	-31%	3.3
Constr. Credits	0.5	138%	0.2	-22%	0.3	-87%	2.1
Eff. Tax Rate	31%	—	33%	—	34%	—	37%
Net Inc.	20.7	9%	19.0	-1%	19.2	-35%	29.5

Balance Sheet & Other Fin. Data (Million $)

	1994	1993	1992	1991	1990	1989
Gross Prop.	880	846	822	797	769	720
Cap. Exp.	41.0	34.0	32.5	35.6	53.0	27.5
Net Prop.	501	488	482	478	469	439
Capitalization:						
LT Debt	189	203	194	205	181	191
% LT Debt	45	48	46	47	45	47
Pfd.	34.8	34.7	35.3	36.7	37.6	38.6
% Pfd.	8.30	8.10	8.40	8.40	9.30	9.40
Common	193	190	190	193	186	181
% Common	46	44	45	45	46	44
Total Cap.	524	530	488	499	467	471

Ratio Analysis

	1994	1993	1992	1991	1990	1989
Oper. Ratio	88.4	88.7	87.7	84.9	85.1	83.6
% Earn. on Net Prop.	7.2	7.2	7.3	9.3	8.9	10.1
% Ret. on Revs.	6.7	6.1	6.7	10.2	9.9	10.6
% Ret. On Invest.Cap	7.1	7.0	7.3	9.3	8.9	9.8
% Return On Com.Eqty	9.5	8.5	8.5	13.9	13.1	14.4

Dividend Data —Dividends have been paid since 1948. A dividend reinvestment plan is available.

Amt. of Div. $	Date Decl.	Ex-Div. Date	Stock of Record	Payment Date
0.520	Jul. 21	Aug. 16	Aug. 22	Sep. 20 '94
0.520	Oct. 20	Nov. 15	Nov. 21	Dec. 20 '94
0.520	Feb. 02	Feb. 14	Feb. 21	Mar. 20 '95
0.520	Apr. 20	May. 15	May. 19	Jun. 20 '95
0.520	Jul. 27	Aug. 17	Aug. 21	Sep. 20 '95

Data as orig. reptd.; bef. results of disc opers. and/or spec. items. Per share data adj. for stk. divs. as of ex-div. date. E-Estimated. NA-Not Available. NM-Not Meaningful. NR-Not Ranked.

Office—1000 Main St., P.O. Box 769, Dubuque, IA 52004-0769. **Tel**—(319) 582-5421. **Chrmn, Pres & CEO**—W. H. Stoppelmoor. **Secy, Treas & Investor Contact**—J. C. McGowan. **Dirs**—A. B. Arends, J. E. Byrns, A. D. Cordes, J. L. Hanes, G. L. Kopischke, N. J. Schrup, W. H. Stoppelmoor. **Transfer Agent & Registrar**—Co. itself. **Incorporated** in Delaware in 1925. **Empl-978.** **S&P Analyst:** Ronald J. Gross

STANDARD & POOR'S
STOCK REPORTS

InterVoice, Inc.

NASDAQ Symbol **INTV**
In S&P SmallCap 600

15-AUG-95 **Industry:** Electronics/Electric

Summary: This company develops, sells and services automated call processing solutions with an emphasis on interactive voice response.

Quantitative Evaluations
Outlook (1 Lowest—5 Highest) • **NA**
Fair Value • **NA**
Risk • **High**
Earn./Div. Rank • **B**

Technical Eval. • **Bullish** since 9/94
Rel. Strength Rank (1 Lowest—99 Highest) • **83**
Insider Activity • **Neutral**

Recent Price • 21
52 Wk Range • 24-8⅝
Yield • Nil
12-Mo. P/E • 87.5

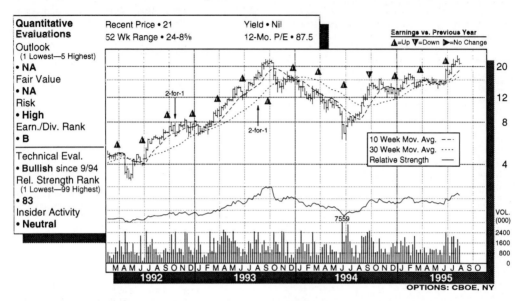

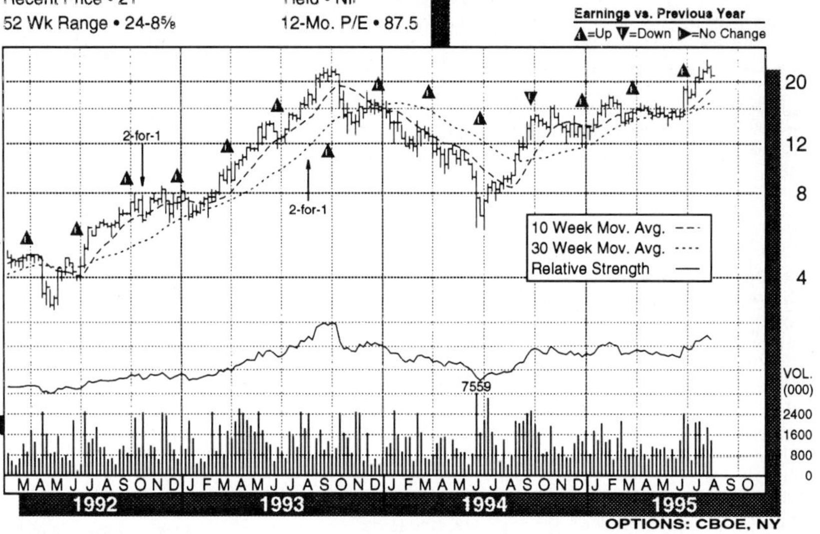

OPTIONS: CBOE, NY

Business Profile - 15-AUG-95

InterVoice is a leading global supplier of automated call processing solutions with the number of installed systems totaling more than 5,300 in 44 countries. INTV systems are used in inbound and outbound call centers across virtually all industry sectors to increase revenues and customer service levels, with lower associated call processing costs. In August 1994, INTV acquired VoicePlex Corp., which develops and sells UNIX-based voice processing systems.

Operational Review - 15-AUG-95

Earnings advanced in fiscal 1995-96's first quarter, reflecting higher international and domestic sales, and wider gross margins due to a more favorable product mix. Operating expenses were up as the company continued to invest in R&D and selling, general and administrative expenses. Other income fell, but share earnings were helped by the completion of a stock repurchase program which resulted in about 12% fewer shares outstanding.

Stock Performance - 11-AUG-95

In the past 30 trading days, INTV's shares have increased 20%, compared to a 2% rise in the S&P 500. Average trading volume for the past five days was 268,380 shares, compared with the 40-day moving average of 349,728 shares.

Key Stock Statistics

Dividend Rate/Share	Nil	Shareholders	400
Shs. outstg. (M)	15.5	Market cap. (B)	$0.330
Avg. daily vol. (M)	0.304	Inst. holdings	59%
Tang. Bk. Value/Share	3.32	Insider holdings	NA
Beta	1.11		

Value of $10,000 invested 5 years ago: $ 31,550

Fiscal Year Ending Feb. 28

	1996	% Change	1995	% Change	1994	% Change
Revenues ()						
1Q	22.02	33%	16.60	20%	13.80	33%
2Q	—	—	18.00	24%	14.50	33%
3Q	—	—	20.10	25%	16.10	52%
4Q	—	—	21.60	31%	16.50	30%
Yr.	—	—	76.30	25%	60.90	37%
Income ()						
1Q	3.99	39%	2.87	7%	2.67	64%
2Q	—	—	-7.60	NM	2.87	58%
3Q	—	—	3.46	12%	3.09	64%
4Q	—	—	3.81	24%	3.08	23%
Yr.	—	—	2.53	-78%	11.71	50%
Earnings Per Share ()						
1Q	0.25	56%	0.16	7%	0.15	50%
2Q	—	—	-0.47	NM	0.16	45%
3Q	—	—	0.22	29%	0.17	55%
4Q	—	—	0.24	41%	0.17	13%
Yr.	—	—	0.15	-77%	0.64	42%

Next earnings report expected: late September

InterVoice, Inc.

Business Summary - 15-AUG-95

InterVoice, Inc. develops, sells and services call automation systems under the trade name OneVoice that allow individuals to interact with a computer database using the keys on their touch-tone telephones, the keyboards of their personal computers, credit card terminals or their voices. Applications are currently functioning in industries including insurance, banking, higher education, help desk, government, utilities, health care, cable TV, retail, distribution, transportation and operator services. The OneVoice System comprised more than 90% of the company's total sales in fiscal 1995. A typical application of this system would be a request for available credit under a credit card account.

The company's InterDial System can provide both inbound and outbound call processing. A typical application of this system would permit a company to improve the productivity of its telemarketing operators by automatically dialing phone numbers and only transferring a call to an operator if the call is answered and the call recipient remains on the phone.

The OneVoice CallCenter was introudced in fiscal 1994, and is targeted for regional or branch offices of large businesses, providing them integrated call automation systems without replacing their existing telecommunications equipment.

INTV's VoicePlex System is an open architecture platform based on the UNIX operating system that has been marketed primarily to telecommunications companies to provide their networks with enhanced features such as voice mail and call forwarding.

In 1994-95, 65% of sales were direct sales to end-users and 35% to distributors. MCI Telecommunications accounted for 11.7% of sales in 1994-95 and international sales accounted for 14% of the total.

Important Developments

Jul. '95—Sprint Corp. signed an agreement to offer INTV's portfolio of interactive voice response products to its business customers in order to provide them with call-processing functions like interactive voice response, audiotext, voice messaging and conferencing.
Jun. '95—INTV received a notice of allowance from the U.S. Patent and Trademark Office for a patent relating to Intelligent Peripheral and Service Node architecture. Separately, InterVoice signed a distribution agreement with Fujitsu Business Communication Systems that allows Fujitsu's direct sales force to market INTV's line of interactive voice response systems.

Capitalization

Long Term Debt: None (5/95).
Options: To buy 1,933,426 shs. (2/95).

Per Share Data () (Year Ended Feb. 28)

	1995	1994	1993	1992	1991	1990
Tangible Bk. Val.	3.05	3.56	2.77	2.54	2.51	2.41
Cash Flow	0.29	0.73	0.54	0.20	0.21	0.38
Earnings	0.15	0.64	0.45	0.16	0.19	0.37
Dividends	Nil	Nil	Nil	Nil	Nil	Nil
Payout Ratio	Nil	Nil	Nil	Nil	Nil	Nil
Cal. Yrs.	1994	1993	1992	1991	1990	1989
Prices - High	17	22 1/2	8 1/2	5	7 1/8	8 1/2
- Low	5 7/8	6 3/8	3 1/8	1 13/16	1 13/16	2 3/8
P/E Ratio - High	113	35	19	32	39	23
- Low	39	10	7	12	10	7

Income Statement Analysis ()

	1995	%Chg	1994	%Chg	1993	%Chg	1992
Revs.	76.3	25%	60.9	37%	44.6	48%	30.2
Oper. Inc.	22.2	18%	18.8	49%	12.6	193%	4.3
Depr.	2.3	31%	1.8	8%	1.6	105%	0.8
Int. Exp.	Nil	—	Nil	—	Nil	—	Nil
Pretax Inc.	9.7	-45%	17.7	54%	11.5	167%	4.3
Eff. Tax Rate	74%	—	34%	—	32%	—	31%
Net Inc.	2.5	-79%	11.7	50%	7.8	167%	2.9

Balance Sheet & Other Fin. Data ()

	1995	1994	1993	1992	1991	1990
Cash	10.3	36.2	25.0	25.9	27.9	41.9
Curr. Assets	40.0	58.7	41.1	40.1	39.5	50.4
Total Assets	62.7	74.2	52.6	49.6	46.8	56.1
Curr. Liab.	15.9	11.1	8.6	5.0	2.5	2.2
LT Debt	Nil	Nil	Nil	Nil	Nil	Nil
Common Eqty.	46.8	63.2	44.1	44.7	44.3	54.0
Total Cap.	46.8	63.2	44.1	44.7	44.3	54.0
Cap. Exp.	9.2	5.6	0.9	2.0	1.3	4.8
Cash Flow	4.8	13.5	9.5	3.7	4.3	7.2

Ratio Analysis

	1995	1994	1993	1992	1991	1990
Curr. Ratio	2.5	5.3	4.8	8.1	15.6	23.5
% LT Debt of Cap.	Nil	Nil	Nil	Nil	Nil	Nil
% Net Inc.of Revs.	3.3	19.2	17.6	9.7	18.4	28.5
% Ret. on Assets	4.0	17.6	16.1	6.1	8.4	18.8
% Ret. on Equity	5.0	20.8	18.6	6.6	8.8	20.3

Dividend Data (No cash dividends have been paid. A shareholder rights plan was adopted in April 1991. Two-for-one stock splits were effected in October 1992 and August 1993.)

Data as orig. reptd.; bef. results of disc. opers. and/or spec. items. Per share data adj. for stk. divs. as of ex-div. date. E-Estimated. NA-Not Available. NM-Not Meaningful. NR-Not Ranked.

Office—17811 Waterview Parkway, Dallas, TX 75252. **Tel**—(214) 669-3988. **Chrmn & CEO**—D. D. Hammond. **Pres & COO**—M. W. Barker. **CFO, Secy & Investor Contact**—Rob-Roy J. Graham. **Dirs**—M. W. Barker, D. D. Hammond, G. F. Montry, J. J. Pietropaolo, G. C. Platt. **Transfer Agent**—KeyCorp Shareholder Svcs., Dallas. **Incorporated** in Texas in 1984. **Empl-520. S&P Analyst:** Ronald J. Gross

Invacare Corp.

NASDAQ Symbol **IVCR**
In S&P SmallCap 600

04-OCT-95

Industry: Medical equipment/ supply

Summary: This company is a leading maker and distributor of manual and motorized wheelchairs and many other durable medical products.

Quantitative Evaluations

Outlook
(1 Lowest—5 Highest)
• **4+**

Fair Value
• **49**

Risk
• **Average**

Earn./Div. Rank
• **B**

Technical Eval.
• **Bullish** since 12/93

Rel. Strength Rank
(1 Lowest—99 Highest)
• **61**

Insider Activity
• **NA**

Recent Price • 48
52 Wk Range • 48-27¼
Yield • 0.2%
12-Mo. P/E • 24.7

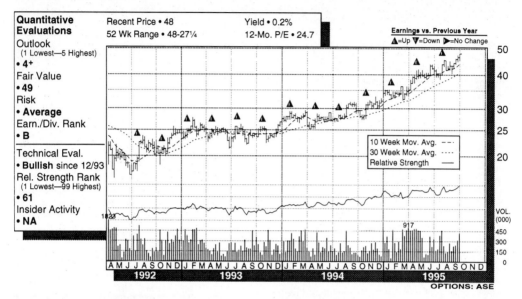

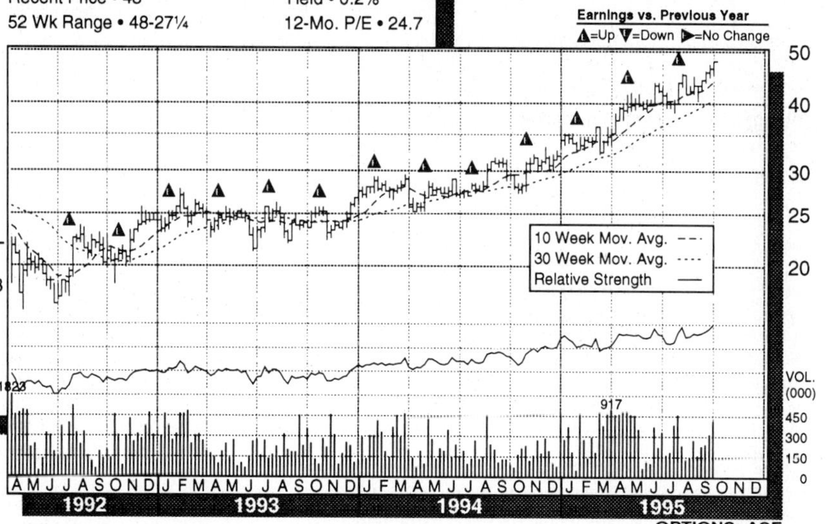

OPTIONS: ASE

Business Profile - 04-OCT-95

Despite a difficult health care environment due to pressures to contain medical expenditures, this company has grown by focusing on the home health care market, developing innovative new products and expanding into new geographic markets. Profitability gains reflect manufacturing efficiencies and tight expense controls. Dividends were initiated in 1994.

Operational Review - 04-OCT-95

Net sales continued to climb in the first half of 1995, reflecting further strong gains in domestic and European sales. Exceptional increases occurred in power wheelchairs, respiratory and therapeutic support products. Wider margins due to manufacturing efficiencies and productivity improvements were partly offset by rising raw material costs and higher SG&A expenses due to additional sales personnel, product specialists and marketing programs. Net income continued to advance.

Stock Performance - 29-SEP-95

In the past 30 trading days, IVCR's shares have increased 14%, compared to a 5% rise in the S&P 500. Average trading volume for the past five days was 82,460 shares, compared with the 40-day moving average of 48,097 shares.

Key Stock Statistics

Dividend Rate/Share	0.10	Shareholders	1,500
Shs. outstg. (M)	14.6	Market cap. (B)	$0.654
Avg. daily vol. (M)	0.067	Inst. holdings	46%
Tang. Bk. Value/Share	6.58	Insider holdings	NA
Beta	1.33		

Value of $10,000 invested 5 years ago: $ 87,474

Fiscal Year Ending Dec. 31

	1995	% Change	1994	% Change	1993	% Change
Revenues (Million $)						
1Q	107.7	23%	87.90	12%	78.77	25%
2Q	122.3	24%	98.89	10%	90.31	21%
3Q	—	—	109.0	14%	95.68	20%
4Q	—	—	115.3	15%	100.7	15%
Yr.	—	—	411.1	12%	365.5	20%
Income (Million $)						
1Q	4.80	32%	3.65	15%	3.18	33%
2Q	7.71	24%	6.23	19%	5.24	24%
3Q	—	—	7.48	22%	6.13	22%
4Q	—	—	9.02	19%	7.55	24%
Yr.	—	—	26.38	19%	22.11	25%
Earnings Per Share ($)						
1Q	0.32	28%	0.25	14%	0.22	29%
2Q	0.51	21%	0.42	17%	0.36	20%
3Q	—	—	0.50	19%	0.42	17%
4Q	—	—	0.61	20%	0.51	21%
Yr.	—	—	1.78	19%	1.50	20%

Next earnings report expected: late October

Invacare Corp.

Business Summary - 04-OCT-95

Invacare Corporation designs, manufactures and distributes an extensive line of durable medical equipment for the home health care and extended care markets. Products include standard manual wheelchairs, motorized and lightweight prescription wheelchairs, motorized scooters, patient aids, home care beds, low air loss therapy products, home respiratory products and seating and positioning products. The company continuously revises and expands its product lines to meet changing market demands.

The company makes and markets a complete line of wheelchairs, including standard wheelchairs and prescription wheelchairs custom built for long-term use by one individual, based on specifications prescribed by a medical professional. Retail prices of Invacare's wheelchairs generally range from about $350 for standard, manually operated chairs to $8,220 for advanced power-driven prescription models.

Invacare also makes and markets three and four-wheeled motorized scooters; ambulatory aids such as crutches, canes, walkers and wheeled walkers; bath safety aids such as tub transfer benches, shower chairs and grab bars; patient care products such as commodes, lift-out chairs, traction equipment, trapeze bars and foam products; a wide variety of manual, semi-electric and fully electric hospital-type beds; home respiratory products; seating and positioning products; low air loss therapy products; and various institutional and accessory products. Invacare also distributes medical care products made by others.

Products are marketed in the U.S. primarily to home health care and medical equipment dealers, which in turn sell or rent these products directly to end-users or to health care institutions. Although the company's primary customer is the dealer, it also markets its products to medical professionals, including physical, occupational and respiratory therapists, who refer their patients to dealers to purchase specific types of home medical equipment. International operations (excluding Mexico, classified as domestic) accounted for 26% of net sales and 8% of pretax profits in 1994.

Important Developments

Sep. '95—The company agreed to acquire Paratec AG, a Swiss manufacturer of manual wheelchairs.
Jul. '95—IVCR acquired Thompson Rehab, New Zealand's leading manufacturer of manual and power wheelchairs from Salmond Smith Biolab Ltd.
Jun. '95—Invacare acquired Bancraft, a manufacturer of wheelchairs headquartered in Birmingham, England.
May '95—The company acquired PinDot Products Inc., a manufacturer of seating products, and Patient Solutions Inc., a manufacturer of ambulatory infusion pumps.

Capitalization

Long Term Obligations: $103,010,000 (12/94).
Class B Common Stock: 2,584,525 shs. (no par). 10 votes ea.; conv. sh.-for-sh. into com.

Per Share Data ($) (Year Ended Dec. 31)

	1994	1993	1992	1991	1990	1989
Tangible Bk. Val.	6.27	5.18	4.43	6.35	3.63	2.85
Cash Flow	2.63	2.33	1.95	1.66	1.22	0.66
Earnings	1.78	1.50	1.25	1.06	0.65	0.23
Dividends	0.04	Nil	Nil	Nil	Nil	Nil
Payout Ratio	2%	Nil	Nil	Nil	Nil	Nil
Prices - High	36¼	27¾	31	32¼	11	8¾
- Low	25¼	21¼	16½	9⅜	4¼	4⅜
P/E Ratio - High	20	19	25	30	17	38
- Low	14	14	13	9	7	19

Income Statement Analysis (Million $)

	1994	%Chg	1993	%Chg	1992	%Chg	1991
Revs.	411	13%	365	20%	305	16%	263
Oper. Inc.	56.4	15%	49.1	31%	37.6	19%	31.7
Depr.	12.7	3%	12.3	23%	10.0	24%	8.1
Int. Exp.	8.2	-4%	8.6	87%	4.6	7%	4.3
Pretax Inc.	41.9	25%	33.5	21%	27.6	21%	22.9
Eff. Tax Rate	37%	—	34%	—	36%	—	38%
Net Inc.	26.4	19%	22.1	25%	17.7	26%	14.1

Balance Sheet & Other Fin. Data (Million $)

	1994	1993	1992	1991	1990	1989
Cash	10.4	13.5	10.7	3.2	3.9	3.2
Curr. Assets	180	156	152	120	104	92.0
Total Assets	337	286	262	162	138	123
Curr. Liab.	70.4	60.9	68.2	42.1	42.8	29.7
LT Debt	103	90.4	78.6	31.8	51.5	58.8
Common Eqty.	164	135	114	86.7	41.9	32.1
Total Cap.	267	225	194	120	96.0	93.0
Cap. Exp.	10.9	12.0	14.5	12.0	8.7	10.9
Cash Flow	39.1	34.4	27.7	22.2	14.2	7.6

Ratio Analysis

	1994	1993	1992	1991	1990	1989
Curr. Ratio	2.6	2.6	2.2	2.8	2.4	3.1
% LT Debt of Cap.	38.5	40.1	40.5	26.4	53.9	63.1
% Net Inc.of Revs.	6.4	6.1	5.8	5.4	3.3	1.4
% Ret. on Assets	8.4	8.0	8.2	8.7	5.8	2.3
% Ret. on Equity	17.6	17.7	17.3	20.7	20.4	8.4

Dividend Data —Quarterly cash dividends were initiated in July 1994. A "poison pill" stock purchase rights plan was adopted in July 1995.

Amt. of Div. $	Date Decl.	Ex-Div. Date	Stock of Record	Payment Date
0.013	Apr. 05	Apr. 24	Apr. 28	May. 15 '95
0.013	May. 22	Jun. 29	Jul. 03	Jul. 17 '95
.005 Spl.	—	Jul. 13	Jul. 17	Jul. 17 '95
0.013	Aug. 21	Sep. 28	Oct. 02	Oct. 16 '95
2-for-1	Aug. 21	Oct. 17	Oct. 02	Oct. 16 '95

Data as orig. reptd.; bef. results of disc. opers. and/or spec. items. Per share data adj. for stk. divs. as of ex-div. date. E-Estimated. NA-Not Available. NM-Not Meaningful. NR-Not Ranked.

Office—899 Cleveland St., P.O. Box 4028, Elyria, OH 44036. **Tel**—(216) 329-6000. **Chrmn, Pres & CEO**—A. M. Mixon III. **CFO, Treas, Secy & Investor Contact**—T. R. Miklich. **Dirs**—F. J. Callahan, F. B. Carr, M. F. Delaney, W. Evans, A. M. Mixon III, D. T. Moore III, E. P. Nalley, J. B. Richey II, W. M. Weber. **Transfer Agent**—National City Bank, Cleveland. **Incorporated** in Ohio in 1971. **Empl**-3,293. **S&P Analyst:** Philip J. Birbara

STANDARD & POOR'S

STOCK REPORTS

Ionics, Inc.

NYSE Symbol **ION**
In S&P SmallCap 600

06-NOV-95 **Industry:** Pollution Control

Summary: Ionics manufactures and sells or leases products, systems and services for the treatment of water and other liquids. Applications include water desalination and bottled water.

S&P Opinion: Hold (★★★)

Recent Price • 41
52 Wk Range • 42-26¼
Yield • Nil
12-Mo. P/E • 32.3

Quantitative Evaluations

Outlook (1 Lowest—5 Highest) • **3+**

Fair Value • **40¼**

Risk • **Average**

Earn./Div. Rank • **B+**

Technical Eval. • **Bullish** since 8/94

Rel. Strength Rank (1 Lowest—99 Highest) • **74**

Insider Activity • **NA**

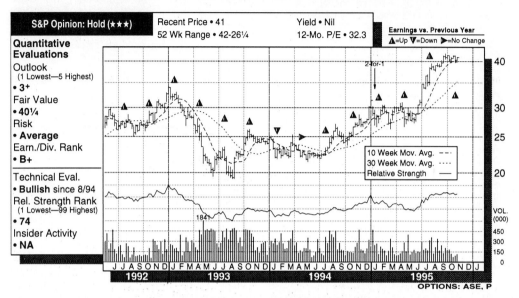

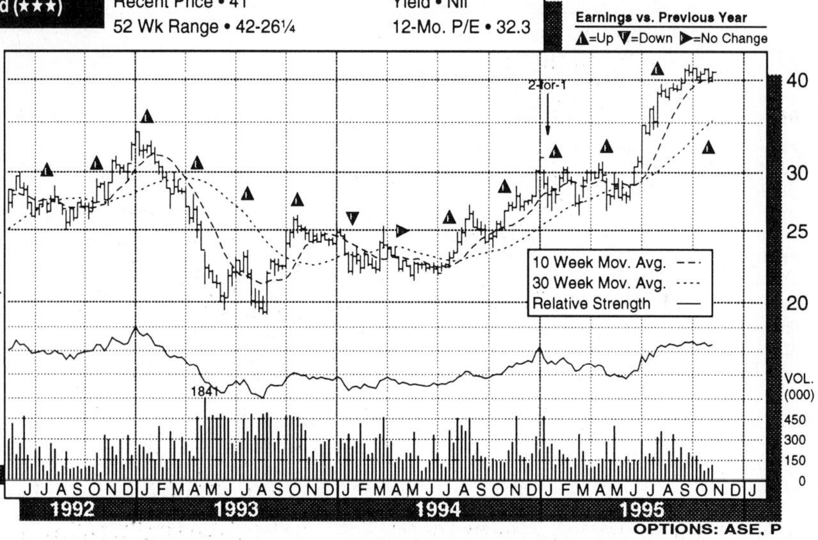

OPTIONS: ASE, P

Overview - 06-NOV-95

Revenues should continue to grow through the balance of 1995 and into 1996, fueled by a growing water purification market. The largest gains are expected to come from the membranes and related equipment area, reflecting the acquisition of Resources Conservation Co. (RCC). Revenue increases are also projected for the consumer water products segment, due to continued volume growth at Aqua Cool and the probable expansion of the bottled water and bleach business. Water and chemical segment revenues should advance at an annual rate of 15% to 20%. Bookings were strong again in the third quarter, and profitability is expected to benefit from the inclusion of RCC, stable margins and well controlled operating expenses.

Valuation - 06-NOV-95

Although revenues and earnings have been in a long uptrend, and results should continue to benefit from an improved water purification market, the shares appear to be fairly valued, having climbed more than 80% since mid-1994. The shares were recently trading at 31X our 1995 EPS projection of $1.30, and 25X our 1996 EPS estimate of $1.60, P/E multiples above that of ION's industry group, as well as that of the S&P SmallCap 600. As a result, we suggest holding the shares until the projected EPS growth of 15% exceeds the P/E ratio.

Key Stock Statistics

S&P EPS Est. 1995	1.30	Tang. Bk. Value/Share	16.34
P/E on S&P Est. 1995	31.5	Beta	1.01
S&P EPS Est. 1996	1.60	Shareholders	1,800
Dividend Rate/Share	Nil	Market cap. (B)	$0.576
Shs. outstg. (M)	14.0	Inst. holdings	57%
Avg. daily vol. (M)	0.019	Insider holdings	NA

Value of $10,000 invested 5 years ago: $ 34,345

Fiscal Year Ending Dec. 31

	1995	% Change	1994	% Change	1993	% Change
Revenues (Million $)						
1Q	56.87	7%	53.04	29%	41.16	14%
2Q	56.54	13%	49.83	9%	45.62	14%
3Q	62.95	12%	56.45	32%	42.79	15%
4Q	—	—	63.06	38%	45.71	9%
Yr.	—	—	222.4	27%	175.3	13%
Income (Million $)						
1Q	4.13	21%	3.40	1%	3.36	29%
2Q	4.62	29%	3.58	2%	3.52	11%
3Q	5.28	27%	4.17	18%	3.52	4%
4Q	—	—	4.30	26%	3.41	-7%
Yr.	—	—	15.45	12%	13.81	8%
Earnings Per Share ($)						
1Q	0.29	21%	0.24	NM	0.24	20%
2Q	0.32	23%	0.26	4%	0.25	11%
3Q	0.36	24%	0.29	16%	0.25	4%
4Q	E0.33	10%	0.30	25%	0.24	-8%
Yr.	E1.30	19%	1.09	11%	0.98	6%

Next earnings report expected: late February

Ionics, Inc.

Business Summary - 27-OCT-95

Ionics Inc. designs, manufactures and sells or leases products and services for the desalination, treatment and analysis of water and other liquids, principally using separations technology. Contributions to revenues by geographic area in recent years were:

	1994	1993	1992
U.S.	78%	71%	66%
Europe	17%	24%	27%
Other	5%	5%	7%

The company's products and services are used by ION or its customers to desalt brackish water and seawater, to purify and supply bottled water, to treat water in the home, to manufacture and supply water treatment chemicals and ultrapure water, to process food products, recycle and reclaim process water and wastewater, and to measure levels of water-borne contaminants and pollutants.

ION's membranes and related equipment business accounted for 54% of revenues in 1994. Products include reverse osmosis systems and instruments for monitoring and on-line detection of pollution levels.

Consumer products, which accounted for 22% of revenues in 1994, include bottled water, over- and under-the-sink point-of-use devices, and point-of-entry systems for treating the entire home water supply. The company has about 21 Aqua Cool distribution centers in the U.S. and overseas.

The water, food and chemical supply business accounted for 24% of revenues in 1994. Operations in this segment include sale of desalted water for municipal and industrial use, sale of ultrapure water for electronics and other industries, processing of food products, and sale of sodium hypochlorite and related chemicals.

In January 1994, the company acquired Resources Conservation Co. (RCC), a unit of Halliburton NUS Corp., for $11 million in cash, plus contingent payments of up to $3 million.

At September 30, 1995, backlog totaled $173 million, up 5.2% from the level a year earlier.

In early 1995, the company's Australian unit, Elite Chemicals Pty. Ltd., expanded the capacity of its sodium hypochlorite production facility by 33%.

Important Developments

Oct. '95—Bookings in the third quarter of 1995 totaled $71.2 million, up 16% from the previous quarter.

Jun. '95—The company expanded its Aqua Cool pure bottled water operations in England with the start-up of a new bottling facility in London.

Capitalization

Long Term Debt: $85,000 (9/95).

Per Share Data ($)

(Year Ended Dec. 31)

	1994	1993	1992	1991	1990	1989
Tangible Bk. Val.	13.94	12.67	13.77	11.05	8.84	8.00
Cash Flow	2.36	2.06	1.83	1.44	1.35	1.18
Earnings	1.09	0.98	0.93	0.73	0.55	0.43
Dividends	Nil	Nil	Nil	Nil	Nil	Nil
Payout Ratio	Nil	Nil	Nil	Nil	Nil	Nil
Prices - High	31⅜	34	34¼	24¼	16	13⅜
- Low	21⅜	19¼	21⅛	13¼	9⅞	7¾
P/E Ratio - High	29	35	37	33	29	31
- Low	20	20	23	18	18	18

Income Statement Analysis (Million $)

	1994	%Chg	1993	%Chg	1992	%Chg	1991
Revs.	222	27%	175	13%	155	12%	138
Oper. Inc.	39.1	21%	32.4	18%	27.4	49%	18.4
Depr.	18.1	18%	15.3	21%	12.6	54%	8.2
Int. Exp.	0.1	-44%	0.2	-75%	0.7	-73%	2.7
Pretax Inc.	22.7	15%	19.7	8%	18.2	57%	11.6
Eff. Tax Rate	32%	—	30%	—	29%	—	28%
Net Inc.	15.4	12%	13.8	8%	12.8	55%	8.3

Balance Sheet & Other Fin. Data (Million $)

	1994	1993	1992	1991	1990	1989
Cash	20.6	30.1	41.8	7.8	3.9	8.1
Curr. Assets	113	110	109	72.3	66.6	67.0
Total Assets	277	250	225	178	144	135
Curr. Liab.	54.9	46.1	30.5	36.5	51.7	44.8
LT Debt	0.1	0.1	0.4	5.6	8.0	14.4
Common Eqty.	219	200	190	128	76.0	68.0
Total Cap.	222	203	194	141	91.0	88.0
Cap. Exp.	38.2	30.1	24.7	36.7	8.7	13.7
Cash Flow	33.5	29.1	25.4	16.4	11.6	10.0

Ratio Analysis

	1994	1993	1992	1991	1990	1989
Curr. Ratio	2.1	2.4	3.6	2.0	1.3	1.5
% LT Debt of Cap.	Nil	0.1	0.2	4.0	8.8	16.4
% Net Inc.of Revs.	6.9	7.9	8.3	6.0	3.7	3.3
% Ret. on Assets	5.8	5.8	5.8	4.4	3.4	2.8
% Ret. on Equity	7.4	7.1	7.4	7.2	6.6	5.4

Dividend Data —No cash dividends have been paid. The shares were split three for two in June 1985, and two-for-one in January 1995. A "poison pill" stock purchase rights plan was adopted in 1987.

Amt. of Div. $	Date Decl.	Ex-Div. Date	Stock of Record	Payment Date
2-for-1	Nov. 21	Jan. 09	Dec. 14	Jan. 06 '95

Data as orig. reptd.; bef. results of disc. opers. and/or spec. items. Per share data adj. for stk. divs. as of ex-div. date. E-Estimated. NA-Not Available. NM-Not Meaningful. NR-Not Ranked.

Office—65 Grove St, Watertown, MA 02172. **Tel**—(617) 926-2500. **Chrmn, Pres & CEO**—A. L. Goldstein. **VP-Fin & CFO**—R. Halliday. **VP, Treas & Investor Contact**—Theodore G. Papastavros. **Dirs**—A. de Vitry d'Avaucourt, W. L. Brown, L. E. Fouraker, S. A. Goldblith, A. L. Goldstein, K. Kachadurian, W. E. Katz, R. B. Luick, J. J. Shields, C. S. Sloane, M. S. Wrighton, A. S. Wyett. **Transfer Agent & Registrar**—State Street Bank and Trust Co., Boston. **Incorporated** in Massachusetts in 1948. **Empl**-1,300. **S&P Analyst:** Stewart Scharf

STANDARD & POOR'S

STOCK REPORTS

J & J Snack Foods

NASDAQ Symbol **JJSF**
In S&P SmallCap 600

02-OCT-95 **Industry:** Food

Summary: This company manufactures and markets snack foods and baked goods, and distributes frozen beverage products to the food service, retail grocery and supermarket industries.

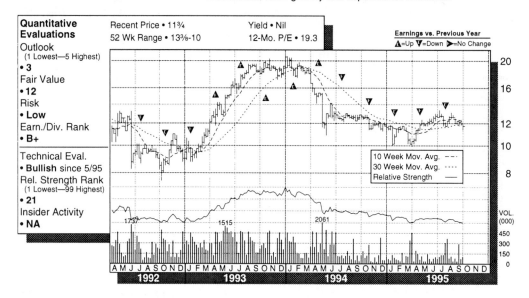

Quantitative Evaluations

Outlook
(1 Lowest—5 Highest)
• 3

Fair Value
• 12

Risk
• Low

Earn./Div. Rank
• B+

Technical Eval.
• Bullish since 5/95

Rel. Strength Rank
(1 Lowest—99 Highest)
• 21

Insider Activity
• NA

Recent Price • 11¾ | Yield • Nil
52 Wk Range • 13⅜-10 | 12-Mo. P/E • 19.3

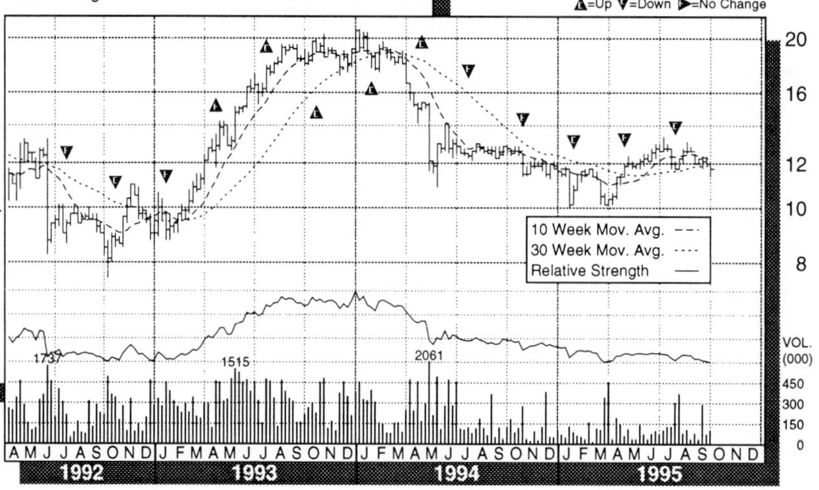

Business Profile - 02-OCT-95

More than 40% of revenues are derived from the sale of soft pretzels. Earnings fell in the first nine months of fiscal 1995, as results were hurt by increased competition in the retail supermarket business, the impact of Mexico's economic problems, and raw material cost increases. Analysts project a decline in EPS to $0.64 for fiscal 1995, with a rebound to $0.80 in fiscal 1996.

Operational Review - 15-AUG-95

Net sales in the 39 weeks ended June 24, 1995, advanced, year to year, reflecting growth in the food service group. Margins narrowed sharply, reflecting increased competition in the supermarket business, raw material and packaging cost increases, weak results in the frozen carbonated beverage business, and Mexico's economic problems. Net income plunged.

Stock Performance - 29-SEP-95

In the past 30 trading days, JJSF's shares have declined 7%, compared to a 5% rise in the S&P 500. Average trading volume for the past five days was 19,820 shares, compared with the 40-day moving average of 19,803 shares.

Key Stock Statistics

Dividend Rate/Share	Nil	Shareholders	400
Shs. outstg. (M)	9.3	Market cap. (B)	$0.110
Avg. daily vol. (M)	0.025	Inst. holdings	40%
Tang. Bk. Value/Share	9.33	Insider holdings	NA
Beta	1.62		

Value of $10,000 invested 5 years ago: $ 9,494

Fiscal Year Ending Sep. 30

	1995	% Change	1994	% Change	1993	% Change
Revenues (Million $)						
1Q	41.22	7%	38.41	25%	30.79	14%
2Q	40.32	NM	40.27	23%	32.73	15%
3Q	47.88	6%	45.17	15%	39.42	18%
4Q	—	—	50.58	14%	44.25	17%
Yr.	—	—	174.4	19%	147.2	16%
Income (Million $)						
1Q	0.55	-58%	1.31	147%	0.53	-36%
2Q	0.47	-71%	1.61	18%	1.37	41%
3Q	1.98	-23%	2.56	-30%	3.64	98%
4Q	—	—	3.06	9%	2.81	23%
Yr.	—	—	8.53	2%	8.35	41%
Earnings Per Share ($)						
1Q	0.06	-50%	0.12	140%	0.05	-38%
2Q	0.05	-67%	0.15	15%	0.13	44%
3Q	0.21	-16%	0.25	-7%	0.27	59%
4Q	—	—	0.30	-12%	0.34	55%
Yr.	—	—	0.82	3%	0.80	45%

Next earnings report expected: early November

J & J Snack Foods

Business Summary - 02-OCT-95

J & J Snack Foods Corporation manufactures and markets snack foods and baked goods and distributes frozen beverages to the food service and retail supermarket industries. Sales in recent fiscal years were derived as follows:

	1994	1993	1992
Soft pretzels	43%	39%	38%
Frozen carbonated beverages	24%	29%	29%
Frozen juice treats & desserts	12%	13%	12%
Churros	6%	6%	5%
Baked cookies, muffins & other	15%	13%	16%

The company's soft-pretzel products are sold under the Superpretzel, Dutchie, Mr. Twister, Soft Pretzel Bites, Softstix, Bavarian Soft Pretzels and Soft Pretzel Buns brand names and, to a lesser extent, under private labels. The pretzels are sold to food service industry customers and, since 1986, to the retail grocery and supermarket industries.

J & J markets frozen carbonated beverages to the food service industry under the ICEE name in 15 western states, Mexico and Canada, and under the name FROZEN COKE and ARCTIC BLAST in midwestern and eastern states.

The company's frozen juice treats and desserts are marketed to the food service (primarily the school segment) and retail supermarket industries under the Super Juice, Frostar, Shape-ups and Luigi's brand names.

In addition, J & J sells frozen churros (an Hispanic pastry) under the Tio Pepe brand name, primarily in the western and southwestern U.S., to the food service and retail supermarket industries.

Baked products, including cookies, muffins and other baked goods, are manufactured by the company and sold under its Pride O' The Farm, Mrs. Goodcookie and Mrs. Goodmuffin labels and under private labels for others.

J & J also markets whipped fruit drinks, soft drinks, funnel cakes under the Funnel Cake Factory brand name, popcorn and dessert toppings.

Important Developments

Jul. '95—J & J said profitability in the fiscal 1995 third quarter declined from year-earlier levels. Results were hurt by higher manufacturing costs, lower frozen carbonated beverage sales, and increased marketing expenses for products sold to supermarkets.

Capitalization

Long Term Debt: $5,016,000 (6/95).
Options: To buy 832,078 shs. at $2.50 to $15.75 ea.
G.B. Shreiber owns 27%.

Per Share Data ($) (Year Ended Sep. 30)

	1994	1993	1992	1991	1990	1989
Tangible Bk. Val.	9.18	8.59	7.68	7.07	4.65	4.45
Cash Flow	2.14	1.93	1.39	1.45	1.10	1.45
Earnings	0.82	0.80	0.55	0.67	0.44	0.81
Dividends	Nil	Nil	Nil	Nil	Nil	Nil
Payout Ratio	Nil	Nil	Nil	Nil	Nil	Nil
Prices - High	20¾	20¾	14¾	15⅞	13¼	17⅛
- Low	10⅞	8¾	7½	7⅝	4⅞	10¾
P/E Ratio - High	25	26	27	24	30	21
- Low	13	11	14	11	11	13

Income Statement Analysis (Million $)

	1994	%Chg	1993	%Chg	1992	%Chg	1991
Revs.	174	18%	147	16%	127	15%	110
Oper. Inc.	26.2	9%	24.0	40%	17.1	4%	16.5
Depr.	13.8	17%	11.8	30%	9.1	26%	7.2
Int. Exp.	0.4	22%	0.4	NM	0.4	-51%	0.8
Pretax Inc.	13.7	5%	13.1	45%	9.0	-3%	9.3
Eff. Tax Rate	38%	—	36%	—	34%	—	35%
Net Inc.	8.5	2%	8.4	41%	5.9	-2%	6.1

Balance Sheet & Other Fin. Data (Million $)

	1994	1993	1992	1991	1990	1989
Cash	11.1	15.8	15.7	23.7	2.4	6.8
Curr. Assets	41.4	43.5	41.0	46.3	22.7	24.2
Total Assets	127	121	112	104	75.0	67.0
Curr. Liab.	16.4	13.6	12.9	11.2	15.0	9.9
LT Debt	5.0	5.0	5.1	2.4	5.9	6.7
Common Eqty.	101	98.0	90.1	86.4	50.5	47.5
Total Cap.	110	108	100	93.2	60.2	56.7
Cap. Exp.	18.6	15.4	21.8	13.2	12.4	8.1
Cash Flow	22.3	20.2	15.0	13.3	9.3	10.6

Ratio Analysis

	1994	1993	1992	1991	1990	1989
Curr. Ratio	2.5	3.2	3.2	4.1	1.5	2.4
% LT Debt of Cap.	4.6	4.7	5.1	2.6	9.7	11.8
% Net Inc.of Revs.	4.9	5.7	4.7	5.5	3.8	6.8
% Ret. on Assets	7.0	7.2	5.5	6.0	5.2	7.9
% Ret. on Equity	8.8	8.9	6.8	8.0	7.6	15.3

Dividend Data —The company has not paid any cash dividends.

Data as orig. reptd.; bef. results of disc. opers. and/or spec. items. Per share data adj. for stk. divs. as of ex-div. date. E-Estimated. NA-Not Available. NM-Not Meaningful. NR-Not Ranked.

Office—6000 Central Hwy., Pennsauken, NJ 08109. **Tel**—(609) 665-9533. **Chrmn, Pres & CEO**—G. B. Shreiber. **SVP, CFO, Secy & Treas**—D. G. Moore. **Dirs**—S. N. Frankel, L. M. Lodish, G. B. Shreiber, P. G. Stanley. **Transfer Agent & Registrar**—Midlantic National Bank, Edison, NJ. **Incorporated** in New Jersey in 1971. **Empl**-1,700. **S&P Analyst:** Efraim Levy

Jan Bell Marketing

ASE Symbol JBM Options on ASE, CBOE (Jan-Apr-Jul-Oct) In S&P SmallCap 600

Price	Range	P–E Ratio	Dividend	Yield	S&P Ranking	Beta
Oct. 10'95	1995					
3 9/16	4¼–2 9/16	NM	None	None	B–	0.77

Summary

Jan Bell markets fine jewelry, watches and other consumer products primarily through leased departments of Sam's Club stores. The company's wholesale watch division was discontinued in 1994. A new credit facility and terms to pay notes that were in default were finalized on May 31, 1995. The net loss narrowed in the first twenty-six weeks of 1995-96.

Business Summary

Jan Bell Marketing, Inc. markets fine jewelry, watches and other non-jewelry consumer products (including perfumes, sunglasses, writing instruments, and collectible and giftware items). The company markets its products primarily through Sam's Club, a division of Wal-Mart, Inc., pursuant to an arrangement whereby JBM operates an exclusive leased department at all of Sam's existing and future domestic locations through February 1, 2001. Sales through Sam's accounted for 85% of sales in the fiscal year ended January 28, 1995. Contributions by product type in recent fiscal years (calendar 1993 & 1992):

	1994–95	1993	1992
Gold jewelry with diamonds and/or other precious and semi–precious stones	35%	39%	29%
Gold jewelry	19%	25%	28%
Watches	22%	26%	38%
Other	24%	10%	5%

Each Sam's location is staffed by Jan Bell employees with the inventory owned by JBM until sold to Sam's members. In exchange for the right to opertate the department and the use of retail space, Jan Bell pays a tenancy fee of 9% of net sales. While Sam's is responsible for paying utility costs, maintenance and certain other expenses associated with operation of the departments, JBM provides and maintains all fixtures and other equipment necessary to operate the departments.

Prior to begining its arrangement with Sam's in the fourth quarter of 1993, the company operated primarily as a wholesale vendor to the warehouse club industry. During late 1994, the company decided to close its wholesale watch operations, and took related charges of $47.2 million in 1994-95.

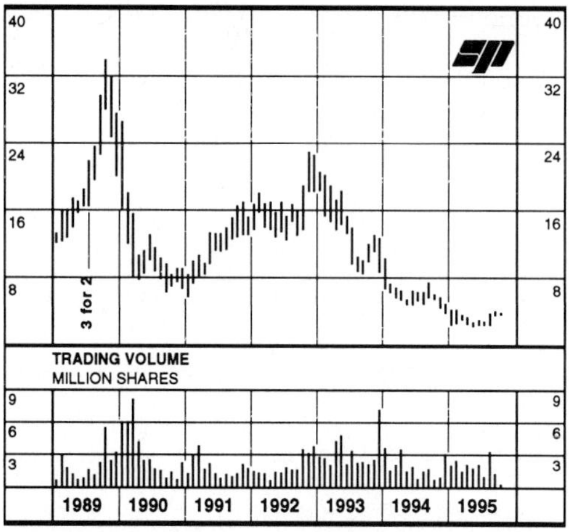

Jan Bell also sells to a limited number of department stores, supermarkets, discount stores, wholesalers and jewelry chains. In fiscal 1994, these customers accounted for approximately 10% of net sales. Due to the closing of the wholesale watch division and the focus on the retail operations at Sam's, it is not anticipated that sales to other customers will continue in any significant manner other than the continued balancing of inventory and selected sales of goods.

Important Developments

Aug. '95— The company reported net retail sales for the four week period ended August 26, 1995 of $13.4 million, an increase of 1.3% from the $13.2 million in the similar period in the prior year. Comparable retail sales for the four week period were up 1.8%.

Next earnings report expected in early December.

Per Share Data ($)

Yr. End Jan. 31[2]	1995	1994	1993	1992	1991	1990	1989	1988	1987
Tangible Bk. Val.	**4.84**	6.87	8.10	7.28	8.11	7.81	2.95	1.57	0.47
Cash Flow	**d2.57**	d1.14	0.79	0.51	0.37	0.86	0.61	0.35	0.20
Earnings[1]	**d2.92**	[3]d1.40	0.59	0.33	0.30	0.80	0.57	0.33	0.19
Dividends	**Nil**	Nil	Nil	Nil	Nil	Nil	Nil	Nil	Nil
Payout Ratio	**Nil**	Nil	Nil	Nil	Nil	Nil	Nil	Nil	Nil
Calendar Years	**1994**	1993	1992	1991	1990	1989	1988	1987	1986
Prices—High	**10⅜**	20⅝	23	17	26⅝	34	13⅜	6¾	NA
Low	**3 13/16**	8½	12½	5¾	6¼	12⅛	3⅝	2⅜	NA
P/E Ratio—	**NM**	NM	38–21	52–17	89–20	43–15	24–6	20–7	NA

Data as orig. reptd. Adj. for stk. divs. of 50% Jul. 1989, 50% Oct. 1988. **1.** Bef. spec. item of +0.06 in 1988. **2.** Yrs. end. Dec. 31 of preceding cal yr. pr. to 1995. **3.** Co. reported a loss of $0.17 a share for the 30 day transition period of Jan. 1'94 to Jan. 30'94. d-Deficit. NM-Not Meaningful. NA-Not Available.

Income Data (Million $)

Year Ended Jan. 31[4]	Revs.	Oper. Inc.	% Oper. Inc. of Revs.	Cap. Exp.	Depr.	Int. Exp.	Net Bef. Taxes	Eff. Tax Rate	[3]Net Inc.	% Net Inc. of Revs.	Cash Flow
1995	**306**	**d9.2**	**NM**	**6.3**	**9.15**	**3.53**	**d74.7**	**NM**	**d75.1**	**NM**	**d65.9**
1994	175	10.9	6.2	[1]12.6	6.76	3.20	d47.4	NM	d35.7	NM	d29.0
1993	334	26.9	8.1	[1]6.7	5.08	0.92	21.5	31.1%	14.8	4.4	19.9
1992	224	21.0	9.4	[1]4.4	3.89	2.42	11.3	26.9%	7.5	3.4	11.4
1991	177	12.3	6.9	5.9	1.79	0.76	13.2	30.2%	6.6	3.7	8.4
1990	181	25.0	13.8	10.2	1.16	0.39	25.6	37.5%	16.0	8.8	17.2
1989	120	14.9	12.4	3.7	0.65	0.03	14.8	37.3%	[2]9.3	7.7	9.9
1988	73	8.2	11.3	0.9	0.30	0.30	7.9	43.5%	4.4	6.1	4.7
1987	47	5.0	10.8	0.5	0.14	0.37	4.8	48.5%	2.3	4.9	2.5
1986	28	3.0	10.6	0.1	0.09	0.26	2.9	46.9%	1.5	5.2	NA

Balance Sheet Data (Million $)

		Curr.									
Jan. 31[4]	Cash	Assets	Liab.	Ratio	Total Assets	% Ret. on Assets	Long Term Debt	Common Equity	Total Cap.	% LT Debt of Cap.	% Ret. on Equity
1995	**28.2**	**148**	**59.4**	**2.5**	**187**	**NM**	**Nil**	**127**	**127**	**Nil**	**NM**
1994	30.2	248	73.4	3.4	312	NM	33.50	205	239	14.0	NM
1993	49.6	232	33.9	6.8	302	5.6	33.00	235	268	12.3	6.7
1992	17.4	161	20.4	7.9	228	3.2	Nil	208	208	Nil	3.7
1991	51.2	186	32.9	5.7	207	3.4	Nil	172	175	Nil	3.9
1990	46.6	179	19.8	9.1	193	11.4	Nil	173	173	Nil	13.4
1989	18.0	62	16.7	3.7	67	17.5	Nil	50	50	Nil	24.3
1988	9.4	33	11.4	2.9	35	14.9	Nil	23	23	Nil	29.4
1987	1.9	18	13.6	1.3	19	14.1	2.65	5	10	27.3	56.3
1986	1.9	14	10.9	1.2	14	11.4	4.80	3	9	54.9	65.8

Data as orig. reptd. **1.** Net. **2.** Refl. acctg. change. **3.** Bef. spec. items. **4.** Yrs. end. Dec. 31 of preceding cal yr. pr. to 1995. d-Deficit. NM-Not Meaningful.

[1]Net Sales (Million $)

Quarter:	1995–96	1994–95	1993–94	1992–93
Apr.	50.0	63.0	45.6	40.0
Jul.	55.5	60.1	49.8	60.7
Oct.		68.6	42.6	80.0
Jan.		114.0	137.2	152.8
		305.7	275.2	333.5

For the twenty-six weeks ended July 29, 1995, net sales declined 14%, year to year, reflecting the elimination of the wholesale division and the reduction in business in Mexico as a result of the peso devaluation. Gross margins widened, and a currency exchange loss from the peso devaluation was offset by higher interest and other income. After taxes of $86,000 versus $205,000, the net loss narrowed to $7,661,000 ($0.30 a share) from $10,911,000 ($0.43).

[1]Common Share Earnings ($)

Quarter:	1995–96	1994–95	1993–94	1992–93
Apr.	d0.22	d0.23	d0.40	0.06
Jul.	d0.07	d0.19	0.01	0.12
Oct.		d0.18	d0.11	0.19
Jan.		d2.32	d0.90	0.23
		d2.92	d1.40	0.59

Dividend Data

No cash dividends have been paid on the common stock. Three-for-two stock splits were effected in 1989 and 1988.

Finances

On May 31, 1995, Jan Bell secured a two year $30 million working capital facility with Gordon Brothers/Foothill Capital. The company also reached an agreement with its senior noteholders which provided a payment schedule for its 6.99% senior notes, which had been in default. Jan Bell agreed to pay $8.5 million of the $35 million outstanding and shortened the maturity date on the remaining balance to February 1, 1998, from October 8, 1999. In addition, the noteholders received warrants to purchase 1,732,520 shares of common stock at an initial price of $2.25.

Capitalization

Long Term Debt: $17,500,000 (4/95).

Common Stock: 25,748,358 shs. ($0.0001 par).
Institutions hold 41%.
A group including Cumberland Associates owns 6.1%.
Shareholders: 942 of record (4/95).

1. Quarters ended Mar., Jun., Sep., Dec., prior to 1994-95. d-Deficit.

Office—13801 N.W. 14th St., Sunrise, FL 33323. **Tel**—(305) 846-2705. **Chrmn**—I. Arguetty. **Pres & CEO**—J. Pennacchio. **Sr EVP & Secy**—R. W. Bowers. **Investor Contact**—Rosemary B. Trudeau. **Dirs**—I. Arguetty, R. W. Bowers, J. Burden, C. Edelstein, T. Epstein, S. Feltenstein, D. Groussman, J. Pennacchio. **Transfer Agent & Registrar**—Sun Bank, Miami. **Incorporated** in Delaware in 1987. **Empl**—1,816.

 Stephen Madonna, CFA

STANDARD & POOR'S

STOCK REPORTS

Johnston Industries

NYSE Symbol **JII**
In S&P SmallCap 600

06-SEP-95 **Industry:** Textiles

Summary: This company, 41% owned by Redlaw Industries, makes woven and nonwoven textile fabrics for industrial, home furnishings and apparel markets.

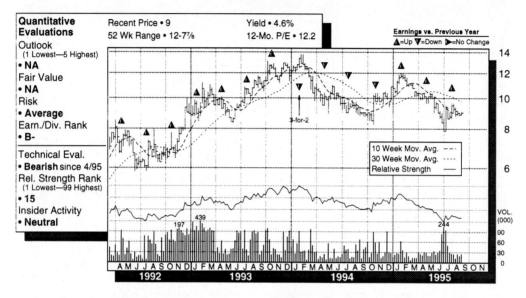

Quantitative Evaluations

Outlook (1 Lowest—5 Highest)
• **NA**

Fair Value
• **NA**

Risk
• **Average**

Earn./Div. Rank
• **B-**

Technical Eval.
• **Bearish** since 4/95

Rel. Strength Rank (1 Lowest—99 Highest)
• **15**

Insider Activity
• **Neutral**

Recent Price • 9
52 Wk Range • 12-7⅞
Yield • 4.6%
12-Mo. P/E • 12.2

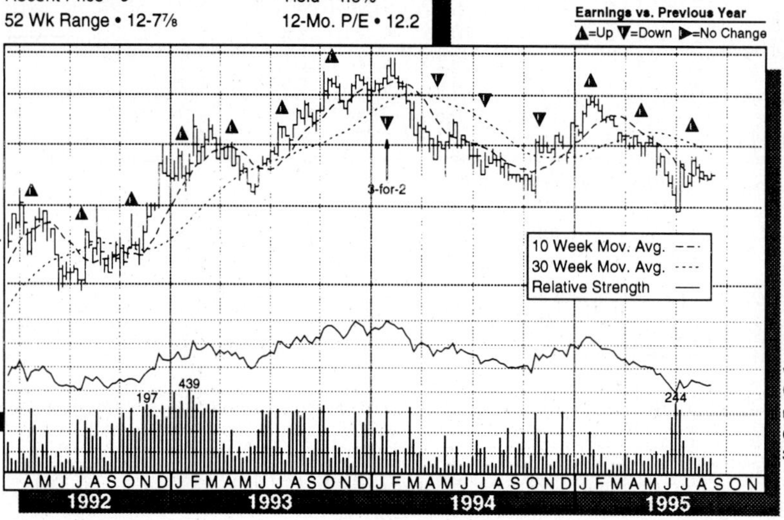

Business Profile - 06-SEP-95

This company makes woven and nonwoven textile fabrics for industrial, home furnishings and apparel markets. It recently agreed to buy the remaining 45% interest in Jupiter National that it does not already own; Jupiter and its Wellington Sears unit will remain separate companies. Johnston's newest venture, Tech Textiles, USA, makes VECTORPLY and other sophisticated multiaxial non-crimp reinforcing fabrics used in engineering composites and other applications.

Operational Review - 06-SEP-95

Net sales in the fiscal year ended June 30, 1995, climbed 65% from those of the preceding year. Despite operating performances of major divisions that were on target, results were hurt by sharply rising raw material costs, especially for cotton and polyester. Although the company was still experiencing increases in raw material costs at the start of fiscal 1996, with an anticipated negative impact on results early in the year, it expects strong earnings for the third and fourth quarters.

Stock Performance - 01-SEP-95

In the past 30 trading days, JII's shares have increased 3%, compared to a 2% rise in the S&P 500. Average trading volume for the past five days was 4,720 shares, compared with the 40-day moving average of 5,065 shares.

Key Stock Statistics

Dividend Rate/Share	0.40	Shareholders	2,000
Shs. outstg. (M)	10.6	Market cap. (B)	$0.092
Avg. daily vol. (M)	0.004	Inst. holdings	19%
Tang. Bk. Value/Share	5.67	Insider holdings	NA
Beta	0.62		

Value of $10,000 invested 5 years ago: $ 22,997

Fiscal Year Ending Jun. 30

	1995	% Change	1994	% Change	1993	% Change
Revenues (Million $)						
1Q	40.77	14%	35.70	NM	35.80	10%
2Q	44.20	15%	38.30	14%	33.73	3%
3Q	91.00	114%	42.60	7%	39.80	10%
4Q	87.36	102%	43.32	-3%	44.71	21%
Yr.	263.3	65%	159.9	4%	154.1	11%
Income (Million $)						
1Q	1.68	-22%	2.15	14%	1.88	100%
2Q	2.51	137%	1.06	-46%	1.97	49%
3Q	2.63	7%	2.45	-2%	2.51	NM
4Q	1.05	21%	0.87	-65%	2.52	24%
Yr.	7.88	21%	6.53	-26%	8.88	31%
Earnings Per Share ($)						
1Q	0.16	-20%	0.20	15%	0.17	100%
2Q	0.24	140%	0.10	-44%	0.18	50%
3Q	0.25	9%	0.23	-1%	0.23	3%
4Q	0.10	25%	0.08	-65%	0.23	21%
Yr.	0.74	23%	0.60	-26%	0.81	31%

Next earnings report expected: late October

Johnston Industries

Business Summary - 06-SEP-95

Johnston Industries is a diversified manufacturer of woven and nonwoven textile fabrics principally for the industrial and home furnishings markets and, to a lesser extent, for the apparel and automotive industries. Sales contributions in recent fiscal years were:

	1994	1993	1992
Home furnishings	57%	48%	45%
Industrial	24%	24%	26%
Automotive	10%	10%	13%
Apparel	7%	14%	12%
Miscellaneous	2%	4%	4%

The company manufactures textiles through its Southern Phenix Textiles, Inc. and Opp and Micolas Mills, Inc. subsidiaries, which together have 1,477,000 sq. ft. of manufacturing, warehouse and administrative facilities. The mills have an annual capacity of 170 million linear yards of fabric (about 82 million pounds).

Southern Phenix (72 million yards capacity) manufactures woven fabrics from 100% polyester fiber for use in the automotive industry, in the bedding and furniture industries, in the coating and laminating trades, and by other fabricators. Its products are used as backing for foam car seat cushions, tufted upholstery and marine coating products, mattress ticking, and products for soft furniture. In fiscal 1994, the unit's facilities operated at about 80% of rated capacity.

Opp and Micolas (93 million yards capacity) manufactures more than 69 different styles (in the greige state) of all-cotton fabric and cotton/polyester blended fabrics for the coating, home furnishings and apparel markets. It also produces fabrics for the footwear and building supplies industries and for various industrial operations. Its fabrics are used in a broad range of coated products including wall coverings, coated fabrics for autos such as convertible tops, cloth roof coverings and felt window liners, rubber coated products such as automotive V-belts and other belts for industrial machinery, apparel, industrial protective clothing, and specialty items. The unit operated at 93% of rated capacity in fiscal 1994.

Johnston recently agreed to acquire the remaining 42.5% interest in ASE-listed Jupiter National that it does not already own. In November 1992, Jupiter bought West Point Pepperell's custom fabrics division (renamed Wellington Sears Co.).

Important Developments

Aug. '95—Johnston agreed to acquire the remaining 45% of the shares (about 867,000) of ASE-listed Jupiter National, Inc. that it did not already own. The cash price of $32.875 a share is subject to certain adjustments at closing, expected in the fall of 1995.

Capitalization

Long Term Debt: $102,573,000 (3/95).

Per Share Data ($) (Year Ended Jun. 30)

	1995	1994	1993	1992	1991	1990
Tangible Bk. Val.	NA	5.33	5.37	4.93	4.70	5.00
Cash Flow	NA	1.54	1.68	1.45	0.66	0.73
Earnings	0.74	0.60	0.81	0.62	-0.10	0.17
Dividends	0.39	0.35	0.32	0.24	0.22	0.22
Payout Ratio	53%	58%	39%	39%	NM	128%
Prices - High	12	13¾	13⅛	10	5⅝	4⅞
- Low	7⅞	8¼	8⅜	5⅜	3	2⅞
P/E Ratio - High	16	23	16	16	NM	29
- Low	11	14	10	9	NM	17

Income Statement Analysis (Million $)

	1994	%Chg	1993	%Chg	1992	%Chg	1991
Revs.	160	4%	154	12%	138	18%	117
Oper. Inc.	25.3	19%	21.2	8%	19.7	99%	9.9
Depr.	10.2	7%	9.5	6%	9.0	11%	8.1
Int. Exp.	3.0	2%	2.9	7%	2.7	5%	2.6
Pretax Inc.	10.6	-25%	14.1	33%	10.6	NM	-1.3
Eff. Tax Rate	39%	—	37%	—	36%	—	NM
Net Inc.	6.5	-27%	8.9	31%	6.8	NM	-1.0

Balance Sheet & Other Fin. Data (Million $)

	1994	1993	1992	1991	1990	1989
Cash	3.9	4.1	3.9	4.5	5.1	10.7
Curr. Assets	48.8	49.1	50.6	39.9	41.0	42.0
Total Assets	141	134	128	112	101	94.0
Curr. Liab.	23.3	34.7	26.9	21.7	20.8	12.1
LT Debt	36.2	22.5	30.0	25.0	11.5	13.0
Common Eqty.	60.1	61.3	57.7	53.1	56.7	59.5
Total Cap.	100	90.3	91.7	81.2	72.0	76.5
Cap. Exp.	12.7	10.4	9.4	18.0	12.6	13.8
Cash Flow	16.7	18.4	15.7	7.1	8.3	13.0

Ratio Analysis

	1994	1993	1992	1991	1990	1989
Curr. Ratio	2.1	1.4	1.9	1.8	2.0	3.5
% LT Debt of Cap.	36.0	24.9	32.7	30.8	16.0	17.0
% Net Inc.of Revs.	4.1	5.8	4.9	NM	1.6	6.7
% Ret. on Assets	4.7	6.8	5.6	NM	1.9	8.5
% Ret. on Equity	10.8	15.0	12.1	NM	3.3	14.1

Dividend Data —Dividends were initiated in fiscal 1988 with the payment of a special dividend. Regular quarterly dividends were initiated in September 1990.

Amt. of Div. $	Date Decl.	Ex-Div. Date	Stock of Record	Payment Date
0.095	Aug. 24	Sep. 01	Sep. 08	Sep. 23 '94
0.095	Oct. 20	Oct. 28	Nov. 03	Nov. 17 '94
0.100	Jan. 24	Feb. 01	Feb. 07	Feb. 21 '95
0.100	Apr. 26	May. 04	May. 10	May. 24 '95
0.100	Aug. 24	Sep. 05	Sep. 07	Sep. 21 '95

Data as orig. reptd.; bef. results of disc. opers. and/or spec. items. Per share data adj. for stk. divs. as of ex-div. date. E-Estimated. NA-Not Available. NM-Not Meaningful. NR-Not Ranked.

Office—105 Thirteenth St., Columbus, GA 31901. **Tel**—(706) 641-3140. **Chrmn & CEO**—D. L. Chandler. **Pres & COO**—G. B. Andrews. **VP, CFO & Investor Contact**—John W. Johnson. **Secy & Treas**—F. F. Walton. **Dirs**—G. B. Andrews, J. R. Bingham, R. H. Bosselmann, D. L. Chandler, W. J. Hart, G. R. Jeffcoat, C. J. Kjorlien. **Transfer Agent & Registrar**—Bank of New York, NYC. **Incorporated** in New York in 1948; reincorporated in Delaware in 1987. **Empl**-1,470. **S&P Analyst:** Philip D. Wohl

STANDARD & POOR'S
STOCK REPORTS

Juno Lighting

NASDAQ Symbol **JUNO**
In S&P SmallCap 600

17-AUG-95 **Industry:** Electronics/Electric

Summary: This company designs, manufactures and markets a full line of recessed and track lighting fixtures for use in commercial, institutional and residential buildings.

Quantitative Evaluations
Outlook
(1 Lowest—5 Highest)
• 3-
Fair Value
• 16⅜
Risk
• Low
Earn./Div. Rank
• A-

Technical Eval.
• **Bullish** since 7/95
Rel. Strength Rank
(1 Lowest—99 Highest)
• 26
Insider Activity
• **Neutral**

Recent Price • 16½
52 Wk Range • 21-15¾
Yield • 1.9%
12-Mo. P/E • 13.6

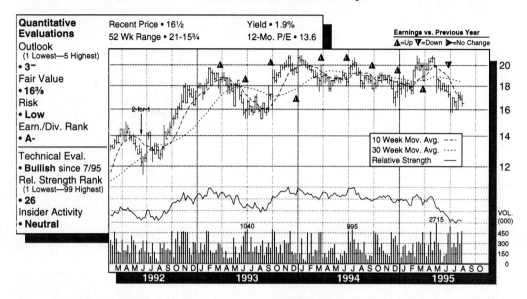

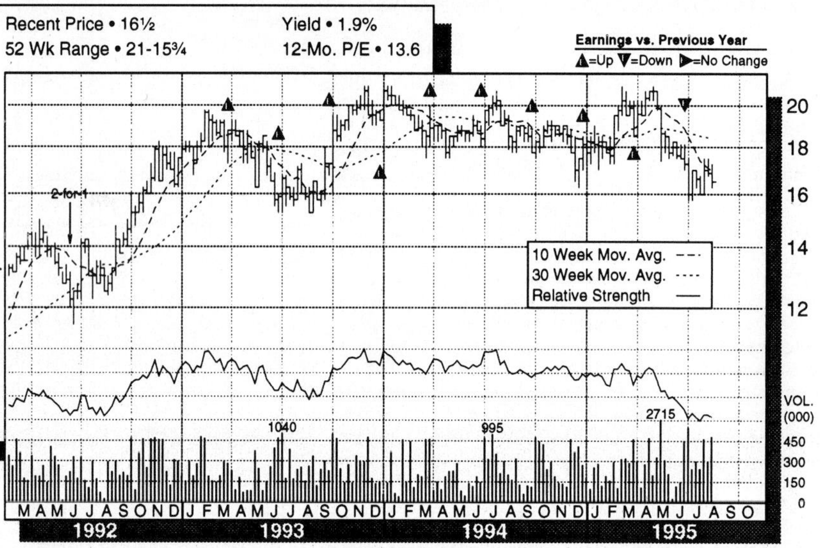

Business Profile - 11-AUG-95

Juno's strategy is to continually introduce new products while anticipating customer needs. The company then provides comprehensive promotional support through a variety of special marketing programs. Juno expects to gain additional market share in 1995 through its aggressive efforts. Results have begun to be affected recently by a slowing economy, though Juno will continue to accelerate product development and sales programs.

Operational Review - 11-AUG-95

Net sales in the first half of fiscal 1995 advanced modestly, aided by stronger sales through Indy Lighting and new product introductions. However, profitability was hampered by significant pricing pressures, and net income fell slightly. Juno's balance sheet is very strong, with a current ratio of 9.5 at fiscal 1994 year-end at its highest since fiscal 1991.

Stock Performance - 11-AUG-95

In the past 30 trading days, JUNO's shares have increased 3%, compared to a 2% rise in the S&P 500. Average trading volume for the past five days was 155,940 shares, compared with the 40-day moving average of 119,787 shares.

Key Stock Statistics

Dividend Rate/Share	0.32	Shareholders	300
Shs. outstg. (M)	18.5	Market cap. (B)	$0.314
Avg. daily vol. (M)	0.123	Inst. holdings	85%
Tang. Bk. Value/Share	7.09	Insider holdings	NA
Beta	0.88		

Value of $10,000 invested 5 years ago: $ 18,473

Fiscal Year Ending Nov. 30

	1995	% Change	1994	% Change	1993	% Change
Revenues (Million $)						
1Q	31.50	14%	27.70	13%	24.60	17%
2Q	33.26	NM	33.30	27%	26.20	11%
3Q	—	—	34.20	16%	29.60	15%
4Q	—	—	31.55	10%	28.70	9%
Yr.	—	—	126.8	16%	109.1	13%
Income (Million $)						
1Q	5.34	12%	4.76	13%	4.23	26%
2Q	5.27	-14%	6.12	41%	4.35	20%
3Q	—	—	6.16	27%	4.85	19%
4Q	—	—	5.87	23%	4.79	13%
Yr.	—	—	22.91	26%	18.21	19%
Earnings Per Share ($)						
1Q	0.29	12%	0.26	13%	0.23	28%
2Q	0.28	-15%	0.33	43%	0.23	15%
3Q	—	—	0.33	27%	0.26	18%
4Q	—	—	0.32	23%	0.26	13%
Yr.	—	—	1.23	26%	0.98	18%

Next earnings report expected: late September

Juno Lighting

Business Summary - 17-AUG-95

Juno Lighting, Inc. designs, manufactures and markets a full line of recessed and track lighting fixtures for use in commercial, institutional and residential buildings. It also produces linear low-voltage and fluorescent strip lighting fixtures. Sales are made primarily to electrical distributors and certain wholesale lighting outlets.

The company's principal products use incandescent and fluorescent light sources and are designed for attractive appearance, reliable and flexible function, efficient operation and simple installation and servicing. Recessed lighting fixtures are generally used for down-lighting, although special frames may be used for wall-washing and spot lighting. Juno has also designed recessed lighting fixtures, sold under the Sloped Ceiling Down-Lites name, that provide lighting perpendicular to a floor from a sloped ceiling, and produces a series of recessed lighting fixtures, sold under the Air-Loc name, that are designed to restrict the passage of air into and out of a residence through the fixture to minimize energy loss.

Juno's principal track lighting system, sold under the Trac-Master name, consists of an electrified extruded aluminum channel and a wide variety of spot lights that can be connected at any point on the track. Track lighting products were originally developed for use in store displays, although they have also become popular in the remodeling and do-it-yourself markets.

Through Indy Lighting, Inc., the company designs, manufactures and markets other lighting products with applications in the commercial lighting market, primarily in department and chain stores. Such products include incandescent, fluorescent, high-intensity-discharge and compact fluorescent light sources to provide specialty and general-purpose lighting.

Through D.W. Barton & Associates, Inc., the company also manufactures low-voltage halogen and fluorescent linear strip lighting fixtures used in merchandise showcases, cove lighting and a variety of display applications.

New products introduced in fiscal 1994 included a line of energy conserving Compact Fluorescent trac fixtures, two new design-patented series of halogen trac fixtures marketed under the names Delta 200 and Flyback; and additional trac and recessed products incorporating White Baffles.

Important Developments

Jun. '95—Juno said that the lighting industry and its financial results for the 1995 second quarter were affected by a general decline in construction activity. Although the company believes it has continued to build market share and recent product introductions and promotions have been successful, second quarter sales did not show typical Juno growth.

Capitalization

Long Term Liabs.: $8,214,000 (5/95).

Per Share Data ($) (Year Ended Nov. 30)

	1994	1993	1992	1991	1990	1989
Tangible Bk. Val.	6.63	5.62	4.84	4.25	3.90	3.29
Cash Flow	1.41	1.10	0.95	0.81	0.88	0.80
Earnings	1.23	0.98	0.83	0.70	0.77	0.70
Dividends	0.26	0.22	0.17	0.14	0.12	0.09
Payout Ratio	21%	22%	20%	20%	16%	13%
Prices - High	21	21	18¼	12⅞	11⅝	10⅛
- Low	16¼	15¼	10	8¼	6	6½
P/E Ratio - High	17	21	22	17	15	15
- Low	13	16	12	12	8	9

Income Statement Analysis (Million $)

	1994	%Chg	1993	%Chg	1992	%Chg	1991
Revs.	127	17%	109	12%	97.0	21%	80.0
Oper. Inc.	36.9	30%	28.4	21%	23.4	20%	19.5
Depr.	3.2	46%	2.2	-4%	2.3	2%	2.2
Int. Exp.	0.3	3%	0.3	29%	0.2	-8%	0.3
Pretax Inc.	36.4	28%	28.5	22%	23.3	21%	19.2
Eff. Tax Rate	37%	—	36%	—	34%	—	34%
Net Inc.	22.9	26%	18.2	19%	15.3	20%	12.8

Balance Sheet & Other Fin. Data (Million $)

	1994	1993	1992	1991	1990	1989
Cash	58.4	45.3	44.0	38.2	32.5	23.6
Curr. Assets	100	81.5	75.8	63.6	56.7	48.0
Total Assets	146	125	111	93.0	86.0	73.0
Curr. Liab.	10.6	9.2	8.6	6.4	8.8	6.5
LT Debt	6.4	6.9	7.3	3.8	4.1	4.5
Common Eqty.	127	108	94.0	82.0	72.0	60.0
Total Cap.	135	116	103	87.0	76.0	65.0
Cap. Exp.	4.4	10.1	5.8	1.8	2.5	2.9
Cash Flow	26.1	20.4	17.6	15.0	16.1	14.7

Ratio Analysis

	1994	1993	1992	1991	1990	1989
Curr. Ratio	9.5	8.9	8.8	9.9	6.5	7.4
% LT Debt of Cap.	4.7	5.9	7.1	4.3	5.4	7.0
% Net Inc.of Revs.	18.1	16.7	15.9	16.1	16.5	16.6
% Ret. on Assets	16.9	15.4	15.0	14.2	17.7	19.0
% Ret. on Equity	19.5	18.0	17.4	16.7	21.3	23.3

Dividend Data —Cash dividends have been paid since 1987.

Amt. of Div. $	Date Decl.	Ex-Div. Date	Stock of Record	Payment Date
0.070	Apr. 26	Jun. 09	Jun. 15	Jul. 15 '94
0.070	Sep. 06	Sep. 09	Sep. 15	Oct. 14 '94
0.070	Dec. 07	Dec. 12	Dec. 16	Jan. 16 '95
0.070	Mar. 03	Mar. 09	Mar. 15	Apr. 14 '95
0.080	Apr. 25	Jun. 13	Jun. 15	Jul. 14 '95

Data as orig. reptd.; bef. results of disc. opers. and/or spec. items. Per share data adj. for stk. divs. as of ex-div. date. E-Estimated. NA-Not Available. NM-Not Meaningful. NR-Not Ranked.

Office—2001 South Mt. Prospect Ave., Des Plaines, IL 60017-5065. **Tel**—(708) 827-9880. **Fax**—(708) 827-1340. **Chrmn & CEO**—R. S. Fremont. **Pres & COO**—R. W. Giedt. **VP-Fin, Treas & Investor Contact**—George J. Bilek. **Secy**—J. Lewis. **Dirs**—G. M. Ball, A. Coleman, R. S. Fremont, R. W. Giedt, J. Lewis, T. W. Tomsovic. **Transfer Agent**—First Chicago Trust Co., NYC. **Incorporated** in Delaware in 1983. **Empl**-915. **S&P Analyst:** Alan Aaron

STANDARD & POOR'S

STOCK REPORTS

Justin Industries

NASDAQ Symbol **JSTN**
In S&P SmallCap 600

04-NOV-95 **Industry:** Leather/shoes

Summary: This company produces western-style footwear, face brick, concrete blocks and other building materials.

Quantitative Evaluations
Outlook
(1 Lowest—5 Highest)
• **2**
Fair Value
• **9⅞**
Risk
• **Average**
Earn./Div. Rank
• **B+**

Technical Eval.
• **Bearish** since 10/93
Rel. Strength Rank
(1 Lowest—99 Highest)
• **45**
Insider Activity
• **NA**

Recent Price • 10½
52 Wk Range • 13¼-9½
Yield • 1.5%
12-Mo. P/E • 10.2

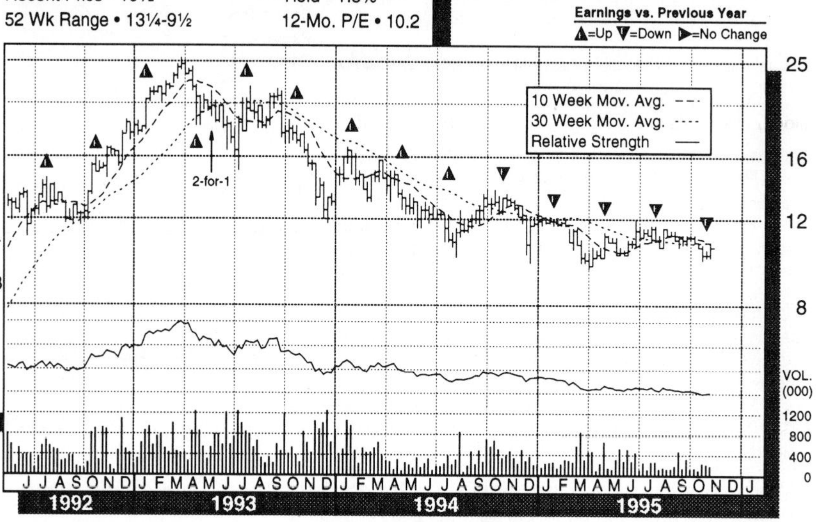

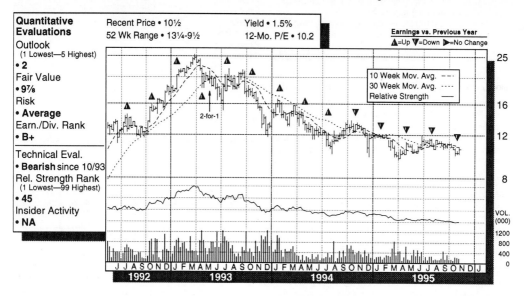

Business Profile - 02-NOV-95

After posting record profits in 1994, the building materials segment has stumbled in recent periods due to slower residential construction. The footwear group continues to be negatively affected by a general malaise in the retail apparel industry. All three major footwear units have taken steps to streamline operations and develop new markets. The program, which includes consolidation of various administrative and accounting functions should be completed in late 1995, with savings seen in 1996.

Operational Review - 02-NOV-95

Total revenues in the nine months ended September 30, 1995 declined 2.5%, year to year, as an 8.0% gain in the building materials segment was outweighed by a 12% drop in footwear sales. Brick shipments were restricted by higher interest rates, which slowed residential construction. However, year-to-year comparisons were aided by the August 1994 acquisition of American Tile. Lower company-wide margins and higher interest expense led to a 33% decline in net income.

Stock Performance - 03-NOV-95

In the past 30 trading days, JSTN's shares have declined 5%, compared to a 2% rise in the S&P 500. Average trading volume for the past five days was 34,500 shares, compared with the 40-day moving average of 34,310 shares.

Key Stock Statistics

Dividend Rate/Share	0.16	Shareholders	5,300
Shs. outstg. (M)	26.9	Market cap. (B)	$0.282
Avg. daily vol. (M)	0.034	Inst. holdings	26%
Tang. Bk. Value/Share	8.45	Insider holdings	NA
Beta	0.54		

Value of $10,000 invested 5 years ago: $ 22,166

Fiscal Year Ending Dec. 31

	1995	% Change	1994	% Change	1993	% Change
Revenues (Million $)						
1Q	113.7	3%	109.9	NM	110.1	13%
2Q	109.9	-4%	114.9	-1%	116.1	11%
3Q	112.4	-6%	119.7	1%	118.3	5%
4Q	—	—	138.5	6%	130.4	-6%
Yr.	—	—	483.0	2%	474.9	5%
Income (Million $)						
1Q	5.27	-21%	6.67	18%	5.63	81%
2Q	6.03	-36%	9.45	20%	7.86	49%
3Q	5.78	-39%	9.44	-4%	9.81	31%
4Q	—	—	11.34	-11%	12.74	14%
Yr.	—	—	36.91	2%	36.04	33%
Earnings Per Share ($)						
1Q	0.19	-21%	0.24	20%	0.20	74%
2Q	0.22	-35%	0.34	21%	0.28	47%
3Q	0.21	-38%	0.34	-3%	0.35	30%
4Q	—	—	0.41	-11%	0.46	15%
Yr.	—	—	1.33	3%	1.29	32%

Next earnings report expected: late January

Justin Industries

Business Summary - 03-NOV-95

Justin Industries, Inc., which traces its history to a company that began making boots in 1879, today produces western-style personal and outdoor products, building materials and evaporative coolers.

Sales and operating profits in 1994 were derived as follows:

	Sales	Profits
Footwear	54%	34%
Building materials	46%	66%

In the footwear segment, Justin is a leading producer of western-style safety, work and sports boots and shoes. It also makes western and dress belts. Footwear products, made by Justin Boot Co., Nocona Boot Co. and Tony Lama Co., are sold primarily in the U.S. under the trade names Justin, Chippewa, Nocona and Diamond J.

Building materials include clay brick (primarily face brick) manufactured by Acme Brick Co. for use in residential and commercial construction; concrete building block sold under the trade name Featherlite Building Products Corp.; and cut limestone manufactured under the name Texas Quarries. The company also represents other manufacturers as a distributor of clay brick, glass block, glazed and unglazed tile and masonry units, fireplace equipment and masonry tools and related items. Justin also provides evaporative coolers produced by Tradewind Technologies Inc., which are used primarily for central residential, light commercial and spot cooling.

In August 1994, the Acme Brick unit acquired American Tile Supply, a Dallas-based distributor of ceramic tile and marble, for about $16 million in cash and notes. American had annual revenues of about $32 million.

In December 1991, Justin sold Ceramic Cooling Tower Co., which was engaged in the design, installation and marketing of water-cooling systems, at a gain of approximately $9.8 million. As a result, Justin's industrial segment was eliminated and operations of Tradewind Technologies were incorporated into the building materials segment.

Northland Publishing Co., based in Flagstaff, Ariz., publishes books about the history and art of the West.

Important Developments

Oct. '95—Higher sales in the building materials segment in the first nine months of 1995 primarily reflected the August 1994 acquisition of American Tile Supply.

Capitalization

Long Term Debt: $71,379,000 (9/95).
Preferred Stock: 100 shs. ($2.50 par); no divd. reqd.; conv. into an aggregate of 2,826 com. shs.; all owned by J. S. Justin.
Options: To buy 1,481,286 shs. at $2.42 to $18.00 ea. (12/94).

Per Share Data ($) (Year Ended Dec. 31)

	1994	1993	1992	1991	1990	1989
Tangible Bk. Val.	8.15	6.95	5.75	4.92	4.31	4.15
Cash Flow	1.83	1.77	1.48	0.80	0.68	0.69
Earnings	1.33	1.29	0.98	0.32	0.28	0.28
Dividends	0.16	0.16	0.14	0.13	0.13	0.10
Payout Ratio	12%	12%	14%	41%	47%	36%
Prices - High	16¾	25⅜	19	6⅛	6	5⅝
- Low	9¾	11¾	5⅝	3⅝	3¾	3⅛
P/E Ratio - High	13	20	19	19	21	20
- Low	7	9	6	11	13	11

Income Statement Analysis (Million $)

	1994	%Chg	1993	%Chg	1992	%Chg	1991
Revs.	483	2%	475	5%	453	23%	368
Oper. Inc.	75.4	3%	73.5	20%	61.4	71%	36.0
Depr.	13.9	3%	13.5	-2%	13.8	8%	12.8
Int. Exp.	4.1	1%	4.0	-23%	5.2	-45%	9.5
Pretax Inc.	57.5	3%	56.0	32%	42.4	NM	13.7
Eff. Tax Rate	36%	—	36%	—	36%	—	38%
Net Inc.	36.9	3%	36.0	33%	27.1	NM	8.5

Balance Sheet & Other Fin. Data (Million $)

	1994	1993	1992	1991	1990	1989
Cash	6.1	10.6	2.4	4.1	1.5	3.3
Curr. Assets	260	240	224	201	199	137
Total Assets	375	347	316	296	293	211
Curr. Liab.	73.8	54.9	54.1	44.9	47.9	38.9
LT Debt	65.0	89.0	100	116	125	56.0
Common Eqty.	222	189	155	128	111	106
Total Cap.	301	292	262	251	245	172
Cap. Exp.	18.6	17.3	12.0	11.0	13.2	9.0
Cash Flow	50.8	49.5	40.9	21.3	18.0	17.7

Ratio Analysis

	1994	1993	1992	1991	1990	1989
Curr. Ratio	3.5	4.4	4.1	4.5	4.1	3.5
% LT Debt of Cap.	21.7	30.3	38.3	46.2	50.9	32.6
% Net Inc.of Revs.	7.6	7.6	6.0	2.3	2.3	2.6
% Ret. on Assets	10.2	10.8	8.7	2.9	2.9	3.3
% Ret. on Equity	17.9	20.9	18.8	7.1	6.7	6.9

Dividend Data —Dividends, paid each year from 1972 until omission in 1982, were resumed in 1984. A dividend reinvestment plan is available.

Amt. of Div. $	Date Decl.	Ex-Div. Date	Stock of Record	Payment Date
0.040	Dec. 15	Dec. 19	Dec. 26	Jan. 04 '95
0.040	Mar. 17	Mar. 21	Mar. 27	Apr. 05 '95
0.040	Jun. 21	Jun. 29	Jul. 03	Jul. 12 '95
0.040	Sep. 13	Sep. 21	Sep. 25	Oct. 04 '95

Data as orig. reptd.; bef. results of disc. opers. and/or spec. items. Per share data adj. for stk. divs. as of ex-div. date. E-Estimated. NA-Not Available. NM-Not Meaningful. NR-Not Ranked.

Office—2821 W. 7th St., P.O. Box 425, Fort Worth, TX 76107. **Tel**—(817) 336-5125. **Chrmn & CEO**—J. S. Justin. **Pres & COO**—J. T. Dickenson. **VP & Secy**—J. M. Bennett. **VP-Fin, CFO & Investor Contact**—Richard J. Savitz (817-390-2412). **Dirs**—J. T. Dickenson, B. H. Friedman, M. Gearhart, R. E. Glaze, J. S. Justin, D. J. Kelly, J. R. Musolino, J. V. Roach, W. E. Tucker. **Transfer Agent**—Society National Bank, Dallas. **Incorporated** in Texas in 1916. **Empl-** 5,007. **S&P Analyst:** Maureen C. Carini

KCS Energy

NYSE Symbol **KCS**
In S&P SmallCap 600

16-SEP-95

Industry: Utilities-Gas

Summary: KCS is engaged in oil and gas exploration and production, natural gas transportation and marketing, and energy services.

Quantitative Evaluations

Outlook
(1 Lowest—5 Highest)
• **5**

Fair Value
• **27⅝**

Risk
• **High**

Earn./Div. Rank
• **NR**

Technical Eval.
• **Bearish** since 8/95

Rel. Strength Rank
(1 Lowest—99 Highest)
• **5**

Insider Activity
• **NA**

Recent Price • 15
52 Wk Range • 22¼-12¼
Yield • 0.8%
12-Mo. P/E • 7.8

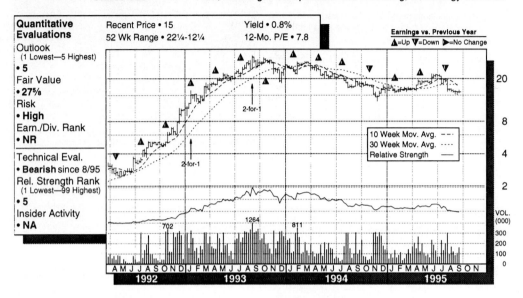

Earnings vs. Previous Year
▲=Up ▼=Down ▶=No Change

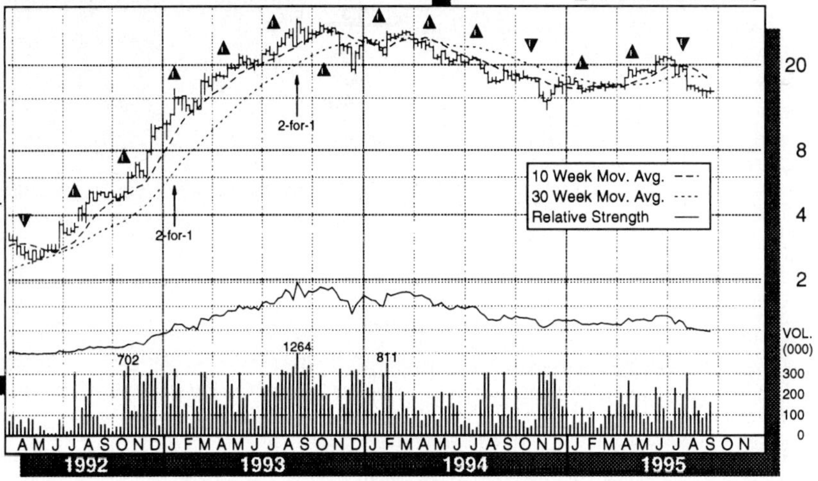

Business Profile - 15-SEP-95

KCS Energy is a vertically integrated energy company with three main businesses: oil and gas exploration and production, natural gas transportation, and energy marketing and services. Its sharp earnings improvement beginning in fiscal 1993 resulted from its above-market-price gas purchase contract, which runs through January 1999, with Tennessee Gas Pipeline Co. (TGP). TGP has contested the validity of the contract, but the arrangement has thus far been upheld by the Texas courts.

Operational Review - 13-SEP-95

Revenues in the nine months ended June 30, 1995, rose 23%, year to year, reflecting increased gas and oil production; a higher percentage of gas production was from non-TGP contract property. Margins narrowed on lower realized prices from non-TGP gas sales, which also produced higher depreciation and depletion. Net interest and other income advanced, as did interest expense. With taxes at 35.3%, versus 34.4%, net income fell 3.2%, to $18,691,000 ($1.59 a share), from $19,304,000 ($1.63).

Stock Performance - 15-SEP-95

In the past 30 trading days, KCS's shares have declined 6%, compared to a 4% rise in the S&P 500. Average trading volume for the past five days was 31,680 shares, compared with the 40-day moving average of 31,226 shares.

Key Stock Statistics

Dividend Rate/Share	0.12	Shareholders	1,500
Shs. outstg. (M)	11.5	Market cap. (B)	$0.172
Avg. daily vol. (M)	0.023	Inst. holdings	38%
Tang. Bk. Value/Share	8.03	Insider holdings	NA
Beta	-0.50		

Value of $10,000 invested 5 years ago: $ 87,019

Fiscal Year Ending Sep. 30

	1995	% Change	1994	% Change	1993	% Change
Revenues (Million $)						
1Q	91.31	7%	85.19	62%	52.60	25%
2Q	96.04	13%	85.17	63%	52.27	68%
3Q	126.6	50%	84.49	9%	77.28	127%
4Q	—	—	80.74	-10%	89.55	145%
Yr.	—	—	335.6	24%	271.7	89%
Income (Million $)						
1Q	7.10	14%	6.22	NM	1.29	111%
2Q	6.22	NM	6.17	108%	2.96	NM
3Q	5.38	-22%	6.91	69%	4.10	NM
4Q	—	—	3.98	-25%	5.33	NM
Yr.	—	—	23.28	70%	13.68	NM
Earnings Per Share ($)						
1Q	0.60	13%	0.53	NM	0.11	109%
2Q	0.53	2%	0.52	100%	0.26	NM
3Q	0.46	-21%	0.58	63%	0.36	NM
4Q	—	—	0.34	-24%	0.45	NM
Yr.	—	—	1.97	66%	1.19	NM

Next earnings report expected: mid November

KCS Energy

Business Summary - 15-SEP-95

KCS Energy (formerly KCS Group) is a vertically integrated energy company that operates three main businesses: oil and gas exploration and production, natural gas transportation, and energy marketing and services. Contributions by business segment in fiscal 1994:

	Revs.	Profits
Energy marketing & services	77%	6%
Oil & gas exploration & production	17%	90%
Natural gas transportation	6%	4%

The company's sharp improvement in earnings beginning in fiscal 1993 was due to the above-market-price gas purchase contract, which runs through January 1999, with Tennessee Gas Pipeline Co. (TGP). TGP legally challenged the contract, but in July 1992, a Texas court ordered TGP to honor it. The decision was upheld in part and remanded for review in part by the Texas Court of Appeals. In June 1994, the Texas Supreme Court agreed to hear the case with respect to output, among other issues. In August 1995, the Texas Supreme Court upheld the validity of the TGP contract, but remanded to the District Court for trial the issues of good faith and whether deliveries by KCS are proportionate to prior or comparable output.

The contract has stimulated an aggressive well development program. In fiscal 1994, total production was 200,000 bbl. of oil and 9,236,000 Mcf of gas. Average sales prices were $15.20 per bbl. of oil ($18.52 the year before) and $5.29 per Mcf of gas ($4.79); the TGP contract price in fiscal 1994 was $7.34 per Mcf. Proved reserves at year end were estimated at 2,576,000 bbl. of oil and 86,362,000 Mcf of natural gas. The present value of future net revenues (discounted at 10%) was estimated at $182.0 million, versus $185.5 million a year earlier. At September 30, 1994, the company had 120 gross (46 net) oil wells and 417 gross (185) gas wells.

The company's major transportation asset is a 150 mile intrastate pipeline located in Texas. It also owns and operates seven gas gathering systems in Texas and Louisiana, with 53 miles of gathering pipelines.

The energy marketing and services segment consists of four major business activities: natural gas marketing, volumetric production payments, energy management services, and energy risk management.

Important Developments

Aug. '95—KCS announced the dual completion of the Baker #3 well, located in the Oletha East Field in Limestone County, Texas, and the completion of a discovery well in Iberville Parish, Louisiana.

Capitalization

Long Term Debt: $80,400,000 (6/95).

Per Share Data ($) (Year Ended Sep. 30)

	1994	1993	1992	1991	1990	1989
Tangible Bk. Val.	6.45	4.52	2.69	2.41	2.18	1.96
Cash Flow	3.25	1.71	0.65	0.51	0.40	0.29
Earnings	1.97	1.19	0.31	0.24	0.23	0.11
Dividends	0.08	0.04	0.03	Nil	Nil	Nil
Payout Ratio	4%	3%	8%	Nil	Nil	Nil
Prices - High	29	32¾	11⅝	2¼	2 5/16	2½
- Low	12¼	9	2 1/16	1½	1¾	1⅛
P/E Ratio - High	15	28	38	9	10	22
- Low	6	8	7	6	8	10

Income Statement Analysis (Million $)

	1994	%Chg	1993	%Chg	1992	%Chg	1991
Revs.	336	24%	272	89%	144	45%	99
Oper. Inc.	51.4	97%	26.1	188%	9.1	37%	6.6
Depr.	15.2	153%	6.0	54%	3.9	35%	2.9
Int. Exp.	2.4	34%	1.8	35%	1.3	10%	1.2
Pretax Inc.	35.0	84%	19.0	NM	4.7	39%	3.3
Eff. Tax Rate	34%	—	28%	—	28%	—	26%
Net Inc.	23.3	70%	13.7	NM	3.3	34%	2.5

Balance Sheet & Other Fin. Data (Million $)

	1994	1993	1992	1991	1990	1989
Cash	5.1	11.3	3.2	2.2	3.2	25.3
Curr. Assets	47.7	70.3	27.4	18.9	17.3	31.8
Total Assets	181	153	74.7	60.5	51.1	42.2
Curr. Liab.	42.1	65.0	23.2	15.5	14.4	18.0
LT Debt	48.6	30.9	17.8	16.0	10.7	0.2
Common Eqty.	73.8	51.4	29.0	25.7	23.1	20.8
Total Cap.	137	87.1	50.2	42.8	34.6	21.5
Cap. Exp.	66.1	41.3	9.8	9.0	26.8	3.8
Cash Flow	38.4	19.7	7.2	5.4	4.3	3.2

Ratio Analysis

	1994	1993	1992	1991	1990	1989
Curr. Ratio	1.1	1.1	1.2	1.2	1.2	1.8
% LT Debt of Cap.	35.5	35.5	35.4	37.4	31.0	0.8
% Net Inc.of Revs.	6.9	5.0	2.3	2.5	3.3	1.7
% Ret. on Assets	13.9	11.8	4.9	4.5	5.1	3.6
% Ret. on Equity	37.2	33.4	12.2	10.2	10.9	7.9

Dividend Data —Cash dividends were initiated in December 1991.

Amt. of Div. $	Date Decl.	Ex-Div. Date	Stock of Record	Payment Date
0.020	Sep. 29	Oct. 07	Oct. 14	Nov. 18 '94
0.030	Dec. 01	Jan. 10	Jan. 17	Feb. 21 '95
0.030	Feb. 27	Apr. 07	Apr. 13	May. 19 '95
0.030	May. 04	Jul. 12	Jul. 14	Aug. 21 '95

Data as orig. reptd.; bef. results of disc. opers. and/or spec. items. Per share data adj. for stk. divs. as of ex-div. date. E-Estimated. NA-Not Available. NM-Not Meaningful. NR-Not Ranked.

Office—379 Thornall St., Edison, NJ 08837. **Tel**—(908) 632-1770. **Chrmn**—S. B. Kean. **Pres & CEO**—J. W. Christmas. **VP-Secy & Treas**—H. A. Jurand. **Dirs**—J. W. Christmas, G. S. Geary, S. B. Kean, J. Kean Jr., J. E. Murphy, Jr., J. D. Siegel, C. A. Viggiano. **Transfer Agent & Registrar**—Registrar & Transfer Co., Cranford, N.J. **Incorporated** in Delaware in 1988. **Empl-** 86. **S&P Analyst:** Michael C. Barr

STANDARD & POOR'S

STOCK REPORTS

KN Energy

NYSE Symbol **KNE**

In S&P SmallCap 600

07-OCT-95

Industry:
Utilities-Gas

Summary: This company is a natural gas energy products and services provider serving communities in Colorado, Kansas, Nebraska and Wyoming.

Quantitative Evaluations

Outlook
(1 Lowest—5 Highest)
• **3+**

Fair Value
• **26½**

Risk
• **Low**

Earn./Div. Rank
• **B**

Technical Eval.
• **Bearish** since 8/95

Rel. Strength Rank
(1 Lowest—99 Highest)
• **62**

Insider Activity
• **NA**

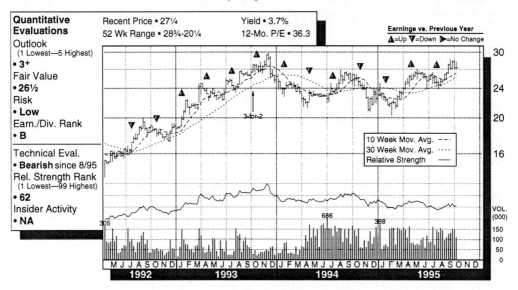

Recent Price • 27¼
52 Wk Range • 28¾-20¼

Yield • 3.7%
12-Mo. P/E • 36.3

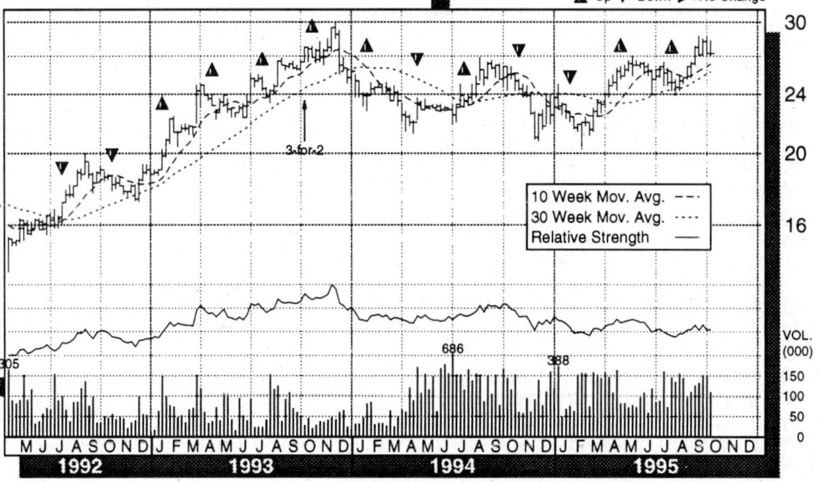

Business Profile - 06-OCT-95

KNE's business strategy involves building on its extensive Rocky Mountain, Mid-Continent and Texas natural gas pipeline systems, in an attempt to provide broader gas supply access while achieving lower gas supply costs. Earnings in the first half of 1995 benefited from expense savings and new business opportunities resulting from the July 1994 acquisition of American Oil & Gas, which significantly expanded KNE's operations. The company adopted a stockholder rights plan in August 1995.

Operational Review - 06-OCT-95

Mild winter weather and lower natural gas prices adversely affected operating revenues in the six months ended June 30, 1995, resulting in a 10% decline. However, stringent cost controls, realized expense savings from the acquisition of American Oil & Gas, contributions from the February 1995 acquisition of transmission and storage assets in Texas and the impact of 1994 rate increases contributed to a 44% gain in net income to $21.4 million ($0.75 a share) from $14.9 million ($0.52) a year ago.

Stock Performance - 06-OCT-95

In the past 30 trading days, KNE's shares have increased 4%, compared to a 4% rise in the S&P 500. Average trading volume for the past five days was 21,620 shares, compared with the 40-day moving average of 26,436 shares.

Key Stock Statistics

Dividend Rate/Share	1.00	Shareholders	8,900
Shs. outstg. (M)	27.9	Market cap. (B)	$0.759
Avg. daily vol. (M)	0.028	Inst. holdings	47%
Tang. Bk. Value/Share	14.28	Insider holdings	NA
Beta	0.42		

Value of $10,000 invested 5 years ago: $ 20,467

Fiscal Year Ending Dec. 31

	1995	% Change	1994	% Change	1993	% Change
Revenues (Million $)						
1Q	291.7	-16%	349.0	129%	152.2	23%
2Q	233.9	-2%	238.7	158%	92.60	38%
3Q	—	—	230.7	149%	92.70	42%
4Q	—	—	265.6	70%	155.9	15%
Yr.	—	—	1,084	120%	493.4	26%
Income (Million $)						
1Q	14.52	21%	11.96	—	—	—
2Q	6.92	138%	2.91	—	—	—
3Q	—	—	-12.46	—	—	—
4Q	—	—	12.91	—	—	—
Yr.	—	—	15.32	-50%	30.87	58%
Earnings Per Share ($)						
1Q	0.51	21%	0.42	-53%	0.89	13%
2Q	0.24	140%	0.10	NM	-0.09	NM
3Q	—	—	-0.45	NM	0.02	NM
4Q	—	—	0.45	-40%	0.75	10%
Yr.	—	—	0.52	-67%	1.57	23%

Next earnings report expected: early November

KN Energy

Business Summary - 06-OCT-95

KN Energy is a natural gas energy products and services provider whose activities consist of developing, producing, gathering, processing, storing, transporting, selling, and marketing natural gas; processing, selling, and marketing NGLs (natural gas liquids); and developing and processing crude oil. Operations were expanded significantly through the July 1994 acquisition of American Oil & Gas Corp. Business segment contributions in 1994:

	Revs.	Profits
Retail natural gas services	19%	23%
Interstate transportation & storage services	5%	30%
Gathering, processing & marketing services	75%	41%
Gas & oil production	1%	5%

Retail natural gas services are provided to residential, commercial, agricultural, and industrial customers for space heating, crop irrigation and drying, and processing of agricultural products. Revenues from this segment are derived primarily from natural gas sales and transportation services. As of year-end 1994, 237,000 retail customers were being served in 302 communities in Colorado, Kansas, Nebraska, and Wyoming through distribution pipelines totaling almost 8,200 miles. This segment also operated over 1,300 miles of intrastate natural gas pipeline sytems in Colorado and Wyoming.

Interstate transportation and storage services are provided to affiliates, third-party natural gas distribution utilities, and shippers. At year-end 1994, interstate pipeline properties included transmission, gathering and storage lines totaling over 6,500 miles and one products extraction plant. Gas storage was being provided by four underground facilities.

KNE also provides natural gas gathering, processing and marketing and supply services, including transportation and storage, to a variety of customers. As of year-end 1994, this segment owned and operated about 11,000 miles of pipeline in seven states; operated 14 gas processing plants with a total processing capacity of about 730 MMcf per day; and a gas storage facility in West Texas.

Gas and oil production involves the development and production of gas and oil reserves. As of year-end 1994, total net reserves for this segment were approximately 50 Bcf equivalent of natural gas.

Important Developments

Aug. '95—KNE entered into an agreement to acquire gathering and processing assets from Parker & Parsley Petroleum (NYSE: PDP) for an undisclosed amount. Separately, the company's directors authorized the adoption of a stockholder rights plan.

Capitalization

Long Term Debt: $321,602,000 (6/95).
Red. Cum. Preferred Stock: $1,143,000.
Cum. Preferred Stock: $7,000,000

Per Share Data ($) (Year Ended Dec. 31)

	1994	1993	1992	1991	1990	1989
Tangible Bk. Val.	14.28	13.41	12.59	12.13	12.74	10.44
Earnings	0.52	1.57	1.27	1.41	1.22	0.93
Dividends	0.76	0.92	0.85	0.79	0.71	0.67
Payout Ratio	147%	59%	67%	56%	58%	71%
Prices - High	26⅞	30	20	18¾	17⅝	16⅞
- Low	20¾	18⅝	13⅞	13⅞	14⅛	11¾
P/E Ratio - High	52	19	16	13	14	18
- Low	40	12	11	10	12	12

Income Statement Analysis (Million $)

	1994	%Chg	1993	%Chg	1992	%Chg	1991
Revs.	1,084	120%	493	26%	392	NM	395
Depr.	50.3	92%	26.2	8%	24.2	13%	21.4
Maint.	NA	—	7.7	5%	7.3	-1%	7.4
Fxd. Chgs. Cov.	1.8	-35%	2.7	9%	2.5	-12%	2.8
Constr. Credits	NA	—	NA	—	NA	—	NA
Eff. Tax Rate	38%	—	37%	—	38%	—	39%
Net Inc.	15.3	-37%	24.3	24%	19.6	-9%	21.6

Balance Sheet & Other Fin. Data (Million $)

	1994	1993	1992	1991	1990	1989
Gross Prop.	1,312	877	769	712	696	658
Cap. Exp.	70.6	63.1	60.1	59.4	47.0	36.3
Net Prop.	851	507	455	412	405	384
Capitalization:						
LT Debt	335	232	220	159	141	138
% LT Debt	45	53	53	46	41	45
Pfd.	8.7	9.9	11.5	13.6	18.3	20.4
% Pfd.	1.20	2.20	2.80	3.90	5.40	6.70
Common	394	202	185	175	182	147
% Common	53	46	44	50	53	48
Total Cap.	846	501	466	391	393	358

Ratio Analysis

	1994	1993	1992	1991	1990	1989
Oper. Ratio	96.0	91.0	90.2	90.5	90.7	91.8
% Earn. on Net Prop.	6.4	9.2	8.9	9.5	9.3	7.5
% Ret. on Revs.	1.4	4.9	5.0	5.5	4.8	4.2
% Ret. On Invest.Cap	5.6	9.8	9.1	10.0	9.5	9.4
% Return On Com.Eqty	3.7	12.1	10.3	11.3	10.6	9.2

Dividend Data —Dividends have been paid since 1937. A dividend reinvestment plan is available.

Amt. of Div. $	Date Decl.	Ex-Div. Date	Stock of Record	Payment Date
0.250	Dec. 05	Dec. 09	Dec. 15	Dec. 30 '94
0.250	Feb. 06	Mar. 09	Mar. 15	Mar. 31 '95
0.250	May. 16	Jun. 13	Jun. 15	Jun. 30 '95
0.250	Aug. 18	Sep. 13	Sep. 15	Sep. 29 '95

Data as orig. reptd.; bef. results of disc opers. and/or spec. items. Per share data adj. for stk. divs. as of ex-div. date. E-Estimated. NA-Not Available. NM-Not Meaningful. NR-Not Ranked.

Office—370 Van Gordon St., P.O. Box 281304, Lakewood, CO 80228-8304. **Tel**—(303) 989-1740. **Chrmn**—C. W. Battey. **Pres & CEO**—L. D. Hall. **VP-Treas**—J. A. Aden. **Secy**—W. S. Garner, Jr. **Investor Contact**—Richard Buxton. **Dirs**—E. H. Austin, Jr., C. W. Battey, S. A. Bliss, D. W. Burkholder, D. M. Carmichael, R. H. Chitwood, H. P. Coghlan, R. B. Daugherty, J. L. Haines, L. D. Hall, W. J. Hybl, E. Randall III, J. C. Taylor, H. A. True III. **Transfer Agent & Registrar**—Chemical Bank, NYC; company's office. **Incorporated** in Kansas in 1927. **Empl-** 2,014. **S&P Analyst:** N. Rosenberg

STANDARD & POOR'S

STOCK REPORTS

K-Swiss Inc.

NASDAQ Symbol **KSWS**

In S&P SmallCap 600

02-NOV-95 **Industry:** Leather/shoes

Summary: This company designs, develops and markets high-performance and casual athletic footwear.

Quantitative Evaluations

Recent Price • 11½ | Yield • 0.7%
52 Wk Range • 22-10½ | 12-Mo. P/E • 9.6

Outlook
(1 Lowest—5 Highest)
• **NA**

Fair Value
• **NA**

Risk
• **Average**

Earn./Div. Rank
• **B**

Technical Eval.
• **Bullish** since 12/94

Rel. Strength Rank
(1 Lowest—99 Highest)
• **21**

Insider Activity
• **NA**

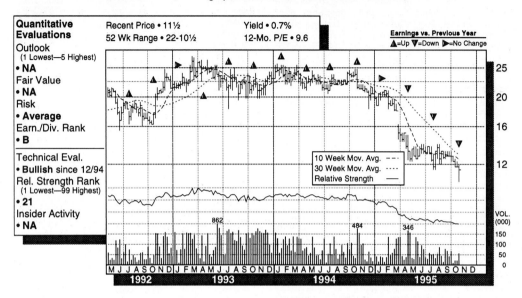

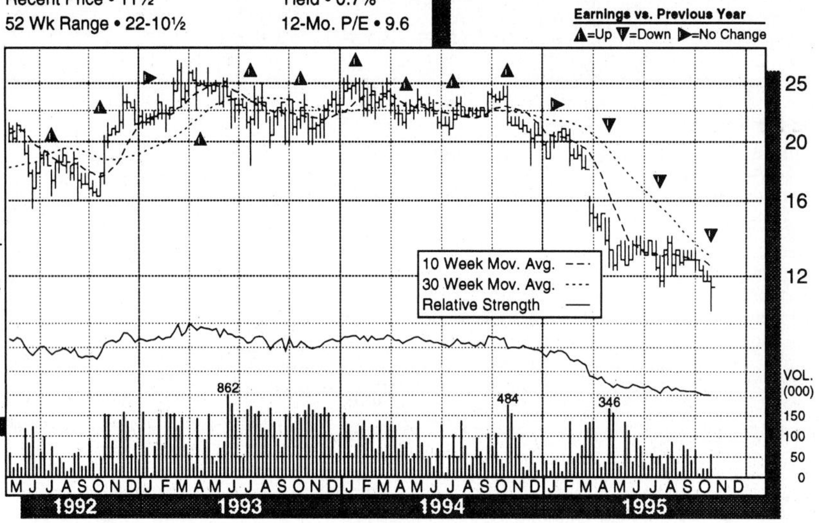

Business Profile - 02-NOV-95

This athletic shoe concern has conducted an ambitious expansion of international operations, with foreign sales accounting for 24% of revenues in 1994. More than 89% of production capacity is now located in China and Indonesia. A new strategy to better manage product sourcing includes reducing the number of factories producing footwear in order to become a more substantial customer of each remaining factory, and employing more experienced personnel to manage overseas operations.

Operational Review - 02-NOV-95

Revenues, which had been in a long uptrend, declined in the first nine months of 1995, as a 2.7% increase in internation sales was outweighed by a 28% drop in domestic sales. With narrower gross margins, and a rise in SG&A expense as a percentage of sales, EPS fell 51%, to $0.98, from $1.98. At September 30, 1995, backlog and futures levels were significantly lower than those a year earlier, a potential sign of weaker results in coming periods.

Stock Performance - 27-OCT-95

In the past 30 trading days, KSWS's shares have declined 10%, compared to a 0.63% fall in the S&P 500. Average trading volume for the past five days was 10,920 shares, compared with the 40-day moving average of 8,938 shares.

Key Stock Statistics

Dividend Rate/Share	0.08	Shareholders	200
Shs. outstg. (M)	6.6	Market cap. (B)	$0.074
Avg. daily vol. (M)	0.006	Inst. holdings	47%
Tang. Bk. Value/Share	11.77	Insider holdings	NA
Beta	1.14		

Value of $10,000 invested 5 years ago: NA

Fiscal Year Ending Dec. 31

	1995	% Change	1994	% Change	1993	% Change
Revenues (Million $)						
1Q	42.76	-6%	45.55	5%	43.56	19%
2Q	29.73	-18%	36.27	-5%	38.30	17%
3Q	29.36	-40%	48.74	11%	43.92	18%
4Q	—	—	24.38	2%	23.79	12%
Yr.	—	—	154.9	4%	149.6	17%
Income (Million $)						
1Q	4.03	-13%	4.62	34%	3.45	28%
2Q	1.50	-57%	3.52	15%	3.07	41%
3Q	1.02	-81%	5.25	16%	4.53	24%
4Q	—	—	1.49	NM	1.48	15%
Yr.	—	—	14.88	19%	12.52	28%
Earnings Per Share ($)						
1Q	0.60	-12%	0.68	31%	0.52	27%
2Q	0.23	-56%	0.52	13%	0.46	39%
3Q	0.15	-81%	0.78	16%	0.67	22%
4Q	—	—	0.22	NM	0.22	10%
Yr.	—	—	2.20	18%	1.87	26%

Next earnings report expected: mid February

K-Swiss Inc.

Business Summary - 02-NOV-95

K-Swiss Inc. develops and markets a growing array of athletic footwear for high-performance sports use and fitness activities. It was founded in 1966 by two Swiss brothers, who introduced one of the first leather tennis shoes in the U.S. The company was acquired December 30, 1986, in a leveraged transaction by an investment group led by the current chairman and president. Subsequently, several new footwear products were introduced, and manufacturing was shifted to independent suppliers in China, Indonesia, Malaysia, Taiwan and the Philippines.

Revenues in recent years were derived as follows:

	1994	1993	1992
Classic (leather)	43%	38%	30%
Tennis/court shoes	21%	31%	35%
Nautical	8%	13%	18%
Children's	14%	11%	9%
Outdoor	11%	5%	6%
Apparel/accessories	3%	2%	2%

K-Swiss derives the bulk of sales from its Classic leather tennis shoes. The Classic, little changed from its original design, has become popular as a casual shoe for men and women, while continuing to sell well as a tennis shoe (2,677,000 pairs were sold in 1994, up from 2,247,000 in 1993). In recent years, the company has developed new product categories whose initial styles were extensions of the Classic. It believes that the use of classic styling reduces the effect of changes in consumer preferences.

In 1994, men's footwear accounted for 46% of revenues, and women's footwear 37%.

The company sells a line of apparel and accessories manufactured by third parties. The line consists of warm-ups, skirts, shorts and shirts, fleece tops and pants, T-shirts, caps, bags and socks. All apparel and accessories carry the K-Swiss logo and name.

K-Swiss sells its products in the U.S. through independent sales representatives, primarily to specialty athletic footwear stores, pro shops, sporting goods stores and upscale department stores. It also sells to a number of foreign distributors. The Foot Locker group of stores accounted for 16% of total revenues in 1994 (17% in 1993), while international sales provided 24% (25%).

Important Developments

Oct. '95—A 40% decline in total revenues in the 1995 third quarter reflected an 11% decrease in international revenues and a 47% drop domestically.

Capitalization

Long Term Debt: $560,000 (6/95), incl. lease obligs.
Cl. B Conv. Com. Stk.: 2,495,251 shs. ($0.01 par).
Cl. A Com. Stk.: 4,082,251 shs. ($0.01 par).

Per Share Data ($) (Year Ended Dec. 31)

	1994	1993	1992	1991	1990	1989
Tangible Bk. Val.	11.77	9.50	7.40	6.00	4.64	0.90
Cash Flow	2.39	2.06	1.68	1.51	1.34	1.05
Earnings	2.20	1.87	1.49	1.34	1.22	0.91
Dividends	0.08	Nil	Nil	Nil	Nil	Nil
Payout Ratio	4%	Nil	Nil	Nil	Nil	Nil
Prices - High	25¾	27¼	24¾	28⅞	30¼	NA
- Low	18¼	18¼	14¼	11¼	10½	NA
P/E Ratio - High	12	15	17	22	25	NA
- Low	8	10	10	8	9	NA

Income Statement Analysis (Million $)

	1994	%Chg	1993	%Chg	1992	%Chg	1991
Revs.	155	3%	150	17%	128	8%	119
Oper. Inc.	25.8	22%	21.1	17%	18.1	1%	17.9
Depr.	1.2	-2%	1.3	NM	1.3	16%	1.1
Int. Exp.	NA	—	0.4	-81%	2.0	-31%	2.9
Pretax Inc.	24.8	28%	19.4	31%	14.8	6%	13.9
Eff. Tax Rate	40%	—	36%	—	34%	—	37%
Net Inc.	14.9	19%	12.5	28%	9.8	11%	8.8

Balance Sheet & Other Fin. Data (Million $)

	1994	1993	1992	1991	1990	1989
Cash	15.8	14.4	10.6	1.1	0.1	0.6
Curr. Assets	90.1	75.7	68.3	54.8	57.7	43.9
Total Assets	100	86.9	80.2	67.1	68.5	52.7
Curr. Liab.	12.9	15.1	23.2	10.9	17.0	26.8
LT Debt	0.5	0.6	1.4	10.9	13.8	16.3
Common Eqty.	82.8	68.0	53.7	45.0	36.1	8.5
Total Cap.	87.4	71.8	57.0	56.2	51.5	25.9
Cap. Exp.	0.7	0.8	0.7	1.6	1.0	0.4
Cash Flow	16.1	13.8	11.1	9.9	7.9	5.5

Ratio Analysis

	1994	1993	1992	1991	1990	1989
Curr. Ratio	7.0	5.0	2.9	5.0	3.4	1.6
% LT Debt of Cap.	0.6	0.9	2.5	19.5	26.7	63.0
% Net Inc.of Revs.	9.6	8.4	7.7	7.4	8.0	6.9
% Ret. on Assets	15.9	14.9	13.3	13.0	9.4	11.3
% Ret. on Equity	19.7	20.4	19.8	21.7	29.0	77.3

Dividend Data —Quarterly cash dividends were initiated in April 1994.

Amt. of Div. $	Date Decl.	Ex-Div. Date	Stock of Record	Payment Date
0.020	Nov. 14	Dec. 23	Dec. 30	Jan. 13 '95
0.020	Mar. 02	Mar. 27	Mar. 31	Apr. 14 '95
0.020	May. 30	Jun. 28	Jun. 30	Jul. 14 '95
0.020	Sep. 14	Sep. 27	Sep. 29	Oct. 13 '95

Data as orig. reptd.; bef. results of disc. opers. and/or spec. items. Per share data adj. for stk. divs. as of ex-div. date. E-Estimated. NA-Not Available. NM-Not Meaningful. NR-Not Ranked.

Office—20664 Bahama St., Chatsworth, CA 91311. **Tel**—(818) 998-3388. **Chrmn & Pres**—S. Nichols. **VP-Fin, CFO, Secy & Investor Contact**—George Powlick. **Dirs**—S. Bernstein, L. Feldman, S. Fine, J. K. Layne, S. Nichols, G. Powlick, M. Wilford. **Transfer Agent & Registrar**—Bank of New York, NYC. **Incorporated** in Delaware in 1990. **Empl**-297. **S&P Analyst:** M.C.C.

STANDARD & POOR'S

STOCK REPORTS

Kaman Corporation

NASDAQ Symbol **KAMNA**

In S&P SmallCap 600

13-NOV-95

Industry: Conglomerate/diversified

Summary: This company provides products and services for defense markets, and distributes industrial and commercial products including musical instruments.

Quantitative Evaluations

Recent Price • 11⅛ | Yield • 4.0%

52 Wk Range • 13⅜-9½ | 12-Mo. P/E • NM

Outlook
(1 Lowest—5 Highest)
• **NA**

Fair Value
• **NA**

Risk
• **Low**

Earn./Div. Rank
• **B**

Technical Eval.
• **Neutral** since 11/95

Rel. Strength Rank
(1 Lowest—99 Highest)
• **32**

Insider Activity
• **NA**

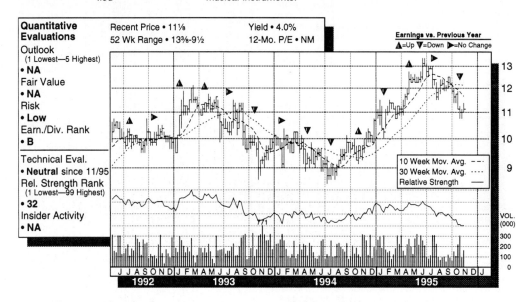

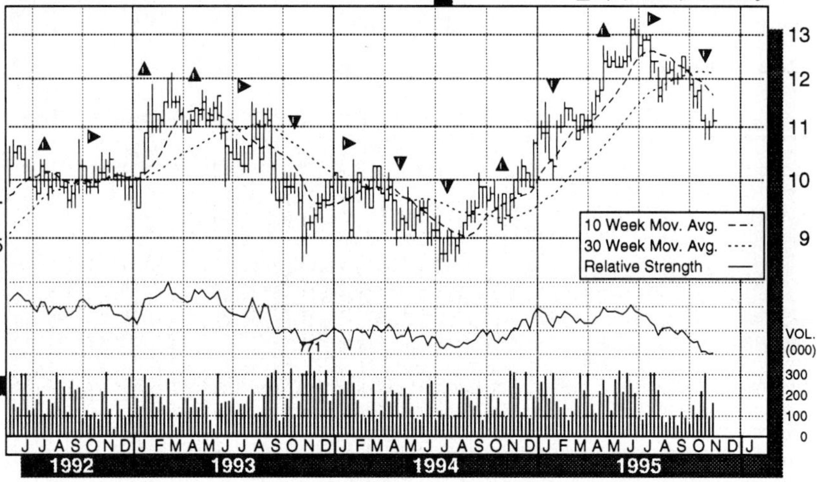

Business Profile - 13-NOV-95

This company's diversified technologies segment continues to feel the effects of declining defense and weak commercial aviation markets. Nevertheless, Kaman believes that it is well positioned to compete in a defense environment that emphasizes advanced technology smart weapons programs. The company continues to be successful in maintaining revenues in this area, although competition for such contracts is increasing.

Operational Review - 13-NOV-95

Revenues in the first nine months of 1995 rose 8.5%, year to year, on gains for industrial technologies, despite a slowdown in international markets for Kaman Music, and growth in diversified technologies. With a $1.8 million pretax gain on the sale of certain real estate, after taxes at 39.9% versus 37.5%. net income was up 7.6%. EPS, after preferred dividends, increased to $0.65, from $0.60.

Stock Performance - 10-NOV-95

In the past 30 trading days, KAMNA's shares have declined 6%, compared to a 1% rise in the S&P 500. Average trading volume for the past five days was 32,120 shares, compared with the 40-day moving average of 30,150 shares.

Key Stock Statistics

Dividend Rate/Share	0.44	Shareholders	6,900
Shs. outstg. (M)	18.4	Market cap. (B)	$0.204
Avg. daily vol. (M)	0.041	Inst. holdings	49%
Tang. Bk. Value/Share	7.72	Insider holdings	NA
Beta	0.20		

Value of $10,000 invested 5 years ago: $ 15,778

Fiscal Year Ending Dec. 31

	1995	% Change	1994	% Change	1993	% Change
Revenues (Million $)						
1Q	210.0	6%	198.0	NM	197.9	-4%
2Q	221.9	6%	208.6	7%	194.9	4%
3Q	226.0	14%	198.9	-2%	202.5	7%
4Q	—	—	21.04	-89%	197.9	-2%
Yr.	—	—	820.8	3%	794.1	1%
Income (Million $)						
1Q	5.55	31%	4.24	6%	4.01	3%
2Q	4.66	1%	4.60	-4%	4.78	NM
3Q	4.57	-7%	4.90	NM	-42.50	NM
4Q	—	—	-26.92	NM	4.91	17%
Yr.	—	—	-13.18	NM	-28.80	NM
Earnings Per Share ($)						
1Q	0.25	39%	0.18	-18%	0.22	5%
2Q	0.20	NM	0.20	-23%	0.26	NM
3Q	0.20	-9%	0.22	NM	-2.36	NM
4Q	—	—	-1.53	NM	0.23	NM
Yr.	—	—	-0.93	NM	-1.63	NM

Next earnings report expected: early February

Kaman Corporation

Business Summary - 13-NOV-95

Kaman Corporation and its subsidiaries serve defense, industrial and commercial markets in two industry segments: diversified technologies and distribution. Segment contributions to sales and operating profits (in 000) in 1994 were:

	Sales	Profits
Diversified technologies	46%	-$17,226
Distribution	54%	19,558

The diversified technologies segment provides design and manufacture of advanced technology products and systems, mostly for use on aircraft; and advanced technology services to customers including all branches of the armed forces, government agencies, defense contractors and industrial organizations, including software engineering and maintenance. The segment also provides aircraft manufacturing, including the development and manufacture of helicopters and the integration of systems related to helicopters. The company is the prime contractor for the SH-2 series helicopter, a multi-mission aircraft for the U.S. Navy.

Kaman is a national distributor of industrial products, operating through more than 150 service centers located in 29 states and British Columbia. It supplies a broad range of industries with original equipment, repair and replacement products needed to maintain traditional manufacturing processes and, increasingly, with products of higher technological content that are required to support automated production processes. This segment serves nearly every sector of heavy and light industry, including automobile, agriculture, food processing, pulp and paper, mining, chemicals and electronics. Products include bearings, power transmission equipment, motors, belts and pulleys. It also distributes more than 13,000 music instruments and accessories to independent retailers in the U.S. and U.K. and to international distributors worldwide. Principal brand names include Ovation, Hamer and Trace Elliot.

Important Developments

Oct. '95—The company said that during the third quarter, the K-MAX aerial truck was chosen as the winner of the U.S. Navy Vertical Replenishment demonstration competetion, which could lead to the Navy evaluating the concept of charter lease for aircraft in non-combat roles. Kaman is currently flying two K-MAX helicopters with the Navy for an evaluation period.

Capitalization

Long Term Debt: $61,805,000 (6/95).
Options: To buy 864,589 Cl. A shs. at $7.50 to $13.83 ea. (12/94).

Per Share Data ($)

(Year Ended Dec. 31)

	1994	1993	1992	1991	1990	1989
Tangible Bk. Val.	7.60	7.83	9.88	9.33	8.81	8.19
Cash Flow	-0.21	-0.88	1.68	1.67	1.79	1.19
Earnings	-0.93	-1.63	0.95	0.93	1.06	0.48
Dividends	0.44	0.44	0.44	0.44	0.44	0.44
Payout Ratio	NM	NM	46%	47%	42%	92%
Prices - High	11⅛	12⅛	10¾	9⅝	9½	14⅞
- Low	8½	8⅝	7⅞	7⅜	6	7⅝
P/E Ratio - High	NM	NM	11	10	9	31
- Low	NM	NM	8	8	6	16

Income Statement Analysis (Million $)

	1994	%Chg	1993	%Chg	1992	%Chg	1991
Revs.	819	3%	793	1%	783	NM	778
Oper. Inc.	46.6	6%	44.1	-8%	48.0	-1%	48.6
Depr.	13.1	-3%	13.5	NM	13.4	-1%	13.6
Int. Exp.	4.7	-33%	7.0	-1%	7.1	-13%	8.2
Pretax Inc.	-14.2	NM	-40.5	NM	29.0	2%	28.3
Eff. Tax Rate	NM	—	NM	—	40%	—	40%
Net Inc.	-13.2	NM	-28.8	NM	17.4	2%	17.0

Balance Sheet & Other Fin. Data (Million $)

	1994	1993	1992	1991	1990	1989
Cash	3.7	3.8	2.5	3.3	3.2	8.7
Curr. Assets	339	317	335	310	327	319
Total Assets	443	440	443	422	444	441
Curr. Liab.	193	167	122	111	117	119
LT Debt	37.0	38.0	101	102	123	131
Common Eqty.	147	171	210	202	193	183
Total Cap.	241	266	317	307	323	321
Cap. Exp.	21.6	20.4	10.6	8.6	9.6	12.4
Cash Flow	-3.8	-16.0	30.7	30.6	32.7	21.5

Ratio Analysis

	1994	1993	1992	1991	1990	1989
Curr. Ratio	1.8	1.9	2.7	2.8	2.8	2.7
% LT Debt of Cap.	15.5	14.3	31.8	33.2	38.2	40.7
% Net Inc.of Revs.	NM	NM	2.2	2.2	2.3	1.1
% Ret. on Assets	NM	NM	4.0	3.9	4.3	2.0
% Ret. on Equity	NM	NM	8.5	8.6	10.2	4.8

Dividend Data —Cash has been paid each year since 1972. A dividend reinvestment plan is available.

Amt. of Div. $	Date Decl.	Ex-Div. Date	Stock of Record	Payment Date
0.110	Nov. 28	Dec. 23	Jan. 02	Jan. 17 '95
0.110	Feb. 14	Mar. 28	Apr. 03	Apr. 17 '95
0.110	Jun. 13	Jun. 29	Jul. 03	Jul. 17 '95
0.110	Sep. 12	Sep. 28	Oct. 02	Oct. 16 '95

Data as orig. reptd.; bef. results of disc. opers. and/or spec. items. Per share data adj. for stk. divs. as of ex-div. date. E-Estimated. NA-Not Available. NM-Not Meaningful. NR-Not Ranked.

Office—1332 Blue Hills Ave., P.O. Box 1, Bloomfield, CT 06002. **Tel**—(203) 243-7100. **Chrmn & CEO**—C. H. Kaman. **Pres & COO**—H. S. Levenson. **SVP & CFO**—R. M. Garneau. **VP & Secy**—G. M. Messemer. **Investor Contact**—J. Kenneth Nasshan (203-243-7319). **Dirs**—E. R. Callaway, III, F. C. Carlucci, J. A. DiBiaggio, E. J. Gaines, H. Hardisty, C. H. Kaman, C. W. Kaman, II, E. S. Kraus, H. Z. Lebed, H. S. Levenson, W. H. Monteith, Jr., J. S. Murtha, W. L. Rogers. **Transfer Agent**—Chemical Bank, NYC. **Incorporated** in Connecticut in 1945. **Empl**-5,239. **S&P Analyst:** J.C.

STANDARD & POOR'S

STOCK REPORTS

Kasler Holding Co.

NYSE Symbol **KAS**
In S&P SmallCap 600

01-NOV-95 **Industry:** Building

Summary: Kasler performs general contracting work, specializing in the construction of concrete roadways, bridges and other public works projects.

Quantitative Evaluations

Outlook
(1 Lowest—5 Highest)
• **NA**

Fair Value
• **NA**

Risk
• **High**

Earn./Div. Rank
• **B-**

Technical Eval.
• **Bearish** since 7/95

Rel. Strength Rank
(1 Lowest—99 Highest)
• **40**

Insider Activity
• **Neutral**

Recent Price • 5¾
52 Wk Range • 6¾-3⅞
Yield • Nil
12-Mo. P/E • 38.3

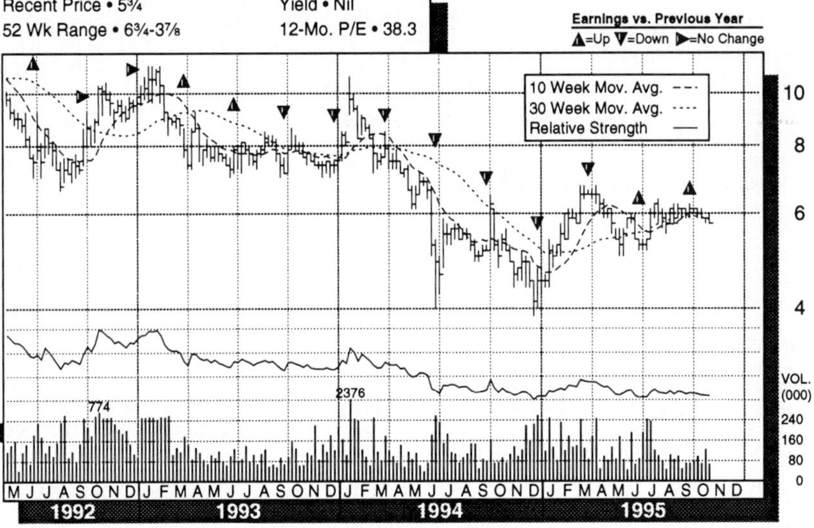

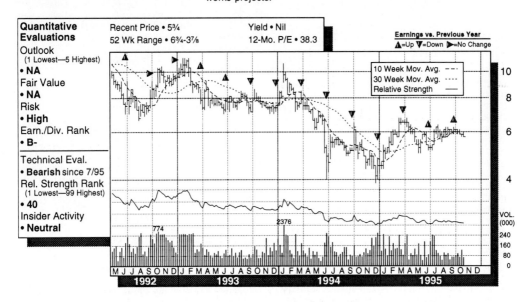

Business Profile - 01-NOV-95

In 1994, Kasler began to implement new business strategies aimed at improving profitability. New budgeting and cost-control programs were put in place to make the company more cost-effective and competitive, and greater profit and loss accountability was assigned to individual operating units. The estimating staff was strengthened and expanded. The programs contributed to greater profitability in the first nine months of fiscal 1995 (Nov.), despite lower revenues.

Operational Review - 01-NOV-95

Revenues in the first nine months of fiscal 1995 fell 17%, year to year, reflecting weather delays and reducted large-scale earthquake repair activity. Results benefited from new cost-control programs, a more favorable project mix, greater investment income, and larger gains on the sale of equipment. Net income rose 2.4-fold, to $5.2 million ($0.18 a share), from $1.5 million ($0.05). Backlog at August 31, 1995, totaled $284 million, up from $207 million a year earlier.

Stock Performance - 27-OCT-95

In the past 30 trading days, KAS's shares have declined 4%, compared to a 0.63% fall in the S&P 500. Average trading volume for the past five days was 12,680 shares, compared with the 40-day moving average of 15,421 shares.

Key Stock Statistics

Dividend Rate/Share	Nil	Shareholders	1,100
Shs. outstg. (M)	29.5	Market cap. (B)	$0.170
Avg. daily vol. (M)	0.018	Inst. holdings	9%
Tang. Bk. Value/Share	3.63	Insider holdings	NA
Beta	1.80		

Value of $10,000 invested 5 years ago: $ 10,063

Fiscal Year Ending Nov. 30

	1995	% Change	1994	% Change	1993	% Change
Revenues (Million $)						
1Q	36.78	-27%	50.50	NM	14.80	-63%
2Q	51.60	-19%	63.75	116%	29.50	-23%
3Q	71.87	-8%	78.49	6%	74.20	89%
4Q	—	—	65.96	-28%	91.70	107%
Yr.	—	—	258.7	23%	210.2	-29%
Income (Million $)						
1Q	0.66	-37%	1.05	18%	0.89	-43%
2Q	1.57	NM	-2.22	NM	0.91	-41%
3Q	3.01	11%	2.70	-11%	3.03	88%
4Q	—	—	-0.87	NM	0.28	-84%
Yr.	—	—	0.66	-93%	8.98	-53%
Earnings Per Share ($)						
1Q	0.02	-50%	0.04	-76%	0.17	6%
2Q	0.06	NM	-0.08	NM	0.17	13%
3Q	0.10	11%	0.09	-36%	0.14	-13%
4Q	—	—	-0.03	NM	0.01	-94%
Yr.	—	—	0.02	-95%	0.39	-40%

Next earnings report expected: mid January

Kasler Holding Co.

Business Summary - 01-NOV-95

Kasler Holding Company (formerly Kasler Corp.) is a diversified heavy-construction company that concentrates on the infrastructure, environmental remediation and contract mining markets. It acts as prime contractor or in joint ventures with other contractors on construction projects in California and other western states. The July 1993 combination of Washington Contractors Group Inc. with Kasler Corp. to form Kasler Holding allowed the company to expand into markets in western states and private-sector projects. Revenue contribution by major lines of business in recent years were:

	1994	1993
Infrastructure	82%	62%
Environmental remediation	9%	17%
Contract mining	9%	21%

Kasler is licensed to do business in 23 western states and operates in the geographic area west of the Mississippi River.

For roadways and bridges, the company acts as prime contractor in most of the construction projects it undertakes. Although the majority of projects are completed within two years, Kasler also engages in projects of longer duration. As prime contractor, it manages the project and is responsible for the performance of all principal construction and other aspects of the project. Company construction crews typically prepare the roadbed, lay the concrete roadway, install drainage facilities and construct bridges, overpasses and other crossing structures.

With respect to airport projects, Kasler has constructed roadways, bridges, runways and taxiways in connection with construction or expansion projects at major airports throughout the U.S. The company's concrete paving capability also lends itself to the construction of these and other large surface concrete placements.

The company also provides contract mining services for such diverse surface mining operations as phosphate, gold, molybdenum, silica and limestone. In addition, KAS contracts to construct waste disposal sites and removes, transports and deposits contaminated materials according to customer designs and specifications developed in accordance with governmental procedures and regulations.

Important Developments

Sep. '95—Kasler said its Washington Contractors Group had been awarded six new contracts totaling $31 million, boosting total backlog over $300 million. Separately, the company said it had obtained a new $60 million bank credit facility, for general corporate purposes.

Capitalization

Long Term Debt: $5,389,000 (2/95).

Per Share Data ($) (Year Ended Nov. 30)

	1994	1993	1992	1991	1990	1989
Tangible Bk. Val.	3.53	3.53	4.31	3.68	2.50	2.11
Cash Flow	0.34	0.96	0.90	0.91	0.68	0.48
Earnings	0.02	0.39	0.65	0.61	0.39	0.18
Dividends	0.05	0.10	0.10	0.09	0.07	0.07
Payout Ratio	NM	33%	15%	16%	17%	38%
Prices - High	10$\frac{3}{4}$	11$\frac{1}{4}$	13$\frac{3}{8}$	15$\frac{1}{2}$	9$\frac{1}{8}$	7$\frac{1}{2}$
- Low	3$\frac{7}{8}$	7	6$\frac{5}{8}$	7$\frac{3}{8}$	5$\frac{5}{8}$	5
P/E Ratio - High	NM	38	21	25	23	42
- Low	NM	23	10	12	14	28

Income Statement Analysis (Million $)

	1994	%Chg	1993	%Chg	1992	%Chg	1991
Revs.	259	23%	210	30%	162	-17%	195
Oper. Inc.	6.7	-65%	18.9	77%	10.7	13%	9.5
Depr.	9.2	-9%	10.1	NM	2.5	-11%	2.8
Int. Exp.	0.1	-25%	0.1	—	Nil	—	0.3
Pretax Inc.	1.0	-91%	11.2	13%	9.9	14%	8.7
Eff. Tax Rate	35%	—	38%	—	35%	—	35%
Net Inc.	0.7	-90%	6.9	7%	6.5	14%	5.7

Balance Sheet & Other Fin. Data (Million $)

	1994	1993	1992	1991	1990	1989
Cash	44.9	53.0	45.1	47.5	44.9	33.0
Curr. Assets	114	118	66.4	73.9	67.9	55.3
Total Assets	182	181	78.8	85.9	79.8	65.4
Curr. Liab.	46.4	52.5	32.9	46.9	46.3	28.1
LT Debt	5.5	Nil	Nil	Nil	11.2	18.5
Common Eqty.	120	120	43.3	36.7	19.9	16.5
Total Cap.	136	129	45.8	39.0	33.4	37.4
Cap. Exp.	14.8	35.2	3.4	3.9	4.0	1.9
Cash Flow	9.9	17.0	9.0	8.5	5.3	3.7

Ratio Analysis

	1994	1993	1992	1991	1990	1989
Curr. Ratio	2.5	2.3	2.0	1.6	1.5	2.0
% LT Debt of Cap.	4.0	Nil	Nil	Nil	33.5	49.5
% Net Inc.of Revs.	0.3	3.3	4.0	2.9	2.0	1.2
% Ret. on Assets	0.4	3.4	7.8	6.1	4.2	2.3
% Ret. on Equity	0.5	5.6	16.1	18.4	16.9	8.7

Dividend Data —Cash distributions, omitted in 1985, resumed in 1989 on a semiannual basis. In July 1994, the company said it would omit its semiannual dividend payable in August 1994, because of a loss in the fiscal 1994 second quarter. Kasler plans to reinstate common dividends once it is prudent to do so.

Data as orig. reptd.; bef. results of disc. opers. and/or spec. items. Per share data adj. for stk. divs. as of ex-div. date. E-Estimated. NA-Not Available. NM-Not Meaningful. NR-Not Ranked.

Office—27400 E. 5th St., Highland, CA 92346. **Tel**—(909) 884-4811. **Fax**—(909) 862-8433. **Chrmn**—D. Parkinson. **Pres & CEO**—J. H. Wimberly. **VP, CFO & Investor Contact**—G. J. Rutherford. **VP & Secy**—E. D. Hughes. **Investor Contact**—Richard Guiss. **Dirs**—D. H. Batchelder, R. G. Hunt, L. R. Judd, D. Parkinson, T. W. Payne, R. G. Reid, V. O. Smith, R. G. Wallace, J. H. Wimberly. **Transfer Agent & Registrar**—Chemical Trust Co. of California, LA. **Incorporated** in California in 1961; reincorporated in Delaware in 1993. **Empl**-212. **S&P Analyst:** J.C.

STANDARD & POOR'S

STOCK REPORTS

Kellwood Co.

NYSE Symbol **KWD**
In S&P SmallCap 600

29-SEP-95

Industry: Textiles

Summary: Kellwood is a global manufacturer and marketer of apparel and recreational camping products, offering 170 brands as well as private label products.

S&P Opinion: Accumulate (★★★★)

Recent Price • 20⅝
52 Wk Range • 24⅛-16½
Yield • 2.9%
12-Mo. P/E • 71.1

Quantitative Evaluations

Outlook (1 Lowest—5 Highest)
• **3+**

Fair Value
• **20½**

Risk
• **Average**

Earn./Div. Rank
• **B**

Technical Eval.
• **Bearish** since 9/93

Rel. Strength Rank (1 Lowest—99 Highest)
• **44**

Insider Activity
• **Neutral**

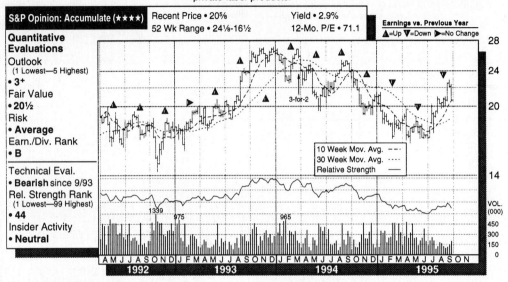

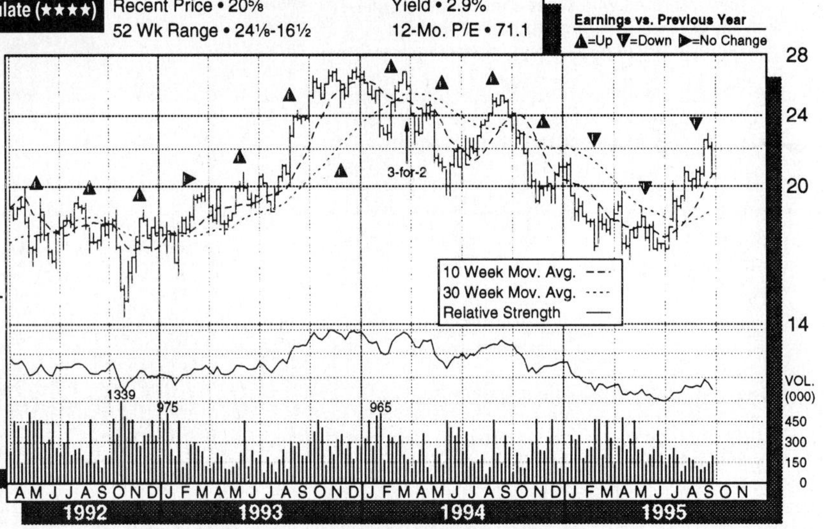

Overview - 29-SEP-95

Despite the weak apparel retail environment, sales should continue in an uptrend on greater volume of brand name merchandise (the company plans to have 75% of its total sales consist of branded apparel), increased market penetration, new divisions, global expansion, licensing agreements, and a wider array of product offerings. Acquisitions made in 1994-95 will contribute to sales growth, as well higher sales of the new Kathie Lee Collection by Halmode in Wal-Mart. Margins should widen on the increased volume, higher sales of more profitable brand name merchandise, more efficient sourcing and plant utilization, and the absence of a one-time after tax charge of $14 million ($0.65 a share). Over the longer term, KWD hopes to grow sales at 10%-12% and earnings at 15%-20% annually.

Valuation - 29-SEP-95

We continue to recommend the shares, based on our view that KWD is quickly gaining market share. We expect 1994-95's problems, including a one-time $14 after tax million charge to close a Smart Shirts plant in Saipan, will be absent in 1995-96, and earnings growth should resume. Thanks to strategies to diversify its product mix into brands, broaden distribution, and increase its domestic and overseas sourcing, KWD is one of the best-positioned apparel makers to benefit from mass merchandisers' and discounters' push to broaden and upgrade their apparel offerings. We think these shares are significantly undervalued and recommend them for capital appreciation.

Key Stock Statistics

S&P EPS Est. 1996	1.90	Tang. Bk. Value/Share	8.69
P/E on S&P Est. 1996	10.9	Beta	1.65
S&P EPS Est. 1997	2.30	Shareholders	1,800
Dividend Rate/Share	0.60	Market cap. (B)	$0.433
Shs. outstg. (M)	21.1	Inst. holdings	81%
Avg. daily vol. (M)	0.033	Insider holdings	NA

Value of $10,000 invested 5 years ago: $ 16,950

Fiscal Year Ending Apr. 30

	1996	% Change	1995	% Change	1994	% Change
Revenues (Million $)						
1Q	340.6	13%	300.9	NM	298.5	19%
2Q	—	—	376.0	10%	342.1	21%
3Q	—	—	291.5	16%	251.6	7%
4Q	—	—	396.3	27%	311.0	NM
Yr.	—	—	1,365	13%	1,203	12%
Income (Million $)						
1Q	5.64	-47%	10.71	8%	9.91	—
2Q	—	—	11.12	4%	10.71	—
3Q	—	—	-2.02	NM	3.51	42%
4Q	—	—	-8.71	NM	11.49	11%
Yr.	—	—	11.10	-69%	35.61	24%
Earnings Per Share ($)						
1Q	0.27	-47%	0.51	6%	0.48	18%
2Q	E0.55	4%	0.53	4%	0.51	42%
3Q	E0.25	NM	-0.10	NM	0.17	42%
4Q	E0.84	NM	-0.41	NM	0.55	10%
Yr.	E1.90	NM	0.53	-69%	1.71	23%

Next earnings report expected: late November

Kellwood Co.

Business Summary - 29-SEP-95

Kellwood primarily manufactures and markets apparel, but also produces recreational camping products. In late 1994, the company sold its home fashions division. During the second half of the 1980s, the company implemented a strategy to expand its branded label products, broaden its customer base, increase its channels of distribution, and further develop its global product sourcing capability. In line with this strategy, Kellwood has acquired over 14 domestic companies since 1985 (excluding those made in 1995-96). As a result of these efforts, sales to Sears declined to 8% of total sales in 1994-95, from 50% in 1984-85. Sales to J. C. Penney Company, Inc. made up about 10% of 1994-95's sales.

Kellwood conducts its business through three business portfolios - brand name apparel (70% of 1994-95 sales), private label apparel (17%), and the Hong Kong-based Smart Shirts division (13%). Smart Shirts produces private label shirts sold mainly in North America. Women's apparel is mainly produced, but also some men's and children's apparel. Apparel is produced through company owned-plants in the U.S. or overseas, or through outside contractors in the U.S. and overseas.

Kellwood's products are sold in over 25,000 stores in the U.S., and in an increasing number of outlets in Mexico and Canada. The company's output is sold through department stores, specialty stores, discounters, national chains, mail order, and miscellaneous outlets.

Kellwood also makes recreational products through American Recreational Products Inc.

Important Developments

Aug. '95—Despite a 13% rise in sales for the first quarter of 1995-96, earnings fell 47%, to $0.27 a share from $0.51 in the year-earlier period. The company attributed this decline to poor results posted by business units that were consolidated and repositioned during the second half of 1994-95. The company also said that margin pressure and higher interest charges associated with KWD's last two acquisitions affected first quarter earnings. Looking ahead, the company said that it was optimistic that earnings growth would return for the remainder of 1995-96. KWD said that it had completed various steps to improve profitability, including closing the unprofitable Smart Shirts' Saipan facility, and acquiring the license to produce dress shirts under the Nautica name.

Capitalization

Long Term Debt: $141,405,000 (7/31/95), incl. $852,000 of 9% debs. due 1999, conv. into com. at $6.33 a sh.

Per Share Data ($) (Year Ended Apr. 30)

	1995	1994	1993	1992	1991	1990
Tangible Bk. Val.	8.36	9.51	8.87	9.40	7.68	7.51
Cash Flow	1.87	2.91	2.42	2.29	1.70	1.78
Earnings	0.53	1.71	1.39	1.26	0.71	0.80
Dividends	0.60	0.55	0.53	0.53	0.53	0.53
Payout Ratio	113%	32%	38%	48%	76%	67%
Cal. Yrs.	1994	1993	1992	1991	1990	1989
Prices - High	26 7/8	27 1/8	22 1/8	17 7/8	15 1/4	23 5/8
- Low	19 1/8	15 7/8	14 1/4	6 1/4	3 1/2	13 5/8
P/E Ratio - High	51	16	16	14	22	29
- Low	36	9	10	5	5	17

Income Statement Analysis (Million $)

	1995	%Chg	1994	%Chg	1993	%Chg	1992
Revs.	1,365	13%	1,203	12%	1,078	18%	915
Oper. Inc.	87.4	-9%	96.1	20%	80.0	21%	66.0
Depr.	28.3	13%	25.1	18%	21.3	15%	18.5
Int. Exp.	19.1	22%	15.6	13%	13.8	-3%	14.2
Pretax Inc.	28.5	-53%	61.0	18%	51.9	25%	41.5
Eff. Tax Rate	61%	—	42%	—	45%	—	45%
Net Inc.	11.1	-69%	35.6	24%	28.7	26%	22.8

Balance Sheet & Other Fin. Data (Million $)

	1995	1994	1993	1992	1991	1990
Cash	11.1	17.7	39.2	40.8	41.3	44.1
Curr. Assets	511	413	426	364	321	310
Total Assets	768	642	636	538	484	469
Curr. Liab.	274	151	228	145	143	128
LT Debt	145	153	103	111	120	128
Common Eqty.	308	307	280	260	200	197
Total Cap.	491	490	407	389	338	337
Cap. Exp.	11.7	12.5	16.8	12.6	10.4	9.7
Cash Flow	39.4	60.7	50.0	41.4	30.0	31.3

Ratio Analysis

	1995	1994	1993	1992	1991	1990
Curr. Ratio	1.9	2.7	1.9	2.5	2.2	2.4
% LT Debt of Cap.	29.5	31.2	25.3	28.4	35.5	38.0
% Net Inc.of Revs.	0.8	3.0	2.7	2.5	1.5	1.8
% Ret. on Assets	1.6	5.5	4.9	4.2	2.6	3.0
% Ret. on Equity	3.6	12.1	10.6	9.3	6.3	7.2

Dividend Data —Dividends have been paid since 1962. A dividend reinvestment plan is available. A "poison pill" stock purchase rights plan was adopted in 1986.

Amt. of Div. $	Date Decl.	Ex-Div. Date	Stock of Record	Payment Date
0.150	Nov. 22	Nov. 28	Dec. 02	Dec. 16 '94
0.150	Feb. 23	Feb. 28	Mar. 06	Mar. 17 '95
0.150	Jun. 01	Jun. 08	Jun. 12	Jun. 23 '95
0.150	Aug. 24	Aug. 31	Sep. 05	Sep. 18 '95

Data as orig. reptd.; bef. results of disc. opers. and/or spec. items. Per share data adj. for stk. divs. as of ex-div. date. E-Estimated. NA-Not Available. NM-Not Meaningful. NR-Not Ranked.

Office—600 Kellwood Parkway (P.O. Box 14374), St. Louis, MO 63178. **Tel**—(314) 576-3100. **Chrmn Emeritus**—F. W. Wenzel. **Chrmn & CEO**—W. J. McKenna. **Vice Chrmn**—J. C. Jacobsen. **Pres & COO**—H. J. Upbin. **VP-Secy**—T. H. Pollihan. **Dirs**—R. F. Bentele, E. S. Bottum, K. G. Dickerson, W. Y. Fung, L. Genovese, J. M. Hunter, J. C. Jacobsen, J. S. Marcus, W. J. McKenna, H. J. Upbin, F. W. Wenzel. **Transfer Agent & Registrar**—KeyCorp. Shareholder Services, Inc., Cleveland, Ohio. **Incorporated** in Delaware in 1961. **Empl**-17,300. **S&P Analyst:** Elizabeth Vandeventer

STANDARD & POOR'S

STOCK REPORTS

KEMET Corp.

NASDAQ Symbol **KMET**

In S&P SmallCap 600

12-OCT-95

Industry: Electronics/Electric

Summary: KEMET is the largest manufacturer and supplier of solid tantalum capacitors and the second largest manufacturer and supplier of multi-layer ceramic capacitors in the U.S.

Quantitative Evaluations

Outlook
(1 Lowest—5 Highest)
• **NA**

Fair Value
• **NA**

Risk
• **Average**

Earn./Div. Rank
• **NR**

Technical Eval.
• **Bullish** since 4/94

Rel. Strength Rank
(1 Lowest—99 Highest)
• **21**

Insider Activity
• **Unfavorable**

Recent Price • 29¼ | Yield • Nil
52 Wk Range • 35¾-10⅛ | 12-Mo. P/E • 30.8

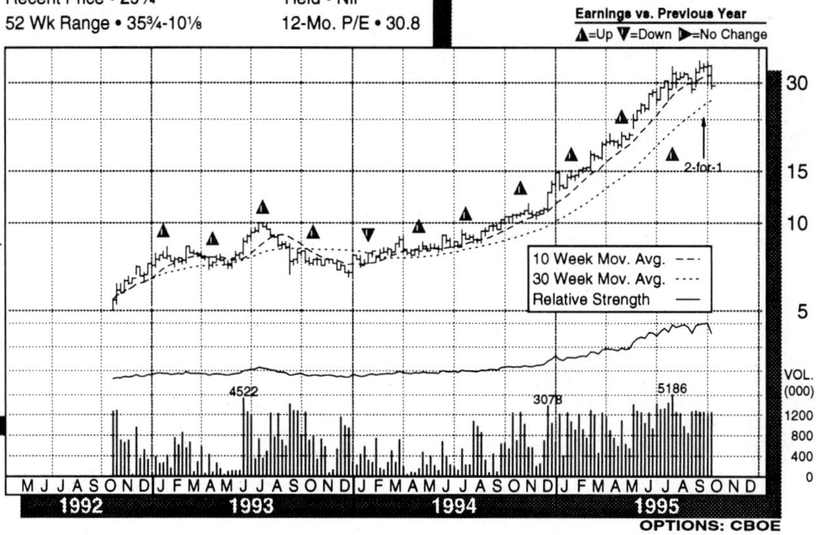

OPTIONS: CBOE

Business Profile - 12-OCT-95

The largest manufacturer of solid tantalum capacitors and second largest manufacturer of multi-layer ceramic capacitors in the U.S., KEMET has been experiencing strong demand for its products both in the U.S. and abroad. To meet that demand, KEMET expanded its surface-mount capacity in fiscal 1994-95 to more than 9.5 billion units annually, up 35% from the year before. Further capacity expansion is planned for 1995-96, with capital expenditures expected to increase 82%.

Operational Review - 12-OCT-95

Net sales for the first quarter of fiscal 1995-96 advanced 38%, year to year, to record levels, led by a 55% gain in sales of surface-mount capacitors. Sales of leaded capacitors were up 14%, while export sales rose 54%. Profitability benefited from the higher volume and manufacturing efficiencies stemming from ongoing capacity expansions. Net income increased 96%. Earnings per share were equal to $0.32, versus $0.17, both adjusted for the September 1995 2-for-1 stock split.

Stock Performance - 06-OCT-95

In the past 30 trading days, KMET's shares have declined 6%, compared to a 4% rise in the S&P 500. Average trading volume for the past five days was 339,160 shares, compared with the 40-day moving average of 320,774 shares.

Key Stock Statistics

Dividend Rate/Share	Nil	Shareholders	200
Shs. outstg. (M)	38.1	Market cap. (B)	$ 1.1
Avg. daily vol. (M)	0.385	Inst. holdings	55%
Tang. Bk. Value/Share	2.28	Insider holdings	NA
Beta	NA		

Value of $10,000 invested 5 years ago: NA

Fiscal Year Ending Mar. 31

	1996	% Change	1995	% Change	1994	% Change
Revenues (Million $)						
1Q	152.5	38%	110.2	15%	96.20	16%
2Q	—	—	110.2	22%	90.50	7%
3Q	—	—	112.3	18%	95.04	11%
4Q	—	—	140.4	36%	103.4	9%
Yr.	—	—	473.2	23%	385.1	11%
Income (Million $)						
1Q	12.74	96%	6.49	60%	4.05	27%
2Q	—	—	6.38	109%	3.05	-3%
3Q	—	—	6.84	79%	3.82	17%
4Q	—	—	11.26	93%	5.83	27%
Yr.	—	—	30.97	85%	16.75	51%
Earnings Per Share ($)						
1Q	0.32	91%	0.17	36%	0.13	39%
2Q	—	—	0.17	106%	0.08	23%
3Q	—	—	0.17	75%	0.10	-9%
4Q	—	—	0.29	93%	0.15	7%
Yr.	—	—	0.80	76%	0.46	3%

Next earnings report expected: late October

KEMET Corp.

Business Summary - 11-OCT-95

KEMET manufactures solid tantalum and monolithic ceramic capacitors. It is the largest manufacturer and supplier of solid tantalum capacitors and the second largest manufacturer and supplier of multilayer ceramic capacitors in the U.S.

In 1994-95, about 7% of capacitors were sold under military specification standards for both military and commercial uses. Foreign sales (primarily Europe and Asia) accounted for about 39% of sales in 1994-95.

Capacitors store, filter and regulate energy and current flow and are used in a wide variety of electronic applications, including communication systems, data processing, personal computers, automotive electronic systems and military and aerospace systems.

KEMET's capacitors use two types of dielectrics--solid tantalum and multilayer ceramic--each accounting for about 50% of net sales. The choice of capacitor dielectric is determined by the engineering specifications and application of the component product into which the capacitor is incorporated. Tantalum and ceramic capacitors are commonly used in conjunction with integrated circuits and are best suited for applications requiring lower- to medium-capacitance values. Generally, ceramic capacitors are more cost-effective at lower capacitance values, while tantalum capacitors are more cost-effective at medium capacitance values.

The company's leaded capacitors are attached to a circuit board using lead wires. Its surface-mount capacitors are attached directly to a circuit board without wires. Demand has generally been evolving from leaded to surface-mount capacitors, which are more commonly used in new product designs that rely on higher-density circuit boards. Surface-mount capacitors accounted for 62% of net sales in 1994-95, up from 57% the year before.

Products are sold to a variety of original equipment manufacturers (OEMs) in a broad range of industries, including the computer, communications, automotive and military and aerospace industries. Some of KEMET's largest customers are AT&T, Ford Motor, General Motors, Hewlett-Packard, IBM, Motorola and TTI, Inc.

Important Developments

Jul. '95—KEMET said that the record sales and earnings reported for three consecutive quarters reflected the results of its increased capacity expansions over the past year. Separately, the company announced that it expected to increase capital expenditures for fiscal 1995-96 to $75 million from the $55 million previously planned, substantially all of which will be used to increase surface-mount manufacturing capacity.

Capitalization

Long Term Debt: $76,542,000 (3/95).

Per Share Data ($)

(Year Ended Mar. 31)

	1995	1994	1993	1992	1991	1990
Tangible Bk. Val.	1.92	1.09	1.68	-2.03	NA	NA
Cash Flow	2.97	1.11	1.43	1.84	NA	NA
Earnings	0.80	0.46	0.44	-2.20	NA	NA
Dividends	Nil	Nil	Nil	Nil	NA	NA
Payout Ratio	Nil	Nil	Nil	Nil	NA	NA
Cal. Yrs.	1994	1993	1992	1991	1990	1989
Prices - High	14⅞	10	7¼	NA	NA	NA
- Low	7	6½	5	NA	NA	NA
P/E Ratio - High	18	22	16	NA	NA	NA
- Low	9	14	11	NA	NA	NA

Income Statement Analysis (Million $)

	1995	%Chg	1994	%Chg	1993	%Chg	1992
Revs.	473	23%	385	11%	348	18%	294
Oper. Inc.	89.5	46%	61.3	-1%	62.2	36%	45.7
Depr.	26.3	7%	24.5	5%	23.3	-57%	54.0
Int. Exp.	6.9	-22%	8.9	-53%	19.1	-22%	24.6
Pretax Inc.	50.3	91%	26.4	26%	20.9	NM	-35.4
Eff. Tax Rate	39%	—	37%	—	37%	—	NM
Net Inc.	31.0	86%	16.7	50%	11.1	NM	-28.2

Balance Sheet & Other Fin. Data (Million $)

	1995	1994	1993	1992	1991	1990
Cash	4.2	2.6	2.3	1.7	NA	NA
Curr. Assets	128	115	103	86.0	NA	NA
Total Assets	387	362	353	339	NA	NA
Curr. Liab.	97.7	71.2	78.2	60.8	NA	NA
LT Debt	77.0	107	147	188	NA	NA
Common Eqty.	139	108	52.5	-29.5	NA	NA
Total Cap.	246	250	232	229	NA	NA
Cap. Exp.	42.8	29.3	23.1	23.3	NA	NA
Cash Flow	57.3	41.3	33.6	24.6	NA	NA

Ratio Analysis

	1995	1994	1993	1992	1991	1990
Curr. Ratio	1.3	1.6	1.3	1.4	NA	NA
% LT Debt of Cap.	31.1	43.0	63.3	82.2	NA	NA
% Net Inc.of Revs.	6.5	4.3	3.2	NM	NA	NA
% Ret. on Assets	8.3	4.3	2.1	NM	NA	NA
% Ret. on Equity	25.1	19.5	NM	NM	NA	NA

Dividend Data —No cash dividends have been paid. The company has said it does not expect to pay cash dividends in the foreseeable future.

Amt. of Div. $	Date Decl.	Ex-Div. Date	Stock of Record	Payment Date
2-for-1	Sep. 06	Sep. 21	Sep. 13	Sep. 20 '95

Data as orig. reptd.; bef. results of disc. opers. and/or spec. items. Per share data adj. for stk. divs. as of ex-div. date. E-Estimated. NA-Not Available. NM-Not Meaningful. NR-Not Ranked.

Office—2835 Kemet Way, Simpsonville, SC 29681. **Tel**—(803) 963-6300. **Chrmn & CEO**—D. E. Maguire. **Pres & COO**—C. E. Volpe. **CFO-Treas**—J. J. Jerozal. **VP-Secy & Investor Contact**—Glenn H. Spears (803-963-6674). **Dirs**—C. E. Corpening, S. A. Kohl, E. E. Maddrey II, D. E. Maguire, C. E. Volpe. **Transfer Agent & Registrar**—Wachovia Corp., Winston-Salem, N.C. **Incorporated** in Delaware in 1990. **Empl**-8,390. **S&P Analyst:** JJS

STANDARD & POOR'S STOCK REPORTS

Kent Electronics

NYSE Symbol **KNT**
In S&P SmallCap 600

01-OCT-95 **Industry:** Electronics/Electric

Summary: This Texas-based firm is a national specialty electronics distributor and a multi-plant custom contract manufacturer.

Quantitative Evaluations
Outlook
(1 Lowest—5 Highest)
• **NA**
Fair Value
• **NA**
Risk
• **Low**
Earn./Div. Rank
• **B+**

Technical Eval.
• **Bullish** since 9/93
Rel. Strength Rank
(1 Lowest—99 Highest)
• **81**
Insider Activity
• **Neutral**

Recent Price • 43⅞
52 Wk Range • 45-22⅜
Yield • Nil
12-Mo. P/E • 29.4

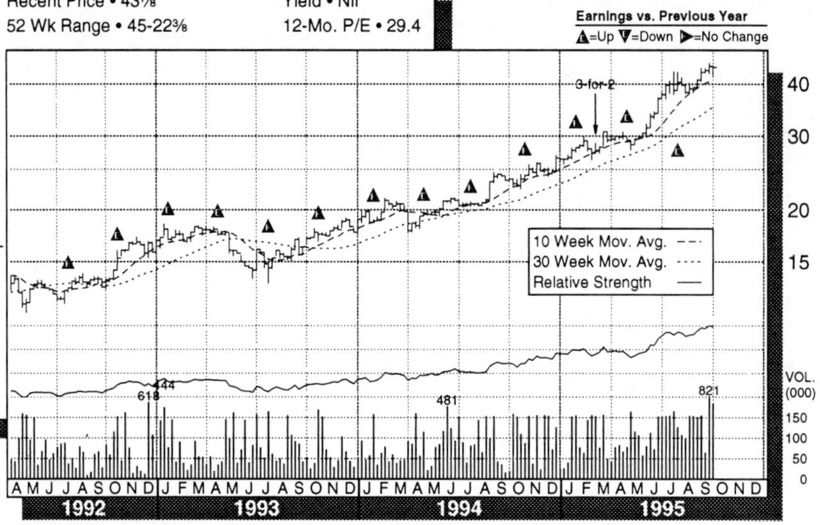

Business Profile - 27-SEP-95

This rapidly growing specialty electronics distributor and contract manufacturer is benefiting from strong growth in the electronics industry and an increase in its market share. It recently completed the sale of 2 million shares of common stock that will be used to extend its growth. The shares have risen steadily since 1991 and were recently trading near their all-time high.

Operational Review - 01-OCT-95

Net sales in the quarter ended July 1, 1995, increased 37%, year to year, reflecting a 46% increase in contract manufacturing and a 32% advance in the distribution business. The entire growth was internally generated, reflecting increased market share and a dynamic growing market. Margins widened on the higher volume, and pretax income soared 69%. After taxes at 40.0%, versus 38.5%, net income was up 65%.

Stock Performance - 29-SEP-95

In the past 30 trading days, KNT's shares have increased 13%, compared to a 5% rise in the S&P 500. Average trading volume for the past five days was 113,640 shares, compared with the 40-day moving average of 57,295 shares.

Key Stock Statistics

Dividend Rate/Share	Nil	Shareholders	1,100
Shs. outstg. (M)	11.8	Market cap. (B)	$0.519
Avg. daily vol. (M)	0.085	Inst. holdings	56%
Tang. Bk. Value/Share	10.27	Insider holdings	NA
Beta	1.24		

Value of $10,000 invested 5 years ago: $ 78,582

Fiscal Year Ending Mar. 31

	1996	% Change	1995	% Change	1994	% Change
Revenues (Million $)						
1Q	77.59	37%	56.53	31%	43.25	25%
2Q	—	—	60.34	29%	46.91	27%
3Q	—	—	64.46	31%	49.24	26%
4Q	—	—	72.16	35%	53.49	22%
Yr.	—	—	253.5	31%	192.9	25%
Income (Million $)						
1Q	4.68	65%	2.83	37%	2.07	12%
2Q	—	—	3.22	41%	2.29	20%
3Q	—	—	3.47	38%	2.51	29%
4Q	—	—	3.87	45%	2.66	31%
Yr.	—	—	13.39	40%	9.54	24%
Earnings Per Share ($)						
1Q	0.45	61%	0.28	31%	0.21	10%
2Q	—	—	0.32	37%	0.23	17%
3Q	—	—	0.34	34%	0.25	27%
4Q	—	—	0.38	42%	0.27	29%
Yr.	—	—	1.32	36%	0.97	21%

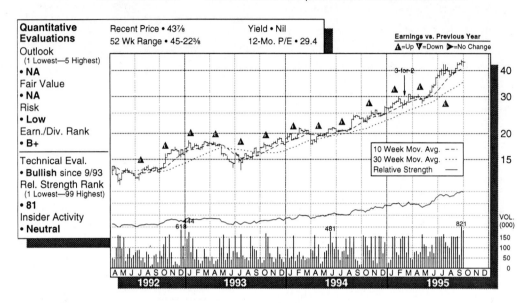

Next earnings report expected: mid October

Kent Electronics

Business Summary - 01-OCT-95

Kent Electronics is a leading national distributor of electronic products and a manufacturer of custom-made electronic assemblies. Sales contributions in recent fiscal years were:

	1994-95	1993-94	1992-93
Distribution	62%	66%	67%
Manufacturing	38%	34%	33%

The principal focus of the company's distribution business, conducted through its Components division, is to provide its industrial and original equipment manufacturer (OEM) customers with rapid and reliable deliveries of specialty wiring and connector products and other electronic components and assembled parts as well as a variety of material management services. Primary products include connectors, receptacles and sockets (19% of total company sales in 1994-95) and other electronic connecting components, such as cable and wiring products (8%).

Through Datacomm, the company serves the voice and data communications aftermarket. Datacomm offers a broad range of premise wiring products to commercial end-users and professionals who install or service voice and data communications networks. Through such a marketing approach, the company believes it is able to participate directly in the large and rapidly growing market for connection devices, reflecting the increasing use of microcomputers in LANs and the continued growth in networking and cabling needs of minicomputer and mainframe users.

Wholly owned K*TEC Electronics Corp. manufactures wiring harnesses, cable assemblies, other subassemblies and custom battery power packs, all of which are made to the specifications of individual customers.

Kent's customers are primarily industrial users and OEMs, served through 21 sales offices and distribution centers in Texas, California, Minnesota and 14 other states, and by manufacturing facilities in Texas and California. Kent has expanded its West Coast operations through a series of acquisitions. KNT's OEM customers serve many industries, including the computer and data processing, telecommunications, medical instrumentation, aerospace systems and energy industries.

Important Developments

Sep. '95—Kent sold in a public offering 2,000,000 shares of its common stock at $44.25 per share. The net proceeds from the offering are expected to be used for construction of new facilities, development and implementation of new information systems, working capital, general corporate purposes, and acquisitions of complementary businesses or assets.

Capitalization

Long Term Debt: None (7/95).

Per Share Data ($) (Year Ended Mar. 31)

	1995	1994	1993	1992	1991	1990
Tangible Bk. Val.	9.75	8.15	6.66	5.69	3.86	3.12
Cash Flow	1.70	1.29	1.09	0.89	0.85	0.68
Earnings	1.32	0.97	0.80	0.69	0.63	0.53
Dividends	Nil	Nil	Nil	Nil	Nil	Nil
Payout Ratio	Nil	Nil	Nil	Nil	Nil	Nil
Cal. Yrs.	1994	1993	1992	1991	1990	1989
Prices - High	27	19 1/8	17 1/4	13 5/8	9 7/8	6 1/4
- Low	17 5/8	13 3/8	11 3/8	7 1/8	4 7/8	3 3/4
P/E Ratio - High	20	20	22	20	16	12
- Low	13	14	14	10	8	7

Income Statement Analysis (Million $)

	1995	%Chg	1994	%Chg	1993	%Chg	1992
Revs.	253	31%	193	25%	155	64%	94.7
Oper. Inc.	24.8	39%	17.8	24%	14.3	48%	9.7
Depr.	3.8	19%	3.2	13%	2.8	62%	1.8
Int. Exp.	0.0	NM	0.0	NM	0.0	-50%	0.0
Pretax Inc.	22.1	44%	15.4	26%	12.2	33%	9.2
Eff. Tax Rate	39%	—	38%	—	37%	—	37%
Net Inc.	13.4	40%	9.5	24%	7.7	34%	5.8

Balance Sheet & Other Fin. Data (Million $)

	1995	1994	1993	1992	1991	1990
Cash	21.3	26.6	22.2	22.9	6.1	4.7
Curr. Assets	91.1	77.9	63.1	55.7	23.0	18.9
Total Assets	134	115	100	85.9	35.9	30.6
Curr. Liab.	24.8	22.0	16.7	13.6	6.7	5.9
LT Debt	Nil	Nil	Nil	Nil	0.7	0.8
Common Eqty.	109	92.5	81.7	71.6	28.1	23.7
Total Cap.	109	92.5	83.0	72.4	29.2	24.7
Cap. Exp.	10.0	5.8	9.2	5.7	1.9	2.0
Cash Flow	17.2	12.7	10.6	7.5	5.1	3.8

Ratio Analysis

	1995	1994	1993	1992	1991	1990
Curr. Ratio	3.7	3.5	3.8	4.1	3.4	3.2
% LT Debt of Cap.	Nil	Nil	Nil	Nil	2.5	3.2
% Net Inc.of Revs.	5.3	4.9	5.0	6.1	5.3	6.2
% Ret. on Assets	10.7	8.9	8.2	8.1	11.3	10.7
% Ret. on Equity	13.2	10.9	10.0	9.9	14.4	13.4

Dividend Data —The company has not paid any dividends. A 3-for-2 stock split was paid March 1, 1995 to shareholders of record February 15.

Amt. of Div. $	Date Decl.	Ex-Div. Date	Stock of Record	Payment Date
3-for-2	Jan. 18	Mar. 02	Feb. 15	Mar. 01 '95

Data as orig. reptd.; bef. results of disc. opers. and/or spec. items. Per share data adj. for stk. divs. as of ex-div. date. E-Estimated. NA-Not Available. NM-Not Meaningful. NR-Not Ranked.

Office—7433 Harwin Drive, Houston, TX 77036-2015. **Tel**—(713) 780-7770. **Chrmn, Pres & CEO**—M. K. Abramson. **VP-Treas, Secy & Investor Contact**—Stephen J. Chapko. **Dirs**—M. K. Abramson, M. S. Levit, D. Siegel, R. C. Webb, A. L. Zimmerman. **Transfer Agent & Registrar**—Society National Bank, Dallas, Texas. **Incorporated** in Texas in 1973. **Empl**-957. **S&P Analyst:** P.H.V.

STANDARD & POOR'S

STOCK REPORTS

Kirby Corp.

ASE Symbol **KEX**
In S&P SmallCap 600

04-NOV-95 **Industry:** Shipping/shipbuilding

Summary: This company provides inland and offshore marine transportation, performs marine and rail diesel engine services, and has a 58% interest in Universal Insurance Co.

Quantitative Evaluations

Outlook
(1 Lowest—5 Highest)
• **NA**
Fair Value
• **NA**
Risk
• **Average**
Earn./Div. Rank
• **B-**

Technical Eval.
• **Bullish** since 10/95
Rel. Strength Rank
(1 Lowest—99 Highest)
• **85**
Insider Activity
• **NA**

Recent Price • 16⅝
52 Wk Range • 19¾-13
Yield • Nil
12-Mo. P/E • 46.2

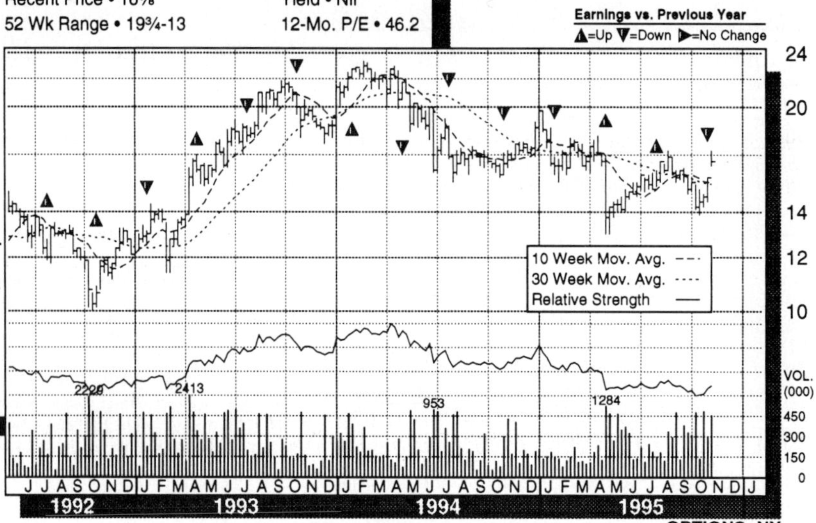

OPTIONS: NY

Overview - 12-JUL-95

Profits in 1995 will be paced by a stronger performance at Kirby's inland barge chemical division, reflecting the acquisition of the Dow Chemical fleet, increased fleet utilization, and the absence of 1994's difficult operating conditions. The inland refined products division will be plagued by weak spot market rates. After a weak first half reflecting reduced movements of heating oil to the Northeast, the offshore tanker fleet should experience a stronger second half performance as demand for reformulated gasoline absorbs excess industry capacity. The offshore dry bulk market should improve later in 1995, reflecting increased government cargo. Diesel repair services will benefit from improved industry conditions and the opening of a new facility in New Jersey. Contributions from insurance should grow, reflecting increased auto sales in Puerto Rico.

Valuation - 12-JUL-95

Shares of this marine transportation and insurance concern have underperformed the market since early 1994. Though barge industry fundamentals have improved, KEX has been unable to maintain its earlier growth rate that had been facilitated by 11 acquisitions since 1989. The long-term picture is favorable as more refiners and chemical processors are expected to outsource their transportation needs and increased demand for reformulated gasoline absorbs barge capacity. Though the company has begun to purchase shares, we still believe KEX will be only an average performer near term.

Key Stock Statistics

S&P EPS Est.	NA	Tang. Bk. Value/Share	7.78
P/E on S&P Est.	NM	Beta	1.15
Dividend Rate/Share	Nil	Shareholders	2,700
Shs. outstg. (M)	26.9	Market cap. (B)	$0.447
Avg. daily vol. (M)	0.085	Inst. holdings	60%
		Insider holdings	NA

Value of $10,000 invested 5 years ago: $ 17,733

Fiscal Year Ending Dec. 31

	1995	% Change	1994	% Change	1993	% Change
Revenues (Million $)						
1Q	118.6	16%	101.8	37%	74.38	51%
2Q	123.0	17%	104.7	11%	94.35	36%
3Q	104.3	-4%	108.1	10%	97.94	34%
4Q	—	—	118.5	6%	111.9	44%
Yr.	—	—	433.1	18%	368.6	42%
Income (Million $)						
1Q	4.81	66%	2.90	-25%	3.85	31%
2Q	5.08	59%	3.19	-51%	6.50	49%
3Q	-6.60	NM	3.61	-29%	5.05	2%
4Q	—	—	6.96	-6%	7.44	NM
Yr.	—	—	16.65	-27%	22.83	68%
Earnings Per Share ($)						
1Q	0.17	70%	0.10	-41%	0.17	31%
2Q	0.18	64%	0.11	-31%	0.16	-20%
3Q	-0.24	NM	0.13	-28%	0.18	-18%
4Q	E0.28	17%	0.24	-8%	0.26	NM
Yr.	—	—	0.58	-33%	0.86	43%

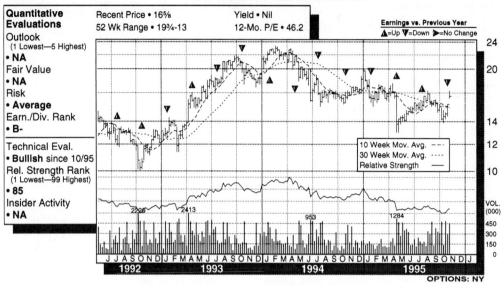

Next earnings report expected: late February

Kirby Corp.

Business Summary - 23-AUG-95

Kirby provides marine transportation and diesel engine repair services, and writes property and casualty insurance in Puerto Rico. Contributions to operating profits by business segment:

	1994	1993	1992
Transportation	79%	87%	88%
Diesel repair	8%	4%	8%
Insurance	13%	9%	4%

Kirby's marine transportation activities consist of inland barge operations and offshore barge, tanker, breakbulk and container services. The inland division operates a fleet of 505 tank barges, the nation's largest, and 130 tow and tugboats. About two-thirds of the inland division's revenues is derived from the transport of industrial and agricultural chemicals and petrochemical feedstock. The inland division also transports refined petroleum products and provides fleeting and shifting services. The offshore fleet consists of 11 tankers or tank barges and nine breakbulk or dry cargo vessels and nine tugboats. The offshore division transports petroleum products along the Gulf of Mexico and the Atlantic Coast and to international ports in the Caribbean Basin, provides dry bulk cargo service to ports in the U.S. Caribbean Basin and West Africa, and transports internationally dry bulk and containerized cargo primarily for U.S. government agencies.

Marine Systems, Inc. repairs and overhauls diesel engines used in the inland and offshore marine industries, at facilities in Louisiana, Virginia and Illinois, Washington and California. Parts sales provided 40% of 1994 revenues for these operations. In 1994, KEX launched a locomotive repair operation serving short line and industrial rail operators.

Universal Insurance Co. (58% owned) is a major writer of property and casualty insurance in the Commonwealth of Puerto Rico. In 1994, 43% of net premiums written were for automobile physical damage. Universal has been rated A+ by A.M. Best for the past 11 years.

Important Developments

Jun. '95—KEX reported that recent flooding conditions in the U.S. Midwest had resulted in the temporary closure of the upper Mississippi River. About 10% of KEX's inland tank barge fleet suffered disruptions because of the floods.

Jun. '95—KEX reported that it had repurchased 715,000 KEX common shares during 1995's second quarter under a 2,000,000 share (7%) buyback plan authorized in August 1994.

Nov. '94—KEX purchased 65 inland tank barges and three other vessels from Dow Chemical Co. for $24 million. It also assumed the leases on an additional 31 tank barges and two towboats.

Capitalization

Long Term Debt: $142,999,000 (3/95).

Per Share Data ($)

(Year Ended Dec. 31)

	1994	1993	1992	1991	1990	1989
Tangible Bk. Val.	7.41	7.04	4.96	4.99	4.31	3.65
Cash Flow	1.75	1.78	1.45	1.21	1.16	0.82
Earnings	0.58	0.86	0.60	0.61	0.60	0.39
Dividends	Nil	Nil	Nil	Nil	Nil	0.10
Payout Ratio	Nil	Nil	Nil	Nil	Nil	25%
Prices - High	23⅜	22	15½	16⅛	11⅛	9¾
- Low	15½	11⅜	10	7	6⅛	4⅜
P/E Ratio - High	40	26	26	26	19	25
- Low	27	13	17	11	10	11

Income Statement Analysis (Million $)

	1994	%Chg	1993	%Chg	1992	%Chg	1991
Revs.	433	15%	378	41%	269	44%	187
Oper. Inc.	74.6	8%	69.3	49%	46.6	34%	34.8
Depr.	33.8	38%	24.5	27%	19.3	45%	13.3
Int. Exp.	8.8	5%	8.4	-10%	9.4	57%	6.0
Pretax Inc.	30.3	-18%	36.9	97%	18.7	5%	17.8
Eff. Tax Rate	34%	—	34%	—	27%	—	26%
Net Inc.	16.7	-27%	22.8	68%	13.6	2%	13.3

Balance Sheet & Other Fin. Data (Million $)

	1994	1993	1992	1991	1990	1989
Cash	35.9	40.1	20.3	30.1	28.9	49.3
Curr. Assets	NA	NA	NA	NA	NA	NA
Total Assets	667	563	446	286	254	247
Curr. Liab.	NA	NA	NA	35.5	33.9	31.4
LT Debt	149	110	148	80.0	67.0	76.0
Common Eqty.	223	212	123	112	97.0	88.0
Total Cap.	432	377	309	199	169	165
Cap. Exp.	31.0	71.0	128	37.2	18.1	73.9
Cash Flow	50.5	47.3	32.9	26.6	26.4	18.8

Ratio Analysis

	1994	1993	1992	1991	1990	1989
Curr. Ratio	NA	NA	NA	NA	NA	NA
% LT Debt of Cap.	34.4	29.1	47.8	40.0	39.8	45.9
% Net Inc.of Revs.	3.8	6.0	5.1	7.1	7.8	6.4
% Ret. on Assets	2.7	4.1	3.7	4.9	5.5	4.3
% Ret. on Equity	7.6	12.5	11.4	12.8	14.9	10.7

Dividend Data —Special cash dividends of $0.10 a share were paid in 1988 and 1989.

Data as orig. reptd.; bef. results of disc. opers. and/or spec. items. Per share data adj. for stk. divs. as of ex-div. date. E-Estimated. NA-Not Available. NM-Not Meaningful. NR-Not Ranked.

Office—1775 St. James Place (P.O. Box 1745), Houston, TX 77251-1745. **Tel**—(713) 629-9370. **Chrmn**—G. A. Peterkin, Jr. **Pres & CEO**—J. H. Pyne. **SVP & Treas**—B. K. Harrington. **VP, Cont & Investor Contact**—G. S. Holcomb. **Secy**—H. Gilchrist. **Dirs**—G. F. Clements, Jr., J. P. Kleifgen, W. M. Lamont, Jr., C. W. Murchison III, G. A. Peterkin, Jr., J. H. Pyne, R. G. Stone, Jr., J. V. Waggoner. **Transfer Agent & Registrar**—Bank of Boston. **Incorporated** in Nevada in 1969. **Empl-** 2,300. **S&P Analyst:** Stephen R. Klein

Komag, Inc.

NASDAQ Symbol **KMAG**
In S&P SmallCap 600

24-OCT-95

Industry: Data Processing

Summary: This company is the largest independent maker of sputtered thin-film media used in Winchester disk drives.

S&P Opinion: Buy (★★★★★)

Recent Price • 67¾	Yield • Nil
52 Wk Range • 74⅞-22¼	12-Mo. P/E • 19.9

Quantitative Evaluations

Outlook
(1 Lowest—5 Highest)
• **NA**

Fair Value
• **NA**

Risk
• **Average**

Earn./Div. Rank
• **B-**

Technical Eval.
• **Bullish** since 9/95

Rel. Strength Rank
(1 Lowest—99 Highest)
• **89**

Insider Activity
• **Neutral**

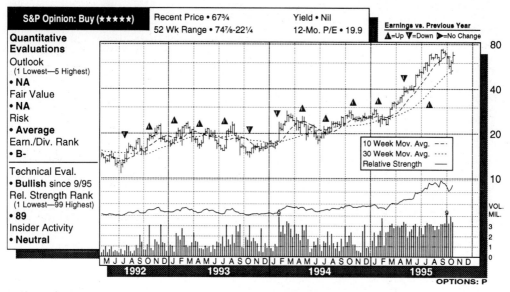

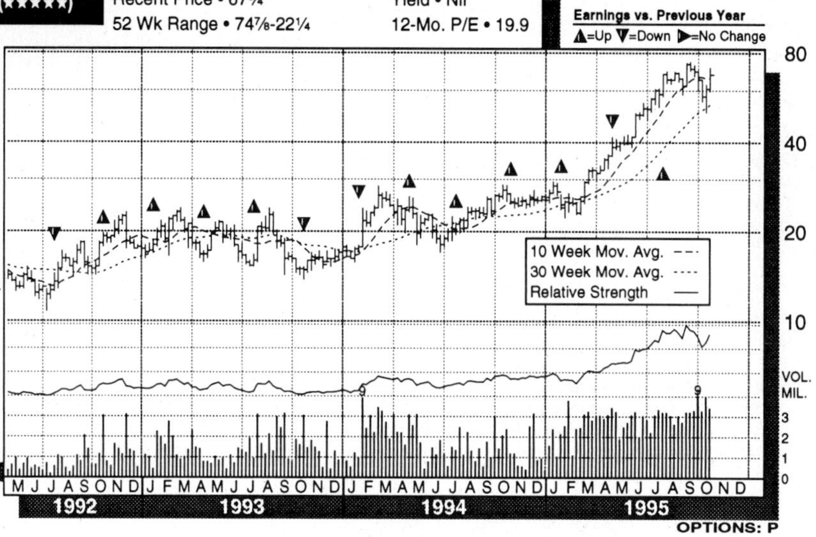

Overview - 24-OCT-95

Sales are expected to rise through 1996, reflecting higher unit shipments of thin-film media, as well as favorable pricing trends, aided by a more favorable mix of higher performance and more profitable media products. Revenue growth accelerated in the second quarter of 1995 and should continue to expand, reflecting the shipment of new products, increased efficiency of new media production lines and the installation of additional production lines. Margins are expected to benefit from the higher volume and a more favorable product mix, but should be restrained by large capital expenditures to increase Komag's manufacturing capabilities.

Valuation - 24-OCT-95

The shares of this leading vendor of magnetic media shot up this year on strong demand for its high-end media products. Komag has invested heavily over the years in increasing its production capacity as well as continuing to enhance the capabilities of its media offerings. It is well positioned in the high performance media market, and the company is poised to benefit from continued strong demand for its products. Earnings are projected to grow rapidly through 1996. The earnings multiple is modest and could continue to expand as investors gain confidence in Komag's successful execution of its business plan, which includes continued expansion of its manufacturing capabilities. The shares are expected to outperform the market in the months ahead.

Key Stock Statistics

S&P EPS Est. 1995	4.00	Tang. Bk. Value/Share	16.29
P/E on S&P Est. 1995	16.9	Beta	1.60
S&P EPS Est. 1996	5.00	Shareholders	400
Dividend Rate/Share	Nil	Market cap. (B)	$ 1.7
Shs. outstg. (M)	25.1	Inst. holdings	73%
Avg. daily vol. (M)	1.523	Insider holdings	NA

Value of $10,000 invested 5 years ago: $ 74,246

Fiscal Year Ending Dec. 31

	1995	% Change	1994	% Change	1993	% Change
Revenues (Million $)						
1Q	105.1	8%	97.70	4%	93.56	32%
2Q	120.8	24%	97.77	-5%	103.2	35%
3Q	132.8	35%	98.17	NM	97.45	18%
4Q	—	—	98.74	8%	91.19	-5%
Yr.	—	—	392.4	2%	385.4	18%
Income (Million $)						
1Q	14.88	-4%	15.44	102%	7.63	153%
2Q	23.36	67%	13.95	73%	8.06	139%
3Q	30.40	102%	15.02	NM	4.11	-33%
4Q	—	—	14.11	NM	-29.70	NM
Yr.	—	—	58.52	NM	-9.90	NM
Earnings Per Share ($)						
1Q	0.63	-7%	0.68	94%	0.35	150%
2Q	0.96	57%	0.61	65%	0.37	147%
3Q	1.21	86%	0.65	NM	0.19	-34%
4Q	E1.20	100%	0.60	NM	-1.37	NM
Yr.	E4.00	57%	2.54	NM	-0.46	NM

Next earnings report expected: early February

Komag, Inc.

Business Summary - 24-OCT-95

Komag develops, manufactures and markets sputtered thin-film media for use in high-capacity, high-performance 5.25-inch and smaller disk drive storage devices. The company believes it is the largest supplier of sputtered thin-film media used in disk drives and makes the highest-density disks commercially available for the 5.25-inch, 3.5-inch and smaller form factors. Komag exited the thin-film recording head business in the third quarter of 1994. Revenues by product segment in recent years were:

	1994	1993	1992
Media	100%	87%	86%
Heads	---	13%	14%

Media products are the disks or platters within a disk drive onto which information is recorded and stored, and from which it is retrieved. High density media are essential to the performance of high-capacity hard disk drives, which are in strong demand owing to the ever-greater processing power of computers, more sophisticated operating systems and application software, higher resolution graphics and larger databases.

Komag's production volume of media products depends on available capacity, utilization of capacity and production yield performance. In July 1995, the company had nine thin-film media sputtering lines operating in California, and four such lines in Malaysia, with a fifth line expected to be installed in the third quarter of 1995.

The company's 50%-owned Asahi Komag Co. joint venture is one of the three largest manufacturers of thin-film media in Japan and has four production lines in operation, with a fifth expected to begin operation in the third quarter of 1995.

The company sells its products to independent OEM disk drive manufacturers for incorporation into rigid disk drives marketed under the manufacturers' own labels. It also sells media to computer system manufacturers that produce their own disk drives.

Important Developments

Oct. '95—The company said sales of high performance 1800 Oe products made up 78% of unit shipments in the third quarter of 1995, versus 61% in the prior quarter. Komag also said it had started ramping higher performance 2000 Oe products.

Sep. '95—Komag sold publicly 1,750,000 common shares at $73 each. Proceeds from the offering will be used for capital expenditures to increase manufacturing capacity, and for general corporate purposes, including working capital.

Capitalization

Long Term Debt: None (10/1/95).
Minority Interest: $5,159,000.

Per Share Data ($) (Year Ended Dec. 31)

	1994	1993	1992	1991	1990	1989
Tangible Bk. Val.	14.46	11.73	11.80	9.86	7.85	5.84
Cash Flow	4.61	1.83	2.48	2.17	2.08	0.53
Earnings	2.54	-0.46	0.79	0.74	0.88	-0.46
Dividends	Nil	Nil	Nil	Nil	Nil	Nil
Payout Ratio	Nil	Nil	Nil	Nil	Nil	Nil
Prices - High	28⅞	24	23¼	24½	16⅛	11½
- Low	15¾	13¾	10¾	10¾	8½	6⅜
P/E Ratio - High	11	NM	29	33	18	NM
- Low	6	NM	14	15	10	NM

Income Statement Analysis (Million $)

	1994	%Chg	1993	%Chg	1992	%Chg	1991
Revs.	392	2%	385	18%	327	17%	279
Oper. Inc.	125	51%	82.7	46%	56.6	-4%	59.0
Depr.	47.6	-3%	49.0	35%	36.3	23%	29.4
Int. Exp.	2.9	-47%	5.5	45%	3.8	-33%	5.6
Pretax Inc.	82.8	NM	-2.5	NM	25.8	-16%	30.7
Eff. Tax Rate	28%	—	NM	—	71%	—	48%
Net Inc.	58.5	NM	-9.9	NM	16.9	12%	15.1

Balance Sheet & Other Fin. Data (Million $)

	1994	1993	1992	1991	1990	1989
Cash	93.9	91.6	89.3	91.0	45.2	37.8
Curr. Assets	172	178	153	149	82.0	64.0
Total Assets	424	382	356	277	163	122
Curr. Liab.	53.3	85.9	55.5	51.7	24.0	19.3
LT Debt	16.3	29.5	27.6	16.5	19.9	21.8
Common Eqty.	331	255	249	202	115	77.0
Total Cap.	370	296	300	225	138	102
Cap. Exp.	102	86.0	109	60.2	40.3	24.7
Cash Flow	106	39.1	53.2	44.5	31.6	7.0

Ratio Analysis

	1994	1993	1992	1991	1990	1989
Curr. Ratio	3.2	2.1	2.8	2.9	3.4	3.3
% LT Debt of Cap.	4.4	10.0	9.2	7.3	14.4	21.4
% Net Inc.of Revs.	14.9	NM	5.2	5.4	8.9	NM
% Ret. on Assets	14.2	NM	5.3	6.0	9.0	NM
% Ret. on Equity	19.5	NM	7.4	8.3	13.3	NM

Dividend Data —No cash dividends have been paid.

Data as orig. reptd.; bef. results of disc. opers. and/or spec. items. Per share data adj. for stk. divs. as of ex-div. date. E-Estimated. NA-Not Available. NM-Not Meaningful. NR-Not Ranked.

Office—275 South Hillview Dr., Milpitas, CA 95035. **Tel**—(408) 946-2300. **Pres & CEO**—S. C. Johnson. **Chrmn**—T. Chen. **VP-CFO & Secy**—W. L. Potts, Jr. **Investor Contact**—David H. Allen. **Dirs**—C. R. Barrett, T. Chen, C. A. Eyre, I. Federman, S. C. Johnson, G. A. Neil, M. Palevsky, A. Sun, M. Takebayashi. **Transfer Agent & Registrar**—Chemical Trust Co. of California, SF. **Incorporated** in Delaware in 1986. **Empl**-2,635. **S&P Analyst:** Peter C. Wood, CFA

Kuhlman Corp.

NYSE Symbol **KUH**
In S&P SmallCap 600

03-AUG-95 **Industry:** Electronics/Electric

Summary: This holding company primarily manufactures electrical transformers, wire and cable products, and, through the May 1995 acquisition of Schwitzer Inc., engine components.

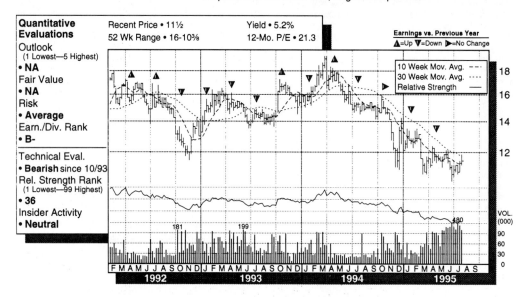

Quantitative Evaluations
Outlook
(1 Lowest—5 Highest)
• NA
Fair Value
• NA
Risk
• Average
Earn./Div. Rank
• B-

Technical Eval.
• Bearish since 10/93
Rel. Strength Rank
(1 Lowest—99 Highest)
• 36
Insider Activity
• Neutral

Recent Price • 11½ | Yield • 5.2%
52 Wk Range • 16-10⅜ | 12-Mo. P/E • 21.3

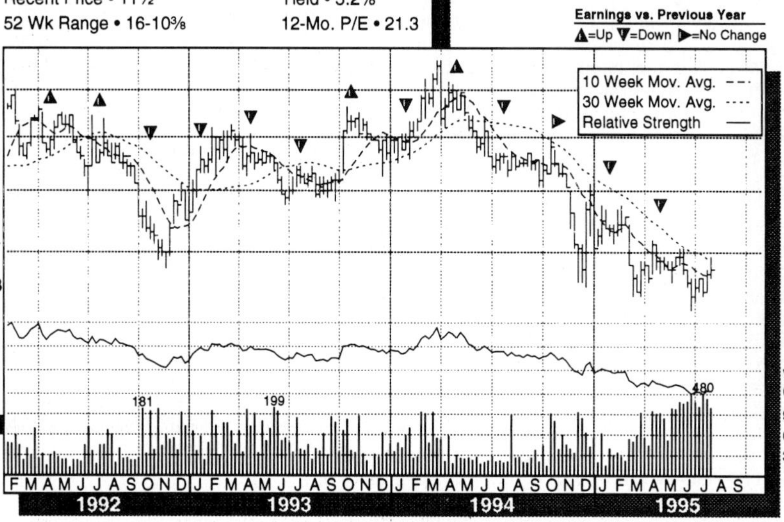

Business Profile - 03-AUG-95

This manufacturer of electric transformers and wire and cable products significantly expanded the scope of its operations with the May 1995 acquisition of Schwitzer Inc., a maker of engine components. KUH issued about 6.9 million new shares for Schwitzer, doubling the number of Kuhlman shares outstanding. The merger should benefit Kuhlman immediately, as SCZ earned $7.3 million more than KUH in 1994 on lower revenues.

Operational Review - 03-AUG-95

Net sales in the six months ended June 30, 1995, rose 7.6%, year to year, as restated for Schwitzer, reflecting continuing strong demand for the company's products. Gross margins narrowed, and results were further penalized by $4.5 million of merger expenses. Income fell to $0.21 a share from $0.40, excluding a special charge of $1.8 million ($0.14 a share). The shares, which are currently trading at about 21X trailing 12 months pro forma earnings, have fallen sharply since early 1994.

Stock Performance - 28-JUL-95

In the past 30 trading days, KUH's shares have increased 3%, compared to a 4% rise in the S&P 500. Average trading volume for the past five days was 40,980 shares, compared with the 40-day moving average of 68,095 shares.

Key Stock Statistics

Dividend Rate/Share	0.60	Shareholders	4,300
Shs. outstg. (M)	13.2	Market cap. (B)	$0.155
Avg. daily vol. (M)	0.070	Inst. holdings	29%
Tang. Bk. Value/Share	1.64	Insider holdings	NA
Beta	0.88		

Value of $10,000 invested 5 years ago: $ 12,955

Fiscal Year Ending Dec. 31

	1995	% Change	1994	% Change	1993	% Change
Revenues (Million $)						
1Q	107.0	71%	62.42	129%	27.24	-17%
2Q	103.0	81%	56.99	97%	28.95	-11%
3Q	—	—	64.13	114%	29.99	5%
4Q	—	—	59.31	86%	31.92	15%
Yr.	—	—	242.9	106%	118.1	-3%
Income (Million $)						
1Q	3.58	NM	1.14	NM	-4.67	NM
2Q	-0.73	NM	0.30	-62%	0.78	-59%
3Q	—	—	1.29	2%	1.27	26%
4Q	—	—	-1.10	NM	0.92	-13%
Yr.	—	—	1.62	NM	-1.71	NM
Earnings Per Share ($)						
1Q	0.27	42%	0.19	NM	-0.80	NM
2Q	-0.06	NM	0.05	-62%	0.13	-59%
3Q	—	—	0.21	NM	0.21	24%
4Q	—	—	-0.18	NM	0.15	-17%
Yr.	—	—	0.27	NM	-0.29	NM

Next earnings report expected: early November

Kuhlman Corp.

Business Summary - 03-AUG-95

Kuhlman Corp. is a holding company whose subsidiaries are involved in the manufacture of distribution, power and instrument transformers; electrical and electronic wire and cable products; spring products; and, through the recent acquisition of Schwitzer Inc., turbochargers, fan drives, vibration dampers and other engine components used to improve the performance of diesel and gasoline engines.

Kuhlman Electric Corp., based in Versailles, Ky., and its wholly owned subsidiary Associated Engineering Co. manufacture and market electric utility and industrial-type transformers used in electric distribution systems serving residences and commercial and industrial buildings. These transformers range from small instrument transformers used in the metering and switching of electricity and pole-mounted, surface-mounted or underground transformers serving from one to eight residences, up to medium-size power transformers used in utility substations or commercial-type electrical power centers serving shopping centers, apartment complexes, factories and other users of electric power. These products are sold primarily to electric utilities throughout the U.S.

Coleman Holding Co. was acquired by the company in December 1993. Through its subsidiaries (primarily Coleman Cable Systems, Inc.), Coleman manufactures a wide range of commercial and consumer wire products, including bare copper and aluminum wire for utilities, portable wiring systems for the construction industry, and wire for security, heating and air conditioning. Coleman is divided into five divisions: Cable and Wire, Cord Products, Signal, Baron Wire & Cable Corp., and Nehring Electrical Works Co.

Emtec Products Corp., headquartered in Coldwater, Mich., manufactures a variety of springs and spring assembly products, as well as a limited number of marine products. Annual sales are about $8 million.

Backlog at December 31, 1994, totaled $28,775,000, down from $38,633,000 at year end 1993. The company expects substantially all of the backlog to be shipped during the year.

Important Developments

May '95—The company acquired Schwitzer, Inc. (NYSE;SCZ), a producer of advanced engine components based in Asheville, N.C. Schwitzer earned $8.9 million on $153 million in revenues in 1994. A total of approximately 6.9 million new shares of Kuhlman were issued in the merger.

Capitalization

Long Term Debt: $56,009,000 (3/95).

Per Share Data ($) (Year Ended Dec. 31)

	1994	1993	1992	1991	1990	1989
Tangible Bk. Val.	1.54	1.39	9.15	8.71	8.06	6.88
Cash Flow	1.18	0.18	1.51	1.78	1.84	1.94
Earnings	0.27	-0.29	1.05	1.21	1.03	0.92
Dividends	0.60	0.60	0.60	0.60	0.31	0.03
Payout Ratio	NM	NM	55%	48%	30%	3%
Prices - High	19⅜	17¼	18	18	12⅝	16½
- Low	11	13¼	11½	9¾	8½	9
P/E Ratio - High	72	NM	17	15	12	18
- Low	41	NM	11	8	8	10

Income Statement Analysis (Million $)

	1994	%Chg	1993	%Chg	1992	%Chg	1991
Revs.	243	106%	118	-3%	122	-3%	126
Oper. Inc.	11.8	157%	4.6	-60%	11.6	-21%	14.7
Depr.	5.6	101%	2.8	NM	2.8	-19%	3.4
Int. Exp.	4.2	NM	1.0	91%	0.5	-45%	1.0
Pretax Inc.	2.9	NM	-5.1	NM	10.3	-16%	12.3
Eff. Tax Rate	45%	—	NM	—	40%	—	42%
Net Inc.	1.6	NM	-1.7	NM	6.2	-14%	7.2

Balance Sheet & Other Fin. Data (Million $)

	1994	1993	1992	1991	1990	1989
Cash	0.6	18.4	21.6	18.6	15.1	1.5
Curr. Assets	68.7	87.5	54.0	54.0	55.1	46.7
Total Assets	147	164	77.0	75.0	75.0	83.0
Curr. Liab.	40.7	45.6	15.5	15.4	17.1	21.4
LT Debt	55.0	67.4	8.5	9.1	9.5	20.4
Common Eqty.	48.7	48.9	52.7	49.8	46.0	39.0
Total Cap.	104	116	61.2	59.2	58.3	61.8
Cap. Exp.	7.0	2.8	5.2	6.5	5.2	5.2
Cash Flow	7.2	1.1	9.0	10.6	10.4	10.8

Ratio Analysis

	1994	1993	1992	1991	1990	1989
Curr. Ratio	1.7	1.9	3.5	3.5	3.2	2.2
% LT Debt of Cap.	53.0	57.9	13.9	15.3	16.3	33.0
% Net Inc.of Revs.	0.7	NM	5.1	5.7	4.9	3.1
% Ret. on Assets	1.0	NM	8.2	9.6	7.3	5.7
% Ret. on Equity	3.3	NM	12.1	15.0	13.6	14.1

Dividend Data (Quarterly dividends were reinstated in 1989. A "poison pill" stock purchase rights plan was adopted in 1987.)

Amt. of Div. $	Date Decl.	Ex-Div. Date	Stock of Record	Payment Date
0.150	Jul. 29	Sep. 06	Sep. 12	Oct. 11 '94
0.150	Nov. 17	Dec. 06	Dec. 12	Jan. 10 '95
0.150	Feb. 22	Mar. 07	Mar. 13	Apr. 11 '95
0.150	May. 31	Jun. 08	Jun. 12	Jul. 11 '95

Data as orig. reptd.; bef. results of disc. opers. and/or spec. items. Per share data adj. for stk. divs. as of ex-div. date. E-Estimated. NA-Not Available. NM-Not Meaningful. NR-Not Ranked.

Office—One Skidaway Village Walk, Suite 201, Savannah, GA 31411. **Tel**—(912) 598-7809. **Chrmn & CEO**—R. S. Jepson, Jr. **Pres & COO**—C. G. Anderson, **VP & Secy**—R. A. Walker. **EVP, CFO, Treasurer & Investor Contact**—Vernon J. Nagle. **Dirs**—C. G. Anderson, W. E. Burch, S. Cenko, G. D. Dillon, A. W. Dreyfoos, Jr., R. S. Jepson, Jr., W. M. Kearns, Jr., R. D. Kilpatrick, J. Marcellus Jr., G. J. Michel Jr., H. N. Schwarzkopf, **Transfer Agent & Registrar**—Harris Trust, Chicago. **Incorporated** in Mich. in 1915, reincorporated in Delaware. in 1993. **Empl**-1,235. **S&P Analyst:** M.T.C.

STANDARD & POOR'S

STOCK REPORTS

Kysor Industrial

NYSE Symbol **KZ**

In S&P SmallCap 600

26-SEP-95 **Industry:** Manufacturing/Distr

Summary: Kysor manufactures refrigerated display cases. It also produces original equipment components for heavy-duty trucks, other commercial vehicles, and marine equipment.

Quantitative Evaluations

Recent Price • 21 3/8 | Yield • 2.8%

52 Wk Range • 24 1/4-20 | 12-Mo. P/E • 8.3

Outlook (1 Lowest—5 Highest)
• **NA**

Fair Value
• **NA**

Risk
• **Low**

Earn./Div. Rank
• **B-**

Technical Eval.
• **Bearish** since 8/95

Rel. Strength Rank (1 Lowest—99 Highest)
• **34**

Insider Activity
• **Unfavorable**

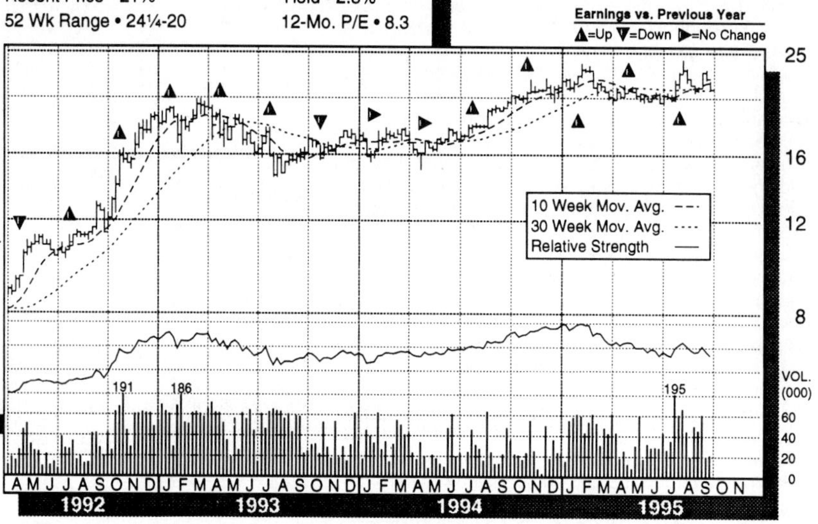

Business Profile - 26-SEP-95

Kysor operates in two segments: commercial products and transportation products. Revenues and earnings advanced in the first six months of 1995, as results improved in both divisions. The commercial products division's European unit has been a disappointment, however, and the company is exploring various options regarding this subsidiary. Institutions hold roughly 46% of the approximately 5.5 million common shares outstanding.

Operational Review - 26-SEP-95

Revenues in the first half of 1995, rose 27%, year to year, reflecting the strong performance of the company's commercial products segment, as well as improved results for the transportation products division. Margins widened on the higher volume, and operating income advanced 37%. With lower interest and other expenses, and despite taxes at 44.2%, versus 40.7%, net income surged 56%, to $7.9 million ($1.26 a share; $1.10 fully diluted) from $5.1 million ($0.81; $0.69).

Stock Performance - 22-SEP-95

In the past 30 trading days, KZ's shares have declined 4%, compared to a 5% rise in the S&P 500. Average trading volume for the past five days was 4,140 shares, compared with the 40-day moving average of 9,836 shares.

Key Stock Statistics

Dividend Rate/Share	0.60	Shareholders	1,300
Shs. outstg. (M)	5.5	Market cap. (B)	$0.120
Avg. daily vol. (M)	0.007	Inst. holdings	46%
Tang. Bk. Value/Share	11.41	Insider holdings	NA
Beta	0.66		

Value of $10,000 invested 5 years ago: $ 21,665

Fiscal Year Ending Dec. 31

	1995	% Change	1994	% Change	1993	% Change
Revenues (Million $)						
1Q	90.60	29%	70.31	10%	63.90	15%
2Q	95.26	24%	76.53	9%	69.93	8%
3Q	—	—	84.54	14%	74.44	3%
4Q	—	—	83.00	27%	65.58	-7%
Yr.	—	—	314.4	15%	273.9	4%
Income (Million $)						
1Q	3.30	57%	2.10	NM	2.11	97%
2Q	4.63	54%	3.00	8%	2.78	19%
3Q	—	—	4.33	32%	3.27	-13%
4Q	—	—	3.84	97%	1.95	NM
Yr.	—	—	13.28	31%	10.10	11%
Earnings Per Share ($)						
1Q	0.51	55%	0.33	NM	0.33	106%
2Q	0.75	56%	0.48	7%	0.45	13%
3Q	—	—	0.70	30%	0.54	-18%
4Q	—	—	0.61	103%	0.30	NM
Yr.	—	—	2.12	31%	1.62	7%

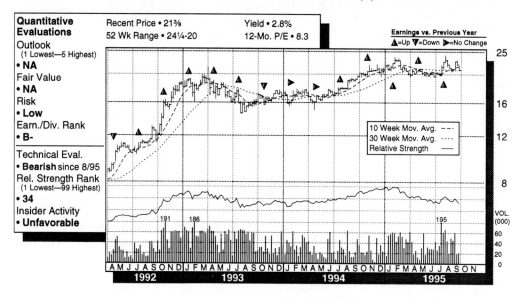

Next earnings report expected: late October

Kysor Industrial

Business Summary - 26-SEP-95

Kysor Industrial manufactures a variety of refrigerated display cases and building systems, as well as components and accessories for heavy duty vehicles and marine equipment. Industry segment contributions in 1994 (profits in million $) were:

	Sales	Profits
Commercial products		
U.S.	47%	$16.7
Europe	6%	-1.7
Transportation products		
U.S.	44%	20.0
Europe	3%	0.1

Commercial products include refrigerated display cases, condensing units, insulated panels for refrigerated building systems and walk-in coolers. Principal markets include supermarkets, convenience stores, food processors and restaurants. Refrigerated display equipment, refrigerated building systems, and sundry food store equipment are sold directly to supermarkets and convenience stores, and through independent commercial refrigeration distributors.

Transportation products include engine performance systems consisting of radiator shutters, fan clutches and plastic fans; engine monitoring devices, truck fuel tanks and marine instruments; commercial vehicle heating, ventilating and air-conditioning (HVAC) units; and truck trailer supports. Products are used by truck, bus, off-road vehicle and marine equipment manufacturers, and in the aftermarket. The majority of the group's sales are made directly to manufacturers; in addition, the company utilizes a network of independent distributors to provide aftermarket and replacement parts service to end users. Ford Motor Co. accounted for about 10% of revenues in 1994.

At December 31, 1994, the commercial products group had order backlogs of $64 million, up from $42 million a year earlier. The transportation products group had backlogs of $31 million, compared to $22 million at December 31, 1993.

Important Developments

Aug. '95—Kysor said that although incoming truck orders softened during the second quarter of 1995, truck manufacturers' current backlogs should be sufficient to provide increased overall production levels in 1995.

Capitalization

Long Term Debt: $29,565,000 (6/95), incl. $20 million guarantee of ESOP debt.
Series A Conv. Voting Preferred Stock: 800,870 shs. ($24.375 stated value); held by ESOP.
Options: To buy 1,731,000 shs. at $7.25 to $21.44 ea. (12/94).

Per Share Data ($)

(Year Ended Dec. 31)

	1994	1993	1992	1991	1990	1989
Tangible Bk. Val.	10.46	8.84	8.82	4.13	4.87	4.81
Cash Flow	3.67	2.98	2.96	1.16	1.99	0.18
Earnings	2.12	1.62	1.52	-0.35	0.72	-0.94
Dividends	0.50	0.42	0.40	0.60	0.60	0.60
Payout Ratio	24%	26%	26%	NM	79%	NM
Prices - High	22⅜	21¾	19⅛	12¾	12⅞	21⅛
- Low	15	14½	6⅞	5¾	6¾	12⅜
P/E Ratio - High	11	13	13	NM	18	NM
- Low	7	9	5	NM	9	NM

Income Statement Analysis (Million $)

	1994	%Chg	1993	%Chg	1992	%Chg	1991
Revs.	313	15%	273	4%	262	17%	224
Oper. Inc.	32.3	13%	28.6	6%	26.9	86%	14.5
Depr.	9.0	17%	7.7	NM	7.7	NM	7.7
Int. Exp.	2.0	-9%	2.2	-17%	2.6	-31%	3.8
Pretax Inc.	21.3	18%	18.0	13%	16.0	NM	-0.1
Eff. Tax Rate	38%	—	44%	—	43%	—	NM
Net Inc.	13.3	32%	10.1	11%	9.1	NM	-0.7

Balance Sheet & Other Fin. Data (Million $)

	1994	1993	1992	1991	1990	1989
Cash	15.9	21.3	6.9	4.3	6.1	7.3
Curr. Assets	108	93.2	80.5	74.7	87.6	87.9
Total Assets	178	156	136	133	148	151
Curr. Liab.	56.6	48.1	38.9	34.6	37.1	39.9
LT Debt	30.4	33.7	36.5	45.5	53.4	51.1
Common Eqty.	63.6	51.1	50.1	24.6	29.3	32.1
Total Cap.	98.0	88.0	91.0	92.0	105	106
Cap. Exp.	8.5	8.7	3.9	5.0	4.8	7.3
Cash Flow	21.3	16.8	15.7	5.9	11.1	1.1

Ratio Analysis

	1994	1993	1992	1991	1990	1989
Curr. Ratio	1.9	1.9	2.1	2.2	2.4	2.2
% LT Debt of Cap.	30.9	38.1	40.3	49.7	50.7	48.2
% Net Inc.of Revs.	4.2	3.7	3.5	NM	2.2	NM
% Ret. on Assets	7.8	6.8	6.7	NM	3.6	NM
% Ret. on Equity	21.1	17.8	17.2	NM	13.8	NM

Dividend Data —Dividends have been paid since 1936. A dividend reinvestment plan is available.

Amt. of Div. $	Date Decl.	Ex-Div. Date	Stock of Record	Payment Date
0.130	Jul. 29	Oct. 05	Oct. 12	Oct. 27 '94
0.130	Oct. 28	Jan. 05	Jan. 11	Jan. 26 '95
0.150	Jan. 27	Apr. 06	Apr. 12	Apr. 27 '95
0.150	Apr. 28	Jul. 10	Jul. 12	Jul. 27 '95
0.150	Sep. 08	Oct. 06	Oct. 11	Oct. 26 '95

Data as orig. reptd.; bef. results of disc. opers. and/or spec. items. Per share data adj. for stk. divs. as of ex-div. date. E-Estimated. NA-Not Available. NM-Not Meaningful. NR-Not Ranked.

Office—One Madison Ave., Cadillac, MI 49601-9785. **Tel**—(616) 779-2200. **Chrmn & CEO**—G. R. Kempton. **Pres & COO**—P. W. Gravelle. **VP & CFO**—T. M. Murphy. **VP & Secy**—D. W. Crooks. **Dirs**—T. J. Campbell, S. I. D'Agostino, P. K. Gaston, G. C. Gentry, P. W. Gravelle, G. R. Kempton, P. LeBoutillier, Jr., R. W. Navarre, R. J. Ratliff, F. W. Schwier, R. A. Weigel. **Transfer Agent & Registrar**—NBD Bank, Detroit. **Incorporated** in Michigan in 1925; reincorp. in Delaware in 1970; reincorp. in Michigan in 1985. **Empl**-2,236. **S&P Analyst:** N. Rosenberg

STANDARD & POOR'S

STOCK REPORTS

L.A. Gear

NYSE Symbol **LA**
In S&P SmallCap 600

30-OCT-95 **Industry:** Leather/shoes

Summary: L.A. Gear designs, develops and markets athletic, casual and children's footwear.

S&P Opinion: Sell (★)

Recent Price • 2⅜
52 Wk Range • 7-2
Yield • Nil
12-Mo. P/E • NM

Quantitative Evaluations
Outlook
(1 Lowest—5 Highest)
• **NA**
Fair Value
• **NA**
Risk
• **High**
Earn./Div. Rank
• **C**

Technical Eval.
• **Bearish** since 9/95
Rel. Strength Rank
(1 Lowest—99 Highest)
• **22**
Insider Activity
• **NA**

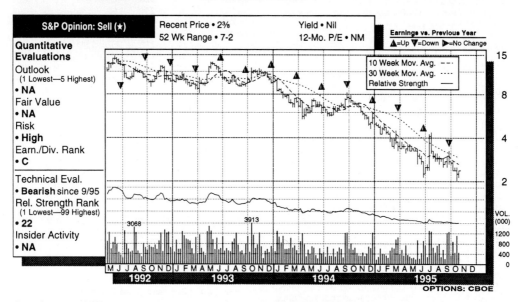

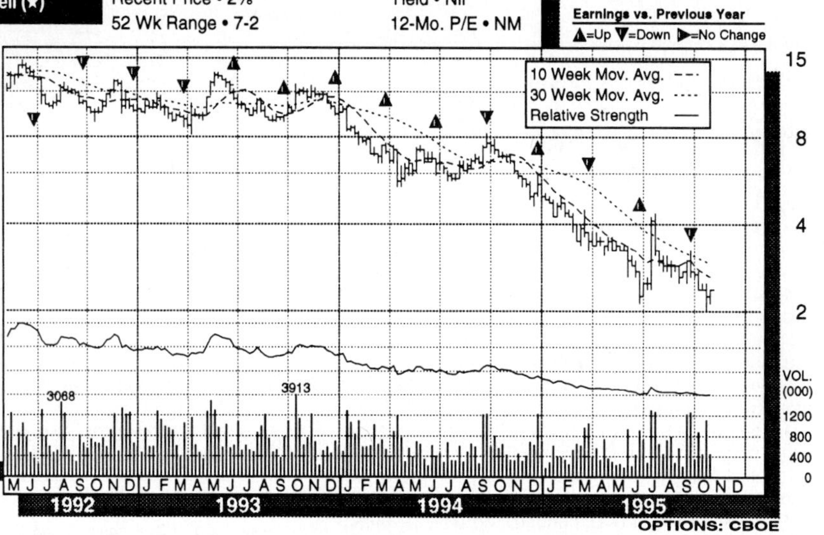

Overview - 30-OCT-95

Despite the company's efforts to become a premier designer and marketer of women's and children's shoes, we expect sales to continue to decline in fiscal 1996, reflecting increased competition and a significant drop in demand for children's lighted footwear. The largest customer, Wal-Mart, could purchase up to $80 million of footwear; however, Wal-Mart may not fulfill its commitment to purchase, which could put further pressure on sales. L.A. Gear may incur a loss in fiscal 1996, but it should be considerably smaller that the loss expected for fiscal 1995, reflecting continuing efforts to cut operating costs.

Valuation - 30-OCT-95

After reaching a high in mid-1990, capping five years of rapid sales and earnings growth, the shares subsequently fell sharply, as sales declined and losses were incurred. Efforts to refinance and restructure have not yet produced the desired results. From fiscal 1991 through the third quarter of fiscal 1995, the company has mostly reported larger than expected losses. Although it expects to improve operating results in fiscal 1995, we remain skeptical, given its weak order backlog at September 30, 1995, and a history of disappointing results. We recommend selling the shares, which present a significant risk of further price erosion.

Key Stock Statistics

S&P EPS Est. 1995	-1.15	Tang. Bk. Value/Share	NM
P/E on S&P Est. 1995	NM	Beta	0.19
Dividend Rate/Share	Nil	Shareholders	19,400
Shs. outstg. (M)	22.9	Market cap. (B)	$0.054
Avg. daily vol. (M)	0.142	Inst. holdings	12%
		Insider holdings	NA

Value of $10,000 invested 5 years ago: $ 763

Fiscal Year Ending Nov. 30

	1995	% Change	1994	% Change	1993	% Change
Revenues (Million $)						
1Q	69.39	-42%	120.4	58%	76.30	-30%
2Q	79.01	-6%	84.25	NM	84.57	-19%
3Q	94.35	-25%	126.6	-11%	143.0	5%
4Q	—	—	84.73	-10%	94.49	19%
Yr.	—	—	416.0	4%	398.4	-7%
Income (Million $)						
1Q	-11.64	NM	-2.03	NM	-11.56	NM
2Q	-5.91	NM	-11.77	NM	-13.16	NM
3Q	0.42	-94%	6.53	-10%	7.22	NM
4Q	—	—	-14.93	NM	-15.01	NM
Yr.	—	—	-22.20	NM	-32.51	NM
Earnings Per Share ($)						
1Q	-0.59	NM	-0.17	NM	-0.59	NM
2Q	-0.34	NM	-0.59	NM	-0.66	NM
3Q	-0.07	NM	0.20	-13%	0.23	NM
4Q	E-0.15	NM	-0.73	NM	-0.74	NM
Yr.	E-1.15	NM	-1.29	NM	-1.75	NM

Next earnings report expected: late February

L.A. Gear

Business Summary - 30-OCT-95

L.A. Gear designs, develops and markets a broad range of quality athletic and casual/lifestyle footwear for men (23% of fiscal 1994 domestic sales), women (21%) and children (56%), primarily under the L.A. Gear brand name. About 28% of fiscal 1994 sales were made overseas.

From 1985 through 1990, the company experienced rapid growth. However, in 1991, sales began to decline, and the company's financial condition deteriorated. After receiving a $100 million investment from Trefoil Investors, L.P. in September 1991, L.A. Gear assembled a new management team and began a restructuring program that included reducing domestic operating expenses and inventories. In mid-1994, the company realigned its management and made plans to redirect sales and marketing efforts to step up sales of women's shoes, focus on expanding its children's business, and re-energize the L.A. Gear brand name through increased visability. In addition, the company made plans to implement a strategy and expand its product lines and distribution channels.

Products are organized into three separate lines: athletic, casual and children's. About 90% of the company's footwear styles available domestically are priced below $55 each. Footwear products are sold in the U.S. to 3,900 accounts that include department, shoe, sporting goods and athletic footwear stores, mass market department stores and mass merchandisers. Internationally, products are sold in 55 countries. L.A. Gear's five largest customers worldwide accounted for 27% of fiscal 1994 total sales.

Important Developments

Oct. '95—L.A. Gear attributed a decline in fiscal 1995 third quarter sales to a 27% drop in U.S. sales, mainly reflecting reduced demand for lighted children's footwear, and to a 22% decrease in international sales, on reduced volume in Latin America. At September 30, 1995, backlog totaled $108.2 million, down from $126.6 million at September 30, 1994. About $38 million of the current backlog was scheduled to ship in October and November, and $58 million in the first quarter of fiscal 1996.
Sep. '95—The company announced a restructuring plan to streamline its company's organization and reduce operating expenses.

Capitalization

Long Term Debt: $50,000,000 (8/95) of 7.75% conv. sub. debs. due 2002, conv. into com. at $12.30 a sh.
7.5% Series A Cum. Conv. Preferred Stock: 1,000,000 shs. ($100 stated value); conv. into 10,000,000 com. shs. Held by Trefoil Capital Investors, L.P.

Per Share Data ($)

(Year Ended Nov. 30)

	1994	1993	1992	1991	1990	1989
Tangible Bk. Val.	0.25	1.56	3.82	6.74	10.61	8.80
Cash Flow	-0.91	-1.38	-3.42	-2.03	1.73	3.07
Earnings	-1.29	-1.75	-3.76	-2.40	1.56	3.01
Dividends	Nil	Nil	Nil	Nil	Nil	Nil
Payout Ratio	Nil	Nil	Nil	Nil	Nil	Nil
Prices - High	10¼	13⅜	16¾	14⅝	50⅜	46¾
- Low	4⅝	8⅛	9	9	9¾	10¾
P/E Ratio - High	NM	NM	NM	NM	32	16
- Low	NM	NM	NM	NM	6	4

Income Statement Analysis (Million $)

	1994	%Chg	1993	%Chg	1992	%Chg	1991
Revs.	416	5%	398	-5%	420	-32%	618
Oper. Inc.	-9.0	NM	-22.0	NM	-43.0	NM	-20.0
Depr.	8.8	2%	8.6	22%	7.1	NM	7.2
Int. Exp.	4.4	10%	4.0	186%	1.4	-89%	13.2
Pretax Inc.	-22.3	NM	-32.5	NM	-85.5	NM	-67.7
Eff. Tax Rate	NM	—	NM	—	NM	—	NM
Net Inc.	-22.2	NM	-32.5	NM	-71.9	NM	-45.0

Balance Sheet & Other Fin. Data (Million $)

	1994	1993	1992	1991	1990	1989
Cash	49.7	27.8	84.0	1.0	3.0	1.0
Curr. Assets	194	220	230	297	338	257
Total Assets	224	255	250	326	364	267
Curr. Liab.	47.0	58.0	62.0	94.0	158	98.0
LT Debt	50.0	50.0	Nil	Nil	Nil	Nil
Common Eqty.	18.0	47.0	87.0	132	206	168
Total Cap.	178	197	187	232	206	168
Cap. Exp.	4.0	5.3	4.9	14.2	18.9	6.2
Cash Flow	-20.9	-31.5	-72.5	-39.4	34.7	56.3

Ratio Analysis

	1994	1993	1992	1991	1990	1989
Curr. Ratio	4.2	3.8	3.7	3.2	2.1	2.6
% LT Debt of Cap.	28.1	25.4	Nil	Nil	Nil	Nil
% Net Inc.of Revs.	NM	NM	NM	NM	3.5	8.9
% Ret. on Assets	NM	NM	NM	NM	9.9	26.4
% Ret. on Equity	NM	NM	NM	NM	16.6	50.9

Dividend Data —No cash dividends have ever been paid.

Data as orig. reptd.; bef. results of disc. opers. and/or spec. items. Per share data adj. for stk. divs. as of ex-div. date. E-Estimated. NA-Not Available. NM-Not Meaningful. NR-Not Ranked.

Office—2850 Ocean Park Blvd., Santa Monica, CA 90405. **Tel**—(310) 452-4327. **Chrmn & CEO**—S. P. Gold. **Pres & COO**—W. L. Benford. **VP & Secy**—T. F. Larkin. **Investor Contact**—Bill Benford. **Dirs**—W. L. Benford, W. C. Bladstrom, A. E. Dalshaug, W. D. Davis, S. P. Gold, S. A. Koffler, A. E. Meyers, C. A. Miller, R. G. Moskowitz, V. A. Ravindran. **Transfer Agent & Registrar**—Chemical Trust Company of California, LA. **Incorporated** in California in 1979. **Empl**-726. **S&P Analyst:** Elizabeth Vandeventer

STANDARD & POOR'S

STOCK REPORTS

LSB Industries

NYSE Symbol **LSB**
In S&P SmallCap 600

10-OCT-95 **Industry:** Manufacturing/Distr

Summary: This diversified manufacturing, engineering and marketing company primarily makes and sells chemicals and air conditioning, automotive and industrial products.

Quantitative Evaluations

Outlook (1 Lowest—5 Highest)
• **NA**

Fair Value
• **NA**

Risk
• **Average**

Earn./Div. Rank
• **B-**

Technical Eval.
• **Bearish** since 8/95

Rel. Strength Rank (1 Lowest—99 Highest)
• **11**

Insider Activity
• **Neutral**

Recent Price • 5
52 Wk Range • 7¾-4⅞
Yield • 1.2%
12-Mo. P/E • NM

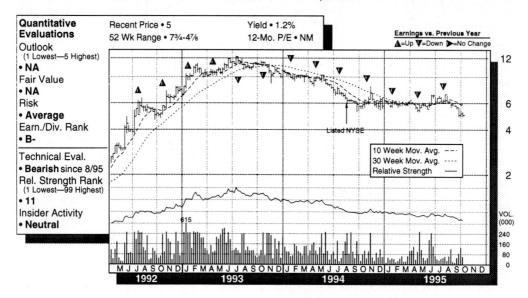

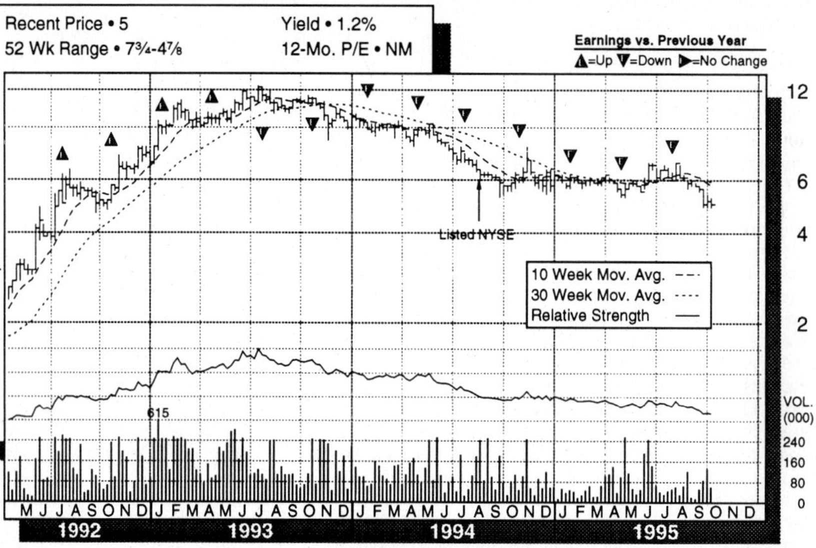

Business Profile - 10-OCT-95

LSB is a diversified manufacturer of chemical products, commercial and residential air conditioning products, and automotive and industrial products. Its financial services unit was sold in May 1994 for a $25 million gain. LSB recently announced its intention to focus on its Chemical and Environmental Control businesses and to reduce its investment in other divisions. In June 1995, LSB's $3.25 convertible exchangeable Class C preferred shares were listed on the New York Stock Exchange.

Operational Review - 10-OCT-95

Revenues were up 8.8%, year to year, in 1995's first half. Gross margins widened slightly as a result of greater production volumes and higher prices. However, with an 18% increase in SG&A costs and a 48% rise in interest expense, share earnings fell 52%, on 6.0% fewer shares. Results for the 1994 period exclude income from discontinued operations of $1.72 a share.

Stock Performance - 06-OCT-95

In the past 30 trading days, LSB's shares have declined 15%, compared to a 4% rise in the S&P 500. Average trading volume for the past five days was 11,420 shares, compared with the 40-day moving average of 13,564 shares.

Key Stock Statistics

Dividend Rate/Share	0.06	Shareholders	1,500
Shs. outstg. (M)	12.9	Market cap. (B)	$0.065
Avg. daily vol. (M)	0.015	Inst. holdings	26%
Tang. Bk. Value/Share	2.90	Insider holdings	NA
Beta	0.08		

Value of $10,000 invested 5 years ago: $ 29,281

Fiscal Year Ending Dec. 31

	1995	% Change	1994	% Change	1993	% Change
Revenues (Million $)						
1Q	65.93	2%	64.35	1%	63.42	12%
2Q	79.93	15%	69.74	-11%	78.42	11%
3Q	—	—	60.14	-12%	68.73	13%
4Q	—	—	55.73	-16%	66.03	13%
Yr.	—	—	250.0	-10%	276.6	12%
Income (Million $)						
1Q	1.45	-22%	1.86	-30%	2.66	140%
2Q	1.50	-94%	27.26	NM	5.76	35%
3Q	—	—	-0.91	NM	2.42	15%
4Q	—	—	-2.78	NM	1.56	-12%
Yr.	—	—	0.98	-92%	12.40	34%
Earnings Per Share ($)						
1Q	0.05	-38%	0.08	-68%	0.25	150%
2Q	0.05	-71%	0.17	-58%	0.40	-18%
3Q	—	—	-0.12	NM	0.09	-53%
4Q	—	—	-0.27	NM	0.05	-69%
Yr.	—	—	-0.16	NM	0.77	-18%

Next earnings report expected: mid November

LSB Industries

Business Summary - 10-OCT-95

LSB Industries, Inc. is a holding company that operated four major divisions at year-end 1994. In May 1994, LSB's financial services unit, Equity Bank for Savings, was sold to Bank IV Oklahoma, a subsidiary of Fourth Financial Corp., for $92 million in cash. Contributions (profits in millions) in 1994 were:

	Sales	Profits
Chemical	54%	$12.8
Environmental Control	28%	3.5
Automotive	13%	-1.5
Industrial	5%	-4.2

The Chemical division makes and sells sulfuric and concentrated nitric acids and ammonium nitrate-based fertilizer and blasting products for the agricultural, mining and other industries. It also markets emulsions that it purchases from others for resale to the mining industry. In 1995's third quarter, LSB expected to complete the construction of a plant in Wilmington, N.C., that will produce a mixed acid product.

The Environmental Control division manufactures and sells a broad range of fan coil, air handling, air conditioning, heating, heat pump and dehumidification products targeted to both new building construction and renovation, as well as industrial applications.

The Automotive division makes a line of antifriction bearings, including straight-thrust, radial-thrust and angular contact ball bearings and certain other automotive replacement parts for automotive, truck, industrial and agricultural applications.

The Industrial Products division manufactures, purchases and markets a proprietary line of machine tools, including milling, drilling, turning, grinding and fabricating equipment. Most machine tools are made by foreign companies to LSB's specifications. This division also manufactures CNC bed mills and electrical control panels for machine tools.

Important Developments

Sep. '95—LSB said it plans to focus on its two core business units, the Chemical business and the Environmental Control business. The company plans to substantially expand both of these businesses over the next 36 months. LSB also intends to reduce its investment or take other action regarding those businesses that are not generating a satisfactory return.

Jun. '95—New Alloy Co., a subsidiary of LSB, acquired the manufacturing equipment, inventory and trademarks of Alloy Industries Inc., a manufacturer of universal joints for cars, trucks and farm equipment, as well as CV boots for front-wheel drives.

Capitalization

Long Term Debt: $98,211,000 (6/95).
Red. Conv. Pfd. Stock: 1,588 shs. ($100 par).
Series B 12% Cum. Conv. Pfd. Stock: 20,000 shs. ($100 par); all controlled by the Golsen family.
Series 2 $3.25 Cum. Conv. Exch. Class C Pfd stock: 920,000 shs. (no par).

Per Share Data ($) (Year Ended Dec. 31)

	1994	1993	1992	1991	1990	1989
Tangible Bk. Val.	2.90	0.34	-2.27	-5.34	-5.22	-3.35
Cash Flow	0.42	1.61	1.99	0.91	-0.79	1.13
Earnings	-0.16	0.77	0.94	-0.48	-2.30	0.32
Dividends	0.03	0.06	Nil	Nil	Nil	Nil
Payout Ratio	NM	8%	Nil	Nil	Nil	Nil
Prices - High	10	12 3/8	7 3/4	2 3/8	1 7/8	3 1/4
- Low	5 1/4	6 3/4	1 1/4	1	1	1 1/2
P/E Ratio - High	NM	16	8	NM	NM	10
- Low	NM	9	1	NM	NM	5

Income Statement Analysis (Million $)

	1994	%Chg	1993	%Chg	1992	%Chg	1991
Revs.	245	-12%	277	12%	247	6%	234
Oper. Inc.	13.9	-59%	34.0	7%	31.9	34%	23.8
Depr.	8.1	-28%	11.2	26%	8.9	3%	8.6
Int. Exp.	7.4	-22%	9.5	-28%	13.2	-18%	16.1
Pretax Inc.	0.3	-98%	13.3	36%	9.8	NM	-1.0
Eff. Tax Rate	NM	—	6.60%	—	5.30%	—	NM
Net Inc.	1.0	-92%	12.4	33%	9.3	NM	-1.1

Balance Sheet & Other Fin. Data (Million $)

	1994	1993	1992	1991	1990	1989
Cash	2.6	13.0	33.7	24.1	50.0	7.7
Curr. Assets	111	NA	NA	NA	NA	NA
Total Assets	221	598	582	606	652	662
Curr. Liab.	48.6	NA	NA	NA	NA	NA
LT Debt	82.0	19.6	41.1	47.7	55.6	39.2
Common Eqty.	42.6	26.9	3.1	-7.0	-3.8	7.1
Total Cap.	173	95.0	60.0	58.0	68.0	233
Cap. Exp.	15.6	10.5	5.3	3.9	16.3	14.9
Cash Flow	5.8	21.6	16.3	5.5	-1.9	8.3

Ratio Analysis

	1994	1993	1992	1991	1990	1989
Curr. Ratio	2.3	NA	NA	NA	NA	NA
% LT Debt of Cap.	47.5	20.8	69.0	81.9	76.2	89.1
% Net Inc.of Revs.	0.4	4.5	3.8	NM	NM	1.5
% Ret. on Assets	0.2	1.5	1.3	NM	NM	0.7
% Ret. on Equity	NM	63.6	NM	NM	NM	31.7

Dividend Data —Semiannual dividends were initiated in 1993.

Amt. of Div. $	Date Decl.	Ex-Div. Date	Stock of Record	Payment Date
0.030	Nov. 16	Dec. 09	Dec. 15	Jan. 01 '95
0.030	Jun. 02	Jun. 13	Jun. 15	Jul. 01 '95

Data as orig. reptd.; bef. results of disc. opers. and/or spec. items. Per share data adj. for stk. divs. as of ex-div. date. E-Estimated. NA-Not Available. NM-Not Meaningful. NR-Not Ranked.

Office—16 South Pennsylvania Ave., Oklahoma City, OK 73107. **Tel**—(405) 235-4546. **Chrmn & Pres**—J. E. Golsen. **Sr VP-Fin, CFO & Investor Contact**—Tony M. Shelby. **VP & Treas**—J. D. Jones. **VP & Secy**—D. M. Shear. **Dirs**—R. B. Ackerman, R. C. Brown, B. H. Golsen, J. E. Golsen, D. R. Goss, B. G. Ille, J. D. Shaffer, T. M. Shelby, C. L. Thurman. **Transfer Agent & Registrar**—Liberty National Bank, Oklahoma City. **Reincorporated** in Delaware in 1977. **Empl**-1,446. **S&P Analyst:** R.J.G.

La-Z-Boy Chair

NYSE Symbol **LZB**
In S&P SmallCap 600

28-SEP-95 **Industry:** Home Furnishings

Summary: La-Z-Boy manufactures residential and office furniture upholstered seating products, including recliners and motion chairs, and solid wood bedroom/dining room products.

S&P Opinion: Hold (★★★)

Recent Price • 30¼
52 Wk Range • 32¾-25⅝
Yield • 2.6%
12-Mo. P/E • 15.5

Quantitative Evaluations

Outlook
(1 Lowest—5 Highest)
• **2+**
Fair Value
• **28⅞**
Risk
• **Low**
Earn./Div. Rank
• **A-**

Technical Eval.
• **Bullish** since 9/95
Rel. Strength Rank
(1 Lowest—99 Highest)
• **65**
Insider Activity
• **Favorable**

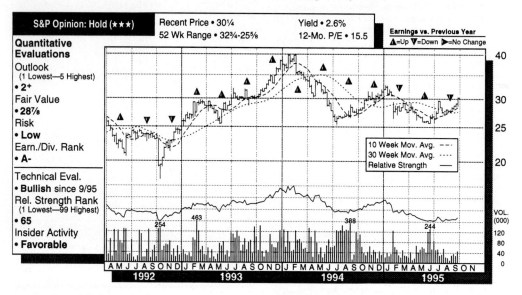

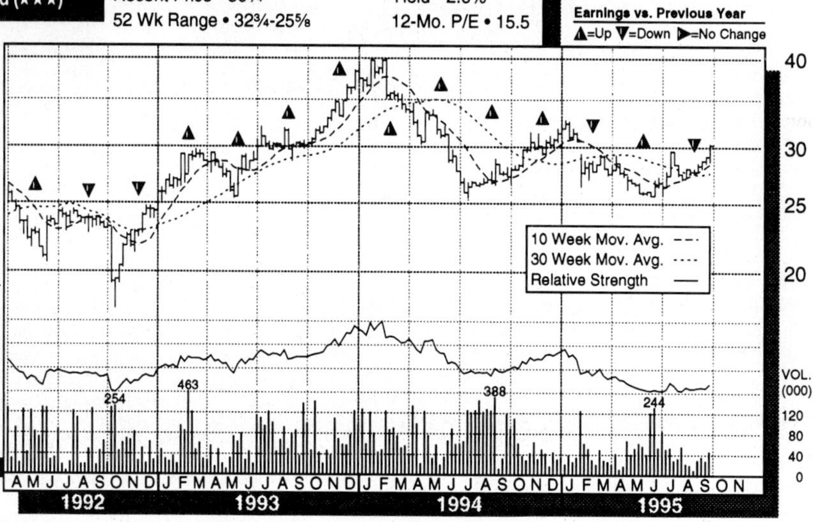

Overview - 28-SEP-95

Sales from ongoing businesses are expected to grow about 3% in fiscal 1995-96. Gains will reflect higher sales of existing product lines, mainly through the expansion of La-Z-Boy Showcase stores, which currently sell about 50% of LZB's residential furniture. The early 1995 acquisition of England/Corsair, a diversified furniture manufacturer whose 1994 sales were about $100 million, should further boost sales. Margins are expected to narrow, reflecting higher advertising expenses and a less profitable product mix due to the acquisition of England/Corsair. Over the long term, the company is aiming to increase its sales at about two times faster than those of the industry.

Valuation - 28-SEP-95

The shares have been under pressure for most of 1995, reflecting concerns over weak industrywide demand for furniture and the general low level of profitability within the domestic furniture industry. In fact, LZB's first quarter earnings were lower than expected, and caused us to lower our estimate for 1995-96. While LZB should show faster growth than that of the industry, we expect the company's income growth could be slower than that over the past several years. As a result, we are retaining our neutral opinion on the shares for the time being.

Key Stock Statistics

S&P EPS Est. 1996	1.95	Tang. Bk. Value/Share	15.13
P/E on S&P Est. 1996	15.5	Beta	0.54
S&P EPS Est. 1997	2.30	Shareholders	12,700
Dividend Rate/Share	0.76	Market cap. (B)	$0.542
Shs. outstg. (M)	18.5	Inst. holdings	24%
Avg. daily vol. (M)	0.007	Insider holdings	NA

Value of $10,000 invested 5 years ago: $ 19,496

Fiscal Year Ending Apr. 30

	1996	% Change	1995	% Change	1994	% Change
Revenues (Million $)						
1Q	195.8	12%	174.4	8%	162.1	16%
2Q	—	—	230.6	10%	209.0	19%
3Q	—	—	210.8	9%	192.6	13%
4Q	—	—	234.5	-3%	241.1	22%
Yr.	—	—	850.3	6%	804.9	18%
Income (Million $)						
1Q	3.17	-26%	4.27	8%	3.97	43%
2Q	—	—	12.08	16%	10.41	60%
3Q	—	—	7.22	-10%	7.99	25%
4Q	—	—	12.73	3%	12.34	6%
Yr.	—	—	36.30	5%	34.72	27%
Earnings Per Share ($)						
1Q	0.17	-26%	0.23	5%	0.22	47%
2Q	E0.65	-3%	0.67	18%	0.57	58%
3Q	E0.44	10%	0.40	-9%	0.44	26%
4Q	E0.69	-3%	0.71	6%	0.67	5%
Yr.	E1.95	-3%	2.01	6%	1.90	27%

Next earnings report expected: mid November

La-Z-Boy Chair

Business Summary - 28-SEP-95

La-Z-Boy manufactures residential and office furniture seating products at 29 manufacturing plants in the U.S. and Canada. The company believes it ranks third in the U.S. in dollar volume of sales within the residential furniture industry, and is the world's largest single-seat recliner manufacturer. Approximately 76% of its fiscal 1994-95 sales consisted of residential upholstery furniture, 18% residential wood furniture, and 6% contract furniture. About 6% of 1994-95 sales were made in Canada and other foreign markets. In early 1995, LZB acquired England/Corsair, Inc., a manufacturer of upholstered furniture.

The La-Z-Boy Residential division, which accounts for the majority of total sales, markets stationary chairs, sofas and loveseats, recliners, reclining sofas, sleep sofas, and modular seating groups through better-quality department stores, furniture stores and regional furniture chains, and through a national network of La-Z-Boy proprietary stores.

The Hammary division manufactures occasional tables, living room cabinets, wall entertainment units, and upholstered furniture.

Kincaid makes solid-wood dining room and bedroom furniture and occasional furniture.

La-Z-Boy Canada produces and markets residential seating in that country.

The La-Z-Boy Contract division produces commercial furniture sold to businesses, hospitality companies and health care users.

Important Developments

Aug. '95—LZB attributed the 12% sales increase for the first quarter of fiscal 1995-96 to the acquisition of England/Corsair, Inc. Sales excluding this acquisition declined 1%, reflecting industrywide softness in residential furniture. LZB reported that sales declined at all of the company's divisions, except the contract furniture and Canadian businesses. Net margins were hurt by a less profitable product mix due to the acquisition, higher national television advertising expenditures, and an increase in interest charges. Looking ahead, the company said that although incoming sales orders and backlogs were slightly behind the levels a year ago, second quarter sales should exceed those of a year ago.

Capitalization

Long Term Debt: $71,218,000 (7/29/95), incl. capital leases.

Per Share Data ($) (Year Ended Apr. 30)

	1995	1994	1993	1992	1991	1990
Tangible Bk. Val.	15.19	14.77	13.29	12.32	11.43	10.61
Cash Flow	2.86	2.67	2.28	2.21	2.08	2.35
Earnings	2.01	1.90	1.50	1.39	1.30	1.58
Dividends	0.68	0.64	0.60	0.58	0.56	0.54
Payout Ratio	34%	34%	40%	42%	43%	34%
Cal. Yrs.	1994	1993	1992	1991	1990	1989
Prices - High	40	$38\frac{7}{8}$	$28\frac{3}{4}$	$25\frac{1}{8}$	22	$23\frac{1}{4}$
- Low	$25\frac{1}{4}$	$25\frac{1}{8}$	$17\frac{3}{4}$	$15\frac{1}{8}$	$12\frac{3}{8}$	$16\frac{7}{8}$
P/E Ratio - High	20	20	19	18	17	15
- Low	13	13	12	11	10	11

Income Statement Analysis (Million $)

	1995	%Chg	1994	%Chg	1993	%Chg	1992
Revs.	850	6%	805	18%	684	11%	619
Oper. Inc.	78.0	6%	73.3	20%	60.9	4%	58.4
Depr.	15.2	9%	14.0	NM	14.1	-5%	14.8
Int. Exp.	3.3	18%	2.8	-13%	3.3	-39%	5.3
Pretax Inc.	62.0	7%	58.2	28%	45.3	14%	39.9
Eff. Tax Rate	42%	—	40%	—	40%	—	37%
Net Inc.	36.3	5%	34.7	27%	27.3	9%	25.1

Balance Sheet & Other Fin. Data (Million $)

	1995	1994	1993	1992	1991	1990
Cash	27.0	25.9	28.8	21.7	13.0	6.7
Curr. Assets	325	296	279	254	238	240
Total Assets	504	430	401	377	363	362
Curr. Liab.	88.1	71.5	77.5	69.1	65.2	70.1
LT Debt	76.4	52.5	55.4	55.9	62.2	69.1
Common Eqty.	324	291	263	246	229	215
Total Cap.	407	350	324	308	298	292
Cap. Exp.	19.0	17.5	12.2	12.2	21.4	22.4
Cash Flow	51.5	48.7	41.3	39.9	37.4	42.0

Ratio Analysis

	1995	1994	1993	1992	1991	1990
Curr. Ratio	3.7	4.1	3.6	3.7	3.7	3.4
% LT Debt of Cap.	18.8	15.0	17.1	18.2	20.9	23.7
% Net Inc.of Revs.	4.3	4.3	4.0	4.1	3.8	4.8
% Ret. on Assets	7.8	8.3	7.0	6.8	6.4	7.9
% Ret. on Equity	11.9	12.5	10.7	10.5	10.5	13.8

Dividend Data —Cash has been paid in each year since 1963. A dividend reinvestment plan is available.

Amt. of Div. $	Date Decl.	Ex-Div. Date	Stock of Record	Payment Date
0.170	Oct. 10	Nov. 10	Nov. 17	Dec. 09 '94
0.170	Jan. 09	Feb. 07	Feb. 13	Mar. 10 '95
0.170	May. 09	May. 15	May. 19	Jun. 09 '95
0.190	Jul. 31	Aug. 15	Aug. 17	Sep. 08 '95

Data as orig. reptd.; bef. results of disc. opers. and/or spec. items. Per share data adj. for stk. divs. as of ex-div. date. E-Estimated. NA-Not Available. NM-Not Meaningful. NR-Not Ranked.

Office—1284 North Telegraph Rd., Monroe, MI 48161-3390. **Tel**—(313) 242-1444. **Chrmn & Pres**—C. T. Knabusch. **Secy, Treas & Investor Contact**—Gene M. Hardy. **VP-Fin**—F. H. Jackson. **Dirs**—W. W. Gruber, G. M. Hardy, D. K. Hehl, F. H. Jackson, J. W. Johnston, C. T. Knabusch, R. E. Lipford, P. H. Norton, E. J. Shoemaker, L. G. Stevens, J. F. Weaver. **Transfer Agent & Registrar**—American Stock Transfer & Trust, NYC. **Incorporated** in Michigan in 1941. **Empl**-11,149. **S&P Analyst:** Elizabeth Vandeventer

STANDARD & POOR'S

STOCK REPORTS

Landmark Graphics

NASDAQ Symbol **LMRK**

In S&P SmallCap 600

17-AUG-95

Industry: Data Processing

Summary: LMRK supplies interactive computer-aided exploration systems to geoscientists, enabling them to analyze subsurface data for the exploration and production of petroleum resources.

Quantitative Evaluations

Outlook
(1 Lowest—5 Highest)
• **5+**

Fair Value
• **31⅛**

Risk
• **Average**

Earn./Div. Rank
• **B-**

Technical Eval.
• **Bearish** since 7/95

Rel. Strength Rank
(1 Lowest—99 Highest)
• **58**

Insider Activity
• **Neutral**

Recent Price • 26¼
52 Wk Range • 28¼-16

Yield • Nil
12-Mo. P/E • 34.1

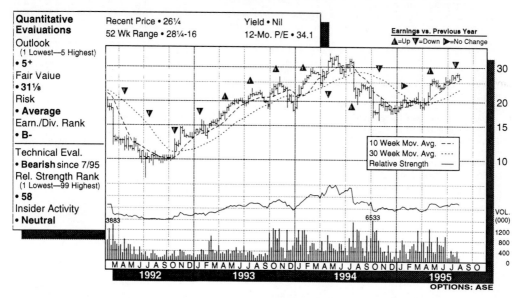

Earnings vs. Previous Year
▲=Up ▼=Down ▶=No Change

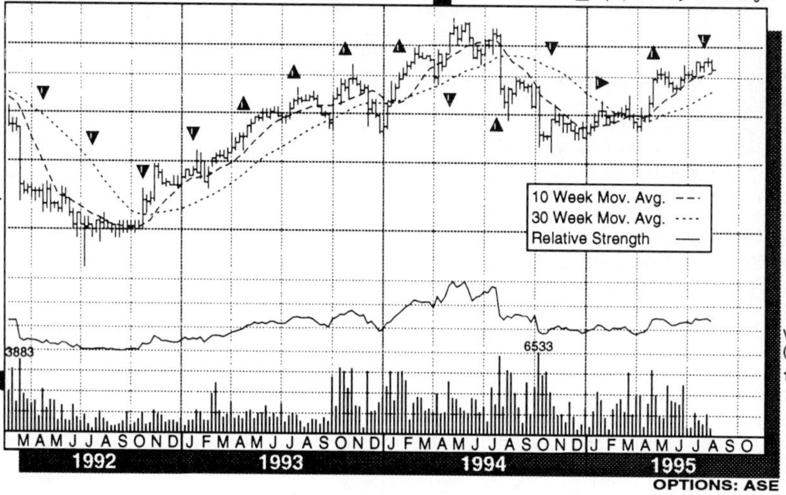

OPTIONS: ASE

Business Profile - 17-AUG-95

LMRK has been growing through acquisition, having acquired Stratamodel, Inc., MGI Associates, Inc., DRD Corp. and GeoGraphix, Inc. during fiscal 1995. Depressed oil and gas prices present both opportunities and threats. On the one hand, low oil and gas prices hurt Landmark's customers' profitability, indirectly affecting the company as well. However, with industry margins dwindling, LMRK's products, designed to improve drilling decisions and maximize exploitable reserves, become more valuable.

Operational Review - 17-AUG-95

Based on a preliminary report, sales increased 20% in the fiscal year ended June 30, 1995, as restated, reflecting strong growth in software product and maintenance revenues; hardware product sales were flat. With substantially lower merger costs outweighing acquired research and development costs and restructuring charges, net income more than doubled, to $13.5 million ($0.77 a share) from $5.8 million ($0.36).

Stock Performance - 11-AUG-95

In the past 30 trading days, LMRK's shares have increased 3%, compared to a 2% rise in the S&P 500. Average trading volume for the past five days was 29,080 shares, compared with the 40-day moving average of 72,377 shares.

Key Stock Statistics

Dividend Rate/Share	Nil	Shareholders	300
Shs. outstg. (M)	17.1	Market cap. (B)	$0.454
Avg. daily vol. (M)	0.050	Inst. holdings	74%
Tang. Bk. Value/Share	8.88	Insider holdings	NA
Beta	1.57		

Value of $10,000 invested 5 years ago: $ 15,217

Fiscal Year Ending Jun. 30

	1995	% Change	1994	% Change	1993	% Change
Revenues (Million $)						
1Q	30.19	12%	27.02	54%	17.60	-17%
2Q	43.35	20%	36.25	78%	20.40	-18%
3Q	43.44	26%	34.52	46%	23.62	18%
4Q	49.22	43%	34.50	33%	25.86	65%
Yr.	171.2	29%	132.3	51%	87.57	7%
Income (Million $)						
1Q	-1.08	NM	1.76	—	—	—
2Q	5.61	9%	5.14	NM	0.66	-79%
3Q	3.29	NM	-8.59	NM	1.88	NM
4Q	5.52	-23%	7.15	184%	2.52	NM
Yr.	13.51	147%	5.46	5%	5.22	NM
Earnings Per Share ($)						
1Q	-0.07	NM	0.13	NM	0.02	-89%
2Q	0.34	NM	0.34	NM	0.06	-80%
3Q	0.20	NM	-0.56	NM	0.18	NM
4Q	0.31	-28%	0.43	87%	0.23	NM
Yr.	0.77	114%	0.36	-27%	0.49	NM

Next earnings report expected: late October

Landmark Graphics

Business Summary - 17-AUG-95

Landmark Graphics Corporation develops and markets interactive computer-aided exploration (CAEX) graphics systems and associated software used by geoscientists to analyze subsurface data in the process of exploring for and producing petroleum resources.

Landmark's software enables geoscientists to create maps and spatial representations of subsurface structures in a fraction of the time required by, and in much greater detail than, traditional methods of analysis. This is important in light of reduced exploration and production budgets, a greater volume of data available to geoscientists, and increased drilling risks. The company's products are designed to improve drilling decisions and maximize exploitable reserves.

The company's systems incorporate a user interface designed specifically for geoscientists, which permits use without extensive computer training. The systems use Landmark's proprietary applications software and hardware platforms, primarily the Sun SparcStation or the IBM RS6000 line of workstations. At the end of fiscal 1994, LMRK was in the process of porting its software applications to Silicon Graphics workstations. A typical system consists of a RISC CPU with memory, mass storage and imaging hardware. Systems operate as stand-alone workstations or may be integrated into a work group environment.

All of Landmark's new application software programs are being developed under its OpenWorks software framework (released commercially in 1989), which allows geoscientists to rapidly integrate and utilize different data types and multiple applications on a stand-alone or networked basis.

Most of the company's systems have been sold to international energy companies. About 36% of fiscal 1994 revenues came from export sales.

In order to more fully satisfy the needs of its diverse customer base, Landmark provides a variety of service and support programs. These include training courses for users of Landmark's software; customized consulting services in data loading and management; and consulting and networking services to help customers design, build and integrate the most effective computer environment for their needs.

Important Developments

Jun. '95—Landmark completed the acquisition of Denver-based GeoGraphix, Inc. in exchange for 654,000 shares of LMRK common stock.

Capitalization

Long Term Debt: $13,655,000 (6/95).
Options: To buy 2,099,332 shs. at $0.60 to $34.13 ea. (6/94).

Per Share Data ($) (Year Ended Jun. 30)

	1995	1994	1993	1992	1991	1990
Tangible Bk. Val.	NA	8.88	7.31	6.73	7.27	6.69
Cash Flow	NA	0.82	1.10	0.03	1.63	1.13
Earnings	0.77	0.36	0.49	-0.67	0.94	0.68
Dividends	Nil	Nil	Nil	Nil	Nil	Nil
Payout Ratio	Nil	Nil	Nil	Nil	Nil	Nil
Prices - High	28	35¼	26¾	25¼	26	23¾
- Low	17¾	16	12¾	8	13	12¾
P/E Ratio - High	36	98	55	NM	28	35
- Low	23	44	26	NM	14	19

Income Statement Analysis (Million $)

	1994	%Chg	1993	%Chg	1992	%Chg	1991
Revs.	132	51%	87.6	7%	81.9	-9%	89.9
Oper. Inc.	27.3	102%	13.5	99%	6.8	-65%	19.3
Depr.	7.2	10%	6.5	-14%	7.5	21%	6.2
Int. Exp.	0.9	NM	0.2	-16%	0.2	-24%	0.3
Pretax Inc.	8.2	15%	7.1	NM	-7.3	NM	14.4
Eff. Tax Rate	34%	—	26%	—	NM	—	32%
Net Inc.	5.5	5%	5.2	NM	-7.2	NM	9.8

Balance Sheet & Other Fin. Data (Million $)

	1994	1993	1992	1991	1990	1989
Cash	73.7	18.0	15.9	14.1	18.9	12.0
Curr. Assets	133	64.9	62.6	64.2	46.5	29.4
Total Assets	184	95.2	91.0	91.9	67.8	37.3
Curr. Liab.	26.8	16.1	17.9	13.9	7.2	5.9
LT Debt	12.0	Nil	1.1	1.5	Nil	Nil
Common Eqty.	141	77.3	70.3	76.0	60.0	30.9
Total Cap.	157	79.0	73.1	78.0	60.5	30.9
Cap. Exp.	25.0	7.4	8.9	6.3	13.3	3.0
Cash Flow	12.6	11.7	0.3	16.0	9.7	6.9

Ratio Analysis

	1994	1993	1992	1991	1990	1989
Curr. Ratio	4.9	4.0	3.5	4.6	6.4	5.0
% LT Debt of Cap.	7.7	Nil	1.5	1.9	Nil	Nil
% Net Inc.of Revs.	4.1	6.0	NM	10.9	10.3	11.6
% Ret. on Assets	3.3	5.6	NM	11.4	10.4	7.6
% Ret. on Equity	4.2	7.0	NM	13.7	12.0	30.4

Dividend Data —No cash dividends have been paid.

Data as orig. reptd.; bef. results of disc. opers. and/or spec. items. Per share data adj. for stk. divs. as of ex-div. date. E-Estimated. NA-Not Available. NM-Not Meaningful. NR-Not Ranked.

Office—15150 Memorial Drive, Houston, TX 77079-4304. **Tel**—(713) 560-1000. **Chrmn**—S. K. Smith. **Pres, CEO & COO**—R. P. Peebler. **VP-Fin & CFO**—W. H. Seippel. **Secy**—P. L. Massaro. **Dirs**—C. L. Blackburn, S. R. Bridges, J. A. Downing II, L. L. Lanza, T. Levitt, R. P. Peebler, S. K. Smith. **Transfer Agent & Registrar**—Ameritrust Texas, Dallas. **Reincorporated** in Delaware in 1982. **Empl**-613. **S&P Analyst:** N. Rosenberg

STANDARD & POOR'S

Lattice Semiconductor

STOCK REPORTS

NASDAQ Symbol **LSCC**
In S&P SmallCap 600

16-SEP-95

Industry: Electronics/Electric

Summary: This company designs, develops and markets both high- and low-density high-speed in-system programmable logic devices (PLDs).

Quantitative Evaluations

Outlook (1 Lowest—5 Highest)
• **5**

Fair Value
• **48⅝**

Risk
• **Average**

Earn./Div. Rank
• **NR**

Technical Eval.
• **Bullish** since 7/95

Rel. Strength Rank (1 Lowest—99 Highest)
• **60**

Insider Activity
• **NA**

Recent Price • 36¼
52 Wk Range • 43-15½
Yield • Nil
12-Mo. P/E • 23.5

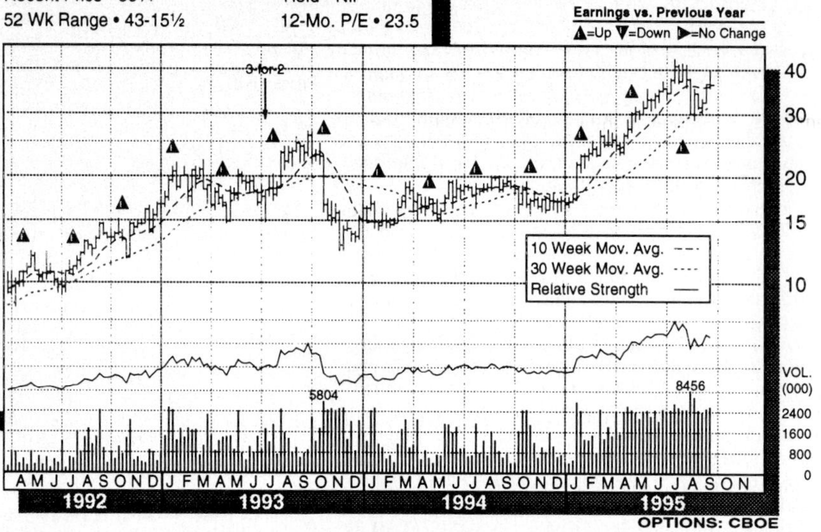

OPTIONS: CBOE

Business Profile - 14-SEP-95

LSCC is pursuing a strategy of transitioning its base business from low-density generic array logic (GAL) products to the high growth, high-density PLD market. At the beginning of fiscal 1995, the low-density GAL business accounted for 90% of total quarterly revenue. However, by the end of the year, 26% of revenues were being generated by the high-density business. During fiscal 1995, LSCC released two high-density product families and added 15 products to its software design tool portfolio.

Operational Review - 14-SEP-95

Revenues rose in fiscal 1996's first quarter, primarily reflecting increased sales of new high density products. Gross margins narrowed as higher period costs associated with increased production of high density products offset improved capacity utilization and other manufacturing cost reductions. Results benefited from a 52% rise in other income. LSCC has a strong balance sheet with no long-term debt as of June 1995, and $98.3 million in cash and short-term investments (49% of total assets).

Stock Performance - 15-SEP-95

In the past 30 trading days, LSCC's shares have declined 4%, compared to a 4% rise in the S&P 500. Average trading volume for the past five days was 888,800 shares, compared with the 40-day moving average of 899,333 shares.

Key Stock Statistics

Dividend Rate/Share	Nil	Shareholders	6,500
Shs. outstg. (M)	19.2	Market cap. (B)	$0.696
Avg. daily vol. (M)	0.714	Inst. holdings	93%
Tang. Bk. Value/Share	8.96	Insider holdings	NA
Beta	1.31		

Value of $10,000 invested 5 years ago: $ 85,294

Fiscal Year Ending Mar. 31

	1996	% Change	1995	% Change	1994	% Change
Revenues (Million $)						
1Q	45.01	37%	32.91	-1%	33.35	62%
2Q	—	—	34.56	1%	34.14	41%
3Q	—	—	36.29	27%	28.57	5%
4Q	—	—	40.32	34%	30.19	-4%
Yr.	—	—	144.1	14%	126.2	22%
Income (Million $)						
1Q	8.85	48%	6.00	6%	5.67	67%
2Q	—	—	6.42	5%	6.10	49%
3Q	—	—	6.85	35%	5.08	10%
4Q	—	—	7.70	37%	5.64	7%
Yr.	—	—	26.97	20%	22.49	29%
Earnings Per Share ($)						
1Q	0.45	41%	0.32	7%	0.30	61%
2Q	—	—	0.34	6%	0.32	45%
3Q	—	—	0.36	33%	0.27	9%
4Q	—	—	0.40	33%	0.30	7%
Yr.	—	—	1.41	18%	1.19	27%

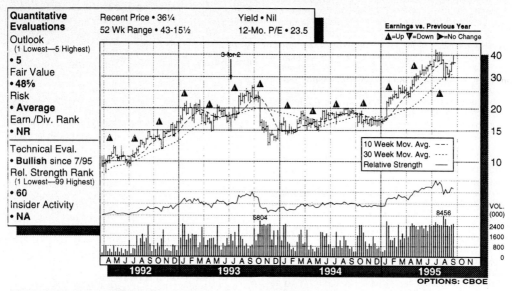

Next earnings report expected: mid October

Lattice Semiconductor

Business Summary - 14-SEP-95

Lattice Semiconductor Corporation is the world's leading supplier of in-system programmable (ISP) logic devices. The company pioneered the application of electrically erasable CMOS (E2CMOS) technology to programmable logic. LSCC designs, develops and markets both high- and low-density, high performance E2CMOS programmable logic devices (PLDs) and related development system software. PLDs are standard semiconductor components that can be custom configured by the customer to perform specific logic functions. PLDs enable the customer to shorten design cycle times and reduce development costs. Its proprietary generic array logic (GAL), pLSI (programmable large scale integration), and ispLSI (in-system programmable large scale integration) devices provide customers with quickly designed, easily configured components.

Lattice products are marketed worldwide through a network of independent sales representatives and indirectly through a network of distributors, primarily to original equipment manufacturers in the fields of data processing, telecommunications, data communications, computer peripherals, instrumentation, industrial controls and military systems.

In 1992-93, Lattice entered the high-density PLD market by releasing to production all eight of the original devices in its pLSI and ispLSI 1000 product families. The ispLSI family allows real-time programming, reduced manufacturing costs, improved testing and end-use reconfiguration. During 1993-94, the company introduced two new pLSI and ispLSI families--the 2000 and 3000 series--each initially containing three devices. During 1994-95, LSCC extended its GAL line by introducing a family of 3.3 volt industry standard architectures. All of LSCC's high-density products are supported by the company's pDS (programmable development system) and pDS+ development systems which allows the customer to verify the design, perform logic minimization, assign pins and critical speed paths, and execute automatic place and route tasks. In 1994-95, the company released new verisons of all its existing pDS and pDS+ software development tools.

Important Developments

Aug. '95—LSCC said it is sampling the world's fastest 3.3-volt, 16V8 programmable logic device (PLD), the 7.5 ns GAL16LV86.

May '95—LSCC announced the release of its pDS+ Mentor Fitter and Libraries software to support designs with Lattice's high density programmable logic in-system programmable ispLSI device family.

Capitalization

Long Term Debt: None (7/1/95).

Options: To buy 2,220,487 shs. at $3.67 to $23.50 ea. (4/95).

Per Share Data ($)

(Year Ended Mar. 31)

	1995	1994	1993	1992	1991	1990
Tangible Bk. Val.	8.57	6.79	5.49	4.44	3.79	2.09
Cash Flow	1.73	1.49	1.20	0.77	0.79	0.65
Earnings	1.41	1.19	0.94	0.61	0.61	0.51
Dividends	Nil	Nil	Nil	Nil	Nil	Nil
Payout Ratio	Nil	Nil	Nil	Nil	Nil	Nil
Cal. Yrs.	1994	1993	1992	1991	1990	1989
Prices - High	20⅛	26¾	17¼	10	11½	4⅝
- Low	14	12¼	7¼	3⅝	3¼	3⅜
P/E Ratio - High	14	22	18	16	19	9
- Low	10	10	8	6	5	7

Income Statement Analysis (Million $)

	1995	%Chg	1994	%Chg	1993	%Chg	1992
Revs.	144	14%	126	22%	103	45%	71.0
Oper. Inc.	43.3	21%	35.8	30%	27.5	71%	16.1
Depr.	6.0	4%	5.8	23%	4.7	70%	2.8
Int. Exp.	NA	—	0.0	-50%	0.0	-50%	0.1
Pretax Inc.	40.6	25%	32.6	29%	25.2	61%	15.7
Eff. Tax Rate	34%	—	31%	—	31%	—	31%
Net Inc.	27.0	20%	22.5	29%	17.4	60%	10.9

Balance Sheet & Other Fin. Data (Million $)

	1995	1994	1993	1992	1991	1990
Cash	88.7	93.6	80.9	63.3	51.3	23.8
Curr. Assets	141	126	110	80.1	67.1	35.1
Total Assets	193	146	129	91.7	79.1	40.8
Curr. Liab.	35.0	21.0	30.4	15.8	15.3	9.6
LT Debt	Nil	Nil	Nil	0.2	0.6	1.2
Common Eqty.	158	125	99	75.6	63.2	29.9
Total Cap.	158	125	99	75.8	63.8	31.2
Cap. Exp.	6.3	7.2	11.7	2.4	9.2	3.5
Cash Flow	33.0	28.3	22.1	13.6	13.1	8.6

Ratio Analysis

	1995	1994	1993	1992	1991	1990
Curr. Ratio	4.0	6.0	3.6	5.1	4.4	3.7
% LT Debt of Cap.	Nil	Nil	Nil	0.3	0.9	3.9
% Net Inc.of Revs.	18.8	17.8	16.8	15.3	16.0	17.5
% Ret. on Assets	15.9	16.2	15.4	12.6	16.3	5.7
% Ret. on Equity	19.1	19.9	19.5	15.5	21.0	34.1

Dividend Data —No cash dividends have been paid. A three-for-two stock split was effected July 6, 1993, for stockholders of record June 14.

Data as orig. reptd.; bef. results of disc. opers. and/or spec. items. Per share data adj. for stk. divs. as of ex-div. date. E-Estimated. NA-Not Available. NM-Not Meaningful. NR-Not Ranked.

Office—5555 N.E. Moore Ct., Hillsboro, OR 97124-6421. **Tel**—(503) 681-0118. **Fax**—(503) 681-0347. **Chrmn, Pres & CEO**—C. Y. Tsui. **VP-Fin, Secy & Investor Contact**—Rodney F. Sloss. **Dirs**—D. S. Hauer, H. A. Merlo, L. W. Sonsini, D. C. Strain, C. Y. Tsui. **Transfer Agent & Registrar**—First Interstate Bank, Seattle, Washington. **Incorporated** in Delaware in 1985. **Empl-** 438. **S&P Analyst:** Ronald J. Gross

STANDARD & POOR'S

STOCK REPORTS

Lechters, Inc.

NASDAQ Symbol **LECH**

In S&P SmallCap 600

19-SEP-95

Industry: Retail Stores

Summary: This retailer operates about 620 stores, mainly in regional malls, featuring a large selection of basic housewares, tabletop items and kitchen textiles at competitive prices.

Quantitative Evaluations

Outlook (1 Lowest—5 Highest)
• **NA**

Fair Value
• **NA**

Risk
• **Average**

Earn./Div. Rank
• **B**

Technical Eval.
• **Bullish** since 5/95

Rel. Strength Rank (1 Lowest—99 Highest)
• **7**

Insider Activity
• **Neutral**

Recent Price • 11⅞
52 Wk Range • 19-10

Yield • Nil
12-Mo. P/E • 27.0

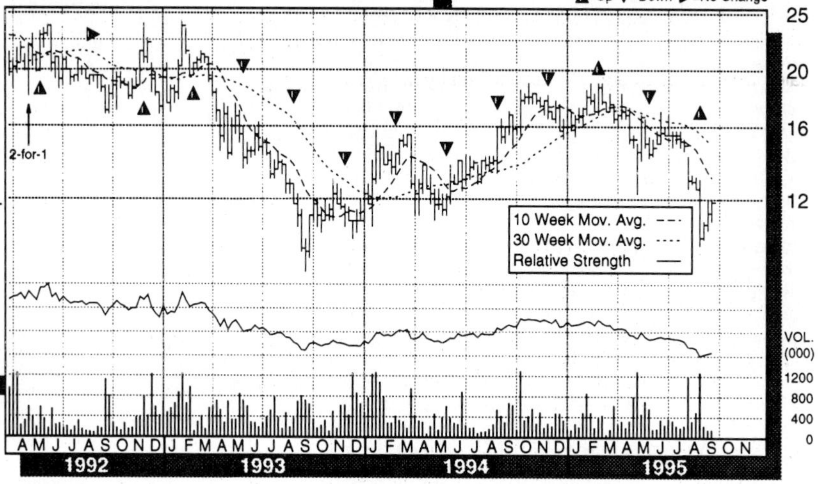

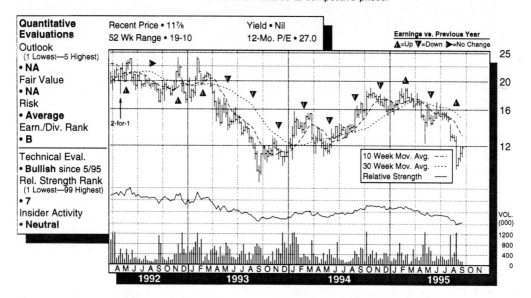

Business Profile - 19-SEP-95

Although new store openings have boosted top line growth of this retailer, profitability has been hurt by lower same-store sales, margin pressures, and higher expenses. LECH embarked upon a restructuring program in mid-1994, aimed at remerchandising stores, and reviewing store formats and the efficiency of central operations. A $11 million pretax charge was posted in 1994-95's second quarter, reflecting the closing of 10 stores, the writedown of certain assets, and personnel-related costs.

Operational Review - 19-SEP-95

Net sales in the 26 weeks ended July 29, 1995, rose 8.8%, year to year, primarily reflecting a greater number of stores in operation. Same-store sales slid 0.3%. Profitability was hurt by lower markups on merchandise, higher freight rates and increased costs associated with 39 additional stores. In the absence of an $11 million restructuring charge, and after a 27% decline in other expenses, the net loss narrowed to $0.24 per share, on 1.8% more shares, from $0.48.

Stock Performance - 15-SEP-95

In the past 30 trading days, LECH's shares have declined 8%, compared to a 4% rise in the S&P 500. Average trading volume for the past five days was 27,940 shares, compared with the 40-day moving average of 117,836 shares.

Key Stock Statistics

Dividend Rate/Share	Nil	Shareholders	800
Shs. outstg. (M)	17.1	Market cap. (B)	$0.204
Avg. daily vol. (M)	0.124	Inst. holdings	56%
Tang. Bk. Value/Share	8.26	Insider holdings	NA
Beta	1.72		

Value of $10,000 invested 5 years ago: $ 12,025

Fiscal Year Ending Jan. 31

	1996	% Change	1995	% Change	1994	% Change
Revenues (Million $)						
1Q	80.32	9%	73.70	14%	64.44	22%
2Q	88.67	9%	81.58	14%	71.33	19%
3Q	—	—	91.08	13%	80.71	16%
4Q	—	—	152.9	14%	133.7	8%
Yr.	—	—	399.3	14%	350.2	14%
Income (Million $)						
1Q	-2.34	NM	-1.27	NM	0.36	-27%
2Q	-1.87	NM	-6.96	NM	0.21	-68%
3Q	—	—	1.22	-26%	1.64	-40%
4Q	—	—	10.37	17%	8.87	-23%
Yr.	—	—	3.36	-69%	11.00	-29%
Earnings Per Share ($)						
1Q	-0.13	NM	-0.07	NM	0.02	-33%
2Q	-0.11	NM	-0.41	NM	0.01	-75%
3Q	—	—	0.07	-30%	0.10	-38%
4Q	—	—	0.60	15%	0.52	-22%
Yr.	—	—	0.20	-69%	0.65	-28%

Next earnings report expected: late November

Lechters, Inc.

Business Summary - 19-SEP-95

Lechters, Inc. is a specialty retailer of primarily brand name basic (non-electric) housewares, tabletop items and kitchen textiles. As of August 30, 1995, the company was operating 620 stores in 42 states. The large majority of the stores were being operated under the Lechters, Lechters Housewares or Super Lechters names, with the remainder operating under the names The Kitchen Place and Famous Brands Housewares Outlet. Most of the stores are located in shopping malls.

Sales by product category in recent fiscal years were:

	1994-95	1993-94	1992-93
Basic housewares	57.3%	54.9%	54.5%
Decorative housewares	42.7%	45.1%	45.5%

Lechters stores (383 at January 28, 1995), averaging about 3,000 sq. ft. in size, offer a large, attractively presented assortment of merchandise at prices below those customarily charged by department stores. Each unit stocks more than 6,000 items categorized as basic housewares (which include cookware, gadgets and closet and storage goods), tabletop items (glassware, frames, ceramics and wooden accessories) and kitchen textiles (towels, napkins, placemats, rugs and aprons). Products range in price from $1.00 to $200, with most items selling for less than $10.

The company also operates city center Lechters stores (23 at January 28, 1995), which offer merchandise similar to its traditional stores, plus certain products oriented toward more affluent apartment dwellers. The Kitchen Place stores (18), averaging 3,800 sq. ft., also feature merchandise similar to the traditional stores, but at lower prices. In May 1990, Lechters introduced its Famous Brands Housewares Outlet format. These stores (128) average about 4,000 sq. ft., and represent an entry into the growing manufacturers' outlet business.

During 1992, the company introduced its Super Lechters stores (76), which average 6,000 sq. ft. and incorporate expansions of frames, closet shop, bath, cookware, glass and tabletop.

Lechters opened 49 stores in 1994-95, and closed 11 stores. It expects to open about 50 stores in 1995-96, including 25 Famous Brands stores, five strip centers and 20 mall units. Ten stores are expected to be closed, and another 15 to 20 stores will be expanded or relocated.

Important Developments

Aug. '95—During the first half of 1995-96, Lechters opened 16 new stores, remodeled seven stores and closed three, bringing the total number of stores in operation at July 29, 1995, to 618.

Capitalization

Long Term Debt: $78,262,000 (7/95).

Per Share Data ($)

(Year Ended Jan. 31)

	1995	1994	1993	1992	1991	1990
Tangible Bk. Val.	8.38	8.14	7.48	6.55	4.71	4.00
Cash Flow	1.03	1.30	1.36	1.18	1.03	0.95
Earnings	0.20	0.65	0.90	0.80	0.70	0.68
Dividends	Nil	Nil	Nil	Nil	Nil	Nil
Payout Ratio	Nil	Nil	Nil	Nil	Nil	Nil
Cal. Yrs.	1994	1993	1992	1991	1990	1989
Prices - High	19	24¼	25¼	22	13⅞	12⅛
- Low	10¾	9	16¾	7¼	5⅝	8⅝
P/E Ratio - High	95	37	28	28	20	18
- Low	54	14	19	9	8	13

Income Statement Analysis (Million $)

	1995	%Chg	1994	%Chg	1993	%Chg	1992
Revs.	399	14%	350	14%	306	31%	234
Oper. Inc.	36.8	6%	34.8	NM	34.9	23%	28.4
Depr.	14.3	29%	11.1	39%	8.0	29%	6.2
Int. Exp.	7.2	-1%	7.3	NM	7.2	77%	4.1
Pretax Inc.	5.7	-70%	18.7	-23%	24.2	19%	20.3
Eff. Tax Rate	41%	—	41%	—	37%	—	36%
Net Inc.	3.4	-69%	11.1	-28%	15.4	18%	13.0

Balance Sheet & Other Fin. Data (Million $)

	1995	1994	1993	1992	1991	1990
Cash	58.1	48.1	64.6	97.9	7.3	14.2
Curr. Assets	167	157	158	163	57.0	57.0
Total Assets	271	257	240	220	102	90.0
Curr. Liab.	31.9	19.1	20.1	20.1	15.5	14.7
LT Debt	77.8	85.9	85.0	84.2	15.0	15.0
Common Eqty.	144	137	125	109	67.0	57.0
Total Cap.	235	222	210	194	82.0	72.0
Cap. Exp.	20.6	29.2	32.7	16.3	16.4	10.7
Cash Flow	17.6	22.2	23.4	19.2	14.9	12.7

Ratio Analysis

	1995	1994	1993	1992	1991	1990
Curr. Ratio	5.2	8.2	7.9	8.1	3.7	3.9
% LT Debt of Cap.	33.1	38.6	40.5	43.5	18.2	20.8
% Net Inc.of Revs.	0.8	3.2	5.0	5.6	5.4	5.8
% Ret. on Assets	1.3	4.5	6.7	7.7	10.5	11.9
% Ret. on Equity	2.4	8.5	13.1	13.9	16.2	21.3

Dividend Data —No cash dividends have been paid.

Data as orig. reptd.; bef. results of disc. opers. and/or spec. items. Per share data adj. for stk. divs. as of ex-div. date. E-Estimated. NA-Not Available. NM-Not Meaningful. NR-Not Ranked.

Office—One Cape May St., Harrison, NJ 07029-9998. **Tel**—(201) 481-1100. **Chrmn**—D. Jonas. **Vice-Chrmn & CEO**—S. Kanter. **VP & CFO**—J. W. Smolak. **VP & Secy**—I. S. Rosenberg. **Treas**—H. Penner. **Dirs**—M. S. Begun, C. A. Davis, B. D. Fischman, D. Jonas, S. Kanter, R. Knox, A. Lechter, A. E. Malkin, R. S. Maneker, N. Matthews, L. Pfeffer, J. Wolff. **Transfer Agent**—Harris Trust Co. of New York. **Incorporated** in New Jersey in 1975. **Empl**-6,911. **S&P Analyst:** Maureen C. Carini

Legg Mason

NYSE Symbol **LM**
In S&P SmallCap 600

21-SEP-95 **Industry:** Securities

Summary: This holding company is a multi-regional broker-dealer and investment banking concern serving individual and institutional investors through 93 offices in 21 states.

Quantitative Evaluations

Outlook (1 Lowest—5 Highest)
• **NA**
Fair Value
• **NA**
Risk
• **Low**
Earn./Div. Rank
• **B+**

Technical Eval.
• **Bullish** since 7/95
Rel. Strength Rank (1 Lowest—99 Highest)
• **57**
Insider Activity
• **Favorable**

Recent Price • 30
52 Wk Range • 30⅝-19¾
Yield • 1.6%
12-Mo. P/E • 19.9

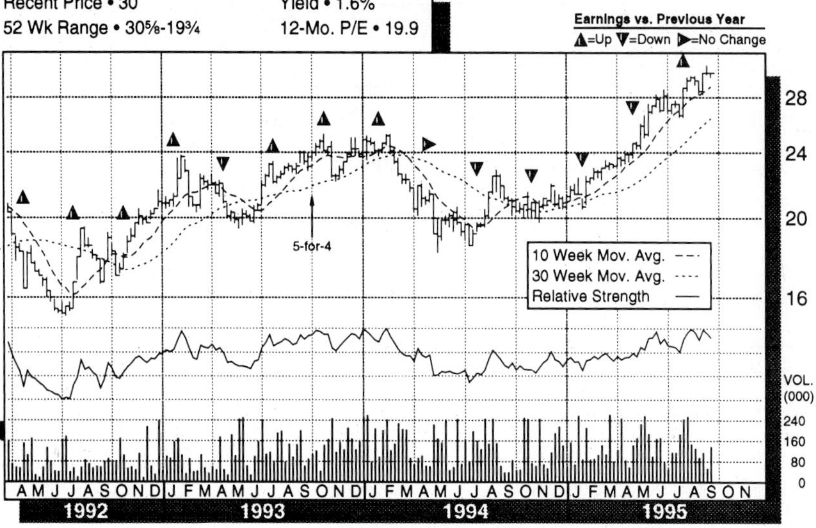

Business Profile - 19-SEP-95

LM has established niche businesses in the securities industry. Demand for LM's value-oriented research, brokerage and investment advisory activities should continue to expand in tandem with the growth in the number of high-net-worth individuals and "do-it-yourself" retirement planners. LM focuses its corporate finance activities on the middle market, which is underserved by most large investment banks.

Operational Review - 17-SEP-95

Revenues in the three months ended June 30, 1995, rose 24%, year to year, as declining interest rates, which contrasted with rising interest rates in the corresponding period last year, resulted in higher investment banking and securities brokerage volume. Total expenses increased 20%, reflecting growth in commission-based revenue and additional office occupancy costs. Net income advanced 56%, to $7.8 million ($0.61 a share; $0.50 fully diluted), from $5.0 million ($0.40; $0.35).

Stock Performance - 15-SEP-95

In the past 30 trading days, LM's shares have increased 2%, compared to a 4% rise in the S&P 500. Average trading volume for the past five days was 26,940 shares, compared with the 40-day moving average of 33,867 shares.

Key Stock Statistics

Dividend Rate/Share	0.48	Shareholders	1,900
Shs. outstg. (M)	13.9	Market cap. (B)	$0.370
Avg. daily vol. (M)	0.020	Inst. holdings	55%
Tang. Bk. Value/Share	13.22	Insider holdings	NA
Beta	1.40		

Value of $10,000 invested 5 years ago: $ 33,399

Fiscal Year Ending Mar. 31

	1996	% Change	1995	% Change	1994	% Change
Revenues (Million $)						
1Q	111.3	24%	89.84	-2%	91.35	12%
2Q	—	—	88.45	-17%	106.8	37%
3Q	—	—	92.89	-10%	103.1	21%
4Q	—	—	100.4	4%	96.29	4%
Yr.	—	—	371.6	-7%	397.5	18%
Income (Million $)						
1Q	7.83	57%	5.00	-38%	8.13	7%
2Q	—	—	3.10	-73%	11.36	66%
3Q	—	—	4.13	-58%	9.89	40%
4Q	—	—	4.02	-40%	6.67	-23%
Yr.	—	—	16.26	-55%	36.05	19%
Earnings Per Share ($)						
1Q	0.61	53%	0.40	-41%	0.68	2%
2Q	—	—	0.25	-73%	0.94	59%
3Q	—	—	0.33	-59%	0.81	33%
4Q	—	—	0.32	-42%	0.55	NM
Yr.	—	—	1.30	-56%	2.98	14%

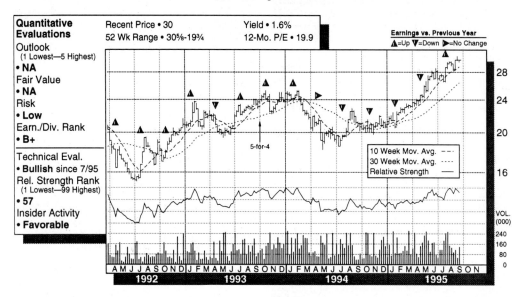

Next earnings report expected: late October

Legg Mason

Business Summary - 17-SEP-95

Legg Mason is a holding company with subsidiaries engaged in securities brokerage and trading, investment management of mutual funds and individual and institutional accounts, underwriting of corporate and municipal securities and other investment banking activities, the sale of annuity and insurance products, commercial mortgage banking, and the provision of other financial services. Principal units are Baltimore-based Legg Mason Wood Walker Inc. and New Orleans-based Howard, Weil, Labouisse, Friedrichs Inc. Total revenues in recent fiscal years were derived as follows:

	1994-95	1993-94	1992-93
Commissions	33%	39%	35%
Principal transactions	16%	18%	16%
Investment advisory	24%	15%	15%
Investment banking	9%	14%	20%
Interest income	11%	9%	7%
Other	7%	5%	7%

Growth in recent years has been spurred by acquisitions of regional broker-dealers. As of March 31, 1995, some 945 investment brokers provided brokerage services through 98 offices in 21 states, the District of Columbia, and Paris, France. Financial planning services are offered to individuals.

Legg Mason as principal is a market maker and distributor of municipal bonds, and makes a market in about 460 equity securities primarily traded over-the-counter. Securities to a large extent are those of entities located in the regions LM serves.

Investment banking activities include underwriting of public offerings of corporate debt and equity and municipal securities, M&A advisory services, and the sale of private and public limited partnership investments.

At March 31, 1995, the company sponsored 15 mutual funds with $4.1 billion in assets. Investment advisory units, in addition to serving as adviser to LM funds, managed assets of $23 billion.

LM Real Estate Services (formerly Latimer & Buck, Inc.) and Dorman & Wilson, Inc. are primarily engaged in commercial mortgage banking and commercial loan servicing.

Important Developments

Jan. '95—LM completed its acquisition of Batterymarch Financial Management, a Boston investment firm with $5.7 billion under management, for $60 million in cash, with up to an additional $60 million payable in 1998 contingent on achievement of certain revenue targets. In April 1994, LM acquired investment consulting firm Gray, Seifert & Co.

Capitalization

Long Term Debt: $68,000,000 of sub. debs. conv. into 2,635,659 com. shs. (8/95).

Options: To buy 1,530,394 shs. at $8.22 to $24.75 a sh.

Per Share Data ($) (Year Ended Mar. 31)

	1995	1994	1993	1992	1991	1990
Tangible Bk. Val.	12.57	16.02	13.44	10.82	9.05	8.81
Cash Flow	NA	NA	NA	NA	NA	NA
Earnings	1.30	2.98	2.61	1.86	1.22	1.10
Dividends	0.43	0.38	0.31	0.28	0.25	0.22
Payout Ratio	33%	13%	12%	15%	20%	20%
Cal. Yrs.	1994	1993	1992	1991	1990	1989
Prices - High	25¼	25¼	21⅝	19½	13⅜	13
- Low	18⅛	19⅜	15¼	10⅛	8⅜	8¼
P/E Ratio - High	19	8	8	11	11	12
- Low	14	7	6	5	7	8

Income Statement Analysis (Million $)

	1995	%Chg	1994	%Chg	1993	%Chg	1992
Commissions	121	-14%	141	21%	117	4%	113
Int. Inc.	39.3	31%	30.0	25%	24.0	-6%	25.6
Total Revs.	372	-7%	398	18%	336	15%	292
Int. Exp.	17.1	11%	15.4	33%	11.6	-13%	13.4
Pretax Inc.	27.7	-53%	59.2	21%	49.0	40%	35.0
Eff. Tax Rate	41%	—	39%	—	38%	—	40%
Net Inc.	16.3	-55%	36.0	19%	30.2	43%	21.1

Balance Sheet & Other Fin. Data (Million $)

	1995	1994	1993	1992	1991	1990
Total Assets	817	811	640	580	496	433
Cash Items	87.0	167	131	145	139	22.0
Receivables	371	353	305	259	216	291
Secs. Owned	51.9	57.6	112	94.6	64.6	53.3
Sec. Borrowed	120	96.0	90.0	100	48.0	17.0
Due Brokers & Cust.	325	310	282	243	248	212
Other Liabs.	58.6	64.1	56.6	53.4	39.2	52.3
Capitalization:						
Debt	103	103	34.6	35.0	35.1	35.1
Equity	226	212	177	148	126	116
Total	329	314	212	183	161	151

Ratio Analysis

	1995	1994	1993	1992	1991	1990
% Ret. on Revs.	4.4	9.1	9.0	7.2	5.3	4.9
% Ret. on Assets	2.0	5.0	4.9	3.9	2.8	2.8
% Ret. on Equity	7.4	18.6	18.6	15.2	10.7	10.6

Dividend Data —Cash dividends on the publicly held shares were initiated in 1983.

Amt. of Div. $	Date Decl.	Ex-Div. Date	Stock of Record	Payment Date
0.110	Jul. 28	Sep. 16	Sep. 22	Oct. 17 '94
0.110	Oct. 18	Dec. 09	Dec. 15	Jan. 09 '95
0.110	Jan. 19	Mar. 10	Mar. 16	Apr. 10 '95
0.110	Apr. 20	Jun. 13	Jun. 15	Jul. 10 '95
0.120	Jun. 27	Sep. 19	Sep. 21	Oct. 16 '95

Data as orig. reptd.; bef. results of disc opers. and/or spec. items. Per share data adj. for stk. divs. as of ex-div. date. E-Estimated. NA-Not Available. NM-Not Meaningful. NR-Not Ranked.

Office—111 South Calvert St., Baltimore, MD 21203-1476. **Tel**—(410) 539-0000. **Chrmn, Pres & CEO**—R. A. Mason. **Vice Chrmn & Investor Contact**—John F. Curley, Jr. **VP-Fin**—F. B. Bilson. **SVP & Secy**—C. A. Bacigalupo. **VP & Treas**—T. C. Scheve. **Dirs**—H. L. Adams, C. A. Bacigalupo, K. S. Battye, J. W. Brinkley, E. J. Cashman, Jr., J. F. Curley, Jr., H. M. Ford, Jr., R. J. Himelfarb, J. E. Koerner, III, J. B. Levert, Jr., W. C. Livingston, R. A. Mason, E. I. O'Brien, P. F. O'Malley, N. J. St. George, R. W. Schipke, M. DeB. Tutwiler, J. E. Ukrop, W. Wirth. **Transfer Agent**—First Union National Bank of North Carolina, Charlotte. **Incorporated** in Maryland in 1981. **Empl**-2,900. **S&P Analyst:** Robert Schpoont

STANDARD & POOR'S

STOCK REPORTS

Levitz Furniture

NYSE Symbol **LFI**
In S&P SmallCap 600

16-NOV-95 **Industry:** Retail Stores

Summary: This company is the largest U.S. specialty furniture retailer, serving customers in major metropolitan areas in 25 states.

Quantitative Evaluations
Outlook
(1 Lowest—5 Highest)
• **NA**
Fair Value
• **NA**
Risk
• **High**
Earn./Div. Rank
• **NR**

Technical Eval.
• **Neutral** since 11/95
Rel. Strength Rank
(1 Lowest—99 Highest)
• **3**
Insider Activity
• **NA**

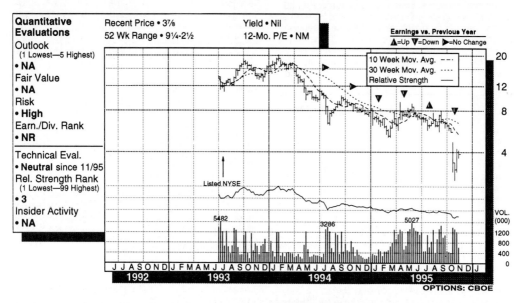

Recent Price • 3⅞
52 Wk Range • 9¼-2½
Yield • Nil
12-Mo. P/E • NM

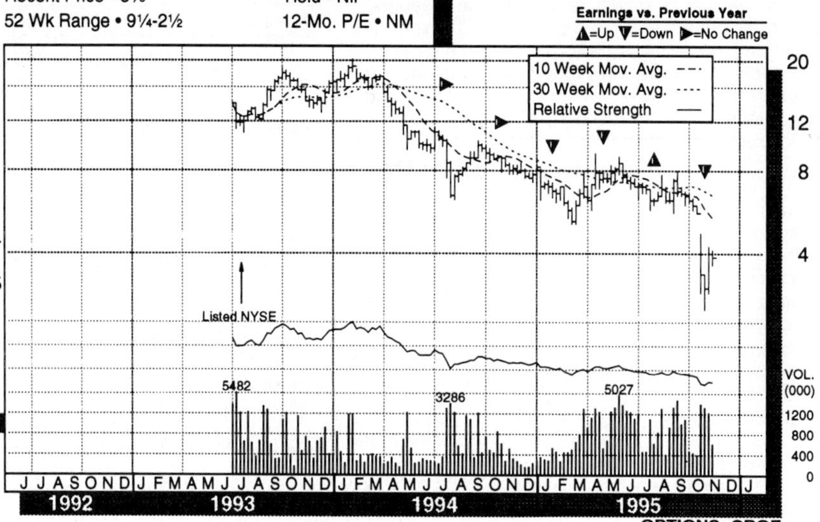

OPTIONS: CBOE

Business Profile - 16-NOV-95

This specialty retailer of furniture has outlets concentrated in California, Texas and Florida. The company, formerly listed on the NYSE, was taken private in 1985, returning to the equity market with a July 1993 IPO. Results in recent periods were hurt by a weak retailing environment. A restructuring has been initiated in an effort to reduce headcount and inventory levels. LFI is highly leveraged, with long term debt accounting for a large part of total capitalization.

Operational Review - 16-NOV-95

Sales in the first half of fiscal 1996 (Mar.) declined 2.8%, year to year, as a 9.5% drop in same-store sales outweighed the inclusion of additional stores. Results were hurt by $4 million of restructuring expenses and higher net interest costs; a loss of $8,604,000 ($0.29 a share) contrasted with net income of $3,977,000 ($0.13). Results exclude an extraordinary charge of $0.05 a share in the fiscal 1995 period.

Stock Performance - 10-NOV-95

In the past 30 trading days, LFI's shares have declined 38%, compared to a 1% rise in the S&P 500. Average trading volume for the past five days was 119,520 shares, compared with the 40-day moving average of 250,220 shares.

Key Stock Statistics

Dividend Rate/Share	Nil	Shareholders	300
Shs. outstg. (M)	29.6	Market cap. (B)	$0.111
Avg. daily vol. (M)	0.299	Inst. holdings	21%
Tang. Bk. Value/Share	NM	Insider holdings	NA
Beta	NA		

Value of $10,000 invested 5 years ago: NA

Fiscal Year Ending Mar. 31

	1996	% Change	1995	% Change	1994	% Change
Revenues (Million $)						
1Q	241.9	5%	230.6	NM	230.6	10%
2Q	251.3	5%	239.0	-1%	241.9	11%
3Q	—	—	268.4	-3%	276.1	7%
4Q	—	—	245.1	4%	235.1	NM
Yr.	—	—	1,047	6%	983.6	7%
Income (Million $)						
1Q	-5.47	NM	-0.44	NM	-0.44	—
2Q	-3.13	NM	0.51	-73%	1.88	—
3Q	—	—	3.46	-63%	9.37	—
4Q	—	—	-5.05	NM	6.00	—
Yr.	—	—	3.95	-77%	17.40	NM
Earnings Per Share ($)						
1Q	-0.18	NM	-0.29	NM	-0.29	—
2Q	-0.11	NM	0.02	NM	0.02	—
3Q	—	—	0.11	-66%	0.32	—
4Q	—	—	-0.17	NM	0.22	—
Yr.	—	—	0.13	-73%	0.48	NM

Next earnings report expected: mid January

Levitz Furniture

Business Summary - 16-NOV-95

Levitz Furniture Incorporated is a furniture retailer. At the end of fiscal 1995 (Mar.), it had 134 stores in operation. The stores, concentrated in California, Texas and Florida, serve customers in 22 of the largest 25 metropolitan statistical areas. The company is the largest U.S. specialty furniture retailer in terms of market share.

The number of stores in operation at the end of recent fiscal years was: 135 in 1995, 121 in 1994, 118 in 1993, 116 in 1992, 116 in 1991, 115 in 1990 and 107 in 1989.

Value-oriented customers are offered a wide selection of furniture and accessories, nationally advertised brands, competitively low prices, instant in-store credit and immediate availability of merchandise. Brands include Armstrong, Ashley, Bassett, Benchcraft, Berkline, Douglas, Klaussner, Lane, Lea Industries, Lexington, Palliser, Rowe, Simmons, Stanton, Stratford and Universal.

Warehouse showrooms are located within access of major highways and expressways and range in size from 62,000 to 250,000 sq. ft., with selling space of 30,000 to 83,000 sq. ft. Merchandise is typically displayed in some 175 to 260 model room settings.

Satellite stores are freestanding showrooms of 25,000 to 60,000 sq. ft. and utilize the warehouse and delivery functions of nearby warehouse-showrooms.

The merchandise sales mix in fiscal 1995 was: upholstery/seating 41%, bedroom 22%, occasional 13%, dining room 6%, bedding 9% and other 9%. LFI believes that its customer base includes the middle 80% of consumers who buy furniture. Some 40% of advertising spending is for direct-mail campaigns targeted at specific customer groups.

The company has developed strong partnerships with principal vendors from whom it purchases large quantities of merchandise, often at, what the company believes are, substantial savings.

In June 1994, LFI acquired John M. Smyth Co. for $46.8 million. Smyth, which operates six retail furniture stores in the Chicago area, had sales of $61 million in the fiscal year ended January 31, 1994.

Important Developments

Oct. '95—LFI and Montgomery Ward terminated discussions regarding a proposed investment by Montgomery in the company. The companies said that a detailed evaluation and analysis of LFI revealed that the goals and objectives of the proposed transaction could not be achieved.

Capitalization

Long Term Debt: $436,675,000 (3/95), incl. $87.8 million of lease obligs.

Per Share Data ($) (Year Ended Mar. 31)

	1995	1994	1993	1992	1991	1990
Tangible Bk. Val.	-3.08	-2.37	-2.71	NA	NA	NA
Cash Flow	1.10	1.45	0.94	NA	NA	NA
Earnings	0.13	0.48	0.03	NA	NA	NA
Dividends	Nil	Nil	NA	NA	NA	NA
Payout Ratio	Nil	Nil	NA	NA	NA	NA
Cal. Yrs.	1994	1993	1992	1991	1990	1989
Prices - High	20¼	18¾	NA	NA	NA	NA
- Low	6¼	10⅞	NA	NA	NA	NA
P/E Ratio - High	NM	39	NA	NA	NA	NA
- Low	NM	23	NA	NA	NA	NA

Income Statement Analysis (Million $)

	1995	%Chg	1994	%Chg	1993	%Chg	1992
Revs.	1,047	6%	984	7%	922	—	NA
Oper. Inc.	82.6	-16%	98.0	26%	77.9	—	NA
Depr.	28.5	15%	24.8	-2%	25.4	—	NA
Int. Exp.	47.8	-2%	48.6	6%	45.7	—	NA
Pretax Inc.	6.3	-74%	24.4	NM	6.8	—	NA
Eff. Tax Rate	38%	—	29%	—	73%	—	NA
Net Inc.	4.0	-77%	17.4	NM	1.9	—	NA

Balance Sheet & Other Fin. Data (Million $)

	1995	1994	1993	1992	1991	1990
Cash	6.3	6.1	NA	NA	NA	NA
Curr. Assets	205	195	NA	NA	NA	NA
Total Assets	651	576	NA	NA	NA	NA
Curr. Liab.	170	164	NA	NA	NA	NA
LT Debt	437	377	386	NA	NA	NA
Common Eqty.	-44.3	-47.0	-62.8	NA	NA	NA
Total Cap.	457	388	NA	NA	NA	NA
Cap. Exp.	80.3	41.0	22.6	NA	NA	NA
Cash Flow	32.4	37.2	27.3	NA	NA	NA

Ratio Analysis

	1995	1994	1993	1992	1991	1990
Curr. Ratio	1.2	1.2	NA	NA	NA	NA
% LT Debt of Cap.	95.6	97.0	NA	NA	NA	NA
% Net Inc.of Revs.	0.4	1.8	0.2	NA	NA	NA
% Ret. on Assets	0.6	2.2	NA	NA	NA	NA
% Ret. on Equity	NM	NM	NA	NA	NA	NA

Dividend Data —The company does not intend to pay dividends in the foreseeable future.

Data as orig. reptd.; bef. results of disc. opers. and/or spec. items. Per share data adj. for stk. divs. as of ex-div. date. E-Estimated. NA-Not Available. NM-Not Meaningful. NR-Not Ranked.

Office—6111 Broken Sound Parkway, N.W., Boca Raton, FL 33487-2799. **Tel**—(407) 994-6006. **Chrmn & CEO**—M. Bozic. **Pres & COO**—R. A. Kaplan. **SVP-Fin, CFO & Investor Contact**—Patrick J. Nolan. **VP & Secy**—E. P. Zimmer. **Dirs**—M. Bozic, R. M. Cashin, R. M. Harrell, B. C. Leadbetter, K. D. Moelis, H. B. Reiling, W. W. Wright. **Transfer Agent & Registrar**—American Stock Transfer & Trust Co., NYC. **Incorporated** in Delaware in 1980. **Empl**-6,018. **S&P Analyst:** S.R.B.

STANDARD & POOR'S

STOCK REPORTS

Liberty Bancorp

NASDAQ Symbol **LBNA**

In S&P SmallCap 600

05-SEP-95

Industry: Banking

Summary: This holding company (formerly Banks of Mid-America) owns Liberty Bank & Trust Co. of Oklahoma City and Liberty Bank & Trust Co. of Tulsa, two of the largest banks in Oklahoma.

Quantitative Evaluations

Outlook
(1 Lowest—5 Highest)
• **1-**

Fair Value
• **27**

Risk
• **Low**

Earn./Div. Rank
• **B-**

Technical Eval.
• **Bearish** since 7/95

Rel. Strength Rank
(1 Lowest—99 Highest)
• **70**

Insider Activity
• **Neutral**

Recent Price • 36¾ Yield • 2.2%

52 Wk Range • 37-27¾ 12-Mo. P/E • 13.5

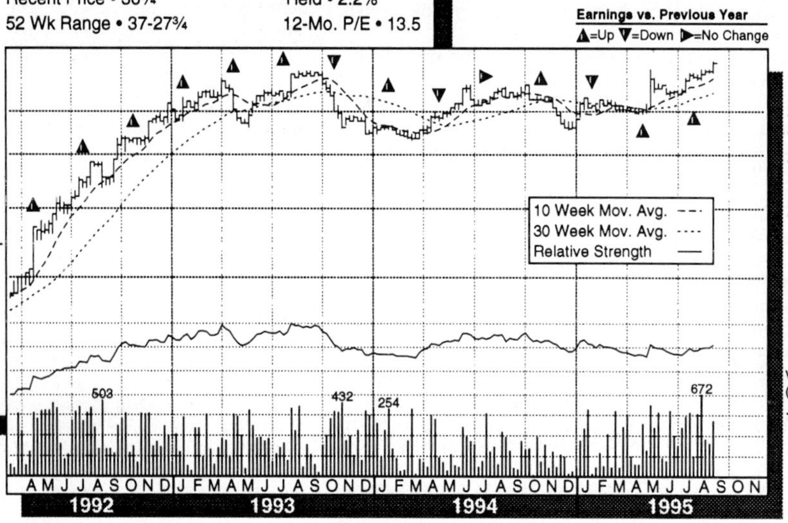

Business Profile - 05-SEP-95

LBNA, which operates 32 banking offices, is continuing to focus on loan growth and expense controls. In 1993, LBNA expanded its asset base by $277 million with five acquisitions. LBNA grew its loan portfolio by 27% in 1994, while reducing noninterest expenses by 6%, with much of the improvement coming from lower personnel costs. In 1995, LBNA is aiming to bring its overall efficiency measures in line with its peers through nonpersonnnel expense reductions and technology enhancements.

Operational Review - 05-SEP-95

Net interest income rose 6.0% in the first half of 1995 from the year-earlier period, reflecting a 5.7% increase in earning assets and a flat net interest margin (3.64%). There was no provision for loan losses in either period. Noninterest income was up 11%, primarily due to the sale of equity securities. Following flat noninterest expense, and higher taxes, net income climbed 19%. LBNA projects loan growth and an increase in its net interest margin for the remainder of 1995.

Stock Performance - 01-SEP-95

In the past 30 trading days, LBNA's shares have increased 5%, compared to a 2% rise in the S&P 500. Average trading volume for the past five days was 21,620 shares, compared with the 40-day moving average of 34,760 shares.

Key Stock Statistics

Dividend Rate/Share	0.80	Shareholders	2,600
Shs. outstg. (M)	9.5	Market cap. (B)	$0.349
Avg. daily vol. (M)	0.046	Inst. holdings	59%
Tang. Bk. Value/Share	25.70	Insider holdings	NA
Beta	0.53		

Value of $10,000 invested 5 years ago: $ 38,531

Fiscal Year Ending Dec. 31

	1995	% Change	1994	% Change	1993	% Change
Revenues (Million $)						
1Q	59.33	26%	47.27	3%	45.84	NM
2Q	NA	—	49.08	9%	44.91	4%
3Q	—	—	49.06	10%	44.55	5%
4Q	—	—	54.99	10%	49.82	20%
Yr.	—	—	200.4	8%	185.1	7%
Income (Million $)						
1Q	5.91	19%	4.95	-32%	7.29	117%
2Q	6.10	18%	5.16	-3%	5.30	37%
3Q	—	—	10.61	NM	3.43	-6%
4Q	—	—	5.16	-18%	6.26	139%
Yr.	—	—	25.88	16%	22.28	65%
Earnings Per Share ($)						
1Q	0.60	18%	0.51	-34%	0.77	103%
2Q	0.62	17%	0.53	NM	0.53	23%
3Q	—	—	1.08	NM	0.35	-13%
4Q	—	—	0.53	-17%	0.64	121%
Yr.	—	—	2.64	16%	2.28	53%

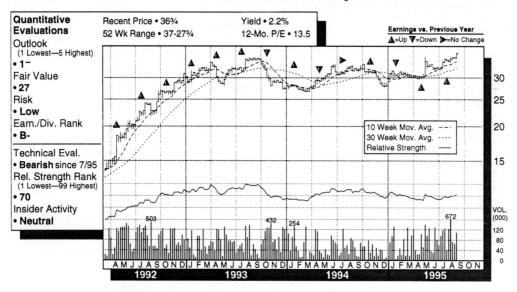

Next earnings report expected: late October

Liberty Bancorp

Business Summary - 05-SEP-95

Liberty Bancorp, Inc. (formerly Banks of Mid-America, Inc.) was formed in 1984 through the consolidation of Liberty National Corp. and First Tulsa Bancorporation, Inc. The company's two principal subsidiaries are Liberty Bank & Trust Co. of Oklahoma City (which had assets of $1.9 billion at the end of 1994) and Liberty Bank & Trust Co. of Tulsa ($964 million), which together operate 31 full-service banking locations in Oklahoma.

At December 31, 1994, gross loans outstanding totaled $1.18 billion, and were divided:

Commercial	41%
Energy	6%
Real estate	31%
Correspondent	2%
Personal	20%

The reserve for possible loan losses at 1994 year end amounted to $19,081,000 ($19,986,000 a year earlier), or 1.62% (2.14%) of loans outstanding. There were net chargeoffs of $905,000 (0.09% of average loans) in 1994, versus a net recovery of $527,000 (0.07%) in 1993. As of December 31, 1994, nonperforming loans (consisting of nonaccrual and restructured loans and loans past due 90 days or more) aggregated $11,556,000 (0.98% of total loans), down from $13,451,000 (1.44%) a year earlier.

Average deposits in 1994 of $2.10 billion were divided: 29% noninterest-bearing demand, 27% interest-bearing demand, 7% savings, and 37% time deposits.

Interest on loans provided 41% of total income in 1994, interest on investments 28%, other interest income 1%, trust fees 8%, service charges on deposits 7%, and other noninterest income 15%.

On a taxable-equivalent basis, the average yield on interest-earning assets in 1994 was 6.56% (6.39% in 1993), while the average rate paid on interest-bearing liabilities was 3.73% (3.40%), for a net spread of 2.83% (2.99%).

Important Developments

Jul. '95—Liberty continued to expand its loan portfolio in the second quarter of 1995, reflecting the favorable business climate in its market territory. Loans outstanding at June 30, 1995, amounted to $1.28 billion, up 17% from $1.04 billion a year earlier.

Capitalization

Long Term Debt: None (12/94).

Per Share Data ($)

(Year Ended Dec. 31)

	1994	1993	1992	1991	1990	1989
Tangible Bk. Val.	23.04	22.51	18.79	16.65	17.42	16.92
Earnings	2.64	2.28	1.49	0.57	0.25	0.13
Dividends	0.60	0.30	Nil	Nil	Nil	Nil
Payout Ratio	23%	13%	Nil	Nil	Nil	Nil
Prices - High	33½	35½	31	14¾	12	11
- Low	26½	27	12¾	6¾	7	9
P/E Ratio - High	13	16	21	26	48	85
- Low	10	12	9	12	28	69

Income Statement Analysis (Million $)

	1994	%Chg	1993	%Chg	1992	%Chg	1991
Net Int. Inc.	77.7	4%	74.6	17%	63.9	16%	55.1
Tax Equiv. Adj.	2.2	-3%	2.3	-12%	2.6	-10%	2.9
Non Int. Inc.	57.9	7%	54.0	11%	48.7	10%	44.1
Loan Loss Prov.	Nil	—	-7.4	NM	1.8	-22%	2.3
% Exp/Op Revs.	81%	—	91%	—	80%	—	89%
Pretax Inc.	25.0	26%	19.9	9%	18.2	NM	5.9
Eff. Tax Rate	3.60%	—	NM	—	26%	—	16%
Net Inc.	25.9	16%	22.3	65%	13.5	170%	5.0
% Net Int. Marg.	3.65%	—	3.76%	—	3.66%	—	3.25%

Balance Sheet & Other Fin. Data (Million $)

	1994	1993	1992	1991	1990	1989
Earning Assets:						
Money Mkt.	74.0	29.0	346	323	437	216
Inv. Securities	1,091	1,249	1,013	846	699	677
Com'l Loans	488	434	340	454	386	354
Other Loans	692	497	346	396	397	468
Total Assets	2,884	2,660	2,428	2,490	2,452	2,275
Demand Deposits	728	689	666	676	624	616
Time Deposits	1,646	1,436	1,263	1,233	1,225	1,134
LT Debt	Nil	Nil	7.5	9.8	10.9	12.0
Common Eqty.	234	227	179	160	153	150

Ratio Analysis

	1994	1993	1992	1991	1990	1989
% Ret. on Assets	1.0	0.9	0.6	0.2	0.1	0.1
% Ret. on Equity	11.3	10.7	7.9	3.1	1.4	0.7
% Loan Loss Resv.	1.6	2.2	3.7	3.1	3.2	3.9
% Loans/Deposits	49.7	43.8	35.5	44.6	42.4	47.0
% Equity to Assets	8.9	8.6	7.9	7.3	7.2	7.3

Dividend Data —Cash dividends, paid by the company or its predecessors since 1935, were omitted in 1986 and resumed in June 1993. A 1-for-10 reverse stock split was effected October 18, 1988.

Amt. of Div. $	Date Decl.	Ex-Div. Date	Stock of Record	Payment Date
0.150	Oct. 19	Oct. 25	Oct. 31	Nov. 14 '94
0.200	Jan. 18	Jan. 30	Feb. 03	Feb. 17 '95
0.200	Apr. 26	May. 01	May. 05	May. 19 '95
0.200	Jul. 21	Aug. 02	Aug. 04	Aug. 18 '95

Data as orig. reptd.; bef. results of disc opers. and/or spec. items. Per share data adj. for stk. divs. as of ex-div. date. E-Estimated. NA-Not Available. NM-Not Meaningful. NR-Not Ranked.

Office—100 N. Broadway, Oklahoma City, OK 73102. **Tel**—(405) 231-6000. **Chrmn & CEO**—C. E. Nelson. **Pres**—W. H. Thompson Jr. **Sr VP, CFO & Investor Contact**—Mischa Gorkuscha. **SVP & Secy**—K. R. Brown. **Dirs**—D. L. Brawner, T. G. Donnell, R. S. Ellis, W. F. Fisher Jr., C. W. Flint Jr., J. L. Hall Jr., R. H. Hefner Jr., W. H. Helmerich III, J. S. Jankowsky, J. E. Kirkpatrick, J. Z. Kishner, D. L. Kyle, E. C. Lawson Jr., H. Mee Jr., C. E. Nelson, W. G. Paul, V. L. Powell, J. R. Stuart, R. E. Torray, J. S. Zink. **Transfer Agent & Registrar**—Liberty Bank & Trust Co., Oklahoma City. **Incorporated** in Delaware in 1984; reincorporated in Oklahoma in 1992. **Empl**-1,364. **S&P Analyst:** Robert Schpoont

STANDARD & POOR'S

STOCK REPORTS

Life Partners Group

NYSE Symbol **LPG**
In S&P SmallCap 600

26-SEP-95

Industry:
Insurance

Summary: Life Partners Group sells mainly universal life insurance and, to a lesser extent, annuity products, through its Massachusetts General Life, Philadelphia Life and Lamar Life units.

Quantitative Evaluations
Outlook
(1 Lowest—5 Highest)
• **NA**
Fair Value
• **NA**
Risk
• **Average**
Earn./Div. Rank
• **NR**

Technical Eval.
• **Neutral** since 8/95
Rel. Strength Rank
(1 Lowest—99 Highest)
• **14**
Insider Activity
• **NA**

Recent Price • 17⅛
52 Wk Range • 23¼-15⅝
Yield • 0.7%
12-Mo. P/E • 18.8

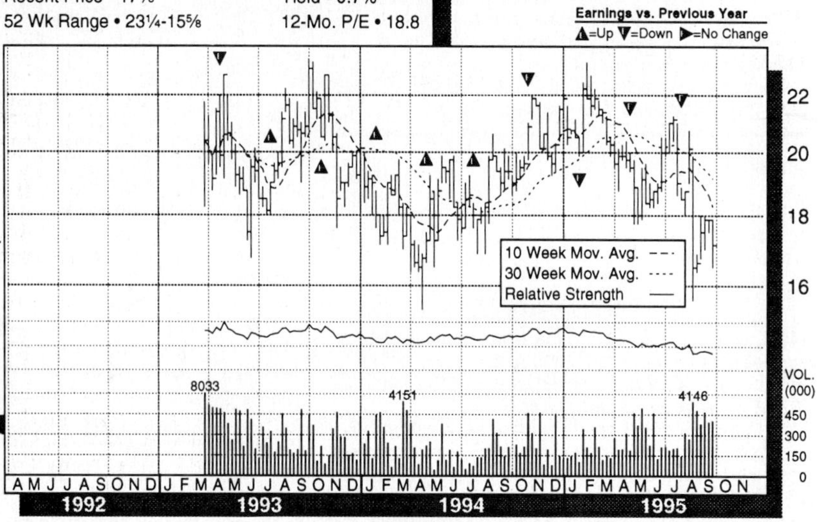

Business Profile - 21-SEP-95

The company expects to grow internally through product design, operations management and distribution, and externally through strategic acquisitions and third-party, fee-for-service arrangements. While disappointed with results in the second quarter of 1995, management noted that it was encouraged by the marketing results and the consolidation of the operations of Lamar Financial, which was acquired in April 1995.

Operational Review - 21-SEP-95

Total revenues in the first half of 1995 advanced 25%, year to year, aided by higher premium income following the acquisition of Lamar Financial and greater net investment income. Results were hurt by mortality experience in the second quarter that was higher than actuarially expected and a $2 million write-off of certain agent debit balances. Net income fell to $11.3 million ($0.42 a share), from $24.6 million ($0.94).

Stock Performance - 22-SEP-95

In the past 30 trading days, LPG's shares have declined 15%, compared to a 5% rise in the S&P 500. Average trading volume for the past five days was 80,180 shares, compared with the 40-day moving average of 185,823 shares.

Key Stock Statistics

Dividend Rate/Share	0.12	Shareholders	1,100
Shs. outstg. (M)	27.8	Market cap. (B)	$0.477
Avg. daily vol. (M)	0.089	Inst. holdings	66%
Tang. Bk. Value/Share	10.73	Insider holdings	NA
Beta	NA		

Value of $10,000 invested 5 years ago: NA

Fiscal Year Ending Dec. 31

	1995	% Change	1994	% Change	1993	% Change
Revenues (Million $)						
1Q	122.1	7%	114.2	NM	114.2	—
2Q	153.9	45%	106.4	-6%	113.4	—
3Q	—	—	113.4	6%	107.5	—
4Q	—	—	98.42	-12%	112.2	—
Yr.	—	—	432.5	-6%	462.0	4%
Income (Million $)						
1Q	6.90	-48%	13.15	30%	10.10	—
2Q	4.60	-60%	11.44	3%	11.10	—
3Q	—	—	17.79	NM	17.80	—
4Q	—	—	-0.40	NM	12.70	—
Yr.	—	—	37.21	-28%	51.99	20%
Earnings Per Share ($)						
1Q	0.26	-49%	0.51	24%	0.41	-33%
2Q	0.16	-64%	0.44	2%	0.43	19%
3Q	—	—	0.50	-26%	0.68	84%
4Q	—	—	-0.01	NM	0.49	53%
Yr.	—	—	1.43	-29%	2.01	21%

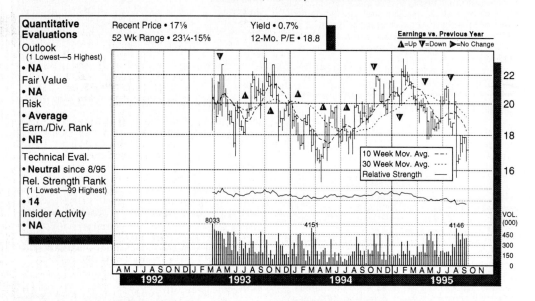

Next earnings report expected: mid November

Life Partners Group

Business Summary - 25-SEP-95

Life Partners Group is an insurance holding company which, through its two principal subsidiaries-- Massachusetts General Life Insurance Co. and Philadelphia Life Insurance Co. --sells a diverse portfolio of universal life insurance and, to a lesser extent, annuity products. Unlike many products currently offered by its competitors, LPG's life insurance products and annuities have been designed to ensure their profitability by shifting the costs of early policy termination to the policyholder rather than the company. The company's traditional and universal life insurance in force amounted to $45.1 billion as of December 31, 1994. Direct collected premiums by product category in recent years were:

	1994	1993
Universal life	68.9%	56.8%
Individual whole & term life	10.8%	10.4%
Tax-qualified annuities	15.2%	25.3%
Non-tax qualified annuities	5.1%	7.5%

LPG's in-force life insurance business consists of a diverse portfolio of universal life and whole life insurance policies, as well as term life insurance policies. Currently, however, predominantly all life insurance sales consist of universal life insurance policies sold to individuals. LPG's universal life insurance policies provide permanent life insurance with adjustable rates of return based on current interest rates. Its universal life insurance policies provide advantages generally not available to its whole life and term life policyholders, such as flexibility in available coverages and timing and amount of premium payments.

LPG began to offer flexible premium and single-premium deferred annuities in September 1990. Its single premium deferred annuities require a one-time lump sum premium payment and are frequently sold as an alternative to certificates of deposit. Flexible premium deferred annuities permit annual premium payments in such amounts as the holder deems appropriate.

The company's insurance subsidiaries are collectively licensed to market its insurance products in all states except New York, and in the District of Columbia and certain U.S. protectorates.

Important Developments

Apr. '95—The company said it acquired Lamar Financial Group, Inc., a national insurer licensed in 46 states and with $8.2 billion of individual life insurance in force, for $39.2 million in stock and $83.7 million in cash.

Capitalization

Long Term Debt: $206,263,000 (12/94).

Per Share Data ($)

(Year Ended Dec. 31)

	1994	1993	1992	1991	1990	1989
Tangible Bk. Val.	8.21	8.84	7.78	NA	NA	NA
Oper. Earnings	NA	1.76	1.32	NA	NA	NA
Earnings	1.43	2.01	1.66	NA	NA	NA
Dividends	0.08	0.04	NA	NA	NA	NA
Payout Ratio	6%	2%	NA	NA	NA	NA
Prices - High	22	23⅜	NA	NA	NA	NA
- Low	15⅝	16¾	NA	NA	NA	NA
P/E Ratio - High	15	12	NA	NA	NA	NA
- Low	11	8	NA	NA	NA	NA

Income Statement Analysis (Million $)

	1994	%Chg	1993	%Chg	1992	%Chg	1991
Life Ins. In Force	45,063	12%	40,331	—	NA	—	NA
Premium Income Life	222	2%	217	12%	194	—	NA
Prem.Inc A & H	Nil	—	Nil	—	Nil	—	NA
Premium Income Other	Nil	—	Nil	—	Nil	—	NA
Net Invest. Inc.	225	2%	221	1%	218	—	NA
Total Revs.	432	-6%	462	4%	443	—	NA
Pretax Inc.	58.5	-29%	81.9	25%	65.7	—	NA
Net Oper. Inc.	NA	—	NA	—	NA	—	NA
Net Inc.	37.2	-28%	52.0	20%	43.5	—	NA

Balance Sheet & Other Fin. Data (Million $)

	1994	1993	1992	1991	1990	1989
Cash & Equiv.	88.0	268	NA	NA	NA	NA
Premiums Due	20.6	18.4	NA	NA	NA	NA
Inv Assets Bonds	2,629	2,347	2,198	NA	NA	NA
Inv. Assets Stock	27.5	29.8	71.0	NA	NA	NA
Inv. Assets Loans	44.0	224	247	NA	NA	NA
Inv. Assets Total	2,944	2,647	2,574	NA	NA	NA
Deferred Policy Cost	277	200	NA	NA	NA	NA
Total Assets	3,749	3,589	3,207	NA	NA	NA
Debt	210	210	263	NA	NA	NA
Common Eqty.	292	311	286	NA	NA	NA

Ratio Analysis

	1994	1993	1992	1991	1990	1989
% Ret. on Revs.	8.6	11.3	9.8	NA	NA	NA
% Ret. on Assets	1.0	1.5	NA	NA	NA	NA
% Ret. on Equity	12.3	22.7	NA	NA	NA	NA
% Invest. Yield	8.1	8.7	9.0	NA	NA	NA

Dividend Data —Cash dividends were initiated with the June 1993 payment.

Amt. of Div. $	Date Decl.	Ex-Div. Date	Stock of Record	Payment Date
0.020	Nov. 16	Nov. 23	Nov. 30	Dec. 15 '94
0.020	Feb. 14	Feb. 17	Feb. 24	Mar. 15 '95
0.030	May. 17	May. 22	May. 26	Jun. 15 '95
0.030	Aug. 16	Aug. 25	Aug. 29	Sep. 15 '95

Data as orig. reptd.; bef. results of disc. opers. and/or spec. items. Per share data adj. for stk. divs. as of ex-div. date. E-Estimated. NA-Not Available. NM-Not Meaningful. NR-Not Ranked.

Office—7887 East Belleview Ave., Englewood, CO 80111. **Tel**—(303) 779-1111. **Chrmn & CEO**—J. H. Massey. **Pres**—D. Gubbay. **EVP & CFO**—G. Paz. **Dirs**—G. H. Bishop, J. W. Gardiner, T. O. Hicks, J. H. Massey, J. R. Muse, B. W. Schnitzer, R. T. Staubach, R. E. Witt. **Transfer Agent & Registrar**—Society National Bank, Dallas. **Incorporated** in Delaware in 1989. **Empl-540. S&P Analyst:** S.R.B.

STANDARD & POOR'S

STOCK REPORTS

Life Re Corp.

NYSE Symbol **LRE**
In S&P SmallCap 600

22-SEP-95 **Industry:** Insurance

Summary: Life Re Corp. is a leading provider of life and health reinsurance in the United States through its subsidiary, Life Reassurance Corp. of America.

Quantitative Evaluations

Outlook
(1 Lowest—5 Highest)
• **NA**

Fair Value
• **NA**

Risk
• **Average**

Earn./Div. Rank
• **NR**

Technical Eval.
• **Bearish** since 8/95

Rel. Strength Rank
(1 Lowest—99 Highest)
• **73**

Insider Activity
• **NA**

Recent Price • 21½
52 Wk Range • 22½-14⅞
Yield • 1.3%
12-Mo. P/E • 10.3

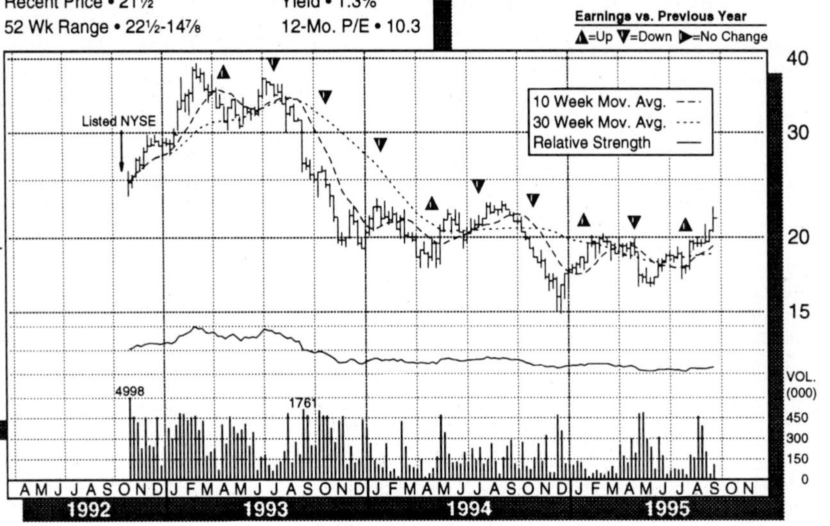

Business Profile - 22-SEP-95

LRE's target growth rate for policy revenues is 15%. Management believes opportunities in the U.S. are sufficient to achieve this goal, but continues to consider other reinsurance markets; in 1994, policy revenues grew at 21%. LRE's investment portfolio is conservative, with investment grade fixed maturity securities accounting for 96% of fixed investment assets. In the quarter ended June 30, 1995, operating earnings increased 13% over those of the previous year, to $0.62 per common share.

Operational Review - 22-SEP-95

In the six months ended June 30, 1995, total revenues rose 9.3%, year to year, reflecting a 9.8% increase in policy revenues and 10% higher investment income. Expenses advanced 12%, as policy claims and benefits climbed 16%, and reinsurance commissions and allowances grew 8.4%. Pretax income fell 14%, while taxes were unchanged at 35.0%. Net income decreased to $14,118,000 ($0.92 a share) from $16,334,000 ($1.05).

Stock Performance - 15-SEP-95

In the past 30 trading days, LRE's shares have increased 10%, compared to a 4% rise in the S&P 500. Average trading volume for the past five days was 21,420 shares, compared with the 40-day moving average of 42,415 shares.

Key Stock Statistics

Dividend Rate/Share	0.28	Shareholders	2,600
Shs. outstg. (M)	14.8	Market cap. (B)	$0.314
Avg. daily vol. (M)	0.032	Inst. holdings	76%
Tang. Bk. Value/Share	16.62	Insider holdings	NA
Beta	NA		

Value of $10,000 invested 5 years ago: NA

Fiscal Year Ending Dec. 31

	1995	% Change	1994	% Change	1993	% Change
Revenues (Million $)						
1Q	114.5	12%	102.2	20%	85.20	3%
2Q	116.3	7%	108.8	20%	90.54	7%
3Q	—	—	106.6	-5%	112.2	11%
4Q	—	—	115.8	21%	95.35	10%
Yr.	—	—	433.4	13%	383.3	8%
Income (Million $)						
1Q	4.55	-39%	7.46	53%	4.88	9%
2Q	9.57	8%	8.87	-8%	9.66	18%
3Q	—	—	7.93	-53%	16.87	-25%
4Q	—	—	10.05	29%	7.82	-22%
Yr.	—	—	34.32	-12%	39.22	-13%
Earnings Per Share ($)						
1Q	0.29	-40%	0.48	55%	0.31	15%
2Q	0.63	11%	0.57	-7%	0.61	-2%
3Q	—	—	0.51	-52%	1.07	-46%
4Q	—	—	0.65	30%	0.50	-23%
Yr.	—	—	2.21	-12%	2.50	-28%

Next earnings report expected: early November

Life Re Corp.

Business Summary - 18-SEP-95

LRE, through its Life Reassurance subsidiary, provides reinsurance for life and health risks in the U.S. and Canada. Life Re serves as a holding company for TexasRe Life Insurance Co., which in turn holds all of the common stock of Life Reassurance.

Revenues in 1994 were derived as follows:

	1994	1993
Premium income	81%	75%
Net investment income	19%	19%
Realized investment gains	Nil	6%

Life Re's reinsurance agreements cover a portfolio of ordinary life insurance products, including term, universal and whole life, as well as group life, group health and special risk insurance. Life Re writes reinsurance predominantly on a direct basis under automatic treaties with primary life insurance companies, but does not currently write primary insurance or surplus relief reinsurance. Net premiums in 1994 totaled $350.9 million, 64% of which was ordinary life reinsurance and 36% group life, health and special risk.

Most of Life Re's ordinary life business is structured as coinsurance written on a quota share basis. The company generally requires ceding companies to retain at least 10% of every risk, whether the business is written on an excess or quota share basis. Life Re generally limits its own net liability on any one ordinary life risk to $1 million.

As of December 31, 1994, Life Re reinsured ordinary life business under treaties with nearly 500 ceding companies. Thirty-six ceding companies each accounted for at least $1.0 million of ordinary life gross policy revenues and in the aggregate represented about 88.4% of its 1994 ordinary life gross premiums. The company markets its ordinary life reinsurance to a broad cross-section of client companies varying in size, corporate structure and geographic location.

In 1994, Primerica Life, Liberty and Guardian Life Insurance Co. of America and Nicolah together represented 36% of Life Re's total policy revenues.

Important Developments

Jul. '95—Life Reassurance acquired 100% of the outstanding stock of John Deere Life Insurance Co. Terms of the transaction were not disclosed. John Deere Life, formed in 1937, is licensed in 48 states and primarily writes life insurance and annuities; it has traditionally focused on the rural marketplace. At closing, John Deere Life had approximately $340 million in assets on a statutory basis. In 1994, its revenues included $9.7 million of ordinary life insurance premiums and approximately $24 million of annuity deposits. LRE believes the acquisition will help it attain its policy revenue growth objectives.

Capitalization

Loans Payable: $140,000,000 (6/95).

Per Share Data ($)

(Year Ended Dec. 31)

	1994	1993	1992	1991	1990	1989
Tangible Bk. Val.	9.61	11.71	7.58	-0.16	NA	NA
Oper. Earnings	2.21	NA	1.88	NA	NA	NA
Earnings	2.21	2.50	3.45	1.72	NA	NA
Dividends	0.24	0.20	Nil	NA	NA	NA
Payout Ratio	11%	8%	Nil	NA	NA	NA
Prices - High	23¼	39¼	29¾	NA	NA	NA
- Low	14⅞	19⅛	22	NA	NA	NA
P/E Ratio - High	11	16	9	NA	NA	NA
- Low	7	8	6	NA	NA	NA

Income Statement Analysis (Million $)

	1994	%Chg	1993	%Chg	1992	%Chg	1991
Life Ins. In Force	81.0	2%	79.4	7%	74.1	-9%	81.1
Premium Income Life	351	21%	289	—	NA	—	NA
Prem.Inc A & H	Nil	—	Nil	—	Nil	—	Nil
Premium Income Other	Nil	—	Nil	—	Nil	—	Nil
Net Invest. Inc.	82.4	12%	73.5	1%	72.6	9%	66.6
Total Revs.	433	13%	383	8%	355	15%	310
Pretax Inc.	52.8	-13%	60.6	-12%	68.6	77%	38.7
Net Oper. Inc.	34.2	—	NA	—	27.2	—	NA
Net Inc.	34.3	-13%	39.2	-13%	45.1	70%	26.6

Balance Sheet & Other Fin. Data (Million $)

	1994	1993	1992	1991	1990	1989
Cash & Equiv.	21.4	23.1	22.1	18.9	NA	NA
Premiums Due	NA	NA	NA	NA	NA	NA
Inv Assets Bonds	847	908	777	752	NA	NA
Inv. Assets Stock	12.1	11.8	48.1	14.4	NA	NA
Inv. Assets Loans	24.0	25.2	20.6	18.8	NA	NA
Inv. Assets Total	999	945	845	785	NA	NA
Deferred Policy Cost	119	96.0	NA	NA	NA	NA
Total Assets	1,442	1,340	1,078	1,021	NA	NA
Debt	140	150	165	165	NA	NA
Common Eqty.	195	231	171	125	NA	NA

Ratio Analysis

	1994	1993	1992	1991	1990	1989
% Ret. on Revs.	7.9	10.2	12.7	8.6	NA	NA
% Ret. on Assets	2.5	3.2	NA	NA	NA	NA
% Ret. on Equity	16.1	19.5	30.5	NA	NA	NA
% Invest. Yield	8.1	8.2	8.9	9.4	NA	NA

Dividend Data —Quarterly dividends were initiated with the March 1993 payment.

Amt. of Div. $	Date Decl.	Ex-Div. Date	Stock of Record	Payment Date
0.060	Aug. 09	Sep. 02	Sep. 09	Sep. 30 '94
0.060	Nov. 04	Nov. 25	Dec. 01	Dec. 20 '94
0.070	Mar. 08	Mar. 17	Mar. 23	Mar. 31 '95
0.070	May. 04	Jun. 06	Jun. 09	Jun. 30 '95
0.070	Aug. 02	Aug. 30	Sep. 01	Sep. 22 '95

Data as orig. reptd.; bef. results of disc. opers. and/or spec. items. Per share data adj. for stk. divs. as of ex-div. date. E-Estimated. NA-Not Available. NM-Not Meaningful. NR-Not Ranked.

Office—969 High Ridge Rd., Stamford, CT 06905. **Tel**—(203) 321-3000. **Chrmn & CEO**—R. A. Hawes Jr. **Pres & COO**—J. E. Dubois. **VP-CFO**—S. V. Filoromo. **VP-Secy**—W. W. Wilson. **Investor Contact**—Tracy L. Rudolph. **Dirs**—J. E. Dubois, S. V. Filoromo, R. A. Hawes Jr., C. K. McCandless, D. M. Schair, K. F. Skousen, T. B. Woodbury II. **Transfer Agent**—Bank of New York, NYC. **Incorporated** in Delaware in 1988. **Empl**-99. **S&P Analyst:** Thomas C. Ferguson

Lillian Vernon

ASE Symbol LVC In S&P SmallCap 600

Price	Range	P-E Ratio	Dividend	Yield	S&P Ranking	Beta
Oct. 10'95	1995					
13⅜	22¼–13⅛	13	0.28	2.1%	B	0.93

Summary

Lillian Vernon is a direct-mail marketer of household, decorative, gardening, Christmas and children's products. In September 1995, LVC's proposed acquisition by Freeman Spogli & Co. at $19 a share was terminated because of failure to obtain financing.

Business Summary

Lillian Vernon Corporation is primarily a direct-mail marketer of gift, household, gardening, decorative, Christmas and children's items, specializing in products that can be differentiated from competitive ones either by design, price or personalization. The Special Markets division sells premium and incentive products to wholesalers. The company also operates a chain of eight outlet stores that offer Lillian Vernon merchandise.

The company uses its proprietary database, containing customer information such as order frequency, size and date of last order and type of items purchased, to determine most likely buyers of products from its catalogs. The database contains information on about 18 million persons. A portion of income is derived from rental of the customer list to other direct-mail marketers.

Catalog and order activity (in millions) in recent years (ended on or about February 28):

	1995	1994	1993
Catalogs mailed..........	179.4	150.8	141.0
Orders received..........	4.9	4.6	4.4
Avg. revenue/order......	$44.61	$42.86	$40.09

In fiscal 1994-5, more than 179 million catalogs in 26 editions were mailed. There were five Spring, five Fall, five Sale, four Lilly's Kids, three Christmas Memories and two Welcome catalogs (targeted at people who have recently moved, offering home decor, organizational products and housewares). The company also issued one edition each of its Personalization and Lillian Vernon's Kitchen catalogs. The Spring catalog typically offers 500 to 600 items; Fall catalogs offer 550 to 725 items. Sale catalogs, issued to sell season overstocks, offer 400 to 500 items. The Lilly's Kids catalog offers 200 to 400 items, and Christmas Memories 250 to 350 items. The Personalization, Lillian Vernon's Kitchen and Wellcome catalogs each offer 300 items for sale. Free monogramming is available for 50% of items offered.

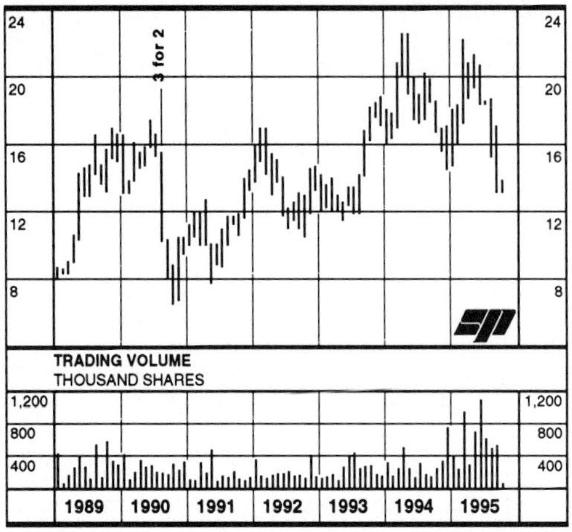

Orders are executed from and products are stored in LVC's national distribution center in Virginia Beach, Va. Products are obtained from more than 850 suppliers, with 80% of the items sold purchased abroad, mostly in the Far East. Business is seasonal, with volume heaviest from September through February.

Important Developments

Oct. '95— LVC's board authorized the repurchase of up to one million common shares. Separately, LVC said it would expand its national distribution center in Virginia Beach, Va., by adding 335,000 sq. ft. to this 486,000 sq. ft. facility. Completion is scheduled for the summer of 1997.

Sep. '95— LVC said that financing for its proposed acquisition, for $19 a share by the private investment firm of Freeman Spogli & Co., could not be obtained. The merger was therefore terminated.

Next earnings report expected in early January.

Per Share Data ($)

Yr. End Feb. 28	1995	1994	1993	1992	1991	1990	1989	1988	1987	1986
Tangible Bk. Val.	**11.44**	[1]10.22	[1]9.07	8.10	7.08	6.06	4.89	3.96	2.01	1.42
Cash Flow	**1.77**	1.68	1.45	1.29	1.28	1.47	1.11	1.14	0.79	NA
Earnings	**1.38**	1.35	1.15	1.02	1.00	1.17	0.88	0.83	0.59	0.28
Dividends	**0.26**	0.20	0.20	Nil	Nil	Nil	Nil	Nil	Nil	Nil
Payout Ratio	**19%**	15%	17%	Nil	Nil	Nil	Nil	Nil	Nil	Nil
Calendar Years	**1994**	1993	1992	1991	1990	1989	1988	1987	1986	1985
Prices—High	**22⅝**	18⅞	17	14½	17½	17	8¹¹⁄₁₆	10³⁄₁₆	NA	NA
Low	**14½**	11½	10½	7¾	6½	8¹⁄₁₆	5⁵⁄₁₆	4¹⁄₁₆	NA	NA
P/E Ratio—	**16–11**	14–9	15–9	14–8	18–7	15–7	10–6	12–5	NA	NA

Data as orig. reptd. Adj. for stk. div. of 50% Aug. 1990. 1. Includes intangibles. NA-Not Available.

Income Data (Million $)

Year Ended Feb. 28	Revs.	Oper. Inc.	% Oper. Inc. of Revs.	Cap. Exp.	Depr.	Int. Exp.	Net Bef. Taxes	Eff. Tax Rate	Net Inc.	% Net Inc. of Revs.	Cash Flow
1995	**222**	**22.6**	**10.2**	**6.3**	**3.90**	**0.73**	**19.1**	**28.8%**	**13.6**	**6.1**	**17.5**
1994	196	22.5	11.5	1.8	3.10	0.88	19.5	34.5%	12.8	6.5	15.9
1993	173	18.9	10.9	7.5	2.81	1.20	16.3	34.0%	10.8	6.2	13.6
1992	162	16.4	10.1	1.8	2.55	1.45	14.3	33.7%	9.5	5.8	12.0
1991	160	16.5	10.3	1.5	2.62	1.98	13.9	33.3%	9.3	5.8	11.9
1990	155	20.6	13.3	2.3	2.84	2.32	17.2	37.0%	10.8	7.0	13.6
1989	141	16.6	11.8	8.0	2.08	2.18	12.9	37.0%	8.1	5.8	10.2
1988	126	15.0	11.9	15.3	1.56	1.02	11.3	29.1%	8.0	6.3	9.5
1987	115	10.7	9.3	1.9	1.47	0.61	8.6	48.5%	4.4	3.8	5.9
1986	100	6.3	6.3	0.5	1.39	1.24	3.7	42.8%	2.1	2.1	NA

Balance Sheet Data (Million $)

Feb. 28	Cash	Curr. Assets	Curr. Liab.	Curr. Ratio	Total Assets	% Ret. on Assets	Long Term Debt	Common Equity	Total Cap.	% LT Debt of Cap.	% Ret. on Equity
1995	**38.8**	**99.0**	**19.4**	**5.1**	**138**	**10.1**	**4.3**	**110.2**	**115.0**	**3.8**	**13.1**
1994	52.9	101.0	26.6	3.8	131	10.3	5.8	97.3	104.0	5.5	13.9
1993	51.1	83.6	20.7	4.0	115	9.8	7.2	85.1	94.3	7.6	13.4
1992	43.5	76.6	15.9	4.8	105	9.2	11.0	75.5	88.7	12.4	13.4
1991	35.7	72.9	20.9	3.5	102	9.2	12.5	65.8	80.9	15.5	15.2
1990	36.8	68.9	21.8	3.2	99	11.5	18.9	56.2	77.6	24.4	21.3
1989	23.4	55.8	19.0	2.9	88	9.8	21.6	45.1	69.2	31.3	19.9
1988	24.4	53.3	23.3	2.3	78	12.9	14.8	36.6	52.4	28.2	29.0
1987	2.7	28.2	16.3	1.7	37	13.0	5.2	15.1	20.7	25.2	34.5
1986	1.4	22.2	15.4	1.4	31	5.8	4.3	10.6	15.7	27.5	21.8

Data as orig. reptd. NA-Not Available.

Revenues (Million $)

13 Weeks:	1995-96	1994-95	1993-94	1992-93
May	29.6	26.0	20.8	18.7
Aug.	36.9	33.7	29.7	26.8
Nov.		91.9	83.2	72.6
Feb.		70.6	62.6	54.8
		222.2	196.3	172.9

Revenues for the six months ended August 26, 1995, advanced 12%, year to year. However, higher paper and postage expenses, as well as a $1 million merger related expense in the 1995 period, led to a widening of the pretax loss to $5.0 million, from $331,000. After tax credits in both periods, the net loss amounted to $3.3 million ($0.34 a share), compared with a loss of $215,000 ($0.02).

Common Share Earnings ($)

13 Weeks:	1995-96	1994-95	1993-94	1992-93
May	d0.29	d0.10	d0.14	d0.16
Aug.	d0.05	0.08	0.06	0.05
Nov.		0.98	0.95	0.88
Feb.		0.42	0.48	0.38
		1.38	1.35	1.15

Finances

The company has $12 million in lines of credit, of which $10 million may be converted into a five-year term loan.

Dividend Data

Cash dividends were initiated in 1992.

Amt. of Divd. $	Date Decl.	Ex-divd. Date	Stock of Record	Payment Date
0.07	Jan. 25	Feb. 9	Feb. 15	Mar. 1'95
0.07	Apr. 24	May 9	May 15	Jun. 1'95
0.07	Jul. 20	Aug. 8	Aug. 10	Sep. 1'95
0.07	Oct. 10	---	Nov. 15	Dec. 1'95

Capitalization

Long Term Debt: $3,660,000 (5/95).

Common Stock: 9,732,000 shs. ($0.01 par).
Lillian Vernon and sons Fred and David Hochberg control 40%.
Institutions own 28%.
Shareholders: 434 of record (5/95).

Options: To buy 1,253,500 shs. at $8.00 to $18.50 ea. (2/95).

d-Deficit.

Office—543 Main St., New Rochelle, NY 10801. **Tel**—(914) 576-6400. **Chrmn & CEO**—Lillian Vernon. **Pres & COO**—S.S. Marks. **VP, CFO & Investor Contact**—Andrew Gregor. **VP & Secy**—Susan N. Cortazzo. **Dirs**—L. H. Affinito, D. C. Hochberg, F. P. Hochberg, W. E. Phillips, L. Salon, L. Vernon, B. W. Wasserman. **Transfer Agent & Registrar**—Continental Stock Transfer & Trust Co., NYC. **Incorporated** in New York in 1965; reincorporated in Delaware in 1987. **Empl**—1,400.

 N.J. DeVita

Lilly Industries

NYSE Symbol LI In S&P SmallCap 600

Price	Range	P-E Ratio	Dividend	Yield	S&P Ranking	Beta
Nov. 3'95	1995					
12½	15–11	13	0.32	2.6%	A–	1.03

Summary

This company is a leading producer of industrial paints and coatings for use on furniture, automotive parts, business machines, appliances and a wide variety of metal products. The company achieved record earnings in fiscal 1993 and fiscal 1994, reflecting the May 1993 acquisition of ICI/Glidden's North American liquid industrial coatings business and gains from ongoing businesses. In the first nine month of fiscal 1995, results have been hurt by lower volume and increased raw material costs. In October 1995, the company's shares shifted to the New York Stock Exchange from the Nasdaq system.

Business Summary

Lilly Industries and its subsidiaries formulate, manufacture and sell industrial coatings, including paints, stains, lacquers and similar products used by a variety of manufacturers to coat wood, plastic and metal products. In May 1993, it exchanged its packaging coating business for ICI/Glidden's North American liquid industrial coatings business.

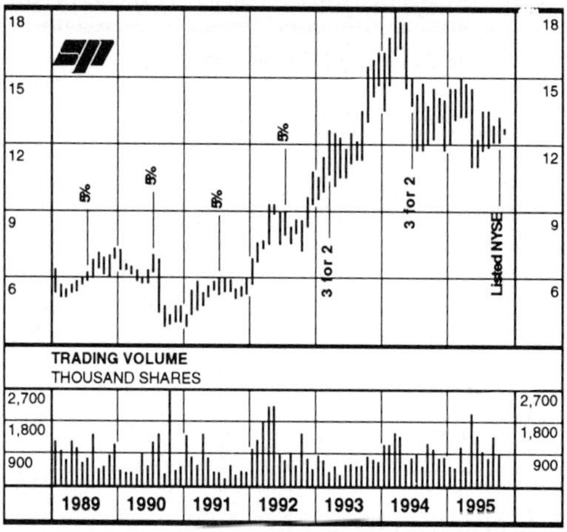

The industrial coatings business is very competitive, with more than 750 manufacturers in the U.S. and Canada. Principal markets for industrial coatings include wood coatings for furniture, flooring, kitchen cabinets and paneling; coil coatings for appliances, aluminum siding and components, automotive parts, doors, windows and metal buildings; general metal coatings for a variety of metal products including extrusions, appliances, caskets, office furniture and truck trailers; and plastics coatings for business machines, computer enclosures and automotive parts.

The company also sells specialty coatings, including gelcoats, mold release agents and adhesives in the fiberglass-reinforced products industry, silver and copper plating chemicals for nonconductive surfaces (such as mirrors), automotive finishes in the automotive aftermarket, and trade sales coatings for professional contractors and homeowners.

Lilly maintains laboratories at its major facilities, to develop manufacturing techniques and product finishes specifically adapted to customer requirements. In fiscal 1994, Lilly spent $13.0 million (3.9% of net sales) on R&D, compared to $12.3 million (4.3%) in fiscal 1993.

The company has 19 manufacturing plants, including facilities in Canada, Germany, Malaysia and Taiwan. Non-U.S. sales accounted for 14% of total revenues in fiscal 1994 (13% in fiscal 1993) and 23% of pretax profits (30%).

Important Developments

Oct. '95— In its review of the third quarter of fiscal 1995, Lilly said its 37% decline in operating income, on an 8% decline in sales, was the result of the lower volume and increased raw material costs.

Jun. '95— The company said it expects its new manufacturing plant in Bowling Green, KY, to be operational by early 1996.

Next earnings report expected in early January.

Per Share Data ($)

Yr. End Nov. 30	1994	[1]1993	1992	1991	1990	1989	1988	[1]1987	1986	1985
Tangible Bk. Val.	**2.13**	1.14	1.98	[2]3.16	[2]3.09	[2]3.00	[2]2.65	[2]2.34	[2]2.11	[2]1.91
Cash Flow	**1.39**	1.01	0.86	0.44	0.57	0.64	0.58	0.51	0.42	0.43
Earnings	**1.00**	0.70	0.55	0.27	0.40	0.50	0.45	0.40	0.33	0.34
Dividends	**0.280**	0.238	0.223	0.212	0.199	0.174	0.154	0.141	0.131	0.113
Payout Ratio	**28%**	33%	41%	78%	47%	35%	34%	34%	39%	32%
Prices[3]—High	**18**	16 5/32	10 25/32	6 1/16	7 9/32	7 11/32	6 27/32	7 9/32	5⅝	4 25/32
Low	**11¾**	9 9/16	5 23/32	3 27/32	3 27/32	5⅛	4 21/32	4 9/16	4⅛	3 9/32
P/E Ratio—	**18–12**	23–14	20–11	22–14	18–9	15–10	15–10	18–11	17–12	14–9

Data as orig. reptd. Adj. for stk. divs. of 50% Jun. 1994, 50% Mar. 1993, 5% Jul. 1992, 5% Jul. 1991, 5% Jul. 1990, 5% Jul. 1989, 5% Jul. 1988, 5% Jul. 1987, 5% Jul. 1986. **1.** Refl. merger or acq. **2.** Incl. intangibles. **3.** Cal. yr.

Income Data (Million $)

Year Ended Nov. 30	Revs.	Oper. Inc.	% Oper. Inc. of Revs.	Cap. Exp.	Depr.	Int. Exp.	Net Bef. Taxes	Eff. Tax Rate	Net Inc.	% Net Inc. of Revs.	Cash Flow
1994	**331**	**51.0**	**15.4**	**6.69**	**8.97**	**2.92**	**39.7**	**41.2%**	**23.3**	**7.0**	**32.3**
[1]1993	284	36.5	12.8	7.60	6.89	1.93	27.9	42.2%	16.2	5.7	23.0
1992	236	29.6	12.5	3.26	6.79	1.66	21.9	42.0%	12.7	5.4	19.5
1991	213	16.4	7.7	1.93	4.04	2.44	10.8	41.0%	6.4	3.0	10.4
1990	232	21.3	9.2	4.11	4.02	2.64	16.9	40.6%	10.0	4.3	14.0
1989	212	23.7	11.2	2.49	3.39	1.40	20.7	40.6%	12.6	5.9	16.0
1988	197	21.0	10.7	2.93	3.13	0.81	18.5	40.9%	11.3	5.7	14.4
[1]1987	184	21.2	11.6	7.54	2.79	0.71	18.8	45.8%	10.3	5.6	13.1
1986	143	18.0	12.6	5.83	2.21	0.09	16.7	46.6%	[2]8.5	6.0	10.7
1985	145	17.7	12.2	9.41	2.25	Nil	16.6	45.4%	8.7	6.0	10.9

Balance Sheet Data (Million $)

Nov. 30	Cash	Curr. Assets	Curr. Liab.	Curr. Ratio	Total Assets	% Ret. on Assets	Long Term Debt	Common Equity	Total Cap.	% LT Debt of Cap.	% Ret. on Equity
1994	**26.6**	**93.1**	**51.5**	**1.8**	**190**	**13.0**	**28.0**	**99.4**	**127.0**	**22.0**	**25.7**
1993	7.5	70.2	37.0	1.9	167	11.3	40.6	81.1	122.0	33.4	21.2
1992	10.8	55.3	28.2	2.0	117	10.7	10.4	70.1	81.5	12.7	18.1
1991	14.1	60.7	30.3	2.0	127	5.0	16.6	74.2	92.0	18.1	8.7
1990	5.0	56.5	22.0	2.6	125	8.1	23.0	73.2	98.2	23.4	13.9
1989	10.6	67.2	26.8	2.5	129	10.9	21.1	74.5	97.9	21.6	17.9
1988	11.9	56.4	20.0	2.8	101	11.4	5.8	66.0	77.2	7.6	18.2
1987	8.6	51.6	25.5	2.0	97	11.9	3.1	58.8	67.6	4.6	18.4
1986	8.8	44.2	12.4	3.6	76	11.6	1.0	53.4	61.6	1.6	16.7
1985	12.6	46.5	13.6	3.4	69	13.2	0.9	47.7	55.5	1.6	19.2

Data as orig. reptd. **1.** Refl. merger or acq. **2.** Refl. acctg. change.

Net Sales (Million $)

Quarter:	1994–95	1993–94	1992–93
Feb.	80.5	74.0	54.5
May	85.4	84.5	65.8
Aug.	79.7	86.6	82.8
Nov.		86.2	81.2
		331.3	284.3

Net sales for the nine months ended August 31, 1994, were up fractionally, as volume growth declined after a solid first quarter advance. Margins narrowed, on rising raw material costs; operating income fell 9.8%. Following a 35% reduction in interest and other expenses (net), and after taxes at 40.0%, versus 41.6%, net income was down 5.4%, to $15,032,000 ($0.65 a share), from $15,900,000 ($0.68).

Common Share Earnings ($)

Quarter:	1994–95	1993–94	1992–93
Feb.	0.20	0.13	0.10
May	0.25	0.25	0.18
Aug.	0.20	0.30	0.20
Nov.		0.32	0.22
		1.00	0.70

Dividend Data

Cash has been paid each year since 1939.

Amt of Divd. $	Date Decl.	Ex-divd. Date	Stock of Record	Payment Date
0.08	Jan. 27	Mar. 6	Mar. 10	Apr. 3'95
0.08	Mar. 31	Jun. 8	Jun. 12	Jul. 3'95
0.08	Jun. 23	Sep. 7	Sep. 11	Oct. 2'95
0.08	Sep. 29	Dec. 8	Dec. 12	Jan. 2'96

Finances

The company's shares began trading on the New York Stock Exchange October 25, 1995, under the symbol LI.

Capitalization

Long Term Debt: $21,000,000 (8/95).

Class A Common Stock: 22,300,000 shs. (no par); elects four directors.
Institutions hold about 48%.
Shareholders of record: 2,080 (11/94).

Class B Common Stock: 350,000 shs. (no par); elects six directors; ownership restricted to employees.
Officers and directors hold 26%.
Shareholders of record: 78 (11/94).

Office—733 South West St., P.O. Box 946, Indianapolis, IN 46225. **Tel**—(317) 687-6700. **Chrmn, Pres & CEO**—D. W. Huemme. **VP-Fin, CFO, Secy & Investor Contact**—Roman J. Klusas. **Treas & Asst Secy**—K. L. Mills. **Dirs**—H. J. Baker, W. C. Dorris, D. W. Huemme, R. J. Klusas, R. H. McKinney, J. D. Peterson, T. E. Reilly, Jr., V. P. Smith, R. A. Steele. **Transfer Agent & Registrar**—Bank One, Indianapolis. **Incorporated** in Indiana in 1888. **Empl**—1,180.

 Justin McCann

STANDARD & POOR'S

STOCK REPORTS

Lindsay Manufacturing

NASDAQ Symbol **LINZ**

In S&P SmallCap 600

15-NOV-95 **Industry:** Machinery

Summary: Lindsay is one of the two leading manufacturers and marketers of automated, center pivot and lateral move irrigation systems. It also provides outsource manufacturing.

S&P Opinion: Hold (★★★)

Recent Price • 35⅛ | 52 Wk Range • 35¾-28¼ | Yield • Nil | 12-Mo. P/E • 14.2

Quantitative Evaluations

Outlook (1 Lowest—5 Highest)
• 2+

Fair Value
• 34⅜

Risk
• Low

Earn./Div. Rank
• NR

Technical Eval.
• Neutral since 11/95

Rel. Strength Rank (1 Lowest—99 Highest)
• 63

Insider Activity
• NA

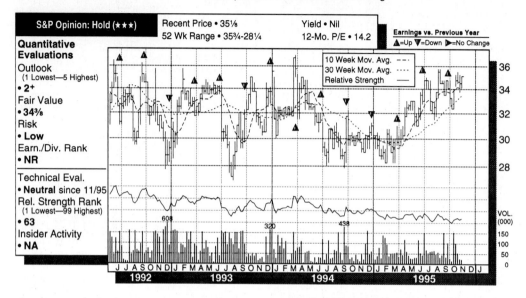

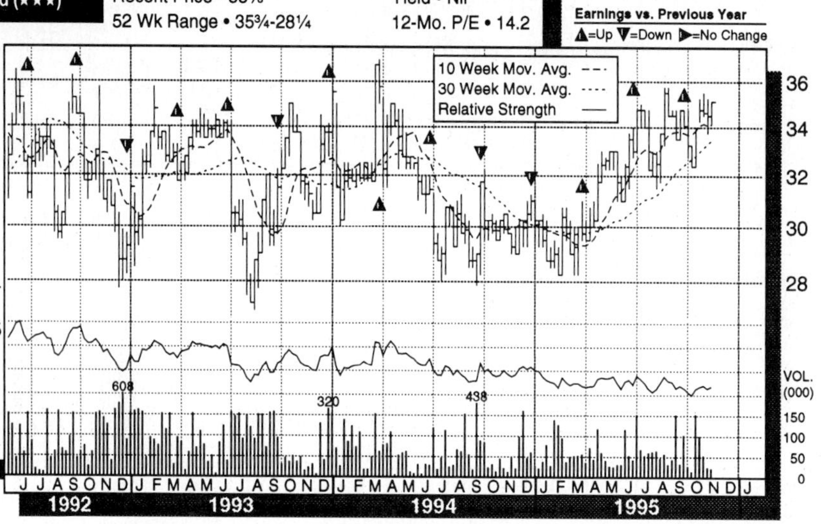

Overview - 11-OCT-95

Revenues are expected to show modest growth in fiscal 1996. With commodity prices up and farmers in good shape financially, domestic irrigation equipment sales should remain strong. Diversified products will continue to gain from the growing demand of its major outsource manufacturing customers. However, increased exports to Western Europe, Australia and Latin America will not be able to replace the loss of sales to Saudi Arabia, where orders will remain limited to replacement parts. Although costs for raw materials have stabilized, an increase in capital expenditures (mainly for automated technologies) and greater administrative expenses will keep margins essentially flat. The stock repurchase program should continue to benefit results.

Valuation - 11-OCT-95

Although down approximately 10% from their early 1994 high, the shares have returned about 9% since the beginning of the year. With steady domestic irrigation equipment sales growth (expected to average 5% to 8% per year for the next five years) providing a solid base, Lindsay's prospects will depend on the growth achieved in diversified products and exports. With no long term debt and over $57 million in cash and marketable securities, LINZ will seek additional growth in a significant acquisition. Based on near term prospects, the shares seem to be fairly valued.

Key Stock Statistics

S&P EPS Est. 1996	2.65	Tang. Bk. Value/Share	15.96
P/E on S&P Est. 1996	13.3	Beta	0.39
Dividend Rate/Share	Nil	Shareholders	200
Shs. outstg. (M)	4.5	Market cap. (B)	$0.156
Avg. daily vol. (M)	0.009	Inst. holdings	62%
		Insider holdings	NA

Value of $10,000 invested 5 years ago: $ 35,519

Fiscal Year Ending Aug. 31

	1996	% Change	1995	% Change	1994	% Change
Revenues (Million $)						
1Q	—	—	22.14	-13%	25.57	3%
2Q	—	—	30.35	10%	27.56	28%
3Q	—	—	37.45	NM	37.72	37%
4Q	—	—	21.90	NM	21.84	-22%
Yr.	—	—	111.8	NM	112.7	10%
Income (Million $)						
1Q	—	—	2.00	-19%	2.48	8%
2Q	—	—	3.00	10%	2.73	23%
3Q	—	—	4.84	8%	4.47	22%
4Q	—	—	1.86	20%	1.55	-38%
Yr.	—	—	11.70	4%	11.23	5%
Earnings Per Share ($)						
1Q	E0.46	12%	0.41	-20%	0.51	6%
2Q	E0.68	6%	0.64	14%	0.56	22%
3Q	E1.09	6%	1.03	12%	0.92	23%
4Q	E0.42	5%	0.40	25%	0.32	-38%
Yr.	E2.65	7%	2.48	7%	2.31	5%

Next earnings report expected: early January

Lindsay Manufacturing

Business Summary - 27-OCT-95

Lindsay Manufacturing Co. is a leading designer, manufacturer, and international and domestic marketer of electrically powered automatic continuous move systems for the irrigation of agricultural crops and related products and services.

Revenues in recent fiscal years were derived as follows:

	1994	1993	1992	1991
Irrigation:				
Domestic	70%	52%	46%	48%
Export	14%	35%	44%	37%
Diversified	16%	13%	10%	15%

Domestic irrigation systems market share has ranged from 35% to 40%. Average annual domestic unit growth of 6% to 8% is seen over the next five years. Major market areas have included the Pacific Northwest, Idaho, Texas, eastern Colorado, Nebraska, southeastern Georgia and Alabama. Saudi Arabia, the most important international customer, accounted for 52% of fiscal 1994 export revenues.

More than 95% of Lindsay's irrigation system sales are of the center-pivot type, which is lower in price and simpler to operate than the lateral-move type. Both products are automatic continuous-move systems that consist of sprinklers mounted on a water-carrying pipeline supported about 11 ft. off the ground by a truss system suspended between moving towers.

A typical center-pivot system, fully installed, requires an investment of up to $60,000. About half of the cost is for the pivot itself, with the remainder for installation of additional equipment such as wells, pumps, underground water pipe, electrical supply and a concrete pad upon which the pivot is anchored. The company also has a significant replacement-parts business.

Lindsay believes that its systems can aid farmers who switch from nonirrigation and other irrigation methods, such as flood irrigation, the primary method. The systems conserve water and energy, offer labor and variable cost saving, and help ensure reliability of crop production. Only about 25% of currently irrigated U.S. acreage is served by center pivot systems.

The diversified products segment manufactures large-diameter tubing and performs outsource manufacturing. Lindsay offers agricultural and industrial capital goods makers services that include welding, machining, painting, punching, forming, galvanizing and hydraulic, electrical and mechanical assembly.

Important Developments

Oct. '95—Lindsay said it repurchased nearly 8% of its outstanding shares in fiscal 1995 and, with cash and marketable securities of more than $57 million, will continue to repurchase shares in fiscal 1996.

Capitalization

Long Term Debt: None (8/95).

Per Share Data ($) (Year Ended Aug. 31)

	1995	1994	1993	1992	1991	1990
Tangible Bk. Val.	NA	14.45	11.86	9.52	7.06	5.16
Cash Flow	NA	2.56	2.46	2.49	2.12	2.01
Earnings	2.48	2.31	2.21	2.28	1.91	1.81
Dividends	Nil	Nil	Nil	Nil	Nil	Nil
Payout Ratio	Nil	Nil	Nil	Nil	Nil	Nil
Prices - High	35¾	37	35¾	44	30¼	17
- Low	28¼	27⅞	27	27¼	10⅞	8
P/E Ratio - High	14	16	16	19	16	9
- Low	11	12	12	12	6	4

Income Statement Analysis (Million $)

	1994	%Chg	1993	%Chg	1992	%Chg	1991
Revs.	113	11%	102	-6%	109	10%	99
Oper. Inc.	15.4	8%	14.3	3%	13.9	16%	12.0
Depr.	1.2	NM	1.2	18%	1.0	8%	0.9
Int. Exp.	NM	—	Nil	—	Nil	—	Nil
Pretax Inc.	16.8	7%	15.7	NM	15.7	25%	12.6
Eff. Tax Rate	33%	—	32%	—	30%	—	29%
Net Inc.	11.2	5%	10.7	-3%	11.0	24%	8.9

Balance Sheet & Other Fin. Data (Million $)

	1994	1993	1992	1991	1990	1989
Cash	13.6	15.6	18.3	18.7	16.9	12.8
Curr. Assets	36.4	39.5	35.8	39.3	38.7	27.3
Total Assets	88.4	79.9	71.4	60.4	46.9	31.7
Curr. Liab.	19.0	23.7	26.2	26.9	22.2	15.2
LT Debt	Nil	Nil	Nil	Nil	Nil	Nil
Common Eqty.	68.1	55.5	44.4	32.8	24.0	16.0
Total Cap.	68.1	55.5	44.4	32.8	24.0	16.0
Cap. Exp.	1.3	0.9	1.7	1.7	1.2	0.8
Cash Flow	12.5	11.9	12.0	9.9	9.3	8.4

Ratio Analysis

	1994	1993	1992	1991	1990	1989
Curr. Ratio	1.9	1.7	1.4	1.5	1.7	1.8
% LT Debt of Cap.	Nil	Nil	Nil	Nil	Nil	Nil
% Net Inc.of Revs.	10.0	10.5	10.1	9.0	8.2	8.0
% Ret. on Assets	13.3	14.2	16.7	16.6	21.3	26.5
% Ret. on Equity	18.1	21.4	28.5	31.3	41.9	61.5

Dividend Data —No cash has been paid.

Data as orig. reptd.; bef. results of disc. opers. and/or spec. items. Per share data adj. for stk. divs. as of ex-div. date. E-Estimated. NA-Not Available. NM-Not Meaningful. NR-Not Ranked.

Office—E. Hwy 91, P.O. Box 156, Lindsay, NE 68644. **Tel**—(402) 428-2131. **Chrmn, Pres & CEO**—G. D. Parker. **VP-Fin, Treas & Secy**—Bruce C. Karsk (402) 428-7250. **Dirs**—H. G. Buffett, J. W. Croghan, J. D. Dunn, G. D. Parker, G. W. Plossl, C. Yeutter. **Transfer Agent & Registrar**—First National Bank of Omaha. **Incorporated** in Nebraska in 1969; reincorporated in Delaware in 1974. **Empl-** 481. **S&P Analyst:** Justin McCann

STANDARD & POOR'S

STOCK REPORTS

Liposome Co.

NASDAQ Symbol **LIPO**
In S&P SmallCap 600

12-OCT-95

Industry:
Drugs-Generic and OTC

Summary: This company develops proprietary liposome and lipid-complex based pharmaceuticals for the treatment, prevention and diagnosis of life-threatening illnesses.

Quantitative Evaluations

Outlook
(1 Lowest—5 Highest)
• **NA**

Fair Value
• **NA**

Risk
• **High**

Earn./Div. Rank
• **C**

Technical Eval.
• **Bullish** since 5/95

Rel. Strength Rank
(1 Lowest—99 Highest)
• **74**

Insider Activity
• **Unfavorable**

Recent Price • 15⅝
52 Wk Range • 17¾-7⅝

Yield • Nil
12-Mo. P/E • NM

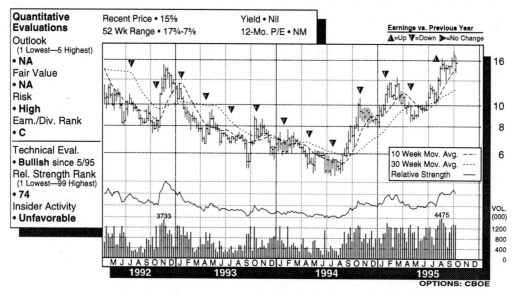

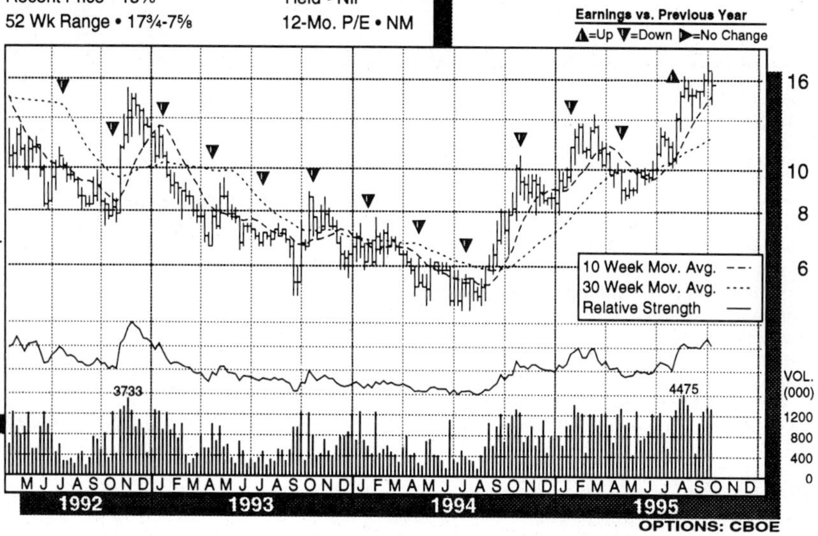

OPTIONS: CBOE

Business Profile - 12-OCT-95

Liposome filed a New Drug Application for ABLC for the treatment of severe fungal infections. Its other lead product, TLC D-99 (for first-line treatments of metastatic breast cancer) is in late Phase III trials. In February 1995, ABLC received regulatory approval in the UK. A third drug candidate, TLC C-53, began Phase III studies in September 1995 to treat acute respiratory distress syndrome. Liposome completed stock offerings in May and July of 1995, raising approximately $44 million.

Operational Review - 12-OCT-95

Revenues in the six months ended June 30, 1995, declined 7%, year to year, chiefly due to lower investment and interest income. Operating costs continued to outpace revenues, reflecting both higher R&D spending and SG&A expenses. The net loss widened to $19.1 million from $15.0 million. After preferred dividends, losses per share were $0.87 and $0.74, respectively.

Stock Performance - 06-OCT-95

In the past 30 trading days, LIPO's shares have increased 5%, compared to a 4% rise in the S&P 500. Average trading volume for the past five days was 511,880 shares, compared with the 40-day moving average of 475,420 shares.

Key Stock Statistics

Dividend Rate/Share	Nil	Shareholders	1,500
Shs. outstg. (M)	29.3	Market cap. (B)	$0.435
Avg. daily vol. (M)	0.489	Inst. holdings	46%
Tang. Bk. Value/Share	0.74	Insider holdings	NA
Beta	NM		

Value of $10,000 invested 5 years ago: $ 113,636

Fiscal Year Ending Dec. 31

	1995	% Change	1994	% Change	1993	% Change
Revenues (Million $)						
1Q	1.85	-39%	3.04	7%	2.85	12%
2Q	3.72	27%	2.94	-17%	3.56	25%
3Q	—	—	2.45	-30%	3.48	25%
4Q	—	—	2.02	-36%	3.16	16%
Yr.	—	—	10.89	-16%	13.04	20%
Income (Million $)						
1Q	-10.33	NM	-6.84	NM	-3.51	NM
2Q	-8.83	NM	-8.14	NM	-3.66	NM
3Q	—	—	-8.68	NM	-7.32	NM
4Q	—	—	-9.91	NM	-7.99	NM
Yr.	—	—	-33.65	NM	-22.48	NM
Earnings Per Share ($)						
1Q	-0.49	NM	-0.34	NM	-0.21	NM
2Q	-0.38	NM	-0.40	NM	-0.21	NM
3Q	—	—	-0.42	NM	-0.37	NM
4Q	—	—	-0.47	NM	-0.39	NM
Yr.	—	—	-1.64	NM	-1.18	NM

Next earnings report expected: early November

Liposome Co.

Business Summary - 03-OCT-95

The Liposome Company Inc., both independently and in collaboration with others, is a leading developer of proprietary liposome and lipid-complex based pharmaceuticals for the treatment, prevention and diagnosis of serious illnesses. Leading products are focused on cancer treatments and fungal infections in immunocompromised patients.

Liposomes are microscopic man-made spheres composed of lipids (fat molecules) that can be engineered to entrap drugs or other biologically active molecules within the lipid membranes of the spheres or in the aqueous spaces between them.

LIPO's research activities focus on developing enhanced liposomal drugs for the treatment of cancer, infections and inflammatory diseases. The company's lead drug is ABLC (Amphotericin B Lipid Complex), currently in Phase III studies for the treatment of fungal infections in cancer and bone marrow transplant patients. Applications for marketing approval have been filed in 18 countries. In February 1995, ABLC (referred to as Abelcet in European markets) was approved for marketing in the U.K. for patients with cryptococcal meningitis and treatment of fungal infections in cases not responding to conventional amphotericin. LIPO submitted a New Application to the FDA for ABLC in May 1995.

Along with Pfizer Inc., the company is conducting Phase III clinical trials of a drug (TLC D-99) for first line treatment of metastatic breast cancer. In January 1995, LIPO commenced a Phase II trial of TLC C-53 for treatment of acute myocardial infarction (heart attack). Phase II trials have already been completed on TLC C-53 for Acute Respiratory Distress Syndrome.

In March 1995, development of TLC A-60, an influenza vaccine, and TLC I-16, for use in diagnosing primary and secondary liver tumors, was discontinued as LIPO's research partners (Wyeth-Ayerst and Schering AG, respectively) terminated funding.

Important Developments

Sep. '95—A Phase III trial demonstrated that ABLC was as effective as amphotericin B in the treatment of systemic fungal infections, but safer. Separately, the company began a Phase III trial for TLC C-53 for acute respiratory distress syndrome.

Jul. '95—LIPO completed a private placement with the State of Wisconsin Investment Board which purchased 1.5 million common shares at $10.00 per share. Earlier, in May, the company sold 3 million common shares at $9 a share in a public offering. Proceeds from both transcations totaled approximately $44 million.

Capitalization

Long Term Debt: $5,015,000 (6/95).
Options: To buy 4,226,105 shs. (12/94).

Per Share Data ($) (Year Ended Dec. 31)

	1994	1993	1992	1991	1990	1989
Tangible Bk. Val.	0.37	4.87	3.54	2.38	0.52	0.86
Cash Flow	-1.50	-1.11	-0.40	-0.19	-0.29	-0.48
Earnings	-1.64	-1.18	-0.43	-0.22	-0.35	-0.54
Dividends	Nil	Nil	Nil	Nil	Nil	Nil
Payout Ratio	Nil	Nil	Nil	Nil	Nil	Nil
Prices - High	10¾	12½	27⅜	14⅜	3¼	3½
- Low	4¾	5⅛	7⅜	2¾	⅞	⅞
P/E Ratio - High	NM	NM	NM	NM	NM	NM
- Low	NM	NM	NM	NM	NA	NA

Income Statement Analysis (Million $)

	1994	%Chg	1993	%Chg	1992	%Chg	1991
Revs.	5.9	8%	5.4	-11%	6.1	-3%	6.3
Oper. Inc.	-34.8	NM	-28.2	NM	-13.6	NM	-6.0
Depr.	3.2	94%	1.6	102%	0.8	23%	0.6
Int. Exp.	0.3	24%	0.3	NM	0.1	NM	0.0
Pretax Inc.	-33.7	NM	-22.5	NM	-9.7	NM	-4.1
Eff. Tax Rate	NM	—	NM	—	NM	—	Nil
Net Inc.	-33.7	NM	-22.5	NM	-9.7	NM	-4.1

Balance Sheet & Other Fin. Data (Million $)

	1994	1993	1992	1991	1990	1989
Cash	58.0	110	75.4	45.7	7.7	10.6
Curr. Assets	61.0	112	78.5	46.9	8.2	11.4
Total Assets	93.0	140	92.8	50.8	11.0	14.9
Curr. Liab.	8.9	9.6	6.6	3.3	2.9	2.0
LT Debt	5.9	7.7	2.4	Nil	0.0	0.1
Common Eqty.	9.0	115	83.2	46.9	7.4	12.2
Total Cap.	84.0	130	85.6	46.9	7.5	12.3
Cap. Exp.	2.9	7.7	9.8	1.3	0.3	0.3
Cash Flow	-35.9	-26.2	-8.9	-3.4	-4.1	-6.7

Ratio Analysis

	1994	1993	1992	1991	1990	1989
Curr. Ratio	6.8	11.7	11.9	14.1	2.8	5.8
% LT Debt of Cap.	7.0	5.9	2.8	Nil	0.2	1.0
% Net Inc.of Revs.	NM	NM	NM	NM	NM	NM
% Ret. on Assets	NM	NM	NM	NM	NM	NM
% Ret. on Equity	NM	NM	NM	NM	NM	NM

Dividend Data —No cash dividends have been paid.

Data as orig. reptd.; bef. results of disc. opers. and/or spec. items. Per share data adj. for stk. divs. as of ex-div. date. Revs. in Income Statement Analysis tbl. excl. other income. E-Estimated. NA-Not Available. NM-Not Meaningful. NR-Not Ranked.

Office—One Research Way, Princeton Forrestal Center, Princeton, NJ 08540. **Tel**—(609) 452-7060. **Chrmn & CEO**—C. A. Baker. **EVP & COO**—E. G. Silverman. **VP-Fin, CFO & Treas**—B. Boveroux. **VP & Secy**—C. Gillespie. **Dirs**—J. G. Andress, C. A. Baker, M. Collins, S. F. Feiner, R. F. Hendrickson, B. Samuelsson, J. T. Stewart Jr., G. Weissmann, H. Witzel. **Transfer Agent & Registrar**—Midlantic National Bank, Edison, NJ. **Incorporated** in Delaware in 1981. **Empl**-230. **S&P Analyst:** Thomas Tirney

STANDARD & POOR'S

Living Centers of America

STOCK REPORTS

NYSE Symbol **LCA**
In S&P SmallCap 600

31-AUG-95 **Industry:** Health Care Centers

Summary: This company, which operates long-term healthcare facilities in nine states, is one of the largest providers of long-term care in Texas and Colorado.

Quantitative Evaluations
Outlook
(1 Lowest—5 Highest)
• **NA**
Fair Value
• **NA**
Risk
• **Average**
Earn./Div. Rank
• **NR**

Technical Eval.
• **Bullish** since 8/95
Rel. Strength Rank
(1 Lowest—99 Highest)
• **13**
Insider Activity
• **Neutral**

Recent Price • 29⅜
52 Wk Range • 38¼-25¼
Yield • Nil
12-Mo. P/E • 15.0

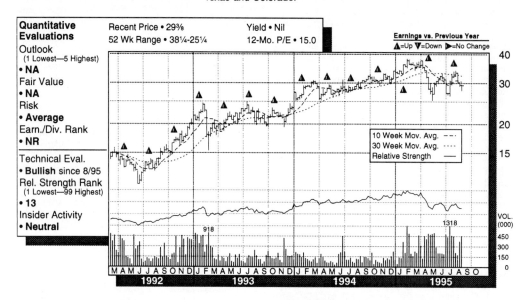

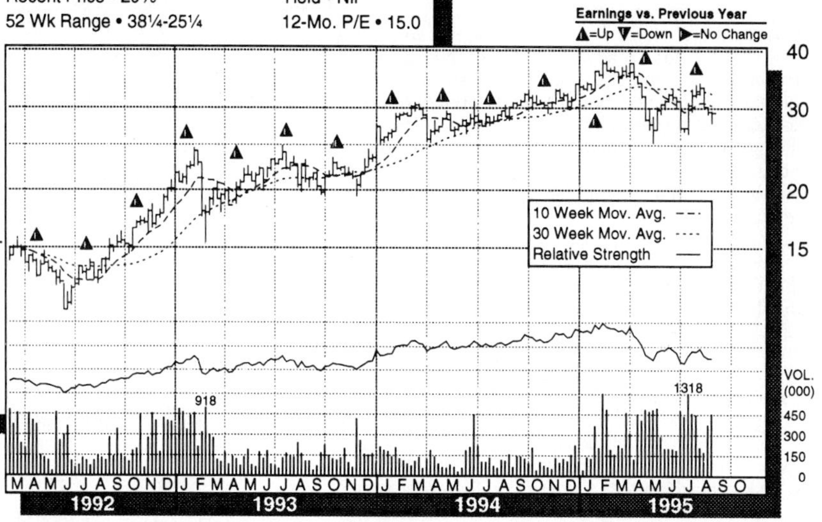

Business Profile - 31-AUG-95

LCA is now focusing on specialized services, including pharmacy, therapy and medical supply services. It acquired the remaining interest in American Pharmaceutical Services in late 1994, and acquired The Brian Center Corp., as well as Rehability Corp., in mid-1995. Demand for company services should remain strong, reflecting LCA's cost effective delivery of specialized health care services and a steady increase in the elderly population.

Operational Review - 31-AUG-95

Net revenues continue to advance, on increases in Medicare and ancillary services, as well as the acquisition of American Pharmaceutical. Wider margins reflect growth in more profitable rehabilitation and ancillary services, and in pharmacy services. Despite charges for mergers and acquisitions, earnings rose strongly in the first nine month of fiscal 1995. Share earnings gains were restricted somewhat by more shares outstanding.

Stock Performance - 25-AUG-95

In the past 30 trading days, LCA's shares have declined 4%, compared to a 0.04% rise in the S&P 500. Average trading volume for the past five days was 94,760 shares, compared with the 40-day moving average of 100,221 shares.

Key Stock Statistics

Dividend Rate/Share	Nil	Shareholders	600
Shs. outstg. (M)	19.9	Market cap. (B)	$0.575
Avg. daily vol. (M)	0.072	Inst. holdings	59%
Tang. Bk. Value/Share	10.39	Insider holdings	NA
Beta	NA		

Value of $10,000 invested 5 years ago: NA

Fiscal Year Ending Sep. 30

	1995	% Change	1994	% Change	1993	% Change
Revenues (Million $)						
1Q	148.4	25%	118.8	28%	92.58	9%
2Q	153.5	25%	122.8	30%	94.42	11%
3Q	160.3	28%	125.6	27%	99.2	15%
4Q	—	—	131.5	28%	102.7	8%
Yr.	—	—	498.6	28%	388.9	11%
Income (Million $)						
1Q	4.88	29%	3.78	40%	2.70	27%
2Q	6.32	31%	4.84	36%	3.56	34%
3Q	6.88	34%	5.13	34%	3.83	22%
4Q	—	—	4.97	39%	3.57	24%
Yr.	—	—	18.72	37%	13.65	30%
Earnings Per Share ($)						
1Q	0.46	28%	0.36	24%	0.29	16%
2Q	0.52	16%	0.45	18%	0.38	27%
3Q	0.51	6%	0.48	17%	0.41	24%
4Q	—	—	0.47	24%	0.38	23%
Yr.	—	—	1.77	21%	1.46	26%

Next earnings report expected: mid November

Business Summary - 31-AUG-95

Living Centers of America, Inc. (LCA) is the fifth largest U.S. operator of long-term healthcare centers, and the largest provider of long-term care in Texas and Colorado, its principal states of operation. As of January 1995, the company was operating 240 centers with 21,174 licensed beds in Texas, Colorado, Florida, Oklahoma, Alabama, Louisiana, Nebraska, Wyoming, Arizona and Mississippi. There were 168 long-term care centers and 72 centers for the developmentally disabled. LCA centers are generally located in non-urban areas that typically have limited local competition. Contributions to resident care revenues in recent fiscal years were as follows:

	1994	1993	1992
Medicaid	60%	64%	67%
Private pay sources	22%	23%	24%
Medicare	18%	13%	9%

The average annual occupancy level for owned or leased centers (excluding divested centers) was 83.0% in fiscal 1994 and 82.3% in fiscal 1993.

LCA's long-term care centers provide healthcare services emphasizing nursing and specialty care. In addition, the centers provide daily dietary, social and recreational services, pharmaceutical and medical supplies, as well as other basic services such as housekeeping and laundry. The company also offers services to developmentally disabled clients through 72 centers in Texas and Florida and long-term care to patients with Alzheimer's disease through 52 Alzheimer's care units with 1,527 beds. LCA has also established other specialty care units and programs in centers where it perceives a need for such services.

Wholly owned American Pharmaceutical Services, Inc. (formerly Abbey Pharmaceutical, when it was 49% owned, prior to November 1994) provides specialty pharmaceutical and infusion therapy services and distributes specialized patient care products to long-term care providers.

Important Developments

Aug. '95—The company acquired The Brian Center Corp., which operates 49 long-term care facilities that provide skilled specialty nursing and ancillary health care services, in exchange for 6,479,000 common shares. Separately, the company acquired privately held Therapy Management Innovations, which provides consulting and contract rehabilitation services, in a stock-for-stock transaction.

Jun. '95—LCA acquired Rehability Corp., one of the largest U.S. providers of rehabilitation services, for approximately $88.3 million in cash.

Feb. '95—In a public offering, 2,875,000 LCA common shares were sold at $36.25 each.

Capitalization

Long Term Debt: $139,416,000 (6/95).

Per Share Data ($)

(Year Ended Sep. 30)

	1994	1993	1992	1991	1990	1989
Tangible Bk. Val.	10.07	8.95	7.57	5.63	NA	NA
Cash Flow	3.98	3.06	2.59	2.21	NA	NA
Earnings	1.77	1.46	1.16	0.90	NA	NA
Dividends	Nil	Nil	Nil	NA	NA	NA
Payout Ratio	Nil	Nil	Nil	NA	NA	NA
Prices - High	32⅞	27¾	22½	NA	NA	NA
- Low	25⅛	15¼	11	NA	NA	NA
P/E Ratio - High	19	19	19	NA	NA	NA
- Low	14	10	9	NA	NA	NA

Income Statement Analysis (Million $)

	1994	%Chg	1993	%Chg	1992	%Chg	1991
Revs.	499	28%	389	11%	351	15%	306
Oper. Inc.	56.8	43%	39.7	15%	34.5	20%	28.8
Depr.	23.5	57%	15.0	15%	13.0	16%	11.2
Int. Exp.	10.6	53%	6.9	-10%	7.7	17%	6.5
Pretax Inc.	28.8	30%	22.2	29%	17.2	56%	11.0
Eff. Tax Rate	35%	—	39%	—	39%	—	37%
Net Inc.	18.7	38%	13.6	30%	10.5	35%	7.8

Balance Sheet & Other Fin. Data (Million $)

	1994	1993	1992	1991	1990	1989
Cash	8.5	5.8	12.6	0.1	NA	NA
Curr. Assets	105	63.7	64.5	44.4	NA	NA
Total Assets	410	244	226	208	NA	NA
Curr. Liab.	96.4	62.9	57.3	45.1	NA	NA
LT Debt	111	60.0	69.3	84.2	NA	NA
Common Eqty.	154	107	97.3	75.4	NA	NA
Total Cap.	265	167	167	160	NA	NA
Cap. Exp.	91.2	30.9	11.6	NA	NA	NA
Cash Flow	42.2	28.6	23.5	19.1	NA	NA

Ratio Analysis

	1994	1993	1992	1991	1990	1989
Curr. Ratio	1.1	1.0	1.1	1.0	NA	NA
% LT Debt of Cap.	41.9	35.7	41.6	52.8	NA	NA
% Net Inc.of Revs.	3.8	3.5	3.0	2.6	NA	NA
% Ret. on Assets	5.4	5.9	4.4	NA	NA	NA
% Ret. on Equity	13.5	13.5	11.2	NA	NA	NA

Dividend Data —LCA does not intend to pay cash dividends on its common stock, and its bank credit facilities contain covenants that effectively limit the payment of cash dividends. A "poison pill" stock purchase rights plan was adopted in 1994.

Data as orig. reptd.; bef. results of disc. opers. and/or spec. items. Per share data adj. for stk. divs. as of ex-div. date. E-Estimated. NA-Not Available. NM-Not Meaningful. NR-Not Ranked.

Office—15415 Katy Freeway, Suite 800, Houston, TX 77094. **Tel**—(713) 578-4600. **Chrmn, Pres & CEO**—E. L. Kuntz. **CFO**—C. W. Frank. **EVP & COO**—L. D. Williams. **VP & Secy**—Susan Thomas Whittle. **VP & Investor Contact**—Dorothy M. Wiley (713-578-4650). **Dirs**—R. L. Bulger, A. M. Frank, A. H. Hurlbut, E. L. Kuntz, E. J. Rogers, Jr., L. D. Williams. **Transfer Agent & Registrar**—Chemical Shareholder Services Group, Inc., Dallas. **Incorporated** in Delaware in 1977. **Empl**-17,800. **S&P Analyst:** Philip J. Birbara

Loyola Capital

NASDAQ Symbol **LOYC**
In S&P SmallCap 600

16-OCT-95 **Industry:** Banking

Summary: This holding company offers retail banking and other financial services from over 30 offices in Maryland and Washington, D.C., through wholly owned Loyola Federal Savings Bank.

Quantitative Evaluations

Outlook
(1 Lowest—5 Highest)
• **NA**

Fair Value
• **NA**

Risk
• **Average**

Earn./Div. Rank
• **NR**

Technical Eval.
• **Bearish** since 9/95

Rel. Strength Rank
(1 Lowest—99 Highest)
• **84**

Insider Activity
• **NA**

Recent Price • 36⅛
52 Wk Range • 36½-15⅞
Yield • 1.3%
12-Mo. P/E • 19.2

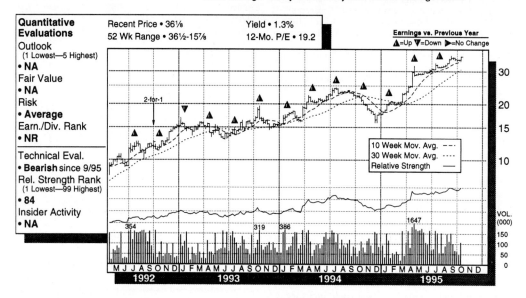

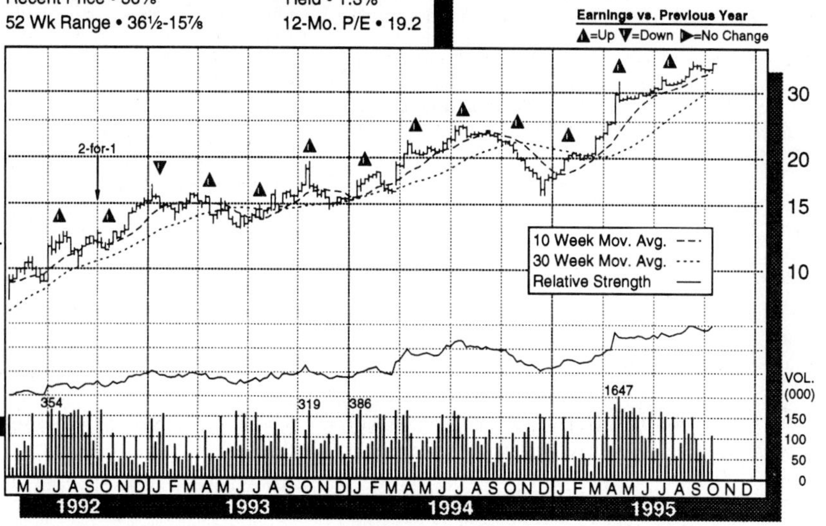

Business Profile - 11-OCT-95

This holding company provides retail banking services and other financial services through wholly owned Loyola Federal Savings Bank, which has more than 30 offices in Maryland and Washington, D.C. In May, Loyola agreed to be acquired by Crestar Financial Corp. (NYSE: CF). Under the terms of the transaction, which is expected to close around year-end 1995, each share of LOYC will be exchanged for 0.69 shares of CF (a value of about $39 a share based on CF's current stock price).

Operational Review - 16-OCT-95

Net interest income advanced 7.1% for the six months ended June 30, 1995, year to year, mainly on growth in the loan portfolio. The provision for loan losses increased 21% to $437,000. Noninterest income fell 13%, hurt by lower service fees and commissions and losses replacing gains on the sale of loans. Following a 3.3% decrease in noninterest expense and higher taxes, net income expanded 18% to $8,449,000 ($0.97 a share) from $7,131,000 ($0.82).

Stock Performance - 13-OCT-95

In the past 30 trading days, LOYC's shares have increased 4%, compared to a 4% rise in the S&P 500. Average trading volume for the past five days was 21,220 shares, compared with the 40-day moving average of 20,249 shares.

Key Stock Statistics

Dividend Rate/Share	0.48	Shareholders	4,000
Shs. outstg. (M)	8.1	Market cap. (B)	$0.293
Avg. daily vol. (M)	0.014	Inst. holdings	1%
Tang. Bk. Value/Share	21.66	Insider holdings	NA
Beta	1.33		

Value of $10,000 invested 5 years ago: $ 51,424

Fiscal Year Ending Dec. 31

	1995	% Change	1994	% Change	1993	% Change
Revenues (Million $)						
1Q	48.39	12%	43.28	22%	35.49	-25%
2Q	49.94	15%	43.57	20%	36.24	-13%
3Q	—	—	45.25	16%	39.05	-2%
4Q	—	—	41.98	2%	41.33	3%
Yr.	—	—	174.1	14%	152.1	-10%
Income (Million $)						
1Q	4.07	17%	3.49	16%	3.01	NM
2Q	4.38	20%	3.64	15%	3.16	3%
3Q	—	—	3.76	25%	3.01	3%
4Q	—	—	4.15	35%	3.08	28%
Yr.	—	—	15.04	23%	12.27	8%
Earnings Per Share ($)						
1Q	0.47	15%	0.41	17%	0.35	3%
2Q	0.50	19%	0.42	17%	0.36	3%
3Q	—	—	0.43	23%	0.35	3%
4Q	—	—	0.48	33%	0.36	33%
Yr.	—	—	1.74	23%	1.42	9%

Next earnings report expected: late October

Loyola Capital

Business Summary - 11-OCT-95

Loyola Capital Corporation is the holding company for Loyola Federal Savings Bank., a community banking and financial services enterprise headquartered in Maryland. Based on consolidated assets of $2.5 billion at 1994 year end, Loyola Federal was the second largest thrift institution headquartered in Maryland. Business is conducted through a network of 35 offices in Maryland and one in Washington, D.C. Loyola Federal converted from a federally chartered mutual to a stock savings and loan association in 1986. In April 1992, Loyola changed its charter and became a federal savings bank. Nonbanking subsidiaries are engaged in real estate investment and development, insurance brokerage, mortgage banking and real estate appraisal services.

Gross loans outstanding of $2.04 billion at December 31, 1994, were divided:

Construction loans	8%
Mortgage--single-family	67%
Mortgage--multifamily	2%
Mortgage--commercial	4%
Consumer loans	18%
Commercial and other	1%

The allowance for loan losses at December 31, 1994, was $13.7 million (0.67% of total loans), down from $14.6 million (0.89%) at 1993 year end. Net charge-offs in 1994 were $1.6 milion (0.09% of average loans), versus $3.6 million (0.25%) in 1993. Total nonperforming assets at 1994 year end were $28.9 million (1.17% of total assets), compared with $39.2 million (1.66%) a year earlier

Interest on loans receivable provided 79% of total income in 1994, interest on mortgage-backed securities 8%, interest on investments 5%, service fees on loans 4%, and other noninterest income 4%.

Total deposits of $1.47 billion at December 31, 1994, were apportioned: 54% certificates, 28% money market, 10% passbook and statement savings, 6% NOW, and 2% noninterest-bearing.

The average yield on interest-earning assets in 1994 was 7.25% (7.45% in 1993), while the average rate paid on interest-bearing liabilities was 4.45% (4.37%), for a net interest rate spread of 2.80% (3.08%).

Important Developments

May '95—LOYC agreed to be acquired by Crestar Financial Corp. (NYSE: CF). Under the terms of the acquisition, which is expected to close around year-end 1995, each LOYC share would be exchanged, subject to adjustments, for 0.69 shares of CF stock (valued at about $39 a share as of mid-October).

Capitalization

Notes Payable & Other Borrowings: $805,968,000 (6/95).

Per Share Data ($) (Year Ended Dec. 31)

	1994	1993	1992	1991	1990	1989
Tangible Bk. Val.	20.90	19.51	18.22	16.59	14.98	13.56
Earnings	1.73	1.42	1.30	1.18	0.91	1.04
Dividends	0.40	0.24	0.22	Nil	Nil	Nil
Payout Ratio	23%	17%	17%	Nil	Nil	Nil
Prices - High	24½	19½	15¾	8¼	7⅝	9¾
- Low	15⅜	12⅞	6⅞	3¾	3¾	5⅞
P/E Ratio - High	14	14	12	7	8	9
- Low	9	9	5	3	4	6

Income Statement Analysis (Million $)

	1994	%Chg	1993	%Chg	1992	%Chg	1991
Net Int. Inc.	66.9	9%	61.6	-6%	65.8	6%	62.1
Loan Loss Prov.	0.7	-79%	3.1	-56%	7.1	-38%	11.4
Non Int. Inc.	12.7	10%	11.5	-28%	16.0	17%	13.7
Non Int. Exp.	53.9	9%	49.6	-11%	55.9	22%	45.7
Pretax Inc.	25.1	23%	20.4	8%	18.9	1%	18.7
Eff. Tax Rate	40%	—	40%	—	40%	—	43%
Net Inc.	15.0	22%	12.3	8%	11.4	8%	10.6
% Net Int. Marg.	3.01%	—	3.26%	—	3.73%	—	3.12%

Balance Sheet & Other Fin. Data (Million $)

	1994	1993	1992	1991	1990	1989
Total Assets	2,469	2,367	1,785	2,002	2,080	2,113
Loans	2,213	1,969	1,391	1,800	1,897	1,904
Deposits	1,466	1,425	1,466	1,614	1,566	1,522
Capitalization:						
Debt	778	728	126	185	332	427
Equity	169	157	149	141	136	130
Total	947	885	275	326	468	557

Ratio Analysis

	1994	1993	1992	1991	1990	1989
% Ret. on Assets	0.6	0.6	0.6	0.5	0.4	0.5
% Ret. on Equity	9.3	8.0	7.9	7.7	6.4	8.3
% Loan Loss Resv.	0.6	0.7	1.1	0.8	0.7	0.4
% Risk Based Capital	10.2	10.3	11.8	8.8	8.0	NA
Price Times Book Value:						
High	1.2	1.0	0.9	0.5	0.5	0.7
Low	0.7	0.7	0.4	0.2	0.3	0.4

Dividend Data —Cash dividends were initiated in 1992.

Amt. of Div. $	Date Decl.	Ex-Div. Date	Stock of Record	Payment Date
0.100	Oct. 18	Dec. 09	Dec. 15	Dec. 30 '94
0.120	Jan. 18	Mar. 09	Mar. 15	Mar. 31 '95
0.120	Apr. 18	Jun. 13	Jun. 15	Jun. 30 '95
0.120	Jul. 18	Sep. 13	Sep. 15	Sep. 29 '95
0.120	Aug. 16	Nov. 02	Nov. 06	Nov. 21 '95

Data as orig. reptd.; bef. results of disc opers. and/or spec. items. Per share data adj. for stk. divs. as of ex-div. date. E-Estimated. NA-Not Available. NM-Not Meaningful. NR-Not Ranked.

Office—1300 N. Charles St., Baltimore, MD 21201. **Tel**—(410) 787-3100. **Chrmn & CEO**—J. W. Mosmiller. **Pres**—J. C. Johnson. **EVP, CFO, Treas & Investor Contact**—James V. McAveney. **Secy**—Linda A. Stadtler. **Dirs**—C. G. Haines, J. C. Johnson, M. J. Macks, J. W. Mosmiller, W. G. Scaggs, J. T. Stinson, H. M. Turner, H. K. Wells. **Transfer Agent & Registrar**—American Stock Transfer & Trust Co., NYC. **Incorporated** in Delaware in 1986. **Empl**-824. **S&P Analyst:** Robert Schpoont

STANDARD & POOR'S

STOCK REPORTS

Lydall, Inc.

NYSE Symbol **LDL**
In S&P SmallCap 600

19-SEP-95

Industry: Manufacturing/Distr

Summary: Lydall's fiber-based materials are used in demanding specialty applications, including filtration media, thermal barriers, electrical insulation, and materials handling products.

Quantitative Evaluations

Outlook (1 Lowest—5 Highest)
• **NA**

Fair Value
• **NA**

Risk
• **Average**

Earn./Div. Rank
• **B+**

Technical Eval.
• **Bullish** since 11/93

Rel. Strength Rank (1 Lowest—99 Highest)
• **60**

Insider Activity
• **NA**

Recent Price • 24⅜
52 Wk Range • 26¼-14¾
Yield • Nil
12-Mo. P/E • 23.0

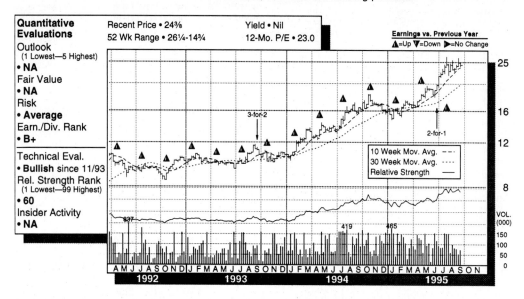

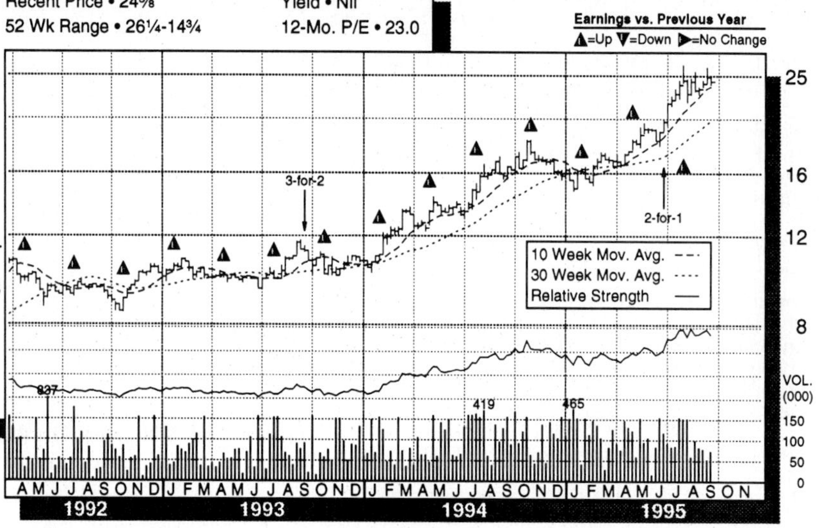

Business Profile - 19-SEP-95

Lydall's products fall into five basic categories: thermal barriers, air and liquid filtration media, materials handling systems, electrical insulation and other products and services. Thermal barriers sales accounted for about one-third of revenues in 1994. During 1994, the company acquired the operations and certain assets of the Clecon Molding division of Standard Packaging, Inc., and also acquired certain assets of the laminates operation of Riverwood International Georgia, Inc.

Operational Review - 19-SEP-95

Sales in the six months ended June 30, 1995, increased 26%, year to year, boosted by acquisitions made in 1994, and by strength in all product segments. Margins widened on the higher volume, and operating income rose significantly. With lower other expenses, and after taxes at 39.0%, versus 41.6%, net income advanced 53%, to $11.2 million ($0.61 a share), from $7.3 million ($0.41, as adjusted).

Stock Performance - 15-SEP-95

In the past 30 trading days, LDL's shares have increased 6%, compared to a 4% rise in the S&P 500. Average trading volume for the past five days was 14,260 shares, compared with the 40-day moving average of 19,167 shares.

Key Stock Statistics

Dividend Rate/Share	Nil	Shareholders	1,900
Shs. outstg. (M)	17.3	Market cap. (B)	$0.421
Avg. daily vol. (M)	0.015	Inst. holdings	58%
Tang. Bk. Value/Share	3.90	Insider holdings	NA
Beta	1.24		

Value of $10,000 invested 5 years ago: $ 46,615

Fiscal Year Ending Dec. 31

	1995	% Change	1994	% Change	1993	% Change
Revenues (Million $)						
1Q	62.74	30%	48.12	26%	38.20	-1%
2Q	65.55	22%	53.56	33%	40.42	4%
3Q	—	—	54.45	40%	38.84	7%
4Q	—	—	56.95	43%	39.93	7%
Yr.	—	—	213.1	35%	157.4	4%
Income (Million $)						
1Q	5.31	50%	3.53	38%	2.55	12%
2Q	5.87	56%	3.76	51%	2.49	8%
3Q	—	—	3.88	70%	2.28	4%
4Q	—	—	4.34	61%	2.69	19%
Yr.	—	—	15.50	55%	10.01	11%
Earnings Per Share ($)						
1Q	0.29	45%	0.20	38%	0.15	12%
2Q	0.32	52%	0.21	50%	0.14	5%
3Q	—	—	0.22	65%	0.13	3%
4Q	—	—	0.24	55%	0.15	19%
Yr.	—	—	0.86	51%	0.57	10%

Next earnings report expected: late October

Lydall, Inc.

Business Summary - 19-SEP-95

Lydall, Inc. makes engineered fiber materials and fiber components that customers use in finished products. Using a broad spectrum of available fibers and several material forming processes, the company has developed a broad range of high performance materials. Lydall operates 10 U.S. manufacturing facilities, and one in France. Segment contributions to revenues in recent years were:

	1994	1993
Thermal barriers	34%	23%
Filtration media	20%	24%
Materials handling	14%	15%
Electrical insulation	8%	11%
Other	24%	27%

Foreign and export sales accounted for 21% of the total in each of 1993 and 1994.

The company makes materials that serve as heat or thermal barriers. Products include composites using unusual materials, in both rigid and flexible forms, manufactured by various processes. They can withstand temperatures from -459 degrees to +3,000 degrees Fahrenheit, and are used to line for ovens, kilns and furnaces, and in glass and metal manufacturing. Cryogenic insulation materials are used to insulate tanker trucks transporting liquid gases.

High efficiency microfiber glass air filtering media are used in applications where clean air is vital, such as semiconductor manufacturing and industrial clean rooms, and biotechnology laboratories. Biomedical materials are used in blood filtration and autotransfusion filters. Liquid filtration media are used in high efficiency hydraulic oil and lubrication oil elements for off-road vehicles, trucks and heavy equipment, and coolant filtration media are used in metalworking applications. A lower efficiency air filtration product is used in residential and commercial water purification units.

Materials handling products include slipsheets and separator sheets used to ship food, pharmaceuticals and chemicals; they offer certain advantages over wooden pallets, including cost and space reduction.

Electrical insulation products are used in personal computers, consumer appliances, utility power transformers, electric motors and other wiring devices. These materials, made of closely engineered celluloid fiber and polymer formulations, meet moisture and electrical resistance, flame retardancy, formability and thermal aging specifications. Products and services also include freight hauling, paperboard, fiberboard and wood replacement products, and gasketing materials.

Capitalization

Long Term Debt: $7,839,000 (6/95).

Per Share Data ($) (Year Ended Dec. 31)

	1994	1993	1992	1991	1990	1989
Tangible Bk. Val.	3.90	3.63	3.08	2.50	2.34	1.83
Cash Flow	1.28	0.90	0.82	0.68	0.65	0.61
Earnings	0.87	0.57	0.52	0.47	0.47	0.45
Dividends	Nil	Nil	Nil	Nil	Nil	Nil
Payout Ratio	Nil	Nil	Nil	Nil	Nil	Nil
Prices - High	18⅝	11¾	11⅛	8¼	5⅜	6⅛
- Low	10⅛	9⅜	8	4⅛	3⅝	2½
P/E Ratio - High	22	21	21	17	11	14
- Low	12	16	15	9	8	6

Income Statement Analysis (Million $)

	1994	%Chg	1993	%Chg	1992	%Chg	1991
Revs.	213	36%	157	4%	151	12%	135
Oper. Inc.	36.2	51%	23.9	6%	22.6	18%	19.2
Depr.	7.5	27%	5.9	13%	5.3	39%	3.8
Int. Exp.	1.3	-9%	1.5	-31%	2.1	-4%	2.2
Pretax Inc.	26.5	57%	16.9	16%	14.6	10%	13.3
Eff. Tax Rate	42%	—	41%	—	38%	—	36%
Net Inc.	15.5	55%	10.0	11%	9.0	6%	8.5

Balance Sheet & Other Fin. Data (Million $)

	1994	1993	1992	1991	1990	1989
Cash	14.6	16.8	9.1	1.5	10.2	5.9
Curr. Assets	64.1	53.2	46.7	40.4	40.9	37.0
Total Assets	137	108	99	93.2	83.1	74.7
Curr. Liab.	33.3	21.4	22.1	20.6	14.8	15.9
LT Debt	10.6	11.2	16.2	22.7	20.4	20.6
Common Eqty.	76.2	60.1	50.1	39.1	38.5	30.1
Total Cap.	99	81.6	72.3	67.8	65.1	56.6
Cap. Exp.	8.0	6.3	6.2	4.1	8.2	6.4
Cash Flow	23.0	15.9	14.3	13.0	12.3	11.2

Ratio Analysis

	1994	1993	1992	1991	1990	1989
Curr. Ratio	1.9	2.5	2.1	2.0	2.8	2.3
% LT Debt of Cap.	10.8	13.7	22.4	33.6	31.3	36.4
% Net Inc.of Revs.	7.3	6.4	6.0	6.3	6.8	6.2
% Ret. on Assets	12.6	9.6	9.2	9.9	10.6	11.2
% Ret. on Equity	22.7	18.0	19.9	22.5	24.3	30.1

Dividend Data —Cash dividends were omitted in 1982, following substantial charges related to plant closings and reorganizations. Several stock splits have been effected,

Amt. of Div. $	Date Decl.	Ex-Div. Date	Stock of Record	Payment Date
2-for-1	May. 10	Jun. 22	May. 24	Jun. 21 '95

Data as orig. reptd.; bef. results of disc. opers. and/or spec. items. Per share data adj. for stk. divs. as of ex-div. date. E-Estimated. NA-Not Available. NM-Not Meaningful. NR-Not Ranked.

Office—One Colonial Rd. (P.O. Box 151), Manchester, CT 06045-0151. **Tel**—(203) 646-1233. **Chrmn, Pres & CEO**—L. R. Jaskol. **VP-Fin & Treas**—J. E. Hanley. **Secy**—Mary Adamowicz. **Investor Contact**—Carole F. Butenas. **Dirs**—L. A. Asseo, P. S. Buddenhagen, C. Buteras, S. P. Cooley, W. L. Duffy, L. R. Jaskol, W. P. Lyons, J. Schiavone, R. M. Widmann, A. E. Wolf. **Transfer Agent**—American Stock Transfer & Trust Co., NYC. **Incorporated** in Connecticut in 1913; reincorporated in Delaware in 1987. **Empl**-1,307. **S&P Analyst:** N. Rosenberg

STANDARD & POOR'S

STOCK REPORTS

M.D.C. Holdings

NYSE Symbol **MDC**

In S&P SmallCap 600

12-SEP-95 **Industry:** Building

Summary: The seventh largest publicly traded homebuilder in the U.S., MDC supports its building activities by originating, buying and servicing mortgages for its customers and others.

Quantitative Evaluations

Outlook (1 Lowest—5 Highest)
• **3**

Fair Value
• **7⅝**

Risk
• **Average**

Earn./Div. Rank
• **B-**

Technical Eval.
• **Bullish** since 5/95

Rel. Strength Rank (1 Lowest—99 Highest)
• **69**

Insider Activity
• **Neutral**

Recent Price • 7⅝
52 Wk Range • 8⅛-4½
Yield • 1.6%
12-Mo. P/E • 8.7

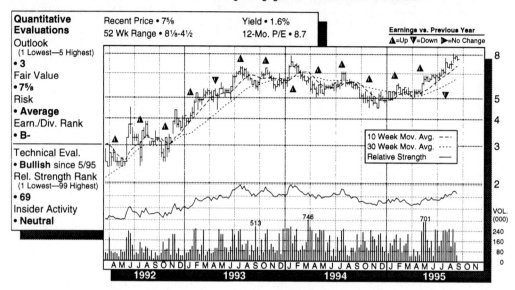

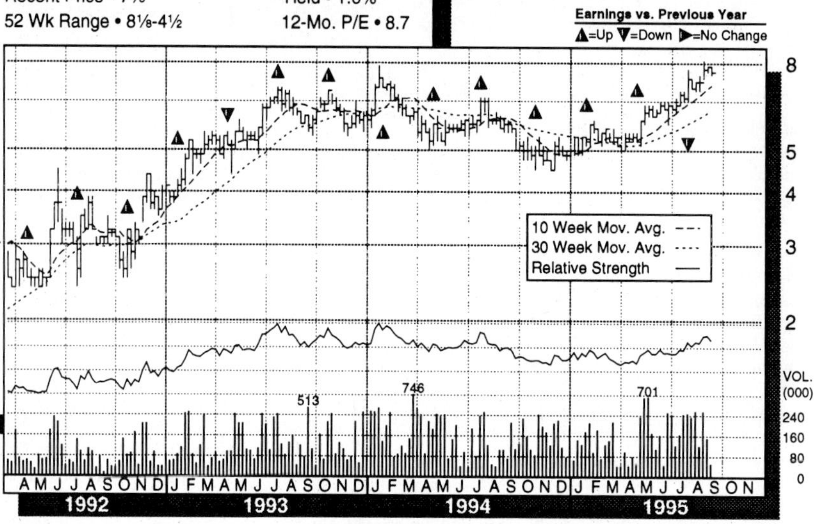

Business Profile - 12-SEP-95

In the first half of 1995, the volume of home closings was at its highest level since 1988. Lower mortgage rates and sales incentives contributed to the improvement; however, homebuilding conditions remained weak nationally. Although adversely affected by poor weather in certain regions, MDC has maintained profitability by carefully controlling costs. The company retains positions in leading housing markets and has the capital and liquidity to expand its share as buyers return to the market.

Operational Review - 12-SEP-95

For the six months ended June 30, 1995, revenues rose 11% year to year, reflecting a substantial increase in the number of home closures. Homebuilding operating margins narrowed, due to incentives offered buyers in order to stimulate sales and costs associated with efforts to reduce the inventory of unsold homes under construction. After taxes at 35.4%, versus 39.5%, net income declined 12%, to $8,399,000 ($0.41 a share; $0.38 fully diluted), from $9,510,000 ($0.47; $0.43).

Stock Performance - 08-SEP-95

In the past 30 trading days, MDC's shares have increased 3%, compared to a 2% rise in the S&P 500. Average trading volume for the past five days was 12,275 shares, compared with the 40-day moving average of 50,249 shares.

Key Stock Statistics

Dividend Rate/Share	0.12	Shareholders	2,300
Shs. outstg. (M)	19.2	Market cap. (B)	$0.147
Avg. daily vol. (M)	0.036	Inst. holdings	43%
Tang. Bk. Value/Share	10.23	Insider holdings	NA
Beta	2.07		

Value of $10,000 invested 5 years ago: $ 56,708

Fiscal Year Ending Dec. 31

	1995	% Change	1994	% Change	1993	% Change
Revenues (Million $)						
1Q	192.5	14%	168.7	44%	117.3	14%
2Q	215.3	9%	197.8	23%	161.2	23%
3Q	—	—	214.3	11%	192.7	37%
4Q	—	—	244.2	32%	185.3	33%
Yr.	—	—	824.9	26%	652.1	27%
Income (Million $)						
1Q	4.07	7%	3.81	NM	0.92	-55%
2Q	4.33	-24%	5.70	89%	3.01	101%
3Q	—	—	5.42	68%	3.22	NM
4Q	—	—	4.33	49%	2.90	NM
Yr.	—	—	19.26	91%	10.06	111%
Earnings Per Share ($)						
1Q	0.20	5%	0.19	NM	0.04	-56%
2Q	0.21	-25%	0.28	100%	0.14	100%
3Q	—	—	0.26	86%	0.14	NM
4Q	—	—	0.21	62%	0.13	NM
Yr.	—	—	0.94	109%	0.45	105%

Next earnings report expected: early November

M.D.C. Holdings

Business Summary - 12-SEP-95

M.D.C. Holdings, Inc. is engaged in the construction and sale of residential housing, with major operations in Colorado, Virginia, Maryland and northern California and smaller operations in Arizona, Nevada and southern California; the acquisition and development of land for use in its homebuilding activities and for sale to others; and mortgage banking and financing activities. The company is Colorado's largest homebuilder and is among the top five builders in the Washington, D.C.-Baltimore metro area and in Sacramento.

MDC supervises the development and construction of all of its projects (through its Richmond American Homes and Richmond Homes subsidiaries) and employs subcontractors for site development and home construction. It emphasizes the building of affordable, single-family detached homes generally for the move-up buyer. Homes are constructed according to basic designs based on customer preferences. A particular design may allow for the selection of optional features.

In part as a result of its geographic diversity of operations and the number of subdivisions in which it builds in certain states, the construction of a significant number of the company's homes, particularly in Colorado, commences prior to the execution of a sales contract. MDC monitors and controls the levels of inventory and construction in each of its subdivisions in order to attempt to match the number of unsold homes with anticipated demand.

The base price for homes sold by MDC generally ranges from approximately $90,000 to $400,000, although the company builds homes in certain of its markets with prices as high as $700,000. Sales prices in 1994 averaged $186,000.

The company acquires unimproved land, which it develops into platted lots for use in homebuilding activities and for sale to others, and purchases platted, rough and finished lots from others. It also originates and services mortgage loans through mortgage operations in each of the areas in which it has homebuilding operations.

The Residual Holdings subsidiary owns interests in issuances of collateralized mortgage obligations. MDC also manages the day-to-day operations of Asset Investors Corp., a NYSE-listed REIT, and Commercial Assets, Inc., an ASE-listed REIT.

Important Developments

Jun. '95—MDC's order backlog at June 30, 1995, had a sales value of about $320,800,000 (1,719 homes), versus $288,700,000 (1,559) at March 31, 1995, and $390,000,000 (2,061) at June 30, 1994.

Capitalization

Total Debt: $306,770,000 (6/95).

Per Share Data ($)

(Year Ended Dec. 31)

	1994	1993	1992	1991	1990	1989
Tangible Bk. Val.	10.19	9.64	8.08	8.00	8.25	7.89
Cash Flow	1.44	0.81	0.59	-0.23	-0.06	-4.68
Earnings	0.94	0.45	0.22	-0.62	-0.63	-5.66
Dividends	0.06	Nil	Nil	Nil	Nil	Nil
Payout Ratio	6%	Nil	Nil	Nil	Nil	Nil
Prices - High	$7\frac{7}{8}$	7	$4\frac{1}{2}$	$2\frac{1}{4}$	$1\frac{1}{2}$	$3\frac{3}{4}$
- Low	$4\frac{1}{2}$	$3\frac{3}{4}$	$1\frac{3}{4}$	$\frac{1}{4}$	$\frac{1}{8}$	1
P/E Ratio - High	8	16	20	NM	NM	NM
- Low	5	8	8	NM	NM	NM

Income Statement Analysis (Million $)

	1994	%Chg	1993	%Chg	1992	%Chg	1991
Revs.	825	27%	652	26%	517	23%	422
Oper. Inc.	58.4	2%	57.4	-32%	84.5	15%	73.2
Depr.	10.1	26%	8.0	-2%	8.2	1%	8.1
Int. Exp.	44.0	-2%	45.0	-42%	77.0	-25%	103
Pretax Inc.	31.0	107%	15.0	114%	7.0	NM	-14.0
Eff. Tax Rate	38%	—	33%	—	27%	—	NM
Net Inc.	19.3	91%	10.1	110%	4.8	NM	-12.9

Balance Sheet & Other Fin. Data (Million $)

	1994	1993	1992	1991	1990	1989
Cash	49.0	82.0	106	91.0	83.0	91.0
Curr. Assets	NA	NA	NA	NA	NA	NA
Total Assets	725	777	859	1,316	1,477	1,664
Curr. Liab.	NA	NA	NA	NA	NA	NA
LT Debt	322	412	510	976	1,131	1,297
Common Eqty.	192	176	164	160	157	150
Total Cap.	515	587	676	1,163	1,315	1,464
Cap. Exp.	Nil	Nil	Nil	Nil	Nil	Nil
Cash Flow	29.4	18.1	12.9	-4.8	-1.1	-74.5

Ratio Analysis

	1994	1993	1992	1991	1990	1989
Curr. Ratio	NA	NA	NA	NA	NA	NA
% LT Debt of Cap.	62.6	70.1	75.4	83.9	86.0	88.6
% Net Inc.of Revs.	2.3	1.5	0.9	NM	NM	NM
% Ret. on Assets	2.5	1.3	0.4	NM	NM	NM
% Ret. on Equity	10.3	6.2	2.9	NM	NM	NM

Dividend Data —Dividends, omitted in 1988 after having been paid since 1979, were resumed in 1994.

Amt. of Div. $	Date Decl.	Ex-Div. Date	Stock of Record	Payment Date
0.020	Aug. 31	Sep. 02	Sep. 09	Sep. 19 '94
0.020	Nov. 21	Nov. 28	Dec. 02	Dec. 12 '94
0.020	Jan. 26	Jan. 31	Feb. 06	Feb. 17 '95
0.030	May. 02	May. 08	May. 12	May. 22 '95
0.030	Jul. 25	Aug. 02	Aug. 04	Aug. 14 '95

Data as orig. reptd.; bef. results of disc. opers. and/or spec. items. Per share data adj. for stk. divs. as of ex-div. date. E-Estimated. NA-Not Available. NM-Not Meaningful. NR-Not Ranked.

Office—3600 South Yosemite St., Suite 900, Denver, CO 80237. **Tel**—(303) 773-1100. **Chrmn & CEO**—L. A. Mizel. **Pres & COO**—S. I. Browne. **Sr VP, CFO & Secy**—P. G. Reece III. **Dirs**—S. J. Borick, S. I. Browne, H. T. Buchwald, G. Goldstein, W. B. Kemper, D. D. Mandarich, L. A. Mizel. **Transfer Agent**—Society National Bank, Denver. **Incorporated** in Colorado; reincorporated in Delaware in 1985. **Empl**-1,124. **S&P Analyst:** Thomas C. Ferguson

STANDARD & POOR'S

STOCK REPORTS

M.S. Carriers

NASDAQ Symbol **MSCA**

In S&P SmallCap 600

12-OCT-95 **Industry:** Trucking

Summary: This irregular-route truckload carrier transports a wide range of general commodities, primarily in the eastern two-thirds of the U.S. and in parts of Canada and Mexico.

Quantitative Evaluations

Outlook (1 Lowest—5 Highest)
• **5−**

Fair Value
• **18¼**

Risk
• **Average**

Earn./Div. Rank
• **B+**

Technical Eval.
• **Bearish** since 7/95

Rel. Strength Rank (1 Lowest—99 Highest)
• **9**

Insider Activity
• **Neutral**

Recent Price • 15¾ Yield • Nil
52 Wk Range • 25¾-15½ 12-Mo. P/E • 13.5

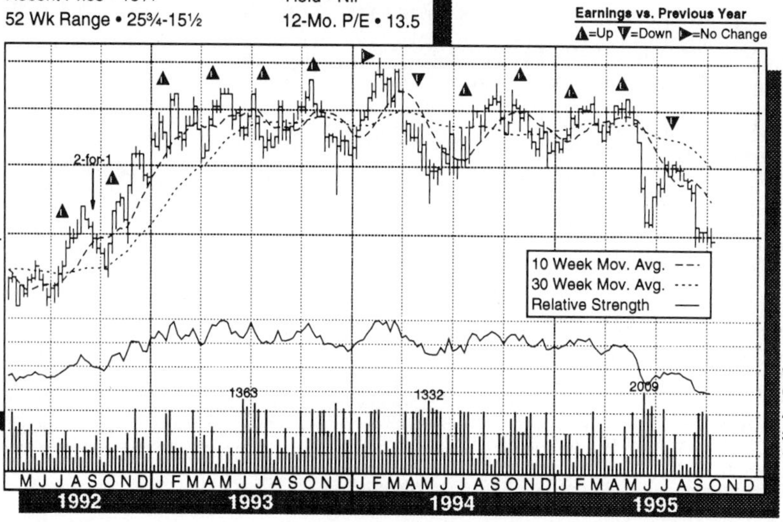

Business Profile - 26-JUN-95

This company's growth is being fueled by increased demand for its shipping services, due to a high level of customer satisfaction and greater capacity. The company has made productivity improvements through the use of technology, and has one of the lowest driver turnover rates in the industry. M.S. Carriers is developing its logistics operations to improve customers' supply chains. The company plans to expand in the western part of the U.S. and to further development existing territories.

Operational Review - 12-OCT-95

Based on a brief report, revenues in the nine months ended September 30, 1995, rose 19%, year to year, reflecting increases in all of the company's business segments. However, expenses grew more rapidly than revenues, and with sharply higher interest expense, pretax income fell 20%. After taxes at 36.1% versus 39.5%, net income declined 15% to $10.4 million ($0.79 a share) from $12.2 million ($0.93).

Stock Performance - 06-OCT-95

In the past 30 trading days, MSCA's shares have declined 16%, compared to a 4% rise in the S&P 500. Average trading volume for the past five days was 59,900 shares, compared with the 40-day moving average of 61,803 shares.

Key Stock Statistics

Dividend Rate/Share	Nil	Shareholders	300
Shs. outstg. (M)	12.9	Market cap. (B)	$0.196
Avg. daily vol. (M)	0.087	Inst. holdings	61%
Tang. Bk. Value/Share	12.08	Insider holdings	NA
Beta	0.93		

Value of $10,000 invested 5 years ago: $ 15,000

Fiscal Year Ending Dec. 31

	1995	% Change	1994	% Change	1993	% Change
Revenues (Million $)						
1Q	81.70	35%	60.42	21%	49.90	21%
2Q	84.54	22%	69.56	26%	55.20	22%
3Q	84.33	5%	80.30	35%	59.30	28%
4Q	—	—	82.59	37%	60.43	25%
Yr.	—	—	292.9	30%	224.7	24%
Income (Million $)						
1Q	3.76	55%	2.42	-9%	2.67	73%
2Q	4.02	-9%	4.42	30%	3.41	14%
3Q	2.58	-52%	5.35	39%	3.86	27%
4Q	—	—	4.96	47%	3.38	12%
Yr.	—	—	17.15	26%	13.60	29%
Earnings Per Share ($)						
1Q	0.29	61%	0.18	-25%	0.24	71%
2Q	0.31	-9%	0.34	10%	0.31	11%
3Q	0.20	-51%	0.41	37%	0.30	7%
4Q	—	—	0.38	36%	0.28	NM
Yr.	—	—	1.31	16%	1.13	16%

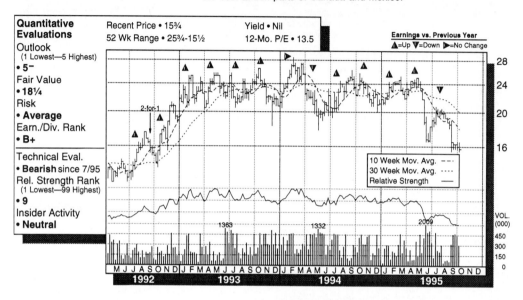

Next earnings report expected: early February

M.S. Carriers

Business Summary - 11-OCT-95

M.S. Carriers, Inc. is a Memphis, Tenn.-based irregular-route truckload carrier, transporting a wide range of general commodities in the eastern two-thirds of the U.S. and in Quebec and Ontario, Canada. The company also provides interline service to and from Mexico.

The company's main traffic flows are between the Middle South and the Southwest, Midwest, Central States, Southeast and Northeast. The average length of a trip (one-way) was about 617 miles in 1994 and 618 in 1993.

Principal types of freight transported are packages, retail goods, nonperishable foodstuffs, paper and paper products, household appliances, furniture and packaged petroleum products.

M.S. has targeted the service-sensitive segment of the truckload market, rather than price-sensitive customers. Premium service is provided and compensating rates are charged.

The company believes that the main characteristics of its premium service are dependable late-model equipment that allows timely deliveries, multiple and appointment pickups and deliveries, assistance in loading and unloading, the availability of extra trailers that can be placed in service for the convenience of customers and sufficient equipment to respond promptly to varying customer requirements. MSCA's 25 largest customers accounted for approximately 57% of revenues in 1994.

Marketing efforts are focused on customers that ship multiple loads from numerous locations complementing M.S.'s existing traffic flows. The company publishes its own freight rates instead of using those provided by rate publishing bureaus. This allows it to offer rates that are more responsive to market conditions and the level of service provided for a particular customer.

At December 31, 1994, the company owned and operated 2,106 tractors (consisting of 2,065 over-the-road and 41 local tractors) and 6,481 van trailers. It also leased 207 tractors owned by independent contractors (owner-operators).

Important Developments

Oct. '95—In announcing third quarter earnings, M.S. Carriers said that revenue growth was less than expected due to sluggish economic conditions in the company's markets. In response to the ongoing softness in these markets, the company intends to continue its short-term strategy of aggressive target marketing, while focusing on process improvements, cost control measures and improved productivity.

Capitalization

Long Term Debt: $38,339,181 (9/95).

Per Share Data ($) (Year Ended Dec. 31)

	1994	1993	1992	1991	1990	1989
Tangible Bk. Val.	11.49	10.25	6.74	5.75	5.02	4.43
Cash Flow	3.88	3.40	2.97	2.44	2.10	1.95
Earnings	1.31	1.13	0.97	0.73	0.60	0.79
Dividends	Nil	Nil	Nil	Nil	Nil	Nil
Payout Ratio	Nil	Nil	Nil	Nil	Nil	Nil
Prices - High	28½	26½	22¾	16	10¾	12
- Low	17¾	18¼	12½	6¾	4⅝	8
P/E Ratio - High	22	23	23	22	18	15
- Low	14	16	13	9	8	10

Income Statement Analysis (Million $)

	1994	%Chg	1993	%Chg	1992	%Chg	1991
Revs.	293	30%	225	24%	181	18%	153
Oper. Inc.	63.4	21%	52.4	24%	42.2	26%	33.6
Depr.	33.7	23%	27.4	25%	21.9	20%	18.2
Int. Exp.	1.8	-15%	2.1	-18%	2.6	-15%	3.0
Pretax Inc.	28.0	21%	23.1	28%	18.0	38%	13.0
Eff. Tax Rate	39%	—	41%	—	41%	—	40%
Net Inc.	17.2	26%	13.6	28%	10.6	37%	7.8

Balance Sheet & Other Fin. Data (Million $)

	1994	1993	1992	1991	1990	1989
Cash	30.8	0.1	0.1	0.1	0.0	0.1
Curr. Assets	73.8	32.0	25.0	20.3	17.0	16.4
Total Assets	276	199	151	122	111	95.0
Curr. Liab.	44.9	22.7	24.6	16.7	17.7	17.6
LT Debt	51.2	18.0	32.7	26.8	25.6	18.2
Common Eqty.	148	132	72.0	61.3	53.4	46.8
Total Cap.	231	176	126	106	94.0	77.0
Cap. Exp.	100	70.1	46.5	35.3	36.9	39.9
Cash Flow	50.8	41.0	32.4	25.9	22.3	20.6

Ratio Analysis

	1994	1993	1992	1991	1990	1989
Curr. Ratio	1.6	1.4	1.0	1.2	1.0	0.9
% LT Debt of Cap.	22.1	10.2	25.9	25.4	27.4	23.6
% Net Inc.of Revs.	5.9	6.1	5.8	5.1	5.2	8.6
% Ret. on Assets	7.2	7.1	7.7	6.6	6.2	10.5
% Ret. on Equity	12.3	12.4	15.9	13.5	12.7	19.5

Dividend Data —No cash dividends have been paid, and the company has expressed its intention to retain earnings to finance expansion of its business. Two-for-one stock splits were effected in 1992 and 1987.

Data as orig. reptd.; bef. results of disc. opers. and/or spec. items. Per share data adj. for stk. divs. as of ex-div. date. E-Estimated. NA-Not Available. NM-Not Meaningful. NR-Not Ranked.

Office—3171 Directors Row, Memphis, TN 38116. **Tel**—(901) 332-2500. **Chrmn, Pres & CEO**—M. S. Starnes. **Sr VP-Fin, Secy & Treas**—M. J. Barrow. **Dirs**—M. J. Barrow, M. H. Fair, G. L. Hardeman, R. P. Hurt, J. H. Morris III, C. Mungenast, M. S. Starnes, J. W. Welch. **Transfer Agent & Registrar**—Trust Co. Bank, Atlanta. **Incorporated** in Tennessee in 1977. **Empl**-3,238. **S&P Analyst:** N. Rosenberg

STANDARD & POOR'S

STOCK REPORTS

Magma Copper

NYSE Symbol **MCU**
In S&P SmallCap 600

11-SEP-95

Industry: Mining/Diversified

Summary: This fully integrated producer of electrolytic copper is one of the largest U.S. copper producers. It also produces gold- and silver-bearing residues and molybdenum disulfide.

Quantitative Evaluations

Outlook
(1 Lowest—5 Highest)
• **2+**

Fair Value
• **16 7/8**

Risk
• **Average**

Earn./Div. Rank
• **NR**

Technical Eval.
• **Bullish** since 6/95

Rel. Strength Rank
(1 Lowest—99 Highest)
• **64**

Insider Activity
• **NA**

Recent Price • 19 5/8
52 Wk Range • 20 7/8-13 7/8

Yield • Nil
12-Mo. P/E • 6.3

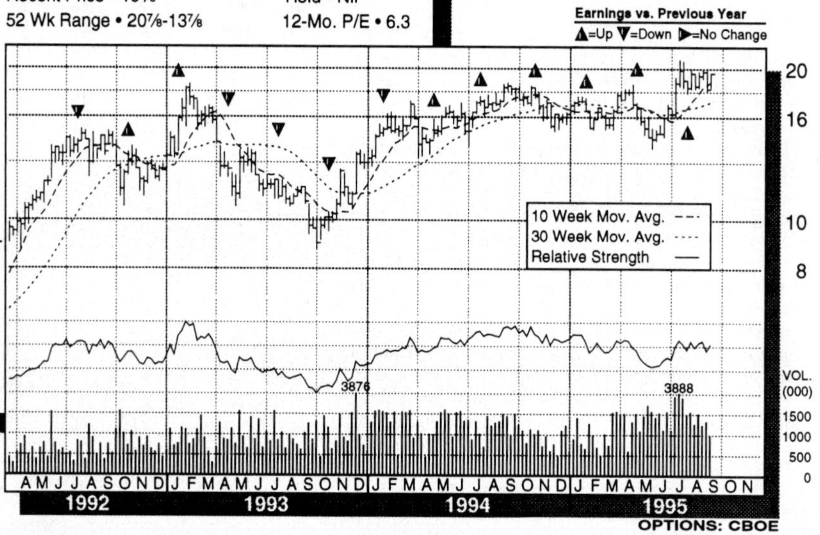

OPTIONS: CBOE

Business Profile - 11-SEP-95

With its 1994 acquisition of the huge, low-cost Tintaya copper mine in Peru, Magma should be able to fully capitalize on the extremely favorable conditions now existing in the copper industry. Copper prices reached a five-year high in 1994 and, with world economic expansion continuing to drain the already low level of inventories, should remain strong for the next few years. Tintaya, which is expected to account for 20% of Magma's 1995 production, will have a major impact on earnings.

Operational Review - 11-SEP-95

Sales advanced 67%, year to year, in the first half of 1995, as the Tintaya acquisition added 60 million pounds (18% of the total) of low-cost copper production. Operating income rose 257%, with a sharp increase (from $0.90 to $1.30 realized per pound) in copper prices. Despite higher interest and other expenses (net), earnings more than quadrupled, to $2.05 a share. MCU should continue to benefit from the low level of world copper inventories and the high-margin sales of its Tintaya operation.

Stock Performance - 08-SEP-95

In the past 30 trading days, MCU's shares have increased 7%, compared to a 2% rise in the S&P 500. Average trading volume for the past five days was 240,050 shares, compared with the 40-day moving average of 346,451 shares.

Key Stock Statistics

Dividend Rate/Share	Nil	Shareholders	4,700
Shs. outstg. (M)	46.1	Market cap. (B)	$0.906
Avg. daily vol. (M)	0.273	Inst. holdings	50%
Tang. Bk. Value/Share	12.15	Insider holdings	NA
Beta	1.31		

Value of $10,000 invested 5 years ago: $ 38,292

Fiscal Year Ending Dec. 31

	1995	% Change	1994	% Change	1993	% Change
Revenues (Million $)						
1Q	297.5	70%	175.5	-10%	194.6	-3%
2Q	361.5	65%	219.5	15%	190.1	-7%
3Q	—	—	227.1	7%	211.9	-3%
4Q	—	—	267.5	37%	195.8	NM
Yr.	—	—	889.6	12%	792.4	-3%
Income (Million $)						
1Q	51.77	NM	7.61	NM	0.28	-97%
2Q	54.42	164%	20.61	NM	4.71	-69%
3Q	—	—	22.32	155%	8.76	-62%
4Q	—	—	36.85	NM	9.05	-11%
Yr.	—	—	87.40	NM	22.80	-61%
Earnings Per Share ($)						
1Q	0.99	NM	0.10	NM	0.01	-96%
2Q	1.05	192%	0.36	NM	0.10	-71%
3Q	—	—	0.39	129%	0.17	-71%
4Q	—	—	0.69	NM	0.16	-24%
Yr.	—	—	1.54	NM	0.42	-69%

Next earnings report expected: late October

Magma Copper

Business Summary - 11-SEP-95

Magma Copper Company is a fully integrated producer of electrolytic copper and ranks among the largest U.S copper producers. MCU sold 774.3 million pounds of copper (77% produced by Magma sources) in 1994, 764.4 million pounds (73%) the year before and 725.4 million pounds (78%) in 1992.

The company's principal products are high-quality copper cathode and copper rod. Magma's copper operations also produce gold- and silver-bearing residues, molybdenum disulfide and sulfuric acid as by-products.

MCU owns and operates underground and open-pit copper mines at its San Manuel, Pinto Valley and Superior mining divisions, located in southeastern Arizona. In situ leaching operations are also conducted at the San Manuel and Pinto Valley divisions.

In October 1994, Magma acquired 98.43% of the Tintaya open-pit mine in Peru, with an ore reserve of 58 million tonnes of 1.78% sulfide copper ore. Tintaya increased MCU's recoverable copper by nearly two billion pounds (25%). At January 1, 1995, estimated ore reserves consisted of 9.66 billion pounds of recoverable copper and 1.94 million ounces of recoverable gold.

MCU's smelter has a capacity rated at 1.3 million tons of copper concentrate annually, which represents some 25% of U.S. smelting and refining capacity. In addition to smelting and refining its own copper concentrate production, Magma smelts and refines a substantial amount of copper concentrates on a custom basis, the profits from which reduce the company's overall break-even production costs.

In late 1994, the company began developing the Robinson Mining District, near Ely, Nev., which has 252 million tons of proven/probable sulfide ore reserves. Magma completed the detailed engineering phase for its development and has received all necessary permits. MCU expects gold and copper production to begin in the first quarter of 1996. Based on year-end estimates, development of the property could require capital expenditures of $300 million.

Important Developments

Jul. '95—The company said Magma Tintaya S.A. and the Tintaya unions ratified a five-year labor contract through June 30, 2000. Separately, MCU said it expected to spend $22 million on exploration and feasibility work during 1995 to develop new copper ore reserves.

Capitalization

Long Term Debt: $583,148,000 (6/95).
$3.00 Series E Conv. Preferred Stock: 2,000,000 shs. ($50 liquid. pref.); ea. conv. into 3.5945 com.
$2.8125 Series D Conv. Preferred Stock: 2,000,000 shs. ($50 liquid. pref.); ea. conv. into 3.448 com..

Per Share Data ($) (Year Ended Dec. 31)

	1994	1993	1992	1991	1990	1989
Tangible Bk. Val.	14.32	12.69	10.21	10.48	15.15	12.64
Cash Flow	3.07	1.77	3.02	-2.30	3.66	2.58
Earnings	1.54	0.42	1.37	-3.76	2.51	1.48
Dividends	Nil	Nil	Nil	Nil	Nil	Nil
Payout Ratio	Nil	Nil	Nil	Nil	Nil	Nil
Prices - High	18¾	18⅝	15⅛	7½	6¾	8⅞
- Low	12¾	8¾	5¼	3⅞	3¾	4⅝
P/E Ratio - High	12	44	11	NM	3	6
- Low	8	21	4	NM	1	3

Income Statement Analysis (Million $)

	1994	%Chg	1993	%Chg	1992	%Chg	1991
Revs.	890	12%	792	-3%	819	13%	725
Oper. Inc.	199	64%	121	-28%	168	38%	122
Depr.	75.1	16%	64.9	17%	55.4	25%	44.3
Int. Exp.	42.8	NM	42.8	-6%	45.3	-15%	53.2
Pretax Inc.	110	NM	32.0	-60%	81.0	NM	-168
Eff. Tax Rate	20%	—	28%	—	28%	—	NM
Net Inc.	87.0	NM	23.0	-60%	58.0	NM	-106

Balance Sheet & Other Fin. Data (Million $)

	1994	1993	1992	1991	1990	1989
Cash	88.0	339	242	91.0	114	49.4
Curr. Assets	341	480	370	249	271	231
Total Assets	1,577	1,351	1,157	1,016	1,004	954
Curr. Liab.	226	120	143	114	69.2	89.7
LT Debt	387	392	395	341	363	385
Common Eqty.	660	580	465	316	441	356
Total Cap.	1,282	1,169	959	842	919	845
Cap. Exp.	149	148	74.0	77.0	54.0	47.0
Cash Flow	151	85.0	101	-70.0	107	73.0

Ratio Analysis

	1994	1993	1992	1991	1990	1989
Curr. Ratio	1.5	4.0	2.6	2.2	3.9	2.6
% LT Debt of Cap.	30.2	33.6	41.2	40.5	39.5	45.5
% Net Inc.of Revs.	9.8	2.9	7.1	NM	10.5	7.5
% Ret. on Assets	5.9	1.8	4.3	NM	8.1	5.2
% Ret. on Equity	12.2	3.9	9.7	NM	18.3	12.8

Dividend Data —No cash dividends have been paid on the common stock.

Data as orig. reptd.; bef. results of disc. opers. and/or spec. items. Per share data adj. for stk. divs. as of ex-div. date. E-Estimated. NA-Not Available. NM-Not Meaningful. NR-Not Ranked.

Office—7400 North Oracle Rd., Suite 200, Tucson, AZ 85704. **Tel**—(520) 575-5600 **Chrmn**—D. J. Donahue. **Pres & CEO**—J. B. Winter. **VP & CFO**—D. J. Purdom. **Treas & Investor Contact**—Richard P. Johnson. **VP & Secy**—A. A. Brodkey. **Dirs**—C. W. Brody, J. R. Cool, D. J. Donahue, J. W. Goth, J. R. Kennedy, P. P. Kuczynski, T. W. Rollins, H. B. Sargent, S. D. Strauss, H. W. Sundt, J. L. Vogelstein, J. B. Winter. **Transfer Agent & Registrar**—Mellon Securities Trust Co., Ridgefield Park, N.J. **Reincorporated** in Delaware in 1969. **Empl**-4,200. **S&P Analyst:** Justin McCann

STANDARD & POOR'S

STOCK REPORTS

Magna Group

NASDAQ Symbol **MAGI**

In S&P SmallCap 600

05-SEP-95

Industry: Banking

Summary: MAGI is a St. Louis-based bank holding company with $4.7 billion in assets. It operates over 100 community banking locations in Illinois and Missouri.

Quantitative Evaluations

Outlook (1 Lowest—5 Highest)
• **NA**

Fair Value
• **NA**

Risk
• **Low**

Earn./Div. Rank
• **B+**

Technical Eval.
• **Bullish** since 8/95

Rel. Strength Rank (1 Lowest—99 Highest)
• **59**

Insider Activity
• **Favorable**

Recent Price • 23⅛ | Yield • 3.5%
52 Wk Range • 23⅜-16¾ | 12-Mo. P/E • 12.8

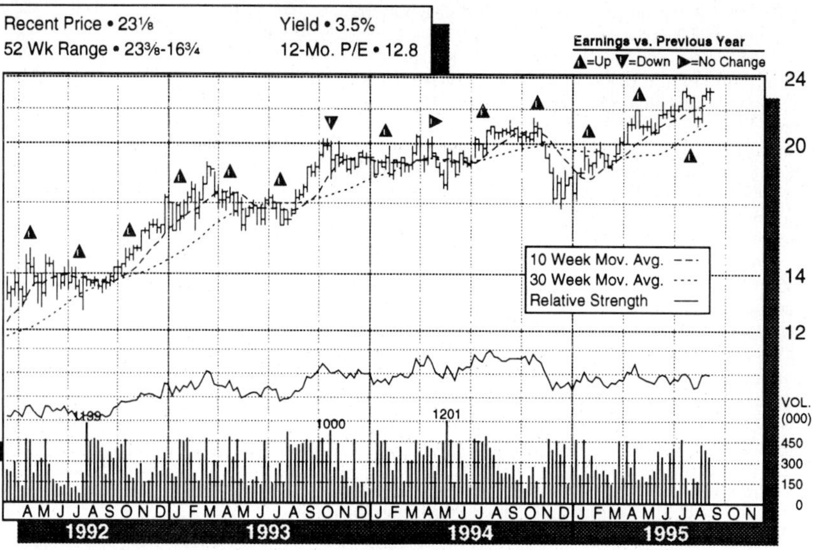

Business Profile - 04-SEP-95

Retail lending, Magna's traditional focus, remains the key to its business strategy. In 1994, MAGI experienced strong loan growth in its indirect auto line and in small business lending. More than 80% of the portfolio consists of loans under $500,000, while the average commercial loan is $87,000. Loans grew 16% in 1994; nonperforming assets fell 28%. The development of a higher proportion of fee-based revenue is being emphasized. In 1994, noninterest income accounted for 21% of total revenues.

Operational Review - 04-SEP-95

In the six months ended June 30, 1995, net interest income rose 12%, year to year, primarily reflecting strong loan growth. The provision for loan losses advanced to $3.9 million, from $2.1 million. Non-interest income declined by 3.9%, while non-interest expense was marginally higher. After taxes at 31.0%, versus 30.2%, net income was up 22% to $24,034,000 ($0.87 a share; $0.85 fully diluted) from $19,756,000 ($0.76; $0.75).

Stock Performance - 01-SEP-95

In the past 30 trading days, MAGI's shares have increased 1%, compared to a 2% rise in the S&P 500. Average trading volume for the past five days was 67,240 shares, compared with the 40-day moving average of 59,385 shares.

Key Stock Statistics

Dividend Rate/Share	0.80	Shareholders	8,900
Shs. outstg. (M)	27.7	Market cap. (B)	$0.640
Avg. daily vol. (M)	0.065	Inst. holdings	35%
Tang. Bk. Value/Share	14.25	Insider holdings	NA
Beta	0.74		

Value of $10,000 invested 5 years ago: $ 18,779

Fiscal Year Ending Dec. 31

	1995	% Change	1994	% Change	1993	% Change
Revenues (Million $)						
1Q	93.28	21%	76.99	6%	72.81	-10%
2Q	96.85	19%	81.41	11%	73.04	-8%
3Q	—	—	86.31	22%	70.51	-9%
4Q	—	—	91.99	25%	73.77	NM
Yr.	—	—	337.1	16%	290.1	-7%
Income (Million $)						
1Q	11.64	26%	9.21	6%	8.68	137%
2Q	12.40	18%	10.54	15%	9.13	30%
3Q	—	—	12.42	32%	9.44	-7%
4Q	—	—	12.86	26%	10.24	25%
Yr.	—	—	45.03	20%	37.49	29%
Earnings Per Share ($)						
1Q	0.42	17%	0.36	NM	0.36	100%
2Q	0.45	13%	0.40	5%	0.38	6%
3Q	—	—	0.46	18%	0.39	-15%
4Q	—	—	0.47	15%	0.41	21%
Yr.	—	—	1.69	10%	1.53	13%

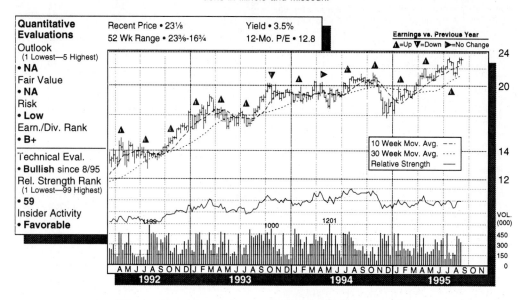

Next earnings report expected: late October

Magna Group

Business Summary - 05-SEP-95

Magna Group, Inc. is a multibank holding company with two chartered banks and a trust company operating from more than 100 locations in Missouri and Illinois, including approximately 70 within the St. Louis metropolitan area. Through its bank and nonbank subsidiaries, the company conducts commercial, retail and correspondent banking and, through an affiliate, provides trust services. At December 31, 1994, custodial trust assets were approximately $4.2 billion. During 1994, Magna introduced a family of mutual funds marketed through its financial services subsidiary, the MGI Group. Since 1991, Magna has shifted its focus to the St. Louis metropolitan area.

Total loans outstanding of $2.97 billion at 1994 year end were divided: Real estate--commercial

	31.4%
Real estate--residential	30.4%
Real estate--construction	4.4%
Commercial, financial & agricultural	16.6%
Other consumer	17.2%

The allowance for loan losses at 1994 year end totaled $44.0 million (1.48% of gross loans outstanding), up from $40.1 million (1.57%) a year earlier. Net chargeoffs during 1994 amounted to $3.7 million (0.14% of average total loans), down from $13.6 million (0.59%) in 1993. Nonperforming assets at December 31, 1994, amounted to $44.1 million (0.95% of total assets), down from $60.9 million (1.48%) a year earlier.

Interest and fees on loans in 1994 amounted to 65% of total income, interest on securities 21%, loan service charges 6%, trust services 3%, and other 5%.

Average deposits of $3.67 billion in 1994 were divided: 44% time, 25% savings and market rate, 16% noninterest-bearing demand, and 15% interest-bearing demand.

The average yield on total interest-earning assets in 1994 was 7.44% (7.37% in 1993), while the average rate paid on total interest-bearing liabilities was 3.48% (3.48%), for an interest rate spread of 3.96% (3.89%).

Important Developments

Jul. '95—In announcing record second quarter results, management reported a 10% annualized rate of loan growth for the period, and an improvement in the efficiency ratio to 65% from 69% in the comparable period of 1994. The return on equity advanced to 12.42% from 11.93%, while the return on assets advanced to 1.08% from 1.01%.

Capitalization

Long Term Debt: $68,928,000 (6/95).

Per Share Data ($) (Year Ended Dec. 31)

	1994	1993	1992	1991	1990	1989
Tangible Bk. Val.	12.71	14.02	13.39	12.72	13.83	13.17
Earnings	1.69	1.53	1.36	0.28	1.27	1.57
Dividends	0.76	0.72	0.68	0.68	0.65	0.62
Payout Ratio	45%	47%	50%	243%	51%	39%
Prices - High	21½	20¼	17⅜	13½	16⅜	17⅛
- Low	16¾	15¾	10⅝	8½	8⅝	13⅛
P/E Ratio - High	13	13	13	48	13	11
- Low	10	10	8	30	7	8

Income Statement Analysis (Million $)

	1994	%Chg	1993	%Chg	1992	%Chg	1991
Net Int. Inc.	173	19%	145	-1%	147	65%	89.1
Tax Equiv. Adj.	5.1	-7%	5.4	-15%	6.4	5%	6.1
Non Int. Inc.	47.5	4%	45.8	24%	36.9	74%	21.2
Loan Loss Prov.	4.9	-49%	9.6	-53%	20.5	-31%	29.5
% Exp/Op Revs.	67%	—	69%	—	68%	—	67%
Pretax Inc.	65.2	30%	50.2	45%	34.6	NM	3.4
Eff. Tax Rate	31%	—	25%	—	16%	—	NM
Net Inc.	45.0	20%	37.5	29%	29.1	NM	3.8
% Net Int. Marg.	4.49%	—	4.45%	—	4.47%	—	4.56%

Balance Sheet & Other Fin. Data (Million $)

	1994	1993	1992	1991	1990	1989
Earning Assets:						
Money Mkt.	17.5	15.0	42.9	65.3	35.6	90.4
Inv. Securities	1,217	1,214	1,088	933	630	566
Com'l Loans	1,553	1,420	1,284	1,444	788	748
Other Loans	1,419	1,149	999	1,054	714	683
Total Assets	4,639	4,128	3,729	3,777	2,320	2,249
Demand Deposits	595	529	497	452	259	283
Time Deposits	3,078	2,966	2,728	2,883	1,726	1,666
LT Debt	105	32.1	33.5	35.0	24.3	32.7
Common Eqty.	371	361	322	250	186	171

Ratio Analysis

	1994	1993	1992	1991	1990	1989
% Ret. on Assets	1.0	1.0	0.8	0.2	0.8	0.9
% Ret. on Equity	12.4	11.3	10.9	2.0	10.3	12.5
% Loan Loss Resv.	1.5	1.6	1.7	2.3	1.1	1.1
% Loans/Deposits	80.9	73.0	69.9	74.0	74.1	71.7
% Equity to Assets	8.5	9.1	7.5	8.3	7.7	7.5

Dividend Data —Cash has been paid each year since 1980. A "poison pill" stock purchase rights plan was adopted in 1988.

Amt. of Div. $	Date Decl.	Ex-Div. Date	Stock of Record	Payment Date
0.190	Jul. 20	Aug. 09	Aug. 15	Sep. 10 '94
0.190	Oct. 21	Nov. 08	Nov. 15	Dec. 10 '94
0.200	Jan. 19	Feb. 09	Feb. 15	Mar. 10 '95
0.200	Apr. 20	May. 09	May. 15	Jun. 10 '95
0.200	Jul. 19	Aug. 11	Aug. 15	Sep. 10 '95

Data as orig. reptd.; bef. results of disc opers. and/or spec. items. Per share data adj. for stk. divs. as of ex-div. date. E-Estimated. NA-Not Available. NM-Not Meaningful. NR-Not Ranked.

Office—One Magna Place, 1401 S. Brentwood Blvd., St. Louis, MO 63144-1401. **Tel**—(314) 963-2500. **Chrmn, Pres & CEO**—G. Thomas Andes. **EVP & CFO**—L. G. Maynard. **Secy**—L. G. Burger. **Investor Contact**—Gary D. Hemmer (314) 963-3016. **Dirs**—G. T. Andes, J. A. Auffenberg, Jr., W. E. Cribbin, W. T. Ewing, D. P. Gallop, C. E. Heiligenstein, C. G. Hogan Sr., F. A. Jacobs, W. J. Kelley, S. L. Kling, R. Korte, J. R. Lowery, R. E. McGlynn, F. R. Trulaske, D. A. Vogt, G. T. Wilkins — Jr. **Transfer Agent**—Magna Trust Co., Belleville, Ill. **Incorporated** in Delaware in 1974. **Empl-** 2,447. **S&P Analyst:** Thomas C. Ferguson

STANDARD & POOR'S

STOCK REPORTS

Mail Boxes Etc.

NASDAQ Symbol **MAIL**
In S&P SmallCap 600

14-SEP-95 **Industry:** Services

Summary: Mail Boxes Etc., is the world's largest franchisor of postal, business and communications retail service centers, with over 2,700 locations worldwide.

Quantitative Evaluations

Recent Price • 13⅝
52 Wk Range • 14¼-7⅞
Yield • Nil
12-Mo. P/E • 21.3

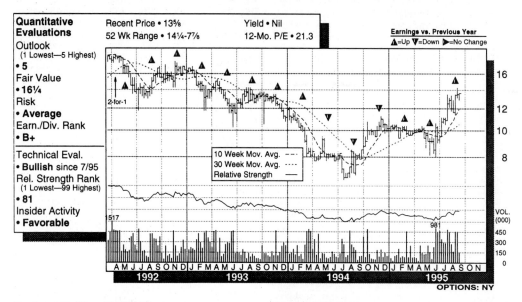

Outlook
(1 Lowest—5 Highest)
• **5**
Fair Value
• **16¼**
Risk
• **Average**
Earn./Div. Rank
• **B+**

Technical Eval.
• **Bullish** since 7/95
Rel. Strength Rank
(1 Lowest—99 Highest)
• **81**
Insider Activity
• **Favorable**

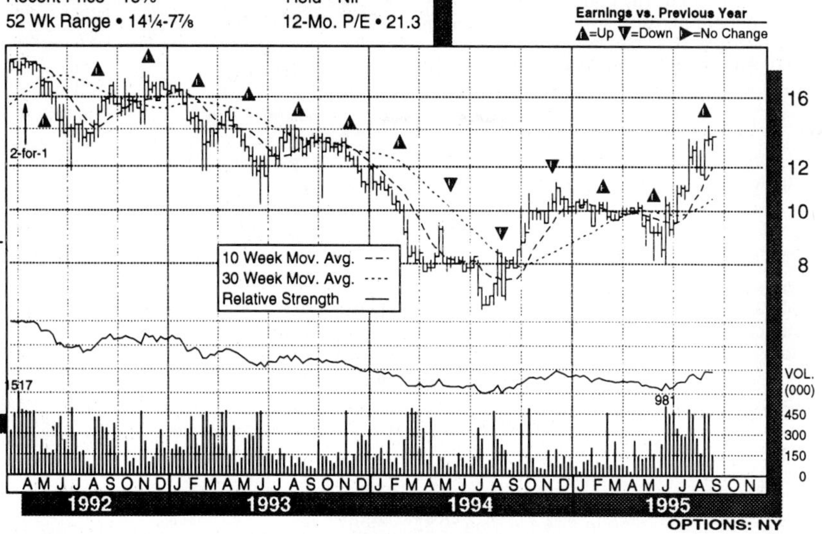

Business Profile - 14-SEP-95

The company plans to grow through increasing individual franchise sales, higher same store sales, and international expansion. In fiscal 1994-95, the company opened 312 centers in the U.S. and 148 internationally, raising the total number of centers to over 2,700. In June 1995, the company authorized the repurchase of 1,000,000 additional common shares, raising the amount of shares eligible for repurchase to 2,500,000. Since March 1994, the company has repurchased 1.3 million shares.

Operational Review - 14-SEP-95

Earnings rebounded in fiscal 1995 from a disappointing 1994, and this positive trend continued in the first quarter of fiscal 1996. Results for the quarter benefited from an increase in individual franchise sales to 65 from 56; a 33% rise in royalties from U.S. centers; and a 23% jump in same store sales. MAIL has become less dependent on revenues generated from franchise fees, which management views as positive.

Stock Performance - 08-SEP-95

In the past 30 trading days, MAIL's shares have increased 9%, compared to a 2% rise in the S&P 500. Average trading volume for the past five days was 36,875 shares, compared with the 40-day moving average of 78,364 shares.

Key Stock Statistics

Dividend Rate/Share	Nil	Shareholders	1,000
Shs. outstg. (M)	11.1	Market cap. (B)	$0.150
Avg. daily vol. (M)	0.063	Inst. holdings	26%
Tang. Bk. Value/Share	4.40	Insider holdings	NA
Beta	0.97		

Value of $10,000 invested 5 years ago: $ 17,722

Fiscal Year Ending Apr. 30

	1996	% Change	1995	% Change	1994	% Change
Revenues (Million $)						
1Q	12.80	32%	9.73	-7%	10.44	13%
2Q	—	—	12.83	7%	12.02	17%
3Q	—	—	14.71	18%	12.43	17%
4Q	—	—	13.08	45%	9.01	-3%
Yr.	—	—	50.35	15%	43.90	12%
Income (Million $)						
1Q	1.62	46%	1.11	-42%	1.93	—
2Q	—	—	1.59	-13%	1.83	—
3Q	—	—	2.32	5%	2.20	6%
4Q	—	—	1.75	NM	0.07	-96%
Yr.	—	—	6.77	12%	6.03	-12%
Earnings Per Share ($)						
1Q	0.14	40%	0.10	-38%	0.16	23%
2Q	—	—	0.14	-7%	0.15	15%
3Q	—	—	0.20	11%	0.18	6%
4Q	—	—	0.16	NM	0.01	-93%
Yr.	—	—	0.60	22%	0.49	-13%

Next earnings report expected: mid November

Mail Boxes Etc.

Business Summary - 14-SEP-95

Mail Boxes Etc. grants franchises for the operation of service centers called Mail Boxes Etc. (MBE) Service Centers specialize in postal, packaging, business, communications and convenience items and services. The company provides franchisees with a system of business training, site selection, marketing, advertising programs and management support designed to assist franchisees in opening and operating service centers. Revenues in recent fiscal years were derived as follows:

	1994-5	1993-4
Royalty & marketing fees	49%	46%
Sales of supplies & equipment	20%	25%
Franchise fees	17%	17%
Interest income & other	11%	10%
Company center	3%	2%

In 1994-5, the company opened 312 MBE Service Centers in the U.S. and 148 internationally. At July 31, 1995, the company has 2,435 domestic and 354 international centers. The company has entered into master license agreements for the development of centers in 47 foreign countries.

Domestically, the company offers area franchises which grant area franchisees exclusive rights to sell individual franchises in their protected areas and provide start-up assistance and continuing support to the individual franchise owners in those areas. In foreign countries, the company sells master licenses that give the master licensee the exclusive right to develop and operate centers in foreign countries and the right to sell franchisees to others who, in turn, own and operate individual MBE service centers.

Major services and products offered at all centers include mail box rentals (a typical center can service an unlimited number of mail service customers at rates ranging from $10 to $30 a month); private mail and parcel receiving services (including value added services that allow customers to check the status of their mail by phone and request that specific pieces of mail be forwarded to them at another location); business support products and services (such as telephone message service, notary public, word processing, copying and printing services, and office supplies); communications services (such as FAX, voice mail, pagers, and wire transfers of funds); and convenience items and services (such as stamps, envelopes, rubber stamps, passport photos, film processing and keys).

Important Developments

Aug. '95—MAIL reported that individual franchise sales in the first quarter increased to 65 from 56 in the prior year period; Royalties from domestic MBE centers were up 33%; and same store sales rose 23%.

Capitalization

Long Term Debt: $1,336,627 (4/95).

Per Share Data ($) (Year Ended Apr. 30)

	1995	1994	1993	1992	1991	1990
Tangible Bk. Val.	4.40	4.30	4.00	3.17	2.46	1.28
Cash Flow	0.69	0.57	0.62	0.50	0.41	0.18
Earnings	0.60	0.49	0.56	0.46	0.37	0.15
Dividends	Nil	Nil	Nil	Nil	Nil	Nil
Payout Ratio	Nil	Nil	Nil	Nil	Nil	Nil
Cal. Yrs.	1994	1993	1992	1991	1990	1989
Prices - High	12	17	21	18¼	10	9½
- Low	6⅝	10¼	11¾	6⅝	5⅞	3⅜
P/E Ratio - High	20	35	38	40	27	63
- Low	11	17	21	14	16	22

Income Statement Analysis (Million $)

	1995	%Chg	1994	%Chg	1993	%Chg	1992
Revs.	50.4	15%	43.9	12%	39.3	9%	36.0
Oper. Inc.	11.8	11%	10.6	-4%	11.0	28%	8.6
Depr.	1.0	-3%	1.0	24%	0.9	57%	0.5
Int. Exp.	Nil	—	Nil	—	Nil	—	Nil
Pretax Inc.	11.2	10%	10.2	-12%	11.6	27%	9.1
Eff. Tax Rate	40%	—	41%	—	41%	—	40%
Net Inc.	6.8	12%	6.0	-12%	6.9	26%	5.5

Balance Sheet & Other Fin. Data (Million $)

	1995	1994	1993	1992	1991	1990
Cash	12.0	12.1	19.5	12.5	10.3	2.3
Curr. Assets	33.4	29.2	33.3	25.5	20.6	9.4
Total Assets	64.3	55.2	56.1	44.1	32.0	18.1
Curr. Liab.	10.8	5.1	6.6	6.0	3.5	4.4
LT Debt	1.3	Nil	Nil	Nil	Nil	Nil
Common Eqty.	52.1	50.1	49.5	38.1	28.5	13.6
Total Cap.	53.5	50.1	49.5	38.2	28.6	13.7
Cap. Exp.	0.5	0.4	1.1	5.9	0.8	0.6
Cash Flow	7.8	7.1	7.7	6.0	4.4	1.8

Ratio Analysis

	1995	1994	1993	1992	1991	1990
Curr. Ratio	3.1	5.7	5.1	4.3	5.9	2.1
% LT Debt of Cap.	2.5	Nil	Nil	Nil	Nil	Nil
% Net Inc.of Revs.	13.5	13.7	17.5	15.2	13.3	5.9
% Ret. on Assets	11.4	11.2	13.5	14.1	15.4	9.3
% Ret. on Equity	13.3	12.5	15.5	16.1	18.4	11.9

Dividend Data —No cash has been paid. A three-for-two stock split was effected in 1989, a four-for-three split in 1991, and a two-for-one split in 1992.

Data as orig. reptd.; bef. results of disc. opers. and/or spec. items. Per share data adj. for stk. divs. as of ex-div. date. E-Estimated. NA-Not Available. NM-Not Meaningful. NR-Not Ranked.

Office—6060 Cornerstone Ct. West, San Diego, CA 92121. **Tel**—(619) 455-8800. **Chrmn**—M. Dooling. **Vice Chrm, Pres & CEO**—A. W. DeSio. **VP-Fin & CFO**—G. S. Grahn. **VP & Secy**—B. M. Rosenberg. **Dirs**—H. Casari, A. W. DeSio, R. J. DeSio, M. Dooling, J. F. Kelly, D. L. LaMarche, J. Rossman. **Transfer Agent & Registrar**—First Interstate Bank, LA. **Incorporated** in California in 1983. **Empl**-175. **S&P Analyst:** Stephen Madonna, CFA

Manitowoc Co.

NYSE Symbol MTW

Price	Range	P–E Ratio	Dividend	Yield	S&P Ranking	Beta
Aug. 25'95	1995					
26⅞	30⅛–21	NM	1.00	3.7%	B	0.67

Summary

This company makes heavy-lift cranes, produces ice-making machines, and operates a shipyard. Earnings in the first half of 1995 were aided by a dramatic improvement in the marine segment. The crane segment is starting to turn around, with the current consolidation expected to show results by the fourth quarter. The fiscal year end has been changed to December 31 from June 30.

Business Summary

Manitowoc Co. makes cranes and excavators and ice cube machines, and provides marine vessel conversion and repair services. Revenue contributions in calendar 1994 were:

	Sales
Cranes & related products	55%
Foodservice	36%
Marine	9%

Exports totaled $57 million (21% of shipments) in the fiscal year ended June 30, 1994, down from $65 million (23%) in fiscal 1993.

A diversified line of crawler, truck, fixed-base mounted and hydraulically powered cranes, sold under the Manitowoc, Manitex, Orley Meyer and West-Manitowoc, Inc. names, is designed for use by the utility, petroleum exploration and production, mining, construction and other industries. Cranes have lifting capabilities ranging from 10 to 1,500 tons and excavating capacities of three to 15 cubic yards. The company has developed a line of hydraulically driven, electronically controlled M-Series cranes, which are easier to transport, operate and maintain. Six models have been introduced to date, with capacities ranging from 65 to 1,500 tons. MTW also remanufactures older cranes and performs machining and assembly subcontract work. Through West-Manitowoc, it serves smaller independent contractors and rental-fleet customers who need less complicated, easily transportable and more versatile cranes. Replacement parts for cranes, draglines and other heavy equipment are produced by Femco Machine Co. Cranes and related equipment are sold throughout North America and foreign countries through independent distributors and by company-owned sales subsidiaries in four states and in England and Switzerland.

MTW is the leading manufacturer of commercial ice cube machines. It also makes ice and bever-

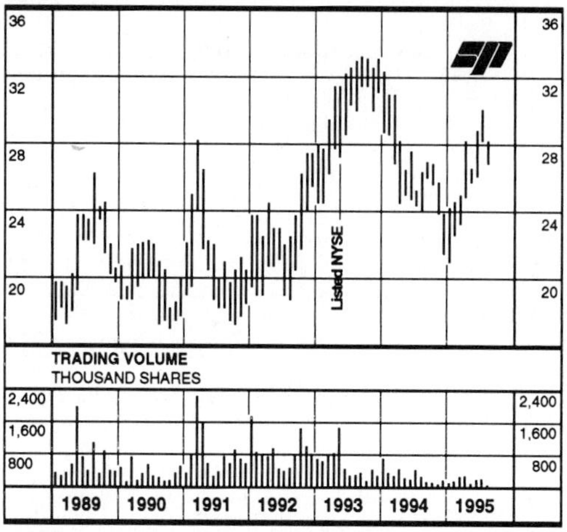

age dispensing machines and related accessories including water filtration systems, reach-in refrigerators and freezers for the foodservice, lodging, convenience store and health care industries. Several products incorporate a self-cleaning feature.

The Bay Shipbuilding Corp. unit operates a shipyard at Sturgeon Bay, Wis., where it performs inspection, repair, reconstruction and conversion work on existing vessels. Merce Industries, which operates ship repair facilities in Toledo and Cleveland, Ohio, was acquired in January 1992.

Important Developments

Jul. '95— Manitowoc said the $297,000 operating loss in its crane segment in the second quarter included $1.8 million in costs related to the consolidation of its large crane plant. With a crane backlog of $96 million, MTW expects full capacity production to be achieved by the fourth quarter.

Next earnings report expected in mid-October.

Per Share Data ($)

Yr. End Jun. 30	1994	1993	1992	1991	1990	1989	1988	1987	1986	[1]1985
Tangible Bk. Val.	**11.09**	12.78	[4]16.04	16.15	15.60	15.53	14.75	15.70	15.39	17.35
Cash Flow	**2.32**	1.25	1.41	2.05	2.50	2.09	0.63	1.70	d0.59	1.82
Earnings[5]	**1.61**	0.65	0.80	1.50	2.04	1.64	0.01	1.08	d1.27	1.12
Dividends	**1.00**	1.00	1.00	1.00	[2]2.00	0.80	0.80	0.80	0.80	0.80
Payout Ratio	**62%**	145%	125%	67%	98%	49%	991%	74%	NM	71%
Prices[3]—High	**32⅜**	33¼	27½	28¼	22¼	26¼	22½	23¾	22¾	24½
Low	**24⅛**	24½	18¾	17¼	17	17¼	16½	13¾	15¾	18½
P/E Ratio—	**20–15**	51–38	34–23	19–12	11–8	16–11	NM	22–13	NM	22–17

Data as orig. reptd. **1.** Refl. merger or acq. **2.** Incl. special. **3.** Cal. yr. **4.** Incl. intangibles. **5.** Bef. spec. item of -1.05 in 1993. d-Deficit. NM-Not Meaningful.

Income Data (Million $)

Year Ended Jun. 30	Revs.	Oper. Inc.	% Oper. Inc. of Revs.	Cap. Exp.	Depr.	Int. Exp.	Net Bef. Taxes	Eff. Tax Rate	[3]Net Inc.	% Net Inc. of Revs.	Cash Flow
1994	**275**	**27.4**	**9.9**	**13.9**	**6.27**	**Nil**	**22.6**	**37.8%**	**14.0**	**5.1**	**20.3**
1993	279	31.5	11.3	11.2	5.86	Nil	8.9	29.3%	6.3	2.3	12.2
1992	246	16.8	6.8	5.1	6.30	Nil	11.6	28.6%	8.3	3.4	14.6
1991	236	24.0	10.2	6.3	5.72	Nil	20.5	24.7%	15.4	6.5	21.1
1990	226	23.2	10.3	4.3	4.73	NA	30.4	30.7%	21.0	9.3	25.8
1989	201	24.4	12.2	2.7	4.69	NA	24.2	30.3%	16.9	8.4	21.6
1988	172	13.3	7.7	3.1	6.65	NA	d1.2	NM	0.1	0.1	6.7
1987	223	9.7	4.3	3.0	6.69	NA	16.6	29.3%	11.8	5.3	18.5
1986	222	6.8	3.1	6.1	7.43	0.24	d32.4	NM	d13.8	NM	d6.4
[1]1985	145	14.8	10.2	5.1	7.63	0.21	[2]18.7	35.0%	12.2	8.4	19.8

Balance Sheet Data (Million $)

		Curr.									
Jun. 30	Cash	Assets	Liab.	Ratio	Total Assets	% Ret. on Assets	Long Term Debt	Common Equity	Total Cap.	% LT Debt of Cap.	% Ret. on Equity
1994	**30**	**118**	**63.6**	**1.8**	**186**	**7.6**	**Nil**	**94**	**95**	**Nil**	**14.1**
1993	49	148	58.4	2.5	208	3.1	Nil	119	122	Nil	4.7
1992	37	168	43.8	3.8	225	3.7	Nil	166	169	Nil	5.0
1991	29	165	42.6	3.9	219	7.1	Nil	167	170	Nil	9.4
1990	39	159	41.4	3.9	213	9.8	Nil	162	164	Nil	13.0
1989	50	163	36.5	4.5	217	7.9	Nil	161	162	Nil	10.7
1988	67	154	35.5	4.3	211	NM	Nil	154	156	Nil	0.1
1987	82	171	45.0	3.8	232	4.8	Nil	171	174	Nil	7.0
1986	124	192	74.4	2.6	260	NM	Nil	167	170	Nil	NM
1985	101	169	44.2	3.8	244	5.2	Nil	188	200	Nil	6.5

Data as orig. reptd. **1.** Refl. merger or acq. **2.** Incl. equity in earns. of nonconsol. subs. **3.** Bef. spec. items. d-Deficit. NA-Not Available. NM-Not Meaningful.

Net Sales (Million $)

[1]Quarter:	1995	1994	1993	1992
Mar.	69.1	60.1	62.9	74.5
Jun.	82.3	86.0	100.6	74.4
Sep.		66.0	61.1	61.8
Dec.		57.9	67.8	53.3
		---	---	---

Effective January 1, 1995, MTW's fiscal year end was changed from June 30 to December 31.

Net sales in the six months ended June 30, 1995, rose 3.3%, year to year, as lower crane sales were outweighed by strong marine gains. Operating income advanced 16%, as exceptional marine margins more than offset losses in cranes and foodservice. Following net other losses, compared with a gain, pretax income increased 3.4%. After taxes of 37.5%, versus 38.0%, net income was up 4.2%, to $0.93 a share from $0.83.

Common Share Earnings ($)

[1]Quarter:	1995	1994	1993	1992
Mar.	0.23	0.19	d0.49	0.04
Jun.	0.70	0.64	d0.84	0.43
Sep.		0.49	d0.45	0.37
Dec.		d1.16	0.35	d0.07
		---	---	---

Dividend Data

Cash has been paid each year since 1945. A dividend reinvestment plan was instituted in 1993.

Amt. of Divd. $	Date Decl.	Ex-divd. Date	Stock of Record	Payment Date
0.25	Nov. 1	Nov. 25	Dec. 1	Dec. 10'94
0.25	Jan. 31	Feb. 23	Mar. 1	Mar. 10'95
0.25	May 22	May 25	Jun. 1	Jun. 10'95
0.25	Jul. 25	Aug. 30	Sep. 1	Sep. 10'95

Finances

Capital spending totaled $13 million in the first half of 1995, compared to $3.4 million in the first six months of 1994, and are projected to reach $18 to $20 million for the full year. The expenditures are primarily for the consolidation of the large-crane plant and the expansion of the food service facility.

In October 1994, MTW signed a joint venture contract to produce ice machines with China's Hangzhou Household Electrical Appliance Industrial Corp. In early 1994, the Femco Machine Co. was acquired for $10.7 million.

Capitalization

Long Term Debt: None (6/95).

Common Stock: 7,674,475 shs. ($0.01 par).
Institutions hold 71%.
Shareholders of record: 2,400 (6/94).

1. Reflects 1995 change in fiscal year end to Dec. 31 from Jun. 30. d-Deficit.

Office—700 E. Magnolia Ave., Suite B, Manitowoc, WI 54220. **Tel**—(414) 684-4410. **Pres & CEO**—F. M. Butler. **EVP & COO**—R. K. Silva, **VP, CFO & Investor Contact**—Robert R. Friedl. **Secy**—E. D. Flynn. **Dirs**—D. H. Anderson, F. M. Butler, J. P. McCann, G. T. McCoy, G. R. Rahr, Jr., G. F. Rankin, Jr., R. K. Silva, R. S. Throop. **Transfer Agent & Registrar**—First Chicago Trust Co. of New York, Jersey City, NJ. **Incorporated** in Wisconsin in 1920. **Empl**—1,900.

Marcus Corporation

NYSE Symbol **MCS**
In S&P SmallCap 600

02-AUG-95 **Industry:** Hotels/Motels/Inns

Summary: This company operates restaurants, movie theatres, and hotels and motels, primarily in the Midwest.

Quantitative Evaluations

Outlook
(1 Lowest—5 Highest)
• **5**

Fair Value
• **34**

Risk
• **Low**

Earn./Div. Rank
• **A**

Technical Eval.
• **Bullish** since 5/92

Rel. Strength Rank
(1 Lowest—99 Highest)
• **67**

Insider Activity
• **NA**

Recent Price • 31½
52 Wk Range • 31½-24
Yield • 1.3%
12-Mo. P/E • 17.1

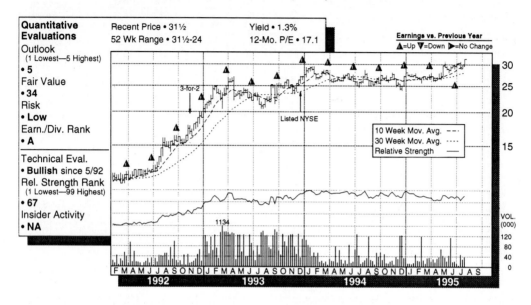

Earnings vs. Previous Year
▲=Up ▼=Down ▶=No Change

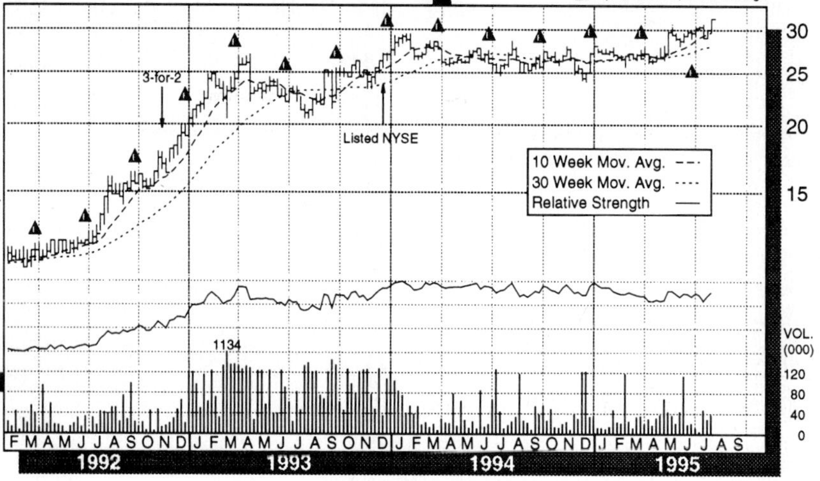

Business Profile - 02-AUG-95

Record sales and net income were reported for fiscal 1994-95, as all four divisions achieved increased revenues and three had higher profits. Marcus recently sold its Marc's Cafe and Coffee Mills restaurant operation, as well as 18 Applebee's restaurants. It plans a significant expansion of its KFC restaurants. Expansion plans over the next five years are expected to cost up to $400 million. The annual cash dividend on the common stock has been raised for seven consecutive years.

Operational Review - 02-AUG-95

Revenues for the fiscal year ended May 25, 1995 (preliminary) increased, reflecting growth in all four divisions. Net income rose strongly, paced by the Budgetel Inns unit, which benefited from increased average daily room rates, additional new properties and a strong summer travel season. Results for fiscal 1993-94, exclude a $0.14 a share special credit from the cumulative effect of an accounting change.

Stock Performance - 28-JUL-95

In the past 30 trading days, MCS's shares have increased 6%, compared to a 4% rise in the S&P 500. Average trading volume for the past five days was 7,180 shares, compared with the 40-day moving average of 7,036 shares.

Key Stock Statistics

Dividend Rate/Share	0.40	Shareholders	1,700
Shs. outstg. (M)	13.0	Market cap. (B)	$0.408
Avg. daily vol. (M)	0.007	Inst. holdings	40%
Tang. Bk. Value/Share	14.88	Insider holdings	NA
Beta	0.99		

Value of $10,000 invested 5 years ago: $ 29,581

Fiscal Year Ending May 31

	1995	% Change	1994	% Change	1993	% Change
Revenues (Million $)						
1Q	76.85	19%	64.75	20%	54.06	5%
2Q	65.38	18%	55.46	17%	47.30	6%
3Q	59.82	16%	51.75	12%	46.31	7%
4Q	77.64	4%	74.36	12%	66.34	2%
Yr.	278.0	13%	246.3	15%	214.0	5%
Income (Million $)						
1Q	9.09	17%	7.80	34%	5.81	22%
2Q	5.50	22%	4.49	27%	3.53	32%
3Q	2.55	15%	2.22	37%	1.62	22%
4Q	6.99	7%	6.54	18%	5.53	22%
Yr.	24.14	15%	21.05	28%	16.48	24%
Earnings Per Share ($)						
1Q	0.69	15%	0.60	18%	0.51	21%
2Q	0.42	24%	0.34	10%	0.31	35%
3Q	0.19	12%	0.17	21%	0.14	27%
4Q	0.53	6%	0.50	14%	0.44	10%
Yr.	1.84	15%	1.60	13%	1.42	20%

Next earnings report expected: early October

Marcus Corporation

Business Summary - 02-AUG-95

Marcus Corp. operates limited-menu restaurants, motion picture theatres, and hotel/resorts and motels, primarily in the Midwest. Segment contributions in 1993-94 were:

	Revs.	Profits
Motels	36%	$25,971
Theatres	21%	12,378
Restaurants	29%	2,203
Hotels/Resorts	13%	2,611
Corporate	1%	-8,509

Marcus owns and operates the Pfister Hotel in Milwaukee and the Milwaukee Hilton (formerly the Marc Plaza Hotel), and The Grand Geneva Resort & Spa, a full facility resort in Lake Geneva, Wisconsin. It also operates the Sheraton Mayfair Inn in Wauwatosa, Wis., the Mead Inn in Wisconsin Rapids, Wis. and the Crowne-Plaza Northstar in Minneapolis, Minn. At July 24, 1995, the company also owned or franchised 113 economy motels in 27 states, under the name Budgetel Inn. During 1993-94, Marcus opened new Woodfield Suites in Denver, Colo., and Milwaukee, Wis., bringing to three the number of all-suite motor inns operated under the Woodfield Suites name.

At July 24, 1995, the company was operating a total of 200 movie screens in theatres located in Milwaukee and its suburbs and in Gurnee, Ill. Nearly all the theatres show only first run movies. Marcus plans to expand to at least 400 screens by 2000.

At July 24, 1995, the restaurant segment was operating 34 KFC (Kentucky Fried Chicken) locations. The company owns nonexclusive franchise rights to operate Kentucky Fried Chicken carryout stores and restaurants in the greater Manitowoc area in Wisconsin.

Important Developments

Jul. '95—The annual dividend was increased 18% with the July 31, 1995, payment.
Jun. '95—Marcus sold 18 Applebee's Neighborhood Grill & Bar restaurants, as well as exclusive franchise rights in Northern Illinois and Wisconsin, to Apple South, Inc. Proceeds of $48 million will be used to expand motel, hotel, movie theatre and KFC operations. Earlier, the company closed its only Original Gino's East of Chicago restaurant.
Feb. '95—The company divested 11 Marc's Cafe & Coffee Mill restaurants in Wisconsin by leasing the locations to key managers. It also closed its remaining Marc's Cafe restaurant in Fond du Lac, Wis., and its last Big Boy restaurant, on West Capitol Drive in Milwaukee.

Capitalization

Long Term Debt: $118,344,000 (2/2/95).
Cl. B Common Stock: 6,113,209 shs. ($1 par). Each sh. has 10 votes; 93% held by Marcus family.

Per Share Data ($)

(Year Ended May 31)

	1995	1994	1993	1992	1991	1990
Tangible Bk. Val.	NA	14.88	13.40	11.19	10.22	9.37
Cash Flow	NA	3.15	2.97	2.73	2.39	2.21
Earnings	1.84	1.60	1.42	1.18	1.02	0.94
Dividends	0.34	0.28	0.26	0.22	0.20	0.18
Payout Ratio	18%	18%	18%	18%	20%	19%
Cal. Yrs.	1994	1993	1992	1991	1990	1989
Prices - High	29½	27½	20½	11⅞	12	13⅛
- Low	24	19¾	10⅞	7½	6½	9
P/E Ratio - High	16	17	14	10	12	14
- Low	13	12	8	7	6	10

Income Statement Analysis (Million $)

	1994	%Chg	1993	%Chg	1992	%Chg	1991
Revs.	233	9%	214	5%	204	9%	188
Oper. Inc.	48.5	14%	42.5	-1%	43.0	19%	36.2
Depr.	20.3	12%	18.2	4%	17.5	12%	15.6
Int. Exp.	7.7	5%	7.3	-20%	9.2	-4%	9.6
Pretax Inc.	34.7	29%	27.0	23%	22.0	16%	18.9
Eff. Tax Rate	39%	—	39%	—	40%	—	38%
Net Inc.	21.0	27%	16.5	24%	13.3	15%	11.6

Balance Sheet & Other Fin. Data (Million $)

	1994	1993	1992	1991	1990	1989
Cash	10.0	15.8	8.1	7.4	10.2	6.4
Curr. Assets	27.4	33.4	24.7	19.5	22.1	16.7
Total Assets	362	309	274	255	231	198
Curr. Liab.	40.7	37.2	34.0	29.8	24.1	22.2
LT Debt	108	79.0	100	96.0	86.0	64.0
Common Eqty.	194	174	125	115	107	98.0
Total Cap.	318	269	239	225	207	176
Cap. Exp.	75.8	47.2	41.8	39.9	42.4	35.7
Cash Flow	41.3	34.7	30.8	27.2	25.3	23.9

Ratio Analysis

	1994	1993	1992	1991	1990	1989
Curr. Ratio	0.7	0.9	0.7	0.7	0.9	0.8
% LT Debt of Cap.	33.9	29.4	41.8	42.8	41.4	36.5
% Net Inc.of Revs.	9.0	8.1	6.8	6.5	6.4	6.3
% Ret. on Assets	6.3	5.2	5.0	4.8	5.0	5.3
% Ret. on Equity	11.4	10.3	11.1	10.6	10.5	10.6

Dividend Data (Dividends were resumed on an annual basis in 1983 after omission in 1979.)

Amt. of Div. $	Date Decl.	Ex-Div. Date	Stock of Record	Payment Date
0.400	Jun. 22	Jul. 13	Jul. 17	Jul. 31 '95

Data as orig. reptd.; bef. results of disc. opers. and/or spec. items. Per share data adj. for stk. divs. as of ex-div. date. E-Estimated. NA-Not Available. NM-Not Meaningful. NR-Not Ranked.

Office—250 E. Wisconsin Ave., Milwaukee, WI 53202-4220. **Tel**—(414) 272-6020. **Fax**—(414) 272-3421. **Chrmn, Pres & CEO**—S. H. Marcus. **CFO, Treas & Investor Contact**—Kenneth MacKenzie (414-274-0503). **Secy**—T. F. Kissinger. **Dirs**—L. S. Dreyfus, D. M. Gershowitz, T. E. Hoeksema, B. Marcus, S. H. Marcus, D. F. McKeithan Jr., J. L. Murray, A. H. Selig, G. R. Slater. **Transfer Agent**—Firstar Trust Co., Milwaukee. **Reincorporated** in Wisconsin in 1992. **Empl**-7,500. **S&P Analyst:** Efraim Levy

STANDARD & POOR'S

STOCK REPORTS

Mark Twain Bancshares

NASDAQ Symbol **MTWN**

In S&P SmallCap 600

14-AUG-95 **Industry:** Banking

Summary: This Missouri-based bank holding company, with $2.75 billion in assets, operates 34 banking offices in three states, and 27 brokerage offices in four states.

Quantitative Evaluations

Recent Price • 32¼ | Yield • 3.3%
52 Wk Range • 33¼-25½ | 12-Mo. P/E • 11.7

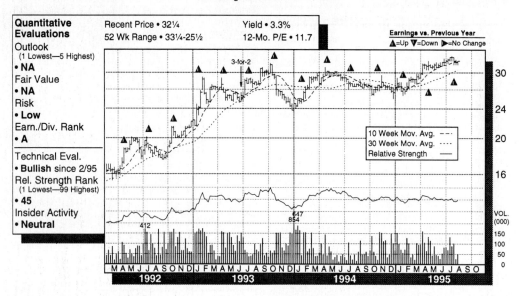

Outlook
(1 Lowest—5 Highest)
• NA

Fair Value
• NA

Risk
• Low

Earn./Div. Rank
• A

Technical Eval.
• Bullish since 2/95

Rel. Strength Rank
(1 Lowest—99 Highest)
• 45

Insider Activity
• Neutral

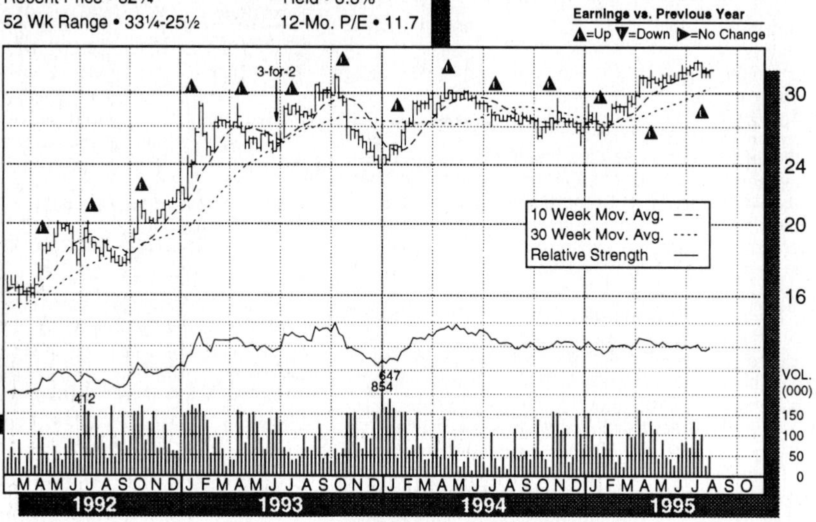

Business Profile - 14-AUG-95

MTWN's principal focus is on private, middle market companies with up to $50 million in annual sales and on retail banking customers. In 1994, improving local economies contributed to 8% growth in the bank's commercial loan portfolio, particularly within segments that included: construction, home building, health care, and manufacturing. During that period, the efficiency ratio was 56.23%, and MTWN raised its dividend for the 29th time since it went public in 1969.

Operational Review - 14-AUG-95

For the six months ended June 30, 1995, net interest income rose 6.1%, year to year, reflecting a 10% increase in loans outstanding. The net interest margin widened to 5.16%, from 5.01%, and the provision for loan losses fell to $2,631,000, from $3,459,000. Noninterest income dropped 5.7%, and noninterest expense was down 5.1%. After taxes at 36.1%, versus 35.5%, net income rose to $23.0 million ($1.42 a share; $1.38 fully diluted), from $19.5 million ($1.21; $1.18).

Stock Performance - 11-AUG-95

In the past 30 trading days, MTWN's shares were unchanged, compared to a 2% rise in the S&P 500. Average trading volume for the past five days was 9,540 shares, compared with the 40-day moving average of 15,815 shares.

Key Stock Statistics

Dividend Rate/Share	1.08	Shareholders	2,400
Shs. outstg. (M)	16.1	Market cap. (B)	$0.518
Avg. daily vol. (M)	0.013	Inst. holdings	22%
Tang. Bk. Value/Share	15.29	Insider holdings	NA
Beta	0.84		

Value of $10,000 invested 5 years ago: $ 33,446

Fiscal Year Ending Dec. 31

	1995	% Change	1994	% Change	1993	% Change
Revenues (Million $)						
1Q	62.76	19%	52.83	7%	49.30	-4%
2Q	65.51	21%	53.95	3%	52.43	3%
3Q	—	—	54.75	7%	51.34	4%
4Q	—	—	67.58	27%	53.37	7%
Yr.	—	—	230.1	11%	206.4	2%
Income (Million $)						
1Q	11.37	19%	9.57	22%	7.83	28%
2Q	11.63	17%	9.92	21%	8.19	24%
3Q	—	—	10.37	24%	8.37	20%
4Q	—	—	11.12	28%	8.68	20%
Yr.	—	—	40.98	24%	33.07	22%
Earnings Per Share ($)						
1Q	0.70	17%	0.60	9%	0.55	21%
2Q	0.72	16%	0.62	9%	0.57	17%
3Q	—	—	0.64	12%	0.57	11%
4Q	—	—	0.69	17%	0.59	12%
Yr.	—	—	2.54	11%	2.28	15%

Next earnings report expected: mid October

Mark Twain Bancshares

Business Summary - 14-AUG-95

Mark Twain Bancshares, Inc. is a multibank holding company that owns or controls four core banks: Mark Twain Bank (which operates 20 locations in the metropolitan St. Louis area); Mark Twain Kansas City Bank (five locations in metropolitan Kansas City); Mark Twain Kansas Bank (five locations in metropolitan Kansas City); and Mark Twain Illinois Bank (four locations in Belleville and Edwardsville, Ill.).

Consolidated gross loans outstanding of $1.86 billion at December 31, 1994, were divided:

Commercial & industrial	45%
Real estate--mortgage	34%
Real estate--construction	13%
Installment	8%

At December 31, 1994, the allowance for loan losses was $28.9 million (1.55% of gross loans outstanding), against $27.0 million (1.57%) a year earlier. Net chargeoffs during 1994 were $3.6 million (0.21% of average loans outstanding), compared with $5.7 million (0.35%) in 1993. Nonperforming assets at the end of 1994 were $17.8 million (0.66% of total assets), down from $20.1 million (0.80%) a year earlier.

Average deposits of $2.20 billion in 1994 were divided: noninterest-bearing demand 18%, interest-bearing demand 12%, savings and money market 33%, time deposits (under $100,000) 30% and other time 7%.

Interest and fees on loans contributed 64% of total income for 1994, interest on investment securities 11%, other interest income 10%, service charges 3% and other noninterest income 12%.

On a taxable-equivalent basis, the average yield on interest-earning assets in 1994 was 7.96% (7.74% in 1993), while the average rate paid on interest-bearing liabilities was 3.54% (3.39%), for a net spread of 4.42% (4.35%).

In addition to providing traditional commercial and personal banking services, the company operates 27 discount brokerage offices in four states; a bond sales office in Chicago, Ill.; a trust services division; a residential mortgage company; and leasing and property management divisions.

Important Developments

Apr. '95—Directors approved a stock repurchase program under which MTWN is authorized to purchase up to one million shares, or approximately 6% of its outstanding shares, from time to time, in open market or private transactions. The company expects to purchase shares under this program, over the next several years, to fund commitments for its employee stock ownership plans.

Capitalization

Long Term Debt: $19,876,000 (6/95).

Per Share Data ($)

(Year Ended Dec. 31)

	1994	1993	1992	1991	1990	1989
Tangible Bk. Val.	14.65	13.78	12.40	11.07	9.98	9.35
Earnings	2.54	2.28	1.98	1.55	1.35	1.37
Dividends	0.96	0.81	0.68	0.61	0.59	0.52
Payout Ratio	38%	35%	34%	39%	44%	38%
Prices - High	31	31¾	22⅜	16⅜	12⅜	13⅝
- Low	24	21½	15⅝	7	7¼	11⅝
P/E Ratio - High	12	14	11	11	9	10
- Low	9	9	8	5	5	8

Income Statement Analysis (Million $)

	1994	%Chg	1993	%Chg	1992	%Chg	1991
Net Int. Inc.	124	18%	105	14%	92.1	11%	83.2
Tax Equiv. Adj.	1.4	13%	1.2	-16%	1.4	-27%	2.0
Non Int. Inc.	35.2	—	NA	—	34.7	12%	30.9
Loan Loss Prov.	5.5	-6%	5.9	-28%	8.2	-42%	14.1
% Exp/Op Revs.	56%	—	61%	—	62%	—	64%
Pretax Inc.	63.7	25%	51.0	26%	40.5	49%	27.2
Eff. Tax Rate	36%	—	35%	—	33%	—	28%
Net Inc.	41.0	24%	33.1	23%	27.0	38%	19.6
% Net Int. Marg.	5.10%	—	5.00%	—	4.60%	—	4.30%

Balance Sheet & Other Fin. Data (Million $)

	1994	1993	1992	1991	1990	1989
Earning Assets:						
Money Mkt.	34.6	44.5	53.0	8.5	48.0	64.1
Inv. Securities	582	474	385	446	385	279
Com'l Loans	842	762	614	609	662	467
Other Loans	1,019	930	849	912	841	913
Total Assets	2,689	2,408	2,213	2,170	2,128	1,949
Demand Deposits	462	395	346	282	287	285
Time Deposits	1,810	1,638	1,546	1,562	1,570	1,384
LT Debt	20.4	22.4	26.3	27.4	32.2	33.1
Common Eqty.	234	201	167	149	117	107

Ratio Analysis

	1994	1993	1992	1991	1990	1989
% Ret. on Assets	1.5	1.4	1.2	0.9	0.8	0.9
% Ret. on Equity	18.5	17.9	17.2	15.1	14.4	15.8
% Loan Loss Resv.	1.5	1.5	1.6	1.4	1.5	1.2
% Loans/Deposits	81.9	83.2	80.0	825.0	81.2	82.7
% Equity to Assets	8.5	8.0	7.2	6.1	6.2	5.7

Dividend Data —Cash has been paid each year since 1970. A dividend reinvestment plan is available.

Amt. of Div. $	Date Decl.	Ex-Div. Date	Stock of Record	Payment Date
0.240	Jul. 05	Jul. 18	Jul. 22	Aug. 12 '94
0.240	Oct. 05	Oct. 17	Oct. 21	Nov. 14 '94
0.270	Jan. 04	Jan. 23	Jan. 27	Feb. 10 '95
0.270	Apr. 04	Apr. 17	Apr. 21	May. 12 '95
0.270	Jul. 05	Jul. 19	Jul. 21	Aug. 11 '95

Data as orig. reptd.; bef. results of disc opers. and/or spec. items. Per share data adj. for stk. divs. as of ex-div. date. E-Estimated. NA-Not Available. NM-Not Meaningful. NR-Not Ranked.

Office—8820 Ladue Road, St. Louis, MO 63124. **Tel**—(314) 727-1000. **Chrmn**—A. J. Siteman. **Pres & CEO**—J. P. Dubinsky. **SVP & Secy**—C. A. Wattenberg, Jr. **SVP, CFO & Investor Contact**—Keith Miller (314-889-0799). **Dirs**—R. J. Baudendistel, P. F. Benoist, R. A. Bernstein, R. C. Butler, G. B. Desloge, J. Deutsch, J. P. Dubinsky, H. J. Givens, Jr., B. D. Hunter, M. M. McCarthy, J. N. Millard, J. J. Murphy, Jr., A. J. Siteman. **Transfer Agent & Registrar**—KeyCorp Shareholder Services, Inc., Cleveland. **Incorporated** in Missouri in 1967. **Empl**-1,000. **S&P Analyst:** Thomas C. Ferguson

STANDARD & POOR'S

STOCK REPORTS

Marshall Industries

NYSE Symbol **MI**
In S&P SmallCap 600

08-SEP-95 **Industry:** Electronics/Electric

Summary: This company is the fourth largest domestic distributor of electronic components and industrial production supplies.

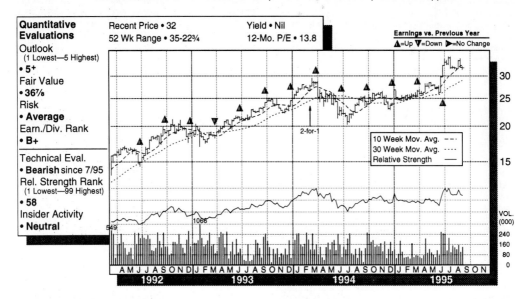

Quantitative Evaluations

Outlook
(1 Lowest—5 Highest)
• **5+**

Fair Value
• **36⅞**

Risk
• **Average**

Earn./Div. Rank
• **B+**

Technical Eval.
• **Bearish** since 7/95

Rel. Strength Rank
(1 Lowest—99 Highest)
• **58**

Insider Activity
• **Neutral**

Recent Price • 32
52 Wk Range • 35-22¾

Yield • Nil
12-Mo. P/E • 13.8

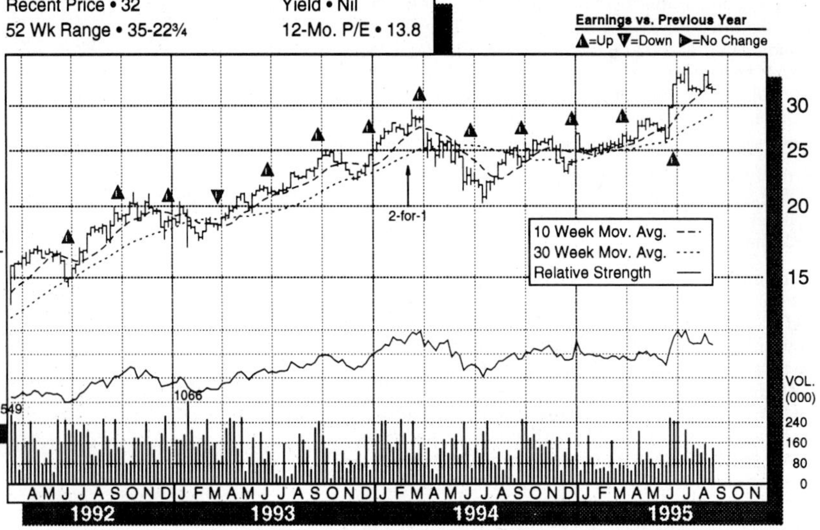

Business Profile - 08-SEP-95

This company focuses on obtaining franchises with the leading manufacturers in product categories that it distributes, in order to meet rising customer demand in the face of product shortages. Revenues and earnings increased in 1994-5, aided primarily by growth in the semiconductor products segment, which has traditionally provided about 70% of total revenues.

Operational Review - 08-SEP-95

Revenues in the fiscal year ended May 31, 1995, rose 23% from those of the preceding year, reflecting increased semiconductor products sales. Margins narrowed, restricted by a less favorable product mix and pricing pressures; operating income was up 19%. With lower depreciation charges, despite taxes at 41.9%, versus 41.1%, net income advanced 22%, to $40.4 million ($2.32 a share), from $33.2 million ($1.91).

Stock Performance - 01-SEP-95

In the past 30 trading days, MI's shares were unchanged, compared to a 2% rise in the S&P 500. Average trading volume for the past five days was 27,480 shares, compared with the 40-day moving average of 27,273 shares.

Key Stock Statistics

Dividend Rate/Share	Nil	Shareholders	6,000
Shs. outstg. (M)	17.3	Market cap. (B)	$0.574
Avg. daily vol. (M)	0.022	Inst. holdings	85%
Tang. Bk. Value/Share	13.85	Insider holdings	NA
Beta	1.02		

Value of $10,000 invested 5 years ago: $ 33,905

Fiscal Year Ending May 31

	1995	% Change	1994	% Change	1993	% Change
Revenues (Million $)						
1Q	223.1	12%	199.8	32%	151.9	10%
2Q	243.8	22%	200.6	30%	154.7	11%
3Q	261.6	32%	197.6	26%	156.3	10%
4Q	280.8	25%	224.5	18%	190.1	22%
Yr.	1,009	23%	822.5	26%	652.9	14%
Income (Million $)						
1Q	8.74	17%	7.49	—	—	—
2Q	9.39	9%	8.64	—	—	—
3Q	10.09	29%	7.82	67%	4.67	-3%
4Q	12.19	32%	9.22	29%	7.17	13%
Yr.	40.41	22%	33.17	39%	23.89	24%
Earnings Per Share ($)						
1Q	0.50	16%	0.43	23%	0.35	49%
2Q	0.54	8%	0.50	43%	0.35	46%
3Q	0.58	29%	0.45	67%	0.27	-4%
4Q	0.70	32%	0.53	29%	0.41	11%
Yr.	2.32	21%	1.91	38%	1.38	22%

Next earnings report expected: mid September

Marshall Industries

Business Summary - 08-SEP-95

Marshall Industries, the fourth largest domestic distributor of electronic components and industrial production supplies, operates a network of 37 sales and distribution centers and three regional support centers in the U.S. and Canada. Contributions to revenues in recent years by segment were:

	1994-5	1993-4
Semiconductors	73%	70%
Passive components	11%	13%
Computer systems/peripherals	10%	11%
Industrial production supplies	6%	6%

Semiconductor products distributed include memory, logic and programmable logic devices, microprocessors and microperipheral components. Texas Instruments, the company's largest supplier of semiconductors, accounted for 14% of sales in 1994-5. Marshall is a major distributor of Japanese semiconductors made by Fujitsu, Hitachi, NEC and Toshiba America; these products accounted for 22% of sales in 1994-5. In addition, the company distributes components made by European suppliers such as Siemens, Philips Semiconductors (formerly Signetics) and SGS-Thomson Microelectronics Inc. Major domestic suppliers are Atmel Corp., Cypress Semiconductor, IBM Technology Products, Lattice Semiconductor, Linear Technology and Xilinx.

Passive components include multilayer ceramic, tantalum and foil capacitors, as well as resistor networks; suppliers include AVX Corp. (a subsidiary of Kyocera), and Bourns, Inc. Connectors and interconnect products include surface-mount sockets, fiber-optic systems, and printed circuit board connectors; suppliers include AMP, Inc. and T&B/Ansley Corp.

Computer systems and peripherals include printers, keyboards, disk drives (optical, hard and floppy), monitors, personal computer motherboards, power supplies, and other system components. Major suppliers include Computer Products, Fujitsu, IBM, NEC, Sharp Electronics, Sony and Toshiba America.

Industrial production supplies include hand tools, static control products, soldering supplies and equipment, test equipment and workstations. The company believes that it is the largest domestic distributor in sales volume of industrial production supplies to the electronics industry.

Important Developments

Jun. '95—Marshall said market pressures on the pricing of most products, and an increased proportion of sales of lower margin products restricted margins in fiscal 1995, and may continue to have an adverse effect in the near-term.

Capitalization

Long Term Debt: $45,205,000 (5/95).

Per Share Data ($) (Year Ended May 31)

	1995	1994	1993	1992	1991	1990
Tangible Bk. Val.	NA	13.85	11.90	10.49	9.34	8.32
Cash Flow	NA	2.28	1.76	1.51	1.42	1.40
Earnings	2.32	1.91	1.38	1.13	1.02	1.13
Dividends	Nil	Nil	Nil	Nil	Nil	Nil
Payout Ratio	Nil	Nil	Nil	Nil	Nil	Nil
Cal. Yrs.	1994	1993	1992	1991	1990	1989
Prices - High	$29\frac{1}{2}$	25	$21\frac{1}{8}$	$13\frac{3}{8}$	$15\frac{1}{8}$	$9\frac{3}{4}$
- Low	$20\frac{1}{4}$	$16\frac{7}{8}$	$12\frac{3}{4}$	10	$8\frac{1}{2}$	7
P/E Ratio - High	13	13	15	12	15	9
- Low	9	9	9	9	8	6

Income Statement Analysis (Million $)

	1994	%Chg	1993	%Chg	1992	%Chg	1991
Revs.	823	26%	653	14%	575	-1%	583
Oper. Inc.	65.4	36%	48.0	17%	41.2	3%	40.1
Depr.	6.3	-2%	6.4	-2%	6.6	-7%	7.0
Int. Exp.	1.9	-4%	2.0	-25%	2.7	-49%	5.3
Pretax Inc.	56.3	43%	39.5	24%	31.9	11%	28.7
Eff. Tax Rate	41%	—	40%	—	40%	—	40%
Net Inc.	33.2	39%	23.9	24%	19.3	12%	17.3

Balance Sheet & Other Fin. Data (Million $)

	1994	1993	1992	1991	1990	1989
Cash	3.7	1.6	1.8	1.9	2.0	1.8
Curr. Assets	314	275	210	200	194	180
Total Assets	364	331	268	254	250	224
Curr. Liab.	84.8	67.6	53.2	48.8	57.9	48.9
LT Debt	34.7	54.5	36.2	47.0	51.5	40.5
Common Eqty.	239	203	178	158	141	135
Total Cap.	279	263	215	205	192	175
Cap. Exp.	1.8	3.2	6.4	7.2	16.3	7.1
Cash Flow	39.5	30.3	25.9	24.3	25.0	25.8

Ratio Analysis

	1994	1993	1992	1991	1990	1989
Curr. Ratio	3.7	4.1	3.9	4.1	3.4	3.7
% LT Debt of Cap.	12.5	20.7	16.9	22.9	26.8	23.1
% Net Inc.of Revs.	4.0	3.7	3.4	3.0	3.7	4.0
% Ret. on Assets	9.5	8.0	7.4	6.8	8.8	10.1
% Ret. on Equity	14.9	12.5	11.4	11.5	15.2	17.3

Dividend Data —No cash dividends have been paid. The stock was split two for one in 1983, 1986 and March 1994.

Data as orig. reptd.; bef. results of disc. opers. and/or spec. items. Per share data adj. for stk. divs. as of ex-div. date. E-Estimated. NA-Not Available. NM-Not Meaningful. NR-Not Ranked.

Office—9320 Telstar Ave., El Monte, CA 91731-2895. **Tel.**—(818) 307-6000. **Chrmn**—G. S. Marshall. **Pres & CEO**—R. Rodin. **VP-Fin, CFO, Secy & Investor Contact**—Henry W. Chin. **Dirs**—R. D. Bentley, R. C. Colyear, J. Fribourg, L. Hoffman, G. S. Marshall, J. Menendez, R. G. Rinehart, R. Rodin, H. C. White. **Transfer Agent & Registrar**—First Union National Bank, Charlotte, NC. **Incorporated** in California in 1954. **Empl**-1,370. **S&P Analyst:** N. Rosenberg

STANDARD & POOR'S

STOCK REPORTS

Material Sciences

NYSE Symbol **MSC**

In S&P SmallCap 600

16-NOV-95

Industry: Coatings, paint, varnishes

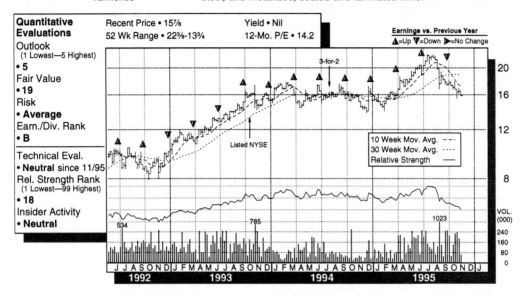

Summary: This company produces advanced materials technologies such as coil-coated and composite materials, electroplated sheet steel, and metallized, coated and laminated films.

Quantitative Evaluations

Outlook (1 Lowest—5 Highest) • **5**

Fair Value • **19**

Risk • **Average**

Earn./Div. Rank • **B**

Technical Eval. • **Neutral** since 11/95

Rel. Strength Rank (1 Lowest—99 Highest) • **18**

Insider Activity • **Neutral**

Recent Price • 15⅞ | 52 Wk Range • 22⅜-13¾ | Yield • Nil | 12-Mo. P/E • 14.2

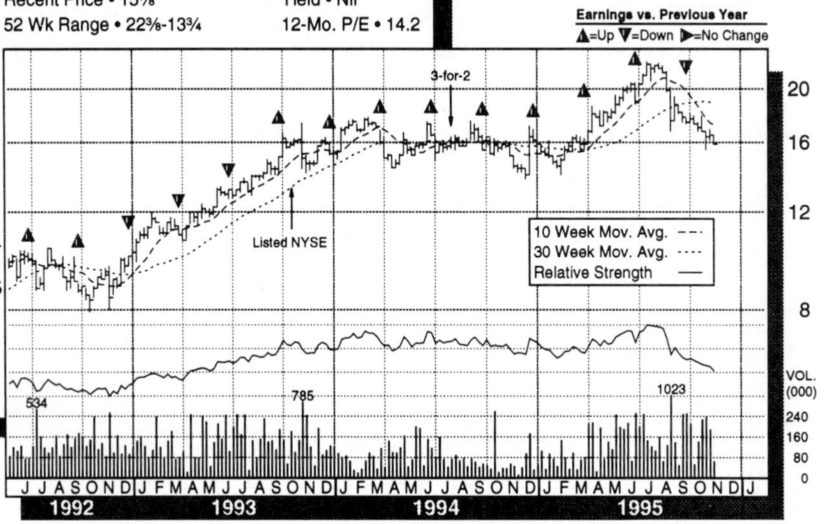

Business Profile - 16-NOV-95

Revenue growth has slowed in the first half of 1995-96. Although electrogalvanizing sales have been strong, metallizing-coating and coil coating revenues were down. In mid-November, the company said that due to continued weak demand in many key markets it expects FY 96 second half and full year earnings to be below last year. MSC plans to record a $2.6 million ($0.16 a share) charge in the third quarter, to implement a reorganization that is expected to reduce costs by $4 million annually.

Operational Review - 16-NOV-95

Net sales in the six months ended August 31, 1995, were flat year to year, as gains in laminates/composites (+1.9%) and electrogalvinizing (+11%) were offset by lower metallizing coating (-4.5%) and coil coating revenues (-3.6%). Margins widened, principally due a better product mix; operating income grew 6.8%. Following equity and interest income, and taxes at 38.5%, versus 38.0%, net income increased 4.5%, to $8.9 million ($0.58 a share), from $8.5 million ($0.56).

Stock Performance - 10-NOV-95

In the past 30 trading days, MSC's shares have declined 10%, compared to a 1% rise in the S&P 500. Average trading volume for the past five days was 12,620 shares, compared with the 40-day moving average of 36,528 shares.

Key Stock Statistics

Dividend Rate/Share	Nil	Shareholders	1,100
Shs. outstg. (M)	15.4	Market cap. (B)	$0.240
Avg. daily vol. (M)	0.057	Inst. holdings	71%
Tang. Bk. Value/Share	7.45	Insider holdings	NA
Beta	0.88		

Value of $10,000 invested 5 years ago: $ 22,861

Fiscal Year Ending Feb. 28

	1996	% Change	1995	% Change	1994	% Change
Revenues (Million $)						
1Q	60.41	3%	58.80	41%	41.62	5%
2Q	58.65	-1%	59.42	25%	47.66	19%
3Q	—	—	56.80	18%	48.28	31%
4Q	—	—	52.62	5%	50.15	26%
Yr.	—	—	227.7	21%	187.7	20%
Income (Million $)						
1Q	4.87	19%	4.08	62%	2.52	8%
2Q	4.07	-9%	4.46	42%	3.13	16%
3Q	—	—	4.60	66%	2.77	63%
4Q	—	—	3.60	6%	3.40	57%
Yr.	—	—	16.74	42%	11.80	33%
Earnings Per Share ($)						
1Q	0.32	19%	0.27	56%	0.17	-13%
2Q	0.26	-10%	0.29	36%	0.21	3%
3Q	—	—	0.30	61%	0.19	56%
4Q	—	—	0.24	9%	0.22	50%
Yr.	—	—	1.10	39%	0.79	18%

Next earnings report expected: early December

Material Sciences

Business Summary - 15-NOV-95

Material Sciences develops and manufactures continuously pressed, coated, and laminated materials. Sales contributions by product group in the past two fiscal years were:

	1994-95	1993-94
Coil coating	45%	42%
Laminates and composites	25%	25%
Electrogalvanizing	22%	24%
Metallizing and coatings	8%	9%

MSC's coil coated products are used by manufacturers in building products, motor vehicles, appliances, lighting products, above-ground swimming pools, furniture and fixtures, packaging and other products. The company's strategy has been to produce high volume coated products at low cost and to develop and produce niche products for special requirements. Coil coating technology reduces the environmental impact of painting and reduces energy needs of manufacturers. This saves significant waste resulting from overspray in most post-fabrication painting. The company believes it processed 10% of the total coated coil produced in the U.S. in 1994.

Laminates and composites combine layers of steel or other metal with layers of polymers or other organic compounds to achieve certain properties, such as noise and vibration reduction, thermal insulation or high reflectivity in lighting. These products, which happen to be MSC's fastest growing product group, are designed to meet specific customer needs. Major products include disc brake noise dampers, Polycore Composites and Specular+.

The company participates in the electrogalvanizing market through a 50% interest in the Walbridge Coatings partnership with Bethlehem Steel and Inland Steel.

Metallizing and coating sales consist mainly of solar control window films for use in the automotive aftermarket and building applications. These products are sold through nine distributors, two of which accounted for 61% of 1994-5 metallizing/coating sales. Products also include silver-sputtered, coated film used in Specular+. In addition, during 1993-4, the company began supplying the market for security seals and tamper evident packaging through its sputtering of transparent holographic film.

Important Developments

Sep. '95—Material Sciences acquired all of the outstanding capital stock of Florida-based Solar-Gard International, Inc. Solar-Gard, the largest independent distributor of professional grade solar control and safety film products, was purchased for approximately $8.6 million.

Capitalization

Long Term Debt: $7,337,000 (8/95).

Per Share Data ($) (Year Ended Feb. 28)

	1995	1994	1993	1992	1991	1990
Tangible Bk. Val.	6.75	5.81	5.00	3.57	2.71	2.29
Cash Flow	1.67	1.27	1.15	1.20	0.93	-2.27
Earnings	1.10	0.79	0.67	0.63	0.42	-2.71
Dividends	Nil	Nil	Nil	Nil	Nil	Nil
Payout Ratio	Nil	Nil	Nil	Nil	Nil	Nil
Cal. Yrs.	1994	1993	1992	1991	1990	1989
Prices - High	17⅝	17⅜	10⅝	7⅞	7⅝	7¾
- Low	13⅝	9¾	7¼	4⅜	4⅛	6⅜
P/E Ratio - High	16	22	16	12	18	NM
- Low	13	12	11	7	10	NM

Income Statement Analysis (Million $)

	1995	%Chg	1994	%Chg	1993	%Chg	1992
Revs.	228	21%	188	21%	156	9%	143
Oper. Inc.	35.2	38%	25.6	26%	20.3	9%	18.6
Depr.	8.8	20%	7.3	13%	6.5	1%	6.4
Int. Exp.	0.1	9%	0.1	-69%	0.3	-72%	1.2
Pretax Inc.	27.2	43%	19.0	35%	14.1	21%	11.7
Eff. Tax Rate	39%	—	38%	—	37%	—	39%
Net Inc.	16.7	42%	11.8	33%	8.9	25%	7.1

Balance Sheet & Other Fin. Data (Million $)

	1995	1994	1993	1992	1991	1990
Cash	5.8	11.9	23.5	Nil	0.9	3.5
Curr. Assets	61.8	62.3	62.1	35.1	40.5	49.4
Total Assets	172	152	129	101	104	111
Curr. Liab.	39.1	33.2	24.4	25.8	23.2	30.7
LT Debt	6.9	8.9	10.7	13.8	29.4	42.4
Common Eqty.	105	86.5	73.3	42.0	30.9	25.5
Total Cap.	123	108	96.0	69.0	73.0	78.0
Cap. Exp.	29.4	49.4	7.6	8.4	7.6	23.0
Cash Flow	25.5	19.1	15.4	13.5	10.4	-25.5

Ratio Analysis

	1995	1994	1993	1992	1991	1990
Curr. Ratio	1.6	1.9	2.5	1.4	1.7	1.6
% LT Debt of Cap.	5.6	8.2	11.2	20.1	40.4	54.6
% Net Inc.of Revs.	7.4	6.3	5.7	5.0	3.4	NM
% Ret. on Assets	10.3	8.5	7.0	6.9	4.3	NM
% Ret. on Equity	17.4	14.9	14.2	19.3	16.5	NM

Dividend Data —No cash dividends have been paid. The shares were split three-for-two in July 1994 and April 1992.

Data as orig. reptd.; bef. results of disc. opers. and/or spec. items. Per share data adj. for stk. divs. as of ex-div. date. E-Estimated. NA-Not Available. NM-Not Meaningful. NR-Not Ranked.

Office—2300 East Pratt Blvd., Elk Grove Village, IL 60007. **Tel**—(708) 439-8270. **Chrmn & CEO**—G. R. Evans. **Pres & COO**—G. G. Nadig. **SVP, CFO & Secy**—W. H. Vrba. **VP & Investor Contact**—R. J. Mataya. **Dirs**—J. B. Cohen, R. J. Decyk, E. W. Emmerich, G. R. Evans, E. F. Heizer, Jr., J. F. Leach, I. P. Pochter. **Transfer Agent & Registrar**—Mellon Securities Transfer Services, Ridgefield Park, NJ. **Incorporated** in Delaware in 1983 to succeed to the business of a company founded in 1971. **Empl**-925. **S&P Analyst:** TT

Maxim Integrated Products

NASDAQ Symbol **MXIM**
In S&P SmallCap 600

06-SEP-95 **Industry:** Electronics/Electric

Summary: This company is a worldwide leader in design, development and manufacture of linear and mixed-signal integrated circuits.

Quantitative Evaluations

Outlook
(1 Lowest—5 Highest)
• NA
Fair Value
• NA
Risk
• Average
Earn./Div. Rank
• B

Technical Eval.
• Bullish since 8/92
Rel. Strength Rank
(1 Lowest—99 Highest)
• 96
Insider Activity
• Neutral

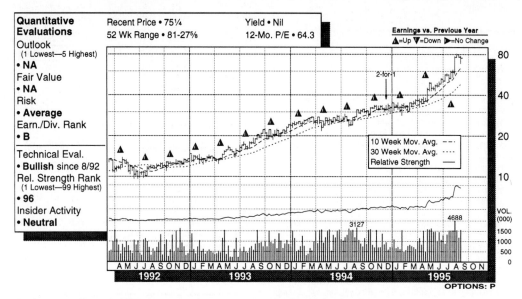

Recent Price • 75¼
52 Wk Range • 81-27⅝
Yield • Nil
12-Mo. P/E • 64.3

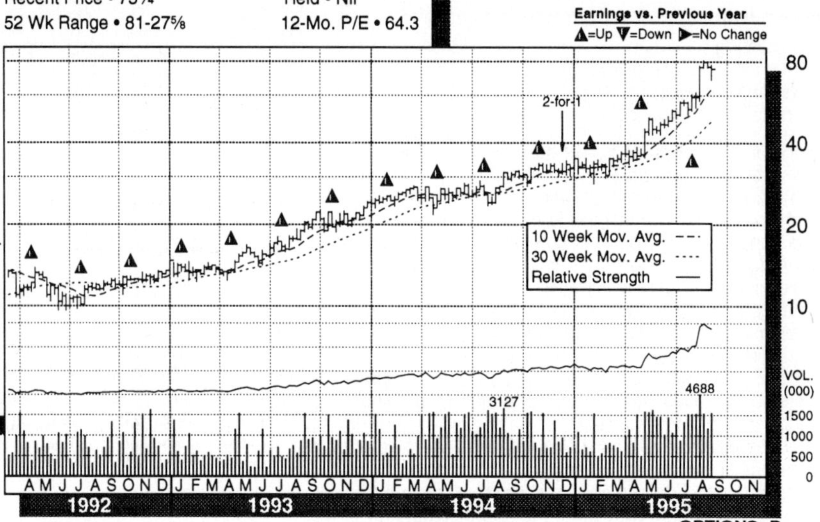

OPTIONS: P

Business Profile - 06-SEP-95

Revenues and earnings of this international supplier of analog products have been in a long uptrend. In August 1995, Maxim said that its revenues and earnings for fiscal 1996's third and fourth quarter would exceed analysts' expectations. In May 1994, Tektronix Inc.'s integrated circuit operations were acquired for $26 million in cash, plus warrants to buy 150,000 common shares at $60 a share. The two companies also formed Maxtek, a joint venture to run Tektronix's hybrid circuit operations.

Operational Review - 06-SEP-95

Based on a preliminary report, net revenues in fiscal 1995, surged 63% from those of the prior year, reflecting new product introductions and the inclusion of the integrated circuit operations acquired from Tektronix in May 1994. Gross margins widened, and despite a significant increase in R&D spending and SG&A expenses, a $16.6 million charge related to modernization of equipment and manufacturing facilities, and 4.5% more shares outstanding, share earnings soared 54%.

Stock Performance - 01-SEP-95

In the past 30 trading days, MXIM's shares have increased 41%, compared to a 2% rise in the S&P 500. Average trading volume for the past five days was 408,980 shares, compared with the 40-day moving average of 402,930 shares.

Key Stock Statistics

Dividend Rate/Share	Nil	Shareholders	500
Shs. outstg. (M)	29.9	Market cap. (B)	$ 2.3
Avg. daily vol. (M)	0.490	Inst. holdings	93%
Tang. Bk. Value/Share	4.54	Insider holdings	NA
Beta	1.84		

Value of $10,000 invested 5 years ago: $ 182,424

Fiscal Year Ending Jun. 30

	1995	% Change	1994	% Change	1993	% Change
Revenues (Million $)						
1Q	52.00	57%	33.09	32%	25.00	23%
2Q	56.18	55%	36.14	35%	26.70	27%
3Q	66.63	64%	40.57	43%	28.38	28%
4Q	76.00	72%	44.12	47%	30.10	29%
Yr.	250.8	63%	153.9	40%	110.2	27%
Income (Million $)						
1Q	8.30	57%	5.30	—	—	—
2Q	8.93	57%	5.69	36%	4.18	26%
3Q	10.12	60%	6.32	45%	4.36	23%
4Q	11.55	70%	6.78	43%	4.73	29%
Yr.	38.91	62%	24.08	39%	17.28	26%
Earnings Per Share ($)						
1Q	0.25	50%	0.17	26%	0.13	23%
2Q	0.27	50%	0.18	29%	0.14	22%
3Q	0.30	54%	0.19	34%	0.15	21%
4Q	0.34	62%	0.21	35%	0.15	24%
Yr.	1.17	56%	0.75	30%	0.57	22%

Next earnings report expected: early November

Maxim Integrated Products

Business Summary - 06-SEP-95

Maxim Integrated Products, Inc. designs, develops, makes and markets a broad range of linear and mixed-signal integrated circuits known as analog circuits. Linear devices process signals representing real-world phenomena (such as temperature, pressure, sound or speed). Mixed-signal devices combine linear and digital functions.

Maxim initially generated substantially all revenues from sales of products that were second sources of a single competitor's integrated circuits, with distribution primarily to European customers. Subsequently, many products have been added (728 introduced as of June 30, 1994)--both second sources to industry standard parts and proprietary designs, and geographical markets were expanded. Although second-sourcing continues to be an important component of the company's product development program, current research emphasizes proprietary circuits.

Through the end of fiscal 1994, Maxim was offering 728 products. During fiscal 1994, the company introduced 132 new products, 45 more than were introduced in fiscal 1993. Of the 728 products introduced, 448 (or 62%) are proprietary. R&D totaled $22,561,000 (14.7% of total sales) in fiscal 1994, versus $16,426,000 (14.9% of total sales) in fiscal 1993 and $13,106,000 (15.1%) in fiscal 1992.

Maxim has recruited its own circuit design staff, and uses its own wafer fabrication facility as well as three outside silicon foundries (utilizing eight different fabrication processes) for wafer manufacturing. Most processed wafers are shipped to subcontractors in the Far East for separation and packaging. Both processed wafers and finished products are tested at the company's Sunnyvale, Calif., headquarters.

Products include data converters, interface circuits, microprocessor supervisors, amplifiers, power supplies, multiplexers, switches, battery chargers, and voltage references. Users include major firms in the instrumentation, industrial control, communications, data processing and other industries. In fiscal 1994, the U.S. accounted for 48% of total revenues, Europe for 24%, Japan 15%, and other 13%.

Important Developments

Aug. '95—Maxim said the shipping of a large delinquent portion of its backlog should cause revenues and earnings for the second and third quarters of fiscal 1996 to exceed analysts' expectations by material amounts. Also, Maxim said it plans to return its revenues to more normal levels consistent with its historic trend line. The plan calls for a reduction in fiscal 1996's fourth quarter revenues and earnings below those of the third quarter.

Capitalization

Long Term Debt: None (3/95).
Options: To buy 5,231,799 shs. at $1.50 to $53.00 ea. (6/94).

Per Share Data ($)

(Year Ended Jun. 30)

	1995	1994	1993	1992	1991	1990
Tangible Bk. Val.	NA	4.54	3.49	2.70	2.01	1.55
Cash Flow	NA	0.99	0.75	0.65	0.55	0.46
Earnings	1.17	0.76	0.57	0.47	0.37	0.29
Dividends	Nil	Nil	Nil	Nil	Nil	Nil
Payout Ratio	Nil	Nil	Nil	Nil	Nil	Nil
Prices - High	70	$29\frac{1}{8}$	$24\frac{1}{2}$	$14\frac{7}{8}$	$11\frac{3}{4}$	$6\frac{3}{4}$
- Low	$28\frac{1}{4}$	$21\frac{3}{4}$	$12\frac{1}{4}$	$9\frac{5}{8}$	$5\frac{1}{2}$	$3\frac{3}{4}$
P/E Ratio - High	60	39	43	32	32	23
- Low	24	29	21	20	15	13

Income Statement Analysis (Million $)

	1994	%Chg	1993	%Chg	1992	%Chg	1991
Revs.	154	40%	110	26%	87.0	18%	73.8
Oper. Inc.	42.8	39%	30.7	20%	25.6	23%	20.8
Depr.	7.2	37%	5.2	3%	5.1	5%	4.9
Int. Exp.	0.1	-54%	0.1	-67%	0.4	-49%	0.8
Pretax Inc.	37.6	41%	26.6	27%	21.0	35%	15.6
Eff. Tax Rate	36%	—	35%	—	35%	—	35%
Net Inc.	24.1	39%	17.3	26%	13.7	36%	10.1

Balance Sheet & Other Fin. Data (Million $)

	1994	1993	1992	1991	1990	1989
Cash	48.4	49.1	33.7	14.9	4.9	7.7
Curr. Assets	100	91.3	67.9	42.1	29.2	24.7
Total Assets	179	127	95.5	71.8	60.7	46.7
Curr. Liab.	43.4	27.2	20.2	15.9	17.1	12.9
LT Debt	0.0	0.2	0.7	2.8	4.9	4.6
Common Eqty.	130	97.3	72.3	51.2	37.7	28.5
Total Cap.	135	100	75.3	56.0	43.6	33.8
Cap. Exp.	50.9	12.9	4.2	4.6	12.3	9.0
Cash Flow	31.3	22.5	18.8	15.0	12.2	8.8

Ratio Analysis

	1994	1993	1992	1991	1990	1989
Curr. Ratio	2.3	3.4	3.4	2.7	1.7	1.9
% LT Debt of Cap.	Nil	0.2	0.9	4.9	11.3	13.6
% Net Inc.of Revs.	15.6	15.7	15.7	13.7	13.6	13.0
% Ret. on Assets	15.6	15.2	16.0	14.9	13.8	13.2
% Ret. on Equity	20.9	20.0	21.6	22.3	22.4	21.3

Dividend Data —No cash dividends have been paid. A two-for-one stock split was effected in December 1994.

Amt. of Div. $	Date Decl.	Ex-Div. Date	Stock of Record	Payment Date
2-for-1	Nov. 14	Dec. 08	Nov. 23	Dec. 07 '94

Data as orig. reptd.; bef. results of disc. opers. and/or spec. items. Per share data adj. for stk. divs. as of ex-div. date. E-Estimated. NA-Not Available. NM-Not Meaningful. NR-Not Ranked.

Office—120 San Gabriel Dr., Sunnyvale, CA 94086. **Tel**—(408) 737-7600. **Chrmn, Pres & CEO**—J. F. Gifford. **VP, CFO & Secy**—M. J. Byrd. **VP & Investor Contact**—Richard Slater. **Dirs**—J. R. Bergman, J. F. Gifford, R. F. Graham, A. R. F. Wazzan. **Transfer Agent & Registrar**—First National Bank of Boston, Canton, MA. **Incorporated** in Delaware in 1988. **Empl**-1,016. **S&P Analyst:** Ronald J. Gross

STANDARD & POOR'S

STOCK REPORTS

Maxtor Corp.

NASDAQ Symbol **MXTR**
In S&P SmallCap 600

15-NOV-95

Industry: Data Processing

Summary: This manufacturer of disk drives and other computer mass storage products has tentatively agreed to be acquired by Hyundai Electronics for $6.70 a share.

S&P Opinion: Hold (★★★)

Recent Price • 6¼
52 Wk Range • 7¼-3¾
Yield • Nil
12-Mo. P/E • NM

Quantitative Evaluations
Outlook (1 Lowest—5 Highest) • 1
Fair Value • 3½
Risk • **High**
Earn./Div. Rank • C

Technical Eval. • **Neutral** since 11/95
Rel. Strength Rank (1 Lowest—99 Highest) • 98
Insider Activity • NA

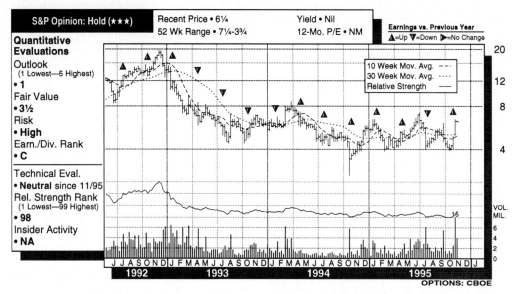

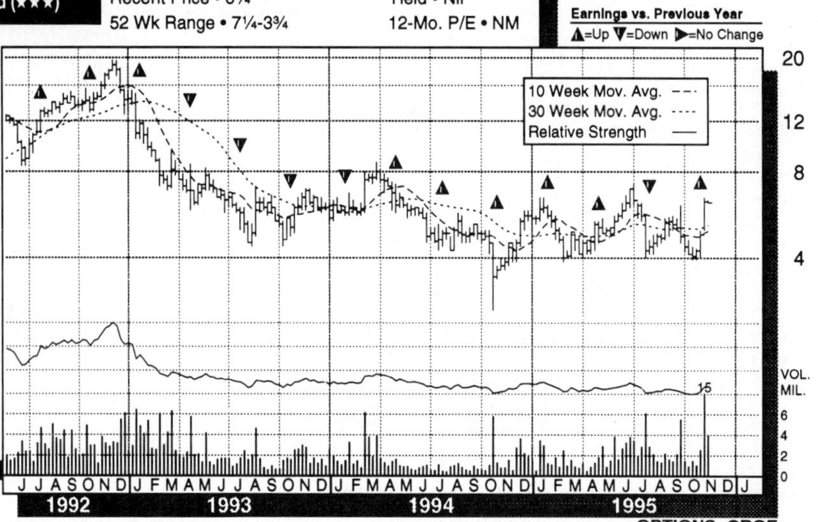

OPTIONS: CBOE

Overview - 15-NOV-95

Revenues for Maxtor as an independent company are expected to rise in the second half of FY96 on increased unit volume, despite continued price pressures. The company has replaced older drive products with new drives developed on lower cost platforms and undertaken cost reduction actions. Still, losses are expected. The company has secured adequate liquidity for continued operations over the intermediate term. We believe Hyundai's $6.70 a share acquisition proposal will be accepted and finalized by early 1996.

Valuation - 15-NOV-95

Maxtor's stock rose sharply in late October on news of Hyundai Electronics Industries' first acquisition proposal. Acceptance of a sweetened offer by a Maxtor directors' committee drove the stock higher still in early November. We believe that Hyundai (owner of about 37% of MXTR's common stock) will complete its acquisition of Maxtor, which has struggled for profitability for the past two years. Maxtor has failed to execute its business plan as well as its competitors, and we remain skeptical the company would outperform its competitors in the near term as an independent entity. However, final acceptance of the $6.70 takeover offer appears assured; we recommend existing holders tender their shares.

Key Stock Statistics

S&P EPS Est. 1996	-1.75	Tang. Bk. Value/Share	0.64
P/E on S&P Est. 1996	NM	Beta	0.14
Dividend Rate/Share	Nil	Shareholders	1,800
Shs. outstg. (M)	53.0	Market cap. (B)	$0.334
Avg. daily vol. (M)	1.160	Inst. holdings	24%
		Insider holdings	NA

Value of $10,000 invested 5 years ago: $ 7,161

Fiscal Year Ending Mar. 31

	1996	% Change	1995	% Change	1994	% Change
Revenues (Million $)						
1Q	315.9	45%	218.3	-16%	260.6	-23%
2Q	281.4	61%	174.4	-44%	313.5	-12%
3Q	—	—	238.2	-25%	318.1	-21%
4Q	—	—	276.0	6%	260.4	-25%
Yr.	—	—	906.8	-21%	1,153	-20%
Income (Million $)						
1Q	-13.83	NM	-12.19	NM	-72.18	NM
2Q	-44.49	NM	-54.72	NM	-59.62	NM
3Q	—	—	-16.44	NM	-121.3	NM
4Q	—	—	1.12	NM	-4.48	NM
Yr.	—	—	-82.22	NM	-257.6	NM
Earnings Per Share ($)						
1Q	-0.27	NM	-0.24	NM	-2.50	NM
2Q	-0.84	NM	-1.09	NM	-2.02	NM
3Q	E-0.40	NM	-0.32	NM	-4.12	NM
4Q	E-0.24	NM	0.02	NM	-0.11	NM
Yr.	E-1.75	NM	-1.63	NM	-8.00	NM

Next earnings report expected: mid January

Maxtor Corp.

Business Summary - 15-NOV-95

Maxtor Corporation develops, manufactures and markets mass storage products, primarily Winchester disk drive storage products used to record, store and retrieve digital information that cannot be stored entirely in a computer system's central memory unit.

The company offers a range of disk drive products in the 1.8-inch and 3.5-inch form factors. Maxtor's 7000 Series of 3.5-inch drives, which include a broad range of capacity points ranging from 270 megabytes (MBs) to 1.2 gigabytes (GBs), accounts for a substantial portion of the company's revenues, and are used primarily for desktop personal computer applications.

The MobileMax line of data storage products, targeted toward the mobile computing market, includes hard drives and flash memory cards for use with notebook, sub-notebook and smaller mobile computers as well as for emerging non-computer applications. In the FY95 fourth quarter, the company curtailed R&D efforts related to the MobileMax product family.

MXTR manufactures all of its high-volume magnetic drive products at facilities in Singapore and all printed circuit boards at a plant in Hong Kong.

Export sales provided 48% of total revenues in FY95 (43% in FY94).

R&D spending in FY95 and FY94 totaled $60,769,000 (6.7% of sales) and $97,168,000 (8.4%), respectively.

Hyundai Electronics Industries Co. Ltd. of Korea owns 19,480,000 shares (some 37%) of Maxtor's outstanding common stock.

Important Developments

Nov. '95—A special committee of the company's board of directors approved an acquisition proposal by Hyundai Electronics America, on behalf of Hyundai Electronics Industries Co. Ltd. (HEI; owner of about 37% of MXTR's common stock), to acquire all of the outstanding shares of Maxtor not already owned by HEI or its affiliates, for $6.70 a share in cash. The acquisition, which is subject, among other things, to approval of various government authorities, is expected to be completed by early 1996.

May '95—Maxtor finalized an agreement for a manufacturing partnership with Hyundai Electronics Industries (HEI), under which HEI will manufacture Maxtor-designed disk drives in a production facility operated by HEI.

Apr. '95—The company announced a fourth quarter gain of $10.2 million ($0.19 a share) on the sale of its 67% interest in Maxoptix, and a charge of $6.4 million for the writedown of inventory, equipment and other costs associated with its 1.8-inch product line.

Capitalization

Long Term Debt: $100,664,000 (9/95).

Per Share Data ($) (Year Ended Mar. 31)

	1995	1994	1993	1992	1991	1990
Tangible Bk. Val.	0.85	2.39	7.62	6.49	6.05	7.48
Cash Flow	-0.94	-5.37	3.36	2.20	0.41	2.05
Earnings	-1.63	-8.00	1.46	0.27	-1.89	0.90
Dividends	Nil	Nil	Nil	Nil	Nil	Nil
Payout Ratio	Nil	Nil	Nil	Nil	Nil	Nil
Cal. Yrs.	1994	1993	1992	1991	1990	1989
Prices - High	8⅝	15⅜	19⅝	6¼	17	12¼
- Low	2⅝	4⅜	5¼	1⅝	4	7½
P/E Ratio - High	NM	NM	13	23	NM	14
- Low	NM	NM	4	6	NM	8

Income Statement Analysis (Million $)

	1995	%Chg	1994	%Chg	1993	%Chg	1992
Revs.	907	-21%	1,153	-19%	1,426	39%	1,029
Oper. Inc.	-51.4	NM	-75.0	NM	97.7	82%	53.7
Depr.	34.9	-59%	84.6	41%	59.8	16%	51.7
Int. Exp.	8.4	-17%	10.1	NM	10.1	-20%	12.6
Pretax Inc.	-80.0	NM	-255	NM	46.4	NM	1.1
Eff. Tax Rate	NM	—	NM	—	2.80%	—	NM
Net Inc.	-82.0	NM	-257	NM	46.1	NM	7.1

Balance Sheet & Other Fin. Data (Million $)

	1995	1994	1993	1992	1991	1990
Cash	109	219	135	76.0	42.0	102
Curr. Assets	318	423	451	342	316	286
Total Assets	382	492	579	445	454	385
Curr. Liab.	236	266	239	178	178	90.0
LT Debt	102	107	120	111	128	127
Common Eqty.	44.0	119	220	156	140	156
Total Cap.	146	227	341	268	276	294
Cap. Exp.	32.6	29.7	92.2	37.5	97.0	51.4
Cash Flow	-47.0	-172	106	58.9	9.9	42.9

Ratio Analysis

	1995	1994	1993	1992	1991	1990
Curr. Ratio	1.3	1.6	1.9	1.9	1.8	3.2
% LT Debt of Cap.	69.9	47.4	35.2	41.4	46.4	43.0
% Net Inc.of Revs.	NM	NM	3.2	0.7	NM	3.9
% Ret. on Assets	NM	NM	8.3	1.6	NM	5.3
% Ret. on Equity	NM	NM	22.7	4.8	NM	13.0

Dividend Data —No cash has been paid.

Data as orig. reptd.; bef. results of disc. opers. and/or spec. items. Per share data adj. for stk. divs. as of ex-div. date. E-Estimated. NA-Not Available. NM-Not Meaningful. NR-Not Ranked.

Office—211 River Oaks Pkwy., San Jose, CA 95134. **Tel**—(408) 432-1700. **Chrmn**—M. H. Chung. **Pres & CEO**—C. S. Park **VP-Fin**—N. Kawaye. **Dirs**—R. Balanson, C. F. Christ, M. H. Chung, G. M. Gallo, C. Hill, I. B. Jeon, C. S. Park. **Transfer Agent & Registrar**—First National Bank of Boston. **Incorporated** in California in 1983; reincorporated in Delaware in 1986. **Empl**-7,700. **S&P Analyst:** Peter C. Wood, CFA

STANDARD & POOR'S

McWhorter Technologies

STOCK REPORTS

NYSE Symbol **MWT**

In S&P SmallCap 600

22-OCT-95

Industry: Chemicals

Summary: This company is a leading specialty chemical manufacturer of liquid and powder resins for the coatings industry and of composite polymers for the fiberglass industry.

Quantitative Evaluations

Outlook (1 Lowest—5 Highest) • **NA**

Fair Value • **NA**

Risk • **Low**

Earn./Div. Rank • **NR**

Technical Eval. • **Bullish** since 7/95

Rel. Strength Rank (1 Lowest—99 Highest) • **38**

Insider Activity • **NA**

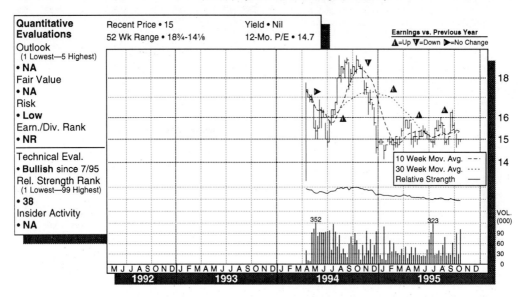

Recent Price • 15

52 Wk Range • 18¾-14⅛

Yield • Nil

12-Mo. P/E • 14.7

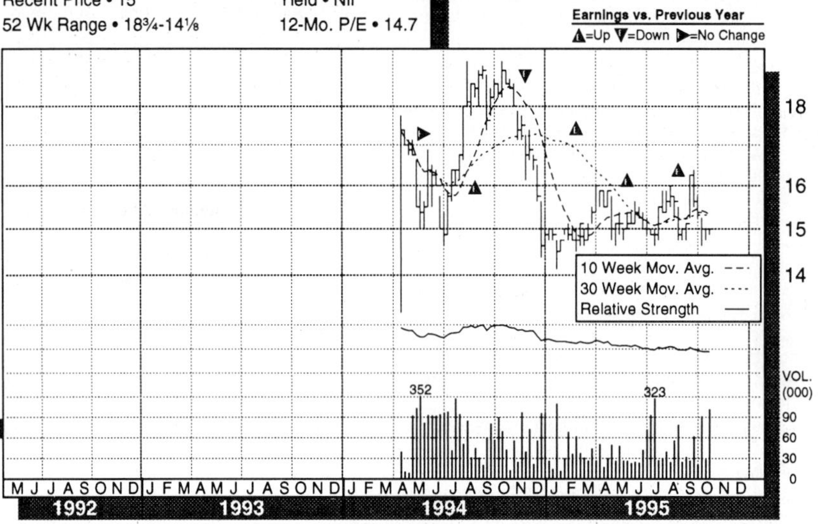

Business Profile - 19-OCT-95

McWhorter, formerly a subsidiary of Valspar Corp., acquired Cargill's Resin Products division in February 1994, and became an independent company in April 1994, when Valspar distributed all MWT stock to its shareholders. McWhorter purchased Shell Chemical's specialty acrylic business in June 1994, and acquired a resin production plant from Glidden Co. in September 1995.

Operational Review - 19-OCT-95

On a pro forma basis, net sales in the first nine months of fiscal 1995 rose 11%, year to year, on strength in composite polymers. Earnings comparisons in the 1995 interim were boosted by the absence of a $0.14 a share charge for the writedown of the Los Angeles resin facility. While the substantial increase in MTW's raw material costs is expected to become less significant, its use of the LIFO method of inventory valuation reduced nine month earnings (up 14%, pro forma) by $0.08 a share.

Stock Performance - 20-OCT-95

In the past 30 trading days, MWT's shares have declined 0.83%, compared to a 3% rise in the S&P 500. Average trading volume for the past five days was 41,080 shares, compared with the 40-day moving average of 12,446 shares.

Key Stock Statistics

Dividend Rate/Share	Nil	Shareholders	1,800
Shs. outstg. (M)	11.0	Market cap. (B)	$0.164
Avg. daily vol. (M)	0.017	Inst. holdings	52%
Tang. Bk. Value/Share	5.72	Insider holdings	NA
Beta	NA		

Value of $10,000 invested 5 years ago: NA

Fiscal Year Ending Oct. 31

	1995	% Change	1994	% Change	1993	% Change
Revenues (Million $)						
1Q	67.31	165%	25.39	-55%	55.90	—
2Q	79.12	25%	63.11	-7%	67.70	—
3Q	82.97	5%	79.24	6%	74.70	—
4Q	—	—	74.59	6%	70.70	—
Yr.	—	—	242.3	-10%	269.0	—
Income (Million $)						
1Q	1.82	NM	-0.26	—	—	—
2Q	2.79	13%	2.46	—	—	—
3Q	3.29	3%	3.19	—	—	—
4Q	—	—	3.06	—	—	—
Yr.	—	—	8.44	-16%	10.10	—
Earnings Per Share ($)						
1Q	0.16	NM	-0.03	NM	0.01	—
2Q	0.26	13%	0.23	NM	0.23	—
3Q	0.30	3%	0.29	16%	0.25	—
4Q	—	—	0.28	-36%	0.44	—
Yr.	—	—	0.78	-16%	0.93	—

Next earnings report expected: early December

McWhorter Technologies

Business Summary - 19-OCT-95

McWhorter Technologies, formerly a subsidiary of Valspar Corp., is one of the leading manufacturers of surface coating resins in the U.S. and a manufacturer of resins used in the reinforced fiberglass plastics industry. The company acquired the Resin Products division of Cargill Inc. in February 1994 and was spun off by Valspar Corp. in April.

The company produces various products including alkyds, modified alkyds, oil modified urethanes, saturated and unsaturated polyesters, powder resins, acrylic emulsions, vinyl-emulsions, solution acrylics, curing agents and a number of small volume specialty resins. Various types of resins are required by customers due to differing application and product performance characteristics.

McWhorter sells its surface coatings resin products primarily to customers in the paint and coatings industry through a direct sales force, with the balance sold through agents or distributors. The majority of sales of unsaturated polyester resins to the fiberglass resin products industry are sold through distributors. McWhorter's business has been focused in North America. International sales have not been significant.

The paint and coatings industry is a mature market growing at an estimated 1%-1.5% per annum, or about the same rate as durable goods. McWhorter believes there are over 900 active companies purchasing resins and selling paint and coatings for a variety of end uses. Although a number of paint and coating manufacturers have captive resin manufacturing capabilities, increasing costs of product reformulation and updating of resin manufacturing processes to comply with environmental regulations are causing a shift from captive manufacturing to out-sourcing. MWT believes this trend will increase its opportunities in future years.

McWhorter's research and development activities have emphasized emerging technologies in the paint and coatings industry, focusing on developing products designed to comply with environmental laws.

McWhorter's business is somewhat seasonal, with sales volume traditionally highest during the third quarter of the fiscal year.

Although an FTC consent agreement restricts interactions between McWhorter and Valspar, certain relationships exist. These include a technology license agreement that gives McWhorter access to all resin technology owned by Valspar prior to the spinoff, a buying cooperative to purchase raw materials, and certain tolling arrangements.

Important Developments

Sep. '95—McWhorter acquired the Columbus, Ga., resin production plant of Glidden Co., a unit of Imperial Chemical Industries. Earlier, MWT said it would not proceed with its letter of intent to buy Ruco Polymer Corp. and its Ruco Polymer Co. affiliate.

Capitalization

Long Term Debt: $30,060,000 (7/95).

Per Share Data ($) (Year Ended Oct. 31)

	1994	1993	1992	1991	1990	1989
Tangible Bk. Val.	5.72	4.94	NA	NA	NA	NA
Cash Flow	1.35	1.70	NA	NA	NA	NA
Earnings	0.78	0.93	NA	NA	NA	NA
Dividends	Nil	Nil	NA	NA	NA	NA
Payout Ratio	Nil	Nil	NA	NA	NA	NA
Prices - High	19¼	NA	NA	NA	NA	NA
- Low	13¼	NA	NA	NA	NA	NA
P/E Ratio - High	25	NA	NA	NA	NA	NA
- Low	17	NA	NA	NA	NA	NA

Income Statement Analysis (Million $)

	1994	%Chg	1993	%Chg	1992	%Chg	1991
Revs.	242	-10%	269	—	NA	—	NA
Oper. Inc.	24.1	-10%	26.7	—	NA	—	NA
Depr.	6.2	-26%	8.3	—	NA	—	NA
Int. Exp.	1.1	-44%	2.0	—	NA	—	NA
Pretax Inc.	14.0	-14%	16.3	—	NA	—	NA
Eff. Tax Rate	40%	—	38%	—	NA	—	NA
Net Inc.	8.4	-16%	10.1	—	NA	—	NA

Balance Sheet & Other Fin. Data (Million $)

	1994	1993	1992	1991	1990	1989
Cash	1.4	1.6	NA	NA	NA	NA
Curr. Assets	67.1	30.7	NA	NA	NA	NA
Total Assets	139	103	NA	NA	NA	NA
Curr. Liab.	40.2	13.2	NA	NA	NA	NA
LT Debt	30.1	34.1	NA	NA	NA	NA
Common Eqty.	62.1	53.6	NA	NA	NA	NA
Total Cap.	95.6	88.4	NA	NA	NA	NA
Cap. Exp.	4.7	NA	NA	NA	NA	NA
Cash Flow	14.6	18.5	NA	NA	NA	NA

Ratio Analysis

	1994	1993	1992	1991	1990	1989
Curr. Ratio	1.7	2.3	NA	NA	NA	NA
% LT Debt of Cap.	31.5	38.6	NA	NA	NA	NA
% Net Inc.of Revs.	3.5	3.8	NA	NA	NA	NA
% Ret. on Assets	NA	NA	NA	NA	NA	NA
% Ret. on Equity	NA	NA	NA	NA	NA	NA

Dividend Data —No dividends have been paid. A "poison pill" stock purchase rights plan was adopted at the time of the spinoff from Valspar.

Data as orig. reptd.; bef. results of disc. opers. and/or spec. items. Per share data adj. for stk. divs. as of ex-div. date. E-Estimated. NA-Not Available. NM-Not Meaningful. NR-Not Ranked.

Office—400 East Cottage Place, Carpentersville, IL 60110. **Tel**—(708) 428-2657. **Pres & CEO**—J. R. Stevenson. **EVP-COO, Secy, Treas & Investor Contact**—Jeffrey M. Nodland. **Dirs**—M. L. Collins, E.M. Giles, D. G. Harris, J. M. Nodland, J. R. Stevenson, H. F. Tomfohrde III, N. L. Zutty. **Transfer Agent & Registrar**—Chemical Bank, NYC. **Incorporated** in Delaware in 1994. **Empl**-550. **S&P Analyst:** Justin McCann

STANDARD & POOR'S

STOCK REPORTS

Medicine Shoppe International

NASDAQ Symbol **MSII**

In S&P SmallCap 600

10-AUG-95

Industry:
Retail Stores

Summary: This company is the largest U.S. franchisor of pharmacies, with 1,096 stores at June 30, 1995, including a total of 109 units in Canada, Malaysia, Taiwan and Mexico.

Quantitative Evaluations

Outlook
(1 Lowest—5 Highest)
• **5+**

Fair Value
• **42¼**

Risk
• **Low**

Earn./Div. Rank
• **B+**

Technical Eval.
• **Bullish** since 3/93

Rel. Strength Rank
(1 Lowest—99 Highest)
• **77**

Insider Activity
• **Neutral**

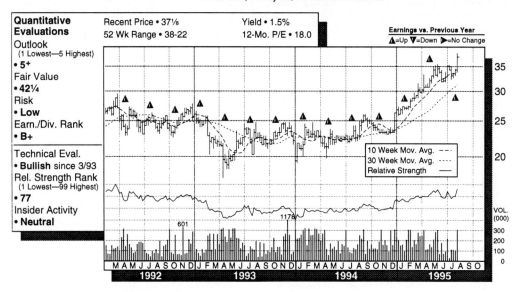

Recent Price • 37⅛

52 Wk Range • 38-22

Yield • 1.5%

12-Mo. P/E • 18.0

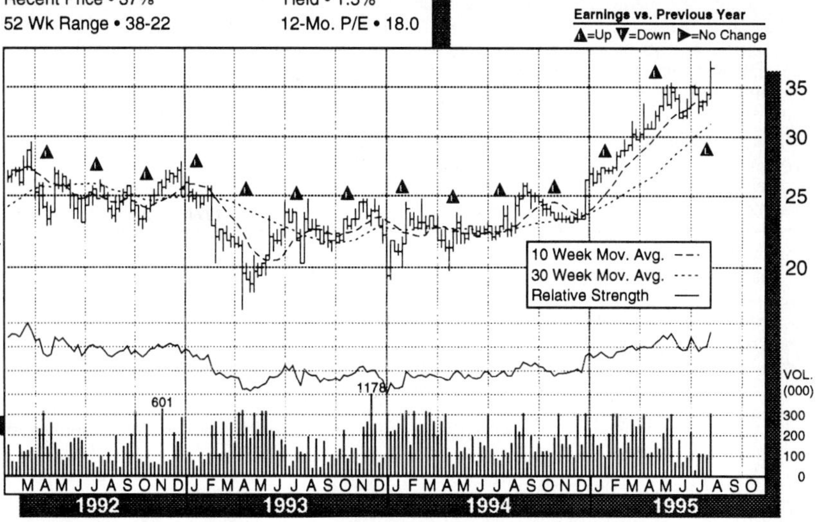

Business Profile - 10-AUG-95

This company operates a system of franchised pharmacies that derive more than 90% of revenues from the fulfillment of doctors' prescriptions. Through Medicine Shoppe InterNet, MSII has over 160 master agreements with managed care plan sponsors, enabling the company's pharmacies to participate in the growth of the managed care pharmacy business. Newly formed Managed Pharmacy Benefits Inc. provides pharmacy benefit management services for corporations, health plans and other health care payers.

Operational Review - 10-AUG-95

Revenues and earnings maintained their long upward trend in the first nine months of fiscal 1995, fueled by additional stores in operation and higher franchise fees and sales at existing stores. We expect this momentum to continue, aided by MSII's expansion into new international markets, and its entry into the managed health care business. The company's balance sheet is strong, with no long-term debt. An ongoing share repurchase program should further enhance earnings comparisons.

Stock Performance - 04-AUG-95

In the past 30 trading days, MSII's shares have increased 13%, compared to a 2% rise in the S&P 500. Average trading volume for the past five days was 71,160 shares, compared with the 40-day moving average of 27,395 shares.

Key Stock Statistics

Dividend Rate/Share	0.56	Shareholders	1,000
Shs. outstg. (M)	7.8	Market cap. (B)	$0.287
Avg. daily vol. (M)	0.033	Inst. holdings	57%
Tang. Bk. Value/Share	10.44	Insider holdings	NA
Beta	1.10		

Value of $10,000 invested 5 years ago: $ 19,082

Fiscal Year Ending Sep. 30

	1995	% Change	1994	% Change	1993	% Change
Revenues (Million $)						
1Q	13.40	9%	12.28	8%	11.40	10%
2Q	13.28	6%	12.48	16%	10.80	6%
3Q	13.71	11%	12.36	9%	11.33	11%
4Q	—	—	13.44	22%	11.04	5%
Yr.	—	—	50.56	13%	44.56	8%
Income (Million $)						
1Q	4.07	15%	3.55	13%	3.13	14%
2Q	4.08	13%	3.62	14%	3.17	11%
3Q	4.20	16%	3.62	8%	3.34	11%
4Q	—	—	3.68	12%	3.28	NM
Yr.	—	—	14.47	12%	12.91	9%
Earnings Per Share ($)						
1Q	0.52	16%	0.45	15%	0.39	15%
2Q	0.53	15%	0.46	15%	0.40	14%
3Q	0.54	17%	0.46	10%	0.42	14%
4Q	—	—	0.47	15%	0.41	3%
Yr.	—	—	1.84	14%	1.62	11%

Next earnings report expected: late September

Medicine Shoppe International

Business Summary - 10-AUG-95

Medicine Shoppe International, Inc. is the largest franchisor of pharmacies in the U.S., with 1,096 units in operation at June 30, 1995, including 109 stores in Canada, Taiwan, Malaysia and Mexico. Revenues in recent fiscal years were derived as follows:

	1994	1993	1992
Sales to franchisees	21%	19%	20%
Franchise fees	69%	71%	70%
Origination fees	3%	2%	3%
Other	7%	8%	7%

In fiscal 1994, 108 pharmacies were opened and 39 closed, for a net increase of 69.

Each Medicine Shoppe unit is operated by a licensed pharmacist under a 20-year franchise agreement, with 10-year renewal terms at the franchisee's option. Franchisees pay the company an initial franchise, or origination, fee of $18,000 ($12,000 for an additional pharmacy or $12,000 for the conversion of an existing drug store). The remaining investment ranges from $65,000 to $116,000 for leasehold improvements, equipment, inventory, supplies and initial working capital. Franchisees also pay Medicine Shoppe an ongoing franchise fee that escalates during the first six months of operation from 2% to 4%, 4 1/2%, 5% or 5 1/2% of all revenues. Combined sales reported by franchised units totaled $851 million in fiscal 1994, up from $765 million in fiscal 1993.

A typical pharmacy is a 1,000- to 1,500-sq.-ft. compact prescription center, located in a freestanding building, or in a small neighborhood strip shopping center. The company seeks to position its pharmacies as the most economic and professional sources of prescription drugs in their areas.

Medicine Shoppe provides pharmacist-franchisees with a comprehensive system of business training, site location, marketing and advertising programs and management support designed to help build a successful business. Because prescription drugs account for the bulk of sales (approximately 94% in fiscal 1994), the company's concept permits pharmacists to concentrate on supplying professional service and working closely with customers in rendering advice on pharmaceutical matters. Nonprescription merchandise is generally limited to over-the-counter drugs, vitamins and health care products, primarily Medicine Shoppe private label items.

Important Developments

Jul. '95—In the third quarter of 1994-95, MSII opened 17 stores and closed six. Separately, the company repurchased 51,275 common shares during the quarter, at an average cost of $32.05 per share, pursuant to a January 1995 authorization to repurchase up to 500,000 common shares.

Capitalization

Long Term Debt: None (6/95).

Per Share Data ($)

(Year Ended Sep. 30)

	1994	1993	1992	1991	1990	1989
Tangible Bk. Val.	9.93	8.71	7.67	6.88	5.83	4.88
Cash Flow	1.92	1.70	1.53	1.36	1.16	0.96
Earnings	1.84	1.62	1.46	1.30	1.11	0.91
Dividends	0.48	0.44	0.36	0.26	0.18	0.07
Payout Ratio	26%	27%	24%	20%	16%	7%
Prices - High	26	26½	30¾	28¾	26¾	23⅛
- Low	19¼	17½	22½	18½	15½	14⅞
P/E Ratio - High	14	16	21	22	24	25
- Low	10	11	15	14	14	16

Income Statement Analysis (Million $)

	1994	%Chg	1993	%Chg	1992	%Chg	1991
Revs.	50.6	13%	44.6	8%	41.4	12%	37.1
Oper. Inc.	22.4	14%	19.7	14%	17.3	15%	15.1
Depr.	0.6	NM	0.6	10%	0.6	7%	0.5
Int. Exp.	Nil	—	Nil	—	Nil	—	Nil
Pretax Inc.	22.5	14%	19.8	11%	17.9	13%	15.8
Eff. Tax Rate	36%	—	35%	—	34%	—	33%
Net Inc.	14.5	12%	12.9	8%	11.9	12%	10.6

Balance Sheet & Other Fin. Data (Million $)

	1994	1993	1992	1991	1990	1989
Cash	16.1	11.2	19.5	19.3	20.3	17.9
Curr. Assets	32.8	28.5	34.9	33.9	31.8	27.1
Total Assets	82.9	72.9	67.8	60.3	50.6	43.6
Curr. Liab.	4.0	3.1	6.0	3.9	2.8	3.2
LT Debt	Nil	Nil	Nil	Nil	Nil	Nil
Common Eqty.	78.0	69.1	61.5	56.1	47.4	39.6
Total Cap.	78.0	69.1	61.5	56.1	47.4	39.6
Cap. Exp.	0.6	0.3	0.4	0.5	0.7	0.3
Cash Flow	15.1	13.6	12.4	11.1	9.4	7.8

Ratio Analysis

	1994	1993	1992	1991	1990	1989
Curr. Ratio	8.3	9.2	5.8	8.8	11.4	8.4
% LT Debt of Cap.	Nil	Nil	Nil	Nil	Nil	Nil
% Net Inc.of Revs.	28.6	29.0	28.7	28.5	27.8	25.8
% Ret. on Assets	18.7	18.4	18.7	19.0	19.0	18.5
% Ret. on Equity	19.8	19.9	20.3	20.4	20.6	20.5

Dividend Data (Recent payments were:)

Amt. of Div. $	Date Decl.	Ex-Div. Date	Stock of Record	Payment Date
0.140	Nov. 09	Nov. 16	Nov. 22	Dec. 08 '94
0.140	Jan. 20	Jan. 27	Feb. 02	Feb. 16 '95
0.140	Apr. 28	May. 08	May. 12	May. 25 '95
0.140	Jul. 25	Aug. 03	Aug. 07	Aug. 17 '95

Data as orig. reptd.; bef. results of disc. opers. and/or spec. items. Per share data adj. for stk. divs. as of ex-div. date. E-Estimated. NA-Not Available. NM-Not Meaningful. NR-Not Ranked.

Office—1100 N. Lindbergh, St. Louis, MO 63132. **Tel**—(314) 993-6000. **Chrmn**—M. Yanow. **Pres, CEO & Investor Contact**—D. A. Abrahamson. **VP-Fin & CFO**—D. C. Schreiber. **Secy**—K. B. Friedman. **Dirs**—D. A. Abrahamson, F. Brown, M. F. Brown, I. C. Gall, D. P. Gallop, A. Katzman, L. F. Loewe, M. Weidenbaum, M. Yanow. **Transfer Agent**—Boatmen's Trust Co., St. Louis. **Incorporated** in Delaware in 1970. **Empl**-260. **S&P Analyst:** Maureen C. Carini

STANDARD & POOR'S

STOCK REPORTS

MedImmune, Inc.

NASDAQ Symbol **MEDI**

In S&P SmallCap 600

12-OCT-95

Industry: Drugs-Generic and OTC

Summary: This company develops, manufactures and markets therapeutics and vaccines to treat and prevent certain infectious diseases and cancer.

Quantitative Evaluations

Outlook (1 Lowest—5 Highest)
• **NA**

Fair Value
• **NA**

Risk
• **High**

Earn./Div. Rank
• **NR**

Technical Eval.
• **Bearish** since 8/95

Rel. Strength Rank (1 Lowest—99 Highest)
• **26**

Insider Activity
• **Neutral**

Recent Price • 10⅞
52 Wk Range • 15¼-3⅜

Yield • Nil
12-Mo. P/E • NM

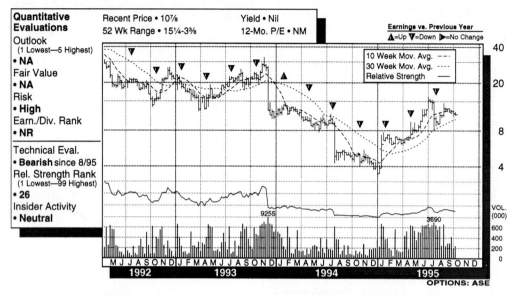

Earnings vs. Previous Year
▲=Up ▼=Down ▶=No Change

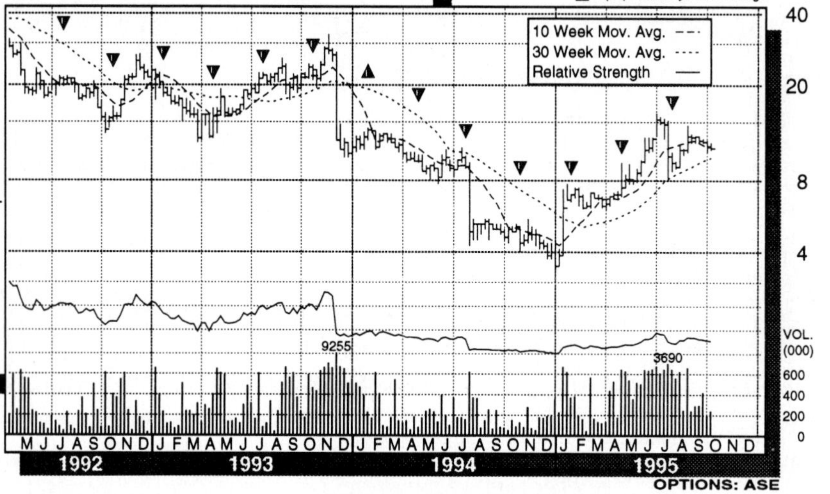

OPTIONS: ASE

Business Profile - 12-OCT-95

Although CytoGam sales have been gaining steam recently, losses continue to widen as the company expands its R&D programs. A second drug, RespiGam completed Phase III trials for the prevention of respiratory syncytial virus (RSV) infection in infants and results were submitted to the FDA in July 1995. FDA approval of RespiGam would provide a substantial boost, as 90,000+ children are hospitalized by RSV annually in the U.S. Two major corporate alliances were reached in the second quarter.

Operational Review - 12-OCT-95

Revenues for the six months ended June 30, 1995, advanced 88%, year to year, mainly reflecting substantially more contract revenue and, to a lesser extent, increased CytoGam sales ($7.3 million, versus $5.6 million). Margins narrowed, due to higher expenditures for RespiGam clinical studies and development of MEDI-500. With lower interest income, the net loss widened to $10.3 million ($0.69 a share) from $8.7 million ($0.60).

Stock Performance - 06-OCT-95

In the past 30 trading days, MEDI's shares have declined 11%, compared to a 4% rise in the S&P 500. Average trading volume for the past five days was 47,180 shares, compared with the 40-day moving average of 85,844 shares.

Key Stock Statistics

Dividend Rate/Share	Nil	Shareholders	3,000
Shs. outstg. (M)	14.6	Market cap. (B)	$0.153
Avg. daily vol. (M)	0.054	Inst. holdings	30%
Tang. Bk. Value/Share	2.34	Insider holdings	NA
Beta	NA		

Value of $10,000 invested 5 years ago: NA

Fiscal Year Ending Dec. 31

	1995	% Change	1994	% Change	1993	% Change
Revenues (Million $)						
1Q	5.93	81%	3.28	58%	2.08	-45%
2Q	7.86	97%	4.00	70%	2.35	-43%
3Q	—	—	3.89	44%	2.71	1%
4Q	—	—	7.41	-7%	7.94	NM
Yr.	—	—	18.86	25%	15.08	16%
Income (Million $)						
1Q	-5.47	NM	-4.54	NM	-3.67	NM
2Q	-4.87	NM	-4.19	NM	-3.36	NM
3Q	—	—	-4.07	NM	-3.65	NM
4Q	—	—	-6.02	NM	-2.54	NM
Yr.	—	—	-18.83	NM	-13.22	NM
Earnings Per Share ($)						
1Q	-0.37	NM	-0.31	NM	-0.27	NM
2Q	-0.32	NM	-0.29	NM	-0.25	—
3Q	—	—	-0.28	NM	-0.26	NM
4Q	—	—	-0.41	NM	-0.17	NM
Yr.	—	—	-1.29	NM	-0.96	NM

Next earnings report expected: early November

MedImmune, Inc.

Business Summary - 12-OCT-95

MedImmune was founded in 1988 to develop, manufacture and market immunotherapeutics and vaccines. Its focus is on products for infectious diseases and transplantation medicine.

Cytomegalovirus (CMV) is a major cause of illness and death in patients with weakened immune systems associated with organ transplantation or immunosuppressive diseases such as AIDS. MedImmune's first commercial product for CMV infections, CytoGam, is an injectible immune globulin made from human plasma containing high concentrations of naturally occurring antibodies to CMV. CytoGam is approved by the FDA for the prevention of disease caused by CMV infection in kidney transplant patients. In 1994, sales of CytoGam amounted to $12.1 million, up from $8.4 million in 1993 and $2.6 million in 1992.

RespiGam (also known as RSVIG-IV) submitted Phase III data for the prevention of respiratory syncytial virus (RSV) in infants in July 1995. RSV causes annual epidemics of bronchiolitis and pneumonia and can be fatal, especially in infants under the age of two. RespiGam is an injectible immune globulin made from human plasma containing high concentrations of naturally occurring antibodies to RSV.

In December 1994, the company began a Phase I clinical trial to evaluate MEDI-493, a humanized monoclonal antibody that has demonstrated in preclinical studies an ability to neutralize RSV. Also in December 1994, Phase I trials began on MEDI-490 rBGC, a Lyme disease vaccine that utilizes recombinant BCG (Bacille Calmette-Guerin) technology.

A Phase III trial of MEDI-500, an anti-T-cell monoclonal antibody, was launched in 1995's first quarter for prevention of graft-versus-host disease. A Phase II study for reversal of graft rejection is expected to commence in the fourth quarter.

The company has a co-promotion agreement with American Home Products for the marketing of Zosyn, an antibiotic of certain bacterial infections. Sales began in 1993.

Important Developments

Jul. '95—The company and Human Genome Sciences (NASDAQ: HGSI) announced a collaboration to create anti-bacterial vaccines and immunotherapeutics. MedImmune will use research from HGSI based on the complete genome sequence of Haemophilus influenzae. Earlier, in June, MEDI formed an alliance with Baxter Healthcare Corp. to market RespiGam outside North America. Baxter purchased 826,536 shares of MedImmune common stock in a private placement for $9.5 million.

Capitalization

Long Term Debt: $2,038,000 (6/95).

Per Share Data ($)

(Year Ended Dec. 31)

	1994	1993	1992	1991	1990	1989
Tangible Bk. Val.	2.34	3.63	3.49	4.15	-12.08	NA
Cash Flow	-1.19	-0.88	-0.46	0.13	-0.94	-0.64
Earnings	-1.29	-0.96	-0.51	0.11	-1.02	-0.69
Dividends	Nil	Nil	Nil	Nil	Nil	NA
Payout Ratio	Nil	Nil	Nil	Nil	Nil	NA
Prices - High	13¼	32⅝	50½	55	NA	NA
- Low	3⅜	10	12½	10	NA	NA
P/E Ratio - High	NM	NM	NM	NM	NA	NA
- Low	NM	NM	NM	NA	NA	NA

Income Statement Analysis (Million $)

	1994	%Chg	1993	%Chg	1992	%Chg	1991
Revs.	18.9	25%	15.1	15%	13.1	-6%	14.0
Oper. Inc.	-18.5	NM	-13.9	NM	-3.9	NM	0.8
Depr.	1.5	41%	1.1	45%	0.7	103%	0.4
Int. Exp.	0.3	-4%	0.3	-7%	0.3	NM	0.1
Pretax Inc.	-18.8	NM	-13.2	NM	-8.4	NM	1.7
Eff. Tax Rate	NM	—	NM	—	NM	—	2.20%
Net Inc.	-18.8	NM	-13.2	NM	-8.5	NM	1.6

Balance Sheet & Other Fin. Data (Million $)

	1994	1993	1992	1991	1990	1989
Cash	22.5	44.4	46.9	55.8	4.6	0.5
Curr. Assets	32.3	51.9	52.6	59.6	6.0	0.5
Total Assets	44.7	61.2	60.2	65.3	7.5	1.8
Curr. Liab.	7.8	5.7	11.1	7.9	5.9	1.9
LT Debt	2.1	2.2	2.2	2.2	0.1	0.3
Common Eqty.	34.2	53.0	46.8	55.1	-18.6	-0.5
Total Cap.	36.3	55.2	48.9	57.3	1.1	-0.2
Cap. Exp.	1.4	3.8	2.2	4.2	0.3	0.1
Cash Flow	-17.3	-12.2	-7.7	1.9	-3.8	-2.6

Ratio Analysis

	1994	1993	1992	1991	1990	1989
Curr. Ratio	4.1	9.2	4.7	7.5	1.0	0.2
% LT Debt of Cap.	5.8	4.0	4.4	3.8	12.0	NM
% Net Inc.of Revs.	NM	NM	NM	11.6	NM	NM
% Ret. on Assets	NM	NM	NM	1.6	NM	NM
% Ret. on Equity	NM	NM	NM	NM	NM	NM

Dividend Data —Cash dividends have never been paid.

Data as orig. reptd.; bef. results of disc. opers. and/or spec. items. Per share data adj. for stk. divs. as of ex-div. date. E-Estimated. NA-Not Available. NM-Not Meaningful. NR-Not Ranked.

Office—35 West Watkins Mill Rd., Gaithersburg, MD 20878. **Tel**—(301) 417-0770. **Fax**—(301) 527-4200. **Chrmn & CEO**—W. T. Hockmeyer. **Sr VP-Fin & CFO**—E. O. DiCataldo. **Dirs**—M. J. Barrett, J. H. Cavanaugh, W. T. Hockmeyer, L. C. Hoff, G. S. Macklin, F. H. Top Jr., W. H. Steinberg. **Transfer Agent & Registrar**—American Stock Transfer & Trust Co., NYC. **Incorporated** in Delaware in 1987. **Empl**-130. **S&P Analyst:** Thomas Tirney

STANDARD & POOR'S
STOCK REPORTS

Medusa Corp.

NYSE Symbol **MSA**
In S&P SmallCap 600

12-OCT-95 **Industry:** Building

Summary: Medusa Corp. produces portland cement, a building material used to make concrete. It also produces and sells aggregates and provides construction services for highway safety.

Quantitative Evaluations

Outlook
(1 Lowest—5 Highest)
• **5+**
Fair Value
• **33¼**
Risk
• **Average**
Earn./Div. Rank
• **NR**

Technical Eval.
• **Bearish** since 7/95
Rel. Strength Rank
(1 Lowest—99 Highest)
• **30**
Insider Activity
• **NA**

Recent Price • 27⅛
52 Wk Range • 28½-18⅜
Yield • 1.9%
12-Mo. P/E • 13.2

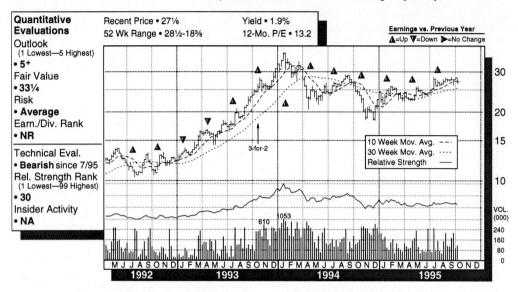

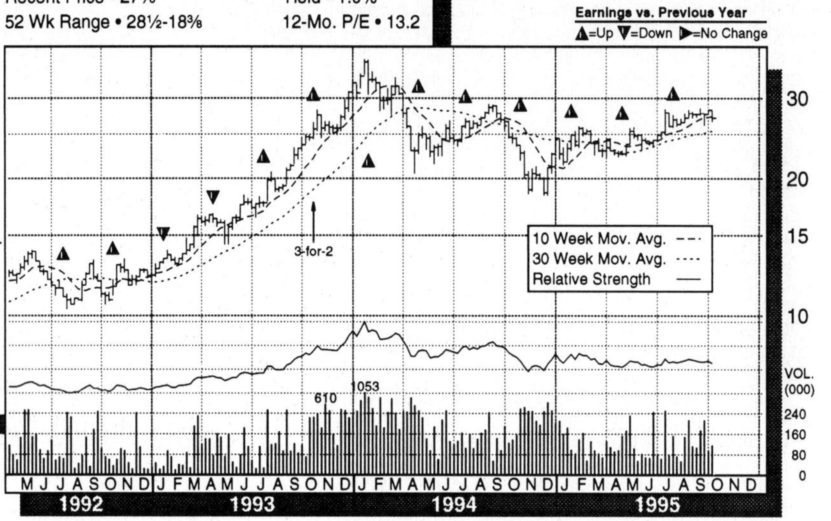

Business Profile - 13-JUL-95

Medusa is one of the leading domestic producers of grey portland cement, the essential building material used in making concrete. Higher housing starts helped MSA generate strong revenue and earnings gains in 1994, and the company expects that anticipated growth in 1995 will reflect both increased demand and rising cement prices in a tight supply market. MSA announced cement price hikes of 5% to 10% in April 1995; the increases should stick given the current strong demand industrywide.

Operational Review - 12-OCT-95

Revenues in the six months ended June 30, 1995, rose 10% year to year, reflecting a 14% increase in cement prices resulting from price increases implemented in April 1994, August 1994 and April 1995. Margins widened, due primarily to the higher cement prices, and operating income advanced 27%. With lower net interest expense, pretax income surged 47%. After taxes at 34.5% versus 33.6%, net income was up 45% to $12.4 million ($0.77 a share) from $8.5 million ($0.52).

Stock Performance - 06-OCT-95

In the past 30 trading days, MSA's shares have declined 2%, compared to a 4% rise in the S&P 500. Average trading volume for the past five days was 22,880 shares, compared with the 40-day moving average of 29,923 shares.

Key Stock Statistics

Dividend Rate/Share	0.50	Shareholders	5,100
Shs. outstg. (M)	16.3	Market cap. (B)	$0.419
Avg. daily vol. (M)	0.029	Inst. holdings	52%
Tang. Bk. Value/Share	2.89	Insider holdings	NA
Beta	0.85		

Value of $10,000 invested 5 years ago: $ 31,364

Fiscal Year Ending Dec. 31

	1995	% Change	1994	% Change	1993	% Change
Revenues (Million $)						
1Q	45.62	22%	37.38	22%	30.70	31%
2Q	80.17	5%	76.53	22%	62.96	17%
3Q	—	—	88.33	4%	84.61	41%
4Q	—	—	74.05	6%	69.76	58%
Yr.	—	—	276.3	11%	248.0	36%
Income (Million $)						
1Q	-0.30	NM	-1.79	NM	-4.21	NM
2Q	12.70	23%	10.31	67%	6.19	48%
3Q	—	—	12.80	30%	9.84	74%
4Q	—	—	8.56	34%	6.39	144%
Yr.	—	—	29.88	64%	18.20	100%
Earnings Per Share ($)						
1Q	-0.02	NM	-0.11	NM	-0.25	NM
2Q	0.79	25%	0.63	66%	0.38	46%
3Q	—	—	0.77	28%	0.60	70%
4Q	—	—	0.53	36%	0.39	144%
Yr.	—	—	1.81	62%	1.12	100%

Next earnings report expected: late October

Medusa Corp.

Business Summary - 11-OCT-95

Medusa Corp. produces and sells gray portland cement and masonry cement and, through subsidiaries, mines, processes and sells coarse aggregates, fine aggregates and high calcium limestone products. The company also provides construction services for highway safety.

For the five years through 1994, cement accounted for about 70% to 79% of sales; aggregates and limestone for about 15% to 20%; and highway safety for generally less than 10%.

With 3.4 million tons of clinker capacity, Medusa is the fourth largest domestically owned cement company in the U.S. Its four plants and six sales offices serve over 1,500 customers, principally ready-mix producers from 20 distribution terminals in the Great Lakes, Western Pennsylvania/Northeastern Ohio and Southeastern regions. At February 28, 1995, MSA had a total annual capacity (finish) of 3,470,000 tons of cement at four plants: Charlevoix, Mich. (1,365,000 tons), Demopolis, Ala. (814,000 tons), Clinchfield, Ga. (599,000) and Wampum, Pa. (692,000). Limestone reserves at each of the four plants are estimated in excess of 50 years, based on production at full rated capacity. In 1994, MSA's cement plants operated at 91.2% annual rated clinker capacity, up from 89.9% the year before.

The aggregates business consists of nine crushed stone quarries, one sand-and-gravel operation and two resale yards. These operations mine, crush, process and sell coarse aggregates (crushed stone) and fine aggregates (aglime). Contruction aggregates are building materials used in all types of concrete, and in blacktop surfaces for highways and parking lots. Finely crushed limestone, called aglime, is used for agricultural purposes as a soil sweetener to make fertilizer more effective and to reduce soil acidity. Limestone products include: industrial limestone, white stone and chemical stone.

The James H. Drew Corp. subsidiary installs highway safety systems such as guardrail, traffic signals, signs, highway lighting and raised pavement markers. Although Drew functions primarily as a subcontractor to paving and bridge contractors, about 30% of its work is bid directly to state highway departments and municipalities.

Important Developments

Aug. '95—Medusa announced that its wholly owned Medusa Aggregates Company subsidiary plans to discontinue its sand and dredging operations at Edinburg, Penn. The operation, which had sales of $1.35 million in 1994, has been unprofitable, and will be liquidated or sold. The company expects costs associated with the closure to reduce third quarter earnings by about $0.05 a share.

Capitalization

Long Term Debt: $61,300,000 (6/95).

Per Share Data ($)

(Year Ended Dec. 31)

	1994	1993	1992	1991	1990	1989
Tangible Bk. Val.	3.90	2.75	1.96	1.55	1.85	0.75
Cash Flow	2.68	1.98	1.31	1.13	1.53	1.36
Earnings	1.81	1.12	0.56	0.50	0.92	0.72
Dividends	0.50	0.27	0.27	0.13	Nil	Nil
Payout Ratio	28%	24%	48%	27%	Nil	Nil
Prices - High	36½	32¾	13⅞	11⅞	12⅞	10¼
- Low	18⅜	12⅛	10⅜	7⅝	7⅜	7⅝
P/E Ratio - High	20	29	25	24	14	14
- Low	10	11	18	16	8	11

Income Statement Analysis (Million $)

	1994	%Chg	1993	%Chg	1992	%Chg	1991
Revs.	276	11%	248	36%	182	5%	173
Oper. Inc.	65.9	40%	47.1	59%	29.6	4%	28.4
Depr.	13.8	-1%	14.0	16%	12.1	21%	10.0
Int. Exp.	7.5	22%	6.2	51%	4.1	-13%	4.7
Pretax Inc.	45.8	72%	26.7	105%	13.0	7%	12.2
Eff. Tax Rate	35%	—	32%	—	30%	—	34%
Net Inc.	29.9	64%	18.2	100%	9.1	12%	8.1

Balance Sheet & Other Fin. Data (Million $)

	1994	1993	1992	1991	1990	1989
Cash	48.5	31.2	7.6	3.3	2.0	5.1
Curr. Assets	100	84.2	49.4	42.9	39.6	39.0
Total Assets	219	204	119	109	108	100
Curr. Liab.	66.9	26.4	19.4	17.1	25.7	22.9
LT Debt	61.3	96.3	38.8	38.9	38.9	49.1
Common Eqty.	60.0	51.5	35.0	28.2	33.7	17.0
Total Cap.	121	148	73.8	67.0	81.0	75.0
Cap. Exp.	14.7	15.4	11.5	7.4	18.3	4.7
Cash Flow	43.7	32.2	21.2	18.1	24.6	21.7

Ratio Analysis

	1994	1993	1992	1991	1990	1989
Curr. Ratio	1.5	3.2	2.5	2.5	1.5	1.7
% LT Debt of Cap.	50.5	65.2	52.6	58.0	48.0	65.2
% Net Inc.of Revs.	10.8	7.3	5.0	4.7	7.7	6.2
% Ret. on Assets	14.7	11.2	7.9	7.4	14.1	10.8
% Ret. on Equity	55.6	41.7	28.6	26.0	58.0	110.9

Dividend Data —The company initiated quarterly dividends in August 1991. A "poison pill" stock purchase right was adopted in 1988.

Amt. of Div. $	Date Decl.	Ex-Div. Date	Stock of Record	Payment Date
0.125	Oct. 24	Nov. 23	Nov. 30	Dec. 09 '94
0.125	Feb. 27	Mar. 02	Mar. 08	Mar. 17 '95
0.125	May. 08	May. 24	May. 31	Jun. 09 '95
0.125	Aug. 21	Sep. 01	Sep. 06	Sep. 15 '95

Data as orig. reptd.; bef. results of disc. opers. and/or spec. items. Per share data adj. for stk. divs. as of ex-div. date. E-Estimated. NA-Not Available. NM-Not Meaningful. NR-Not Ranked.

Office—3008 Monticello Blvd., Cleveland Heights, OH 44118. **Tel**—(216) 371-4000. **Chrmn & CEO**—R. S. Evans. **Pres & COO**—G. E. Uding Jr. **VP-Fin & Treas**—R. P. Denny. **VP-Secy**—J. P. Siegfried. **Dirs**—M. Anathan III, E. T. Bigelow Jr., R. S. Evans, R. S. Forte, J. Ganlin, D. R. Gardner, D. C. Minton, C. J. Queenan Jr., G. E. Uding Jr., B. Yavitz. **Transfer Agent & Registrar**—National City Bank, Cleveland, Ohio. **Incorporated** in Ohio in 1916. **Empl**-1,100. **S&P Analyst:** N. Rosenberg

STANDARD & POOR'S

STOCK REPORTS

Merisel, Inc.

NASDAQ Symbol **MSEL**
In S&P SmallCap 600

16-NOV-95 **Industry:** Data Processing

Summary: This company is the largest, publicly held wholesale distributor of microcomputer hardware and software products in the world.

Quantitative Evaluations

Recent Price • 5⅝
52 Wk Range • 9⅝-3⅞
Yield • Nil
12-Mo. P/E • NM

Outlook
(1 Lowest—5 Highest)
• 4

Fair Value
• 6⅜

Risk
• **High**

Earn./Div. Rank
• **B**

Technical Eval.
• **Neutral** since 11/95

Rel. Strength Rank
(1 Lowest—99 Highest)
• **11**

Insider Activity
• **Neutral**

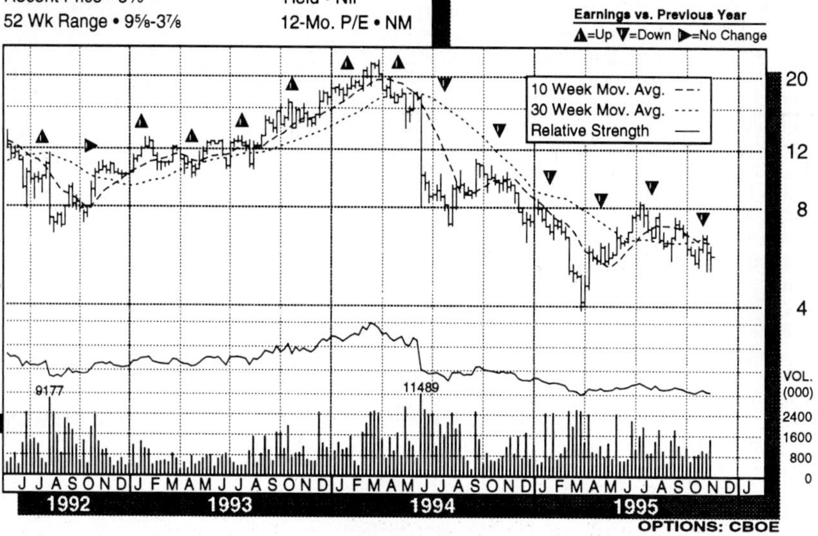

Business Profile - 02-AUG-95

This company is the computer industry's largest distributor of microcomputer hardware and software. In 1994, Merisel purchased the franchise and distribution businesses of ComputerLand, which makes the company the industry's first "Master Distributor", a combination of a full-line distributor and master reseller. Its business strategy is to offer the largest range of products possible to take advantage of resellers' general preference for buying from one source.

Operational Review - 16-NOV-95

Net sales rose 22% in the first nine months of 1995, reflecting growth in all geographic regions, the August 1995 launch of Windows 95, and one extra month of sales for Computerland (acquired January 31, 1994). Gross margins narrowed primarily as a result of worldwide pricing pressures and, to a lesser extent, the release of Windows 95. After a $9.3 million restructuring charge, a net loss of $6,655,000 ($0.22 a share, on 2.9% fewer shares) contrasted with net income of $14,109,000 ($0.46).

Stock Performance - 10-NOV-95

In the past 30 trading days, MSEL's shares have declined 5%, compared to a 1% rise in the S&P 500. Average trading volume for the past five days was 287,480 shares, compared with the 40-day moving average of 188,383 shares.

Key Stock Statistics

Dividend Rate/Share	Nil	Shareholders	1,000
Shs. outstg. (M)	29.8	Market cap. (B)	$0.156
Avg. daily vol. (M)	0.211	Inst. holdings	44%
Tang. Bk. Value/Share	4.12	Insider holdings	NA
Beta	1.21		

Value of $10,000 invested 5 years ago: $ 9,284

Fiscal Year Ending Dec. 31

	1995	% Change	1994	% Change	1993	% Change
Revenues (Million $)						
1Q	1,455	26%	1,155	67%	692.5	42%
2Q	1,380	14%	1,211	70%	713.4	39%
3Q	1,544	25%	1,231	68%	731.4	32%
4Q	—	—	1,423	50%	948.5	39%
Yr.	—	—	5,019	63%	3,086	38%
Income (Million $)						
1Q	-1.79	NM	8.60	35%	6.35	53%
2Q	-4.61	NM	2.72	-55%	6.07	37%
3Q	-0.25	NM	2.79	-54%	6.11	73%
4Q	—	—	-2.50	NM	11.91	58%
Yr.	—	—	11.61	-62%	30.44	55%
Earnings Per Share ($)						
1Q	-0.06	NM	0.28	33%	0.21	31%
2Q	-0.16	NM	0.09	-55%	0.20	33%
3Q	-0.01	NM	0.09	-55%	0.20	67%
4Q	—	—	-0.08	NM	0.39	56%
Yr.	—	—	0.38	-62%	1.00	49%

Next earnings report expected: late February

Merisel, Inc.

Business Summary - 09-NOV-95

Merisel, Inc. is the largest worldwide, publicly held wholesale distributor of microcomputer hardware and software products. Following the ComputerLand acquisition in February 1994 (see below), Merisel became the industry's first "master distributor", which combines the strengths of an aggregator and a full-line distributor. In this unique role, Merisel can offer a wider range of products to a more diverse group of customers.

Sales by product category in recent years were:

	1994	1993	1992
Hardware & accessories	75%	60%	50%
Software products	25%	40%	50%

The company stocks more than 25,000 products, including those for the MS-DOS, OS/2, Macintosh, Apple and UNIX operating environments, from over 850 microcomputer hardware and software manufacturers. Software and hardware products are offered from vendors such as Microsoft, WordPerfect, Lotus, Novell, IBM, Apple, and Epson. Sales of products manufactured by Microsoft accounted for 12% of net sales in 1994, compared to 16% in 1993, and 17% in 1992. Merisel sells to more than 65,000 computer resellers worldwide. The company's customers include value-added resellers, large hardware and software retail chains, mass merchants and OEMs.

Merisel operates subsidiaries in Canada, the U.K., France, Germany, Australia, Switzerland, Austria and Mexico, and it has a unit in Miami, Fla., that sells primarily to customers in Latin America. The company maintains 20 distribution centers that serve North America, Europe, Latin America and Australia. In 1994, European, Canadian and other international sales accounted for 32% of revenues.

In February 1994, Merisel acquired the franchise and distribution division of ComputerLand (sales of $1.1 billion in 1993) for $80 million ($20 million of which will be converted to Merisel common stock at $18.13 a share) plus up to an additional $30 million over two years based on performance.

Important Developments

Nov. '95—MSEL opened its new European Distribution Center (EDC) as part of its long-term strategy to centralize and integrate its European operations. The company closed its German warehouse in August 1995, and now ships to Germany from the EDC, located in Helmond, The Netherlands.

Oct. '95—MSEL increased its working capital facilities by entering into a new five year, $300 million accounts receivable asset securitiztion agented and arranged by GE Capital. The new facility replaces the existing $150 million asset securitization.

Capitalization

Long Term Debt: $282,600,000 (6/95).

Per Share Data ($)

(Year Ended Dec. 31)

	1994	1993	1992	1991	1990	1989
Tangible Bk. Val.	4.14	6.45	5.62	3.73	3.25	3.89
Cash Flow	0.90	1.34	0.99	0.77	0.30	0.96
Earnings	0.38	1.00	0.67	0.43	0.03	0.81
Dividends	Nil	Nil	Nil	Nil	Nil	Nil
Payout Ratio	Nil	Nil	Nil	Nil	Nil	Nil
Prices - High	22½	18½	14⅞	9⅜	6⅜	7⅞
- Low	6¼	9¾	6⅝	1¾	1⅝	5½
P/E Ratio - High	59	18	22	22	NM	10
- Low	16	10	10	4	NM	7

Income Statement Analysis (Million $)

	1994	%Chg	1993	%Chg	1992	%Chg	1991
Revs.	5,019	63%	3,086	38%	2,239	41%	1,585
Oper. Inc.	76.8	-6%	81.9	35%	60.7	30%	46.7
Depr.	16.1	53%	10.5	14%	9.2	9%	8.4
Int. Exp.	29.0	63%	17.8	13%	15.7	-2%	16.0
Pretax Inc.	20.0	-61%	50.9	48%	34.5	60%	21.5
Eff. Tax Rate	42%	—	40%	—	43%	—	50%
Net Inc.	11.6	-62%	30.4	54%	19.7	82%	10.8

Balance Sheet & Other Fin. Data (Million $)

	1994	1993	1992	1991	1990	1989
Cash	3.5	0.0	0.1	0.5	0.8	1.0
Curr. Assets	998	860	607	450	370	205
Total Assets	1,192	936	667	509	432	216
Curr. Liab.	598	500	312	358	157	116
LT Debt	358	209	153	25.0	159	51.0
Common Eqty.	236	224	199	126	114	49.0
Total Cap.	594	436	355	151	275	100
Cap. Exp.	40.2	24.6	10.0	5.9	9.0	4.6
Cash Flow	27.7	40.9	28.9	19.2	6.5	12.1

Ratio Analysis

	1994	1993	1992	1991	1990	1989
Curr. Ratio	1.7	1.7	1.9	1.3	2.4	1.8
% LT Debt of Cap.	60.2	47.8	43.2	16.8	57.9	51.4
% Net Inc.of Revs.	0.2	1.0	0.9	0.7	0.1	1.6
% Ret. on Assets	1.1	3.8	3.1	2.3	0.1	5.5
% Ret. on Equity	5.0	14.3	11.3	9.0	0.6	23.9

Dividend Data —No cash dividends have been paid. The company intends to retain earnings for the development and expansion of its business.

Data as orig. reptd.; bef. results of disc. opers. and/or spec. items. Per share data adj. for stk. divs. as of ex-div. date. E-Estimated. NA-Not Available. NM-Not Meaningful. NR-Not Ranked.

Office—200 Continental Blvd., El Segundo, CA 90245-0984. **Tel**—(310) 615-3080. **Chrmn & CEO**—M. D. Pickett. **Pres & COO**—R. A. Rittenmeyer. **SVP-Fin, CFO, Secy**—James L. Brill. **Investor Contact**—Susan Stillings. **Dirs**—J. Abrams, J. L. Brill, D. L. House, A. Miller, M. D. Pickett, L. J. Schoenberg, D. A. Steffensen, D. S. Wagman. **Transfer Agent & Registrar**—U.S. Stock Transfer Corp., Glendale, CA. **Organized** in California in 1980; incorporated in Delaware in 1988. **Empl**-2,502. **S&P Analyst:** Ronald J. Gross

STANDARD & POOR'S

STOCK REPORTS

Merrill Corp.

NASDAQ Symbol **MRLL**
In S&P SmallCap 600

03-OCT-95

Industry: Graphic Arts

Summary: MRLL is a leading provider of on-demand, 24 hour-a-day typesetting, printing, document reproduction and distribution services to financial, legal and corporate markets worldwide.

Quantitative Evaluations
Outlook
(1 Lowest—5 Highest)
• **5-**
Fair Value
• **21½**
Risk
• **Average**
Earn./Div. Rank
• **B**

Technical Eval.
• **Bullish** since 6/95
Rel. Strength Rank
(1 Lowest—99 Highest)
• **17**
Insider Activity
• **Unfavorable**

Recent Price • 18½
52 Wk Range • 21¼-13¾
Yield • 0.7%
12-Mo. P/E • 19.1

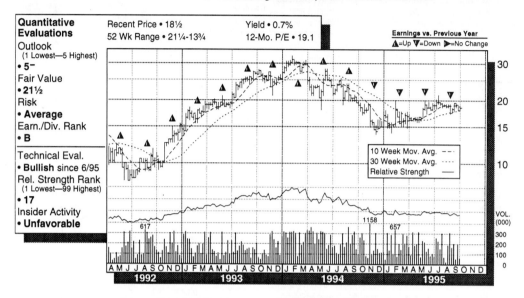

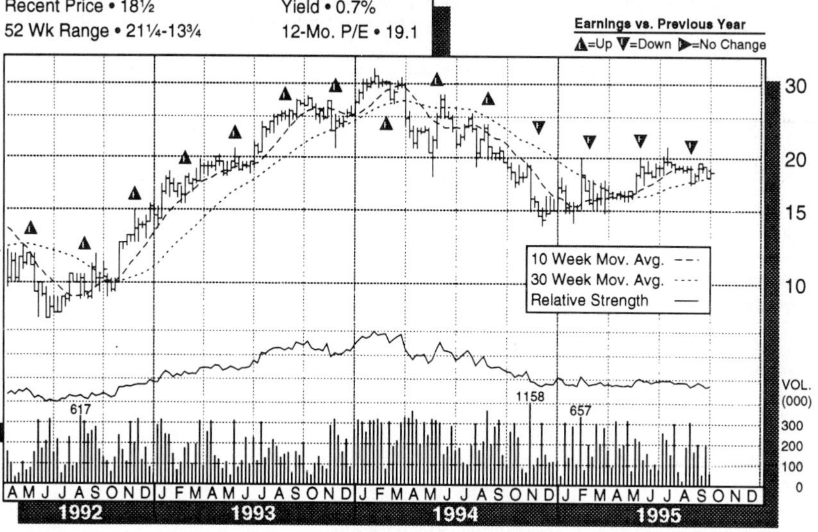

Business Profile - 22-SEP-95

Merrill is seeking to gain market share both domestically and internationally. To achieve this goal, the company has expanded its sales force and is aggressively pursuing foreign accounts. Management sees opportunity in the growth of mutual funds and plans to increase its client base in that industry. Demand for MRLL's services could also increase as the SEC contiunes to implement its Electronic Data Gathering, Analysis and Retrieval (EDGAR) System.

Operational Review - 03-OCT-95

Earnings did not fall as much in the second quarter as the first, due to an increased number of financial transactions. However, the financial printing segment's margins are being pressured by high capacity in the industry which has led to competitive pricing. Lower volume and price competition in the corporate segment and reductions in election-related printing are also negatively impacting results.

Stock Performance - 29-SEP-95

In the past 30 trading days, MRLL's shares have declined 2%, compared to a 5% rise in the S&P 500. Average trading volume for the past five days was 11,320 shares, compared with the 40-day moving average of 32,336 shares.

Key Stock Statistics

Dividend Rate/Share	0.12	Shareholders	400
Shs. outstg. (M)	7.8	Market cap. (B)	$0.136
Avg. daily vol. (M)	0.025	Inst. holdings	50%
Tang. Bk. Value/Share	7.78	Insider holdings	NA
Beta	2.41		

Value of $10,000 invested 5 years ago: $ 57,840

Fiscal Year Ending Jan. 31

	1996	% Change	1995	% Change	1994	% Change
Revenues (Million $)						
1Q	57.43	-7%	61.46	49%	41.24	19%
2Q	62.70	-2%	63.68	42%	44.91	17%
3Q	—	—	57.47	35%	42.54	14%
4Q	—	—	54.26	3%	52.89	41%
Yr.	—	—	236.9	30%	181.6	23%
Income (Million $)						
1Q	2.08	-56%	4.70	43%	3.28	53%
2Q	2.71	-38%	4.40	25%	3.52	39%
3Q	—	—	2.21	-27%	3.03	42%
4Q	—	—	0.68	-80%	3.34	87%
Yr.	—	—	11.98	-9%	13.17	53%
Earnings Per Share ($)						
1Q	0.26	-55%	0.58	38%	0.42	50%
2Q	0.34	-38%	0.55	25%	0.44	33%
3Q	—	—	0.28	-26%	0.38	36%
4Q	—	—	0.09	-78%	0.41	78%
Yr.	—	—	1.50	-9%	1.65	47%

Next earnings report expected: late November

Merrill Corp.

Business Summary - 03-OCT-95

Merrill Corporation provides on-demand, 24-hour-a-day typesetting, printing, document reproduction, distribution and marketing communication services for financial, legal, insurance and corporate markets. Advanced computer and telecommunications technology is applied to the production and distribution of time-sensitive financial documents, such as registration statements, prospectuses and other printed materials related to corporate financings and acquisitions. Merrill's corporate printing business involves typesetting and printing of annual and quarterly reports and proxy materials. In its commercial printing business, the company produces price catalogs, directories, insurance industry annual reports, sample ballots and technical manuals from electronic information supplied by customers. The company's May Printing subsidiary provides demand printing and distribution services. Operating revenues by category of service:

	1994-95	1993-94
Financial printing	34%	42%
Corporate printing	33%	34%
Commercial/other printing	33%	24%

The company's central computerized production facility is in St. Paul, Minn., and its 18 service facilities are located throughout the U.S. and Canada. By concentrating equipment and typesetting personnel in St. Paul and linking its service facilities electronically to the St. Paul hub, Merrill is able to reduce overhead and labor expenses, implement more effective training programs and respond quickly to changing demand in each of its markets.

Merrill meets the fluctuating demand for financial printing services by associating with several qualified commercial printers that provide press time on an "as required" basis, reducing fixed corporate overhead expenses. For its increasing and recurring corporate and commercial business, the company operates printing plants in Minneapolis/St. Paul, Los Angeles, Chicago, Dallas and New Jersey. In September 1992, the company entered into a joint marketing arrangement to provide international financial printing services with London-based Burrups, Ltd., a financial printing company with service facilities in Europe and Asia.

Important Developments

Aug. '95—In reporting second quarter results, the company said that financial market activity improved from the first quarter, but continued margin pressure from competitive pricing and business mix were still affecting earnings.

Capitalization

Long Term Debt: $5,295,000 (7/95).

Per Share Data ($) (Year Ended Jan. 31)

	1995	1994	1993	1992	1991	1990
Tangible Bk. Val.	7.18	5.60	5.36	4.11	3.20	2.82
Cash Flow	2.72	2.34	1.65	1.27	0.86	0.11
Earnings	1.50	1.65	1.12	0.86	0.37	-0.17
Dividends	0.12	0.10	Nil	Nil	Nil	Nil
Payout Ratio	8%	6%	Nil	Nil	Nil	Nil
Cal. Yrs.	1994	1993	1992	1991	1990	1989
Prices - High	32½	28	15¾	13⅛	5½	5¾
- Low	13¾	13½	8¼	3½	2¾	3⅛
P/E Ratio - High	22	17	14	15	15	NM
- Low	9	8	7	4	7	NM

Income Statement Analysis (Million $)

	1995	%Chg	1994	%Chg	1993	%Chg	1992
Revs.	237	30%	182	23%	148	18%	125
Oper. Inc.	31.5	15%	27.5	51%	18.2	28%	14.2
Depr.	9.8	77%	5.5	36%	4.1	30%	3.1
Int. Exp.	1.1	NM	0.3	28%	0.3	-54%	0.5
Pretax Inc.	21.2	-4%	22.0	55%	14.2	31%	10.8
Eff. Tax Rate	43%	—	40%	—	39%	—	40%
Net Inc.	12.0	-9%	13.2	53%	8.6	32%	6.5

Balance Sheet & Other Fin. Data (Million $)

	1995	1994	1993	1992	1991	1990
Cash	10.0	2.6	9.6	6.3	1.2	1.2
Curr. Assets	63.5	59.4	48.0	37.7	30.6	24.3
Total Assets	106	100	66.0	53.0	46.9	40.6
Curr. Liab.	31.9	36.9	23.3	21.0	21.2	16.4
LT Debt	7.5	8.7	2.1	2.2	2.3	2.4
Common Eqty.	66.1	53.6	39.3	29.1	22.5	20.5
Total Cap.	73.6	62.9	42.7	32.0	25.7	24.2
Cap. Exp.	10.1	7.9	7.4	2.6	2.8	5.0
Cash Flow	21.8	18.7	12.7	9.7	6.2	0.8

Ratio Analysis

	1995	1994	1993	1992	1991	1990
Curr. Ratio	2.0	1.6	2.0	1.8	1.4	1.5
% LT Debt of Cap.	10.2	13.8	5.0	7.0	9.0	9.9
% Net Inc.of Revs.	5.1	7.3	5.8	5.2	2.6	NM
% Ret. on Assets	11.5	15.7	14.2	13.0	6.2	NM
% Ret. on Equity	19.9	28.1	24.8	25.2	12.6	NM

Dividend Data —Cash dividends were initiated in 1993. A two-for-one stock split was effected in March 1992.

Amt. of Div. $	Date Decl.	Ex-Div. Date	Stock of Record	Payment Date
0.030	Sep. 19	Sep. 26	Sep. 30	Oct. 14 '94
0.030	Dec. 16	Dec. 23	Dec. 30	Jan. 13 '95
0.030	Mar. 21	Mar. 27	Mar. 31	Apr. 14 '95
0.030	Jun. 20	Jun. 28	Jun. 30	Jul. 14 '95
0.030	Sep. 20	Sep. 27	Sep. 29	Oct. 13 '95

Data as orig. reptd.; bef. results of disc. opers. and/or spec. items. Per share data adj. for stk. divs. as of ex-div. date. E-Estimated. NA-Not Available. NM-Not Meaningful. NR-Not Ranked.

Office—One Merrill Circle, St. Paul, MN 55108. **Tel**—(612) 646-4501. **Chrmn**—K. F. Merrill. **Pres & CEO**—J. W. Castro. **VP-Fin, CFO & Treas**—J. B. McCain. **Secy**—S. J. Machov. **Dirs**—R. R. Atterbury, J. R. Campbell, J. W. Castro, R. N. Hoge, R. G. Lareau, K. F. Merrill, P. G. Miller, R. F. Nienhouse. **Transfer Agent & Registrar**—First Trust Co. Inc., St. Paul. **Incorporated** in Minnesota in 1968. **Empl**-1,721. **S&P Analyst:** Stephen Madonna, CFA

STANDARD & POOR'S

STOCK REPORTS

MESA Inc.

NYSE Symbol **MXP**

In S&P SmallCap 600

11-SEP-95

Industry: Oil and Gas

Summary: MESA is one of the nation's largest independent natural gas producers, with production primarily in Kansas and Texas.

S&P Opinion: Sell (★)

Recent Price • 4¾

52 Wk Range • 6⅛-3½

Yield • Nil

12-Mo. P/E • NM

Quantitative Evaluations

Outlook (1 Lowest—5 Highest) • **NA**

Fair Value • **NA**

Risk • **High**

Earn./Div. Rank • **C**

Technical Eval. • **Bullish** since 6/95

Rel. Strength Rank (1 Lowest—99 Highest) • **21**

Insider Activity • **Neutral**

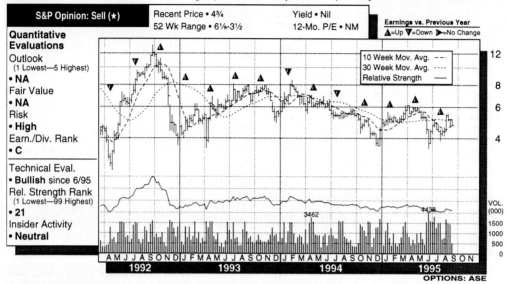

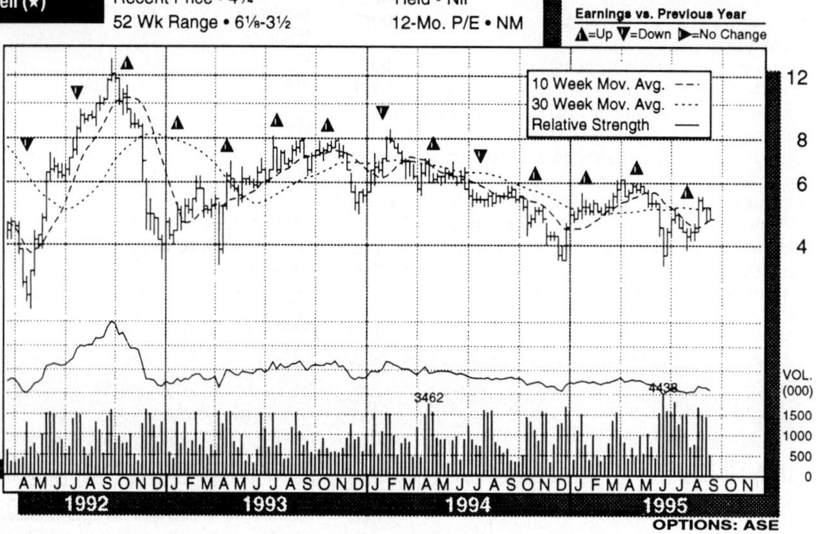

OPTIONS: ASE

Overview - 07-SEP-95

Revenues are predicted to remain stable over the next six months, reflecting higher levels of oil production, while natural gas wellhead prices are anticipated to trend higher in the remainder of 1995 and should average $1.55 per mcf, rising to $1.70 in 1996, reflecting increased demand as well as pipeline capacity contraints in Canada. Planned restructuring moves include the sale of the company's prized natural gas assets in the Hugoton field. The ability to meet scheduled debt payments will depend on the successful sale of smaller pieces of this property. Volatile natural gas markets and limited access to debt markets, with the majority of Mesa's debt tied to specific oil and gas assets, make profitability in the near-term unlikely. However, if the company can complete its contemplated asset sales, and is able to refinance its debt, prospects may improve.

Valuation - 11-SEP-95

A proxy solicitation battle with dissident shareholders and negotiations surrounding asset sales have led to volatility in the shares. We believe that based solely on the company's earnings and cash flow outlook, MESA's shares are overvalued. Exploration activities in 1995 and 1996 will suffer as a result of high-cost debt, debt covenants and limited access to additional borrowings. Lehman Brothers has been hired to examine the possibility of the sale of the company. Under this scenario, MESA might fetch as much as $6.25 a share, reflecting the cash flow potential of the company, assuming a sharply lower cost of capital and conservative estimates of commodity prices.

Key Stock Statistics

S&P EPS Est. 1995	-1.05	Tang. Bk. Value/Share	1.60
P/E on S&P Est. 1995	NM	Beta	-0.31
Dividend Rate/Share	Nil	Shareholders	26,700
Shs. outstg. (M)	64.1	Market cap. (B)	$0.304
Avg. daily vol. (M)	0.334	Inst. holdings	25%
		Insider holdings	NA

Value of $10,000 invested 5 years ago: $ 1,257

Fiscal Year Ending Dec. 31

	1995	% Change	1994	% Change	1993	% Change
Revenues (Million $)						
1Q	62.25	2%	61.08	-4%	63.80	8%
2Q	59.17	11%	53.36	5%	50.83	-1%
3Q	—	—	45.73	8%	42.38	-12%
4Q	—	—	68.57	5%	65.18	-17%
Yr.	—	—	228.7	3%	222.2	-6%
Income (Million $)						
1Q	-7.89	NM	-17.77	NM	-17.09	NM
2Q	-13.95	NM	-25.34	NM	-14.45	NM
3Q	—	—	-25.91	NM	-27.48	NM
4Q	—	—	-14.34	NM	-43.44	NM
Yr.	—	—	-83.35	NM	-102.4	NM
Earnings Per Share ($)						
1Q	-0.12	NM	-0.37	NM	-0.44	NM
2Q	-0.22	NM	-0.43	NM	-0.37	NM
3Q	E-0.33	NM	-0.40	NM	-0.71	NM
4Q	E-0.38	NM	-0.22	NM	-1.06	NM
Yr.	E-1.05	NM	-1.42	NM	-2.61	NM

Next earnings report expected: late September

MESA Inc.

Business Summary - 19-JUL-95

MESA Inc., the successor corporation to Mesa Limited Partnership (MLP) formed in 1964 and reorganized in 1985, is a leading U.S. independent natural gas and oil producer. MXP shares began NYSE trading January 2, 1992, following MLP's conversion to a corporation, effective December 31, 1991. During 1994, MESA resumed exploration and development in the Gulf of Mexico. MXP is pioneering the use of natural gas vehicles through its MESA Environmental subsidiary.

As of December 31, 1994, estimated proved reserves amounted to 1,303,187 Mmcf of natural gas (1,204,444 a year earlier) and 89,428,000 bbl. of crude oil, condensate and gas liquids (82,446,000). Production in 1994 was estimated at 82,339 MMcf of gas (79,820 MMcf in 1993) and 546 MBls of oil (738 MBls), condensate and gas liquids 6,911 MBls (5,050 MBls).

To alleviate a severe liquidity drain, MXP has initiated a number of restructuring moves, in April 1994, it sold 15 million new common shares, and in August 1993, a total of $586.3 million principal amount of subordinated notes (and $28.6 million of related accrued interest claims payable at May 1, 1993) was replaced by a combination of $572.4 million of initial accreted value of new secured and unsecured 12.75% discount notes, $29.3 million of new convertible notes that were later converted, and $13.2 million in cash.

Important Developments

Jul. '95—Mesa said it will shortly call a special meeting of its board to consider the possible sale or merger of the company. Earlier, dissident minority shareholders had urged the board to explore all possible strategic alternatives to enhance shareholder value.

Jun. '95—MESA did not accept any of the bids on its Hugoton field properties, since the highest bid amounted to $750 million, or about $0.65 mcf. This fell short of company expectations, and therefore none of the bids were successful. The sale of these properties will be pursued, and efforts will be directed towards selling the property in smaller pieces. The company said that cash reserves and flow from operating activities are forecasted to provide for principal and interest payments on its debt up to June 30, 1996, when additional funding will be necessary. Having hired Lehman Brothers as its advisers, the company is evaluating options related to refinancing its Hugoton Capital Limited Partnership debt through either bank debt or high-yield debt, or a combination of both. The refinancing is intended to facilitate the sale of the Hugoton properties.

Capitalization

Long Term Debt: $1,189,837,000 (3/95).

Per Share Data ($) (Year Ended Dec. 31)

	1994	1993	1992	1991	1990	1989
Tangible Bk. Val.	1.94	2.41	4.78	7.09	NA	NA
Cash Flow	0.15	-0.06	0.64	1.03	-11.15	-1.55
Earnings	-1.42	-2.61	-2.31	-2.05	-10.10	-1.20
Dividends	Nil	Nil	Nil	Nil	1.88	9.38
Payout Ratio	Nil	Nil	Nil	Nil	NM	NM
Prices - High	8½	8⅛	13⅜	17½	40⅝	67½
- Low	3⅝	3½	2½	5	10	34⅜
P/E Ratio - High	NM	NM	NM	NM	NM	NM
- Low	NM	NM	NM	NM	NM	NM

Income Statement Analysis (Million $)

	1994	%Chg	1993	%Chg	1992	%Chg	1991
Revs.	229	3%	222	-6%	237	-5%	250
Oper. Inc.	121	NM	122	-13%	140	-8%	153
Depr. Depl. & Amort.	92.0	-8%	100	-12%	114	-4%	119
Int. Exp.	145	2%	142	NM	143	-5%	151
Pretax Inc.	-83.0	NM	-106	NM	-93.0	NM	-83.0
Eff. Tax Rate	NM	—	NM	—	NM	—	NM
Net Inc.	-83.0	NM	-101	NM	-89.0	NM	-79.0

Balance Sheet & Other Fin. Data (Million $)

	1994	1993	1992	1991	1990	1989
Cash	163	150	169	260	174	351
Curr. Assets	205	196	219	310	244	420
Total Assets	1,484	1,533	1,677	1,833	2,168	2,626
Curr. Liab.	89.0	120	116	93.0	242	276
LT Debt	1,193	1,174	1,242	1,304	1,361	1,520
Common Eqty.	125	112	184	274	NA	NA
Total Cap.	1,317	1,288	1,434	1,590	NA	NA
Cap. Exp.	33.0	28.0	63.0	34.0	35.0	42.0
Cash Flow	9.0	-2.0	25.0	40.0	-176	-24.0

Ratio Analysis

	1994	1993	1992	1991	1990	1989
Curr. Ratio	2.3	1.6	1.9	3.3	1.0	1.5
% LT Debt of Cap.	90.5	91.1	86.6	82.0	NA	NA
% Ret. on Assets	NM	NM	NM	NM	NM	NM
% Ret. on Equity	NM	NM	NM	NA	NA	NA

Dividend Data —Payment of a common dividend can not be expected, because of the company's severe liquidity requirements and debt burden.

Data as orig. reptd.; bef. results of disc opers. and/or spec. items. Per share data adj. for stk. divs. as of ex-div. date. E-Estimated. NA-Not Available. NM-Not Meaningful. NR-Not Ranked.

Office—1400 Williams Square West, 5205 North O'Connor Bouleveard, Irving, TX 75039. **Tel**—(214) 402-7087. **Chrmn & CEO**—B. Pickens. **CFO**—S. K. Gardner. **Investor Contact**—Malcolm Gorrie. **Dirs**—D. Batchelder, P. W. Cain, J. L. Cox, J. S. Herrington, W. H. Madden Jr., D. Parkinson, B. Pickens, F. S. Sarofim, R. L. Stillwell, J. R. Walsh Jr. **Transfer Agent**—American Stock Transfer & Trust Co., NYC. **Incorporated** in Texas in 1991. **Empl**-399. **S&P Analyst:** Raymond J. Deacon

STANDARD & POOR'S

STOCK REPORTS

Michaels Stores

NASDAQ Symbol **MIKE**
In S&P SmallCap 600

11-SEP-95

Industry:
Retail Stores

Summary: This company is the leading arts and crafts retailer in the U.S., with a chain of over 470 stores in 41 states, Canada and Puerto Rico.

Quantitative Evaluations

Outlook
(1 Lowest—5 Highest)
• **5-**

Fair Value
• **34**

Risk
• **High**

Earn./Div. Rank
• **B**

Technical Eval.
• **Bearish** since 5/95

Rel. Strength Rank
(1 Lowest—99 Highest)
• **1**

Insider Activity
• **NA**

Recent Price • 17½
52 Wk Range • 45¾-15¼

Yield • Nil
12-Mo. P/E • 67.3

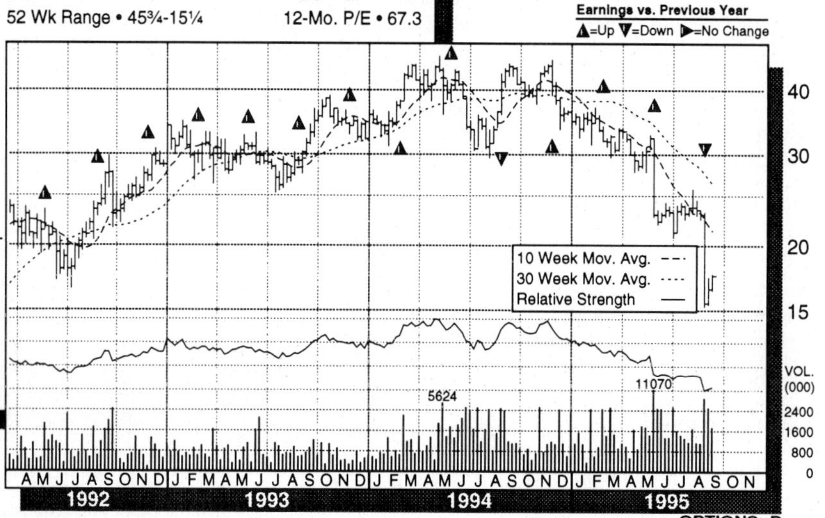

OPTIONS: P

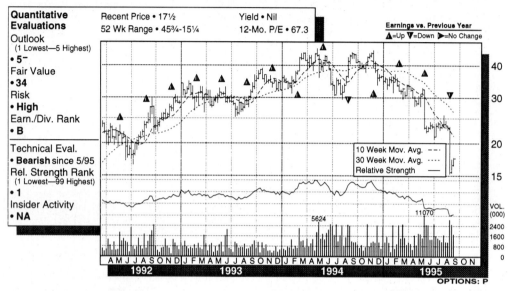

Business Profile - 11-SEP-95

This company is the leading specialty retailer in the U.S. dedicated to serving the arts and crafts marketplace. It has nearly doubled its store base over the past year through the acquisition of five arts and crafts chains. However, concerns about the soft retail climate are leading to highly promotional activities and resulting gross margin pressures. To improve results, MIKE said it would focus on profits rather than on sales by reducing inventory levels, and slowing its rate of store growth.

Operational Review - 11-SEP-95

Sales soared 57%, year to year, for the first six months of 1995-96, mainly reflecting more stores in operation and 9% higher same-store sales. Margins were squeezed by higher levels of promotional activity. Results were further penalized by costs associated with the retail markdown of inventory to be eliminated as part of an inventory reduction program. With sharply higher net interest and other expense, and 17% more shares, a net loss of $1.20 per share contrasted with income of $0.31.

Stock Performance - 08-SEP-95

In the past 30 trading days, MIKE's shares have declined 26%, compared to a 2% rise in the S&P 500. Average trading volume for the past five days was 426,575 shares, compared with the 40-day moving average of 488,826 shares.

Key Stock Statistics

Dividend Rate/Share	Nil	Shareholders	1,100
Shs. outstg. (M)	21.4	Market cap. (B)	$0.375
Avg. daily vol. (M)	0.708	Inst. holdings	69%
Tang. Bk. Value/Share	10.35	Insider holdings	NA
Beta	1.29		

Value of $10,000 invested 5 years ago: $ 34,146

Fiscal Year Ending Jan. 31

	1996	% Change	1995	% Change	1994	% Change
Revenues (Million $)						
1Q	265.5	66%	159.8	41%	113.0	20%
2Q	259.9	49%	174.2	51%	115.4	24%
3Q	—	—	283.1	82%	155.8	26%
4Q	—	—	377.5	60%	235.6	29%
Yr.	—	—	994.6	60%	619.7	26%
Income (Million $)						
1Q	7.56	52%	4.97	31%	3.80	25%
2Q	-33.12	NM	0.71	-80%	3.64	38%
3Q	—	—	7.81	61%	4.85	34%
4Q	—	—	22.15	58%	14.00	26%
Yr.	—	—	35.65	36%	26.29	29%
Earnings Per Share ($)						
1Q	0.35	25%	0.28	27%	0.22	22%
2Q	-1.55	NM	0.04	-86%	0.28	75%
3Q	—	—	0.36	29%	0.28	33%
4Q	—	—	1.01	35%	0.75	15%
Yr.	—	—	1.77	16%	1.53	25%

Next earnings report expected: late November

Michaels Stores

Business Summary - 11-SEP-95

Michaels Stores, Inc. is the largest nationwide specialty retailer of arts, crafts and decorative items. Its stores offer a selection of over 30,000 competitively priced items, including picture framing materials and services, silk and dried flowers and related floral items, hobby and art supplies, creative crafts and party, seasonal and holiday merchandise. The company targets as its primary customer base women aged 25 to 54 with above-average household incomes.

Revenues by product line in recent years were:

	1994-95	1993-94
Picture framing	15%	15%
Silk, dried flowers & plants	22%	21%
Art materials	10%	11%
Crafts & wearable art	20%	21%
Seasonal/promotional items	14%	14%
Other	195	18%

As of August 30, 1995, Michaels was operating 420 stores in 43 states and Canada. The stores contain an average of 15,600 sq. ft. of selling space. In the fiscal year ended January 1995, stores open for the full year averaged $3,180,000 in sales or roughly $204 per sq. ft. of selling space.

Stores are located on a cluster or single-store basis in geographic areas where rent, freight and advertising expenditures are cost-effective; stores currently in operation are located primarily in strip shopping centers in areas easily accessible to customer traffic with ample parking.

Substantially all of the products sold in Michaels stores are manufactured in the U.S., the Far East and Mexico. Goods manufactured in the Far East generally require long lead times and are ordered four to six months in advance of delivery. The company operates three distribution centers, in Irving, Texas, Buena Park, Calif., and Lexington, Ky., and a bulk warehouse in Phoenix, Ariz.

At 1994-95 year-end, MIKE was operating five Michaels Craft and Floral Warehouse (CFW) superstores. CFW stores occupy up to 40,000 sq. ft. of selling space and carry a wider selection of certain categories of merchandise at discounted prices. The company expects to open three new CFW stores in 1995-96.

Aaron Brothers, acquired in March 1995, operates 69 stores, primarily in California, selling frames, framing materials, custom framing services and art supplies.

Important Developments

Aug. '95—The company reported that sales in August 1995 increased 13%, year to year; same-store sales slid 1%. Total year-to-date sales rose 49%, on an 8% gain in same-store sales.

Capitalization

Long Term Debt: $273,340,000 (7/95).

Per Share Data ($) (Year Ended Jan. 31)

	1995	1994	1993	1992	1991	1990
Tangible Bk. Val.	11.17	9.70	7.96	6.90	2.39	1.70
Cash Flow	2.84	2.25	1.83	1.65	1.34	0.68
Earnings	1.76	1.53	1.22	0.90	0.57	Nil
Dividends	Nil	Nil	Nil	Nil	Nil	Nil
Payout Ratio	Nil	Nil	Nil	Nil	Nil	Nil
Cal. Yrs.	1994	1993	1992	1991	1990	1989
Prices - High	46½	39	34	17⅛	6½	10¼
- Low	29½	25¼	16	3⅝	2⅞	4⅞
P/E Ratio - High	26	25	28	19	11	NM
- Low	17	17	13	4	5	NM

Income Statement Analysis (Million $)

	1995	%Chg	1994	%Chg	1993	%Chg	1992
Revs.	995	60%	620	26%	493	20%	411
Oper. Inc.	92.6	72%	53.8	21%	44.4	29%	34.5
Depr.	21.5	72%	12.5	23%	10.2	15%	8.9
Int. Exp.	9.1	43%	6.4	NM	0.3	-96%	7.0
Pretax Inc.	57.2	34%	42.6	27%	33.5	88%	17.8
Eff. Tax Rate	38%	—	38%	—	39%	—	40%
Net Inc.	35.6	35%	26.3	29%	20.4	91%	10.7

Balance Sheet & Other Fin. Data (Million $)

	1995	1994	1993	1992	1991	1990
Cash	16.9	68.8	42.1	27.4	0.1	1.2
Curr. Assets	419	291	170	126	85.0	92.0
Total Assets	686	398	322	181	144	151
Curr. Liab.	186	109	65.6	51.1	40.5	33.5
LT Debt	138	97.8	97.8	Nil	54.2	74.2
Common Eqty.	356	185	155	126	47.0	40.0
Total Cap.	494	283	253	126	104	117
Cap. Exp.	68.1	46.8	19.8	5.5	6.8	9.5
Cash Flow	57.2	38.8	30.5	19.6	13.7	7.2

Ratio Analysis

	1995	1994	1993	1992	1991	1990
Curr. Ratio	2.2	2.7	2.6	2.5	2.1	2.8
% LT Debt of Cap.	27.9	34.5	38.6	Nil	52.2	63.3
% Net Inc.of Revs.	3.6	4.2	4.1	2.6	1.6	NM
% Ret. on Assets	6.0	7.3	7.8	5.4	4.0	NM
% Ret. on Equity	12.0	15.3	13.9	10.9	13.4	NM

Dividend Data —No dividends have been paid.

Data as orig. reptd.; bef. results of disc. opers. and/or spec. items. Per share data adj. for stk. divs. as of ex-div. date. E-Estimated. NA-Not Available. NM-Not Meaningful. NR-Not Ranked.

Office—5931 Campus Circle Drive, Las Colinas Business Park, Irving, TX 75063; P.O. Box 619566, DFW, TX 75261-9566. **Tel**—(214) 714-7000. **Chrmn & CEO**—S. Wyly. **Vice Chrmn**—C. J. Wyly Jr. **Pres & COO**—D. Sullivan. **Exec VP, CFO & Investor Contact**—R. Don Morris. **VP & Secy**—M. V. Beasley. **Dirs**—J. E. Bush, M. C. French, R. E. Hanlon, D. R. Miller Jr., F. J. Taylor, C. J. Wyly Jr., E. A. Wyly, S. Wyly. **Transfer Agent & Registrar**—Society National Bank, Dallas. **Incorporated** in Delaware in 1983. **Empl**-17,440. **S&P Analyst:** Maureen C. Carini

MicroAge, Inc.

NASDAQ Symbol **MICA**
In S&P SmallCap 600

17-OCT-95

Industry:
Retail Stores

Summary: This franchisor of computer stores and distributor of microcomputer systems has an international network of outlets that sell, support and service office information products.

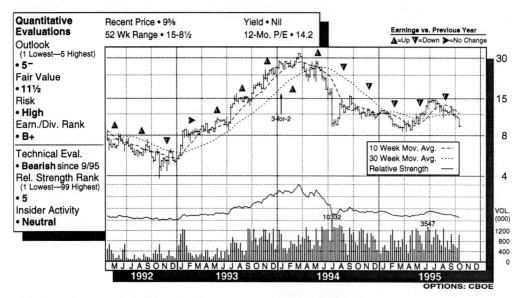

Quantitative Evaluations

Outlook
(1 Lowest—5 Highest)
• **5-**

Fair Value
• **11½**

Risk
• **High**

Earn./Div. Rank
• **B+**

Technical Eval.
• **Bearish** since 9/95

Rel. Strength Rank
(1 Lowest—99 Highest)
• **5**

Insider Activity
• **Neutral**

Recent Price • 9⅜
52 Wk Range • 15-8½
Yield • Nil
12-Mo. P/E • 14.2

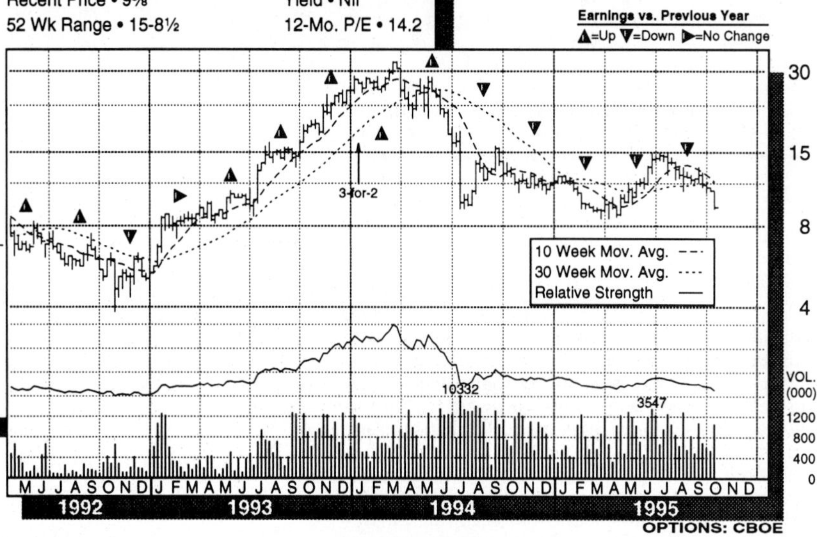

OPTIONS: CBOE

Business Profile - 11-OCT-95

MicroAge is a leading master reseller that markets, distributes and integrates information technology products and services through a growing international network of resellers. The goals of a recently-formed business unit, MicroAge Data Services, include examining ways to use the Internet for business transactions, expanding and extending MICA's existing Electronic Data Interchange systems, and investigating creative ways to package technology information through CD-ROMS and other platforms.

Operational Review - 17-OCT-95

Revenues for the 39 weeks ended July 29, 1995, climbed 37% year to year, driven by continued growth in sales to large accounts and value added resellers. However, profitability was hurt by heightened price competition and costs related to capacity expansion. With sharply higher other expense and taxes at 43.7% versus 39.6%, net income fell 53% to $5,965,000 ($0.42 per share, based on 10% more shares) from $12,794,000 ($0.98).

Stock Performance - 13-OCT-95

In the past 30 trading days, MICA's shares have declined 21%, compared to a 4% rise in the S&P 500. Average trading volume for the past five days was 209,440 shares, compared with the 40-day moving average of 147,167 shares.

Key Stock Statistics

Dividend Rate/Share	Nil	Shareholders	500
Shs. outstg. (M)	14.3	Market cap. (B)	$0.138
Avg. daily vol. (M)	0.144	Inst. holdings	48%
Tang. Bk. Value/Share	11.12	Insider holdings	NA
Beta	1.59		

Value of $10,000 invested 5 years ago: $ 19,397

Fiscal Year Ending Oct. 31

	1995	% Change	1994	% Change	1993	% Change
Revenues (Million $)						
1Q	674.3	43%	470.4	43%	328.0	33%
2Q	743.5	40%	529.6	45%	365.0	57%
3Q	759.1	30%	583.4	49%	392.1	54%
4Q	—	—	637.4	50%	425.2	50%
Yr.	—	—	2,221	47%	1,510	48%
Income (Million $)						
1Q	2.87	-37%	4.53	157%	1.76	34%
2Q	2.43	-53%	5.16	146%	2.10	69%
3Q	0.66	-79%	3.11	2%	3.04	100%
4Q	—	—	3.55	-1%	3.60	NM
Yr.	—	—	16.34	56%	10.50	124%
Earnings Per Share ($)						
1Q	0.20	-44%	0.36	80%	0.20	NM
2Q	0.17	-59%	0.41	76%	0.23	40%
3Q	0.05	-78%	0.23	-31%	0.33	92%
4Q	—	—	0.25	-34%	0.38	NM
Yr.	—	—	1.22	6%	1.15	95%

Next earnings report expected: early December

MicroAge, Inc.

Business Summary - 11-OCT-95

MicroAge, Inc. is a leading franchisor of computer stores and a distributor of microcomputers, workstations, peripherals and software. The MicroAge Computer Store Network specializes in the sale, support and servicing of information technology products, consisting primarily of stand-alone and multiuser microcomputer systems and software, networking and telecommunication equipment and related services for business applications.

At October 31, 1994, the company had 2,514 locations in operation (up from 1,555 a year earlier), consisting of 753 franchised reseller locations, nine company-owned locations and 1,752 affiliated resellers. The stores provide products and services to businesses of all sizes. Sales to large national businesses are developed by combined efforts of company-owned sales locations, franchised locations and/or MICA's National Accounts division.

MICA features a variety of franchise and other programs designed to meet market demands and industry conditions. In 1989, the company introduced MicroAge 2000, which requires franchisees to purchase certain vendor products only through MicroAge. It also established an Affiliated Reseller (AR) program, which provides that resellers purchase certain vendors' products from the company and not directly from such vendors. Under each of these programs, MICA receives a markup on products purchased from it, but does not receive any royalty fees.

The company also provides a wide variety of services to the Network, including product assortment and distribution, technical support, sales and marketing training and support, financial management and administration of financing programs.

Established distribution agreements exist with selected vendors, including IBM, COMPAQ, Apple, Hewlett-Packard (HP), AT&T, NCR, Novell, Microsoft, NEC, AST and Toshiba. Volume discounts are received from most vendors, allowing the sale of products to franchisees and ARs on a more favorable basis than they could obtain on their own. In fiscal 1994, sales of COMPAQ, HP, IBM and Apple products accounted respectively for 22%, 19%, 19% and 12% of revenue from sales of merchandise.

In June 1995, MICA formed a new unit, MicroAge Data Services, designed to capture, manage and deliver product and market information to technology manufacturers, resellers, consultants and end-users.

Important Developments

Aug. '95—MICA increased its working capital financing facilities to $500 million through a three-year agreement with Deutsche Financial Services and IBM Credit Corp., which included an accounts receivable sale facility, a working capital revolver and inventory financing facilities.

Capitalization

Long Term Debt: $3,835,000 (7/95).

Per Share Data ($) (Year Ended Oct. 31)

	1994	1993	1992	1991	1990	1989
Tangible Bk. Val.	11.11	13.48	6.32	4.87	4.27	3.66
Cash Flow	1.91	2.77	1.20	1.05	1.41	0.98
Earnings	1.22	1.15	0.59	0.50	0.97	0.64
Dividends	Nil	Nil	Nil	Nil	Nil	Nil
Payout Ratio	Nil	Nil	Nil	Nil	Nil	Nil
Prices - High	32½	26⅝	10½	10⅛	12⅜	7⅛
- Low	9¼	5⅜	3⅞	3⅞	4⅛	4⅛
P/E Ratio - High	27	23	18	20	13	11
- Low	8	5	6	8	4	6

Income Statement Analysis (Million $)

	1994	%Chg	1993	%Chg	1992	%Chg	1991
Revs.	2,221	47%	1,510	48%	1,017	29%	787
Oper. Inc.	41.8	67%	25.1	87%	13.4	34%	10.0
Depr.	9.3	45%	6.4	32%	4.8	36%	3.5
Int. Exp.	1.3	88%	0.7	-58%	1.6	-2%	1.6
Pretax Inc.	27.0	54%	17.5	124%	7.8	34%	5.8
Eff. Tax Rate	39%	—	40%	—	40%	—	44%
Net Inc.	16.3	55%	10.5	124%	4.7	44%	3.2

Balance Sheet & Other Fin. Data (Million $)

	1994	1993	1992	1991	1990	1989
Cash	11.1	20.2	23.2	14.7	2.5	3.0
Curr. Assets	456	298	205	141	100	82.0
Total Assets	510	323	227	162	113	92.0
Curr. Liab.	342	214	161	117	74.0	58.0
LT Debt	2.1	1.2	9.3	11.0	8.8	6.4
Common Eqty.	166	108	56.9	33.5	29.7	27.0
Total Cap.	168	109	66.2	44.5	38.5	33.4
Cap. Exp.	17.6	7.9	4.9	8.4	4.9	1.6
Cash Flow	25.6	16.9	9.5	6.8	9.4	6.3

Ratio Analysis

	1994	1993	1992	1991	1990	1989
Curr. Ratio	1.3	1.4	1.3	1.2	1.3	1.4
% LT Debt of Cap.	1.2	1.1	14.1	24.7	22.9	19.2
% Net Inc.of Revs.	0.7	0.7	0.5	0.4	1.1	1.2
% Ret. on Assets	3.7	3.3	2.1	2.4	6.4	5.7
% Ret. on Equity	11.1	11.3	9.1	10.2	23.1	16.5

Dividend Data —No cash has been paid. Under its credit agreements, MicroAge is prohibited from paying any dividend without the bank's consent. A three-for-two stock split was effected in January 1994.

Data as orig. reptd.; bef. results of disc. opers. and/or spec. items. Per share data adj. for stk. divs. as of ex-div. date. E-Estimated. NA-Not Available. NM-Not Meaningful. NR-Not Ranked.

Tel—(602) 804-2000. **Chrmn & CEO**—J. D. McKeever. **Pres**—R. K. Waters. **Vice Chrmn & Secy**—A. P. Hald. **SVP, CFO & Treas**—J. R. Daniel. **Investor Contact**—Curtis J. Scheel (602-929-2414). **Dirs**—K. Eguchi, A. P. Hald, F. Israel, J. D. McKeever, W. H. Mallender, S. G. Mihaylo. **Transfer Agent & Registrar**—First Interstate Bank of Arizona, Phoenix. **Incorporated** in Delaware in 1987. **Empl**-1,729. **S&P Analyst:** Maureen C. Carini

Mohawk Industries

NASDAQ Symbol **MOHK**
In S&P SmallCap 600

31-OCT-95

Industry: Home Furnishings

Summary: This producer of woven and tufted broadloom carpeting for residential and commercial applications is among the world's largest manufacturers of carpeting.

Quantitative Evaluations

Outlook (1 Lowest—5 Highest)
• **5**

Fair Value
• **19**

Risk
• **High**

Earn./Div. Rank
• **NR**

Technical Eval.
• **Bullish** since 4/95

Rel. Strength Rank (1 Lowest—99 Highest)
• **16**

Insider Activity
• **Neutral**

Recent Price • 15⅜
52 Wk Range • 19¼-10¾
Yield • Nil
12-Mo. P/E • 21.4

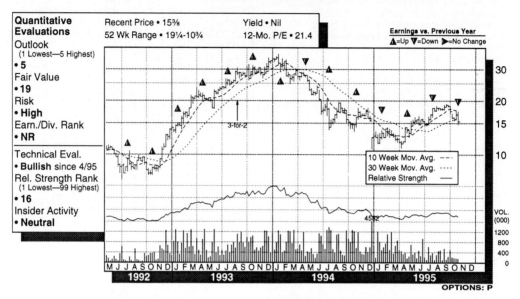

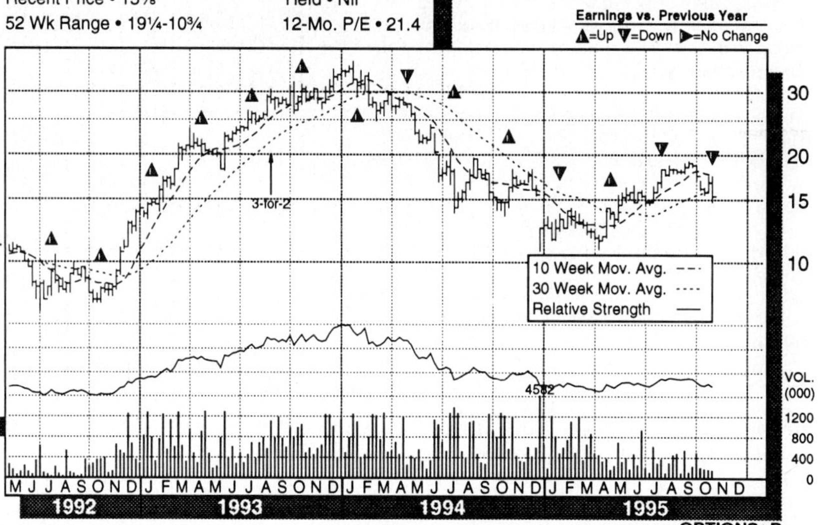

OPTIONS: P

Business Profile - 26-OCT-95

This company produces carpet for residential and commercial applications, and is among the world's largest carpet makers. Two 1993 purchases and the early 1994 acquisition of Aladdin Mills approximately tripled the sales base. Although the company had stressed products in the medium-to-high price rango, the purchase of Aladdin expanded its presence in the low-to-medium price segment. Operations were further expanded by the early 1995 acquisition of Galaxy Carpet Mills.

Operational Review - 31-OCT-95

Net sales in the first nine months of 1995 advanced 15%, year to year, reflecting the acquisition of Galaxy Carpet Mills, as well as strong sales growth of Aladdin and American Rug. However, net income declined 35% due to soft market conditions and continued high raw material costs, which the company was unable to pass through to customers. Mohawk has been consolidating various operations in an effort to improve results.

Stock Performance - 27-OCT-95

In the past 30 trading days, MOHK's shares have declined 19%, compared to a 0.63% fall in the S&P 500. Average trading volume for the past five days was 28,340 shares, compared with the 40-day moving average of 51,485 shares.

Key Stock Statistics

Dividend Rate/Share	Nil	Shareholders	600
Shs. outstg. (M)	33.0	Market cap. (B)	$0.495
Avg. daily vol. (M)	0.031	Inst. holdings	50%
Tang. Bk. Value/Share	6.37	Insider holdings	NA
Beta	NA		

Value of $10,000 invested 5 years ago: NA

Fiscal Year Ending Dec. 31

	1995	% Change	1994	% Change	1993	% Change
Revenues (Million $)						
1Q	379.8	16%	327.1	133%	140.5	120%
2Q	429.8	16%	370.5	136%	156.9	101%
3Q	425.3	13%	377.6	74%	216.9	179%
4Q	—	—	362.1	65%	219.7	66%
Yr.	—	—	1,437	96%	734.0	108%
Income (Million $)						
1Q	4.31	NM	-0.43	NM	5.76	—
2Q	5.62	-55%	12.46	25%	9.94	—
3Q	6.63	-50%	13.36	14%	11.67	—
4Q	—	—	7.61	-37%	12.15	117%
Yr.	—	—	33.01	-16%	39.52	NM
Earnings Per Share ($)						
1Q	0.13	NM	-0.01	NM	0.12	NM
2Q	0.17	-54%	0.37	19%	0.31	55%
3Q	0.20	-50%	0.40	11%	0.36	33%
4Q	—	—	0.23	-36%	0.36	16%
Yr.	—	—	0.99	-15%	1.16	35%

Next earnings report expected: late January

Mohawk Industries

Business Summary - 31-OCT-95

Mohawk Industries, Inc. is a leading maker of both woven and tufted broadloom carpets and rugs for residential and commercial markets. It is the second largest U.S. carpet and rug manufacturer. Operations are organized into four business units: Residential Business; Commercial Business; American Rug; and Aladdin.

The company designs, makes and markets hundreds of carpet styles in a broad range of colors, textures and patterns, with the products positioned in all price ranges. It also offers a broad line of washable accent and bath rugs and area rugs. Products are sold primarily through specialty retailers and commercial dealers and to selected end-users.

The residential business sells hundreds of carpet styles, with most shipments consisting of tufted broadloom carpet. The division has positioned its premier brand names, Mohawk, Alexander Smith, Horizon, Karastan and Bigelow, to sell mainly in the medium-to-high price range in the residential market, and also sells the lines under private labels.

The commercial market is segmented into several sub-markets: educational institutions, corporate office space, hospitality facilities, retail space and health care facilities. In addition, Mohawk sells carpet for the export market, the federal government and other niche markets. Brand names include Mohawk Commercial, Harbinger, Helios and Karastan Bigelow.

American Rug is a rapidly growing manufacturer of household rugs and mats, offering one of the broadest lines of any domestic supplier. American maintains a capability for the production of about 1,200 proprietary designs.

Aladdin is a leading maker of tufted broadloom carpet and washable accent and bath rugs in the U.S. Aladdin's carpet products, sold under the Aladdin, Townhouse, Ciboney, Modesto and Hamilton brand names, and under private labels, generally compete in middle-to-low-end retail markets.

In January 1995, Mohawk acquired the Galaxy Carpet Mills unit (annual sales of about $200 million) of Peerless Carpet Corp. for $43.3 million in cash. Galaxy makes broadloom carpet for sale mainly in the mid-to-upper price points of the residential market.

Important Developments

Oct. '95—Management said it has been challenged by soft market conditions and continued raw material cost increases that could not be passed on to consumers. The company noted that it began to see some relief from the cost pressures at the end of the third quarter, when polypropylene and latex costs decreased slightly, but it still expects results to be restricted in future periods by the adverse market conditions.

Capitalization

Long Term Debt: $438,400,000 (9/95).

Per Share Data ($)

(Year Ended Dec. 31)

	1994	1993	1992	1991	1990	1989
Tangible Bk. Val.	6.37	5.79	4.35	1.45	NA	NA
Cash Flow	2.47	2.32	1.33	0.99	NA	NA
Earnings	0.99	1.16	0.86	0.51	NA	NA
Dividends	Nil	Nil	Nil	Nil	NA	NA
Payout Ratio	Nil	Nil	Nil	Nil	NA	NA
Prices - High	36½	34¾	14⅜	NA	NA	NA
- Low	10¾	13⅛	7¼	NA	NA	NA
P/E Ratio - High	37	30	17	NA	NA	NA
- Low	11	11	8	NA	NA	NA

Income Statement Analysis (Million $)

	1994	%Chg	1993	%Chg	1992	%Chg	1991
Revs.	1,437	96%	734	108%	353	27%	279
Oper. Inc.	148	99%	74.4	122%	33.5	29%	25.9
Depr.	49.5	118%	22.7	NM	7.1	34%	5.3
Int. Exp.	27.1	98%	13.7	161%	5.2	-47%	9.9
Pretax Inc.	58.2	48%	39.3	82%	21.6	106%	10.5
Eff. Tax Rate	43%	—	42%	—	40%	—	39%
Net Inc.	33.0	45%	22.7	73%	13.1	105%	6.4

Balance Sheet & Other Fin. Data (Million $)

	1994	1993	1992	1991	1990	1989
Cash	Nil	Nil	Nil	2.9	NA	NA
Curr. Assets	454	287	166	78.0	NA	NA
Total Assets	855	561	278	116	NA	NA
Curr. Liab.	162	134	67.9	33.4	NA	NA
LT Debt	394	244	114	59.0	NA	NA
Common Eqty.	264	159	89.3	15.9	NA	NA
Total Cap.	691	426	208	81.0	NA	NA
Cap. Exp.	78.0	33.9	7.7	4.8	NA	NA
Cash Flow	82.5	45.4	20.0	11.0	NA	NA

Ratio Analysis

	1994	1993	1992	1991	1990	1989
Curr. Ratio	2.8	2.2	2.4	2.3	NA	NA
% LT Debt of Cap.	57.0	57.2	54.7	72.1	NA	NA
% Net Inc.of Revs.	2.3	3.1	3.7	2.3	NA	NA
% Ret. on Assets	3.6	5.1	5.8	5.3	NA	NA
% Ret. on Equity	12.3	17.1	23.0	43.7	NA	NA

Dividend Data —No cash dividends have been paid. A three-for-two stock split was effected in August 1993.

Data as orig. reptd.; bef. results of disc. opers. and/or spec. items. Per share data adj. for stk. divs. as of ex-div. date. E-Estimated. NA-Not Available. NM-Not Meaningful. NR-Not Ranked.

Office—1755 The Exchange, Atlanta, GA 30339. **Tel**—(404) 951-6000. **Chrmn & CEO**—D. L. Kolb. **Pres & COO**—J. S. Lorberbaum. **VP-Fin, CFO, Secy & Investor Contact**—John D. Swift (404-951-6221). **Dirs**—L. Benatar, B. C. Bruckmann, D. L. Kolb, A. S. Lorberbaum, J. S. Lorberbaum, L. W. McCurdy, R. N. Pokelwaldt, R. W. Schipke. **Transfer Agent & Registrar**—First Union National Bank of North Carolina, Charlotte. **Incorporated** in Delaware in 1988. **Empl**-15,065. **S&P Analyst:** Philip D. Wohl

STANDARD & POOR'S

STOCK REPORTS

Molecular Biosystems

NYSE Symbol **MB**

In S&P SmallCap 600

13-SEP-95

Industry: Medical equipment/ supply

Summary: This company is developing ultrasound contrast agents for medical imaging.

Quantitative Evaluations

Recent Price • 9¾ | Yield • Nil

52 Wk Range • 14¼-5¼ | 12-Mo. P/E • NM

Outlook (1 Lowest—5 Highest)
• NA

Fair Value
• NA

Risk
• High

Earn./Div. Rank
• C

Technical Eval.
• Bearish since 12/93

Rel. Strength Rank (1 Lowest—99 Highest)
• 90

Insider Activity
• NA

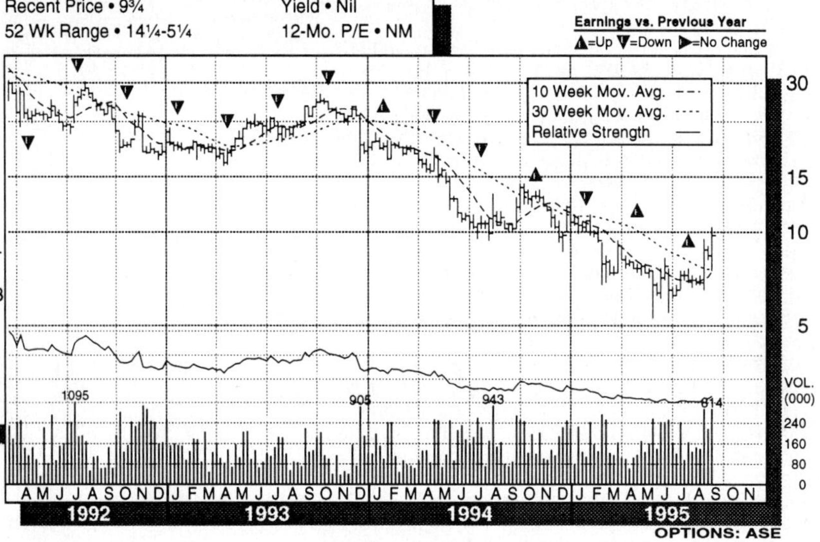

Business Profile - 13-SEP-95

The company reached a major new marketing arrangement in September 1995 with Mallinckrodt Group, potentially worth $47.5 million. In early 1995, MB restructured operations to focus on ultrasound-related products. The company significantly reduced staff and research expenditures. Although product revenues rose sharply in 1994-5, they accounted for 10% of total revenues. Revenue gains mainly reflected milestone payments. Quarterly losses are likely to continue through 1995-6.

Operational Review - 13-SEP-95

Revenues for the three months ended June 30, 1995, declined 34%, year to year, representing lower product sales ($28,000 versus $509,000) and, to a lesser extent, reduced license fees. Total costs were down 27%, aided by substantially lower R&D expenses and workforce reductions. The net loss narrowed to $4,518,000 ($0.37 a share), from $5,913,000 ($0.49).

Stock Performance - 08-SEP-95

In the past 30 trading days, MB's shares have increased 39%, compared to a 2% rise in the S&P 500. Average trading volume for the past five days was 203,525 shares, compared with the 40-day moving average of 64,138 shares.

Key Stock Statistics

Dividend Rate/Share	Nil	Shareholders	3,300
Shs. outstg. (M)	12.2	Market cap. (B)	$0.111
Avg. daily vol. (M)	0.104	Inst. holdings	32%
Tang. Bk. Value/Share	2.89	Insider holdings	NA
Beta	1.28		

Value of $10,000 invested 5 years ago: $ 4,309

Fiscal Year Ending Mar. 31

	1996	% Change	1995	% Change	1994	% Change
Revenues (Million $)						
1Q	0.35	-34%	0.53	-78%	2.36	134%
2Q	—	—	8.79	NM	0.37	-71%
3Q	—	—	6.91	25%	5.53	NM
4Q	—	—	0.71	37%	0.52	-4%
Yr.	—	—	16.94	93%	8.78	138%
Income (Million $)						
1Q	-4.52	NM	-5.91	NM	-2.77	NM
2Q	—	—	2.08	NM	-5.81	NM
3Q	—	—	-2.24	NM	-1.12	NM
4Q	—	—	-6.12	NM	-9.10	NM
Yr.	—	—	-12.18	NM	-18.80	NM
Earnings Per Share ($)						
1Q	-0.37	NM	-0.49	NM	-0.23	NM
2Q	—	—	0.17	NM	-0.49	NM
3Q	—	—	-0.19	NM	-0.09	NM
4Q	—	—	-0.51	NM	-0.76	NM
Yr.	—	—	-1.02	NM	-1.58	NM

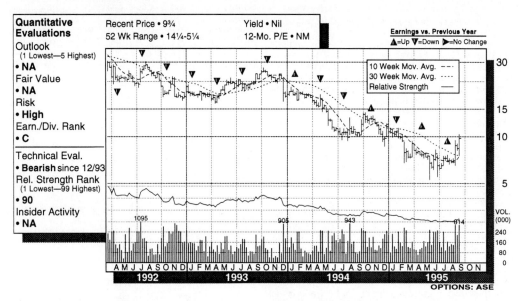

Next earnings report expected: early November

Molecular Biosystems

Business Summary - 13-SEP-95

Molecular Biosystems, Inc. is a leading developer and manufacturer of contrast agents used in medical imaging. Its research focuses on products for use with ultrasound equipment.

The principal focus of the company's development of diagnostic imaging products has been on the contrast agent Albunex. Albunex, based on MB's proprietary technology, is capable of transpulmonary passage after intravenous admission (i.e., to pass from the right side of the heart through the lungs and into the left side of the heart). When injected, Albunex reflects ultrasound waves in the blood approximately 100 times more strongly than blood alone. The company believes that the product can also enhance ultrasound imaging applications that rely on the Doppler effect.

In August 1994 (following FDA approval), Albunex became the first transpulmonary ultrasound imaging agent available for U.S. sale. The product is being sold by Mallinckrodt Medical Inc. in the U.S., by Shionogi & Co. Ltd. in Japan and by Hafslund Nycomed AS in Europe.

The company plans to pursue further applications of Albunex in cardiovascular ultrasound imaging, including myocardial perfusion (the assessment of blood flow in the heart muscle tissue) and as an intra-arterial agent to use with cardiac catheterization. Phase I/II trials are under way to investigate the safety and efficacy of Albunex delivered intra-arterially following the surgical implantation of coronary artery grafts.

MB is also developing Oralex, an orally administered agent to enhance ultrasound imaging of the gastrointestinal tract and surrounding organs. A second ultrasound contrasting agent, FS069, is in Phase I clinical trials.

In February 1995, the company initiated a restructuring by terminating the development of non-ultrasound products and reducing its staff by 24%. As a result, MB expects annual operating costs to be cut by about $6 million.

Important Developments

Sep. '95—MB and Mallinckrodt Group entered into a new distribution and investment agreement for Albunex. Mallinckrodt will purchase $13 million of MB common stock (10% ownership), pay $20 million over four years to support FS069 clinical trials and potentially pay up to an additional $14.5 million for further clinical funding and milestone achievements. In exchange, Mallinckrodt will have expanded marketing and sales rights on Albunex and FS069.

Capitalization

Long Term Debt: $8,333,000 (6/95).

Per Share Data ($)

(Year Ended Mar. 31)

	1995	1994	1993	1992	1991	1990
Tangible Bk. Val.	NA	3.88	5.38	6.62	3.58	3.53
Cash Flow	NA	-1.46	-0.89	0.03	0.05	0.63
Earnings	-1.02	-1.58	-1.01	-0.05	-0.02	0.43
Dividends	Nil	Nil	Nil	Nil	Nil	Nil
Payout Ratio	Nil	Nil	Nil	Nil	Nil	Nil
Cal. Yrs.	1994	1993	1992	1991	1990	1989
Prices - High	20¾	27⅝	40⅞	39¼	24⅜	26¼
- Low	8⅝	16¼	17	13⅛	13⅛	15⅜
P/E Ratio - High	NM	NM	NM	NM	NM	61
- Low	NM	NM	NM	NM	NM	36

Income Statement Analysis (Million $)

	1994	%Chg	1993	%Chg	1992	%Chg	1991
Revs.	8.8	138%	3.7	-65%	10.7	NM	10.6
Oper. Inc.	-15.3	NM	-14.4	NM	-3.3	NM	-1.0
Depr.	1.4	-6%	1.5	73%	0.8	15%	0.7
Int. Exp.	0.3	-3%	0.3	-26%	0.5	-10%	0.5
Pretax Inc.	-18.8	NM	-13.0	NM	-0.9	NM	-0.4
Eff. Tax Rate	NM	—	NM	—	NM	—	NM
Net Inc.	-18.8	NM	-11.8	NM	-0.6	NM	-0.2

Balance Sheet & Other Fin. Data (Million $)

	1994	1993	1992	1991	1990	1989
Cash	29.5	51.2	67.5	24.4	27.9	25.6
Curr. Assets	32.6	54.7	71.0	26.7	30.7	27.9
Total Assets	56.5	71.8	87.0	43.2	47.6	38.8
Curr. Liab.	4.5	2.9	5.9	2.7	7.2	5.6
LT Debt	3.9	4.0	4.0	4.6	4.6	4.6
Common Eqty.	48.1	64.9	77.2	34.4	33.4	27.2
Total Cap.	52.0	68.9	81.2	39.4	38.0	31.9
Cap. Exp.	8.2	1.8	1.1	0.7	1.9	8.5
Cash Flow	-17.4	-10.4	0.3	0.5	6.1	2.6

Ratio Analysis

	1994	1993	1992	1991	1990	1989
Curr. Ratio	7.3	18.8	12.1	10.0	4.3	5.0
% LT Debt of Cap.	7.5	5.8	4.9	11.7	12.1	14.6
% Net Inc.of Revs.	NM	NM	NM	NM	24.9	24.9
% Ret. on Assets	NM	NM	NM	NM	9.6	7.2
% Ret. on Equity	NM	NM	NM	NM	13.6	9.0

Dividend Data —No cash dividend has ever been paid.

Data as orig. reptd.; bef. results of disc. opers. and/or spec. items. Per share data adj. for stk. divs. as of ex-div. date. E-Estimated. NA-Not Available. NM-Not Meaningful. NR-Not Ranked.

Office—10030 Barnes Canyon Rd., San Diego, CA 92121. **Tel**—(619) 452-0681. **Chrmn & CEO**—K. J. Widder. **VP & Acting COO**—J. L. Barnhart. **VP-Fin & CFO**—G. A. Wills. **Investor Contact**—Beth Wallace. **Dirs**—R. W. Brightfelt, C. C. Edwards, V. A. Frank, G. C. Luce, D. Rubinfien, K. J. Widder. **Transfer Agent & Registrar**—Continental Stock Transfer & Trust Co., NYC. **Incorporated** in Delaware in 1980. **Empl**-115. **S&P Analyst:** Thomas Tirney

STANDARD & POOR'S

STOCK REPORTS

Mosinee Paper

NASDAQ Symbol **MOSI**

In S&P SmallCap 600

14-NOV-95 **Industry:** Paper/Products

Summary: This company manufactures and markets industrial specialty paper products, and converts towel and tissue paper products.

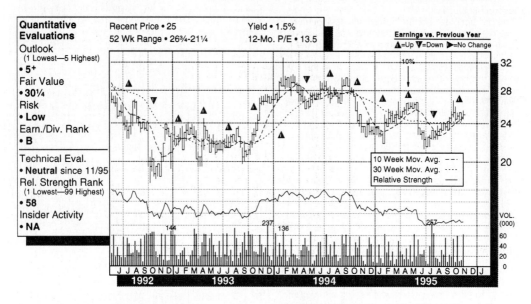

Quantitative Evaluations

Outlook (1 Lowest—5 Highest) • 5+

Fair Value • 30¼

Risk • Low

Earn./Div. Rank • B

Technical Eval. • **Neutral** since 11/95

Rel. Strength Rank (1 Lowest—99 Highest) • 58

Insider Activity • NA

Recent Price • 25

52 Wk Range • 26¾-21¼

Yield • 1.5%

12-Mo. P/E • 13.5

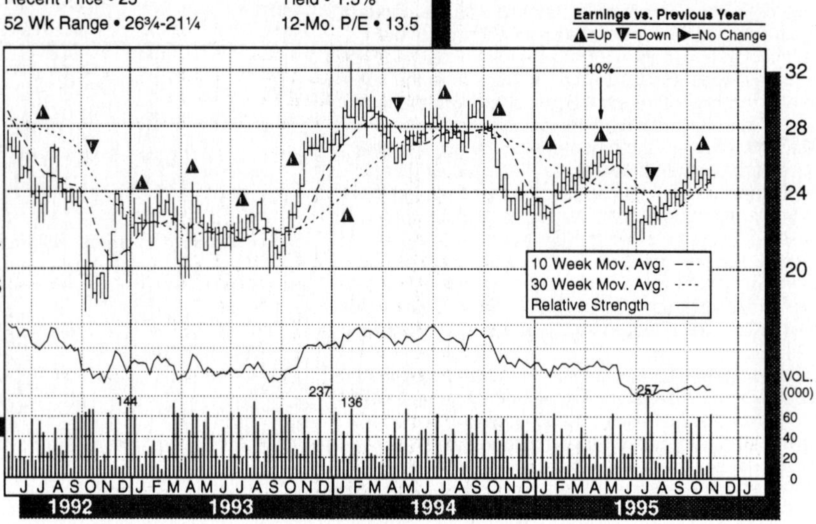

Business Profile - 14-NOV-95

MOSI's growth strategy continues to focus on marketing, productivity and capital investment. The company has benefited from recent price increases and cost reductions, although some softening in the economy has adversely affected the towel and tissue market in recent periods. Industry experts are predicting a shorter supply of towel and tissue, which should help MOSI continue its positive trend into 1996. Long term goals include a 20% return on equity and a 6% return on sales.

Operational Review - 14-NOV-95

Net sales advanced 16%, year to year, in the first nine months of 1995, primarily reflecting improved pricing and, to a lesser extent, increased volume. Operating costs and expenses were well controlled, and despite much higher interest expense, income was up 19%. The company recently noted that selling price increases and lower wastepaper costs have begun to aid margins.

Stock Performance - 10-NOV-95

In the past 30 trading days, MOSI's shares were unchanged, compared to a 1% rise in the S&P 500. Average trading volume for the past five days was 16,280 shares, compared with the 40-day moving average of 6,578 shares.

Key Stock Statistics

Dividend Rate/Share	0.36	Shareholders	4,600
Shs. outstg. (M)	7.9	Market cap. (B)	$0.194
Avg. daily vol. (M)	0.013	Inst. holdings	51%
Tang. Bk. Value/Share	11.92	Insider holdings	NA
Beta	0.23		

Value of $10,000 invested 5 years ago: $ 16,685

Fiscal Year Ending Dec. 31

	1995	% Change	1994	% Change	1993	% Change
Revenues (Million $)						
1Q	72.58	17%	62.00	9%	57.10	9%
2Q	74.67	15%	64.78	7%	60.33	5%
3Q	79.42	17%	67.81	4%	65.35	9%
4Q	—	—	72.12	16%	62.13	11%
Yr.	—	—	266.7	9%	244.8	9%
Income (Million $)						
1Q	3.41	35%	2.52	-45%	4.60	NM
2Q	2.89	NM	2.88	113%	1.35	85%
3Q	3.79	24%	3.06	52%	2.01	NM
4Q	—	—	4.58	173%	1.68	NM
Yr.	—	—	13.04	35%	9.64	NM
Earnings Per Share ($)						
1Q	0.43	35%	0.32	-45%	0.58	NM
2Q	0.36	NM	0.36	111%	0.17	90%
3Q	0.48	26%	0.38	50%	0.25	NM
4Q	—	—	0.58	178%	0.21	NM
Yr.	—	—	1.65	35%	1.22	NM

Next earnings report expected: early February

Mosinee Paper

Business Summary - 14-NOV-95

Mosinee Paper Corporation manufactures and markets paper and paper products, principally industrial specialty kraft papers and converted papers. In 1994, specialty paper production capacity was about 138,900 tons, towel and tissue production capacity totaled 83,000 tons, pulp production capacity amounted to 86,000 tons, and deink pulp capacity was approximately 86,000 tons. The company's Bay West and Mosinee Converted Products divisions had the capacity to convert a total of 121,000 tons of paper.

The Pulp and Paper division manufactures more than 300 different types of industrial specialty kraft papers for direct sale to paper converters for further processing into end-use items. Principal products include industrial crepe paper, masking paper, converting and waxing papers, gumming paper, foil laminating paper, flame-resistant paper, specialty metal interleaver, cable wrap, electrical insulation, pressure-sensitive backing, water base and film coating, ink-jet printing papers, toweling and packaging papers. Customers include companies in the housing, automotive, metals, consumer packaging, food processing, home appliance, consumer goods and printing industries.

Sorg Paper makes a variety of highly technical specialty papers, including: menu, blotting, latex label and construction papers; facial tissue, napkin and tablecloth papers; filter paper for vacuum bags; and decorative laminates.

The Mosinee Converted Products division produces printed papers used primarily for product wrapping, protective food papers, laminated fiber can-body stock and moisture barrier wrappers. Markets include the corrugated container, household products, battery, composite can, building materials and packaging industries.

The Bay West division produces a "washroom system," including towels, tissues, hand soap and dispensers, primarily for the commercial and institutional wash room product market, including recreation, health care, food service, manufacturing, education and automotive customers.

Mosinee Industrial Forest supplies pulpwood for the Pulp and Paper divison. In 1994, a harvest of 31,520 cords of pulpwood was produced on some 87,145 acres of natural and plantation woodlands.

Important Developments

Oct. '95—Mosinee said it expects near-term margins to benefit from higher selling prices and lower wastepaper costs. It also projected strong results for 1996.

Capitalization

Long Term Debt: $91,333,000 (6/95).
Subsidiary Preferred Stock: $1,255,000.

Per Share Data ($) (Year Ended Dec. 31)

	1994	1993	1992	1991	1990	1989
Tangible Bk. Val.	11.11	10.00	9.10	10.35	10.59	9.25
Cash Flow	3.45	2.99	1.94	1.45	2.66	1.42
Earnings	1.65	1.22	-0.01	0.11	1.55	0.20
Dividends	0.33	0.33	0.33	0.32	0.28	0.25
Payout Ratio	20%	27%	NM	297%	18%	122%
Prices - High	32¾	27½	34½	31⅛	19½	21⅞
- Low	22½	19½	18⅛	16⅞	14½	14⅜
P/E Ratio - High	20	23	NM	NM	13	NM
- Low	14	16	NM	NM	9	NM

Income Statement Analysis (Million $)

	1994	%Chg	1993	%Chg	1992	%Chg	1991
Revs.	267	9%	245	8%	226	15%	197
Oper. Inc.	40.2	24%	32.3	45%	22.3	39%	16.1
Depr.	14.2	2%	13.9	-9%	15.2	46%	10.4
Int. Exp.	5.1	-10%	5.7	-27%	7.8	69%	4.6
Pretax Inc.	21.5	24%	17.4	NM	0.1	-95%	2.0
Eff. Tax Rate	40%	—	45%	—	37%	—	55%
Net Inc.	13.0	35%	9.6	—	NM	—	0.8

Balance Sheet & Other Fin. Data (Million $)

	1994	1993	1992	1991	1990	1989
Cash	1.6	1.5	0.8	1.8	4.2	2.6
Curr. Assets	63.0	57.7	53.7	50.1	55.9	49.0
Total Assets	265	252	248	249	152	127
Curr. Liab.	36.7	36.4	40.2	34.2	31.6	33.1
LT Debt	91.0	96.0	100	110	14.0	1.0
Common Eqty.	88.9	79.1	72.1	80.9	81.7	72.1
Total Cap.	203	195	186	209	112	87.0
Cap. Exp.	20.0	13.0	14.0	114	26.0	13.0
Cash Flow	27.2	23.5	15.1	11.2	20.6	11.2

Ratio Analysis

	1994	1993	1992	1991	1990	1989
Curr. Ratio	1.7	1.6	1.3	1.5	1.8	1.5
% LT Debt of Cap.	45.0	49.4	53.6	52.8	12.4	1.2
% Net Inc.of Revs.	4.9	3.9	NM	0.4	5.7	0.7
% Ret. on Assets	5.0	3.8	NM	0.4	8.6	1.3
% Ret. on Equity	15.4	12.7	NM	1.0	15.6	2.2

Dividend Data —Cash has been paid each year since 1942.

Amt. of Div. $	Date Decl.	Ex-Div. Date	Stock of Record	Payment Date
0.090	Dec. 15	Jan. 06	Jan. 12	Jan. 26 '95
0.090	Apr. 20	Apr. 28	May. 04	May. 18 '95
10% Stk.	Apr. 20	Apr. 28	May. 04	May. 18 '95
0.090	Jun. 22	Jul. 18	Jul. 20	Aug. 03 '95
0.090	Oct. 19	Oct. 31	Nov. 02	Nov. 16 '95

Data as orig. reptd.; bef. results of disc. opers. and/or spec. items. Per share data adj. for stk. divs. as of ex-div. date. E-Estimated. NA-Not Available. NM-Not Meaningful. NR-Not Ranked.

Office—1244 Kronenwetter Dr., Mosinee, WI 54455-9099. **Tel**—(715) 693-4470. **Chrmn**—S. W. Orr, Jr. **Pres & CEO**—D. R. Olvey. **SVP-Fin, CFO, Secy, Treas & Investor Contract**—Gary P. Peterson. **Dirs**—W. Alexander, R. G. Jacobus, D. R. Olvey, S. W. Orr, Jr., R. L. Radt. **Transfer Agent & Registrar**—Norwest Bank Minnesota, South St. Paul. **Incorporated** in Wisconsin in 1910. **Empl**-1,295. **S&P Analyst:** Stewart Scharf

STANDARD & POOR'S

STOCK REPORTS

Mueller Industries

NYSE Symbol **MLI**
In S&P SmallCap 600

07-SEP-95

Industry:
Metal

Summary: Through subsidiaries, this company fabricates brass, bronze, copper, plastic and aluminum products, owns a short line railroad, and mines gold.

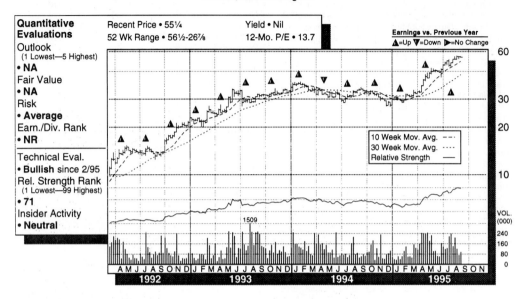

Quantitative Evaluations
Outlook
(1 Lowest—5 Highest)
• **NA**
Fair Value
• **NA**
Risk
• **Average**
Earn./Div. Rank
• **NR**

Technical Eval.
• **Bullish** since 2/95
Rel. Strength Rank
(1 Lowest—99 Highest)
• **71**
Insider Activity
• **Neutral**

Recent Price • 55¼
52 Wk Range • 56½-26⅞
Yield • Nil
12-Mo. P/E • 13.7

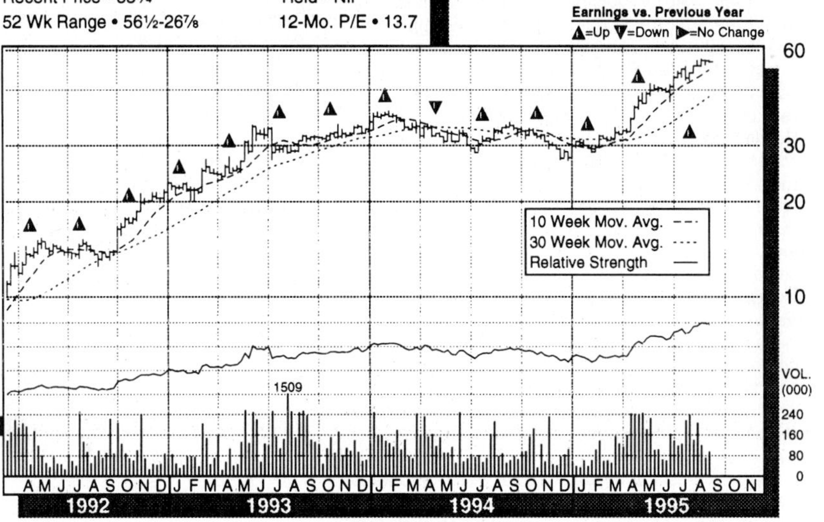

Business Profile - 07-SEP-95

Results have rebounded strongly since the company emerged from bankruptcy in 1990. Profitability was restored in 1992, and earnings have continued to advance through the first half of 1995. The shares, which surged nearly eight-fold since early 1992, were recently trading at about 13X the analyst EPS estimate of $4.25 for 1995, and at less than 11X the 1996 estimate of $5.20. A two-for-one stock split was declared in August.

Operational Review - 07-SEP-95

Net sales in the six months ended July 1, 1995, rose 37%, year to year, as higher sales volume reflected in part the September 1994 acquisition of two plastic manufacturing facilities, as well as price increases in the manufacturing segment. Margins widened, aided by the higher volume and productivity improvements; operating income advanced 61%. After taxes at 31.6%, versus 36.9%, net income more than doubled, to $20.7 miilion ($2.18 a share), from $10.0 million ($0.97).

Stock Performance - 01-SEP-95

In the past 30 trading days, MLI's shares have increased 13%, compared to a 2% rise in the S&P 500. Average trading volume for the past five days was 18,540 shares, compared with the 40-day moving average of 29,925 shares.

Key Stock Statistics

Dividend Rate/Share	Nil	Shareholders	4,200
Shs. outstg. (M)	8.6	Market cap. (B)	$0.478
Avg. daily vol. (M)	0.018	Inst. holdings	57%
Tang. Bk. Value/Share	30.18	Insider holdings	NA
Beta	NA		

Value of $10,000 invested 5 years ago: NA

Fiscal Year Ending Dec. 31

	1995	% Change	1994	% Change	1993	% Change
Revenues (Million $)						
1Q	171.8	42%	120.8	-8%	131.0	11%
2Q	181.4	33%	136.6	7%	127.3	-3%
3Q	—	—	138.0	13%	122.1	-17%
4Q	—	—	154.6	27%	121.4	NM
Yr.	—	—	550.0	10%	501.9	-3%
Income (Million $)						
1Q	10.05	140%	4.18	NM	4.21	18%
2Q	10.66	84%	5.78	9%	5.31	33%
3Q	—	—	8.52	51%	5.64	34%
4Q	—	—	9.45	58%	5.98	35%
Yr.	—	—	27.93	32%	21.14	30%
Earnings Per Share ($)						
1Q	1.06	165%	0.40	-2%	0.41	11%
2Q	1.12	96%	0.57	12%	0.51	28%
3Q	—	—	0.90	67%	0.54	29%
4Q	—	—	1.00	75%	0.57	33%
Yr.	—	—	2.87	42%	2.02	25%

Next earnings report expected: mid October

Mueller Industries

Business Summary - 07-SEP-95

Mueller Industries (formerly Sharon Steel Corp.) primarily fabricates and sells brass, bronze, copper, plastic and aluminum products through its Mueller Brass Co. subsidiary. Mueller Brass operates 12 prodction facilities in five states and Canada, and has distribution facilities nationwide and sales representation worldwide. The company's natural resource subsidiaries are Arava Natural Resources Co., Inc. which engages principally in the operation of a short line railroad; and 85% owned Alaska Gold Co. Prior to emerging from bankruptcy in December 1990, Mueller also engaged in the fabrication and sale of steel products. Manufacturing provided 97% of total sales and operating income in 1994.

The manufacturing segment produces industrial and standard products. Industrial products include brass rod, nonferrous forgings and impact extrusions, which are sold primarily to other manufacturers and distributors. Standard products include copper and red brass pipe, "Streamline" copper tube, wrought and cast fittings and related components for the plumbing and heating industry, and air conditioning refrigeration tubes and dehydrated tubes, valves, wrought copper and brass fittings, filter driers and other related assemblies for the commercial air conditioning and refrigeration industry. A major portion of these products is ultimately used in domestic residential and commercial construction markets and, to a lesser extent, in the automotive and heavy on- and off-road vehicle markets.

Utah Railway Co., a wholly owned subsidiary of Arava, operates about 100 miles of railroad track in Utah. It serves four major customers pursuant to long-term contracts, and transports nearly 4 million tons of coal a year. Alaska Gold mines placer gold in Nome, Alaska. It produced 14,173 net oz. of gold in 1994, down from 22,440 net oz. in 1993. Properties consist of 14,500 acres in and adjacent to Nome. Alaska Gold also owns or has claims on 10,400 acres in the Fairbanks area and 3,000 acres in the Hogatza, Alaska, area. Arava's U.S. Fuel unit, which sold 68,000 net tons of coal in 1993, entered into an agreement in 1994 to sell the majority of its assets.

Important Developments

Jul. '95—MLI said that the sale of the majority of U.S. Fuel's assets, agreed upon in 1994, had not yet been consumated. Extensions have been granted to give the purchaser additional time to finalize financing. U.S. Fuel intends to resume full-scale remediation at its mining site if the sale is not completed.

Capitalization

Long Term Debt: $69,151,000 (7/95).

Per Share Data ($) (Year Ended Dec. 31)

	1994	1993	1992	1991	1990	1989
Tangible Bk. Val.	27.81	23.18	21.21	15.80	20.00	21.50
Cash Flow	4.05	3.30	2.86	-3.12	NA	2.85
Earnings	2.82	2.02	1.61	-4.49	NA	1.54
Dividends	Nil	Nil	Nil	Nil	NA	NA
Payout Ratio	Nil	Nil	Nil	Nil	NA	NA
Prices - High	38⅝	37¼	23⅛	13⅞	NA	NA
- Low	26⅞	20	7	7	NA	NA
P/E Ratio - High	14	18	14	NM	NA	NA
- Low	10	10	4	NM	NA	NA

Income Statement Analysis (Million $)

	1994	%Chg	1993	%Chg	1992	%Chg	1991
Revs.	550	10%	502	-3%	517	17%	441
Oper. Inc.	56.0	9%	51.3	23%	41.8	NM	11.7
Depr.	12.1	-9%	13.3	6%	12.5	-6%	13.3
Int. Exp.	6.7	16%	5.8	2%	5.7	-5%	6.0
Pretax Inc.	41.0	24%	33.0	38%	24.0	NM	-50.0
Eff. Tax Rate	32%	—	37%	—	33%	—	NM
Net Inc.	28.0	33%	21.0	31%	16.0	NM	-44.0

Balance Sheet & Other Fin. Data (Million $)

	1994	1993	1992	1991	1990	1989
Cash	34.5	77.3	44.0	8.0	41.0	39.0
Curr. Assets	184	194	182	152	201	229
Total Assets	431	370	373	335	416	385
Curr. Liab.	67.0	51.0	62.0	89.0	113	84.0
LT Debt	76.1	54.3	62.0	45.0	54.0	55.0
Common Eqty.	242	222	204	153	200	215
Total Cap.	321	280	271	211	261	269
Cap. Exp.	48.2	11.1	11.0	11.8	9.9	NA
Cash Flow	40.0	34.0	29.0	-30.0	21.0	29.0

Ratio Analysis

	1994	1993	1992	1991	1990	1989
Curr. Ratio	2.7	3.8	3.0	1.7	1.8	2.7
% LT Debt of Cap.	23.7	19.4	23.0	21.4	20.7	20.2
% Net Inc.of Revs.	5.1	4.2	3.1	NM	1.6	3.0
% Ret. on Assets	7.3	5.7	4.6	NM	NM	NA
% Ret. on Equity	12.6	9.9	9.1	NM	NM	NA

Dividend Data —No dividends have been paid. The company's ability to pay dividends is limited by financial coverage covenants and restrictions. A poison pill stock purchase rights plan was adopted in November 1994

Amt. of Div. $	Date Decl.	Ex-Div. Date	Stock of Record	Payment Date
2-for-1	Aug. 14	Oct. 02	Sep. 06	Sep. 29 '95

Data as orig. reptd.; bef. results of disc. opers. and/or spec. items. Per share data adj. for stk. divs. as of ex-div. date. E-Estimated. NA-Not Available. NM-Not Meaningful. NR-Not Ranked.

Office—2959 N. Rock Rd., Wichita, KS 67226-1191. **Tel**—(316) 636-6300. **Chrmn**—H. L. Karp. **Pres & CEO**—W. D. O'Hagan. **EVP & CFO**—E. W. Bunkers. **VP & Secy**—W. H. Hensley. **Treas & Investor Contact**—Kent A. McKee. **Dirs**—R.B. Hodes, H. L. Karp, J. A. Mactier, W. D. O'Hagan, R. J. Pasquarelli. **Transfer Agent & Registrar**—Continental Stock Transfer & Trust Co., NYC. **Incorporated** in Pennsylvania in 1900; reincorporated in Delaware in 1990. **Empl**-2,250. **S&P Analyst:** N. Rosenberg

Musicland Stores

NYSE Symbol **MLG**
In S&P SmallCap 600

03-NOV-95 **Industry:** Retail Stores

Summary: This company is the largest U.S. specialty retailer of prerecorded music and video home entertainment products, with more than 1,450 stores in operation.

Quantitative Evaluations
Outlook (1 Lowest—5 Highest) • **5**
Fair Value • **10⅜**
Risk • **High**
Earn./Div. Rank • **NR**
Technical Eval. • **Bearish** since 10/95
Rel. Strength Rank (1 Lowest—99 Highest) • **5**
Insider Activity • **Neutral**

Recent Price • 7⅜
52 Wk Range • 16⅜-6¾
Yield • Nil
12-Mo. P/E • NM

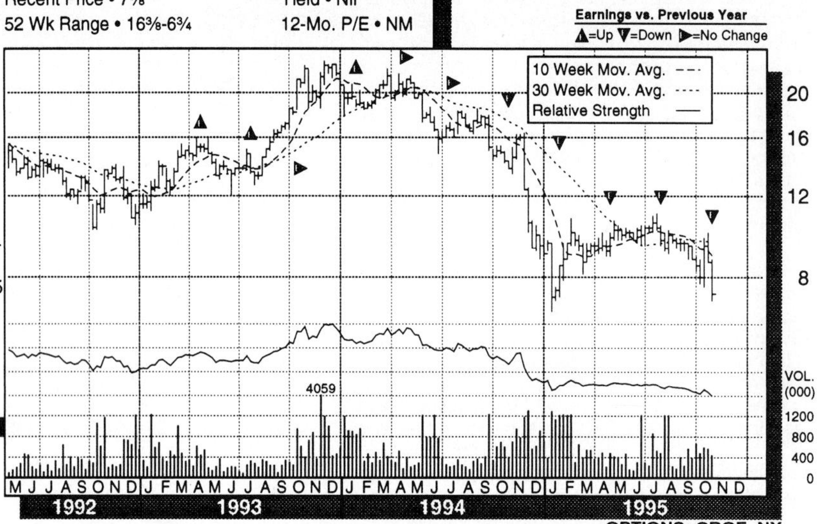

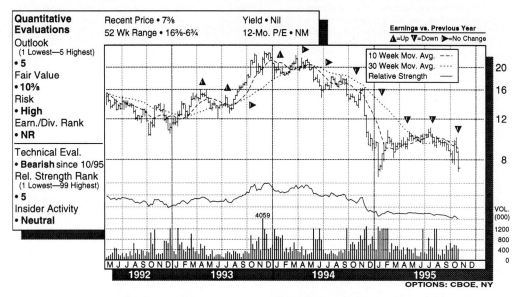

OPTIONS: CBOE, NY

Business Profile - 03-NOV-95

Musicland is the largest retailer of prerecorded music and video home entertainment products in the U.S. The company has been aggressively expanding its store base, mainly through its new specialty formats that feature music, books, entertainment computer software and videos. MLG will continue to focus on the superstore format, with an additional 30 to 40 Media Play and 65 to 75 On Cue stores planned for 1996, while closing some of its mall music stores.

Operational Review - 03-NOV-95

Sales in the nine months ended September 30, 1995, rose 23%, year to year, reflecting growth of 166% for superstores, aided by a 17% increase in comparable store sales. Mall-based stores grew only 0.9%. Margins were hurt by the shift toward the low-price superstores and costs related to new store openings. Following a pretax write-down of goodwill totaling $138 million ($4.09 a share after taxes), the net loss widened to $158.4 million ($4.65 a share) from $6.9 million ($0.20).

Stock Performance - 27-OCT-95

In the past 30 trading days, MLG's shares have declined 21%, compared to a 0.63% fall in the S&P 500. Average trading volume for the past five days was 86,080 shares, compared with the 40-day moving average of 98,833 shares.

Key Stock Statistics

Dividend Rate/Share	Nil	Shareholders	500
Shs. outstg. (M)	34.3	Market cap. (B)	$0.240
Avg. daily vol. (M)	0.107	Inst. holdings	60%
Tang. Bk. Value/Share	2.57	Insider holdings	NA
Beta	NA		

Value of $10,000 invested 5 years ago: NA

Fiscal Year Ending Dec. 31

	1995	% Change	1994	% Change	1993	% Change
Revenues (Million $)						
1Q	346.4	29%	269.4	20%	223.7	21%
2Q	331.7	21%	273.1	23%	222.2	11%
3Q	357.6	18%	302.5	20%	251.3	17%
4Q	—	—	633.9	31%	484.5	15%
Yr.	—	—	1,479	25%	1,182	16%
Income (Million $)						
1Q	-6.31	NM	-2.11	NM	-1.79	NM
2Q	-7.53	NM	-2.20	NM	-1.70	NM
3Q	-144.6	NM	-2.55	NM	0.08	-33%
4Q	—	—	24.24	-30%	34.76	19%
Yr.	—	—	17.38	-45%	31.35	29%
Earnings Per Share ($)						
1Q	-0.18	NM	-0.06	NM	-0.06	NM
2Q	-0.22	NM	-0.06	NM	-0.06	NM
3Q	-4.28	NM	-0.07	—	Nil	—
4Q	—	—	0.71	-35%	1.10	13%
Yr.	—	—	0.51	-50%	1.03	24%

Next earnings report expected: late January

Musicland Stores

Business Summary - 02-NOV-95

Musicland Stores is a leading specialty retailer of home entertainment products, principally in the United States. The company is the largest specialty retailer of prerecorded home entertainment products. At September 30, 1995, it was operating a total of 1,468 retail stores. The stores are located in 49 states, Puerto Rico, the United Kingdom and the Virgin Islands.

The number of stores in operation at the end of recent years was:

	1994	1993	1992	1991
Music	869	875	861	816
Video sell-through	378	320	252	220
Media Play	46	13	1	Nil
On Cue	77	32	13	Nil
United Kingdom	15	10	8	5
Readwell's	1	1	Nil	Nil
Total	1,386	1,251	1,135	1,041

Audio cassettes and other provided 21% of total sales in 1994, compact discs 36%, prerecorded video cassettes 28%, books, 4% and accessories, apparel, blank tapes, and electronic equipment 11%.

Music stores, operated principally under the names Musicland and Sam Goody, offer a full line of music, video and home entertainment products and generally range from moderate sized mall stores to large free-standing, downtown, and mall locations.

Suncoast Motion Picture Co. is the largest chain of stores in the U.S. whose primary focus is video sell-through. The stores, which primarily sell video recordings, also offer special order video cassette and laser disk recordings, movie and video related apparel, and gift products, blank audio and video tapes and other accessories.

International operations (started in April 1990) consist of 18 stores located in the U.K.

In 1992, the company introduced two new specialty store concepts: Media Play and On Cue. Media Play is a 50,000 sq. ft. store selling music, books, videos and entertainment computer software. On Cue sells music, books and videos in smaller markets. At September 30, 1995, there were 70 Media Play stores and 135 On Cue stores.

Important Developments

Nov. '95—MLG reported that its total sales for the four weeks ended October 28, 1995, rose 11.1%, year to year, aided by a 95% increase from superstores.

Oct. '95—The company said that during 1995's third quarter it opened six Media Play stores, 26 On Cue stores, eight Suncoast Motion Picture Company stores and eight Sam Goody music stores, and closed five music stores.

Capitalization

Long Term Debt: $446,000,000 (9/95).

Per Share Data ($)

(Year Ended Dec. 31)

	1994	1993	1992	1991	1990	1989
Tangible Bk. Val.	2.87	2.14	-1.09	NA	NA	NA
Cash Flow	1.60	1.98	1.70	1.37	NA	NA
Earnings	0.51	1.03	0.83	0.58	NA	NA
Dividends	Nil	Nil	Nil	NA	NA	NA
Payout Ratio	Nil	Nil	Nil	NA	NA	NA
Prices - High	22½	23⅜	17⅛	NA	NA	NA
- Low	8¾	11⅛	10⅛	NA	NA	NA
P/E Ratio - High	44	23	21	NA	NA	NA
- Low	17	11	12	NA	NA	NA

Income Statement Analysis (Million $)

	1994	%Chg	1993	%Chg	1992	%Chg	1991
Revs.	1,479	25%	1,182	16%	1,021	10%	932
Oper. Inc.	94.0	-11%	106	12%	94.5	10%	85.6
Depr.	37.2	28%	29.1	18%	24.7	6%	23.3
Int. Exp.	19.6	-1%	19.8	-19%	24.4	-42%	42.4
Pretax Inc.	34.5	-39%	56.8	25%	45.3	27%	35.6
Eff. Tax Rate	50%	—	47%	—	47%	—	48%
Net Inc.	17.4	-45%	31.4	30%	24.2	31%	18.5

Balance Sheet & Other Fin. Data (Million $)

	1994	1993	1992	1991	1990	1989
Cash	38.6	95.8	16.1	NA	NA	NA
Curr. Assets	556	453	282	NA	NA	NA
Total Assets	1,080	906	689	635	NA	NA
Curr. Liab.	583	432	351	NA	NA	NA
LT Debt	110	110	79.0	104	NA	NA
Common Eqty.	340	323	224	193	NA	NA
Total Cap.	456	442	310	308	NA	NA
Cap. Exp.	120	77.1	36.1	NA	NA	NA
Cash Flow	54.6	60.4	48.2	40.5	NA	NA

Ratio Analysis

	1994	1993	1992	1991	1990	1989
Curr. Ratio	1.0	1.1	0.8	NA	NA	NA
% LT Debt of Cap.	24.1	24.9	25.3	33.6	NA	NA
% Net Inc.of Revs.	1.2	2.7	2.4	2.0	NA	NA
% Ret. on Assets	1.8	3.7	3.0	NA	NA	NA
% Ret. on Equity	5.2	10.9	14.2	NA	NA	NA

Dividend Data —Musicland does not plan to pay cash dividends on its common stock in the foreseeable future, but intends to reinvest earnings in the operation and expansion of its business. A "poison pill" stock purchase right was adopted in 1995.

Data as orig. reptd.; bef. results of disc. opers. and/or spec. items. Per share data adj. for stk. divs. as of ex-div. date. E-Estimated. NA-Not Available. NM-Not Meaningful. NR-Not Ranked.

Office—10400 Yellow Circle Drive, Minnetonka, MN 55343. **Tel**—(612) 931-8000. **Chrmn, Pres & CEO**—J. W. Eugster. **EVP & CFO**—R. Johnson. **VP, Treas & Investor Contact**—J. D. Nermyr. **Dirs**—K. A. Benson, J. W. Eugster, K. F. Gorman, W. A. Hodder, L. P. Johnson, J. O. Low III, T. F. Weyl, M. W. Wright. **Transfer Agent & Registrar**—Norwest Stock Transfer Services, Minn. **Incorporated** in 1988 in Delaware. **Empl**-16,000. **S&P Analyst:** Michael V. Pizzi

Mutual Risk Management

NYSE Symbol **MM**
In S&P SmallCap 600

24-AUG-95 **Industry:** Insurance

Summary: MM provides risk management services to clients seeking alternatives to traditional commercial insurance for certain risk exposure, especially workers' compensation.

Quantitative Evaluations
Outlook
(1 Lowest—5 Highest)
• **NA**
Fair Value
• **NA**
Risk
• **Low**
Earn./Div. Rank
• **NR**

Technical Eval.
• **Bearish** since 7/95
Rel. Strength Rank
(1 Lowest—99 Highest)
• **77**
Insider Activity
• **NA**

Recent Price • 36¼
52 Wk Range • 36⅜-24⅜
Yield • 0.9%
12-Mo. P/E • 18.1

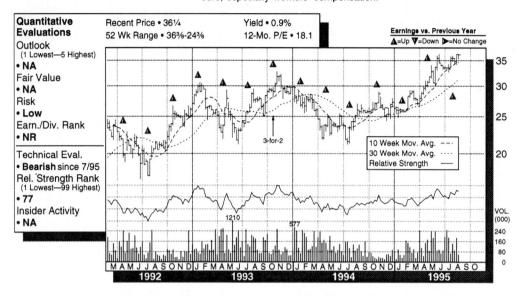

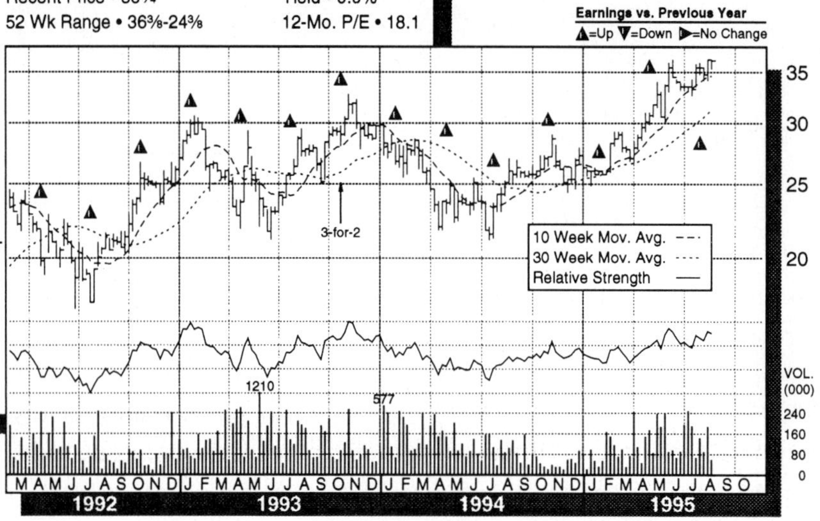

Business Profile - 24-AUG-95

MM is a leader in the alternative insurance market, which is one of the fastest growing segments of the insurance industry. It includes self-insurance and captive insurance programs, representing about one-third of the commercial lines insurance market in the U.S. MM's income is principally derived from fees for the services it provides to clients; typically, it earns between 11% and 13% of a client's premium in fee income. Pretax profit margins on these fees are stable at 46%.

Operational Review - 24-AUG-95

For the six months ended June 30, 1995, revenues rose 1.8%, year to year, due to 18% higher risk management fees and a 36% increase in net investment income, which were partly offset by an 18% decline in premiums earned. Expenses fell 5.5%, led by a 27% drop in losses and loss expenses incurred. Pretax income increased 22%. After taxes at 23.7%, versus 26.2%, and minority interest, net income was up 25%, to $14,537,000 ($1.07 a share), from $11,584,00 ($0.87).

Stock Performance - 18-AUG-95

In the past 30 trading days, MM's shares have increased 8%, compared to a 0.51% rise in the S&P 500. Average trading volume for the past five days was 11,320 shares, compared with the 40-day moving average of 31,631 shares.

Key Stock Statistics

Dividend Rate/Share	0.32	Shareholders	200
Shs. outstg. (M)	12.9	Market cap. (B)	$0.483
Avg. daily vol. (M)	0.021	Inst. holdings	0%
Tang. Bk. Value/Share	10.13	Insider holdings	NA
Beta	NA		

Value of $10,000 invested 5 years ago: NA

Fiscal Year Ending Dec. 31

	1995	% Change	1994	% Change	1993	% Change
Revenues (Million $)						
1Q	28.58	-3%	29.53	14%	26.01	47%
2Q	32.52	7%	30.49	46%	20.82	6%
3Q	—	—	33.47	7%	31.38	—
4Q	—	—	35.18	26%	27.93	NM
Yr.	—	—	128.7	21%	106.1	16%
Income (Million $)						
1Q	6.63	13%	5.85	31%	4.46	22%
2Q	7.86	36%	5.79	22%	4.75	21%
3Q	—	—	6.23	9%	5.72	46%
4Q	—	—	6.18	7%	5.77	40%
Yr.	—	—	24.05	16%	20.73	33%
Earnings Per Share ($)						
1Q	0.49	11%	0.44	32%	0.33	19%
2Q	0.58	35%	0.43	19%	0.36	23%
3Q	—	—	0.47	9%	0.43	47%
4Q	—	—	0.46	7%	0.43	40%
Yr.	—	—	1.80	16%	1.55	31%

Next earnings report expected: early November

Mutual Risk Management

Business Summary - 24-AUG-95

Mutual Risk Management provides risk management services to clients seeking alternatives to traditional commercial insurance for certain risk exposures, especially workers' compensation. Risk management involves a process of analyzing loss exposure and developing risk financing methods to reduce exposure. The use of loss financing methods in place of traditional insurance, known as the alternative market, involves client self-funding of a significant amount of loss exposure, transferring only unpredictable excess risk to insurers. Contributions to pretax earnings (in million $) in recent years were:

	1994	1993	1992
Risk management	$25.8	$21.3	$15.6
Underwriting	-0.7	-0.7	-0.3
Invest. income	10.1	8.9	8.5

The company's principal source of profits is fees received for services provided to clients in connection with its programs. The structure of MM's programs places most underwriting risk with the client. For regulatory and other reasons, however, the company is required to assume a limited amount of risk. It does not seek to earn income from underwriting risk, but from fees for services provided. MM markets services in the U.S., Canada and Europe to retail insurance brokers and consultants representing clients.

In connection with many programs, Legion Insurance Co., licensed in 49 states and the District of Columbia, issues an insurance policy to the client and reinsures the premium and liability related to the client's chosen retention. For most programs, Legion retains only the relatively small portion of the premium associated with its retention of a portion of the specific and aggregate excess risk, ceding the majority of premiums and risk to the clients' IPC (Insurance Profit Center) Program and the balance to unaffiliated excess reinsurers. The IPC Program allows the client to retain a significant portion of its own loss exposure.

Subsidiaries include Park International Ltd., a wholesale insurance broker; MRM Hancock Ltd., a reinsurance broker; Captive Managers, which provide a full range of administrative and accounting services to unaffiliated captive insurers; The Worksafe Group, Inc., which operates a proprietary loss control system; IPC Companies, which are multiple-line insurance and reinsurance companies; Commonwealth Risk Services, Inc., a marketing subsidiary; and Legion Insurance Co.

Important Developments

Aug. '95—MM announced that it had completed the acquisition of Shoreline Mutual Management (Bermuda) Ltd., a Bermuda-based shipping insurance company, during the first quarter of the year. Terms were not disclosed.

Capitalization

Loans Payable: $14,000,000 (3/95).

Per Share Data ($) (Year Ended Dec. 31)

	1994	1993	1992	1991	1990	1989
Tangible Bk. Val.	9.13	8.61	7.07	5.20	3.34	2.31
Oper. Earnings	1.84	1.54	1.17	0.91	NA	NA
Earnings	1.80	1.55	1.18	0.92	0.60	0.41
Dividends	0.29	0.21	0.16	0.07	Nil	Nil
Payout Ratio	16%	14%	14%	7%	Nil	Nil
Prices - High	29¾	32¾	27	23½	NA	NA
- Low	21⅛	21⅛	17⅛	11⅜	NA	NA
P/E Ratio - High	17	21	23	26	NA	NA
- Low	12	14	15	12	NA	NA

Income Statement Analysis (Million $)

	1994	%Chg	1993	%Chg	1992	%Chg	1991
Premium Income	68.2	24%	55.2	10%	50.4	107%	24.4
Net Invest. Inc.	11.4	21%	9.5	3%	9.2	40%	6.6
Oth. Revs.	49.0	18%	41.4	31%	31.7	36%	23.3
Total Revs.	129	21%	106	16%	91.4	68%	54.3
Pretax Inc.	32.3	19%	27.2	25%	21.7	39%	15.6
Net Oper. Inc.	24.5	20%	20.5	33%	15.4	55%	10.0
Net Inc.	24.0	16%	20.7	33%	15.6	51%	10.3

Balance Sheet & Other Fin. Data (Million $)

	1994	1993	1992	1991	1990	1989
Cash & Equiv.	48.0	32.4	51.7	24.8	25.5	13.7
Premiums Due	19.0	15.9	10.1	6.2	3.3	2.9
Inv Assets Bonds	235	205	148	120	65.0	41.0
Inv. Assets Stock	Nil	Nil	Nil	Nil	Nil	Nil
Inv. Assets Loans	Nil	Nil	0.6	0.6	1.2	1.5
Inv. Assets Total	235	205	149	120	66.0	43.0
Deferred Policy Cost	9.5	8.0	6.8	3.6	1.5	1.0
Total Assets	1,018	859	499	405	310	253
Debt	3.0	6.0	8.0	9.0	10.0	4.0
Common Eqty.	122	114	95.6	62.6	34.0	23.9

Ratio Analysis

	1994	1993	1992	1991	1990	1989
Prop&Cas Loss	56.4	73.0	84.4	93.4	99.2	95.4
Prop&Cas Expense	83.9	64.7	45.7	51.6	72.7	81.4
Prop&Cas Comb.	140.3	137.7	130.1	145.0	171.9	176.8
% Ret. on Revs.	18.6	19.5	17.1	19.0	14.1	13.4
% Return on Equity	20.2	19.8	19.6	20.9	18.2	16.5

Dividend Data —Quarterly payments were initiated in 1992; previously, an initial semiannual dividend of $0.10 was paid in November 1991.

Amt. of Div. $	Date Decl.	Ex-Div. Date	Stock of Record	Payment Date
0.070	Jul. 13	Aug. 02	Aug. 08	Aug. 22 '94
0.080	Sep. 28	Nov. 03	Nov. 09	Nov. 23 '94
0.080	Jan. 12	Feb. 01	Feb. 07	Feb. 21 '95
0.080	Apr. 18	May. 02	May. 08	May. 22 '95
0.080	Jul. 31	Aug. 09	Aug. 11	Aug. 23 '95

Data as orig. reptd.; bef. results of disc. opers. and/or spec. items. Per share data adj. for stk. divs. as of ex-div. date. E-Estimated. NA-Not Available. NM-Not Meaningful. NR-Not Ranked.

Office—44 Church St., Hamilton HM 12, Bermuda. **Tel**—(809) 295-5688. **Chrmn & CEO**—R. A. Mulderig. **Pres**—J. Kessock, Jr. **VP & CFO**—James C. Kelly. **Investor Contact**—Diane H. Newman. **Dirs**—R. E. Dailey, D. J. Doyle, A. E. Engel, A. W. Fulkerson, W. F. Galtney, Jr., J. Kessock, Jr., R. A. Mulderig, G. R. Partridge, B. H. Patrick, J. S. Rosenbloom, J. D. Sargent, R. G. Turner. **Transfer Agent & Registrar**—First National Bank of Boston. **Incorporated** in Bermuda in 1977. **Empl**-222. **S&P Analyst:** Thomas C. Ferguson

STANDARD & POOR'S

STOCK REPORTS

Myers Industries

ASE Symbol **MYE**
In S&P SmallCap 600

07-NOV-95

Industry:
Auto parts/equipment

Summary: This diversified maker of polymer and metal products is also a specialized distributor of tools, equipment and supplies for the tire service and transportation industries.

Quantitative Evaluations

Recent Price • 14 | Yield • 1.1%
52 Wk Range • 15¼-11¾ | 12-Mo. P/E • 14.0

Outlook
(1 Lowest—5 Highest)
• **2⁻**
Fair Value
• **13⅞**
Risk
• **Average**
Earn./Div. Rank
• **A**

Technical Eval.
• **Neutral** since 11/95
Rel. Strength Rank
(1 Lowest—99 Highest)
• **37**
Insider Activity
• **Neutral**

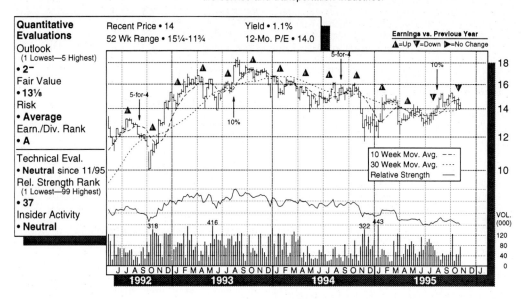

Earnings vs. Previous Year
▲=Up ▼=Down ▶=No Change

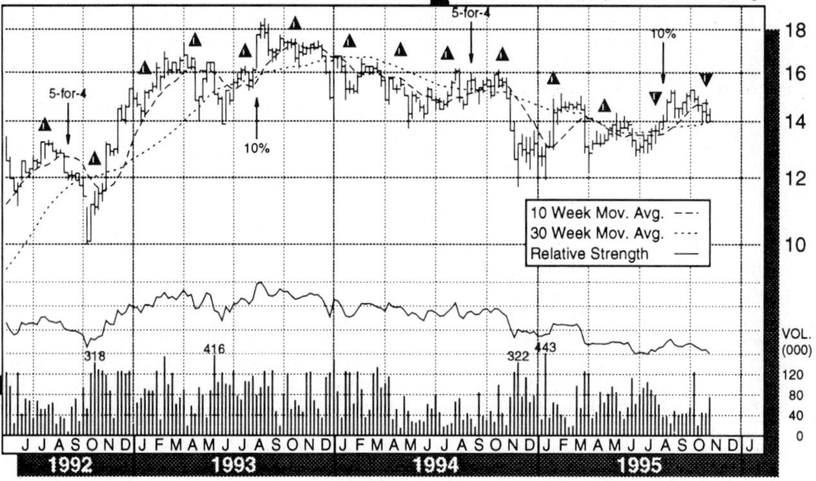

Business Profile - 07-NOV-95

Myers anticipates annual capital spending of $12 million to $15 million over the next five years, primarily for increased polymer manufacturing capacity. The company believes that available credit and anticipated cash flow from operations will be sufficient to meet its needs. The dividend has been raised for 19 consecutive years; a 10% stock dividend was paid in August 1995.

Operational Review - 03-NOV-95

Net sales rose 12%, year to year, in the first nine months of 1995, on increased volume in both the manufacturing and distribution segments. Gross margins narrowed, restricted by rising raw material costs, and with higher operating expenses, net income declined 8.5%. Margins are likely to continue under pressure from higher operating costs in the near-term.

Stock Performance - 03-NOV-95

In the past 30 trading days, MYE's shares have declined 7%, compared to a 2% rise in the S&P 500. Average trading volume for the past five days was 14,880 shares, compared with the 40-day moving average of 11,860 shares.

Key Stock Statistics

Dividend Rate/Share	0.16	Shareholders	1,500
Shs. outstg. (M)	16.9	Market cap. (B)	$0.236
Avg. daily vol. (M)	0.009	Inst. holdings	41%
Tang. Bk. Value/Share	7.47	Insider holdings	NA
Beta	1.02		

Value of $10,000 invested 5 years ago: $ 20,784

Fiscal Year Ending Dec. 31

	1995	% Change	1994	% Change	1993	% Change
Revenues (Million $)						
1Q	67.50	13%	59.69	10%	54.40	12%
2Q	75.58	10%	68.44	8%	63.56	6%
3Q	74.65	13%	66.19	8%	61.19	7%
4Q	—	—	79.73	21%	65.98	4%
Yr.	—	—	274.0	12%	245.1	7%
Income (Million $)						
1Q	3.77	8%	3.50	14%	3.06	21%
2Q	4.35	-15%	5.14	17%	4.38	14%
3Q	3.32	-14%	3.87	24%	3.13	17%
4Q	—	—	5.32	15%	4.62	14%
Yr.	—	—	17.83	16%	15.39	17%
Earnings Per Share ($)						
1Q	0.23	8%	0.21	7%	0.20	20%
2Q	0.25	-17%	0.31	11%	0.28	13%
3Q	0.20	-12%	0.23	20%	0.19	9%
4Q	—	—	0.32	15%	0.28	5%
Yr.	—	—	1.06	13%	0.94	11%

Next earnings report expected: late January

Myers Industries

Business Summary - 07-NOV-95

Myers Industries, Inc., founded in 1933, is a leading manufacturer and distributor of tire service equipment and supplies, and also makes and distributes plastic and metal products. Contributions by business segment in 1994 were:

	Sales	Profits
Aftermarket repair products & services	43%	32%
Polymer & metal products	57%	68%

The aftermarket repair and services segment sells more than 12,000 products to a large portion of the automotive aftermarket, including independent and affiliated tire dealers, retreaders, auto service specialists, rubber and tire manufacturers, and general industrial customers. Products include air compressors, tire changers, high-speed digital wheel balancers, mechanics' hand tools, valves, buffing equipment, matrices for tire presses, tire repair materials, tread stock and molded rubber products. The company's distribution network consists of 53 branch/warehouses--42 in the U.S. and 11 foreign distributors (including Canada and Puerto Rico)

The plastic and metal products segment manufactures and distributes consumer products, including reusable plastic containers and metal storage/organizer systems. The segment also makes molded rubber products consisting of air intake hoses, rubber boots, rubber adhesives, and tread stock and molded patches.

In a May 1993 public offering, 1,240,250 common shares were sold at $15.21 each (as adjusted), through underwriters led by Smith Barney, Harris Upham & Co. and Kidder Peabody & Co.

Important Developments

Oct. '95—The company's Buckhorn unit purchased a 174,000-sq.-ft. factory in Bluffton, Ind., for an undisclosed amount. The new plant, which is expected to be operational in mid- to late 1996, will allow Buckhorn to expand its manufacturing capacity for its plastic reusable material-handling products.
Jun. '95—Myers acquired privately held Ameri-Kart Corp., a maker of plastic residential waste carts, material handling containers, recreational vehicle parts, and hydraulic dumping devices, for an undisclosed amount of cash. Ameri-Kart had 1994 sales of $19 million.

Capitalization

Long Term Debt: $6,886,369 (6/95).
Options: To purchase 186,807 shs. at $7.95 to $19.30 ea. (12/94).

Per Share Data ($) (Year Ended Dec. 31)

	1994	1993	1992	1991	1990	1989
Tangible Bk. Val.	7.04	6.08	4.53	4.04	3.39	2.68
Cash Flow	1.62	1.42	1.26	1.08	1.08	1.09
Earnings	1.06	0.94	0.85	0.69	0.71	0.63
Dividends	0.15	0.13	0.11	0.10	0.09	0.08
Payout Ratio	15%	13%	13%	15%	13%	13%
Prices - High	16¾	18½	15¼	8⅞	9	8⅜
- Low	11¾	13⅞	8⅛	6	6⅛	6⅝
P/E Ratio - High	16	20	18	13	13	13
- Low	11	15	10	9	9	10

Income Statement Analysis (Million $)

	1994	%Chg	1993	%Chg	1992	%Chg	1991
Revs.	274	12%	245	7%	229	17%	196
Oper. Inc.	40.1	17%	34.2	16%	29.5	15%	25.6
Depr.	9.4	23%	7.6	21%	6.3	5%	6.0
Int. Exp.	0.8	-35%	1.2	-21%	1.5	-25%	2.0
Pretax Inc.	30.0	18%	25.4	17%	21.8	22%	17.8
Eff. Tax Rate	41%	—	40%	—	40%	—	41%
Net Inc.	17.8	16%	15.4	18%	13.1	25%	10.5

Balance Sheet & Other Fin. Data (Million $)

	1994	1993	1992	1991	1990	1989
Cash	1.8	1.7	3.4	3.2	2.5	2.5
Curr. Assets	94.7	78.9	74.9	60.7	63.3	61.5
Total Assets	172	152	142	113	116	111
Curr. Liab.	34.1	24.4	31.7	25.3	26.3	26.4
LT Debt	4.2	10.7	24.9	14.6	25.4	29.8
Common Eqty.	131	115	83.9	72.5	63.2	53.3
Total Cap.	138	128	110	88.0	90.0	85.0
Cap. Exp.	12.5	14.1	16.7	6.3	11.0	6.4
Cash Flow	27.2	23.0	19.4	16.5	16.5	15.0

Ratio Analysis

	1994	1993	1992	1991	1990	1989
Curr. Ratio	2.8	3.2	2.4	2.4	2.4	2.3
% LT Debt of Cap.	3.0	8.3	22.6	16.6	28.2	35.2
% Net Inc.of Revs.	6.5	6.3	5.7	5.4	5.3	4.9
% Ret. on Assets	11.0	10.0	10.2	9.2	9.4	8.7
% Ret. on Equity	14.5	14.9	16.7	15.5	18.5	19.6

Dividend Data —Dividends have been paid since 1966.

Amt. of Div. $	Date Decl.	Ex-Div. Date	Stock of Record	Payment Date
0.040	Jan. 18	Mar. 06	Mar. 10	Apr. 03 '95
0.040	Apr. 27	Jun. 06	Jun. 09	Jul. 03 '95
10%	Jul. 28	Aug. 07	Aug. 09	Aug. 31 '95
0.040	Jul. 28	Sep. 06	Sep. 08	Oct. 02 '95
0.040	Oct. 26	Dec. 06	Dec. 08	Jan. 02 '96

Data as orig. reptd.; bef. results of disc. opers. and/or spec. items. Per share data adj. for stk. divs. as of ex-div. date. E-Estimated. NA-Not Available. NM-Not Meaningful. NR-Not Ranked.

Office—1293 S. Main St., Akron, OH 44301. **Tel**—(216) 253-5592. **Pres & CEO**—S. E. Myers. **SVP & Secy**—M. I. Wiskind. **VP-Fin, CFO & Investor Contact**—Gregory J. Stodnick. **Dirs**—K. S. Hay, R. P. Johnston, S. E. Myers, R. L. Osborne, J. H. Outcalt, S. Salem, E. P. Schrank, M. I. Wiskind. **Transfer Agent & Registrar**—First Chicago Trust of New York, NYC. **Incorporated** in Ohio in 1955. **Empl**-1,813. **S&P Analyst:** Stewart Scharf

STANDARD & POOR'S

STOCK REPORTS

NBTY, Inc.

NASDAQ Symbol **NBTY**
In S&P SmallCap 600

26-SEP-95

Industry:
Drugs-Generic and OTC

Summary: NBTY (formerly Nature's Bounty) manufactures and distributes vitamins, food supplements and health and beauty aids under its own and private labels.

Quantitative Evaluations
Outlook
(1 Lowest—5 Highest)
• **NA**
Fair Value
• **NA**
Risk
• **High**
Earn./Div. Rank
• **B-**

Technical Eval.
• **Bearish** since 8/95
Rel. Strength Rank
(1 Lowest—99 Highest)
• **30**
Insider Activity
• **NA**

Recent Price • 6
52 Wk Range • 11⅜-4¾

Yield • Nil
12-Mo. P/E • 26.1

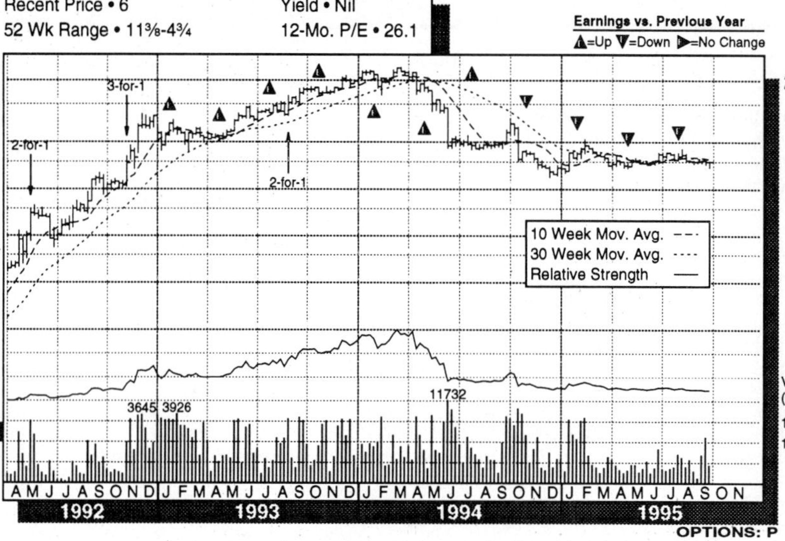

OPTIONS: P

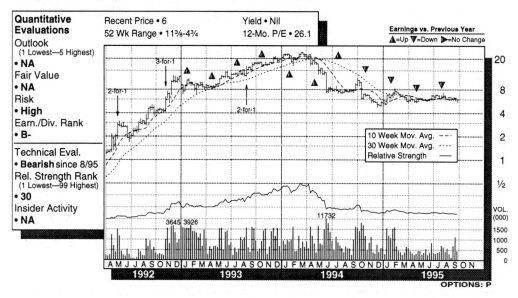

Business Profile - 20-SEP-95

NBTY's share price has been depressed since late 1994, as net income has declined sharply in the last four quarters. The company's strategy for growth includes new product introductions, the addition of new retail accounts and the building of customer loyalty. NBTY's employee stock ownership plan holds 5%. The shares recently traded at about 1.5X times book value.

Operational Review - 25-SEP-95

Net sales in the nine months ended June 30, 1995, advanced 13%, year to year, led by strengthening sales in the core vitamin operations. Margins narrowed on increased marketing and merchandising efforts; income from operations declined 34%. With net other expenses, versus net other income, and after taxes at 41.9%, versus 38.0%, net income plunged 40%.

Stock Performance - 22-SEP-95

In the past 30 trading days, NBTY's shares have declined 2%, compared to a 5% rise in the S&P 500. Average trading volume for the past five days was 85,760 shares, compared with the 40-day moving average of 107,338 shares.

Key Stock Statistics

Dividend Rate/Share	Nil	Shareholders	900
Shs. outstg. (M)	17.9	Market cap. (B)	$0.108
Avg. daily vol. (M)	0.118	Inst. holdings	41%
Tang. Bk. Value/Share	4.13	Insider holdings	NA
Beta	1.95		

Value of $10,000 invested 5 years ago: $ 136,986

Fiscal Year Ending Sep. 30

	1995	% Change	1994	% Change	1993	% Change
Revenues (Million $)						
1Q	37.48	14%	32.74	28%	25.60	33%
2Q	50.95	8%	47.00	28%	36.65	28%
3Q	41.65	16%	35.86	5%	34.06	41%
4Q	—	—	40.45	-4%	42.13	46%
Yr.	—	—	156.1	13%	138.4	37%
Income (Million $)						
1Q	0.94	-43%	1.65	94%	0.85	NM
2Q	2.55	-39%	4.17	67%	2.50	NM
3Q	1.15	-41%	1.94	-57%	4.49	NM
4Q	—	—	0.01	-100%	4.49	111%
Yr.	—	—	7.78	-20%	9.77	156%
Earnings Per Share ($)						
1Q	0.05	-38%	0.08	45%	0.06	NM
2Q	0.13	-38%	0.21	56%	0.13	108%
3Q	0.06	-40%	0.10	5%	0.09	90%
4Q	—	—	Nil	—	0.22	100%
Yr.	—	—	0.38	-28%	0.53	89%

Next earnings report expected: late November

NBTY, Inc.

Business Summary - 25-SEP-95

NBTY, Inc. (formerly Nature's Bounty, Inc.) is engaged primarily in the manufacture and distribution of vitamins, food supplements, and health and beauty aids. The company emphasizes sales of its own products and, to a lesser extent, sales under private label. Products are distributed through direct mail, wholesale and retail channels.

NBTY markets a full range of vitamin products and other nutritional supplements including beta carotene, vitamin C, vitamin E, folic acid, magnesium and potassium under several brand names. The company also offers personal care products including shampoos, soaps, cosmetics, skin creams, fresheners and lotions.

The company believes it is the largest volume U.S. mail order provider of vitamins and other nutritional supplements. NBTY sells through its catalogs mailed about eight times annually under the name Puritan's Pride. Personal care and other selected products are sold under the Beautiful Visions name at discount prices. Puritan's Pride and Beautiful Visions have about 3 million active customers. In late fiscal 1994, it began production of cosmetic pencils.

The Nature's Bounty line, the company's leading brand, is distributed to drug store chains and supermarkets, independent pharmacies, health food stores, health food store wholesalers and other retailers such as mass merchandisers. Clients include Genovese Drug Stores, Walgreens, Lucky Stores and Bergen Brunswig. NBTY also offers private label products under the brand name Natural Wealth. In addition, a comprehensive line of over-the-counter products such as cold remedies and analgesic formulas are sold to independent pharmacies under the Hudson brand name.

The company operates 31 retail stores and kiosks in eight states under the name Vitamin World, which offer a comprehensive line of products.

Over 65% to 70% of NBTY's tablets and capsules sold through all divisions are produced by the Starlen Laboratories division.

Important Developments

Jul. '95—Earnings in the first nine months of fiscal 1995 declined 40%, year to year, despite higher sales, primarily reflecting losses from non-vitamin operations and a signficant increase in marketing costs.
May '95—The company changed its corporate name to NBTY, Inc., from Nature's Bounty, Inc. The action was taken to keep the identity of each nutritional supplement brand separate from the "Nature's Bounty" brand.
Jan. '95—NBTY said it was exploring alternatives with respect to the Beautiful Visions operation.

Capitalization

Long Term Debt: $10,382,115 (6/95).
Options: To purchase 2,825,000 shs. at $0.50 to $0.92 ea.

Per Share Data ($)

(Year Ended Sep. 30)

	1994	1993	1992	1991	1990	1989
Tangible Bk. Val.	4.13	3.64	1.00	0.93	0.76	0.58
Cash Flow	0.59	0.75	0.50	0.32	0.33	0.20
Earnings	0.38	0.53	0.28	0.09	0.07	0.02
Dividends	Nil	Nil	Nil	Nil	Nil	Nil
Payout Ratio	Nil	Nil	Nil	Nil	Nil	Nil
Prices - High	24¼	21½	12⅛	¾	13/16	⅝
- Low	4¾	7	½	5/16	⅜	5/16
P/E Ratio - High	64	41	43	8	12	32
- Low	13	13	2	3	6	16

Income Statement Analysis (Million $)

	1994	%Chg	1993	%Chg	1992	%Chg	1991
Revs.	156	13%	138	37%	101	36%	74.0
Oper. Inc.	17.7	-12%	20.2	92%	10.5	81%	5.8
Depr.	4.2	7%	4.0	29%	3.1	21%	2.5
Int. Exp.	0.9	-26%	1.2	-7%	1.3	-4%	1.4
Pretax Inc.	12.5	-20%	15.7	167%	5.9	NM	1.7
Eff. Tax Rate	38%	—	38%	—	35%	—	40%
Net Inc.	7.8	-20%	9.8	156%	3.8	NM	1.0

Balance Sheet & Other Fin. Data (Million $)

	1994	1993	1992	1991	1990	1989
Cash	5.9	10.8	2.4	2.4	0.3	0.2
Curr. Assets	66.6	63.7	32.7	24.2	17.1	20.0
Total Assets	115	102	58.3	43.5	36.3	35.8
Curr. Liab.	27.2	21.7	19.6	15.5	12.4	13.1
LT Debt	7.6	8.3	21.0	14.2	11.4	11.2
Common Eqty.	78.0	70.0	16.5	12.8	11.8	11.4
Total Cap.	87.5	79.2	38.0	27.6	23.8	22.7
Cap. Exp.	11.6	14.2	5.1	3.1	6.4	2.4
Cash Flow	12.0	13.7	6.9	3.6	3.7	2.4

Ratio Analysis

	1994	1993	1992	1991	1990	1989
Curr. Ratio	2.5	2.9	1.7	1.6	1.4	1.5
% LT Debt of Cap.	8.7	10.4	55.3	51.4	48.0	49.5
% Net Inc.of Revs.	5.0	7.1	3.8	1.4	1.0	0.4
% Ret. on Assets	7.2	10.0	7.5	2.6	2.1	0.7
% Ret. on Equity	10.5	20.2	26.2	8.3	6.4	2.1

Dividend Data —No cash dividends have been paid. Two-for-one stock splits were effected in August 1993 and May 1992, and a three-for-one stock split was effected in November 1992.

Data as orig. reptd.; bef. results of disc. opers. and/or spec. items. Per share data adj. for stk. divs. as of ex-div. date. E-Estimated. NA-Not Available. NM-Not Meaningful. NR-Not Ranked.

Office—90 Orville Dr., Bohemia, NY 11716. **Tel**—(516) 567-9500. **Chrmn & CEO**—S. Rudolph **EVP, Secy & Investor Contact**—Harvey Kamil. **Dirs**—G. Cohen, M. Daly, A. Garabedian, B. G. Owen, N. Rosenblatt, A. Rudolph, S. Rudolph, A. Sacks, B. Solk. **Transfer Agent & Registrar**—American Stock Transfer Co., NYC. **Incorporated** in Delaware in 1980. **Empl**-1,100. **S&P Analyst:** Efraim Levy

STANDARD & POOR'S

STOCK REPORTS

NS Group

NYSE Symbol **NSS**
In S&P SmallCap 600

18-OCT-95 **Industry:** Steel-Iron

Summary: This holding company's subsidiaries are primarily low-cost producers of tubular and bar steel products; NSS also owns an adhesives producer.

Quantitative Evaluations

Outlook (1 Lowest—5 Highest)
• **NA**

Fair Value
• **NA**

Risk
• **High**

Earn./Div. Rank
• **C**

Technical Eval.
• **Bearish** since 7/94

Rel. Strength Rank (1 Lowest—99 Highest)
• **7**

Insider Activity
• **Neutral**

Recent Price • 2¼ | Yield • Nil
52 Wk Range • 6-1⅞ | 12-Mo. P/E • NM

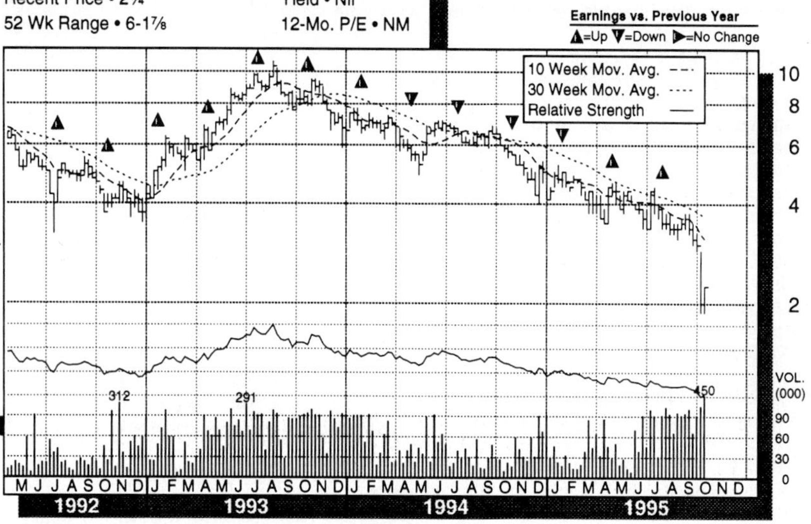

Business Profile - 18-OCT-95

Demand for domestic tubular steel is mostly affected by U.S. oil & gas drilling activity, the level of foreign imports and general economic conditions. In 1994, NS Group resolved to position itself as the premier producer of welded and seamless tubular products in the U.S. by divesting its non-tubular steelmaking facility. NSS used some of the proceeds to purchase capital equipment for its tubular steel segment, in order to reduce production costs, expand its product line and increase capacity.

Operational Review - 18-OCT-95

Revenues in fiscal 1995's first nine months advanced 30%, year to year, mostly reflecting higher average selling prices and increased steel shipments in all three specialty steel segments, from greater demand and new product introductions. Margins widened significantly, due to much improved production efficiencies from the higher volume and prices; operating income soared 107%. In the absence of a $35.3 million gain from the sale of Kentucky Steel, net income was down 92%.

Stock Performance - 13-OCT-95

In the past 30 trading days, NSS's shares have declined 36%, compared to a 4% rise in the S&P 500. Average trading volume for the past five days was 90,000 shares, compared with the 40-day moving average of 37,885 shares.

Key Stock Statistics

Dividend Rate/Share	Nil	Shareholders	300
Shs. outstg. (M)	13.8	Market cap. (B)	$0.036
Avg. daily vol. (M)	0.046	Inst. holdings	41%
Tang. Bk. Value/Share	5.55	Insider holdings	NA
Beta	0.14		

Value of $10,000 invested 5 years ago: $ 2,044

Fiscal Year Ending Sep. 30

	1995	% Change	1994	% Change	1993	% Change
Revenues (Million $)						
1Q	93.49	30%	71.96	-8%	77.80	27%
2Q	97.06	47%	66.01	-24%	86.70	29%
3Q	94.80	17%	80.81	-15%	95.36	27%
4Q	—	—	84.60	-9%	93.21	20%
Yr.	—	—	303.4	-14%	353.1	26%
Income (Million $)						
1Q	0.08	-100%	20.03	NM	-3.36	NM
2Q	0.45	NM	-5.83	NM	-2.12	NM
3Q	0.53	NM	-5.58	NM	0.01	NM
4Q	—	—	-0.96	NM	-1.53	NM
Yr.	—	—	11.49	NM	-5.90	NM
Earnings Per Share ($)						
1Q	0.01	-99%	1.46	NM	-0.25	NM
2Q	0.03	NM	-0.40	NM	-0.16	NM
3Q	0.04	NM	-0.14	—	Nil	—
4Q	—	—	-0.07	NM	-0.03	NM
Yr.	—	—	0.84	NM	-0.44	NM

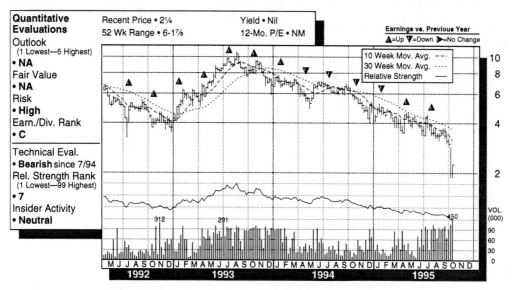

Next earnings report expected: early November

NS Group

Business Summary - 18-OCT-95

NS Group, Inc. is the holding company for two specialty steel mini-mills, a finishing facility and an adhesives producer. Contributions to sales and operating profit in fiscal 1994 were:

	Sales	Profit
Specialty steel products	89%	72%
Imperial Adhesives	11%	28%

Newport Steel Corp. (44% of fiscal 1994 sales) makes welded tubular steel products, primarily used as casing for oil and gas drilling or as pipe by utilities in transporting gas and other fluids, and hot rolled coils. Shipments were 321,000 tons in fiscal 1994, down from 324,000 tons the year before.

Koppel Steel (45% of sales) makes special bar quality (SBQ), seamless tubular and semifinished steel products. Seamless tubular products are used in oil and natural gas drilling and production operations and in the transmission of oil, natural gas and other fluids. SBQ products are primarily used by forgers and OEMs of heavy equipment and off-road vehicles. Shipments totaled 240,000 tons in fiscal 1994, up from 179,000 in fiscal 1993. In July 1994, Koppel acquired the tubular products processing facility formerly owned by Hoesch Tubular Products.

Erlanger Tubular Corp. processes and finishes tubular steel products for Newport Steel, Koppel Steel and other manufacturers.

Imperial Adhesives (8% of sales) manufactures water-based, solvent-based and hot-melt adhesives.

Important Developments

Sep. '95—NSS expects to incur a fourth quarter fiscal 1995 operating loss substantially greater than earlier analysts' estimates. NSS noted the loss is due to higher costs and curtailed shipments from production breakdowns of new and existing equipment at its Newport facility. Additionally, power curtailments from adverse weather, at both Newport and Koppel steel plants, also negatively impacted production and shipments in the fourth quarter of fiscal 1995.

Aug. '95—NSS will incur an aftertax extraordinary charge of about $5.4 million ($0.39 a share) in fourth quarter 1995, reflecting costs incurred from a debt refinancing. Earlier, in July 1995, NSS completed a senior secured note and warrant offering, in which total proceeds of $120.8 million were used to retire a large portion of existing debt.

Capitalization

Long Term Debt: $121,803,000 (7/1/95), incl. $29 million of 11% sub. debs. conv. into 1,706,000 com. shs.

Warrants: To buy some 772,000 shs. at $8 ea., and 1,500,000 shs. at $4 ea.

Options: To buy 1,048,705 shs. at $3.25 to $14.125 ea.

Per Share Data ($) (Year Ended Sep. 30)

	1994	1993	1992	1991	1990	1989
Tangible Bk. Val.	5.54	4.57	5.08	6.33	7.98	7.13
Cash Flow	2.14	0.90	0.35	-0.41	1.47	1.41
Earnings	0.84	-0.44	-0.99	-1.53	0.97	0.95
Dividends	Nil	Nil	0.06	0.12	0.11	0.05
Payout Ratio	Nil	NM	NM	NM	11%	5%
Prices - High	7¾	10¾	8⅜	12⅛	14⅜	11½
- Low	4	4⅛	3¼	5⅛	6⅛	7
P/E Ratio - High	9	NM	NM	NM	15	12
- Low	5	NM	NM	NM	6	7

Income Statement Analysis (Million $)

	1994	%Chg	1993	%Chg	1992	%Chg	1991
Revs.	303	-14%	353	26%	281	33%	212
Oper. Inc.	18.7	-37%	29.8	53%	19.5	NM	-3.1
Depr.	18.0	NM	18.1	NM	18.1	21%	15.0
Int. Exp.	20.0	-5%	21.1	-3%	21.8	NM	21.7
Pretax Inc.	18.9	NM	-9.3	NM	-19.4	NM	-32.0
Eff. Tax Rate	39%	—	NM	—	NM	—	NM
Net Inc.	11.5	NM	-5.9	NM	-13.4	NM	-20.6

Balance Sheet & Other Fin. Data (Million $)

	1994	1993	1992	1991	1990	1989
Cash	44.5	9.3	12.4	11.1	17.4	26.4
Curr. Assets	136	127	114	110	99	99
Total Assets	315	317	319	330	221	177
Curr. Liab.	91.0	87.7	73.4	61.3	34.2	42.8
LT Debt	138	156	164	169	66.0	25.0
Common Eqty.	76.0	63.0	69.0	85.0	107	95.0
Total Cap.	224	230	246	269	187	134
Cap. Exp.	12.0	6.0	6.0	125	96.0	37.0
Cash Flow	29.5	12.2	4.8	-5.6	19.8	18.8

Ratio Analysis

	1994	1993	1992	1991	1990	1989
Curr. Ratio	1.5	1.4	1.6	1.8	2.9	2.3
% LT Debt of Cap.	61.6	68.0	66.8	62.9	35.3	18.6
% Net Inc.of Revs.	3.8	NM	NM	NM	5.2	5.8
% Ret. on Assets	3.6	NM	NM	NM	6.5	7.7
% Ret. on Equity	16.5	NM	NM	NM	12.9	14.3

Dividend Data —The dividend was omitted in May 1992. A "poison pill" stock purchase rights plan was adopted in 1988.

Data as orig. reptd.; bef. results of disc. opers. and/or spec. items. Per share data adj. for stk. divs. as of ex-div. date. E-Estimated. NA-Not Available. NM-Not Meaningful. NR-Not Ranked.

Office—Ninth & Lowell Sts., P.O. Box 1670, Newport, KY 41072. **Tel**—(606) 292-6809. **Pres & CEO**—C. R. Borland. **VP-CFO & Treas**—J. R. Parker. **VP-Secy**—R. R. Noel. **Investor Contact**—Linda A. Pleiman. **Dirs**—C. R. Borland, P. J. B. Donnelly, J. B. Lally, R. G. Mayfield, R. R. Noel. **Transfer Agent & Registrar**—Registrar & Transfer Co., Cranford, NJ. **Incorporated** in Kentucky in 1980. **Empl**-1,568. **S&P Analyst:** Robert E. Friedman

NTN Communications

ASE Symbol **NTN**
In S&P SmallCap 600

03-AUG-95 **Industry:** Broadcasting

Summary: This company's 24-hour-a-day television broadcast network features interactive sports and trivia game programming that allows viewers to electronically respond and participate.

Quantitative Evaluations
Outlook (1 Lowest—5 Highest)
• **NA**
Fair Value
• **NA**
Risk
• **High**
Earn./Div. Rank
• **C**

Technical Eval.
• **Bearish** since 6/94
Rel. Strength Rank (1 Lowest—99 Highest)
• **5**
Insider Activity
• **NA**

Recent Price • 4½
52 Wk Range • 8⅝-4
Yield • Nil
12-Mo. P/E • NM

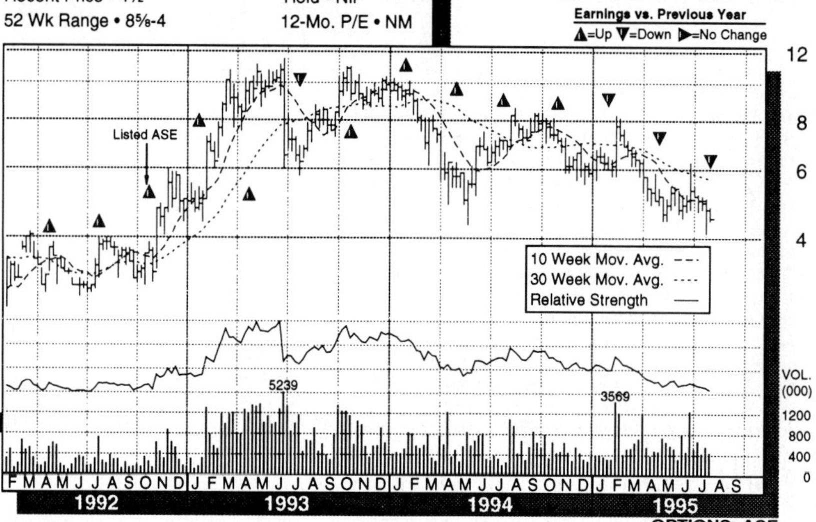

OPTIONS: ASE

Business Profile - 02-AUG-95

NTN hired Donaldson, Lufkin and Jenrette in July 1995 to help prepare a long-term financial strategy and maximize shareholder value. The company signed up a record number of subscriber locations and advertisers in 1994, and at the end of the year had 8 million monthly participants/viewers. The company has been forming alliances to develop interactive services for the gaming and horse racing industries. NTN will also be providing interactive programming to T.G.I. Friday's restaurants.

Operational Review - 02-AUG-95

After several years of losses, NTN realized a profit in 1994, aided by sharply higher sales and improved gross margins. In the first half of 1995, despite a 24% increase in revenues, a loss was incurred, reflecting higher first quarter legal expenses and new product development costs and increased marketing expenditures at the New World Computing Inc. subsidiary. A small profit was realized in the second quarter.

Stock Performance - 28-JUL-95

In the past 30 trading days, NTN's shares have declined 10%, compared to a 4% rise in the S&P 500. Average trading volume for the past five days was 84,780 shares, compared with the 40-day moving average of 139,285 shares.

Key Stock Statistics

Dividend Rate/Share	Nil	Shareholders	1,800
Shs. outstg. (M)	19.9	Market cap. (B)	$0.089
Avg. daily vol. (M)	0.090	Inst. holdings	6%
Tang. Bk. Value/Share	1.24	Insider holdings	NA
Beta	NA		

Value of $10,000 invested 5 years ago: NA

Fiscal Year Ending Dec. 31

	1995	% Change	1994	% Change	1993	% Change
Revenues (Million $)						
1Q	5.74	34%	4.29	157%	1.67	101%
2Q	6.23	17%	5.34	153%	2.11	13%
3Q	—	—	6.99	140%	2.91	66%
4Q	—	—	8.03	-19%	9.95	NM
Yr.	—	—	24.65	43%	17.26	185%
Income (Million $)						
1Q	-1.90	NM	0.09	NM	-0.66	-12%
2Q	0.13	-68%	0.40	NM	-0.52	117%
3Q	—	—	0.33	NM	-0.50	-24%
4Q	—	—	-0.11	NM	0.38	NM
Yr.	—	—	0.71	NM	-1.30	NM
Earnings Per Share ($)						
1Q	-0.10	NM	0.02	NM	-0.05	NM
2Q	0.01	-50%	0.02	NM	-0.03	NM
3Q	—	—	0.02	NM	-0.03	NM
4Q	—	—	-0.03	NM	0.03	NM
Yr.	—	—	0.03	NM	-0.08	NM

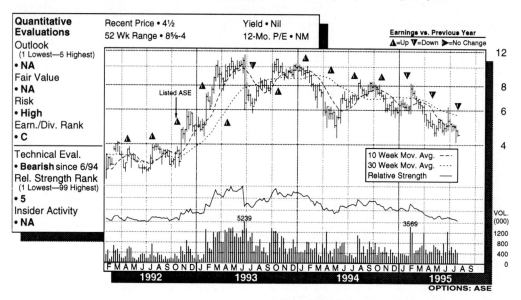

Next earnings report expected: mid October

NTN Communications

Business Summary - 02-AUG-95

NTN Communications, Inc. operates the NTN network, a 24-hour-a-day television broadcast network featuring interactive sports and trivia game programming that allows viewers to electronically respond and participate. As of year-end 1994, it had over 2,000 location subscribers in the U. S. and Canada, with eight million monthly participants.

NTN Network Programming consists of 31 interactive sports and trivia game programs including QB1, Diamondball, PowerPlay, Showdown, Trivia Countdown, Sports Trivia Challenge and Nightside. Sports game programs are played by viewing two television screens, one featuring the live telecast of the sporting event and the other displaying the broadcast of the NTN Network programming, including descriptions of previous plays and players' scores. Participants make decisions on various plays by using a Playmaker, a hand-held wireless response unit that transmits a radio signal to a personal computer located at the subscriber location. The computer compiles data from all players at the location and then transmits it to the company's offices. NTN's central computers tabulate the players' scores and transmit data back to individual locations. Trivia game programs are played in a similar manner.

To date, the primary market for the NTN Network has been the 330,000 bars and restaurants in North America. Potential subscribers include hotels, military bases, college campuses, hospitals, country clubs, fraternal organizations and bowling centers. Subscribers generally have a one-year broadcast services agreement under which they pay a monthly subscriber fee of approximately $600 per location. Subscribers must also purchase or lease a system consisting of a two-foot satellite dish, signal decoder, personal computer and 10 or more Playmakers from the company.

The company also provides interactive programming for a variety of computer-based on-line services and in-room hotel use. Corporate customers are provided interactive programs for trade shows, conventions, corporate training and auctions.

Broadcast service contract revenues provided 50% of 1994 revenues, equipment sales 18%, computer and video game products 21%, licensing 8%, and other 3%.

Important Developments

Jul. '95—NTN Communications hired Donaldson, Lufkin and Jenrette (DLJ) to act as the company's investment banking firm. DLJ will assist NTN in establishing a long-term financial plan and maximizing shareholder value.

Capitalization

Long Term Debt: $12,000 (3/95).
Cum. Conv. Pfd. Stock: 192,612 shs. ($0.005 par).

Per Share Data ($) (Year Ended Dec. 31)

	1994	1993	1992	1991	1990	1989
Tangible Bk. Val.	1.32	1.24	0.55	0.06	-6.78	-7.53
Cash Flow	0.07	-0.06	-0.22	-0.41	-1.17	-1.22
Earnings	0.03	-0.08	-0.23	-0.43	-1.20	-1.20
Dividends	Nil	Nil	Nil	Nil	Nil	Nil
Payout Ratio	Nil	Nil	Nil	Nil	Nil	Nil
Prices - High	10¼	11½	6	5⅝	6¼	10
- Low	4¼	4⅜	2⅛	2¾	⅛	2½
P/E Ratio - High	NM	NM	NM	NM	NM	NM
- Low	NM	NM	NM	NA	NA	NA

Income Statement Analysis (Million $)

	1994	%Chg	1993	%Chg	1992	%Chg	1991
Revs.	24.6	42%	17.3	186%	6.1	72%	3.5
Oper. Inc.	1.1	NM	-1.2	NM	-2.3	NM	-1.6
Depr.	0.8	NM	0.3	65%	0.2	70%	0.1
Int. Exp.	0.1	-29%	0.1	-22%	0.1	-86%	0.6
Pretax Inc.	0.7	NM	-1.0	NM	-2.4	NM	-2.3
Eff. Tax Rate	Nil	—	NM	—	NM	—	Nil
Net Inc.	0.7	NM	-1.3	NM	-2.4	NM	-2.3

Balance Sheet & Other Fin. Data (Million $)

	1994	1993	1992	1991	1990	1989
Cash	3.4	10.8	5.0	2.4	0.3	0.2
Curr. Assets	22.1	22.9	7.6	4.3	1.7	1.8
Total Assets	31.2	27.2	8.6	4.6	1.9	2.0
Curr. Liab.	5.0	2.9	1.3	2.1	11.2	9.8
LT Debt	0.0	0.2	0.0	Nil	0.8	0.8
Common Eqty.	25.3	23.4	6.7	0.6	-12.4	-10.9
Total Cap.	23.5	23.8	7.2	2.5	-9.3	-7.7
Cap. Exp.	0.9	0.7	0.2	0.2	0.0	0.1
Cash Flow	1.5	-1.0	-2.2	-2.2	-1.9	-1.6

Ratio Analysis

	1994	1993	1992	1991	1990	1989
Curr. Ratio	4.5	7.8	6.1	2.1	0.2	0.2
% LT Debt of Cap.	Nil	0.7	0.0	Nil	NM	NM
% Net Inc.of Revs.	2.9	NM	NM	NM	NM	NM
% Ret. on Assets	2.4	NM	NM	NM	NM	NM
% Ret. on Equity	2.9	NM	NM	NM	NM	NM

Dividend Data (No cash dividends have been paid.)

Data as orig. reptd.; bef. results of disc. opers. and/or spec. items. Per share data adj. for stk. divs. as of ex-div. date. E-Estimated. NA-Not Available. NM-Not Meaningful. NR-Not Ranked.

Office—2121 Palomar Airport Rd., Second Fl., Carlsbad, CA 92009. **Tel**—(619) 438-7400. **Chrmn. & CEO**—P. J. Downs. **Pres. & COO**—D. C. Downs. **SVP-Fin, CFO & Secy**—R. E. Hogan. **Dirs**—D. C. Downs, P. J. Downs, K. Hamlet, D. C. Klosterman, A. P. Magerman, A. R. Rozelle. **Transfer Agent & Registrar**—American Stock Transfer & Trust Co., NYC. **Incorporated** in Delaware in 1984. **Empl-210. S&P Analyst:** Stephen Madonna, CFA

STANDARD & POOR'S

STOCK REPORTS

Nash-Finch Co.

NASDAQ Symbol **NAFC**

In S&P SmallCap 600

17-AUG-95 **Industry:** Food

Summary: This company is a leading food wholesaler, supplying products to more than 5,700 supermarkets and convenience stores and other retail outlets and institutional accounts.

Quantitative Evaluations

Outlook
(1 Lowest—5 Highest)
• **NA**

Fair Value
• **NA**

Risk
• **Low**

Earn./Div. Rank
• **A-**

Technical Eval.
• **Bullish** since 3/95

Rel. Strength Rank
(1 Lowest—99 Highest)
• **88**

Insider Activity
• **NA**

Recent Price • 19¼ Yield • 3.6%
52 Wk Range • 19¼-15 12-Mo. P/E • 12.9

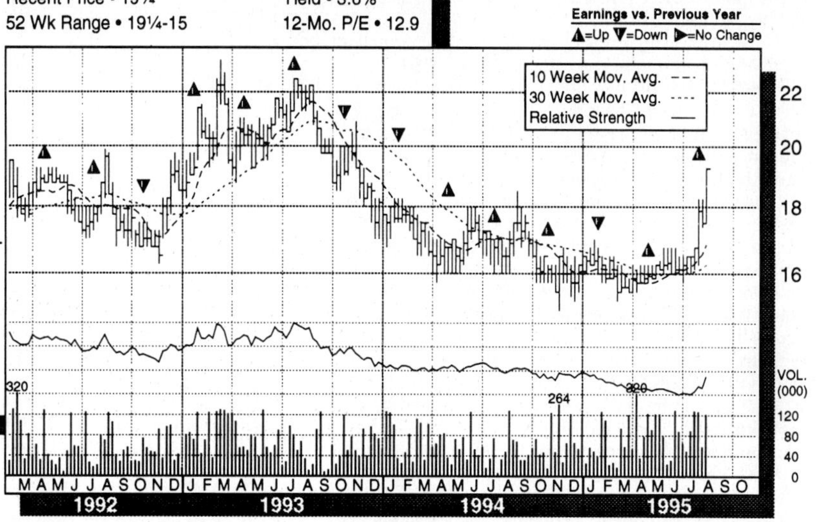

Business Profile - 30-MAY-95

This leading food wholesaler has suffered in recent years from weak sales growth, intense competition in certain retail markets, and low margins in the convenience store wholesale business. The company hopes to offset these trends by pursuing growth through strategic acquisitions, store expansion, and productivity improvements in all phases of its operations.

Operational Review - 10-AUG-95

Total revenues in the 24 weeks ended June 17, 1995, rose marginally, year to year, as improvement in the wholesale segment from the addition of new accounts was offset by a reduction in retail sales, reflecting the sale or closing of a number of retail stores; same-store sales declined 3.0%. Improved operating results at both wholesale and corporate retail stores led to an increase in net income.

Stock Performance - 11-AUG-95

In the past 30 trading days, NAFC's shares have increased 18%, compared to a 2% rise in the S&P 500. Average trading volume for the past five days was 24,660 shares, compared with the 40-day moving average of 21,592 shares.

Key Stock Statistics

Dividend Rate/Share	0.72	Shareholders	2,100
Shs. outstg. (M)	10.9	Market cap. (B)	$0.215
Avg. daily vol. (M)	0.025	Inst. holdings	41%
Tang. Bk. Value/Share	18.74	Insider holdings	NA
Beta	0.48		

Value of $10,000 invested 5 years ago: $ 9,719

Fiscal Year Ending Dec. 31

	1995	% Change	1994	% Change	1993	% Change
Revenues (Million $)						
1Q	623.6	NM	618.2	3%	601.0	13%
2Q	676.5	NM	670.4	6%	631.3	11%
3Q	—	—	887.0	4%	856.5	9%
4Q	—	—	656.5	3%	634.7	NM
Yr.	—	—	2,832	4%	2,724	8%
Income (Million $)						
1Q	2.69	5%	2.57	5%	2.45	8%
2Q	5.85	12%	5.21	4%	5.01	5%
3Q	—	—	4.05	34%	3.02	-52%
4Q	—	—	3.65	-32%	5.39	-21%
Yr.	—	—	15.48	-2%	15.87	-21%
Earnings Per Share ($)						
1Q	0.25	4%	0.24	4%	0.23	10%
2Q	0.54	12%	0.48	4%	0.46	5%
3Q	—	—	0.37	37%	0.27	-53%
4Q	—	—	0.33	-34%	0.50	-21%
Yr.	—	—	1.42	-3%	1.46	-21%

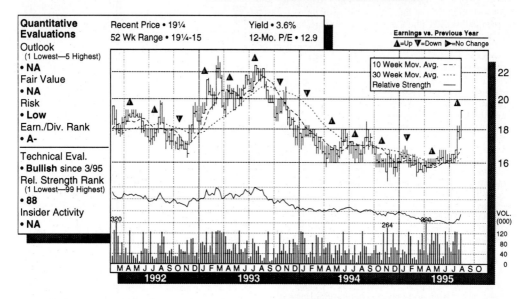

Next earnings report expected: mid October

Nash-Finch Co.

Business Summary - 17-AUG-95

Nash-Finch Company and its subsidiaries are engaged principally in the wholesale and retail distribution of food and nonfood products typically found in supermarkets. Its wholesale operations sell to independently owned retail food stores and institutional customers, while its retail operations sell to the public. The company's 18 distribution centers supply corporate, affiliated and nonaffiliated independent and institutional customers. It also owns a produce marketing subsidiary. Contributions in 1994:

	Revs.	Profits
Wholesale distribution	66%	71%
Retail distribution	33%	26%

Wholesale operations are conducted from strategically located distribution centers that maintain complete inventories of a full line of both national and private branded products, including dry groceries, fresh fruits and vegetables, fresh meats and poultry, dairy and delicatessen products, frozen foods and general merchandise items. On a wholesale basis, Nash-Finch distributes food and nonfood products to more than 700 affiliated and unaffiliated supermarkets and 5,000 convenience stores and other retail outlets and institutional accounts. As part of its wholesale operations, Nash-Finch offers various types of services and assistance to the affiliated independent store owner, such as promotion, advertising and merchandising programs, the installation of computerized inventory and accounting systems, store development services and insurance programs.

As of 1994 year end, the company owned and operated 122 retail outlets: 83 supermarkets operating principally under the names Sun Mart, Easter Foods, Food Folks and Jack & Jill; 35 warehouse stores using the names Econofoods and Food Bonanza; and four combination general merchandise/food stores under the name Family Thrift Center.

Through wholly owned Nash-DeCamp Co., the company grows, packs, ships and markets fresh fruits and vegetables from locations in California and Chile to customers across the U.S., Canada and overseas.

Part of the company's growth strategy includes the acquisition of profitable wholesale operations outside the Midwest to broaden its geographic reach. Recent acquisitions included the July 1993 purchase of a 16-store supermarket group in the Midwest for $27.1 million and the January 1994 buyout of Food Folks, Inc., a 23-store supermarket chain.

Important Developments

Mar. '95—The company announced plans to convert its Sioux Falls grocery warehouse to a more specialized function.

Capitalization

Long Term Debt: $94,002,000 (6/17/95).

Per Share Data ($)

(Year Ended Dec. 31)

	1994	1993	1992	1991	1990	1989
Tangible Bk. Val.	18.25	17.45	17.59	16.45	15.40	14.43
Cash Flow	4.35	4.12	4.31	4.13	4.20	3.32
Earnings	1.42	1.46	1.85	1.75	1.64	1.21
Dividends	0.73	0.72	0.71	0.70	0.69	0.67
Payout Ratio	51%	49%	38%	40%	42%	55%
Prices - High	18½	23¼	19⅞	20¼	25¼	26
- Low	15	17	16¼	16⅛	15¾	21
P/E Ratio - High	13	16	11	12	15	21
- Low	11	12	9	9	10	17

Income Statement Analysis (Million $)

	1994	%Chg	1993	%Chg	1992	%Chg	1991
Revs.	2,822	4%	2,716	8%	2,509	7%	2,338
Oper. Inc.	59.3	2%	57.9	-8%	62.7	5%	59.9
Depr.	31.8	10%	28.9	8%	26.8	4%	25.8
Int. Exp.	11.4	13%	10.1	9%	9.3	4%	9.0
Pretax Inc.	25.8	-3%	26.7	-18%	32.6	6%	30.8
Eff. Tax Rate	40%	—	41%	—	38%	—	38%
Net Inc.	15.5	-3%	15.9	-21%	20.1	5%	19.1

Balance Sheet & Other Fin. Data (Million $)

	1994	1993	1992	1991	1990	1989
Cash	1.1	0.9	0.8	0.6	0.6	12.8
Curr. Assets	310	295	310	240	234	212
Total Assets	532	522	514	430	416	381
Curr. Liab.	220	215	214	155	158	128
LT Debt	96.0	97.9	94.1	82.5	74.3	78.0
Common Eqty.	206	199	191	179	167	157
Total Cap.	302	297	285	263	246	240
Cap. Exp.	35.0	52.0	46.3	36.8	43.8	34.6
Cash Flow	47.3	44.8	46.8	44.9	45.6	36.1

Ratio Analysis

	1994	1993	1992	1991	1990	1989
Curr. Ratio	1.4	1.4	1.4	1.5	1.5	1.7
% LT Debt of Cap.	31.8	32.9	33.0	31.3	30.3	32.5
% Net Inc.of Revs.	0.5	0.6	0.8	0.8	0.8	0.6
% Ret. on Assets	2.9	3.1	4.3	4.5	4.5	3.4
% Ret. on Equity	7.6	8.1	10.8	11.0	11.0	8.5

Dividend Data —Cash dividends, paid since 1926, have been increased for 26 consecutive years. A dividend reinvestment plan is available.

Amt. of Div. $	Date Decl.	Ex-Div. Date	Stock of Record	Payment Date
0.010	Nov. 17	Nov. 18	Nov. 25	Dec. 09 '94
0.180	Nov. 17	Nov. 18	Nov. 25	Dec. 09 '94
0.180	Feb. 14	Feb. 17	Feb. 24	Mar. 10 '95
0.180	May. 12	May. 22	May. 26	Jun. 09 '95
0.180	Jul. 18	Aug. 23	Aug. 25	Sep. 08 '95

Data as orig. reptd.; bef. results of disc. opers. and/or spec. items. Per share data adj. for stk. divs. as of ex-div. date. E-Estimated. NA-Not Available. NM-Not Meaningful. NR-Not Ranked.

Office—7600 France Ave. South, P.O. Box 355, Minneapolis, MN 55440-0355. **Tel**—(612) 832-0534. **Chair**—D. R. Miller. **Pres, CEO & COO**—A. N. Flaten Jr. **VP, Secy & Investor Contact**—Norman R. Soland. **VP & Treas**—R. F. Nash. **Dirs**—C. F. Bitter, R. A. Fisher, A. N. Flaten Jr., A. P. Graham, J. H. Grunewald, R. G. Lareau, R. N. Mammel, D. E. Marsh, D. R. Miller, R. F. Nash, J. O. Rodysill, A. C. Wangaard Jr. **Transfer Agent & Registrar**—Norwest Bank Minnesota, South St. Paul. **Incorporated** in Delaware in 1921. **Empl**-13,090. **S&P Analyst:** Efraim Levy

STANDARD & POOR'S

STOCK REPORTS

Nashua Corp.

NYSE Symbol **NSH**
In S&P SmallCap 600

05-NOV-95 **Industry:** Office Equipment

Summary: This company provides a diverse mix of products and services that include coated paper products, office supplies, photofinishing services and precision materials.

Quantitative Evaluations

Outlook
(1 Lowest—5 Highest)
• **3-**
Fair Value
• **12⅞**
Risk
• **Low**
Earn./Div. Rank
• **B-**

Technical Eval.
• **Bearish** since 10/95
Rel. Strength Rank
(1 Lowest—99 Highest)
• **6**
Insider Activity
• **NA**

Recent Price • 12¾
52 Wk Range • 22⅝-12¼
Yield • 5.6%
12-Mo. P/E • NM

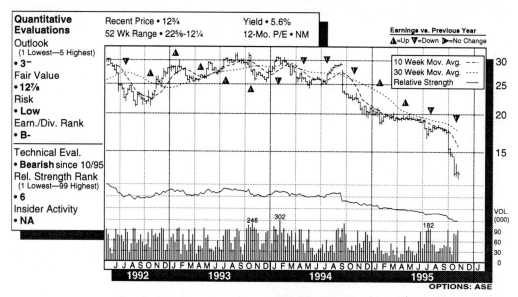

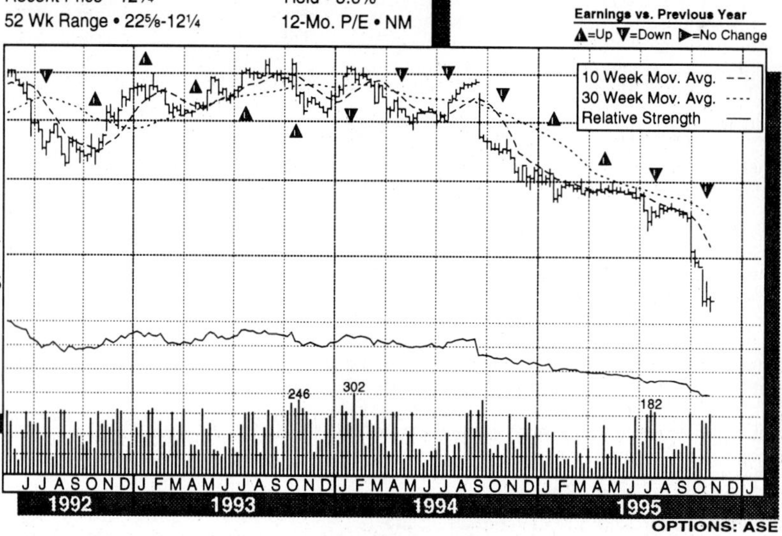

Business Profile - 05-NOV-95

Nashua is still undergoing major changes in its corporate structure. After reorganizing operations in late 1993 and divesting the bulk of its computer unit in 1994, the company announced that it would incur $8.3 million of restructuring charges in 1995's third quarter. Specifically, Nashua is trying to revitalize its commercial products unit, which has experienced operating losses in recent quarters. It expects to record additional charges of about $7.5 million in the fourth quarter of 1995.

Operational Review - 05-NOV-95

Net sales in the nine months ended September 30, 1995, advanced 9.4%, year to year, as rising revenues in the Precision Technologies and Photofinishing units more than offset a sales decline in commercial products. Margins narrowed, and after restructuring charges of $8.3 million, a loss of $5.3 million ($0.84 a share) replaced income of $4.1 million ($0.65). Results in 1994 do not include a $0.36 loss from discontinued operations.

Stock Performance - 03-NOV-95

In the past 30 trading days, NSH's shares have declined 27%, compared to a 2% rise in the S&P 500. Average trading volume for the past five days was 24,960 shares, compared with the 40-day moving average of 14,213 shares.

Key Stock Statistics

Dividend Rate/Share	0.72	Shareholders	1,700
Shs. outstg. (M)	6.4	Market cap. (B)	$0.081
Avg. daily vol. (M)	0.015	Inst. holdings	73%
Tang. Bk. Value/Share	14.55	Insider holdings	NA
Beta	1.20		

Value of $10,000 invested 5 years ago: $ 4,374

Fiscal Year Ending Dec. 31

	1995	% Change	1994	% Change	1993	% Change
Revenues (Million $)						
1Q	124.3	10%	112.8	-20%	141.1	17%
2Q	137.1	12%	122.7	-13%	141.7	5%
3Q	136.2	7%	127.8	-14%	147.9	-2%
4Q	—	—	115.2	-8%	125.1	-14%
Yr.	—	—	478.6	-14%	555.7	NM
Income (Million $)						
1Q	0.07	NM	-1.16	NM	2.64	NM
2Q	1.86	-36%	2.92	-24%	3.86	NM
3Q	-7.27	NM	2.36	-46%	4.39	57%
4Q	—	—	0.32	NM	-32.57	NM
Yr.	—	—	4.44	NM	-21.68	NM
Earnings Per Share ($)						
1Q	0.01	NM	-0.18	NM	0.42	NM
2Q	0.29	-37%	0.46	-25%	0.61	NM
3Q	-1.14	NM	0.37	-46%	0.69	57%
4Q	—	—	0.05	NM	-5.14	NM
Yr.	—	—	0.70	NM	-3.42	NM

Next earnings report expected: early February

Nashua Corp.

Business Summary - 05-NOV-95

Nashua Corp. is a leading manufacturer and provider of coated products, office supplies, photofinishing services and precision materials.

Contributions in 1994 (profits in million $ net of restructuring and other unusual charges) were as follows:

	Sales	Profits
Commercial products	67%	-$0.6
Photofinishing	30%	16.4
Precision Technologies	3%	-0.2

The commercial products unit was formed in 1994 to combine coated products and office supplies.

The coated products segment consists of graphic products (thermosensitive label papers, dry gummed label papers, carbonless papers and facsimile and other thermal papers), labels (electronic data processing and thermal pressure sensitive labels and roll stock for those labels) and tapes (duct, masking, foil and strapping).

The office supplies segment markets toners, developers, facsimile paper, copying paper, remanufactured laser printer cartridges and other supplies used in the office equipment industry. Certain of these products are manufactured by Nashua.

Nashua provides mail order photofinishing services, including developing, printing and enlarging, and sells film and related products to amateur photographers. It operates under the trade name York Photo Labs in the U.S., Truprint and York Photo Labs in the U.K. and Scot Foto and York Photo Labs in Canada, and is the leading mail-order film processor in all three markets.

In May 1994, the company divested its thin-film disk, oxide disk and head-disk assembly operations. Cash proceeds of $11.1 million and a $4.9 million note were realized from the transaction. Nashua retained the materials finishing operation formerly included in its Computer Products group and renamed it Precision Technologies.

Important Developments

Oct. '95—The company posted a third-quarter loss of $0.84 primarily due to restructuring charges of $8.3 million. The charges include a write-down of excess inventory, severance payments, management realignment, and a $3 million valuation allowance against tax assets. The loss caused Nashua to be out of compliance with certain financial covenants in credit agreements with lenders. The company said it was discussing correcting the issues associated with its non-compliance.

Jul. '95—A group of investors, including asset manager Mario Gabelli, raised its stake in Nashua to 9.94%.

Capitalization

Long Term Debt: $68,600,000 (9/95).

Per Share Data ($) (Year Ended Dec. 31)

	1994	1993	1992	1991	1990	1989
Tangible Bk. Val.	12.25	12.25	14.74	15.60	15.83	23.84
Cash Flow	3.10	0.07	4.56	3.47	5.63	4.13
Earnings	0.70	-3.42	0.84	0.09	2.73	1.84
Dividends	0.72	0.72	0.72	0.72	0.69	0.57
Payout Ratio	103%	NM	86%	NM	21%	30%
Prices - High	30⅞	31¾	31¼	37	44⅞	42⅞
- Low	19⅝	25¼	21	18	30½	28¾
P/E Ratio - High	44	NM	37	NM	16	23
- Low	28	NM	25	NM	11	16

Income Statement Analysis (Million $)

	1994	%Chg	1993	%Chg	1992	%Chg	1991
Revs.	479	-14%	556	NM	552	5%	526
Oper. Inc.	27.2	-34%	41.0	22%	33.6	29%	26.0
Depr.	15.3	-31%	22.1	-6%	23.6	10%	21.4
Int. Exp.	2.5	19%	2.1	-22%	2.7	59%	1.7
Pretax Inc.	7.5	NM	-31.4	NM	10.5	NM	3.5
Eff. Tax Rate	41%	—	NM	—	49%	—	84%
Net Inc.	4.4	NM	-21.7	NM	5.3	NM	0.6

Balance Sheet & Other Fin. Data (Million $)

	1994	1993	1992	1991	1990	1989
Cash	10.2	5.9	12.2	30.0	7.5	10.8
Curr. Assets	108	110	111	113	104	178
Total Assets	228	219	237	243	239	319
Curr. Liab.	61.0	86.0	71.0	77.0	87.0	64.0
LT Debt	49.2	20.3	27.9	25.4	10.4	19.4
Common Eqty.	93.0	93.0	117	130	134	236
Total Cap.	142	113	145	155	145	255
Cap. Exp.	16.8	35.7	23.6	33.1	49.8	36.8
Cash Flow	19.7	0.5	28.9	22.0	42.9	39.4

Ratio Analysis

	1994	1993	1992	1991	1990	1989
Curr. Ratio	1.8	1.3	1.6	1.5	1.2	2.8
% LT Debt of Cap.	34.7	17.9	19.2	16.4	7.2	7.6
% Net Inc.of Revs.	0.9	NM	1.0	0.1	3.5	3.2
% Ret. on Assets	2.0	NM	2.2	0.2	9.1	4.6
% Ret. on Equity	4.8	NM	4.3	0.4	14.1	7.7

Dividend Data —Omitted in 1983, cash dividends were resumed in 1986. A dividend reinvestment plan is available.

Amt. of Div. $	Date Decl.	Ex-Div. Date	Stock of Record	Payment Date
0.180	Oct. 28	Dec. 08	Dec. 14	Jan. 04 '95
0.180	Feb. 24	Mar. 08	Mar. 14	Apr. 04 '95
0.180	Apr. 28	Jun. 13	Jun. 15	Jul. 06 '95
0.180	Aug. 29	Sep. 08	Sep. 12	Oct. 03 '95

Data as orig. reptd.; bef. results of disc. opers. and/or spec. items. Per share data adj. for stk. divs. as of ex-div. date. E-Estimated. NA-Not Available. NM-Not Meaningful. NR-Not Ranked.

Office—44 Franklin St., Nashua, NH 03061-2002. **Tel**—(603) 880-2323. **Chrmn**—J. A. Baute. **Pres & CEO**—F. J. Lunger. **VP-Fin & CFO**—D. Junius. **Secy**—P. Buffum. **Treas & Investor Contact**—D. M. Junius. **Dirs**—J. A. Baute, S. A. Buckler, R. E. Carter, T. W. Eagar, C. S. Hoppin, J. M. Kucharski, W. E. Mitchell, J. F. Orr III, J. B. Quinn. **Transfer Agent & Registrar**—First National Bank of Boston. **Incorporated** in Delaware in 1957. **Empl**-3,100. **S&P Analyst:** TT

STANDARD & POOR'S
STOCK REPORTS

National Auto Credit

NYSE Symbol **NAK**
In S&P SmallCap 600

20-OCT-95 **Industry:** Auto rental/service

Summary: This company (formerly Agency Rent-A-Car) recently sold its Agency Rent-A-Car auto rental replacement business to focus on its auto finance business.

Quantitative Evaluations

Outlook (1 Lowest—5 Highest)
• **5-**

Fair Value
• **23⅛**

Risk
• **Average**

Earn./Div. Rank
• **B**

Technical Eval.
• **NA**

Rel. Strength Rank (1 Lowest—99 Highest)
• **94**

Insider Activity
• **Neutral**

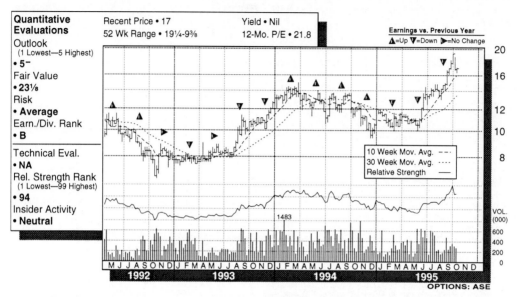

Recent Price • 17
52 Wk Range • 19¼-9⅜
Yield • Nil
12-Mo. P/E • 21.8

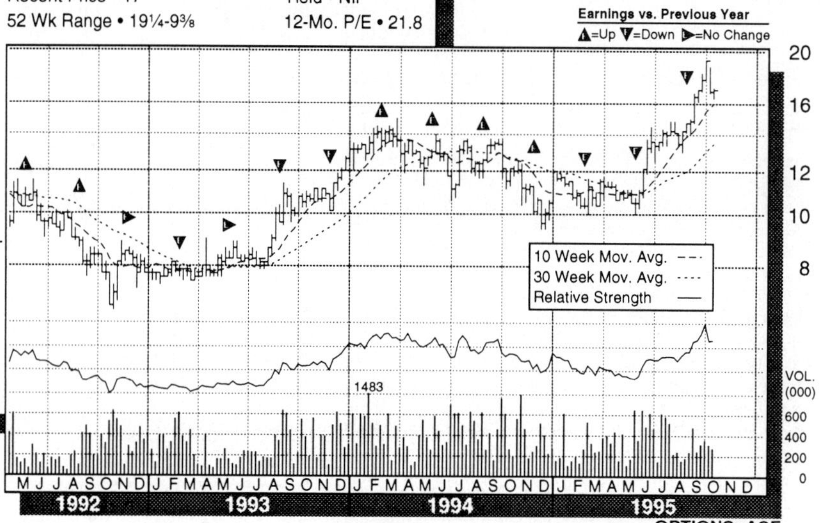

OPTIONS: ASE

Business Profile - 20-OCT-95

NAK, which recently moved to the New York Stock Exchange from the NASDAQ Stock Market, sold its Agency Rent-A-Car business to Avis, Inc. in October 1995 in order to focus its resources on its more profitable financial subsidiary. The company expects the growth pattern experienced during the first half of 1995-96 in its auto financing segment to continue through the remainder of the fiscal year and 1996-97. NAK sees its gross receivables reaching $350 million by January 31, 1996.

Operational Review - 20-OCT-95

Total revenues from continuing operations in the six months ended July 31, 1995, rose 24%, year to year, primarily reflecting sharply higher financial services revenue. Operating costs and expenses were well controlled, and income from continuing operations more than doubled. Per share results exclude a charge of $0.02 in the 1995-96 interim, and a gain of $0.27 in 1994-95, from the discontinued Agency Rent-A-Car business.

Stock Performance - 13-OCT-95

In the past 30 trading days, NAK's shares have increased 14%, compared to a 4% rise in the S&P 500. Average trading volume for the past five days was 53,700 shares, compared with the 40-day moving average of 60,213 shares.

Key Stock Statistics

Dividend Rate/Share	Nil	Shareholders	1,500
Shs. outstg. (M)	25.8	Market cap. (B)	$0.474
Avg. daily vol. (M)	0.055	Inst. holdings	30%
Tang. Bk. Value/Share	8.09	Insider holdings	NA
Beta	1.57		

Value of $10,000 invested 5 years ago: $ 15,355

Fiscal Year Ending Jan. 31

	1996	% Change	1995	% Change	1994	% Change
Revenues (Million $)						
1Q	28.91	-50%	58.30	-28%	81.50	9%
2Q	26.18	-54%	57.30	-31%	83.50	-3%
3Q	—	—	51.40	-32%	75.70	-17%
4Q	—	—	48.00	-22%	61.90	-22%
Yr.	—	—	219.2	-28%	303.2	-9%
Income (Million $)						
1Q	4.03	-13%	4.63	33%	3.48	-5%
2Q	4.85	-27%	6.65	31%	5.06	-20%
3Q	—	—	6.09	41%	4.32	NM
4Q	—	—	5.03	-7%	5.38	173%
Yr.	—	—	22.40	23%	18.24	9%
Earnings Per Share ($)						
1Q	0.16	-11%	0.18	29%	0.14	NM
2Q	0.19	-27%	0.26	30%	0.20	-20%
3Q	—	—	0.24	41%	0.17	-11%
4Q	—	—	0.20	-5%	0.21	163%
Yr.	—	—	0.87	21%	0.72	9%

Next earnings report expected: late November

National Auto Credit

Business Summary - 12-OCT-95

National Auto Credit, Inc. (formerly Agency Rent-A-Car) operates two segments: financial services and dealership operations. The rental replacement business was sold in October 1995.

The financial services business is conducted by NAC, Inc. (formerly National Auto Credit, Inc.), which was created during 1992-93. As of April 1995, NAC conducted business with over 1,600 dealerships in 40 states, and has built an installment receivable portfolio of over $215 million. NAC enables member dealers to capture the sale that may have been lost as a result of unavailable credit. The unit charges qualified dealers a $3,500 fee for enrollment into the NAC Dealer Acceptance Program, which provides a source of funds for the buyer. The installment notes generally have initial terms ranging from 12 to 42 months. NAC receives 20% of all cash receipts for the management and collection of outstanding debt.

NAC utilizes national direct marketing campaigns, trade shows and print advertising to build its image in an effort to stimulate more enrollments and generate increased contract volume.

During 1994-95, NAC operated up to six branch locations which were responsible for the review of loan applications, credit scoring and disbursement of advances to member dealers on approved loans. In late 1994-95, NAC decided to consolidate this loan processing function into one location at its corporate headquarters in Solon, Ohio. By the first quarter of 1995-96, all of the branches had been consolidated.

The dealership operations segment supplies and sells front-line ready vehicles to NAC member dealers through National Motors, Inc. (NMI). Dealership operations generated $64.7 million in revenue from the sale of 9,000 vehicles in 1994-95. More than 80% of these vehicles were sold to NAC member dealers.

Important Developments

Oct. '95—The company sold its Agency Rent-A-Car automobile rental replacement business to Avis, Inc. Terms were not disclosed. Agency had contributed $132 million of the company's $219 million in revenue in 1994-95. NAK said it would focus on expanding its more profitable auto financing business, which is growing significantly faster than its vehicle replacement insurance business. In August, the company moved to the New York Stock Exchange from the NASDAQ Stock Market, and changed its symbol to "NAK" from "NACC".

Capitalization

Notes Payable: $13,254,000 (4/95).

Per Share Data ($)

(Year Ended Jan. 31)

	1995	1994	1993	1992	1991	1990
Tangible Bk. Val.	7.74	6.90	6.18	6.70	6.15	5.63
Cash Flow	NA	2.95	3.43	3.32	4.17	3.75
Earnings	0.87	0.72	0.66	0.68	0.53	0.66
Dividends	Nil	Nil	Nil	Nil	Nil	Nil
Payout Ratio	Nil	Nil	Nil	Nil	Nil	Nil
Cal. Yrs.	1994	1993	1992	1991	1990	1989
Prices - High	15	13½	13½	12½	15½	22⅜
- Low	9⅜	7⅜	6⅝	6⅝	6⅜	9½
P/E Ratio - High	17	19	20	18	29	34
- Low	11	10	10	10	12	14

Income Statement Analysis (Million $)

	1995	%Chg	1994	%Chg	1993	%Chg	1992
Revs.	219	-28%	303	-9%	332	23%	269
Oper. Inc.	75.0	-18%	92.0	-15%	108	5%	103
Depr.	36.7	-36%	57.0	-19%	70.4	5%	67.2
Int. Exp.	2.2	-52%	4.6	-35%	7.1	-7%	7.6
Pretax Inc.	36.4	19%	30.6	14%	26.8	-5%	28.2
Eff. Tax Rate	39%	—	40%	—	37%	—	39%
Net Inc.	22.4	23%	18.2	8%	16.8	-2%	17.2

Balance Sheet & Other Fin. Data (Million $)

	1995	1994	1993	1992	1991	1990
Cash	0.4	0.8	1.4	1.6	4.4	3.3
Curr. Assets	179	100	41.0	36.0	39.0	42.0
Total Assets	321	350	406	378	334	344
Curr. Liab.	37.0	95.0	174	208	NA	142
LT Debt	Nil	Nil	Nil	Nil	Nil	1.3
Common Eqty.	199	177	157	170	158	147
Total Cap.	222	207	185	170	158	201
Cap. Exp.	17.0	67.0	191	191	156	139
Cash Flow	59.0	75.0	87.0	84.0	109	98.0

Ratio Analysis

	1995	1994	1993	1992	1991	1990
Curr. Ratio	4.8	1.1	0.2	0.2	NA	0.3
% LT Debt of Cap.	Nil	Nil	Nil	Nil	Nil	0.7
% Net Inc.of Revs.	10.2	6.0	5.1	6.4	4.9	6.2
% Ret. on Assets	6.7	4.8	4.3	4.8	4.1	4.9
% Ret. on Equity	11.9	10.9	10.3	10.5	9.1	12.4

Dividend Data —No cash dividends have been paid on the publicly traded shares.

Data as orig. reptd.; bef. results of disc. opers. and/or spec. items. Per share data adj. for stk. divs. as of ex-div. date. E-Estimated. NA-Not Available. NM-Not Meaningful. NR-Not Ranked.

Office—30000 Aurora Rd., Solon, OH 44139. **Tel**—(216) 349-1000. **Chrmn**—S. J. Frankino. **Pres & CEO**—R. J. Bronchetti. **VP-Fin**—D. S. Howard. **VP, Secy & Investor Contact**—Thomas J. Dostart. **Dirs**—R. J. Bronchetti, E. A. Burkhart, S. J. Frankino, J. P. Henley, N. T. Herndon, P. Hoel, E. N. Leszczynski. **Transfer Agent & Registrar**—Chemcial Bank, NYC. **Incorporated** in Delaware in 1971. **Empl**-1,000. **S&P Analyst:** Stewart Scharf

STANDARD & POOR'S

STOCK REPORTS

National Data Corp.

NYSE Symbol **NDC**

In S&P SmallCap 600

06-SEP-95 **Industry:** Data Processing

Summary: This company is a leading provider of high-volume transaction processsing services and application systems to the health care and payment markets.

Quantitative Evaluations

Recent Price • 25⅞ | Yield • 1.1%

52 Wk Range • 26⅝-12⅞ | 12-Mo. P/E • 34.0

Outlook
(1 Lowest—5 Highest)
• **3+**

Fair Value
• **25½**

Risk
• **Average**

Earn./Div. Rank
• **B**

Technical Eval.
• **Bullish** since 8/94

Rel. Strength Rank
(1 Lowest—99 Highest)
• **71**

Insider Activity
• **Unfavorable**

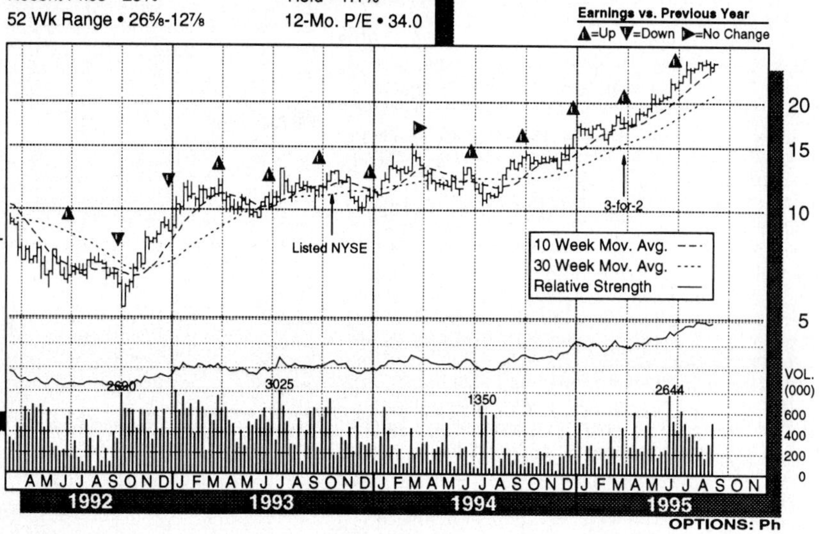

OPTIONS: Ph

Business Profile - 05-SEP-95

As the transition from paper-based to electronic information continues, the most significant penetration of electronic information processing has occurred in the areas of credit card authorization and settlement of medical related transactions. NDC's focus on these two expanding areas should allow it to continue its growth pattern. The company's strategy of acquiring other electronic processing firms will serve to broaden NDC's geographic reach.

Operational Review - 05-SEP-95

Revenue growth in recent periods has been driven by increased demand in the health care application systems and services segment. Gross margins have widened, bolstered by productivity gains. Recent contract wins with the Texas Medical Association (38,000 members) and Randalls Food Markets (122 stores) are examples of the growing popularity of NDC's services. Future revenue growth should be aided by strategic acquisitions of other processing companies.

Stock Performance - 01-SEP-95

In the past 30 trading days, NDC's shares have increased 4%, compared to a 2% rise in the S&P 500. Average trading volume for the past five days was 100,060 shares, compared with the 40-day moving average of 69,303 shares.

Key Stock Statistics

Dividend Rate/Share	0.30	Shareholders	2,100
Shs. outstg. (M)	22.6	Market cap. (B)	$0.591
Avg. daily vol. (M)	0.057	Inst. holdings	76%
Tang. Bk. Value/Share	2.30	Insider holdings	NA
Beta	1.13		

Value of $10,000 invested 5 years ago: $ 13,412

Fiscal Year Ending May 31

	1995	% Change	1994	% Change	1993	% Change
Revenues (Million $)						
1Q	55.97	11%	50.20	-3%	51.60	-4%
2Q	59.81	19%	50.30	NM	50.00	-9%
3Q	62.16	23%	50.40	2%	49.50	-11%
4Q	64.09	21%	53.00	NM	53.50	-2%
Yr.	242.0	19%	204.0	NM	204.6	-7%
Income (Million $)						
1Q	3.08	46%	2.11	—	—	—
2Q	3.52	54%	2.28	32%	1.73	-13%
3Q	3.86	46%	2.64	9%	2.42	13%
4Q	4.94	29%	3.83	20%	3.19	128%
Yr.	15.39	38%	11.16	31%	8.49	15%
Earnings Per Share ($)						
1Q	0.15	32%	0.11	70%	0.07	-37%
2Q	0.17	28%	0.13	43%	0.09	-18%
3Q	0.19	43%	0.13	NM	0.13	11%
4Q	0.24	24%	0.19	12%	0.17	136%
Yr.	0.76	33%	0.57	22%	0.47	13%

Next earnings report expected: late September

National Data Corp.

Business Summary - 05-SEP-95

National Data Corporation is a worldwide provider of value-added information systems and services for health care, government and retail markets. Revenue contributions in recent fiscal years were:

	1993-4	1992-3
Integrated payment systems	55%	56%
Health care application systems & services	31%	28%
Gov't./corp. information systems & services	10%	10%
Other	4%	6%

The integrated payment systems segment provides a wide range of payment alternatives to the retail, health care and government markets. Services provided include credit card, debit card and check processing and verification services, data capture and product and customer support functions, primarily for VISA and MasterCard bank cards. NDC markets its retail application products and services principally through bank relationships and its own personnel. During 1993-4, NDC announced its new procurement card service aimed at corporate purchases of high-volume, small-dollar items.

The health care application systems and services segment offers NDC's DataStat pharmacy practice management systems, which provide solutions for independent and chain pharmacies, HMOs, clinics and hospitals. DataStat systems enable users to manage and perform patient registration, private and third-party billing, inventory, automatic price updating, management reporting and drug record keeping. The company's EasyClaim services, offered to pharmacies, dentists, hospitals, preferred provider organizations and HMOs, include eligibility verification, patient-specific benefit coverage, claims data capture and adjudication and drug utilization review. The number of claims processed through EasyClaim increased 50% in 1993-4 from those of the preceding year. During 1993-4, NDC introduced its Dental System, which incorporates the business automation functions of the DataStat dental system with advanced clinical functionality.

The government and corporate information systems and services segment provides cash management, tax payment and filing, information reporting and electronic data interchange services to corporate and government institutions worldwide.

Important Developments

Jun. '95—NDC sold 2,750,000 common shares at $21.25 each. Proceeds were earmarked for general corporate purposes, including acquisitions. Seperately, in May 1995, the company acquired Claim*Net, a nationwide electronic medical claims clearing house, from Physicians Practice Management.

Capitalization

Long Term Debt: $18,025,000 (2/95), incl. $4,440,000 of capital lease obligations.

Per Share Data ($)

(Year Ended May 31)

	1995	1994	1993	1992	1991	1990
Tangible Bk. Val.	NA	3.60	3.00	2.41	2.16	2.63
Cash Flow	NA	1.51	1.55	1.63	0.74	2.03
Earnings	0.76	0.57	0.47	0.41	-0.80	0.11
Dividends	0.30	0.29	0.29	0.29	0.29	0.29
Payout Ratio	39%	51%	63%	71%	NM	263%
Cal. Yrs.	1994	1993	1992	1991	1990	1989
Prices - High	17⅝	13	11⅞	10	23	23⅜
- Low	10⅜	8⅞	5⅜	6⅛	5⅜	15⅜
P/E Ratio - High	23	23	25	24	NM	NM
- Low	14	15	11	15	NM	NM

Income Statement Analysis (Million $)

	1994	%Chg	1993	%Chg	1992	%Chg	1991
Revs.	204	NM	205	-6%	219	-5%	230
Oper. Inc.	36.6	5%	34.7	-4%	36.2	-6%	38.7
Depr.	18.2	-8%	19.7	-9%	21.6	-21%	27.2
Int. Exp.	1.5	-33%	2.2	-47%	4.2	-25%	5.6
Pretax Inc.	17.4	19%	14.6	14%	12.8	NM	-23.9
Eff. Tax Rate	36%	—	42%	—	42%	—	NM
Net Inc.	11.2	32%	8.5	15%	7.4	NM	-14.1

Balance Sheet & Other Fin. Data (Million $)

	1994	1993	1992	1991	1990	1989
Cash	38.0	17.8	2.9	5.4	4.0	4.1
Curr. Assets	100	86.0	74.0	83.0	108	87.0
Total Assets	183	175	195	212	277	236
Curr. Liab.	51.0	45.0	58.0	83.0	112	75.0
LT Debt	16.3	14.1	20.8	13.3	12.8	12.8
Common Eqty.	109	101	96.0	93.0	111	110
Total Cap.	127	126	128	118	145	151
Cap. Exp.	15.4	8.1	7.3	13.0	25.3	25.7
Cash Flow	29.4	28.2	29.0	13.1	36.0	43.1

Ratio Analysis

	1994	1993	1992	1991	1990	1989
Curr. Ratio	2.0	1.9	1.3	1.0	1.0	1.2
% LT Debt of Cap.	12.8	11.2	16.3	11.3	8.8	8.5
% Net Inc.of Revs.	5.5	4.2	3.4	NM	0.7	8.9
% Ret. on Assets	6.1	4.5	3.6	NM	0.8	10.1
% Ret. on Equity	10.4	8.5	7.8	NM	1.8	19.9

Dividend Data —Cash payments began in 1977.

Amt. of Div. $	Date Decl.	Ex-Div. Date	Stock of Record	Payment Date
0.110	Sep. 26	Nov. 08	Nov. 15	Nov. 30 '94
0.110	Jan. 18	Feb. 13	Feb. 17	Feb. 28 '95
3-for-2	Feb. 01	Mar. 21	Feb. 20	Mar. 20 '95
0.075	Apr. 20	May. 16	May. 22	May. 31 '95
0.075	Aug. 04	Aug. 17	Aug. 21	Aug. 31 '95

Data as orig. reptd.; bef. results of disc. opers. and/or spec. items. Per share data adj. for stk. divs. as of ex-div. date. E-Estimated. NA-Not Available. NM-Not Meaningful. NR-Not Ranked.

Office—National Data Plaza, Corporate Square, Atlanta, GA 30329-2010. **Tel**—(404) 728-2000. **Chrmn & CEO**—R. A. Yellowlees. **VP-CFO & Investor Contact**—Jerry W. Braxton. **Sr VP & Secy**—E. M. Ingram. **Dirs**—E. L. Barlow, J. B. Edwards, I. C. Herbert, D. W. Sands, L. N. Williams Jr., R. A. Yellowlees. **Transfer Agent**—Wachovia Bank of North Carolina, Winston-Salem. **Incorporated** in Delaware in 1967. **Empl**-1,525. **S&P Analyst:** Steven A. Jaworski

STANDARD & POOR'S

STOCK REPORTS

National Re Corp.

NYSE Symbol **NRE**
In S&P SmallCap 600

20-SEP-95 **Industry:** Insurance

Summary: Through its wholly owned National Reinsurance Corp. subsidiary, NRE provides property and casualty reinsurance to primary insurers on a direct basis.

Quantitative Evaluations

Outlook
(1 Lowest—5 Highest)
• **NA**
Fair Value
• **NA**
Risk
• **Low**
Earn./Div. Rank
• **NR**

Technical Eval.
• **Bullish** since 1/95
Rel. Strength Rank
(1 Lowest—99 Highest)
• **57**
Insider Activity
• **NA**

Recent Price • 34 3/8
52 Wk Range • 34 7/8-22 1/4
Yield • 0.5%
12-Mo. P/E • 19.6

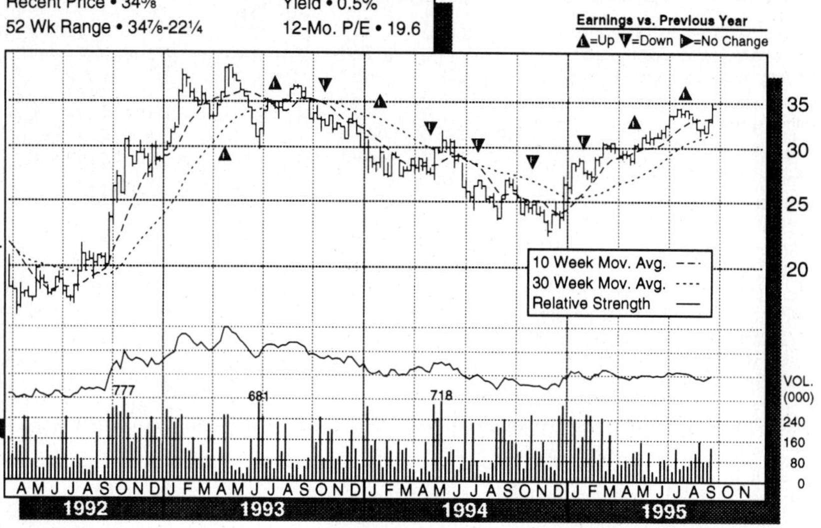

Business Profile - 20-SEP-95

NRE is the sixth largest direct reinsurer in the U.S. Its concentration on casualty over property reinsurance has enabled it to avoid severe losses from major catastrophes in recent years. NRE maintains strict underwriting standards and refrains from underwriting lines it considers highly volatile and inadequately priced. It has consistently achieved underwriting results surpassing those of the industry.

Operational Review - 20-SEP-95

For the six months ended June 30, 1995, total revenues declined 8.0%, year to year, principally reflecting 12% lower net premiums earned. Total expenses were down 11%, as loss and loss expenses fell 15% and underwriting costs declined 6.1%. Pretax operating income rose 19%. After taxes at 23.1%, versus 18.9%, income was up 13%, to $21.3 million ($1.27 a share), from $18.9 million ($1.11). Results for the 1994 period exclude a charge of $0.08 a share from the early retirement of debt.

Stock Performance - 15-SEP-95

In the past 30 trading days, NRE's shares have increased 2%, compared to a 4% rise in the S&P 500. Average trading volume for the past five days was 26,160 shares, compared with the 40-day moving average of 19,254 shares.

Key Stock Statistics

Dividend Rate/Share	0.16	Shareholders	200
Shs. outstg. (M)	16.9	Market cap. (B)	$0.576
Avg. daily vol. (M)	0.021	Inst. holdings	61%
Tang. Bk. Value/Share	20.51	Insider holdings	NA
Beta	NA		

Value of $10,000 invested 5 years ago: NA

Fiscal Year Ending Dec. 31

	1995	% Change	1994	% Change	1993	% Change
Revenues (Million $)						
1Q	96.20	-9%	105.6	2%	103.3	19%
2Q	96.20	-7%	103.5	-6%	109.6	39%
3Q	—	—	88.30	-7%	95.20	2%
4Q	—	—	80.42	-14%	93.20	9%
Yr.	—	—	377.8	-6%	401.3	17%
Income (Million $)						
1Q	11.50	22%	9.40	-41%	15.90	NM
2Q	9.80	3%	9.50	-45%	17.20	125%
3Q	—	—	9.40	-22%	12.10	-4%
4Q	—	—	-1.00	NM	13.50	42%
Yr.	—	—	27.29	-54%	58.70	85%
Earnings Per Share ($)						
1Q	0.68	24%	0.55	-41%	0.93	NM
2Q	0.58	4%	0.56	-45%	1.01	124%
3Q	—	—	0.55	-23%	0.71	-3%
4Q	—	—	-0.06	NM	0.78	39%
Yr.	—	—	1.59	-54%	3.42	85%

Next earnings report expected: mid October

National Re Corp.

Business Summary - 20-SEP-95

National Re Corporation, through wholly owned National Reinsurance Corp., provides property and casualty reinsurance directly to primary insurers without the assistance of reinsurance brokers. The company is one of only six major direct underwriters of property and casualty reinsurance in the U.S. Reinsurance is a form of insurance in which a reinsurer indemnifies a primary insurer against all or a part of the liability assumed by the primary insurer.

NRE's business includes the reinsurance of automobile liability and collision, homeowners, fire, general liability, umbrella, commercial multi-peril, and workers' compensation coverage. In 1994, approximately three-fourths of net premiums written were derived from casualty risks and the remaining one-fourth were property risks. The company reinsures primarily "main street" commercial property and casualty risks, such as small and medium-size businesses with limited sites, local retail establishments and light industrial manufacturers. National Reinsurance Corp. is licensed in 23 states and the District of Columbia. It ultimately expects to be licensed in all 50 states.

The company believes that one of its principal competitive advantages is its position as a direct writer of reinsurance. By working directly with its clients, the company believes that it can better evaluate clients and their respective underwriting risks, helping to limit adverse risks and improve overall underwriting results. In 1994 and 1993, approximately 79% and 83%, respectively, of net premiums written were written on a treaty basis, which, compared with facultative reinsurance, is a lower-risk, lower-cost form of reinsurance.

NRE's business strategy has been to capitalize on its position as a direct writer of reinsurance, building long-term relationships with clients to provide relative stability in its sources of revenue, adhering to underwriting practices designed to limit exposure to more volatile risks and catastrophic losses, and adjusting its mix of business and contract terms to take advantage of market conditions.

At December 31, 1994, the company's investments had a fair value of $1.09 billion. Municipal bonds accounted for 34% of the portfolio, U.S. Government and government agency bonds 29%, corporate bonds 16%, preferred stock 13% and short-term investments 8%.

Important Developments

Jul. '95—NRE issued $25 million of 7.5% notes due 2005. Net proceeds were contributed to the statutory surplus of the National Reinsurance Corp. subsidiary.

Capitalization

Long Term Debt: $185,500,000 (6/95).

Per Share Data ($) (Year Ended Dec. 31)

	1994	1993	1992	1991	1990	1989
Tangible Bk. Val.	17.18	18.28	12.61	NA	5.91	NA
Oper. Earnings	NA	2.12	1.11	1.39	1.24	NA
Earnings	1.59	3.42	1.85	2.29	1.08	NA
Dividends	0.16	0.12	0.12	NA	NA	NA
Payout Ratio	10%	3%	6%	NA	NA	NA
Prices - High	31¾	39⅝	31	NA	NA	NA
- Low	22¼	29¼	17	NA	NA	NA
P/E Ratio - High	20	12	17	NA	NA	NA
- Low	14	8	9	NA	NA	NA

Income Statement Analysis (Million $)

	1994	%Chg	1993	%Chg	1992	%Chg	1991
Premium Income	334	11%	300	20%	250	-7%	270
Net Invest. Inc.	63.4	-4%	66.2	-9%	73.1	-3%	75.0
Oth. Revs.	-19.7	NM	35.2	71%	20.6	-11%	23.2
Total Revs.	378	-6%	401	17%	344	-7%	368
Pretax Inc.	30.6	-62%	80.7	76%	45.9	-22%	58.9
Net Oper. Inc.	NA	—	36.2	99%	18.2	—	NA
Net Inc.	27.3	-53%	58.7	85%	31.7	-19%	39.2

Balance Sheet & Other Fin. Data (Million $)

	1994	1993	1992	1991	1990	1989
Cash & Equiv.	111	37.1	53.2	NA	32.6	NA
Premiums Due	194	199	188	NA	NA	NA
Inv Assets Bonds	878	901	849	NA	NA	NA
Inv. Assets Stock	126	156	100	NA	NA	NA
Inv. Assets Loans	Nil	Nil	Nil	NA	NA	NA
Inv. Assets Total	1,004	1,077	958	NA	917	NA
Deferred Policy Cost	25.0	35.1	19.0	NA	19.4	NA
Total Assets	1,523	1,535	1,325	1,283	1,270	NA
Debt	186	187	200	200	200	NA
Common Eqty.	290	313	243	203	196	NA

Ratio Analysis

	1994	1993	1992	1991	1990	1989
Prop&Cas Loss	70.4	63.8	72.0	NA	73.2	NA
Prop&Cas Expense	28.0	36.0	31.3	NA	28.9	NA
Prop&Cas Comb.	98.4	99.8	103.3	NA	102.1	NA
% Ret. on Revs.	5.8	14.6	9.2	10.7	5.7	NA
% Return on Equity	9.1	21.1	14.2	NA	NA	NA

Dividend Data —Payments began in 1992.

Amt. of Div. $	Date Decl.	Ex-Div. Date	Stock of Record	Payment Date
0.040	Sep. 07	Sep. 09	Sep. 15	Sep. 30 '94
0.040	Dec. 07	Dec. 09	Dec. 15	Dec. 30 '94
0.040	Feb. 01	Mar. 09	Mar. 15	Mar. 31 '95
0.040	May. 17	Jun. 13	Jun. 15	Jun. 30 '95
0.040	Sep. 14	Sep. 15	Sep. 19	Sep. 29 '95

Data as orig. reptd.; bef. results of disc. opers. and/or spec. items. Per share data adj. for stk. divs. as of ex-div. date. E-Estimated. NA-Not Available. NM-Not Meaningful. NR-Not Ranked.

Office—777 Long Ridge Rd., P.O. Box 10167, Stamford, CT 06904-2167. **Tel**—(203) 329-7700. **Chrmn, Pres & CEO**—W. D. Warren. **Exec VP & CFO**—P. A. Cheney. **VP, Secy & Investor Contact**—Anne M. Quinn. **Dirs**—T. M. Bancroft Jr., R. T. Barnum, D. Bonderman, J. A. Boscia, R. W. Bruce III, P. A. Cheney, J. T. Crandall, D. L. Doctoroff, R. W. Eager Jr., S. B. Gruber, G. B. Kent, T. T. McCaffrey, R. A. Spass, W. D. Warren. **Transfer Agent & Registrar**—Chemical Bank, NYC. **Incorporated** in Delaware in 1989. **Empl**-279. **S&P Analyst:** Thomas C. Ferguson

Nature's Sunshine Products

NASDAQ Symbol **NATR**
In S&P SmallCap 600

12-OCT-95

Industry:
Retail merchandiser

Summary: This company is a leading international manufacturer and marketer of encapsulated and tableted herbal products, high-quality natural vitamins and other complementary products.

Quantitative Evaluations

Outlook
(1 Lowest—5 Highest)
• **NA**
Fair Value
• **NA**
Risk
• **Average**
Earn./Div. Rank
• **B+**

Technical Eval.
• **Bearish** since 9/95
Rel. Strength Rank
(1 Lowest—99 Highest)
• **89**
Insider Activity
• **Neutral**

Recent Price • 21½
52 Wk Range • 27-9¾
Yield • 0.9%
12-Mo. P/E • 28.3

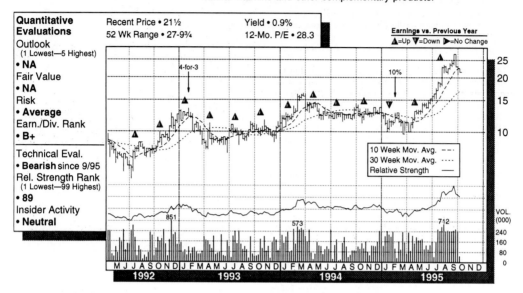

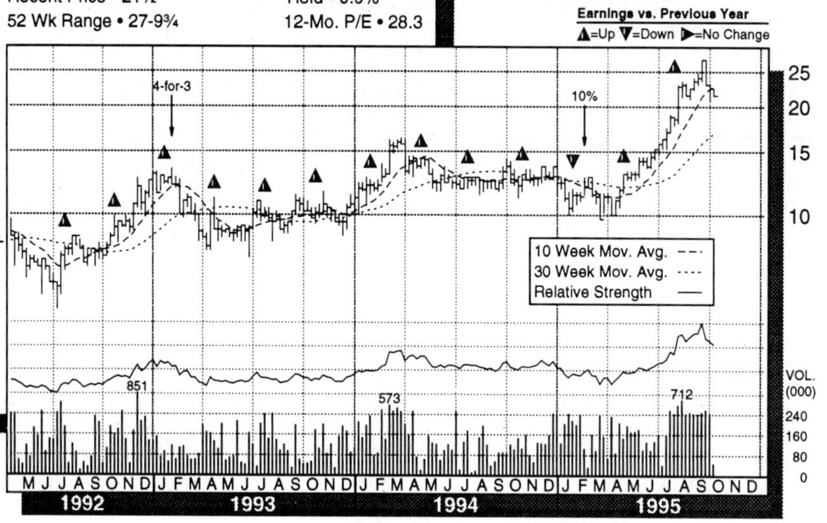

Business Profile - 12-OCT-95

Nature's Sunshine has expanded its revenue base substantially in recent years, primarily by increasing its number of independent sales managers, reaching a total of about 10,400 in the 1995 first half. Sales and earnings growth has been impressive, aided by healthy demand for both nutritional and herbal products as well as momentum in international markets. NATR has distributors in the rapidly growing markets of Japan, Colombia, Venezuela, Brazil, Costa Rica, and Malaysia.

Operational Review - 12-OCT-95

Sales for the six months ended June 30, 1995, rose 29%, year to year, reflecting expansion of the company's independent sales force and increased penetration in international markets. Margins narrowed, as volume incentive costs and SG&A expenses were much higher; operating income gains were 14%. After other income of about $834,000, versus income of $347,000, and a slightly lower tax rate, net income advanced 27%, to $5.0 million ($0.40 a share), from $3.9 million ($0.31).

Stock Performance - 06-OCT-95

In the past 30 trading days, NATR's shares have declined 4%, compared to a 4% rise in the S&P 500. Average trading volume for the past five days was 9,240 shares, compared with the 40-day moving average of 56,421 shares.

Key Stock Statistics

Dividend Rate/Share	0.20	Shareholders	800
Shs. outstg. (M)	12.2	Market cap. (B)	$0.283
Avg. daily vol. (M)	0.053	Inst. holdings	29%
Tang. Bk. Value/Share	2.88	Insider holdings	NA
Beta	0.84		

Value of $10,000 invested 5 years ago: $ 39,435

Fiscal Year Ending Dec. 31

	1995	% Change	1994	% Change	1993	% Change
Revenues (Million $)						
1Q	47.06	26%	37.34	25%	29.83	36%
2Q	50.73	32%	38.31	21%	31.62	28%
3Q	—	—	41.00	26%	32.46	22%
4Q	—	—	44.25	33%	33.29	20%
Yr.	—	—	160.9	27%	127.2	26%
Income (Million $)						
1Q	2.01	18%	1.70	47%	1.16	25%
2Q	2.97	33%	2.24	14%	1.97	33%
3Q	—	—	2.23	6%	2.11	20%
4Q	—	—	2.29	3%	2.22	27%
Yr.	—	—	8.45	13%	7.46	26%
Earnings Per Share ($)						
1Q	0.16	17%	0.14	50%	0.09	25%
2Q	0.24	32%	0.18	18%	0.15	31%
3Q	—	—	0.18	5%	0.17	19%
4Q	—	—	0.18	NM	0.18	25%
Yr.	—	—	0.67	12%	0.60	25%

Next earnings report expected: late December

Nature's Sunshine Products

Business Summary - 12-OCT-95

Nature's Sunshine Products, Inc. primarily manufactures and sells nutritional and personal care products. Nutritional products include herbs, vitamins, beverages, diet and weight loss plans, and mineral and food supplements. Personal care products include natural skin, hair and beauty care items. The company also sells a line of homeopathic remedies and a reverse-osmosis water purification system ("Nature's Spring").

The company sells its products primarily through an independent sales force of managers and distributors; managers numbered 10,396 at June 30, 1995 (7,928 a year earlier), distributors numbered 280,830 (172,420). For domestic sales, NATR generally sells its products on a cash or credit card basis. For certain international operations, the company uses independent distribution centers and offers credit terms consistent with industry standards. Managers resell the products to the distributors in their sales group, to consumers, or use the products themselves. Many distributors sell on a part-time basis to friends or associates or consume the products themselves. Demand for the products is created largely by the 262,453 active members (as of March 1995) of its independent distributor sales force.

NATR buys herbs and other raw materials in bulk and, after quality control testing, encapsulates, tabulates or concentrates them, and then packages them for shipment. Most products are made at the company headquarters in Spanish Fork, Utah. Certain personal care products are manufactured for the company by contract manufacturers in accordance with company specifications. NATR also operates regional warehouses in Columbus, Ohio, Dallas, Texas, and Atlanta, Georgia.

The company's direct sales of nutritional and personal care products are established internationally in Mexico, Canada, the U.K., Colombia, Venezuela, Japan, Brazil, Costa Rica and Malaysia. NATR also exports its products to other countries, including Australia, New Zealand, Norway, the Philippines and, most recently, the Peoples Republic of China. International sales accounted for 30% of revenues in 1994, up from 27% in 1993 and 24% in 1992.

Important Developments

Jul. '95—The company reported record sales and increased earnings for 1995's first half. Although Mexico sales continued to lag, attributed to the currency devaluation, domestic sales were strong and other international markets exhibited high demnad.

Capitalization

Long Term Debt: None (6/95).
Minority Interest: $194,879.

Per Share Data ($) (Year Ended Dec. 31)

	1994	1993	1992	1991	1990	1989
Tangible Bk. Val.	2.72	2.36	1.97	1.61	1.35	1.18
Cash Flow	0.92	0.75	0.61	0.47	0.37	0.39
Earnings	0.67	0.60	0.48	0.37	0.29	0.32
Dividends	0.18	0.18	0.14	0.11	0.10	0.10
Payout Ratio	27%	30%	28%	28%	34%	31%
Prices - High	16⅜	13⅞	13⅛	9⅛	6⅞	6⅞
- Low	10	7⅝	5½	3⅛	2½	2½
P/E Ratio - High	24	22	27	24	21	20
- Low	15	13	11	8	8	8

Income Statement Analysis (Million $)

	1994	%Chg	1993	%Chg	1992	%Chg	1991
Revs.	161	27%	127	26%	101	39%	72.6
Oper. Inc.	17.3	29%	13.4	33%	10.1	32%	7.7
Depr.	3.1	59%	1.9	19%	1.6	43%	1.1
Int. Exp.	0.1	—	Nil	—	0.1	NM	0.0
Pretax Inc.	13.9	14%	12.2	23%	9.9	36%	7.3
Eff. Tax Rate	44%	—	40%	—	40%	—	36%
Net Inc.	8.4	13%	7.5	26%	5.9	28%	4.6

Balance Sheet & Other Fin. Data (Million $)

	1994	1993	1992	1991	1990	1989
Cash	11.2	8.7	6.3	9.1	8.5	7.3
Curr. Assets	36.6	26.5	20.5	17.8	14.6	13.0
Total Assets	52.5	41.5	34.0	27.4	22.0	20.1
Curr. Liab.	17.8	12.3	9.4	7.6	5.1	5.3
LT Debt	Nil	Nil	Nil	Nil	0.0	0.0
Common Eqty.	33.3	28.9	23.9	19.6	16.5	14.4
Total Cap.	34.7	29.3	24.6	19.8	16.9	14.8
Cap. Exp.	2.6	2.9	2.8	1.5	1.5	1.3
Cash Flow	11.5	9.4	7.5	5.8	4.6	4.8

Ratio Analysis

	1994	1993	1992	1991	1990	1989
Curr. Ratio	2.1	2.2	2.2	2.3	2.9	2.5
% LT Debt of Cap.	Nil	Nil	Nil	Nil	0.1	0.2
% Net Inc.of Revs.	5.3	5.9	5.9	6.4	6.0	7.6
% Ret. on Assets	18.0	19.7	19.3	18.7	17.1	21.2
% Ret. on Equity	27.2	28.2	27.2	25.6	23.3	29.3

Dividend Data —Cash payments began in 1988.

Amt. of Div. $	Date Decl.	Ex-Div. Date	Stock of Record	Payment Date
0.050	Nov. 02	Nov. 14	Nov. 18	Nov. 30 '94
10%	Jan. 26	Feb. 13	Feb. 17	Feb. 27 '95
0.050	Feb. 27	Mar. 06	Mar. 10	Mar. 24 '95
0.050	May. 05	May. 11	May. 17	May. 30 '95
0.050	Aug. 08	Aug. 16	Aug. 18	Aug. 29 '95

Data as orig. reptd.; bef. results of disc. opers. and/or spec. items. Per share data adj. for stk. divs. as of ex-div. date. E-Estimated. NA-Not Available. NM-Not Meaningful. NR-Not Ranked.

Office—75 E. 1700 S., Provo, UT 84606. **Tel**—(801) 342-4300. **Fax**—(801) 342-4305. **Chrmn**—Kristine F. Hughes. **Pres & CEO**—A. D. Kennedy. **Exec VP & COO**—W. E. Spears. **VP & Secy**—B. F. Ashworth. **CFO, Treas & Investor Contact**—Douglas Faggioli. **Dirs**—M. Gappmayer, E. L. Hughes, K. F. Hughes, P. T. Hughes, A. D. Kennedy. **Transfer Agent & Registrar**—American Stock Transfer & Trust Co., NYC. **Incorporated** in Utah in 1976. **Empl**-720. **S&P Analyst:** Thomas Tirney

STANDARD & POOR'S STOCK REPORTS

Network Equipment Tech.

NYSE Symbol **NWK**
In S&P SmallCap 600

28-SEP-95

Industry: Telecommunications

Summary: This company is a leading supplier of multiservice backbone networks for information-intensive organizations worldwide.

Quantitative Evaluations

Outlook
(1 Lowest—5 Highest)
• **1+**

Fair Value
• **30¾**

Risk
• **High**

Earn./Div. Rank
• **C**

Technical Eval.
• **Bullish** since 6/95

Rel. Strength Rank
(1 Lowest—99 Highest)
• **95**

Insider Activity
• **Unfavorable**

Recent Price • 36⅞
52 Wk Range • 39¾-12½
Yield • Nil
12-Mo. P/E • 21.9

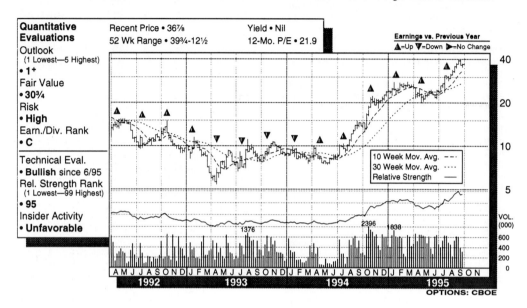

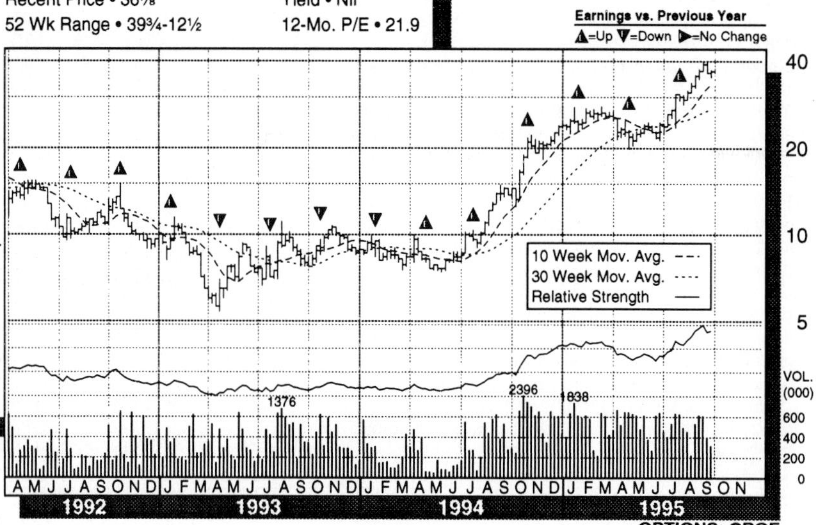

OPTIONS: CBOE

Business Profile - 28-SEP-95

NWK's products and services provide sophisticated, high-value added transmission, network management and connectivity applications and solutions. The company believes that it must continue to focus its product lines to meet the needs of its strategic markets through internal development or the acquisition of additional technology. A recent trend of a decline in first quarter revenues from those of the preceding fourth quarter is expected to continue.

Operational Review - 28-SEP-95

Revenues in the three months ended June 30, 1995, climbed 29%, year to year, reflecting growth in both product and service revenues. Product sales benefited from strong international sales and sales to network service providers, while service revenues were up on increased systems integration services in support of product sales to the U.S. government. Operating expenses rose less rapidly, and net income soared more than four-fold.

Stock Performance - 22-SEP-95

In the past 30 trading days, NWK's shares have increased 18%, compared to a 5% rise in the S&P 500. Average trading volume for the past five days was 63,080 shares, compared with the 40-day moving average of 96,115 shares.

Key Stock Statistics

Dividend Rate/Share	Nil	Shareholders	700
Shs. outstg. (M)	19.1	Market cap. (B)	$0.740
Avg. daily vol. (M)	0.111	Inst. holdings	84%
Tang. Bk. Value/Share	5.79	Insider holdings	NA
Beta	1.99		

Value of $10,000 invested 5 years ago: $ 11,706

Fiscal Year Ending Mar. 31

	1996	% Change	1995	% Change	1994	% Change
Revenues (Million $)						
1Q	79.61	29%	61.54	13%	54.58	6%
2Q	—	—	66.85	22%	55.01	2%
3Q	—	—	73.84	21%	61.25	9%
4Q	—	—	81.81	22%	66.84	17%
Yr.	—	—	284.0	20%	237.7	9%
Income (Million $)						
1Q	6.42	NM	1.43	NM	-1.01	NM
2Q	—	—	2.92	NM	-1.55	NM
3Q	—	—	5.26	NM	0.33	-72%
4Q	—	—	17.47	NM	-4.10	NM
Yr.	—	—	27.07	NM	-6.32	NM
Earnings Per Share ($)						
1Q	0.32	NM	0.08	NM	-0.06	NM
2Q	—	—	0.16	NM	-0.09	NM
3Q	—	—	0.27	NM	0.02	-75%
4Q	—	—	0.87	NM	-0.24	NM
Yr.	—	—	1.44	NM	-0.38	NM

Next earnings report expected: late October

Network Equipment Tech.

Business Summary - 28-SEP-95

Network Equipment Technologies is a leading supplier of multiservice backbone networks for information-intensive organizations and value-added network service providers worldwide. Customers include financial, transportation, manufacturing, service, government, telecommunications service and other organizations.

The company believes that large organizations have a wide range of communication requirements that determine their networking needs. Its sales strategy is to reach the top 1,000 communications users worldwide by employing a highly trained direct sales force in the U.S. and the U.K., and by selling through additional distribution channels worldwide. In addition, NWK is developing its products and distribution capabilities to more fully address targeted domestic and international markets.

The IDNX Transmission Resource Managers product family combines multiplexing, routing and network management functions and is designed to allow the largest users of voice and data communications to achieve the full potential from wide-area networks in a highly cost-effective manner.

Other products include Internetworking Communications Resource Managers (enhance connectivity among devices that transmit information between local area networks across wide area networks); Broadband Communications Resources Managers (broadband networking systems for communication intensive enterprises); SPX Statistical Muliplexers (providing low capacity networking for independent low-to-medium volume data networks with an upgrade path to higher capacity and functionality; ADNX/48 Integrated Access Muliplexer (based on Intelligent Channel Bank technology); and ATMX switch (a high performance Asynchronous Transfer Mode, or ATM, swich designed for LAN).

NWK has agreements with IBM that give IBM non-exclusive, worldwide marketing, installation and service rights for current and future releases of the company's IDNX and ADNX Communications Resource Managers and certain related products. During 1994-5, IBM accounted for 8% of total revenues. International sales accounted for 28%.

Important Developments

Aug. '95—NWK and Singapore-based Datacraft Asia, a data communications system integrator, received a contract to provide the multiservice public digital data network to Cellular Communications Net of Malaysia. The company said the initial phase of the network is valued at $3 million.

Capitalization

Long Term Debt: $68,625,000 of 7.25% sub. debs., conv. into com. at $31.50 a sh. (6/95).
Options: To purchase 3,012,462 com. shs. at $4.00 to $29.88 each (3/95).

Per Share Data ($) (Year Ended Mar. 31)

	1995	1994	1993	1992	1991	1990
Tangible Bk. Val.	5.43	3.45	3.82	4.15	4.29	7.45
Cash Flow	2.23	0.56	0.28	0.17	-2.65	1.55
Earnings	1.44	-0.38	-0.71	-0.76	-3.47	0.93
Dividends	Nil	Nil	Nil	Nil	Nil	Nil
Payout Ratio	Nil	Nil	NA	Nil	Nil	Nil
Cal. Yrs.	1994	1993	1992	1991	1990	1989
Prices - High	24¾	11½	18¼	15⅞	34⅜	31⅞
- Low	7⅜	5⅜	8⅞	4	5	16½
P/E Ratio - High	17	NM	NA	NM	NM	34
- Low	5	NM	NA	NM	NM	18

Income Statement Analysis (Million $)

	1995	%Chg	1994	%Chg	1993	%Chg	1992
Revs.	284	19%	238	9%	219	21%	181
Oper. Inc.	40.8	NM	13.5	-47%	25.4	46%	17.4
Depr.	14.8	-6%	15.8	2%	15.5	13%	13.7
Int. Exp.	5.2	-1%	5.3	NM	5.3	-9%	5.8
Pretax Inc.	23.3	NM	-6.3	NM	-11.1	NM	-12.6
Eff. Tax Rate	NM	—	NM	—	NM	—	NM
Net Inc.	27.1	NM	-6.3	NM	-11.1	NM	-11.2

Balance Sheet & Other Fin. Data (Million $)

	1995	1994	1993	1992	1991	1990
Cash	86.6	41.6	52.1	44.8	49.8	66.6
Curr. Assets	190	137	132	118	111	159
Total Assets	232	187	187	177	170	234
Curr. Liab.	61.8	59.1	54.8	42.9	34.6	42.7
LT Debt	68.6	68.6	68.7	69.8	71.5	80.3
Common Eqty.	102	59.0	61.0	64.0	62.0	105
Total Cap.	170	128	132	134	135	191
Cap. Exp.	8.3	14.2	15.2	11.1	10.1	20.7
Cash Flow	41.9	9.4	4.4	2.4	-38.0	22.6

Ratio Analysis

	1995	1994	1993	1992	1991	1990
Curr. Ratio	3.1	2.3	2.4	2.8	3.2	3.7
% LT Debt of Cap.	40.3	53.7	52.1	52.2	52.8	42.1
% Net Inc.of Revs.	9.5	NM	NM	NM	NM	7.5
% Ret. on Assets	12.4	NM	NM	NM	NM	7.4
% Ret. on Equity	32.6	NM	NM	NM	NM	14.0

Dividend Data —No cash has been paid. A poison pill stock purchase rights plan was adopted in 1989.

Data as orig. reptd.; bef. results of disc. opers. and/or spec. items. Per share data adj. for stk. divs. as of ex-div. date. E-Estimated. NA-Not Available. NM-Not Meaningful. NR-Not Ranked.

Office—800 Saginaw Drive, Redwood City, CA 94063. **Tel**—(415) 366-4400. **Pres & CEO**—J. J. Francesconi. **SVP, CFO, Secy & Investor Contact**—Craig M. Gentner. **Dirs**—J. B Arnold, R. H. B. Baldwin, D. R. Doll, J. J. Francesconi, W. J. Gill, F. S. Vigilante., H. A. Wolf. **Transfer Agent & Registrar**—First National Bank of Boston. **Incorporated** in California in 1983; reincorporated in Delaware in 1987. **Empl**-1,189. **S&P Analyst:** S.S.

Network General Corp.

NASDAQ Symbol **NETG**
In S&P SmallCap 600

25-SEP-95

Industry: Data Processing

Summary: Network General is a leading supplier of software-based monitoring and analysis tools that help troubleshoot and maintain enterprise networks.

Quantitative Evaluations
Outlook
(1 Lowest—5 Highest)
• **NA**
Fair Value
• **NA**
Risk
• **Average**
Earn./Div. Rank
• **NR**

Technical Eval.
• **Bearish** since 8/95
Rel. Strength Rank
(1 Lowest—99 Highest)
• **93**
Insider Activity
• **Neutral**

Recent Price • 41
52 Wk Range • 44¾-17⅛

Yield • Nil
12-Mo. P/E • 32.8

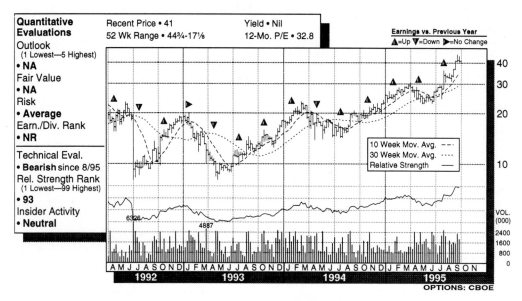

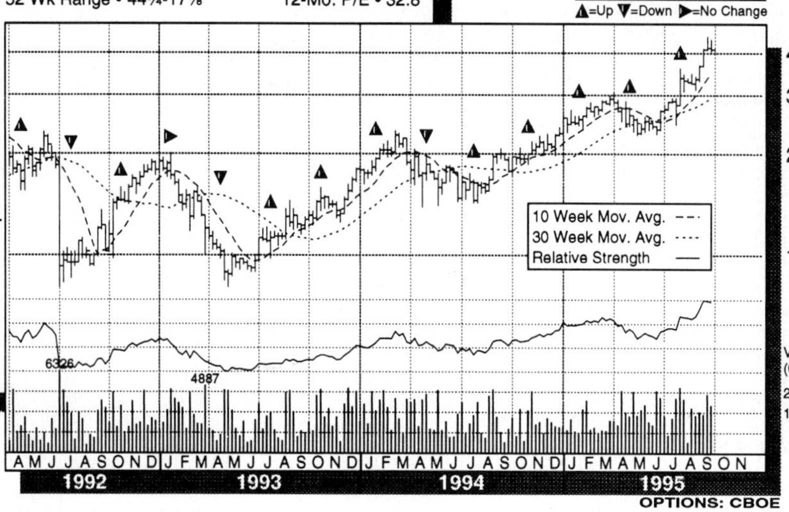

Business Profile - 25-SEP-95

This network management provider is well-positioned to benefit from trends occurring throughout worldwide organizations, mainly the increasing implementation of networked computing and decentralized client-server architectures in place of centralized mainframe structures. As these networks grow in size, quantity and complexity, there is an increasing need for centralized management tools such as those offered by NETG to monitor these platforms.

Operational Review - 25-SEP-95

Revenues for the first quarter of fiscal 1995-96 grew 32%, year to year, due to strong demand for the company's products. Margins improved on well-controlled costs, and net income surged 57% to $0.32 a share. The company has a strong balance sheet, with nearly $19 million in cash, a 4.6 current ratio, and no long term debt. The shares, currently trading at about 33 times trailing 12 month earnings, have doubled since the third quarter of 1994-5.

Stock Performance - 22-SEP-95

In the past 30 trading days, NETG's shares have increased 25%, compared to a 5% rise in the S&P 500. Average trading volume for the past five days was 372,540 shares, compared with the 40-day moving average of 332,487 shares.

Key Stock Statistics

Dividend Rate/Share	Nil	Shareholders	400
Shs. outstg. (M)	21.8	Market cap. (B)	$0.895
Avg. daily vol. (M)	0.373	Inst. holdings	76%
Tang. Bk. Value/Share	7.74	Insider holdings	NA
Beta	1.85		

Value of $10,000 invested 5 years ago: $ 38,139

Fiscal Year Ending Mar. 31

	1996	% Change	1995	% Change	1994	% Change
Revenues (Million $)						
1Q	39.74	32%	30.05	34%	22.40	45%
2Q	—	—	32.38	30%	24.93	24%
3Q	—	—	37.53	30%	28.80	20%
4Q	—	—	39.80	17%	33.95	44%
Yr.	—	—	139.8	22%	114.9	38%
Income (Million $)						
1Q	7.19	57%	4.57	107%	2.21	96%
2Q	—	—	5.23	54%	3.40	22%
3Q	—	—	7.41	54%	4.82	35%
4Q	—	—	8.21	NM	2.16	-23%
Yr.	—	—	25.41	125%	11.28	10%
Earnings Per Share ($)						
1Q	0.32	52%	0.21	75%	0.12	100%
2Q	—	—	0.24	33%	0.18	20%
3Q	—	—	0.33	32%	0.25	32%
4Q	—	—	0.36	NM	0.10	-33%
Yr.	—	—	1.14	115%	0.53	-4%

Next earnings report expected: late October

Network General Corp.

Business Summary - 25-SEP-95

Network General Corporation designs, manufactures, markets and supports software-based analysis and monitoring tools primarily for managing enterprise-wide computer networks.

The company's network analysis product line consists of portable tools and centralized systems that use artificial intelligence-based software to facilitate real-time indentification, diagnosis and resolution of network problems. The company also provides product support, training, and network troubleshooting service.

NETG's portable tools are designed to monitor and analyze individual local area network (LAN) and internetwork segments. The flagship tool prcduct is the Expert Sniffer Network Analyzer.

The company's system product is the Distributed Sniffer System (DSS), which is designed for monitoring and troubleshooting distributed enterprise and client/server networks. DSS consists of centralized console software that displays information received from distributed hardware-based servers, hardware-based probes of software-only agents.

NETG's analysis software utilizes artificial intelligence technology called "expert analysis", which learns network configurations automatically. By automating identification and analysis of network problems, the software provides faster problem resolution.

In January 1994, NETG acquired ProTools in exchange for 2,000,000 of its common shares. ProTools is a maker of products that offer standards-based Remote Monitoring (RMON) technology that enables proactive monitoring and performance analysis of network segments.

Other products include the Progressive Computing (PCI) line of WAN analysis products. The company also derives revenues from professional services, which include software support and maintenance contracts, training and consulting services, as well as product rentals and royalties from license agreements.

International sales accounted for 22% of revenues in 1994-5 and 1993-4.

Important Developments

Sep. '95—NETG announced that it will acquire AIM Technology, a California-based provider of UNIX-based systems management solutions. The company will acquire all of the outstanding stock of AIM for approximately $7.1 million.

Capitalization

Long Term Debt: None (3/95).
Options: To buy 3,192,330 shs. at $4.375 to $28.44 ea. (3/95).

Per Share Data ($) (Year Ended Mar. 31)

	1995	1994	1993	1992	1991	1990
Tangible Bk. Val.	7.59	6.31	5.97	3.42	2.88	2.34
Cash Flow	1.45	0.82	0.70	0.71	0.63	0.51
Earnings	1.14	0.53	0.55	0.56	0.50	0.43
Dividends	Nil	Nil	Nil	Nil	Nil	Nil
Payout Ratio	Nil	Nil	Nil	Nil	Nil	Nil
Cal. Yrs.	1994	1993	1992	1991	1990	1989
Prices - High	26⅛	20⅛	25½	17¼	14⅝	10¾
- Low	13⅞	8	8	6¼	4	4
P/E Ratio - High	23	38	46	31	29	25
- Low	12	15	15	11	8	9

Income Statement Analysis (Million $)

	1995	%Chg	1994	%Chg	1993	%Chg	1992
Revs.	140	22%	115	38%	83.3	30%	64.0
Oper. Inc.	38.6	50%	25.8	76%	14.7	-8%	16.0
Depr.	6.8	11%	6.2	121%	2.8	16%	2.4
Int. Exp.	Nil	—	Nil	—	Nil	—	Nil
Pretax Inc.	37.1	114%	17.3	14%	15.2	10%	13.8
Eff. Tax Rate	32%	—	35%	—	33%	—	35%
Net Inc.	25.4	125%	11.3	10%	10.3	14%	9.0

Balance Sheet & Other Fin. Data (Million $)

	1995	1994	1993	1992	1991	1990
Cash	92.9	55.6	30.2	35.4	29.6	26.7
Curr. Assets	130	91.9	60.3	58.2	41.3	33.7
Total Assets	196	161	130	58.0	45.0	37.0
Curr. Liab.	28.4	26.4	18.5	10.6	4.2	3.5
LT Debt	Nil	Nil	Nil	Nil	Nil	0.1
Common Eqty.	166	132	110	53.0	41.0	33.0
Total Cap.	166	132	110	54.0	41.0	33.0
Cap. Exp.	8.8	7.5	6.3	4.5	2.8	3.1
Cash Flow	32.2	17.5	13.1	11.4	9.1	6.9

Ratio Analysis

	1995	1994	1993	1992	1991	1990
Curr. Ratio	4.6	3.5	3.3	5.5	9.9	9.7
% LT Debt of Cap.	Nil	Nil	Nil	Nil	Nil	0.2
% Net Inc.of Revs.	18.2	9.8	12.3	14.0	16.3	20.1
% Ret. on Assets	14.2	7.3	9.9	16.1	17.7	16.1
% Ret. on Equity	17.1	8.8	11.9	18.9	19.6	17.9

Dividend Data —No cash dividends have been paid, and NETG does not expect to pay dividends in the foreseeable future. A two-for-one stock split was effected in August 1990.

Data as orig. reptd.; bef. results of disc. opers. and/or spec. items. Per share data adj. for stk. divs. as of ex-div. date. E-Estimated. NA-Not Available. NM-Not Meaningful. NR-Not Ranked.

Office—4200 Bohannon Dr., Menlo Park, CA 94025. **Tel**—(415) 473-2000. **Chrmn**—H. J. Saal. **Pres & CEO**—L. G. Denend. **SVP, CFO & Secy**—J. T. Richardson. **Dirs**—C. J. Abbe, D. C. Chance, L. G. Denend, H. Frank, G. M. Gallo, L. R. Hootnick, J. L. Hyland, H. J. Saal. **Transfer Agent & Registrar**—Chemical Tust Co. of California. **Incorporated** in Delaware in 1987. **Empl**-572. **S&P Analyst:** Mike Cavanaugh

New England Business Service

NYSE Symbol **NEB**
In S&P SmallCap 600

07-NOV-95 **Industry:** Office Equipment

Summary: NEB supplies standardized business forms, software and related printed products, selling primarily by mail order to small businesses throughout the U.S., Canada and the U.K.

Quantitative Evaluations

Outlook
(1 Lowest—5 Highest)
• **3+**
Fair Value
• **19**
Risk
• **Low**
Earn./Div. Rank
• **A-**

Technical Eval.
• **Bullish** since 10/95
Rel. Strength Rank
(1 Lowest—99 Highest)
• **53**
Insider Activity
• **NA**

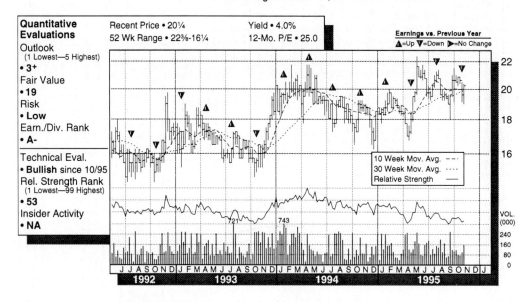

Recent Price • 20¼
52 Wk Range • 22⅜-16¼
Yield • 4.0%
12-Mo. P/E • 25.0

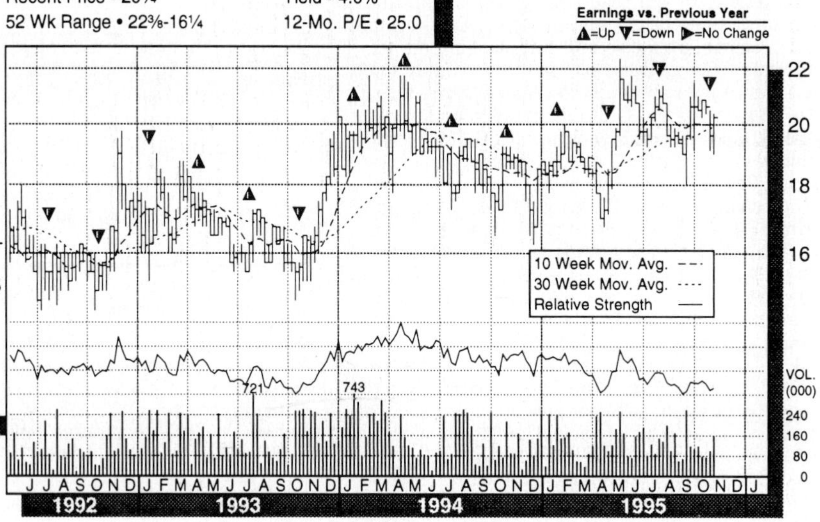

Business Profile - 07-NOV-95

NEB has announced plans for a major operational restructuring designed to reduce costs. The company opened an additional 33 custom print desks in Kinko's stores during the first quarter of FY 96 (Jun.), and now has print desks in 55 Kinko's. NEB released an enhanced version of its Page Magic desktop publishing software in June. A Windows version of the company's One-Write Plus software is being tested and was scheduled for release in the second quarter of FY 96.

Operational Review - 07-NOV-95

Sales rose 2.7% year to year in the first quarter of FY 96 (Jun.). While an improvement over the 1% increase in fourth quarter of FY 95, this was still lower than growth rates realized over the past two years. Margins widened on cost cutting efforts. After an $8,372,000 pretax restructuring charge, EPS declined to $0.04 from $0.30; absent the charge, EPS would have been $0.38. NEB's balance sheet at June 30, 1995, was strong, with no long term debt and about $23 million in cash and investments.

Stock Performance - 03-NOV-95

In the past 30 trading days, NEB's shares have declined 2%, compared to a 2% rise in the S&P 500. Average trading volume for the past five days was 31,420 shares, compared with the 40-day moving average of 29,403 shares.

Key Stock Statistics

Dividend Rate/Share	0.80	Shareholders	5,600
Shs. outstg. (M)	14.9	Market cap. (B)	$0.299
Avg. daily vol. (M)	0.019	Inst. holdings	79%
Tang. Bk. Value/Share	6.16	Insider holdings	NA
Beta	0.97		

Value of $10,000 invested 5 years ago: $ 13,972

Fiscal Year Ending Jun. 30

	1996	% Change	1995	% Change	1994	% Change
Revenues (Million $)						
1Q	63.79	3%	62.08	4%	59.82	4%
2Q	—	—	69.48	6%	65.55	9%
3Q	—	—	68.83	9%	63.42	7%
4Q	—	—	63.33	1%	62.46	4%
Yr.	—	—	263.7	5%	251.3	6%
Income (Million $)						
1Q	0.54	-88%	4.63	NM	0.76	—
2Q	—	—	5.26	6%	4.97	49%
3Q	—	—	2.57	-48%	4.92	46%
4Q	—	—	3.84	-22%	4.92	14%
Yr.	—	—	16.30	5%	15.56	9%
Earnings Per Share ($)						
1Q	0.04	-87%	0.30	NM	0.05	-76%
2Q	—	—	0.34	6%	0.32	45%
3Q	—	—	0.17	-47%	0.32	45%
4Q	—	—	0.26	-19%	0.32	14%
Yr.	—	—	1.07	6%	1.01	9%

Next earnings report expected: late January

New England Business Service

Business Summary - 07-NOV-95

New England Business Service, Inc. markets office and business products primarily by mail order to small businesses. Products include more than 1,000 standardized imprinted manual and computer business forms, check writing systems, stationery, color-coordinated papers, forms and stationery, custom forms, other printed products and a line of software designed to meet small business needs.

Additionally, NEB offers the Company Colors line of printed products. Company Colors offers a select line of two-color stationery, marketing products and business forms imprinted on the customer's choice of high quality papers. NEB also offers Company Colors customers a logo design service. In fiscal 1995, the company commenced distribution of the Company Colors line and other products through custom print desks located in selected Kinko's retail stores. At September 30, 1995, there were 55 custom print desks in Kinko's stores.

The company's line of proprietary software consists of checkwriting, billing, and mailing application packages, easy to use forms-filling packages, and the One-Write Plus line of accounting software. NEB also distributes and supports the Page Magic line of desktop marketing software. The company's software is compatible with the full range of business forms and laser products offered by NEB.

Products are sold to a large but geographically scattered market of small businesses, or branches of larger businesses, typically employing fewer than 20 people. Customers are divided into market segments to carry out specialized market research, product development and sales promotion. Typical market segments are small contractors, such as plumbers, electricians and general building contractors; retailers, such as hardware stores, clothing stores and gift shops; and small professional offices, such as those of dentists, physicians and attorneys.

The company's objective is to produce and ship product within two days from receipt of a customer's order. During FY 95 (Jun.), over 50% of products were produced and shipped within two days and 90% within five days of order.

Important Developments

Sep. '95—The company announced it would implement a major operational restructuring in order to reduce costs, and incurred a related pretax charge of $8.4 million in the first quarter of FY 96 (Jun.). The restructuring included plans to improve manufacturing efficiency, to outsource non-critical corporate functions and to reduce fixed costs. The restructuring will result in a 5% reduction of the company's workforce and the closure of NEB's Flagstaff, AZ, manufacturing facility.

Capitalization

Long Term Debt: None (6/95).

Per Share Data ($)

(Year Ended Jun. 30)

	1995	1994	1993	1992	1991	1990
Tangible Bk. Val.	6.16	6.43	6.19	6.18	6.61	6.27
Cash Flow	1.90	1.77	1.58	1.63	1.73	1.81
Earnings	1.07	1.01	0.93	1.02	1.24	1.23
Dividends	0.80	0.80	0.80	0.80	0.80	0.76
Payout Ratio	75%	79%	86%	77%	64%	61%
Prices - High	22⅜	21¾	20¼	19¾	20¼	19¾
- Low	16¾	17¼	14¾	13½	12¼	10½
P/E Ratio - High	21	22	22	19	16	16
- Low	16	17	16	13	10	9

Income Statement Analysis (Million $)

	1995	%Chg	1994	%Chg	1993	%Chg	1992
Revs.	264	5%	251	6%	237	2%	232
Oper. Inc.	41.8	-4%	43.4	32%	32.8	2%	32.2
Depr.	12.7	9%	11.6	17%	9.9	4%	9.5
Int. Exp.	Nil	—	Nil	—	0.0	-93%	0.3
Pretax Inc.	28.1	2%	27.6	15%	24.1	-3%	24.9
Eff. Tax Rate	42%	—	44%	—	41%	—	36%
Net Inc.	16.3	4%	15.6	10%	14.2	-11%	15.9

Balance Sheet & Other Fin. Data (Million $)

	1995	1994	1993	1992	1991	1990
Cash	23.0	41.0	28.1	31.6	45.2	39.1
Curr. Assets	77.5	85.3	69.0	74.8	87.5	84.3
Total Assets	125	132	121	121	134	130
Curr. Liab.	32.2	30.1	25.3	25.6	24.1	21.6
LT Debt	Nil	Nil	Nil	Nil	Nil	3.3
Common Eqty.	92.0	99	95.0	94.0	108	104
Total Cap.	92.0	101	95.0	95.0	109	108
Cap. Exp.	10.8	6.1	6.5	9.7	9.2	8.8
Cash Flow	29.0	27.2	24.2	25.5	28.2	28.2

Ratio Analysis

	1995	1994	1993	1992	1991	1990
Curr. Ratio	2.4	2.8	2.7	2.9	3.6	3.9
% LT Debt of Cap.	Nil	Nil	Nil	Nil	Nil	3.1
% Net Inc.of Revs.	6.2	6.2	6.0	6.9	8.8	8.8
% Ret. on Assets	13.0	12.3	11.7	13.0	15.5	16.0
% Ret. on Equity	17.4	15.9	15.0	16.4	19.3	20.3

Dividend Data —Cash has been paid each year since 1965.

Amt. of Div. $	Date Decl.	Ex-Div. Date	Stock of Record	Payment Date
0.200	Oct. 28	Nov. 04	Nov. 11	Nov. 25 '94
0.200	Jan. 20	Feb. 01	Feb. 03	Feb. 17 '95
0.200	May. 05	May. 08	May. 12	May. 26 '95
0.200	Jul. 31	Aug. 09	Aug. 11	Aug. 25 '95
0.200	Oct. 31	Nov. 08	Nov. 10	Nov. 24 '95

Data as orig. reptd.; bef. results of disc. opers. and/or spec. items. Per share data adj. for stk. divs. as of ex-div. date. E-Estimated. NA-Not Available. NM-Not Meaningful. NR-Not Ranked.

Office—500 Main St., Groton, MA 01471. **Tel**—(508) 448-6111. **Chrmn**—R. H. Rhoads. **Pres & CEO**—W. C. Lowe. **Secy & Treas**—J. F. Fairbanks. **VP, CFO & Investor Contact**—Russell V. Corsini, Jr. **Dirs**—P. A. Brooke, B. H. Lacy, W. C. Lowe, R. J. Murray, F. L. Randall, Jr., J. R. Rhoads, Jr., R. H. Rhoads, B. E. Stern. **Transfer Agent & Registrar**—First National Bank of Boston. **Incorporated** in Massachusetts in 1955; reincorporated in Delaware in 1986. **Empl**-2,055. **S&P Analyst:** Stephen Madonna, CFA

New Jersey Resources

NYSE Symbol **NJR**
In S&P SmallCap 600

27-JUL-95

Industry: Utilities-Gas

Summary: Through New Jersey Natural Gas Co., this utility holding company supplies gas to more than 345,000 customers in Monmouth, Morris, Middlesex and Ocean counties of New Jersey.

Quantitative Evaluations
Outlook
(1 Lowest—5 Highest)
• 3+
Fair Value
• 23⅛
Risk
• Low
Earn./Div. Rank
• B+

Technical Eval.
• **Bearish** since 6/95
Rel. Strength Rank
(1 Lowest—99 Highest)
• 52
Insider Activity
• NA

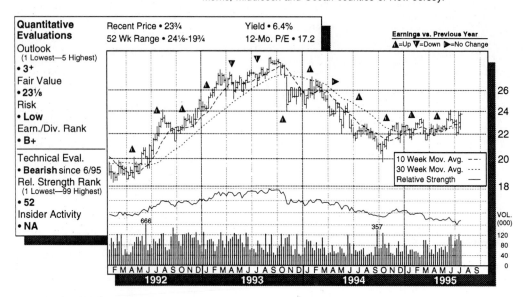

Recent Price • 23¾
52 Wk Range • 24⅛-19¾

Yield • 6.4%
12-Mo. P/E • 17.2

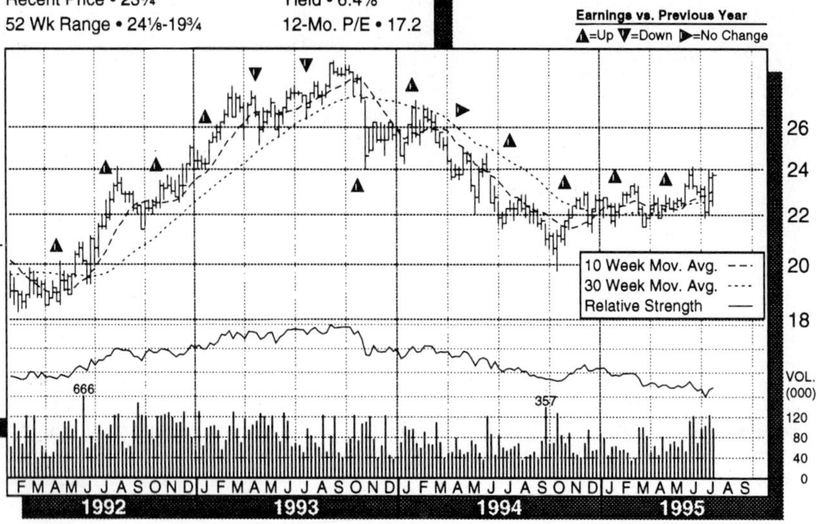

Business Profile - 26-JUL-95

In May 1995, in order to pursue strategies more in line with its core utility business, NJR announced its decision to exit the oil and gas production business. The company continues to experience strong customer growth, making it one of the fastest-growing natural gas utilities in the nation, with a projected growth rate of more than 3% in fiscal 1995. New Jersey Natural Energy Co. was recently created to market gas services to commercial, industrial and electric generation users.

Operational Review - 25-JUL-95

Revenues from continuing operations in the first nine months of fiscal 1995 fell modestly, reflecting warm winter weather and a decline in average customer usage, despite continued customer growth and increased sales to non-core markets. During the third quarter, NJR's oil and gas production business was classified as a discontinued operation following the company's decision to exit this business, and a one-time, after-tax charge of $8.7 million was taken.

Stock Performance - 21-JUL-95

In the past 30 trading days, NJR's shares were unchanged, compared to a 5% rise in the S&P 500. Average trading volume for the past five days was 19,620 shares, compared with the 40-day moving average of 21,482 shares.

Key Stock Statistics

Dividend Rate/Share	1.52	Shareholders	18,500
Shs. outstg. (M)	17.7	Market cap. (B)	$0.420
Avg. daily vol. (M)	0.024	Inst. holdings	31%
Tang. Bk. Value/Share	15.81	Insider holdings	NA
Beta	0.27		

Value of $10,000 invested 5 years ago: $ 16,722

Fiscal Year Ending Sep. 30

	1995	% Change	1994	% Change	1993	% Change
Revenues (Million $)						
1Q	129.9	-5%	136.1	3%	132.6	23%
2Q	194.3	-13%	222.8	18%	189.5	9%
3Q	76.26	NM	75.61	NM	75.70	-2%
4Q	—	—	64.22	13%	56.90	4%
Yr.	—	—	498.8	10%	454.7	10%
Income (Million $)						
1Q	11.24	8%	10.44	-1%	10.55	56%
2Q	25.49	10%	23.27	NM	23.16	14%
3Q	1.19	-64%	3.30	NM	0.97	3%
4Q	—	—	-4.82	NM	-4.99	8%
Yr.	—	—	33.94	19%	28.50	21%
Earnings Per Share ($)						
1Q	0.65	5%	0.62	2%	0.61	27%
2Q	1.45	6%	1.37	NM	1.37	-4%
3Q	0.07	-63%	0.19	NM	0.06	-14%
4Q	—	—	-0.28	NM	-0.30	NM
Yr.	—	—	1.89	10%	1.72	5%

Next earnings report expected: late October

New Jersey Resources

Business Summary - 27-JUL-95

New Jersey Resources is the holding company for New Jersey Natural Gas Co. (NJNG), which distributes natural gas to more than 345,000 customers in Monmouth and Ocean and parts of Morris and Middlesex counties. Subsidiaries are also engaged in real estate development, and the development of cogeneration and independent power production. In May 1995, the company said it would exit the oil and natural gas production business. NJNG operating revenues by customer class in recent fiscal years were:

	1993-94	1992-93	1991-92
Residential	75%	74%	74%
Commercial, industrial & other	21%	21%	21%
JCP&L and PSE&G	2%	3%	2%
Interruptible	2%	2%	3%

Therm sales to firm customers in fiscal 1994 rose to 504 million versus 474 million a year earlier. Average use per residential customer was 1,211 therms and 5,287 therms per commercial customer.

Natural gas requirements in fiscal 1994 were met mainly through eight federally regulated suppliers, with the predominant supplier being Alberta Northeast, and through unbundled supplies. Total gas volumes purchased in 1994 were 846,404,000 therms versus 765,458,000 in 1993. The average cost per therm was $0.33 versus $0.36.

In fiscal 1994, NJR added 11,222 new natural gas customers, representing a growth rate of over 3%, which is expected to continue over the next five years.

Commercial Realty & Resources Corp. develops and owns office and mixed use real estate projects in Monmouth and Atlantic counties. At September 30, 1994, NJR had completed 17 buildings totaling 914,200 sq. ft., with an occupancy rate of 97%.

Paradigm Power, Inc. was formed in April 1992 to pursue investment opportunities in natural gas-fueled cogeneration and independent power projects.

In May 1995, NJR said it planned to exit the oil and natural gas production business and pursue the sale of the reserves and related assets of its NJR Energy and New Jersey Natural Resources units. Such subsidiaries were classified as discontinued operations and NJR recorded a related after-tax charge of $8.7 million ($0.42 a share) in fiscal 1995's third quarter.

Important Developments

Jul. '95—NJR said it formed a new non-regulated subsidiary, New Jersey Natural Energy Co., during fiscal 1995's third quarter to market gas services to commercial, industrial and electric generation users in New Jersey and neighboring states.

Capitalization

Long Term Debt: $323,877,000 (3/95).
Subsid. Red. Preferred Stock: $21,285,000.

Per Share Data ($) (Year Ended Sep. 30)

	1994	1993	1992	1991	1990	1989
Tangible Bk. Val.	14.46	14.72	14.16	12.85	13.27	13.65
Earnings	1.89	1.72	1.64	0.83	0.97	1.45
Dividends	1.52	1.52	1.52	1.50	1.44	1.36
Payout Ratio	80%	88%	93%	181%	148%	94%
Prices - High	27⅜	29½	25⅛	21⅛	20⅞	21½
- Low	19¾	24	18¼	17	17⅛	17⅛
P/E Ratio - High	14	17	15	25	22	15
- Low	10	14	11	20	18	12

Income Statement Analysis (Million $)

	1994	%Chg	1993	%Chg	1992	%Chg	1991
Revs.	499	10%	455	10%	412	23%	335
Depr.	27.6	9%	25.4	5%	24.3	12%	21.7
Maint.	NA	—	NA	—	6.4	-12%	7.3
Fxd. Chgs. Cov.	3.0	5%	2.8	15%	2.5	43%	1.7
Constr. Credits	Nil	—	3.2	-3%	3.3	-8%	3.6
Eff. Tax Rate	30%	—	30%	—	31%	—	31%
Net Inc.	33.9	19%	28.5	21%	23.5	108%	11.3

Balance Sheet & Other Fin. Data (Million $)

	1994	1993	1992	1991	1990	1989
Gross Prop.	859	831	770	725	673	588
Cap. Exp.	58.6	70.4	47.6	57.4	83.2	84.8
Net Prop.	640	633	592	567	533	463
Capitalization:						
LT Debt	324	311	252	263	228	209
% LT Debt	54	54	49	55	54	52
Pfd.	22.1	22.3	32.6	32.9	13.2	13.4
% Pfd.	3.70	3.90	6.30	6.90	3.10	3.30
Common	250	248	231	179	179	180
% Common	42	43	45	38	43	45
Total Cap.	661	642	577	529	475	451

Ratio Analysis

	1994	1993	1992	1991	1990	1989
Oper. Ratio	89.2	89.0	88.7	89.6	89.5	89.5
% Earn. on Net Prop.	8.7	8.2	8.0	6.3	6.8	8.1
% Ret. on Revs.	6.8	6.3	5.7	3.4	4.0	5.0
% Ret. On Invest.Cap	8.6	8.4	8.6	7.0	7.4	8.8
% Return On Com.Eqty	13.4	11.9	11.4	6.3	7.2	10.4

Dividend Data (Dividends have been paid since 1951. A dividend reinvestment plan is available.)

Amt. of Div. $	Date Decl.	Ex-Div. Date	Stock of Record	Payment Date
0.380	Sep. 14	Sep. 19	Sep. 23	Oct. 03 '94
0.380	Dec. 01	Dec. 09	Dec. 15	Jan. 02 '95
0.380	Jan. 16	Mar. 09	Mar. 15	Apr. 03 '95
0.380	May. 22	Jun. 13	Jun. 15	Jul. 03 '95
0.380	Jul. 13	Sep. 13	Sep. 15	Oct. 02 '95

Data as orig. reptd.; bef. results of disc opers. and/or spec. items. Per share data adj. for stk. divs. as of ex-div. date. E-Estimated. NA-Not Available. NM-Not Meaningful. NR-Not Ranked.

Office—1415 Wyckoff Road, P.O. Box 1468, Wall, NJ 07719. **Tel**—(908) 938-1480. **Chrmn**—B. C. Coe. **Pres & CEO**—L. M. Downes. **SVP & Secy**—Oleta J. Harden. **Dirs**—R. E. Birk, B. G. Coe, L. M. Downes, J. B. Foster, W. R. Haas, S. A. Jackson, D. K. Light, D. E. O'Neill, R. S. Sambol, C. G. Stalon, T. B Toohey, J. J. Unkles, Jr. **Transfer Agent & Registrar**—The First National Bank of Boston. **Incorporated** in New Jersey in 1922. **Empl**-864. **S&P Analyst:** A.M.A.

STANDARD & POOR'S

STOCK REPORTS

Newfield Exploration

NYSE Symbol **NFX**
In S&P SmallCap 600

08-OCT-95 **Industry:** Oil and Gas

Summary: Newfield Exploration is a small independent oil and natural gas exploration and production company working primarily in the Gulf of Mexico offshore Louisiana and Texas.

Quantitative Evaluations

Outlook (1 Lowest—5 Highest)
• **NA**
Fair Value
• **NA**
Risk
• **Average**
Earn./Div. Rank
• **NR**

Technical Eval.
• **Bullish** since 8/95
Rel. Strength Rank (1 Lowest—99 Highest)
• **70**
Insider Activity
• **Unfavorable**

Recent Price • 30⅜
52 Wk Range • 32⅛-18
Yield • Nil
12-Mo. P/E • 34.5

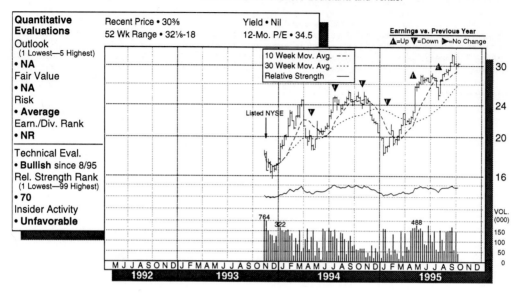

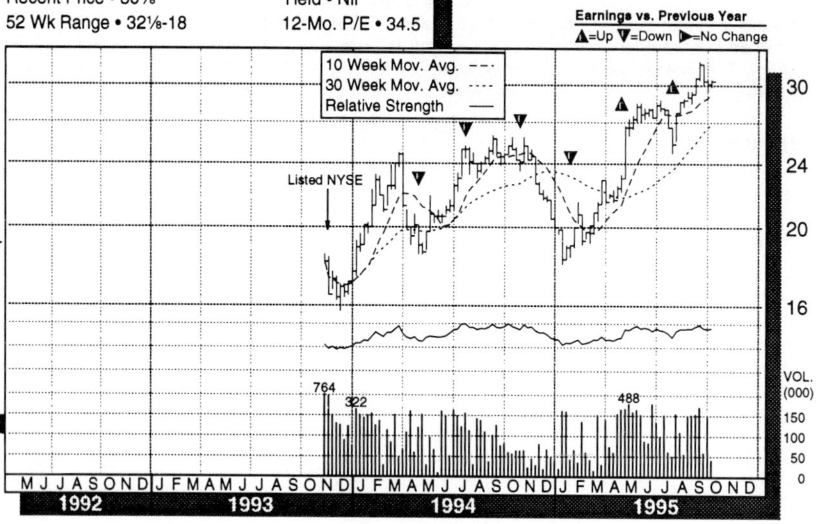

Business Profile - 05-JUL-95

This independent oil and gas producer has focused its operations in the Gulf of Mexico offshore Louisiana and Texas. Newfield's revenues, profitability and future rate of growth are highly dependent upon prevailing prices for natural gas and oil. NFX ranks among the lowest-cost domestic E&P concerns, and has little long term debt. NFX plans to continue to expand its reserve base and increase its cash flow through exploration, acquistition of proved properties and development of its properties.

Operational Review - 06-OCT-95

Oil and gas revenues in the six months ended June 30, 1995, advanced 45%, year to year, reflecting sharply higher production (up 62% to 21.8 billion cubic feet of natural gas equivalent) and increased oil prices, which outweighed lower gas prices. While other expenses were well controlled, DD&A was up 66%, and the gain in pretax income was held to 20%. After taxes at 35.0%, versus 36.4%, net income rose 23%, to $7,820,000 ($0.44 a share) from $6,376,000 ($0.36).

Stock Performance - 06-OCT-95

In the past 30 trading days, NFX's shares have increased 5%, compared to a 4% rise in the S&P 500. Average trading volume for the past five days was 7,980 shares, compared with the 40-day moving average of 30,236 shares.

Key Stock Statistics

Dividend Rate/Share	Nil	Shareholders	3,400
Shs. outstg. (M)	17.1	Market cap. (B)	$0.519
Avg. daily vol. (M)	0.032	Inst. holdings	56%
Tang. Bk. Value/Share	10.73	Insider holdings	NA
Beta	1.23		

Value of $10,000 invested 5 years ago: NA

Fiscal Year Ending Dec. 31

	1995	% Change	1994	% Change	1993	% Change
Revenues (Million $)						
1Q	19.03	37%	13.86	7%	12.94	—
2Q	24.81	51%	16.40	NM	16.43	—
3Q	—	—	18.95	34%	14.17	—
4Q	—	—	20.53	23%	16.65	—
Yr.	—	—	69.73	16%	60.18	NM
Income (Million $)						
1Q	3.40	16%	2.94	2%	2.89	—
2Q	4.42	28%	3.44	NM	3.46	—
3Q	—	—	4.32	18%	3.66	—
4Q	—	—	3.75	-6%	4.01	—
Yr.	—	—	14.44	3%	14.03	8%
Earnings Per Share ($)						
1Q	0.19	19%	0.16	-27%	0.22	—
2Q	0.24	26%	0.19	-21%	0.24	—
3Q	—	—	0.24	-8%	0.26	—
4Q	—	—	0.21	-16%	0.25	—
Yr.	—	—	0.80	-18%	0.98	NM

Next earnings report expected: early November

Newfield Exploration

Business Summary - 06-OCT-95

Newfield Exploration is a small independent oil and gas company engaged in the exploration, development and acquisition of oil and natural gas properties located in the Gulf of Mexico, primarily offshore Louisiana in water depths of less than 300 feet. Seismic and other geologic data for the shallow water areas of the Gulf of Mexico are readily available at reasonable costs, and there is also a substantial existing infrastructure. The company prefers exploration prospects and property acquisitions that allow it to operate the properties in order to manage production and control operating expenses.

NFX discovered and acquired its first oil and gas reserves in 1990 and has grown rapidly since that time. Through December 31, 1994, NFX drilled 41 exploratory wells and acquired interests in 68 leases in fields offshore Louisiana and Texas. Approximately 75% of proved reserves were natural gas and 92% were proved developed.

Production of oil and condensate in 1994 was 1,394,000 barrels, up from 901,000 bbls. in 1993. Natural gas production was 24,267 MMcf, compared with 22,540 MMcf in 1993. The average sales price for oil was $15.73 per bbl. in 1994 and $16.92 in 1993. In 1994, the average sales price per Mcf of natural gas was $1.97, versus $1.99 in 1993. Total production, in equivalent Mcf, in 1994 was 32,631 MMcfe, versus 27,946 MMcfe in 1993. Proved oil reserves at year-end 1994 were 8,610,000 bbls, versus 6,414,000 bbls a year before. Natural gas reserves at year-end 1994 were 153,967 MMcf, and 102,261 MMcf in 1993. Total equivalent natural gas reserves at year-end 1994 were 205,627 MMcfe, compared with 140,742 MMcfe in 1993.

In order to increase both the size and number of prospects that it has been able to pursue, NFX has entered into agreements with several institutional and corporate investors which have participated in substantially all of the exploration and acquisition activities through direct working interests. Program participants has agreed to commit a fixed percentage of the company's $20 million per year exploration budget. Collectively, as of January 1, 1994, 25% of the company's exploration program was for the account of program participants, with the remaining 75% for the account of NFX.

Important Developments

Jul. '95—NFX noted that during 1995's second quarter five exploratory wells were drilled, four of which were successsful. Of five development wells drilled during the period, four were successful, bringing the total number of wells drilled during 1995 to 18.

Capitalization

Long Term Debt: $10,292,000, including $292,000 of capital lease obligations (6/95).

Per Share Data ($) (Year Ended Dec. 31)

	1994	1993	1992	1991	1990	1989
Tangible Bk. Val.	10.17	9.24	8.57	NA	NA	NA
Cash Flow	2.70	2.73	3.14	NA	NA	NA
Earnings	0.80	0.98	0.98	NA	NA	NA
Dividends	Nil	Nil	NA	NA	NA	NA
Payout Ratio	Nil	Nil	NA	NA	NA	NA
Prices - High	26	18½	NA	NA	NA	NA
- Low	17⅞	15¾	NA	NA	NA	NA
P/E Ratio - High	32	19	NA	NA	NA	NA
- Low	22	16	NA	NA	NA	NA

Income Statement Analysis (Million $)

	1994	%Chg	1993	%Chg	1992	%Chg	1991
Revs.	69.7	16%	60.2	1%	59.6	—	NA
Oper. Inc.	56.4	14%	49.4	NM	49.7	—	NA
Depr. Depl. & Amort.	34.1	36%	25.1	-12%	28.6	—	NA
Int. Exp.	0.4	NM	0.1	-97%	1.5	—	NA
Pretax Inc.	22.5	3%	21.8	11%	19.7	—	NA
Eff. Tax Rate	36%	—	36%	—	34%	—	NA
Net Inc.	14.4	3%	14.0	8%	13.0	—	NA

Balance Sheet & Other Fin. Data (Million $)

	1994	1993	1992	1991	1990	1989
Cash	18.6	65.0	NA	NA	NA	NA
Curr. Assets	35.9	88.3	NA	NA	NA	NA
Total Assets	216	184	NA	NA	NA	NA
Curr. Liab.	24.9	18.1	NA	NA	NA	NA
LT Debt	0.6	0.4	0.6	NA	NA	NA
Common Eqty.	169	153	137	NA	NA	NA
Total Cap.	190	165	NA	NA	NA	NA
Cap. Exp.	115	43.8	NA	NA	NA	NA
Cash Flow	48.6	39.1	41.6	NA	NA	NA

Ratio Analysis

	1994	1993	1992	1991	1990	1989
Curr. Ratio	1.4	4.9	NA	NA	NA	NA
% LT Debt of Cap.	0.3	0.3	NA	NA	NA	NA
% Ret. on Assets	7.2	9.1	NA	NA	NA	NA
% Ret. on Equity	8.9	11.1	NA	NA	NA	NA

Dividend Data —The company said in its initial offering prospectus dated November 1993 that it did not intend to pay cash dividends on its common stock in the foreseeable future, but to retain any earnings for the future operation and development of the business.

Data as orig. reptd.; bef. results of disc opers. and/or spec. items. Per share data adj. for stk. divs. as of ex-div. date. E-Estimated. NA-Not Available. NM-Not Meaningful. NR-Not Ranked.

Office—363 North Sam Houston Parkway East, Suite 2020, Houston, TX 77060. **Tel**—(713) 847-6000. **Chrmn, CEO & Pres**—J. B. Foster. **VP-CFO & Secy**—T. W. Rathert. **Dirs**—C. W. Duncan, Jr., J. B. Foster, J. A. Harris, H. H. Newman, T. G. Ricks, C. E. Schultz, R. W. Waldrup, D. E. Zand. **Transfer Agent & Registrar**—Chemical Bank, NYC. **Incorporated** in Delaware in 1988. **Empl-** 50. **S&P Analyst:** N. Rosenberg

Noble Drilling

NASDAQ Symbol NDCO In S&P SmallCap 600 (Incl. in Nat'l Market)

Price	Range	P-E Ratio	Dividend	Yield	S&P Ranking	Beta
Sep. 28'95	1995					
7⅝	8⅜–5	NM	None	None	NR	0.21

Summary

This company is engaged principally in providing contract drilling services for the oil and gas industry worldwide. After eight consecutive years of losses, profitability was restored in 1993. Despite higher operating revenues, share earnings fell in 1994 as a result of nonrecurring charges and higher preferred dividends. A net loss was reported in 1995's first half, reflecting a decline in contract drilling services and narrower margins.

Current Outlook

A per-share loss of $0.02 is projected for 1995, versus share earnings of $0.11 in 1994.

No dividends have been paid on the common stock.

The loss projected for 1995 should reflect deterioration of day rates in the U.S. Gulf during 1995's first half. Day rates and utilization rates should remain under pressure for the rest of 1995, as no significant improvement in natural gas prices or rig demand outside the U.S. Gulf should be seen. However, share earnings should improve to $0.25 in 1996, reflecting improving day rates and international operations.

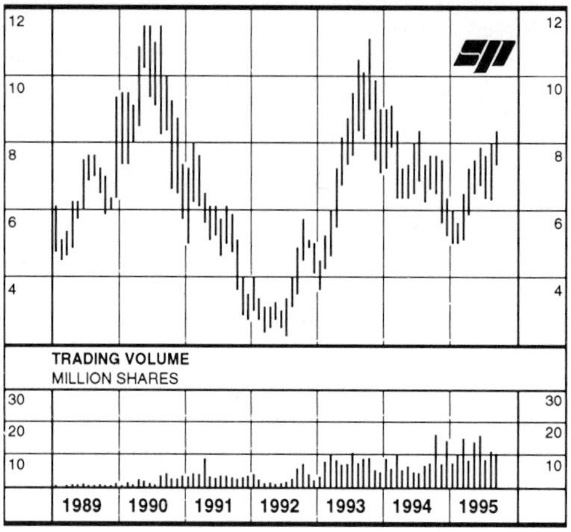

Revenues (Million $)

Quarter:	1995	1994	1993	1992
Mar.	85.1	78.9	52.2	35.9
Jun.	87.6	71.6	39.5	32.9
Sep.		98.1	44.8	33.3
Dec.		87.4	58.5	37.7
		352.0	194.9	139.7

Revenues for the first half of 1995 fell 4.5%, year to year, as a decrease in offshore contract drilling services was partially offset by revenues from Triton Engineering. Gross margins from contract drilling narrowed, due to fewer operating days and lower average dayrates, a gross loss was incurred at the turnkey drilling operations. A net loss of $5.0 million ($0.13 a share based on 9.3% more shares) contrasted with net income of $20.5 million ($0.18).

Common Share Earnings ($)

Quarter:	1995	1994	1993	1992
Mar.	d0.06	0.06	0.05	d0.15
Jun.	d0.07	0.05	0.07	d0.12
Sep.	E0.02	d0.01	0.12	d0.09
Dec.	E0.09	d0.06	0.09	d0.07
	Ed0.02	0.11	0.32	d0.43

Important Developments

Jul. '95— Noble signed long-term drilling contracts for five of its offshore jackup drilling rigs in Venezuela and Nigeria. Two of Noble's four jackup rigs on Lake Maracaibo in Venezuela received five-year contracts from Lagoven, an affiliate of Petroleos de Venezuela, the state oil company. The Dick Favor and Carl Norberg jackups began their new contracts in May and June 1995, respectively, and will be under contract until the year 2000. Both rigs previously were contracted with Lagoven. Also in Venezuela, a contract has been secured for the Charles Copeland jackup with Shell Venezuela S.A. The unit will be under contract until August 1997. In Nigeria, the jackup Don Walker and the jackup Percy Johns both received three-year contracts with Mobil Producing Nigeria Unlimited.

Next earnings report expected in mid-October.

Per Share Data ($)

Yr. End Dec. 31	[1]1994	1993	1992	1991	1990	1989	[1]1988	1987	1986	1985
Tangible Bk. Val.	**4.53**	5.35	3.99	4.61	5.08	5.02	5.63	5.21	6.28	10.19
Cash Flow	**0.62**	0.85	0.08	0.17	0.36	0.16	0.18	0.31	d1.41	NA
Earnings[2]	**0.11**	0.32	d0.43	d0.42	d0.35	d0.50	d0.42	d0.71	d3.90	NA
Dividends	**Nil**	Nil	Nil	Nil	Nil	Nil	Nil	Nil	Nil	Nil
Payout Ratio	**Nil**	Nil	Nil	Nil	Nil	Nil	Nil	Nil	Nil	Nil
Prices—High	**9⅛**	11⅛	5¾	8	11½	9⅜	6⅜	7⅝	3¾	4½
Low	**5¼**	3⅝	2¼	2¾	5¾	4½	3½	2¼	1½	2½
P/E Ratio—	**83–48**	35–11	NM	NM	NM	NM	NM	NM	NM	NM

Data as orig. reptd. **1.** Refl. merger or acq. **2.** Bef. results of disc. ops. of -0.10 in 1992, -0.05 in 1991 & spec. item(s) of +0.05 in 1993, +0.15 in 1991, +0.16 in 1989. d-Deficit. E-Estimated. NM-Not Meaningful. NA-Not Available.

Income Data (Million $)

Year Ended Dec. 31	Revs.	Oper. Inc.	% Oper. Inc. of Revs.	Cap. Exp.	Depr.	Int. Exp.	Net Bef. Taxes	Eff. Tax Rate	[3]Net Inc.	% Net Inc. of Revs.	Cash Flow
[2]1994	**352**	**66.5**	**18.9**	**56**	**39.5**	**12.4**	**[4]27.0**	**21.0%**	**21.5**	**6.1**	**48.3**
1993	195	43.8	22.5	170	20.4	5.4	[4]21.4	11.6%	19.1	9.8	32.8
1992	140	13.3	9.5	5	17.7	7.8	d5.8	NM	d8.1	NM	2.9
[1]1991	177	21.8	12.3	104	19.9	14.5	d11.2	NM	d13.4	NM	5.8
1990	136	10.8	8.0	65	18.3	2.5	d7.6	NM	d8.8	NM	9.6
1989	106	4.3	4.1	10	14.2	2.7	d9.7	NM	d10.5	NM	3.6
[2]1988	44	d0.7	NM	70	12.1	0.7	d13.3	NM	d8.4	NM	3.7
1987	29	d1.1	NM	7	14.5	0.5	d16.9	NM	d10.1	NM	4.4
1986	35	d1.1	NM	4	28.0	3.0	d82.0	NM	d44.0	NM	d15.9
1985	71	7.7	10.8	4	34.7	4.4	d31.0	NM	d16.5	NM	18.2

Balance Sheet Data (Million $)

		Curr.									
Dec. 31	Cash	Assets	Liab.	Ratio	Total Assets	% Ret. on Assets	Long Term Debt	Common Equity	Total Cap.	% LT Debt of Cap.	% Ret. on Equity
1994	**145.0**	**240**	**82.3**	**2.9**	**740**	**2.8**	**127.0**	**352**	**655**	**19.3**	**2.3**
1993	44.1	117	42.3	2.8	500	4.1	127.0	254	456	27.9	5.6
1992	27.5	80	55.1	1.4	310	NM	41.3	137	253	16.3	NM
1991	56.1	118	71.4	1.6	377	NM	71.2	156	302	23.6	NM
1990	48.8	82	39.4	2.1	271	NM	59.5	169	231	25.8	NM
1989	7.1	43	24.4	1.8	177	NM	20.0	115	151	13.3	NM
1988	1.4	25	16.7	1.5	175	NM	21.2	122	158	13.4	NM
1987	2.1	10	5.2	1.9	104	NM	6.1	87	98	6.2	NM
1986	7.7	12	4.7	2.6	116	NM	27.3	71	110	24.8	NM
1985	10.9	22	10.8	2.0	202	NA	27.6	115	190	14.5	NA

Data as orig. reptd. **1.** Excl. disc. ops. **2.** Refl. merger or acq. **3.** Bef. spec. items. **4.** Incl. equity in earns. of nonconsol. subs. d-Deficit. NM-Not Meaningful. NA-Not Available.

Business Summary

Noble Drilling Corporation is primarily engaged in contract drilling services for the oil and gas industry. In September 1994, Noble acquired Chiles Offshore Corp. Contributions to revenues were:

	1994	1993	1992	1991
Drilling:				
International offshore	30%	30%	46%	23%
Domestic offshore	33%	45%	22%	40%
International land	5%	7%	3%	10%
Domestic land	3%	3%	5%	5%
Labor contract drilling	10%	13%	19%	17%
Turnkey drilling	16%	---	---	---
Engineering and consulting	1%	1%	2%	4%
Other	2%	1%	3%	1%

Offshore operations are conducted primarily in the Gulf of Mexico, West Africa, Venezuela and, to a lesser extent, India. At December 31, 1994, the company's offshore fleet totaled 44 rigs, consisting of 32 jackup drilling rigs, eight submersible rigs and four posted barges. The average age of the offshore fleet was 14 years, with 34 of the 44 offshore rigs having been built or rebuilt since 1980. Noble also has labor contracts for drilling and workover activities covering 16 offshore rigs operating in the U.K. North Sea and one offshore rig operating in the Middle East. These rigs are not owned or leased by the company.

Land drilling operations are conducted in Canada, Texas and Louisiana. The land fleet consists of 46 rigs, of which 19 are active.

Through wholly owned Triton Engineering Services, Noble provides turnkey drilling, drilling project management, drilling and completion planning and design, specialized drilling tools and services, and contract engineering and consulting manpower. Engineering design services are provided through Noble Engineering Services Ltd.

Dividend Data

No dividends have been paid on the common stock. Debt agreements prohibit payments. A stockholder rights plan was adopted in June 1995.

Capitalization

Long Term Debt: $126,286,000 (6/95).

Minority Interest: $419,000.

$1.50 Conv. Exch. Pfd. Stk.: 4,025,000 shs. ($1 par); $25 liq. pref.; conv. into 2.4446 com. shs.

Common Stock: 94,436,609 shs. ($0.10 par). Institutions hold about 72%. Shareholders: 2,393 of record (3/8/95).

Options: To buy 1,810,472 shs. at $2.50 to $7.69 ea. (12/94).

d-Deficit.

Office—10370 Richmond Ave., Suite 400, Houston, TX 77042. **Tel**—(713) 974-3131. **Chrmn, Pres & CEO**—J. C. Day. **SVP-Fin, Treas & Investor Contact**—Byron L. Welliver. **Secy**—J. J. Robertson. **Dirs**—M. A. Cawley, L. J. Chazen, T. C. Craighead, J. C. Day, J. L. Fishel, J. W. Hoffman, E. Holt, M. E. Leland, J. F. Snodgrass, B. M. Thompson. **Transfer Agent & Registrar**—Liberty National Bank & Trust Co. of Oklahoma City. **Incorporated** in Delaware in 1939. **Empl**—2,673.

 Ronald J. Gross

North American Mortgage

NYSE Symbol NAC In S&P SmallCap 600

Price	Range	P-E Ratio	Dividend	Yield	S&P Ranking	Beta
Sep. 7'95	1995					
24¼	25⅞–14½	28	0.24	1.0%	NR	NA

Summary

This mortgage banking company is the tenth largest originator of residential mortgage loans in the U.S.—principally first lien mortgage loans secured by single-family residences. Earnings in 1994 fell sharply due to a significant decline in loan origination fee income, which was related to rising interest rates. However, earnings improved in the first half of 1995, as results were boosted by a decline in expenses.

Business Summary

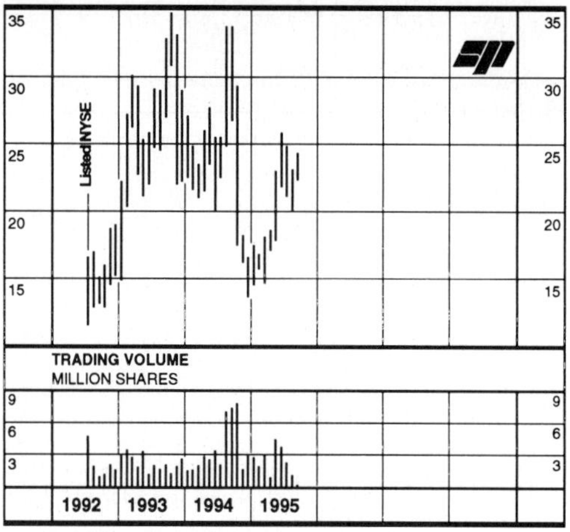

North American Mortgage originates, acquires, sells and services mortgage loans, principally first lien mortgage loans secured by one- to four-family residences. It also sells servicing rights associated with a portion of such loans. As of February 28, 1995, NAC operated through 93 loan origination offices in 28 states and D.C., and was a leading residential lender in California, Texas, Maryland, Virginia, Colorado, Hawaii, Oregon, New Mexico, Florida and Arizona. NAC originated $9.8 billion of mortgage loans in 1994, versus $17.6 billion the year before.

Sources of revenues in recent years:

	1994	1993
Gain on sales of servicing rights	45%	27%
Loan origination fees	28%	39%
Loan servicing fees	19%	12%
Gain/Loss on sale of loans	–5%	12%
Net interest income	11%	8%
Other	2%	2%

The company's mortgage loan originations are generated from three primary sources: wholesale, which represents loans solicited from loan brokers (accounting for 61% of originations in 1994); retail, which represents loans generated principally through builders and real estate brokers (32%); and telemarketing, which represents loans generated by telephone and mail (7%). NAC's significant loan origination markets are California, Texas and Maryland. The company customarily sells all of its mortgage loan originations, retaining servicing rights. The majority of conventional loans are sold under purchase and guarantee programs sponsored by the Federal Home Loan Mortgage Corp. (Freddie Mac) and the Federal National Mortgage Association (Fannie Mae).

Mortgage loan servicing entails collecting payments from borrowers and remitting such funds to investors, accounting for principal and interest payments, holding escrow funds for the payment of taxes and insurance and other administrative duties. The company's owned loan servicing portfolio at year-end 1994 amounted to $14.8 billion, with NAC having primary servicing responsibility for approximately 99.5% of its owned loans.

In August 1994, NAC retained Morgan Stanley & Co. to advise it on strategic alternatives to enhance shareholder value. Rising intest rates reduced originations in the latter half ot the year and precluded the sale of NAC at a premium to market value. Management continues to explore ways to increase shareholder value.

Important Developments

Sep. '95— NAC reported that its August 1995 loan applications were $1.23 billion, a 19% increase over August 1994 applications of $1.03 billion; loan fundings were up 29%. August marked the fourth consecutive month in which loan applications increased over the same month from the prior year. The most significant increase was in the Midwest region, established during NAC's 1994 geographic expansion, where applications grew 130%, year to year.

Next earnings report expected in October.

Per Share Data ($)

Yr. End Dec. 31	1994	1993	1992	[1]1991	[1]1990	[1]1989
Tangible Bk. Val.	**9.76**	9.63	4.16	[2]3.07	NA	NA
Earnings	**0.53**	3.17	2.37	1.19	0.36	0.98
Dividends	**0.24**	0.21	0.05	NA	NA	NA
Payout Ratio	**45%**	7%	2%	NA	NA	NA
Prices—High	**33¾**	34¾	19	NA	NA	NA
Low	**13⅝**	14⅞	11½	NA	NA	NA
P/E Ratio—	**64–26**	11–5	8–5	NA	NA	NA

Data as orig. reptd. **1.** Pro forma. **2.** As of 3-31-92. NA-Not Available.

Income Data (Million $)

Year Ended Dec. 31	Loan Fees	Invest. Inc.	Total Revs.	Int. Exp.	% Exp./ Op. Revs.	Net Bef. Taxes	Eff. Tax Rate	Net Inc.	% Return On Revs.	% Return On Assets	% Return On Equity
1994	**126**	**29.5**	**268**	**10.81**	**95.8**	**11.2**	**27.2%**	**8.2**	**3.1**	**0.7**	**5.2**
1993	165	26.0	325	6.19	77.4	73.4	35.1%	47.7	3.6	3.9	39.6
1992	107	21.3	213	5.17	77.8	42.0	22.7%	32.5	15.2	4.0	66.4
[1]1991	60	12.0	127	2.86	81.2	23.9	35.8%	15.3	12.0	NA	NA
[1]1990	46	5.9	88	3.22	93.3	5.8	20.2%	4.7	5.3	NA	NA
[1]1989	40	3.6	97	6.20	80.7	18.8	32.6%	12.7	12.7	NA	NA

Balance Sheet Data (Million $)

Dec. 31	[2]Loans Serviced	Total Assets	Cash & Secs.	Loans	Loans/ Equity	Capitalization [4]Debt	Capitalization Equity	Capitalization Total	Price Times Book Value HI LO
1994	**14,836**	**765**	**102.0**	**542**	**6.4–1**	**382**	**153.1**	**535**	**3.5–1.4**
1993	17,276	1,627	11.7	1,495	10.1–1	371	165.4	536	3.6–1.5
1992	11,620	1,021	5.2	930	14.7–1	121	75.4	197	4.6–2.8
[3]1991	10,507	628	0.3	543	NA	45	46.4	92	NA

Data as orig. reptd. **1.** Pro forma. **2.** Portfolio of loans serviced. **3.** As of 3-31-92, pro forma. **4.** Incl. curr. portion. NA-Not Available.

Review of Operations

In the six months ended June 30, 1995, total revenues fell 24%, principally due to a 39% decline in loan origination fees, and a 68% drop in gains from sales of servicing. Total expenses were down 32%, paced by a 36% reduction in personnel costs and a 34% decline in other operating expenses. After taxes at 36.2%, versus 37.2%, net income advanced 40% to $15,707,000 ($1.05 a share on 4.0% fewer shares) from $11,224,000 ($0.72).

Common Share Earnings ($)

Quarter:	1995	1994	1993	1992
Mar.	0.38	0.71	0.61	0.48
Jun.	0.67	0.01	0.88	0.57
Sep.		d0.27	0.83	0.64
Dec.		0.07	0.84	0.68
		0.53	3.17	2.37

Dividend Data

North American's certificate of incorporation prohibits the payment of dividends in excess of $1.00 a share per year until June 30, 1995. Credit agreements restrict the amount of dividends that may be paid by the company in any quarter to an amount which, when added to all other dividends and restricted payments during such quarter and the preceding three quarters, does not exceed one third of the company's net earnings for the preceding four quarters. A "poison pill" stock purchase right was adopted in October 1992.

Amt of Divd. $	Date Decl.	Ex–divd. Date	Stock of Record	Payment Date
0.06	Oct. 14	Oct. 18	Oct. 24	Nov. 15'94
0.06	Feb. 14	Feb. 17	Feb. 24	Mar. 08'95
0.06	May 03	May 09	May 15	May 22'95
0.06	Jul. 12	Jul. 28	Aug. 01	Aug. 15'95

Finances

On January 23, 1995, NAC entered into two new warehouse line of credit facilities totaling $800 million. These lines of credit are renewable annually and $320 million expires on January 22, 1996, and $480 million expires on January 23, 1997. Management expects this facility to continue to be available in the future.

In February 1994, directors of North American Mortgage authorized the repurchase of up to 1.5 million shares, or about 9.5% of its common stock outstanding. As of December 31, 1994, the company had repurchased 1.0 million shares at an aggregate cost of $19.2 million.

Capitalization

Total Debt: $565,390,000 (6/95).

Common Stock: 15,080,170 shs. ($0.01 par).
Officers & directors control about 6%.
Institutions hold about 61%.
Shareholders: 1,013 of record (3/95).

d-Deficit.

Office—3883 Airway Drive, Santa Rosa, CA 95403. **Tel**—(707) 523-5000. **Chrmn & CEO**—J. F. Farrell Jr. **Pres & COO**—T. G. Hodel. **EVP, Treas-CFO & Investor Contact**—Martin S. Hughes. **Dirs**—W. L. Brown, W. F. Connell, J. F. Farrell Jr., T. G. Hodel, W. O. Murphy, R. J. Murray, J. B. Nicholson. **Transfer Agent & Registrar**—Bank of New York, NYC. **Incorporated** in Delaware in 1991. **Empl**—2,355.

 Thomas C. Ferguson

North American Vaccine

ASE Symbol **NVX**
In S&P SmallCap 600

21-SEP-95

Industry: Medical equipment/ supply

Summary: This company, both directly and through subsidiaries, is engaged in research, development and manufacture of vaccines to prevent human infectious diseases.

Quantitative Evaluations
Outlook (1 Lowest—5 Highest)
• **NA**
Fair Value
• **NA**
Risk
• **High**
Earn./Div. Rank
• **NR**

Technical Eval.
• **Bearish** since 7/95
Rel. Strength Rank (1 Lowest—99 Highest)
• **73**
Insider Activity
• **NA**

Recent Price • 10½
52 Wk Range • 13⅞-5¼
Yield • Nil
12-Mo. P/E • 61.8

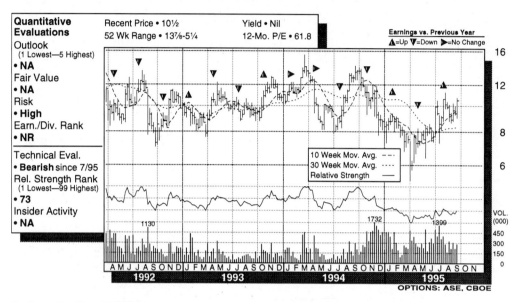

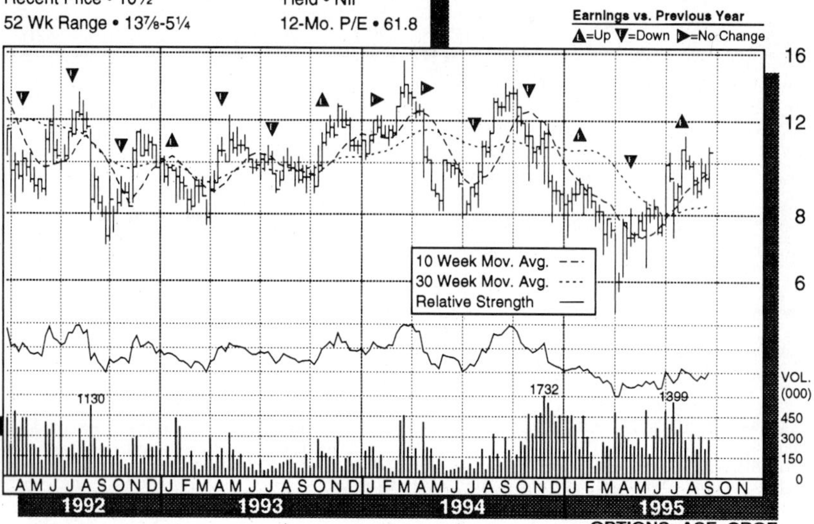

OPTIONS: ASE, CBOE

Business Profile - 21-SEP-95

NVX is developing a new vaccine for whooping cough, and also holds licenses to develop, manufacture and sell vaccines against meningitis and other bacterial infections. To date, the company's only source of revenue has been from contracts with the National Institute of Child Health and Development. It expects quarterly losses to continue, increasing to about $8.5 million in the 1995 fourth quarter, reflecting costs for clinical trials and the production of its DTaP vaccine.

Operational Review - 21-SEP-95

There were no contract revenues in the first half of 1995. R&D spending increased, and the operating loss widened, but with a $10.9 million gain on the sale of an investment in BioChem Pharma in the second quarter, net income replaced a net loss. NVX expects operating costs to increase moderately in the first two quarters of 1996 from the level in the 1995 fourth quarter, but expects production costs to rise significantly during 1996, as it boosts its vaccine inventory.

Stock Performance - 15-SEP-95

In the past 30 trading days, NVX's shares have increased 4%, compared to a 4% rise in the S&P 500. Average trading volume for the past five days was 55,400 shares, compared with the 40-day moving average of 55,295 shares.

Key Stock Statistics

Dividend Rate/Share	Nil	Shareholders	500
Shs. outstg. (M)	29.8	Market cap. (B)	$0.301
Avg. daily vol. (M)	0.052	Inst. holdings	26%
Tang. Bk. Value/Share	1.24	Insider holdings	NA
Beta	1.70		

Value of $10,000 invested 5 years ago: NA

Fiscal Year Ending Dec. 31

	1995	% Change	1994	% Change	1993	% Change
Revenues (Million $)						
1Q	Nil	—	Nil	—	0.04	—
2Q	—	—	Nil	—	Nil	—
3Q	—	—	Nil	—	0.08	—
4Q	—	—	Nil	—	0.03	-85%
Yr.	—	—	Nil	—	0.14	-91%
Income (Million $)						
1Q	-3.61	NM	-3.12	NM	-2.90	NM
2Q	0.01	NM	-3.73	NM	-3.15	NM
3Q	—	—	-5.30	NM	-3.14	NM
4Q	—	—	8.23	NM	-2.97	NM
Yr.	—	—	-3.93	NM	-12.13	NM
Earnings Per Share ($)						
1Q	-0.12	NM	-0.11	NM	-0.11	NM
2Q	0.18	NM	-0.13	NM	-0.11	NM
3Q	—	—	-0.18	NM	-0.11	NM
4Q	—	—	0.24	NM	-0.11	NM
Yr.	—	—	-0.14	NM	-0.44	NM

Next earnings report expected: early November

North American Vaccine

Business Summary - 21-SEP-95

North American Vaccine Inc. (NAVA) is engaged in research, development and manufacture of vaccines, with an emphasis on vaccines to prevent childhood infectious diseases.

The company has developed a new generation acellular pertussis vaccine that has been combined with diphtheria and tetanus toxoids for use in a DTaP (diphtheria, tetanus and acellular pertussis) vaccine. In July 1994, Phase III clinical trials in Sweden of the DTaP vaccine were concluded.

NVX also intends to combine its DTaP vaccine with other pediatric vaccines currently under development for use in standard immunization programs. The first such vaccine, DTap-IPV, being developed in conjunction with Statens Seruminstitut (SSI), which is owned by the government of Denmark, combines the company's acellular pertussis toxoid with SSI's diphtheria and tetanus toxoid and injectible enhanced inactivated polio vaccine. Phase III trials began in Denmark in May 1993. Phase II clinical trials in the U.S. are expected to be completed in 1996.

The company is in the preclinical stage of developing a vaccine that combines its DTaP vaccine with a vaccine against meningitis caused by HIB, as well as a DTaP-IPV-HIB vaccine. These include vaccines against meningococcal B; meningococcal C; meningococcal A/C; meningococcal A/B/C; Haemophilus influenzae type b; group B streptococcal; group A streptococcal; and pneumococcal infections.

In the 1995 second quarter of 1995, NVX sold all its entire holding of 695,936 BioChem Pharma Inc. common shares for $11.5 million, realizing a gain of $10.9 million. In October 1994, it had placed privately 1.1 million BioChem shares for $10.2 million, realizing a gain of $9.3 million.

Important Developments

Aug. '95—The company said it filed for U.K. approval to start a Phase I clinical trial for its conjugate vaccine against Group C Meningococcal infection. Upon completion of the adult study, a Phase II study will be initiated in infants. Clinical trials are expected to be completed within 18 months.

Capitalization

Long Term Debt: None (6/95).
Series A Conv. Preferred Stock: 2,000,000 shs. (no par). Conv. sh.-for-sh. into com.
BioChem Pharma Inc. and IVAX Corp. own 50% each.
Options: To buy 2,476,993 shs. at $1.19 to $13.63 ea. (12/94).

Per Share Data ($) (Year Ended Dec. 31)

	1994	1993	1992	1991	1990	1989
Tangible Bk. Val.	1.38	2.07	1.29	1.63	0.23	0.34
Cash Flow	-0.06	-0.36	-0.32	-0.17	0.03	-0.13
Earnings	-0.14	-0.44	-0.40	-0.26	-0.11	-0.14
Dividends	Nil	Nil	Nil	Nil	Nil	Nil
Payout Ratio	Nil	Nil	Nil	Nil	Nil	Nil
Prices - High	15½	12⅞	17⅛	14	3⅛	NA
- Low	7¾	7⅝	7	1⅛	1	NA
P/E Ratio - High	NM	NM	NM	NM	NM	NA
- Low	NM	NM	NA	NA	NA	NA

Income Statement Analysis (Million $)

	1994	%Chg	1993	%Chg	1992	%Chg	1991
Revs.	Nil	—	0.1	-91%	1.5	72%	0.9
Oper. Inc.	-12.5	NM	-10.6	NM	-9.7	NM	-4.5
Depr.	2.2	2%	2.2	NM	2.1	2%	2.1
Int. Exp.	Nil	—	Nil	—	0.0	-97%	0.3
Pretax Inc.	-3.9	NM	-12.1	NM	-10.7	NM	-5.8
Eff. Tax Rate	NM	—	NM	—	NM	—	NM
Net Inc.	-3.9	NM	-12.1	NM	-10.7	NM	-5.8

Balance Sheet & Other Fin. Data (Million $)

	1994	1993	1992	1991	1990	1989
Cash	20.9	17.2	28.2	39.9	1.0	5.5
Curr. Assets	21.5	17.9	29.3	40.3	1.7	6.2
Total Assets	49.6	63.8	42.6	51.0	13.2	19.1
Curr. Liab.	5.4	2.1	2.5	3.2	3.4	5.9
LT Debt	Nil	Nil	Nil	Nil	0.5	2.0
Common Eqty.	40.4	57.5	35.7	43.1	4.4	6.2
Total Cap.	43.9	61.3	39.6	47.4	9.3	12.5
Cap. Exp.	6.4	1.6	4.7	1.5	8.5	4.8
Cash Flow	-1.7	-10.0	-8.6	-3.7	0.5	-2.3

Ratio Analysis

	1994	1993	1992	1991	1990	1989
Curr. Ratio	4.0	8.5	11.6	12.8	0.5	1.1
% LT Debt of Cap.	Nil	Nil	Nil	Nil	5.8	15.9
% Net Inc.of Revs.	NM	NM	NM	NM	NM	NM
% Ret. on Assets	NM	NM	NM	NM	NM	NM
% Ret. on Equity	NM	NM	NM	NM	NM	NM

Dividend Data —No cash dividends have been paid. A two-for-one stock split was effected in January 1992.

Data as orig. reptd.; bef. results of disc. opers. and/or spec. items. Per share data adj. for stk. divs. as of ex-div. date. E-Estimated. NA-Not Available. NM-Not Meaningful. NR-Not Ranked.

Offices—12103 Indian Creek Court, Beltsville, MD 20705. **Tel**—(301) 470-6100. **Chrmn**—N. W. Flanzraich. **Co-Vice Chrmn**—F. Bellini, P. Frost. **Pres**—Sharon Mates. **SVP & COO**—A. Y. Elliott. **VP-Fin**—L. J. Hineline. **SVP & Secy**—D. J. Abdun-Nabi. **Dirs**—F. Bellini, A. Cousineau, J. Deitcher, D. Dionne, N. Flanzraich, R. R. Grey, P. Frost, L. Kasprick, S. Mates, R. Pfenniger, L. R. Wilson. **Transfer Agent**—American Stock Transfer & Trust Co., NYC. **Incorporated** in Canada in 1989. **Empl**-118. **S&P Analyst:** S.S.

STANDARD & POOR'S

STOCK REPORTS

Northwest Natural Gas

NASDAQ Symbol **NWNG**

In S&P SmallCap 600

10-OCT-95 **Industry:** Utilities-Gas

Summary: This company is one of the largest distributors of natural gas in the Pacific Northwest. NWNG is also engaged in natural gas exploration and production.

Quantitative Evaluations

Outlook
(1 Lowest—5 Highest)
• **3+**

Fair Value
• **30¾**

Risk
• **Low**

Earn./Div. Rank
• **B+**

Technical Eval.
• **Bullish** since 7/95

Rel. Strength Rank
(1 Lowest—99 Highest)
• **56**

Insider Activity
• **Neutral**

Recent Price • 31 | Yield • 5.8%
52 Wk Range • 32¼-27½ | 12-Mo. P/E • 12.7

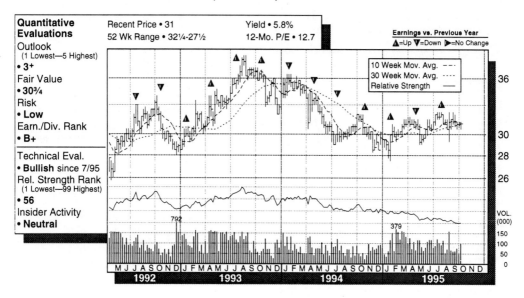

Earnings vs. Previous Year
▲=Up ▼=Down ▶=No Change

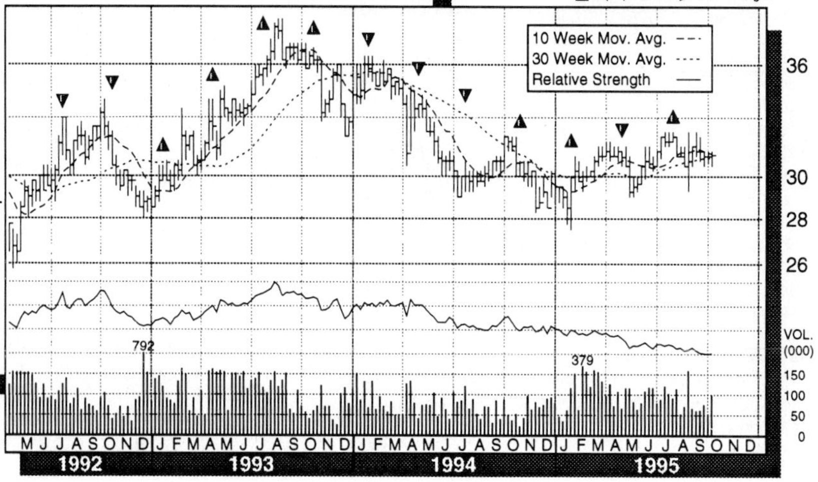

Business Profile - 10-OCT-95

This company is one of the largest distributors of natural gas in the Pacific Northwest, serving customers in most of Oregon and parts of Washington, and is also involved in natural gas exploration and production. Earnings for the first half of 1995 improved sharply, due to cooler weather, a larger customer base, and increased transportation revenues. NWNG raised the quarterly cash dividend in 1995, marking the 40th consecutive annual increase.

Operational Review - 10-OCT-95

Revenues for the six months ended June 30, 1995, rose 0.7%, year to year. Gas sales to weather-sensitive residential and commercial customers were up 1.0%. Weather conditions were 2.0% cooler than last year, but 9.0% warmer than the average. Although the customer base grew 5.2%, a comparatively rapid pace, rates declined due to lower gas prices. Industrial and transportation revenues rose 7.6%, and margins widened on fewer tariffs. Net income was up 6.2%.

Stock Performance - 06-OCT-95

In the past 30 trading days, NWNG's shares have increased 1%, compared to a 4% rise in the S&P 500. Average trading volume for the past five days was 19,680 shares, compared with the 40-day moving average of 18,421 shares.

Key Stock Statistics

Dividend Rate/Share	1.80	Shareholders	12,300
Shs. outstg. (M)	14.7	Market cap. (B)	$0.461
Avg. daily vol. (M)	0.014	Inst. holdings	28%
Tang. Bk. Value/Share	21.69	Insider holdings	NA
Beta	0.22		

Value of $10,000 invested 5 years ago: $ 17,474

Fiscal Year Ending Dec. 31

	1995	% Change	1994	% Change	1993	% Change
Revenues (Million $)						
1Q	125.4	-2%	128.5	NM	128.7	43%
2Q	71.03	7%	66.51	8%	61.79	29%
3Q	—	—	48.47	2%	47.45	22%
4Q	—	—	124.8	3%	120.8	24%
Yr.	—	—	368.3	3%	358.7	31%
Income (Million $)						
1Q	19.05	1%	18.78	-24%	24.65	88%
2Q	3.51	42%	2.47	-11%	2.77	NM
3Q	—	—	-3.77	NM	-4.42	NM
4Q	—	—	17.99	23%	14.65	7%
Yr.	—	—	35.46	-6%	37.65	139%
Earnings Per Share ($)						
1Q	1.32	-4%	1.37	-25%	1.82	72%
2Q	0.19	46%	0.13	-13%	0.15	NM
3Q	—	—	-0.34	NM	-0.40	NM
4Q	—	—	1.29	23%	1.05	-3%
Yr.	—	—	2.44	-7%	2.61	135%

Next earnings report expected: late October

Northwest Natural Gas

Business Summary - 10-OCT-95

Northwest Natural Gas Company distributes natural gas to customers in western Oregon and southwestern Washington. Its service area covers 15,000 sq. mi., with a population of nearly 2.7 million, including 78% of Oregon's population. Gas service is provided in 94 cities and neighboring communities in 16 Oregon counties and in nine regions in three Washington counties.

Gas revenues in recent years were derived as follows:

	1994	1993	1992
Residential	51%	52%	53%
Commercial	31%	32%	33%
Industrial--firm	10%	10%	11%
Industrial--interruptible	8%	6%	3%

Natural gas for NWNG's core market is transported by Northwest Pipeline Corp. (NPC) under a contract expiring in September 2013, providing for the delivery of firm sales of up to 2,460,440 therms per day. An additional contract, expiring in April 2008, allows for 500,000 therms per day of firm transportation capacity as a result of NPC's 612 mile pipeline expansion.

The company has two active subsidiaries. Oregon Natural Gas Development Corp. conducts exploration, development and production of natural gas and oil in the U.S. and Canada, as well as marketing and transportation in several western states. NNG Financial Corp. holds limited partnership investments in electric generation projects and real estate.

The most recent rate cases in Oregon (1989) and in Washington (1986) authorized a return on common equity of 13.25%. NWNG's return on average common equity for utility operations was 11.3% in 1994, versus 15.9% in 1993. For the consolidated company, returns were 12.2% in 1994, compared to 13.7%. The decline in 1994 is primarily attributable to weather that was 10% warmer than in 1993.

Important Developments

Jul. '95—A jury in Oregon found the company guilty in a case wherein Chase Gardens, Inc. filed a counter-claim to NWNG's proposed lien for unpaid gas service, charging NWNG with breach of contract and intentional interference with Chase's business relationship with its bank. NWNG is seeking to reduce the verdict to judgment, and will appeal if unsuccessful. The settlement could reach $4.9 million ($0.20 a share).

Feb. '95—NWNG sold 1.5 million common shares in 1995's first quarter. Net proceeds of $33 million are being used primarily to fund the utility construction program, and to repay short term debt.

Capitalization

Long Term Debt: $276,066,000 (6/95).
Red. Cum. Preferred Stock: 148,400 shs. of $4.68-$7.125 stk. in three series ($100 par).
Preference Stock: 250,000 shs. of $6.95 stk.

Per Share Data ($)

(Year Ended Dec. 31)

	1994	1993	1992	1991	1990	1989
Tangible Bk. Val.	3.20	19.62	18.62	18.35	18.91	18.06
Earnings	2.44	2.61	1.11	1.01	2.43	2.37
Dividends	1.76	1.75	1.72	1.69	1.65	1.61
Payout Ratio	72%	67%	155%	167%	68%	68%
Prices - High	36½	38¾	34	33½	26⅞	26⅞
- Low	28¼	28½	25¾	24¾	20⅞	18¾
P/E Ratio - High	15	15	31	33	11	11
- Low	12	11	23	25	9	8

Income Statement Analysis (Million $)

	1994	%Chg	1993	%Chg	1992	%Chg	1991
Revs.	368	3%	359	31%	274	-7%	296
Depr.	38.1	-4%	39.7	20%	33.0	-2%	33.6
Maint.	NA	—	NA	—	NA	—	NA
Fxd. Chgs. Cov.	2.9	-4%	3.0	76%	1.7	14%	1.5
Constr. Credits	0.3	50%	0.2	—	NM	—	Nil
Eff. Tax Rate	37%	—	37%	—	31%	—	14%
Net Inc.	35.5	-6%	37.6	138%	15.8	10%	14.4

Balance Sheet & Other Fin. Data (Million $)

	1994	1993	1992	1991	1990	1989
Gross Prop.	908	840	779	722	669	623
Cap. Exp.	77.7	70.4	60.7	58.4	50.5	57.6
Net Prop.	629	585	546	515	485	459
Capitalization:						
LT Debt	291	273	254	253	215	221
% LT Debt	48	48	46	51	46	48
Pfd.	42.2	44.0	55.0	31.0	32.1	33.9
% Pfd.	6.90	7.60	10	6.20	6.90	7.30
Common	274	259	242	216	219	206
% Common	45	45	44	43	47	45
Total Cap.	734	694	601	552	524	519

Ratio Analysis

	1994	1993	1992	1991	1990	1989
Oper. Ratio	85.9	82.8	84.4	86.6	81.6	82.4
% Earn. on Net Prop.	8.5	10.9	9.4	7.9	11.6	10.5
% Ret. on Revs.	9.6	10.5	5.7	4.9	10.4	10.9
% Ret. On Invest.Cap	8.5	9.7	8.6	7.6	10.5	9.7
% Return On Com.Eqty	12.2	13.7	5.8	5.4	13.1	13.3

Dividend Data —Cash has been paid each year since 1952. A dividend reinvestment plan is available.

Amt. of Div. $	Date Decl.	Ex-Div. Date	Stock of Record	Payment Date
0.440	Oct. 11	Oct. 25	Oct. 31	Nov. 15 '94
0.440	Jan. 05	Jan. 25	Jan. 31	Feb. 15 '95
0.440	Apr. 18	Apr. 24	Apr. 28	May. 15 '95
0.440	Jul. 07	Jul. 27	Jul. 31	Aug. 15 '95
0.450	Oct. 04	Oct. 27	Oct. 31	Nov. 15 '95

Data as orig. reptd.; bef. results of disc opers. and/or spec. items. Per share data adj. for stk. divs. as of ex-div. date. E-Estimated. NA-Not Available. NM-Not Meaningful. NR-Not Ranked.

Office—One Pacific Square, 220 N.W. Second Ave., Portland, OR 97209. **Tel**—(503) 226-4211. **Chrmn, Pres & CEO**—R. L. Ridgley. **Secy**—C. J. Rue. **SVP-Fin & CFO**—B. R. De Bolt. **Investor Contact**—Virginia V. Burgess (503) 226-4211 Ext. 3427. **Dirs**—M. A. Arnstad, T. E. Dewey, Jr., T. R. Hamachek, R. B. Keller, W. D. Kuni, R. L. Ridgley, D. A. Sangrey, M. C. Teppola, R. F. Tromley, B. R. Whiteley, W. R. Wiley, C. Woodard. **Transfer Agent and Registrar**—Co.'s office. **Incorporated** in Oregon in 1910. **Empl**-1,338. **S&P Analyst:** J. Santoriello

STANDARD & POOR'S

STOCK REPORTS

Novellus Systems

NASDAQ Symbol **NVLS**

In S&P SmallCap 600

10-OCT-95

Industry: Electronics/Electric

Summary: This company manufactures, markets, and services automated wafer fabrication systems for chemical vapor deposition (CVD) of thin films used in semiconductor manufacturing.

Quantitative Evaluations

Outlook (1 Lowest—5 Highest) • **5+**

Fair Value • **85**

Risk • **Average**

Earn./Div. Rank • **NR**

Technical Eval. • **Bearish** since 7/95

Rel. Strength Rank (1 Lowest—99 Highest) • **1**

Insider Activity • **Neutral**

Recent Price • 57

52 Wk Range • 87¼-42¾

Yield • Nil

12-Mo. P/E • 15.2

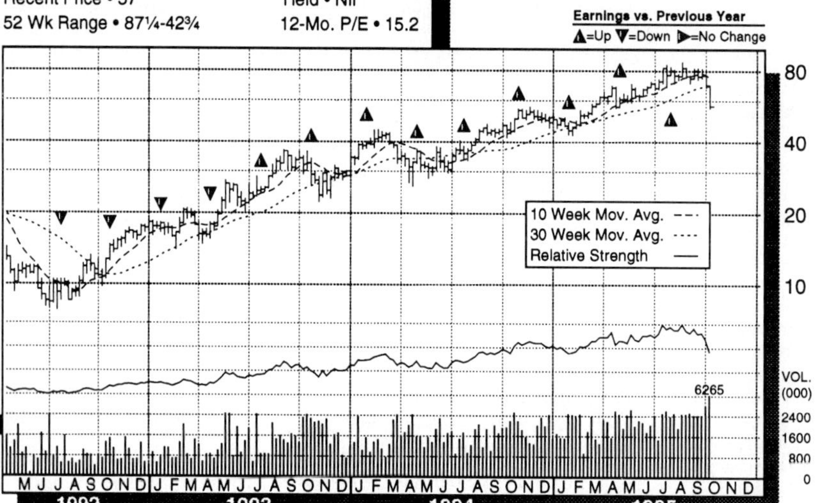

OPTIONS: CBOE, NY, P

Business Profile - 10-OCT-95

Novellus designs, manufactures, markets and services equipment used in the fabrication of integrated circuits. In the fiercely competitive semiconductor equipment market, NVLS tries to differentiate its systems with high levels of throughput, yield, and film quality, flexibility, low-cost, and strong customer support. The recent strength in demand for semiconductors has led to record revenues and profits in 1994; and based on the first half of 1995, a new record should be reached by year end.

Operational Review - 10-OCT-95

Net sales in the six months ended June 30, 1995, rose 75%, year to year, reflecting higher unit shipments, especially for the Concept Two Altus Tungsten and Sequel dielectric systems. Margins widened on improved manufacturing efficiencies. Higher interest rates and larger cash balances from exercised options and a March 1994 stock offering, combined to cause net interest income to nearly triple. Net income increased 109%, to $2.10 a share, on 7% more shares.

Stock Performance - 06-OCT-95

In the past 30 trading days, NVLS's shares have declined 25%, compared to a 4% rise in the S&P 500. Average trading volume for the past five days was 1,252,939 shares, compared with the 40-day moving average of 750,723 shares.

Key Stock Statistics

Dividend Rate/Share	Nil	Shareholders	200
Shs. outstg. (M)	16.4	Market cap. (B)	$0.857
Avg. daily vol. (M)	0.909	Inst. holdings	91%
Tang. Bk. Value/Share	15.48	Insider holdings	NA
Beta	1.89		

Value of $10,000 invested 5 years ago: $ 82,909

Fiscal Year Ending Dec. 31

	1995	% Change	1994	% Change	1993	% Change
Revenues (Million $)						
1Q	76.13	79%	42.44	102%	20.96	-3%
2Q	87.40	71%	51.03	102%	25.28	74%
3Q	—	—	59.53	99%	29.97	84%
4Q	—	—	71.68	92%	37.33	115%
Yr.	—	—	224.7	98%	113.5	63%
Income (Million $)						
1Q	16.61	129%	7.24	NM	2.10	-49%
2Q	19.18	95%	9.86	171%	3.64	NM
3Q	—	—	12.55	167%	4.70	NM
4Q	—	—	15.28	169%	5.68	NM
Yr.	—	—	44.93	179%	16.12	158%
Earnings Per Share ($)						
1Q	0.98	109%	0.47	NM	0.15	-46%
2Q	1.12	87%	0.60	140%	0.25	NM
3Q	—	—	0.75	134%	0.32	NM
4Q	—	—	0.90	137%	0.38	NM
Yr.	—	—	2.72	147%	1.10	150%

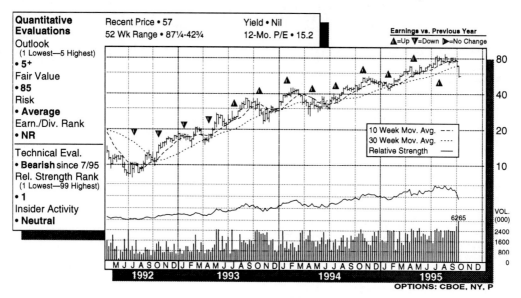

Next earnings report expected: mid October

Novellus Systems

Business Summary - 10-OCT-95

Novellus Systems, Inc. designs, manufactures, markets and services chemical vapor deposition (CVD) and physical vapor deposition (PVD) equipment used in the fabrication of integrated circuits. The company focuses on advanced CVD systems that provide superior film quality and yield while attaining the high levels of productivity required to meet the semiconductor industry's need for high volume, low cost wafer production. There are currently three primary products: the Concept One-Dielectric; the Concept One-W; and the Concept Two.

The Concept One-Dielectric (first shipped in 1987) is used in the fabrication process to deposit a variety of insulating or dielectric films on wafers. This is accomplished through a process known as chemical vapor deposition, in which the surface of the wafer is exposed to various gases containing the material to be deposited on the wafer. The Concept One-W (introduced in September 1990) deposits blanket tungsten metal films, which are increasingly utilized in advanced semiconductor devices to connect multiple metal layers in the integrated circuit.

The Concept Two (introduced in November 1991) is a modular CVD system with greater levels of wafer processing integration, higher volume production, and increased factory automation. In 1993, Novellus introduced the Concept Two-ALTUS, which combines the modular architecture of the Concept Two system with an advanced tungsten CVD process chamber. In 1994, Novellus introduced the Concept Two-Dual ALTUS, with a dual advanced tungsten CVD process chamber, which has significant throughput power to dramatically lower the cost of tungsten deposition.

Products are marketed worldwide to semiconductor manufacturers, primarily through a direct sales force. NVLS has sold one or more systems to the 20 largest semiconductor manufacturers in the world, and is currently seeking a larger presence in the growing Asian market. Export sales rose to 54% of the total in 1994, up from 44% in 1993 and 46% in 1992.

R&D spending in 1994 totaled $26.0 million (12% of net sales), compared to $16.9 million (15%) in 1993, and $12.3 million (18%) in 1992.

Important Developments

Jul. '95—The company reported record revenues and net income for the first six months of 1995. Bookings for the second quarter were at record levels and the backlog increased over the prior quarter. In July, Novellus introduced the new Maxus system, which can deposit silicon nitride films and a new fluorine doped TEOS film.

Capitalization

Long Term Debt: None (6/95).
Options: To buy 1,835,000 shs. at $0.40 to $53.38 ea. (12/94).

Per Share Data ($) (Year Ended Dec. 31)

	1994	1993	1992	1991	1990	1989
Tangible Bk. Val.	13.25	7.44	6.04	5.73	4.18	3.07
Cash Flow	2.96	1.35	0.66	1.28	1.11	0.94
Earnings	2.72	1.10	0.44	1.15	1.01	0.87
Dividends	Nil	Nil	Nil	Nil	Nil	Nil
Payout Ratio	Nil	Nil	Nil	Nil	Nil	Nil
Prices - High	56½	37	26½	27¼	18	9⅞
- Low	25¾	14	7¾	10½	5½	4⅜
P/E Ratio - High	21	34	60	24	18	11
- Low	9	13	18	9	5	5

Income Statement Analysis (Million $)

	1994	%Chg	1993	%Chg	1992	%Chg	1991
Revs.	225	97%	114	63%	69.8	-13%	80.0
Oper. Inc.	67.7	150%	27.1	149%	10.9	-56%	24.7
Depr.	4.0	7%	3.7	15%	3.2	70%	1.9
Int. Exp.	0.3	164%	0.1	-56%	0.3	NM	0.1
Pretax Inc.	68.1	175%	24.8	164%	9.4	-63%	25.4
Eff. Tax Rate	34%	—	35%	—	34%	—	34%
Net Inc.	44.9	179%	16.1	160%	6.2	-63%	16.8

Balance Sheet & Other Fin. Data (Million $)

	1994	1993	1992	1991	1990	1989
Cash	137	48.6	43.0	40.5	39.8	30.0
Curr. Assets	234	109	79.2	79.3	62.8	45.6
Total Assets	265	131	97.3	94.7	68.9	50.5
Curr. Liab.	50.8	25.7	13.9	12.8	12.4	10.1
LT Debt	Nil	Nil	0.8	1.0	0.4	0.8
Common Eqty.	214	105	82.7	80.9	56.1	39.5
Total Cap.	214	105	83.4	81.9	56.5	40.3
Cap. Exp.	6.9	6.6	5.1	10.2	2.5	2.5
Cash Flow	48.9	19.8	9.5	18.7	15.5	12.2

Ratio Analysis

	1994	1993	1992	1991	1990	1989
Curr. Ratio	4.6	4.3	5.7	6.2	5.1	4.5
% LT Debt of Cap.	Nil	Nil	0.9	1.2	0.7	1.9
% Net Inc.of Revs.	20.0	14.2	8.9	21.0	20.9	22.1
% Ret. on Assets	21.7	13.9	6.6	20.1	23.1	28.6
% Ret. on Equity	26.9	16.9	7.7	24.0	28.8	38.0

Dividend Data —No cash dividends have been paid. The shares were split two for one in 1990.

Data as orig. reptd.; bef. results of disc. opers. and/or spec. items. Per share data adj. for stk. divs. as of ex-div. date. E-Estimated. NA-Not Available. NM-Not Meaningful. NR-Not Ranked.

Office—81 Vista Montana, San Jose, CA 95134. **Tel**—(408) 943-9700. **Chrmn**—R. F. Graham. **Pres & CEO**—R. S. Hill. **VP, CFO & Secy**—W. J. Wall. **Treas.**—J. Root. **Dirs**—J. Dox, R. F. Graham, D. J. Guzy, R. S. Hill, G. Possley, E. van de Ven, J. Van Poppelen. **Transfer Agent & Registrar**—Chemical Trust Co. of California, SF. **Incorporated** in California in 1984. **Empl**-530. **S&P Analyst:** J. Santoriello

STANDARD & POOR'S

STOCK REPORTS

OHM Corp.

NYSE Symbol **OHM**
In S&P SmallCap 600

30-OCT-95 **Industry:** Pollution Control

Summary: This leading environmental services company provides hazardous waste remediation services to industrial and government clients.

Quantitative Evaluations

Outlook (1 Lowest—5 Highest)
• **NA**
Fair Value
• **NA**
Risk
• **High**
Earn./Div. Rank
• **C**

Technical Eval.
• **Bullish** since 12/94
Rel. Strength Rank (1 Lowest—99 Highest)
• **9**
Insider Activity
• **Neutral**

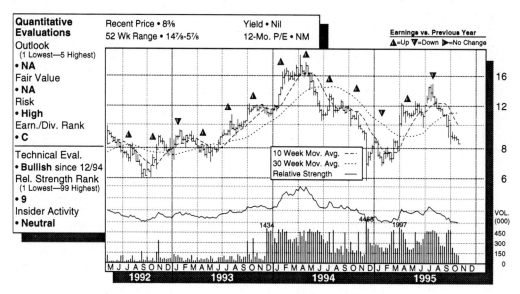

Recent Price • 8⅜
52 Wk Range • 14⅞-5⅞
Yield • Nil
12-Mo. P/E • NM

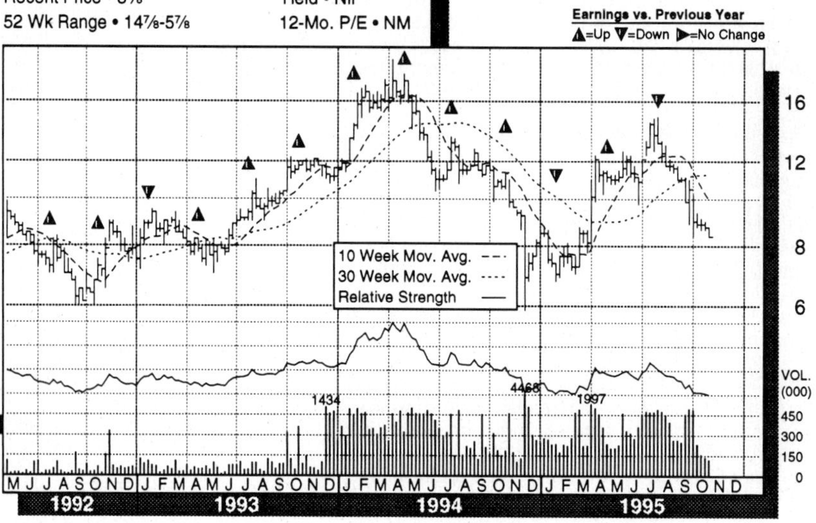

Business Profile - 29-OCT-95

Following the acquisition of Rust International in May 1995, OHM became the largest U.S. company totally focused on the remediation of hazardous wastes. The integration of the two companies provided cost savings by consolidating offices and eliminating redundant positions, and provided expanded resources to pursue additional contracts. The company expects to benefit from a market shift from studies to cleanups of environmental problems.

Operational Review - 29-OCT-95

Net revenues in the first half of 1995 rose 5.9%, year to year, reflecting higher spending by the Department of Defense to clean up environmental problems at military bases, which offset weak demand from the private sector. Operating income benefited from the increased revenues and improved gross margins. However with a charge for costs associated with the acquisition of Rust International, net income fell 47%. Per share results were further restricted by 14% more shares outstanding.

Stock Performance - 27-OCT-95

In the past 30 trading days, OHM's shares have declined 15%, compared to a 0.63% fall in the S&P 500. Average trading volume for the past five days was 23,300 shares, compared with the 40-day moving average of 83,208 shares.

Key Stock Statistics

Dividend Rate/Share	Nil	Shareholders	900
Shs. outstg. (M)	26.5	Market cap. (B)	$0.222
Avg. daily vol. (M)	0.031	Inst. holdings	22%
Tang. Bk. Value/Share	4.77	Insider holdings	NA
Beta	1.31		

Value of $10,000 invested 5 years ago: $ 7,790

Fiscal Year Ending Dec. 31

	1995	% Change	1994	% Change	1993	% Change
Revenues (Million $)						
1Q	56.55	9%	51.81	51%	34.37	-28%
2Q	70.61	9%	65.03	58%	41.16	-24%
3Q	—	—	69.33	48%	46.77	-17%
4Q	—	—	34.10	-36%	53.43	4%
Yr.	—	—	220.3	25%	175.7	-16%
Income (Million $)						
1Q	1.29	59%	0.81	145%	0.33	NM
2Q	0.23	-89%	2.07	68%	1.23	50%
3Q	—	—	2.62	50%	1.75	42%
4Q	—	—	-13.11	NM	1.10	NM
Yr.	—	—	-7.62	NM	4.41	NM
Earnings Per Share ($)						
1Q	0.08	60%	0.05	67%	0.03	NM
2Q	0.01	-92%	0.13	30%	0.10	43%
3Q	—	—	0.16	14%	0.14	40%
4Q	—	—	-0.84	NM	0.08	NM
Yr.	—	—	-0.49	NM	0.35	NM

Next earnings report expected: late October

Business Summary - 30-OCT-95

OHM Corp. (formerly Environmental Treatment and Technologies) is a leading provider of hazardous waste remediation services to industrial and government clients. The company was formed in 1986 to facilitate the merger of O.H. Materials Corp. and Environmental Testing and Certification Corp.

Gross revenues from federal government agencies accounted for 55% of the 1994 total, while revenues from state and local government agencies accounted for 10%.

The company primarily provides on-site environmental remediation services, but also offers other services, including site assessment, engineering, remedial design and analytical testing. Service is provided through 29 regional offices, one fixed laboratory and nine mobile laboratories, and more than 3,000 pieces of mobile treatment and related field equipment.

NSC Corp. (40% owned) provides asbestos abatement and restoration services to private and public sector clients primarily through asbestos abatement service centers. NSC removes hazards associated with asbestos insulation and asbestos-containing materials in large commercial and public buildings, and in connection with large industrial facility decontamination and decommissioning projects.

In 1993, the company sold its investment in Concord Resources Group, Inc. (a joint venture with Conrail, formed in 1989) which sites, designs, develops and operates a network of fixed-base recovery, treatment and disposal facilities for solid and hazardous waste.

Important Developments

Sep. '95—OHM projected third quarter earnings of $0.10 to $0.14 a share, as Rust's results were substantially below expectations.
Jun. '95—Total contract backlog at the end of the second quarter of 1995 totaled $2.0 billion, a 48% increase over the contract backlog at June 30, 1994. Separately, the company entered into a new five-year revolving bank credit agreement to provide up to $150 million.
May '95—The company acquired Rust International Inc. for 9,668,000 shares of common stock, creating the largest company focused on the remediation of hazardous wastes. Additionally, WMX Technologies, Inc., which owned a majority of Rust, agreed to provide a credit enhancement in exchange for warrants to purchase 700,000 shares of OHM common stock at $15.00 a share exercisable over the next five years.

Capitalization

Long Term Debt: $122,578,000 (6/95).

Per Share Data ($)

(Year Ended Dec. 31)

	1994	1993	1992	1991	1990	1989
Tangible Bk. Val.	4.92	5.36	3.64	4.00	4.55	4.06
Cash Flow	-0.01	0.92	0.52	0.35	2.12	0.92
Earnings	-0.49	0.35	-0.26	-0.57	1.20	0.14
Dividends	Nil	Nil	Nil	Nil	Nil	Nil
Payout Ratio	Nil	Nil	Nil	Nil	Nil	Nil
Prices - High	19½	12¼	9⅞	13¾	14	14⅞
- Low	5⅞	7	6	5⅞	8	10⅛
P/E Ratio - High	NM	35	NM	NM	12	NM
- Low	NM	20	NM	NM	7	NM

Income Statement Analysis (Million $)

	1994	%Chg	1993	%Chg	1992	%Chg	1991
Revs.	220	25%	176	-16%	209	19%	175
Oper. Inc.	27.2	36%	20.0	21%	16.5	11%	14.9
Depr.	7.4	4%	7.1	-24%	9.4	-15%	11.1
Int. Exp.	10.1	20%	8.4	23%	6.9	NM	6.9
Pretax Inc.	-14.1	NM	6.5	NM	-5.5	NM	-7.9
Eff. Tax Rate	NM	—	32%	—	NM	—	NM
Net Inc.	-7.6	NM	4.4	NM	-3.1	NM	-6.9

Balance Sheet & Other Fin. Data (Million $)

	1994	1993	1992	1991	1990	1989
Cash	4.9	5.0	2.8	4.7	9.1	7.9
Curr. Assets	181	128	134	103	91.7	79.3
Total Assets	273	215	213	190	194	180
Curr. Liab.	64.9	57.7	50.6	42.3	49.9	36.3
LT Debt	127	71.0	102	81.5	71.5	85.6
Common Eqty.	76.9	82.7	43.8	48.3	54.7	48.7
Total Cap.	207	157	161	147	143	143
Cap. Exp.	13.4	17.8	14.1	7.2	14.4	23.7
Cash Flow	-0.2	11.5	6.3	4.3	25.5	11.3

Ratio Analysis

	1994	1993	1992	1991	1990	1989
Curr. Ratio	2.8	2.2	2.6	2.4	1.8	2.2
% LT Debt of Cap.	61.6	45.4	63.3	55.7	50.1	59.8
% Net Inc.of Revs.	NM	2.5	NM	NM	7.7	0.8
% Ret. on Assets	NM	1.8	NM	NM	7.7	1.0
% Ret. on Equity	NM	6.3	NM	NM	27.8	3.4

Dividend Data —No dividends have ever been paid.

Data as orig. reptd.; bef. results of disc. opers. and/or spec. items. Per share data adj. for stk. divs. as of ex-div. date. E-Estimated. NA-Not Available. NM-Not Meaningful. NR-Not Ranked.

Office—16406 U.S. Route 224 East, Findlay, OH 45839-0551. **Tel**—(419) 423-3529. **Chrmn, Pres & CEO**—J. L. Kirk. **VP-Fin & CFO**—D. P. Buettin. **Treas & Investor Contact**—Pamela K. M. Beall. **VP & Secy**—R. M. Walters. **Dirs**—H. A. Getz, R. C. Gilbert, I. W. Gorr, C. D. Hollister, J. L. Kirk, J. R. Kirk, J. E. Koenig, R. W. Pogue, C. W. Schmidt. **Transfer Agent & Registrar**—Midlantic National Bank, Iselin, NJ. **Incorporated** in Delaware in 1981. **Empl**-3,100. **S&P Analyst:** PJB

STANDARD & POOR'S

STOCK REPORTS

Oak Industries

NYSE Symbol **OAK**
In S&P SmallCap 600

08-AUG-95 **Industry:** Electronics/Electric

Summary: This company makes components and controls, primarily for cable TV and consumer appliances; it also makes railroad repair equipment.

Quantitative Evaluations
Outlook
(1 Lowest—5 Highest)
• **4-**
Fair Value
• **27⅞**
Risk
• **Average**
Earn./Div. Rank
• **B-**

Technical Eval.
• **Bullish** since 7/95
Rel. Strength Rank
(1 Lowest—99 Highest)
• **35**
Insider Activity
• **NA**

Recent Price • 26½
52 Wk Range • 30⅜-22⅜
Yield • Nil
12-Mo. P/E • 10.6

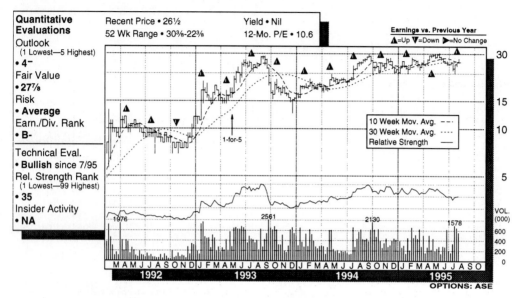

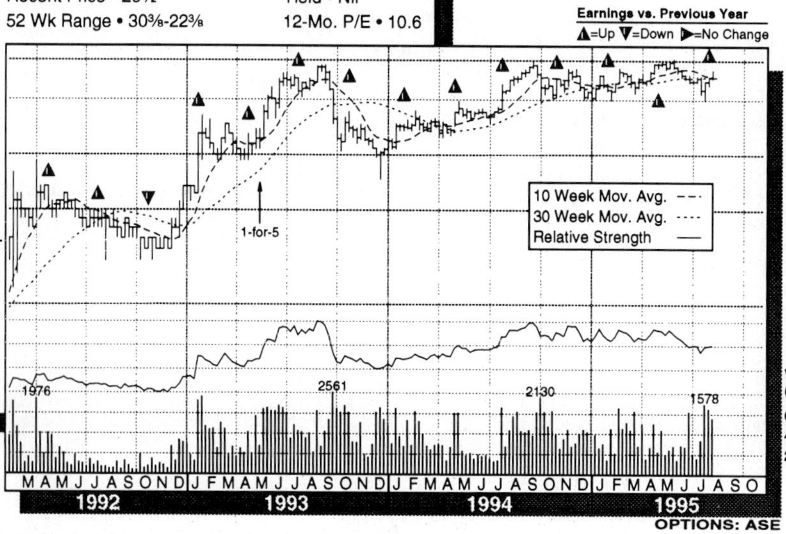

OPTIONS: ASE

Business Profile - 08-AUG-95

This company primarily makes and sells communications components, including cable TV specialty connectors and frequency control devices, and control components such as electronic and mechanical controls for consumer appliances and industrial testing equipment. Since 1992, Oak has made four acquisitions, most recently the June 1994 purchase of Cabel-Con A/S (for $9.2 million). Future results should benefit from expansion and upgrading of U.S. cable TV systems.

Operational Review - 08-AUG-95

Revenues in the first half of 1995 rose 8.7%, year to year, as increased communications components business outweighed a decline in the controls business. Margins widened on the higher volume; EPS increased to $1.16, from $0.97. The shares have been in an uptrend since early 1994.

Stock Performance - 04-AUG-95

In the past 30 trading days, OAK's shares have increased 3%, compared to a 2% rise in the S&P 500. Average trading volume for the past five days was 110,480 shares, compared with the 40-day moving average of 127,995 shares.

Key Stock Statistics

Dividend Rate/Share	Nil	Shareholders	13,000
Shs. outstg. (M)	17.5	Market cap. (B)	$0.466
Avg. daily vol. (M)	0.179	Inst. holdings	67%
Tang. Bk. Value/Share	6.56	Insider holdings	NA
Beta	0.83		

Value of $10,000 invested 5 years ago: $ 53,000

Fiscal Year Ending Dec. 31

	1995	% Change	1994	% Change	1993	% Change
Revenues (Million $)						
1Q	71.60	16%	61.79	4%	59.22	65%
2Q	66.93	2%	65.68	13%	58.22	52%
3Q	—	—	58.40	13%	51.58	55%
4Q	—	—	63.14	25%	50.54	41%
Yr.	—	—	249.0	13%	219.6	53%
Income (Million $)						
1Q	10.82	46%	7.39	47%	5.02	102%
2Q	10.72	4%	10.29	85%	5.57	129%
3Q	—	—	7.37	14%	6.45	NM
4Q	—	—	17.40	81%	9.63	124%
Yr.	—	—	42.45	59%	26.66	157%
Earnings Per Share ($)						
1Q	0.58	45%	0.40	43%	0.28	87%
2Q	0.58	4%	0.56	81%	0.31	107%
3Q	—	—	0.40	14%	0.35	NM
4Q	—	—	0.94	77%	0.53	112%
Yr.	—	—	2.31	57%	1.47	145%

Next earnings report expected: late October

Oak Industries

Business Summary - 08-AUG-95

Oak Industries Inc., through subsidiaries, makes and sells communications components such as cable TV specialty connectors and frequency controls, as well as mechanical and electronic controls and switches. It also manufactures and sells railway maintenance equipment.

Communications components include specialty connectors for use in CATV and other precision applications and devices that control radio frequencies such as quartz crystals, filters and oscillators and their related bases and enclosures. Communications components accounted for 55% of 1994 revenues.

Gilbert Engineering Co., based in Glendale, Ariz., Vordingsborg, Denmark, and Amboise, France, manufactures connectors for the cable television and high-end microwave markets. It is the leading U.S. maker of aluminum connectors, and a leading manufacturer of brass connectors to the cable industry. In June 1994, the company acquired Cabel-Com A/S, a Danish manufacturer of connectors, for $9.2 million.

Through its frequency control devices business units, McCoy/Ovenaire/Spectrum, Croven Crystals and H.E.S. International, Oak offers frequency control devices, such as crystals and crystal oscillators, to OEMs for both commercial and military products.

The company also makes glass-to-metal hermetically sealed packages. These are manufactured in Kansas City, Kan., and are used in a variety of products such as semiconductors and frequency controls.

Oak's control products include electronic, electro-mechanical and mechanical controls, switches and components sold to various consumer and industrial manufacturers. The Harper-Wyman subsidiary manufactures controls for gas and electric range appliances, for sale to OEMs. The Harpco division manufactures replacement parts for outdoor grills and appliances.

The company's OakGrigsby subsidiary makes switches and switch products, which are sold to test equipment OEMs. Nordco Inc., based in Milwaukee, supplies a broad line of maintenance-of-way equipment to U.S. railroads and their contractors. Revenues from this business accounted for 8% of the total in each of 1994 and 1993.

Important Developments

Jun. '95—Responding to reports of weakness in the cable television and telecommunications industries, the company said it did not expect a slowdown at Gilbert Engineering.

Capitalization

Long Term Debt: $26,327,000 (6/95).

Per Share Data ($) (Year Ended Dec. 31)

	1994	1993	1992	1991	1990	1989
Tangible Bk. Val.	5.23	3.25	1.55	5.10	4.75	4.05
Cash Flow	2.89	2.04	0.95	0.60	0.35	-0.85
Earnings	2.31	1.47	0.60	0.35	0.10	-1.15
Dividends	Nil	Nil	Nil	Nil	Nil	Nil
Payout Ratio	Nil	Nil	Nil	Nil	Nil	Nil
Prices - High	29⅞	29	14⅜	5⅝	6⅞	8¾
- Low	15⅝	10⅝	4⅜	3⅛	1¼	3¾
P/E Ratio - High	13	20	24	16	69	NM
- Low	7	7	7	9	16	NM

Income Statement Analysis (Million $)

	1994	%Chg	1993	%Chg	1992	%Chg	1991
Revs.	249	13%	220	54%	143	15%	124
Oper. Inc.	61.0	30%	47.0	NM	10.1	51%	6.7
Depr.	10.6	3%	10.3	94%	5.3	15%	4.6
Int. Exp.	6.6	-15%	7.8	NM	1.4	-22%	1.8
Pretax Inc.	43.4	65%	26.3	192%	9.0	NM	2.0
Eff. Tax Rate	NM	—	NM	—	NM	—	NM
Net Inc.	42.4	59%	26.7	167%	10.0	100%	5.0

Balance Sheet & Other Fin. Data (Million $)

	1994	1993	1992	1991	1990	1989
Cash	37.6	27.4	24.9	37.6	44.5	21.8
Curr. Assets	120	96.0	90.0	82.0	93.0	82.0
Total Assets	282	238	229	125	131	131
Curr. Liab.	47.5	27.0	35.0	20.0	29.0	33.0
LT Debt	34.0	62.0	77.0	11.0	11.0	17.0
Common Eqty.	167	127	98.1	84.0	78.0	67.0
Total Cap.	228	203	182	95.0	90.0	84.0
Cap. Exp.	6.8	7.0	4.1	4.7	6.5	5.4
Cash Flow	53.1	37.0	16.0	10.0	6.0	-14.0

Ratio Analysis

	1994	1993	1992	1991	1990	1989
Curr. Ratio	2.5	3.6	2.6	4.0	3.2	2.5
% LT Debt of Cap.	15.1	30.3	42.2	11.8	12.6	20.7
% Net Inc.of Revs.	17.0	12.1	7.3	4.2	1.0	NM
% Ret. on Assets	16.2	11.2	5.9	4.1	1.1	NM
% Ret. on Equity	28.7	23.3	11.4	6.5	1.9	NM

Dividend Data (Cash dividends, paid since 1934, were omitted in 1983. A one-for-five reverse stock split was effected in May 1993.)

Data as orig. reptd.; bef. results of disc. opers. and/or spec. items. Per share data adj. for stk. divs. as of ex-div. date. E-Estimated. NA-Not Available. NM-Not Meaningful. NR-Not Ranked.

Office—1000 Winter St., Waltham, MA 02154. **Tel**—(617) 890-0400. **Chrmn**—Lord David Stevens. **Vice Chrmn**—R. M. Hills. **Pres & CEO**—W. S Antle III. **SVP, CFO & Investor Contact**—William C. Weaver. **SVP & Secy**—P. J. Halas. **Dirs**—W. S. Antle III, D. W. Derbes, R. M. Hills, G. W. Leisz, G. E. Matthews, C. H. B. Mills, E. L. Richardson, Lord David Stevens. **Transfer Agent & Registrar**—Bank of Boston. **Incorporated** in Delaware in 1960. **Empl**-2,847. **S&P Analyst:** M.T.C.

STANDARD & POOR'S

Oakwood Homes

STOCK REPORTS

NYSE Symbol **OH**
In S&P SmallCap 600

10-NOV-95 **Industry:** Mobile/Modular Homes

Summary: This vertically integrated producer and retailer of manufactured homes also derives substantial profits from related financial services.

S&P Opinion: Accumulate (★★★★)

Recent Price • 37¼
52 Wk Range • 38-20⅝
Yield • 0.2%
12-Mo. P/E • 18.9

Quantitative Evaluations
Outlook (1 Lowest—5 Highest) • 3+
Fair Value • 37½
Risk • Average
Earn./Div. Rank • A-

Technical Eval. • **Bullish** since 10/95
Rel. Strength Rank (1 Lowest—99 Highest) • 84
Insider Activity • Neutral

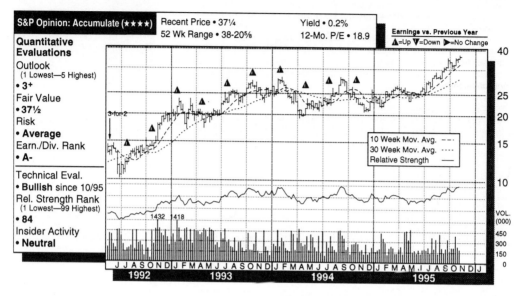

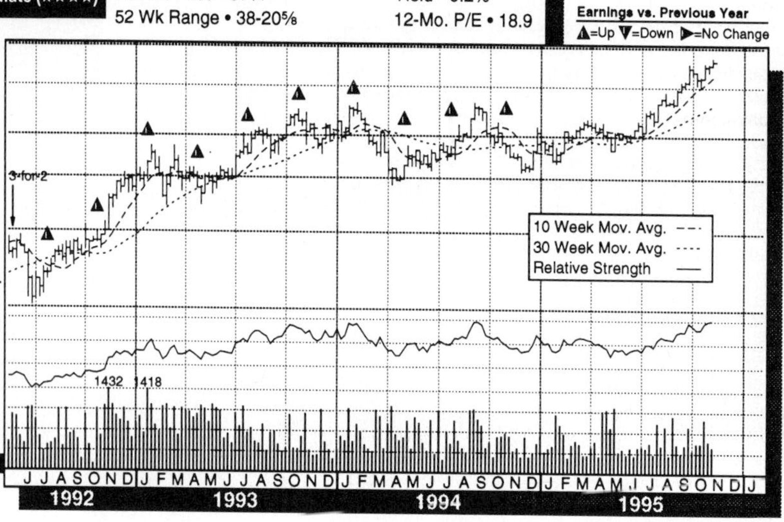

Overview - 09-NOV-95

Sales should be solidly higher through fiscal 1996, aided largely by Oakwood's aggressive expansion of its retail sales network. The expansion will be concentrated in Northwestern and Deep South markets served by Golden West Homes (acquired in September 1994) and Destiny Industries (June 1995), respectively, which had sold homes strictly to independent dealers prior to their acquisitions. Top line growth should also benefit from continued positive industry trends, along with OH's ongoing efforts to gain market share. Margins are likely to benefit from greater internal sourcing of homes and a variety of cost containment measures, including the recent sale of Golden West's Sacramento plant, whose low capacity utilization had been hurting profitability. The growing size of Oakwood's business should also provide it with greater operating leverage.

Valuation - 09-NOV-95

Oakwood's shares, which have risen dramatically since 1990, resumed their upward trend in late 1994 after a period of correction during that year. With solid sales and earnings growth expected to continue in upcoming periods, the shares appear to have room for further appreciation, given their recent trading range of about 15X our fiscal 1996 EPS estimate. Although the stock price could be hurt if interest rates resume an upward path or the economy slows dramatically, neither appears likely in the foreseeable future.

Key Stock Statistics

S&P EPS Est. 1996	2.40	Tang. Bk. Value/Share	13.68
P/E on S&P Est. 1996	15.5	Beta	2.07
Dividend Rate/Share	0.08	Shareholders	1,000
Shs. outstg. (M)	22.1	Market cap. (B)	$0.808
Avg. daily vol. (M)	0.049	Inst. holdings	76%
		Insider holdings	NA

Value of $10,000 invested 5 years ago: $ 107,945

Fiscal Year Ending Sep. 30

	1996	% Change	1995	% Change	1994	% Change
Revenues (Million $)						
1Q	—	—	--	—	113.0	100%
2Q	—	—	--	—	129.7	91%
3Q	—	—	580.3	NM	164.2	84%
4Q	—	—	241.1	40%	172.1	58%
Yr.	—	—	821.4	42%	579.1	80%
Income (Million $)						
1Q	—	—	—	—	6.63	80%
2Q	—	—	18.07	142%	7.46	47%
3Q	—	—	12.24	22%	10.00	45%
4Q	—	—	15.00	53%	9.82	11%
Yr.	—	—	45.32	34%	33.91	38%
Earnings Per Share ($)						
1Q	E0.43	—	—	—	0.30	20%
2Q	E0.50	-37%	0.79	132%	0.34	36%
3Q	E0.70	32%	0.53	18%	0.45	36%
4Q	E0.77	18%	0.65	44%	0.45	10%
Yr.	E2.40	22%	1.97	28%	1.54	22%

Next earnings report expected: mid January

Oakwood Homes

Business Summary - 01-NOV-95

Oakwood Homes is a producer and retailer of manufactured homes. Most of OH's sales are financed through installment contracts with its finance unit, and it also acts as agent on homeowners' and credit life insurance written for buyers of its homes. Segment contributions in fiscal 1994:

	Revs.	Profits
Manufactured homes	88%	69%
Financial services	10%	30%
Land development	2%	-1%
Investment income	Nil	2%

OH makes 14- and 16-foot wide single section homes and 24- and 28-foot wide multi-section homes, ranging from 50 feet to 80 feet in length. In fiscal 1994 (including Golden West), OH sold 16,006 new homes (13,034 at retail and 2,972 at wholesale), with 74% of the homes sold at retail manufactured by Oakwood; OH produced 13,934 units in fiscal 1994. It also sold 1,675 used homes at retail, most of which had been acquired as trade-ins. As of the end of fiscal 1994, OH was selling manufactured homes through 152 company-owned sales centers (198 at the end of fiscal 1995), located primarily in the Southeast and Southwest. Through the acquisitions of Destiny Industries (June 1995) and Golden West Homes (September 1994), Oakwood was also selling homes to independent dealers located primarily in California, the Pacific Northwest and the Southeast.

The retail sales price for new single section homes sold by OH in fiscal 1994 ranged from $12,000 to $40,000, with a mean sales price of about $23,900. Multi-section homes (excluding those sold by Golden West) ranged from $23,000 to $65,000, with a mean price of $42,800. Multi-section homes sold by Golden West ranged from $40,000 to $150,000, with a mean of $56,500.

Important Developments

Oct. '95—The company's very strong year over year earnings growth in the fourth quarter of fiscal 1995 was attributed to a 14% gain in same store retail home sales (on a 4.1% volume increase and higher average prices), the addition of 46 net new sales centers in fiscal 1995 and the favorable integration of Golden West Homes (acquired in September 1994) and Destiny Industries (acquired in June 1995 for 925,000 common shares). Oakwood also noted that it sold a total of 21,370 new homes in fiscal 1995 (16,711 at retail and 4,659 at wholesale) up from 18,093 (13,034 at retail and 5,059 at wholesale) in the prior year, which was restated for the Destiny acquisition. OH's mean retail sales prices in fiscal 1995 were $25,900 for new single section homes and $46,500 for new multi-section homes.

Capitalization

Notes & Bonds Payable: $208,675,000 (6/95).

Per Share Data ($) (Year Ended Sep. 30)

	1995	1994	1993	1992	1991	1990
Tangible Bk. Val.	NA	12.85	11.25	7.91	6.99	5.91
Cash Flow	NA	1.73	1.40	1.27	1.05	0.87
Earnings	1.97	1.54	1.26	1.00	0.77	0.56
Dividends	0.08	0.08	0.08	0.06	0.05	0.04
Payout Ratio	4%	5%	7%	6%	7%	8%
Prices - High	37¾	29⅞	28¾	21⅜	11	6⅜
- Low	21⅝	19¼	17⅛	10⅛	5¾	3⅜
P/E Ratio - High	19	19	23	21	14	11
- Low	11	13	14	10	7	6

Income Statement Analysis (Million $)

	1994	%Chg	1993	%Chg	1992	%Chg	1991
Revs.	575	81%	317	39%	228	43%	160
Oper. Inc.	56.1	50%	37.4	-21%	47.2	35%	35.0
Depr.	4.3	49%	2.8	-23%	3.7	18%	3.1
Int. Exp.	24.3	-7%	26.1	3%	25.3	25%	20.3
Pretax Inc.	53.9	39%	38.9	82%	21.4	50%	14.3
Eff. Tax Rate	37%	—	37%	—	34%	—	38%
Net Inc.	33.9	38%	24.5	75%	14.0	58%	8.9

Balance Sheet & Other Fin. Data (Million $)

	1994	1993	1992	1991	1990	1989
Cash	12.6	23.9	17.2	16.3	12.8	14.8
Curr. Assets	NA	NA	NA	NA	NA	NA
Total Assets	575	557	432	345	275	229
Curr. Liab.	NA	NA	NA	NA	NA	NA
LT Debt	173	223	258	182	169	122
Common Eqty.	271	229	104	89.7	57.9	52.7
Total Cap.	444	452	364	274	232	179
Cap. Exp.	27.2	13.0	5.3	2.3	3.4	6.3
Cash Flow	38.2	27.4	17.7	12.0	8.5	5.3

Ratio Analysis

	1994	1993	1992	1991	1990	1989
Curr. Ratio	NA	NA	NA	NA	NA	NA
% LT Debt of Cap.	39.0	49.3	70.8	66.3	73.1	68.1
% Net Inc.of Revs.	5.9	7.7	6.1	5.5	4.1	2.8
% Ret. on Assets	5.9	4.0	3.6	2.5	2.2	1.6
% Ret. on Equity	13.3	12.6	14.3	10.7	9.9	5.5

Dividend Data —Cash has been paid since 1976. A "poison pill" stock purchase rights plan was adopted in 1991.

Amt. of Div. $	Date Decl.	Ex-Div. Date	Stock of Record	Payment Date
0.020	Oct. 19	Nov. 02	Nov. 08	Nov. 23 '94
0.020	Feb. 01	Feb. 07	Feb. 13	Feb. 27 '95
0.020	Apr. 19	May. 03	May. 09	May. 24 '95
0.020	Jul. 19	Aug. 04	Aug. 08	Aug. 23 '95
0.020	Oct. 19	Nov. 03	Nov. 07	Nov. 22 '95

Data as orig. reptd.; bef. results of disc. opers. and/or spec. items. Per share data adj. for stk. divs. as of ex-div. date. Revs. in Inc. Statement excl. certain oth. inc. E-Estimated. NA-Not Available. NM-Not Meaningful. NR-Not Ranked.

Office—7025 Albert Pick Rd., Greensboro, NC 27409. **Mailing Address**—P.O. Box 7386, Greensboro, NC 27417. **Tel**—(910) 855-2400. **Chrmn**—R. L. Darling. **Pres & CEO**—N. J. St. George. **EVP & CFO**—C. M. Kilbourne. **Dirs**—R. L. Darling, R. D. Harvey Sr., D. I. Meyer, A. S. Michael, K. G. Phillips II, N. J. St. George, S. G. Steifel Jr., S. C. Streeter, F. T. Vincent Jr., C. W. Walker, H. M. Weaver. **Transfer Agent & Registrar**—Wachovia Bank of North Carolina, Winston-Salem. **Incorporated** in North Carolina in 1971. **Empl**-3,586. **S&P Analyst:** Michael W. Jaffe

STANDARD & POOR'S

Oceaneering International

STOCK REPORTS

NYSE Symbol **OII**
In S&P SmallCap 600

22-AUG-95 **Industry:** Oil and Gas

Summary: Oceaneering International is one of the world's largest suppliers of underwater services, as well as mobile offshore production systems, to the offshore oil and gas industry.

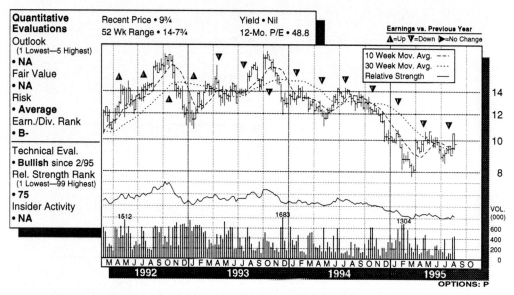

Quantitative Evaluations

Outlook
(1 Lowest—5 Highest)
• **NA**

Fair Value
• **NA**

Risk
• **Average**

Earn./Div. Rank
• **B-**

Technical Eval.
• **Bullish** since 2/95

Rel. Strength Rank
(1 Lowest—99 Highest)
• **75**

Insider Activity
• **NA**

Recent Price • 9¾
52 Wk Range • 14-7¾
Yield • Nil
12-Mo. P/E • 48.8

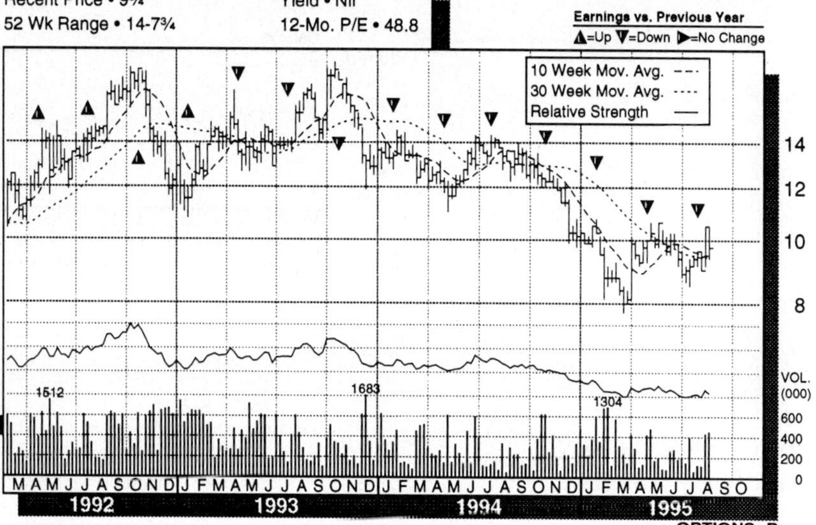

OPTIONS: P

Business Profile - 22-AUG-95

The company's primary market--oil and gas--is a cyclical and volatile industry. Potentially large fluctuations in demand for OII's primary services can translate into significant changes in revenues and profits. Although oil and gas continues to be its principal market, OII also performs services for the U.S. and foreign governments and the telecommunications, aerospace, insurance and environmental remediation industries.

Operational Review - 22-AUG-95

Revenues rose 13%, year to year, in the first quarter of 1995-96, as greater oilfield service activity was only partially offset by weakness in the advanced technologies sector. Margins narrowed, in part reflecting costs associated with entry into the environmental services business. After taxes at 42.0%, versus 34.5%, net income fell 24%, to $2,787,000 ($0.12 a share, on 4.2% fewer shares), from $3,666,000 ($0.15).

Stock Performance - 18-AUG-95

In the past 30 trading days, OII's shares have increased 8%, compared to a 0.51% rise in the S&P 500. Average trading volume for the past five days was 89,120 shares, compared with the 40-day moving average of 48,218 shares.

Key Stock Statistics

Dividend Rate/Share	Nil	Shareholders	800
Shs. outstg. (M)	23.1	Market cap. (B)	$0.239
Avg. daily vol. (M)	0.056	Inst. holdings	76%
Tang. Bk. Value/Share	4.43	Insider holdings	4%
Beta	0.91		

Value of $10,000 invested 5 years ago: $ 9,069

Fiscal Year Ending Mar. 31

	1996	% Change	1995	% Change	1994	% Change
Revenues (Million $)						
1Q	71.54	13%	63.37	7%	59.39	17%
2Q	—	—	66.90	2%	65.54	9%
3Q	—	—	55.20	NM	55.49	-2%
4Q	—	—	54.47	10%	49.34	4%
Yr.	—	—	239.9	4%	229.8	7%
Income (Million $)						
1Q	2.79	-24%	3.67	-22%	4.72	-11%
2Q	—	—	4.26	-11%	4.78	-12%
3Q	—	—	-2.85	NM	3.89	-31%
4Q	—	—	0.42	-73%	1.55	-49%
Yr.	—	—	5.50	-63%	14.93	-23%
Earnings Per Share ($)						
1Q	0.12	-20%	0.15	-25%	0.20	-9%
2Q	—	—	0.18	-10%	0.20	-13%
3Q	—	—	-0.12	NM	0.16	-33%
4Q	—	—	0.02	-67%	0.06	-54%
Yr.	—	—	0.23	-63%	0.62	-24%

Next earnings report expected: early November

Oceaneering International

22-AUG-95

Business Summary - 22-AUG-95

Oceaneering International is one of the world's largest underwater services contractors. It supplies a comprehensive range of integrated technical services, primarily to the offshore oil and gas industry, including subsea construction, drilling support, production systems, maintenance and repair, surveys and positioning, and onshore and offshore engineering, design and inspection. The company also offers a wide range of above-water inspection services to customers required to obtain third-party inspections. OII's first mobile offshore production system was deployed in December 1991. The company also provides project management, engineering services and equipment to non-oilfield customers for applications in harsh environments, including space. Contributions by business segment in 1994-95:

	Revs.	Gross Profits
Oilfield marine services	44%	-19%
Offshore field development	26%	52%
Advanced technologies	30%	67%

Operations are conducted in the U.S. and 28 other countries. International operations, principally in the North Sea, Far East and Africa, accounted for 51% of revenues and 77% of profits before taxes in 1994-95.

In May 1993, OII acquired the assets of the ILC Space Systems division (SSD) of ILC Dover. This business designs, develops and fabricates spacecraft hardware and high temperature insulation products.

In July 1994, OII formed an Environmental Industrial Services Group, which will apply robotic intervention, computer-aided inspection techniques and advanced sensor technology to process decontamination projects. In October 1994, OII introduced a new generation of work class remotely operated vehicle (ROV), the Hydra MAGNUM. It is available in 1,000 and 3,000 meter configurations with 75 to 150hp propulsion systems.

OII's floating production, storage and offloading system operates offshore Angola under a contract that has been extended until January 1996. In January 1995, the company received a letter of intent from Soekor (Proprietary) Limited, the national oil and gas exploration/production company of the Republic of South Africa, to develop and produce Soekor's offshore E-BT oil field and adjacent discoveries.

Important Developments

Aug. '95—OII reported that the "Ocean Developer" was lost at sea off the west coast of Africa; it had been recently acquired and was being towed to South Africa to be converted to a floating production system.

Capitalization

Long Term Debt: $21,000,000 (6/95).

Per Share Data ($) (Year Ended Mar. 31)

	1995	1994	1993	1992	1991	1990
Tangible Bk. Val.	4.43	4.14	4.17	3.78	3.08	2.23
Cash Flow	0.90	1.13	1.30	1.01	1.00	0.76
Earnings	0.23	0.62	0.82	0.70	0.72	0.47
Dividends	Nil	Nil	Nil	Nil	Nil	Nil
Payout Ratio	Nil	Nil	Nil	Nil	Nil	Nil
Cal. Yrs.	1994	1993	1992	1991	1990	1989
Prices - High	14⅝	18½	18⅛	14⅛	18⅞	11⅜
- Low	9¾	10¾	8⅞	8½	8¾	2½
P/E Ratio - High	64	30	22	20	26	24
- Low	42	17	11	12	12	5

Income Statement Analysis (Million $)

	1995	%Chg	1994	%Chg	1993	%Chg	1992
Revs.	240	4%	230	6%	216	29%	168
Oper. Inc.	29.0	-12%	33.1	-14%	38.4	44%	26.7
Depr.	16.2	33%	12.2	6%	11.5	60%	7.2
Int. Exp.	0.7	-26%	0.9	-30%	1.4	—	NM
Pretax Inc.	12.5	-40%	20.8	-18%	25.4	15%	22.0
Eff. Tax Rate	56%	—	28%	—	23%	—	26%
Net Inc.	5.5	-63%	14.9	-23%	19.4	22%	15.9

Balance Sheet & Other Fin. Data (Million $)

	1995	1994	1993	1992	1991	1990
Cash	12.9	26.5	34.0	23.3	40.1	37.8
Curr. Assets	75.8	80.8	88.8	66.9	72.1	71.6
Total Assets	188	172	155	136	113	96.0
Curr. Liab.	52.7	46.4	46.3	38.3	30.3	32.5
LT Debt	9.5	0.2	0.2	0.3	0.4	Nil
Common Eqty.	115	113	98.3	85.2	68.9	49.6
Total Cap.	126	115	101	89.5	73.2	52.6
Cap. Exp.	32.1	36.7	12.0	34.6	19.9	11.5
Cash Flow	21.7	27.1	30.9	23.1	22.6	16.7

Ratio Analysis

	1995	1994	1993	1992	1991	1990
Curr. Ratio	1.4	1.7	1.9	1.7	2.4	2.2
% LT Debt of Cap.	7.5	0.1	0.2	0.4	0.6	Nil
% Net Inc.of Revs.	2.3	6.5	9.0	9.5	11.1	5.6
% Ret. on Assets	3.1	9.1	13.1	12.7	15.5	11.6
% Ret. on Equity	4.8	14.1	20.7	20.6	27.4	24.9

Dividend Data —No dividends have been paid since 1977. A "poison pill" stock purchase rights plan was adopted in November 1992.

Data as orig. reptd.; bef. results of disc. opers. and/or spec. items. Per share data adj. for stk. divs. as of ex-div. date. E-Estimated. NA-Not Available. NM-Not Meaningful. NR-Not Ranked.

Office—16001 Park Ten Place, Suite 600, P.O. Box 218130, Houston, TX 77218-8130. **Tel**—(713) 578-8868. **Chrmn, Pres & CEO**—J. R. Huff. **SVP-CFO**—M. J. Migura. **VP-Secy**—G. R. Haubenreich, Jr. **Investor Contact**—Jack Jurkoshek. **Dirs**—G. M. Anderson, C. B. Evans, D. S. Hooker, J. R. Huff, D. M. Hughes. **Transfer Agent & Registrar**—First Chicago Trust Co. of New York, Jersey City, N.J. **Incorporated** in Delaware in 1969. **Empl**-1,900. **S&P Analyst:** Michael C. Barr

STANDARD & POOR'S

STOCK REPORTS

Offshore Logistics

NASDAQ Symbol **OLOG**

In S&P SmallCap 600

17-SEP-95

Industry: Oil and Gas

Summary: This company provides helicopter transportation and related services to the offshore oil and gas industry worldwide, principally in the Gulf of Mexico.

Quantitative Evaluations

Outlook
(1 Lowest—5 Highest)
• **5**

Fair Value
• **15⅞**

Risk
• **Average**

Earn./Div. Rank
• **B-**

Technical Eval.
• **Bullish** since 7/95

Rel. Strength Rank
(1 Lowest—99 Highest)
• **48**

Insider Activity
• **NA**

Recent Price • 14⅛
52 Wk Range • 15⅛-11¾

Yield • Nil
12-Mo. P/E • 14.7

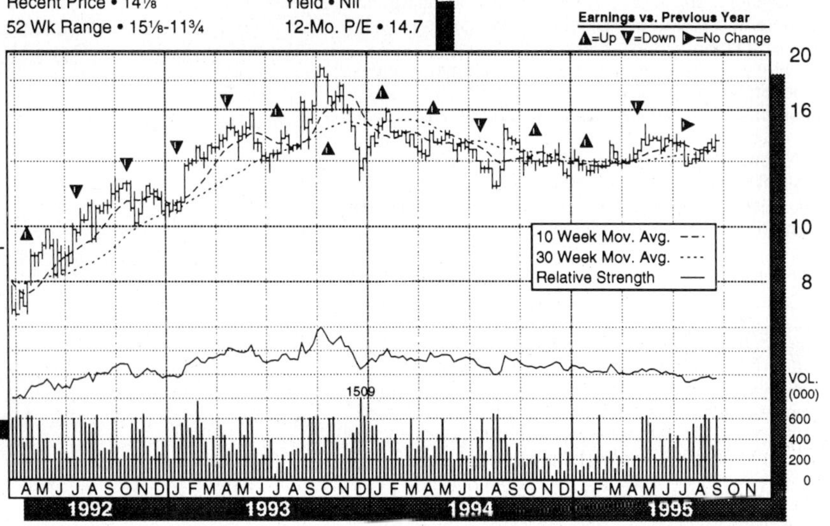

Business Profile - 14-SEP-95

OLOG provides helicopter transportation services to the worldwide offshore oil and gas industry. Beginning in 1992, OLOG expanded its operations to encompass production management services. In October 1994, OLOG acquired 75% of Cathodic Protection Services, which manufactures, installs and maintains cathodic protection services to arrest corrosion in oil and gas drilling and production facilities, pipelines, oil and gas well casings, hydrocarbon processing plants and other metal structures.

Operational Review - 14-SEP-95

Revenues (preliminary) for the fiscal year ended June 30, 1995 rose 52% from those of the previous year. The consolidation of Grasso Production Management and Cathodic Protection Services after the first quarter was responsible for the increase in revenue. Helicopter flight activity and revenues generated in the Gulf of Mexico were relatively unchanged, but stringent cost controls resulted in net income advancing 7.0% to $18,450,000 ($0.96 a share, on 7.3% more shares), from $17,247,000 ($0.96).

Stock Performance - 15-SEP-95

In the past 30 trading days, OLOG's shares have increased 8%, compared to a 4% rise in the S&P 500. Average trading volume for the past five days was 182,400 shares, compared with the 40-day moving average of 118,538 shares.

Key Stock Statistics

Dividend Rate/Share	Nil	Shareholders	1,500
Shs. outstg. (M)	19.4	Market cap. (B)	$0.275
Avg. daily vol. (M)	0.157	Inst. holdings	75%
Tang. Bk. Value/Share	8.04	Insider holdings	NA
Beta	1.24		

Value of $10,000 invested 5 years ago: $ 12,021

Fiscal Year Ending Jun. 30

	1995	% Change	1994	% Change	1993	% Change
Revenues (Million $)						
1Q	26.23	19%	21.98	9%	20.20	-18%
2Q	41.70	81%	23.03	19%	19.29	-6%
3Q	36.51	42%	25.79	26%	20.41	5%
4Q	39.80	67%	23.88	9%	21.98	10%
Yr.	144.2	52%	94.68	16%	81.88	-3%
Income (Million $)						
1Q	5.02	13%	4.43	4%	4.27	-19%
2Q	5.22	27%	4.10	11%	3.69	-7%
3Q	3.88	-19%	4.81	51%	3.18	-12%
4Q	4.33	10%	3.92	-21%	4.95	5%
Yr.	18.45	7%	17.25	8%	16.04	-9%
Earnings Per Share ($)						
1Q	0.28	12%	0.25	4%	0.24	-20%
2Q	0.27	17%	0.23	10%	0.21	-9%
3Q	0.20	-26%	0.27	50%	0.18	-14%
4Q	0.22	NM	0.22	-21%	0.28	4%
Yr.	0.96	NM	0.96	7%	0.90	-10%

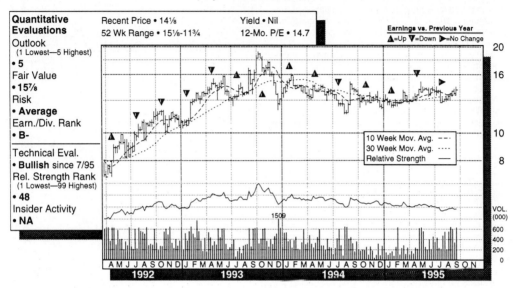

Next earnings report expected: early November

Offshore Logistics

Business Summary - 15-SEP-95

Offshore Logistics, Inc., whose business was organized in 1969, supplies helicopter transportation and production management services to the offshore oil and gas industry in the U.S. and about 10 other countries. The company also provides technical support and assistance for various joint-venture affiliated companies. As of June 1994, OLOG operated 162 aircraft, of which it owned 150. In fiscal 1994, operating revenues and profits by geographic area were:

	Revs.	Profits
U.S.	82%	79%
International	18%	21%

Historically, demand for the company's services has been influenced by the level of worldwide offshore oil and gas production and drilling activity. Domestic helicopter services are provided primarily from facilities along the Gulf of Mexico, where 137 aircraft were being operated as of June 30, 1994. OLOG was also operating 11 aircraft in Alaska. Although OLOG's business is oriented to oil and gas, a secondary market for its fleet includes emergency medical transportation, agricultural and forestry support and general aviation activities. Domestic operations contributed revenues of $75 million in fiscal 1994, up 24% from the fiscal 1993 total, and operating profit of $19 million, up 23%.

Internationally, the company operated 14 helicopters as of June 30, 1994. Locations included Brazil, Colombia and Mexico. In addition, there were service agreements with, and, in some cases, equity interests in entities operating 29 aircraft in Egypt and Mexico. International operations contributed revenues of $16 million in fiscal 1994, down 15% from the fiscal 1993 total, and operating profit of $5.2 million, down 23%.

During 1993, OLOG expanded its operations to include production management services through the acquisition of 50% of PPI-Seahawk Services. Following a merger of Seahawk into Grasso Corp., the company gained an interest in Grasso, which was also engaged in the production management services business, and in September 1994, OLOG acquired all the remaining outstanding stock of Grasso.

In October 1994, OLOG acquired 75% of Cathodic Protection Services Co., which manufactures, installs and maintains cathodic systems to arrest corrosion in oil and gas drilling and production facilities, pipelines, oil and gas well casings, hydrocarbon processing plants and other metal structures, for $7.5 million.

Important Developments

Aug. '95—The company remains optimistic about the potential for 1994 acquisitions Grasso Production Management and Cathodic Protection Services, although neither made significant contributions in fiscal 1995.

Capitalization

Long Term Debt: $6,600,000 (12/94).
Minority Interest: $1,513,000.

Per Share Data ($) (Year Ended Jun. 30)

	1995	1994	1993	1992	1991	1990
Tangible Bk. Val.	NA	8.04	7.06	6.09	5.10	3.81
Cash Flow	NA	1.38	1.27	1.36	1.31	1.34
Earnings	0.96	0.96	0.90	1.00	0.97	0.98
Dividends	Nil	Nil	Nil	Nil	Nil	Nil
Payout Ratio	Nil	Nil	Nil	Nil	Nil	Nil
Prices - High	15⅛	16⅛	19¼	12⅛	10¾	14¾
- Low	12¼	11⅝	10⅜	7	6⅜	6⅝
P/E Ratio - High	16	17	21	12	11	15
- Low	13	12	12	7	7	7

Income Statement Analysis (Million $)

	1994	%Chg	1993	%Chg	1992	%Chg	1991
Revs.	92.0	15%	80.0	-2%	82.0	-14%	95.0
Oper. Inc.	25.5	6%	24.1	-7%	25.9	2%	25.4
Depr.	7.5	15%	6.5	2%	6.4	5%	6.1
Int. Exp.	1.1	-27%	1.5	-21%	1.9	-10%	2.1
Pretax Inc.	23.6	10%	21.5	-12%	24.3	14%	21.3
Eff. Tax Rate	27%	—	25%	—	28%	—	20%
Net Inc.	17.2	8%	16.0	-9%	17.5	3%	17.0

Balance Sheet & Other Fin. Data (Million $)

	1994	1993	1992	1991	1990	1989
Cash	47.2	46.9	40.7	30.2	16.1	10.6
Curr. Assets	87.3	82.2	72.3	64.7	54.7	42.7
Total Assets	174	164	145	138	112	97.0
Curr. Liab.	10.0	16.0	19.0	27.0	17.0	17.0
LT Debt	2.0	9.3	10.0	19.0	25.0	31.0
Common Eqty.	142	124	107	88.9	66.4	18.2
Total Cap.	162	146	123	112	93.0	78.0
Cap. Exp.	12.0	7.9	9.2	33.4	11.8	12.3
Cash Flow	24.8	22.0	24.0	23.1	23.5	17.3

Ratio Analysis

	1994	1993	1992	1991	1990	1989
Curr. Ratio	8.6	5.2	3.8	2.4	3.2	2.5
% LT Debt of Cap.	1.2	6.4	8.2	17.0	26.4	39.8
% Net Inc.of Revs.	18.8	20.0	21.4	17.9	17.6	14.5
% Ret. on Assets	10.2	10.4	12.4	13.6	14.9	11.8
% Ret. on Equity	13.0	13.9	17.9	21.9	38.9	95.7

Dividend Data —No cash dividends have been paid on the common shares since 1984.

Data as orig. reptd.; bef. results of disc. opers. and/or spec. items. Per share data adj. for stk. divs. as of ex-div. date. E-Estimated. NA-Not Available. NM-Not Meaningful. NR-Not Ranked.

Office—224 Rue de Jean, P.O. Box 5C, Lafayette, LA 70505. **Tel**—(318) 233-1221. **Chrmn**—H. Wolf. **Pres & CEO**—J. B. Clement. **VP, CFO, Treas, Secy & Investor Contact**—George M. Small. **Dirs**—J. B. Clement, L. F. Crane, D. S. Foster, D. M. Johnson, K. M. Jones, H. L. Luther Jr., H. C. Sager, G. M. Small, H. Wolf. **Transfer Agent & Registrar**—Chemical Bank, NYC. **Reincorporated** in Delaware in 1988. **Empl-** 619. **S&P Analyst:** Michael C. Barr

STANDARD & POOR'S

STOCK REPORTS

Omega Environmental

NASDAQ Symbol **OMEG**

In S&P SmallCap 600

02-NOV-95

Industry: Manufacturing/Distr

Summary: This company provides products and services related to underground storage tanks, including soil and groundwater remediation.

Quantitative Evaluations

Outlook (1 Lowest—5 Highest) • **NA**

Fair Value • **NA**

Risk • **High**

Earn./Div. Rank • **NR**

Technical Eval. • **Bearish** since 5/94

Rel. Strength Rank (1 Lowest—99 Highest) • **80**

Insider Activity • **NA**

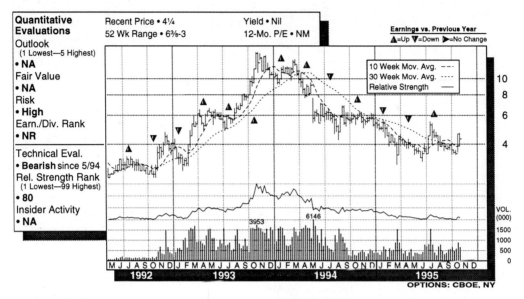

Recent Price • 4¼

52 Wk Range • 6⅜-3

Yield • Nil

12-Mo. P/E • NM

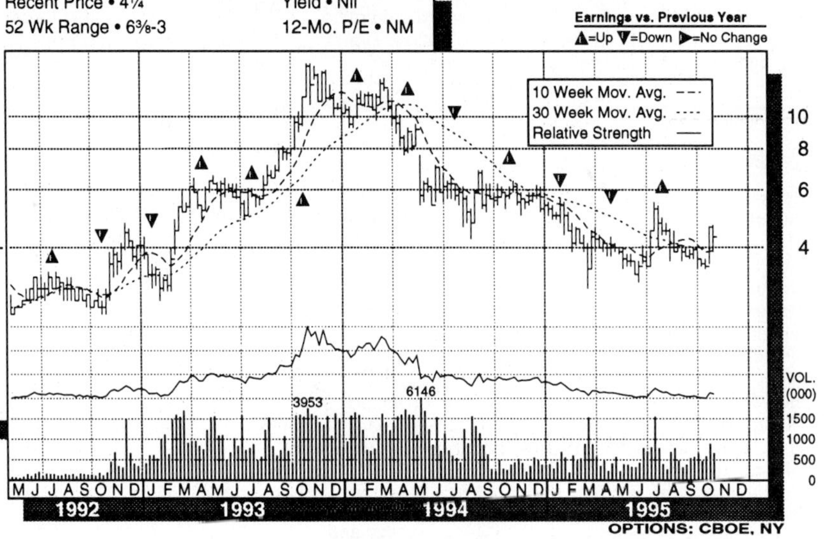

OPTIONS: CBOE, NY

Business Profile - 02-NOV-95

Omega has completed the first phase of its acquisition program, having purchased 17 UST companies. It will continue to make acquisitions, but at a slower rate and without the cost of an acquisition staff. A Mexican subsidiary has been expanding operations outside the U.S. In February 1995, the company agreed, without admitting wrongdoing, to a $5.6 million class-action settlement. Losses have been incurred since inception.

Operational Review - 02-NOV-95

Revenues in the first quarter of fiscal 1996 (Mar.) advanced 49%, year to year, with acquisitions accounting for 86% of the increase. The operating loss narrowed to $187,000, from $3,078,000, as gross margins widened and acquisition-related SG&A declined to 19% of sales, from 27%. Despite net interest and other expense of $156,000, versus net income of $201,000, the net loss was cut to $0.01 a share, on 9% more shares, from $0.10.

Stock Performance - 27-OCT-95

In the past 30 trading days, OMEG's shares have increased 13%, compared to a 0.63% fall in the S&P 500. Average trading volume for the past five days was 128,820 shares, compared with the 40-day moving average of 117,592 shares.

Key Stock Statistics

Dividend Rate/Share	Nil	Shareholders	500
Shs. outstg. (M)	34.6	Market cap. (B)	$0.143
Avg. daily vol. (M)	0.121	Inst. holdings	6%
Tang. Bk. Value/Share	0.84	Insider holdings	NA
Beta	NA		

Value of $10,000 invested 5 years ago: NA

Fiscal Year Ending Mar. 31

	1996	% Change	1995	% Change	1994	% Change
Revenues (Million $)						
1Q	40.41	49%	27.10	NM	5.34	NM
2Q	—	—	34.20	NM	7.73	NM
3Q	—	—	39.76	132%	17.14	NM
4Q	—	—	35.98	119%	16.40	NM
Yr.	—	—	137.0	194%	46.64	NM
Income (Million $)						
1Q	-0.34	NM	-2.88	NM	-1.60	NM
2Q	—	—	-0.63	NM	-1.49	NM
3Q	—	—	-7.36	NM	-1.53	NM
4Q	—	—	-6.31	NM	-4.30	NM
Yr.	—	—	-17.17	NM	-8.91	NM
Earnings Per Share ($)						
1Q	-0.01	NM	-0.10	NM	-0.08	NM
2Q	—	—	-0.02	NM	-0.06	NM
3Q	—	—	-0.23	NM	-0.06	NM
4Q	—	—	-0.19	NM	-0.14	NM
Yr.	—	—	-0.55	NM	-0.35	NM

Next earnings report expected: early November

Omega Environmental

Business Summary - 02-NOV-95

Omega Environmental, Inc. provides turnkey products and services to owners of underground storage tank (UST) systems, which are required to be in compliance with U.S. EPA, state and local regulations governing USTs. As a result of acquisitions and internal expansion, the company has subsidiaries in 31 states and one in Mexico, with limited operations in Argentina and Spain.

The company derives its revenues from a range of products and services, including removal of leaking and outdated USTs, construction, soil and groundwater remediation services, the sale and installation of new UST systems and the distribution and servicing of petroleum storage and dispensing equipment.

According to May 1995 EPA data, about 25% of the more than 1.14 million active USTs registered with the EPA are currently leaking and must be removed and replaced immediately according to the law. The EPA also estimates that there are several million more unregistered USTs. Because the major source of groundwater contamination is leaking UST systems, EPA regulations have required, since December 1993, that a leak detection program be in place for existing tank systems. Omega expects to benefit from this large and increasingly regulated market.

The company's patented Leak Prevention Technology is designed to prevent leaks in double-walled containment storage tank systems and related piping, through creating and maintaining a "curtain" of compressed air or an inert gas in the space between the inner and outer walls.

Under EPA regulations, a UST owner must satisfy financial assurance requirements. This can be accomplished through various means, including pollution liability insurance. However, because of the lack of effective UST monitoring capability in the past, such insurance has been expensive and difficult to obtain.

Omega developed a Total Compliance Program to provide a "one stop shopping" solution for UST compliance upgrades. The program includes site assessment, environment analysis, removal and installation of tanks, soil remediation, and the facilitation of financing.

Important Developments

Aug. '95—Omega said it plans to pursue additional acquisitions during the current fiscal year (Mar.), but noted that acquisition-related expenses have been reduced because targeted companies are larger and fewer in number.

Jul. '95—The company received a commitment from BNY Financial Corp. for senior secured term and revolving credit facilities totaling $30 million.

Capitalization

Long Term Debt: $2,458,000 (6/95).

Per Share Data ($)

(Year Ended Mar. 31)

	1995	1994	1993	1992	1991	1990
Tangible Bk. Val.	0.82	1.43	0.55	0.12	-0.18	0.06
Cash Flow	-0.43	-0.28	-0.84	-0.60	-0.54	-0.24
Earnings	-0.55	-0.35	-0.89	-0.66	-0.57	-0.25
Dividends	Nil	Nil	Nil	Nil	Nil	Nil
Payout Ratio	Nil	Nil	Nil	Nil	Nil	Nil
Cal. Yrs.	1994	1993	1992	1991	1990	1989
Prices - High	13⅛	14½	4¾	2⅝	NA	NA
- Low	4¼	2¾	2⅛	1½	NA	NA
P/E Ratio - High	NM	NM	NM	NM	NM	NM
- Low	NM	NM	NM	NA	NA	NA

Income Statement Analysis (Million $)

	1995	%Chg	1994	%Chg	1993	%Chg	1992
Revs.	137	194%	46.6	NM	7.7	57%	4.9
Oper. Inc.	-5.0	NM	-6.7	NM	-5.1	NM	-2.9
Depr.	3.8	114%	1.8	NM	0.4	52%	0.3
Int. Exp.	1.1	174%	0.4	NM	0.1	-65%	0.2
Pretax Inc.	-17.2	NM	-8.9	NM	-8.2	NM	-3.3
Eff. Tax Rate	NM	—	NM	—	NM	—	Nil
Net Inc.	-17.2	NM	-8.9	NM	-8.2	NM	-3.3

Balance Sheet & Other Fin. Data (Million $)

	1995	1994	1993	1992	1991	1990
Cash	2.2	30.7	10.3	0.6	0.3	0.0
Curr. Assets	61.6	58.0	14.1	1.8	0.3	0.0
Total Assets	110	85.6	22.0	3.6	0.6	0.2
Curr. Liab.	39.4	19.2	4.6	1.4	1.1	0.2
LT Debt	2.3	2.1	1.9	0.3	0.2	0.2
Common Eqty.	63.3	64.0	15.2	2.0	-0.7	-0.2
Total Cap.	65.6	66.2	17.1	2.3	-0.5	-0.1
Cap. Exp.	2.0	1.9	0.3	1.0	0.0	Nil
Cash Flow	-13.3	-7.1	-7.8	-3.0	-0.9	-0.2

Ratio Analysis

	1995	1994	1993	1992	1991	1990
Curr. Ratio	1.6	3.0	3.1	1.3	0.3	0.1
% LT Debt of Cap.	2.5	3.2	11.2	13.5	NM	NM
% Net Inc.of Revs.	NM	NM	NM	NM	NM	NM
% Ret. on Assets	NM	NM	NM	NM	NM	NM
% Ret. on Equity	NM	NM	NM	NM	NM	NM

Dividend Data —No cash dividends have been paid. The company intends to retain any earnings to provide funds for the growth of its business.

Data as orig. reptd.; bef. results of disc. opers. and/or spec. items. Per share data adj. for stk. divs. as of ex-div. date. E-Estimated. NA-Not Available. NM-Not Meaningful. NR-Not Ranked.

Office—19805 Northcreek Parkway, P.O. Box 3005, Bothell, WA 98041-3005. **Tel**—(206) 486-4800. **Chrmn**—D.C. Kravitz. **Pres & CEO**—L. J. Tedesco. **CFO**—D. E. Steigerwald. **Investor Contact**—Joseph Allen, South Coast Communications Group (714-252-8440). **Dirs**—L. L. Azure, Jr., E. S. Brower, D. C. Kravitz, E. J. O'Sullivan, D. R. Rogers, S. Sarich, Jr, L. J. Tedesco. **Transfer Agent & Registrar**—Continental Stock Transfer & Trust Co., NYC. **Incorporated** in Delaware in 1990. **Empl**-900. **S&P Analyst:** Justin McCann

STANDARD & POOR'S

Omnicare, Inc.

STOCK REPORTS

NYSE Symbol **OCR**
In S&P SmallCap 600

02-NOV-95 **Industry:** Health Care Centers

Summary: This company is a leading provider of professional pharmacy management and related consulting services for long-term care institutions.

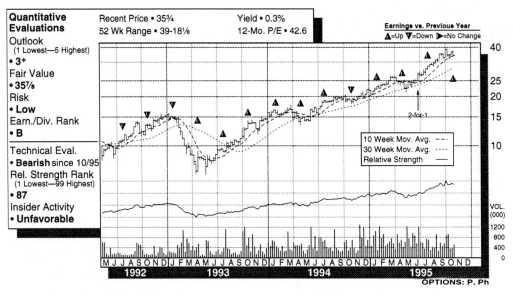

Quantitative Evaluations
Outlook (1 Lowest—5 Highest) • **3+**
Fair Value • **35⅞**
Risk • **Low**
Earn./Div. Rank • **B**

Technical Eval. • **Bearish** since 10/95
Rel. Strength Rank (1 Lowest—99 Highest) • **87**
Insider Activity • **Unfavorable**

Recent Price • 35¾
52 Wk Range • 39-18⅛
Yield • 0.3%
12-Mo. P/E • 42.6

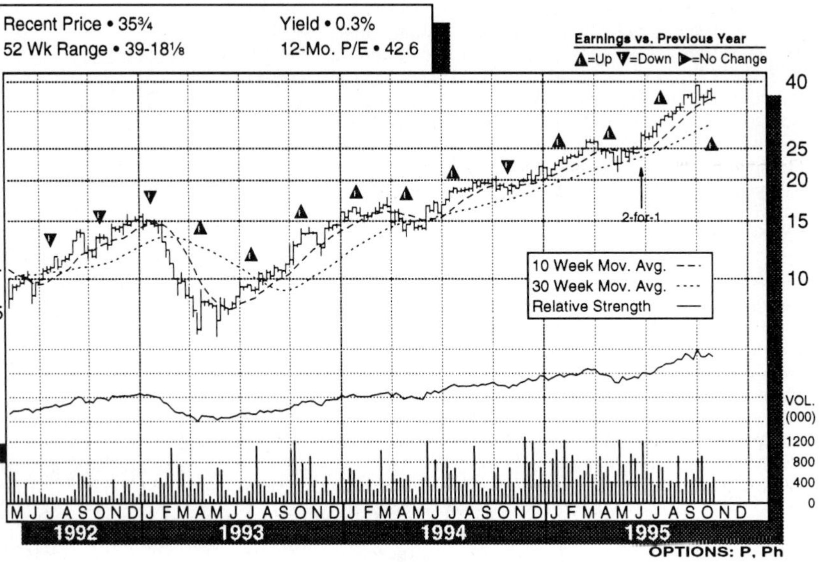

OPTIONS: P, Ph

Business Profile - 02-NOV-95

This company is benefiting from an aggressive acquisition program and internal growth generated through increased market penetration and expansion of services. By acquiring independent pharmacies, Omnicare achieves greater economies of scale in purchasing and distribution, and improves efficiency through the consolidation of administrative functions. Sales gains are being further fueled by the efforts of the new Omnicare National Sales and Marketing Group, established in late 1994.

Operational Review - 02-NOV-95

Revenues have risen in recent periods, aided by several acquisitions and internal growth through the addition of new clients, an increase in drug utilization, and expansion of infusion therapy services. Operating margins widened on the greater volume. Results in the second quarter of 1995 and third quarter of 1994 were penalized by acquisition related charges. Net income in the nine months ended September 30, 1995, rose 89% year to year.

Stock Performance - 27-OCT-95

In the past 30 trading days, OCR's shares have declined 2%, compared to a 0.63% fall in the S&P 500. Average trading volume for the past five days was 98,740 shares, compared with the 40-day moving average of 116,526 shares.

Key Stock Statistics

Dividend Rate/Share	0.10	Shareholders	1,800
Shs. outstg. (M)	26.3	Market cap. (B)	$0.971
Avg. daily vol. (M)	0.107	Inst. holdings	94%
Tang. Bk. Value/Share	2.34	Insider holdings	NA
Beta	0.55		

Value of $10,000 invested 5 years ago: $ 87,040

Fiscal Year Ending Dec. 31

	1995	% Change	1994	% Change	1993	% Change
Revenues (Million $)						
1Q	82.47	36%	60.70	73%	35.07	85%
2Q	97.13	47%	66.09	74%	37.98	67%
3Q	102.1	43%	71.41	77%	40.26	52%
4Q	—	—	77.46	67%	46.26	33%
Yr.	—	—	275.7	73%	159.6	55%
Income (Million $)						
1Q	5.19	54%	3.38	113%	1.59	161%
2Q	4.90	38%	3.54	90%	1.86	124%
3Q	6.93	NM	2.05	-21%	2.59	176%
4Q	—	—	4.44	65%	2.69	151%
Yr.	—	—	13.41	54%	8.73	153%
Earnings Per Share ($)						
1Q	0.21	32%	0.15	82%	0.08	143%
2Q	0.19	15%	0.17	65%	0.10	122%
3Q	0.26	174%	0.09	-32%	0.14	180%
4Q	—	—	0.19	31%	0.15	142%
Yr.	—	—	0.60	28%	0.47	147%

Next earnings report expected: early February

Omnicare, Inc.

Business Summary - 24-OCT-95

Omnicare, Inc. is a leading provider of professional pharmacy management and related consulting services for long-term care institutions. The Veratex Group of subsidiaries (medical, dental and veterinary supplies), was sold in December 1992.

The company's institutional pharmacy business purchases, repackages and dispenses pharmaceuticals, both prescription and nonprescription, and provides computerized medical record-keeping and third-party billing for patients in long-term care facilities such as nursing homes, retirement centers and other institutional healthcare settings. Omnicare also provides consultant pharmacist services, including but not limited to monthly patient drug therapy evaluation; monitoring of the control, distribution and administration of drugs within the nursing facility; and compliance with state and federal regulations. In addition, the company provides infusion therapy services and medical supplies to its client nursing homes.

As of July 1995, Omnicare was providing its services to approximately 194,200 nursing facility residents in 16 states.

Following sweeping changes in federal reimbursement programs for healthcare costs under Medicare in the 1980s, the company undertook a restructuring program in which it redeployed capital invested in businesses it believed were lacking in attractive growth potential to businesses that provide attractive returns on investment and favorable prospects for long-term growth, primarily the long-term care pharmacy business. The company completed the restructuring plan with the sale of its Veratex Group of businesses in December 1992 for $62 million in cash. As a result, Omnicare now operates principally in one business, institutional pharmacy services for the long-term care market.

Important Developments

Sep. '95—OCR acquired Dynatran Computer Systems, which develops computerized care plan systems for long-term care facilities to maintain and report federally required data on their residents, for 47,244 shares of Omnicare. Separately, the company acquired the nursing home pharmacy business of Rite Aid, which provides pharmaceuticals and related services to about 15,000 residents in nursing facilities.
Jul. '95—Omnicare acquired CPM Datascript Corp., a provider of comprehensive pharmacy services to over 3,400 residents in long-term care facilities in the New York City area, for an undisclosed amount of cash.
Jun. '95—The company completed the acquisition of Pharmacy Services Inc., the largest provider of pharmaceuticals and related clinical and consulting services for residents of long-term care institutions in Michigan, for 403,185 OCR shares.

Capitalization

Long Term Debt: $82,720,000 (6/95).

Per Share Data ($) (Year Ended Dec. 31)

	1994	1993	1992	1991	1990	1989
Tangible Bk. Val.	2.41	0.36	1.09	2.39	3.20	3.38
Cash Flow	0.95	0.71	0.35	0.40	0.31	0.21
Earnings	0.60	0.47	0.19	0.25	0.19	0.09
Dividends	0.09	0.08	0.07	0.06	0.05	0.04
Payout Ratio	15%	17%	38%	24%	27%	43%
Prices - High	$22\frac{5}{8}$	$16\frac{1}{8}$	$15\frac{3}{4}$	$11\frac{1}{4}$	$4\frac{1}{2}$	$4\frac{3}{4}$
- Low	$13\frac{1}{2}$	$6\frac{5}{8}$	$8\frac{1}{8}$	$3\frac{3}{4}$	3	$3\frac{7}{8}$
P/E Ratio - High	37	34	83	45	24	52
- Low	22	14	43	15	16	43

Income Statement Analysis (Million $)

	1994	%Chg	1993	%Chg	1992	%Chg	1991
Revs.	276	73%	160	55%	103	-11%	116
Oper. Inc.	36.5	85%	19.7	67%	11.8	36%	8.7
Depr.	7.4	69%	4.4	55%	2.8	1%	2.8
Int. Exp.	5.8	180%	2.1	3%	2.0	NM	0.5
Pretax Inc.	22.5	62%	13.9	111%	6.6	-3%	6.8
Eff. Tax Rate	40%	—	37%	—	48%	—	35%
Net Inc.	13.4	53%	8.7	157%	3.4	-23%	4.4

Balance Sheet & Other Fin. Data (Million $)

	1994	1993	1992	1991	1990	1989
Cash	79.6	63.3	13.3	3.4	13.0	11.0
Curr. Assets	162	111	52.2	51.7	56.4	57.4
Total Assets	306	219	131	108	90.0	88.0
Curr. Liab.	37.2	34.2	31.6	19.4	13.5	10.6
LT Debt	83.0	83.5	3.4	6.5	3.7	4.7
Common Eqty.	179	96.6	88.7	74.6	68.9	70.4
Total Cap.	263	180	95.0	84.0	75.0	77.0
Cap. Exp.	8.6	3.4	2.2	3.6	5.8	5.4
Cash Flow	20.8	13.1	6.3	7.2	5.3	3.8

Ratio Analysis

	1994	1993	1992	1991	1990	1989
Curr. Ratio	4.4	3.3	1.6	2.7	4.2	5.4
% LT Debt of Cap.	31.5	46.3	3.5	7.8	4.9	6.1
% Net Inc.of Revs.	4.9	5.5	3.3	3.8	3.2	1.7
% Ret. on Assets	4.4	5.0	2.8	4.4	3.7	1.9
% Ret. on Equity	8.7	9.4	4.2	6.1	4.7	2.4

Dividend Data —Dividends, initiated in 1981, were suspended in 1984 and resumed in 1989. A dividend reinvestment plan is available. A two-for-one stock split was effected in June 1995.

Amt. of Div. $	Date Decl.	Ex-Div. Date	Stock of Record	Payment Date
0.050	Feb. 02	Feb. 17	Feb. 24	Mar. 10 '95
0.050	May. 15	May. 23	May. 30	Jun. 09 '95
2-for-1	May. 15	Jun. 22	May. 31	Jun. 21 '95
0.025	Aug. 03	Aug. 17	Aug. 21	Sep. 07 '95
0.025	Nov. 01	Nov. 16	Nov. 20	Dec. 07 '95

Data as orig. reptd.; bef. results of disc. opers. and/or spec. items. Per share data adj. for stk. divs. as of ex-div. date. E-Estimated. NA-Not Available. NM-Not Meaningful. NR-Not Ranked.

Office—2800 Chemed Center, 255 E. Fifth Street, Cincinnati, OH 45202. **Tel**—(513) 762-6666. **Chrmn**—E. L. Hutton. **Pres**—J. F. Gemunder. **Sr VP & CFO**—K. H. Stump. **Sr VP-Secy & Investor Contact**—Cheryl D. Hodges. **VP & Treas**—T. R. Marsh. **Dirs**—R. K. Baur, K. W. Chesterman, C. H. Erhart Jr., M. Fox, J. F. Gemunder, J. P. Grace Jr., C. D. Hodges, E. L. Hutton, T. C. Hutton, P. E. Keefe, S. E. Laney, A. R. Lindell, S. Margen, K. J. McNamara, J. M. Mount, T. S. O'Toole, D. W. Robbins. **Transfer Agent & Registrar**—Mellon Securities Transfer Services, Pittsburgh. **Incorporated** in Delaware in 1981. **Empl**-2,466. **S&P Analyst:** Philip J. Birbara

Orange & Rockland Utilities

NYSE Symbol **ORU**
In S&P SmallCap 600

30-AUG-95

Industry:
Util.-Diversified

Summary: This electric-gas utility serves areas to the north of New York City, with nonregulated subsidiaries engaged in natural gas marketing and land development.

Quantitative Evaluations

Outlook
(1 Lowest—5 Highest)
• **1-**

Fair Value
• **25⅝**

Risk
• **Low**

Earn./Div. Rank
• **A**

Technical Eval.
• **Bearish** since 8/95

Rel. Strength Rank
(1 Lowest—99 Highest)
• **41**

Insider Activity
• **NA**

Recent Price • 32⅞
52 Wk Range • 34⅞-28⅜

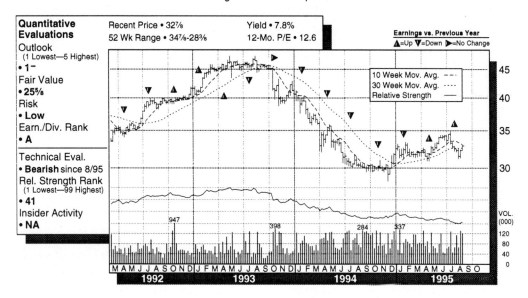

Yield • 7.8%
12-Mo. P/E • 12.6

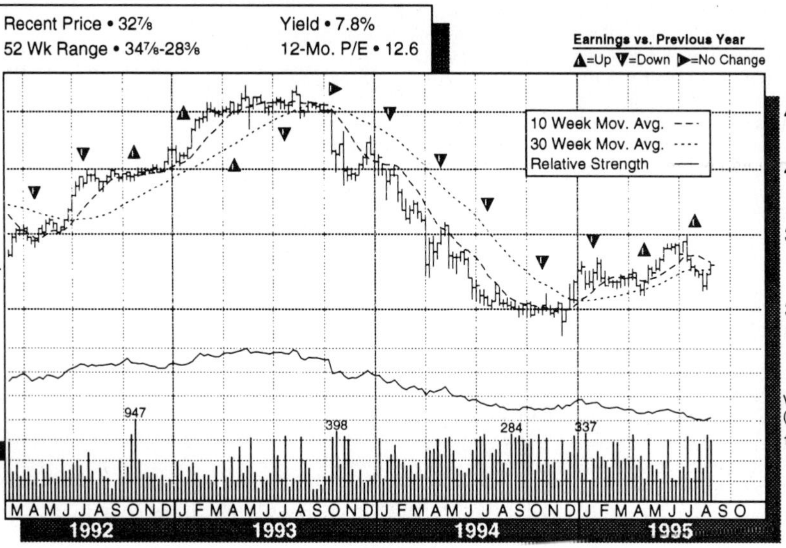

Business Profile - 30-AUG-95

This electric-gas utility also operates nonregulated subsidiaries engaged in gas marketing, real estate development and oil and gas production. In June 1994, chairman and CEO James F. Smith was removed from the board in the course of an investigation into misappropriation of funds. The company has since installed a new senior management team and sold the six radio stations that it owned. ORU has also reduced the size of its work force and terminated certain power production contracts.

Operational Review - 30-AUG-95

Operating revenues rose 7.1%, year to year, during the first half of 1995, as substantially greater diversified activities outweighed declining utility sales. Income from operations fell 13%, primarily as a result of increased non-utility gas marketing purchases. With lower investigation costs, other income replaced a loss, and total interest charges decreased. Net income advanced 9.1%, to $19,042,880 ($1.28 a share, after preferred dividends), from $17,447,763 ($1.17).

Stock Performance - 25-AUG-95

In the past 30 trading days, ORU's shares have declined 1%, compared to a 0.04% rise in the S&P 500. Average trading volume for the past five days was 24,320 shares, compared with the 40-day moving average of 23,441 shares.

Key Stock Statistics

Dividend Rate/Share	2.58	Shareholders	23,300
Shs. outstg. (M)	13.7	Market cap. (B)	$0.449
Avg. daily vol. (M)	0.025	Inst. holdings	20%
Tang. Bk. Value/Share	26.36	Insider holdings	NA
Beta	0.33		

Value of $10,000 invested 5 years ago: $ 15,070

Fiscal Year Ending Dec. 31

	1995	% Change	1994	% Change	1993	% Change
Revenues (Million $)						
1Q	311.9	7%	292.7	11%	264.0	10%
2Q	245.4	7%	229.7	7%	215.1	17%
3Q	—	—	239.2	NM	237.6	24%
4Q	—	—	255.3	NM	254.7	11%
Yr.	—	—	1,017	5%	971.4	15%
Income (Million $)						
1Q	15.32	9%	14.07	-7%	15.08	25%
2Q	3.72	10%	3.38	-49%	6.60	-7%
3Q	—	—	16.38	-5%	17.31	NM
4Q	—	—	3.39	-42%	5.82	-39%
Yr.	—	—	37.22	-17%	44.82	-2%
Earnings Per Share ($)						
1Q	1.06	8%	0.98	-7%	1.05	25%
2Q	0.22	16%	0.19	-56%	0.43	-7%
3Q	—	—	1.14	-7%	1.22	NM
4Q	—	—	0.19	-47%	0.36	-43%
Yr.	—	—	2.50	-18%	3.06	-3%

Next earnings report expected: late October

Orange & Rockland Utilities

Business Summary - 30-AUG-95

Orange & Rockland Utilities and its subsidiaries (Rockland Electric Co. in New Jersey and Pike County Light & Power Co. in Pennsylvania) supply electric service to more than 260,000 customers and gas service to 111,000 customers in a 1,350 sq. mi. area north of New York City that includes parts of southeastern New York, northern New Jersey and northeastern Pennsylvania. Electric revenues accounted for 47% of revenues and 80% of operating income in 1994, gas for 15% and 20%, and non-utility operations for 38% and less than 1%. In October 1994, the company decided to sell its six radio outlets and it signed the last sale contract in April 1995. Electric revenue contributions by customer class in recent years were:

	1994	1993	1992	1991
Residential	44%	43%	42%	44%
Commercial	43%	44%	45%	44%
Industrial	11%	11%	10%	10%
Other	2%	2%	3%	2%

Sources of electricity available for sale in 1994 were oil 6%, natural gas 23%, coal 36%, hydro 3%, and purchased power 32%. Peak load in 1994 was 1,022 mw; net capability at peak hours was 1,289 mw, for a capacity margin of 26.1%. Average residential rates were $0.1291 per kwh ($0.1310 in 1993); average annual usage was 7,357 kwh (7,214).

The company buys capacity and energy from other utilities as needed to meet its load and reserve requirements. It belongs to the New York Power Pool and has agreements with the New York Power Authority and other utilities to purchase power.

In 1994, ORU sold 21,471,000 Mcf of natural gas, up from 21,217,000 Mcf in 1993. Total maximum daily capacity at December 31, 1994, was 225,800 Mcf. The company has firm, long-term contracts for the supply of natural gas with seven gas producers. In addition to purchased gas, ORU manufactures gas at its propane air gas plants located in New York, which have a combined capacity of 30,600 Mcf per day.

Construction spending for 1995-1999 is estimated at $229.4 million, including $61.5 million for 1995. The company's forecasted construction expenditures consist primarily of routine production, transmission and distribution projects and do not include any additions to generating capacity.

Important Developments

Aug. '95—The NY State Public Service Commission approved a stipulated agreement for a 1.8% electric rate reduction, effective immediately. The agreement also increases the base return on common equity to 10.8% from 10.6%, effective January 1.

Capitalization

Long Term Debt: $359,454,000 (6/95).
Red. Cum Preferred Stock: $2,774,000.
Non-Red. Cum. Pfd. Stk.: $43,261,000.

Per Share Data ($) (Year Ended Dec. 31)

	1994	1993	1992	1991	1990	1989
Tangible Bk. Val.	26.98	27.08	25.18	24.12	22.89	21.36
Earnings	2.50	3.06	3.15	3.12	2.99	3.14
Dividends	2.54	2.49	2.43	2.37	2.32	2.28
Payout Ratio	102%	81%	77%	76%	78%	73%
Prices - High	41¼	47½	41⅞	39	32⅜	32
- Low	28⅜	38⅝	32⅜	30⅞	26⅛	27¼
P/E Ratio - High	17	16	13	13	11	10
- Low	11	13	10	10	9	9

Income Statement Analysis (Million $)

	1994	%Chg	1993	%Chg	1992	%Chg	1991
Revs.	1,017	5%	971	15%	844	15%	732
Depr.	35.9	4%	34.5	NM	34.5	7%	32.1
Maint.	44.0	3%	42.9	NM	42.5	5%	40.3
Fxd. Chgs. Cov.	2.6	-9%	2.8	9%	2.6	1%	2.6
Constr. Credits	0.5	86%	0.3	-35%	0.4	-72%	1.5
Eff. Tax Rate	35%	—	33%	—	32%	—	29%
Net Inc.	37.2	-17%	44.8	-2%	45.8	2%	44.9

Balance Sheet & Other Fin. Data (Million $)

	1994	1993	1992	1991	1990	1989
Gross Prop.	1,255	1,204	1,163	1,118	1,067	1,013
Cap. Exp.	61.0	54.0	56.0	60.5	63.7	54.8
Net Prop.	856	832	815	792	765	722
Capitalization:						
LT Debt	360	381	381	379	374	293
% LT Debt	46	47	48	49	49	44
Pfd.	46.0	47.4	48.8	50.3	51.7	57.1
% Pfd.	5.90	5.90	6.10	6.50	6.80	8.60
Common	379	376	368	351	334	313
% Common	48	47	46	45	44	47
Total Cap.	975	999	918	894	872	776

Ratio Analysis

	1994	1993	1992	1991	1990	1989
Oper. Ratio	92.5	91.5	90.6	89.4	86.7	86.0
% Earn. on Net Prop.	9.0	10.0	9.9	9.9	10.0	10.6
% Ret. on Revs.	3.7	4.6	5.4	6.1	7.6	8.2
% Ret. On Invest.Cap	7.2	8.2	9.0	8.9	9.3	9.9
% Return On Com.Eqty	9.0	11.2	11.9	12.1	14.5	13.4

Dividend Data —Dividends have been paid since 1908. A dividend reinvestment plan is available.

Amt. of Div. $	Date Decl.	Ex-Div. Date	Stock of Record	Payment Date
0.640	Oct. 06	Oct. 11	Oct. 17	Nov. 01 '94
0.640	Jan. 05	Jan. 09	Jan. 16	Feb. 01 '95
0.640	Apr. 06	Apr. 10	Apr. 17	May. 01 '95
0.645	Jun. 29	Jul. 13	Jul. 17	Aug. 01 '95

Data as orig. reptd.; bef. results of disc opers. and/or spec. items. Per share data adj. for stk. divs. as of ex-div. date. E-Estimated. NA-Not Available. NM-Not Meaningful. NR-Not Ranked.

Office—One Blue Hill Plaza, Pearl River, NY 10965. **Tel**—(914) 352-6000. **Chrmn**—H. K. Vanderhoef. **Vice Chrmn & CEO**—D. L. Peoples. **VP & CFO**—R. L. Hanley. **Secy**—G. D. Caliendo. **Treas & Investor Contact**—Robert J. McBennett. **Dirs**—R. M. Baruch, J. F. Creamer, M. J. Del Giudice, K. D. McPherson, J. F. O'Grady, Jr., D. L. Peoples, F. V. Salerno, L. C. Taliaferro, H. K. Vanderhoef. **Transfer Agent & Registrar**—Chemical Bank, NYC. **Incorporated** in New York in 1926. **Empl**-1,640. **S&P Analyst:** Michael C. Barr

STANDARD & POOR'S

STOCK REPORTS

Orion Capital

NYSE Symbol **OC**
In S&P SmallCap 600

11-OCT-95 **Industry:** Insurance

Summary: Through wholly owned subsidiaries, this insurance holding company is engaged in the specialty property and casualty insurance business.

Quantitative Evaluations
Outlook
(1 Lowest—5 Highest)
• **3+**
Fair Value
• **43**
Risk
• **Low**
Earn./Div. Rank
• **B**

Technical Eval.
• **Bearish** since 8/95
Rel. Strength Rank
(1 Lowest—99 Highest)
• **74**
Insider Activity
• **Neutral**

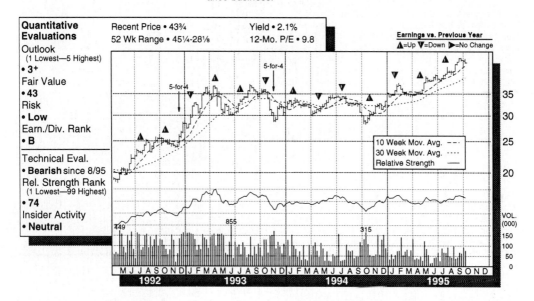

Recent Price • 43¾
52 Wk Range • 45¼-28⅛
Yield • 2.1%
12-Mo. P/E • 9.8

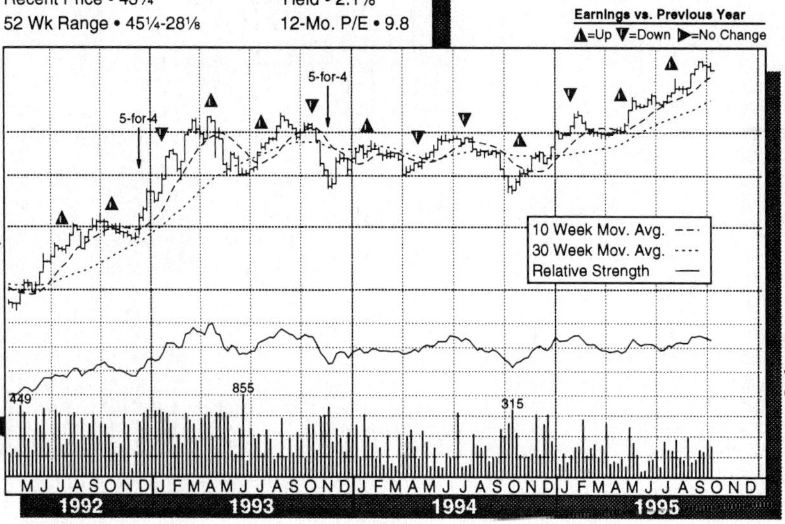

Business Profile - 04-OCT-95

Orion Capital, the parent to the 64th-largest property and casualty insurance group, had a combined ratio of 101.2% at year end 1994, which was significantly better than the industry average of 109.4%. Over the past several years the property/casualty industry has seen an unusually high number of catastrophes. Orion believes that this difficult operating environment will force many companies to seek out merger partners, providing OC the opportunity to choose attractive acquisition candidates.

Operational Review - 11-OCT-95

Revenues for the six months ended June 30, 1995, rose 11%, year to year, primarily due to higher net investment income and an increase in net written premiums. Operating earnings advanced 29%, and following sharply higher after-tax investment gains, net income was up 33% to $33,111,000 ($2.33 a share, based on 1.9% fewer shares) from $24,807,000 ($1.72).

Stock Performance - 06-OCT-95

In the past 30 trading days, OC's shares have increased 6%, compared to a 4% rise in the S&P 500. Average trading volume for the past five days was 14,860 shares, compared with the 40-day moving average of 12,869 shares.

Key Stock Statistics

Dividend Rate/Share	0.92	Shareholders	2,000
Shs. outstg. (M)	14.1	Market cap. (B)	$0.616
Avg. daily vol. (M)	0.014	Inst. holdings	65%
Tang. Bk. Value/Share	27.71	Insider holdings	NA
Beta	0.52		

Value of $10,000 invested 5 years ago: $ 35,399

Fiscal Year Ending Dec. 31

	1995	% Change	1994	% Change	1993	% Change
Revenues (Million $)						
1Q	201.8	7%	188.7	7%	176.1	—
2Q	212.1	16%	183.6	2%	180.8	16%
3Q	—	—	204.8	17%	175.4	—
4Q	—	—	203.8	8%	187.9	12%
Yr.	—	—	781.0	8%	720.2	11%
Income (Million $)						
1Q	17.06	29%	13.24	-8%	14.33	34%
2Q	16.05	39%	11.57	-17%	13.91	40%
3Q	—	—	15.33	19%	12.87	NM
4Q	—	—	15.11	-5%	15.89	29%
Yr.	—	—	55.24	-3%	56.99	24%
Earnings Per Share ($)						
1Q	1.20	32%	0.91	-6%	0.97	9%
2Q	1.13	41%	0.80	-16%	0.95	22%
3Q	—	—	1.07	22%	0.88	-16%
4Q	—	—	1.07	-2%	1.09	22%
Yr.	—	—	3.85	NM	3.88	7%

Next earnings report expected: early November

Orion Capital

Business Summary - 11-OCT-95

Orion Capital Corporation is an insurance holding company whose subsidiaries concentrate in niche insurance markets, particularly the underwriting of workers' compensation, architect and engineer professional liability and nonstandard automobile insurance. Contributions to net written premiums:

	1994	1993	1992
Workers' compensation	43%	49%	58%
Liability (non-auto)	28%	23%	22%
Private passenger automobile	9%	11%	6%
Commercial automobile	10%	10%	8%
Other	10%	7%	6%

In 1994, 12% of direct premiums written by OC units were generated in Pennsylvania, with an additional 38% in California, Wisconsin, Texas, Florida and Illinois. OC's insurance subsidiaries obtain substantially all of their business from about 830 independent insurance agents and brokers.

The EBI Companies--making up the Regional Operations segment, which sells and underwrites workers' compensation insurance through independent agents and brokers--emphasize intensive loss control and claims management services.

The Reinsurance/Special Programs segment, through the DPIC Companies, writes professional liability insurance for engineers, architects and accountants, marketed through an exclusive network of 53 specialized agencies. The segment also includes the Connecticut Specialty Insurance Group, through which it administers the operation of about 30 various specialty programs, including workers' compensation for coal miners and truckers. SecurityRe Companies, another part of this segment, underwrites a diverse book of property and casualty business using reinsurers.

Guaranty National Corp. (GNC, 49.9% owned) primarily writes nonstandard automobile insurance, which accounted for 83% of its net written premiums in 1994. Private passenger coverage is marketed through 1,950 independent agents in 21 western states. Commercial insurance, including nonstandard automobile, general liability, umbrella, miscellaneous professional and property insurance, is sold through 68 general agents.

Important Developments

Jul. '95—Orion Capital reported that the combined ratio, after policyholders' dividends, improved to 100.1% for the second quarter of 1995 from 102.2% in the second quarter of 1994. For the first six months of 1995, the combined ratio improved to 100.6% from 101.9% in the year-ago period.

Capitalization

Notes Payable: $149,000,000 (3/95).

Per Share Data ($) (Year Ended Dec. 31)

	1994	1993	1992	1991	1990	1989
Tangible Bk. Val.	23.91	25.29	19.16	15.67	7.38	8.13
Oper. Earnings	3.68	3.23	3.33	4.12	2.51	2.13
Earnings	3.85	3.88	3.61	3.75	1.78	2.22
Dividends	0.76	0.68	0.60	0.59	0.58	0.53
Payout Ratio	20%	18%	17%	16%	32%	24%
Prices - High	35¼	37½	28¾	21⅜	15⅜	18¼
- Low	28⅛	27¼	18⅝	10½	8¼	9¾
P/E Ratio - High	9	10	8	6	9	8
- Low	7	7	5	3	5	4

Income Statement Analysis (Million $)

	1994	%Chg	1993	%Chg	1992	%Chg	1991
Premium Income	691	12%	617	10%	560	-20%	701
Net Invest. Inc.	84.9	-8%	91.8	11%	82.5	-18%	100
Oth. Revs.	4.8	-56%	10.9	98%	5.5	-85%	35.8
Total Revs.	781	8%	720	11%	648	-23%	837
Pretax Inc.	71.5	-1%	72.5	55%	46.7	1%	46.1
Net Oper. Inc.	52.8	11%	47.5	11%	42.7	-8%	46.5
Net Inc.	55.2	-3%	57.0	24%	45.8	2%	44.7

Balance Sheet & Other Fin. Data (Million $)

	1994	1993	1992	1991	1990	1989
Cash & Equiv.	23.6	24.1	30.9	29.3	30.7	29.5
Premiums Due	125	111	102	96.0	113	114
Inv Assets Bonds	1,002	1,029	934	915	1,005	970
Inv. Assets Stock	264	243	186	130	105	104
Inv. Assets Loans	Nil	Nil	Nil	2.0	4.0	4.0
Inv. Assets Total	1,319	1,322	1,157	1,075	1,134	1,102
Deferred Policy Cost	70.1	57.5	56.1	58.9	64.9	70.3
Total Assets	2,113	2,117	1,554	1,455	1,500	1,471
Debt	152	160	130	142	175	175
Common Eqty.	365	394	283	188	130	141

Ratio Analysis

	1994	1993	1992	1991	1990	1989
Prop&Cas Loss	72.1	74.4	75.7	79.1	77.0	77.8
Prop&Cas Expense	27.0	26.8	27.3	30.2	28.7	28.1
Prop&Cas Comb.	99.1	101.2	103.0	109.3	105.7	105.9
% Ret. on Revs.	7.1	7.9	7.1	5.3	3.2	3.7
% Return on Equity	14.5	16.8	19.7	20.2	12.9	15.6

Dividend Data —Dividends were initiated in 1978. A "poison pill" stock purchase right was issued in 1989.

Amt. of Div. $	Date Decl.	Ex-Div. Date	Stock of Record	Payment Date
0.200	Dec. 07	Dec. 09	Dec. 15	Jan. 03 '95
0.200	Feb. 10	Mar. 09	Mar. 15	Apr. 03 '95
0.200	May. 31	Jun. 13	Jun. 15	Jul. 03 '95
0.230	Sep. 11	Sep. 20	Sep. 22	Oct. 02 '95

Data as orig. reptd.; bef. results of disc. opers. and/or spec. items. Per share data adj. for stk. divs. as of ex-div. date. E-Estimated. NA-Not Available. NM-Not Meaningful. NR-Not Ranked.

Office—30 Rockefeller Plaza, New York, NY 10112. **Tel**—(212) 332-8080. **Chrmn & CEO**—A. R. Gruber. **Vice Chrmn**—R. B. Sanborn. **Pres & COO**—L. D. Hollen. **VP-Secy**—M. P. Maloney. **VP-Treas & Investor Contact**—Vincent T. Papa. **Dirs**—B. J. Cohn, J. C. Colman, A. R. Gruber, L. D. Hollen, R. H. Jeffrey, W. R. Lyons, J. K. McWilliams, R. W. Moore, R. B. Sanborn, W. J. Shepherd, J. R. Thorne, R. B. Ware. **Transfer Agent & Registrar**—Chemical Bank, NYC. **Incorporated** in Delaware in 1976. **Empl**-1,500. **S&P Analyst:** Brad Ohlmuller

STANDARD & POOR'S

STOCK REPORTS

Oshkosh B'Gosh

NASDAQ Symbol **GOSHA**

In S&P SmallCap 600

07-AUG-95 **Industry:** Textiles

Summary: Oshkosh B'Gosh produces children's high-quality apparel, youth wear and men's and women's casual and workwear clothing.

S&P Opinion: Avoid (★★)

Recent Price • 16¾	Yield • 1.7%
52 Wk Range • 17-13	12-Mo. P/E • 30.5

Quantitative Evaluations

Outlook (1 Lowest—5 Highest)
• **1+**

Fair Value
• **15**

Risk
• **Low**

Earn./Div. Rank
• **B**

Technical Eval.
• **Bullish** since 8/94

Rel. Strength Rank (1 Lowest—99 Highest)
• **59**

Insider Activity
• **NA**

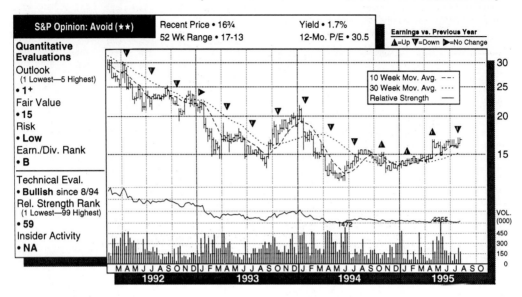

Overview - 07-AUG-95

Sales for 1995 could rise moderately, on increased store openings in 1995, and full-year contributions from stores opened in 1994. Wholesale sales will remain under pressure due to greater competition, including children's clothes made in the Far East, V.F. Corp's Healthtex division, Reebok and Nike. Growth of GOSHA's target market, infants to seven-year-olds, has also been slowing, which could limit sales increases. Wholesale sales to GOSHA's non-traditional distributors, such as J. C. Penney and Sears, should increase, however, reflecting marketing efforts, more efficient distribution, a more varied product assortment and volume discounts. Overseas sales are also expected to make a higher contribution to wholesale sales. Margins should remain under some pressure as the company changes its product mix from more profitable apparel wholesaling to less profitable retailing.

Valuation - 07-AUG-95

These shares have recovered somewhat since reaching a near-term low of 12 1/4 in 1994. However, they remain substantially below their all-time high of 44, reached in 1989, which we attribute to volatile sales and, for the most part, declining earnings. It now appears earnings are finally beginning to grow again, mainly reflecting the company's strategy to de-emphasize wholesaling and focus on retailing. But we think investors should continue avoiding this stock for now, until the company re-establishes a consistent earnings pattern and meets earnings expectations.

Key Stock Statistics

S&P EPS Est. 1995	0.75	Tang. Bk. Value/Share	11.50
P/E on S&P Est. 1995	22.3	Beta	1.31
S&P EPS Est. 1996	0.85	Shareholders	2,300
Dividend Rate/Share	0.28	Market cap. (B)	$0.214
Shs. outstg. (M)	12.8	Inst. holdings	58%
Avg. daily vol. (M)	0.030	Insider holdings	NA

Value of $10,000 invested 5 years ago: $ 4,592

Fiscal Year Ending Dec. 31

	1995	% Change	1994	% Change	1993	% Change
Revenues (Million $)						
1Q	108.5	24%	87.39	-6%	93.23	-6%
2Q	74.93	13%	66.16	5%	63.31	-11%
3Q	—	—	118.4	15%	103.1	3%
4Q	—	—	91.41	14%	80.53	11%
Yr.	—	—	363.4	7%	340.2	-2%
Income (Million $)						
1Q	2.72	NM	0.90	-77%	3.94	-47%
2Q	-1.88	NM	-0.74	NM	1.35	-42%
3Q	—	—	5.27	-2%	5.39	-17%
4Q	—	—	1.61	NM	-6.16	NM
Yr.	—	—	7.04	56%	4.52	-71%
Earnings Per Share ($)						
1Q	0.20	NM	0.06	-78%	0.27	-47%
2Q	-0.14	NM	-0.05	NM	0.09	-44%
3Q	E0.55	—	0.38	3%	0.37	-16%
4Q	E0.14	—	0.12	NM	-0.42	NM
Yr.	E0.75	—	0.50	61%	0.31	-71%

Next earnings report expected: late October

Oshkosh B'Gosh

Business Summary - 02-AUG-95

Oshkosh B'Gosh designs, manufactures and markets a broad range of children's clothing, as well as lines of youth wear and men's casual and workwear clothing. Children's wear is for girls' sizes up to 6X and boys' sizes up to seven, and youth wear is for girls' sizes seven to 14 and boys' sizes eight to 20. Men's clothing is in adult sizes. Approximately 94% of 1994 sales were of children's wear, versus 16% in 1979. Products are marketed primarily under the Oshkosh, Oshkosh B'Gosh, Baby B'Gosh, Genuine Kids, Our Stuff and Oshkosh Men's Wear labels.

Primary offerings for children in any given season will typically consist of a variety of clothing items, including bib overalls, pants, jeans, shorts and shortalls, shirts, blouses and knit tops, skirts, jumpers, sweaters, dresses, playwear and fleece. The men's wear line consists of bib overalls; several styles of waistband work, carpenter, and painters pants; five pocket jeans; work and flannel shirts; and coats and jackets.

The company's products are sold primarily through better-quality department and specialty stores, own stores, direct mail catalogs, foreign retailers, and through the company's own outlets including 137 retail factory stores, a retail showcase store, and the company proprietary mail order catalog.

The company's business is increasingly seasonal, with highest sales and income in the third quarter which is the company's peak retail selling season at its retail outlet stores. Second quarter sales and earnings are the lowest both because of relatively low domestic wholesale unit shipments and relatively modest retail outlet store sales during this period.

Important Developments

Jul. '95—GOSHA attributed the loss of $0.14 per share in 1995's second quarter to the increasingly seasonal nature of the company's business.
May '95—GOSHA announced that its board authorized the addition of up to 325,000 shares of its Class A common stock to its previously announced stock repurchase program of up to 1,500,000 shares in the open market. As of May 5, 1995, GOSHA had purchased 1,442,500 shares of its Class A common stock under its repurchase program.

Capitalization

Long Term Debt: $33,996,000 (6/95).
Cl. A Common Stock: 11,513,287 shs. ($0.01 par); holders elect 25% of directors but may not vote on other matters except as required by law.
Institutions hold about 57%.The Wyman/Hyde group holds 14%.
Cl. B Common Stock: 1,267,513 shs. ($0.01 par); holders elect 75% of directors & vote on all other matters.
Some 79.3% is held by the Wyman/Hyde group.
Shareholders: 2,081 Cl. A; 203. Cl. B.

Per Share Data ($) (Year Ended Dec. 31)

	1994	1993	1992	1991	1990	1989
Tangible Bk. Val.	11.76	11.79	12.01	11.48	10.36	8.82
Cash Flow	1.25	0.89	1.62	2.04	2.37	2.87
Earnings	0.50	0.31	1.08	1.62	2.03	2.58
Dividends	0.38	0.51	0.51	0.51	0.49	0.43
Payout Ratio	75%	165%	48%	32%	24%	17%
Prices - High	21¾	22½	30¾	42¼	43½	44
- Low	12¼	13½	19¼	22½	17	20
P/E Ratio - High	43	73	28	26	21	17
- Low	24	44	18	14	8	8

Income Statement Analysis (Million $)

	1994	%Chg	1993	%Chg	1992	%Chg	1991
Revs.	363	7%	340	-2%	346	-5%	365
Oper. Inc.	19.7	-22%	25.2	-11%	28.2	-40%	47.0
Depr.	10.7	27%	8.4	7%	7.9	29%	6.1
Int. Exp.	1.3	106%	0.6	-21%	0.8	-27%	1.1
Pretax Inc.	13.0	40%	9.3	-65%	26.5	-32%	39.1
Eff. Tax Rate	46%	—	51%	—	41%	—	41%
Net Inc.	7.0	-84%	45.0	187%	15.7	-33%	23.6

Balance Sheet & Other Fin. Data (Million $)

	1994	1993	1992	1991	1990	1989
Cash	10.5	17.9	21.1	14.4	6.8	3.3
Curr. Assets	142	152	146	141	129	116
Total Assets	217	229	226	215	189	163
Curr. Liab.	39.8	40.1	35.2	33.9	28.7	27.2
LT Debt	0.5	0.8	1.3	2.4	3.5	4.5
Common Eqty.	159	172	175	167	151	129
Total Cap.	162	176	180	174	155	134
Cap. Exp.	9.9	9.0	14.4	19.6	15.5	7.3
Cash Flow	17.7	12.9	23.6	29.7	34.5	41.9

Ratio Analysis

	1994	1993	1992	1991	1990	1989
Curr. Ratio	3.6	3.8	4.2	4.1	4.5	4.3
% LT Debt of Cap.	0.3	0.4	0.7	1.4	2.2	3.4
% Net Inc.of Revs.	1.9	1.3	4.5	6.5	9.1	11.9
% Ret. on Assets	3.3	2.0	7.1	11.7	16.8	24.9
% Ret. on Equity	4.4	2.6	9.2	14.8	21.1	33.3

Dividend Data (Prior to its 1985 recapitalization, the company paid some cash on its old common shares in each year since 1936. When any cash payment is made on the Class B, a dividend equal to 115% of such amount per share must be paid on the Class A.)

Amt. of Div. $	Date Decl.	Ex-Div. Date	Stock of Record	Payment Date
0.103	Aug. 08	Aug. 15	Aug. 19	Sep. 01 '94
0.070	Nov. 07	Nov. 14	Nov. 18	Dec. 01 '94
0.070	Jan. 21	Feb. 13	Feb. 17	Mar. 01 '95
0.070	May. 05	May. 15	May. 19	Jun. 01 '95

Data as orig. reptd.; bef. results of disc. opers. and/or spec. items. Per share data adj. for stk. divs. as of ex-div. date. E-Estimated. NA-Not Available. NM-Not Meaningful. NR-Not Ranked.

Office—112 Otter Ave., Oshkosh, WI 54901. **Tel**—(414) 231-8800. **Chrmn**—C. F. Hyde. **Vice Chrmn**—T. R. Wyman. **Pres & CEO**—D. W. Hyde. **COO**—M. D. Wachtel. **VP-Fin & CFO**—D. L. Omachinski. **Secy**—S. R. Duback. **Dirs**—O. J. Bradley, S. R. Duback, J. M. Hiegel, C. F. Hyde, D. W. Hyde, W. P. Jacobsen, D. L. Omachinski, J. D. Pyle, M. D. Wachtel, T. R. Wyman. **Transfer Agent**—Harris Trust & Savings Bank, Chicago. **Incorporated** in Delaware in 1929. **Empl**-6,600. **S&P Analyst:** Elizabeth Vandeventer

STANDARD & POOR'S

STOCK REPORTS

O'Sullivan Corp.

ASE Symbol **OSL**
In S&P SmallCap 600

12-OCT-95 **Industry:** Plastic/Products

Summary: OSL produces smooth rolled plastic products for a variety of applications, and also produces consumer lawn and garden products. The automotive trim unit was sold in late 1994.

Quantitative Evaluations

Recent Price • 11¾ Yield • 2.8%
52 Wk Range • 12⅜-8⅝ 12-Mo. P/E • 15.1

Outlook
(1 Lowest—5 Highest)
• **NA**
Fair Value
• **NA**
Risk
• **Low**
Earn./Div. Rank
• **B**

Technical Eval.
• **Bearish** since 6/95
Rel. Strength Rank
(1 Lowest—99 Highest)
• **61**
Insider Activity
• **Neutral**

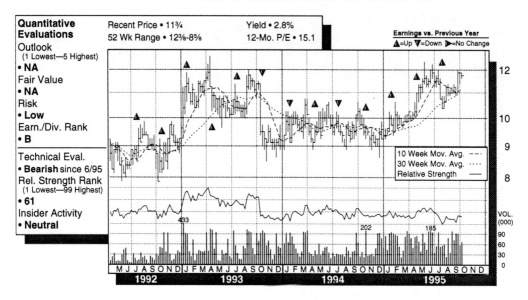

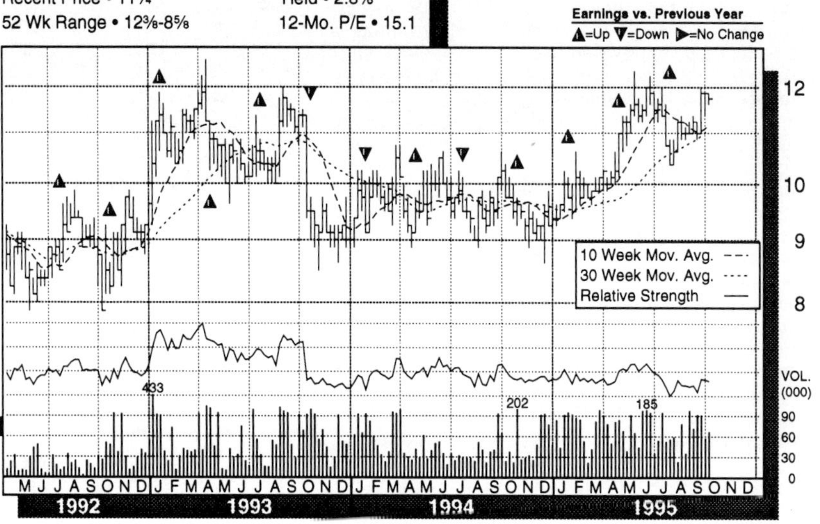

Business Profile - 03-JUL-95

O'Sullivan, following the sale of its automotive trim unit, has significantly downsized its operations and strengthened its balance sheet. The company's core business is now premium vinyl coverstock for the automotive, medical and office supply products. OSL's Melnor Inc. subsidiary is a leading producer of lawn and garden watering products. The company has indicated it may use some of the cash from the sale of the automotive trim division to pursue startegic acquisitions.

Operational Review - 12-OCT-95

Based on a brief report, net sales from continuing operations for the nine months ended September 30, 1995, rose 7.7% year to year, as increased sales in the company's plastics division offset lower than expected sales from the consumer products division's Melnor subsidiary. Net income was up 19% to $10,832,107 ($0.66 a share) from $9,072,113. Results for the 1994 period exclude a net loss from discontinued operations of $8,345,126 ($0.51).

Stock Performance - 06-OCT-95

In the past 30 trading days, OSL's shares have increased 7%, compared to a 4% rise in the S&P 500. Average trading volume for the past five days was 13,180 shares, compared with the 40-day moving average of 17,403 shares.

Key Stock Statistics

Dividend Rate/Share	0.32	Shareholders	3,000
Shs. outstg. (M)	16.5	Market cap. (B)	$0.190
Avg. daily vol. (M)	0.014	Inst. holdings	25%
Tang. Bk. Value/Share	6.78	Insider holdings	NA
Beta	0.31		

Value of $10,000 invested 5 years ago: $ 13,604

Fiscal Year Ending Dec. 31

	1995	% Change	1994	% Change	1993	% Change
Revenues (Million $)						
1Q	55.05	16%	47.41	-33%	70.80	35%
2Q	57.07	NM	57.03	-29%	80.24	42%
3Q	48.55	9%	44.70	-33%	66.51	26%
4Q	—	—	45.85	-39%	74.66	32%
Yr.	—	—	195.0	-33%	292.3	34%
Income (Million $)						
1Q	4.08	44%	2.84	24%	2.29	34%
2Q	3.96	3%	3.83	-11%	4.28	33%
3Q	2.78	15%	2.41	23%	1.96	-33%
4Q	—	—	1.90	28%	1.48	-50%
Yr.	—	—	10.97	10%	10.01	-7%
Earnings Per Share ($)						
1Q	0.25	47%	0.17	21%	0.14	40%
2Q	0.24	4%	0.23	-12%	0.26	30%
3Q	0.17	13%	0.15	25%	0.12	-33%
4Q	—	—	0.12	33%	0.09	-50%
Yr.	—	—	0.67	14%	0.59	-11%

Next earnings report expected: mid February

O'Sullivan Corp.

Business Summary - 11-OCT-95

O'Sullivan Corporation, founded in 1896 by Humphrey O'Sullivan (the inventor of the rubber heel), manufactures calendered plastic products for automobile producers and a variety of other users. The company also produces and distributes a wide range of lawn and garden products for the consumer market. In late 1994, OSL sold its injection plastics molding operations, which primarily produced automotive trim. Contribution to sales in recent years:

	1994	1993	1992
Plastics Products	77%	77%	98%
Consumer Products	23%	23%	2%

Calendered (smooth rolled) plastic products made by the plastics division include vinyl sheeting for automobile dashboard pads, swimming pool linings and covers, notebook binders, luggage, upholstered furniture, golf bags, floor tile, pond liners, protective clothing, mine curtains, boat and automobile windows and medical-grade materials.

The Consumer Products segment is primarily the result of the November 1992 acquisition of Melnor Industries Inc. Now known as Melnor Inc., this segment produces and sells oscillating, rotary and traveling sprinklers, hose storage units, watering timers, aqua guns, air spray tanks and snow shovels. Other products include humidification systems and distribution of ceiling fans and thermostats.

O'Sullivan's properties include 663,000 sq. ft. of manufacturing, warehouse and office space on 123 acres of land in Winchester, Va., 76,000 sq. ft. of manufacturing, warehouse and office space on 6 acres in Lebanon, Pa, 110,000 sq. ft. of manufacturing and warehouse space on five acres in Newton Upper Falls, Massachusetts and 347,000 sq. ft. of leased manufacturing, warehousing and office space in Moonachie, N.J.

In December 1994, the company completed the sale of its Gulfstream and Capital Plastics automotive trim operations to Automotive Industries Holdings, Inc. Proceeds to the company were $46.5 million cash and a $4.0 million unsecured promissory note. O'Sullivan recorded an after-tax loss on disposal of $8.2 million.

Important Developments

Oct. '95—In reporting third quarter earnings, O'Sullivan said that the August 1995 relocation of its Melnor Inc. subsidiary's U.S. operations were more costly than forecast, reducing earnings per share for the quarter by about $0.06. However, the company expects the relocation to reduce operating costs by about $1 million annually. The company also said that the outlook for its businesses in the fourth quarter and beyond is optimistic, and improved earnings are anticipated.

Capitalization

Long Term Debt: $1,764,470 (6/95).

Per Share Data ($) (Year Ended Dec. 31)

	1994	1993	1992	1991	1990	1989
Tangible Bk. Val.	6.42	6.54	6.23	5.88	6.09	5.48
Cash Flow	1.32	1.28	1.33	0.69	1.30	1.30
Earnings	0.67	0.61	0.66	0.09	0.89	0.98
Dividends	0.28	0.28	0.28	0.28	0.28	0.27
Payout Ratio	42%	46%	43%	300%	31%	27%
Prices - High	10¾	12⅝	9⅞	11½	11¼	16¼
- Low	8⅝	8½	7½	6⅝	7⅜	10
P/E Ratio - High	16	21	15	NM	13	17
- Low	13	14	11	NM	8	10

Income Statement Analysis (Million $)

	1994	%Chg	1993	%Chg	1992	%Chg	1991
Revs.	195	-33%	292	34%	218	11%	196
Oper. Inc.	29.5	NM	29.4	2%	28.8	62%	17.8
Depr.	10.9	-4%	11.4	3%	11.1	13%	9.9
Int. Exp.	0.9	-64%	2.5	NM	0.8	-50%	1.6
Pretax Inc.	18.1	8%	16.8	-4%	17.5	NM	2.4
Eff. Tax Rate	39%	—	42%	—	38%	—	36%
Net Inc.	11.0	13%	9.7	-10%	10.8	NM	1.5

Balance Sheet & Other Fin. Data (Million $)

	1994	1993	1992	1991	1990	1989
Cash	9.7	3.1	3.5	2.0	1.0	2.5
Curr. Assets	89.0	103	76.9	60.2	58.3	53.7
Total Assets	145	205	172	151	157	140
Curr. Liab.	30.7	47.6	35.6	32.6	27.6	27.1
LT Debt	1.7	39.6	25.5	13.7	19.8	16.5
Common Eqty.	107	109	104	97.0	100	90.0
Total Cap.	112	156	135	116	127	113
Cap. Exp.	8.8	17.3	14.5	7.5	16.5	33.7
Cash Flow	21.8	21.1	21.9	11.4	21.4	21.4

Ratio Analysis

	1994	1993	1992	1991	1990	1989
Curr. Ratio	2.9	2.2	2.2	1.8	2.1	2.0
% LT Debt of Cap.	1.5	25.4	18.9	11.8	15.6	14.6
% Net Inc.of Revs.	5.6	3.3	4.9	0.8	7.4	7.4
% Ret. on Assets	6.3	5.2	6.7	1.0	9.9	12.5
% Ret. on Equity	10.2	9.1	10.7	1.6	15.4	19.0

Dividend Data —Cash has been paid each year since 1960.

Amt. of Div. $	Date Decl.	Ex-Div. Date	Stock of Record	Payment Date
0.070	Jul. 26	Sep. 12	Sep. 16	Oct. 14 '94
0.070	Oct. 25	Dec. 12	Dec. 16	Jan. 13 '95
0.070	Feb. 08	Mar. 06	Mar. 10	Apr. 14 '95
0.080	Apr. 25	Jun. 06	Jun. 09	Jun. 14 '95
0.080	Jul. 25	Sep. 13	Sep. 15	Oct. 13 '95

Data as orig. reptd.; bef. results of disc. opers. and/or spec. items. Per share data adj. for stk. divs. as of ex-div. date. E-Estimated. NA-Not Available. NM-Not Meaningful. NR-Not Ranked.

Office—1944 Valley Ave., P.O. Box 3510, Winchester, VA 22601. **Tel**—(540) 667-6666. **Chrmn**—A. H. Bryant II. **Pres & CEO**—J. T. Holland. **Treas, VP, Secy & CFO**—C. B. Nickerson. **Dirs**—J. J. Armstrong, C. H. Bloom Jr., A. H. Bryant II, M. O. Bryant, R. L. Burrus Jr., M. C. Chapman Jr., J. T. Holland, R. M. McCullough, S. P. Munn. **Transfer Agent & Registrar**—Mellon Securities Trust Co., Pittsburgh. **Incorporated** in Virginia in 1945. **Empl**-1,100. **S&P Analyst:** N. Rosenberg

STANDARD & POOR'S

STOCK REPORTS

Owens & Minor

NYSE Symbol **OMI**
In S&P SmallCap 600

08-SEP-95

Industry:
Medical equipment/ supply

Summary: This company is a wholesale distributor of medical and surgical supplies, pharmaceuticals and related products throughout the U.S.

Quantitative Evaluations

Outlook
(1 Lowest—5 Highest)
• **3⁻**

Fair Value
• **14⅛**

Risk
• **Average**

Earn./Div. Rank
• **A-**

Technical Eval.
• **Bearish** since 11/94

Rel. Strength Rank
(1 Lowest—99 Highest)
• **42**

Insider Activity
• **NA**

Recent Price • 14½
52 Wk Range • 16¾-11⅝
Yield • 1.3%
12-Mo. P/E • 63.0

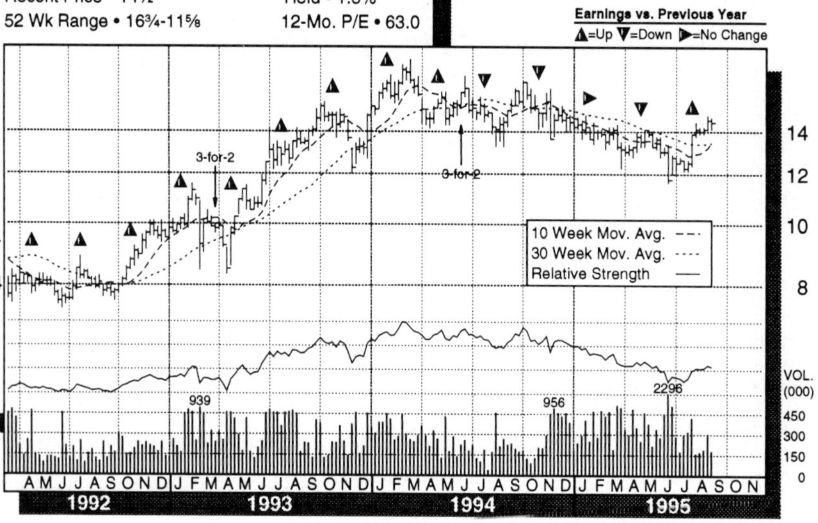

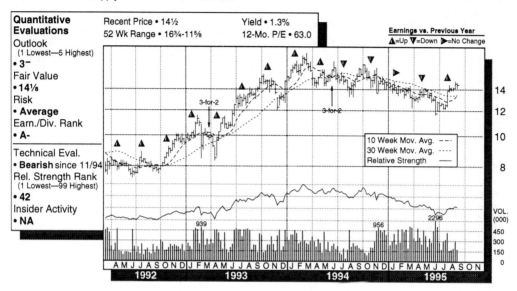

Business Profile - 08-SEP-95

Owens & Minor grew significantly in 1994, as it acquired Stuart Medical Inc., another large distributor of medical supplies. Although the acquisition gave rise to substantial restructuring costs, the consolidation of Stuart's operations into OMI should bolster future performance, reflecting greater economies of scale. In addition to increasing its revenue base, OMI is focused on cutting selling, general and administrative expenses, which it plans to reduce by 20% to 25% over two years.

Operational Review - 08-SEP-95

Net sales rose sharply in recent periods, reflecting the inclusion of Stuart Medical and the addition of new contracts with large health care providers such as Columbia/HCA. Margins narrowed as a result of cost containment pressures and higher SG&A expenses. Results in both 1994 and 1995 were penalized by nonrecurring restructuring costs, high interest expense and new dividends on preferred stock. First half earnings from recurring operations were $0.25 versus $0.32.

Stock Performance - 01-SEP-95

In the past 30 trading days, OMI's shares have increased 16%, compared to a 2% rise in the S&P 500. Average trading volume for the past five days was 34,980 shares, compared with the 40-day moving average of 50,258 shares.

Key Stock Statistics

Dividend Rate/Share	0.18	Shareholders	12,000
Shs. outstg. (M)	30.8	Market cap. (B)	$0.431
Avg. daily vol. (M)	0.045	Inst. holdings	57%
Tang. Bk. Value/Share	NM	Insider holdings	NA
Beta	0.99		

Value of $10,000 invested 5 years ago: $ 41,087

Fiscal Year Ending Dec. 31

	1995	% Change	1994	% Change	1993	% Change
Revenues (Million $)						
1Q	747.1	91%	390.8	23%	318.0	13%
2Q	743.7	28%	581.8	70%	341.2	18%
3Q	—	—	693.0	91%	362.0	21%
4Q	—	—	730.2	94%	376.0	23%
Yr.	—	—	2,396	71%	1,397	19%
Income (Million $)						
1Q	4.61	-3%	4.76	29%	3.69	19%
2Q	0.39	NM	-5.13	NM	4.27	18%
3Q	—	—	1.49	-69%	4.79	21%
4Q	—	—	6.80	21%	5.64	18%
Yr.	—	—	7.92	-57%	18.52	20%
Earnings Per Share ($)						
1Q	0.11	-28%	0.15	21%	0.13	19%
2Q	0.01	NM	-0.19	NM	0.14	17%
3Q	—	—	0.01	-93%	0.15	15%
4Q	—	—	0.18	NM	0.18	13%
Yr.	—	—	0.15	-75%	0.60	15%

Next earnings report expected: mid October

Owens & Minor

Business Summary - 08-SEP-95

Owens & Minor, Inc. is a wholesale distributor of medical and surgical supplies to hospitals and alternate medical care facilities. It also distributes pharmaceuticals and other products to independent pharmacies and chain drug stores in South Florida. In May 1994, OMI acquired Stuart Medical Inc., which had annual sales of about $890 million, for $40.2 million in cash, plus $115 million of convertible preferred stock. The acquisition enabled the company to provide products and services in all 50 states.

The medical/surgical division is a wholesale distributor of supplies such as urological products, dressings, needles and syringes, surgical packs and gowns, sterile procedure trays, sutures, intravenous products and endoscopic products. These products are disposable and are generally used in high volume by customers. These supplies are supplemented by sales of other products, including incontinence products, feeding tubes, surgical staples, blood collection devices and surgical gloves. The division carries more than 163,000 products, obtained from approximately 3,000 different manufacturers, and operates 53 distribution centers serving hospitals, nursing homes, alternate medical care facilities and other institutions nationwide. Products purchased from Johnson & Johnson Inc. accounted for approximately 19% of 1994 medical/surgical net sales.

Hospital customers (including members of hospital buying groups) represent the majority of medical/surgical sales. The remaining sales are made to nursing homes, physicians and other purchasers. The emphasis on hospitals reflects a strategy of concentrating on hospital customers in the belief that hospitals will remain the primary focus of the health care industry. Important elements of this strategy have been to maintain the company's status as a low-cost distributor of high-volume disposable commodity products and to operate in a decentralized manner to provide customers with a high level of service on a local basis.

Important Developments

Jul. '95—In 1994 and the first half of 1995, the company incurred $29.6 million and $6.8 million, respectively, of nonrecurring restructuring expenses in connection with the company's combination with Stuart and a decision to contract out the management and operation of its mainframe computer system.

Oct. '94—OMI acquired substantially all the assets of Emery Medical Supply, Inc. With $29 million in sales in 1993, Emery is a pioneer in stockless operations for fully integrated health care systems.

Capitalization

Long Term Debt: $323,304,000 (3/95).
$4.50 Conv. Pfd. Stock: 1,150,000 shs. ($100 par); ea. conv. into about 6.1 com. shs.

Per Share Data ($)

(Year Ended Dec. 31)

	1994	1993	1992	1991	1990	1989
Tangible Bk. Val.	-1.13	3.93	3.46	2.87	2.62	2.34
Cash Flow	0.57	0.84	0.72	0.50	0.49	0.22
Earnings	0.15	0.60	0.52	0.33	0.31	0.09
Dividends	0.19	0.14	0.11	0.09	0.08	0.08
Payout Ratio	125%	23%	21%	26%	25%	87%
Prices - High	18⅛	15⅝	10⅛	10¾	4½	4¾
- Low	13¼	8⅜	7⅜	4⅛	3⅛	3⅜
P/E Ratio - High	NM	26	19	32	15	53
- Low	NM	14	14	12	10	38

Income Statement Analysis (Million $)

	1994	%Chg	1993	%Chg	1992	%Chg	1991
Revs.	2,396	72%	1,397	19%	1,177	15%	1,027
Oper. Inc.	68.7	68%	40.9	19%	34.3	32%	25.9
Depr.	13.0	71%	7.6	30%	5.9	18%	5.0
Int. Exp.	12.1	NM	2.9	19%	2.5	-44%	4.4
Pretax Inc.	14.0	-54%	30.4	17%	25.9	57%	16.5
Eff. Tax Rate	43%	—	39%	—	41%	—	41%
Net Inc.	7.9	-57%	18.5	20%	15.4	58%	9.8

Balance Sheet & Other Fin. Data (Million $)

	1994	1993	1992	1991	1990	1989
Cash	0.5	2.0	7.1	0.8	3.3	3.3
Curr. Assets	641	282	229	267	249	226
Total Assets	869	334	275	312	290	259
Curr. Liab.	359	143	129	144	131	93.0
LT Debt	248	50.8	25.0	67.7	71.3	85.3
Common Eqty.	141	137	117	97.1	85.0	77.6
Total Cap.	505	188	142	165	156	163
Cap. Exp.	6.6	6.3	5.0	5.9	4.8	5.3
Cash Flow	17.6	26.1	21.3	14.7	14.1	6.1

Ratio Analysis

	1994	1993	1992	1991	1990	1989
Curr. Ratio	1.8	2.0	1.8	1.9	1.9	2.4
% LT Debt of Cap.	49.2	27.0	17.6	41.1	45.6	52.4
% Net Inc.of Revs.	0.3	1.3	1.3	0.9	0.7	0.3
% Ret. on Assets	1.3	6.0	5.2	3.2	3.2	1.1
% Ret. on Equity	3.3	14.4	14.4	10.6	10.8	3.2

Dividend Data —Cash dividends have been paid in each year since 1926. A "poison pill" stock purchase rights plan was adopted in 1988.

Amt. of Div. $	Date Decl.	Ex-Div. Date	Stock of Record	Payment Date
0.045	Jul. 25	Sep. 09	Sep. 15	Sep. 30 '94
0.045	Oct. 25	Dec. 09	Dec. 15	Dec. 30 '94
0.045	Feb. 27	Mar. 09	Mar. 15	Mar. 31 '95
0.045	May. 02	Jun. 13	Jun. 15	Jun. 30 '95
0.045	Jul. 25	Sep. 13	Sep. 15	Sep. 29 '95

Data as orig. reptd.; bef. results of disc. opers. and/or spec. items. Per share data adj. for stk. divs. as of ex-div. date. E-Estimated. NA-Not Available. NM-Not Meaningful. NR-Not Ranked.

Office—4800 Cox Rd., Glen Allen, VA 23060. **Tel**—(804) 747-9794. **Chrmn, Pres & CEO**—G. G. Minor III. **Sr VP & Secy**—D. St. J. Carneal. **Sr VP, CFO & Investor Contact**—Glenn J. Dozier (804-965-2945). **Dirs**—R. E. Cabell Jr., J. B. Farinholt Jr., W. F. Fife, C. G. Grefenstette, V. W. Henley, E. M. Massey, G. G. Minor III, P. M. Minor, J. E. Rogers, J. E. Ukrop, A. M. Whittemore. **Transfer Agent**—Wachovia Bank of North Carolina, Winston-Salem. **Incorporated** in Virginia in 1926. **Empl**-3,000. **S&P Analyst:** Philip J. Birbara

STANDARD & POOR'S

STOCK REPORTS

Oxford Industries

NYSE Symbol **OXM**

In S&P SmallCap 600

28-SEP-95

Industry: Textiles

Summary: Oxford manufactures and distributes brand name and private label apparel for men and women in the medium- to higher-price range.

S&P Opinion: Hold (★★★)

Recent Price • 17¾

52 Wk Range • 28¾-17¼

Yield • 4.5%

12-Mo. P/E • 25.7

Quantitative Evaluations

Outlook (1 Lowest—5 Highest)
• **5⁻**

Fair Value
• **20½**

Risk
• **Average**

Earn./Div. Rank
• **B+**

Technical Eval.
• **Bearish** since 12/94

Rel. Strength Rank (1 Lowest—99 Highest)
• **28**

Insider Activity
• **NA**

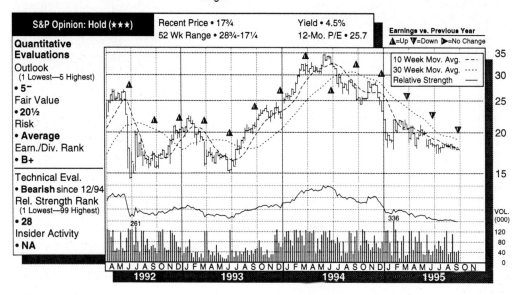

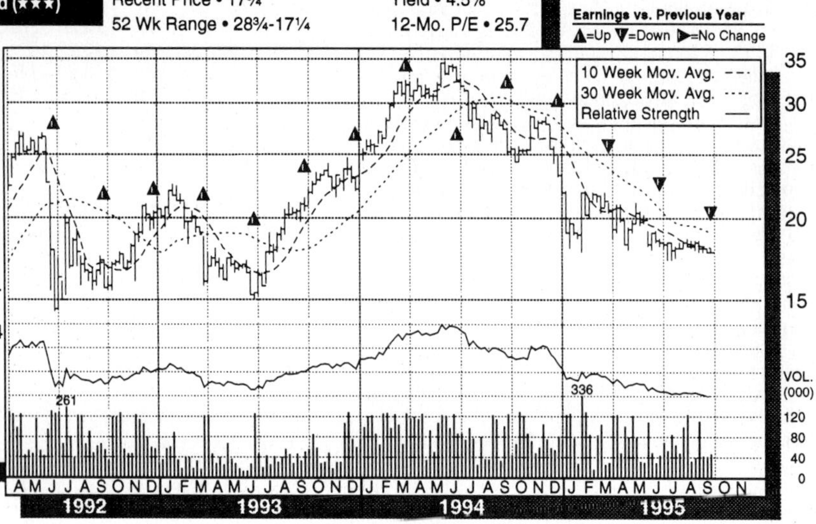

Overview - 28-SEP-95

Despite the weak apparel market, sales for fiscal 1995-96 could improve slightly, on higher sales of moderately-priced men's tailored clothing sold under the Oscar de la Renta label, dress shirts sold under the Tommy Hilfiger brand, and greater demand for wrinkle-resistant men's apparel. Marketshare should expand in most product categories, and sales will be enhanced by quick-response programs with customers. Margins should widen somewhat from 1994-95's depressed levels, mainly in the absence of one-time expenses related to expanding wrinkle-resistant capacity. Earnings will be hurt by a one-time $0.31 charge. Longer term, OXM hopes to increase sales at 7% to 8% and earnings at about 15% a year.

Valuation - 28-SEP-95

Oxford's shares have been under pressure for some time, mainly reflecting the weak retail market, narrower gross margins and a significant slowdown in earnings growth. Assuming that consumer apparel spending may remain stagnant in the near future, we have some concern that Oxford's sales and earnings could continue to be under pressure. On the positive side, however, we think this company is one of the best positioned in its markets. Mass merchandisers are rapidly increasing apparel offerings and relying on well-capitalized suppliers such as Oxford. Nevertheless, we are retaining a neutral opinion on these shares until a return to earnings growth is clearly in sight.

Key Stock Statistics

S&P EPS Est. 1996	1.45	Tang. Bk. Value/Share	15.25
P/E on S&P Est. 1996	12.2	Beta	0.62
Dividend Rate/Share	0.80	Shareholders	900
Shs. outstg. (M)	8.7	Market cap. (B)	$0.155
Avg. daily vol. (M)	0.011	Inst. holdings	57%
		Insider holdings	NA

Value of $10,000 invested 5 years ago: $ 17,443

Fiscal Year Ending May 31

	1996	% Change	1995	% Change	1994	% Change
Revenues (Million $)						
1Q	189.3	14%	165.3	11%	148.7	11%
2Q	—	—	192.2	8%	178.7	9%
3Q	—	—	153.1	7%	143.1	2%
4Q	—	—	146.4	-5%	154.0	15%
Yr.	—	—	657.0	5%	624.6	9%
Income (Million $)						
1Q	0.28	-94%	4.86	22%	3.98	28%
2Q	—	—	6.07	4%	5.83	26%
3Q	—	—	1.82	-59%	4.47	29%
4Q	—	—	-2.17	NM	4.92	37%
Yr.	—	—	10.58	-45%	19.20	30%
Earnings Per Share ($)						
1Q	0.03	-95%	0.56	22%	0.46	28%
2Q	E0.45	-36%	0.70	3%	0.68	28%
3Q	E0.47	124%	0.21	-60%	0.52	30%
4Q	E0.50	NM	-0.25	NM	0.57	39%
Yr.	E1.45	19%	1.22	-45%	2.23	31%

Next earnings report expected: late September

Oxford Industries

Business Summary - 28-SEP-95

Oxford Industries is a leading manufacturer of brand-name and private-label apparel products in the popular to better price range. Contributions to sales in recent fiscal years were:

	1994-95	1993-94	1992-93
Menswear	74%	73%	73%
Womenswear	26%	27%	27%

Menswear products include men's suits, vests, dress slacks, sportcoats, and men's and boys' sportswear, dress shirts, woven and knitted sport shirts, sweaters, slacks, shorts and jeans. Womenswear products include women's and girls' sportswear, dresses, suits, sweaters, shirts, blouses, T-shirts, swimsuits, sweatshirts, vests, jackets, skirts, shorts, jeans and pants. Sportswear products are marketed as coordinates or as separates.

Principal trademarks are Lanier, Oxford Shirtings, Travelers Worsted, Everset, Everpress, 928, RENNY, B.J. Design Concepts, MBC, and Koala Blue. Oxford licenses its trademark Merona to the Target Stores and Mervyn's divisions of Dayton Hudson Corp. In addition, Oxford also has the right to use trademarks under license including Polo by Ralph Lauren, Robert Stock, Oscar de le Renta, Tommy Hilfiger, Savane, Process 2000, Done Art & Design, Peanuts and Jump Start.

The company manufactures its products primarily in the U.S. through its own facilities as well as independent contractors. Oxford also uses Far East sourcing and has apparel operations in the Caribbean and in Mexico.

There are approximately 3,481 customers, including national and regional chain stores, mail-order and catalog firms, discount stores, department stores and chain and independent specialty stores. The 50 largest customers accounted for over 91% of 1994-95 sales. JCPenney Company, Inc. accounted for 20% of 1994-95 sales.

Important Developments

Aug. '95—OXM announced that it would incur a one-time $4.5 million charge (equal to about $0.31 a share) against earnings for the first quarter of the fiscal year ending May 1996. The charge is related to a past unauthorized disposal of a substance believed to be dry cleaning fluid on one of the company's properties. Based on the advice of the company's environmental experts, the maximum expenditures for remediation of this property over the next 30 years is estimated at $4.5 million.

Capitalization

Long Term Debt: $47,011,000 (6/2/95).

Per Share Data ($)

(Year Ended May 31)

	1995	1994	1993	1992	1991	1990
Tangible Bk. Val.	15.25	14.79	13.28	12.28	11.43	11.19
Cash Flow	2.12	3.05	2.45	2.13	1.30	1.50
Earnings	1.22	2.23	1.70	1.42	0.62	0.82
Dividends	0.94	0.69	0.63	0.55	0.50	0.50
Payout Ratio	77%	31%	37%	39%	80%	58%
Cal. Yrs.	1994	1993	1992	1991	1990	1989
Prices - High	34¾	25⅜	27⅛	18⅜	13	13⅜
- Low	21⅞	15	14⅜	6⅞	6½	10½
P/E Ratio - High	28	11	16	13	21	16
- Low	18	7	8	5	10	13

Income Statement Analysis (Million $)

	1995	%Chg	1994	%Chg	1993	%Chg	1992
Revs.	657	5%	625	9%	573	9%	528
Oper. Inc.	29.6	-29%	41.6	25%	33.3	17%	28.5
Depr.	7.8	11%	7.0	9%	6.5	3%	6.3
Int. Exp.	4.1	78%	2.3	2%	2.3	33%	1.7
Pretax Inc.	17.6	-46%	32.3	32%	24.5	20%	20.5
Eff. Tax Rate	40%	—	41%	—	40%	—	39%
Net Inc.	10.6	-45%	19.2	30%	14.8	18%	12.5

Balance Sheet & Other Fin. Data (Million $)

	1995	1994	1993	1992	1991	1990
Cash	2.2	3.2	3.3	8.4	19.2	2.5
Curr. Assets	269	205	186	167	154	175
Total Assets	309	240	218	199	187	208
Curr. Liab.	126	96.1	81.8	66.2	56.8	70.0
LT Debt	47.0	12.4	17.8	22.7	27.3	32.0
Common Eqty.	133	128	115	108	101	104
Total Cap.	183	144	136	133	130	138
Cap. Exp.	14.8	9.4	8.1	5.4	6.4	5.8
Cash Flow	18.4	26.2	21.2	18.8	11.7	14.5

Ratio Analysis

	1995	1994	1993	1992	1991	1990
Curr. Ratio	2.1	2.1	2.3	2.5	2.7	2.5
% LT Debt of Cap.	25.7	8.6	13.0	17.1	20.9	23.1
% Net Inc.of Revs.	1.6	3.1	2.6	2.4	1.1	1.4
% Ret. on Assets	3.9	8.4	7.1	6.5	2.9	3.9
% Ret. on Equity	8.1	15.8	13.3	12.0	5.5	7.8

Dividend Data —Dividends have been paid since 1960.

Amt. of Div. $	Date Decl.	Ex-Div. Date	Stock of Record	Payment Date
0.180	Oct. 03	Nov. 07	Nov. 14	Dec. 03 '94
0.200	Jan. 09	Feb. 09	Feb. 15	Mar. 04 '95
0.200	Apr. 03	May. 11	May. 17	Jun. 03 '95
0.200	Jul. 18	Aug. 16	Aug. 18	Sep. 02 '95

Data as orig. reptd.; bef. results of disc. opers. and/or spec. items. Per share data adj. for stk. divs. as of ex-div. date. E-Estimated. NA-Not Available. NM-Not Meaningful. NR-Not Ranked.

Office—222 Piedmont Ave. NE, Atlanta, GA 30308. **Tel**—(404) 659-2424. **Chrmn & Pres**—J. H. Lanier. **Exec VP-Fin & Investor Contact**—B. B. Blount Jr. **Secy**—D. K. Ginn. **Dirs**—B. B. Blount Jr., C. D. Conlee, J. B. Ellis, T. Gallagher, C. M. Kirtland Jr., J. H. Lanier, J. R. Lanier, R. W. Lee Jr., K. J. O'Reilly, C. B. Rogers Jr., R. E. Shaw, E. J. Wood. **Transfer Agent & Registrar**—Trust Company Bank, Atlanta. **Incorporated** in Georgia in 1960. **Empl**-8,577. **S&P Analyst:** Elizabeth A. Vandeventer

STANDARD & POOR'S
STOCK REPORTS

Pacific Scientific

NYSE Symbol **PSX**
In S&P SmallCap 600

09-NOV-95 **Industry:** Electronics/Electric

Summary: This company designs, makes and markets technology-based proprietary electrical and safety equipment.

Quantitative Evaluations
Outlook
(1 Lowest—5 Highest)
• 3
Fair Value
• 23¼
Risk
• High
Earn./Div. Rank
• B-

Technical Eval.
• **Bullish** since 10/95
Rel. Strength Rank
(1 Lowest—99 Highest)
• 71
Insider Activity
• **Neutral**

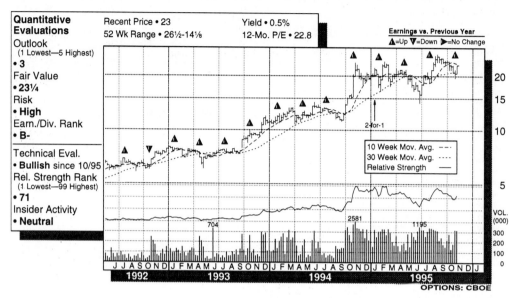

Recent Price • 23
52 Wk Range • 26½-14⅛
Yield • 0.5%
12-Mo. P/E • 22.8

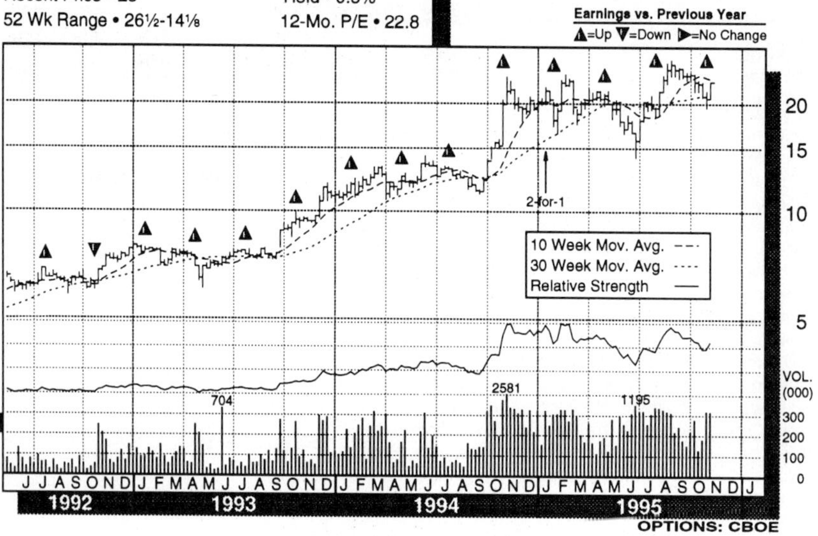

OPTIONS: CBOE

Business Profile - 09-NOV-95

PSX expects its core businesses to continue to grow through 1996. Development, production and introduction of the Solium product line cut EPS by $0.07 through the 1995 third quarter, but is expected to contribute to net income in 1996. The company is comfortable with EPS projections of $1.10 for 1995 (before Solium startup costs). Backlog at September 29, 1995, came to $99 million, up from $92 million a year earlier.

Operational Review - 09-NOV-95

Net sales in the nine months ended September 29, 1995, advanced 19%, reflecting 24% growth in electrical equipment. Margins widened, as selling and administrative expense rose less rapidly. Despite increased R&D and other expenses for the startup of the Solium product line, after taxes at 37.5%, versus 40.0%, net income rose 34%, to $8,303,000 ($0.72 a share), from $6,199,000 ($0.56, as adjusted).

Stock Performance - 03-NOV-95

In the past 30 trading days, PSX's shares have declined 4%, compared to a 2% rise in the S&P 500. Average trading volume for the past five days was 89,940 shares, compared with the 40-day moving average of 50,885 shares.

Key Stock Statistics

Dividend Rate/Share	0.12	Shareholders	1,600
Shs. outstg. (M)	11.0	Market cap. (B)	$0.254
Avg. daily vol. (M)	0.072	Inst. holdings	36%
Tang. Bk. Value/Share	4.74	Insider holdings	NA
Beta	0.83		

Value of $10,000 invested 5 years ago: $ 31,060

Fiscal Year Ending Dec. 31

	1995	% Change	1994	% Change	1993	% Change
Revenues (Million $)						
1Q	64.84	26%	51.59	25%	41.40	NM
2Q	68.89	20%	57.19	15%	49.93	15%
3Q	66.24	11%	59.84	25%	47.93	14%
4Q	—	—	66.12	17%	56.32	22%
Yr.	—	—	234.7	20%	195.6	13%
Income (Million $)						
1Q	2.54	52%	1.67	48%	1.13	2%
2Q	2.90	29%	2.24	37%	1.63	34%
3Q	2.86	25%	2.28	5%	2.17	49%
4Q	—	—	3.32	44%	2.31	43%
Yr.	—	—	9.52	31%	7.24	34%
Earnings Per Share ($)						
1Q	0.22	47%	0.15	43%	0.10	5%
2Q	0.25	25%	0.20	33%	0.15	30%
3Q	0.25	22%	0.21	3%	0.20	48%
4Q	—	—	0.29	38%	0.21	40%
Yr.	—	—	0.85	28%	0.66	33%

Next earnings report expected: mid February

Pacific Scientific

Business Summary - 09-NOV-95

Pacific Scientific Company manufactures electrical and safety equipment. Principal markets served include factory automation, aviation, electric utilities, semiconductor manufacturers and pharmaceutical companies. Contributions in 1994 were:

	Sales	Profits
Electrical equipment	71%	72%
Safety equipment	29%	28%

Exports accounted for 21% of sales in 1994, and U.S. defense contracts for about 16%.

Electrical equipment includes motors and controls, particle detection instruments and products for the electric utility industry. Electric motors and controls are used in manufacturing, packaging, shipping, sorting and vending, mostly for industrial applications. Half of the motor and control sales are of DC brushless motors and controls. The company believes that it has a leading share in this emerging market. In 1993, PSX bought Powertec Industrial Corp. and Automation Intelligence, Inc., enabling it to move its brushless technology into such markets as packaging, plastic extruding and wire drawing.

PSX's products for electric utilities include a broad line of fault indicators, as well as distribution automation sensors, load management devices and metering equipment. Distribution products allow for greater efficiency of power distribution for utilities. The company has a major share of the U.S. market for controls used in street lighting.

The company believes that it has a leading market position for sensing particulate contamination in liquid, air and vacuum environments. Products include instruments that detect and measure contaminating particles during semiconductor manufacturing and instruments that measure contaminant particles in pharmaceutical manufacturing, water supply and food packaging.

In October 1994, PSX formed Solium Inc. to market a family of electronic lighting controls and electronic ballasts.

Major markets for safety equipment include fire detection and suppression, restraints and pyrotechnics. The company is a leading supplier of aircraft safety equipment and electrical components to major aircraft makers. Its fire suppression systems protect aircraft engines and cargo compartments. Other products include fire detection and warning products, restraints for commercial aircraft crews and lightweight lap belts.

Important Developments

Oct. '95—PSX said it had made a small initial shipment of Solium electronic lighting systems from its Randolph, MA facility. Annual production capacity of 8 million Solium devices is expected for the facility, beginning in early 1996.

Capitalization

Long Term Debt: $55,431,000 (6/95).

Per Share Data ($) (Year Ended Dec. 31)

	1994	1993	1992	1991	1990	1989
Tangible Bk. Val.	8.33	7.50	6.78	6.32	5.59	5.45
Cash Flow	1.90	1.64	1.21	1.45	0.73	0.84
Earnings	0.85	0.66	0.50	0.73	0.10	0.28
Dividends	0.06	0.06	0.06	0.02	Nil	Nil
Payout Ratio	7%	9%	12%	2%	Nil	Nil
Prices - High	23¾	12	8	6¼	8¼	9¼
- Low	10¾	6⅛	4⅞	3⅝	3¾	4⅞
P/E Ratio - High	28	18	16	9	82	33
- Low	13	9	10	5	37	17

Income Statement Analysis (Million $)

	1994	%Chg	1993	%Chg	1992	%Chg	1991
Revs.	235	20%	196	13%	173	NM	173
Oper. Inc.	30.6	40%	21.9	29%	17.0	34%	12.7
Depr.	11.8	12%	10.5	39%	7.6	-1%	7.7
Int. Exp.	3.2	23%	2.6	-2%	2.7	-31%	3.8
Pretax Inc.	15.7	40%	11.2	38%	8.1	-33%	12.1
Eff. Tax Rate	39%	—	35%	—	33%	—	33%
Net Inc.	9.5	31%	7.2	34%	5.4	-33%	8.0

Balance Sheet & Other Fin. Data (Million $)

	1994	1993	1992	1991	1990	1989
Cash	3.4	4.0	6.0	7.4	7.5	7.3
Curr. Assets	90.4	79.7	69.4	69.0	79.4	88.5
Total Assets	173	161	135	136	143	149
Curr. Liab.	35.1	31.1	27.7	27.7	35.8	41.8
LT Debt	42.3	44.1	28.0	32.9	39.0	37.6
Common Eqty.	91.1	81.0	72.4	67.5	59.6	60.7
Total Cap.	135	127	103	103	102	102
Cap. Exp.	NA	NA	NA	NA	NA	11.7
Cash Flow	21.3	17.8	12.9	15.5	8.0	9.3

Ratio Analysis

	1994	1993	1992	1991	1990	1989
Curr. Ratio	2.6	2.6	2.5	2.5	2.2	2.1
% LT Debt of Cap.	31.3	34.8	27.2	31.8	38.2	37.0
% Net Inc.of Revs.	4.1	3.7	3.1	4.7	0.8	2.0
% Ret. on Assets	5.7	4.9	4.0	5.8	1.0	2.3
% Ret. on Equity	11.0	9.4	7.7	12.2	1.9	5.3

Dividend Data —Cash dividends, omitted in 1988, were resumed in 1991. A poison pill stock purchase rights plan was adopted in 1988.

Amt. of Div. $	Date Decl.	Ex-Div. Date	Stock of Record	Payment Date
2-for-1	Dec. 08	Jan. 10	Dec. 16	Jan. 09 '95
0.030	Feb. 23	Mar. 06	Mar. 10	Apr. 03 '95
0.030	Apr. 27	Jun. 14	Jun. 16	Jul. 03 '95
0.030	Aug. 24	Sep. 13	Sep. 15	Oct. 02 '95
0.030	Oct. 26	Dec. 13	Dec. 15	Jan. 02 '96

Data as orig. reptd.; bef. results of disc. opers. and/or spec. items. Per share data adj. for stk. divs. as of ex-div. date. Bk. val. figs. in Per Share Data tbl. incl. intangibles. E-Estimated. NA-Not Available. NM-Not Meaningful. NR-Not Ranked.

Office—620 Newport Center Drive, Suite 700, Newport Beach, CA 92660. **Tel**—(714) 720-1714. **Fax**—(714) 720-1083. **Chrmn, Pres & CEO**—E. S. Brower. **EVP-Fin, Secy & Investor Contact**—Richard V. Plat. **Dirs**—W. F. Beran, R. O. Briscoe, E. S. Brower, R. D. Ketchum, W. A. Preston, M. H. Pryor, Jr., T. P. Stafford, H. W. Todd. **Transfer Agent & Registrar**—Chemical Trust Co. of California, LA. **Incorporated** in California in 1937. **Empl**-1,848. **S&P Analyst:** J.C.

STANDARD & POOR'S

STOCK REPORTS

Paragon Trade Brands

NYSE Symbol **PTB**
In S&P SmallCap 600

25-OCT-95 **Industry:** Cosmetics/Toiletries

Summary: This company is a leading manufacturer of store brand disposable diapers in the U.S. and Canada.

Quantitative Evaluations

Outlook (1 Lowest—5 Highest)
• **NA**
Fair Value
• **NA**
Risk
• **High**
Earn./Div. Rank
• **NR**

Technical Eval.
• **Bullish** since 8/95
Rel. Strength Rank (1 Lowest—99 Highest)
• **67**
Insider Activity
• **NA**

Recent Price • 15¼ Yield • Nil
52 Wk Range • 25⅜-11⅝ 12-Mo. P/E • 9.2

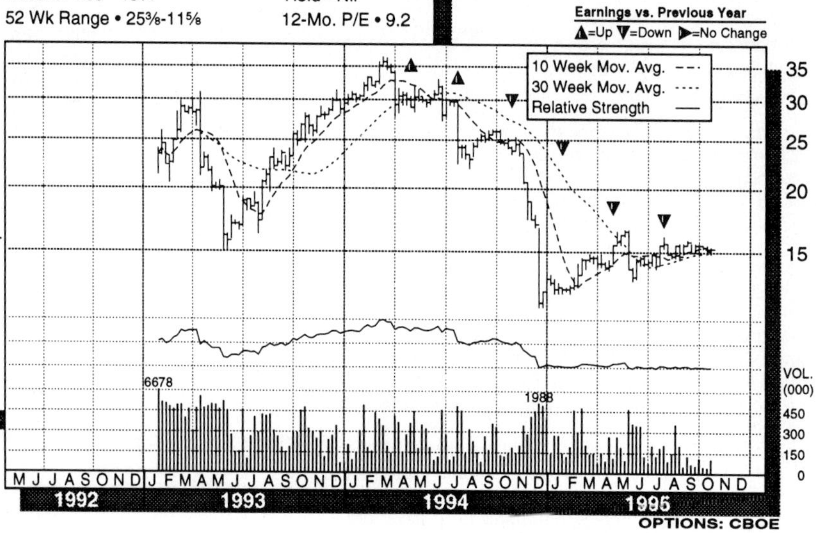

OPTIONS: CBOE

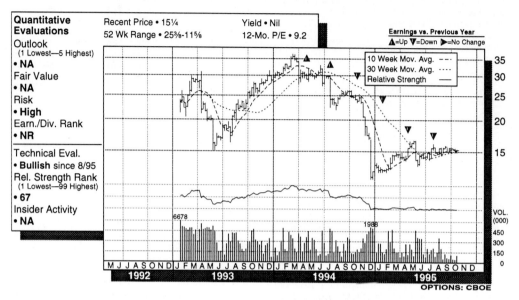

Business Profile - 25-OCT-95

In response to competition, this maker of private label disposable diapers closed its California diaper manufacturing facility and reduced its corporate staff by 10%. Benefits of these actions were seen in the 1995 third quarter , and further improvement is expected. Capital spending in 1995 has focused on the move to a thin pad diaper and other product quality improvements. The company has repurchased about 252,900 shares under a plan to buy back up to one million shares.

Operational Review - 25-OCT-95

Net sales in the 39 weeks ended September 24, 1995, fell 12%, year to year. Recent results were penalized by lower volume and sales prices, higher raw material costs, and greater legal costs and depreciation charges. Although Paragon expects sales and earnings to improve in the remainder of 1995, volume and margins will continue to be restricted by competitive pricing and promotional pressure from national diaper brands, and by rising fluff pulp prices.

Stock Performance - 20-OCT-95

In the past 30 trading days, PTB's shares have declined 3%, compared to a 3% rise in the S&P 500. Average trading volume for the past five days was 19,680 shares, compared with the 40-day moving average of 14,277 shares.

Key Stock Statistics

Dividend Rate/Share	Nil	Shareholders	300
Shs. outstg. (M)	11.8	Market cap. (B)	$0.185
Avg. daily vol. (M)	0.014	Inst. holdings	84%
Tang. Bk. Value/Share	15.86	Insider holdings	NA
Beta	NA		

Value of $10,000 invested 5 years ago: NA

Fiscal Year Ending Dec. 31

	1995	% Change	1994	% Change	1993	% Change
Revenues (Million $)						
1Q	126.6	-12%	143.2	NM	141.9	30%
2Q	127.3	-13%	146.0	5%	138.4	17%
3Q	131.4	-12%	149.4	3%	144.9	7%
4Q	—	—	140.0	2%	137.8	12%
Yr.	—	—	578.6	3%	563.0	16%
Income (Million $)						
1Q	-9.36	NM	7.88	9%	7.24	—
2Q	-0.36	NM	7.55	14%	6.63	—
3Q	-2.64	NM	7.71	-15%	9.04	—
4Q	—	—	1.90	-73%	7.14	—
Yr.	—	—	24.99	-17%	30.04	69%
Earnings Per Share ($)						
1Q	-0.80	NM	0.68	8%	0.63	—
2Q	-0.03	NM	0.65	12%	0.58	—
3Q	-0.22	NM	0.66	-69%	2.14	—
4Q	—	—	0.16	-74%	0.62	—
Yr.	—	—	2.16	-46%	3.97	158%

Next earnings report expected: late January

Paragon Trade Brands

Business Summary - 25-OCT-95

Paragon Trade Brands (formerly a unit of Weyerhaeuser Co.) is the leading maker of private label infant disposable diapers in the U.S and Canada. Infant disposable diapers are designed to allow moisture to pass through a soft inner layer, in contact with a baby's skin, into a highly absorbent inner core, from which the moisture is prevented from escaping by an outer moisture-proof backsheet. The principal product lines are a premium quality Ultra line, an economy line, and a training pant diaper line. Shipments of a new thin pad diaper line began in April 1994. The distribution of sales in recent years was:

	1994	1993	1992
Ultra	83%	82%	84%
Economy	11%	14%	15%
Training	6%	4%	1%

Ultra diapers combine wood pulp with a super-absorbent polymer (SAP) in the absorbent inner core. The Ultra diaper incorporates a number of product innovations comparable to those introduced by the national branded manufacturers to enhance performance and appearance. Elasticized leg cuffs, inner-leg gathers and gender-specific absorbency zones improve the diaper's ability to prevent leakage and retain moisture.

The economy diaper is designed to satisfy the needs of the more cost-conscious value segment shopper. The training pant is designed for use primarily during the transition out of diapers.

Products are distributed throughout the U.S. and Canada primarily through grocery and food stores, mass merchandisers, warehouse clubs, toy stores and drug stores, which market the products under their own store brands. The vast majority of sales are in the U.S., with about 5% of 1994 sales to trade customers in Canada (down from 6% in 1993). Although Paragon does not sell diapers directly in Mexico, it believes that in 1994 about 7% of its diapers were sold to trade customers in the U.S. for use by consumers in Mexico.

Important Developments

Jul. '95—Paragon said its loss in the 1995 third quarter of 1995 reflected lower volume and sales prices, as well as higher costs, primarily for raw materials (pulp prices were significantly higher) and promotional spending. The company noted that sales were up sequentially, aided by strategic initiatives begun earlier in the year.

Capitalization

Long Term Debt: None (9/95).

Per Share Data ($) (Year Ended Dec. 31)

	1994	1993	1992	1991	1990	1989
Tangible Bk. Val.	16.73	14.38	10.81	9.35	NA	NA
Cash Flow	4.84	5.87	2.90	2.97	NA	NA
Earnings	2.16	3.97	1.54	1.62	NA	NA
Dividends	Nil	Nil	NA	NA	NA	NA
Payout Ratio	Nil	Nil	NA	NA	NA	NA
Prices - High	36½	31⅜	NA	NA	NA	NA
- Low	11⅝	15	NA	NA	NA	NA
P/E Ratio - High	17	8	NA	NA	NA	NA
- Low	5	4	NA	NA	NA	NA

Income Statement Analysis (Million $)

	1994	%Chg	1993	%Chg	1992	%Chg	1991
Revs.	579	3%	563	16%	485	22%	396
Oper. Inc.	73.6	4%	71.1	54%	46.2	8%	42.8
Depr.	31.1	43%	21.8	40%	15.6	16%	13.5
Int. Exp.	1.2	—	Nil	—	1.2	-65%	3.5
Pretax Inc.	40.3	-17%	48.4	69%	28.6	10%	25.9
Eff. Tax Rate	38%	—	5.10%	—	38%	—	38%
Net Inc.	25.0	-46%	45.9	158%	17.8	10%	16.2

Balance Sheet & Other Fin. Data (Million $)

	1994	1993	1992	1991	1990	1989
Cash	2.7	8.8	0.1	0.0	NA	NA
Curr. Assets	90.2	97.8	67.7	74.2	NA	NA
Total Assets	275	244	166	165	NA	NA
Curr. Liab.	73.6	77.1	30.2	33.4	NA	NA
LT Debt	6.0	Nil	9.2	36.0	NA	NA
Common Eqty.	196	167	126	96.0	NA	NA
Total Cap.	202	167	136	132	NA	NA
Cap. Exp.	74.9	53.7	NA	NA	NA	NA
Cash Flow	56.1	67.7	33.4	29.7	NA	NA

Ratio Analysis

	1994	1993	1992	1991	1990	1989
Curr. Ratio	1.2	1.3	2.2	2.2	NA	NA
% LT Debt of Cap.	3.0	Nil	6.8	27.3	NA	NA
% Net Inc.of Revs.	4.3	8.2	3.7	4.1	NA	NA
% Ret. on Assets	9.6	NA	NA	NA	NA	NA
% Ret. on Equity	13.7	NA	NA	NA	NA	NA

Dividend Data —No dividends have been paid, and none are anticipated in the foreseeable future. A shareholder rights plan was adopted in late 1994.

Data as orig. reptd.; bef. results of disc. opers. and/or spec. items. Per share data adj. for stk. divs. as of ex-div. date. E-Estimated. NA-Not Available. NM-Not Meaningful. NR-Not Ranked.

Office—33325 8th Avenue South, Federal Way, WA 98003. **Tel**—(206) 815-7000. **Chrmn & CEO**—B. V. Abraham. **Pres & COO**—D. W. Cole. **CFO**—A. J. Cyron. **VP**—R. Hirschey. **VP-Secy**—S. Barley. **Dirs**—B. V. Abraham, T. B. Boklund, G. D. Hoffman, W. I. Savel, R. Schuyler. **Transfer Agent & Registrar**—Chemical Bank, NYC. **Incorporated** in Delaware in 1992. **Empl**-1,575. **S&P Analyst:** Philip D. Wohl

STANDARD & POOR'S

STOCK REPORTS

PAXAR Corp.

NYSE Symbol **PXR**
In S&P SmallCap 600

22-AUG-95 **Industry:** Graphic Arts

Summary: PAXAR manufactures bar-code tag and labeling systems, as well as printed labels, woven labels and merchandise tags for the apparel and textile industries.

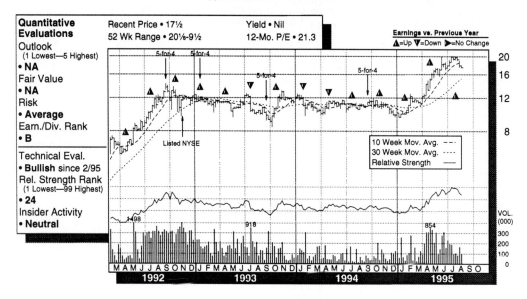

Quantitative Evaluations

Outlook
(1 Lowest—5 Highest)
• **NA**

Fair Value
• **NA**

Risk
• **Average**

Earn./Div. Rank
• **B**

Technical Eval.
• **Bullish** since 2/95

Rel. Strength Rank
(1 Lowest—99 Highest)
• **24**

Insider Activity
• **Neutral**

Recent Price • 17½
52 Wk Range • 20⅛-9½

Yield • Nil
12-Mo. P/E • 21.3

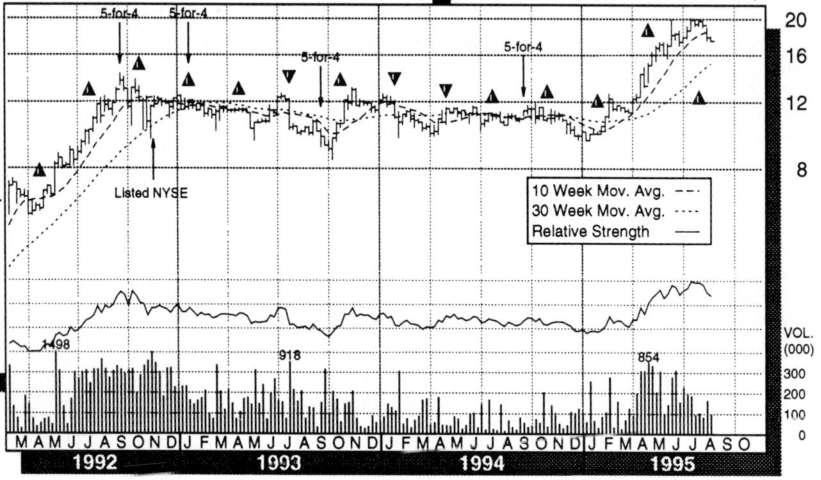

Business Profile - 22-AUG-95

PAXAR attributes its strong growth in recent years to its strategy of focusing on apparel and textile customers. In June 1995, the company and Odyssey Partners L.P. reached an agreement to acquire Pitney Bowes' Monarch Marketing Systems and related operations for $127 million in cash. Monarch is a manufacturer of bar code systems and supplies with 1994 revenues of approximately $250 million. In August 1995, the company declared a 25% stock dividend payable on the 9th of September.

Operational Review - 22-AUG-95

PAXAR's sales and earnings have risen four consecutive years, and this positive trend continued in the first half of 1995. Revenues increased 32%, reflecting strong internal growth, acquisitions, and greater foreign and export sales. Margins rose on the higher volume. A decline in the company's tax rate due to tax incentives stemming from 1994 acquisitions also contributed to the 49% increase in net income.

Stock Performance - 18-AUG-95

In the past 30 trading days, PXR's shares have declined 6%, compared to a 0.51% rise in the S&P 500. Average trading volume for the past five days was 19,160 shares, compared with the 40-day moving average of 28,921 shares.

Key Stock Statistics

Dividend Rate/Share	Nil	Shareholders	800
Shs. outstg. (M)	17.6	Market cap. (B)	$0.309
Avg. daily vol. (M)	0.025	Inst. holdings	40%
Tang. Bk. Value/Share	3.87	Insider holdings	0%
Beta	0.78		

Value of $10,000 invested 5 years ago: $ 59,491

Fiscal Year Ending Dec. 31

	1995	% Change	1994	% Change	1993	% Change
Revenues (Million $)						
1Q	50.52	40%	35.98	NM	36.20	17%
2Q	52.90	25%	42.46	17%	36.34	NM
3Q	—	—	41.01	26%	32.62	5%
4Q	—	—	47.16	40%	33.69	-2%
Yr.	—	—	166.6	20%	138.9	5%
Income (Million $)						
1Q	3.94	81%	2.18	-19%	2.69	42%
2Q	4.41	29%	3.41	24%	2.76	8%
3Q	—	—	2.74	34%	2.05	-16%
4Q	—	—	3.27	75%	1.87	25%
Yr.	—	—	11.60	24%	9.36	12%
Earnings Per Share ($)						
1Q	0.22	83%	0.12	-22%	0.15	14%
2Q	0.25	32%	0.19	19%	0.16	-4%
3Q	—	—	0.16	33%	0.12	44%
4Q	—	—	0.19	83%	0.10	-26%
Yr.	—	—	0.66	22%	0.54	4%

Next earnings report expected: late October

PAXAR Corp.

Business Summary - 22-AUG-95

PAXAR Corporation is a fully integrated manufacturer and distributor of label systems, bar-code systems, labels, tags and related supplies and services for apparel manufacturers and retailers. To broaden its product line and enhance its market position, the company has developed several new products and completed several aquisitions since 1986. In May 1994, it acquired majority interests in Collitex and Astria, two related Italian companies in the woven label business. Subsequently, PAXAR effectively acquired 100% of Collitex and Astria. In October 1994, the company acquired an 80% interest (with an option to acquire the remaining 20%) in Orvafin, an Italian company engaged in the production and distribution of inks and coated fabrics for labeling systems.

The company's tag and label systems consist primarily of bar-code tag systems and hot-stamp label printers. These systems enable customers to print, cut and batch large volumes of tags and labels in their own plants. The bar-code tag systems made by PAXAR include personal computers, electronic bar-code printers, thermal ink, pre-printed tag stock and supporting software. Hot-stamp printing systems include hot-stamp printers, fabrics, inks and printing accessories, which are used by manufacturers for in-house printing of care labels and labels that carry brand logo, size and other information for the retail customer. Tag and label systems and supplies accounted for 53% and 56% of net sales in 1994 and 1993, respectively.

PAXAR also designs and produces finished tags and woven and printed labels in its manufacturing facilities in the U.S., England, Italy and Hong Kong and ships them to domestic and international apparel manufacturers. Its labels are printed on a wide range of fabrics and other materials. Labels are often attatched to garments early in the manufacturing process and must withstand all production processes and remain legible through washing and dry cleaning by the consumer. To a limited extent, tags and labels are also produced for sheets, towels and pillowcases.

The company has more than 10,000 customers, including major retailers and apparel manufacturers such as Levi Strauss, Sears, and J.C. Penney. In 1994, Levi Strauss represented approximately 11% of PAXAR's total sales.

Important Developments

Jun. '95—Paxar Corp. and Odyssey Partners L.P. acquired Pitney Bowes Inc.'s Monarch Marking Systems and related operations for $127 million in cash. Monarch Marking is a manufacturer and marketer of bar code marking, tracking and control systems and supplies, with 1994 revenues of about $250 million. Paxar and Odyssey, a private investment firm, plan to operate Monarch on a stand-alone basis.

Capitalization

Long Term Debt: $24,930,000 (6/95).

Per Share Data ($)

(Year Ended Dec. 31)

	1994	1993	1992	1991	1990	1989
Tangible Bk. Val.	3.64	3.59	3.03	1.78	1.54	1.41
Cash Flow	1.05	0.81	0.74	0.46	0.29	0.52
Earnings	0.66	0.54	0.52	0.25	0.08	0.30
Dividends	Nil	Nil	Nil	Nil	Nil	Nil
Payout Ratio	Nil	Nil	Nil	Nil	Nil	Nil
Prices - High	$12\frac{5}{8}$	$13\frac{1}{8}$	$14\frac{1}{4}$	$4\frac{5}{8}$	$3\frac{1}{8}$	$3\frac{7}{8}$
- Low	$9\frac{1}{2}$	$8\frac{3}{8}$	$4\frac{1}{2}$	$1\frac{13}{16}$	$1\frac{11}{16}$	$1\frac{11}{16}$
P/E Ratio - High	19	24	28	19	36	13
- Low	14	16	9	7	20	6

Income Statement Analysis (Million $)

	1994	%Chg	1993	%Chg	1992	%Chg	1991
Revs.	167	20%	139	5%	133	50%	88.9
Oper. Inc.	24.8	27%	19.6	7%	18.3	85%	9.9
Depr.	6.8	45%	4.7	29%	3.6	28%	2.8
Int. Exp.	0.9	88%	0.5	-40%	0.8	-26%	1.1
Pretax Inc.	17.1	18%	14.5	4%	13.9	133%	6.0
Eff. Tax Rate	32%	—	35%	—	40%	—	42%
Net Inc.	11.6	24%	9.4	12%	8.4	143%	3.4

Balance Sheet & Other Fin. Data (Million $)

	1994	1993	1992	1991	1990	1989
Cash	4.5	0.7	0.3	0.3	1.2	0.3
Curr. Assets	64.0	47.8	42.4	30.3	26.6	27.3
Total Assets	129	85.5	72.8	51.1	43.0	44.3
Curr. Liab.	25.0	17.6	14.1	13.1	9.1	10.2
LT Debt	13.8	0.7	2.1	10.2	10.9	13.0
Common Eqty.	77.9	62.5	52.8	25.0	20.8	19.2
Total Cap.	102	67.9	58.6	38.0	34.0	34.1
Cap. Exp.	11.2	12.6	8.5	6.6	3.2	1.5
Cash Flow	18.4	14.0	12.0	6.3	3.9	6.4

Ratio Analysis

	1994	1993	1992	1991	1990	1989
Curr. Ratio	2.6	2.7	3.0	2.3	2.9	2.7
% LT Debt of Cap.	13.5	1.1	3.6	27.0	32.1	38.0
% Net Inc.of Revs.	7.0	6.7	6.3	3.9	1.6	5.6
% Ret. on Assets	10.7	11.8	12.2	7.2	2.6	9.4
% Ret. on Equity	16.4	16.2	19.9	14.8	5.7	24.2

Dividend Data —PAXAR has never paid a cash dividend. However, it has paid at least one stock dividend or effected a stock split in each year since 1976, except for 1984. A 5-for-4 stock split will be effected in September 1995.

Amt. of Div. $	Date Decl.	Ex-Div. Date	Stock of Record	Payment Date
5-for-4	Aug. 15	Sep. 12	Aug. 30	Sep. 09 '94
5-for-4	Aug. 09	Sep. 12	Aug. 23	Sep. 11 '95

Data as orig. reptd.; bef. results of disc. opers. and/or spec. items. Per share data adj. for stk. divs. as of ex-div. date. E-Estimated. NA-Not Available. NM-Not Meaningful. NR-Not Ranked.

Office—105 Corporate Park Drive, White Plains, NY 10604-3814. **Tel**—(914) 697-6800. **Fax**—(914) 696-4128. **Chrmn & CEO**—A. Hershaft. **Pres & COO**—V. Hershaft. **VP, CFO, Secy & Investor Contact**—Jack R. Plaxe. **Dirs**—J. Becker, A. Hershaft, V. Hershaft, R. G. Laidlaw, T. R. Loemker, D. E. McKinney, S. Merians, R. T. Puopolo. W. W. Williams. **Transfer Agent & Registrar**—Chemical Bank, NYC. **Incorporated** in New York in 1946. **Empl**-1,891. **S&P Analyst:** Stephen Madonna

Payless Cashways

NYSE Symbol **PCS**
In S&P SmallCap 600

11-OCT-95 **Industry:** Retail Stores

Summary: This company is the fourth largest U.S. retailer of building materials and home improvement products, with more than 200 stores in 24 states.

Quantitative Evaluations
Outlook
(1 Lowest—5 Highest)
• **NA**
Fair Value
• **NA**
Risk
• **Average**
Earn./Div. Rank
• **NR**

Technical Eval.
• **Bearish** since 2/95
Rel. Strength Rank
(1 Lowest—99 Highest)
• **1**
Insider Activity
• **NA**

Recent Price • 4⅝
52 Wk Range • 10-4
Yield • Nil
12-Mo. P/E • 8.9

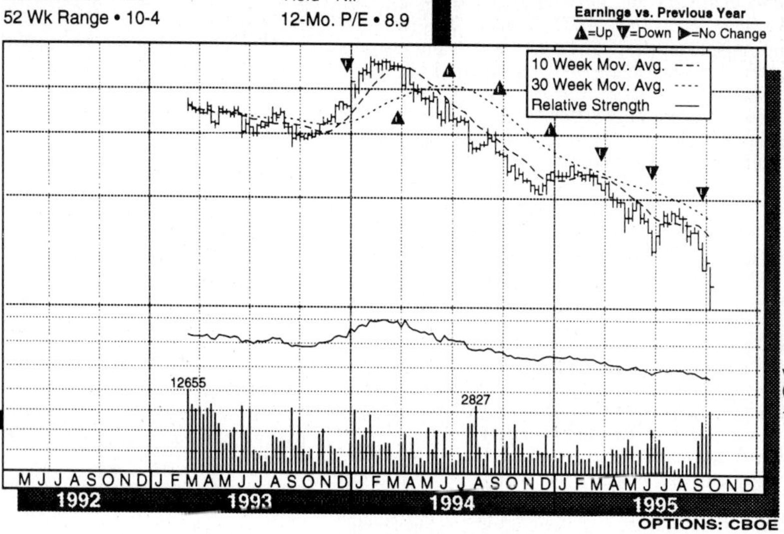

Business Profile - 11-OCT-95

This highly-leveraged retailer operates more than 200 stores that cater mainly to serious do-it-yourselfers and professional home builders. It has substantially completed a comprehensive recapitalization plan designed to increase equity, reduce debt and interest expense, and improve access to capital markets. This added operating and financial flexibility will be essential if PCS is to retain its position (currently fourth) in the increasingly competitive home building materials industry.

Operational Review - 11-OCT-95

Net sales in the 39 weeks ended August 26, 1995, declined fractionally, year to year, as contributions from new stores in operation were outweighed by 3.6% lower same-store sales. Profitability was hurt by a slower housing environment, lower lumber costs, and a softening in consumer spending. Results were further restricted by pricing initiatives and costs associated with new stores, and by a $3.5 million loss related to the company's Mexican joint venture.

Stock Performance - 06-OCT-95

In the past 30 trading days, PCS's shares have declined 27%, compared to a 4% rise in the S&P 500. Average trading volume for the past five days was 333,320 shares, compared with the 40-day moving average of 131,708 shares.

Key Stock Statistics

Dividend Rate/Share	Nil	Shareholders	900
Shs. outstg. (M)	39.9	Market cap. (B)	$0.175
Avg. daily vol. (M)	0.208	Inst. holdings	65%
Tang. Bk. Value/Share	NM	Insider holdings	NA
Beta	NA		

Value of $10,000 invested 5 years ago: NA

Fiscal Year Ending Nov. 30

	1995	% Change	1994	% Change	1993	% Change
Revenues (Million $)						
1Q	556.2	3%	542.0	10%	492.8	5%
2Q	711.7	-3%	734.2	5%	699.0	2%
3Q	737.2	NM	744.1	4%	716.8	3%
4Q	—	—	702.2	1%	693.0	7%
Yr.	—	—	2,723	5%	2,601	4%
Income (Million $)						
1Q	-3.86	NM	-0.68	NM	-3.98	—
2Q	4.61	-73%	16.96	8%	15.70	—
3Q	8.15	-56%	18.35	7%	17.12	—
4Q	—	—	17.51	—	—	—
Yr.	—	—	52.13	NM	9.67	-74%
Earnings Per Share ($)						
1Q	-0.13	NM	-0.05	NM	-0.13	NM
2Q	0.08	-79%	0.38	6%	0.36	—
3Q	0.17	-60%	0.42	8%	0.39	—
4Q	—	—	0.40	3%	0.39	-64%
Yr.	—	—	1.17	18%	0.99	9%

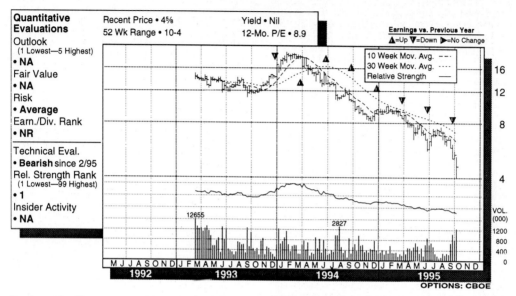

Next earnings report expected: late December

Payless Cashways

Business Summary - 11-OCT-95

Payless Cashways is the fourth largest U.S. retailer of building materials and home improvement products, as measured by sales. The company operates 201 full-line stores in 24 states in the Midwest, Southwest, Pacific Coast, Rocky Mountains and New England, under the names Payless Cashways Building Materials, Furrow Building Materials and four other names. The heaviest concentrations of stores are in Texas (42), Colorado (18), Indiana (17) and California (16).

Each full-line store is designed as a one-stop source that provides customers with a complete selection of quality products and services needed to build, improve, and maintain their home, business, farm or ranch properties. PCS's merchandise assortment includes about 24,000 items in the following categories: lumber and building materials, millwork, tools, hardware, electrical and plumbing products, paint, lighting, home decore, kitchens, decorative plumbing, heating, ventilating and cooling (HVAC), and seasonal items. Sales contributions by business unit in fiscal 1994 were: lumberyard 49%, hardware 34%, and showroom 17%.

Primary customers include serious do-it-yourselfers, who engage in more frequent and complex repair or improvement projects, and spendg over $1,000 annually on home improvement products; and professionals, who include remodelers, residential contractors, and specialty tradesmen along with enterprises which purchase large quantities of building materials for facility maintenance.

The company seeks to enlarge its market share through existing stores; to continue to increase professional sales as a percentage of total sales, and to acquire new customers through implementation of a store expansion program and the development of new, complementary retail concepts.

PCS's business mix as a percentage of sales was about 50% do-it-yourself and 50% professional in fiscal 1994, versus 54% and 46%, respectively, in fiscal 1993. Reflecting the company's focus on expanding its professional business and the higher rate of increase anticipated for that segment, it expects to maintain this balance in the future.

Important Developments

Sep. '95—In the third quarter of 1994-95, Payless Cashways opened five new stores, and in the fourth quarter to date had opened one store. Additionally, in June, 1995, Total Home, the company's Mexican joint venture, opened a second store located in Mexico City.

Capitalization

Long Term Debt: $641,458,000 (8/95).
Conv. Preferred Stock: 406,000 shs. ($1 par); conv. into 5.9994 com. shs.
Masco Capital owns 100%.
Nonvoting Common Stock: 2,250,000 shs. ($0.01 par).

Per Share Data ($) (Year Ended Nov. 30)

	1994	1993	1992	1991	1990	1989
Tangible Bk. Val.	-1.78	-3.19	-6.71	NA	NA	NA
Cash Flow	2.63	2.00	2.45	NA	NA	NA
Earnings	1.17	0.16	0.91	NA	NA	NA
Dividends	Nil	Nil	NA	NA	NA	NA
Payout Ratio	Nil	Nil	NA	NA	NA	NA
Prices - High	19⅝	16¾	NA	NA	NA	NA
- Low	8¼	11	NA	NA	NA	NA
P/E Ratio - High	17	NM	NA	NA	NA	NA
- Low	7	NM	NA	NA	NA	NA

Income Statement Analysis (Million $)

	1994	%Chg	1993	%Chg	1992	%Chg	1991
Revs.	2,723	5%	2,601	4%	2,496	—	NA
Oper. Inc.	210	2%	206	NM	205	—	NA
Depr.	58.7	4%	56.2	1%	55.4	—	NA
Int. Exp.	66.0	-47%	125	45%	86.3	—	NA
Pretax Inc.	93.9	NM	25.8	-62%	67.6	—	NA
Eff. Tax Rate	45%	—	63%	—	45%	—	NA
Net Inc.	52.1	NM	9.7	-74%	37.0	—	NA

Balance Sheet & Other Fin. Data (Million $)

	1994	1993	1992	1991	1990	1989
Cash	2.7	3.7	5.5	NA	NA	NA
Curr. Assets	450	423	397	NA	NA	NA
Total Assets	1,496	1,454	1,443	NA	NA	NA
Curr. Liab.	311	338	306	NA	NA	NA
LT Debt	654	640	775	NA	NA	NA
Common Eqty.	369	325	261	NA	NA	NA
Total Cap.	1,162	1,092	1,077	NA	NA	NA
Cap. Exp.	82.0	50.0	NA	NA	NA	NA
Cash Flow	106	61.2	88.1	NA	NA	NA

Ratio Analysis

	1994	1993	1992	1991	1990	1989
Curr. Ratio	1.4	1.3	1.3	NA	NA	NA
% LT Debt of Cap.	56.3	58.6	72.0	NA	NA	NA
% Net Inc.of Revs.	1.9	0.4	1.5	NA	NA	NA
% Ret. on Assets	3.5	0.2	NA	NA	NA	NA
% Ret. on Equity	13.5	NM	NA	NA	NA	NA

Dividend Data —The company does not expect to pay dividends for the foreseeable future.

Data as orig. reptd.; bef. results of disc. opers. and/or spec. items. Per share data adj. for stk. divs. as of ex-div. date. E-Estimated. NA-Not Available. NM-Not Meaningful. NR-Not Ranked.

Office—Two Pershing Sq., 2300 Main, P.O. Box 419466, Kansas City, MO 64141-0466. **Tel**—(816) 234-6000. **Chrmn & CEO**—D. Stanley. **Pres & COO**—S. M. Stanton. **SVP-Fin & Treas**—S. A. Lightstone. **SVP & Secy**—Linda J. French. **Investor Contact**—Brenda Nolte. **Dirs**—H. Cohen, S. G. Fossel, W. A. Hall, L. P. Kunz, G. Latimer, W. B. Lyon, G. D. Rose, D. Stanley, S. M. Stanton, R. Strangis, J. H. Weitnauer, Jr. **Transfer Agent & Registrar**—First Chicago Trust Co. of New York, NYC. **Incorporated** in Iowa in 1968. **Empl**-18,400. **S&P Analyst:** Maureen C. Carini

STANDARD & POOR'S

STOCK REPORTS

Pennsylvania Enterprises

NYSE Symbol **PNT**

In S&P SmallCap 600

01-OCT-95 **Industry:** Utilities-Gas

Summary: This company's Pennsylvania Gas and Water unit distributes natural gas and water. Gas utility operations account for about 70% of revenues.

Quantitative Evaluations

Outlook (1 Lowest—5 Highest)
• **NA**

Fair Value
• **NA**

Risk
• **Low**

Earn./Div. Rank
• **B**

Technical Eval.
• **Bearish** since 4/95

Rel. Strength Rank (1 Lowest—99 Highest)
• **66**

Insider Activity
• **NA**

Recent Price • 34½
52 Wk Range • 34⅝-26⅞

Yield • 6.4%
12-Mo. P/E • 75.0

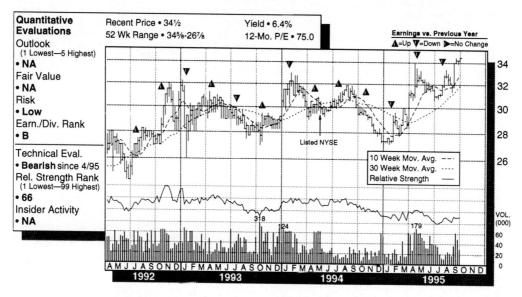

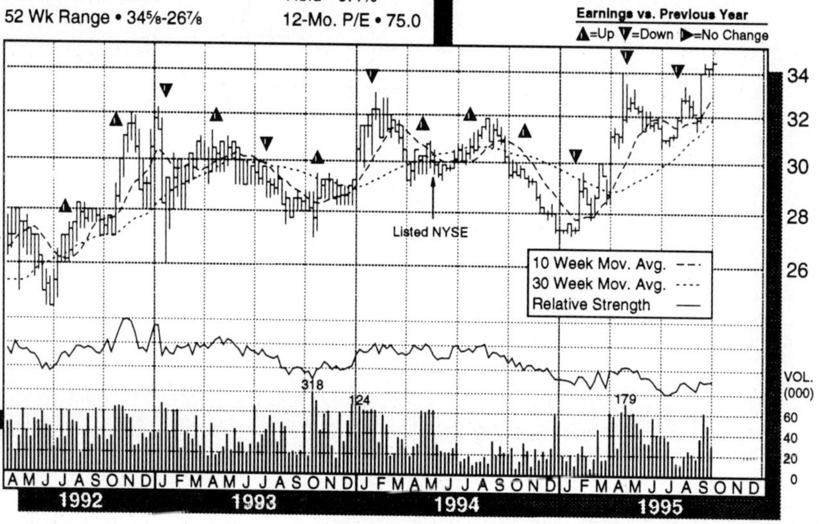

Business Profile - 01-OCT-95

This company distributes, through its Pennsylvania Gas and Water subsidiary, natural gas to approximately 140,000 customers in a 10 county area in northeastern Pennsylvania. The company's water operations provide water service to approximately 133,000 customers. Gas operations accounted for over 70% of revenues in 1994, and water for the balance. In April 1995, PNT agreed to sell all of its water operations to Pennsylvania-American Water Company. The sale is expected to close in December 1995.

Operational Review - 01-OCT-95

Operating revenues from continuing operations the six months ended June 30, 1995, fell 13%, year to year, primarily due to a decrease in sales to residential and commercial heating customers. Margins widened, and operating income was off 7.7%. With higher interest charges, income from continuing operations fell 29%, to $4,919,000 ($0.62 a share, on 5.1% more shares), from $6,883,000 ($0.78). Results for the 1994 period exclude income from discontinued water operations.

Stock Performance - 29-SEP-95

In the past 30 trading days, PNT's shares have increased 6%, compared to a 5% rise in the S&P 500. Average trading volume for the past five days was 5,720 shares, compared with the 40-day moving average of 6,913 shares.

Key Stock Statistics

Dividend Rate/Share	2.20	Shareholders	6,200
Shs. outstg. (M)	5.7	Market cap. (B)	$0.198
Avg. daily vol. (M)	0.010	Inst. holdings	27%
Tang. Bk. Value/Share	30.20	Insider holdings	NA
Beta	0.41		

Value of $10,000 invested 5 years ago: $ 11,511

Fiscal Year Ending Dec. 31

	1995	% Change	1994	% Change	1993	% Change
Revenues (Million $)						
1Q	68.24	-29%	96.29	23%	78.30	11%
2Q	25.18	-42%	43.48	17%	37.30	10%
3Q	—	—	31.86	14%	28.00	10%
4Q	—	—	63.09	NM	63.20	2%
Yr.	—	—	234.7	14%	206.7	8%
Income (Million $)						
1Q	6.36	-26%	8.55	35%	6.32	17%
2Q	-2.13	NM	0.42	NM	-1.45	NM
3Q	—	—	-1.12	NM	-1.96	NM
4Q	—	—	4.98	-2%	5.07	17%
Yr.	—	—	12.82	60%	7.99	24%
Earnings Per Share ($)						
1Q	1.00	-37%	1.58	3%	1.53	3%
2Q	-0.37	NM	-0.02	NM	-0.35	NM
3Q	—	—	-0.21	NM	-0.47	NM
4Q	—	—	0.82	-17%	0.99	-6%
Yr.	—	—	2.17	19%	1.82	13%

Next earnings report expected: early November

Pennsylvania Enterprises

Business Summary - 01-OCT-95

Pennsylvania Enterprises is a holding company whose principal subsidiary, Pennsylvania Gas and Water Co. (PG&W), distributes natural gas and water in northeastern Pennsylvania, including Scranton and Wilkes-Barre. Contributions by business segment in 1994 were as follows:

	Revs.	Profits
Gas utility operations	72%	46%
Water utility operations	28%	54%

PG&W distributes natural gas purchased from others to an area of northeastern Pennsylvania lying within the counties of Lackawanna, Luzerne, Wyoming, Susquehanna, Columbia, Montour, Northumberland, Lycoming, Union and Snyder. It also transports natural gas for those eligible customers that elect to make purchases from parties other than PG&W.

As of December 31, 1994, PG&W had 139,300 natural gas customers, 91.6% of which were residential, 8.1% commercial, 0.2% industrial, and 0.1% other users. Of total natural gas revenues of $168.0 million in 1994, 63.8% was derived from residential customers, 23.8% from commercial customers, 10.8% from industrial customers, and 1.6% from other users.

During 1994, PG&W delivered an estimated total of 44,400,000 Mcf of natural gas to its customers, of which 56.3% was sold at normal tariff rates, 2.8% was sold under the Alternate Fuel Rate, and 40.9% represented gas transported for customers. PG&W transported 18,155,000 Mcf of natural gas in 1994, and it expects to transport 16,672,000 Mcf of natural gas in 1995.

PG&W also distributes water from an extensive PG&W-owned reservoir system to an area in northeastern Pennsylvania lying within the counties of Wayne, Susquehanna, Lackawanna and Luzerne. As of December 31, 1994, PG&W had about 132,500 water customers, 91.6% of which were residential, 7.1% commercial, 0.3% industrial, and 1.0% municipal and other users.

Important Developments

Apr. '95—Pennsylvania Enterprises, Inc. and its Pennsylvania Gas & Water subsidiary (PG&W) agreed to sell all of the assets, properties and rights of PG&W's water utility operations to Pennsylvania-American Water Company (PAWC), a wholly owned subsidiary of American Water Works Company, Inc. Under the terms of the agreement, PAWC will pay approximately $409 million, consisting of $254 million in cash and the assumption of $255 million in PG&W's liabilities. Until the closing of the sale, which is expected to be in December 1995, PG&W will continue to operate the water utility operations.

Capitalization

Long Term Debt: $157,893,000 (6/95).
Subsidiary Preferred Stock: $35,295,000 (6/95).

Per Share Data ($)

(Year Ended Dec. 31)

	1994	1993	1992	1991	1990	1989
Tangible Bk. Val.	30.96	30.60	32.95	40.10	40.84	42.84
Cash Flow	4.98	4.62	4.32	5.10	3.14	5.18
Earnings	2.17	1.82	1.61	1.53	0.25	2.68
Dividends	2.20	2.20	2.20	2.20	2.20	2.20
Payout Ratio	101%	121%	137%	144%	880%	82%
Prices - High	33	32¼	32	37¼	47	58½
- Low	26⅞	29¾	22	22¼	30	43½
P/E Ratio - High	15	18	20	24	NM	22
- Low	12	14	14	15	NM	16

Income Statement Analysis (Million $)

	1994	%Chg	1993	%Chg	1992	%Chg	1991
Revs.	235	14%	207	8%	192	5%	183
Oper. Inc.	69.2	21%	57.4	8%	53.1	13%	46.8
Depr.	14.3	16%	12.3	13%	10.9	11%	9.8
Int. Exp.	26.7	2%	26.2	2%	25.6	-4%	26.6
Pretax Inc.	29.1	29%	22.5	19%	18.9	51%	12.5
Eff. Tax Rate	40%	—	36%	—	39%	—	33%
Net Inc.	17.5	22%	14.4	25%	11.5	37%	8.4

Balance Sheet & Other Fin. Data (Million $)

	1994	1993	1992	1991	1990	1989
Cash	2.9	2.8	1.1	0.7	2.2	0.7
Curr. Assets	75.0	85.6	62.7	58.3	59.8	61.8
Total Assets	735	719	633	543	518	488
Curr. Liab.	39.0	79.0	78.0	129	125	91.0
LT Debt	362	296	276	195	178	181
Common Eqty.	172	166	135	110	111	116
Total Cap.	675	623	530	398	380	387
Cap. Exp.	36.8	45.9	57.1	28.5	36.4	70.5
Cash Flow	27.2	20.3	17.3	14.0	8.5	14.0

Ratio Analysis

	1994	1993	1992	1991	1990	1989
Curr. Ratio	1.9	1.1	0.8	0.5	0.5	0.7
% LT Debt of Cap.	53.6	47.5	52.1	48.9	46.8	46.9
% Net Inc.of Revs.	7.4	7.0	6.0	4.6	3.0	6.4
% Ret. on Assets	2.4	1.9	1.9	1.6	1.0	2.6
% Ret. on Equity	7.5	4.7	5.3	3.8	0.6	6.3

Dividend Data —Cash dividends have been paid by the company or its predecessor since 1946.

Amt. of Div. $	Date Decl.	Ex-Div. Date	Stock of Record	Payment Date
0.550	Oct. 19	Nov. 25	Dec. 01	Dec. 15 '94
0.550	Jan. 20	Feb. 23	Mar. 01	Mar. 15 '95
0.550	Apr. 26	May. 25	Jun. 01	Jun. 15 '95
0.550	Jul. 27	Aug. 30	Sep. 01	Sep. 15 '95

Data as orig. reptd.; bef. results of disc. opers. and/or spec. items. Per share data adj. for stk. divs. as of ex-div. date. E-Estimated. NA-Not Available. NM-Not Meaningful. NR-Not Ranked.

Office—39 Public Square, Wilkes-Barre, PA 18711-0601. **Tel**—(717) 829-8843. **Chrmn**—K. L. Pollock. **Pres & CEO**—D. T. Casaday. **Treas**—R. N. Marshall. **Secy**—T. J. Ward. **Investor Contact**—Robert J. Lopatto. **Dirs**—D. T. Casaday, W. D. Davis, R. J. Keating, J. D. McCarthy, K. L. Pollock, K. M. Pollock, J. A. Ross, R. W. Simms. **Transfer Agent & Registrar**—Chemical Bank, NYC. **Incorporated** in Pennsylvania in 1974. **Empl**-965. **S&P Analyst:** B.O.

STANDARD & POOR'S

STOCK REPORTS

PENWEST, LTD.

NASDAQ Symbol **PENW**

In S&P SmallCap 600

05-SEP-95 **Industry:** Chemicals

Summary: This company manufactures specialty carbohydrate and synthetic polymer chemicals for papermaking and also produces pharmaceutical products and food ingredients.

Quantitative Evaluations

Recent Price • 25 | Yield • 0.8%

52 Wk Range • 26¼-17½ | 12-Mo. P/E • 23.1

Outlook
(1 Lowest—5 Highest)
• 3−

Fair Value
• 25

Risk
• Average

Earn./Div. Rank
• B

Technical Eval.
• Bearish since 7/95

Rel. Strength Rank
(1 Lowest—99 Highest)
• 66

Insider Activity
• Neutral

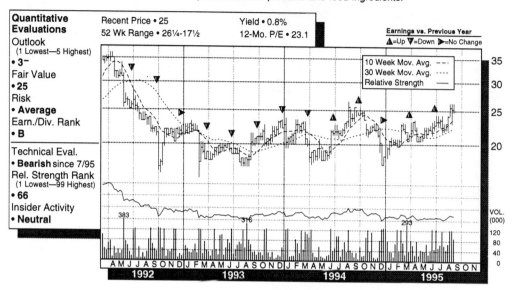

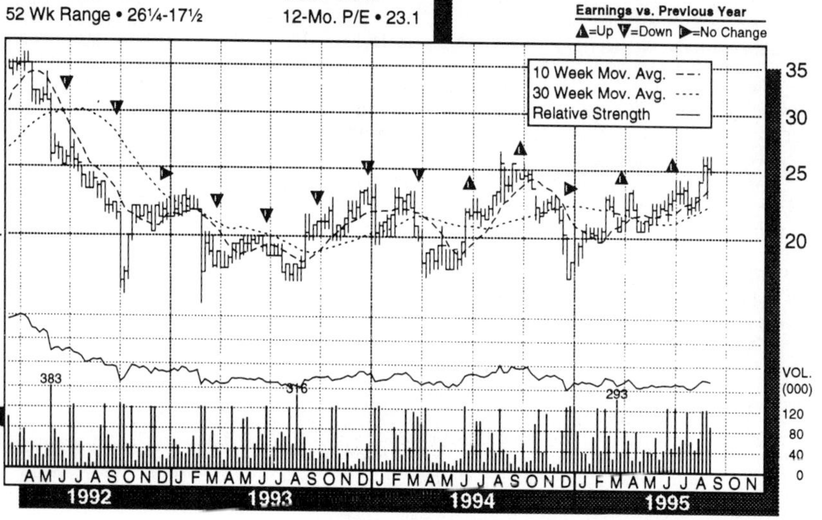

Business Profile - 05-SEP-95

As a producer of specialty chemicals for papermaking, PENW sees its primary growth coming from paper companies making the conversion from acid to alkaline-based papers. Recent results have benefited from the recovery in the paper industry, as well as from growth in the pharmaceutical and food groups. TIMERx Technology is developing a product that controls the release of pharmaceuticals. While not expected to generate revenues before 1996 or 1997, it has the potential to offer attractive returns.

Operational Review - 05-SEP-95

Revenues grew 12% for the first nine months of fiscal 1995, reflecting strong demand at all business units. Operating income jumped 47%, as margins widened on the greater volume and improved production efficiencies, and, aided by other income, pretax income soared 62%. However, with a sharply higher tax rate, earnings advanced just 35%, to $0.84 a share. PENW said fourth quarter earnings will drop to between $0.19 and $0.22, due to repeated power blackouts at its specialty starch plant in Iowa.

Stock Performance - 01-SEP-95

In the past 30 trading days, PENW's shares have increased 13%, compared to a 2% rise in the S&P 500. Average trading volume for the past five days was 17,800 shares, compared with the 40-day moving average of 18,075 shares.

Key Stock Statistics

Dividend Rate/Share	0.20	Shareholders	2,000
Shs. outstg. (M)	6.8	Market cap. (B)	$0.169
Avg. daily vol. (M)	0.022	Inst. holdings	25%
Tang. Bk. Value/Share	9.86	Insider holdings	NA
Beta	0.77		

Value of $10,000 invested 5 years ago: $ 14,108

Fiscal Year Ending Aug. 31

	1995	% Change	1994	% Change	1993	% Change
Revenues (Million $)						
1Q	42.77	13%	37.82	13%	33.50	14%
2Q	42.43	18%	35.84	13%	31.80	NM
3Q	43.62	5%	41.35	20%	34.50	9%
4Q	—	—	43.79	23%	35.68	7%
Yr.	—	—	158.8	17%	135.5	8%
Income (Million $)						
1Q	1.76	NM	1.76	-6%	1.87	-2%
2Q	2.15	150%	0.86	-48%	1.65	-20%
3Q	2.00	13%	1.77	27%	1.39	-15%
4Q	—	—	1.72	22%	1.41	-26%
Yr.	—	—	6.12	-3%	6.32	-16%
Earnings Per Share ($)						
1Q	0.25	NM	0.25	-4%	0.26	NM
2Q	0.31	158%	0.12	-48%	0.23	-15%
3Q	0.29	16%	0.25	25%	0.20	-9%
4Q	—	—	0.24	20%	0.20	-23%
Yr.	—	—	0.86	-2%	0.88	-13%

Next earnings report expected: early November

PENWEST, LTD.

05-SEP-95

Business Summary - 27-AUG-95

PENWEST, LTD. develops, manufactures and markets specialty carbohydrate and synthetic polymer chemicals for papermaking. Its basic chemistry is applied to four carbohydrate groups through six distinct technologies. The company operates in three market lines: carbohydrate-based specialty chemicals, pharmaceutical excipients and food ingredient products.

PENWEST's principal source of revenue is Penford Products Co., which supplies specially modified starches to the paper industry. These products improve strength, quality and runnability of coated and uncoated paper. Specialty starches are also supplied to the textile industry for bonding yarn and finished fabric and for providing body and stiffness to textiles. This segment's primary source of growth are paper companies that convert from acid to alkaline-based papers.

The Penwest Pharmaceuticals Group includes Edward Mendell Co. and TIMERx Technologies. Mendell makes and markets the non-active ingredients in tablet and capsule pharmaceuticals, over-the-counter drugs and vitamins. These ingredients, including binders, lubricants, fillers and disintegrants, provide bulk for concentrated medicines, ease of manufacture, product integrity and disintegration, which aids release of the active drug in the body. TIMERx is developing a controlled release technology for pharmaceuticals. Although the company does not expect to see any revenues from the subsidiary's principal product until 1996 or 1997, it described the economics of a success as fairly dramatic. The pharmaceutical group contributed 14% of fiscal 1994 revenues.

Penwest Foods Co., formed in 1991, develops, manufactures and markets corn-based specialty dextrose and dextrose-like products, along with food-grade potato-starch-based products and plant nutrition supplements. It is the only value-added food-grade potato starch producer in North America. Sales in fiscal 1994 were less than 10% of total sales.

Penwest owns a cogeneration facility which it expects to sell in the second quarter of fiscal 1995. The Pacific Cogeneration subsidiary sells heat to Canada Malting, and sells the by-product electrical energy to a local public utility district.

Important Developments

Jun. '95—Penwest said its Penford Products subsidiary had received one of the largest orders in its history, to supply a major North American paper producer with Penford Gums for its conversion to alkaline-based chemistry.

Capitalization

Long Term Debt: $61,600,000 (5/95).

Per Share Data ($)

(Year Ended Aug. 31)

	1994	1993	1992	1991	1990	1989
Tangible Bk. Val.	9.57	8.84	8.37	8.16	7.20	7.02
Cash Flow	2.25	2.12	2.05	2.09	1.79	1.28
Earnings	0.86	0.88	1.01	1.17	1.06	0.68
Dividends	0.20	0.20	0.15	Nil	Nil	Nil
Payout Ratio	23%	22%	15%	Nil	Nil	Nil
Prices - High	26½	23½	36¼	37¼	35½	18½
- Low	17½	16	16½	19¼	17	11⅝
P/E Ratio - High	31	27	36	32	33	11
- Low	20	18	16	16	16	17

Income Statement Analysis (Million $)

	1994	%Chg	1993	%Chg	1992	%Chg	1991
Revs.	159	17%	136	8%	126	14%	111
Oper. Inc.	20.8	16%	18.0	-2%	18.3	-6%	19.5
Depr.	9.9	11%	8.9	14%	7.8	12%	7.0
Int. Exp.	3.5	NM	3.5	29%	2.7	-4%	2.8
Pretax Inc.	8.1	7%	7.6	-25%	10.1	-19%	12.5
Eff. Tax Rate	24%	—	17%	—	26%	—	30%
Net Inc.	6.1	-3%	6.3	-16%	7.5	-15%	8.8

Balance Sheet & Other Fin. Data (Million $)

	1994	1993	1992	1991	1990	1989
Cash	Nil	11.9	18.4	29.8	31.3	38.8
Curr. Assets	42.1	41.5	44.1	52.1	48.0	53.6
Total Assets	164	156	131	121	102	96.0
Curr. Liab.	20.7	20.1	15.3	17.7	15.7	13.0
LT Debt	42.9	47.0	30.9	31.6	23.1	23.7
Common Eqty.	67.2	63.0	61.6	60.1	51.1	49.6
Total Cap.	110	110	93.0	92.0	74.0	73.0
Cap. Exp.	14.3	42.1	20.2	14.0	13.5	7.6
Cash Flow	16.0	15.2	15.3	15.8	13.5	10.5

Ratio Analysis

	1994	1993	1992	1991	1990	1989
Curr. Ratio	2.0	2.1	2.9	2.9	3.1	4.1
% LT Debt of Cap.	39.0	42.7	33.4	34.4	31.1	32.3
% Net Inc.of Revs.	3.9	4.7	6.0	7.9	8.6	7.0
% Ret. on Assets	3.8	4.5	6.0	7.9	8.0	5.5
% Ret. on Equity	9.4	10.3	12.3	15.8	15.8	13.0

Dividend Data —Cash dividends have been paid since early 1992.

Amt. of Div. $	Date Decl.	Ex-Div. Date	Stock of Record	Payment Date
0.050	Jun. 29	Aug. 15	Aug. 19	Sep. 02 '94
0.050	Oct. 25	Nov. 02	Nov. 08	Dec. 05 '94
0.050	Jan. 24	Feb. 13	Feb. 17	Mar. 03 '95
0.050	Apr. 28	May. 15	May. 19	Jun. 02 '95
0.050	Jun. 27	Aug. 16	Aug. 18	Sep. 01 '95

Data as orig. reptd.; bef. results of disc. opers. and/or spec. items. Per share data adj. for stk. divs. as of ex-div. date. E-Estimated. NA-Not Available. NM-Not Meaningful. NR-Not Ranked.

Office—777-108th Ave., NE, Suite 2390, Bellevue, WA **Tel**—(206) 462-6000. **Chrmn**—N. S. Rogers. **Pres & CEO**—T. R. Hamachek. **VP-Fin & CFO**—J. T. Cook. **VP-Secy**—F. E. Olsen Jr. **Dirs**—R. E. Engebrecht, T. R. Hamachek, P. H. Hatfield, C. C. Knudsen, H. L. Mullikin, S. G. Narodick, W. G. Parzybok Jr., N. S. Rogers, W. K. Street, J. H. Wiborg. **Transfer Agent & Registrar**—First Interstate Bank of Washington, Calabasas, Calif. **Incorporated** in Delaware in 1983. **Empl**-482. **S&P Analyst:** Justin McCann

STANDARD & POOR'S
STOCK REPORTS

Pharmaceutical Resources

NYSE Symbol **PRX**
In S&P SmallCap 600

03-NOV-95

Industry: Drugs-Generic and OTC

Summary: Pharmaceutical Resources is the parent company of Par Pharmaceutical, a generic drug producer, which manufactures and distributes a line of about 91 products.

Quantitative Evaluations

Outlook
(1 Lowest—5 Highest)
• **4-**

Fair Value
• **9⅛**

Risk
• **High**

Earn./Div. Rank
• **B-**

Technical Eval.
• **Bearish** since 6/95

Rel. Strength Rank
(1 Lowest—99 Highest)
• **17**

Insider Activity
• **Favorable**

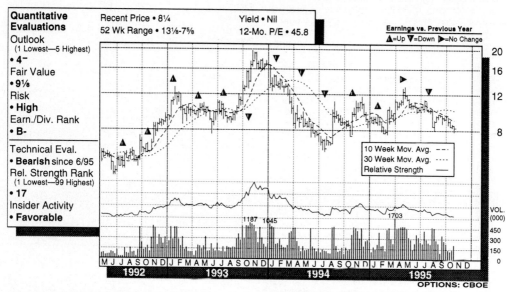

Recent Price • 8¼
52 Wk Range • 13⅛-7⅝
Yield • Nil
12-Mo. P/E • 45.8

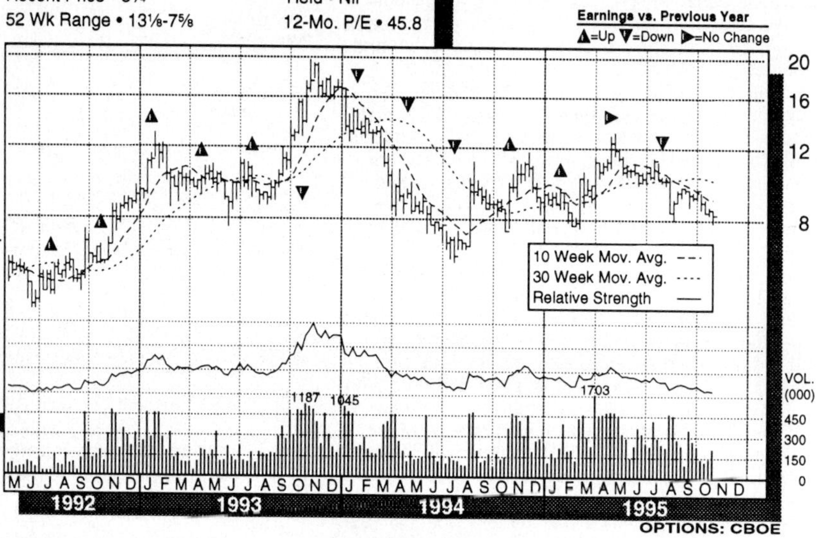

OPTIONS: CBOE

Business Profile - 03-NOV-95

Results in recent years were hurt by litigation-related charges and disputes with federal regulators. However, the company substantially cleared up its FDA problems in mid-1995. PRX formed a joint venture with Clal Pharmaceuticals in March 1995 to develop generic drugs and won marketing approval for a cardiovascular product, Metoprolol, in April 1995. Recently, the company obtained FDA approval for generic drugs cimetidine, Amiloride, and Glipizide in October 1995.

Operational Review - 03-NOV-95

Revenues in the nine months ended July 1, 1995, fell 4.5%, year to year, reflecting reduced sales of distributed products and price erosion from increased competition. Gross margins were unchanged, but total costs declined slightly due to receipt of a $2 million legal settlement. After taxes at 25.6%, versus 33.8%, net income declined to $1,792,000 ($0.11 a share), from $3,054,000 ($0.19, before $0.03 of income from discontinued operations and an $0.87 gain from an accounting change).

Stock Performance - 27-OCT-95

In the past 30 trading days, PRX's shares have declined 11%, compared to a 0.63% fall in the S&P 500. Average trading volume for the past five days was 42,200 shares, compared with the 40-day moving average of 39,131 shares.

Key Stock Statistics

Dividend Rate/Share	Nil	Shareholders	5,000
Shs. outstg. (M)	18.2	Market cap. (B)	$0.148
Avg. daily vol. (M)	0.031	Inst. holdings	14%
Tang. Bk. Value/Share	3.24	Insider holdings	NA
Beta	0.80		

Value of $10,000 invested 5 years ago: $ 13,750

Fiscal Year Ending Sep. 30

	1995	% Change	1994	% Change	1993	% Change
Revenues (Million $)						
1Q	17.03	-5%	17.92	-24%	23.70	106%
2Q	16.15	-2%	16.44	-19%	20.36	60%
3Q	15.83	-7%	17.09	13%	15.15	12%
4Q	—	—	17.79	16%	15.35	4%
Yr.	—	—	69.17	-7%	74.54	42%
Income (Million $)						
1Q	2.11	47%	1.44	-48%	2.78	NM
2Q	0.42	-26%	0.57	-50%	1.15	95%
3Q	-0.74	NM	1.05	-23%	1.36	-27%
4Q	—	—	1.18	NM	-5.17	NM
Yr.	—	—	4.23	NM	0.11	-97%
Earnings Per Share ($)						
1Q	0.13	44%	0.09	-44%	0.16	NM
2Q	0.03	NM	0.03	-57%	0.07	75%
3Q	-0.04	NM	0.07	-22%	0.09	13%
4Q	—	—	0.07	NM	-0.32	NM
Yr.	—	—	0.26	NM	0.01	-96%

Next earnings report expected: mid December

Pharmaceutical Resources

Business Summary - 03-NOV-95

Pharmaceutical Resources, primarily operating through its Par Pharmaceutical subsidiary, manufactures and markets a broad line of generic prescription and over-the-counter drugs.

The company's drugs are principally in oral solid (tablet, caplet and capsule) form with a smaller number manufactured in dosage forms such as topical creams. PRX currently has FDA approval to manufacture and market about 125 products, representing various dosage strengths of about 48 drugs. About 88 of these products (34 drugs) were being marketed in the first half of fiscal 1995. The company's oral solid products fall into six therapeutic categories, including central nervous system, cardiovascular, anti-inflammatory, anti-infective, anti-cancer and other. During fiscal 1994, sales of three drugs accounted for 46% of net sales.

The company also has distribution agreements with two manufacturers of generic drugs: Genpharm Inc. (Canada) and its affiliate, Alphapharm Inc. (Australia). Pursuant to the agreement with Genpharm, the company is the exclusive U.S. distributor of three FDA-approved generic drugs; Piroxicam (nonsteroidal anti-inflammatory), Pindolol (hypertension), and Atenolol (beta blocker). Under the agreement with Alphapharm, PRX is the exclusive U.S. distributor for Triazolam (anxiety).

In February 1994, the company and Par Pharmaceutical agreed to distribute generic pharmaceuticals utilizing transdermal drug delivery systems in an exclusive 10-year agreement with Sano Corp. As of May 1995, the company had invested approximately $3.5 million in Sano.

In March 1995, PRX formed an alliance with Clal Pharmaceuticals to develop and manufacture generic pharmaceuticals through an Israel-based joint venture. Clal plans to purchase 2,027,272 PRX common shares (about 12%) for $20 million with warrants to purchase up to 1,649,000 additional shares.

Important Developments

Oct. '95—Pharmaceutical Resources commenced shipment of generic drugs cimetidine (brand name: Tagamet; '94 U.S. market: $466 million) and Amilioride HCl (Midamor; $2.4 million), and planned to ship Glipizide (Glucotrol; $215 million) in late October.
Jul. '95—PRX exercised its option to convert all outstanding Series A convertible preferred shares into common stock. Each Series A share was converted into 1.1 common shares. Earlier, in April, the company received FDA approval to market generic drug Metoprolol, a cardiovascular product.

Capitalization

Long Term Debt: $4,525,000 (7/95).

Per Share Data ($) (Year Ended Sep. 30)

	1994	1993	1992	1991	1990	1989
Tangible Bk. Val.	2.98	1.19	0.90	1.01	3.80	5.20
Cash Flow	0.38	0.15	0.42	-1.23	-0.99	0.61
Earnings	0.26	0.01	0.28	-1.54	-1.31	0.36
Dividends	Nil	Nil	Nil	Nil	Nil	0.04
Payout Ratio	Nil	Nil	Nil	Nil	Nil	11%
Prices - High	16¾	19¾	9⅝	5⅞	8¼	11⅞
- Low	6¼	7⅝	4¾	2⅝	3⅜	3⅞
P/E Ratio - High	64	NM	34	NM	NM	33
- Low	24	NM	17	NM	NM	11

Income Statement Analysis (Million $)

	1994	%Chg	1993	%Chg	1992	%Chg	1991
Revs.	69.0	-8%	75.0	44%	52.0	53%	34.0
Oper. Inc.	8.4	-34%	12.7	21%	10.5	NM	-3.7
Depr.	2.4	6%	2.3	-2%	2.3	-11%	2.6
Int. Exp.	0.5	-22%	0.6	-35%	0.9	-22%	1.2
Pretax Inc.	6.0	NM	0.8	-87%	6.2	NM	-19.7
Eff. Tax Rate	30%	—	85%	—	34%	—	NM
Net Inc.	4.2	NM	0.1	-98%	4.1	NM	-17.9

Balance Sheet & Other Fin. Data (Million $)

	1994	1993	1992	1991	1990	1989
Cash	3.3	13.3	4.6	6.3	7.9	2.1
Curr. Assets	33.6	36.2	24.2	21.5	35.3	58.3
Total Assets	69.0	57.0	45.0	47.0	75.0	103
Curr. Liab.	13.9	23.0	16.1	18.6	14.2	19.8
LT Debt	5.5	5.8	7.5	12.6	14.0	14.7
Common Eqty.	44.0	16.7	11.1	12.3	44.0	57.7
Total Cap.	54.8	29.9	28.6	24.9	60.5	82.5
Cap. Exp.	5.7	2.7	0.7	0.6	2.2	10.7
Cash Flow	6.3	2.4	6.3	-15.3	-11.2	6.8

Ratio Analysis

	1994	1993	1992	1991	1990	1989
Curr. Ratio	2.4	1.6	1.5	1.2	2.5	2.9
% LT Debt of Cap.	10.0	19.5	26.3	50.5	23.1	17.8
% Net Inc.of Revs.	6.1	0.1	7.8	NM	NM	4.0
% Ret. on Assets	6.5	0.2	8.9	NM	NM	4.2
% Ret. on Equity	12.7	0.8	33.5	NM	NM	7.2

Dividend Data —Dividends were paid only in fiscal 1988 and 1989.

Data as orig. reptd.; bef. results of disc. opers. and/or spec. items. Per share data adj. for stk. divs. as of ex-div. date. E-Estimated. NA-Not Available. NM-Not Meaningful. NR-Not Ranked.

+ffice—One Ram Ridge Rd., Spring Valley, NY 10977. **Tel**—(914) 425-7100. **Chrmn, Pres & CEO**—K. I. Sawyer. **VP-CFO & Secy**—R. I. Edinger. **Dirs**—M. Auerbach, M. Ben-Dor, A. Maguire, H. S. Matthews, R. O. Motz, K. I. Sawyer, M. H. Van Woert. **Transfer Agent**—Midlantic National Bank, Edison, NJ. **Organized** in New Jersey in 1978. **Empl**-430. **S&P Analyst:** Thomas Tirney

STANDARD & POOR'S

STOCK REPORTS

Philadelphia Suburban

NYSE Symbol **PSC**
In S&P SmallCap 600

28-SEP-95 **Industry:** Utilities-Water

Summary: This company's principal operating unit is Philadelphia Suburban Water Co., a regulated public utility that provides water to about 250,000 customers in the Philadelphia suburbs.

Quantitative Evaluations

Outlook
(1 Lowest—5 Highest)
• **3+**

Fair Value
• **17 7/8**

Risk
• **Low**

Earn./Div. Rank
• **B+**

Technical Eval.
• **Bearish** since 8/94

Rel. Strength Rank
(1 Lowest—99 Highest)
• **36**

Insider Activity
• **NA**

Recent Price • 17 7/8 Yield • 6.5%
52 Wk Range • 18 3/4-17 1/4 12-Mo. P/E • 12.7

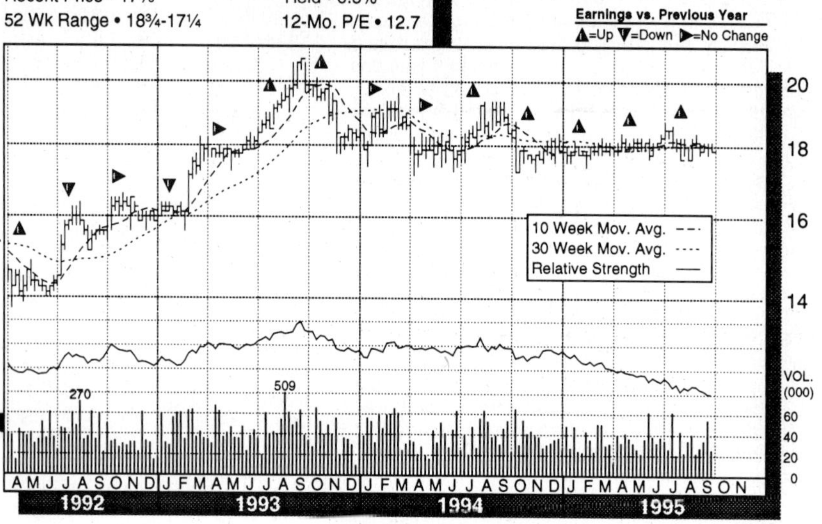

Business Profile - 28-SEP-95

This company supplies water to about 250,000 customers in suburban Philadelphia. It completed the sale of its nonwater services operations in February 1993, and plans to concentrate future activities on water services. Expansion efforts have picked up, and in May 1995 PSC acquired Media Borough for $25.7 million. Media's 23 square mile service territory is contiguous to PSC's. The quarterly dividend was increased 3.6% with the September 1995 payment, and now provides a yield of over 6%.

Operational Review - 28-SEP-95

Revenues for the first half of 1995 rose 5.7%, year to year, mainly reflecting the June 1994 9.05% rate increase and additional revenues from the Media water system, though customer consumption declined. Somewhat higher operating and depreciation costs should continue, though earnings will likely rise at a faster rate possibly leading to further dividend hikes.

Stock Performance - 22-SEP-95

In the past 30 trading days, PSC's shares have increased 1%, compared to a 5% rise in the S&P 500. Average trading volume for the past five days was 4,960 shares, compared with the 40-day moving average of 6,546 shares.

Key Stock Statistics

Dividend Rate/Share	1.16	Shareholders	11,300
Shs. outstg. (M)	12.0	Market cap. (B)	$0.214
Avg. daily vol. (M)	0.008	Inst. holdings	15%
Tang. Bk. Value/Share	12.49	Insider holdings	NA
Beta	0.49		

Value of $10,000 invested 5 years ago: $ 18,572

Fiscal Year Ending Dec. 31

	1995	% Change	1994	% Change	1993	% Change
Revenues (Million $)						
1Q	25.71	3%	24.85	9%	22.73	NM
2Q	28.83	8%	26.73	7%	25.05	8%
3Q	—	—	28.85	3%	27.95	15%
4Q	—	—	28.21	11%	25.52	11%
Yr.	—	—	108.6	7%	101.2	8%
Income (Million $)						
1Q	3.32	13%	2.95	14%	2.59	23%
2Q	4.66	15%	4.04	12%	3.60	37%
3Q	—	—	4.90	15%	4.26	39%
4Q	—	—	3.76	11%	3.39	20%
Yr.	—	—	15.64	13%	13.84	30%
Earnings Per Share ($)						
1Q	0.28	8%	0.26	NM	0.26	NM
2Q	0.39	11%	0.35	6%	0.33	3%
3Q	—	—	0.42	11%	0.38	9%
4Q	—	—	0.32	7%	0.30	NM
Yr.	—	—	1.35	6%	1.27	3%

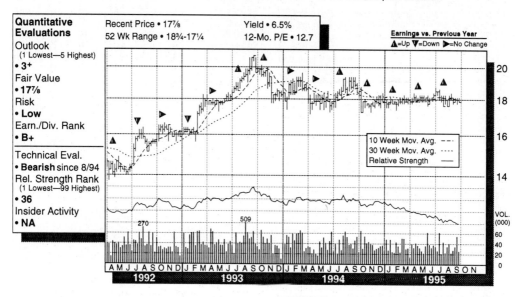

Next earnings report expected: early November

Philadelphia Suburban

Business Summary - 28-SEP-95

This company's principal operating unit is Philadelphia Suburban Water Co. (PSWC), a regulated public utility that provides water to about 250,000 customers in the suburbs of Philadelphia. Between 1991 and early 1993, PSC completed the divestiture of its nonwater services operations, which had included data processing services, telemarketing, computer modeling and engineering businesses.

Contributions to water revenues in recent years:

	1994	1993	1992	1991
Residential	65%	67%	66%	67%
Commercial	22%	20%	21%	21%
Industrial	5%	5%	5%	5%
Fire protection	7%	6%	6%	5%
Other	1%	2%	2%	2%

Water sales in 1994 totaled 27,106 million gallons, versus 26,910 million gallons in 1993. Average daily sendout was 89.8 million gallons per day in 1994, against 89.1 million in 1993. PSWC derives its principal water supplies from the Schuylkill River and tributaries of the Schuylkill and Delaware Rivers and Upper Merion Reservoir, supplemented by 40 wells. PSWC also has interconnections with the Chester Water Authority and the Bucks County Water and Sewer Authority, which brings its systems capability (minimum safe yield) to 123.5 million gallons of water per day.

During 1994, PSC acquired the privately-owned Grandstaff and Chesterdale water companies in Chester County, Pa., the fastest growing region in PSC's service territory. PSC also integrated the Malvern municipal system (acquired in December 1993 for $1.3 million) with its own. Together, these additions led to a 5,000 resident increase in the company's service area.

Projected construction expenditures for 1996 through 1999 are estimated at $110 million.

Important Developments

Aug. '95—In reporting its second quarter results, the company said that it would continue to pursue acquisitions that fit well within existing infrastructure. Three local water systems were acquired within the past eight months. PSC has also recently acquired two community water systems, and is in negotiations to acquire six additional systems.

Capitalization

Long Term Debt: $174,735,000 (6/95).
Subsidiary Red. Preferred Stock: $5,714,000.

Per Share Data ($) (Year Ended Dec. 31)

	1994	1993	1992	1991	1990	1989
Tangible Bk. Val.	12.23	11.89	10.88	10.66	13.06	12.45
Earnings	1.35	1.27	1.23	1.29	1.27	1.05
Dividends	1.10	1.07	1.04	1.00	1.00	0.94
Payout Ratio	81%	84%	85%	78%	79%	90%
Prices - High	19⅝	20¾	16⅝	16⅜	15	14½
- Low	17⅛	15⅝	13¾	11¾	10⅜	12¾
P/E Ratio - High	15	16	14	13	12	14
- Low	13	12	11	9	8	12

Income Statement Analysis (Million $)

	1994	%Chg	1993	%Chg	1992	%Chg	1991
Revs.	109	8%	101	9%	93.0	4%	89.0
Depr.	10.5	5%	9.9	15%	8.6	13%	7.6
Maint.	NA	—	NA	—	NA	—	NA
Fxd. Chgs. Cov.	3.0	8%	2.7	27%	2.2	6%	2.0
Constr. Credits	0.1	-84%	0.8	NM	0.3	-78%	1.2
Eff. Tax Rate	43%	—	43%	—	43%	—	41%
Net Inc.	15.6	13%	13.8	30%	10.6	4%	10.2

Balance Sheet & Other Fin. Data (Million $)

	1994	1993	1992	1991	1990	1989
Gross Prop.	463	433	402	371	350	332
Cap. Exp.	28.0	29.3	30.8	22.3	30.8	33.8
Net Prop.	386	366	346	321	307	288
Capitalization:						
LT Debt	152	145	154	168	176	163
% LT Debt	50	50	57	64	67	66
Pfd.	7.1	10.0	10.0	10.0	Nil	Nil
% Pfd.	2.30	3.40	3.70	3.80	Nil	Nil
Common	144	136	107	85.6	85.5	85.9
% Common	48	47	40	33	33	35
Total Cap.	371	382	291	283	279	266

Ratio Analysis

	1994	1993	1992	1991	1990	1989
Oper. Ratio	73.1	73.4	71.8	72.3	88.2	83.9
% Earn. on Net Prop.	7.8	7.6	7.9	7.8	7.4	7.8
% Ret. on Revs.	14.4	13.7	11.4	11.5	11.8	5.8
% Ret. On Invest.Cap	10.9	12.4	12.0	11.3	8.0	8.6
% Return On Com.Eqty	11.2	11.4	11.0	11.9	4.8	9.3

Dividend Data —Dividends have been paid since 1939. A dividend reinvestment plan is available. A "poison pill" stock purchase right was adopted in 1988.

Amt. of Div. $	Date Decl.	Ex-Div. Date	Stock of Record	Payment Date
0.280	Nov. 01	Nov. 08	Nov. 15	Dec. 01 '94
0.280	Jan. 30	Feb. 07	Feb. 13	Mar. 01 '95
0.280	Apr. 26	May. 09	May. 15	Jun. 01 '95
0.290	Aug. 01	Aug. 11	Aug. 15	Sep. 01 '95

Data as orig. reptd.; bef. results of disc opers. and/or spec. items. Per share data adj. for stk. divs. as of ex-div. date. E-Estimated. NA-Not Available. NM-Not Meaningful. NR-Not Ranked.

Office—762 Lancaster Ave., Bryn Mawr, PA 19010-3489. **Tel**—(610) 527-8000. **Chrmn & Pres**—N. DeBenedictis. **SVP-Fin, Treas & Investor Contact**—Michael P. Graham (215-645-1087). **Secy**—P. M. Mycek. **Dirs**—J. H. Austin Jr., J. W. Boyer Jr., M. C. Carroll, N. DeBenedictis, G. F. DiBona Jr., C. Elia, R. H. Glanton, J.C. Ladd, J. F. McCaughan, H. J. Wilson. **Transfer Agent & Registrar**—Mellon Securities Transfer Services, Ridgefield Park, N.J. **Incorporated** in Pennsylvania in 1968. **Empl**-525. **S&P Analyst:** R.J.D.

STANDARD & POOR'S

STOCK REPORTS

Phillips-Van Heusen

NYSE Symbol **PVH**
In S&P SmallCap 600

27-SEP-95

Industry:
Textiles

Summary: This company produces a broad range of well known brand name apparel and shoes, some of which it sells through its own 872 outlets.

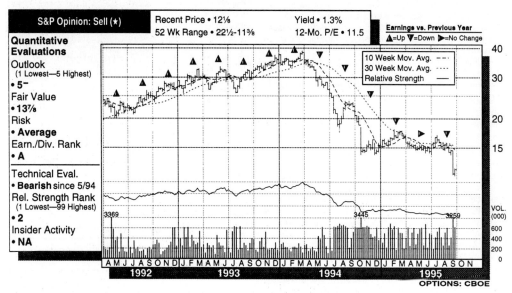

S&P Opinion: Sell (★)

Recent Price • 12⅛
52 Wk Range • 22½-11⅜
Yield • 1.3%
12-Mo. P/E • 11.5

Quantitative Evaluations

Outlook
(1 Lowest—5 Highest)
• **5⁻**

Fair Value
• **13⅞**

Risk
• **Average**

Earn./Div. Rank
• **A**

Technical Eval.
• **Bearish** since 5/94

Rel. Strength Rank
(1 Lowest—99 Highest)
• **2**

Insider Activity
• **NA**

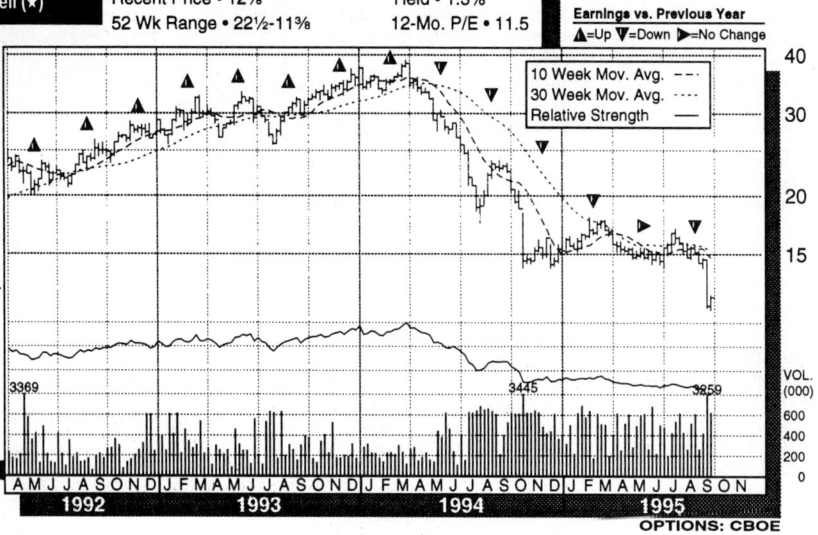

Overview - 27-SEP-95

Sales from continuing operations in 1995-96 could be under pressure reflecting weak industry demand for apparel and shoes. Contributions from the acquisition of Crystal Brands, whose major brands include Salty Dog, Gant and Izod, could offset some of the sales decline, however. Comparable store sales at the outlet shops are likely to decline. Despite the absence of start--up costs for wrinkle-free shirts, a problem that hurt results for most of 1994-95, margins are expected to contract on the weak volume and ongoing promotional selling environment. Interest charges will be higher due to the Crystal Brands acquisition. Earnings will also be hurt by a one-time restructuring charge aimed at closing three plants and 200 outlet stores.

Valuation - 27-SEP-95

After trading in a relatively narrow range for most of 1995, these shares plunged in September on news that the company expected to report lower earnings in the second half of 1995-96 than those in 1994-95, which were already depressed. In response to the ongoing weakness in the apparel and shoe sector and the threat of rapidly increasing imports, PVH also announced a restructuring program to close three plants and 200 outlet stores. We believe consumers may continue to refrain from making all but necessary apparel and shoe purchases in the near future. This could cause PVH to disappoint the investment community once again and drive the shares down. As a result, we would sell this stock.

Key Stock Statistics

S&P EPS Est. 1996	0.20	Tang. Bk. Value/Share	5.61
P/E on S&P Est. 1996	60.6	Beta	1.06
S&P EPS Est. 1997	0.75	Shareholders	2,100
Dividend Rate/Share	0.15	Market cap. (B)	$0.314
Shs. outstg. (M)	26.7	Inst. holdings	61%
Avg. daily vol. (M)	0.247	Insider holdings	NA

Value of $10,000 invested 5 years ago: $ 15,992

Fiscal Year Ending Jan. 31

	1996	% Change	1995	% Change	1994	% Change
Revenues (Million $)						
1Q	283.0	18%	239.0	8%	221.9	7%
2Q	349.5	23%	283.8	7%	264.0	10%
3Q	—	—	379.4	6%	357.4	11%
4Q	—	—	353.4	14%	309.1	14%
Yr.	—	—	1,255	9%	1,152	10%
Income (Million $)						
1Q	-3.36	NM	-3.53	NM	-2.21	NM
2Q	3.89	-32%	5.74	-26%	7.76	20%
3Q	—	—	17.85	-27%	24.52	12%
4Q	—	—	9.96	-24%	13.18	36%
Yr.	—	—	30.02	-31%	43.25	14%
Earnings Per Share ($)						
1Q	-0.13	NM	-0.13	NM	-0.08	NM
2Q	0.15	-29%	0.21	-28%	0.29	21%
3Q	E-0.07	NM	0.66	-27%	0.91	12%
4Q	E0.25	-32%	0.37	-23%	0.48	33%
Yr.	E0.20	-82%	1.11	-3%	1.15	-19%

Next earnings report expected: mid November

Phillips-Van Heusen

Business Summary - 20-SEP-95

Phillips-Van Heusen Corp. is a vertically integrated manufacturer, marketer and retailer of men's and women's apparel and men's, women's and children's footwear. In early 1995, the company acquired the Apparel Group of Crystal Brands, Inc. for $115 million. Major brand names in the Apparel Group include Izod, Gant and Salty Dog. In early 1995, PVH also entered into a licensing agreement to make and market Jantzen branded men's sweaters. Segment contributions in 1994-5 were:

	Sales	Profits
Apparel	70%	48%
Footwear	30%	52%

Apparel is manufactured domestically and abroad. Operations are conducted principally under company brand names. Van Heusen apparel includes men's traditional dress and sport shirts. Geoffrey Beene apparel consists of dress shirts produced under a licensing agreement with that designer. Bass apparel includes casual dress shirts. Jantzen apparel consists of men's sweaters, sport shirts and related bottoms under a licensing agreement. Izod branded apparel includes men's and women's sportswear and golf apparel. Gant and Salty Dog apparel consists of men's sportswear.

PVH also makes private-label men's dress and sport shirts for major national retail chains, department stores and catalog merchants. The private-label knitwear division sells men's sweaters and golf apparel to department and specialty stores, national retail chains and catalog merchants.

Bass (acquired 1987) makes men's and women's shoes domestically and through international sources.

PVH also operates 872 stores, located primarily in manufacturers' outlet malls, called Van Heusen, Geoffrey Beene, Windsor Shirt, Cape Isle Knitters and Bass. Expansion plans call for additional store openings in 1995-6.

Important Developments

Sep. '95—PVH announced that it would take a non-recurring restructuring charge of $23 milliion (pre-tax) in the third quarter of 1995-96. The restructuring would primarily entail closing three domestic plants and 200 outlet stores. The company said the plant closures were necessary due to rising, more competitively priced imports, while the store closings reflect the weak retail environment. PVH added that these moves would allow it to focus more on expanding its brand name apparel offerings. Separately, PVH said its second half earnings in 1995-96 would fall below those in 1994-95.

Capitalization

Long Term Debt: $219,682,000 (7/30/95).

Per Share Data ($) (Year Ended Jan. 31)

	1995	1994	1993	1992	1991	1990
Tangible Bk. Val.	9.69	8.64	7.42	3.50	2.32	2.35
Cash Flow	2.00	2.30	2.01	1.76	1.47	1.22
Earnings	1.11	1.60	1.42	1.15	0.95	0.84
Dividends	0.15	0.15	0.15	0.14	0.14	0.14
Payout Ratio	14%	9%	11%	12%	14%	16%
Cal. Yrs.	1994	1993	1992	1991	1990	1989
Prices - High	39	37½	29¼	21	11⅝	12½
- Low	14	25¾	16½	7	5¼	6⅞
P/E Ratio - High	35	23	21	18	12	15
- Low	13	16	12	6	5	8

Income Statement Analysis (Million $)

	1995	%Chg	1994	%Chg	1993	%Chg	1992
Revs.	1,255	9%	1,152	10%	1,043	15%	904
Oper. Inc.	81.0	-19%	99	13%	88.1	19%	74.1
Depr.	24.3	27%	19.1	27%	15.0	24%	12.1
Int. Exp.	12.8	-23%	16.7	NM	16.8	-6%	17.8
Pretax Inc.	36.9	-42%	63.6	17%	54.5	24%	44.0
Eff. Tax Rate	19%	—	32%	—	31%	—	29%
Net Inc.	30.0	-31%	43.3	14%	37.9	22%	31.1

Balance Sheet & Other Fin. Data (Million $)

	1995	1994	1993	1992	1991	1990
Cash	80.5	68.1	77.1	7.0	5.8	6.6
Curr. Assets	430	419	411	303	285	267
Total Assets	596	555	517	399	377	333
Curr. Liab.	114	109	115	105	90.7	84.2
LT Debt	170	170	170	121	140	119
Common Eqty.	275	247	211	85.0	62.0	46.0
Total Cap.	445	417	382	280	275	238
Cap. Exp.	53.1	47.9	36.8	21.1	22.2	12.8
Cash Flow	54.3	62.4	50.8	35.1	28.0	23.3

Ratio Analysis

	1995	1994	1993	1992	1991	1990
Curr. Ratio	3.8	3.8	3.6	2.9	3.1	3.2
% LT Debt of Cap.	38.1	40.8	44.6	43.4	50.9	50.0
% Net Inc.of Revs.	2.4	3.8	3.6	3.4	3.3	3.3
% Ret. on Assets	5.2	8.0	7.1	8.0	7.4	7.4
% Ret. on Equity	11.5	18.7	21.7	30.9	33.4	40.7

Dividend Data —Dividends have been paid since 1970. A "poison pill" stock purchase right was issued in 1986.

Amt. of Div. $	Date Decl.	Ex-Div. Date	Stock of Record	Payment Date
0.038	Sep. 13	Dec. 05	Dec. 10	Jan. 03 '95
0.038	Feb. 14	Mar. 06	Mar. 10	Mar. 16 '95
0.038	Apr. 18	Jun. 01	Jun. 07	Jun. 29 '95
0.038	Jun. 13	Aug. 10	Aug. 14	Sep. 06 '95
0.038	Sep. 12	Nov. 08	Nov. 10	Dec. 04 '95

Data as orig. reptd.; bef. results of disc. opers. and/or spec. items. Per share data adj. for stk. divs. as of ex-div. date. E-Estimated. NA-Not Available. NM-Not Meaningful. NR-Not Ranked.

Office—1290 Avenue of the Americas, New York, NY 10104. **Tel**—(212) 541-5200. **Chrmn, Pres & CEO**—B. J. Klatsky. **VP-CFO**—I. W. Winter. **Dirs**— E. H. Cohen, E. Ellis, J. B. Fuller, B. J. Klatsky, M. E. Lagomasino, H. N. S. Lee, B. Maggin, E. E. Meredith, S. L. Osterweis, W. S. Scolnick, P. J. Solomon, I. W. Winter. **Transfer Agent & Registrar**—The Bank of New York, NYC. **Incorporated** in New York in 1919; reincorporated in Delaware in 1976. **Empl**-13,800. **S&P Analyst:** Elizabeth Vandeventer

STANDARD & POOR'S

Phoenix Resource Cos.

STOCK REPORTS

ASE Symbol **PHN**
In S&P SmallCap 600

08-OCT-95 **Industry:** Oil and Gas

Summary: This independent oil and gas concern is engaged primarily in the production, sale and exploration of crude oil and natural gas in Egypt.

Quantitative Evaluations
Outlook
(1 Lowest—5 Highest)
• **NA**
Fair Value
• **NA**
Risk
• **Average**
Earn./Div. Rank
• **NR**

Technical Eval.
• **Bearish** since 6/95
Rel. Strength Rank
(1 Lowest—99 Highest)
• **83**
Insider Activity
• **NA**

Recent Price • 19⅛
52 Wk Range • 20½-6⅝
Yield • 0.4%
12-Mo. P/E • 23.3

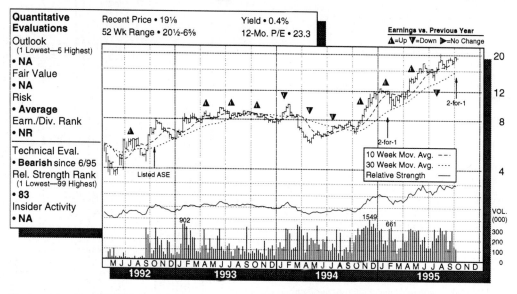

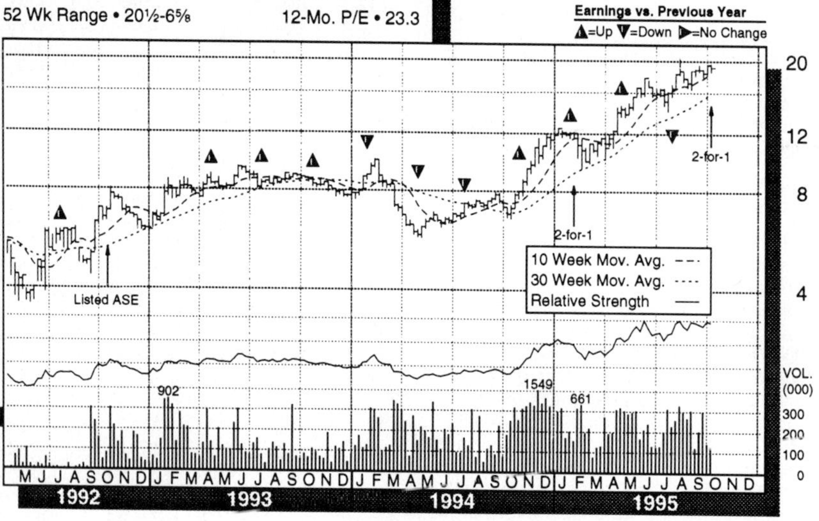

Business Profile - 07-MAY-95

The only long-established, successful independent oil and gas company operating in Egypt, Phoenix continues to set new records for oil production rates, reserves, earnings and shareholders' equity. Each of the exploratory and development wells drilled in 1994 in the Khalda Concession, its principal asset, was successful, and a highly prospective block of acreage, South Khalda, was recently acquired. Phoenix remains debt-free, and has recently repurchased over 7% of its stock.

Operational Review - 03-OCT-95

Revenues in the six months ended June 30, 1995 rose 14%, year to year. Earnings increased 4.9%, but were constrained by a $0.5 million ($0.035 per common share), non-cash charge for depreciation, depletion and amortization, due to inclusion of costs from the Qarun Concession. Share earnings of $0.38, versus $0.36, were enhanced by PHN's stock repurchase program. Future results should reflect a higher rate of production from the Khalda Concession, and new drilling in both Qarun and Khalda.

Stock Performance - 06-OCT-95

In the past 30 trading days, PHN's shares have increased 12%, compared to a 4% rise in the S&P 500. Average trading volume for the past five days was 24,880 shares, compared with the 40-day moving average of 45,428 shares.

Key Stock Statistics

Dividend Rate/Share	0.08	Shareholders	700
Shs. outstg. (M)	15.6	Market cap. (B)	$0.298
Avg. daily vol. (M)	0.038	Inst. holdings	40%
Tang. Bk. Value/Share	2.14	Insider holdings	NA
Beta	1.76		

Value of $10,000 invested 5 years ago: NA

Fiscal Year Ending Dec. 31

	1995	% Change	1994	% Change	1993	% Change
Revenues (Million $)						
1Q	8.69	25%	6.94	-16%	8.23	7%
2Q	9.31	6%	8.80	-33%	13.07	7%
3Q	—	—	9.19	8%	8.51	5%
4Q	—	—	8.92	14%	7.81	-16%
Yr.	—	—	33.84	-10%	37.61	NM
Income (Million $)						
1Q	3.08	26%	2.44	-11%	2.74	18%
2Q	3.00	-11%	3.36	-52%	6.97	17%
3Q	—	—	3.67	22%	3.01	10%
4Q	—	—	3.42	34%	2.56	-25%
Yr.	—	—	12.89	-16%	15.26	5%
Earnings Per Share ($)						
1Q	0.19	34%	0.15	-9%	0.16	16%
2Q	0.19	-10%	0.21	-49%	0.40	13%
3Q	—	—	0.23	30%	0.18	9%
4Q	—	—	0.22	43%	0.15	-26%
Yr.	—	—	0.79	-12%	0.89	3%

Next earnings report expected: early November

Phoenix Resource Cos.

08-OCT-95

Business Summary - 06-OCT-95

The Phoenix Resource Companies, Inc. is an independent oil and gas concern engaged primarily in production, sale and exploration of crude oil and natural gas in Egypt.

The company's principal producing asset is its nonoperated interest in the Khalda Concession in the Western Desert of Egypt. Production from the concession accounts for virtually all of the company's oil and gas revenues. Phoenix, Repsol and Samsung comprise the joint contractor. Under the Khalda agreement, the contractor pays all capital and operating costs, while production is split between Egyptian General Petroleum Corp. (EGPC) and the contractor. Up to 40% of the crude oil is available to the contractor to recover costs; capital costs are amortized over four years, and operating expenses are recovered on a current basis. The remaining crude oil is divided 75% to EGPC and 25% to the contractor until crude oil production levels exceed 25,000 bbl. per day or natural gas sales exceed 12 billion BTUs per day, at which time EGPC's share rises to 77%. Contractor rights and obligations are generally split 50% to Repsol, 40% to Phoenix and 10% to Samsung, except Repsol is obligated to pay 100% of the capital expenditures that generally pertain to crude oil.

In September 1992, Phoenix was awarded exploration rights in Egypt's Qarun Concession area, which contains 1.9 million acres and is located in the Western Desert of Egypt. In April 1993, the Egyptian Parliament approved the Qarun concession agreement, under which Phoenix of Qarun, as operator, holds 50% of the contractor interest, while Apache Corp. holds 25%, and Global Natural Resources holds 25%. PHN, Apache and Global are committed to drill at least one exploratory well in the initial three-year exploration phase, and have the option to extend exploration for two successive extensions of two years each, by committing to drill two additional wells for each extension.

At December 31, 1994, the present value (discounted at 10%) of total proved reserves amounted to $80,039,000 ($73,524,000 a year earlier).

Important Developments

Sep. '95—PHN announced the discovery of a new gas and condensate field on the Khalda Concession in Egypt. During initial testing, the well produced up to 17.2 million cubic feet of gas and 950 barrels of condensate per day. The discovery well is being temporarily abandoned until such time as this field and other shut-in gas fields in the Khalda Concession and other Western Desert Concessions are connected to the Egyptian gas grid.

Capitalization

Long Term Debt: None (6/95).

Per Share Data ($) (Year Ended Dec. 31)

	1994	1993	1992	1991	1990	1989
Tangible Bk. Val.	2.14	2.05	1.15	0.31	-0.71	-2.21
Cash Flow	0.92	1.03	1.01	0.02	0.91	0.37
Earnings	0.79	0.89	0.87	-0.15	0.68	0.08
Dividends	0.05	Nil	Nil	Nil	Nil	Nil
Payout Ratio	6%	Nil	Nil	Nil	Nil	Nil
Prices - High	12	$9\frac{1}{2}$	$8\frac{1}{8}$	$7\frac{1}{4}$	$2\frac{1}{2}$	$\frac{1}{2}$
- Low	$5\frac{3}{4}$	$6\frac{1}{8}$	$3\frac{1}{2}$	$1\frac{7}{16}$	$\frac{1}{16}$	$\frac{1}{16}$
P/E Ratio - High	15	11	9	NM	NM	6
- Low	7	7	4	6	NM	1

Income Statement Analysis (Million $)

	1994	%Chg	1993	%Chg	1992	%Chg	1991
Revs.	32.7	2%	32.0	45%	22.0	47%	15.0
Oper. Inc.	25.1	9%	23.0	69%	13.6	172%	5.0
Depr.	2.2	-4%	2.3	-8%	2.5	19%	2.1
Int. Exp.	Nil	—	0.1	-92%	1.3	-82%	7.4
Pretax Inc.	24.0	-7%	25.8	4%	24.7	NM	-1.6
Eff. Tax Rate	46%	—	41%	—	42%	—	NM
Net Inc.	12.9	-16%	15.3	6%	14.5	NM	-1.8

Balance Sheet & Other Fin. Data (Million $)

	1994	1993	1992	1991	1990	1989
Cash	26.5	25.2	11.5	32.4	16.1	6.2
Curr. Assets	40.0	37.0	40.0	37.0	21.0	24.0
Total Assets	56.0	54.0	60.0	51.0	38.0	39.0
Curr. Liab.	13.0	10.0	28.0	33.0	7.0	16.0
LT Debt	Nil	Nil	1.0	12.0	34.0	33.0
Common Eqty.	34.0	35.0	20.0	5.0	-5.0	-15.0
Total Cap.	43.0	43.0	31.0	17.0	29.0	18.0
Cap. Exp.	2.9	2.6	0.5	1.0	3.0	4.0
Cash Flow	15.1	17.5	16.9	0.2	6.3	2.5

Ratio Analysis

	1994	1993	1992	1991	1990	1989
Curr. Ratio	3.2	3.6	1.4	1.1	2.9	1.5
% LT Debt of Cap.	Nil	Nil	2.3	69.2	116.8	184.3
% Net Inc.of Revs.	39.4	47.0	64.4	NM	20.5	1.8
% Ret. on Assets	24.1	26.6	25.6	NM	12.0	1.8
% Ret. on Equity	39.2	56.3	117.0	NM	NM	NM

Dividend Data —Quarterly cash dividends, omitted since 1982, were resumed in early 1994.

Amt. of Div. $	Date Decl.	Ex-Div. Date	Stock of Record	Payment Date
2-for-1	Jan. 03	Feb. 01	Jan. 17	Jan. 31 '95
0.040	Feb. 21	Mar. 09	Mar. 15	Mar. 31 '95
0.040	May. 11	Jun. 13	Jun. 15	Jun. 30 '95
0.040	Aug. 08	Sep. 13	Sep. 15	Sep. 29 '95
2-for-1	Aug. 16	Oct. 02	Sep. 15	Sep. 29 '95

Data as orig. reptd.; bef. results of disc. opers. and/or spec. items. Per share data adj. for stk. divs. as of ex-div. date. E-Estimated. NA-Not Available. NM-Not Meaningful. NR-Not Ranked.

Office—6525 N. Meridian Ave., Oklahoma City, OK 73116-1491. **Tel**—(405) 728-5100. **Chrmn**—J. A. Pardo. **Pres & CEO**—G. D. Lawrence, Jr. **VP & CFO**—Cheryl A. Rich. **Secy**—Patricia J. Murano. **Investor Contact**—Debora Bingham. **Dirs**—G. P. Doss, F. L. Durand, G. D. Lawrence, Jr., L. M. Miller, J. A. Pardo, R. A. Sebastian. **Transfer Agent & Registrar**—Chemical Bank, NYC. **Incorporated** in Delaware in 1930. **Empl-** 22. **S&P Analyst:** T.C.F.

STANDARD & POOR'S

STOCK REPORTS

PhyCor, Inc.

NASDAQ Symbol **PHYC**

In S&P SmallCap 600

15-OCT-95

Industry:
Health Care Centers

Summary: PhyCor acquires and operates multi-specialty medical clinics and develops and manages independent practice associations (IPAs).

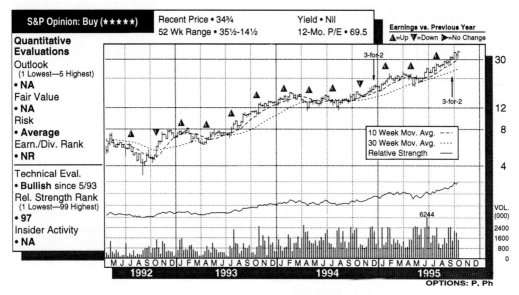

S&P Opinion: Buy (★★★★★)

Recent Price • 34¾

52 Wk Range • 35½-14½

Yield • Nil

12-Mo. P/E • 69.5

Quantitative Evaluations

Outlook
(1 Lowest—5 Highest)
• NA

Fair Value
• NA

Risk
• Average

Earn./Div. Rank
• NR

Technical Eval.
• Bullish since 5/93

Rel. Strength Rank
(1 Lowest—99 Highest)
• 97

Insider Activity
• NA

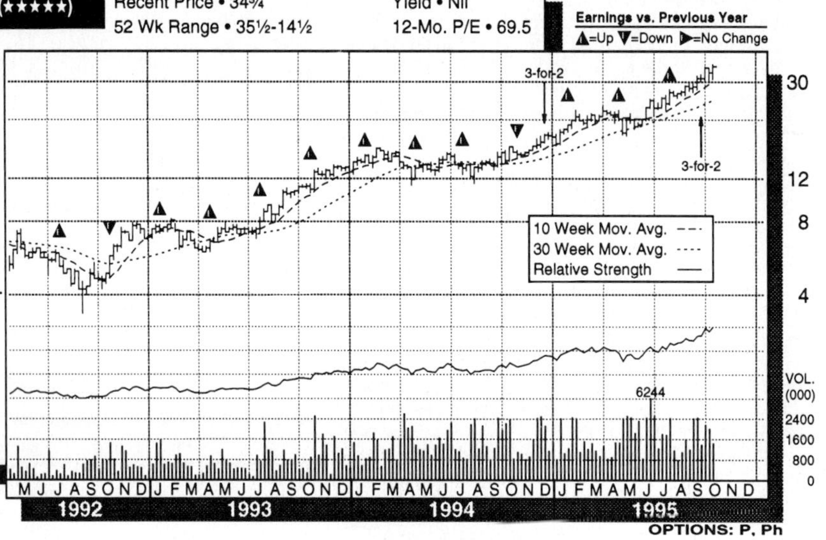

OPTIONS: P, Ph

Overview - 11-OCT-95

PhyCor is a leading participant in one of the most dynamic areas of the healthcare services sector -- physician practice management. By offering its administrative expertise, and by grouping together previously unaffiliated doctors, the company is able to negotiate favorable contracts with managed care entities and other payers. Acquisitions have generally added to earnings from the outset, and we expect PhyCor to add about 10 new clinics by the end of 1995. Additionally, the percentage of primary care physicians in the company's network should reach 60% of the total, up from the current 50%, another important factor in obtaining managed care contracts.

Valuation - 11-OCT-95

PhyCor has generated strong growth as a result of successful multi-specialty clinic acquisitions. These transactions have been accretive to earnings, and we expect more acquisitions as this sector continues to consolidate. The underlying fundamentals of the physician practice management sector are strong, and leading players such as PhyCor will benefit as physicians seek to join forces in order to effectively negotiate with large payers such as HMOs. We remain confident in our 1995 EPS estimate of $0.60, and look for $0.80 in 1996 (both as adjusted for the recent 3-for-2 split). Despite the recent runup and lofty P/E, we believe the shares of PhyCor will continue to generate interest and expect further appreciation in the coming months.

Key Stock Statistics

S&P EPS Est. 1995	0.60	Tang. Bk. Value/Share	3.93
P/E on S&P Est. 1995	57.9	Beta	1.30
S&P EPS Est. 1996	0.80	Shareholders	500
Dividend Rate/Share	Nil	Market cap. (B)	$ 1.2
Shs. outstg. (M)	34.6	Inst. holdings	83%
Avg. daily vol. (M)	0.348	Insider holdings	NA

Value of $10,000 invested 5 years ago: NA

Fiscal Year Ending Dec. 31

	1995	% Change	1994	% Change	1993	% Change
Revenues (Million $)						
1Q	92.76	86%	49.77	25%	39.90	25%
2Q	99.2	96%	50.46	27%	39.62	25%
3Q	—	—	63.18	51%	41.81	23%
4Q	—	—	79.08	72%	46.00	21%
Yr.	—	—	242.5	45%	167.4	23%
Income (Million $)						
1Q	4.18	79%	2.33	108%	1.12	56%
2Q	4.62	50%	3.09	158%	1.20	67%
3Q	—	—	2.70	108%	1.30	NM
4Q	—	—	3.55	134%	1.52	18%
Yr.	—	—	11.68	127%	5.14	NM
Earnings Per Share ($)						
1Q	0.13	11%	0.12	29%	0.09	91%
2Q	0.14	5%	0.13	43%	0.09	110%
3Q	E0.16	57%	0.10	-4%	0.11	NM
4Q	E0.17	32%	0.13	6%	0.12	59%
Yr.	E0.60	25%	0.48	16%	0.41	NM

Next earnings report expected: late October

PhyCor, Inc.

Business Summary - 12-SEP-95

PhyCor Inc. acquires and operates multi-specialty medical clinics and develops and manages independent practice associations (IPAs). Its strategy is to position its affiliated clinics and IPAs to be the physician component of an integrated health care system. The company targets for acquisition primary care-oriented multi-specialty clinics with significant market shares and established reputations for providing quality medical care. As of late August 1995, PHyCor operated 27 clinics with about 1,400 physicians in 18 states, and managed IPAs with more than 4,700 physicians in 14 markets.

A multi-specialty clinic provides a wide range of primary and specialty physician care and ancillary services through an organized physician group practice representing various medical specialties. The company believes that such clinics will continue to grow, reflecting their attractiveness to managed care organizations; their cost-effective treatment of patients in a subacute setting; their ability to increase the competitive position of physicians within organized health care networks; general recognition that they deliver high quality health care; and their ability to pool physicians' resources to obtain sophisticated medical equipment, technology and support services.

PhyCor's IPAs, which are networks of independent physicians, provide capitated medical services to about 152,000 members, including 28,000 Medicare members. The company has been expanding its IPA management business, and believes that significant opportunities exist in this sector. IPAs enable previously unaffiliated doctors to assume and more effectively manage capitated risk. The combination of PhyCor's multi-specialty medical clinic management services and IPA management services allow the company to offer physician practice management services to substantially all types of physician organizations.

Important Developments

Aug. '95—PhyCor acquired certain assets of the Arnett Clinic, a multi-specialty physican clinic in Lafayette, Indiana, and subsequently entered into a long term service agreement with the 113 physician group associated with the clinic.

Jun. '95—In a public offering through underwriters Alex Brown & Sons, Robertson, Stephens & Co., Smith Barney and Equitable Securities, 3,250,000 common shares (including 158,671 for existing shareholders) were sold at $37.75 each. Net proceeds to PhyCor of $111 million were earmarked for the repayment of bank debt, for potential acquisitions, and for general corporate purposes.

Capitalization

Long Term Debt: $103,674,000 (3/95), incl. $24,589,000 of conv. sub. debs., and cap. lease obligs. of $1,069,000.

Per Share Data ($)

(Year Ended Dec. 31)

	1994	1993	1992	1991	1990	1989
Tangible Bk. Val.	7.29	4.34	3.67	2.76	NM	NA
Cash Flow	0.99	0.77	-0.58	0.37	0.31	-0.16
Earnings	0.42	0.41	-0.86	0.08	0.00	-0.34
Dividends	Nil	Nil	Nil	Nil	Nil	Nil
Payout Ratio	Nil	Nil	Nil	Nil	Nil	Nil
Prices - High	18⅝	13⅝	7⅞	NA	NA	NA
- Low	11¼	6	3⅜	NA	NA	NA
P/E Ratio - High	44	46	NM	NA	NA	NA
- Low	27	20	NM	NA	NA	NA

Income Statement Analysis (Million $)

	1994	%Chg	1993	%Chg	1992	%Chg	1991
Revs.	242	45%	167	23%	136	51%	90.0
Oper. Inc.	31.4	75%	17.9	32%	13.6	79%	7.6
Depr.	12.2	99%	6.1	37%	4.5	64%	2.7
Int. Exp.	4.0	2%	3.9	-13%	4.5	17%	3.8
Pretax Inc.	16.5	101%	8.2	NM	-13.3	NM	1.3
Eff. Tax Rate	29%	—	13%	—	NM	—	43%
Net Inc.	11.7	65%	7.1	NM	-13.7	NM	0.8

Balance Sheet & Other Fin. Data (Million $)

	1994	1993	1992	1991	1990	1989
Cash	6.5	3.2	9.1	2.6	3.6	2.1
Curr. Assets	145	77.5	69.4	39.6	33.5	13.4
Total Assets	351	171	141	93.0	79.0	34.0
Curr. Liab.	64.3	30.5	33.5	17.7	15.5	6.0
LT Debt	84.9	66.8	51.2	49.3	38.9	20.0
Common Eqty.	184	70.0	53.9	2.4	1.3	NA
Total Cap.	269	137	105	75.0	63.0	28.0
Cap. Exp.	17.5	13.9	13.6	6.3	4.3	0.5
Cash Flow	23.9	13.3	-9.3	3.5	2.8	-0.8

Ratio Analysis

	1994	1993	1992	1991	1990	1989
Curr. Ratio	2.3	2.5	2.1	2.2	2.2	2.2
% LT Debt of Cap.	31.6	48.8	48.7	66.0	61.5	71.0
% Net Inc.of Revs.	4.8	4.3	NM	0.8	0.1	NM
% Ret. on Assets	3.8	4.4	NM	0.9	1.0	NM
% Ret. on Equity	7.9	11.1	NM	41.4	3.6	NM

Dividend Data —No cash dividends have been paid on the common stock. A poison pill stock purchase rights plan was adopted in February 1994.

Amt. of Div. $	Date Decl.	Ex-Div. Date	Stock of Record	Payment Date
3-for-2	Nov. 21	Dec. 16	Dec. 01	Dec. 15 '94
3-for-2	Aug. 21	Sep. 18	Sep. 01	Sep. 15 '95

Data as orig. reptd.; bef. results of disc. opers. and/or spec. items. Per share data adj. for stk. divs. as of ex-div. date. E-Estimated. NA-Not Available. NM-Not Meaningful. NR-Not Ranked.

Office—30 Burton Hills Blvd., Suite 340, Nashville, TN 37215. **Tel**—(615) 665-9066. **Chrmn, Pres & CEO**—J. C. Hutts. **EVP & Secy**—T. S. Dent. **VP, Treas & CFO**—J.K. Crawford. **Dirs**—R.B. Ashworth, S.A. Brooks, Jr., T.S. Dent, W. Dunn, C.S. Givens, J.A. Hill, J.C. Hutts, J.A. Moncrief, D.W. Reeves, R.D. Wright. **Transfer Agent & Registrar**—First Union National Bank of North Carolina, Charlotte. **Incorporated** in Tennessee in 1988. **Empl-** 3,000. **S&P Analyst:** Robert M. Gold

STANDARD & POOR'S

Piedmont Natural Gas

STOCK REPORTS

NYSE Symbol **PNY**
In S&P SmallCap 600

10-OCT-95 **Industry:** Utilities-Gas

Summary: This company is involved principally in the transportation and sale of natural gas and propane to 560,000 customers in North Carolina, South Carolina and Tennessee.

Quantitative Evaluations
Outlook (1 Lowest—5 Highest)
• **2-**
Fair Value
• **19**
Risk
• **Low**
Earn./Div. Rank
• **A-**

Technical Eval.
• **Bearish** since 9/95
Rel. Strength Rank (1 Lowest—99 Highest)
• **55**
Insider Activity
• **Neutral**

Recent Price • 20½
52 Wk Range • 21¾-18
Yield • 5.4%
12-Mo. P/E • 15.0

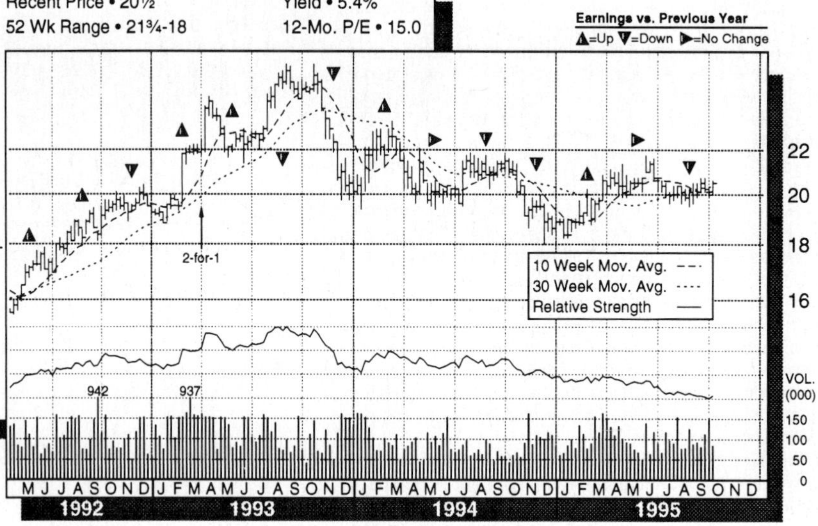

Business Profile - 10-OCT-95

The company intends to sustain an approximate 6% annual growth rate in its customer base. As such, its capital expansion program and ability to generate required funds are important in meeting the growing demand for natural gas. Proceeds from a March 1995 public offering of common shares will be used in part to construct additional facilities. The company has also filed for a rate increase in South Carolina, its first in four years, to improve its overall rate of return on invested capital.

Operational Review - 10-OCT-95

Operating revenues in the nine months ended July 31, 1995, fell 13%, year to year, reflecting warmer winter weather in the company's service territory. However, the cost of gas dropped 27%, aided by reduced commodity gas costs, a lower demand cost component, and a more favorable sales mix, and margins increased 9.3%. After higher utility interest charges, net income was up 4.5%, to $45.4 million ($1.65 a share, on 5.0% more average shares outstanding) from $43.5 million ($1.65).

Stock Performance - 06-OCT-95

In the past 30 trading days, PNY's shares have increased 2%, compared to a 4% rise in the S&P 500. Average trading volume for the past five days was 16,880 shares, compared with the 40-day moving average of 21,174 shares.

Key Stock Statistics

Dividend Rate/Share	1.10	Shareholders	12,500
Shs. outstg. (M)	28.7	Market cap. (B)	$0.586
Avg. daily vol. (M)	0.022	Inst. holdings	20%
Tang. Bk. Value/Share	13.29	Insider holdings	NA
Beta	0.41		

Value of $10,000 invested 5 years ago: $ 19,741

Fiscal Year Ending Oct. 31

	1995	% Change	1994	% Change	1993	% Change
Revenues (Million $)						
1Q	202.5	-13%	233.1	15%	202.6	17%
2Q	179.4	-12%	204.8	NM	205.1	36%
3Q	61.65	-13%	70.64	-5%	74.65	14%
4Q	—	—	66.80	-5%	70.50	NM
Yr.	—	—	575.3	4%	552.8	20%
Income (Million $)						
1Q	30.23	9%	27.74	2%	27.20	11%
2Q	24.03	5%	22.99	2%	22.57	13%
3Q	-8.83	NM	-7.24	NM	-5.28	NM
4Q	—	—	-7.99	NM	-6.96	NM
Yr.	—	—	35.51	-5%	37.53	6%
Earnings Per Share ($)						
1Q	1.13	7%	1.06	NM	1.05	6%
2Q	0.87	NM	0.87	NM	0.87	10%
3Q	-0.31	NM	-0.27	NM	-0.20	NM
4Q	—	—	-0.30	NM	-0.27	NM
Yr.	—	—	1.35	-7%	1.45	4%

Next earnings report expected: early December

Piedmont Natural Gas

Business Summary - 06-OCT-95

Piedmont Natural Gas is engaged mainly in the distribution of natural gas in the Piedmont region of North Carolina and South Carolina, and in the Nashville, Tenn., area. Revenue contributions in recent years were:

	1994	1993	1992	1991
Residential	41%	40%	40%	38%
Commercial	29%	28%	27%	29%
Industrial	29%	31%	32%	32%
Other	1%	1%	1%	1%

Gas volumes delivered in fiscal 1994 totaled 126.1 million dekatherms, versus 120.2 million dekatherms in fiscal 1993.

Customers billed averaged 478,961 in fiscal 1994, versus 452,612 in fiscal 1993. Degree days amounted to 3,567 (3,659). Average revenue per dekatherm on sales to residential customers was $6.68, up from $6.48. The cost of gas per dekatherm in fiscal 1994 was $3.29 ($3.11).

The company purchases or transports gas from five interstate pipeline suppliers: Columbia Gas Transmission Co., Transcontinental Gas Pipe Line Corp. (Transco), Tennessee Gas Pipeline Co., Texas Eastern Transmission Corp., and Columbia Gulf Transmission Corp. As of November 1, 1993, suppliers had contracted to supply a total of 459,200 dekatherms per day to PNY, with additional daily peaking capacity avaliable. The company uses underground storage for peaking purposes.

Nonutility subsidiaries are involved in acquiring, marketing and arranging for the transportation of natural gas to large volume purchasers; in retailing gas appliances; and in the sale of propane and propane appliances to 47,000 propane customers. Nonutility activities accounted for 8% of total revenues and 12% of total net income in fiscal 1994 (8% and 7% in fiscal 1993).

In October 1994, PNY received an order from the North Carolina Utilities Commission approving a 1.51% overall increase in its natural gas service rates for its customers in North Carolina, effective November 1, 1994. The increase was the first general increase in rates for the company in North Carolina in three years.

Important Developments

Aug. '95—PNY filed a notice of appeal of an order by the North Carolina Utilities Commission that granted a certificate to a competing applicant to serve a four county area of the state. Piedmont was originally granted the certificate in June, but was prohibited from financing the expansion with funds set aside for expansion into unserved areas.

Capitalization

Long Term Debt: $312,000,000 (7/95).

Per Share Data ($)

(Year Ended Oct. 31)

	1994	1993	1992	1991	1990	1989
Tangible Bk. Val.	11.36	10.79	10.24	9.62	9.10	8.67
Earnings	1.35	1.45	1.39	0.88	1.22	1.21
Dividends	1.02	0.96	0.91	0.87	0.83	0.79
Payout Ratio	76%	67%	65%	98%	68%	65%
Prices - High	23⅜	26⅜	20½	16⅞	14⅞	14¾
- Low	18⅝	18¾	15½	13	12¾	11½
P/E Ratio - High	17	18	15	19	12	12
- Low	14	13	11	15	10	10

Income Statement Analysis (Million $)

	1994	%Chg	1993	%Chg	1992	%Chg	1991
Revs.	575	4%	553	20%	460	12%	412
Depr.	24.6	11%	22.2	10%	20.1	12%	18.0
Maint.	15.5	3%	15.0	13%	13.3	2%	13.1
Fxd. Chgs. Cov.	3.2	-12%	3.7	5%	3.5	50%	2.3
Constr. Credits	1.3	18%	1.1	29%	0.8	9%	0.8
Eff. Tax Rate	36%	—	38%	—	38%	—	36%
Net Inc.	35.5	-5%	37.5	6%	35.3	71%	20.6

Balance Sheet & Other Fin. Data (Million $)

	1994	1993	1992	1991	1990	1989
Gross Prop.	978	877	796	723	658	591
Cap. Exp.	106	84.0	74.0	69.1	71.0	65.9
Net Prop.	735	655	593	538	488	434
Capitalization:						
LT Debt	313	278	231	221	174	186
% LT Debt	51	49	47	48	47	51
Pfd.	Nil	Nil	Nil	Nil	Nil	Nil
% Pfd.	Nil	Nil	Nil	Nil	Nil	Nil
Common	302	285	265	239	196	181
% Common	49	51	53	52	53	49
Total Cap.	697	653	576	534	442	437

Ratio Analysis

	1994	1993	1992	1991	1990	1989
Oper. Ratio	90.3	89.8	88.4	90.3	89.1	90.2
% Earn. on Net Prop.	8.0	9.1	9.4	7.8	9.5	10.1
% Ret. on Revs.	6.2	6.8	7.7	5.0	6.4	5.9
% Ret. On Invest.Cap	8.9	9.7	10.2	8.8	10.8	10.9
% Return On Com.Eqty	12.1	13.7	14.0	9.5	13.6	14.2

Dividend Data —Dividends have been paid since 1956. A dividend reinvestment plan is available.

Amt. of Div. $	Date Decl.	Ex-Div. Date	Stock of Record	Payment Date
0.260	Aug. 26	Sep. 19	Sep. 23	Oct. 14 '94
0.260	Dec. 13	Dec. 16	Dec. 22	Jan. 13 '95
0.275	Mar. 01	Mar. 27	Mar. 31	Apr. 14 '95
0.275	Jun. 07	Jun. 21	Jun. 23	Jul. 14 '95
0.275	Aug. 25	Sep. 20	Sep. 22	Oct. 13 '95

Data as orig. reptd.; bef. results of disc opers. and/or spec. items. Per share data adj. for stk. divs. as of ex-div. date. E-Estimated. NA-Not Available. NM-Not Meaningful. NR-Not Ranked.

Office—1915 Rexford Rd, Charlotte, NC 28211. **Tel**—(704) 364-3120. **Chrmn, Pres & CEO**—J. H. Maxheim. **SVP-Fin & CFO**—D. J. Dzuricky. **VP, Treas & Investor Contact**—Ted C. Coble. **Dirs**—J. W. Amos, J. C. Bolinger, Jr., C. M. Butler III, S. J. DiGiovanni, M. W. Helms, J. H. Maxheim, J. F. McNair III, W. S. Montgomery, Jr., D. S. Russell, Jr., J. E. Simkins, Jr. **Transfer Agent & Registrar**—Wachovia Bank of North Carolina, Winston-Salem, NC. **Incorporated** in North Carolina in 1994; previously incorporated in New York in 1950. **Empl**-1,968. **S&P Analyst:** N. Rosenberg

Pier 1 Imports

NYSE Symbol **PIR**
In S&P SmallCap 600

05-OCT-95

Industry: Retail Stores

Summary: This specialty retailer operates over 645 stores that sell a wide variety of home furnishings and related items imported primarily from Asian countries.

Quantitative Evaluations

Recent Price • 10 1/8 | Yield • 1.1%
52 Wk Range • 10 5/8-7 | 12-Mo. P/E • 25.3

Outlook
(1 Lowest—5 Highest)
• **4-**

Fair Value
• **10 3/8**

Risk
• **Average**

Earn./Div. Rank
• **B**

Technical Eval.
• **Bearish** since 7/95

Rel. Strength Rank
(1 Lowest—99 Highest)
• **86**

Insider Activity
• **Unfavorable**

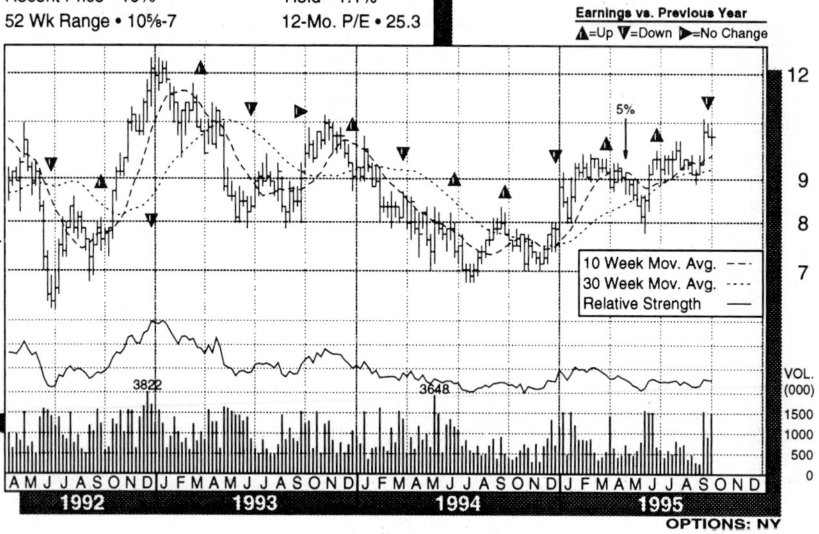

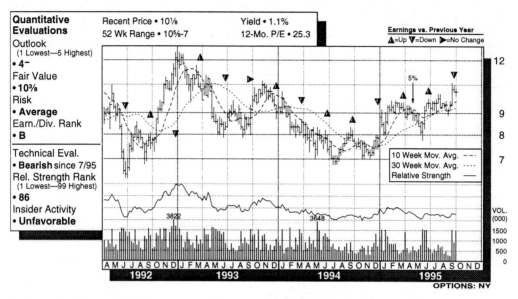

Business Profile - 05-OCT-95

Pier 1 is North America's largest specialty retailer of imported decorative home furnishings, gifts and related items, with over 645 stores in 47 states, Puerto Rico and Canada, and international operations in England and Mexico. Sales are expected to top $800 million in 1995-96, with earnings estimated to grow by 12% to 15%. To enhance shareholder value, PIR plans to use surplus cash to purchase up to $16.5 million principal amount of its 6 7/8% convertible notes due 2002.

Operational Review - 05-OCT-95

Net sales for the six months ended August 26, 1995, advanced 8.5%, year to year, benefiting from more stores in operation and a 2.4% gain in same-store sales. Gross margins widened and operating costs were well-controlled. However, following an aftertax charge of $9.6 million ($0.24 per share) related to the disengagement of financial support of Sunbelt Nursery Group, net earnings declined 57% to $6,159,000 ($0.16 per share), from $14,191,000 ($0.36).

Stock Performance - 29-SEP-95

In the past 30 trading days, PIR's shares have increased 8%, compared to a 5% rise in the S&P 500. Average trading volume for the past five days was 298,500 shares, compared with the 40-day moving average of 159,305 shares.

Key Stock Statistics

Dividend Rate/Share	0.12	Shareholders	16,000
Shs. outstg. (M)	39.6	Market cap. (B)	$0.416
Avg. daily vol. (M)	0.245	Inst. holdings	59%
Tang. Bk. Value/Share	5.69	Insider holdings	NA
Beta	0.55		

Value of $10,000 invested 5 years ago: $ 11,511

Fiscal Year Ending Feb. 28

	1996	% Change	1995	% Change	1994	% Change
Revenues (Million $)						
1Q	176.8	10%	161.0	2%	158.6	4%
2Q	199.5	8%	185.4	2%	181.4	9%
3Q	—	—	165.8	1%	163.5	13%
4Q	—	—	199.3	10%	181.9	10%
Yr.	—	—	712.0	4%	685.4	9%
Income (Million $)						
1Q	6.24	13%	5.54	18%	4.70	-42%
2Q	-0.07	NM	8.66	18%	7.34	-1%
3Q	—	—	0.22	-95%	4.04	80%
4Q	—	—	10.45	NM	-10.15	NM
Yr.	—	—	24.86	NM	5.93	-74%
Earnings Per Share ($)						
1Q	0.16	12%	0.14	25%	0.11	-45%
2Q	Nil	—	0.22	15%	0.19	NM
3Q	—	—	0.01	-90%	0.10	84%
4Q	—	—	0.28	NM	-0.26	NM
Yr.	—	—	0.63	NM	0.15	-74%

Next earnings report expected: early December

Pier 1 Imports

Business Summary - 05-OCT-95

Pier 1 Imports, Inc. sells a wide variety of imported home furnishings and related items. As of September 12, 1995, the company was operating 648 stores in 47 states, Puerto Rico and Canada, with international operations in England and Mexico. The number of stores in operation (excluding franchised stores) at fiscal year end was as follows:

1995	628
1994	636
1993	605
1992	585
1991	568

Rattan and willow furniture, decorative home furnishings, accessories and other specialty items for the home, as well as casual clothing and fashion accessories, are part of a diverse selection of more than 5,000 items available in the stores. Customers tend to be primarily women 25 to 44 years old, college educated, with a household income of about $40,000. Sales by principal merchandise category in recent fiscal years were:

	1995	1994	1993
Decorative home furnishings	26%	24%	24%
Furniture	28%	27%	26%
Housewares & kitchen goods	15%	14%	14%
Textiles	13%	14%	14%
Clothing, jewelry & accessories	9%	12%	14%

A majority of the items sold are imported directly by Pier 1, mostly from Asian countries. Most items require a significant degree of handcraftedness. Company-operated stores range from 3,300 to 15,600 sq. ft. of selling space, with the typical store averaging 7,500 sq. ft. Stores are generally located in strip shopping centers or are freestanding units near or in suburbs of metropolitan areas.

During 1994-95, Pier 1 opened 42 stores, including one test of a mall-based concept, and closed 50 unprofitable locations. PIR estimated that it would open up to 55 new Pier 1 Imports stores and six to ten mall-based stores in 1995-96.

Important Developments

Jul. '95—PIR completed a settlement agreement with Sunbelt Nursery Group, Inc. concerning Sunbelt's default on 13 Sunbelt store leases. As part of the agreement, Sunbelt agreed to pay the company $14.7 million, and will continue to lease the 13 stores at market rates for up to three years or until Pier 1 is able to find a buyer for the properties. Additionally, Sunbelt will make future deferred payments, up to a total of $8 million, out of its cash flow.

Capitalization

Long Term Debt: $143,032,000 (5/95).

Per Share Data ($)

(Year Ended Feb. 28)

	1995	1994	1993	1992	1991	1990
Tangible Bk. Val.	5.69	5.10	5.11	4.59	3.44	4.64
Cash Flow	0.98	0.59	0.97	1.07	0.64	1.03
Earnings	0.63	0.15	0.59	0.68	0.16	0.65
Dividends	0.10	0.09	0.06	Nil	0.14	0.12
Payout Ratio	16%	59%	11%	Nil	88%	18%
Cal. Yrs.	1994	1993	1992	1991	1990	1989
Prices - High	10⅛	12½	12½	9⅜	11⅞	12⅞
- Low	6¾	7⅞	6¼	3⅞	2⅞	8¾
P/E Ratio - High	16	82	21	14	73	20
- Low	11	52	11	6	17	13

Income Statement Analysis (Million $)

	1995	%Chg	1994	%Chg	1993	%Chg	1992
Revs.	712	4%	685	9%	629	7%	587
Oper. Inc.	71.6	9%	65.9	NM	66.0	18%	56.0
Depr.	16.0	-9%	17.6	17%	15.1	NM	15.0
Int. Exp.	14.2	-15%	16.8	12%	15.0	-10%	16.6
Pretax Inc.	36.0	NM	8.4	-74%	32.3	-8%	35.0
Eff. Tax Rate	31%	—	29%	—	29%	—	25%
Net Inc.	24.9	NM	5.9	-74%	23.0	-13%	26.3

Balance Sheet & Other Fin. Data (Million $)

	1995	1994	1993	1992	1991	1990
Cash	54.2	17.1	73.6	9.0	18.8	16.3
Curr. Assets	353	321	318	240	270	210
Total Assets	489	463	460	386	454	350
Curr. Liab.	85.0	92.0	93.0	80.0	141	72.0
LT Debt	154	145	147	107	142	93.0
Common Eqty.	225	201	200	177	155	180
Total Cap.	382	350	348	289	301	279
Cap. Exp.	17.5	21.7	12.6	6.2	62.2	32.6
Cash Flow	40.8	23.5	38.1	41.3	24.4	40.5

Ratio Analysis

	1995	1994	1993	1992	1991	1990
Curr. Ratio	4.1	3.5	3.4	3.0	1.9	2.9
% LT Debt of Cap.	40.4	41.5	42.3	37.0	47.3	33.2
% Net Inc.of Revs.	3.5	0.9	3.7	4.5	1.1	4.9
% Ret. on Assets	5.2	1.3	5.4	6.2	1.6	7.3
% Ret. on Equity	11.6	2.9	12.1	15.8	3.8	16.2

Dividend Data —Cash dividends were reinstated in March 1992, after having been omitted in early 1991. A "poison pill" stock purchase rights plan was adopted in December 1994.

Amt. of Div. $	Date Decl.	Ex-Div. Date	Stock of Record	Payment Date
0.030	Dec. 07	Feb. 02	Feb. 08	Feb. 22 '95
5%	Mar. 15	Apr. 25	May. 01	May. 17 '95
0.030	Mar. 15	May. 02	May. 08	May. 17 '95
0.030	Jun. 23	Jul. 31	Aug. 02	Aug. 16 '95
0.030	Sep. 28	Oct. 30	Nov. 01	Nov. 15 '95

Data as orig. reptd.; bef. results of disc. opers. and/or spec. items. Per share data adj. for stk. divs. as of ex-div. date. E-Estimated. NA-Not Available. NM-Not Meaningful. NR-Not Ranked.

Office—301 Commerce St., Suite 600, Fort Worth, TX 76102. **Tel**—(817) 878-8000. **Chrmn & CEO**—C. A. Johnson. **Pres**—M. J. Girouard. **Sr VP & Secy**—J. R. Lawrence. **Exec VP, CFO & Investor Contact**—Robert G. Herndon. **Dirs**—M. J. Girouard, C. G. Gordon, J. M. Hoak Jr., C. A. Johnson, S. F. McKenzie, C. R. Scott. **Transfer Agent**—Society National Bank, Dallas. **Incorporated** in Georgia in 1978; reincorporated in Delaware in 1986. **Empl**-8,671. **S&P Analyst:** Maureen C. Carini

Pillowtex Corp.

NYSE Symbol **PTX**
In S&P SmallCap 600

24-OCT-95 **Industry:** Home Furnishings

Summary: Pillowtex is a leading manufacturer and marketer of bed pillows, blankets, mattress pads, down comforters, comforter covers, and a full line of bedroom textile furnishings.

Quantitative Evaluations

Recent Price • 11¼ | Yield • Nil
52 Wk Range • 13⅛-8 | 12-Mo. P/E • 18.1

Outlook
(1 Lowest—5 Highest)
• **NA**
Fair Value
• **NA**
Risk
• **High**
Earn./Div. Rank
• **NR**

Technical Eval.
• **Bullish** since 7/95
Rel. Strength Rank
(1 Lowest—99 Highest)
• **22**
Insider Activity
• **NA**

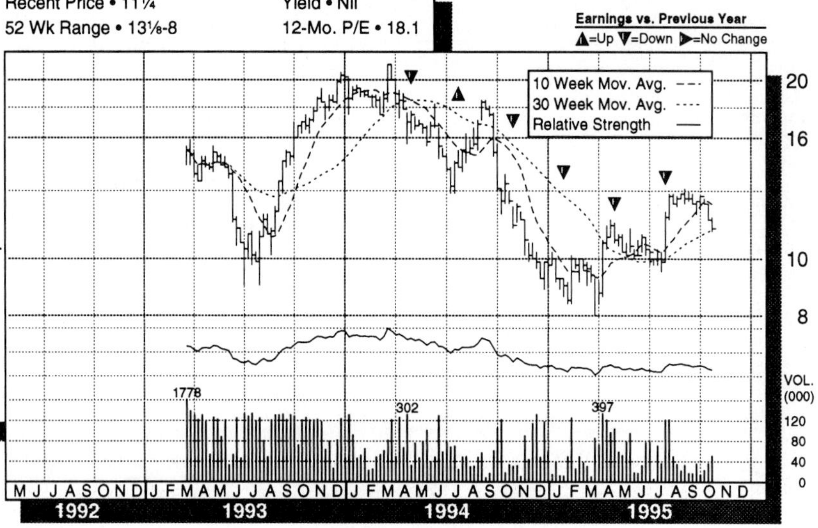

Business Profile - 24-OCT-95

Pillotex, one of the largest U.S. makers of bedroom textile furnishings, has launched a company-wide profit improvement and cost reduction plan, and has combined its three blanket subsidiaries into a new woven products division. Problems at two blanket facilities were expected to be substantially resolved in the second half of 1995. The company believes that the market for blankets and throws remains strong.

Operational Review - 24-OCT-95

Net sales in the first half of 1995 advanced 34%, year to year, spurred by the acquisition of Beacon Manufacturing in December 1994. Despite cost cutting efforts, results were penalized by much greater interest expense; net income fell 33%. The company plans to use a recently purchased cotton yarn spinning plant to centralize cotton yarn spinning and reduce raw materials costs for blanket production by eliminating more expensive outside purchases.

Stock Performance - 20-OCT-95

In the past 30 trading days, PTX's shares have declined 11%, compared to a 3% rise in the S&P 500. Average trading volume for the past five days was 10,060 shares, compared with the 40-day moving average of 5,621 shares.

Key Stock Statistics

Dividend Rate/Share	Nil	Shareholders	NA
Shs. outstg. (M)	10.6	Market cap. (B)	$0.118
Avg. daily vol. (M)	0.006	Inst. holdings	30%
Tang. Bk. Value/Share	2.57	Insider holdings	NA
Beta	NA		

Value of $10,000 invested 5 years ago: NA

Fiscal Year Ending Dec. 31

	1995	% Change	1994	% Change	1993	% Change
Revenues (Million $)						
1Q	94.74	32%	71.82	29%	55.48	—
2Q	90.79	36%	66.58	31%	50.86	—
3Q	—	—	102.0	11%	92.03	—
4Q	—	—	111.5	19%	93.81	—
Yr.	—	—	351.9	20%	292.2	7%
Income (Million $)						
1Q	1.16	-46%	2.13	18%	1.81	—
2Q	1.09	-12%	1.24	97%	0.63	—
3Q	—	—	3.35	-36%	5.27	—
4Q	—	—	0.98	-81%	5.17	—
Yr.	—	—	7.69	-40%	12.88	54%
Earnings Per Share ($)						
1Q	0.11	-45%	0.20	-20%	0.25	—
2Q	0.10	-17%	0.12	100%	0.06	—
3Q	—	—	0.32	-36%	0.50	—
4Q	—	—	0.09	-82%	0.49	—
Yr.	—	—	0.73	-45%	1.32	57%

Next earnings report expected: late October

Pillowtex Corp.

Business Summary - 24-OCT-95

Pillowtex Corp. designs and manufactures bed pillows, mattress pads, down comforters, blankets and other bedroom textile furnishings. Its products are marketed to department and specialty stores, mass merchants, wholesale clubs, catalogs and institutions. Pillowtex believes that it is among the largest North American suppliers in all of its major product lines.

Pillowtex makes a broad line of traditional bed pillows, as well as specialty bed pillows such as body, side sleeper and neck roll pillows. The company offers products at various quality and price levels, from synthetic pillows sold at retail prices as low as $5 to fine white goose down pillows sold at about $100.

The company's line of mattress pads consists of sizes for adults and children, and includes natural and synthetic filled, flat, fitted and skirted pads. Pillowtex also makes the patented Adjust-A-Fit adjustable fit mattress pad.

Pillowtex was also a pioneer in marketing down comforters in the U.S.

The company added blankets to its product line through two acquisitions in the second half of 1993. Pillowtex produces both conventional and thermal weave blankets, and is the exclusive supplier of blankets for the Ralph Lauren Home Collection. In December 1994, it acquired Beacon Manufacturing Co., a blanket producer.

To complement its four principal product lines, Pillowtex also offers other home fashion furnishings, including comforter covers, featherbeds, pillow protectors, decorative pillows, bedspreads, synthetic comforters, pillow shams, dust ruffles and window treatments.

The company is one of the principal suppliers of bedroom textile furnishings to almost all of the largest department stores in the U.S. Its 10 largest customers accounted for 58% of sales in 1994, with Dayton Hudson Corp. contributing 13%.

Products are marketed under company-owned trademarks and trade names and customer-owned private labels, as well as certain licensed trademarks and tradenames.

Important Developments

Sep. '95—Pillowtex said its Beacon Manufacturing subsidiary purchased Dixie Yarn, Inc.'s Newton, NC, cotton yarn spinning plant for $5.8 million. The company said the plant is ready for integration, and should be fully on line by the end of 1995.

Capitalization

Long Term Debt: $172,328,000 (4/95).

Per Share Data ($) (Year Ended Dec. 31)

	1994	1993	1992	1991	1990	1989
Tangible Bk. Val.	2.43	5.11	5.00	NA	NA	NA
Cash Flow	1.33	1.69	1.15	NA	NA	NA
Earnings	0.73	1.32	0.84	NA	NA	NA
Dividends	Nil	Nil	NA	NA	NA	NA
Payout Ratio	Nil	Nil	NA	NA	NA	NA
Prices - High	21¼	20⅝	NA	NA	NA	NA
- Low	8⅞	9	NA	NA	NA	NA
P/E Ratio - High	29	16	NA	NA	NA	NA
- Low	12	7	NA	NA	NA	NA

Income Statement Analysis (Million $)

	1994	%Chg	1993	%Chg	1992	%Chg	1991
Revs.	352	21%	292	7%	273		NA
Oper. Inc.	24.8	-11%	27.9	35%	20.6	—	NA
Depr.	6.4	75%	3.6	17%	3.1	—	NA
Int. Exp.	6.4	109%	3.0	—	NA	—	NA
Pretax Inc.	12.4	-42%	21.2	—	NA	—	NA
Eff. Tax Rate	38%	—	39%	—	NA	—	NA
Net Inc.	7.7	-40%	12.9	54%	8.4	—	NA

Balance Sheet & Other Fin. Data (Million $)

	1994	1993	1992	1991	1990	1989
Cash	0.6	2.6	NA	NA	NA	NA
Curr. Assets	185	124	NA	NA	NA	NA
Total Assets	320	181	130	NA	NA	NA
Curr. Liab.	62.3	45.6	NA	NA	NA	NA
LT Debt	177	63.7	52.4	NA	NA	NA
Common Eqty.	76.5	69.3	48.5	NA	NA	NA
Total Cap.	257	135	102	NA	NA	NA
Cap. Exp.	10.5	15.1	5.9	NA	NA	NA
Cash Flow	14.1	16.5	11.5	NA	NA	NA

Ratio Analysis

	1994	1993	1992	1991	1990	1989
Curr. Ratio	3.0	2.7	NA	NA	NA	NA
% LT Debt of Cap.	68.9	47.1	51.5	NA	NA	NA
% Net Inc.of Revs.	2.2	4.4	3.1	NA	NA	NA
% Ret. on Assets	3.1	6.5	NA	NA	NA	NA
% Ret. on Equity	10.5	31.6	NA	NA	NA	NA

Dividend Data —Pillowtex does not plan to pay cash dividends to shareholders in the foreseeable future, except in respect of certain of its shareholders' remaining federal and state income tax liabilities attributable to Subchapter S earnings for periods prior to March 25, 1993.

Data as orig. reptd.; bef. results of disc. opers. and/or spec. items. Per share data adj. for stk. divs. as of ex-div. date. E-Estimated. NA-Not Available. NM-Not Meaningful. NR-Not Ranked.

Office—4111 Mint Way, Dallas, TX 75237. **Tel**—(214) 333-3225. **Chrmn, Pres & CEO**—C. M. Hansen, Jr. **EVP & CFO**—J. D. Cordes. **Dirs**—C. N. Baker, J. D. Cordes, P. G. Gillease, C. M. Hansen, Jr., W. B. Madden, M. J. McHugh, J. D. Miller, M. R. Silverthorne. **Transfer Agent & Registrar**—Chemical Bank, NYC. **Incorporated** in Illinois in 1954; reincorporated in Texas in 1986. **Empl**-3,770. **S&P Analyst:** Philip D. Wohl

Pioneer Group

NASDAQ Symbol **PIOG**
In S&P SmallCap 600

07-NOV-95 **Industry:** Securities

Summary: This mutual fund manager, venture capital investor and shareholder servicing agent also has a majority interest in a gold-mining venture in Ghana.

Quantitative Evaluations

Outlook
(1 Lowest—5 Highest)
• **1-**

Fair Value
• **20⅞**

Risk
• **Average**

Earn./Div. Rank
• **A-**

Technical Eval.
• **Bullish** since 12/93

Rel. Strength Rank
(1 Lowest—99 Highest)
• **32**

Insider Activity
• **Neutral**

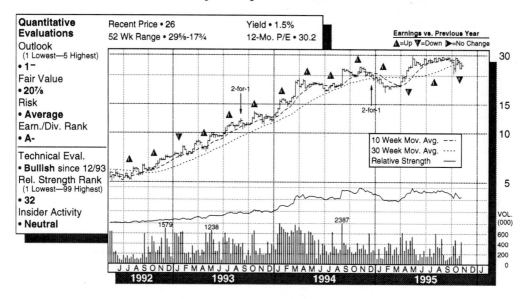

Recent Price • 26
52 Wk Range • 29⅝-17¾
Yield • 1.5%
12-Mo. P/E • 30.2

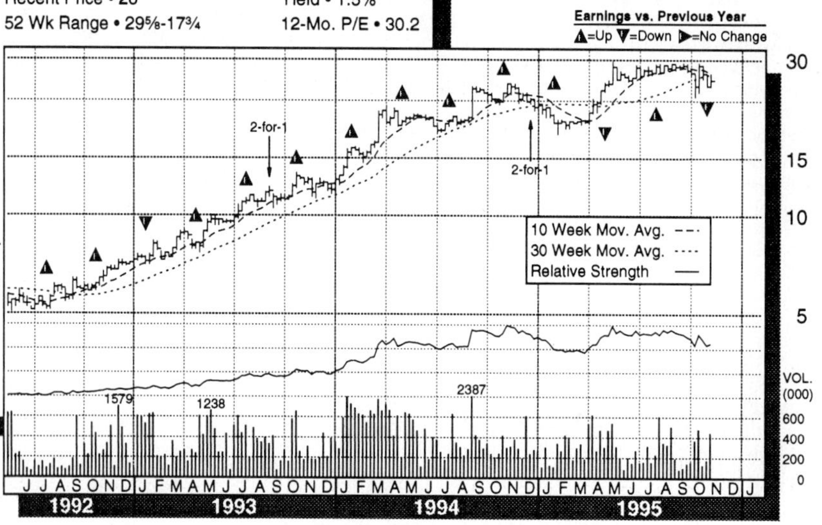

Business Profile - 07-NOV-95

This company is engaged in mutual fund and related services businesses in the U.S., operates a gold mine in Ghana and participates as owner or joint venturer in several asset management and natural resources operations. Earnings fell 28% in the first nine months of 1995, despite 12% higher revenues, due to the absence of a foreign income tax credit. The shares were recently trading at 22X the consensus EPS estimate of $1.16 for 1996, with a projected annualized five-year growth rate of 15%.

Operational Review - 07-NOV-95

Total revenues for the nine months ended September 30, 1995, rose 12%, year to year, as increased gold sales offset lower revenues from financial services businesses. With a 32% increase in total costs and expenses, pretax income fell 13%. After taxes at 41.3%, versus 28.4% (reduced in the 1994 period by a $4.4 million adjustment related to the gold-mining subsidiary), net income fell 28%, to $19,399,000 ($0.77 a share), from $27,018,000 ($1.07).

Stock Performance - 03-NOV-95

In the past 30 trading days, PIOG's shares have declined 7%, compared to a 2% rise in the S&P 500. Average trading volume for the past five days was 88,460 shares, compared with the 40-day moving average of 48,663 shares.

Key Stock Statistics

Dividend Rate/Share	0.40	Shareholders	4,000
Shs. outstg. (M)	24.8	Market cap. (B)	$0.645
Avg. daily vol. (M)	0.060	Inst. holdings	49%
Tang. Bk. Value/Share	4.81	Insider holdings	NA
Beta	0.83		

Value of $10,000 invested 5 years ago: $ 53,920

Fiscal Year Ending Dec. 31

	1995	% Change	1994	% Change	1993	% Change
Revenues (Million $)						
1Q	45.68	7%	42.60	43%	29.70	27%
2Q	46.55	17%	39.82	29%	30.90	27%
3Q	51.24	13%	45.31	38%	32.90	27%
4Q	—	—	44.02	23%	35.90	27%
Yr.	—	—	171.7	33%	129.4	27%
Income (Million $)						
1Q	5.80	-51%	11.89	NM	3.74	17%
2Q	7.33	7%	6.85	69%	4.05	11%
3Q	6.27	-24%	8.28	73%	4.79	24%
4Q	—	—	6.44	16%	5.55	42%
Yr.	—	—	29.03	60%	18.13	24%
Earnings Per Share ($)						
1Q	0.23	-26%	0.31	107%	0.15	15%
2Q	0.29	7%	0.27	64%	0.17	10%
3Q	0.25	-24%	0.33	74%	0.19	23%
4Q	—	—	0.25	14%	0.22	38%
Yr.	—	—	1.16	60%	0.73	23%

Next earnings report expected: late January

Pioneer Group

Business Summary - 07-NOV-95

The Pioneer Group, Inc. is a financial services company that operates as an investment manager for open-end investment companies, a distributor of mutual fund shares, a venture capital investor and manager, and a shareholder servicing agent for mutual funds. The company also holds a 90% interest in Teberebie Goldfields Ltd., a gold-mining venture in Ghana, through its wholly owned Pioneer Goldfields Ltd. subsidiary.

Revenues in recent years were derived as follows:

	1994	1993
Investment management fees	38%	31%
Underwriting commissions	7%	10%
Shareholder services fees	12%	13%
Trustee fees & other	4%	---
Gold sales	39%	46%

Through its Pioneering Management Corp. subsidiary, the company acts as investment manager for a family of 31 diversified mutual funds. At March 3, 1995, the funds had total net assets with a market value of $10.4 billion.

Through Pioneer Funds Distributor, Inc., the company acts as principal underwriter and distributor of the mutual fund shares. In 1994, Pioneer Funds sold mutual fund shares with an aggregate offering price of $1.3 billion and received aggregate commissions of $48.1 million.

Pioneer Capital Corp. makes venture capital investments and manages venture capital. In 1986, it organized Pioneer SBIC Corp., the general partner of Pioneer Ventures Limited Partnership (PVLP), a Small Business Investment Company. At 1994 year-end, Pioneer Capital and PVLP had about $17.2 million of investments in 24 privately held companies and $1.0 million in six publicly held companies.

Through Pioneer Services Corp., the company acts as shareholder servicing agent for the mutual funds, which had nearly 929,000 active accounts, including 338,000 IRAs and other qualified retirement accounts, at December 31, 1994.

Teberebie Goldfields Ltd. (TGL--90% owned) is engaged in exploration, mining and processing of gold ore in the western region of the Republic of Ghana. TGL shipped approximately 176,000 oz. of gold in 1994, up from 165,000 oz. in 1993.

Important Developments

Oct. '95—Pioneer Group said it received a certification from an independent technical consultant regarding the Teberebie mine's gold reserves. At August 31, 1995, remaining proven and probable reserves totaled about 9.2 million ounces, consisting of some 8.2 million ounces of heap leached ore and one million ounces of run-of-mine ore.

Capitalization

Notes Payable: $14,075,000 (6/95).
Minority Interest: $5,489,000.
Options: To buy 1,769,500 shs. at $4.188 to $21.25 ea. (6/95).

Per Share Data ($)

(Year Ended Dec. 31)

	1994	1993	1992	1991	1990	1989
Tangible Bk. Val.	4.43	3.25	3.68	3.32	2.91	2.59
Earnings	1.16	0.73	0.59	0.59	0.50	0.58
Dividends	0.32	0.22	0.21	0.21	0.20	0.19
Payout Ratio	27%	31%	36%	35%	40%	34%
Prices - High	25⅜	13½	7⅜	6⅜	7⅛	6¼
- Low	12⅜	7⅛	5⅛	4	3¾	4½
P/E Ratio - High	22	19	12	11	14	11
- Low	11	10	9	7	7	8

Income Statement Analysis (Million $)

	1994	%Chg	1993	%Chg	1992	%Chg	1991
Mgt. Fees	64.3	63%	39.5	23%	32.2	6%	30.3
Gold Sales	67.6	14%	59.2	35%	43.8	89%	23.2
Total Revs.	172	33%	129	26%	102	26%	81.0
Int. Exp.	1.3	-45%	2.4	67%	1.4	-9%	1.6
Net Bef. Taxes	47.6	38%	34.5	25%	27.5	8%	25.4
Eff. Tax Rate	30%	—	47%	—	47%	—	43%
Net Inc.	29.0	60%	18.1	24%	14.6	1%	14.4

Balance Sheet & Other Fin. Data (Million $)

	1994	1993	1992	1991	1990	1989
Total Assets	203	172	135	124	109	100
Cash Items	23.1	21.5	47.8	46.9	38.5	44.2
Rec.	22.0	20.2	9.2	8.4	4.5	8.8
Secs. Owned	6.5	15.8	9.2	5.4	4.9	1.3
Sec. Borrowed	13.6	6.0	4.5	4.8	4.3	1.8
Due Brokers & Cust.	7.1	7.9	2.8	3.2	1.3	5.1
Other Liabs.	33.2	35.0	21.0	13.3	8.2	8.8
Capitalization:						
Debt	9.1	13.3	12.0	17.1	20.3	17.3
Equity	134	107	93.0	85.0	75.0	67.0
Total	148	123	106	103	95.0	84.0

Ratio Analysis

	1994	1993	1992	1991	1990	1989
% Exp./Op. Revs.	72.3	73.1	74.4	73.4	67.0	59.9
% Ret. on Revs.	16.9	14.0	14.3	17.8	20.4	23.3
% Ret. on Assets	15.5	11.8	11.3	12.4	11.7	16.8
% Ret. on Equity	24.1	18.1	16.4	18.1	17.3	22.9

Dividend Data —Cash dividends have been paid since 1979.

Amt. of Div. $	Date Decl.	Ex-Div. Date	Stock of Record	Payment Date
2-for-1	Nov. 11	Dec. 12	Dec. 01	Dec. 09 '94
0.100	Jan. 30	Feb. 23	Mar. 01	Mar. 09 '95
0.100	May. 04	May. 25	Jun. 01	Jun. 09 '95
0.100	Jul. 26	Aug. 30	Sep. 01	Sep. 08 '95
0.100	Nov. 01	Nov. 29	Dec. 01	Dec. 08 '95

Office—60 State St., Boston, MA 02109. **Tel**—(617) 742-7825. **Chrmn & Pres**—J. F. Cogan Jr. **Sr VP, CFO, Treas & Investor Contact**—William H. Keough. **Secy**—J. P. Barri. **Dirs**—R. L. Butler, P. L. Carret, J. F. Cogan Jr., M. Engleman, J. S. Teja, D. D. Tripple, J. H. Valentine. **Transfer Agent**—State Street Bank & Trust Co., Boston. **Incorporated** in Delaware in 1956. **Empl**-1,324. **S&P Analyst:** Brad Ohlmuller

Pioneer-Standard Electronics

NASDAQ Symbol **PIOS**
In S&P SmallCap 600

09-NOV-95 **Industry:** Electronics/Electric

Summary: Pioneer-Standard is the third largest distributor of industrial and end-user electronic products in the U.S.

Quantitative Evaluations
Outlook
(1 Lowest—5 Highest)
• **5−**
Fair Value
• **21⅜**
Risk
• **Average**
Earn./Div. Rank
• **B+**

Technical Eval.
• **Bullish** since 11/95
Rel. Strength Rank
(1 Lowest—99 Highest)
• **25**
Insider Activity
• **NA**

Recent Price • 15⅛
52 Wk Range • 19¼-9½
Yield • 0.8%
12-Mo. P/E • 13.0

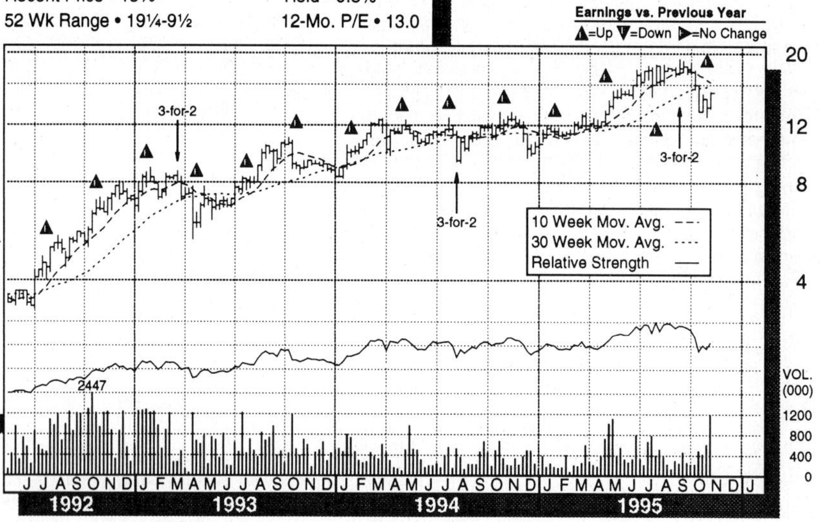

Business Profile - 09-NOV-95

This company is the third largest electronics distributor in the U.S., serving 19,000 customers with products from over 100 different manufacturers. The company has been aggressively expanding its presence in North America; two elements of this growth are its FutureStart total quality management program, and an increase in the value added services provided by Pioneer. The company believes that results will benefit from the continued development of new electronic technologies and products.

Operational Review - 09-NOV-95

Net sales rose 22% in fiscal 1996's first half, reflecting strong demand for electronic products and computer systems due to a rapid technology change in the electronic industry. Margins widened slightly on the higher volume, but results were penalized by an 80% increase in interest expense. After a 6.1% rise in equity earnings (Pioneer Technologies Group), net income was up 16% to $13,521,000 ($0.58 a share) from $11,614,000 ($0.51, as adjusted for the September 1995 three-for-two stock split).

Stock Performance - 03-NOV-95

In the past 30 trading days, PIOS's shares have declined 15%, compared to a 2% rise in the S&P 500. Average trading volume for the past five days was 235,280 shares, compared with the 40-day moving average of 95,233 shares.

Key Stock Statistics

Dividend Rate/Share	0.12	Shareholders	500
Shs. outstg. (M)	22.4	Market cap. (B)	$0.331
Avg. daily vol. (M)	0.182	Inst. holdings	70%
Tang. Bk. Value/Share	5.65	Insider holdings	NA
Beta	1.27		

Value of $10,000 invested 5 years ago: $ 67,517

Fiscal Year Ending Mar. 31

	1996	% Change	1995	% Change	1994	% Change
Revenues (Million $)						
1Q	224.7	22%	183.8	37%	134.5	31%
2Q	234.9	21%	194.4	42%	137.3	37%
3Q	—	—	212.4	42%	149.8	37%
4Q	—	—	241.5	52%	159.2	35%
Yr.	—	—	832.2	43%	580.8	35%
Income (Million $)						
1Q	6.82	14%	5.97	34%	4.47	46%
2Q	6.70	19%	5.65	18%	4.79	65%
3Q	—	—	6.13	25%	4.89	48%
4Q	—	—	7.27	31%	5.53	52%
Yr.	—	—	25.01	27%	19.68	52%
Earnings Per Share ($)						
1Q	0.29	12%	0.26	31%	0.20	22%
2Q	0.29	18%	0.25	18%	0.21	38%
3Q	—	—	0.27	25%	0.21	45%
4Q	—	—	0.32	31%	0.24	49%
Yr.	—	—	1.09	26%	0.87	38%

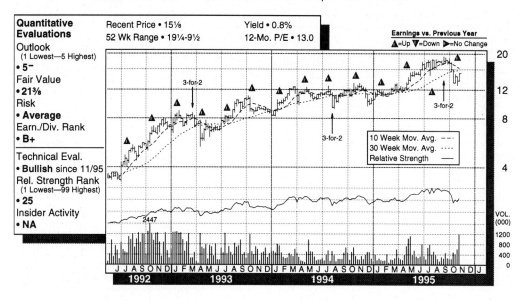

Next earnings report expected: mid January

Pioneer-Standard Electronics

Business Summary - 07-NOV-95

Pioneer-Standard Electronics, Inc. distributes industrial and end-user electronic products in the United States. Through a 50% owned subsidiary, Pioneer Technologies Group, Inc., it also distributes electronic products.

The company distributes a wide range of electronic components and computer products manufactured by other firms. The products are sold to value-added resellers, research laboratories, government agencies, and end users, such as manufacturing companies. The products the company offers are grouped into three basic categories: semiconductors, computer products, and passive and electromechanical components. Semiconductor products, which accounted for 37% of Pioneer's sales in fiscal 1995 (compared to 41% in 1994 and 37% in 1993), include microprocessors and memory devices. Computer products include mini and personal computers and disk drives; they accounted for 38% of the company's sales in fiscal 1995 (33%, 39%). Passive and electromechanical products accounted for 22% of sales in 1995 (24%, 21%), and consist of resistors, connectors, and other products.

The company and its affiliate, Pioneer Technologies Group, Inc. (a 50%-owned unconsolidated subsidiary), serve most of the major markets in the U.S., and have over 19,000 customers. In March 1989, the company gained a West Coast presence through the acquistion of California-based Compumech Electronics, Inc., which provides application engineering services and sells power conditioning equipment and uninterruptible power supplies. In December 1990, the company entered the southern California market with the acquisition of Lex Electronics USA, a distributor of electronic components. During 1991, it expanded its technical support and sales staff in California and plans to continue to expand there.

During the second quarter of 1992-93, the company forced conversion of all of its $13.2 million principal amount of 9% convertible subordinated debentures due 1998. A total of 1,025,305 shares plus $913,000 in cash were issued to retire the debentures.

Important Developments

Oct. '95—TelCom Semiconductor Inc. said Pioneer Technology was chosen to distribute its analog integrated circuits. Financial terms were not disclosed.
Sep. '95—A three-for-two stock split was effected on September 6, 1995. Separately, the company raised its quarterly dividend 29% with the September 1995 declaration.

Capitalization

Long Term Debt: $80,313,000 (9/95).

Per Share Data ($)

(Year Ended Mar. 31)

	1995	1994	1993	1992	1991	1990
Tangible Bk. Val.	5.65	4.60	3.82	3.11	2.87	2.46
Cash Flow	1.37	1.10	0.85	0.51	0.64	0.47
Earnings	1.09	0.87	0.63	0.29	0.45	0.31
Dividends	0.16	0.07	0.05	0.05	0.04	0.04
Payout Ratio	15%	8%	8%	16%	10%	13%
Cal. Yrs.	1994	1993	1992	1991	1990	1989
Prices - High	13⅛	11	8⅛	5¼	4½	3⅜
- Low	8¼	5⅜	3⅛	2⅝	2⅛	2⅛
P/E Ratio - High	12	13	13	18	10	11
- Low	8	6	5	9	5	7

Income Statement Analysis (Million $)

	1995	%Chg	1994	%Chg	1993	%Chg	1992
Revs.	832	43%	581	35%	430	19%	362
Oper. Inc.	50.0	36%	36.7	43%	25.7	56%	16.5
Depr.	6.2	18%	5.3	13%	4.7	13%	4.1
Int. Exp.	4.0	48%	2.7	-25%	3.6	-21%	4.5
Pretax Inc.	42.2	33%	31.7	59%	20.0	135%	8.5
Eff. Tax Rate	41%	—	38%	—	35%	—	38%
Net Inc.	25.0	27%	19.7	53%	12.9	142%	5.3

Balance Sheet & Other Fin. Data (Million $)

	1995	1994	1993	1992	1991	1990
Cash	9.6	5.9	1.9	1.9	2.5	3.5
Curr. Assets	274	178	136	116	114	114
Total Assets	327	220	172	151	146	145
Curr. Liab.	142	93.0	64.8	47.1	47.8	49.7
LT Debt	56.3	22.3	21.3	44.7	44.3	49.4
Common Eqty.	126	105	84.1	57.5	52.9	44.8
Total Cap.	185	127	107	104	99	95.0
Cap. Exp.	11.3	7.6	4.2	5.1	4.1	10.3
Cash Flow	31.2	29.9	17.6	9.5	11.8	8.6

Ratio Analysis

	1995	1994	1993	1992	1991	1990
Curr. Ratio	1.9	1.9	2.1	2.5	2.4	2.3
% LT Debt of Cap.	30.4	17.5	19.9	43.1	45.0	51.8
% Net Inc.of Revs.	3.0	3.4	3.0	1.5	2.4	1.8
% Ret. on Assets	9.1	10.0	7.3	3.6	5.7	4.1
% Ret. on Equity	21.8	20.9	16.9	9.6	16.9	13.6

Dividend Data —Cash has been paid each year since 1965. A "poison pill" rights plan was adopted in 1989.

Amt. of Div. $	Date Decl.	Ex-Div. Date	Stock of Record	Payment Date
0.030	Dec. 21	Dec. 28	Jan. 04	Feb. 01 '95
0.035	Mar. 15	Mar. 30	Apr. 05	May. 01 '95
0.035	Jun. 21	Jun. 30	Jul. 05	Aug. 01 '95
3-for-2	Jul. 25	Sep. 07	Aug. 16	Sep. 06 '95
0.030	Sep. 21	Oct. 02	Oct. 04	Nov. 01 '95

Data as orig. reptd.; bef. results of disc. opers. and/or spec. items. Per share data adj. for stk. divs. as of ex-div. date. E-Estimated. NA-Not Available. NM-Not Meaningful. NR-Not Ranked.

Tel—(216) 587-3600. **Chrmn**—P. B. Heller Jr. **Pres & CEO**—J. L. Bayman. **Secy**—W. A. Papenbrock. **VP, Treas, Asst Secy & Investor Contact**—John V. Goodger. **Dirs**—J. L. Bayman, F. A. Downey, V. Gelb, G. E. Heffern, P. B. Heller Jr., A. Rhein, E. Z. Singer, T. C. Sullivan, K. E. Ware. **Transfer Agent & Registrar**—KeyCorp Shareholder Services Inc., Cleveland. **Incorporated** in Ohio in 1963. **Empl**-1,379. **S&P Analyst:** Ronald J. Gross

STANDARD & POOR'S
STOCK REPORTS

Piper Jaffray

NYSE Symbol **PJC**
In S&P SmallCap 600

17-SEP-95 **Industry:** Securities

Summary: This major securities firm, based in Minneapolis, offers individual investors and businesses a full array of investment services through 77 branch offices in 17 states.

Quantitative Evaluations
Outlook (1 Lowest—5 Highest) • **NA**
Fair Value • **NA**
Risk • **Average**
Earn./Div. Rank • **B+**

Technical Eval. • **Bearish** since 9/95
Rel. Strength Rank (1 Lowest—99 Highest) • **22**
Insider Activity • **NA**

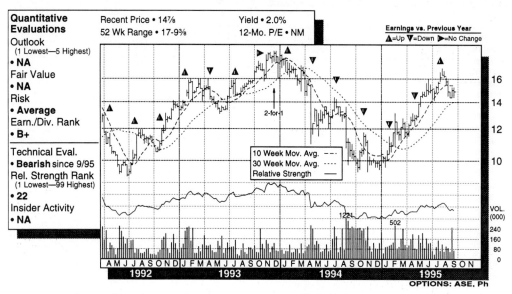

Recent Price • 14⅞ Yield • 2.0%
52 Wk Range • 17-9⅜ 12-Mo. P/E • NM

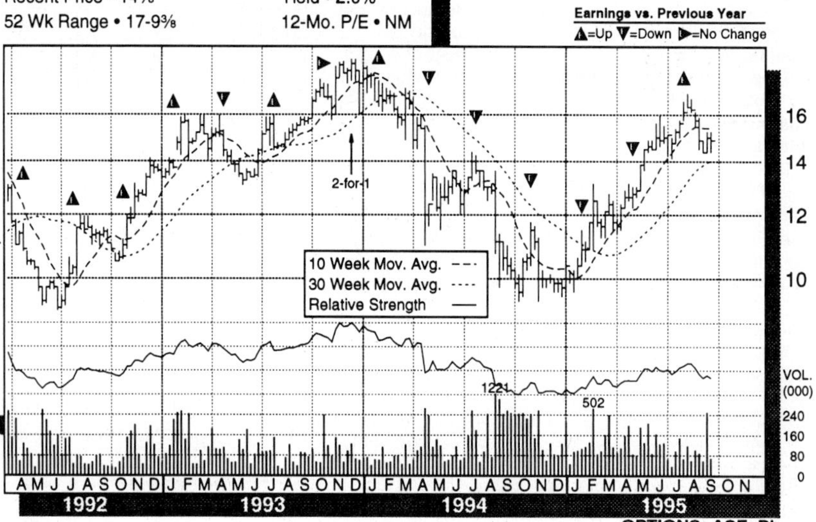

OPTIONS: ASE, Ph

Business Profile - 15-SEP-95

Earnings in the first nine months of fiscal 1995 were adversely affected by charges for the proposed settlement of litigation arising from derivative-related losses in one of PJC's mutual funds. While investment banking and commission revenues remain weak, shares of PJC and other securities firms have rebounded recently, due to a more favorable interest rate environment and the resulting bond market rally. Investors could see a turnaround in earnings if interest rates continue to trend downward.

Operational Review - 15-SEP-95

Revenues in the nine months ended June 30, 1995, fell slightly, year to year, as higher profits on principal transactions were outweighed by lower commissions and investment banking revenues. Following 25% higher expenses (including a $56,090,000 litigation charge), a pretax loss contrasted with pretax income. After a tax benefit of $11,994,000, against taxes at 39.0%, there was a loss of $19,529,000 ($1.13 a share, on fewer shares), versus income of $21,714,000 ($1.20).

Stock Performance - 15-SEP-95

In the past 30 trading days, PJC's shares have declined 9%, compared to a 4% rise in the S&P 500. Average trading volume for the past five days was 13,020 shares, compared with the 40-day moving average of 22,315 shares.

Key Stock Statistics

Dividend Rate/Share	0.30	Shareholders	1,000
Shs. outstg. (M)	17.4	Market cap. (B)	$0.259
Avg. daily vol. (M)	0.028	Inst. holdings	23%
Tang. Bk. Value/Share	8.65	Insider holdings	NA
Beta	1.60		

Value of $10,000 invested 5 years ago: $ 47,374

Fiscal Year Ending Sep. 30

	1995	% Change	1994	% Change	1993	% Change
Revenues (Million $)						
1Q	92.50	-13%	106.2	18%	89.90	19%
2Q	97.86	-5%	102.8	-5%	108.1	8%
3Q	109.2	19%	91.80	-7%	98.92	19%
4Q	—	—	96.66	-15%	113.8	12%
Yr.	—	—	397.5	-3%	410.7	14%
Income (Million $)						
1Q	4.65	-53%	9.98	12%	8.93	21%
2Q	-37.27	NM	6.90	-38%	11.19	4%
3Q	13.09	170%	4.84	-46%	9.03	9%
4Q	—	—	3.56	-70%	11.84	7%
Yr.	—	—	25.28	-38%	40.99	9%
Earnings Per Share ($)						
1Q	0.27	-51%	0.55	6%	0.52	18%
2Q	-2.17	NM	0.38	-40%	0.63	NM
3Q	0.73	170%	0.27	-46%	0.50	5%
4Q	—	—	0.20	-69%	0.65	NM
Yr.	—	—	1.41	-38%	2.28	4%

Next earnings report expected: early November

Piper Jaffray

Business Summary - 15-SEP-95

Piper Jaffray Companies Inc. is a Minneapolis-based holding company that offers individual investor, investment banking and investment management services through various subsidiaries. Contributions to revenues in recent fiscal years:

	1994	1993	1992
Commissions	37%	31%	29%
Principal transactions	26%	23%	24%
Investment banking	15%	28%	28%
Asset management	13%	10%	8%
Interest	6%	5%	5%
Other	3%	3%	6%

The principal subsidiary, Piper Jaffray Inc., provides individual and capital markets services. Its individual investor services are provided through 77 retail sales offices in 17 Midwest, Mountain, Southwest and Pacific Coast states. PJC's capital markets businesses, including its corporate and public finance departments and institutional sales, trading and research operations, are conducted from its head office in Minneapolis and offices in San Francisco, Seattle, Portland, Los Angeles, Kansas City, St. Louis, Denver, Des Moines, Lincoln, Great Falls, Spokane, Milwaukee and London. Piper Jaffray is among the leaders in several markets including retail brokerage in the northwest quadrant of the U.S., investment banking in selected industries, public finance, and over-the-counter trading of equity securities.

PJC's principal investment management subsidiary, Piper Capital Management Inc., is the investment adviser to 22 closed-end and 12 open-end mutual funds, the Piper Institutional Funds series of three open-end funds, and the Piper Global Funds with one global open-end fund. In fiscal 1994, Piper Capital introduced two new funds and now has a total of 38 closed and open-end funds. From commencement of operations in 1985, Piper Capital's total assets under management had grown to about $11.6 billion at September 30, 1994. Piper Trust Co., established in 1989, provides trust services to individuals and institutions. Piper Trust had about $800 million in client assets at September 30, 1994.

Important Developments

Sep. '95—PJC announced that it had reached an agreement in principle to settle, for $1.95 million, a class action litigation brought on the behalf of purchasers of PJC common stock during the period of May 12, 1993, through August 24, 1994. The settlement will be comprised of a combination of $450,000 in cash, $700,000 in PJC common stock to be delivered on the effective date of the settlement, and a note for $800,000 to be paid 12 months after the settlement date.

Capitalization

Long Term Debt: None (6/95).

Per Share Data ($) (Year Ended Sep. 30)

	1994	1993	1992	1991	1990	1989
Tangible Bk. Val.	9.76	9.01	7.05	5.21	4.31	4.82
Cash Flow	NA	NA	NA	NA	NA	NA
Earnings	1.41	2.29	2.21	1.16	0.63	0.73
Dividends	0.70	0.50	0.35	0.28	1.25	0.16
Payout Ratio	50%	22%	16%	24%	198%	22%
Prices - High	18⅜	15½	15½	13⅞	5½	7⅜
- Low	9⅜	9⅛	9⅛	4⅛	3⅛	4
P/E Ratio - High	13	7	7	12	9	10
- Low	7	4	4	4	5	5

Income Statement Analysis (Million $)

	1994	%Chg	1993	%Chg	1992	%Chg	1991
Commissions	148	14%	129	25%	103	26%	82.3
Int. Inc.	24.8	30%	19.1	6%	18.0	NM	17.9
Total Revs.	398	-3%	411	14%	360	34%	268
Int. Exp.	7.2	52%	4.8	20%	4.0	-29%	5.6
Pretax Inc.	40.1	-41%	68.3	11%	61.4	99%	30.8
Eff. Tax Rate	37%	—	40%	—	39%	—	37%
Net Inc.	25.3	-38%	41.0	9%	37.5	94%	19.3

Balance Sheet & Other Fin. Data (Million $)

	1994	1993	1992	1991	1990	1989
Total Assets	584	535	481	615	592	539
Cash Items	12.1	19.9	14.0	17.3	19.0	NA
Receivables	424	367	286	209	169	NA
Secs. Owned	49.1	77.8	116	82.3	83.5	NA
Sec. Borrowed	108	45.6	57.3	46.0	82.5	NA
Due Brokers & Cust.	193	203	179	132	105	NA
Other Liabs.	111	122	108	77.3	54.3	NA
Capitalization:						
Debt	4.0	7.0	16.0	272	279	NA
Equity	168	158	120	87.5	71.3	77.5
Total	172	164	136	360	350	NA

Ratio Analysis

	1994	1993	1992	1991	1990	1989
% Ret. on Revs.	6.4	10.0	10.4	7.2	5.1	6.0
% Ret. on Assets	4.5	8.1	6.9	3.2	1.8	2.5
% Ret. on Equity	15.5	29.4	36.1	24.3	13.8	16.1

Dividend Data —In July 1991, PJC revised its dividend payment policy so that regular quarterly dividends are now paid in March, June, September and December; previously, dividends were paid on a semiannual basis, and an extra dividend in January provided a total payout of 25%-30% of the preceding year's earnings.

Amt. of Div. $	Date Decl.	Ex-Div. Date	Stock of Record	Payment Date
0.075	Nov. 08	Nov. 16	Nov. 22	Dec. 06 '94
0.075	Jan. 25	Feb. 22	Feb. 28	Mar. 14 '95
0.075	Apr. 19	May. 17	May. 23	Jun. 06 '95
0.075	Jul. 19	Aug. 18	Aug. 22	Sep. 05 '95

Data as orig. reptd.; bef. results of disc opers. and/or spec. items. Per share data adj. for stk. divs. as of ex-div. date. E-Estimated. NA-Not Available. NM-Not Meaningful. NR-Not Ranked.

Office—Piper Jaffray Tower, 222 South Ninth St., Minneapolis, MN 55402-3804. **Tel**—(612) 342-6000. **Chrmn & CEO**—A. L. Piper. **Pres & COO**—W. H. Ellis. **Secy**—D. E. Rosedahl. **CFO**—D. K. Roesler. **VP-Investor Contact**—Marge Proell (612) 342-6084. **Dirs**—E. N. Bennett, K. M. Bohn, R. W. Burnet, D. P. Crosby, W. H. Ellis, K. Halbreich, D. L. Lastavich, R. J. Magnuson, J. L. McElroy, Jr., G. M. Petrucci, A. L. Piper, R. S. Slifka, D. Stanley, D. V. Steenson, R. J. Stream. **Transfer Agent & Registrar**—Norwest Bank Minnesota, South St. Paul. **Incorporated** in Delaware in 1974. **Empl-** 2,878. **S&P Analyst:** Brad Ohlmuller

STANDARD & POOR'S

STOCK REPORTS

Plains Resources

ASE Symbol **PLX**
In S&P SmallCap 600

12-OCT-95 **Industry:** Oil and Gas

Summary: This company acquires, explores for, develops and produces crude oil and natural gas primarily in the U.S.

Quantitative Evaluations

Outlook (1 Lowest—5 Highest) • **NA**
Fair Value • **NA**
Risk • **Average**
Earn./Div. Rank • **C**

Technical Eval. • **Bearish** since 4/95
Rel. Strength Rank (1 Lowest—99 Highest) • **12**
Insider Activity • **NA**

Recent Price • 7⅝
52 Wk Range • 11-5⅜
Yield • Nil
12-Mo. P/E • 48.0

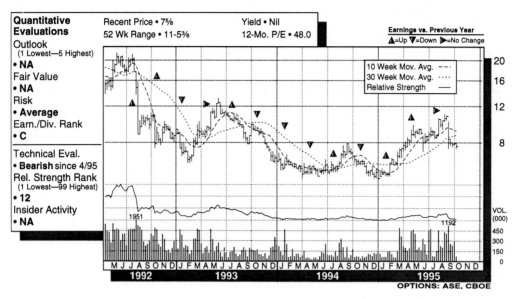

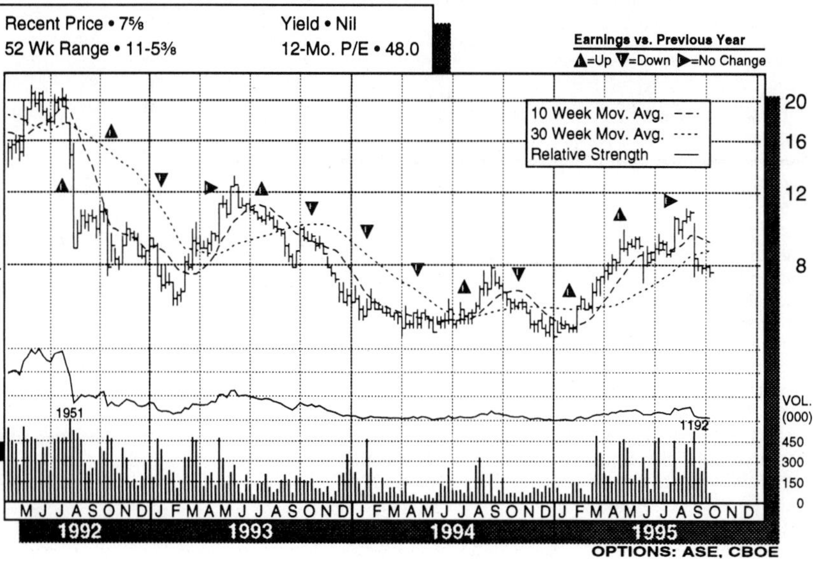

OPTIONS: ASE, CBOE

Business Profile - 11-OCT-95

This company acquires, explores for, develops and produces crude oil and natural gas. Through subsidiaries, it is engaged in the downstream activities of marketing, transportation, storage, and terminalling of crude oil. Plains has steadily increased its proved oil and natural gas reserves, from 0.6 million BOE at December 31, 1981, to 70 million BOE at December 31, 1994.

Operational Review - 12-OCT-95

Total revenues in the six months ended June 30, 1995, rose 60% year to year, reflecting increased crude oil marketing, transportation storage and terminalling revenues, as well as increased oil production and prices, which outweighed lower natural gas production and prices. Net income of $1,233,000 ($0.08 a share, on 36% more average shares outstanding) replaced a loss of $428,000 ($0.04).

Stock Performance - 06-OCT-95

In the past 30 trading days, PLX's shares have declined 27%, compared to a 4% rise in the S&P 500. Average trading volume for the past five days was 13,600 shares, compared with the 40-day moving average of 78,474 shares.

Key Stock Statistics

Dividend Rate/Share	Nil	Shareholders	1,900
Shs. outstg. (M)	15.3	Market cap. (B)	$0.114
Avg. daily vol. (M)	0.038	Inst. holdings	55%
Tang. Bk. Value/Share	4.48	Insider holdings	NA
Beta	0.37		

Value of $10,000 invested 5 years ago: $ 12,945

Fiscal Year Ending Dec. 31

	1995	% Change	1994	% Change	1993	% Change
Revenues (Million $)						
1Q	93.65	85%	50.58	14%	44.20	84%
2Q	95.26	42%	67.20	40%	48.00	63%
3Q	—	—	66.22	37%	48.39	48%
4Q	—	—	72.69	54%	47.30	2%
Yr.	—	—	256.7	38%	186.0	40%
Income (Million $)						
1Q	0.32	NM	-1.18	NM	-0.85	NM
2Q	0.91	21%	0.75	142%	0.31	NM
3Q	—	—	0.21	-51%	0.43	-60%
4Q	—	—	0.79	NM	-20.09	NM
Yr.	—	—	0.57	NM	-20.20	NM
Earnings Per Share ($)						
1Q	0.02	NM	-0.10	NM	-0.08	NM
2Q	0.06	NM	0.06	NM	0.02	NM
3Q	—	—	0.02	-33%	0.03	-67%
4Q	—	—	0.07	NM	-1.74	NM
Yr.	—	—	0.04	NM	-1.77	NM

Next earnings report expected: early November

Plains Resources

Business Summary - 12-OCT-95

Plains Resources Inc. is engaged in the acquisition, exploration, development and production of crude oil and natural gas and the marketing, transportation, storage and terminalling of crude oil. Its oil and natural gas producing activities are concentrated in California, Florida, the Gulf Coast areas of Texas and Louisiana, and Utah. Downstream activities are concentrated in Oklahoma, Kansas, Texas and Louisiana. The number of producing wells at recent year-ends was:

	1994	1993	1992	1991
Gross	453	462	355	216
Net	413	387	307	74

Proved reserves at December 31, 1994, were estimated at 61,459,000 bbl. of oil and 51,009,000 Mcf of gas, versus 38,810,000 bbl. and 49,397,000 Mcf a year earlier.

At the end of 1994, Plains had working interests in 381 gross (378 net) active oil wells and 72 gross (35 net) producing gas wells. Drilling activities in 1994 resulted in 1 gross (1.00 net) development oil wells. The company held 44,107 gross (33,558 net) developed acres and 163,277 gross (134,531 net) undeveloped acres at 1994 year-end, not including undeveloped land in Pakistan and Australia. About 33% of gross developed acres were in Utah and 52% of gross undeveloped acres were in Florida. In 1994, Plains produced 3,835,000 bbl. of crude oil and natural gas liquids (3,556,000 in 1993) and 3,569,000 Mcf of natural gas (4,176,000). Chevron and Phibro Energy accounted for 16% and 19%, respectively, of total revenues in 1994.

In December 1993, the company completed construction on the first phase of an above-ground crude oil storage and terminalling facility in Cushing, Okla. Total cost of the first phase was $30.6 million.

Important Developments

Sep. '95—The company called for the redemption of all 48,070 outstanding shares of its $1.30 cumulative convertible preferred stock on October 31, 1995. Each share of the preferred stock is convertible into approximately 0.89 share of PLX common stock. All unconverted shares will be redeemed for $10 per share plus unpaid and accrued dividends of $0.325 a share.

Capitalization

Long Term Debt: $156,996,000 (6/95).
$1.30 Cum. Conv. Pfd. Stock: 48,070 shs. ($10 liq. pref.); ea. conv. into com. at $11.25 a sh.

Per Share Data ($) (Year Ended Dec. 31)

	1994	1993	1992	1991	1990	1989
Tangible Bk. Val.	3.97	3.83	5.58	3.67	4.54	4.49
Cash Flow	1.45	-0.38	0.78	-0.71	0.85	1.25
Earnings	0.04	-1.77	-0.32	-1.59	-0.36	-0.10
Dividends	Nil	Nil	Nil	Nil	Nil	Nil
Payout Ratio	Nil	Nil	Nil	Nil	Nil	Nil
Prices - High	8	13⅛	21¾	30¾	8⅜	7¾
- Low	5⅜	6⅜	7½	4⅞	5⅜	3⅛
P/E Ratio - High	NM	NM	NM	NM	NM	NM
- Low	NM	NM	NM	NM	NM	NM

Income Statement Analysis (Million $)

	1994	%Chg	1993	%Chg	1992	%Chg	1991
Revs.	256	38%	186	41%	132	67%	79.3
Oper. Inc.	29.2	NM	4.4	-68%	13.6	NM	-2.6
Depr. Depl. & Amort.	16.3	1%	16.1	39%	11.6	62%	7.2
Int. Exp.	15.3	33%	11.5	128%	5.0	32%	3.8
Pretax Inc.	0.6	NM	-20.2	NM	-3.3	NM	-12.8
Eff. Tax Rate	Nil	—	NM	—	NM	—	NM
Net Inc.	0.6	NM	-20.2	NM	-3.3	NM	-12.9

Balance Sheet & Other Fin. Data (Million $)

	1994	1993	1992	1991	1990	1989
Cash	2.8	4.9	25.1	3.4	2.4	2.4
Curr. Assets	41.7	35.1	46.3	16.7	11.8	6.6
Total Assets	267	237	199	96.8	94.8	69.3
Curr. Liab.	46.2	49.1	33.3	20.1	22.4	12.4
LT Debt	145	136	100	42.2	36.5	28.8
Common Eqty.	46.0	44.3	62.6	33.3	33.0	22.4
Total Cap.	212	181	163	76.3	70.8	52.9
Cap. Exp.	41.7	84.1	78.4	33.9	29.2	22.3
Cash Flow	16.9	-4.3	8.2	-5.8	5.4	5.3

Ratio Analysis

	1994	1993	1992	1991	1990	1989
Curr. Ratio	0.9	0.7	1.4	0.8	0.5	0.5
% LT Debt of Cap.	68.3	75.1	61.2	55.3	51.5	54.5
% Ret. on Assets	0.2	NM	NM	NM	NM	0.2
% Ret. on Equity	1.3	NM	NM	NM	NM	NM

Dividend Data —No cash has been paid on the common. A one-for-five reverse stock split was effected in 1990.

Data as orig. reptd.; bef. results of disc opers. and/or spec. items. Per share data adj. for stk. divs. as of ex-div. date. E-Estimated. NA-Not Available. NM-Not Meaningful. NR-Not Ranked.

Office—1600 Smith St., Suite 1500, Houston, TX 77002. **Tel**—(713) 654-1414. **Chrmn**—D. M. Krausse. **Pres & CEO**—G. L. Armstrong. **VP, CFO, Treas & Investor Contact**—Phillip D. Kramer. **VP & Secy**—M. R. Patterson. **Dirs**—G. L. Armstrong, R. A. Bezuch, T. H. Delimitros, W. H. Hitchcock, D. M. Krausse, D. I. Obrow, G. F. Rome, R. V. Sinnott, J. T. Symonds. **Transfer Agent & Registrar**—Liberty National Bank & Trust Co., Oklahoma City. **Incorporated** in Delaware in 1976. **Empl**-217. **S&P Analyst:** N. Rosenberg

STANDARD & POOR'S

STOCK REPORTS

PLATINUM technology

NASDAQ Symbol **PLAT**
In S&P SmallCap 600

08-OCT-95 **Industry:** Data Processing

Summary: PLAT develops, markets and supports software and related educational programs and publications for use with DB2, IBM's MVS mainframe relational database management system.

S&P Opinion: Accumulate (★★★★)

Recent Price • 18⅞
52 Wk Range • 26-13½
Yield • Nil
12-Mo. P/E • NM

Quantitative Evaluations

Outlook (1 Lowest—5 Highest)
• **NA**
Fair Value
• **NA**
Risk
• **High**
Earn./Div. Rank
• **NR**

Technical Eval.
• **Bullish** since 7/95
Rel. Strength Rank (1 Lowest—99 Highest)
• **7**
Insider Activity
• **NA**

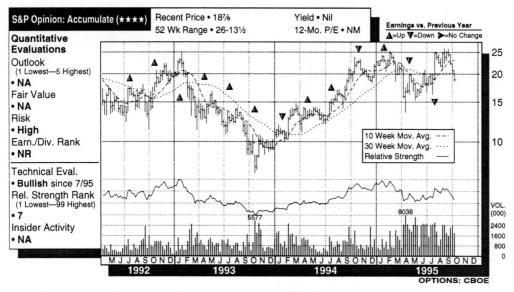

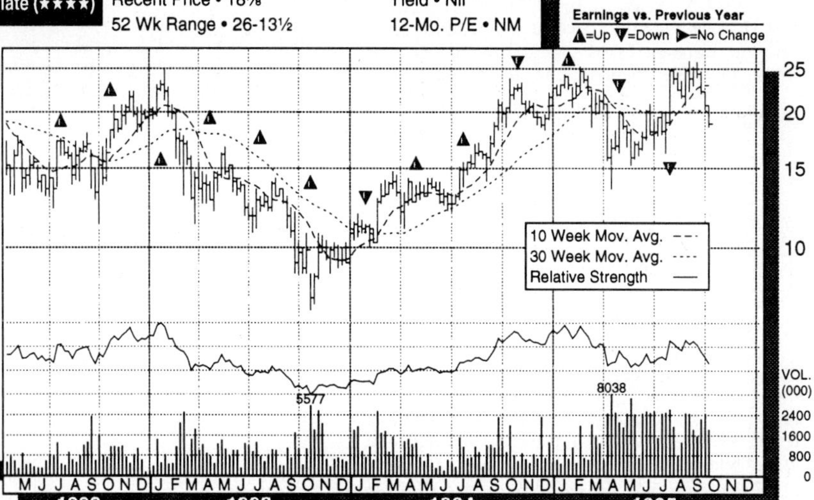

OPTIONS: CBOE

Overview - 05-OCT-95

With its string of acquisitions completed, PLAT has become a $300 million revenue company. We expect revenue growth will continue to exceed 20% annually. Fundamentals remain strong, with the company reporting strong demand for DB2 and client-server products. International sales have increased as a percentage of revenues, a trend that is expected to continue. First half results were penalized by $21 million (pre-tax) in merger related charges, a portion of which was not tax deductable. Additional merger related costs are expected to be recorded in the third quarter. To take advantage of its substantial product offerings, PLAT will embark on an aggressive sales program later in the year. Related costs could restrict earnings growth in the near term.

Valuation - 22-SEP-95

The shares have rebounded after a sharp drop caused by unfounded concerns over the acquisition of Trinzic Corp. The addition of Trinzic and other 13 other companies during the past 20 months has placed PLAT in an enviable position within the open systems management and data warehousing niches. Only the pending Computer Associates/Legent combination (expected to close by year-end) can challange PLAT's broad base of relational and open architecture technology. The synergies from PLAT's one-stop shopping coupled with an international salesforce, a luxury that many of its acquired firms could not support, presents an exciting picture for future growth.

Key Stock Statistics

S&P EPS Est. 1995	-0.31	Tang. Bk. Value/Share	4.14
P/E on S&P Est. 1995	NM	Beta	0.37
S&P EPS Est. 1996	1.15	Shareholders	200
Dividend Rate/Share	Nil	Market cap. (B)	$0.641
Shs. outstg. (M)	33.9	Inst. holdings	49%
Avg. daily vol. (M)	0.414	Insider holdings	NA

Value of $10,000 invested 5 years ago: NA

Fiscal Year Ending Dec. 31

	1995	% Change	1994	% Change	1993	% Change
Revenues (Million $)						
1Q	26.61	60%	16.61	40%	11.90	55%
2Q	36.41	64%	22.19	45%	15.34	32%
3Q	—	—	23.37	61%	14.50	12%
4Q	—	—	33.58	65%	20.38	21%
Yr.	—	—	95.75	54%	62.17	27%
Income (Million $)						
1Q	-14.70	NM	1.69	34%	1.26	58%
2Q	-1.27	NM	3.20	46%	2.19	15%
3Q	—	—	-8.49	NM	2.53	4%
4Q	—	—	0.40	NM	-2.98	NM
Yr.	—	—	-3.20	NM	3.00	-68%
Earnings Per Share ($)						
1Q	-0.61	NM	0.08	33%	0.06	50%
2Q	-0.05	NM	0.15	50%	0.10	11%
3Q	E0.15	NM	-0.38	NM	0.12	9%
4Q	E0.20	NM	0.02	NM	-0.14	NM
Yr.	E-0.31	NM	-0.16	NM	0.14	-67%

Next earnings report expected: mid October

PLATINUM technology

Business Summary - 28-JUN-95

PLATINUM technology, inc. develops, markets and supports an integrated line of system software products and educational programs and publications for use with DB2, IBM's MVS mainframe relational database management system. In 1993, it moved to expand its products to include software products for non-mainframe client/server (c/s) and distributed systems. Its products and services enable data center personnel of large organizations to operate their mainframes and central databases, as well as PCs, minicomputers and networks, more efficiently.

The company believes that the role of the mainframe will evolve in many computing environments into that of a central repository for data and an enterprise server in a c/s architecture. PLAT also believes that non-mainframe client server relational database management systems will continue to increase in importance as users move toward distributed database management. Its strategy is to provide continued support of DB2 while expanding its products to include software that supports non-mainframe c/s relational database management systems and that allows for movement and management of data across distributed environments. Software accounted for 63% and 61% of total revenues in 1994 and 1993, respectively.

The PLATINUM Open Enterprise Management System (P.O.E.M.S.) lets clients manage, distribute and access misson-critical data anywhere on MVS, UNIX and Windows-based systems, as well as on MVS AS/400, OS/2 and others. P.O.E.M.S. helps information systems professionals manage open enterprise environments through a single point of control.

PLAT is also involved with data warehousing construction, a process that stores data but allows users full access to periodically consolidate historical data for making business decisions without jeopardizing the performance of mission-critical operations. The company believes that following its acquisition of Trinzic Corp., it will be the only software concern able to offer comprehensive data warehousing solutions.

Important Developments

May '95—PLAT agreed to acquire Houston-based Software Interfaces Inc. for about $20 million in stock, adding to its warehousing offerings. Earlier, in March, it agreed to purchase Trinzic Corp. for about $150 million of stock. The addition of Trinzic, a provider of application development software tools (1994 sales of $44 million) will broaden the company's data warehousing offerings and strengthen its move into the open enterprise systems management market.

Capitalization

Long Term Debt: None (3/95).
Options: To buy 5,078,958 shs. at $0.0025 to $23.50 ea. (12/94).

Per Share Data ($)

(Year Ended Dec. 31)

	1994	1993	1992	1991	1990	1989
Tangible Bk. Val.	5.01	3.46	3.13	2.58	-1.53	NA
Cash Flow	-0.07	0.18	0.44	0.26	0.15	0.02
Earnings	-0.16	0.14	0.43	0.25	0.15	0.02
Dividends	Nil	Nil	Nil	Nil	Nil	Nil
Payout Ratio	Nil	Nil	Nil	Nil	Nil	Nil
Prices - High	23¾	25	25¼	23½	NA	NA
- Low	10	7¼	11¼	7½	NA	NA
P/E Ratio - High	NM	NM	59	94	NA	NA
- Low	NM	NM	26	30	NA	NA

Income Statement Analysis (Million $)

	1994	%Chg	1993	%Chg	1992	%Chg	1991
Revs.	95.7	54%	62.2	27%	49.0	70%	28.8
Oper. Inc.	22.9	58%	14.5	16%	12.5	74%	7.2
Depr.	1.8	112%	0.8	163%	0.3	129%	0.1
Int. Exp.	Nil	—	Nil	—	Nil	—	Nil
Pretax Inc.	-1.2	NM	6.9	-51%	14.2	80%	7.9
Eff. Tax Rate	NM	—	56%	—	34%	—	36%
Net Inc.	-3.2	NM	3.0	-68%	9.3	83%	5.1

Balance Sheet & Other Fin. Data (Million $)

	1994	1993	1992	1991	1990	1989
Cash	79.4	28.7	21.5	25.1	2.0	0.5
Curr. Assets	124	58.7	43.1	39.1	8.1	2.8
Total Assets	190	102	77.8	55.7	8.9	2.9
Curr. Liab.	45.4	26.5	15.3	8.0	4.6	1.4
LT Debt	8.4	2.0	Nil	Nil	Nil	Nil
Common Eqty.	131	68.4	61.0	46.6	-10.9	1.6
Total Cap.	140	73.7	62.5	47.7	4.3	1.6
Cap. Exp.	8.3	2.8	2.2	0.7	0.2	0.1
Cash Flow	-1.4	3.8	9.7	5.2	2.3	0.3

Ratio Analysis

	1994	1993	1992	1991	1990	1989
Curr. Ratio	2.7	2.2	2.8	4.9	1.8	2.0
% LT Debt of Cap.	6.0	2.7	Nil	Nil	Nil	Nil
% Net Inc.of Revs.	NM	4.8	19.1	17.7	14.8	3.6
% Ret. on Assets	NM	3.3	13.6	13.0	38.0	12.5
% Ret. on Equity	NM	4.6	16.8	NM	NM	28.5

Dividend Data —The company has never paid a cash dividend.

Data as orig. reptd.; bef. results of disc. opers. and/or spec. items. Per share data adj. for stk. divs. as of ex-div. date. E-Estimated. NA-Not Available. NM-Not Meaningful. NR-Not Ranked.

Office—1815 South Meyers Rd., Oakbrook Terrace, IL 60181. **Tel**—(708) 620-5000. **Chrmn, Pres & CEO**—A. J. Filipowski. **EVP & COO**—P. L. Humenansky. **CFO, Secy, Treas & Investor Contact**—Michael P. Cullinane. **Dirs**—C. G. Cowell, J. E. Cowie, M. P. Cullinane, S. D. Devick, A. J. Filipowski, G. Fulgoni, P. L. Humenansky. **Transfer Agent & Registrar**—Harris Trust & Savings Bank, Chicago. **Incorporated** in Delaware in 1987. **Empl-** 613. **S&P Analyst:** Steven A. Jaworski

STANDARD & POOR'S

STOCK REPORTS

Plexus Corp.

NASDAQ Symbol **PLXS**
In S&P SmallCap 600

14-NOV-95 **Industry:** Electronics/Electric

Summary: This company provides contract design, manufacturing, and testing of electronic products.

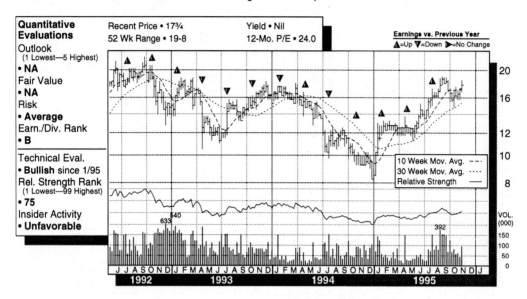

Quantitative Evaluations
Outlook
(1 Lowest—5 Highest)
• **NA**
Fair Value
• **NA**
Risk
• **Average**
Earn./Div. Rank
• **B**

Technical Eval.
• **Bullish** since 1/95
Rel. Strength Rank
(1 Lowest—99 Highest)
• **75**
Insider Activity
• **Unfavorable**

Recent Price • 17¾
52 Wk Range • 19-8
Yield • Nil
12-Mo. P/E • 24.0

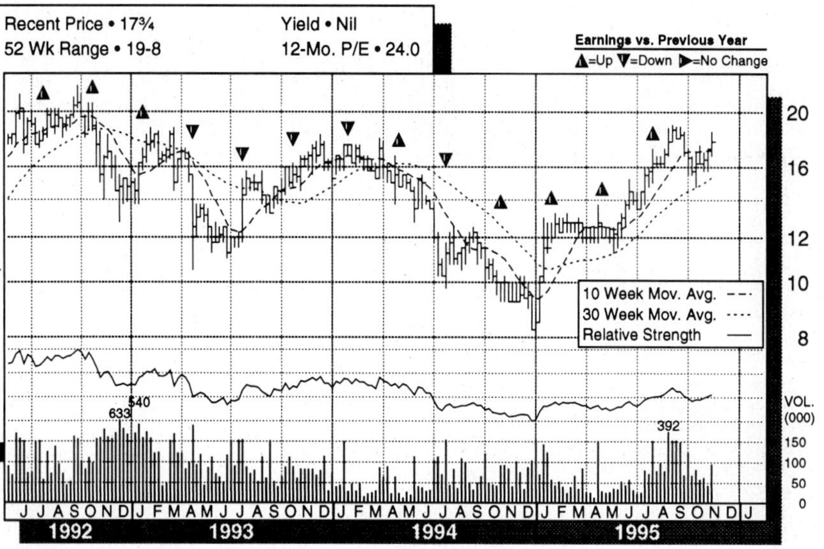

Business Profile - 13-NOV-95

Plexus provides contract electronics manufacturing and product testing services to major corporations. In 1994, the company sold its services to about 94 customers, with its two largest, IBM and GE, accounting for over 50% of revenues. Recent emphasis has been on pursuing new manufacturing relationships, as the company seeks to reduce its dependence on IBM and GE. Management believes that the electronics manufacturing services segment will continue to grow rapidly.

Operational Review - 14-NOV-95

Revenues rose 20% year to year in the first nine months of fiscal 1995, reflecting new strategic relationships, as well as a strong electronics manufacturing services sector. Margins widened on the higher volume, and net income more than doubled, to $4,188,000 ($0.59 a share, on 10% more shares) from $2,031,000 ($0.32). The company expects continued revenue growth and margin improvement as production commences on additional new programs.

Stock Performance - 10-NOV-95

In the past 30 trading days, PLXS's shares have increased 7%, compared to a 1% rise in the S&P 500. Average trading volume for the past five days was 18,640 shares, compared with the 40-day moving average of 14,633 shares.

Key Stock Statistics

Dividend Rate/Share	Nil	Shareholders	1,100
Shs. outstg. (M)	6.5	Market cap. (B)	$0.112
Avg. daily vol. (M)	0.013	Inst. holdings	21%
Tang. Bk. Value/Share	5.96	Insider holdings	NA
Beta	0.99		

Value of $10,000 invested 5 years ago: $ 39,444

Fiscal Year Ending Sep. 30

	1995	% Change	1994	% Change	1993	% Change
Revenues (Million $)						
1Q	65.34	17%	55.94	33%	42.10	14%
2Q	69.38	13%	61.32	68%	36.58	-6%
3Q	72.35	32%	55.00	41%	38.97	-6%
4Q	—	—	70.21	67%	41.95	4%
Yr.	—	—	242.5	52%	159.6	1%
Income (Million $)						
1Q	0.90	29%	0.70	-42%	1.21	21%
2Q	1.47	44%	1.02	NM	0.29	-73%
3Q	1.82	NM	0.30	-60%	0.75	-46%
4Q	—	—	1.03	NM	0.32	-80%
Yr.	—	—	3.06	19%	2.57	-49%
Earnings Per Share ($)						
1Q	0.13	18%	0.11	-42%	0.19	19%
2Q	0.21	31%	0.16	NM	0.05	-71%
3Q	0.26	NM	0.05	-58%	0.12	-45%
4Q	—	—	0.15	NM	0.05	-80%
Yr.	—	—	0.46	15%	0.40	-50%

Next earnings report expected: late November

Plexus Corp.

Business Summary - 14-NOV-95

Plexus Corp., through its wholly owned subsidiaries, provides services related to the design of electronic components and assemblies; the manufacture, programming and testing of such assemblies; and the design and manufacture of related test equipment. Design and production services are provided under various arrangements and, other than test equipment products, Plexus does not design or manufacture its own proprietary products.

Designed and manufactured products include printed circuit boards, power supplies, telecommunications terminals, microprocessor-based equipment, test equipment, electronic meters and intelligent burn-in chambers. These products are used in a wide variety of goods, including computers, telecommunications equipment, production control equipment, medical equipment, word processing equipment and automobiles.

Product design and engineering services provided by Plexus include software development, circuit design, printed circuit board layout and packaging design. Design services provide customers with a product capable of performing an intended function and manufactured in an efficient and economical manner. The company's technologies involve the design of electronic systems, including printed circuit boards, and the arrangement of electronic components thereon, and the development and/or programming of the application software necessary to control the functions of those components.

Plexus manufactures nonproprietary electronic products and assemblies for use in a wide variety of industries and applications. Assembly processes involve the fabrication of products from components manufactured to specification by others. Plexus purchases electronic components such as memory chips, microprocessing units, integrated circuits, resistors, capacitors, transformers, switches, wire and related items from various manufacturers and distributors.

Plexus also makes test equipment used for testing customers' products. Test equipment includes functional fixtures for testing printed circuit assemblies; in-circuit component measurement testers; and intelligent burn-in chambers, which temperature-cycle products under load.

During fiscal 1994, the company' services were sold to approximately 94 customers, including IBM, which accounted for 39% of total sales (versus 37% the year before), and General Electric, which accounted for 16% (19%).

Capitalization

Long Term Debt: $37,911,000 (6/95).

Per Share Data ($) (Year Ended Sep. 30)

	1994	1993	1992	1991	1990	1989
Tangible Bk. Val.	5.39	3.85	3.59	2.67	2.09	1.84
Cash Flow	0.91	0.79	1.18	0.91	0.55	0.81
Earnings	0.46	0.40	0.80	0.59	0.25	0.47
Dividends	Nil	Nil	Nil	Nil	Nil	Nil
Payout Ratio	Nil	Nil	Nil	Nil	Nil	Nil
Prices - High	18	18¾	22¼	13¼	5¼	6½
- Low	8	10½	12⅛	2¾	2⅞	3
P/E Ratio - High	39	47	28	23	21	14
- Low	17	26	15	5	12	6

Income Statement Analysis (Million $)

	1994	%Chg	1993	%Chg	1992	%Chg	1991
Revs.	242	51%	160	2%	157	31%	120
Oper. Inc.	11.0	24%	8.9	-25%	11.9	25%	9.5
Depr.	3.1	21%	2.6	6%	2.4	20%	2.0
Int. Exp.	3.2	72%	1.8	27%	1.4	-24%	1.9
Pretax Inc.	4.9	19%	4.1	-50%	8.2	43%	5.8
Eff. Tax Rate	38%	—	38%	—	39%	—	37%
Net Inc.	3.1	19%	2.6	-49%	5.1	39%	3.6

Balance Sheet & Other Fin. Data (Million $)

	1994	1993	1992	1991	1990	1989
Cash	1.1	0.8	0.9	0.3	1.3	0.8
Curr. Assets	109	74.9	49.8	41.3	31.2	25.2
Total Assets	122	95.1	62.7	54.5	43.4	36.5
Curr. Liab.	46.0	29.7	18.5	17.9	13.7	10.2
LT Debt	40.7	40.1	20.5	19.7	16.4	14.5
Common Eqty.	34.8	24.8	23.1	16.6	13.0	11.3
Total Cap.	76.0	65.5	44.2	36.7	29.7	26.3
Cap. Exp.	5.3	8.2	2.0	3.4	2.7	1.2
Cash Flow	6.1	5.1	7.5	5.7	3.4	5.0

Ratio Analysis

	1994	1993	1992	1991	1990	1989
Curr. Ratio	2.4	2.5	2.7	2.3	2.3	2.5
% LT Debt of Cap.	53.5	61.2	46.3	53.8	55.1	55.1
% Net Inc.of Revs.	1.3	1.6	3.2	3.0	2.0	3.7
% Ret. on Assets	2.8	3.3	8.5	7.4	3.9	8.4
% Ret. on Equity	10.1	10.7	25.0	24.6	12.9	27.6

Dividend Data —No dividends have been paid. Plexus has reinvested earnings to support its working capital and expansion requirements, and it does not expect to pay cash dividends in the foreseeable future. A 50% stock dividend was paid in March 1992.

Data as orig. reptd.; bef. results of disc. opers. and/or spec. items. Per share data adj. for stk. divs. as of ex-div. date. E-Estimated. NA-Not Available. NM-Not Meaningful. NR-Not Ranked.

Office—55 Jewelers Park Dr., Neenah, WI 54957-0156. **Tel**—(414) 722-3451. **Chrmn & CEO**—P. Strandwitz. **Pres**—J. L. Nussbaum. **VP-Fin, Treas & Investor Contact**—Thomas N. Turriff. **VP & Secy**—J. D. Kaufman. **Dirs**—R. A. Cooper, R. T. Hoppe, H. R. Miller, J. L. Nussbaum, G. A. Pitner, T. J. Prosser, P. Strandwitz. **Transfer Agent & Registrar**—Firstar Trust Co., Milwaukee. **Incorporated** in Wisconsin in 1979. **Empl**-2,165. **S&P Analyst:** Ronald J. Gross

STANDARD & POOR'S

STOCK REPORTS

Ply Gem Industries

NYSE Symbol **PGI**
In S&P SmallCap 600

03-OCT-95 **Industry:** Building

Summary: This company makes and distributes specialty products for the home improvement industry.

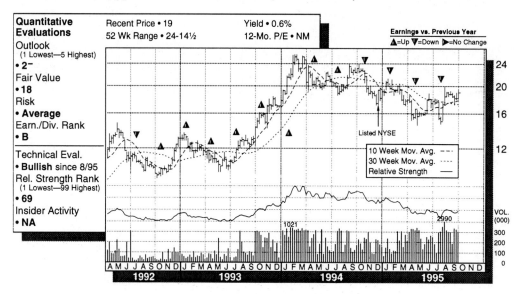

Quantitative Evaluations

Outlook
(1 Lowest—5 Highest)
• **2-**

Fair Value
• **18**

Risk
• **Average**

Earn./Div. Rank
• **B**

Technical Eval.
• **Bullish** since 8/95

Rel. Strength Rank
(1 Lowest—99 Highest)
• **69**

Insider Activity
• **NA**

Recent Price • 19
52 Wk Range • 24-14½

Yield • 0.6%
12-Mo. P/E • NM

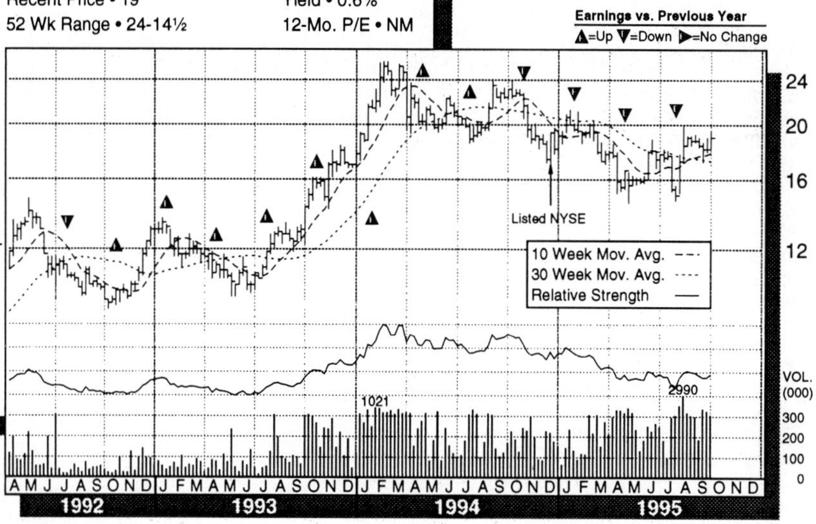

Business Profile - 03-OCT-95

Ply Gem sells high-margin products in the rapidly expanding do-it-yourself home improvement market. A loss in 1994 reflected $41 million of charges for a restructuring that, when completed, is expected to produce annual pretax savings of $12 million. However, in 1995's first six months, PGI reported a net loss, due to unexpected higher expenses from the restructuring. PGI retained Bear Stearns to explore options to optimize shareholder value, including possible sale of the company.

Operational Review - 03-OCT-95

Revenues in 1995's first six months fell 6.1%, year to year, mostly due to the elimination of certain lower-margin products. Margins eroded as a result of restructuring and new product start-up costs, as well as higher training and moving expenses; operating income fell 61%. Despite slightly lower net other expenses, a pretax loss of $2,976,000 contrasted with income of $9,004,000. At July 1, 1995, the operating cash flow deficit decreased 36% year to year, to $17,297,000.

Stock Performance - 29-SEP-95

In the past 30 trading days, PGI's shares were unchanged, compared to a 5% rise in the S&P 500. Average trading volume for the past five days was 69,600 shares, compared with the 40-day moving average of 154,923 shares.

Key Stock Statistics

Dividend Rate/Share	0.12	Shareholders	4,000
Shs. outstg. (M)	14.6	Market cap. (B)	$0.275
Avg. daily vol. (M)	0.102	Inst. holdings	48%
Tang. Bk. Value/Share	7.02	Insider holdings	NA
Beta	0.91		

Value of $10,000 invested 5 years ago: $ 17,938

Fiscal Year Ending Dec. 31

	1995	% Change	1994	% Change	1993	% Change
Revenues (Million $)						
1Q	160.2	-2%	163.4	12%	146.4	14%
2Q	199.6	-9%	219.8	19%	184.4	10%
3Q	—	—	219.0	5%	209.0	18%
4Q	—	—	194.2	6%	182.9	20%
Yr.	—	—	796.4	10%	722.7	16%
Income (Million $)						
1Q	-2.67	NM	-1.31	NM	-2.05	NM
2Q	1.03	-84%	6.27	82%	3.45	24%
3Q	—	—	-13.98	NM	5.26	20%
4Q	—	—	0.49	-84%	2.99	66%
Yr.	—	—	-8.53	NM	9.65	53%
Earnings Per Share ($)						
1Q	-0.18	NM	-0.11	NM	-0.19	NM
2Q	0.07	-83%	0.40	29%	0.31	29%
3Q	—	—	-0.95	NM	0.44	13%
4Q	—	—	0.03	-87%	0.23	44%
Yr.	—	—	-0.62	NM	0.76	36%

Next earnings report expected: early November

Ply Gem Industries

Business Summary - 03-OCT-95

Ply Gem Industries, Inc. is a national manufacturer and distributor of specialty home improvement products, with 10 independent operating companies in more than 40 locations throughout the U.S. and Canada.

The Specialty Wood Products group manufactures and distributes pressure treated wood products; decorative wall coverings made from plywood, hardboard and wood composition boards; melamine-coated tileboard; ceramic tile; solid-wood planking; and furniture components, laminates and board products.

The Windows, Doors and Siding group makes and distributes vinyl siding, soffits and other custom-made vinyl products for the home improvement and new construction markets. It also manufactures a full line of wood and vinyl windows and patio doors, glass and polycarbonate skylights, and wooden interior bifold doors and shutters. The 1989 acquisition of SNE Enterprises, the fourth largest U.S. window manufacturer, expanded the product line to include wood windows and patio doors. In 1992, Ply Gem acquired Richwood Building Products, Inc., a maker of siding accessories.

The Distribution group, through the Allied Plywood Corp. unit , is a national distributor of specialty wood products supplied to customers via an extensive branch network. Allied is also a major importer of Russian wood products into North America.

The Home Products division, through Studley Products, Inc., is the largest independent U.S. maker of disposable paper vacuum cleaner bags in the U.S. Its products include a new hypo-allergenic line. Studley also manufactures grass catcher bags and other products for the lawn and garden market.

Ply Gem has pursued an aggressive acquisition program. During the 1980s, it acquired 14 companies. In 1990, it launched a strategic growth plan (Teamwork 90s) that relies on internal development for continued growth. Under Teamwork 90s, the company consolidated its filtration and distribution business to streamline operations.

Important Developments

Aug. '95—In the second quarter of 1995, PGI reported a 9% decline in revenues; if discontinued product lines were excluded, the decline was 3%. Net income was down 84%, year to year. PGI said the poor results were from unexpected higher expenses from the restructuring, primarily in its window subsidiaries. PGI said it retained Bear Stearns to explore several options to increase shareholder value, including possible sale of the company.

Capitalization

Long Term Debt: $101,146,000, incl. $7,133,000 of cap. lease obligs. (7/1/95).
Options: To buy 4,479,027 shs. at $5.63 to $25.50 ea. (12/94).

Per Share Data ($) (Year Ended Dec. 31)

	1994	1993	1992	1991	1990	1989
Tangible Bk. Val.	7.14	5.77	4.41	3.42	2.85	2.43
Cash Flow	0.35	1.53	1.60	1.55	1.48	1.87
Earnings	-0.62	0.76	0.56	0.39	0.31	0.90
Dividends	Nil	0.12	0.12	0.12	0.12	0.12
Payout Ratio	Nil	16%	21%	31%	39%	12%
Prices - High	25 7/8	18 3/8	14 3/4	9 3/8	11 3/8	15
- Low	17	9 7/8	8 3/4	5 1/4	4 1/4	10 7/8
P/E Ratio - High	NM	24	26	24	37	17
- Low	NM	13	16	13	14	12

Income Statement Analysis (Million $)

	1994	%Chg	1993	%Chg	1992	%Chg	1991
Revs.	796	10%	723	16%	623	11%	562
Oper. Inc.	50.3	29%	39.0	13%	34.4	4%	33.2
Depr.	13.4	10%	12.2	3%	11.8	-3%	12.2
Int. Exp.	7.5	-26%	10.1	5%	9.6	-32%	14.1
Pretax Inc.	-11.9	NM	17.5	54%	11.4	46%	7.8
Eff. Tax Rate	NM	—	45%	—	45%	—	48%
Net Inc.	-8.5	NM	9.7	54%	6.3	58%	4.0

Balance Sheet & Other Fin. Data (Million $)

	1994	1993	1992	1991	1990	1989
Cash	16.2	14.4	4.5	7.4	5.8	11.9
Curr. Assets	185	197	164	148	176	167
Total Assets	346	345	314	281	330	303
Curr. Liab.	74.7	61.0	70.1	54.7	63.7	45.9
LT Debt	87.0	150	120	108	153	144
Common Eqty.	162	129	118	111	108	108
Total Cap.	248	280	240	223	265	256
Cap. Exp.	23.0	20.5	17.1	9.7	27.3	12.1
Cash Flow	4.9	21.8	18.1	16.2	15.3	21.1

Ratio Analysis

	1994	1993	1992	1991	1990	1989
Curr. Ratio	2.5	3.2	2.3	2.7	2.8	3.6
% LT Debt of Cap.	34.9	53.6	49.9	48.4	57.7	56.5
% Net Inc.of Revs.	NM	1.3	1.0	0.7	0.6	2.0
% Ret. on Assets	NM	2.9	2.1	1.3	1.0	3.9
% Ret. on Equity	NM	7.7	5.4	3.6	3.0	9.8

Dividend Data —Cash has been paid each year since 1977.

Amt. of Div. $	Date Decl.	Ex-Div. Date	Stock of Record	Payment Date
0.030	Oct. 20	Nov. 04	Nov. 10	Dec. 02 '94
0.030	Jan. 19	Feb. 03	Feb. 09	Mar. 03 '95
0.030	Apr. 20	May. 05	May. 11	Jun. 02 '95
0.030	Jul. 20	Aug. 08	Aug. 10	Sep. 01 '95

Data as orig. reptd.; bef. results of disc. opers. and/or spec. items. Per share data adj. for stk. divs. as of ex-div. date. E-Estimated. NA-Not Available. NM-Not Meaningful. NR-Not Ranked.

Office—777 Third Ave., New York, NY 10017. **Tel**—(212) 832-1550. **Chrmn & CEO**—J. S. Silverman. **Pres & COO**—D. R. Snyder. **VP & Treas**—P. Bogutsky. **Investor Contact**—Diane M. Cady. **Dirs**—H. P. Dooskin, J. M. Goldenberg, A. Hersh, W. Lilley, III, E. H. Modlin, J. S. Silverman, D. R. Snyder. **Transfer Agent & Registrar**—Harris Trust Co. of New York, NYC. **Incorporated** in New York in 1946. Reincorporated in Delaware in 1987. **Empl**-4,200. **S&P Analyst:** Robert E. Friedman

STANDARD & POOR'S

STOCK REPORTS

Pogo Producing

NYSE Symbol **PPP**
In S&P SmallCap 600

24-SEP-95

Industry:
Oil and Gas

Summary: This independent oil and gas company explores for, develops and produces oil and gas onshore and offshore the U.S. and, since 1991, offshore Thailand.

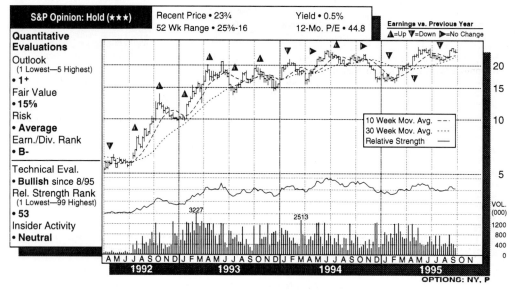

S&P Opinion: Hold (★★★)

Recent Price • 23¾
52 Wk Range • 25⅝-16
Yield • 0.5%
12-Mo. P/E • 44.8

Quantitative Evaluations

Outlook
(1 Lowest—5 Highest)
• 1+

Fair Value
• 15⅝

Risk
• Average

Earn./Div. Rank
• B-

Technical Eval.
• Bullish since 8/95

Rel. Strength Rank
(1 Lowest—99 Highest)
• 53

Insider Activity
• Neutral

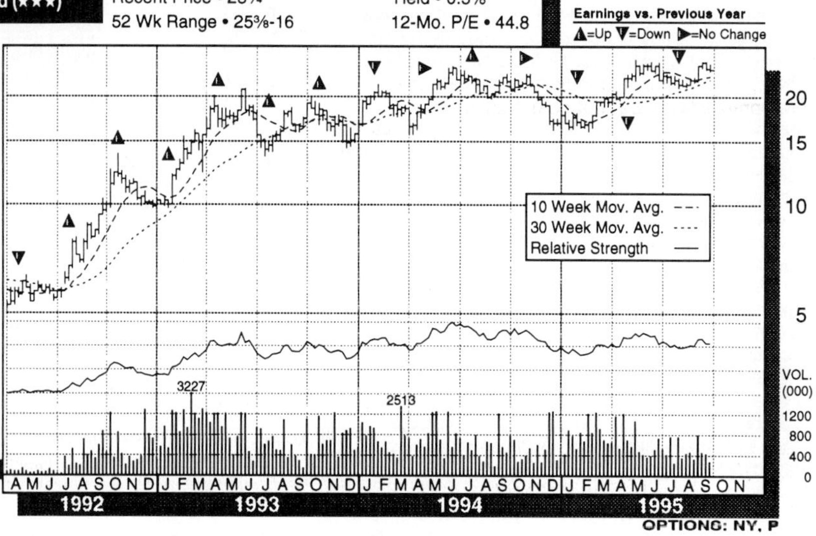

Overview - 22-SEP-95

This company's major focus is in the Gulf of Mexico, a prime offshore exploratory and production area, where the company is adding working interests and continuing its successful drilling efforts. Prospects are also positive in the Gulf of Thailand, where PPP is a joint-venture partner in a 2.6-million-acre concession and production facilities are to be installed by 1996. The company has made progress in reducing its debt load and consequent annual interest obligations. Along with increasing both net liquids and natural gas production, PPP's cash flow has risen steadily, as have earnings. With higher capital expenditures projected for 1995, the ongoing upward trend in the company's results should resume when gas prices rebound.

Valuation - 22-SEP-95

The shares appear to be fully valued. Oil prices rallied earlier in the year, but have again weakened on overproduction, although worldwide demand remains robust and prices should rebound by year-end. The U.S. embargo of oil from Iran continues to favor domestic production. PPP is well positioned to take advantage of this situation through its Gulf of Mexico offshore concessions. However, the company's stock is selling at a significant multiple to its underlying earnings. While income can be expected to improve from the lows experienced at the beginning of the year, it is unlikely to do so in a dramatic fashion. Consequently, future price movements of the shares will be limited.

Key Stock Statistics

S&P EPS Est. 1995	0.55	Tang. Bk. Value/Share	2.03
P/E on S&P Est. 1995	43.2	Beta	0.62
S&P EPS Est. 1996	0.80	Shareholders	5,100
Dividend Rate/Share	0.12	Market cap. (B)	$0.779
Shs. outstg. (M)	32.8	Inst. holdings	81%
Avg. daily vol. (M)	0.099	Insider holdings	NA

Value of $10,000 invested 5 years ago: $ 23,337

Fiscal Year Ending Dec. 31

	1995	% Change	1994	% Change	1993	% Change
Revenues (Million $)						
1Q	41.81	10%	37.89	9%	34.68	23%
2Q	41.74	-16%	49.73	44%	34.53	1%
3Q	—	—	46.45	25%	37.21	7%
4Q	—	—	39.53	19%	33.13	-24%
Yr.	—	—	173.6	24%	139.6	NM
Income (Million $)						
1Q	3.43	-53%	7.28	2%	7.16	NM
2Q	4.35	-56%	9.90	77%	5.60	71%
3Q	—	—	7.43	4%	7.16	29%
4Q	—	—	2.76	-46%	5.14	-53%
Yr.	—	—	27.37	9%	25.06	35%
Earnings Per Share ($)						
1Q	0.10	-55%	0.22	NM	0.22	NM
2Q	0.13	-57%	0.30	76%	0.17	42%
3Q	E0.15	-32%	0.22	NM	0.22	10%
4Q	E0.17	113%	0.08	-50%	0.16	-58%
Yr.	E0.55	-33%	0.82	8%	0.76	15%

Next earnings report expected: late October

Pogo Producing

Business Summary - 22-SEP-95

Pogo Producing Company is an independent oil and gas company that explores for, develops and produces oil and gas primarily on properties located offshore the Gulf of Mexico and onshore the U.S. The company also has interests in 2.6 million acres offshore Thailand.

Historically, the company's interests have been concentrated in the Gulf of Mexico, where approximately 81% of PPP's domestic proved reserves and 63% of its total proved reserves are now located. During 1994, approximately 82% of both natural gas equivalent production and consolidated oil and gas revenues were from the company's domestic offshore properties.

In 1991, PPP, together with its joint-venture partners, was awarded a license from the Kingdom of Thailand to explore for and produce oil and gas in a 2.6-million-acre tract in the Gulf of Thailand. In March 1995, the company reached an agreement with its partners under which its working interest would increase to about 46.3%, from 31.7%.

At December 31, 1994, estimated proved reserves totaled 242,890 MMcf of gas (73% developed) and 33,862,000 bbl. of oil, condensate and natural gas liquids (73%), compared with 232,866 MMcf of gas (79%) and 28,268,000 bbl. of oil (74%) at year-end 1993. About 77% of the oil and condensate reserves and 77% of the natural gas reserves are domestic, with the remaining portion located in Thailand.

As of year-end 1994, company properties included 262,195 gross (85,362 net) developed acres, primarily offshore Louisiana and Texas and onshore Texas and New Mexico. PPP also had undeveloped acreage totaling 2,805,650 gross acres, located mostly on concessions in Thailand. The company drilled 97 gross (49.2 net) wells in 1994, of which 86 (43.3 net) were successful.

In 1994, average daily production amounted to 144,800 Mcf of gas and 11,100 bbl. of oil and condensate, versus 91,700 Mcf of gas per day and 9,851 bbl. of oil daily in 1993. Average sales prices were $1.88 per Mcf and $16.08 per bbl. in 1994, versus $1.98 per Mcf and $17.81 per bbl. the year before.

The company's $100 million 1995 capital and exploration budget will be used to explore and develop oil and gas properties in the Gulf of Mexico, for development and further exploration of PPP's offshore Thailand discoveries and to expand the company's oil drilling program in southeastern New Mexico.

Important Developments

Sep. '95—PPP and various partners bid on six tracts and won four of them at two oil and gas lease sales covering waters offshore Louisiana and Texas.

Capitalization

Long Term Debt: $158,249,000 (6/95).

Per Share Data ($) (Year Ended Dec. 31)

	1994	1993	1992	1991	1990	1989
Tangible Bk. Val.	1.95	1.04	0.18	-2.06	1.90	0.58
Cash Flow	2.72	2.00	2.18	1.90	3.26	2.51
Earnings	0.82	0.76	0.66	0.37	0.70	-0.23
Dividends	0.06	Nil	Nil	Nil	Nil	Nil
Payout Ratio	7%	Nil	Nil	Nil	Nil	Nil
Prices - High	24¼	21	13⅞	8¼	10⅛	10¼
- Low	15⅝	9¾	5⅛	4⅝	5¾	4
P/E Ratio - High	30	28	21	22	14	NM
- Low	19	13	8	13	8	NM

Income Statement Analysis (Million $)

	1994	%Chg	1993	%Chg	1992	%Chg	1991
Revs.	174	27%	137	NM	137	13%	121
Oper. Inc.	115	29%	89.0	3%	86.0	13%	76.0
Depr. Depl. & Amort.	63.0	54%	41.0	-2%	42.0	NM	42.0
Int. Exp.	10.1	-8%	11.0	-42%	19.0	-24%	24.9
Pretax Inc.	43.0	8%	40.0	38%	29.0	93%	15.0
Eff. Tax Rate	36%	—	37%	—	36%	—	29%
Net Inc.	27.4	9%	25.1	36%	18.5	80%	10.3

Balance Sheet & Other Fin. Data (Million $)

	1994	1993	1992	1991	1990	1989
Cash	2.9	6.7	5.0	5.2	7.1	17.3
Curr. Assets	49.7	40.5	33.6	30.6	66.2	43.4
Total Assets	299	240	206	214	425	421
Curr. Liab.	38.7	37.6	32.2	30.1	37.1	41.8
LT Debt	149	131	144	222	260	311
Common Eqty.	64.0	34.0	6.0	-57.0	52.0	14.0
Total Cap.	250	194	167	174	380	372
Cap. Exp.	118	73.0	39.0	51.0	45.0	32.0
Cash Flow	90.7	66.0	61.0	52.0	85.0	60.0

Ratio Analysis

	1994	1993	1992	1991	1990	1989
Curr. Ratio	1.3	1.1	1.0	1.0	1.8	1.0
% LT Debt of Cap.	59.8	67.3	86.2	127.3	68.5	83.6
% Ret. on Assets	10.1	11.2	8.1	3.2	4.0	NM
% Ret. on Equity	55.7	126.9	NM	NM	53.3	NM

Dividend Data —Common dividends, initiated in 1978, were omitted in 1987, then resumed August 1994.

Amt. of Div. $	Date Decl.	Ex-Div. Date	Stock of Record	Payment Date
0.030	Oct. 25	Nov. 02	Nov. 08	Nov. 30 '94
0.030	Jan. 24	Feb. 06	Feb. 10	Feb. 28 '95
0.030	Apr. 26	May. 02	May. 08	May. 31 '95
0.030	Jul. 25	Aug. 09	Aug. 11	Aug. 31 '95

Data as orig. reptd.; bef. results of disc opers. and/or spec. items. Per share data adj. for stk. divs. as of ex-div. date. E-Estimated. NA-Not Available. NM-Not Meaningful. NR-Not Ranked.

Office—5 Greenway Plaza, Suite 2700, P.O. Box 2504, Houston, TX 77252-2504. **Tel**—(713) 297-5000. **Fax**—(713) 297-5100. **Chrmn, Pres, CEO & Investor Contact**—Paul G. Van Wagenen. **Sr VP & CFO**—D. S. Slack. **VP & Treas**—J. W. Elsenhans. **Secy**—R. B. Manning. **Dirs**—T. Armstrong, J. S. Blanton, W. M. Brumley Jr., J. B. Carter Jr., W. L. Fisher, W. E. Gipson, G. W. Gong, J. S. Hunt, F. A. Klingenstein, N. R. Petry, D. S. Slack, P. G. Van Wagenen, J. A. Vickers. **Transfer Agents & Registrars**—Harris Trust Co. of New York, NYC; KeyCorp Shareholder Services, Inc. **Incorporated** in Delaware in 1970. **Empl-** 108. **S&P Analyst:** Michael C. Barr

STANDARD & POOR'S

STOCK REPORTS

Pool Energy Services Co.

NASDAQ Symbol **PESC**

In S&P SmallCap 600

08-OCT-95

Industry: Oil and Gas

Summary: One of the world's largest well servicing firms, Pool Energy concentrates on the maintenance and repair of existing oil and natural gas wells.

Quantitative Evaluations

Outlook (1 Lowest—5 Highest)
• **NA**

Fair Value
• **NA**

Risk
• **Average**

Earn./Div. Rank
• **NR**

Technical Eval.
• **Bearish** since 3/95

Rel. Strength Rank (1 Lowest—99 Highest)
• **53**

Insider Activity
• **NA**

Recent Price • 9
52 Wk Range • 9⅞-6¼
Yield • Nil
12-Mo. P/E • NM

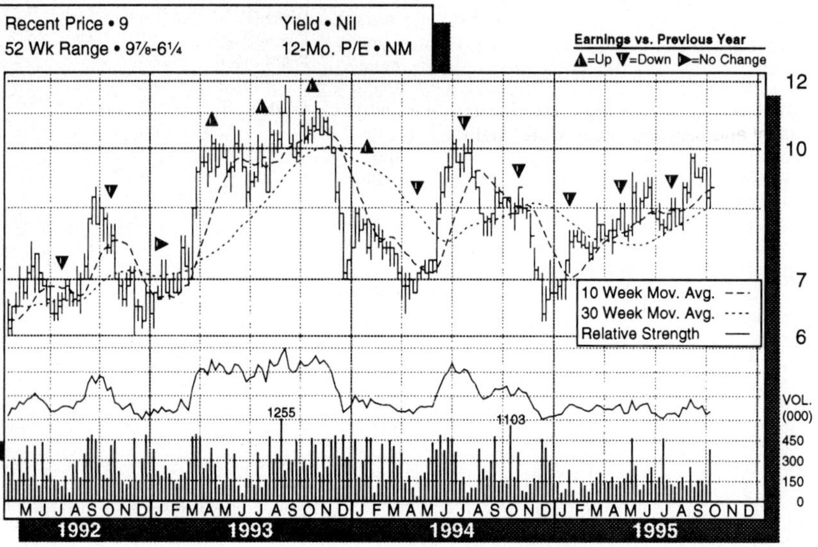

Business Profile - 06-OCT-95

One of the world's largest well servicing firms, Pool Energy was established in 1988 with the disposal of oilfield services operations by ENSERCH Corp. The company has expanded in recent years. In late 1994, Pool acquired the 60.7% of Pool Arctic Alaska it did not already own, while in June 1995, Pool completed the acquisition of Golden Pacific Corp., a California well servicing company. Pool is considering further consolidation in the U.S. and penetration of markets in Argentina and Venezuela.

Operational Review - 06-OCT-95

Total revenues in the six months ended June 30, 1995, advanced 15%, year to year, as increased onshore activity in the lower 48 states offset lower rig rates in Alaska and the Gulf of Mexico. The higher revenues also reflected the acquisitions of Pool Arctic Alaska and Golden Pacific. Following higher operating expenses and interest payments, share earnings fell to $0.06 from $0.11.

Stock Performance - 06-OCT-95

In the past 30 trading days, PESC's shares have increased 1%, compared to a 4% rise in the S&P 500. Average trading volume for the past five days was 75,580 shares, compared with the 40-day moving average of 36,903 shares.

Key Stock Statistics

Dividend Rate/Share	Nil	Shareholders	3,900
Shs. outstg. (M)	14.1	Market cap. (B)	$0.127
Avg. daily vol. (M)	0.040	Inst. holdings	67%
Tang. Bk. Value/Share	9.50	Insider holdings	NA
Beta	0.73		

Value of $10,000 invested 5 years ago: NA

Fiscal Year Ending Dec. 31

	1995	% Change	1994	% Change	1993	% Change
Revenues (Million $)						
1Q	62.85	12%	55.98	-7%	60.19	20%
2Q	63.80	18%	54.26	-6%	57.63	20%
3Q	—	—	56.17	-5%	59.01	9%
4Q	—	—	62.77	5%	59.88	NM
Yr.	—	—	229.2	-3%	236.7	11%
Income (Million $)						
1Q	0.22	-67%	0.67	-56%	1.51	NM
2Q	0.56	-32%	0.82	-38%	1.33	NM
3Q	—	—	0.57	-65%	1.62	NM
4Q	—	—	-14.79	NM	1.75	NM
Yr.	—	—	-12.73	NM	6.20	NM
Earnings Per Share ($)						
1Q	0.02	-60%	0.05	-55%	0.11	NM
2Q	0.04	-33%	0.06	-40%	0.10	NM
3Q	—	—	0.04	-67%	0.12	NM
4Q	—	—	-1.09	NM	0.13	NM
Yr.	—	—	-0.94	NM	0.46	NM

Next earnings report expected: early November

Pool Energy Services Co.

Business Summary - 06-OCT-95

Pool Energy Services Co. is one of the world's largest well servicing firms. Maintenance, workover and completion services are provided for oil and gas wells, onshore and offshore, both domestically and internationally. Pool also performs contract drilling offshore domestically and internationally and onshore in Alaska, as well as overseas. Additional services include onsite temporary fluid storage facilities, the provision, removal and disposal of specialized fluids used during certain completion and workover operations and the removal and disposal of salt water that is often produced in conjunction with the production of oil and gas. Other specialized rig services include the plugging of depleted oil and gas wells.

Operating revenues in recent years were derived as follows:

	1994	1993
Domestic onshore well servicing and production services	68%	67%
Gulf offshore workover/drilling	16%	16%
Pacific offshore and Alaska drilling/ Workover	5%	5%
International Drilling/Workover	11%	12%

A significant portion of operations is conducted through unconsolidated affiliates. Such affiliates' contribution is important to bottom line results.

Pool was formed in November 1988 to purchase from NYSE-listed ENSERCH Corp. all of the oilfield services business that had been conducted by Pool Co. and its subsidiaries and affiliates (Old Pool). Old Pool was purchased with proceeds from the initial public stock offering and a private placement. Among Pool's current arrangements with ENSERCH is a contingent support agreement intended to enhance the ability of Pool to borrow funds and fulfill various obligations.

Pool's equipment as of December 31, 1994, included a worldwide fleet of 574 rigs. Average 1994 rig utilization rates were: 48% U.S. (land) Operations (51% in 1993), 53% Gulf Offshore Operations (77%), 53% International Operations (51%), and 44% Alaska (49%). Domestic onshore operations, which do not include Alaska, are conducted in 14 states within the U.S. The company has 19 rigs in the offshore producing areas of the Gulf of Mexico. Operations are also undertaken in 10 other countries. Large international oil and gas companies, foreign national oil companies and independent producers are the major customers.

Important Developments

Jun. '95—PESC completed the acquisition of Golden Pacific Corp. for approximately $18 million of cash, notes and stock. Golden Pacific's principal subsidiary has a fleet of 155 land rigs in California.

Capitalization

Long Term Debt: $17,303,000 (6/95).

Per Share Data ($) (Year Ended Dec. 31)

	1994	1993	1992	1991	1990	1989
Tangible Bk. Val.	9.49	10.43	9.99	10.13	9.94	10.33
Cash Flow	0.08	1.66	1.11	1.55	1.74	1.37
Earnings	-0.94	0.46	-0.22	0.19	0.44	-0.21
Dividends	Nil	Nil	Nil	Nil	Nil	Nil
Payout Ratio	Nil	Nil	Nil	Nil	Nil	Nil
Prices - High	10½	11⅞	9	13⅛	18⅛	NA
- Low	6¼	6⅛	5¾	5¼	8⅝	NA
P/E Ratio - High	NM	26	NM	69	41	NM
- Low	NM	13	NM	28	20	NM

Income Statement Analysis (Million $)

	1994	%Chg	1993	%Chg	1992	%Chg	1991
Revs.	229	-3%	237	11%	213	-5%	225
Oper. Inc.	10.2	-33%	15.3	94%	7.9	-48%	15.1
Depr.	13.8	-15%	16.3	-9%	18.0	-2%	18.3
Int. Exp.	0.3	-51%	0.5	-45%	0.9	31%	0.7
Pretax Inc.	-21.1	NM	7.6	NM	-6.7	NM	1.8
Eff. Tax Rate	NM	—	18%	—	NM	—	NM
Net Inc.	-12.7	NM	6.2	NM	-3.0	NM	2.5

Balance Sheet & Other Fin. Data (Million $)

	1994	1993	1992	1991	1990	1989
Cash	2.7	4.7	3.2	8.1	30.4	10.8
Curr. Assets	68.5	69.7	65.9	62.0	89.5	87.5
Total Assets	208	193	196	198	214	238
Curr. Liab.	36.1	29.2	37.6	31.9	47.1	74.6
LT Debt	0.4	Nil	Nil	Nil	Nil	Nil
Common Eqty.	129	141	135	137	134	129
Total Cap.	131	144	138	141	138	130
Cap. Exp.	11.4	20.4	12.7	26.1	11.9	NA
Cash Flow	1.0	22.5	15.1	20.9	23.5	17.1

Ratio Analysis

	1994	1993	1992	1991	1990	1989
Curr. Ratio	1.9	2.4	1.8	1.9	1.9	1.2
% LT Debt of Cap.	0.3	Nil	Nil	Nil	Nil	Nil
% Net Inc.of Revs.	NM	2.6	NM	1.1	2.6	NM
% Ret. on Assets	NM	3.2	NM	1.2	2.7	NM
% Ret. on Equity	NM	4.5	NM	1.9	4.6	NM

Dividend Data —No cash dividends have been paid, and terms of Pool's credit line preclude such payments. A shareholder rights plan was adopted in June 1994.

Data as orig. reptd.; bef. results of disc. opers. and/or spec. items. Per share data adj. for stk. divs. as of ex-div. date. E-Estimated. NA-Not Available. NM-Not Meaningful. NR-Not Ranked.

Office—10375 Richmond Ave., P.O. Box 4271, Houston, TX 77210. **Tel**—(713) 954-3000. **Chrmn, Pres & CEO**—J. T. Jongebloed. **Sr VP-Fin**—E. J. Spillard. **VP & Secy**—G. G. Arms. **Investor Contact**—D. C. Oatman. **Dirs**—P. M. Geren Jr., J. T. Jongebloed, W. C. McCord, W. H. Mobley, J. R. Musolino, J. L. Payne, F. M. Pool, D. D. Sykora. **Transfer Agent & Registrar**—First National Bank of Boston. **Incorporated** in Texas in 1988. **Empl**- 4,449. **S&P Analyst:** D.J.B.

STANDARD & POOR'S

STOCK REPORTS

Pope & Talbot

NYSE Symbol **POP**
In S&P SmallCap 600

13-SEP-95 **Industry:** Paper/Products

Summary: This company is a diversified producer of lumber, private-label consumer tissue and disposable diapers, and market pulp.

Quantitative Evaluations

Recent Price • 15¾ | Yield • 4.8%
52 Wk Range • 21¾-15⅛ | 12-Mo. P/E • NM

Outlook
(1 Lowest—5 Highest)
• **2⁻**

Fair Value
• **14⅝**

Risk
• **Low**

Earn./Div. Rank
• **B-**

Technical Eval.
• **Bearish** since 7/95

Rel. Strength Rank
(1 Lowest—99 Highest)
• **23**

Insider Activity
• **NA**

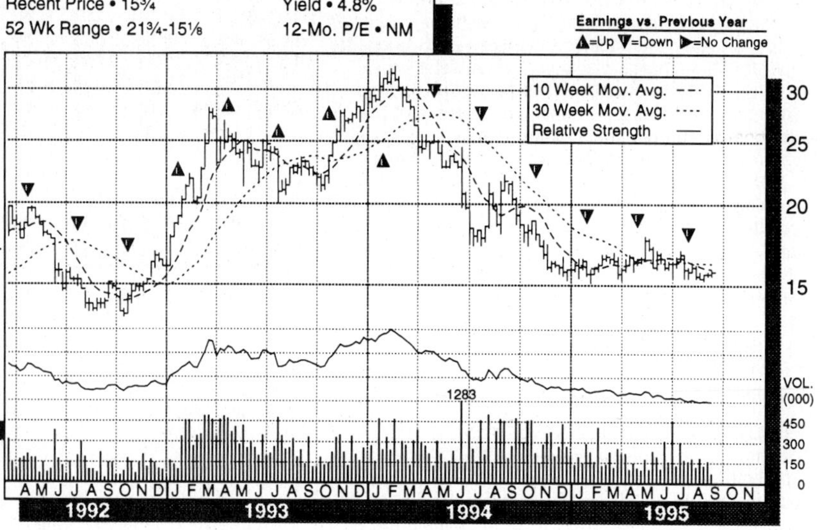

Business Profile - 13-SEP-95

Pope & Talbot is an integrated wood-fiber products company that produces pulp, consumer tissue, disposable diapers and softwood lumber. A large net loss was recorded for the first half of 1995, on difficulties in all businesses with the exception of pulp operations. Upcoming prospects appear better, as wood products should benefit from lower interest rates, diaper offerings have been adapted to battle competition, wastepaper costs have declined from their peak and pulp operations remain strong.

Operational Review - 13-SEP-95

POP sustained a loss of $0.77 a share for the first half of 1995, on a 1.7% gain in revenues. The poor results reflected depressed lumber prices and high log costs in the wood products division, competitive pressures in the disposable diaper area (with price and package-count reductions initiated by national brands) and higher raw materials costs and a tissue mill strike in the consumer tissue business. Those factors easily outweighed continued demand and pricing strength in the pulp business.

Stock Performance - 08-SEP-95

In the past 30 trading days, POP's shares were unchanged, compared to a 2% rise in the S&P 500. Average trading volume for the past five days was 16,200 shares, compared with the 40-day moving average of 29,003 shares.

Key Stock Statistics

Dividend Rate/Share	0.76	Shareholders	1,400
Shs. outstg. (M)	13.4	Market cap. (B)	$0.210
Avg. daily vol. (M)	0.028	Inst. holdings	59%
Tang. Bk. Value/Share	15.74	Insider holdings	NA
Beta	1.72		

Value of $10,000 invested 5 years ago: $ 7,821

Fiscal Year Ending Dec. 31

	1995	% Change	1994	% Change	1993	% Change
Revenues (Million $)						
1Q	173.1	3%	168.7	NM	167.6	32%
2Q	159.0	NM	157.9	4%	151.2	17%
3Q	—	—	171.3	13%	150.9	5%
4Q	—	—	162.0	2%	159.2	11%
Yr.	—	—	659.9	5%	628.9	16%
Income (Million $)						
1Q	-1.23	NM	8.59	-22%	11.03	NM
2Q	-9.01	NM	2.80	-40%	4.67	NM
3Q	—	—	0.92	-30%	1.31	NM
4Q	—	—	3.59	-21%	4.56	61%
Yr.	—	—	15.90	-26%	21.58	NM
Earnings Per Share ($)						
1Q	-0.09	NM	0.70	-26%	0.95	NM
2Q	-0.68	NM	0.21	-48%	0.40	NM
3Q	—	—	0.07	-36%	0.11	NM
4Q	—	—	0.27	-31%	0.39	56%
Yr.	—	—	1.21	-35%	1.85	NM

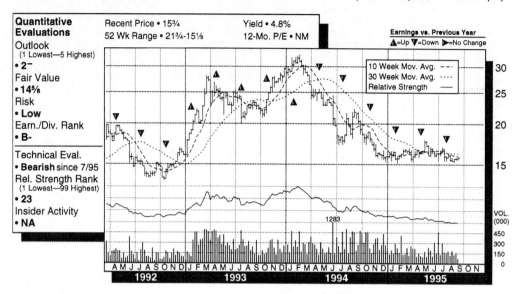

Next earnings report expected: mid October

Pope & Talbot

Business Summary - 13-SEP-95

Pope & Talbot is engaged mainly in the wood products and pulp and paper businesses. Segment contributions in 1994 (profits in millions) were:

	Sales	Profits
Wood products	46%	$55.2
Pulp & paper products	54%	-23.2

The wood products segment manufactures standardized and specialty lumber and wood chips. POP produces boards and dimension lumber, including specialty items such as stress-rated lumber. Lumber products are sold mainly to wholesalers. The company sells wood chips to pulp and paper producers, while logs are sold to other domestic and Canadian forest products companies.

The company's wood products operations obtain raw materials through open market log purchases, long-term cutting licenses on public land, sales by federal and state agencies and private sources, and timber purchased under contracts to cut timber on private land. Approximately 80% of POP's lumber capacity is located in regions of relatively stable timber supply, including Canada and the Black Hills region of South Dakota and Wyoming.

The paper products segment produces a full line of private-label consumer tissue products, including towels, napkins, bathroom and facial tissue and disposable diapers. Approximately 44% of pulp and paper sales in 1994 were disposable diapers, while tissue products represented 30%. Tissue and diaper products are sold to supermarkets, drugstores, mass merchandisers, and food and drug distribution companies.

Bleached kraft pulp, which accounted for 22% of 1994 paper segment revenues, is sold in the open market and to newsprint manufacturers and a writing paper manufacturer in the Northwest. The remaining 4% of pulp and paper revenues were generated by the brokering of pulp chips, mainly in the export market.

Important Developments

Aug. '95—POP announced that it would permanently close its Port Gamble, Wash., sawmill in October (96 workers), after the mill had sustained almost continuous losses in recent years and endured numerous temporary shutdowns. The troubles were attributed to an insufficient supply of logs at competitive prices, which was brought on by government restrictions.

Jul. '95—In reporting a $0.68 a share loss in the second quarter of 1995, POP expressed some optimism about upcoming prospects. The company noted that pulp markets remained strong and that conditions seemed to be improving in its lumber and consumer products segments. However, still posing problems was the ongoing strike at its Ransom, Pa., tissue mill, which affects 50% of tissue capacity.

Capitalization

Long Term Debt: $177,260,000 (6/95).

Per Share Data ($) (Year Ended Dec. 31)

	1994	1993	1992	1991	1990	1989
Tangible Bk. Val.	16.76	15.36	14.46	15.68	17.42	16.48
Cash Flow	4.19	4.35	2.27	1.97	3.95	5.74
Earnings	1.21	1.85	-0.19	-0.44	1.70	3.70
Dividends	0.76	0.76	0.76	0.76	0.72	0.60
Payout Ratio	63%	41%	NM	NM	42%	16%
Prices - High	32⅝	29⅞	19¾	19	27½	29¾
- Low	15¼	16	13⅜	12¾	10¼	17⅞
P/E Ratio - High	27	16	NM	NM	16	8
- Low	13	9	NM	NM	6	5

Income Statement Analysis (Million $)

	1994	%Chg	1993	%Chg	1992	%Chg	1991
Revs.	660	5%	629	16%	544	8%	502
Oper. Inc.	61.2	-18%	74.4	123%	33.3	25%	26.7
Depr.	39.1	33%	29.3	2%	28.6	3%	27.9
Int. Exp.	12.0	15%	10.4	74%	6.0	37%	4.4
Pretax Inc.	26.7	-27%	36.4	NM	-2.5	NM	-7.1
Eff. Tax Rate	40%	—	41%	—	NM	—	NM
Net Inc.	15.9	-26%	21.6	NM	-2.3	NM	-5.1

Balance Sheet & Other Fin. Data (Million $)

	1994	1993	1992	1991	1990	1989
Cash	6.8	3.8	4.3	3.8	9.0	2.1
Curr. Assets	223	170	138	122	132	130
Total Assets	539	456	370	347	354	355
Curr. Liab.	104	101	79.7	64.5	53.8	68.5
LT Debt	177	135	89.5	69.0	77.5	67.6
Common Eqty.	228	184	172	187	207	199
Total Cap.	407	327	266	266	300	287
Cap. Exp.	55.6	82.6	32.3	37.3	41.9	52.1
Cash Flow	55.0	50.9	26.3	22.9	46.2	67.7

Ratio Analysis

	1994	1993	1992	1991	1990	1989
Curr. Ratio	2.2	1.7	1.7	1.9	2.4	1.9
% LT Debt of Cap.	43.6	41.2	33.7	26.0	25.8	23.5
% Net Inc.of Revs.	2.4	3.4	NM	NM	3.5	7.1
% Ret. on Assets	3.0	5.2	NM	NM	5.6	12.9
% Ret. on Equity	7.3	12.0	NM	NM	9.9	24.1

Dividend Data —Dividends have been paid since 1948. A "poison pill" stock purchase rights plan was adopted in 1988.

Amt. of Div. $	Date Decl.	Ex-Div. Date	Stock of Record	Payment Date
0.190	Sep. 16	Nov. 01	Nov. 07	Nov. 15 '94
0.190	Jan. 24	Jan. 31	Feb. 06	Feb. 15 '95
0.190	Apr. 19	Apr. 25	May. 01	May. 15 '95
0.190	Jul. 18	Aug. 02	Aug. 04	Aug. 15 '95

Data as orig. reptd.; bef. results of disc. opers. and/or spec. items. Per share data adj. for stk. divs. as of ex-div. date. E-Estimated. NA-Not Available. NM-Not Meaningful. NR-Not Ranked.

Office—1500 S.W. First Ave., Portland, OR 97201. **Tel**—(503) 228-9161. **Chrmn, Pres & CEO**—P. T. Pope. **SVP-Fin, Treas, Secy & CFO**—C. M. Lamadrid. **Investor Contact**—Bob Wulf. **Dirs**—G. P. Andrews, H. W. Budge, C. Crocker, W. E. McCain, R. S. Miller Jr., P. T. Pope, H. G. L. Powell, B. Walker Jr. **Transfer Agent & Registrar**—Chemical Trust Co. of California, San Francisco. **Incorporated** in California in 1940; reincorporated in Delaware in 1979. **Empl**-3,000. **S&P Analyst:** Michael W. Jaffe

STANDARD & POOR'S

STOCK REPORTS

Premier Bancorp

NASDAQ Symbol **PRBC**

In S&P SmallCap 600

20-OCT-95

Industry: Banking

Summary: This one bank holding company, with total assets of $5.5 billion, has 150 retail outlets serving seven of the eight major metropolitan areas in Louisiana.

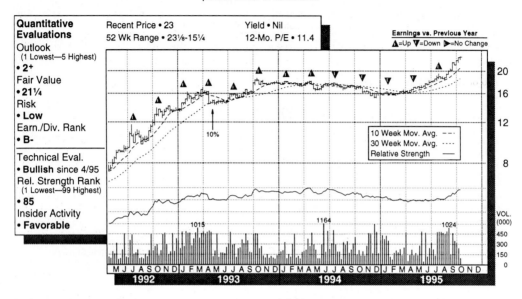

Quantitative Evaluations

Outlook (1 Lowest—5 Highest)
• **2+**

Fair Value
• **21¼**

Risk
• **Low**

Earn./Div. Rank
• **B-**

Technical Eval.
• **Bullish** since 4/95

Rel. Strength Rank (1 Lowest—99 Highest)
• **85**

Insider Activity
• **Favorable**

Recent Price • 23 | Yield • Nil
52 Wk Range • 23⅛-15¼ | 12-Mo. P/E • 11.4

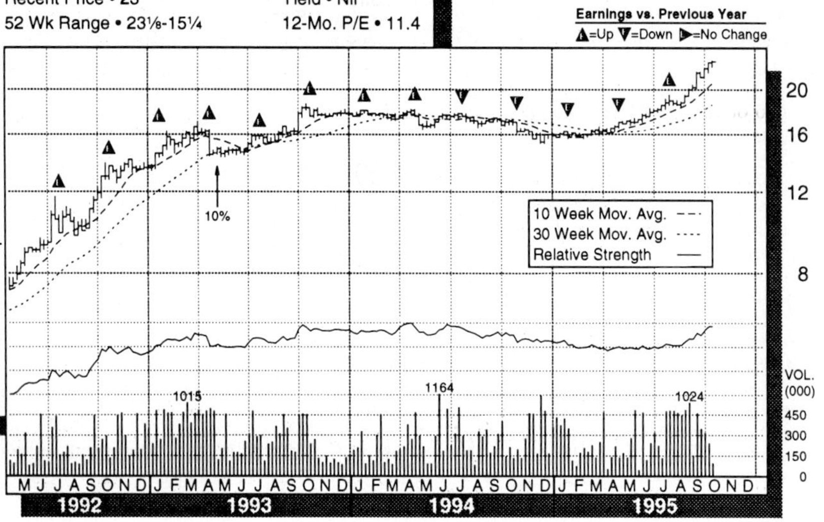

Business Profile - 11-OCT-95

Premier Bancorp recently agreed to be acquired by Banc One Corp. The merger is expected to be completed prior to year-end 1995. PRBC, formed by the 1985 merger of three Louisiana banks, operates 150 offices in seven of Louisiana's eight major metropolitan areas. Premier's total assets grew to $5.4 billion at year end 1994, up 29% from the previous year, with 75% of this growth achieved through the acquisitions of National Bank of Commerce, Heritage Financial Corp., and Red River Valley Bank.

Operational Review - 18-OCT-95

Net interest income for the nine months ended September 30, 1995, rose 4.9% year to year. There was no provision for loan losses, versus a negative provision of $5,828,000. Noninterest income (excluding securities transactions) climbed 14%, and noninterest expense was up 4.4%; pretax income advanced 4.0%. After taxes at 33.7% versus 31.9%, net income was up 1.3% to $52,349,000 ($1.51 a share, on 5.2% more shares) from $51,699,000 ($1.57).

Stock Performance - 13-OCT-95

In the past 30 trading days, PRBC's shares have increased 15%, compared to a 4% rise in the S&P 500. Average trading volume for the past five days was 17,880 shares, compared with the 40-day moving average of 90,867 shares.

Key Stock Statistics

Dividend Rate/Share	Nil	Shareholders	10,600
Shs. outstg. (M)	33.8	Market cap. (B)	$0.760
Avg. daily vol. (M)	0.057	Inst. holdings	37%
Tang. Bk. Value/Share	11.19	Insider holdings	NA
Beta	0.60		

Value of $10,000 invested 5 years ago: $ 56,832

Fiscal Year Ending Dec. 31

	1995	% Change	1994	% Change	1993	% Change
Revenues (Million $)						
1Q	115.4	22%	94.70	15%	82.10	-8%
2Q	123.0	22%	100.8	20%	84.15	-4%
3Q	—	—	106.4	24%	85.53	-2%
4Q	—	—	115.6	38%	83.73	-7%
Yr.	—	—	417.4	24%	335.5	-5%
Income (Million $)						
1Q	14.29	-8%	15.58	17%	13.36	56%
2Q	19.58	21%	16.13	-12%	18.27	101%
3Q	18.48	-8%	19.99	14%	17.58	39%
4Q	—	—	17.77	-3%	18.37	-8%
Yr.	—	—	69.47	3%	67.59	34%
Earnings Per Share ($)						
1Q	0.41	-15%	0.48	7%	0.45	65%
2Q	0.57	16%	0.49	-23%	0.64	171%
3Q	0.53	-10%	0.59	-6%	0.63	78%
4Q	—	—	0.51	-23%	0.66	19%
Yr.	—	—	2.08	-13%	2.38	69%

Next earnings report expected: mid January

Premier Bancorp

Business Summary - 18-OCT-95

Premier Bancorp, Inc. is a Louisiana-based bank holding company that was organized in early 1985. On December 30, 1988, all of the company's subsidiary banks were merged into one statewide national banking unit operating as Premier Bank. Premier operates 150 offices in seven of Louisiana's eight major metropolitan areas. Through nonbank affiliates, the company also offers discount brokerage and asset management services.

Total loans and leases, net of unearned income, at the end of 1994 of $2.76 billion ($2.38 billion at year-end 1993) were divided:

	1994	1993
Commercial	32%	34%
Commercial real estate	9%	12%
Retail-other	42%	38%
Retail-mortgage	13%	13%
Construction	4%	3%

The reserve for possible loan losses at 1994 year-end totaled $63,776,000 (2.31% of loans and leases outstanding), compared with $70,237,000 (2.96%) a year earlier. Net loan chargeoffs in 1994 were $382,000 (0.02% of average loans and leases), versus $9,256,000 (0.43%) in 1993. As of December 31, 1994, nonperforming loans totaled $19,557,000 (0.71% of loans and leases outstanding), compared with $22,604,000 (0.95%) a year earlier.

At year-end 1994, average deposits of $3.99 billion were apportioned: noninterest-bearing demand 22%, interest-bearing demand 14%, money market 13%, time deposits of $100,000 or more 12%, and savings and other time 39%.

On a tax-equivalent basis, the average yield on interest-earning assets was 7.65% in 1994 (7.85% in 1993), while the average rate paid on interest-bearing liabilities was 3.47% (3.22%), for a net spread of 4.18% (4.63%).

Important Developments

Oct. '95—Premier Bancorp reported a return on average assets of 1.34% and a return on average shareholders' equity of 15.20% for the third quarter of 1995. The return on average assets was 1.28% and the return on average shareholders' equity was 15.26% for the nine months ended September 30, 1995.

Capitalization

Long Term Debt: $284,794,000 (9/95).
Options: To purchase 1,149,610 shs. at $4.21 to $11.03 ea. (12/94).

Per Share Data ($) (Year Ended Dec. 31)

	1994	1993	1992	1991	1990	1989
Tangible Bk. Val.	11.19	12.23	8.16	6.39	5.34	5.40
Earnings	2.08	2.38	1.41	0.54	0.27	-3.90
Dividends	Nil	Nil	Nil	Nil	Nil	Nil
Payout Ratio	Nil	Nil	Nil	Nil	Nil	Nil
Prices - High	$18\frac{1}{8}$	$18\frac{5}{8}$	$14\frac{1}{8}$	$6\frac{7}{8}$	$4\frac{3}{4}$	$6\frac{1}{8}$
- Low	$15\frac{1}{4}$	$13\frac{1}{4}$	$5\frac{3}{4}$	$2\frac{5}{8}$	$2\frac{1}{4}$	$3\frac{3}{4}$
P/E Ratio - High	9	8	10	13	18	NM
- Low	7	6	4	5	8	NM

Income Statement Analysis (Million $)

	1994	%Chg	1993	%Chg	1992	%Chg	1991
Net Int. Inc.	216	19%	182	6%	172	19%	144
Tax Equiv. Adj.	2.8	27%	2.2	-15%	2.6	-21%	3.3
Non Int. Inc.	72.6	15%	63.2	6%	59.8	15%	52.2
Loan Loss Prov.	8.0	—	NM	—	11.0	-39%	18.0
% Exp/Op Revs.	67%	—	67%	—	71%	—	80%
Pretax Inc.	103	6%	97.0	64%	59.0	195%	20.0
Eff. Tax Rate	33%	—	30%	—	32%	—	26%
Net Inc.	69.0	1%	68.0	70%	40.0	167%	15.0
% Net Int. Marg.	4.83%	—	5.31%	—	5.05%	—	4.23%

Balance Sheet & Other Fin. Data (Million $)

	1994	1993	1992	1991	1990	1989
Earning Assets:						
Money Mkt.	249	291	410	222	121	NA
Inv. Securities	1,851	1,369	1,171	1,386	1,191	1,176
Com'l Loans	898	812	755	760	700	794
Other Loans	1,860	1,337	1,140	1,069	1,335	1,481
Total Assets	5,420	4,216	3,897	3,852	3,940	4,227
Demand Deposits	936	833	750	700	704	684
Time Deposits	3,398	2,642	2,536	2,658	2,774	3,064
LT Debt	311	87.7	66.3	44.9	45.8	47.9
Common Eqty.	424	331	221	173	155	146

Ratio Analysis

	1994	1993	1992	1991	1990	1989
% Ret. on Assets	1.4	1.8	1.1	0.4	0.2	NM
% Ret. on Equity	17.6	22.7	19.2	8.9	4.9	NM
% Loan Loss Resv.	2.3	3.1	4.4	4.8	4.3	4.2
% Loans/Deposits	63.6	61.8	57.7	54.4	58.5	59.2
% Equity to Assets	7.9	7.6	5.2	4.2	3.7	4.6

Dividend Data —Cash dividends were omitted in October 1986. Before declaring a cash dividend, Premier must receive permission from the Federal Reserve Bank of Atlanta.

Amt. of Div. $	Date Decl.	Ex-Div. Date	Stock of Record	Payment Date
0.250	Jul. 19	Aug. 11	Aug. 15	Aug. 31 '95

Data as orig. reptd.; bef. results of disc opers. and/or spec. items. Per share data adj. for stk. divs. as of ex-div. date. E-Estimated. NA-Not Available. NM-Not Meaningful. NR-Not Ranked.

Office—451 Florida St. (P.O. Box 1511), Baton Rouge, LA 70801 (70821). **Tel**—(504) 332-7277. **Chrmn & CEO**—G. L. Griffin. **Pres**—F. W. Lockett, Jr. **Exec VP & Secy**—J. H. Napper, II. **Vice Chrmn & CFO**—R. N. Williams. **Dirs**—F. M. Biedenharn, J. C. Blackman IV, D. T. Bollinger, V. G. Dean, G. L. Griffin, F. W. Harrison, Jr., F. W. Lockett, Jr., W. A. Marbury, Jr., M. V. Marmande, C. B. McCoy, H. B. McElveen, G. M. Millet, G. D. Nelson, Jr., J. B. Noland, J. B. Nowery, E. H. Owen, C. R. Patterson, Jr., B. M. Peters, T. H. Turner, R. N. Williams, R. E. Zuschlag. **Transfer Agent & Registrar**—Co. itself. **Incorporated** in Louisiana in 1985. **Empl**-2,948. **S&P Analyst:** Brad Ohlmuller

STANDARD & POOR'S

Pride Petroleum Services

STOCK REPORTS

NASDAQ Symbol **PRDE**

In S&P SmallCap 600

14-NOV-95 **Industry:** Oil and Gas

Summary: The second largest well servicing contractor in the world, Pride provides services in the U.S., Argentina, Venezuela and Russia.

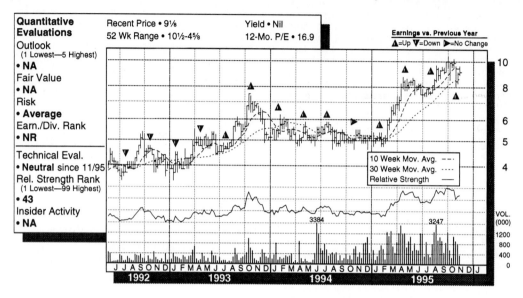

Quantitative Evaluations

Outlook (1 Lowest—5 Highest) • **NA**

Fair Value • **NA**

Risk • **Average**

Earn./Div. Rank • **NR**

Technical Eval. • **Neutral** since 11/95

Rel. Strength Rank (1 Lowest—99 Highest) • **43**

Insider Activity • **NA**

Recent Price • 9⅛

52 Wk Range • 10½-4⅝

Yield • Nil

12-Mo. P/E • 16.9

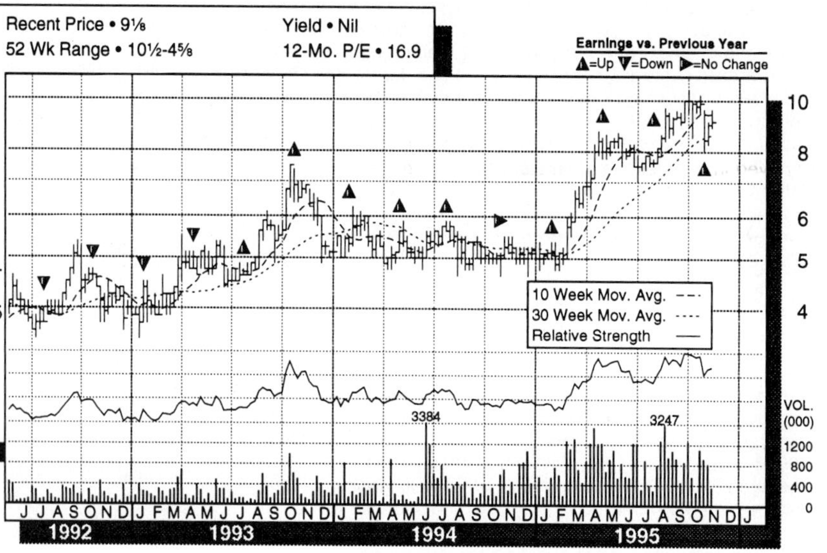

Business Profile - 14-NOV-95

Pride is the second largest well servicing contractor in the world, performing the maintenance and workovers on oil and gas rigs necessary to keep them operating efficiently. The company has actively sought to diversify away from the domestic onshore market, which has suffered recently; in 1994, international and domestic offshore operations accounted for 35% and 13%, respectively, of total revenues.

Operational Review - 14-NOV-95

Revenues in the first nine months of 1995 advanced 55%, year to year. Net income rose sharply to $11,227,000 ($0.44 a share, on 29% more shares), from $3,836,000 ($0.20). The company attributed its improved results to expanded operations and better performance in each of its operating regions, as well as to a $0.03 a share gain from insurance proceeds received from the loss of one of its U.S. land rigs.

Stock Performance - 10-NOV-95

In the past 30 trading days, PRDE's shares have declined 9%, compared to a 1% rise in the S&P 500. Average trading volume for the past five days was 69,620 shares, compared with the 40-day moving average of 162,125 shares.

Key Stock Statistics

Dividend Rate/Share	Nil	Shareholders	2,400
Shs. outstg. (M)	24.2	Market cap. (B)	$0.218
Avg. daily vol. (M)	0.162	Inst. holdings	84%
Tang. Bk. Value/Share	4.62	Insider holdings	NA
Beta	1.18		

Value of $10,000 invested 5 years ago: $ 14,313

Fiscal Year Ending Dec. 31

	1995	% Change	1994	% Change	1993	% Change
Revenues (Million $)						
1Q	62.51	70%	36.81	47%	25.09	5%
2Q	68.86	71%	40.26	52%	26.50	11%
3Q	67.14	32%	50.97	37%	37.25	44%
4Q	—	—	54.30	42%	38.26	38%
Yr.	—	—	182.3	43%	127.1	25%
Income (Million $)						
1Q	3.01	NM	0.93	NM	-0.70	NM
2Q	3.58	NM	0.98	104%	0.48	NM
3Q	4.63	140%	1.93	47%	1.31	NM
4Q	—	—	2.38	133%	1.02	NM
Yr.	—	—	6.21	194%	2.11	NM
Earnings Per Share ($)						
1Q	0.12	100%	0.06	NM	-0.04	NM
2Q	0.14	133%	0.06	100%	0.03	NM
3Q	0.18	125%	0.08	NM	0.08	NM
4Q	—	—	0.10	67%	0.06	NM
Yr.	—	—	0.30	131%	0.13	NM

Next earnings report expected: late February

Pride Petroleum Services

Business Summary - 14-NOV-95

Pride Petroleum Services, Inc., which became a publicly traded company on August 31, 1988, as a result of the restructuring of DEKALB Corp. (subsequently renamed and continuing business as DEKALB Energy Co.), is the second largest well servicing contractor in the world, providing well servicing, workover, completion and plugging and abandonment services for the domestic and international oil and gas industry. Pride's fleet of 482 owned rigs (as of year-end 1994) consisted of 400 rigs in the United States, 58 rigs deployed in international markets, and 22 offshore platform rigs located in the Gulf of Mexico and off the coast of Venezuela.

Domestically, the company operates its rigs and other equipment from 21 service stations located in three general geographic areas. These are the Southern area, which includes the Texas Gulf Coast, East Texas and Louisiana; the Central area, which is comprised of the Permian Basin of West Texas and New Mexico; and the Western area, principally California.

In the United States, the company's customers range from major integrated oil companies to small independent operators. Approximately 60% of domestic onshore revenues in 1994 were generated from Pride's 20 largest U.S. customers, with no one customer accounting for more than 8% of revenues. However, Shell Oil accounted for approximately 40% of domestic offshore revenues in 1994.

International operations are an increasingly important source of revenue for the company, comprising over 35% of revenues in 1994. In this market, Pride works for government-owned companies, multinationals and local independents. In Argentina, 67% of business is with YPF (which accounted for 18% of total revenues in 1994), and the remainder with multinational and local companies. Pride provides services for three subsidiaries of Petroleos de Venezuela, and in Russia, the company's current contracts are with a joint venture entity.

The well servicing industry is driven in large part by the direction of oil and gas prices. As prices decline, producers are more apt to postpone servicing activities or shut down marginal wells.

Important Developments

Nov. '95—Pride said it completed the acquisition of Marlin Colombia Drilling Co., which owns six drilling/workover rigs in the Republic of Colombia, from Shell Overseas Trading Limited for an undisclosed amount.

Capitalization

Long Term Debt: $58,207,000 (3/95).

Per Share Data ($) (Year Ended Dec. 31)

	1994	1993	1992	1991	1990	1989
Tangible Bk. Val.	4.49	4.24	3.85	3.92	3.69	3.36
Cash Flow	0.76	0.49	0.27	0.55	0.56	0.29
Earnings	0.30	0.13	-0.05	0.22	0.29	0.05
Dividends	Nil	Nil	Nil	Nil	Nil	Nil
Payout Ratio	Nil	Nil	Nil	Nil	Nil	Nil
Prices - High	6¼	7½	5⅜	7	8⅝	6⅝
- Low	4⅝	3½	3⅜	3⅝	4	2⅝
P/E Ratio - High	21	58	NM	32	30	NM
- Low	15	27	NM	16	14	NM

Income Statement Analysis (Million $)

	1994	%Chg	1993	%Chg	1992	%Chg	1991
Revs.	182	43%	127	26%	101	-10%	112
Oper. Inc.	17.6	100%	8.8	193%	3.0	-71%	10.3
Depr.	9.6	61%	5.9	14%	5.2	-5%	5.5
Int. Exp.	0.7	NM	0.0	—	Nil	—	0.0
Pretax Inc.	8.1	145%	3.3	NM	-1.4	NM	5.7
Eff. Tax Rate	23%	—	37%	—	NM	—	39%
Net Inc.	6.2	194%	2.1	NM	-0.8	NM	3.5

Balance Sheet & Other Fin. Data (Million $)

	1994	1993	1992	1991	1990	1989
Cash	9.0	15.2	24.1	17.0	8.9	21.8
Curr. Assets	60.3	46.0	43.5	35.4	29.6	35.6
Total Assets	205	110	94.8	89.8	85.6	72.5
Curr. Liab.	33.6	24.3	18.4	12.1	10.0	8.3
LT Debt	42.1	0.2	3.7	4.9	5.9	2.0
Common Eqty.	111	69.1	61.8	62.4	58.9	53.1
Total Cap.	166	80.6	76.4	77.7	75.6	64.1
Cap. Exp.	59.2	23.8	4.1	5.9	14.7	4.6
Cash Flow	15.8	8.1	4.4	9.0	9.1	3.4

Ratio Analysis

	1994	1993	1992	1991	1990	1989
Curr. Ratio	1.8	1.9	2.4	2.9	2.9	4.3
% LT Debt of Cap.	25.3	0.2	4.8	6.3	7.9	3.0
% Net Inc.of Revs.	3.4	1.7	NM	3.1	4.6	0.8
% Ret. on Assets	3.4	2.0	NM	4.0	5.9	0.8
% Ret. on Equity	5.8	3.2	NM	5.8	8.3	1.1

Dividend Data —No cash dividends have been paid. On September 2, 1988, in a tax-free spinoff, holders of DEKALB Corp. Class A and Class B common stock received one share of Pride Petroleum common stock for each share of DEKALB common held. DEKALB also spun off its agricultural genetics business, which began to trade publicly as DEKALB Genetics.

Data as orig. reptd.; bef. results of disc. opers. and/or spec. items. Per share data adj. for stk. divs. as of ex-div. date. E-Estimated. NA-Not Available. NM-Not Meaningful. NR-Not Ranked.

Office—1500 City West Blvd., Suite 400, Houston, TX 77042. **Tel**—(713) 789-1400. **Chrmn, Pres & CEO**—R. H. Tolson. **VP-CFO & Treas**—P. A. Bragg. **Dirs**—J. B. Clement, J. E. Estrada M., T. H. Roberts, Jr., J. T. Sneed, R. H. Tolson. **Transfer Agent & Registrar**—American Stock Transfer & Trust Co., NYC. **Incorporated** in Louisiana in 1988. **Empl**-3,850. **S&P Analyst:** S.R.B.

Primark Corp.

NYSE Symbol **PMK**
In S&P SmallCap 600

11-OCT-95 **Industry:** Publishing

Summary: Through its wholly owned subsidiaries, this holding company is primarily engaged in providing high-technology global information services.

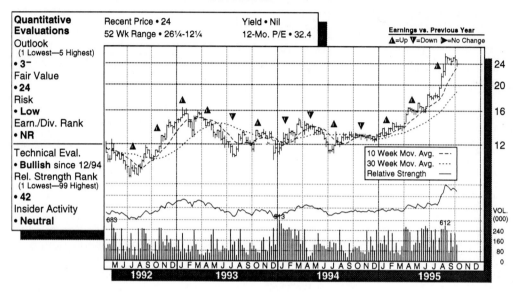

Quantitative Evaluations

Outlook (1 Lowest—5 Highest) • **3-**

Fair Value • **24**

Risk • **Low**

Earn./Div. Rank • **NR**

Technical Eval. • **Bullish** since 12/94

Rel. Strength Rank (1 Lowest—99 Highest) • **42**

Insider Activity • **Neutral**

Recent Price • 24 | Yield • Nil

52 Wk Range • 26¼-12¼ | 12-Mo. P/E • 32.4

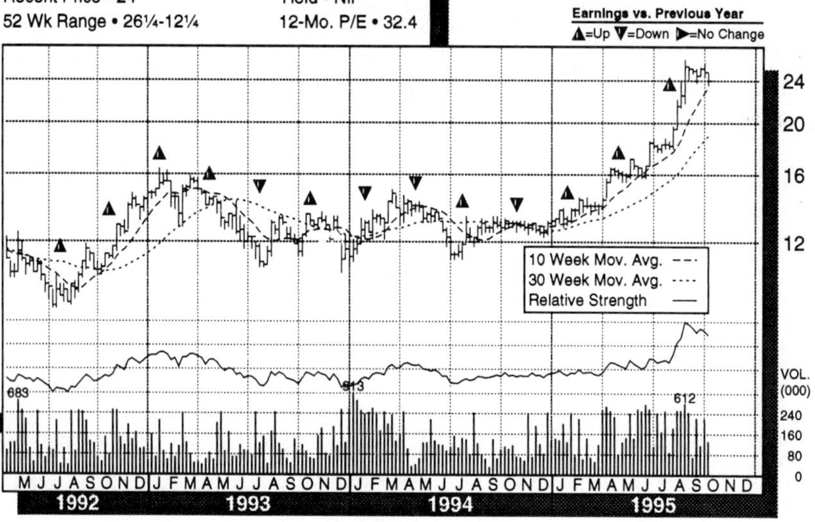

Business Profile - 06-OCT-95

This global information services company recently acquired Disclosure, Inc. and certain of its affiliates, including I/B/E/S, Inc. The acquisition is expected to significantly increase PMK's role in the financial information services industry and dramatically improve the range of products and services offered to institutional investment and money management professionals worldwide. Looking forward, the company will continue to focus on expanding its information services outside the U.S.

Operational Review - 11-OCT-95

Operating revenues for the six months ended June 30, 1995, rose 21%, year to year, led by higher revenues from the core information services segment and the transportation services segment. Operating margins widened, and operating income increased 33%. Following a $2.1 million foreign currency loss and lower interest expense, pretax income advanced 37%. After taxes at 44.3% versus 43.4% net income was up 35% to $9,030,000 ($0.42 a share, after preferred dividends) from $6,701,000 ($0.30).

Stock Performance - 06-OCT-95

In the past 30 trading days, PMK's shares have declined 6%, compared to a 4% rise in the S&P 500. Average trading volume for the past five days was 25,820 shares, compared with the 40-day moving average of 51,964 shares.

Key Stock Statistics

Dividend Rate/Share	Nil	Shareholders	11,200
Shs. outstg. (M)	18.9	Market cap. (B)	$0.421
Avg. daily vol. (M)	0.046	Inst. holdings	50%
Tang. Bk. Value/Share	NM	Insider holdings	NA
Beta	0.94		

Value of $10,000 invested 5 years ago: $ 25,263

Fiscal Year Ending Dec. 31

	1995	% Change	1994	% Change	1993	% Change
Revenues (Million $)						
1Q	135.9	21%	112.4	3%	108.9	59%
2Q	143.0	20%	119.0	7%	111.5	53%
3Q	—	—	121.0	8%	112.2	51%
4Q	—	—	124.6	12%	111.4	18%
Yr.	—	—	477.0	7%	444.0	43%
Income (Million $)						
1Q	4.45	42%	3.14	-16%	3.76	54%
2Q	4.58	29%	3.56	NM	0.84	-3%
3Q	—	—	3.28	-13%	3.78	104%
4Q	—	—	3.77	13%	3.35	-13%
Yr.	—	—	13.75	17%	11.73	30%
Earnings Per Share ($)						
1Q	0.20	43%	0.14	-18%	0.17	55%
2Q	0.21	31%	0.16	NM	0.02	-33%
3Q	—	—	0.15	-12%	0.17	113%
4Q	—	—	0.17	13%	0.15	-17%
Yr.	—	—	0.62	19%	0.52	30%

Next earnings report expected: mid November

Primark Corp.

Business Summary - 11-OCT-95

Primark Corp. is now primarily engaged, through wholly owned subsidiaries, in providing high-technology and financial information services, following two major acquisitions in 1991 and 1992, and a number of divestitures including the sale of its mortgage banking business and the liquidation of its life insurance unit during 1993. Industry segment contributions in 1994:

	Revs.	Profits
Information services	89%	83%
Transportation services	10%	7%
Financial services	2%	10%

TASC, Inc. provides high-technology information services mainly to the U.S. government, and also to business organizations. Revenues from U.S. government contracts represented approximately 88%, 89% and 89% of TASC's revenues in 1994, 1993 and 1992, respectively. TASC's business is performed under two contract forms: cost reimbursement plus a fee, and fixed price. About 83% of the contracts are cost reimbursement, which virtually guarantees a profit, and 17% are more risky fixed price contracts.

Datastream International, acquired in September 1992, is a worldwide financial information services firm headquartered in London that provides on-line investment research products and services to financial institutions and investment professionals in 41 countries worldwide.

Primark Storage Leasing Corp. owns and leases to ANR Pipeline Co. eight underground natural gas storage fields and related facilities, and explores for and develops mineral resources underneath the storage fields through farmout agreements with exploration companies.

Triad International Maintenance Corp. (TIMCO) provides major maintenance services to operators and owners of aircraft. It currently has two anchor customers, ABX Air, Inc. and Emery Worldwide Airlines.

Important Developments

Sep. '95—PMK announced that its Disclosure Inc. subsidiary will be further extending its reach to individual investors by making data on over 25,000 publicly traded companies worldwide available over America Online.

Aug. '95—PMK announced that data from four of its financial data subsidiaries will be available over The Microsoft Network (MSN). The subsidiaries include Disclosure, Inc.; Datastream Intl.; Vestek; and I/B/E/S. The company also announced that its WSI Corp. subsidiary has joined with NBC News to be the primary source of local and worldwide weather on MSN.

Capitalization

Long Term Debt: $269,016,000 (6/95).
Red. Preferred Stock: $16,874,000.

Per Share Data ($) (Year Ended Dec. 31)

	1994	1993	1992	1991	1990	1989
Tangible Bk. Val.	-3.29	-4.42	-5.83	4.68	10.66	10.34
Cash Flow	2.00	1.84	0.98	0.23	0.10	0.41
Earnings	0.62	0.52	0.40	0.02	0.03	0.23
Dividends	Nil	Nil	Nil	Nil	Nil	Nil
Payout Ratio	Nil	Nil	Nil	Nil	Nil	Nil
Prices - High	15	16³/₈	14³/₄	14³/₄	9¹/₂	10¹/₄
- Low	11	10¹/₂	9	6	5⁵/₈	6¹/₂
P/E Ratio - High	24	31	37	NM	NM	45
- Low	18	20	23	NM	NM	28

Income Statement Analysis (Million $)

	1994	%Chg	1993	%Chg	1992	%Chg	1991
Revs.	477	7%	444	43%	310	103%	153
Oper. Inc.	65.6	3%	63.5	96%	32.3	NM	1.6
Depr.	27.5	5%	26.2	132%	11.3	166%	4.3
Int. Exp.	14.2	-3%	14.6	147%	5.9	96%	3.0
Pretax Inc.	23.5	10%	21.3	31%	16.2	NM	1.3
Eff. Tax Rate	42%	—	45%	—	44%	—	30%
Net Inc.	13.8	18%	11.7	30%	9.0	NM	0.9

Balance Sheet & Other Fin. Data (Million $)

	1994	1993	1992	1991	1990	1989
Cash	20.0	18.0	23.1	48.0	115	112
Curr. Assets	135	125	142	153	157	170
Total Assets	508	497	523	335	219	254
Curr. Liab.	97.0	102	109	83.0	13.6	27.8
LT Debt	146	148	171	31.5	1.0	0.5
Common Eqty.	225	208	202	195	193	205
Total Cap.	401	386	403	249	201	216
Cap. Exp.	22.6	12.7	6.9	NA	NA	NA
Cash Flow	39.9	36.5	19.0	4.6	1.9	8.1

Ratio Analysis

	1994	1993	1992	1991	1990	1989
Curr. Ratio	1.4	1.2	1.3	1.8	11.5	6.1
% LT Debt of Cap.	36.4	38.3	42.5	12.6	0.5	0.2
% Net Inc.of Revs.	2.9	2.6	2.9	0.6	2.4	11.6
% Ret. on Assets	2.7	2.3	1.9	0.3	0.3	1.7
% Ret. on Equity	5.7	5.0	3.6	0.2	0.3	2.2

Dividend Data —Dividends, which were initiated in 1982, ceased following PMK's spinoff to shareholders of Michigan Consolidated Gas in 1988. A "poison pill" stock purchase rights plan was adopted in 1988.

Data as orig. reptd.; bef. results of disc. opers. and/or spec. items. Per share data adj. for stk. divs. as of ex-div. date. E-Estimated. NA-Not Available. NM-Not Meaningful. NR-Not Ranked.

Office—1000 Winter Street, Suite 4300N, Waltham, MA 02154. **Tel**—(617) 466-6611. **Chrmn, Pres & CEO**—J. E. Kasputys. **SVP-Secy**—M. R. Kargula. **SVP, CFO & Treas**—S. H. Curran. **EVP**—J. C. Holt. **Investor Contact**—Steven L. Schneider (617-487-2131). **Dirs**—K. J. Bradley, J. C. Holt, J. E. Kasputys, S. Lazarus, C. R. Montgomery, R. W. Stewart, C. K. Weaver. **Transfer Agent & Registrar**—Bank of Boston. **Incorporated** in Michigan in 1981. **Empl**-3,789. **S&P Analyst:** Brad Ohlmuller

STANDARD & POOR'S

STOCK REPORTS

Prime Hospitality

NYSE Symbol **PDQ**

04-OCT-95 **Industry:** Hotels/Motels/Inns

Summary: This company owns or manages hotels throughout the U.S. under its proprietary trade names and under franchise agreements with national hotel chains.

Quantitative Evaluations

Outlook (1 Lowest—5 Highest)
• **NA**

Fair Value
• **NA**

Risk
• **Average**

Earn./Div. Rank
• **NR**

Technical Eval.
• **Bullish** since 8/95

Rel. Strength Rank (1 Lowest—99 Highest)
• **16**

Insider Activity
• **NA**

Recent Price • 10¼
52 Wk Range • 11-6⅞

Yield • Nil
12-Mo. P/E • 19.0

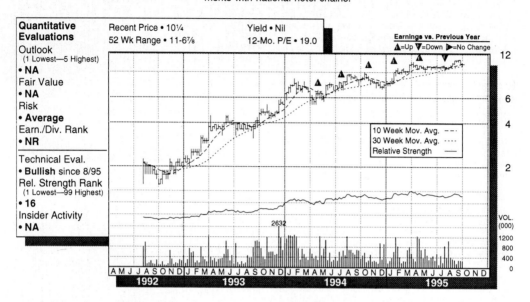

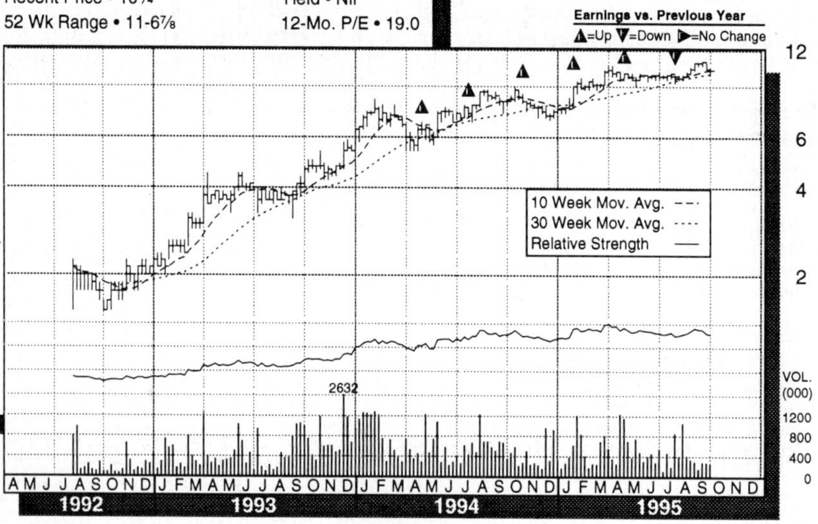

Business Profile - 04-OCT-95

This company plans to accelerate the growth of its AmeriSuites all-suite hotel chain and focus on full-service hotel acquisitions. To this end, it recently retained an investment advisor to explore the sale of its limited-service Wellesley Inn hotel chain. The company believes that hotel industry conditions are currently favorable, with demand growth outpacing new hotel supply, resulting in higher occupancy levels and improved room rates.

Operational Review - 04-OCT-95

Revenues in the first half of 1995 advanced 63% year to year, aided by growth in room rates and the addition of 13 hotels through acquisition or construction. Hurt by the absence of a $4.1 million non-recurring gain on the settlement of a note receivable, net income declined to $9,123,000 ($0.28 share) from $9,709,000 ($0.30). Results exclude an extraordinary gain of $0.01 a share in the 1994 period for the discharge of indebtedness.

Stock Performance - 29-SEP-95

In the past 30 trading days, PDQ's shares have increased 3%, compared to a 5% rise in the S&P 500. Average trading volume for the past five days was 49,760 shares, compared with the 40-day moving average of 77,146 shares.

Key Stock Statistics

Dividend Rate/Share	Nil	Shareholders	2,900
Shs. outstg. (M)	30.9	Market cap. (B)	$0.293
Avg. daily vol. (M)	0.060	Inst. holdings	70%
Tang. Bk. Value/Share	7.06	Insider holdings	NA
Beta	NM		

Value of $10,000 invested 5 years ago: NA

Fiscal Year Ending Dec. 31

	1995	% Change	1994	% Change	1993	% Change
Revenues (Million $)						
1Q	48.24	72%	28.08	13%	24.79	—
2Q	51.70	56%	33.19	24%	26.69	—
3Q	—	—	36.06	22%	29.48	—
4Q	—	—	36.97	32%	27.91	—
Yr.	—	—	134.3	23%	108.9	-19%
Income (Million $)						
1Q	4.21	48%	2.84	184%	1.00	—
2Q	4.91	-29%	6.87	NM	1.59	—
3Q	—	—	4.12	22%	3.38	—
4Q	—	—	4.43	100%	2.21	—
Yr.	—	—	18.26	123%	8.18	NM
Earnings Per Share ($)						
1Q	0.13	63%	0.08	167%	0.03	—
2Q	0.14	-36%	0.22	NM	0.05	—
3Q	—	—	0.13	30%	0.10	—
4Q	—	—	0.14	133%	0.06	—
Yr.	—	—	0.57	138%	0.24	NM

Next earnings report expected: mid October

Prime Hospitality

Business Summary - 04-OCT-95

Prime Hospitality (formerly Prime Motor Inns, Inc.) owns, develops, leases and sells full-service, limited-service and all-suite hotel properties, manages hotels owned or leased by third parties, and manages a portfolio of mortgages, notes and other financial assets. The company emerged from Chapter 11 bankruptcy proceedings in July 1992. Occupancy and average daily room rates for all owned hotels in recent years (ended December 31):

	1994	1993	1992
Occupancy	73.1%	70.0%	68.0%
Average daily room rate	$61.16	$56.02	$54.83

Prime hotels are operated or managed by the company pursuant to franchise agreements with national hotel chains such as Howard Johnson, Ramada, Marriott, Holiday Inn, Sheraton and Radisson. In addition, the company owns the trademarks Wellesley Inns and AmeriSuites. The hotels are located primarily in secondary markets in 19 states and the U.S. Virgin Islands.

At December 31, 1994, the company's portfolio consisted of 87 hotels with 12,743 rooms. Prime owns or leases 50 hotels and manages 37 hotels for third parties. In addition, it holds financial interests in the form of mortgages or profit participations in 17 of the managed hotels. In total, the company has equity or financial interests in 67 hotels with about 10,000 rooms.

About 53% of the rooms are in full-service hotels. The AmeriSuites, which are mid-priced, all-suite hotels, comprise 12% of total rooms. The company also competes in the limited-service segment primarily through its economically-priced Wellesley Inns, which comprise about 35% of hotel rooms.

Important Developments

Aug. '95—The company announced the acquisition of the all-suite St. Tropez Hotel & Shopping Center in Las Vegas, which is comprised of 149 suites and a 34,000 sq. ft. shopping center, for $15.2 million. Separately, Prime said it retained Smith Barney Inc. to explore the sale of its Wellesley Inn chain, citing plans to accelerate the growth of its all-suite hotel chain and to focus on full-service hotel acquisitions.

Aug. '95—Prime said it entered into an agreement to purchase four Bradbury Suites Hotels, comprised of 459 rooms, for $18.9 million. The company plans to convert the hotels to its proprietary AmeriSuites brand.

Capitalization

Long Term Debt: $178,545,000 (12/94).

Per Share Data ($)

(Year Ended Dec. 31)

	1994	1993	1992	1991	1990	1989
Tangible Bk. Val.	6.71	5.18	NM	NA	NA	12.59
Cash Flow	0.86	0.45	NM	NA	NA	2.67
Earnings	0.57	0.24	NM	NA	NA	2.35
Dividends	Nil	Nil	Nil	Nil	0.08	0.08
Payout Ratio	Nil	Nil	Nil	Nil	NA	3%
Prices - High	9	6⅜	2¼	2	23¾	37½
- Low	5⅜	2	1½	3/16	⅜	21⅝
P/E Ratio - High	16	27	NM	NA	NA	16
- Low	9	8	NM	NA	NA	9

Income Statement Analysis (Million $)

	1994	%Chg	1993	%Chg	1992	%Chg	1991
Revs.	134	23%	109	NM	109	-36%	171
Oper. Inc.	42.7	34%	31.9	NM	3.9	NM	-20.6
Depr.	9.3	33%	7.0	1%	6.9	-13%	7.9
Int. Exp.	14.8	-8%	16.1	92%	8.4	-59%	20.3
Pretax Inc.	30.0	114%	14.0	NM	-71.0	NM	-259
Eff. Tax Rate	40%	—	41%	—	NM	—	NM
Net Inc.	18.0	125%	8.0	NM	-72.0	NM	-245

Balance Sheet & Other Fin. Data (Million $)

	1994	1993	1992	1991	1990	1989
Cash	22.0	53.0	60.0	61.0	NA	40.0
Curr. Assets	39.0	68.0	134	115	NA	270
Total Assets	435	411	554	680	NA	1,144
Curr. Liab.	29.0	42.0	32.0	33.0	NA	196
LT Debt	179	169	9.0	3.0	NA	423
Common Eqty.	204	171	-228	-156	NA	452
Total Cap.	383	340	-219	-153	NA	922
Cap. Exp.	63.4	23.4	14.1	21.9	NA	73.0
Cash Flow	28.0	15.0	-65.0	-237	NA	88.0

Ratio Analysis

	1994	1993	1992	1991	1990	1989
Curr. Ratio	1.3	1.6	4.2	3.5	NA	1.4
% LT Debt of Cap.	46.7	49.6	NM	NM	NA	45.8
% Net Inc.of Revs.	13.6	7.5	NM	NM	NA	24.6
% Ret. on Assets	4.5	1.7	NM	NA	NA	7.5
% Ret. on Equity	10.1	NM	NM	NA	NA	18.7

Dividend Data —No cash dividends have been paid. The company does not anticipate paying any dividends on the common stock in the foreseeable future.

Data as orig. reptd.; bef. results of disc. opers. and/or spec. items. Per share data adj. for stk. divs. as of ex-div. date. E-Estimated. NA-Not Available. NM-Not Meaningful. NR-Not Ranked.

Office—700 Route 46 East, Fairfield, NJ 07004. **Tel**—(201) 882-1010. **Chrmn, Pres & CEO**—D. A. Simon. **EVP-CFO**—J. Elwood. **SVP-Secy**—J. Bernadino. **VP-Treas**—D. Vicari. **Dirs**—J. M. Elwood, H. M. Lorber, H. Lust II, J. H. Nusbaum, A. J. Ostroff, A. F. Petrocelli, D. A. Simon. **Transfer Agent & Registrar**—Continental Stock Transfer & Trust Co., NYC. **Incorporated** in Delaware in 1985. **Empl**-5,000. **S&P Analyst:** S.R.B.

STANDARD & POOR'S

STOCK REPORTS

Production Operators

NASDAQ Symbol **PROP**

In S&P SmallCap 600

10-OCT-95 **Industry:** Oil and Gas

Summary: This oilfield service company specializes in the handling of gases for maximizing the recovery of hydrocarbon resources. Services include compression and processing of natural gas.

Quantitative Evaluations

Outlook (1 Lowest—5 Highest) • **NA**

Fair Value • **NA**

Risk • **Low**

Earn./Div. Rank • **B+**

Technical Eval. • **Bullish** since 12/94

Rel. Strength Rank (1 Lowest—99 Highest) • **64**

Insider Activity • **NA**

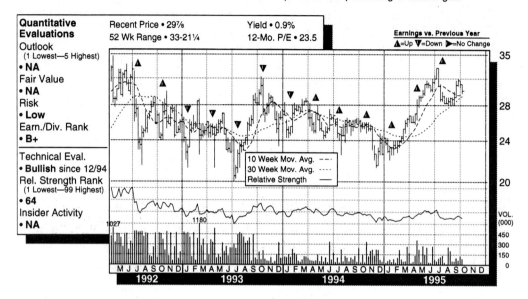

Recent Price • 29⅞ Yield • 0.9%

52 Wk Range • 33-21¼ 12-Mo. P/E • 23.5

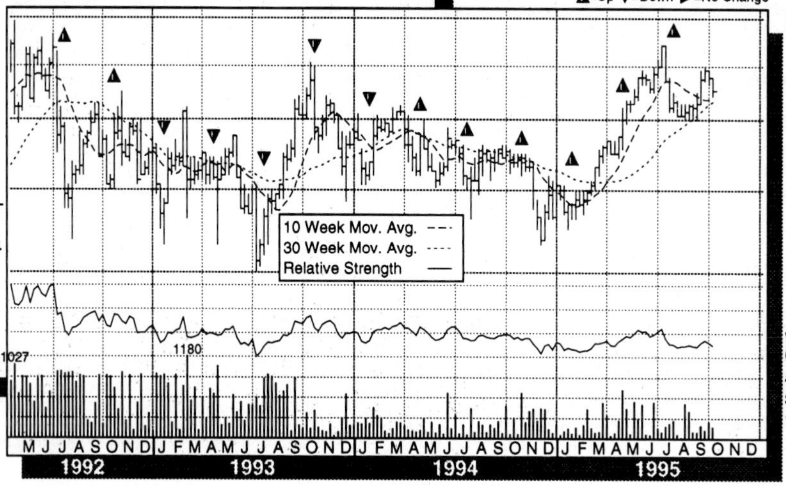

Business Profile - 10-OCT-95

Production Operators Corp is an oilfield service company that compresses and processes natural gas to maximize the recovery of hydrocarbon resources and performs specialized enhanced oil recovery services. In July 1995, the company announced that it was exiting the oil and gas production business. Earnings rose slightly during fiscal 1994, on a moderate upturn in revenues. Capital spending was increased significantly in fiscal 1994.

Operational Review - 10-OCT-95

For the nine months ended June 30, 1995, revenues rose 5.6%, year to year. Most costs and expenses were well controlled, but interest expense was sharply higher. Net income advanced 11%. Share earnings were $0.95, versus $0.86. Results exclude a $0.02 a share special credit from an accounting change in the fiscal 1994 period.

Stock Performance - 06-OCT-95

In the past 30 trading days, PROP's shares have increased 3%, compared to a 4% rise in the S&P 500. Average trading volume for the past five days was 17,360 shares, compared with the 40-day moving average of 23,272 shares.

Key Stock Statistics

Dividend Rate/Share	0.28	Shareholders	1,000
Shs. outstg. (M)	10.1	Market cap. (B)	$0.306
Avg. daily vol. (M)	0.018	Inst. holdings	56%
Tang. Bk. Value/Share	14.01	Insider holdings	NA
Beta	0.12		

Value of $10,000 invested 5 years ago: $ 18,651

Fiscal Year Ending Sep. 30

	1995	% Change	1994	% Change	1993	% Change
Revenues (Million $)						
1Q	19.43	1%	19.20	7%	17.90	-6%
2Q	19.86	5%	18.89	7%	17.58	-5%
3Q	20.97	11%	18.97	6%	17.88	-4%
4Q	—	—	18.41	-2%	18.82	NM
Yr.	—	—	75.47	5%	72.15	-4%
Income (Million $)						
1Q	3.08	8%	2.85	-8%	3.10	23%
2Q	3.04	7%	2.84	2%	2.79	4%
3Q	3.53	17%	3.03	10%	2.76	-17%
4Q	—	—	3.28	16%	2.82	-33%
Yr.	—	—	12.00	5%	11.47	-10%
Earnings Per Share ($)						
1Q	0.30	7%	0.28	-10%	0.31	-3%
2Q	0.30	7%	0.28	4%	0.27	-10%
3Q	0.35	17%	0.30	11%	0.27	-18%
4Q	—	—	0.32	14%	0.28	-32%
Yr.	—	—	1.18	4%	1.13	-18%

Next earnings report expected: mid November

Production Operators

Business Summary - 10-OCT-95

Production Operators Corp is engaged in oil and gas production services through its Production Operators, Inc. (POI) subsidiary. The company principally provides two kinds of services on a contract basis to oil and gas producers and pipeline companies: compression, treating and processing of gases, primarily natural gas, and specialized enhanced oil recovery services. It also engages in contract operations of customer-owned equipment and the production of oil and gas through its Kamlok Oil & Gas, Inc. subsidiary.

Operating revenues and profits in fiscal 1994 were derived as follows:

	Revs.	Profits.
Contract gas handling services	76%	86%
Oil & gas operations	18%	9%
Enhanced oil recovery	6%	5%

POI designs, fabricates, installs, operates and services gas compression units specifically designed to meet customer requirements. These units are typically owned and operated by the company. Gas compression services are needed to increase the pressure of gas for its transmission in pipelines and to compress gas for injection into oilfields in secondary recovery operations. At the end of fiscal 1994, the company's fleet of compressors totaled 322,000 horsepower, over 80% of which were revenue producing, and was installed at more than 200 locations in North America, the Gulf of Mexico and Venezuela. In its gas-processing operations, usually performed in conjunction with gas compression, POI designs, installs and operates specialized processing or treating equipment that recovers liquid hydrocarbons from associated gas streams or removes undesirable impurities.

The company's enhanced oil recovery operations include gathering, transporting, compressing and injecting carbon dioxide gases used in enhanced oil recovery projects. POI is engaged in various enhanced oil recovery projects, including the operation of the wholly owned Comanche Creek Pipeline System in west Texas.

As of September 30, 1994, the company operated 76 gross (75.9 net) productive oil wells 49 gross (48.0 net) gas wells. During fiscal 1994, the company produced 576 Mbbl of oil and 2,379 Mmcf of gas.

Important Developments

Jul. '95—PROP said that it plans to exit the oil and gas production businesss. The company indicated that it had not been successful in adding to its reserves in recent years and the segment (which represents 8.6% of total assets) no longer justifies retention on a stand-alone basis.

Capitalization

Senior Term Notes: $43,000,000 (6/95).

Per Share Data ($) (Year Ended Sep. 30)

	1994	1993	1992	1991	1990	1989
Tangible Bk. Val.	13.27	12.23	11.67	6.71	4.93	4.25
Cash Flow	2.53	2.38	2.72	2.54	2.20	2.01
Earnings	1.18	1.13	1.37	0.99	0.76	0.65
Dividends	0.24	0.21	0.19	0.16	0.16	0.16
Payout Ratio	20%	19%	15%	17%	20%	24%
Prices - High	28⅞	31¾	34¾	26	21¼	16⅞
- Low	21¼	20	21½	12½	13¼	4⅝
P/E Ratio - High	24	28	25	26	28	26
- Low	18	18	16	13	17	7

Income Statement Analysis (Million $)

	1994	%Chg	1993	%Chg	1992	%Chg	1991
Revs.	73.4	4%	70.6	-3%	73.1	10%	66.4
Oper. Inc.	30.3	9%	27.8	-7%	30.0	19%	25.3
Depr.	13.7	8%	12.7	2%	12.5	11%	11.3
Int. Exp.	0.3	NM	0.0	-97%	1.4	-62%	3.7
Pretax Inc.	18.3	11%	16.5	-9%	18.1	65%	11.0
Eff. Tax Rate	35%	—	31%	—	30%	—	34%
Net Inc.	12.0	4%	11.5	-9%	12.7	74%	7.3

Balance Sheet & Other Fin. Data (Million $)

	1994	1993	1992	1991	1990	1989
Cash	3.6	17.0	16.3	0.3	0.5	1.5
Curr. Assets	27.6	43.2	38.2	21.1	12.4	12.5
Total Assets	168	150	139	120	84.0	73.0
Curr. Liab.	12.3	12.3	9.5	12.5	7.9	5.8
LT Debt	6.0	0.4	1.3	47.2	34.3	32.3
Common Eqty.	134	123	116	51.0	34.0	29.0
Total Cap.	156	138	129	108	76.0	68.0
Cap. Exp.	46.0	19.7	15.6	39.7	26.1	16.5
Cash Flow	25.7	24.2	25.2	18.6	15.8	14.0

Ratio Analysis

	1994	1993	1992	1991	1990	1989
Curr. Ratio	2.2	3.5	4.0	1.7	1.6	2.2
% LT Debt of Cap.	3.9	0.3	1.0	43.9	45.4	47.8
% Net Inc.of Revs.	16.3	16.2	17.3	10.9	9.7	8.5
% Ret. on Assets	7.5	7.9	8.6	6.9	6.9	6.5
% Ret. on Equity	9.3	9.6	13.9	16.5	17.2	15.7

Dividend Data —Cash has been paid each year since 1976.

Amt. of Div. $	Date Decl.	Ex-Div. Date	Stock of Record	Payment Date
0.060	Sep. 30	Oct. 07	Oct. 14	Nov. 15 '94
0.060	Dec. 30	Jan. 09	Jan. 13	Feb. 15 '95
0.060	Mar. 31	Apr. 07	Apr. 14	May. 15 '95
0.070	Jun. 30	Jul. 12	Jul. 14	Aug. 15 '95
0.070	Sep. 29	Oct. 11	Oct. 13	Nov. 15 '95

Data as orig. reptd.; bef. results of disc. opers. and/or spec. items. Per share data adj. for stk. divs. as of ex-div. date. E-Estimated. NA-Not Available. NM-Not Meaningful. NR-Not Ranked.

Offices—11302 Tanner Rd., Houston, TX 77041; 515 One Piedmont Center, 3565 Piedmont Road, N.E., Atlanta, GA 30305. **Tels**—(713) 466-0980; (404) 231-1550. **Chrmn**—C. W. Knobloch Jr. **Pres**—D. J. Ogren. **CFO & Treas**—W. S. Robinson Jr. **Secy & Investor Contact**—Carla Knobloch. **Dirs**—F. E. Ellis, J. E. Estrada M., C. R. George, J. R. Huff, C. W. Knobloch Jr., H. E. Longley, D. J. Ogren, L. Varn Jr. **Transfer Agent & Registrar**—Bank of New York, NYC. **Reincorporated** in Delaware in 1969. **Empl**-414. **S&P Analyst:** D.J.B

Protective Life Corp.

NYSE Symbol PL

Price	Range	P-E Ratio	Dividend	Yield	S&P Ranking	Beta
Aug. 30'95	1995					
27⅞	29 9/16–21⅜	10	0.62	2.3%	B+	0.35

Summary

This holding company provides individual and group life and health products and annuities throughout the U.S. It has followed a policy of acquiring small, inactive or troubled companies, or of assuming blocks of insurance in force from such companies. A two-for-one stock split was recently effected in conjunction with a boost in the cash dividend.

Business Summary

Protective Life Corporation is a holding company whose subsidiaries provide individual and group life and health insurance, annuities and guaranteed investment contracts. The company's principal operating subsidiary is Protective Life Insurance Co. The breakdown of revenues and pretax operating profit by business segment in 1994 was:

	Revs.	Profit
Acquisitions	20.1%	36.9%
Financial institutions	12.8%	9.0%
Group	17.5%	10.4%
Guaranteed investment contracts	21.6%	28.4%
Individual life	14.5%	16.0%
Investment products	10.3%	–1.5%
Corporate & other	2.6%	–4.2%
Realized invest. gains	0.6%	5.0%

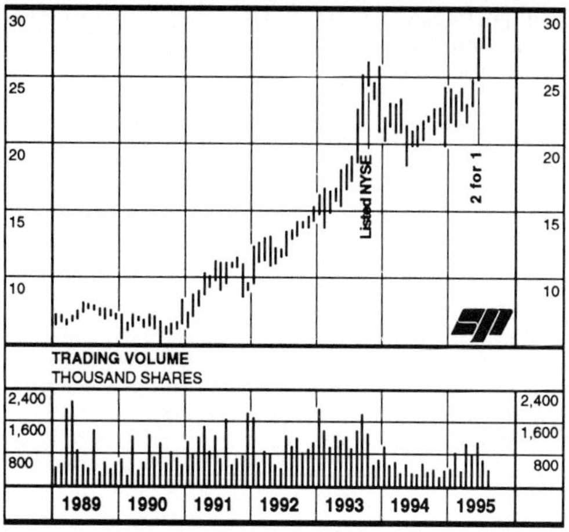

The Individual Life division (formerly the Agency division) markets individual insurance products primarily in the Sun Belt states through independent personal producing general agents. Its main products are universal life policies that combine traditional life insurance coverage with the ability to tailor a flexible payment schedule to the individual's needs and accumulate cash values on a tax-deferred basis. It also serves the payroll-deduction market by offering universal life and cancer insurance products. The division includes ProEquities, Inc., a securities broker-dealer.

The Group division markets life, accident and health insurance packages, including hospital and medical coverages, as well as dental and disability coverages, primarily in the southeastern and southwestern U.S. through full-time field representatives that market to employers and associations through agents and brokers. Group policies are directed primarily at employers and associations with between 25 and 1,000 employees.

The Financial Institutions division specializes in marketing life and health insurance products, most of which are used to secure consumer and mortgage loans, through commercial banks, savings and loan associations and mortgage bankers primarily in the southeastern U.S.

The Investment Products division markets annuity products through the Individual Life division, financial insitutions and broker-dealer channels.

In 1989, the company began marketing guaranteed investment contracts, which are generally issued to 401(k) or other retirement savings plans.

The company actively seeks to acquire blocks of insurance policies through acquisitions of companies or the assumption or reinsurance of policies. Recent, larger acquisitions include Wisconsin National Life Insurance Co. in 1993 and a coinsured block of 130,000 policies in late 1994.

At December 31, 1994, total consolidated life insurance in force was $49.9 billion ($42.5 billion a year earlier), consisting of $38.9 billion individual and $11.0 billion group policies.

Next earnings report expected in mid-October.

Per Share Data ($)

Yr. End Dec. 31	1994	1993	1992	1991	1990	1989	[2]1988	1987	1986	1985
Tangible Bk. Val.[1]	**9.86**	11.95	10.28	9.22	8.15	7.75	7.27	8.63	8.26	7.76
Oper. Earnings	**2.380**	1.990	1.555	1.385	1.110	0.785	0.075	0.510	0.775	0.865
Earnings[3,4]	**2.57**	2.07	1.56	1.31	1.04	0.79	0.05	0.70	0.85	0.89
Dividends	**0.550**	0.505	0.450	0.410	0.365	0.350	0.350	0.350	0.345	0.325
Payout Ratio	**21%**	24%	29%	31%	35%	44%	NM	50%	41%	37%
Prices—High	**24 5/16**	26 3/16	15⅜	11½	8⅜	8⅛	7 9/16	10⅝	12¾	12½
Low	**18 7/16**	13¾	9½	6¼	5⅛	6 7/16	6⅛	5 11/16	8 13/16	8¼
P/E Ratio—[5]	**9–7**	13–7	10–6	9–5	8–5	10–8	NM	21–11	16–11	14–10

Data as orig. reptd. Adj. for stk. divs. of 100% Jun. 1995, 100% Jan. 1985. **1.** As reptd. by co. prior to 1993. **2.** Refl. acctg. change. **3.** Bef. spec. item of -0.04 in 1992. **4.** Aft. gains/losses on sec. trans. **5.** Based on oper. earns. prior to 1988. NM-Not Meaningful.

Income Data (Million $)

Year Ended Dec. 31	Life Ins. In Force	Premium Income Life	Premium Income A & H	Premium Income Other	Net Invest. Inc.	Total Revs.	Net Bef. Taxes	[4]Net Oper. Inc.	[4]Net Inc.	% Return On Revs.	% Return On Assets	% Return On [3]Equity
1994	**49,878**	**242**	**161**	**Nil**	**418**	**848**	**106.0**	**65.2**	**70.4**	**8.3**	**1.2**	**20.1**
1993	42,451	201	170	Nil	362	760	85.0	54.5	56.6	7.4	1.2	18.6
1992	34,477	[2]323	NA	Nil	284	626	59.9	42.5	42.5	6.8	1.2	15.5
1991	30,578	[2]274	NA	Nil	234	516	51.7	37.8	35.8	6.9	1.3	15.1
1990	28,277	[2]248	NA	Nil	137	390	40.3	30.2	28.1	7.2	1.6	13.0
1989	25,145	124	113	Nil	82	325	32.3	21.7	21.8	6.7	1.9	10.5
[1]1988	23,542	124	121	Nil	76	326	2.6	2.0	1.2	0.4	0.1	0.6
1987	23,236	174	89	Nil	76	343	22.5	14.6	20.2	4.3	1.3	8.3
1986	22,424	167	64	Nil	71	306	29.1	22.5	24.4	7.3	2.2	10.6
1985	22,605	151	72	Nil	65	289	27.7	24.1	24.7	8.3	2.6	11.8

Balance Sheet Data (Million $)

Dec. 31	Cash & Equiv.	[5]Premiums Due	Investment Assets [6]Bonds	Investment Assets Stocks	Investment Assets Loans	Investment Assets Total	[7]Invest. Yield	Deferred Policy Costs	Total Assets	Debt	Common Equity
1994	**60.1**	**152.6**	**3,553**	**45.0**	**1,635**	**5,302**	**8.3**	**434**	**6,130**	**98.0**	**270**
1993	78.5	128.9	3,135	40.6	1,549	4,767	8.7	300	5,316	137.6	361
1992	56.0	32.8	2,238	26.6	1,296	3,597	8.9	275	4,007	31.0	281
1991	41.5	25.5	1,607	31.2	1,106	2,796	9.7	215	3,120	23.5	252
1990	48.5	21.9	1,161	23.2	793	2,029	9.0	193	2,331	2.1	222
1989	23.7	25.5	458	20.7	497	1,006	8.8	136	1,232	2.1	212
1988	12.7	20.9	387	16.9	432	859	8.9	127	1,065	2.1	203
1987	11.4	26.3	406	16.6	400	844	9.2	184	1,116	0.1	242
1986	13.2	26.4	372	18.9	395	802	9.4	186	1,078	NM	239
1985	18.6	32.4	335	38.2	317	702	9.6	168	971	0.1	224

Data as orig. reptd. **1.** Refl. acctg. change. **2.** Combined life, A&H premium income and policy fees. **3.** As reptd. by co. **4.** Bef. spec. items. **5.** Incl. other rec. **6.** Incl. short-term invest. **7.** Based on avg. invest. assets. NA-Not Available. NM-Not Meaningful.

Review of Operations

Based on a brief report, net income advanced 12%, year to year, in the six months ended June 30, 1995, to $36.9 million ($1.31 a share), from $33.0 million ($1.21, as adjusted), as growth in the investment base resulted in higher net investment income.

Common Share Earnings ($)

Quarter:	1995	1994	1993	1992
Mar.	0.69	0.61	0.44	0.37
Jun.	0.62	0.60	0.50	0.39
Sep.		0.68	0.45	0.40
Dec.		0.69	0.69	0.41
		2.57	2.07	1.56

Finances

In March 1995, PL acquired National Health Care Systems of Florida, Inc., a dental health maintenance organization based in the southeast with over 260,000 members, for $38.3 million. In connection with the transaction, PL reissued 658,229 shares of common stock held as treasury shares.

At March 31, 1995, the company had borrowed $23 million under lines of credit totaling $60 million.

In August 1993, the company sold its ownership interest in Southeast Health Plan, Inc., a Birmingham-based health maintenance organization, for a gain of $2.7 million. Earlier, in July 1993, PL acquired Wisconsin National Life Insurance Co. of Oshkosh, Wis. ($3.9 billion of life insurance in force), for $67.8 million.

Dividend Data

Cash has been paid in each year since 1926. A revised shareholder rights plan was adopted in August 1995.

Amt. of Divd. $	Date Decl.	Ex-divd. Date	Stock of Record	Payment Date
0.28	Nov. 7	Nov. 14	Nov. 18	Dec. 1'94
0.28	Feb. 6	Feb. 13	Feb. 17	Mar. 1'95
0.32	May 1	May 8	May 12	Jun. 1'95
2-for-1	May 1	Jun. 2	May 12	Jun. 1'95
0.15½	Aug. 7	Aug. 16	Aug. 18	Sep. 1'95
0.005 Spl.	Aug. 7	Aug. 16	Aug. 18	Sep. 1'95

Capitalization

Debt: $124,000,000 (3/95).

Common Stock: 28,762,906 shs. ($0.50 par).
Institutions hold about 61%.
Shareholders: About 2,100 of record (2/95).

Office—2801 Highway 280 South, Birmingham, AL 35223. **Tel**—(205) 879-9230. **Chrmn, Pres & CEO**—D. Nabers Jr. **EVP, CFO & Investor Contact**—John D. Johns (205-868-4400). **VP & Secy**—J. K. Wright. **SVP & Treas**—A. S. Williams III. **Dirs**—E. L. Addison, W. J. Cabaniss, A. W. Dahlberg, R. T. David, R. L. Kuehn Jr., J. J. McMahon Jr., D. Nabers Jr., H. G. Pattillo, J. W. Rouse Jr., W. J. Rushton III, H. A. Sklenar, J. W. Woods. **Transfer Agent**—AmSouth Bank, Birmingham. **Incorporated** in Alabama in 1907. **Empl**—1,094.

 Robert Schpoont

STANDARD & POOR'S **STOCK REPORTS**

Public Service of No. Carolina

NYSE Symbol **PGS**
In S&P SmallCap 600

29-OCT-95

Industry: Utilities-Gas

Summary: This company distributes natural gas to about 280,000 customers in 90 cities and communities in a 26-county territory in North Carolina.

Quantitative Evaluations

Outlook
(1 Lowest—5 Highest)
• **2+**

Fair Value
• **15**

Risk
• **Low**

Earn./Div. Rank
• **B+**

Technical Eval.
• **Bearish** since 8/95

Rel. Strength Rank
(1 Lowest—99 Highest)
• **68**

Insider Activity
• **Neutral**

Recent Price • 15⅞ | Yield • 5.4%
52 Wk Range • 16¾-13¾ | 12-Mo. P/E • 13.1

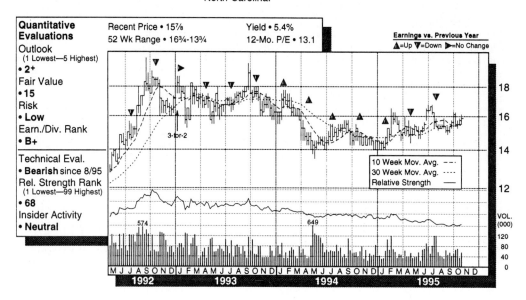

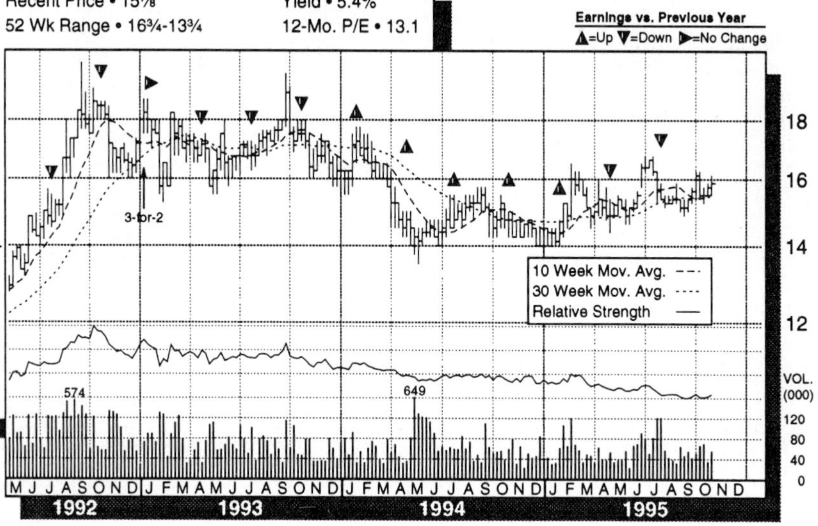

Business Profile - 25-OCT-95

PGS principally delivers natural gas products and services to residential, commercial, industrial, transportation and electric power generation customers. In October 1994, PGS was granted permission to increase annual revenues by $10.8 million, or about 3.6%. The company raised its quarterly dividend 3.7% with the April 1995 declaration. In March 1995, trading in the common shares shifted to the New York Stock Exchange from the Nasdaq Stock Market.

Operational Review - 28-JUL-95

Gross margin for the first nine months of fiscal 1995 rose 11%, year to year, reflecting the recent general rate increase, the Cardinal Pipeline rate hike and an increase in the number of customers served. PGS's weather adjustment mechanism offset the impact of 12% warmer than normal weather. Share earnings for the fiscal 1994 period included a $0.09 capital gain, and average common shares outstanding that were 11% higher due to a May 1994 public offering of 1.7 million shares.

Stock Performance - 27-OCT-95

In the past 30 trading days, PGS's shares have increased 3%, compared to a 0.63% fall in the S&P 500. Average trading volume for the past five days was 10,880 shares, compared with the 40-day moving average of 10,595 shares.

Key Stock Statistics

Dividend Rate/Share	0.85	Shareholders	11,700
Shs. outstg. (M)	18.7	Market cap. (B)	$0.296
Avg. daily vol. (M)	0.011	Inst. holdings	18%
Tang. Bk. Value/Share	8.82	Insider holdings	NA
Beta	0.42		

Value of $10,000 invested 5 years ago: $ 19,982

Fiscal Year Ending Sep. 30

	1995	% Change	1994	% Change	1993	% Change
Revenues (Million $)						
1Q	66.80	-6%	71.40	-7%	77.00	NM
2Q	112.7	-9%	123.2	5%	117.3	21%
3Q	41.65	-14%	48.20	-13%	55.30	23%
4Q	—	—	30.90	1%	30.50	NM
Yr.	—	—	273.7	-2%	280.0	16%
Income (Million $)						
1Q	6.66	33%	5.02	12%	4.47	NM
2Q	18.50	10%	16.86	14%	14.82	-3%
3Q	0.60	-64%	1.67	NM	0.02	-97%
4Q	—	—	-3.56	NM	-5.09	NM
Yr.	—	—	19.98	41%	14.22	-15%
Earnings Per Share ($)						
1Q	0.36	16%	0.31	11%	0.28	NM
2Q	1.00	-4%	1.04	11%	0.94	-5%
3Q	0.03	-70%	0.10	—	Nil	—
4Q	—	—	-0.20	NM	-0.32	NM
Yr.	—	—	1.17	30%	0.90	-17%

Next earnings report expected: mid November

Public Service of No. Carolina

Business Summary - 27-OCT-95

Public Service Company of North Carolina, Incorporated supplies natural gas to 89 communities in that state. The area served, with a population exceeding 2.3 million, includes the Raleigh-Durham area, with the Research Triangle Park, sections of the Piedmont and western parts of the state. PGS's strong industrial base in its service territory includes the manufacture of textiles, chemicals, ceramics and clay products, glass, automotive products, minerals, pharmaceuticals, plastics, fabricated metals, electronic equipment and furniture, and a variety of food and tobacco processing.

The delivery mix in recent fiscal years was:

	1994	1993	1992
Residential	32%	32%	29%
Commercial	21%	23%	23%
Industrial	22%	37%	38%
Gas transported for others	25%	8%	10%

At September 30, 1994, PGS was serving 263,139 customers (250,153 a year earlier), of which 234,948 were residential, 25,942 commercial and 2,249 industrial. Total volume of natural gas sold and transported in fiscal 1994 was 58,888,322 dekatherms (dt), compared with 57,179,381 dt the year before (dt=1 Mcf at 1,000 BTU/cu. ft.). The average amount of gas used per residential customer in fiscal 1994 was 79.94 dt (80.98 dt in fiscal 1993), with revenues per dt of $7.35 ($7.04) and average revenues of $587.31 ($570.05).

PGS purchases for resale to its customers most of the natural gas it distributes, while the balance distributed is natural gas purchased by certain large-volume commercial and industrial customers directly from various producers and marketers. Natural gas purchased directly from Transcontinental Gas Pipe Line Corp. (Transco) accounted for 30% and 33%, respectively, of PGS's supply in fiscal 1994 and 1993.

In June 1994, PGS sold its propane operations for about $12.8 million.

Important Developments

Sep. '95—PGS, Transcontinental Gas Pipe Line Corp. (Transco), Piedmont Natural Gas Co., Inc., and North Carolina Natural Gas Corp. (NCNG) signed a letter of intent to form a limited liability company to purchase and extend the existing 24-inch diameter, 37-mile Cardinal Pipeline in North Carolina. The proposed purchase and extension will be project-financed and has an estimated cost of $97 million. It is anticipated that Transco will own about 45%, PGS will own 33%, Piedmont will own 17% and NCNG will own 5%. Pending a definitive agreement and regulatory approval, construction is scheduled to begin in early 1999 with service anticipated to begin before November 1, 1999.

Capitalization

Long Term Debt: $109,140,000 (6/95).

Per Share Data ($)

(Year Ended Sep. 30)

	1994	1993	1992	1991	1990	1989
Tangible Bk. Val.	8.82	7.73	7.40	6.92	6.87	6.66
Earnings	1.17	0.90	1.08	0.70	0.84	0.93
Dividends	0.80	0.77	0.75	0.73	0.72	0.69
Payout Ratio	69%	86%	69%	105%	86%	74%
Prices - High	17¾	19¾	20⅛	12¼	11½	11⅛
- Low	13½	15¼	11¼	10⅛	9¾	9½
P/E Ratio - High	15	22	19	17	14	12
- Low	12	17	10	14	12	10

Income Statement Analysis (Million $)

	1994	%Chg	1993	%Chg	1992	%Chg	1991
Revs.	274	-2%	280	17%	240	24%	193
Depr.	15.2	8%	14.1	8%	13.1	7%	12.2
Maint.	4.7	-5%	4.9	-7%	5.2	21%	4.3
Fxd. Chgs. Cov.	2.5	24%	2.0	-10%	2.2	25%	1.8
Constr. Credits	0.2	NM	0.1	-17%	0.1	-81%	0.3
Eff. Tax Rate	34%	—	35%	—	38%	—	36%
Net Inc.	20.0	41%	14.2	-15%	16.8	58%	10.6

Balance Sheet & Other Fin. Data (Million $)

	1994	1993	1992	1991	1990	1989
Gross Prop.	520	478	442	414	380	351
Cap. Exp.	45.5	40.1	31.1	36.5	32.3	42.9
Net Prop.	367	338	310	293	271	250
Capitalization:						
LT Debt	114	125	130	104	109	85.0
% LT Debt	42	50	53	50	51	47
Pfd.	Nil	Nil	Nil	1.7	2.0	2.2
% Pfd.	Nil	Nil	Nil	0.80	0.90	1.20
Common	161	124	115	104	101	95.0
% Common	59	50	47	50	48	52
Total Cap.	328	300	296	257	255	224

Ratio Analysis

	1994	1993	1992	1991	1990	1989
Oper. Ratio	85.9	89.9	87.3	87.5	88.5	89.3
% Earn. on Net Prop.	8.1	8.7	10.1	8.6	8.9	9.8
% Ret. on Revs.	7.3	5.1	7.0	5.5	6.1	6.2
% Ret. On Invest.Cap	10.6	9.4	10.9	9.4	10.6	10.5
% Return On Com.Eqty	14.1	11.9	15.2	10.2	12.5	14.4

Dividend Data —Common dividends have been paid in each year since 1958. A dividend reinvestment plan is available.

Amt. of Div. $	Date Decl.	Ex-Div. Date	Stock of Record	Payment Date
0.205	Nov. 03	Dec. 05	Dec. 09	Jan. 01 '95
0.205	Jan. 27	Mar. 06	Mar. 10	Apr. 01 '95
0.213	Apr. 20	Jun. 06	Jun. 09	Jul. 01 '95
0.213	Jul. 27	Sep. 07	Sep. 11	Oct. 01 '95

Data as orig. reptd.; bef. results of disc opers. and/or spec. items. Per share data adj. for stk. divs. as of ex-div. date. E-Estimated. NA-Not Available. NM-Not Meaningful. NR-Not Ranked.

Office—400 Cox Rd., P.O. Box 1398, Gastonia, NC 28053-1398. **Tel**—(704) 864-6731. **Chrmn, Pres & CEO**—C. E. Zeigler Jr. **Sr VP-Corp. Dev. & CFO**—R. D. Voigt. **Investor Contact**—Jack G. Mason. **VP & Secy**—J. P. Douglas. **Dirs**—W. C. Burkhardt, W. A. V. Cecil, B. Collins, H. M. Craig Jr., V. E. Eure, B. F. Matthews II, W. L. O'Brien Jr., P. P. Pearson Jr., G. S. York, C. E. Zeigler Jr., C. E. Zeigler Sr. **Transfer Agent & Registrar**—First Union National Bank of North Carolina, Charlotte. **Incorporated** in North Carolina in 1938. **Empl-** 1,130. **S&P Analyst:** Ronald J. Gross

Quaker Chemical

NASDAQ Symbol **QCHM**
In S&P SmallCap 600

28-SEP-95 **Industry:** Chemicals

Summary: This company produces and markets worldwide a broad range of specialty chemical products for various heavy industrial, institutional and manufacturing applications.

Quantitative Evaluations
Outlook
(1 Lowest—5 Highest)
• 3−
Fair Value
• 17
Risk
• Average
Earn./Div. Rank
• B+

Technical Eval.
• **Bearish** since 7/95
Rel. Strength Rank
(1 Lowest—99 Highest)
• 76
Insider Activity
• Neutral

Recent Price • 17¼
52 Wk Range • 19-14½
Yield • 3.9%
12-Mo. P/E • 16.4

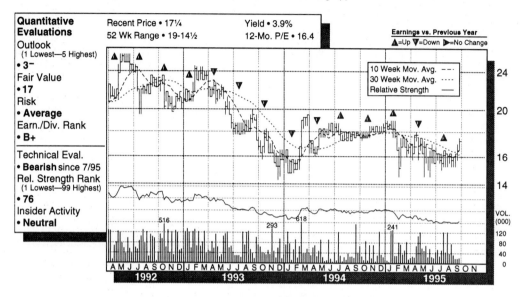

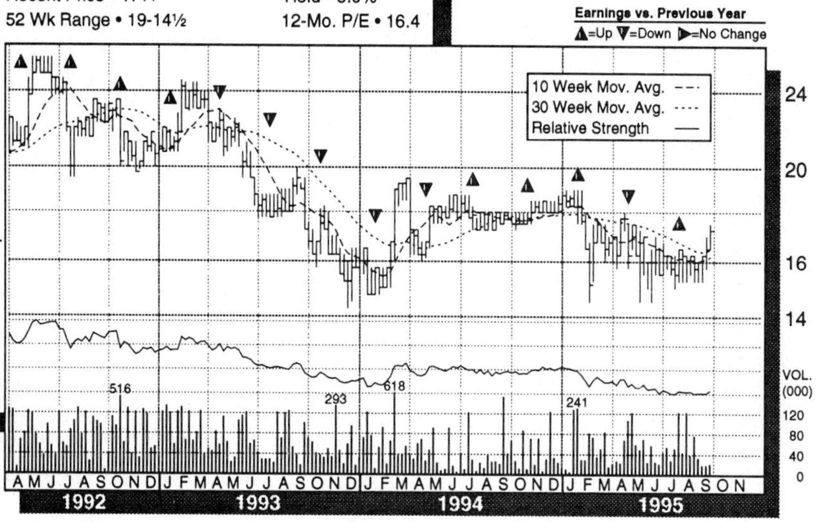

Business Profile - 28-SEP-95

With the 1994 divestiture of its Quaker Construction Products businesses, this international manufacturer and marketer of specialty chemical products refocused its priorities to its Total Fluid Management and Chemical Management Services programs. Although results have been hampered by the difficulty in passing along higher raw material costs, QCHM plans to capitalize on the growth opportunities it sees in South America and the Asia/Pacific area, while building on its current strength in Europe.

Operational Review - 28-SEP-95

Revenues grew 23% in the first half of 1995, year to year, on strong market conditions in Europe and the positive impact of a weaker dollar. Operating income, however, was up only 5.9% as margins were hurt (particularly in the first quarter) by the higher costs of raw materials. Following lower interest income and reduced equity in income of associated companies, net income declined 1.2%, while earnings per share increased 4.2% (on 4.8% fewer shares) to $0.50.

Stock Performance - 22-SEP-95

In the past 30 trading days, QCHM's shares have increased 7%, compared to a 5% rise in the S&P 500. Average trading volume for the past five days was 3,960 shares, compared with the 40-day moving average of 9,838 shares.

Key Stock Statistics

Dividend Rate/Share	0.68	Shareholders	1,000
Shs. outstg. (M)	8.8	Market cap. (B)	$0.152
Avg. daily vol. (M)	0.003	Inst. holdings	38%
Tang. Bk. Value/Share	9.33	Insider holdings	NA
Beta	-0.17		

Value of $10,000 invested 5 years ago: $ 15,354

Fiscal Year Ending Dec. 31

	1995	% Change	1994	% Change	1993	% Change
Revenues (Million $)						
1Q	54.53	21%	45.09	-7%	48.36	-12%
2Q	59.78	26%	47.35	-8%	51.34	-8%
3Q	—	—	50.12	3%	48.44	-10%
4Q	—	—	52.12	11%	46.86	-2%
Yr.	—	—	194.7	NM	195.0	-8%
Income (Million $)						
1Q	1.92	-15%	2.25	-17%	2.72	-27%
2Q	2.47	13%	2.19	NM	-0.45	NM
3Q	—	—	2.35	NM	0.73	-77%
4Q	—	—	2.61	NM	-4.76	NM
Yr.	—	—	9.40	NM	-1.76	NM
Earnings Per Share ($)						
1Q	0.22	-8%	0.24	-20%	0.30	-27%
2Q	0.28	17%	0.24	NM	-0.05	NM
3Q	—	—	0.26	NM	0.08	-77%
4Q	—	—	0.29	NM	-0.52	NM
Yr.	—	—	1.03	NM	-0.19	NM

Next earnings report expected: early November

Quaker Chemical

Business Summary - 28-SEP-95

Quaker Chemical Corporation develops and produces a broad range of specialty chemicals for the steel, metalworking, aerospace, automotive, bearing, can, construction, fluid power and pulp and paper industries. Sales by market in recent years were:

	1994	1993	1992
Steel production	46%	46%	44%
Metalworking	30%	30%	28%
Pulp and Paper	7%	6%	7%
Other	17%	18%	21%

In 1994, the company divested the business units of its Quaker Construction Products, Inc., and acquired the Perstorp AB cutting fluid business in Scandanavia.

The company's principal products include: (1) rolling lubricants, used in the hot and cold rolling of steel; (2) corrosion preventives, used by steel and metalworking customers to protect metal during manufacture, storage and shipment; (3) metal finishing compounds used to prepare metal surfaces for special treatments such as galvanizing and tin plating and to ready metals for further processing; (4) machining and grinding compounds, used by metalworking customers in cutting, shaping and grinding metal parts that require special treatment to tolerate the manufacturing process; (5) forming compounds used to facilitate the drawing and extrusion of metal products; (6) paper production products, used as defoamers, release agents, softeners, debonders and dispersants; (7) hydraulic fluids, used to operate hydraulically activated equipment; (8) products for the removal of hydrogen sulfide in various industrial applications; and (9) programs to provide recycling and chemical management services.

The company's subsidiary, AC Products, develops and manufactures chemical milling maskants for the aerospace industry, as well as flexible sealants and exterior protective coatings for roofs and walls for the construction industry.

R&D spending totaled $9,919,000, $11,037,000 and $11,134,000 in 1994, 1993 and 1992, respectively.

Important Developments

Jul. '95—Quaker Chemical said that the 25% increase in sales for the second quarter (23% for the first half) of 1995 was the result of increased volume, 9% (11%); the positive effect of currency translation, 7% (7%); price/mix and acquisitions in Europe, 6% (3%), and Latin America, 3% (2%). Currency translation added approximately $0.03 ($0.06) a share to net income.

Capitalization

Long Term Debt: $11,875,000 (6/95), incl. lease obligs.
Minority Interest: $2,704,000.

Per Share Data ($) (Year Ended Dec. 31)

	1994	1993	1992	1991	1990	1989
Tangible Bk. Val.	9.23	8.32	10.03	10.05	10.14	8.64
Cash Flow	1.74	0.52	2.03	1.78	2.01	1.75
Earnings	1.03	-0.19	1.33	1.20	1.51	1.35
Dividends	0.62	0.60	0.56	0.52	0.46	0.40
Payout Ratio	60%	NM	43%	44%	29%	30%
Prices - High	19½	24⅝	26	22¼	19¼	15⅝
- Low	14¾	14¼	18¾	15	12	12½
P/E Ratio - High	19	NM	20	19	13	12
- Low	14	NM	14	13	8	9

Income Statement Analysis (Million $)

	1994	%Chg	1993	%Chg	1992	%Chg	1991
Revs.	195	NM	195	-8%	212	11%	191
Oper. Inc.	19.5	31%	14.9	-37%	23.6	23%	19.2
Depr.	6.5	NM	6.6	2%	6.4	24%	5.2
Int. Exp.	1.3	-12%	1.5	-5%	1.5	-13%	1.8
Pretax Inc.	15.7	NM	-1.2	NM	19.5	13%	17.3
Eff. Tax Rate	38%	—	NM	—	36%	—	35%
Net Inc.	9.4	NM	-1.8	NM	12.1	12%	10.8

Balance Sheet & Other Fin. Data (Million $)

	1994	1993	1992	1991	1990	1989
Cash	11.3	20.3	24.5	23.8	26.4	22.6
Curr. Assets	83.4	84.4	85.6	82.7	84.8	75.4
Total Assets	170	171	167	156	152	131
Curr. Liab.	43.4	42.6	28.1	36.6	40.3	27.8
LT Debt	12.2	16.1	18.6	5.2	5.4	5.7
Common Eqty.	94.0	91.0	102	99	99	90.4
Total Cap.	112	113	125	106	108	99
Cap. Exp.	NA	9.0	7.2	8.4	12.7	7.6
Cash Flow	15.9	4.8	18.5	16.0	18.8	16.7

Ratio Analysis

	1994	1993	1992	1991	1990	1989
Curr. Ratio	1.9	2.0	3.0	2.3	2.1	2.7
% LT Debt of Cap.	10.9	14.3	14.9	4.9	5.1	5.7
% Net Inc.of Revs.	4.8	NM	5.7	5.6	7.0	7.1
% Ret. on Assets	5.6	NM	7.4	7.0	10.2	10.3
% Ret. on Equity	10.4	NM	12.0	10.8	15.3	15.0

Dividend Data —Cash has been paid each year since 1954.

Amt. of Div. $	Date Decl.	Ex-Div. Date	Stock of Record	Payment Date
0.155	Sep. 14	Oct. 07	Oct. 14	Oct. 30 '94
0.170	Dec. 14	Jan. 09	Jan. 13	Jan. 30 '95
0.170	Apr. 04	Apr. 07	Apr. 13	Apr. 30 '95
0.170	Jun. 09	Jul. 12	Jul. 14	Jul. 30 '95
0.170	Sep. 12	Oct. 11	Oct. 13	Oct. 30 '95

Data as orig. reptd.; bef. results of disc. opers. and/or spec. items. Per share data adj. for stk. divs. as of ex-div. date. E-Estimated. NA-Not Available. NM-Not Meaningful. NR-Not Ranked.

Office—Elm and Lee Streets, Conshohocken, PA 19428-0809. **Tel**—(610) 832-4000. **Chrmn**—P. A. Benoliel. **Pres & CEO**—R. J. Naples. **VP-Secy & Investor Contact**—Karl H. Spaeth. **Contr & Acting Treas**—R. J. Fagan. **Dirs**—J. B. Anderson, Jr., P. C. Barron, W. L. Batchelor, P. A. Benoliel, L. K. Black, E. J. Delattre, F. J. Dunleavy, R. P. Hauptfuhrer, F. Heldring, R. J. Naples, A. Satinsky. **Transfer Agent & Registrar**—American Stock Transfer & Trust Co., NYC. **Incorporated** in Pennsylvania in 1930. **Empl**-955. **S&P Analyst:** Justin McCann

STANDARD & POOR'S

STOCK REPORTS

Quanex Corp.

NYSE Symbol **NX**
In S&P SmallCap 600

20-SEP-95 **Industry:** Steel-Iron

Summary: Quanex produces hot rolled special bar quality carbon and alloy steel bars, cold finished bars, seamless and welded steel tubing. It also makes aluminum building products.

S&P Opinion: Accumulate (★★★★)

Recent Price • 23¾
52 Wk Range • 27-20
Yield • 2.6%
12-Mo. P/E • 12.3

Quantitative Evaluations

Outlook
(1 Lowest—5 Highest)
• **4−**

Fair Value
• **26¼**

Risk
• **Average**

Earn./Div. Rank
• **B**

Technical Eval.
• **Bearish** since 9/94

Rel. Strength Rank
(1 Lowest—99 Highest)
• **14**

Insider Activity
• **Neutral**

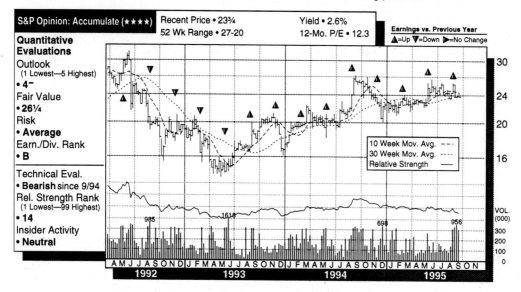

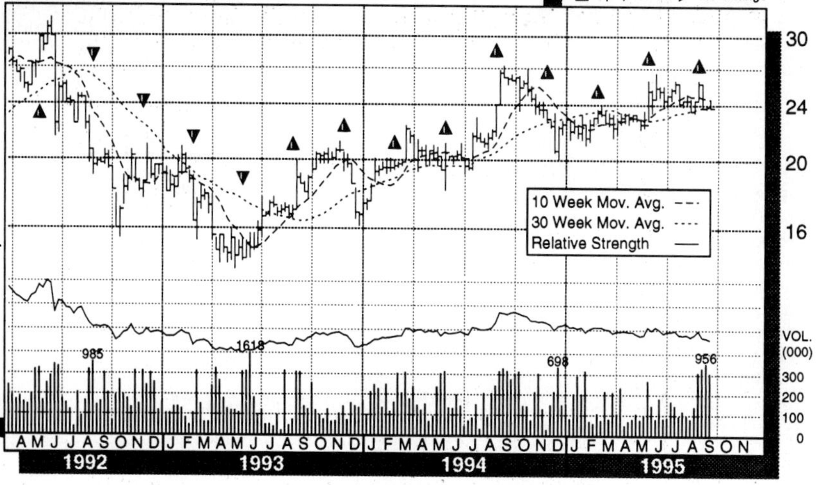

Overview - 19-SEP-95

Assuming 2.6% GDP growth in 1996, we anticipate a 12% sales increase for fiscal 1996, mostly reflecting higher prices and volume in the hot rolled bar and higher volume in the aluminum segment. We look for flat sales and earnings in both the cold finished bar and tubes units. Sales of hot rolled bar will benefit from strong demand for utility vehicles; aluminum sales will rise on market share gains in the service center sector. High operating rates, only modest increases in raw material costs and higher prices for hot rolled bar should lead to increased earnings in fiscal 1996. Further penetration of aluminum sheet mill markets, contributions from the Phase II program at MacSteel and possible acquisitions should boost long-term sales and EPS.

Valuation - 20-SEP-95

Shares of this specialty metals producer have underperformed the market thus far in 1995. rising 1.1%, versus a 24% gain for the S&P 500. With most other steel stock also down in the period, NX's performance relative to its peers has been good. We are maintaining our accumulate rating on the shares, based on their attractive P/E, as well as the company's solid long-term growth prospects. At 9.2X our fiscal 1996 EPS estimate, and only 4.5X projected cash flow, the stock offers good value. With a strong balance sheet and only moderate capital spending, cash flow is available for acquisitions or to fund programs to upgrade existing products.

Key Stock Statistics

S&P EPS Est. 1995	2.00	Tang. Bk. Value/Share	8.95
P/E on S&P Est. 1995	11.9	Beta	1.68
S&P EPS Est. 1996	2.50	Shareholders	3,900
Dividend Rate/Share	0.60	Market cap. (B)	$0.312
Shs. outstg. (M)	13.4	Inst. holdings	72%
Avg. daily vol. (M)	0.129	Insider holdings	NA

Value of $10,000 invested 5 years ago: $ 18,650

Fiscal Year Ending Oct. 31

	1995	% Change	1994	% Change	1993	% Change
Revenues (Million $)						
1Q	199.9	34%	149.6	6%	141.4	13%
2Q	234.4	36%	172.2	7%	161.4	9%
3Q	228.2	26%	181.1	18%	153.5	8%
4Q	—	—	196.5	23%	159.9	2%
Yr.	—	—	699.3	13%	616.2	8%
Income (Million $)						
1Q	4.65	163%	1.77	NM	0.49	-11%
2Q	9.82	160%	3.78	99%	1.90	-40%
3Q	9.60	66%	5.78	116%	2.68	20%
4Q	—	—	7.53	124%	3.36	NM
Yr.	—	—	18.85	124%	8.43	36%
Earnings Per Share ($)						
1Q	0.23	NM	0.02	NM	-0.07	NM
2Q	0.62	NM	0.17	NM	0.03	-88%
3Q	0.63	97%	0.32	NM	0.09	13%
4Q	E0.52	16%	0.45	NM	0.13	NM
Yr.	E2.00	108%	0.96	NM	0.18	-36%

Next earnings report expected: early December

Quanex Corp.

Business Summary - 20-SEP-95

Quanex produces hot rolled special bar quality carbon and alloy steel bars, cold finished bars, seamless and welded steel tubing and aluminum building products. Segment contributions in fiscal 1994 were:

	Sales	Profits
Hot rolled bars	33%	56%
Cold finished bars	23%	15%
Steel tubes	15%	12%
Aluminum products	29%	17%

The MacSteel division makes hot rolled bars, including hot rolled steel bar quality carbon and steel bars used for camshafts, transmission gears, bearing cages, steering components, hydraulic mechanisms, seamless tube production, and track components for military vehicles.

NX's cold finished steel bars are used for production of clutch shafts, gear box shafts, ball joints, socket and drive mechanisms.

The tubes unit produces carbon and alloy tubing, boiler and condenser tubing, and pipe. It also produces seamless and welded tubular products primarily for markets in the Southwest.

Through Nichols-Homeshield, the company makes aluminum products for the home improvement, new construction, light commercial construction, and lawn and garden markets. Principal products include aluminum window screens, patio door screens, window frames, window and screen components, rain carrying systems, exterior trim, and mill finish sheet. Aluminum reroll coil is produced by a Davenport, Iowa, minimill.

At October 31, 1994, backlog stood at $182.7 million, up from $154.9 million a year earlier.

Important Developments

Aug. '95— NX reported fiscal 1995 third quarter EPS of $0.63, on a 26% sales gain, versus $0.32 in fiscal 1994. The company attributed its large EPS gain to record operating profits in three of its four business segments. Earlier, NX exchanged 6.88% convertible debentures for 6.88% convertible preferred stock, in a move that is expected to boost EPS $0.17 on an annualized basis.

Jul. '95—The company announced that the International Trade Commission had made a unanimous final determination affirming NX's contention that imports of small-diameter seamless carbon and alloy standard line and pressure pipe from four countries caused injury to the U.S. industry. Pursuant to the decision, the Commerce Department imposed duties of 108.13% for Argentina, 124.96% for Brazil, 57.72% for Germany, and 3.31% for Italy.

Capitalization

Long Term Debt: $134,192,000 (7/95), incl. $86.3 million of 6.88% debs. due 2007, conv. into com. at $31.50 a sh.

Per Share Data ($)

(Year Ended Oct. 31)

	1994	1993	1992	1991	1990	1989
Tangible Bk. Val.	8.12	7.76	8.54	9.94	9.24	8.56
Cash Flow	3.01	2.23	2.36	3.17	3.88	3.51
Earnings	0.96	0.18	0.28	1.02	2.03	2.11
Dividends	0.56	0.56	0.52	0.48	0.40	0.30
Payout Ratio	58%	NM	200%	47%	19%	14%
Prices - High	$27\frac{1}{4}$	$21\frac{1}{4}$	$31\frac{3}{4}$	$23\frac{1}{8}$	$18\frac{1}{2}$	19
- Low	17	14	$15\frac{1}{2}$	$11\frac{3}{8}$	$9\frac{1}{8}$	$13\frac{1}{8}$
P/E Ratio - High	28	NM	NM	23	9	9
- Low	18	NM	NM	11	4	6

Income Statement Analysis (Million $)

	1994	%Chg	1993	%Chg	1992	%Chg	1991
Revs.	699	13%	616	8%	572	-3%	589
Oper. Inc.	69.2	36%	50.9	-3%	52.5	-13%	60.2
Depr.	27.8	NM	27.7	5%	26.4	5%	25.1
Int. Exp.	13.9	-8%	15.1	-3%	15.5	-12%	17.7
Pretax Inc.	32.5	124%	14.5	36%	10.7	-50%	21.4
Eff. Tax Rate	42%	—	42%	—	42%	—	42%
Net Inc.	18.9	125%	8.4	35%	6.2	-50%	12.4

Balance Sheet & Other Fin. Data (Million $)

	1994	1993	1992	1991	1990	1989
Cash	88.1	89.9	96.9	31.1	24.1	24.8
Curr. Assets	259	243	250	164	170	166
Total Assets	564	529	535	446	451	400
Curr. Liab.	135	95.1	96.0	95.0	96.0	90.0
LT Debt	107	128	129	156	131	93.0
Common Eqty.	146	140	151	152	147	133
Total Cap.	363	372	383	341	344	298
Cap. Exp.	44.6	37.0	52.5	57.0	31.9	13.8
Cash Flow	40.7	30.2	30.0	37.0	47.4	43.5

Ratio Analysis

	1994	1993	1992	1991	1990	1989
Curr. Ratio	1.9	2.6	2.6	1.7	1.8	1.8
% LT Debt of Cap.	29.6	34.5	33.6	45.8	38.2	31.3
% Net Inc.of Revs.	2.7	1.4	1.1	2.1	4.3	5.8
% Ret. on Assets	3.4	1.6	1.2	2.8	6.7	8.3
% Ret. on Equity	9.0	1.7	2.2	8.0	18.0	21.3

Dividend Data —Dividends, paid since 1939 and omitted in 1982, were resumed in 1988. A dividend reinvestment plan is available. A new poison pill stock purchase rights plan was adopted in 1989.

Amt. of Div. $	Date Decl.	Ex-Div. Date	Stock of Record	Payment Date
0.140	Aug. 25	Sep. 12	Sep. 16	Sep. 30 '94
0.140	Dec. 08	Dec. 13	Dec. 19	Dec. 30 '94
0.150	Mar. 02	Mar. 13	Mar. 17	Mar. 31 '95
0.150	May. 25	Jun. 15	Jun. 19	Jun. 30 '95
0.150	Aug. 25	Sep. 13	Sep. 15	Sep. 29 '95

Data as orig. reptd.; bef. results of disc. opers. and/or spec. items. Per share data adj. for stk. divs. as of ex-div. date. E-Estimated. NA-Not Available. NM-Not Meaningful. NR-Not Ranked.

Office—1900 West Loop South, Suite 1500, Houston, TX 77027. **Tel**—(713) 961-4600. **Chrmn**—R. C. Snyder. **Pres & CEO**—V. E. Oechsle. **VP & CFO**—W. M. Rose. **Secy**—M. W. Conlon. **Investor Contact**—Jeff Galow (800-231-8176). **Dirs**—F. J. Broad, G. B. Haeckel, D. J. Morfee, J. D. O'Connell, V. E. Oechsle, C. E. Pfeiffer, M. J. Sebastian, R. C. Synder, R. L. Walker. **Transfer Agent & Registrar**—Chemical Bank, NYC. **Incorporated** in Michigan in 1927; reincorporated in Delaware in 1968. **Empl**-2,536. **S&P Analyst:** Leo Larkin

STANDARD & POOR'S

Quantum Health Resources

STOCK REPORTS

NASDAQ Symbol **QHRI**

In S&P SmallCap 600

12-AUG-95 **Industry:** Health Care Centers

Summary: Quantum provides therapies and support services to patients with certain chronic disorders. The hemophilia business accounts for about 60% of revenues.

S&P Opinion: Hold (★★★)

Recent Price • 11½

52 Wk Range • 42¾-11¼

Yield • Nil

12-Mo. P/E • 9.8

Quantitative Evaluations

Outlook (1 Lowest—5 Highest)
• **5**

Fair Value
• **32½**

Risk
• **High**

Earn./Div. Rank
• **NR**

Technical Eval.
• **Bullish** since 5/95

Rel. Strength Rank (1 Lowest—99 Highest)
• **NA**

Insider Activity
• **NA**

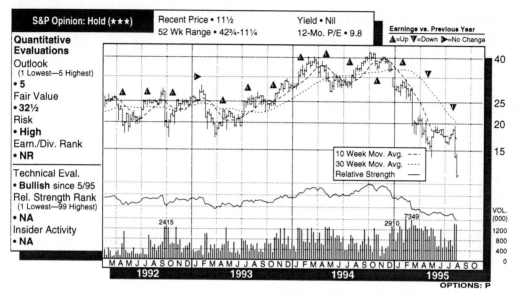

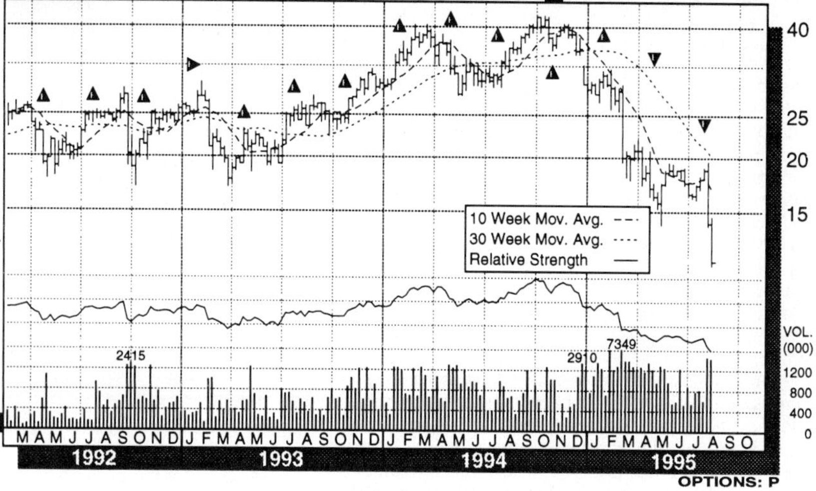

Overview - 10-AUG-95

Although demand for hemophilia services and therapies should remain strong, revenue gains from this business are likely to be restricted by the new reimbursement rates for anti-hemophilic factor, as well as increasing price competition. Revenue comparisons in the second half of 1995 will also be hurt by the nearly completed phase-out of Ceredase to Gaucher disease patients. Margins are also under pressure due to continued operating losses at Quantum Disease Management and the inclusion of OptimalCare Inc. (acquired in February 1995). The extent of the EPS shortfall in the second quarter of 1995 was surprising, and highlighted some significant operational problems which management must overcome in order to resume strong earnings growth.

Valuation - 10-AUG-95

Quantum Health's shares lost nearly 25% of their value following the release of 1995 second quarter EPS of $0.20, significantly below analyst forecasts of $0.27. Year-to-year revenue comparisons were hurt by the elimination of services related to Ceredase (a treatment for Gaucher disease), as well as a dispute over reimbursement issues for hemophilia patients enrolled in California government-sponsored programs. Our recent EPS revision reflected concerns that these issues may drag on for several quarters, and the stock appears likely to trade in a tight range over the next several months.

Key Stock Statistics

S&P EPS Est. 1995	1.00	Tang. Bk. Value/Share	7.12
P/E on S&P Est. 1995	11.5	Beta	1.71
S&P EPS Est. 1996	1.20	Shareholders	500
Dividend Rate/Share	Nil	Market cap. (B)	$0.181
Shs. outstg. (M)	15.7	Inst. holdings	96%
Avg. daily vol. (M)	0.539	Insider holdings	NA

Value of $10,000 invested 5 years ago: NA

Fiscal Year Ending Dec. 31

	1995	% Change	1994	% Change	1993	% Change
Revenues (Million $)						
1Q	71.31	16%	61.59	46%	42.30	78%
2Q	72.17	4%	69.19	42%	48.77	73%
3Q	—	—	72.06	36%	53.08	69%
4Q	—	—	72.14	25%	57.58	65%
Yr.	—	—	275.0	36%	201.7	71%
Income (Million $)						
1Q	3.92	-19%	4.83	50%	3.21	53%
2Q	3.16	-41%	5.38	29%	4.17	71%
3Q	—	—	5.78	36%	4.24	55%
4Q	—	—	5.65	19%	4.76	142%
Yr.	—	—	21.64	31%	16.57	79%
Earnings Per Share ($)						
1Q	0.25	-17%	0.30	43%	0.21	40%
2Q	0.20	-39%	0.33	22%	0.27	50%
3Q	E0.25	—	0.35	21%	0.29	45%
4Q	E0.30	—	0.34	10%	0.31	121%
Yr.	E1.00	—	1.37	28%	1.07	60%

Next earnings report expected: early October

Quantum Health Resources

Business Summary - 11-AUG-95

Quantum Health Resources Inc. provides therapies and support services to individuals with chronic disorders including hemophilia (60% of 1994 revenues); alpha1-antitrypsin deficiency (a hereditary condition which may cause emphysema); primary immunodeficiency and autoimmune disorders; Cystic Fibrosis; and growth hormone disorders. For certain patients and those with other diseases, Quantum offers infusion therapies such as antibiotic, and parenteral and enteral nutrition. Therapies and services are provided through four licensed regional centers, 20 licensed branches, and 17 service branches throughout the U.S.

The company offers a range of therapies and support services to assist patients affected by certain long-term chronic disorders who have clinical and related needs that differ markedly from those with more acute or short-term illnesses. Quantum focuses on rare chronic disorders for which it has the opportunity to be the leader in terms of the therapy provided and number of patients served. The company delivers pharmaceuticals, coordinates medication during travel, helps establish an inventory management and record-keeping system, coordinates backup care in the event of an acute episode and provides information on advances in technology and treatment regimens.

The Quantum Disease Management unit (formed in 1994) seeks to manage select chronic disease populations (hemophilia, CF and others) on behalf of HMOs, fully capitated independent practice associations and medical groups, government payors, state high risk insurance pools and other payors.

In February 1995, Quantum acquired a controlling stake in OptimalCare Inc., a software developer dealing with workers' compensation, case management, encounters-based data for specific disease states and related services.

Revenues in 1994 were derived from private insurance and other private payors (59%); Medicaid and other state programs (28%); and Medicare and other federal programs (13%).

Important Developments

May '95—Quantum sued the California Department of Health Services seeking to enjoin the enforcement of a new reimbursement rate for services involving anti-hemophilic factor (AHF) of net cost plus 1%. In a related matter, the California State Controller's office said that Quantum's billing procedures for AHF supplied from 1991 to 1994 to patients reimbursed under Medi-Cal and two other state programs may have resulted in an overpayment of $2.4 million. Gross margins on about $27.5 million in aggregate revenues could be affected.

Capitalization

Long Term Debt: $86,250,000 (12/94) of 4.75% sub. debs. due 10/1/2000; conv. into com. at $30.31 a sh.

Per Share Data ($) (Year Ended Dec. 31)

	1994	1993	1992	1991	1990	1989
Tangible Bk. Val.	7.25	6.10	5.05	4.12	0.47	NA
Cash Flow	1.62	1.22	0.75	0.50	0.16	0.04
Earnings	1.37	1.07	0.67	0.45	0.13	0.03
Dividends	Nil	Nil	Nil	Nil	Nil	Nil
Payout Ratio	Nil	Nil	Nil	Nil	Nil	Nil
Prices - High	42¾	32	28¾	24¾	NA	NA
- Low	26½	17	17	13½	NA	NA
P/E Ratio - High	31	30	43	55	NA	NA
- Low	19	16	25	30	NA	NA

Income Statement Analysis (Million $)

	1994	%Chg	1993	%Chg	1992	%Chg	1991
Revs.	275	36%	202	71%	118	53%	77.0
Oper. Inc.	40.5	32%	30.7	86%	16.5	92%	8.6
Depr.	3.9	70%	2.3	110%	1.1	72%	0.6
Int. Exp.	4.5	NM	1.0	—	Nil	—	0.2
Pretax Inc.	35.8	28%	27.9	89%	14.8	66%	8.9
Eff. Tax Rate	40%	—	41%	—	37%	—	38%
Net Inc.	21.6	30%	16.6	79%	9.3	68%	5.5

Balance Sheet & Other Fin. Data (Million $)

	1994	1993	1992	1991	1990	1989
Cash	73.5	94.5	30.7	28.4	0.2	0.2
Curr. Assets	176	182	82.6	61.0	18.0	7.1
Total Assets	236	210	87.8	63.9	19.7	8.0
Curr. Liab.	22.2	30.0	18.9	11.7	9.0	3.9
LT Debt	86.3	86.3	Nil	Nil	Nil	Nil
Common Eqty.	123	93.5	68.9	52.2	2.2	4.1
Total Cap.	214	180	68.9	52.2	10.7	4.1
Cap. Exp.	8.3	5.6	3.3	1.7	1.2	0.9
Cash Flow	25.6	18.9	10.4	6.2	1.5	0.3

Ratio Analysis

	1994	1993	1992	1991	1990	1989
Curr. Ratio	7.9	6.1	4.4	5.2	2.0	1.8
% LT Debt of Cap.	40.3	48.0	Nil	Nil	Nil	Nil
% Net Inc.of Revs.	7.9	8.2	7.8	7.2	3.0	1.5
% Ret. on Assets	9.6	10.7	11.8	9.4	8.7	3.9
% Ret. on Equity	19.8	19.4	14.8	19.0	16.3	7.4

Dividend Data (No cash dividends have been paid. A shareholder rights plan was adopted in February 1994.)

Data as orig. reptd.; bef. results of disc. opers. and/or spec. items. Per share data adj. for stk. divs. as of ex-div. date. E-Estimated. NA-Not Available. NM-Not Meaningful. NR-Not Ranked.

Office—9100 Keystone Crossing, Suite 500, Indianapolis, IN 46240 **Tel**—(317) 580-6830. **Chrmn & CEO**—D. H. Stickney. **Pres & COO**—J. M. DeStefanis. **SVP, CFO & Treas**—K. T. Coleman. **Dirs**—S. B. Epstein, R. J. Erra, W. R. Hawley, A. J. Lazos, D. L. Lucas. **Transfer Agent**—U.S. Stock Transfer Corp., Glendale, CA. **Incorporated** in Delaware in 1988. **Empl-** 1,216. **S&P Analyst:** Robert M. Gold

STANDARD & POOR'S

STOCK REPORTS

Quick & Reilly

NYSE Symbol **BQR**
In S&P SmallCap 600

07-SEP-95 **Industry:** Securities

Summary: This holding company owns one of the largest discount brokerages in the U.S.; it also provides securities clearing services and acts as a specialist on the floor of the NYSE.

Quantitative Evaluations

Outlook
(1 Lowest—5 Highest)
• **NA**

Fair Value
• **NA**

Risk
• **Average**

Earn./Div. Rank
• **A-**

Technical Eval.
• **Bearish** since 8/95

Rel. Strength Rank
(1 Lowest—99 Highest)
• **53**

Insider Activity
• **Unfavorable**

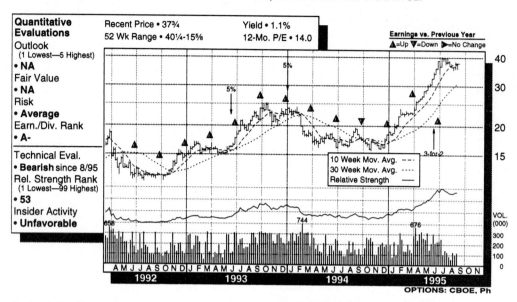

Recent Price • 37¾
52 Wk Range • 40¼-15⅝
Yield • 1.1%
12-Mo. P/E • 14.0

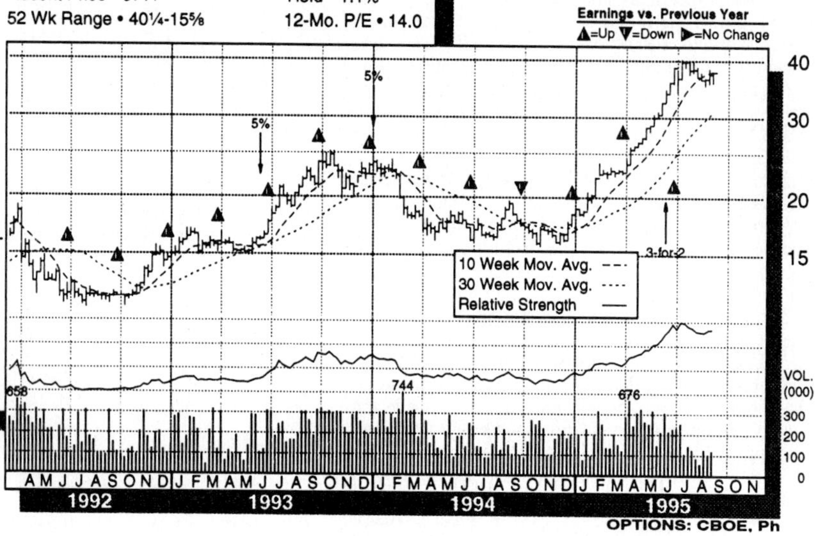

OPTIONS: CBOE, Ph

Business Profile - 07-SEP-95

BQR's earnings are directly related to interest rate movements, stock borrowing and lending activities, and trading volume. Its assets are highly liquid and not significantly affected by inflation; however, inflation may impact the company's performance through its effect on securities markets activities. At 1995 fiscal year-end, BQR far exceeded its aggregate minimum capital requirements. The company has been consistently profitable since its inception in 1974.

Operational Review - 07-SEP-95

In the three months ended May 26, 1995 total revenues rose 36% year to year, due principally to an 89% increase in interest income. Interest expense rose sharply; net revenues were up 14%. Non-interest expenses advanced 7.6%, partially reflecting 5.1% higher employee compensation and benefits costs. After taxes at 45.7%, versus 48.2%, net income was up 31% to $13,567,000 ($0.82 a share) from $10,320,000 ($0.62).

Stock Performance - 01-SEP-95

In the past 30 trading days, BQR's shares have declined 0.98%, compared to a 2% rise in the S&P 500. Average trading volume for the past five days was 23,120 shares, compared with the 40-day moving average of 20,905 shares.

Key Stock Statistics

Dividend Rate/Share	0.40	Shareholders	900
Shs. outstg. (M)	16.6	Market cap. (B)	$0.619
Avg. daily vol. (M)	0.021	Inst. holdings	36%
Tang. Bk. Value/Share	14.97	Insider holdings	NA
Beta	2.39		

Value of $10,000 invested 5 years ago: $ 50,556

Fiscal Year Ending Feb. 28

	1996	% Change	1995	% Change	1994	% Change
Revenues (Million $)						
1Q	102.7	36%	75.44	26%	60.10	29%
2Q	—	—	73.06	19%	61.33	43%
3Q	—	—	80.00	16%	68.70	54%
4Q	—	—	86.67	16%	75.03	21%
Yr.	—	—	315.2	19%	265.2	35%
Income (Million $)						
1Q	13.57	31%	10.32	NM	10.22	51%
2Q	—	—	8.52	-14%	9.95	91%
3Q	—	—	10.14	NM	10.18	82%
4Q	—	—	12.48	3%	12.14	9%
Yr.	—	—	41.46	-2%	42.49	48%
Earnings Per Share ($)						
1Q	0.82	32%	0.62	2%	0.61	48%
2Q	—	—	0.51	-13%	0.59	86%
3Q	—	—	0.61	NM	0.60	76%
4Q	—	—	0.75	5%	0.72	7%
Yr.	—	—	2.49	-2%	2.53	NM

Next earnings report expected: early October

Quick & Reilly

Business Summary - 07-SEP-95

The Quick & Reilly Group is a holding company engaged, through its principal subsidiaries, in providing discount brokerage services primarily to retail customers across the U.S.; clearing securities transactions for its own customers and for other brokerage firms and banks; and acting as a specialist on the floor of the New York Stock Exchange. Revenues were derived as follows in the past two fiscal years:

	1994-95	1993-94
Commissions	44%	58%
Interest	41%	26%
Specialist trading & commissions	13%	14%
Other	2%	2%

BQR's brokerage unit became the first NYSE member organization to offer substantially discounted commissions to individual investors following the elimination of fixed commission rates by the SEC in 1975. The discount service is based on the principle that many investors prefer to conduct their own research and make their own investment decisions and, therefore, do not wish to pay for such assistance provided by full-service brokers.

At 1994-95 year end, BQR's branch network consisted of 103 offices throughout the U.S., including the District of Columbia. The company serves a client base of more than 825,000 investors, and plans to open 10 new offices in fiscal 1996.

U.S. Clearing Corp., wholly owned, provides securities clearing for BQR's customers and also carries accounts and clears transactions for 233 other brokerage firms.

Specialist operations are conducted through wholly owned JJC Specialist Corp. Through 1988, JJC was registered as a specialist in 12 NYSE-listed stocks. Operations were expanded in 1988-89 through the acquisition of Conklin, Cahill & Co., specialists in 42 NYSE-listed stocks. In February 1990, BQR acquired the specialist operations of Drexel Burnham Lambert, which made a market in 28 NYSE stocks. In 1992, BQR combined the NYSE operations of Stokes, Hoyt & Co., a specialist in 34 listed companies, with JJC Specialist Corp. At February 28, 1995, JJC made markets in 162 listed companies and was among the leading specialist units on the NYSE.

Important Developments

Jun. '95—BQR's wholly owned subsidiary, JJC Specialist Corp., entered into an agreement in principle to acquire the NYSE specialist activities of Murphey, Marseilles, Smith & Nammack, Inc., pending approval by the NYSE. The acquisition would firmly establish JJC as the second largest specialist on the floor of the NYSE. MMS&N currently makes markets in 106 issues.

Capitalization

Long Term Debt: None (5/95)

Per Share Data ($) (Year Ended Feb. 28)

	1995	1994	1993	1992	1991	1990
Tangible Bk. Val.	14.26	12.23	9.78	8.47	6.41	5.63
Cash Flow	NA	NA	NA	NA	NA	NA
Earnings	2.49	2.53	1.75	1.47	0.76	0.73
Dividends	0.43	0.30	0.28	0.24	0.17	0.19
Payout Ratio	17%	12%	16%	16%	22%	26%
Cal. Yrs.	1994	1993	1992	1991	1990	1989
Prices - High	24⅛	25¼	19⅜	17	10	11
- Low	15⅝	14¾	11⅜	6	5½	6⅝
P/E Ratio - High	10	14	11	12	13	15
- Low	6	8	7	4	7	9

Income Statement Analysis (Million $)

	1995	%Chg	1994	%Chg	1993	%Chg	1992
Commissions	149	-3%	154	24%	124	22%	102
Int. Inc.	129	89%	68.3	44%	47.3	33%	35.6
Total Revs.	315	19%	265	35%	196	27%	154
Int. Exp.	83.8	116%	38.8	60%	24.2	75%	13.8
Pretax Inc.	80.4	NM	79.9	53%	52.2	24%	42.0
Eff. Tax Rate	48%	—	47%	—	45%	—	46%
Net Inc.	41.5	-2%	42.5	48%	28.7	26%	22.7

Balance Sheet & Other Fin. Data (Million $)

	1995	1994	1993	1992	1991	1990
Total Assets	2,582	2,477	1,377	1,030	435	525
Cash Items	40.9	41.8	46.2	29.3	10.6	27.8
Receivables	2,407	2,342	1,245	926	361	430
Secs. Owned	106	64.8	55.8	52.8	47.1	45.6
Sec. Borrowed	8.0	38.0	28.1	2.6	1.1	71.2
Due Brokers & Cust.	2,265	2,182	1,130	850	304	334
Other Liabs.	72.0	52.0	47.8	38.1	21.9	18.7
Capitalization:						
Debt	Nil	Nil	0.4	0.4	3.1	3.1
Equity	237	205	169	138	105	98.1
Total	237	205	170	139	108	101

Ratio Analysis

	1995	1994	1993	1992	1991	1990
% Ret. on Revs.	13.2	16.0	14.6	14.7	10.6	10.8
% Ret. on Assets	1.6	2.2	2.4	3.1	2.4	2.6
% Ret. on Equity	18.8	22.7	18.6	18.7	11.6	12.2

Dividend Data —Quarterly dividends on the publicly held shares were initiated in 1984. A dividend reinvestment plan was introduced in 1994.

Amt. of Div. $	Date Decl.	Ex-Div. Date	Stock of Record	Payment Date
0.150	Dec. 22	Feb. 23	Mar. 01	Apr. 03 '95
0.140	Dec. 22	Feb. 23	Mar. 01	Apr. 03 '95
3-for-2	Mar. 28	Jun. 08	May. 15	Jun. 07 '95
0.100	May. 23	Jun. 12	Jun. 14	Jul. 03 '95
0.100	Jul. 17	Aug. 30	Sep. 01	Oct. 02 '95

Data as orig. reptd.; bef. results of disc opers. and/or spec. items. Per share data adj. for stk. divs. as of ex-div. date. E-Estimated. NA-Not Available. NM-Not Meaningful. NR-Not Ranked.

Office—230 South County Rd., Palm Beach, FL 33480. **Tel**—(407) 655-8000. **Chrmn & CEO**—L. C. Quick Jr. **Pres & COO**—P. Quick. **Investor Contact**—Leslie Zuke (212) 747-6876. **Dirs**—A. Benisatto, R. G. Brodrick, T. C. Christman, A. B. Fryer, H. P. Kilroy, C. W. Mays, P. J. Mercurio, C. C. Quick, L. C. Quick Jr., L. C. Quick III, P. Quick, T. C. Quick. **Transfer Agent & Registrar**—First National Bank of Boston. **Reincorporated** in Delaware in 1987. **Empl**-848. **S&P Analyst:** Thomas C. Ferguson

STANDARD & POOR'S

STOCK REPORTS

RCSB Financial Inc.

NASDAQ Symbol **RCSB**

In S&P SmallCap 600

05-OCT-95 **Industry:** Banking

Summary: This unitary savings and loan holding company for Rochester Community Savings Bank serves primarily the Rochester and Buffalo regions through 30 retail offices.

Quantitative Evaluations

Outlook
(1 Lowest—5 Highest)
• **NA**

Fair Value
• **NA**

Risk
• **Average**

Earn./Div. Rank
• **NR**

Technical Eval.
• **Neutral** since 9/95

Rel. Strength Rank
(1 Lowest—99 Highest)
• **64**

Insider Activity
• **NA**

Recent Price • 24⅛
52 Wk Range • 25⅞-15¼
Yield • 2.0%
12-Mo. P/E • 11.2

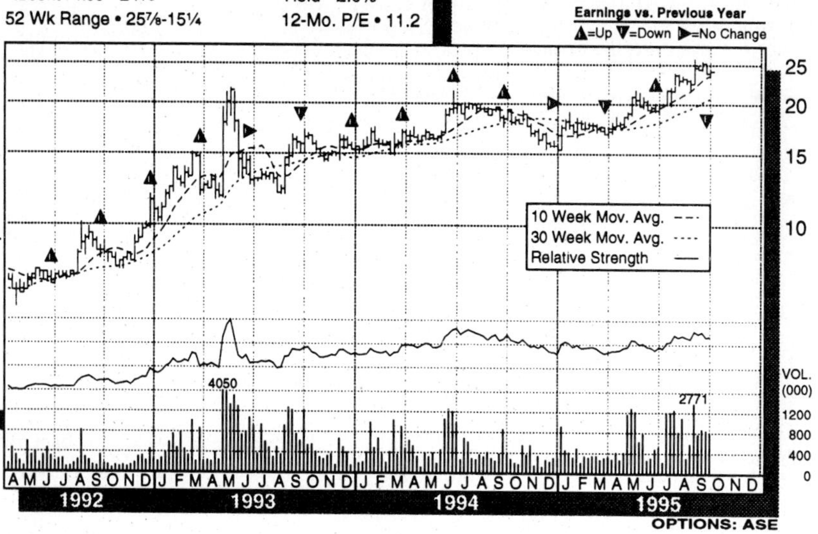

OPTIONS: ASE

Business Profile - 05-OCT-95

RCSB is focusing on its balance sheet and franchise strength, additional efficiency improvements, and the productive use of capital to enhance shareholder value. The sale of Shadow Lawn Savings Bank improved reserve coverages, and increased the bank's equity capital position. RCSB is looking to expand its New York franchise around Buffalo, and might enter nearby states. In September 1995, RCSB reorganized into a holding company structure to facilitate stock repurchases and operational matters.

Operational Review - 05-OCT-95

Net interest income in the six months ended May 31, 1995, fell 4.5%, year to year, reflecting the sale of Shadow Lawn Savings Bank. The loan loss provision contracted 70%, to $3.0 million. A soft mortgage origination market and the sale of Shadow Lawn helped push noninterest income down 46%. Following 25% lower operating expenses, and taxes of 27.0%, versus 10.0%, net income dropped 3.6%, to $17.6 million ($1.07 a share; $0.94 fully diluted), from $17.0 million ($1.04; $0.92).

Stock Performance - 29-SEP-95

In the past 30 trading days, RCSB's shares have increased 5%, compared to a 5% rise in the S&P 500. Average trading volume for the past five days was 154,020 shares, compared with the 40-day moving average of 203,818 shares.

Key Stock Statistics

Dividend Rate/Share	0.48	Shareholders	18,000
Shs. outstg. (M)	14.0	Market cap. (B)	$0.330
Avg. daily vol. (M)	0.150	Inst. holdings	32%
Tang. Bk. Value/Share	18.60	Insider holdings	NA
Beta	0.20		

Value of $10,000 invested 5 years ago: $ 23,666

Fiscal Year Ending Nov. 30

	1995	% Change	1994	% Change	1993	% Change
Revenues (Million $)						
1Q	76.42	-9%	83.85	9%	76.99	-16%
2Q	76.42	-5%	80.48	NM	80.17	-15%
3Q	84.72	-13%	97.89	NM	21.79	-75%
4Q	—	—	73.35	19%	61.46	-33%
Yr.	—	—	335.6	40%	240.4	-34%
Income (Million $)						
1Q	8.27	-8%	9.02	NM	2.48	22%
2Q	9.32	17%	7.96	199%	2.66	2%
3Q	9.72	-49%	19.18	NM	-72.72	NM
4Q	—	—	8.17	NM	8.15	131%
Yr.	—	—	44.32	NM	-59.43	NM
Earnings Per Share ($)						
1Q	0.50	-11%	0.56	NM	0.18	20%
2Q	0.57	19%	0.48	153%	0.19	NM
3Q	0.60	-53%	1.29	NM	-5.37	NM
4Q	—	—	0.49	NM	0.49	88%
Yr.	—	—	2.81	NM	-4.50	NM

Next earnings report expected: late January

RCSB Financial Inc.

Business Summary - 05-OCT-95

RCSB Financial, Inc. is the unitary savings and loan holding company for Rochester Community Savings Bank, a New York State-chartered stock savings bank formed in 1983 through the merger of Rochester Savings Bank and Community Savings Bank. The bank serves consumers as well as businesses through 30 full-service banking offices in western New York (22 branches in the Rochester area, and eight branches in the Buffalo market).

Gross loans receivable totaled $1.88 billion as of November 30, 1994, and were divided:

Mortgage loans:	
One- to four-family	30%
Home equity	13%
Multifamily & commercial	5%
FHA-insured/ VA-guaranteed	1%
Mtge. loans held for sale	5%
Auto loans & leases	40%
Other	6%

The loan loss allowance was $26.2 million at November 30, 1994 ($26.0 million a year earlier), equal to 1.41% of loans receivable (1.02%). Net chargeoffs were $11.2 million in fiscal 1994 ($25.1 million), or 0.51% of average loans (1.05%). Nonperforming assets totaled $28.5 million (0.83% of total assets) at November 30, 1994, down from $97.5 million (2.33%) at fiscal 1993 year end.

Total deposits of $2.09 billion as of November 30, 1994, were apportioned: noninterest-bearing checking accounts 1%, NOW accounts 8%, savings accounts 28%, money-market accounts 16%, and certificate accounts 47%.

The average yield on total interest-earning assets was 7.22% in fiscal 1994 (7.50% in fiscal 1993), while the average rate paid on total interest-bearing liabilities was 3.88% (4.18%), for a net spread of 3.34% (3.32%).

Subsidiaries of the bank engage in mortgage banking, automobile financing, insurance sales, and securities brokerage.

Important Developments

Sep. '95—The reorganization of Rochester Community Savings Bank into a RCSB Financial, Inc., a unitary savings and loan holding company, was completed. Management said the new structure would improve its flexibility in financial and operational matters, including the repurchase of shares and an expansion of its consumer business.

Aug. '95—Directors authorized a program to repurchase up to one million common or preferred shares in the open market.

Capitalization

FHLB Advances: $789,932,000 (11/94).
Other Borrowings: $47,007,000.
Preference Stock: 2,990,000 shs.

Per Share Data ($) (Year Ended Nov. 30)

	1994	1993	1992	1991	1990	1989
Tangible Bk. Val.	18.60	17.12	21.82	20.93	23.39	23.57
Earnings	2.81	-4.50	0.80	-2.24	0.57	1.45
Dividends	0.10	Nil	Nil	0.42	0.53	0.44
Payout Ratio	4%	Nil	Nil	NM	93%	30%
Prices - High	21½	21¾	11⅞	10¾	14⅜	19⅜
- Low	14¾	10⅛	6	5¼	6¼	10⅞
P/E Ratio - High	8	NM	15	NM	25	13
- Low	5	NM	8	NM	11	8

Income Statement Analysis (Million $)

	1994	%Chg	1993	%Chg	1992	%Chg	1991
Net Int. Inc.	128	15%	111	20%	92.7	2%	90.8
Loan Loss Prov.	16.1	24%	13.0	-10%	14.4	-78%	65.8
Non Int. Inc.	76.7	NM	-9.7	NM	82.5	42%	58.3
Non Int. Exp.	132	-13%	151	6%	142	17%	121
Pretax Inc.	55.7	NM	-63.3	NM	18.8	NM	-38.0
Eff. Tax Rate	21%	—	NM	—	41%	—	NM
Net Inc.	44.3	NM	-59.4	NM	11.0	NM	-30.9
% Net Int. Marg.	3.56%	—	3.32%	—	2.77%	—	2.35%

Balance Sheet & Other Fin. Data (Million $)

	1994	1993	1992	1991	1990	1989
Total Assets	3,426	4,189	3,829	3,963	4,316	3,977
Loans	1,857	3,465	3,010	3,166	3,417	3,085
Deposits	2,077	2,690	2,760	2,844	2,816	2,625
Capitalization:						
Debt	863	956	625	701	1,039	859
Equity	272	238	301	289	323	326
Total	1,210	1,268	926	990	1,362	1,185

Ratio Analysis

	1994	1993	1992	1991	1990	1989
% Ret. on Assets	1.2	NM	0.3	NM	0.2	0.5
% Ret. on Equity	15.3	NM	3.7	NM	2.4	6.3
% Loan Loss Resv.	1.4	0.8	1.3	1.3	0.7	0.3
% Risk Based Capital	15.8	11.4	10.5	10.2	9.8	NA
Price Times Book Value:						
High	1.2	1.3	0.5	0.5	0.6	0.8
Low	0.8	0.6	0.3	0.3	0.3	0.5

Dividend Data —Cash dividends, initiated in 1987 and omitted in September 1991, were reinstated in September 1994.

Amt. of Div. $	Date Decl.	Ex-Div. Date	Stock of Record	Payment Date
0.100	Sep. 28	Oct. 07	Oct. 15	Nov. 01 '94
0.100	Dec. 21	Jan. 09	Jan. 13	Feb. 01 '95
0.100	Mar. 29	Apr. 07	Apr. 15	May. 01 '95
0.100	Jun. 28	Jul. 12	Jul. 15	Aug. 01 '95
0.120	Sep. 27	Oct. 11	Oct. 15	Nov. 01 '95

Data as orig. reptd.; bef. results of disc opers. and/or spec. items. Per share data adj. for stk. divs. as of ex-div. date. E-Estimated. NA-Not Available. NM-Not Meaningful. NR-Not Ranked.

Office—40 Franklin St., Rochester, NY 14604. **Tel**—(716) 258-3000. **Chrmn, Pres & CEO**—L. S. Simon. **SVP-CFO**—P. R. Wuest. **Secy**—R. Craig. **Investor Contact**—Richard Dye (716-423-7363). **Dirs**—M. Augustine, B. B. Bates, K. N. Hanson, J. D. Hostutler, G. G. Kaufman, S. R. Martoche, M. P. Morley, R. F. Poe, L. Schutzman, K. D. Shaw, L. S. Simon. **Transfer Agent**—State Street Bank and Trust Company, Boston. **Chartered** in New York in 1983. **Empl**-1,380. **S&P Analyst:** Robert Schpoont

STANDARD & POOR'S

Raymond James Financial

STOCK REPORTS

NYSE Symbol **RJF**
In S&P SmallCap 600

30-AUG-95 **Industry:** Securities

Summary: This holding company is engaged, through subsidiaries, in securities brokerage, investment banking, financial planning, and investment advisory and related financial services.

Quantitative Evaluations

Outlook
(1 Lowest—5 Highest)
• **NA**
Fair Value
• **NA**
Risk
• **Average**
Earn./Div. Rank
• **A-**

Technical Eval.
• **Bullish** since 8/95
Rel. Strength Rank
(1 Lowest—99 Highest)
• **71**
Insider Activity
• **NA**

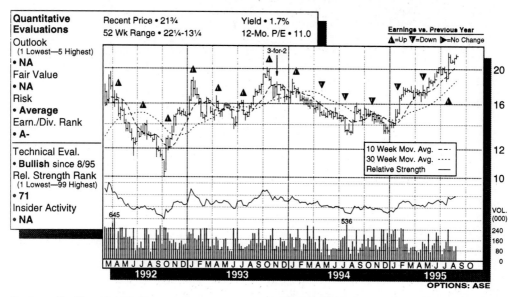

Recent Price • 21¾ | Yield • 1.7%
52 Wk Range • 22¼-13¼ | 12-Mo. P/E • 11.0

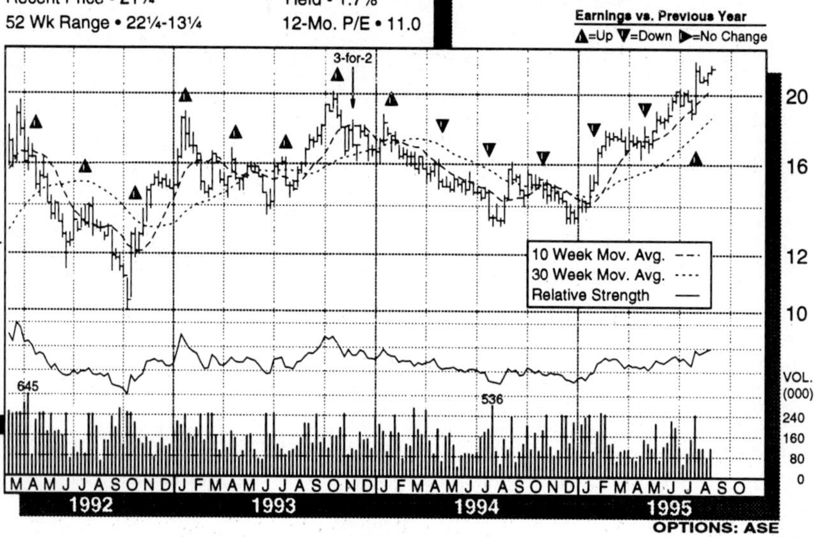

OPTIONS: ASE

Business Profile - 28-AUG-95

In May 1994, this holding company formed Raymond James Bank after its acquisition from the Resolution Trust Corp. of three Security Federal Savings Association branches in Florida. RJF's earnings are subject to wide fluctuations, reflecting the volatile nature of securities markets. Fiscal 1994 income was negatively affected as the rate of corporate equity issuances and corporate debt underwritings declined due to higher interest rates. The James family owns 38% of the common stock.

Operational Review - 30-AUG-95

Revenues in the nine months ended June 30, 1995, were up 2.1%, year to year. Sharply higher interest income was largely offset by lower investment banking and investment advisory fees. Expenses rose 3.2%, reflecting higher interest, occupancy and equipment costs. Income before taxes and minority interests dropped 4.4%. After taxes at 37.0%, versus 37.4%, net income was down 3.8%, to $31,829,000 ($1.54 a share), from $33,074,000 ($1.54).

Stock Performance - 25-AUG-95

In the past 30 trading days, RJF's shares have increased 11%, compared to a 0.04% rise in the S&P 500. Average trading volume for the past five days was 22,500 shares, compared with the 40-day moving average of 25,328 shares.

Key Stock Statistics

Dividend Rate/Share	0.36	Shareholders	7,500
Shs. outstg. (M)	20.6	Market cap. (B)	$0.445
Avg. daily vol. (M)	0.020	Inst. holdings	34%
Tang. Bk. Value/Share	12.31	Insider holdings	NA
Beta	1.55		

Value of $10,000 invested 5 years ago: $ 51,855

Fiscal Year Ending Sep. 30

	1995	% Change	1994	% Change	1993	% Change
Revenues (Million $)						
1Q	115.7	-14%	134.4	44%	93.31	15%
2Q	125.7	-3%	130.1	16%	112.4	16%
3Q	148.9	26%	117.7	3%	114.1	25%
4Q	—	—	124.9	-35%	192.0	108%
Yr.	—	—	507.1	12%	451.8	25%
Income (Million $)						
1Q	7.89	-41%	13.28	29%	10.33	23%
2Q	10.10	-18%	12.35	-3%	12.68	10%
3Q	13.84	86%	7.45	-37%	11.77	9%
4Q	—	—	9.00	-38%	14.56	43%
Yr.	—	—	42.07	-15%	49.35	20%
Earnings Per Share ($)						
1Q	0.38	-39%	0.62	29%	0.48	24%
2Q	0.49	-14%	0.57	-2%	0.58	10%
3Q	0.67	91%	0.35	-35%	0.54	9%
4Q	—	—	0.43	-36%	0.67	44%
Yr.	—	—	1.97	-14%	2.28	21%

Next earnings report expected: mid November

Raymond James Financial

Business Summary - 30-AUG-95

Raymond James Financial is a financial services holding company that, through operating subsidiaries, is engaged in securities brokerage, investment banking, investment advisory services, financial planning, and management of limited partnerships. Segment contributions to revenues in recent fiscal years were:

	1994	1993
Securities commissions	60%	61%
Limited partnerships & investment banking	12%	13%
Investment advisory fees	10%	10%
Interest	12%	8%
Net trading & investment profits	1%	3%
Other	5%	5%

The company's principal subsidiary, Raymond James & Associates, Inc. (RJA), is a regional brokerage with 47 offices (the majority in Florida). RJA is Florida's largest brokerage and investment concern. It serves both retail and institutional customers. Activities include trading of securities; sales of mutual funds; institutional sales and research; corporate finance; origination, syndication and marketing of limited partnerships (primarily in the real estate, equipment leasing and telecommunications industries); and distribution and underwriting of municipal securities.

Other operating subsidiaries include Investment Management & Research Inc., an independent financial planning organization that also distributes all securities offered by RJA to its retail customers through 455 offices and satellites in all 50 states; Robert Thomas Securities Inc., which operates 293 branch offices and satellites in 43 states and Puerto Rico; Eagle Asset Management Inc., which provides investment advisory services and had $6.1 billion under management at September 30, 1994; and Heritage Asset Management Inc., which manages six RJF-sponsored mutual funds with assets of about $1.5 billion at September 30, 1994.

The investment banking group is involved in public and private debt and equity financing for corporate clients, merger and acquisition consulting services. It also originates, syndicates and markets public and private limited partnerships, primarily in the real estate and equipment leasing industries. In May 1994, the company formed Raymond James Bank, whose three branches, located in Hudson, Spring Hill and Crystal River, Fla., were purchased for an undisclosed amount from the Resolution Trust Corp.

Important Developments

Jun. '95—RJA said the quarter ended June 30, 1995, was the second most profitable in its history. Favorable results were attributed to a resurgence of equity capital markets and improved investment banking activity.

Capitalization

Mortgage Note Payable: $13,125,000 (6/95).

Per Share Data ($)

(Year Ended Sep. 30)

	1994	1993	1992	1991	1990	1989
Tangible Bk. Val.	11.10	9.64	7.58	5.86	4.58	3.67
Cash Flow	NA	NA	NA	NA	NA	NA
Earnings	1.97	2.28	1.89	1.26	0.91	0.66
Dividends	0.32	0.21	0.16	0.10	0.07	0.06
Payout Ratio	16%	9%	8%	8%	8%	9%
Prices - High	18¾	20¼	19⅝	14¼	6⅝	5⅝
- Low	13⅛	13⅝	10	4⅞	4¼	3⅛
P/E Ratio - High	10	9	10	11	7	9
- Low	7	6	5	4	5	5

Income Statement Analysis (Million $)

	1994	%Chg	1993	%Chg	1992	%Chg	1991
Commissions	303	10%	276	35%	204	36%	150
Int. Inc.	58.5	74%	33.6	-8%	36.4	-34%	55.0
Total Revs.	507	12%	452	25%	361	26%	286
Int. Exp.	36.2	110%	17.2	-20%	21.4	-47%	40.3
Pretax Inc.	67.2	-16%	80.3	22%	65.8	51%	43.5
Eff. Tax Rate	37%	—	39%	—	38%	—	39%
Net Inc.	42.1	-15%	49.3	20%	41.0	54%	26.7

Balance Sheet & Other Fin. Data (Million $)

	1994	1993	1992	1991	1990	1989
Total Assets	1,698	1,448	806	1,060	948	830
Cash Items	296	208	231	334	275	251
Receivables	1,124	1,088	482	655	608	522
Secs. Owned	179	72.1	33.5	31.8	32.5	26.5
Sec. Borrowed	Nil	Nil	Nil	Nil	Nil	Nil
Due Brokers & Cust.	1,359	1,142	573	869	810	709
Other Liabs.	99	86.8	58.6	54.6	27.9	21.9
Capitalization:						
Debt	13.2	13.4	13.5	13.6	13.7	27.8
Equity	227	206	161	122	97.0	72.0
Total	240	219	174	136	111	99

Ratio Analysis

	1994	1993	1992	1991	1990	1989
% Ret. on Revs.	8.3	10.9	11.4	9.3	7.0	5.5
% Ret. on Assets	2.7	4.4	4.4	2.7	2.0	1.8
% Ret. on Equity	19.4	26.9	29.0	24.4	21.3	19.0

Dividend Data —Cash dividends were initiated in 1985.

Amt. of Div. $	Date Decl.	Ex-Div. Date	Stock of Record	Payment Date
0.080	Aug. 26	Sep. 06	Sep. 12	Oct. 06 '94
0.090	Dec. 16	Jan. 03	Jan. 09	Jan. 30 '95
0.090	Feb. 21	Mar. 07	Mar. 13	Apr. 03 '95
0.090	May. 23	Jun. 08	Jun. 12	Jul. 03 '95
0.090	Aug. 23	Sep. 07	Sep. 11	Oct. 03 '95

Data as orig. reptd.; bef. results of disc opers. and/or spec. items. Per share data adj. for stk. divs. as of ex-div. date. E-Estimated. NA-Not Available. NM-Not Meaningful. NR-Not Ranked.

Office—880 Carillon Parkway, St. Petersburg, FL 33716. **Tel**—(813) 573-3800. **Chrmn & CEO**—T. A. James. **Pres**—F. S. Godbold. **Secy-Treas**—L. Pippenger. **VP-Fin & CFO**—J. P. Julien. **VP & Investor Contact**—Lawrence A. Silver. **Dirs**—J. A. Bulkley, H. E. Ehlers, T. S. Franke, F. S. Godbold, M. A. Greene, H. H. Hill, Jr., C. W. James, T. A. James, P. W. Marshall, J. S. Putnam, R. F. Shuck. **Transfer Agent & Registrar**—Mellon Financial Services, Pittsburgh. **Incorporated** in Florida in 1974. **Empl**-2,513. **S&P Analyst:** Thomas C. Ferguson

STANDARD & POOR'S
STOCK REPORTS

Read-Rite Corp.

NASDAQ Symbol **RDRT**
In S&P SmallCap 600

11-SEP-95

Industry: Data Processing

Summary: This company is the leading independent supplier of magnetic recording heads for rigid disk drives.

Quantitative Evaluations
Outlook
(1 Lowest—5 Highest)
• 5
Fair Value
• 49⅞
Risk
• High
Earn./Div. Rank
• NR

Technical Eval.
• **Bullish** since 8/94
Rel. Strength Rank
(1 Lowest—99 Highest)
• 97
Insider Activity
• Neutral

Recent Price • 48
52 Wk Range • 49½-14
Yield • Nil
12-Mo. P/E • 24.4

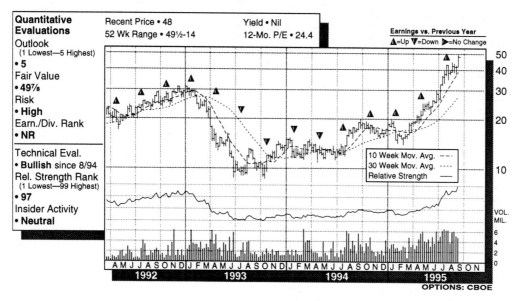

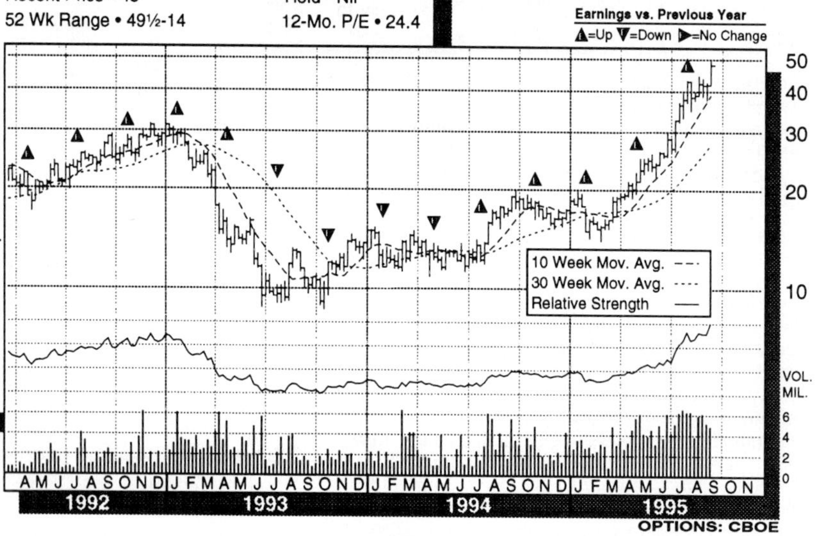

Business Profile - 11-SEP-95

This company manufactures heads and headstack assemblies for disk drives and heads for tape drives. Operations were significantly expanded through the August 1994 acquisition of Sunward Technologies, Inc. (in exchange for about 9 million shares). Because the disk drive market is characterized by rapid technology changes, short product life, and price erosion, Read-Rite seeks continuous technological improvement, coupled with product quality and cost efficiency.

Operational Review - 11-SEP-95

Revenues in the first nine months of fiscal 1995 soared 62%, year to year, reflecting strong sales of heads and headstacks. Margins widened, as improved manufacturing efficiency reduced unit costs. EPS surged to $1.63, from $0.09. An agreement in principle to obtain $100 million from a group of insurance companies would provide funds to expand operations to meet increasing product demand.

Stock Performance - 08-SEP-95

In the past 30 trading days, RDRT's shares have increased 12%, compared to a 2% rise in the S&P 500. Average trading volume for the past five days was 1,190,725 shares, compared with the 40-day moving average of 1,393,035 shares.

Key Stock Statistics

Dividend Rate/Share	Nil	Shareholders	17,000
Shs. outstg. (M)	45.3	Market cap. (B)	$ 2.2
Avg. daily vol. (M)	1.128	Inst. holdings	82%
Tang. Bk. Value/Share	9.39	Insider holdings	NA
Beta	NA		

Value of $10,000 invested 5 years ago: NA

Fiscal Year Ending Sep. 30

	1995	% Change	1994	% Change	1993	% Change
Revenues (Million $)						
1Q	219.5	66%	132.0	-5%	139.4	106%
2Q	241.8	73%	139.5	-7%	150.2	59%
3Q	253.1	49%	170.1	41%	120.8	14%
4Q	—	—	197.0	174%	71.91	-41%
Yr.	—	—	638.6	32%	482.4	24%
Income (Million $)						
1Q	19.58	NM	-2.30	NM	17.23	95%
2Q	25.00	NM	-4.46	NM	18.77	54%
3Q	32.30	192%	11.06	NM	1.33	—
4Q	—	—	15.39	NM	-36.44	—
Yr.	—	—	19.69	NM	0.88	-98%
Earnings Per Share ($)						
1Q	0.42	NM	-0.05	NM	0.52	58%
2Q	0.53	NM	-0.10	NM	0.52	41%
3Q	0.68	183%	0.24	NM	0.04	-90%
4Q	—	—	0.33	NM	-1.05	NM
Yr.	—	—	0.43	NM	0.02	-99%

Next earnings report expected: late October

Read-Rite Corp.

Business Summary - 11-SEP-95

Read-Rite Corporation is the leading independent supplier of magnetic recording heads for rigid disk drives. It supplies magnetic recording heads as head gimbal assemblies (HGAs), and for certain customers incorporates multiple HGAs into headstack assemblies (HSAs). The company's products are sold primarily to independent manufacturers of small form factor rigid disk drives. Read-Rite believes that it supplies heads for a broader range of disk drive products than any other independent supplier.

In August 1994, the company acquired Sunward Technologies, Inc., a leading supplier of ferrite metal-in-gap (MIG) and double MIG recording heads and HSAs for rigid disk drives. The acquisition of Sunward's ferrite HGA and HSA capabilities allowed Read-Rite to offer customers a full range of HGAs and HSAs incorporating advanced MIG and thin film technologies.

The principal components of rigid disk drives are HGAs, disks, an actuator for positioning HGAs, a motor/spindle assembly to rotate the disk, control electronics and software. An HGA consists of a magnetic recording head attached to a flexure, or suspension arm, and a wire/tubing assembly. Several HGAs can be combined with other components to form an HSA. One or more rigid disks coated with a thin layer of magnetic material are attached to the motor/spindle assembly, which rotates the disks at high speed within a sealed enclosure. The heads, attached to and positioned by the movable actuator, "fly" above both sides of each disk. The head position is controlled by drive electronics based on a servo pattern previously written on the surface of at least one disk. The heads record or retrieve data from tracks pre-formatted in the magnetic layer of each disk.

Product development efforts are directed toward the development of next-generation products and technologies related to existing business, enhancement of existing products, and manufacturing process developments that boost product yields. R&D spending totaled $25,524,000 (4.0% of total sales) in fiscal 1994, up from $20,053,000 (3.4%) in fiscal 1993 and $14,359,000 (3.0%) in fiscal 1992.

In fiscal 1994, Western Digital, Quantum, Conner Peripherals and Maxtor accounted for 34%, 23%, 15% and 13% of net sales, respectively.

Important Developments

Aug. '95—Read-Rite announced an agreement to obtain $100 million from a group of insurance companies. The company said that the loan was not needed immediately, but would enable it to respond to increasing unit demand for its products.

Capitalization

Long Term Debt: $48,026,000 (6/95).

Per Share Data ($) (Year Ended Sep. 30)

	1994	1993	1992	1991	1990	1989
Tangible Bk. Val.	8.45	10.02	6.84	2.47	-4.22	NA
Cash Flow	1.48	0.99	2.25	1.34	0.52	NA
Earnings	0.43	0.02	1.59	1.04	0.33	NA
Dividends	Nil	Nil	Nil	Nil	Nil	NA
Payout Ratio	Nil	Nil	Nil	Nil	Nil	NA
Prices - High	19⅞	31¼	32	15⅞	NA	NA
- Low	10⅞	8⅝	14⅛	11¾	NA	NA
P/E Ratio - High	46	NM	20	15	NA	NA
- Low	25	NM	9	11	NA	NA

Income Statement Analysis (Million $)

	1994	%Chg	1993	%Chg	1992	%Chg	1991
Revs.	639	33%	482	24%	389	120%	177
Oper. Inc.	82.9	38%	60.2	-21%	76.6	89%	40.5
Depr.	48.7	43%	34.1	76%	19.4	194%	6.6
Int. Exp.	4.8	NM	1.2	-32%	1.8	NM	1.8
Pretax Inc.	28.8	NM	-1.9	NM	58.8	109%	28.2
Eff. Tax Rate	16%	—	NM	—	20%	—	17%
Net Inc.	19.7	NM	0.9	-98%	47.0	103%	23.1

Balance Sheet & Other Fin. Data (Million $)

	1994	1993	1992	1991	1990	1989
Cash	111	124	50.8	63.2	3.0	NA
Curr. Assets	260	228	174	99	17.0	NA
Total Assets	631	516	345	154	36.0	NA
Curr. Liab.	130	84.6	85.5	49.9	21.6	NA
LT Debt	52.4	46.5	28.7	26.7	5.8	NA
Common Eqty.	397	350	195	13.0	-24.0	NA
Total Cap.	500	431	259	104	14.0	NA
Cap. Exp.	113	170	112	42.0	8.0	NA
Cash Flow	68.4	35.0	66.4	29.7	10.3	NA

Ratio Analysis

	1994	1993	1992	1991	1990	1989
Curr. Ratio	2.0	2.7	2.0	2.0	0.8	NA
% LT Debt of Cap.	10.5	10.8	11.1	25.7	41.4	NA
% Net Inc.of Revs.	3.1	0.2	12.1	13.0	8.9	NA
% Ret. on Assets	3.0	0.2	7.8	24.9	21.3	NA
% Ret. on Equity	4.6	0.3	35.4	NM	NM	NA

Dividend Data —No cash dividends have been paid.

Data as orig. reptd.; bef. results of disc. opers. and/or spec. items. Per share data adj. for stk. divs. as of ex-div. date. E-Estimated. NA-Not Available. NM-Not Meaningful. NR-Not Ranked.

Office—345 Los Coches St., Milpitas, CA 95035. **Tel**—(408) 262-6700. **Chrmn & CEO**—C. J. Yansouni. **Pres & COO**—F. Schwettman. **VP-Fin & CFO**—L. Holland. **Secy**—R. S. Jackson. **Dirs**—W. J. Almon, H. V. Blaxter III, J. G. Linvill, F. Schwettman, C. J. Yansouni. **Transfer Agent & Registrar**—Chemical Trust Co. of California, SF. **Incorporated** in California in 1981; reincorporated in Delaware in 1985. **Empl**-18,472. **S&P Analyst:** Mike Cavanaugh

STANDARD & POOR'S
STOCK REPORTS

Regal-Beloit Corp.

ASE Symbol **RBC**
In S&P SmallCap 600

07-NOV-95 **Industry:** Machinery

Summary: This company is one of the leading U.S. producers of power transmission systems and expendable cutting tools.

Quantitative Evaluations

Outlook (1 Lowest—5 Highest)
• **4+**

Fair Value
• **19⅛**

Risk
• **Average**

Earn./Div. Rank
• **B+**

Technical Eval.
• **Neutral** since 11/95

Rel. Strength Rank (1 Lowest—99 Highest)
• **77**

Insider Activity
• **NA**

Recent Price • 18⅞
52 Wk Range • 21⅛-11¼
Yield • 2.1%
12-Mo. P/E • 12.5

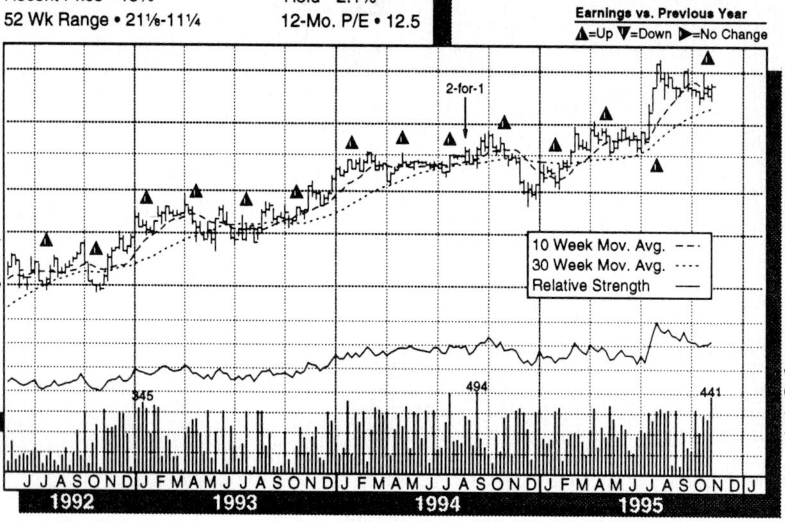

Business Profile - 07-NOV-95

Continuing to expand through acquisitions, RBC has steadily improved its earnings since 1992. The company's cash flow continues to be very strong, enabling it to reduce its debt. Sales of agricultural products slowed during 1995, but demand from the heavy industries has remained strong, and foreign operations have been performing well. RBC has been adding capital equipment, which should benefit its productivity. The dividend was boosted 13% in June 1995.

Operational Review - 07-NOV-95

Net sales rose 23%, year to year, in the first nine months of 1995, aided by recent acquisitions, increased order levels at all divisions in both the power transmission and cutting tool groups, and improving foreign operations. Results benefited from the greater volume, cost controls, improved productivity, lower interest expense and higher interest income; net income was up 49%. Near-term results should continue to benefit from strong incoming orders.

Stock Performance - 03-NOV-95

In the past 30 trading days, RBC's shares have increased 0.67%, compared to a 2% rise in the S&P 500. Average trading volume for the past five days was 88,280 shares, compared with the 40-day moving average of 32,405 shares.

Key Stock Statistics

Dividend Rate/Share	0.40	Shareholders	1,300
Shs. outstg. (M)	20.5	Market cap. (B)	$0.395
Avg. daily vol. (M)	0.047	Inst. holdings	59%
Tang. Bk. Value/Share	6.00	Insider holdings	NA
Beta	0.73		

Value of $10,000 invested 5 years ago: $ 27,015

Fiscal Year Ending Dec. 31

	1995	% Change	1994	% Change	1993	% Change
Revenues (Million $)						
1Q	74.34	26%	58.85	9%	54.20	30%
2Q	76.27	27%	60.04	9%	55.32	7%
3Q	71.55	17%	61.19	12%	54.77	3%
4Q	—	—	62.57	13%	55.61	5%
Yr.	—	—	242.6	10%	219.9	10%
Income (Million $)						
1Q	7.38	59%	4.63	51%	3.06	67%
2Q	8.38	52%	5.52	50%	3.68	55%
3Q	8.43	38%	6.13	72%	3.56	47%
4Q	—	—	6.85	68%	4.08	44%
Yr.	—	—	23.13	62%	14.25	51%
Earnings Per Share ($)						
1Q	0.36	60%	0.22	50%	0.15	67%
2Q	0.41	52%	0.27	50%	0.18	57%
3Q	0.41	37%	0.30	71%	0.17	46%
4Q	—	—	0.33	65%	0.20	43%
Yr.	—	—	1.13	61%	0.70	51%

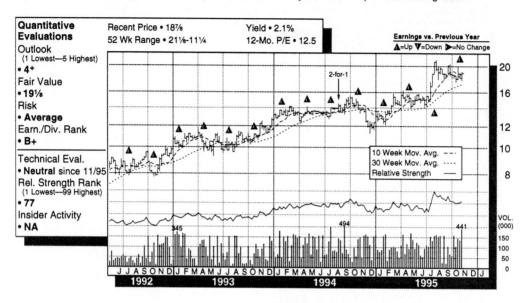

Next earnings report expected: early February

Regal-Beloit Corp.

Business Summary - 06-NOV-95

Regal-Beloit manufactures a diversified line of power transmission products, as well as expendable, high-speed, rotary cutting tools. Contributions by business segment in 1994 were:

	Sales	Profits
Power transmission systems	86%	90%
Cutting tools	14%	10%

European operations accounted for 5.8% of total sales in 1994.

The Power Transmission Group makes products that are used to transfer power from a single source to one or more end uses, usually decreasing the speed. Products include standard and custom gearboxes, rigid forklift axles, custom gearing, mini-gear motors and manual valve actuators.

Typical applications for power transmission products include material handling systems such as conveyors, palletizers and packaging equipment; off-highway vehicular equipment such as street pavers, graders, airport/fire/crash rescue equipment; farm implements; center pivot irrigation systems; gas and liquid pipeline transmission systems and civic water and waste treatment facilities; open-pit mining; paper-making machinery; and high-performance, after-market automotive transmissions and ring-pinion sets.

In July 1991, power transmission products operations were expanded by the acquisition of Opperman Mastergear, which has facilities in the U.K. and Germany, as well as in the U.S. In April 1992, Hub City, Inc., Aberdeen, S.D., was acquired. Hub City manufactures a broad line of enclosed worm and bevel gear drives and mounted bearings. In November 1992, Terrell Gear Drives Inc., Charlotte, N.C., was purchased. In early 1995, the company acquired the Velvet Drive Transmission division and, in late 1994, C.M.L. of Italy.

The Cutting Tool Group's products consist of a complete line of expendable high-speed steel rotary cutting tools. Principal products include taps, drills, end mills, reamers and gages in about 25,000 styles and sizes.

In January 1995, the company acquired certain assets of Borg-Warner Automotive's Marine & Industrial Transmission business. The division, which had 1993 sales of about $28 million, manufactures marine and industrial transmission products in New Bedford, Mass.

Important Developments

Oct. '95—Regal-Beloit said it expects its 1995 fourth quarter shipments to be better than those of the third quarter. RBC added that it sees improved earnings for the period as well.

Capitalization

Long Term Debt: $4,419,000 (6/95).
Options: To buy 955,420 shs. at $3.56 to $13.87 a sh. (12/94).

Per Share Data ($) (Year Ended Dec. 31)

	1994	1993	1992	1991	1990	1989
Tangible Bk. Val.	5.40	4.55	4.13	4.04	3.95	3.69
Cash Flow	1.57	1.14	0.81	0.50	0.73	0.75
Earnings	1.13	0.70	0.46	0.28	0.53	0.57
Dividends	0.31	0.26	0.26	0.26	0.26	0.24
Payout Ratio	27%	38%	56%	95%	49%	42%
Prices - High	15½	13¼	11	7⅜	8⅜	9½
- Low	11¼	9¼	6½	5⅜	4⅝	6½
P/E Ratio - High	14	19	24	27	16	17
- Low	10	13	14	20	9	11

Income Statement Analysis (Million $)

	1994	%Chg	1993	%Chg	1992	%Chg	1991
Revs.	243	10%	220	10%	200	32%	152
Oper. Inc.	48.0	42%	33.8	41%	23.9	67%	14.3
Depr.	9.0	3%	8.8	26%	7.0	55%	4.5
Int. Exp.	1.0	-37%	1.5	-20%	1.9	39%	1.4
Pretax Inc.	38.2	61%	23.7	56%	15.2	69%	9.0
Eff. Tax Rate	39%	—	39%	—	38%	—	38%
Net Inc.	23.1	60%	14.4	52%	9.5	73%	5.5

Balance Sheet & Other Fin. Data (Million $)

	1994	1993	1992	1991	1990	1989
Cash	13.4	2.2	5.2	7.2	10.0	3.2
Curr. Assets	91.7	71.7	77.5	68.7	73.4	72.4
Total Assets	168	139	145	118	114	111
Curr. Liab.	36.6	22.5	24.1	19.7	14.7	17.3
LT Debt	16.0	19.6	34.4	13.8	16.6	17.3
Common Eqty.	111	92.7	83.9	81.8	80.0	74.2
Total Cap.	131	117	121	98.0	99	94.0
Cap. Exp.	7.5	8.5	6.5	7.5	7.6	13.4
Cash Flow	32.1	23.1	16.4	10.0	14.6	15.1

Ratio Analysis

	1994	1993	1992	1991	1990	1989
Curr. Ratio	2.5	3.2	3.2	3.5	5.0	4.2
% LT Debt of Cap.	12.2	16.8	28.5	14.1	16.8	18.5
% Net Inc.of Revs.	9.5	6.5	4.7	3.6	6.4	6.9
% Ret. on Assets	15.1	10.1	7.2	4.8	9.5	11.2
% Ret. on Equity	22.7	16.3	11.4	6.8	13.8	16.3

Dividend Data —Cash has been paid each year since 1961.

Amt. of Div. $	Date Decl.	Ex-Div. Date	Stock of Record	Payment Date
0.080	Oct. 21	Dec. 23	Dec. 30	Jan. 13 '95
0.090	Jan. 30	Mar. 27	Mar. 31	Apr. 14 '95
0.100	Apr. 18	Jun. 28	Jun. 30	Jul. 14 '95
0.100	Jul. 24	Sep. 27	Sep. 30	Oct. 13 '95
0.100	Oct. 31	Dec. 27	Dec. 29	Jan. 15 '96

Data as orig. reptd.; bef. results of disc. opers. and/or spec. items. Per share data adj. for stk. divs. as of ex-div. date. E-Estimated. NA-Not Available. NM-Not Meaningful. NR-Not Ranked.

Office—200 State St., Beloit, WI 53511-6254. **Tel**—(608) 364-8800. **Chrmn, Pres & CEO**—J. L. Packard. **VP, & Secy**—G. J. Berres. **VP, CFO & Investor Contact**—Robert C. Burress. **Dirs**—F. E. Bauchiero, J. R. Coleman, J. M. Eldred, G. F. Kasten Jr., W. W. Keefer, H. W. Knueppel, J. A. McKay, E. H. Neese, H. R. Odell, J. L. Packard. **Transfer Agent & Registrar**—Bank of Boston. **Incorporated** in Delaware in 1955; reincorporated in Wisconsin in 1994. **Empl**-2,400. **S&P Analyst:** Stewart Scharf

Regal Cinemas

NASDAQ Symbol **REGL**
In S&P SmallCap 600

02-OCT-95 **Industry:** Filmed Entertainment

Summary: This regional motion picture exhibitor acquires, develops and operates multi-screen theatres in the eastern U.S. It was recently operating more than 860 screens.

Quantitative Evaluations

Outlook (1 Lowest—5 Highest)
• **NA**
Fair Value
• **NA**
Risk
• **Average**
Earn./Div. Rank
• **NR**

Technical Eval.
• **Bullish** since 3/95
Rel. Strength Rank (1 Lowest—99 Highest)
• **91**
Insider Activity
• **Neutral**

Recent Price • 41⅛
52 Wk Range • 43-17
Yield • Nil
12-Mo. P/E • 33.7

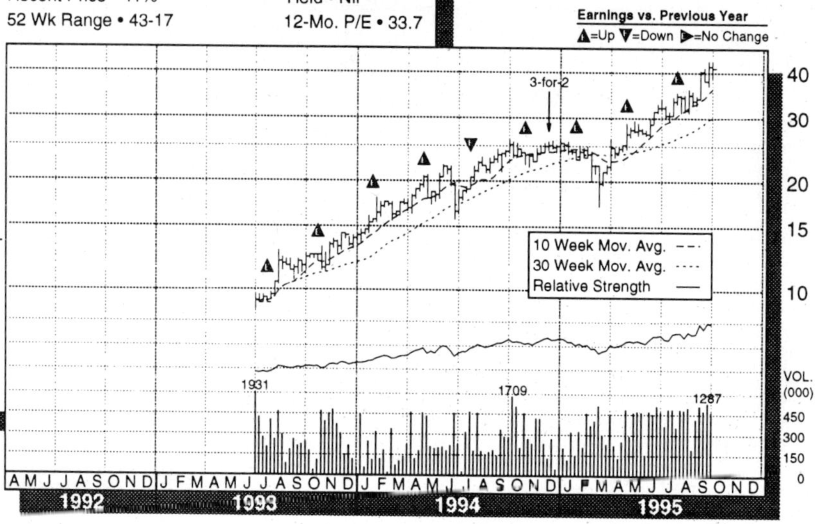

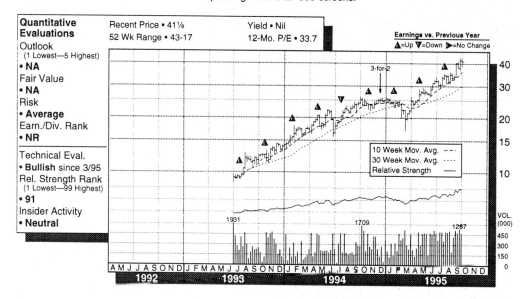

Business Profile - 02-OCT-95

This rapidly expanding regional motion picture exhibitor's focuses on mid-sized metropolitan markets and suburban growth areas that can support a clustering of multi-screen theaters. Its primary expansion vehicle will be controlled internal development of new screens. Secondary methods include acquisitions and additions of screens to existing theatres. In August 1995, Regal opened its first Funscape family entertainment center. Funscape is designed to complement the company's theatres.

Operational Review - 02-OCT-95

Revenues in the first half of 1995, as restated for the April 1995 acquisition Neighborhood Entertainment, Inc., advanced 25%, year to year, primarily reflecting more screens in operation. Profitability was boosted by greater economies of scale, more efficient operation of acquired properties, and a reduction in merger-related expenses; net income replaced a net loss. Future growth is expected to reflect both internal expansion and acquisitions.

Stock Performance - 29-SEP-95

In the past 30 trading days, REGL's shares have increased 18%, compared to a 5% rise in the S&P 500. Average trading volume for the past five days was 115,260 shares, compared with the 40-day moving average of 155,818 shares.

Key Stock Statistics

Dividend Rate/Share	Nil	Shareholders	4,400
Shs. outstg. (M)	11.7	Market cap. (B)	$0.479
Avg. daily vol. (M)	0.192	Inst. holdings	51%
Tang. Bk. Value/Share	7.57	Insider holdings	NA
Beta	NA		

Value of $10,000 invested 5 years ago: NA

Fiscal Year Ending Dec. 31

	1995	% Change	1994	% Change	1993	% Change
Revenues (Million $)						
1Q	32.54	28%	25.36	151%	10.10	17%
2Q	44.90	52%	29.49	146%	12.00	24%
3Q	—	—	44.98	135%	19.10	101%
4Q	—	—	35.87	126%	15.90	38%
Yr.	—	—	135.7	137%	57.20	46%
Income (Million $)						
1Q	2.63	79%	1.47	NM	0.42	—
2Q	2.68	NM	-1.45	NM	0.53	—
3Q	—	—	5.46	142%	2.26	—
4Q	—	—	3.26	130%	1.42	—
Yr.	—	—	8.73	89%	4.62	—
Earnings Per Share ($)						
1Q	0.23	64%	0.14	27%	0.11	38%
2Q	0.22	NM	-0.13	NM	0.13	8%
3Q	—	—	0.51	46%	0.35	NM
4Q	—	—	0.28	33%	0.21	5%
Yr.	—	—	0.80	-8%	0.87	74%

Next earnings report expected: late October

Business Summary - 02-OCT-95

Regal Cinemas, Inc. is a leading regional motion picture exhibitor. It acquires, develops and operates multi-screen theatres in the eastern U.S. Revenues from theatre operations in recent years were derived as follows:

	1994	1993	1992
Admissions	70%	69%	70%
Concessions	28%	29%	28%
Other	2%	2%	2%

At December 29, 1994, the company operated 92 multi-screen theatres with an aggregate of 704 screens in 10 states, up from 45 theatres with 359 screens a year earlier.

Regal's multi-screen theatre complexes, which typically contain auditoriums with seating capacities of 100 to 500, feature wall-to-wall screens, digital stereo surround-sound, multi-station concessions, computerized ticketing systems, plush seating with cup holders, neon-enhanced interiors and exteriors, and video game areas adjacent to the theatre lobby.

The company operates certain theatres as discount theatres, exhibiting second-run movies and charging lower admission prices. It plans to divest these discount theatres.

Regal's theatres offer a wide range of concession products, although popcorn, candy and soft drinks remain the best selling concession items. Certain existing theatres and those under construction feature specialty concession cafes serving cappuccino, fruit juices, cookies and muffins, soft pretzels and yogurt.

In August 1995, the company opened its first 95,000 sq. ft. Funscape family entertainment center, in Chesapeake, Va. Funscape includes a 13-screen theatre with an attached two-level, year-round indoor family entertainment center.

Important Developments

Jul. '95—Regal recorded net charges totaling about $1.1 million ($0.09 a share) in the 1995 second quarter, related to the acquisition of Neighborhood Entertainment, Inc. (for 362,113 common shares). Neighborhood Entertainment operates of 25 theatres with 99 screens in the Tidewater and Richmond areas of Virginia. Separately, the company agreed to acquire four Florida theatres with 30 screens.
Apr. '95—The company purchased three companies that held a total of four theatres with 40 screens, in exchange for 107,250 common shares and $14.3 million in cash and other consideration.
Mar. '95—Regal announced plans to construct and open 210 new screens over the next 18 months.

Capitalization

Long Term Debt: $74,250,000 (6/95).

Per Share Data ($) (Year Ended Dec. 31)

	1994	1993	1992	1991	1990	1989
Tangible Bk. Val.	6.95	6.17	2.57	NA	NA	NA
Cash Flow	1.35	1.67	1.89	NA	NA	NA
Earnings	0.80	1.07	0.85	NA	NA	NA
Dividends	Nil	Nil	Nil	NA	NA	NA
Payout Ratio	Nil	Nil	Nil	NA	NA	NA
Prices - High	26¼	14⅜	NA	NA	NA	NA
- Low	13½	8⅝	NA	NA	NA	NA
P/E Ratio - High	33	13	NA	NA	NA	NA
- Low	17	8	NA	NA	NA	NA

Income Statement Analysis (Million $)

	1994	%Chg	1993	%Chg	1992	%Chg	1991
Revs.	136	138%	57.2	46%	39.3	—	NA
Oper. Inc.	28.8	153%	11.4	81%	6.3	—	NA
Depr.	5.9	148%	2.4	49%	1.6	—	NA
Int. Exp.	2.9	117%	1.3	-20%	1.7	—	NA
Pretax Inc.	15.1	98%	7.6	138%	3.2	—	NA
Eff. Tax Rate	42%	—	40%	—	38%	—	NA
Net Inc.	8.7	89%	4.6	133%	2.0	—	NA

Balance Sheet & Other Fin. Data (Million $)

	1994	1993	1992	1991	1990	1989
Cash	5.6	7.3	6.5	NA	NA	NA
Curr. Assets	9.8	8.8	7.6	NA	NA	NA
Total Assets	138	59.5	44.0	NA	NA	NA
Curr. Liab.	17.7	8.3	6.7	NA	NA	NA
LT Debt	38.3	10.2	22.1	NA	NA	NA
Common Eqty.	77.2	38.9	3.3	NA	NA	NA
Total Cap.	117	51.2	37.4	NA	NA	NA
Cap. Exp.	59.2	16.5	8.8	NA	NA	NA
Cash Flow	14.7	6.6	2.9	NA	NA	NA

Ratio Analysis

	1994	1993	1992	1991	1990	1989
Curr. Ratio	0.6	1.1	1.1	NA	NA	NA
% LT Debt of Cap.	32.6	19.9	59.2	NA	NA	NA
% Net Inc.of Revs.	6.4	8.1	5.0	NA	NA	NA
% Ret. on Assets	7.2	3.4	NA	NA	NA	NA
% Ret. on Equity	12.0	15.4	NA	NA	NA	NA

Dividend Data —No cash dividends have been paid. The company intends to retain its earnings to support operations and finance expansion. A three-for-two stock split was effected in December 1994.

Data as orig. reptd.; bef. results of disc. opers. and/or spec. items. Per share data adj. for stk. divs. as of ex-div. date. E-Estimated. NA-Not Available. NM-Not Meaningful. NR-Not Ranked.

Office—7132 Commercial Park Dr., Knoxville, TN 37918. **Tel**—(615) 922-1123. **Chrmn, Pres & CEO**—M. L. Campbell. **EVP**—G. Dunn. **VP, CFO, Treas & Investor Contact**—Lewis Frazer III. **VP & Secy**—R. N. Melton. **Dirs**—P. D. Borack, M. L. Campbell, M. E. Gellert, J. D. Grissom, W. H. Lomicka, R. N. Melton, H. S. Sanger, Jr., J. Tyrrell. **Transfer Agent & Registrar**—Bank of Boston. **Incorporated** in Tennessee in 1989. **Empl**-1,120. **S&P Analyst:** Efraim Levy

Regeneron Pharmaceuticals

NASDAQ Symbol **REGN**
In S&P SmallCap 600

19-SEP-95 **Industry:** Drugs-Generic and OTC

Summary: This biotechnology company focuses on discovery and development of nerve growth factors to treat neurological conditions, including Lou Gehrig's disease and Alzheimer's disease.

Quantitative Evaluations
Outlook
(1 Lowest—5 Highest)
• **NA**
Fair Value
• **NA**
Risk
• **High**
Earn./Div. Rank
• **NR**

Technical Eval.
• **Bearish** since 7/95
Rel. Strength Rank
(1 Lowest—99 Highest)
• **84**
Insider Activity
• **Neutral**

Recent Price • 12½
52 Wk Range • 16½-3
Yield • Nil
12-Mo. P/E • NM

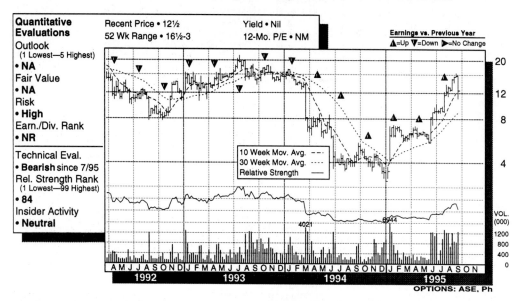

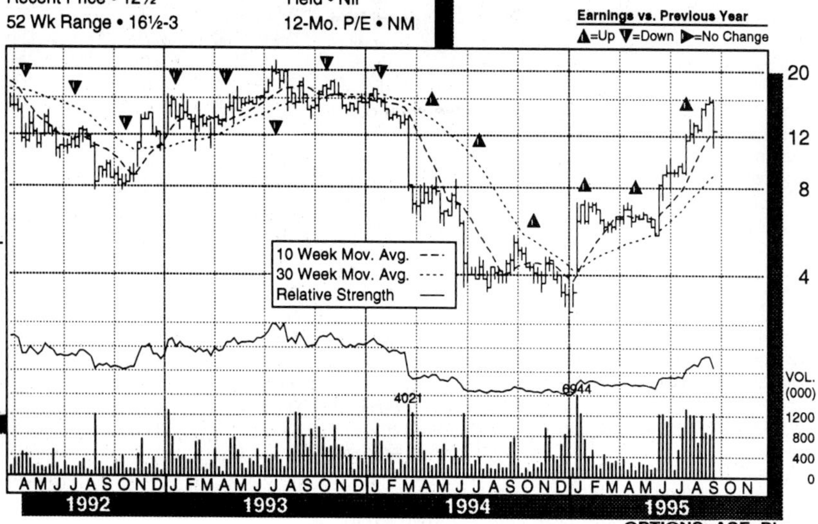

OPTIONS: ASE, Ph

Business Profile - 13-SEP-95

Regeneron has formed collaborative partnerships with Amgen and Sumitomo Pharmaceuticals to develop brain-derived neurotrophic factor (BDNF) to treat neurological diseases (most notably ALS, or Lou Gehrig's disease). Phase III trials of BDNF in the treatment of Lou Gehrig's disease (being developed with Amgen) are expected to begin in the third quarter of 1995. Research payments comprise the bulk of revenues, and the company does not expect to receive product revenues at least for several years.

Operational Review - 13-SEP-95

Revenues in the six months ended June 30, 1995, more than doubled, year to year, on higher contract income from Sumitomo Pharmaceuticals. Operating expenses declined 18% on lower R&D due to the discontinuance of the ciliary neurotrophic factor program. The net loss narrowed to $8.6 million ($0.44 a share) from $21.0 million ($1.11). At June 30, 1995, the company had about $50 million in cash and equivalents.

Stock Performance - 15-SEP-95

In the past 30 trading days, REGN's shares have increased 2%, compared to a 4% rise in the S&P 500. Average trading volume for the past five days was 370,080 shares, compared with the 40-day moving average of 281,292 shares.

Key Stock Statistics

Dividend Rate/Share	Nil	Shareholders	1,200
Shs. outstg. (M)	19.5	Market cap. (B)	$0.268
Avg. daily vol. (M)	0.277	Inst. holdings	16%
Tang. Bk. Value/Share	3.27	Insider holdings	NA
Beta	NA		

Value of $10,000 invested 5 years ago: NA

Fiscal Year Ending Dec. 31

	1995	% Change	1994	% Change	1993	% Change
Revenues (Million $)						
1Q	7.83	162%	2.99	40%	2.14	-39%
2Q	7.62	110%	3.62	85%	1.96	-39%
3Q	—	—	8.90	149%	3.58	46%
4Q	—	—	7.69	167%	2.88	22%
Yr.	—	—	23.19	120%	10.56	-8%
Income (Million $)						
1Q	-4.17	NM	-10.73	NM	-9.32	—
2Q	12.00	NM	-10.25	NM	-9.43	NM
3Q	—	—	-3.97	NM	-9.63	NM
4Q	—	—	-5.71	NM	-11.50	NM
Yr.	—	—	-30.65	NM	-39.88	NM
Earnings Per Share ($)						
1Q	-0.22	NM	-0.57	NM	-0.61	NM
2Q	-0.22	NM	-0.54	NM	-0.61	NM
3Q	—	—	-0.21	NM	-0.58	NM
4Q	—	—	-0.30	NM	-0.61	NM
Yr.	—	—	-1.62	NM	-2.41	NM

Next earnings report expected: early November

Regeneron Pharmaceuticals

Business Summary - 19-SEP-95

Regeneron Pharmaceuticals Inc. is developing compounds to treat neurodegenerative diseases, peripheral neuropathies and nerve injury. It has discovered and characterized certain naturally occurring human proteins that may lead to drugs to treat neurological diseases.

Neurodegenerative diseases are incurable conditions in which there is progressive loss of neurons crucial for functions such as learning and memory, sensation, control of movement, muscle strength and coordination. More than six million Americans have such conditions, including amyotrophic lateral sclerosis (ALS, or Lou Gehrig's disease), Parkinson's disease and Alzheimer's disease.

Regeneron has focused on the discovery and development of brain-derived neurotrophic factor (BDNF), which has been shown to promote survival of motor neurons in several preclinical models of injury or disease, including ALS. The company completed a Phase I/II trial of BDNF with Amgen Inc. (Amgen-Regeneron Partners). In Japan, it is developing BDNF with Sumitomo Pharmaceuticals.

Clinical studies are being conducted by Amgen-Regeneron Partners on Neurotrophin-3 (NT-3), a potential agent to treat toxic and diabetic neuropathies, trauma to spinal cord, disorders of the cerebellum, Parkinson's disease, Huntington's disease, Alzheimer's disease and retinal diseases. The company is also developing Neurotrophin-4/5 (NT-4/5) for retinal diseases, peripheral neuropathies, Parkinson's disease and Alzheimer's disease.

Amgen-Regeneron Partners was created in 1990 when Amgen Inc. invested $15,000,000 in the company. Amgen also agreed to provide a total of $25 million of development funding over five years, and to make $13 million in progress payments. As of December 1994, $29,612,000 had been received in connection with the partnership.

In October 1994, the company entered into a collaborative agreement with Sumitomo Pharmaceuticals to develop BDNF in Japan. Sumitomo paid $1.6 million, and agreed to provide up to $40 million, including $25 million in research payments (of which $16 million has been received) and $15 million in progress payments. Regeneron will also receive royalties from Sumitomo on BDNF sales in Japan.

Important Developments

Jun. '95—The company, along with Amgen, reported favorable ressults for its Phase I/II trials of BDNF in the treatment of Lou Gehrig's disease. Phase III trials, which will be conducted by Amgen, are expected to commence in the third quarter of 1995.

Capitalization

Long Term Liabilities: $9,046,359 (6/95), of cap. lease oblgs.

Class A Stock: 5,575,499 shs. ($0.001 par); 10 votes per sh. Officers and directors own 70%.

Per Share Data ($) (Year Ended Dec. 31)

	1994	1993	1992	1991	1990	1989
Tangible Bk. Val.	3.55	5.22	5.68	6.92	1.69	NA
Cash Flow	-1.42	-2.24	-1.12	-0.24	-0.29	NA
Earnings	-1.62	-2.41	-1.24	-0.29	-0.32	NA
Dividends	Nil	Nil	Nil	Nil	Nil	NA
Payout Ratio	Nil	Nil	Nil	Nil	Nil	NA
Prices - High	17⅞	21½	23¼	23¼	NA	NA
- Low	3	10½	7¾	9¾	NA	NA
P/E Ratio - High	NM	NM	NM	NM	NM	NA
- Low	NM	NM	NM	NM	NA	NA

Income Statement Analysis (Million $)

	1994	%Chg	1993	%Chg	1992	%Chg	1991
Revs.	20.6	NM	6.1	-7%	6.6	-10%	7.3
Oper. Inc.	-27.5	NM	-40.5	NM	-21.4	NM	-8.8
Depr.	3.9	39%	2.8	45%	2.0	151%	0.8
Int. Exp.	1.4	33%	1.0	42%	0.7	NM	0.1
Pretax Inc.	-30.7	NM	-39.9	NM	-19.1	NM	-4.5
Eff. Tax Rate	NM	—	NM	—	NM	—	Nil
Net Inc.	-30.7	NM	-39.9	NM	-19.1	NM	-4.5

Balance Sheet & Other Fin. Data (Million $)

	1994	1993	1992	1991	1990	1989
Cash	50.0	88.0	83.0	104	22.0	11.0
Curr. Assets	52.0	92.0	85.0	107	22.0	12.0
Total Assets	94.0	118	98.0	114	25.0	13.0
Curr. Liab.	17.9	13.1	4.6	3.3	1.8	0.3
LT Debt	9.3	5.9	5.8	2.4	Nil	5.0
Common Eqty.	67.0	98.0	87.0	106	-7.0	1.0
Total Cap.	76.0	104	93.0	109	19.0	13.0
Cap. Exp.	NA	10.2	2.1	1.0	1.6	0.4
Cash Flow	-26.7	-37.0	-17.2	-3.7	-3.0	-2.5

Ratio Analysis

	1994	1993	1992	1991	1990	1989
Curr. Ratio	2.9	7.0	18.6	32.3	12.4	41.8
% LT Debt of Cap.	12.1	5.7	6.3	2.2	Nil	40.2
% Net Inc.of Revs.	NM	NM	NM	NM	NM	NM
% Ret. on Assets	NM	NM	NM	NM	NM	NM
% Ret. on Equity	NM	NM	NM	NM	NA	NM

Dividend Data —No cash dividends have been paid.

Data as orig. reptd.; bef. results of disc. opers. and/or spec. items. Per share data adj. for stk. divs. as of ex-div. date. E-Estimated. NA-Not Available. NM-Not Meaningful. NR-Not Ranked.

Office—777 Old Saw Mill River Rd., Tarrytown, NY 10591-6707. **Tel**—(914) 347-7000. **Chrmn**—P. R. Vagelos. **Pres & CEO**—L. S. Schleifer. **VP-Fin, CFO & Treas**—M. A. Goldberg. **VP & Secy**—P. Lubetkin. **Dirs**—C. A. Baker, M. S. Brown, J. W. Fordyce, A. G. Gilman, J. L. Goldstein, F. A. Middleton, L. S. Schleifer, E. M. Shooter, G. L. Sing, P. R. Vagelos. **Transfer Agent & Registrar**—Chemical Bank, NYC. **Incorporated** in New York in 1988. **Empl**-193. **S&P Analyst:** Thomas Tirney

STANDARD & POOR'S

STOCK REPORTS

Republic Gypsum

NYSE Symbol **RGC**
In S&P SmallCap 600

18-OCT-95 **Industry:** Paper/Products

Summary: Republic Gypsum makes paperboard and gypsum wallboard for distribution throughout the U.S.

Quantitative Evaluations

Outlook (1 Lowest—5 Highest)
• **NA**

Fair Value
• **NA**

Risk
• **Average**

Earn./Div. Rank
• **B**

Technical Eval.
• **Bullish** since 9/95

Rel. Strength Rank (1 Lowest—99 Highest)
• **49**

Insider Activity
• **Neutral**

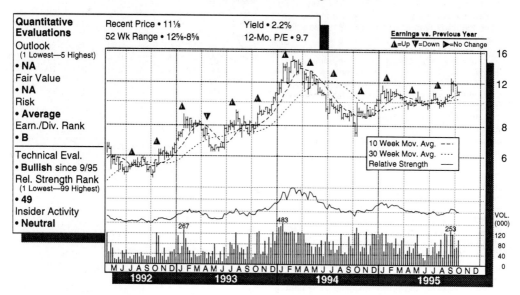

Recent Price • 11⅛
52 Wk Range • 12⅝-8⅝
Yield • 2.2%
12-Mo. P/E • 9.7

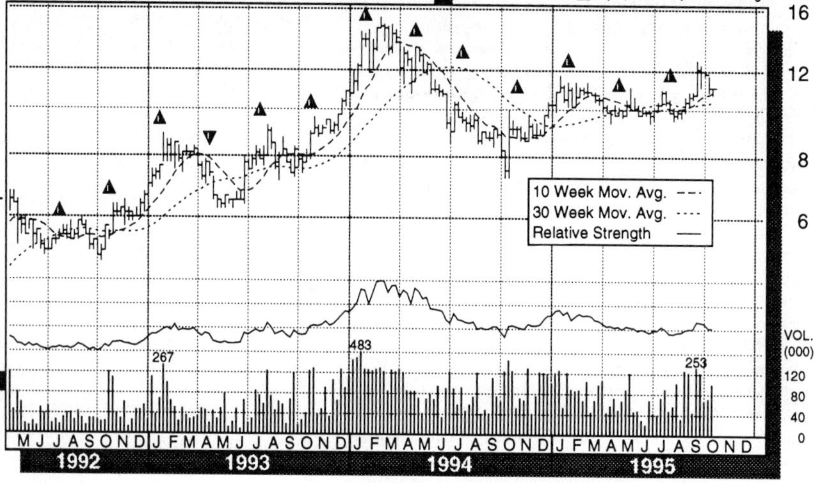

Business Profile - 18-OCT-95

Sales and earnings of this manufacturer of gypsum wallboard and paperboard have been in an uptrend since profitability was restored in fiscal 1992. The June 1995 acquisiton of Halltown Paperboard Co. furthers RGC's strategic objective of becoming a national, premier manufacturer of 100% recycled paperboard. Directors have proposed a change in the company's name to Republic Group Inc. Officers & directors control about 25% of the common shares outstanding.

Operational Review - 18-OCT-95

Net sales and net income for the three months ended September 30, 1995, climbed 55% and 18%, respectively, year to year. These improvements reflected the June 1995 acquisition of Halltown Paperboard and falling raw material costs, mainly reclaimed paper fiber costs. Share earnings were $0.30, versus $0.25. RGC's debt ratio rose to 31% at year-end fiscal 1995, from zero a year earlier, due primarily to long term financing for the Halltown Paperboard acquisition.

Stock Performance - 13-OCT-95

In the past 30 trading days, RGC's shares have increased 5%, compared to a 4% rise in the S&P 500. Average trading volume for the past five days was 19,700 shares, compared with the 40-day moving average of 25,310 shares.

Key Stock Statistics

Dividend Rate/Share	0.24	Shareholders	1,000
Shs. outstg. (M)	10.6	Market cap. (B)	$0.116
Avg. daily vol. (M)	0.018	Inst. holdings	34%
Tang. Bk. Value/Share	4.79	Insider holdings	NA
Beta	1.58		

Value of $10,000 invested 5 years ago: $ 25,618

Fiscal Year Ending Jun. 30

	1996	% Change	1995	% Change	1994	% Change
Revenues (Million $)						
1Q	32.27	55%	20.85	44%	14.48	13%
2Q	—	—	22.35	51%	14.82	20%
3Q	—	—	26.53	58%	16.80	42%
4Q	—	—	26.68	56%	17.10	40%
Yr.	—	—	96.41	53%	63.20	28%
Income (Million $)						
1Q	3.17	18%	2.68	75%	1.53	—
2Q	—	—	2.85	94%	1.47	58%
3Q	—	—	3.23	23%	2.62	NM
4Q	—	—	2.92	38%	2.11	NM
Yr.	—	—	11.68	51%	7.74	139%
Earnings Per Share ($)						
1Q	0.30	20%	0.25	79%	0.14	40%
2Q	—	—	0.27	93%	0.14	56%
3Q	—	—	0.30	20%	0.25	NM
4Q	—	—	0.27	35%	0.20	NM
Yr.	—	—	1.10	51%	0.73	135%

Next earnings report expected: mid January

Republic Gypsum

Business Summary - 17-OCT-95

Republic Gypsum manufactures recycled paperboard, reclaimed paper fiber, and gypsum wallboard. Business segment contributions in fiscal 1995:

	Revs.	Profits
Recycled paperboard	51%	37%
Gypsum wallboard	49%	63%

Recycled paperboard is sold to converter customers that manufacture composite cans, cores, tubes and other consumer and industrial packaging products. RGC also uses its recycled paperboard as a raw material in the production of gypsum wallboard, and also sells gypsum-grade paperboard to other gypsum wallboard manufacturers. Reclaimed paper fiber is a raw material sold to and used by other recycled paper and paperboard mills as well as by RGC's mills. Recycled paperboard is the principal component used in the production of recycled paper and recycled paperboard.

Part of RGC's strategy over the years has been to increase its emphasis on recycled paperboard so that the company would become less subject to the cyclical construction and housing industries. In fiscal 1995, RGC completed the third year of a five-year plan to expand and develop recycled paperboard operations. Spending for capital improvements and expansion at two recycled paperboard mills was estimated at $14 million to $18 million for the five fiscal years ending in 1997. Capital expenditures of $9.4 million were budgeted for fiscal 1996.

In fiscal 1995, about 16% of RGC's paperboard production was consumed by its own wallboard production operations, 18% purchased by other wallboard manufacturers, and 66% purchased by about 100 converter customers. A litle over 10% of output was sold to Sonoco Products Inc.

Gypsum wallboard is a primary building material used by the residential and commercial construction industries. Gypsum wallboard is sold directly to building materials dealers and to contractors and applicators. During fiscal 1995, 58% of wallboard shipments was to customers in Texas, Oklahoma, Colorado and Kansas. The remaining 42% was made in other areas, especially in the Midwestern and Southeastern U.S.

Important Developments

Oct. '95—Republic Gypsum said that the integration of Halltown Paperboard Co. (HP; acquired in June 1995) into its operations has gone smoothly. For the fiscal 1996 first quarter, HP's facility contributed favorably to consolidated net sales and earnings.

Oct. '95—RGC said that stockholders would vote at the annual meeting, on October 26, 1995, regarding a proposed name change for the company to Republic Group Incorporated, from Republic Gypsum Company.

Capitalization

Long Term Debt: $24,840,000 (6/95).

Per Share Data ($) (Year Ended Jun. 30)

	1995	1994	1993	1992	1991	1990
Tangible Bk. Val.	4.79	3.87	3.30	3.17	3.00	2.98
Cash Flow	1.44	0.99	0.53	0.39	0.19	0.49
Earnings	1.10	0.73	0.31	0.18	-0.04	0.04
Dividends	0.23	0.17	0.21	0.02	Nil	0.14
Payout Ratio	21%	23%	68%	11%	NM	376%
Prices - High	11¾	15⅝	11⅛	7	5¼	5
- Low	9⅜	8½	6¼	4¼	2⅜	2¼
P/E Ratio - High	11	21	26	39	NM	NM
- Low	9	12	20	24	NM	NM

Income Statement Analysis (Million $)

	1995	%Chg	1994	%Chg	1993	%Chg	1992
Revs.	96.4	53%	63.2	28%	49.2	17%	42.1
Oper. Inc.	22.6	53%	14.8	124%	6.6	53%	4.3
Depr.	3.6	29%	2.8	19%	2.4	7%	2.2
Int. Exp.	0.0	-50%	0.0	100%	0.0	—	Nil
Pretax Inc.	19.2	55%	12.4	176%	4.5	55%	2.9
Eff. Tax Rate	39%	—	38%	—	27%	—	33%
Net Inc.	11.7	51%	7.7	139%	3.2	66%	2.0

Balance Sheet & Other Fin. Data (Million $)

	1995	1994	1993	1992	1991	1990
Cash	6.1	1.4	5.6	6.1	1.3	8.1
Curr. Assets	27.0	14.6	15.8	15.4	11.8	21.2
Total Assets	95.4	53.0	44.1	41.3	38.9	47.9
Curr. Liab.	13.5	7.3	5.2	4.5	4.6	6.1
LT Debt	24.8	Nil	Nil	Nil	Nil	6.1
Common Eqty.	50.6	41.2	35.1	33.6	31.8	31.6
Total Cap.	81.2	44.9	38.3	36.5	34.4	41.9
Cap. Exp.	8.8	13.3	5.6	2.7	2.3	4.2
Cash Flow	15.3	10.5	5.6	4.1	2.0	5.2

Ratio Analysis

	1995	1994	1993	1992	1991	1990
Curr. Ratio	2.0	2.0	3.0	3.4	2.6	3.5
% LT Debt of Cap.	30.6	Nil	Nil	Nil	Nil	14.5
% Net Inc.of Revs.	12.2	12.2	6.6	4.6	NM	0.9
% Ret. on Assets	15.7	15.9	7.6	4.9	NM	0.8
% Ret. on Equity	25.5	20.3	9.4	6.0	NM	1.3

Dividend Data —Cash dividends were resumed in May 1992 after omission in May 1990. A 5% stock dividend was paid in May 1990.

Amt. of Div. $	Date Decl.	Ex-Div. Date	Stock of Record	Payment Date
0.060	Oct. 28	Nov. 23	Nov. 30	Dec. 15 '94
0.060	Jan. 20	Feb. 22	Feb. 28	Mar. 15 '95
0.060	Apr. 25	May. 24	May. 31	Jun. 15 '95
0.060	Aug. 08	Aug. 29	Aug. 31	Sep. 15 '95

Data as orig. reptd.; bef. results of disc. opers. and/or spec. items. Per share data adj. for stk. divs. as of ex-div. date. E-Estimated. NA-Not Available. NM-Not Meaningful. NR-Not Ranked.

Office—811 East 30th Ave., Hutchinson, KS 67502. **Tel**—(316) 727-2700. **Chrmn & Pres**—P. Simpson. **VP-CFO & Investor Contact**—Doyle R. Ramsey. **Treas & Secy**—J. L. Sowell. **Dirs**—S. L. Gagnon, B. A. Nelson, T. Rain, G. L. Ray, R. F. Sexton, D. P. Simpson, P. Simpson, L. L. Wallace, D. B. Yarbrough. **Transfer Agent & Registrar**—Continental Stock & Transfer Co., NYC. **Incorporated** in Delaware in 1961. **Empl-600.**
S&P Analyst: N.J. DeVita

STANDARD & POOR'S

STOCK REPORTS

Respironics, Inc.

NASDAQ Symbol **RESP**

In S&P SmallCap 600

24-SEP-95

Industry: Medical equipment/ supply

Summary: This company makes respiratory medical products for use in the home, hospitals and in emergency care situations.

Quantitative Evaluations

Outlook (1 Lowest—5 Highest) • **NA**

Fair Value • **NA**

Risk • **Average**

Earn./Div. Rank • **B**

Technical Eval. • **Bullish** since 3/95

Rel. Strength Rank (1 Lowest—99 Highest) • **64**

Insider Activity • **NA**

Recent Price • 18 | Yield • Nil

52 Wk Range • 19¾-9¾ | 12-Mo. P/E • 26.9

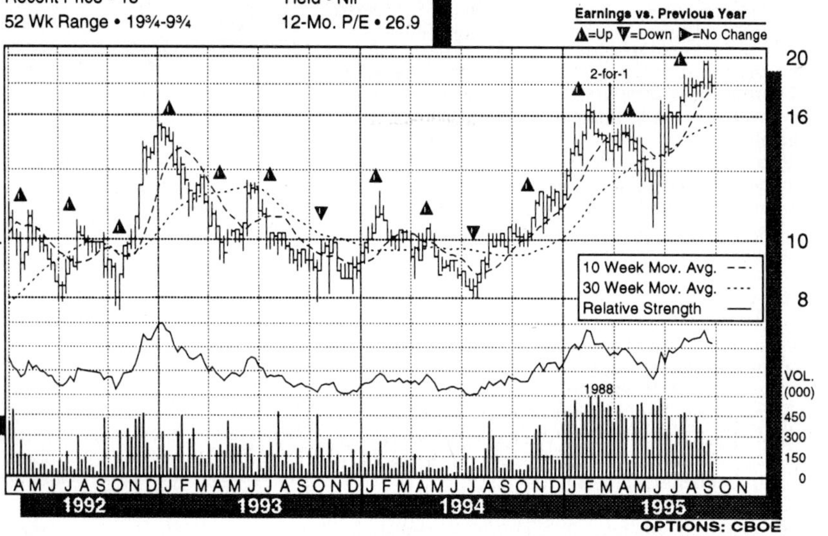

OPTIONS: CBOE

Business Profile - 18-SEP-95

This company has experienced rapid growth, due to strong demand for its sleep disorder products and resuscitators. Respironics is increasing its investment in research and development and expects to introduce several new products. Shipments of the BigEasy manual resuscitators began in the third quarter of fiscal 1995, and next generation Continuous Positive Airway Pressure and BiPAP Ventilation Systems are on the horizon. Cost control measures are also aiding profitability.

Operational Review - 21-SEP-95

Net sales advanced in fiscal 1995, boosted by rising demand for obstructive sleep apnea products, ventilation products, and patient interface accessories and components. Margins widened due to well controlled production and overhead costs, and operating income rose. Net income comparisons further benefited from the absence of charges of $7.1 million taken during fiscal 1994 for a writeoff of an acquisition of distribution rights and expenses related to discontinuing a line of resuscitators.

Stock Performance - 22-SEP-95

In the past 30 trading days, RESP's shares have increased 4%, compared to a 5% rise in the S&P 500. Average trading volume for the past five days was 23,080 shares, compared with the 40-day moving average of 68,913 shares.

Key Stock Statistics

Dividend Rate/Share	Nil	Shareholders	1,400
Shs. outstg. (M)	16.7	Market cap. (B)	$0.301
Avg. daily vol. (M)	0.054	Inst. holdings	45%
Tang. Bk. Value/Share	3.22	Insider holdings	NA
Beta	1.44		

Value of $10,000 invested 5 years ago: $ 82,285

Fiscal Year Ending Jun. 30

	1995	% Change	1994	% Change	1993	% Change
Revenues (Million $)						
1Q	21.67	19%	18.23	20%	15.20	55%
2Q	23.87	28%	18.60	8%	17.20	58%
3Q	25.60	33%	19.31	8%	17.92	38%
4Q	28.31	28%	22.04	16%	19.01	24%
Yr.	99.4	27%	78.17	13%	69.29	41%
Income (Million $)						
1Q	2.42	178%	0.87	—	—	—
2Q	2.70	31%	2.06	17%	1.76	57%
3Q	3.07	37%	2.24	17%	1.91	34%
4Q	3.49	NM	-0.44	NM	2.16	25%
Yr.	11.68	146%	4.74	-36%	7.38	38%
Earnings Per Share ($)						
1Q	0.14	180%	0.05	-44%	0.09	38%
2Q	0.15	29%	0.12	20%	0.10	54%
3Q	0.17	31%	0.13	18%	0.11	38%
4Q	0.20	NM	-0.03	NM	0.13	25%
Yr.	0.67	148%	0.27	-36%	0.43	35%

Next earnings report expected: early November

Respironics, Inc.

Business Summary - 13-SEP-95

Respironics Inc. designs, produces and sells medical products which address a wide range of respiratory and pulmonary problems by assisting patient breathing. These products are used in the home, in hospitals and in emergency medical situtations.

RESP's principal product, the REMstar Choice Nasal CPAP system (retail price of $1,100 to $1,300), is designed to treat a sleeping disorder known as obstructive sleep apnea (the repeated cessation of breathing during sleep caused by anatomical disorders). The disorder is commonly found in obese individuals, and consumption of alcohol and tranquilizers can make the problem worse. The REMStar system consists of a small, portable air pressurization device, air pressure controls and a nasal mask worn by the patient at home during sleep, and uses a pulmonary procedure known as Continuous Positive Airway Pressure (CPAP). Sales of obstructive sleep apnea therapy products and related accessories and replacement parts accounted for 64% of net sales in fiscal 1994.

The company's primary ventilatory product is the BiPAP Ventilatory Support System (priced at $3,000 to $6,000), a low-pressure, electrically driven flow generator with an electronic pressure control designed to augment patient ventilation by supplying pressurized air through a nasal mask. The Hospital BiPAP Ventilatory Support System, which includes accessories such as an airway pressure monitor, a detachable control panel, a disposable circuit and a mounting stand, was introduced in May 1992. Sales of ventilatory products and related accessories accounted for 27% of fiscal 1994 net sales.

Four types of face masks are provided by RESP: air-filled cushion anesthesia masks primarily for use during surgery; SealEasy and Circle Seal resuscitation masks for use in emergency medical situations; Nasal Sealing FlapMasks, used with REMstar and BiPAP; and CPAP masks for respiratory therapy following surgery. These masks are designed as single-use patient ventilation products.

Important Developments

Apr. '95—The company acquired Vitalog Monitoring Inc., a designer, manufacturer, and marketer of sleep monitoring and diagnostic equipment.
Dec. '94—RESP received a warning letter from the FDA related to alleged deficiencies in the company's complaint handling and reporting processes and claims that certain modifications to its BiPAP non-continuous ventilator systems were not reviewed by the FDA under its 510(k) review process. Requested company responses to the letter include refinements to systems and processes, as well as the filing of additional reports and additional 510(k) documents for certain device improvements and claims.

Capitalization

Long Term Debt: $5,605,936 (3/95).

Per Share Data ($) (Year Ended Jun. 30)

	1995	1994	1993	1992	1991	1990
Tangible Bk. Val.	NA	2.71	2.41	1.95	1.61	0.77
Cash Flow	NA	0.48	0.65	0.44	0.35	0.19
Earnings	0.67	0.28	0.43	0.32	0.26	0.15
Dividends	Nil	Nil	Nil	Nil	Nil	Nil
Payout Ratio	Nil	Nil	Nil	Nil	Nil	Nil
Prices - High	$19\frac{3}{4}$	$12\frac{1}{4}$	$15\frac{1}{2}$	$15\frac{3}{8}$	$7\frac{1}{4}$	$5\frac{3}{8}$
- Low	$10\frac{1}{2}$	8	$7\frac{7}{8}$	$6\frac{1}{4}$	$4\frac{1}{4}$	$2\frac{1}{8}$
P/E Ratio - High	29	44	36	41	28	35
- Low	16	29	19	20	17	14

Income Statement Analysis (Million $)

	1994	%Chg	1993	%Chg	1992	%Chg	1991
Revs.	78.2	13%	69.3	41%	49.0	36%	36.0
Oper. Inc.	17.0	16%	14.6	51%	9.7	42%	6.8
Depr.	3.6	-8%	3.9	84%	2.1	63%	1.3
Int. Exp.	0.2	-6%	0.2	-10%	0.2	-33%	0.3
Pretax Inc.	6.8	-39%	11.1	38%	8.1	45%	5.6
Eff. Tax Rate	30%	—	34%	—	34%	—	32%
Net Inc.	4.7	-36%	7.4	38%	5.4	42%	3.8

Balance Sheet & Other Fin. Data (Million $)

	1994	1993	1992	1991	1990	1989
Cash	12.4	14.6	10.2	11.3	2.2	2.4
Curr. Assets	40.2	36.4	27.8	21.9	11.7	8.1
Total Assets	58.9	54.6	43.5	36.1	19.8	9.9
Curr. Liab.	9.2	11.2	7.8	5.8	5.9	1.8
LT Debt	4.9	4.3	4.3	4.5	3.6	Nil
Common Eqty.	44.2	39.1	31.4	25.8	10.3	8.1
Total Cap.	49.7	43.4	35.7	30.3	13.9	8.1
Cap. Exp.	8.4	6.7	3.5	3.1	5.8	0.9
Cash Flow	8.3	11.2	7.5	5.1	2.7	1.7

Ratio Analysis

	1994	1993	1992	1991	1990	1989
Curr. Ratio	4.4	3.2	3.6	3.8	2.0	4.6
% LT Debt of Cap.	9.8	9.9	12.0	15.0	25.6	Nil
% Net Inc.of Revs.	6.1	10.7	11.0	10.5	9.4	7.8
% Ret. on Assets	8.3	15.0	13.4	12.6	14.4	13.6
% Ret. on Equity	11.3	20.9	18.7	19.8	23.2	17.6

Dividend Data —Cash dividends have never been paid. A two-for-one stock split was effected in March 1995.

Amt. of Div. $	Date Decl.	Ex-Div. Date	Stock of Record	Payment Date
2-for-1	Feb. 15	Mar. 20	Mar. 03	Mar. 17 '95

Data as orig. reptd.; bef. results of disc. opers. and/or spec. items. Per share data adj. for stk. divs. as of ex-div. date. E-Estimated. NA-Not Available. NM-Not Meaningful. NR-Not Ranked.

Office—1001 Murry Ridge Dr., Murrysville, PA 15668. **Tel**—(412) 733-0200. **Chrmn**—G. E. McGinnis. **Pres & CEO**—D. S. Meteny. **Contr & CFO**—D. J. Bevevino. **Treas**—J. C. Woll. **Secy & Investor Contact**—D. A. Pishko (412-733-0209). **Dirs**—D. P. Barry, D. A. Cotter, J. H. Hardie, J. C. Lawyer, G. J. Magovern, G. E. McGinnis, D. S. Meteny, B. Shou-Chung Zau. **Transfer Agent & Registrar**—Mellon Financial Services, Pittsburgh. **Incorporated** in Pennsylvania in 1976; reincorporated in Delaware in 1984. **Empl-** 1,078. **S&P Analyst:** Philip J. Birbara

Rexel, Inc.

NYSE Symbol RXL In S&P SmallCap 600

Price	Range	P-E Ratio	Dividend	Yield	S&P Ranking	Beta
Oct. 10'95	1995					
10⅜	10⅞–5¾	18	None	None	C	1.45

Summary

This company (formerly Willcox & Gibbs) is the fifth largest U.S. distributor of electrical parts and supplies. A restructuring program begun several years ago was largely completed in 1994, with the disposal of all other operations and substantial changes in management. Paris-based Rexel, S.A., holds a 47% stake in the company.

Business Summary

Rexel, Inc. (formerly Willcox & Gibbs) is the fifth largest U.S. distributor of electrical parts and supplies, based on 1994 sales. In recent years, it undertook a major restructuring that included the spinoff of its covered yarn business (Worldtex, Inc.) and the disposal of its data communications equipment distribution unit, both in 1992, and the 1994 sale of its remaining apparel parts and supplies distribution business (accounted for as a discontinued operation in 1993). Several acquisitions were also made, greatly expanding the company's interests in the electrical parts and supplies business.

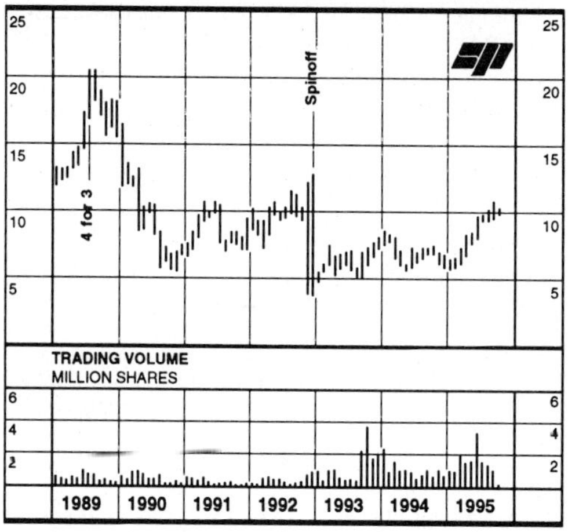

Through Consolidated Electric Supply, Southern Electric Supply Co. (acquired in late 1992), Sacks Electrical Supply Co. (April 1993) and Summers Group Inc. (December 1993), the company operates 171 electrical distribution centers in 19 states (principally in the Southeast, South, Southern California and Ohio) and the Bahamas. In 1994, the company served over 75,000 customers, with the ten largest customers accounting for about 7.5% of total revenues. Approximately 50% of sales in 1994 were from the construction-based electrical contractor market, with the balance of sales coming from the industrial, government, municipal and utility customers.

The average branch has about 400 customers, makes deliveries within a 50-mile radius, and stocks over 15,000 items. The extensive product line includes electrical supplies, such as wire, cable, cords, boxes, covers, wiring devices, conduit, raceway duct, safety switches, motor controls, breakers, panels, lamps, fuses and related supplies and accessories, residential, commercial and industrial electrical fixtures, as well as materials and special cables for computers and advanced communications systems.

In May 1995, the company changed its name from Willcox & Gibbs, Inc., to Rexel, Inc. Paris-based Rexel, S.A., the world's largest electrical parts distributor, owns about 47% of the company.

Important Developments

Sep. '95— Directors approved the repurchase of up to 2 million RXL common shares on the open market.

Aug. '95— The company redeemed its entire issue of 7% Convertible Subordinated Debentures due 2014 totaling $50 million on August 11. The redemption price was 102.8% of principal, plus accrued and unpaid interest to the redemption date.

Next earnings report expected mid-October.

Per Share Data ($)

Yr. End Dec. 31	1994	[1]1993	[1]1992	1991	[1]1990	[1]1989	1988	1987	1986	1985
Tangible Bk. Val.	**2.96**	2.17	2.61	4.54	4.21	5.08	4.91	4.29	3.78	3.23
Cash Flow	**0.80**	0.57	d0.25	0.70	0.88	1.71	1.33	0.99	0.80	0.75
Earnings[2]	**0.39**	0.33	d0.82	0.12	0.40	1.30	1.03	0.75	0.62	0.59
Dividends	**Nil**	Nil	Nil	0.100	0.100	0.093	0.085	0.064	0.054	0.021
Payout Ratio	**Nil**	Nil	Nil	81%	25%	7%	8%	8%	9%	4%
Prices—High	**8⅝**	8⅛	12⅞	10¾	16½	20½	14⅞	15	7⅞	6¼
Low	**5⅝**	4¾	3¾	6⅝	5½	11⅞	8¾	5⅝	5⅛	3⅝
P/E Ratio—	**21–14**	25–14	NM	90–55	41–14	16–9	14–8	20–7	13–8	11–6

Data as orig. reptd. Adj. for stk. divs. of 33⅓% Jul. 1989, 33⅓% Jul. 1988, 33⅓% Jul. 1987. **1.** Refl. merger or acq. **2.** Bef. results of disc. ops. of +0.07 in 1993, and spec. items of +0.01 in 1994, +0.03 in 1993, -0.10 1991, +0.50 in 1985. d-Deficit. NM-Not Meaningful.

Income Data (Million $)

Year Ended Dec. 31	Revs.	Oper. Inc.	% Oper. Inc. of Revs.	Cap. Exp.	Depr.	Int. Exp.	Net Bef. Taxes	Eff. Tax Rate	[5]Net Inc.	% Net Inc. of Revs.	Cash Flow
1994	**1,066**	**34.8**	**3.3**	**12.1**	**9.72**	**9.6**	**16.5**	**44.0%**	**9.26**	**0.9**	**19.0**
[1,2]1993	522	22.3	4.3	5.4	5.16	5.9	[4]11.9	42.2%	6.90	1.3	12.1
[1,2]1992	438	21.2	4.8	11.2	8.40	9.4	[4]d16.9	NM	d0.12	NM	d3.7
1991	600	34.9	5.8	10.9	7.93	16.3	[4]4.5	62.6%	1.70	0.3	9.6
[1]1990	568	34.7	6.1	8.7	6.60	12.7	[4]8.8	37.1%	5.50	1.0	12.1
[1]1989	548	43.1	7.9	8.8	5.67	10.9	27.1	34.0%	17.90	3.3	23.6
1988	381	30.4	8.0	10.0	4.08	6.7	20.0	29.7%	14.00	3.7	18.1
1987	317	24.1	7.6	[3]10.6	3.22	5.6	15.6	35.5%	10.10	3.2	13.3
[1]1986	262	20.3	7.8	[3]16.3	2.12	4.5	14.1	46.0%	7.60	2.9	9.8
1985	225	18.0	8.0	[3]4.5	1.68	5.3	11.4	47.6%	6.00	2.7	7.6

Balance Sheet Data (Million $)

Dec. 31	Cash	Curr. Assets	Curr. Liab.	Curr. Ratio	Total Assets	% Ret. on Assets	Long Term Debt	Common Equity	Total Cap.	% LT Debt of Cap.	% Ret. on Equity
1994	**23.84**	**292**	**181**	**1.6**	**414**	**2.2**	**95**	**131**	**226**	**42.0**	**8.3**
1993	19.10	278	207	1.3	429	1.9	126	93	218	57.7	7.7
1992	28.40	209	87	2.4	285	NM	109	84	193	56.5	NM
1991	8.07	223	139	1.6	365	0.5	113	112	227	50.1	1.5
1990	7.28	222	168	1.3	365	1.7	83	113	197	42.4	5.0
1989	4.80	197	105	1.9	296	6.8	80	109	190	42.2	17.8
1988	3.63	149	102	1.5	224	6.7	29	91	122	24.0	16.6
1987	4.13	123	79	1.5	186	5.9	30	75	106	27.7	14.3
1986	0.75	98	55	1.8	149	5.1	31	64	95	32.4	13.2
1985	1.28	84	48	1.8	113	5.5	26	40	65	39.1	17.7

Data as orig. reptd. **1.** Refl. merger or acq. **2.** Excl. disc. ops. **3.** Net of curr. yr. retirement and disposals. **4.** Incl. equity in earns. of nonconsol. subs. **5.** Bef. spec. items. d-Deficit. NM-Not Meaningful.

Net Sales (Million $)

Quarter:	1995	1994	1993	1992
Mar.	278.8	244.6	111.8	100.5
Jun.	288.7	264.5	126.4	104.9
Sep.		275.8	138.7	109.8
Dec.		280.1	144.6	122.9
		1,065	521.5	438.1

Revenues for the first six months of 1995 rose 12%, year to year. Gross margins narrowed slightly due to a less favorable product mix, but this was offset by the effects of cost cutting measures instituted in 1994; operating income surged 70%. Following taxes at 44.0% in both periods, net income was up 100%, to $9,172,000 ($0.38 a share; $0.34 fully diluted) from $4,575,000 ($0.20; no dilution). Results for the 1994 period exclude income from discontinued operations of $0.02 a share.

Common Share Earnings ($)

Quarter:	1995	1994	1993	1992
Mar.	0.18	0.08	0.06	0.03
Jun.	0.20	0.12	0.06	0.06
Sep.		0.11	0.10	0.01
Dec.		0.08	0.11	d0.77
		0.39	0.33	d0.82

Dividend Data

Dividends, paid since 1985, were omitted in March 1992. In December 1992, one Worldtex, Inc. common share was distributed for each WG share held.

Finances

In December 1993, the company acquired Summers Group Inc., an electrical parts and supplies distributor, for $60 million cash and a $25 million three-year note, plus consideration based on Summers' operating profits for 1993 and 1994, subject to a maximum purchase price of $120 million. In April 1993, it acquired Sacks Electrical Supply Co. for $13.6 million.

Capitalization

Long Term Debt: $87,353,000 (6/95).

Common Stock: 24,114,138 shs. ($1 par).
Rexel, S.A. owns 47%.
Institutions hold 28%.
Shareholders of record: 1,389 (3/95).

d-Deficit.

Office—150 Alhambra Circle, Coral Gables, FL 33134. **Tel**—(305) 446-8000. **Chrmn**—E. Lomas. **Pres & CEO**—A. Viry. **VP & CFO**— S. M. Hitt. **Secy**—J. O. Fullerton. **VP & Investor Contact**—Allan M. Gonopolsky. **Dirs**—F. de Castro, J. B. Fraser, R. G. Gentles, A. List, E. Lomas, G. E. Morris, N. Sokolow, A. Viry, S. Weinberg. **Transfer Agent & Registrar**—Chemical Bank, NYC. **Incorporated** in New York in 1866. **Empl**—2,800.

STANDARD & POOR'S

STOCK REPORTS

Riggs National Corp.

NASDAQ Symbol **RIGS**

In S&P SmallCap 600

18-SEP-95

Industry: Banking

Summary: This bank holding company's principal subsidiary is Riggs National Bank, the largest in Washington, D.C., with approximately $4.9 billion in assets.

Quantitative Evaluations

Outlook (1 Lowest—5 Highest)
• **1−**

Fair Value
• **10⅝**

Risk
• **Average**

Earn./Div. Rank
• **C**

Technical Eval.
• **Bearish** since 5/95

Rel. Strength Rank (1 Lowest—99 Highest)
• **91**

Insider Activity
• **Neutral**

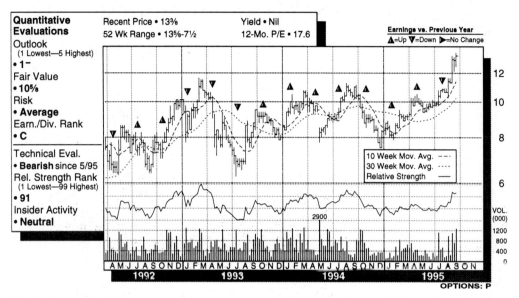

Recent Price • 13⅜

52 Wk Range • 13⅝-7½

Yield • Nil

12-Mo. P/E • 17.6

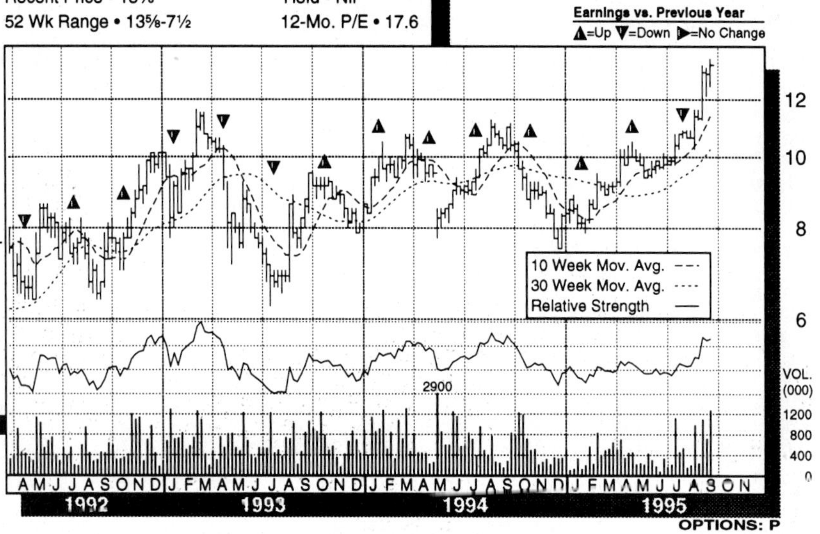

OPTIONS: P

Business Profile - 18-SEP-95

Riggs' strategy is to provide customers with the breadth of financial products and services typical of a regional bank, while providing the personalized customer service of a community bank. The bank is exploring new and more efficient ways to deliver traditional banking products to its customers, whether it is through an ATM, the telephone or home computer. Riggs recently established the RIMCO Monument Mutual Funds, which will give non-trust customers access to professional money management.

Operational Review - 18-SEP-95

Net interest income in the six months ended June 30, 1995, rose 1.1%, year to year. There was no provision for loan losses, versus a provision of $4,200,000 in the year earlier period. Following 26% lower noninterest income and an 8.8% decline in noninterest expense, pretax income advanced 6.8%. After taxes at 1.0%, versus a tax benefit of $563,000, net income was up 13% to $18,163,000 ($0.42 a share, after preferred dividends), from $17,746,000 ($0.38).

Stock Performance - 15-SEP-95

In the past 30 trading days, RIGS's shares have increased 26%, compared to a 4% rise in the S&P 500. Average trading volume for the past five days was 388,880 shares, compared with the 40-day moving average of 148,277 shares.

Key Stock Statistics

Dividend Rate/Share	Nil	Shareholders	3,700
Shs. outstg. (M)	30.3	Market cap. (B)	$0.405
Avg. daily vol. (M)	0.207	Inst. holdings	31%
Tang. Bk. Value/Share	6.79	Insider holdings	NA
Beta	1.08		

Value of $10,000 invested 5 years ago: $ 7,531

Fiscal Year Ending Dec. 31

	1995	% Change	1994	% Change	1993	% Change
Revenues (Million $)						
1Q	90.22	NM	90.67	NM	90.03	-23%
2Q	94.81	9%	86.99	-23%	112.6	-6%
3Q	—	—	86.21	3%	83.85	-33%
4Q	—	—	87.66	5%	83.16	-14%
Yr.	—	—	351.5	-5%	369.6	-19%
Income (Million $)						
1Q	8.80	11%	7.91	NM	-27.62	NM
2Q	9.37	-5%	9.83	NM	-72.63	NM
3Q	—	—	8.23	178%	2.96	143%
4Q	—	—	8.04	161%	3.08	NM
Yr.	—	—	34.02	NM	-94.21	NM
Earnings Per Share ($)						
1Q	0.20	33%	0.15	NM	-1.11	NM
2Q	0.22	-4%	0.23	NM	-2.89	NM
3Q	—	—	0.17	70%	0.10	100%
4Q	—	—	0.17	89%	0.09	NM
Yr.	—	—	0.72	NM	-3.65	NM

Next earnings report expected: early November

Riggs National Corp.

Business Summary - 18-SEP-95

Riggs National Corporation is the parent of Riggs National Bank, founded in 1836 and the largest commercial bank in Washington, D.C., with 1994 year-end deposits of $3.60 billion. The bank operates 33 branches in the district's metropolitan area and has an Edge Act subsidiary in Miami, Fla. Riggs National Bank also has branch offices in London, England; Nassau, Bahamas; Paris, France; and owns Riggs AP Bank, Ltd., London. The bank also operates an investment advisory subsidiary in Washington, D.C. and a Bahamian bank and trust company.

Through the acquisitions of Guaranty Bank and Trust Company of Fairfax, Va., and First Fidelity Bank, Rockville, Md., Riggs now operates Riggs National Bank of Virginia (17 offices in northern Virginia) and Riggs National Bank of Maryland (10 offices).

Loans at year-end 1994 broke down as follows:

Commercial and financial	16%
Real estate-commercial/construction	13%
Residential mortgage	52%
Home equity	9%
Consumer	3%
Foreign	8%

At 1994 year-end, the reserve for loan losses totaled $97,039,000 ($86,513,000 a year earlier), equal to 3.81% (3.42%) of loans outstanding. There was a net loan recovery of $3,028,000 in 1994 (a net loan chargeoff of $66,413,000 the year before), or -12% (3.04%) of average loans outstanding. Nonperforming assets at 1994 year-end were $75,701,000 (1.71% of total assets), versus $213,276,000 (4.46%) a year earlier.

Consolidated deposits of $3.60 billion at 1994 year-end consisted of noninterest bearing demand 23%, savings and NOW 25%, money market 27%, domestic time 17%, and foreign time 8%.

On a tax-equivalent basis, the average yield on interest-earning assets was 6.68% in 1994 (6.06% in 1993), while the average rate paid on interest-bearing liabilities was 3.34% (3.18%), for a net spread of 3.34% (2.88%).

Important Developments

Aug. '95—Riggs said its nonperforming assets totaled $57.6 million at June 30, 1995, down 24% from the $75.7 million at December 31, 1994, and down 55% from the $127.5 million level a year ago. The latest improvement resulted from collection and asset management efforts as well as improved economic conditions domestically and in the United Kingdom.

Capitalization

Long Term Debt: $217,625,000 (6/95).

Per Share Data ($)

(Year Ended Dec. 31)

	1994	1993	1992	1991	1990	1989
Tangible Bk. Val.	5.53	4.81	7.58	11.99	16.58	23.79
Earnings	0.72	-3.65	-0.86	-4.79	-4.41	2.86
Dividends	Nil	Nil	Nil	0.20	1.09	1.25
Payout Ratio	Nil	Nil	Nil	NM	NM	44%
Prices - High	11¼	11⅝	10⅛	13	22½	28
- Low	7½	6¼	4¼	3¾	7¾	18⅜
P/E Ratio - High	16	NM	NM	NM	NM	10
- Low	10	NM	NM	NM	NM	6

Income Statement Analysis (Million $)

	1994	%Chg	1993	%Chg	1992	%Chg	1991
Net Int. Inc.	153	13%	135	-2%	138	-11%	155
Tax Equiv. Adj.	3.4	-26%	4.6	-29%	6.5	-8%	7.1
Non Int. Inc.	85.5	-3%	88.5	-8%	96.2	4%	92.9
Loan Loss Prov.	6.3	-91%	69.3	39%	50.0	14%	44.0
% Exp/Op Revs.	82%	—	117%	—	100%	—	114%
Pretax Inc.	33.5	NM	-88.6	NM	-22.1	NM	-72.1
Eff. Tax Rate	NM	—	NM	—	NM	—	NM
Net Inc.	34.0	NM	-94.2	NM	-21.1	NM	-66.0
% Net Int. Marg.	3.89%	—	3.23%	—	3.15%	—	3.04%

Balance Sheet & Other Fin. Data (Million $)

	1994	1993	1992	1991	1990	1989
Earning Assets:						
Money Mkt.	388	406	1,264	1,142	1,387	2,293
Inv. Securities	1,041	1,368	955	585	961	417
Com'l Loans	401	412	500	606	869	1,043
Other Loans	2,142	2,110	1,642	2,398	2,946	2,797
Total Assets	4,426	4,780	5,078	5,536	7,051	7,337
Demand Deposits	827	865	884	1,011	1,086	935
Time Deposits	2,276	2,909	2,670	3,902	5,025	5,042
LT Debt	NA	213	213	232	246	309
Common Eqty.	NA	174	245	205	278	342

Ratio Analysis

	1994	1993	1992	1991	1990	1989
% Ret. on Assets	0.8	NM	NM	NM	NM	0.6
% Ret. on Equity	NA	NM	NM	NM	NM	11.9
% Loan Loss Resv.	NA	3.4	3.9	3.5	2.9	1.0
% Loans/Deposits	NA	67.0	48.3	60.9	62.0	63.7
% Equity to Assets	NA	3.1	5.0	4.2	4.3	5.0

Dividend Data —Prior to suspension in July 1991, cash had been paid in each year since 1899.

Data as orig. reptd.; bef. results of disc opers. and/or spec. items. Per share data adj. for stk. divs. as of ex-div. date. E-Estimated. NA-Not Available. NM-Not Meaningful. NR-Not Ranked.

Office—1503 Pennsylvania Ave., NW, Washington, DC 20005. **Tel**—(202) 835-6000. **Chrmn & CEO**—J. L. Allbritton. **Pres**—T. C. Coughlin. **Vice Chrmn**—R. L. Sloan. **EVP & CFO**—J. L. Davis. **Treas**—J. E. Hans. **Secy**—A. C. Baker. **Investor Contact**—J. E. Day (202 835-5156). **Dirs**—J. L. Allbritton, B. B. Allbritton, R. L. Allbritton, F. L. Bollerer, C. Cafritz, C. A. Camilier, III, T. C. Coughlin, R. E. Cuneo, F. E. Davis, III, J. C. Duchange, M. A. English, J. E. Fitzgerald, D. J. Gladstone, L. I. Hebert, M. J. Jackson, L. J. O'Donovan, S. B. Pfeiffer, J. A. Sargent, R. L. Sloan, J. W. Symington, J. Valenti, E. N. Williams. **Transfer Agent & Registrar**—Riggs National Bank. **Incorporated** in Delaware in 1980; chartered in 1896; founded in 1836. **Empl**-1,624. **S&P Analyst:** Brad Ohlmuller

STANDARD & POOR'S

STOCK REPORTS

Roadmaster Industries

NYSE Symbol **RDM**
In S&P SmallCap 600

03-SEP-95 **Industry:** Leisure/Amusement

Summary: This leading maker of bicycles, fitness equipment, toys and lamps is also the exclusive U.S. retail distributor of MacGregor team sports and inflatable sporting goods.

Quantitative Evaluations

Outlook
(1 Lowest—5 Highest)
• **NA**
Fair Value
• **NA**
Risk
• **Average**
Earn./Div. Rank
• **NR**

Technical Eval.
• **Bullish** since 8/95
Rel. Strength Rank
(1 Lowest—99 Highest)
• **15**
Insider Activity
• **NA**

Recent Price • 2¾
52 Wk Range • 4⅜-2¼

Yield • Nil
12-Mo. P/E • NM

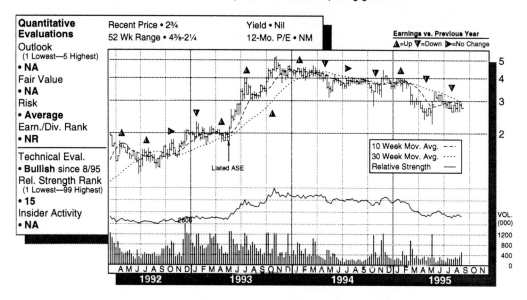

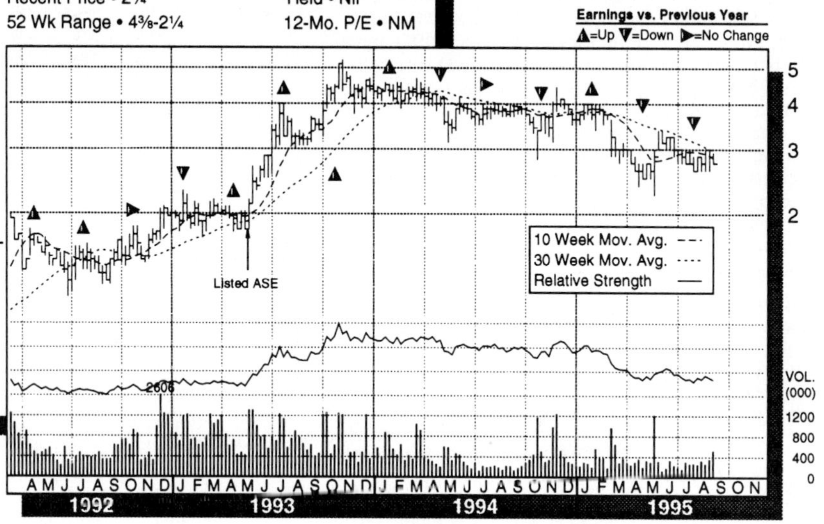

Business Profile - 03-SEP-95

Roadmaster is a leading maker of bicycles (under the Roadmaster name), fitness equipment (Vitamaster), junior products (Flexible Flyer and Roadmaster), trampolines (American Playworld) and lamps (Hamilton), and the exclusive U.S. retail distributor of MacGregor team sports and inflatable sporting goods. The acquisition of Actava Group's sporting goods segment in late 1994 should provide significant manufacturing synergies and complement Roadmaster's current product offerings.

Operational Review - 03-SEP-95

Net sales in the six months ended July 1, 1995, soared 73%, year to year, primarily reflecting the acquisition of the sporting goods operations of Actava Group. Gross margins were hurt by increased material costs and increased competition. Profitability was further restricted by sharply higher interest charges. A net loss of $0.14 per share, based on 61% more shares outstanding, contrasted with income of $0.06.

Stock Performance - 01-SEP-95

In the past 30 trading days, RDM's shares were unchanged, compared to a 2% rise in the S&P 500. Average trading volume for the past five days was 100,800 shares, compared with the 40-day moving average of 60,135 shares.

Key Stock Statistics

Dividend Rate/Share	Nil	Shareholders	1,700
Shs. outstg. (M)	49.8	Market cap. (B)	$0.137
Avg. daily vol. (M)	0.070	Inst. holdings	5%
Tang. Bk. Value/Share	0.47	Insider holdings	NA
Beta	0.50		

Value of $10,000 invested 5 years ago: $ 22,559

Fiscal Year Ending Dec. 31

	1995	% Change	1994	% Change	1993	% Change
Revenues (Million $)						
1Q	175.6	79%	98.29	48%	66.31	28%
2Q	172.7	68%	102.6	55%	66.34	70%
3Q	—	—	103.1	45%	70.89	34%
4Q	—	—	151.7	40%	108.6	32%
Yr.	—	—	455.7	46%	312.2	38%
Income (Million $)						
1Q	-1.48	NM	0.78	-26%	1.06	33%
2Q	-5.58	NM	1.05	38%	0.76	NM
3Q	—	—	2.99	15%	2.60	35%
4Q	—	—	0.17	-95%	3.22	137%
Yr.	—	—	5.00	-34%	7.63	77%
Earnings Per Share ($)						
1Q	-0.03	—	Nil	—	0.04	33%
2Q	-0.11	NM	0.03	NM	0.03	NM
3Q	—	—	0.03	-67%	0.09	13%
4Q	—	—	0.10	11%	0.09	NM
Yr.	—	—	0.16	-38%	0.26	73%

Next earnings report expected: early November

Roadmaster Industries

Business Summary - 03-SEP-95

Roadmaster Industries, Inc. is one of the largest makers of bicycles and a leading manufacturer of fitness equipment and toy products in the U.S. It also manufactures trampolines (through the February 1994 acquisition of American Playworld), makes lamp and related products, and in late 1993 became the exclusive U.S. retail distributor of MacGregor team sports and inflatable sporting goods. Actava Group's sporting goods segment was acquired in December 1994.

The company's line of bicycles includes virtually all types and sizes of bicycles for the juvenile, teen and adult markets. Roadmaster currently focuses on all-terrain bicycles, which the Bicycle Manufacturers' Association estimates accounted for 52% of bicycles sold in the U.S. in 1994.

Fitness equipment, sold under the Vitamaster and DP names, consists of free weights, weight benches, other resistance systems and stationary aerobic equipment, such as exercise bicycles, treadmills, ski machines and stair steppers.

Bicycle and fitness products together accounted for 78% of the company net sales in 1994.

Toy products include tricycles, wagons, 10-inch sidewalk bikes, and swing sets (expanded considerably through the September 1993 acquisition of Flexible Flyer Co.), many of which use licensed Walt Disney characters, and, through the Flexible Flyer purchase, toy horses, molded plastic toys, wood and steel sleds and a broad assortment of snow toys.

The company also makes Hamilton lamps, replacement shades and related products with an emphasis beginning in late 1992 on children's lamps utilizing popular licensed children's characters and themes.

Roadmaster's international division distributes and markets a broad range of recreation and fitness products in Canada (the majority produced by Roadmaster), as well as a variety of Flexible Flyer products in Europe (through the September 1993 acquisition of Flexible Flyer Europe). International sales represented 4.0% of revenues in 1994.

In December 1994, RDM acquired the sporting goods operations of NYSE-listed Actava Group in exchange for 19.2 million common shares (a 39% interest). Actava's sporting goods segment manufactures, imports and distributes camping and outdoor recreation products; sporting goods equipment such as footballs, basketballs and children's athletic outfits; athletic hosiery; and DP fitness and recreation equipment.

Important Developments

Mar. '95—Roadmaster's Hutch Sports, USA unit acquired the sporting goods division of Forster Manufacturing Co., a Wilton, Maine-based maker of various backyard and lawn games, including croquet, bocce ball and volleyball. Forster had revenues of approximately $11 million in 1994.

Capitalization

Long Term Debt: $144,687,000 (7/1/95).

Per Share Data ($) (Year Ended Dec. 31)

	1994	1993	1992	1991	1990	1989
Tangible Bk. Val.	0.94	0.32	0.52	0.43	0.37	0.59
Cash Flow	0.39	0.38	0.23	0.15	-0.17	0.09
Earnings	0.16	0.26	0.15	0.07	-0.22	0.05
Dividends	Nil	Nil	Nil	Nil	Nil	Nil
Payout Ratio	Nil	Nil	Nil	Nil	NM	Nil
Prices - High	4⅝	5¼	2⅜	1¼	1½	2⅛
- Low	2¾	1¾	⅞	⅜	⅜	1
P/E Ratio - High	29	20	16	18	NM	43
- Low	18	7	6	6	NM	21

Income Statement Analysis (Million $)

	1994	%Chg	1993	%Chg	1992	%Chg	1991
Revs.	456	46%	312	38%	226	7%	212
Oper. Inc.	36.3	36%	26.6	64%	16.2	22%	13.3
Depr.	7.5	102%	3.7	65%	2.3	15%	2.0
Int. Exp.	21.3	105%	10.4	64%	6.4	-19%	7.8
Pretax Inc.	7.9	-32%	11.7	53%	7.7	178%	2.8
Eff. Tax Rate	37%	—	35%	—	44%	—	27%
Net Inc.	5.0	-34%	7.6	77%	4.3	113%	2.0

Balance Sheet & Other Fin. Data (Million $)

	1994	1993	1992	1991	1990	1989
Cash	6.4	41.7	6.3	5.3	0.7	1.0
Curr. Assets	358	223	118	114	86.0	103
Total Assets	517	282	145	137	110	123
Curr. Liab.	182	101	68.0	109	91.0	84.0
LT Debt	227	159	59.9	16.2	8.7	22.5
Common Eqty.	103	16.4	15.8	11.2	9.5	15.5
Total Cap.	330	178	76.3	28.0	18.7	38.8
Cap. Exp.	14.2	9.6	3.1	1.8	2.8	3.5
Cash Flow	12.5	11.4	6.6	4.0	-4.3	2.4

Ratio Analysis

	1994	1993	1992	1991	1990	1989
Curr. Ratio	2.0	2.2	1.7	1.1	0.9	1.2
% LT Debt of Cap.	68.8	89.3	78.4	58.0	46.5	58.0
% Net Inc.of Revs.	1.1	2.4	1.9	1.0	NM	0.7
% Ret. on Assets	1.0	3.7	3.0	1.6	NM	1.1
% Ret. on Equity	7.5	51.3	31.4	19.6	NM	8.2

Dividend Data —No dividends have been paid.

Data as orig. reptd.; bef. results of disc. opers. and/or spec. items. Per share data adj. for stk. divs. as of ex-div. date. E-Estimated. NA-Not Available. NM-Not Meaningful. NR-Not Ranked.

Office—250 Spring Street NW, Atlanta, GA 30303. **Tel**—(404) 586-9000. **Fax**—(303) 796-9762. **Chrmn, Pres & CEO**—H. Fong. **Secy**—C. E. Sanders. **Dirs**—S. P. Bradley, L. J. Conti, H. Fong, C. C. Long, M. P. Marshall, J. D. Phillips, J. H. Rand, C. E. Sanders, E. E. Shake. **Transfer Agent & Registrar**—American Securities Transfer Inc., Denver. **Incorporated** in Delaware in 1987. **Empl**-5,800. **S&P Analyst:** M.C.C.

STANDARD & POOR'S

STOCK REPORTS

Roberts Pharmaceutical

NASDAQ Symbol **RPCX**

In S&P SmallCap 600

30-AUG-95 **Industry:** Drugs-Generic and OTC

Summary: This international pharmaceutical company acquires, develops and markets prescription drug products.

S&P Opinion: Hold (★★★)

Recent Price • 19¼
52 Wk Range • 46½-15½
Yield • Nil
12-Mo. P/E • NM

Quantitative Evaluations

Outlook
(1 Lowest—5 Highest)
• **NA**

Fair Value
• **NA**

Risk
• **High**

Earn./Div. Rank
• **B-**

Technical Eval.
• **Bullish** since 7/95

Rel. Strength Rank
(1 Lowest—99 Highest)
• **6**

Insider Activity
• **Neutral**

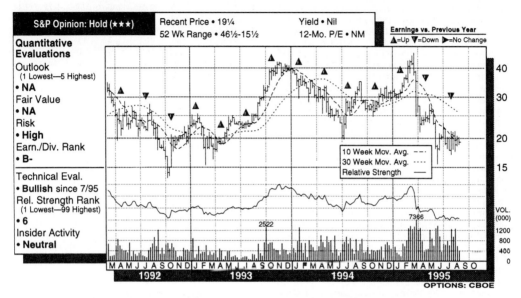

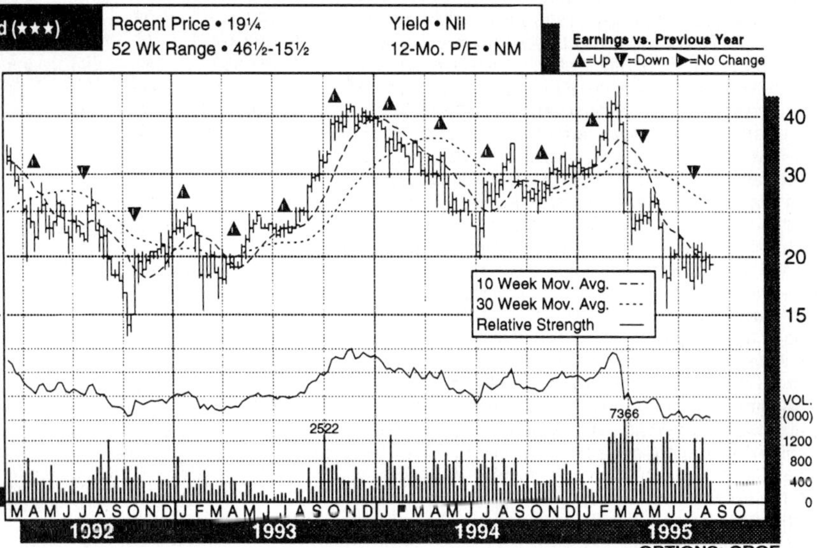

OPTIONS: CBOE

Overview - 30-AUG-95

Roberts incurred $12 million of losses from discontinued operations in 1995's second quarter. The losses stemmed from the company's decision to divest its Home Care and Medical Products operations in order to focus on its core pharmaceutical business. Sales of new product Noroxin, a treatment for urinary tract infections, have penalized gross margins, which fell to 59% in the six months ended June 30, 1995, from 77% in the year-earlier period. Recently, Roberts initiated cost-cutting programs, included layoffs (about 5% of the workforce) and the possibility of selling certain drug lines.

Valuation - 30-AUG-95

The company's stock price has suffered in the past eight months, losing more than half of its value as growth prospects and margins have diminished. Losses from the company's discontinued operations will likely continue into 1995's second half. FDA approvals of Pro-Amatine and Agrelin could have a favorable effect on the stock valuation; however, the company will not speculate on when, or if, approvals might be received. Although the company is addressing its problems, in the midst of corporate retrenchment, we believe the shares are fairly valued.

Key Stock Statistics

S&P EPS Est. 1995	0.45	Tang. Bk. Value/Share	0.74
P/E on S&P Est. 1995	42.8	Beta	NM
S&P EPS Est. 1996	1.15	Shareholders	900
Dividend Rate/Share	Nil	Market cap. (B)	$0.336
Shs. outstg. (M)	18.1	Inst. holdings	34%
Avg. daily vol. (M)	0.180	Insider holdings	NA

Value of $10,000 invested 5 years ago: NA

Fiscal Year Ending Dec. 31

	1995	% Change	1994	% Change	1993	% Change
Revenues (Million $)						
1Q	20.23	-21%	25.72	52%	16.90	NM
2Q	31.53	23%	25.64	24%	20.66	192%
3Q	—	—	30.77	31%	23.48	187%
4Q	—	—	30.06	5%	28.60	124%
Yr.	—	—	112.2	25%	89.66	172%
Income (Million $)						
1Q	-1.19	NM	4.16	NM	0.72	NM
2Q	1.05	-76%	4.43	NM	0.88	NM
3Q	—	—	4.92	NM	1.15	NM
4Q	—	—	5.91	31%	4.50	NM
Yr.	—	—	19.41	168%	7.23	NM
Earnings Per Share ($)						
1Q	-0.06	NM	0.23	NM	0.05	NM
2Q	0.06	-75%	0.24	NM	0.06	NM
3Q	E0.20	-26%	0.27	NM	0.08	NM
4Q	E0.25	-22%	0.32	28%	0.25	NM
Yr.	E0.45	-57%	1.04	126%	0.46	NM

Next earnings report expected: early November

Roberts Pharmaceutical

Business Summary - 15-AUG-95

Roberts Pharmaceutical Corporation acquires and develops high-potential, undervalued, late-stage-development pharmaceuticals and acquires currently marketed prescription and nonprescription products.

In recent years, the company acquired prescription drugs from manufacturers such as Upjohn, Procter & Gamble, Bristol-Myers Squibb, Glaxo Canada, Du Pont Merck, Wyeth-Ayerst and G.D. Searle. Robert's broad portfolio consists of 28 products primarily in six major therapeutic areas: cardiovascular, gynecology/endocrinology, respiratory, urology, oncology, and gastroenterology. Sales of Salutensin (a cardiovascular product), Colace and Peri-Colace (both used in gastrointestinal disorders) added approximately $21 million to 1994 revenues. These three drugs were acquired from Bristol-Myers Squibb in 1993. Acquisitions in early 1995 included Noroxin, an antibiotic to treat urinary tract infections; Replens, a vaginal moisturizer; Tigan, to control nausea and vomiting; and Eminase, a thrombolytic agent for heart attacks.

Drugs in clinical development include Amatine, in Phase II studies for the treatment of stress urinary incontinence; Maxivent, in Phase III studies for asthma; Somagard, in Phase III studies for central precocious puberty and prostate cancer; Radinyl, in Phase III trials as a radiosensitizer; Dirame, in Phase III trials for pain management; and Stanate, in Phase III studies for neonatal jaundice. Applications for FDA marketing approval have been filed for Agrelin (bone cancer), Pro-Banthine (urinary incontinence) and Amatine (orthostatic hypotension).

In 1994, Roberts reorganized its homecare and medical products businesses under the name Pronetics Health Care Group. Pronetics distributes high-value prescription-injectable and biotechnology drug products for physician office use.

Through wholly owned VRG International Inc. and National Clinical Research Centers Inc., Roberts provides contract clinical research for pharmaceutical companies. Roberts also acquires and sells nonprescription pharmaceuticals and actively engages in the development of product line extensions for its nonprescription pharmaceuticals.

Important Developments

Aug. '95—In reporting 1995 first-half results, Roberts said it would divest its Home Care and Medical Products businesses in order to grow its pharmaceutical operations. The company charged current operations with an estimated loss of $0.64 a share on the discontinued operations.

Capitalization

Long Term Debt: $36,478,000 (6/95).

Per Share Data ($)

(Year Ended Dec. 31)

	1994	1993	1992	1991	1990	1989
Tangible Bk. Val.	1.95	2.18	0.33	2.55	1.45	0.06
Cash Flow	1.41	0.79	-0.53	-0.49	-0.82	0.01
Earnings	1.04	0.46	-0.68	-0.58	-0.85	Nil
Dividends	Nil	Nil	Nil	Nil	Nil	Nil
Payout Ratio	Nil	Nil	Nil	Nil	Nil	Nil
Prices - High	40	42½	36¾	33	8	NA
- Low	19¾	15¼	13½	4	2½	NA
P/E Ratio - High	38	92	NM	NM	NM	NA
- Low	19	33	NM	NA	NA	NA

Income Statement Analysis (Million $)

	1994	%Chg	1993	%Chg	1992	%Chg	1991
Revs.	112	25%	89.7	172%	33.0	144%	13.5
Oper. Inc.	31.3	128%	13.7	NM	-8.9	NM	-3.8
Depr.	7.1	40%	5.0	155%	2.0	151%	0.8
Int. Exp.	4.0	22%	3.3	190%	1.1	9%	1.0
Pretax Inc.	23.3	NM	7.2	NM	-8.6	NM	-4.9
Eff. Tax Rate	17%	—	Nil	—	NM	—	NM
Net Inc.	19.4	168%	7.2	NM	-9.3	NM	-5.1

Balance Sheet & Other Fin. Data (Million $)

	1994	1993	1992	1991	1990	1989
Cash	36.5	91.6	43.9	14.2	11.8	0.8
Curr. Assets	96.0	128	58.3	19.8	12.5	1.9
Total Assets	336	343	185	44.0	13.0	3.0
Curr. Liab.	53.9	57.7	34.0	9.8	1.0	0.6
LT Debt	22.4	45.7	29.0	9.2	0.4	0.5
Common Eqty.	259	239	122	25.0	10.0	Nil
Total Cap.	282	285	151	34.0	12.0	2.0
Cap. Exp.	1.0	6.6	9.4	0.3	0.0	0.1
Cash Flow	26.5	12.3	-7.3	-4.3	-4.7	0.1

Ratio Analysis

	1994	1993	1992	1991	1990	1989
Curr. Ratio	1.8	2.2	1.7	2.0	12.7	3.4
% LT Debt of Cap.	8.0	16.0	19.2	26.9	3.6	26.3
% Net Inc.of Revs.	17.3	8.1	NM	NM	NM	1.8
% Ret. on Assets	5.7	2.5	NM	NM	NM	NA
% Ret. on Equity	7.8	3.7	NM	NM	NM	NA

Dividend Data —Cash dividends have never been paid.

Data as orig. reptd.; bef. results of disc. opers. and/or spec. items. Per share data adj. for stk. divs. as of ex-div. date. E-Estimated. NA-Not Available. NM-Not Meaningful. NR-Not Ranked.

Office—6 Industrial Way West, Eatontown, NJ 07724. **Tel**—(908) 389-1182. **Chrmn, Pres & CEO**—R. A. Vukovich. **VP & COO**—R. W. Loy. **VP, Treas & CFO**—A. P. Maris. **VP & Secy**—A. A. Rascio. **Dirs**—D. W. Barrios, Y. Brozen, W. R. Fowler, R. W. Loy, A. P. Maris, A. Matsubara, T. Miyamoto, A. A. Rascio, R. A. Vukovich. **Transfer Agent & Registrar**—Continental Stock Transfer & Trust Co., NYC. **Incorporated** in New Jersey in 1982. **Empl**-568. **S&P Analyst:** Thomas Tirney

STANDARD & POOR'S

STOCK REPORTS

Rollins Truck Leasing

NYSE Symbol **RLC**
In S&P SmallCap 600

24-JUL-95 **Industry:** Finance

Summary: This firm is the nation's third largest provider of truck leasing and commercial vehicle rental services. Rollins also provides dedicated contract carriage and logistics services.

S&P Opinion: Accumulate (★★★★) | Recent Price • 10⅞ | 52 Wk Range • 14½-10⅜ | Yield • 1.5% | 12-Mo. P/E • 11.4

Quantitative Evaluations
Outlook
(1 Lowest—5 Highest)
• **5⁻**
Fair Value
• **13½**
Risk
• **Low**
Earn./Div. Rank
• **A-**

Technical Eval.
• **Bearish** since 4/95
Rel. Strength Rank
(1 Lowest—99 Highest)
• **25**
Insider Activity
• **Neutral**

Earnings vs. Previous Year
▲=Up ▼=Down ▶=No Change

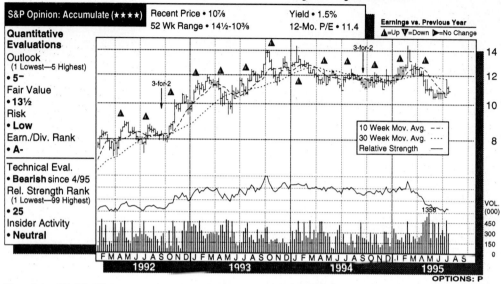

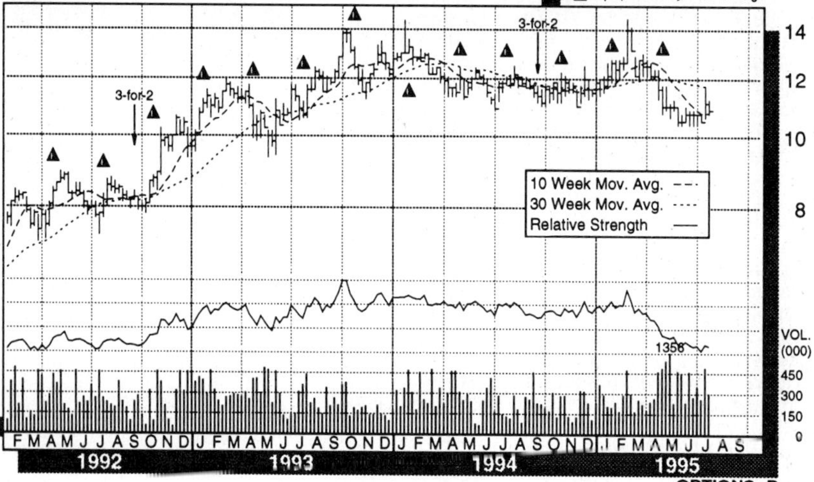

OPTIONS: P

Overview - 24-JUL-95

While higher profits are projected from RLC's commercial truck rental business in fiscal 1995, the rate of growth could slow in the second half as the economy cools down. Increased demand is also anticipated for guaranteed maintenance services. Contract carriage will post rapid growth reflecting new accounts and expanded business with existing clients. RLC's full-service truck lease business will continue to benefit from private fleet operators' outsourcing their transportation needs and geographic expansion. Despite an aggressive marketing program, margins should widen as RLC experiences lower maintenance and repair costs for new vehicles. Aiding comparisons will be the absence of weather-related costs in fiscal 1994. Heavier depreciation charges will be balanced by higher disposition gains. Higher interest expense will be offset by a lower tax rate.

Valuation - 24-JUL-95

Shares of this leading truck lessor, after successfully testing the lower level of a two-year trading range in the second quarter, moved higher in July on a good third quarter profit report. Though business conditions have slowed, we believe RLC's shares have already discounted this and perhaps worse. Given Rollins outstanding long-term growth record, stemming from acquisitions and internal expansion, we believe the shares are presently undervalued. Rollins long-term fundamental position is favorable given the desire of private fleet operators to transfer their operations to professional distribution/logistics companies.

Key Stock Statistics

S&P EPS Est. 1995	1.00	Tang. Bk. Value/Share	5.23
P/E on S&P Est. 1995	10.9	Beta	1.64
S&P EPS Est. 1996	1.15	Shareholders	2,600
Dividend Rate/Share	0.16	Market cap. (B)	$0.499
Shs. outstg. (M)	45.9	Inst. holdings	59%
Avg. daily vol. (M)	0.090	Insider holdings	NA

Value of $10,000 invested 5 years ago: $ 30,216

Fiscal Year Ending Sep. 30

	1995	% Change	1994	% Change	1993	% Change
Revenues (Million $)						
1Q	119.1	11%	107.4	7%	100.1	12%
2Q	116.7	9%	107.1	10%	97.04	6%
3Q	122.7	6%	115.8	11%	104.6	6%
4Q	—	—	120.5	13%	107.1	6%
Yr.	—	—	450.9	10%	408.8	7%
Income (Million $)						
1Q	11.51	22%	9.47	26%	7.50	54%
2Q	11.23	38%	8.16	26%	6.49	14%
3Q	11.23	7%	10.45	18%	8.86	35%
4Q	—	—	11.75	55%	7.57	NM
Yr.	—	—	39.83	31%	30.42	24%
Earnings Per Share ($)						
1Q	0.25	21%	0.21	29%	0.16	26%
2Q	0.20	15%	0.17	24%	0.14	31%
3Q	0.25	10%	0.23	17%	0.19	38%
4Q	E0.30	—	0.25	50%	0.17	4%
Yr.	E1.00	—	0.86	30%	0.66	25%

Next earnings report expected: late October

Rollins Truck Leasing

Business Summary - 21-JUL-95

Rollins Truck Leasing Corp., the third largest full-service lessor of over-the-road tractors, trucks and trailers in the U.S., operates through a network of 198 facilities in 43 states. A Rollins full-service lease includes vehicles custom-engineered to clients' requirements, fuel, oil and tire purchases, maintenance and repairs, licenses, insurance, 24-hour emergency road service and driver training and safety programs. Full-service leases typically cover a three- to eight-year period.

Rollins' commercial rental service is provided through a fleet of some 7,000 trucks, tractors and trailers, which are used to supplement customers' peak, seasonal or emergency transportation needs. Rental periods may be as short as one day or for several months.

For private fleet operators that own their vehicles, RLC offers guaranteed maintenance services. Clients receive preventive maintenance, fuel procurement, tax reporting, permitting, licensing and 24-hour road service.

Rollins' dedicated contract service is a customized distribution and transportation package, including vehicles, management and road personnel and state-of-the-art information systems.

Important Developments

Jul. '95—Rollins reported that during the three months ended June 30, 1995 it had repurchased and retired some 379,900 RLC common shares (0.8%) for an undisclosed sum.

May '95—RLC sold $50 million face amount of 7.2% collateral trust debentures due May 15, 2005. In March the company privately placed $100 million of 8.27% collateral trust debentures due March 15, 2002. Proceeds will be used to refinance certain existing debt and for new equipment purchases.

Jan. '95—RLC said that during fiscal 1995 it would construct new full-service truck leasing facilities in Tulsa, Okla., Southborough, Mass. and Los Angeles, Calif. In fiscal 1994 RLC opened new facilities in Springfield, MO., Cedartown, GA., Lafayette, LA., Bozeman, Mont., and Clearwater, Fla. Total capital outlays for fiscal 1995 were projected at $300 million, versus $297 million in fiscal 1994. Some $268 million of fiscal 1995's budget was allocated for equipment, $30 million for facilities and $2 million for computers.

Capitalization

Long Term Debt: $565,435,000 (6/95), incl. $564.8 million of equipment obligations.

Per Share Data ($) (Year Ended Sep. 30)

	1994	1993	1992	1991	1990	1989
Tangible Bk. Val.	5.23	4.49	3.95	3.48	2.89	2.57
Cash Flow	3.49	3.08	2.85	2.74	2.57	2.45
Earnings	0.86	0.66	0.53	0.45	0.43	0.40
Dividends	0.13	0.12	0.11	0.09	0.09	0.09
Payout Ratio	15%	18%	20%	21%	21%	22%
Prices - High	14⅜	14	10⅝	7¾	4⅛	5⅝
- Low	10⅞	9⅜	7⅛	3⅛	2½	3¼
P/E Ratio - High	17	21	20	17	10	14
- Low	13	14	13	7	6	8

Income Statement Analysis (Million $)

	1994	%Chg	1993	%Chg	1992	%Chg	1991
Revs.	451	10%	409	8%	380	11%	342
Oper. Inc.	225	12%	201	10%	183	10%	167
Depr.	122	9%	112	6%	106	9%	97.0
Int. Exp.	37.4	5%	35.5	-4%	36.8	-9%	40.5
Pretax Inc.	66.4	21%	54.7	34%	40.7	29%	31.5
Eff. Tax Rate	40%	—	44%	—	39%	—	40%
Net Inc.	39.8	31%	30.4	24%	24.6	29%	19.0

Balance Sheet & Other Fin. Data (Million $)

	1994	1993	1992	1991	1990	1989
Cash	15.1	15.1	17.6	21.9	18.9	16.8
Curr. Assets	102	90.0	91.0	80.0	81.0	77.0
Total Assets	910	781	708	656	658	631
Curr. Liab.	78.0	68.0	72.0	73.0	91.0	84.0
LT Debt	469	404	367	351	377	376
Common Eqty.	251	217	191	169	133	120
Total Cap.	823	704	627	577	561	541
Cap. Exp.	297	243	203	146	170	185
Cash Flow	162	142	131	116	108	103

Ratio Analysis

	1994	1993	1992	1991	1990	1989
Curr. Ratio	1.3	1.3	1.3	1.1	0.9	0.9
% LT Debt of Cap.	57.0	57.4	58.5	60.8	67.1	69.4
% Net Inc.of Revs.	8.8	7.4	6.5	5.5	5.4	5.4
% Ret. on Assets	4.7	4.1	3.6	2.8	2.8	2.7
% Ret. on Equity	17.0	14.9	13.6	12.1	14.2	12.6

Dividend Data (Dividends were initiated in 1976. A dividend reinvestment plan is available. A "poison pill" stock purchase rights plan was adopted in 1989.)

Amt. of Div. $	Date Decl.	Ex-Div. Date	Stock of Record	Payment Date
0.050	Jul. 29	Aug. 09	Aug. 15	Sep. 15 '94
0.040	Oct. 31	Nov. 08	Nov. 15	Dec. 15 '94
0.040	Jan. 31	Feb. 09	Feb. 15	Mar. 15 '95
0.040	Apr. 27	May. 09	May. 15	Jun. 15 '95

Data as orig. reptd.; bef. results of disc. opers. and/or spec. items. Per share data adj. for stk. divs. as of ex-div. date. E-Estimated. NA-Not Available. NM-Not Meaningful. NR-Not Ranked.

Office—One Rollins Plaza, Wilmington, DE 19803. **Tel**—(302) 426-2700. **Chrmn & CEO**—J. W. Rollins. **Pres**—J. W. Rollins Jr. **VP-Treas & Investor Contact**—Patrick J. Bagley. **VP-Secy**—M. B. Kinnard. **Dirs**—W. B. Philipbar Jr., G. W. Rollins, J. W. Rollins, J. W. Rollins Jr., H. B. Tippie. **Transfer Agent & Registrar**—Registrar & Transfer Co., Cranford, N.J. **Incorporated** in Delaware in 1954. **Empl**-2,924. **S&P Analyst:** Stephen R. Klein

STANDARD & POOR'S

STOCK REPORTS

Roper Industries

NASDAQ Symbol **ROPR**

In S&P SmallCap 600

16-NOV-95 **Industry:** Manufacturing/Distr

Summary: This company is an international manufacturer of fluid handling and industrial control products.

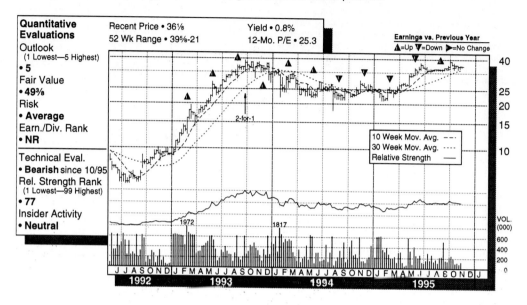

Quantitative Evaluations

Recent Price • 36⅛
52 Wk Range • 39⅝-21
Yield • 0.8%
12-Mo. P/E • 25.3

Outlook
(1 Lowest—5 Highest)
• **5**

Fair Value
• **49⅜**

Risk
• **Average**

Earn./Div. Rank
• **NR**

Technical Eval.
• **Bearish** since 10/95

Rel. Strength Rank
(1 Lowest—99 Highest)
• **77**

Insider Activity
• **Neutral**

Earnings vs. Previous Year
▲=Up ▼=Down ▶=No Change

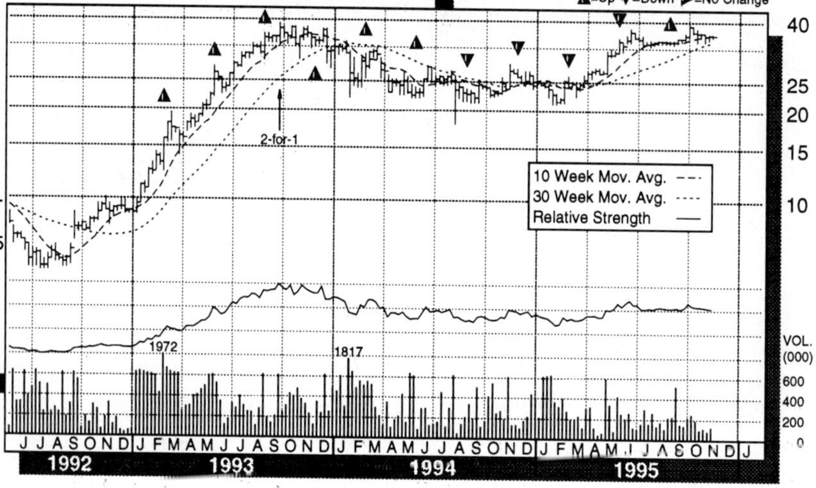

Business Profile - 16-NOV-95

Roper continues to strive for its goal of achieving higher margins by increasing market share, introducing new products and product improvements, acquiring attractive growth companies, and focusing on the maintenance and improvement of high operating margins. The completed negotiation of long-term financing by Gazprom should provide financial support for future Roper product shipments to Gazprom. Roper recently completed its third acquisition of a controls company in the past 12 months.

Operational Review - 16-NOV-95

Net revenues in the first nine months of FY 95 (Oct.), climbed 16% year to year. Margins narrowed, mostly due to a rise in selling, general and administrative expenses; operating income rose 8.1%. After a sharp rise in interest expense from higher debt, the increase in net income was limited to 4.2%, to $14,120,000 ($0.94 a share), from $13,555,000 ($0.90).

Stock Performance - 10-NOV-95

In the past 30 trading days, ROPR's shares have declined 7%, compared to a 1% rise in the S&P 500. Average trading volume for the past five days was 24,160 shares, compared with the 40-day moving average of 29,265 shares.

Key Stock Statistics

Dividend Rate/Share	0.30	Shareholders	NA
Shs. outstg. (M)	14.9	Market cap. (B)	$0.552
Avg. daily vol. (M)	0.023	Inst. holdings	63%
Tang. Bk. Value/Share	2.28	Insider holdings	NA
Beta	NA		

Value of $10,000 invested 5 years ago: NA

Fiscal Year Ending Oct. 31

	1995	% Change	1994	% Change	1993	% Change
Revenues (Million $)						
1Q	34.40	3%	33.50	70%	19.70	36%
2Q	39.82	4%	38.40	35%	28.50	63%
3Q	47.09	44%	32.70	-20%	41.10	138%
4Q	—	—	43.10	NM	43.30	111%
Yr.	—	—	147.7	11%	132.5	90%
Income (Million $)						
1Q	3.24	-16%	3.86	NM	1.24	176%
2Q	4.21	-36%	6.55	121%	2.97	NM
3Q	6.67	112%	3.15	-56%	7.24	NM
4Q	—	—	7.31	-4%	7.61	NM
Yr.	—	—	20.86	9%	19.06	NM
Earnings Per Share ($)						
1Q	0.22	-15%	0.26	NM	0.08	60%
2Q	0.28	-36%	0.44	120%	0.20	NM
3Q	0.44	110%	0.21	-57%	0.49	NM
4Q	—	—	0.49	-4%	0.51	NM
Yr.	—	—	1.39	8%	1.29	NM

Next earnings report expected: mid December

Roper Industries

Business Summary - 07-NOV-95

Roper Industries, Inc. designs, makes and distributes specialty industrial controls and fluid handling products worldwide, mostly serving the oil and gas, agricultural, chemical, diesel engine and turbine/compressor control manufacturing, trucking, utilities, semiconductor and petrochemical refining industries.

ROPR's businesses are grouped into two segments: Industrial Controls and Fluid Handling, whose contributions to net sales and operating profit in fiscal 1994 were as follows:

	Sales	Profits
Industrial Controls	62%	63%
Fluid Handling	38%	37%

Sales outside the U.S. contributed 52% of the total in fiscal 1994, versus 56% in 1993.

The Industrial Controls segment's products are made and distributed by Amot Controls Corp., Richmond, Calif.; Amot Controls Ltd., Bury St. Edmonds, England; Compressor Controls Corp., Des Moines, Iowa; ISL, Verson, France (acquired in August 1994); and Uson Corp., Houston, TX (acquired March 1995). Products include thermostatic valves, pneumatic panel components, pressure and temperature sensors, microprocessor-based control systems and associated engineering services, and petroleum product test equipment. Some 37% of the segment's sales in fiscal 1994 were from Gazprom, the Russian natural gas production and distribution company, under an early 1993 multiyear agreement for the supply of turbomachinery control systems and engineering services in connection with a pipeline system retrofit project.

The Fluid Handling segment's products are made and distributed by Roper Pump Co., Commerce, Ga.; Cornell Pump Co., Portland, Ore.; and Integrated Designs, Inc., Dallas, Texas. Products include various types of industrial pumps and precision chemical dispensing products for the semiconductor industry.

Important Developments

Oct. '95—Roper acquired Metrix Instrument Co. for $11.9 million in cash (5.7X pretax earnings). Houston-based Metrix, with estimated 1995 sales of $8 million and operating profits of 26%, is a vibration detection and analysis equipment maker for the rotating machinery industry. ROPR said Metrix's offerings will complement Amot Controls' and Compressor Controls' existing product lines. Results will be reported in the Industrial Controls segment.

Jun. '95—ROPR said Gazprom agreed to purchase $166.5 million of control systems over five years, including $15.5 million in FY 1995, from ROPR's Industrial Controls segment.

Capitalization

Long Term Debt: $22,495,000 (7/95).

Per Share Data ($)

(Year Ended Oct. 31)

	1994	1993	1992	1991	1990	1989
Tangible Bk. Val.	2.33	1.39	0.55	-0.14	NA	NA
Cash Flow	1.59	1.49	0.58	0.71	NA	NA
Earnings	1.39	1.29	0.37	0.47	NA	NA
Dividends	0.14	0.09	0.06	Nil	NA	NA
Payout Ratio	10%	7%	19%	Nil	NA	NA
Prices - High	34	39	10½	NA	NA	NA
- Low	18	8⅞	5¾	NA	NA	NA
P/E Ratio - High	24	30	28	NA	NA	NA
- Low	13	7	16	NA	NA	NA

Income Statement Analysis (Million $)

	1994	%Chg	1993	%Chg	1992	%Chg	1991
Revs.	148	11%	133	90%	70.0	-7%	75.0
Oper. Inc.	36.0	8%	33.4	134%	14.3	-6%	15.2
Depr.	3.0	NM	3.0	12%	2.7	13%	2.4
Int. Exp.	1.5	-26%	2.0	-13%	2.3	-54%	5.0
Pretax Inc.	31.6	11%	28.4	NM	7.5	-5%	7.9
Eff. Tax Rate	34%	—	33%	—	37%	—	37%
Net Inc.	20.9	9%	19.1	NM	4.7	-4%	4.9

Balance Sheet & Other Fin. Data (Million $)

	1994	1993	1992	1991	1990	1989
Cash	2.0	1.2	1.7	2.9	NA	NA
Curr. Assets	53.2	34.4	32.2	25.9	NA	NA
Total Assets	122	94.0	81.0	48.0	NA	NA
Curr. Liab.	20.8	20.5	10.5	11.2	NA	NA
LT Debt	16.7	9.9	28.4	31.8	NA	NA
Common Eqty.	82.9	62.4	40.5	3.7	NA	NA
Total Cap.	100	73.2	70.2	37.0	NA	NA
Cap. Exp.	4.1	3.9	0.9	4.3	NA	NA
Cash Flow	23.9	22.1	7.4	7.0	NA	NA

Ratio Analysis

	1994	1993	1992	1991	1990	1989
Curr. Ratio	2.6	1.7	3.1	2.3	NA	NA
% LT Debt of Cap.	16.8	13.5	40.4	85.9	NA	NA
% Net Inc.of Revs.	14.1	14.4	6.8	6.6	NA	NA
% Ret. on Assets	19.3	21.7	6.2	NA	NA	NA
% Ret. on Equity	28.7	36.9	20.5	NA	NA	NA

Dividend Data —Quarterly dividends have been paid since the company's initial public stock offering in early 1992.

Amt. of Div. $	Date Decl.	Ex-Div. Date	Stock of Record	Payment Date
0.050	Jan. 03	Jan. 09	Jan. 13	Jan. 27 '95
0.050	Mar. 21	Apr. 26	Apr. 18	Apr. 28 '95
0.050	Jun. 22	Jul. 05	Jul. 07	Jul. 28 '95
0.075	Sep. 28	Oct. 11	Oct. 13	Oct. 27 '95

Data as orig. reptd.; bef. results of disc. opers. and/or spec. items. Per share data adj. for stk. divs. as of ex-div. date. E-Estimated. NA-Not Available. NM-Not Meaningful. NR-Not Ranked.

Office—160 Ben Burton Rd., Bogart, GA 30622. **Tel**—(706) 369-7170. **Fax**—(706) 353-6496. **Chrmn, Pres & CEO**—D. N. Key. **VP, CFO & Investor Contact**—A. Donald O'Steen. **VP & Treas**—Z. E. Metcalf. **Dirs**—W. L. Banks, L. von Braun, D. G. Calder, E. D. Kenna, D. N. Key, D. C. Mecum, G. L. Ohrstrom Jr., G. G. Schall-Riaucour, E. R. Scocimara, P. A. Uzielli, C. Wright. **Transfer Agent & Registrar**—Trust Company Bank, Atlanta. **Incorporated** in Delaware in 1981. **Empl**-961. **S&P Analyst:** Robert E. Friedman

Ross Stores

NASDAQ Symbol **ROST**
In S&P SmallCap 600

21-SEP-95

Industry:
Retail Stores

Summary: This national chain of off-price retail stores offers first quality in-season branded apparel and apparel-related merchandise through 282 stores in 18 states.

Quantitative Evaluations
Outlook
(1 Lowest—5 Highest)
• **3⁻**
Fair Value
• **16 3/8**
Risk
• **Average**
Earn./Div. Rank
• **B**

Technical Eval.
• **Bullish** since 2/95
Rel. Strength Rank
(1 Lowest—99 Highest)
• **83**
Insider Activity
• **Unfavorable**

Recent Price • 16 3/8
52 Wk Range • 16½-9½
Yield • 1.5%
12-Mo. P/E • 10.6

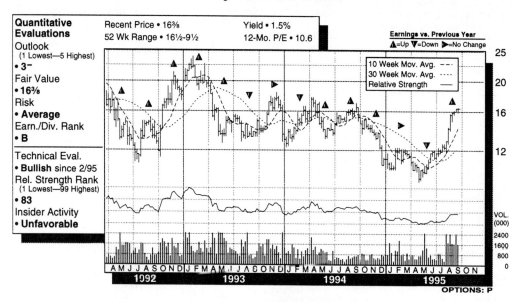

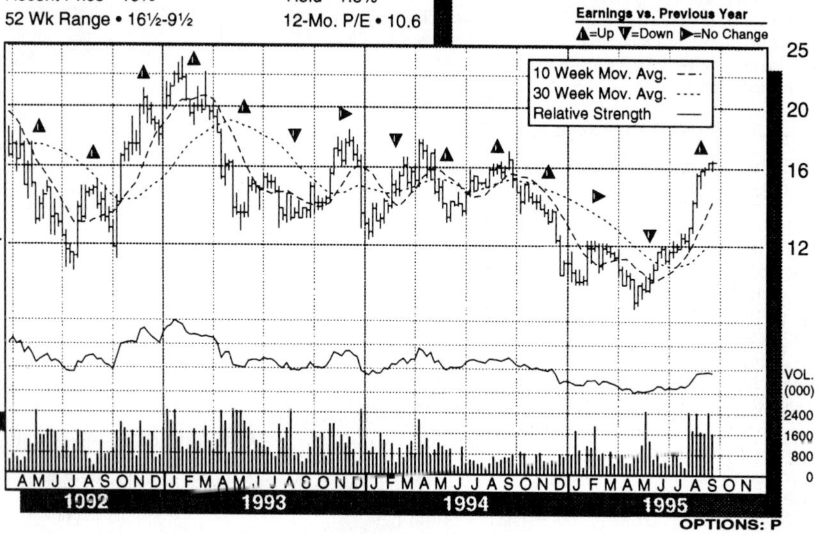

OPTIONS: P

Business Profile - 21-SEP-95

This company operates 282 off-price retail stores that feature first-quality, in-season apparel, shoes, fragrances and apparel-related accessories. A highly competitive climate for apparel retailers has led to an aggressive pricing environment in recent periods. However, future results should benefit from an ambitious expansion program, and new technological systems to improve the company's distribution process and store-based systems to speed up, simplify and automate most transactions.

Operational Review - 21-SEP-95

Net sales for the 26 weeks ended July 29, 1995, advanced 13%, year to year, primarily reflecting 25 additional stores in operation. Same-store sales grew only 1%, restricted by the general lackluster environment for apparel sales. Gross margins narrowed, but SG&A expenses benefited from strict expense controls and economies of scale. After taxes at 40.0% in each period, net income was up 7.2%.

Stock Performance - 15-SEP-95

In the past 30 trading days, ROST's shares have increased 27%, compared to a 4% rise in the S&P 500. Average trading volume for the past five days was 321,160 shares, compared with the 40-day moving average of 378,872 shares.

Key Stock Statistics

Dividend Rate/Share	0.24	Shareholders	1,200
Shs. outstg. (M)	24.6	Market cap. (B)	$0.393
Avg. daily vol. (M)	0.397	Inst. holdings	55%
Tang. Bk. Value/Share	10.42	Insider holdings	NA
Beta	1.47		

Value of $10,000 invested 5 years ago: $ 11,808

Fiscal Year Ending Jan. 31

	1996	% Change	1995	% Change	1994	% Change
Revenues (Million $)						
1Q	297.4	13%	264.0	10%	239.6	8%
2Q	351.2	12%	312.3	13%	276.0	9%
3Q	—	—	295.0	12%	262.2	6%
4Q	—	—	391.1	14%	344.3	7%
Yr.	—	—	1,263	13%	1,122	8%
Income (Million $)						
1Q	3.87	-12%	4.41	23%	3.59	10%
2Q	10.34	17%	8.85	9%	8.15	-16%
3Q	—	—	11.09	132%	4.79	-3%
4Q	—	—	12.48	-2%	12.79	-21%
Yr.	—	—	36.82	26%	29.32	-14%
Earnings Per Share ($)						
1Q	0.16	-11%	0.18	29%	0.14	8%
2Q	0.42	17%	0.36	16%	0.31	-18%
3Q	—	—	0.45	137%	0.19	NM
4Q	—	—	0.51	NM	0.51	-16%
Yr.	—	—	1.49	31%	1.14	-14%

Next earnings report expected: mid November

Ross Stores

Business Summary - 21-SEP-95

As of August 26, 1995, Ross Stores, Inc. operated 282 off-price retail stores, up from 260 a year earlier. The stores feature first-quality, in-season apparel, shoes, fragrances and apparel-related accessories. The company targets its sales to 25- to 54-year-old men and women in middle- to upper-income households, which are believed to be the fastest growing portion of the population and largest customer segment in the retailing industry. California had the most stores, with the balance in Texas, Arizona, Washington, Colorado, Florida, Oklahoma, Utah, Georgia, Nevada, Oregon, New Mexico, Virginia, New Jersey, Maryland, Pennsylvania, Idaho and Hawaii.

Emphasizing the ROSS-Dress for Less theme in TV, direct mail, radio and newspaper advertising, the company offers a wide selection within each of its merchandise categories, at prices 20% to 60% below those charged by most department and specialty stores for identical goods. Ross seeks to purchase directly from manufacturers at advantageous prices. It can obtain favorable pricing by purchasing closer to and during the selling season, and by not requiring that manufacturers provide promotional and markdown allowances, return privileges and delayed deliveries. It also tries to minimize operating costs. In 1994-95, 95% of the sales mix consisted of first quality merchandise and 5% irregulars.

A Home Accents department, featuring china, crystal, glassware, framed art and other decorative items for the home, was introduced in 1992. Most of the chain featured this department at the end of 1994-95. Ross further expanded into the home merchandising segment in 1994-95 with the addition of a Bed and Bath department in 72 stores, featuring soft goods for the home, including tabletop, bed and bath linens and bath accessories.

The average Ross store has 22,300 sq. ft. of selling space. All of the stores except one occupy leased facilities and are located predominantly in neighborhood or strip shopping centers in heavily populated urban and suburban areas. The company owns a 494,000 sq. ft. distribution center in Newark, Cal., and a 424,000 sq. ft. center in Carlisle, Pa.

Important Developments

Aug. '95—Sales in the four weeks ended August 26, 1995, advanced 9%, year to year; same-store sales were up 2%. For the seven months ended August 26, total sales rose 12%, on a 1% gain in same-store sales.

May '95—Directors authorized the repurchase of an additional 1,000,000 common shares, representing a continuation of the 1993 and 1994 repurchase programs in which the company bought back a total of two million shares.

Capitalization

Long Term Debt: $45,940,000 (7/95).

Per Share Data ($)

(Year Ended Jan. 31)

	1995	1994	1993	1992	1991	1990
Tangible Bk. Val.	10.42	9.01	7.99	6.36	5.00	4.18
Cash Flow	2.46	1.94	2.06	1.78	1.29	1.74
Earnings	1.49	1.14	1.32	1.13	0.72	1.25
Dividends	0.20	Nil	Nil	Nil	Nil	Nil
Payout Ratio	13%	Nil	Nil	Nil	Nil	Nil
Cal. Yrs.	1994	1993	1992	1991	1990	1989
Prices - High	17$\frac{3}{4}$	24	23	18$\frac{3}{8}$	14$\frac{5}{8}$	24$\frac{5}{8}$
- Low	10$\frac{3}{4}$	12$\frac{5}{8}$	10$\frac{7}{8}$	4$\frac{3}{4}$	4$\frac{3}{8}$	10$\frac{1}{8}$
P/E Ratio - High	12	21	17	16	20	20
- Low	7	11	8	4	6	8

Income Statement Analysis (Million $)

	1995	%Chg	1994	%Chg	1993	%Chg	1992
Revs.	1,263	13%	1,122	8%	1,043	13%	926
Oper. Inc.	78.5	9%	71.7	-8%	78.3	18%	66.5
Depr.	24.0	17%	20.5	9%	18.8	17%	16.0
Int. Exp.	3.5	52%	2.3	-24%	3.1	-43%	5.4
Pretax Inc.	61.4	26%	48.9	-14%	56.7	25%	45.4
Eff. Tax Rate	40%	—	40%	—	40%	—	39%
Net Inc.	36.8	26%	29.3	-14%	34.0	23%	27.7

Balance Sheet & Other Fin. Data (Million $)

	1995	1994	1993	1992	1991	1990
Cash	23.6	32.3	40.5	16.4	5.3	2.5
Curr. Assets	316	280	278	216	179	146
Total Assets	506	437	420	358	310	250
Curr. Liab.	185	155	157	139	112	86.0
LT Debt	46.1	33.3	33.5	40.7	57.6	48.9
Common Eqty.	255	228	210	163	123	104
Total Cap.	301	262	243	203	181	153
Cap. Exp.	52.1	40.2	22.4	29.4	40.7	30.8
Cash Flow	60.8	49.9	52.8	43.7	30.0	41.8

Ratio Analysis

	1995	1994	1993	1992	1991	1990
Curr. Ratio	1.7	1.8	1.8	1.6	1.6	1.7
% LT Debt of Cap.	15.3	12.7	13.8	20.0	31.9	32.0
% Net Inc.of Revs.	2.9	2.6	3.3	3.0	2.1	4.1
% Ret. on Assets	7.8	6.9	8.6	8.1	5.9	12.3
% Ret. on Equity	15.3	13.6	18.0	18.9	14.6	28.8

Dividend Data —Dividend payments were initiated in 1994.

Amt. of Div. $	Date Decl.	Ex-Div. Date	Stock of Record	Payment Date
0.050	Aug. 25	Sep. 02	Sep. 09	Oct. 01 '94
0.050	Nov. 01	Dec. 05	Dec. 09	Jan. 01 '95
0.060	Jan. 27	Mar. 06	Mar. 10	Apr. 03 '95
0.060	May. 25	Jun. 06	Jun. 09	Jul. 03 '95
0.060	Aug. 24	Sep. 06	Sep. 08	Oct. 02 '95

Data as orig. reptd.; bef. results of disc. opers. and/or spec. items. Per share data adj. for stk. divs. as of ex-div. date. E-Estimated. NA-Not Available. NM-Not Meaningful. NR-Not Ranked.

Office—8333 Central Ave., Newark, CA 94560-3433. **Tel**—(510) 505-4400. **Chrmn Emeritus**—S. G. Moldaw. **Chrmn & CEO**—N. A. Ferber. **Pres**—M. A. Wilmore. **SVP, CFO, Secy & Investor Contact**—Earl T. Benson. **Dirs**—N. A. Ferber, S. G. Moldaw, G. P. Orban, P. Schlein, D. H. Seiler, D. L. Weaver, M. A. Wilmore. **Transfer Agent & Registrar**—Chemical Trust Co. of California, SF. **Incorporated** in California in 1957; reincorporated in Delaware in 1989. **Empl**-10,574. **S&P Analyst:** Maureen C. Carini

STANDARD & POOR'S

STOCK REPORTS

Royal Appliance Mfg.

NYSE Symbol **RAM**

In S&P SmallCap 600

23-OCT-95

Industry: Electronics/Electric

Summary: This company markets plastic and metal vacuum cleaners for home and commercial use under the Dirt Devil and Royal brand names.

Quantitative Evaluations

Recent Price • 3⅜

52 Wk Range • 5¼-2⅝

Yield • Nil

12-Mo. P/E • 84.4

Outlook
(1 Lowest—5 Highest)
• **NA**

Fair Value
• **NA**

Risk
• **High**

Earn./Div. Rank
• **NR**

Technical Eval.
• **Bullish** since 7/95

Rel. Strength Rank
(1 Lowest—99 Highest)
• **20**

Insider Activity
• **Neutral**

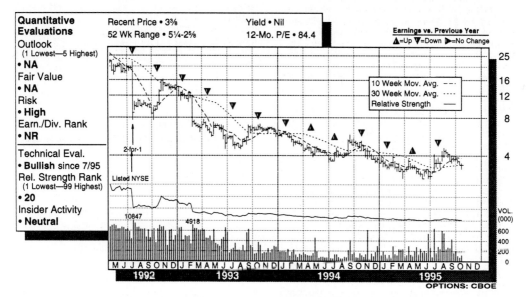

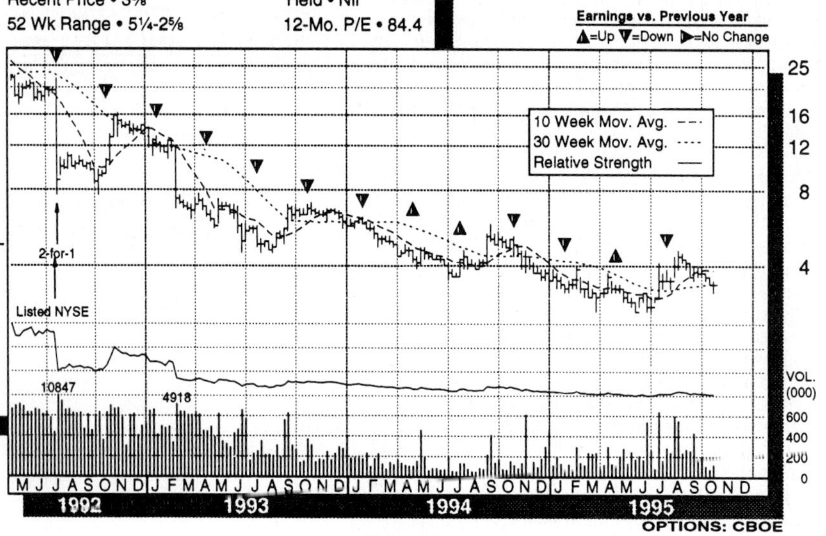

Business Profile - 20-OCT-95

RAM competes in the domestic vacuum cleaner industry, a mature marketplace with modest overall growth prospects. Competition is dependent on price, quality, extension of product lines, and advertising and promotion expenditures. Management's goal is to provide retailers with new and innovative products and support those products with advertising. Royal hopes to see benefits from its refocused advertising campaign, additional product placements at retail and the introduction of new products.

Operational Review - 20-OCT-95

Net sales in first half of 1995 fell 6.7%, year to year, reflecting lower sales of the Dirt Devil Hand Vac and the Dirt Devil Broom Vac. A 5.5% increase in comparable second quarter net sales was due to unit sales growth of upright vacuum cleaners, particularly the Dirt Devil MVP. A lower loss from European operations, which accounted for about 25% of the total loss in the 1995 first half, was attributable to a reduction in advertising and promotional expenditures.

Stock Performance - 20-OCT-95

In the past 30 trading days, RAM's shares have declined 7%, compared to a 3% rise in the S&P 500. Average trading volume for the past five days was 22,480 shares, compared with the 40-day moving average of 40,308 shares.

Key Stock Statistics

Dividend Rate/Share	Nil	Shareholders	1,900
Shs. outstg. (M)	24.0	Market cap. (B)	$0.081
Avg. daily vol. (M)	0.023	Inst. holdings	15%
Tang. Bk. Value/Share	2.34	Insider holdings	NA
Beta	NA		

Value of $10,000 invested 5 years ago: NA

Fiscal Year Ending Dec. 31

	1995	% Change	1994	% Change	1993	% Change
Revenues (Million $)						
1Q	49.02	-18%	59.79	-15%	70.40	-9%
2Q	58.26	5%	55.24	4%	53.24	-31%
3Q	—	—	69.06	-24%	91.21	-8%
4Q	—	—	96.03	-3%	99.1	-30%
Yr.	—	—	280.1	-11%	313.9	-21%
Income (Million $)						
1Q	-2.45	NM	-2.58	NM	-6.78	NM
2Q	-1.89	NM	-1.32	NM	-9.62	NM
3Q	—	—	2.94	-10%	3.27	-32%
4Q	—	—	2.51	-48%	4.81	-51%
Yr.	—	—	1.56	NM	-8.32	NM
Earnings Per Share ($)						
1Q	-0.10	NM	-0.11	NM	-0.28	NM
2Q	-0.08	NM	-0.05	NM	-0.40	NM
3Q	—	—	0.12	-14%	0.14	-22%
4Q	—	—	0.10	-50%	0.20	-51%
Yr.	—	—	0.06	NM	-0.35	NM

Next earnings report expected: late October

Royal Appliance Mfg.

Business Summary - 23-OCT-95

Royal Appliance Mfg. develops, assembles and markets a full line of plastic and metal hand-held, upright and canister vacuum cleaners under the Dirt Devil and Royal brand names. Its Dirt Devil vacuum cleaners are intended for home use, while its metal (Royal) and certain enhanced versions of its Dirt Devil vacuum cleaners are intended for home and commercial use. Sales contributions by product line in recent years were:

	1994	1993	1992
Dirt Devil & related products	89%	88%	89%
Metal vacuum cleaners	4%	4%	4%
Accessories & other	7%	8%	7%

Royal's primary retail products are sold under the Dirt Devil name. The first product in this line, the Hand-Vac, a corded, hand-held vacuum cleaner, was introduced in 1984. The line has since been expanded to include the Broom-Vac, a lightweight upright vacuum cleaner; the Can-Vac, a lightweight canister vacuum cleaner; the Upright Deluxe, a full-size upright vacuum cleaner that includes a set of attachments; the Sweeper, a nonelectric carpet sweeper, and the CanVac Power Pak, which adds a power nozzle to the basic Can-Vac; the Upright Plus, an upright vacuum cleaner with a set of on-board attachments, and the lower-priced Upright; and the Upright Plus XF, an enhanced version of the Upright Plus, the Stick-Vac, a lightweight stick vacuum, and the Car Vac hand-held vacuum that plugs into a vehicle's 12 volt cigarette lighter. Subsequent introductions included the Cyclone deep cleaner, Wet-Dry vacs and Electric Leaf Blowers. The company recently reintroduced the Dirt Devil Upright Deluxe under the name Dirt Devil MVP, and will introduce the Dust Devil, a cordless rechargeable hand vacuum, and the Dirt Devil Impulse, a lightweight upright.

Dirt Devil products are marketed primarily through major retailers, including mass merchants, warehouse clubs, catalog showrooms and regional chains and department stores. Wal-Mart accounted for 23% of sales in 1994 (20% in 1993), while Kmart contributed 14% (17%). The company sells its metal vacuum cleaners exclusively through a network of independent dealers. Accessories, attachments and replacement parts for each of the product lines are sold through retailers and dealers, and are also available directly from Royal.

Important Developments

Aug. '95—Royal Appliance said that the decrease in net sales in the first half of 1995 was due primarily to decreased unit sales of the Dirt Devil Hand Vac and Dirt Devil Broom Vac.

Capitalization

Long Term Debt: $46,485,000 (6/95), incl. $7,358,000 of cap. lease obligs.

Per Share Data ($) (Year Ended Dec. 31)

	1994	1993	1992	1991	1990	1989
Tangible Bk. Val.	2.52	2.45	2.79	2.39	0.67	NA
Cash Flow	0.57	0.07	1.05	1.20	0.33	NA
Earnings	0.06	-0.35	0.81	1.09	0.27	NA
Dividends	Nil	Nil	Nil	Nil	NA	NA
Payout Ratio	Nil	Nil	Nil	Nil	NA	NA
Prices - High	6¼	14¼	31	23⅞	NA	NA
- Low	3¼	4½	7⅝	7¾	NA	NA
P/E Ratio - High	NM	NM	38	22	NA	NA
- Low	NM	NM	9	7	NA	NA

Income Statement Analysis (Million $)

	1994	%Chg	1993	%Chg	1992	%Chg	1991
Revs.	280	-11%	314	-21%	395	45%	273
Oper. Inc.	19.5	NM	4.1	-90%	42.3	-17%	51.2
Depr.	12.1	22%	9.9	62%	6.1	113%	2.9
Int. Exp.	4.5	-19%	5.6	70%	3.3	18%	2.8
Pretax Inc.	2.5	NM	-13.0	NM	33.0	-27%	45.4
Eff. Tax Rate	37%	—	NM	—	39%	—	40%
Net Inc.	1.6	NM	-8.3	NM	20.2	-26%	27.4

Balance Sheet & Other Fin. Data (Million $)

	1994	1993	1992	1991	1990	1989
Cash	Nil	Nil	Nil	Nil	1.3	0.0
Curr. Assets	86.0	93.0	134	94.3	54.2	24.7
Total Assets	142	154	188	121	62.0	30.0
Curr. Liab.	34.1	35.7	53.3	41.5	17.8	8.6
LT Debt	46.9	59.6	68.1	19.4	31.2	14.9
Common Eqty.	60.5	58.7	66.9	60.2	12.8	6.0
Total Cap.	107	118	135	79.6	43.9	20.9
Cap. Exp.	5.9	21.1	32.1	9.5	4.7	1.6
Cash Flow	13.6	1.6	26.3	30.2	8.3	2.9

Ratio Analysis

	1994	1993	1992	1991	1990	1989
Curr. Ratio	2.5	2.6	2.5	2.3	3.0	2.9
% LT Debt of Cap.	43.7	50.4	50.4	24.4	70.9	71.2
% Net Inc.of Revs.	0.6	NM	5.1	10.0	5.7	3.2
% Ret. on Assets	1.1	NM	13.3	29.9	14.9	7.3
% Ret. on Equity	2.6	NM	32.4	75.1	73.0	41.6

Dividend Data —Royal intends to retain earnings to finance the expansion of its business. The shares were split 2-for-1 in July 1992. A shareholder rights plan was adopted in October 1993.

Data as orig. reptd.; bef. results of disc. opers. and/or spec. items. Per share data adj. for stk. divs. as of ex-div. date. E-Estimated. NA-Not Available. NM-Not Meaningful. NR-Not Ranked.

Office—650 Alpha Drive, Cleveland, OH 44143. **Tel**—(216) 449-6150. **Chrmn & CEO**—J. A. Balch. **Pres, COO & Investor Contact**—M. J. Merriman. **Secy**—R. Vasek. **Treas**—P. LoPiccolo. **Dirs**—J. Kahl, Jr., M. J. Merriman, E. P. Nalley, J. B. Richey II, J. P. Rochon, R. L. Schneeberger. **Transfer Agent**—National City Bank, Cleveland. **Incorporated** in Ohio. **Empl**-685. **S&P Analyst:** Philip D. Wohl

Russ Berrie

NYSE Symbol **RUS**
In S&P SmallCap 600

03-NOV-95

Industry:
Retail merchandiser

Summary: This company designs, manufactures through third parties, and markets to retail stores throughout the U.S. and elsewhere a wide variety of impulse gift and toy items.

Quantitative Evaluations

Outlook
(1 Lowest—5 Highest)
• **NA**

Fair Value
• **NA**

Risk
• **Average**

Earn./Div. Rank
• **B**

Technical Eval.
• **Bearish** since 9/95

Rel. Strength Rank
(1 Lowest—99 Highest)
• **20**

Insider Activity
• **Neutral**

Recent Price • 14
52 Wk Range • 15⅞-12
Yield • 4.6%
12-Mo. P/E • 19.4

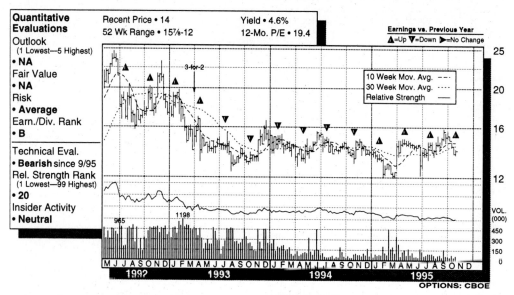

Earnings vs. Previous Year
▲=Up ▼=Down ▶=No Change

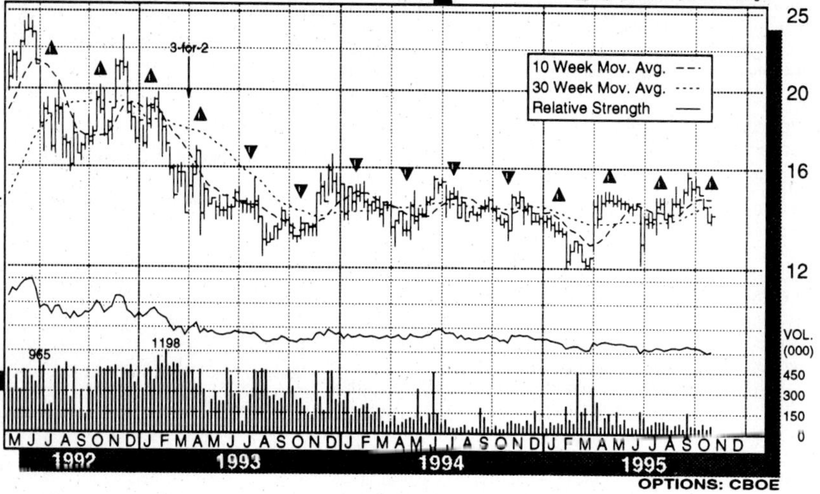

OPTIONS: CBOE

Business Profile - 03-NOV-95

Russ Berrie's two major business segments are impulse gift items and toys. The company's toy segment was formed through the acquisitions of Cap Toys, Inc. and OddzOn Products, Inc. in October 1993 and 1994, respectively. The toy segment's performance has recently helped earnings. RUS also operates two retail store chains that sell its own products and the products of other companies. In August 1995, the company signed a letter of intent to sell its Papel/Freelance gift and stationery subsidiary.

Operational Review - 03-NOV-95

Results improved through the first nine months of 1995, after plunging sales of Trolls products harmed profitability in 1994. Sales for 1995's first nine months rose 26%, year to year, reflecting the OddzOn acquisition and a strong performance in the core business. Margins widened, and net income soared to $13,497,000 ($0.63 a share) from $3,437,000 ($0.16). RUS's financial position is strong, with over $35 million in cash and no debt as of June 30, 1995.

Stock Performance - 27-OCT-95

In the past 30 trading days, RUS's shares have declined 10%, compared to a 0.63% fall in the S&P 500. Average trading volume for the past five days was 11,900 shares, compared with the 40-day moving average of 12,895 shares.

Key Stock Statistics

Dividend Rate/Share	0.60	Shareholders	800
Shs. outstg. (M)	21.5	Market cap. (B)	$0.283
Avg. daily vol. (M)	0.012	Inst. holdings	36%
Tang. Bk. Value/Share	8.48	Insider holdings	NA
Beta	0.53		

Value of $10,000 invested 5 years ago: $ 17,926

Fiscal Year Ending Dec. 31

	1995	% Change	1994	% Change	1993	% Change
Revenues (Million $)						
1Q	80.12	25%	64.17	-33%	96.30	NM
2Q	74.26	29%	57.55	15%	49.89	-42%
3Q	104.0	26%	82.85	17%	70.74	-53%
4Q	—	—	73.54	18%	62.18	-43%
Yr.	—	—	278.1	NM	279.1	-37%
Income (Million $)						
1Q	4.08	NM	1.02	-93%	13.63	6%
2Q	0.15	NM	-3.33	NM	-3.00	NM
3Q	9.26	61%	5.74	-9%	6.32	-78%
4Q	—	—	1.89	NM	-3.77	NM
Yr.	—	—	5.33	-60%	13.18	-78%
Earnings Per Share ($)						
1Q	0.19	NM	0.05	-92%	0.62	9%
2Q	0.01	NM	-0.16	NM	-0.14	NM
3Q	0.43	59%	0.27	-10%	0.30	-77%
4Q	—	—	0.09	NM	-0.18	NM
Yr.	—	—	0.25	-59%	0.61	-77%

Next earnings report expected: mid February

Russ Berrie

Business Summary - 02-NOV-95

Russ Berrie and Company, Inc. designs and markets a line of more than 10,000 impulse gift items in the U.S. and abroad. A diverse customer base includes more than 75,000 retail stores such as card and gift shops, florists, pharmacies, party shops and stationery stores, as well as hotel, airport and hospital gift shops. The company also sells toys through two recently acquired companies, Cap Toys, Inc., and OddzOn Products, Inc. Cap Toys and OddzOn were acquired in October 1993 and October 1994, respectively. Revenue breakdown by business segment in recent years was:

	1994	1993	1992
Gift	67%	95%	100%
Toys	33%	5%	-

Gift/Expression products include stuffed animals, picture frames, ceramic mugs, porcelain gifts, figurines, kitchen magnets, stationery products and National Football League and Major League Baseball merchandise. Sales of the Trolls product line accounted for 4% of total gift sales in 1994, down from 33% in 1993 and 56% in 1992. Most items are priced between $1 and $30.

The company's toy line includes a variety of innovative toys, novelty candies and sports-related products. Toy products include proprietary items such as Stretch Armstrong, Vac-Man, Kattie Kiss 'N' Giggles, Shout 'N' Shoot and Koosh Ball and related Koosh products. Toy products generally have suggested retail prices between $3 and $25. During 1994, sales of Stretch Armstrong and related products accounted for 31% of the company's total toy sales.

The Bright of America, Inc. subsidiary markets gift products directly to mass merchandisers. The company also operates a chain of retail stores under the name Russ and a chain of outlet stores, Fluf N' Stuf, Inc. The retail stores sell the company's products and products of unrelated companies.

In addition to its everyday product line, RUS produces specially designed products for individual seasons during the year, including Christmas, Graduation, Halloween and Thanksgiving. Such products accounted for 44% of total gift sales in 1994.

Important Developments

Aug. '95—The company signed a letter of intent to sell its Papel/Freelance subsidiary, which markets back-to-school, gift and stationery items, to Zebra Captial Corp. Papel/Freelance generated revenues in excess of $25 million in the past year.

Capitalization

Long Term Debt: None (6/95).

Per Share Data ($) (Year Ended Dec. 31)

	1994	1993	1992	1991	1990	1989
Tangible Bk. Val.	8.49	9.69	10.82	8.89	8.34	8.21
Cash Flow	0.58	0.91	2.99	1.27	1.06	0.76
Earnings	0.25	0.61	2.70	0.98	0.77	0.43
Dividends	0.60	0.60	0.47	0.40	0.70	0.27
Payout Ratio	NM	98%	17%	40%	91%	62%
Prices - High	15⅝	19⅞	24⅝	13⅛	12¼	14¼
- Low	12¾	12⅜	12	8¾	9¼	9½
P/E Ratio - High	62	33	9	13	16	33
- Low	51	20	4	9	12	22

Income Statement Analysis (Million $)

	1994	%Chg	1993	%Chg	1992	%Chg	1991
Revs.	278	NM	279	-37%	444	66%	268
Oper. Inc.	12.0	-54%	26.0	-75%	104	197%	35.0
Depr.	7.0	10%	6.4	-3%	6.6	NM	6.5
Int. Exp.	0.2	-61%	0.6	32%	0.5	-38%	0.8
Pretax Inc.	7.0	-60%	17.6	-81%	93.0	193%	31.7
Eff. Tax Rate	24%	—	25%	—	35%	—	31%
Net Inc.	5.3	-60%	13.2	-78%	60.3	174%	22.0

Balance Sheet & Other Fin. Data (Million $)

	1994	1993	1992	1991	1990	1989
Cash	48.0	82.9	92.7	51.4	38.5	78.3
Curr. Assets	189	213	264	194	178	192
Total Assets	255	259	299	226	216	217
Curr. Liab.	36.4	35.1	57.6	27.0	23.6	28.9
LT Debt	Nil	Nil	Nil	3.0	4.5	2.7
Common Eqty.	218	224	241	196	188	186
Total Cap.	218	224	241	199	193	188
Cap. Exp.	2.4	5.2	10.1	3.5	19.6	6.8
Cash Flow	12.4	19.5	66.9	28.6	23.9	17.2

Ratio Analysis

	1994	1993	1992	1991	1990	1989
Curr. Ratio	5.2	6.1	4.6	7.2	7.6	6.6
% LT Debt of Cap.	Nil	Nil	Nil	1.5	2.3	1.4
% Net Inc.of Revs.	1.9	4.7	13.6	8.2	7.0	4.0
% Ret. on Assets	2.1	4.8	22.9	10.1	8.0	4.6
% Ret. on Equity	2.4	5.8	27.5	11.6	9.3	5.3

Dividend Data —Dividends were initiated in 1986.

Amt. of Div. $	Date Decl.	Ex-Div. Date	Stock of Record	Payment Date
0.150	Oct. 25	Nov. 16	Nov. 22	Dec. 02 '94
0.150	Feb. 09	Feb. 27	Mar. 03	Mar. 17 '95
0.150	Apr. 25	May. 16	May. 22	Jun. 07 '95
0.150	Jul. 25	Aug. 11	Aug. 15	Sep. 05 '95
0.150	Oct. 26	Nov. 20	Nov. 22	Dec. 01 '95

Data as orig. reptd.; bef. results of disc. opers. and/or spec. items. Per share data adj. for stk. divs. as of ex-div. date. E-Estimated. NA-Not Available. NM-Not Meaningful. NR-Not Ranked.

Office—111 Bauer Drive, Oakland, NJ 07436. **Tel**—(201) 337-9000. **Chrmn & CEO**—R. Berrie. **Pres**—A. C. Cooke. **VP & Secy**—A. S. Bloom. **VP, CFO & Investor Contact**—Paul Cargotch. **Dirs**—R. Benaroya, R. Berrie, A. C. Cooke, J. Hsu, I. Kaufthal, C. Klatskin, J. Kling, W. Landman, S. Slauson, B. Tenenbaum. **Transfer Agent & Registrar**—Midlantic National Bank, Edison, N.J. **Incorporated** in New Jersey in 1966. **Empl**-1,850. **S&P Analyst:** Stephen Madonna, CFA

STANDARD & POOR'S

STOCK REPORTS

Rykoff-Sexton

NYSE Symbol **RYK**

In S&P SmallCap 600

15-NOV-95 **Industry:** Food

Summary: This company is a nationwide distributor and manufacturer of food and related products for U.S. foodservice markets.

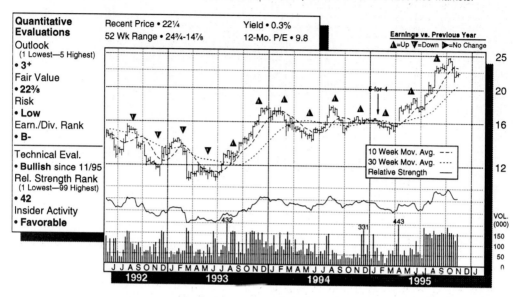

Quantitative Evaluations

Outlook (1 Lowest—5 Highest) • **3+**

Fair Value • **22⅜**

Risk • **Low**

Earn./Div. Rank • **B-**

Technical Eval. • **Bullish** since 11/95

Rel. Strength Rank (1 Lowest—99 Highest) • **42**

Insider Activity • **Favorable**

Recent Price • 22¼

52 Wk Range • 24¾-14⅞

Yield • 0.3%

12-Mo. P/E • 9.8

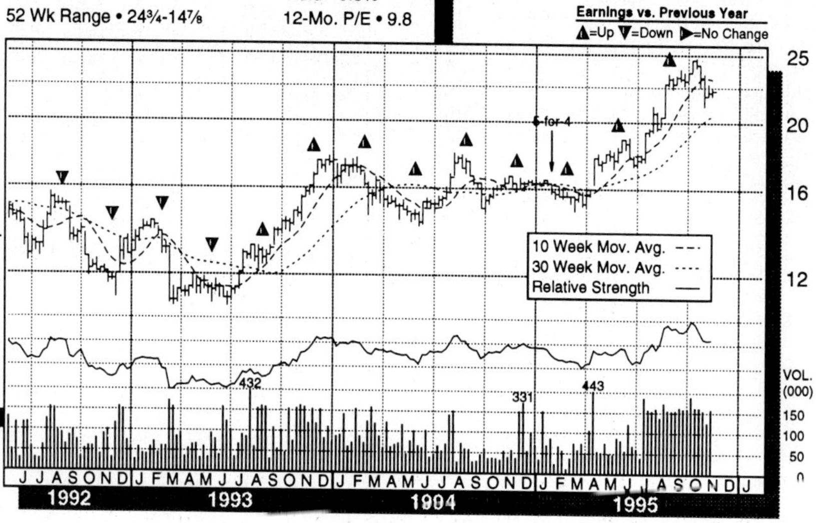

Business Profile - 15-NOV-95

RYK has stated a long-term objective of generating a 15% return on equity. Analysts project a five-year earnings growth rate of 13% and earnings per share of $1.01 in fiscal 1995-96. RYK effected a 5-for-4 stock split in January 1995, and reinstated a semiannual dividend at an annual rate of $0.06 a share, beginning with the February 1995 payment. The company recently completed the acquisition of H&O Foods, Inc. ($117 million in annual sales), a Las Vegas-based foodservice distributor.

Operational Review - 15-NOV-95

Net sales in the three months ended July 29, 1995, rose 11%, year to year, reflecting new sales and marketing strategies and product line introductions. Margins benefited from lower operating expenses and improved operating efficiencies. After taxes at 40.0%, versus 41.0%, net income increased 25%, to $2.6 million ($0.18 a share) from $2.1 million ($0.15, adjusted). Results exclude a loss from discontinued operations of $0.01 a share in the 1994-95 period.

Stock Performance - 10-NOV-95

In the past 30 trading days, RYK's shares have declined 6%, compared to a 1% rise in the S&P 500. Average trading volume for the past five days was 44,200 shares, compared with the 40-day moving average of 49,303 shares.

Key Stock Statistics

Dividend Rate/Share	0.06	Shareholders	8,300
Shs. outstg. (M)	14.7	Market cap. (B)	$0.322
Avg. daily vol. (M)	0.032	Inst. holdings	73%
Tang. Bk. Value/Share	12.23	Insider holdings	NA
Beta	0.68		

Value of $10,000 invested 5 years ago: $ 13,338

Fiscal Year Ending Apr. 30

	1996	% Change	1995	% Change	1994	% Change
Revenues (Million $)						
1Q	421.8	11%	380.4	4%	366.4	-2%
2Q	—	—	392.8	NM	390.8	NM
3Q	—	—	379.6	2%	372.8	4%
4Q	—	—	416.3	5%	394.7	9%
Yr.	—	—	1,569	3%	1,525	2%
Income (Million $)						
1Q	2.65	25%	2.12	86%	1.14	NM
2Q	—	—	3.99	6%	3.78	48%
3Q	—	—	0.90	150%	0.36	NM
4Q	—	—	2.37	14%	2.08	NM
Yr.	—	—	9.38	27%	7.36	NM
Earnings Per Share ($)						
1Q	0.18	20%	0.15	88%	0.08	NM
2Q	—	—	0.27	6%	0.26	45%
3Q	—	—	0.06	150%	0.02	NM
4Q	—	—	0.16	11%	0.14	NM
Yr.	—	—	0.64	28%	0.50	NM

Next earnings report expected: late November

Rykoff-Sexton

Business Summary - 15-NOV-95

Rykoff-Sexton is a leading distributor and manufacturer of processed foods and related non-food products to the foodservice industry throughout the U.S. Sales contributions by customer type in fiscal 1994-95:

	1994-95
Restaurants	61.1%
Hospitals, nursing homes & health care	12.7%
Schools & colleges	7.4%
Hotels & motels	8.2%
Distributors	1.5%
Retail	3.7%
Other	5.4%

With 25 distribution centers nationwide, RYK offers a single source of supply for about 41,000 products to some 100,000 foodservice establishments. Food products include a full line of the company's own private labels (56% of 1994-95 sales), as well as nationally branded domestic and imported items such as canned fruits and vegetables, tomatoes and tomato products, juices, relishes, pickles and condiments, dry package foods, syrups, mayonnaise, dressings and salad oils, baking supplies, seasonings and sauces, jellies, preserves, coffee, tea and fountain goods, prepared convenience entrees, meats, desserts, puddings, dietary foods, imported and domestic cheeses and specialty gourmet items. Frozen foods include soups, entrees, bakery products, and fruits and vegetables. Fresh meats, produce and other perishables were added in fiscal 1994-95. RYK purchases from approximately 7,500 suppliers.

Related non-food items include a broad line of janitorial supplies such as detergents and cleaning compounds, refuse container liners, cutlery, straws and sandwich bags; and paper products such as napkins, cups, hats, coasters, lace doilies and placemats. Restaurant supplies and equipment such as cookware, glassware and dinnerware, and other commercial kitchen equipment, are offered through the company's facilities.

Important Developments

Nov. '95—The company acquired H&O Foods, Inc., a privately-owned, Las Vegas-based foodservice distributor. Terms were not disclosed. H&O had nearly $117 million in sales in 1994.

Aug. '95—Rykoff-Sexton said first quarter profitability benefited from new sales and marketing strategies and operating efficiencies.

Feb. '95—The company acquired Continental Foods Inc., a privately owned, Baltimore-based foodservice distributor for $27 million plus the assumption of liabilities. Continental had approximately $100 million in sales in 1994. The transaction is part of Rykoff-Sexton's goal of becoming one of the top three distributors in each of its markets.

Capitalization

Long Term Debt: $188,546,000 (7/95).

Per Share Data ($)

(Year Ended Apr. 30)

	1995	1994	1993	1992	1991	1990
Tangible Bk. Val.	14.15	11.91	11.50	13.09	12.86	12.39
Cash Flow	1.78	2.13	0.02	2.49	2.48	2.26
Earnings	0.64	0.50	-1.35	0.87	0.95	0.77
Dividends	0.03	Nil	0.26	0.48	0.48	0.48
Payout Ratio	5%	Nil	NM	55%	50%	62%
Cal. Yrs.	1994	1993	1992	1991	1990	1989
Prices - High	18	17¾	16⅞	19¼	19¼	23⅝
- Low	14⅛	10¾	11⅛	12¼	11⅜	15⅞
P/E Ratio - High	28	35	NM	22	20	31
- Low	22	21	NM	14	12	21

Income Statement Analysis (Million $)

	1995	%Chg	1994	%Chg	1993	%Chg	1992
Revs.	1,569	3%	1,525	2%	1,488	-2%	1,519
Oper. Inc.	43.4	-12%	49.3	48%	33.2	-40%	55.6
Depr.	16.9	-29%	23.7	19%	20.0	-15%	23.5
Int. Exp.	13.8	-3%	14.2	6%	13.4	21%	11.1
Pretax Inc.	15.6	26%	12.4	NM	-31.3	NM	21.0
Eff. Tax Rate	40%	—	41%	—	NM	—	40%
Net Inc.	9.3	26%	7.4	NM	-19.7	NM	12.6

Balance Sheet & Other Fin. Data (Million $)

	1995	1994	1993	1992	1991	1990
Cash	4.9	9.3	7.6	14.7	9.7	12.8
Curr. Assets	319	305	281	305	282	280
Total Assets	524	487	461	483	405	407
Curr. Liab.	159	145	131	141	117	108
LT Debt	147	151	145	139	91.0	107
Common Eqty.	207	173	167	190	186	180
Total Cap.	364	332	316	341	289	298
Cap. Exp.	53.9	37.5	28.4	78.4	18.6	26.1
Cash Flow	26.2	31.0	0.4	36.1	36.0	33.3

Ratio Analysis

	1995	1994	1993	1992	1991	1990
Curr. Ratio	2.0	2.1	2.1	2.2	2.4	2.6
% LT Debt of Cap.	40.4	45.6	45.7	40.8	31.5	35.9
% Net Inc.of Revs.	0.6	0.5	NM	0.8	0.9	0.8
% Ret. on Assets	1.8	1.6	NM	2.8	3.4	2.8
% Ret. on Equity	4.9	4.3	NM	6.7	7.6	6.3

Dividend Data —Dividends were resumed with a $0.03 semiannual payment on February 16, 1995. Previously, quarterly dividends had been omitted in 1993 after having been paid since 1972. A dividend reinvestment plan is available. A "poison pill" stock purchase right was adopted in 1986.

Amt. of Div. $	Date Decl.	Ex-Div. Date	Stock of Record	Payment Date
5-for-4	Dec. 05	Jan. 25	Dec. 21	Jan. 24 '95
0.030	Dec. 05	Jan. 27	Feb. 02	Feb. 16 '95
0.030	Jun. 19	Jun. 28	Jun. 30	Jul. 18 '95

Data as orig. reptd.; bef. results of disc. opers. and/or spec. items. Per share data adj. for stk. divs. as of ex-div. date. E-Estimated. NA-Not Available. NM-Not Meaningful. NR-Not Ranked.

Office—1050 Warrenville Rd., Lisle, IL 60532. **Tel**—(708) 964-1414. **Pres & CEO**—M. Van Stekelenburg. **SVP-CFO & Investor Contact**—Richard J. Martin. **Secy**—N. I. Sell. **Dirs**—R. B. Gookin, J. W. Jeurgens, J. I. Maslon, J. P. Miscoll, N. I. Sell, M. Van Stekelenburg, B. Sweet, R. G. Zeller. **Transfer Agent & Registrar**—Chemical Trust Co. of California, NYC. **Incorporated** in Delaware in 1961. **Empl**-5,400. **S&P Analyst:** Efraim Levy

Ryland Group

NYSE Symbol **RYL**
In S&P SmallCap 600

31-OCT-95 **Industry:** Building

Summary: Ryland is one of the largest homebuilders in the U.S., operating in 19 states across the nation, and also has extensive mortgage lending operations.

S&P Opinion: Hold (★★★)

Recent Price • 14½
52 Wk Range • 17½-12⅞
Yield • 4.1%
12-Mo. P/E • 10.7

Quantitative Evaluations

Outlook
(1 Lowest—5 Highest)
• 2⁻

Fair Value
• 14¼

Risk
• **Average**

Earn./Div. Rank
• **B+**

Technical Eval.
• **Bearish** since 5/95

Rel. Strength Rank
(1 Lowest—99 Highest)
• **34**

Insider Activity
• **Neutral**

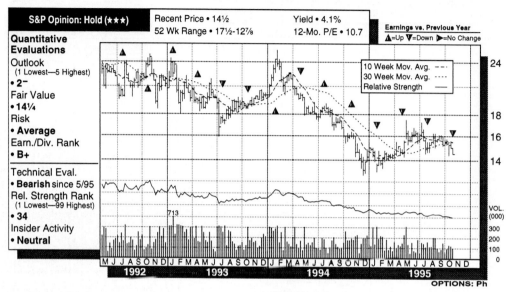

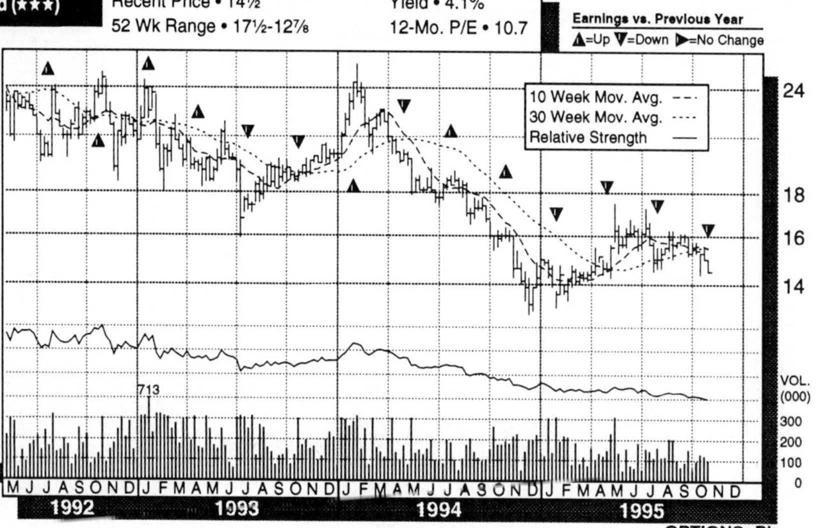

OPTIONS: Ph

Overview - 31-OCT-95

Revenues in 1996 should improve over the sluggish levels recorded to date in 1995, with gains anticipated in both operating segments. Homebuilding sales should begin to derive benefits from the declining mortgage rate environment, while the sector should also receive some assistance from repositioning efforts in the difficult mid-Atlantic market and entry into new markets. The more favorable domestic housing conditions should also benefit the financial services division, which is likely to experience a pick-up in mortgage originations. Margins should benefit from the better business conditions, the likely completion of efforts to close-out older communities in the mid-Atlantic (expected by 1995 year-end) and cost cutting measures. Those factors should outweigh the continued negative impact of the build-out of inventory in market weakened California.

Valuation - 31-OCT-95

Ryland's shares fell sharply during the tight credit period of 1994, and outside of a bounce after long-term interest rates fell sharply in the spring of 1995, have had a rather lackluster performance to date in 1995. Although we expect RYL's profits to improve considerably in 1996 from the very weak 1995 performance, earnings are still likely to remain at modest levels, as a result of Ryland's substantial presence in difficult mid-Atlantic markets and its continued need to build-out inventories in California. Given those factors, we believe that Ryland's shares are fairly valued.

Key Stock Statistics

S&P EPS Est. 1995	0.10	Tang. Bk. Value/Share	19.55
P/E on S&P Est. 1995	NM	Beta	1.45
S&P EPS Est. 1996	0.75	Shareholders	3,500
Dividend Rate/Share	0.60	Market cap. (B)	$0.228
Shs. outstg. (M)	15.6	Inst. holdings	79%
Avg. daily vol. (M)	0.022	Insider holdings	NA

Value of $10,000 invested 5 years ago: $ 9,384

Fiscal Year Ending Dec. 31

	1995	% Change	1994	% Change	1993	% Change
Revenues (Million $)						
1Q	345.2	4%	332.5	12%	297.0	2%
2Q	389.2	-7%	416.7	11%	375.4	3%
3Q	402.6	-10%	447.8	18%	378.8	-3%
4Q	—	—	445.7	4%	430.2	9%
Yr.	—	—	1,643	11%	1,474	2%
Income (Million $)						
1Q	-1.48	NM	4.16	-36%	6.55	151%
2Q	-0.92	NM	7.58	32%	5.74	-31%
3Q	0.68	-92%	8.39	NM	-22.56	NM
4Q	—	—	2.27	-70%	7.61	10%
Yr.	—	—	22.39	NM	-2.66	NM
Earnings Per Share ($)						
1Q	-0.13	NM	0.23	-39%	0.38	153%
2Q	-0.09	NM	0.45	36%	0.33	-31%
3Q	0.01	-98%	0.50	NM	-1.50	NM
4Q	E0.31	182%	0.11	-76%	0.45	13%
Yr.	E0.10	-92%	1.29	NM	-0.34	NM

Next earnings report expected: early February

Ryland Group

Business Summary - 31-OCT-95

The Ryland Group, the nation's third largest homebuilder, constructs single-family attached and detached housing and condominiums. It also markets mortgage-related products and services. Segment contributions in 1994 (profits in million $):

	Revenues	Profits
Homebuilding	88%	$10.9
Financial services	9%	43.5
Limited-purpose subsidiaries	3%	0.1

The homebuilding segment constructs homes in six regions containing the following metropolitan areas: Mid-Atlantic--Baltimore, Delaware Valley, Philadelphia, Washington D.C.; Midwest--Chicago, Cincinnati, Columbus, Indianapolis; Southeast--Atlanta, Charlotte, Columbia, Greenville, Orlando; Southwest--Austin, Dallas, Houston, San Antonio; West--Denver, Phoenix, Salt Lake City; and California-- Los Angeles, Sacramento, San Diego. RYL's homes vary in size and price range, but are generally marketed to customers purchasing their first home or first move-up home. In 1994, RYL's average settlement price was $160,000. Substantially all construction work is performed by subcontractors monitored by RYL supervisors.

Financial services activities include mortgage origination, loan servicing and title and escrow services. During 1994, RYL originated 16,740 mortgage loans (down from 27,872 in 1993) totaling $2.1 billion ($3.6 billion), of which 72% (80%) were for buyers of homes built by other companies or for refinancings. RYL services loans that it originates as well as loans originated by others.

Important Developments

Oct. '95—The company's sharp year-to-year earnings decline in the third quarter of 1995 reflected much lower profits in both the homebuilding and financial services segments. Homebuilding results were hurt by a reduced level of closings, along with the negative impact of efforts to sell older inventories in California and the mid-Atlantic; while weakness in financial services was related to lower activity in all areas. Ryland also experienced flat new home orders in the quarter, as weakness in the mid-Atlantic offset gains in all other geographic regions.

Jul. '95—RYL reported that during the second quarter of 1995, it completed the sale of its institutional financial services business to Norwest Bank Minnesota. A net gain of $19.5 million ($1.24 a share) was recorded on the sale of the discontinued operation.

Capitalization

Long Term Debt: $811,335,000 (9/95), incl. $381,682,000 subsid. debt not guaranteed by parent.
ESOP $2.2094 Conv. Preferred Stock: 964,920 shs., conv. sh.-for-sh. into com.

Per Share Data ($) (Year Ended Dec. 31)

	1994	1993	1992	1991	1990	1989
Tangible Bk. Val.	18.88	17.86	18.51	16.32	15.49	16.19
Cash Flow	2.93	1.36	3.71	2.17	3.13	4.45
Earnings	1.29	-0.34	1.66	0.53	1.53	3.25
Dividends	0.60	0.60	0.60	0.60	0.60	0.60
Payout Ratio	47%	NM	37%	111%	38%	17%
Prices - High	25⅝	24½	28	25¼	22	25¾
- Low	12⅞	15⅞	18½	13¾	9½	18¼
P/E Ratio - High	20	NM	17	48	14	8
- Low	10	NM	11	26	6	6

Income Statement Analysis (Million $)

	1994	%Chg	1993	%Chg	1992	%Chg	1991
Revs.	1,643	11%	1,474	2%	1,442	19%	1,214
Oper. Inc.	168	-9%	185	-44%	328	-7%	353
Depr.	25.6	-2%	26.1	-15%	30.6	49%	20.5
Int. Exp.	117	-30%	167	-33%	249	-18%	302
Pretax Inc.	37.3	NM	-4.7	NM	42.3	196%	14.3
Eff. Tax Rate	40%	—	NM	—	35%	—	34%
Net Inc.	22.4	NM	-2.7	NM	27.5	189%	9.5

Balance Sheet & Other Fin. Data (Million $)

	1994	1993	1992	1991	1990	1989
Cash	26.8	44.3	10.4	3.5	4.5	13.3
Curr. Assets	NA	NA	NA	NA	NA	NA
Total Assets	1,704	2,316	2,897	3,559	3,860	4,212
Curr. Liab.	NA	NA	NA	NA	NA	522
LT Debt	837	1,130	1,704	2,822	3,270	3,466
Common Eqty.	327	312	329	245	236	235
Total Cap.	1,150	1,423	2,010	3,041	3,486	3,690
Cap. Exp.	19.0	12.6	14.0	3.7	10.1	9.0
Cash Flow	45.6	20.8	55.5	27.2	38.9	59.0

Ratio Analysis

	1994	1993	1992	1991	1990	1989
Curr. Ratio	NA	NA	NA	NA	NA	NA
% LT Debt of Cap.	72.8	79.4	84.8	92.8	93.8	93.9
% Net Inc.of Revs.	1.4	NM	1.9	0.8	1.7	3.1
% Ret. on Assets	1.1	NM	0.8	0.3	0.5	1.1
% Ret. on Equity	6.2	NM	7.8	2.8	8.2	21.6

Dividend Data —Dividends were initiated in 1975. A "poison pill" stock purchase right was adopted in 1986.

Amt. of Div. $	Date Decl.	Ex-Div. Date	Stock of Record	Payment Date
0.150	Aug. 18	Oct. 07	Oct. 14	Oct. 28 '94
0.150	Dec. 21	Jan. 09	Jan. 13	Jan. 30 '95
0.150	Feb. 15	Apr. 07	Apr. 14	Apr. 28 '95
0.150	Jun. 15	Jul. 12	Jul. 14	Jul. 31 '95
0.150	Aug. 31	Oct. 11	Oct. 13	Oct. 30 '95

Data as orig. reptd.; bef. results of disc. opers. and/or spec. items. Per share data adj. for stk. divs. as of ex-div. date. E-Estimated. NA-Not Available. NM-Not Meaningful. NR-Not Ranked.

Office—11000 Broken Land Parkway, Columbia, MD 21044. **Tel**—(410) 715-7000. **Chrmn, Pres & CEO**—R. C. Dreier. **EVP-CFO**—M. D. Mangan. **EVP-Secy**—D. Lesser. **Investor Contact**—Lawrence P. Cates. **Dirs**—A. W. Brewster, R. C. Dreier, J. A. Flick, Jr., R. J. Gaw, L. M. Harlan, L. C. Heist, W. L. Jews, W. G. Kagler, J. H. Mullin III, J. O. Wilson. **Transfer Agent & Registrar**—Chemical Bank, NYC. **Incorporated** in Maryland in 1967. **Empl**-3,259. **S&P Analyst:** Michael W. Jaffe

SCI Systems

NASDAQ Symbol **SCIS**
In S&P SmallCap 600

18-SEP-95 **Industry:** Electronics/Electric

Summary: SCI, is one of the world's largest electronic contract manufacturers, with the greatest surface mount technology production capacity in the merchant market.

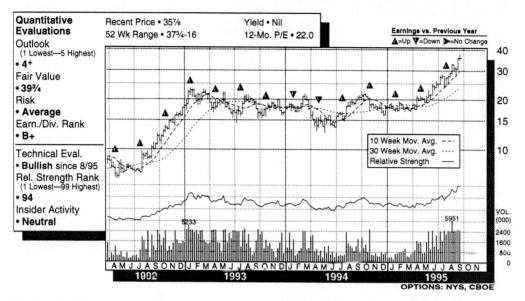

Quantitative Evaluations
Outlook
(1 Lowest—5 Highest)
• 4+
Fair Value
• 39¾
Risk
• Average
Earn./Div. Rank
• B+

Technical Eval.
• Bullish since 8/95
Rel. Strength Rank
(1 Lowest—99 Highest)
• 94
Insider Activity
• Neutral

Recent Price • 35⅞
52 Wk Range • 37¾-16
Yield • Nil
12-Mo. P/E • 22.0

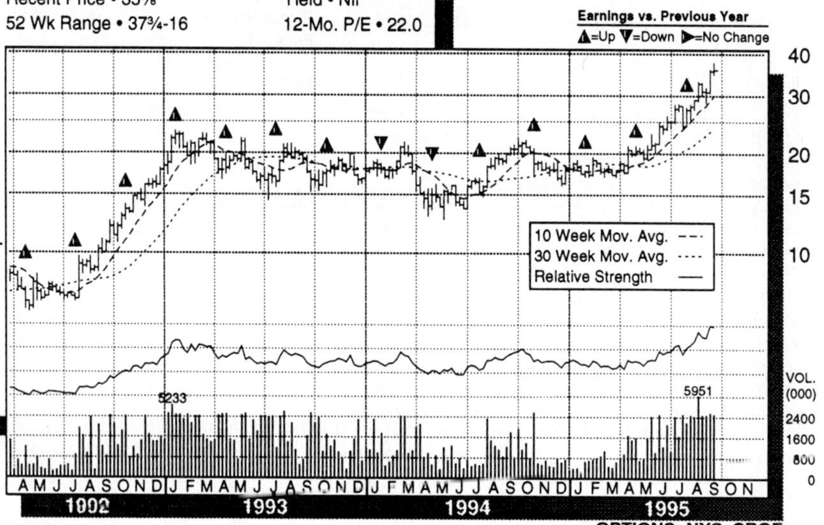

OPTIONS: NYS, CBOE

Business Profile - 18-SEP-95

This major electronics manufacturer designs, distributes, and services electronic products for the aerospace, computer, defense and other industries. In March 1994, it acquired Hewlett-Packard's Grenoble, France, surface mount center. Backlog at June 30, 1995, totaled $2.1 billion, up from $1.2 billion a year earlier. SCI has been adding to its work force, reflecting continued strong product demand.

Operational Review - 18-SEP-95

Higher revenues in fiscal 1995 reflected strong demand for the company's products. Margins widened, and EPS surged to $1.63, from $$.108. Future results should benefit from continuing industry trends toward the outsourcing of components and increased supplier participation in engineering and distribution.

Stock Performance - 15-SEP-95

In the past 30 trading days, SCIS's shares have increased 29%, compared to a 4% rise in the S&P 500. Average trading volume for the past five days was 701,840 shares, compared with the 40-day moving average of 707,038 shares.

Key Stock Statistics

Dividend Rate/Share	Nil	Shareholders	3,200
Shs. outstg. (M)	27.4	Market cap. (B)	$0.981
Avg. daily vol. (M)	0.756	Inst. holdings	60%
Tang. Bk. Value/Share	11.02	Insider holdings	NA
Beta	0.99		

Value of $10,000 invested 5 years ago: $ 41,594

Fiscal Year Ending Jun. 30

	1995	% Change	1994	% Change	1993	% Change
Revenues (Million $)						
1Q	618.4	47%	421.0	20%	350.0	46%
2Q	621.5	47%	422.9	-6%	451.0	104%
3Q	591.5	39%	424.1	-7%	455.6	75%
4Q	842.3	44%	584.5	32%	441.4	36%
Yr.	2,674	44%	1,852	9%	1,697	62%
Income (Million $)						
1Q	10.06	10%	9.17	—	—	—
2Q	10.20	11%	9.21	—	—	—
3Q	10.94	NM	0.48	—	—	—
4Q	14.05	27%	11.07	—	—	—
Yr.	45.20	51%	29.94	13%	26.60	NM
Earnings Per Share ($)						
1Q	0.36	9%	0.33	65%	0.20	150%
2Q	0.37	12%	0.33	-3%	0.34	NM
3Q	0.39	NM	0.02	-94%	0.34	NM
4Q	0.50	25%	0.40	29%	0.31	107%
Yr.	1.63	51%	1.08	NM	1.09	NM

Next earnings report expected: late October

SCI Systems

Business Summary - 18-SEP-95

SCI Systems, Inc. is an international provider of electronic products to the computer, aerospace, telecommunications, medical and banking industries, as well as the U.S. Government. The company operates through two divisions: Commercial and Government.

The Commercial division is the leading international supplier of full-service contract manufacturing for the electronics industry. A steady shift to outsourcing is continuing, as original equipment manufacturers (OEMs) seek solutions to the problems of rapid change in manufacturing technologies, new product proliferation, short product life cycles, intense cost pressures and heightened user reliability and quality expectations. SCI makes printed circuit boards using pin-in-hole (PIH) and surface mount technology (SMT). SMT is the production technique of growing preference, offering smaller size, lower cost and higher reliability. The company operates 112 automated SMT assembly lines in eight countries, making it one of the world's largest SMT producers and a leader in the merchant market.

The Government division provides a wide range of high-performance systems and subsystems for use by the U.S. and foreign governments and by the defense and aerospace industries. The division designs and manufactures electronic systems and subsystems for launch vehicle, satellite, aircraft and surface applications, with emphasis on the instrumentation, communication and computer disciplines. During 1994, production of mission critical voice and communication control systems continued in support of the F-15, F-16, F-18 and AV-8B aircraft, as well as the Digital Non-Secure Voice Terminal and the FAA Rapid Deployment Voice System. Contract manufacturing was expanded in fiscal 1994 by adding new programs in missile electronics and ruggedized electronics for a major transportation customer.

Hewlett-Packard and IBM accounted for 24% and 18% of fiscal 1994 net sales, respectively, while Conner Peripherals and Dell Computer accounted for 16% and 13%, respectively, in fiscal 1993. International sales totaled $697 million (38% of net sales) in fiscal 1994, down from $739 million (44%) in fiscal 1993.

Important Developments

Apr. '95—The company said it obtained a contract from NEC Technologies, Inc. to produce a family of computer products. The contract was valued at about $100 million. Separately, SCI purchased Digital Equipment Corp.'s contract manufacturing business, including international accounts and an Augusta, Me., manufacturing facility.

Capitalization

Long Term Debt: $194,315,000 (3/95).

Per Share Data ($) (Year Ended Jun. 30)

	1995	1994	1993	1992	1991	1990
Tangible Bk. Val.	NA	11.02	9.98	8.62	8.26	7.93
Cash Flow	NA	2.84	2.45	2.00	1.89	1.74
Earnings	1.63	1.08	1.09	0.18	0.16	0.11
Dividends	Nil	Nil	Nil	Nil	Nil	Nil
Payout Ratio	Nil	Nil	Nil	Nil	Nil	Nil
Prices - High	28⅜	22¼	23⅜	18½	10⅛	13⅛
- Low	17	12⅝	14⅜	6½	5⅞	5¼
P/E Ratio - High	17	21	21	NM	63	NM
- Low	10	12	13	NM	37	NM

Income Statement Analysis (Million $)

	1994	%Chg	1993	%Chg	1992	%Chg	1991
Revs.	1,852	9%	1,697	62%	1,045	-7%	1,129
Oper. Inc.	119	25%	95.0	82%	52.3	-26%	70.5
Depr.	48.6	19%	40.9	7%	38.2	6%	36.2
Int. Exp.	15.4	-8%	16.8	8%	15.5	-31%	22.4
Pretax Inc.	46.9	25%	37.4	NM	1.0	-58%	2.4
Eff. Tax Rate	36%	—	29%	—	NM	—	NM
Net Inc.	29.9	12%	26.6	NM	3.8	9%	3.5

Balance Sheet & Other Fin. Data (Million $)

	1994	1993	1992	1991	1990	1989
Cash	36.0	16.0	39.0	26.0	28.0	32.0
Curr. Assets	721	580	449	382	451	487
Total Assets	920	780	613	551	630	624
Curr. Liab.	326	244	194	128	135	171
LT Debt	278	249	219	234	318	278
Common Eqty.	305	278	192	186	176	170
Total Cap.	584	531	415	423	495	453
Cap. Exp.	46.5	84.1	29.8	30.3	62.7	50.7
Cash Flow	78.6	67.4	42.0	39.7	36.4	46.5

Ratio Analysis

	1994	1993	1992	1991	1990	1989
Curr. Ratio	2.2	2.4	2.3	3.0	3.3	2.8
% LT Debt of Cap.	47.7	46.9	52.8	55.2	64.3	61.5
% Net Inc.of Revs.	1.6	1.6	0.4	0.3	0.2	2.1
% Ret. on Assets	3.5	3.4	0.7	0.6	0.4	3.8
% Ret. on Equity	10.2	10.1	2.0	1.9	1.3	13.0

Dividend Data —A loan agreement limits cash payments. A three-for-two stock split was effected in 1987.

Data as orig. reptd.; bef. results of disc. opers. and/or spec. items. Per share data adj. for stk. divs. as of ex-div. date. E-Estimated. NA-Not Available. NM-Not Meaningful. NR-Not Ranked.

Office—2101 West Clinton Ave., Huntsville, AL 35805. **Tel**—(302) 998-0592. **Chrmn & CEO**—O. B. King. **Pres & COO**—A. E. Sapp Jr. **Secy**—M. M. Sullivan. **Dirs**—H. H. Callaway, W. E. Fruhan, Jr., O. B. King, J. C. Moquin, A. E. Sapp, Jr., W. Shortridge, G. R. Tod, J. M. Ward. **Transfer Agent & Registrar**—Mellon Bank, Pittsburgh. **Incorporated** in Delaware in 1961. **Empl**-12,027. **S&P Analyst:** Mike Cavanaugh

STANDARD & POOR'S

STOCK REPORTS

SEI Corp.

NASDAQ Symbol **SEIC**
In S&P SmallCap 600

05-SEP-95 **Industry:** Data Processing

Summary: SEI provides accounting and management information services to bank trust departments and investment performance services to investment managers.

Quantitative Evaluations

Outlook
(1 Lowest—5 Highest)
• **5-**

Fair Value
• **27⅜**

Risk
• **Average**

Earn./Div. Rank
• **B+**

Technical Eval.
• **Bearish** since 7/95

Rel. Strength Rank
(1 Lowest—99 Highest)
• **37**

Insider Activity
• **Neutral**

Recent Price • 21¾
52 Wk Range • 24½-16¾
Yield • 0.9%
12-Mo. P/E • 22.9

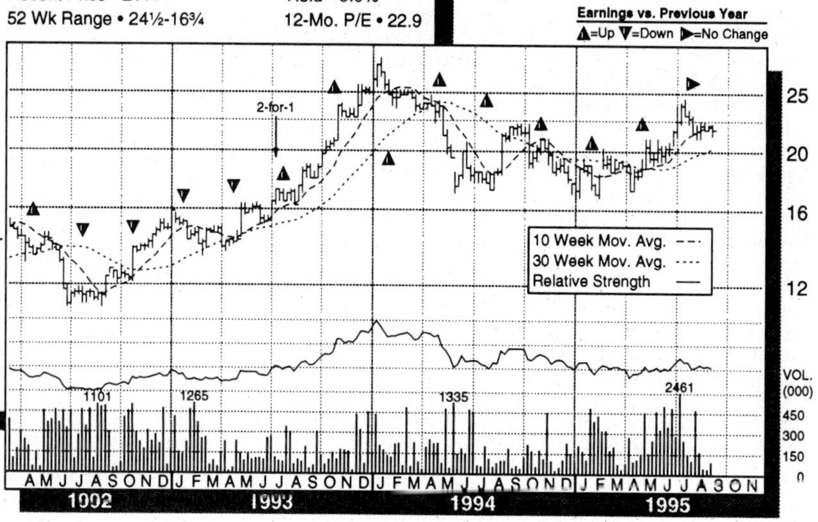

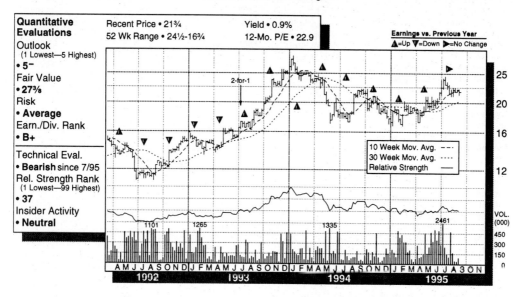

Business Profile - 05-SEP-95

With the recent announcement that it plans to divest itself of its investment consulting business, SEI will focus on providing trust and investment technology and asset management services. Continued growth in the mutual fund and trust sectors will aid future results. The company will also seek to grow through international expansion.

Operational Review - 05-SEP-95

Technology and service related revenues have improved in recent periods, aided by the company's broad product base. Sales growth is expected to continue for the remainder of 1995. Revenues from the investment management sector have remained relatively flat, due to run-off in de-emphasized products. This segment should begin to show improvement by the end of the year as a result of growth in SEI's asset management and cash management businesses.

Stock Performance - 01-SEP-95

In the past 30 trading days, SEIC's shares have declined 4%, compared to a 2% rise in the S&P 500. Average trading volume for the past five days was 17,940 shares, compared with the 40-day moving average of 37,560 shares.

Key Stock Statistics

Dividend Rate/Share	0.20	Shareholders	1,100
Shs. outstg. (M)	18.8	Market cap. (B)	$0.409
Avg. daily vol. (M)	0.016	Inst. holdings	64%
Tang. Bk. Value/Share	2.59	Insider holdings	NA
Beta	1.01		

Value of $10,000 invested 5 years ago: $ 25,332

Fiscal Year Ending Dec. 31

	1995	% Change	1994	% Change	1993	% Change
Revenues (Million $)						
1Q	64.73	2%	63.69	10%	57.74	12%
2Q	55.74	-14%	64.68	8%	59.65	17%
3Q	—	—	66.11	3%	64.04	25%
4Q	—	—	69.29	5%	65.74	20%
Yr.	—	—	263.8	7%	247.2	18%
Income (Million $)						
1Q	4.88	12%	4.37	40%	3.13	-25%
2Q	4.52	-2%	4.62	27%	3.65	9%
3Q	—	—	4.92	13%	4.35	157%
4Q	—	—	5.34	6%	5.02	139%
Yr.	—	—	19.25	19%	16.14	42%
Earnings Per Share ($)						
1Q	0.25	19%	0.21	40%	0.15	-21%
2Q	0.23	NM	0.23	28%	0.18	20%
3Q	—	—	0.25	19%	0.21	163%
4Q	—	—	0.27	12%	0.24	140%
Yr.	—	—	0.96	23%	0.78	50%

Next earnings report expected: early November

SEI Corp.

Business Summary - 05-SEP-95

SEI Corporation provides information, financial, evaluation and benefits services to the financial community. The company organizes its operations around the markets to which it delivers products and services: Trust and Banking (71% of 1994's total revenues) and Fund Sponsor/Investment Advisory (29%).

The company's Trust and Banking segment provides accounting and management information services primarily to bank trust departments with its 3000 product line. SEI's IBM-based 3000 systems automate a significant portion of a trust department's reporting and accounting functions, such as client administration, portfolio analysis, trade-order processing, performance measurement, and a centralized securities and financial information database. The company's market consists primarily of bank trust departments managing assets between $10 million and $100 billion. SEI estimates that there are approximately 1,500 trust departments of this size. As of December 31, 1994, it had under contract 221 trust departments in 46 states, the District of Columbia and Canada.

The investment products and services business offers a "family of funds," including equity, fixed income, and tax-exempt products. These products include several open-end investment companies: SEI Liquid Asset Trust, SEI Tax Exempt Trust, SEI Daily Income Trust, SEI Index Funds, SEI Institutional Managed Trust, and SEI International Trust. SEI traditionally provided administration and distribution services to banks that act as advisor for their own proprietary mutual funds. In 1994, SEI became the investment advisor for several portfolios. This change is consistant with the company's move toward becoming an asset management firm with in-house allocation and investment expertise.

SEI's Fund Sponsor/Investment Advisory segment provides performance services to sponsors of tax-exempt benefit plans and other institutional investors. To complement these services, SEI also offers investment solutions to its benefit plan and money manager clients that provide clients sophisticated investment vehicles and investment strategies.

The company's defined contribution benefits services business provides administrative & processing services and software systems for use by employee benefit, trust and human resource departments of corporations and banks.

Important Developments

May '95—SEI hired an investment firm to help it divest its U.S.-based pension and investment consulting business. Additionally, the company announced that it will outsource its defined contribution recordkeeping business.

Capitalization

Long Term Debt: None (6/95).

Per Share Data ($)

(Year Ended Dec. 31)

	1994	1993	1992	1991	1990	1989
Tangible Bk. Val.	2.34	2.21	1.97	1.75	1.79	0.97
Cash Flow	1.74	1.56	1.17	1.38	1.27	1.12
Earnings	0.96	0.78	0.52	0.70	0.54	0.53
Dividends	0.16	0.12	0.08	0.06	0.05	0.05
Payout Ratio	17%	14%	13%	8%	9%	8%
Prices - High	28½	27¼	16	13¾	11⅛	10
- Low	16¾	13⅜	11	8⅞	7¼	8
P/E Ratio - High	30	35	31	20	21	19
- Low	17	17	21	13	13	15

Income Statement Analysis (Million $)

	1994	%Chg	1993	%Chg	1992	%Chg	1991
Revs.	264	7%	247	18%	209	11%	188
Oper. Inc.	46.9	12%	41.9	31%	32.1	-22%	40.9
Depr.	15.7	-3%	16.2	NM	16.1	3%	15.7
Int. Exp.	Nil	—	Nil	—	Nil	—	Nil
Pretax Inc.	31.6	22%	26.0	42%	18.3	-30%	26.0
Eff. Tax Rate	39%	—	38%	—	38%	—	39%
Net Inc.	19.3	20%	16.1	42%	11.3	-29%	16.0

Balance Sheet & Other Fin. Data (Million $)

	1994	1993	1992	1991	1990	1989
Cash	20.2	17.9	17.5	13.7	19.4	2.1
Curr. Assets	59.1	55.7	43.6	37.3	39.4	22.9
Total Assets	102	100	86.0	83.0	84.0	76.0
Curr. Liab.	49.7	45.0	33.4	32.2	26.1	27.7
LT Debt	Nil	Nil	Nil	Nil	Nil	4.1
Common Eqty.	51.3	51.5	49.4	47.9	53.1	36.5
Total Cap.	52.7	55.4	52.6	50.6	57.9	47.3
Cap. Exp.	15.5	16.9	18.0	18.7	8.9	7.3
Cash Flow	34.9	32.3	25.6	31.7	28.4	25.7

Ratio Analysis

	1994	1993	1992	1991	1990	1989
Curr. Ratio	1.2	1.2	1.3	1.2	1.5	0.8
% LT Debt of Cap.	Nil	Nil	Nil	Nil	Nil	8.6
% Net Inc.of Revs.	7.3	6.5	5.4	8.5	7.0	8.1
% Ret. on Assets	19.2	17.5	13.6	19.6	14.8	16.9
% Ret. on Equity	37.8	32.4	23.6	32.6	26.4	30.5

Dividend Data —Semiannual cash distributions were initiated with the July 1988 payment. In July 1993, a two-for-one stock split was effected.

Amt. of Div. $	Date Decl.	Ex-Div. Date	Stock of Record	Payment Date
0.080	Dec. 15	Dec. 19	Dec. 23	Jan. 19 '95
0.100	May. 18	Jun. 02	Jun. 08	Jun. 29 '95

Data as orig. reptd.; bef. results of disc. opers. and/or spec. items. Per share data adj. for stk. divs. as of ex-div. date. E-Estimated. NA-Not Available. NM-Not Meaningful. NR-Not Ranked.

Office—680 E. Swedesford Rd., Wayne, PA 19087. **Tel**—(610) 254-1000. **Chrmn & CEO**—A. P. West Jr. **Pres & COO**—H. H. Greer. **EVP, CFO & Treas**—C. V. Romeo. **Secy**—W. M. Doran. **Dirs**—D. C. Carroll, W. M. Doran, H. H. Greer, R. B. Lieb, H. H. Porter Jr., C. V. Romeo, A. P. West Jr. **Transfer Agent & Registrar**—American Stock Transfer & Trust Co., NYC. **Incorporated** in Pennsylvania in 1968. **Empl**-1,277. **S&P Analyst:** SAJ

SPS Technologies

NYSE Symbol **ST**
In S&P SmallCap 600

07-SEP-95 **Industry:** Machinery

Summary: This company manufactures high-strength fastening and assembly systems, superalloys in ingot form, and magnetic materials.

Quantitative Evaluations
Outlook (1 Lowest—5 Highest)
• **NA**
Fair Value
• **NA**
Risk
• **Low**
Earn./Div. Rank
• **C**

Technical Eval.
• **Bullish** since 12/93
Rel. Strength Rank (1 Lowest—99 Highest)
• **33**
Insider Activity
• **Favorable**

Recent Price • 38⅝
52 Wk Range • 41-22
Yield • Nil
12-Mo. P/E • 20.2

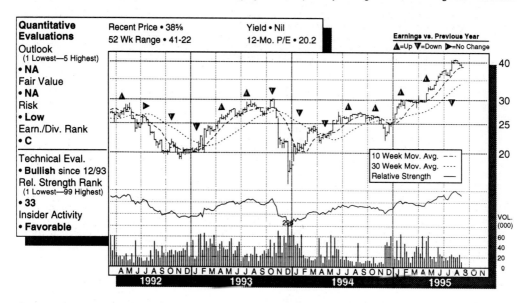

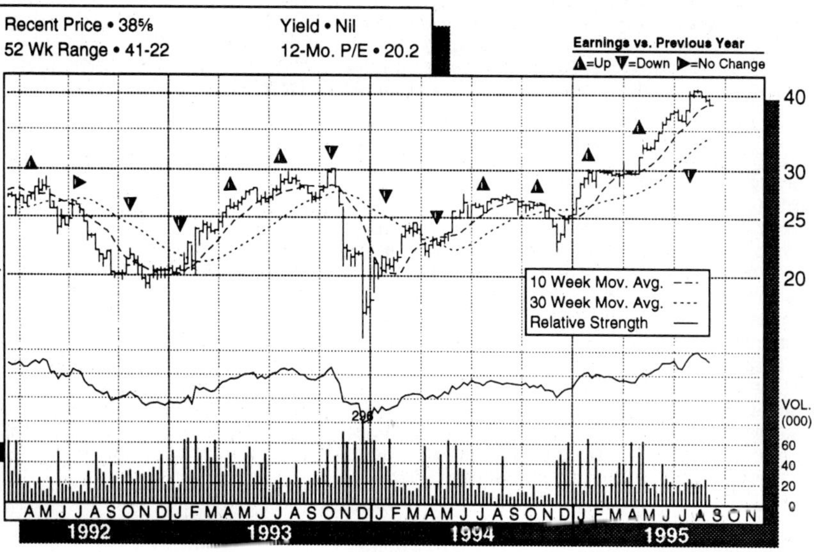

Business Profile - 06-SEP-95

SPS Technologies is engaged in the design, manufacture and marketing of fasteners and superalloys. In 1994, the company completed programs that reduced its cost structure and improved its operating performance. SPS completed a 10% reduction in its non-direct workforce, which included significant reductions in corporate and executive staff. The company also relocated its corporate offices to a smaller leased facility, sold its corporate headquarters and exited unprofitable lines of business.

Operational Review - 06-SEP-95

Sales for the six months ended June 30, 1995, rose 20%, year to year. Gross margins widened on the increased volume, and SG&A expenses were well controlled. In the absence of a $6.6 million unusual charge, pretax income rose 12-fold. After taxes at 31.3%, versus taxes of $1,250,000, net income of $6,975,000 ($1.20 a share based on 13% more shares) contrasted with a net loss of $440,000 ($0.09).

Stock Performance - 01-SEP-95

In the past 30 trading days, ST's shares have increased 2%, compared to a 2% rise in the S&P 500. Average trading volume for the past five days was 2,100 shares, compared with the 40-day moving average of 3,908 shares.

Key Stock Statistics

Dividend Rate/Share	Nil	Shareholders	1,700
Shs. outstg. (M)	5.7	Market cap. (B)	$0.217
Avg. daily vol. (M)	0.004	Inst. holdings	54%
Tang. Bk. Value/Share	23.51	Insider holdings	NA
Beta	1.56		

Value of $10,000 invested 5 years ago: $ 11,596

Fiscal Year Ending Dec. 31

	1995	% Change	1994	% Change	1993	% Change
Revenues (Million $)						
1Q	102.4	26%	81.58	-7%	87.28	4%
2Q	100.6	14%	87.87	3%	85.45	NM
3Q	—	—	88.47	19%	74.39	-3%
4Q	—	—	90.99	26%	71.96	-4%
Yr.	—	—	348.9	9%	319.1	NM
Income (Million $)						
1Q	3.05	NM	-4.14	NM	1.63	4%
2Q	3.93	6%	3.70	168%	1.38	3%
3Q	—	—	1.99	NM	-6.84	NM
4Q	—	—	1.65	NM	-27.16	NM
Yr.	—	—	3.20	NM	-31.00	NM
Earnings Per Share ($)						
1Q	0.54	NM	-0.81	NM	0.32	3%
2Q	0.67	-7%	0.72	167%	0.27	4%
3Q	—	—	0.39	NM	-1.34	NM
4Q	—	—	0.32	NM	-5.32	NM
Yr.	—	—	0.62	NM	-6.07	NM

Next earnings report expected: late October

SPS Technologies

Business Summary - 06-SEP-95

SPS Technologies is a multinational manufacturer of high-strength, precision mechanical fasteners, precision components, fastening systems and assembly systems (fasteners); and superalloys in ingot form and magnetic materials (materials). Business segment contributions (operating profits in million $) in 1994:

	Sales	Profits
Fasteners	69%	-$2.7
Materials	31%	10.7

Foreign business accounted for 26% of sales in 1994.

Principal fastener markets include aerospace, machine tool and industrial machinery and automotive and off-highway equipment. Principal markets for materials include the precision investment casting and powdered metal industries, and the aerospace, medical equipment, automotive, computer and communication industries.

Fastener products include SPS aerospace, Multiphase alloy fasteners; Unbrako socket screws, hex keys, dowel pins, shaft collars, spring pins and pressure plugs; engineered fasteners for gasoline and diesel engines, other critical automotive applications and off-highway equipment; Hi-Life thread roll dies and other metal-working tools; and SPS Joint Control System computer-controlled tightening equipment and systems.

Materials products include air and vacuum-melted iron, cobalt and nickel-based superalloys; and metallic and ceramic permanent magnets, wound and pressed powder magnetic components and ultra-thin foil and strip products.

The company sells directly to original equipment manufacturers and industrial, commercial and governmental users, and also sells through independent stocking distributors and dealers.

Important Developments

Aug. '95—SPS raised its interest in Metalec SA Industria e Comercio, of San Paolo, Brazil, to 95%. Metalec is a manufacturer and distributor of industrial and automotive fasteners in Brazil.

Jul. '95—The company acquired Unbrako K.K., a distributor of Unbrako and SPS aerospace products in the Japanese market.

Nov. '94—SPS Technologies distributed to its shareholders of record November 28, 1994, transferable rights to subscribe for the purchase of approximately 515,000 common shares currently held in the company's treasury at a subscription price of $24.50 a share. Shareholders received one right to subscribe for the purchase of one share of common stock for each 10 shares held.

Capitalization

Long Term Debt: $68,233,000 (6/95).

Per Share Data ($) (Year Ended Dec. 31)

	1994	1993	1992	1991	1990	1989
Tangible Bk. Val.	20.33	17.67	27.42	35.27	35.62	34.70
Cash Flow	3.17	-3.40	0.99	3.68	0.75	5.43
Earnings	0.62	-6.07	-1.37	1.10	-1.98	3.21
Dividends	Nil	0.96	1.28	1.28	1.28	1.22
Payout Ratio	Nil	NM	NM	116%	NM	38%
Prices - High	27⅞	30⅛	29½	37	44	60⅛
- Low	18¾	15¾	19	20⅝	20½	41
P/E Ratio - High	44	NM	NM	34	NM	19
- Low	30	NM	NM	19	NM	13

Income Statement Analysis (Million $)

	1994	%Chg	1993	%Chg	1992	%Chg	1991
Revs.	349	9%	319	NM	321	-14%	374
Oper. Inc.	24.5	44%	17.0	-7%	18.3	-42%	31.5
Depr.	13.1	-4%	13.6	12%	12.1	-8%	13.1
Int. Exp.	6.9	17%	5.9	9%	5.4	-30%	7.7
Pretax Inc.	6.1	NM	-33.6	NM	-8.3	NM	10.7
Eff. Tax Rate	48%	—	NM	—	NM	—	48%
Net Inc.	3.2	NM	-31.0	NM	-7.0	NM	5.6

Balance Sheet & Other Fin. Data (Million $)

	1994	1993	1992	1991	1990	1989
Cash	9.5	6.8	2.9	3.8	5.2	6.8
Curr. Assets	160	161	152	157	218	195
Total Assets	289	286	290	311	369	324
Curr. Liab.	71.9	66.5	59.9	60.1	86.8	68.4
LT Debt	56.4	81.8	63.1	60.6	91.3	74.9
Common Eqty.	124	103	143	179	180	174
Total Cap.	191	194	215	251	282	256
Cap. Exp.	17.6	12.2	14.5	11.1	24.2	18.9
Cash Flow	16.3	-17.4	5.0	18.7	3.7	27.2

Ratio Analysis

	1994	1993	1992	1991	1990	1989
Curr. Ratio	2.2	2.4	2.5	2.6	2.5	2.9
% LT Debt of Cap.	29.5	42.2	29.4	24.2	32.4	29.3
% Net Inc.of Revs.	0.9	NM	NM	1.5	NM	3.8
% Ret. on Assets	1.1	NM	NM	1.6	NM	4.9
% Ret. on Equity	2.7	NM	NM	3.1	NM	9.3

Dividend Data —Dividends were omitted in December 1993 after having been paid since 1972. The most recent payment was $0.32 a share in October 1993. A "poison pill" stock purchase right was adopted in 1988.

Data as orig. reptd.; bef. results of disc. opers. and/or spec. items. Per share data adj. for stk. divs. as of ex-div. date. E-Estimated. NA-Not Available. NM-Not Meaningful. NR-Not Ranked.

Office—101 Greenwood Avenue, Suite 470, Jenkintown PA 19046. **Tel**—(215) 517-2000. **Chrmn & CEO**—C. W. Grigg. **Pres & COO**—H. J. Wilkinson. **VP-CFO**—W. M. Shockley. **VP-Secy**—A. Nerenberg. **Treas**—J. M. Morrash. **Investor Contact**—Peter Lawton (215-860-3038). **Dirs**—C. W. Grigg, H. T. Hallowell III, J. F. Lubin, P. F. Miller Jr., E. M. Ruttenberg, R. P. Sharp, H. J. Wilkinson. **Transfer Agent & Registrar**—Mellon Bank, N.A., Pittsburgh. **Incorporated** in Pennsylvania in 1903. **Empl**-3,573. **S&P Analyst:** K.J.G.

SPX Corp.

NYSE Symbol **SPW**
In S&P SmallCap 600

09-AUG-95 **Industry:** Auto parts/equipment

Summary: This leading manufacturer of automotive specialty service tools and equipment and original equipment components also owns 70% of Sealed Power Technologies L.P. Europe.

S&P Opinion: Avoid (★★)

Recent Price • 14⅜
52 Wk Range • 18½-10¾
Yield • 2.7%
12-Mo. P/E • 23.2

Quantitative Evaluations
Outlook (1 Lowest—5 Highest) • **3⁻**
Fair Value • **14⅛**
Risk • **Low**
Earn./Div. Rank • **B-**

Technical Eval. • **Bullish** since 5/95
Rel. Strength Rank (1 Lowest—99 Highest) • **78**
Insider Activity • **Favorable**

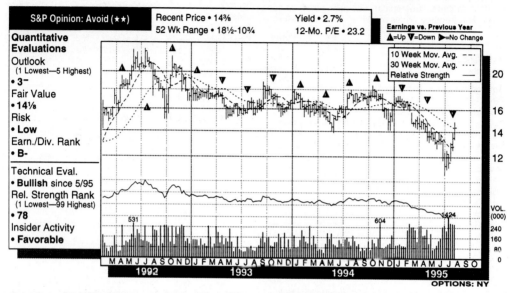

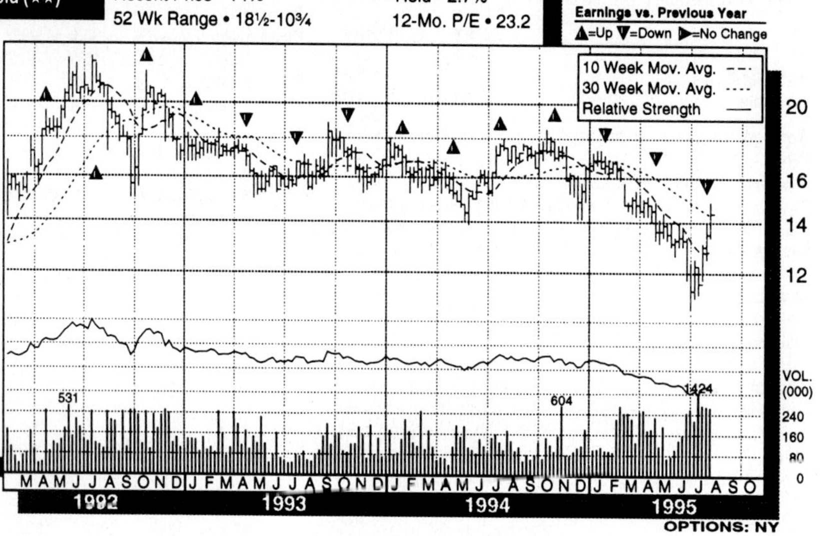

Overview - 09-AUG-95

Sales of original equipment motor vehicle components could decline in 1996 as vehicle assemblies in North America may peak in 1995. Refrigerant recycling system sales should begin to improve, as independent repair shops upgrade their equipment, and demand for specialty repair tools should grow, spurred by the need for increasingly sophisticated equipment. A partial offset will be a trend to commonization of parts across vehicle models, particularly at General Motors. The long-term outlook is enhanced by mandates for more stringent vehicle emissions inspections, which should boost demand for emissions test and diagnostic equipment. However, delays in the start of such programs have shut down sales in 1995 and only a gradual ramp-up is expected beginning in 1996.

Valuation - 09-AUG-95

We rank the shares avoid due to the weak earnings outlook for 1995 following delayed implementation of a new generation of emissions inspection programs. The delay has frozen sales of emissions test equipment to repair shops. The company must also deal with its aggressive capital structure, which looks increasingly risky in light of a maturing economic cycle and the sales delay. The expected sale of SPX Credit Corp. should lighten the company's debt load, but restructuring charges are likely as SPW finally moves to eliminate redundant costs due to operation of separate administrative and engineering functions for each of its specialty service tools brandnames.

Key Stock Statistics

S&P EPS Est. 1995	0.85	Tang. Bk. Value/Share	NM
P/E on S&P Est. 1995	16.9	Beta	1.15
S&P EPS Est. 1996	1.00	Shareholders	7,900
Dividend Rate/Share	0.40	Market cap. (B)	$0.188
Shs. outstg. (M)	12.8	Inst. holdings	66%
Avg. daily vol. (M)	0.164	Insider holdings	NA

Value of $10,000 invested 5 years ago: $ 6,145

Fiscal Year Ending Dec. 31

	1995	% Change	1994	% Change	1993	% Change
Revenues (Million $)						
1Q	278.8	NM	277.5	55%	178.7	2%
2Q	293.4	1%	289.0	37%	210.8	-3%
3Q	—	—	253.0	32%	191.8	-19%
4Q	—	—	273.3	61%	169.4	NM
Yr.	—	—	1,093	45%	756.2	-6%
Income (Million $)						
1Q	0.25	-92%	3.10	NM	0.80	-60%
2Q	3.57	-48%	6.90	30%	5.30	-35%
3Q	—	—	3.20	NM	-19.60	NM
4Q	—	—	0.90	NM	-29.67	NM
Yr.	—	—	14.10	-7%	15.20	-31%
Earnings Per Share ($)						
1Q	0.02	-92%	0.24	NM	0.06	-57%
2Q	0.28	-48%	0.54	42%	0.38	-36%
3Q	E0.30	—	0.25	NM	-1.41	NM
4Q	E0.25	—	0.07	-97%	2.34	NM
Yr.	E0.85	—	1.10	-8%	1.20	-25%

Next earnings report expected: mid October

SPX Corp.

Business Summary - 09-AUG-95

Following a 1993 realignment, SPX Corp. produces specialty service tools and original equipment vehicle components (OEC). Sales as reported in recent years were divided:

	1994	1993
Specialty service tools	50%	66.6%
Original equipment components	48%	3.5%
SPX Credit Corp.	2%	1.2%
Businesses sold in 1993	Nil	28.7%

Specialty service tools and diagnostic products are sold under brand names such as Kent-Moore, OTC, Bear Automotive, Allen Testproducts, Robinair, Power Team and V.L. Churchill. Products include handtools, gauges, battery testers and air-conditioning refrigerant and anti-freeze recycling systems. Automotive Diagnostics was formed in 1993 to combine newly acquired Allen Testproducts with SPW's Bear Automotive. The unit produces engine diagnostic and emissions test equipment. SPX Credit Corp. (acquired with Allen) was designated for divestiture in April 1995.

OEC was formed after the reacquisition (on December 31, 1993) of a 51% interest in Sealed Power Technologies L.P. (SPT). SPT was formed in 1989 when SPW sold a 51% interest in four businesses. OEC includes proprietary solenoid valves that interface between vehicle electronic and hydraulic systems, die castings, transmission filters, tappets, lash adjusters and roller rocker arms. Sealed Power is a world leader in piston rings and cylinder liners.

In 1993, SPW sold Truth, a window and door hardware maker, and Sealed Power Replacement, a distributor of aftermarket parts.

Important Developments

Jul. '95—SPW said delays by states in implementing federally mandated emissions testing programs had resulted in little or no sales of a new generation of emissions test equipment in the 1995 first half. Commencement of sales is contingent upon states receiving approval from the EPA of modified proposals. SPW believes that the modified approach will result in a greater level of sales but timing is uncertain. The EPA had originally advised states that they must adopt centralized vehicle test programs as mandated by the Clean Air Act of 1990. Tests were to begin in 27 states and the District of Columbia in 1995 and 1996, and would have required the use of centralized testing stations. The EPA is now permitting hybrid alternatives that combine initial centralized testing with decentralized repair and certification by independent shops.

Capitalization

Long Term Debt: $417,229,000 (6/95).

Per Share Data ($) (Year Ended Dec. 31)

	1994	1993	1992	1991	1990	1989
Tangible Bk. Val.	-2.65	-4.14	7.24	6.57	8.70	7.71
Cash Flow	4.11	2.99	3.26	0.32	2.65	2.98
Earnings	1.10	1.20	1.59	-1.40	1.28	1.66
Dividends	0.40	0.40	0.40	0.70	1.00	14.10
Payout Ratio	36%	41%	25%	NM	78%	849%
Prices - High	18½	18⅞	23	16¾	30½	42
- Low	13⅞	15	12⅛	10⅞	12⅝	25
P/E Ratio - High	17	16	14	NM	24	25
- Low	13	12	8	NM	10	15

Income Statement Analysis (Million $)

	1994	%Chg	1993	%Chg	1992	%Chg	1991
Revs.	1,093	45%	756	-6%	801	19%	673
Oper. Inc.	98.0	56%	63.0	-22%	81.0	93%	42.0
Depr.	38.5	71%	22.5	-2%	23.0	-3%	23.8
Int. Exp.	40.9	111%	19.4	28%	15.1	-11%	16.9
Pretax Inc.	21.7	-51%	44.7	23%	36.4	NM	-25.2
Eff. Tax Rate	45%	—	66%	—	39%	—	NM
Net Inc.	14.1	-7%	15.2	-31%	22.1	NM	-19.4

Balance Sheet & Other Fin. Data (Million $)

	1994	1993	1992	1991	1990	1989
Cash	10.0	118	0.7	11.1	12.5	22.1
Curr. Assets	406	518	308	331	377	340
Total Assets	932	1,024	560	579	624	575
Curr. Liab.	222	399	126	123	117	154
LT Debt	414	336	160	200	226	153
Common Eqty.	162	146	196	189	216	205
Total Cap.	589	502	416	457	508	420
Cap. Exp.	48.5	15.1	20.4	19.4	26.7	41.0
Cash Flow	52.6	37.7	45.1	4.4	36.6	42.5

Ratio Analysis

	1994	1993	1992	1991	1990	1989
Curr. Ratio	1.8	1.3	2.5	2.7	3.2	2.2
% LT Debt of Cap.	70.3	66.9	38.5	43.8	44.6	36.3
% Net Inc.of Revs.	1.3	2.0	2.8	NM	2.5	3.7
% Ret. on Assets	1.4	1.9	3.9	NM	2.9	3.5
% Ret. on Equity	9.1	8.9	11.5	NM	8.4	8.4

Dividend Data (Dividends have been paid since 1939. A dividend reinvestment plan is available.)

Amt. of Div. $	Date Decl.	Ex-Div. Date	Stock of Record	Payment Date
0.100	Oct. 28	Nov. 14	Nov. 18	Dec. 09 '94
0.100	Dec. 14	Feb. 13	Feb. 17	Mar. 10 '95
0.100	Apr. 26	May. 15	May. 19	Jun. 09 '95
0.100	Jun. 28	Aug. 16	Aug. 18	Sep. 08 '95

Data as orig. reptd.; bef. results of disc. opers. and/or spec. items. Per share data adj. for stk. divs. as of ex-div. date. E-Estimated. NA-Not Available. NM-Not Meaningful. NR-Not Ranked.

Office—700 Terrace Point Drive, Muskegon, MI 49443. **Tel**—(616) 724-5000. **Acting Chrmn & CEO**—C. E. Johnson II. **Pres & COO**—C. T. Atkisson, Jr. **SVP & CFO**—W. L. Trubeck. **VP & Secy**—J. M. Sheridan. **Investor Contact**—John D. Tyson. **Dirs**—C. T. Atkisson, Jr., J. K. Campbell, S. R. Coffin, F. A. Ehmann, E. D. Hopkins, C. E. Johnson II, R. L. Kerber, P. H. Merlin, D. P. Williams. **Transfer Agent & Registrar**—Bank of New York, NYC. **Incorporated** in Michigan in 1912; reincorporated in Delaware in 1968. **Empl**-8,500. **S&P Analyst:** Joshua M. Harari, CFA

STANDARD & POOR'S

STOCK REPORTS

S3 Incorporated

NASDAQ Symbol **SIII**
In S&P SmallCap 600

28-AUG-95 **Industry:** Data Processing

Summary: S3 supplies high-performance accelerator solutions for the graphical user interface environments created by Microsoft Windows, IBM OS/2 and other advanced PC operating systems.

Quantitative Evaluations

Outlook
(1 Lowest—5 Highest)
• **NA**
Fair Value
• **NA**
Risk
• **High**
Earn./Div. Rank
• **NR**

Technical Eval.
• **Bullish** since 2/95
Rel. Strength Rank
(1 Lowest—99 Highest)
• **78**
Insider Activity
• **Neutral**

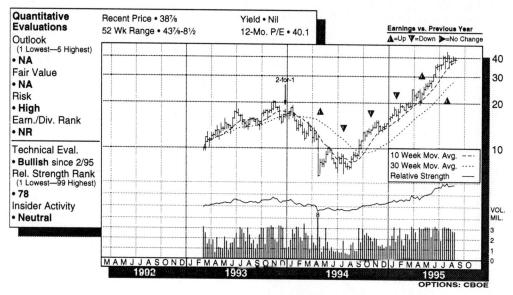

Recent Price • 38⅞
52 Wk Range • 43⅞-8½
Yield • Nil
12-Mo. P/E • 40.1

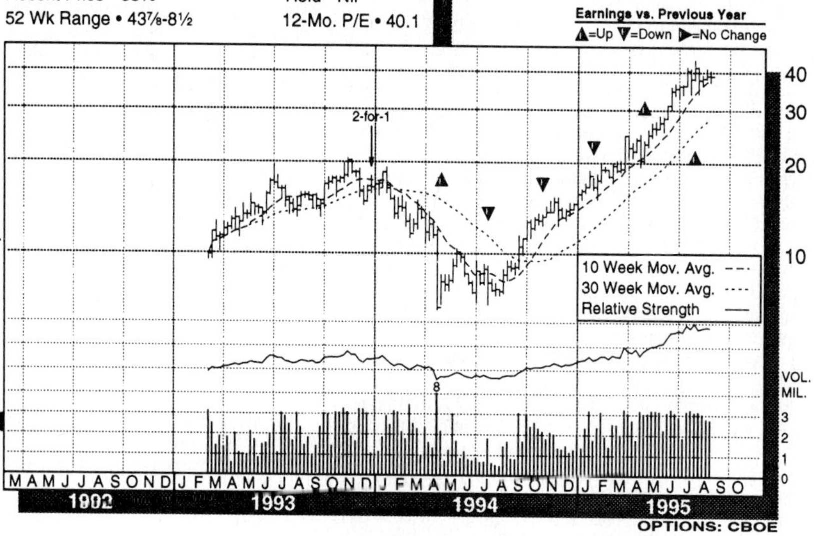

Business Profile - 28-AUG-95

The rapid spread of 486 and Pentium chip technologies, coupled with more powerful software packages, has created a need for high performance graphic tools in both the desktop and portable computer markets. S3's leading edge technology has placed it in a leadership position for meeting current end user requirements. The company's focus on developing products that will allow computers to utilize multimedia tools should aid future growth.

Operational Review - 28-AUG-95

Sales nearly doubled in the first half of 1995, year to year, reflecting increased manufacturing capacity and robust demand for the company's products. Gross margins widened on the higher sales volume. New product launches, a strong emphasis on product development, and the recent acquisition of Floreat, Inc., a company specializing in communications software, will allow S3 to broaden its product offerings and enter new market segments.

Stock Performance - 25-AUG-95

In the past 30 trading days, SIII's shares have declined 4%, compared to a 0.04% rise in the S&P 500. Average trading volume for the past five days was 546,320 shares, compared with the 40-day moving average of 749,346 shares.

Key Stock Statistics

Dividend Rate/Share	Nil	Shareholders	300
Shs. outstg. (M)	21.9	Market cap. (B)	$0.852
Avg. daily vol. (M)	0.652	Inst. holdings	80%
Tang. Bk. Value/Share	4.07	Insider holdings	NA
Beta	NA		

Value of $10,000 invested 5 years ago: NA

Fiscal Year Ending Dec. 31

	1995	% Change	1994	% Change	1993	% Change
Revenues (Million $)						
1Q	57.42	53%	37.53	113%	17.60	NM
2Q	70.56	157%	27.47	10%	25.02	NM
3Q	—	—	30.89	-7%	33.17	NM
4Q	—	—	44.42	19%	37.22	NM
Yr.	—	—	140.3	24%	113.0	NM
Income (Million $)						
1Q	6.09	58%	3.86	92%	2.01	—
2Q	7.97	NM	-4.68	NM	3.51	—
3Q	—	—	1.92	-58%	4.57	—
4Q	—	—	4.40	-13%	5.03	—
Yr.	—	—	5.50	-64%	15.12	NM
Earnings Per Share ($)						
1Q	0.30	50%	0.20	60%	0.13	—
2Q	0.35	NM	-0.26	NM	0.18	—
3Q	—	—	0.10	-57%	0.24	—
4Q	—	—	0.22	-15%	0.26	—
Yr.	—	—	0.28	-65%	0.81	161%

Next earnings report expected: late October

S3 Incorporated

Business Summary - 28-AUG-95

S3 Incorporated is a supplier of high-performance accelerator solutions for the graphical user interface environments created by Microsoft Windows, IBM OS/2 and other advanced personal computer (PC) operating systems. The company's integrated accelerator solutions relieve a computer's central processing unit of primary responsibility for graphics processing and significantly improve the graphics performance of PC.

The company's accelerators implement in silicon the most frequently used graphics functions native to Windows, OS/2 and other advanced PC operating systems. S3's first product, the 86C911 graphics accelerator chip, began shipping in volume in September 1991. In 1992, the company introduced its second generation of products, a family of single-chip, DRAM and VRAM based graphics accelerators. These products featured 32-bit graphics engines that provided higher resolutions than earlier products. In November 1993, S3 introduced its third generation of products, 64-bit graphics accelerators, which are also DRAM and VRAM based, but offer significant performance improvement over 32-bit products.

In 1994, S3 expanded its product offerings by introducing its latest generation of 64-bit multimedia accelerators, the Vision868 and Vision968. Additionally, the company launched its Trio family of integrated graphics accelerators which addressed the need for high performance graphics in entry-level systems.

Recently, S3 unveiled its Cooperative Accelerator Architecture (CAA) solution. The CAA is the industry's first graphics, audio and MPEG (Motion Picture Expert's Group standard) solution designed to improve quality and affordability for multimedia on commercial and home desktop PCs. The chipset is the industry's first multimedia acceleration solution with hardware support for the Microsoft Windows 95 Direct Draw feature set.

R&D efforts are currently focused on enhancing the company's existing family of graphics accelerators and developing new accelerator products for multimedia, home and mobile products.

Important Developments

Jul. '95—The company entered into a joint venture with United Microelectronics Corp. and Alliance Semiconductor Corp. to form a separate Taiwanese company for the purpose of building and managing a semiconductor manufacturing facility. The new fabrication facility is scheduled to begin production in late 1996.

May '95—S3 completed a secondary offering of 4,025,000 common shares. Net proceeds of $90 million were earmarked for capacity expansion.

Capitalization

Long Term Debt: None (6/95).

Per Share Data ($) (Year Ended Dec. 31)

	1994	1993	1992	1991	1990	1989
Tangible Bk. Val.	3.78	3.45	0.58	NA	NA	NA
Cash Flow	0.48	0.89	0.38	NA	NA	NA
Earnings	0.28	0.81	0.31	NA	NA	NA
Dividends	Nil	Nil	Nil	NA	NA	NA
Payout Ratio	Nil	Nil	Nil	NA	NA	NA
Prices - High	19¼	20⅝	NA	NA	NA	NA
- Low	6½	7½	NA	NA	NA	NA
P/E Ratio - High	69	25	NA	NA	NA	NA
- Low	23	9	NA	NA	NA	NA

Income Statement Analysis (Million $)

	1994	%Chg	1993	%Chg	1992	%Chg	1991
Revs.	140	24%	113	NM	30.6	NM	3.3
Oper. Inc.	10.1	-60%	25.0	NM	5.7	NM	-4.2
Depr.	4.0	134%	1.7	78%	0.9	16%	0.8
Int. Exp.	0.0	-78%	0.2	50%	0.1	-65%	0.3
Pretax Inc.	6.9	-72%	24.4	NM	4.7	NM	-4.9
Eff. Tax Rate	21%	—	38%	—	4.70%	—	Nil
Net Inc.	5.5	-64%	15.1	NM	4.4	NM	-4.9

Balance Sheet & Other Fin. Data (Million $)

	1994	1993	1992	1991	1990	1989
Cash	34.6	44.5	5.8	5.2	NA	NA
Curr. Assets	79.5	75.3	14.2	7.5	NA	NA
Total Assets	89.5	81.7	15.8	8.3	NA	NA
Curr. Liab.	19.8	20.3	7.6	4.9	NA	NA
LT Debt	0.4	0.1	1.2	1.2	NA	NA
Common Eqty.	68.9	61.0	7.0	14.3	NA	NA
Total Cap.	69.7	61.4	8.2	-1.1	NA	NA
Cap. Exp.	7.6	6.3	1.7	0.1	0.1	NA
Cash Flow	9.5	16.8	5.4	-4.1	-6.2	NA

Ratio Analysis

	1994	1993	1992	1991	1990	1989
Curr. Ratio	4.0	3.7	1.9	1.5	NA	NA
% LT Debt of Cap.	0.6	0.2	14.4	NM	NA	NA
% Net Inc.of Revs.	3.9	13.4	14.5	NM	NM	NA
% Ret. on Assets	6.4	14.8	36.9	NM	NA	NA
% Ret. on Equity	8.5	NM	NM	NM	NA	NA

Dividend Data —No cash dividends have been paid. The company intends to retain earnings for use in the development of its business, and does not expect to pay cash dividends in the foreseeable future. A two-for-one stock split was effected in December 1993.

Data as orig. reptd.; bef. results of disc. opers. and/or spec. items. Per share data adj. for stk. divs. as of ex-div. date. E-Estimated. NA-Not Available. NM-Not Meaningful. NR-Not Ranked.

Office—2770 San Tomas Expressway, Santa Clara, CA 95051-0968. **Tel**—(408) 980-5400. **Chrmn**—D. P. Banatao. **Pres & CEO**—T. N. Holdt. **VP-Fin & CFO**—G. A. Hervey. **VP & Secy**—R. T. Yara. **Dirs**—D. P. Banatao, J. C. Colligan, T. N. Holdt, R. P. Lee, C. J. Santoro, R. T. Yara. **Transfer Agent & Registrar**—First National Bank of Boston, Canton, MA. **Incorporated** in Delaware in 1989. **Empl**-217. **S&P Analyst:** Steven A. Jaworski

STANDARD & POOR'S

STOCK REPORTS

St. John Knits

NYSE Symbol **SJK**
In S&P SmallCap 600

19-OCT-95 **Industry:** Textiles

Summary: This company designs and manufactures women's clothing and accessories, sold through speciality retailers and its own retail boutiques and outlets.

Quantitative Evaluations

Outlook
(1 Lowest—5 Highest)
• **NA**
Fair Value
• **NA**
Risk
• **Low**
Earn./Div. Rank
• **NR**

Technical Eval.
• **Bullish** since 8/94
Rel. Strength Rank
(1 Lowest—99 Highest)
• **48**
Insider Activity
• **NA**

Recent Price • 46½
52 Wk Range • 50-28½
Yield • 0.4%
12-Mo. P/E • 20.7

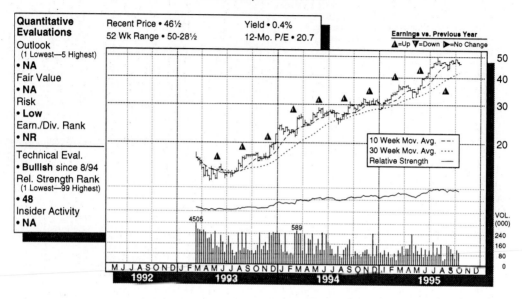

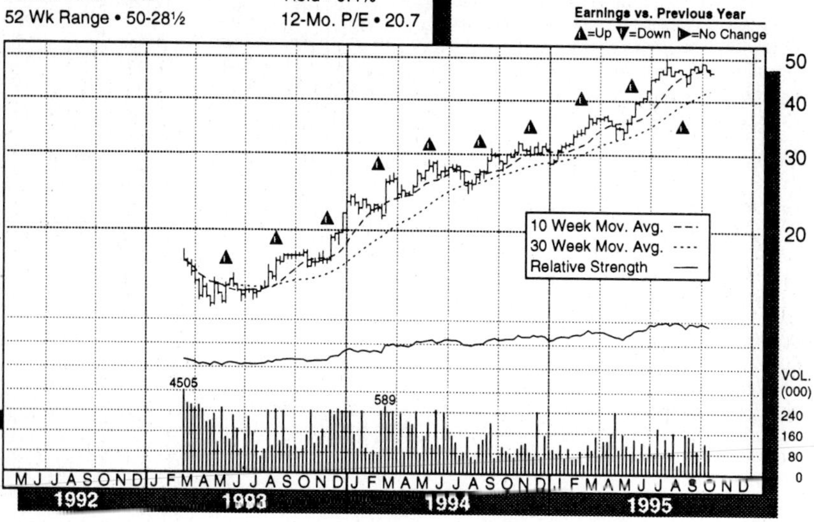

Business Profile - 19-OCT-95

This company is a vertically integrated designer, maker and marketer of women's clothing and accessories, sold mainly under the St. John tradename through specialty retailers and its own retail boutiques and outlet stores. Three national specialty retailers (Saks Fifth Avenue, Neiman-Marcus and Nordstrom) accounted for 55% of fiscal 1994 sales. SJK also has 16 retail boutiques and four outlet stores for off-price inventory (21% of total sales).

Operational Review - 19-OCT-95

Net sales in the 39 weeks ended July 30, 1995, advanced 28%, year to year, reflecting continued strong demand from retail customers, expansion of the company's network of retail boutiques and outlet stores, and higher international retail sales. Results were strong relative to other women's apparel manufacturers and specialty retailers, which experienced another period of soft demand. The opening of additional retail boutiques and outlet stores enhances future growth prospects.

Stock Performance - 13-OCT-95

In the past 30 trading days, SJK's shares have increased 5%, compared to a 4% rise in the S&P 500. Average trading volume for the past five days was 19,540 shares, compared with the 40-day moving average of 21,503 shares.

Key Stock Statistics

Dividend Rate/Share	0.20	Shareholders	300
Shs. outstg. (M)	8.2	Market cap. (B)	$0.382
Avg. daily vol. (M)	0.016	Inst. holdings	74%
Tang. Bk. Value/Share	7.69	Insider holdings	NA
Beta	NA		

Value of $10,000 invested 5 years ago: NA

Fiscal Year Ending Oct. 31

	1995	% Change	1994	% Change	1993	% Change
Revenues (Million $)						
1Q	36.30	33%	27.27	31%	20.80	26%
2Q	40.62	26%	32.23	30%	24.84	20%
3Q	36.95	25%	29.67	18%	25.04	33%
4Q	—	—	38.78	31%	29.60	22%
Yr.	—	—	127.9	28%	100.3	25%
Income (Million $)						
1Q	3.98	43%	2.79	42%	1.96	—
2Q	5.10	45%	3.52	29%	2.72	—
3Q	4.30	21%	3.55	40%	2.53	—
4Q	—	—	5.09	32%	3.86	—
Yr.	—	—	14.95	35%	11.06	33%
Earnings Per Share ($)						
1Q	0.48	41%	0.34	42%	0.24	NM
2Q	0.62	44%	0.43	30%	0.33	38%
3Q	0.52	21%	0.43	39%	0.31	11%
4Q	—	—	0.62	32%	0.47	7%
Yr.	—	—	1.82	35%	1.35	32%

Next earnings report expected: late December

St. John Knits

Business Summary - 19-OCT-95

St. John Knits is a leading designer, maker and marketer of women's clothing and accessories, sold primarily under the St. John tradename. The St. John name has been associated with high quality and a specific look in knitwear, with vibrant colors and classic, timeless styling. Sales contributions by division in recent fiscal years were:

	1994	1993
Knitwear	75%	79%
Co. owned retail stores	19%	17%
Accessories	5%	4%
Other	1%	---

The collection line consists of elegant ready-to-wear styles for which the company is best known. The day-time knit fashions, with suggested retail prices of $600 to $1,300, include sophisticated dresses and suits with a tailored look, aimed at active women.

The sportswear line consists of separates, including jackets, pants, skirts, coats, novelty sweaters and jeans, with suggested retail prices of $150 to $800. This more casual and modern line represents a departure from SJK's classic styles.

The dressy line includes dresses, theater suits and dressy separates at $670 to $1,700. The basic look is one of understated elegance, enhanced by innovative, often luxurious touches.

The basics line includes seasonless products, such as classic jackets, skirts and pants, that are an integral part of women's wardrobes, in solid black, white and navy. Suggested retail prices range from $150 to $690.

The accessories line, priced from $50 to $675, consists of fine fashion jewelry, silk scarves, suede belts and handbags. The fragrance line includes perfume, body cream, lotion, body powder and soap as an accessory to the St. John label. Suggested retail prices range from $45 to $250.

The Griffith & Gray product line was introduced in late fiscal 1994, with suggested retail prices of $180 to $1,290 for suits, coats, dresses, separates and eveningwear.

Saks Fifth Avenue, Neiman-Marcus and Nordstrom accounted for 55% of fiscal 1994 sales.

Important Developments

Sep. '95—The company said it would begin shipping a line of fur coats under the name Tyber by St. John, and a collection of dressy warm-ups under the name St. John Sport, in the fourth quarter.

Capitalization

Long Term Debt: None (4/95).

Per Share Data ($) (Year Ended Oct. 31)

	1994	1993	1992	1991	1990	1989
Tangible Bk. Val.	6.16	4.46	3.07	NA	NA	NA
Cash Flow	2.27	1.68	1.27	0.81	0.40	NA
Earnings	1.82	1.35	1.02	0.64	0.22	0.63
Dividends	0.15	Nil	NA	NA	NA	NA
Payout Ratio	8%	Nil	NA	NA	NA	NA
Prices - High	32¼	23¼	NA	NA	NA	NA
- Low	21¼	13¼	NA	NA	NA	NA
P/E Ratio - High	18	17	NA	NA	NA	NA
- Low	12	10	NA	NA	NA	NA

Income Statement Analysis (Million $)

	1994	%Chg	1993	%Chg	1992	%Chg	1991
Revs.	128	28%	100	25%	80.2	22%	65.9
Oper. Inc.	29.2	36%	21.5	37%	15.7	65%	9.5
Depr.	3.7	34%	2.7	31%	2.1	53%	1.4
Int. Exp.	Nil	—	Nil	—	Nil	—	Nil
Pretax Inc.	25.8	35%	19.1	37%	13.9	58%	8.8
Eff. Tax Rate	42%	—	42%	—	40%	—	40%
Net Inc.	14.9	34%	11.1	33%	8.3	59%	5.3

Balance Sheet & Other Fin. Data (Million $)

	1994	1993	1992	1991	1990	1989
Cash	15.0	11.5	3.5	NA	NA	NA
Curr. Assets	43.3	31.4	21.7	NA	NA	NA
Total Assets	62.6	46.3	33.2	NA	NA	NA
Curr. Liab.	11.9	9.1	7.3	NA	NA	NA
LT Debt	Nil	Nil	Nil	NA	NA	NA
Common Eqty.	50.5	36.6	25.5	NA	NA	NA
Total Cap.	50.8	37.1	26.0	NA	NA	NA
Cap. Exp.	7.8	5.7	5.6	4.2	2.7	NA
Cash Flow	18.6	13.8	10.4	6.6	3.3	NA

Ratio Analysis

	1994	1993	1992	1991	1990	1989
Curr. Ratio	3.6	3.4	3.0	NA	NA	NA
% LT Debt of Cap.	Nil	Nil	Nil	NA	NA	NA
% Net Inc.of Revs.	11.7	11.0	10.4	8.0	3.0	11.2
% Ret. on Assets	27.4	26.2	NA	NA	NA	NA
% Ret. on Equity	34.3	33.0	NA	NA	NA	NA

Dividend Data —The company initiated quarterly distributions in May 1994.

Amt. of Div. $	Date Decl.	Ex-Div. Date	Stock of Record	Payment Date
0.050	Dec. 20	Jan. 12	Jan. 19	Feb. 17 '95
0.050	Mar. 06	Mar. 31	Apr. 06	May. 03 '95
0.050	Jun. 13	Jul. 03	Jul. 06	Aug. 04 '95
0.050	Sep. 06	Oct. 03	Oct. 05	Nov. 03 '95

Data as orig. reptd.; bef. results of disc. opers. and/or spec. items. Per share data adj. for stk. divs. as of ex-div. date. E-Estimated. NA-Not Available. NM-Not Meaningful. NR-Not Ranked.

Office—17422 Derian Ave., Irvine, CA 92714. **Tel**—(714) 863-1171. **Chrmn & CEO**—R. E. Gray. **Vice Chrmn & Secy**—M. St. John Gray. **Pres & COO**—R. C. Davis. **SVP-Fin, CFO & Investor Contact**—R. G. Ruppert. **Dirs**—R. C. Davis, R. A. Gadbois III, K. A. Gray, M. St. John Gray, R. E. Gray, D. A. Krinsky, R. G. Ruppert. **Transfer Agent & Registrar**—Harris Trust Co. of California, LA. **Incorporated** in California in 1962. **Empl**-2,420. **S&P Analyst:** Philip D. Wohl

STANDARD & POOR'S

STOCK REPORTS

St. Paul Bancorp

NASDAQ Symbol **SPBC**

In S&P SmallCap 600

08-OCT-95

Industry: Banking

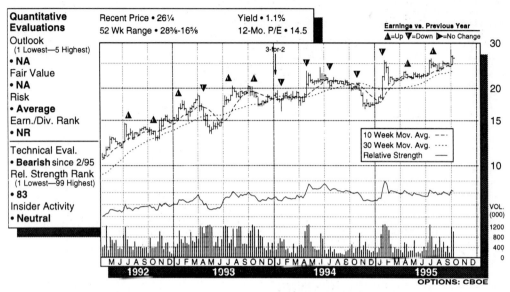

Summary: This bank holding company owns St. Paul Federal Bank For Savings, the largest Illinois-based thrift, with 52 retail banking offices in metropolitan Chicago.

Quantitative Evaluations

Outlook (1 Lowest—5 Highest)
• **NA**

Fair Value
• **NA**

Risk
• **Average**

Earn./Div. Rank
• **NR**

Technical Eval.
• **Bearish** since 2/95

Rel. Strength Rank (1 Lowest—99 Highest)
• **83**

Insider Activity
• **Neutral**

Recent Price • 26¼
52 Wk Range • 28⅜-16⅝

Yield • 1.1%
12-Mo. P/E • 14.5

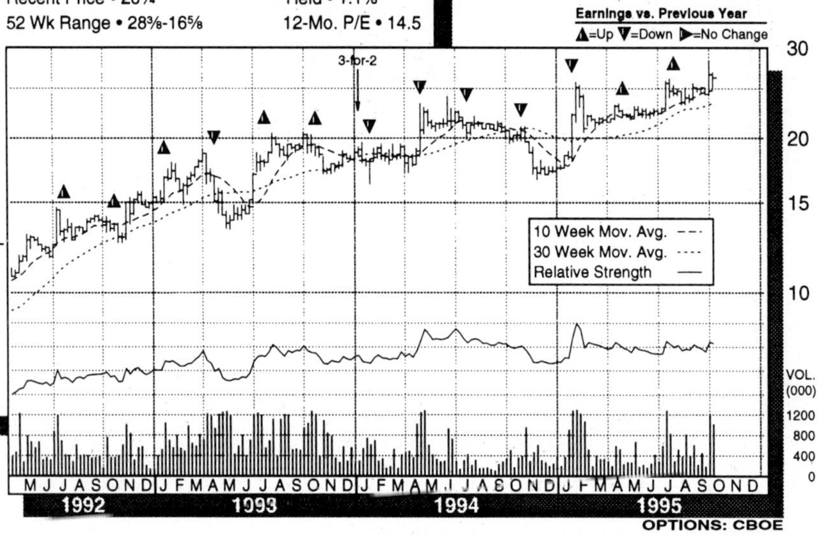

Business Profile - 07-JUL-95

SPBC is turning to technology to boost its sales and efficiency. A teller system installed in 1994 should streamline transactions, provide more customer information and benefit cross-selling opportunities. Also, a new digital telephone system aims to free branch staff for face-to-face sales efforts. Seeking to exploit its fragmented market, SPBC is expanding its direct mail/ telemarketing campaigns as well as the number of in-store branches (which require a low initial capital investment).

Operational Review - 18-JUL-95

Net interest income in the six months ended June 30, 1995, was flat, year to year, as higher earning assets were offset by a narrower net interest margin. The net interest margin contracted due to increases in borrowing costs and the need to compete for deposits. The provision for loan losses was 59% lower, reflecting improved credit quality. Following higher ATM and other fee income, a moderate rise in operating expenses, and share repurchases, per share income advanced 12% to $0.93.

Stock Performance - 06-OCT-95

In the past 30 trading days, SPBC's shares have increased 10%, compared to a 4% rise in the S&P 500. Average trading volume for the past five days was 200,900 shares, compared with the 40-day moving average of 128,303 shares.

Key Stock Statistics

Dividend Rate/Share	0.30	Shareholders	7,500
Shs. outstg. (M)	18.6	Market cap. (B)	$0.489
Avg. daily vol. (M)	0.150	Inst. holdings	33%
Tang. Bk. Value/Share	19.70	Insider holdings	NA
Beta	1.95		

Value of $10,000 invested 5 years ago: $ 26,288

Fiscal Year Ending Dec. 31

	1995	% Change	1994	% Change	1993	% Change
Revenues (Million $)						
1Q	77.07	16%	66.48	-5%	69.83	-14%
2Q	78.00	13%	69.18	-5%	72.68	-7%
3Q	—	—	72.24	-4%	75.36	1%
4Q	—	—	75.14	5%	71.56	-2%
Yr.	—	—	283.0	-2%	289.4	-6%
Income (Million $)						
1Q	9.00	10%	8.20	-11%	9.24	NM
2Q	9.03	5%	8.62	-25%	11.52	18%
3Q	—	—	9.01	-19%	11.11	23%
4Q	—	—	8.68	-9%	9.52	-1%
Yr.	—	—	34.51	-17%	41.39	10%
Earnings Per Share ($)						
1Q	0.46	15%	0.40	-15%	0.47	-6%
2Q	0.46	10%	0.42	-26%	0.57	9%
3Q	—	—	0.44	-19%	0.54	12%
4Q	—	—	0.44	-4%	0.46	-9%
Yr.	—	—	1.70	-16%	2.03	2%

Next earnings report expected: mid October

St. Paul Bancorp

Business Summary - 06-OCT-95

St. Paul Bancorp, Inc. is the holding company for St. Paul Federal Bank For Savings, the largest independent savings institution headquartered in Illinois. Following the February 1993 acquisition of Elm Financial Services, Inc., the company operates 52 retail branches in the Chicago metropolitan area. In April 1995, SPBC applied to the Comptroller of the Currency for a national commercial bank charter so that it would benefit from the FDIC's planned reduction in deposit insurance premiums.

Total loans of $2.61 billion at 1994 year-end were divided:

First mortgage one-to four-family	58%
First mortgage multifamily	38%
Commercial mortgage	3%
Consumer	1%

The allowance for possible loan losses at 1994 year-end was $42,196,000 (1.62% of total loans), versus $46,574,000 (1.98%) a year earlier. Net charge-offs in 1994 totaled $9,528,000 (0.41% of average loans), versus $13,786,000 (0.69%) in 1993. At December 31, 1994, total nonperforming assets came to $27.1 million (0.66% of total assets), versus $49.6 million (1.34%) a year earlier.

Total deposits at 1994 year end of $3.23 billion were apportioned: checking accounts 12%, regular savings 24%, money market 8% and certificates of deposit 56%.

Interest income on loans receivable accounted for about 64% of total income for 1994, interest income on mortgage-backed securities 21%, other interest income 4%, loan servicing fees 1%, other fee income 6%, discount brokerage commissions 1% and other noninterest income 3%.

The average yield on interest-earning assets in 1994 was 6.75% (7.17% in 1993), while the average rate paid on interest-bearing liabilities was 3.84% (3.95%), for a net interest rate spread of 2.91% (3.22%).

Nonbank subsidiaries include Investment Network, Inc., which provides discount brokerage services; St. Paul Service, Inc., a full-service insurance agency; St. Paul Financial Development Corp., a real estate developer; and Annuity Network, Inc., a distributor of annuities.

Important Developments

May '95—The company, the largest operator of supermarket branch banks in the Chicago area, said it was negotiating to open three branches in high-volume grocery superstores. The new branches are scheduled to open through the end of 1996.

Capitalization

FHLB Advances: $331,959,000 (3/95).
Other Borrowings: $155,110,000.

Per Share Data ($)

(Year Ended Dec. 31)

	1994	1993	1992	1991	1990	1989
Tangible Bk. Val.	18.63	17.65	15.74	14.01	11.99	12.41
Earnings	1.70	2.03	2.00	1.51	-0.30	0.58
Dividends	0.30	0.27	0.27	0.27	0.27	0.25
Payout Ratio	18%	13%	13%	18%	NM	43%
Prices - High	24⅛	20⅝	15¾	10⅞	12⅛	13¼
- Low	16¼	13¼	8⅝	4¾	3¾	7⅛
P/E Ratio - High	14	10	8	7	NM	23
- Low	10	7	4	3	NM	12

Income Statement Analysis (Million $)

	1994	%Chg	1993	%Chg	1992	%Chg	1991
Net Int. Inc.	118	-5%	124	10%	113	14%	99
Loan Loss Prov.	5.2	-52%	10.8	2%	10.6	-5%	11.1
Non Int. Inc.	29.8	-8%	32.5	15%	28.3	25%	22.6
Non Int. Exp.	87.2	5%	82.7	16%	71.2	7%	66.7
Pretax Inc.	53.5	-11%	60.4	4%	58.0	33%	43.7
Eff. Tax Rate	36%	—	32%	—	35%	—	38%
Net Inc.	34.5	-17%	41.4	10%	37.7	39%	27.2
% Net Int. Marg.	3.15%	—	3.46%	—	3.27%	—	2.84%

Balance Sheet & Other Fin. Data (Million $)

	1994	1993	1992	1991	1990	1989
Total Assets	4,132	3,705	3,500	3,663	3,417	3,345
Loans	3,737	3,085	2,914	3,133	3,121	3,019
Deposits	3,233	3,253	2,985	3,004	2,648	2,560
Capitalization:						
Debt	272	63.0	100	168	234	206
Equity	351	347	287	253	216	223
Total	623	410	387	421	450	429

Ratio Analysis

	1994	1993	1992	1991	1990	1989
% Ret. on Assets	0.9	1.1	1.1	0.8	NM	0.3
% Ret. on Equity	9.7	12.8	14.0	11.3	NM	4.8
% Loan Loss Resv.	1.1	1.5	1.6	1.5	1.5	0.5
% Risk Based Capital	16.7	16.7	12.8	11.0	NA	NA
Price Times Book Value:						
High	1.3	0.7	1.0	0.8	1.0	1.1
Low	0.9	1.2	0.5	0.3	0.3	0.6

Dividend Data —Quarterly payments were initiated in 1987.

Amt. of Div. $	Date Decl.	Ex-Div. Date	Stock of Record	Payment Date
0.075	Oct. 12	Oct. 25	Oct. 31	Nov. 16 '94
0.075	Jan. 12	Jan. 25	Jan. 31	Feb. 16 '95
0.075	Apr. 12	Apr. 24	Apr. 28	May. 10 '95
0.075	Jul. 12	Jul. 26	Jul. 28	Aug. 15 '95

Data as orig. reptd.; bef. results of disc opers. and/or spec. items. Per share data adj. for stk. divs. as of ex-div. date. E-Estimated. NA-Not Available. NM-Not Meaningful. NR-Not Ranked.

Office—6700 W. North Ave., Chicago, IL 60635. **Tel**—(312) 622-5000. **Chrmn & CEO**—J. C. Scully. **Pres & COO**—P. J. Agnew. **SVP, CFO & Investor Contact**—Robert N. Parke (312-804-2360). **Dirs**—P. J. Agnew, W. A. Anderson, J. W. Croghan, A. J. Fredian, K. J. James, J. C. Murray, M. R. Notaro, J. C. Scully, J. J. Viera, J. B. Wood. **Transfer Agent & Registrar**—First National Bank of Boston. **Incorporated** in Delaware in 1987. **Empl-** 1,103. **S&P Analyst:** Robert Schpoont

STANDARD & POOR'S

STOCK REPORTS

Sanifill, Inc.

NYSE Symbol **FIL**
In S&P SmallCap 600

22-AUG-95

Industry: Pollution Control

Summary: This company owns, operates and develops nonhazardous solid waste disposal facilities, and provides waste collection services.

S&P Opinion: Hold (★★★)

Recent Price • 32⅛
52 Wk Range • 33⅛-20½
Yield • Nil
12-Mo. P/E • 25.5

Quantitative Evaluations

Outlook (1 Lowest—5 Highest) • **NA**
Fair Value • **NA**
Risk • **Low**
Earn./Div. Rank • **NR**

Technical Eval. • **Bearish** since 7/95
Rel. Strength Rank (1 Lowest—99 Highest) • **71**
Insider Activity • **Unfavorable**

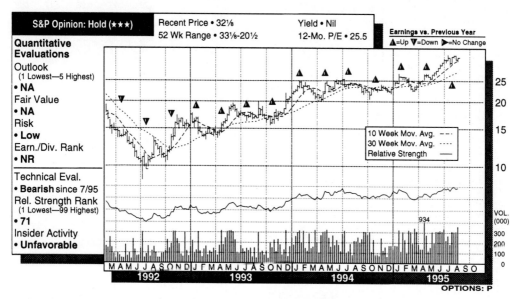

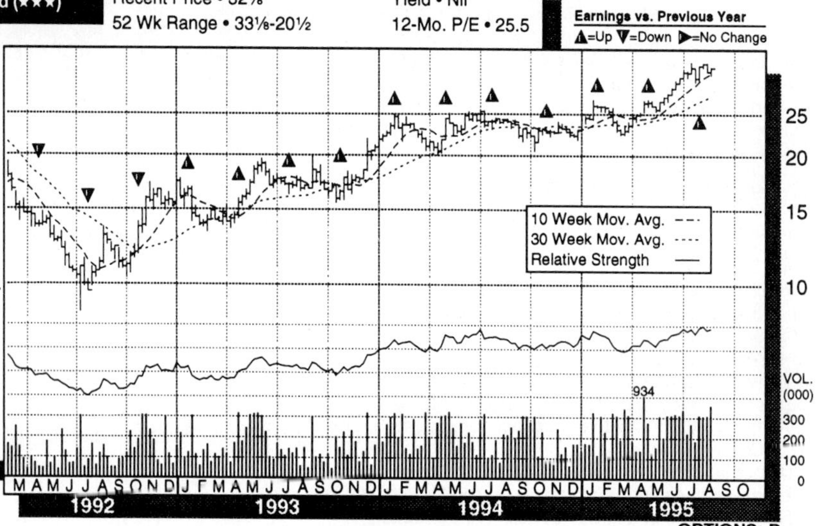

OPTIONS: P

Overview - 22-AUG-95

FIL should post strong revenue growth in 1995 primarily reflecting acquisitions of independent landfill operators. Dry waste volumes may be flat as FIL had to curtail deliveries at its Delaware facility until approval was obtained to construct a new cell. Prices should continue to trend modestly upward. Collection revenues will benefit from the expansion of service in the Houston area. Volumes of non-hazardous oilfield waste will benefit from a full-year operation of the Lacassine facility, offset by reduced oil and gas drilling in the Gulf of Mexico. Despite higher costs related to the implementation of Subtitle D regulations, margins should widen as administrative costs drop as a percentage of revenue. Limiting per share comparisons will be an 18% increase in shares outstanding.

Valuation - 22-AUG-95

Shares of the waste services company have outperformed the market and its peers. Sanifill's strategy of growth through absorbtion of independent landfill and collection companies has paid off handsomely. FIL also will benefit from the trend to privatize municipal waste collection; FIL was awarded a major contract from the City of Houston in July 1995. Near-term industry fundamentals are positive, we dropped FIL to a hold in August as we think market valuations are less attractive. Confirming our view was the firm's sale of 1,825,000 (10.5%) new FIL common shares at $31.625 through a public offering.

Key Stock Statistics

S&P EPS Est. 1995	1.35	Tang. Bk. Value/Share	7.92
P/E on S&P Est. 1995	23.8	Beta	0.41
S&P EPS Est. 1996	1.60	Shareholders	400
Dividend Rate/Share	Nil	Market cap. (B)	$0.571
Shs. outstg. (M)	17.4	Inst. holdings	64%
Avg. daily vol. (M)	0.101	Insider holdings	0%

Value of $10,000 invested 5 years ago: NA

Fiscal Year Ending Dec. 31

	1995	% Change	1994	% Change	1993	% Change
Revenues (Million $)						
1Q	48.81	36%	35.93	46%	24.60	45%
2Q	61.06	44%	42.49	47%	28.99	46%
3Q	—	—	48.32	46%	33.06	57%
4Q	—	—	46.08	33%	34.70	46%
Yr.	—	—	172.8	42%	121.3	49%
Income (Million $)						
1Q	4.71	34%	3.52	38%	2.55	29%
2Q	6.23	37%	4.55	83%	2.49	25%
3Q	—	—	5.60	47%	3.82	43%
4Q	—	—	5.16	44%	3.59	47%
Yr.	—	—	18.83	51%	12.44	37%
Earnings Per Share ($)						
1Q	0.27	23%	0.22	22%	0.18	20%
2Q	0.32	19%	0.27	59%	0.17	13%
3Q	E0.40	21%	0.33	32%	0.25	25%
4Q	E0.36	20%	0.30	30%	0.23	35%
Yr.	E1.35	21%	1.12	35%	0.83	24%

Next earnings report expected: mid October

Sanifill, Inc.

Business Summary - 22-AUG-95

Sanifill, Inc. owns, operates and develops nonhazardous waste disposal facilities and provides waste collection services. Historically, the company has grown solely through the acquisition and construction of landfills and treatment facilities. Businesses acquired consisted primarily of those owned by independent operators lacking the capital or other resources necessary to comply with stricter environmental regulation of disposal facilities. Although Sanifill will continue to acquire and develop additional landfills and facilities, it will also focus on acquiring or developing complementary businesses such as waste collection, transfer and recycling services.

At December 31, 1994, the company operated 35 disposal facilities in 17 states. Facilities consisted of 15 municipal solid waste (MSW) landfills, 12 dry waste landfills, two special waste facilities, five nonhazardous oilfield waste (NOW) disposal facilities, and one facility that accepts NOW containing naturally occurring radioactive material (NORM). MSW landfills are permitted to receive residential garbage, while dry waste landfills receive construction and demolition debris, rubbish, paper and yard waste and nonhazardous industrial waste. One special waste facility is permitted to receive a variety of nonhazardous industrial and oilfield wastes; the other is solely for asbestos waste. NOW disposal facilities are permitted to receive nonhazardous oilfield waste, including saltwater (brines), drilling fluids (muds), drilling cuttings and sludges from drilling activities. Sanifill also operates collection and transfer station operations to enhance its disposal operations, and provides sludge treatment and organic recycling services. The company also conducts waste collection and landfilling operations in six cities in Mexico.

The MSW and dry waste landfills accept waste from municipalities, private waste collection companies and the general public. NOW facilities accept waste companies in the oil and gas industry. Sanifill also sells sand, clay and other earthen materials excavated from its disposal facilities to create landfill air space.

In 1994, the company acquired 17 collection businesses and one landfill, with expected annual revenues of $28 million. In 1993, Sanifill acquired five landfills, 11 collection businesses, and two transfer stations.

Important Developments

Aug. '95—Sanifill sold 1,825,000 new FIL common shares (10.5%) at $31.625 each through a public offering.

Jul. '95—FIL commenced work under a five-year contract with the City of Houston to collect municipal solid waste and recyclables from some 32,000 homes (10% of the residential market).

Capitalization

Long Term Debt: $225,484,000 (6/95), incl. $58.1 million of 7.5% sub. debs. due 2006, conv. into com. at $28.82 a sh.

Per Share Data ($) (Year Ended Dec. 31)

	1994	1993	1992	1991	1990	1989
Tangible Bk. Val.	6.91	6.08	6.08	4.64	2.98	0.68
Cash Flow	2.90	2.36	1.80	1.58	1.05	0.39
Earnings	1.12	0.83	0.67	0.91	0.80	0.20
Dividends	Nil	Nil	Nil	Nil	Nil	Nil
Payout Ratio	Nil	Nil	Nil	Nil	Nil	Nil
Prices - High	25 5/8	22 1/8	19 1/2	33 3/8	29 3/8	NA
- Low	20	13 1/4	8 5/8	13 1/8	9 1/2	NA
P/E Ratio - High	23	27	29	37	37	NA
- Low	18	16	13	14	12	NA

Income Statement Analysis (Million $)

	1994	%Chg	1993	%Chg	1992	%Chg	1991
Revs.	173	43%	121	49%	81.6	25%	65.2
Oper. Inc.	68.6	41%	48.7	46%	33.3	11%	29.9
Depr.	30.2	31%	23.1	49%	15.5	78%	8.7
Int. Exp.	14.2	45%	9.8	48%	6.6	58%	4.2
Pretax Inc.	31.2	54%	20.2	41%	14.3	-26%	19.2
Eff. Tax Rate	40%	—	38%	—	36%	—	39%
Net Inc.	18.8	52%	12.4	36%	9.1	-22%	11.7

Balance Sheet & Other Fin. Data (Million $)

	1994	1993	1992	1991	1990	1989
Cash	2.8	6.4	6.1	19.5	4.6	1.9
Curr. Assets	40.9	31.7	22.2	33.0	11.8	3.5
Total Assets	500	410	312	214	59.0	12.0
Curr. Liab.	39.8	31.3	19.9	15.2	7.2	3.1
LT Debt	188	144	103	84.0	14.0	2.0
Common Eqty.	179	145	101	76.0	30.0	3.0
Total Cap.	417	337	252	165	46.0	5.0
Cap. Exp.	69.0	72.0	69.0	112	31.0	Nil
Cash Flow	49.0	35.6	24.6	20.4	10.2	2.4

Ratio Analysis

	1994	1993	1992	1991	1990	1989
Curr. Ratio	1.0	1.0	1.1	2.2	1.6	0.7
% LT Debt of Cap.	45.0	42.7	40.8	50.6	31.3	38.7
% Net Inc.of Revs.	10.9	10.3	11.2	18.0	19.8	10.0
% Ret. on Assets	4.0	3.3	3.4	8.1	15.1	10.9
% Ret. on Equity	11.3	9.6	10.0	20.4	37.6	47.3

Dividend Data —No cash dividends have been paid. A poison pill stock purchase rights plan was adopted in 1991.

Data as orig. reptd.; bef. results of disc. opers. and/or spec. items. Per share data adj. for stk. divs. as of ex-div. date. E-Estimated. NA-Not Available. NM-Not Meaningful. NR-Not Ranked.

Office—2777 Allen Parkway, Suite 700, Houston, TX 77019-2155. **Tel**—(713) 942-6200. **Chrmn & CEO**—L. D. Bain. **Pres & COO**—R. R. Proto. **VP-Fin, CFO & Investor Contact**—J. Chris Brewster. **VP-Secy**—H. S. Walton. **Dirs**—L. D. Bain, R. F. Cox, R. G. Jones, R. C. Loehr, W. J. Lynch, L. J. Martin, R. R. Proto, W. J. Razzouk, A. C. Warrington IV. **Transfer Agent & Registrar**—Chemical Shareholder Services Group, Inc., Dallas. **Incorporated** in Texas in 1989; reincorporated in Delaware in 1991. **Empl**-1,300. **S&P Analyst:** Stephen R. Klein

STANDARD & POOR'S

STOCK REPORTS

Sanmina Corp.

NASDAQ Symbol **SANM**
In S&P SmallCap 600

14-NOV-95 **Industry:** Electronics/Electric

Summary: This company is a leading provider of customized integrated manufacturing services to OEMs in the electronics industry.

Quantitative Evaluations

Outlook (1 Lowest—5 Highest) • **NA**

Fair Value • **NA**

Risk • **Average**

Earn./Div. Rank • **NR**

Technical Eval. • **Bearish** since 10/95

Rel. Strength Rank (1 Lowest—99 Highest) • **82**

Insider Activity • **NA**

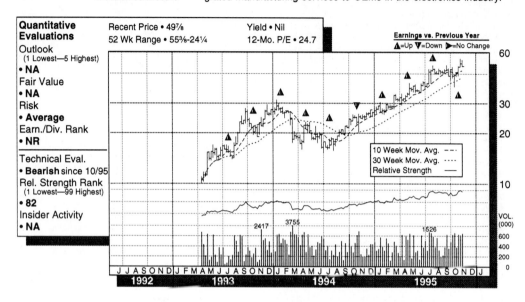

Recent Price • 49⅞
52 Wk Range • 55⅜-24¼
Yield • Nil
12-Mo. P/E • 24.7

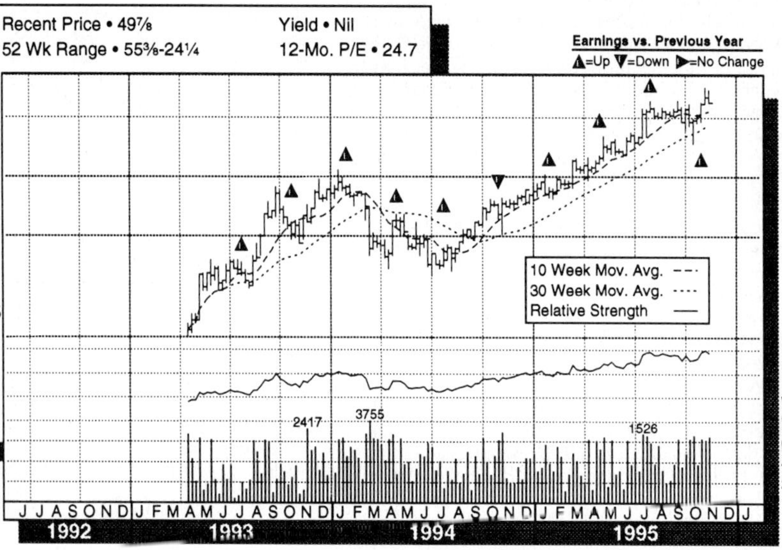

Business Profile - 14-NOV-95

During fiscal 1994, SANM completed its transition from a manufacturer of complex printed circuit boards to a leading supplier in the contract assembly business. As part of this strategy, SANM expanded its contract manufacturing capacity by acquiring a sophisticated surface mount assembly facility in San Jose, CA. SANM's goal is to build long-term relationships with its customers by focusing on state-of-the-art technology, quick-turn manufacturing and materials management and support.

Operational Review - 14-NOV-95

Based on a preliminary report, sales in FY 95 (Sep.) rose 46%, reflecting continued demand from the company's key customers. Gross margins narrowed, but results benefited from the absence of $14,819,000 of charges for the write-off of goodwill and for plant closing costs. After taxes at 39.4%, versus taxes of $6,704,000, net income of $16,954,000 ($2.02 a share based on 8.5% more shares), contrasted with a net loss of $3,109,000 ($0.40).

Stock Performance - 10-NOV-95

In the past 30 trading days, SANM's shares have increased 4%, compared to a 1% rise in the S&P 500. Average trading volume for the past five days was 212,680 shares, compared with the 40-day moving average of 145,545 shares.

Key Stock Statistics

Dividend Rate/Share	Nil	Shareholders	200
Shs. outstg. (M)	8.5	Market cap. (B)	$0.421
Avg. daily vol. (M)	0.156	Inst. holdings	96%
Tang. Bk. Value/Share	5.82	Insider holdings	NA
Beta	NA		

Value of $10,000 invested 5 years ago: NA

Fiscal Year Ending Sep. 30

	1995	% Change	1994	% Change	1993	% Change
Revenues (Million $)						
1Q	34.75	24%	28.04	37%	20.40	47%
2Q	39.30	41%	27.89	31%	21.30	31%
3Q	44.59	54%	28.90	31%	22.10	39%
4Q	49.11	62%	30.30	23%	24.70	29%
Yr.	167.8	46%	115.1	30%	88.47	36%
Income (Million $)						
1Q	3.33	25%	2.67	NM	0.86	—
2Q	3.90	49%	2.61	158%	1.01	—
3Q	4.55	64%	2.77	54%	1.80	—
4Q	5.20	NM	-11.16	NM	2.25	—
Yr.	16.95	NM	-3.11	NM	5.92	NM
Earnings Per Share ($)						
1Q	0.40	14%	0.35	84%	0.19	NM
2Q	0.47	47%	0.32	39%	0.23	NM
3Q	0.54	59%	0.34	31%	0.26	NM
4Q	0.61	NM	-1.40	NM	0.32	NM
Yr.	2.02	NM	-0.40	NM	1.03	NM

Next earnings report expected: mid January

Sanmina Corp.

Business Summary - 14-NOV-95

Sanmina Corporation is a leading independent provider of customized integrated manufacturing services to a diversified base of original equipment manufacturers (OEMs) in the telecommunications (60% of net sales in fiscal 1994), data communications (20%), industrial and medical instrumentation (11%), computer systems (8%) and contract assembly (1%) segments of the electronics industry. Sanmina also provides sophisticated electronic assembly and turnkey manufacturing management services.

The company's electronic assembly services involve the manufacture of complex printed circuit board assemblies using surface mount (SMT) and pin through-hole (PTH) interconnections technologies, the manufacture of custom designed backplane assemblies, the manufacture of complex multi-layer printed circuit boards, and the testing and assembly of electronic sub-systems and systems. Turnkey manufacturing involves procurement and materials management, as well as consultation on board design and manufacturability.

SMT and PTH printed circuit board assemblies are printed circuit boards on which various electronic components, such as integrated circuits, capacitors, microprocessors and resistors have been mounted. Backplane assemblies are large printed circuit boards on which connectors are mounted to receive and interconnect printed circuit boards and other electronic components. Printed circuit boards are the basic platform used to interconnect the microprocessors, capacitors, resistor networks and other components essential to the functioning of electronic products. In fiscal 1994, about 71% of sales consisted of assembly revenues and about 29% consisted of printed circuit boards.

In fiscal 1994, DSC Communications and SynOptics Communications (now known as Bay Networks) accounted for 29% and 11% of net sales, respectively.

Sanmina manufactures its products in seven decentralized plants, each with its own production expertise and profit responsibility. Facilities are in San Jose, Milpitas, Santa Clara and Fremont, CA, and Richardson, TX.

Important Developments

Sep. '95—Sanmina completed the expansion of its Richardson, TX backplane facility. Separately, the company announced plans to build a 72,000 square foot contract manufacturing facility in Manchester, NH. **May '95**—Sanmina acquired Assembly Solutions Inc. (ASI), a contract manufacturer headquartered in Manchester, NH. ASI had 1994 revenue of about $6 million.

Capitalization

Subordinated Notes: $86,250,000, convertible into common stock at $56.385 a share (9/95).

Per Share Data ($)

(Year Ended Sep. 30)

	1995	1994	1993	1992	1991	1990
Tangible Bk. Val.	NA	5.84	1.83	1.13	NA	NA
Cash Flow	NA	0.17	1.75	0.51	NA	NA
Earnings	2.02	-0.40	1.03	-0.01	NA	NA
Dividends	Nil	Nil	Nil	Nil	NA	NA
Payout Ratio	Nil	Nil	Nil	Nil	NA	NA
Prices - High	50½	31½	29½	NA	NA	NA
- Low	25¾	15¼	10	NA	NA	NA
P/E Ratio - High	25	NM	29	NA	NA	NA
- Low	13	NM	10	NA	NA	NA

Income Statement Analysis (Million $)

	1994	%Chg	1993	%Chg	1992	%Chg	1991
Revs.	115	30%	88.5	36%	65.1	—	NA
Oper. Inc.	22.4	36%	16.5	169%	6.1	—	NA
Depr.	4.4	8%	4.1	17%	3.5	—	NA
Int. Exp.	0.1	-97%	2.6	63%	1.6	—	NA
Pretax Inc.	3.6	-64%	9.9	—	NA	—	NA
Eff. Tax Rate	187%	—	40%	—	NA	—	NA
Net Inc.	-3.1	NM	5.9	NM	0.0	—	NA

Balance Sheet & Other Fin. Data (Million $)

	1994	1993	1992	1991	1990	1989
Cash	25.9	0.6	NA	NA	NA	NA
Curr. Assets	55.8	23.4	NA	NA	NA	NA
Total Assets	64.5	45.6	41.7	NA	NA	NA
Curr. Liab.	17.7	15.0	NA	NA	NA	NA
LT Debt	Nil	4.4	8.8	NA	NA	NA
Common Eqty.	46.7	26.1	20.9	NA	NA	NA
Total Cap.	46.7	30.6	29.6	NA	NA	NA
Cap. Exp.	4.1	3.1	NA	NA	NA	NA
Cash Flow	1.3	10.0	3.4	NA	NA	NA

Ratio Analysis

	1994	1993	1992	1991	1990	1989
Curr. Ratio	3.1	1.6	NA	NA	NA	NA
% LT Debt of Cap.	Nil	14.5	29.6	NA	NA	NA
% Net Inc.of Revs.	NM	6.7	NM	NA	NA	NA
% Ret. on Assets	NM	10.2	NA	NA	NA	NA
% Ret. on Equity	NM	45.1	NA	NA	NA	NA

Dividend Data —No cash has been paid. Sanmina intends to retain earnings for use in its business and does not expect to pay cash dividends in the foreseeable future. A bank credit agreement currently prohibits the payment of cash dividends.

Data as orig. reptd.; bef. results of disc. opers. and/or spec. items. Per share data adj. for stk. divs. as of ex-div. date. E-Estimated. NA-Not Available. NM-Not Meaningful. NR-Not Ranked.

Office—2121 O'Toole Ave., San Jose, CA 95131. **Tel**—(408) 435-8444. **Chrmn, Pres & CEO**—J. Sola. **VP-Fin, CFO & Investor Contact**—Randy W. Furr. **Dirs**—J. Bolger, N. Bonke, J. Sola, B. Vonderschmitt. **Transfer Agent & Registrar**—Norwest Bank Minnesota, South St. Paul. **Incorporated** in Delaware in 1989. **Empl**-727. **S&P Analyst:** R.J.G.

STANDARD & POOR'S

SciClone Pharmaceuticals

STOCK REPORTS

NASDAQ Symbol **SCLN**

In S&P SmallCap 600

14-AUG-95 **Industry:** Drugs-Generic and OTC

Summary: This company is developing therapeutics for infectious diseases, cancer and immune system disorders.

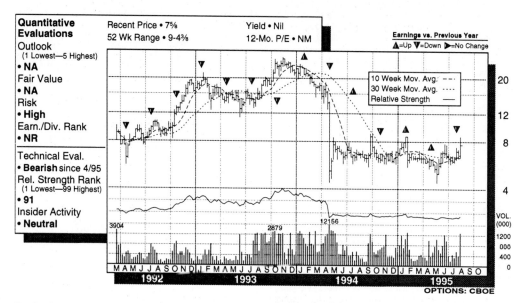

Quantitative Evaluations

Outlook (1 Lowest—5 Highest)
• **NA**

Fair Value
• **NA**

Risk
• **High**

Earn./Div. Rank
• **NR**

Technical Eval.
• **Bearish** since 4/95

Rel. Strength Rank (1 Lowest—99 Highest)
• **91**

Insider Activity
• **Neutral**

Recent Price • 7⅝
52 Wk Range • 9-4¾
Yield • Nil
12-Mo. P/E • NM

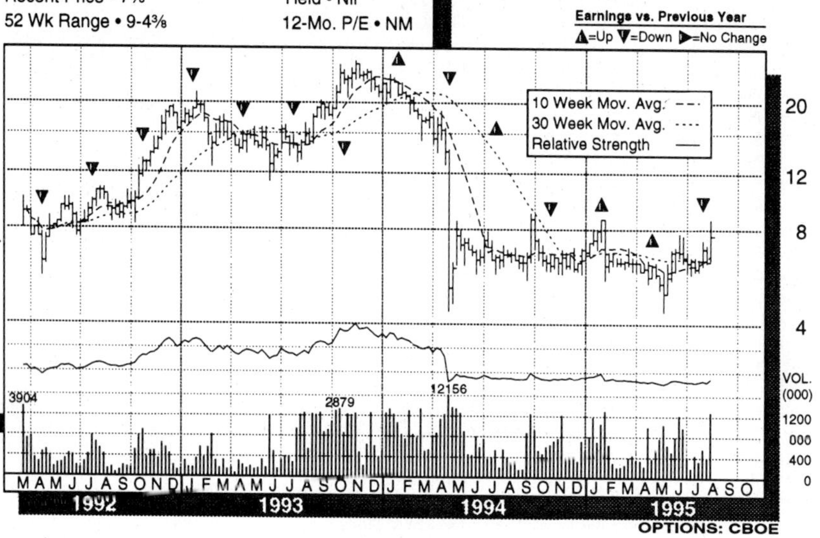

Business Profile - 14-AUG-95

During the second quarter of 1995, the SciClone began overseas shipments of its lead drug, Zadaxin thymosin alpha 1, recording its first product revenues ever. However, the company said that it does not expect significant sales from Zadaxin in 1995. Going forward, R&D expenditures are expected to rise as SciClone will begin more rigorous late stage hepatitis trials for Zadaxin in the United States and Europe.

Operational Review - 14-AUG-95

Revenues in the six months ended June 30, 1995, were $45,198, compared to none, year to year, based on the first Zadaxin product shipments. Total costs were relatively unchanged, as cost of goods sold and higher R&D expenditures offset savings in SG&A. The net loss equaled $7,252,006 ($0.43 a share), compared to a deficit of $7,502,683 ($0.42).

Stock Performance - 11-AUG-95

In the past 30 trading days, SCLN's shares have increased 22%, compared to a 2% rise in the S&P 500. Average trading volume for the past five days was 412,400 shares, compared with the 40-day moving average of 134,985 shares.

Key Stock Statistics

Dividend Rate/Share	Nil	Shareholders	NA
Shs. outstg. (M)	17.0	Market cap. (B)	$0.129
Avg. daily vol. (M)	0.165	Inst. holdings	17%
Tang. Bk. Value/Share	3.52	Insider holdings	NA
Beta	NA		

Value of $10,000 invested 5 years ago: NA

Fiscal Year Ending Dec. 31

	1995	% Change	1994	% Change	1993	% Change
Revenues (Million $)						
1Q	Nil	—	Nil	—	Nil	—
2Q	0.05	—	Nil	—	Nil	—
3Q	—	—	Nil	—	Nil	—
4Q	—	—	Nil	—	Nil	—
Yr.	—	—	Nil	—	Nil	—
Income (Million $)						
1Q	-3.57	NM	-3.99	NM	-2.11	109%
2Q	-3.68	NM	-3.51	NM	-2.57	136%
3Q	—	—	-6.78	NM	-3.01	117%
4Q	—	—	-3.60	NM	-3.99	-5%
Yr.	—	—	-17.88	NM	-11.68	NM
Earnings Per Share ($)						
1Q	-0.21	NM	-0.23	NM	-0.18	NM
2Q	-0.22	NM	-0.20	NM	-0.22	NM
3Q	—	—	-0.39	NM	-0.22	NM
4Q	—	—	-0.21	NM	-0.25	NM
Yr.	—	—	-1.02	NM	-0.89	NM

Next earnings report expected: late October

SciClone Pharmaceuticals

Business Summary - 03-AUG-95

SciClone Pharmaceuticals, Inc. engages primarily in the acquisition and development of drugs that it intends to market in targeted countries worldwide for the treatment of infectious diseases, immune system disorders and cancer.

The company's lead product is Zadaxin, a chemically synthesized version of thymosin alpha 1, a naturally occurring peptide produced primarily by the thymus gland. In September 1993, SciClone received approval in Singapore for the sale of Zadaxin to treat chronic hepatitis B. Zadaxin is also under development for the treatment of hepatitis B in Taiwan (Phase III) and in Japan (Phase II). Phase III trials being conducted in Mexico and Latin America for chronic hepatitis B were halted in early 1995. In China and Hong Kong, the company has filed for regulatory marketing approval.

SciClone is reviewing its clinical trial strategy with respect to studies in the United States and Europe for hepatitis B and C. Both of these Phase III, which were completed in 1995, use a Zadaxin treatment in combination with interferon alpha-2B. The two studies exhibited favorable trends in the drug's respective treatments, however, additional studies will be needed in order to obtain regulatory approval for these indications. SciClone expects its R&D expenses to increase significantly during 1995 and 1996.

In August 1994, SciClone acquired from Alpha 1 Biomedicals, Inc. additional rights to manufacture, and market Zadaxin in the United States, most of Europe, Israel and Canada. In other areas (Italy, Portugal and Spain), rights are held by other Alpha 1 licensees. Additionally, the company is now in control of Alpha 1 Biomedical's thymosin alpha 1 patent portfolio. Under a revised royalty structure, Alpha 1 will receive 6%-7% of the company's Zadaxin revenue in newly licensed territory; in the company's existing territories, royalties were reduced to 3%-3.5%.

The company has a long-term finished product supply agreement for Zadaxin with Sclavo S.p.A. In addition, a Schering-Plough unit has certain rights to develop and market Zadaxin in Japan.

Important Developments

Jul. '95—SciClone received product revenues for the first time in 1995's second quarter from overseas shipments of its Zadaxin thymosin alpha 1. However, the company said that it does not anticipate significant sales growth this year. Earlier, in March, SciClone announced that its R&D expenditures are expected to increase significantly in 1995 and 1996.

Capitalization

Long Term Debt: None (6/95).

Per Share Data ($) (Year Ended Dec. 31)

	1994	1993	1992	1991	1990	1989
Tangible Bk. Val.	3.67	2.88	1.58	1.71	NM	NM
Cash Flow	-0.99	-0.83	-0.64	-0.40	-0.18	-0.03
Earnings	-1.02	-0.89	-0.73	-0.41	-0.18	-0.03
Dividends	Nil	Nil	Nil	Nil	Nil	Nil
Payout Ratio	Nil	Nil	Nil	Nil	Nil	Nil
Prices - High	24⅝	19½	19½	NA	NA	NA
- Low	4⅜	5⅝	5⅝	NA	NA	NA
P/E Ratio - High	NM	NM	NM	NM	NM	NM
- Low	NM	NM	NM	NA	NA	NA

Income Statement Analysis (Million $)

	1994	%Chg	1993	%Chg	1992	%Chg	1991
Revs.	Nil	—	Nil	—	Nil	—	0.3
Oper. Inc.	-16.8	NM	-12.0	NM	-4.8	NM	-1.8
Depr.	0.6	-23%	0.8	-15%	1.0	NM	0.0
Int. Exp.	Nil	—	NM	—	0.4	NM	0.1
Pretax Inc.	-17.9	NM	-11.7	NM	-7.7	NM	-3.0
Eff. Tax Rate	NM	—	Nil	—	NM	—	NM
Net Inc.	17.9	NM	-11.7	NM	-7.7	NM	-3.0

Balance Sheet & Other Fin. Data (Million $)

	1994	1993	1992	1991	1990	1989
Cash	46.5	45.3	19.4	0.6	NM	NA
Curr. Assets	49.1	47.6	19.9	0.8	NM	NA
Total Assets	67.0	48.1	20.2	1.5	0.1	NA
Curr. Liab.	0.3	2.6	2.1	1.4	NM	NA
LT Debt	Nil	Nil	Nil	0.9	0.7	NA
Common Eqty.	62.8	45.5	18.0	-3.3	-1.5	NA
Total Cap.	62.8	45.5	18.0	0.1	-0.8	NA
Cap. Exp.	0.1	0.2	0.2	0.1	0.0	NM
Cash Flow	-17.2	-10.9	-6.7	-3.0	-1.3	-0.2

Ratio Analysis

	1994	1993	1992	1991	1990	1989
Curr. Ratio	11.5	18.5	9.3	0.6	NM	NA
% LT Debt of Cap.	Nil	Nil	Nil	NM	NM	NA
% Net Inc.of Revs.	NM	NM	NM	NM	NM	NM
% Ret. on Assets	NM	NM	NM	NM	NM	NA
% Ret. on Equity	NM	NM	NM	NM	NM	NA

Dividend Data —No cash dividends have been paid. A shareholder rights plan was adopted in April 1994.

Data as orig. reptd.; bef. results of disc. opers. and/or spec. items. Per share data adj. for stk. divs. as of ex-div. date. E-Estimated. NA-Not Available. NM-Not Meaningful. NR-Not Ranked.

Office—901 Mariner's Island Blvd., San Mateo, CA 94404. **Tel**—(415) 358-3456. **Chrmn & CEO**—T. E. Moore. **Pres & COO**—P. Vander Werf. **VP-Fin & CFO**— M. A. Culhane. **Dirs**—J. D. Baxter, E. C. Cadman, J. E. Goyan, T. E. Moore, P. Vander Werf. **Transfer Agent & Registrar**—Continental Stock Transfer, NYC. **Incorporated** in California in 1990. **Empl**-37. **S&P Analyst:** Thomas Tirney

STANDARD & POOR'S

STOCK REPORTS

Score Board

NASDAQ Symbol **BSBL**

In S&P SmallCap 600

01-SEP-95 **Industry:** Leisure/Amusement

Summary: This company designs, markets and distributes sports and entertainment-related products, including trading cards and memorabilia.

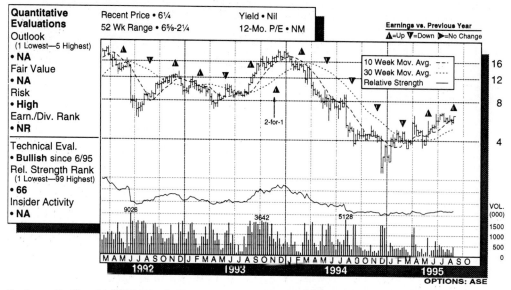

Quantitative Evaluations

Outlook (1 Lowest—5 Highest)
• **NA**

Fair Value
• **NA**

Risk
• **High**

Earn./Div. Rank
• **NR**

Technical Eval.
• **Bullish** since 6/95

Rel. Strength Rank (1 Lowest—99 Highest)
• **66**

Insider Activity
• **NA**

Recent Price • 6¼ | Yield • Nil
52 Wk Range • 6⅝-2¼ | 12-Mo. P/E • NM

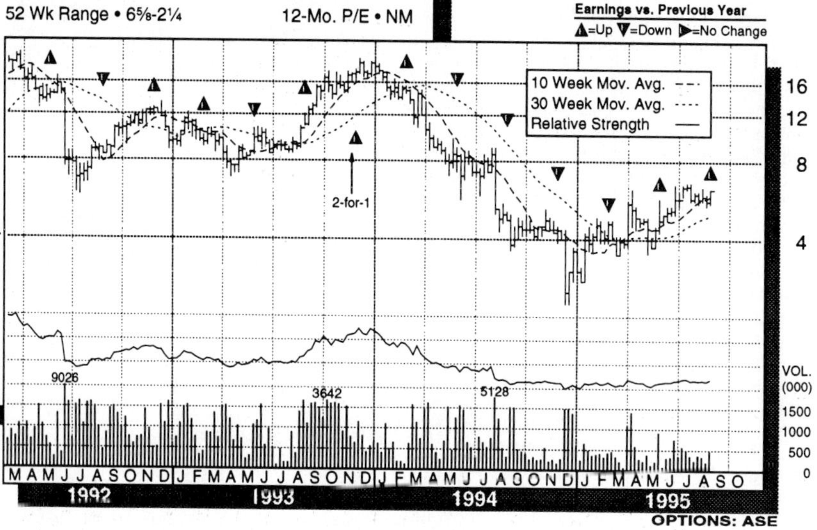

OPTIONS: ASE

Business Profile - 01-SEP-95

This company designs and markets sports and entertainment-related products, including sports and other trading cards and memorabilia. During 1994-5, BSBL initiated a restructuring of its Classic Games unit and a realignment of other operations; less successful product lines were discontinued. The shares, which have been volatile, were recently down nearly 70% from their 1994 high, reflecting BSBL's operating difficulties including an oversaturated sports card market and labor disputes.

Operational Review - 01-SEP-95

Net sales in the six months ended July 31, 1995, declined 10%, year to year. Recent sales have been down in virtually all categories due to an oversupply of trading cards, higher than normal returns, labor strife in baseball and hockey, the discontinuance of several product lines and a reduction of inventory through alternative distribution programs. The company disposed of approximately $11 million of inventory through January 31, 1995 and an additional $3.5 million through March 1995.

Stock Performance - 25-AUG-95

In the past 30 trading days, BSBL's shares have declined 3%, compared to a 0.04% rise in the S&P 500. Average trading volume for the past five days was 90,660 shares, compared with the 40-day moving average of 75,082 shares.

Key Stock Statistics

Dividend Rate/Share	Nil	Shareholders	1,600
Shs. outstg. (M)	11.3	Market cap. (B)	$0.067
Avg. daily vol. (M)	0.056	Inst. holdings	41%
Tang. Bk. Value/Share	1.06	Insider holdings	NA
Beta	1.59		

Value of $10,000 invested 5 years ago: $ 20,272

Fiscal Year Ending Jan. 31

	1996	% Change	1995	% Change	1994	% Change
Revenues (Million $)						
1Q	15.56	39%	11.20	-42%	19.30	86%
2Q	16.50	-32%	24.41	11%	22.03	104%
3Q	—	—	18.02	-50%	35.89	52%
4Q	—	—	19.14	-39%	31.38	3%
Yr.	—	—	72.80	-33%	108.6	44%
Income (Million $)						
1Q	0.53	NM	-6.79	NM	1.33	-1%
2Q	-1.53	NM	-8.21	NM	1.73	88%
3Q	—	—	-13.83	NM	3.87	39%
4Q	—	—	-5.00	NM	3.59	20%
Yr.	—	—	-33.82	NM	10.51	31%
Earnings Per Share ($)						
1Q	0.05	NM	-0.58	NM	0.13	-4%
2Q	-0.14	NM	-0.72	NM	0.16	78%
3Q	—	—	-1.23	NM	0.35	32%
4Q	—	—	-0.44	NM	0.31	11%
Yr.	—	—	-3.01	NM	0.95	25%

Next earnings report expected: late November

Business Summary - 01-SEP-95

The Score Board, Inc. designs, markets and distributes sports and entertainment-related products, primarily trading cards, games and memorabilia, for sale to television shopping networks, national retailers and the hobby market. Reflecting unsatisfactory operating results in recent periods, in September 1994, BSBL initiated a realignment of its operating strategy, and decided to discontinue all comic book memorabilia, Elvis Presley and John Lennon products, historical, space and general movie/entertainment memorabilia, trivia and other games and minor league baseball cards. Contributions to sales in recent fiscal years (including lines being discontinued) were:

	1994-95	1993-94
Trading cards		
Draft pick cards	31%	49%
Minor league cards	3%	2%
Pro-Line football cards	11%	5%
Repackaged premium cards, sets & cases & collecting kits	3%	3%
Trivia card & other games	3%	4%
Memorabilia	41%	32%
Racing cards	4%	---
Comic books & other	4%	5%

In September 1990, the company introduced a baseball draft pick trading card set. It subsequently developed football, basketball and hockey draft pick sets, and a four-sport set.

Since January 1993, BSBL has held a license for NFL Properties' Pro-Line Football cards.

The company introduced "Classic Finish Line Racing" trading cards in fiscal 1995.

Sports-related products and memorabilia include autographed baseballs, bats, uniform jerseys, hockey sticks, footballs, basketballs, trading cards, limited-edition or specially commissioned lithographs, posters, plaques, ceramic plates, ceramic and pewter figurines and ceramic trading cards.

BSBL has licenses and/or personal service contracts to market a wide variety of entertainment memorabilia products featuring Star Trek, Star Wars, Indiana Jones, Gone With The Wind, The Wizard of Oz and other celebrities, characters and trademarks. In early 1994, the company reached agreements to offer memorabilia products of a broad portfolio of top pop, rock and country recording artists.

Important Developments

Aug. '95—BSBL said its product line is finding strong acceptance in both the phone card and trading card collector markets and has proven effective in introducing sports card collectors to the emerging prepaid phone card collector market.

Capitalization

Long Term Debt: $10,682,000 (4/95).

Per Share Data ($) (Year Ended Jan. 31)

	1995	1994	1993	1992	1991	1990
Tangible Bk. Val.	1.06	4.07	2.73	1.78	0.79	0.39
Cash Flow	-2.88	1.03	0.81	0.65	0.32	0.19
Earnings	-3.01	0.95	0.76	0.63	0.31	0.15
Dividends	Nil	Nil	Nil	Nil	Nil	Nil
Payout Ratio	Nil	Nil	Nil	Nil	Nil	Nil
Cal. Yrs.	1994	1993	1992	1991	1990	1989
Prices - High	18⅞	19¾	20⅝	16⅝	4⅜	3¼
- Low	2¼	6⅞	5⅞	2¹⁄₁₆	1⁹⁄₁₆	1
P/E Ratio - High	NM	21	27	27	14	21
- Low	NM	7	8	3	5	7

Income Statement Analysis (Million $)

	1995	%Chg	1994	%Chg	1993	%Chg	1992
Revs.	73.0	-33%	109	44%	75.4	29%	58.6
Oper. Inc.	-13.8	NM	18.0	36%	13.2	33%	9.9
Depr.	1.4	50%	0.9	62%	0.6	152%	0.2
Int. Exp.	2.4	61%	1.5	70%	0.9	118%	0.4
Pretax Inc.	-40.3	NM	15.7	26%	12.5	34%	9.4
Eff. Tax Rate	NM	—	33%	—	36%	—	36%
Net Inc.	-33.8	NM	10.5	30%	8.1	33%	6.0

Balance Sheet & Other Fin. Data (Million $)

	1995	1994	1993	1992	1991	1990
Cash	0.1	3.7	3.4	1.0	0.9	0.6
Curr. Assets	48.3	79.1	56.5	26.2	13.7	8.5
Total Assets	53.7	86.8	62.6	28.4	14.9	9.2
Curr. Liab.	31.0	30.2	22.7	10.1	8.0	5.1
LT Debt	10.7	10.7	11.0	0.2	0.3	0.3
Common Eqty.	11.9	45.6	28.6	17.9	6.6	3.8
Total Cap.	22.6	56.3	39.6	18.1	6.9	4.1
Cap. Exp.	0.4	2.4	1.2	0.7	0.3	0.1
Cash Flow	-32.4	11.5	8.6	6.3	2.9	1.6

Ratio Analysis

	1995	1994	1993	1992	1991	1990
Curr. Ratio	1.6	2.6	2.5	2.6	1.7	1.7
% LT Debt of Cap.	47.4	19.1	27.7	1.2	4.6	8.1
% Net Inc.of Revs.	NM	9.7	10.7	10.3	8.3	6.3
% Ret. on Assets	NM	13.7	17.5	26.0	22.8	19.1
% Ret. on Equity	NM	27.6	34.1	46.7	53.1	40.9

Dividend Data —Cash dividends have not been paid. A two-for-one stock split was effected in November 1993. A three-for-two stock split was effected in 1991.

Data as orig. reptd.; bef. results of disc. opers. and/or spec. items. Per share data adj. for stk. divs. as of ex-div. date. E-Estimated. NA-Not Available. NM-Not Meaningful. NR-Not Ranked.

Office—1951 Old Cuthbert Rd., Cherry Hill, NJ 08034. **Tel**—(609) 354-9000. **Fax**—(609) 354-8402. **Chrmn, Pres & CEO**—K. Goldin. **SVP-Fin, CFO & Investor Contact**—N. T. Schelle. **SVP-Secy**—Christine M. Dolce. **Dirs**—K. Goldin, A. R. Lyons, G. B. Shreiber, F. A. Shabel, R. C. Yancey. **Transfer Agent**—American Stock Transfer & Trust Co., NYC. **Incorporated** in New Jersey in 1986. **Empl**-196. **S&P Analyst:** Philip D. Wohl

Scotts Co.

NASDAQ Symbol **SCTT**
In S&P SmallCap 600

27-SEP-95

Industry:
Chemicals

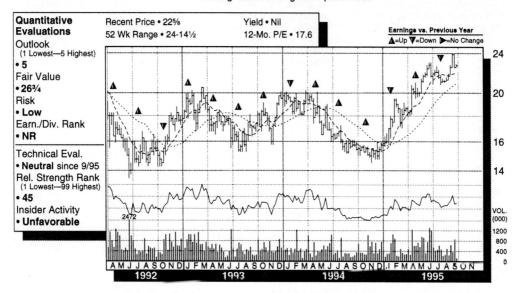

Summary: This company is the leading U.S. producer of consumer do-it-yourself lawn care and commercial turf care products, and the leading marketer of garden plant foods.

Quantitative Evaluations

Outlook
(1 Lowest—5 Highest)
• **5**

Fair Value
• **26¾**

Risk
• **Low**

Earn./Div. Rank
• **NR**

Technical Eval.
• **Neutral** since 9/95

Rel. Strength Rank
(1 Lowest—99 Highest)
• **45**

Insider Activity
• **Unfavorable**

Recent Price • 22⅝
52 Wk Range • 24-14½

Yield • Nil
12-Mo. P/E • 17.6

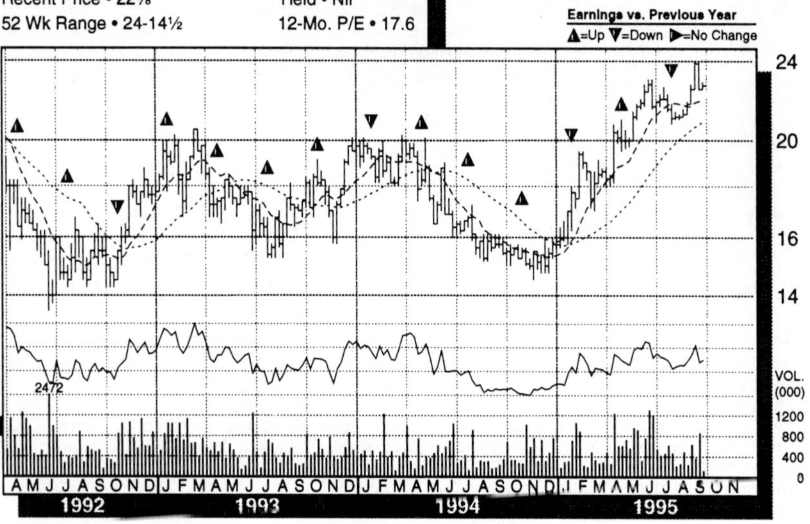

Business Profile - 27-SEP-95

With its December 1993 acquisition of Grace-Sierra, Scotts became the largest turf and horticultural products company in the world. The recent merger with Miracle-Gro, which markets the leading brands of garden plant foods, will make SCTT even stronger. The consumer business segment should continue to benefit from growth in the "do it yourself" market, while the professional business segment is expected to gain from the increasing demand for golf course maintenance products and services.

Operational Review - 27-SEP-95

Revenues grew 18% in the first nine months of fiscal 1995, on strength in international business and the Miracle-Gro merger. Excluding the merger, sales rose 15%. Margins narrowed (despite a decline in SG&A) on higher distribution and marketing expenses, and, with interest expense up 68%, pretax income was down 0.9%. Due to the delay in closing the Miracle-Gro merger, EPS declined 1.8% to $1.09 a share, as the impact on earnings could not match the effect of an 8% increase in shares outstanding.

Stock Performance - 22-SEP-95

In the past 30 trading days, SCTT's shares have increased 7%, compared to a 5% rise in the S&P 500. Average trading volume for the past five days was 22,720 shares, compared with the 40-day moving average of 79,333 shares.

Key Stock Statistics

Dividend Rate/Share	Nil	Shareholders	6,400
Shs. outstg. (M)	18.7	Market cap. (B)	$0.415
Avg. daily vol. (M)	0.082	Inst. holdings	59%
Tang. Bk. Value/Share	NM	Insider holdings	NA
Beta	NA		

Value of $10,000 invested 5 years ago: NA

Fiscal Year Ending Sep. 30

	1995	% Change	1994	% Change	1993	% Change
Revenues (Million $)						
1Q	98.02	43%	68.33	NM	67.80	10%
2Q	236.1	14%	207.4	29%	161.1	7%
3Q	229.0	14%	200.9	29%	156.3	20%
4Q	—	—	129.7	60%	80.86	14%
Yr.	—	—	606.3	30%	466.0	13%
Income (Million $)						
1Q	-3.14	NM	-1.56	NM	-0.01	NM
2Q	14.81	14%	13.01	16%	11.17	20%
3Q	10.54	12%	9.41	13%	8.31	14%
4Q	—	—	3.01	12%	2.69	122%
Yr.	—	—	23.88	13%	21.05	40%
Earnings Per Share ($)						
1Q	-0.17	NM	-0.08	—	Nil	—
2Q	0.79	14%	0.69	25%	0.55	6%
3Q	0.45	-10%	0.50	14%	0.44	29%
4Q	—	—	0.16	14%	0.14	133%
Yr.	—	—	1.27	19%	1.07	27%

Next earnings report expected: mid November

Scotts Co.

Business Summary - 18-SEP-95

The Scotts Company is the leading U.S. producer and marketer of consumer do-it-yourself lawn care and professional golf course turf care products. The company's long history of innovative products and its reputation for quality and service have enabled it to maintain the leading positions in both of these markets. Sales in recent years were:

	1994	1993
Consumer	69.2%	79.4%
Professional	30.0%	20.1%
Other	0.8%	0.5%

In December 1993, Scotts acquired Grace-Sierra Horticultural Products ("Sierra"), which accounted for approximately 17% of fiscal 1994 sales. Sierra derives about 25% of its sales from outside the U.S., with its products being marketed worldwide under brand names that include Osmocote, Once, and Terra-Lite.

Through its consumer products line, the company provides lawn fertilizers, fertilizer/control combination products, potting soils and other organic products, grass seed, lawn spreaders, indoor and garden products and garden tools. The Ultra Turf Builder products--patented, controlled-release, granular lawn fertilizers that are easy to apply and supply up to two months of controlled feeding for consumers' lawns--are the most popular lawn care fertilizers and fertilizer/control combinations in the U.S. The Hyponex subsidiary sells the leading line of organic products--top soils, potting soils, composted manures and mulches.

Scotts sells its professional products directly to golf courses, sports fields, nurseries, lawn care service companies and growers of specialty agricultural crops. Its ProTurf fertilizer and control products have the leading share of the noncommodity golf course turf care market. SCTT also produces controlled-release fertilizers and weed controls for commercial nurseries.

In fiscal 1991, the company began a program with municipalities and waste haulers to compost yard waste. Scotts operates a nationwide network of 15 composting facilities. In addition to the service fees it receives, SCTT substitutes the resulting compost for raw materials in its products.

Important Developments

Jul. '95—The company divested its Peters U.S. consumer water-soluble fertilizer business to Peters Acquisition Co. for approximately $10 million. The purchaser will be licensed to utilize the Peters trademark and Scotts will continue to manufacture the products. The transaction follows an FTC consent order in connection with SCTT's May 1995 merger with Stern's Miracle-Gro Products, Inc.

Capitalization

Long Term Debt: $243,041,000 (7/95).

Per Share Data ($)

(Year Ended Sep. 30)

	1994	1993	1992	1991	1990	1989
Tangible Bk. Val.	1.86	7.66	8.35	4.19	NA	NA
Cash Flow	2.36	1.93	1.64	1.75	NA	NA
Earnings	1.27	1.07	0.84	0.89	-0.58	0.07
Dividends	Nil	Nil	Nil	Nil	Nil	Nil
Payout Ratio	Nil	Nil	Nil	Nil	Nil	Nil
Prices - High	20¼	20½	24½	NA	NA	NA
- Low	14½	15¼	13½	NA	NA	NA
P/E Ratio - High	16	19	29	NA	NA	NA
- Low	11	14	16	NA	NA	NA

Income Statement Analysis (Million $)

	1994	%Chg	1993	%Chg	1992	%Chg	1991
Revs.	606	30%	466	13%	413	6%	388
Oper. Inc.	82.0	33%	61.5	8%	56.9	3%	55.3
Depr.	20.5	21%	17.0	18%	14.4	-19%	17.8
Int. Exp.	17.8	109%	8.5	-47%	15.9	-49%	30.9
Pretax Inc.	41.8	18%	35.4	35%	26.2	—	NA
Eff. Tax Rate	43%	—	41%	—	43%	—	NA
Net Inc.	23.9	14%	21.0	39%	15.1	-18%	18.4

Balance Sheet & Other Fin. Data (Million $)

	1994	1993	1992	1991	1990	1989
Cash	10.7	2.3	0.9	2.9	NA	NA
Curr. Assets	250	144	116	110	NA	NA
Total Assets	529	322	269	261	NA	NA
Curr. Liab.	110	64.9	60.9	88.4	NA	NA
LT Debt	220	87.0	32.0	54.0	NA	NA
Common Eqty.	168	143	176	147	NA	NA
Total Cap.	388	230	208	201	NA	NA
Cap. Exp.	54.9	15.2	19.9	8.8	8.5	6.7
Cash Flow	44.3	38.1	29.5	36.2	13.6	20.5

Ratio Analysis

	1994	1993	1992	1991	1990	1989
Curr. Ratio	2.3	2.2	1.9	1.2	NA	NA
% LT Debt of Cap.	56.7	37.8	15.3	26.6	NA	NA
% Net Inc.of Revs.	3.9	4.5	3.7	4.7	NM	NM
% Ret. on Assets	5.6	7.5	3.6	6.9	NA	NA
% Ret. on Equity	15.3	14.1	NM	12.5	NA	NA

Dividend Data —No dividends have been paid.

Data as orig. reptd.; bef. results of disc. opers. and/or spec. items. Per share data adj. for stk. divs. as of ex-div. date. E-Estimated. NA-Not Available. NM-Not Meaningful. NR-Not Ranked.

Office—14111 Scottslawn Rd., Marysville, OH 43041. **Tel**—(513) 644-0011. **Chrmn & CEO**—T. C. Seitz. **Pres & COO**—T. J. Host. **EVP-CFO & Investor Contact**—Paul D. Yeager. **VP-Secy**—C. D. Walley. **Dirs**—J. B. Beard, J. S. Chamberlin, J. P. Flannery, H. Hagedorn, J. Hagedorn, T. J. Host, J. Kenlon, K. G. Mills, T. C. Seitz, D. A. Sherman, J. M. Sullivan, L. J. Van Fossen. **Transfer Agent & Registrar**—Bank One Indianapolis. **Organized** in Delaware in 1986. **Empl**-2,500. **S&P Analyst:** Justin McCann

STANDARD & POOR'S

STOCK REPORTS

Seitel, Inc.

NYSE Symbol **SEI**
In S&P SmallCap 600

02-OCT-95 **Industry:** Oil and Gas

Summary: Seitel is a leading provider of seismic data and corollary geophysical services to the petroleum industry.

Quantitative Evaluations
Outlook
(1 Lowest—5 Highest)
• **NA**
Fair Value
• **NA**
Risk
• **High**
Earn./Div. Rank
• **B**

Technical Eval.
• **Bullish** since 9/95
Rel. Strength Rank
(1 Lowest—99 Highest)
• **47**
Insider Activity
• **NA**

Recent Price • 28¼
52 Wk Range • 34¾-18⅞
Yield • Nil
12-Mo. P/E • 21.2

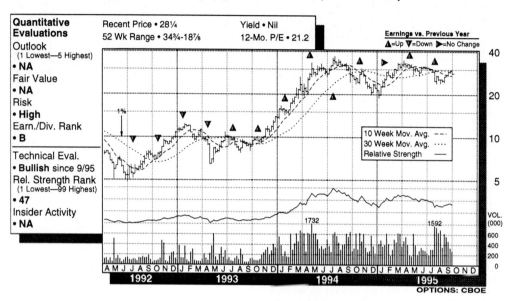

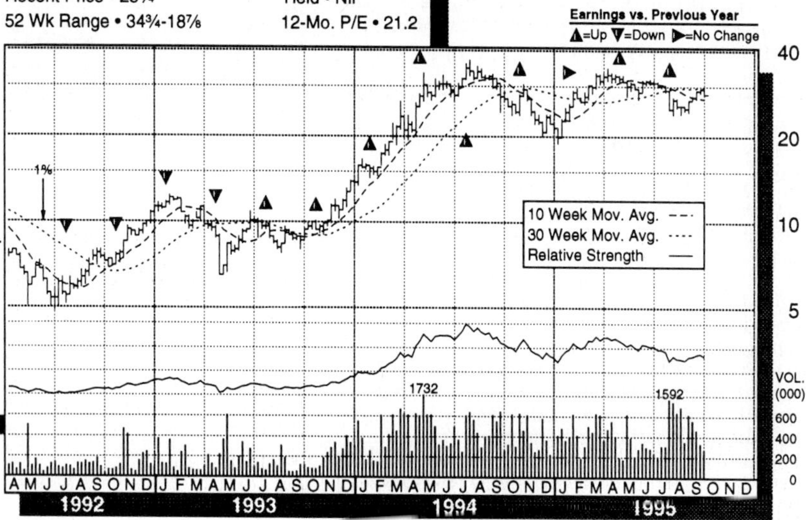

OPTIONS: CBOE

Business Profile - 02-OCT-95

Seitel owns and aggressively markets the second largest publicly available seismic library in North America, with a primary focus on the U.S. Gulf Coast. The company also provides advanced geophysical technology services, including 3D seismic recording systems and crews. Its wholly owned DDD Energy subsidiary participates directly in petroleum exploration and development through partnership arrangements. Another subsidiary markets natural gas to large-volume consumers.

Operational Review - 02-OCT-95

Revenues for the six months ended June 30, 1995, rose 59%, year to year, reflecting increased sales of both 2D and 3D seismic data; oil and gas production and gas marketing activities also improved. Data bank amortization charges decreased as a percentage of revenues, and pretax income advanced 69%. After taxes at 37.0%, versus 35.0%, net income was up 64%, to $6,315,000 ($0.65 a share, based on 39% more shares), from $3,850,000 ($0.55).

Stock Performance - 29-SEP-95

In the past 30 trading days, SEI's shares have increased 10%, compared to a 5% rise in the S&P 500. Average trading volume for the past five days was 53,440 shares, compared with the 40-day moving average of 126,495 shares.

Key Stock Statistics

Dividend Rate/Share	Nil	Shareholders	1,300
Shs. outstg. (M)	9.3	Market cap. (B)	$0.263
Avg. daily vol. (M)	0.097	Inst. holdings	62%
Tang. Bk. Value/Share	12.43	Insider holdings	NA
Beta	1.17		

Value of $10,000 invested 5 years ago: $ 40,288

Fiscal Year Ending Dec. 31

	1995	% Change	1994	% Change	1993	% Change
Revenues (Million $)						
1Q	21.16	68%	12.60	94%	6.49	10%
2Q	24.54	52%	16.15	116%	7.46	73%
3Q	—	—	18.79	75%	10.76	22%
4Q	—	—	26.23	18%	22.15	82%
Yr.	—	—	73.77	57%	46.87	50%
Income (Million $)						
1Q	2.97	80%	1.65	136%	0.70	-30%
2Q	3.34	52%	2.20	147%	0.89	85%
3Q	—	—	2.07	46%	1.42	10%
4Q	—	—	3.70	37%	2.71	73%
Yr.	—	—	9.62	68%	5.72	31%
Earnings Per Share ($)						
1Q	0.31	24%	0.25	108%	0.12	-33%
2Q	0.34	13%	0.30	100%	0.15	67%
3Q	—	—	0.25	4%	0.24	9%
4Q	—	—	0.41	NM	0.41	58%
Yr.	—	—	1.23	34%	0.92	21%

Next earnings report expected: early November

Seitel, Inc.

Business Summary - 02-OCT-95

Seitel, Inc. creates and owns a proprietary seismic data library and markets proprietary seismic surveys to oil and gas companies under license agreements. It focuses operations on the U.S. Gulf Coast, but also pursues international and other domestic opportunities. Through its wholly owned Seitel Geophysical, Inc. subsidiary, SEI started advanced 3D seismic recording and crew operations in 1993. SEI also buys seismic information from third parties to add to its database. At December 31, 1994, SEI had approximately 730,000 linear miles of 2D and 4,500 square miles of 3D seismic data in its library. In addition, it exclusively markets 400,000 miles of seismic data owned by Texaco, U.S.A.

SEI's geophysical staff determines the optimum parameters for a proposed seismic data creation program. Analysis of seismic data for identification and definition of underground geological structures is the main technique used in oil and gas exploration and development to determine the existence and location of subsurface hydrocarbons. SEI had 374 seismic data customers in 1994, up from 333 in 1993 and 207 in 1992.

In March 1993, SEI formed DDD Energy, Inc. to participate directly in exploration and production and ownership of petroleum reserves through working-interest partnerships established with oil and gas producers. As of December 31, 1994, DDD owned interests in 15 gross (2.94 net) oil wells and 22 gross (6.30 net) gas wells, with oil and gas rights in leases comprising 9,368 gross (2,871 net) developed acres and 93,435 gross (24,117 net) undeveloped acres. Net production totaled 54,000 bbl. of oil and 268,000 Mcf of gas during 1994, with respective average sales prices of $12.32 and $1.76. In February 1994, SEI added a seismic data processing center to accommodate advanced 3D seismic surveys conducted for DDD.

In the fall of 1993, SEI formed a gas marketing subsidiary, Seitel Gas & Energy Corp. (SG&E), to provide large-volume consumers of natural gas with significant savings. SG&E accomplishes this through the elimination of various middle distributors, by securing its gas supplies directly. It is initially concentrating on customers in the Northeast.

Important Developments

Sep. '95—DDD Energy reported its fourth successful discovery well, in which it has a 10% working interest, in the Yegua gas zone. Previously, in July, DDD Energy announced that it had formed a second petroleum exploration and production partnership project, with Louisiana Land & Exploration Co.

Capitalization

Debt: $32,799,000 (6/95), incl. lease obligs.
Warrants: To buy 1,834,000 shs. at $5.38-$30.13 ea. (12/94).

Per Share Data ($) (Year Ended Dec. 31)

	1994	1993	1992	1991	1990	1989
Tangible Bk. Val.	11.48	6.95	5.96	5.65	4.66	3.12
Cash Flow	4.72	3.71	3.12	2.86	2.85	2.41
Earnings	1.23	0.92	0.76	1.14	1.02	0.73
Dividends	Nil	Nil	0.05	0.10	0.09	Nil
Payout Ratio	Nil	Nil	7%	9%	9%	Nil
Prices - High	37	14⅜	11½	15⅛	15⅞	9⅜
- Low	13⅜	6½	4⅞	8	6¾	3⅜
P/E Ratio - High	30	16	15	13	16	13
- Low	11	7	6	7	7	5

Income Statement Analysis (Million $)

	1994	%Chg	1993	%Chg	1992	%Chg	1991
Revs.	73.8	70%	43.5	39%	31.2	12%	27.8
Oper. Inc.	45.7	66%	27.6	36%	20.3	10%	18.5
Depr.	27.2	37%	19.9	47%	13.5	47%	9.2
Int. Exp.	3.5	50%	2.3	45%	1.6	79%	0.9
Pretax Inc.	15.3	70%	9.0	39%	6.5	-29%	9.1
Eff. Tax Rate	37%	—	36%	—	33%	—	34%
Net Inc.	9.6	68%	5.7	31%	4.3	-28%	6.0

Balance Sheet & Other Fin. Data (Million $)

	1994	1993	1992	1991	1990	1989
Cash	1.5	1.8	3.5	1.1	1.9	1.1
Curr. Assets	NA	NA	NA	18.7	21.3	13.5
Total Assets	169	92.6	73.1	52.0	42.8	25.2
Curr. Liab.	45.6	18.4	10.5	8.0	9.9	6.4
LT Debt	14.6	30.7	26.2	11.5	7.4	4.5
Common Eqty.	101	41.6	35.6	31.4	24.8	13.5
Total Cap.	119	73.3	62.2	43.2	32.5	18.4
Cap. Exp.	52.6	22.9	22.0	20.0	0.3	0.0
Cash Flow	36.8	25.6	17.8	15.2	14.5	10.5

Ratio Analysis

	1994	1993	1992	1991	1990	1989
Curr. Ratio	NA	NA	NA	2.3	2.2	2.1
% LT Debt of Cap.	12.3	41.9	42.2	26.5	22.8	24.4
% Net Inc.of Revs.	13.0	13.2	14.4	22.0	20.8	17.6
% Ret. on Assets	6.3	6.9	6.7	12.4	14.0	13.5
% Ret. on Equity	11.8	14.8	12.5	21.0	24.9	26.5

Dividend Data —Quarterly cash dividends were discontinued in 1992.

Data as orig. reptd.; bef. results of disc. opers. and/or spec. items. Per share data adj. for stk. divs. as of ex-div. date. E-Estimated. NA-Not Available. NM-Not Meaningful. NR-Not Ranked.

Office—50 Briar Hollow Lane, West Bldg., 7th Fl., Houston, TX 77027. **Tel**—(713) 627-1990. **Chrmn**—H. M. Pearlman. **Pres & CEO**—P. A. Frame. **Exec VP & COO**—H. A. Calvert. **VP-Fin, CFO, Treas & Secy**—Debra D. Valice. **Investor Contact**—Jay M. Green (203) 629-0633. **Dirs**—H. A. Calvert, W. M. Craig Jr., P. A. Frame, D. S. Lawi, W. Lerner, H. M. Pearlman, J. C. Rives Jr., J. E. Steiglitz. **Transfer Agent & Registrar**—American Stock Transfer & Trust Co., NYC. **Incorporated** in Delaware in 1982. **Empl**-87. **S&P Analyst:** Michael C. Barr

Selective Insurance Group

NASDAQ Symbol **SIGI**
In S&P SmallCap 600

22-AUG-95 **Industry:** Insurance

Summary: Through subsidiaries, this eastern regional insurance holding company offers a broad range of property and casualty insurance products principally to customers in suburban locales.

Quantitative Evaluations
Outlook
(1 Lowest—5 Highest)
• 3+
Fair Value
• 32¼
Risk
• Low
Earn./Div. Rank
• B

Technical Eval.
• Bearish since 5/95
Rel. Strength Rank
(1 Lowest—99 Highest)
• 59
Insider Activity
• Neutral

Recent Price • 32½
52 Wk Range • 33¾-23¼
Yield • 3.4%
12-Mo. P/E • 9.9

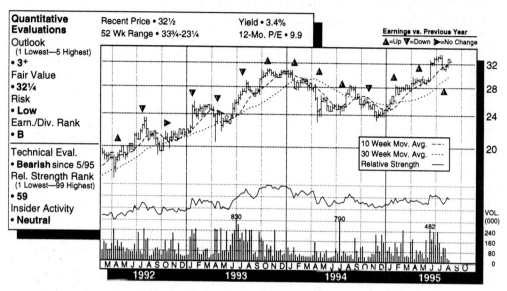

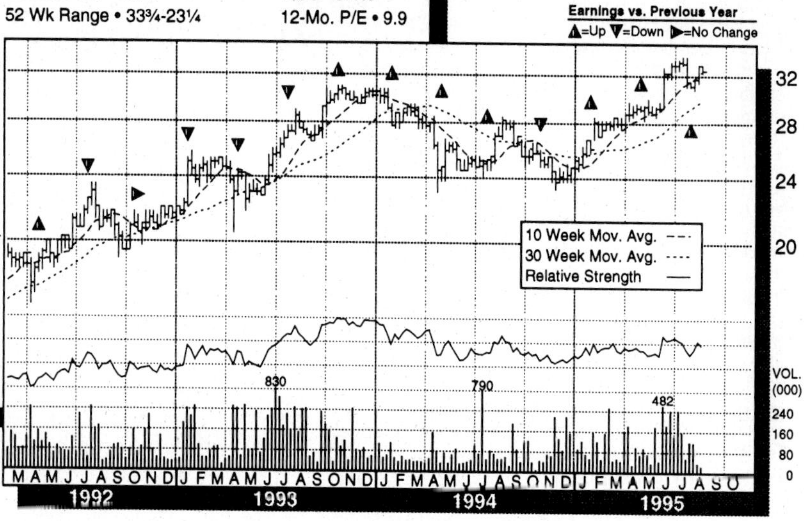

Business Profile - 22-AUG-95

SIGI sells to individuals and small commercial customers in rural and suburban New Jersey and neighboring states. Strategic plans call for reducing underwriting expenses by paring the work force and increasing automation; increasing commercial line premium volume; and expanding business outside New Jersey. SIGI's statutory underwriting expense and operating expenses to premiums written ratios continue to improve; they were 29.4% and 10.7%, respectively, in the six months ended June 30, 1995.

Operational Review - 22-AUG-95

In the six months ended June 30, 1995, total premiums written increased 16.5%, year to year, while net premiums earned and net investment income rose 13%. Underwriting losses fell sharply to $7,615,000 from $21,944,000, in the absence of catastrophic losses. A capital loss of $400,000 compared with a gain of $3,665,000. After taxes, earnings grew 46% to $25,150,000 ($1.77 per share, primary; 1.72, fully diluted) from $17,201,000 ($1.25; $1.20).

Stock Performance - 18-AUG-95

In the past 30 trading days, SIGI's shares have declined 2%, compared to a 0.51% rise in the S&P 500. Average trading volume for the past five days was 4,620 shares, compared with the 40-day moving average of 22,800 shares.

Key Stock Statistics

Dividend Rate/Share	1.12	Shareholders	2,900
Shs. outstg. (M)	14.2	Market cap. (B)	$0.470
Avg. daily vol. (M)	0.014	Inst. holdings	53%
Tang. Bk. Value/Share	24.26	Insider holdings	0%
Beta	0.65		

Value of $10,000 invested 5 years ago: $ 22,818

Fiscal Year Ending Dec. 31

	1995	% Change	1994	% Change	1993	% Change
Revenues (Million $)						
1Q	201.0	10%	182.7	13%	162.0	12%
2Q	208.4	13%	184.4	11%	166.8	13%
3Q	—	—	200.4	16%	172.8	9%
4Q	—	—	200.8	13%	177.6	7%
Yr.	—	—	768.3	13%	679.6	10%
Income (Million $)						
1Q	12.85	68%	7.64	132%	3.30	-54%
2Q	12.30	29%	9.56	NM	0.31	-95%
3Q	—	—	9.34	-16%	11.17	23%
4Q	—	—	11.74	49%	7.89	52%
Yr.	—	—	38.28	69%	22.68	-17%
Earnings Per Share ($)						
1Q	0.91	63%	0.56	133%	0.24	-56%
2Q	0.86	25%	0.69	NM	0.02	-96%
3Q	—	—	0.67	-18%	0.82	21%
4Q	—	—	0.84	45%	0.58	49%
Yr.	—	—	2.76	66%	1.66	-19%

Next earnings report expected: late October

Selective Insurance Group

Business Summary - 22-AUG-95

Selective Insurance Group, Inc. is a holding company for six multi-line property/casualty insurance companies, two premium finance companies and a real estate holding company. During 1992, SIGI added two property/casualty insurers and a premium finance company through the acquisition of Niagara Exchange Corp. of Buffalo, N.Y. With the addition of Niagara, Selective is now licensed to do business in 27 jurisdictions throughout the U.S.

In 1994, net premiums earned and pretax loss from underwriting operations (in millions) were:

	Prems. Earned	Underw. Income
Commercial	69%	-$23.7
Personal & other	31%	-$11.6

Selective's commercial lines of insurance include workers' compensation, commercial automobile, liability, property, umbrella and commercial bonds. Personal lines included automobile, homeowners, umbrella and flood coverages.

In 1994, the company's premium distribution by state was: New Jersey 60.8%, Pennsylvania 9.8%, New York 6.1%, Maryland 5.1%, Virginia 5.0%, and other 13.2%.

Through subsidiaries, Selective writes liability and physical damage insurance for private passenger and commercial automobiles, multi-peril property insurance primarily for homeowners, political entities and small and medium-size businesses, workers' compensation insurance, general liability insurance principally in the Northeast, and most forms of fidelity and surety bonds. In 1994, personal automobile net premiums earned represented 88.5% of SIGI's personal insurance net premiums earned. New Jersey automobile underwriting results account for 86% of the company's personal net premiums written; this segment's statutory combined ratio improved to 100.8% in 1994 from 111.9% in 1993, and should benefit from the elimination of certain state assesment and surtax charges in 1996.

At December 31, 1994, the company's investment portfolio's carried value totaled $1.3 billion, and consisted of held-to-maturity debt securities 52.9%, available-for-sale debt securities 36.9%, equity securities 7.0%, short-term investments 2.4%, and other 0.8%.

Important Developments

Aug. '95—SIGI reported a 32% year-to-year increase in operating income for the second quarter, in part reflecting the ongoing reduction of the statutory expense ratio, which fell 2.1 percentage points, and a lower than anticipated assessment from the New Jersey Unsatisfied Claim & Judgement Fund. The lower UCJF assessment increased primary operating earnings by approximately $0.08 per share for the quarter.

Capitalization

Notes Payable: $111,000,000 (3/95).

Per Share Data ($)

(Year Ended Dec. 31)

	1994	1993	1992	1991	1990	1989
Tangible Bk. Val.	23.22	22.64	23.19	20.34	18.91	18.36
Oper. Earnings	2.56	1.45	1.86	1.85	1.89	2.90
Earnings	2.76	1.66	2.06	2.07	2.50	3.05
Dividends	1.12	1.12	1.10	1.04	1.02	0.92
Payout Ratio	41%	67%	53%	50%	41%	30%
Prices - High	30¾	31	23½	18	20¼	20
- Low	23	20½	16	13	12½	14½
P/E Ratio - High	11	19	11	9	8	7
- Low	8	12	8	6	5	5

Income Statement Analysis (Million $)

	1994	%Chg	1993	%Chg	1992	%Chg	1991
Premium Income	680	14%	595	11%	536	8%	497
Net Invest. Inc.	80.7	4%	77.3	5%	73.5	7%	68.5
Oth. Revs.	7.4	NM	7.4	19%	6.2	9%	5.7
Total Revs.	768	13%	680	10%	616	8%	571
Pretax Inc.	43.4	103%	21.4	-32%	31.5	NM	31.6
Net Oper. Inc.	NA	—	NA	—	NA	—	NA
Net Inc.	38.3	69%	22.7	-17%	27.4	NM	27.3

Balance Sheet & Other Fin. Data (Million $)

	1994	1993	1992	1991	1990	1989
Cash & Equiv.	21.8	20.7	20.3	18.4	17.0	16.7
Premiums Due	274	283	132	109	124	118
Inv Assets Bonds	1,170	1,053	1,034	870	786	739
Inv. Assets Stock	91.6	88.2	86.3	70.2	72.8	91.1
Inv. Assets Loans	10.7	10.1	10.0	8.4	3.1	3.0
Inv. Assets Total	1,303	1,196	1,130	948	863	833
Deferred Policy Cost	81.0	78.6	76.4	53.0	53.0	49.5
Total Assets	1,867	1,739	1,479	1,211	1,139	1,074
Debt	111	61.3	63.7	14.5	15.2	35.8
Common Eqty.	329	323	312	270	248	230

Ratio Analysis

	1994	1993	1992	1991	1990	1989
Prop&Cas Loss	71.7	71.8	69.5	67.9	70.5	69.4
Prop&Cas Expense	32.6	36.7	37.0	38.1	35.0	32.2
Prop&Cas Comb.	104.3	108.5	107.9	107.6	108.0	103.4
% Ret. on Revs.	5.0	3.3	4.5	5.5	6.0	7.9
% Return on Equity	11.7	7.1	9.4	10.5	13.5	18.3

Dividend Data —Cash has been paid each year since 1929. A dividend reinvestment plan is available.

Amt. of Div. $	Date Decl.	Ex-Div. Date	Stock of Record	Payment Date
0.280	Aug. 05	Aug. 09	Aug. 15	Sep. 01 '94
0.280	Nov. 04	Nov. 08	Nov. 15	Dec. 01 '94
0.280	Jan. 30	Feb. 09	Feb. 15	Mar. 01 '95
0.280	May. 05	May. 09	May. 15	Jun. 01 '95
0.280	Aug. 01	Aug. 11	Aug. 15	Sep. 01 '95

Data as orig. reptd.; bef. results of disc. opers. and/or spec. items. Per share data adj. for stk. divs. as of ex-div. date. E-Estimated. NA-Not Available. NM-Not Meaningful. NR-Not Ranked.

Office—40 Wantage Ave., Branchville, NJ 07890. **Tel**—(201) 948-3000. **Chrmn, Pres & CEO**—J. W. Entringer. **SVP-Fin**—G. E. Murphy. **Secy**—S. R. Perretta. **Dirs**—W. A. Dolan II, J. W. Entringer, W. C Gray, C. E. Herder, F. H. Jarvis, W. M. Kearns Jr., J. Lamm-Tennant, S. G. McClellan III, R. R. Moffett, W. M. Rue, T. D. Sayles Jr., L. P. Thebault. **Transfer Agent & Registrar**—First Chicago Trust Co. of N.Y., Jersey City, NJ. **Incorporated** in New Jersey in 1977. **Empl**-1,810. **S&P Analyst:** Thomas C. Ferguson

SEQUUS Pharmaceuticals, Inc.

NASDAQ Symbol SEQU In S&P SmallCap 600 (Incl. in Nat'l Market)

Price	Range	P–E Ratio	Dividend	Yield	S&P Ranking	Beta
Aug. 21'95	1995					
13⅞	14⅜–5½	NM	None	None	C	3.18

Summary

This company (formerly Liposome Technology) is developing proprietary liposome and lipid-based pharmaceuticals to treat life-threatening diseases. Its first commercially available product, Amphocil, was launched in the U.K. and Ireland in 1994. In February 1995, an FDA advisory committee recommended conditional approval for DOX-SL as a second-line treatment of AIDS-related Kaposi's sarcoma. Private placements in 1995 have raised approximately $25.5 million.

Business Summary

SEQUUS Pharmaceuticals, Inc. (formerly Liposome Technology) is engaged in the development, production, marketing and sale of proprietary liposome and lipid-based products to treat life-threatening illnesses. It has emphasized injectable pharmaceuticals designed to improve the efficacy and reduce the toxicity of selected existing and new drugs used to treat cancer, infectious diseases and other illnesses.

Products being developed involve the entrapment of therapeutics by liposomes or in a colloidal dispersion of liquids. SEQUUS has developed proprietary methods to lower the natural defense mechanism's recognition of injected liposomes. These methods form the technology base for the company's Stealth liposomes, and can increase the blood circulation time of such liposomes to several days, from a few hours for traditional liposomes.

The proprietary Amphocil product is a lipid-based colloidal dispersion of amphotericin B, an off-patent antibiotic approved for sale in the U.S. and elsewhere as a standard therapy for the treatment of severe systemic fungal infections. Despite its effectiveness, the use of free amphotericin B is limited by its acute and chronic toxicities. SEQUUS began marketing the product in the U.K. for this indication in May 1994; the product was approved in Ireland in October 1994. The company is currently analyzing the results of four Phase III trials conducted in patients with disseminated fungal disease to provide the basis for a New Drug Application.

SEQUUS has developed stealth liposomes to improve the chemotherapeutic approach to treating solid tumors and certain lymphomas by increasing the amount of drug available at the site of disease while reducing the exposure of healthy tissues to a cytotoxic drug. DOX-SL is a long-circulating stealth liposome formulation of the anticancer drug doxorubicin hydrochloride, an off-patent chemotherapeutic used to treat many solid tumors and leukemias. Following analysis of positive data from Phase III trials using DOX-SL to treat AIDS-related Kaposi's sarcoma, in February 1995 an FDA advisory committee recommended conditional approval for this indication. In May 1995, preliminary Phase III data comparing DOX-SL with standard combination chemotherapies in AIDS patients were positive. Phase II trials of DOX-SL in patients with various solid tumors are continuing.

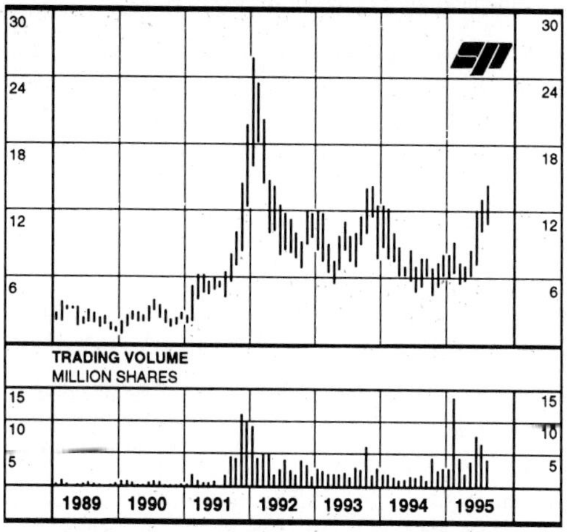

Important Developments

May '95— SEQUUS closed a private placement of Units (consisting of one share of common stock and a warrant to purchase one-half share of common at $7.43) priced at $6.7571 each, which raised over $14.5 million. Earlier, in March, the company closed another placement, issuing 436,000 shares of convertible preferred stock with warrants to purchase 734,000 additional shares, which raised appoximately $11 million.

Next earnings report expected in late October.

Per Share Data ($)

Yr. End Dec. 31[1]	1994	1993	1992	1991	1990	1989	1988	1987	1986
Tangible Bk. Val.	**0.56**	2.05	3.08	2.38	0.82	1.71	2.99	3.51	d1.36
Cash Flow	**d1.44**	d0.97	d0.77	d0.57	d0.69	d0.96	d0.44	d0.40	d0.26
Earnings	**d1.54**	d1.05	d0.84	d0.66	d0.80	d1.04	d0.48	d0.45	d0.32
Dividends	**Nil**	Nil	Nil	Nil	Nil	Nil	Nil	Nil	Nil
Payout Ratio	**Nil**	Nil	Nil	Nil	Nil	Nil	Nil	Nil	Nil
Prices—High	**12½**	14¼	25¾	19¾	3¹⁵⁄₁₆	3¾	5⅞	11⅛	NA
Low	**4½**	5½	6⅞	1⅞	⅞	1⅛	1⅞	2¾	NA
P/E Ratio—	**NM**	NM	NM	NM	NM	NM	NM	NM	NM

Data as orig. reptd. Adj. for stk. div. of 10% Jul. 1988. **1.** Prior to 1989, yrs. ended Sep. 30. d-Deficit. NM-Not Meaningful. NA-Not Available.

Income Data (Million $)

Year Ended Dec. 31[1]	Revs.	Oper. Inc.	% Oper. Inc. of Revs.	Cap. Exp.	Depr.	Int. Exp.	Net Bef. Taxes	Eff. Tax Rate	Net Inc.	% Net Inc. of Revs.	Cash Flow
1994	**3.76**	**d28.3**	**NM**	**1.28**	**1.90**	**0.03**	**d29.2**	**NM**	**d29.2**	**NM**	**d27.3**
1993	6.76	d19.8	NM	1.86	1.44	NA	d19.7	NM	d19.7	NM	d18.2
1992	0.72	d16.6	NM	1.84	1.24	0.03	d15.4	Nil	d15.4	NM	d14.2
1991	0.33	d7.6	NM	0.28	1.11	0.08	d8.2	Nil	d8.2	NM	d7.1
1990	1.40	d6.9	NM	0.33	1.06	0.14	d7.5	Nil	d7.5	NM	d6.4
1989	0.85	d7.0	NM	2.67	0.59	0.09	d7.3	Nil	d7.3	NM	d6.7
1988	3.38	d4.4	NM	1.61	0.30	0.10	[2]d3.3	Nil	d3.3	NM	d3.0
1987	3.42	d3.0	NM	0.59	0.22	0.06	[2]d2.5	Nil	d2.5	NM	d2.3
1986	3.58	d1.3	NM	0.26	0.24	0.06	[2]d1.3	Nil	d1.3	NM	d1.1

Balance Sheet Data (Million $)

Dec. 31	Cash	Curr. Assets	Curr. Liab.	Curr. Ratio	Total Assets	% Ret. on Assets	Long Term Debt	Common Equity	Total Cap.	% LT Debt of Cap.	% Ret. on Equity
1994	**11.8**	**13.5**	**7.26**	**1.9**	**18.2**	**NM**	**Nil**	**10.9**	**10.9**	**Nil**	**NM**
1993	34.7	37.7	5.86	6.4	45.2	NM	Nil	39.3	39.3	Nil	NM
1992	41.3	43.2	1.95	22.2	60.5	NM	Nil	58.6	58.6	Nil	NM
1991	32.2	32.5	1.82	17.9	41.0	NM	0.10	39.1	39.2	0.3	NM
1990	4.8	5.0	1.60	5.1	10.5	NM	0.45	8.5	8.9	5.0	NM
1989	8.5	9.0	1.52	5.9	15.3	NM	0.90	12.9	13.8	6.6	NM
1988	19.5	20.1	1.47	13.7	23.9	NM	1.29	21.1	22.4	5.7	NM
1987	23.5	24.0	1.00	24.1	26.2	NM	0.76	24.3	25.1	3.0	NM
1986	6.6	7.5	1.02	7.4	9.3	NM	0.45	d2.3	8.2	5.4	NM

Data as orig reptd. 1. Prior to 1989, yrs. ended Sep. 30. 2. Incl. equity in earns. of nonconsol. subs. d-Deficit. NM-Not Meaningful. NA-Not Available.

[1]Total Revenues (Million $)

Quarter:	1995	1994	1993	1992
Mar.	0.99	0.64	0.83	0.57
Jun.	0.19	0.94	0.73	0.99
Sep.		1.71	5.74	0.72
Dec.		1.46	1.10	0.86
		4.76	8.40	3.14

Total revenues in the six months ended June 30, 1995, rose 9.3% year to year, aided by increased sales of Amphocil. However, results were penalized by expenses related to the termination of the employment of certain officers. The net loss widened to $15,919,000 ($0.80 a share, based on 5.1% more shares) from $15,358,000 ($0.81).

Common Share Earnings ($)

Quarter:	1995	1994	1993	1992
Mar.	d0.48	d0.40	d0.30	d0.17
Jun.	d0.33	d0.41	d0.33	d0.19
Sep.		d0.35	d0.06	d0.24
Dec.		d0.38	d0.36	d0.24
		d1.54	d1.05	d0.84

Dividend Data

No cash dividends have been paid.

Finances

In August 1993, SEQU entered into an agreement under which Zeneca Ltd. will market and sell Amphocil in most European countries. In the 1993 third quarter, the company received and recognized a $5.25 million signing fee and milestone payment earned upon receipt of a product license authorizing the sale of Amphocil in the U.K. Additional milestone payments will be received upon receipt of product licenses in certain other European countries and the achievement of certain cumulative sales totals.

The company plans to fund from its own cash resources preclinical and clinical development of two of its proprietary products, Amphocil and DOX-SL, and to continue R&D of additional Stealth liposome products in the anticancer, antibiotic, anti-inflammatory and other areas. In addition to increased levels of operating activities, this strategy will require significant capital expenditures, including a pilot production facility in the planning phase. SEQU believed that existing cash balances and interest earned theron, along with sales revenues, will be adequate to fund its planned activities through the fourth quarter of 1995, and intends to seek additional financing if market conditions are favorable. The company said it will need additional financing to support full commercialization of its products.

Capitalization

Long Term Debt: None (3/95).

Common Stock: 19,146,132 shs. ($0.001 par). Institutions hold about 43%. Shareholders of record: 532 (1/95).

1. Incl. int. inc. d-Deficit.

Office—1050 Hamilton Ct., Menlo Park, CA 94025. **Tel**—(415) 323-9011. **Chrmn & CEO**—I. C. Henderson. **Pres & COO**—L. S. Minick. **VP-Fin**—D. J. Stewart. **Dirs**—R. G. Faris, I. C. Henderson, L. S. Minick, R. C. E. Morgan, R. B. Shapiro, E. D. Thomas. **Transfer Agent & Registrar**—Chemical Trust Co. of California, SF. **Incorporated** in Delaware in 1987. **Empl**—154.

 Thomas Tirney

STANDARD & POOR'S

STOCK REPORTS

ShopKo Stores

NYSE Symbol **SKO**

In S&P SmallCap 600

22-OCT-95

Industry: Retail Stores

Summary: This Wisconsin-based regional discount store chain operates about 129 stores in 15 states, serving small and mid-sized markets.

Quantitative Evaluations

Outlook (1 Lowest—5 Highest)
• **NA**

Fair Value
• **NA**

Risk
• **Average**

Earn./Div. Rank
• **NR**

Technical Eval.
• **Bearish** since 5/95

Rel. Strength Rank (1 Lowest—99 Highest)
• **21**

Insider Activity
• **NA**

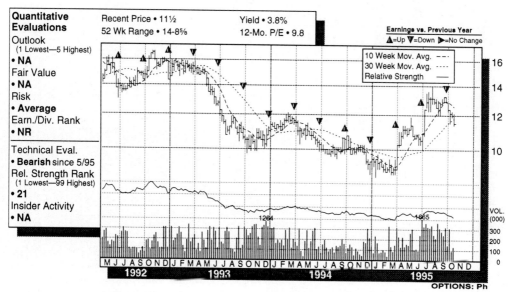

Recent Price • 11½

52 Wk Range • 14-8⅝

Yield • 3.8%

12-Mo. P/E • 9.8

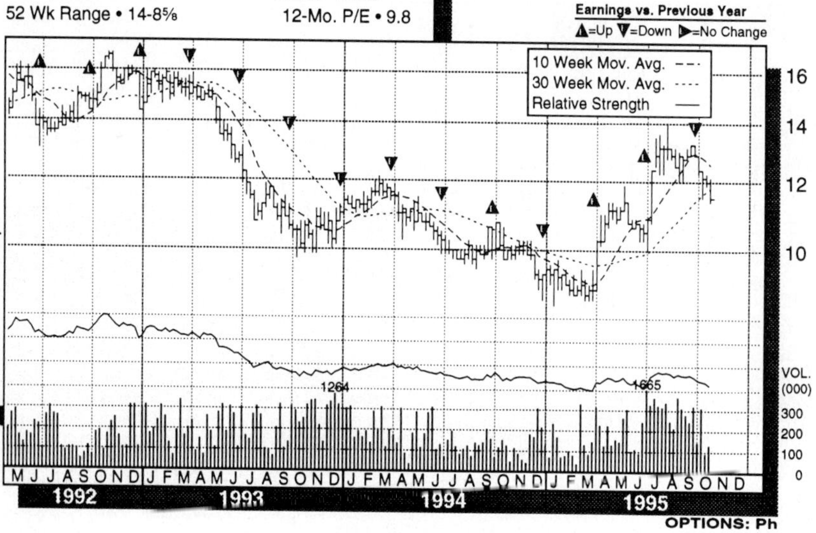

OPTIONS: Ph

Business Profile - 18-OCT-95

This discount retailer (46% owned by Super Value Stores) continues to make substantial investments in its Vision 2000 concept by remodeling stores using upscale merchandising techniques that emphasize a better quality, higher margin product mix. Approximately 75% of the stores will feature Vision 2000 by the end of 1995-96. SKO also expects significant growth from its new prescription benefit management division and has intensified marketing efforts in fast growth areas.

Operational Review - 18-OCT-95

Net sales in the 28 weeks ended September 9, 1995, advanced 9.2%, year to year, aided by more stores in operation and a 1.9% gain in same-store sales. Gross margins narrowed on the impact of less profitable prescription benefit management (PBM) sales and increased promotional sales. Operating expenses were well controlled, but after a 33% jump in interest expense, and taxes at 39.3%, versus 37.7%, net income slid 6.4%, to $7,237,000 ($0.23 per share), from $7,730,000 ($0.24).

Stock Performance - 20-OCT-95

In the past 30 trading days, SKO's shares have declined 11%, compared to a 3% rise in the S&P 500. Average trading volume for the past five days was 25,840 shares, compared with the 40-day moving average of 56,397 shares.

Key Stock Statistics

Dividend Rate/Share	0.44	Shareholders	2,700
Shs. outstg. (M)	32.0	Market cap. (B)	$0.368
Avg. daily vol. (M)	0.038	Inst. holdings	36%
Tang. Bk. Value/Share	12.36	Insider holdings	NA
Beta	NA		

Value of $10,000 invested 5 years ago: NA

Fiscal Year Ending Feb. 28

	1996	% Change	1995	% Change	1994	% Change
Revenues (Million $)						
1Q	560.5	9%	514.9	8%	474.6	1%
2Q	418.2	10%	381.3	7%	355.3	NM
3Q	—	—	470.9	6%	446.3	3%
4Q	—	—	485.8	5%	463.0	8%
Yr.	—	—	1,853	7%	1,739	3%
Income (Million $)						
1Q	5.37	8%	4.98	-13%	5.72	-48%
2Q	1.87	-32%	2.75	29%	2.13	-52%
3Q	—	—	11.30	-20%	14.06	-19%
4Q	—	—	18.76	84%	10.22	-41%
Yr.	—	—	37.79	18%	32.12	-36%
Earnings Per Share ($)						
1Q	0.17	6%	0.16	-11%	0.18	-47%
2Q	0.06	-33%	0.09	29%	0.07	-50%
3Q	—	—	0.35	-20%	0.44	-19%
4Q	—	—	0.59	84%	0.32	-42%
Yr.	—	—	1.18	18%	1.00	-36%

Next earnings report expected: mid December

ShopKo Stores

Business Summary - 18-OCT-95

ShopKo Stores, Inc. is a regional discount store chain in the upper Midwest, with a growing presence in the Mountain and Pacific Northwest states. As of October 5, 1995, the company was operating 129 stores in small and mid-size markets in 15 states. Comparable-store sales gains and the number of stores in operation at the end of recent fiscal years were:

	1995	1994	1993	1992
Comp. sales	0.7%	1.2%	1.5%	1.7%
Stores	128	117	111	109

The stores carry a full assortment of value-priced general merchandise consisting of both branded and private-label nondurable hard goods (housewares, music/videos, health and beauty aids, toys and sporting goods) and soft goods (home textiles, men's, women's and children's apparel, shoes, jewelry, cosmetics and accessories). Most stores carry more than 75,000 items of merchandise. A majority of the stores also include pharmacy and optical departments.

Sales by product category in recent fiscal years:

	1995	1994	1993
Hardline goods	54%	55%	55%
Softline goods	26%	26%	28%
Health services	20%	19%	17%

SKO's average store size is about 90,000 sq. ft., with 84% of the stores greater than 74,000 sq. ft. New stores are expected to be larger. Competitors include national general merchandise discount chains such as Wal-Mart, K mart and Target. The company opened seven new stores in 1994-95, and remodeled 32 stores. In the first quarter of 1995-96, it opened four new stores, with plans to open one additional store and remodel 13 stores during the remainder of the year. New stores and remodels are formatted with SKO's new Vision 2000 merchandising concept, which is geared toward better quality, service and a higher level of taste.

In 1994-95, the company launched its prescription benefit management division, ProVantage Mail Service, initially a mail service pharmacy offered to companies across the country. With the acquisition of Bravell Inc., a national claims processor, the company firmly established ProVantage as a prescription benefit manager.

Important Developments

Oct. '95—SKO reported that total sales in the five weeks ended September 30, 1995, rose 11%, year to year; same-store sales were up 2.4%. In the 35 weeks ended September 30, total sales advanced 8.9%, on a 1.8% increase in same-store sales.

Capitalization

Long Term Debt: $413,234,000 (9/9/95).

Per Share Data ($) (Year Ended Feb. 28)

	1995	1994	1993	1992	1991	1990
Tangible Bk. Val.	12.41	11.67	11.11	9.98	8.88	7.14
Cash Flow	2.85	2.48	2.92	2.81	2.66	2.43
Earnings	1.18	1.00	1.56	1.55	1.44	1.33
Dividends	0.44	0.44	0.44	0.11	NA	NA
Payout Ratio	37%	44%	28%	7%	NA	NA
Cal. Yrs.	1994	1993	1992	1991	1990	1989
Prices - High	12⅛	16	17¼	15⅛	NA	NA
- Low	8¾	9¾	12⅞	11¾	NA	NA
P/E Ratio - High	10	16	11	10	NA	NA
- Low	7	10	8	8	NA	NA

Income Statement Analysis (Million $)

	1995	%Chg	1994	%Chg	1993	%Chg	1992
Revs.	1,853	7%	1,739	3%	1,683	2%	1,648
Oper. Inc.	133	21%	110	-16%	131	2%	128
Depr.	53.5	13%	47.3	10%	43.0	6%	40.4
Int. Exp.	30.3	29%	23.5	21%	19.4	6%	18.3
Pretax Inc.	62.4	18%	52.9	-35%	81.5	NM	81.2
Eff. Tax Rate	40%	—	39%	—	39%	—	39%
Net Inc.	37.8	18%	32.1	-36%	50.1	1%	49.6

Balance Sheet & Other Fin. Data (Million $)

	1995	1994	1993	1992	1991	1990
Cash	12.6	2.6	2.8	2.1	2.0	1.8
Curr. Assets	469	371	296	260	273	236
Total Assets	1,110	953	792	706	705	648
Curr. Liab.	281	252	215	182	217	177
LT Debt	414	310	209	192	192	235
Common Eqty.	397	374	355	320	284	228
Total Cap.	828	701	577	524	488	471
Cap. Exp.	95.0	134	91.1	55.3	59.1	80.1
Cash Flow	91.3	79.5	93.3	90.0	85.1	77.8

Ratio Analysis

	1995	1994	1993	1992	1991	1990
Curr. Ratio	1.7	1.5	1.4	1.4	1.3	1.3
% LT Debt of Cap.	49.9	44.1	36.2	36.6	39.4	49.8
% Net Inc.of Revs.	2.0	1.8	3.0	3.0	3.0	3.0
% Ret. on Assets	3.7	3.7	6.7	7.1	6.5	7.0
% Ret. on Equity	9.8	8.8	14.8	16.7	NA	20.6

Dividend Data —Dividends were initiated in December 1991. A "poison pill" stock purchase rights plan was adopted in 1992.

Amt. of Div. $	Date Decl.	Ex-Div. Date	Stock of Record	Payment Date
0.110	Oct. 25	Nov. 25	Dec. 01	Dec. 15 '94
0.110	Jan. 13	Feb. 23	Mar. 01	Mar. 15 '95
0.110	Apr. 13	May. 25	Jun. 01	Jun. 15 '95
0.110	Jun. 29	Aug. 30	Sep. 01	Sep. 15 '95
0.110	Sep. 21	Nov. 29	Dec. 01	Dec. 15 '95

Data as orig. reptd.; bef. results of disc. opers. and/or spec. items. Per share data adj. for stk. divs. as of ex-div. date. E-Estimated. NA-Not Available. NM-Not Meaningful. NR-Not Ranked.

Office—700 Pilgrim Way, Green Bay, WI 54304. **Tel**—(414) 497-2211. **Chrmn**—M. W. Wright. **Vice Chrmn**—W. J. Tyrell. **Pres & CEO**—D. P. Kramer. **SVP & CFO**—J. A. Jones. **SVP & Secy**—D. A. Liebergen. **Investor Contacts**—Gene Bankers (414-496-4158); Amy Ludwig (212-986-5900). **Dirs**—J. W. Eugster, J. C. Girard, D. P. Kramer, W. J. Tyrrell, M. W. Wright. **Transfer Agent & Registrar**—Norwest Bank Minnesota, Minneapolis. **Incorporated** in Minnesota in 1961. **Empl**-19,200. **S&P Analyst:** Maureen C. Carini

STANDARD & POOR'S

Shorewood Packaging

STOCK REPORTS

NASDAQ Symbol **SHOR**

In S&P SmallCap 600

15-OCT-95

Industry: Containers

Summary: This company prints and manufactures packaging for the cosmetics, home video, music, software, tobacco, toiletries and general consumer markets.

Quantitative Evaluations

Recent Price • 17⅞

52 Wk Range • 20½-14⅜

Yield • Nil

12-Mo. P/E • 15.3

Outlook (1 Lowest—5 Highest)
• **5+**

Fair Value
• **20⅞**

Risk
• **Average**

Earn./Div. Rank
• **B**

Technical Eval.
• **Bullish** since 7/95

Rel. Strength Rank (1 Lowest—99 Highest)
• **59**

Insider Activity
• **NA**

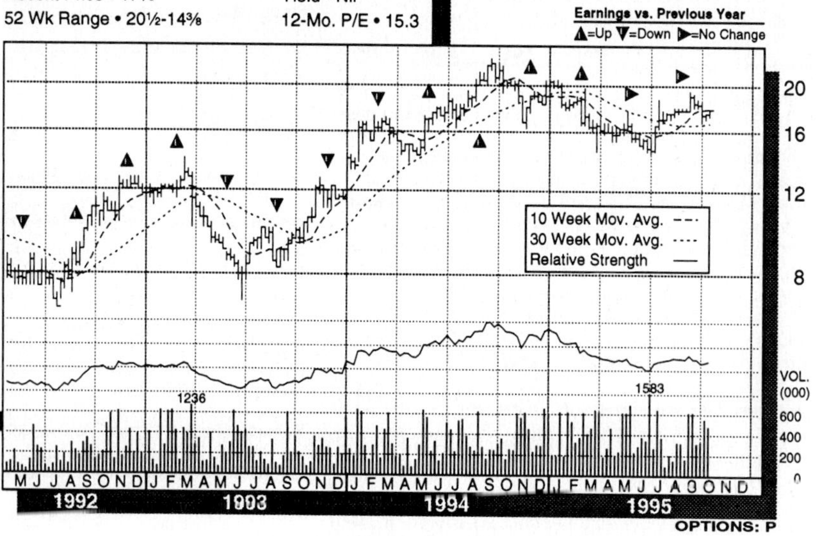

OPTIONS: P

Business Profile - 10-OCT-95

SHOR recently closed its Pittsford, N.Y. plant, as the facility failed to achieve adequate production levels, and commenced operations at a new facility in Oregon, which will produce packaging for the CD-ROM and interactive entertainment marketplace. The company said it expects continued growth with existing customers, as well as in new geographic and emerging product markets, including China, Europe and Latin America. Earnings are seen growing at a rate of 18% a year for the next five years.

Operational Review - 10-OCT-95

Sales in the three months ended July 29, 1995, rose 7.0%, year to year, as growth from the continued penetration of existing markets was offset somewhat by certain major customers deferring orders due to maintenance shutdowns. Operating costs and expenses were well controlled, and net income was up 7.2%. Per share earnings were unchanged, on 7.6% more shares outstanding.

Stock Performance - 13-OCT-95

In the past 30 trading days, SHOR's shares have increased 0.70%, compared to a 4% rise in the S&P 500. Average trading volume for the past five days was 94,800 shares, compared with the 40-day moving average of 90,569 shares.

Key Stock Statistics

Dividend Rate/Share	Nil	Shareholders	300
Shs. outstg. (M)	19.2	Market cap. (B)	$0.344
Avg. daily vol. (M)	0.082	Inst. holdings	61%
Tang. Bk. Value/Share	2.73	Insider holdings	NA
Beta	0.14		

Value of $10,000 invested 5 years ago: $ 28,336

Fiscal Year Ending Apr. 30

	1996	% Change	1995	% Change	1994	% Change
Revenues (Million $)						
1Q	90.70	7%	84.77	110%	40.37	-12%
2Q	—	—	97.05	111%	46.08	-11%
3Q	—	—	85.65	63%	52.43	21%
4Q	—	—	89.56	15%	77.59	79%
Yr.	—	—	357.0	65%	216.5	18%
Income (Million $)						
1Q	5.86	7%	5.47	159%	2.11	-48%
2Q	—	—	6.77	117%	3.12	-36%
3Q	—	—	5.52	NM	-0.21	NM
4Q	—	—	4.75	9%	4.37	100%
Yr.	—	—	22.51	140%	9.39	-36%
Earnings Per Share ($)						
1Q	0.30	NM	0.30	150%	0.12	-45%
2Q	—	—	0.36	100%	0.18	-31%
3Q	—	—	0.28	NM	-0.01	NM
4Q	—	—	0.24	NM	0.24	100%
Yr.	—	—	1.17	125%	0.52	-33%

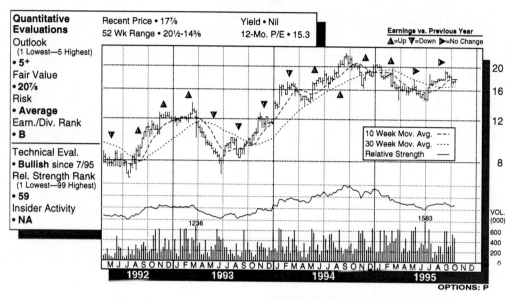

Next earnings report expected: late November

Shorewood Packaging

Business Summary - 04-AUG-95

Shorewood Packaging Corporation prints and manufactures high-quality paperboard packaging for the cosmetics, home video, music, software, tobacco, toiletries and general consumer markets in the U.S. and Canada. The company expects its future sales growth to be derived from the continued penetration of its existing markets and from the exploitation of new, emerging markets such as the expanding market for CD-ROM packaging.

For the home entertainment industry, the company's principal products are packaging for prerecorded cassettes and compact discs and packaging for videocassettes. In addition to Sony, customers include most of the major record production and distribution companies in the U.S. For the cosmetics and toiletries and other general consumer markets, Shorewood produces specialized packaging for customers requiring sophisticated precision graphic packaging for their products.

Shorewood manufactures its products on state-of-the-art sheet-fed and web printing presses. A printing and manufacturing web system, known as JOSH, has been developed over many years. The system, believed by the company to be unique (but not patented), combines offset lithographic and gravure printing, which were previously considered incompatible.

In January 1994, Shorewood acquired the premium packaging business of Somerville Packaging ($139 million in revenues) for $97 million cash and the assumption of certain liabilities, plus contingent compensation of up to $5 million. The Somerville operations make folding cartons for the tobacco, cosmetics and toiletries and general consumer industries.

Operations in Canada accounted for some 34% of sales in 1993-4, up from 25% in 1992-3.

Important Developments

Jun. '95—Shorewood said it will close its Pittsford, N.Y. plant in the fall of 1995. The facility employs 140 people. SHOR said the plant's production level is lower than the company's other facilities. SHOR noted that it does not expect to lose any significant accounts or sales as a result of the closing.

Mar. '95—Shorewood said it began construction of a new 120,000-sq.-ft., $20 million manufacturing facility in Springfield, Ore., which will produce packaging for the CD-ROM and interactive entertainment marketplace and other packaging products. The plant will commence operations in September 1995.

Capitalization

Long Term Debt: $101,912,000 (1/95).

Per Share Data ($)

(Year Ended Apr. 30)

	1995	1994	1993	1992	1991	1990
Tangible Bk. Val.	2.73	1.52	1.43	0.92	3.65	3.23
Cash Flow	1.86	1.06	1.19	0.93	1.04	1.10
Earnings	1.17	0.52	0.78	0.52	0.67	0.82
Dividends	Nil	Nil	Nil	3.25	Nil	Nil
Payout Ratio	Nil	Nil	Nil	621%	Nil	Nil
Cal. Yrs.	1994	1993	1992	1991	1990	1989
Prices - High	22¾	14¼	12¾	13⅞	18½	19
- Low	13¼	7	6¾	6½	5¾	10⅝
P/E Ratio - High	19	27	16	27	28	23
- Low	11	13	9	13	9	13

Income Statement Analysis (Million $)

	1995	%Chg	1994	%Chg	1993	%Chg	1992
Revs.	357	65%	216	17%	184	15%	160
Oper. Inc.	58.5	68%	34.9	-3%	35.8	21%	29.5
Depr.	13.3	36%	9.8	25%	7.9	3%	7.7
Int. Exp.	9.0	31%	6.9	24%	5.5	1%	5.5
Pretax Inc.	36.2	129%	15.8	-32%	23.4	44%	16.2
Eff. Tax Rate	38%	—	41%	—	38%	—	40%
Net Inc.	22.5	139%	9.4	-36%	14.6	49%	9.8

Balance Sheet & Other Fin. Data (Million $)

	1995	1994	1993	1992	1991	1990
Cash	4.1	2.7	12.5	5.7	12.2	11.3
Curr. Assets	96.9	78.2	50.8	42.3	48.1	44.5
Total Assets	245	220	113	100	111	104
Curr. Liab.	65.0	46.8	28.9	22.7	22.1	18.3
LT Debt	100	138	49.4	52.5	13.2	15.2
Common Eqty.	67.4	27.1	26.1	17.3	68.0	63.8
Total Cap.	179	174	83.9	77.3	88.8	86.0
Cap. Exp.	15.6	9.2	12.4	3.9	7.9	15.3
Cash Flow	35.8	19.2	22.5	17.5	19.8	21.7

Ratio Analysis

	1995	1994	1993	1992	1991	1990
Curr. Ratio	1.5	1.7	1.8	1.9	2.2	2.4
% LT Debt of Cap.	55.8	79.5	58.9	67.9	14.9	17.7
% Net Inc.of Revs.	6.3	4.3	7.9	6.1	9.0	11.6
% Ret. on Assets	9.6	5.7	13.9	9.3	12.3	16.7
% Ret. on Equity	47.6	35.7	68.2	22.9	20.0	29.1

Dividend Data —In July 1991, the company paid a special dividend of $3.25 a share.

Data as orig. reptd.; bef. results of disc. opers. and/or spec. items. Per share data adj. for stk. divs. as of ex-div. date. E-Estimated. NA-Not Available. NM-Not Meaningful. NR-Not Ranked.

Office—55 Engineers Lane, Farmingdale, NY 11735. **Tel**—(516) 694-2900. **Chrmn & CEO**—P. B. Shore. **Vice Chrmn & Pres**—M. P. Shore. **EVP, CFO & Investor Contact**—Howard M. Liebman. **Secy**—Joan Matheis. **Dirs**—K. J. Bannon, M. L. Braun, F. S. Glinert, S. Leslie, R. T. O'Donnell, M. P. Shore, P. B. Shore. **Transfer Agent**—Bank of New York, NYC. **Incorporated** in Delaware in 1985. **Empl-** 2,200. **S&P Analyst:** Stewart Scharf

STANDARD & POOR'S

STOCK REPORTS

Showboat, Inc.

NYSE Symbol **SBO**

In S&P SmallCap 600

28-SEP-95

Industry: Leisure/Amusement

Summary: This gaming company owns and operates a casino/hotel in Atlantic City and another in Las Vegas.

Quantitative Evaluations

Outlook
(1 Lowest—5 Highest)
• **5+**

Fair Value
• **27⅞**

Risk
• **Average**

Earn./Div. Rank
• **B-**

Technical Eval.
• **Bullish** since 7/95

Rel. Strength Rank
(1 Lowest—99 Highest)
• **38**

Insider Activity
• **Unfavorable**

Recent Price • 22¼ | Yield • 0.5%

52 Wk Range • 24⅜-11½ | 12-Mo. P/E • 25.6

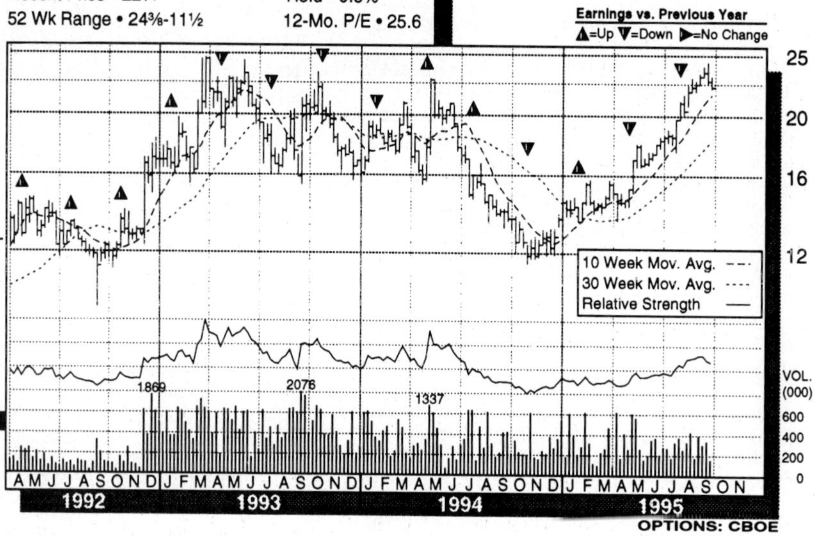

Business Profile - 28-SEP-95

Lower earnings are expected for 1995, reflecting the sale of the Star Casino, competitive pressures, and disruptions from remodeling in Las Vegas. However, the opening of a casino in Australia, anticipated benefits from property improvements, and the opening (pending licensing) of a riverboat casino in East Chicago, Ind., in early 1996, should boost 1996 profitability. The shares have advanced in anticipation of a 1996 EPS rebound to a projected $1.38, from $0.59 seen for 1995.

Operational Review - 28-SEP-95

Net revenues in the first half of 1995 advanced 10%, year to year, as record revenues at the Atlantic City Showboat outweighed weaker results in Las Vegas. Costs and expenses increased less rapidly; income from operations climbed strongly. However, with equity in the loss of an unconsolidated affiliate, versus equity in income, greater interest expense, a loss on the sale of the Star Casino in New Orleans, and higher taxes, net income declined 23%.

Stock Performance - 22-SEP-95

In the past 30 trading days, SBO's shares have increased 2%, compared to a 5% rise in the S&P 500. Average trading volume for the past five days was 30,320 shares, compared with the 40-day moving average of 59,754 shares.

Key Stock Statistics

Dividend Rate/Share	0.10	Shareholders	1,900
Shs. outstg. (M)	15.4	Market cap. (B)	$0.327
Avg. daily vol. (M)	0.064	Inst. holdings	48%
Tang. Bk. Value/Share	9.62	Insider holdings	NA
Beta	1.34		

Value of $10,000 invested 5 years ago: $ 25,528

Fiscal Year Ending Dec. 31

	1995	% Change	1994	% Change	1993	% Change
Revenues (Million $)						
1Q	98.68	12%	88.43	3%	85.50	NM
2Q	111.9	9%	102.4	10%	92.71	4%
3Q	—	—	113.2	5%	108.0	9%
4Q	—	—	97.28	9%	89.52	10%
Yr.	—	—	401.3	7%	375.7	6%
Income (Million $)						
1Q	1.78	-48%	3.44	79%	1.92	-27%
2Q	4.96	-7%	5.35	43%	3.75	-6%
3Q	—	—	5.92	-20%	7.36	-13%
4Q	—	—	0.99	125%	0.44	-47%
Yr.	—	—	15.70	17%	13.46	-15%
Earnings Per Share ($)						
1Q	0.12	-48%	0.23	77%	0.13	-43%
2Q	0.32	-9%	0.35	46%	0.24	-29%
3Q	—	—	0.38	-21%	0.48	-34%
4Q	—	—	0.06	100%	0.03	-57%
Yr.	—	—	1.02	15%	0.89	-35%

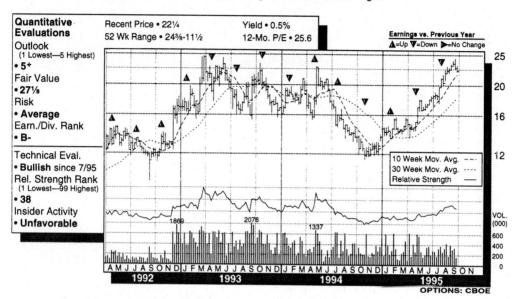

Next earnings report expected: early November

Showboat, Inc.

Business Summary - 28-SEP-95

Showboat, Inc. owns and operates the Showboat Casino Hotel in Atlantic City, N.J., and the Showboat Hotel, Casino and Bowling Center in Las Vegas, Nev. A 26%-owned affiliate holds a license to construct, manage and operate the Sydney Harbour Casino in Sydney, Australia; an interim casino opened in September 1995. The company is pursuing gaming opportunities in Indiana and Missouri.

The Atlantic City facility, opened in 1987, provides most operating revenues. It includes a 516-room, 24-story casino hotel featuring a 95,000 sq. ft. casino containing about 3,000 slot machines and 116 table games, a bowling center, 32,000 sq. ft. of meeting and exhibition space, and parking facilities. In 1994, slot machines accounted for 73.6% of casino revenues. With the November 1994 completion of a 284-room hotel tower, the company finished a $97 million expansion that included the addition of 20,000 sq. ft. of casino space and a horse racing simulcasting facility.

The Las Vegas Showboat, which began operations in 1954, is located on the eastern edge of the city, about two and one-half miles from downtown Las Vegas and from the Strip, where most of Las Vegas's major casino/hotel operations are located. The facility is a 453-room, 18-story casino hotel featuring a 106-lane bowling center, a 78,000 sq. ft. casino with 1,900 slot machines, 33 table games, and a 1,300-seat bingo parlor. It also includes a 408-seat buffet, a 194-seat coffee shop, and two specialty restaurants. An $18 to $19 million renovation of the Las Vegas Showboat was planned for 1995.

Through a subsidiary, Showboat owns a 55% interest in the Showboat Marina Partnership, the only applicant for the sole riverboat gaming license allocated to East Chicago, Ind.

Important Developments

Sep. '95—Showboat opened its A$60 million interim Sydney Harbor Casino in Australia. The main gaming area has 118 gaming tables and 500 gaming machines.

Jun. '95—The company was named the preferred developer/operator of a $110 million riverboat casino in Lemay, Mo.. It holds a 35% interest in the casino.

Apr. '95—Showboat sold Showboat Star Partnership, the operator of a New Orleans riverboat casino, to Players International Inc., for $52 million. Separately, it projected lower earnings for 1995, reflecting the sale, competitive pressures, and renovation-related disruptions at the Las Vegas Showboat. Results in 1996 are expected to benefit from contributions from the Syndey Harbor Casino and from a new East Chicago, Ind., casino, expected to open in early 1996, pending licensing.

Capitalization

Long Term Debt: $392,000,000 (6/95).

Per Share Data ($) (Year Ended Dec. 31)

	1994	1993	1992	1991	1990	1989
Tangible Bk. Val.	9.98	9.02	8.51	5.65	5.18	4.89
Cash Flow	2.87	2.44	3.27	2.78	2.07	2.34
Earnings	1.02	0.89	1.37	0.53	0.10	0.62
Dividends	0.10	0.10	0.10	0.10	0.10	0.24
Payout Ratio	10%	11%	9%	19%	105%	38%
Prices - High	22⅞	24⅝	18¼	11¾	9¾	15⅝
- Low	11½	15⅜	8¼	3¾	3	8½
P/E Ratio - High	22	28	14	22	98	25
- Low	11	17	6	7	30	14

Income Statement Analysis (Million $)

	1994	%Chg	1993	%Chg	1992	%Chg	1991
Revs.	401	7%	376	6%	355	7%	331
Oper. Inc.	67.4	-3%	69.6	2%	68.5	13%	60.4
Depr.	28.4	22%	23.3	6%	22.0	-14%	25.7
Int. Exp.	32.8	27%	25.8	2%	25.3	-8%	27.5
Pretax Inc.	27.2	14%	23.9	6%	22.6	124%	10.1
Eff. Tax Rate	42%	—	44%	—	30%	—	41%
Net Inc.	15.7	16%	13.5	-15%	15.9	165%	6.0

Balance Sheet & Other Fin. Data (Million $)

	1994	1993	1992	1991	1990	1989
Cash	90.0	123	100	38.7	37.6	46.3
Curr. Assets	144	140	115	50.0	51.6	63.5
Total Assets	624	471	385	320	332	323
Curr. Liab.	50.3	43.5	91.1	42.9	38.1	38.8
LT Debt	392	277	155	204	227	223
Common Eqty.	157	135	126	64.1	58.8	55.7
Total Cap.	568	427	294	277	294	284
Cap. Exp.	72.0	71.0	21.0	14.0	41.0	23.0
Cash Flow	44.1	36.8	37.9	31.7	23.5	26.7

Ratio Analysis

	1994	1993	1992	1991	1990	1989
Curr. Ratio	2.9	3.2	1.3	1.2	1.4	1.6
% LT Debt of Cap.	69.0	64.9	52.8	73.6	77.3	78.5
% Net Inc.of Revs.	3.9	3.6	4.5	1.8	0.3	2.1
% Ret. on Assets	2.8	3.1	4.0	1.8	0.3	2.2
% Ret. on Equity	10.6	10.3	15.1	9.8	1.9	13.2

Dividend Data —Dividends have been paid since 1970.

Amt. of Div. $	Date Decl.	Ex-Div. Date	Stock of Record	Payment Date
0.025	Aug. 31	Sep. 09	Sep. 15	Oct. 10 '94
0.025	Dec. 05	Dec. 09	Dec. 15	Jan. 10 '95
0.025	Feb. 22	Mar. 09	Mar. 15	Apr. 10 '95
0.025	May. 31	Jun. 13	Jun. 15	Jul. 10 '95
0.025	Aug. 30	Sep. 13	Sep. 15	Oct. 10 '95

Data as orig. reptd.; bef. results of disc. opers. and/or spec. items. Per share data adj. for stk. divs. as of ex-div. date. E-Estimated. NA-Not Available. NM-Not Meaningful. NR-Not Ranked.

Office—2800 Fremont St., Las Vegas, NV 89104. **Tel**—(702) 385-9141. **Chrmn**—J. K. Houssels. **Pres & CEO**—J. K. Houssels III. **VP-Fin, CFO & Investor Contact**—Leann Schneider. **EVP & Secy**—H. G. Nasky. **Dirs**—M. A. Clayton, J. D. Gaughan, J. K. Houssels, J. K. Houssels III, F. A. Modica, H. G. Nasky, W. C. Richardson, C. M. Sparks, J. S. Stewart, G. A. Zettler. **Transfer Agent & Registrar**—American Stock Transfer & Trust Co., NYC. **Incorporated** in Nevada in 1960. **Empl**-6,116. **S&P Analyst:** Efraim Levy

STANDARD & POOR'S

STOCK REPORTS

Sierra Health Services

NYSE Symbol **SIE**

In S&P SmallCap 600

03-OCT-95 **Industry:** Health Care Centers

Summary: This company provides and administers the delivery of health care programs through its health maintenance organization and other managed medical plans, primarily in Nevada.

Quantitative Evaluations

Outlook
(1 Lowest—5 Highest)
• **NA**

Fair Value
• **NA**

Risk
• **Average**

Earn./Div. Rank
• **B-**

Technical Eval.
• **Bullish** since 7/95

Rel. Strength Rank
(1 Lowest—99 Highest)
• **17**

Insider Activity
• **NA**

Recent Price • 25

52 Wk Range • 33⅝-22⅛

Yield • Nil

12-Mo. P/E • 13.7

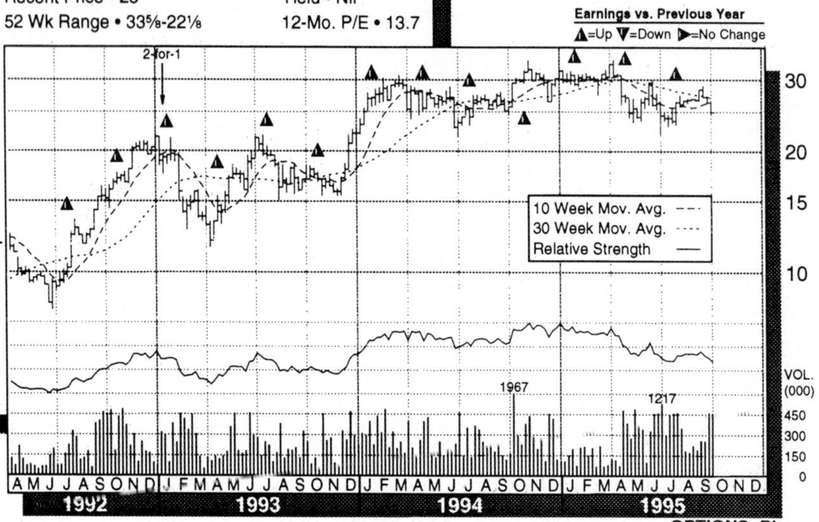

OPTIONS: Ph

Business Profile - 03-OCT-95

This managed care company is experiencing rapid growth resulting from strong membership increases and the implementation of operating efficiencies. The company has increased its product portfolio, including a point of service and individual plan, to meet the needs of as many clients as possible. During 1995, the company hopes that Nevada will move its Medicaid program into the managed care arena, which will provide further expansion opportunities.

Operational Review - 03-OCT-95

Revenues continued to climb in the first half of 1995, reflecting HMO membership gains and higher revenues from administrative services, workers' compensation services and Medicare supplement products. Margins widened as smaller increase in G&A expense offset a higher medical loss ratio and expenses associated with opening the Texas HMO. Results benefited further from a lower tax rate. EPS gains were restricted by more shares outstanding.

Stock Performance - 29-SEP-95

In the past 30 trading days, SIE's shares have declined 7%, compared to a 5% rise in the S&P 500. Average trading volume for the past five days was 98,500 shares, compared with the 40-day moving average of 58,497 shares.

Key Stock Statistics

Dividend Rate/Share	Nil	Shareholders	200
Shs. outstg. (M)	14.8	Market cap. (B)	$0.370
Avg. daily vol. (M)	0.079	Inst. holdings	56%
Tang. Bk. Value/Share	8.99	Insider holdings	NA
Beta	1.76		

Value of $10,000 invested 5 years ago: $ 57,964

Fiscal Year Ending Dec. 31

	1995	% Change	1994	% Change	1993	% Change
Revenues (Million $)						
1Q	83.63	21%	69.40	9%	63.80	14%
2Q	86.64	19%	72.68	14%	63.67	8%
3Q	—	—	75.33	14%	65.83	9%
4Q	—	—	78.38	20%	65.43	9%
Yr.	—	—	295.8	14%	258.7	10%
Income (Million $)						
1Q	6.25	40%	4.48	23%	3.65	19%
2Q	7.04	28%	5.50	32%	4.16	41%
3Q	—	—	5.83	28%	4.56	22%
4Q	—	—	6.40	26%	5.08	33%
Yr.	—	—	22.20	27%	17.44	28%
Earnings Per Share ($)						
1Q	0.43	19%	0.36	20%	0.30	15%
2Q	0.48	9%	0.44	29%	0.34	36%
3Q	—	—	0.46	24%	0.37	19%
4Q	—	—	0.45	10%	0.41	28%
Yr.	—	—	1.71	20%	1.42	25%

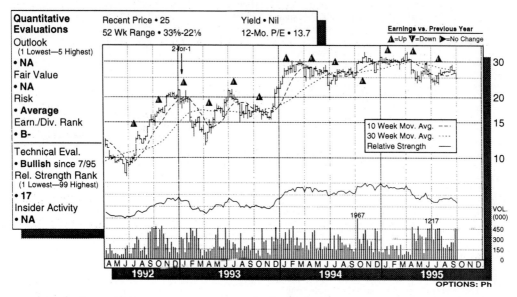

Next earnings report expected: late October

Sierra Health Services

Business Summary - 26-SEP-95

Sierra Health Services is a managed health care company that provides and administers the delivery of comprehensive health care programs through its health maintenance organization, managed indemnity plans, a third party administrative services company for employee funded health benefit plans and workers' compensation medical management programs, primarily in Nevada.

Sierra's HMO, Health Plan of Nevada (HPN), provided health services to 126,460 members as of December 31, 1994. HPN's members were served by 113 providers employed by the company's own multi-specialty medical group, Southwest Medical Associates, as well as by 750 additional contracted health care providers and 11 hospitals. HPN generally contracts with its primary care physicians and specialists on a modified fee-for-service basis and with its hospitals on a discounted per diem basis. In addition to its commercial plan, the company offers a prepaid health care program for Medicare-eligible beneficiaries. As of December 31, 1994, 19,760 (16%) of the company's HMO members were enrolled in this program.

The company also offers health insurance through its preferred provider organization (PPO), which offers members the option of receiving their medical care from either non-contracted or contracted providers. As of December 31, 1994, 24,428 persons were enrolled in the company's managed indemnity plans. The company also offers a triple option benefit program pursuant to which covered members can elect indemnity plan coverage, PPO coverage or HMO coverage.

The company's administrative services products provide utilization review and PPO services to large employer groups that are usually self insured. As of December 31, 1994, 65,454 persons were enrolled in administrative services plans. In January 1994, the company began providing workers' compansation medical management services in Nevada. As of December 31, 1994, enrollment in this program was 78,868.

The company also provides home health care services, a hospice program and mental health and substance abuse services.

Important Developments

Jun. '95—Sierra agreed to acquire CII Financial, an underwriter of workers' compensation insurance in California and four other western and midwestern states for about $86 million in SIE stock. Separately, SIE acquired Northern Nevada Health Network, a provider of utilization review services.

Feb. '95—The company received a license to operate an HMO in Texas.

Capitalization

Long Term Debt: $18,083,000 (6/95).
Minority Interest: $355,000.

Per Share Data ($)

(Year Ended Dec. 31)

	1994	1993	1992	1991	1990	1989
Tangible Bk. Val.	8.99	4.87	3.36	1.92	0.90	0.61
Cash Flow	2.28	1.85	1.53	1.30	0.58	0.52
Earnings	1.71	1.42	1.14	0.91	0.28	0.28
Dividends	Nil	Nil	Nil	Nil	Nil	Nil
Payout Ratio	Nil	Nil	Nil	Nil	Nil	Nil
Prices - High	33½	22⅝	21⅝	14¾	7	4⅞
- Low	21¼	11½	8⅛	5⅝	2¾	¾
P/E Ratio - High	20	16	19	16	25	17
- Low	12	8	7	6	10	3

Income Statement Analysis (Million $)

	1994	%Chg	1993	%Chg	1992	%Chg	1991
Revs.	296	14%	259	10%	236	13%	209
Oper. Inc.	43.5	40%	31.1	21%	25.6	19%	21.5
Depr.	7.4	41%	5.3	11%	4.7	5%	4.5
Int. Exp.	1.9	NM	0.1	-88%	0.8	-26%	1.0
Pretax Inc.	34.2	32%	25.9	33%	19.5	29%	15.1
Eff. Tax Rate	35%	—	32%	—	29%	—	29%
Net Inc.	22.2	28%	17.4	28%	13.6	26%	10.8

Balance Sheet & Other Fin. Data (Million $)

	1994	1993	1992	1991	1990	1989
Cash	105	48.5	45.2	32.1	39.4	17.2
Curr. Assets	119	60.8	55.9	41.2	46.2	23.2
Total Assets	223	144	108	85.5	82.4	56.2
Curr. Liab.	59.1	55.0	46.7	43.3	52.0	30.2
LT Debt	18.4	16.0	7.7	6.3	6.1	8.4
Common Eqty.	134	62.1	42.3	24.1	11.9	8.5
Total Cap.	154	78.7	50.6	30.8	18.4	17.3
Cap. Exp.	11.2	32.0	9.3	8.5	3.2	7.7
Cash Flow	29.6	22.7	18.3	15.3	6.7	6.0

Ratio Analysis

	1994	1993	1992	1991	1990	1989
Curr. Ratio	2.0	1.1	1.2	1.0	0.9	0.8
% LT Debt of Cap.	12.0	20.3	15.1	20.5	33.2	48.5
% Net Inc.of Revs.	7.5	6.7	5.8	5.1	1.9	2.4
% Ret. on Assets	11.3	13.7	13.9	12.7	4.7	6.4
% Ret. on Equity	21.4	33.2	40.5	59.6	31.8	47.4

Dividend Data —No cash dividends have been paid, and Sierra plans to retain earnings for development of its business. A two-for-one stock split was effected in January 1993. A "poison pill" stock purchase rights plan was adopted in June 1994.

Data as orig. reptd.; bef. results of disc. opers. and/or spec. items. Per share data adj. for stk. divs. as of ex-div. date. E-Estimated. NA-Not Available. NM-Not Meaningful. NR-Not Ranked.

Office—2724 N. Tenaya Way, Las Vegas, NV 89128 (P.O. Box 15645, Las Vegas 89114-5645). **Tel**—(702) 242-7000. **Chrmn & CEO**—A. M. Marlon. **Pres & COO**— E. E. McDonald. **VP, CFO & Treas**—J. L. Starr. **Secy**—F. E. Collins. **Dirs**—T. Y. Hartley, A. M. Marlon, E. E. MacDonald, W. J. Raggio, C. L. Ruthe. **Transfer Agent & Registrar**—Continental Stock Transfer & Trust Co., NYC. **Incorporated** in Nevada in 1984. **Empl**-1,600. **S&P Analyst:** Philip J. Birbara

STANDARD & POOR'S

Sierra Pacific Resources

STOCK REPORTS

NYSE Symbol **SRP**
In S&P SmallCap 600

07-SEP-95

Industry:
Util.-Diversified

Summary: This utility holding company provides electric, gas and water services to western, cental and northeastern parts of Nevada and the Lake Tahoe region of California.

Quantitative Evaluations

Outlook
(1 Lowest—5 Highest)
• **1+**

Fair Value
• **18¾**

Risk
• **Low**

Earn./Div. Rank
• **B**

Technical Eval.
• **Bullish** since 12/94

Rel. Strength Rank
(1 Lowest—99 Highest)
• **41**

Insider Activity
• **NA**

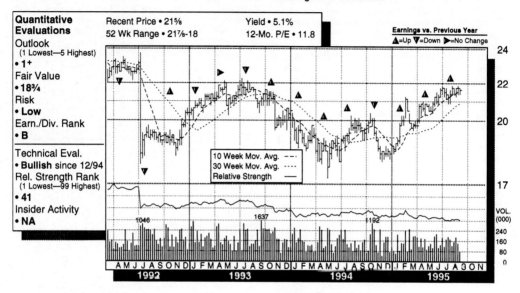

Recent Price • 21⅝
52 Wk Range • 21⅞-18

Yield • 5.1%
12-Mo. P/E • 11.8

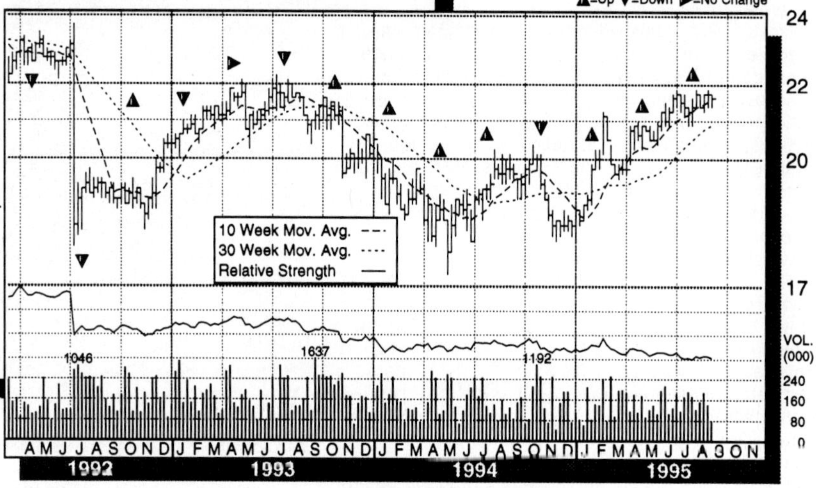

Business Profile - 07-SEP-95

This holding company for Sierra Pacific Power Co. operates electric, gas and water utilities. In November 1994, shareholders of SRP and Washington Water Power Co. (WWP) approved the June 1994 merger proposal under which SRP and WWP will combine to form Resources West Energy Corp. The merger is expected to be completed in the fall of 1995. As a result of the pending merger, SRP has proposed a freeze on Nevada electric and gas prices until January 2000, with one limited price increase in 1997.

Operational Review - 01-SEP-95

Revenues advanced in 1995's first half, reflecting increased electric and natural gas sales as a result of cooler-than-normal weather, and a small water price increase. Expenses were up only 3.3%, aided by lower fuel and purchased power prices. However, these savings were partially offset by a one-time requirement to refund $2.9 million related to a 1978 coal contract. SRP's Lands of Sierra subsidiary had improved performance due to sales of real estate properties and lower operating costs.

Stock Performance - 01-SEP-95

In the past 30 trading days, SRP's shares have increased 2%, compared to a 2% rise in the S&P 500. Average trading volume for the past five days was 15,020 shares, compared with the 40-day moving average of 30,090 shares.

Key Stock Statistics

Dividend Rate/Share	1.12	Shareholders	28,500
Shs. outstg. (M)	29.8	Market cap. (B)	$0.648
Avg. daily vol. (M)	0.030	Inst. holdings	31%
Tang. Bk. Value/Share	17.38	Insider holdings	NA
Beta	0.11		

Value of $10,000 invested 5 years ago: $ 12,494

Fiscal Year Ending Dec. 31

	1995	% Change	1994	% Change	1993	% Change
Revenues (Million $)						
1Q	160.1	4%	154.0	11%	139.3	10%
2Q	142.2	5%	135.9	10%	123.1	10%
3Q	—	—	158.2	22%	130.1	10%
4Q	—	—	178.2	31%	135.6	9%
Yr.	—	—	626.3	19%	528.1	10%
Income (Million $)						
1Q	15.25	2%	14.90	16%	12.90	NM
2Q	12.77	33%	9.63	71%	5.64	-24%
3Q	—	—	13.38	NM	13.47	34%
4Q	—	—	14.46	12%	12.88	NM
Yr.	—	—	52.37	17%	44.89	59%
Earnings Per Share ($)						
1Q	0.52	2%	0.51	2%	0.50	NM
2Q	0.37	12%	0.33	50%	0.22	-24%
3Q	—	—	0.46	-10%	0.51	31%
4Q	—	—	0.49	11%	0.44	NM
Yr.	—	—	1.79	7%	1.67	53%

Next earnings report expected: late October

Sierra Pacific Resources

Business Summary - 01-SEP-95

Sierra Pacific Resources, a holding company for Sierra Pacific Power Co. (SPPC), provides electric services (83% of 1994 revenues) to about 263,000 customers in a total service area of about 50,000 square miles in western, central and northeastern parts of Nevada and the Lake Tahoe area of California. SPPC also provides gas services (11% of 1994 revenues) to about 88,000 gas customers in a total area of about 600 square miles in Reno-Sparks, Nevada, and the surrounding area, and water service (6%) to 60,000 customers in a total area of 160 square miles in the Reno-Sparks metropolitan area. The mining industry is the single largest source of the company's revenue, accounting for 21% of total 1994 electric revenue. Total revenues by customer class in recent years were:

	1994	1993	1992	1991
Residential	35%	38%	37%	37%
Small comm'l & ind'l	31%	31%	32%	33%
Large comm'l & ind'l	26%	26%	26%	24%
Other	8%	5%	5%	6%

Sources of electric generation in 1994 were coal (23%), gas and oil (30%), and purchased power and other (47%). Peak demand in 1994 was 1,130 mw, and capability at peak totaled 1,309 mw, for a capacity margin of 14%.

Estimated construction expenditures for 1995 through 1999 total $647 million, with 87.5% of the funds slated for electric facilities.

Important Developments

Nov. '94—Shareholders of both SRP and Washington Water Power Co. (WWP) approved the June 1994 merger proposal under which SRP and WWP will combine to form Resources West Energy Corp. SRP shareholders will receive 1.44 common shares in Resources West for each SRP common share, while WWP shareholders will receive one Resources West common share for each WWP common share. Each share of the two firms' preferred stock will be converted into the right to receive one share of preferred stock of the new company with equal stated value, dividends, redemption provisions and rights upon liquidation. The firms said that their combined revenues totaled about $1.2 billion in 1993, with earnings of $119.0 million and assets of $3.4 billion. The merger is subject to the approval of federal and state regualtory agencies. The process is expected to be completed in the fall of 1995. In October, the Montana Public Service Commission approved the merger.

Capitalization

Long Term Debt: $565,708,000 (3/95).
Subsid. Cum. Pfd. Stk.: $93,515,000.

Per Share Data ($)

(Year Ended Dec. 31)

	1994	1993	1992	1991	1990	1989
Tangible Bk. Val.	17.27	16.85	15.85	16.83	16.39	17.77
Earnings	1.79	1.67	1.09	1.75	1.93	2.05
Dividends	1.12	1.12	1.48	1.84	1.84	1.81
Payout Ratio	63%	67%	136%	105%	95%	88%
Prices - High	20⅜	22¼	24⅜	24¼	25½	25⅞
- Low	17¼	19½	17⅞	20⅛	18⅜	22⅜
P/E Ratio - High	11	13	22	14	13	13
- Low	10	12	16	12	10	11

Income Statement Analysis (Million $)

	1994	%Chg	1993	%Chg	1992	%Chg	1991
Revs.	626	19%	528	10%	482	3%	469
Depr.	52.6	5%	49.9	4%	48.1	7%	44.8
Maint.	16.2	-2%	16.6	-3%	17.2	3%	16.7
Fxd. Chgs. Cov.	2.6	10%	2.4	20%	2.0	-15%	2.3
Constr. Credits	3.5	NM	3.5	133%	1.5	114%	0.7
Eff. Tax Rate	33%	—	32%	—	33%	—	33%
Net Inc.	52.4	17%	44.9	33%	33.8	-19%	41.9

Balance Sheet & Other Fin. Data (Million $)

	1994	1993	1992	1991	1990	1989
Gross Prop.	1,836	1,736	1,586	1,485	1,417	1,328
Cap. Exp.	125	166	115	81.0	99	81.0
Net Prop.	1,331	1,271	1,160	1,094	1,064	1,009
Capitalization:						
LT Debt	562	551	562	506	490	462
% LT Debt	48	48	52	51	53	50
Pfd.	93.5	107	107	57.1	57.0	57.1
% Pfd.	8.00	9.30	9.90	5.80	6.20	6.20
Common	509	490	412	429	376	399
% Common	44	43	38	43	41	44
Total Cap.	1,367	1,357	1,259	1,216	1,140	1,148

Ratio Analysis

	1994	1993	1992	1991	1990	1989
Oper. Ratio	84.3	83.4	82.2	82.1	81.6	81.2
% Earn. on Net Prop.	7.6	7.2	6.2	7.8	8.4	8.4
% Ret. on Revs.	8.4	8.5	7.0	8.9	9.3	10.1
% Ret. On Invest.Cap	7.6	7.4	6.3	7.8	8.0	8.2
% Return On Com.Eqty	10.5	10.0	6.8	10.4	11.3	11.7

Dividend Data —Dividends have been paid since 1916. A dividend reinvestment plan is available. A "poison pill" stock purchase rights plan was adopted in 1989.

Amt. of Div. $	Date Decl.	Ex-Div. Date	Stock of Record	Payment Date
0.280	Sep. 29	Oct. 12	Oct. 18	Nov. 01 '94
0.280	Dec. 01	Jan. 11	Jan. 18	Feb. 01 '95
0.280	Mar. 21	Apr. 11	Apr. 18	May. 01 '95
0.280	May. 15	Jul. 14	Jul. 18	Aug. 01 '95

Data as orig. reptd.; bef. results of disc opers. and/or spec. items. Per share data adj. for stk. divs. as of ex-div. date. E-Estimated. NA-Not Available. NM-Not Meaningful. NR-Not Ranked.

Office—6100 Neil Rd., Reno, NV 89511. **Tel**—(702) 689-3600. **Chrmn, Pres & CEO**—W. M. Higgins. **VP & Secy**—W. E. Peterson. **SVP-CFO**—M. K. Malquist. **Treas & Investor Contact**—Steven C. Oldham. **Dirs**—E. P. Bliss, K. M. Corbin, T. J. Day, H. P. Dayton, Jr., J. R. Donnelley, R. N. Fulstone, W. M. Higgins, J. L. Murphy, D. E. Wheeler, R. B. Whittington. **Transfer Agent & Registrar**—First Chicago Trust Co., Jersey City, NJ. **Incorporated** in Maine in 1912; reincorporated in Nevada in 1965 and 1983. **Empl**-1,779. **S&P Analyst:** Ronald J. Gross

STANDARD & POOR'S
STOCK REPORTS

Simpson Industries

NASDAQ Symbol **SMPS**
In S&P SmallCap 600

06-NOV-95 **Industry:** Auto parts/equipment

Summary: This company makes machined components and assemblies for OEMs in the automotive, truck and heavy-duty equipment industries in North America, Europe and Japan.

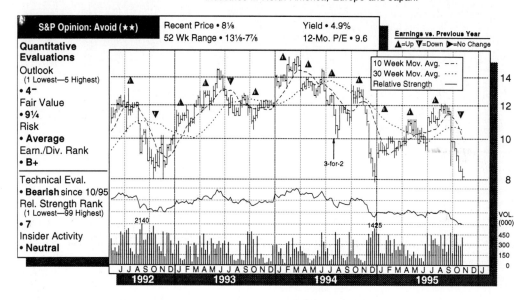

S&P Opinion: Avoid (★★)

Recent Price • 8⅛
52 Wk Range • 13⅛-7⅞
Yield • 4.9%
12-Mo. P/E • 9.6

Quantitative Evaluations
Outlook
(1 Lowest—5 Highest)
• **4-**
Fair Value
• **9¼**
Risk
• **Average**
Earn./Div. Rank
• **B+**

Technical Eval.
• **Bearish** since 10/95
Rel. Strength Rank
(1 Lowest—99 Highest)
• **7**
Insider Activity
• **Neutral**

Earnings vs. Previous Year
▲=Up ▼=Down ▶=No Change

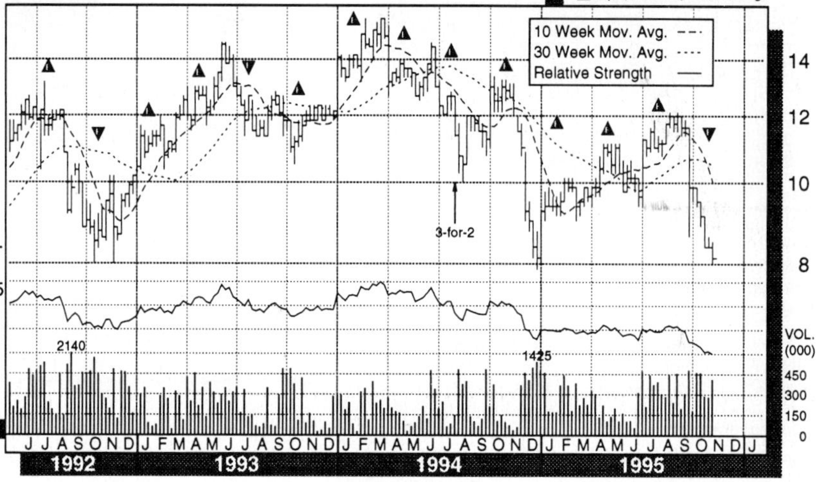

Overview - 06-NOV-95

Sales for 1995 should be unchanged from those of last year, with modest growth expected for 1996, reflecting softening North American automobile and light-truck production schedules. The company's heavy-duty business continues to grow as mid-range and off-road heavy-duty diesel engine production remains strong and business with Caterpillar, Inc. continues to expand. Despite decreased new program launch costs, operating margins will be penalized by higher fixed costs of engineering, development and geographic expansion. Long-term results should benefit somewhat from improving domestic and foreign markets and higher prices. The new Mexican unit should not be affected by currency fluctuations, as transactions are in dollars. Growth is expected in Europe and Japan, with sales to Japan rising rapidly.

Valuation - 06-NOV-95

The shares, which fell 50% during 1994, have dropped more than 30% in 1995, as production schedules for North American vehicles have softened. Weak demand for automobiles and light trucks is expected to continue into 1996. The shares, trading at 10X our 1995 EPS estimate of $0.85 and under 10X our projection of $0.90 for 1996, are at a discount to projected multiples for the S&P SmallCap 600 and on par with those of company peers. With production schedules softening, we suggest avoiding purchase at this time.

Key Stock Statistics

S&P EPS Est. 1995	0.85	Tang. Bk. Value/Share	5.47
P/E on S&P Est. 1995	9.6	Beta	0.99
S&P EPS Est. 1996	0.90	Shareholders	1,800
Dividend Rate/Share	0.40	Market cap. (B)	$0.146
Shs. outstg. (M)	18.0	Inst. holdings	60%
Avg. daily vol. (M)	0.074	Insider holdings	NA

Value of $10,000 invested 5 years ago: $ 17,024

Fiscal Year Ending Dec. 31

	1995	% Change	1994	% Change	1993	% Change
Revenues (Million $)						
1Q	107.2	30%	82.70	27%	65.13	25%
2Q	103.6	13%	91.32	36%	67.31	10%
3Q	86.34	NM	85.88	48%	57.87	10%
4Q	—	—	96.75	34%	72.18	27%
Yr.	—	—	356.6	36%	262.5	18%
Income (Million $)						
1Q	5.56	36%	4.08	22%	3.35	86%
2Q	4.91	10%	4.48	51%	2.97	-11%
3Q	1.43	-42%	2.47	NM	0.66	32%
4Q	—	—	3.34	36%	2.46	5%
Yr.	—	—	14.37	52%	9.44	18%
Earnings Per Share ($)						
1Q	0.31	35%	0.23	23%	0.19	56%
2Q	0.27	8%	0.25	50%	0.17	-14%
3Q	0.08	-43%	0.14	NM	0.04	50%
4Q	E0.19	6%	0.18	29%	0.14	5%
Yr.	E0.85	6%	0.80	51%	0.53	13%

Next earnings report expected: late January

Simpson Industries

Business Summary - 06-NOV-95

Simpson Industries, Inc. makes precision machined components principally on a sole-source basis for original equipment manufacturers (OEMs) in the automotive, truck and heavy-duty equipment industries.

Simpson's products include a broad range of vibration control devices, air-conditioning compressors, and transmissions and drive trains, precision machined to customer specifications.

Engine products include vibration control products such as dampers, isolators and balance shafts and modular assemblies for automobile, light-truck and medium-truck OEMs.

The company's transmission and chassis products include hubs, brake components, transmission components, yokes, flanges, brackets and compressor components.

In the area of heavy-duty products, Simpson manufactures water pump and fly wheel assemblies, engine covers, manifolds, dampers and brackets for diesel engines.

Sales to the four largest customers accounted for 80% of the total in 1994, apportioned as follows: GM 31%, Ford 25%, Chrysler 15% and Consolidated Diesel Co. 9%.

The company has 11 manufacturing units located throughout the Midwest, as well as in North Carolina, Ontario and Mexico.

In January 1995, the company borrowed $20 million at an interest rate of 8.45% payable quarterly. In addition, Simpson's Mexican subsidiary borrowed $4,050,000 at an interest rate of 8.82%, payable monthly.

Important Developments

Oct. '95—Simpson completed the purchase of a 111,000-sq.-ft. plant near Mexico City. The company's Mexican operation currently manufactures engine components for Chrysler's 2.4 liter engine. SMPS' work force in Mexico consists of approximately 50 company trained Mexican citizens. The company noted that even if North American vehicle production is relatively flat in 1996, its sales should rise modestly due to volume from new programs. The company is structured to continue to reduce costs throughout its facilities. Simpson added that through the first nine months of 1995, it has gained new business which will result in annual volume of over $40 million at the maturity of the programs, expected from 1997 through 1999.

Capitalization

Long Term Debt: $62,000,000 (9/95).

Per Share Data ($) (Year Ended Dec. 31)

	1994	1993	1992	1991	1990	1989
Tangible Bk. Val.	5.45	5.09	5.16	4.39	4.45	4.37
Cash Flow	1.71	1.32	1.26	1.15	1.17	1.38
Earnings	0.80	0.53	0.47	0.31	0.42	0.75
Dividends	0.48	0.37	0.37	0.37	0.37	0.37
Payout Ratio	60%	71%	83%	120%	89%	50%
Prices - High	15 5/8	14 5/8	13 1/8	9 1/8	7 5/8	9 7/8
- Low	7 7/8	10 3/8	8	4 5/8	4 5/8	6
P/E Ratio - High	20	28	28	30	18	13
- Low	10	20	17	15	11	8

Income Statement Analysis (Million $)

	1994	%Chg	1993	%Chg	1992	%Chg	1991
Revs.	357	36%	262	17%	223	16%	192
Oper. Inc.	43.1	28%	33.6	12%	30.1	34%	22.5
Depr.	16.3	15%	14.2	6%	13.4	8%	12.4
Int. Exp.	4.3	20%	3.6	-4%	3.8	40%	2.7
Pretax Inc.	23.1	42%	16.3	16%	14.0	97%	7.1
Eff. Tax Rate	38%	—	42%	—	43%	—	36%
Net Inc.	14.4	53%	9.4	17%	8.0	78%	4.5

Balance Sheet & Other Fin. Data (Million $)

	1994	1993	1992	1991	1990	1989
Cash	4.8	18.1	43.0	21.1	8.7	8.3
Curr. Assets	70.5	70.9	76.9	51.3	38.7	41.2
Total Assets	207	187	170	138	123	124
Curr. Liab.	38.9	36.4	27.2	20.9	17.6	20.9
LT Debt	50.4	39.0	37.0	38.5	25.0	25.0
Common Eqty.	98.0	91.5	91.8	64.1	64.8	63.8
Total Cap.	158	141	141	116	104	102
Cap. Exp.	38.2	37.5	22.4	15.8	14.1	22.6
Cash Flow	30.7	23.7	21.4	16.9	17.0	19.9

Ratio Analysis

	1994	1993	1992	1991	1990	1989
Curr. Ratio	1.8	1.9	2.8	2.5	2.2	2.0
% LT Debt of Cap.	31.9	27.7	26.2	33.2	24.0	24.6
% Net Inc.of Revs.	4.0	3.6	3.6	2.4	3.2	5.4
% Ret. on Assets	7.3	5.3	4.7	3.5	4.9	8.9
% Ret. on Equity	15.1	10.3	9.4	7.0	9.5	17.6

Dividend Data —Cash has been paid each year since 1947. A dividend reinvestment plan is available.

Amt. of Div. $	Date Decl.	Ex-Div. Date	Stock of Record	Payment Date
0.100	Oct. 25	Nov. 25	Dec. 01	Dec. 22 '94
0.100	Jan. 24	Feb. 24	Mar. 02	Mar. 23 '95
0.100	Apr. 28	May. 25	Jun. 01	Jun. 22 '95
0.100	Jul. 25	Sep. 05	Sep. 07	Sep. 28 '95
0.100	Oct. 23	Nov. 28	Nov. 30	Dec. 21 '95

Data as orig. reptd.; bef. results of disc. opers. and/or spec. items. Per share data adj. for stk. divs. as of ex-div. date. E-Estimated. NA-Not Available. NM-Not Meaningful. NR-Not Ranked.

Office—47603 Halyard Dr., Plymouth, MI 48170-2429. **Tel**—(313) 207-6200. **Fax**—(313) 207-6500. **Chrmn**—R. W. Navarre. **Pres & CEO**—R. E. Parrott. **VP-Fin, CFO, Treas & Investor Contact**—Kathryn L. Williams. **Secy**—F. K. Zinn. **Dirs**—J. M. Bakken, S. Haka, G. R. Kempton, W. J. Kirchberger, R. W. Navarre, R. E. Parrott, R. L. Roudebush, F. L. Weaver, F. K. Zinn. **Transfer Agent & Registrar**—State Street Bank & Trust Co., Boston. **Incorporated** in Michigan in 1945. **Empl**-2,135. **S&P Analyst:** Stewart Scharf

STANDARD & POOR'S

STOCK REPORTS

Skyline Corp.

NYSE Symbol **SKY**

In S&P SmallCap 600

03-AUG-95 **Industry:** Mobile/Modular Homes

Summary: Skyline is one of the largest producers of manufactured housing and recreational vehicles.

S&P Opinion: Hold (★★★)	Recent Price • 16⅝	Yield • 2.9%
	52 Wk Range • 22⅛-16⅜	12-Mo. P/E • 12.0

Quantitative Evaluations

Outlook (1 Lowest—5 Highest)
• **NA**

Fair Value
• **NA**

Risk
• **Low**

Earn./Div. Rank
• **B+**

Technical Eval.
• **Bullish** since 12/94

Rel. Strength Rank (1 Lowest—99 Highest)
• **8**

Insider Activity
• **NA**

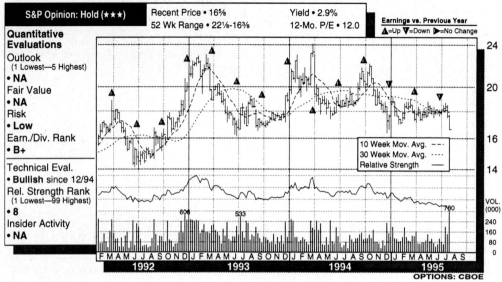

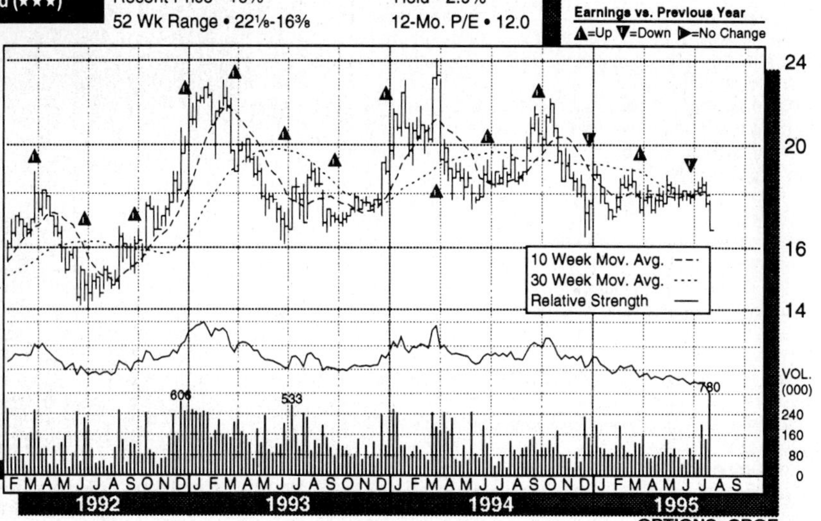

OPTIONS: CBOE

Overview - 03-AUG-95

Modest sales growth is expected in 1995-96, with most of the increase likely to be derived from ongoing gains in the manufactured housing segment, even if SKY's volume growth continues to trail the industry. The division should be aided by wider acceptance of factory-built homes as a lower cost housing option, along with a growing number of individuals looking to make their first home purchase, who account for the largest proportion of manufactured home purchases. However, although industry demand has remained strong, the moderating economy will likely reduce the growth pace. The recent slowdown in the RV segment is also likely to continue, as consumers tend to reduce discretionary spending in a less robust economy. Margins are expected to be relatively unchanged, with the cost of greater sales efforts offset by increased manufacturing efficiencies.

Valuation - 03-AUG-95

Skyline's shares, which have been volatile in recent years, have followed a mostly downward path since the fall of 1994. With earnings disappointing investors since the second quarter of 1994-95, and SKY's volume growth of manufactured homes below the industry norm, the shares have not mirrored the strong appreciation of many manufactured housing stocks in the first half of 1995. Although our forecast of only modest sales and earnings growth in 1995-96 does not bode particularly well for Skyline's upcoming stock performance, prospects could get a lift if the recent drop in long-term interest rates provides a spark to the economy.

Key Stock Statistics

S&P EPS Est. 1996	1.50	Tang. Bk. Value/Share	15.27
P/E on S&P Est. 1996	11.1	Beta	0.63
Dividend Rate/Share	0.48	Shareholders	2,300
Shs. outstg. (M)	11.1	Market cap. (B)	$0.189
Avg. daily vol. (M)	0.075	Inst. holdings	49%
		Insider holdings	NA

Value of $10,000 invested 5 years ago: $ 13,150

Fiscal Year Ending May 31

	1995	% Change	1994	% Change	1993	% Change
Revenues (Million $)						
1Q	155.3	14%	136.2	18%	115.7	37%
2Q	164.5	13%	145.3	14%	127.6	68%
3Q	150.7	15%	130.7	18%	110.4	51%
4Q	171.7	2%	167.9	22%	138.0	31%
Yr.	642.1	11%	580.1	18%	491.7	45%
Income (Million $)						
1Q	4.03	34%	3.00	23%	2.44	39%
2Q	4.05	-5%	4.27	49%	2.87	156%
3Q	2.58	6%	2.44	66%	1.47	NM
4Q	4.69	-11%	5.28	67%	3.16	9%
Yr.	15.34	2%	14.99	45%	10.31	78%
Earnings Per Share ($)						
1Q	0.36	33%	0.27	8%	0.25	56%
2Q	0.36	-5%	0.38	46%	0.26	160%
3Q	0.23	5%	0.22	69%	0.13	—
4Q	0.42	-11%	0.47	68%	0.28	8%
Yr.	1.38	3%	1.34	46%	0.92	77%

Next earnings report expected: mid September

Skyline Corp.

Business Summary - 25-JUL-95

Skyline Corp. produces manufactured housing and recreational vehicles. It operates through 27 divisions in 13 states across the U.S. Segment contributions in 1993-94 were:

	Sales	Profits
Manufactured housing	76%	80%
Recreational vehicles	24%	20%

The company produced and shipped 19,467 manufactured homes in 1993-94, up from 18,001 units shipped in 1992-93. Homes are marketed under a number of trademarks, and range from 36 ft. to 80 ft. long and 12 ft. to 28 ft. wide. Primary markets for manufactured homes are the suburban and rural areas of the continental U.S. Principal buyers are generally young couples and senior citizens, although the market tends to broaden when conventional housing becomes more difficult to purchase and finance. SKY's manufactured homes are distributed by 1,250 dealers at 1,900 locations throughout the U.S. These dealerships also sell the products of other producers. The company's share of the manufactured housing market was over 7% in 1993-94.

SKY produces towable recreational vehicles (travel trailers and fifth wheels) that are sold under the Aljo, Layton, Mountainview, Outland and Nomad trademarks. The company's RVs are sold through 600 dealers at 750 locations. RV sales are generally highest in the spring and summer months.

The company assembles components purchased from outside sources, ranging in size from large national companies to very small local suppliers. Major components used in home construction are lumber, plywood, steel, aluminum, insulation, appliances, furnaces, plumbing fixtures, hardware, floor coverings and furniture.

Important Developments

Jun. '95—The company reported an 11% year over year earnings decline in the fourth quarter of 1994-95, on a 2.2% increase in revenues. The earnings weakness was related to a downturn in SKY's recreational vehicle segment, which experienced softening demand (sales were down 19%) and increased marketing costs. Those difficulties outweighed continued favorable results in the manufactured housing segment, which sustained an 11% sales gain.

Capitalization

Long Term Debt: None (5/95).

Per Share Data ($) (Year Ended May 31)

	1995	1994	1993	1992	1991	1990
Tangible Bk. Val.	NA	15.27	14.43	14.02	13.98	14.00
Cash Flow	NA	1.59	1.16	0.75	0.70	1.09
Earnings	1.38	1.34	0.92	0.52	0.47	0.87
Dividends	0.48	0.48	0.48	0.48	0.48	0.48
Payout Ratio	35%	36%	52%	92%	103%	55%
Cal. Yrs.	1994	1993	1992	1991	1990	1989
Prices - High	$24\frac{1}{8}$	23	$21\frac{5}{8}$	$18\frac{1}{4}$	$15\frac{7}{8}$	$20\frac{1}{4}$
- Low	$16\frac{3}{8}$	$16\frac{1}{8}$	14	$13\frac{7}{8}$	$12\frac{3}{8}$	$13\frac{7}{8}$
P/E Ratio - High	17	17	24	35	34	23
- Low	12	12	15	27	26	16

Income Statement Analysis (Million $)

	1994	%Chg	1993	%Chg	1992	%Chg	1991
Revs.	580	18%	492	45%	339	3%	328
Oper. Inc.	22.1	67%	13.2	128%	5.8	100%	2.9
Depr.	2.9	7%	2.7	1%	2.7	NM	2.6
Int. Exp.	Nil	—	Nil	—	Nil	—	Nil
Pretax Inc.	25.0	48%	16.9	80%	9.4	11%	8.5
Eff. Tax Rate	40%	—	39%	—	38%	—	38%
Net Inc.	15.0	46%	10.3	78%	5.8	12%	5.2

Balance Sheet & Other Fin. Data (Million $)

	1994	1993	1992	1991	1990	1989
Cash	17.0	14.0	17.0	111	109	111
Curr. Assets	84.0	68.0	61.0	146	150	149
Total Assets	209	189	180	176	179	177
Curr. Liab.	35.8	24.7	21.3	18.1	20.7	23.6
LT Debt	Nil	Nil	Nil	Nil	Nil	Nil
Common Eqty.	170	162	157	157	157	153
Total Cap.	170	162	157	157	157	153
Cap. Exp.	8.1	4.1	2.4	3.9	3.2	3.7
Cash Flow	17.9	13.0	8.4	7.9	12.2	19.5

Ratio Analysis

	1994	1993	1992	1991	1990	1989
Curr. Ratio	2.3	2.8	2.9	8.0	7.2	6.3
% LT Debt of Cap.	Nil	Nil	Nil	Nil	Nil	Nil
% Net Inc.of Revs.	2.6	2.1	1.7	1.6	2.7	4.5
% Ret. on Assets	7.6	5.6	3.2	2.9	5.5	10.1
% Ret. on Equity	9.0	6.5	3.7	3.3	6.3	11.7

Dividend Data (Dividends have been paid since 1960.)

Amt. of Div. $	Date Decl.	Ex-Div. Date	Stock of Record	Payment Date
0.120	Jul. 21	Sep. 06	Sep. 12	Oct. 01 '94
0.120	Dec. 01	Dec. 12	Dec. 16	Jan. 02 '95
0.120	Mar. 01	Mar. 10	Mar. 16	Apr. 01 '95
0.120	Jun. 01	Jun. 14	Jun. 18	Jul. 01 '95

Data as orig. reptd.; bef. results of disc. opers. and/or spec. items. Per share data adj. for stk. divs. as of ex-div. date. E-Estimated. NA-Not Available. NM-Not Meaningful. NR-Not Ranked.

Office—2520 By-Pass Rd. (P.O. Box 743), Elkhart, IN 46515. **Tel**—(219) 294-6521. **Chrmn & CEO**—A. J. Decio. **Vice Chrmn**—R. F. Kloska. **Pres & COO**—W. H. Murschel. **Secy**—R. M. Treckelo. **VP-Fin, Treas & CFO**—J. B. Fanchi. **Dirs**—T. P. Bergin, A. J. Decio, T. M. Decio, J. Hammes, R. F. Kloska, W. H. Lawson, A. J. McKenna, W. H. Murschel, D. Swikert. **Transfer Agent & Registrar**—Harris Trust and Savings, Chicago. **Incorporated** in Indiana in 1959. **Empl**-3,600. **S&P Analyst:** Michael W. Jaffe

STANDARD & POOR'S

STOCK REPORTS

SkyWest, Inc.

NASDAQ Symbol **SKYW**
In S&P SmallCap 600

01-OCT-95 **Industry:** Air Transport

Summary: This company's SkyWest Airlines subsidiary is one of the largest regional airlines in the U.S.

Quantitative Evaluations

Recent Price • 19 | 52 Wk Range • 25⅜-11⅛ | Yield • 0.4% | 12-Mo. P/E • 17.9

Outlook
(1 Lowest—5 Highest)
• **NA**

Fair Value
• **NA**

Risk
• **High**

Earn./Div. Rank
• **B**

Technical Eval.
• **Bullish** since 4/95

Rel. Strength Rank
(1 Lowest—99 Highest)
• **9**

Insider Activity
• **Neutral**

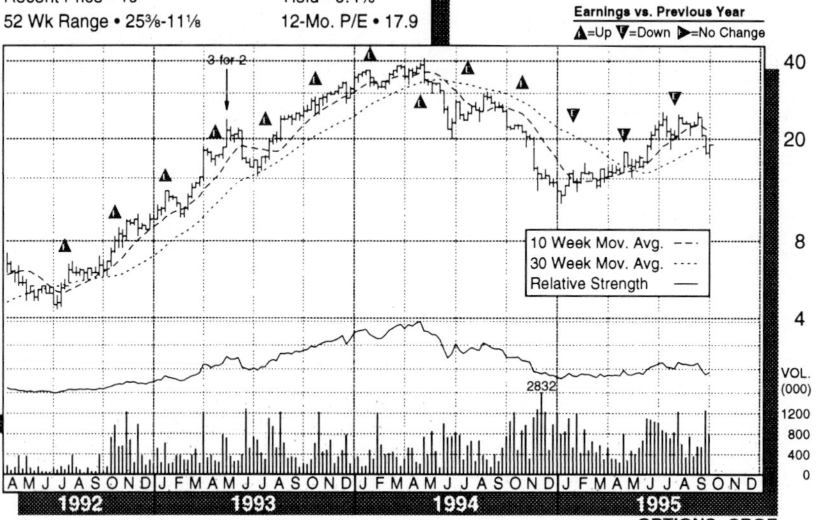

OPTIONS: CBOE

Business Profile - 01-OCT-95

SkyWest's strategy is to maximize profits by becoming both a Delta and Continental connecting carrier, continually upgrading its fleet, and providing full service. SKYW is replacing its older turboprops with larger, more efficient turboprops. SKYW is also operating more jets; it believes the jets' faster cruising speed and longer range will help SKYW expand into longer routes. In 1994-5, SKYW repurchased 1.15 million shares, and authorized the buyback of 0.5 million additional shares.

Operational Review - 01-OCT-95

Revenues in the 1995-6 first quarter rose 2.6%, year to year, mostly on a rise in revenue passenger miles (RPMs) from the addition of four jets, which more than offset a decrease in yield (passenger revenues per RPM) from an increase in the average trip length of the jets. Margins eroded, primarily due to a lower volume of passengers, and higher wages; operating income fell 25%. After a sharp rise in interest expense, and higher depreciation, pretax income dropped 43%.

Stock Performance - 29-SEP-95

In the past 30 trading days, SKYW's shares have declined 17%, compared to a 5% rise in the S&P 500. Average trading volume for the past five days was 154,360 shares, compared with the 40-day moving average of 143,126 shares.

Key Stock Statistics

Dividend Rate/Share	0.08	Shareholders	1,100
Shs. outstg. (M)	10.3	Market cap. (B)	$0.196
Avg. daily vol. (M)	0.180	Inst. holdings	48%
Tang. Bk. Value/Share	11.53	Insider holdings	NA
Beta	1.25		

Value of $10,000 invested 5 years ago: $ 46,809

Fiscal Year Ending Mar. 31

	1996	% Change	1995	% Change	1994	% Change
Revenues (Million $)						
1Q	60.38	3%	58.87	46%	40.37	14%
2Q	—	—	65.55	26%	51.99	35%
3Q	—	—	51.45	11%	46.53	29%
4Q	—	—	49.53	NM	49.10	33%
Yr.	—	—	225.4	20%	188.0	28%
Income (Million $)						
1Q	3.09	-42%	5.37	88%	2.85	73%
2Q	—	—	6.86	40%	4.89	122%
3Q	—	—	1.42	-52%	2.98	122%
4Q	—	—	0.06	-98%	3.68	144%
Yr.	—	—	13.70	-5%	14.40	115%
Earnings Per Share ($)						
1Q	0.30	-36%	0.47	38%	0.34	70%
2Q	—	—	0.60	25%	0.48	71%
3Q	—	—	0.13	-55%	0.29	81%
4Q	—	—	0.01	-97%	0.34	70%
Yr.	—	—	1.23	-16%	1.46	72%

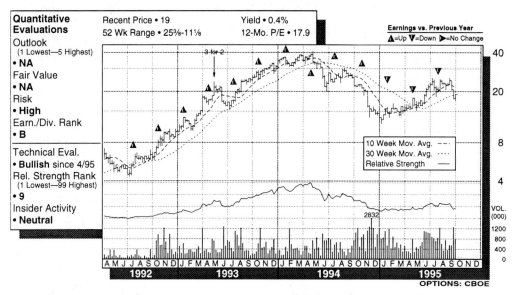

Next earnings report expected: early November

SkyWest, Inc.

Business Summary - 01-OCT-95

SkyWest, Inc., through its wholly owned SkyWest Airlines subsidiary, provides service to 49 cities in the western U.S., including Delta Air Lines' hubs in Salt Lake City and Los Angeles. About half its passengers connect with flights offered by Delta.

SKYW's strategy is to maximize profitability by increasing its opportunities as a Delta Connection carrier, continually upgrading its fleet, while preserving customer service. SkyWest offers a frequent flight schedule, with more than 550 daily flights. Operating data for recent fiscal years:

	1994-5	1993-4
Passengers carried	2,073,885	1,730,993
Rev. passenger miles (000)	488,901	345,414
Load factor	50.1%	47.5%
Breakeven load factor	45.5%	41.2%
Available seat miles (000)	976,095	727,059
Rev. per passenger mile	$0.363	$0.439
Cost per avail. seat mile	$0.171	$0.188
No. of aircraft at year end	60	55

Under a joint marketing and code-sharing agreement entered into effective April 1, 1987, with Delta Air Lines, Inc., SkyWest operates as "The Delta Connection," coordinating with Delta to provide the maximum number of connections at the hub airports of Los Angeles and Salt Lake City and, to a lesser extent, Las Vegas, Reno and Phoenix. SkyWest has maintained control over its routes, equipment and pricing.

As of June 21, 1995, SKYW operated 25 19-passenger Metroliner turboprops (average age 8.3 years), 29 30-passenger Brasilia turboprops (4.0 years) and eight jets (0.8 years). SKYW believes the faster cruising speed and longer range of the jets will help it expand into longer routes, and it plans to acquire two more in 1995-6. The Brasilia aircraft are replacing the Metroliners, offering greater capacity and operating efficiencies. At the end of 1996-7, SKYW expects its turboprop fleet to consist only of Brasilias.

SKYW has two other wholly owned subsidiaries: Scenic Airlines Inc., which operates 57 aircraft and provides general aviation services and scenic air tours, and National Parks Transportation Inc., which operates car rental franchises. These units accounted for about 19% of total 1994-5 revenues.

Important Developments

Aug. '95—SkyWest signed a code share agreement with Continental Airlines (CA), effective in the third quarter of 1995-6. SKYW will carry both CA and Delta codes on all 115 daily departures from Los Angeles. CA offers 27 departures. The new agreement will not affect the company's partnership with Delta.

Capitalization

Long Term Debt: $28,472,000 (6/95).

Per Share Data ($)

(Year Ended Mar. 31)

	1995	1994	1993	1992	1991	1990
Tangible Bk. Val.	11.41	10.73	5.31	4.49	4.29	4.12
Cash Flow	2.49	2.49	1.89	1.23	1.09	1.35
Earnings	1.23	1.46	0.85	0.25	0.26	0.61
Dividends	0.28	0.15	0.06	0.06	0.12	0.10
Payout Ratio	23%	12%	6%	22%	47%	16%
Cal. Yrs.	1994	1993	1992	1991	1990	1989
Prices - High	41	34½	10⅛	5⅛	6	6⅝
- Low	11½	9⅝	3¾	2½	3⅜	3⅜
P/E Ratio - High	33	24	12	20	23	11
- Low	9	7	5	10	13	5

Income Statement Analysis (Million $)

	1995	%Chg	1994	%Chg	1993	%Chg	1992
Revs.	225	20%	188	28%	147	18%	125
Oper. Inc.	34.3	-2%	34.9	77%	19.7	73%	11.4
Depr.	14.0	37%	10.2	24%	8.3	8%	7.6
Int. Exp.	1.1	-44%	2.0	40%	1.4	6%	1.3
Pretax Inc.	22.2	-7%	23.8	127%	10.5	NM	3.1
Eff. Tax Rate	38%	—	40%	—	36%	—	37%
Net Inc.	13.7	-5%	14.4	115%	6.7	NM	2.0

Balance Sheet & Other Fin. Data (Million $)

	1995	1994	1993	1992	1991	1990
Cash	48.7	68.0	12.0	10.0	9.8	13.0
Curr. Assets	71.6	87.1	28.2	24.3	24.0	25.3
Total Assets	188	184	86.9	72.4	73.3	69.2
Curr. Liab.	25.6	20.5	15.9	13.0	11.9	10.8
LT Debt	29.6	26.6	18.4	13.8	16.5	13.8
Common Eqty.	118	123	42.8	35.3	33.5	32.5
Total Cap.	160	160	67.1	54.6	55.8	51.5
Cap. Exp.	39.3	45.6	20.9	10.1	14.9	8.1
Cash Flow	27.7	24.6	15.0	9.6	8.6	10.5

Ratio Analysis

	1995	1994	1993	1992	1991	1990
Curr. Ratio	2.8	4.3	1.8	1.9	2.0	2.4
% LT Debt of Cap.	18.4	16.6	27.4	25.2	29.6	26.7
% Net Inc.of Revs.	6.1	7.7	4.6	1.6	1.8	4.7
% Ret. on Assets	7.7	9.4	8.3	2.7	2.8	7.0
% Ret. on Equity	12.0	15.7	17.0	5.8	6.1	15.5

Dividend Data —Cash dividends were initiated in 1987.

Amt. of Div. $	Date Decl.	Ex-Div. Date	Stock of Record	Payment Date
0.080	Nov. 17	Dec. 23	Dec. 31	Jan. 13 '95
.17 Spl	May. 30	Jun. 14	Jun. 16	Jul. 03 '95

Data as orig. reptd.; bef. results of disc. opers. and/or spec. items. Per share data adj. for stk. divs. as of ex-div. date. E-Estimated. NA-Not Available. NM-Not Meaningful. NR-Not Ranked.

Office—444 S. River Rd., St. George, UT 84770. **Tel**—(801) 634-3600. **Chrmn, Pres & CEO**—J. C. Atkin. **Vice Chrmn**—S. J. Atkin. **Exec VP & COO**—R. B. Reber. **Exec VP-Fin, CFO, Treas & Investor Contact**—Bradford R. Rich (801-634-3300). **Dirs**—B. V. Atkin, J. C. Atkin, J. R. Atkin, L. C. Atkin, S. J. Atkin, W. M. Braham, M. K. Cox, I. M. Cumming, D. C. Stout, S. F. Udvar-Hazy. **Transfer Agent & Registrar**—Zions First National Bank, Salt Lake City. **Incorporated** in Utah in 1972. **Empl-2,369. S&P Analyst:** Robert E. Friedman

Smith (A. O.)

NYSE Symbol **AOS**
In S&P SmallCap 600

02-AUG-95 **Industry:** Auto parts/equipment

Summary: AOS primarily produces automotive structural components, in addition to electric motors, water heaters, and fiberglass piping systems.

Quantitative Evaluations

Recent Price • 27¼ | Yield • 2.2%
52 Wk Range • 28½-19⅛ | 12-Mo. P/E • 9.2

Outlook
(1 Lowest—5 Highest)
• **4-**

Fair Value
• **26⅞**

Risk
• **Average**

Earn./Div. Rank
• **B**

Technical Eval.
• **Bearish** since 5/94

Rel. Strength Rank
(1 Lowest—99 Highest)
• **75**

Insider Activity
• **NA**

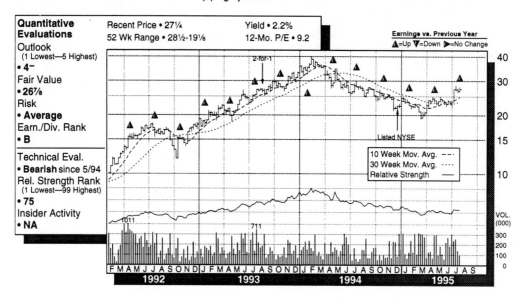

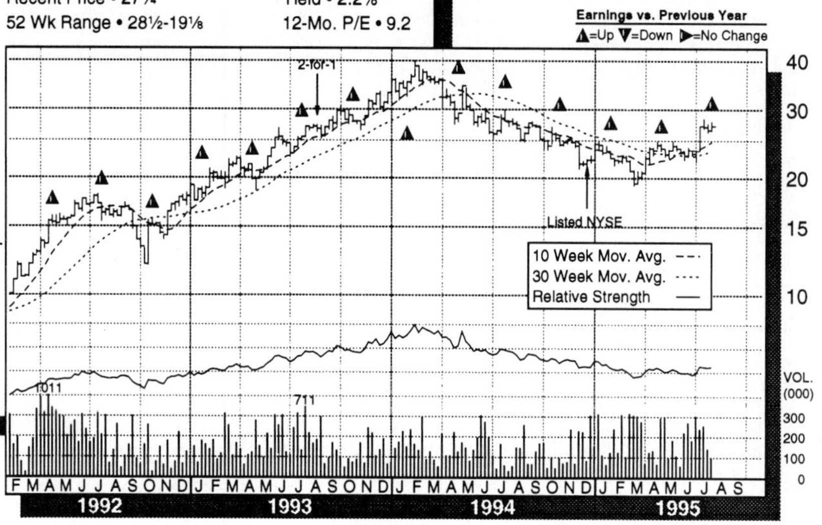

Business Profile - 30-JUL-95

This manufacturer of automotive structural components, as well as electric motors, water heaters and fiberglass piping systems, met its objective of a 15% return on common equity in both 1993 and 1994. The company is emphasizing new product introductions and productivity improvements. Its automotive business should benefit from increased market penetration and sales of the vehicles launched in 1994 and 1995. The company's common shares were relisted on the NYSE in late 1994.

Operational Review - 01-AUG-95

Net revenues in the first half of 1995 advanced 15%, year to year, reflecting strong sales gains for most segments. Operating profit was up 16%. After larger other expenses (net), taxes at 38.3%, versus 37.8%, and greater equity in earnings of affiliates, net income increased 14%. Future results should benefit from product launches scheduled for the 1995 third quarter: the Ford Taurus/Mercury Sable engine cradle and the Dodge Ram extended cab frame.

Stock Performance - 28-JUL-95

In the past 30 trading days, AOS's shares have increased 15%, compared to a 4% rise in the S&P 500. Average trading volume for the past five days was 19,240 shares, compared with the 40-day moving average of 43,721 shares.

Key Stock Statistics

Dividend Rate/Share	0.60	Shareholders	200
Shs. outstg. (M)	20.9	Market cap. (B)	$0.578
Avg. daily vol. (M)	0.037	Inst. holdings	60%
Tang. Bk. Value/Share	15.74	Insider holdings	NA
Beta	0.70		

Value of $10,000 invested 5 years ago: $ 49,658

Fiscal Year Ending Dec. 31

	1995	% Change	1994	% Change	1993	% Change
Revenues (Million $)						
1Q	393.0	16%	339.8	15%	296.1	17%
2Q	399.8	14%	350.2	11%	315.8	10%
3Q	—	—	332.7	22%	272.8	13%
4Q	—	—	350.8	13%	309.1	17%
Yr.	—	—	1,374	15%	1,194	14%
Income (Million $)						
1Q	18.36	17%	15.71	21%	13.03	177%
2Q	20.03	12%	17.96	19%	15.08	25%
3Q	—	—	10.13	85%	5.47	31%
4Q	—	—	13.55	49%	9.11	47%
Yr.	—	—	57.35	34%	42.68	57%
Earnings Per Share ($)						
1Q	0.88	16%	0.76	19%	0.64	167%
2Q	0.96	12%	0.86	16%	0.74	16%
3Q	—	—	0.48	78%	0.27	29%
4Q	—	—	0.65	48%	0.44	42%
Yr.	—	—	2.75	32%	2.08	49%

Next earnings report expected: mid October

Smith (A. O.)

Business Summary - 01-AUG-95

A. O. Smith Corporation, founded in 1874, makes and supplies products and services for the following industries: transportation, water heating, water supply, air-conditioning, refrigeration, agricultural, financial, chemical, power generation, wastewater and petroleum. Business segment contributions (profits in millions) in 1994:

	Sales	Profits
OEM products	73%	$92.2
Water products	20%	30.1
Fiberglass products	4%	9.2
Agricultural products	3%	-5.8

Ford, Chrysler and GM accounted for 24%, 13% and 9.9% of 1994 sales, respectively.

The OEM products segment makes automotive and electrical products. Smith produces truck frames and components (41% of total 1994 sales) and other automotive structural components. It holds the largest market share (over 30% in 1994) in truck frame manufacturing in the U.S. and Canada. AOS also supplies engine cradles for Ford and other manufacturers.

Also included in the OEM segment is Smith's electrical products unit, the third largest U.S. producer of hermetic electric motors (20% of total 1994 sales), mainly for air movement, water pumping, refrigeration and air conditioning.

The water products segment is the largest U.S. maker of commercial water heaters and the fourth largest maker of residential water heaters. The Smith Fiberglass Products subsidiary makes reinforced thermosetting resin pipe.

The agricultural segment includes A.O. Smith Harvestore Products, which supplies glass-lined storage structures, automated equipment, and replacement parts for municipal, industrial, and agricultural customers. Applications include storage of potable water, free-flowing dry industrial materials, animal feed, and animal waste; and waste water and waste water treatment.

Important Developments

Jul. '95—Smith said that its automotive products unit has two major new product programs: the Ford Taurus/Mercury Sable engine cradle and the Dodge Ram extended cab frame assembly. Both product launches were scheduled for the third quarter of 1995.

Jul. '95—Smith said that although the automotive industry and some of its electric motor markets appeared to be cooling off, efforts to gain market share and secure new customers were paying off.

Dec. '94—Trading in AO Smith shares shifted from the American Stock Exchange back to the New York Stock Exchange on December 14 after an absence of 10 years.

Capitalization

Long Term Debt: $163,072,000 (6/95).

Per Share Data ($)

(Year Ended Dec. 31)

	1994	1993	1992	1991	1990	1989
Tangible Bk. Val.	13.90	11.85	10.72	14.93	16.38	15.42
Cash Flow	5.10	4.15	3.49	2.39	3.82	1.45
Earnings	2.75	2.08	1.39	0.10	1.70	-0.54
Dividends	0.50	0.62	0.40	0.40	0.40	0.40
Payout Ratio	18%	32%	29%	439%	24%	NM
Prices - High	40	35¾	19⅛	10⅞	10	9¼
- Low	21⅛	17⅜	8⅞	7½	5⅞	6¼
P/E Ratio - High	15	17	14	NM	6	NM
- Low	8	8	6	NM	3	NM

Income Statement Analysis (Million $)

	1994	%Chg	1993	%Chg	1992	%Chg	1991
Revs.	1,374	15%	1,194	14%	1,046	14%	916
Oper. Inc.	152	22%	125	29%	96.6	56%	61.8
Depr.	49.2	15%	42.6	8%	39.5	4%	37.8
Int. Exp.	12.9	-11%	14.5	-22%	18.7	-22%	23.9
Pretax Inc.	92.1	30%	70.8	67%	42.3	NM	4.0
Eff. Tax Rate	38%	—	40%	—	36%	—	14%
Net Inc.	57.3	34%	42.7	57%	27.2	NM	3.5

Balance Sheet & Other Fin. Data (Million $)

	1994	1993	1992	1991	1990	1989
Cash	8.5	11.9	6.0	8.9	3.2	4.8
Curr. Assets	330	304	234	209	258	271
Total Assets	848	823	769	754	788	796
Curr. Liab.	216	223	172	172	206	197
LT Debt	166	191	237	249	156	155
Common Eqty.	313	270	245	265	282	269
Total Cap.	533	501	509	547	452	438
Cap. Exp.	76.1	54.7	46.9	59.3	64.9	45.9
Cash Flow	107	85.3	65.8	37.8	60.4	23.0

Ratio Analysis

	1994	1993	1992	1991	1990	1989
Curr. Ratio	1.5	1.4	1.4	1.2	1.3	1.4
% LT Debt of Cap.	31.1	38.0	46.4	45.5	34.5	35.3
% Net Inc.of Revs.	4.2	3.6	2.6	0.4	3.3	NM
% Ret. on Assets	6.8	5.3	3.1	0.4	3.8	NM
% Ret. on Equity	19.6	16.5	9.0	NM	9.7	NM

Dividend Data (Cash has been paid since 1940.)

Amt. of Div. $	Date Decl.	Ex-Div. Date	Stock of Record	Payment Date
0.130	Oct. 11	Oct. 25	Oct. 31	Nov. 15 '94
0.130	Jan. 20	Jan. 25	Jan. 31	Feb. 15 '95
0.150	Apr. 06	Apr. 24	Apr. 28	May. 15 '95
0.150	Jun. 06	Jul. 27	Jul. 31	Aug. 15 '95

Data as orig. reptd.; bef. results of disc. opers. and/or spec. items. Per share data adj. for stk. divs. as of ex-div. date. E-Estimated. NA-Not Available. NM-Not Meaningful. NR-Not Ranked.

Office—11270 W. Park Place, Milwaukee, WI 53224-3690 (P.O. Box 23972, Milwaukee 53223-0972). **Tel**—(414) 359-4000. **Chrmn & Pres**—R. J. O'Toole. **VP-CFO**—G. R. Bomberger. **Treas**—J. J. Kita. **VP-Secy**—W. D. Romoser. **Dirs**—T. H. Barrett, G. R. Bomberger, R. G. Cleary, T. I. Dolan, L. W. Jennings, R. O'Toole, A. Pytte, D. J. Schuenke, A. O. Smith, B. M. Smith. **Transfer Agent & Registrar**—Firstar Trust Co., Milwaukee. **Incorporated** in New York in 1916; reincorporated in Delaware in 1986. **Empl**-12,100. **S&P Analyst:** N.J. DeVita

STANDARD & POOR'S
STOCK REPORTS

Smithfield Foods

NASDAQ Symbol **SFDS**
In S&P SmallCap 600

09-NOV-95 **Industry:** Food

Summary: This regional meat packer, the largest producer of "genuine Smithfield" hams, also produces fresh pork and markets a wide variety of processed meats.

Quantitative Evaluations
Outlook
(1 Lowest—5 Highest)
• **5⁻**
Fair Value
• **37⅝**
Risk
• **Average**
Earn./Div. Rank
• **B**

Technical Eval.
• **Bullish** since 10/95
Rel. Strength Rank
(1 Lowest—99 Highest)
• **90**
Insider Activity
• **Neutral**

Recent Price • 26½
52 Wk Range • 34¼-19½
Yield • Nil
12-Mo. P/E • 22.3

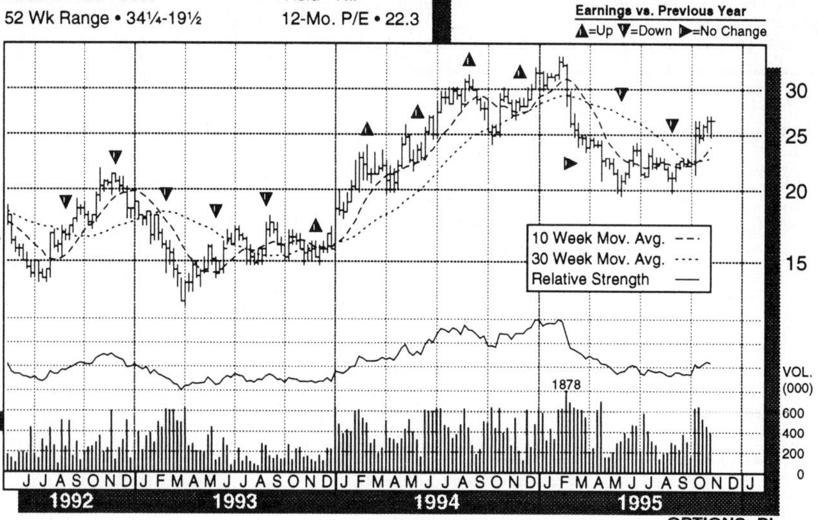

OPTIONS: Ph

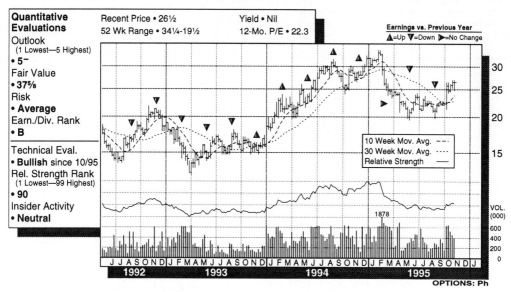

Business Profile - 09-NOV-95

Earnings advanced in 1994-95, on higher sales volumes, wider margins for both fresh pork and processed meat, and a change in the estimated useful lives of certain assets. The company said it anticipates pressure on margins in 1995-96, but is optimistic about the long term. Smithfield expects significant future sales from an agreement with Sumitomo Corp. to distribute Smithfield's premium pork products in Japan and from the rollout of its Smithfield Lean Generation Pork Program.

Operational Review - 09-NOV-95

Sales in the 13 weeks ended July 30, 1995, rose 11%, year to year, reflecting greater volume. Margins narrowed due to increased hog prices and higher SG&A expenses and interest costs; a pretax loss contrasted with income. Following a tax benefit of $1,144,000, versus taxes at 37.2%, there was a net loss of $2.6 million ($0.16 a share), versus net income of $2.5 million ($0.14). Results exclude losses from discontinued operations of $0.11 a share and $0.01 in the respective periods.

Stock Performance - 03-NOV-95

In the past 30 trading days, SFDS's shares have increased 18%, compared to a 2% rise in the S&P 500. Average trading volume for the past five days was 79,560 shares, compared with the 40-day moving average of 107,278 shares.

Key Stock Statistics

Dividend Rate/Share	Nil	Shareholders	1,600
Shs. outstg. (M)	16.4	Market cap. (B)	$0.435
Avg. daily vol. (M)	0.093	Inst. holdings	31%
Tang. Bk. Value/Share	10.93	Insider holdings	NA
Beta	0.89		

Value of $10,000 invested 5 years ago: $ 43,265

Fiscal Year Ending Apr. 30

	1996	% Change	1995	% Change	1994	% Change
Revenues (Million $)						
1Q	367.3	11%	331.8	11%	299.2	31%
2Q	—	—	373.8	5%	354.9	33%
3Q	—	—	439.4	2%	429.0	27%
4Q	—	—	381.6	5%	364.2	18%
Yr.	—	—	1,527	5%	1,447	27%
Income (Million $)						
1Q	-2.59	NM	2.55	NM	-0.37	NM
2Q	—	—	8.08	NM	0.92	NM
3Q	—	—	18.05	54%	11.75	NM
4Q	—	—	3.24	-56%	7.40	NM
Yr.	—	—	31.91	62%	19.70	NM
Earnings Per Share ($)						
1Q	-0.16	NM	0.14	NM	-0.03	NM
2Q	—	—	0.47	NM	0.04	100%
3Q	—	—	1.04	NM	1.04	NM
4Q	—	—	0.18	-58%	0.43	NM
Yr.	—	—	1.83	62%	1.13	NM

Next earnings report expected: mid November

Smithfield Foods

Business Summary - 09-NOV-95

Smithfield Foods, Inc. produces and markets a wide variety of processed and fresh meats. Subsidiaries include Smithfield Packing Co., Gwaltney of Smithfield Ltd., Patrick Cudahy Inc., Brown's of Carolina Inc., and Smithfield-Carroll's, a joint hog production arrangement between the company and Carroll's Foods of Virginia.

The company produces fresh and processed meats. Unprocessed meats include fresh pork cuts, pork loins (including roasts and chops), butts, picnics, and ribs. The processed products, which include ham, bacon, sausage, hot dogs, deli and luncheon meats, are marketed under various brandnames, including Smithfield, Luter's, Hamilton, Gwaltney, Patrick Cudahy, Esskay, Mash's and Valleydale. Profit margins on processed meats are greater than those on fresh meats and other products. In response to growing consumer preferences for more nutritious and healthful meats, the company has emphasized production of more closely trimmed, leaner and lower-salt processed products.

Sales in recent years were derived as follows:

	1994-5	1993-4	1992-3
Processed meats	45%	49%	55%
Fresh pork	51%	48%	41%
Other products	4%	3%	4%

Sales are concentrated in the Eastern Seaboard states. Smithfield's marketing strategy is to sell large quantities of medium-priced processed products to national and regional supermarket chains, wholesale distributors and the foodservice industry.

The company is the largest producer of "genuine Smithfield" hams, a label that under Virginia statute may be used only on hams processed within the Town of Smithfield.

The company's business is based on four strategic initiatives: (1) to market highly differentiated pork products by using the leanest genetics available, (2) vertical integration, (3) operation of highly efficient processing facilities, and (4) plant locations that reduce freight expense and permit rapid delivery and response to customers.

Important Developments

Oct. '95—Smithfield privately sold a new series of preferred stock to Sumitomo Corp. of America for $20 million in cash. The shares are convertible into approximately 666,667 SFDS common shares, or about 4% of the company's outstanding shares, at $30 a share. In addition, Sumitomo will now distibute Smithfield products in Japan through 2005.

Capitalization

Long Term Debt: $155,047,000 (4/95), incl. capitalized lease obligs.

Per Share Data ($) (Year Ended Apr. 30)

	1995	1994	1993	1992	1991	1990
Tangible Bk. Val.	11.22	9.52	8.35	7.53	5.67	3.54
Cash Flow	2.99	2.43	1.29	2.18	2.78	1.15
Earnings	1.83	1.13	0.15	1.37	1.99	0.48
Dividends	Nil	Nil	Nil	Nil	Nil	Nil
Payout Ratio	Nil	Nil	Nil	Nil	Nil	Nil
Cal. Yrs.	1994	1993	1992	1991	1990	1989
Prices - High	34	19½	22¼	25¼	10⅛	9⅜
- Low	17¾	12½	13¾	9⅛	5	5¾
P/E Ratio - High	19	17	NM	18	5	20
- Low	10	11	NM	7	3	12

Income Statement Analysis (Million $)

	1995	%Chg	1994	%Chg	1993	%Chg	1992
Revs.	1,527	6%	1,447	27%	1,142	9%	1,051
Oper. Inc.	84.2	22%	69.0	101%	34.3	-28%	47.4
Depr.	19.7	-9%	21.7	16%	18.7	46%	12.8
Int. Exp.	14.9	16%	12.8	50%	8.6	57%	5.5
Pretax Inc.	50.4	44%	35.1	NM	5.4	-84%	33.4
Eff. Tax Rate	37%	—	37%	—	27%	—	35%
Net Inc.	31.9	62%	19.7	NM	2.9	-87%	21.6

Balance Sheet & Other Fin. Data (Million $)

	1995	1994	1993	1992	1991	1990
Cash	14.8	12.4	3.1	1.7	2.7	1.1
Curr. Assets	233	226	178	125	112	89.0
Total Assets	550	452	400	278	201	165
Curr. Liab.	172	145	113	99	77.2	74.3
LT Debt	155	119	125	49.1	37.4	28.2
Common Eqty.	184	155	136	114	71.0	45.0
Total Cap.	367	299	279	172	118	84.0
Cap. Exp.	91.9	28.2	88.0	75.7	26.5	19.6
Cash Flow	51.0	40.7	21.1	34.4	40.0	17.0

Ratio Analysis

	1995	1994	1993	1992	1991	1990
Curr. Ratio	1.4	1.6	1.6	1.3	1.5	1.2
% LT Debt of Cap.	42.2	39.7	44.7	28.5	31.7	33.4
% Net Inc.of Revs.	2.1	1.4	0.2	2.1	2.7	0.8
% Ret. on Assets	6.3	4.6	0.8	8.3	15.8	4.6
% Ret. on Equity	18.4	13.1	1.9	21.7	49.6	16.5

Dividend Data —No cash has been paid. A two-for-one stock split was effected in 1991.

Data as orig. reptd.; bef. results of disc. opers. and/or spec. items. Per share data adj. for stk. divs. as of ex-div. date. E-Estimated. NA-Not Available. NM-Not Meaningful. NR-Not Ranked.

Office—501 N. Church St., Smithfield, VA 23430. **Tel**—(804) 357-4321. **Chrmn & CEO**—J. W. Luter III. **Pres & COO**—J. O. Nielson. **VP, Secy, Treas & Investor Contact**—Aaron D. Trub. **Dirs**—F. J. Faison, Jr., J. W. Greenberg, C. W. Gwaltney, G. E. Hamilton, Jr., R. J. Holland, R. R. Kapella, L. R. Little, J. W. Luter III, R. W. Manly, W. H. Murphy, J. O. Nielson, W. H. Prestage. A. D. Trub. **Transfer Agent & Registrar**—First Union National Bank, Charlotte, NC. **Incorporated** in Delaware in 1971. **Empl**-9,000. **S&P Analyst:** Efraim Levy

STANDARD & POOR'S

STOCK REPORTS

Snyder Oil

NYSE Symbol **SNY**

In S&P SmallCap 600

11-SEP-95 **Industry:** Oil and Gas

Summary: This independent oil company engages in the acquisition, production, development and exploration of primarily domestic oil and gas properties.

Recent Price • 13¼ | Yield • 2.0%

52 Wk Range • 18⅝-10¾ | 12-Mo. P/E • NM

Quantitative Evaluations

Outlook
(1 Lowest—5 Highest)
• NA

Fair Value
• NA

Risk
• Average

Earn./Div. Rank
• NR

Technical Eval.
• Bearish since 7/94

Rel. Strength Rank
(1 Lowest—99 Highest)
• 66

Insider Activity
• Neutral

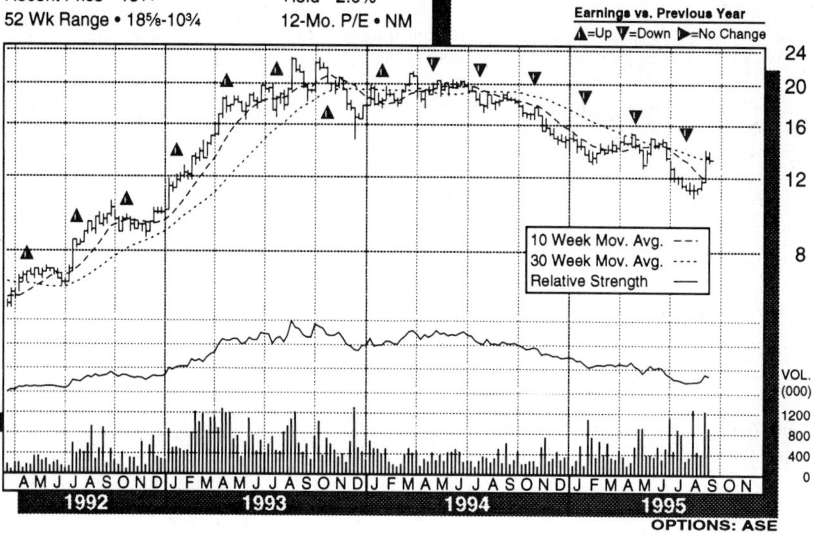

Business Profile - 11-SEP-95

This independent oil company acquires, produces, develops and explores for domestic oil and gas properties and gathers, transports, processes and markets natural gas. Prior to 1994 SNY emphasized development in the Wattenberg Field; it currently concentrates in Texas and Rocky Mountain basins. SNY participates in joint ventures in Russia and Mongolia and has invested in an Australian company with interests in the Southwestern Pacific Rim and the North Sea.

Operational Review - 11-SEP-95

Revenues during the first half of 1995, decreased 14%, year to year, reflecting the suspension of third party gas marketing, even though production of both oil and gas was on the rise. Also, on an equivalent barrel basis, prices declined 10%. Interest and direct operating expenses rose. SNY incurred a special provision related to a litigation settlement of $4.4 million. As a result, a net loss of $5,456,000 ($0.28 a share, on 29% more shares), replaced net income of $8,241,000 ($0.12).

Stock Performance - 08-SEP-95

In the past 30 trading days, SNY's shares have increased 18%, compared to a 2% rise in the S&P 500. Average trading volume for the past five days was 225,325 shares, compared with the 40-day moving average of 173,574 shares.

Key Stock Statistics

Dividend Rate/Share	0.26	Shareholders	3,200
Shs. outstg. (M)	30.2	Market cap. (B)	$0.400
Avg. daily vol. (M)	0.179	Inst. holdings	67%
Tang. Bk. Value/Share	9.11	Insider holdings	NA
Beta	0.54		

Value of $10,000 invested 5 years ago: NA

Fiscal Year Ending Dec. 31

	1995	% Change	1994	% Change	1993	% Change
Revenues (Million $)						
1Q	53.02	-16%	63.46	41%	44.87	67%
2Q	57.47	-11%	64.58	11%	58.28	109%
3Q	—	—	71.05	16%	61.29	104%
4Q	—	—	63.24	-3%	65.45	85%
Yr.	—	—	262.3	14%	229.9	91%
Income (Million $)						
1Q	-5.98	NM	4.58	-28%	6.37	93%
2Q	0.52	-86%	3.66	-44%	6.54	115%
3Q	—	—	5.00	-24%	6.62	46%
4Q	—	—	1.87	-77%	8.08	34%
Yr.	—	—	12.37	-55%	27.61	64%
Earnings Per Share ($)						
1Q	-0.25	NM	0.08	-65%	0.23	156%
2Q	-0.03	NM	0.04	-78%	0.18	125%
3Q	—	—	-0.02	NM	0.17	13%
4Q	—	—	-0.03	NM	0.23	10%
Yr.	—	—	0.07	-91%	0.80	51%

Next earnings report expected: early November

Snyder Oil

Business Summary - 11-SEP-95

Snyder Oil, formerly a limited partnership which converted to corporate form in 1990, is an independent oil corporation engaged in the acquisition, production, development and, to a lesser degree, exploration of primarily domestic oil and gas properties. The company is also engaged in a small but growing international development and exploration program, including a Russian joint venture in which it has a 21% interest and a partial ownership in an Australian company with interests in the Southwestern Pacific Rim and an interest in a Dutch company that has assets in the North Sea. In addition, with interests in gas transportation and processing facilities, the company engages in the gathering, processing, transportation and marketing of natural gas. SNY holds interests in producing properties in 15 states and in the Gulf of Mexico.

As of December 31, 1994, estimated proved reserves were 34,977,000 bbl. of oil (75% developed) and 511.3 Bcf of natural gas (69%). Production in 1994 totaled 4,366,000 bbl. of oil and 43,809 Mcf of gas, compared with 3,451,000 bbl. and 35,080 Mcf in 1993. Average sales prices for 1994 were $14.80 per bbl. and $1.67 per Mcf, versus $15.41 per bbl. and $1.94 per Mcf the year before.

As of December 31, 1994, SNY held 529,000 gross (234,000 net) developed acres and 7,110,000 gross (3,772,000 net) undeveloped acres in several producing areas, both domestically and internationally, including Russia, Thailand and Mongolia, overseas. There were 3,109 gross (1,590 net) productive oil wells and 2,160 (1,061) productive gas wells at year-end 1994.

Prior to 1994, drilling was focused in the Wattenberg Field of the Denver-Julesburg basin of Colorado, where the company has drilled over 1,000 wells since 1991. In late 1994, the company curtailed drilling in Wattenberg as a result of declining gas prices and disappointing drilling results in certain outlying areas of the Field. Currently, SNY's primary emphasis is on development drilling in several Rocky Mountain basins and in southeast Texas. Assuming no material changes in energy prices, the company plans to spend $70 million on development drilling in 1995, down from $157 million in 1994.

Important Developments

Aug. '95—SNY completed the sale of its West Plant gas processing facility in Weld County, Colo., for approximately $18.5 million, to an undisclosed buyer. Also, the company signed a letter of intent to sell its remaining Weld County gas facilities to Associated Natural Gas Corp. for $63.5 million.

Capitalization

Long Term Debt: $332,242,000 (6/95).
Minority Interest: $4,712,000.
$1.50 Depositary Stock: 4,140,000 shs. ($25 liq. pref.); conv. into com. at $21 a sh.
Options: To purchase 1,800,000 shs. at $6.00 to $20.13.

Per Share Data ($)

(Year Ended Dec. 31)

	1994	1993	1992	1991	1990	1989
Tangible Bk. Val.	8.25	9.12	5.44	5.02	4.98	NA
Cash Flow	3.30	3.02	1.94	1.48	1.20	1.26
Earnings	0.07	0.80	0.53	0.37	0.36	0.25
Dividends	0.25	0.22	0.20	0.20	0.12	NA
Payout Ratio	480%	27%	47%	55%	37%	NA
Prices - High	21 3/8	23	10 1/2	8 1/2	9 1/2	NA
- Low	13 7/8	10	5 7/8	4 3/4	4 3/4	NA
P/E Ratio - High	NM	29	20	23	26	NA
- Low	NM	12	11	13	13	NA

Income Statement Analysis (Million $)

	1994	%Chg	1993	%Chg	1992	%Chg	1991
Revs.	245	12%	219	89%	116	34%	86.8
Oper. Inc.	85.3	3%	83.0	64%	50.7	25%	40.5
Depr. Depl. & Amort.	76.6	50%	51.2	61%	31.9	26%	25.4
Int. Exp.	NA	—	5.3	6%	5.0	-41%	8.4
Pretax Inc.	13.5	-61%	34.9	102%	17.3	52%	11.4
Eff. Tax Rate	7.20%	—	21%	—	2.50%	—	23%
Net Inc.	12.4	-55%	27.6	63%	16.9	92%	8.8

Balance Sheet & Other Fin. Data (Million $)

	1994	1993	1992	1991	1990	1989
Cash	21.7	10.9	20.5	24.7	16.8	10.2
Curr. Assets	72.4	61.8	52.3	48.3	40.3	40.0
Total Assets	673	480	347	252	227	206
Curr. Liab.	71.7	60.5	44.6	31.0	28.2	39.0
LT Debt	319	115	115	42.1	81.2	48.5
Common Eqty.	248	212	124	115	115	119
Total Cap.	598	412	300	221	198	167
Cap. Exp.	244	167	130	48.0	172	NA
Cash Flow	78.1	69.7	44.0	33.7	24.7	29.8

Ratio Analysis

	1994	1993	1992	1991	1990	1989
Curr. Ratio	1.0	1.0	1.2	1.6	1.4	1.0
% LT Debt of Cap.	53.2	27.9	38.5	19.1	41.1	28.9
% Ret. on Assets	1.9	6.6	5.6	3.7	NA	NA
% Ret. on Equity	0.6	10.9	10.1	7.3	NA	NA

Dividend Data —SNY initiated dividends following the March, 1990 consolidation of Snyder Oil Partners L.P. and SOCO Holdings Inc.

Amt. of Div. $	Date Decl.	Ex-Div. Date	Stock of Record	Payment Date
0.065	Sep. 01	Sep. 09	Sep. 15	Sep. 30 '94
0.065	Dec. 05	Dec. 09	Dec. 15	Dec. 30 '94
0.065	Mar. 03	Mar. 09	Mar. 15	Mar. 31 '95
0.065	Jun. 02	Jun. 13	Jun. 15	Jun. 30 '95
0.065	Sep. 01	Sep. 13	Sep. 15	Sep. 29 '95

Data as orig. reptd.; bef. results of disc opers. and/or spec. items. Per share data adj. for stk. divs. as of ex-div. date. E-Estimated. NA-Not Available. NM-Not Meaningful. NR-Not Ranked.

Office—777 Main St., Suite 2500, Fort Worth, TX 76102. **Tel**—(817) 338-4043. **Chrmn & CEO**—J. C. Snyder. **Pres**—T. J. Edelman. **EVP**—J. A. Fanning. **SVP-Secy**—P. E. Lorenzen. **VP & Investor Contact**—Diana K. Ten Eyck. **Dirs**—R. W. Brittain, T. J. Edelman, J. A. Fanning, J. A. Hill, W. J. Johnson, B. J. Kellenberger, J. H. Lichtblau, J. E. McCormick, A. M. Micallef, J. C. Snyder. **Transfer Agent**—Society National Bank, Dallas. **Incorporated** in Delaware in 1989. **Empl**-473. **S&P Analyst:** Michael C. Barr

STANDARD & POOR'S

Sonat Offshore Drilling

STOCK REPORTS

NYSE Symbol **RIG**

In S&P SmallCap 600

02-NOV-95 **Industry:** Oil and Gas

Summary: This former subsidiary of Sonat Inc. is a worldwide offshore contract drilling company serving most of the leading international oil companies.

Quantitative Evaluations

Outlook (1 Lowest—5 Highest)
- **NA**

Fair Value
- **NA**

Risk
- **Average**

Earn./Div. Rank
- **NR**

Technical Eval.
- **Bullish** since 8/95

Rel. Strength Rank (1 Lowest—99 Highest)
- **32**

Insider Activity
- **NA**

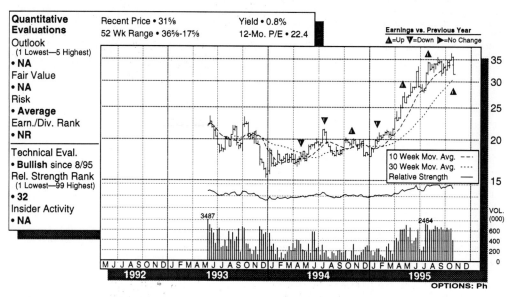

Recent Price • 31⅝ | Yield • 0.8%

52 Wk Range • 36⅝-17⅝ | 12-Mo. P/E • 22.4

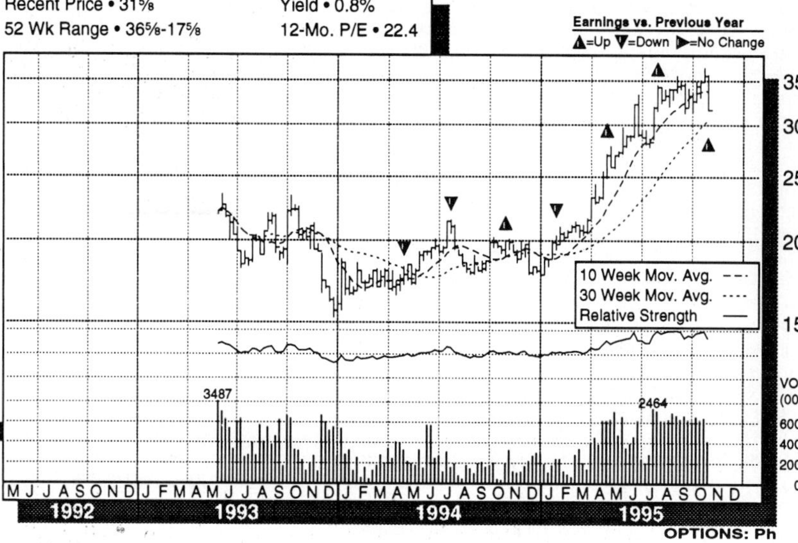

OPTIONS: Ph

Business Profile - 30-OCT-95

Sonat is engaged in offshore contract drilling throughout the world. RIG's strategy is to achieve higher dayrates and rig utilization by being a leader in the technically demanding segments of the industry, particularly the deep water and harsh environment markets. Sonat has implemented its strategy by operating seven technically advanced semisubmersibles and drillships, employing experienced personnel and investing substantial capital to maintain and upgrade its fleet.

Operational Review - 02-NOV-95

Revenues for the nine months ended September 30, 1995, climbed 33%, year to year, as higher overall utilization was accompanied by improved dayrates. Margins widened, and operating income advanced 159%. Following a $16 million pretax gain from the sale of five bottom-supported rigs, equity in earnings of joint ventures, versus losses, and a lower tax rate, net income rose to $35.8 million ($1.26 per share), from $8.5 million ($0.30).

Stock Performance - 27-OCT-95

In the past 30 trading days, RIG's shares have declined 0.78%, compared to a 0.63% fall in the S&P 500. Average trading volume for the past five days was 82,480 shares, compared with the 40-day moving average of 189,964 shares.

Key Stock Statistics

Dividend Rate/Share	0.24	Shareholders	1,600
Shs. outstg. (M)	28.4	Market cap. (B)	$0.893
Avg. daily vol. (M)	0.155	Inst. holdings	53%
Tang. Bk. Value/Share	11.77	Insider holdings	NA
Beta	NA		

Value of $10,000 invested 5 years ago: NA

Fiscal Year Ending Dec. 31

	1995	% Change	1994	% Change	1993	% Change
Revenues (Million $)						
1Q	70.73	7%	66.10	29%	51.34	—
2Q	85.51	45%	58.92	-27%	80.36	—
3Q	83.28	53%	54.55	5%	51.94	—
4Q	—	—	63.38	-28%	87.63	—
Yr.	—	—	242.9	-10%	271.3	29%
Income (Million $)						
1Q	7.28	71%	4.25	—	—	—
2Q	8.19	NM	2.17	—	—	—
3Q	20.38	NM	2.06	27%	1.62	—
4Q	—	—	4.24	-49%	8.33	—
Yr.	—	—	12.72	-47%	24.05	119%
Earnings Per Share ($)						
1Q	0.26	73%	0.15	-72%	0.53	—
2Q	0.29	NM	0.08	-33%	0.12	—
3Q	0.72	NM	0.07	17%	0.06	—
4Q	—	—	0.15	-48%	0.29	—
Yr.	—	—	0.45	-55%	1.00	163%

Next earnings report expected: late January

Sonat Offshore Drilling

Business Summary - 02-NOV-95

Sonat Offshore Drilling is engaged in contract drilling of oil and gas wells in offshore areas throughout the world. The company operates a fleet of 21 mobile offshore drilling rigs (19 of which are wholly owned), which are currently located mainly in the North Sea, the Gulf of Mexico, the Middle East, Italy and South America.

Revenue and profit contributions (in million $) by geographic area in 1994:

	Revs.	Profits
United States	38%	$17.6
Middle East	12%	10.4
Europe	34%	10.3
Western Hemisphere (excl.U.S.)	15%	2.0
Other foreign areas	1%	d1.1

RIG operates five of the world's 13 "fourth generation" semisubmersibles (larger semisubmersibles built after 1984 and having advanced features). Its fleet of three semisubmersibles includes two of the three drilling rigs certified by the Norwegian government to work year-round above the Arctic Circle in the North Sea. RIG also operates two dynamically positioned drillships, 10 jack-ups (including four operating in the Gulf of Mexico and five operating in Egypt), and one submersible.

Sonat Offshore's drilling equipment is normally engaged in both exploration and development drilling. Its rigs are mobile and can be moved to new locations in response to customer demand. In 1994, average fleet utilization was 77%, unchanged from 1993. Utilization of the strategic fleet reached 89% in 1994.

During the past five years, the company has engaged in offshore drilling for most of the leading international oil companies as well as for many government controlled and independent oil companies. Sonat's four largest customers in 1994 were Shell (accounting for 34% of revenues), Gulf of Suez Petroleum Co. (12%), Norsk Hydro (10%), and Pemex (10%).

Important Developments

Oct. '95—Sonat received contracts for two of its fourth-generation, deep-water semisubmersibles from Shell Offshore Inc. The contracts are guaranteed for at least two years beginning in mid-1996, and are expected to generate revenue in excess of $114 million.
Oct. '95—Directors authorized the repurchase of up to $50 million of RIG common shares in open market or privately negotiated transactions.
Sep. '95—The company sold five bottom suppported rigs to Falcon Drilling Inc. for $37,950,000. A pretax gain of $16 million was recorded in 1995's third quarter.

Capitalization

Notes Payable: $30,000,000 (6/95).

Per Share Data ($) (Year Ended Dec. 31)

	1994	1993	1992	1991	1990	1989
Tangible Bk. Val.	11.32	11.11	10.34	NA	NA	NA
Cash Flow	1.31	1.87	1.38	NA	NA	NA
Earnings	0.45	1.00	0.38	NA	NA	NA
Dividends	0.24	0.06	NA	NA	NA	NA
Payout Ratio	53%	6%	NA	NA	NA	NA
Prices - High	21½	23½	NA	NA	NA	NA
- Low	15⅝	15¼	NA	NA	NA	NA
P/E Ratio - High	48	23	NA	NA	NA	NA
- Low	35	15	NA	NA	NA	NA

Income Statement Analysis (Million $)

	1994	%Chg	1993	%Chg	1992	%Chg	1991
Revs.	243	-10%	271	29%	210	—	NA
Oper. Inc.	45.4	NM	45.2	28%	35.4	—	NA
Depr.	24.5	17%	21.0	-25%	28.1	—	NA
Int. Exp.	2.0	-76%	8.5	NM	0.6	—	NA
Pretax Inc.	20.2	NM	-41.1	NM	14.0	—	NA
Eff. Tax Rate	37%	—	42%	—	21%	—	NA
Net Inc.	12.7	-47%	24.0	118%	11.0	—	NA

Balance Sheet & Other Fin. Data (Million $)

	1994	1993	1992	1991	1990	1989
Cash	46.8	21.6	NA	NA	NA	NA
Curr. Assets	128	144	97.0	NA	NA	NA
Total Assets	493	472	433	NA	NA	NA
Curr. Liab.	48.5	65.4	50.0	NA	NA	NA
LT Debt	30.0	Nil	Nil	NA	NA	NA
Common Eqty.	321	314	292	NA	NA	NA
Total Cap.	424	386	355	NA	NA	NA
Cap. Exp.	59.2	9.7	12.9	NA	NA	NA
Cash Flow	37.2	45.0	39.1	NA	NA	NA

Ratio Analysis

	1994	1993	1992	1991	1990	1989
Curr. Ratio	2.6	2.2	1.9	NA	NA	NA
% LT Debt of Cap.	7.1	Nil	Nil	NA	NA	NA
% Net Inc.of Revs.	5.2	8.9	5.2	NA	NA	NA
% Ret. on Assets	2.6	3.4	NA	NA	NA	NA
% Ret. on Equity	4.0	8.6	NA	NA	NA	NA

Dividend Data —Quarterly dividends were initiated with the November 1993 payment.

Amt. of Div. $	Date Decl.	Ex-Div. Date	Stock of Record	Payment Date
0.060	Oct. 28	Nov. 07	Nov. 14	Nov. 28 '94
0.060	Jan. 27	Feb. 08	Feb. 14	Feb. 28 '95
0.060	Apr. 28	May. 08	May. 12	May. 30 '95
0.060	Jul. 28	Aug. 09	Aug. 11	Aug. 28 '95
0.060	Oct. 27	Nov. 10	Nov. 14	Nov. 28 '95

Data as orig. reptd.; bef. results of disc. opers. and/or spec. items. Per share data adj. for stk. divs. as of ex-div. date. E-Estimated. NA-Not Available. NM-Not Meaningful. NR-Not Ranked.

Office—4 Greenway Plaza, Houston, TX 77046. **Tel**—(713) 871-7500. **Chrmn & CEO**—J. M. Talbert. **Pres & COO**—W. D. Heagney. **Treas**—F. E. Wylie. **VP-Secy**—P. J. Williamson. **Investor Contact**—Jeffrey L. Chastain. **Dirs**—P. Cortina del Valle, R. D. Kinder, R. L. Kuehn Jr., R. J. Lanigan, M. L. Lukens, M. B. McNamara, G. M. A. Portal, D. G. Russell, J. M. Talbert. **Transfer Agent & Registrar**—Trust Company Bank. **Incorporated** in Delaware in 1953. **Empl**-2,100. **S&P Analyst:** M.C.C.

Sonic Corp.

NASDAQ Symbol **SONC**
In S&P SmallCap 600

06-OCT-95 **Industry:** Food serving

Summary: Sonic operates and franchises more than 1,450 drive-in restaurants featuring fast service and a limited menu of moderately priced, cooked-to-order items.

Quantitative Evaluations
Outlook
(1 Lowest—5 Highest)
• **5**
Fair Value
• **28⅝**
Risk
• **Average**
Earn./Div. Rank
• **NR**

Technical Eval.
• **Bullish** since 9/95
Rel. Strength Rank
(1 Lowest—99 Highest)
• **82**
Insider Activity
• **NA**

Recent Price • 22¾
52 Wk Range • 23⅜-12
Yield • Nil
12-Mo. P/E • 23.2

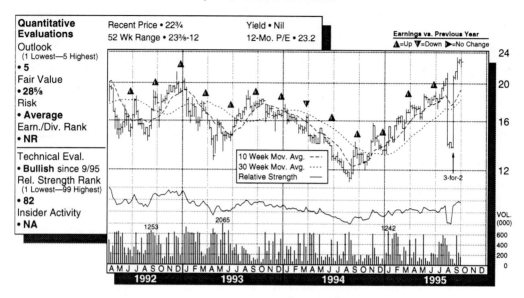

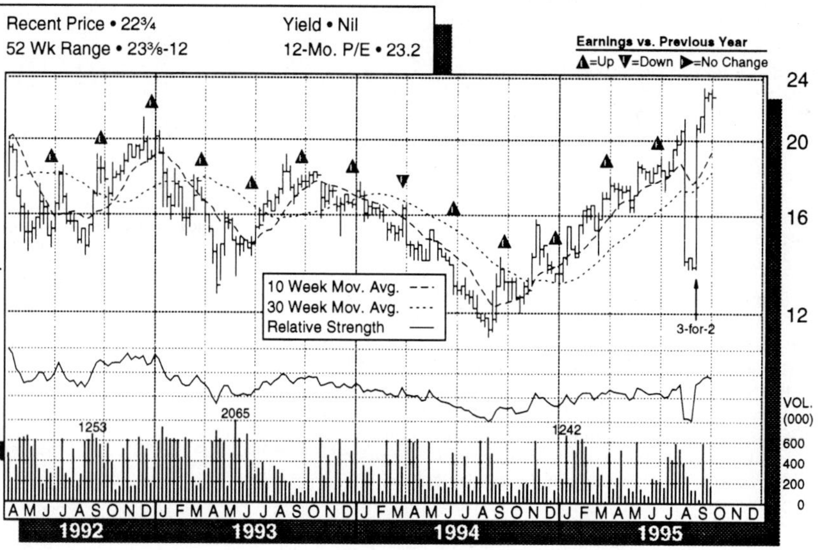

Business Profile - 06-OCT-95

Sales and earnings in recent periods benefited from additional restaurants in operation and higher comparable-store sales. Further expansion and improving comparable-store sales are expected to fuel continued earnings growth. In an October public offering, 2,170,000 common shares (including 750,000 sold by the former CEO) were sold at $21.25. Company proceeds will be used to fund expansion. The shares were split three for two in August.

Operational Review - 28-SEP-95

Revenues in the nine months ended May 31, 1995, advanced, year to year, reflecting additional units in operation and higher same-store sales; comparable system-wide and company-owned restaurant sales had year-to-year increases of 3.9% and 1.0%, respectively. With lower provisions for writedowns, partly offset by higher interest expense, net income nearly doubled.

Stock Performance - 29-SEP-95

In the past 30 trading days, SONC's shares have increased 61%, compared to a 5% rise in the S&P 500. Average trading volume for the past five days was 31,480 shares, compared with the 40-day moving average of 48,705 shares.

Key Stock Statistics

Dividend Rate/Share	Nil	Shareholders	300
Shs. outstg. (M)	13.0	Market cap. (B)	$0.248
Avg. daily vol. (M)	0.175	Inst. holdings	56%
Tang. Bk. Value/Share	3.18	Insider holdings	NA
Beta	NA		

Value of $10,000 invested 5 years ago: NA

Fiscal Year Ending Aug. 31

	1995	% Change	1994	% Change	1993	% Change
Revenues (Million $)						
1Q	27.57	19%	23.10	18%	19.60	29%
2Q	26.02	23%	21.09	23%	17.15	27%
3Q	33.77	22%	27.57	25%	22.02	24%
4Q	—	—	27.99	12%	25.03	24%
Yr.	—	—	99.7	19%	83.79	26%
Income (Million $)						
1Q	2.86	19%	2.40	22%	1.97	29%
2Q	2.21	NM	-0.76	NM	1.56	36%
3Q	3.38	24%	2.72	18%	2.30	26%
4Q	—	—	3.29	17%	2.81	21%
Yr.	—	—	7.64	-12%	8.64	27%
Earnings Per Share ($)						
1Q	0.24	20%	0.20	20%	0.17	32%
2Q	0.19	NM	-0.07	NM	0.13	33%
3Q	0.29	26%	0.23	17%	0.19	26%
4Q	—	—	0.27	17%	0.23	17%
Yr.	—	—	0.64	-11%	0.72	24%

Next earnings report expected: mid October

Sonic Corp.

Business Summary - 06-OCT-95

Sonic Corp. operates and franchises drive-in restaurants under the name Sonic, featuring fast service and a limited menu of moderately priced, cooked-to-order items. Sonic restaurants, located principally in the south central U.S., form the largest chain of quick-service, drive-in restaurants in the country. At May 31, 1995, there were 1,438 restaurants in the chain, of which 1,269 were owned by independent franchisees and 169 were owned by the company. Restaurant data for recent fiscal years (sales per unit in 000):

	1993-94	1992-93	1991-92
Company-owned			
Avg. unit sales	$558	$547	$526
No. of units	142	120	91

At a typical Sonic restaurant, the customer drives into one of 24 covered parking spaces, orders through an intercom from a menu featuring hamburgers, hot dogs, french fries, onion rings and specialty beverages, and has the food delivered by a carhop within an average of five minutes.

Each restaurant, including those owned by the company, operates under a franchise agreement that provides for payments to the company of a graduated percentage of gross revenues. About 75% of the restaurants are subject to a form of franchise agreement adopted in 1984 that provides for a royalty beginning at 1% of gross revenues and increasing to 3%. The recent average royalty rate for franchisees operating under the 1984 agreement was 2.1%. A new franchise agreement adopted in 1988 provides for graduated rates that begin at 1% and increase to 4%. Restaurants opened since September 1, 1989, have been paying average royalties of 2.75%.

The current average cost to start a new Sonic restaurant is about $605,000. Average first-year sales of a new restaurant were $750,000 for the 12-month period ending August 31, 1994.

The company also sells restaurant equipment to existing Sonic restaurants and to a majority of new Sonic units.

Important Developments

Oct. '95—In a public offering, 2,170,000 common shares (including 750,000 shares sold by Sonic's former CEO) were sold at $21.25 each. Company proceeds were to be used to fund expansion and acquisitions.

Jul. '95—In the quarter ended May 31, 1995, company-owned and systemwide comparable store sales rose 2.6% and 3.9%, respectively. At least 30 new company-operated restaurants were expected to be opened in the fiscal year ending August 31, 1995.

Capitalization

Long Term Debt: $20,000,000 (5/95).

Per Share Data ($)

(Year Ended Aug. 31)

	1994	1993	1992	1991	1990	1989
Tangible Bk. Val.	4.59	3.95	3.08	2.49	-0.72	-2.61
Cash Flow	1.17	0.92	0.75	0.56	0.30	0.06
Earnings	0.64	0.72	0.58	0.39	0.13	-0.27
Dividends	Nil	Nil	Nil	Nil	Nil	Nil
Payout Ratio	Nil	Nil	Nil	Nil	Nil	Nil
Prices - High	17⅝	20½	22	21	NA	NA
- Low	11⅛	12⅝	14⅛	8⅛	NA	NA
P/E Ratio - High	28	28	38	54	NA	NA
- Low	17	18	24	21	NA	NA

Income Statement Analysis (Million $)

	1994	%Chg	1993	%Chg	1992	%Chg	1991
Revs.	100	19%	83.8	26%	66.7	24%	53.9
Oper. Inc.	26.2	33%	19.7	20%	16.4	37%	12.0
Depr.	6.3	162%	2.4	14%	2.1	26%	1.7
Int. Exp.	1.1	35%	0.8	19%	0.7	-68%	2.1
Pretax Inc.	15.0	-8%	16.3	17%	13.9	64%	8.5
Eff. Tax Rate	31%	—	31%	—	32%	—	30%
Net Inc.	7.6	-12%	8.6	27%	6.8	83%	3.7

Balance Sheet & Other Fin. Data (Million $)

	1994	1993	1992	1991	1990	1989
Cash	6.0	5.4	9.0	10.3	2.5	2.8
Curr. Assets	14.1	13.6	14.2	14.7	6.5	6.4
Total Assets	77.0	63.5	50.3	41.9	31.6	31.6
Curr. Liab.	6.8	6.2	4.7	4.6	5.1	5.0
LT Debt	12.7	6.6	6.0	5.3	29.9	31.0
Common Eqty.	54.4	46.8	36.0	29.1	-5.2	-5.8
Total Cap.	69.4	56.2	44.3	36.2	26.2	25.9
Cap. Exp.	16.7	14.8	9.1	4.8	2.2	13.0
Cash Flow	13.9	11.0	8.9	5.4	2.2	-0.5

Ratio Analysis

	1994	1993	1992	1991	1990	1989
Curr. Ratio	2.1	2.2	3.0	3.2	1.3	1.3
% LT Debt of Cap.	18.3	11.7	13.5	14.7	114.1	119.8
% Net Inc.of Revs.	7.7	10.3	10.2	6.9	2.1	NM
% Ret. on Assets	10.9	15.1	14.8	8.0	NA	NM
% Ret. on Equity	15.1	20.8	20.9	NM	NA	NM

Dividend Data —Sonic has not paid cash dividends on its common stock, and intends to retain all earnings for working capital and general corporate purposes.

Amt. of Div. $	Date Decl.	Ex-Div. Date	Stock of Record	Payment Date
3-for-2	Jul. 19	Aug. 11	Jul. 31	Aug. 10 '95

Data as orig. reptd.; bef. results of disc. opers. and/or spec. items. Per share data adj. for stk. divs. as of ex-div. date. E-Estimated. NA-Not Available. NM-Not Meaningful. NR-Not Ranked.

Office—101 Park Ave., Oklahoma City, OK 73102. **Tel**—(405) 280-7654. **Chrmn**—E. D. Werries. **CEO**—J. C. Hudson. **SVP, CFO & Treas**—L. B. Kilbourne. **VP & Secy**—M. T. Folks. **Dirs**—D. H. Clark, R. P. Flack, J.C. Hudson, E. L. Hutton, L. Lieberman, F. E. Richardson III, R. M. Rosenberg, E. D. Werries. **Transfer Agent & Registrar**—Liberty Bank & Trust, Oklahoma City. **Reincorporated** in Delaware in 1991. **Empl**-141. **S&P Analyst:** Efraim Levy

Southern California Water

NYSE Symbol **SCW**
In S&P SmallCap 600

08-NOV-95 **Industry:** Utilities-Water

Summary: This water supply company serves customers in areas of southern and northern California and provides electric service to a small section of San Bernardino County.

Quantitative Evaluations

Recent Price • 18 5/8 — Yield • 6.5%
52 Wk Range • 19 7/8-15 1/4 — 12-Mo. P/E • 13.0

Outlook (1 Lowest—5 Highest)
• **3**

Fair Value
• **18 5/8**

Risk
• **Low**

Earn./Div. Rank
• **B+**

Technical Eval.
• **Bullish** since 7/95

Rel. Strength Rank (1 Lowest—99 Highest)
• **63**

Insider Activity
• **Favorable**

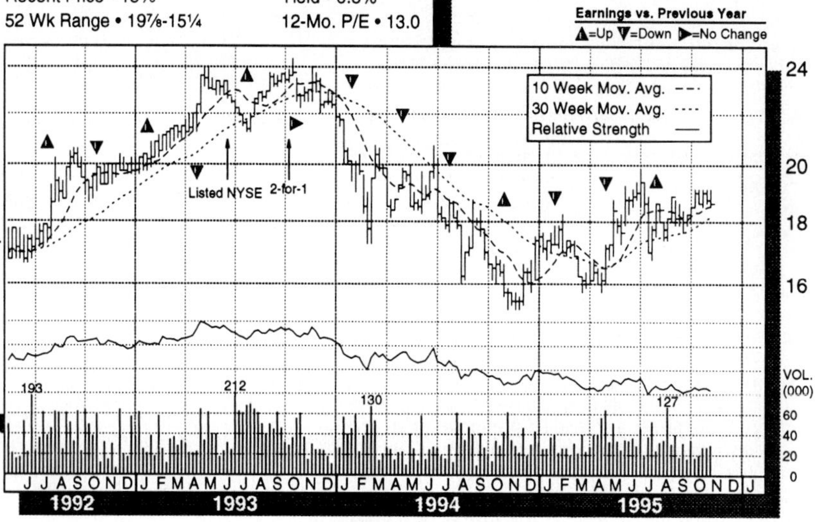

Business Profile - 08-NOV-95

SCW is the second largest investor-owned water company in California, and the fifth largest in the U.S. The company also provides electric service to more than 20,000 customers in the Bear Valley mountain communities. As of June 30, 1995, the company provided water service in 21 customer service areas in California. SCW operates in Northern California under the names Arden-Cordova Water Service and California Cities Water.

Operational Review - 08-NOV-95

Operating revenues for 1995's first half rose 4.7%, year to year, primarily reflecting a 5.1% gain in water revenues due to general, step and attrition rate increases, as well as about $13 million in supply cost offset rate increases. Electric revenues rose 1.1%, due to a slight shift in volumes from industrial customers to residential and commercial customers who have a higher unit rate. After a 25% increase in interest charges, net income was down fractionally (0.9%).

Stock Performance - 03-NOV-95

In the past 30 trading days, SCW's shares have increased 2%, compared to a 2% rise in the S&P 500. Average trading volume for the past five days was 5,760 shares, compared with the 40-day moving average of 4,930 shares.

Key Stock Statistics

Dividend Rate/Share	1.22	Shareholders	4,100
Shs. outstg. (M)	7.8	Market cap. (B)	$0.147
Avg. daily vol. (M)	0.005	Inst. holdings	23%
Tang. Bk. Value/Share	18.44	Insider holdings	NA
Beta	0.09		

Value of $10,000 invested 5 years ago: $ 18,218

Fiscal Year Ending Dec. 31

	1995	% Change	1994	% Change	1993	% Change
Revenues (Million $)						
1Q	24.84	3%	24.18	9%	22.20	6%
2Q	32.40	6%	30.49	7%	28.61	19%
3Q	—	—	38.69	22%	31.73	5%
4Q	—	—	29.31	13%	25.99	2%
Yr.	—	—	122.7	13%	108.5	8%
Income (Million $)						
1Q	0.57	-51%	1.17	-24%	1.54	-20%
2Q	2.89	24%	2.33	-22%	2.99	22%
3Q	—	—	5.21	20%	4.34	15%
4Q	—	—	2.64	-16%	3.16	-20%
Yr.	—	—	11.34	-6%	12.03	NM
Earnings Per Share ($)						
1Q	0.07	-53%	0.15	-35%	0.23	-19%
2Q	0.37	28%	0.29	-34%	0.44	21%
3Q	—	—	0.66	16%	0.57	NM
4Q	—	—	0.33	-21%	0.42	-29%
Yr.	—	—	1.43	-14%	1.66	-9%

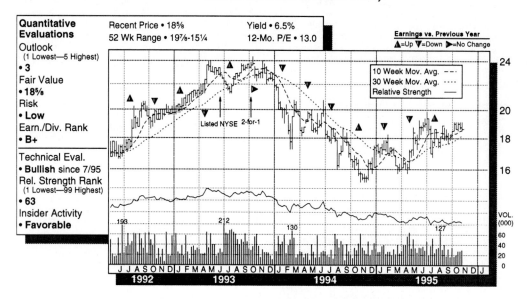

Next earnings report expected: early November

Southern California Water

Business Summary - 08-NOV-95

Southern California Water Company is engaged principally in the purchase, production, distribution, and sale of water. It also distributes electricity in one community. In recent years, more than 90% of revenues have been derived from supplying water.

At December 31, 1994, the company was serving 237,905 water customers and 20,331 electric customers, for a total of 258,236 customers, compared with 257,116 customers at the end of 1993.

Service is provided in 17 separate customer service areas and one electric service area, in 10 California counties. Total population of the service area is around 1.0 million. About 67% of the company's water customers are located in the greater metropolitan areas of Los Angeles and Orange Counties. Electric service is supplied around Big Bear Lake in San Bernardino County. All electric energy sold is purchased from Southern California Edison Co.

In 1994, the company produced 55.5% of its water needs from its own wells located in various service areas, purchased 43.0% from others, mainly member agencies of the Metropolitan Water District of Southern California, and received 1.5% from the Bureau of Reclamation under contract, at no cost, for the company's Arden-Cordova and Clearlake customer service areas.

As of December 31, 1994, the company's principal physical properties included more than 2,550 miles of pipeline and approximately 437 parcels of land on which are located wells, pumping plants, reservoirs and other utility facilities. SCW owned and operated 271 active wells equipped with pumps with an aggregate capacity of about 180 million gallons per day.

The company's electric properties are all located in the Big Bear area of San Bernardino County. At 1994 year-end, the company operated 28.7 miles of overhead 34.5 KV transmission lines, 0.6 miles of underground 34.5 KV transmission lines, 172.4 miles of 4.16 KV or 2.4-KV distribution lines, 39.5 miles of underground cable and 14 substations. SCW's system has no generating plants.

Important Developments

Jun. '95—SCW filed a registration statement with the SEC for the proposed sale to the public of up to $70 million in securities. Also, the company anticipates that it will be necessary to issue additional common equity in 1996.

Capitalization

Long Term Debt: $77,645,000 (6/95).
$1.0625 Cum. Pfd. Stk.: 32,000 shs. ($25 par); red. at $26.50.
$1 Cum. Pfd. Stk.: 32,000 shs. ($25 par); red. at $27.
$1.25 Cum. Pfd. Stk.: 24,000 shs. ($25 par); red. at $25.25.

Per Share Data ($) (Year Ended Dec. 31)

	1994	1993	1992	1991	1990	1989
Tangible Bk. Val.	18.42	14.92	13.28	12.58	11.31	10.97
Earnings	1.43	1.66	1.82	2.34	1.40	1.38
Dividends	1.20	1.19	1.15	1.10	1.08	1.04
Payout Ratio	84%	125%	63%	47%	77%	75%
Prices - High	22	24⅜	20⅝	17⅞	15¾	15⅝
- Low	15¼	19⅝	16	13⅝	12⅝	12⅛
P/E Ratio - High	15	15	11	8	11	11
- Low	11	12	9	6	9	9

Income Statement Analysis (Million $)

	1994	%Chg	1993	%Chg	1992	%Chg	1991
Revs.	123	13%	109	8%	101	11%	90.7
Depr.	8.1	9%	7.4	13%	6.5	8%	6.0
Maint.	6.9	7%	6.4	27%	5.1	-1%	5.2
Fxd. Chgs. Cov.	3.5	16%	3.0	-12%	3.5	16%	3.0
Constr. Credits	Nil	—	Nil	—	Nil	—	Nil
Eff. Tax Rate	45%	—	24%	—	41%	—	36%
Net Inc.	11.3	-6%	12.0	NM	12.1	-21%	15.4

Balance Sheet & Other Fin. Data (Million $)

	1994	1993	1992	1991	1990	1989
Gross Prop.	408	380	355	331	300	275
Cap. Exp.	30.9	28.1	28.2	32.5	27.1	25.7
Net Prop.	315	295	278	259	236	214
Capitalization:						
LT Debt	92.9	84.3	84.2	82.6	67.3	67.8
% LT Debt	43	42	48	49	48	49
Pfd.	2.2	2.2	2.2	2.3	2.3	2.4
% Pfd.	1.00	1.10	1.30	1.40	1.60	1.70
Common	119	117	88.2	83.2	71.1	68.6
% Common	56	57	51	50	51	50
Total Cap.	279	267	214	206	171	170

Ratio Analysis

	1994	1993	1992	1991	1990	1989
Oper. Ratio	84.6	81.5	81.0	81.4	83.7	82.7
% Earn. on Net Prop.	6.2	7.0	7.1	6.8	6.5	6.9
% Ret. on Revs.	9.2	11.1	12.1	16.9	9.9	10.2
% Ret. On Invest.Cap	7.0	8.5	9.5	12.2	9.0	9.6
% Return On Com.Eqty	9.5	11.7	14.1	19.9	12.6	12.8

Dividend Data —Cash has been paid each year since 1931. A dividend reinvestment plan is available. A 2-for-1 stock split was effected in October 1993.

Amt. of Div. $	Date Decl.	Ex-Div. Date	Stock of Record	Payment Date
0.300	Oct. 24	Nov. 07	Nov. 14	Dec. 01 '94
0.300	Jan. 30	Feb. 07	Feb. 13	Mar. 01 '95
0.300	Apr. 24	May. 08	May. 12	Jun. 01 '95
0.300	Jul. 24	Aug. 10	Aug. 14	Sep. 01 '95
0.305	Oct. 23	Nov. 09	Nov. 13	Dec. 01 '95

Data as orig. reptd.; bef. results of disc opers. and/or spec. items. Per share data adj. for stk. divs. as of ex-div. date. E-Estimated. NA-Not Available. NM-Not Meaningful. NR-Not Ranked.

Office—630 East Foothill Blvd., San Dimas, CA 91773. **Tel**—(909) 394-3600. **Chrmn**—W. V. Caveney. **Pres & CEO**—F. E. Wicks. **CFO, Treas, Secy, & Investor Contact**—J. B. Gallagher. **Dirs**—J. E. Auer, W. V. Caveney, R. B. Clark, N. P. Dodge Jr., R. F. Kathol, L. E. Ross, F. E. Wicks. **Transfer Agent & Registrar**—First Interstate Bank of California, Los Angeles. **Incorporated** in California in 1929. **Empl**-467. **S&P Analyst:** R.J.G.

STANDARD & POOR'S

STOCK REPORTS

Southwest Gas

NYSE Symbol **SWX**

In S&P SmallCap 600

31-AUG-95 **Industry:** Utilities-Gas

Summary: SWX conducts natural gas distribution operations, mainly in Nevada and Arizona, and nonutility operations through PriMerit Bank, a Nevada-based savings bank.

Quantitative Evaluations

Recent Price • 15¼ | Yield • 5.3%

52 Wk Range • 17⅞-13⅝ | 12-Mo. P/E • 18.2

Outlook (1 Lowest—5 Highest)
• **2-**

Fair Value
• **14⅜**

Risk
• **Low**

Earn./Div. Rank
• **B**

Technical Eval.
• **Bullish** since 10/94

Rel. Strength Rank (1 Lowest—99 Highest)
• **66**

Insider Activity
• **NA**

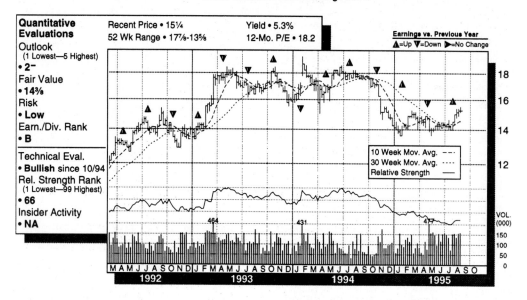

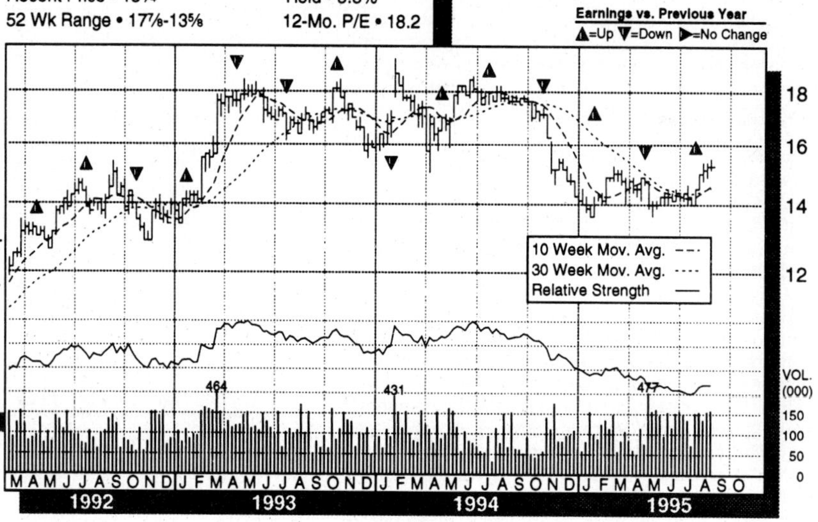

Business Profile - 30-AUG-95

The company anticipates that customer growth will continue at a rapid pace in 1995, since the western states in which it operates are expected to lead the U.S. in population growth, job growth and housing activity. However, an imbalance between the rates charged customers and expenses incurred to serve new customers is expected to negatively impact operating results in the short run. The timeliness of rate relief and the effects of weather will remain pivotal factors in future earnings.

Operational Review - 30-AUG-95

Revenues in the first half of 1995 rose 4.8%, year to year. Results were hurt by increased operating costs and net interest deductions incurred as a result of a continued expansion and upgrading of the gas system to accommodate customer growth, and net income declined to $5,304,000 ($0.23 a share), from $12,929,000 ($0.60).

Stock Performance - 25-AUG-95

In the past 30 trading days, SWX's shares have increased 7%, compared to a 0.04% rise in the S&P 500. Average trading volume for the past five days was 46,280 shares, compared with the 40-day moving average of 32,090 shares.

Key Stock Statistics

Dividend Rate/Share	0.82	Shareholders	23,900
Shs. outstg. (M)	23.6	Market cap. (B)	$0.366
Avg. daily vol. (M)	0.040	Inst. holdings	34%
Tang. Bk. Value/Share	13.70	Insider holdings	NA
Beta	0.29		

Value of $10,000 invested 5 years ago: $ 12,993

Fiscal Year Ending Dec. 31

	1995	% Change	1994	% Change	1993	% Change
Revenues (Million $)						
1Q	238.9	NM	239.0	8%	221.0	-8%
2Q	158.5	13%	140.2	2%	138.0	-4%
3Q	—	—	124.3	-1%	126.0	NM
4Q	—	—	224.5	10%	205.0	-1%
Yr.	—	—	728.2	6%	690.0	-4%
Income (Million $)						
1Q	14.65	-35%	22.71	33%	17.13	16%
2Q	-9.34	NM	-9.78	NM	-13.07	NM
3Q	—	—	-11.17	NM	-7.34	NM
4Q	—	—	24.54	31%	18.70	-24%
Yr.	—	—	26.30	113%	12.36	-30%
Earnings Per Share ($)						
1Q	0.68	-36%	1.07	60%	0.67	-6%
2Q	-0.41	NM	-0.47	NM	-0.64	NM
3Q	—	—	-0.54	NM	-0.37	NM
4Q	—	—	1.15	28%	0.90	-24%
Yr.	—	—	1.22	118%	0.56	-31%

Next earnings report expected: early November

Southwest Gas

Business Summary - 30-AUG-95

Southwest Gas distributes natural gas in portions of Nevada, Arizona and California. The company also conducts savings and loan operations through PriMerit Bank (formerly Nevada Savings and Loan Association), acquired in December 1986. Contributions to revenues and operating profits (in millions) by business segment in 1994 were:

	Revs.	Profits
Gas	82%	86%
Financial services	18%	14%

Gas sales volume in 1994 was 881.9 million therms, up from 850.6 million in 1993. Gas transported for others in 1994 amounted to 914.8 million therms, up from 725.0 million in 1993. Degree days in 1994 totaled 2,427, versus 2,470 the year before and 1.7% higher than the 10-year average.

At 1994 year-end, SWX served 980,000 customers, up from 932,000 a year earlier. Paiute Pipeline Co. (wholly owned) provides transportation service of gas from the Idaho-Nevada border to communities in northern and western Nevada.

Operating margins by major customer class in 1994 were derived: residential and small commercial 79%; large commercial, industrial and other 7%; and electric generation, resale and transportation 14%.

PriMerit Bank is a federally chartered savings bank with branch offices in Nevada. Its Arizona operations were sold in the second quarter of 1993. Since 1989 year-end, the balance sheet has been restructured to more effectively operate under regulatory guidelines; downsizing of operations is also part of a strategy to optimize the bank's size. Assets of $1.8 billion at 1994 year-end were divided: 52% loans receivable, debt securities 35%, 7% cash and cash equivalents, 5% non-interest earning and 1% FHLB stock. In 1994, the net yield on interest-earning assets was 3.69%, versus 3.15% in 1993.

Important Developments

Aug. '95—In reporting earnings for the second quarter of 1995, the company noted that gas operations reported a net loss of $10.0 million, versus a loss of $10.7 million a year earlier. The improvement was attributed primarily to higher operating margin partially offset by increased operating expenses and net interest deductions. At the financial services segment, net income declined to $2.1 million, from $2.2 million.

Capitalization

Long Term Debt: $901,688,000 (6/95), includes current maturities.
Preferred Stock: $4,000,000.

Per Share Data ($)

(Year Ended Dec. 31)

	1994	1993	1992	1991	1990	1989
Tangible Bk. Val.	12.85	12.87	12.14	11.83	12.89	12.14
Cash Flow	4.81	3.63	3.75	1.95	4.44	4.77
Earnings	1.22	0.56	0.81	-0.76	1.81	2.15
Dividends	0.60	0.74	0.70	1.05	1.40	1.37
Payout Ratio	50%	132%	87%	NM	77%	64%
Prices - High	19⅜	18½	15⅜	17½	18½	20⅜
- Low	13¾	13⅜	10⅜	9	11¾	16⅝
P/E Ratio - High	16	33	19	NM	10	9
- Low	11	24	13	NM	6	8

Income Statement Analysis (Million $)

	1994	%Chg	1993	%Chg	1992	%Chg	1991
Revs.	728	6%	690	-4%	720	-10%	800
Oper. Inc.	168	11%	151	-39%	249	NM	247
Depr.	65.1	2%	63.6	5%	60.7	10%	55.3
Int. Exp.	58.0	16%	50.1	-68%	157	-24%	207
Pretax Inc.	44.0	86%	23.6	-26%	32.1	NM	-13.5
Eff. Tax Rate	40%	—	48%	—	45%	—	NM
Net Inc.	26.3	112%	12.4	-30%	17.7	NM	-14.2

Balance Sheet & Other Fin. Data (Million $)

	1994	1993	1992	1991	1990	1989
Cash	166	136	133	113	70.0	41.0
Curr. Assets	NA	NA	NA	NA	NA	NA
Total Assets	3,090	2,944	3,342	3,463	3,764	3,706
Curr. Liab.	NA	NA	NA	NA	NA	NA
LT Debt	786	648	614	598	817	830
Common Eqty.	339	340	329	327	353	334
Total Cap.	1,262	1,147	1,062	1,058	1,313	1,302
Cap. Exp.	145	115	105	86.0	105	114
Cash Flow	90.9	75.2	77.3	39.8	87.2	90.7

Ratio Analysis

	1994	1993	1992	1991	1990	1989
Curr. Ratio	NA	NA	NA	NA	NA	NA
% LT Debt of Cap.	62.2	56.5	57.8	56.5	62.2	63.8
% Net Inc.of Revs.	3.6	1.8	2.5	NM	4.3	5.0
% Ret. on Assets	0.9	0.4	0.5	NM	1.0	1.1
% Ret. on Equity	7.5	3.5	5.1	NM	10.2	12.5

Dividend Data —Dividends have been paid since 1956. A dividend reinvestment plan is available.

Amt. of Div. $	Date Decl.	Ex-Div. Date	Stock of Record	Payment Date
0.205	May. 11	Aug. 10	Aug. 16	Sep. 01 '94
0.205	Sep. 20	Nov. 08	Nov. 15	Dec. 01 '94
0.205	Jan. 18	Feb. 09	Feb. 15	Mar. 01 '95
0.205	Apr. 13	May. 09	May. 15	Jun. 01 '95
0.205	Jul. 19	Aug. 11	Aug. 15	Sep. 01 '95

Data as orig. reptd.; bef. results of disc. opers. and/or spec. items. Per share data adj. for stk. divs. as of ex-div. date. E-Estimated. NA-Not Available. NM-Not Meaningful. NR-Not Ranked.

Office—5241 Spring Mountain Rd., P.O. Box 98510, Las Vegas, NV 89193-8510. **Tel**—(702) 876-7237. **Chrmn**—K. C. Guinn. **Pres & CEO**—M. O. Maffie. **SVP & CFO**—G. C. Biehl. **SVP-Secy**—T. J. Trimble. **Investor Contact**—Laura Hobbs. **Dirs**—R.C. Batastini, M. J. Cortez, L. T. Dyer, K. C. Guinn, T. Y. Hartley, M. B. Jager, L. R. Judd, J. R. Lincicome, M. O. Maffie, C. M. Sparks, R. S. Sundt. **Transfer Agent & Registrar**—Co. itself. **Incorporated** in California in 1931. **Empl**-2,945. **S&P Analyst:** S.R.B.

Southwestern Energy

NYSE Symbol **SWN**
In S&P SmallCap 600

11-OCT-95 **Industry:** Utilities-Gas

Summary: Through its wholly owned subsidiaries, Southwestern Energy explores for and produces oil and natural gas, and is involved in the transmission and distribution of natural gas.

Quantitative Evaluations
Outlook
(1 Lowest—5 Highest)
• 3-
Fair Value
• 13⅝
Risk
• Average
Earn./Div. Rank
• A-

Technical Eval.
• Bearish since 7/95
Rel. Strength Rank
(1 Lowest—99 Highest)
• 61
Insider Activity
• NA

Recent Price • 13½
52 Wk Range • 17¾-11¾
Yield • 1.8%
12-Mo. P/E • 23.3

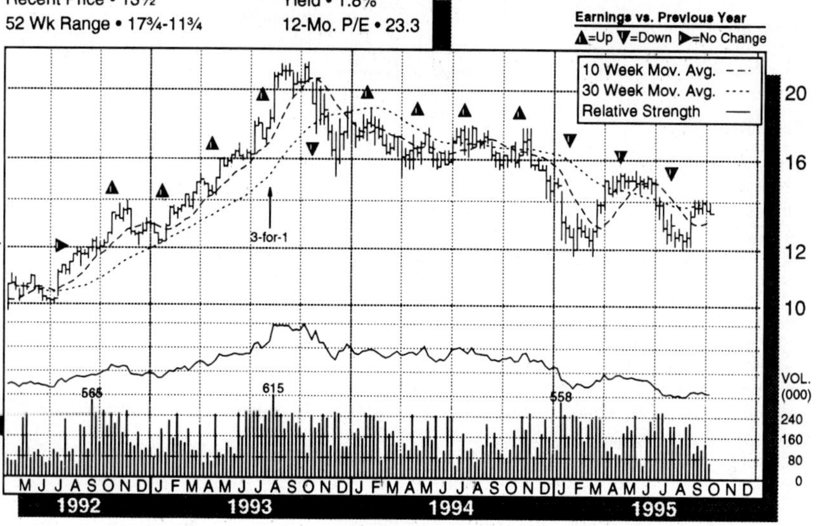

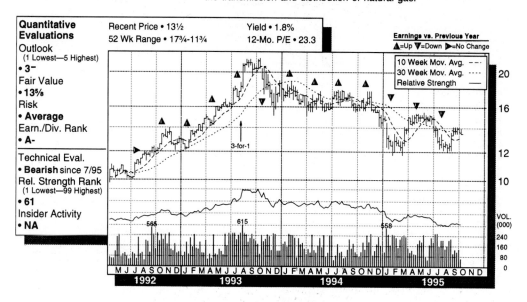

Business Profile - 11-OCT-95

Southwestern Energy operates natural gas transmission and distribution systems that serve over 160,000 customers in northern Arkansas and southeastern Missouri, and explores for, produces and markets natural gas and oil, supplying over 50% of the systems' gas requirements. Lower natural gas prices have had a negative impact on earnings, which declined 58% for the first six months of 1995. In February 1995, directors authorized the repurchase of up to $30 million of the company's common shares.

Operational Review - 11-OCT-95

Operating revenues for the six months ended June 30, 1995, fell 18%, year to year, reflecting lower gas prices, a decrease in gas production and warmer heating weather. Margins narrowed on the lower volume, and operating income was down 44%. After higher interest expense, and taxes at 38.5% in both periods, net income declined 58%, to $7.5 million ($0.30 a share) from $17.8 million ($0.69).

Stock Performance - 06-OCT-95

In the past 30 trading days, SWN's shares have increased 8%, compared to a 4% rise in the S&P 500. Average trading volume for the past five days was 11,860 shares, compared with the 40-day moving average of 28,385 shares.

Key Stock Statistics

Dividend Rate/Share	0.24	Shareholders	28,800
Shs. outstg. (M)	24.7	Market cap. (B)	$0.336
Avg. daily vol. (M)	0.020	Inst. holdings	61%
Tang. Bk. Value/Share	7.20	Insider holdings	NA
Beta	0.41		

Value of $10,000 invested 5 years ago: $ 13,830

Fiscal Year Ending Dec. 31

	1995	% Change	1994	% Change	1993	% Change
Revenues (Million $)						
1Q	51.75	-21%	65.40	10%	59.20	21%
2Q	30.64	-11%	34.60	2%	34.00	35%
3Q	—	—	27.81	-2%	28.50	36%
4Q	—	—	42.34	-20%	53.20	9%
Yr.	—	—	170.2	-3%	174.8	22%
Income (Million $)						
1Q	7.10	-45%	12.99	14%	11.37	29%
2Q	0.44	-91%	4.83	31%	3.70	103%
3Q	—	—	2.13	48%	1.44	-19%
4Q	—	—	5.17	-51%	10.54	7%
Yr.	—	—	25.12	-7%	27.05	21%
Earnings Per Share ($)						
1Q	0.28	-45%	0.51	16%	0.44	29%
2Q	0.02	-89%	0.18	20%	0.15	114%
3Q	—	—	0.09	80%	0.05	-29%
4Q	—	—	0.20	-51%	0.41	8%
Yr.	—	—	0.98	-7%	1.05	21%

Next earnings report expected: early November

Southwestern Energy

Business Summary - 11-OCT-95

Southwestern Energy operates, through subsidiaries, an integrated gas transmission and distribution system serving northern Arkansas and southeastern Missouri. Other subsidiaries explore for, produce and market natural gas and oil.

Gas exploration and production is conducted in Arkansas by wholly owned SEECO, Inc., with most production used to serve SWN's utility customers. Southwestern Energy Production Co. conducts oil and gas exploration and production outside Arkansas, primarily in the Gulf Coast areas of Texas and Louisiana; its production is sold to unaffiliated companies. Exploration and production activities accounted for 39% of revenues and 74% of operating income in 1994.

Production in 1994 amounted to 37,700,000 thousand cubic feet (Mcf) of gas (35,700,000 Mcf in 1993) at an average price of $2.04 per Mcf ($2.18), and 200,000 bbl. of oil (97,000) at an average price of $15.89 per bbl. ($17.20). Net proved reserves at year-end 1994 were estimated at 316,098,000 Mcf of gas (318,776,000 Mcf a year earlier) and 1,231,000 bbl. of oil (479,000). Independent petroleum engineers estimated the present value of future cash flows of reserves at $189.5 million at December 31, 1994.

The company's gas utility, Arkansas Western Gas Co. (AWG), operates 5,893 miles of pipeline, including gathering, transmission and distribution systems. An average of 159,897 customers were served during 1994, up from 155,944 in 1993. Gas sales and transportation revenues of $124.7 million in 1994 were divided as follows: residential 50%, commercial 26%, industrial 20% and transportation 4%. AWG contributed 61% of revenues and 26% of operating income in 1994.

SWN operates and also owns a 47.93% general partnership interest in the NOARK Pipeline System, a 258-mile-long intrastate natural gas transmission system across northern Arkansas. The system was placed in service in September 1992. NOARK has an estimated transportation capacity of 141,000 Mcf on its main line. A lateral line to augment supply for existing markets and serve new markets was placed in service in November 1992. The company's gas distribution subsidiary has a 10-year transportation contract for firm capacity of 41,000 Mcf per day.

Wholly owned A.W. Realty Co. owns some 170 acres in Arkansas for mixed-use development.

Important Developments

Jul. '95—Gas production for the first six months of 1995 was 17,700 Mcf, down 7.8% from the 19,200 Mcf produced in the first six months of 1994. Average sales price for gas was $1.73 per Mcf, versus $2.26. Oil production increased to 95,731 bbl. from 87,703 bbl.

Capitalization

Long Term Debt: $146,029,000 (6/95).

Per Share Data ($) (Year Ended Dec. 31)

	1994	1993	1992	1991	1990	1989
Tangible Bk. Val.	7.92	7.18	5.97	5.30	4.70	4.15
Cash Flow	2.36	2.26	1.80	1.49	1.16	1.21
Earnings	0.98	1.05	0.87	0.78	0.57	0.56
Dividends	Nil	0.22	0.20	0.19	0.19	0.19
Payout Ratio	Nil	21%	23%	24%	33%	33%
Prices - High	18⅞	21½	14	12¾	12⅛	11⅛
- Low	14	12⅛	9¼	9⅛	9½	5¾
P/E Ratio - High	19	21	16	16	21	20
- Low	14	12	11	12	16	10

Income Statement Analysis (Million $)

	1994	%Chg	1993	%Chg	1992	%Chg	1991
Revs.	170	-3%	175	22%	144	6%	136
Oper. Inc.	87.6	-1%	88.5	27%	69.9	16%	60.4
Depr.	35.5	15%	30.9	29%	23.9	31%	18.2
Int. Exp.	10.5	NM	10.6	-8%	11.5	3%	11.2
Pretax Inc.	40.9	-13%	46.9	32%	35.6	11%	32.2
Eff. Tax Rate	39%	—	42%	—	37%	—	38%
Net Inc.	25.1	-7%	27.1	22%	22.3	11%	20.1

Balance Sheet & Other Fin. Data (Million $)

	1994	1993	1992	1991	1990	1989
Cash	1.1	0.8	1.1	2.2	1.2	1.1
Curr. Assets	48.0	46.3	45.1	41.5	34.7	34.6
Total Assets	485	445	427	392	366	347
Curr. Liab.	39.0	38.7	31.3	31.4	32.7	32.5
LT Debt	136	124	143	131	123	126
Common Eqty.	203	185	153	136	121	103
Total Cap.	442	405	394	359	332	313
Cap. Exp.	76.3	59.2	49.3	38.5	36.9	39.0
Cash Flow	60.7	58.0	46.1	38.3	29.3	30.3

Ratio Analysis

	1994	1993	1992	1991	1990	1989
Curr. Ratio	1.2	1.2	1.4	1.3	1.1	1.1
% LT Debt of Cap.	30.8	30.6	36.3	36.5	36.9	40.1
% Net Inc.of Revs.	14.8	15.5	15.5	14.7	12.4	11.1
% Ret. on Assets	3.4	6.2	5.4	5.3	4.0	4.2
% Ret. on Equity	13.0	16.0	15.4	15.6	12.8	14.2

Dividend Data —Dividends have been paid since 1939. The company has a dividend reinvestment plan. A "poison pill" stock purchase rights plan was adopted in 1989.

Amt. of Div. $	Date Decl.	Ex-Div. Date	Stock of Record	Payment Date
0.060	Oct. 06	Oct. 14	Oct. 20	Nov. 04 '94
0.060	Jan. 06	Jan. 13	Jan. 20	Feb. 03 '95
0.060	Apr. 06	Apr. 13	Apr. 20	May. 05 '95
0.060	Jul. 11	Jul. 18	Jul. 20	Aug. 04 '95
0.060	Oct. 05	Oct. 18	Oct. 20	Nov. 03 '95

Data as orig. reptd.; bef. results of disc. opers. and/or spec. items. Per share data adj. for stk. divs. as of ex-div. date. E-Estimated. NA-Not Available. NM-Not Meaningful. NR-Not Ranked.

Office—1083 Sain St., P.O.B. 1408, Fayetteville, AR 72702-1408. **Tel**—(501) 521-1141. **Chrmn & CEO**—C. E. Scharlau. **Pres & COO**—D. B. Grubb. **Exec VP-Fin & CFO**—S. D. Green. **VP, Secy & Treas**—G. D. Kerley. **Dirs**—E. J. Ball, J. B. Coffman, J. P. Hammerschmidt, C. E. Sanders, C. E. Scharlau. **Transfer Agent & Registrar**—First Chicago Trust Co. of New York, NYC. **Incorporated** in Arkansas in 1929. **Empl-661.** **S&P Analyst:** N. Rosenberg

SpaceLabs Medical

NASDAQ Symbol **SLMD**

In S&P SmallCap 600

17-SEP-95

Industry: Medical equipment/ supply

Summary: This company is a leading manufacturer of clinical information systems, patient monitoring equipment and diagnostic monitoring products.

Quantitative Evaluations

Outlook
(1 Lowest—5 Highest)
• **NA**

Fair Value
• **NA**

Risk
• **Average**

Earn./Div. Rank
• **NR**

Technical Eval.
• **Bearish** since 10/94

Rel. Strength Rank
(1 Lowest—99 Highest)
• **70**

Insider Activity
• **NA**

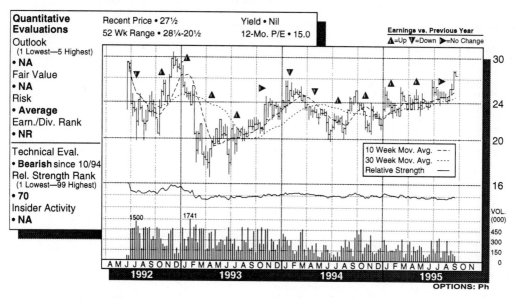

Recent Price • 27½

52 Wk Range • 28¼-20½

Yield • Nil

12-Mo. P/E • 15.0

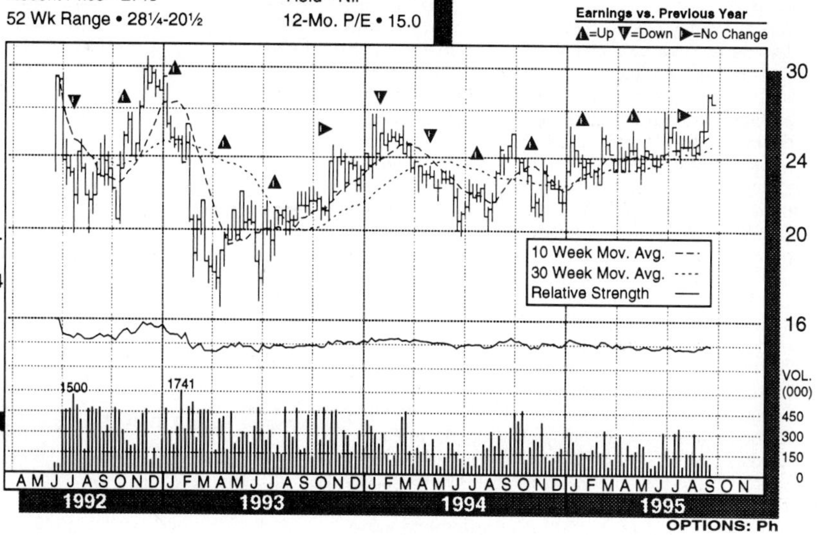

OPTIONS: Ph

Business Profile - 15-SEP-95

SpaceLabs is coping with a difficult domestic market, as consolidation in the hospital industry is limiting capital spending for patient-monitoring systems. The company is expanding internationally to offset weakness in the U.S. market. It has also taken restructuring charges to consolidate several locations into one facility. New products and product enhancements as well as the integration of products from the acquisition of JRS Clinical Technologies could help future results.

Operational Review - 15-SEP-95

Revenues were stable in the first half of 1995, as lower domestic demand was offset by increased sales in foreign markets (about 25% of total revenues). Slightly lower gross profit margins, higher SG&A expenses, and restructuring and reorganization charges were offset by higher net interest income. Also, results 1994 were hurt by costs related to earthquake damage.

Stock Performance - 15-SEP-95

In the past 30 trading days, SLMD's shares have increased 11%, compared to a 4% rise in the S&P 500. Average trading volume for the past five days was 16,640 shares, compared with the 40-day moving average of 28,608 shares.

Key Stock Statistics

Dividend Rate/Share	Nil	Shareholders	9,700
Shs. outstg. (M)	10.5	Market cap. (B)	$0.289
Avg. daily vol. (M)	0.027	Inst. holdings	74%
Tang. Bk. Value/Share	16.80	Insider holdings	NA
Beta	0.24		

Value of $10,000 invested 5 years ago: NA

Fiscal Year Ending Dec. 31

	1995	% Change	1994	% Change	1993	% Change
Revenues (Million $)						
1Q	63.14	3%	61.24	-6%	65.20	6%
2Q	64.02	1%	63.26	NM	62.70	NM
3Q	—	—	60.03	1%	59.40	-5%
4Q	—	—	62.67	2%	61.31	-6%
Yr.	—	—	247.2	NM	248.7	-1%
Income (Million $)						
1Q	4.47	59%	2.81	-35%	4.31	23%
2Q	4.58	NM	4.62	NM	4.59	56%
3Q	—	—	5.14	1%	5.08	NM
4Q	—	—	5.50	6%	5.19	-9%
Yr.	—	—	18.06	-6%	19.17	11%
Earnings Per Share ($)						
1Q	0.41	58%	0.26	-32%	0.38	15%
2Q	0.43	NM	0.43	5%	0.41	52%
3Q	—	—	0.48	7%	0.45	NM
4Q	—	—	0.51	9%	0.47	-6%
Yr.	—	—	1.68	-2%	1.71	9%

Next earnings report expected: late October

SpaceLabs Medical

Business Summary - 15-SEP-95

SpaceLabs Medical, Inc. develops, manufactures, markets and services patient monitoring and clinical information systems products for use in critical-care situations worldwide. Its principal product line is the Patient Care Information System (PCIS), which, as an integrated whole, forms an advanced and comprehensive critical-care patient monitoring system and the foundation for a clinical information system.

In the critical-care patient monitoring market, the company's principal product line is the PCIS, both as an entire system and in its component parts. The PCIS product line includes both the company's long-established Patient Care Management System (PCMS) monitoring products and its evolving clinical information products. PCMS products address the hospital's principal monitoring needs, from adult and neonatal intensive care units to out-patient surgery, step-down units and patient transport, and at the same time provide the flexible architecture to accommodate future advances in monitoring and the transition to clinical information systems. Sales of these products to hospitals vary over a wide range, depending on the size and configuration of the system. A typical eight-bed hardwired system sells for about $170,000, while a typical 12-bed telemetry system sells for about $85,000. PCMS products represent the major portion of current business.

In late 1993, the company introduced the PC Scout, a portable monitor compatible with PCMS modules, designed for the transport market and stand-alone applications. During 1994, the company introduced the module configuration manager, which allows clinicians to customize and save selected monitoring protocols and default functions. SpaceLabs has greatly expanded its library of PCIS modules and their features from only two modules to 15. Through the use of an Ethernet based local area network, the company connects PCIS bedside monitors to each other and to central station monitors. By linking monitoring products with evolving clinical information products, the PCIS interactive network in the foundation for the Patient Care Information System.

SpaceLabs also develops, produces, markets and services ambulatory ECG and ambulatory noninvasive blood pressure monitoring products, which enable a medical professional to determine how a patient's ECG or blood pressure reacts to normal daily activity, with or without medications, over a 24- to 48-hour period.

Important Developments

Feb. '95—SpaceLabs Medical agreed to acquire JRS Clinical Technologies, Inc., which makes a patient focused point-of-care system. Spacelabs plans to integrate the system into PCIS.

Capitalization

Long Term Debt: $10,850,000 (7/95).

Per Share Data ($)

(Year Ended Dec. 31)

	1994	1993	1992	1991	1990	1989
Tangible Bk. Val.	16.89	15.26	13.68	9.98	NA	NA
Cash Flow	2.48	2.47	2.43	2.24	1.78	NA
Earnings	1.68	1.71	1.57	1.54	1.19	0.89
Dividends	Nil	Nil	Nil	Nil	Nil	Nil
Payout Ratio	Nil	Nil	Nil	Nil	Nil	Nil
Prices - High	26¾	28¾	30¾	NA	NA	NA
- Low	19¾	16½	19¾	NA	NA	NA
P/E Ratio - High	16	17	20	NA	NA	NA
- Low	12	10	13	NA	NA	NA

Income Statement Analysis (Million $)

	1994	%Chg	1993	%Chg	1992	%Chg	1991
Revs.	247	NM	249	-1%	252	12%	225
Oper. Inc.	37.7	NM	37.6	14%	33.0	30%	25.4
Depr.	8.6	2%	8.4	-11%	9.4	32%	7.2
Int. Exp.	NA	—	NA	—	0.9	-5%	0.9
Pretax Inc.	28.9	-6%	30.9	4%	29.6	15%	25.8
Eff. Tax Rate	37%	—	38%	—	42%	—	39%
Net Inc.	18.1	-6%	19.2	12%	17.2	9%	15.8

Balance Sheet & Other Fin. Data (Million $)

	1994	1993	1992	1991	1990	1989
Cash	49.1	55.4	38.5	1.0	NA	NA
Curr. Assets	180	170	158	114	NA	NA
Total Assets	234	219	209	168	138	117
Curr. Liab.	36.3	34.9	34.0	36.9	NA	NA
LT Debt	11.2	11.9	12.6	13.3	Nil	Nil
Common Eqty.	185	171	161	116	100	88.0
Total Cap.	198	184	175	131	100	88.0
Cap. Exp.	14.9	7.2	6.7	15.7	8.1	NA
Cash Flow	26.7	27.6	26.6	22.9	18.2	NA

Ratio Analysis

	1994	1993	1992	1991	1990	1989
Curr. Ratio	5.0	4.9	4.6	3.1	NA	NA
% LT Debt of Cap.	5.7	6.5	7.2	10.2	Nil	Nil
% Net Inc.of Revs.	7.3	7.7	6.8	7.0	6.1	5.3
% Ret. on Assets	8.0	9.1	9.1	10.3	9.5	8.4
% Ret. on Equity	10.2	11.8	12.4	14.6	12.9	11.1

Dividend Data —No cash dividends have been paid on the common shares, and no payments are expected in the foreseeable future.

Data as orig. reptd.; bef. results of disc. opers. and/or spec. items. Per share data adj. for stk. divs. as of ex-div. date. E-Estimated. NA-Not Available. NM-Not Meaningful. NR-Not Ranked.

Office—15220 N.E. 40th St., Redmond, WA 98052. **Tel**—(206) 882-3700. **Chrmn & CEO**—C. A. Lombardi. **VP & CFO**—Barbara Sherrill. **Secy**—Mary Brodd. **Dirs**—T. J. Dudley, H. Feigenbaum, D. C. Fill, C. A. Lombardi, P. M. Nudelman, H. Woolf. **Transfer Agent & Registrar**—First Chicago Trust Co. of New York, NYC. **Incorporated** in Delaware in 1958. **Empl-** 1,525. **S&P Analyst:** Philip J. Birbara

STANDARD & POOR'S

STOCK REPORTS

Spartan Motors

NASDAQ Symbol **SPAR**

In S&P SmallCap 600

14-AUG-95

Industry: Auto parts/equipment

Summary: Spartan makes custom-designed heavy truck chassis for motorhome, fire apparatus and utility applications, and also produces vehicles for special applications.

Quantitative Evaluations

Outlook (1 Lowest—5 Highest)
• **5-**

Fair Value
• **12½**

Risk
• **Average**

Earn./Div. Rank
• **B+**

Technical Eval.
• **Bullish** since 7/94

Rel. Strength Rank (1 Lowest—99 Highest)
• **13**

Insider Activity
• **NA**

Recent Price • 9⅜
52 Wk Range • 17⅝-8⅝

Yield • 0.5%
12-Mo. P/E • 14.0

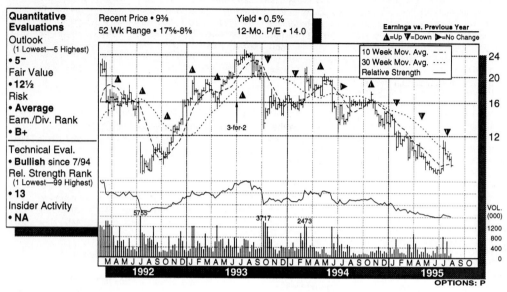

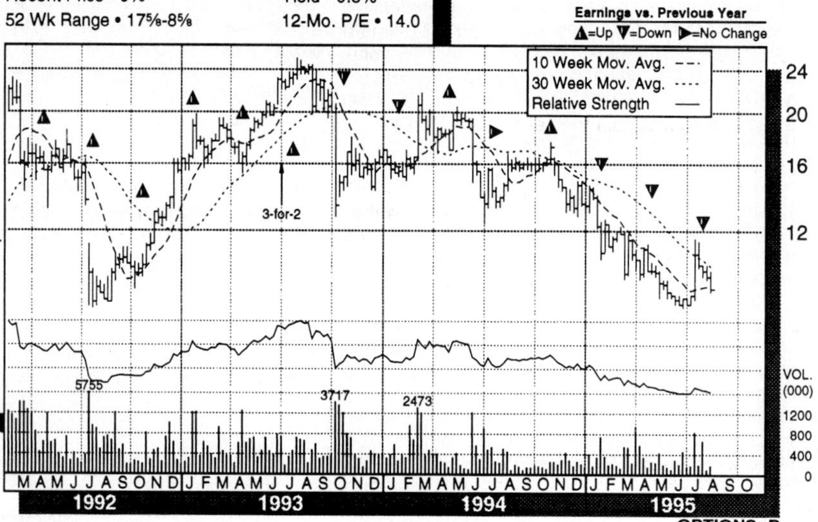

OPTIONS: P

Business Profile - 07-AUG-95

This maker of custom heavy-duty chassis sees substantial growth opportunities ahead in each of its markets. In the fire truck market, new industry standards and new products and technologies available from component suppliers bode well for custom chassis manufacturers such as SPAR. Spartan believes it can continue to penetrate larger portions of the motorhome and bus/specialty market. Spartan paid its eighth consecutive $0.05 a share (unadjusted) special annual cash dividend in July 1995.

Operational Review - 14-AUG-95

Revenues dropped sharply in the first half of 1995, year to year, as a large decline in sales of RV chassis units outweighed higher sales of fire truck chassis. The reduced volume, which was attributed to continuing softness in the North American RV market, led to a second quarter net loss and lower income for the half. Nevertheless, SPAR sees signs of improvement in the RV industry in the second half. Directors recently authorized the repurchase of an additional 1,000,000 SPAR common shares.

Stock Performance - 11-AUG-95

In the past 30 trading days, SPAR's shares have increased 7%, compared to a 2% rise in the S&P 500. Average trading volume for the past five days was 33,660 shares, compared with the 40-day moving average of 68,872 shares.

Key Stock Statistics

Dividend Rate/Share	0.05	Shareholders	1,100
Shs. outstg. (M)	13.1	Market cap. (B)	$0.122
Avg. daily vol. (M)	0.055	Inst. holdings	44%
Tang. Bk. Value/Share	4.84	Insider holdings	NA
Beta	1.29		

Value of $10,000 invested 5 years ago: $ 56,014

Fiscal Year Ending Dec. 31

	1995	% Change	1994	% Change	1993	% Change
Revenues (Million $)						
1Q	44.20	-19%	54.76	31%	41.70	65%
2Q	28.79	-38%	46.36	6%	43.92	42%
3Q	—	—	44.77	11%	40.27	23%
4Q	—	—	45.64	12%	40.78	16%
Yr.	—	—	191.5	15%	166.7	34%
Income (Million $)						
1Q	1.77	-51%	3.62	18%	3.08	74%
2Q	-0.22	NM	3.15	1%	3.11	36%
3Q	—	—	2.97	39%	2.13	-17%
4Q	—	—	0.87	-60%	2.18	-16%
Yr.	—	—	10.61	1%	10.50	14%
Earnings Per Share ($)						
1Q	0.14	-48%	0.27	17%	0.23	57%
2Q	-0.02	NM	0.24	NM	0.24	38%
3Q	—	—	0.23	44%	0.16	-20%
4Q	—	—	0.06	-65%	0.17	-15%
Yr.	—	—	0.80	NM	0.80	11%

Next earnings report expected: early November

Spartan Motors

Business Summary - 14-AUG-95

Spartan Motors, Inc. produces custom-designed heavy truck chassis for specialized applications. The company sells to three principal markets--fire truck, motorhome and bus-specialty--with the majority of sales derived from the motorhome segment.

The direct customers for Spartan's designed and manufactured chassis are the original equipment manufacturers that finish the building of the specialty vehicle by mounting the body or apparatus on the chassis. Spartan does not sell standard commercial truck chassis, but focuses on certain market niches within its principal markets. The company manufactures its chassis with components purchased from outside supplier, which allows for easier serviceability of finished products, reduces production costs and expedites the development of new products. Sales in 1994 to three major customers amounted to 36% of total sales.

The company estimates that 4,000 fire trucks were sold domestically in 1994, with 2,600 utilizing standard commercial truck chassis and 1,400 utilizing customized chassis.

In 1994, the company introduced the M-11 Mountain Master Chassis to offer recreational vehicle owners the option of using a higher-horsepower engine. In 1993, the company introduced the new-generation Global Truck-One (GT-ONE) chassis, a rear-engine fire truck chassis offering a lower-cost chassis with many custom chassis features.

In January 1993, the company launched its first foreign venture, 80%-owned Spartan de Mexico S.A. In March 1994, the company said long-term prospects for the unit are good, and it was striving to contribute positive revenues and earnings during 1995, subject to the stabilization of the Mexican economy and further growth into Latin American markets.

During 1994, the company began developing electric vehicles, which consisted of commercial pickups converted to electric for use in meter reading applications by utility companies. SPAR is also continuing to allocate resources to the development of a "Custom Low Floor" bus chassis.

Important Developments

Aug. '95—SPAR said that there were signs that the RV industry was beginning to recover following a weak first half of 1995, noting increased production orders going into the third and fourth quarters. Spartan expected improved revenues in the third quarter and beyond, on higher volume production schedules, new revenues from school bus chassis, and increases in transit bus volume.

Jul. '95—Directors authorized the additional repurchase of 1,000,000 SPAR common shares. SPAR had completed the buyback of 150,000 shares authorized by the board in March. In the last three years, SPAR has repurchased about 400,000 shares.

Capitalization

Long Term Debt: $6,079,487 (3/95).

Per Share Data ($)

(Year Ended Dec. 31)

	1994	1993	1992	1991	1990	1989
Tangible Bk. Val.	4.72	4.11	3.29	1.85	0.84	0.62
Cash Flow	0.93	0.86	0.77	0.61	0.28	0.15
Earnings	0.80	0.80	0.72	0.58	0.24	0.11
Dividends	0.05	0.05	0.03	0.02	0.02	0.02
Payout Ratio	6%	6%	5%	4%	9%	20%
Prices - High	$21\frac{3}{4}$	$25\frac{1}{4}$	$23\frac{1}{8}$	$16\frac{1}{2}$	$2\frac{5}{8}$	$3\frac{3}{8}$
- Low	$12\frac{3}{8}$	$12\frac{3}{4}$	$8\frac{5}{8}$	$1\frac{9}{16}$	$1\frac{7}{16}$	$1\frac{9}{16}$
P/E Ratio - High	27	32	32	28	11	29
- Low	15	16	12	3	6	13

Income Statement Analysis (Million $)

	1994	%Chg	1993	%Chg	1992	%Chg	1991
Revs.	189	14%	166	35%	123	31%	94.0
Oper. Inc.	16.5	3%	16.0	16%	13.8	31%	10.5
Depr.	1.6	81%	0.9	36%	0.7	61%	0.4
Int. Exp.	0.5	9%	0.4	114%	0.2	-60%	0.5
Pretax Inc.	16.5	4%	15.8	15%	13.7	38%	9.9
Eff. Tax Rate	36%	—	34%	—	33%	—	34%
Net Inc.	10.6	NM	10.5	14%	9.2	41%	6.5

Balance Sheet & Other Fin. Data (Million $)

	1994	1993	1992	1991	1990	1989
Cash	14.2	11.3	12.1	0.9	0.2	0.5
Curr. Assets	65.5	56.2	46.9	27.3	19.2	12.9
Total Assets	81.1	71.3	56.4	34.7	23.7	17.2
Curr. Liab.	13.2	12.8	10.8	8.7	12.5	7.2
LT Debt	6.2	4.7	2.9	3.7	2.5	3.5
Common Eqty.	61.6	53.8	42.7	22.3	8.7	6.5
Total Cap.	67.8	58.4	45.6	26.0	11.2	10.0
Cap. Exp.	4.7	4.1	4.4	1.7	0.5	2.0
Cash Flow	12.2	11.4	9.9	6.9	2.9	1.5

Ratio Analysis

	1994	1993	1992	1991	1990	1989
Curr. Ratio	5.0	4.4	4.4	3.2	1.5	1.8
% LT Debt of Cap.	9.2	8.0	6.4	14.3	22.0	35.3
% Net Inc.of Revs.	5.6	6.3	7.5	6.9	4.9	3.3
% Ret. on Assets	13.9	16.4	19.7	21.0	12.2	6.9
% Ret. on Equity	18.4	21.7	27.7	40.3	32.8	19.7

Dividend Data (A three-for-two stock split was effected in 1993. A special cash dividend of $0.05 a share was paid July 8, 1995. Special dividends of $0.05 a share (not adjusted) were also paid in each of the preceding seven years.)

Amt. of Div. $	Date Decl.	Ex-Div. Date	Stock of Record	Payment Date
0.050	May. 08	Jun. 02	Jun. 08	Jul. 08 '95

Data as orig. reptd.; bef. results of disc. opers. and/or spec. items. Per share data adj. for stk. divs. as of ex-div. date. E-Estimated. NA-Not Available. NM-Not Meaningful. NR-Not Ranked.

Office—1000 Reynolds Rd., Charlotte, MI 48813. **Tel**—(517) 543-6400. **Chrmn & CEO**—G. W. Sztykiel. **Pres & COO**—J. E. Sztykiel. **Exec VP & CFO**—A. G. Sommer. **Secy-Treas**—J. R. Jenks. **Dirs**—M. A. Coon, W. F. Foster, C. E. Nihart, A. G. Sommer, G. W. Sztykiel, J. E. Sztykiel, G. Tesseris. **Transfer Agent**—American Stock Transfer & Trust Co., NYC. **Incorporated** in Michigan in 1975. **Empl**-540. **S&P Analyst:** Stewart Scharf

Sports & Recreation

NYSE Symbol **WON**
In S&P SmallCap 600

25-OCT-95 **Industry:** Retail Stores

Summary: This specialty retailer of name brand sporting equipment and athletic footwear and apparel operates a rapidly growing chain of over 70 large format sporting goods superstores.

Quantitative Evaluations

Recent Price • 7½ | Yield • Nil
52 Wk Range • 28⅜-7 | 12-Mo. P/E • 9.7

Outlook
(1 Lowest—5 Highest)
• **NA**
Fair Value
• **NA**
Risk
• **High**
Earn./Div. Rank
• **NR**

Technical Eval.
• **Bullish** since 7/95
Rel. Strength Rank
(1 Lowest—99 Highest)
• **1**
Insider Activity
• **NA**

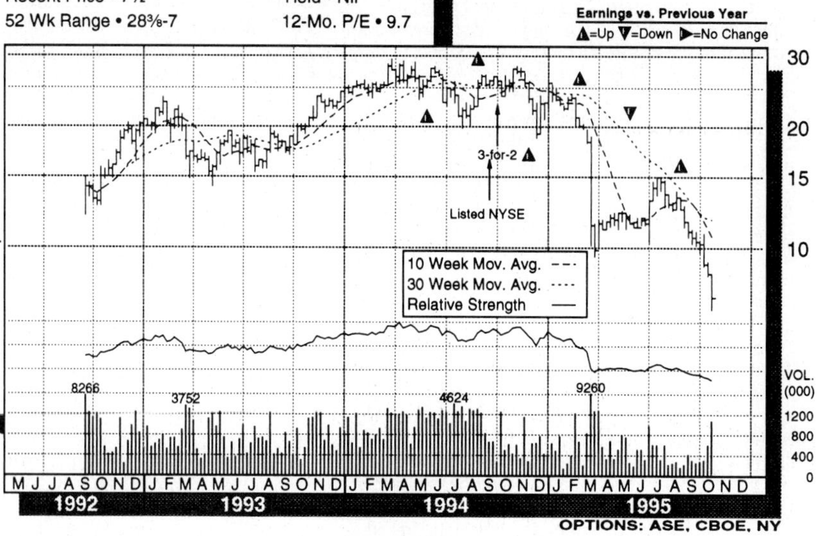

OPTIONS: ASE, CBOE, NY

Business Profile - 20-OCT-95

Sports & Recreation plans to continue its rapid expansion through the opening of 23 to 25 new stores in fiscal 1995-96. By the end of 1996, WON intends to operate in nearly every region in the U.S. Following a weak first quarter in 1995-96, earnings growth resumed in the second quarter, reflecting new store openings, and analysts' estimates call for good earnings growth through 1996-97. However, comparable store sales growth has been restricted by the soft economy.

Operational Review - 20-OCT-95

Sales for the 26 weeks ended July 30, 1995, advanced 44%, year to year, reflecting an increase in the number of stores as well as a 4.6% increase in comparable store sales. Margins narrowed significantly, due primarily to lower merchandise margins in the first quarter resulting from the clearance of seasonal goods. Profitability was penalized further by higher interest charges stemming from greater borrowings. Net income fell 12% to $0.27 a share (on 10% more shares) from $0.34 (adjusted).

Stock Performance - 20-OCT-95

In the past 30 trading days, WON's shares have declined 32%, compared to a 3% rise in the S&P 500. Average trading volume for the past five days was 214,660 shares, compared with the 40-day moving average of 86,379 shares.

Key Stock Statistics

Dividend Rate/Share	Nil	Shareholders	300
Shs. outstg. (M)	19.8	Market cap. (B)	$0.143
Avg. daily vol. (M)	0.118	Inst. holdings	65%
Tang. Bk. Value/Share	8.53	Insider holdings	NA
Beta	NA		

Value of $10,000 invested 5 years ago: NA

Fiscal Year Ending Jan. 31

	1996	% Change	1995	% Change	1994	% Change
Revenues (Million $)						
1Q	110.7	47%	75.50	70%	44.50	—
2Q	124.9	41%	88.50	70%	52.00	—
3Q	—	—	90.30	67%	54.10	—
4Q	—	—	129.4	46%	88.70	—
Yr.	—	—	383.6	60%	239.3	43%
Income (Million $)						
1Q	1.72	-41%	2.92	78%	1.64	—
2Q	3.74	14%	3.27	43%	2.29	—
3Q	—	—	2.79	54%	1.81	—
4Q	—	—	6.91	24%	5.58	—
Yr.	—	—	15.89	40%	11.32	107%
Earnings Per Share ($)						
1Q	0.09	-44%	0.16	78%	0.09	—
2Q	0.19	6%	0.18	38%	0.13	—
3Q	—	—	0.15	50%	0.10	—
4Q	—	—	0.34	10%	0.31	—
Yr.	—	—	0.84	33%	0.63	62%

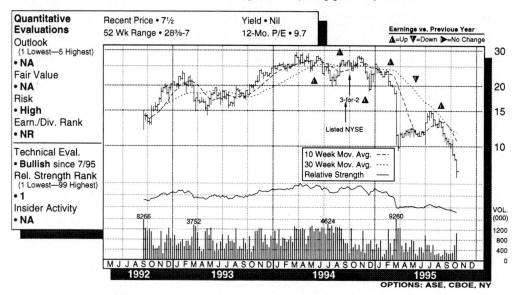

Next earnings report expected: mid November

Sports & Recreation

Business Summary - 24-OCT-95

Sports & Recreation is a specialty retailer of quality name brand sporting equipment and athletic footwear and apparel. As of October 1995, the company was operating 73 large format sporting goods superstores in 27 states, primarily under the names Sports Unlimited, Sports and Sports & Rec in conjunction with the local community name (such as Jacksonville Sports Unlimited, Tampa Sports or Suncoast Sports & Rec).

As of January 29, 1995, WON was operating 56 retail stores with 2,626,600 total gross sq. ft. of store space in 22 states primarily in the south, up from 39 stores (1,699,450 sq. ft.) a year earlier. Comparable store sales increased 9.6% in fiscal 1994-95, and rose 8.0% the year before. The company's superstores average 46,904 gross sq. ft., and are destination stores (free standing or shopping center anchor).

The merchandising strategy of the company is to offer the largest breadth of selection in quality name brand sporting goods in each of its product categories at everyday low prices. Each of its stores offers about 125,000 stock keeping units (SKUs) across nine major departments and over 100 subdepartments. WON believes that its customer service levels and merchandise presentation allow it to offer quality name brands, some of which are not currently carried by other large format sporting goods competitors. The company's target customer ranges from the frequent shopping sports enthusiasts to the casual sporting goods customer. WON believes that its sales penetration among sports enthusiasts is generally higher than other large format sporting goods competitors.

The company has experienced significant growth over the past five fiscal years through fiscal 1994-95, with the store base more than tripling from 18 to 56. During fiscal 1994-95, it opened 17 new stores. WON's planned expansion strategy includes increasing new store openings in smaller to mid-size markets, as well as opening new stores in larger metropolitan markets on an opportunistic basis. The company planned to increase its store base by about 45% in fiscal 1995-96; WON intends to build a majority of its new store sites and projects capital expenditures to be about $70 to $80 million.

Important Developments

Oct. '95—The company announced the opening of its 73rd store, Detroit Sports & Rec, a 60,000 sq. ft. sporting goods superstore located in Roseville, Michigan, and the first of four new stores planned for that state in fiscal 1995-96. To date, WON had executed 17 of its 23 to 25 planned store openings for 1995-96. Separately, the company reported its sales for September 1995 increased 29%, year to year, to $44.6 million, although comparable store sales were flat.

Capitalization

Long Term Liabilities: $216,521,000 (7/95); incl. $74,750,000 of 4.25% sub. notes due 2000 & conv. into com. at $25.50 a share.

Per Share Data ($) (Year Ended Jan. 31)

	1995	1994	1993	1992	1991	1990
Tangible Bk. Val.	8.53	5.95	5.27	1.71	NA	NA
Cash Flow	1.08	0.79	0.56	0.41	NA	NA
Earnings	0.84	0.63	0.39	0.23	NA	NA
Dividends	Nil	Nil	Nil	Nil	NA	NA
Payout Ratio	Nil	Nil	Nil	Nil	NA	NA
Cal. Yrs.	1994	1993	1992	1991	1990	1989
Prices - High	29½	25	20⅞	NA	NA	NA
- Low	18¾	14⅛	12	NA	NA	NA
P/E Ratio - High	35	40	53	NA	NA	NA
- Low	22	23	31	NA	NA	NA

Income Statement Analysis (Million $)

	1995	%Chg	1994	%Chg	1993	%Chg	1992
Revs.	384	61%	239	43%	167	20%	139
Oper. Inc.	35.0	56%	22.4	47%	15.2	41%	10.8
Depr.	4.5	48%	3.1	32%	2.3	21%	1.9
Int. Exp.	6.7	NM	0.9	-74%	3.3	-32%	4.8
Pretax Inc.	25.7	40%	18.4	111%	8.7	112%	4.1
Eff. Tax Rate	38%	—	39%	—	37%	—	39%
Net Inc.	15.9	41%	11.3	105%	5.5	120%	2.5

Balance Sheet & Other Fin. Data (Million $)

	1995	1994	1993	1992	1991	1990
Cash	4.9	6.2	17.4	1.3	NA	NA
Curr. Assets	207	138	93.0	59.0	NA	NA
Total Assets	390	234	134	94.0	NA	NA
Curr. Liab.	39.4	35.3	23.5	19.0	NA	NA
LT Debt	168	78.5	4.1	41.5	NA	NA
Common Eqty.	180	117	105	32.0	NA	NA
Total Cap.	349	197	110	75.0	NA	NA
Cap. Exp.	89.6	55.3	5.0	3.1	NA	NA
Cash Flow	20.4	14.4	7.8	4.4	NA	NA

Ratio Analysis

	1995	1994	1993	1992	1991	1990
Curr. Ratio	5.3	3.9	4.0	3.1	NA	NA
% LT Debt of Cap.	48.1	39.8	3.7	55.3	NA	NA
% Net Inc.of Revs.	4.1	4.7	3.3	1.8	NA	NA
% Ret. on Assets	4.9	6.1	3.9	NA	NA	NA
% Ret. on Equity	10.2	10.1	7.0	NA	NA	NA

Dividend Data —No dividends have been paid. The company's $200 million revolving credit facility contains prohibitions on the payment of dividends. A 3-for-2 stock split was distributed in September 1994.

Data as orig. reptd.; bef. results of disc. opers. and/or spec. items. Per share data adj. for stk. divs. as of ex-div. date. E-Estimated. NA-Not Available. NM-Not Meaningful. NR-Not Ranked.

Office—4701 W. Hillsborough Ave., Tampa, FL 33614. **Tel**—(813) 886-9688. **Chrmn & CEO**—J. W. Bradke. **Pres & COO**—T. H. Wirkus. **Vice Chrmn & EVP-Fin**—R. T. Welch. **EVP, CFO & Treas**—S. E. Skarda. **Dirs**—J. W. Bradke, R. B. Martin, S. A. Raymund, C. T. Sullivan, R. T. Welch. **Transfer Agent & Registrar**—Chemical Bank, NYC. **Incorporated** in Delaware in 1988. **Empl-** 4,500. **S&P Analyst:** Michael V. Pizzi

STANDARD & POOR'S

STOCK REPORTS

Standard Microsystems

NASDAQ Symbol **SMSC**

In S&P SmallCap 600

05-AUG-95 **Industry:** Data Processing

Summary: This company is a leading worldwide supplier of PC LAN system products.

Quantitative Evaluations

Outlook
(1 Lowest—5 Highest)
• **NA**

Fair Value
• **NA**

Risk
• **High**

Earn./Div. Rank
• **B-**

Technical Eval.
• **Bearish** since 7/95

Rel. Strength Rank
(1 Lowest—99 Highest)
• **20**

Insider Activity
• **NA**

Recent Price • 17 | Yield • Nil
52 Wk Range • 31⅝-12½ | 12-Mo. P/E • 13.5

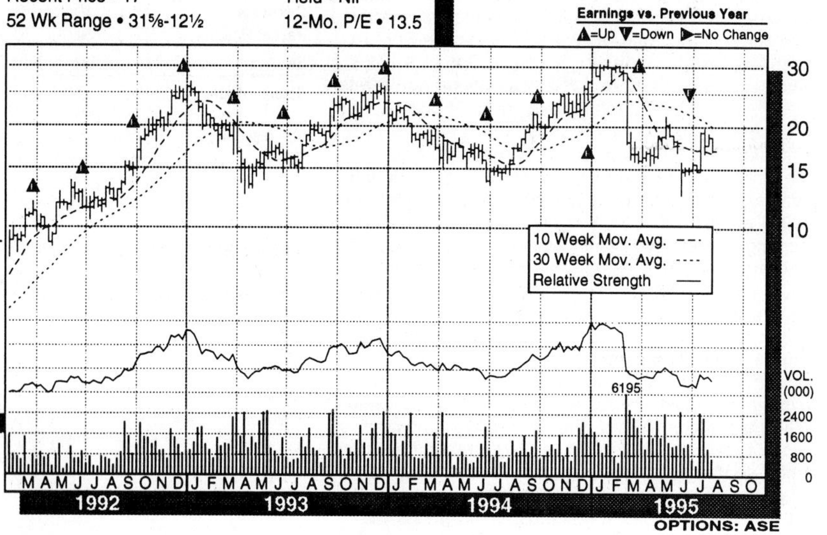

Business Profile - 04-AUG-95

SMSC is one of the world's largest suppliers of products used to connect PCs over local area networks (LANs). As part of its efforts to secure an adequate supply of semiconductor manufacturing capacity, during fiscal 1994-95, SMSC agreed to invest $16 million in equipment for an AT&T Microelectronics semiconductor production line in Madrid, Spain. Products which are slated for introduction in 1995-96 should significantly expand SMSC's ability to provide comprehensive networking solutions.

Operational Review - 04-AUG-95

A net loss was reported for 1995-96's first quarter, reflecting a loss at the System Products Division due to lower revenues from both the Desktop Networks and Enterprise Networks units. Revenues and gross margins declined, primarily as a result of a program to reduce excessive inventory levels at a number of major distributors. Results were also penalized by spending on product development, sales and marketing. However, profits at the Component Products Division improved substantially.

Stock Performance - 04-AUG-95

In the past 30 trading days, SMSC's shares have increased 14%, compared to a 2% rise in the S&P 500. Average trading volume for the past five days was 130,240 shares, compared with the 40-day moving average of 267,008 shares.

Key Stock Statistics

Dividend Rate/Share	Nil	Shareholders	1,200
Shs. outstg. (M)	13.3	Market cap. (B)	$0.226
Avg. daily vol. (M)	0.353	Inst. holdings	38%
Tang. Bk. Value/Share	11.15	Insider holdings	NA
Beta	1.75		

Value of $10,000 invested 5 years ago: $ 27,200

Fiscal Year Ending Feb. 28

	1996	% Change	1995	% Change	1994	% Change
Revenues (Million $)						
1Q	72.21	-10%	80.00	17%	68.44	15%
2Q	—	—	91.96	28%	72.03	26%
3Q	—	—	104.8	18%	88.89	37%
4Q	—	—	101.9	9%	93.21	35%
Yr.	—	—	378.7	17%	322.6	29%
Income (Million $)						
1Q	-3.00	NM	5.36	22%	4.39	31%
2Q	—	—	5.58	34%	4.16	20%
3Q	—	—	6.82	26%	5.43	27%
4Q	—	—	7.41	25%	5.93	25%
Yr.	—	—	25.17	26%	19.91	26%
Earnings Per Share ($)						
1Q	-0.22	NM	0.41	21%	0.34	21%
2Q	—	—	0.42	31%	0.32	14%
3Q	—	—	0.51	24%	0.41	21%
4Q	—	—	0.55	22%	0.45	22%
Yr.	—	—	1.89	24%	1.52	20%

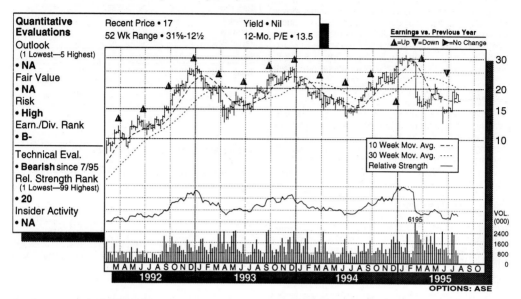

Next earnings report expected: mid September

Standard Microsystems

Business Summary - 04-AUG-95

Standard Microsystems Corp. manufactures products used to connect PCs over LANs through its System Products Division and produces standard and custom metal-oxide-semiconductor/very-large-scale integrated (MOS/VLSI) circuits through its Component Products Division. Revenues in recent fiscal years were derived as follows:

	1994-1995	1993-1994	1992-1993
System Products	69%	82%	90%
Component Products	31%	18%	10%

Export sales, primarily to the Far East, Europe and Canada, accounted for 46.8% of revenues in 1994-95, up from 44.0% in 1993-94.

In 1993-94, the company formed two business units within its System Products Division: Desktop Networks, responsible for SMSC's line of network interface cards (NICs), and Enterprise Networks, responsible for the company's line of workgroup wiring hubs and switches. The company offers a full line of ARCNET, Token-Ring and Ethernet NICs along with wiring hubs, internetworking platforms, and a variety of network management hardware and software products. SMSC's high performance LAN switch combines internetworking and hub functions into one modular chassis.

The Component Product Division's circuits are designed for the computer peripheral market, with a primary focus on PC I/O and networking markets. The company's products are sold primarily to original equipment manufacturers and distributors.

In March 1995, the company purchased a minority equity interest in Singapore-based Chartered Semiconductor Pte Ltd. for about $14 million. An additional $6.0 million will be invested in early 1996-97.

The December 1992 acquisition of Sigma Network Systems, for a total of 350,000 common shares, accelerated the company's entry into the internetworking market. In October 1991, SMSC acquired Western Digital's LAN business for a total cost of approximately $34 million.

Important Developments

Jun. '95—SMSC reported the filing of class action lawsuits by certain shareholders seeking damages against the company and certain of its officers and directors. The complaints allege that between December 20, 1994, and June 2, 1995, the price of the company's stock was artificially inflated by false and misleading statements issued by the defendants. SMSC believes these suits are without merit and intends to defend against them vigorously.

Capitalization

Long Term Debt: $10,000,000 (5/95).
Minority Interest: $11,215,000 (5/95).

Per Share Data ($) (Year Ended Feb. 28)

	1995	1994	1993	1992	1991	1990
Tangible Bk. Val.	11.16	11.18	6.59	4.73	7.65	7.43
Cash Flow	3.00	2.17	2.23	0.88	0.78	1.16
Earnings	1.89	1.52	1.27	0.05	0.10	0.41
Dividends	Nil	Nil	Nil	Nil	Nil	Nil
Payout Ratio	Nil	Nil	Nil	Nil	Nil	Nil
Cal. Yrs.	1994	1993	1992	1991	1990	1989
Prices - High	30⅜	27	26¼	7¼	9⅞	7⅝
- Low	13⅜	12½	6⅜	3⅝	4⅛	4½
P/E Ratio - High	16	18	21	NM	99	19
- Low	7	8	5	NM	41	11

Income Statement Analysis (Million $)

	1995	%Chg	1994	%Chg	1993	%Chg	1992
Revs.	379	17%	323	29%	250	88%	133
Oper. Inc.	55.4	26%	44.0	3%	42.8	NM	12.2
Depr.	14.8	74%	8.5	-29%	12.0	25%	9.6
Int. Exp.	1.3	-24%	1.6	-29%	2.3	91%	1.2
Pretax Inc.	41.3	23%	33.5	20%	27.9	NM	1.9
Eff. Tax Rate	39%	—	41%	—	45%	—	75%
Net Inc.	25.2	27%	19.9	26%	15.8	NM	0.6

Balance Sheet & Other Fin. Data (Million $)

	1995	1994	1993	1992	1991	1990
Cash	29.5	32.1	35.9	17.9	31.1	38.9
Curr. Assets	163	140	111	79.7	75.2	76.3
Total Assets	229	206	184	154	112	113
Curr. Liab.	43.4	41.8	41.0	35.1	8.1	11.1
LT Debt	Nil	9.2	12.1	18.2	1.8	1.9
Common Eqty.	174	144	120	89.3	88.0	85.0
Total Cap.	185	164	143	119	104	102
Cap. Exp.	13.6	8.6	5.4	6.5	7.9	2.0
Cash Flow	40.0	28.4	27.8	10.2	9.0	13.2

Ratio Analysis

	1995	1994	1993	1992	1991	1990
Curr. Ratio	3.7	3.4	2.7	2.3	9.3	6.9
% LT Debt of Cap.	Nil	5.6	8.5	15.3	1.7	1.8
% Net Inc.of Revs.	6.6	6.2	6.3	0.4	1.4	6.1
% Ret. on Assets	11.4	10.1	9.4	0.4	1.1	4.2
% Ret. on Equity	15.6	15.0	14.8	0.7	1.4	5.6

Dividend Data (No cash has been paid. A "poison pill" rights plan was adopted in January 1988.)

Data as orig. reptd.; bef. results of disc. opers. and/or spec. items. Per share data adj. for stk. divs. as of ex-div. date. E-Estimated. NA-Not Available. NM-Not Meaningful. NR-Not Ranked.

Office—80 Arkay Drive, Hauppauge, NY 11788. **Tel**—(516) 273-3100. **Chrmn & CEO**—P. Richman. **SVP-Fin & Treas**—A. M. D'Agostino. **Secy**—H. I. Kahen. **Investor Contact**—James R. Frankenthaler (516-434-2816). **Dirs**—E. Berezin, R. M. Brill, P. F. Dicks, H. Fialkov, R. Frankel, I. T. Frisch, P. Richman. **Transfer Agent**—Mellon Securities Trust Co., Ridgefield, N.J. **Incorporated** in Delaware in 1971. **Empl-** 861. **S&P Analyst:** Ronald J. Gross

STANDARD & POOR'S

STOCK REPORTS

Standard Motor Products

NYSE Symbol **SMP**
In S&P SmallCap 600

12-OCT-95 **Industry:** Auto parts/equipment

Summary: This company derives the bulk of its sales from ignition, engine control, fuel system, wire and cable, brake and temperature control parts for the automotive aftermarket.

Quantitative Evaluations

Outlook
(1 Lowest—5 Highest)
• **3**

Fair Value
• **18⅛**

Risk
• **Low**

Earn./Div. Rank
• **B**

Technical Eval.
• **Bearish** since 9/95

Rel. Strength Rank
(1 Lowest—99 Highest)
• **20**

Insider Activity
• **NA**

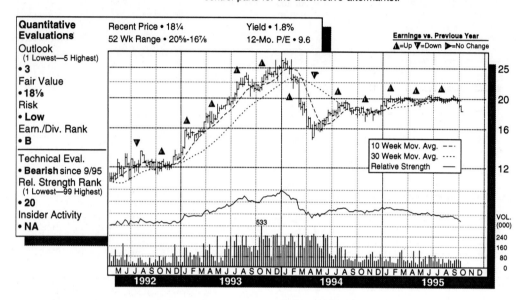

Recent Price • 18¼
52 Wk Range • 20⅝-16⅞
Yield • 1.8%
12-Mo. P/E • 9.6

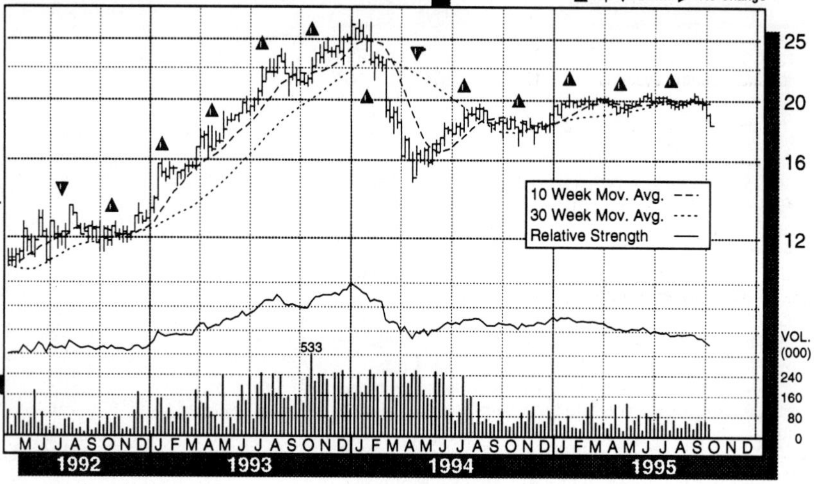

Business Profile - 12-OCT-95

SMP achieved improved sales and profits in 1994, despite price reductions in several product lines. The company has said that it is committed to ongoing cost reduction programs to meet challenges in its increasingly competitive market, and it expects the positive effects of these efforts, as well as a reduced level of new business expense, to continue for the foreseeable future. In early 1995, SMP acquired Pik-A-Nut, a leading aftermarket supplier of nuts, bolts, screws and other fasteners.

Operational Review - 12-OCT-95

Net sales edged up 2.7%, year to year, in the first half of 1995, as slightly lower sales at most divisions due to certain customers carrying inventories into the second quarter, offset strong orders for temperature control products and new sales from acquisitions. Profitability benefited from the increased volume and cost reduction efforts and, despite higher interest expense, net income rose 11%.

Stock Performance - 06-OCT-95

In the past 30 trading days, SMP's shares have declined 8%, compared to a 4% rise in the S&P 500. Average trading volume for the past five days was 10,060 shares, compared with the 40-day moving average of 10,372 shares.

Key Stock Statistics

Dividend Rate/Share	0.32	Shareholders	2,200
Shs. outstg. (M)	13.1	Market cap. (B)	$0.236
Avg. daily vol. (M)	0.014	Inst. holdings	43%
Tang. Bk. Value/Share	15.78	Insider holdings	NA
Beta	1.11		

Value of $10,000 invested 5 years ago: $ 13,850

Fiscal Year Ending Dec. 31

	1995	% Change	1994	% Change	1993	% Change
Revenues (Million $)						
1Q	159.7	9%	147.1	15%	127.8	NM
2Q	184.0	-2%	187.6	16%	161.2	7%
3Q	—	—	168.3	4%	161.3	17%
4Q	—	—	137.8	4%	132.6	13%
Yr.	—	—	640.8	10%	582.8	9%
Income (Million $)						
1Q	3.89	41%	2.75	-4%	2.85	166%
2Q	8.30	NM	8.22	21%	6.78	NM
3Q	—	—	7.73	36%	5.70	103%
4Q	—	—	4.97	52%	3.26	9%
Yr.	—	—	23.67	27%	18.60	109%
Earnings Per Share ($)						
1Q	0.30	43%	0.21	-5%	0.22	175%
2Q	0.63	2%	0.62	22%	0.51	NM
3Q	—	—	0.59	37%	0.43	95%
4Q	—	—	0.38	52%	0.25	9%
Yr.	—	—	1.80	28%	1.41	107%

Next earnings report expected: late October

Standard Motor Products

Business Summary - 11-OCT-95

Standard Motor Products, Inc. is primarily a manufacturer of replacement parts for the electrical, fuel, brake, steering and temperature control systems of motor vehicles. Its parts are used in cars, trucks and marine and industrial engines. Sales distribution in recent years:

	1994	1993	1992
Ignition parts	36%	34%	34%
Brake parts	26%	28%	29%
Temperature control systems	17%	15%	15%
Wires & cables	8%	9%	9%
Fuel system parts	7%	8%	9%
Champ general service line	6%	6%	5%

The company's manufactured parts are sold to distributors and jobbers under the brand names Standard, Blue Streak, Champ, Hygrade, Four Seasons, EIS Brake Parts and GP/Sorensen; parts of other manufacturers are also distributed. SMP sells replacement parts only and does not sell to automotive manufacturers. Products are sold to 1,600 warehouse distributors, who distribute at wholesale to 23,000 retail jobber outlets.

Automotive ignition parts include distributor caps and rotors, electronic ignition modules, voltage regulators, coils and switches. Emission control parts, including throttle position sensors, air pump check valves, coolant temperature sensors, air charge temperature sensors and MAP sensors, are also sold. EIS Brake Parts makes a full line of brake system parts and also markets many special tools and fluids used by mechanics who perform brake service. Wire and cable parts include ignition spark plugs, wires, battery cables and a wide range of electrical wire, terminals, connectors and tools. The fuel systems segment is making the transition from carburetor-related parts to fuel injection parts and replacement fuel injectors; it also supplies fuel pumps. SMP also offers replacement parts for automotive temperature control systems and power steering products. The Champ division markets more than 8,000 automotive-related items, ranging from mirrors, window cranks and antennas to cleaning and polishing materials, specialty tools and maintenance supplies.

In 1994, the five largest customers accounted for 27% of sales. Export sales (mainly to Canada) were 7.9% of the total in 1994.

Important Developments

Jun. '95—SMP acquired Automotive Dryers, Inc. and Air Parts, Inc. for an undisclosed amount. The two Cumming, Ga.-based companies had combined 1994 revenues of almost $6 million. ADI makes receiver filter driers and accumulators for mobile air-conditioning systems. API distributes parts for the systems.

Capitalization

Long Term Debt: $105,734,000 (6/95).

Per Share Data ($)

(Year Ended Dec. 31)

	1994	1993	1992	1991	1990	1989
Tangible Bk. Val.	14.29	12.77	12.20	11.78	11.46	11.10
Cash Flow	2.63	2.20	1.41	1.18	1.20	1.56
Earnings	1.80	1.41	0.68	0.51	0.59	1.00
Dividends	0.32	0.32	0.32	0.32	0.32	0.32
Payout Ratio	18%	23%	47%	63%	54%	32%
Prices - High	26⅞	26⅞	13⅝	13⅞	15⅝	20
- Low	14¾	13⅛	9½	7⅜	5⅞	13¾
P/E Ratio - High	15	19	20	27	26	20
- Low	8	9	14	14	10	14

Income Statement Analysis (Million $)

	1994	%Chg	1993	%Chg	1992	%Chg	1991
Revs.	641	10%	583	9%	536	NM	535
Oper. Inc.	54.2	7%	50.8	58%	32.2	-4%	33.4
Depr.	11.0	5%	10.5	8%	9.7	9%	8.9
Int. Exp.	12.3	NM	12.3	NM	12.3	-28%	17.2
Pretax Inc.	35.4	32%	26.8	148%	10.8	38%	7.8
Eff. Tax Rate	33%	—	31%	—	18%	—	15%
Net Inc.	23.7	27%	18.6	109%	8.9	33%	6.7

Balance Sheet & Other Fin. Data (Million $)

	1994	1993	1992	1991	1990	1989
Cash	8.8	12.4	17.0	24.0	15.8	13.8
Curr. Assets	329	304	265	291	321	313
Total Assets	462	423	375	393	422	406
Curr. Liab.	140	100	74.0	160	175	149
LT Debt	110	131	136	73.0	90.0	103
Common Eqty.	195	178	161	155	151	146
Total Cap.	310	312	301	232	247	257
Cap. Exp.	12.6	12.3	15.3	12.0	16.2	23.2
Cash Flow	34.7	29.1	18.6	15.5	15.8	20.5

Ratio Analysis

	1994	1993	1992	1991	1990	1989
Curr. Ratio	2.4	3.1	3.6	1.8	1.8	2.1
% LT Debt of Cap.	35.5	41.8	45.3	31.6	36.5	40.1
% Net Inc.of Revs.	3.7	3.2	1.7	1.2	1.5	3.1
% Ret. on Assets	5.4	4.6	2.3	1.6	1.9	3.5
% Ret. on Equity	12.8	10.9	5.6	4.4	5.2	8.8

Dividend Data —Dividends have been paid since 1960.

Amt. of Div. $	Date Decl.	Ex-Div. Date	Stock of Record	Payment Date
0.080	Oct. 20	Nov. 08	Nov. 15	Dec. 01 '94
0.080	Jan. 13	Feb. 09	Feb. 15	Mar. 01 '95
0.080	Apr. 20	May. 09	May. 15	Jun. 01 '95
0.080	Jul. 21	Aug. 09	Aug. 11	Sep. 01 '95

Data as orig. reptd.; bef. results of disc. opers. and/or spec. items. Per share data adj. for stk. divs. as of ex-div. date. E-Estimated. NA-Not Available. NM-Not Meaningful. NR-Not Ranked.

Office—37-18 Northern Blvd., Long Island City, NY 11101. **Tel**—(718) 392-0200. **Co-Chrmn**—B. Fife, N. L. Sills. **Pres & COO**—L. I. Sills. **VP-Fin, CFO & Investor Contact**—Michael J. Bailey. **VP & Secy**—S. Kay. **Dirs**—A. D. Davis, A. R. Fife, B. Fife, J. L. Kelsey, L. I. Sills, N. L. Sills, R. F. Sills, R. J. Swartz, W. H. Turner. **Transfer Agent & Registrar**—Registrar & Transfer Co., Cranford, N.J. **Incorporated** in New York in 1926. **Empl**-3,300. **S&P Analyst:** Stewart Scharf

Standard Pacific

NYSE Symbol **SPF**
In S&P SmallCap 600

12-OCT-95 **Industry:** Building

Summary: This company operates primarily as a geographically diversified builder of medium-priced single family homes throughout major metropolitan markets in California and Texas.

Quantitative Evaluations

Recent Price • 6⅞
52 Wk Range • 8⅜-4⅞
Yield • 1.9%
12-Mo. P/E • 32.7

Outlook
(1 Lowest—5 Highest)
• **4⁻**

Fair Value
• **7½**

Risk
• **High**

Earn./Div. Rank
• **NR**

Technical Eval.
• **Bearish** since 8/95

Rel. Strength Rank
(1 Lowest—99 Highest)
• **22**

Insider Activity
• **NA**

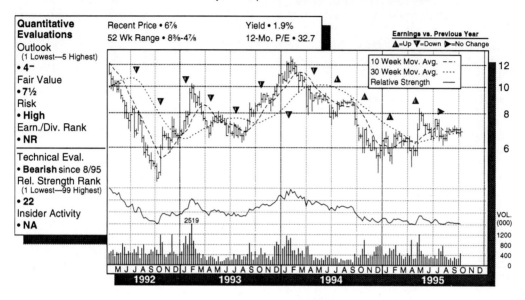

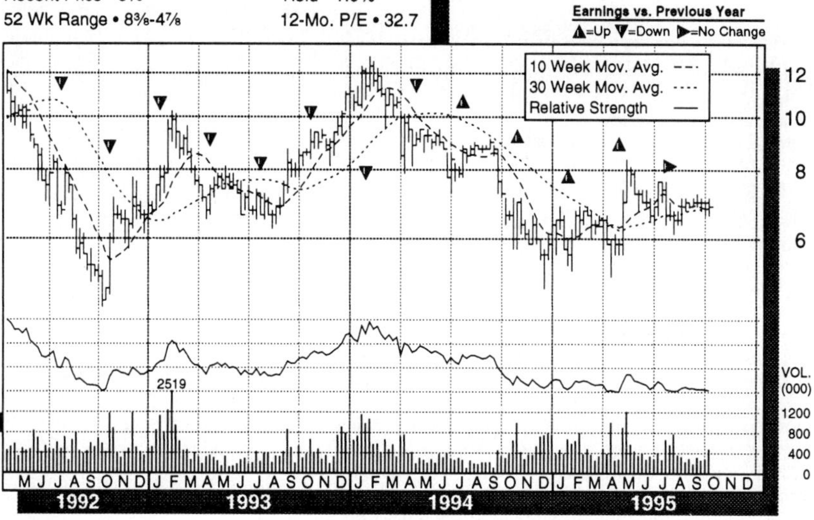

Business Profile - 12-OCT-95

This company builds medium-priced single family homes, primarily throughout the major metropolitan areas in California and Texas. It focuses its efforts on acquiring land suitable for the construction and sale of homes generally ranging in price from $150,000 to $300,000. In 1995, SPF expects to concentrate its additional growth in Northern California. Standard Pacific also owns a savings and loan, and a manufacturer and marketer of high quality office furniture systems.

Operational Review - 12-OCT-95

Revenues in the six months ended June 30, 1995, declined 9.0% year to year, reflecting lower average new home selling prices. The number of new homes delivered was flat and net new home orders fell 4% from the year-earlier level, restricted by higher interest rates and unusually heavy and constant rains throughout California. However, costs were well controlled, and net income rose 34% to $2.3 million ($0.08 a share) from $1.7 million ($0.06).

Stock Performance - 06-OCT-95

In the past 30 trading days, SPF's shares have declined 2%, compared to a 4% rise in the S&P 500. Average trading volume for the past five days was 92,440 shares, compared with the 40-day moving average of 57,441 shares.

Key Stock Statistics

Dividend Rate/Share	0.12	Shareholders	3,000
Shs. outstg. (M)	30.6	Market cap. (B)	$0.195
Avg. daily vol. (M)	0.072	Inst. holdings	34%
Tang. Bk. Value/Share	9.55	Insider holdings	NA
Beta	2.61		

Value of $10,000 invested 5 years ago: $ 6,964

Fiscal Year Ending Dec. 31

	1995	% Change	1994	% Change	1993	% Change
Revenues (Million $)						
1Q	77.99	-1%	78.94	51%	52.20	-17%
2Q	91.86	-15%	107.7	53%	70.24	-13%
3Q	—	—	111.5	58%	70.73	-12%
4Q	—	—	122.3	22%	100.6	25%
Yr.	—	—	420.5	43%	293.8	-4%
Income (Million $)						
1Q	1.10	112%	0.52	-54%	1.14	-33%
2Q	1.21	NM	1.21	NM	0.18	-88%
3Q	—	—	2.09	NM	0.03	-94%
4Q	—	—	2.07	NM	0.47	-41%
Yr.	—	—	5.89	NM	1.82	-60%
Earnings Per Share ($)						
1Q	0.04	100%	0.02	-50%	0.04	-33%
2Q	0.04	NM	0.04	NM	0.01	-80%
3Q	—	—	0.07	—	Nil	—
4Q	—	—	0.07	NM	0.02	-33%
Yr.	—	—	0.19	NM	0.06	-60%

Next earnings report expected: mid October

Standard Pacific

Business Summary - 12-OCT-95

Standard Pacific constructs and sells medium-priced single-family homes in Orange, San Diego and Ventura counties and the San Francisco Bay area in California, and in Houston, Dallas and Austin, Texas. It also arranges financing and related financial services for its homebuyers through its savings and loan subsidiary, and manufactures office furniture. After converting from corporate form to a limited partnership in December 1966, SPF reorganized as a corporation on December 31, 1991. Contributions to revenues in recent years:

	1994	1993	1992
Residential housing	89%	85%	81%
Manufacturing	4%	4%	6%
Savings & loan	6%	10%	11%
Builder bonds & other	1%	1%	2%

At December 31, 1994, SPF had single-family home projects at 50 locations in California (267 homes under construction), six in Houston (27) and 10 in Dallas (43). In 1994, the company delivered 1,368 homes, compared with 942 in 1993. The average home selling price in 1994 was $295,772, versus $264,930 in 1993. Backlog at June 30, 1995, was 447 homes, down from 501 homes a year earlier.

Most SPF homes are single-family detached dwellings, but some 7% to 15% sold during the past several years were townhouses or condominiums attached in configurations of two, three, four or six dwelling units. Work is done by subcontractors.

During 1994, about 1% of the homes delivered by SPF were financed with funds provided through its Standard Pacific Savings, F.A., subsidiary. However, in response to competitive market forces, mortgage banking oeprations were significantly reduced and, as a result, no loans have been originated for its portfolio for SPF homebuyers since June 1994.

Panel Concepts, Inc., makes moveable and acoustical office partitions and furniture components such as shelves, work surfaces and drawers which can be attached to its panels; and specialized modular work stations for light industrial applications.

Important Developments

Aug. '95—The company's Standard Pacific Savings, F.A. subsidiary announced that a pretax charge of approximately $2.8 million would be recorded during the third quarter in connection with asset disposal and liability refinancing.

Jul. '95—Standard Pacific's directors authorized the repurchase of up to $10 million of its common stock, depending on market conditions.

Capitalization

Long Term Debt: $193,706,000 (6/95).
FHLB Advances: $165,000,000.

Per Share Data ($)

(Year Ended Dec. 31)

	1994	1993	1992	1991	1990	1989
Tangible Bk. Val.	9.51	9.49	9.52	9.35	9.32	9.54
Cash Flow	0.22	0.08	0.18	0.44	1.83	4.07
Earnings	0.19	0.06	0.15	0.40	1.77	3.87
Dividends	0.12	0.12	0.09	0.30	2.00	2.10
Payout Ratio	63%	200%	61%	74%	112%	53%
Prices - High	12⅞	11⅜	14	12	16	19⅞
- Low	4⅞	6¼	4½	5⅛	4¾	11⅞
P/E Ratio - High	68	NM	93	30	9	5
- Low	26	NM	30	13	3	3

Income Statement Analysis (Million $)

	1994	%Chg	1993	%Chg	1992	%Chg	1991
Revs.	416	41%	294	-4%	305	2%	299
Oper. Inc.	16.0	78%	9.0	-50%	18.0	-45%	33.0
Depr.	0.8	10%	0.7	-15%	0.8	-21%	1.1
Int. Exp.	28.8	7%	26.8	-23%	34.9	-15%	41.3
Pretax Inc.	10.0	NM	3.0	-50%	6.0	-50%	12.0
Eff. Tax Rate	41%	—	39%	—	30%	—	4.90%
Net Inc.	6.0	NM	2.0	-60%	5.0	-55%	11.0

Balance Sheet & Other Fin. Data (Million $)

	1994	1993	1992	1991	1990	1989
Cash	16.5	18.6	82.7	56.9	26.5	25.9
Curr. Assets	NA	NA	NA	NA	NA	NA
Total Assets	923	858	953	972	934	896
Curr. Liab.	NA	NA	NA	NA	NA	NA
LT Debt	365	321	353	413	436	398
Common Eqty.	291	290	291	254	253	259
Total Cap.	656	612	644	669	689	657
Cap. Exp.	0.4	NA	1.0	0.7	0.6	2.0
Cash Flow	7.0	3.0	5.0	12.0	50.0	111

Ratio Analysis

	1994	1993	1992	1991	1990	1989
Curr. Ratio	NA	NA	NA	NA	NA	NA
% LT Debt of Cap.	55.6	52.5	54.8	61.8	63.3	60.6
% Net Inc.of Revs.	1.4	0.6	1.5	3.7	12.6	21.9
% Ret. on Assets	0.7	0.2	0.4	1.2	5.3	12.9
% Ret. on Equity	2.0	0.6	1.6	4.3	18.9	45.3

Dividend Data —SPF paid a final partnership quarterly distribution on December 31, 1991. Most recent payments:

Amt. of Div. $	Date Decl.	Ex-Div. Date	Stock of Record	Payment Date
0.030	Oct. 18	Nov. 08	Nov. 15	Nov. 30 '94
0.030	Jan. 24	Feb. 09	Feb. 15	Feb. 28 '95
0.030	Apr. 18	May. 08	May. 12	May. 26 '95
0.030	Jul. 18	Aug. 10	Aug. 14	Aug. 28 '95

Data as orig. reptd.; bef. results of disc. opers. and/or spec. items. Per share data adj. for stk. divs. as of ex-div. date. E-Estimated. NA-Not Available. NM-Not Meaningful. NR-Not Ranked.

Office—1565 West MacArthur Blvd., Costa Mesa, CA 92626. **Tel**—(714) 668-4300. **Chrmn & CEO**—A. E. Svendsen. **Pres**—R. R. Foell. **VP-Fin, Secy & Investor Contact**—April J. Morris (714) 668-4303. **Treas**—A. H. Parnes. **Dirs**—J. L. Doti, R. R. Foell, H. Van Jacobsen, K. D. Koeller, W. H. Langenberg, R. E. Morgan, A. J. Morris, T. L. Roquemore, R. J. St. Lawrence, D. H. Spengler, A. E. Svendsen. **Transfer Agent & Registrar**—Chemical Trust Co. of California, Los Angeles. **Incorporated** in California in 1961; organized in Delaware in 1986; reincorporated in Delaware in 1991. **Empl**-430. **S&P Analyst:** N. Rosenberg

STANDARD & POOR'S

STOCK REPORTS

Standard Products

NYSE Symbol **SPD**
In S&P SmallCap 600

08-NOV-95 **Industry:** Rubber

Summary: This company makes rubber and plastic parts for the automotive industry and magnetic door seals for appliances.

Quantitative Evaluations
Outlook
(1 Lowest—5 Highest)
• **4-**
Fair Value
• **16⅜**
Risk
• **Average**
Earn./Div. Rank
• **B-**

Technical Eval.
• **Neutral** since 11/95
Rel. Strength Rank
(1 Lowest—99 Highest)
• **11**
Insider Activity
• **Neutral**

Recent Price • 15⅜
52 Wk Range • 24⅝-15
Yield • 4.4%
12-Mo. P/E • 34.2

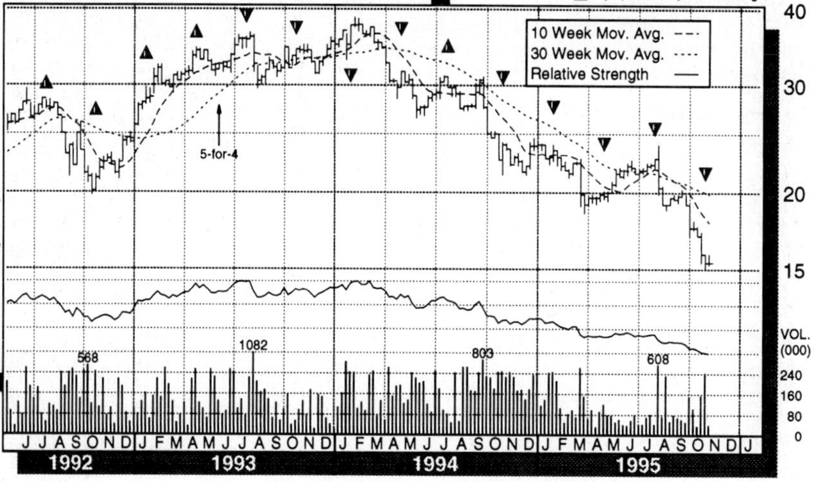

Business Profile - 08-NOV-95

SPD continues to look for ways to streamline its operations through organizational changes and realignments of its manufacturing capacity. The company noted that new business typically comes in at lower margins than the business it is replacing, and it takes time to bring down the start-up production costs. Additionally, SPD has incurred substantial launch costs for the Ford Taurus/Sable. The company is currently constructing plants in Brazil and Mexico for those respective markets.

Operational Review - 08-NOV-95

Sales for the three months ended September 30, 1995, rose 8.1%, year to year, reflecting generally improved European volume. Results were penalized by launch costs related to the new Taurus and Sable models, and seasonally lower activity throughout the company's operations. Following a retroactive 10% increase in the tax rate in France, a net loss was incurred, in contrast to net income. With softening production schedules continuing, SPD projects earnings of $1.00 per share for fiscal 1996.

Stock Performance - 03-NOV-95

In the past 30 trading days, SPD's shares have declined 20%, compared to a 2% rise in the S&P 500. Average trading volume for the past five days was 7,520 shares, compared with the 40-day moving average of 20,713 shares.

Key Stock Statistics

Dividend Rate/Share	0.68	Shareholders	1,000
Shs. outstg. (M)	16.7	Market cap. (B)	$0.258
Avg. daily vol. (M)	0.024	Inst. holdings	64%
Tang. Bk. Value/Share	11.68	Insider holdings	NA
Beta	0.32		

Value of $10,000 invested 5 years ago: $ 10,542

Fiscal Year Ending Jun. 30

	1996	% Change	1995	% Change	1994	% Change
Revenues (Million $)						
1Q	238.8	8%	220.9	10%	201.7	23%
2Q	—	—	243.8	23%	198.3	13%
3Q	—	—	265.0	19%	222.7	11%
4Q	—	—	266.2	7%	249.7	12%
Yr.	—	—	995.9	14%	872.4	14%
Income (Million $)						
1Q	-9.78	NM	2.90	-40%	4.85	—
2Q	—	—	5.33	-14%	6.19	-21%
3Q	—	—	6.85	-16%	8.18	-19%
4Q	—	—	4.99	-64%	13.82	25%
Yr.	—	—	20.07	-39%	33.03	-1%
Earnings Per Share ($)						
1Q	-0.58	NM	0.17	-41%	0.29	-2%
2Q	—	—	0.32	-14%	0.37	-29%
3Q	—	—	0.41	-16%	0.49	-27%
4Q	—	—	0.30	-64%	0.83	14%
Yr.	—	—	1.20	-40%	1.99	-10%

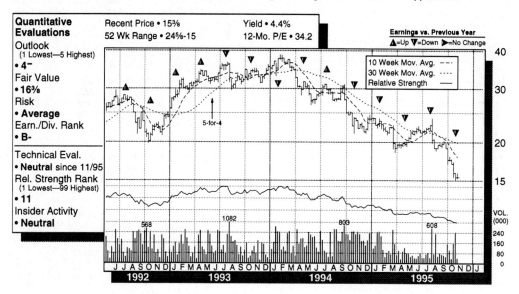

Next earnings report expected: mid January

Standard Products

Business Summary - 08-NOV-95

Standard Products manufactures rubber and plastic parts for the automotive, construction and marine industries, tread rubber for tire retreading, and appliance door magnetic seals. A unit producing rubberized track for military vehicles was discontinued in fiscal 1992. Segment contributions in fiscal 1995:

	Sales	Profits
Transportation equipment	87%	96%
Tread rubber	13%	4%

The U.S. accounted for 56% of sales and 57% of income from operations in fiscal 1995, Canada for 20% and 9%, respectively, and Europe for 24% and 34%.

Transportation equipment includes extruded and molded rubber and plastic products for the automotive, building and marine industries. Approximately 56%, 56% and 65% of revenues in fiscal 1995, 1994 and 1993, respectively, were attributable to original equipment sales to GM, Ford and Chrysler. SPD has a 50% interest (boosted from 40% in 1992) in Nisco, a joint venture with Nishikawa Rubber Co. of Japan that supplies sponge door seals to North American motor vehicle manufacturers from two Indiana plants.

The company's Oliver Rubber Co. subsidiary makes precure and mold cure tread rubber, bonding gum, cement, repair materials and equipment for the worldwide tire retreading industry. In October 1992, the unit formed a joint venture with Myers Industries to make retreading molds.

Holm Industries produces rubber and plastic trim seals for the automotive replacement, construction and marine industries and a variety of plastic and magnetic parts for appliance manufacturers and exterior door and window manufacturers.

In May 1995, the company acquired the remaining 80% of Itatiaia Standard of Brazil. Additionally, during 1995, the company was building new plants in Brazil and Mexico. Operations should begin in late 1996.

Important Developments

Oct. '95—Standard Products said that it expects earnings for the second quarter of fiscal 1996 to be at breakeven or slightly better, and full year earnings to reach $1.00 a share. SPD noted that weakness is continuing in the automotive components industry, and the company is experiencing price and quality pressures, while also coping with softening production schedules worldwide.

Capitalization

Long Term Debt: $190,522,000 (6/95).

Per Share Data ($)

(Year Ended Jun. 30)

	1995	1994	1993	1992	1991	1990
Tangible Bk. Val.	11.68	10.80	9.82	11.24	7.29	12.05
Cash Flow	4.00	4.39	4.26	3.70	0.30	2.49
Earnings	1.20	1.99	2.21	1.79	-1.65	0.93
Dividends	0.68	0.64	0.48	0.38	0.56	0.74
Payout Ratio	57%	32%	24%	25%	NM	79%
Prices - High	24⅛	38¾	36⅝	29⅝	20⅜	21
- Low	18½	21⅜	25¾	19⅛	9⅝	9⅝
P/E Ratio - High	20	19	17	17	NM	23
- Low	15	11	12	11	NM	10

Income Statement Analysis (Million $)

	1995	%Chg	1994	%Chg	1993	%Chg	1992
Revs.	996	14%	872	14%	764	16%	657
Oper. Inc.	77.3	-21%	97.7	9%	89.8	16%	77.4
Depr.	47.0	17%	40.0	29%	31.0	24%	24.9
Int. Exp.	13.0	44%	9.0	-7%	9.7	-35%	15.0
Pretax Inc.	17.3	-66%	50.2	NM	50.2	29%	38.8
Eff. Tax Rate	NM	—	34%	—	34%	—	40%
Net Inc.	20.0	-39%	33.0	-1%	33.4	43%	23.3

Balance Sheet & Other Fin. Data (Million $)

	1995	1994	1993	1992	1991	1990
Cash	19.5	Nil	5.5	44.3	19.3	15.7
Curr. Assets	307	271	234	218	182	183
Total Assets	702	624	565	399	368	362
Curr. Liab.	189	183	155	121	121	93.0
LT Debt	191	135	116	69.0	113	99
Common Eqty.	260	243	224	178	102	153
Total Cap.	451	378	340	247	216	252
Cap. Exp.	55.0	61.0	115	19.9	21.2	39.2
Cash Flow	66.9	73.0	64.4	48.2	3.8	31.8

Ratio Analysis

	1995	1994	1993	1992	1991	1990
Curr. Ratio	1.6	1.5	1.5	1.8	1.5	2.0
% LT Debt of Cap.	42.3	36.0	34.0	28.0	52.5	39.4
% Net Inc.of Revs.	2.1	3.8	4.4	3.5	NM	1.8
% Ret. on Assets	3.1	5.6	6.7	5.6	NM	3.4
% Ret. on Equity	8.0	14.2	15.9	15.6	NM	7.7

Dividend Data —Dividends have been paid since 1949.

Amt. of Div. $	Date Decl.	Ex-Div. Date	Stock of Record	Payment Date
0.170	Dec. 05	Jan. 09	Jan. 13	Jan. 27 '95
0.170	Mar. 20	Apr. 07	Apr. 14	Apr. 28 '95
0.170	Jun. 26	Jul. 06	Jul. 10	Jul. 24 '95
0.170	Aug. 21	Oct. 05	Oct. 10	Oct. 24 '95

Data as orig. reptd.; bef. results of disc. opers. and/or spec. items. Per share data adj. for stk. divs. as of ex-div. date. E-Estimated. NA-Not Available. NM-Not Meaningful. NR-Not Ranked.

Office—2130 West 110 St., Cleveland, OH 44102. **Tel**—(216) 281-8300. **Chrmn & CEO**—J. S. Reid Jr. **Pres & COO**—T. K. Zampetis. **VP-Fin, CFO & Investor Contact**—Donald R. Sheley, Jr. **Secy**—J. R. Hamilton. **Dirs**—J. C. Baillie, E. B. Brandon, J. Doddridge, J. D. Drinko, C. E. Moll, M. R. Myers, L. H. Perkins, A. M. Rankin Jr., J. S. Reid Jr., A. E. Riedel, J. D. Sigel, W. H. Thompson, T. K. Zampetis. **Transfer Agent & Registrar**—National City Bank, Cleveland. **Incorporated** in Ohio in 1927. **Empl**-10,308. **S&P Analyst:** S.S.

STANDARD & POOR'S

Stock Reports

Standex International

NYSE Symbol **SXI**

29-AUG-95

Industry: Conglomerate/diversified

Summary: This company is a diversified manufacturer of institutional, graphics/mail order, industrial and other products.

Quantitative Evaluations

Outlook
(1 Lowest—5 Highest)
• **NA**

Fair Value
• **NA**

Risk
• **Low**

Earn./Div. Rank
• **A**

Technical Eval.
• **Bullish** since 1/92

Rel. Strength Rank
(1 Lowest—99 Highest)
• **35**

Insider Activity
• **NA**

Recent Price • 33¾
52 Wk Range • 35⅝-26¼

Yield • 2.0%
12-Mo. P/E • 12.8

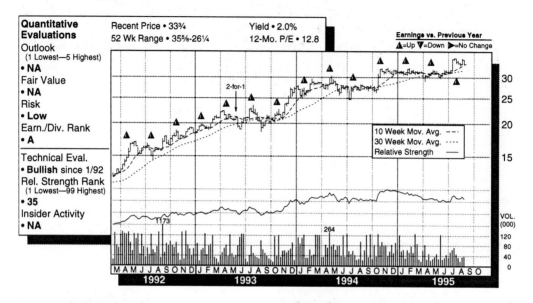

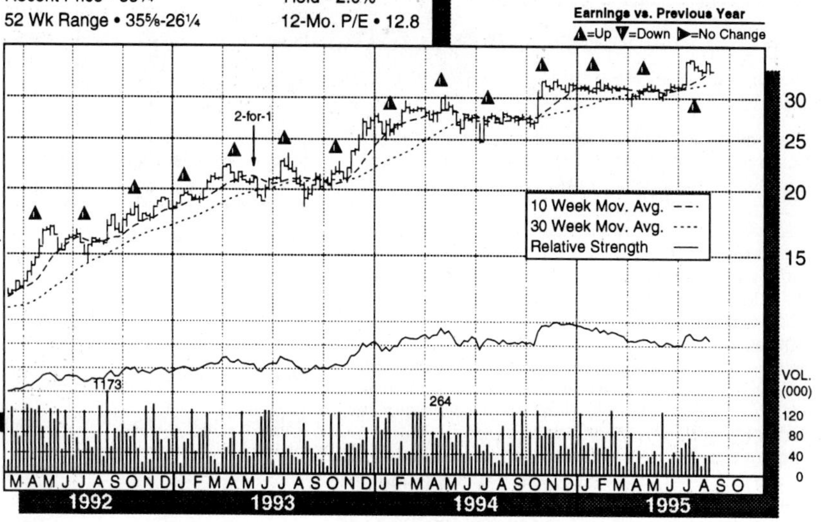

Business Profile - 25-AUG-95

Standex seeks growth by acquiring companies that complement and expand current operations. Backlog at the end of fiscal 1995 totaled $80 million, up 8% from the level a year earlier. A share repurchase program is in progress; during fiscal 1995, the company bought back $23.9 million of stock. A 6% dividend hike in April 1995 marked the 31st dividend increase in 31 years.

Operational Review - 25-AUG-95

Sales advanced moderately in the fiscal year ended June 30, 1995, reflecting strong U.S. order rates and improving economic conditions in Europe. Results benefited from the increased volume, and with a $5.1 million pretax gain, primarily related to the sale of a German subsidiary, net income climbed 48%. The company expects strong growth to continue in fiscal 1996, spurred by increased sales in Europe and contributions from acquisitions.

Stock Performance - 25-AUG-95

In the past 30 trading days, SXI's shares have declined 4%, compared to a 0.04% rise in the S&P 500. Average trading volume for the past five days was 7,700 shares, compared with the 40-day moving average of 9,210 shares.

Key Stock Statistics

Dividend Rate/Share	0.68	Shareholders	5,900
Shs. outstg. (M)	14.1	Market cap. (B)	$0.471
Avg. daily vol. (M)	0.008	Inst. holdings	59%
Tang. Bk. Value/Share	7.04	Insider holdings	NA
Beta	0.52		

Value of $10,000 invested 5 years ago: $ 32,620

Fiscal Year Ending Jun. 30

	1995	% Change	1994	% Change	1993	% Change
Revenues (Million $)						
1Q	140.6	10%	127.3	NM	127.0	12%
2Q	143.9	8%	133.5	-2%	136.0	7%
3Q	141.6	8%	130.9	11%	118.0	NM
4Q	143.2	4%	137.7	10%	125.6	5%
Yr.	569.3	8%	529.4	5%	506.3	6%
Income (Million $)						
1Q	11.80	87%	6.31	15%	5.50	18%
2Q	9.03	27%	7.09	7%	6.61	8%
3Q	8.06	29%	6.23	18%	5.28	7%
4Q	9.44	26%	7.52	14%	6.62	6%
Yr.	38.32	41%	27.15	13%	24.01	10%
Earnings Per Share ($)						
1Q	0.80	95%	0.41	24%	0.33	29%
2Q	0.62	35%	0.46	15%	0.40	19%
3Q	0.56	37%	0.41	26%	0.32	16%
4Q	0.66	32%	0.50	19%	0.42	17%
Yr.	2.64	48%	1.78	21%	1.47	20%

Next earnings report expected: late October

Standex International

Business Summary - 25-AUG-95

Standex International Corporation is a diversified manufacturer, producing and marketing a wide variety of products. Contributions by industry segment (profits in millions) in fiscal 1994 were:

	Sales	Profits
Institutional products	46%	$28.4
Graphics/mail order	26%	11.5
Industrial products	28%	17.0
Corporate & other	---	-14.6

The institutional products segment custom-designs and manufactures casters and wheels, chiropractic tables, HVAC pipe duct and fittings, feeding systems for hospitals, nursing homes, schools and correctional institutions; makes or distributes a variety of electric slicing, mixing, meat grinding and vegetable cutting machines for commercial use, as well as heavy-duty food waste disposers for schools, hospitals, hotels and restaurants; manufactures a broad line of refrigerated storage and display cabinets; fabricates and installs walk-in coolers and freezers, as well as large refrigerated warehouses; and makes commercial barbecue ovens, hot-food display merchandisers and a wide variety of metal fabricated products and specialty hardware.

The graphics/mail order segment manufactures mechanical binding systems; designs and builds punching, binding and collating equipment; and produces a broad range of custom continuous forms for business, as well as specialized forms and election supplies for municipal governments. It also publishes nondenominational religious curricula and Vacation Bible School (VBS) material.

The industrial products segment manufactures hydraulic cylinders and metal spinning components, engraved embossing rolls and plates for the texturization of paper, plastics, metals and other materials; and produces machinery used to emboss ferrous and nonferrous metals.

In August 1994, the company sold its Standex International Engraving GmbH subsidiary to a German producer of brass and steel press plates, for $19 million.

Important Developments

Aug. '95—Standex acquired DSC Technologies, Inc. The recently formed Crystal Lakes, Ill., company will develop monitoring, data-acquisition and radio frequency indentification systems for the transportation industry. Terms were not disclosed.

Apr. '95—Portland, Ore.-based Metal Products Manufacturing, Inc. was purchased for an undisclosed amount of cash. Metal Products makes HVAC pipe, duct and fittings for the home building industry in the Northwest.

Capitalization

Long Term Debt: $121,974,000 (3/95).

Per Share Data ($)

(Year Ended Jun. 30)

	1995	1994	1993	1992	1991	1990
Tangible Bk. Val.	NA	7.04	6.85	7.11	6.69	6.44
Cash Flow	NA	2.54	2.25	1.89	1.62	1.62
Earnings	2.64	1.78	1.47	1.23	1.05	1.07
Dividends	0.63	0.52	0.43	0.38	0.36	0.33
Payout Ratio	24%	29%	29%	28%	32%	30%
Prices - High	35⅝	30⅜	27¾	19	13⅝	13⅞
- Low	29	24⅝	18½	11	10⅛	10⅜
P/E Ratio - High	13	17	19	15	13	13
- Low	11	14	13	9	10	10

Income Statement Analysis (Million $)

	1994	%Chg	1993	%Chg	1992	%Chg	1991
Revs.	529	5%	506	6%	477	-1%	482
Oper. Inc.	58.1	5%	55.3	12%	49.2	-4%	51.1
Depr.	11.8	-9%	12.9	8%	11.9	NM	12.0
Int. Exp.	6.9	24%	5.6	-15%	6.6	-17%	7.9
Pretax Inc.	42.2	13%	37.5	11%	33.7	3%	32.6
Eff. Tax Rate	36%	—	36%	—	35%	—	38%
Net Inc.	27.1	13%	24.0	10%	21.9	8%	20.2

Balance Sheet & Other Fin. Data (Million $)

	1994	1993	1992	1991	1990	1989
Cash	5.0	7.5	10.9	7.3	8.0	7.9
Curr. Assets	197	182	186	177	182	170
Total Assets	324	309	317	297	298	277
Curr. Liab.	70.2	73.2	74.5	72.9	66.8	61.8
LT Debt	113	94.4	86.7	70.1	73.0	65.0
Common Eqty.	119	122	137	139	142	137
Total Cap.	246	229	236	220	225	211
Cap. Exp.	13.2	10.7	15.7	13.8	12.7	12.7
Cash Flow	38.9	36.9	33.8	32.2	33.1	32.6

Ratio Analysis

	1994	1993	1992	1991	1990	1989
Curr. Ratio	2.8	2.5	2.5	2.4	2.7	2.7
% LT Debt of Cap.	46.0	41.2	36.7	31.9	32.4	30.8
% Net Inc.of Revs.	5.1	4.7	4.6	4.2	4.7	5.0
% Ret. on Assets	8.8	8.0	7.4	7.0	7.8	8.5
% Ret. on Equity	23.1	19.4	16.6	14.9	16.0	16.0

Dividend Data —Dividends have been paid since 1964. A poison pill stock purchase rights plan was adopted in 1989.

Amt. of Div. $	Date Decl.	Ex-Div. Date	Stock of Record	Payment Date
0.140	Jul. 27	Aug. 02	Aug. 08	Aug. 25 '94
0.160	Oct. 25	Oct. 28	Nov. 03	Nov. 25 '94
0.160	Jan. 25	Jan. 31	Feb. 06	Feb. 25 '95
0.170	Apr. 26	May. 02	May. 08	May. 25 '95
0.170	Jul. 26	Aug. 03	Aug. 07	Aug. 25 '95

Data as orig. reptd.; bef. results of disc. opers. and/or spec. items. Per share data adj. for stk. divs. as of ex-div. date. E-Estimated. NA-Not Available. NM-Not Meaningful. NR-Not Ranked.

Office—6 Manor Parkway, Salem, NH 03079. **Tel**—(603) 893-9701. **Chrmn**—T. L. King. **Pres, CEO & COO**—E. J. Trainor. **VP, Treas & Investor Contact**—Lindsay M. Sedwick. **Secy**—R. H. Booth. **Dirs**—J. Bolten, Jr., W. L. Brown, D. R. Crichton, S. S. Dennis III, T. H. DeWitt, W. F. Greeley, D. B. Hogan, T. L. King, C. K. Landry, H. N. Muller III, S. Sackel, L. M. Sedwick. E. J. Trainor. **Transfer Agent & Registrar**—First National Bank of Boston. **Incorporated** in Ohio in 1955; reincorporated in Delaware in 1975. **Empl**-5,100. **S&P Analyst:** S.S.

STANDARD & POOR'S

STOCK REPORTS

Steel Technologies

NASDAQ Symbol **STTX**

In S&P SmallCap 600

02-NOV-95

Industry: Steel-Iron

Summary: This intermediate steel processor purchases flat-rolled steel produced by major steel mills and processes it to specifications required by industrial end-users.

Quantitative Evaluations

Outlook (1 Lowest—5 Highest)
• **5-**

Fair Value
• **13½**

Risk
• **High**

Earn./Div. Rank
• **B+**

Technical Eval.
• **Bearish** since 9/95

Rel. Strength Rank (1 Lowest—99 Highest)
• **54**

Insider Activity
• **Neutral**

Recent Price • 9¾ | Yield • 0.8%
52 Wk Range • 14¼-6¼ | 12-Mo. P/E • 16.0

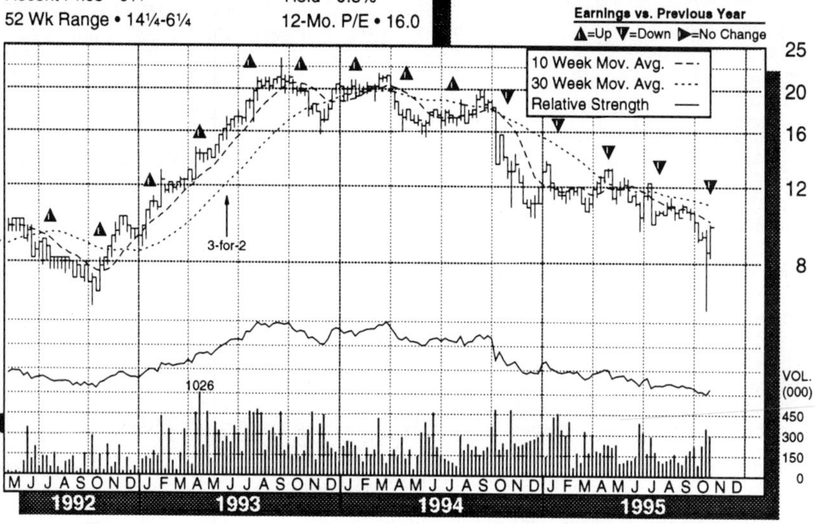

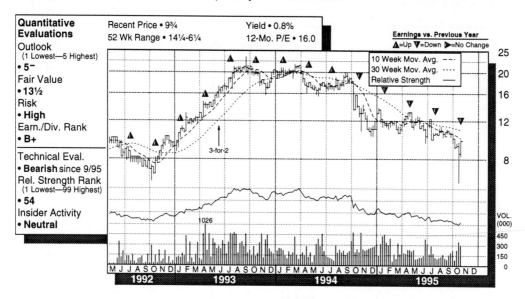

Business Profile - 02-NOV-95

This intermediate steel processor purchases flat-rolled steel produced by major steel mills and processes it to specifications required by industrial end-users. In addition to its six plants in Kentucky, Indiana, Maryland, Michigan and Mexico, STTX operates four joint venture facilities in Tennessee, Indiana and Ohio. Earnings declined in fiscal 1995, but the company expects improved results in fiscal 1996, reflecting capacity additions made during 1995 and increased demand from auto makers.

Operational Review - 02-NOV-95

Based on a preliminary report, net sales in the fiscal year ended September 30, 1995, rose 4.8% from those of the previous year. However, results were penalized by foreign currency exchange losses, substantially higher interest expense, and the absence of a gain on the sale of certain assets, and net income declined 29%, to $7.4 million ($0.61 a share) from $10.5 million ($0.87).

Stock Performance - 27-OCT-95

In the past 30 trading days, STTX's shares have declined 8%, compared to a 0.63% fall in the S&P 500. Average trading volume for the past five days was 59,180 shares, compared with the 40-day moving average of 40,444 shares.

Key Stock Statistics

Dividend Rate/Share	0.08	Shareholders	700
Shs. outstg. (M)	12.1	Market cap. (B)	$0.121
Avg. daily vol. (M)	0.053	Inst. holdings	32%
Tang. Bk. Value/Share	7.62	Insider holdings	NA
Beta	-0.24		

Value of $10,000 invested 5 years ago: $ 16,220

Fiscal Year Ending Sep. 30

	1995	% Change	1994	% Change	1993	% Change
Revenues (Million $)						
1Q	64.25	19%	54.06	29%	41.80	18%
2Q	71.50	14%	62.73	21%	52.02	36%
3Q	60.15	-5%	63.29	19%	53.06	32%
4Q	56.84	-6%	60.67	19%	50.92	25%
Yr.	252.7	5%	240.8	22%	197.8	28%
Income (Million $)						
1Q	2.02	-15%	2.38	33%	1.79	34%
2Q	2.66	-9%	2.92	12%	2.61	102%
3Q	2.06	-35%	3.17	10%	2.87	89%
4Q	0.67	-67%	2.05	-23%	2.67	43%
Yr.	7.42	-29%	10.51	6%	9.95	66%
Earnings Per Share ($)						
1Q	0.17	-15%	0.20	36%	0.15	29%
2Q	0.22	-8%	0.24	9%	0.22	106%
3Q	0.17	-35%	0.26	8%	0.24	89%
4Q	—	—	0.17	-26%	0.23	50%
Yr.	0.61	-30%	0.87	5%	0.83	66%

Next earnings report expected: mid January

Steel Technologies

02-NOV-95

Business Summary - 24-OCT-95

Steel Technologies Inc. is an intermediate steel processor. The company purchases commercial-tolerance steel from major steel mills and processes it to the precise thickness, width, temper and finish specified by customers, generally end-product manufacturers that purchase steel with closer tolerances on shorter lead-times and requiring more reliable and more frequent deliveries than the primary steel producers can efficiently provide.

The company maintains a substantial inventory of commercial-tolerance steel, which is a continuous sheet typically 36 to 72 inches wide, between 0.015 and 0.625 inches thick, and rolled into a 10- to 25-ton coil. The first processing function typically involves slitting coils into specified widths subject to close tolerances. The slitting lines maintain a width tolerance of +/-0.002 inches. Many orders also involve a process known as cold reduction, which reduces the thickness of the steel to customer specification by passing it through a set of rolls under pressure. The edges are conditioned to partially or fully rounded or squared shapes. Shipments rose to 408,000 tons in fiscal 1994 from 357,000 tons in fiscal 1993.

Major customer industries include automotive, auto supply, appliance, communications, electrical, machinery and office equipment. Sales to the automotive supply industry accounted for 59% of total sales in fiscal 1994; sales to the automotive industry directly provided 16%, while sales to GM were 8.0%. There are about 600 active accounts, mostly located within 300 miles of one of STTX's six plants in Kentucky, Indiana, Michigan, Maryland and Mexico.

STTX has joint ventures that operate four plants to process mill material.

Important Developments

Aug. '95—STTX signed a letter of intent to acquire the assets of Vincent Industrial Plastics, Inc., a Kentucky-based plastic injection molding company with about $10 million in annual revenues, for an undisclosed amount.

Capitalization

Long Term Debt: $63,867,000 (6/95).

Per Share Data ($) (Year Ended Sep. 30)

	1995	1994	1993	1992	1991	1990
Tangible Bk. Val.	NA	7.21	6.42	5.63	5.17	4.91
Cash Flow	NA	1.28	1.19	0.85	0.57	0.78
Earnings	0.61	0.87	0.83	0.50	0.29	0.53
Dividends	0.08	0.07	0.05	0.04	0.03	0.03
Payout Ratio	13%	8%	6%	8%	9%	5%
Prices - High	13¾	21¾	23½	10⅝	9⅛	9⅞
- Low	6¼	10⅛	10½	6⅜	6	6
P/E Ratio - High	23	25	28	21	31	18
- Low	10	12	13	13	20	11

Income Statement Analysis (Million $)

	1994	%Chg	1993	%Chg	1992	%Chg	1991
Revs.	241	22%	198	29%	154	18%	130
Oper. Inc.	21.5	3%	20.8	43%	14.5	42%	10.2
Depr.	5.0	14%	4.4	6%	4.2	21%	3.4
Int. Exp.	1.3	44%	0.9	-1%	0.9	-26%	1.2
Pretax Inc.	16.6	5%	15.8	66%	9.5	67%	5.7
Eff. Tax Rate	37%	—	37%	—	37%	—	38%
Net Inc.	10.5	6%	9.9	66%	6.0	72%	3.5

Balance Sheet & Other Fin. Data (Million $)

	1994	1993	1992	1991	1990	1989
Cash	1.0	0.1	0.6	1.6	0.7	0.4
Curr. Assets	118	82.1	53.0	43.5	55.3	37.0
Total Assets	200	144	107	95.0	99	74.0
Curr. Liab.	47.3	31.9	20.7	21.0	17.8	10.8
LT Debt	60.8	30.0	15.6	8.7	18.9	8.9
Common Eqty.	88.0	78.0	67.8	62.3	59.2	52.8
Total Cap.	153	112	86.7	74.1	81.2	63.7
Cap. Exp.	24.5	11.5	7.0	10.1	9.0	12.5
Cash Flow	15.5	14.3	10.2	6.9	9.4	8.1

Ratio Analysis

	1994	1993	1992	1991	1990	1989
Curr. Ratio	2.5	2.6	2.6	2.1	3.1	3.4
% LT Debt of Cap.	39.7	26.8	18.0	11.7	23.3	13.9
% Net Inc.of Revs.	4.4	5.0	3.9	2.7	4.6	4.8
% Ret. on Assets	6.1	7.9	5.9	3.6	7.4	7.8
% Ret. on Equity	12.7	13.6	9.2	5.8	11.5	13.1

Dividend Data —Cash dividends are paid on a semiannual basis.

Amt. of Div. $	Date Decl.	Ex-Div. Date	Stock of Record	Payment Date
0.040	Nov. 11	Nov. 21	Nov. 28	Dec. 09 '94
0.040	Apr. 21	May. 01	May. 05	May. 19 '95

Data as orig. reptd.; bef. results of disc. opers. and/or spec. items. Per share data adj. for stk. divs. as of ex-div. date. E-Estimated. NA-Not Available. NM-Not Meaningful. NR-Not Ranked.

Office—15415 Shelbyville Rd., Louisville, KY 40245. **Tel**—(502) 245-2110. **Chrmn & CEO**—M. J. Ray. **Pres & COO**—B. T. Ray. **VP-Fin, CFO, Secy, Treas and Investor Contact**—Kenneth R. Bates. **Dirs**—D. L. Armstrong, H. F. Bates, Jr., M. J. Carroll, J. D. Conner, W. E. Hellmann, C. A. Mays, R. W. McIntyre, B. T. Ray, M. J. Ray. **Transfer Agent & Registrar**—Mid-America Bank of Louisville & Trust Co. **Incorporated** in Kentucky in 1971. **Empl**-498. **S&P Analyst:** N. Rosenberg

STANDARD & POOR'S

STOCK REPORTS

Sterling Software

NYSE Symbol **SSW**
In S&P SmallCap 600

25-OCT-95

Industry:
Data Processing

Summary: This company provides systems software, application development tools, and electronic data interchange (EDI) products, as well as contract services for the federal government.

S&P Opinion: Buy (★★★★★)

Recent Price • 48¾
52 Wk Range • 49½-29
Yield • Nil
12-Mo. P/E • NM

Quantitative Evaluations
Outlook
(1 Lowest—5 Highest)
• **3+**
Fair Value
• **49**
Risk
• **Average**
Earn./Div. Rank
• **B-**

Technical Eval.
• **Bearish** since 8/95
Rel. Strength Rank
(1 Lowest—99 Highest)
• **87**
Insider Activity
• **Neutral**

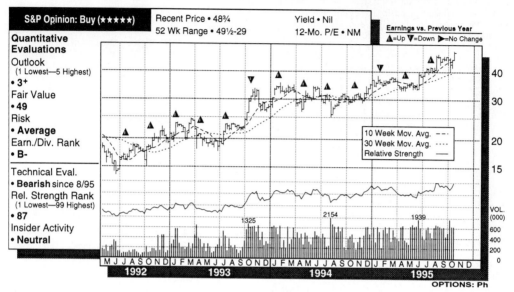

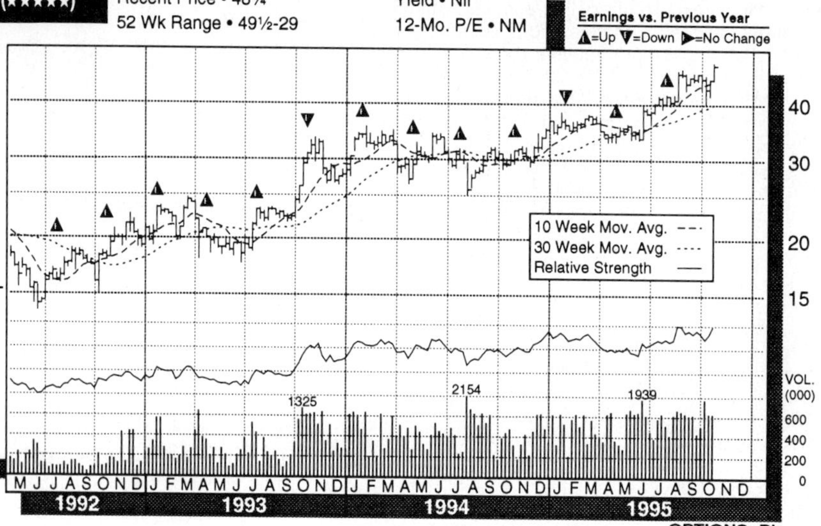

OPTIONS: Ph

Overview - 20-OCT-95

Revenues should rise sharply through fiscal 1996, aided by the KnowledgeWare acquisition, strength in the electronic commerce segment and new products. Operating profitability should benefit from the greater volume, a more favorable revenue mix of electronic commerce products, wider margins on federal contracts, merger-related synergies and tight expense controls. While results in the first quarter of fiscal 1995 were penalized by a $3.43 a share charge, operating earnings should continue to advance through fiscal 1996 year end.

Valuation - 20-OCT-95

Sterling's growth has been highly consistent: the company has recorded 27 consecutive quarters of revenue and operating earnings gains. However, the shares trade at a slight discount to the market, after adjusting for nonrecurring charges, owing to uncertainties over SSW's continued success in providing non-mainframe-based software solutions, uncertainty related to the smooth integration of KnowledgeWare, and accounting methods which are more aggressive than average. Still, revenues derived from mainframe-based products continue to decrease as a percentage of total revenues, the company is entrenched as a leader in the growing electronic commerce market, and its accounting practices continue to become more conservative. In light of the earnings growth we expect, the stock is expected to outperform the market in the coming months.

Key Stock Statistics

S&P EPS Est. 1995	-0.45	Tang. Bk. Value/Share	6.59
P/E on S&P Est. 1995	NM	Beta	2.00
S&P EPS Est. 1996	3.45	Shareholders	1,500
Dividend Rate/Share	Nil	Market cap. (B)	$ 1.2
Shs. outstg. (M)	25.1	Inst. holdings	81%
Avg. daily vol. (M)	0.232	Insider holdings	NA

Value of $10,000 invested 5 years ago: $ 53,424

Fiscal Year Ending Sep. 30

	1995	% Change	1994	% Change	1993	% Change
Revenues (Million $)						
1Q	126.4	15%	110.0	11%	98.78	76%
2Q	138.2	20%	115.5	18%	97.85	57%
3Q	150.9	30%	116.5	12%	104.5	58%
4Q	—	—	131.4	19%	110.7	48%
Yr.	—	—	473.4	15%	411.8	59%
Income (Million $)						
1Q	-61.66	NM	11.02	186%	3.85	41%
2Q	20.16	51%	13.36	192%	4.58	52%
3Q	22.29	47%	15.15	170%	5.62	52%
4Q	—	—	18.99	NM	-48.63	NM
Yr.	—	—	58.34	NM	-33.35	NM
Earnings Per Share ($)						
1Q	-2.87	NM	0.48	50%	0.32	33%
2Q	0.72	22%	0.59	64%	0.36	33%
3Q	0.79	22%	0.65	51%	0.43	30%
4Q	E0.91	11%	0.82	NM	-2.75	NM
Yr.	E-0.45	NM	2.54	NM	-2.00	NM

Next earnings report expected: early December

Sterling Software

Business Summary - 23-OCT-95

Sterling Software acquires, develops, markets and supports a broad range of computer software products and services.

The electronic commerce segment, which accounts for about 37% of revenues, aids in the computer-to-computer transmission of business documents, such as purchase orders, invoices, freight bills and remittance advices. Primary industries for the company's electronic commerce software and services, which include network services, interchange software, and communications software, are the healthcare, hardlines, grocery, retail, transportation, automotive, chemical, petroleum, paper, packaging, banking and government markets. SSW also provides software for the check processing operations of major financial institutions.

The systems management segment (26% or revenues), includes a range of software products to improve the operations of large data processing centers in three major areas: operating software products, which manage and control data processing centers; storage management products which facilitate the storage requirements of computers; and VM software products, which enhance the management of the VM operating system.

The applications management segment (18% of revenues), assists programming personnel with time-saving applications development and reengineering tools.

The federal systems segment (18% of revenues), provides technical professional services in support of both defense and civilian projects for the federal government, generally under long-term contract. Major customers include NASA and agencies of the Department of Defense.

The international group is responsible for the sales, marketing and primary support of all Sterling Software products outside the U.S.

Important Developments

Jan. '95—During the first quarter of fiscal 1995, the company completed the acquisition of KnowledgeWare, a developer of applications management and development tools, for about 2,421,000 SSW common shares. In the first quarter of fiscal 1995, Sterling recorded charges totaling $81,512,000 ($3.43 a share after tax) in connection with the acquisition, consisting of a $62,000,000 write-off for purchased R&D and a $19,512,000 restructuring charge to integrate KnowledgeWare's business into the company's operations.

Capitalization

Long Term Debt: $116,424,000 (6/95), mostly 5.75% sub. debs. due 2003, conv. into com. at $28.35 a sh.
Series B Jr. Preferred Stock: 200,000 shs. (liquid. pref. $8.93 per sh.); owned by the Wyly family.

Per Share Data ($) (Year Ended Sep. 30)

	1994	1993	1992	1991	1990	1989
Tangible Bk. Val.	8.45	5.37	9.96	10.84	0.93	-1.74
Cash Flow	3.16	-1.31	1.96	1.75	1.48	1.21
Earnings	2.31	-2.00	1.23	1.09	0.92	0.73
Dividends	Nil	Nil	Nil	Nil	Nil	Nil
Payout Ratio	Nil	NM	Nil	Nil	Nil	Nil
Prices - High	35⅝	33⅝	25¼	24⅞	11	9⅜
- Low	25	17⅝	13¾	7⅜	5½	5
P/E Ratio - High	15	NM	21	23	12	13
- Low	11	NM	11	7	6	7

Income Statement Analysis (Million $)

	1994	%Chg	1993	%Chg	1992	%Chg	1991
Revs.	473	15%	412	59%	259	16%	224
Oper. Inc.	110	91%	57.6	60%	36.1	13%	31.9
Depr.	14.4	22%	11.8	46%	8.1	19%	6.8
Int. Exp.	6.7	-13%	7.7	57%	4.9	2%	4.8
Pretax Inc.	92.6	NM	-48.3	NM	23.9	13%	21.2
Eff. Tax Rate	37%	—	NM	—	42%	—	40%
Net Inc.	58.3	NM	-33.4	NM	13.8	9%	12.7

Balance Sheet & Other Fin. Data (Million $)

	1994	1993	1992	1991	1990	1989
Cash	144	81.1	35.7	21.4	14.1	21.2
Curr. Assets	297	215	125	88.0	80.0	83.0
Total Assets	489	398	252	209	189	182
Curr. Liab.	172	164	78.9	46.2	41.6	38.1
LT Debt	116	117	53.0	59.0	59.0	66.0
Common Eqty.	174	95.4	99	69.4	61.7	43.1
Total Cap.	292	214	164	152	142	139
Cap. Exp.	16.4	13.0	7.2	8.2	4.9	4.1
Cash Flow	72.5	-22.6	21.5	16.1	13.9	11.5

Ratio Analysis

	1994	1993	1992	1991	1990	1989
Curr. Ratio	1.7	1.3	1.6	1.9	1.9	2.2
% LT Debt of Cap.	39.7	54.6	32.2	38.8	41.7	47.9
% Net Inc.of Revs.	12.3	NM	5.3	5.6	5.3	4.8
% Ret. on Assets	12.3	NM	4.8	6.3	5.6	4.5
% Ret. on Equity	40.9	NM	12.9	14.0	14.0	13.8

Dividend Data —Dividends were paid on the common stock only in 1984 and 1985.

Data as orig. reptd.; bef. results of disc. opers. and/or spec. items. Per share data adj. for stk. divs. as of ex-div. date. E-Estimated. NA-Not Available. NM-Not Meaningful. NR-Not Ranked.

Office—8080 North Central Expressway, Suite 1100, Dallas, TX 75206-1895. **Tel**—(214) 891-8600. **Chrmn**—S. Wyly. **Vice Chrmn**—C. J. Wyly, Jr. **Pres & CEO**—S. L. Williams. **EVP & Secy**—J. P. Meier. **EVP-Fin & CFO**—G. H. Ellis. **VP & Investor Contact**—Anne Vahala. **Dirs**—R. E. Cook, R. J. Donachie, M. C. French, D. R. Miller, Jr., P. A. Moore, F. A. Tarkenton, S. L. Williams, C. J. Wyly, Jr., E. A. Wyly, S. Wyly. **Transfer Agent & Registrar**—Bank of Boston. **Incorporated** in Delaware in 1983. **Empl-** 3,500. **S&P Analyst:** Peter C. Wood, CFA

Stone & Webster

NYSE Symbol **SW**
In S&P SmallCap 600

06-OCT-95 **Industry:** Building

Summary: This company is primarily a worldwide engineering, design, construction, and consulting firm. Other smaller subsidiaries participate in cold storage and other diverse operations.

Quantitative Evaluations

Outlook (1 Lowest—5 Highest) • **NA**

Fair Value • **NA**

Risk • **Low**

Earn./Div. Rank • **B-**

Technical Eval. • **Bearish** since 9/95

Rel. Strength Rank (1 Lowest—99 Highest) • **87**

Insider Activity • **Unfavorable**

Recent Price • 37¾ | 52 Wk Range • 40-27¼ | Yield • 1.6% | 12-Mo. P/E • 25.5

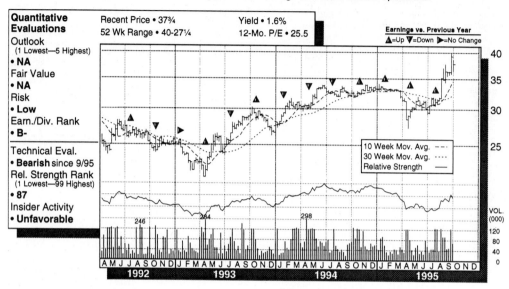

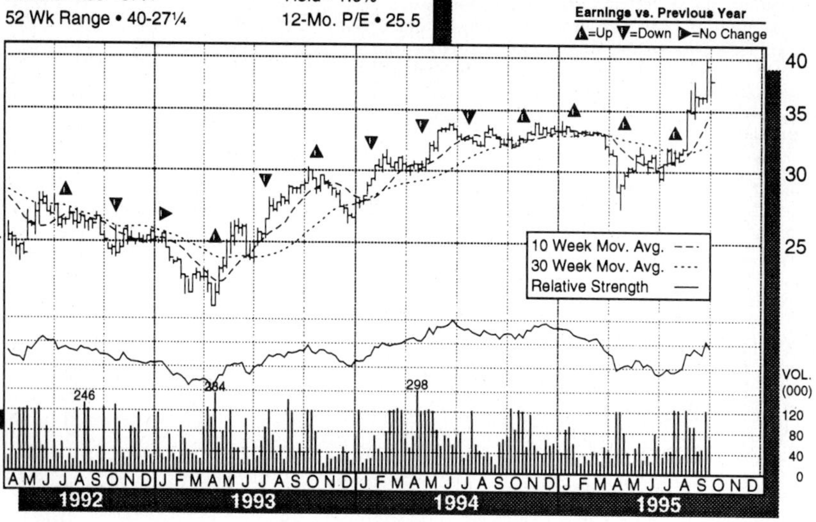

Business Profile - 06-OCT-95

Stone & Webster is a worldwide engineering, design, construction and consulting company which also provides cold storage warehousing services, owns oil and gas properties, and develops real estate. The company has been reducing its workforce in an attempt to reduce costs. SW returned to profitability for the first six months of 1995, aided by improved results in its core engineering, construction and consulting business. Employees own some 35% of the 14.4 million shares outstanding.

Operational Review - 06-OCT-95

Revenues for the six months ended June 30, 1995, rose 19%, year to year, reflecting strength in the core engineering, construction and consulting business, led by increased materials procurement contract revenues. Cost control programs and the absence of $8.6 million in severance costs resulting from workforce reductions lowered expenses, and after taxes at 39.1%, versus a $7.3 million tax credit, net income of $12.7 million ($0.87 a share) contrasted with a net loss of $16.9 million ($1.13).

Stock Performance - 29-SEP-95

In the past 30 trading days, SW's shares have increased 7%, compared to a 5% rise in the S&P 500. Average trading volume for the past five days was 13,760 shares, compared with the 40-day moving average of 18,297 shares.

Key Stock Statistics

Dividend Rate/Share	0.60	Shareholders	6,500
Shs. outstg. (M)	14.4	Market cap. (B)	$0.546
Avg. daily vol. (M)	0.017	Inst. holdings	29%
Tang. Bk. Value/Share	26.25	Insider holdings	NA
Beta	0.77		

Value of $10,000 invested 5 years ago: $ 11,392

Fiscal Year Ending Dec. 31

	1995	% Change	1994	% Change	1993	% Change
Revenues (Million $)						
1Q	222.5	15%	192.7	165%	72.83	11%
2Q	230.7	21%	190.4	143%	78.22	3%
3Q	—	—	205.4	NM	65.44	-5%
4Q	—	—	229.7	NM	63.30	-13%
Yr.	—	—	818.2	192%	279.8	-1%
Income (Million $)						
1Q	4.70	NM	-12.92	NM	0.38	NM
2Q	7.95	NM	-3.99	NM	0.08	-99%
3Q	—	—	5.18	NM	1.21	89%
4Q	—	—	3.92	NM	-2.04	NM
Yr.	—	—	-7.81	NM	-0.37	NM
Earnings Per Share ($)						
1Q	0.32	NM	-0.86	NM	0.02	—
2Q	0.55	NM	-0.27	NM	0.01	-97%
3Q	—	—	0.35	NM	0.08	100%
4Q	—	—	0.26	NM	-0.14	NM
Yr.	—	—	-0.52	NM	-0.03	NM

Next earnings report expected: late October

Stone & Webster

Business Summary - 06-OCT-95

Stone & Webster is primarily engaged in providing professional engineering, construction and consulting services. It also has much less significant operations in cold storage warehousing, as well as interests in real estate and oil and natural gas.

Engineering, construction & consulting services include complete engineering, design, construction, and full environmental services which are provided for power, process, industrial, governmental, transportation, and civil works projects. SW also constructs from plans developed by others, makes engineering reports and business examinations, undertakes consulting engineering work, and offers information management and computer systems expertise to clients. SW offers a full range of services in environmental engineering and sciences, including complete execution of environmental projects.

Other activities that come under the heading of engineering, construction & consulting services include advanced computer systems development services and products for plant scheduling, information systems, systems integration, computer-aided design, expert systems, and database management; projects in the power and other industries in which SW may take an ownership position and for which it may provide engineering, construction, management and operation and maintenance services; management consulting and financial services for business and industry (including public utility, transportation, pipeline, land development, banking, petroleum and manufacturing companies and government agencies); and appraisals for industrial companies and utilities. Engineering, construction and consulting services accounted for approximately 90% of total revenues in 1994.

Public cold storage warehousing, blast-freeze and other refrigeration and consolidation services are offered from three facilities near Atlanta, Ga. Other subsidiaries participate in oil and gas exploration, production, gathering and transportation, and in real estate operations.

Foreign operations accounted for 11% of total revenues in 1994.

Important Developments

Aug. '95—In response to a statement by the Lens fund, owners of approximately 3% of SW's shares, calling for the sale or merger of the company, Stone & Webster reaffirmed its strategy to reinvest available capital in the company's core engineering, construction and consulting business, invest in new development projects and periodically repurchase shares of the company's common stock. In August, under pressure from Lens and other shareholders, who feel that management is not maximizing shareholder value, Bruce Coles resigned as SW's Chairman and CEO .

Capitalization

Long Term Debt: $95,818,000 (6/95).

Per Share Data ($) (Year Ended Dec. 31)

	1994	1993	1992	1991	1990	1989
Tangible Bk. Val.	25.69	28.40	26.93	26.29	25.22	24.97
Cash Flow	0.80	1.32	1.96	2.34	1.64	2.57
Earnings	-0.52	-0.03	0.62	1.08	0.50	1.37
Dividends	0.60	0.60	0.60	0.60	1.05	1.20
Payout Ratio	NM	NM	97%	56%	210%	87%
Prices - High	34	30¼	31	36¼	41¾	45¾
- Low	27¼	21¼	23¾	26⅛	25⅛	34⅛
P/E Ratio - High	NM	NM	50	34	84	33
- Low	NM	NM	38	24	50	25

Income Statement Analysis (Million $)

	1994	%Chg	1993	%Chg	1992	%Chg	1991
Revs.	766	192%	262	-2%	266	4%	257
Oper. Inc.	-37.0	NM	26.5	-10%	29.4	-14%	34.3
Depr.	19.7	-2%	20.1	NM	20.1	7%	18.8
Int. Exp.	5.3	73%	3.0	NM	3.0	-18%	3.7
Pretax Inc.	-8.8	NM	8.5	-64%	23.6	-16%	28.1
Eff. Tax Rate	NM	—	104%	—	60%	—	42%
Net Inc.	-7.8	NM	-0.4	NM	9.3	-43%	16.4

Balance Sheet & Other Fin. Data (Million $)

	1994	1993	1992	1991	1990	1989
Cash	130	119	104	81.0	70.0	103
Curr. Assets	278	292	286	306	296	314
Total Assets	678	680	615	602	569	566
Curr. Liab.	141	118	116	119	126	120
LT Debt	89.6	47.7	24.8	28.0	11.4	21.6
Common Eqty.	375	425	403	395	380	378
Total Cap.	514	538	475	461	422	425
Cap. Exp.	52.3	31.7	26.9	26.6	18.4	21.7
Cash Flow	11.9	19.8	29.5	35.2	24.8	38.9

Ratio Analysis

	1994	1993	1992	1991	1990	1989
Curr. Ratio	2.0	2.5	2.5	2.6	2.4	2.6
% LT Debt of Cap.	17.5	8.9	5.2	6.1	2.7	5.1
% Net Inc.of Revs.	NM	NM	3.5	6.4	3.2	8.6
% Ret. on Assets	NM	NM	1.5	2.8	1.3	3.7
% Ret. on Equity	NM	NM	2.3	4.2	2.0	5.6

Dividend Data —Dividends have been paid since 1939. A dividend reinvestment plan is available.

Amt. of Div. $	Date Decl.	Ex-Div. Date	Stock of Record	Payment Date
0.150	Sep. 21	Sep. 26	Oct. 01	Nov. 15 '94
0.150	Dec. 21	Dec. 27	Jan. 03	Feb. 15 '95
0.150	Mar. 15	Mar. 27	Apr. 01	May. 15 '95
0.150	Jun. 21	Jun. 28	Jul. 01	Aug. 15 '95
0.150	Sep. 20	Sep. 28	Oct. 02	Nov. 15 '95

Data as orig. reptd.; bef. results of disc. opers. and/or spec. items. Per share data adj. for stk. divs. as of ex-div. date. E-Estimated. NA-Not Available. NM-Not Meaningful. NR-Not Ranked.

Office—250 W. 34th St., New York, NY 10119. **Tel**—(212) 290-7500. **Chrmn**—K. F. Hansen. **Pres & CEO**—E. J. Walsh. **Secy**—J. A. Skidmore. **EVP-Fin & Investor Contact**—William M. Egan (212) 290-7490. **Dirs**—W. L. Brown, F. J. A. Cilluffo, B. C. Coles, W. M. Egan, D. R. Fitzpatrick, J. P. Grace, K. F. Hansen, E. R. Heiberg III, J. A. Hooper, J. A. McKee, B. W. Reznicek, K. G. Ryder, E. J. Walsh. **Transfer Agent & Registrar**—Chemical Bank, NYC. **Incorporated** in Delaware in 1929. **Empl**-5,000. **S&P Analyst:** N. Rosenberg

STANDARD & POOR'S

STOCK REPORTS

StrataCom, Inc.

NASDAQ Symbol **STRM**

In S&P SmallCap 600

07-AUG-95 **Industry:** Data Processing

Summary: This company designs, manufactures, markets and services IPX FastPacket cell switching systems for private wide area networks and public carrier high-speed data service offerings.

Quantitative Evaluations

Recent Price • 50⅝ | Yield • Nil
52 Wk Range • 57½-15⅜ | 12-Mo. P/E • 51.7

Outlook
(1 Lowest—5 Highest)
• NA
Fair Value
• NA
Risk
• High
Earn./Div. Rank
• NR

Technical Eval.
• Bullish since 4/95
Rel. Strength Rank
(1 Lowest—99 Highest)
• 61
Insider Activity
• Unfavorable

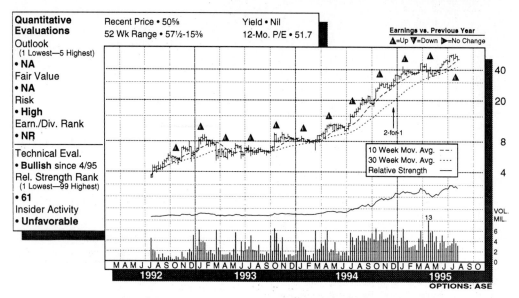

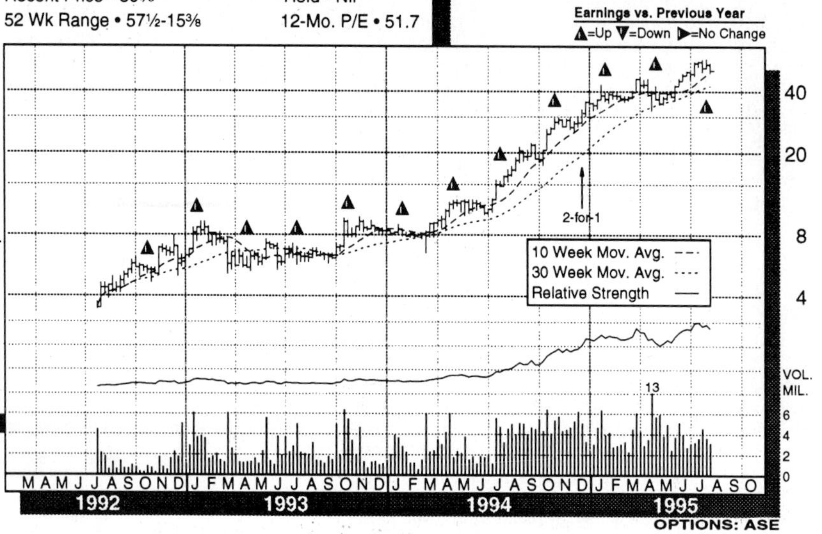

OPTIONS: ASE

Business Profile - 07-AUG-95

StrataCom is a leader in worldwide, high-speed wide area network solutions. The company supplies some of the world's largest telecommunications service providers with the equipment to offer both frame relay and asynchronous transfer mode (ATM) services. StrataCom's FastPacket products are widely used by private wide area networks (WANs), public carriers and value added networks (VANs) around the world to provide commercial frame relay, voice, video, data and ATM services.

Operational Review - 07-AUG-95

Total revenues for the six months ended July 1, 1995, nearly tripled, year to year, reflecting increases in products and services. Gross margins widened on the increased volume, and despite significant increases in R&D and SG&A, operating income rose more than fourfold. With sharply higher interest income (net), and after taxes at 36.0%, versus 30.0%, net income soared to $23,901,000 ($0.60 a share based on 18% more shares), from $5,800,000 ($0.17).

Stock Performance - 04-AUG-95

In the past 30 trading days, STRM's shares have increased 2%, compared to a 2% rise in the S&P 500. Average trading volume for the past five days was 612,840 shares, compared with the 40-day moving average of 703,095 shares.

Key Stock Statistics

Dividend Rate/Share	Nil	Shareholders	500
Shs. outstg. (M)	36.0	Market cap. (B)	$ 1.8
Avg. daily vol. (M)	0.736	Inst. holdings	80%
Tang. Bk. Value/Share	4.62	Insider holdings	NA
Beta	NA		

Value of $10,000 invested 5 years ago: NA

Fiscal Year Ending Dec. 31

	1995	% Change	1994	% Change	1993	% Change
Revenues (Million $)						
1Q	71.59	NM	23.11	36%	17.00	40%
2Q	80.03	176%	29.02	61%	18.02	38%
3Q	—	—	41.03	116%	19.02	31%
4Q	—	—	61.09	NM	20.31	27%
Yr.	—	—	154.2	107%	74.36	34%
Income (Million $)						
1Q	11.15	NM	2.47	45%	1.70	NM
2Q	12.75	NM	3.33	84%	1.81	79%
3Q	—	—	5.27	176%	1.91	43%
4Q	—	—	8.70	NM	2.11	29%
Yr.	—	—	19.77	163%	7.53	67%
Earnings Per Share ($)						
1Q	0.28	NM	0.08	50%	0.05	150%
2Q	0.32	NM	0.10	82%	0.06	57%
3Q	—	—	0.15	150%	0.06	33%
4Q	—	—	0.23	NM	0.07	30%
Yr.	—	—	0.55	139%	0.23	53%

Next earnings report expected: mid October

Business Summary - 07-AUG-95

StrataCom, Inc. designs, manufactures, markets and supports FastPacket networking systems based on frame relay and Asynchronous Transfer Mode (ATM) technologies for both public carrier service offerings and private wide area networks (WANs). The company has been a pioneer in the development of cell switching which it believes offers superior performance over prior generation circuit switching or packet switching alternatives. Cell switching is the basis of ATM, which many industry experts expect to be the next generation internetworking standard. StrataCom's family of products, including FastPAD, IPX and BPX, are used to integrate and transport a wide variety of corporate information, including voice, data, video, local area networks (LANs), image and multimedia traffic at speeds which range from 9.6Kbps to over 45Mbps. The company believes FastPacket networking systems can lower the cost, increase the performance and reduce the complexity of WANs. Revenues in recent years were derived as follows:

	1994	1993	1992
Products	89%	87%	88%
Service & other	11%	13%	12%

The company has broadened its product family to offer Multiband ATM solutions, such as the BPX product family at broadband speeds, the IPX product family at narrowband speeds, and the FastPAD product family for lower speed lines, subrate networks and frame relay devices. These products integrate multimedia communications over high-speed transmission facilities to allow users to build efficient, flexible, reliable and manageable WANs. During 1994, approximately 98% of the company's product revenue was from the IPX product line. The IPX supports a wide variety of networking options through the use of flexible topologies, setting of preferred routes and a wide variety of access interfaces.

StrataCom markets its products in North America primarily through a direct sales force and internationally primarily through a network of distributors with expertise in selling WAN solutions. Several public carriers and Value Added Networks (VANs) including AT&T, British Telecom, CompuServe, Japan Telecom and Unitel offer frame relay services based on the company's FastPacket family of products.

Important Developments

May '95—STRM introduced StrataSphere, a scalable, robust network management architecture designed to meet business requirements for operation of wide area ATM networks.

Capitalization

Long Term Debt: $294,000 (7/95) of cap. lease obligs.

Per Share Data ($) (Year Ended Dec. 31)

	1994	1993	1992	1991	1990	1989
Tangible Bk. Val.	4.22	1.44	1.14	-4.02	0.57	NA
Cash Flow	0.80	0.35	0.22	0.07	-0.24	-0.11
Earnings	0.55	0.23	0.15	Nil	-0.29	-0.15
Dividends	Nil	Nil	Nil	Nil	Nil	Nil
Payout Ratio	Nil	Nil	Nil	Nil	Nil	Nil
Prices - High	37¼	9⅞	7⅞	NA	NA	NA
- Low	6½	5⅛	3½	NA	NA	NA
P/E Ratio - High	68	43	53	NA	NA	NA
- Low	12	22	23	NA	NA	NA

Income Statement Analysis (Million $)

	1994	%Chg	1993	%Chg	1992	%Chg	1991
Revs.	154	107%	74.4	34%	55.6	41%	39.5
Oper. Inc.	37.2	NM	11.7	75%	6.7	NM	1.5
Depr.	9.2	133%	3.9	83%	2.2	21%	1.8
Int. Exp.	0.1	-18%	0.1	-58%	0.3	-24%	0.3
Pretax Inc.	29.9	NM	8.9	77%	5.0	NM	0.1
Eff. Tax Rate	34%	—	15%	—	10%	—	42%
Net Inc.	19.8	163%	7.5	67%	4.5	NM	0.1

Balance Sheet & Other Fin. Data (Million $)

	1994	1993	1992	1991	1990	1989
Cash	104	35.8	30.2	16.5	12.4	NA
Curr. Assets	148	51.6	42.1	25.2	18.9	NA
Total Assets	187	60.4	46.8	28.3	22.0	20.3
Curr. Liab.	36.3	14.6	11.9	11.7	6.4	NA
LT Debt	0.3	0.4	0.3	1.2	1.3	1.4
Common Eqty.	150	44.8	34.7	15.4	14.3	11.3
Total Cap.	150	45.2	35.0	16.6	15.6	12.7
Cap. Exp.	21.5	7.2	3.8	0.7	1.0	0.7
Cash Flow	29.0	11.5	6.7	1.8	-5.5	-2.5

Ratio Analysis

	1994	1993	1992	1991	1990	1989
Curr. Ratio	4.1	3.5	3.6	2.2	2.9	NA
% LT Debt of Cap.	0.2	0.9	0.7	7.4	8.2	10.8
% Net Inc.of Revs.	12.8	10.1	8.1	0.1	NM	NM
% Ret. on Assets	15.4	13.9	4.5	0.2	NM	NM
% Ret. on Equity	19.7	18.7	NM	0.4	NM	NM

Dividend Data (No cash dividends have been paid. The company intends to retain its earnings for use in its business. A "poison pill" stock purchase right was adopted in September 1994. A two-for-one stock split was distributed December 15, 1994, to shareholders of record December 1.)

Amt. of Div. $	Date Decl.	Ex-Div. Date	Stock of Record	Payment Date
2-for-1	Nov. 18	Dec. 16	Dec. 01	Dec. 15 '94

Data as orig. reptd.; bef. results of disc. opers. and/or spec. items. Per share data adj. for stk. divs. as of ex-div. date. E-Estimated. NA-Not Available. NM-Not Meaningful. NR-Not Ranked.

Office—1400 Parkmoor Ave., San Jose, CA 95126. **Tel**—(408) 294-7600. **Chrmn, Pres & CEO**—R. M. Moley. **VP-Fin & CFO**—S. Subhedar. **Dirs**—J. M. Drazan, P. T. Gianos, J. A. Graziano, R. M. Moley, M. K. Oshman, A. Sun. **Transfer Agent & Registrar**—First National Bank of Boston. **Incorporated** in California in 1986; reincorporated in Delaware in 1988. **Empl**-626. **S&P Analyst:** Kevin J. Gooley

STANDARD & POOR'S

STOCK REPORTS

Strawbridge & Clothier

NASDAQ Symbol **STRWA**

In S&P SmallCap 600

06-OCT-95

Industry:
Retail Stores

Summary: This retailer operates 13 department stores, a home furnishings store and 27 Clover discount stores, primarily in Philadelphia and the surrounding Delaware Valley area.

Quantitative Evaluations

Outlook
(1 Lowest—5 Highest)
• **3-**

Fair Value
• **19**

Risk
• **Low**

Earn./Div. Rank
• **B+**

Technical Eval.
• **Bullish** since 2/95

Rel. Strength Rank
(1 Lowest—99 Highest)
• **34**

Insider Activity
• **NA**

Recent Price • 19
52 Wk Range • 23½-18¼

Yield • 5.9%
12-Mo. P/E • 35.2

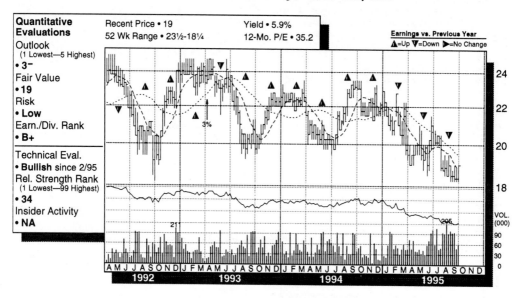

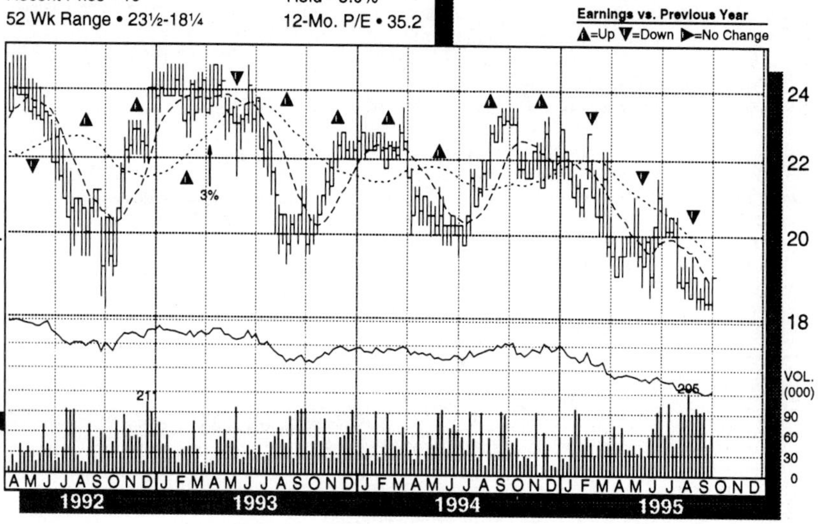

Business Profile - 06-OCT-95

The company expects to spend approximately $70.2 million this year and next for expansion efforts, including the recent opening of a new home furnishings store and three new Clover stores, and the renovation of four existing Clover locations and one department store. Future earnings gains will depend upon the strength of the economy and Strawbridge's ability to successfully meet the challenge of increased competition from a host of retailers, including Wal-Mart.

Operational Review - 06-OCT-95

Strawbridge attributed its reduced sales in the first half of 1995-96 to a 14-day public transit strike, a weaker overall economic climate, and ongoing sluggishness in female apparel sales. Profitability was hurt by increased markdowns, higher costs associated with new stores, and $3.2 million of costs incurred in connnection with an unsuccessful attempt to acquire six John Wanamaker stores. Despite tax credits of $8.3 million, versus $383,000, the net loss widened.

Stock Performance - 29-SEP-95

In the past 30 trading days, STRWA's shares have increased 3%, compared to a 5% rise in the S&P 500. Average trading volume for the past five days was 11,620 shares, compared with the 40-day moving average of 26,421 shares.

Key Stock Statistics

Dividend Rate/Share	1.10	Shareholders	5,500
Shs. outstg. (M)	10.6	Market cap. (B)	$0.196
Avg. daily vol. (M)	0.016	Inst. holdings	33%
Tang. Bk. Value/Share	23.05	Insider holdings	NA
Beta	0.41		

Value of $10,000 invested 5 years ago: $ 9,057

Fiscal Year Ending Jan. 31

	1996	% Change	1995	% Change	1994	% Change
Revenues (Million $)						
1Q	198.6	-5%	209.0	6%	197.0	-4%
2Q	218.6	-2%	222.9	NM	225.0	5%
3Q	—	—	226.6	1%	223.6	4%
4Q	—	—	345.8	2%	338.8	2%
Yr.	—	—	1,004	2%	984.6	2%
Income (Million $)						
1Q	-6.06	NM	-0.99	NM	-4.26	NM
2Q	-9.08	NM	0.24	NM	-1.43	NM
3Q	—	—	0.53	NM	0.07	NM
4Q	—	—	20.25	-13%	23.34	5%
Yr.	—	—	20.03	13%	17.73	-2%
Earnings Per Share ($)						
1Q	-0.58	NM	-0.10	NM	-0.41	NM
2Q	-0.86	NM	0.02	NM	-0.14	NM
3Q	—	—	0.05	NM	0.01	NM
4Q	—	—	1.93	-14%	2.25	4%
Yr.	—	—	1.92	12%	1.71	-3%

Next earnings report expected: late November

Strawbridge & Clothier

Business Summary - 06-OCT-95

Strawbridge & Clothier operates a large department store in downtown Philadelphia, 13 suburban branch department stores and 27 self-service Clover outlets. In addition to Philadelphia, the stores serve the surrounding Delaware Valley area of Pennsylvania, Delaware and New Jersey, as well as the Lehigh Valley and Lancaster areas of Pennsylvania. The majority of the suburban department stores are in shopping centers. Of the 27 self-service stores, 19 are in Pennsylvania, six in New Jersey and two in Delaware.

Strawbridge & Clothier stores carry full lines of general merchandise and provide standard department store services. Clover stores offer a broad range of general merchandise but do not sell major appliances or furniture; no services are provided except for cafeteria-style restaurant service in several stores, snack bars in all stores, pharmacies in eight stores and beauty salons in nine stores.

In the fiscal year ended January 28, 1995, 35% of sales were on a cash basis and 65% on credit. The business is seasonal, with 29% of annual sales and a major portion of profits recorded in the peak November-December period.

Merchandise is sold under a broad variety of brand names, including the company's own brand names, manufacturers' brand names and several names owned by Associated Merchandising Corp., of which Strawbridge & Clothier is a member.

The downtown Philadelphia store contains more than 1,065,000 sq. ft. of floor area, and the branch department stores range from 150,000 to 255,000 sq. ft. Clover units range from 70,000 to 157,000 sq. ft., excluding adjoining space that is leased to third parties.

The company maintains a 705,000 sq. ft. warehouse and distribution facility in Philadelphia and a 262,000 sq. ft. Clover warehouse facility in Howell Township, N.J.

Important Developments

Aug. '95—The company opened a new Clover store in the Gallery Mall in Philadelphia.

May '95—STRWA opened a new Clover store in New Castle County, Del. Previously, on April 21, 1995, it opened its first home furnishings store at the Concord Mall, north of Wilmington, Del. The store carries furniture, bedding, floor coverings, curtains, draperies, lamps and a full-service interior design studio.

Capitalization

Long Term Debt: $205,059,000 (7/95), incl. lease obligs.

Common Ser. A Stock: 7,412,685 shs. ($1 par).

Common Ser. B Stock: 3,159,281 shs. ($1 par); 10 votes per sh.; not traded on public market; conv. sh.-for-sh. into Ser. A.

Per Share Data ($) (Year Ended Jan. 31)

	1995	1994	1993	1992	1991	1990
Tangible Bk. Val.	25.08	24.38	24.38	25.38	24.40	23.68
Cash Flow	4.76	4.51	4.53	4.18	4.51	5.59
Earnings	1.92	1.71	1.76	1.34	1.71	3.12
Dividends	1.10	1.09	1.05	1.03	0.99	0.93
Payout Ratio	57%	64%	60%	75%	58%	29%
Cal. Yrs.	1994	1993	1992	1991	1990	1989
Prices - High	$23\frac{1}{2}$	$24\frac{3}{4}$	$25\frac{1}{4}$	27	$31\frac{3}{8}$	$34\frac{3}{8}$
- Low	$19\frac{1}{2}$	$19\frac{1}{4}$	$18\frac{1}{4}$	$16\frac{3}{4}$	$16\frac{3}{4}$	26
P/E Ratio - High	12	14	14	20	18	11
- Low	10	11	10	12	10	8

Income Statement Analysis (Million $)

	1995	%Chg	1994	%Chg	1993	%Chg	1992
Revs.	1,004	2%	985	2%	968	NM	968
Oper. Inc.	76.0	3%	74.0	-3%	76.0	4%	73.0
Depr.	29.6	3%	28.8	2%	28.3	-1%	28.7
Int. Exp.	19.6	-6%	20.9	-2%	21.4	-7%	23.0
Pretax Inc.	30.1	12%	26.8	-1%	27.2	31%	20.7
Eff. Tax Rate	33%	—	34%	—	34%	—	35%
Net Inc.	20.0	13%	17.7	-2%	18.0	32%	13.6

Balance Sheet & Other Fin. Data (Million $)

	1995	1994	1993	1992	1991	1990
Cash	1.6	2.9	5.4	2.8	1.3	1.9
Curr. Assets	323	356	342	314	312	308
Total Assets	640	663	654	632	646	619
Curr. Liab.	117	147	130	130	141	119
LT Debt	202	206	224	212	218	226
Common Eqty.	262	252	243	251	244	235
Total Cap.	465	462	472	463	463	462
Cap. Exp.	38.0	22.1	22.6	16.4	43.9	46.8
Cash Flow	49.6	46.5	46.3	42.2	45.1	55.7

Ratio Analysis

	1995	1994	1993	1992	1991	1990
Curr. Ratio	2.8	2.4	2.6	2.4	2.2	2.6
% LT Debt of Cap.	43.5	44.6	47.4	45.7	47.1	49.0
% Net Inc.of Revs.	2.0	1.8	1.9	1.4	1.8	3.3
% Ret. on Assets	3.1	2.6	2.8	2.1	2.7	5.1
% Ret. on Equity	7.8	7.0	7.3	5.5	7.1	13.9

Dividend Data —Cash dividends have been paid on the common in each year since 1947. Annual stock dividends, paid for 31 consecutive years, were suspended in 1994-5.

Amt. of Div. $	Date Decl.	Ex-Div. Date	Stock of Record	Payment Date
0.275	Sep. 21	Sep. 27	Oct. 03	Nov. 01 '94
0.275	Dec. 21	Dec. 27	Jan. 03	Feb. 01 '95
0.275	Mar. 22	Mar. 28	Apr. 03	May. 01 '95
0.275	Jun. 21	Jun. 29	Jul. 03	Aug. 01 '95
0.275	Sep. 20	Sep. 28	Oct. 02	Nov. 01 '95

Data as orig. reptd.; bef. results of disc. opers. and/or spec. items. Per share data adj. for stk. divs. as of ex-div. date. E-Estimated. NA-Not Available. NM-Not Meaningful. NR-Not Ranked.

Office—801 Market St., Philadelphia, PA 19107-3199. **Tel**—(215) 629-6000. **Chrmn**—F. R. Strawbridge III. **Pres**—P. S. Strawbridge. **VP, Treas, Secy & Investor Contact**—Steven L. Strawbridge. **Dirs**—J. S. Braxton, I. H. Clothier IV, R. H. Hall, T. B. Harvey, Jr., A. C. Longstreth, P. E. Shipley, D. W. Strawbridge, F. R. Strawbridge III, P. S. Strawbridge, S. L. Strawbridge, N. B. Weintraub, W. W. White. **Transfer Agent**—Mellon Bank N.A., Pittsburgh. **Incorporated** in Pennsylvania in 1922. **Empl**-7,282. **S&P Analyst:** Maureen C. Carini

STANDARD & POOR'S

STOCK REPORTS

Sturm, Ruger

NYSE Symbol **RGR**
In S&P SmallCap 600

08-OCT-95 **Industry:** Arms/Ammunition

Summary: This leading manufacturer of rifles and handguns for sporting and law enforcement purposes also produces ferrous and nonferrous investment castings.

Quantitative Evaluations

Recent Price • 27⅝ Yield • 5.1%
52 Wk Range • 35⅝-25⅜ 12-Mo. P/E • 12.1

Outlook
(1 Lowest—5 Highest)
• **NA**

Fair Value
• **NA**

Risk
• **Average**

Earn./Div. Rank
• **A-**

Technical Eval.
• **Bearish** since 7/95

Rel. Strength Rank
(1 Lowest—99 Highest)
• **8**

Insider Activity
• **NA**

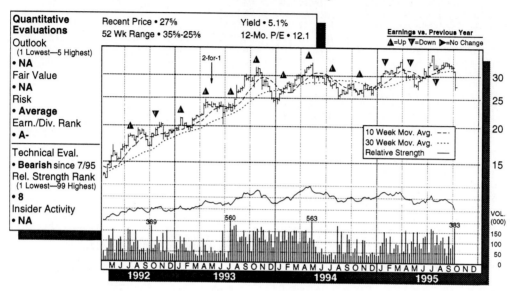

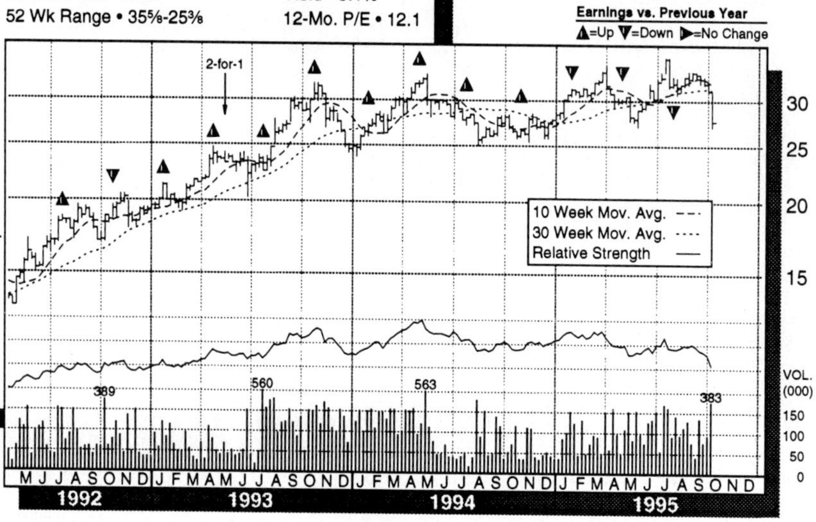

Business Profile - 21-JUN-95

Despite recent softness, RGR has historically increased sales and earnings through higher unit sales of firearms, introduction of new products and selective price increases. In recent years, demand for RGR's products has outstripped supply capacity. However, a 65,000 square foot addition to the company's Newport, N.H., manufacturing facility will substantially increase firearms capacity. Product liability cases add uncertainty, but these suits have abated.

Operational Review - 05-OCT-95

Net sales in the six months ended June 30, 1995, fell 4.1%, year to year, reflecting weakening customer demand for pistols. Sales in the other firearm categories (revolvers, rifles and shotguns) remained strong, with demand in excess of current plant capacity. Margins narrowed, due to a less favorable firearm sales mix and a higher proportion of lower margin casting sales, and operating income decreased 21%. Net income declined 18%, to $15,039,000 ($1.12 a share) from $18,387,000 ($1.37).

Stock Performance - 06-OCT-95

In the past 30 trading days, RGR's shares have declined 16%, compared to a 4% rise in the S&P 500. Average trading volume for the past five days was 76,620 shares, compared with the 40-day moving average of 26,605 shares.

Key Stock Statistics

Dividend Rate/Share	1.40	Shareholders	1,400
Shs. outstg. (M)	13.5	Market cap. (B)	$0.372
Avg. daily vol. (M)	0.034	Inst. holdings	48%
Tang. Bk. Value/Share	9.81	Insider holdings	NA
Beta	0.26		

Value of $10,000 invested 5 years ago: $ 24,099

Fiscal Year Ending Dec. 31

	1995	% Change	1994	% Change	1993	% Change
Revenues (Million $)						
1Q	50.30	-1%	51.05	-1%	51.68	30%
2Q	45.20	-7%	48.55	NM	48.25	25%
3Q	—	—	44.94	7%	41.95	13%
4Q	—	—	51.89	NM	52.31	28%
Yr.	—	—	196.4	1%	194.2	24%
Income (Million $)						
1Q	8.56	-13%	9.85	15%	8.58	29%
2Q	6.48	-24%	8.53	NM	8.52	59%
3Q	—	—	6.89	22%	5.64	35%
4Q	—	—	8.77	-16%	10.49	76%
Yr.	—	—	34.05	2%	33.23	50%
Earnings Per Share ($)						
1Q	0.64	-12%	0.73	14%	0.64	29%
2Q	0.48	-25%	0.64	2%	0.63	58%
3Q	—	—	0.51	21%	0.42	35%
4Q	—	—	0.65	-17%	0.78	77%
Yr.	—	—	2.53	2%	2.47	50%

Next earnings report expected: early January

Sturm, Ruger

Business Summary - 20-JUL-95

Sturm, Ruger & Company, Inc. primarily manufactures pistols, revolvers, rifles and shotguns for a variety of sporting and law enforcement purposes. The company also produces ferrous and nonferrous investment castings.

Business segment contributions in 1994 were:

	Sales	Profits
Firearms	92%	94%
Investment castings	8%	6%

The company believes it is the largest U.S. firearms manufacturer and the only one offering products in all four industry categories (pistols, revolvers, rifles and shotguns).

Firearms, which are sold under the Ruger trademark, consist of .22-caliber target pistols; single-action revolvers in various calibers from .22 to .44 magnum; .22 caliber sporting carbines; single shot and bolt-action rifles in a variety of calibers; hunting rifles in .223 and 7.62 x 39mm calibers; various models of double-action revolvers; 9mm, .40 and .45 caliber pistols; police and military automatic rifles; and over-and-under shotguns in 12, 20 and 28 gauges.

Sturm, Ruger seeks to position its products at the high end of their respective markets and does not manufacture inexpensive concealable firearms, sometimes known as "Saturday Night Specials." In addition, the company does not manufacture any firearm considered an "assault weapon" by the 1994 crime bill.

Many of the firearms introduced by the company over the years are said to have retained their popularity for decades and are sought by collectors. These firearms include the single-action Single-Six revolvers, the Number One Single-Shot rifles, the Blackhawk and Redhawk revolvers, the Model 10/22 rifles, the M77 rifles and the Red Label over-and-under shotguns.

New variations of the company's models introduced in 1994 included the P94 centerfire autoloading pistol and the 77/22 bolt-action rifle in .22 hornet caliber. In 1995, the company plans more product introductions including the Ruger Woodside over-and-under shotgun in both 12 and 20 gauges.

Ferrous, aluminum and titanium investment casting facilities produce parts used in the company's firearms, as well as for outside commercial customers in several different industries.

Important Developments

Apr. '95—Sturm, Ruger announced that Gerald W. Bersett, president of the Winchester division of Olin Corp., will join RGR as president and chief operating officer on August 1. In addition, William B. Ruger, Jr. will become senior executive officer and vice chairman.

Capitalization

Long Term Debt: None (3/95).

Per Share Data ($) (Year Ended Dec. 31)

	1994	1993	1992	1991	1990	1989
Tangible Bk. Val.	9.39	8.06	6.67	6.28	5.80	5.33
Cash Flow	2.92	2.79	1.95	1.43	1.33	1.66
Earnings	2.53	2.47	1.65	1.08	1.01	1.35
Dividends	1.20	1.05	1.25	0.60	0.55	0.75
Payout Ratio	47%	43%	76%	55%	55%	56%
Prices - High	33¼	32	20½	14⅞	15¾	18¼
- Low	23⅞	19⅛	13	10⅜	10¾	9¾
P/E Ratio - High	13	13	12	14	16	14
- Low	9	8	8	10	11	7

Income Statement Analysis (Million $)

	1994	%Chg	1993	%Chg	1992	%Chg	1991
Revs.	196	1%	194	24%	156	14%	137
Oper. Inc.	59.6	1%	58.8	47%	40.0	33%	30.0
Depr.	5.3	21%	4.3	5%	4.1	-12%	4.7
Int. Exp.	Nil	—	Nil	—	Nil	—	Nil
Pretax Inc.	57.0	2%	56.0	51%	37.1	53%	24.3
Eff. Tax Rate	40%	—	41%	—	40%	—	40%
Net Inc.	34.0	2%	33.2	50%	22.2	52%	14.6

Balance Sheet & Other Fin. Data (Million $)

	1994	1993	1992	1991	1990	1989
Cash	66.4	59.6	31.4	22.3	9.0	14.6
Curr. Assets	119	106	85.5	77.0	66.4	62.5
Total Assets	169	150	124	116	107	100
Curr. Liab.	24.7	24.6	18.5	16.0	13.9	12.3
LT Debt	Nil	Nil	Nil	Nil	Nil	Nil
Common Eqty.	126	108	89.7	84.4	78.0	71.6
Total Cap.	126	108	89.7	84.4	78.0	71.6
Cap. Exp.	12.4	7.3	3.5	3.0	7.1	8.2
Cash Flow	39.3	37.6	26.3	19.2	17.9	22.3

Ratio Analysis

	1994	1993	1992	1991	1990	1989
Curr. Ratio	4.8	4.3	4.6	4.8	4.8	5.1
% LT Debt of Cap.	Nil	Nil	Nil	Nil	Nil	Nil
% Net Inc.of Revs.	17.3	17.1	14.2	10.7	10.0	13.6
% Ret. on Assets	21.3	24.2	18.4	13.1	13.0	19.0
% Ret. on Equity	29.0	33.5	25.4	18.0	18.1	26.8

Dividend Data —Dividends have been paid since 1955.

Amt. of Div. $	Date Decl.	Ex-Div. Date	Stock of Record	Payment Date
0.300	Oct. 25	Nov. 25	Dec. 01	Dec. 15 '94
0.350	Jan. 20	Feb. 23	Mar. 01	Mar. 15 '95
0.350	Apr. 25	May. 25	Jun. 01	Jun. 15 '95
0.350	Jul. 18	Aug. 30	Sep. 01	Sep. 15 '95

Data as orig. reptd.; bef. results of disc. opers. and/or spec. items. Per share data adj. for stk. divs. as of ex-div. date. E-Estimated. NA-Not Available. NM-Not Meaningful. NR-Not Ranked.

Office—Lacey Place, Southport, CT 06490. **Tel**—(203) 259-7843. **Chrmn, CEO & Treas**—W. B. Ruger. **Pres**—W. B. Ruger Jr. **Exec VP-CFO**—J. M. Kingsley Jr. **Secy**—Leslie M. Gasper. **Dirs**—N. Anderson Jr., R. T. Cunniff, T. Hornor, P. X. Kelley, J. M. Kingsley Jr., W. B. Ruger, W. B. Ruger Jr., J. E. Service, S. B. Terhune. **Transfer Agent & Registrar**—Harris Trust Co. of New York, NYC. **Incorporated** in Delaware in 1969. **Empl-** 1,910. **S&P Analyst:** D.J.B.

STANDARD & POOR'S

STOCK REPORTS

Summit Bancorporation

NASDAQ Symbol **SUBN**

In S&P SmallCap 600

18-SEP-95 **Industry:** Banking

Summary: Summit Bancorporation is a $5.5 billion-asset, New Jersey bank holding company that recently signed a definitive agreement to be acquired by UJB Financial Corp.

S&P Opinion: Hold (★★★)

Recent Price • 28 3/8 | Yield • 3.0%

52 Wk Range • 29 1/8-18 | 12-Mo. P/E • 29.9

Quantitative Evaluations

Outlook (1 Lowest—5 Highest) • **2+**

Fair Value • **24 7/8**

Risk • **Low**

Earn./Div. Rank • **A-**

Technical Eval. • **Bullish** since 7/95

Rel. Strength Rank (1 Lowest—99 Highest) • **90**

Insider Activity • **NA**

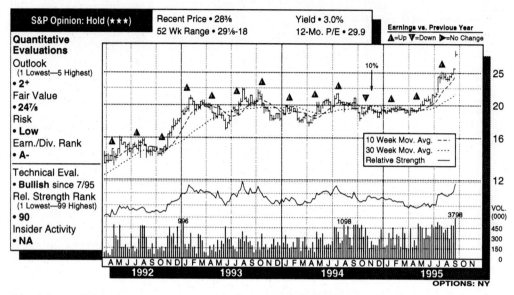

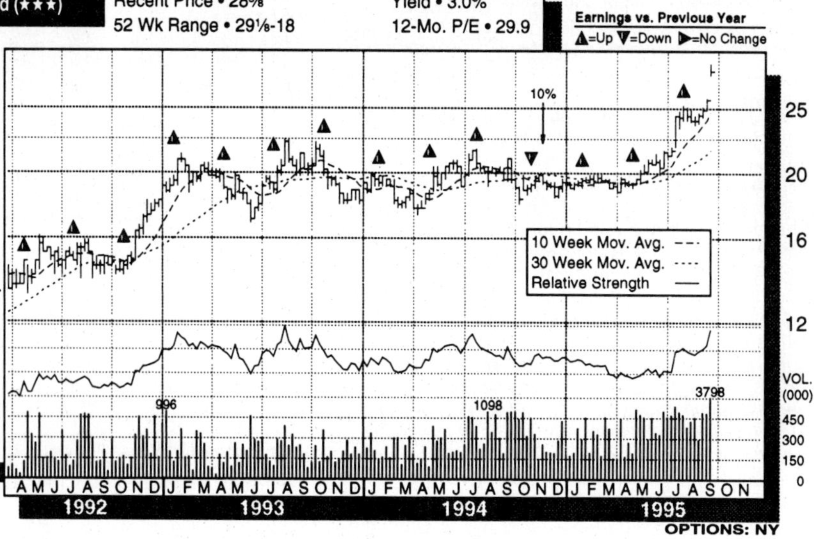

OPTIONS: NY

Overview - 18-SEP-95

Summit's aggressive cost containment and growth strategies favorably impacted earnings in the first six months of 1995, as it reported record net income for the period. Earnings of $1.03 a share were 32% higher than those of 1994's first half. Much of the gain was due to a 21% rise in total interest income, wider net interest margins, and declining noninterest expenses. The efficiency ratio improved to 55.9% in the second quarter of 1995. Net interest margins should continue to recover as a result of the current favorable interest rate environment. Asset quality has improved due to the sale of $33.9 million of non-performing real estate loans in 1994, and the loan loss provision is not expected to be a drag on earnings.

Valuation - 18-SEP-95

SUBN shares rose sharply on news of its agreement to merge with UJB Financial Corp. At 2.2 times tangible book value, and 12.5 times estimated 1996 earnings, SUBN stock currently trades at a premium, and is not expected to outperform the overall market. Given a 6% discount to the acquisition price, which at current levels approximates $30.15 a share, SUBN is a worthwhile hold for modest capital gains until completion of the merger, expected in the first quarter of 1996. The transaction still faces regulatory and shareholder approval.

Key Stock Statistics

S&P EPS Est. 1995	2.10	Tang. Bk. Value/Share	13.00
P/E on S&P Est. 1995	13.5	Beta	0.46
S&P EPS Est. 1996	2.30	Shareholders	8,000
Dividend Rate/Share	0.84	Market cap. (B)	$0.953
Shs. outstg. (M)	33.6	Inst. holdings	37%
Avg. daily vol. (M)	0.304	Insider holdings	NA

Value of $10,000 invested 5 years ago: $ 24,382

Fiscal Year Ending Dec. 31

	1995	% Change	1994	% Change	1993	% Change
Revenues (Million $)						
1Q	106.9	13%	94.30	26%	74.89	-6%
2Q	112.8	17%	96.10	23%	78.22	-1%
3Q	—	—	100.2	31%	76.61	-2%
4Q	—	—	103.2	39%	74.23	-4%
Yr.	—	—	393.8	30%	304.0	-3%
Income (Million $)						
1Q	17.28	34%	12.86	29%	9.94	62%
2Q	17.93	33%	13.47	27%	10.62	46%
3Q	—	—	-18.47	NM	10.74	39%
4Q	—	—	16.54	49%	11.12	33%
Yr.	—	—	24.40	-42%	42.42	44%
Earnings Per Share ($)						
1Q	0.51	34%	0.38	7%	0.35	39%
2Q	0.52	30%	0.40	7%	0.37	37%
3Q	E0.52	NM	-0.57	NM	0.38	35%
4Q	E0.55	12%	0.49	25%	0.39	30%
Yr.	E2.10	NM	0.70	-53%	1.50	35%

Next earnings report expected: late October

Summit Bancorporation

Business Summary - 13-SEP-95

The Summit Bancorporation, a New Jersey bank holding company ($5.5 billion in assets), owns Summit Bank, a commercial bank operating a total of 90 retail banking offices throughout the state. The consolidation of three former subsidiary banks into Summit Bank was consummated during 1993. The company also operates specialized financial service affiliates, including Summit Mortgage Co., which provides mortgage origination services and Beechwood Insurance Agency, Inc.

Total average loans for 1994 of $3.23 billion ($3.03 billion for 1993) was divided as follows:

	1994	1993
Real estate-residential	40%	36%
Real estate-commercial	24%	24%
Commercial	19%	22%
Consumer	14%	15%
Real estate-construction	3%	3%

The allowance for possible loan losses at December 31, 1994, totaled $91.2 million (2.64% of gross loans outstanding), down from $94.9 million (3.02%) a year earlier. Net loan chargeoffs during 1994 amounted to $11.8 million (0.36% of average loans), versus $19.5 million (0.64%) in 1993. Nonperforming assets totaled $50.3 million (1.45% of total loans and other real estate owned) at December 31, 1994, down from $114.6 million (3.61%) a year earlier.

Total deposits of $4.41 billion at December 31, 1994 were 18% demand, 37% savings and NOW accounts, 17% money market, 5% certificates of deposit of $100,000 and more and 23% other time. On a tax-equivalent basis, the average yield on interest-earning assets was 6.86% in 1994 (7.03% in 1993), while the average rate paid on interest-bearing liabilities was 3.12% (3.15%), for a net spread of 3.74% (3.88%).

Important Developments

Sep. '95—Summit signed a definitive agreement to merge with UJB Financial Corp. (UJB) in a stock-for-stock exchange whereby SUBN shareholders will receive 0.90 shares of UJB common stock for each share of Summit in a tax-free exchange. Based on the recent average closing price of UJB common stock, the transaction has a value of $31.95 per share for a total of $1.2 billion. The new corporation will operate under the Summit Bank Corp. name, and the transaction is expected to close in the first quarter of 1996.

Capitalization

Long Term Debt: $317,187,000 (6/95).
Adjustable-Rate Cum. Pfd. Stk.: 504,000 shs. (no par; $25 stated value).

Per Share Data ($)

(Year Ended Dec. 31)

	1994	1993	1992	1991	1990	1989
Tangible Bk. Val.	12.01	12.29	11.44	10.95	10.55	12.26
Earnings	0.70	1.50	1.11	0.91	-0.65	2.34
Dividends	0.78	0.74	0.73	0.73	0.73	0.67
Payout Ratio	112%	49%	66%	80%	NM	29%
Prices - High	21¾	22½	19⅜	13	15⅞	20
- Low	17¼	16⅞	11⅛	7	8⅛	14⅜
P/E Ratio - High	31	15	17	14	NM	9
- Low	25	11	10	8	NM	6

Income Statement Analysis (Million $)

	1994	%Chg	1993	%Chg	1992	%Chg	1991
Net Int. Inc.	211	23%	171	5%	163	9%	149
Tax Equiv. Adj.	4.1	-10%	4.6	10%	4.2	-16%	4.9
Non Int. Inc.	51.7	10%	47.1	18%	39.9	19%	33.5
Loan Loss Prov.	8.0	-39%	13.2	-44%	23.5	2%	23.0
% Exp/Op Revs.	80%	—	64%	—	65%	—	69%
Pretax Inc.	41.0	-35%	63.0	41%	44.7	52%	29.5
Eff. Tax Rate	41%	—	33%	—	34%	—	28%
Net Inc.	24.4	-42%	42.4	44%	29.4	39%	21.2
% Net Int. Marg.	4.30%	—	4.60%	—	4.70%	—	4.50%

Balance Sheet & Other Fin. Data (Million $)

	1994	1993	1992	1991	1990	1989
Earning Assets:						
Money Mkt.	NA	240	148	128	86.0	155
Inv. Securities	1,631	1,160	1,089	791	690	542
Com'l Loans	727	597	543	626	697	990
Other Loans	2,722	2,024	1,935	1,873	1,931	1,869
Total Assets	5,467	4,312	4,059	3,764	3,718	3,865
Demand Deposits	781	662	635	551	524	562
Time Deposits	3,628	2,948	2,942	2,790	2,723	2,713
LT Debt	339	162	16.0	21.0	51.0	123
Common Eqty.	412	351	318	247	230	268

Ratio Analysis

	1994	1993	1992	1991	1990	1989
% Ret. on Assets	0.5	1.0	0.8	0.6	NM	1.2
% Ret. on Equity	5.5	12.5	9.8	8.5	NM	16.6
% Loan Loss Resv.	2.6	3.2	3.4	3.3	3.1	1.6
% Loans/Deposits	78.2	72.6	69.3	74.8	80.9	87.3
% Equity to Assets	7.9	8.1	7.5	6.4	7.0	7.0

Dividend Data —The company or its predecessors have paid cash dividends in each year since 1911. A dividend reinvestment plan is available.

Amt. of Div. $	Date Decl.	Ex-Div. Date	Stock of Record	Payment Date
0.210	Oct. 18	Nov. 16	Nov. 22	Dec. 15 '94
10%	Oct. 18	Nov. 16	Nov. 22	Dec. 15 '94
0.210	Jan. 17	Feb. 13	Feb. 17	Mar. 15 '95
0.210	Apr. 18	May. 17	May. 23	Jun. 15 '95
0.210	Jul. 18	Aug. 21	Aug. 23	Sep. 15 '95

Data as orig. reptd.; bef. results of disc opers. and/or spec. items. Per share data adj. for stk. divs. as of ex-div. date. E-Estimated. NA-Not Available. NM-Not Meaningful. NR-Not Ranked.

Office—One Main St., Chatham, NJ 07928. **Tel**—(201) 701-2666. **Chrmn**—T. D. Sayles, Jr. **Pres & CEO**—R. G. Cox. **EVP, CFO & Investor Contact**—John R. Feeney. **VP-Secy**—J. F. Kuntz. **Dirs**—A. G. Anderson, S. R. Benjamin, J. C. Brady, Jr., R. G. Cox, S. V. Gilman, Jr., P. Hardin, W. B. Lum, S. G. McClellan III, R. W. Parsons, Jr., T. D. Sayles, Jr., R. Schley III, O. R. Smith, D. G. Watson, K. B. Wood. **Transfer Agent & Registrar**—Chemical Bank, NYC. **Incorporated** in New Jersey in 1973. **Empl**-1,623. **S&P Analyst:** Thomas C Ferguson

STANDARD & POOR'S

STOCK REPORTS

Summit Technology

NASDAQ Symbol **BEAM**

In S&P SmallCap 600

04-OCT-95

Industry: Medical equipment/ supply

Summary: This company develops, makes and sells ophthalmic laser systems used to treat common refractive vision disorders.

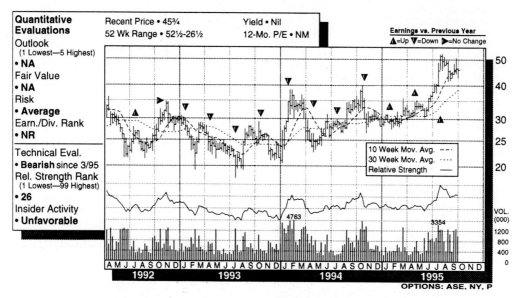

Quantitative Evaluations

Outlook (1 Lowest—5 Highest)
• **NA**

Fair Value
• **NA**

Risk
• **Average**

Earn./Div. Rank
• **NR**

Technical Eval.
• **Bearish** since 3/95

Rel. Strength Rank (1 Lowest—99 Highest)
• **26**

Insider Activity
• **Unfavorable**

Recent Price • 45¾
52 Wk Range • 52½-26½

Yield • Nil
12-Mo. P/E • NM

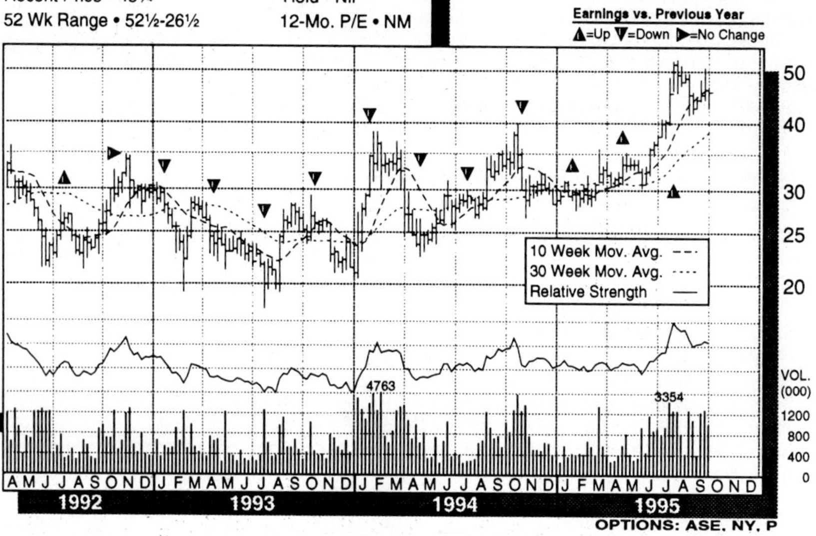

OPTIONS: ASE, NY, P

Business Profile - 04-OCT-95

Summit obtained final FDA marketing approval in March 1995 for its excimer laser system for use with a procedure called phototherapeutic keratectomy (PTK) in the treatment of nearsightedness. The company now believes it has a significant lead over its competitors in bringing products to the marketplace. Summit plans to increase sales and marketing efforts to promote vision correction procedures and plans to operate clinics that will perform laser vision correction.

Operational Review - 04-OCT-95

Revenues, which declined in 1994 due to lower international sales, advanced sharply in the first half of 1995, reflecting higher sales of the excimer system in the U.S. and product upgrade revenue. Gross margins widened on the higher sales volume, but were partly offset by increased costs incurred for product upgrades and revisions. The net loss, which widened during 1994, narrowed significantly.

Stock Performance - 29-SEP-95

In the past 30 trading days, BEAM's shares have declined 6%, compared to a 5% rise in the S&P 500. Average trading volume for the past five days was 197,060 shares, compared with the 40-day moving average of 230,141 shares.

Key Stock Statistics

Dividend Rate/Share	Nil	Shareholders	4,300
Shs. outstg. (M)	16.8	Market cap. (B)	$0.715
Avg. daily vol. (M)	0.256	Inst. holdings	17%
Tang. Bk. Value/Share	1.84	Insider holdings	NA
Beta	2.09		

Value of $10,000 invested 5 years ago: $ 55,454

Fiscal Year Ending Dec. 31

	1995	% Change	1994	% Change	1993	% Change
Revenues (Million $)						
1Q	7.11	94%	3.66	-41%	6.20	-5%
2Q	9.26	58%	5.86	-32%	8.66	NM
3Q	—	—	6.50	-8%	7.09	-12%
4Q	—	—	8.19	67%	4.90	-39%
Yr.	—	—	24.21	-10%	26.80	-14%
Income (Million $)						
1Q	-1.99	NM	-4.22	NM	-1.06	NM
2Q	-1.98	NM	-4.27	NM	-0.80	NM
3Q	—	—	-3.19	NM	-1.80	NM
4Q	—	—	-3.70	NM	-5.20	NM
Yr.	—	—	-15.38	NM	-9.15	NM
Earnings Per Share ($)						
1Q	-0.12	NM	-0.26	NM	-0.07	NM
2Q	-0.12	NM	-0.26	NM	-0.05	NM
3Q	—	—	-0.19	NM	-0.11	NM
4Q	—	—	-0.22	NM	-0.32	NM
Yr.	—	—	-0.94	NM	-0.59	NM

Next earnings report expected: early November

Summit Technology

Business Summary - 04-OCT-95

Summit Technology is a worldwide leader in the development, manufacture and sale of ophthalmic laser systems designed to correct common refractive vision disorders, such as nearsightedness, farsightedness and astigmatism. The company believes that outpatient procedures performed with its products will make it possible for many of the more than 100 million people in the U.S. who use eyeglasses or contact lenses to correct refractive vision disorders, to eliminate or reduce their reliance on corrective eyewear.

Summit's principal product is OmniMed, a fully integrated ophthalmic surgical workstation (which incorporates an excimer or a holmium laser system) for use by ophthalmologists to perform procedures to treat refractive and other ophthalmic disorders.

The primary use of the OmniMed/Excimer has been to treat myopia (nearsightedness) using a procedure called Photorefractive Keratectomy (PRK). It is estimated that 60 million people in the U.S. suffer from myopia. Summit's Excimer Laser Systems have been used to perform PRK to treat myopia on more than 2,500 eyes in the U.S., pursuant to clinical trials approved by the FDA. Its products are also used to treat hyperopia (farsightedness), astigmatism and other ophthalmic disorders, including: the use of the OmniMed/Excimer (used with Summit's erodible mask) to treat hyperopia, astigmatism and certain combinations of refractive disorders; the use of the OmniMed/Holmium to treat hyperobia and astigmatism; the use of the OmniMed/Excimer to treat corneal pathologies with Phototherapeutic Keratectomy (PTK); and the use of the OmniMed/Holmium to treat symptoms of glaucoma.

Summit has sold over 300 systems worldwide. Sales of systems outside the U.S. is currently unrestricted in over 40 countries, including most of Europe. In addition to the U.S., the company is seeking to obtain regulatory approval to sell the system in Japan, Mexico, and Taiwan.

Important Developments

Sep. '95—The company received a formal notice of approvability from the FDA for its excimer laser to treat nearsightedness with the PRK procedure. Summit is the only company to reach this regulatory milestone, which is generally the last step in the approval process before the FDA grants final approval of the device. Separately, Summit filed a registration statement to offer 2.2 million common shares in a public offering.

Mar. '95—Summit received FDA approval to commercially market its excimer laser systems in the U.S. for PTK. Summit is the only company authorized to sell excimer laser systems in the U.S. for ophthamic applications.

Capitalization

Long Term Debt: $1,228,000 (6/95).

Per Share Data ($)

(Year Ended Dec. 31)

	1994	1993	1992	1991	1990	1989
Tangible Bk. Val.	2.26	2.48	1.98	2.04	0.80	1.02
Cash Flow	-0.80	-0.48	0.06	0.08	-0.02	-0.15
Earnings	-0.94	-0.59	-0.03	0.04	-0.05	-0.17
Dividends	Nil	Nil	Nil	Nil	Nil	Nil
Payout Ratio	Nil	Nil	Nil	Nil	Nil	Nil
Prices - High	40	$30\frac{3}{4}$	$38\frac{1}{2}$	$28\frac{3}{4}$	$18\frac{5}{8}$	$15\frac{7}{8}$
- Low	$20\frac{1}{2}$	18	$21\frac{1}{4}$	$9\frac{7}{8}$	$5\frac{7}{8}$	$2\frac{3}{8}$
P/E Ratio - High	NM	NM	NM	NM	NM	NM
- Low	NM	NM	NM	NM	NA	NA

Income Statement Analysis (Million $)

	1994	%Chg	1993	%Chg	1992	%Chg	1991
Revs.	24.2	-10%	26.8	-14%	31.1	41%	22.0
Oper. Inc.	-13.2	NM	-7.2	NM	1.0	NM	1.0
Depr.	2.3	35%	1.7	31%	1.3	79%	0.7
Int. Exp.	NA	—	0.1	9%	0.1	83%	0.1
Pretax Inc.	-15.4	NM	-9.1	NM	-0.4	NM	1.0
Eff. Tax Rate	NM	—	NM	—	NM	—	47%
Net Inc.	15.4	NM	-9.1	NM	-0.4	NM	0.5

Balance Sheet & Other Fin. Data (Million $)

	1994	1993	1992	1991	1990	1989
Cash	17.2	10.9	8.6	17.1	5.9	7.3
Curr. Assets	35.5	36.6	32.7	31.0	11.4	10.5
Total Assets	51.2	50.5	38.8	35.5	13.7	11.5
Curr. Liab.	12.1	10.0	8.2	5.4	3.4	1.4
LT Debt	1.2	0.2	0.7	0.4	0.1	0.0
Common Eqty.	37.9	40.4	29.9	29.7	10.1	10.1
Total Cap.	39.1	40.5	30.6	30.1	10.3	10.1
Cap. Exp.	1.2	3.1	1.8	2.0	1.2	0.8
Cash Flow	-13.1	-7.5	0.9	1.2	-0.3	-1.3

Ratio Analysis

	1994	1993	1992	1991	1990	1989
Curr. Ratio	2.9	3.7	4.0	5.8	3.4	7.7
% LT Debt of Cap.	3.0	0.4	2.4	1.3	1.2	0.1
% Net Inc.of Revs.	NM	NM	NM	2.4	NM	NM
% Ret. on Assets	NM	NM	NM	2.0	NM	NM
% Ret. on Equity	NM	NM	NM	2.5	NM	NM

Dividend Data —No dividends have been paid.

Data as orig. reptd.; bef. results of disc. opers. and/or spec. items. Per share data adj. for stk. divs. as of ex-div. date. E-Estimated. NA-Not Available. NM-Not Meaningful. NR-Not Ranked.

Office—21 Hickory Drive, Waltham, MA 02154. **Tel**—(617) 890-1234. **Chrmn, Pres & CEO**—D. F. Muller. **SVP & COO**—R. H. Krauss. **CFO**—R. Bhatt. **Investor Contact**—Paula Elliott. **Dirs**—J. A. Bernfeld, R. F. Miller, D. F. Muller, J. A. Norris, R. M. Traskos. **Transfer Agent & Registrar**—American Stock Transfer & Trust Co., NYC. **Incorporated** in Massachusetts in 1985. **Empl**-211. **S&P Analyst:** Philip J. Birbara

STANDARD & POOR'S

STOCK REPORTS

SunGard Data Systems

NASDAQ Symbol **SNDT**

In S&P SmallCap 600

11-OCT-95 **Industry:** Data Processing

Summary: The only large specialized provider of proprietary investment support systems, this company is also the pioneer of comprehensive computer disaster recovery services.

Quantitative Evaluations

Outlook (1 Lowest—5 Highest)
• 3+

Fair Value
• 28⅝

Risk
• Average

Earn./Div. Rank
• B+

Technical Eval.
• Bearish since 8/95

Rel. Strength Rank (1 Lowest—99 Highest)
• 44

Insider Activity
• Neutral

Recent Price • 28½
52 Wk Range • 31¾-17
Yield • Nil
12-Mo. P/E • 23.4

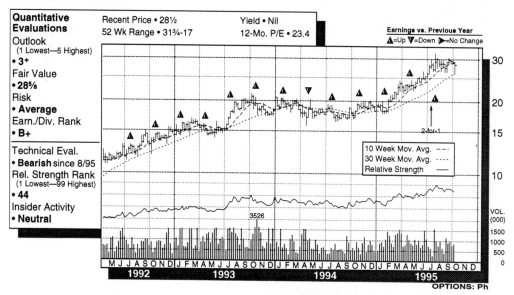

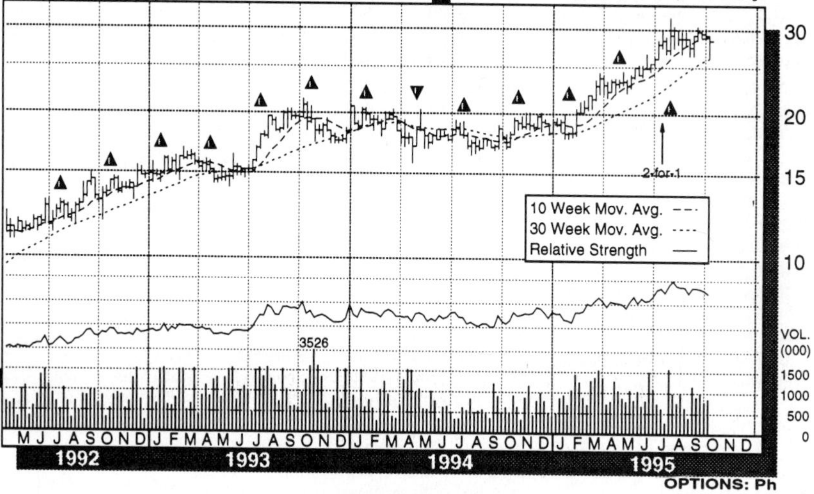

OPTIONS: Ph

Business Profile - 11-OCT-95

SunGard's business strategy involves developing long-term customer relationships, spending heavily on product development, acquiring companies that broaden or complement its existing products and markets, and rewarding its autonomous business units for their performance. The shares were split two-for-one in July 1995. The company's outlook for fully diluted earnings per share for 1995 is in the range of $1.28 to $1.31.

Operational Review - 11-OCT-95

Revenues in the six months ended June 30, 1995, rose 19%, year to year, reflecting acquisitions, increases in software licenses, professional services, data processing and software maintenance, new disaster recovery contract signings and contract renewals and increased volume in remote-access computer services and mailing services. Margins narrowed due to computer equipment upgrades and facility improvements. With higher investment income, net income was up 18%, to $0.61 a share, from $0.51.

Stock Performance - 06-OCT-95

In the past 30 trading days, SNDT's shares have declined 0.87%, compared to a 4% rise in the S&P 500. Average trading volume for the past five days was 168,440 shares, compared with the 40-day moving average of 169,508 shares.

Key Stock Statistics

Dividend Rate/Share	Nil	Shareholders	2,200
Shs. outstg. (M)	37.8	Market cap. (B)	$ 1.0
Avg. daily vol. (M)	0.170	Inst. holdings	85%
Tang. Bk. Value/Share	6.34	Insider holdings	NA
Beta	0.71		

Value of $10,000 invested 5 years ago: $ 24,000

Fiscal Year Ending Dec. 31

	1995	% Change	1994	% Change	1993	% Change
Revenues (Million $)						
1Q	121.5	19%	102.2	17%	87.50	18%
2Q	125.1	20%	104.6	11%	94.65	25%
3Q	—	—	109.9	17%	94.03	14%
4Q	—	—	120.5	15%	105.2	14%
Yr.	—	—	437.2	15%	381.4	17%
Income (Million $)						
1Q	11.12	18%	9.42	-7%	10.14	75%
2Q	12.22	17%	10.42	24%	8.39	34%
3Q	—	—	10.74	15%	9.33	41%
4Q	—	—	12.50	18%	10.61	48%
Yr.	—	—	43.09	12%	38.47	49%
Earnings Per Share ($)						
1Q	0.29	18%	0.24	-23%	0.32	73%
2Q	0.32	19%	0.27	12%	0.24	20%
3Q	—	—	0.28	14%	0.24	17%
4Q	—	—	0.32	18%	0.28	20%
Yr.	—	—	1.12	5%	1.07	30%

Next earnings report expected: late October

SunGard Data Systems

Business Summary - 06-OCT-95

SunGard Data Systems Inc. provides specialized computer services, mainly proprietary investment support systems for the financial services industry and disaster recovery services. Operating revenues in recent years were derived as follows:

	1994	1993	1992
Investment support systems	62%	64%	60%
Disaster recovery services	32%	30%	29%
Computer services & other	6%	6%	11%

Investment accounting and portfolio systems maintain the books of record of all types of large investment portfolios such as those managed by banks, mutual funds, employee retirement plans and insurance companies. The primary functions of these systems are to accept investment transactions, value portfolios using security prices received from various worldwide sources, perform complex accounting calculations and general ledger postings, and generate various accounting, audit, tax and regulatory reports. In addition to performing many investment accounting functions, the securities and derivatives systems maintain inventories of unsold securities, process trade activities, provide risk management capabilities and assist users in determining hedging strategies. SunGard also provides systems to handle trust and global custody operations, shareholder accounting, retirement plan accounting, investment reporting and analysis and document-imaging and work-flow.

SunGard's disaster recovery services include alternate-site backup, testing and recovery services for IBM, DEC, Hewlett Packard, NCR, Prime, Sequent, Stratus, Sun Microsystems, Tandem and Unisys computer installations. The company also offers recovery planning software and related consulting and educational services.

The company's computer services unit provides remote-access computer services, direct marketing and automated mass mailing and printing services.

Important Developments

Oct. '95—SNDT announced the acquisition of two health care information systems companies, Intellus Corp. (acquisition completed on Aug. 31) and MACESS Corp. (definitive agreement signed on Sep. 29), for a total of about 2.8 million SNDT common shares. Figures for the purchase price of each individual company were not disclosed.

Sep. '95—SunGard entered into a definitive agreement to acquire Renaissance Software, Inc., a provider of risk management and derivatives trading software systems, for approximately 1.5 million SNDT common shares, subject to adjustment.

Capitalization

Long Term Debt: $3,027,000 (6/95).

Per Share Data ($)

(Year Ended Dec. 31)

	1994	1993	1992	1991	1990	1989
Tangible Bk. Val.	5.60	5.18	2.70	2.28	1.50	1.46
Cash Flow	2.05	1.85	1.58	1.36	1.26	0.99
Earnings	1.12	1.07	0.82	0.70	0.68	0.61
Dividends	Nil	Nil	Nil	Nil	Nil	Nil
Payout Ratio	Nil	Nil	Nil	Nil	Nil	Nil
Prices - High	20½	21⅜	15⅝	10¼	13	11⅞
- Low	15¾	14	9	5	4¾	6¼
P/E Ratio - High	18	20	19	15	19	19
- Low	14	13	11	7	7	10

Income Statement Analysis (Million $)

	1994	%Chg	1993	%Chg	1992	%Chg	1991
Revs.	437	15%	381	17%	325	14%	284
Oper. Inc.	106	20%	88.2	19%	74.0	17%	63.0
Depr.	35.9	28%	28.0	18%	23.7	16%	20.5
Int. Exp.	0.7	-80%	3.4	-57%	7.8	-3%	8.1
Pretax Inc.	72.5	15%	63.2	39%	45.4	19%	38.3
Eff. Tax Rate	41%	—	39%	—	43%	—	44%
Net Inc.	43.1	12%	38.5	49%	25.8	20%	21.5

Balance Sheet & Other Fin. Data (Million $)

	1994	1993	1992	1991	1990	1989
Cash	103	84.8	83.4	69.5	71.5	35.6
Curr. Assets	222	191	171	145	133	86.0
Total Assets	486	418	366	313	303	193
Curr. Liab.	113	91.0	77.7	60.0	69.6	55.4
LT Debt	4.9	3.4	86.6	87.1	87.4	17.4
Common Eqty.	359	317	190	163	140	116
Total Cap.	372	327	288	253	233	138
Cap. Exp.	34.3	35.1	24.0	15.3	14.7	11.2
Cash Flow	79.0	66.5	49.5	42.0	38.2	27.8

Ratio Analysis

	1994	1993	1992	1991	1990	1989
Curr. Ratio	2.0	2.1	2.2	2.4	1.9	1.6
% LT Debt of Cap.	1.3	1.0	30.1	34.4	37.5	12.6
% Net Inc.of Revs.	9.9	10.1	8.0	7.6	7.8	8.5
% Ret. on Assets	9.5	8.9	7.6	7.0	7.9	9.6
% Ret. on Equity	12.8	14.0	14.6	14.1	15.2	15.1

Dividend Data —No cash dividends have been paid on the common shares. A two-for-one stock split is payable July 7, 1995.

Amt. of Div. $	Date Decl.	Ex-Div. Date	Stock of Record	Payment Date
2-for-1	Jun. 02	Jul. 10	Jun. 15	Jul. 07 '95

Data as orig. reptd.; bef. results of disc. opers. and/or spec. items. Per share data adj. for stk. divs. as of ex-div. date. E-Estimated. NA-Not Available. NM-Not Meaningful. NR-Not Ranked.

Office—1285 Drummers Lane, Wayne, PA 19087. **Tel**—(610) 341-8700. **Chrmn, Pres & CEO**—J. L. Mann. **VP-Fin, CFO & Investor Contact**—Michael J. Ruane. **VP & Secy**—L. A. Gross. **Dirs**—G. S. Bentley, M. C. Brooks, A. A. Eisenstat, B. Goldstein, J. L. Mann, M. Roth, M. I. Ruddock, L. J. Schoenberg. **Transfer Agent & Registrar**—Norwest Bank Minnesota, S. St. Paul. **Incorporated** in Delaware in 1982. **Empl**-2,500. **S&P Analyst:** N. Rosenberg

STANDARD & POOR'S

STOCK REPORTS

Sunrise Medical

NYSE Symbol **SMD**

In S&P SmallCap 600

20-SEP-95

Industry: Medical equipment/ supply

Summary: This company manufactures a broad line of medical products used to address rehabilitation, recovery and home respiratory needs.

Quantitative Evaluations

Outlook (1 Lowest—5 Highest)
• **5+**

Fair Value
• **32¼**

Risk
• **Average**

Earn./Div. Rank
• **B**

Technical Eval.
• **Bearish** since 7/95

Rel. Strength Rank (1 Lowest—99 Highest)
• **10**

Insider Activity
• **Neutral**

Recent Price • 25⅛

52 Wk Range • 36¾-24

Yield • Nil

12-Mo. P/E • 15.4

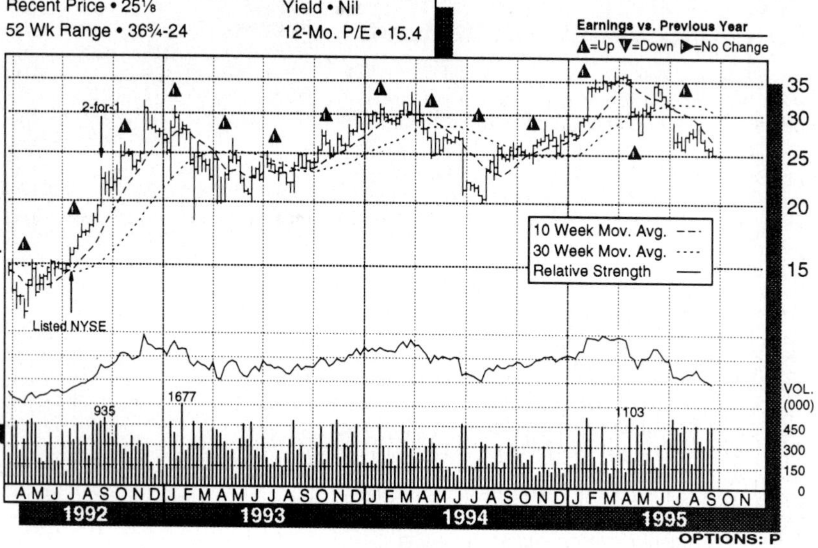

OPTIONS: P

Business Profile - 15-SEP-95

This company's rapid growth reflects contributions from acquisitions and steady market-share gains in most product areas. Acquisitions have expanded the product line as well as provided new international distribution networks. Although margins have been under pressure from recent cost containment efforts in the healthcare industry, profit growth should be sustained as the company continues to increase its revenue base. Sunrise Medical's goal is to surpass $1 billion in sales by the year 2000.

Operational Review - 15-SEP-95

Net sales advanced sharply in fiscal 1995, reflecting both internal growth and contributions from acquisitions. Margins narrowed with higher raw material costs and increased corporate expenses. Results were further penalized by higher interest expense and a higher effective tax rate, but per-share income continued its upward trend.

Stock Performance - 15-SEP-95

In the past 30 trading days, SMD's shares have declined 9%, compared to a 4% rise in the S&P 500. Average trading volume for the past five days was 90,360 shares, compared with the 40-day moving average of 79,474 shares.

Key Stock Statistics

Dividend Rate/Share	Nil	Shareholders	300
Shs. outstg. (M)	18.7	Market cap. (B)	$0.484
Avg. daily vol. (M)	0.093	Inst. holdings	58%
Tang. Bk. Value/Share	3.50	Insider holdings	NA
Beta	1.22		

Value of $10,000 invested 5 years ago: $ 52,202

Fiscal Year Ending Jun. 30

	1995	% Change	1994	% Change	1993	% Change
Revenues (Million $)						
1Q	140.6	41%	99.9	39%	71.70	38%
2Q	146.9	32%	111.1	50%	74.30	40%
3Q	148.6	24%	120.0	48%	80.98	30%
4Q	167.9	23%	137.0	49%	92.19	20%
Yr.	604.0	29%	467.9	47%	319.2	31%
Income (Million $)						
1Q	6.32	11%	5.70	—	—	—
2Q	7.03	36%	5.16	61%	3.21	70%
3Q	7.93	19%	6.68	44%	4.65	48%
4Q	9.39	13%	8.31	34%	6.19	35%
Yr.	30.68	19%	25.86	43%	18.09	51%
Earnings Per Share ($)						
1Q	0.34	6%	0.32	7%	0.30	58%
2Q	0.38	36%	0.28	22%	0.23	53%
3Q	0.42	17%	0.36	24%	0.29	21%
4Q	0.49	9%	0.45	22%	0.37	6%
Yr.	1.63	16%	1.41	17%	1.21	29%

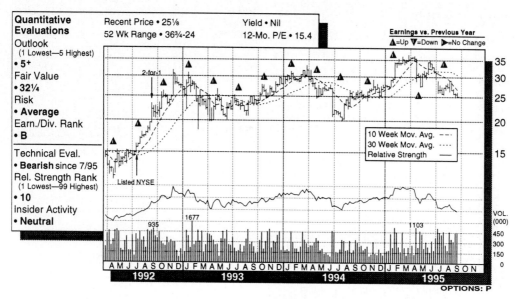

Next earnings report expected: late October

Sunrise Medical

Business Summary - 19-SEP-95

Sunrise Medical Inc. designs, manufactures and markets internationally a broad line of medical products used in institutional and homecare settings that address the recovery, rehabilitation and respiratory needs of the patient. Its products are designed to address the needs of five primary groups: the elderly, the disabled, the recovering patient, the respiratory sufferer and the health-conscious consumer.

The company's rehabilitation products (50% of fiscal 1994 sales) are designed to address the equipment needs of the elderly and disabled in an outpatient setting. The two core product lines within the rehabilitation products group are custom wheelchairs, which are individually manufactured to meet the specifications of each end-user, and patient aids, which are medical products designed to assist in walking, bathing, toileting and patient lifting. Sunrise believes it is the U.S. market leader in ultralight manual wheelchairs and that its ambulatory aids and crutches hold a leadership position in the domestic homecare and hospital markets.

Recovery products (30% of fiscal 1994 sales) promote recovery from illness and foster ease of care in institutional settings, such as hospitals and extended-care centers. The two core product lines are pressure management products, such as air therapy systems and foam mattress overlays, and healthcare beds and nursing home furniture. Sunrise is the U.S. market leader in disposable foam overlays and also in nursing home beds and furniture.

Home respiratory products, which are manufactured through DeVilbiss Healthcare Inc. (acquired in July 1993), are in three categories: aerosols, oxygen concentrators and sleep therapy. Aerosols, made up primarily of compressor nebulizers, convert liquid medicine into airborne particles to treat breathing disorders such as asthma and cystic fibrosis. Oxygen concentrators enrich normal room air up to 95% purity for patients suffering from chronic obstructive lung diseases such as emphysema and bronchitis. Sleep products are intended to help sufferers of obstructive sleep apnea by supplying continuous positive airway pressure while they are sleeping.

Important Developments

Jul. '95—SMD completed the acquisition of Coopers Healthcare Plc, a leading United Kingdom-based manufacturer of patient aids.
Jul. '95—Sunrise Medical aquired its Swiss distributor, Rospo AG.
May '95—Sunrise Medical acquired Cozy Craft, a manufacturer of a specialized line of seating products.
Apr. '95—The company acquired the Corona Group of Tours, France, for $37 million in cash and 175,000 SMD shares. Corona is a French market leader in beds for home care, nursing homes and hospitals.

Capitalization

Long Term Debt: $182,029,000 (6/95).

Per Share Data ($) (Year Ended Jun. 30)

	1995	1994	1993	1992	1991	1990
Tangible Bk. Val.	NA	3.40	6.98	1.65	2.92	0.12
Cash Flow	NA	2.37	1.86	1.53	1.31	1.10
Earnings	1.63	1.41	1.21	0.94	0.79	0.58
Dividends	Nil	Nil	Nil	Nil	Nil	Nil
Payout Ratio	Nil	Nil	Nil	Nil	Nil	Nil
Prices - High	36¾	33¼	31	31¾	19⅛	11½
- Low	24⅞	20	18⅜	11⅝	9	4
P/E Ratio - High	23	24	26	34	24	20
- Low	15	14	15	12	11	7

Income Statement Analysis (Million $)

	1994	%Chg	1993	%Chg	1992	%Chg	1991
Revs.	468	47%	319	31%	244	20%	204
Oper. Inc.	66.2	52%	43.6	42%	30.7	35%	22.7
Depr.	17.6	81%	9.7	28%	7.6	43%	5.3
Int. Exp.	6.1	43%	4.3	46%	2.9	-20%	3.7
Pretax Inc.	42.6	43%	29.7	47%	20.2	47%	13.7
Eff. Tax Rate	39%	—	39%	—	41%	—	41%
Net Inc.	25.9	43%	18.1	51%	12.0	48%	8.1

Balance Sheet & Other Fin. Data (Million $)

	1994	1993	1992	1991	1990	1989
Cash	2.6	40.0	1.3	0.1	0.2	1.0
Curr. Assets	196	146	82.9	55.6	50.3	46.8
Total Assets	478	284	202	120	115	113
Curr. Liab.	92.9	53.5	50.8	33.4	29.7	24.4
LT Debt	119	32.5	56.0	16.9	48.1	58.8
Common Eqty.	264	195	92.3	67.4	34.6	28.2
Total Cap.	385	231	151	87.0	85.0	89.0
Cap. Exp.	25.6	18.3	21.5	7.0	4.7	3.4
Cash Flow	43.4	27.8	19.6	13.4	10.0	8.4

Ratio Analysis

	1994	1993	1992	1991	1990	1989
Curr. Ratio	2.1	2.7	1.6	1.7	1.7	1.9
% LT Debt of Cap.	30.8	14.1	37.1	19.5	56.7	66.1
% Net Inc.of Revs.	5.5	5.7	4.9	4.0	3.1	2.4
% Ret. on Assets	6.8	6.7	7.3	5.9	4.6	3.1
% Ret. on Equity	11.3	11.6	14.7	14.2	16.7	13.5

Dividend Data —No cash dividends have been paid. A two-for-one stock split was effected in 1992.

Data as orig. reptd.; bef. results of disc. opers. and/or spec. items. Per share data adj. for stk. divs. as of ex-div. date. E-Estimated. NA-Not Available. NM-Not Meaningful. NR-Not Ranked.

Office—2382 Faraday Ave., Suite 200, Carlsbad, CA 92008. **Tel**—(619) 930-1500. **Chrmn & CEO**—R. H. Chandler. **Pres & COO**—L. C. Buckelew. **Sr VP-Fin, CFO & Investor Contact**—Ted N. Tarbet. **Dirs**—L. A. Ault III, L. C. Buckelew, R. H. Chandler, L. E. Cotsen, B. Heimbuch, M. H. Hutchison, W. L. Pierpoint, J. Stemler, J. R. Woodhull. **Transfer Agent & Registrar**—Chemical Trust Co. of California, Los Angeles. **Incorporated** in Delaware in 1983. **Empl**-3,586. **S&P Analyst:** Philip J. Birbara

STANDARD & POOR'S

Sunshine Mining and Refining

STOCK REPORTS

NYSE Symbol **SSC**

In S&P SmallCap 600

10-AUG-95 **Industry:** Mining/Diversified

Summary: This company mines, refines, and markets to industrial customers silver and limited quantities of antimony and copper.

Quantitative Evaluations

Outlook (1 Lowest—5 Highest)
• **NA**

Fair Value
• **NA**

Risk
• **High**

Earn./Div. Rank
• **C**

Technical Eval.
• **Bullish** since 3/94

Rel. Strength Rank (1 Lowest—99 Highest)
• **10**

Insider Activity
• **NA**

Recent Price • 1⅞ Yield • Nil
52 Wk Range • 2½-1½ 12-Mo. P/E • NM

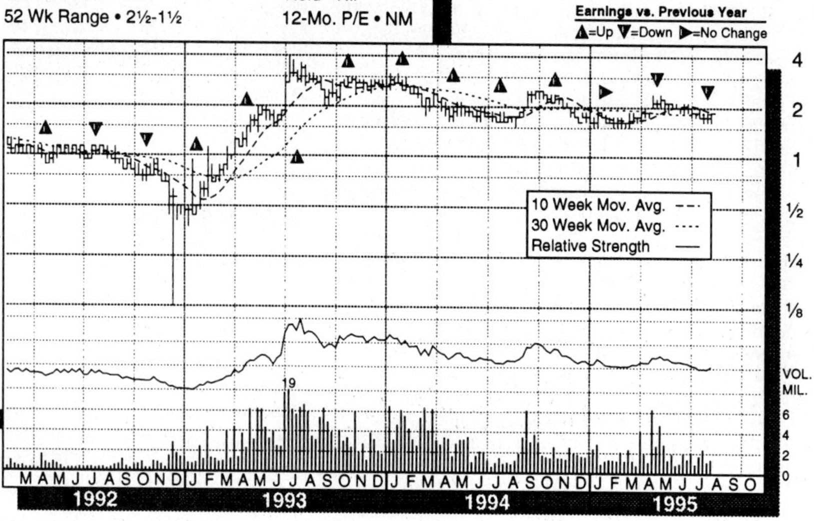

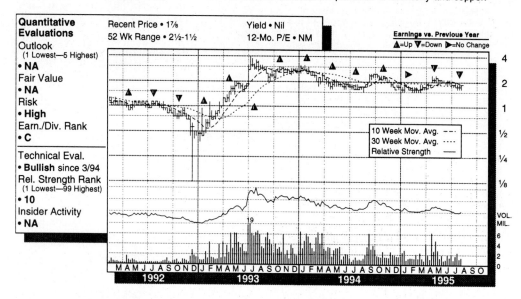

Business Profile - 10-AUG-95

SSC is pursuing three strategies for developing new properties to achieve positive earnings and cash flow. The company plans to explore previously undeveloped areas of the Sunshine Mine, utilize its patented refining technology to develop joint venture mining opportunities, and attempt to develop new sources of reserves and cash flow at other locations. As a result, SSC is active in Argentina, Peru and Colorado.

Operational Review - 08-AUG-95

Operating revenues advanced modestly in the first half of 1995, year to year. Despite the higher volume, in the absence of a $6.9 million gain from the elimination of retiree medical benefits, the net loss widened to $8,206,000 ($0.07 a share, on 6% more shares; after preferred dividends) from $2,136,000 ($0.02).

Stock Performance - 04-AUG-95

In the past 30 trading days, SSC's shares have declined 6%, compared to a 2% rise in the S&P 500. Average trading volume for the past five days was 268,260 shares, compared with the 40-day moving average of 321,728 shares.

Key Stock Statistics

Dividend Rate/Share	Nil	Shareholders	42,000
Shs. outstg. (M)	193.0	Market cap. (B)	$0.338
Avg. daily vol. (M)	0.301	Inst. holdings	8%
Tang. Bk. Value/Share	NM	Insider holdings	NA
Beta	-0.73		

Value of $10,000 invested 5 years ago: $ 5,769

Fiscal Year Ending Dec. 31

	1995	% Change	1994	% Change	1993	% Change
Revenues (Million $)						
1Q	4.56	13%	4.03	38%	2.91	—
2Q	3.47	NM	3.46	-22%	4.41	—
3Q	—	—	5.01	59%	3.15	-63%
4Q	—	—	4.92	-31%	7.11	65%
Yr.	—	—	17.41	NM	17.58	36%
Income (Million $)						
1Q	-3.63	NM	3.20	NM	-5.32	-8%
2Q	-4.58	NM	-1.06	NM	-4.37	-43%
3Q	—	—	-2.83	NM	-17.41	-13%
4Q	—	—	-4.23	NM	-1.51	-75%
Yr.	—	—	-4.92	NM	-28.61	NM
Earnings Per Share ($)						
1Q	-0.03	—	Nil	—	-0.05	NM
2Q	-0.04	NM	-0.02	NM	-0.05	NM
3Q	—	—	-0.03	NM	-0.13	NM
4Q	—	—	-0.03	NM	-0.03	NM
Yr.	—	—	-0.08	NM	-0.25	NM

Next earnings report expected: early November

Sunshine Mining and Refining

Business Summary - 10-AUG-95

Sunshine Mining and Refining Co. (formerly Sunshine Mining Co.) is a natural resource holding company which, through its Sunshine Precious Metals subsidiary, mines, refines, and markets to industrial customers silver and limited quantities of antimony and copper. In March 1992, Sunshine Precious Metals filed for protection under Chapter 11 of the U.S. Bankruptcy Code. A plan of reorganization was approved later in the year, essentially completing SSC's planned downsizing and restructuring.

The company's principal facilities are the Sunshine Mine and Refining Complex located in the Coeur d'Alene mining district, near Kellogg, Idaho, which consists primarily of the Sunshine Mine, a 1,000 ton per day mill, an antimony recovery plant, a silver refinery and related facilities. Operations were at full production until May 1991 when production was cut by 50% due to depressed silver prices.

Normal annual silver production at the Sunshine Mine exceeds 5.0 million oz. of silver, 1.8 million lbs. of copper, and 1.3 million lbs. of antimony. Pursuant to the reduced operating plan instituted during 1991, production in 1994 was 2.1 million oz. of silver, 826,000 lbs. of copper, and 474,000 lbs. of antimony. At January 1, 1995, proven and probable ore reserves at the Sunshine Mine were estimated to contain 28.8 million oz. of silver and 10.8 million lbs. of copper.

Management has stated that operating losses and cash flow deficiencies are likely to continue until silver prices recover or the company is successful in adding significant new reserves at a higher grade than has been mined in recent years.

In 1994, Sunshine processed over 800,000 ounces of custom material. In 1995, the company began phasing out its custom refining operation. In 1994, custom refining generated $3.8 million of revenues.

Important Developments

Apr. '95—SSC began suspending operation of its silver refinery during the first quarter of 1995. As a result, sales of silver and copper concentrate were made to a third-party smelter instead of refining silver bullion and copper metal for sales to commercial and industrial customers. This resulted in a shorter processing time before sales recognition, causing a drawdown of work-in-process inventories versus an inventory buildup in the first quarter of 1994.

Capitalization

Long Term Debt: $1,519,000 (3/95).
$1.19 Cum. Preferred Stock: 7,200,000 shs. ($1 par); red. at $11.94. Divd. payable in cash or stk. Divd. suspended 2/91.
Warrants: To purchase 10,100,000 com. shs. at $2.145.

Per Share Data ($) (Year Ended Dec. 31)

	1994	1993	1992	1991	1990	1989
Tangible Bk. Val.	-0.07	-0.22	-0.18	-0.26	-0.01	0.92
Cash Flow	-0.06	-0.22	-0.38	-0.41	-0.78	-0.17
Earnings	-0.08	-0.25	-0.44	-0.47	-0.88	-0.56
Dividends	Nil	Nil	Nil	Nil	Nil	Nil
Payout Ratio	Nil	Nil	Nil	Nil	Nil	Nil
Prices - High	3 1/8	4	1 1/2	2 1/8	4	4 1/4
- Low	1 1/2	3/8	1/8	3/4	1 1/4	2 7/8
P/E Ratio - High	NM	NM	NM	NM	NM	NM
- Low	NM	NM	NM	NM	NM	NM

Income Statement Analysis (Million $)

	1994	%Chg	1993	%Chg	1992	%Chg	1991
Revs.	17.0	-6%	18.0	38%	13.0	-46%	24.0
Oper. Inc.	-8.7	NM	-4.3	NM	-8.6	NM	-11.7
Depr.	4.2	-29%	5.9	-6%	6.3	-5%	6.6
Int. Exp.	1.2	-80%	6.1	-53%	13.1	-6%	14.0
Pretax Inc.	-5.0	NM	-29.0	NM	-40.0	NM	-40.0
Eff. Tax Rate	NM	—	NM	—	NM	—	NM
Net Inc.	-5.0	NM	-29.0	NM	-40.0	NM	-40.0

Balance Sheet & Other Fin. Data (Million $)

	1994	1993	1992	1991	1990	1989
Cash	27.7	5.8	8.2	16.1	21.9	75.2
Curr. Assets	41.0	20.0	20.0	32.0	86.0	109
Total Assets	117	100	113	154	222	419
Curr. Liab.	2.0	4.0	7.0	10.0	46.0	41.0
LT Debt	2.0	9.0	20.0	4.0	80.0	195
Common Eqty.	-14.0	-37.0	-26.0	-29.0	-1.0	93.0
Total Cap.	102	77.0	87.0	59.0	159	364
Cap. Exp.	Nil	1.0	Nil	1.0	2.0	17.0
Cash Flow	-11.2	-33.5	-45.5	-46.1	-75.0	-16.0

Ratio Analysis

	1994	1993	1992	1991	1990	1989
Curr. Ratio	16.5	4.7	3.0	3.2	1.9	2.6
% LT Debt of Cap.	1.5	12.4	22.6	6.7	50.7	53.6
% Net Inc.of Revs.	NM	NM	NM	NM	NM	NM
% Ret. on Assets	NM	NM	NM	NM	NM	NM
% Ret. on Equity	NM	NM	NM	NM	NM	NM

Dividend Data (No dividends have been paid since 1981.)

Data as orig. reptd.; bef. results of disc. opers. and/or spec. items. Per share data adj. for stk. divs. as of ex-div. date. E-Estimated. NA-Not Available. NM-Not Meaningful. NR-Not Ranked.

Office—877 W. Main St., Suite 600, Boise, ID 83702. **Tel**—(208) 345-0660. **CEO & Pres**—J. S. Simko. **SVP-CFO & Investor Contact**—William W. Davis. **Secy**—R. L. Saunders. **Dirs**—G. C. Andersen, V. D. Babbitt, G. M. Elvin, F. Humphreys, D. D. Jackson, H. Kaback, O. Shaffer, J. S. Simko, R. B. Smith, D. K. Stewart. **Transfer Agent & Registrar**—American Stock Transfer & Trust Co., NYC. **Incorporated** in Wash. in 1918; reincorp. in Del. in 1980. **Empl**-229. **S&P Analyst:** S.S.

STANDARD & POOR'S
STOCK REPORTS

Super Food Services

NYSE Symbol **SFS**
In S&P SmallCap 600

02-AUG-95 **Industry:** Food

Summary: This leading publicly owned food wholesaler distributes a complete line of food and non-food products to supermarkets in the south central U.S.

Quantitative Evaluations

Outlook
(1 Lowest—5 Highest)
• **2-**

Fair Value
• **11¼**

Risk
• **Average**

Earn./Div. Rank
• **B+**

Technical Eval.
• **Bearish** since 6/95

Rel. Strength Rank
(1 Lowest—99 Highest)
• **59**

Insider Activity
• **NA**

Recent Price • 12 | Yield • 3.2%
52 Wk Range • 14¼-10 | 12-Mo. P/E • 14.6

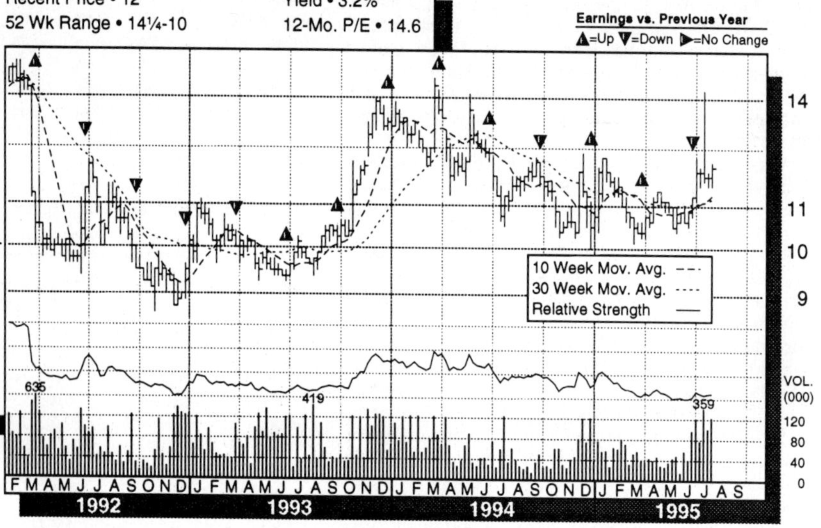

Business Profile - 31-JUL-95

This company is one of the largest food wholesalers in the U.S., distributing a complete line of food and non-food products to more than 845 supermarkets in Ohio, Michigan, Indiana, Kentucky, Tennessee and West Virginia. A decline in revenue and income over the past three years has led SFS to concentrate on expense control and productivity. The company has continued to borrow to support high inventory and receivables levels and the expenses necessary to generate new business.

Operational Review - 31-JUL-95

Sales in the 36 weeks ended May 6, 1995, were up 0.9%, year to year, reflecting increased sales to existing customers. Margins widened as a result of a more favorable product mix, which outweighed higher payroll and employee benefits costs; operating income rose 5.1%. Following a 31% rise in net interest expense due to higher interest rates and an increase in borrowings, net income edged up 1.7%, to $6,170,100 ($0.56 a share), from $6,069,221 ($0.55).

Stock Performance - 28-JUL-95

In the past 30 trading days, SFS's shares have increased 10%, compared to a 4% rise in the S&P 500. Average trading volume for the past five days was 28,740 shares, compared with the 40-day moving average of 25,441 shares.

Key Stock Statistics

Dividend Rate/Share	0.38	Shareholders	2,100
Shs. outstg. (M)	10.9	Market cap. (B)	$0.131
Avg. daily vol. (M)	0.038	Inst. holdings	54%
Tang. Bk. Value/Share	12.42	Insider holdings	NA
Beta	0.45		

Value of $10,000 invested 5 years ago: $ 6,932

Fiscal Year Ending Aug. 31

	1995	% Change	1994	% Change	1993	% Change
Revenues (Million $)						
1Q	271.2	NM	271.1	-4%	283.0	-36%
2Q	257.5	NM	257.4	-2%	262.5	-36%
3Q	260.2	3%	253.2	-4%	265.1	-26%
4Q	—	—	348.3	-2%	355.3	-2%
Yr.	—	—	1,130	-3%	1,166	-26%
Income (Million $)						
1Q	2.38	5%	2.26	10%	2.06	-17%
2Q	2.06	4%	1.99	9%	1.82	-10%
3Q	1.73	-5%	1.82	6%	1.72	NM
4Q	—	—	2.76	-24%	3.62	65%
Yr.	—	—	8.83	-4%	9.22	NM
Earnings Per Share ($)						
1Q	0.22	5%	0.21	11%	0.19	-17%
2Q	0.19	6%	0.18	6%	0.17	-11%
3Q	0.16	-6%	0.17	6%	0.16	NM
4Q	—	—	0.25	-24%	0.33	65%
Yr.	—	—	0.81	-5%	0.85	NM

Next earnings report expected: late October

Super Food Services

Business Summary - 31-JUL-95

Super Food Services is engaged in the wholesale grocery distribution business. It holds IGA (Independent Grocers' Alliance Distributing Co.) franchises for each of its warehouse locations except for Lexington, Ky. The company distributes a wide variety of food products, health and beauty aids, general merchandise and related nonfood items to about 270 independently owned IGA retail food stores, 605 other retail food stores, including independently owned stores not licensed as IGA stores, and several major chains and convenience stores, located primarily in Ohio, Michigan, Indiana, Kentucky, Tennessee and West Virginia.

SFS operates five computerized distribution centers located in Ohio (three), Michigan (one) and Kentucky (one). Each warehouse serves as a central source of supply for affiliated retailers within its operating area, handling a full line of products ranging from 10,000 to 15,000 items. Retailers order at regular intervals through direct links with the distribution center computer. The company operates about 140 tractors, 195 refrigerated trailers and 190 dry trailers.

Company operations include procurement of food products and allied items; development and administration of promotion, advertising, merchandising and insurance programs, as well as retail accounting and payroll systems; installation of computerized inventory control and ordering systems; store development services; personnel management assistance; and employee training.

SFS primarily distributes and sells nationally advertised brand products purchased directly from manufacturers, processors and suppliers or through manufacturers' representatives and brokers. It also sells IGA, Better Valu and Saver's Choice brand products and various products using its own registered trademarks: Fame, Table Treat, Table King and Gard. About 12% of fiscal 1994 sales were from private label and IGA and Better Valu brand products.

Albertson's Inc. accounted for about 22% of sales in fiscal 1992, but in June 1992 it ceased purchasing goods from SFS. As a result, the company closed its Florida division and recorded a charge of $23 million. In April 1992, the company announced the filing of a lawsuit against Albertson's, following the latter's notification to the company that it would no longer pursue the purchase of the Florida division.

Important Developments

Jun. '95—The company reported that arguments were still being heard in its case against Albertson's Inc. SFS's request for a rehearing was denied in January 1995, and Albertson's motion to recover certain costs from SFS was being heard.

Capitalization

Long Term Debt: $57,587,135 (5/95), incl. $22.2 million of capital lease obligations.

Per Share Data ($) (Year Ended Aug. 31)

	1994	1993	1992	1991	1990	1989
Tangible Bk. Val.	11.74	11.29	10.79	12.03	11.12	9.82
Cash Flow	1.47	1.51	0.30	1.85	2.24	2.05
Earnings	0.81	0.85	-0.51	1.13	1.60	1.47
Dividends	0.36	0.34	0.34	0.34	0.32	0.29
Payout Ratio	44%	40%	NM	30%	20%	20%
Prices - High	14⅝	14	16	18½	20¾	22
- Low	10¼	9¼	8⅝	12¾	14¾	17
P/E Ratio - High	18	16	NM	16	13	15
- Low	13	11	NM	11	9	12

Income Statement Analysis (Million $)

	1994	%Chg	1993	%Chg	1992	%Chg	1991
Revs.	1,130	-3%	1,166	-26%	1,573	-14%	1,826
Oper. Inc.	24.3	-5%	25.7	-9%	28.1	-20%	35.3
Depr.	7.3	NM	7.2	-18%	8.8	12%	7.8
Int. Exp.	6.3	-9%	7.0	-12%	7.9	-18%	9.7
Pretax Inc.	14.3	-6%	15.2	NM	-8.9	NM	20.1
Eff. Tax Rate	38%	—	39%	—	NM	—	39%
Net Inc.	8.8	-4%	9.2	NM	-5.5	NM	12.2

Balance Sheet & Other Fin. Data (Million $)

	1994	1993	1992	1991	1990	1989
Cash	15.8	14.4	15.6	12.9	12.9	10.5
Curr. Assets	160	153	163	216	196	183
Total Assets	258	248	252	304	271	248
Curr. Liab.	67.0	55.0	65.5	85.9	70.5	74.0
LT Debt	56.0	60.3	54.0	87.4	78.3	67.2
Common Eqty.	133	128	122	130	122	106
Total Cap.	189	188	177	218	200	174
Cap. Exp.	18.0	5.2	NA	NA	12.0	7.4
Cash Flow	16.1	16.4	3.2	20.0	24.1	22.1

Ratio Analysis

	1994	1993	1992	1991	1990	1989
Curr. Ratio	2.4	2.8	2.5	2.5	2.8	2.5
% LT Debt of Cap.	29.6	32.1	30.6	40.0	39.1	38.6
% Net Inc.of Revs.	0.8	0.8	NM	0.7	1.0	0.9
% Ret. on Assets	3.5	3.7	NM	4.2	6.6	6.7
% Ret. on Equity	6.8	7.4	NM	9.6	15.0	15.8

Dividend Data (Dividends have been paid since 1971. A "poison pill" stock purchase rights plan was adopted in 1989.)

Amt. of Div. $	Date Decl.	Ex-Div. Date	Stock of Record	Payment Date
0.095	Oct. 21	Nov. 15	Nov. 21	Dec. 15 '94
0.095	Dec. 13	Feb. 13	Feb. 20	Mar. 15 '95
0.095	Mar. 27	May. 16	May. 22	Jun. 15 '95
0.095	May. 24	Aug. 18	Aug. 22	Sep. 15 '95

Data as orig. reptd.; bef. results of disc. opers. and/or spec. items. Per share data adj. for stk. divs. as of ex-div. date. E-Estimated. NA-Not Available. NM-Not Meaningful. NR-Not Ranked.

Office—3233 Newmark Drive, Dayton, OH 45342 (Kettering Box 2323, Dayton, OH 45429). **Tel**—(513) 439-7500. **Chrmn & CEO**—J. Twyman. **Vice Chrmn & Secy**—J. Demos. **Pres & COO**—S. Robinson. **SVP-Fin, Treas & Investor Contact**—Robert F. Koogler. **Dirs**—J. W. Berry, J. H. Covington, J. Demos, T. S. Haggai, E. H. Jennings, S. Robinson, C. E. Shaffer, J. Twyman. **Transfer Agent & Registrar**—Mellon Securities Transfer Services, Ridgefield Park, N.J. **Incorporated** in Delaware in 1957. **Empl**-1,700. **S&P Analyst:** Julie Santoriello

STANDARD & POOR'S

STOCK REPORTS

Sybron International

NYSE Symbol **SYB**

In S&P SmallCap 600

11-OCT-95 **Industry:** Medical equipment/ supply

Summary: Through its operating subsidiaries, this company designs, makes and markets laboratory and dental supply products worldwide.

Quantitative Evaluations

Outlook (1 Lowest—5 Highest)
• **NA**

Fair Value
• **NA**

Risk
• **Low**

Earn./Div. Rank
• **NR**

Technical Eval.
• **Bullish** since 8/94

Rel. Strength Rank (1 Lowest—99 Highest)
• **22**

Insider Activity
• **Unfavorable**

Recent Price • 37⅞ | 52 Wk Range • 43¼-31 | Yield • Nil | 12-Mo. P/E • 18.0

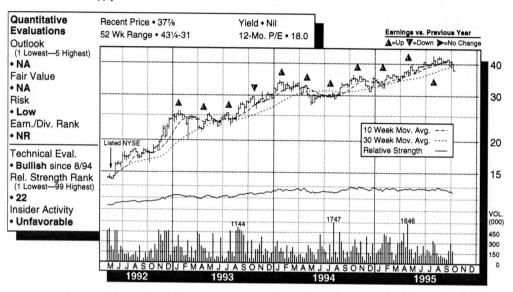

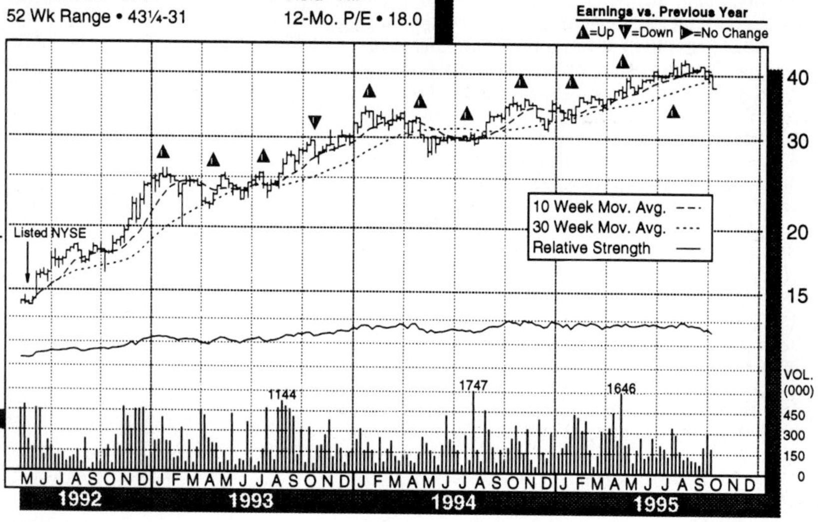

Business Profile - 05-OCT-95

Sybron's 1995 acquisitions, including Metrex Research (March), Excellence in Endodontics (April), the lab products division of Richard-Allan Medical Industries (May), and BTR's group of Nunc plastic laboratory companies (July), should expand its position in the dental and laboratory markets. Weakness in the dollar has also helped revenue growth as exports account for over a third of total sales. Continued cost reduction efforts have helped boost operating margins as well.

Operational Review - 11-OCT-95

Net sales in the nine months ended June 30, 1995, rose 14% year to year, aided by strong international growth, favorable exchange rates and recent acquisitions. Margins improved, reflecting process improvements and the introduction of new products; operating profit increased 18%. After taxes at 39.4% versus 39.3%, net income advanced 21% to $37.3 million ($1.59 a share) from $30.9 million ($1.33). Results for the prior-year period exclude a special charge of $0.02 a share.

Stock Performance - 06-OCT-95

In the past 30 trading days, SYB's shares have declined 7%, compared to a 4% rise in the S&P 500. Average trading volume for the past five days was 36,940 shares, compared with the 40-day moving average of 29,787 shares.

Key Stock Statistics

Dividend Rate/Share	Nil	Shareholders	400
Shs. outstg. (M)	23.2	Market cap. (B)	$0.859
Avg. daily vol. (M)	0.037	Inst. holdings	72%
Tang. Bk. Value/Share	NM	Insider holdings	NA
Beta	NA		

Value of $10,000 invested 5 years ago: NA

Fiscal Year Ending Sep. 30

	1995	% Change	1994	% Change	1993	% Change
Revenues (Million $)						
1Q	111.7	7%	104.0	11%	93.80	8%
2Q	127.9	19%	107.5	8%	99.7	2%
3Q	129.8	14%	113.3	12%	101.0	3%
4Q	—	—	114.9	14%	100.9	NM
Yr.	—	—	439.7	11%	395.4	3%
Income (Million $)						
1Q	9.95	22%	8.15	73%	4.72	141%
2Q	13.51	21%	11.20	37%	8.19	45%
3Q	13.80	20%	11.53	71%	6.73	1%
4Q	—	—	12.10	95%	6.20	-13%
Yr.	—	—	43.00	67%	25.79	21%
Earnings Per Share ($)						
1Q	0.43	23%	0.35	67%	0.21	NM
2Q	0.58	21%	0.48	33%	0.36	NM
3Q	0.59	18%	0.50	67%	0.30	58%
4Q	—	—	0.52	93%	0.27	-16%
Yr.	—	—	1.85	64%	1.13	85%

Next earnings report expected: mid November

Sybron International

Business Summary - 11-OCT-95

Sybron International Corporation is a leading maker of value-added products for the laboratory and professional orthodontic and dental markets in the U.S. and abroad. Through its operating subsidiaries, the company designs, produces and markets laboratory microscope slides, reusable and disposable plastic labware, precision heating and stirring apparatus, water purification systems and orthodontic products and dental materials.

Foreign and U.S. export sales provided 35% of revenues in both fiscal 1994 and 1993.

The laboratory segment operates through three subsidiaries. Nalge Co. (26% of fiscal 1994 revenues) develops, manufactures and markets a diversified line of reusable products (bottles, carboys, graduated ware, beakers and flasks) and disposable products (microfiltration and cryogenic storage products). Erie Scientific Co. (13%) develops, makes and markets microscope slides and cover glass, both of which are disposable. Barnstead/Thermolyne Corp. (11%) develops, manufactures and markets precision heating, stirring and temperature control apparatus, water purification systems, liquid handling equipment and replacement parts for such products.

The Sybron Dental Specialties division (49% of fiscal 1994 revenues) consists of two subsidiaries. Kerr Manufacturing Co. develops, manufactures and markets a broad range of consumable dental products, including restorative materials (amalgam alloys, composites, cavity liners and ancillary products), impression materials, endodontic instruments and materials, dental burs, preventive products, laboratory products and industrial jewelry products. Ormco Corp. develops, makes and markets a broad line of orthodontic appliances and related products, including bands, brackets, wires, adhesives and ancillary supplies and equipment used during the course of orthodontic treatment. It also manufactures and sells a line of orthodontic chairs.

Important Developments

Jul. '95—The company purchased BTR plc's Nunc group of companies, which make disposable plastic lab equipment, for approximately $170 million. Funding was provided by Sybron's credit facility. The Nunc companies expect sales of about $70 million in 1995. **May '95**—SYB's Erie Scientific unit agreed to acquire the assets of the laboratory products division of Richard-Allan Medical Industries, which has annual sales of about $9.0 million. Earlier, SYB acquired Excellence in Endodontics (4/95; $2.5 million annual sales), Metrex Research Corp. (3/95; $7 million), Owl Scientific (1/95; $4.2 million) and Sani-Tech (1/95; $12 million).

Capitalization

Long Term Debt: $249,469,000 (6/95).

Per Share Data ($)

(Year Ended Sep. 30)

	1994	1993	1992	1991	1990	1989
Tangible Bk. Val.	7.62	5.48	5.23	-8.56	NA	NA
Cash Flow	3.00	2.15	2.16	1.56	NA	NA
Earnings	1.85	1.13	0.61	0.24	NA	NA
Dividends	Nil	Nil	Nil	NA	NA	NA
Payout Ratio	Nil	Nil	Nil	NA	NA	NA
Prices - High	36¼	32	24⅜	NA	NA	NA
- Low	27½	20	14	NA	NA	NA
P/E Ratio - High	20	28	41	NA	NA	NA
- Low	15	18	23	NA	NA	NA

Income Statement Analysis (Million $)

	1994	%Chg	1993	%Chg	1992	%Chg	1991
Revs.	440	11%	395	3%	383	9%	350
Oper. Inc.	119	11%	107	10%	97.4	11%	87.5
Depr.	26.9	15%	23.3	NM	23.2	-17%	28.0
Int. Exp.	20.6	-36%	32.4	-16%	38.7	-13%	44.3
Pretax Inc.	71.2	53%	46.6	28%	36.3	116%	16.8
Eff. Tax Rate	39%	—	44%	—	40%	—	70%
Net Inc.	43.0	67%	25.8	21%	21.4	NM	5.1

Balance Sheet & Other Fin. Data (Million $)

	1994	1993	1992	1991	1990	1989
Cash	11.2	19.5	8.3	7.3	5.9	NA
Curr. Assets	179	156	140	123	120	NA
Total Assets	558	480	472	469	480	481
Curr. Liab.	95.6	91.9	88.8	79.7	71.2	NA
LT Debt	224	249	270	316	340	349
Common Eqty.	177	126	101	59.3	60.3	NA
Total Cap.	449	376	372	376	402	NA
Cap. Exp.	20.6	16.7	13.7	13.3	10.6	9.1
Cash Flow	70.0	49.1	32.3	33.1	30.2	22.3

Ratio Analysis

	1994	1993	1992	1991	1990	1989
Curr. Ratio	1.9	1.7	1.7	1.5	1.7	NA
% LT Debt of Cap.	49.8	66.3	72.7	84.0	84.6	NA
% Net Inc.of Revs.	9.8	6.5	5.6	1.4	0.7	NM
% Ret. on Assets	8.3	5.0	2.7	0.5	0.5	NM
% Ret. on Equity	28.3	20.9	NM	NM	NM	NM

Dividend Data—Debt agreements prohibit the payment of cash dividends or other cash distributions on the company's common stock. Subject to these restrictions, any future payments will depend on, among other factors, Sybron's earnings, financial condition and capital requirements.

Data as orig. reptd.; bef. results of disc. opers. and/or spec. items. Per share data adj. for stk. divs. as of ex-div. date. Bk. val. figs. for 1994, 1993, 1992 in Per Share Data tbl. incl. intangibles. E-Estimated. NA-Not Available. NM-Not Meaningful. NR-Not Ranked.

Office—411 East Wisconsin Ave., Milwaukee, WI 53202. **Tel**—(414) 274-6600. **Chrmn, Pres & CEO**—K. F. Yontz. **VP-Fin, CFO & Treas**—D. Brown. **VP-Secy**—R. J. Harris. **Dirs**—D. H. Davis Jr., R. B. Haas, T. O. Hicks, J. L. Roby, R. W. Vieser, K. F. Yontz. **Transfer Agent & Registrar**—Bank of Boston. **Incorporated** in Delaware in 1987; reincorporated in Wisconsin in 1994. **Empl**-3,900. **S&P Analyst:** Thomas Tirney

Symmetricom

NASDAQ Symbol **SYMM**

In S&P SmallCap 600

18-OCT-95 **Industry:** Electronics/Electric

Summary: SYMM manufactures specialized transmission equipment for telephone companies and private network operators, as well as semiconductors for power management applications.

Quantitative Evaluations

Outlook (1 Lowest—5 Highest)
• **NA**

Fair Value
• **NA**

Risk
• **Average**

Earn./Div. Rank
• **B**

Technical Eval.
• **Bullish** since 9/94

Rel. Strength Rank (1 Lowest—99 Highest)
• **13**

Insider Activity
• **Neutral**

Recent Price • 19¾
52 Wk Range • 26⅝-10⅞

Yield • Nil
12-Mo. P/E • 28.2

Earnings vs. Previous Year
▲=Up ▼=Down ▶=No Change

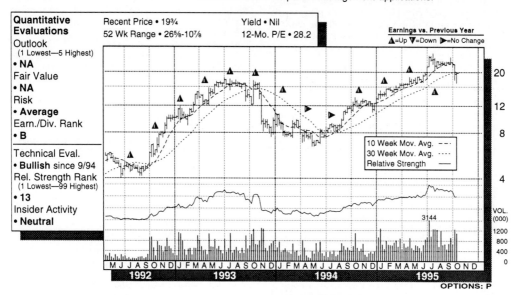

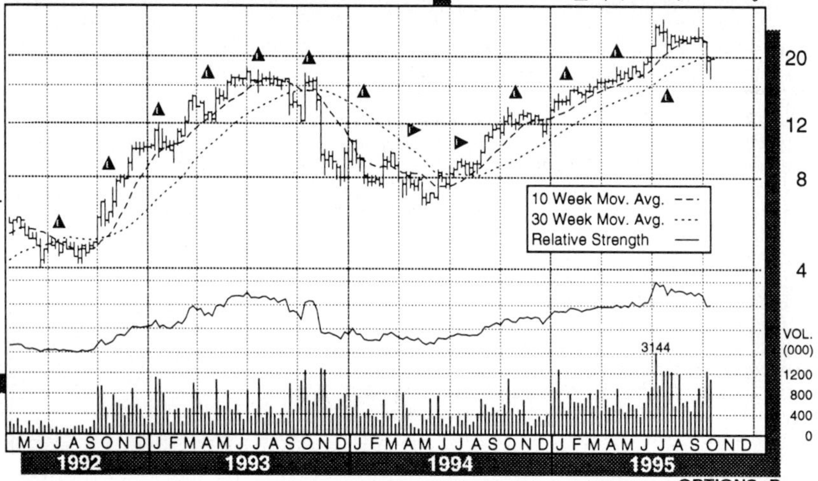

OPTIONS: P

Business Profile - 17-OCT-95

This manufacturer of specialized transmission equipment for telephone companies and private network operators also makes semiconductors for power management applications. After bottoming in fiscal 1992, share earnings have been in an uptrend. New products introduced in recent years and currently under development should provide the basis for potential future sales growth. The balance sheet is strong, with long term debt at less than 10% of capitalization at fiscal year-end 1995.

Operational Review - 17-OCT-95

Net sales for the three months ended September 30, 1995, advanced 14%, year to year. Improved gross margins and well controlled selling, general, & administrative expenses enabled operating profit to move ahead 48%. After higher other income (net) and a higher tax rate, net income was up 39%, to $0.17 a share on 5.1% more shares, from $0.13. Future results will be affected by SYMM's ability to develop new products, changes in product mix, and manufacturing efficiencies.

Stock Performance - 13-OCT-95

In the past 30 trading days, SYMM's shares have declined 11%, compared to a 4% rise in the S&P 500. Average trading volume for the past five days was 215,620 shares, compared with the 40-day moving average of 172,308 shares.

Key Stock Statistics

Dividend Rate/Share	Nil	Shareholders	1,500
Shs. outstg. (M)	15.4	Market cap. (B)	$0.295
Avg. daily vol. (M)	0.220	Inst. holdings	23%
Tang. Bk. Value/Share	3.98	Insider holdings	NA
Beta	0.36		

Value of $10,000 invested 5 years ago: $ 112,857

Fiscal Year Ending Jun. 30

	1996	% Change	1995	% Change	1994	% Change
Revenues (Million $)						
1Q	27.68	14%	24.18	NM	24.03	14%
2Q	—	—	25.59	2%	25.01	16%
3Q	—	—	26.26	8%	24.37	10%
4Q	—	—	27.08	8%	24.97	8%
Yr.	—	—	103.1	5%	98.39	12%
Income (Million $)						
1Q	2.77	39%	2.00	16%	1.72	32%
2Q	—	—	2.41	44%	1.67	14%
3Q	—	—	2.79	90%	1.47	-3%
4Q	—	—	3.15	86%	1.69	-1%
Yr.	—	—	10.35	58%	6.55	9%
Earnings Per Share ($)						
1Q	0.17	31%	0.13	18%	0.11	22%
2Q	—	—	0.15	36%	0.11	10%
3Q	—	—	0.18	80%	0.10	NM
4Q	—	—	0.20	82%	0.11	NM
Yr.	—	—	0.66	53%	0.43	7%

Next earnings report expected: mid January

Symmetricom

Business Summary - 16-OCT-95

Symmetricom, Inc. (formerly Silicon General, Inc.) conducts its business through two separate operations: Telecom Solutions (formerly the Telecom Group) and Linfinity Microelectronics, Inc. (formerly the Silicon General Semiconductor Group). Telecom Solutions designs, manufactures and markets specialized transmission, synchronization and intelligent access systems for both domestic and international telecommunications service providers. Linfinity Microelectronics designs, manufactures and markets linear and mixed signal integrated circuits used in intelligent power management, motion control, and signal conditioning applications in commercial, industrial, and defense and space markets.

Sales contributions in recent fiscal years:

	1995	1994	1993	1992
Telecom Solutions	61%	60%	65%	61%
Linfinity Microelec.	39%	40%	35%	39%

Exports (mostly to the Far East, Canada and Western Europe) accounted for 24% of net sales in fiscal 1995.

Telecom Solutions (TS) offers a broad range of time reference, or synchronization, products and digital terminal products for the telecommunications industry. Reliable synchronization is fundamental to telecommunications services as the orderly and error free transmission of data would be impossible without it.

During 1994, TS developed a new synchronization platform, the DCD500 Series, in response to evolving network requirements, such as new digital services being provided, the Synchronous Optical Network (SONET) and the Signaling System Seven (SS7) network.

TS synchronization systems are typically priced from $3,000 to $40,000.

Linfinity Microelectronics' products consist principally of linear and mixed signal, standard and custom integrated circuits (ICs) primarily for use in intelligent power management, motion control, and signal conditioning applications in the commercial, industrial, defense, and space markets.

Linfinity manufactures linear and mixed signal ICs utilizing bipolar and bipolar complementary metal oxide silicon (BiCMOS) wafer fabrication processes. Linfinity also sells ICs utilizing CMOS wafer fabrication processes. Its strategy is to continue development of more market driven standard products for use in computer and data storage, lighting, and other industries.

Important Developments

Oct. '95—SYMM said that new products are now being released to production on a regular basis at Linfinity. These new products are being designed into customers' systems.

Capitalization

Long Term Debt: $5,752,000 (9/95).

Per Share Data ($) (Year Ended Jun. 30)

	1995	1994	1993	1992	1991	1990
Tangible Bk. Val.	3.98	3.32	2.78	2.35	2.18	2.04
Cash Flow	0.99	0.80	0.73	0.37	0.37	0.34
Earnings	0.66	0.43	0.40	0.10	0.11	0.07
Dividends	Nil	Nil	Nil	Nil	Nil	Nil
Payout Ratio	Nil	Nil	Nil	Nil	Nil	Nil
Prices - High	26⅝	10⅝	18¼	10⅜	4¼	3
- Low	13⅛	6½	8⅞	3⅛	2	1¼
P/E Ratio - High	40	25	46	NM	47	43
- Low	20	15	22	NM	22	18

Income Statement Analysis (Million $)

	1995	%Chg	1994	%Chg	1993	%Chg	1992
Revs.	103	5%	98.4	12%	87.9	28%	68.8
Oper. Inc.	16.1	14%	14.1	9%	12.9	90%	6.8
Depr.	5.3	-9%	5.8	17%	4.9	33%	3.7
Int. Exp.	0.6	2%	0.6	-2%	0.6	NM	0.6
Pretax Inc.	11.6	43%	8.1	6%	7.7	175%	2.8
Eff. Tax Rate	11%	—	19%	—	22%	—	52%
Net Inc.	10.3	57%	6.6	9%	6.0	NM	1.3

Balance Sheet & Other Fin. Data (Million $)

	1995	1994	1993	1992	1991	1990
Cash	33.2	21.3	18.2	10.1	7.5	1.0
Curr. Assets	66.6	51.7	42.3	31.3	24.3	20.3
Total Assets	85.3	69.1	59.0	48.2	43.1	41.3
Curr. Liab.	15.9	13.2	12.9	10.6	8.2	9.5
LT Debt	5.8	5.8	5.9	5.9	5.9	4.9
Common Eqty.	60.1	46.8	38.1	30.2	27.3	25.1
Total Cap.	69.2	55.4	45.4	36.9	34.0	30.7
Cap. Exp.	6.6	3.6	4.6	1.9	1.0	1.5
Cash Flow	15.6	12.3	10.9	5.1	4.7	4.3

Ratio Analysis

	1995	1994	1993	1992	1991	1990
Curr. Ratio	4.2	3.9	3.3	3.0	3.0	2.1
% LT Debt of Cap.	8.3	10.5	12.9	16.0	17.5	15.9
% Net Inc.of Revs.	10.0	6.7	6.8	2.0	2.2	1.5
% Ret. on Assets	13.3	10.2	10.9	2.9	3.2	2.0
% Ret. on Equity	19.4	15.4	17.1	4.6	5.1	3.5

Dividend Data —No cash dividends have been paid, and the company does not intend to pay any in the foreseeable future.

Data as orig. reptd.; bef. results of disc. opers. and/or spec. items. Per share data adj. for stk. divs. as of ex-div. date. E-Estimated. NA-Not Available. NM-Not Meaningful. NR-Not Ranked.

Office—85 West Tasman Dr., San Jose, CA 95134-1703. **Tel**—(408) 943-9403. **Chrmn & CEO**—W. D. Rasdal. **Vice Chrmn**—P. N. Risinger. **VP-Fin, CFO, Secy & Investor Contact**—J. Scott Kamsler. **Dirs**—H. Anderson, W. D. Rasdal, P. N. Risinger, R. A. Strauch, R. M. Wolfe. **Transfer Agent & Registrar**—Chemical Trust Co. of California, SF. **Incorporated** in California in 1973. **Empl**-651. **S&P Analyst:** N.J. DeVita

STANDARD & POOR'S

STOCK REPORTS

Syncor International

NASDAQ Symbol **SCOR**

In S&P SmallCap 600

15-NOV-95

Industry: Drugs-Generic and OTC

Summary: This distributor of radiopharmaceuticals operates a network of more than 115 nuclear pharmacy centers throughout the U.S., servicing hospitals, clinics and physicians.

Quantitative Evaluations

Outlook (1 Lowest—5 Highest) • **3-**

Fair Value • **8**

Risk • **High**

Earn./Div. Rank • **B**

Technical Eval. • **Neutral** since 11/95

Rel. Strength Rank (1 Lowest—99 Highest) • **13**

Insider Activity • **NA**

Recent Price • 8 | Yield • Nil

52 Wk Range • 12⅛-6⅝ | 12-Mo. P/E • 27.6

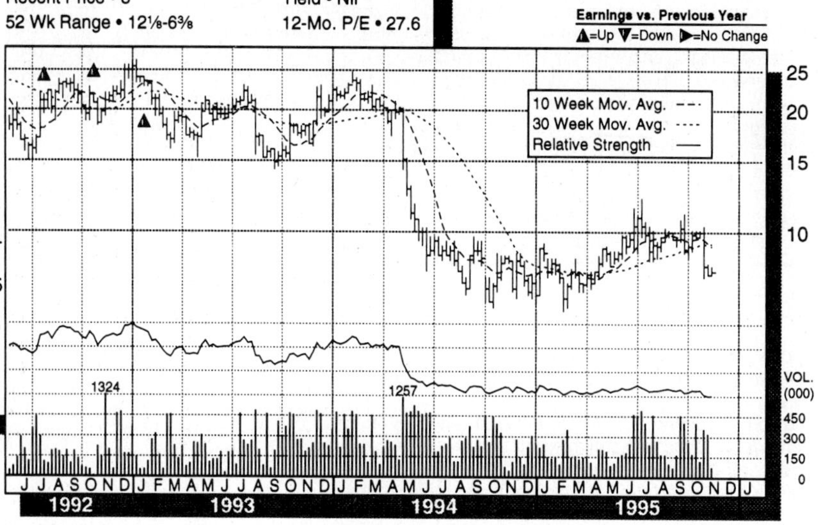

Business Profile - 14-NOV-95

Syncor returned to profitability in the first quarter of 1995 following losses throughout the second half of 1994. SCOR is continuing its profit improvement programs, initiated in late 1994, to bolster market share and strengthen its financial position. A 500,000-share repurchase program was announced in June 1995, after the completion of a similar program the year before. Results in 1996 may be adversely affected by the impending launch of a competing technetium-based heart imaging agent.

Operational Review - 14-NOV-95

For the nine months ended September 30, 1995, sales increased 3.8%, year to year, despite the loss of a supplier, which diminished revenues in the third quarter by approximately $4.5 million. Gross margins grew fractionally and, after 2.4% higher SG&A costs, operating income rose to $5.5 million, from $2.5 million. Following a near-doubling in other income ($401,000 vs. $231,000) and taxes at 40.0%, vs. 37.0%, net income increased to $3.5 million ($0.34 a share), from $1.8 million ($0.16).

Stock Performance - 10-NOV-95

In the past 30 trading days, SCOR's shares have declined 14%, compared to a 1% rise in the S&P 500. Average trading volume for the past five days was 14,360 shares, compared with the 40-day moving average of 51,840 shares.

Key Stock Statistics

Dividend Rate/Share	Nil	Shareholders	2,200
Shs. outstg. (M)	10.6	Market cap. (B)	$0.085
Avg. daily vol. (M)	0.061	Inst. holdings	49%
Tang. Bk. Value/Share	5.96	Insider holdings	NA
Beta	1.24		

Value of $10,000 invested 5 years ago: $ 10,158

Fiscal Year Ending Dec. 31

	1995	% Change	1994	% Change	1993	% Change
Revenues (Million $)						
1Q	83.00	11%	74.80	—	--	—
2Q	83.30	2%	81.90	—	--	—
3Q	81.01	NM	81.60	—	--	—
4Q	—	—	81.67	—	--	—
Yr.	—	—	320.0	125%	142.2	-36%
Income (Million $)						
1Q	1.02	-51%	2.09	—	—	—
2Q	1.28	73%	0.74	-65%	2.11	-9%
3Q	1.24	NM	-1.08	NM	2.16	NM
4Q	—	—	-0.54	NM	3.27	NM
Yr.	—	—	1.21	-68%	3.84	-62%
Earnings Per Share ($)						
1Q	0.10	-47%	0.19	—	--	—
2Q	0.12	71%	0.07	—	--	—
3Q	0.12	NM	-0.10	—	--	—
4Q	—	—	-0.05	—	--	—
Yr.	—	—	0.11	-31%	0.16	-83%

Next earnings report expected: mid February

Syncor International

Business Summary - 15-NOV-95

Syncor International Corporation is a pharmacy services company that operates through a network of nuclear pharmacy service centers throughout the U.S. (117 centers as of March 1995); there are also six international centers. The company compounds, dispenses and distributes patient-specific intravenous drugs and solutions for use in diagnostic imaging and a complete range of high-technology pharmacy services. Syncor's home healthcare pharmacy business was sold in 1993.

The company's nuclear pharmacies dispense radiopharmaceuticals on prescription to more than 7,000 hospitals, clinics and physicians' offices in unit and multiple doses. Radiopharmaceuticals are used by physicians in conjunction with nuclear imaging cameras and computers to obtain images of organs and body functions for diagnostic purposes. Syncor also provides services related to the sale of radiopharmaceuticals, including radiopharmaceutical record keeping required by federal and state government agencies and radiopharmaceutical technical consulting. In each of the past three fiscal years, the pharmacies contributed more than 95% of consolidated net sales.

Syncor provides Positron Emission Tomography (PET) services at four of its pharmacies. PET is a new technology that enables physicians to view a metabolic process as it occurs within the body. The company also serves the research community by assisting in monoclonal antibody clinical trials.

Other activities include the marketing and distribution of imaging cold kits, isotopes and medical reference sources, in addition to nuclear and home care pharmacy equipment and accessories.

In 1994, Syncor extended its long-term contracts with VHA Inc., Columbia/HCA Healthcare Corp. and the Radiopharmaceutical division of DuPont Merck Pharmaceutical Co. The company said the contracts had a combined annual value of over $130 million.

Important Developments

Oct. '95—After announcing 1995's nine-month results, Syncor expressed concern about the impending launch of a competing heart imaging agent in early 1996.

Aug. '95—The company filed a lawsuit seeking to overturn the U.S. FDA's attempt to regulate pharmacy compounding of positron emission tomography (PET) drugs. The FDA proposes to require state-licensed pharmacies that formulate PET drugs to receive FDA premarket approval.

Capitalization

Long Term Debt: $6,583,000 (6/95).
Options: To buy 1,625,000 shs. at $4.75 to $21.88 ea. (12/94).

Per Share Data ($) (Year Ended Dec. 31)

	1994	1993	1992	1991	1990	1989
Tangible Bk. Val.	5.96	5.51	5.15	3.89	2.93	2.32
Cash Flow	1.08	0.64	1.62	1.13	0.85	0.66
Earnings	0.11	0.16	0.95	0.63	0.46	0.32
Dividends	Nil	Nil	Nil	Nil	Nil	Nil
Payout Ratio	Nil	Nil	Nil	Nil	Nil	Nil
Prices - High	24¾	26½	34½	27¼	10½	8¼
- Low	6½	14¼	15	9⅛	6¼	4⅜
P/E Ratio - High	NM	NM	36	43	23	26
- Low	NM	NM	16	14	14	14

Income Statement Analysis (Million $)

	1994	%Chg	1993	%Chg	1992	%Chg	1991
Revs.	320	125%	142	-39%	231	10%	210
Oper. Inc.	12.2	58%	7.7	-67%	23.4	40%	16.7
Depr.	10.6	102%	5.3	-27%	7.2	33%	5.4
Int. Exp.	0.8	142%	0.3	-49%	0.6	-27%	0.8
Pretax Inc.	2.1	-25%	2.8	-83%	16.9	46%	11.6
Eff. Tax Rate	42%	—	39%	—	40%	—	41%
Net Inc.	1.2	-29%	1.7	-84%	10.2	48%	6.9

Balance Sheet & Other Fin. Data (Million $)

	1994	1993	1992	1991	1990	1989
Cash	18.0	18.7	20.9	10.0	9.3	9.6
Curr. Assets	76.3	63.7	60.7	52.0	42.8	37.7
Total Assets	129	115	104	90.8	74.6	65.7
Curr. Liab.	49.7	36.6	33.3	31.8	22.6	20.4
LT Debt	5.2	6.8	4.5	6.0	7.9	8.5
Common Eqty.	73.9	71.2	65.8	52.4	42.8	35.8
Total Cap.	79.0	78.0	70.7	59.7	52.0	45.3
Cap. Exp.	9.2	5.5	10.6	10.5	5.3	2.0
Cash Flow	11.8	6.9	17.3	12.3	8.7	6.7

Ratio Analysis

	1994	1993	1992	1991	1990	1989
Curr. Ratio	1.5	1.7	1.8	1.6	1.9	1.8
% LT Debt of Cap.	6.5	8.8	6.4	10.2	15.2	18.7
% Net Inc.of Revs.	0.4	1.2	4.4	3.3	3.0	2.5
% Ret. on Assets	1.0	NA	10.4	8.3	6.7	5.4
% Ret. on Equity	1.7	NA	17.1	14.4	12.0	8.6

Dividend Data —No cash has been paid on the common shares.

Data as orig. reptd.; bef. results of disc. opers. and/or spec. items. Per share data adj. for stk. divs. as of ex-div. date. E-Estimated. NA-Not Available. NM-Not Meaningful. NR-Not Ranked.

Office—20001 Prairie St., Chatsworth, CA 91311. **Tel**—(818) 886-7400. **Chrmn**—M. Fu. **Pres & CEO**—G. R. McGrevin. **Exec VP & COO**—R. G. Funari. **VP & CFO**—M. E. Mikity. **VP & Secy**—H. Bagerdjian. **Dirs**—M. Fu, R. G. Funari, S. B. Gerber, J. Kleiman, G. R. McGrevin, G. S. Oki, A. E. Spangler, H. N. Wagner Jr., G. R. Wilensky. **Transfer Agent & Registrar**—American Stock Transfer & Trust Co., NYC. **Incorporated** in New Mexico in 1974; reincorporated in Delaware in 1985. **Empl**-2,048. **S&P Analyst:** Thomas Tirney

System Software Associates

NASDAQ Symbol **SSAX**
In S&P SmallCap 600

25-SEP-95

Industry: Data Processing

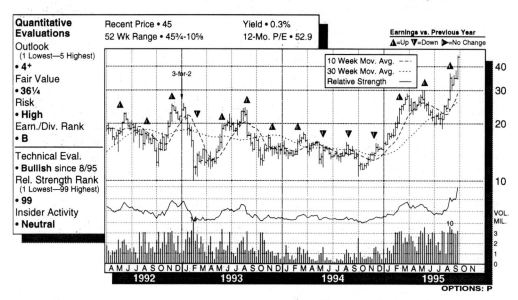

Summary: This company develops and supports an integrated line of business application, maintenance management, computer-aided systems engineering and electronic data interchange software.

Quantitative Evaluations

Outlook (1 Lowest—5 Highest) • **4+**
Fair Value • **36¼**
Risk • **High**
Earn./Div. Rank • **B**

Technical Eval. • **Bullish** since 8/95
Rel. Strength Rank (1 Lowest—99 Highest) • **99**
Insider Activity • **Neutral**

Recent Price • 45
52 Wk Range • 45¾-10⅝
Yield • 0.3%
12-Mo. P/E • 52.9

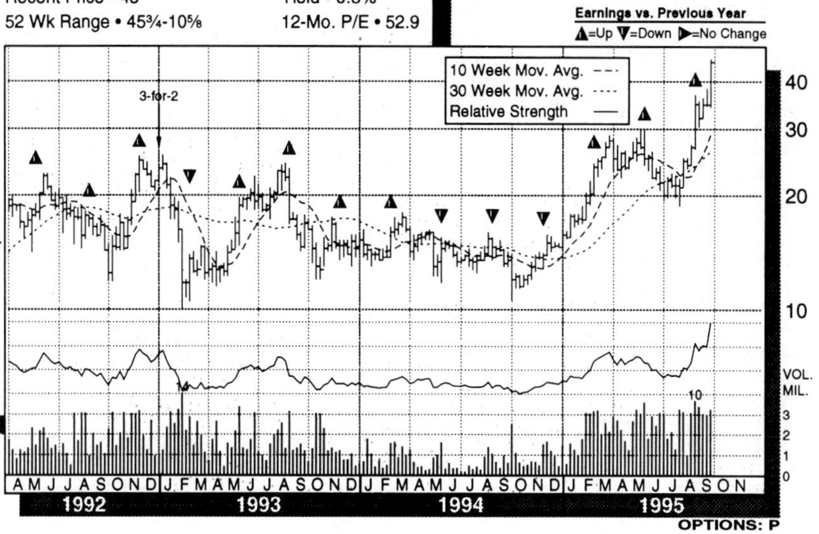

OPTIONS: P

Business Profile - 25-SEP-95

This company's primary product line consists of over 40 integrated software products designed for manufacturing, distribution, financial, electronic data interchange, and toolset applications. SSAX is delivering on its technology strategy of offering platform independent products. In addition, SSAX continues to make progress on both the development and use of its new object oriented tools.

Operational Review - 25-SEP-95

Total revenues in the first nine months of fiscal 1995 rose 19%, year to year, reflecting higher license fees, initial shipments of the BPCS Unix Client/Server software and continued gains in the worldwide client services business. Margins widened on the higher volume and well-controlled operating expenses, despite higher investments in R&D, and net income soared 87%, to $17.2 million ($0.62 a share), from $9.2 million ($0.34).

Stock Performance - 22-SEP-95

In the past 30 trading days, SSAX's shares have increased 88%, compared to a 5% rise in the S&P 500. Average trading volume for the past five days was 1,128,160 shares, compared with the 40-day moving average of 974,892 shares.

Key Stock Statistics

Dividend Rate/Share	0.12	Shareholders	600
Shs. outstg. (M)	27.4	Market cap. (B)	$ 1.2
Avg. daily vol. (M)	0.977	Inst. holdings	63%
Tang. Bk. Value/Share	3.79	Insider holdings	NA
Beta	0.63		

Value of $10,000 invested 5 years ago: $ 52,619

Fiscal Year Ending Oct. 31

	1995	% Change	1994	% Change	1993	% Change
Revenues (Million $)						
1Q	77.40	17%	66.40	37%	48.60	-6%
2Q	84.30	17%	72.00	14%	62.90	27%
3Q	105.0	22%	86.20	25%	68.70	24%
4Q	—	—	109.8	32%	83.20	16%
Yr.	—	—	334.4	27%	263.4	15%
Income (Million $)						
1Q	1.80	50%	1.20	33%	0.90	-88%
2Q	4.20	62%	2.60	-57%	6.00	20%
3Q	11.20	107%	5.40	-23%	7.00	21%
4Q	—	—	6.20	-35%	9.50	17%
Yr.	—	—	15.40	-34%	23.40	-12%
Earnings Per Share ($)						
1Q	0.07	75%	0.04	33%	0.03	-90%
2Q	0.15	50%	0.10	-55%	0.22	16%
3Q	0.40	100%	0.20	-23%	0.26	24%
4Q	—	—	0.23	-34%	0.35	17%
Yr.	—	—	0.57	-34%	0.86	-13%

Next earnings report expected: late November

System Software Associates

Business Summary - 22-SEP-95

System Software Associates develops, markets and supports an integrated line of business application, maintenance management, computer-aided systems engineering (CASE) and electronic data interchange software. Revenue contributions in recent fiscal years:

	1994	1993	1992
License fees & hardware	72%	71%	78%
Client services & other	28%	29%	22%

The primary product line is known as the Business Planning and Control System (BPCS), which consists of over 40 integrated software products designed for manufacturing, distribution, financial, electronic data interchange and toolset applications. Historically, SSAX's software was primarily designed to operate on IBM Application System 400 computers. However, in March 1995, SSAX began delivering on its open systems strategy and shipped a Unix version of BCPS. The strategy includes platform independence (supporting the IBM AS/400, the IBM RS/6000 and the Hewlett-Packard HP 9000) in addition to configurable business processes that can be customized according to each client's needs.

The BCPS product line is comprised of a variety of products including: manufacturing products; supply chain management products; electronic data interchange products; financial products; and retrieval products.

The CASE products line, which is known as AS/SET (Application System/Solution Engineering Technology) is designed to help users develop and maintain applications.

R&D expenses totaled $64.1 million (8.7% of revenues) in fiscal 1994, compared with $37.3 million (7.2%) in fiscal 1993.

Important Developments

Sep. '95—The company announced a strategic partnership with Harbinger Corp., under which Harbinger acquired SSAX's AS/400 line of electronic data interchange (EDI) products, as well as its development organization. As part of the partnership, SSAX gained the right to market, sell and support Harbinger's complete line of EDI products and services including products for the MVS, UNIX and Windows platforms.
Mar. '95—SSAX announced that it began shipping its BPCS Unix Client/Server software, which operates on HP 9000 server platforms under HP-UX version 9.0.4, Informix database version 7.1 and Windows 3.1 client platforms.

Capitalization

Long Term Debt: $34,700,000 (7/95).
Minority Interest: $1,100,000.

Per Share Data ($) (Year Ended Oct. 31)

	1994	1993	1992	1991	1990	1989
Tangible Bk. Val.	3.66	3.24	2.66	2.35	1.90	1.21
Cash Flow	0.96	1.14	1.20	0.82	0.74	0.51
Earnings	0.57	0.86	0.99	0.63	0.61	0.42
Dividends	0.12	0.12	0.12	0.11	Nil	Nil
Payout Ratio	21%	14%	12%	18%	Nil	Nil
Prices - High	18	25½	25⅜	16½	12¾	9¼
- Low	10⅝	10	11⅞	5½	5⅝	5⅛
P/E Ratio - High	32	30	26	26	21	22
- Low	19	12	12	9	9	12

Income Statement Analysis (Million $)

	1994	%Chg	1993	%Chg	1992	%Chg	1991
Revs.	334	27%	263	15%	229	54%	149
Oper. Inc.	35.2	-19%	43.5	-7%	46.8	58%	29.7
Depr.	10.4	41%	7.4	28%	5.8	12%	5.2
Int. Exp.	2.8	155%	1.1	22%	0.9	100%	0.4
Pretax Inc.	23.8	-33%	35.7	-14%	41.6	61%	25.9
Eff. Tax Rate	36%	—	36%	—	36%	—	36%
Net Inc.	15.4	-34%	23.4	-12%	26.6	59%	16.7

Balance Sheet & Other Fin. Data (Million $)

	1994	1993	1992	1991	1990	1989
Cash	60.2	57.6	23.4	23.2	28.4	20.5
Curr. Assets	238	215	151	99	84.3	58.4
Total Assets	333	280	200	136	114	77.0
Curr. Liab.	145	124	101	55.4	46.2	34.2
LT Debt	32.7	34.0	3.5	2.5	1.3	1.5
Common Eqty.	115	101	80.0	67.8	55.9	37.9
Total Cap.	158	145	87.9	72.5	59.9	39.5
Cap. Exp.	14.7	5.0	7.0	5.0	8.5	2.0
Cash Flow	25.8	30.8	32.4	24.4	19.8	13.5

Ratio Analysis

	1994	1993	1992	1991	1990	1989
Curr. Ratio	1.6	1.7	1.5	1.8	1.8	1.7
% LT Debt of Cap.	20.7	23.4	4.0	3.5	2.2	3.7
% Net Inc.of Revs.	4.6	8.9	11.6	11.2	13.2	11.7
% Ret. on Assets	5.0	9.7	15.7	13.4	17.0	17.1
% Ret. on Equity	14.2	25.6	35.6	27.2	34.7	34.2

Dividend Data —SSAX initiated annual cash dividend payments in January 1991. Several stock splits have been effected, most recently a three-for-two split in December 1992.

Amt. of Div. $	Date Decl.	Ex-Div. Date	Stock of Record	Payment Date
0.120	Dec. 08	Dec. 20	Dec. 27	Jan. 06 '95

Data as orig. reptd.; bef. results of disc. opers. and/or spec. items. Per share data adj. for stk. divs. as of ex-div. date. E-Estimated. NA-Not Available. NM-Not Meaningful. NR-Not Ranked.

Office—500 West Madison St., Chicago, IL 60661. **Tel**—(312) 641-2900. **Chrmn & CEO**—R. E. Covey. **Pres & COO**—T. H. Osborne. **VP & CFO**—J. J. Skadra. **Investor Contact**—Margo Wories. **Dirs**—R. E. Covey, W. L. Hayford, J. W. Puth, W. N. Weaver Jr. **Transfer Agent & Registrar**—First National Bank of Chicago. **Incorporated** in Delaware in 1981. **Empl**-1,800. **S&P Analyst:** A.M.A.

STANDARD & POOR'S

STOCK REPORTS

TBC Corp.

NASDAQ Symbol **TBCC**
In S&P SmallCap 600

10-SEP-95

Industry:
Auto parts/equipment

Summary: TBC, one of the largest U.S. distributors of replacement tires, also distributes replacement automotive parts.

S&P Opinion: Accumulate (★★★★)

Recent Price • 9½
52 Wk Range • 11¾-8½
Yield • Nil
12-Mo. P/E • 13.0

Quantitative Evaluations

Outlook
(1 Lowest—5 Highest)
• **2⁻**

Fair Value
• **9⅛**

Risk
• **Low**

Earn./Div. Rank
• **B+**

Technical Eval.
• **Bearish** since 7/95

Rel. Strength Rank
(1 Lowest—99 Highest)
• **14**

Insider Activity
• **Neutral**

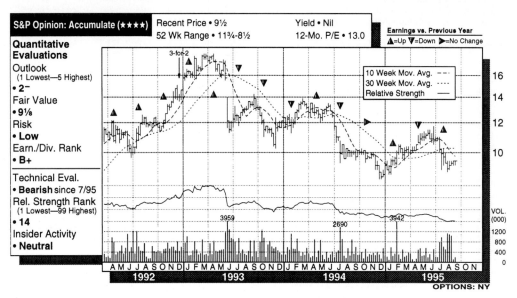

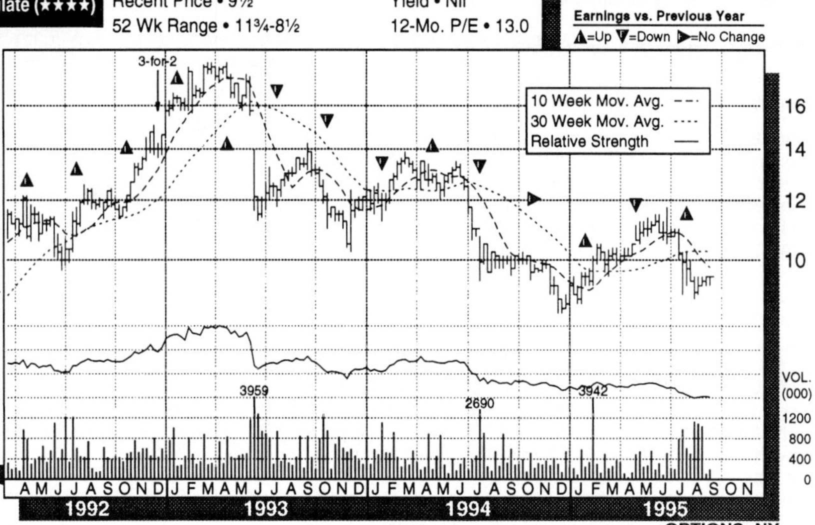

OPTIONS: NY

Overview - 07-SEP-95

Although sales should rise due to a series of industry-wide price increases which were the result of higher raw materials costs, unit tire shipments are likely to decline about 2% in 1995. Little increase is also expected from non-tire products, despite a restructuring of the unit in 1994. With cost controls and higher net interest income, and in the absence of a $2.5 million charge for previously unaccrued pension benefit obligations, net income should advance in 1995. EPS will benefit from fewer shares outstanding, as a result of an active long-term share repurchase program. We look for a stronger performance from TBCC in 1996, as economic growth should lead to more domestic vehicle miles traveled and greater demand for replacement tires.

Valuation - 07-SEP-95

The shares have been out of favor since mid-year, as demand for replacement tires softened and unit sales declined 2.2% in the first half. Nevertheless, TBCC's earnings should rise in 1995, in the absence of a nonrecurring charge realized in 1994. The company has no long term debt, very moderate capital needs and remains one of the largest factors in replacement tire distribution. Its strong cash flow is largely directed to the repurchase of shares, providing strong support for EPS and the stock price. The stock is very modestly valued at 11X our 1996 EPS estimate, and is an attractive portfolio addition for long-term capital gains. Initiation of a cash dividend is not expected.

Key Stock Statistics

S&P EPS Est. 1995	0.78	Tang. Bk. Value/Share	4.34
P/E on S&P Est. 1995	12.2	Beta	1.11
S&P EPS Est. 1996	0.87	Shareholders	6,000
Dividend Rate/Share	Nil	Market cap. (B)	$0.235
Shs. outstg. (M)	24.8	Inst. holdings	71%
Avg. daily vol. (M)	0.129	Insider holdings	NA

Value of $10,000 invested 5 years ago: $ 16,602

Fiscal Year Ending Dec. 31

	1995	% Change	1994	% Change	1993	% Change
Revenues (Million $)						
1Q	130.3	-3%	133.8	6%	125.7	3%
2Q	132.2	NM	132.9	-14%	154.4	NM
3Q	—	—	157.5	NM	159.0	3%
4Q	—	—	127.7	-1%	129.6	-7%
Yr.	—	—	551.9	-3%	568.7	NM
Income (Million $)						
1Q	4.28	-16%	5.09	1%	5.02	20%
2Q	4.04	12%	3.60	-35%	5.55	-9%
3Q	—	—	5.66	-4%	5.90	-6%
4Q	—	—	5.19	6%	4.91	-17%
Yr.	—	—	19.55	-9%	21.38	-5%
Earnings Per Share ($)						
1Q	0.17	-6%	0.18	6%	0.17	21%
2Q	0.16	23%	0.13	-32%	0.19	-5%
3Q	E0.22	5%	0.21	NM	0.21	-5%
4Q	E0.23	15%	0.20	18%	0.17	-15%
Yr.	E0.78	10%	0.71	-4%	0.74	-3%

Next earnings report expected: mid October

TBC Corp.

Business Summary - 07-SEP-95

TBC Corporation is one of the largest U.S. distributors of products for the automotive replacement market. Its lines of tires, tubes, custom wheels, batteries, shock absorbers, brake parts, filters and other items, which are made by others to company specifications, are marketed under TBC's own brand names.

Sales of tires accounted for 89% of the total in 1994, versus 88% in 1993, 87% in 1992, 84% in 1991 and 81% in 1990. The company believes that it is the largest independent wholesale distributor of replacement tires in the U.S. The Kelly-Springfield Tire Co. subsidiary of Goodyear Tire & Rubber Co. manufactured more than half of TBC's tires in recent years; Cooper Tire & Rubber manufactured most of the balance.

TBC offers three complete lines of tires under its Cordovan, Multi-Mile and Sigma brands. Each line includes tires for passenger, truck, farm, industrial, recreational and other applications. It also markets automotive replacement parts under the brandnames Grand Am, Grand Prix, Grand Sport, Astro-Lite, Harvest King and Power King.

Most products are sold through a nationwide network of 185 regional distributors, most of which act as wholesalers or operate retail outlets, with some functioning in both capacities. The company estimates that its products are distributed to more than 20,000 retail outlets, consisting primarily of independent tire dealers. The 10 largest distributors accounted for 52% of gross sales in 1994 and 1993, including 15% for Carroll's Inc. The company has an on-line information system to permit continuous contact with distributors and facilitate just-in-time service to retail dealers.

Battery Associates sells through its own network of 140 wholesale and retail distributors. In 1993 and 1994, TBC closed its 10 company-owned branches. The company furnishes batteries and related accessories for motor vehicles nationwide.

Important Developments

Jul. '95—TBCC said that second quarter tire shipments were down 2.2%, despite a 13% rise in unit sales in June which TBCC believes was related to an expansion of inventories by customers ahead of price increases planned for July by most major tire manufacturers. Several price increases were implemented over the past year, due to rapidly rising raw materials prices and each of these price changes has resulted in a similar shift in orders.

Feb. '95—Directors approved the purchase of an additional 1.5 million common shares, following the acquisition of 1.2 million shares in early 1995, nearly completing the repurchase of 1.5 million shares authorized in August 1994. Future EPS comparisons should benefit from fewer shares outstanding.

Capitalization

Long Term Debt: None (6/95).

Per Share Data ($) (Year Ended Dec. 31)

	1994	1993	1992	1991	1990	1989
Tangible Bk. Val.	4.31	4.09	3.52	3.01	2.50	2.15
Cash Flow	0.85	0.87	0.87	0.68	0.61	0.55
Earnings	0.71	0.74	0.76	0.59	0.52	0.47
Dividends	Nil	Nil	Nil	Nil	Nil	Nil
Payout Ratio	Nil	Nil	Nil	Nil	Nil	Nil
Prices - High	13⅞	18¼	16	9¼	6	5⅞
- Low	8½	10¼	9⅛	5	3⅜	3⅞
P/E Ratio - High	20	25	21	16	11	12
- Low	12	14	12	8	7	8

Income Statement Analysis (Million $)

	1994	%Chg	1993	%Chg	1992	%Chg	1991
Revs.	552	-3%	569	NM	570	14%	499
Oper. Inc.	33.8	-10%	37.7	NM	37.4	24%	30.1
Depr.	4.1	4%	3.9	20%	3.3	23%	2.7
Int. Exp.	1.3	-28%	1.8	67%	1.1	-36%	1.7
Pretax Inc.	31.4	-9%	34.6	-3%	35.6	27%	28.1
Eff. Tax Rate	38%	—	38%	—	37%	—	37%
Net Inc.	19.5	-9%	21.4	-5%	22.5	27%	17.7

Balance Sheet & Other Fin. Data (Million $)

	1994	1993	1992	1991	1990	1989
Cash	Nil	Nil	1.9	0.3	Nil	0.5
Curr. Assets	146	145	155	117	126	119
Total Assets	170	167	177	135	137	131
Curr. Liab.	55.0	50.2	73.9	44.7	59.9	59.6
LT Debt	Nil	Nil	Nil	Nil	Nil	Nil
Common Eqty.	114	117	103	90.0	76.7	70.8
Total Cap.	114	117	103	91.0	77.0	71.4
Cap. Exp.	3.6	3.1	6.8	10.3	1.8	2.4
Cash Flow	23.6	25.3	25.7	20.3	19.3	19.0

Ratio Analysis

	1994	1993	1992	1991	1990	1989
Curr. Ratio	2.7	2.9	2.1	2.6	2.1	2.0
% LT Debt of Cap.	Nil	Nil	Nil	Nil	Nil	Nil
% Net Inc.of Revs.	3.5	3.8	3.9	3.5	3.3	3.4
% Ret. on Assets	12.1	12.6	14.6	13.1	12.8	12.7
% Ret. on Equity	17.6	19.7	23.5	21.3	23.3	24.0

Dividend Data —No cash has been paid. A three-for-two stock split was effected in December 1992. A poison pill stock purchase rights plan expires in 1998.

Data as orig. reptd.; bef. results of disc. opers. and/or spec. items. Per share data adj. for stk. divs. as of ex-div. date. E-Estimated. NA-Not Available. NM-Not Meaningful. NR-Not Ranked.

Office—4770 Hickory Hill Rd., Memphis, TN 38141. **Tel**—(901) 363-8030. **Chrmn**—M. E. Bruce. **Pres & CEO**—L. S. DiPasqua. **SVP & Investor Contact**—Ronald E. McCollough. **VP & Treas**—C. B. Quinn, Jr. **Secy**—S. A. Freedman. **Dirs**—M. E. Bruce, R. E. Carroll, Jr., L. S. DiPasqua, R. H. Dunlap, S. A. Freedman, D. W. Higginbotham, R. A. McStay, R. M. O'Hara, R. R. Schoeberl, N. F. Taubman. **Transfer Agent & Registrar**—First National Bank of Boston. **Incorporated** in Delaware in 1970. **Empl-** 215. **S&P Analyst:** Joshua M. Harari, CFA

STANDARD & POOR'S

STOCK REPORTS

TCBY Enterprises

NYSE Symbol **TBY**
In S&P SmallCap 600

04-OCT-95 **Industry:** Retail Stores

Summary: This Arkansas-based company is the largest franchisor, licensor and operator of soft-serve frozen yogurt stores in the world.

Quantitative Evaluations

Outlook
(1 Lowest—5 Highest)
• **1⁻**

Fair Value
• **4⅛**

Risk
• **Average**

Earn./Div. Rank
• **B**

Technical Eval.
• **Bearish** since 9/95

Rel. Strength Rank
(1 Lowest—99 Highest)
• **7**

Insider Activity
• **Neutral**

Recent Price • 4⅝
52 Wk Range • 6½-4⅛
Yield • 4.4%
12-Mo. P/E • 57.8

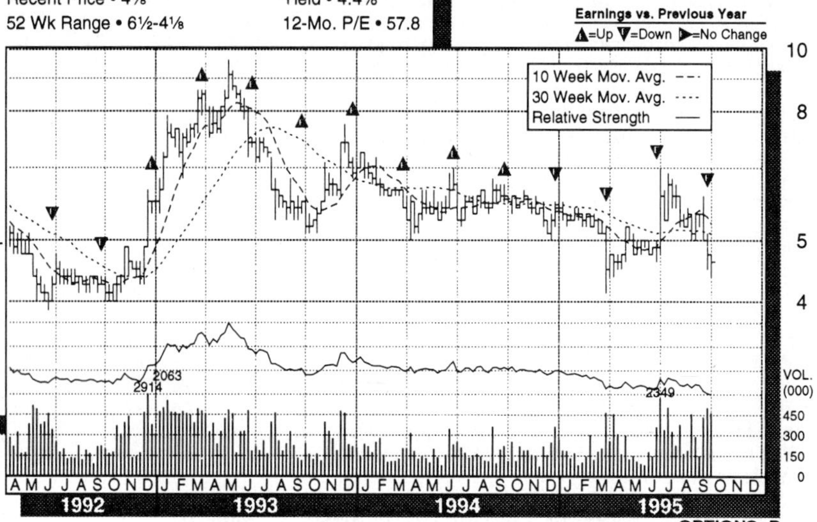

OPTIONS: P

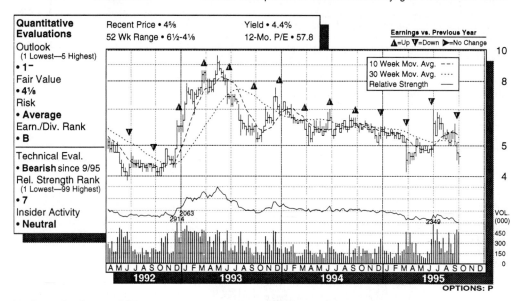

Business Profile - 04-OCT-95

TCBY Enterprises franchises--and to a lesser extent operates--soft-serve frozen yogurt stores and produces yogurt for those stores and other customers. In an effort to improve earnings, TCBY has been focusing on cost-cutting efforts, testing and introducing new menu items, and emphasizing marketing and customer service. The company recently hired the investment banking firm of Stephens Inc. to explore strategic alternatives for TCBY with the intent of maximizing shareholder value.

Operational Review - 04-OCT-95

The 15% decline in total sales and franchising revenues for the nine months ended August 31, 1995, year to year, reflected the sale of the TCBY refrigerated yogurt product line to Mid-American Dairymen, fewer stores in operation and lower equipment sales. Gross margins widened, but SG&A expenses were sharply higher to support the introduction and expansion of the hardpack frozen yogurt products. Despite a $1.6 million gain from the sale of the refrigerated yogurt line, a net loss was incurred.

Stock Performance - 29-SEP-95

In the past 30 trading days, TBY's shares have declined 16%, compared to a 5% rise in the S&P 500. Average trading volume for the past five days was 112,780 shares, compared with the 40-day moving average of 86,077 shares.

Key Stock Statistics

Dividend Rate/Share	0.20	Shareholders	6,200
Shs. outstg. (M)	25.5	Market cap. (B)	$0.115
Avg. daily vol. (M)	0.116	Inst. holdings	18%
Tang. Bk. Value/Share	3.89	Insider holdings	NA
Beta	0.54		

Value of $10,000 invested 5 years ago: $ 3,041

Fiscal Year Ending Nov. 30

	1995	% Change	1994	% Change	1993	% Change
Revenues (Million $)						
1Q	26.04	7%	24.26	NM	24.30	31%
2Q	32.78	-24%	43.30	26%	34.24	-2%
3Q	39.24	-23%	50.67	36%	37.23	-5%
4Q	—	—	34.20	30%	26.21	NM
Yr.	—	—	152.5	27%	120.5	1%
Income (Million $)						
1Q	-2.82	NM	-0.62	NM	-0.79	NM
2Q	2.44	-31%	3.56	30%	2.74	10%
3Q	2.19	-51%	4.48	12%	4.00	7%
4Q	—	—	0.13	-72%	0.46	100%
Yr.	—	—	7.55	18%	6.41	26%
Earnings Per Share ($)						
1Q	-0.11	NM	-0.02	NM	-0.03	NM
2Q	0.10	-29%	0.14	27%	0.11	10%
3Q	0.09	-50%	0.18	13%	0.16	7%
4Q	—	—	0.01	-50%	0.02	100%
Yr.	—	—	0.30	20%	0.25	25%

Next earnings report expected: mid January

TCBY Enterprises

Business Summary - 04-OCT-95

TCBY Enterprises franchises and operates soft-serve frozen yogurt stores and produces yogurt for those stores and other customers. The company is the largest franchisor of soft-serve frozen yogurt in the U.S. At August 31, 1995, 2,773 TCBY stores (1,231 domestic franchised, 184 international licensed, 85 owned and 1,273 non-traditional locations) were operating in 50 states, as well as in Canada and overseas. The company also markets refrigerated yogurt through the retail grocery trade and manufactures and sells equipment related to the foodservice industry. Revenues in recent fiscal years were derived as follows:

	1994	1993	1992	1991
Sales	92%	91%	91%	91%
Franchise	8%	9%	9%	9%

The number of stores in operation at recent fiscal year-ends:

	1994	1993	1992	1991
Owned	96	121	147	136
Non-traditional	1,319	989	292	140
Franchised	1,386	1,364	1,401	1,574
Total	2,801	2,474	1,840	1,850

The stores, which operate under the name TCBY The Country's Best Yogurt, are located in shopping centers, free standing locations, and shopping malls. They generally occupy 800 to 1,600 sq. ft., seat 24 to 44 customers, and accommodate eat-in and carry-out business. Non-traditional locations include airports, schools, hospitals, sports arenas, travel plazas and convenience stores. A bakery program offering gourmet coffee and freshly baked cookies, muffins and brownies has been introduced in many of the domestic stores. The company is in the process of testing an expanded breakfast and lunch menu, featuring soups salads, sandwiches etc.

Franchisees pay an initial fee of $20,000, a weekly royalty and service fee of 4% of net revenues and up to 3% of net revenues for advertising. The total initial investment required to establish a franchised unit ranges from $113,500 to $341,900. The company offers franchisees a complete package of equipment. As of November 30, 1994, franchise agreements had been executed for 80 stores to be opened in the United States, only some of which are expected to open in 1995.

Important Developments

Aug. '95—TCBY said that its new "Treats" concept has been well-received by franchisees and consumers. To date, 358 stores have converted to the concept, and 125 are in the process of converting. Same-store sales results for these locations have exceeded those for non-Treats locations.

Capitalization

Long Term Debt: $13,400,591 (8/95).

Per Share Data ($) (Year Ended Nov. 30)

	1994	1993	1992	1991	1990	1989
Tangible Bk. Val.	3.73	3.89	3.87	3.92	4.07	3.61
Cash Flow	0.67	0.57	0.50	0.62	1.00	1.28
Earnings	0.30	0.25	0.20	0.31	0.75	1.10
Dividends	0.20	0.20	0.20	0.35	0.18	0.07
Payout Ratio	67%	80%	101%	113%	24%	6%
Prices - High	6⅞	9⅝	6⅞	9¼	24¾	29
- Low	5	5⅛	3⅞	4½	4⅛	11⅛
P/E Ratio - High	23	39	34	30	33	26
- Low	17	21	19	15	6	10

Income Statement Analysis (Million $)

	1994	%Chg	1993	%Chg	1992	%Chg	1991
Revs.	152	27%	120	NM	119	-8%	129
Oper. Inc.	20.6	18%	17.5	2%	17.2	-10%	19.2
Depr.	9.5	15%	8.3	6%	7.8	-6%	8.3
Int. Exp.	0.6	-23%	0.8	-30%	1.2	-35%	1.8
Pretax Inc.	11.3	16%	9.7	33%	7.3	-40%	12.2
Eff. Tax Rate	33%	—	34%	—	30%	—	35%
Net Inc.	7.6	19%	6.4	25%	5.1	-36%	8.0

Balance Sheet & Other Fin. Data (Million $)

	1994	1993	1992	1991	1990	1989
Cash	20.2	25.0	27.8	22.8	24.5	29.9
Curr. Assets	59.0	53.8	51.5	52.8	55.8	54.8
Total Assets	142	129	132	135	142	134
Curr. Liab.	12.5	8.8	9.3	8.1	10.3	11.9
LT Debt	15.9	11.5	14.8	17.3	19.7	21.3
Common Eqty.	108	105	105	106	109	98.0
Total Cap.	130	120	123	127	131	122
Cap. Exp.	11.4	6.5	7.6	4.2	13.4	28.1
Cash Flow	17.0	14.7	12.9	16.3	26.7	34.5

Ratio Analysis

	1994	1993	1992	1991	1990	1989
Curr. Ratio	4.7	6.1	5.5	6.5	5.4	4.6
% LT Debt of Cap.	12.3	9.6	12.1	13.7	15.0	17.5
% Net Inc.of Revs.	5.0	5.3	4.3	6.2	13.2	20.4
% Ret. on Assets	5.6	4.9	3.8	5.8	14.6	26.0
% Ret. on Equity	7.1	6.1	4.8	7.5	19.4	35.1

Dividend Data —Cash dividends were initiated in 1988.

Amt. of Div. $	Date Decl.	Ex-Div. Date	Stock of Record	Payment Date
0.050	Sep. 15	Sep. 20	Sep. 26	Oct. 11 '94
0.050	Dec. 16	Dec. 23	Dec. 30	Jan. 13 '95
0.050	Mar. 15	Mar. 21	Mar. 27	Apr. 07 '95
0.050	Jun. 21	Jun. 28	Jun. 30	Jul. 14 '95
0.050	Sep. 21	Sep. 27	Sep. 29	Oct. 13 '95

Data as orig. reptd.; bef. results of disc. opers. and/or spec. items. Per share data adj. for stk. divs. as of ex-div. date. E-Estimated. NA-Not Available. NM-Not Meaningful. NR-Not Ranked.

Office—425 West Capitol Ave. (Suite 1100), Little Rock, AR 72201. **Tel**—(501) 688-8229. **Chrmn & CEO**—F. D. Hickingbotham. **Pres**—H. C. Hickingbotham. **SVP-Treas & CFO**—G. Law. **SVP-Secy**—B. D. Clay. **Investor Contact**—Stacy Duckett. **Dirs**—W. H. Bowen, D. R. Grant, F. D. Hickingbotham, F. T. Hickingbotham, H. C. Hickingbotham, D. O. Kirkpatrick, G. Law, M. D. Loyd, H. H. Pollard. **Transfer Agent & Registrar**—Wachovia Bank & Trust Co., Winston-Salem, NC. **Incorporated** in Delaware in 1984. **Empl**-1,150. **S&P Analyst:** Maureen C. Carini

STANDARD & POOR'S
STOCK REPORTS

TCF Financial

NYSE Symbol **TCB**
In S&P SmallCap 600

25-OCT-95 **Industry:** Banking

Summary: This savings bank holding company, with about $7.3 billion in assets, operates some 268 retail financial services offices in Minnesota, Illinois, Wisconsin, Michigan and Ohio.

Quantitative Evaluations
Outlook
(1 Lowest—5 Highest)
• **1**
Fair Value
• **54⅜**
Risk
• **Low**
Earn./Div. Rank
• **B**

Technical Eval.
• **Bearish** since 7/95
Rel. Strength Rank
(1 Lowest—99 Highest)
• **79**
Insider Activity
• **Neutral**

Recent Price • 60½
52 Wk Range • 61⅝-35⅜
Yield • 2.1%
12-Mo. P/E • 20.7

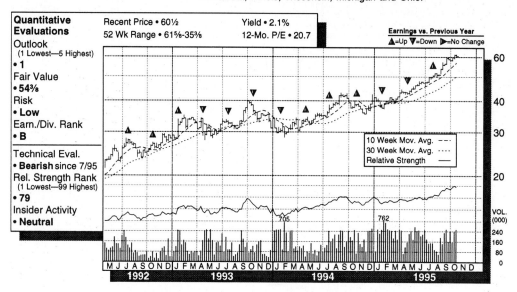

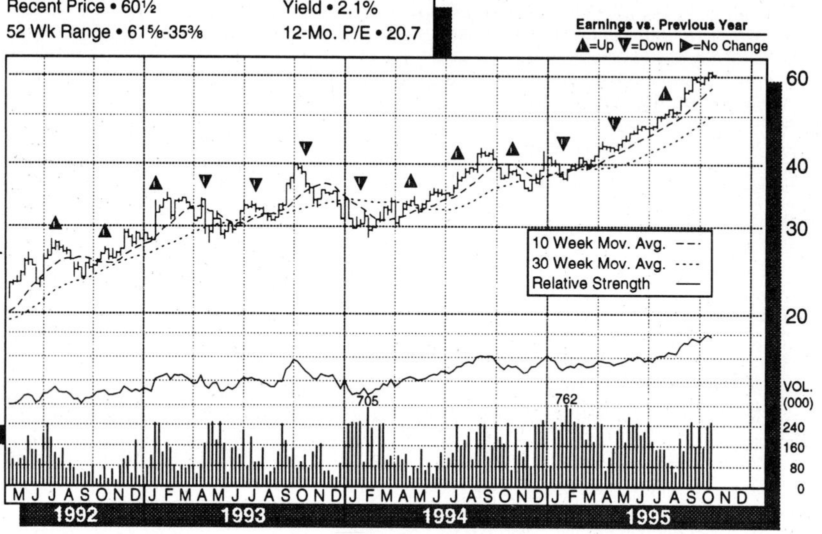

Business Profile - 25-OCT-95

TCF Financial's February 1995 merger with Great Lakes Bancorp ($2.8 billion in assets and 39 offices in Michigan and five in western Ohio) significantly expanded TCF's franchise in attractive Midwest markets. Excluding $32.8 million in aftertax merger-related charges, TCF's income rose 27% in the first nine months of 1995. Looking forward, TCF should continue to benefit from strong consumer loan growth, improving credit quality and an increased level of fee income.

Operational Review - 25-OCT-95

Net interest income for the nine months ended September 30, 1995, rose 15%, year to year. The provision for loan losses increased 73%, to $12,563,000. Merger-related charges led to a 20% decline in noninterest income and a 17% increase in noninterest expense; pretax income fell 33%. After taxes at 39.4%, versus 39.7%, income was down 32%, to $36,168,000 ($1.99 a share, after preferred dividends), from $53,428,000 ($2.98). Results exclude a special charge of $963,000 ($0.05 a share) in 1995.

Stock Performance - 20-OCT-95

In the past 30 trading days, TCB's shares have increased 7%, compared to a 3% rise in the S&P 500. Average trading volume for the past five days was 76,800 shares, compared with the 40-day moving average of 50,085 shares.

Key Stock Statistics

Dividend Rate/Share	1.25	Shareholders	9,600
Shs. outstg. (M)	17.7	Market cap. (B)	$ 1.1
Avg. daily vol. (M)	0.051	Inst. holdings	58%
Tang. Bk. Value/Share	27.08	Insider holdings	NA
Beta	1.87		

Value of $10,000 invested 5 years ago: $ 51,866

Fiscal Year Ending Dec. 31

	1995	% Change	1994	% Change	1993	% Change
Revenues (Million $)						
1Q	157.7	-4%	163.4	66%	98.36	-4%
2Q	185.8	12%	166.3	21%	137.8	33%
3Q	188.2	9%	173.2	43%	121.0	18%
4Q	—	—	174.8	46%	120.1	18%
Yr.	—	—	677.7	42%	477.2	16%
Income (Million $)						
1Q	-11.64	NM	16.23	72%	9.46	16%
2Q	23.39	32%	17.76	47%	12.06	35%
3Q	24.41	26%	19.43	61%	12.06	22%
4Q	—	—	16.76	38%	12.14	-4%
Yr.	—	—	70.18	85%	37.97	-4%
Earnings Per Share ($)						
1Q	-0.72	NM	0.90	15%	0.78	-7%
2Q	1.31	32%	0.99	NM	0.32	-64%
3Q	1.36	25%	1.09	14%	0.96	-2%
4Q	—	—	0.93	-4%	0.97	-22%
Yr.	—	—	3.91	29%	3.04	-24%

Next earnings report expected: mid January

TCF Financial

Business Summary - 25-OCT-95

TCF Financial Corporation owns TCF Bank Minnesota fsb, that state's largest thrift and third largest banking institution. At March 1, 1995, TCF Bank operated, directly and through subsidiaries, more than 250 retail financial services offices in Minnesota, Illinois, Wisconsin, Michigan and Ohio. Other TCF subsidiaries include mortgage banking, consumer finance, title insurance, annuity and mutual fund companies.

Loans outstanding totaling $3.08 billion at December 31, 1994, and $2.75 billion at the end of 1993, were divided:

	1994	1993
Real estate--residential	41%	39%
Consumer loans	36%	33%
Real estate--commercial	21%	25%
Commercial loans	3%	3%

Loans originated during 1994 amounted to $1.37 billion, down from $1.89 billion a year earlier. Loans and mortgage-backed securities purchased amounted to $896.6 million ($1.49 billion), while loans and mortgage-backed securities sold totaled $1.01 billion ($1.77 billion). Principal payments and other reductions aggregated $1.10 billion ($1.36 billion).

At December 31, 1994, nonperforming assets (mainly nonaccrual loans and real estate acquired through foreclosure) totaled $26.1 million (0.86% of net loans), down from $45.0 million (1.66%) a year earlier. At year-end 1994, the allowance for loan losses was $31.6 million (1.02% of loans), versus $26.1 million (0.95%) a year earlier.

Deposits of $3.82 billion at year-end 1994 were apportioned: checking 21%, passbook and statement 20%, money market 11% and certificates 48%.

The weighted average yield on interest-earning assets at December 31, 1994, was 8.48% (7.50% a year earlier), while the weighted average rate paid on interest-bearing liabilities was 4.24% (3.90%), for a net spread of 4.24% (3.60%).

Important Developments

Oct. '95—The company reported that record third-quarter earnings were highlighted by a widening net interest margin. The net interest margin increased 60 basis points in the quarter, to 4.71%, due primarily to strong consumer loan growth. Average loans were $5.33 billion in the third quarter of 1995, a 9.9% increase from average loans of $4.85 billion in the year-earlier period.

Capitalization

FHLB Advances: $809,770,000 (9/95).
Subordinated debt: $48,020,000 (9/95).

Per Share Data ($) (Year Ended Dec. 31)

	1994	1993	1992	1991	1990	1989
Tangible Bk. Val.	24.76	21.40	19.37	14.34	11.40	11.66
Earnings	4.63	3.04	3.98	1.51	-2.86	1.53
Dividends	1.00	0.69	0.47	0.40	0.40	0.40
Payout Ratio	22%	23%	12%	26%	NM	26%
Prices - High	43⅛	40	29½	21¼	14⅜	17⅜
- Low	28½	27¾	17½	7	5½	8⅞
P/E Ratio - High	9	13	7	14	NM	11
- Low	6	9	4	5	NM	6

Income Statement Analysis (Million $)

	1994	%Chg	1993	%Chg	1992	%Chg	1991
Net Int. Inc.	205	11%	184	32%	139	19%	117
Loan Loss Prov.	10.9	-50%	21.9	119%	10.0	-30%	14.3
Non Int. Inc.	117	-3%	120	32%	91.2	7%	85.2
Non Int. Exp.	214	NM	215	26%	171	2%	167
Pretax Inc.	97.7	47%	66.6	36%	48.9	129%	21.4
Eff. Tax Rate	41%	—	43%	—	19%	—	46%
Net Inc.	57.4	51%	38.0	-4%	39.6	NM	11.7
% Net Int. Marg.	4.59%	—	4.04%	—	3.72%	—	3.18%

Balance Sheet & Other Fin. Data (Million $)

	1994	1993	1992	1991	1990	1989
Total Assets	5,068	5,026	4,050	4,037	4,186	4,657
Loans	4,365	4,378	2,195	3,371	3,524	3,871
Deposits	3,820	4,103	3,204	3,232	3,317	3,363
Capitalization:						
Debt	698	446	499	484	519	643
Equity	327	296	210	173	153	176
Total	1,025	741	709	657	672	819

Ratio Analysis

	1994	1993	1992	1991	1990	1989
% Ret. on Assets	1.1	0.8	1.0	0.5	NM	0.4
% Ret. on Equity	18.4	13.7	21.7	11.7	NM	11.4
% Loan Loss Resv.	0.7	0.6	0.7	0.6	0.7	0.4
% Risk Based Capital	12.0	12.3	11.9	8.7	7.6	NA
Price Times Book Value:						
High	1.7	1.9	1.5	1.5	1.3	1.5
Low	1.2	1.3	0.9	0.5	0.5	0.8

Dividend Data —Dividends were initiated in 1988. A dividend reinvestment plan is available. A "poison pill" stock purchase rights plan was adopted in 1989.

Amt. of Div. $	Date Decl.	Ex-Div. Date	Stock of Record	Payment Date
0.250	Jan. 24	Feb. 06	Feb. 10	Feb. 28 '95
0.313	Apr. 18	May. 08	May. 12	May. 31 '95
0.313	Jul. 25	Aug. 09	Aug. 11	Aug. 31 '95
0.313	Oct. 24	Nov. 08	Nov. 10	Nov. 30 '95
2-for-1	Oct. 16	Dec. 01	Nov. 10	Nov. 30 '95

Data as orig. reptd.; bef. results of disc opers. and/or spec. items. Per share data adj. for stk. divs. as of ex-div. date. E-Estimated. NA-Not Available. NM-Not Meaningful. NR-Not Ranked.

Office—801 Marquette Ave., Suite 302, Minneapolis, MN 55402. **Tel**—(612) 661-6500. **Chrmn & CEO**—W. A. Cooper. **Vice Chrmn & Secy**—G. J. Pulles. **Pres, COO & Treas**—Lynn A. Nagorske. **Investor Contact**—Cynthia W. Lee (612) 661-8859. **Dirs**—B. G. Allbright, R. E. Boschwitz, J. P. Clifford, W. A. Cooper, T. A. Cusick, R. J. Delonis, J. M. Eggemeyer III, R. E. Evans, L. G. Goldberg, D. F. May, T. J. McGough, M. K. Rosenfeld, R. Strangis, R. A. Ward, R. E. Weber. **Transfer Agent & Registrar**—First National Bank of Boston. **Incorporated** in Delaware in 1987. **Empl**-4,000. **S&P Analyst:** Brad Ohlmuller

STANDARD & POOR'S

STOCK REPORTS

TJ International

NASDAQ Symbol **TJCO**

In S&P SmallCap 600

17-OCT-95 **Industry:** Building

Summary: This manufacturer of structural components for the light construction industry also produces high-quality wood windows and patio doors.

Quantitative Evaluations	Recent Price • 18¾	Yield • 1.2%
	52 Wk Range • 21½-14¼	12-Mo. P/E • NM

Outlook (1 Lowest—5 Highest) **• 2−**

Fair Value **• 17**

Risk **• Average**

Earn./Div. Rank **• B**

Technical Eval. **• Bearish** since 10/95

Rel. Strength Rank (1 Lowest—99 Highest) **• 26**

Insider Activity **• Neutral**

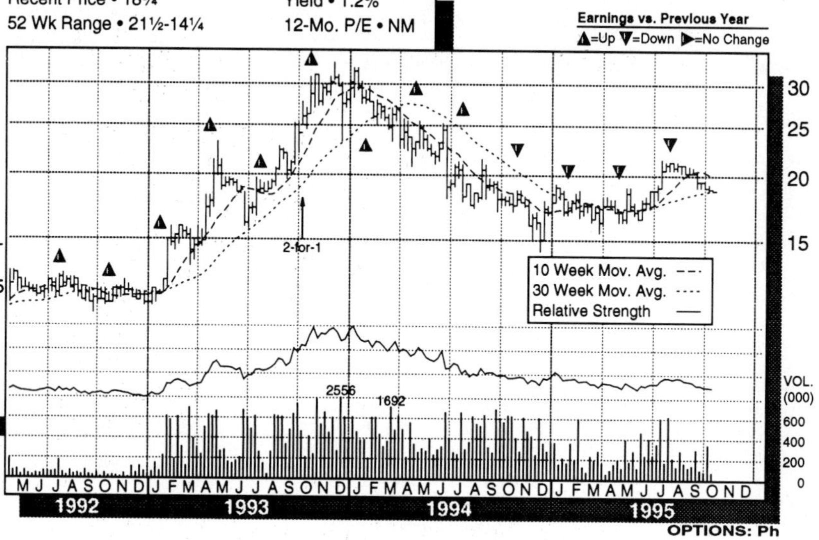

OPTIONS: Ph

Business Profile - 17-OCT-95

This company is primarily a producer of laminated structural lumber products, mostly for use in new home building. TJCO believes its engineered lumber business will grow, due to the increasing acceptance of lumber laminates as a substitute for traditional lumber in homebuilding. However, TJCO expects greater pricing pressure on manufactured lumber for the foreseeable future. In late 1993, TJCO began building two lumber product plants to expand capacity and broaden TJ's product lines.

Operational Review - 17-OCT-95

Revenues for 1995's first half fell 7.0%, year to year, reflecting lower selling prices of lumber products, and a decrease in window and door volume, both from slowing housing starts. Operating income declined 40%, mostly due to a decline in gross profit margins from the lower selling price of lumber products, and $3.8 million in start-up costs at two new plants. Despite a sharp increase in net investment income, net income fell 63%, to $3,100,000 from $8,281,000.

Stock Performance - 13-OCT-95

In the past 30 trading days, TJCO's shares have declined 7%, compared to a 4% rise in the S&P 500. Average trading volume for the past five days was 14,000 shares, compared with the 40-day moving average of 32,664 shares.

Key Stock Statistics

Dividend Rate/Share	0.22	Shareholders	1,800
Shs. outstg. (M)	16.9	Market cap. (B)	$0.313
Avg. daily vol. (M)	0.030	Inst. holdings	44%
Tang. Bk. Value/Share	11.17	Insider holdings	NA
Beta	0.94		

Value of $10,000 invested 5 years ago: $ 16,727

Fiscal Year Ending Dec. 31

	1995	% Change	1994	% Change	1993	% Change
Revenues (Million $)						
1Q	129.1	-4%	135.1	18%	114.1	51%
2Q	148.6	-9%	163.5	17%	139.6	26%
3Q	—	—	171.7	12%	152.7	35%
4Q	—	—	148.6	3%	144.7	44%
Yr.	—	—	618.9	12%	551.2	38%
Income (Million $)						
1Q	0.51	-80%	2.56	NM	-0.57	NM
2Q	2.59	-55%	5.72	34%	4.26	29%
3Q	—	—	4.21	-28%	5.83	69%
4Q	—	—	-3.64	NM	3.01	NM
Yr.	—	—	8.85	-29%	12.53	95%
Earnings Per Share ($)						
1Q	0.02	-85%	0.13	NM	-0.06	NM
2Q	0.14	-56%	0.32	7%	0.30	40%
3Q	—	—	0.23	-44%	0.41	67%
4Q	—	—	-0.23	NM	0.17	NM
Yr.	—	—	0.46	-44%	0.82	116%

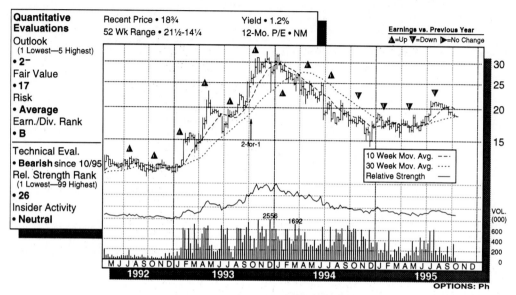

Next earnings report expected: late October

TJ International

Business Summary - 17-OCT-95

TJ International, Inc. (formerly Trus Joist Corporation) manufactures and markets specialty building products. It is the 51% owner and managing partner of Trus Joist MacMillan, A Limited Partnership, a joint venture with MacMillan Bloedel Ltd. that makes structural composite lumber. TJCO also owns a 64% interest in a window and patio door limited partnership.

The company is an industry leader in developing and commercializing proprietary technologies that enable the manufacturing of engineered lumber products from wood that has been regarded as not sufficiently large, strong, straight or free of defects to be sawn into structural lumber. TJ's three engineered lumber technologies are: laminated veneer lumber (LVL), parallel strand lumber (PSL) and laminated strand lumber (LSL). Both PSL and LSL are proprietary to the company. TJ's engineered products are sold mostly to the new-housing market. In addition, it makes wood and steel web trusses for light commercial and industrial products, such as scaffold planking and concrete forming, and engineered lumber core material for windows, doors and furniture.

TJ's proprietary Microllam LVL product, consisting of many layers of thin, dried veneer, is used mainly as a raw material for TJ's joists and is also sold directly to industrial users as a structural component for manufactured housing, scaffold planking and other uses. Parallam PSL, a high-strength structural composite lumber produced from small-diameter, second- and third-growth trees, is sold mainly as headers, beams, columns and posts. TimberStrand LSL is an environmentally friendly, high-performance window and door core material.

In 1994, TJ decided to reduce its investment in and exposure to the window business. In October 1994, TJCO formed the Outlook Window Partnership L.P., (64% interest), and combined its U.S. subsidiary, Norco Windows, Inc., with SealRite Windows, Inc. and Oldach Window Corp.

TJ also makes a full line of unfinished, primed, aluminum-clad and vinyl-encapsulated wood windows and doors--all sold primarily to the new-housing market.

Important Developments

Aug. '95—Commenting on 1995's second quarter results, TJCO said that the 9% decline in revenues mainly reflected a reduction in window and door sales. The erosion in margins stemmed from TJCO's decision to lower prices on lumber products in order to retain market position.

Capitalization

Long Term Debt: $117,456,000 (7/1/95).
Minority Interest: $192,974,000.
ESOP Conv. Pfd. Stk.: 1,193,122 shs. ($1 par).

Per Share Data ($) (Year Ended Dec. 31)

	1994	1993	1992	1991	1990	1989
Tangible Bk. Val.	11.17	12.38	7.85	6.66	5.94	6.55
Cash Flow	2.09	2.47	2.01	0.84	1.71	1.88
Earnings	0.46	0.82	0.38	-0.32	0.82	1.06
Dividends	0.22	0.22	0.21	0.21	0.21	0.20
Payout Ratio	48%	31%	54%	NM	25%	19%
Prices - High	32¼	33	13	15	13¼	18⅛
- Low	14¼	11⅛	8	7¾	7⅛	11½
P/E Ratio - High	70	40	34	NM	16	17
- Low	31	14	21	NM	9	11

Income Statement Analysis (Million $)

	1994	%Chg	1993	%Chg	1992	%Chg	1991
Revs.	619	12%	551	38%	400	41%	283
Oper. Inc.	69.6	23%	56.5	NM	13.0	6%	12.3
Depr.	28.3	20%	23.6	8%	21.8	46%	14.9
Int. Exp.	5.3	55%	3.4	-4%	3.5	48%	2.4
Pretax Inc.	43.6	45%	30.1	NM	-11.0	NM	-12.4
Eff. Tax Rate	18%	—	25%	—	NM	—	NM
Net Inc.	8.9	-29%	12.5	95%	6.4	NM	-3.2

Balance Sheet & Other Fin. Data (Million $)

	1994	1993	1992	1991	1990	1989
Cash	73.7	73.3	0.2	0.5	3.1	3.3
Curr. Assets	188	183	80.9	68.9	59.1	66.3
Total Assets	614	454	345	335	167	173
Curr. Liab.	62.4	57.1	56.8	54.7	27.7	35.4
LT Debt	102	30.9	33.1	26.4	28.9	30.3
Common Eqty.	238	231	127	112	78.0	92.0
Total Cap.	540	382	274	276	137	135
Cap. Exp.	152	34.0	27.0	145	14.0	37.0
Cash Flow	36.3	35.3	26.9	10.9	24.3	27.2

Ratio Analysis

	1994	1993	1992	1991	1990	1989
Curr. Ratio	3.0	3.2	1.4	1.3	2.1	1.9
% LT Debt of Cap.	19.0	8.1	12.1	9.6	21.1	22.4
% Net Inc.of Revs.	1.1	2.3	1.6	NM	3.6	4.3
% Ret. on Assets	1.6	2.8	1.9	NM	7.3	9.5
% Ret. on Equity	3.4	5.9	4.0	NM	14.3	17.8

Dividend Data —Cash has been paid each year since 1977.

Amt. of Div. $	Date Decl.	Ex-Div. Date	Stock of Record	Payment Date
0.055	Aug. 30	Sep. 19	Sep. 23	Oct. 19 '94
0.055	Dec. 15	Dec. 19	Dec. 23	Jan. 11 '95
0.055	Feb. 16	Mar. 20	Mar. 24	Apr. 19 '95
0.055	May. 24	Jun. 21	Jun. 23	Jul. 21 '95
0.055	Aug. 24	Sep. 20	Sep. 22	Oct. 18 '95

Data as orig. reptd.; bef. results of disc. opers. and/or spec. items. Per share data adj. for stk. divs. as of ex-div. date. E-Estimated. NA-Not Available. NM-Not Meaningful. NR-Not Ranked.

Office—200 E. Mallard Dr., Boise, ID 83706. **Tel**—(208) 364-3300. **Chrmn**—H. E. Thomas. **Pres & CEO**—T. Denig. **VP-Fin & CFO**—V. A. Heusinkveld. **Secy & Treas**—R. B. Drury. **Dirs**—T. H. Denig, R. B. Findlay, R. V. Hansberger, J. L. Scott, H. E. Thomas, A. L. Troutner, J. R. Tullis, S. C. Wheelwright, W. J. White. **Transfer Agent & Registrar**—West One Bank, Boise. **Incorporated** in Idaho in 1960; reincorporated in Nevada in 1973; reincorporated in Delaware in 1987. **Empl**-4,000. **S&P Analyst:** Robert E. Friedman

STANDARD & POOR'S

STOCK REPORTS

TNP Enterprises

NYSE Symbol **TNP**
In S&P SmallCap 600

03-AUG-95 **Industry:** Utilities-Electric

Summary: TNP is the holding company for Texas-New Mexico Power, which distributes electricity to diverse areas of Texas and New Mexico.

Quantitative Evaluations

Outlook (1 Lowest—5 Highest) • **4+**
Fair Value • **16½**
Risk • **Low**
Earn./Div. Rank • **B**
Technical Eval. • **Bullish** since 9/92
Rel. Strength Rank (1 Lowest—99 Highest) • **43**
Insider Activity • **NA**

Recent Price • 16⅜
52 Wk Range • 16¾-13⅛
Yield • 4.9%
12-Mo. P/E • 9.5

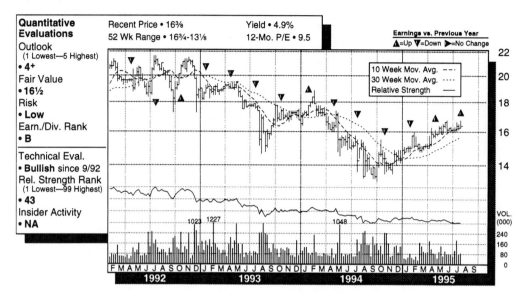

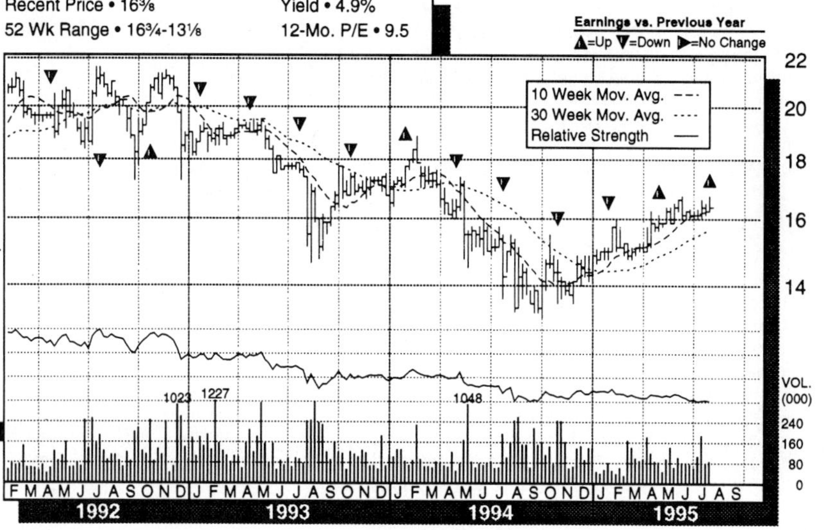

Business Profile - 03-AUG-95

In 1994, TNP implemented a reorganization, which included a 14% staff reduction that it expects will result in annual cost savings of about $7 million in payroll and payroll-related expenses. In October 1994, a settlement was negotiated in TNP's Texas rate case that resolved virtually all outstanding issues related to the regulatory treatment of TNP One. TNP agreed to freeze its base rates at current levels for five years and to pursue the sale of its properties in the Texas Panhandle.

Operational Review - 03-AUG-95

Revenues for the second quarter of 1995 rose 9%, year to year, reflecting higher residential and commercial sales, partially offset by lower industrial sales. Following a $31.5 million loss from the recognition of regulatory disallowances in 1994, net income contrasted with a large net loss. During the second quarter, TNP changed its method of accounting for operating revenues from cycle billing to full accrual, and applied this method retroactively to January 1, 1995.

Stock Performance - 28-JUL-95

In the past 30 trading days, TNP's shares have increased 0.77%, compared to a 4% rise in the S&P 500. Average trading volume for the past five days was 16,760 shares, compared with the 40-day moving average of 19,033 shares.

Key Stock Statistics

Dividend Rate/Share	0.80	Shareholders	6,300
Shs. outstg. (M)	10.7	Market cap. (B)	$0.175
Avg. daily vol. (M)	0.023	Inst. holdings	45%
Tang. Bk. Value/Share	17.26	Insider holdings	NA
Beta	0.42		

Value of $10,000 invested 5 years ago: $ 11,967

Fiscal Year Ending Dec. 31

	1995	% Change	1994	% Change	1993	% Change
Revenues (Million $)						
1Q	107.6	NM	107.6	4%	103.2	5%
2Q	121.2	9%	111.1	3%	107.5	2%
3Q	—	—	149.9	NM	150.1	9%
4Q	—	—	109.5	-4%	113.5	11%
Yr.	—	—	478.0	NM	474.2	7%
Income (Million $)						
1Q	-1.04	NM	-2.88	NM	-1.87	143%
2Q	6.13	NM	-21.65	NM	-0.41	NM
3Q	—	—	11.92	-12%	13.58	7%
4Q	—	—	-4.82	NM	0.30	NM
Yr.	—	—	-17.44	NM	11.61	6%
Earnings Per Share ($)						
1Q	-0.11	NM	-0.29	NM	-0.20	NM
2Q	0.54	NM	-2.04	NM	-0.06	NM
3Q	—	—	1.09	-13%	1.25	-14%
4Q	—	—	-0.47	NM	0.01	NM
Yr.	—	—	-1.70	NM	1.01	-14%

Next earnings report expected: early November

TNP Enterprises

Business Summary - 03-AUG-95

TNP Enterprises is the holding company for Texas-New Mexico Power Co. (TNMP), a utility that engages in the production, transmission and distribution of electricity. It serves areas in Texas (about 83% of utility revenues) and New Mexico with a population of some 630,000. About 50% of utility revenues are derived from the Gulf Coast area of Texas, between Houston and Galveston, where the economy is supported by the oil, petrochemical and agriculture industries and the general commercial activity of the Houston area. Contributions to revenues:

	1994	1993	1992	1991
Residential	41%	41%	40%	40%
Commercial	30%	29%	29%	27%
Industrial	25%	26%	27%	29%
Other	4%	4%	4%	4%

Sales of electricity in 1994 totaled 6,471 million kwh, up 2.9% from 1993. Average residential rates were 9.35 cents per kwh (9.45 cents in 1993) on average annual usage of 11,354 kwh (11,362 kwh).

TNP purchased about 66% (65% in 1993) of its electric requirements in 1994. The utility reduced its dependence on other sources of energy when it purchased the first 150-megawatt unit of a lignite-fired power plant in 1990 and the second 150-megawatt unit in 1991. The two units (which began commercial operation in September 1990 and October 1991, respectively) on an annualized basis are expected to continue providing about 30% of TNP's electric capacity requirements in Texas.

At December 31, 1994, the costs of Unit 1 and Unit 2 totaled about $357 million and $283 million, respectively. The company expects 1995-1999 capital requirements for utility plant additions, bond sinking fund and retirements, and preferred stock redemptions to aggregate $511 million. Utility plant financings and additions account for about $157 million of the requirements. TNP anticipates funding the utility plant additions with operating cash flow.

In October 1994, TNP resolved substantially all of its outstanding court appeals with the Public Utilities Commission of Texas (PUCT) for rate filings associated with two previous rate cases. The settlement required a writeoff of $35 million of the $61.4 million in TNP One plant costs which previously had been disallowed by PUCT. Earlier, in May 1994, TNP successfully resolved its rate filing case with New Mexico.

Important Developments

Nov. '94—TNP agreed in principle to sell its Texas Panhandle area properties to Southwestern Public Service Co. for $29 million. Closing is expected in the summer of 1995.

Capitalization

Long Term Debt: $689,841,000 (3/95).
Red. Cum. Preferred Stock: $8,380,000.

Per Share Data ($)

(Year Ended Dec. 31)

	1994	1993	1992	1991	1990	1989
Tangible Bk. Val.	17.01	19.97	20.55	21.35	20.76	20.55
Earnings	-1.70	1.01	1.17	2.23	1.84	1.90
Dividends	1.21	1.63	1.63	1.63	1.63	1.55
Payout Ratio	NM	161%	139%	73%	89%	82%
Prices - High	$18\frac{7}{8}$	$19\frac{1}{2}$	$21\frac{5}{8}$	21	$22\frac{1}{2}$	$22\frac{3}{8}$
- Low	$13\frac{1}{8}$	$14\frac{5}{8}$	$17\frac{1}{4}$	$15\frac{7}{8}$	$14\frac{1}{2}$	19
P/E Ratio - High	NM	19	18	9	12	12
- Low	NM	14	15	7	8	10

Income Statement Analysis (Million $)

	1994	%Chg	1993	%Chg	1992	%Chg	1991
Revs.	478	NM	474	7%	444	NM	441
Depr.	36.8	2%	36.0	3%	35.1	25%	28.0
Maint.	12.0	4%	11.5	2%	11.3	NM	11.2
Fxd. Chgs. Cov.	0.6	-50%	1.2	4%	1.2	-26%	1.6
Constr. Credits	0.3	-7%	0.3	100%	0.2	-97%	4.6
Eff. Tax Rate	NM	—	30%	—	22%	—	29%
Net Inc.	-17.4	NM	11.6	6%	10.9	-44%	19.5

Balance Sheet & Other Fin. Data (Million $)

	1994	1993	1992	1991	1990	1989
Gross Prop.	1,196	1,209	1,189	1,162	853	475
Cap. Exp.	29.0	26.0	22.1	29.9	40.8	24.0
Net Prop.	967	1,006	1,016	1,017	729	363
Capitalization:						
LT Debt	683	679	742	525	350	135
% LT Debt	78	75	76	73	66	42
Pfd.	8.7	9.6	10.4	11.3	12.6	13.9
% Pfd.	1.00	1.10	1.10	1.60	2.40	4.40
Common	185	214	219	178	172	169
% Common	21	24	23	25	32	53
Total Cap.	940	1,007	1,085	819	630	387

Ratio Analysis

	1994	1993	1992	1991	1990	1989
Oper. Ratio	83.7	83.5	82.7	85.8	90.7	92.5
% Earn. on Net Prop.	7.9	7.7	7.6	7.2	6.8	7.9
% Ret. on Revs.	NM	2.4	2.5	4.4	4.1	4.4
% Ret. On Invest.Cap	6.0	7.6	8.3	8.7	7.3	8.0
% Return On Com.Eqty	NM	5.0	5.0	10.5	8.9	9.3

Dividend Data (Dividends have been paid since 1936. A dividend reinvestment plan is available. A "poison pill" stock purchase rights plan was adopted in 1988.)

Amt. of Div. $	Date Decl.	Ex-Div. Date	Stock of Record	Payment Date
0.200	Aug. 16	Aug. 23	Aug. 29	Sep. 15 '94
0.200	Nov. 15	Nov. 21	Nov. 28	Dec. 15 '94
0.200	Feb. 10	Feb. 22	Feb. 28	Mar. 15 '95
0.200	Apr. 28	May. 16	May. 22	Jun. 15 '95

Data as orig. reptd.; bef. results of disc opers. and/or spec. items. Per share data adj. for stk. divs. as of ex-div. date. E-Estimated. NA-Not Available. NM-Not Meaningful. NR-Not Ranked.

Office—4100 International Plaza, P.O. Box 2943, Fort Worth, TX 76113. **Tel**—(817) 731-0099. **Chrmn, Pres & CEO**—K. R. Joyce. **Secy**—M. D. Blanchard. **VP-CFO, Treas & Investor Contact**—Manjit S. Cheema. **Dirs**—R. D. Alexander, C. O. Edwards II, J. A. Fanning, S. M. Gutierrez, K. R. Joyce, H. L. Kempner Jr., D. R. Spurlock, R. D. Woofter. **Transfer Agent & Registrar**—Society National Bank, Dallas. **Incorporated** in Texas in 1963; reincorporated in Texas in 1984. **Empl**-894. **S&P Analyst:** A.M.A.

STANDARD & POOR'S

STOCK REPORTS

TPI Enterprises

NASDAQ Symbol **TPIE**

In S&P SmallCap 600

02-NOV-95

Industry: Food serving

Summary: In September 1995 this operator of 187 Shoney's and 69 Captain D's restaurants signed a letter of intent to be acquired by Shoney's Inc.

Quantitative Evaluations

Outlook (1 Lowest—5 Highest)
• **NA**

Fair Value
• **NA**

Risk
• **High**

Earn./Div. Rank
• **C**

Technical Eval.
• **Bearish** since 9/95

Rel. Strength Rank (1 Lowest—99 Highest)
• **37**

Insider Activity
• **NA**

Recent Price • 3⅜

52 Wk Range • 6⅝-3⅜

Yield • Nil

12-Mo. P/E • NM

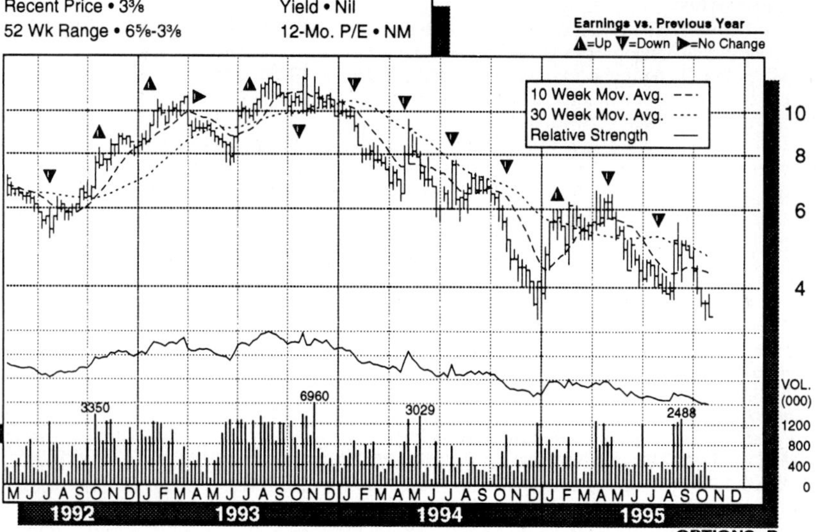

OPTIONS: P

Business Profile - 02-NOV-95

In September 1995, TPI agreed to be acquired by Shoney's Inc. TPI is the largest U.S. franchisee of Shoney's and Captain D's restaurants. To combat declining sales in the Shoney's system, the company has undertaken a restructuring program that includes consumer research studies, advertising adjustments, enhanced employee training, restructured bonus programs, remodeling of restaurants and modification of the menu.

Operational Review - 02-NOV-95

A net loss was incurred in 1995's first half. Revenues fell 4.4% as same-store sales declines outweighed increased contributions from new restaurants. Comparable-store sales decreased 5.2% in the Shoney's units and increased 0.7% in Captain D's restaurants. Margins narrowed on the lower sales volumes and price increases in several high-volume commodities. Results were further penalized by an increase in interest rates, resulting in higher interest costs.

Stock Performance - 27-OCT-95

In the past 30 trading days, TPIE's shares have declined 29%, compared to a 0.63% fall in the S&P 500. Average trading volume for the past five days was 40,000 shares, compared with the 40-day moving average of 130,674 shares.

Key Stock Statistics

Dividend Rate/Share	Nil	Shareholders	2,100
Shs. outstg. (M)	20.5	Market cap. (B)	$0.082
Avg. daily vol. (M)	0.082	Inst. holdings	44%
Tang. Bk. Value/Share	0.46	Insider holdings	NA
Beta	0.73		

Value of $10,000 invested 5 years ago: $ 4,740

Fiscal Year Ending Dec. 31

	1995	% Change	1994	% Change	1993	% Change
Revenues (Million $)						
1Q	83.74	-4%	87.40	3%	85.10	1%
2Q	67.24	-2%	68.73	-2%	69.85	2%
3Q	—	—	67.33	-4%	70.33	7%
4Q	—	—	63.93	NM	64.13	5%
Yr.	—	—	287.4	NM	289.4	4%
Income (Million $)						
1Q	-1.51	NM	0.85	-13%	0.98	1%
2Q	-0.76	NM	0.34	-70%	1.13	18%
3Q	—	—	-1.25	NM	0.49	-60%
4Q	—	—	-3.65	NM	-39.08	NM
Yr.	—	—	-3.72	NM	-36.49	NM
Earnings Per Share ($)						
1Q	-0.07	NM	0.04	-20%	0.05	NM
2Q	-0.04	NM	0.02	-67%	0.06	20%
3Q	—	—	-0.06	NM	0.02	-71%
4Q	—	—	-0.18	NM	-1.93	NM
Yr.	—	—	-0.18	NM	-1.81	NM

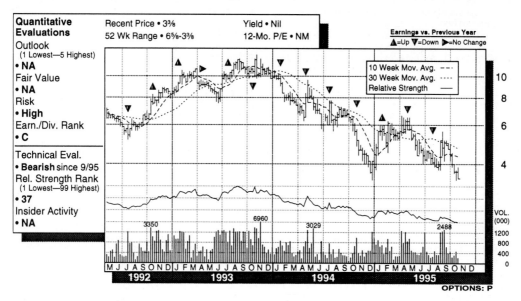

Next earnings report expected: early November

TPI Enterprises

Business Summary - 02-NOV-95

Since the 1988 acquisition of Shoney's South, Inc., the business of TPI Enterprises, Inc. (formerly Telecom Plus International) has consisted primarily of the operation of moderately priced restaurants. As of March 15, 1995, TPI operated 256 restaurants--187 Shoney's and 69 Captain D's.

The company is the largest franchisee of Shoney's restaurants, which are full-service, family-style restaurants that generally are open 18 hours per day, seven days a week, serving breakfast, lunch and dinner. The varied menu of steaks, seafood, hamburgers, chicken and sandwiches, as well as the availability of salad and breakfast bars, is designed to appeal to a broad spectrum of customers. The average check was $5.84 in 1994. The company has the right to develop Shoney's restaurants in more than 80% of Texas, and in the Orlando, Broward and Palm Beach areas of Florida.

Captain D's are fast-service restaurants specializing in seafood and are generally open 11 hours per day, seven days a week. The menu emphasizes fish fillets, shrimp, clams, stuffed crab in a natural shell, and salads. Hamburgers, chicken fillets, french fries, hush-puppies and country-style vegetables are also served. Take-out service including drive-through windows accounted for about 44% of the chain's sales in 1994. The average check in 1994 was $4.63.

During 1994, the company opened five newly constructed Shoney's, closed 15 underperforming Shoney's, and relocated one restaurant. Three new Captain D's were opened during 1994, and TPI closed one underperforming restaurant. Comparable-store sales for Shoney's in 1994 were down 4.3%, while Captain D's comparable-store sales rose 6.0%.

TPI adopted a restructuring plan at the end of 1993 that included closing or relocating 31 of its restaurants by the end of 1994. TPI recorded $19.8 million of restructuring charges in 1993. As of December 25, 1994, the company had closed 22 restaurants, and planned to close an additional four restaurants during the first half of 1995.

Important Developments

Sep. '95—Shoney's Inc. signed a letter of intent to merge a unit with TPI. Shoney's will exchange 0.28 shares for each outstanding TPI share, and a warrant for every 3.125 outstanding TPI shares. The five-year warrants entitle the holder to acquire Shoney's stock at $21.50 a share. Also, Shoney's agreed to assume $95 million of TPI debt. The transaction is expected to close by the end of 1995, subject to the requisite approvals.

Capitalization

Long Term Debt: $83,675,000 (7/9/95).
Warrants: To buy 1,000,000 shs. at $11 a sh.

Per Share Data ($) (Year Ended Dec. 31)

	1994	1993	1992	1991	1990	1989
Tangible Bk. Val.	0.50	3.48	4.60	5.38	5.07	-0.23
Cash Flow	0.76	-1.02	0.84	0.22	1.23	0.57
Earnings	-0.18	-1.81	0.04	-0.63	0.07	-0.39
Dividends	Nil	Nil	Nil	Nil	Nil	Nil
Payout Ratio	Nil	Nil	Nil	Nil	Nil	Nil
Prices - High	10⅝	12½	8⅞	7½	7½	7¾
- Low	3⅜	7½	5⅛	3½	4	3¾
P/E Ratio - High	NM	NM	NM	NM	NM	NM
- Low	NM	NM	NM	NM	NM	NM

Income Statement Analysis (Million $)

	1994	%Chg	1993	%Chg	1992	%Chg	1991
Revs.	287	NM	289	4%	279	6%	263
Oper. Inc.	24.4	-9%	26.7	-11%	29.9	52%	19.7
Depr.	19.2	19%	16.1	10%	14.7	-10%	16.3
Int. Exp.	10.2	-3%	10.5	-27%	14.3	-21%	18.2
Pretax Inc.	-3.7	NM	-42.3	NM	0.9	NM	-16.4
Eff. Tax Rate	NM	—	NM	—	29%	—	NM
Net Inc.	-3.7	NM	-36.5	NM	0.7	NM	-12.1

Balance Sheet & Other Fin. Data (Million $)

	1994	1993	1992	1991	1990	1989
Cash	17.0	17.0	21.0	64.0	41.0	38.0
Curr. Assets	39.0	41.0	48.0	91.0	113	123
Total Assets	254	259	259	283	427	445
Curr. Liab.	57.0	52.0	49.0	63.0	95.0	111
LT Debt	108	107	113	108	214	207
Common Eqty.	68.0	71.0	84.0	97.0	110	111
Total Cap.	181	184	206	216	328	330
Cap. Exp.	19.1	51.8	30.9	17.1	22.1	17.9
Cash Flow	15.5	-20.4	15.4	4.3	26.9	13.1

Ratio Analysis

	1994	1993	1992	1991	1990	1989
Curr. Ratio	0.7	0.8	1.0	1.4	1.2	1.1
% LT Debt of Cap.	59.5	58.0	55.0	50.0	65.2	62.8
% Net Inc.of Revs.	NM	NM	0.2	NM	0.4	NM
% Ret. on Assets	NM	NM	0.2	NM	0.4	NM
% Ret. on Equity	NM	NM	0.7	NM	1.4	NM

Dividend Data —No cash dividends have been paid.

Data as orig. reptd.; bef. results of disc. opers. and/or spec. items. Per share data adj. for stk. divs. as of ex-div. date. E-Estimated. NA-Not Available. NM-Not Meaningful. NR-Not Ranked.

Office—3950 RCA Boulevard, Suite 5001, Palm Beach Gardens, FL 33410. **Tel**—(407) 691-8800. **Pres & CEO**—J. G. Sharp. **EVP & CFO**—F. W. Burford. **EVP & Secy**—R. A. Kennedy. **Dirs**—D. K. Bratton, F. W. Burford, O. Cisneros, L. W. Levy, J. L. Marion Jr., J. G. Sharp, P. J. Siu, E. B. Spievack, T. M. Taylor. **Transfer Agent**—American Stock Transfer & Trust Co., NYC. **Incorporated** in New Jersey in 1970. **Empl**-10,300. **S&P Analyst:** SAJ

Tech Data Corp.

NASDAQ Symbol **TECD**
In S&P SmallCap 600

01-OCT-95

Industry:
Data Processing

Summary: This company is a leading distributor of microcomputer-related hardware and software to VARs and computer retailers throughout the U.S., Canada, Latin America and the Caribbean.

Quantitative Evaluations

Outlook
(1 Lowest—5 Highest)
• **5+**

Fair Value
• **15⅝**

Risk
• **High**

Earn./Div. Rank
• **B**

Technical Eval.
• **Bullish** since 9/95

Rel. Strength Rank
(1 Lowest—99 Highest)
• **87**

Insider Activity
• **Neutral**

Recent Price • 14⅛
52 Wk Range • 20-8¼
Yield • Nil
12-Mo. P/E • 25.2

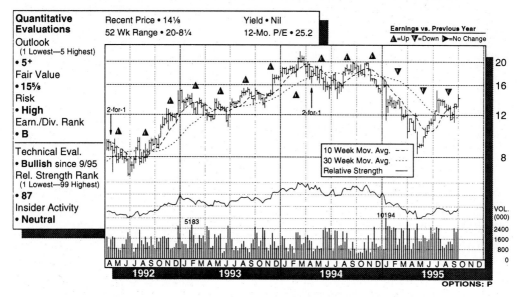

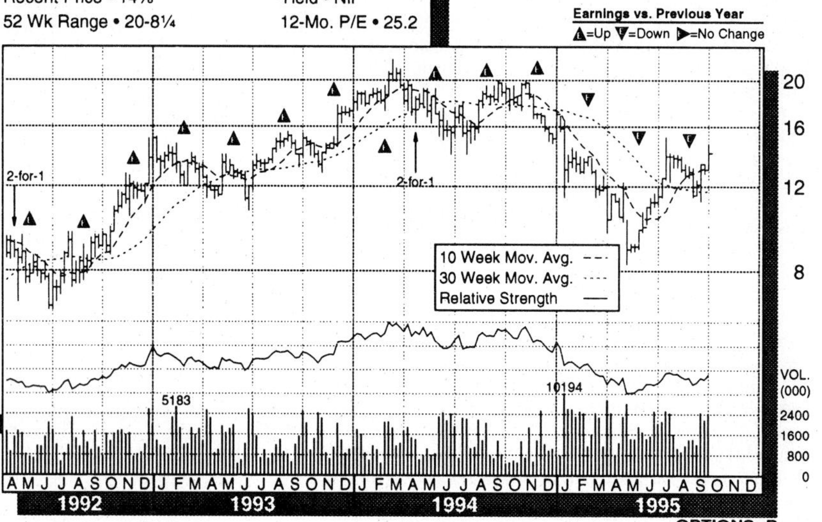

OPTIONS: P

Business Profile - 28-SEP-95

Tech Data is a leading distributor of microcomputer-related hardware and software products to VARs and computer retailers throughout the U.S., Canada, Latin America and the Caribbean. The company has introduced several new services to increase its competitiveness, including a computerized online data system through which customers can get product availability, pricing and ordering information; and Tech Data Elect, which offers selected resellers competitive cost-plus pricing and discounts.

Operational Review - 28-SEP-95

Revenues in the first half of fiscal 1996 rose 22%, year to year, reflecting increased sales in all product segments, especially software and computer systems, which increased 34% and 27%, respectively. International sales also grew 31% during the first half. Margins narrowed, mainly due to increased competition, and net income plunged 72% to $0.14 a share from $0.49 in the first half last year.

Stock Performance - 29-SEP-95

In the past 30 trading days, TECD's shares have increased 12%, compared to a 5% rise in the S&P 500. Average trading volume for the past five days was 513,440 shares, compared with the 40-day moving average of 344,815 shares.

Key Stock Statistics

Dividend Rate/Share	Nil	Shareholders	15,000
Shs. outstg. (M)	37.8	Market cap. (B)	$0.535
Avg. daily vol. (M)	0.443	Inst. holdings	51%
Tang. Bk. Value/Share	6.84	Insider holdings	NA
Beta	1.22		

Value of $10,000 invested 5 years ago: $ 72,884

Fiscal Year Ending Jan. 31

	1996	% Change	1995	% Change	1994	% Change
Revenues (Million $)						
1Q	633.5	20%	530.0	59%	332.3	65%
2Q	708.8	24%	569.7	62%	352.0	54%
3Q	—	—	658.3	63%	404.0	52%
4Q	—	—	659.9	49%	444.0	56%
Yr.	—	—	2,418	58%	1,532	57%
Income (Million $)						
1Q	1.85	-80%	9.23	43%	6.45	65%
2Q	3.45	-64%	9.60	38%	6.98	54%
3Q	—	—	10.30	29%	7.98	42%
4Q	—	—	5.79	-34%	8.80	54%
Yr.	—	—	34.91	16%	30.21	53%
Earnings Per Share ($)						
1Q	0.05	-79%	0.24	33%	0.18	44%
2Q	0.09	-64%	0.25	32%	0.19	31%
3Q	—	—	0.27	26%	0.22	19%
4Q	—	—	0.15	-38%	0.24	33%
Yr.	—	—	0.91	10%	0.83	32%

Next earnings report expected: mid December

Tech Data Corp.

Business Summary - 29-SEP-95

Tech Data Corporation distributes microcomputers and microcomputer-related hardware and software products, such as local area networks, disk drives and peripherals, to value-added resellers (VARs) and computer retailers throughout the U.S., Canada, Latin America and the Caribbean. It purchases directly from manufacturers in large quantities, maintains a stocking inventory in excess of 18,000 products from more than 600 manufacturers, and sells to an active base of more than 50,000 customers. As a distributor, the company offers manufacturers of microcomputer hardware the ability to reach low-volume customers on a cost-efficient basis.

The company delivers products from distribution centers in Miami, Fla., Atlanta, Ga., Ft. Worth, Tex., Paulsboro, N.J., South Bend, Ind., Ontario and Union City, Calif., Twinsburg, Ohio, Mississauga, Ont., Richmond, B.C., and Bobigny (Paris), France.

Tech Data's suppliers include Apple, Compaq, IBM, Adobe, Aldus, Novell, Borland, Computer Associates, Microsoft, 3Com, Intel, Lotus, NEC Technologies, Toshiba and Conner Peripherals. In addition, it began to distribute certain application software during the first quarter of 1992-3. In recent years, no single vendor accounted for over 10% of net sales, and no single customer for more than 3%.

The company has introduced a variety of new services to complement its products. The Advanced Technology Systems Engineers group was formed to assist customers with high-end network configurations and emerging technology needs. The SMARTSupport program was initiated to aid resellers with post-sales technical support needs. Tech Data also offers credit services and educational services.

Tech Data's operations are structured to realize operating efficiencies both for itself and for its customers, to benefit from economies of scale in product purchasing, financing and working capital management, and to provide an efficient distribution system that focuses on ease of order placement, speed of delivery, facilitation of product returns and reduction of freight costs. VARs currently represent about 70% of total sales.

Important Developments

Jul. '95—Tech Data announced the formation of a new business unit called Tech Data Elect. This unit offers qualified resellers of PC products a competitive cost-plus pricing structure on systems, and discounts on all other products. Participating vendors include Apple, Compaq, Acer, and IBM.

Capitalization

Long Term Debt: $9,358,000 (7/95).

Per Share Data ($) (Year Ended Jan. 31)

	1995	1994	1993	1992	1991	1990
Tangible Bk. Val.	6.63	5.56	3.66	3.02	2.03	1.76
Cash Flow	1.15	0.98	0.74	0.55	0.39	0.22
Earnings	0.91	0.82	0.63	0.44	0.27	0.13
Dividends	Nil	Nil	Nil	Nil	Nil	Nil
Payout Ratio	Nil	Nil	Nil	Nil	Nil	Nil
Cal. Yrs.	1994	1993	1992	1991	1990	1989
Prices - High	22⅛	30¼	15⅛	7⅞	2¾	4⅜
- Low	14	13¼	6⅝	1¾	1	1⅞
P/E Ratio - High	24	24	24	18	10	35
- Low	15	11	11	4	4	15

Income Statement Analysis (Million $)

	1995	%Chg	1994	%Chg	1993	%Chg	1992
Revs.	2,418	58%	1,532	62%	947	46%	647
Oper. Inc.	80.4	33%	60.6	54%	39.4	51%	26.1
Depr.	9.1	64%	5.6	63%	3.4	14%	3.0
Int. Exp.	13.8	175%	5.0	26%	4.0	-3%	4.1
Pretax Inc.	57.6	15%	50.0	56%	32.0	68%	19.0
Eff. Tax Rate	39%	—	40%	—	38%	—	38%
Net Inc.	34.9	16%	30.2	53%	19.8	66%	11.9

Balance Sheet & Other Fin. Data (Million $)

	1995	1994	1993	1992	1991	1990
Cash	0.5	0.7	0.4	3.9	3.1	0.6
Curr. Assets	697	449	292	175	124	97.0
Total Assets	784	507	327	200	149	122
Curr. Liab.	514	284	202	96.1	84.5	63.8
LT Debt	9.7	9.5	9.6	9.8	13.0	13.1
Common Eqty.	261	213	115	94.5	51.5	44.9
Total Cap.	271	223	125	104	65.0	58.0
Cap. Exp.	40.0	19.5	13.3	4.2	3.3	8.7
Cash Flow	44.0	35.8	23.2	14.9	9.6	5.3

Ratio Analysis

	1995	1994	1993	1992	1991	1990
Curr. Ratio	1.4	1.6	1.4	1.8	1.5	1.5
% LT Debt of Cap.	3.6	4.2	7.7	9.4	20.2	22.6
% Net Inc.of Revs.	1.4	2.0	2.0	1.8	1.5	0.9
% Ret. on Assets	5.4	6.8	7.5	6.2	4.9	2.9
% Ret. on Equity	14.7	17.3	18.9	15.0	13.8	7.1

Dividend Data —The company has not paid any cash dividends since fiscal 1983. Two-for-one stock splits were effected in April 1994 and 1992.

Data as orig. reptd.; bef. results of disc. opers. and/or spec. items. Per share data adj. for stk. divs. as of ex-div. date. E-Estimated. NA-Not Available. NM-Not Meaningful. NR-Not Ranked.

Office—5350 Tech Data Dr., Clearwater, FL 34620. **Tel**—(813) 539-7429. **Chrmn & CEO**—S. A. Raymund. **Pres & COO**—A. T. Godwin. **SVP-Fin & CFO**—J. P. Howells. **VP, Treas & Secy**—A. W. Singleton. **Dirs**—C. E. Adair, D. M. Doyle, D. F. Dunn, L. J. Dunn, A. T. Godwin, E. C. Raymund, S. A. Raymund, J. Y. Williams. **Transfer Agent**—Mellon Securities Trust Co., Pittsburgh. **Incorporated** in Florida in 1974. **Empl-** 2,265. **S&P Analyst:** Mike Cavanaugh

Telxon Corp.

NASDAQ Symbol **TLXN**
In S&P SmallCap 600

12-OCT-95 **Industry:** Data Processing

Summary: This company is a leading manufacturer of portable tele-transaction computers (PTCs) that gather, process and store on-site real-time data.

Quantitative Evaluations

Outlook (1 Lowest—5 Highest)
• **3+**
Fair Value
• **21¾**
Risk
• **High**
Earn./Div. Rank
• **B**

Technical Eval.
• **Bullish** since 2/95
Rel. Strength Rank (1 Lowest—99 Highest)
• **41**
Insider Activity
• **Neutral**

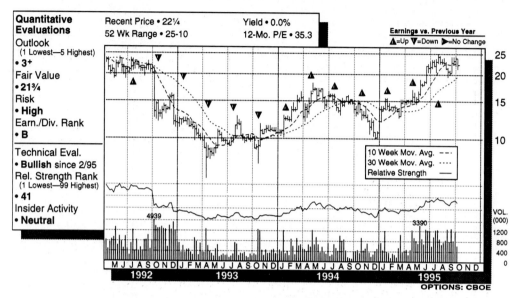

Recent Price • 22¼ | Yield • 0.0%
52 Wk Range • 25-10 | 12-Mo. P/E • 35.3

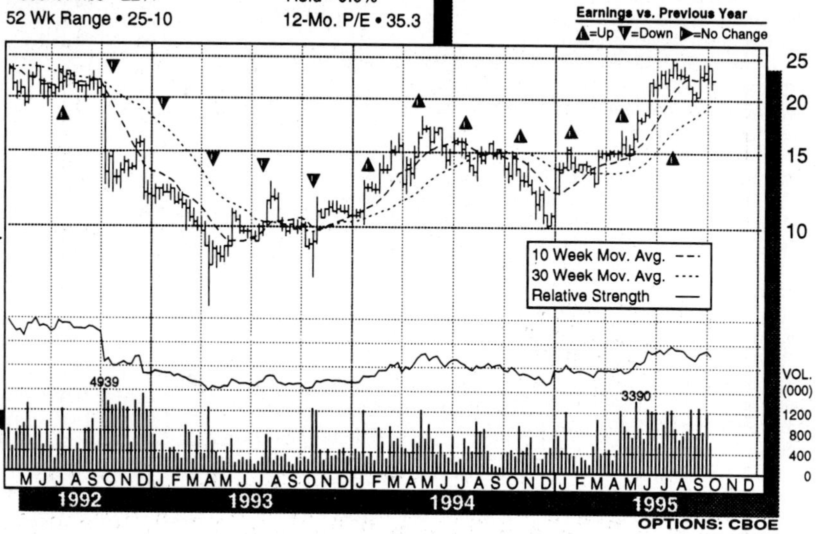

OPTIONS: CBOE

Business Profile - 03-OCT-95

Telxon is one of the leading providers of portable and wireless tele-transaction systems. The company integrates advanced portable teletransaction computers (PTCs) with wireless and network communication technology, a wide array of peripherals, and application-specific software for a diverse group of vertical markets. The company recently formed an alliance with Wireless Access, Inc. (WA) to integrate WA's wireless PCS technology into its PTC systems.

Operational Review - 12-OCT-95

Revenues for the first quarter of 1994-95 increased 18%, year to year, reflecting strong demand for the company's products; margins were essentially flat for the period. Results benefited from the disbursement of $1 million in R & D expenses from a customer, and net income advanced to $0.14 a share. The shares, which have risen sharply since early 1995, are currently trading at about 24 times the consensus 1995-96 EPS estimate of $0.91 a share.

Stock Performance - 06-OCT-95

In the past 30 trading days, TLXN's shares have increased 4%, compared to a 4% rise in the S&P 500. Average trading volume for the past five days was 123,320 shares, compared with the 40-day moving average of 243,262 shares.

Key Stock Statistics

Dividend Rate/Share	0.01	Shareholders	1,600
Shs. outstg. (M)	15.8	Market cap. (B)	$0.342
Avg. daily vol. (M)	0.183	Inst. holdings	60%
Tang. Bk. Value/Share	7.73	Insider holdings	NA
Beta	1.76		

Value of $10,000 invested 5 years ago: $ 27,925

Fiscal Year Ending Mar. 31

	1996	% Change	1995	% Change	1994	% Change
Revenues (Million $)						
1Q	103.5	18%	87.43	55%	56.54	-16%
2Q	—	—	91.89	46%	63.09	-5%
3Q	—	—	98.20	28%	76.97	57%
4Q	—	—	102.0	3%	99.4	78%
Yr.	—	—	379.5	28%	296.0	24%
Income (Million $)						
1Q	2.23	76%	1.27	NM	-1.98	NM
2Q	—	—	1.62	NM	-1.09	NM
3Q	—	—	2.46	NM	-0.62	NM
4Q	—	—	3.66	NM	0.89	NM
Yr.	—	—	9.02	NM	-2.80	NM
Earnings Per Share ($)						
1Q	0.14	75%	0.08	NM	-0.13	NM
2Q	—	—	0.10	NM	-0.07	NM
3Q	—	—	0.16	NM	-0.04	NM
4Q	—	—	0.23	NM	0.06	NM
Yr.	—	—	0.57	NM	-0.18	NM

Next earnings report expected: late October

Telxon Corp.

12-OCT-95

Business Summary - 12-OCT-95

Telxon Corporation designs, manufactures, and sells portable, batch, and wireless tele-transaction computers and systems. TLXN integrates its portable tele-transaction computers (PTCs) with wired and wireless local area networks, and links these networks to customers' specific enterprise networks. International sales in 1994-95 accounted for 25% of revenues, compared to 28% in 1993-94.

The company's Vertical Systems Group (VSG) is composed of five industry-specific marketing groups--Retail, Industrial, Logistics & Transportation, Healthcare and Insurance & Financial Services--to provide specific customer solutions. Retail applications accounted for 50% of 1994-95 revenues.

An important element of Telxon's approach to selling application systems is in the support provided to the customer. Revenues from customer service accounted for 15% of the company's total revenues in each of the two preceding years.

In January 1994, the company formed Metanetics, which develops two-dimensional bar code encoding and autodiscriminating decode software. It also formed AIRONET Wireless Communications to continue development and marketing of wireless local area networks (LANs) and wide area networks (WANs). AIRONET has developed one of the first commercial applications for spread spectrum radio technology and currently designs and develops universal modular LAN and WAN radio products and networks.

In January 1994, Telxon purchased certain assets of PenRight! Corp., a provider of character recognition and operating software for pen-based products, from AST Research, Inc. In March 1993, it acquired Itronix Corp., a leading maker of ruggedized portable microcomputers specifically for the mobile workforce and field service automation markets. In February 1993, TLXN acquired Teletransaction, Inc., a manufacturer of pen and touch-screen wireless, mobile workslates.

Important Developments

Sep. '95—TLXN announced that it had formed an alliance with Wireless Access, Inc. (WA) which allows Telxon to integrate WA's two-way PCS wireless technology into its portable teletransaction computers and systems.

Jul. '95—The company acquired Virtual Vision, Inc., a developer of digital head mounted systems (DHMS) technology, for an undisclosed price.

Capitalization

Long Term Debt: $31,292,000 (6/95); incl. $24,734,000 of debs. conv. into com. at $26.75 a sh.

Per Share Data ($)

(Year Ended Mar. 31)

	1995	1994	1993	1992	1991	1990
Tangible Bk. Val.	7.73	6.59	6.33	8.94	7.57	6.19
Cash Flow	1.91	0.99	0.07	1.67	1.39	-0.64
Earnings	0.57	-0.18	-0.79	1.13	0.91	-1.09
Dividends	0.02	0.01	0.01	0.01	0.01	0.01
Payout Ratio	4%	NM	NM	1%	1%	NM
Cal. Yrs.	1994	1993	1992	1991	1990	1989
Prices - High	18¼	12¾	28¼	28⅛	15½	20¼
- Low	10	6½	11¼	13⅜	4¾	6⅜
P/E Ratio - High	32	NM	NM	25	17	NM
- Low	18	NM	NM	12	5	NM

Income Statement Analysis (Million $)

	1995	%Chg	1994	%Chg	1993	%Chg	1992
Revs.	380	28%	296	24%	238	11%	215
Oper. Inc.	42.3	136%	17.9	NM	-0.3	NM	31.9
Depr.	21.0	17%	18.0	42%	12.7	66%	7.6
Int. Exp.	4.3	77%	2.5	8%	2.3	3%	2.2
Pretax Inc.	17.2	NM	-1.9	NM	-15.7	NM	25.0
Eff. Tax Rate	48%	—	NM	—	NM	—	37%
Net Inc.	9.0	NM	-2.8	NM	-11.6	NM	15.9

Balance Sheet & Other Fin. Data (Million $)

	1995	1994	1993	1992	1991	1990
Cash	31.4	24.8	27.2	42.3	44.7	55.5
Curr. Assets	205	186	138	162	138	140
Total Assets	276	260	213	199	167	167
Curr. Liab.	104	106	53.2	45.3	35.7	43.5
LT Debt	31.7	27.5	24.9	25.6	26.0	36.5
Common Eqty.	139	125	128	124	102	83.0
Total Cap.	170	152	153	151	129	122
Cap. Exp.	15.2	21.7	16.4	9.0	7.6	7.7
Cash Flow	30.4	15.2	1.1	23.5	18.7	-8.4

Ratio Analysis

	1995	1994	1993	1992	1991	1990
Curr. Ratio	2.0	1.8	2.6	3.6	3.9	3.2
% LT Debt of Cap.	18.6	18.1	16.3	16.9	20.1	29.9
% Net Inc.of Revs.	2.4	NM	NM	7.4	6.7	NM
% Ret. on Assets	3.4	NM	NM	8.5	7.4	NM
% Ret. on Equity	6.9	NM	NM	13.8	13.3	NM

Dividend Data —Telxon has made only nominal cash payments. The most recent annual dividend was $0.01 on March 30, 1995, to shareholders of record March 23.

Amt. of Div. $	Date Decl.	Ex-Div. Date	Stock of Record	Payment Date
0.010	Mar. 09	Mar. 17	Mar. 23	Mar. 30 '95

Data as orig. reptd.; bef. results of disc. opers. and/or spec. items. Per share data adj. for stk. divs. as of ex-div. date. E-Estimated. NA-Not Available. NM-Not Meaningful. NR-Not Ranked.

Office—3330 W. Market St., Akron, OH 44333. **Tel**—(216) 867-3700. **Chrmn & CEO**—R. F. Meyerson. **Vice Chrmn**—J. H. Cribb. **Pres & COO**—W. J. Murphy. **SVP & CFO**—K. W. Haver. **Dirs**—J. R. Anderson, J. H. Cribb, R. A. Goodman, R. F. Meyerson, W. J. Murphy, R. Reddy, N. W. Rose, W. J. Salmon. **Transfer Agent & Registrar**—Society National Bank, Cleveland. **Incorporated** in Delaware in 1969. **Empl**-1,850. **S&P Analyst:** M.T.C

STANDARD & POOR'S

STOCK REPORTS

TETRA Technologies

NASDAQ Symbol **TTRA**

In S&P SmallCap 600

17-SEP-95 **Industry:** Pollution Control

Summary: This company provides recycling and treatment services for environmentally sensitive byproduct and waste streams, and markets chemicals extracted from such streams.

Quantitative Evaluations

Outlook
(1 Lowest—5 Highest)
• **NA**

Fair Value
• **NA**

Risk
• **Average**

Earn./Div. Rank
• **NR**

Technical Eval.
• **Bullish** since 9/95

Rel. Strength Rank
(1 Lowest—99 Highest)
• **81**

Insider Activity
• **Neutral**

Recent Price • 14¾
52 Wk Range • 14⅞-7¾

Yield • Nil
12-Mo. P/E • 24.6

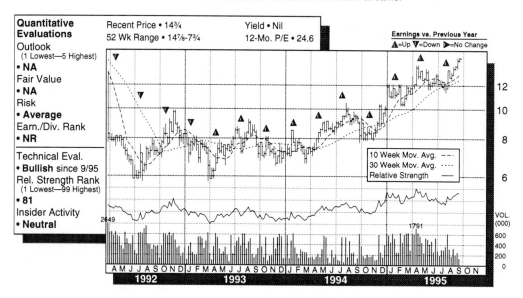

Earnings vs. Previous Year
▲=Up ▼=Down ▶=No Change

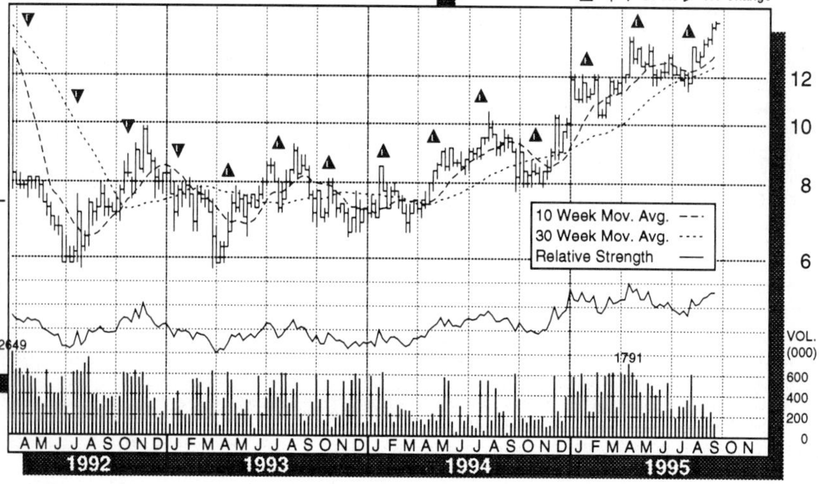

Business Profile - 15-SEP-95

During the past two years, TETRA has shifted strategy to focus on the sale of process packages and technology licenses, while de-emphasizing construction projects. For 1995 and beyond, the company expects a return to its long-term annual earnings growth rate of 20% to 25%. TETRA also plans to seek acquisition opportunities in the chemical industry and in the oil and gas service sector.

Operational Review - 15-SEP-95

Revenues in the first half of 1995 rose sharply, reflecting increased oil and gas related revenues resulting from 1994 acquisitions, and higher liquid calcium chloride and performance chemicals sales. Results benefited from the greater volume, higher prices at calcium chloride operations, and improved operating efficiencies; net income was up significantly. Near-term results are expected to continue to grow rapidly.

Stock Performance - 15-SEP-95

In the past 30 trading days, TTRA's shares have increased 9%, compared to a 4% rise in the S&P 500. Average trading volume for the past five days was 26,160 shares, compared with the 40-day moving average of 62,679 shares.

Key Stock Statistics

Dividend Rate/Share	Nil	Shareholders	3,400
Shs. outstg. (M)	12.7	Market cap. (B)	$0.187
Avg. daily vol. (M)	0.046	Inst. holdings	91%
Tang. Bk. Value/Share	6.03	Insider holdings	NA
Beta	0.93		

Value of $10,000 invested 5 years ago: NA

Fiscal Year Ending Dec. 31

	1995	% Change	1994	% Change	1993	% Change
Revenues (Million $)						
1Q	25.27	41%	17.91	20%	14.98	18%
2Q	26.08	38%	18.93	33%	14.21	14%
3Q	—	—	23.06	46%	15.77	21%
4Q	—	—	28.60	60%	17.90	-6%
Yr.	—	—	88.51	41%	62.85	10%
Income (Million $)						
1Q	1.94	100%	0.97	185%	0.34	NM
2Q	1.97	58%	1.25	NM	0.39	NM
3Q	—	—	1.32	106%	0.64	NM
4Q	—	—	2.52	NM	-0.51	NM
Yr.	—	—	6.06	NM	0.86	NM
Earnings Per Share ($)						
1Q	0.15	88%	0.08	167%	0.03	NM
2Q	0.15	50%	0.10	NM	0.03	NM
3Q	—	—	0.10	100%	0.05	NM
4Q	—	—	0.20	NM	-0.04	NM
Yr.	—	—	0.48	NM	0.07	NM

Next earnings report expected: late October

TETRA Technologies

Business Summary - 15-SEP-95

TETRA Technologies, Inc. provides recycling and treatment services for environmentally sensitive by-product and waste streams, and it markets chemicals extracted from such streams. Revenue contributions in recent years were:

	1993	1992
Product sales	86%	81%
Services	12%	17%
Rentals	2%	2%

Activities of the Specialty Chemicals division include conversion of low-cost chemical byproduct and waste streams into high-quality commercial products that are marketed by TETRA. The division manufactures and recycles chemicals, primarily calcium chloride, calcium bromide, zinc bromide and zinc chloride, from by-product and waste streams produced by other chemical plants. The calcium chloride, zinc bromide and other clear brine fluids (CBFs) are sold to oil and gas operators completing and reworking wells located mainly offshore in the Gulf of Mexico.

The company's process technologies group (formerly the Waste Treatment division) provides engineered systems and services that treat industrial and municipal wastewater, and solid waste streams. These systems employ the company's patented and proprietary biological filtration, metals removal and resource recovery processes. The resources of the old Waste Treatment division have been integrated into the Specialty Chemicals division.

The Oil and Gas division provides well operators with substantial fluid engineering assistance, on-site fluid management services and fluid handling services. TETRA also repurchases recycled calcium bromide and zinc bromide CBF's from operators.

In May 1994, the company purchased the remaining 50% stake in its Inteq/TETRA joint venture from Baker Hughes, Inc.'s Inteq unit for about $8.5 million.

Important Developments

Aug. '95—TETRA said that the dry calcium chloride expansion at its Lake Charles, La., facility was on target for the 1995 fourth quarter, and would begin to yield significant production in early 1996. In the 1995 second quarter, dry calcium chloride production increased 40%, year to year. The company noted that the oil field service sector continues to be robust, with strong increases in activity both in the Gulf of Mexico and in selected international markets.

Capitalization

Long Term Debt: $1,890,000 (6/95), incl. $620,000 of lease obligs.

Per Share Data ($) (Year Ended Dec. 31)

	1994	1993	1992	1991	1990	1989
Tangible Bk. Val.	5.87	5.58	5.51	5.84	4.04	-0.35
Cash Flow	0.84	0.46	0.04	0.99	0.85	0.63
Earnings	0.48	0.07	-0.31	0.70	0.62	0.49
Dividends	Nil	Nil	Nil	Nil	Nil	Nil
Payout Ratio	Nil	Nil	Nil	Nil	Nil	Nil
Prices - High	12¼	9¼	15¾	21¾	16¼	NA
- Low	6⅝	5¾	5¾	13½	9¼	NA
P/E Ratio - High	26	NM	NM	31	26	NA
- Low	14	NM	NM	19	15	NA

Income Statement Analysis (Million $)

	1994	%Chg	1993	%Chg	1992	%Chg	1991
Revs.	88.5	41%	62.8	10%	57.2	-33%	85.3
Oper. Inc.	12.6	107%	6.1	NM	1.2	-93%	16.2
Depr.	4.6	-6%	4.9	13%	4.4	18%	3.7
Int. Exp.	0.4	-30%	0.6	-21%	0.7	-19%	0.9
Pretax Inc.	9.0	NM	1.3	NM	-6.2	NM	13.8
Eff. Tax Rate	33%	—	32%	—	NM	—	37%
Net Inc.	6.1	NM	0.9	NM	-3.9	NM	8.7

Balance Sheet & Other Fin. Data (Million $)

	1994	1993	1992	1991	1990	1989
Cash	13.3	16.6	16.4	32.4	18.3	0.8
Curr. Assets	55.7	46.9	50.3	66.5	43.4	19.3
Total Assets	103	89.2	88.2	99	65.7	36.9
Curr. Liab.	18.4	10.8	9.7	17.2	10.5	17.1
LT Debt	2.3	3.2	4.7	5.8	6.9	5.8
Common Eqty.	77.7	71.4	70.3	73.4	45.6	13.8
Total Cap.	84.2	77.9	77.8	81.6	54.3	19.7
Cap. Exp.	6.0	5.3	10.2	10.4	7.0	4.2
Cash Flow	10.7	5.8	0.5	12.4	9.2	5.3

Ratio Analysis

	1994	1993	1992	1991	1990	1989
Curr. Ratio	3.0	4.3	5.2	3.9	4.1	1.1
% LT Debt of Cap.	2.7	4.1	6.0	7.2	12.8	29.9
% Net Inc.of Revs.	6.8	1.4	NM	10.2	11.5	8.5
% Ret. on Assets	6.3	1.0	NM	10.1	5.4	13.2
% Ret. on Equity	8.1	1.2	NM	14.0	22.5	16.8

Dividend Data —No cash dividends have been paid on the common shares, and TETRA does not expect to pay such dividends in the foreseeable future.

Data as orig. reptd.; bef. results of disc. opers. and/or spec. items. Per share data adj. for stk. divs. as of ex-div. date. E-Estimated. NA-Not Available. NM-Not Meaningful. NR-Not Ranked.

Office—25025 I-45 North, The Woodlands, TX 77380. **Tel**—(713) 367-1983. **Fax**—(713) 364-2240. **Chrmn**—J. T. Symonds. **Pres & CEO**—M. L. Jeane. **Exec VP-Fin, CFO, Secy & Investor Contact**—Geoffrey M. Hertel. **Treas**—J. R. Hale. **Dirs**—P. D. Coombs, T. H. Delimitros, S. T. Harcrow, G. M. Hertel, M. L. Jeane, A. T. McInnes, J. T. Symonds, T. H. Wentzler. **Transfer Agent & Registrar**—Society National Bank, Houston. **Incorporated** in Delaware in 1981. **Empl-** 433. **S&P Analyst:** Stewart Scharf

STANDARD & POOR'S

STOCK REPORTS

Texas Industries

NYSE Symbol **TXI**
In S&P SmallCap 600

27-JUL-95 **Industry:** Building

Summary: This company is a leading producer of cement, aggregate and concrete products, primarily in Texas and Louisiana, and of carbon steel products through 81%-owned Chaparral Steel.

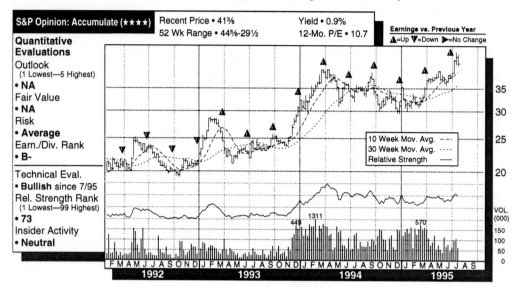

S&P Opinion: Accumulate (★★★★)
Recent Price • 41⅜
52 Wk Range • 44⅝-29½
Yield • 0.9%
12-Mo. P/E • 10.7

Quantitative Evaluations
Outlook (1 Lowest—5 Highest) • **NA**
Fair Value • **NA**
Risk • **Average**
Earn./Div. Rank • **B-**

Technical Eval. • **Bullish** since 7/95
Rel. Strength Rank (1 Lowest—99 Highest) • **73**
Insider Activity • **Neutral**

Overview - 27-JUL-95

Sales should rise solidly in fiscal 1995-96, as strong demand for cement and concrete is combined with a rapidly improving steel market. Both businesses are expected to benefit from a Texas economy which has improved steadily over the last few years. Demand continues to outstrip supply in the markets for cement and concrete, which should bolster pricing over the next few years. In addition, Chaparral Steel should see strong demand for special bar quality and structural products. Margins are expected to widen on the higher prices and volumes and well-controlled operating expenses. Aided by lower interest costs, a share repurchase plan, and the recent repurchase of 1.2 million shares from Co-Steel, earnings should advance strongly in fiscal 1995-96.

Valuation - 27-JUL-95

TXI's shares are up over 30% since we initiated coverage in November 1994 with an accumulate rating. The shares have been strong in recent months, reflecting a combination of a rebound in cyclical shares due to the prospects of a recovering economy from recent weakness and excellent earnings gains in the past year. The cement and concrete segment is benefiting from soaring prices and should see significant earnings gains from excellent operating leverage. Chaparral Steel should also continue to profit from moderate volume gains and higher prices. Upside potential still exists for the shares, which trade at only slightly over 7x our fiscal 1996 estimate.

Key Stock Statistics

S&P EPS Est. 1996	5.65	Tang. Bk. Value/Share	22.35
P/E on S&P Est. 1996	7.3	Beta	0.79
Dividend Rate/Share	0.40	Shareholders	5,100
Shs. outstg. (M)	10.7	Market cap. (B)	$0.456
Avg. daily vol. (M)	0.017	Inst. holdings	74%
		Insider holdings	NA

Value of $10,000 invested 5 years ago: $ 20,140

Fiscal Year Ending May 31

	1995	% Change	1994	% Change	1993	% Change
Revenues (Million $)						
1Q	201.0	19%	168.8	9%	155.5	-5%
2Q	201.1	16%	173.1	13%	153.4	NM
3Q	199.0	17%	170.1	20%	142.3	5%
4Q	229.5	18%	195.2	20%	163.1	9%
Yr.	830.5	17%	707.2	15%	614.3	2%
Income (Million $)						
1Q	10.77	NM	1.43	NM	-0.94	NM
2Q	12.01	115%	5.59	NM	0.26	-90%
3Q	6.88	140%	2.87	NM	-4.47	-31%
4Q	18.37	16%	15.87	156%	6.20	NM
Yr.	48.00	86%	25.75	NM	1.06	-44%
Earnings Per Share ($)						
1Q	0.85	NM	0.13	NM	-0.08	NM
2Q	0.96	88%	0.51	NM	0.03	-88%
3Q	0.55	112%	0.26	NM	-0.40	NM
4Q	1.56	17%	1.33	138%	0.56	NM
Yr.	3.88	69%	2.29	NM	0.11	-42%

Next earnings report expected: mid September

Texas Industries

Business Summary - 19-JUL-95

Texas Industries manufactures steel and cement and concrete products. Business segment contributions in fiscal 1993-94:

	Revs.	Profits
Steel	65%	43%
Cement/concrete	35%	57%

Through its 81%-owned Chaparral Steel Co. (NYSE: CSM), TXI produces concrete reinforcing steel, merchant bar, angles, flats, light, medium and large-size beams and other structural sections. In 1990-91, a large-section mill was added that produces structural steel beams up to 24 inches wide. Melting capacity at the end of 1993-94 exceeded 1.5 million tons per year, while rolling capacity totaled 2.0 million tons; shipments in 1993-94 totaled 1,362,000 tons.

The cement/concrete unit makes cement, aggregates, ready-mix concrete, concrete pipe, block and brick. Cement production is conducted at two plants in Texas with a combined annual rated capacity of 1.95 million tons of clinker. Production totaled about 2.1 million tons in 1993-94, versus 1.7 million tons of finished cement in 1992-93. Annual shipments of finished cement to outside trade customers were about 1.6 million tons in 1993-94, versus 1.2 million tons in 1992-93.

The aggregate business, which includes sand, gravel, crushed limestone and lightweight aggregate, is conducted from plants mainly in Texas and Louisiana. The lightweight aggregate plants operated at 80% of capacity in 1993-94, with sales of about 928,000 cubic yards. Production for the remaining aggregate facilities was 79% of practical capacity, and sales totaled 10.8 million tons. Ready-mix concrete operations are conducted at 18 plants in Texas and 11 in Louisiana.

Important Developments

Jul. '95—In reporting results for fiscal 1995, TXI said that cement supply and demand in the Texas region remained in balance as increased construction in the commercial and manufacturing sectors served to offset a decline in residential building. Cement, concrete and aggregate pricing continued to improve from the depressed levels of recent years. Overall, prices still remain low by national and international standards. Shipments for all product lines increased during the year. At Chaparral, during the last quarter of the year, profitability began to accelerate as volumes and margins expanded. Four price increases on structural beams since March will serve to further expand margins in fiscal 1996.

Capitalization

Long Term Debt: $185,274,000 (5/95).
Minority Interest: $39,323,000.
$5 Cum. Pfd. Stk.: 5,976 shs. (no par).

Per Share Data ($) (Year Ended May 31)

	1995	1994	1993	1992	1991	1990
Tangible Bk. Val.	NA	22.35	18.76	18.66	18.47	23.74
Cash Flow	NA	6.12	4.31	4.47	6.08	3.29
Earnings	3.88	2.29	0.11	0.19	1.97	-0.84
Dividends	0.30	0.20	0.20	0.20	0.20	0.77
Payout Ratio	8%	9%	182%	105%	10%	NM
Cal. Yrs.	1994	1993	1992	1991	1990	1989
Prices - High	39¾	32½	25¼	25	23½	35½
- Low	29½	21⅛	19¼	14	10¾	21⅛
P/E Ratio - High	10	14	NM	NM	12	NM
- Low	8	9	NM	NM	5	NM

Income Statement Analysis (Million $)

	1994	%Chg	1993	%Chg	1992	%Chg	1991
Revs.	716	15%	621	2%	606	-9%	664
Oper. Inc.	113	43%	79.0	22%	65.0	-8%	71.0
Depr.	43.6	-7%	46.8	-1%	47.5	6%	45.0
Int. Exp.	26.2	-20%	32.6	-6%	34.5	1%	34.0
Pretax Inc.	43.6	—	Nil	—	5.0	-87%	39.4
Eff. Tax Rate	36%	—	NM	—	35%	—	35%
Net Inc.	25.8	NM	1.1	-42%	1.9	-91%	22.1

Balance Sheet & Other Fin. Data (Million $)

	1994	1993	1992	1991	1990	1989
Cash	31.8	33.1	20.7	23.2	42.3	73.4
Curr. Assets	277	261	240	227	261	289
Total Assets	749	757	777	789	703	731
Curr. Liab.	116	101	105	111	108	113
LT Debt	171	267	289	293	260	260
Common Eqty.	352	282	281	282	239	253
Total Cap.	560	645	657	661	578	546
Cap. Exp.	23.3	17.9	21.6	98.4	50.4	43.4
Cash Flow	69.3	47.8	49.4	67.0	36.4	62.5

Ratio Analysis

	1994	1993	1992	1991	1990	1989
Curr. Ratio	2.4	2.6	2.3	2.0	2.4	2.6
% LT Debt of Cap.	30.6	41.4	44.0	44.3	44.9	47.6
% Net Inc.of Revs.	3.6	0.2	0.3	3.3	NM	2.7
% Ret. on Assets	3.2	0.1	0.2	2.8	NM	2.7
% Ret. on Equity	7.7	0.4	0.7	8.0	NM	7.3

Dividend Data (Dividends have been paid each year since 1951. A "poison pill" stock purchase right was adopted in 1986.)

Amt. of Div. $	Date Decl.	Ex-Div. Date	Stock of Record	Payment Date
0.050	Jul. 15	Jul. 25	Jul. 29	Aug. 31 '94
0.050	Oct. 18	Oct. 31	Nov. 04	Nov. 30 '94
0.100	Jan. 18	Jan. 30	Feb. 03	Feb. 24 '95
0.100	Apr. 24	Apr. 25	May. 01	May. 31 '95
0.100	Jul. 14	Jul. 28	Aug. 01	Aug. 31 '95

Data as orig. reptd.; bef. results of disc. opers. and/or spec. items. Per share data adj. for stk. divs. as of ex-div. date. E-Estimated. NA-Not Available. NM-Not Meaningful. NR-Not Ranked.

Office—1341 W. Mockingbird Lane, Dallas, TX 75247. **Tel**—(214) 647-6700. **Chrmn**—R. B. Rogers. **Pres & CEO**— R. D. Rogers. **VP-Fin**—R. M. Fowler. **VP-Secy**—R. C. Moore. **Treas & Investor Contact**—Kenneth R. Allen. **Dirs**—R. Alpert, G. E. Forward, R. I. Galland, J. M. Hoak, G. R. Heffernan, R. B. Rogers, R. D. Rogers, I. Wachtmeister, E. C. Williams. **Transfer Agent & Registrar**—Chemical Bank, NYC. **Incorporated** in Delaware in 1951. **Empl**-2,700. **S&P Analyst:** Alan Aaron

STANDARD & POOR'S

STOCK REPORTS

TheraTech, Inc.

NASDAQ Symbol **THRT**

In S&P SmallCap 600

31-OCT-95

Industry: Medical equipment/ supply

Summary: This company develops advanced, controlled-release drug delivery products that administer drugs through the skin, through tissue in the oral cavity and by other means.

Quantitative Evaluations

Outlook
(1 Lowest—5 Highest)
• **NA**

Fair Value
• **NA**

Risk
• **Average**

Earn./Div. Rank
• **NR**

Technical Eval.
• **Bullish** since 2/95

Rel. Strength Rank
(1 Lowest—99 Highest)
• **94**

Insider Activity
• **Neutral**

Recent Price • 18¾ | Yield • Nil
52 Wk Range • 20½-8¾ | 12-Mo. P/E • NM

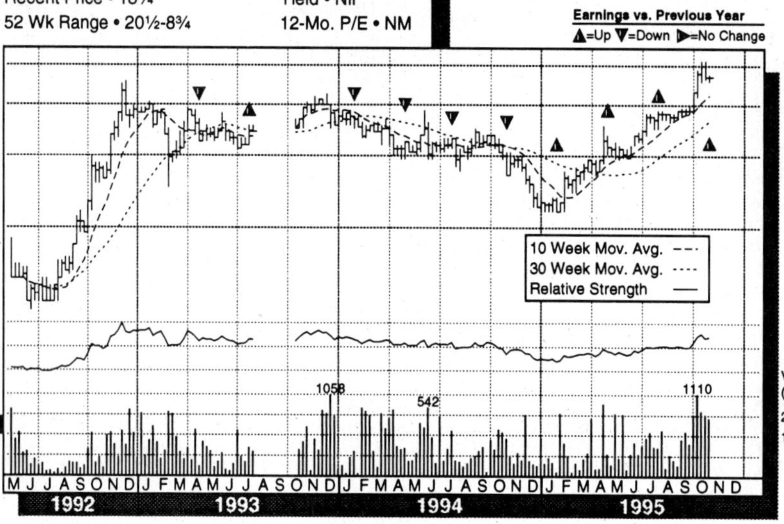

Business Profile - 31-OCT-95

TheraTech's research efforts are funded primarily through equity offerings and corporate partnerships. Lead products include two hormonal transdermal patches currently registered with the FDA. In October 1995, TheraTech received FDA marketing approval for its Androderm testosterone patch for hypogonadism. Androderm will be distributed by SmithKline Beecham. In March 1995, a research agreement was signed with Procter & Gamble for the development of female hormone products.

Operational Review - 31-OCT-95

Revenues for the six months ended June 30, 1995, rose to $7,991,063, from $1,560,619 in the year-earlier period, due principally to upfront and milestone payments received from Procter & Gamble and Astra AB. Total expenses increased nearly 50%, reflecting higher R&D outlays from ongoing clinical study costs and validation of manufacturing processes. The net loss narrowed to $4,437,126 ($0.34 a share, based on 6.3% more shares), from $6,511,772 ($0.53).

Stock Performance - 27-OCT-95

In the past 30 trading days, THRT's shares have increased 21%, compared to a 0.63% fall in the S&P 500. Average trading volume for the past five days was 45,440 shares, compared with the 40-day moving average of 69,313 shares.

Key Stock Statistics

Dividend Rate/Share	Nil	Shareholders	200
Shs. outstg. (M)	13.2	Market cap. (B)	$0.252
Avg. daily vol. (M)	0.072	Inst. holdings	36%
Tang. Bk. Value/Share	2.78	Insider holdings	NA
Beta	NA		

Value of $10,000 invested 5 years ago: NA

Fiscal Year Ending Dec. 31

	1995	% Change	1994	% Change	1993	% Change
Revenues (Million $)						
1Q	3.04	NM	0.52	-27%	0.71	65%
2Q	4.95	NM	1.04	68%	0.62	13%
3Q	3.11	77%	1.76	-47%	3.29	NM
4Q	—	—	4.22	NM	0.85	-13%
Yr.	—	—	7.54	38%	5.47	114%
Income (Million $)						
1Q	-2.07	NM	-3.13	—	—	—
2Q	-2.37	NM	-3.38	—	—	—
3Q	-2.80	NM	-3.00	NM	0.28	NM
4Q	—	—	-2.13	NM	-4.50	NM
Yr.	—	—	-11.64	NM	-7.87	NM
Earnings Per Share ($)						
1Q	-0.16	NM	-0.26	NM	-0.17	NM
2Q	-0.18	NM	-0.26	NM	-0.18	NM
3Q	-0.21	NM	-0.23	NM	0.03	NM
4Q	—	—	-0.16	NM	-0.42	NM
Yr.	—	—	-0.92	NM	-0.75	NM

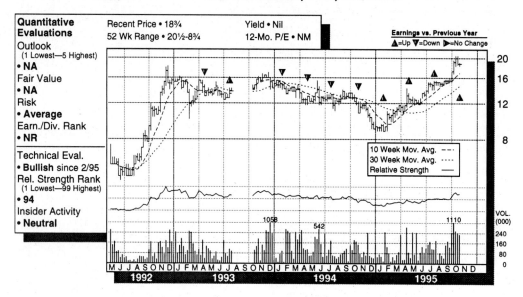

Next earnings report expected: early November

TheraTech, Inc.

Business Summary - 31-OCT-95

TheraTech, Inc. develops advanced, controlled-release drug delivery products that administer drugs through the skin, by oral delivery to the gastrointestinal tract, through tissues in the oral cavity and by other means. The company focuses its research and development efforts on the design and development of improved delivery systems for off-patent and proprietary drugs, thus avoiding much of the risk associated with new drug discovery.

TheraTech currently has two products in registration with the FDA. In February 1993, the company submitted an application to market a transdermal nitroglycerin product for the treatment of angina. In September 1994, the company filed a New Drug Application (NDA) for its Androderm testosterone patch. Additionally, efficacy and safety studies were completed for the estradiol matrix patch in 1994. TheraTech expects to submit an NDA for this product in the latter half of 1995.

As of December 31, 1994, THRT had approximately 20 drug delivery products in various stages of development, of which eight products were in clinical testing.

The company has focused the majority of its efforts on transdermal patch drug delivery systems that release drugs through the skin at controlled rates over extended periods. TheraTech's liquid reservoir patches are designed to deliver a wide range of drugs, including testosterone for the treatment of male hypogonadism and ketorolac tromethamine (marketed in the U.S. as Toradol), a non-narcotic proprietary drug for the treatment of pain. The company's matrix patches also deliver a variety of drugs, including estrogen for post-menopausal women and nitroglycerin for angina patients.

The company is involved in several marketing agreements with large drug companies, including SmithKline Beecham, Pfizer, Sam Yang Co., Ltd., Solvay Pharmaceuticals, Syntex, Astra AB and Wyeth-Ayerst. In March 1995, TheraTech agreed with Procter & Gamble to develop and market new hormone replacement products for women.

Important Developments

Oct. '95—TheraTech received FDA approval to market its Androderm testosterone patch for hypogonadism in the U.S. The company has marketing agreements for Androderm with SmithKline Beecham (rights to U.S., Canada and Australia), Grelan Pharmaceutical Co. (Japan) and Wyeth-Ayerst (Mexico, Central and South America, Africa and the Middle East). TheraTech will receive fees and milestone payments from its marketing partners and retain manufacturing rights.

Capitalization

Long Term Debt: $8,766,501 (6/95), incl. lease obligs.

Per Share Data ($) (Year Ended Dec. 31)

	1994	1993	1992	1991	1990	1989
Tangible Bk. Val.	2.85	2.01	2.55	0.06	NA	NA
Cash Flow	-0.86	-0.70	-0.65	-0.08	NA	NA
Earnings	-0.92	-0.75	-0.70	-0.11	NA	NA
Dividends	Nil	Nil	Nil	Nil	NA	NA
Payout Ratio	Nil	Nil	Nil	Nil	NA	NA
Prices - High	15½	17	18¼	NA	NA	NA
- Low	8¾	10	5	NA	NA	NA
P/E Ratio - High	NM	NM	NM	NA	NA	NA
- Low	NM	NM	NA	NA	NA	NA

Income Statement Analysis (Million $)

	1994	%Chg	1993	%Chg	1992	%Chg	1991
Revs.	7.5	38%	5.5	114%	2.6	-7%	2.7
Oper. Inc.	-11.9	NM	-7.0	NM	-5.5	NM	-0.3
Depr.	0.7	39%	0.5	28%	0.4	111%	0.2
Int. Exp.	0.3	NM	0.1	25%	0.0	NM	0.0
Pretax Inc.	-11.6	NM	-7.9	NM	-5.8	NM	-0.8
Eff. Tax Rate	NM	—	Nil	—	Nil	—	Nil
Net Inc.	-11.6	NM	-7.9	NM	-5.8	NM	-0.8

Balance Sheet & Other Fin. Data (Million $)

	1994	1993	1992	1991	1990	1989
Cash	22.5	18.7	25.7	1.1	NA	NA
Curr. Assets	23.6	19.4	26.4	1.4	NA	NA
Total Assets	49.8	28.1	28.4	2.9	NA	NA
Curr. Liab.	3.7	4.6	1.1	0.3	NA	NA
LT Debt	8.7	0.6	0.4	0.2	NA	NA
Common Eqty.	37.3	22.6	26.7	0.4	NA	NA
Total Cap.	45.9	23.2	27.1	2.6	NA	NA
Cap. Exp.	9.8	5.9	0.6	0.3	NA	NA
Cash Flow	-10.9	-7.4	-5.4	-0.6	NA	NA

Ratio Analysis

	1994	1993	1992	1991	1990	1989
Curr. Ratio	6.5	4.2	23.5	4.3	NA	NA
% LT Debt of Cap.	18.9	2.8	1.5	6.3	NA	NA
% Net Inc.of Revs.	NM	NM	NM	NM	NA	NA
% Ret. on Assets	NM	NM	NM	NM	NA	NA
% Ret. on Equity	NM	NM	NM	NM	NA	NA

Dividend Data —No cash dividends have been paid on the common stock.

Data as orig. reptd.; bef. results of disc. opers. and/or spec. items. Per share data adj. for stk. divs. as of ex-div. date. E-Estimated. NA-Not Available. NM-Not Meaningful. NR-Not Ranked.

Office—417 Wakara Way, Salt Lake City, UT 84108. **Tel**—(801) 588-6200. **Chrmn**—W. I. Higuchi. **Pres & CEO**—D. C. Patel. **Sr VP & CFO**—A. L. Searl. **Dirs**—G. L. Crocker, W. I. Higuchi, J. T. O'Brien, D. C. Patel, J. J. Pisik, B. J. Poulsen. **Transfer Agent & Registrar**—First National Bank of Boston. **Incorporated** in Utah in 1985; reincorporated in Delaware in 1992. **Empl**-215. **S&P Analyst:** Thomas Tirney

STANDARD & POOR'S

STOCK REPORTS

Thomas Industries

NYSE Symbol **TII**
In S&P SmallCap 600

03-OCT-95 **Industry:** Electronics/Electric

Summary: This company designs, produces and sells commercial, industrial and residential lighting products, as well as compressors and vacuum pumps for global OEM applications.

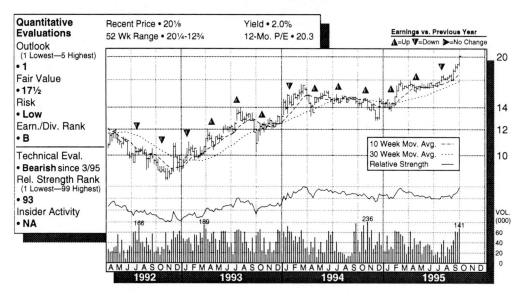

Quantitative Evaluations

Outlook (1 Lowest—5 Highest) • **1**

Fair Value • **17½**

Risk • **Low**

Earn./Div. Rank • **B**

Technical Eval. • **Bearish** since 3/95

Rel. Strength Rank (1 Lowest—99 Highest) • **93**

Insider Activity • **NA**

Recent Price • 20⅛ | Yield • 2.0%
52 Wk Range • 20¼-12¾ | 12-Mo. P/E • 20.3

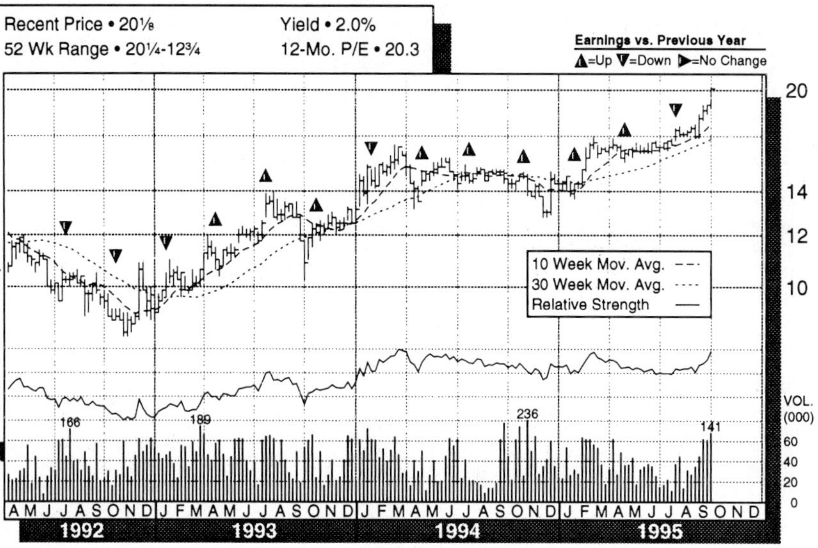

Business Profile - 03-OCT-95

Last year's sales of two non-core operations helped raise $10.9 million for debt reduction and plant expansion. The company hopes to grow its compressor and vacuum pump business to $250 million in sales (versus 1994's $146 million) in five years, through internal expansion and acquisitions. Thomas is looking at greater penetration of international markets as a way to accelerate overall top-line growth.

Operational Review - 03-OCT-95

Revenue growth in the first half of 1995 is a result of strong performances by both the Lighting and Compressor & Vacuum Pump divisions. Both groups achieved record sales for the period. Operating income for the Compressor & Vacuum Group declined modestly, year over year, due to competitive margin pressures and increased fixed costs related to plant expansion. Excluding a net gain of $0.30 a share on the sale of two divisions in the 1994 period earnings per share rose 80%.

Stock Performance - 29-SEP-95

In the past 30 trading days, TII's shares have increased 17%, compared to a 5% rise in the S&P 500. Average trading volume for the past five days was 28,260 shares, compared with the 40-day moving average of 11,295 shares.

Key Stock Statistics

Dividend Rate/Share	0.40	Shareholders	2,700
Shs. outstg. (M)	10.1	Market cap. (B)	$0.207
Avg. daily vol. (M)	0.018	Inst. holdings	53%
Tang. Bk. Value/Share	7.55	Insider holdings	NA
Beta	1.51		

Value of $10,000 invested 5 years ago: $ 12,942

Fiscal Year Ending Dec. 31

	1995	% Change	1994	% Change	1993	% Change
Revenues (Million $)						
1Q	117.6	8%	109.4	-2%	112.1	12%
2Q	127.4	9%	117.3	6%	111.0	7%
3Q	—	—	119.0	1%	117.3	8%
4Q	—	—	110.8	1%	109.8	1%
Yr.	—	—	456.6	1%	450.1	7%
Income (Million $)						
1Q	1.59	57%	1.01	53%	0.66	NM
2Q	3.88	-23%	5.05	NM	1.18	151%
3Q	—	—	2.82	82%	1.55	NM
4Q	—	—	1.67	NM	0.42	-39%
Yr.	—	—	10.54	177%	3.81	NM
Earnings Per Share ($)						
1Q	0.16	60%	0.10	43%	0.07	NM
2Q	0.38	-24%	0.50	NM	0.12	140%
3Q	—	—	0.28	87%	0.15	NM
4Q	—	—	0.17	NM	0.04	-43%
Yr.	—	—	1.05	176%	0.38	NM

Next earnings report expected: mid October

Thomas Industries

Business Summary - 27-SEP-95

Thomas Industries Inc. manufactures a broad range of residential, commercial and industrial outdoor lighting fixtures, as well as compressors and vacuum pumps. Other consumer and commercial products divisions have been divested. Business segment contributions in 1994 were:

	Sales	Profits
Lighting products	67%	14%
Compressors & vacuum pumps	32%	86%
Commercial & consumer products	1%	Nil

The company's residential lighting products include high-style chandeliers and bathroom fixtures and quality lighting products for foyers, dining rooms, living rooms, entertainment areas, kitchens, bedrooms and outdoors. These products are distributed throughout the U.S. by a network of electrical distributors, retail lighting showrooms and home centers, which in turn sell to electrical contractors, builders and consumers. Products are manufactured and sold in the U.S. and Canada under the Day-Bright, Gardco, Capri, Electro/Connect, McPhilben, Omega, Emco, Lumec and Thomas Lighting trade names.

The compressors and vacuum pumps segment consists of air compressors and vacuum pumps manufactured for use in medical equipment, vending machines, photocopiers, computer tape drives, automotive and transportation equipment, liquid dispensing applications and waste disposal equipment. Brand names include Thomas, Sprayit, ASF, Brey, Pneumotive and WISA.

During 1994, the company divested its three remaining disassociated operating units that manufactured commercial construction hardware and consumer fireplaces and fireplaces accessory products.

No single customer accounted for more than 10% of consolidated net sales or more than 10% of any segment's net sales in 1994.

Important Developments

Jul. '95—The company noted that the increase in earnings for the first half of 1995 was primarily attributable to the improved performance by the Lighting Group. The second quarter represented the group's best quarter in both sales and operating income since 1990.

Capitalization

Long Term Debt: $71,197,000 (6/95).

Per Share Data ($) (Year Ended Dec. 31)

	1994	1993	1992	1991	1990	1989
Tangible Bk. Val.	7.07	6.09	6.29	6.87	6.90	6.84
Cash Flow	2.59	2.03	1.43	1.99	2.62	3.15
Earnings	1.05	0.38	-0.20	0.38	1.15	2.02
Dividends	0.40	0.40	0.40	0.76	0.76	0.73
Payout Ratio	38%	NM	NM	201%	65%	36%
Prices - High	16½	14	14⅛	14¾	20⅞	20⅝
- Low	12¾	9⅛	8⅜	9¼	9¼	17⅝
P/E Ratio - High	16	37	NM	39	18	10
- Low	12	24	NM	24	8	9

Income Statement Analysis (Million $)

	1994	%Chg	1993	%Chg	1992	%Chg	1991
Revs.	457	2%	450	7%	421	3%	408
Oper. Inc.	38.7	2%	37.8	17%	32.2	-4%	33.4
Depr.	15.5	-6%	16.5	1%	16.3	1%	16.1
Int. Exp.	9.2	-11%	10.3	NM	10.4	-5%	11.0
Pretax Inc.	18.2	133%	7.8	NM	0.2	-97%	7.2
Eff. Tax Rate	42%	—	51%	—	919%	—	48%
Net Inc.	10.5	176%	3.8	NM	-2.0	NM	3.8

Balance Sheet & Other Fin. Data (Million $)

	1994	1993	1992	1991	1990	1989
Cash	5.1	2.4	3.5	14.2	21.0	30.1
Curr. Assets	155	153	141	142	156	178
Total Assets	305	303	294	303	323	333
Curr. Liab.	77.8	74.4	70.1	66.3	67.5	74.5
LT Debt	80.0	88.0	90.0	93.0	109	117
Common Eqty.	134	125	130	139	142	139
Total Cap.	221	221	221	237	256	259
Cap. Exp.	16.3	13.9	13.2	11.6	21.6	15.5
Cash Flow	26.1	20.3	14.3	19.9	26.7	32.1

Ratio Analysis

	1994	1993	1992	1991	1990	1989
Curr. Ratio	2.0	2.1	2.0	2.1	2.3	2.4
% LT Debt of Cap.	36.0	39.6	40.6	39.4	42.5	45.3
% Net Inc.of Revs.	2.3	0.8	NM	0.9	2.5	4.7
% Ret. on Assets	3.5	1.3	NM	1.2	3.6	7.6
% Ret. on Equity	811.0	3.0	NM	2.7	8.4	15.6

Dividend Data —Dividends have been paid since 1955. A dividend reinvestment plan is available. A "poison pill" stock purchase right was adopted in 1987.

Amt. of Div. $	Date Decl.	Ex-Div. Date	Stock of Record	Payment Date
0.100	Aug. 18	Aug. 29	Sep. 02	Oct. 01 '94
0.100	Oct. 20	Nov. 28	Dec. 02	Jan. 01 '95
0.100	Feb. 09	Feb. 27	Mar. 03	Apr. 01 '95
0.100	Apr. 20	May. 26	Jun. 02	Jul. 01 '95
0.100	Jul. 21	Aug. 30	Sep. 01	Oct. 01 '95

Data as orig. reptd.; bef. results of disc. opers. and/or spec. items. Per share data adj. for stk. divs. as of ex-div. date. E-Estimated. NA-Not Available. NM-Not Meaningful. NR-Not Ranked.

Office—4360 Brownsboro Rd., Louisville, KY 40207. **Tel**—(502) 893-4600. **Pres & CEO**—T. C. Brown. **VP, CFO & Secy**—P. J. Stuecker. **Treas**—C. Barr Schuler. **Investor Contact**—Laurie Lyons. **Dirs**—T. C. Brown, P. P. Donis, W. H. Dunbar, R. P. Eklund, H. J. Ferguson, G. P. Gardner, L. E. Gloyd, R. D. Ketchum, F. J. Lunding, Jr. **Transfer Agent & Registrar**—Wachovia Bank of North Carolina, Winston-Salem. **Empl**-3,200. **S&P Analyst:** SAJ

Thomas Nelson, Inc.

NYSE Symbol TNM In S&P SmallCap 600

Price	Range	P-E Ratio	Dividend	Yield	S&P Ranking	Beta
Sep. 7'95	1995					
25 7/8	25 7/8–17 1/2	29	0.16	0.6%	B	0.60

Summary

This company, believed to be the world's leading Bible publisher, also publishes other primarily religious books and music, and sells gift and stationery items. Recent revenue and earnings gains reflected growth in all major product categories; TNM is optimistic about prospects for 1995-96. A 5-for-4 stock split was effected in March 1995. On June 19, trading in the shares shifted to the NYSE from the Nasdaq Stock Market.

Business Summary

Thomas Nelson Inc., founded in 1798, is a leading publisher, producer and distributor of books and recorded music emphasizing Christian, inspirational and family value themes. It believes it is the largest commercial publisher of English translations of the Bible. The company also designs and markets a broad line of gift and stationery products. Contributions to revenues in recent fiscal years were:

	1994–95	1993–94	1992–93
Bibles	33%	20%	30%
Books	22%	37%	37%
Music	34%	32%	18%
Gifts & other	11%	11%	15%

The company publishes and sells about 700 Bible editions and styles and has a backlist of 1,400 other titles. In each of the last three fiscal years, the company has published at least 300 new titles.

Bible and book products are sold primarily to Christian bookstores, general bookstores and mass-market merchandisers and directly to consumers.

Led by its Word Inc. unit, the company believes it is the leading producer, distributor and publisher of Christian and inspirational music. Word produces recordings and related products under five proprietary labels, and distributes Christian products for other companies under their labels. Its music publishing business is divided into three operations: print music, song and songwriter development, and copyright administration. TNM has additional music and video operations under the Regency Entertainment division, which produces and licenses master recordings for distribution primarily to the mass market.

PPC, Inc. ("Pretty Paper Company") develops and sells gift and stationery items and other products of social expression, sold under the Markings, Pretty Paper, and Markings Inspirational brand

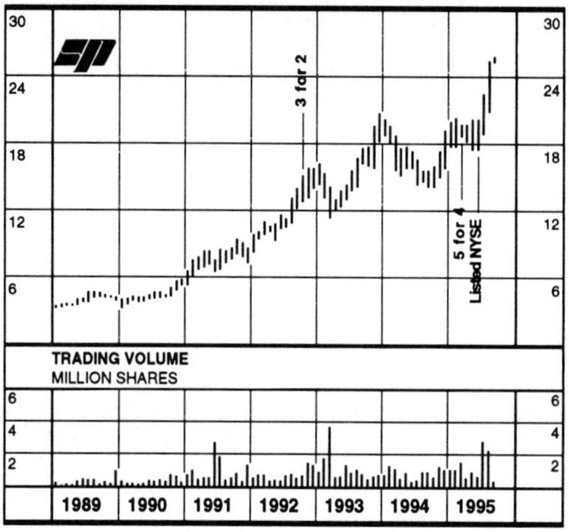

names. Current production lines offered by the company include over 800 separate items, such as journals and blank books, diaries, address books and social stationery products.

In 1994-95, the company formed the Royal Media division, whose existing operations include the Royal Magazine Group and the Morningstar Radio Network. The Royal Magazine Group publishes four magazines. The Morningstar Radio Network features adult contemporary Christian music and "High Country" programming formats to 138 affiliated stations nationwide.

Important Developments

Aug. '95— Management said that it was optimistic about its future prospects and cited continued strength in its core businesses and its new product leases scheduled for the remainder of fiscal 1995-96.

Next earnings report expected early November.

Per Share Data ($)

Yr. End Mar. 31	1995	[1]1994	[1]1993	[1]1992	1991	1990	1989	1988	1987	1986
Tangible Bk. Val.	**2.74**	1.93	0.87	3.68	2.62	2.26	2.10	1.86	1.54	1.43
Cash Flow	**1.31**	0.97	0.67	0.60	0.50	0.41	0.33	0.26	0.20	d0.34
Earnings[2]	**0.88**	0.66	0.49	0.48	0.42	0.32	0.25	0.15	0.02	d0.48
Dividends	**0.128**	0.128	0.106	0.086	0.074	0.032	Nil	Nil	Nil	0.023
Payout Ratio	**15%**	20%	22%	19%	18%	10%	Nil	Nil	Nil	NM
Calendar Years	**1994**	1993	1992	1991	1990	1989	1988	1987	1986	1985
Prices—High	**20 3/16**	20 13/16	15 13/16	9 7/16	5 27/32	4 3/4	3 21/32	6 27/32	5 21/32	3 21/32
Low	**14 3/16**	11 13/32	8 5/16	5 11/32	3 1/4	3 1/4	2 5/32	1 27/32	2 21/32	2 13/16
P/E Ratio—	**23–16**	32–17	32–17	20–11	14–8	15–10	15–9	42–11	NM	NM

Data as orig. reptd. Adj. for stk. divs. of 25% Mar. 1995, 50% Oct. 1992, 5% Sep. 1988, 5% Oct. 1986. **1.** Refl. merger or acq. **2.** Bef. results of disc. opers. of +0.05 in 1988 & spec. item(s) of +0.02 in 1994, +0.02 in 1989, +0.02 in 1987. d-Deficit. NM-Not Meaningful.

Income Data (Million $)

Year Ended Mar. 31	Revs.	Oper. Inc.	% Oper. Inc. of Revs.	Cap. Exp.	Depr.	Int. Exp.	Net Bef. Taxes	Eff. Tax Rate	[3]Net Inc.	% Net Inc. of Revs.	Cash Flow
1995	**265.0**	**31.9**	**12.0**	**2.20**	**5.87**	**8.59**	**18.30**	**36.2%**	**11.70**	**4.4**	**17.60**
[1]1994	228.0	24.2	10.6	3.20	4.18	6.90	13.30	34.2%	8.75	3.8	12.90
[1]1993	138.0	14.6	10.6	11.10	2.43	2.86	9.45	32.7%	6.36	4.6	8.78
[1]1992	93.1	11.0	11.8	3.18	1.47	0.87	9.03	34.5%	5.91	6.4	7.38
1991	73.6	8.5	11.6	2.37	0.98	1.25	6.70	35.5%	4.32	5.6	5.30
1990	59.4	6.9	11.6	0.54	0.90	0.86	5.58	40.5%	3.32	5.6	4.22
1989	49.1	6.0	12.2	0.21	0.87	1.03	4.42	41.5%	2.58	5.3	3.45
[2]1988	44.3	5.1	11.5	0.07	1.13	1.26	2.82	41.0%	1.67	3.8	2.80
1987	69.4	4.6	6.6	1.47	1.97	3.24	0.34	44.6%	0.19	0.3	2.15
1986	72.1	d2.7	NM	5.31	1.80	3.07	d9.76	NM	d5.37	NM	d3.57

Balance Sheet Data (Million $)

Mar. 31	Cash	Curr. Assets	Curr. Liab.	Curr. Ratio	Total Assets	% Ret. on Assets	Long Term Debt	Common Equity	Total Cap.	% LT Debt of Cap.	% Ret. on Equity
1995	**0.78**	**184.0**	**54.2**	**3.4**	**250.0**	**5.0**	**120.0**	**72.7**	**194.0**	**61.8**	**17.3**
1994	0.79	150.0	45.9	3.3	216.0	4.3	103.0	62.7	167.0	62.0	14.7
1993	0.80	119.0	36.7	3.2	192.0	4.7	92.8	55.4	150.0	62.0	12.1
1992	0.67	61.7	17.4	3.5	76.8	7.9	9.7	49.1	59.4	16.3	14.2
1991	1.32	49.7	16.9	2.9	58.4	8.7	13.9	26.9	41.5	33.4	17.2
1990	0.29	35.1	13.2	2.7	41.6	8.3	4.6	23.8	28.4	16.2	14.5
1989	4.76	31.8	12.5	2.5	38.4	7.2	4.0	21.9	25.9	15.5	12.5
1988	3.20	27.2	10.1	2.7	34.5	3.6	4.6	19.8	24.4	18.8	8.9
1987	0.08	39.0	13.1	3.0	58.6	0.3	27.9	17.7	45.5	61.2	1.1
1986	1.01	48.6	13.4	3.6	70.0	NM	40.1	16.5	56.5	70.8	NM

Data as orig. reptd. **1.** Refl. merger or acq. **2.** Excl. disc. ops. **3.** Bef. spec. items & disc. ops. d-Deficit. NM-Not Meaningful.

Net Revenues (Million $)

Quarter:	1995–96	1994–95	1993–94	1992–93
Jun.	61.1	49.1	46.1	19.2
Sep.		70.5	64.4	31.0
Dec.		71.1	60.7	35.1
Mar.		74.4	56.5	52.2
		265.1	227.7	137.5

Net revenues for the three months ended June 30, 1995, advanced 24%, year to year, reflecting increases in all major product categories. Expenses rose less rapidly, and operating income doubled. Interest expense rose 34%, and the seasonal net loss narrowed to $358,000, from $544,000. Per share losses were $0.03, versus $0.04.

Common Share Earnings ($)

Quarter:	1995–96	1994–95	1993–94	1992–93
Jun.	d0.03	d0.04	d0.09	0.05
Sep.		0.42	0.34	0.22
Dec.		0.36	0.24	0.14
Mar.		0.14	0.11	0.07
		0.88	0.66	0.49

Finances

In July 1995, TNM sold publicly 2,875,000 common shares (including 357,000 shares sold through exercise of underwriters' over-allotments) at $20 per share through undwriters led by PaineWebber Inc., Merrill Lynch & Co., and J.C. Bradford & Co. Net proceeds were used to repay debt.

Dividend Data

Omitted in 1985, cash dividends resumed in 1989.

Amt. of Divd. $	Date Decl.	Ex–divd. Date	Stock of Record	Payment Date
0.04	Nov. 22	Jan. 26	Feb. 1	Feb. 15'95
5–for–4	Feb. 23	Mar. 27	Mar. 10	Mar. 24'95
0.04	Feb. 23	May 2	May 8	May 22'95
0.04	May 24	Jul. 27	Jul. 31	Aug. 14'95
0.04	Aug. 24	Nov. 2	Nov. 6	Nov. 20'95

Capitalization

Long Term Debt: About $91,000,000 (6/95; adj.), incl. $55 million of 5 3/4% sub. notes due 1999, conv. into com. at $17 a sh.

Common Stock: 15,237,377 shs. ($1 par). Institutions hold about 47%. Shareholders: 1,147 of record.

Class B Common Stock: 1,067,094 shs. ($1 par). Institutions hold about 20%. Shareholders: 863 of record.

d-Deficit.

Office—Nelson Pl. at Elm Hill Pike, Nashville, TN 37214-1000. **Tel**—(615) 889-9000. **Chrmn, Pres & CEO**—S. Moore. **VP & Secy**—J. L. Powers. **Treas**—P. E. Williams. **Dirs**—B. O. Currey, Jr., W. L. Davis, Jr., S. J. Moore, S. Moore, R. J. Niebel, M. V. Oakley, J. M. Rodgers, C. Turner, Jr., A. Young. **Transfer Agent**—Trust Company Bank, Atlanta, Ga. **Incorporated** in Tennessee in 1961. **Empl**—1,130.

 Efraim Levy

STANDARD & POOR'S

STOCK REPORTS

Thor Industries

NYSE Symbol **THO**
In S&P SmallCap 600

27-JUL-95

Industry: Auto/Truck mfrs.

Summary: This company is the second largest manufacturer of recreational vehicles in the U.S. and Canada, and the largest producer of small and mid-size buses.

Quantitative Evaluations

Outlook (1 Lowest—5 Highest)
• **NA**

Fair Value
• **NA**

Risk
• **Average**

Earn./Div. Rank
• **B**

Technical Eval.
• **Bearish** since 7/95

Rel. Strength Rank (1 Lowest—99 Highest)
• **16**

Insider Activity
• **NA**

Recent Price • 19
52 Wk Range • 23¼-18¾

Yield • 0.6%
12-Mo. P/E • 9.9

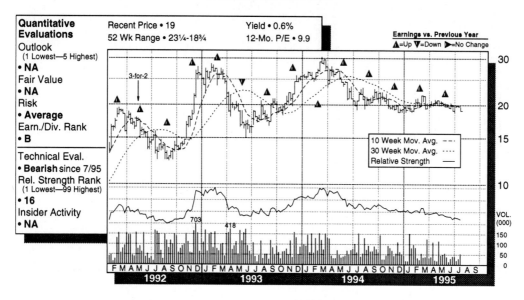

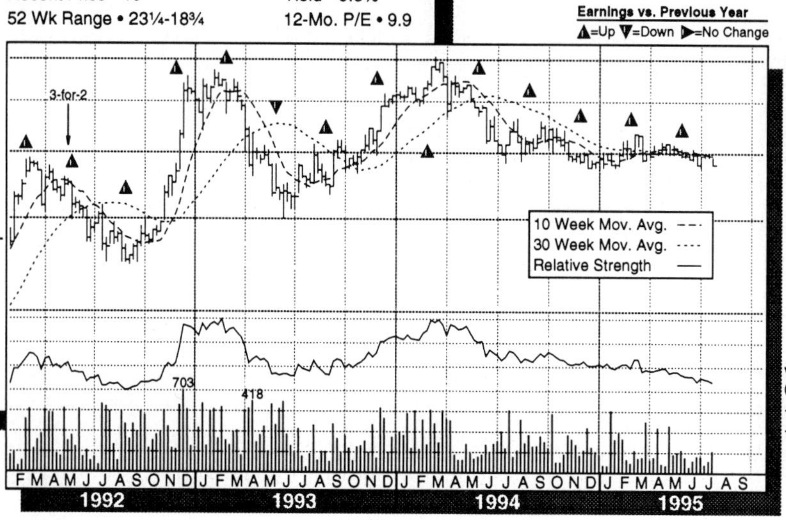

Business Profile - 27-JUL-95

Record earnings in recent periods reflect increased demand for both of the company's product lines. Thor expects continued strong demand, as a result of low RV dealer inventories and improved consumer confidence. In March 1994, the company and Ganis Credit Corp. formed a captive finance company, Thor Credit Corp., allowing dealers to service client financing needs. The balance sheet shows no long term debt. Officers and directors own nearly 50% of the shares.

Operational Review - 27-JUL-95

Net sales in the nine months ended April 30, 1995 jumped 20%, year to year, as sales for recreational vehicles and bus products grew 18% and 30%, respectively. Margins narrowed, reflecting higher material costs and more competitive pricing. Despite a smaller increase in SG&A expenses, with higher other expense, the gain in net income was held to 8.8%. EPS rose to $1.32, from $1.21.

Stock Performance - 21-JUL-95

In the past 30 trading days, THO's shares have declined 3%, compared to a 5% rise in the S&P 500. Average trading volume for the past five days was 10,360 shares, compared with the 40-day moving average of 6,618 shares.

Key Stock Statistics

Dividend Rate/Share	0.12	Shareholders	200
Shs. outstg. (M)	8.9	Market cap. (B)	$0.169
Avg. daily vol. (M)	0.007	Inst. holdings	43%
Tang. Bk. Value/Share	9.81	Insider holdings	NA
Beta	1.11		

Value of $10,000 invested 5 years ago: $ 28,848

Fiscal Year Ending Jul. 31

	1995	% Change	1994	% Change	1993	% Change
Revenues (Million $)						
1Q	139.2	9%	128.2	23%	104.0	61%
2Q	114.4	26%	90.78	13%	80.26	79%
3Q	163.1	26%	129.0	10%	117.2	52%
4Q	—	—	143.1	29%	110.8	27%
Yr.	—	—	491.1	19%	412.2	51%
Income (Million $)						
1Q	5.78	8%	5.35	—	—	—
2Q	2.21	13%	1.96	131%	0.85	67%
3Q	3.74	8%	3.47	16%	2.99	15%
4Q	—	—	5.26	44%	3.66	25%
Yr.	—	—	16.05	42%	11.27	34%
Earnings Per Share ($)						
1Q	0.65	8%	0.60	40%	0.43	30%
2Q	0.25	14%	0.22	120%	0.10	43%
3Q	0.42	8%	0.39	15%	0.34	-6%
4Q	—	—	0.59	47%	0.40	3%
Yr.	—	—	1.80	42%	1.27	10%

Next earnings report expected: mid September

Thor Industries

Business Summary - 27-JUL-95

Thor Industries is the second largest manufacturer of recreational vehicles (RVs) in North America (following its 1991 purchase of Dutchmen Manufacturing), and the largest producer of small and mid-size buses. Contributions to revenues and operating profits in fiscal 1994 were:

	Revs.	Profits
Recreational vehicles	85%	91%
Bus products	15%	9%

Canadian sales from operations in Canada and export sales to Canada from U.S. operations accounted for 5% and 7%, respectively, of total sales in fiscal 1994.

The Airstream subsidiary builds premium- and medium-high-priced travel trailers and motor homes, sold under the names Airstream, Classic, Sovereign and Land Yacht. The company believes that Classic vehicles are the most recognized product in the industry.

Thor Industries of Pennsylvania (Thor PA) is a manufacturer of travel trailers and fifth wheels in the eastern U.S. Fifth-wheel trailers, which are designed to be towed by pickup trucks, are constructed with a raised forward section that allows a bi-level floor plan and more living space. Thor PA sells products in the medium and low price range in both Canada and the U.S. Thor Industries West produces conventional motor homes in the medium price range.

Citair is one of the largest Canadian producers of travel trailers and motor homes, with a broad range of medium-priced products in most industry classifications. Dutchmen Manufacturing, Inc. is a major manufacturer of low-priced travel trailers and fifth wheels. Four Winds International manufactures conventional Class C motor homes and, to a lesser extent, Class A motor homes.

The company also manufactures axles and suspension systems. RV products are marketed through some 600 independent dealers in the U.S. and Canada.

Thor's line of small and mid-size buses are sold under the name ElDorado National. Its buses include airport shuttle buses, intra- and inter-urban mass transportation buses and buses for other purposes such as paramedical and tourist uses. ElDorado is the industry leader and innovator, building new buses fit to run on a variety of alternative fuels.

Important Developments

Jun. '95—Thor said it had received a $3.5 million order from Holiday RV Superstores, Inc., the only publicly held U.S. RV dealer.

Capitalization

Long Term Debt: None (4/95)

Per Share Data ($)

(Year Ended Jul. 31)

	1994	1993	1992	1991	1990	1989
Tangible Bk. Val.	7.98	9.09	8.01	5.70	4.88	4.51
Cash Flow	2.31	1.75	1.56	0.30	0.66	0.61
Earnings	1.80	1.27	1.15	0.08	0.47	0.43
Dividends	0.12	0.12	0.09	0.08	0.08	0.08
Payout Ratio	7%	9%	10%	100%	17%	19%
Prices - High	30³/₈	28⁵/₈	27⁷/₈	15¹/₈	7¹/₈	9³/₈
- Low	18³/₄	15	12¹/₄	6³/₈	4¹/₂	6³/₈
P/E Ratio - High	17	23	24	NM	15	22
- Low	10	12	11	NM	10	15

Income Statement Analysis (Million $)

	1994	%Chg	1993	%Chg	1992	%Chg	1991
Revs.	491	19%	412	51%	273	94%	141
Oper. Inc.	32.0	35%	23.7	32%	17.9	NM	2.3
Depr.	4.5	5%	4.3	42%	3.0	88%	1.6
Int. Exp.	0.3	-76%	1.1	-23%	1.4	NM	0.2
Pretax Inc.	26.8	43%	18.8	31%	14.4	NM	0.9
Eff. Tax Rate	40%	—	40%	—	42%	—	39%
Net Inc.	16.0	42%	11.3	35%	8.4	NM	0.6

Balance Sheet & Other Fin. Data (Million $)

	1994	1993	1992	1991	1990	1989
Cash	13.6	10.6	21.7	19.1	15.2	21.7
Curr. Assets	102	82.9	81.6	51.4	44.1	46.0
Total Assets	142	123	124	74.0	57.0	59.0
Curr. Liab.	45.5	41.0	52.4	32.3	15.3	17.9
LT Debt	Nil	Nil	Nil	Nil	Nil	Nil
Common Eqty.	95.9	80.8	71.1	40.8	40.9	40.5
Total Cap.	95.9	80.8	71.1	41.3	41.5	40.6
Cap. Exp.	4.3	1.8	2.0	1.0	1.6	2.0
Cash Flow	20.6	15.6	11.4	2.2	4.8	4.6

Ratio Analysis

	1994	1993	1992	1991	1990	1989
Curr. Ratio	2.2	2.0	1.6	1.6	2.9	2.6
% LT Debt of Cap.	Nil	Nil	Nil	Nil	Nil	Nil
% Net Inc.of Revs.	3.3	2.7	3.1	0.4	2.1	2.0
% Ret. on Assets	12.1	9.1	7.8	0.9	6.0	5.6
% Ret. on Equity	18.1	14.8	13.8	1.4	8.5	8.4

Dividend Data (Dividends were initiated in 1988.)

Amt. of Div. $	Date Decl.	Ex-Div. Date	Stock of Record	Payment Date
0.030	Sep. 13	Sep. 19	Sep. 23	Oct. 03 '94
0.030	Dec. 06	Dec. 14	Dec. 20	Jan. 03 '95
0.030	Mar. 13	Mar. 16	Mar. 22	Apr. 05 '95
0.030	Jun. 05	Jun. 15	Jun. 19	Jul. 05 '95

Data as orig. reptd.; bef. results of disc. opers. and/or spec. items. Per share data adj. for stk. divs. as of ex-div. date. E-Estimated. NA-Not Available. NM-Not Meaningful. NR-Not Ranked.

Office—419 West Pike St., Jackson Center, OH 45334. **Tel**—(513) 596-6849. **Chrmn, Pres & CEO**—W. F. B. Thompson. **Vice Chrmn & Treas**—P. B. Orthwein. **SVP-Fin & Secy**—W. L. Bennett. **Dirs**—C. D. Hoefer, P. B. Orthwein, A. Siegel, W. F. B. Thompson, W. C. Tomson. **Transfer Agent & Registrar**—Bank One, Indianapolis. **Incorporated** in Delaware in 1983. **Empl**-2,507. **S&P Analyst:** Julie Santoriello

STANDARD & POOR'S
STOCK REPORTS

Three-Five Systems

NYSE Symbol **TFS**
In S&P SmallCap 600

17-SEP-95 **Industry:** Electronics/Electric

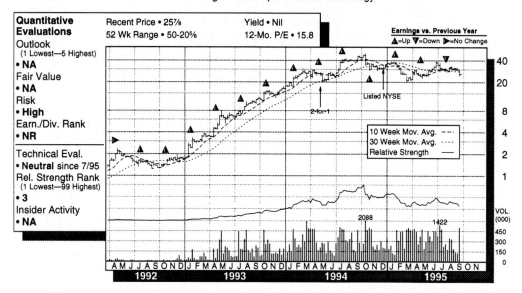

Summary: This company designs and manufactures a wide range of user interface devices that feature liquid crystal display and light emitting diode components and technology.

Quantitative Evaluations
Outlook
(1 Lowest—5 Highest)
• **NA**
Fair Value
• **NA**
Risk
• **High**
Earn./Div. Rank
• **NR**

Technical Eval.
• **Neutral** since 7/95
Rel. Strength Rank
(1 Lowest—99 Highest)
• **3**
Insider Activity
• **NA**

Recent Price • 25⅞
52 Wk Range • 50-20⅝
Yield • Nil
12-Mo. P/E • 15.8

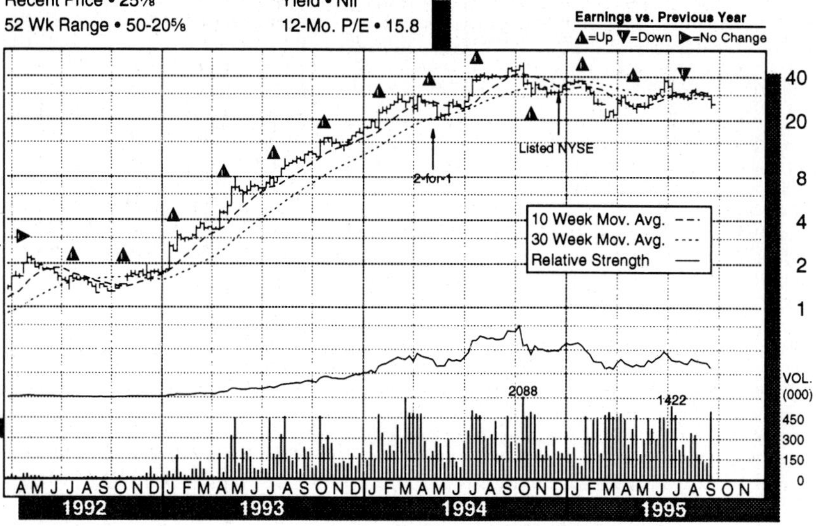

Business Profile - 27-JUN-95

TFS believes it is well positioned for future growth based on its strength in designing, prototyping and producing on a timely and cost-efficient basis a wide range of innovative, distinctive and high quality user interface devices. The recent completion of a manufacturing line in Arizona, the company's first in the U.S., will allow it to pursue additional markets, including laptop computer screens, which require LCD panels larger than those that had been produced by TFS's Asian suppliers.

Operational Review - 27-JUN-95

Net sales in the first quarter of 1995 advanced 49%, year to year, primarily reflecting higher order rates from a major wireless communications customer for existing and new product programs. Gross margins widened, aided by an improved product mix. With well controlled operating expenses, the gain in pretax income was extended to 73%. After taxes at 40.0%, versus 38.2%, net income was up 68%, to $3,314,000 ($0.41 a share, on 11% more shares), from $1,976,000 ($0.27).

Stock Performance - 15-SEP-95

In the past 30 trading days, TFS's shares have declined 9%, compared to a 4% rise in the S&P 500. Average trading volume for the past five days was 206,060 shares, compared with the 40-day moving average of 65,813 shares.

Key Stock Statistics

Dividend Rate/Share	Nil	Shareholders	1,400
Shs. outstg. (M)	7.7	Market cap. (B)	$0.199
Avg. daily vol. (M)	0.077	Inst. holdings	54%
Tang. Bk. Value/Share	6.81	Insider holdings	NA
Beta	0.80		

Value of $10,000 invested 5 years ago: NA

Fiscal Year Ending Dec. 31

	1995	% Change	1994	% Change	1993	% Change
Revenues (Million $)						
1Q	24.48	49%	16.42	126%	7.25	60%
2Q	22.10	4%	21.25	163%	8.07	66%
3Q	—	—	23.67	130%	10.31	105%
4Q	—	—	24.14	95%	12.38	93%
Yr.	—	—	85.48	125%	38.00	82%
Income (Million $)						
1Q	3.31	67%	1.98	NM	0.60	150%
2Q	2.82	-19%	3.49	NM	0.67	NM
3Q	—	—	3.40	NM	1.04	NM
4Q	—	—	3.69	103%	1.82	NM
Yr.	—	—	12.55	NM	4.13	NM
Earnings Per Share ($)						
1Q	0.41	52%	0.27	NM	0.08	183%
2Q	0.35	-19%	0.43	NM	0.09	NM
3Q	—	—	0.42	190%	0.15	NM
4Q	—	—	0.46	80%	0.25	NM
Yr.	—	—	1.59	169%	0.59	NM

Next earnings report expected: mid October

Three-Five Systems

Business Summary - 10-JUL-95

Three-Five Systems (formerly Three-Five Semiconductor), which was formed out of National Semiconductor's Optoelectronics division in 1985, designs and manufactures a wide range of user interface devices for operational control and informational display functions. Custom displays featuring liquid crystal display (LCD) and light emitting diode (LED) components and technology account for a majority of revenues. The company's products are used in cellular telephones and other wireless communication devices, as well as in medical equipment, office automation equipment, industrial process controls, instrumentation, consumer electronic products, automotive equipment, and industrial and military control products.

The company also produces a wide range of standard LCD and LED devices with varied applications. "Visible" standard devices include solid state lamps used for indicators, status lights, on-board circuit monitors and instrumentation; single and dual digit displays and multi-digit numerical displays used for calculators, industrial controls, data terminals, instrumentation timers, hand held instruments, event counters and PCB diagnostics; integrated and alpha numeric displays used for hand held terminals, minicomputers, telecommunications and instrumentation word processors; bar graph displays used for power meters in stereo systems, ham and CB radio meters; multi-digit numeric displays used for industrial controls, data terminals, test equipment, point-of-sale, mini-computer readout and home consumer applications; and clock modules used for clock radio timers, alarm and desk clocks, auto, marine and aviation clocks, portable instruments and time/temperature displays.

Infrared standard devices include emitters and silicon detectors used for TV remote controls, disk and tape drives, printers, encoders, solid state relays, photoelectric controls, switches, intrusion alarms, touch screens and sensors; and optocouplers used for power controls and supplies, solid state relays and logic to power interfaces.

Revenues by geographic region were derived as follows in 1994: North America 40% and Europe 60%. Motorola and Pitney Bowes accounted for 88% of total revenues in 1994.

Important Developments

May '95—The company said it completed a new high-volume LCD manufacturing line in Arizona that will produce a range of passive-matrix LCDs. Production from the line, which is expected to reach full capacity of 40 million square inches of displays per year by the end of 1995, will replace some of the company's supply from Asia.

Capitalization

Long Term Debt: None (3/95).
Options: To buy 465,326 shs. at $0.26 to $34.38 ea. (12/94).

Per Share Data ($) (Year Ended Dec. 31)

	1994	1993	1992	1991	1990	1989
Tangible Bk. Val.	6.03	1.50	0.68	-0.57	-0.73	-1.42
Cash Flow	1.75	0.67	0.19	0.07	0.15	0.08
Earnings	1.59	0.59	0.14	0.03	0.09	0.02
Dividends	Nil	Nil	Nil	Nil	Nil	Nil
Payout Ratio	Nil	Nil	Nil	Nil	Nil	Nil
Prices - High	50	17 5/8	2 3/8	1 7/8	9/16	NA
- Low	16 5/8	1 11/16	1	1/2	3/8	NA
P/E Ratio - High	31	30	17	63	6	NA
- Low	10	3	7	17	4	NA

Income Statement Analysis (Million $)

	1994	%Chg	1993	%Chg	1992	%Chg	1991
Revs.	85.5	125%	38.0	83%	20.8	11%	18.7
Oper. Inc.	21.1	197%	7.1	NM	1.9	105%	0.9
Depr.	1.2	122%	0.6	38%	0.4	33%	0.3
Int. Exp.	NA	—	0.1	-40%	0.2	5%	0.2
Pretax Inc.	20.7	NM	6.2	NM	1.2	NM	0.3
Eff. Tax Rate	39%	—	33%	—	13%	—	7.10%
Net Inc.	12.5	NM	4.1	NM	1.0	NM	0.2

Balance Sheet & Other Fin. Data (Million $)

	1994	1993	1992	1991	1990	1989
Cash	27.1	0.8	0.6	0.6	0.6	0.3
Curr. Assets	47.0	14.4	7.9	6.3	7.2	3.5
Total Assets	56.3	17.5	9.8	8.4	9.2	4.6
Curr. Liab.	9.4	6.9	3.4	3.5	4.5	1.5
LT Debt	0.2	0.2	1.7	0.8	0.7	0.3
Common Eqty.	46.6	10.2	4.7	-2.2	-2.9	-4.3
Total Cap.	46.9	10.5	6.4	4.9	4.6	3.0
Cap. Exp.	7.4	1.9	0.3	0.6	0.4	0.1
Cash Flow	13.8	4.7	1.4	0.5	1.0	0.3

Ratio Analysis

	1994	1993	1992	1991	1990	1989
Curr. Ratio	5.0	2.1	2.3	1.8	1.6	2.4
% LT Debt of Cap.	0.3	1.7	27.0	15.9	14.9	9.3
% Net Inc.of Revs.	14.7	10.9	4.9	1.3	3.7	0.9
% Ret. on Assets	32.8	29.9	9.3	2.7	8.0	NA
% Ret. on Equity	43.0	55.0	NA	NM	NM	NA

Dividend Data —No cash has ever been paid. A two-for-one stock split was effected in May 1994.

Data as orig. reptd.; bef. results of disc. opers. and/or spec. items. Per share data adj. for stk. divs. as of ex-div. date. E-Estimated. NA-Not Available. NM-Not Meaningful. NR-Not Ranked.

Offices—1600 N. Desert Dr., Tempe, AZ 85281. **Tel**—(602) 389-8600. **Chrmn, Pres & CEO**—D. R. Buchanan. **VP-Fin, CFO, Treas & Secy**—R. L. Buness. **Investor Contact**—Peg Breen. **Dirs**—D. R. Buchanan, D. C. Malmberg, B. E. McGillivray, J. A. Wilson. **Transfer Agent & Registrar**—Bank of New York, NYC. **Incorporated** in Delaware in 1990. **Empl-** 168. **S&P Analyst:** S.R.B.

STANDARD & POOR'S

STOCK REPORTS

Timberland Co.

NYSE Symbol **TBL**
In S&P SmallCap 600

12-NOV-95 **Industry:** Leather/shoes

Summary: Timberland manufactures and markets footwear, apparel and accessories; core products consist of waterproof boots, shoes and apparel for outdoor recreational activities.

Quantitative Evaluations
Outlook
(1 Lowest—5 Highest)
• NA
Fair Value
• NA
Risk
• High
Earn./Div. Rank
• NR

Technical Eval.
• Neutral since 11/95
Rel. Strength Rank
(1 Lowest—99 Highest)
• 4
Insider Activity
• NA

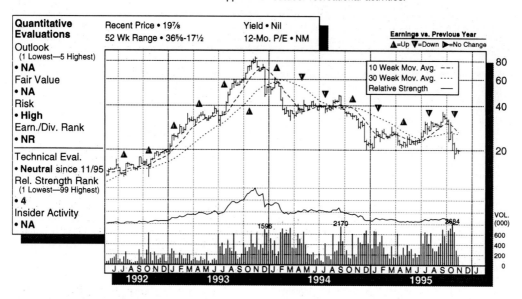

Recent Price • 19⅞
52 Wk Range • 36⅝-17½
Yield • Nil
12-Mo. P/E • NM

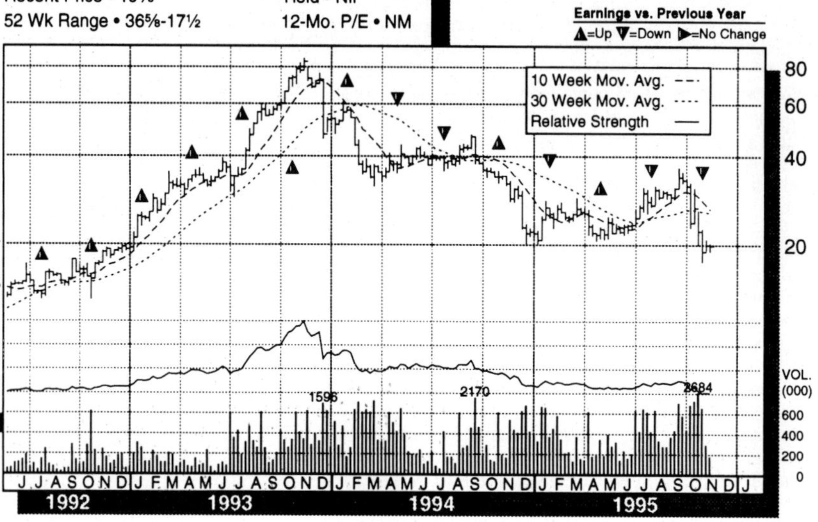

Business Profile - 07-NOV-95

TBL sells its products through independent retailers, and through a smaller number of its own stores. Business is seasonal, with most sales generated in the year's second half. Earnings in recent periods have continued to suffer from a weak retail industry. TBL is currently focusing on improving its balance sheet through tighter asset management and greater operational controls. It has also been evaluating its manufacturing capabilities and sourcing alternatives in order to improve margins.

Operational Review - 07-NOV-95

Revenues rose 4.7%, year to year, for the nine months ended September 29, 1995, reflecting continued demand for the company's products. However, gross margins narrowed as price reductions for certain footwear and apparel lines were not fully offset by product cost reductions. Following a $16 million manufacturing restructuring charge in the second quarter, a net loss of $12.4 million ($1.11 per share), contrasted with income of $14.9 million ($1.32).

Stock Performance - 10-NOV-95

In the past 30 trading days, TBL's shares have declined 37%, compared to a 1% rise in the S&P 500. Average trading volume for the past five days was 33,620 shares, compared with the 40-day moving average of 216,675 shares.

Key Stock Statistics

Dividend Rate/Share	Nil	Shareholders	900
Shs. outstg. (M)	11.0	Market cap. (B)	$0.219
Avg. daily vol. (M)	0.216	Inst. holdings	13%
Tang. Bk. Value/Share	9.82	Insider holdings	NA
Beta	1.26		

Value of $10,000 invested 5 years ago: $ 17,282

Fiscal Year Ending Dec. 31

	1995	% Change	1994	% Change	1993	% Change
Revenues (Million $)						
1Q	141.4	31%	108.1	53%	70.61	34%
2Q	125.1	-1%	126.9	50%	84.85	47%
3Q	212.6	-4%	222.1	58%	140.3	52%
4Q	—	—	180.4	46%	123.2	39%
Yr.	—	—	637.5	52%	418.9	44%
Income (Million $)						
1Q	0.92	NM	-1.62	NM	2.33	174%
2Q	-20.38	NM	0.15	-92%	1.91	NM
3Q	7.07	-57%	16.33	45%	11.24	63%
4Q	—	—	2.86	-59%	7.04	46%
Yr.	—	—	17.71	-21%	22.52	74%
Earnings Per Share ($)						
1Q	0.08	NM	-0.14	NM	0.21	163%
2Q	-1.83	NM	0.01	-94%	0.17	NM
3Q	0.63	-57%	1.45	45%	1.00	59%
4Q	—	—	0.26	-58%	0.62	41%
Yr.	—	—	1.58	-21%	2.01	70%

Next earnings report expected: early February

Timberland Co.

Business Summary - 25-AUG-95

The Timberland Company designs, manufactures and markets footwear and apparel and accessories under the Timberland brand name. Its core products consist of waterproof boots, shoes and apparel designed for outdoor recreational activities. Products are sold primarily through other retailers, as well as through TBL's own retail stores. Contributions to sales in recent years were:

	1994	1993	1992
Footwear	81%	83%	83%
Apparel & accessories	19%	17%	17%

Wholesale operations accounted for about 91% of sales in recent years and retail stores for 9%. International sales accounted for some 26% of 1994 sales, down from 29% in 1993.

A wide range of men's and women's footwear is offered, including boat shoes and sandals, water- resistant and waterproof footwear, casual dress shoes, lightweight moccasins and a variety of boots, including hiking and trail boots. The men's product line includes the HydroTech boat shoe, designed to be both durable and lightweight. During 1994, TBL introduced various new styles in each of its men's and women's line of boots and shoes, including a new line of footwear products in the Timberland Work Division.

Apparel and accessories includes coats, jackets, sweaters, shirts, pants, shorts and skirts. The accessory line, which consists of personals, luggage, briefcases, handbags, belts, caps, hats gloves and socks, is made from such materials as waterproof leather and combinations of leather and canvas.

At March 1995, TBL was operating 23 retail and 20 factory outlet stores. Regional distribution warehouses are located in New Hampshire, California and Kentucky.

Important Developments

Jul. '95—TBL recorded a $16 million pretax charge in 1995's second quarter, to reflect the closing of its manufacturing plants in Boone, N.C. and Mountain City, Tenn., effective June 28, 1995. It also plans to downsize its Dominican Republic operations.
Apr. '95—TBL recorded a $0.41 per share pretax gain in 1995's first quarter to reflect the appointment of Inchcape plc as exclusive Asia/Pacific distributor of Timberland products, and the related sale of two subsidiaries.

Capitalization

Long Term Debt: $206,826,000 (6/95).
Class A Common Stock: 8,219,649 shs. ($0.01 par); elects 25% of dirs.
Class B Common Stock: 2,735,381 shs. ($0.01 par); elects 75% of dirs.; conv. sh.-for-sh. into Cl. A.

Per Share Data ($) (Year Ended Dec. 31)

	1994	1993	1992	1991	1990	1989
Tangible Bk. Val.	11.25	10.16	7.94	6.88	6.12	5.07
Cash Flow	2.95	2.93	1.91	1.33	1.23	0.97
Earnings	1.58	2.01	1.18	0.75	0.73	0.60
Dividends	Nil	Nil	Nil	Nil	Nil	Nil
Payout Ratio	Nil	Nil	Nil	Nil	Nil	Nil
Prices - High	61	85⅜	20	10½	12½	15½
- Low	19⅞	18⅞	8¾	5⅝	5	8¾
P/E Ratio - High	39	42	17	14	17	26
- Low	13	9	7	8	7	15

Income Statement Analysis (Million $)

	1994	%Chg	1993	%Chg	1992	%Chg	1991
Revs.	638	52%	419	44%	291	29%	226
Oper. Inc.	58.4	15%	50.7	50%	33.8	43%	23.7
Depr.	15.3	49%	10.3	29%	8.0	26%	6.3
Int. Exp.	15.1	142%	6.3	13%	5.5	-5%	5.8
Pretax Inc.	28.1	-18%	34.1	79%	19.0	62%	11.7
Eff. Tax Rate	37%	—	34%	—	32%	—	31%
Net Inc.	17.7	-21%	22.5	74%	12.9	59%	8.1

Balance Sheet & Other Fin. Data (Million $)

	1994	1993	1992	1991	1990	1989
Cash	6.4	3.3	1.2	7.5	1.6	5.0
Curr. Assets	374	221	138	119	118	103
Total Assets	473	291	194	173	170	148
Curr. Liab.	107	65.4	43.4	26.3	29.3	17.6
LT Debt	207	90.8	41.5	44.2	46.9	46.7
Common Eqty.	149	128	105	93.4	85.7	74.9
Total Cap.	366	225	151	147	141	131
Cap. Exp.	31.5	21.6	11.8	7.5	9.1	6.9
Cash Flow	33.1	32.8	20.9	14.4	13.1	10.4

Ratio Analysis

	1994	1993	1992	1991	1990	1989
Curr. Ratio	3.5	3.4	3.2	4.5	4.0	5.8
% LT Debt of Cap.	56.5	40.3	27.6	30.1	33.3	35.7
% Net Inc.of Revs.	2.8	5.4	4.4	3.6	4.0	4.1
% Ret. on Assets	4.6	9.3	7.0	4.7	4.9	4.5
% Ret. on Equity	12.7	19.3	13.0	9.0	9.8	8.8

Dividend Data —No dividends have been paid.

Data as orig. reptd.; bef. results of disc. opers. and/or spec. items. Per share data adj. for stk. divs. as of ex-div. date. E-Estimated. NA-Not Available. NM-Not Meaningful. NR-Not Ranked.

Office—200 Domain Drive, Stratham, NH 03885. **Tel**—(603) 772-9500. **Chrmn, Pres & CEO**—S. W. Swartz. **EVP & COO**—J. B. Swartz. **Secy**—J. E. Beard. **Sr VP-CFO**—K. D. Monda. **Investor Contact**—Elizabeth Hunter Lavallee. **Dirs**—R. M. Agate, J. F. Brennan, J. B. Swartz, S. W. Swartz, A. Zaleznik. **Transfer Agent & Registrar**—First National Bank of Boston. **Incorporated** in Delaware in 1978; predecessor firm incorporated in 1933. **Empl-** 6,700. **S&P Analyst:** Maureen C. Carini

STANDARD & POOR'S

STOCK REPORTS

Toll Brothers

NYSE Symbol **TOL**
In S&P SmallCap 600

11-SEP-95 **Industry:** Building

Summary: This company is a builder of luxury homes in the Mid-Atlantic, Northeast, Southeast, Texas and California.

Quantitative Evaluations

Outlook
(1 Lowest—5 Highest)
• **NA**

Fair Value
• **NA**

Risk
• **Average**

Earn./Div. Rank
• **B**

Technical Eval.
• **Bearish** since 6/95

Rel. Strength Rank
(1 Lowest—99 Highest)
• **80**

Insider Activity
• **Unfavorable**

Recent Price • 18⅜
52 Wk Range • 18½-9⅛
Yield • Nil
12-Mo. P/E • 12.8

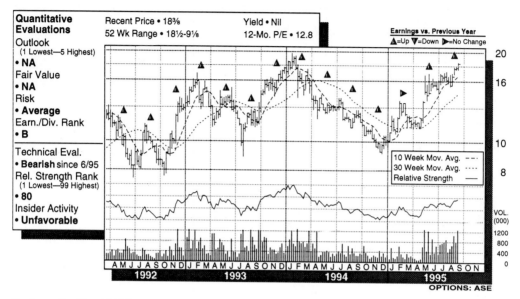

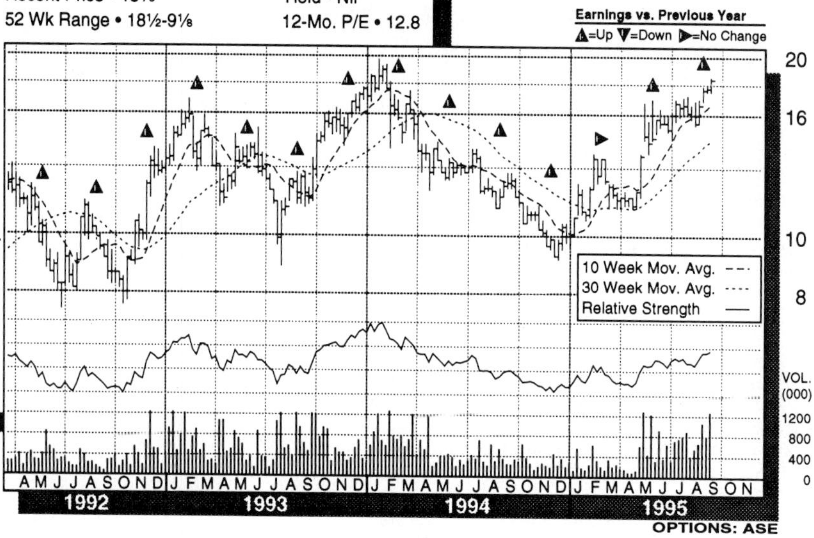

OPTIONS: ASE

Business Profile - 11-SEP-95

Toll focuses on the move-up market, where it believes demographics favor builders of more expensive homes. TOL uses sophisticated building methods that lower production costs, and increase its ability to customize. Due to the company's expansion in Arizona, Texas and Florida, new communities in California and North Carolina and diversification efforts in the Northeast and Mid-Atlantic states, TOL expects another record year in fiscal 1996.

Operational Review - 11-SEP-95

Revenues in fiscal 1995's first nine months climbed 36%, due to higher average selling prices and number of homes delivered. Margins widened significantly, and despite a large increase in net interest expense, pretax income soared 57%, to $52,288,000, from $33,403,000. Signed contracts rose 12%, to $468 million (1,303 homes), from $420 million (1,244). TOL expects fiscal 1996 will be another record year, based on the strong demographics of the move-up market and its geographic diversification.

Stock Performance - 08-SEP-95

In the past 30 trading days, TOL's shares have increased 14%, compared to a 2% rise in the S&P 500. Average trading volume for the past five days was 474,025 shares, compared with the 40-day moving average of 178,392 shares.

Key Stock Statistics

Dividend Rate/Share	Nil	Shareholders	1,400
Shs. outstg. (M)	33.5	Market cap. (B)	$0.616
Avg. daily vol. (M)	0.224	Inst. holdings	45%
Tang. Bk. Value/Share	6.63	Insider holdings	NA
Beta	NM		

Value of $10,000 invested 5 years ago: $ 56,538

Fiscal Year Ending Oct. 31

	1995	% Change	1994	% Change	1993	% Change
Revenues (Million $)						
1Q	122.3	4%	118.1	55%	76.38	47%
2Q	137.5	50%	91.44	23%	74.41	46%
3Q	186.9	56%	120.1	17%	102.8	26%
4Q	—	—	174.4	22%	143.5	42%
Yr.	—	—	504.1	27%	397.0	39%
Income (Million $)						
1Q	8.26	-3%	8.51	74%	4.89	115%
2Q	9.45	117%	4.35	-31%	6.32	NM
3Q	15.24	91%	7.99	26%	6.32	25%
4Q	—	—	15.33	23%	12.50	56%
Yr.	—	—	36.18	32%	27.42	58%
Earnings Per Share ($)						
1Q	0.25	NM	0.25	67%	0.15	114%
2Q	0.28	115%	0.13	18%	0.11	83%
3Q	0.45	87%	0.24	26%	0.19	27%
4Q	—	—	0.46	24%	0.37	54%
Yr.	—	—	1.08	32%	0.82	58%

Next earnings report expected: mid December

Toll Brothers

Business Summary - 11-SEP-95

Toll Brothers, Inc. designs, builds, markets and finances single family detached homes, townhomes and condominiums in middle and high income residential communities located primarily on land the company has developed. The company currently operates mainly in major suburban residential areas in southeastern Pennsylvania, central New Jersey, the Virginia and Maryland suburbs of Washington, D.C., northern Delaware, the Boston metropolitan area, southern Connecticut and Westchester County, N.Y. It is also developing communities in Orange County, Calif., Nassau County, N.Y., the suburbs of Raleigh, N.C. and in Charlotte, N.C. The company has recently acquired property in McKinney, Tex., a northern suburb of Dallas and in Palm Beach County, Fla. and expects to begin offering homes for sale there in the first half of 1995.

Toll markets homes primarily to upper income buyers, emphasizing high quality construction and customer satisfaction. In the five years ended October 31, 1994, it closed 5,329 homes in 111 communities. As of October 31, 1994, the company was offering homes for sale in 80 communities. Single family detached homes were offered at prices, excluding customized options, ranging from $174,900 to $664,900, with an average base sales price of $352,000. Attached home prices, excluding options, ranged from $99,900 to $467,900, with an average base price of $255,000. At October 31, 1994, Toll owned or controlled through options more than 6,100 home sites in communities under development, and land for 5,100 home sites in proposed communities.

Each of TOL's single family home communities offers several home plans, with the opportunity to select various exterior styles. As a result of additional charges for options such as three-car garages, basements and fireplaces, the average sales price for Toll's homes in fiscal 1994 was about 12.8% higher than the base price.

Toll generally attempts to reduce certain risks homebuilders encounter by controlling or purchasing land through options, beginning construction after sales agreements are executed, and by using subcontractors to perform all home construction and site improvement work on a fixed price basis.

Important Developments

Aug. '95—Toll announced it is negotiations to acquire a Phoenix-based, privately-owned, luxury homebuilder.

Capitalization

Total Debt: $298,437,000 (4/95), incl. $4,133,000 of CMOs.

Per Share Data ($) (Year Ended Oct. 31)

	1994	1993	1992	1991	1990	1989
Tangible Bk. Val.	6.11	5.01	4.12	3.59	3.19	2.85
Cash Flow	1.16	0.89	3.58	0.18	0.37	0.51
Earnings	1.08	0.82	0.52	0.12	0.30	0.44
Dividends	Nil	Nil	Nil	Nil	Nil	Nil
Payout Ratio	Nil	Nil	Nil	Nil	Nil	Nil
Prices - High	19¾	17¾	14	12⅝	4	5⅞
- Low	9⅛	8⅞	7½	2⅜	2¼	2⅞
P/E Ratio - High	18	21	27	NM	13	13
- Low	8	11	14	NM	8	7

Income Statement Analysis (Million $)

	1994	%Chg	1993	%Chg	1992	%Chg	1991
Revs.	504	27%	397	39%	285	57%	182
Oper. Inc.	84.7	33%	63.5	35%	47.1	113%	22.1
Depr.	2.7	10%	2.5	8%	2.3	9%	2.1
Int. Exp.	21.7	—	NA	—	NA	—	16.7
Pretax Inc.	56.8	29%	43.9	52%	28.8	NM	6.2
Eff. Tax Rate	36%	—	38%	—	40%	—	41%
Net Inc.	36.2	32%	27.4	57%	17.4	NM	3.7

Balance Sheet & Other Fin. Data (Million $)

	1994	1993	1992	1991	1990	1989
Cash	41.7	34.3	48.9	31.5	10.4	9.2
Curr. Assets	NA	NA	NA	NA	NA	NA
Total Assets	587	476	385	312	317	348
Curr. Liab.	NA	NA	NA	NA	NA	NA
LT Debt	250	210	179	145	179	218
Common Eqty.	204	167	136	118	95.0	85.0
Total Cap.	468	391	333	278	288	315
Cap. Exp.	3.0	1.8	1.4	0.5	0.6	2.5
Cash Flow	38.9	29.9	19.6	5.8	11.1	15.4

Ratio Analysis

	1994	1993	1992	1991	1990	1989
Curr. Ratio	NA	NA	NA	NA	NA	NA
% LT Debt of Cap.	53.5	53.7	53.8	52.2	62.3	69.0
% Net Inc.of Revs.	7.2	6.9	6.1	2.0	4.3	7.1
% Ret. on Assets	6.8	6.4	5.0	1.1	2.7	4.3
% Ret. on Equity	19.5	18.0	13.6	3.3	9.9	16.6

Dividend Data —No cash dividends have ever been paid.

Data as orig. reptd.; bef. results of disc. opers. and/or spec. items. Per share data adj. for stk. divs. as of ex-div. date. E-Estimated. NA-Not Available. NM-Not Meaningful. NR-Not Ranked.

Office—3103 Philmont Ave., Huntingdon Valley, PA 19006-4298. **Tel**—(215) 938-8000. **Chrmn & CEO**—R. I. Toll. **Pres, COO & Secy**—B. E. Toll. **SVP, Treas, & CFO**—Joel H. Rassman. **Investor Contact**—Joseph R. Sicree. **Dirs**—Z. Barzilay, R. S. Blank, R. J. Braemer, R. S. Hillas, C. B. Marbach, P. E. Shapiro, A. A. Toll, B. E. Toll, R. I. Toll. **Transfer Agent & Registrar**—Mellon Securities Trust Co., NYC. **Incorporated** in Delaware in 1986. **Empl**-935. **S&P Analyst:** Robert E. Friedman

Toro Co.

NYSE Symbol **TTC**
In S&P SmallCap 600

18-SEP-95

Industry:
Manufacturing/Distr

Summary: This company is a leading maker of consumer and commercial lawn and turf maintenance equipment, snow removal equipment and irrigation systems.

Quantitative Evaluations

Recent Price • 31⅜ | Yield • 1.5%
52 Wk Range • 32⅛-23⅜ | 12-Mo. P/E • 11.2

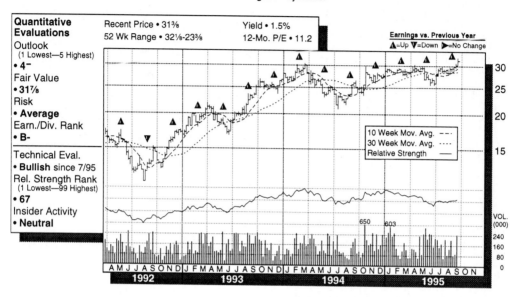

Outlook
(1 Lowest—5 Highest)
• **4-**

Fair Value
• **31⅞**

Risk
• **Average**

Earn./Div. Rank
• **B-**

Technical Eval.
• **Bullish** since 7/95

Rel. Strength Rank
(1 Lowest—99 Highest)
• **67**

Insider Activity
• **Neutral**

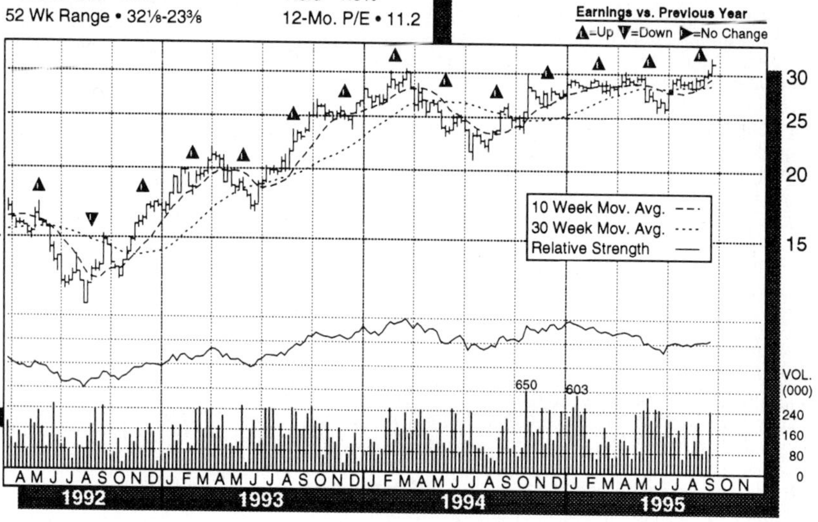

Business Profile - 18-SEP-95

The outdoor maintenance and beautification equipment made by Toro is divided into consumer, commercial and irrigation products, with consumer lines accounting for the majority of sales. The company seeks to immunize its product lines against economic cycles. Management believes the company's plants, warehouses and organizational structure are flexible to changes in demand and volume.

Operational Review - 18-SEP-95

Toro's operating results have traditionally fluctuated with the business cycle. TTC realized record revenues and earnings for the fiscal year ended July 31, 1995, as the company experienced strong sales growth in its three main divisions. Lackluster fourth-quarter results reflected efforts to reduce field inventory. Management believes earnings will rise again in fiscal 1996, which ends October 31. However, first-quarter results may decline, as Toro enjoyed exceptional snowthrower sales in 1995.

Stock Performance - 15-SEP-95

In the past 30 trading days, TTC's shares have increased 8%, compared to a 4% rise in the S&P 500. Average trading volume for the past five days was 51,880 shares, compared with the 40-day moving average of 28,326 shares.

Key Stock Statistics

Dividend Rate/Share	0.48	Shareholders	7,500
Shs. outstg. (M)	12.8	Market cap. (B)	$0.400
Avg. daily vol. (M)	0.032	Inst. holdings	60%
Tang. Bk. Value/Share	15.83	Insider holdings	NA
Beta	0.94		

Value of $10,000 invested 5 years ago: $ 14,319

Fiscal Year Ending Jul. 31

	1995	% Change	1994	% Change	1993	% Change
Revenues (Million $)						
1Q	205.7	52%	135.8	20%	113.0	-3%
2Q	213.9	13%	189.4	24%	153.0	-4%
3Q	310.6	12%	276.5	15%	241.4	8%
4Q	202.6	5%	192.7	9%	176.4	31%
Yr.	932.8	17%	794.3	16%	684.3	8%
Income (Million $)						
1Q	8.30	NM	-1.89	NM	-4.14	NM
2Q	6.80	52%	4.48	146%	1.82	NM
3Q	17.54	12%	15.64	23%	12.74	36%
4Q	4.03	NM	4.01	53%	2.62	NM
Yr.	36.67	65%	22.23	70%	13.04	NM
Earnings Per Share ($)						
1Q	0.64	NM	-0.15	NM	-0.34	NM
2Q	0.51	46%	0.35	133%	0.15	NM
3Q	1.32	11%	1.19	18%	1.01	29%
4Q	0.32	3%	0.31	48%	0.21	NM
Yr.	2.81	64%	1.71	63%	1.05	NM

Next earnings report expected: mid November

Toro Co.

Business Summary - 18-SEP-95

The Toro Company is a leading independent manufacturer of outdoor maintenance and beautification equipment. Sales contributions by product line in recent fiscal years were:

	1995	1994	1993
Consumer	52%	54%	54%
Commercial	33%	32%	30%
Irrigation	15%	14%	16%

International sales accounted for 16% of the total in fiscal 1995 and 1994.

The consumer segment produces a line of walk and riding lawn mowers, tractors, snowthrowers and debris management equipment, electric trimmers and outdoor lighting. Expansion of the product line included the acquisition in fiscal 1987 of Wheel Horse Products, Inc., a manufacturer of consumer lawn and garden equipment, and, in fiscal 1990, Lawn-Boy Inc., which makes outdoor power equipment, including walk powermowers and riding mowers. Products developed since fiscal 1992 contributed over 50% of consumer sales in fiscal 1994.

In 1991, the consumer products business was realigned into four strategic business units--Toro Power Equipment, Lawn-Boy Power Equipment, Toro Electric Outdoor Appliances and ProLine Landscaping Products--in order to increase market share and profitability. In fiscal 1992, the company consolidated Toro and Lawn-Boy manufacturing, marketing and administrative functions into one organization, resulting in significantly lower costs after plant and office closings and staff cuts.

Commercial products include professional-quality riding and walk mowers, debris equipment and grooming and aerating equipment for golf courses, parks, municipalities, landscape contractors and schools.

Irrigation products are automatic underground irrigation systems and components for commercial and residential markets, as well as golf courses, parks and athletic fields.

Products are sold under the Toro, Wheel Horse and Lawn-Boy brand names. Toro and Lawn-Boy products are marketed to 103 domestic and foreign distributors. Distributors resell consumer products to 10,800 independent retail dealers worldwide. However, Toro/Wheel Horse riding mowers and lawn and garden tractors are sold primarily direct to retail dealers, and Toro electrical home appliance and Lawn Boy mowers are sold mainly to mass merchandisers.

Important Developments

Aug. '95—The company announced that president and chief operating officer David H. Morris has tendered his resignation effective November 1, 1995, to pursue other interests.

Capitalization

Long Term Debt: $64,935,000 (7/95).

Per Share Data ($)

(Year Ended Jul. 31)

	1995	1994	1993	1992	1991	1990
Tangible Bk. Val.	NA	13.43	11.78	11.01	13.48	12.92
Cash Flow	NA	3.16	2.61	-0.15	2.38	3.01
Earnings	2.81	1.71	1.05	-1.98	0.81	1.55
Dividends	0.48	0.48	0.48	0.48	0.48	0.48
Payout Ratio	17%	28%	45%	NM	59%	35%
Prices - High	32⅛	30½	26¾	17½	20½	30
- Low	25⅝	20⅞	16½	11⅜	13¼	11
P/E Ratio - High	11	18	25	NM	25	19
- Low	9	12	16	NM	16	7

Income Statement Analysis (Million $)

	1994	%Chg	1993	%Chg	1992	%Chg	1991
Revs.	794	16%	684	8%	635	-11%	712
Oper. Inc.	61.4	12%	54.7	134%	23.4	-49%	46.2
Depr.	18.8	-2%	19.2	-13%	22.0	17%	18.8
Int. Exp.	13.6	-21%	17.2	-8%	18.7	-2%	19.0
Pretax Inc.	37.1	73%	21.4	NM	-34.9	NM	15.3
Eff. Tax Rate	40%	—	39%	—	NM	—	37%
Net Inc.	22.2	71%	13.0	NM	-23.8	NM	9.7

Balance Sheet & Other Fin. Data (Million $)

	1994	1993	1992	1991	1990	1989
Cash	36.2	61.8	25.5	17.0	12.3	19.7
Curr. Assets	364	344	333	319	320	266
Total Assets	444	419	421	415	424	326
Curr. Liab.	189	150	122	108	130	123
LT Debt	81.0	123	164	145	134	97.0
Common Eqty.	169	145	133	161	153	98.0
Total Cap.	250	269	299	307	293	203
Cap. Exp.	18.2	10.2	12.8	11.4	14.6	11.5
Cash Flow	4.1	32.3	-1.8	28.5	31.0	30.5

Ratio Analysis

	1994	1993	1992	1991	1990	1989
Curr. Ratio	1.9	2.3	2.7	3.0	2.5	2.2
% LT Debt of Cap.	32.5	45.7	54.8	47.3	45.9	47.7
% Net Inc.of Revs.	2.8	1.9	NM	1.4	2.2	3.4
% Ret. on Assets	5.1	3.1	NM	2.3	4.1	7.5
% Ret. on Equity	14.0	9.3	NM	6.2	11.9	23.7

Dividend Data —Cash dividends, initiated in 1947 and omitted in 1981, were resumed in 1984. A dividend reinvestment plan is available. A revised "poison pill" stock purchase rights plan was adopted in 1988.

Amt. of Div. $	Date Decl.	Ex-Div. Date	Stock of Record	Payment Date
0.120	Aug. 16	Sep. 19	Sep. 23	Oct. 12 '94
0.120	Dec. 15	Dec. 21	Dec. 28	Jan. 12 '95
0.120	Feb. 21	Mar. 17	Mar. 23	Apr. 12 '95
0.120	Jun. 21	Jun. 28	Jun. 30	Jul. 14 '95
0.120	Aug. 15	Sep. 20	Sep. 22	Oct. 12 '95

Data as orig. reptd.; bef. results of disc. opers. and/or spec. items. Per share data adj. for stk. divs. as of ex-div. date. E-Estimated. NA-Not Available. NM-Not Meaningful. NR-Not Ranked.

Office—8111 Lyndale Ave. South, Bloomington, MN 55420. **Tel**—(612) 888-8801. **Chrmn & CEO**—K. B. Melrose. **Pres**—D. H. Morris. **VP & Secy**—J. L. McIntyre. **VP-Fin & CFO**—G. T. Knight. **VP & Treas**—D. P. Himan. **Asst Treas & Investor Contact**—Stephen D. Keating. **Dirs**—J. K. Cooper, W. W. George, K. B. Melrose, A. A. Meyer, D. H. Morris, R. H. Nassau, D. R. Olseth, E. H. Wingate. **Transfer Agent & Registrar**—Norwest Bank Minnesota, South St. Paul. **Incorporated** in Minnesota in 1935; reincorporated in Delaware in 1984. **Empl**-3,434. **S&P Analyst:** Stephen Madonna, CFA

STANDARD & POOR'S

STOCK REPORTS

Tredegar Industries

NYSE Symbol **TG**
In S&P SmallCap 600

05-OCT-95

Industry: Plastic/Products

Summary: This company has operations in plastics, including films and molded products, as well as molded aluminum products and computer software.

Quantitative Evaluations

Outlook (1 Lowest—5 Highest)
• **NA**

Fair Value
• **NA**

Risk
• **Average**

Earn./Div. Rank
• **NR**

Technical Eval.
• **Bullish** since 1/95

Rel. Strength Rank (1 Lowest—99 Highest)
• **77**

Insider Activity
• **NA**

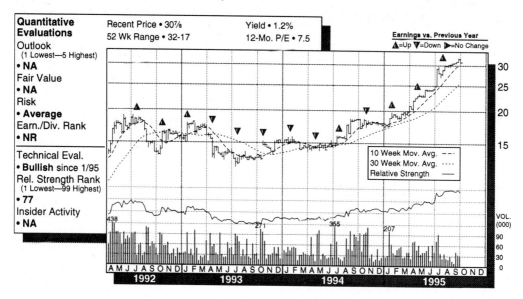

Recent Price • 30⅞
52 Wk Range • 32-17
Yield • 1.2%
12-Mo. P/E • 7.5

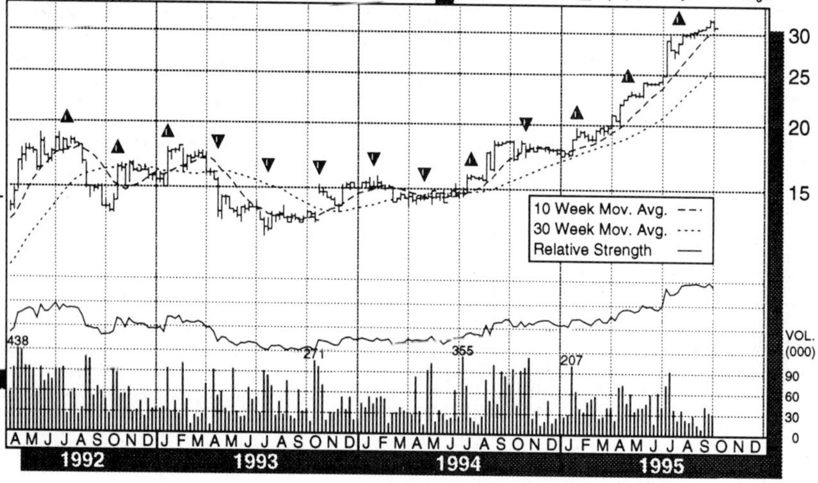

Business Profile - 05-OCT-95

In the last two years, Tredegar exited the energy business, selling coal and oil and natural gas properties. In August, it said it was pursuing the sale of its materials handling subsidiary, Brudi Inc. (book value of $27 million). In July, Tredegar said it would explore the sale of its injection molding business. Core businesses have improved, with plastic and metal products demand boosting profitability. A recent restructuring at APPX should also aid profitability.

Operational Review - 05-OCT-95

Sales in the first half of 1995 advanced 23%, year to year. Increased demand drove raw materials costs higher, and end user prices rose commensurately. Gross margins widened slightly, although operating costs rose at a slower rate than sales. With reduced interest costs and a lower effective tax rate, net income was up 25%, to $10.5 million ($1.16 a share), from $8.4 million ($0.78). Share repurchases in the past year boosted EPS.

Stock Performance - 29-SEP-95

In the past 30 trading days, TG's shares have increased 2%, compared to a 5% rise in the S&P 500. Average trading volume for the past five days was 6,160 shares, compared with the 40-day moving average of 4,987 shares.

Key Stock Statistics

Dividend Rate/Share	0.36	Shareholders	7,200
Shs. outstg. (M)	8.4	Market cap. (B)	$0.262
Avg. daily vol. (M)	0.007	Inst. holdings	24%
Tang. Bk. Value/Share	15.69	Insider holdings	NA
Beta	0.58		

Value of $10,000 invested 5 years ago: $ 21,676

Fiscal Year Ending Dec. 31

	1995	% Change	1994	% Change	1993	% Change
Revenues (Million $)						
1Q	151.1	25%	121.0	9%	111.2	-6%
2Q	149.7	22%	122.9	14%	108.0	-8%
3Q	—	—	132.2	16%	113.9	-10%
4Q	—	—	126.1	9%	116.1	NM
Yr.	—	—	502.2	12%	449.2	-6%
Income (Million $)						
1Q	4.44	NM	-5.09	NM	1.71	-38%
2Q	6.07	98%	3.07	NM	0.67	-82%
3Q	—	—	-0.28	NM	1.15	-72%
4Q	—	—	3.71	NM	0.19	-96%
Yr.	—	—	1.42	-62%	3.72	-76%
Earnings Per Share ($)						
1Q	0.49	NM	-0.47	NM	0.16	-36%
2Q	0.68	134%	0.29	NM	0.06	-83%
3Q	—	—	-0.02	NM	0.10	-74%
4Q	—	—	0.40	NM	0.02	-95%
Yr.	—	—	0.13	-62%	0.34	-76%

Next earnings report expected: mid October

Tredegar Industries

Business Summary - 05-OCT-95

Tredegar Industries is a diversified manufacturer of plastics and aluminum products and has interests in coal, oil and gas. Contributions by industry segment in 1994 (profits in million $) were:

	Sales	Profits
Plastics	$277	$33.2
Metal products	223	11.0
Technology	2.7	-8.9

The plastics segment is composed of the Film Products and Molded Products divisions, which manufacture a wide range of products including specialty films, custom injection molds, and injection molded products. Broad application for such products is found in films for packaging, industrial, agricultural and disposable personal products including diapers, and in molded products for industrial, household and disposable personal products, including diapers. Procter & Gamble, leading disposable diaper maker, is the primary customer for embossed films used as backsheet. Fiberlux Inc. produces vinyl extrusions, windows and patio doors. In 1992, Brazil-based Folium Plasticos Especiais Ltda., a producer of polyethylene and polypropylene films for disposable diapers and other personal care products, was acquired. Plastic products, produced at various U.S. locations, are sold both directly and through distributors. The company has film plants in the Netherlands and Brazil to serve the European and Latin American markets. A new Tacoma, Wash., plant was opened in 1993 to serve Far East customers.

The Metal Products segment, consisting of The William L. Bonnell Co., Capitol Products Corp. and Brudi, produces soft alloy aluminum extrusions primarily for the building and construction industry, and also for transportation and consumer durables markets. During 1992, Brudi acquired Fielden Engineers, a materials handling company in Halifax, U.K.

In December 1992, the company acquired APPX Software Inc., a supplier of flexible software development environments and business applications software. During 1992, Tredegar formed Molecumetics Ltd. to manufacture drug compounds. In August 1993, it acquired privately held Polestar Plastics, a plastic injection molder with annual sales of $8.8 million.

Important Developments

Sep. '95—Directors declared a three-for-two stock split payable January 1, 1996, to shareholders of record December 8, 1995. The quarterly dividend will be maintained at $0.06, an effective 50% boost.

Capitalization

Long Term Debt: $47,000,000 (6/95).

Per Share Data ($) (Year Ended Dec. 31)

	1994	1993	1992	1991	1990	1989
Tangible Bk. Val.	19.11	15.52	14.91	10.26	10.88	13.05
Cash Flow	2.41	2.46	3.60	3.59	0.33	3.74
Earnings	0.13	0.34	1.41	0.52	-2.19	1.44
Dividends	0.24	0.24	0.24	0.24	0.24	0.12
Payout Ratio	185%	70%	17%	46%	NM	8%
Prices - High	$18\frac{5}{8}$	18	19	11	$15\frac{7}{8}$	$17\frac{5}{8}$
- Low	$13\frac{7}{8}$	$12\frac{1}{8}$	$9\frac{3}{4}$	$6\frac{3}{8}$	7	$12\frac{7}{8}$
P/E Ratio - High	NM	53	13	21	NM	19
- Low	NM	36	7	12	NM	14

Income Statement Analysis (Million $)

	1994	%Chg	1993	%Chg	1992	%Chg	1991
Revs.	502	12%	449	-6%	479	1%	474
Oper. Inc.	49.6	38%	35.9	-36%	55.7	9%	50.9
Depr.	23.5	2%	23.1	-3%	23.9	-29%	33.5
Int. Exp.	4.2	-21%	5.4	-22%	6.9	-24%	9.1
Pretax Inc.	5.3	-23%	6.9	-73%	25.5	187%	8.9
Eff. Tax Rate	73%	—	46%	—	40%	—	37%
Net Inc.	1.4	-62%	3.7	-76%	15.3	173%	5.6

Balance Sheet & Other Fin. Data (Million $)

	1994	1993	1992	1991	1990	1989
Cash	9.0	Nil	Nil	0.5	2.3	1.7
Curr. Assets	135	117	125	119	134	127
Total Assets	318	353	359	339	342	368
Curr. Liab.	72.8	54.8	62.5	58.1	62.0	49.3
LT Debt	38.0	97.0	102	100	100	100
Common Eqty.	172	169	162	150	147	185
Total Cap.	230	289	295	280	279	317
Cap. Exp.	15.6	16.5	21.0	36.8	39.7	45.6
Cash Flow	24.9	26.8	39.2	39.1	3.7	44.9

Ratio Analysis

	1994	1993	1992	1991	1990	1989
Curr. Ratio	1.9	2.1	2.0	2.1	2.2	2.6
% LT Debt of Cap.	16.5	33.5	34.4	35.8	35.8	31.5
% Net Inc.of Revs.	0.3	0.8	3.2	1.2	NM	2.7
% Ret. on Assets	0.5	1.0	4.4	1.7	NM	NA
% Ret. on Equity	0.9	2.2	9.8	3.8	NM	NA

Dividend Data —A poison pill stock purchase rights plan was adopted in 1989. Dividends were initiated in 1989.

Amt. of Div. $	Date Decl.	Ex-Div. Date	Stock of Record	Payment Date
0.060	Nov. 21	Dec. 12	Dec. 16	Jan. 01 '95
0.060	Feb. 24	Mar. 13	Mar. 17	Apr. 01 '95
0.060	May. 24	Jun. 14	Jun. 16	Jul. 01 '95
0.060	Jul. 26	Sep. 13	Sep. 15	Oct. 01 '95
0.060	Sep. 28	Dec. 06	Dec. 08	Jan. 01 '96

Data as orig. reptd.; bef. results of disc. opers. and/or spec. items. Per share data adj. for stk. divs. as of ex-div. date. E-Estimated. NA-Not Available. NM-Not Meaningful. NR-Not Ranked.

Office—1100 Boulders Parkway, Richmond, VA 23225. **Tel**—(804) 330-1000. **Pres & CEO**—J. D. Gottwald. **EVP & COO**—R. W. Goodrum. **EVP, CFO & Treas**—N. A. Scher. **Secy**—N. M. Taylor. **Investor Contact**—Edward A. Cunningham (804-330-1598). **Dirs**—A. Brockenbrough III, P. Cothran, R. W. Goodrum, B. C. Gottwald, F. D. Gottwald, Jr., J. D. Gottwald, A. B. Lacy, E. J. Rice, W. T. Rice, N. A. Scher. **Transfer Agent & Registrar**—American Stock Transfer & Trust, NYC. **Incorporated** in Virginia in 1988. **Empl**-3,500. **S&P Analyst:** RJD

STANDARD & POOR'S
STOCK REPORTS

Triarc Cos.

NYSE Symbol **TRY**
In S&P SmallCap 600

17-OCT-95

Industry: Conglomerate/diversified

Summary: This diversified holding company owns the Arby's restaurant chain, produces Royal Crown sodas, manufactures apparel and distributes liquefied petroleum gas.

Quantitative Evaluations

Outlook (1 Lowest—5 Highest)
• **NA**

Fair Value
• **NA**

Risk
• **Average**

Earn./Div. Rank
• **C**

Technical Eval.
• **Bearish** since 8/95

Rel. Strength Rank (1 Lowest—99 Highest)
• **19**

Insider Activity
• **NA**

Recent Price • 13⅛
52 Wk Range • 16¾-9½

Yield • Nil
12-Mo. P/E • NM

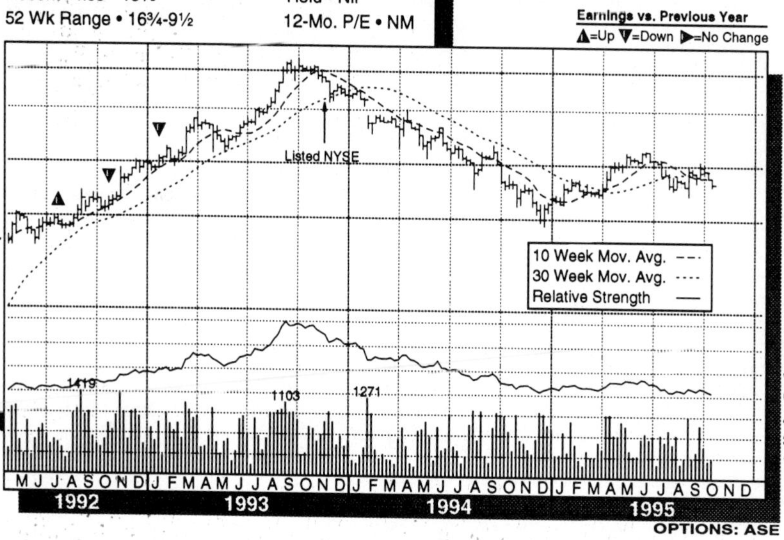

OPTIONS: ASE

Business Profile - 10-OCT-95

Triarc is attempting to relaunch its Arby's and Royal Crown brands with image-building campaigns and substantial capital investment. Except for the liquefied petroleum gas division, most of Triarc's public service businesses have been sold off to concentrate on restaurants, soft drinks and textiles. TRY recently agreed to merge its Graniteville textile unit into Galey & Lord. The company expects the transaction to strengthen its balance sheet and enhance its financial flexibility.

Operational Review - 11-OCT-95

Revenues rose 7.4%, year to year, in the first half of 1995, as solid gains in core businesses (restaurants up 21%; soft drinks 19%) outweighed decreased LP gas sales. Gross margins narrowed in all businesses and, after higher marketing and SG&A expenses and a $1.3 million facilities relocation and corporate restructuring charge, which offset sharply higher other income, net income was up 7.4%.

Stock Performance - 13-OCT-95

In the past 30 trading days, TRY's shares have declined 9%, compared to a 4% rise in the S&P 500. Average trading volume for the past five days was 27,640 shares, compared with the 40-day moving average of 45,551 shares.

Key Stock Statistics

Dividend Rate/Share	Nil	Shareholders	4,700
Shs. outstg. (M)	29.9	Market cap. (B)	$0.389
Avg. daily vol. (M)	0.043	Inst. holdings	16%
Tang. Bk. Value/Share	NM	Insider holdings	NA
Beta	0.64		

Value of $10,000 invested 5 years ago: $ 10,937

Fiscal Year Ending Dec. 31

	1995	% Change	1994	% Change	1993	% Change
Revenues (Million $)						
1Q	298.0	10%	270.0	—	--	—
2Q	279.3	5%	267.0	3%	258.0	2%
3Q	—	—	256.1	-3%	264.0	-5%
4Q	—	—	268.9	5%	257.0	NM
Yr.	—	—	1,063	51%	704.0	-33%
Income (Million $)						
1Q	6.72	-24%	8.79	—	—	—
2Q	1.01	NM	-1.59	NM	-1.23	NM
3Q	—	—	-2.88	NM	-0.94	NM
4Q	—	—	-6.41	NM	-38.31	NM
Yr.	—	—	-2.09	—	—	—
Earnings Per Share ($)						
1Q	0.22	-35%	0.34	—	--	—
2Q	0.03	NM	-0.13	NM	-0.07	NM
3Q	—	—	-0.18	NM	-0.99	NM
4Q	—	—	-0.33	NM	-0.56	NM
Yr.	—	—	-0.34	NM	-1.62	NM

Next earnings report expected: early November

Triarc Cos.

Business Summary - 10-OCT-95

Triarc Companies, Inc. (formerly DWG Corp.) is a holding company that owns 95% of CFC Holdings (which in turn owns 100% of Royal Crown Cola and Arby's Inc.), 100% of National Propane Corp. and 100% of GS Holdings Inc., which has a 51% interest in Graniteville Co. and a 100% stake in Southeastern Public Service Co. Revenue contributions by segment in recent years were:

	1994	1993
Textiles	51%	52%
Restaurants	21%	21%
Soft drinks	14%	14%
LP gas	14%	13%

Arby's is largest restaurant franchise specializing in roast beef sandwices. As of December 31, 1994, Arby's had 2,788 restaurants, including 288 company-operated units and 167 outside the U.S.

Royal Crown is the third largest national brand cola. The company produces soft-drink concentrates that are sold to independent, licensed bottlers who are responsible for the manufacture and distribution of finished beverage products.

National Propane and Public Gas distribute liquefied petroleum gas for household and industrial uses, as well as related appliances and equipment. Operations were conducted through 174 centers in 22 states as of December 31, 1994.

Graniteville Co. is a leading manufacturer of fabrics for utility wear. It also manufactures, dyes and finishes cotton, synthetic and blended fabrics for sportswear, casual wear and outerwear.

Important Developments

Sep. '95—Triarc agreed to merge its Graniteville unit into Galey & Lord, Inc. TRY will receive 35% of GNL's fully diluted shares and GNL will assume $174 million of Graniteville's debt.

Sep. '95—The Arby's unit paid $5 million for a 12.5% interest in ZuZu Inc., a 40-restaurant Mexican fast-food chain based in Dallas. In August, TRY acquired Mistic Beverages Inc. for about $95 million. Mistic had 1994 sales of $130 million. In July, TRY agreed to form a strategic alliance with Saratoga Beverage Group; in return for $6.0 million of direct funding, Triarc will receive a warrant to purchase 51% of Saratoga.

May '95—Royal Crown signed an exclusive bottling agreement with Calcol Inc. to establish a soft-drink plant in Beijing, China, by April 1996.

Capitalization

Long Term Debt: $612,118,000 (6/95).

Per Share Data ($)

(Year Ended Dec. 31)

	1994	1993	1992	1991	1990	1989
Tangible Bk. Val.	-9.79	-11.82	-10.49	-3.84	-3.31	-2.86
Cash Flow	1.40	-0.04	-0.26	1.72	1.21	1.34
Earnings	-0.34	-1.62	-1.73	-0.29	-0.68	-0.51
Dividends	Nil	Nil	Nil	Nil	Nil	Nil
Payout Ratio	Nil	Nil	Nil	Nil	Nil	Nil
Prices - High	26⅛	33	15¼	4⅜	15⅝	16
- Low	9½	14	3	1½	2¾	5⅜
P/E Ratio - High	NM	NM	NM	NM	NM	NM
- Low	NM	NM	NM	NM	NM	NM

Income Statement Analysis (Million $)

	1994	%Chg	1993	%Chg	1992	%Chg	1991
Revs.	1,063	51%	704	-33%	1,058	-17%	1,275
Oper. Inc.	118	115%	55.0	-53%	117	5%	111
Depr.	40.6	62%	25.0	-34%	38.0	-27%	52.0
Int. Exp.	73.0	63%	44.8	-38%	72.8	-3%	75.4
Pretax Inc.	0.8	NM	-22.9	NM	-39.3	NM	-0.1
Eff. Tax Rate	199%	—	NM	—	NM	—	NM
Net Inc.	-2.1	NM	-3.0	NM	-44.5	NM	-7.5

Balance Sheet & Other Fin. Data (Million $)

	1994	1993	1992	1991	1990	1989
Cash	96.0	138	102	55.0	75.0	63.0
Curr. Assets	359	393	359	NA	NA	NA
Total Assets	922	897	911	882	917	929
Curr. Liab.	223	241	226	NA	NA	NA
LT Debt	612	575	489	308	364	425
Common Eqty.	-32.0	-76.0	-35.0	86.0	92.0	109
Total Cap.	675	572	591	468	522	605
Cap. Exp.	61.6	29.0	24.0	48.0	60.0	63.0
Cash Flow	32.6	-9.3	-13.5	44.5	31.3	33.9

Ratio Analysis

	1994	1993	1992	1991	1990	1989
Curr. Ratio	1.6	1.6	1.6	NA	NA	NA
% LT Debt of Cap.	90.7	100.5	82.7	65.8	69.7	70.3
% Net Inc.of Revs.	NM	NM	NM	NM	NM	NM
% Ret. on Assets	NM	NM	NM	NM	NM	NM
% Ret. on Equity	NM	NM	NM	NM	NM	NM

Dividend Data —Cash dividends were omitted in 1974. The most recent stock payment was in 1986.

Data as orig. reptd.; bef. results of disc. opers. and/or spec. items. Per share data adj. for stk. divs. as of ex-div. date. E-Estimated. NA-Not Available. NM-Not Meaningful. NR-Not Ranked.

Office—900 Third Ave., New York, NY 10022. **Tel**—(212) 230-3000. **Chrmn & CEO**—N. Peltz. **Pres & COO**—P. W. May. **Exec VP & CFO**—J. A. Levato. **VP-Secy**—S. I. Rosen. **Investor Contact**—Martin Shea. **Dirs**—H. L Carey, C. Chajet, S. R. Jaffe, L. Kalvaria, H. E. Kelley, R. M. Kerger, M. L. Lowenkron, P. W. May, D. R. McCarthy, N. Peltz, R. S. Troubb, G. Tsai Jr. **Transfer Agent & Registrar**—Harris Trust Co., NYC. **Incorporated** in Ohio in 1929. **Empl**-11,250. **S&P Analyst:** S.S.

STANDARD & POOR'S

STOCK REPORTS

True North Communications

NYSE Symbol **TNO**
In S&P SmallCap 600

17-AUG-95 **Industry:** Advertising/Communications

Summary: Formerly Foote, Cone & Belding Communications, TNO is a global marketing communications company that operates through about 190 offices in 57 countries.

S&P Opinion: Hold (★★★)

Recent Price • 20⅜
52 Wk Range • 23⅜-15¾
Yield • 3.0%
12-Mo. P/E • 25.2

Quantitative Evaluations

Outlook
(1 Lowest—5 Highest)
• **4-**

Fair Value
• **21⅜**

Risk
• **Average**

Earn./Div. Rank
• **B+**

Technical Eval.
• **Bearish** since 7/95

Rel. Strength Rank
(1 Lowest—99 Highest)
• **52**

Insider Activity
• **NA**

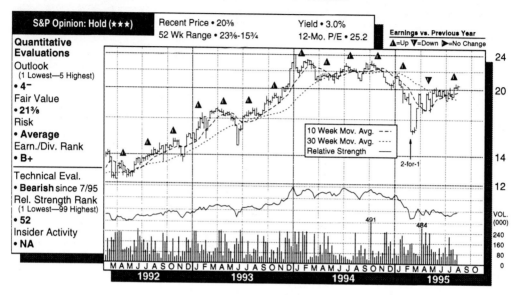

Earnings vs. Previous Year
▲=Up ▼=Down ▶=No Change

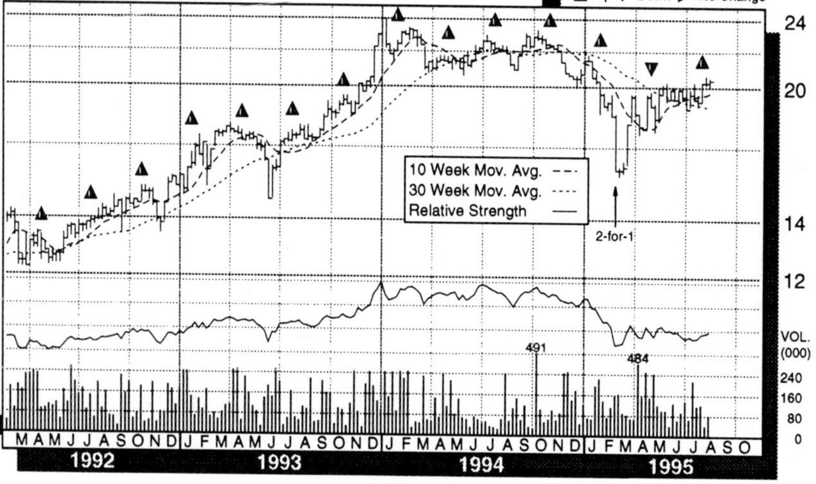

Overview - 17-AUG-95

Commission and fee income for 1995 will be lifted by gains in net new business, as well as growth from most European markets and expansion in Latin America and the Asia-Pacific region, particularly Argentina, Peru, Australia, China and Vietnam. Investments in new technologies and spending to restructure management in key Asian regions are creating some pressure on margins. A weaker U.S. dollar relative to other currencies would boost net income, while a stronger dollar would hurt. The strong pace of revenue growth should continue in 1996, reflecting a healthy advertising market, acquisitions and joint ventures, and geographic expansion. That, plus operating efficiencies and the absence of the $0.60 first-quarter restructuring charge should contribute to strong double-digit earnings growth.

Valuation - 17-AUG-95

The settlement of a dispute with Publicis, TNO's European partner, in mid-May helped TNO's stock price partially recover from a slide that began in the fourth quarter of 1994. The stock has languished in a holding pattern in recent periods however. Excluding a first-quarter one-time restructuring charge of $0.60, TNO should earn about $1.60 a share in 1995. The stock appears reasonably valued for now, but merits holding based on the stronger operating results anticipated longer term, augmented by the generous dividend payout ratio.

Key Stock Statistics

S&P EPS Est. 1995	1.00	Tang. Bk. Value/Share	6.65
P/E on S&P Est. 1995	20.4	Beta	0.59
S&P EPS Est. 1996	1.75	Shareholders	6,800
Dividend Rate/Share	0.60	Market cap. (B)	$0.467
Shs. outstg. (M)	23.0	Inst. holdings	63%
Avg. daily vol. (M)	0.018	Insider holdings	NA

Value of $10,000 invested 5 years ago: $ 17,275

Fiscal Year Ending Dec. 31

	1995	% Change	1994	% Change	1993	% Change
Revenues (Million $)						
1Q	95.39	8%	88.36	12%	79.20	NM
2Q	110.9	9%	102.1	9%	93.70	8%
3Q	—	—	100.5	4%	96.34	8%
4Q	—	—	112.8	9%	103.4	5%
Yr.	—	—	403.7	8%	372.7	5%
Income (Million $)						
1Q	-11.03	NM	1.87	25%	1.50	21%
2Q	11.36	9%	10.46	18%	8.90	17%
3Q	—	—	4.11	24%	3.31	24%
4Q	—	—	13.84	15%	12.00	84%
Yr.	—	—	30.28	18%	25.71	42%
Earnings Per Share ($)						
1Q	-0.49	NM	0.09	29%	0.07	17%
2Q	0.51	11%	0.46	15%	0.40	13%
3Q	E0.21	17%	0.18	20%	0.15	20%
4Q	E0.77	23%	0.63	18%	0.53	80%
Yr.	E1.00	-25%	1.34	17%	1.15	39%

Next earnings report expected: early November

True North Communications

Business Summary - 17-AUG-95

True North Communications (formerly Foote, Cone & Belding Communications) is the third largest advertising agency group in the U.S. and seventh largest worldwide, based on billings. As part of an alliance made with Publicis S.A. in January 1989, the two firms formed a new holding company (49% owned) that included all of TNO's European operations, Publicis' international operations and 30% of Publicis' operations in France. In addition, TNO owns a 21% stake in Publicis, and Publicis owns 20% of TNO.

Through a network of about 190 offices in 57 countries, including the PublicisFCB Group in Europe, the company is engaged in planning and creating advertising for clients and placing the advertising in media such as television, radio, newspapers and magazines. At times, the company also provides public relations services, plans merchandising and sales promotion programs and materials for its clients and performs other services. International operations accounted for 24% of revenues and 1% of pretax earnings (before corporate overhead) in 1994. PublicisFCB ranks as the second largest ad network in Europe, serving 22 countries with $3.3 in billings in 1994. FCB Latin America ranks as the eighth largest network in that region, serving 18 countries. FCB and Mojo operations rank as the third largest agency group in Australia and New Zealand.

In 1994, revenue sources were: 84% general and specialized advertising, 8% direct marketing and sales promotion, 5% healthcare communications, and 3% yellow pages directory. The 10 largest clients in 1994 represented 45% of consolidated revenues, and no one client accounted for more than 10%.

Important Developments

Jun. '95—As part of a strategy to expand its presence in Latin America, TNO boosted its ownership to 60% from 20% in Pragma/FCB Publicidad S.A., the fourth largest agency in Argentina with billings of over $90 million in 1994. FCB, TNO's largest agency subsidiary, entered Peru with the acquisition of a majority stake in Mayo Publicidad, the tenth largest agency in Peru with billings of $8 million.

May '95—TNO agencies achieved strong new business performance in the first quarter, traditionally the slowest period of the year, bolstered by a new venture with Campbell Soup Co. which consolidated planning, buying and media research for Campbell's $120 million domestic advertising billings with True North Media Inc.

Capitalization

Long Term Debt: $5,190,000 (3/95).

Per Share Data ($) (Year Ended Dec. 31)

	1994	1993	1992	1991	1990	1989
Tangible Bk. Val.	6.65	6.46	6.24	5.44	6.13	5.69
Cash Flow	1.99	1.82	1.46	-0.21	1.70	1.57
Earnings	1.34	1.15	0.83	-0.90	1.05	0.97
Dividends	0.60	0.60	0.60	0.60	0.60	0.60
Payout Ratio	45%	54%	77%	NM	61%	65%
Prices - High	24	24	$15\frac{3}{4}$	$13\frac{3}{4}$	$15\frac{1}{8}$	16
- Low	$19\frac{7}{8}$	$14\frac{3}{4}$	$11\frac{1}{2}$	$9\frac{3}{8}$	$8\frac{7}{8}$	$11\frac{1}{4}$
P/E Ratio - High	18	21	18	NM	14	16
- Low	15	13	13	NM	8	12

Income Statement Analysis (Million $)

	1994	%Chg	1993	%Chg	1992	%Chg	1991
Revs.	404	8%	373	6%	353	3%	342
Oper. Inc.	51.9	8%	47.9	20%	39.9	13%	35.4
Depr.	14.9	NM	14.9	9%	13.7	-7%	14.8
Int. Exp.	7.0	-26%	9.4	40%	6.7	-29%	9.4
Pretax Inc.	46.2	41%	32.8	12%	29.3	NM	-16.5
Eff. Tax Rate	35%	—	20%	—	37%	—	NM
Net Inc.	30.3	18%	25.7	43%	18.0	NM	-19.1

Balance Sheet & Other Fin. Data (Million $)

	1994	1993	1992	1991	1990	1989
Cash	77.0	65.0	45.0	63.0	69.0	111
Curr. Assets	383	355	320	326	365	398
Total Assets	674	638	589	591	648	658
Curr. Liab.	400	341	315	326	376	394
LT Debt	5.5	35.4	31.3	37.2	43.1	43.3
Common Eqty.	208	200	183	163	191	178
Total Cap.	221	241	217	207	242	238
Cap. Exp.	9.7	9.0	8.2	9.8	14.9	20.0
Cash Flow	45.2	40.6	31.7	-4.4	35.1	31.7

Ratio Analysis

	1994	1993	1992	1991	1990	1989
Curr. Ratio	1.0	1.0	1.0	1.0	1.0	1.0
% LT Debt of Cap.	2.5	14.7	14.4	18.0	17.8	18.1
% Net Inc.of Revs.	7.5	6.9	5.1	NM	6.4	6.0
% Ret. on Assets	4.7	4.2	3.0	NM	3.3	2.8
% Ret. on Equity	15.0	13.4	10.3	NM	11.6	11.6

Dividend Data —Dividends have been paid since 1963. A dividend reinvestment plan is available. A new "poison pill" stock purchase rights plan was adopted in 1988.

Amt. of Div. $	Date Decl.	Ex-Div. Date	Stock of Record	Payment Date
0.300	Aug. 17	Sep. 12	Sep. 16	Oct. 03 '94
0.300	Nov. 10	Dec. 13	Dec. 19	Jan. 03 '95
2-for-1	Dec. 19	Feb. 21	Jan. 06	Feb. 17 '95
0.150	Feb. 15	Mar. 13	Mar. 17	Apr. 03 '95
0.150	May. 18	Jun. 14	Jun. 16	Jul. 03 '95

Data as orig. reptd.; bef. results of disc. opers. and/or spec. items. Per share data adj. for stk. divs. as of ex-div. date. E-Estimated. NA-Not Available. NM-Not Meaningful. NR-Not Ranked.

Office—101 East Erie St., Chicago, IL 60611-2897. **Tel**—(312) 751-7000. **Chrmn & CEO**—B. Mason. **Pres**—J. B. Balousek. **Exec VP-CFO**—T. M. Ashwill. **VP-Treas**—M. S. Duffey. **VP-Secy**—D. F. Perona. **Dirs**—T. M. Ashwill, J. B. Balousek, G. W. Blaine, R. S. Braddock, L. Cutler, M. Levy, B. Mason, N. N. Minow, J. B. Ryan, W. A. Schreyer, L. E. Scott, S. T. Vehslage, C. R. Wiggins. **Transfer Agent & Registrar**—First Chicago Trust Co. of New York, Jersey City, NJ. **Incorporated** in Delaware in 1942. **Empl**-3,929. **S&P Analyst:** William H. Donald

Tuboscope Vetco Int'l

NASDAQ Symbol **TUBO**
In S&P SmallCap 600

10-OCT-95 **Industry:** Oil and Gas

Summary: This company is the world's largest supplier of coating and inspection services to the petroleum industry.

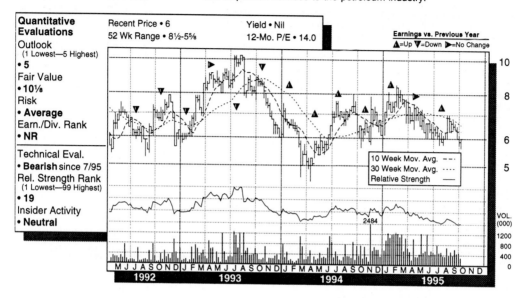

Quantitative Evaluations
Outlook
(1 Lowest—5 Highest)
• 5
Fair Value
• 10⅛
Risk
• Average
Earn./Div. Rank
• NR

Technical Eval.
• Bearish since 7/95
Rel. Strength Rank
(1 Lowest—99 Highest)
• 19
Insider Activity
• Neutral

Recent Price • 6
52 Wk Range • 8½-5⅝
Yield • Nil
12-Mo. P/E • 14.0

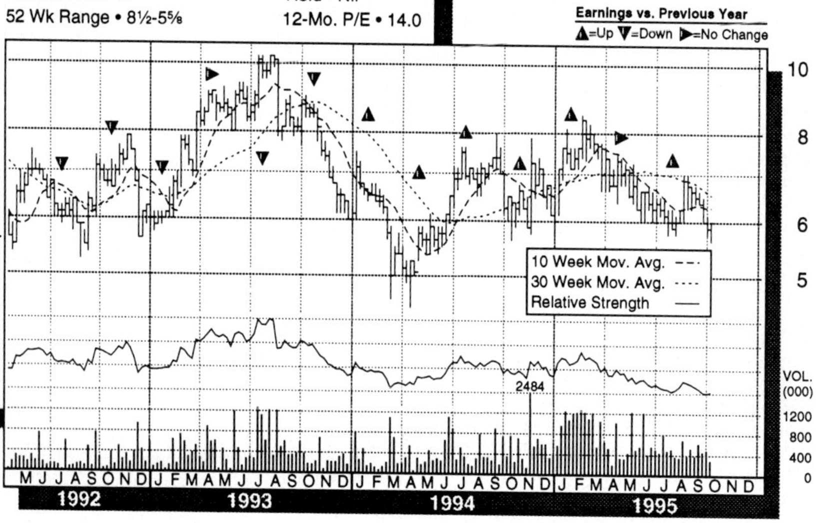

Business Profile - 10-OCT-95

This company is the world's largest supplier of coating and inspection services to the petroleum industry. During 1994, it introduced its TruRes high-resolution digital pig to the pipeline inspection marketplace. In October 1994, Tuboscope acquired the inspection and manufacturing assets of NDT Systems, Inc., a maker of equipment used in the inspection of oil country tubular goods. Also in 1994, the company resumed sales and inspection activity in the former Soviet Union.

Operational Review - 10-OCT-95

Revenues in the six months ended June 30, 1995, fell 1.6%, year to year, as declines in pipeline services and North American coating revenues offset revenue increases from mill systems/services, international coating and oilfield inspection. However, with lower SG&A expenses and higher foreign currency gains and other income, net income rose 12%, to $2.9 million ($0.14 a share) from $2.6 million ($0.12). Results for 1994 exclude an extraordinary charge of $0.04 for the early retirement of debt.

Stock Performance - 06-OCT-95

In the past 30 trading days, TUBO's shares have declined 11%, compared to a 4% rise in the S&P 500. Average trading volume for the past five days was 54,960 shares, compared with the 40-day moving average of 95,567 shares.

Key Stock Statistics

Dividend Rate/Share	Nil	Shareholders	300
Shs. outstg. (M)	18.5	Market cap. (B)	$0.106
Avg. daily vol. (M)	0.091	Inst. holdings	38%
Tang. Bk. Value/Share	1.99	Insider holdings	NA
Beta	0.94		

Value of $10,000 invested 5 years ago: NA

Fiscal Year Ending Dec. 31

	1995	% Change	1994	% Change	1993	% Change
Revenues (Million $)						
1Q	43.69	-4%	45.53	14%	39.79	-1%
2Q	45.65	NM	45.24	NM	45.21	10%
3Q	—	—	49.45	1%	48.78	17%
4Q	—	—	51.95	5%	49.56	18%
Yr.	—	—	192.2	5%	183.3	11%
Income (Million $)						
1Q	1.04	-6%	1.11	73%	0.64	-6%
2Q	1.87	26%	1.49	187%	0.52	-54%
3Q	—	—	2.23	NM	-11.13	NM
4Q	—	—	3.45	116%	1.60	146%
Yr.	—	—	8.29	NM	-8.36	NM
Earnings Per Share ($)						
1Q	0.05	NM	0.05	67%	0.03	NM
2Q	0.09	29%	0.07	NM	0.02	-60%
3Q	—	—	0.11	NM	-0.61	NM
4Q	—	—	0.18	125%	0.08	167%
Yr.	—	—	0.41	NM	-0.49	NM

Next earnings report expected: late October

Tuboscope Vetco Int'l

Business Summary - 06-OCT-95

Tuboscope Vetco International Corporation provides specialized services and products to the oil and gas industry worldwide. Its principal services are coating and inspection of oil-country tubular goods (oilfield services) and in-service inspection of oil and gas pipelines (pipeline services). In addition, the company produces, sells and leases inspection equipment for use by steel mills during the manufacture of oil-country tubulars (mill systems and sales). Tuboscope also provides industrial inspection services to energy-related industries.

Operating revenues in 1994 were derived as follows:

Oilfield services	74%
Pipeline services	11%
Industrial inspection services	9%
Mill systems & sales and other	6%

Tuboscope furnishes inspection and coating services for both new and used oil-country tubular goods (drill pipe, line pipe, casing and tubing) and also sells tubular connections. Before being placed in or returned to use, tubulars are inspected to detect production and transportation- or service-induced flaws to reduce the risk of failures during drilling and completion of wells. The company makes and develops proprietary internal coatings that it applies to tubulars for corrosion protection, reduced frequency of workovers, and greater hydraulic efficiency.

For existing oil and gas pipelines, the company offers in-place inspection without excavation or dismantling and without disrupting product flow.

Through the acquisition of Vetco Services (1991) and CTI Inspection Services (1993), Tuboscope provides industrial inspection and monitoring services, including quality control and quality assurance for construction, operation and maintenance of major energy-related projects.

The mill systems and sales segment fabricates and sells or leases inspection equipment to steel mills.

Important Developments

Sep. '95—TUBO acquired the inspection assets of Argentina-based Operaciones Especiales Argentina S.A. (OEA) through its wholly owned Argentine subsidiary, Tuboscope Vetco International de Argentina, for an undisclosed amount. OEA has been Tuboscope's oil country tubular goods and pipeline inspection agent in Argentina for the past 30 years.

Capitalization

Long Term Debt: $121,920,000 (6/95).
$7 Conv. Pfd. Stock: 100,000 shs. ($101.75 liq. pref.); ea. conv. into 10 com. shs.; red. by co. at prices decreasing to $100 a sh. in 1996.

Per Share Data ($) (Year Ended Dec. 31)

	1994	1993	1992	1991	1990	1989
Tangible Bk. Val.	6.14	5.72	1.83	1.78	3.15	3.56
Cash Flow	1.03	0.10	0.70	0.89	0.87	0.63
Earnings	0.41	-0.49	0.15	0.35	0.34	0.08
Dividends	Nil	Nil	Nil	Nil	Nil	Nil
Payout Ratio	Nil	Nil	Nil	Nil	Nil	Nil
Prices - High	8	10¼	8¼	10	11½	NA
- Low	4½	5¾	4½	6⅜	6	NA
P/E Ratio - High	20	NM	55	29	34	NA
- Low	11	NM	30	18	18	NA

Income Statement Analysis (Million $)

	1994	%Chg	1993	%Chg	1992	%Chg	1991
Revs.	192	5%	183	11%	165	9%	152
Oper. Inc.	38.4	45%	26.5	-2%	27.1	-6%	28.8
Depr.	11.4	6%	10.8	9%	9.9	44%	6.9
Int. Exp.	12.9	13%	11.4	-10%	12.6	12%	11.3
Pretax Inc.	15.0	NM	-9.9	NM	5.3	-29%	7.5
Eff. Tax Rate	40%	—	NM	—	19%	—	37%
Net Inc.	8.3	NM	-8.4	NM	3.5	-23%	4.6

Balance Sheet & Other Fin. Data (Million $)

	1994	1993	1992	1991	1990	1989
Cash	8.5	2.5	5.3	32.9	4.2	7.3
Curr. Assets	81.0	72.3	66.3	95.1	46.8	41.9
Total Assets	317	310	300	327	191	173
Curr. Liab.	45.1	67.0	38.1	45.3	19.6	20.0
LT Debt	124	101	101	118	82.0	69.0
Common Eqty.	113	105	120	115	70.0	66.0
Total Cap.	261	229	250	268	172	153
Cap. Exp.	7.5	20.2	5.3	39.2	9.3	2.5
Cash Flow	18.9	1.8	12.7	11.3	8.9	7.4

Ratio Analysis

	1994	1993	1992	1991	1990	1989
Curr. Ratio	1.8	1.1	1.7	2.1	2.4	2.1
% LT Debt of Cap.	47.5	44.3	40.6	44.1	47.8	44.7
% Net Inc.of Revs.	4.3	NM	2.1	3.0	3.1	0.9
% Ret. on Assets	2.6	NM	1.1	1.5	0.9	0.6
% Ret. on Equity	6.9	NM	2.4	4.1	NM	2.9

Dividend Data —No cash dividends have been paid on the common shares.

Data as orig. reptd.; bef. results of disc. opers. and/or spec. items. Per share data adj. for stk. divs. as of ex-div. date. E-Estimated. NA-Not Available. NM-Not Meaningful. NR-Not Ranked.

Office—2835 Holmes Rd., Houston, TX 77051; P.O. Box 808, Houston, TX 77001. **Tel**—(713) 799-5100. **Chrmn**—M. R. Reid. **Pres & CEO**—W. V. Larkin, Jr. **EVP, Treas & CFO**—R. L. Koons. **VP & Secy**—J. F. Maroney III. **Dirs**—J. R. Baier, M. G. Hubbard, W. V. Larkin, Jr., E. L. Mattson, T. M. Pennington III, M. R. Reid, P. T. Seaver, J. J. Shelton, F. J. Warren. **Transfer Agent & Registrar**—Chemical Shareholder Services Group, Inc., Dallas. **Incorporated** in Delaware in 1988. **Empl**-1,954. **S&P Analyst:** N. Rosenberg

STANDARD & POOR'S

STOCK REPORTS

Tultex Corp.

NYSE Symbol **TTX**
In S&P SmallCap 600

01-NOV-95 **Industry:** Textiles

Summary: This company makes fleece and jersey knit activewear and licensed sports apparel for the physical fitness and leisure time markets.

Quantitative Evaluations
Outlook
(1 Lowest—5 Highest)
• **5-**
Fair Value
• **6⅛**
Risk
• **Average**
Earn./Div. Rank
• **C**

Technical Eval.
• **Neutral** since 10/95
Rel. Strength Rank
(1 Lowest—99 Highest)
• **16**
Insider Activity
• **Neutral**

Recent Price • 4⅞
52 Wk Range • 6½-4⅛
Yield • Nil
12-Mo. P/E • 14.8

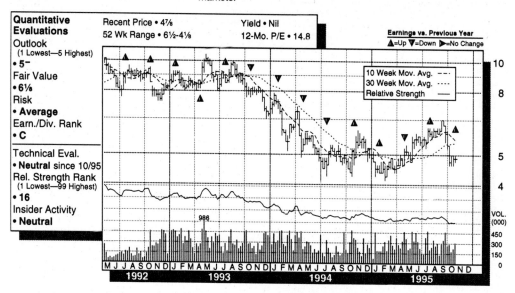

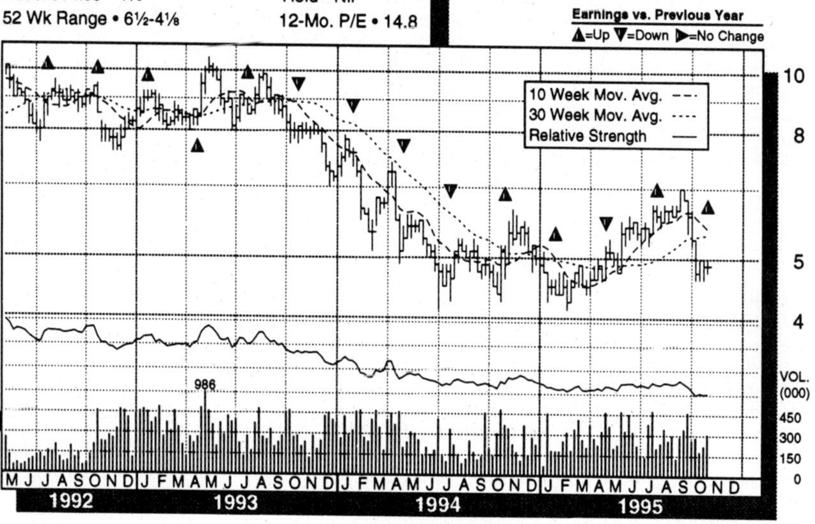

Business Profile - 31-OCT-95

This apparel maker is seeking to boost its competitiveness in licensed sports apparel by developing branded and private label higher-quality and higher-margin products to supplement its strong position in the lower-priced segments. It is developing its own brands, promoting Discus and Logo Athletic for its premium products, and using the Tultex label for the value-oriented segment of the market. TTX is also trying to increase distribution channels and strengthen customer relationships.

Operational Review - 01-NOV-95

Net sales in the first nine months of 1995 rose 4.0%, year to year. A reported $0.02 a share profit (versus a $0.05 loss) excluded a $0.13 loss on early extinguishment of debt. A slow back-to-school season caused a decline in 1995 third quarter sales, but gross margins improved on better pricing and an improved product mix. Fourth quarter strength in licensed apparel may be offset by higher material costs, price reductions and unpredictable consumer demand for the holiday season.

Stock Performance - 27-OCT-95

In the past 30 trading days, TTX's shares have declined 22%, compared to a 0.63% fall in the S&P 500. Average trading volume for the past five days was 60,880 shares, compared with the 40-day moving average of 62,795 shares.

Key Stock Statistics

Dividend Rate/Share	Nil	Shareholders	3,000
Shs. outstg. (M)	29.8	Market cap. (B)	$0.142
Avg. daily vol. (M)	0.045	Inst. holdings	31%
Tang. Bk. Value/Share	4.49	Insider holdings	NA
Beta	0.58		

Value of $10,000 invested 5 years ago: $ 5,763

Fiscal Year Ending Dec. 31

	1995	% Change	1994	% Change	1993	% Change
Revenues (Million $)						
1Q	84.14	-2%	86.29	-5%	91.02	29%
2Q	121.0	19%	101.9	2%	100.2	13%
3Q	207.9	NM	208.9	12%	187.1	3%
4Q	—	—	168.3	8%	155.2	-5%
Yr.	—	—	565.4	6%	533.6	6%
Income (Million $)						
1Q	-7.99	NM	-4.91	NM	-1.44	NM
2Q	-0.06	NM	-3.03	NM	0.44	NM
3Q	9.24	25%	7.39	58%	4.67	-53%
4Q	—	—	9.50	NM	2.24	-81%
Yr.	—	—	8.95	52%	5.90	-66%
Earnings Per Share ($)						
1Q	-0.27	NM	-0.18	NM	-0.06	NM
2Q	-0.01	NM	-0.11	NM	0.01	NM
3Q	0.30	25%	0.24	60%	0.15	-55%
4Q	—	—	0.31	NM	0.06	-85%
Yr.	—	—	0.26	63%	0.16	-71%

Next earnings report expected: mid January

Tultex Corp.

Business Summary - 01-NOV-95

Tultex manufactures fleece and jersey knit activewear and leisure apparel. The acquisitions of Logo 7, Inc. (effective January 1, 1992) and Universal Industries, Inc. (June 1992; subsequently merged into Logo 7) established the company as a major competitor in the imprinted sports apparel market.

Principal products are knitwear items for work and casual wear, such as sweatshirts, jogging suits, hooded jackets, headwear and T-shirts. Products are sold under the Tultex, Tultex Maximum Sweats, Tultex Super Weights, Discus Athletic, Universal, Logo 7, Logo Athletic and Competitor brand labels, and under private labels. In 1991, the company was licensed to make and market adult fleecewear under Levi Strauss & Co.'s Brittania label.

In the imprinted sports apparel segment, Logo 7 decorates garments using silkscreening or embroidery and markets decorated headwear. The unit is a licensee of the NFL, Major League Baseball, the NHL, the NBA and other sports organizations for imprinting sports apparel with team logos and designs. Logo 7's apparel product lines include T-shirts, golf shirts and sweaters, basic fleece products, shorts, fashion fleece, jerseys, wind suits and jackets. Headwear marketed by Logo 7 bears licensed logos of professional sports organizations, major colleges, corporations and toy/character/entertainment entities.

Apparel is sold wholesale through Tultex sales offices and manufacturers' representatives in the U.S. and abroad, primarily to discount and chain stores, mail order houses, silk screen printers and contract customers.

The company's activewear business is vertically integrated, spinning 80% to 85% of the yarn it requires in three yarn plants located in North Carolina and knitting, dyeing and cutting fabric and sewing finished goods in 11 plants in Virginia and North Carolina and one plant in Jamaica. Licensed sports apparel operations are conducted from one plant each in Indiana and Massachusetts.

Tultex also operates 14 retail stores in North Carolina, Virginia and West Virginia, selling surplus company apparel and apparel items of other manufacturers, and 32 retail stores in 19 states selling first quality company-made products.

Capitalization

Long Term Debt: $261,077,000 (7/95).
$5 Cum. Preferred Stock: 1,975 shs. ($100 par).
$7.50 Series B Cum. Conv. Pfd. Stock: 150,000 shs. ($100 stated val.); conv. into 1.5 million com. shs.

Per Share Data ($)

(Year Ended Dec. 31)

	1994	1993	1992	1991	1990	1989
Tangible Bk. Val.	5.33	5.10	5.04	5.37	5.33	4.75
Cash Flow	1.14	1.01	1.32	0.88	1.38	0.69
Earnings	0.26	0.16	0.56	0.26	0.85	0.18
Dividends	0.05	0.20	0.20	0.32	0.36	0.36
Payout Ratio	19%	125%	36%	125%	42%	199%
Prices - High	7⅞	10½	10⅝	9⅜	10⅜	14⅝
- Low	4⅛	6½	6½	6¼	6½	7¾
P/E Ratio - High	30	66	19	36	12	81
- Low	16	41	12	24	8	43

Income Statement Analysis (Million $)

	1994	%Chg	1993	%Chg	1992	%Chg	1991
Revs.	565	6%	534	6%	504	60%	315
Oper. Inc.	53.4	5%	50.7	-18%	62.1	98%	31.4
Depr.	25.2	2%	24.6	12%	22.0	29%	17.1
Int. Exp.	18.2	7%	17.0	26%	13.5	32%	10.2
Pretax Inc.	14.4	58%	9.1	-66%	26.5	155%	10.4
Eff. Tax Rate	38%	—	35%	—	35%	—	32%
Net Inc.	9.0	53%	5.9	-66%	17.2	142%	7.1

Balance Sheet & Other Fin. Data (Million $)

	1994	1993	1992	1991	1990	1989
Cash	5.8	6.8	3.6	2.8	2.4	1.0
Curr. Assets	290	289	247	151	153	145
Total Assets	457	475	433	292	303	289
Curr. Liab.	167	45.1	123	78.9	77.0	71.8
LT Debt	83.0	231	118	52.6	68.9	72.1
Common Eqty.	186	178	176	149	147	131
Total Cap.	285	424	307	211	224	212
Cap. Exp.	8.6	22.3	30.3	14.0	21.9	59.0
Cash Flow	33.9	29.3	38.2	24.2	38.1	19.0

Ratio Analysis

	1994	1993	1992	1991	1990	1989
Curr. Ratio	1.7	6.4	2.0	1.9	2.0	2.0
% LT Debt of Cap.	29.1	54.4	38.6	24.9	30.7	34.0
% Net Inc.of Revs.	1.6	1.1	3.4	2.2	6.6	1.5
% Ret. on Assets	1.9	1.3	4.7	2.4	7.9	1.8
% Ret. on Equity	4.7	2.7	9.7	4.8	16.8	3.7

Dividend Data —Dividends were omitted in May 1994 on both the common and preferred stock; dividends on the common had been paid since 1952. The most recent payment on the common was $0.05 a share on April 1, 1994. A shareholder rights plan was adopted in 1990.

Data as orig. reptd.; bef. results of disc. opers. and/or spec. items. Per share data adj. for stk. divs. as of ex-div. date. E-Estimated. NA-Not Available. NM-Not Meaningful. NR-Not Ranked.

Office—101 Commonwealth Blvd., P.O. Box 5191, Martinsville, VA 24115. **Tel**—(703) 632-2961. **Chrmn**—J. M. Franck. **Pres & CEO**—C. W. Davies, Jr. **EVP & CFO**—O. R. Rollins. **VP-Fin**—D. P. Shook. **VP & Treas**—K. W. Walsh. **Secy**—J. M. Baker. **Investor Contact**—Kathy Rogers. **Dirs**—C. W. Davies, Jr., L. M. Ewers, Jr., J. M. Franck, I. M. Groves, Jr., H. R. Hunnicutt, Jr., F. K. Iverson, B. M. Jacobson, R. M. Simmons, Jr.. **Transfer Agent**—Wachovia Bank of North Carolina, N.A., Winston-Salem. **Incorporated** in Virginia in 1937. **Empl**-6,933. **S&P Analyst:** Philip D. Wohl

STANDARD & POOR'S

STOCK REPORTS

Tyco Toys

NYSE Symbol **TTI**
In S&P SmallCap 600

11-AUG-95 **Industry:** Leisure/Amusement

Summary: Tyco is the third largest toy manufacturer in the U.S. It has valuable interests in radio controlled toys, electric racing, diecast vehicles, activity toys and large dolls.

S&P Opinion: Buy (★★★★★)

Recent Price • 6⅝
52 Wk Range • 8⅝-4¼
Yield • Nil
12-Mo. P/E • NM

Quantitative Evaluations

Outlook
(1 Lowest—5 Highest)
• **2+**

Fair Value
• **6⅜**

Risk
• **High**

Earn./Div. Rank
• **NR**

Technical Eval.
• **Bullish** since 12/93

Rel. Strength Rank
(1 Lowest—99 Highest)
• **41**

Insider Activity
• **NA**

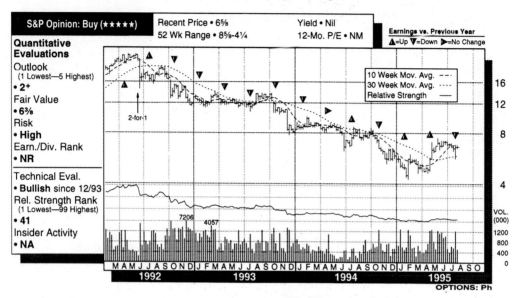

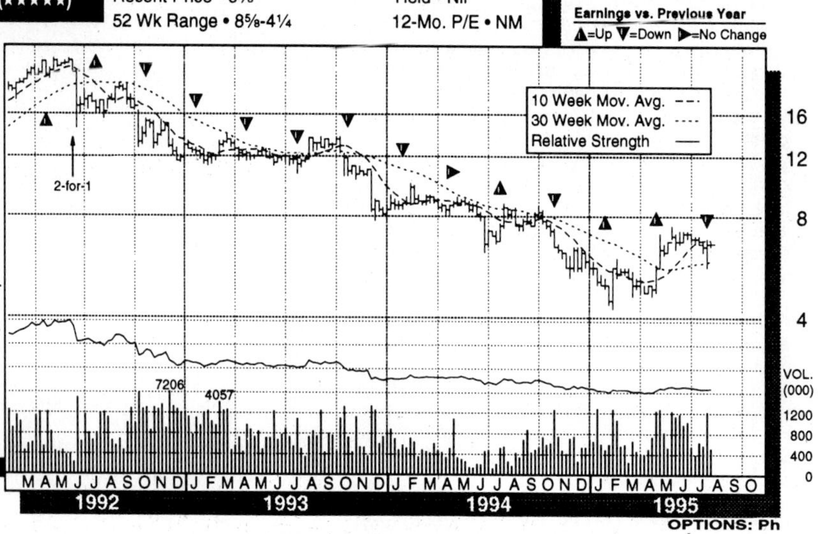

Overview - 11-AUG-95

Sales for 1996 are likely to rise 20%. A well received product line in the U.S. so far in 1995 is especially encouraging since it should provide the company with important momentum going into 1996. The company should also benefit from a consolidation of operations in Europe, as well as from improved economic conditions in that region. Lastly, a new product introduction program focused on the company's core product lines should also be favorable. Margins should widen substantially due to the higher volume, greater focus by management on realizing appropriate margins on its products and a projected annual savings of $10 million on the restructuring undertaken in 1995. The absence of the restructuring charge itself will also benefit comparisons.

Valuation - 11-AUG-95

Tyco Toys is ranked a "buy" because its valuable franchises in radio control, electric racing, diecast vehicles, activity toys and large dolls will either provide the foundation for a turnaround or attract a buyer. These brands should serve as a base for the company to return to profitability 1995 as their sales benefit from new products and more focused marketing. New product lines and reduced costs should provide further momentum. There also remains a significant chance that Tyco's well known brand names could attract a bidder as the consolidation trend in the toy industry continues.

Key Stock Statistics

S&P EPS Est. 1995	0.10	Tang. Bk. Value/Share	1.63
P/E on S&P Est. 1995	66.3	Beta	1.45
S&P EPS Est. 1996	0.80	Shareholders	22,600
Dividend Rate/Share	Nil	Market cap. (B)	$0.230
Shs. outstg. (M)	34.8	Inst. holdings	49%
Avg. daily vol. (M)	0.157	Insider holdings	NA

Value of $10,000 invested 5 years ago: $ 6,094

Fiscal Year Ending Dec. 31

	1995	% Change	1994	% Change	1993	% Change
Revenues (Million $)						
1Q	116.1	9%	106.8	6%	100.3	-25%
2Q	151.7	-4%	158.4	8%	146.7	NM
3Q	—	—	241.1	2%	235.3	34%
4Q	—	—	246.8	NM	247.9	NM
Yr.	—	—	753.1	3%	730.2	-5%
Income (Million $)						
1Q	-6.67	NM	-13.38	NM	-12.95	NM
2Q	-8.84	NM	1.21	NM	-3.53	NM
3Q	—	—	-8.10	NM	4.69	-70%
4Q	—	—	-12.70	NM	-58.15	NM
Yr.	—	—	-32.97	NM	-69.94	NM
Earnings Per Share ($)						
1Q	-0.21	NM	-0.39	NM	-0.39	NM
2Q	-0.28	NM	0.02	NM	-0.11	NM
3Q	E0.32	—	-0.26	NM	0.14	-73%
4Q	E0.27	—	-0.39	NM	-1.68	NM
Yr.	E0.10	—	-1.01	NM	-2.08	NM

Next earnings report expected: late October

Tyco Toys

Business Summary - 08-AUG-95

Tyco Toys is the third largest manufacturer and marketer of toys in the U.S.

Among its toys for boys, the company maintains the largest U.S. market share in radio control toys. Its major new product introduction in this category in 1995 is a radio controlled motorcycle. It also has a dominant market share in the electric racing category. The company participates in the male action figure caregory. Its two introductions in this catagory in 1995 will be BattleTech and Thunderbirds. Through its Matchbox brand the company is a major participant in the die-cast vehicle category.

In girls' toys, the company has a strong market share in the large doll category. Its lead introductions in this category in 1995 will be Flower Magic Mary and Surprise Hat Susie. Small doll introductions in 1995 include Fabulous Hair Friends, The Swan Princess and Liddle Kiddles.

Its major plush products are the Kitty Kitty Kittens and Puppy Puppy Puppies and characters based on Looney Tunes. Playtime Kitties and Doodle Bear will be introduced in 1995.

Activity toys include Magna Doodle, the Doctor Dreadful Food Lab, View-Master viewers, Fashion Magic, the Watch-It-Bake Oven, the 3-Minute Ice Cream Maker and science and craft sets. Sparkle Party will be introduced in 1995.

Toys will also be marketed in 1995 using the Casper license.

The company also sells a line of games, including Lickin' Lizards, Fleas on Fred, Toss Across and the Magic 8 Ball. Its introductions in this category for 1995 include B-Ball Jam, Don't Bug Me and Love It Or Hate It.

Tyco Playtime sells a line of Seasame Street preschool toys, as well as other toys. These are sold on a direct import basis.

International sales accounted for 49% of net sales and a $10.5 million operating profit in 1994.

Important Developments

Jul. '95—The company said that its loss in the second quarter primarily reflected weakness in international operations, which experienced a 17% decrease in sales due primarily to poor results in Europe. Tyco Playtime sales were also 11% lower. Sales in the U.S. were 5.6% higher and operating income was substantially higher. The company added that actions associated with its $4.9 million restructuring charge were anticipated to result in annual savings of $10 million.

Jun. '95—Children's Television Workshop (CTW) announced an agreement with TTI under which TI will nearly double the number of Seasame Street product categories.

Capitalization

Long Term Debt: $147,590,000 (6/95).

6% Conv. Exch. Pfd. Stock: $50,000,000. Conv. into 5 million common shares.

Per Share Data ($) (Year Ended Dec. 31)

	1994	1993	1992	1991	1990	1989
Tangible Bk. Val.	1.84	1.20	3.08	4.20	0.05	0.43
Cash Flow	-0.12	-1.57	1.21	1.67	1.12	1.35
Earnings	-1.01	-2.08	0.60	1.14	0.25	1.19
Dividends	Nil	0.08	0.10	Nil	Nil	Nil
Payout Ratio	Nil	NM	18%	Nil	Nil	Nil
Prices - High	10	14	23⅜	17⅞	14¼	12⅝
- Low	5¼	7¾	11½	3⅞	3⅝	6
P/E Ratio - High	NM	NM	39	15	57	11
- Low	NM	NM	19	3	15	5

Income Statement Analysis (Million $)

	1994	%Chg	1993	%Chg	1992	%Chg	1991
Revs.	753	3%	730	-5%	769	40%	549
Oper. Inc.	36.2	NM	-11.6	NM	65.8	2%	64.7
Depr.	30.9	81%	17.1	-4%	17.9	57%	11.4
Int. Exp.	31.6	28%	24.7	74%	14.2	-30%	20.4
Pretax Inc.	-31.5	NM	-83.3	NM	30.1	11%	27.2
Eff. Tax Rate	NM	—	NM	—	40%	—	29%
Net Inc.	-33.0	NM	-69.9	NM	18.0	-6%	19.2

Balance Sheet & Other Fin. Data (Million $)

	1994	1993	1992	1991	1990	1989
Cash	30.5	32.0	51.2	19.0	11.4	13.0
Curr. Assets	350	389	424	241	181	185
Total Assets	671	715	749	390	319	313
Curr. Liab.	225	257	212	116	104	96.0
LT Debt	147	180	199	91.0	117	118
Common Eqty.	295	277	335	181	97.0	92.0
Total Cap.	443	457	534	272	214	217
Cap. Exp.	21.2	29.7	22.2	11.4	9.0	10.8
Cash Flow	-4.3	-52.8	35.9	30.6	14.9	22.9

Ratio Analysis

	1994	1993	1992	1991	1990	1989
Curr. Ratio	1.6	1.5	2.0	2.1	1.7	1.9
% LT Debt of Cap.	33.1	39.3	37.2	33.4	54.7	54.4
% Net Inc.of Revs.	NM	NM	2.3	3.5	0.7	4.2
% Ret. on Assets	NM	NM	2.6	4.5	1.1	7.0
% Ret. on Equity	NM	NM	5.7	11.9	3.5	21.9

Dividend Data (Dividends, initiated in 1992, were omitted in December 1993.)

Data as orig. reptd.; bef. results of disc. opers. and/or spec. items. Per share data adj. for stk. divs. as of ex-div. date. E-Estimated. NA-Not Available. NM-Not Meaningful. NR-Not Ranked.

Office—6000 Midlantic Drive, Mt. Laurel, NJ 08054. **Tel**—(609) 234-7400. **Chrmn & CEO**—R. E. Grey. **Pres**—G. Baughman. **Vice Chairman & CFO**—H. J. Pearce. **Secy**—R. M. Kennedy Jr. **Investor Contact**—Bruce McQuire (609-840-1384). **Dirs**—G. Baughman, J. A. Canning, T. J. Danis, J. I. Gellman, D. Golub, A. Gratch, R. E. Grey, J. M. Handel, J. Kagan, L. D. Leffall, H. J. Pearce, A. Thaler, A. Vituli. **Transfer Agent & Registrar**—Midlantic National Bank, N.A. **Incorporated** in Delaware in 1980. **Empl**-2,500. **S&P Analyst:** Paul H. Valentine, CFA

STANDARD & POOR'S

STOCK REPORTS

UNC Incorporated

NYSE Symbol **UNC**
In S&P SmallCap 600

10-OCT-95

Industry:
Aircraft manufacturing/components

Summary: This company manufactures and remanufactures jet engine and aircraft components; overhauls aircraft engines and accessories; and provides aircraft maintenance and pilot training.

Quantitative Evaluations

Outlook
(1 Lowest—5 Highest)
• **4**

Fair Value
• **7**

Risk
• **Average**

Earn./Div. Rank
• **B-**

Technical Eval.
• **Bearish** since 7/95

Rel. Strength Rank
(1 Lowest—99 Highest)
• **85**

Insider Activity
• **NA**

Recent Price • 6⅝
52 Wk Range • 6⅞-4⅝
Yield • Nil
12-Mo. P/E • NM

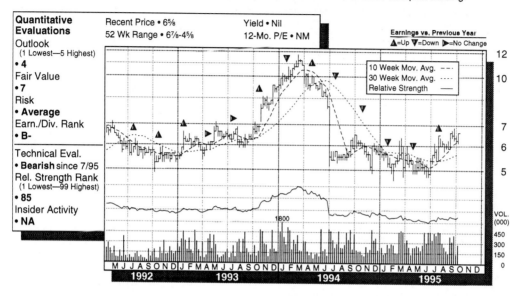

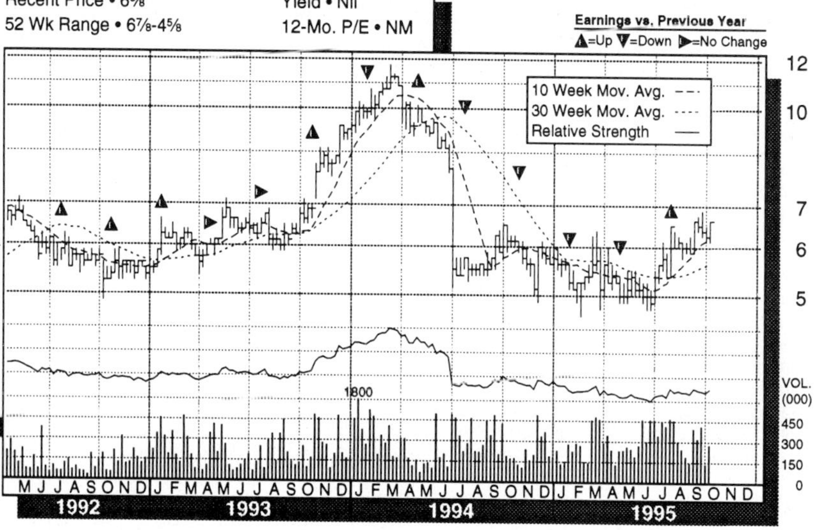

Business Profile - 26-JUN-95

In 1994, UNC began a restructuring program designed to reestablish meaningful levels of profitability during the ongoing industry downcycle. The program includes significantly reducing UNC's cost structure both at the operating expense level and through reduced interest expense. The company feels that the restructuring program will result in gradually improving quarterly financial performance in 1995 and significant full year earnings improvement in 1996 and beyond.

Operational Review - 10-OCT-95

Revenues in the six months ended June 30, 1995, declined slightly, year to year, reflecting lower revenues in the Manufacturing division and Aviation Services division. However, in the absence of a $58.7 million restructuring charge, and with lower expenses resulting from the 1994 restructuring, operating income of $17.9 million contrasted with a $48.4 million operating loss. After taxes at 35.0%, versus a benefit of $13.0 million, net income of $0.05 a share replaced a loss of $2.99 a share.

Stock Performance - 06-OCT-95

In the past 30 trading days, UNC's shares have increased 10%, compared to a 4% rise in the S&P 500. Average trading volume for the past five days was 54,380 shares, compared with the 40-day moving average of 53,528 shares.

Key Stock Statistics

Dividend Rate/Share	Nil	Shareholders	6,700
Shs. outstg. (M)	17.7	Market cap. (B)	$0.115
Avg. daily vol. (M)	0.052	Inst. holdings	49%
Tang. Bk. Value/Share	NM	Insider holdings	NA
Beta	2.04		

Value of $10,000 invested 5 years ago: $ 12,619

Fiscal Year Ending Dec. 31

	1995	% Change	1994	% Change	1993	% Change
Revenues (Million $)						
1Q	125.7	-9%	138.4	67%	82.97	-4%
2Q	131.3	7%	122.3	29%	94.74	8%
3Q	—	—	129.7	23%	105.5	11%
4Q	—	—	135.4	-13%	155.1	61%
Yr.	—	—	525.8	20%	438.3	20%
Income (Million $)						
1Q	0.05	-98%	2.46	11%	2.22	NM
2Q	0.96	NM	-54.63	NM	2.92	1%
3Q	—	—	0.03	-99%	3.70	15%
4Q	—	—	-15.79	NM	2.76	-8%
Yr.	—	—	-67.93	NM	11.59	2%
Earnings Per Share ($)						
1Q	Nil	—	0.14	8%	0.13	NM
2Q	0.05	NM	-3.12	NM	0.17	NM
3Q	—	—	Nil	—	0.21	17%
4Q	—	—	-0.90	NM	0.16	-6%
Yr.	—	—	-3.89	NM	0.67	2%

Next earnings report expected: late October

UNC Incorporated

Business Summary - 10-OCT-95

UNC Incorporated is a diversified supplier of products and services to the aviation industry which includes the overhaul of aircraft accessories, aircraft engines and industrial gas turbine engines. It also manufactures and remanufactures jet engine and aircraft components and provides maintenance and training, repair and logistical contract services.

UNC's Manufacturing division (18% of 1994 revenues) supplies turbine engine and airframe component parts for the prime-engine and aircraft original equipment manufacturers and the military. UNC Manufacturing provides advanced capabilites from design to production that result in high technology, precise tolerance and advanced alloy parts. This division consists of UNC Tri-Manufacturing, UNC Johnson Technology and UNC Aerostructures-Washington and Texas.

UNC Engine Overhaul division (25%) performs turbine engine overhaul and maintenance, provides parts provisioning for business and helicopter operators, regional airlines, helicopter operations, and provides industrial power packages for land based industrial use. This division is comprised of UNC Airwork, UNC Engine & Engine Parts and UNC Metcalf.

UNC Component (10%) Services provides a wide range of repair, remanufacturing and overhaul services for the commercial airline industry as well as for the original equipment manufacturers. This division was formed in 1994 in order to combine all repair services serving the same customer base under one management.

Aviation Services (47%) provides aircraft maintenance, overhaul, logistics support and aviation training services to the U.S. military, as well as domestic and foreign government agencies. The division has three operating units, UNC Federal Services, UNC Contract Field Services and UNC International Services.

In 1994's second quarter, UNC recorded an after-tax restructuring charge of $47 million in connection with a strategic program to reduce its cost structure and asset base in light of the continuing depressed economic conditions in the aviation industry.

Important Developments

Jul. '95—UNC said its UNC Aviation Services division, as the principal member of a team led by Sabreliner Corp., won a contract to provide aircraft maintenance and logistics services for the C-20 Gulfstream aircraft fleet used for senior government command, control and transportation functions. UNC's portion of the $200 million contract is worth about $40 million in revenue.

Capitalization

Long Term Debt: $215,231,000 (6/95).

Per Share Data ($) (Year Ended Dec. 31)

	1994	1993	1992	1991	1990	1989
Tangible Bk. Val.	-2.29	1.37	3.36	2.84	2.07	1.82
Cash Flow	-3.16	1.33	1.26	-0.89	1.03	0.82
Earnings	-3.89	0.67	0.66	-1.49	0.31	Nil
Dividends	Nil	Nil	Nil	Nil	Nil	Nil
Payout Ratio	Nil	Nil	Nil	Nil	Nil	Nil
Prices - High	11¾	9½	8	6⅛	5⅝	9⅜
- Low	4⅞	5⅜	4⅞	2¾	2¾	4⅞
P/E Ratio - High	NM	14	12	NM	18	NM
- Low	NM	8	7	NM	9	NM

Income Statement Analysis (Million $)

	1994	%Chg	1993	%Chg	1992	%Chg	1991
Revs.	526	20%	438	20%	365	1%	361
Oper. Inc.	24.4	-31%	35.4	-5%	37.4	113%	17.6
Depr.	12.7	10%	11.5	11%	10.4	2%	10.2
Int. Exp.	18.5	25%	14.8	21%	12.2	-30%	17.5
Pretax Inc.	-81.4	NM	7.8	-40%	12.9	NM	-24.1
Eff. Tax Rate	NM	—	NM	—	12%	—	NM
Net Inc.	-67.9	NM	11.6	2%	11.4	NM	-25.5

Balance Sheet & Other Fin. Data (Million $)

	1994	1993	1992	1991	1990	1989
Cash	2.6	1.0	2.0	1.0	3.0	2.0
Curr. Assets	248	249	192	257	188	211
Total Assets	468	506	384	455	410	482
Curr. Liab.	148	99	62.0	168	58.0	83.0
LT Debt	171	191	126	100	181	230
Common Eqty.	99	165	156	143	136	131
Total Cap.	270	356	287	249	320	363
Cap. Exp.	10.3	11.3	6.6	7.3	24.2	49.1
Cash Flow	-55.2	23.1	21.7	-15.3	17.6	13.9

Ratio Analysis

	1994	1993	1992	1991	1990	1989
Curr. Ratio	1.7	2.5	3.1	1.5	3.2	2.5
% LT Debt of Cap.	63.4	53.5	43.8	40.2	56.5	63.4
% Net Inc.of Revs.	NM	2.6	3.1	NM	1.5	NM
% Ret. on Assets	NM	2.6	2.7	NM	1.2	NM
% Ret. on Equity	NM	7.2	7.6	NM	3.9	NM

Dividend Data —Cash dividends, initiated in 1978, were omitted in March 1980. A "poison pill" preferred stock purchase rights plan was adopted in 1987, exercisable only if a party acquires at least 20% of the common shares.

Data as orig. reptd.; bef. results of disc. opers. and/or spec. items. Per share data adj. for stk. divs. as of ex-div. date. E-Estimated. NA-Not Available. NM-Not Meaningful. NR-Not Ranked.

Office—175 Admiral Cochrane Drive, Annapolis, MD 21401-7394. **Tel**—(410) 266-7333. **Chrmn & CEO**—D. A. Colussy. **Pres & COO**—G. M. Czarnecki. **SVP & CFO**—R. L. Pevenstein. **SVP & Secy**—R. H. Lange. **VP, Treas & Investor Contact**—Gregory M. Bubb. **Dirs**—B. Bernhard, B. B. Byron, J. K. Castle, D. A. Colussy, G. M. Czarnecki, W. C. Hittinger, J. L. Holloway III, G. V. McGowan, J. Moseley, L. A. Skantze. **Transfer Agent & Registrar**—Chemical Bank, NYC. **Incorporated** in Delaware in 1954; reincorporated in Virginia in 1978; reincorporated in Delaware in 1987. **Empl**-5,410. **S&P Analyst:** N. Rosenberg

USA Waste Services

NYSE Symbol **UW**
In S&P SmallCap 600

21-AUG-95 **Industry:** Pollution Control

Summary: This rapidly growing nonhazardous solid-waste management company performs waste collection and disposal services in multiple locations nationwide.

Quantitative Evaluations
Outlook
(1 Lowest—5 Highest)
• **NA**
Fair Value
• **NA**
Risk
• **Average**
Earn./Div. Rank
• **NR**

Technical Eval.
• **Bullish** since 3/95
Rel. Strength Rank
(1 Lowest—99 Highest)
• **95**
Insider Activity
• **Neutral**

Recent Price • 21⅝ Yield • Nil
52 Wk Range • 21⅝-10 12-Mo. P/E • NM

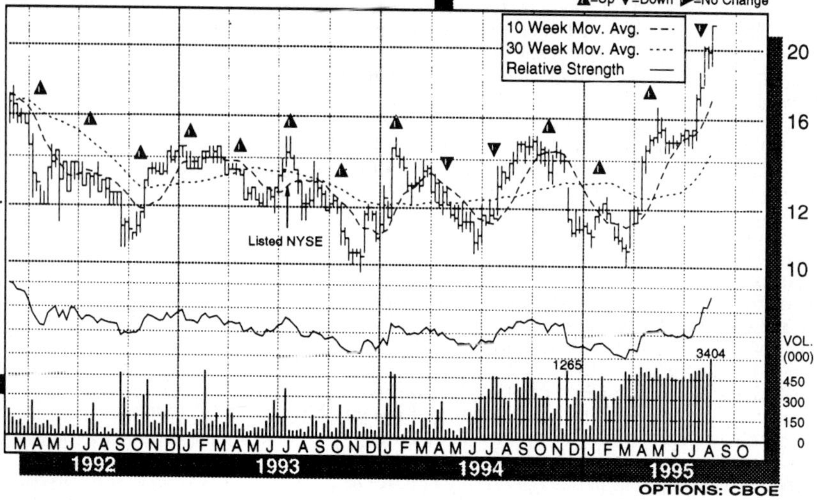

OPTIONS: CBOE

Business Profile - 18-AUG-95

UW's aggressive acquisition strategy has played a major role in the company's substantial earnings and asset growth in recent years. The company acquired Chambers Development Co. in mid-1995; in 1994, it acquired Envirofil, Inc. USA Waste intends to expand its integrated nonhazardous solid-waste management services in selected markets and to improve the operating results of the businesses it acquires. Capital expenditures for 1995 are expected to reach $40 million.

Operational Review - 18-AUG-95

Revenues for the first half of 1995 were up slightly from those of the year-earlier period, as restated for acquisitions. Results were penalized by merger costs, restructuring charges and unusual interest costs. A net loss of $27.7 million ($0.54 a share, based on 5.2% more shares) contrasted with restated income of $2.4 million ($0.05).

Stock Performance - 18-AUG-95

In the past 30 trading days, UW's shares have increased 42%, compared to a 0.51% rise in the S&P 500. Average trading volume for the past five days was 680,900 shares, compared with the 40-day moving average of 295,974 shares.

Key Stock Statistics

Dividend Rate/Share	Nil	Shareholders	1,000
Shs. outstg. (M)	52.3	Market cap. (B)	$ 1.1
Avg. daily vol. (M)	0.399	Inst. holdings	13%
Tang. Bk. Value/Share	1.11	Insider holdings	4%
Beta	0.59		

Value of $10,000 invested 5 years ago: NA

Fiscal Year Ending Dec. 31

	1995	% Change	1994	% Change	1993	% Change
Revenues (Million $)						
1Q	46.51	22%	38.21	142%	15.76	57%
2Q	111.2	148%	44.87	145%	18.34	36%
3Q	—	—	47.13	141%	19.55	37%
4Q	—	—	59.50	143%	24.49	70%
Yr.	—	—	176.2	126%	78.14	50%
Income (Million $)						
1Q	4.79	112%	2.26	—	—	—
2Q	-27.84	NM	1.02	—	—	—
3Q	—	—	4.62	—	—	—
4Q	—	—	5.43	—	—	—
Yr.	—	—	13.83	101%	6.89	-6%
Earnings Per Share ($)						
1Q	0.21	91%	0.11	-42%	0.19	36%
2Q	-0.54	NM	0.04	-80%	0.20	25%
3Q	—	—	0.21	5%	0.20	18%
4Q	—	—	0.27	29%	0.21	17%
Yr.	—	—	0.61	-24%	0.80	23%

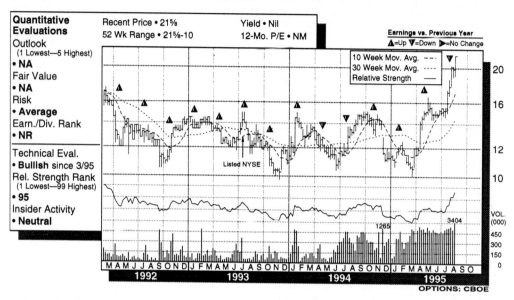

Next earnings report expected: mid November

USA Waste Services

Business Summary - 18-AUG-95

USA Waste Services, Inc. is engaged in the nonhazardous solid-waste management business, providing collection, transfer, disposal and recycling services to municipal, commercial, industrial and residential customers. The company conducts its operations through several subsidiaries, maintaining the integrity of the local service name in each of its market areas. Following the acquisition of Chambers Development Co. in June 1995, the company was providing collection, transfer, disposal and recycling services to about 450,000 customers in 22 states, including California, Texas, Illinois, Indiana, Oklahoma, Missouri, New Jersey, North Dakota, Pennsylvania, Washington, West Virginia and Ohio. The company had 28 landfills, 35 collection operations, 14 transfer stations, 14 recycling operations and two soil remediation facilities.

Solid-waste collection is provided under two primary types of arrangements, depending on the customer being served. Commercial and industrial collection services are generally performed under one- to three-year service agreements, and fees are determined by such factors as collection frequency, type of collection equipment furnished by the company, the type and volume or weight of the waste collected and the distance to the disposal facility and cost of disposal.

As part of its services, the company provides steel containers to most of its commercial and industrial customers to store solid waste. The company often obtains waste collection accounts through acquisitions, including the purchase of customer lists, routes and equipment.

The company operates curbside recycling programs in connection with its residential collection operations in six markets and its transfer station in Crestwood, Ill. The company also owns a 25% interest in Automated Recycling Technologies, Inc., which operates two recycling and sorting facilities in Ocean County, N.J.

In May 1994, the company acquired Envirofil, Inc., for 9.7 million common shares.

Important Developments

Aug. '95—UW said it has acquired six companies and has agreed to acquire three others. The company said the nine companies represent additional annual revenues of $51 million. Terms were not disclosed.

Jun. '95—UW completed the acquisition of Chambers Development Co., an integrated solid-waste management company operating primarily in the eastern U.S., for some 27.8 million common shares. The total value of the transaction, including Chambers debt, was about $725 million. The merger brought UW's annual revenues to about $450 million.

Capitalization

Long Term Debt: $167,715,000 (3/95), incl. $49,000,000 of 8.5% sub. debs. due 2002 & conv. into com. at $13.25 a sh.

Per Share Data ($) (Year Ended Dec. 31)

	1994	1993	1992	1991	1990	1989
Tangible Bk. Val.	0.90	4.04	3.79	2.59	2.07	1.84
Cash Flow	1.47	1.48	1.07	0.49	0.32	0.18
Earnings	0.61	0.80	0.65	0.32	0.08	0.03
Dividends	Nil	Nil	Nil	Nil	Nil	Nil
Payout Ratio	Nil	Nil	Nil	Nil	Nil	Nil
Prices - High	15$\frac{1}{8}$	15	18$\frac{1}{2}$	18	6	3$\frac{1}{8}$
- Low	10$\frac{3}{8}$	9$\frac{3}{4}$	10$\frac{1}{2}$	5$\frac{3}{8}$	1$\frac{3}{8}$	1$\frac{1}{2}$
P/E Ratio - High	25	19	28	56	75	NM
- Low	17	12	16	17	17	NM

Income Statement Analysis (Million $)

	1994	%Chg	1993	%Chg	1992	%Chg	1991
Revs.	176	125%	78.1	50%	52.2	185%	18.3
Oper. Inc.	51.7	85%	27.9	46%	19.1	165%	7.2
Depr.	18.8	129%	8.2	70%	4.8	198%	1.6
Int. Exp.	11.4	90%	6.0	72%	3.5	87%	1.9
Pretax Inc.	21.6	44%	15.0	27%	11.8	168%	4.4
Eff. Tax Rate	36%	—	36%	—	35%	—	32%
Net Inc.	13.8	44%	9.6	31%	7.3	147%	3.0

Balance Sheet & Other Fin. Data (Million $)

	1994	1993	1992	1991	1990	1989
Cash	6.6	3.2	11.7	3.9	2.3	1.2
Curr. Assets	37.0	15.1	20.3	7.5	2.9	1.5
Total Assets	323	166	110	60.0	14.0	7.0
Curr. Liab.	28.4	14.9	10.9	4.7	1.4	0.4
LT Debt	154	93.6	49.3	22.8	2.6	0.7
Common Eqty.	108	46.7	39.9	25.6	9.9	5.3
Total Cap.	278	146	96.4	54.0	12.7	6.3
Cap. Exp.	40.9	49.1	29.6	23.5	3.4	2.3
Cash Flow	32.1	17.8	12.2	4.6	0.9	0.5

Ratio Analysis

	1994	1993	1992	1991	1990	1989
Curr. Ratio	1.3	1.0	1.9	1.6	2.1	3.3
% LT Debt of Cap.	55.4	64.3	51.1	42.3	20.2	11.6
% Net Inc.of Revs.	7.8	12.3	14.1	16.2	6.2	3.5
% Ret. on Assets	4.3	6.7	8.5	6.3	1.9	1.3
% Ret. on Equity	13.3	21.2	21.9	11.8	2.6	1.7

Dividend Data —No cash dividends have been paid.

Data as orig. reptd.; bef. results of disc. opers. and/or spec. items. Per share data adj. for stk. divs. as of ex-div. date. E-Estimated. NA-Not Available. NM-Not Meaningful. NR-Not Ranked.

Office—5000 Quorum Drive, Suite 300, Dallas, TX 75240. **Tel**—(214) 233-4212. **Chrmn**—D. F. Moorehead Jr. **CEO**—J. E. Drury. **Pres & COO**—D. Sutherland-Yoest. **Exec VP, CFO, Secy & Investor Contact**—Earl E. DeFrates. **Dirs**—G. L. Ball, E. E. DeFrates, G. A. Meredith, D. F. Moorehead Jr., R. A. Mosley, T. W. Patrick, N. E. Shepard, R. F. Smith, J. D. Spellman, D. Sutherland-Yoest. **Transfer Agent & Registrar**—First National Bank of Boston, Boston, Mass. **Incorporated** in Oklahoma in 1987. **Empl-** 0. **S&P Analyst:** S.O.S.

STANDARD & POOR'S

STOCK REPORTS

Union Planters

NYSE Symbol **UPC**
In S&P SmallCap 600

29-SEP-95 **Industry:** Banking

Summary: This Tennessee-based bank holding company owns the state's third largest commercial bank, and smaller banks throughout Alabama, Arkansas, Kentucky, Louisiana and Mississippi.

S&P Opinion: Accumulate (★★★★) Recent Price • 29⅝ 52 Wk Range • 31-19½ Yield • 3.4% 12-Mo. P/E • 18.2

Quantitative Evaluations

Outlook (1 Lowest—5 Highest)
• **NA**

Fair Value
• **NA**

Risk
• **Low**

Earn./Div. Rank
• **B**

Technical Eval.
• **Bullish** since 4/95

Rel. Strength Rank (1 Lowest—99 Highest)
• **55**

Insider Activity
• **Neutral**

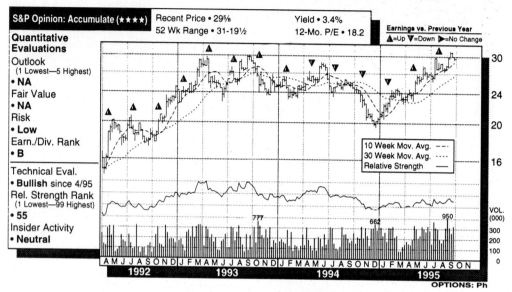

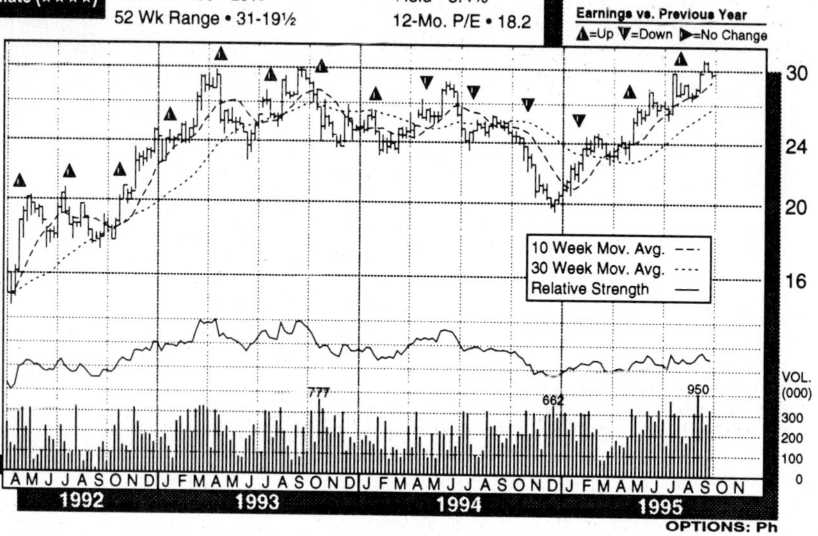

Overview - 29-SEP-95

UPC's market area has experienced above average economic growth over the past several years, which should continue for the foreseeable future. The company's primary focus has been on growth through acquisitions and controlling costs. Earnings in 1994 were restrained by restructuring charges incurred to reduce staff and divest branches. In the six months ended June 30, 1995, UPC had a record 30% increase in net income, or 32% on a per share basis. Results were bolstered by 5.6% higher net interest income, 27% growth in noninterest income, and flat noninterest expenses. Average loans grew 14.7%, year to year, in the second quarter, and the net interest margin widened to 4.66% from 4.42%. Loans should continue growing through 1996 at an annualized rate of about 14%. Asset quality is excellent, as nonperforming assets at June 30, 1995, were just 0.51% of loans and foreclosed properties.

Valuation - 26-SEP-95

Shares of UPC have risen 37% thus far in 1995, keeping pace with the bank indices, and outperforming the broader market. We anticipate that the company will benefit from the continued growth of the regional economy, expense reductions, high credit quality and integration of its acquisitions. Currently selling at 1.8 times book value, and 9 times our 1996 estimated EPS, we see shares of UPC as undervalued given the strength of its franchise.

Key Stock Statistics

S&P EPS Est. 1995	3.02	Tang. Bk. Value/Share	16.70
P/E on S&P Est. 1995	9.8	Beta	1.00
S&P EPS Est. 1996	3.30	Shareholders	4,800
Dividend Rate/Share	1.00	Market cap. (B)	$ 1.2
Shs. outstg. (M)	40.9	Inst. holdings	33%
Avg. daily vol. (M)	0.105	Insider holdings	NA

Value of $10,000 invested 5 years ago: $ 32,769

Fiscal Year Ending Dec. 31

	1995	% Change	1994	% Change	1993	% Change
Revenues (Million $)						
1Q	212.7	17%	181.9	64%	110.7	23%
2Q	223.9	17%	191.1	139%	80.09	-26%
3Q	—	—	--	—	120.2	4%
4Q	—	—	--	—	173.0	51%
Yr.	—	—	757.6	57%	483.4	13%
Income (Million $)						
1Q	33.02	30%	25.39	101%	12.64	40%
2Q	33.87	29%	26.25	90%	13.78	38%
3Q	—	—	23.73	41%	16.82	54%
4Q	—	—	-16.76	NM	16.22	41%
Yr.	—	—	58.61	-4%	61.27	48%
Earnings Per Share ($)						
1Q	0.77	33%	0.58	-3%	0.60	25%
2Q	0.79	32%	0.60	-5%	0.63	26%
3Q	E0.73	35%	0.54	-28%	0.75	36%
4Q	E0.73	NM	-0.47	NM	0.71	25%
Yr.	E3.02	142%	1.25	-54%	2.69	28%

Next earnings report expected: late October

Union Planters

Business Summary - 29-SEP-95

Union Planters Corp., with $9.7 billion in assets at June 30, 1995, is a multi-bank holding company whose largest subsidiary is Union Planters National Bank, the third largest commercial bank in Tennessee. Operations are conducted by the lead bank and 33 smaller "community" banks through a total of 379 offices in Alabama, Arkansas, Kentucky, Louisiana, Mississippi and Tennessee.

Gross loans outstanding totaled $5.98 billion at December 31, 1994, up from $4.68 billion a year earlier, divided as follows:

	1994	1993
Real estate mortgage	53%	53%
Commercial	22%	25%
Consumer	20%	18%
Real estate construction	4%	3%
Lease financing & other	1%	1%

Average earning assets in 1994 totaled $9.25 billion ($8.12 billion in 1993) and were divided: loans 59%, investment securities 39%, and other 2%. Average sources of funds were interest bearing deposits 70%, interest free deposits 14%, stockholders equity 7%, short-term borrowings 4%, and other 5%. On a tax-equivalent basis, the average yield on interest-earning assets was 7.37% (7.32% in 1993), while the average rate paid on interest-bearing liabilities was 3.48% (3.32%), for a net spread of 3.89% (4.00%).

The allowance for loan losses at year-end 1994 was $122.1 million (2.05% of loans outstanding), versus $114.4 million (2.46%) a year earlier. Net loan charge-offs in 1994 were $5.2 million (0.09% of average loans), versus $13.6 million (0.30%) in 1993. Nonperforming assets totaled $25.0 million (0.42% of loans plus foreclosed properties) at December 31, 1994, against $36.4 million (0.78%) at year-end 1993.

Important Developments

Jul. '95—UPC acquired First State Bancorporation, Inc., the parent company of First Exchange Bank in Tiptonville, Tenn., with assets of $110 million. Terms called for UPC to issue 388,497 shares of 8% cumulative convertible preferred stock, Series E.

Jun. '95—The company signed a definitive agreement to acquire Capital Bancorporation, Inc., in a transaction valued at approximately $114 million. Under the terms of the agreement, UPC will exchange 1.185 shares of its common stock for each common share of Capital. Capital is a $1 billion-assets holding company headquartered in Cape Girardeau, Mo., that operates 31 locations through six affiliate banks.

Capitalization

FHLB Advances: $291,630,000 (6/95).
Long Term Debt: $121,793,000 (6/95).
Convertible Preferred Stk.: $87,298,000.

Per Share Data ($)

(Year Ended Dec. 31)

	1994	1993	1992	1991	1990	1989
Tangible Bk. Val.	14.76	16.19	14.33	12.87	11.17	10.87
Earnings	1.25	2.69	2.10	1.59	1.20	-1.19
Dividends	0.88	0.72	0.60	0.48	0.48	0.48
Payout Ratio	70%	27%	29%	30%	40%	NM
Prices - High	28⅞	30	24⅞	16⅞	11⅞	15¾
- Low	19½	22⅜	13½	6½	6½	10⅝
P/E Ratio - High	23	11	12	11	10	NM
- Low	16	8	6	4	5	NM

Income Statement Analysis (Million $)

	1994	%Chg	1993	%Chg	1992	%Chg	1991
Net Int. Inc.	388	65%	235	23%	191	24%	154
Tax Equiv. Adj.	18.0	35%	13.3	49%	8.9	14%	7.8
Non Int. Inc.	93.6	17%	80.0	14%	70.0	11%	63.0
Loan Loss Prov.	3.6	-64%	10.0	-47%	19.0	-24%	25.0
% Exp/Op Revs.	80%	—	68%	—	74%	—	72%
Pretax Inc.	79.4	-7%	85.2	51%	56.6	68%	33.6
Eff. Tax Rate	26%	—	28%	—	27%	—	18%
Net Inc.	58.6	-4%	61.3	48%	41.4	51%	27.5
% Net Int. Marg.	4.39%	—	4.34%	—	4.61%	—	4.63%

Balance Sheet & Other Fin. Data (Million $)

	1994	1993	1992	1991	1990	1989
Earning Assets:						
Money Mkt.	210	233	286	285	258	397
Inv. Securities	2,962	2,617	2,198	1,148	1,155	1,020
Com'l Loans	1,405	690	566	599	776	828
Other Loans	4,576	2,318	1,765	1,366	1,394	1,329
Total Assets	10,015	6,318	5,262	3,787	4,005	4,003
Demand Deposits	1,381	750	627	480	482	473
Time Deposits	7,037	4,501	3,823	2,731	2,860	2,657
LT Debt	341	275	77.2	42.1	48.8	73.7
Common Eqty.	643	373	274	248	233	236

Ratio Analysis

	1994	1993	1992	1991	1990	1989
% Ret. on Assets	0.6	1.0	0.9	0.7	0.6	NM
% Ret. on Equity	7.4	14.9	12.7	11.3	9.3	NM
% Loan Loss Resv.	2.0	2.7	2.8	2.5	2.4	2.2
% Loans/Deposits	71.0	57.0	52.0	60.6	64.1	67.8
% Equity to Assets	6.9	5.7	5.9	6.1	5.9	6.6

Dividend Data —A "poison pill" stock purchase rights plan was adopted in 1989. A dividend reinvestment plan is available.

Amt. of Div. $	Date Decl.	Ex-Div. Date	Stock of Record	Payment Date
0.230	Oct. 27	Nov. 01	Nov. 07	Nov. 18 '94
0.230	Jan. 26	Jan. 31	Feb. 06	Feb. 17 '95
0.250	Apr. 27	May. 02	May. 08	May. 19 '95
0.250	Jul. 27	Aug. 03	Aug. 07	Aug. 18 '95

Data as orig. reptd.; bef. results of disc opers. and/or spec. items. Per share data adj. for stk. divs. as of ex-div. date. E-Estimated. NA-Not Available. NM-Not Meaningful. NR-Not Ranked.

Office—7130 Goodlett Farms Pkwy., Memphis, TN 38018. **Tel**—(901) 383-6000. **Chrmn & CEO**—B. W. Rawlins, Jr. **Pres**—J. W. Moore. **EVP, CFO & Investor Contact**—Jack W. Parker. **Secy**—J. F. Springfield. **Dirs**—A. M. Austin, M. E. Bruce, G. W. Bryan, R. B. Colbert, Jr., C. J. Lowrance III, J. W. Moore, S. D. Overton, C. P. Owen, Jr., B. W. Rawlins, Jr., V. L. Rawlins, M. P. Sturdivant, R. A. Trippeer, Jr., M. J. Womack. **Transfer Agent & Registrar**—Union Planters National Bank. **Incorporated** in Tennessee in 1971; bank chartered in 1869. **Empl**-4,509. **S&P Analyst:** Thomas C. Ferguson

STANDARD & POOR'S

STOCK REPORTS

United Cities Gas

NASDAQ Symbol **UCIT**
In S&P SmallCap 600

12-OCT-95 **Industry:** Utilities-Gas

Summary: This Tennessee-based public utility owns and operates natural gas distribution systems and engages in other energy-related activities.

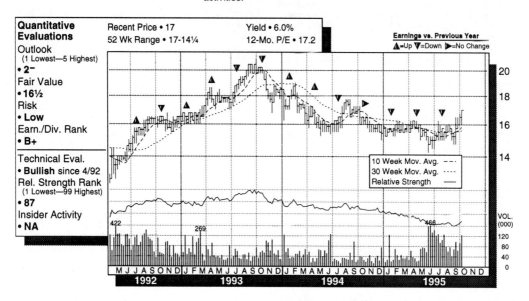

Quantitative Evaluations

Outlook (1 Lowest—5 Highest) • **2-**
Fair Value • **16½**
Risk • **Low**
Earn./Div. Rank • **B+**
Technical Eval. • **Bullish** since 4/92
Rel. Strength Rank (1 Lowest—99 Highest) • **87**
Insider Activity • **NA**

Recent Price • 17
52 Wk Range • 17-14¼
Yield • 6.0%
12-Mo. P/E • 17.2

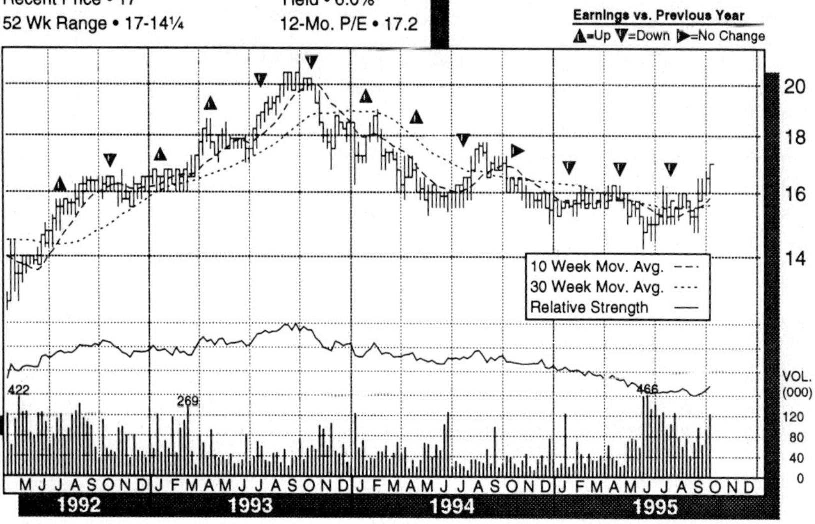

Business Profile - 12-OCT-95

United Cities' customer base has grown substantially over the past several years, reaching over 320,000 customers in 10 states. Results have been negatively affected by warmer than normal weather. UCIT has filed for rate hikes in Tennessee and Virginia. The company traditionally reports a loss for the second and third quarters, as the majority of revenues come during the winter heating season.

Operational Review - 12-OCT-95

Year-to-year revenues have slid in recent periods, primarily reflecting warmer weather. An increased number of natural gas customers and the Palmyra, Missouri acquisition (February 1995) partially offset the effect of the weather on utility revenues. Non-utility revenues also fell as the higher than normal temperature caused propane sales to fall. Additionally, utility service revenues dipped due to decreased gas brokage sales to certain industrial customers. Costs have remained well controlled.

Stock Performance - 06-OCT-95

In the past 30 trading days, UCIT's shares have increased 8%, compared to a 4% rise in the S&P 500. Average trading volume for the past five days was 31,420 shares, compared with the 40-day moving average of 16,623 shares.

Key Stock Statistics

Dividend Rate/Share	1.02	Shareholders	7,100
Shs. outstg. (M)	12.6	Market cap. (B)	$0.215
Avg. daily vol. (M)	0.024	Inst. holdings	15%
Tang. Bk. Value/Share	11.40	Insider holdings	NA
Beta	0.21		

Value of $10,000 invested 5 years ago: $ 15,995

Fiscal Year Ending Dec. 31

	1995	% Change	1994	% Change	1993	% Change
Revenues (Million $)						
1Q	106.0	-15%	124.2	7%	116.5	19%
2Q	42.25	-13%	48.40	-1%	48.90	15%
3Q	—	—	34.10	7%	31.80	-1%
4Q	—	—	74.30	-18%	90.30	-3%
Yr.	—	—	281.0	-2%	287.5	8%
Income (Million $)						
1Q	13.33	-6%	14.24	7%	13.34	25%
2Q	-3.96	NM	-3.32	NM	-3.13	NM
3Q	—	—	-5.21	NM	-5.17	NM
4Q	—	—	6.39	-10%	7.10	4%
Yr.	—	—	12.09	NM	12.15	19%
Earnings Per Share ($)						
1Q	1.25	-9%	1.38	5%	1.32	6%
2Q	-0.35	NM	-0.32	NM	-0.31	NM
3Q	—	—	-0.50	NM	-0.50	NM
4Q	—	—	0.61	-12%	0.69	1%
Yr.	—	—	1.16	-3%	1.19	11%

Next earnings report expected: early November

United Cities Gas

Business Summary - 10-OCT-95

United Cities Gas Company is a public utility that as of 1994 year-end was distributing natural and propane gas in 10 states to 323,000 customers (301,000 natural gas customers in eight states, and 22,000 propane customers in two states). At 1994 year-end, the customer base was 88% residential (accounting for 47% of utility revenues in 1994), 12% commercial (27%), and less than 1% industrial (25%). Nonutility operations include propane distribution, storage services, the sale and installation of gas appliances, and certain appliance service work.

In 1994, revenues and net income available for common from utility and nonutility businesses were derived as follows:

	Revs.	Income
Utility	80%	65%
Nonutility	20%	35%

Utility revenues by geographic operating division in 1994 were: Virginia-East Tennessee 32%, Georgia-South Carolina 22%, Illinois-Tennessee-Missouri 21%, and Kansas-Iowa-Missouri 25%.

UCG Energy Corp. operates retail propane (LP gas) outlets in Tennessee, Virginia and North Carolina. A rental division rents appliances, real estate, vehicles and other equipment. The utility services division is active in energy-related fields, including exploration, and provides brokerage services. United Cities Gas Storage (formed in December 1989) provides natural gas storage services and owns several storage fields. During 1993, additional emphasis was placed on gas marketing, and United Cities Energy Marketing was formed to engage in this activity.

From 1984 through the end of 1994, 178,000 customers were added, with acquisitions accounting for 105,000 of the total.

UCIT's business is seasonal in nature, typically resulting in greater earnings during the winter months.

The company is constructing a 28 mile main that will connect two of its distribution systems in Tennessee, at an estimated cost of $8.2 million. The project is scheduled for completion by the fall of 1995.

Important Developments

Oct. '95—UCIT was granted a rate increase of 7%, about $903,000 in annual revenues, by the Missouri Public Service Commission, for about 14,000 customers in Missouri.

Aug. '95—UCIT was granted a rate increase of $2.7 million in annual revenues by the Kansas State Corporation Commission. The overall rate increase of approximately 5.3% went into effect September 1 for about 72,000 customers in the eastern half of Kansas.

Capitalization

Long Term Debt: $137,637,000 (6/95).

Per Share Data ($)

(Year Ended Dec. 31)

	1994	1993	1992	1991	1990	1989
Tangible Bk. Val.	11.12	10.85	10.57	10.09	9.75	10.17
Earnings	1.16	1.19	1.07	0.97	0.44	1.52
Dividends	1.01	0.99	0.96	0.93	0.92	0.88
Payout Ratio	88%	84%	90%	102%	209%	63%
Prices - High	19	21	16¾	16¼	15⅝	15½
- Low	15	16	12½	12	12⅞	12¼
P/E Ratio - High	16	18	16	17	36	10
- Low	13	13	12	12	29	8

Income Statement Analysis (Million $)

	1994	%Chg	1993	%Chg	1992	%Chg	1991
Revs.	281	-2%	288	9%	265	11%	239
Depr.	13.9	6%	13.1	12%	11.7	-3%	12.1
Maint.	6.0	NM	6.1	-13%	7.0	121%	3.2
Fxd. Chgs. Cov.	2.2	7%	2.0	NM	2.0	23%	1.7
Constr. Credits	NA	—	NA	—	NA	—	NA
Eff. Tax Rate	35%	—	32%	—	35%	—	26%
Net Inc.	12.1	NM	12.2	20%	10.2	29%	7.9

Balance Sheet & Other Fin. Data (Million $)

	1994	1993	1992	1991	1990	1989
Gross Prop.	403	374	349	329	306	NA
Cap. Exp.	30.9	27.0	23.5	28.0	30.0	NA
Net Prop.	263	246	232	221	207	NA
Capitalization:						
LT Debt	144	152	158	127	97.0	78.0
% LT Debt	55	58	60	59	57	NA
Pfd.	Nil	Nil	Nil	1.4	148	NA
% Pfd.	Nil	Nil	Nil	0.60	0.90	NA
Common	118	112	106	86.0	71.1	73.0
% Common	45	42	40	40	42	NA
Total Cap.	292	292	292	242	193	177

Ratio Analysis

	1994	1993	1992	1991	1990	1989
Oper. Ratio	92.1	92.1	93.1	92.7	93.9	NA
% Earn. on Net Prop.	8.7	9.5	8.1	8.2	6.9	NA
% Ret. on Revs.	4.3	4.2	3.8	3.3	1.5	5.3
% Ret. On Invest.Cap	9.2	9.7	8.9	10.3	9.6	NA
% Return On Com.Eqty	10.5	11.1	10.5	9.9	4.4	14.1

Dividend Data —Cash has been paid each year since 1955. A dividend reinvestment plan is available.

Amt. of Div. $	Date Decl.	Ex-Div. Date	Stock of Record	Payment Date
0.255	Oct. 28	Nov. 23	Nov. 30	Dec. 15 '94
0.255	Feb. 01	Feb. 22	Feb. 28	Mar. 15 '95
0.255	Apr. 28	May. 24	May. 31	Jun. 15 '95
0.255	Jul. 28	Aug. 29	Aug. 31	Sep. 15 '95

Data as orig. reptd.; bef. results of disc opers. and/or spec. items. Per share data adj. for stk. divs. as of ex-div. date. E-Estimated. NA-Not Available. NM-Not Meaningful. NR-Not Ranked.

Office—5300 Maryland Way, Brentwood, TN 37027. **Tel**—(615) 373-5310. **Chrmn**—D. C. Baum. **Pres & CEO**—G. C. Koonce. **SVP & Treas**—J. B. Ford. **SVP & Secy**—Shirley M. Hawkins. **Investor Contact**—Linda A. Kelly. **Dirs**—D. C. Baum, T. J. Garland, D. A. Keasling, G. C. Koonce, V. J. Lewis, D. L. Newberry II, S. Oman, Jr., T. W. Triplett, G. C. Woodruff, Jr. **Transfer Agent & Registrar**—Harris Trust and Savings Bank, Chicago. **Incorporated** in Illinois in 1929. **Empl**-1,343. **S&P Analyst:** SAJ

STANDARD & POOR'S

STOCK REPORTS

United Illuminating

NYSE Symbol **UIL**
In S&P SmallCap 600

28-AUG-95 **Industry:** Utilities-Electric

Summary: This Connecticut-based utility has a 17.5% interest in the capacity and output of New Hampshire's Seabrook nuclear plant, which achieved commercial operation in mid-1990.

Quantitative Evaluations
Outlook
(1 Lowest—5 Highest)
• **2+**
Fair Value
• **29⅞**
Risk
• **Low**
Earn./Div. Rank
• **B**

Technical Eval.
• **Bullish** since 6/95
Rel. Strength Rank
(1 Lowest—99 Highest)
• **53**
Insider Activity
• **NA**

Recent Price • 33¾
52 Wk Range • 33¾-28¾
Yield • 8.4%
12-Mo. P/E • 10.5

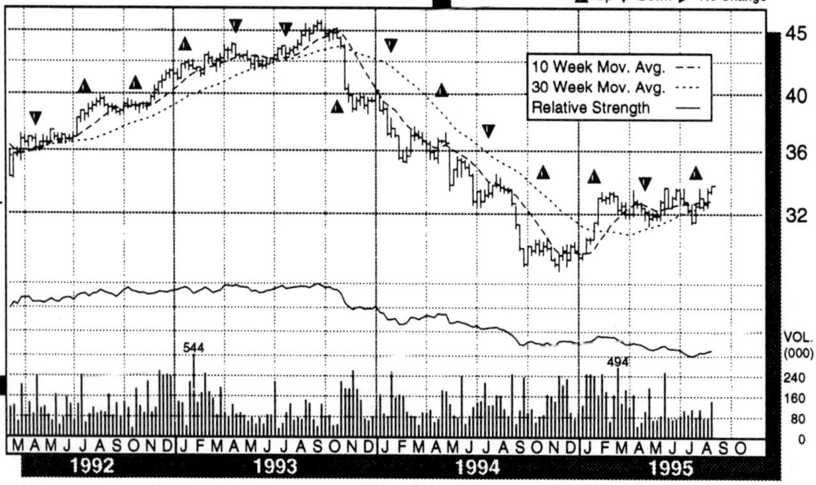

Business Profile - 25-AUG-95

The financial condition of this southwestern Connecticut electric utility is dependent on the level of retail and wholesale sales. The two primary factors affecting sales are economic conditions and weather. Weather is likely to return to more normal levels, while the economy has shown steady but unspectacular growth. Control of expenses is also a major concern, and UIL expects to benefit from a reorganization and retirement program.

Operational Review - 28-AUG-95

Revenues climbed 2.4%, year to year, in the first half of 1995, as retail sales remained unchanged, but wholesale demand increased. Margins narrowed on higher expenses for fuel and energy and capacity purchased, and depreciation and amortization charges; taxes also rose. Despite lower interest expense due to a debt refinancing program and strong cash flows, income fell 12%, to $17,244,000 ($1.29 a share, after preferred dividends), from $19,646,000 ($1.26, before an accounting charge of $0.09).

Stock Performance - 25-AUG-95

In the past 30 trading days, UIL's shares have increased 5%, compared to a 0.04% rise in the S&P 500. Average trading volume for the past five days was 28,240 shares, compared with the 40-day moving average of 19,959 shares.

Key Stock Statistics

Dividend Rate/Share	2.82	Shareholders	17,900
Shs. outstg. (M)	14.1	Market cap. (B)	$0.475
Avg. daily vol. (M)	0.020	Inst. holdings	40%
Tang. Bk. Value/Share	29.87	Insider holdings	NA
Beta	0.36		

Value of $10,000 invested 5 years ago: $ 14,751

Fiscal Year Ending Dec. 31

	1995	% Change	1994	% Change	1993	% Change
Revenues (Million $)						
1Q	165.4	-1%	167.6	3%	161.9	-8%
2Q	163.4	7%	153.4	2%	151.0	-6%
3Q	—	—	184.6	-3%	189.4	8%
4Q	—	—	151.1	NM	150.6	-2%
Yr.	—	—	656.8	NM	653.0	-2%
Income (Million $)						
1Q	9.47	-28%	13.23	5%	12.59	-8%
2Q	7.77	21%	6.41	-38%	10.37	-52%
3Q	—	—	25.79	13%	22.76	42%
4Q	—	—	2.66	—	—	—
Yr.	—	—	48.09	19%	40.48	-29%
Earnings Per Share ($)						
1Q	0.62	-28%	0.86	5%	0.82	-10%
2Q	0.67	68%	0.40	-39%	0.66	-55%
3Q	—	—	1.78	16%	1.54	44%
4Q	—	—	0.14	NM	-0.45	NM
Yr.	—	—	3.18	24%	2.57	-32%

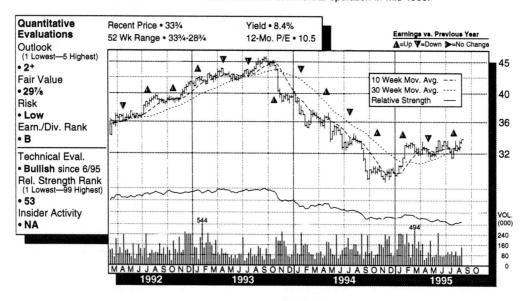

Next earnings report expected: late October

United Illuminating

Business Summary - 28-AUG-95

The United Illuminating Co. is engaged in the production, purchase, transmission, distribution and sale of electricity for residential, commercial and industrial purposes in a service area of about 335 sq. mi. in southwestern Connecticut. The population of the area is 711,000 (22% of the population of the state), and it includes the principal cities of Bridgeport and New Haven. Retail revenues by customer class in recent years were:

	1994	1993	1992	1991
Residential	41%	39%	39%	39%
Commercial	40%	43%	43%	44%
Industrial	17%	16%	16%	16%
Other	2%	2%	2%	1%

UIL has three wholly owned subsidiaries. Research Center participates in development of regulated power production ventures. United Energy International was formed to facilitate participation in a joint venture relating to power production plants abroad. United Resources serves as the parent for several unregulated businesses that complement and enhance UIL's electric utility business.

Peak demand in 1994 was 1,131 mw, and capacity at peak totaled 1,462 mw, for a capacity margin of 23%. Generation in 1994 was from nuclear (32%), coal (35%), oil (14%), and other (19%).

The company burns coal, residual oil and natural gas at fossil fuel generating stations in Bridgeport and New Haven. UIL has a 17.5% interest in the capacity and output of the Seabrook nuclear plant and a 3.7% interest in Millstone Unit 3. The company also owns 9.5% of the common stock of Connecticut Yankee, and is entitled to 9.5% of the generating capability of its nuclear generating unit. Both New Hampshire and Connecticut regulate the decommissioning of nuclear units. The decommissioning cost estimate for Seabrook is $376 million, of which UIL's share at December 31, 1994, was $5.2 million. Current decommissioning cost estimates for Millstone Unit 3 and the Connecticut Yankee unit are $448 million and $357 million, respectively, of which UIL's respective shares were $2.4 million and $14.1 million at December 31, 1994.

UIL has a revolving bank credit agreement that extends to December 14, 1995. The borrowing limit of the facility is $225 million.

Important Developments

Jun. '95—UIL had $49 million in cash at June 30, 1995, an increase of $38 million from December 31, 1994. Also, it said it had entered into a series of interest rate swap agreements for $100 million of floating rate debt, effectively converting it to fixed rate debt.

Capitalization

Long Term Debt: $697,597,000 (6/95).
Cum. Preferred Stock: $11,039,000.

Per Share Data ($)

(Year Ended Dec. 31)

	1994	1993	1992	1991	1990	1989
Tangible Bk. Val.	29.97	27.24	27.61	26.20	24.56	23.72
Earnings	3.18	2.57	3.76	3.14	3.55	-5.87
Dividends	2.76	2.66	2.56	2.44	2.32	2.32
Payout Ratio	87%	104%	68%	78%	65%	NM
Prices - High	40	$45\frac{7}{8}$	42	$39\frac{1}{8}$	$34\frac{1}{8}$	$34\frac{1}{4}$
- Low	$28\frac{3}{4}$	$38\frac{1}{2}$	$34\frac{1}{8}$	30	$26\frac{7}{8}$	$24\frac{5}{8}$
P/E Ratio - High	13	18	11	12	10	NM
- Low	9	15	9	10	8	NM

Income Statement Analysis (Million $)

	1994	%Chg	1993	%Chg	1992	%Chg	1991
Revs.	657	NM	653	-2%	667	NM	673
Depr.	58.2	3%	56.3	11%	50.7	5%	48.2
Maint.	41.8	NM	41.5	8%	38.4	-8%	41.8
Fxd. Chgs. Cov.	2.0	27%	1.6	-14%	1.9	8%	1.7
Constr. Credits	3.5	-15%	4.1	26%	3.2	-38%	5.2
Eff. Tax Rate	47%	—	40%	—	39%	—	38%
Net Inc.	48.1	19%	40.5	-29%	56.8	18%	48.0

Balance Sheet & Other Fin. Data (Million $)

	1994	1993	1992	1991	1990	1989
Gross Prop.	1,851	1,808	1,744	1,712	1,670	1,726
Cap. Exp.	63.0	95.0	70.0	68.0	67.0	142
Net Prop.	1,357	1,361	1,336	1,340	1,337	1,402
Capitalization:						
LT Debt	726	895	917	1,006	998	976
% LT Debt	62	65	66	68	69	69
Pfd.	44.7	60.9	60.9	63.0	70.0	70.0
% Pfd.	3.80	4.40	4.30	4.30	4.80	5.00
Common	428	423	423	402	380	363
% Common	36	31	30	27	26	26
Total Cap.	1,646	1,824	1,710	2,069	2,036	1,959

Ratio Analysis

	1994	1993	1992	1991	1990	1989
Oper. Ratio	80.6	82.4	83.8	84.7	83.4	82.3
% Earn. on Net Prop.	9.4	8.5	8.1	7.7	7.2	6.4
% Ret. on Revs.	7.3	6.2	8.5	7.2	9.1	NM
% Ret. On Invest.Cap	7.5	7.1	9.0	7.0	8.1	NM
% Return On Com.Eqty	12.1	8.6	12.7	11.2	13.3	NM

Dividend Data —Dividends have been paid since 1900. A dividend reinvestment plan is available.

Amt. of Div. $	Date Decl.	Ex-Div. Date	Stock of Record	Payment Date
0.690	Aug. 23	Aug. 30	Sep. 06	Oct. 01 '94
0.690	Nov. 29	Dec. 06	Dec. 12	Jan. 01 '95
0.705	Feb. 27	Mar. 07	Mar. 13	Apr. 01 '95
0.705	May. 19	May. 30	Jun. 05	Jul. 01 '95

Data as orig. reptd.; bef. results of disc opers. and/or spec. items. Per share data adj. for stk. divs. as of ex-div. date. E-Estimated. NA-Not Available. NM-Not Meaningful. NR-Not Ranked.

Office—157 Church St., New Haven, CT 06506. **Tel**—(203) 499-2000. **Chrmn & CEO**—R. J. Grossi. **Pres & CFO**—R. L. Fiscus. **Secy & Treas**—K. D. Mohlman. **Investor Contact**—Frank Maher. **Dirs**—D. E. A. Carson, J. F. Croweak, J. H. Devlin, J. D. Fassett, R. L. Fiscus, R. J. Grossi, B. Henley-Cohn, J. L. Lahey, F. P. McFadden, Jr., F. R. O'Keefe, Jr., J. A. Thomas, W. S. Warner. **Transfer Agent & Registar**—Bank of New York, NYC. **Incorporated** in Connecticut in 1899. **Empl**-1,377. **S&P Analyst:** Michael C. Barr

STANDARD & POOR'S

STOCK REPORTS

United Meridian

NYSE Symbol **UMC**
In S&P SmallCap 600

28-AUG-95

Industry:
Oil and Gas

Summary: This independent energy company acquires, explores and develops oil and natural gas properties in the U.S. and Canada, West Africa's Ivory Coast and Equatorial Guinea.

Quantitative Evaluations

Outlook
(1 Lowest—5 Highest)
• **NA**

Fair Value
• **NA**

Risk
• **Average**

Earn./Div. Rank
• **NR**

Technical Eval.
• **Bullish** since 3/95

Rel. Strength Rank
(1 Lowest—99 Highest)
• **81**

Insider Activity
• **Neutral**

Recent Price • 17⅞
52 Wk Range • 18-10¼

Yield • Nil
12-Mo. P/E • NM

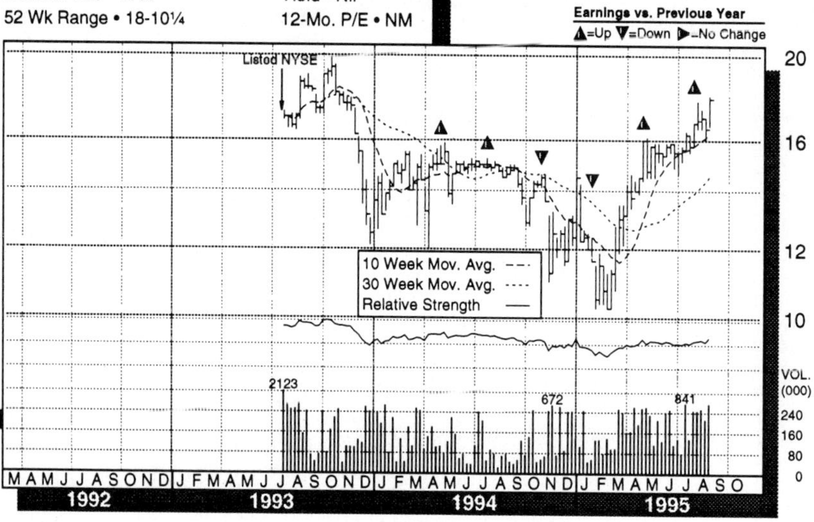

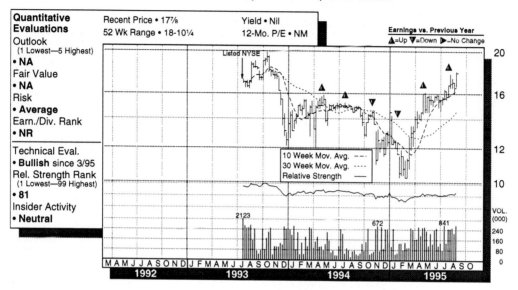

Business Profile - 25-AUG-95

This Houston-based independent energy company is funding acquisitions through the issuance of common and preferred shares. Results in 1995 have been impressive, and output from the Gulf of Mexico and the Ivory Coast in West Africa is expected to continue to grow sharply through 1996. Acquisitions and development of reserves should also accelerate. Results are also expected to benefit from the 1994 acquisition of General Atlantic Resources Inc., a Denver-based oil and gas property developer.

Operational Review - 25-AUG-95

Revenues for 1995's first half rose sharply, year to year, reflecting acquisitions and a stepped-up exploration program. Higher average oil prices and a near doubling of oil production were partly offset by higher depreciation and amortization costs and increased dry hole costs. Discretionary cash flow held steady versus the prior year. The shares are highly leveraged to natural gas prices, which have fallen due to rising capacity utilization at nuclear facilities, and high storage levels.

Stock Performance - 25-AUG-95

In the past 30 trading days, UMC's shares have increased 10%, compared to a 0.04% rise in the S&P 500. Average trading volume for the past five days was 163,140 shares, compared with the 40-day moving average of 79,000 shares.

Key Stock Statistics

Dividend Rate/Share	Nil	Shareholders	200
Shs. outstg. (M)	27.8	Market cap. (B)	$0.497
Avg. daily vol. (M)	0.085	Inst. holdings	52%
Tang. Bk. Value/Share	6.16	Insider holdings	NA
Beta	NA		

Value of $10,000 invested 5 years ago: NA

Fiscal Year Ending Dec. 31

	1995	% Change	1994	% Change	1993	% Change
Revenues (Million $)						
1Q	40.86	71%	23.86	60%	14.90	—
2Q	28.74	18%	24.26	14%	21.20	—
3Q	—	—	22.47	-38%	36.10	—
4Q	—	—	28.56	4%	27.40	—
Yr.	—	—	99.1	NM	99.6	-17%
Income (Million $)						
1Q	3.61	NM	-0.80	—	—	—
2Q	0.46	119%	0.21	-95%	3.91	—
3Q	—	—	-4.36	NM	-0.90	—
4Q	—	—	-76.03	—	—	—
Yr.	—	—	-80.99	NM	-5.71	NM
Earnings Per Share ($)						
1Q	0.12	NM	-0.04	NM	-0.47	—
2Q	0.02	100%	0.01	NM	-0.26	—
3Q	—	—	-0.19	NM	0.77	—
4Q	—	—	-3.01	NM	-0.29	—
Yr.	—	—	-3.47	NM	-0.25	NM

Next earnings report expected: early November

United Meridian

Business Summary - 25-AUG-95

United Meridian is an independent oil and gas firm engaged in the acquisition, exploitation, development and exploration of oil and natural gas properties. Its North American oil and natural gas activities are concentrated in major producing regions along the Gulf Coast, in the Midcontinent, Appalachian and Montana regions of the U.S., and in Alberta and Saskatchewan, Canada. The company is also pursuing offshore international exploration opportunities in the Ivory Coast and Equatorial Guinea in Western Africa.

Estimated proved reserves at December 31, 1994, were 22,667 bbl. of oil and 439.4 Bcf of natural gas or 513.7 Bcfe. UMC's acreage position at 1994 year-end amounted to 6.4 million gross acres (3.8 million net), of which 1.4 million gross acres (454,000 net) were classified as developed. Approximately 76% of the proved reserves were natural gas (81% proved developed); 80% were located in the U.S. and 20% were in Canada. For 1993, the reserve-to-production ratio was 9.3 years, assuming that the company owned the production of the acquired properties for the full year.

The company conducts its North American exploration activities on internally generated prospects preferably operated by itself. During 1994, UMC drilled 30 exploratory wells, of which 13 were producing. Development drilling yielded 108 producers from 129 wells drilled. For 1995, UMC expects to drill about 100 wells, down from 158 in 1994, mainly due to higher cost wells to be drilled in the Gulf of Mexico. The company is also committing a substantial portion of its capital budget for 1995 to develop reserves in the Ivory Coast. Drilling could commence from recently acquired blocks during 1996.

During 1994, the company began a drilling program offshore Equatorial Guinea in West Africa. Two dry holes were drilled. A third well, drilled in March 1995, tested at rates exceeding 10,500 barrels of oil a day, and 3.4 MMCf/d of natural gas. Following the 1994 acquisition of General Atlantic, UMC has a significantly expanded asset base in the Gulf of Mexico.

Important Developments

Jul. '95—United Meridian announced that the two wells most recently tested in the Zafiro area offshore Equatorial Guinea tested a combined 18,055 barrels of oil per day. Also in July, the company reported second quarter earnings of $0.02 a share, versus $0.01 the prior year. In spite of a drop in the average realized gas price from $1.83, to $1.53, discretionary cash flow fell only $200,000 to $11.5 million. Higher oil prices and a near doubling of oil production to 7,550 barrels a day contributed to the higher earnings. Average shares outstanding were up 25% in the quarter.

Capitalization

Long Term Debt: $189,495,000 (6/95).

Per Share Data ($) (Year Ended Dec. 31)

	1994	1993	1992	1991	1990	1989
Tangible Bk. Val.	6.18	8.41	8.73	NA	NA	NA
Cash Flow	-1.30	4.54	2.87	NA	NA	NA
Earnings	-3.47	-0.75	1.22	NA	NA	NA
Dividends	Nil	Nil	NA	NA	NA	NA
Payout Ratio	Nil	Nil	NA	NA	NA	NA
Prices - High	15⅞	19⅞	NA	NA	NA	NA
- Low	11	12⅛	NA	NA	NA	NA
P/E Ratio - High	NM	NM	NA	NA	NA	NA
- Low	NM	NM	NA	NA	NA	NA

Income Statement Analysis (Million $)

	1994	%Chg	1993	%Chg	1992	%Chg	1991
Revs.	99	20%	82.0	-32%	120	—	NA
Oper. Inc.	-63.3	NM	51.2	-27%	70.3	—	NA
Depr. Depl. & Amort.	50.7	-17%	61.4	65%	37.2	—	NA
Int. Exp.	9.4	43%	6.5	-10%	7.3	—	NA
Pretax Inc.	-122	NM	-13.5	NM	26.2	—	NA
Eff. Tax Rate	NM	—	NM	—	5.30%	—	NA
Net Inc.	-81.0	NM	-7.2	NM	27.6	—	NA

Balance Sheet & Other Fin. Data (Million $)

	1994	1993	1992	1991	1990	1989
Cash	11.8	0.5	0.6	NA	NA	NA
Curr. Assets	68.7	32.4	29.8	NA	NA	NA
Total Assets	511	343	345	NA	NA	NA
Curr. Liab.	63.5	37.5	25.4	NA	NA	NA
LT Debt	240	92.0	95.0	NA	NA	NA
Common Eqty.	171	190	197	NA	NA	NA
Total Cap.	431	298	312	NA	NA	NA
Cap. Exp.	53.0	18.0	NA	NA	NA	NA
Cash Flow	-30.3	52.6	64.8	NA	NA	NA

Ratio Analysis

	1994	1993	1992	1991	1990	1989
Curr. Ratio	1.1	0.9	1.2	NA	NA	NA
% LT Debt of Cap.	55.6	30.9	30.5	NA	NA	NA
% Ret. on Assets	NM	NM	NA	NA	NA	NA
% Ret. on Equity	NM	NM	NA	NA	NA	NA

Dividend Data —UMC has never paid dividends on its common stock, and is currently restricted from paying any under terms of its credit facility.

Data as orig. reptd.; bef. results of disc opers. and/or spec. items. Per share data adj. for stk. divs. as of ex-div. date. E-Estimated. NA-Not Available. NM-Not Meaningful. NR-Not Ranked.

Office—1201 Louisiana, Suite 1400, Houston, TX 77002. **Tel**—(713) 654-9110. **Chrmn & CEO**—J. B. Brock. **Pres**—D. D. Wolf. **SVP & CFO**—J. M. Clarkson. **Secy**—L. Mortner. **Investor Contact**—Jeanne Buchanan. **Dirs**—K. A. Alireza, R. G. d'Alviella, R. E. Bailey, J. B. Brock, C. R. Carson, A. M. Cranberg, R. H. Dedman, S. A. Denning, R. V. Lindsay, R. L. MacDonald, Jr., E. L. Mason, W. J. McQuinn, J. L. Murdy, D. K. Newbigging, O. A. Sawaf, M. R. Simmons, D. D. Wolf, W. B. Wriston. **Transfer Agent & Registrar**—Chemical Shareholder Services Group, Dallas. **Incorporated** in Delaware in 1986. **Empl**-292. **S&P Analyst:** R.J.D.

STANDARD & POOR'S

STOCK REPORTS

U.S. Bioscience

ASE Symbol **UBS**
In S&P SmallCap 600

06-SEP-95

Industry: Drugs-Generic and OTC

Summary: This pharmaceutical company develops and sells products to treat cancer, AIDS and allied diseases. Drug products include Hexalen, Ethyol, and NeuTrexin.

Quantitative Evaluations

Recent Price • 4⅝
52 Wk Range • 8½-1⅝
Yield • Nil
12-Mo. P/E • NM

Outlook
(1 Lowest—5 Highest)
• **NA**
Fair Value
• **NA**
Risk
• **High**
Earn./Div. Rank
• **NR**

Technical Eval.
• **Bearish** since 7/95
Rel. Strength Rank
(1 Lowest—99 Highest)
• **85**
Insider Activity
• **NA**

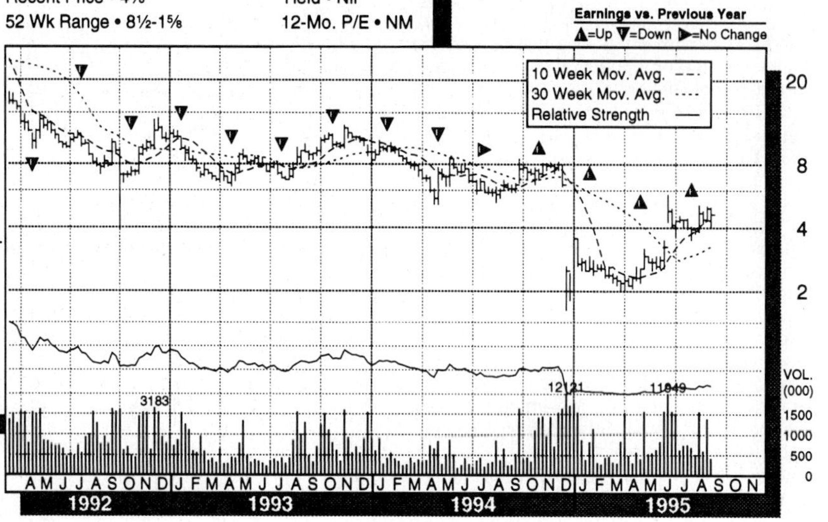

Business Profile - 06-SEP-95

In June, UBS received a recommendation for approval from an FDA advisory committee for Ethyol. The committee's rejection of Ethyol in December 1994 led to dramatic cost-cutting moves by UBS. Ethyol will again be reviewed by the FDA over the next several months. Traditionally, a favorable recommendation is a precursor to full FDA approval. The shares moved up sharply on news of the recommendation. UBS also makes Hexalen and NeuTrexin, which are sold in Europe, Canada and the U.S.

Operational Review - 06-SEP-95

Total revenues in the six months ended June 30, 1995, advanced 50%, due chiefly to gains in product sales (Hexalen and NeuTrexin) and a hefty one-time license fee received from Eli Lilly. Total expenses were reduced by about 30% reflecting an internal restructuring undertaken during early 1995. The net loss narrowed to $6,629,900 ($0.16 a share) from $12,949,700 ($0.33). Cash and marketable securities at the end of June totaled $17.0 million.

Stock Performance - 01-SEP-95

In the past 30 trading days, UBS's shares have increased 16%, compared to a 2% rise in the S&P 500. Average trading volume for the past five days was 79,340 shares, compared with the 40-day moving average of 176,585 shares.

Key Stock Statistics

Dividend Rate/Share	Nil	Shareholders	5,200
Shs. outstg. (M)	40.8	Market cap. (B)	$0.194
Avg. daily vol. (M)	0.221	Inst. holdings	13%
Tang. Bk. Value/Share	0.50	Insider holdings	NA
Beta	2.01		

Value of $10,000 invested 5 years ago: $ 7,474

Fiscal Year Ending Dec. 31

	1995	% Change	1994	% Change	1993	% Change
Revenues (Million $)						
1Q	2.64	10%	2.41	8%	2.23	-3%
2Q	3.61	104%	1.77	-49%	3.48	-6%
3Q	—	—	2.01	50%	1.34	-61%
4Q	—	—	2.36	105%	1.15	-43%
Yr.	—	—	8.55	4%	8.20	-28%
Income (Million $)						
1Q	-4.16	NM	-5.96	NM	-5.13	NM
2Q	-2.47	NM	-6.99	NM	-7.08	NM
3Q	—	—	-5.67	NM	-9.15	NM
4Q	—	—	-5.42	NM	-19.30	NM
Yr.	—	—	-24.04	NM	-40.63	NM
Earnings Per Share ($)						
1Q	-0.10	NM	-0.15	NM	-0.13	NM
2Q	-0.06	NM	-0.18	NM	-0.18	NM
3Q	—	—	-0.14	NM	-0.23	NM
4Q	—	—	-0.13	NM	-0.49	NM
Yr.	—	—	-0.60	NM	-1.03	NM

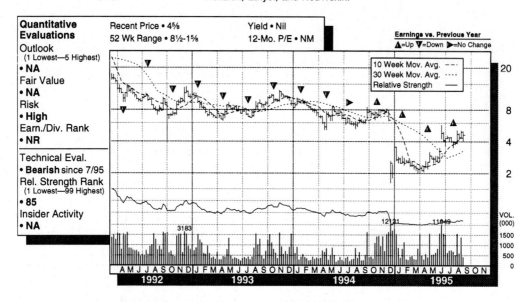

Next earnings report expected: late October

Business Summary - 06-SEP-95

U.S. Bioscience, Inc., develops and markets drugs, principally for the treatment of patients with cancer and allied diseases. UBS's strategy has been to identify, and to acquire exclusive licenses in the U.S. and certain other markets for late stage drugs with an established preclinical or clinical database and for which development will consist largely of further preclinical testing, clinical trials and preparation of applications for regulatory approval.

UBS has acquired, through licensing agreements, rights to 10 drugs, including cancer-attacking cytogens (Hexalen, NeuTrexin, AZQ, third generation platinum anticancer agents and Mitomycin-C analogues); hormonal drugs (rogletimide); cytoprotectors (Ethyol and WR-151327); and modulators (PALA and NeuTrexin).

Hexalen is a cytotoxic drug approved to treat patients with persistent or recurrent ovarian cancer following first-line therapy with a cisplatin and/or alkylating agent-based combination therapy. Hexalen is also approved for the treatment of advanced ovarian cancer in Canada, Sweden, Israel, Australia and the U.K. Hexalen is being evaluated for other tumor types.

NeuTrexin is a lipid-soluble intravenously administrable analog of methotrexate, a commonly used anticancer agent. As of March 1995, NeuTrexin had received regulatory approval in the U.S., Canada, U.K., France, Ireland, Spain, The Netherlands and Luxembourg as a treatment for pneumocystis carinii pneumonia in patients with immune system disorders.

Ethyol, an injectable agent used to protect healthy cells from the harmful effects of chemotherapy (approved for sale in five European countries) is awaiting FDA approval. In June 1995, the Oncologic Drug Advisory committee reviewed Ethyol and gave it a favorable recommendation to the FDA.

SmithKline Beecham (SB) is developing and marketing Ethyol, WR-151327 and PALA in Japan, South Korea and Taiwan. UBS will manufacture the products, while SB has exclusive marketing rights for Ethyol, will co-market the other compounds with UBS in Japan, and will help establish a Japanese marketing organization; Schering-Plough has exclusive marketing rights in Western Europe. Eli Lilly has an exclusive marketing arrangement in Canada for Ethyol, NeuTrexin, and Hexalen.

Important Developments

Jul. '95—The company signed an exclusive agreement with French-based Beaufour Ipsen Group to market Hexalen and NeuTrexin in Europe. UBS will receive an up-front payment and royalties from sales.

Capitalization

Long Term Debt: $2,521,400 (6/95).

Per Share Data ($) (Year Ended Dec. 31)

	1994	1993	1992	1991	1990	1989
Tangible Bk. Val.	0.59	0.96	1.96	2.40	1.04	0.27
Cash Flow	-0.57	-1.01	-0.50	-0.17	-0.15	-0.26
Earnings	-0.60	-1.03	-0.51	-0.18	-0.15	-0.26
Dividends	Nil	Nil	Nil	Nil	Nil	Nil
Payout Ratio	Nil	Nil	Nil	Nil	Nil	Nil
Prices - High	10⅜	12¼	44	40⅞	10½	7
- Low	1⅝	6¼	6⅛	8⅜	4⅜	3¼
P/E Ratio - High	NM	NM	NM	NM	NM	NM
- Low	NM	NM	NM	NA	NA	NA

Income Statement Analysis (Million $)

	1994	%Chg	1993	%Chg	1992	%Chg	1991
Revs.	7.3	65%	4.4	7%	4.1	19%	3.5
Oper. Inc.	-24.2	NM	-33.4	NM	-26.9	NM	-13.8
Depr.	1.0	28%	0.8	29%	0.6	100%	0.3
Int. Exp.	0.1	—	Nil	—	Nil	—	0.1
Pretax Inc.	-24.0	NM	-40.6	NM	-20.2	NM	-6.5
Eff. Tax Rate	NM	—	NM	—	NM	—	Nil
Net Inc.	-24.0	NM	-40.6	NM	-20.2	NM	-6.5

Balance Sheet & Other Fin. Data (Million $)

	1994	1993	1992	1991	1990	1989
Cash	24.4	48.4	77.2	95.5	38.0	13.0
Curr. Assets	28.0	5.9	80.0	97.5	39.0	13.6
Total Assets	34.5	57.8	83.3	99	40.2	14.1
Curr. Liab.	6.4	8.6	5.3	3.8	2.6	2.0
LT Debt	1.0	Nil	Nil	Nil	0.7	4.0
Common Eqty.	23.9	38.1	77.5	94.1	35.0	6.8
Total Cap.	24.9	38.1	77.5	94.1	35.8	10.8
Cap. Exp.	1.3	3.6	2.2	0.8	1.0	0.1
Cash Flow	-23.0	-39.8	-19.6	-6.2	-4.8	-5.7

Ratio Analysis

	1994	1993	1992	1991	1990	1989
Curr. Ratio	4.3	6.1	15.0	25.4	15.2	6.6
% LT Debt of Cap.	4.0	Nil	Nil	Nil	2.0	37.3
% Net Inc.of Revs.	NM	NM	NM	NM	NM	NM
% Ret. on Assets	NM	NM	NM	NM	NM	NM
% Ret. on Equity	NM	NM	NM	NM	NM	NM

Dividend Data —No cash dividends have been paid.

Data as orig. reptd.; bef. results of disc. opers. and/or spec. items. Per share data adj. for stk. divs. as of ex-div. date. Qtrly. and full-yr. figs. in Revs. tbl. incl. other income. E-Estimated. NA-Not Available. NM-Not Meaningful. NR-Not Ranked.

Office—One Tower Bridge, 100 Front St., West Conshohocken, PA 19428. **Tel**—(610) 832-0570. **Chrmn, Pres, CEO & COO**—P. S. Schein. **SVP-Fin & Treas**—R. I. Kriebel. **Secy**—Martha E. Manning. **Dirs**—P. Calabresi, R. L. Capizzi, M. Gordon, R. I. Kriebel, D. J. MacMaster Jr., A. Misher, P. S. Schein, J. Shacknai, B. Wright. **Transfer Agent & Registrar**—Mellon Bank N.A., Pittsburgh. **Incorporated** in Delaware in 1987. **Empl**-113. **S&P Analyst:** Thomas Tirney

U.S. Filter

NYSE Symbol **USF**
In S&P SmallCap 600

16-OCT-95

Industry:
Pollution Control

Summary: USF is a leading provider of water treatment systems, services and replacement parts to industrial and commercial customers.

Quantitative Evaluations

Outlook
(1 Lowest—5 Highest)
• **5**

Fair Value
• **29**

Risk
• **Low**

Earn./Div. Rank
• **B-**

Technical Eval.
• **Bullish** since 7/95

Rel. Strength Rank
(1 Lowest—99 Highest)
• **94**

Insider Activity
• **NA**

Recent Price • 24⅞
52 Wk Range • 24⅞-13⅛
Yield • Nil
12-Mo. P/E • 40.8

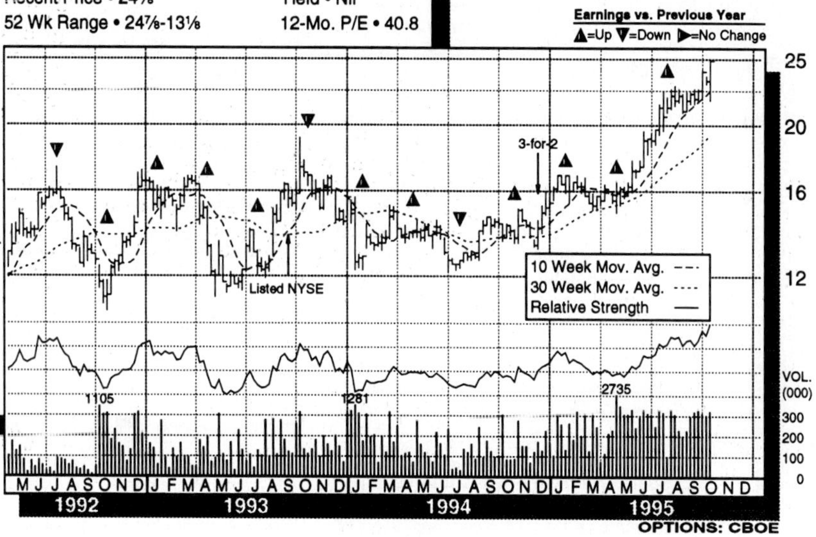

OPTIONS: CBOE

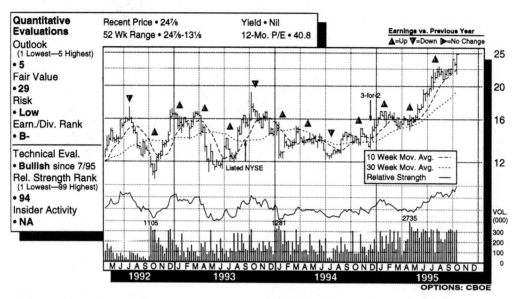

Business Profile - 16-OCT-95

Since mid-1991, USF has acquired and integrated a number of businesses with strong market positions in the manufacture of systems for the filtration, purification and treatment of water and wastewater. The company intends to continue to acquire businesses that provide it with specific technologies and penetration into certain industries and geographic areas. Earnings are expected to grow at an annualized rate of 20% for the next five years.

Operational Review - 16-OCT-95

Revenues for the three months ended June 30, 1995, advanced 66%, year to year, reflecting the acquisitions of Ionpure and Liquipure during 1994-5, as well as continued strength in the core equipment manufacturing business and expansion in the service and parts component. Operating costs and expenses rose less rapidly and, despite sharply higher interest expense, net income more than tripled. Backlog at June 30, 1995, was to $156 million, up from $75 million a year earlier.

Stock Performance - 13-OCT-95

In the past 30 trading days, USF's shares have increased 14%, compared to a 4% rise in the S&P 500. Average trading volume for the past five days was 108,340 shares, compared with the 40-day moving average of 79,056 shares.

Key Stock Statistics

Dividend Rate/Share	Nil	Shareholders	4,000
Shs. outstg. (M)	22.2	Market cap. (B)	$0.553
Avg. daily vol. (M)	0.093	Inst. holdings	46%
Tang. Bk. Value/Share	0.60	Insider holdings	NA
Beta	1.33		

Value of $10,000 invested 5 years ago: $ 79,574

Fiscal Year Ending Mar. 31

	1996	% Change	1995	% Change	1994	% Change
Revenues (Million $)						
1Q	91.54	66%	55.06	97%	27.91	12%
2Q	—	—	67.20	133%	28.86	25%
3Q	—	—	72.19	89%	38.25	65%
4Q	—	—	77.58	47%	52.86	75%
Yr.	—	—	272.0	84%	147.9	46%
Income (Million $)						
1Q	3.36	NM	1.11	29%	0.86	39%
2Q	—	—	1.91	69%	1.13	NM
3Q	—	—	2.41	88%	1.28	-10%
4Q	—	—	2.91	69%	1.72	107%
Yr.	—	—	8.33	67%	4.99	25%
Earnings Per Share ($)						
1Q	0.16	167%	0.06	-18%	0.07	57%
2Q	—	—	0.12	20%	0.10	-12%
3Q	—	—	0.15	41%	0.11	100%
4Q	—	—	0.18	50%	0.12	38%
Yr.	—	—	0.51	24%	0.41	23%

Next earnings report expected: early November

U.S. Filter

Business Summary - 16-OCT-95

United States Filter Corporation designs and manufactures customized and pre-engineered systems and equipment to filter and purify water used in industrial production processes, to treat wastewater effluent before recycling or discharge and for use by municipal water treatment facilities. It also offers products for gas filtration and for separation of dissolved and suspended solids and organic matter from other liquids and operates a centralized industrial hazardous-waste treatment and recovery facility. Sales by product line in recent fiscal years were:

	1994-5	1993-4
Capital equipment	60%	63%
Spare parts, consumables & other	21%	18%
Services	19%	19%

USF offers water purification and treatment technologies that can be integrated and applied to meet customer needs for treatment of incoming water supplies and outgoing wastewater on a cost-effective basis.

In July 1994, the company acquired Liquipure Technologies, Inc. ($34 million in revenues), from Warburg, Pincus Capital Co., L.P., for 1,924,949 (adjusted) common shares. Liquipure owns water systems and makes standard ultrapure water products.

In September 1995, the company privately placed $140 million of 6% convertible subordinated notes due 2005. In April 1995, the company sold 6,000,000 common shares publicly at $15 each.

Important Developments

Oct. '95—U.S. Filter acquired Polymetrics, Inc. ($50 million in revenues), a manufacturer of water treatment systems, from a unit of Compagnie Generale des Eaux of France, for $60 million in cash and stock. In August, USF acquired Interlake Water Systems ($21 million in revenues), a supplier of systems and service to customers in the Midwest.

May '95—USF acquired Arrowhead Industrial Water from BF Goodrich Co. for $80 million. Arrowhead supplies on-site industrial treatment systems in the U.S. In April, the company acquired the Permutit Group ($20 million in revenues), a major provider of service deionization in the U.K., Australia and New Zealand, from Thames Water plc for $10 million.

Capitalization

Long Term Debt: $114,165,000 (6/95); incl. $105 million of conv. sub. debs.

Voting Cum. Conv. Pfd. Stock: 880,000 shs. ($0.10 par); $25 liq. pref.; ea. conv. into 1.5 com. shs.

Series B Conv. Pfd. Stock: 139,518 shs.; ea. conv. into 1.5 com. shs.

Options: To buy 1,671,184 shs. at $3.67 to $16.17 ea. (3/95).

Per Share Data ($) (Year Ended Mar. 31)

	1995	1994	1993	1992	1991	1990
Tangible Bk. Val.	0.71	4.13	3.67	1.13	1.33	-0.33
Cash Flow	1.36	0.92	0.75	-0.57	0.29	0.19
Earnings	0.51	0.41	0.33	-0.71	0.13	Nil
Dividends	Nil	Nil	Nil	Nil	Nil	Nil
Payout Ratio	Nil	Nil	Nil	Nil	Nil	Nil
Cal. Yrs.	1994	1993	1992	1991	1990	1989
Prices - High	16 1/8	19 1/8	17 3/8	15 1/8	9 3/8	37 5/8
- Low	12 1/8	11 1/8	10 3/8	1 9/16	3 1/8	3
P/E Ratio - High	32	47	52	NM	70	NM
- Low	24	27	31	NM	23	NM

Income Statement Analysis (Million $)

	1995	%Chg	1994	%Chg	1993	%Chg	1992
Revs.	272	84%	148	47%	101	145%	41.2
Oper. Inc.	27.4	176%	9.9	22%	8.1	NM	-3.3
Depr.	12.8	134%	5.5	61%	3.4	NM	0.9
Int. Exp.	5.4	NM	1.7	106%	0.8	84%	0.4
Pretax Inc.	11.0	NM	1.8	-59%	4.3	NM	-3.9
Eff. Tax Rate	24%	—	NM	—	6.90%	—	NM
Net Inc.	8.3	67%	5.0	25%	4.0	NM	-4.0

Balance Sheet & Other Fin. Data (Million $)

	1995	1994	1993	1992	1991	1990
Cash	18.6	33.5	2.3	13.2	2.9	2.5
Curr. Assets	175	122	49.2	39.5	10.4	10.7
Total Assets	379	242	102	77.6	14.2	15.0
Curr. Liab.	118	53.7	27.8	29.6	5.2	12.5
LT Debt	114	62.7	2.8	6.3	3.5	0.1
Common Eqty.	110	103	49.2	19.0	4.8	2.4
Total Cap.	259	187	74.0	47.7	8.9	2.5
Cap. Exp.	16.2	6.5	3.3	1.3	0.1	0.1
Cash Flow	20.4	9.8	6.1	-3.4	1.1	0.4

Ratio Analysis

	1995	1994	1993	1992	1991	1990
Curr. Ratio	1.5	2.3	1.8	1.3	2.0	0.9
% LT Debt of Cap.	43.9	33.4	3.8	13.2	39.1	2.5
% Net Inc.of Revs.	3.1	3.4	3.9	NM	2.1	NM
% Ret. on Assets	2.5	2.6	3.9	NM	2.5	NM
% Ret. on Equity	6.5	5.1	7.3	NM	11.2	NM

Dividend Data —No cash dividends have been paid. A three-for-two stock split was effected in December 1994.

Amt. of Div. $	Date Decl.	Ex-Div. Date	Stock of Record	Payment Date
3-for-2	Nov. 08	Dec. 06	Nov. 18	Dec. 05 '94

Data as orig. reptd.; bef. results of disc. opers. and/or spec. items. Per share data adj. for stk. divs. as of ex-div. date. E-Estimated. NA-Not Available. NM-Not Meaningful. NR-Not Ranked.

Office—73-710 Fred Waring Dr., Suite 222, Palm Desert, CA 92260. **Tel**—(619) 340-0098. **Chrmn, Pres & CEO**—R. J. Heckmann. **Exec VP & COO**—M. J. Reardon. **VP, CFO & Treas**—K. L. Spence. **VP & Secy**—D. L. Bergmann. **Dirs**—J. R. Bullock, J. E. Clark, J. L. Diederich, R. J. Heckmann, J. A. Ives, A. B. Laffer, A. E. Osborne, M. J. Reardon, T. L. Traff, C. H. Wilkins Jr. **Transfer Agent & Registrar**—American Stock Transfer & Trust Co., NYC. **Incorporated** in Colorado in 1978; reincorporated in Delaware in 1986. **Empl**-2,047. **S&P Analyst:** S.O.S.

STANDARD & POOR'S STOCK REPORTS

U.S. Trust Corp.

NASDAQ Symbol **USTC**
In S&P SmallCap 600

23-AUG-95 **Industry:** Banking

Summary: This asset management, private banking, fiduciary and securities services company serves affluent individuals and institutions through its principal subsidiary in New York.

S&P Opinion: Accumulate (★★★★) Recent Price • 74¾ Yield • 2.6%
52 Wk Range • 76-51¼ 12-Mo. P/E • 44.2

Quantitative Evaluations
Outlook
(1 Lowest—5 Highest)
• **NA**
Fair Value
• **NA**
Risk
• **Low**
Earn./Div. Rank
• **A-**

Technical Eval.
• **Bullish** since 9/94
Rel. Strength Rank
(1 Lowest—99 Highest)
• **70**
Insider Activity
• **NA**

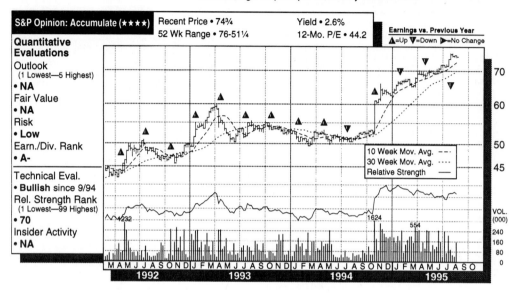

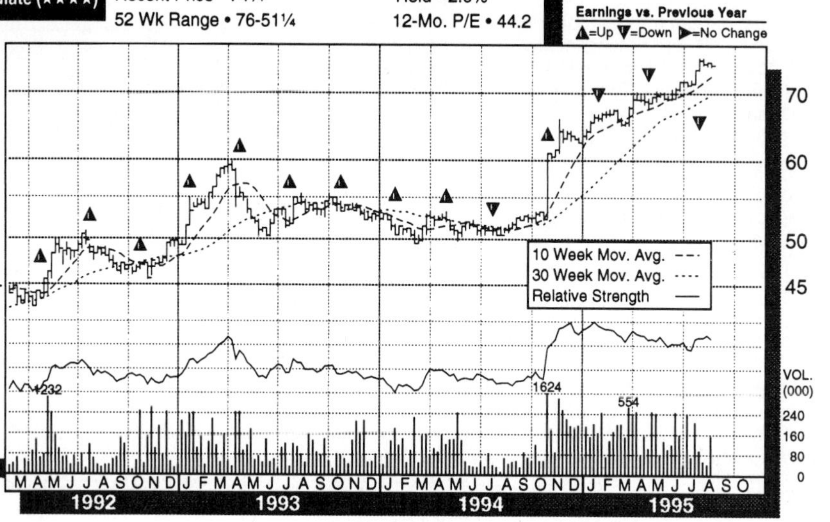

Overview - 23-AUG-95

U.S. Trust and The Chase Manhattan Corporation have set Sept. 1, 1995, as the closing date for the sale of USTC's securities processing business to Chase. The sale of the processing business, which accounted for approximately 36% and 33% of U.S. Trust's revenue and profit, respectively, in 1994, will allow the company to focus on its core asset management and private banking businesses. The company expects fee revenue to grow in the range of 10% to 15% in 1996. Future growth will be achieved through increasing its presence in those regions where it is already established and expanding into new areas of considerable wealth concentration throughout the U.S. After the sale of the processing business, the company should operate more efficiently, due to reductions in overhead and headcount.

Valuation - 23-AUG-95

Based on the purchase price of $363.5 million in Chase common stock and 9.75 million USTC shares outstanding at the closing date, the processing business is being valued at roughly $37 a share. After deducting $37 from USTC's current stock price, the value of the surviving entity is approximately $38 a share. At this price, the shares will be trading at a valuation of around 11 times our earnings estimate for 1996. With fee revenues increasing 10% to 15%, a more efficient cost structure, and favorable demographic trends, USTC is expected to outperform the market over the next six to 12 months.

Key Stock Statistics

S&P EPS Est. 1995	3.20	Tang. Bk. Value/Share	24.99
P/E on S&P Est. 1995	23.4	Beta	0.47
S&P EPS Est. 1996	3.60	Shareholders	2,200
Dividend Rate/Share	2.00	Market cap. (B)	$0.749
Shs. outstg. (M)	9.6	Inst. holdings	62%
Avg. daily vol. (M)	0.020	Insider holdings	3%

Value of $10,000 invested 5 years ago: $ 24,635

Fiscal Year Ending Dec. 31

	1995	% Change	1994	% Change	1993	% Change
Revenues (Million $)						
1Q	127.0	7%	118.6	11%	106.9	3%
2Q	126.4	5%	120.5	12%	107.8	3%
3Q	—	—	127.3	12%	114.2	7%
4Q	—	—	90.87	-22%	116.6	12%
Yr.	—	—	457.3	3%	445.6	6%
Income (Million $)						
1Q	8.63	-32%	12.67	11%	11.42	17%
2Q	5.37	-51%	10.90	11%	9.78	22%
3Q	—	—	12.95	9%	11.92	9%
4Q	—	—	-15.55	NM	9.15	17%
Yr.	—	—	20.97	-50%	42.27	16%
Earnings Per Share ($)						
1Q	0.85	-34%	1.28	10%	1.16	14%
2Q	0.52	-53%	1.10	-90%	11.43	NM
3Q	E0.88	-33%	1.31	9%	1.20	6%
4Q	E0.95	NM	-1.65	NM	0.92	14%
Yr.	E3.20	51%	2.12	-50%	4.26	13%

Next earnings report expected: mid October

U.S. Trust Corp.

Business Summary - 23-AUG-95

U.S. Trust Corporation is the holding company for U.S. Trust Co. of New York and regional subsidiaries in New Jersey, California, Florida, Texas, Connecticut and Oregon. U.S. Trust Co. operates in four core business areas: asset management, private banking, special fiduciary, corporate trust, and securities processing. On November 18, 1994, Chase Manhattan Corp. agreed to purchase USTC's institutional custody, mutual funds servicing, and unit trust businesses (processing business) for $363.5 million in Chase common stock. In 1994, the processing business accounted for approximately 36% of the corporation's revenues and 33% of profits.

With $33.0 billion in assets under management and more than $424.2 billion in assets under supervision, U.S. Trust views itself as a financial services company serving specialty markets, rather than as a traditional bank. Accordingly, it has one of the highest percentages of fee-based revenues among major U.S. banks.

Fiduciary and other fees provided 59% of total income in 1994, interest on loans 19%, interest on investment securities 16%, interest on federal funds sold and securities purchased under agreements to resell 2%, deposits with banks 1%, and other noninterest income 3%.

At December 31, 1994, average loans of $1.63 billion were divided: private banking 78% (67% of which was for residential real estate), short-term trust credit 13%, loans to financial institutions 8% and other 1%. Average deposits in 1994 amounted to $2.44 billion, of which 58% was interest-bearing.

The allowance for loan losses amounted to $14,699,000 at 1994 year-end ($13,393,000 a year earlier), equal to 1.12% (1.22%) of average loans outstanding. Net loan chargeoffs totaled $694,000 in 1994 ($2,283,000 in 1993), or 0.05% (0.21%) of average loans. As of December 31, 1994, nonaccrual and restructured loans totaled $6,371,000 ($6,005,000 a year earlier), or 0.39% (0.43%) of loans outstanding.

The yield on average interest-earning assets was 5.93% in 1994 (5.68% in 1993), while the average rate paid on interest-bearing liabilities was 3.89% (3.14%), for a net interest spread of 2.04% (2.54%).

Important Developments

Jul. '95—U.S. Trust and the Chase Manhattan Corporation set Friday, Sept. 1, 1995, as the closing date for the sale of USTC's processing business to Chase. Shares of the restructured U.S. Trust will begin trading on Nasdaq under the symbol USTDV on a "when-issued" basis ten days prior to the closing date.

Capitalization

Long Term Debt: $57,187,000 (6/95).
Options: To purchase 1,320,009 shs. at $27.75 to $53.88 ea. (12/94).

Per Share Data ($)

(Year Ended Dec. 31)

	1994	1993	1992	1991	1990	1989
Tangible Bk. Val.	23.63	24.42	21.26	20.02	18.13	18.81
Earnings	2.12	4.26	3.76	3.32	1.24	3.08
Dividends	1.97	1.84	1.69	1.60	1.58	1.43
Payout Ratio	94%	43%	45%	48%	127%	46%
Prices - High	66	59¾	50⅞	44½	38	43¼
- Low	49½	49¼	42¼	28	26¾	36½
P/E Ratio - High	32	14	14	13	31	14
- Low	24	12	11	8	22	12

Income Statement Analysis (Million $)

	1994	%Chg	1993	%Chg	1992	%Chg	1991
Net Int. Inc.	108	-7%	116	6%	109	14%	96.0
Tax Equiv. Adj.	4.7	-20%	5.8	-29%	8.2	-19%	10.2
Non Int. Inc.	270	-2%	276	14%	243	15%	212
Loan Loss Prov.	2.0	-50%	4.0	-33%	6.0	NM	6.0
% Exp/Op Revs.	81%	—	80%	—	81%	—	80%
Pretax Inc.	34.4	-53%	72.7	23%	58.9	21%	48.8
Eff. Tax Rate	39%	—	42%	—	38%	—	36%
Net Inc.	21.0	-50%	42.3	16%	36.5	16%	31.4
% Net Int. Marg.	3.49%	—	3.95%	—	4.16%	—	4.35%

Balance Sheet & Other Fin. Data (Million $)

	1994	1993	1992	1991	1990	1989
Earning Assets:						
Money Mkt.	142	298	62.0	400	400	199
Inv. Securities	1,034	923	1,196	1,013	896	866
Com'l Loans	140	58.0	58.0	66.0	676	728
Other Loans	1,487	1,341	1,202	1,098	384	350
Total Assets	3,223	3,186	2,951	2,917	2,778	2,526
Demand Deposits	1,032	1,241	1,221	1,037	969	1,004
Time Deposits	1,409	1,246	1,134	1,071	1,071	983
LT Debt	60.9	65.1	65.1	68.9	70.9	75.2
Common Eqty.	223	229	197	182	166	177

Ratio Analysis

	1994	1993	1992	1991	1990	1989
% Ret. on Assets	0.5	1.1	1.0	1.1	0.4	1.2
% Ret. on Equity	9.2	20.5	19.4	18.1	5.9	15.2
% Loan Loss Resv.	1.1	1.0	0.9	0.7	0.8	0.7
% Loans/Deposits	66.7	56.2	53.5	55.2	52.0	54.3
% Equity to Assets	5.7	5.4	5.4	6.8	7.7	8.2

Dividend Data —Cash has been paid in each year since 1854.

Amt. of Div. $	Date Decl.	Ex-Div. Date	Stock of Record	Payment Date
0.500	Jul. 26	Oct. 26	Oct. 07	Oct. 25 '94
0.500	Oct. 26	Jan. 04	Jan. 10	Jan. 25 '95
0.500	Jan. 24	Apr. 04	Apr. 10	Apr. 25 '95

Data as orig. reptd.; bef. results of disc opers. and/or spec. items. Per share data adj. for stk. divs. as of ex-div. date. E-Estimated. NA-Not Available. NM-Not Meaningful. NR-Not Ranked.

Office—114 W. 47th St., New York, NY 10036. **Tel**—(212) 852-1000. **Chrmn & CEO**—H.M. Schwarz. **Vice Chrmn**—F.S. Wonham, F.B. Taylor. **Pres & COO**—J.S. Maurer. **VP & Secy**—Carol A. Strickland. **Vice Chrmn & Treas**—D.M. Roberts. **Dirs**—E. Baum, S.C. Butler, P.O. Crisp, D.P. Davison, P. de Montebello, P.W. Douglas, E.D. Etherington, A.M. Grumbach, F.C. Hamilton, P.L. Malkin, J.S. Maurer, O.D. Munn, D.M. Roberts, H.M. Schwarz, P.L. Smith, J.H. Stookey, F.B. Taylor, R.F. Tucker, C.L. Wainwright, Jr., R.N. Wilson, F.S. Wonham, R.A. Wooden. **Transfer Agent & Registrar**—Co.'s office. **Incorporated** in New York in 1877. **Empl**-2,558. **S&P Analyst:** Brad Ohlmuller

Universal Health Services

NYSE Symbol **UHS**

In S&P SmallCap 600

02-NOV-95

Industry: Health Care Centers

Summary: This company owns and operates acute-care and psychiatric hospitals and ambulatory surgery and radiation therapy centers, and acts as the adviser to a real estate investment trust.

Quantitative Evaluations

Outlook (1 Lowest—5 Highest)
• **4+**

Fair Value
• **41**

Risk
• **Low**

Earn./Div. Rank
• **B**

Technical Eval.
• **Bullish** since 7/95

Rel. Strength Rank (1 Lowest—99 Highest)
• **95**

Insider Activity
• **NA**

Recent Price • 36¼
52 Wk Range • 37⅜-21¼

Yield • Nil
12-Mo. P/E • 15.4

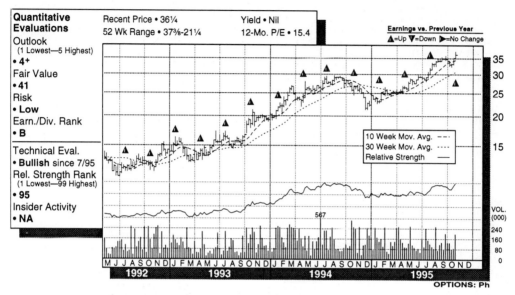

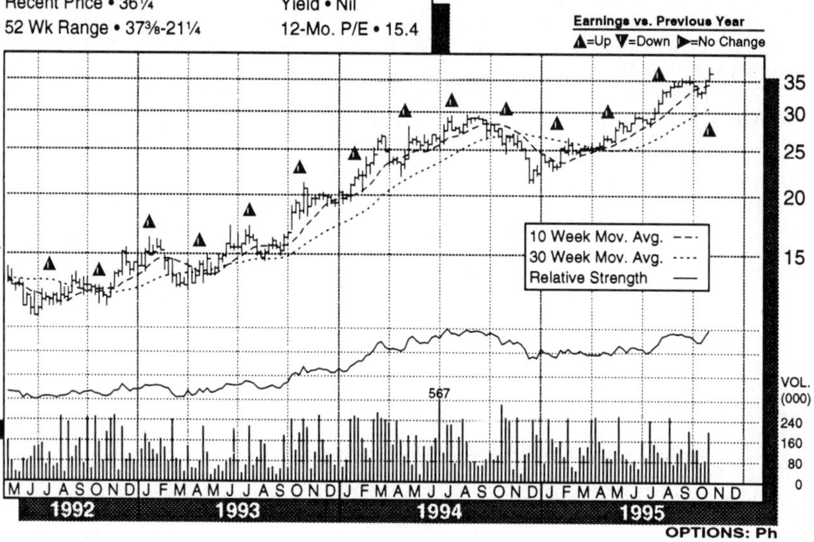

OPTIONS: Ph

Business Profile - 24-OCT-95

UHS has grown by acquiring or building facilities in communities with rapidly rising populations. It has also focused on containing costs and creating alliances with managed care insurers. To capitalize on the trend toward outpatient services, UHS has expanded that segment of its business. UHS has improved its financial condition by lowering its debt to capital ratio, which has enabled it to finance expansion and repurchase shares. Officers and directors control a majority of the voting power.

Operational Review - 02-NOV-95

Net revenues advanced 16% in the first nine months of 1995, year to year, reflecting an increase in the number of facilities operated by the company . Slightly narrower operating margins and higher interest expense were partly offset by only a small increase in lease and rental expenses. With a lower effective tax rate, net income rose 18%. Earnings per share increased to $2.04 from $1.70 on fewer shares outstanding.

Stock Performance - 27-OCT-95

In the past 30 trading days, UHS's shares have increased 4%, compared to a 0.63% fall in the S&P 500. Average trading volume for the past five days was 39,380 shares, compared with the 40-day moving average of 25,862 shares.

Key Stock Statistics

Dividend Rate/Share	Nil	Shareholders	1,000
Shs. outstg. (M)	13.8	Market cap. (B)	$0.538
Avg. daily vol. (M)	0.022	Inst. holdings	69%
Tang. Bk. Value/Share	17.73	Insider holdings	NA
Beta	1.73		

Value of $10,000 invested 5 years ago: $ 39,189

Fiscal Year Ending Dec. 31

	1995	% Change	1994	% Change	1993	% Change
Revenues (Million $)						
1Q	220.7	14%	194.4	NM	195.3	-3%
2Q	214.2	11%	192.2	3%	187.4	7%
3Q	234.1	22%	191.5	3%	186.3	7%
4Q	—	—	204.1	6%	192.4	6%
Yr.	—	—	782.2	3%	761.5	4%
Income (Million $)						
1Q	11.84	15%	10.29	20%	8.61	16%
2Q	9.56	17%	8.15	26%	6.48	6%
3Q	7.23	24%	5.84	13%	5.16	52%
4Q	—	—	4.45	18%	3.77	23%
Yr.	—	—	28.72	20%	24.01	20%
Earnings Per Share ($)						
1Q	0.85	18%	0.72	20%	0.60	15%
2Q	0.68	19%	0.57	24%	0.46	7%
3Q	0.51	24%	0.41	11%	0.37	48%
4Q	—	—	0.32	14%	0.28	22%
Yr.	—	—	2.02	18%	1.71	20%

Next earnings report expected: mid February

Universal Health Services

Business Summary - 02-NOV-95

Universal Health Services, Inc. owns and operates acute-care and psychiatric hospitals. As of October 1995, the company was operating 15 acute-care and 15 psychiatric hospitals and 24 ambulatory surgery and radiation centers. The company has an addictive diseases group within its psychiatric division that operates two substance abuse facilities. UHS owns the ambulatory treatment centers in partnership with physicians.

UHS has also entered into other specialized medical service arrangements, laboratory services, mobile computerized tomography and magnetic resonance imaging services, preferred provider organization arrangements, health maintenance organization contracts, medical office building leasing, construction management services and real estate management and administrative services.

UHS provides capital resources and management services to its hospitals and ambulatory treatment centers, including central purchasing, data processing, finance and control systems, facilities planning, physician recruitment, administrative personnel management, marketing and public relations.

UHS selectively seeks opportunities to expand its operations by acquiring, constructing or leasing additional hospital facilities. In addition, it is the company's objective to increase the operating revenues and profitability of its hospitals by the introduction of new services, improvement of existing services, physician recruitment and the application of financial and operational controls. UHS also continues to examine its facilities and to dispose of those that do not have the potential to contribute to its growth or operating strategy.

The company serves as adviser to Universal Health Realty Income Trust (UHT, NYSE), which leases to UHS the real property of eight UHS facilities and holds interests in properties owned by unrelated companies. UHS receives a fee for its advisory services based on the value of Universal Health Realty's assets and owns 7.7% of its outstanding shares.

Important Developments

Sep. '95—The company acquired Manatee Memorial Hospital, a 512 bed acute care hospital in Bradenton, FL. The company also agreed to sell Universal Medical Center, a 202 bed scute care hospital in Plantation, FL.

Jul. '95—UHS acquired Aiken Regional Medical Centers in Aiken, SC, a 225 bed acute care facility, from Columbia/HCA Healthcare for the assets of UHS's hospitals in Westlake Village, CA, and Dallas, TX, and cash.

Capitalization

Long Term Debt: $75,038,000 (3/95).

Per Share Data ($)

(Year Ended Dec. 31)

	1994	1993	1992	1991	1990	1989
Tangible Bk. Val.	16.09	13.86	12.40	10.36	7.52	6.04
Cash Flow	4.94	4.29	3.71	3.69	4.35	3.35
Earnings	2.02	1.71	1.43	1.45	0.84	0.62
Dividends	Nil	Nil	Nil	Nil	Nil	0.20
Payout Ratio	Nil	Nil	Nil	Nil	Nil	31%
Prices - High	29⅝	21¼	15¾	18⅜	10⅛	11⅝
- Low	19⅛	12½	11⅛	8⅛	6⅜	6⅛
P/E Ratio - High	15	12	11	13	12	19
- Low	9	7	8	6	8	10

Income Statement Analysis (Million $)

	1994	%Chg	1993	%Chg	1992	%Chg	1991
Revs.	781	5%	747	7%	699	2%	686
Oper. Inc.	104	28%	81.0	17%	69.0	1%	68.0
Depr.	42.4	7%	39.6	11%	35.6	2%	35.0
Int. Exp.	6.5	-29%	9.1	-24%	11.9	16%	10.3
Pretax Inc.	46.9	34%	35.1	-14%	41.0	35%	30.3
Eff. Tax Rate	39%	—	32%	—	51%	—	33%
Net Inc.	28.7	20%	24.0	20%	20.0	-1%	20.3

Balance Sheet & Other Fin. Data (Million $)

	1994	1993	1992	1991	1990	1989
Cash	0.8	0.6	6.7	22.7	22.9	21.2
Curr. Assets	118	102	119	141	131	104
Total Assets	521	460	472	501	535	526
Curr. Liab.	104	86.0	85.0	127	93.0	101
LT Debt	85.0	75.0	115	127	206	206
Common Eqty.	261	224	203	184	167	158
Total Cap.	346	303	327	326	408	399
Cap. Exp.	59.0	59.0	44.0	55.0	34.0	35.0
Cash Flow	71.1	63.6	55.6	55.3	60.1	48.7

Ratio Analysis

	1994	1993	1992	1991	1990	1989
Curr. Ratio	1.1	1.2	1.4	1.1	1.4	1.0
% LT Debt of Cap.	24.6	24.7	35.2	39.0	50.4	51.5
% Net Inc.of Revs.	3.7	3.2	2.9	3.0	1.9	1.5
% Ret. on Assets	5.8	5.2	4.1	3.9	2.2	1.7
% Ret. on Equity	11.7	11.3	10.4	11.5	7.2	5.9

Dividend Data —No regular dividends have been paid on the common stock. The company paid a special dividend of $0.20 a share on all classes of stock in October 1989.

Data as orig. reptd.; bef. results of disc. opers. and/or spec. items. Per share data adj. for stk. divs. as of ex-div. date. E-Estimated. NA-Not Available. NM-Not Meaningful. NR-Not Ranked.

Office—367 South Gulph Rd., King of Prussia, PA 19406. **Tel**—(215) 768-3300. **Chrmn, Pres & CEO**—A. B. Miller. **Secy**—S. Miller. **Sr VP-CFO & Investor Contact**—Kirk E. Gorman. **Dirs**—L. W. Cronkhite Jr., J. H. Herrell, R. H. Hotz, M. Meyerson, A. B. Miller, S. Miller, A. Pantaleoni. **Transfer Agent & Registrar**—Mellon Securities Trust Co., Ridgefield Park, N.J. **Incorporated** in Delaware in 1978. **Empl**-9,800. **S&P Analyst:** Philip J. Birbara

STANDARD & POOR'S

STOCK REPORTS

VISX, Inc.

NASDAQ Symbol **VISX**
In S&P SmallCap 600

08-AUG-95 **Industry:** Medical equipment/ supply

Summary: This company develops and manufactures excimer laser surgical systems for use in correcting vision disorders.

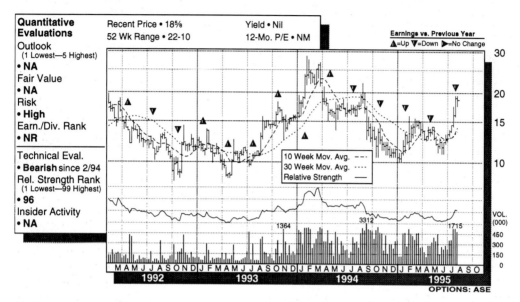

Quantitative Evaluations
Outlook (1 Lowest—5 Highest) • **NA**
Fair Value • **NA**
Risk • **High**
Earn./Div. Rank • **NR**

Technical Eval. • **Bearish** since 2/94
Rel. Strength Rank (1 Lowest—99 Highest) • **96**
Insider Activity • **NA**

Recent Price • 18⅝
52 Wk Range • 22-10
Yield • Nil
12-Mo. P/E • NM

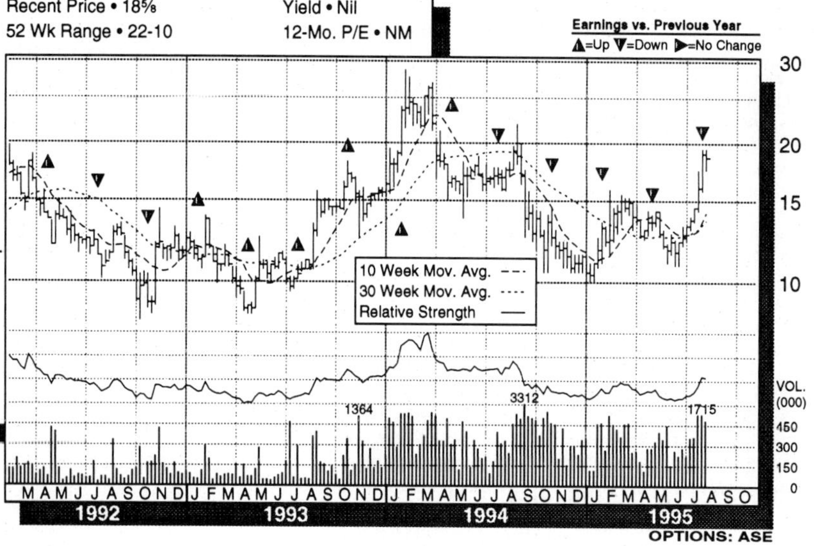

OPTIONS: ASE

Business Profile - 08-AUG-95

This company has been struggling as it is only able to market its laser systems internationally and sales in these markets have been declining. The company, however, hopes to obtain final marketing approval from the FDA in 1995 in the U.S. for one eye procedure, and continue clinical trials and Pre-Market Approval phases with other procedures. Additionally, the company believes that it will benefit from a new laser introduced in March 1995.

Operational Review - 08-AUG-95

Total revenues, which have been declining in recent periods, continued to fall in the most recent quarter reflecting a reduced number of system sales in international markets by Alcon, the company's marketing partner. Margins narrowed due to the lower volume, increased costs associated with the product transition to the STAR Excimer Laser System, and increases in SG&A costs and research and development expenses. The net loss widened significantly.

Stock Performance - 04-AUG-95

In the past 30 trading days, VISX's shares have increased 49%, compared to a 2% rise in the S&P 500. Average trading volume for the past five days was 163,580 shares, compared with the 40-day moving average of 144,579 shares.

Key Stock Statistics

Dividend Rate/Share	Nil	Shareholders	900
Shs. outstg. (M)	12.0	Market cap. (B)	$0.226
Avg. daily vol. (M)	0.233	Inst. holdings	24%
Tang. Bk. Value/Share	2.03	Insider holdings	NA
Beta	2.60		

Value of $10,000 invested 5 years ago: $ 13,796

Fiscal Year Ending Dec. 31

	1995	% Change	1994	% Change	1993	% Change
Revenues (Million $)						
1Q	2.69	-45%	4.87	-10%	5.40	8%
2Q	3.78	-29%	5.36	7%	5.01	95%
3Q	—	—	4.88	-8%	5.29	3%
4Q	—	—	2.78	-56%	6.37	-16%
Yr.	—	—	17.90	-19%	22.07	9%
Income (Million $)						
1Q	-3.60	NM	0.12	NM	-0.21	-32%
2Q	-4.68	NM	-0.38	NM	0.03	NM
3Q	—	—	-2.58	NM	0.06	NM
4Q	—	—	-3.43	NM	0.30	NM
Yr.	—	—	-6.26	NM	0.18	NM
Earnings Per Share ($)						
1Q	-0.32	NM	0.01	NM	-0.02	NM
2Q	-0.39	NM	-0.04	—	Nil	—
3Q	—	—	-0.25	NM	0.01	NM
4Q	—	—	-0.33	NM	0.03	NM
Yr.	—	—	-0.60	NM	0.02	NM

Next earnings report expected: late October

VISX, Inc.

Business Summary - 08-AUG-95

VISX Incorporated designs, develops and manufactures excimer refractive surgical systems designed to recontour the front surface of the cornea of the human eye. The company's current product, the VISX System is undergoing clinical evaluation in the United States and currently is sold only internationally.

The VISX System is designed to enable an ophthalmologist to treat two major categories of vision disorders - phototherapeutic keratectomy (PTK), and photorefractive keratectomy (PRK). The Ophthalmic Devices Advisory Panel of the FDA reviewed the company's application for Pre-Market Approval (PMA) for PTK in March 1994, and recommended that the FDA approve the PMA following receipt and review of certain additional follow-up data. To date the company's PMA for use of the VISX System for PRK has not been scheduled for panel review.

The excimer laser is a type of gas laser that produces ultraviolet light and emits high energy pulses lasting only several billionths of a second. Excimer lesers remove, or ablate, tissue through light rather than with heat, which is typical of many other types of lasers. Excimer lasers therefore have potential to recontour the front surface of the cornea by removing corneal tissue in submicron layers, without significant damage to adjacent cells.

To perform procedures with the VISX System, the physician enters the patient's prescription and the curvature of the cornea into the system's computer. The computer calculates precisely the required corneal correction, which the physician verifies before commencing the laser treatment. The VISX System then performs the treatment, varying automatically the diameter of the laser beam and the number of pulses needed to recontour the front surface of the cornea to correct for the specified prescription. VISX anticipates that procedures will be performed on an out-patient basis.

The company's marketing strategy is to use third parties to market and sell the VISX System. The company granted an exclusive license to Alcon Laboratories, Inc. to market and sell the VISX System in the United States, and to Alcon Pharmaceuticals, Ltd. to market and sell the VISX System outside the U.S.

Important Developments

Jul. '95—The company offered all infringing manufacturers of VISX's proprietary laser technology in Canada, the right to obtain licenses to make and sell these systems in exchange for royalty payments.
May '95—VISX filed additional data with the FDA on PRK performed on almost 2,000 eyes.
Mar. '95—The company introduced an excimer laser system called STAR, which is clinically and functionally equivalent to the original VISX System, but easier and cheaper to operate.

Capitalization

Long Term Debt: None (6/95).

Per Share Data ($)

(Year Ended Dec. 31)

	1994	1993	1992	1991	1990	1989
Tangible Bk. Val.	1.33	1.77	1.60	2.06	0.75	-0.15
Cash Flow	-0.55	0.07	-0.94	-0.19	-0.91	-0.99
Earnings	-0.60	0.02	-0.98	-0.22	-0.94	-1.03
Dividends	Nil	Nil	Nil	Nil	Nil	Nil
Payout Ratio	Nil	Nil	Nil	Nil	Nil	Nil
Prices - High	28¾	18¼	21⅝	18¾	16½	27¾
- Low	10	8½	8¼	4¼	4¼	8
P/E Ratio - High	NM	NM	NM	NM	NM	NM
- Low	NM	NM	NM	NA	NA	NA

Income Statement Analysis (Million $)

	1994	%Chg	1993	%Chg	1992	%Chg	1991
Revs.	17.9	-19%	22.1	9%	20.3	54%	13.2
Oper. Inc.	-5.3	NM	0.3	NM	-4.2	NM	-2.2
Depr.	0.6	11%	0.5	29%	0.4	58%	0.3
Int. Exp.	Nil	—	Nil	—	0.0	—	Nil
Pretax Inc.	-6.3	NM	0.2	NM	-9.6	NM	-1.8
Eff. Tax Rate	NM	—	Nil	—	Nil	—	Nil
Net Inc.	-6.3	NM	0.2	NM	-9.6	NM	-1.8

Balance Sheet & Other Fin. Data (Million $)

	1994	1993	1992	1991	1990	1989
Cash	11.2	11.8	9.1	6.8	4.9	0.9
Curr. Assets	18.1	20.0	20.2	12.5	9.8	1.0
Total Assets	20.6	22.9	23.0	25.2	10.5	1.6
Curr. Liab.	6.2	4.2	6.2	4.9	3.0	0.9
LT Debt	Nil	Nil	Nil	0.0	0.0	Nil
Common Eqty.	14.0	18.0	16.2	19.6	5.9	-0.5
Total Cap.	14.0	18.0	16.2	19.6	6.0	-0.5
Cap. Exp.	0.4	0.6	1.4	0.2	0.4	0.2
Cash Flow	-5.7	0.7	-9.1	-1.6	-7.0	-4.5

Ratio Analysis

	1994	1993	1992	1991	1990	1989
Curr. Ratio	2.9	4.7	3.3	2.6	3.3	1.2
% LT Debt of Cap.	Nil	Nil	NM	0.1	0.3	NM
% Net Inc.of Revs.	NM	0.8	NM	NM	NM	NM
% Ret. on Assets	NM	0.8	NM	NM	NM	NM
% Ret. on Equity	NM	1.0	NM	NM	NM	NM

Dividend Data (No cash dividends have been paid, and VISX does not expect to initiate dividends in the foreseeable future.)

Data as orig. reptd.; bef. results of disc. opers. and/or spec. items. Per share data adj. for stk. divs. as of ex-div. date. E-Estimated. NA-Not Available. NM-Not Meaningful. NR-Not Ranked.

Office—3400 Central Expwy., Santa Clara, CA 95051. **Tel**—(408) 733-2020. **Chrmn, Pres & CEO**—M. B. Logan. **VP & CFO**—T. R. Maier. **VP & Secy**—K. J. Church. **Dirs**—K. Brenner, M. B. Logan, A. R. McMillen, R. R. Montgomery, R. B. Samuels, E. H. Schollmaier, T. R. G. Sear. **Transfer Agent**—American Stock Transfer & Trust Co., NYC. **Incorporated** in California in 1987. **Empl**-104. **S&P Analyst:** Philip J. Birbara

STANDARD & POOR'S

STOCK REPORTS

VLSI Technology

NASDAQ Symbol **VLSI**

In S&P SmallCap 600

02-OCT-95

Industry: Electronics/Electric

Summary: VLSI makes complex application-specific integrated circuits (ASICs), application-specific standard products (ASSPs) and design software tools.

S&P Opinion: Hold (★★★)

Recent Price • 34¼
52 Wk Range • 39⅛-10¼
Yield • Nil
12-Mo. P/E • 46.3

Quantitative Evaluations

Outlook
(1 Lowest—5 Highest)
• **2+**

Fair Value
• **32⅛**

Risk
• **High**

Earn./Div. Rank
• **B-**

Technical Eval.
• **Bullish** since 8/95

Rel. Strength Rank
(1 Lowest—99 Highest)
• **73**

Insider Activity
• **NA**

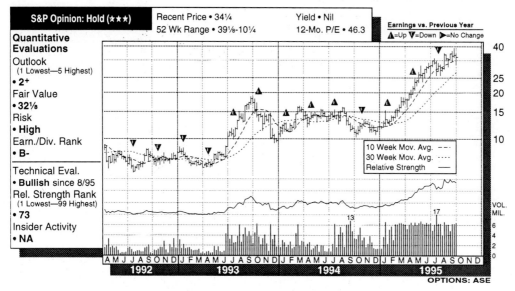

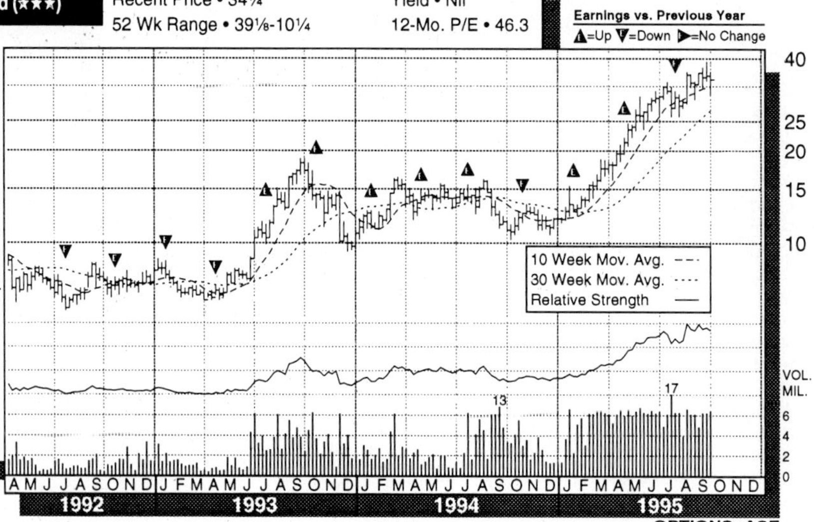

OPTIONS: ASE

Overview - 28-SEP-95

Sales are expected to climb over 25% in 1995, as demand for ASIC products remains strong. Demand from the computer, communications and consumer electronics sectors is expected to continue to grow through 1996. VLSI's cell-based technology gives it a specialized niche in the semiconductor industry. Cell-based technology reduces development time for ASSPs, providing customers with a time-to-market advantage. The company expects to boost its fabrication facility capacity 40% later in the year, and an additional 50% in 1996. Results in the 1995 second quarter include a legal charge of $19.4 million ($0.33 a share, after tax).

Valuation - 28-SEP-95

With additional capacity coming on line by year-end, VLSI appears poised for strong growth in 1996. The company, which has an estimated 30% share in the cellular phone market, will benefit from continuing strong demand. In the computing sector, design wins for Power Macintosh and Pentium-based systems should allow VLSI to maintain its core logic leadership position in the industry. A promising area for the long-term is digital satellite and cable TV set-top boxes. Currently, only the company and LSI Logic have the required technology to meet the requirements of set-top boxes. However, although the long-term outlook is attractive, we see revenue growth in the next two quarters constrained by lack of additional production capacity.

Key Stock Statistics

S&P EPS Est. 1995	1.00	Tang. Bk. Value/Share	6.96
P/E on S&P Est. 1995	34.3	Beta	1.68
S&P EPS Est. 1996	1.85	Shareholders	1,900
Dividend Rate/Share	Nil	Market cap. (B)	$ 1.6
Shs. outstg. (M)	46.7	Inst. holdings	82%
Avg. daily vol. (M)	1.595	Insider holdings	NA

Value of $10,000 invested 5 years ago: $ 46,440

Fiscal Year Ending Dec. 31

	1995	% Change	1994	% Change	1993	% Change
Revenues (Million $)						
1Q	163.0	18%	138.1	18%	117.0	11%
2Q	184.4	25%	148.1	16%	128.0	23%
3Q	0.35	-100%	151.6	10%	137.3	31%
4Q	0.35	-100%	149.3	12%	133.3	16%
Yr.	—	—	587.1	14%	516.0	21%
Income (Million $)						
1Q	110.3	NM	5.36	NM	-2.15	NM
2Q	1.30	-86%	9.34	NM	2.96	NM
3Q	—	—	7.54	NM	7.51	NM
4Q	—	—	9.46	25%	7.57	NM
Yr.	—	—	31.70	100%	15.88	NM
Earnings Per Share ($)						
1Q	0.27	80%	0.15	NM	-0.06	NM
2Q	0.03	-88%	0.25	178%	0.09	NM
3Q	E0.35	75%	0.20	-5%	0.21	NM
4Q	E0.35	40%	0.25	19%	0.21	NM
Yr.	E1.00	18%	0.85	89%	0.45	NM

Next earnings report expected: mid October

VLSI Technology

Business Summary - 29-SEP-95

VLSI Technology designs, makes and markets integrated circuits for single and multiple customer applications in a number of markets.

Contributions (profits in millions) by geographic region in 1994 were:

	Sales	Profits
U.S.	76%	$42.8
Europe	21%	7.6
Japan & Asia-Pacific	3%	-3.7

Export revenues, primarily to the Asia-Pacific region, provided 28% of the 1994 total. Compaq Computer accounted for 22%.

The company designs, makes and sells complex application-specific integrated circuits (ASICs), custom designed chips for an individual customer; and application-specific standard products (ASSPs), semi-custom chips designed for a particular market application that may be used by several customers. Using its cell-based technology, which features a broad range of highly complex, flexible, functional blocks that can be used to as components in custom ASICs, VLSI is able reduce the design cyle for its customers.

The Personal Computer division supplies system-logic chipsets and peripheral components for desktop and portable personal computers based on X86 architectures. The product line consists of high-integration core logic and peripheral input/output (I/O) devices for X86-based systems.

The VLSI Product divisions consist of the Apple Products division, the Computer and Government Products division, the Consumer and Industrial Products division, the Network Products division and the Wireless Products division.

COMPASS Design Automation offers an integrated suite of electronic design automation software tools, foundry-flexible libraries and support services for use by systems and circuit designers.

The company balances wafer production between VLSI facilities in San Jose, Calif, and San Antonio, Tex., and third-party subcontractors.

Important Developments

Sep. '95—The company sold publicly $150 million of 8.25% subordinated notes due 2005, convertible into common at $54.80 a share. Proceeds were earmarked for wafer fabrication capacity expansion and general corporate purposes.

Aug. '95—Intel excercised a warrant to buy 2,677,604 VLSI common shares at $11.69 each (about $31.3 million). Separately, VLSI redeemed all $57.3 million of its 7% convertible subordinated debentures.

Capitalization

Long Term Debt: $47,099,000 (8/95).Shareholders: 1,636 of record (2/94).

Per Share Data ($)

(Year Ended Dec. 31)

	1994	1993	1992	1991	1990	1989
Tangible Bk. Val.	6.96	6.03	5.56	6.10	5.86	6.42
Cash Flow	2.50	1.82	0.56	2.18	1.48	1.61
Earnings	0.85	0.45	-1.12	0.37	-0.52	0.02
Dividends	Nil	Nil	Nil	Nil	Nil	Nil
Payout Ratio	Nil	Nil	Nil	Nil	Nil	Nil
Prices - High	$16\frac{3}{8}$	$18\frac{7}{8}$	$10\frac{1}{2}$	$12\frac{1}{4}$	$12\frac{1}{4}$	$10\frac{1}{8}$
- Low	$10\frac{1}{4}$	$6\frac{1}{2}$	6	$4\frac{1}{4}$	3	$6\frac{3}{8}$
P/E Ratio - High	19	42	NM	33	NM	NM
- Low	12	14	NM	11	NM	NM

Income Statement Analysis (Million $)

	1994	%Chg	1993	%Chg	1992	%Chg	1991
Revs.	587	14%	516	21%	428	4%	413
Oper. Inc.	109	42%	76.6	48%	51.6	-27%	70.4
Depr.	61.8	27%	48.5	NM	48.3	NM	48.4
Int. Exp.	8.7	8%	8.1	-11%	9.1	-2%	9.2
Pretax Inc.	41.7	103%	20.5	NM	-31.6	NM	12.[illegible]
Eff. Tax Rate	24%	—	23%	—	NM	—	23%
Net Inc.	31.7	99%	15.9	NM	-32.2	NM	9.9

Balance Sheet & Other Fin. Data (Million $)

	1994	1993	1992	1991	1990	1989
Cash	103	73.0	70.0	48.0	35.0	55.0
Curr. Assets	266	222	202	186	157	150
Total Assets	490	412	368	364	327	318
Curr. Liab.	128	108	100	110	91.0	78.0
LT Debt	96.8	85.9	83.2	92.6	89.3	84.9
Common Eqty.	255	213	185	162	147	155
Total Cap.	363	304	268	254	236	240
Cap. Exp.	64.6	75.0	41.8	32.8	55.5	56.9
Cash Flow	93.5	64.4	16.1	58.2	36.0	38.3

Ratio Analysis

	1994	1993	1992	1991	1990	1989
Curr. Ratio	2.1	2.1	2.0	1.7	1.7	1.9
% LT Debt of Cap.	26.7	28.2	31.0	36.4	37.8	35.4
% Net Inc.of Revs.	5.4	3.1	NM	2.4	NM	0.2
% Ret. on Assets	6.9	4.0	NM	2.8	NM	0.2
% Ret. on Equity	13.3	7.8	NM	6.2	NM	0.3

Dividend Data —No cash has been paid.

Data as orig. reptd.; bef. results of disc. opers. and/or spec. items. Per share data adj. for stk. divs. as of ex-div. date. Data for 1993 refl. merger or acq. E-Estimated. NA-Not Available. NM-Not Meaningful. NR-Not Ranked.

Office—1109 McKay Dr., San Jose, CA 95131. **Tel**—(408) 434-3000. **Chrmn, Pres & CEO**—A. J. Stein. **VP-Fin & CFO**—G. K. Hinckley. **VP & Secy**—T. F. Mulvaney. **VP, Treas & Investor Contact**—John C. Batty. **Dirs**—P. S. Bonelli, R. P. Dilworth, J. J. Kim, A. J. Stein, H. Tsiang. **Transfer Agent & Registrar**—Bank of Boston. **Incorporated** in California in 1979; reincorporated in Delaware in 1987. **Empl**-2,700. **S&P Analyst:** Steven A. Jaworski

STANDARD & POOR'S

Valassis Communications

STOCK REPORTS

NYSE Symbol **VCI**

In S&P SmallCap 600

03-NOV-95 **Industry:** Graphic Arts

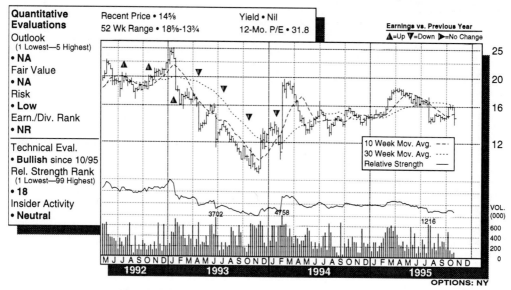

Summary: Valassis is one of the largest printers and publishers of cents-off coupons and other consumer purchase incentives, most of which are featured in Sunday editions of newspapers.

Quantitative Evaluations

Outlook
(1 Lowest—5 Highest)
• **NA**

Fair Value
• **NA**

Risk
• **Low**

Earn./Div. Rank
• **NR**

Technical Eval.
• **Bullish** since 10/95

Rel. Strength Rank
(1 Lowest—99 Highest)
• **18**

Insider Activity
• **Neutral**

Recent Price • 14⅝ | Yield • Nil
52 Wk Range • 18⅝-13¾ | 12-Mo. P/E • 31.8

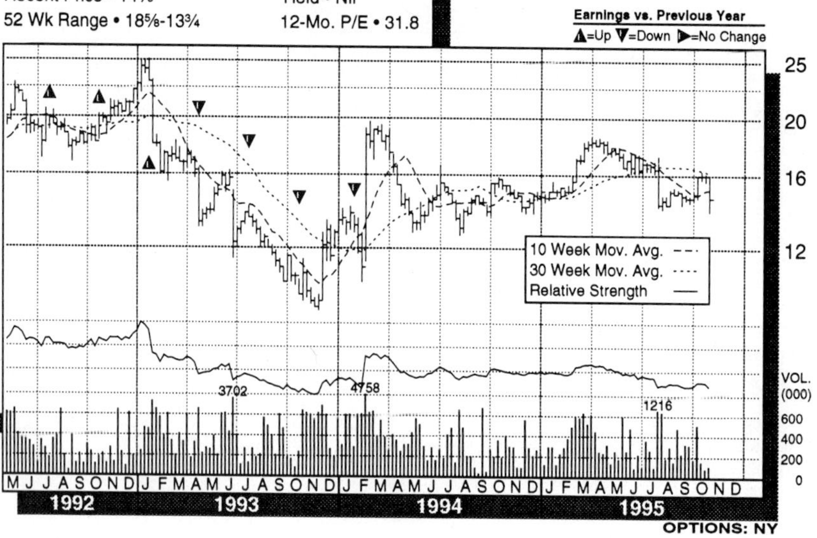

OPTIONS: NY

Business Profile - 27-OCT-95

Valassis core freestanding insert (FSI) business is recovering from a price war which forced deeply discounted sales. The company is seeking to maintain market share and raise prices to offset substantial paper cost increases incurred so far in 1995. These efforts are being complicated by the company's major competitor's strategy to increase its market share. The company's European sales promotion business launched its first co-op FSI test in France during the third quarter.

Operational Review - 27-OCT-95

Valassis changed its reporting period from a June 30 fiscal year to a calendar year, which commenced with a six-month transition period from July 1, 1994 to December 31, 1994. Results in first nine months of 1995 showed a gradual recovery from the industry's 1993-1994 FSI price war; comparable net income increased to $18.9 million from $2.6 million. Higher paper costs have hampered the earnings recovery. Due to price increases, the company is losing market share in FSIs.

Stock Performance - 27-OCT-95

In the past 30 trading days, VCI's shares were unchanged, compared to a 0.63% fall in the S&P 500. Average trading volume for the past five days was 21,100 shares, compared with the 40-day moving average of 47,349 shares.

Key Stock Statistics

Dividend Rate/Share	Nil	Shareholders	300
Shs. outstg. (M)	43.3	Market cap. (B)	$0.601
Avg. daily vol. (M)	0.029	Inst. holdings	42%
Tang. Bk. Value/Share	NM	Insider holdings	NA
Beta	NA		

Value of $10,000 invested 5 years ago: NA

Fiscal Year Ending Dec. 31

	1995	% Change	1994	% Change	1993	% Change
Revenues (Million $)						
1Q	157.4	—	--	—	126.2	-21%
2Q	155.5	—	--	—	132.1	-19%
3Q	138.0	5%	131.3	-7%	141.3	-25%
4Q	—	—	147.8	3%	143.5	-4%
Yr.	—	—	279.0	-49%	542.6	-18%
Income (Million $)						
1Q	8.84	—	—	—	2.59	—
2Q	6.70	—	—	—	0.70	—
3Q	3.33	NM	0.87	NM	0.87	-97%
4Q	—	—	1.01	NM	1.01	-95%
Yr.	—	—	1.88	-64%	5.17	-93%
Earnings Per Share ($)						
1Q	0.20	—	--	—	0.06	-86%
2Q	0.16	—	--	—	0.02	-95%
3Q	0.08	NM	0.02	NM	0.02	-97%
4Q	—	—	0.02	NM	0.02	-95%
Yr.	—	—	0.04	-67%	0.12	-94%

Next earnings report expected: early February

Valassis Communications

Business Summary - 27-OCT-95

Valassis Communications, Inc. is a leading print media company in the consumer promotion industry. The majority of its revenues are generated by printing and publishing cents-off coupons and other consumer purchase incentives primarily for package goods manufacturers. Contributions to revenues in recent fiscal years were:

	1994	1993	1992
Free-standing inserts	82.5%	87.5%	85.7%
Impact printing	10.8%	9.8%	4.0%
Run-of-press	5.2%	2.5%	8.2%
Other	1.5%	0.2%	2.1%

Package goods manufacturers and retail service companies divide their marketing budgets among media advertising, trade promotions and consumer promotions. Marketers use the types of consumer promotions printed and published by Valassis, which includes cents-off coupons, refund offers, premiums, sweepstakes and contests, because they offer certain advantages over trade promotions and media advertising, including direct contact with consumers and the ability to achieve specific marketing objectives.

Most of the consumer purchase incentives published by Valassis are featured in multi-participant (referred to as cooperative) freestanding inserts (FSIs), which are four-color promotional booklets printed by the company at its own facilities. On 46 publishing dates in fiscal 1994, the company's cooperative FSIs were inserted in the Sunday editions of nearly 400 newspapers with a combined average paid circulation of approximately 55 million. Major cooperative FSI customers include companies such as Kellogg, Procter & Gamble and Gerber Products.

The Valassis Impact Printing (VIP) division offers customized design, printing and distribution services primarily for single-participant ("solo") promotional programs. Its promotional product offerings are provided in multiple customized formats such as die-cuts, posters and calendars, as well as traditional FSI formats.

In addition to FSIs, Valassis arranges for the publication of its customers' consumer promotions directly on the pages of newspapers through its run-of-press (ROP) division, which has the capacity to place promotions in any newspaper.

Important Developments

Oct. '95—The number of FSI pages sold/produced continued to decline in the third quarter. The company attributed the decline to the effect of increased FSI prices as well as a 21% reduction in FSI industry publishing dates during the quarter.

Capitalization

Long Term Debt: $418,004,000 (9/95).
Minority Interest: $721,000.

Per Share Data ($)

(Year Ended Dec. 31)

	1994	1993	1992	1991	1990	1989
Tangible Bk. Val.	-9.21	-9.22	-10.00	-11.72	-12.99	NA
Cash Flow	0.27	0.67	2.48	2.54	1.71	NA
Earnings	0.04	0.12	1.89	1.62	0.75	NA
Dividends	Nil	Nil	0.42	0.11	NA	NA
Payout Ratio	Nil	Nil	22%	6%	NA	NA
Prices - High	19¾	19¾	25⅛	22⅞	NA	NA
- Low	10½	10½	9½	16	NA	NA
P/E Ratio - High	NM	NM	13	14	NA	NA
- Low	NM	NM	5	10	NA	NA

Income Statement Analysis (Million $)

	1994	%Chg	1993	%Chg	1992	%Chg	1991
Revs.	278	-49%	540	-18%	660	-1%	669
Oper. Inc.	32.0	-48%	61.0	-69%	199	3%	194
Depr.	9.7	-60%	24.0	-6%	25.4	-29%	35.7
Int. Exp.	19.6	-49%	38.2	-4%	39.9	6%	37.7
Pretax Inc.	4.0	NM	-2.0	NM	135	5%	128
Eff. Tax Rate	56%	—	NM	—	39%	—	42%
Net Inc.	1.9	-63%	5.2	-94%	81.9	10%	74.4

Balance Sheet & Other Fin. Data (Million $)

	1994	1993	1992	1991	1990	1989
Cash	21.2	32.3	39.6	15.3	NA	NA
Curr. Assets	109	118	118	107	122	NA
Total Assets	234	240	275	293	323	NA
Curr. Liab.	131	133	173	207	199	NA
LT Debt	418	419	419	463	550	NA
Common Eqty.	-318	-316	-321	-385	-433	NA
Total Cap.	104	106	102	86.0	NA	NA
Cap. Exp.	9.2	4.1	4.0	4.2	8.0	NA
Cash Flow	12.0	29.0	107	110	74.0	NA

Ratio Analysis

	1994	1993	1992	1991	1990	1989
Curr. Ratio	0.8	0.9	0.7	0.5	0.6	NA
% LT Debt of Cap.	403.1	395.3	410.8	NM	NA	NA
% Net Inc.of Revs.	0.7	9.6	12.4	11.1	5.1	NA
% Ret. on Assets	NA	2.0	28.9	16.4	NA	NA
% Ret. on Equity	NA	NM	NM	NM	NA	NA

Dividend Data —Dividends were omitted in June 1993, after having been paid on a quarterly basis since June 1992.

Data as orig. reptd.; bef. results of disc. opers. and/or spec. items. Per share data adj. for stk. divs. as of ex-div. date. Prior to 1994, data for fiscal yrs. ended Jun. 30 of the fol. cal. yr.; data for 1994 represents six mos. end Dec. 31. E-Estimated. NA-Not Available. NM-Not Meaningful. NR-Not Ranked.

Office—36111 Schoolcraft Rd., Livonia, MI 48150. **Tel**—(313) 591-3000. **Chrmn**—B. M. Powers. **Pres & CEO**—D. A. Brandon. **VP-CFO & Treas**—R. L. Recchia. **Secy**—B. P Hoffman. **VP & Investor Contact**—Lynn M. Liddle. **Dirs**—D. A. Brandon, G. A. Cubbin, M. C. Davis, C. D. DeLoach, J. M. Huntsman Jr., H. G. Kristol, J. D. Packer, B. M. Powers, R. L. Recchia, F. R. Whittlesey. **Transfer Agent & Registrar**—Bank of New York, NYC. **Incorporated** in Delaware in 1986. **Empl**-1,261. **S&P Analyst:** Stephen Madonna, CFA

STANDARD & POOR'S

STOCK REPORTS

Valence Technology

NASDAQ Symbol **VLNC**

In S&P SmallCap 600

22-OCT-95

Industry: Electronics/Electric

Summary: This company is engaged in research and development of advanced rechargeable batteries based on lithium and polymer technologies.

Quantitative Evaluations

Outlook
(1 Lowest—5 Highest)
• NA

Fair Value
• NA

Risk
• High

Earn./Div. Rank
• NR

Technical Eval.
• Bullish since 7/95

Rel. Strength Rank
(1 Lowest—99 Highest)
• 97

Insider Activity
• NA

Recent Price • 5⅞
52 Wk Range • 6½-1⁹⁄₁₆

Yield • Nil
12-Mo. P/E • NM

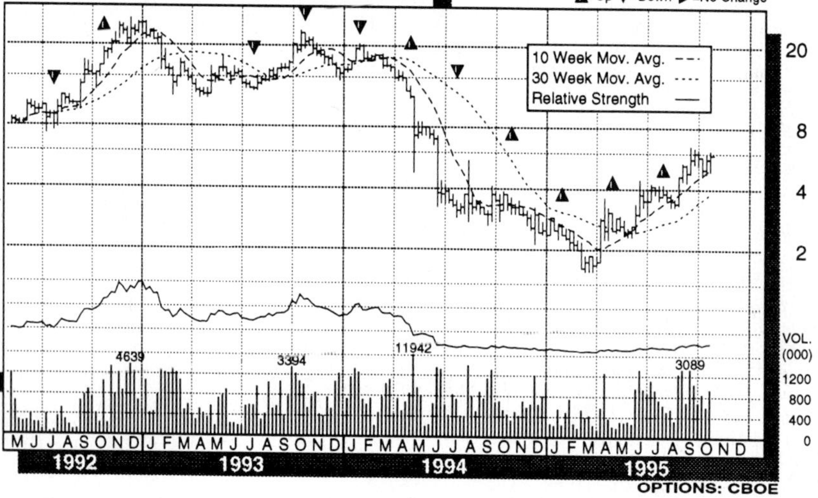

OPTIONS: CBOE

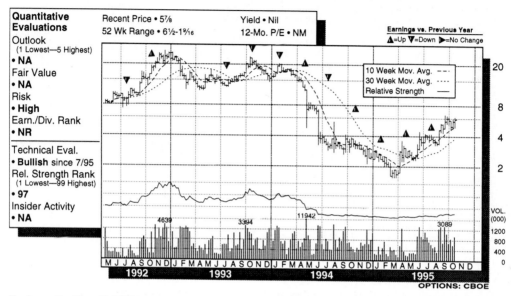

Business Profile - 22-OCT-95

Substantially all of Valence's revenues have been derived from an R&D contract with GM's Delphi Automotive Systems Group (formerly Delco Remy division). However, as a result of a new September 1994 agreement with Delphi, Valence now treats funding as an R&D cost offset rather than as revenue. In August 1994, Valence began refocusing its efforts on R&D and the manufacture of limited quantities of working prototypes instead of volume manufacturing.

Operational Review - 22-OCT-95

The share loss narrowed in fiscal 1996's first quarter, reflecting the absence of charges of $18.9 million ($0.94 a share) for an equipment writedown and consolidation of facilities. However, there were no contract revenues in the quarter, as a result of a September 1994 agreement with Delphi that treats funding as an R&D cost offset rather than as revenue. Comparisons benefited from a 59% drop in R&D and a 17% decrease in marketing expenses, partially offset by a 38% decline in interest income.

Stock Performance - 20-OCT-95

In the past 30 trading days, VLNC's shares have increased 22%, compared to a 3% rise in the S&P 500. Average trading volume for the past five days was 185,720 shares, compared with the 40-day moving average of 275,185 shares.

Key Stock Statistics

Dividend Rate/Share	Nil	Shareholders	900
Shs. outstg. (M)	20.1	Market cap. (B)	$0.118
Avg. daily vol. (M)	0.151	Inst. holdings	13%
Tang. Bk. Value/Share	3.17	Insider holdings	NA
Beta	NA		

Value of $10,000 invested 5 years ago: NA

Fiscal Year Ending Mar. 31

	1996	% Change	1995	% Change	1994	% Change
Revenues (Million $)						
1Q	Nil	—	1.63	9%	1.50	NM
2Q	—	—	1.63	9%	1.50	NM
3Q	—	—	0.45	-78%	2.00	6%
4Q	—	—	0.45	-80%	2.30	53%
Yr.	—	—	4.15	-43%	7.30	14%
Income (Million $)						
1Q	-3.14	NM	-21.81	NM	-2.85	NM
2Q	—	—	-4.21	NM	-4.15	NM
3Q	—	—	-4.02	NM	-5.13	NM
4Q	—	—	-3.60	NM	-6.50	NM
Yr.	—	—	-33.63	NM	-18.65	NM
Earnings Per Share ($)						
1Q	-0.16	NM	-1.09	NM	-0.17	NM
2Q	—	—	-0.21	NM	-0.25	NM
3Q	—	—	-0.20	NM	-0.31	NM
4Q	—	—	-0.18	NM	-0.33	NM
Yr.	—	—	-1.68	NM	-1.08	NM

Next earnings report expected: early November

Valence Technology

Business Summary - 22-OCT-95

Valence Technology, Inc. is engaged in R&D of advanced rechargeable batteries based on lithium ion and polymer technologies. In August 1994, Valence began refocusing its activities on R&D and the manufacture of limited quantities of working prototypes, including developing chemistry improvements, battery designs, manufacturing technology and manufacturing capabilities needed to support commercial introduction of its products.

The company believes that its lithium polymer batteries, when commercially introduced, will offer a number of performance characteristics superior to those of batteries currently in commercial use, including longer operating life, reduced size and weight, and improved recharge characteristics.

Valence believes that its battery technology, although usable in a number of applications, is especially well suited to the portable electronics and equipment market (including portable computers, cellular telephones, camcorders, hand-held power tools and other consumer electronics products), the automotive starting, lighting and ignition market, the electric vehicle market, and the military market.

In March 1991, the company entered into a research and development agreement with GM's Delphi Automotive Systems Group (formerly Delco Remy) to develop lithium polymer batteries for the land, marine and air vehicle and load leveling markets. Under the agreement, Valence obtained a multiyear funding commitment of up to $20 million and, if its batteries are successfully commercialized by Delphi, will receive ongoing royalties. Upon completion of the 1991 agreement, the company and Delphi, in June 1994, extended the agreement until the end of 1994, for an additional fee of $900,000. Both the 1991 agreement and the June 1994 extension have been completed. In September 1994, Valence and Delphi entered into a new five-year agreement that calls for Delphi to fund a majority of the operating expenses at VLNC's Henderson, Nevada, location. This new funding is treated as a research and development cost offset rather than as new revenue.

Important Developments

Jul. '95—Valence received a license for plastic lithium battery technology from Bell Communications Research Co. (Bellcore). Under the agreement, which includes license fees and royalty payments, Bellcore received a minority equity position in Valence. Financial terms were not disclosed.

Capitalization

Long Term Debt: $7,947,000 (6/95).
Options: To buy 2,702,000 shs. at $0.01 to $4.00 ea. (3/95).

Per Share Data ($) (Year Ended Mar. 31)

	1995	1994	1993	1992	1991	1990
Tangible Bk. Val.	3.32	4.98	4.23	3.47	NM	NM
Cash Flow	-1.45	-0.84	-0.46	-0.36	-0.51	-0.04
Earnings	-1.68	-1.08	-0.63	-0.37	-0.52	-0.04
Dividends	Nil	Nil	Nil	Nil	Nil	Nil
Payout Ratio	Nil	Nil	Nil	Nil	Nil	Nil
Cal. Yrs.	1994	1993	1992	1991	1990	1989
Prices - High	20½	26	27	NA	NA	NA
- Low	2⅛	11	7¼	NA	NA	NA
P/E Ratio - High	NM	NM	NM	NM	NM	NM
- Low	NM	NM	NM	NA	NA	NA

Income Statement Analysis (Million $)

	1995	%Chg	1994	%Chg	1993	%Chg	1992
Revs.	4.2	-42%	7.3	14%	6.4	69%	3.8
Oper. Inc.	-13.1	NM	-16.8	NM	-7.3	NM	-1.0
Depr.	4.5	8%	4.2	83%	2.3	NM	0.1
Int. Exp.	0.8	NM	0.3	-17%	0.3	-29%	0.4
Pretax Inc.	-33.6	NM	-18.7	NM	-8.5	NM	-3.8
Eff. Tax Rate	Nil	—	NM	—	NM	—	Nil
Net Inc.	-33.6	NM	-18.7	NM	-8.5	NM	-3.8

Balance Sheet & Other Fin. Data (Million $)

	1995	1994	1993	1992	1991	1990
Cash	59.6	61.0	61.8	0.8	0.1	0.0
Curr. Assets	61.4	62.4	62.4	0.9	0.1	0.0
Total Assets	92.0	121	77.2	3.3	0.4	0.1
Curr. Liab.	16.4	14.1	6.4	5.9	0.8	0.0
LT Debt	8.8	7.3	1.8	7.2	5.1	0.4
Common Eqty.	66.7	100	69.0	-9.8	-5.5	-0.4
Total Cap.	75.5	107	70.8	-2.6	-0.4	0.0
Cap. Exp.	8.8	23.5	6.0	1.7	0.4	0.0
Cash Flow	-29.1	-14.5	-6.2	-3.6	-5.1	-0.4

Ratio Analysis

	1995	1994	1993	1992	1991	1990
Curr. Ratio	3.7	4.4	9.7	0.2	0.1	1.5
% LT Debt of Cap.	11.7	6.8	2.5	NM	NM	NM
% Net Inc.of Revs.	NM	NM	NM	NM	NM	NM
% Ret. on Assets	NM	NM	NM	NM	NM	NM
% Ret. on Equity	NM	NM	NM	NM	NM	NM

Dividend Data —No cash dividends have been paid, and the company does not intend to pay any in the foreseeable future.

Data as orig. reptd.; bef. results of disc. opers. and/or spec. items. Per share data adj. for stk. divs. as of ex-div. date. E-Estimated. NA-Not Available. NM-Not Meaningful. NR-Not Ranked.

Office—301 Conestoga Way, Henderson, NV 89015. **Tel**—(702) 558-1000. **Chrmn, Pres & CEO**—C. L. Reed. **EVP**—W. J. Masuda. **Secy**—B. A. Perkins. **Dirs**—C. E. Berg, C. L. Reed, A. F. Shugart. **Transfer Agent & Registrar**—First National Bank of Boston. **Incorporated** in Delaware in 1989. **Empl**-60. **S&P Analyst:** Ronald J. Gross

Valmont Industries

NASDAQ Symbol **VALM**
In S&P SmallCap 600

11-SEP-95 **Industry:** Manufacturing/Distr

Summary: This company is the world's largest manufacturer of center pivot and linear move irrigation equipment. It also supplies pole structures and energy-efficient lighting ballasts.

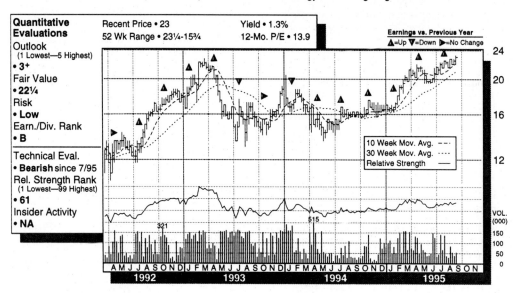

Quantitative Evaluations
Outlook
(1 Lowest—5 Highest)
• **3+**
Fair Value
• **22¼**
Risk
• **Low**
Earn./Div. Rank
• **B**

Technical Eval.
• **Bearish** since 7/95
Rel. Strength Rank
(1 Lowest—99 Highest)
• **61**
Insider Activity
• **NA**

Recent Price • 23
52 Wk Range • 23¼-15¾
Yield • 1.3%
12-Mo. P/E • 13.9

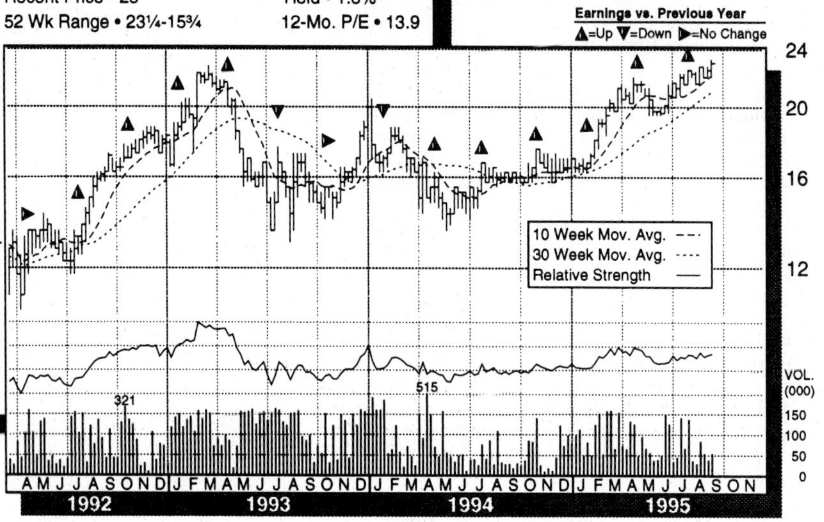

Business Profile - 11-SEP-95

This manufacturer of irrigation and industrial products has benefited from the strong demand for mechanized agricultural irrigation systems. New products have been developed to further enhance electronic and computerized controls. With the global need for infrastructure development, VALM's recent acquisition of Microflect will increase the growth potential for its engineered metal structures. Valmont plans to continue its expansion through acquisitions and joint ventures.

Operational Review - 11-SEP-95

Revenues grew 11% in the first half of 1995, as strength in metal structures and European industrial products outweighed a second quarter decline in irrigation products, which were hurt by wet weather and uncertainty over farm legislation. Despite higher expenses related to future business development, margins widened substantially, on reduced ballast costs and the higher European volume. Pretax income advanced 41%, and, following a lower tax rate, earnings were up 44% to $0.91 a share.

Stock Performance - 08-SEP-95

In the past 30 trading days, VALM's shares have increased 2%, compared to a 2% rise in the S&P 500. Average trading volume for the past five days was 13,075 shares, compared with the 40-day moving average of 12,474 shares.

Key Stock Statistics

Dividend Rate/Share	0.30	Shareholders	3,800
Shs. outstg. (M)	13.5	Market cap. (B)	$0.311
Avg. daily vol. (M)	0.011	Inst. holdings	31%
Tang. Bk. Value/Share	11.99	Insider holdings	NA
Beta	0.82		

Value of $10,000 invested 5 years ago: $ 13,610

Fiscal Year Ending Dec. 31

	1995	% Change	1994	% Change	1993	% Change
Revenues (Million $)						
1Q	133.7	20%	111.2	4%	106.9	-3%
2Q	124.6	2%	122.0	5%	116.0	NM
3Q	—	—	109.8	2%	107.2	13%
4Q	—	—	128.7	18%	108.7	5%
Yr.	—	—	471.8	8%	438.8	3%
Income (Million $)						
1Q	4.76	58%	3.01	8%	2.80	60%
2Q	5.87	36%	4.32	13%	3.83	-6%
3Q	—	—	3.86	45%	2.67	2%
4Q	—	—	4.93	NM	-4.04	NM
Yr.	—	—	16.12	NM	5.27	-60%
Earnings Per Share ($)						
1Q	0.41	58%	0.26	8%	0.24	60%
2Q	0.50	35%	0.37	12%	0.33	-6%
3Q	—	—	0.33	43%	0.23	NM
4Q	—	—	0.42	NM	-0.35	NM
Yr.	—	—	1.38	NM	0.45	-61%

Next earnings report expected: mid October

Valmont Industries

Business Summary - 11-SEP-95

Valmont Industries, Inc. manufactures industrial products and irrigation products. Contributions by segment in 1994 were:

	Sales	Profits
Industrial products	65%	52%
Irrigation products	35%	48%

Foreign sales represented 13% of 1994 revenues (19% in 1993 and 22% in 1992).

The Industrial Products segment produces a broad line of mechanical and structural tubing and manufactures components for the electrical construction industry. Products include lighting and traffic signal poles, high voltage transmission structures, communication towers, utility substations, lighting ballasts and custom steel tubing. Light poles and tubing are distributed through manufacturer's representatives, joint ventures, dealers, distributors, and other arrangements; lighting ballasts are sold through distributors and directly to OEMs.

Valmont is one of the largest producers of automated mechanical move irrigation systems for agricultural applications. The primary products are center-pivot and linear-move models. A center-pivot system travels in a circle, while a linear system operates in a straight line. Products also include computer-aided management systems, agricultural waste handling systems, wastewater management systems, replacement parts, and turn-key projects. In 1994, VALM introduced a new system structure and a family of modular, upgradable control panels.

Irrigation products are being marketed on all six arable continents--North and South America, Europe, Australia, Asia and Africa. Many areas that have historically utilized traditional flood irrigation are converting rapidly to center privot and linear move irrigation. In most regions, yields achieved with mechanized irrigation are superior to those from dryland farming. In recent years, water conservation and water quality concerns have also spurred demand.

In 1994, the company entered into a joint venture to produce pole structures in Shanghai, China for developing lighting, utility and communications markets in China and other parts of Asia.

Important Developments

Jul. '95— Valmont acquired Microflect Co., a producer of structures for the wireless communications industry, in exchange for 1.95 million shares of newly issued VALM common stock. The transaction, accounted for as a pooling of interests, is not expected to dilute 1995 EPS. Microflect anticipates sales of around $40 million in 1995.

Capitalization

Long Term Debt: $34,458,000 (7/95).
Minority Interest: $2,127,000 (7/95).

Per Share Data ($)

(Year Ended Dec. 31)

	1994	1993	1992	1991	1990	1989
Tangible Bk. Val.	11.04	9.83	9.74	8.90	9.91	8.83
Cash Flow	2.27	1.31	2.16	0.31	2.24	2.46
Earnings	1.38	0.45	1.14	-0.69	1.34	1.78
Dividends	0.30	0.29	0.26	0.26	0.26	0.22
Payout Ratio	22%	64%	22%	NM	19%	12%
Prices - High	20½	22¾	18¾	18½	25	20
- Low	13½	13	10⅜	9½	9¼	11
P/E Ratio - High	15	51	16	NM	19	11
- Low	10	29	9	NM	7	6

Income Statement Analysis (Million $)

	1994	%Chg	1993	%Chg	1992	%Chg	1991
Revs.	472	8%	439	3%	425	-1%	430
Oper. Inc.	37.4	10%	34.1	4%	32.8	59%	20.6
Depr.	10.4	4%	10.0	-15%	11.8	2%	11.6
Int. Exp.	4.7	-21%	5.9	-22%	7.5	-12%	8.6
Pretax Inc.	24.9	NM	8.1	-56%	18.4	NM	-12.3
Eff. Tax Rate	35%	—	35%	—	28%	—	NM
Net Inc.	16.1	NM	5.3	-60%	13.2	NM	-4.0

Balance Sheet & Other Fin. Data (Million $)

	1994	1993	1992	1991	1990	1989
Cash	29.6	14.0	12.7	7.3	12.8	20.5
Curr. Assets	171	166	153	159	254	241
Total Assets	266	247	273	281	351	322
Curr. Liab.	90.0	83.0	89.0	94.0	164	143
LT Debt	35.5	38.4	60.4	70.4	55.3	60.9
Common Eqty.	127	113	111	101	112	99
Total Cap.	173	161	182	182	187	179
Cap. Exp.	23.0	16.3	7.9	15.5	23.6	30.3
Cash Flow	26.5	15.3	25.0	3.6	26.1	28.5

Ratio Analysis

	1994	1993	1992	1991	1990	1989
Curr. Ratio	1.9	2.0	1.7	1.7	1.5	1.7
% LT Debt of Cap.	20.5	23.9	33.2	38.7	29.6	34.0
% Net Inc.of Revs.	3.4	1.2	3.1	NM	1.8	2.6
% Ret. on Assets	6.3	2.0	4.8	NM	4.6	7.1
% Ret. on Equity	13.4	4.7	12.4	NM	14.7	22.9

Dividend Data —Cash has been paid in each year since 1980.

Amt. of Div. $	Date Decl.	Ex-Div. Date	Stock of Record	Payment Date
0.075	Sep. 27	Sep. 29	Sep. 30	Oct. 14 '94
0.075	Dec. 12	Dec. 23	Dec. 30	Jan. 13 '95
0.075	Feb. 27	Mar. 27	Mar. 31	Apr. 14 '95
0.075	Jun. 02	Jun. 28	Jun. 30	Jul. 14 '95
0.075	Sep. 07	Sep. 27	Sep. 29	Oct. 16 '95

Data as orig. reptd.; bef. results of disc. opers. and/or spec. items. Per share data adj. for stk. divs. as of ex-div. date. E-Estimated. NA-Not Available. NM-Not Meaningful. NR-Not Ranked.

Office—Valley, NE 68064. **Tel**—(402) 359-2201. **Chrmn**—R. B. Daugherty. **Pres & CEO**—M. C. Bay. **VP & CFO**—T. J. McClain. **VP & Secy**—T. P. Egan, Jr. **VP, Contr & Investor Contact**—Brian C. Stanley. **Dirs**—M. C. Bay, R. B. Daugherty, C. M. Harper. A. F. Jacobson, L. P. Johnson, J. E. Jones, T. F. Madison, W. Scott, Jr., R. G. Wallace. **Transfer Agent & Registrar**—First National Bank of Omaha. **Incorporated** in Delaware in 1974. **Empl**-3,754. **S&P Analyst:** Justin McCann

STANDARD & POOR'S

STOCK REPORTS

Vencor, Inc.

NYSE Symbol **VC**
In S&P SmallCap 600

26-OCT-95 **Industry:** Health Care Centers

Summary: Vencor operates 35 long-term acute-care hospitals, 311 nursing centers, 55 pharmacy outlets and 23 retirement housing communities.

S&P Opinion: Hold (★★★)

Recent Price • 29⅞ | 52 Wk Range • 38-25¾ | Yield • Nil | 12-Mo. P/E • 21.3

Quantitative Evaluations
Outlook (1 Lowest—5 Highest) • **5⁻**
Fair Value • **44**
Risk • **Average**
Earn./Div. Rank • **B**

Technical Eval. • **Bullish** since 9/95
Rel. Strength Rank (1 Lowest—99 Highest) • **21**
Insider Activity • **NA**

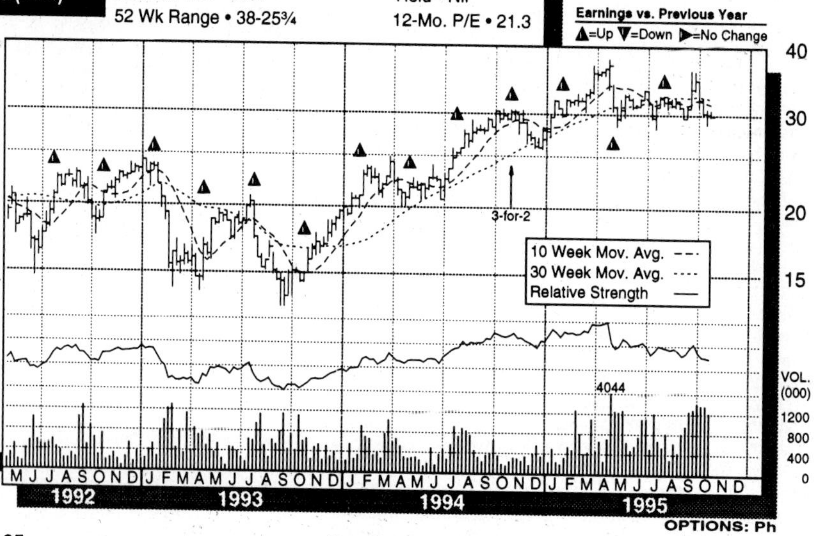

OPTIONS: Ph

Overview - 26-OCT-95

Vencor's acquisition of Hillhaven Corp. was consistent with management's strategy of repositioning the company as a provider of a broad range of long-term healthcare, as opposed to strictly an operator of long-term acute-care hospitals. The transaction should generate upwards of $20 million in annual cost savings and will boost annual revenues past the $2.0 billion mark. Although the merger enhanced the scope of Vencor's operations, we are only modestly positive on the transaction as it appears likely that investors will now view the company as a nursing home operator. With the outlook for nursing home stocks clouded by regulatory issues, we would expect the shares of Vencor to trade in a narrow range for the balance of 1995.

Valuation - 26-OCT-95

Based on our EPS estimate for 1996 of $1.85, the shares of Vencor seem appropriate for more speculative accounts. While earnings forecasts for the company show solid growth, several risk elements could prove these forecasts to be overly optimistic. On the regulatory front, proposed reductions in the growth of Medicare and Medicaid would cause problems for all long-term care and nursing home companies, as over 50% of their revenues are generated from these programs. Specifically, any changes in Medicare reimbursement for catastrophically ill patients would have potentially dramatic effects on Vencor. With earnings visibility clouded by these and other issues, we would not aggressively add to positions at current levels.

Key Stock Statistics

S&P EPS Est. 1995	1.45	Tang. Bk. Value/Share	9.18
P/E on S&P Est. 1995	20.6	Beta	2.18
S&P EPS Est. 1996	1.85	Shareholders	12,000
Dividend Rate/Share	Nil	Market cap. (B)	$ 2.1
Shs. outstg. (M)	73.0	Inst. holdings	30%
Avg. daily vol. (M)	0.507	Insider holdings	NA

Value of $10,000 invested 5 years ago: $ 101,846

Fiscal Year Ending Dec. 31

	1995	% Change	1994	% Change	1993	% Change
Revenues (Million $)						
1Q	120.4	38%	86.96	39%	62.55	33%
2Q	140.7	43%	98.53	47%	66.95	26%
3Q	—	—	103.5	43%	72.42	29%
4Q	—	—	111.0	38%	80.32	38%
Yr.	—	—	400.0	42%	282.2	31%
Income (Million $)						
1Q	9.15	55%	5.92	30%	4.54	37%
2Q	10.81	48%	7.28	36%	5.34	27%
3Q	—	—	8.33	33%	6.24	30%
4Q	—	—	9.88	45%	6.81	34%
Yr.	—	—	31.42	37%	22.92	31%
Earnings Per Share ($)						
1Q	0.34	46%	0.23	40%	0.17	39%
2Q	0.37	32%	0.28	45%	0.19	26%
3Q	E0.36	13%	0.32	41%	0.23	31%
4Q	E0.38	NM	0.38	46%	0.26	39%
Yr.	E1.45	21%	1.20	41%	0.85	34%

Next earnings report expected: early November

Vencor, Inc.

Business Summary - 26-OCT-95

Following its recent acquisition of The Hillhaven Corporation, Vencor, Inc. is one of the largest diversified healthcare providers in the U.S., with operations in 41 states. Its operations include 35 long-term acute-care hospitals, 311 nursing centers, 55 pharmacy outlets and 23 retirement housing communities. The company is also the leading provider of ancillary services to nursing homes and subacute-care providers.

Since its inception in 1985, Vencor has created the largest network of long-term intensive-care hospitals. These facilities primarily offer care to medically complex, chronically ill patients. Vencor's hospitals are able to treat patients who suffer from multiple systemic failures or conditions such as neurological disorders, head injuries, brain stem and spinal cord trauma, cerebral vascular accidents, chemical brain injuries, central nervous system disorders, developmental anomolies and cardiopulmonary disorders. Generally, about 70% of the company's chronic patients are ventilator-dependent for some period of time during their hospitalization.

Through its Vencare Contract Services division (formed in 1993), the company has expanded the scope of its cardiopulmonary care by providing subacute and respiratory care services and supplies to skilled nursing facilities and hospitals.

The nursing centers acquired in the Hillhaven merger provide a wide range of diversified healthcare services, including long-term care and subacute medical and rehabilitative services such as wound care, oncology treatment, brain injury care, stroke therapy and orthopedic therapy. Hillhaven is also a leading provider of rehabilitative services, including physical, occupational and speech therapies, and provides long-term care to residents of its nursing centers with Alzheimer's disease. In addition, Hillhaven provides institutional and retail pharmacy services and operates retirement housing communites in 14 states.

Important Developments

Oct. '95—VC said it plans to call for redemption all of its outstanding $115 million of 6% surbordinated notes (convertible into about 4.4 million Vencor common shares) and $75 million of 7.75% subordinated debentures (convertible into about 4.2 million Vencor common shares; originally issued by Hillhaven). Conversion of these securities would lower annual interest expense by about $14 million.

Sep. '95—Vencor acquired The Hillhaven Corporation, the second largest domestic provider of long-term healthcare (revenues of about $1.6 billion in its fiscal year ended May 31, 1995), in exchangefor Vencor common stock valued at about $1.4 billion and the assumption of approximately $580 million of Hillhaven debt.

Capitalization

Long Term Debt: $144,285,000 (6/95).

Per Share Data ($)

(Year Ended Dec. 31)

	1994	1993	1992	1991	1990	1989
Tangible Bk. Val.	6.70	5.31	5.38	4.79	1.57	1.03
Cash Flow	1.90	1.31	0.90	0.53	0.28	0.13
Earnings	1.20	0.85	0.63	0.42	0.19	0.06
Dividends	Nil	Nil	Nil	Nil	Nil	Nil
Payout Ratio	Nil	Nil	Nil	Nil	Nil	Nil
Prices - High	30⅝	24⅛	26⅝	24⅞	6⅜	3⅛
- Low	19⅛	13	14⅝	5⅝	2 7/16	2 7/16
P/E Ratio - High	25	29	42	59	33	52
- Low	16	15	23	13	13	40

Income Statement Analysis (Million $)

	1994	%Chg	1993	%Chg	1992	%Chg	1991
Revs.	397	43%	277	31%	212	58%	134
Oper. Inc.	76.5	48%	51.8	45%	35.8	90%	18.8
Depr.	20.4	61%	12.7	72%	7.4	172%	2.7
Int. Exp.	7.7	9%	7.1	NM	2.2	NM	0.7
Pretax Inc.	52.6	37%	38.4	34%	28.6	67%	17.1
Eff. Tax Rate	40%	—	40%	—	39%	—	41%
Net Inc.	31.4	37%	22.9	32%	17.4	72%	10.1

Balance Sheet & Other Fin. Data (Million $)

	1994	1993	1992	1991	1990	1989
Cash	3.1	16.6	20.7	43.4	4.5	3.3
Curr. Assets	126	95.8	82.4	91.6	31.8	15.3
Total Assets	390	294	294	148	56.0	34.0
Curr. Liab.	48.7	34.1	27.9	18.8	11.5	8.2
LT Debt	142	116	117	0.9	12.8	9.1
Common Eqty.	184	131	145	126	30.0	16.0
Total Cap.	336	257	262	127	43.0	26.0
Cap. Exp.	51.3	40.9	30.4	32.5	5.8	10.6
Cash Flow	51.8	35.6	24.8	12.8	4.8	1.8

Ratio Analysis

	1994	1993	1992	1991	1990	1989
Curr. Ratio	2.6	2.8	3.0	4.9	2.8	1.9
% LT Debt of Cap.	42.2	45.4	44.7	0.7	29.7	35.6
% Net Inc.of Revs.	7.9	8.3	8.2	7.6	4.2	1.5
% Ret. on Assets	9.0	8.1	7.8	9.0	6.8	2.4
% Ret. on Equity	19.7	17.4	12.8	12.0	13.3	8.4

Dividend Data —No cash dividends have been paid. A stock purchase rights plan was adopted in 1993. Details of a stock split in 1994 follow:

Amt. of Div. $	Date Decl.	Ex-Div. Date	Stock of Record	Payment Date
3-for-2	Sep. 29	Oct. 26	Oct. 10	Oct. 25 '94

Data as orig. reptd.; bef. results of disc. opers. and/or spec. items. Per share data adj. for stk. divs. as of ex-div. date. E-Estimated. NA-Not Available. NM-Not Meaningful. NR-Not Ranked.

Office—3300 Providian Center, 400 West Market St., Louisville, KY 40202. **Tel**—(502) 569-7300. **Chrmn, Pres & CEO**—W. B. Lunsford. **VP-Fin & Investor Contact**—W. Earl Reed III. **Secy**—Jill L. Force. **Dirs**—W. F. Beran, W. C. Ballard Jr., M. R. Barr, B. L. Busby, D. R. Ecton, G. D. Hudson, W. H. Lomicka, W. B. Lunsford, W. E. Reed III, R. G. Smith, J. O. Vance. **Transfer Agent & Registrar**—National City Bank, Cleveland. **Incorporated** in Kentucky in 1983; reincorporated in Delaware in 1987. **Empl**-42,000. **S&P Analyst:** Robert M. Gold

STANDARD & POOR'S

STOCK REPORTS

Venture Stores

NYSE Symbol **VEN**
In S&P SmallCap 600

11-SEP-95 **Industry:** Retail Stores

Summary: Venture Stores operates a chain of 114 retail discount stores in the Midwest and Southwest. The stores feature a broad assortment of branded and unbranded merchandise.

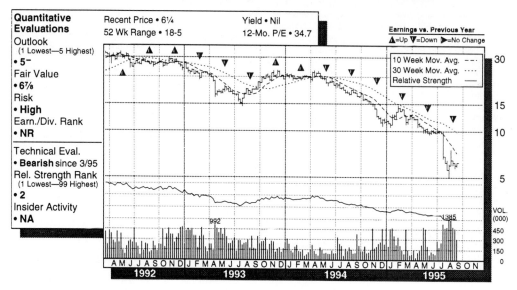

Quantitative Evaluations
Outlook (1 Lowest—5 Highest) • **5⁻**
Fair Value • **6⅞**
Risk • **High**
Earn./Div. Rank • **NR**

Technical Eval. • **Bearish** since 3/95
Rel. Strength Rank (1 Lowest—99 Highest) • **2**
Insider Activity • **NA**

Recent Price • 6¼ | 52 Wk Range • 18-5 | Yield • Nil | 12-Mo. P/E • 34.7

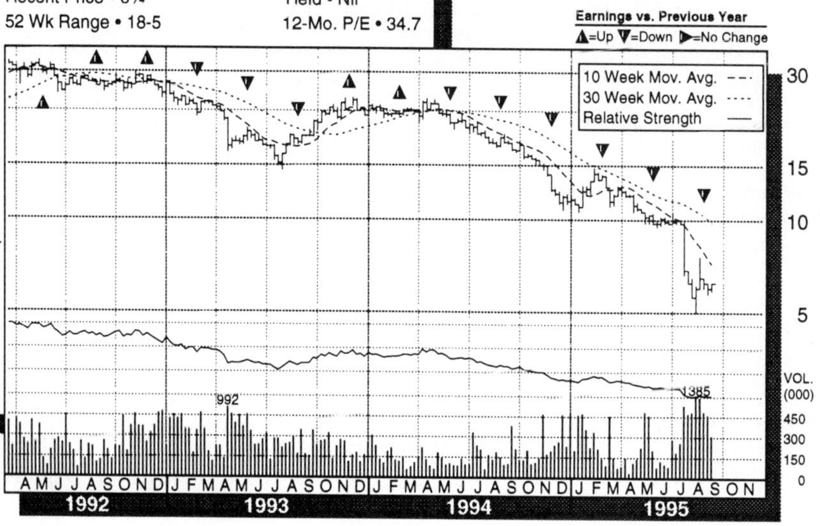

Business Profile - 11-SEP-95

In July 1995, VEN said it would transform itself from a discount general merchandiser to a leading, value-price family apparel, home and leisure retailer, by placing more emphasis on the shopping needs of working women and busy, budget-conscious mothers. The program, which is expected to cost $40 million, should be finished by early February 1996. Other expense saving actions being implemented are expected to save the company $18 million in the second half of 1995-96, and $30 million in 1996-97.

Operational Review - 11-SEP-95

Higher sales in the 26 weeks ended July 29, 1995, primarily reflected more stores in operation; same-store sales dropped 3.9%. Profitability was hurt by weak apparel sales and a highly promotional environment. Per share results for the period included charges of $0.13 to complete the implementation of a merchandise reorganization program initiated in the 1994 fourth quarter, and $0.56 for a repositioning program announced in July 1995. A net loss contrasted with net income.

Stock Performance - 08-SEP-95

In the past 30 trading days, VEN's shares were unchanged, compared to a 2% rise in the S&P 500. Average trading volume for the past five days was 76,100 shares, compared with the 40-day moving average of 176,662 shares.

Key Stock Statistics

Dividend Rate/Share	Nil	Shareholders	24,000
Shs. outstg. (M)	17.3	Market cap. (B)	$0.108
Avg. daily vol. (M)	0.158	Inst. holdings	61%
Tang. Bk. Value/Share	15.21	Insider holdings	NA
Beta	NA		

Value of $10,000 invested 5 years ago: NA

Fiscal Year Ending Jan. 31

	1996	% Change	1995	% Change	1994	% Change
Revenues (Million $)						
1Q	440.9	6%	414.9	14%	363.6	NM
2Q	456.8	4%	439.6	9%	403.1	4%
3Q	—	—	463.6	4%	446.5	14%
4Q	—	—	699.2	8%	649.4	13%
Yr.	—	—	2,017	8%	1,863	8%
Income (Million $)						
1Q	-3.19	NM	1.16	-49%	2.27	-59%
2Q	-17.34	NM	1.61	-63%	4.37	-18%
3Q	—	—	1.61	-76%	6.84	4%
4Q	—	—	24.34	-20%	30.46	-5%
Yr.	—	—	28.71	-35%	43.94	-11%
Earnings Per Share ($)						
1Q	-0.22	NM	0.03	-70%	0.10	-70%
2Q	-1.04	NM	0.06	-73%	0.22	-21%
3Q	—	—	0.06	-83%	0.36	3%
4Q	—	—	1.38	-21%	1.75	27%
Yr.	—	—	1.53	-37%	2.43	-14%

Next earnings report expected: early November

Venture Stores

Business Summary - 06-SEP-95

Venture Stores (which was spun off by May Department Stores Co. in November 1990) operates a regional chain of retail discount stores in the Midwest and Southwest. As of August 3, 1995, it operated 117 stores in nine states. About 78% of the stores were in the Chicago, St. Louis, Kansas City, Houston, Dallas/Fort Worth, Indianapolis and Oklahoma City markets.

The stores offer a broad selection of branded and unbranded merchandise designed to appeal to a wide range of customers. Merchandise includes hardline products such as lifestyle furniture, housewares, consumer electronics, home textiles, toys, sporting goods, hardware, automotive products and household consumables, as well as softline products such as women's, men's and children's clothing, intimate apparel, shoes, jewelry, cosmetics and accessories. Sales by merchandise category in recent years were:

	1994-95	1993-94	1992-93
Hardlines	63%	61%	61%
Softlines	36%	38%	38%
Other	1%.	1%	1%

The average store size is 100,000 sq. ft. Venture operates a 404,000 sq. ft. distribution facility in Chicago, Ill., a 350,000 sq. ft. distribution center in Corsicana, Tex., and a 614,000 sq. ft. facility in O'Fallon, Mo. (this facility includes 235,000 sq. ft. of central offices and a 379,000 sq. ft. distribution center).

Sales are highly seasonal; the fourth quarter contributed 35% of sales and 85% of net earnings in 1994.

Nine stores were opened in 1994: four in Houston, two in Dallas/Fort Worth, and one each in Corpus Christi, Tex., Geneva, Ill., and Edmond, Okla. Openings scheduled for 1995 include three in Houston and one each in Dallas/Fort Worth and Amarillo, Tex. Plans call for two openings in 1995-96 and two annually over the next five years, with the primary focus on Texas.

Important Developments

Aug. '95—Sales in the four weeks ended August 26, 1995, declined 7.6%, year to year; same-store sales fell 13%. In the 30 weeks ended August 26, total sales grew 3.2%, despite a 5.2% drop in same-store sales.

Aug. '95—During the first half of 1995-96, Venture opened four new stores in Texas, one each located in Houston, Amarillo, Fort Worth and Dallas.

Capitalization

Long Term Debt: $151,195,000 (7/95).

$3.25 Depositary Stock: 769,300 shs.; ea. represents 0.10 sh. of $32.50 cum. conv. pfd. stk.; conv. into 1.316 com. shs.

Per Share Data ($) (Year Ended Jan. 31)

	1995	1994	1993	1992	1991	1990
Tangible Bk. Val.	NA	14.48	11.93	7.39	5.43	3.65
Cash Flow	NA	3.78	3.93	3.41	3.20	1.44
Earnings	1.53	2.43	2.82	2.48	2.06	0.57
Dividends	0.58	0.57	0.55	0.54	0.13	NA
Payout Ratio	38%	24%	20%	22%	7%	NA
Cal. Yrs.	1994	1993	1992	1991	1990	1989
Prices - High	24¾	27⅞	33¾	27¼	10	NA
- Low	10¾	14⅜	24½	8	4	NA
P/E Ratio - High	16	11	12	11	5	NA
- Low	7	6	9	3	2	NA

Income Statement Analysis (Million $)

	1994	%Chg	1993	%Chg	1992	%Chg	1991
Revs.	1,863	8%	1,718	13%	1,522	7%	1,421
Oper. Inc.	103	-3%	106	16%	91.0	5%	87.0
Depr.	22.9	22%	18.7	20%	15.6	-19%	19.2
Int. Exp.	11.1	19%	9.3	-22%	11.9	-19%	14.7
Pretax Inc.	71.9	-10%	79.7	21%	65.8	22%	53.8
Eff. Tax Rate	39%	—	38%	—	37%	—	36%
Net Inc.	43.9	-11%	49.4	19%	41.5	20%	34.5

Balance Sheet & Other Fin. Data (Million $)

	1994	1993	1992	1991	1990	1989
Cash	46.7	77.1	75.7	60.9	7.0	NA
Curr. Assets	354	351	319	304	279	NA
Total Assets	669	595	508	451	424	NA
Curr. Liab.	279	258	244	214	182	NA
LT Debt	100	92.0	93.0	93.0	130	NA
Common Eqty.	247	202	124	91.0	61.0	NA
Total Cap.	362	308	233	200	208	NA
Cap. Exp.	97.1	79.1	60.7	21.1	37.3	44.0
Cash Flow	64.3	66.2	57.1	53.7	24.0	59.7

Ratio Analysis

	1994	1993	1992	1991	1990	1989
Curr. Ratio	1.3	1.4	1.3	1.4	1.5	NA
% LT Debt of Cap.	27.7	29.7	39.8	46.6	62.5	NA
% Net Inc.of Revs.	2.4	2.9	2.7	2.4	0.7	2.6
% Ret. on Assets	6.9	8.9	8.7	NA	NA	NA
% Ret. on Equity	18.4	29.1	38.6	NA	NA	NA

Dividend Data —Dividends were eliminated in the second quarter of fiscal 1995. A poison pill stock purchase rights plan was adopted in 1990.

Amt. of Div. $	Date Decl.	Ex-Div. Date	Stock of Record	Payment Date
0.145	Aug. 19	Aug. 29	Sep. 02	Sep. 16 '94
0.145	Nov. 21	Nov. 25	Dec. 01	Dec. 15 '94
0.145	Feb. 02	Feb. 23	Mar. 01	Mar. 15 '95
0.070	May. 19	May. 25	Jun. 01	Jun. 15 '95

Data as orig. reptd.; bef. results of disc. opers. and/or spec. items. Per share data adj. for stk. divs. as of ex-div. date. E-Estimated. NA-Not Available. NM-Not Meaningful. NR-Not Ranked.

Office—2001 East Terra Lane, O'Fallon, MO 63366-0110. **Tel**—(314) 281-5500. **Chrmn**—J. M. Seeherman. **Pres & CEO**—R. N. Wildrick. **SVP & CFO**—J. F. Burtelow. **Secy**—J. A. Rosenblum. **Dirs**—R. L. Berra, D. W. Kemper, J. M. Seeherman, H. E. Trusheim, R. N. Wildrick, L. J. Young. **Transfer Agent & Registrar**—Mellon Securities Transfer Services, Ridgefield Park, NJ. **Incorporated** in Delaware in 1969. **Empl**-17,000. **S&P Analyst:** Maureen C. Carini

Vicor Corp.

NASDAQ Symbol **VICR**
In S&P SmallCap 600

08-OCT-95 **Industry:** Electronics/Electric

Summary: This company designs, develops, manufactures and markets modular power components and complete power systems for use in electronic products.

Quantitative Evaluations

Outlook (1 Lowest—5 Highest)
• **NA**

Fair Value
• **NA**

Risk
• **Average**

Earn./Div. Rank
• **NR**

Technical Eval.
• **Bullish** since 8/95

Rel. Strength Rank (1 Lowest—99 Highest)
• **37**

Insider Activity
• **Neutral**

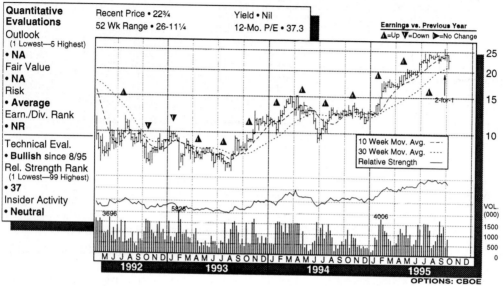

Recent Price • 22¾
52 Wk Range • 26-11¼
Yield • Nil
12-Mo. P/E • 37.3

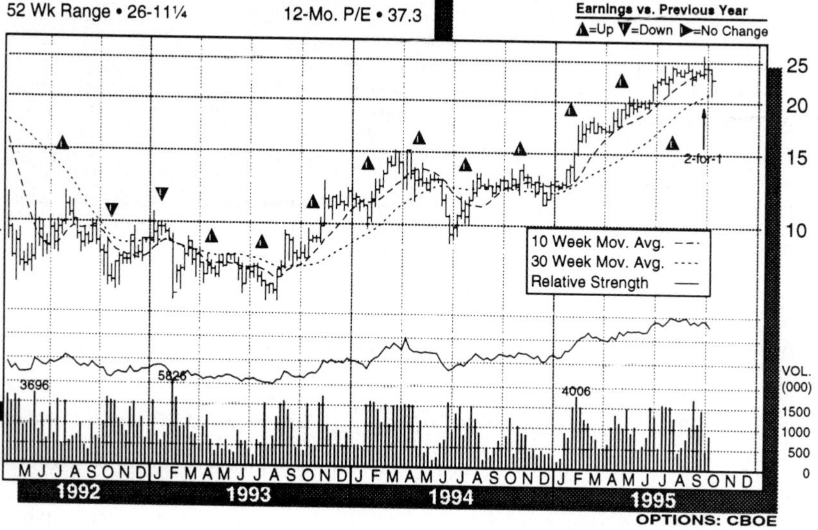

OPTIONS: CBOE

Business Profile - 05-OCT-95

VICR designs, develops, makes and markets modular power components and complete power systems for use in converting electric power into a form suitable for the operation of electronic circuity. Its product lines consist of families of modular power components used as building blocks to configure a power system. Primary customers are the telecommunications, electronic data processing, industrial control and military electronics markets. The common shares were split two-for-one in September 1995.

Operational Review - 05-OCT-95

Based on a brief report, net revenues in the six months ended June 30, 1995, rose 29%, year to year, on continued strong demand for company products. Margins widened on the increased volume, and operating income was up 42%. With sharply higher interest and other income, net income advanced 44%, to $14,419,000 ($0.67 a share), from $10,017,000 ($0.46). The balance sheet is strong, with no long term debt, and a current ratio of better than 8:1 at June 30, 1995.

Stock Performance - 06-OCT-95

In the past 30 trading days, VICR's shares have declined 5%, compared to a 4% rise in the S&P 500. Average trading volume for the past five days was 163,780 shares, compared with the 40-day moving average of 250,895 shares.

Key Stock Statistics

Dividend Rate/Share	Nil	Shareholders	700
Shs. outstg. (M)	42.4	Market cap. (B)	$0.966
Avg. daily vol. (M)	0.191	Inst. holdings	24%
Tang. Bk. Value/Share	3.90	Insider holdings	NA
Beta	1.88		

Value of $10,000 invested 5 years ago: NA

Fiscal Year Ending Dec. 31

	1995	% Change	1994	% Change	1993	% Change
Revenues (Million $)						
1Q	33.79	31%	25.76	38%	18.70	24%
2Q	35.12	27%	27.68	38%	20.09	29%
3Q	—	—	30.05	38%	21.70	32%
4Q	—	—	31.95	36%	23.55	40%
Yr.	—	—	115.4	37%	84.03	32%
Income (Million $)						
1Q	7.04	47%	4.79	38%	3.46	23%
2Q	7.38	41%	5.23	50%	3.48	12%
3Q	—	—	5.78	49%	3.89	27%
4Q	—	—	6.34	47%	4.30	44%
Yr.	—	—	22.14	46%	15.13	26%
Earnings Per Share ($)						
1Q	0.17	50%	0.11	38%	0.08	23%
2Q	0.17	42%	0.12	50%	0.08	14%
3Q	—	—	0.13	50%	0.09	29%
4Q	—	—	0.15	50%	0.10	43%
Yr.	—	—	0.51	47%	0.35	27%

Next earnings report expected: mid October

Vicor Corp.

Business Summary - 13-JUL-95

Vicor Corporation designs, develops, makes and markets modular power components and complete power systems using zero current switching, a patented high-frequency electronic power conversion technology. Company components are used in electronic products to convert power from a primary power source, such as a wall outlet, into direct current required by most electronic circuits.

Modular power converters include five families of component-level DC-DC power converters. Designed to be mounted directly on printed circuit board assemblies, these products are offered in a wide range of input voltages, output voltages and power ratings.

Vicor's configurable products use its standard converters as core elements. The company has developed several product families that provide complete power solutions configured to customer needs. These products use a component-level approach to offer higher performance, higher power densities, lower costs, greater flexibility and faster delivery than traditional offerings.

Accessory power system components, used with the company's component-level converters, integrate other important functions of the power system, facilitating the design of complete power systems by interconnecting several modules. In general, accessory products are used to condition the inputs and outputs of the company's modular power components.

In February 1995, Vicor began prototype production on a new automated manufacturing line designed to make next-generation families of modular power conversion products. The line, which combines flexible robotic workcells into a fully computer-integrated manufacturing environment, will eventually be able to make converters at an average rate of one every 10 seconds.

International sales accounted for 31% of the total sales in 1994, versus 28% in 1993 and 19% in 1992.

Important Developments

Dec. '94—Vicor repurchased $8,912,000 of its common stock in 1994, under an authorization to buy up to $10 million of stock.

Capitalization

Long Term Debt: None (3/95).
Cl. B Com. Stk.: 6,199,711 shs. ($0.01 par); conv. sh.-for-sh. into com.; 10 votes per sh.
P. Vinciarelli owns 89%.
Shareholders: 38 of record (1/95).
Options: To buy 1,474,554 com. shs. at $0.30 to $42.75 ea. (12/94).

Per Share Data ($)

(Year Ended Dec. 31)

	1994	1993	1992	1991	1990	1989
Tangible Bk. Val.	2.73	2.41	2.09	1.68	0.40	0.20
Cash Flow	0.70	0.51	0.39	0.36	0.19	0.10
Earnings	0.51	0.35	0.28	0.29	0.13	0.07
Dividends	Nil	Nil	Nil	Nil	Nil	Nil
Payout Ratio	Nil	Nil	Nil	Nil	Nil	Nil
Prices - High	15⅛	12¾	22⅞	22⅝	4⅜	NA
- Low	9	6½	6⅞	4⅛	1¾	NA
P/E Ratio - High	29	36	83	79	33	NA
- Low	17	19	25	14	13	NA

Income Statement Analysis (Million $)

	1994	%Chg	1993	%Chg	1992	%Chg	1991
Revs.	115	37%	84.0	32%	63.8	15%	55.6
Oper. Inc.	40.9	45%	28.3	30%	21.7	7%	20.3
Depr.	7.6	14%	6.7	37%	4.8	51%	3.2
Int. Exp.	0.0	-67%	0.1	-45%	0.1	-61%	0.3
Pretax Inc.	35.7	48%	24.2	26%	19.2	5%	18.3
Eff. Tax Rate	38%	—	38%	—	38%	—	39%
Net Inc.	22.1	46%	15.1	26%	12.0	7%	11.2

Balance Sheet & Other Fin. Data (Million $)

	1994	1993	1992	1991	1990	1989
Cash	43.2	45.2	42.9	37.4	1.8	1.2
Curr. Assets	77.1	73.4	65.5	60.5	15.7	10.6
Total Assets	126	115	97.0	77.6	27.5	18.7
Curr. Liab.	12.1	10.6	6.7	6.4	8.9	3.5
LT Debt	Nil	0.1	0.5	1.0	2.2	4.7
Common Eqty.	113	102	88.5	70.1	13.0	6.2
Total Cap.	114	104	89.6	71.2	18.6	15.2
Cap. Exp.	15.5	16.1	14.8	8.4	5.5	3.8
Cash Flow	29.7	21.8	16.8	14.4	6.9	3.9

Ratio Analysis

	1994	1993	1992	1991	1990	1989
Curr. Ratio	6.4	6.9	9.7	9.4	1.8	3.0
% LT Debt of Cap.	Nil	0.1	0.6	1.5	11.6	30.7
% Net Inc.of Revs.	19.2	18.0	18.8	20.2	13.8	8.9
% Ret. on Assets	18.5	14.3	13.6	19.9	21.7	15.2
% Ret. on Equity	20.7	15.8	15.0	25.9	52.5	26.3

Dividend Data —No cash payments have been made. For the foreseeable future, the company plans to retain earnings to finance the expansion of its business. A two-for-one stock split was effected in 1991.

Amt. of Div. $	Date Decl.	Ex-Div. Date	Stock of Record	Payment Date
2-for-1	Jul. 28	Sep. 19	Aug. 28	Sep. 18 '95

Data as orig. reptd.; bef. results of disc. opers. and/or spec. items. Per share data adj. for stk. divs. as of ex-div. date. E-Estimated. NA-Not Available. NM-Not Meaningful. NR-Not Ranked.

Office—23 Frontage Rd., Andover, MA 01810. **Tel**—(508) 470-2900. **Chrmn & Pres**—P. Vinciarelli. **VP-Fin, Treas, Secy & Investor Contact**—Mark A. Glazer. **Dirs**—M. M. Ansour, R. E. Beede, E. J. Eichten, J. M. Prager, D. T. Riddiford, P. Vinciarelli. **Transfer Agent**—State Street Bank & Trust Co., Boston. **Incorporated** in Delaware in 1981. **Empl-** 762. **S&P Analyst:** K.J.G.

STANDARD & POOR'S

Video Lottery Technologies

STOCK REPORTS

NASDAQ Symbol **VLTS**

In S&P SmallCap 600

25-JUL-95

Industry: Leisure/Amusement

Summary: This company is a leading supplier of system software, equipment and related services for on-line lotteries, video lotteries and pari-mutuel systems throughout the world.

Quantitative Evaluations

Outlook
(1 Lowest—5 Highest)
• **NA**

Fair Value
• **NA**

Risk
• **High**

Earn./Div. Rank
• **NR**

Technical Eval.
• **Bullish** since 5/94

Rel. Strength Rank
(1 Lowest—99 Highest)
• **9**

Insider Activity
• **NA**

Recent Price • 7
52 Wk Range • 10¾-5½
Yield • Nil
12-Mo. P/E • NM

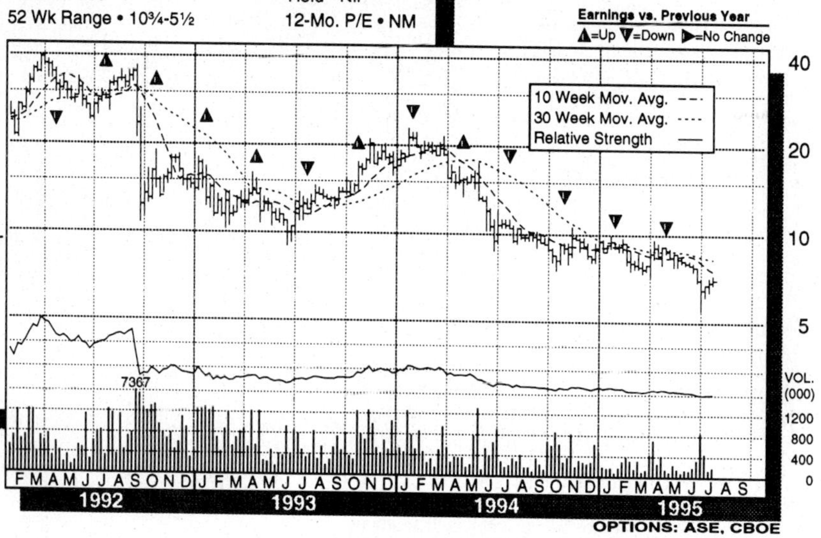

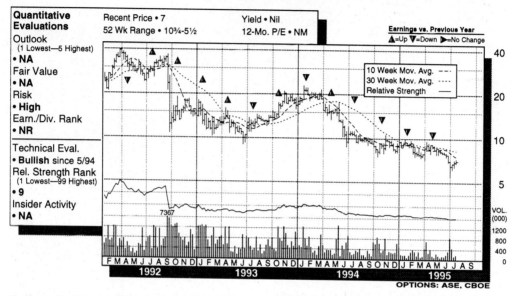

OPTIONS: ASE, CBOE

Business Profile - 24-JUL-95

VLTS's loss in 1994 reflected pretax charges totaling $27.1 million for the impairment of goodwill related to its May 1994 acquisition of United Wagering Systems, restructuring efforts and other unusual adjustments. After reaching a high of nearly $40 a share in early 1992, the stock price has fallen sharply and now hovers in the single digits, reflecting certain jurisdictions' canceling their contracts with the company or awarding contracts to competitors such as Gtech Holdings.

Operational Review - 20-JUL-95

Total revenues in the three months ended March 31, 1995, advanced, year to year, primarily reflecting the acquisition of United Wagering in May 1994. Expenses rose more rapidly; an operating loss replaced income. After sharply higher interest expense and a tax credit of $225,882, versus taxes at 40.6%, a net loss contrasted with net income. Shares outstanding in the 1995 period were 15% lower than in 1994.

Stock Performance - 21-JUL-95

In the past 30 trading days, VLTS's shares have declined 11%, compared to a 5% rise in the S&P 500. Average trading volume for the past five days was 33,300 shares, compared with the average of 59,895 shares. 40-day moving

Key Stock Statistics

Dividend Rate/Share	Nil	Shareholders	700
Shs. outstg. (M)	10.6	Market cap. (B)	$0.074
Avg. daily vol. (M)	0.078	Inst. holdings	18%
Tang. Bk. Value/Share	6.90	Insider holdings	NA
Beta	NA		

Value of $10,000 invested 5 years ago: NA

Fiscal Year Ending Dec. 31

	1995	% Change	1994	% Change	1993	% Change
Revenues (Million $)						
1Q	46.94	19%	39.56	NM	39.26	NM
2Q	—	—	47.46	-4%	49.20	102%
3Q	—	—	51.68	13%	45.61	19%
4Q	—	—	50.08	24%	40.54	6%
Yr.	—	—	188.8	8%	174.6	57%
Income (Million $)						
1Q	-0.29	NM	2.37	—	—	—
2Q	—	—	2.47	—	—	—
3Q	—	—	2.17	—	—	—
4Q	—	—	-23.18	—	—	—
Yr.	—	—	-16.17	NM	4.35	-48%
Earnings Per Share ($)						
1Q	-0.03	NM	0.19	19%	0.16	33%
2Q	—	—	0.20	-17%	0.24	-14%
3Q	—	—	0.18	-33%	0.27	108%
4Q	—	—	-2.19	NM	-0.32	NM
Yr.	—	—	-1.54	NM	0.35	-53%

Next earnings report expected: early August

Video Lottery Technologies

Business Summary - 24-JUL-95

Video Lottery Technologies, Inc., through its Video Lottery Consultants subsidiary, designs, manufactures and markets video terminals, central control system software and related services for the video lottery market. The company, through its Automated Wagering International subsidiary, also provides on-line lottery systems and services to governmental lottery authorities. United Wagering Systems, acquired in May 1994, through its United Tote Company unit, supplies computerized pari-mutuel wagering systems for horse and greyhound racetracks, off-track betting facilities, and jai alai frontons. It also owns and operates a racetrack facility.

Video lottery operations include video terminals on which games, including poker, blackjack, bingo and keno, can be played for low-stakes entertainment. Typically, the amount wagered per game is limited to less than $2.50, and the maximum payout per game is limited to less than $1,000. The terminals are located in age-controlled establishments such as restaurants serving alcoholic beverages and bars.

Video lottery operations have been implemented on a jurisdictionwide basis by four states and certain Canadian and Australian provinces. They have provided substantial incremental sources of revenues to each the jurisdictions without increasing general taxation.

Automated Wagering operates and maintains on-line, computer-based networks for state lotteries in Florida, Pennsylvania, Washington, Minnesota, Delaware, Montana and South Dakota.

United Wagering Systems, Inc. (UWS) designs, manufactures, markets and operates computerized wagering systems and provides services for approximately 140 pari-mutuel wagering facilities in the Americas and abroad. Historically, its primary focus has been the domestic pari-mutuel racing market; however, it has recently entered the international pari-mutuel racing market. UWS operates the on-line OTB computer networks in both the Capital District and Western Region of New York.

Through three subsidiaries, the company operates and services video lottery and amusement machines in approximately 210 business establishments in southern Montana.

Important Developments

Mar. '95—VLT said its losses in the fourth quarter and full year reflected a pretax $17.3 million writedown for the impairment of goodwill related to the company's acquisition of United Wagering Systems and a pretax restructuring charge of $6.7 million due to a revision of the company's domestic and international operations and other unusual pretax adjustments totaling about $3.1 million.

Capitalization

Long Term Debt: $20,723,955 (3/95).
Preferred Stock: 1,912,728 shs. ($0.01 par); held by Electronic Data Systems.

Per Share Data ($) (Year Ended Dec. 31)

	1994	1993	1992	1991	1990	1989
Tangible Bk. Val.	7.50	8.48	8.03	4.08	0.88	0.42
Cash Flow	0.43	1.68	1.53	0.56	0.64	0.37
Earnings	-1.54	0.35	0.74	0.42	0.47	0.24
Dividends	Nil	Nil	Nil	Nil	Nil	Nil
Payout Ratio	Nil	Nil	Nil	Nil	Nil	Nil
Prices - High	23	21	39¾	31½	NA	NA
- Low	7½	9	10¾	14	NA	NA
P/E Ratio - High	NM	60	54	75	NA	NA
- Low	NM	26	15	33	NA	NA

Income Statement Analysis (Million $)

	1994	%Chg	1993	%Chg	1992	%Chg	1991
Revs.	189	8%	175	58%	111	NM	31.5
Oper. Inc.	30.1	-14%	34.8	66%	21.0	NM	6.3
Depr.	20.7	27%	16.3	82%	9.0	NM	1.2
Int. Exp.	1.7	72%	1.0	-13%	1.1	149%	0.4
Pretax Inc.	-14.9	NM	7.5	-39%	12.3	123%	5.5
Eff. Tax Rate	NM	—	42%	—	32%	—	35%
Net Inc.	-16.2	NM	4.3	-48%	8.4	133%	3.6

Balance Sheet & Other Fin. Data (Million $)

	1994	1993	1992	1991	1990	1989
Cash	7.6	37.0	21.0	1.9	1.0	0.8
Curr. Assets	75.8	73.2	64.8	39.6	9.4	4.2
Total Assets	1.7	140	155	48.4	16.1	10.5
Curr. Liab.	56.1	21.7	44.7	4.8	5.8	2.7
LT Debt	15.5	0.9	3.0	0.0	3.0	3.6
Common Eqty.	94.0	108	103	43.0	7.3	4.2
Total Cap.	118	110	110	43.7	10.3	7.7
Cap. Exp.	13.3	5.4	72.7	2.6	1.5	1.6
Cash Flow	4.5	20.6	17.3	4.7	4.5	2.6

Ratio Analysis

	1994	1993	1992	1991	1990	1989
Curr. Ratio	1.4	3.4	1.4	8.3	1.6	1.5
% LT Debt of Cap.	13.1	0.8	2.7	0.1	29.3	46.1
% Net Inc.of Revs.	NM	2.5	7.5	11.4	11.6	9.3
% Ret. on Assets	NM	2.9	7.8	11.1	25.3	19.3
% Ret. on Equity	NM	4.1	10.8	14.2	58.6	57.4

Dividend Data (No dividends have been paid. The company intends to retain earnings to finance the growth and development of its business and does not expect to pay cash dividends on its common stock in the foreseeable future.)

Data as orig. reptd.; bef. results of disc. opers. and/or spec. items. Per share data adj. for stk. divs. as of ex-div. date. E-Estimated. NA-Not Available. NM-Not Meaningful. NR-Not Ranked.

Office—115 Perimeter Center Place, Suite 911, Atlanta, GA 30346. **Tel**—(404) 481-1800. **Chrmn**—R. Burt. **Vice Chrmn**—J. Davey. **Acting CEO**—M. Spagnolo. **Exec VP, CFO & Investor Contact**—Richard M. Haddrill. **Dirs**—P. Becker, R. Burt, J. Davey, W. P. Lyons, M. Spagnolo, W. Spier. **Transfer Agent & Registrar**—Continental Stock Transfer & Trust Co., NYC. **Incorporated** in Delaware in 1991. **Empl**-900. **S&P Analyst:** Efraim Levy

STANDARD & POOR'S

STOCK REPORTS

Viewlogic Systems

NASDAQ Symbol **VIEW**

In S&P SmallCap 600

15-AUG-95

Industry:
Data Processing

Summary: This company develops, markets and supports a comprehensive family of software tools that aid engineers in the design of advanced electronic products.

Quantitative Evaluations

Outlook
(1 Lowest—5 Highest)
• **NA**

Fair Value
• **NA**

Risk
• **High**

Earn./Div. Rank
• **NR**

Technical Eval.
• **Bearish** since 7/95

Rel. Strength Rank
(1 Lowest—99 Highest)
• **35**

Insider Activity
• **NA**

Recent Price • 12¼
52 Wk Range • 24-7⅞
Yield • Nil
12-Mo. P/E • NM

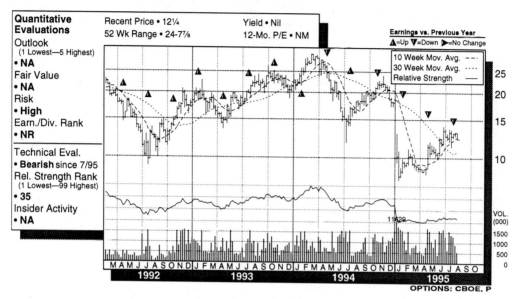

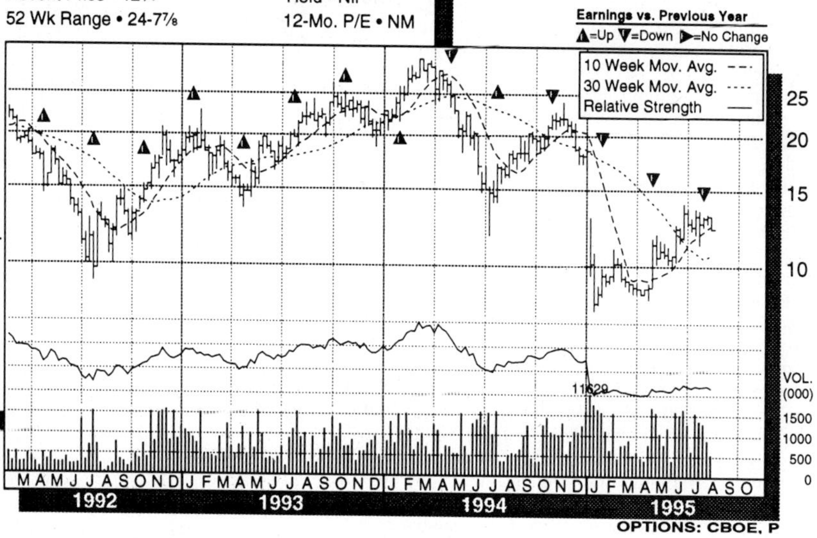

OPTIONS: CBOE, P

Business Profile - 14-AUG-95

After years of reporting mid-single digit growth rates, the EDA sector was able to top 10% in 1994. Industry growth should continue to rise as semiconductor makers demand innovative designs to meet end-user requirements and increased design complexities associated with ever-shrinking integrated circuit geometries. Success will depend on the ability of an EDA company to design open-system tools that will reduce customers' time-to-market.

Operational Review - 14-AUG-95

Revenues in the first half of 1995 were flat, year to year, lagging industry growth. The shortfall is related to a market shift, in late 1994, in design methodology from schematic-based to high-level language-based design, for which VIEW was not prepared. Future growth will be dependent on the success of new product introductions. VIEW's focus on meeting the needs of the PC/EDA designer could allow it to increase its market share in that fragmented sector.

Stock Performance - 11-AUG-95

In the past 30 trading days, VIEW's shares have declined 3%, compared to a 2% rise in the S&P 500. Average trading volume for the past five days was 104,920 shares, compared with the 40-day moving average of 285,272 shares.

Key Stock Statistics

Dividend Rate/Share	Nil	Shareholders	NA
Shs. outstg. (M)	16.7	Market cap. (B)	$0.202
Avg. daily vol. (M)	0.187	Inst. holdings	41%
Tang. Bk. Value/Share	4.24	Insider holdings	NA
Beta	NA		

Value of $10,000 invested 5 years ago: NA

Fiscal Year Ending Dec. 31

	1995	% Change	1994	% Change	1993	% Change
Revenues ()						
1Q	26.26	NM	26.03	35%	19.35	38%
2Q	29.07	NM	28.96	36%	21.36	39%
3Q	—	—	31.95	36%	23.51	40%
4Q	—	—	31.64	8%	29.25	49%
Yr.	—	—	118.6	27%	93.47	42%
Income ()						
1Q	0.32	-52%	0.66	-57%	1.55	29%
2Q	1.50	-62%	3.92	41%	2.79	42%
3Q	—	—	-10.99	NM	3.19	52%
4Q	—	—	0.10	-98%	4.93	148%
Yr.	—	—	-6.32	NM	12.45	72%
Earnings Per Share ()						
1Q	0.02	-50%	0.04	-60%	0.10	25%
2Q	0.09	-61%	0.23	28%	0.18	38%
3Q	—	—	-0.64	NM	0.20	43%
4Q	—	—	0.01	-97%	0.30	131%
Yr.	—	—	-0.36	NM	0.78	56%

Next earnings report expected: late October

Viewlogic Systems

Business Summary - 14-AUG-95

Viewlogic Systems, Inc. develops, markets and supports a comprehensive family of software tools that aid engineers in the design of advanced electronic products. VIEW's products automate the design entry, analysis and verification of integrated circuits (ICs), application-specific integrated circuits (ASICs), field programmable gate arrays (FPGAs), programmable logic devices (PLDs), printed circuit boards (PCBs) and entire electronic systems.

Revenues in recent years were derived as follows:

	1994	1993	1992	1991
Software	74%	77%	80%	78%
Services & other	26%	23%	20%	22%

Prior to 1992, the company's sole product was the Workview family of software products. In June 1992, Viewlogic introduced the Powerview product family, which the company believes to be the most open and flexible computer-aided engineering (CAE) solution available. In April 1993, VIEW introduced the WorkviewPLUS on Windows product line, a comprehensive suite of CAE tools for personal computers. In early 1993, the company announced the PRO Series, a family of products targeted at price sensitive designers.

VIEW's strategy is to provide customers with advanced software tools that enable them to minimize their time to market, differentiate their products and reduce overall costs while improving quality. The Workview family has an open architecture that enables users to integrate the company's software with other vendors' EDA tools, including back-end IC layout and PCB layout systems.

Viewlogic believes that its products operate on a broader range of computer platforms than those of any other major EDA vendor. Workview Series I products are designed for use with the DOS operating system on IBM and IBM-compatible computers. Workview Series II products are designed for use with the UNIX operating system on workstation and server systems from Sun, Hewlett-Packard, IBM and Digital and offer an advanced suite of CAE solutions in a high-performance, multi-tasking environment.

Important Developments

Mar. '95—VIEW made a strategic technology investment in Eagle Design Automation Inc., whose products are used to reduce design time and developemnt costs, and improve the quality of embedded systems design through innovative software tools linking hardware and software development. In addition to a minority investment, other components of the relationaship include technology sharing as well as cooperative product development and distribution.

Capitalization

Long Term Debt: $79,000 of lease obligs. (6/95).

Per Share Data () (Year Ended Dec. 31)

	1994	1993	1992	1991	1990	1989
Tangible Bk. Val.	4.24	4.52	3.55	3.03	2.92	NA
Cash Flow	-0.13	0.95	0.65	0.37	0.22	0.12
Earnings	-0.36	0.78	0.50	0.27	0.14	0.05
Dividends	Nil	Nil	Nil	Nil	Nil	Nil
Payout Ratio	Nil	Nil	Nil	Nil	Nil	Nil
Prices - High	30	26½	25¼	20⅜	NA	NA
- Low	11¾	13½	9⅛	13	NA	NA
P/E Ratio - High	NM	34	51	75	NA	NA
- Low	NM	17	18	48	NA	NA

Income Statement Analysis ()

	1994	%Chg	1993	%Chg	1992	%Chg	1991
Revs.	119	27%	93.5	42%	65.8	56%	42.1
Oper. Inc.	19.6	-4%	20.5	56%	13.1	129%	5.7
Depr.	4.0	43%	2.8	23%	2.3	97%	1.2
Int. Exp.	0.1	-17%	0.1	-40%	0.2	—	Nil
Pretax Inc.	-1.4	NM	18.1	81%	10.0	107%	4.8
Eff. Tax Rate	NM	—	31%	—	28%	—	40%
Net Inc.	-6.3	NM	12.4	71%	7.3	149%	2.9

Balance Sheet & Other Fin. Data ()

	1994	1993	1992	1991	1990	1989
Cash	54.2	44.1	36.3	28.7	7.5	2.8
Curr. Assets	92.0	77.5	59.3	44.6	19.3	10.1
Total Assets	116	93.2	69.5	51.4	23.7	13.4
Curr. Liab.	39.7	22.0	16.7	10.5	8.5	5.4
LT Debt	0.1	0.3	0.5	Nil	Nil	0.3
Common Eqty.	72.4	69.3	50.3	38.7	13.7	6.6
Total Cap.	76.5	71.2	52.6	40.7	15.0	8.1
Cap. Exp.	5.0	5.6	3.2	2.4	1.6	0.5
Cash Flow	-2.3	15.3	9.5	4.1	2.4	1.1

Ratio Analysis

	1994	1993	1992	1991	1990	1989
Curr. Ratio	2.3	3.5	3.5	4.2	2.3	1.9
% LT Debt of Cap.	0.2	0.4	0.9	Nil	Nil	3.5
% Net Inc.of Revs.	NM	13.3	11.0	6.9	4.7	2.4
% Ret. on Assets	NM	14.8	11.1	7.8	7.6	3.4
% Ret. on Equity	NM	20.1	15.1	11.1	13.9	6.5

Dividend Data —No cash dividends have been paid on the common stock. The company intends to retain earnings to finance growth.

Data as orig. reptd.; bef. results of disc. opers. and/or spec. items. Per share data adj. for stk. divs. as of ex-div. date. E-Estimated. NA-Not Available. NM-Not Meaningful. NR-Not Ranked.

Office—293 Boston Post Road West, Marlboro, MA 01752-4615. **Tel**—(508) 480-0881. **Chrmn, Pres & CEO**—A. J. Hanover. **SVP-Fin, CFO, Treas & Investor Contact**—Ronald R. Benanto. **Dirs**—S. F. Alfeld, D. A. Boucher, G. T. George, A. J. Hanover, W. J. Herman, G. B. Hoffman, L. E. Reeder. **Transfer Agent & Registrar**—State Street Bank & Trust Co. **Reincorporated** in Delaware in 1988. **Empl**-568. **S&P Analyst:** Steven A. Jaworski

STANDARD & POOR'S

STOCK REPORTS

Vintage Petroleum

NYSE Symbol **VPI**
In S&P SmallCap 600

13-OCT-95

Industry:
Oil and Gas

Summary: This independent oil and gas company focuses on the acquisition of producing oil and gas properties that contain potential for increased value through exploitation and development.

Quantitative Evaluations

Outlook
(1 Lowest—5 Highest)
• **NA**

Fair Value
• **NA**

Risk
• **Average**

Earn./Div. Rank
• **NR**

Technical Eval.
• **Bullish** since 8/95

Rel. Strength Rank
(1 Lowest—99 Highest)
• **37**

Insider Activity
• **Neutral**

Recent Price • 20⅛
52 Wk Range • 21¾-14¾

Yield • 0.5%
12-Mo. P/E • 34.1

Earnings vs. Previous Year
▲=Up ▼=Down ▶=No Change

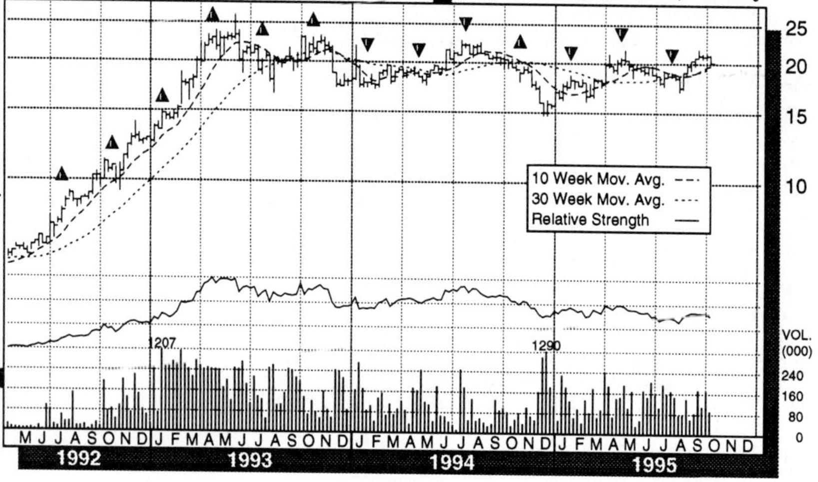

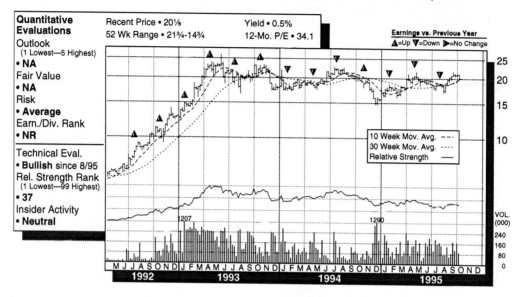

Business Profile - 13-OCT-95

California storms and associated mudslides, which reduced oil and gas production, and a sharp drop in gas prices and higher interest costs, penalized first half 1995 earnings. VPI expects recently acquired Argentina properties to have a strong impact on 1996 production, with more modest increases in 1995's second half. Through October 1995, Vintage had acquired 40.7 million barrels of oil and 39.8 Bcf of gas for $116 million. VPI has registered a planned offering of $125 million of notes.

Operational Review - 13-OCT-95

Revenues for the first half of 1995 declined 7.0%, year to year, mainly reflecting a 35% decline in oil and gas gathering revenues and 38% lower gas marketing revenues. Profitability was hurt by a 25% decrease in average gas prices and 43% higher interest expenses. After taxes at 39.0% in both periods, net income fell 24%. Earnings declined to $0.23 a share from $0.30 in the year-earlier period.

Stock Performance - 06-OCT-95

In the past 30 trading days, VPI's shares have increased 2%, compared to a 4% rise in the S&P 500. Average trading volume for the past five days was 18,180 shares, compared with the 40-day moving average of 22,782 shares.

Key Stock Statistics

Dividend Rate/Share	0.10	Shareholders	100
Shs. outstg. (M)	20.9	Market cap. (B)	$0.407
Avg. daily vol. (M)	0.022	Inst. holdings	38%
Tang. Bk. Value/Share	7.87	Insider holdings	NA
Beta	1.02		

Value of $10,000 invested 5 years ago: NA

Fiscal Year Ending Dec. 31

	1995	% Change	1994	% Change	1993	% Change
Revenues (Million $)						
1Q	41.04	-8%	44.64	20%	37.10	103%
2Q	45.23	-6%	48.09	23%	39.06	91%
3Q	—	—	48.25	20%	40.15	40%
4Q	—	—	44.68	2%	43.71	28%
Yr.	—	—	185.6	16%	160.0	58%
Income (Million $)						
1Q	1.61	-35%	2.47	-40%	4.13	NM
2Q	3.24	-18%	3.94	-23%	5.11	NM
3Q	—	—	4.40	17%	3.75	50%
4Q	—	—	3.12	-18%	3.81	-5%
Yr.	—	—	13.93	-17%	16.79	94%
Earnings Per Share ($)						
1Q	0.08	-33%	0.12	-43%	0.21	NM
2Q	0.15	-21%	0.19	-21%	0.24	140%
3Q	—	—	0.21	17%	0.18	20%
4Q	—	—	0.15	-17%	0.18	-22%
Yr.	—	—	0.66	-19%	0.81	59%

Next earnings report expected: early November

Vintage Petroleum

Business Summary - 13-OCT-95

Vintage Petroleum, Inc. is an independent oil and gas company focused on the acquisition of producing oil and gas properties that contain the potential for increased value through exploitation and development. The company also engages in the purchase, gathering and marketing of natural gas and crude oil and the exploration and development of nonproducing properties. Contributions in 1994 were:

	Revs.	Profits
Exploration & production	63%	87%
Gas marketing	28%	5%
Gathering	8%	3%
Other	1%	5%

In the three years through 1994, VPI acquired 84.5 million barrels of oil equivalent (BOE) of crude oil and natural gas reserves for $261 million. The average acquisition cost was $3.08 per BOE.

At December 31, 1994, estimated proved reserves aggregated 281.6 Bcf of natural gas (78% developed) and 70,789,000 bbl. of oil, condensate and natural gas liquids (78%), compared with 273.1 Bcf of gas (83% developed) and 63,277,000 bbl. of liquids (81%) at December 31, 1993.

Interests were held in 1,758 gross (1,294 net) productive oil wells and 962 gross (286 net) productive gas wells at December 31, 1994. Production in 1994 totaled 28,884,000 Mcf of gas and 6,657,000 bbl. of oil, compared with 22,504,000 Mcf and 4,785,000 bbl. in 1993. Average sales prices were $1.78 per Mcf and $13.53 per bbl. in 1994, versus $2.03 per Mcf and $14.14 per bbl. in 1993.

VPI also owns 100% interests in two crude oil and gas gathering systems in Oklahoma and Texas and a 100% interest in 24 gas gathering systems in Kansas, Texas and Oklahoma. The systems consist of about 275 miles with a combined capacity exceeding 165,000 Mcf per day.

Texaco Trading and Transportation, Inc. was the company's most significant customer in 1994, accounting for about 14% of total revenues.

Important Developments

Oct. '95—VPI acquired 50% working interests in three producing concessions in Argentina from BG Overseas Holding Ltd., an affiliate of British Gas PLC, for $37 million. Total current net daily production from the BG interest is about 2,000 barrels of mid-gravity oil. Separately, VPI agreed to acquire an additional 22.8% stake in Cadipsa, S.A., an Argentine oil and exploration firm, for about $6.6 million; completion of the acquisition would raise its interest in Cadipsa to over 70%.

Capitalization

Long Term Debt: $183,000,000 (3/95).

Per Share Data ($)

(Year Ended Dec. 31)

	1994	1993	1992	1991	1990	1989
Tangible Bk. Val.	7.74	7.12	4.80	4.30	3.90	NA
Cash Flow	2.82	2.40	1.54	1.17	1.13	1.00
Earnings	0.66	0.81	0.51	0.41	0.45	0.37
Dividends	0.07	0.05	0.02	Nil	Nil	Nil
Payout Ratio	11%	6%	4%	Nil	Nil	Nil
Prices - High	22¾	26⅛	14	9⅛	10¾	NA
- Low	14¾	12¼	5⅝	5½	7	NA
P/E Ratio - High	34	32	27	22	24	NA
- Low	22	15	11	13	16	NA

Income Statement Analysis (Million $)

	1994	%Chg	1993	%Chg	1992	%Chg	1991
Revs.	183	17%	157	57%	100	43%	69.9
Oper. Inc.	77.8	18%	65.8	91%	34.5	44%	24.0
Depr. Depl. & Amort.	45.8	38%	33.2	91%	17.4	36%	12.8
Int. Exp.	12.0	74%	6.9	53%	4.5	6%	4.2
Pretax Inc.	22.4	-21%	28.5	108%	13.7	26%	10.9
Eff. Tax Rate	38%	—	41%	—	37%	—	38%
Net Inc.	13.9	-17%	16.8	94%	8.6	27%	6.8

Balance Sheet & Other Fin. Data (Million $)

	1994	1993	1992	1991	1990	1989
Cash	0.4	0.6	0.6	0.3	0.5	0.8
Curr. Assets	39.3	36.6	27.1	16.4	13.6	14.8
Total Assets	408	384	260	144	123	121
Curr. Liab.	34.0	42.6	34.2	23.3	20.4	24.9
LT Debt	187	174	128	36.6	27.6	28.0
Common Eqty.	156	143	78.7	69.8	62.9	57.4
Total Cap.	374	342	226	121	103	96.0
Cap. Exp.	67.0	151	120	32.3	27.6	NA
Cash Flow	59.7	49.9	26.0	19.6	16.9	17.1

Ratio Analysis

	1994	1993	1992	1991	1990	1989
Curr. Ratio	1.2	0.9	0.8	0.7	0.7	0.6
% LT Debt of Cap.	49.9	51.0	56.7	30.3	26.9	29.1
% Ret. on Assets	3.5	4.8	4.3	5.1	4.7	NA
% Ret. on Equity	9.3	14.0	11.6	10.2	16.3	NA

Dividend Data —Dividends were initiated in 1992.

Amt. of Div. $	Date Decl.	Ex-Div. Date	Stock of Record	Payment Date
0.020	Dec. 09	Dec. 14	Dec. 20	Jan. 03 '95
0.020	Mar. 16	Mar. 21	Mar. 27	Apr. 04 '95
0.020	May. 10	Jun. 09	Jun. 13	Jul. 05 '95
0.025	Sep. 12	Sep. 20	Sep. 22	Oct. 04 '95

Data as orig. reptd.; bef. results of disc opers. and/or spec. items. Per share data adj. for stk. divs. as of ex-div. date. E-Estimated. NA-Not Available. NM-Not Meaningful. NR-Not Ranked.

Office—4200 One Williams Center, Tulsa, OK 74172. **Tel**—(918) 592-0101. **Fax**—(918) 584-7282. **Chrmn**—C. C. Stephenson Jr. **Pres & COO**—C. S. George. **Vice-Chrmn & CEO**—J. B. Hille. **EVP-CFO, Secy, Treas & Investor Contact**—William C. Barnes. **Dirs**—W. C. Barnes, S. C. George, J. B. Hille, B. H. Lawrence, J. T. McNabb II, C. C. Stephenson Jr. **Transfer Agent & Registrar**—Mellon Securities Trust Co., Ridgefield Park, N.J. **Incorporated** in Delaware in 1983. **Empl**-284. **S&P Analyst:** JJS

STANDARD & POOR'S

STOCK REPORTS

Vivra Inc.

NYSE Symbol **V**
In S&P SmallCap 600

18-SEP-95

Industry: Health Care Centers

Summary: This company operates dialysis facilities and ambulatory surgical centers. It also provides pharmacy services and diabetes management services.

Quantitative Evaluations

Outlook (1 Lowest—5 Highest)
• **5-**

Fair Value
• **40¼**

Risk
• **Average**

Earn./Div. Rank
• **NR**

Technical Eval.
• **Neutral** since 9/95

Rel. Strength Rank (1 Lowest—99 Highest)
• **58**

Insider Activity
• **Neutral**

Recent Price • 32¾
52 Wk Range • 35⅞-26

Yield • Nil
12-Mo. P/E • 20.9

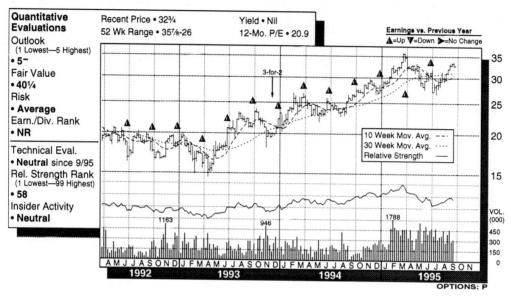

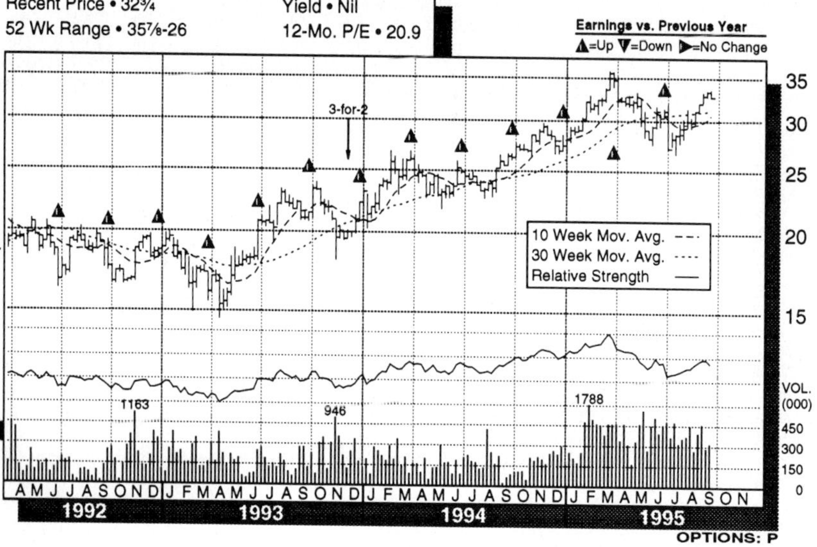

OPTIONS: P

Business Profile - 12-SEP-95

Recent revenue and earnings gains have primarily reflected continued growth in the dialysis business. Vivra plans to continue to supplement internal growth with acquisitions and development of new facilities. Additionally, the company is aggressively expanding its diabetes management and asthma and allergy services. The company believes that strong growth will continue as it delivers a high level of service, while providing savings to payors.

Operational Review - 18-SEP-95

Operating revenues soared in recent periods, reflecting continued growth of the dialysis and rehabilitation therapy businesses. A gain of $2.2 million on the disposition of certain surgery centers was offset by a charge of $2.2 million for non-recurring items. Net income, however, benefitted from a lower effective tax rate, but EPS growth was limited by a greater number of shares outstanding.

Stock Performance - 15-SEP-95

In the past 30 trading days, V's shares have increased 9%, compared to a 4% rise in the S&P 500. Average trading volume for the past five days was 62,740 shares, compared with the 40-day moving average of 74,777 shares.

Key Stock Statistics

Dividend Rate/Share	Nil	Shareholders	3,100
Shs. outstg. (M)	23.9	Market cap. (B)	$0.784
Avg. daily vol. (M)	0.078	Inst. holdings	78%
Tang. Bk. Value/Share	7.50	Insider holdings	NA
Beta	1.25		

Value of $10,000 invested 5 years ago: $ 41,513

Fiscal Year Ending Nov. 30

	1995	% Change	1994	% Change	1993	% Change
Revenues (Million $)						
1Q	83.88	32%	63.50	30%	48.69	23%
2Q	92.06	32%	69.60	33%	52.38	26%
3Q	—	—	74.39	33%	56.12	15%
4Q	—	—	78.23	31%	59.58	17%
Yr.	—	—	286.5	31%	218.0	21%
Income (Million $)						
1Q	8.47	24%	6.84	29%	5.29	19%
2Q	9.92	34%	7.40	26%	5.86	23%
3Q	—	—	7.68	21%	6.36	31%
4Q	—	—	7.82	24%	6.33	25%
Yr.	—	—	29.74	25%	23.84	25%
Earnings Per Share ($)						
1Q	0.40	18%	0.34	21%	0.28	20%
2Q	0.42	17%	0.36	20%	0.30	25%
3Q	—	—	0.37	23%	0.30	22%
4Q	—	—	0.38	23%	0.31	19%
Yr.	—	—	1.45	22%	1.19	21%

Next earnings report expected: late September

Vivra Inc.

Business Summary - 18-SEP-95

Vivra Inc. was formed in 1989 as a spinoff from Community Psychiatric Centers to assume that company's dialysis and home health care businesses. It currently operates principally in two business segments: chronic services, under which it owns and operates hemodialysis centers for persons with chronic kidney disease, provides dialysis patients with pharmacy services, and provides diabetes management services for hospital patients; and other services, which consist of the ownership and operation of ambulatory surgery centers. Home nursing services operations were sold in December 1993. Contributions (profits in 000s) by segment in fiscal 1994 were:

	Revs.	Profits
Chronic services	90%	$54,616
Other services	10%	-$790

Vivra provides dialysis services for chronic end-stage renal disease patients primarily in its outpatient dialysis facilities. The company also provides services for inpatients with acute kidney disorders at hospitals near its outpatient facilities and participates in the instruction process to facilitate the implementation of home dialysis. As of July 1995, Vivra operated 180 dialysis facilities, compared with 150 centers as of December 1994. About 66% of fiscal 1994 dialysis revenues came from Medicare and Medicaid.

Through Associated Health Services, the company operates two pharmacies,in Southern California and Atlanta, providing intradialytic parenteral nutrition pharmacy and support services to dialysis patients. In 1993, Vivra began mail order delivery of oral medications for dialysis and transplant patients from its Southern California pharmacy. Through Health Advantage Inc., the company provides diabetes management services to general hospitals.

In November 1994, Vivra acquired AllergyClinics of America Inc., a provider of outpatient asthma and allergy care with long-term contracts to manage 17 allergy practices in 11 states and the District of Columbia.

Surgical Partners of America was established by the company in February 1992 to acquire, develop and operate ambulatory surgical centers. As of November 1994, Vivra operated five centers. In April 1994, the company established Vivra Physician Services to acquire and manage primary care physician practices.

Important Developments

Jul. '95—Vivra sold its South Coast Rehabilitation Services subsidiary, a contract manager of speech, occupational and physical therapies, to Regency Health Services. Vivra will realize a gain on the transaction.

Capitalization

Long Term Debt: $1,770,000 (5/95).
Minority Interest: $953,000.

Per Share Data ($) (Year Ended Nov. 30)

	1994	1993	1992	1991	1990	1989
Tangible Bk. Val.	7.50	6.73	5.85	5.90	3.72	3.25
Cash Flow	1.91	1.55	1.24	1.04	0.86	0.63
Earnings	1.45	1.19	0.98	0.82	0.65	0.45
Dividends	Nil	Nil	Nil	Nil	Nil	Nil
Payout Ratio	Nil	Nil	Nil	Nil	Nil	Nil
Prices - High	29¾	23⅞	25½	22⅛	12	9⅜
- Low	20¼	14⅝	16¼	10¼	6¾	6¾
P/E Ratio - High	21	20	26	27	19	21
- Low	14	12	17	13	11	15

Income Statement Analysis (Million $)

	1994	%Chg	1993	%Chg	1992	%Chg	1991
Revs.	285	31%	217	20%	181	30%	139
Oper. Inc.	58.6	22%	48.0	30%	36.9	30%	28.3
Depr.	9.6	33%	7.2	42%	5.1	26%	4.0
Int. Exp.	0.5	-43%	0.9	5%	0.9	24%	0.7
Pretax Inc.	50.4	23%	41.1	27%	32.4	29%	25.1
Eff. Tax Rate	41%	—	42%	—	41%	—	40%
Net Inc.	29.7	25%	23.8	25%	19.1	27%	15.0

Balance Sheet & Other Fin. Data (Million $)

	1994	1993	1992	1991	1990	1989
Cash	79.5	52.5	39.9	42.4	1.5	4.6
Curr. Assets	149	113	89.9	88.2	40.1	37.3
Total Assets	276	207	170	141	87.0	72.0
Curr. Liab.	51.6	25.1	17.8	12.4	9.5	6.9
LT Debt	4.9	4.2	7.5	7.2	7.2	5.8
Common Eqty.	212	172	141	118	68.0	58.0
Total Cap.	224	182	152	128	77.0	65.0
Cap. Exp.	20.5	12.1	9.4	8.8	11.8	9.5
Cash Flow	39.3	31.0	24.2	19.1	13.6	10.0

Ratio Analysis

	1994	1993	1992	1991	1990	1989
Curr. Ratio	2.9	4.5	5.0	7.1	4.2	5.4
% LT Debt of Cap.	2.2	2.3	4.9	5.6	9.4	8.9
% Net Inc.of Revs.	10.4	11.0	10.6	10.8	8.8	7.5
% Ret. on Assets	12.1	12.3	12.1	12.4	12.8	NA
% Ret. on Equity	15.2	14.9	14.6	15.2	16.1	NA

Dividend Data —A three-for-two stock split was effected in November 1993.

Data as orig. reptd.; bef. results of disc. opers. and/or spec. items. Per share data adj. for stk. divs. as of ex-div. date. E-Estimated. NA-Not Available. NM-Not Meaningful. NR-Not Ranked.

Office—400 Primrose, Suite 200, Burlingame, CA 94010. **Tel**—(415) 348-8200. **Pres & CEO**—K. J. Thiry. **VP-Fin, Secy & Treas**—LeAnne M. Zumwalt. **Dirs**—D. G. Conner, R. B. Fontaine, J. M. Nehra, S. G. Pagliuca, K. J. Thiry, L. M. Zumwalt. **Transfer Agent & Registrar**—First National Bank of Boston. **Incorporated** in Delaware in 1989. **Empl**-3,490. **S&P Analyst:** Philip J. Birbara

STANDARD & POOR'S

STOCK REPORTS

WD-40 Company

NASDAQ Symbol **WDFC**

In S&P SmallCap 600

05-SEP-95 **Industry:** Chemicals

Summary: This company makes a single product, WD-40, which has multiple uses as a lubricant, rust preventative, penetrant and moisture displacer.

Quantitative Evaluations

Outlook
(1 Lowest—5 Highest)
• **NA**

Fair Value
• **NA**

Risk
• **Low**

Earn./Div. Rank
• **B+**

Technical Eval.
• **Bullish** since 8/95

Rel. Strength Rank
(1 Lowest—99 Highest)
• **21**

Insider Activity
• **NA**

Recent Price • 42¼
52 Wk Range • 45½-38¾
Yield • 5.9%
12-Mo. P/E • 15.5

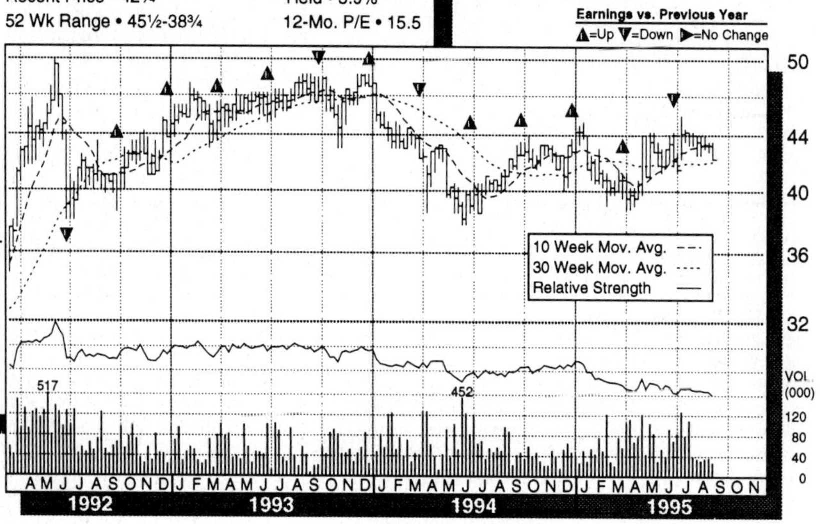

Business Profile - 05-SEP-95

Bearing the name of its sole product, WDFC markets WD-40 through chain stores, hardware and sporting goods stores, automotive parts outlets and industrial distributors and suppliers. Wal-Mart accounted for 11% of fiscal 1994 sales. An earnings uptrend was interrupted in fiscal 1994's second quarter by a $12.6 million charge for legal expenses. Margin pressures have weakened recent results.

Operational Review - 05-SEP-95

Revenues in the first nine months of fiscal 1995 increased 3.7%, year to year, as declines in the U.S., Mexico, and Canada were outweighed by gains in Europe, Latin America, and the Pacific Rim. Despite higher interest expense and in the absence of $12.6 million in legal expenses resulting from an adverse judgment, earnings doubled to $2.08 a share. Excluding the effect of the legal expense, margins narrowed and operating income declined 0.6%.

Stock Performance - 01-SEP-95

In the past 30 trading days, WDFC's shares have declined 4%, compared to a 2% rise in the S&P 500. Average trading volume for the past five days was 5,260 shares, compared with the 40-day moving average of 9,550 shares.

Key Stock Statistics

Dividend Rate/Share	2.48	Shareholders	2,500
Shs. outstg. (M)	7.7	Market cap. (B)	$0.325
Avg. daily vol. (M)	0.006	Inst. holdings	36%
Tang. Bk. Value/Share	5.78	Insider holdings	NA
Beta	0.40		

Value of $10,000 invested 5 years ago: $ 17,826

Fiscal Year Ending Aug. 31

	1995	% Change	1994	% Change	1993	% Change
Revenues (Million $)						
1Q	29.77	3%	28.88	17%	24.60	12%
2Q	29.39	7%	27.56	-6%	29.37	5%
3Q	29.92	2%	29.46	NM	29.31	36%
4Q	—	—	26.27	2%	25.70	-10%
Yr.	—	—	112.2	3%	109.0	9%
Income (Million $)						
1Q	5.52	6%	5.21	6%	4.92	39%
2Q	5.61	NM	-2.71	NM	6.30	13%
3Q	4.90	-7%	5.27	48%	3.55	4%
4Q	—	—	4.91	7%	4.58	-18%
Yr.	—	—	12.68	-34%	19.33	7%
Earnings Per Share ($)						
1Q	0.72	6%	0.68	6%	0.64	36%
2Q	0.73	NM	-0.35	NM	0.82	12%
3Q	0.63	-7%	0.68	48%	0.46	2%
4Q	—	—	0.64	7%	0.60	-18%
Yr.	—	—	1.65	-35%	2.52	6%

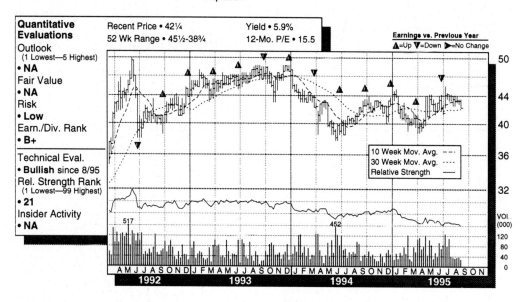

Next earnings report expected: mid December

WD-40 Company

Business Summary - 05-SEP-95

WD-40 Company manufactures and markets a petroleum-based product known as WD-40. Acting as a lubricant, rust preventative, penetrant and moisture displacer, the product has a variety of uses in the home, in protection of sporting goods, marine and automotive equipment and in industrial applications.

WD-40 concentrate for North America is formulated at the company's plant in San Diego, and shipped by rail car or tank wagon to contract packagers in Los Angeles, Georgia, Massachusetts, Texas, Wisconsin and Toronto. Independent subcontractors package WD-40 to specification and, on order from the company, ship the product to customers in their respective areas via common carrier. This system reduces capital requirements by eliminating the need for investment in packaging equipment and finished-product warehousing and limits WD-40's employment needs.

Sold in over 115 countries, WD-40 satisfies a diverse group of end users. In fiscal 1994, North American sales accounted for 74% of net sales (75% in fiscal 1993) and 76% of operating profits (79%). The U.K. subsidiary is responsible for developing business in Europe, the Middle East and Africa. There is an Australian subsidiary that is responsible for marketing WD-40 in Australia and New Zealand, and a Canadian unit that operates in Canada. The San Diego facility oversees providing distributors and licensees in Mexico, the Caribbean, Central America, South America and the Pacific Rim (excluding Australia and New Zealand) with finished product and concentrate.

WD-40 believes that the success of its product in the U.S. has created many imitators. However, the company also believes that end-user brand loyalty has resulted in its withstanding such intrusions. Its product is marketed through chain stores, hardware and sporting goods stores, automotive parts outlets and industrial distributors and suppliers. A direct sales force replaced commissioned sales representatives during 1988. Although there is strong competition from many products similar to WD-40, none is believed to have gained a significant market share.

In fiscal 1994, sales to Wal-Mart Stores, Inc. and Sam's Club amounted to $12,027,000 (10.7% of net sales). With the ongoing consolidation in the marketplace, many of the major retailers are aggressively pursuing additional trade allowances. The company believes that these demands could produce a long-term negative impact on both sales and profits.

Important Developments

Jun. '95—WD-40 said its 9.3% decline in third quarter operating income (on a 1.6% increase in sales) reflected higher packaging costs and increased advertising and promotion expenses.

Capitalization

Long Term Debt: $3,176,000 (5/95).

Per Share Data ($) (Year Ended Aug. 31)

	1994	1993	1992	1991	1990	1989
Tangible Bk. Val.	5.47	5.96	5.91	5.38	5.16	5.01
Cash Flow	1.76	2.60	2.45	2.09	2.11	2.15
Earnings	1.65	2.52	2.38	2.02	2.05	2.08
Dividends	2.30	2.30	2.16	1.72	2.02	1.90
Payout Ratio	139%	91%	91%	85%	99%	91%
Prices - High	48	48¾	50	34	34½	38¼
- Low	37¾	43	30¼	23¾	23½	30½
P/E Ratio - High	29	19	21	17	17	18
- Low	23	17	13	12	11	15

Income Statement Analysis (Million $)

	1994	%Chg	1993	%Chg	1992	%Chg	1991
Revs.	112	3%	109	9%	100	11%	89.8
Oper. Inc.	33.2	-1%	33.6	17%	28.8	19%	24.2
Depr.	0.8	53%	0.6	NM	0.6	17%	0.5
Int. Exp.	NA	—	Nil	—	Nil	—	Nil
Pretax Inc.	20.5	-35%	31.7	7%	29.5	18%	25.1
Eff. Tax Rate	38%	—	39%	—	39%	—	39%
Net Inc.	12.7	-34%	19.3	7%	18.1	18%	15.3

Balance Sheet & Other Fin. Data (Million $)

	1994	1993	1992	1991	1990	1989
Cash	22.7	21.9	19.1	24.9	21.6	22.4
Curr. Assets	45.5	43.2	41.4	43.9	43.2	41.1
Total Assets	54.9	58.8	53.5	47.8	46.8	44.6
Curr. Liab.	8.2	9.7	8.2	6.9	7.6	6.7
LT Debt	3.8	2.7	Nil	Nil	Nil	Nil
Common Eqty.	42.1	45.7	45.2	40.7	39.0	37.8
Total Cap.	45.9	48.3	45.3	40.8	39.2	38.0
Cap. Exp.	0.8	1.4	0.7	1.1	0.4	1.4
Cash Flow	13.5	19.9	18.6	15.8	16.0	16.2

Ratio Analysis

	1994	1993	1992	1991	1990	1989
Curr. Ratio	5.6	4.4	5.1	6.3	5.7	6.1
% LT Debt of Cap.	8.3	5.5	Nil	Nil	Nil	Nil
% Net Inc.of Revs.	11.3	17.7	18.1	17.0	17.0	18.8
% Ret. on Assets	22.3	34.4	35.5	32.4	33.9	35.8
% Ret. on Equity	28.9	42.5	41.8	38.4	40.4	42.4

Dividend Data —Cash has been paid in each year since 1962, with payments on the publicly held shares commencing in 1973.

Amt. of Div. $	Date Decl.	Ex-Div. Date	Stock of Record	Payment Date
0.600	Sep. 26	Oct. 04	Oct. 11	Oct. 28 '94
0.600	Dec. 12	Jan. 04	Jan. 10	Jan. 30 '95
0.600	Apr. 03	Apr. 05	Apr. 10	Apr. 28 '95
0.620	Jun. 27	Jul. 06	Jul. 10	Jul. 28 '95

Data as orig. reptd.; bef. results of disc. opers. and/or spec. items. Per share data adj. for stk. divs. as of ex-div. date. E-Estimated. NA-Not Available. NM-Not Meaningful. NR-Not Ranked.

Office—1061 Cudahy Place, San Diego, CA 92110. **Tel**—(619) 275-1400. **Fax**—(619) 275-5823. **Chrmn**—J. S. Barry. **Pres, CEO & Investor Contact**—Gerald C. Schleif. **Secy**—H. F. Harmsen. **Treas**—R. D. Gal. **Dirs**—J. S. Barry, S. Crivello, D. W. Derbes, H. F. Harmsen, J. L. Heckel, M. L. Roulette, G. C. Schleif, C. F. Sehnert, E. J. Walsh. **Transfer Agent & Registrar**—Harris Trust Co. of California, Los Angeles. **Incorporated** in California in 1953. **Empl**-144. **S&P Analyst:** Justin McCann

STANDARD & POOR'S

STOCK REPORTS

WHX Corp.

NYSE Symbol **WHX**
In S&P SmallCap 600

10-OCT-95 **Industry:** Steel-Iron

Summary: This company (formerly Wheeling-Pittsburgh Corp.) is a major producer of flat rolled and fabricated steel products.

Quantitative Evaluations
Outlook (1 Lowest—5 Highest)
• **NA**
Fair Value
• **NA**
Risk
• **Average**
Earn./Div. Rank
• **NR**

Technical Eval.
• **Bullish** since 5/95
Rel. Strength Rank (1 Lowest—99 Highest)
• **13**
Insider Activity
• **NA**

Recent Price • 10¾
52 Wk Range • 16⅞-9⅝
Yield • Nil
12-Mo. P/E • 4.8

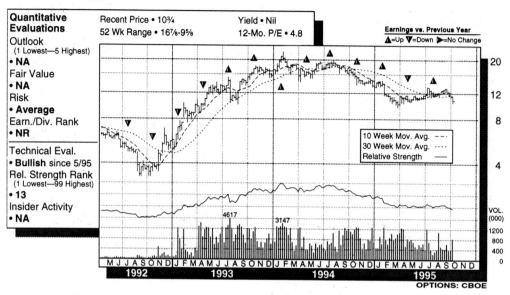

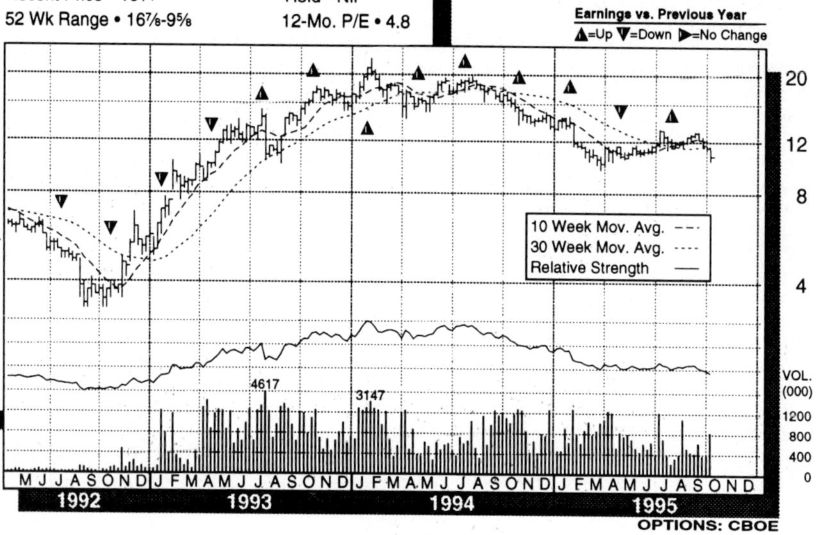

OPTIONS: CBOE

Business Profile - 10-OCT-95

This company (formerly Wheeling-Pittsburgh Corp.) is a major producer of flat rolled and fabricated steel products for the auto, appliance, construction, container markets. WHX expects its product mix to shift to higher value-added products. Profitability was restored in 1993, on increased shipments, bolstered by greater sales and higher prices. Near-term operating earnings are expected to improve, reflecting current pricing levels, acquisitions, and the resumption of normal production.

Operational Review - 10-OCT-95

Sales in the six months ended June 30, 1995, rose 25%, year to year, reflecting higher steel prices and shipment volume, and the acquisition of Unimast, Inc. However, results were hurt by higher raw materials costs. In the absence of a gain from a legal settlement, pretax income fell 15%. After taxes at 22.0%, versus 26.0%, net income declined 10%, to $44.3 million ($1.23 a share) from $49.3 million ($1.54). Prior year results exclude a charge of $0.35 for the effect of an accounting change.

Stock Performance - 06-OCT-95

In the past 30 trading days, WHX's shares have declined 14%, compared to a 4% rise in the S&P 500. Average trading volume for the past five days was 164,720 shares, compared with the 40-day moving average of 118,005 shares.

Key Stock Statistics

Dividend Rate/Share	Nil	Shareholders	10,900
Shs. outstg. (M)	25.8	Market cap. (B)	$0.271
Avg. daily vol. (M)	0.108	Inst. holdings	42%
Tang. Bk. Value/Share	24.91	Insider holdings	NA
Beta	1.79		

Value of $10,000 invested 5 years ago: $ 9,662

Fiscal Year Ending Dec. 31

	1995	% Change	1994	% Change	1993	% Change
Revenues (Million $)						
1Q	324.2	28%	253.8	8%	235.7	-3%
2Q	366.3	22%	300.4	12%	269.0	14%
3Q	—	—	309.8	15%	269.3	14%
4Q	—	—	329.8	21%	272.7	26%
Yr.	—	—	1,194	14%	1,047	13%
Income (Million $)						
1Q	22.83	-37%	36.47	NM	-2.80	NM
2Q	21.52	67%	12.86	40%	9.19	NM
3Q	—	—	18.72	78%	10.54	NM
4Q	—	—	18.32	34%	13.72	NM
Yr.	—	—	86.37	181%	30.72	NM
Earnings Per Share ($)						
1Q	0.61	-48%	1.18	NM	-0.15	—
2Q	0.60	67%	0.36	3%	0.35	NM
3Q	—	—	0.55	83%	0.30	NM
4Q	—	—	0.44	10%	0.40	NM
Yr.	—	—	2.54	149%	1.02	NM

Next earnings report expected: mid October

Business Summary - 10-OCT-95

WHX Corp. (formerly Wheeling-Pittsburgh Corp.), a major U.S. integrated steelmaker, produces flat rolled and fabricated steel products. It emerged from nearly six years of bankruptcy proceedings in January 1991.

Flat rolled products consist of a variety of sheet products, including hot rolled, cold rolled, galvanized and prepainted, and tin mill products. Products are sold to the automotive, appliance, construction, container, converter/processor, and steel service center markets. WHX holds a 36% interest in Wheeling-Nisshin, Inc., a maker of galvanized and aluminized products.

The Wheeling Corrugating division is a leading fabricator of roll formed construction products. Fabricated steel products including roof deck, form deck, and composite deck are sold to the non-residential building market; culvert products are used in highway construction; products sold to the agricultural industry are used for roofing and siding; other products include cut nails used for general construction.

Production in 1994 totaled 2,270,000 net tons of raw steel, and shipments came to 2,400,000 net tons. The company expects its product mix to shift toward increased marketing of higher value-added products during the 1990s. It intends to emphasize product lines in which it has substantial market share, or in which it can use its competitive cost advantages. Product sales in recent years were as follows:

	1994	1993	1992	1991
Hot rolled & semi-finished	31%	36%	32%	40%
Higher value added products:				
Cold rolled	28%	18%	23%	19%
Coated	17%	19%	17%	15%
Tin mill	7%	11%	10%	9%
Wheeling Corrugating	17%	16%	18%	17%

Principal markets in 1994 included steel service centers (32% of total net tons shipped), converters/processors (28%), construction (18%), containers (6%), automotive (6%), agriculture (5%), appliances (3%) and other (2%).

In 1994, WHX's 10 largest customers accounted for 37% of sales.

Important Developments

Oct. '95—WHX's Wheeling-Pittsburgh Steel Corp. unit purchased the assets of the building products division of Namasco, Inc., a division of Klockner Namasco Corp. Terms of the acquisition were not disclosed.

Capitalization

Long Term Debt: $286,100,000 (6/95).
$3.25 Conv. Pfd. Stk.: 3,000,000 shs. ($50 liquid. pref.); conv. into 3.1686 com.
$3.75 Conv. Pfd. Stock: 3,500,000 shs. ($50 liquid. pref.); conv. into 2.451 com.

Per Share Data ($)

(Year Ended Dec. 31)

	1994	1993	1992	1991	1990	1989
Tangible Bk. Val.	25.65	16.65	13.42	15.50	16.92	NA
Cash Flow	4.67	3.26	1.17	2.89	NA	NA
Earnings	2.54	1.02	-1.85	0.27	NA	NA
Dividends	Nil	Nil	Nil	Nil	Nil	NA
Payout Ratio	Nil	Nil	Nil	Nil	Nil	NA
Prices - High	22⅝	18¼	7⅞	8⅞	13¼	NA
- Low	12⅞	4⅞	3¼	5¾	2⅜	NA
P/E Ratio - High	9	18	NM	33	NA	NA
- Low	5	5	NM	21	NA	NA

Income Statement Analysis (Million $)

	1994	%Chg	1993	%Chg	1992	%Chg	1991
Revs.	1,194	14%	1,047	13%	930	-3%	957
Oper. Inc.	141	32%	107	128%	47.0	-19%	58.0
Depr.	61.5	8%	57.1	4%	54.9	22%	45.0
Int. Exp.	31.0	11%	27.9	-7%	29.9	-17%	35.9
Pretax Inc.	111	178%	40.0	NM	-34.0	NM	-3.0
Eff. Tax Rate	22%	—	23%	—	NM	—	NM
Net Inc.	86.0	177%	31.0	NM	-34.0	NM	5.0

Balance Sheet & Other Fin. Data (Million $)

	1994	1993	1992	1991	1990	1989
Cash	402	280	9.0	45.0	65.0	584
Curr. Assets	786	654	337	397	506	892
Total Assets	1,730	1,492	1,117	1,174	1,218	1,486
Curr. Liab.	262	272	232	248	249	176
LT Debt	290	347	214	225	302	2.0
Common Eqty.	698	442	244	281	250	-16.0
Total Cap.	989	789	458	506	552	174
Cap. Exp.	82.0	74.0	67.0	97.0	107	90.0
Cash Flow	135	83.0	21.0	50.0	-224	164

Ratio Analysis

	1994	1993	1992	1991	1990	1989
Curr. Ratio	3.0	2.4	1.5	1.6	2.0	5.1
% LT Debt of Cap.	29.3	44.0	46.7	44.4	54.7	1.2
% Net Inc.of Revs.	7.2	2.9	NM	0.5	NM	11.2
% Ret. on Assets	5.3	2.0	NM	0.4	NM	9.3
% Ret. on Equity	12.7	6.5	NM	1.6	NM	NM

Dividend Data —Directors omitted common dividends in 1979.

Data as orig. reptd.; bef. results of disc. opers. and/or spec. items. Per share data adj. for stk. divs. as of ex-div. date. E-Estimated. NA-Not Available. NM-Not Meaningful. NR-Not Ranked.

Office—110 East 59th St., New York, NY 10022. **Tel**—(212) 355-5200. **Chrmn**—R. LaBow. **Pres**—J. L. Wareham. **Secy**—M. Olshan. **CFO & Investor Contact**—F. G. Chbosky. **Dirs**—N. D. Arnold, P. W. Bucha, R. A. Davidow, W. Goldsmith, R. LaBow, M. Olshan, R. S. Troubh, J. L. Wareham, **Transfer Agent & Registrar**—First National Bank of Boston. **Incorporated** in Delaware in 1920. **Empl**-5,481. **S&P Analyst:** N. Rosenberg

STANDARD & POOR'S

STOCK REPORTS

WICOR, Inc.

NYSE Symbol **WIC**
In S&P SmallCap 600

31-AUG-95 **Industry:** Utilities-Gas

Summary: This holding company's main subsidiary, Wisconsin Gas Co., is the largest gas distributor in Wisconsin. Other subsidiaries produce pumps and filters.

Quantitative Evaluations

Outlook
(1 Lowest—5 Highest)
• **3-**

Fair Value
• **29**

Risk
• **Low**

Earn./Div. Rank
• **B**

Technical Eval.
• **Bearish** since 2/95

Rel. Strength Rank
(1 Lowest—99 Highest)
• **50**

Insider Activity
• **Neutral**

Recent Price • 29¼
52 Wk Range • 30¾-25⅞
Yield • 5.6%
12-Mo. P/E • 15.8

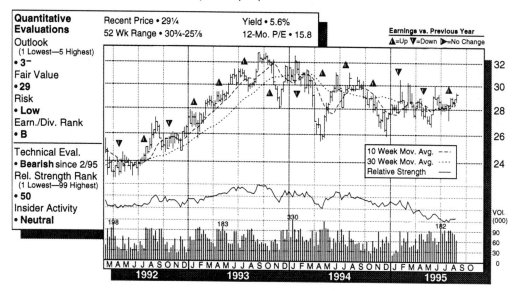

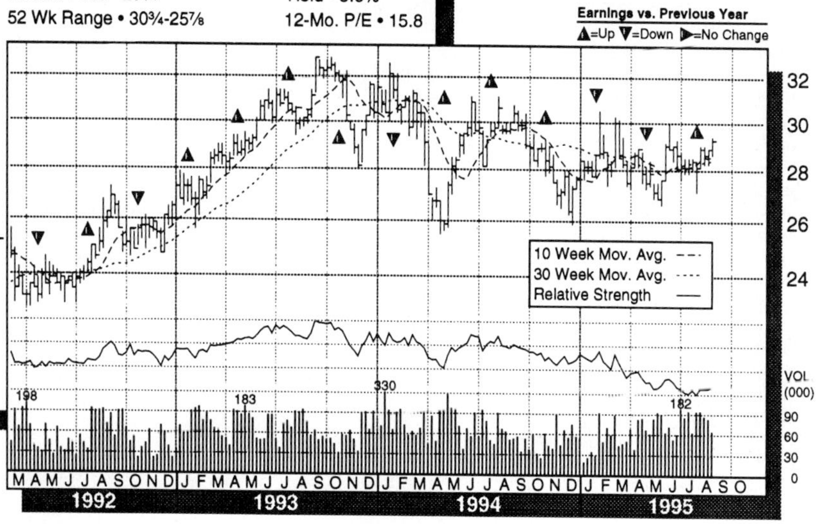

Business Profile - 31-AUG-95

WICOR is a diversified holding company with two principal businesses: natural gas retail distribution in Wisconsin, and manufacturing and sale of pumps and water processing equipment, which occurs on a global scale. The manufactured products include pool and spa pumps, pool filters and accessories, water purifiers and food service and industrial units. While gas distribution is the primary segment, manufacturing has grown in recent years, and now accounts for more than one-third of revenues.

Operational Review - 31-AUG-95

Operating revenues for the first half of 1995 fell 11%, year to year, reflecting the impact on the gas distribution segment of temperatures that were 7.0% warmer than normal and 9.0% warmer than a year earlier. Manufacturing also saw a softening in domestic demand, which was partially offset by a 15% increase in international sales. Expenses were down, and operating income declined 6.6%. Other income rose, and net income decreased 5.9%, to $27,467,000 ($1.62 a share) from $29,200,000 ($1.76).

Stock Performance - 25-AUG-95

In the past 30 trading days, WIC's shares have increased 4%, compared to a 0.04% rise in the S&P 500. Average trading volume for the past five days was 12,800 shares, compared with the 40-day moving average of 20,064 shares.

Key Stock Statistics

Dividend Rate/Share	1.64	Shareholders	16,500
Shs. outstg. (M)	16.9	Market cap. (B)	$0.493
Avg. daily vol. (M)	0.014	Inst. holdings	31%
Tang. Bk. Value/Share	18.09	Insider holdings	NA
Beta	0.45		

Value of $10,000 invested 5 years ago: $ 16,264

Fiscal Year Ending Dec. 31

	1995	% Change	1994	% Change	1993	% Change
Revenues (Million $)						
1Q	269.3	-16%	321.0	18%	273.0	17%
2Q	179.2	-4%	186.1	-2%	190.0	32%
3Q	--	—	151.0	-1%	153.0	34%
4Q	--	—	210.0	-10%	234.0	9%
Yr.	--	—	867.8	2%	850.0	21%
Income (Million $)						
1Q	24.79	-12%	28.20	18%	23.94	38%
2Q	2.68	168%	1.00	72%	0.58	NM
3Q	—	—	-8.07	NM	-8.60	NM
4Q	—	—	12.00	-10%	13.40	6%
Yr.	—	—	33.17	13%	29.31	43%
Earnings Per Share ($)						
1Q	1.46	-15%	1.71	13%	1.51	26%
2Q	0.16	167%	0.06	50%	0.04	NM
3Q	—	—	-0.48	NM	-0.53	NM
4Q	—	—	0.71	-13%	0.82	-4%
Yr.	—	—	1.99	9%	1.82	30%

Next earnings report expected: late October

WICOR, Inc.

Business Summary - 31-AUG-95

WICOR is a utility holding company formed in 1980 to take advantage of opportunities in nonutility diversification. Wisconsin Gas Co., its main subsidiary, is the largest distributor of natural gas in Wisconsin, where all of its utility operations are conducted. Manufacturing consists mostly of pumps and water processing equipment. Contributions (profits in millions) in 1994 were:

	Revs.	Profits
Gas distribution	64.1%	$44.4
Manufacturing	35.9%	22.2

Gas volume sold and transported of 1,196 million therms in 1994, down from 1,205 in 1993, was divided: 39% residential, 16% commercial, 12% industrial firm, 24% industrial interruptible and 9% transported for others. Customers at year-end 1994 were 495,129, a 2.1% increase from 485,103 at year-end 1993. The total number of degree days in 1994 was 6,431, down from 6,775 in 1993. Wisconsin Gas has agreements for firm pipeline and storage capacity that expire at various dates through 2008.

In July 1993, Wisconsin Gas submitted an incentive rate making proposal to the Public Service Commission of Wisconsin ("PSCW"). In its November 1994 rate order, the PSCW significantly modified the proposal, subjecting rates to a three year margin rate cap based on rates approved in November 1993. The rates at December 31, 1994, were at the top of the range.

Sta-Rite Industries, Inc. (30% of 1994 revenues) is a manufacturer of pumps and water processing equipment whose international and export sales (up more than 20% in 1994) are increasing. In November 1993, Sta-Rite acquired Dega Research Pty. Ltd., an Australian manufacturer and marketer of filters, pumps, heaters and other accessories for the pool and spa market.

SHURflo Pump Manufacturing Co. (6%), a Santa Ana, Calif., manufacturer and marketer of fluid-handling equipment and pumps for the beverage, recreational vehicle and marine, industrial and water markets, was acquired in July 1993.

WICOR's interests in Wexco of Delaware, Inc., involved in exploration for natural gas and oil, were sold during the second quarter of 1993.

In March 1994, WICOR recorded a $2.7 million charge for costs associated with a retirement plan. Approximately 131 employees elected to retire.

Important Developments

Aug. '95—WIC acquired Hypro Corp., a manufacturer of pumps, for about $58 million in cash. Also, the PSCW approved the formation of WICOR Gas Marketing to service various gas markets.

Capitalization

Long Term Debt: $167,679,000 (6/95).

Per Share Data ($) (Year Ended Dec. 31)

	1994	1993	1992	1991	1990	1989
Tangible Bk. Val.	17.23	16.47	15.91	16.28	16.64	17.39
Cash Flow	3.75	3.56	3.23	3.31	2.79	4.02
Earnings	1.99	1.82	1.40	1.54	1.04	2.40
Dividends	1.58	1.54	1.50	1.46	1.42	1.37
Payout Ratio	79%	85%	107%	98%	137%	57%
Prices - High	32⅝	32⅞	27⅜	24½	25¼	25½
- Low	25½	25⅝	22⅞	18⅝	18¼	19⅜
P/E Ratio - High	16	18	20	16	24	11
- Low	13	14	16	12	18	8

Income Statement Analysis (Million $)

	1994	%Chg	1993	%Chg	1992	%Chg	1991
Revs.	868	2%	850	21%	705	3%	682
Oper. Inc.	96.0	4%	92.0	21%	76.0	3%	73.8
Depr.	29.4	5%	28.0	5%	26.7	8%	24.8
Int. Exp.	16.7	-4%	17.4	-3%	18.0	8%	16.6
Pretax Inc.	50.5	8%	46.8	44%	32.6	-3%	33.7
Eff. Tax Rate	34%	—	37%	—	37%	—	36%
Net Inc.	33.2	13%	29.3	43%	20.5	-5%	21.5

Balance Sheet & Other Fin. Data (Million $)

	1994	1993	1992	1991	1990	1989
Cash	35.1	23.0	16.5	47.6	16.0	29.7
Curr. Assets	312	315	238	242	210	259
Total Assets	931	934	810	669	638	601
Curr. Liab.	239	256	192	149	166	190
LT Debt	162	165	164	168	128	122
Common Eqty.	291	270	236	235	230	238
Total Cap.	504	490	455	489	443	388
Cap. Exp.	55.1	54.0	80.5	47.9	36.5	39.7
Cash Flow	62.6	57.4	47.1	46.3	38.4	54.7

Ratio Analysis

	1994	1993	1992	1991	1990	1989
Curr. Ratio	1.3	1.2	1.2	1.6	1.3	1.4
% LT Debt of Cap.	32.1	33.7	36.0	34.4	28.9	31.5
% Net Inc.of Revs.	3.8	3.5	2.9	3.2	2.2	4.6
% Ret. on Assets	3.5	3.2	2.8	3.2	2.3	5.7
% Ret. on Equity	11.6	11.0	8.7	9.0	6.1	14.1

Dividend Data —Dividends have been paid since 1960. A dividend reinvestment plan is available. A "poison pill" stock purchase right was adopted in 1989.

Amt. of Div. $	Date Decl.	Ex-Div. Date	Stock of Record	Payment Date
0.400	Oct. 25	Nov. 04	Nov. 10	Nov. 30 '94
0.400	Jan. 24	Feb. 06	Feb. 10	Feb. 28 '95
0.400	Apr. 28	May. 08	May. 12	May. 31 '95
0.410	Jul. 25	Aug. 09	Aug. 11	Aug. 31 '95

Data as orig. reptd.; bef. results of disc. opers. and/or spec. items. Per share data adj. for stk. divs. as of ex-div. date. E-Estimated. NA-Not Available. NM-Not Meaningful. NR-Not Ranked.

Office—626 East Wisconsin Ave., P.O. Box 334, Milwaukee, WI 53201. **Tel**—(414) 291-7026. **Pres & CEO**—G. Wardeberg. **VP-CFO, Treas & Investor Contact**—J. P. Wenzler. **Secy**—R. A. Nuernberg. **Dirs**—W. F. Bueche, W. D. Davis, J. D. McGaffey, D. F. McKeithan, Jr., G. A. Osborn, T. F. Schrader, S. W. Tisdale, G. Wardeberg, E. M. Whitelaw, W. B. Winter. **Transfer Agent & Registrar**—Chemical Bank, NYC. **Incorporated** in Wisconsin in 1852; reincorporated in Wisconsin in 1980. **Empl**-3,214. **S&P Analyst:** Michael C. Barr

STANDARD & POOR'S
STOCK REPORTS

WMS Industries

NYSE Symbol **WMS**
In S&P SmallCap 600

15-NOV-95

Industry:
Leisure/Amusement

Summary: This company designs, manufactures and sells coin-operated amusement games, home video games and gaming devices. It also owns and operates hotels and casinos in Puerto Rico.

Quantitative Evaluations
Outlook
(1 Lowest—5 Highest)
• **5+**
Fair Value
• **24⅝**
Risk
• **Average**
Earn./Div. Rank
• **B-**

Technical Eval.
• **Bullish** since 10/95
Rel. Strength Rank
(1 Lowest—99 Highest)
• **11**
Insider Activity
• **NA**

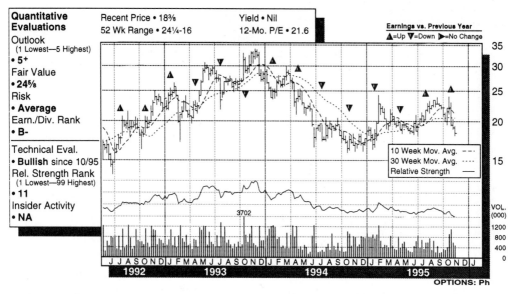

Recent Price • 18⅜
52 Wk Range • 24¼-16
Yield • Nil
12-Mo. P/E • 21.6

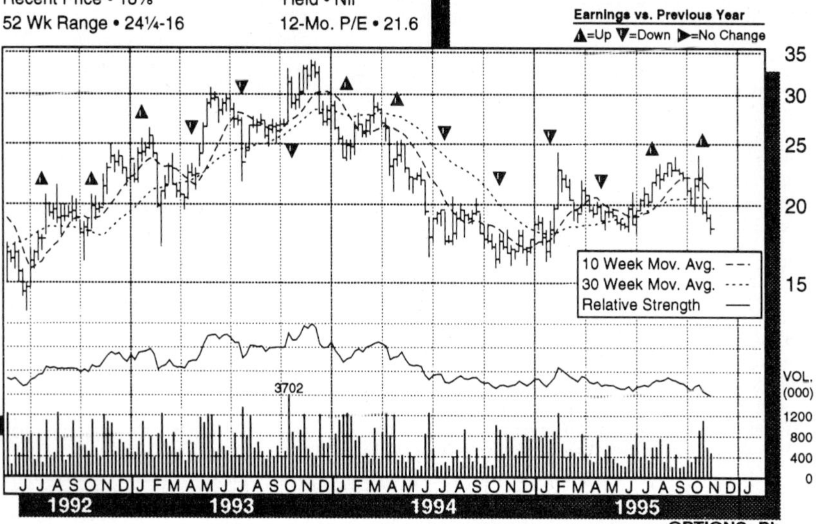

OPTIONS: Ph

Business Profile - 15-NOV-95

WMS intends to expand its video game operations and enter into the video gambling devices business. Its short term goal is to capture 20% of the video gambling devices market. WMS recently announced plans to divest three casino-hotels in Puerto Rico. Ongoing new state legislation authorizing machine-based gambling and state lottery systems should augment the company's long-term growth. Sumner Redstone owns a 24% stake in WMS.

Operational Review - 13-NOV-95

Total revenues in the three months ended September 30, 1995, rose 19%, year to year, primarily due to higher video game sales. Two hurricanes that threatened Puerto Rico and a lower win percentage in the casinos resulted in lower hotel and casino revenues. Higher amusement segment income outweighed losses from the hotel/casino business and increased research and development expenses; operating income climbed nearly ten-fold. After taxes and minority interest, net income replaced a net loss.

Stock Performance - 10-NOV-95

In the past 30 trading days, WMS's shares have declined 13%, compared to a 1% rise in the S&P 500. Average trading volume for the past five days was 93,920 shares, compared with the 40-day moving average of 107,040 shares.

Key Stock Statistics

Dividend Rate/Share	Nil	Shareholders	2,000
Shs. outstg. (M)	24.1	Market cap. (B)	$0.434
Avg. daily vol. (M)	0.156	Inst. holdings	40%
Tang. Bk. Value/Share	7.82	Insider holdings	NA
Beta	1.59		

Value of $10,000 invested 5 years ago: $ 37,692

Fiscal Year Ending Jun. 30

	1996	% Change	1995	% Change	1994	% Change
Revenues (Million $)						
1Q	97.64	19%	82.39	30%	63.19	-6%
2Q	—	—	112.6	11%	101.3	17%
3Q	—	—	93.46	-12%	106.4	21%
4Q	—	—	96.97	11%	87.30	-3%
Yr.	—	—	385.4	8%	358.2	8%
Income (Million $)						
1Q	0.27	NM	-1.07	NM	0.46	-90%
2Q	—	—	6.10	-40%	10.10	6%
3Q	—	—	8.03	-44%	14.23	39%
4Q	—	—	6.15	66%	3.70	-43%
Yr.	—	—	19.21	-33%	28.48	-7%
Earnings Per Share ($)						
1Q	0.01	NM	-0.04	NM	0.02	-89%
2Q	—	—	0.25	-40%	0.42	2%
3Q	—	—	0.33	-44%	0.59	34%
4Q	—	—	0.26	73%	0.15	-46%
Yr.	—	—	0.80	-33%	1.19	-9%

Next earnings report expected: mid January

WMS Industries

Business Summary - 15-NOV-95

WMS Industries Inc. designs, manufactures and sells coin-operated amusement games, home video games, novelty games, video lottery terminals and gaming devices. It also designs and sells home video devices and owns and operates hotels and casinos in Puerto Rico. Contributions (profit in millions) in fiscal 1995 were:

	Revs.	Profits
Amusement games	80.8%	$38.8
Hotel/casino	14.8%	-1.5
Management fees	4.5%	9.2

Export sales accounted for 44% of amusement game sales in fiscal 1995. Nova Games Import-Export GmbH & Co. accounted for 17% of fiscal 1995 game sales.

The company makes pinball games, video games, shuffle-alley bowling simulation games and novelty games under the Williams, Bally, Tradewest and Midway names. Games are also produced for use on home video game systems and on personal computers. The company also sells video lottery terminals, on which games including blackjack, poker, bingo and keno can be played for low-stakes entertainment.

In March 1994, WMS and a unit of Japan's Nintendo jointly formed a company called Williams/Nintendo Inc. to market exclusively for Nintendo's Ultra 64 system and to split the profits. WMS will initially make the games for Ultra 64 machines in arcades and then turn them over to the new company for distribution to the home market.

Hotel and casino operations include: (1) a 95% ownership interest in the 569-room Condado Plaza Hotel & Casino in San Juan, Puerto Rico; (2) a 50% stake in the 388-room El San Juan Hotel & Casino; (3) and 23% of the 750-room El Conquistador luxury resort in Las Croabas, Puerto Rico. The Condado and El San Juan properties have a variety of restaurants, lounges, meeting and conference space, and retail shops and are operated by Williams Hospitality Management Corp., a 62%-owned subsidiary. The El Conquistador includes a casino, golf course and marina.

Important Developments

Oct. '95—The company said it will not contest a merger agreement between Bally Gaming International, Inc. and Alliance Gaming Corp. It has, however, initiated a lawsuit against Bally for failure to pay $4.8 million in break-up fees and additional damages generated by Bally's unilateral termination of a June 1995 agreement to merge with WMS. Separately, WMS said it plans to divest its three hotels in Puerto Rico.

Capitalization

Long Term Debt: $84,428,000 (6/95).
Minority Interests: $16,363,000.

Per Share Data ($)

(Year Ended Jun. 30)

	1995	1994	1993	1992	1991	1990
Tangible Bk. Val.	17.82	6.70	6.06	4.56	0.80	0.12
Cash Flow	1.28	1.58	1.57	1.47	0.75	-0.36
Earnings	0.80	1.19	1.31	1.21	0.47	-0.62
Dividends	Nil	Nil	Nil	Nil	Nil	Nil
Payout Ratio	Nil	Nil	Nil	Nil	Nil	Nil
Prices - High	24¼	29⅞	34	25	14½	5⅝
- Low	16¼	15⅞	17⅛	13⅜	1⅝	1¾
P/E Ratio - High	30	25	26	21	31	NM
- Low	20	13	13	11	3	NM

Income Statement Analysis (Million $)

	1995	%Chg	1994	%Chg	1993	%Chg	1992
Revs.	385	8%	358	8%	331	46%	227
Oper. Inc.	52.6	-15%	62.2	6%	58.7	86%	31.6
Depr.	11.7	25%	9.4	54%	6.1	14%	5.3
Int. Exp.	7.6	-4%	7.9	24%	6.4	2%	6.2
Pretax Inc.	34.0	-27%	46.3	-7%	49.7	96%	25.4
Eff. Tax Rate	35%	—	29%	—	32%	—	6.90%
Net Inc.	19.2	-33%	28.5	-7%	30.7	23%	25.0

Balance Sheet & Other Fin. Data (Million $)

	1995	1994	1993	1992	1991	1990
Cash	46.0	97.0	124	51.5	5.6	4.3
Curr. Assets	203	191	202	119	47.0	51.0
Total Assets	386	343	307	225	121	120
Curr. Liab.	63.9	47.4	38.7	44.0	38.8	44.7
LT Debt	84.4	88.3	89.3	39.7	49.8	56.2
Common Eqty.	209	181	152	115	23.0	11.0
Total Cap.	313	289	259	173	75.0	69.0
Cap. Exp.	19.5	18.9	11.3	8.6	6.3	9.9
Cash Flow	30.9	37.9	36.8	30.4	12.8	-5.9

Ratio Analysis

	1995	1994	1993	1992	1991	1990
Curr. Ratio	3.2	4.0	5.2	2.7	1.2	1.1
% LT Debt of Cap.	26.9	30.5	34.5	23.0	66.6	81.2
% Net Inc.of Revs.	5.0	8.0	9.3	11.0	5.0	NM
% Ret. on Assets	5.3	8.7	11.5	12.8	6.6	NM
% Ret. on Equity	9.8	16.9	22.8	34.3	47.2	NM

Dividend Data —Dividends, initiated in 1982, were omitted in 1984. A two-for-one stock split was effected in February 1992.

Data as orig. reptd.; bef. results of disc. opers. and/or spec. items. Per share data adj. for stk. divs. as of ex-div. date. E-Estimated. NA-Not Available. NM-Not Meaningful. NR-Not Ranked.

Office—3401 North California Ave., Chicago, IL 60618. **Tel**—(312) 728-2300. **Chrmn & Co-CEO**—L. J. Nicastro. **Co-CEO, COO & Pres**—N. D. Nicastro. **CFO, Treas & Investor Contact**—Harold H. Bach Jr. **VP-Secy**—B. M. Norman. **Dirs**—G. R. Baker, W. C. Bartholomay, K. J. Fedesna, W. E. McKenna, N. J. Menell, L. J. Nicastro, N. D. Nicastro, H. Reich, I. R. Sheinfeld. **Transfer Agent & Registrar**—Bank of New York, NYC. **Incorporated** in Delaware in 1974. **Empl**-4,881. **S&P Analyst:** Efraim Levy

STANDARD & POOR'S

STOCK REPORTS

Wabash National

NYSE Symbol **WNC**

In S&P SmallCap 600

02-NOV-95 **Industry:** Auto/Truck mfrs.

Summary: This company is the largest U.S. manufacturer of truck trailers and the leading producer of both fiberglass-reinforced plastic trailers and aluminum plate trailers.

S&P Opinion: Buy (★★★★★)

Recent Price • 27
52 Wk Range • 40½-26¼
Yield • 0.4%
12-Mo. P/E • 18.6

Quantitative Evaluations

Outlook
(1 Lowest—5 Highest)
• 5

Fair Value
• 35¾

Risk
• Average

Earn./Div. Rank
• NR

Technical Eval.
• Bearish since 9/95

Rel. Strength Rank
(1 Lowest—99 Highest)
• 5

Insider Activity
• NA

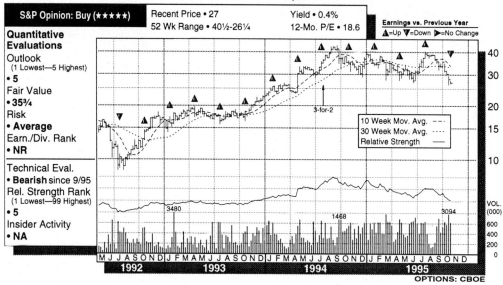

Earnings vs. Previous Year
▲=Up ▼=Down ▶=No Change

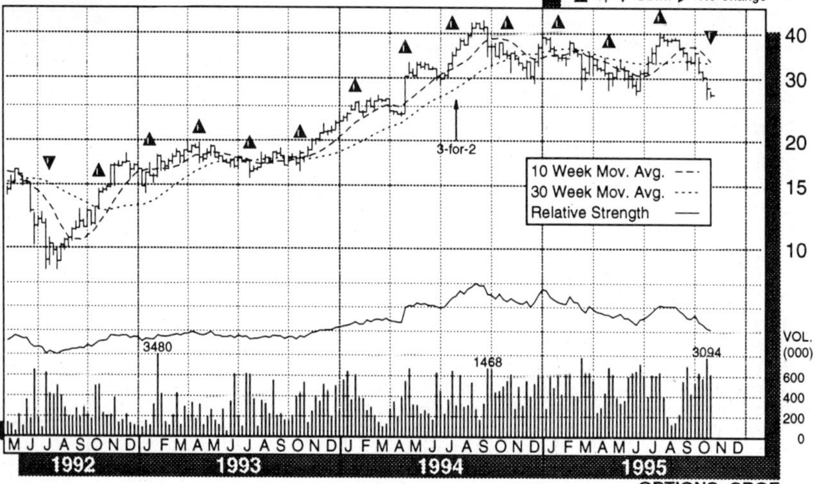

OPTIONS: CBOE

Overview - 02-NOV-95

Revenues are expected to continue to rise through 1996, reflecting increased plate trailer and refrigerated trailer volume, new RoadRailer orders and the introduction of new trailers. WNC should not be affected significantly by market weakness as it ships mostly to end-users. The slowdown primarily involves the non-user segment such as truck leasing and rental companies. Profitability should benefit from the greater volume, higher-margin products and manufacturing efficiencies (the company expects its manufacturing capacity to reach 70,000 units by the end of 1995). With a strong backlog of more than $1.0 billion, we believe the company is well positioned for further growth based on expected demand for new products such as the AutoRailer and AllRailer, and expansion into European markets.

Valuation - 02-NOV-95

The shares are about 36% below their mid-1995 high of 40.5, primarily reflecting a weaker than expected third quarter due to a slowdown in production caused by excessive heat in the summer. However, potential exists for a rebound in the stock price, as earnings are projected to grow at better than 25% annually at least for the next two years. The shares were recently trading at about 16X our $1.65 EPS estimate for 1995, and 12X our $2.25 projection for 1996, a slight discount to that of the SmallCap 600. With limited exposure to the highly cyclical truck-leasing and rental markets, the purchase of Wabash shares is still highly recommended.

Key Stock Statistics

S&P EPS Est. 1995	1.65	Tang. Bk. Value/Share	8.89
P/E on S&P Est. 1995	16.4	Beta	NA
S&P EPS Est. 1996	2.25	Shareholders	700
Dividend Rate/Share	0.10	Market cap. (B)	$0.479
Shs. outstg. (M)	19.0	Inst. holdings	85%
Avg. daily vol. (M)	0.252	Insider holdings	NA

Value of $10,000 invested 5 years ago: NA

Fiscal Year Ending Dec. 31

	1995	% Change	1994	% Change	1993	% Change
Revenues (Million $)						
1Q	177.6	52%	116.6	39%	83.73	42%
2Q	193.4	41%	137.6	51%	91.02	24%
3Q	176.1	19%	147.9	65%	89.76	27%
4Q	—	—	159.7	67%	95.53	12%
Yr.	—	—	561.8	56%	360.0	25%
Income (Million $)						
1Q	6.96	45%	4.79	53%	3.14	80%
2Q	8.05	31%	6.16	66%	3.72	180%
3Q	5.83	-9%	6.38	56%	4.09	85%
4Q	—	—	6.60	43%	4.61	26%
Yr.	—	—	23.93	54%	15.56	74%
Earnings Per Share ($)						
1Q	0.37	35%	0.27	46%	0.19	75%
2Q	0.43	22%	0.35	66%	0.21	167%
3Q	0.31	-9%	0.34	46%	0.23	75%
4Q	E0.54	54%	0.35	31%	0.27	21%
Yr.	E1.65	25%	1.32	47%	0.90	67%

Next earnings report expected: late January

Wabash National

Business Summary - 24-OCT-95

Wabash National Corporation, founded in 1985, believes that it is the largest U.S. manufacturer of truck trailers and the leading manufacturer of both fiberglass-reinforced plastic trailers and aluminum plate trailers. The company is also the exclusive manufacturer of RoadRailer, a patented bimodal technology that consists of trailers and detachable rail bogies that permit a vehicle to run both on the highway and directly on railroad lines. In June 1994, Wabash agreed to enter into joint ventures to manufacture and market its RoadRailer system throughout China and Australia.

The company markets its products directly and through dealers to truckload and less-than-truckoad common carriers, household and package moving companies, leasing companies, package carriers and intermodal carriers including railroads. It has established significant relationships as a supplier to many large customers in the transportation industry. In 1994, the five largest customers accounted for 37% of total sales, with Schneider National accounting for 16%. Sales to leasing companies represented 15% of total new trailer sales in 1994.

Wabash believes that customers historically have replaced trailers in cycles that run from six to eight years. However, economic conditions in prior periods depressed demand for new trailers and led to an overall aging of trailer fleets beyond the typical cycle. Recently, improved economic conditions in the transportation industry have led to increased demand. The industry has begun to consolidate, and both the number of major manufacturers and the number of plants operated have diminished, resulting in extremely competitive product pricing.

New products include AllRailer, a railcar designed to carry larger motor vehicles; AutoRailer, a highway trailer capable of running on rails and carrying six full-size or smaller automobiles; RefrigeRailer, ChassisRailer and the PupRailer trailer.

Important Developments

Oct. '95—Wabash said its third quarter production was affected by excessive heat in July and August. The company said production in September returned to more normal levels and it expects to see continued growth for the balance of the year.
May '95—The company received an order for 30 curtainsided RoadRailer trailers and supporting Mark V rail bogies from Compagnie Nouvelle de Conteneurs. Wabash noted that it is currently shipping units to Germany to start RoadRailer service in Germany, Austria and Italy.
Apr. '95—Directors authorized the repurchase of $30 million of common stock. Separately, Wabash obtained new credit facilities totaling $155 million.

Capitalization

Long Term Debt: $42,309,000 (6/95).

Per Share Data ($) (Year Ended Dec. 31)

	1994	1993	1992	1991	1990	1989
Tangible Bk. Val.	8.14	5.03	3.73	3.21	1.28	0.89
Cash Flow	1.72	1.18	0.71	NA	0.43	NA
Earnings	1.32	0.90	0.54	0.52	0.31	NA
Dividends	0.08	0.07	Nil	Nil	NA	NA
Payout Ratio	6%	7%	Nil	Nil	NA	NA
Prices - High	43½	23⅜	19⅝	16½	NA	NA
- Low	22⅝	14⅛	8⅝	9⅜	NA	NA
P/E Ratio - High	33	25	36	32	NA	NA
- Low	17	15	16	18	NA	NA

Income Statement Analysis (Million $)

	1994	%Chg	1993	%Chg	1992	%Chg	1991
Revs.	562	56%	360	25%	289	51%	191
Oper. Inc.	48.6	52%	31.9	77%	18.0	27%	14.2
Depr.	7.4	51%	4.9	67%	2.9	89%	1.5
Int. Exp.	2.7	93%	1.4	99%	0.7	-57%	1.6
Pretax Inc.	39.6	53%	25.9	79%	14.5	31%	11.1
Eff. Tax Rate	40%	—	40%	—	38%	—	39%
Net Inc.	23.9	53%	15.6	75%	8.9	31%	6.8

Balance Sheet & Other Fin. Data (Million $)

	1994	1993	1992	1991	1990	1989
Cash	39.7	27.6	3.0	14.6	1.9	1.7
Curr. Assets	198	116	94.0	71.4	37.9	35.8
Total Assets	301	180	135	93.4	49.9	47.3
Curr. Liab.	108	59.3	49.9	35.1	20.7	17.0
LT Debt	24.9	24.4	18.1	1.9	13.3	19.6
Common Eqty.	154	87.5	62.1	53.4	15.3	10.7
Total Cap.	193	120	84.5	57.8	28.6	30.3
Cap. Exp.	32.7	20.1	16.5	6.8	1.7	2.0
Cash Flow	31.3	20.5	11.9	8.3	4.0	5.3

Ratio Analysis

	1994	1993	1992	1991	1990	1989
Curr. Ratio	1.8	2.0	1.9	2.0	1.8	2.1
% LT Debt of Cap.	12.9	20.3	21.4	3.2	68.3	64.6
% Net Inc.of Revs.	4.3	4.3	3.1	3.6	1.7	2.8
% Ret. on Assets	9.6	9.7	7.8	12.9	NM	9.4
% Ret. on Equity	19.2	20.4	15.5	28.1	NM	45.7

Dividend Data —Cash dividends were initiated in early 1993.

Amt. of Div. $	Date Decl.	Ex-Div. Date	Stock of Record	Payment Date
0.025	Dec. 09	Jan. 09	Jan. 13	Jan. 27 '95
0.025	Mar. 28	Apr. 07	Apr. 13	Apr. 27 '95
0.025	May. 11	Jul. 11	Jul. 13	Jul. 27 '95
0.025	Sep. 22	Oct. 11	Oct. 13	Oct. 27 '95

Data as orig. reptd.; bef. results of disc. opers. and/or spec. items. Per share data adj. for stk. divs. as of ex-div. date. E-Estimated. NA-Not Available. NM-Not Meaningful. NR-Not Ranked.

Office—1000 Sagamore Parkway South, Lafayette, IN 47905. **Tel**—(317) 448-1591. **Pres & CEO**—D. J. Ehrlich. **VP & CFO**—M. R. Holden. **Secy**—J. R. Gambs. **Dirs**—D. J. Ehrlich, J. T. Hackett, E. H. Harrison, M. R. Holden, L. F. Koci. **Transfer Agent & Registrar**—Bank One, Indianapolis. **Incorporated** in Delaware in 1991. **Empl**-3,400. **S&P Analyst:** Stewart Scharf

STANDARD & POOR'S
STOCK REPORTS

Wall Data

NASDAQ Symbol **WALL**
In S&P SmallCap 600

17-SEP-95

Industry: Data Processing

Summary: This company is engaged primarily in the development and marketing of software products and related services for users of personal computers in business organizations.

Quantitative Evaluations

Outlook
(1 Lowest—5 Highest)
• **NA**
Fair Value
• **NA**
Risk
• **High**
Earn./Div. Rank
• **NR**

Technical Eval.
• **Bearish** since 3/95
Rel. Strength Rank
(1 Lowest—99 Highest)
• **18**
Insider Activity
• **NA**

Recent Price • 19
52 Wk Range • 55½-15
Yield • Nil
12-Mo. P/E • 12.0

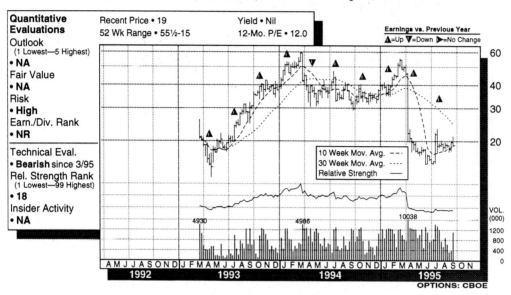

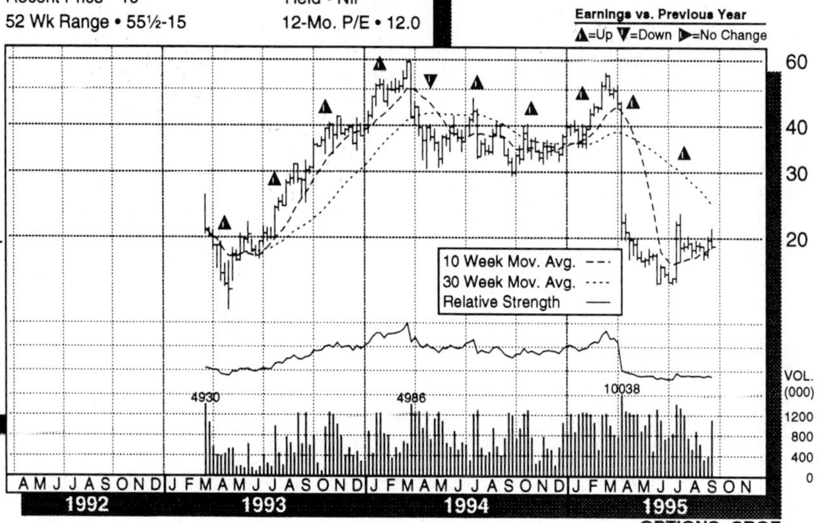

OPTIONS: CBOE

Business Profile - 13-SEP-95

This company develops and markets connectivity software products that give personal computer users access to applications and data residing on enterprise-wide information systems. WALL actively seeks development agreements with other companies such as Apple Computer and Cisco Systems. In April 1995, the company completed the acquisition of Concentric Data Systems Inc., a manufacturer of data access and reporting products for desktop and client/server databases.

Operational Review - 13-SEP-95

Revenues in the first half of 1995 rose 16%, year to year, propelled by increased sales of RUMBA Office, ONESTEP support contracts, and report writer products, which offset reduced sales of single host products. Gross margins were squeezed by higher operating expenses and competitive pressures. Results benefited from a one-time gain of $14.0 million resulting from the sale of an investment, but this was partially offset by acquisition-related charges of $6.8 million.

Stock Performance - 15-SEP-95

In the past 30 trading days, WALL's shares have declined 2%, compared to a 4% rise in the S&P 500. Average trading volume for the past five days was 219,920 shares, compared with the 40-day moving average of 149,254 shares.

Key Stock Statistics

Dividend Rate/Share	Nil	Shareholders	200
Shs. outstg. (M)	9.2	Market cap. (B)	$0.175
Avg. daily vol. (M)	0.133	Inst. holdings	69%
Tang. Bk. Value/Share	8.77	Insider holdings	NA
Beta	0.43		

Value of $10,000 invested 5 years ago: NA

Fiscal Year Ending Dec. 31

	1995	% Change	1994	% Change	1993	% Change
Revenues (Million $)						
1Q	22.10	29%	17.16	70%	10.10	95%
2Q	24.73	7%	23.14	52%	15.20	118%
3Q	—	—	25.01	45%	17.30	121%
4Q	—	—	35.93	63%	22.04	86%
Yr.	—	—	101.2	57%	64.64	103%
Income (Million $)						
1Q	0.02	NM	-0.45	NM	1.07	60%
2Q	4.98	38%	3.60	38%	2.61	95%
3Q	—	—	4.06	NM	1.20	10%
4Q	—	—	6.98	49%	4.67	49%
Yr.	—	—	14.18	48%	9.55	118%
Earnings Per Share ($)						
1Q	Nil	—	-0.04	NM	0.13	63%
2Q	0.49	36%	0.36	38%	0.26	73%
3Q	—	—	0.40	NM	0.12	20%
4Q	—	—	0.69	50%	0.46	84%
Yr.	—	—	1.40	40%	1.00	72%

Next earnings report expected: late October

Business Summary - 14-SEP-95

Wall Data Incorporated develops, markets and supports connectivity software products and associated application tools for Microsoft Windows, Windows NT, IBM OS/2 and Macintosh operating systems. The RUMBA family of software products gives personal computer users easy access and use of applications and data residing in enterprise-wide information systems. The company also offers products that enhance productivity, such as the RUMBA Office, which gives users connectivity to multiple applications from a single workstation.

RUMBA products support the exchange of information between PC applications and host applications operating on IBM and IBM-compatible mainframe computers, IBM AS/400 midrange computers and Digital Equipment Corp. VAX computers. The company also markets a version of RUMBA software that operates with the IBM OS/2 operating system. RUMBA products implement PC-to-host connections using a wide array of network and communication system configurations, including several types of direct and LAN communication hardware, multiple LAN operating systems and a broad range of communications servers and gateways.

The RUMBA software line has several different product packages. The comany's award-winning RUMBA software for connectivity to IBM-compatible computers gives users greater flexibility in bringing host information and applications to PC users. The RUMBA Office's newest release provides Novell LAN users with simultaneous access to multiple hosts from a single geographical environment. In addition, there are French, German and UK language versions of this product. The RUMBA Gateway extends connectivity to the mobile work force with remote access capability.

Products are marketed to national and multinational business organizations and governmental entities with installed host computer systems and PCs using Windows or OS/2 using a combination of direct sales, indirect distribution and OEM arrangements. Indirect channels consist primarily of national software resellers, distributors, regional resellers and system integrators addressing the business market.

Important Developments

Apr. '95—The company said it had completed its previously announced acquisition of Concentric Data Systems Inc. Concentric develops data access and reporting products for desktop and client/server databases.

Capitalization

Long Term Obligations: None (6/95).

Per Share Data ($) (Year Ended Dec. 31)

	1994	1993	1992	1991	1990	1989
Tangible Bk. Val.	8.79	6.99	5.55	NM	NM	NM
Cash Flow	1.76	1.15	0.68	0.25	-2.01	NA
Earnings	1.40	1.00	0.58	0.19	-2.29	-2.15
Dividends	Nil	Nil	Nil	Nil	Nil	Nil
Payout Ratio	Nil	Nil	Nil	Nil	Nil	Nil
Prices - High	60	42½	NA	NA	NA	NA
- Low	29¼	12¾	NA	NA	NA	NA
P/E Ratio - High	43	43	NA	NA	NA	NA
- Low	21	13	NA	NA	NA	NA

Income Statement Analysis (Million $)

	1994	%Chg	1993	%Chg	1992	%Chg	1991
Revs.	101	56%	64.6	103%	31.8	118%	14.6
Oper. Inc.	28.7	50%	19.1	138%	8.0	NM	2.1
Depr.	3.6	150%	1.5	104%	0.7	145%	0.3
Int. Exp.	0.2	17%	0.2	-25%	0.2	50%	0.2
Pretax Inc.	22.8	49%	15.3	126%	6.8	NM	1.7
Eff. Tax Rate	38%	—	38%	—	35%	—	37%
Net Inc.	14.2	49%	9.6	118%	4.4	NM	1.0

Balance Sheet & Other Fin. Data (Million $)

	1994	1993	1992	1991	1990	1989
Cash	48.9	50.3	4.6	1.8	NA	NA
Curr. Assets	80.7	67.3	14.1	6.0	NA	NA
Total Assets	106	74.4	16.1	6.9	2.0	2.2
Curr. Liab.	24.4	12.0	6.1	3.6	NA	NA
LT Debt	Nil	0.1	1.0	0.6	4.5	4.2
Common Eqty.	81.2	62.3	9.0	2.7	-4.6	-3.0
Total Cap.	81.2	62.5	10.0	3.2	-0.1	1.2
Cap. Exp.	10.1	3.8	1.6	0.3	0.1	NA
Cash Flow	17.8	11.0	5.1	1.3	-1.4	NA

Ratio Analysis

	1994	1993	1992	1991	1990	1989
Curr. Ratio	3.3	5.6	2.3	1.6	NA	NA
% LT Debt of Cap.	Nil	0.2	10.1	17.5	NM	NM
% Net Inc.of Revs.	14.0	14.8	13.8	7.2	NM	NM
% Ret. on Assets	15.5	10.8	38.3	23.7	NM	NM
% Ret. on Equity	19.4	19.7	75.3	NM	NM	NM

Dividend Data —No cash dividends have been paid, and the company does not expect to pay any in the foreseeable future. A "poison pill" shareholder rights plan was adopted in 1995.

Data as orig. reptd.; bef. results of disc. opers. and/or spec. items. Per share data adj. for stk. divs. as of ex-div. date. E-Estimated. NA-Not Available. NM-Not Meaningful. NR-Not Ranked.

Office—11332 N.E. 122nd Way, Kirkland, WA 98052. **Tel**—(206) 814-9255. **Chrmn, Pres & CEO**—J. Simpson. **EVP & Secy**—J. R. Wall. **VP-Fin, CFO, Treas & Investor Contact**—Angelo F. Grestoni. **Dirs**—M. A. Ellison, H. N. Lewis, D. F. Millet, L. K. Orr, S. Sarich, Jr., J. Simpson, J. R. Wall. **Transfer Agent & Registrar**—First Interstate Bank of Washington. **Incorporated** in Washington in 1982. **Empl-** 577. **S&P Analyst:** Mike Cavanaugh

STANDARD & POOR'S

STOCK REPORTS

Washington Energy

NYSE Symbol **WEG**

In S&P SmallCap 600

19-OCT-95

Industry: Utilities-Gas

Summary: This company is to merge with Puget Sound & Light Co. Through a subsidiary, it distributes natural gas at retail in western Washington, including the cities of Seattle and Tacoma.

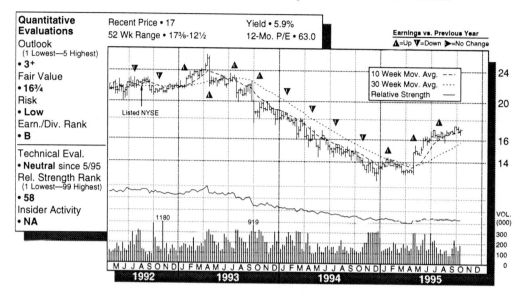

Quantitative Evaluations

Outlook
(1 Lowest—5 Highest)
• **3+**

Fair Value
• **16¾**

Risk
• **Low**

Earn./Div. Rank
• **B**

Technical Eval.
• **Neutral** since 5/95

Rel. Strength Rank
(1 Lowest—99 Highest)
• **58**

Insider Activity
• **NA**

Recent Price • 17
52 Wk Range • 17⅜-12½

Yield • 5.9%
12-Mo. P/E • 63.0

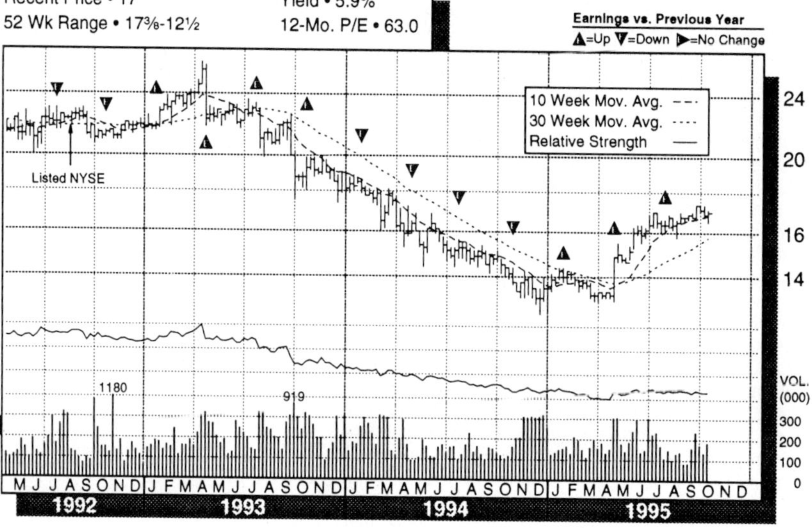

Business Profile - 19-OCT-95

Washington Energy is a holding company whose main subsidiary, Washington Natural Gas Co., is involved in the retail distribution of natural gas. Through other subsidiaries, it is also engaged in the business of selling gas appliances and energy efficiency and security products for the home. In October 1995, Puget Sound Power & Light Co. agreed to acquire WEG in a transaction valued at $488 million. Each WEG share will be exchanged for 0.86 of a share of Puget stock.

Operational Review - 19-OCT-95

Revenues in the first nine months of fiscal 1995 advanced 4.1%, year to year, reflecting more customers and higher utility rates. Operating income rose to $53,507,000 from $29,947,000, as operating and maintenance expenses declined, primarily from a work force reduction. Net income of $18,859,000 ($0.79 a share), replaced a loss of $32,957,000 ($1.44, after preferred dividends and preferred redemption premium). Results exclude losses from discontinued operations of $203,000 in the 1994 interim.

Stock Performance - 13-OCT-95

In the past 30 trading days, WEG's shares have increased 1%, compared to a 4% rise in the S&P 500. Average trading volume for the past five days was 36,360 shares, compared with the 40-day moving average of 29,931 shares.

Key Stock Statistics

Dividend Rate/Share	1.00	Shareholders	12,800
Shs. outstg. (M)	24.0	Market cap. (B)	$0.408
Avg. daily vol. (M)	0.034	Inst. holdings	21%
Tang. Bk. Value/Share	10.82	Insider holdings	NA
Beta	0.45		

Value of $10,000 invested 5 years ago: $ 11,152

Fiscal Year Ending Sep. 30

	1995	% Change	1994	% Change	1993	% Change
Revenues (Million $)						
1Q	156.3	7%	146.7	8%	136.2	14%
2Q	157.5	4%	151.5	-6%	161.0	28%
3Q	78.87	NM	-79.00	NM	91.00	32%
4Q	—	—	54.79	-34%	82.47	35%
Yr.	—	—	432.0	-8%	470.4	25%
Income (Million $)						
1Q	13.26	60%	8.31	-42%	14.24	16%
2Q	11.23	51%	7.45	-54%	16.22	47%
3Q	-5.62	NM	-48.92	NM	-1.05	NM
4Q	—	—	-11.89	NM	-7.42	NM
Yr.	—	—	-44.85	NM	22.04	57%
Earnings Per Share ($)						
1Q	0.56	70%	0.33	-48%	0.63	5%
2Q	0.47	47%	0.32	-54%	0.70	32%
3Q	-0.23	NM	-2.08	NM	-0.04	NM
4Q	—	—	-0.50	NM	-0.32	NM
Yr.	—	—	-1.94	NM	0.95	64%

Next earnings report expected: late October

Business Summary - 19-OCT-95

Washington Energy is a holding company whose main subsidiary distributes natural gas in western Washington. WEG also owns Washington Energy Services Co., which sells natural gas heating equipment, monitored security systems and energy efficient products for the home. Through two other subsidiaries, Thermal Energy, Inc., and ThermRail, Inc., WEG has interests in coal and related transportation.

Segment contributions in fiscal 1994 (operating income in million $):

	Revs.	Operating Income
Gas distribution	92%	$19.1
Merchandising & other	8%	- 1.0

Washington Natural Gas Co. provides natural gas service to customers in the western Washington counties of Snohomish, King, Pierce, Thurston and Lewis, which have a combined population representing 57% of the state total.

Gas sales in fiscal 1994 amounted to 879.6 million therms (901.4 million in fiscal 1993) and were divided as follows: firm (71%) and interruptible (29%). Customers averaged 444,623 (423,142). The number of heating degree days totaled 4,289 in fiscal 1994 (9.6% warmer than normal), versus 4,702 in fiscal 1993 (1.5% warmer than normal).

In 1994, the company shifted its strategic focus back to its utility. In May 1994, WEG sold its Washington Energy Resources Co. (WERC) unit to Cabot Oil & Gas for $180 million, consisting of Cabot common and preferred stock, plus the assumption of debt. WERC is engaged in oil and gas exploration and development in the U.S., Canada and the Gulf of Mexico. The transaction entailed a net loss of $30 million. WEG also restructured and reduced the size of its work force, consolidating work groups, eliminating layers of management, and reducing overall staffing by 12%. The company had to take an after-tax charge of $4.6 million, covering employee severance and the costs of planning a new headquarters facility that is not yet required. In addition, the company sold its biowaste technology business, which had been started in 1984. Earlier, in October 1993, WEG combined its appliance sales, energy efficiency products and home security businesses in a new subsidiary, Washington Energy Services Company.

Important Developments

Oct. '95—Puget Sound Power & Light Co. agreed to acquire WEG in a transaction valued at $488 million, or $19.89 a share. Each WEG share is to be exchanged for 0.86 of a Puget share. The proposed combination will save an estimated $370 million over 10 years.

Capitalization

Long Term Debt: $290,000,000 (6/95).
Preferred Stock: $90,000,000.

Per Share Data ($) (Year Ended Sep. 30)

	1994	1993	1992	1991	1990	1989
Tangible Bk. Val.	10.82	13.85	13.88	14.59	13.65	12.96
Earnings	-1.94	0.95	0.58	1.55	1.17	1.52
Dividends	1.00	1.40	1.40	1.38	1.34	1.30
Payout Ratio	NM	147%	NM	89%	115%	86%
Prices - High	18⅞	26⅜	23½	23½	22	22⅜
- Low	13⅞	17⅜	20	18½	17⅝	13¾
P/E Ratio - High	NM	28	41	15	19	15
- Low	NM	21	34	12	15	9

Income Statement Analysis (Million $)

	1994	%Chg	1993	%Chg	1992	%Chg	1991
Revs.	432	-8%	470	25%	375	-5%	396
Depr.	30.9	-18%	37.9	6%	35.7	8%	33.1
Maint.	NA	—	NA	—	6.2	22%	5.1
Fxd. Chgs. Cov.	1.7	-12%	1.9	44%	1.3	-29%	1.9
Constr. Credits	NA	—	NA	—	NA	—	NA
Eff. Tax Rate	NM	—	31%	—	16%	—	30%
Net Inc.	-44.9	NM	22.0	56%	14.1	-55%	31.0

Balance Sheet & Other Fin. Data (Million $)

	1994	1993	1992	1991	1990	1989
Gross Prop.	1,032	1,147	1,046	938	824	723
Cap. Exp.	86.9	126	123	118	110	85.7
Net Prop.	783	851	778	697	609	532
Capitalization:						
LT Debt	290	353	277	227	224	192
% LT Debt	46	51	48	42	47	47
Pfd.	90.0	17.3	27.5	32.7	33.1	33.5
% Pfd.	14	2.50	4.80	6.00	6.90	8.30
Common	257	323	276	284	220	180
% Common	40	47	48	52	46	44
Total Cap.	637	793	665	627	553	475

Ratio Analysis

	1994	1993	1992	1991	1990	1989
Oper. Ratio	94.0	88.2	88.3	85.7	86.6	86.4
% Earn. on Net Prop.	3.1	6.8	5.9	8.7	8.5	9.7
% Ret. on Revs.	NM	4.7	3.7	7.8	5.7	6.5
% Ret. On Invest.Cap	NM	7.7	7.0	10.2	8.9	10.4
% Return On Com.Eqty	NM	7.3	4.0	11.2	8.9	11.9

Dividend Data —Dividends have been paid each year since 1960. A dividend reinvestment plan is available.

Amt. of Div. $	Date Decl.	Ex-Div. Date	Stock of Record	Payment Date
0.250	Oct. 19	Nov. 14	Nov. 18	Dec. 12 '94
0.250	Dec. 14	Feb. 13	Feb. 17	Mar. 13 '95
0.250	Apr. 19	May. 22	May. 26	Jun. 12 '95
0.250	Aug. 16	Aug. 24	Aug. 28	Sep. 11 '95
0.250	Oct. 18	Nov. 22	Nov. 27	Dec. 11 '95

Data as orig. reptd.; bef. results of disc opers. and/or spec. items. Per share data adj. for stk. divs. as of ex-div. date. E-Estimated. NA-Not Available. NM-Not Meaningful. NR-Not Ranked.

Office—815 Mercer St., Seattle, WA 98109. **Tel**—(206) 622-6767. **Chrmn-CEO & Pres**—W. P. Vititoe. **EVP, CAO & CFO**—J. P. Torgerson. **EVP & COO**—T. J. Hogan. **SVP & Secy**—R. J. Tomlinson. **VP, Treas & Investor Contact**—Betsy J. Moseley. **Dirs**—V. Anderson, R. F. Bailey, D. J. Covey, J. W. Creighton, Jr., R. L. Dryden, T. Moriguchi, S. G. Narodick, W. P. Vititoe. **Transfer Agent & Registrar**—Harris Trust and Savings Bank, Chicago. **Incorporated** in Washington in 1977. **Empl**-1,413. **S&P Analyst:** Michael C. Barr

STANDARD & POOR'S

STOCK REPORTS

Washington National

NYSE Symbol **WNT**
In S&P SmallCap 600

25-OCT-95 **Industry:** Insurance

Summary: This insurance holding company markets and underwrites life insurance, annuities, and health insurance for individuals and groups.

Quantitative Evaluations

Outlook
(1 Lowest—5 Highest)
• **4+**

Fair Value
• **25⅝**

Risk
• **Low**

Earn./Div. Rank
• **B-**

Technical Eval.
• **Bullish** since 5/95

Rel. Strength Rank
(1 Lowest—99 Highest)
• **63**

Insider Activity
• **NA**

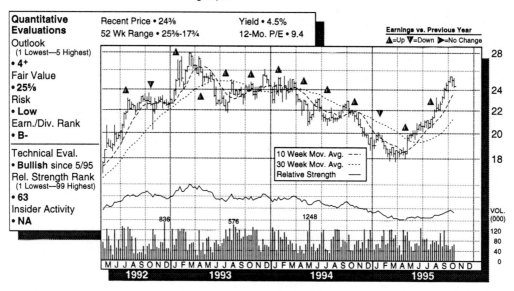

Recent Price • 24⅜
52 Wk Range • 25⅝-17¾
Yield • 4.5%
12-Mo. P/E • 9.4

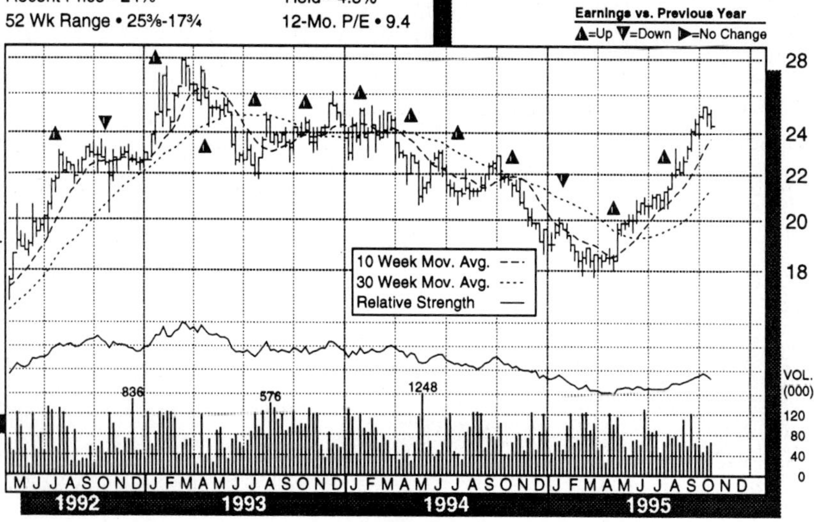

Business Profile - 25-OCT-95

The market for health insurance has become more competitive over the last few quarters, as insurance companies have begun aggressively pricing insurance products to gain market share. WNT will focus on maintaining its margins, sacrificing some growth for profitability. As interest rates rose in the second half of 1994, WNT increased credited interest rates, which narrowed the company's interest rate spreads. The recent declines in rates should help reverse this trend in the latter half of 1995.

Operational Review - 25-OCT-95

Total revenues in the six months ended June 30, 1995, increased 6.7% year to year, reflecting increased premium revenue in the specialty health insurance segment. Total benefits and expenses rose 6.5%, due to a higher benefit ratio as competitors have aggressively priced insurance products in an attempt to gain market share; pretax income rose 9.1%. After taxes at 33.6% versus 30.8%, net income was up 4.7% to $16,187,000 ($1.31 a share; $1.29 fully diluted) from $15,455,000 ($1.25; $1.24).

Stock Performance - 20-OCT-95

In the past 30 trading days, WNT's shares have increased 5%, compared to a 3% rise in the S&P 500. Average trading volume for the past five days was 12,900 shares, compared with the 40-day moving average of 15,021 shares.

Key Stock Statistics

Dividend Rate/Share	1.08	Shareholders	6,000
Shs. outstg. (M)	12.2	Market cap. (B)	$0.293
Avg. daily vol. (M)	0.011	Inst. holdings	66%
Tang. Bk. Value/Share	31.06	Insider holdings	NA
Beta	0.37		

Value of $10,000 invested 5 years ago: $ 12,397

Fiscal Year Ending Dec. 31

	1995	% Change	1994	% Change	1993	% Change
Revenues (Million $)						
1Q	168.4	5%	160.4	6%	151.2	—
2Q	175.6	8%	162.1	1%	160.0	—
3Q	—	—	167.8	6%	158.1	—
4Q	—	—	166.7	4%	159.8	10%
Yr.	—	—	656.9	5%	628.5	12%
Income (Million $)						
1Q	7.29	4%	7.03	48%	4.75	53%
2Q	8.90	6%	8.42	24%	6.79	69%
3Q	—	—	9.13	68%	5.44	105%
4Q	—	—	6.72	-40%	11.23	59%
Yr.	—	—	31.30	11%	28.22	67%
Earnings Per Share ($)						
1Q	0.59	4%	0.57	24%	0.46	53%
2Q	0.72	6%	0.68	3%	0.66	69%
3Q	—	—	0.74	48%	0.50	92%
4Q	—	—	0.54	-41%	0.91	30%
Yr.	—	—	2.53	-2%	2.59	57%

Next earnings report expected: early November

Washington National

Business Summary - 23-OCT-95

Washington National Corp. is a financial services holding company that currently focuses on three core businesses: individual and group health insurance, disability insurance for educators, and individual life insurance and annuities. WNT's main operating companies are Washington National Insurance Co. (WNIC) and United Presidential Life Insurance Co. (UPI). Contributions to revenues by business segment in recent years were:

	1994	1993	1992
Life insurance & annuities	35%	36%	41%
Health insurance	64%	63%	59%
Corporate & other	1%	1%	---

Life insurance in force at December 31, 1994, totaled $21.0 billion.

WNIC, based in Lincolnshire, Illinois, is licensed to do business in all states (except New York) and the District of Columbia. It offers a variety of insurance products including individual health, group employee benefits, and disability insurance for educators. In 1994, 32% of WNT's total revenues were derived from WNIC's group product premiums, which are included in the health insurance segment. Premiums for WNIC's disablility insurance for educators accounted for 10% of WNT's revenues in 1994.

UPI, based in Indiana, is licensed to do business in 45 states and the District of Columbia. Its primary business is the marketing and underwriting of individual life insurance and annuities, with a focus on interest-sensitive products such as universal life insurance, excess interest whole life insurance and annuities.

Investments totaled $2.3 billion at year end 1994, and were divided: fixed maturities 77.1%, mortgage loans on real estate 15.6%, real estate investments 1.2%, equity securities 0.1%, policy loans 2.4%, other long term 1.3%, and short term 2.3%. Of the fixed maturity investments, 94.8% were investment grade, including 41.2% rated AAA.

Important Developments

Aug. '95—Washington National reported that, over the past few quarters, the sales environment for the company's group and individual major medical health insurance products has become more competitive as other insurance companies have priced their products more aggressively in an attempt to gain market share. This sales environment has caused the segment to experience an increase in the level of policy lapses and an increase in the benefit ratio. WNT expects this trend to continue over the remainder of 1995 and into 1996.

Capitalization

Mortgage Payable: $1,631,000 (6/95).
$2.50 Convertible Preferred Stock: 144,608 shs. ($5 par); conv. into 1.875 com. shs.

Per Share Data ($) (Year Ended Dec. 31)

	1994	1993	1992	1991	1990	1989
Tangible Bk. Val.	23.62	26.94	25.81	26.90	26.86	28.55
Oper. Earnings	2.44	2.30	1.84	NA	NA	NA
Earnings	2.53	2.59	1.65	-0.33	-0.84	0.87
Dividends	1.08	1.08	1.08	1.08	1.08	1.08
Payout Ratio	43%	42%	65%	NM	NM	124%
Prices - High	25⅜	28	23⅝	16¼	28¾	29⅛
- Low	18⅜	21¾	15⅞	9⅜	10	24
P/E Ratio - High	10	11	14	NM	NM	33
- Low	7	8	10	NM	NM	28

Income Statement Analysis (Million $)

	1994	%Chg	1993	%Chg	1992	%Chg	1991
Life Ins. In Force	21,035	-5%	22,215	-13%	25,454	5%	24,227
Premium Income Life	102	2%	100	-3%	103	NM	102
Prem.Inc A & H	366	8%	338	25%	270	-3%	278
Premium Income Other	Nil	—	Nil	—	Nil	—	Nil
Net Invest. Inc.	182	-1%	184	-2%	187	-6%	199
Total Revs.	657	4%	629	12%	563	-1%	571
Pretax Inc.	44.6	15%	38.7	47%	26.4	NM	-0.4
Net Oper. Inc.	30.2	20%	25.1	34%	18.8	—	NA
Net Inc.	31.3	11%	28.2	67%	16.9	NM	-3.0

Balance Sheet & Other Fin. Data (Million $)

	1994	1993	1992	1991	1990	1989
Cash & Equiv.	40.4	42.8	43.2	36.0	38.0	48.0
Premiums Due	14.9	25.2	11.4	18.5	19.8	35.7
Inv Assets Bonds	1,763	1,836	1,602	1,401	1,492	1,652
Inv. Assets Stock	13.0	16.0	39.0	82.0	99	109
Inv. Assets Loans	412	444	504	545	632	604
Inv. Assets Total	2,285	2,356	2,234	2,112	2,313	2,447
Deferred Policy Cost	294	257	242	193	202	239
Total Assets	2,811	2,854	2,653	2,487	2,685	2,899
Debt	1.9	2.4	31.2	20.7	23.1	44.7
Common Eqty.	306	348	287	299	307	345

Ratio Analysis

	1994	1993	1992	1991	1990	1989
% Ret. on Revs.	4.8	4.5	3.0	NM	NM	1.2
% Ret. on Assets	1.1	1.0	0.7	NM	NM	0.4
% Ret. on Equity	9.5	8.9	5.6	NM	NM	2.7
% Invest. Yield	7.8	8.0	8.6	9.0	9.0	9.4

Dividend Data —Dividends have been paid since 1923. A dividend reinvestment plan is available. A "poison pill" stock purchase right was issued in 1988.

Amt. of Div. $	Date Decl.	Ex-Div. Date	Stock of Record	Payment Date
0.270	Nov. 23	Nov. 30	Dec. 06	Jan. 03 '95
0.270	Feb. 23	Mar. 01	Mar. 07	Apr. 03 '95
0.270	May. 25	May. 31	Jun. 06	Jul. 03 '95
0.270	Aug. 31	Sep. 08	Sep. 12	Oct. 02 '95

Data as orig. reptd.; bef. results of disc. opers. and/or spec. items. Per share data adj. for stk. divs. as of ex-div. date. E-Estimated. NA-Not Available. NM-Not Meaningful. NR-Not Ranked.

Office—300 Tower Parkway, Lincolnshire, IL 60069. **Tel**—(708) 793-3000. **Chrmn, Pres & CEO**—R. W. Patin. **EVP & CFO**—T. C. Scott. **VP & Secy**—C. R. Edwards. **VP & Treas**—J. K. Cohen. **VP & Investor Contact**—Craig Simundza (708-793-3053). **Dirs**—F. R. Blume, E. R. Bond, R. L. Bornhuetter, W. F. Brennan, L. A. Ellis, J. R. Haire, S. P. Hutchison, G. P. Kendall, Jr., F. L. Klapperich, Jr., L. M. Mitchell, R. W. Patin, R. Reade, P. Y. Tsien. **Transfer Agent & Registrar**—First Chicago Trust Co. of New York. **Incorporated** in Delaware in 1968 (Washington National Insurance was founded in 1911). **Empl**-976. **S&P Analyst:** Brad Ohlmuller

STANDARD & POOR'S **Waterhouse Investor Services**

STOCK REPORTS

NYSE Symbol **WHO**
In S&P SmallCap 600

13-OCT-95 **Industry:** Securities

Summary: This company is the parent of Waterhouse Securities, which provides discount brokerage services to retail customers through a network of over 70 offices in the U.S.

Quantitative Evaluations

Outlook
(1 Lowest—5 Highest)
• **NA**

Fair Value
• **NA**

Risk
• **High**

Earn./Div. Rank
• **B+**

Technical Eval.
• **Bullish** since 2/95

Rel. Strength Rank
(1 Lowest—99 Highest)
• **65**

Insider Activity
• **Neutral**

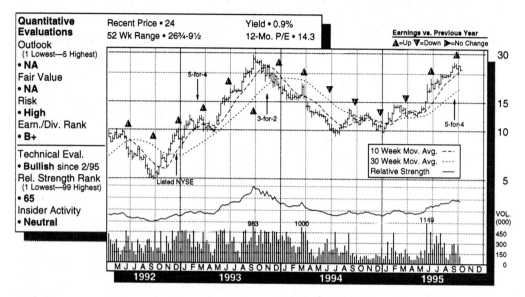

Recent Price • 24 | Yield • 0.9%
52 Wk Range • 26¾-9½ | 12-Mo. P/E • 14.3

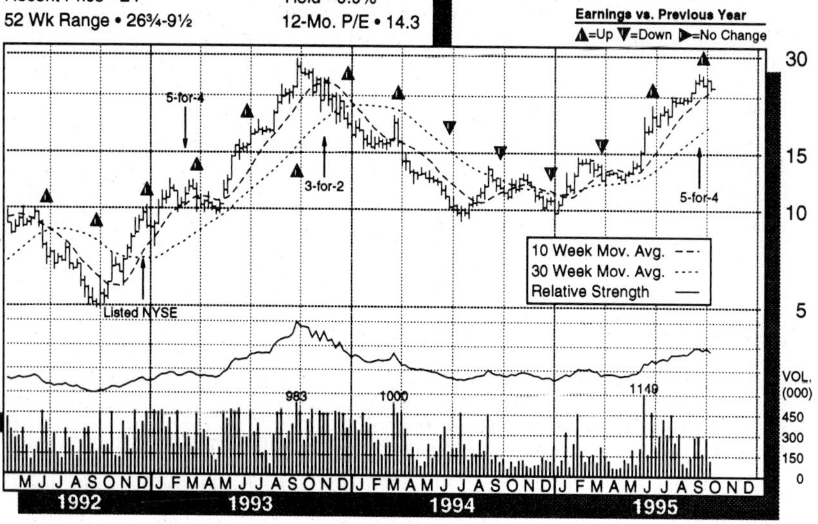

Business Profile - 29-SEP-95

Due to favorable market conditions and increasing participation of individual investors, this discount broker has seen rapid growth in customer accounts, trade processing and revenues over the past several years. WHO continues to expand its branch office network, opening 12 new offices during fiscal 1995. The company plans to continue its growth strategy of expanding its branch office network (12 additional offices are planned for fiscal 1996) and the introduction of new products and services.

Operational Review - 13-OCT-95

Based on a preliminary report, revenues for the fiscal year ended August 31, 1995, rose 33% from those of the prior fiscal year. Margins continued to be penalized by a rise in expenses due to the expansion of the branch office network and introduction of new services. Net income was up 23% to $19,357,000 ($1.68 a share; $1.54 fully diluted) from $15,726,000 ($1.37; $1.30).

Stock Performance - 06-OCT-95

In the past 30 trading days, WHO's shares have increased 9%, compared to a 4% rise in the S&P 500. Average trading volume for the past five days was 22,500 shares, compared with the 40-day moving average of 36,470 shares.

Key Stock Statistics

Dividend Rate/Share	0.20	Shareholders	8,500
Shs. outstg. (M)	11.4	Market cap. (B)	$0.266
Avg. daily vol. (M)	0.040	Inst. holdings	14%
Tang. Bk. Value/Share	5.46	Insider holdings	NA
Beta	NM		

Value of $10,000 invested 5 years ago: $ 256,377

Fiscal Year Ending Aug. 31

	1995	% Change	1994	% Change	1993	% Change
Revenues (Million $)						
1Q	28.15	4%	27.09	79%	15.11	36%
2Q	31.26	8%	28.85	29%	22.29	35%
3Q	36.61	36%	26.99	19%	22.61	59%
4Q	46.98	90%	24.67	2%	24.21	76%
Yr.	143.0	33%	107.6	28%	84.22	52%
Income (Million $)						
1Q	3.67	-26%	4.96	128%	2.18	45%
2Q	4.04	-20%	5.03	17%	4.29	43%
3Q	5.16	51%	3.42	-13%	3.93	83%
4Q	6.50	180%	2.32	-41%	3.96	118%
Yr.	19.36	23%	15.73	10%	14.36	70%
Earnings Per Share ($)						
1Q	0.32	-26%	0.43	125%	0.19	41%
2Q	0.35	-20%	0.44	18%	0.37	41%
3Q	0.45	51%	0.30	-13%	0.34	82%
4Q	0.56	180%	0.20	-42%	0.35	120%
Yr.	1.68	23%	1.37	9%	1.26	69%

Next earnings report expected: late December

Waterhouse Investor Services

Business Summary - 29-SEP-95

Waterhouse Investor Services is a holding company whose principal subsidiary, Waterhouse Securities, Inc., provides discount brokerage and mutual fund services primarily to retail customers. In October 1994, Waterhouse National Bank, a wholly owned subsidiary, registered as a bank holding company.

As of April 1995, the company was operating 66 branches in 33 states and the District of Columbia. A total of 12 offices were opened in fiscal 1994, and 12 more per year were expected to be added in both fiscal 1995 and 1996. At November 17, 1994, Waterhouse had approximately 221,000 active accounts for customers throughout the U.S.

Revenues in recent fiscal years (ended August 31) were derived as follows:

	1994	1993	1992
Commissions	70%	75%	75%
Interest	15%	12%	13%
Mutual fund fees	6%	6%	5%
Other	9%	7%	7%

Waterhouse provides all of the customer contact aspects of discount brokerage services, such as opening accounts, providing price information and taking orders. It is registered as a broker-dealer in all 50 states, the District of Columbia, and Puerto Rico.

The company reaches potential customers through a combination of customer referrals and advertisements that appear almost exclusively in national financial and other newspapers and publications. It has developed a four-part marketing plan that includes a simple, level-discount commission schedule; services of personal account officers in regional offices; free investment and financial publication information (but not investment advice) to customers with active accounts; and no-load mutual funds and fixed income securities.

Waterhouse National Bank, a wholly owned subsidiary, received its charter in October 1994 and said it would take the necessary steps to be operational in the early part of 1995. The bank will offer (if approved) cash management accounts, credit cards and other retail loan products.

Important Developments

Sep. '95—The company announced that it is in the process of establishing its own money market funds under the name Waterhouse Investors Cash Management Fund and that it is planning to introduce additional mutual funds over the next few years. Also, Waterhouse National Bank is planning to expand its banking services by offering a No Fee Investors Prime Credit Card with a low variable interest rate and other consumer loan products in fiscal 1996.

Capitalization

Long Term Debt: $48,500,000 of 6% sub. notes due 2003; conv. into com. at $29.25 a sh. (2/95).

Per Share Data ($)

(Year Ended Aug. 31)

	1995	1994	1993	1992	1991	1990
Tangible Bk. Val.	NA	4.34	3.12	1.85	1.12	0.85
Cash Flow	NA	NA	NA	NA	NA	NA
Earnings	1.68	1.37	1.26	0.75	0.30	0.12
Dividends	0.45	0.16	0.14	0.09	0.05	0.03
Payout Ratio	27%	12%	10%	11%	15%	28%
Prices - High	26¾	19⅝	29¼	12⅜	8⅛	1³⁄₁₆
- Low	9⅞	9¼	7⅝	4⅞	¾	¹¹⁄₁₆
P/E Ratio - High	16	14	23	17	27	10
- Low	6	7	6	7	3	6

Income Statement Analysis (Million $)

	1994	%Chg	1993	%Chg	1992	%Chg	1991
Commissions	75.7	20%	63.2	50%	42.0	87%	22.5
Int. Inc.	15.7	58%	9.9	41%	7.C	38%	5.1
Total Revs.	108	28%	84.2	51%	55.6	77%	31.4
Int. Exp.	5.8	90%	3.0	55%	2.0	41%	1.4
Pretax Inc.	28.0	9%	25.8	70%	15.2	166%	5.7
Eff. Tax Rate	44%	—	44%	—	44%	—	44%
Net Inc.	15.7	9%	14.4	70%	8.5	168%	3.2

Balance Sheet & Other Fin. Data (Million $)

	1994	1993	1992	1991	1990	1989
Total Assets	316	241	149	71.6	60.8	51.8
Cash Items	15.3	5.8	8.2	1.1	0.7	0.5
Receivables	286	226	136	67.1	56.5	47.9
Secs. Owned	Nil	Nil	Nil	0.3	0.0	0.4
Sec. Borrowed	76.3	99	74.0	14.6	25.2	20.4
Due Brokers & Cust.	124	90.4	44.3	40.1	23.0	19.1
Other Liabs.	17.9	16.2	9.6	5.1	3.4	3.4
Capitalization:						
Debt	48.5	Nil	Nil	0.2	0.4	0.6
Equity	49.6	35.6	21.0	11.5	8.9	8.3
Total	98.1	35.6	21.0	11.8	9.3	8.9

Ratio Analysis

	1994	1993	1992	1991	1990	1989
% Ret. on Revs.	14.6	17.0	15.3	10.1	5.4	5.6
% Ret. on Assets	5.6	7.4	7.7	4.8	2.3	2.2
% Ret. on Equity	36.9	50.7	52.0	31.0	14.9	13.7

Dividend Data —Cash dividends have been paid since fiscal 1989, while stock dividends were paid in 1991 to 1993.

Amt. of Div. $	Date Decl.	Ex-Div. Date	Stock of Record	Payment Date
0.250	Jul. 28	Aug. 15	Aug. 17	Sep. 07 '95
5-for-4	Jul. 28	Sep. 15	Aug. 17	Sep. 14 '95

Data as orig. reptd.; bef. results of disc opers. and/or spec. items. Per share data adj. for stk. divs. of 50% Nov. 1993, 25% Mar. 1993, 50% Feb. 1992, 25% Jun. 1991. E-Estimated. NA-Not Available. NM-Not Meaningful. NR-Not Ranked.

Office—100 Wall St., New York, NY 10005. **Tel**—(212) 806-3500. **Chrmn, Pres & CEO**—L. M. Waterhouse, Jr. **SVP-CFO**—B. M. Siegel. **EVP-Secy**—R. H. Neiman. **SVP-Treas & Investor Contact**—Kenneth I. Coco. **Dirs**—J. Belson, W. J. Cardew, J. H. Chapel, K. I. Coco, F. E. Conti, R. H. Neiman, E. J. Nicoll, A. J. Radin, J. F. Rittinger, G. F. Staudter, L. M. Waterhouse Jr., P. A. Wigger. **Transfer Agent & Registrar**—Continental Stock & Transfer Co., NYC. **Incorporated** in Delaware in 1987. **Empl**-756. **S&P Analyst:** Brad Ohlmuller

STANDARD & POOR'S

STOCK REPORTS

Watkins-Johnson

NYSE Symbol **WJ**
In S&P SmallCap 600

29-JUL-95

Industry: Electronics/Electric

Summary: This producer of semiconductor manufacturing equipment also makes electronic products for wireless telecommunications and defense applications.

S&P Opinion: Accumulate (★★★★)

Recent Price • 51⅛
52 Wk Range • 53¼-26⅛
Yield • 0.9%
12-Mo. P/E • 17.7

Quantitative Evaluations

Outlook
(1 Lowest—5 Highest)
• **4**

Fair Value
• **46**

Risk
• **Average**

Earn./Div. Rank
• **B**

Technical Eval.
• **Bullish** since 1/95

Rel. Strength Rank
(1 Lowest—99 Highest)
• **82**

Insider Activity
• **Neutral**

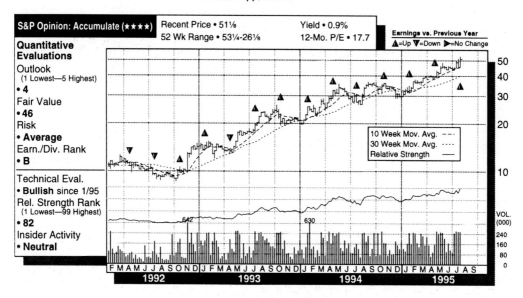

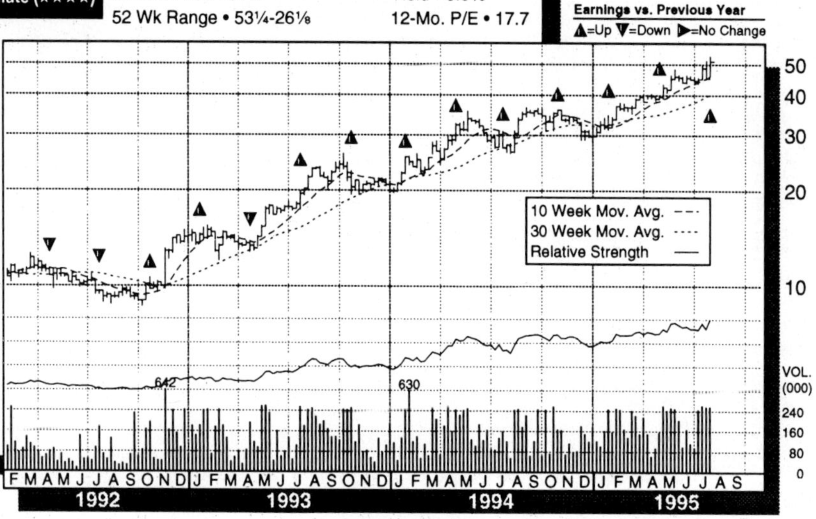

Overview - 28-JUL-95

Sales for 1995 are likely to rise about 20% from those of 1994. Gains will again come from the semiconductor equipment group, which should be up over 50%. Commercial products (primarily wireless communications products) should also experience robust growth. The defense electronics business is projected to continue its steady decline, reflecting the MSS divestiture and the shrinking government defense budget. Margins should benefit from cost-cutting initiatives, including the consolidation of northern California operations, and from a more favorable product mix.

Valuation - 28-JUL-95

With WJ's earnings increasingly attributable to semiconductor manufacturers, its shares will become more closely correlated to events in the semiconductor industry. Although the semiconductor market may begin to slow, we are encouraged by the substantial amounts being spent on R&D. There is strong customer interest in the company's new high-density plasma (HDP) product (to be introduced early 1996), and we see a large potential demand for the TruePosition cellular location system. Sales of defense electronics should experience some relief when government procurement begins to rebound (budgeted for 1997). Given the long-term high growth outlook for WJ, we view the shares as attractive at about 14 times estimated 1995 earnings.

Key Stock Statistics

S&P EPS Est. 1995	3.20	Tang. Bk. Value/Share	20.16
P/E on S&P Est. 1995	16.0	Beta	0.80
S&P EPS Est. 1996	4.00	Shareholders	4,600
Dividend Rate/Share	0.48	Market cap. (B)	$0.396
Shs. outstg. (M)	7.7	Inst. holdings	79%
Avg. daily vol. (M)	0.081	Insider holdings	NA

Value of $10,000 invested 5 years ago: $ 28,459

Fiscal Year Ending Dec. 31

	1995	% Change	1994	% Change	1993	% Change
Revenues (Million $)						
1Q	92.98	15%	80.56	20%	67.08	6%
2Q	102.0	17%	87.37	28%	68.22	2%
3Q	—	—	83.17	14%	72.71	6%
4Q	—	—	81.54	4%	78.28	19%
Yr.	—	—	332.6	16%	286.3	8%
Income (Million $)						
1Q	5.35	48%	3.62	164%	1.37	-7%
2Q	7.78	31%	5.93	124%	2.65	NM
3Q	—	—	5.39	54%	3.51	156%
4Q	—	—	6.02	48%	4.06	196%
Yr.	—	—	21.65	87%	11.60	134%
Earnings Per Share ($)						
1Q	0.63	34%	0.47	161%	0.18	-10%
2Q	0.88	14%	0.77	133%	0.33	NM
3Q	E0.87	—	0.63	50%	0.42	133%
4Q	E0.90	—	0.77	48%	0.52	189%
Yr.	E3.20	—	2.66	83%	1.45	120%

Next earnings report expected: mid October

Watkins-Johnson

Business Summary - 28-APR-95

Watkins-Johnson specializes in semiconductor manufacturing equipment and electronic products. The environmental services unit was divested at the end of 1994. Contributions by segment in 1994 were:

	Sales	Profits
Electronics	57%	27%
Semiconductor equipment	43%	73%

International sales accounted for 45% of the total in 1994, up from 33% in 1993.

The Semiconductor Group produces chemical-vapor-deposition (CVD) equipment for semiconductor manufacturing. The equipment is used by semiconductor manufacturers worldwide in the production of microprocessor, logic and computer memory chips. A related application is in liquid crystal flat-panel display.

The Electronics Group manufactures turnkey systems, integrated subsystems and signal processing components for intelligence collection and general reconnaissance and surveillance purposes, missile-guidance systems and space communications missions. Direct sales to U.S. government agencies totaled $57 million in 1994, down from $60 million in 1993. Sales to Hughes Aircraft Co. came to $35 million in 1994 ($41 million in 1993).

The group also serves customers with wireless-communication requirements. Non-defense contracts include transceivers for cellular base stations, receivers for locating emergency 911 callers and high-dynamic-range mixers for the Japanese manufacturer of "personal handi-phone" base stations.

The environmental services group, which conducted technical consulting for groundwater resources and detection and remediation of aquifer contamination, was divested at the end of 1994.

Important Developments

Apr. '95—The company reported that a 67% increase in sales by semiconductor equipment group offset a 12% decline by the electronics group in the first quarter. The Far East continued to be the strongest geographic area for new semiconductor equipment orders, with 61% of system bookings. Separately, WJ said it is supplying custom-designed receivers and signal processing subsystems to the Associated Group for its TruePosition cellular location system, currently undergoing field testing in Philadelphia.

Mar. '95—Firm order backlog at March 31, 1995, totaled $229.2 million, up 5.2% from the level a year earlier. About 96% of backlog was shippable within a year.

Capitalization

Long Term Debt: $7,823,000 (12/94); incl. capital lease obligs.

Per Share Data ($) (Year Ended Dec. 31)

	1994	1993	1992	1991	1990	1989
Tangible Bk. Val.	19.75	17.62	16.55	15.67	19.15	17.74
Cash Flow	3.72	2.69	2.15	-1.42	3.23	3.68
Earnings	2.66	1.45	0.66	-2.98	1.67	2.23
Dividends	0.48	0.48	0.48	0.48	0.48	0.46
Payout Ratio	18%	33%	73%	NM	28%	21%
Prices - High	36⅝	26¼	15	19½	20⅞	27¼
- Low	19⅝	12	8⅝	9¼	10⅝	19
P/E Ratio - High	14	18	23	NM	13	12
- Low	7	8	13	NM	6	9

Income Statement Analysis (Million $)

	1994	%Chg	1993	%Chg	1992	%Chg	1991
Revs.	333	16%	286	8%	264	-5%	278
Oper. Inc.	39.3	46%	26.9	42%	19.0	40%	13.6
Depr.	8.7	-13%	10.0	-12%	11.3	-3%	11.7
Int. Exp.	1.1	-12%	1.3	-14%	1.5	-1%	1.5
Pretax Inc.	30.9	84%	16.8	133%	7.2	NM	-28.7
Eff. Tax Rate	30%	—	31%	—	31%	—	NM
Net Inc.	21.7	87%	11.6	132%	5.0	NM	-22.4

Balance Sheet & Other Fin. Data (Million $)

	1994	1993	1992	1991	1990	1989
Cash	34.5	45.0	49.1	40.1	17.2	26.6
Curr. Assets	179	169	153	153	159	169
Total Assets	235	221	206	213	223	227
Curr. Liab.	62.8	60.3	52.4	62.8	59.3	55.1
LT Debt	7.8	12.2	12.9	14.8	15.8	19.0
Common Eqty.	150	134	125	118	144	149
Total Cap.	157	146	138	133	160	168
Cap. Exp.	12.5	9.7	5.2	9.9	16.8	11.8
Cash Flow	30.4	21.6	16.3	-10.7	25.2	30.9

Ratio Analysis

	1994	1993	1992	1991	1990	1989
Curr. Ratio	2.9	2.8	2.9	2.4	2.7	3.1
% LT Debt of Cap.	5.0	8.3	9.3	11.2	9.9	11.3
% Net Inc.of Revs.	6.5	4.1	1.9	NM	4.2	6.0
% Ret. on Assets	9.5	5.4	2.4	NM	6.1	8.6
% Ret. on Equity	15.3	8.9	4.1	NM	9.4	13.2

Dividend Data (Dividends have been paid since 1974. A "poison pill" stock purchase right was adopted in 1986.)

Amt. of Div. $	Date Decl.	Ex-Div. Date	Stock of Record	Payment Date
0.120	Jul. 26	Aug. 30	Sep. 06	Sep. 22 '94
0.120	Nov. 28	Dec. 06	Dec. 12	Jan. 02 '95
0.120	Feb. 28	Mar. 07	Mar. 13	Mar. 30 '95
0.120	May. 23	May. 30	Jun. 05	Jun. 22 '95

Data as orig. reptd.; bef. results of disc. opers. and/or spec. items. Per share data adj. for stk. divs. as of ex-div. date. E-Estimated. NA-Not Available. NM-Not Meaningful. NR-Not Ranked.

Office—3333 Hillview Ave., Palo Alto, CA 94304. **Tel**—(415) 493-4141. **Chrmn**—D. A. Watkins. **Vice Chrmn**—H. R. Johnson. **Pres & CEO**—W. K. Kennedy, Jr. **Secy**—Carol H. Roosen. **VP & CFO**—S. G. Buchanan. **Treas**—Joan M. Varrone. **Investor Contact**—Frank E. Emery. **Dirs**—G. M. Cusumano, W. R. Graham, J. J. Hartmann, H. R. Johnson, W. K. Kennedy, Jr., R. F. O'Brien, R. L. Prestel, D. A. Watkins. **Transfer Agent**—Chemical Trust Co. of California, SF. **Incorporated** in California in 1957. **Empl-** 2,220. **S&P Analyst:** Joe Victor Shammas

Watson Pharmaceuticals

NASDAQ Symbol **WATS**
In S&P SmallCap 600

04-OCT-95

Industry: Drugs-Generic and OTC

Summary: Watson manufactures and sells off-patent medications and develops advanced drug delivery systems designed primarily to enhance the therapeutic benefits of pharmaceutical compounds.

Quantitative Evaluations

Outlook
(1 Lowest—5 Highest)
• **NA**

Fair Value
• **NA**

Risk
• **Average**

Earn./Div. Rank
• **NR**

Technical Eval.
• **Bullish** since 2/95

Rel. Strength Rank
(1 Lowest—99 Highest)
• **46**

Insider Activity
• **NA**

Recent Price • 41
52 Wk Range • 44½-20
Yield • Nil
12-Mo. P/E • 30.8

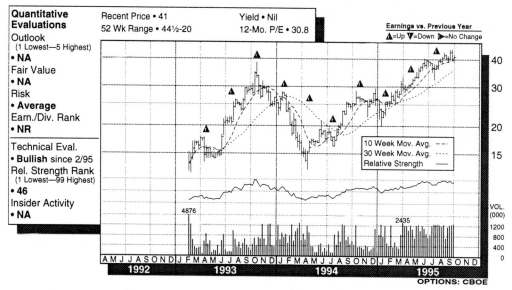

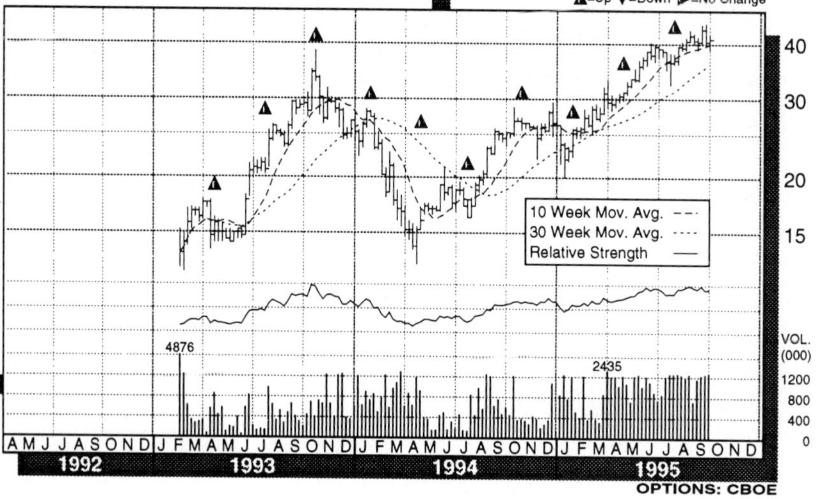

Business Profile - 04-OCT-95

Fueled by the company's pipeline of generic products and aggressive expansion program, Watson's earnings have grown dramatically in recent years. In July 1995, the company acquired ASE-listed Circa Pharmaceuticals, a maker of OTC drug products. Although the acquisition will be accretive to earnings WATS expects to incur a one-time charge of $12 to $14 million in the third quarter of 1995. FDA approvals in 1995 include Glipizide tablets and Fiorinal with Codeine capsules.

Operational Review - 04-OCT-95

Revenues for the six months ended June 30, 1995 (pro forma) advanced 67%, year to year, reflecting contributions from recently acquired Circa Pharmaceuticals. Margins widened, aided by an improved product mix and well controlled costs, boosted; operating income rose to $22.7 million from $6.0 million. Results benefited from equity in joint ventures and after taxes at 27.6%, versus 22.8%, net income increased 68%, to $25.7 million ($0.70 a share) from $15.3 million ($0.42).

Stock Performance - 29-SEP-95

In the past 30 trading days, WATS's shares have increased 0.92%, compared to a 5% rise in the S&P 500. Average trading volume for the past five days was 387,380 shares, compared with the 40-day moving average of 292,336 shares.

Key Stock Statistics

Dividend Rate/Share	Nil	Shareholders	300
Shs. outstg. (M)	36.0	Market cap. (B)	$ 1.4
Avg. daily vol. (M)	0.306	Inst. holdings	34%
Tang. Bk. Value/Share	6.96	Insider holdings	NA
Beta	NA		

Value of $10,000 invested 5 years ago: NA

Fiscal Year Ending Dec. 31

	1995	% Change	1994	% Change	1993	% Change
Revenues (Million $)						
1Q	34.13	77%	19.32	31%	14.70	93%
2Q	36.99	76%	21.03	29%	16.34	112%
3Q	—	—	22.50	25%	18.03	140%
4Q	—	—	24.21	31%	18.45	55%
Yr.	—	—	87.06	29%	67.55	95%
Income (Million $)						
1Q	12.39	NM	4.09	74%	2.35	—
2Q	13.31	198%	4.47	48%	3.02	—
3Q	—	—	4.81	48%	3.25	—
4Q	—	—	5.31	48%	3.60	—
Yr.	—	—	18.69	53%	12.22	NM
Earnings Per Share ($)						
1Q	0.33	43%	0.23	53%	0.15	NM
2Q	0.36	44%	0.25	39%	0.18	NM
3Q	—	—	0.27	42%	0.19	NM
4Q	—	—	0.30	43%	0.21	50%
Yr.	—	—	1.05	42%	0.74	185%

Next earnings report expected: early November

Watson Pharmaceuticals

Business Summary - 29-SEP-95

Watson Pharmaceuticals Inc. is engaged in the manufacture and sale of off-patent medications and the development of advanced drug delivery systems designed primarily to enhance the therapeutic benefits of pharmaceutical compounds.

Off-patent (or generic) drugs, which are sold after the patents on the related brand-name drugs have expired, are typically sold at prices substantially below those of their brand-name equivalents. At 1994 year-end, Watson was manufacturing and marketing 62 dosage forms and strengths representing 20 ethical drugs under 62 approved Abbreviated New Drug Applications (ANDAs). The company also has 7 ANDAs representing 7 ethical drugs pending before the FDA and several ethical drugs under development. Therapeutic products include anti-depressants, tranquilizers, anti-hypertensives, diuretics, oral contraceptives, anti-inflammatories and analgesics, as well as hormone replacement, asthma, anti-spasmodic, pro-motility and anti-diarrheal drugs.

Off-patent products are marketed to drug distributors, pharmaceutcial wholesalers, drugstore chains, hospitals, health maintenance organizations and other drug companies. In 1994, sales of off-patent products to Rugby Laboratories, Inc. (a subsidiary of Marion Merrell Dow Inc.) and Warner Chilcott Laboratories (a division of Warner-Lambert Co.) accounted for 11% and 14%, respectively, of total revenues.

Watson has developed various proprietary polymer-based drug delivery systems for various routes of administration, including transmucosal, oral, vaginal and transdermal. Watson's proprietary buccal, oral and vaginal drug delivery systems permit defined adjustment of release rates.

In July 1995, Watson completed the acquisition of Circa Pharmaceuticals, Inc., a maker of generic drug products, for about 18,700,000 common shares. Circa had 1994 earnings of $17.3 million.

Important Developments

Sep. '95—Watson received approval from the U.S. FDA for an off-patent form of Fiorinal with Codeine, a capsule drug marketed by Sandoz Pharmaceuticals. Branded sales of the drug are estimated at $70 million for 1995.

Aug. '95—The company entered a joint marketing agreement with Creighton Products, a division of Sandoz Pharmaceuticals, in which Watson would provide about 10 of its generic drugs for distribution to Creighton's nursing homes. Creighton will then provide Watson with products for distribution through its wholesaler channels.

Capitalization

Long Term Liabs.: $5,890,000 (6/95).

Per Share Data ($) (Year Ended Dec. 31)

	1994	1993	1992	1991	1990	1989
Tangible Bk. Val.	6.50	5.41	2.97	1.24	0.97	0.81
Cash Flow	1.22	0.87	0.38	0.21	0.17	NA
Earnings	1.05	0.74	0.26	0.12	0.09	0.10
Dividends	Nil	Nil	Nil	Nil	Nil	Nil
Payout Ratio	Nil	Nil	Nil	Nil	Nil	Nil
Prices - High	29½	38½	NA	NA	NA	NA
- Low	12¾	12	NA	NA	NA	NA
P/E Ratio - High	28	52	NA	NA	NA	NA
- Low	12	16	NA	NA	NA	NA

Income Statement Analysis (Million $)

	1994	%Chg	1993	%Chg	1992	%Chg	1991
Revs.	87.1	29%	67.5	95%	34.7	18%	29.5
Oper. Inc.	31.9	46%	21.9	172%	8.0	81%	4.4
Depr.	3.0	39%	2.2	32%	1.6	31%	1.3
Int. Exp.	0.5	44%	0.4	-16%	0.4	NM	0.4
Pretax Inc.	30.0	49%	20.1	NM	6.0	104%	2.9
Eff. Tax Rate	38%	—	39%	—	40%	—	46%
Net Inc.	18.7	53%	12.2	NM	3.6	129%	1.6

Balance Sheet & Other Fin. Data (Million $)

	1994	1993	1992	1991	1990	1989
Cash	56.5	56.4	0.2	1.4	0.5	0.7
Curr. Assets	87.1	78.7	16.0	12.5	NA	NA
Total Assets	130	105	31.2	23.9	18.9	18.4
Curr. Liab.	12.0	10.1	7.4	5.2	NA	NA
LT Debt	5.1	12.1	4.0	2.7	3.0	2.9
Common Eqty.	111	91.2	19.8	16.0	11.8	9.4
Total Cap.	118	105	23.8	18.7	14.8	12.4
Cap. Exp.	20.0	12.8	5.6	3.8	2.0	NA
Cash Flow	21.7	14.4	5.2	2.8	2.3	NA

Ratio Analysis

	1994	1993	1992	1991	1990	1989
Curr. Ratio	7.2	7.8	2.1	2.4	NA	NA
% LT Debt of Cap.	4.3	11.6	16.8	14.6	20.5	23.7
% Net Inc.of Revs.	21.5	18.1	10.4	5.3	5.2	6.0
% Ret. on Assets	15.9	18.0	12.8	7.3	6.5	7.5
% Ret. on Equity	18.5	22.0	20.4	11.2	11.1	14.7

Dividend Data —No cash dividends have been paid, and none are anticipated in the foreseeable future.

Data as orig. reptd.; bef. results of disc. opers. and/or spec. items. Per share data adj. for stk. divs. as of ex-div. date. E-Estimated. NA-Not Available. NM-Not Meaningful. NR-Not Ranked.

Office—311 Bonnie Circle, Corona, CA 91720. **Tel**—(909) 270-1400. **Chrmn**—A. D. Keith. **Pres & CEO**—A. Y. Chao. **Secy**—A. Y. Kung. **Dirs**—H. R. Besch, A. Y. Chao, J. Chao, M. J. Feldman, A. F. Hummel, A. D. Keith, A. Y. Kung, W. Kiang, A. Y. Kung, R. R. Taylor. **Transfer Agent & Registrar**—Chemical Trust Co. of California, LA. **Incorporated** in Nevada in 1985. **Empl**-379. **S&P Analyst:** Thomas Tirney

Westcott Communications

NASDAQ Symbol **WCTV**
In S&P SmallCap 600

18-SEP-95

Industry: Education

Summary: WCTV is a creator and producer of training, educational and informational programming delivered through satellite television networks, videotape and teleconference distribution.

Quantitative Evaluations

Outlook (1 Lowest—5 Highest)
• **NA**

Fair Value
• **NA**

Risk
• **High**

Earn./Div. Rank
• **NR**

Technical Eval.
• **Bullish** since 4/95

Rel. Strength Rank (1 Lowest—99 Highest)
• **41**

Insider Activity
• **NA**

Recent Price • 15⅜
52 Wk Range • 18¼-11⅛
Yield • Nil
12-Mo. P/E • 21.7

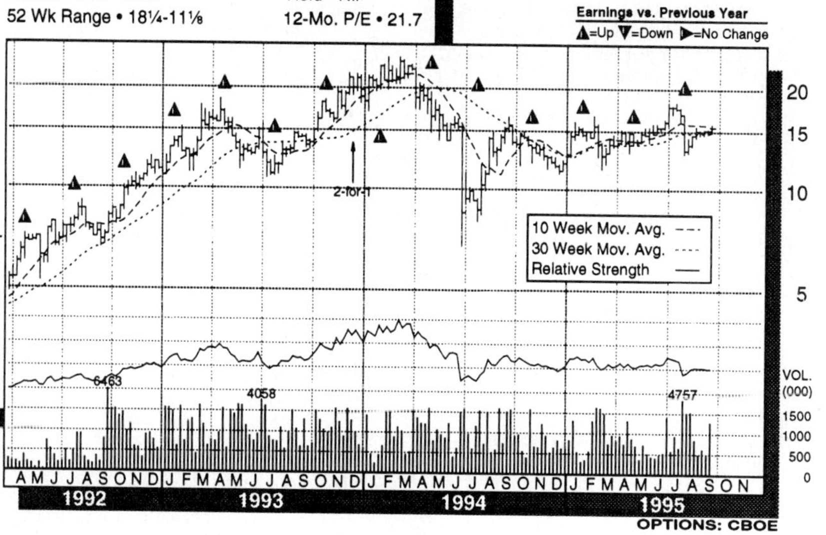

Business Profile - 18-SEP-95

The company intends to grow through developing new networks and services in existing or additional markets, and by the acquisition of new networks and services. In August 1995, the company's Bankers Training and Consulting Co. division acquired Capital Training Corp., a producer of financial educational programs. The company recently launched its Executive Education Network, through which eight business schools will offer corporate managers executive education courses.

Operational Review - 18-SEP-95

WCTV's operations are characterized by recurring revenues from subscribers, the high cost of producing and marketing programs, and the low incremental cost of supplying programs to new customers. The company has realized strong growth in recent years, although the increase in revenues in the second quarter was below historical rates. This was due in part to weakness in sales to Mexico and other Latin American countries. Earnings were helped by well controlled administrative and selling expenses.

Stock Performance - 15-SEP-95

In the past 30 trading days, WCTV's shares have increased 13%, compared to a 4% rise in the S&P 500. Average trading volume for the past five days was 252,400 shares, compared with the 40-day moving average of 301,387 shares.

Key Stock Statistics

Dividend Rate/Share	Nil	Shareholders	5,000
Shs. outstg. (M)	19.7	Market cap. (B)	$0.303
Avg. daily vol. (M)	0.148	Inst. holdings	55%
Tang. Bk. Value/Share	3.33	Insider holdings	NA
Beta	1.38		

Value of $10,000 invested 5 years ago: $ 30,874

Fiscal Year Ending Dec. 31

	1995	% Change	1994	% Change	1993	% Change
Revenues (Million $)						
1Q	24.63	19%	20.64	34%	15.44	56%
2Q	23.48	5%	22.36	33%	16.75	48%
3Q	—	—	22.18	27%	17.53	50%
4Q	—	—	24.52	25%	19.54	58%
Yr.	—	—	89.71	30%	69.26	53%
Income (Million $)						
1Q	3.81	32%	2.89	128%	1.27	28%
2Q	3.44	39%	2.48	24%	2.00	63%
3Q	—	—	3.03	21%	2.50	91%
4Q	—	—	3.44	12%	3.07	92%
Yr.	—	—	11.84	34%	8.84	72%
Earnings Per Share ($)						
1Q	0.20	33%	0.15	114%	0.07	17%
2Q	0.18	38%	0.13	18%	0.11	47%
3Q	—	—	0.16	23%	0.13	63%
4Q	—	—	0.18	13%	0.16	88%
Yr.	—	—	0.61	30%	0.47	52%

Next earnings report expected: late October

Westcott Communications

Business Summary - 18-SEP-95

Westcott Communications, Inc. is a leader in the creation and production of training, educational and informational programming delivered through private satellite television networks, and has expanded its services to include videotape and teleconference distribution.

The company's strategy is to provide quality, industry-specific training, education and information to address the needs of selected, well-defined markets in business, government and education. By combining the talents and knowledge of industry experts with its creative programming, production, marketing and satellite communications expertise, Westcott seeks to produce original, national network-quality programming that meets the training, educational and informational needs of its target markets while retaining the entertaining and visually stimulating character of consumer television and video.

Westcott delivers programming to more than 20,000 subscribers that employ about 3 million professionals. Contributions to 1994 revenues:

Government & public services	20%
Health care	22%
Automotive	12%
Corporate & professional	24%
Education	12%
Financial services	6%
Other	4%

The government and public services market is served through the Law Enforcement Television Network and Fire & Emergency Television Network satellite networks and the American Heat and Pulse videotape subscription services; the automotive market through the Automotive Satellite Television Network satellite network; the health care market through the Health & Sciences Television Network and Long Term Care Network satellite networks, and the American Hospital Association teleconferencing operations; the corporate and professional market through the Professional Security Television Network, Accounting and Financial Television Network and the CPA Report videotape subscription services; the financial services market through the Bankers Training and Consulting Company and BancTraining Video Systems videotape library services; and the primary and secondary education market through the TI-IN Network satellite network.

Important Developments

Aug. '95—The company's Bankers Training and Consulting Co. (BTCC) division acquired Capital Training Corp. With the acquisition, BTCC now offers nearly 500 financial educational programs.

Capitalization

Long Term Debt: $26,508,000 (6/95).

Per Share Data ($)

(Year Ended Dec. 31)

	1994	1993	1992	1991	1990	1989
Tangible Bk. Val.	3.32	2.54	1.11	1.30	1.16	NA
Cash Flow	1.13	0.79	0.65	0.38	0.30	0.08
Earnings	0.61	0.47	0.31	0.12	0.10	-0.06
Dividends	Nil	Nil	Nil	Nil	Nil	Nil
Payout Ratio	Nil	Nil	Nil	Nil	Nil	Nil
Prices - High	24¾	22⅛	12½	5⅛	6½	8
- Low	6¾	10¾	3⅞	2⅛	2	4⅜
P/E Ratio - High	41	47	41	43	62	NM
- Low	11	23	13	18	19	NM

Income Statement Analysis (Million $)

	1994	%Chg	1993	%Chg	1992	%Chg	1991
Revs.	89.7	29%	69.3	53%	45.4	58%	28.7
Oper. Inc.	29.3	42%	20.7	45%	14.3	113%	6.7
Depr.	10.1	66%	6.1	8%	5.7	40%	4.0
Int. Exp.	0.2	-28%	0.3	-47%	0.5	-24%	0.6
Pretax Inc.	19.1	32%	14.5	77%	8.2	187%	2.8
Eff. Tax Rate	38%	—	38%	—	37%	—	34%
Net Inc.	11.8	31%	9.0	75%	5.1	173%	1.9

Balance Sheet & Other Fin. Data (Million $)

	1994	1993	1992	1991	1990	1989
Cash	6.5	5.6	7.1	6.4	5.0	NA
Curr. Assets	39.2	34.2	24.2	15.9	12.5	NA
Total Assets	109	92.0	59.2	36.2	33.7	25.7
Curr. Liab.	23.4	23.7	12.7	6.1	6.0	NA
LT Debt	0.0	0.2	1.1	6.3	6.3	3.5
Common Eqty.	84.3	67.4	31.9	23.1	21.0	19.2
Total Cap.	85.6	68.3	46.5	30.1	27.6	22.7
Cap. Exp.	12.8	15.9	6.5	3.6	4.6	7.0
Cash Flow	21.9	14.9	10.6	5.9	4.7	1.1

Ratio Analysis

	1994	1993	1992	1991	1990	1989
Curr. Ratio	1.7	1.4	1.9	2.6	2.1	NA
% LT Debt of Cap.	Nil	0.3	2.4	20.9	22.8	15.5
% Net Inc.of Revs.	13.2	13.0	11.3	6.6	7.2	NM
% Ret. on Assets	11.7	11.2	10.8	5.4	5.5	NM
% Ret. on Equity	15.5	16.9	18.1	8.5	8.2	NM

Dividend Data —No cash dividends have been paid on the common stock, and the company has no intention of paying any in the foreseeable future. A two-for-one stock split was effected in December 1993.

Data as orig. reptd.; bef. results of disc. opers. and/or spec. items. Per share data adj. for stk. divs. as of ex-div. date. E-Estimated. NA-Not Available. NM-Not Meaningful. NR-Not Ranked.

Office—Galleria Tower Two, 13455 Noel Road, Dallas, TX 75240. **Tel**—(214) 417-4100. **Chrmn & CEO**—C. Westcott. **Pres & COO**—J. T. Smith. **VP, CFO & Secy**—P. Farragut. **Investor Contact**—Rupal Mehta (214-716-5141). **Dirs**—G. J. Fernandes, J. M. Heller, J. T. Smith, S. Turner, C. Westcott, K. Wildenthal. **Transfer Agent & Registrar**—Bank One, Texas. **Incorporated** in Texas in 1986. **Empl**-616. **S&P Analyst:** Stephen Madonna, CFA

STANDARD & POOR'S
STOCK REPORTS

Western Waste Industries

NYSE Symbol **WW**
In S&P SmallCap 600

16-OCT-95 **Industry:** Pollution Control

Summary: This integrated solid-waste service company provides collection, landfill, transfer station and recycling services in California, Texas, Florida, Colorado, Louisiana and Arkansas.

Quantitative Evaluations

Outlook (1 Lowest—5 Highest) • **3+**

Fair Value • **18¾**

Risk • **Average**

Earn./Div. Rank • **B-**

Technical Eval. • **Bullish** since 9/95

Rel. Strength Rank (1 Lowest—99 Highest) • **35**

Insider Activity • **NA**

Recent Price • 20
52 Wk Range • 24½-13⅜
Yield • Nil
12-Mo. P/E • 18.2

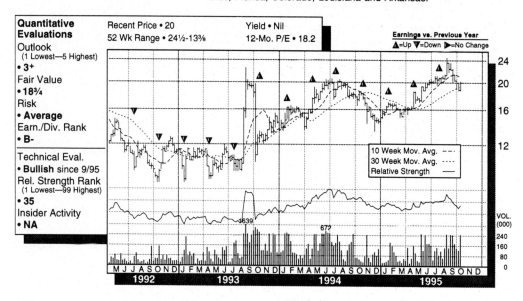

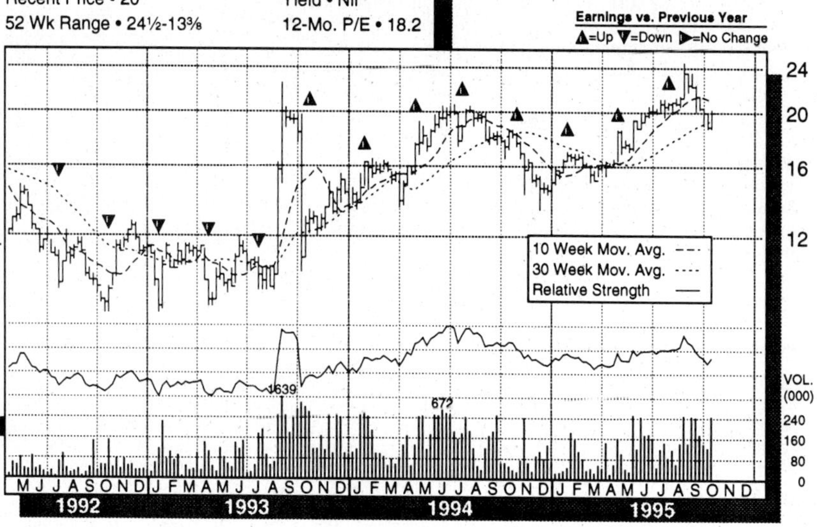

Business Profile - 16-OCT-95

This solid-waste management company serves commercial, industrial and residential customers mainly in California. WW's development program focuses on expanding landfill operations, further penetrating existing collection markets and making acquisitions to complement current operations or expand geographically. WW hopes to win approval of its California InteRail railfill joint venture, which would transport waste by train to a 600-million-ton landfill with a lifespan of 100 years.

Operational Review - 16-OCT-95

Revenues for fiscal 1995 advanced 5.4% from those of fiscal 1994, reflecting price increases obtained for collection services. Margins widened as these higher prices were unmatched by cost increases, and efforts to control costs led to slower growth in SG&A expenses. Despite competitive pressures in the green-waste business and higher dump fees, aftertax income rose 36%, excluding a $0.03-a-share credit from an accounting change in fiscal 1994.

Stock Performance - 13-OCT-95

In the past 30 trading days, WW's shares have declined 11%, compared to a 4% rise in the S&P 500. Average trading volume for the past five days was 58,620 shares, compared with the 40-day moving average of 44,826 shares.

Key Stock Statistics

Dividend Rate/Share	Nil	Shareholders	800
Shs. outstg. (M)	14.6	Market cap. (B)	$0.292
Avg. daily vol. (M)	0.036	Inst. holdings	47%
Tang. Bk. Value/Share	9.09	Insider holdings	NA
Beta	1.26		

Value of $10,000 invested 5 years ago: $ 12,500

Fiscal Year Ending Jun. 30

	1995	% Change	1994	% Change	1993	% Change
Revenues (Million $)						
1Q	67.15	7%	62.91	8%	58.10	13%
2Q	67.67	7%	63.32	11%	57.28	7%
3Q	67.64	4%	64.95	14%	57.07	NM
4Q	68.49	4%	65.82	12%	58.72	2%
Yr.	270.9	5%	257.0	11%	231.2	5%
Income (Million $)						
1Q	4.08	59%	2.56	—	—	—
2Q	4.15	46%	2.84	27%	2.24	-16%
3Q	4.34	28%	3.38	NM	-9.83	NM
4Q	4.53	20%	3.76	NM	-4.89	NM
Yr.	17.09	36%	12.53	NM	-10.12	NM
Earnings Per Share ($)						
1Q	0.26	44%	0.18	6%	0.17	-11%
2Q	0.27	42%	0.19	19%	0.16	-16%
3Q	0.28	27%	0.22	NM	-0.71	NM
4Q	0.29	21%	0.24	NM	-0.35	NM
Yr.	1.10	33%	0.83	NM	-0.73	NM

Next earnings report expected: early November

Western Waste Industries

Business Summary - 16-OCT-95

Western Waste Industries is engaged in the solid-waste management business, providing collection, transfer, recycling and disposal services to commercial, industrial and residential customers. Contributions to revenues by business segment in recent fiscal years were:

	1995	1994	1993
Collection services	83%	85%	86%
Landfill operations	7%	7%	6%
Transfer stations	3%	3%	2%
Recycling	6%	4%	4%
Other	1%	1%	2%

Operations in California accounted for 68%, 68% and 64% of revenues in fiscal 1995, 1994 and 1993, respectively.

WW provides solid-waste collection services to more than 63,000 commercial and industrial customers (55% of total fiscal 1995 revenues) and to about 677,000 homes and residential dwelling units (28%). Services for homes and other residential units generally are performed under exclusive franchises granted by municipalities or regional authorities. On a limited basis, WW offers hazardous waste services, mainly the transportation of non-liquid materials in drums and other containers provided by its customers, to landfills operated by others.

As of June 1995, the company had six landfills in operation, in California, Texas (three), Louisiana and Florida, with additional sites under development or under construction.

WW has three transfer stations in California, which process waste from collection vehicles to transfer trailers that can more efficiently transport waste to distant landfills. The company also operates five recycling facilities in California and is involved in receiving, processing, composting and end-market distributing of green and wood waste material in California and Texas.

The company conducts other waste management-related business activities, including construction support, earth moving, excavation contracting and engineering and consulting services.

Important Developments

Sep. '95—The company announced several new and renewed residential, commercial and recycling contracts, including a $7 million, six-year contract with Kings County in central California.
Jun. '95—WW announced a $15 million, five-year contract with the City of Mission Viejo, Calif.

Capitalization

Long Term Debt: $78,882,000 (6/95).
Options: To buy 3,131,037 shs. at $8 to $22 ea. (6/95).

Per Share Data ($)

(Year Ended Jun. 30)

	1995	1994	1993	1992	1991	1990
Tangible Bk. Val.	9.09	7.53	6.36	6.85	6.98	5.96
Cash Flow	2.84	2.10	0.37	1.15	1.96	1.84
Earnings	1.10	0.83	-0.73	0.17	0.81	0.78
Dividends	Nil	Nil	Nil	Nil	Nil	Nil
Payout Ratio	Nil	Nil	Nil	Nil	Nil	Nil
Prices - High	24½	20⅝	22½	18⅞	23½	21½
- Low	14⅞	13⅜	8¾	8¾	13⅞	14½
P/E Ratio - High	22	25	NM	NM	29	28
- Low	14	16	NM	NM	17	19

Income Statement Analysis (Million $)

	1995	%Chg	1994	%Chg	1993	%Chg	1992
Revs.	271	5%	257	11%	231	5%	219
Oper. Inc.	62.2	37%	45.5	64%	27.7	-16%	32.8
Depr.	27.0	41%	19.1	26%	15.2	10%	13.8
Int. Exp.	5.3	12%	4.8	3%	4.6	-18%	5.7
Pretax Inc.	30.8	36%	22.6	NM	-14.5	NM	4.3
Eff. Tax Rate	45%	—	45%	—	NM	—	44%
Net Inc.	17.1	37%	12.5	NM	-10.1	NM	2.4

Balance Sheet & Other Fin. Data (Million $)

	1995	1994	1993	1992	1991	1990
Cash	6.5	9.9	2.3	0.7	6.4	2.2
Curr. Assets	47.5	54.1	49.6	45.8	49.3	38.9
Total Assets	293	285	268	249	226	196
Curr. Liab.	32.2	33.5	36.3	26.9	20.6	18.9
LT Debt	78.9	91.9	89.9	86.4	73.0	58.0
Common Eqty.	160	139	122	123	116	103
Total Cap.	243	243	214	217	203	175
Cap. Exp.	36.4	35.5	43.7	43.7	33.7	33.2
Cash Flow	44.1	31.6	5.1	16.1	27.2	22.9

Ratio Analysis

	1995	1994	1993	1992	1991	1990
Curr. Ratio	1.5	1.6	1.4	1.7	2.4	2.1
% LT Debt of Cap.	32.5	39.3	42.0	39.8	36.0	33.2
% Net Inc.of Revs.	6.3	4.9	NM	1.1	5.6	5.6
% Ret. on Assets	5.9	4.5	NM	1.0	5.2	5.0
% Ret. on Equity	11.4	9.4	NM	2.0	10.0	10.7

Dividend Data —No cash dividends have been paid. The shares were split two for one in 1990.

Data as orig. reptd.; bef. results of disc. opers. and/or spec. items. Per share data adj. for stk. divs. as of ex-div. date. E-Estimated. NA-Not Available. NM-Not Meaningful. NR-Not Ranked.

Office—21061 S. Western Ave., Torrance, CA 90501. **Tel**—(310) 328-0900. **Chrmn & Pres**—K. Shirvanian. **COO**—R. G. DiLibero. **Exec VP, Secy & Treas**—S. Tufenkian. **Exec VP-Fin & CFO**—L. F. McQuaide. **VP & Investor Contact**—Richard F. Widrig (310) 222-8723. **Dirs**—H. S. Derbyshire, R. G. DiLibero, A. N. Mosich, M. C. Palmer, K. Shirvanian, J. W. Simmons, S. Tufenkian. **Transfer Agent & Registrar**—Chemical Trust Co. of California, Los Angeles. **Incorporated** in California in 1964. **Empl**-1,770. **S&P Analyst:** J. Santoriello

STANDARD & POOR'S

STOCK REPORTS

Whittaker Corp.

NYSE Symbol **WKR**
In S&P SmallCap 600

10-OCT-95 **Industry:** Aerospace

Summary: This company makes a variety of products for aerospace, defense and industrial markets, with increasing emphasis on commercial applications, primarily telecommunications.

S&P Opinion: Buy (★★★★★)	Recent Price • 18⅞	Yield • Nil
	52 Wk Range • 24⅝-16⅛	12-Mo. P/E • 25.2

Quantitative Evaluations

Outlook
(1 Lowest—5 Highest)
• **3**

Fair Value
• **18¾**

Risk
• **Average**

Earn./Div. Rank
• **NR**

Technical Eval.
• **Bullish** since 9/95

Rel. Strength Rank
(1 Lowest—99 Highest)
• **14**

Insider Activity
• **NA**

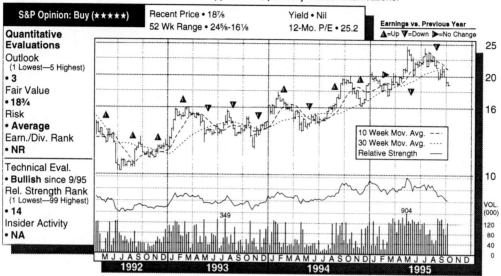

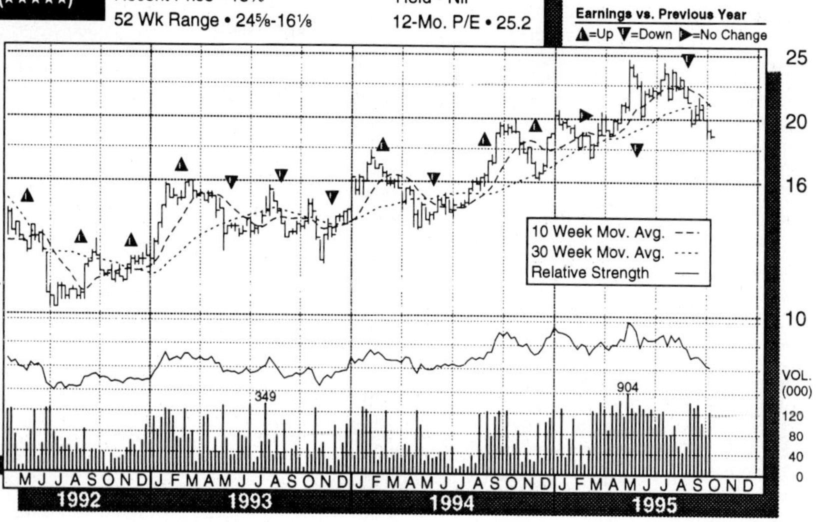

Overview - 06-OCT-95

Sales should grow solidly through fiscal 1996. Though defense appears to have stabilized following a recent downtrend and aerospace is on track for its highest revenues ever in fiscal 1995, communications is where the strong gains will be seen. The acquisition of Hughes LAN Systems (HLS) in April 1995 greatly expanded WKR's presence in the market for ATM computer networking products, which is expected to grow into a $1 billion industry by 1997. HLS brings a complete infrastructure and portfolio of ATM products to WKR that will allow it to provide "complete solutions" to its customers. Operating margins should widen on a more favorable product mix, but earnings in fiscal 1995 will fall below those of fiscal 1994 because of one-time costs associated with HLS. However, we expect earnings to soar in fiscal 1996 on sharply higher sales and the absence of these one-time costs.

Valuation - 06-OCT-95

Whittaker's shares have been in a steady upward trend, more than doubling since mid-1992. WKR is already among the most profitable companies in the defense and aerospace industries, and the acquisition of HLS, with its fast-growing sales and high margins, will only bolster this position. If the ATM market lives up to its current expectations, sales and earnings should increase substantially over the next few years. To realize WKR's full value, we view a spinoff of Whittaker Communications likely in fiscal 1997. We expect to see gains of 30% or more in the stock over the next 12 months.

Key Stock Statistics

S&P EPS Est. 1995	0.75	Tang. Bk. Value/Share	8.49
P/E on S&P Est. 1995	25.2	Beta	0.27
S&P EPS Est. 1996	1.65	Shareholders	5,700
Dividend Rate/Share	Nil	Market cap. (B)	$0.159
Shs. outstg. (M)	8.6	Inst. holdings	68%
Avg. daily vol. (M)	0.032	Insider holdings	NA

Value of $10,000 invested 5 years ago: NA

Fiscal Year Ending Oct. 31

	1995	% Change	1994	% Change	1993	% Change
Revenues (Million $)						
1Q	26.69	4%	25.77	-12%	29.28	NM
2Q	31.68	10%	28.85	-1%	29.26	-21%
3Q	44.35	34%	33.11	24%	26.78	-31%
4Q	—	—	38.72	29%	30.07	-45%
Yr.	—	—	126.4	10%	115.4	-28%
Income (Million $)						
1Q	1.72	NM	1.71	8%	1.59	7%
2Q	0.15	-92%	1.87	-12%	2.13	-27%
3Q	1.75	-40%	2.94	NM	0.80	-76%
4Q	—	—	3.54	11%	3.20	-44%
Yr.	—	—	10.06	31%	7.70	-42%
Earnings Per Share ($)						
1Q	0.18	NM	0.18	6%	0.17	6%
2Q	0.02	-90%	0.20	-9%	0.22	-29%
3Q	0.18	-42%	0.31	NM	0.08	-76%
4Q	E0.37	NM	0.37	9%	0.34	-44%
Yr.	E0.75	-29%	1.06	31%	0.81	-43%

Next earnings report expected: mid December

Whittaker Corp.

Business Summary - 10-OCT-95

Whittaker Corporation develops specialized aerospace and electronic technologies to create products for aircraft, defense, telecommunications and industrial markets. About 49% of sales from continuing operations in fiscal 1994 were from the U.S. Government (68% in fiscal 1993), primarily in the aerospace segment; 20% of sales were to customers outside the U.S.

WKR produces fluid control devices that control hydraulic and pneumatic fluids in military aircraft and commercial applications, including ground refueling devices. Whittaker's fluid controls are used on virtually all commercial aircraft. They are also used on military transports, bombers, helicopters, fighters and landing craft. Both commercial and military applications include aircraft jet engines built by General Electric and Pratt & Whitney. In 1993, the commercial aerospace business was expanded with the acquisition of Thiem Industries, an aircraft refueling equipment maker, and Seaton-Wilson, which makes quick disconnects. Aircraft fluid controls accounted for 42% of fiscal 1994 sales.

The company also designs and manufactures electronic systems for battle command, control and communications, a variety of electronic countermeasure systems, electronic equipment used in antisubmarine warfare systems, radar, tracking and identification systems, high-reliability cable systems and high-energy-density batteries.

Whittaker Communications was expanded through the July 1993 acquisition of Aptec Computer Systems, a commercial maker of ultra-high-speed transmission devices for storage management and data networks. The company is developing a lower-priced version of its Data Manager file/video server with Asynchronous Transfer Mode (ATM) capabilities to provide services for telecommunications markets, including real-time access to full-motion video on demand and other applications requiring access to large amounts of video data. WKR also recently began selling its ATM Enterprise Network Access Switch (ENAS), which was designed for use by business customers and by telephone companies to efficiently transfer data files, video, still images and multimedia files at extremely high speeds among local area networks over telephone companies' fiberoptic wide area networks.

Important Developments

Apr. '95—WKR acquired Hughes LAN Systems for $32.5 million, including $17.5 million in cash and $15 million of convertible subordinated debt plus contingent deferred payments not to exceed $25 million.

Capitalization

Long Term Debt: $77,019,000, incl. $15,000,000 of conv. sub. debt (7/95).

$5 Cum. Conv. Pfd. Stock: 2,185 shs.; ea. conv. into 1.854 com. shs. plus $74.16 cash.

Ser. D Participating Conv. Pfd. Stock: 895.18 shs.; ea. conv. into 326.531 com. shs.

Per Share Data ($)

(Year Ended Oct. 31)

	1994	1993	1992	1991	1990	1989
Tangible Bk. Val.	11.06	7.84	7.92	6.13	3.89	-10.99
Cash Flow	1.68	1.42	2.07	1.85	2.13	1.93
Earnings	1.06	0.81	1.42	1.27	0.66	0.41
Dividends	Nil	Nil	Nil	Nil	Nil	40.25
Payout Ratio	Nil	Nil	Nil	Nil	Nil	NM
Prices - High	20	16¼	14½	24¼	12	53¼
- Low	13½	11⅞	10¼	8⅞	7½	7⅝
P/E Ratio - High	19	20	10	19	18	NM
- Low	13	15	7	7	11	NM

Income Statement Analysis (Million $)

	1994	%Chg	1993	%Chg	1992	%Chg	1991
Revs.	122	6%	115	-28%	160	NM	159
Oper. Inc.	22.4	7%	21.0	-36%	33.0	10%	30.0
Depr.	5.9	4%	5.7	-8%	6.2	19%	5.2
Int. Exp.	4.0	3%	3.9	-30%	5.6	-15%	6.6
Pretax Inc.	16.5	27%	13.0	-41%	22.0	16%	19.0
Eff. Tax Rate	39%	—	39%	—	39%	—	39%
Net Inc.	10.1	31%	7.7	-43%	13.4	18%	11.4

Balance Sheet & Other Fin. Data (Million $)

	1994	1993	1992	1991	1990	1989
Cash	4.0	Nil	3.0	2.0	6.0	10.0
Curr. Assets	118	116	135	113	127	200
Total Assets	209	202	218	199	243	413
Curr. Liab.	37.0	42.0	49.0	54.0	62.0	217
LT Debt	55.0	57.0	67.0	55.0	104	198
Common Eqty.	94.0	84.0	75.0	58.0	39.0	-49.0
Total Cap.	161	150	151	121	154	161
Cap. Exp.	2.5	1.3	2.2	2.0	4.2	5.9
Cash Flow	16.0	13.4	19.5	16.5	17.9	14.6

Ratio Analysis

	1994	1993	1992	1991	1990	1989
Curr. Ratio	3.2	2.8	2.7	2.1	2.1	0.9
% LT Debt of Cap.	34.1	37.8	44.2	45.4	67.4	NM
% Net Inc.of Revs.	8.2	6.7	8.4	7.2	3.0	1.6
% Ret. on Assets	4.9	3.6	6.4	4.9	1.7	0.8
% Ret. on Equity	11.3	9.5	20.0	22.5	NM	3.9

Dividend Data —Dividends, initiated in 1978, were discontinued in February 1989 in connection with a recapitalization and payment of a $40 special distribution in June 1989. A "poison pill" stock purchase rights plan was adopted in 1988.

Data as orig. reptd.; bef. results of disc. opers. and/or spec. items. Per share data adj. for stk. divs. as of ex-div. date. E-Estimated. NA-Not Available. NM-Not Meaningful. NR-Not Ranked.

Office—1955 North Surveyor Ave., Simi Valley, CA 93063. **Tel**—(805) 526-5700. **Chrmn**—J. F. Alibrandi. **Pres, CEO & COO**—T. Brancati. **VP, CFO & Secy**—R. Levin. **Treas**—J. K. Otto. **Dirs**—J. F. Alibrandi, G. H. Benter Jr., T. Brancati, J. L. Hancock, E. R. Muller, G. T. Parkos, M. T. Stamper. **Transfer Agent & Registrar**—Mellon Securities Trust Co., Pittsburgh. **Incorporated** in California in 1947; reincorporated in Delaware in 1986. **Empl**-800. **S&P Analyst:** Alan Aaron

STANDARD & POOR'S

STOCK REPORTS

Whole Foods Market

NASDAQ Symbol **WFMI**

In S&P SmallCap 600

18-SEP-95 **Industry:** Retail Stores

Summary: Whole Foods Market owns and operates the largest chain of natural foods supermarkets in the U.S., with 41 stores in 10 states.

S&P Opinion: Accumulate (★★★★)

Recent Price • 12½
52 Wk Range • 16¾-9½

Yield • Nil
12-Mo. P/E • 22.3

Quantitative Evaluations

Outlook (1 Lowest—5 Highest)
• **5**

Fair Value
• **17⅝**

Risk
• **High**

Earn./Div. Rank
• **NR**

Technical Eval.
• **Bullish** since 1/95

Rel. Strength Rank (1 Lowest—99 Highest)
• **11**

Insider Activity
• **NA**

Earnings vs. Previous Year
▲=Up ▼=Down ▶=No Change

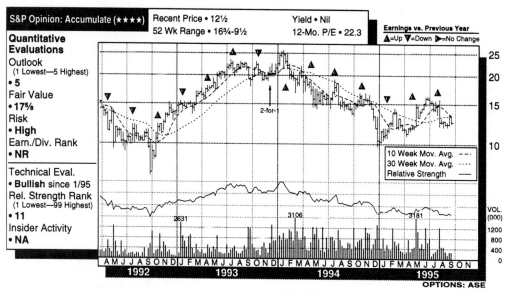

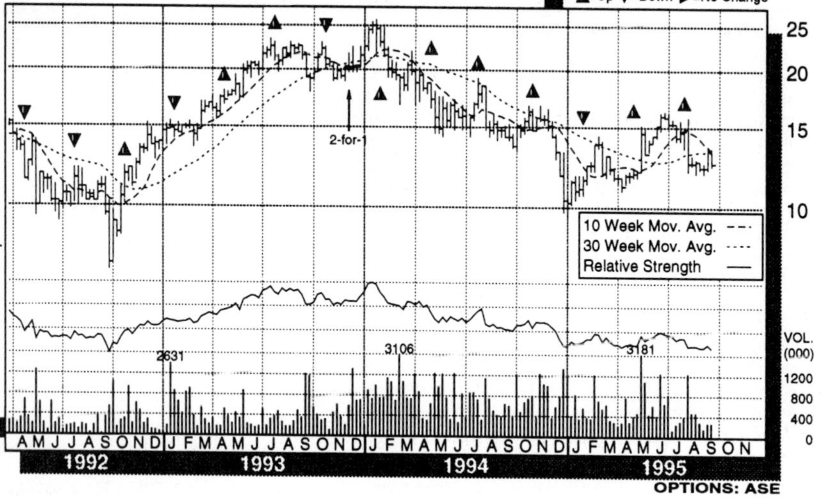

OPTIONS: ASE

Overview - 17-SEP-95

The biggest test for Whole Foods Market will be how quickly and effectively it can beat smaller competitors such as Fresh Fields to the market. Both chains plan to open stores in major markets such as New York, Washington, D.C., and Philadelphia, and are sure to meet in other regions as the scramble for organic supremacy heats up. The company is making a real effort toward prepared foods, and would like customers to be able to do all their weekly shopping in its natural food superstores. Americans have become very environmental and health conscious, but only time will tell if the concept will be successful. Early indications are that WFMI has clearly jumped ahead of its fragmented competitors.

Valuation - 18-SEP-95

The company's shares have recovered as concerns over union problems have been resolved. WFMI's fundamentals and expansion strategy are solid, and it is looking to bank on more upscale, larger locations in major markets that include prepared meals and cafe/ restaurants. Trading at about 15X our fiscal 1996 earnings estimate, the shares of Whole Foods are not cheap, but offer an opportunity to invest in a well run, expansion-oriented company with a specialty food retailing concept that could really catch on if consumers demand more fresh, natural products.

Key Stock Statistics

S&P EPS Est. 1995	0.70	Tang. Bk. Value/Share	4.79
P/E on S&P Est. 1995	17.9	Beta	NA
S&P EPS Est. 1996	0.85	Shareholders	900
Dividend Rate/Share	Nil	Market cap. (B)	$0.173
Shs. outstg. (M)	13.8	Inst. holdings	59%
Avg. daily vol. (M)	0.052	Insider holdings	NA

Value of $10,000 invested 5 years ago: NA

Fiscal Year Ending Sep. 30

	1995	% Change	1994	% Change	1993	% Change
Revenues (Million $)						
1Q	139.0	19%	116.5	31%	88.71	163%
2Q	117.0	26%	92.77	23%	75.48	168%
3Q	119.9	23%	97.36	22%	79.52	186%
4Q	—	—	95.10	21%	78.60	160%
Yr.	—	—	401.6	25%	322.3	169%
Income (Million $)						
1Q	2.35	-4%	2.46	43%	1.72	142%
2Q	2.55	26%	2.02	12%	1.80	134%
3Q	1.05	-52%	2.21	27%	1.74	118%
4Q	—	—	1.95	NM	-1.44	NM
Yr.	—	—	8.64	126%	3.82	24%
Earnings Per Share ($)						
1Q	0.17	-6%	0.18	20%	0.15	-3%
2Q	0.18	29%	0.14	8%	0.13	30%
3Q	0.17	13%	0.15	15%	0.13	30%
4Q	E0.18	29%	0.14	NM	-0.10	NM
Yr.	E0.70	15%	0.61	110%	0.29	-33%

Next earnings report expected: early November

Whole Foods Market

Business Summary - 18-SEP-95

Whole Foods Market, Inc. owns and operates the largest chain of natural foods supermarkets in the U.S. Stores are designed to attract quality-oriented consumers interested in health, nutrition, food safety, and preserving the environment. As of August 1995, the company was operating 41 stores in California (14), Texas (10), Massachusetts (8), Michigan (1), North Carolina (3), Florida (1), Louisiana (1), Illinois (2) and Rhode Island (1).

Product offerings include organically grown and high-grade commercial produce; grocery products and environmentally safe household items; meat, poultry and seafood free of growth hormones and antibiotics; bulk foods, such as nuts, candies, dried fruit and whole unprocessed grains and cereals; specialty gourmet foods such as beer, wine, coffee and cheese; prepared foods, such as fresh bakery goods, soups, salads, hot entrees and sandwiches, vitamins, body care products and cosmetics; and other items including books and magazines emphasizing health and nutrition.

The company's stores contain an average of about 20,000 square feet and offer a selection of 10,000 to 14,000 food and non-food products designed to meet the needs of natural food shoppers as well as gourmet customers.

The company's expansion strategy is to open or acquire stores in existing regions and in metropolitan areas where it believes it can become the leading natural foods supermarket retailer. In fiscal 1994, the company opened stores in Houston and Dallas, Tex., Cambridge, Mass., Chicago, Ill., and Los Gatos, Calif. One new store opened in each of Boston, Mass., Plano, Tex. and Austin, Tex. in fiscal 1995's first half. At May 1, 1995, Whole Foods had stores under development in Austin, Tex., Tustin, Calif., and St. Paul, Minn., all of which are scheduled to open in fiscal 1995. WFMI also expects to close three stores in Austin during the year. The company plans to open 10 to 13 additional locations and relocate three stores in fiscal 1996.

In February 1995, WFMI acquired two Bread of Life natural foods supermarkets in northern California, and a Unicorn Village Ltd. natural foods supermarket in Florida.

Important Developments

Aug. '95—WFMI said same-store sales rose 6.5% and 7.4%, year to year, in the fiscal 1995 second quarter and first half, respectively.

Capitalization

Long Term Debt: $32,282,000 (4/9/95).

Per Share Data ($) (Year Ended Sep. 30)

	1994	1993	1992	1991	1990	1989
Tangible Bk. Val.	4.53	3.20	4.29	1.06	NA	NA
Cash Flow	1.16	0.67	0.73	0.88	NA	NA
Earnings	0.61	0.29	0.43	0.38	NA	NA
Dividends	Nil	Nil	Nil	Nil	NA	NA
Payout Ratio	Nil	Nil	Nil	Nil	NA	NA
Prices - High	25¾	23⅜	17	NA	NA	NA
- Low	9½	13½	7¼	NA	NA	NA
P/E Ratio - High	42	81	39	NA	NA	NA
- Low	16	47	17	NA	NA	NA

Income Statement Analysis (Million $)

	1994	%Chg	1993	%Chg	1992	%Chg	1991
Revs.	402	25%	322	168%	120	30%	92.5
Oper. Inc.	22.8	39%	16.4	146%	6.7	31%	5.1
Depr.	7.9	58%	5.0	137%	2.1	29%	1.6
Int. Exp.	0.5	-36%	0.8	142%	0.3	-68%	1.0
Pretax Inc.	14.7	75%	8.4	70%	4.9	89%	2.6
Eff. Tax Rate	41%	—	55%	—	38%	—	40%
Net Inc.	8.6	126%	3.8	24%	3.1	96%	1.6

Balance Sheet & Other Fin. Data (Million $)

	1994	1993	1992	1991	1990	1989
Cash	4.3	6.8	16.0	2.2	NA	NA
Curr. Assets	31.3	23.7	23.6	8.2	NA	NA
Total Assets	136	106	46.5	23.4	NA	NA
Curr. Liab.	26.0	22.7	7.9	8.3	NA	NA
LT Debt	7.2	3.2	0.3	9.3	NA	NA
Common Eqty.	97.7	75.5	36.3	5.0	NA	NA
Total Cap.	107	80.3	38.0	14.8	NA	NA
Cap. Exp.	28.9	27.8	6.7	2.8	NA	NA
Cash Flow	16.5	8.8	5.1	3.2	NA	NA

Ratio Analysis

	1994	1993	1992	1991	1990	1989
Curr. Ratio	1.2	1.0	3.0	1.0	NA	NA
% LT Debt of Cap.	6.7	4.0	0.9	62.9	NA	NA
% Net Inc.of Revs.	2.2	1.2	2.6	1.7	NA	NA
% Ret. on Assets	6.9	4.1	5.2	NA	NA	NA
% Ret. on Equity	9.7	5.5	11.6	NA	NA	NA

Dividend Data —No cash dividends have been paid. The company intends to retain its earnings for use in its business and therefore does not anticipate paying any cash dividends in the foreseeable future. A 2-for-1 stock split was effected November 29, 1993.

Data as orig. reptd.; bef. results of disc. opers. and/or spec. items. Per share data adj. for stk. divs. as of ex-div. date. E-Estimated. NA-Not Available. NM-Not Meaningful. NR-Not Ranked.

Office—601 N. Lamar, Austin, TX 78703. **Tel**—(512) 477-4455. **Chrmn & CEO**—J. Mackey. **Pres & COO**—P. Roy. **VP, CFO and Investor Contact**—Glenda Flanagan. **Dirs**—C. G. Banks, J. E. Elstrott, A. J. Goldberg, J. Mackey, L. A. Mason, J. R. Moorman, R. Z. Sorenson, J. P. Sud. **Transfer Agent & Registrar**—Securities Transfer Corp. **Incorporated** in Texas in 1980. **Empl**-5,300. **S&P Analyst:** Philip D. Wohl

STANDARD & POOR'S

STOCK REPORTS

Winnebago Industries

NYSE Symbol **WGO**

In S&P SmallCap 600

10-OCT-95 **Industry:** Auto/Truck mfrs.

Summary: WGO primarily produces motor homes, which are used in leisure travel and outdoor recreational activities.

Quantitative Evaluations

Outlook (1 Lowest—5 Highest)
• 3⁻

Fair Value
• 7½

Risk
• **Average**

Earn./Div. Rank
• **B-**

Technical Eval.
• **Bullish** since 6/95

Rel. Strength Rank (1 Lowest—99 Highest)
• **14**

Insider Activity
• **NA**

Recent Price • 7½ | 52 Wk Range • 10¾-7⅜ | Yield • 5.4% | 12-Mo. P/E • 6.0

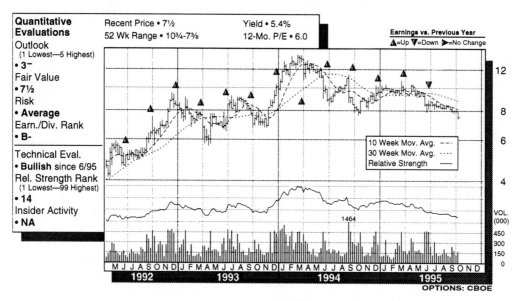

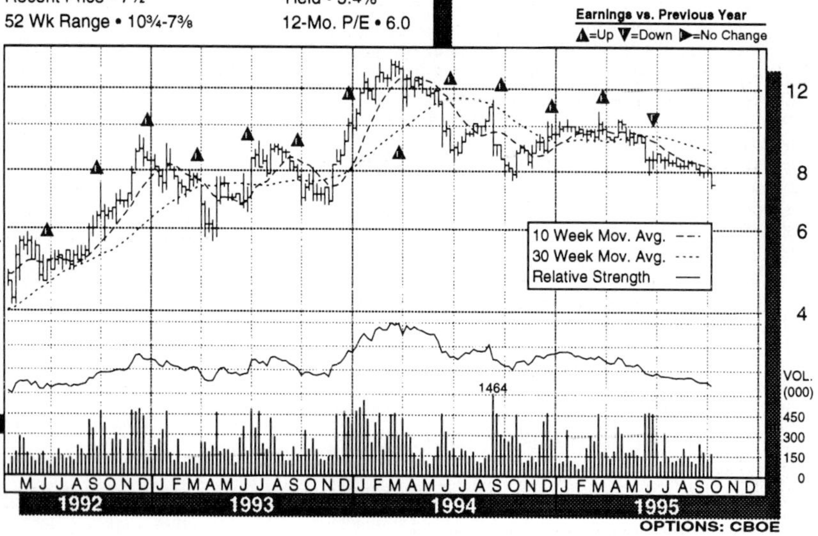

Business Profile - 10-OCT-95

This leading producer of motor homes--self-contained recreational vehicles used primarily for leisure travel and outdoor recreation--also makes component parts and provides satellite courier and tape duplication services. Peak motor home retail selling normally occurs in the spring and summer. The level of interest rates can, at times, have an impact on sales. The balance sheet is strong, with long term debt at only about 5% of total capitalization at fiscal year end-1994 .

Operational Review - 10-OCT-95

Revenues for the 39 weeks ended May 27, 1995, advanced 11%, year to year, reflectng strong demand for 1995 model year products during the first half of fiscal 1995. Profitability benefited from the higher sales, and operating profit advanced 47%. Aided by a tax credit in the 1995 period only, net income more than doubled.

Stock Performance - 06-OCT-95

In the past 30 trading days, WGO's shares have declined 10%, compared to a 4% rise in the S&P 500. Average trading volume for the past five days was 33,980 shares, compared with the 40-day moving average of 32,487 shares.

Key Stock Statistics

Dividend Rate/Share	0.40	Shareholders	13,100
Shs. outstg. (M)	25.3	Market cap. (B)	$0.187
Avg. daily vol. (M)	0.035	Inst. holdings	22%
Tang. Bk. Value/Share	4.01	Insider holdings	NA
Beta	1.80		

Value of $10,000 invested 5 years ago: $ 16,293

Fiscal Year Ending Aug. 31

	1995	% Change	1994	% Change	1993	% Change
Revenues (Million $)						
1Q	130.8	25%	104.6	25%	83.40	39%
2Q	115.4	17%	99.0	28%	77.46	29%
3Q	125.1	-4%	129.7	12%	115.9	30%
4Q	—	—	118.9	11%	107.3	25%
Yr.	—	—	452.1	18%	384.1	30%
Income (Million $)						
1Q	7.61	103%	3.74	NM	1.12	NM
2Q	12.09	NM	1.28	NM	0.41	NM
3Q	6.58	-10%	7.34	60%	4.58	62%
4Q	—	—	5.09	60%	3.18	37%
Yr.	—	—	17.45	88%	9.28	NM
Earnings Per Share ($)						
1Q	0.30	100%	0.15	NM	0.04	NM
2Q	0.48	NM	0.05	150%	0.02	NM
3Q	0.26	-10%	0.29	61%	0.18	64%
4Q	—	—	0.20	54%	0.13	18%
Yr.	—	—	0.69	86%	0.37	NM

Next earnings report expected: mid December

Winnebago Industries

Business Summary - 10-OCT-95

Winnebago Industries manufactures motor homes--self-contained recreational vehicles (RVs) used primarily in leisure travel and outdoor recreation activities. WGO also makes a variety of component parts and provides satellite courier and tape duplication services. Van conversion operations were discontinued subsequent to August 27, 1994, and WGO sold the majority of the assets of its North Iowa Electronics subsidiary in August 1993. Business segment contributions in fiscal 1994:

	Revs.	Profits
Recreational vehicles & other manufactured products	96%	94%
Satellite courier	4%	6%

WGO makes three types of motor homes: Class A, B and C. Class A models are conventional motor homes constructed directly on medium-duty truck chassis, which include the engine and drive components. The living area and driver's compartment are designed and produced by WGO. Class B models are panel-type trucks to which sleeping, kitchen and toilet facilities are added. These models also have a top extension added to them for more head room. Class C models are mini motor homes built on van-type chassis onto which WGO constructs a living area with access to the driver's compartment. Certain Class C units include van-type driver's compartments built by WGO.

Motor homes are sold under the Winnebago, Itasca, Vectra, Rialta and Luxor brand names. The A and C classes of motor homes generally provide living accommodations for four to seven persons and incude kitchen, dining, sleeping and bath areas, and in some models, a lounge. Optional equipment accessories include air conditioning, an electric power plant, and a stereo system. Motor home prices range from $32,000 to more than $170,000, depending on size and model, plus optional equipment and delivery charges.

Peak retail selling occurs in the spring and summer. Attempts are made to maintain low inventory when interest rates are high and/or market conditions uncertain.

The Cycle-Sat (CS) subsidiary (80%-owned) is engaged in the satellite transmission of television and radio commercials. In April 1995, CS acquired Tape Film Inc., a distributor of spot advertising to TV stations. Terms were not disclosed.

Important Developments

Jun. '95—WGO expected consumer confidence to rebound as interest rates become more stable in the near term. Meanwhile, WGO said it was preparing its new 1996 motor home lineup for introduction.

Capitalization

Long Term Debt: $2,228,000 (5/95), incl. capital lease obligations.

Per Share Data ($) (Year Ended Aug. 31)

	1994	1993	1992	1991	1990	1989
Tangible Bk. Val.	3.16	3.26	2.88	3.30	4.49	5.28
Cash Flow	1.00	0.68	0.25	-0.27	-0.21	0.26
Earnings	0.69	0.37	-0.07	-0.65	-0.72	-0.19
Dividends	Nil	Nil	Nil	Nil	0.10	0.40
Payout Ratio	Nil	Nil	Nil	Nil	NM	NM
Prices - High	13⅞	10½	9½	6¾	5¾	9⅜
- Low	7⅞	5⅝	3⅝	2¼	2⅛	4½
P/E Ratio - High	20	28	NM	NM	NM	NM
- Low	11	15	NM	NM	NM	NM

Income Statement Analysis (Million $)

	1994	%Chg	1993	%Chg	1992	%Chg	1991
Revs.	452	18%	384	30%	295	32%	223
Oper. Inc.	25.0	59%	15.7	NM	4.9	NM	-12.1
Depr.	7.7	-1%	7.8	-4%	8.1	-16%	9.6
Int. Exp.	1.4	125%	0.6	50%	0.4	-71%	1.4
Pretax Inc.	16.3	112%	7.7	NM	-2.8	NM	-22.4
Eff. Tax Rate	NM	—	NM	—	NM	—	NM
Net Inc.	17.4	87%	9.3	NM	-1.8	NM	-16.3

Balance Sheet & Other Fin. Data (Million $)

	1994	1993	1992	1991	1990	1989
Cash	4.1	13.5	14.5	7.9	23.6	22.5
Curr. Assets	111	94.0	82.0	77.0	129	200
Total Assets	184	157	140	135	198	286
Curr. Liab.	52.0	50.0	44.0	39.0	64.0	128
LT Debt	4.1	3.2	3.1	3.9	3.5	6.4
Common Eqty.	80.0	82.0	72.0	83.0	111	131
Total Cap.	88.0	89.0	79.0	90.0	129	153
Cap. Exp.	12.0	7.7	3.0	3.8	9.6	12.0
Cash Flow	25.2	17.0	6.3	-6.7	-5.2	6.4

Ratio Analysis

	1994	1993	1992	1991	1990	1989
Curr. Ratio	2.1	1.9	1.8	2.0	2.0	1.6
% LT Debt of Cap.	4.7	3.6	3.9	4.4	2.8	4.2
% Net Inc.of Revs.	3.9	2.4	NM	NM	NM	NM
% Ret. on Assets	10.2	6.2	NM	NM	NM	NM
% Ret. on Equity	21.6	12.1	NM	NM	NM	NM

Dividend Data —Dividends, which were omitted in 1990 after having been paid each year since 1983, were resumed with the January 1995 payment.

Amt. of Div. $	Date Decl.	Ex-Div. Date	Stock of Record	Payment Date
0.100	Oct. 20	Nov. 29	Dec. 05	Jan. 06 '95
0.100	Feb. 03	Feb. 28	Mar. 06	Apr. 07 '95
0.100	May. 05	May. 30	Jun. 05	Jul. 07 '95

Data as orig. reptd.; bef. results of disc. opers. and/or spec. items. Per share data adj. for stk. divs. as of ex-div. date. E-Estimated. NA-Not Available. NM-Not Meaningful. NR-Not Ranked.

Office—605 W. Crystal Lake Rd., P.O. Box 152, Forest City, IA 50436. **Tel**—(515) 582-3535. **Chrmn**—J. K. Hanson. **Pres & CEO**—F. G. Dohrmann. **VP-CFO**—E. F. Barker. **VP-Secy**—R. M. Beebe. **VP-Treas & Investor Contact**—Jerry M. Clouse (515-582-6836). **Dirs**—G. E. Boman, D. G. Croonquist, F. G. Dohrmann, K. D. Elwick, J. K. Hanson, J. M. Shuster, F. M. Zimmerman, F. L. Zrostlik. **Transfer Agent & Registrar**—Norwest Bank Minnesota, St. Paul. **Incorporated** in Iowa in 1958. **Empl**-3,150. **S&P Analyst:** N.J. DeVita

Wiser Oil

NYSE Symbol **WZR**
In S&P SmallCap 600

10-JUL-95

Industry: Oil and Gas

Summary: This independent energy company is engaged in exploration, development, production and acquisition of crude oil and natural gas in the U.S. and Canada.

Quantitative Evaluations

Outlook
(1 Lowest—5 Highest)
• **2+**

Fair Value
• **12⅜**

Risk
• **Low**

Earn./Div. Rank
• **B**

Technical Eval.
• **Bullish** since 6/95

Rel. Strength Rank
(1 Lowest—99 Highest)
• **18**

Insider Activity
• **Neutral**

Recent Price • 13½
52 Wk Range • 17¾-13⅛
Yield • 3.0%
12-Mo. P/E • 11.8

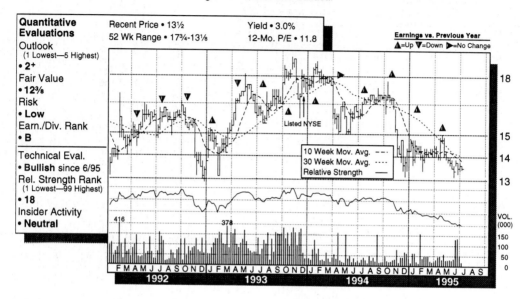

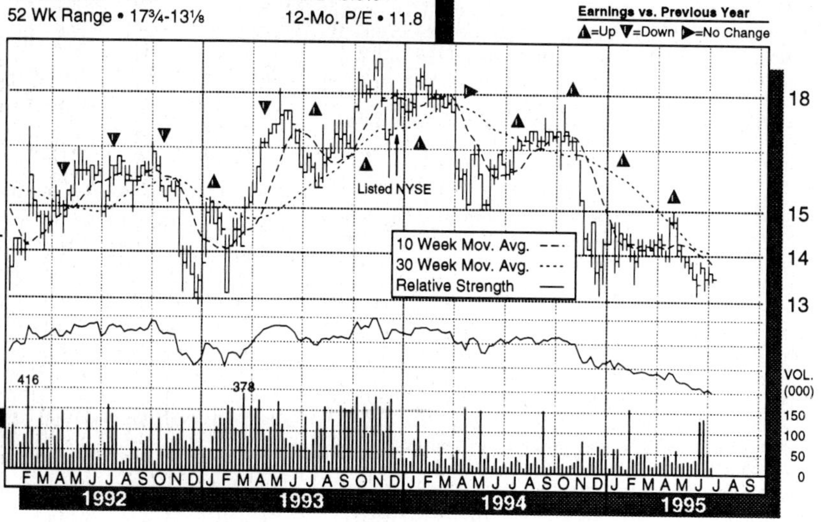

Business Profile - 10-JUL-95

Wizer has recently sold non-strategic properties in 13 states. It boosted production substantially through the 1993 acquisition of properties in the Permian Basin of West Texas and New Mexico. In June 1994, the company established a new core operating area with the purchase of Eagle Resources, Ltd., a Canadian company, most of whose resources are located in Alberta. Wiser continues to evaluate acquisition opportunities, mainly in areas where it currently operates wells.

Operational Review - 10-JUL-95

Total revenues rose strongly in the 1995 first quarter, reflecting increased oil and condensate production from Eagle Resources (acquired in June 1994), offset in part by lower natural gas sales. Profitability was aided by a sharp increase in oil and condensate prices, and despite a significant decline in natural gas prices, net income soared. The company expects 1995 profits to continue to be hurt by low natural gas prices.

Stock Performance - 07-JUL-95

In the past 30 trading days, WZR's shares have declined 2%, compared to a 6% rise in the S&P 500. Average trading volume for the past five days was 4,250 shares, compared with the 40-day moving average of 11,779 shares.

Key Stock Statistics

Dividend Rate/Share	0.40	Shareholders	1,600
Shs. outstg. (M)	8.9	Market cap. (B)	$0.121
Avg. daily vol. (M)	0.017	Inst. holdings	45%
Tang. Bk. Value/Share	11.83	Insider holdings	NA
Beta	0.34		

Value of $10,000 invested 5 years ago: $ 7,563

Fiscal Year Ending Dec. 31

	1995	% Change	1994	% Change	1993	% Change
Revenues (Million $)						
1Q	16.25	29%	12.58	18%	10.70	19%
2Q	—	—	13.51	35%	10.04	4%
3Q	—	—	15.35	77%	8.65	-4%
4Q	—	—	23.92	77%	13.53	9%
Yr.	—	—	65.36	52%	42.92	7%
Income (Million $)						
1Q	1.24	NM	0.07	40%	0.05	-91%
2Q	—	—	0.84	NM	0.07	NM
3Q	—	—	0.68	NM	-0.28	-67%
4Q	—	—	7.41	NM	1.18	51%
Yr.	—	—	8.99	NM	1.02	112%
Earnings Per Share ($)						
1Q	0.14	NM	0.01	NM	0.01	-83%
2Q	—	—	0.09	NM	0.01	—
3Q	—	—	0.08	NM	-0.03	NM
4Q	—	—	0.83	NM	0.12	50%
Yr.	—	—	1.01	NM	0.11	120%

Next earnings report expected: mid August

Wiser Oil

Business Summary - 10-JUL-95

Wiser Oil primarily explores for, produces and wholesales crude oil and natural gas. Revenues in recent years were derived as follows:

	1994	1993	1992
Oil & condensate sales	53%	54%	58%
Natural gas sales	29%	40%	34%
Other	18%	6%	8%

Net liquids production in 1994 amounted to 2,277,000 bbl., up 55% from 1,468,000 bbl. in 1993. Average crude oil prices were $15.60 a bbl. in 1994, versus $16.44 in 1993, while average NGLs prices were $9.00 a bbl. in 1994, versus $9.42 in 1993. Sales of natural gas in 1994 totaled 11,076,000 Mcf, up 34% from 8,296,000 Mcf in 1993. Natural gas prices averaged $1.73 per Mcf ($2.07).

At December 31, 1994, proved reserves amounted to 23.4 million bbl. of oil (80% developed) and 107.9 million Mcf of gas (91%). The present value of future revenues from these reserves was estimated at $159 million. Wiser had undeveloped and developed oil and gas leases covering 291,237 net acres in 11 states and Canada at 1994 year-end. Its main holdings were in Alberta, Canada (123,185 net acres), Kentucky (93,530), Texas (26,119) and New Mexico (20,668).

During 1994, the company participated in drilling 63 gross (25 net) wells, of which 21 were exploratory wells and 42 were development wells. Some 33% of the exploratory wells were successful, while overall the drilling program had a 67% success rate. Spending for drilling and development totaled $17.6 million in 1994, versus $14.5 million in 1993.

In October 1993, Wiser purchased oil and gas properties from Mobil Corp. units, for $59 million in cash. The properties, located in the Permian Basin of West Texas and New Mexico, were expected to boost daily oil and gas production by 60% and 70%, respectively. The company will operate over 80% of production from the properties.

In June 1994, the company's Canadian subsidiary acquired substantially all assets of privately held Eagle Resources, Ltd., a Canadian oil and gas company, for $52 million. The acquired properties, mostly located in Alberta, included 127,000 net undeveloped leasehold acres and 16 exploration prospects. Proved reserves before royalties were 8,400,000 bbl. of oil equivalent.

Important Developments

Mar. '95—Wiser said it had sold its interest in the Agaritta Field in Texas for $6.5 million, and had purchased properties in Louisiana, Texas and West Virginia for a total of $5.9 million, resulting in a net increase of 753,000 BOE of total proved reserves.

Capitalization

Long Term Debt: $76,996,000 (3/95).

Per Share Data ($) (Year Ended Dec. 31)

	1994	1993	1992	1991	1990	1989
Tangible Bk. Val.	11.79	11.76	9.76	10.11	10.39	10.14
Cash Flow	3.05	1.83	1.88	1.81	2.12	2.04
Earnings	1.01	0.11	0.05	0.28	0.74	0.75
Dividends	0.40	0.40	0.40	0.50	0.50	0.50
Payout Ratio	40%	NM	750%	179%	67%	66%
Prices - High	18⅞	19⅛	17	17¼	21½	21⅝
- Low	13⅛	13⅛	12⅞	13⅜	14⅝	13¾
P/E Ratio - High	19	NM	NM	62	29	29
- Low	13	NM	NM	48	20	18

Income Statement Analysis (Million $)

	1994	%Chg	1993	%Chg	1992	%Chg	1991
Revs.	53.6	33%	40.3	8%	37.2	NM	37.2
Oper. Inc.	19.9	63%	12.2	-7%	13.1	10%	11.9
Depr. Depl. & Amort.	18.3	19%	15.4	-6%	16.3	19%	13.7
Int. Exp.	3.9	NM	0.5	—	Nil	—	NM
Pretax Inc.	9.4	NM	-1.1	NM	0.2	-93%	3.0
Eff. Tax Rate	4.70%	—	NM	—	NM	—	17%
Net Inc.	9.0	NM	1.0	104%	0.5	-80%	2.5

Balance Sheet & Other Fin. Data (Million $)

	1994	1993	1992	1991	1990	1989
Cash	2.7	3.5	14.5	16.6	14.8	9.3
Curr. Assets	15.6	14.8	22.3	23.2	21.9	16.5
Total Assets	211	178	102	107	110	106
Curr. Liab.	13.3	8.4	5.9	7.0	6.4	4.8
LT Debt	78.0	46.8	0.1	0.2	0.2	0.3
Common Eqty.	105	105	87.0	90.3	93.8	91.6
Total Cap.	196	168	96.0	99	103	100
Cap. Exp.	71.8	70.9	16.1	11.3	16.3	18.9
Cash Flow	27.3	16.4	16.8	16.2	19.2	18.4

Ratio Analysis

	1994	1993	1992	1991	1990	1989
Curr. Ratio	1.2	1.8	3.8	3.3	3.4	3.5
% LT Debt of Cap.	39.7	27.8	0.1	0.2	0.2	0.3
% Ret. on Assets	4.6	0.7	0.5	2.3	6.2	6.5
% Ret. on Equity	8.5	1.1	0.1	2.7	7.3	7.5

Dividend Data (Cash dividends have been paid by the company or its predecessor in each year since 1941. A stockholder rights plan was adopted in October 1993.)

Amt. of Div. $	Date Decl.	Ex-Div. Date	Stock of Record	Payment Date
0.100	Aug. 16	Aug. 24	Aug. 30	Sep. 09 '94
0.100	Nov. 15	Nov. 23	Nov. 30	Dec. 09 '94
0.100	Feb. 21	Feb. 24	Mar. 02	Mar. 13 '95
0.100	May. 16	May. 23	May. 30	Jun. 09 '95

Data as orig. reptd.; bef. results of disc opers. and/or spec. items. Per share data adj. for stk. divs. as of ex-div. date. E-Estimated. NA-Not Available. NM-Not Meaningful. NR-Not Ranked.

Office—8115 Preston Rd., Suite 400, Dallas, TX 75225. **Tel**—(214) 265-0080. **Chrmn**—J. C. Wright. **Pres & CEO**—A. J. Shoup, Jr. **VP-Fin & CFO**—L. J. Finn. **Secy & Investor Contact**—Richard L. Starkey. **Treas**—R. D. Lee. **Dirs**—J. W. Cushing III, H. G. Hamilton, C. F. Kimball III, R. A. Lenser, J. L. Mosle, Jr., P. D. Neuenschwander, A. W. Schenck III, A. J. Shoup, Jr., J. C. Wright. **Transfer Agent**—Chemical Shareholder Services, Inc., Dallas. **Incorporated** in Delaware in 1970. **Empl**-130. **S&P Analyst:** A.M.A.

STANDARD & POOR'S

STOCK REPORTS

Wolverine Tube

NYSE Symbol **WLV**

In S&P SmallCap 600

15-OCT-95

Industry: Metal

Summary: This leading North American manufacturer and distributor of copper and copper alloy tube focuses on custom-engineered, high-value-added products.

Quantitative Evaluations

Outlook
(1 Lowest—5 Highest)
• **NA**

Fair Value
• **NA**

Risk
• **Average**

Earn./Div. Rank
• **NR**

Technical Eval.
• **Bullish** since 1/95

Rel. Strength Rank
(1 Lowest—99 Highest)
• **44**

Insider Activity
• **NA**

Recent Price • 37¼

52 Wk Range • 43½-22⅝

Yield • Nil

12-Mo. P/E • 17.7

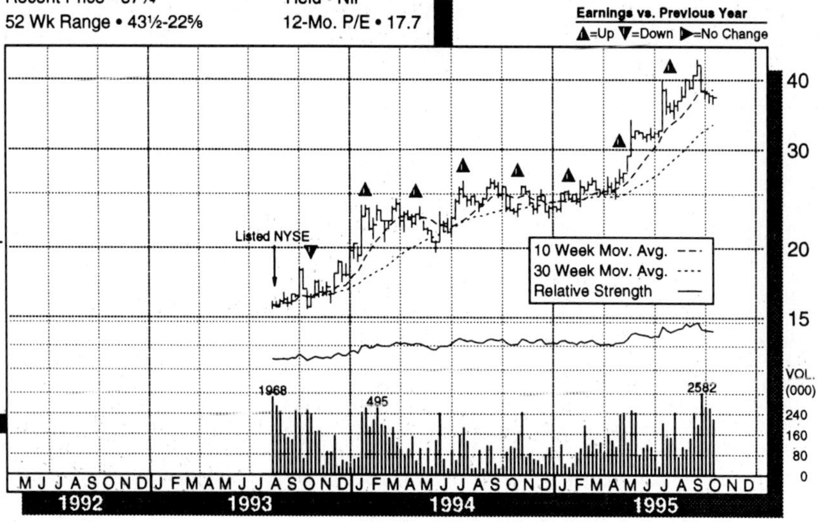

Business Profile - 12-OCT-95

Wolverine Tube continues to implement its strategy of focusing on high-value-added commercial products, cutting costs at its plants, improving operating efficiencies and expanding product offerings. Additionally, the company is growing through acquisitions, most recently the purchase of Small Tube Products, and is evaluating several investment possibilities in Europe and the Far East. WLV expects demand for its high-value-added efficient tubes to increase.

Operational Review - 12-OCT-95

Sales rose 33%, year to year, in the first half of 1995, primarily reflecting higher copper prices, increased volume, a continued shift to higher-margin commercial products and the inclusion of Small Tube Products. Greater operating expenses, principally raw-material costs, and a rise in interest expense, limited the gain in net income to 31%.

Stock Performance - 13-OCT-95

In the past 30 trading days, WLV's shares have declined 4%, compared to a 4% rise in the S&P 500. Average trading volume for the past five days was 43,640 shares, compared with the 40-day moving average of 120,049 shares.

Key Stock Statistics

Dividend Rate/Share	Nil	Shareholders	600
Shs. outstg. (M)	13.6	Market cap. (B)	$0.508
Avg. daily vol. (M)	0.200	Inst. holdings	41%
Tang. Bk. Value/Share	9.55	Insider holdings	NA
Beta	0.46		

Value of $10,000 invested 5 years ago: NA

Fiscal Year Ending Dec. 31

	1995	% Change	1994	% Change	1993	% Change
Revenues (Million $)						
1Q	179.8	39%	129.6	-4%	135.5	—
2Q	164.4	28%	128.3	8%	119.2	-53%
3Q	—	—	132.4	16%	113.8	-9%
4Q	—	—	135.3	35%	100.6	-4%
Yr.	—	—	525.6	12%	469.0	-3%
Income (Million $)						
1Q	9.13	31%	6.95	103%	3.42	—
2Q	8.93	31%	6.80	90%	3.58	—
3Q	—	—	6.01	39%	4.33	—
4Q	—	—	5.29	80%	2.94	—
Yr.	—	—	25.05	56%	16.03	31%
Earnings Per Share ($)						
1Q	0.65	27%	0.51	55%	0.33	—
2Q	0.63	26%	0.50	43%	0.35	-42%
3Q	—	—	0.44	22%	0.36	-3%
4Q	—	—	0.38	81%	0.21	NM
Yr.	—	—	1.82	31%	1.39	42%

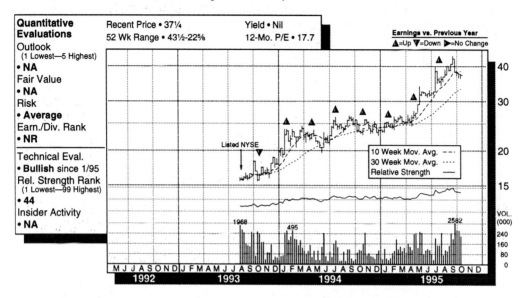

Next earnings report expected: mid October

Wolverine Tube

Business Summary - 20-JUN-95

Wolverine Tube, Inc. is a leading North American manufacturer and distributor of copper and copper alloy tube. It also manufactures and distributes copper and copper alloy rod, bar and strip products. The company focuses on custom-engineered, high-value-added copper and copper alloy tube, which enhances performance and energy efficiency in many applications. WLV groups its products into three major categories, whose contributions to net sales in recent years were:

	1994	1993	1992
Commercial products	67%	64%	60%
Wholesale products	18%	24%	28%
Rod, bar & strip	15%	12%	12%

Commercial products include several types of technically sophisticated tubes that are sold directly to equipment makers and that are generally custom designed and manufactured. Because of the high level of added value, profitability tends to be higher for commercial products than for other products. Commercial products consist of industrial tube made to customer specifications, technical tube used to increase heat transfer in such areas as large commercial air conditioners and power generating plants, and copper alloy tube made for certain severe uses and corrosive environments.

Wholesale products include plumbing tube and refrigeraton service tube produced in standard sizes and lengths primarily for plumbing, air-conditioning and refrigeration applications. Plumbing tube and refrigeration service tube are sold primarily through wholesalers.

Rod, bar and strip products are in two primary categories. Copper and copper alloy rod and bar products include a broad range of copper and copper alloy solid products, including round, rectangular, hexagonal and specialized shapes. Brass rod and bar are used by industrial equipment and machinery makers for valves, fittings and plumbing goods.

WLV's products are sold to a diverse customer base, including residential and commercial air-conditioning and refrigeration equipment makers, appliance manufacturers and utilities.

Important Developments

Apr. '95—The company said that construction at its new Roxboro, N.C., mill is on schedule, and full production capacity is expected during the second half of 1995.

Nov. '94—WLV acquired Small Tube Products Co. (Altoona, Pa.), a producer of copper and alloy tube with 1993 revenues of $67 million, for almost $55 million in cash and 400,000 common shares.

Capitalization

Long Term Debt: $100,715,000 (12/94).

$14 Cum. Preferred Stock: 20,000 shs. ($100 liquid. pref.).

Per Share Data ($) (Year Ended Dec. 31)

	1994	1993	1992	1991	1990	1989
Tangible Bk. Val.	9.55	7.50	4.74	NA	NA	NA
Cash Flow	2.76	2.31	2.11	1.14	NA	NA
Earnings	1.82	1.39	0.98	0.20	NA	NA
Dividends	Nil	Nil	NA	NA	NA	NA
Payout Ratio	Nil	Nil	NA	NA	NA	NA
Prices - High	26⅝	19¾	NA	NA	NA	NA
- Low	18⅞	15½	NA	NA	NA	NA
P/E Ratio - High	15	14	NA	NA	NA	NA
- Low	10	11	NA	NA	NA	NA

Income Statement Analysis (Million $)

	1994	%Chg	1993	%Chg	1992	%Chg	1991
Revs.	526	12%	469	-3%	484	16%	418
Oper. Inc.	61.6	24%	49.5	10%	45.1	54%	29.3
Depr.	12.9	24%	10.4	-13%	11.9	18%	10.1
Int. Exp.	10.3	7%	9.6	2%	9.4	-9%	10.3
Pretax Inc.	40.6	49%	27.2	27%	21.5	NM	6.7
Eff. Tax Rate	38%	—	41%	—	44%	—	39%
Net Inc.	25.0	56%	16.0	31%	12.2	NM	4.0

Balance Sheet & Other Fin. Data (Million $)

	1994	1993	1992	1991	1990	1989
Cash	0.1	55.2	NA	NA	NA	NA
Curr. Assets	126	136	NA	NA	NA	NA
Total Assets	341	276	NA	NA	NA	NA
Curr. Liab.	64.2	37.3	NA	NA	NA	NA
LT Debt	101	100	100	NA	NA	NA
Common Eqty.	129	97.6	92.0	NA	NA	NA
Total Cap.	255	217	NA	NA	NA	NA
Cap. Exp.	34.4	22.3	4.1	2.0	4.2	13.8
Cash Flow	37.7	26.2	22.4	12.4	12.2	20.1

Ratio Analysis

	1994	1993	1992	1991	1990	1989
Curr. Ratio	2.0	3.7	NA	NA	NA	NA
% LT Debt of Cap.	39.5	46.1	NA	NA	NA	NA
% Net Inc.of Revs.	4.8	3.4	2.5	1.0	1.1	2.2
% Ret. on Assets	8.0	5.7	NA	NA	NA	NA
% Ret. on Equity	21.6	21.0	NA	NA	NA	NA

Dividend Data —No dividends have been paid on the common stock. The company intends to retain earnings to support the growth of its business.

Data as orig. reptd.; bef. results of disc. opers. and/or spec. items. Per share data adj. for stk. divs. as of ex-div. date. E-Estimated. NA-Not Available. NM-Not Meaningful. NR-Not Ranked.

Office—1525 Perimeter Parkway, Suite 210, Huntsville, AL 35601. **Tel**—(205) 353-1310. **Chrmn, Pres & CEO**—J. M. Quarles. **COO**—G. M. Trickey. **Exec VP-Fin, Secy & Treas**—J. E. Deason. **Dirs**—M. E. Bandeen, D. C. Blasius, J. L. Duncan, A. A. MacNaughton, R. D. Paterson, J. M. Quarles, G. M. Trickey, R. J. Turner, J. A. West. **Transfer Agent & Registrar**—Society National Bank, Cleveland. **Incorporated** in Delaware in 1987. **Empl-** 2,915. **S&P Analyst:** S.O.S.

STANDARD & POOR'S

Wolverine World Wide

STOCK REPORTS

NYSE Symbol **WWW**
In S&P SmallCap 600

31-OCT-95 **Industry:** Leather/shoes

Summary: WWW makes, imports and markets casual footwear sold under the Hush Puppies, Wolverine and other brand names, and is the largest domestic tanner of pigskins.

Quantitative Evaluations

Outlook
(1 Lowest—5 Highest)
• **1+**

Fair Value
• **25½**

Risk
• **Average**

Earn./Div. Rank
• **B**

Technical Eval.
• **Bullish** since 12/94

Rel. Strength Rank
(1 Lowest—99 Highest)
• **89**

Insider Activity
• **Neutral**

Recent Price • 28⅜ | Yield • 0.5%
52 Wk Range • 31-13½ | 12-Mo. P/E • 22.7

Earnings vs. Previous Year
▲=Up ▼=Down ▶=No Change

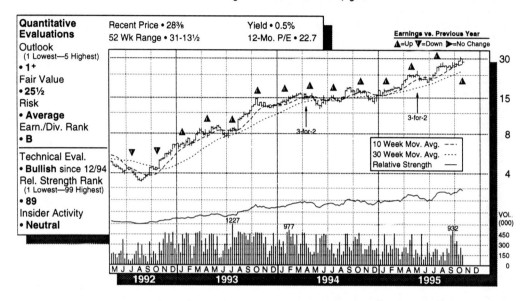

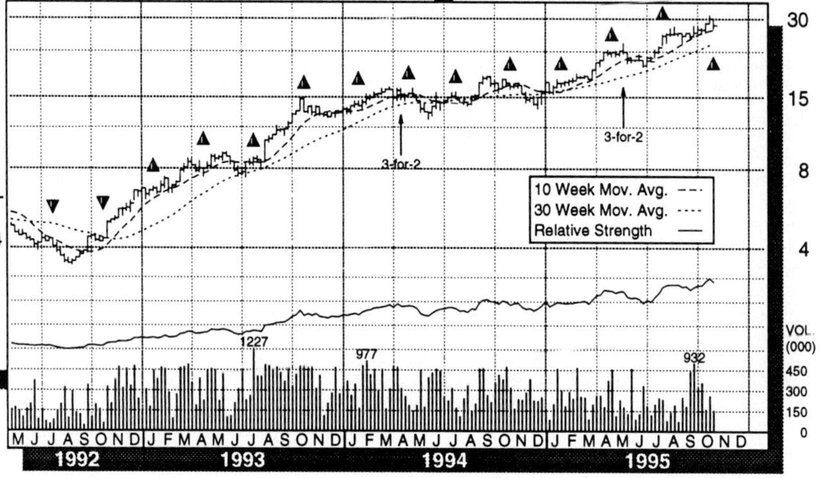

Business Profile - 19-OCT-95

This company is the world's leading marketer of U.S. branded, non-athletic footwear, with 152 marketing partners on six continents. Domestic and international businesses contribute equally to sales and earnings. A decision to focus on the core Hush Puppies and Wolverine brands, the discontinuance of the leased shoe department business, and benefits of additional cost-cutting measures should continue to boost profits for the remainder of 1995.

Operational Review - 31-OCT-95

Sales in the 36 weeks ended September 9, 1995, rose 11%, year to year, fueled by growing global demand for company brands and aggressive domestic sales efforts. Strong international revenues outpaced modest gains in the U.S. despite an extremely weak retail environment for footwear. Gross margins narrowed, but tight expense controls led to a reduction in SG&A costs as a percentage of sales. Earnings per share from continuing operations grew to $0.69, from $0.47.

Stock Performance - 27-OCT-95

In the past 30 trading days, WWW's shares have increased 10%, compared to a 0.63% fall in the S&P 500. Average trading volume for the past five days was 30,160 shares, compared with the 40-day moving average of 71,264 shares.

Key Stock Statistics

Dividend Rate/Share	0.14	Shareholders	2,000
Shs. outstg. (M)	16.4	Market cap. (B)	$0.478
Avg. daily vol. (M)	0.043	Inst. holdings	75%
Tang. Bk. Value/Share	8.82	Insider holdings	NA
Beta	0.87		

Value of $10,000 invested 5 years ago: $ 60,211

Fiscal Year Ending Dec. 31

	1995	% Change	1994	% Change	1993	% Change
Revenues (Million $)						
1Q	76.33	14%	66.78	1%	65.86	23%
2Q	86.29	9%	79.32	20%	65.90	10%
3Q	100.5	9%	91.91	13%	81.31	11%
4Q	—	—	140.5	17%	120.1	13%
Yr.	—	—	378.5	14%	333.1	14%
Income (Million $)						
1Q	2.50	80%	1.39	99%	0.70	NM
2Q	3.90	59%	2.46	128%	1.08	NM
3Q	5.21	39%	3.76	83%	2.05	NM
4Q	—	—	10.44	36%	7.66	20%
Yr.	—	—	18.05	57%	11.49	149%
Earnings Per Share ($)						
1Q	0.15	69%	0.09	95%	0.04	NM
2Q	0.23	50%	0.15	103%	0.08	NM
3Q	0.31	37%	0.23	70%	0.13	NM
4Q	—	—	0.63	32%	0.48	12%
Yr.	—	—	1.10	51%	0.73	133%

Next earnings report expected: late February

Wolverine World Wide

Business Summary - 30-OCT-95

Wolverine World Wide, Inc. manufactures, imports and markets footwear, primarily casual shoes, slippers, moccasins, dress shoes, boots and uniform and work shoes. The company also operates retail shoe stores and leased shoe departments. In addition, it is the largest domestic tanner of pigskins, which are used internally and also sold to others. Footwear and related products accounted for over 90% of total sales in recent years, with pigskin sales accounting for most of the remainder.

Hush Puppies, the company's principal and best known brand, is a line of casual shoes for men, women and children. Other brand names manufactured as well as imported and purchased for resale include Wolverine, Wilderness, Bates, Floaters, Durashocks, Bounce & Design, Comfort Curve, Town & Country, Tru-Stich, Wimzees and Sioux Mox.

WWW also makes shoes for resale under labels of other shoe companies and retailers, and is licensed to market footwear in the U.S. under the Coleman, Caterpillar and Cat trademarks. Pigskin leather is sold under the trademarks Breathin' Brushed Pigskin and Silkee.

Footwear is sold directly to more than 10,000 accounts operating more than 20,000 retail outlets. Sales are also made to large footwear chains (including those owned or operated by other companies in the shoe industry), catalog houses, and independently and company-owned Hush Puppies specialty stores.

At March 25, 1995, WWW was operating about 102 retail shoe stores and leased shoe departments. Approximately 56 stores were factory outlet stores, including 21 operated under the Little Red Shoe House name and 35 under the Hush Puppies Factory Direct name. The company also operated 32 full-price, full-service family leased shoe departments in the Pacific Northwest and Alaska featuring its wholesale brands and 14 mall-based Hush Puppies specialty stores.

In June 1994, the company signed separate licensing agreements to market apparel under the Wolverine Wilderness label: one with The Apparel Group Ltd. for the marketing of a moderately priced men's sportswear line, geared toward an outdoor rugged lifestyle and slated to debut in the fall of 1995; and the other with Rainforest Inc. (debuted in the fall of 1994).

Important Developments

Jun. '95—The company began construction of a new $10 million, 210,000 sq. ft. distribution center in Cedar Springs, Mich. The facility will serve as WWW's global hub for work and rugged outdoor shoes and boots.

Capitalization

Long Term Debt: $80,700,000 (9/95).

Per Share Data ($)

(Year Ended Dec. 31)

	1994	1993	1992	1991	1990	1989
Tangible Bk. Val.	8.19	10.99	6.66	7.48	7.29	7.65
Cash Flow	1.45	1.59	0.66	0.56	-0.04	0.80
Earnings	1.10	0.73	0.31	0.22	-0.38	0.48
Dividends	0.10	0.07	0.07	0.07	0.07	0.07
Payout Ratio	9%	10%	23%	32%	NM	15%
Prices - High	18⅛	14⅞	6¾	5¾	5⅝	7
- Low	12⅜	6⅛	3½	3½	2¾	4¾
P/E Ratio - High	16	20	22	26	NM	14
- Low	11	8	11	16	NM	10

Income Statement Analysis (Million $)

	1994	%Chg	1993	%Chg	1992	%Chg	1991
Revs.	378	14%	333	14%	293	-7%	314
Oper. Inc.	35.0	41%	24.9	40%	17.8	-10%	19.7
Depr.	5.7	9%	5.2	NM	5.2	3%	5.0
Int. Exp.	4.0	-21%	5.1	39%	3.6	-30%	5.2
Pretax Inc.	25.4	60%	15.9	145%	6.5	44%	4.5
Eff. Tax Rate	29%	—	28%	—	29%	—	28%
Net Inc.	18.1	57%	11.5	150%	4.6	39%	3.3

Balance Sheet & Other Fin. Data (Million $)

	1994	1993	1992	1991	1990	1989
Cash	2.9	3.7	2.4	2.2	2.5	3.2
Curr. Assets	169	150	148	155	142	142
Total Assets	230	206	204	208	190	189
Curr. Liab.	43.0	38.3	52.4	61.7	44.4	33.8
LT Debt	43.5	44.9	42.7	31.6	34.3	36.3
Common Eqty.	133	113	100	110	108	116
Total Cap.	178	159	144	142	142	152
Cap. Exp.	9.9	6.6	4.1	6.7	7.2	5.8
Cash Flow	23.7	16.7	9.8	8.3	-0.6	12.2

Ratio Analysis

	1994	1993	1992	1991	1990	1989
Curr. Ratio	3.9	3.9	2.8	2.5	3.2	4.2
% LT Debt of Cap.	24.4	28.2	29.6	22.3	24.2	23.8
% Net Inc.of Revs.	4.8	3.4	1.6	1.0	NM	2.3
% Ret. on Assets	8.1	5.5	2.2	1.6	NM	3.9
% Ret. on Equity	14.4	10.7	4.3	3.0	NM	6.4

Dividend Data —Payments, omitted in 1986, were resumed 1988. A "poison pill" stock purchase rights plan was adopted in 1987.

Amt. of Div. $	Date Decl.	Ex-Div. Date	Stock of Record	Payment Date
0.050	Mar. 10	Mar. 28	Apr. 03	May. 01 '95
3-for-2	Apr. 19	May. 16	May. 01	May. 15 '95
0.035	Apr. 19	Jun. 29	Jul. 03	Aug. 01 '95
0.035	Jul. 12	Sep. 28	Oct. 02	Nov. 01 '95
0.035	Oct. 06	Dec. 28	Jan. 02	Feb. 01 '96

Data as orig. reptd.; bef. results of disc. opers. and/or spec. items. Per share data adj. for stk. divs. as of ex-div. date. E-Estimated. NA-Not Available. NM-Not Meaningful. NR-Not Ranked.

Office—9341 Courtland Dr., Rockford, MI 49351. **Tel**—(616) 866-5500. **Chrmn**—P. D. Matthews. **Pres & CEO**—G. B. Bloom. **Vice Chrmn**—T. D. Gleason. **VP & CFO**—S. L. Gulis, Jr. **VP & Treas**—T. P. Mundt. **VP & Secy**—B. W. Krueger. **Investor Contact**—L. James Lovejoy. **Dirs**—G. B. Bloom, D. T. Carroll, T. D. Gleason, A. L. Grimoldi, D. T. Kolatt, P. D. Matthews, D. P. Mehney, S. J. Northrop, T. J. O'Donovan, J. A. Parini, J. Parker, E. A. Sanders. **Transfer Agent & Registrar**—NBD Bank, Detroit. **Incorporated** in Michigan in 1906; reincorporated in Delaware in 1969. **Empl**-5,205. **S&P Analyst:** Maureen C. Carini

STANDARD & POOR'S

STOCK REPORTS

Wyle Electronics

NYSE Symbol **WYL**
In S&P SmallCap 600

27-OCT-95 **Industry:** Electronics/Electric

Summary: Formerly Wyle Laboratories, this company is a leading distributor of high technology electronic products, specializing in semiconductors, computer systems and value-added services.

Quantitative Evaluations

Outlook
(1 Lowest—5 Highest)
• **1+**

Fair Value
• **36⅞**

Risk
• **Average**

Earn./Div. Rank
• **B+**

Technical Eval.
• **Bearish** since 8/95

Rel. Strength Rank
(1 Lowest—99 Highest)
• **81**

Insider Activity
• **Unfavorable**

Recent Price • 41 | 52 Wk Range • 45⅜-17¼ | Yield • 0.7% | 12-Mo. P/E • 18.0

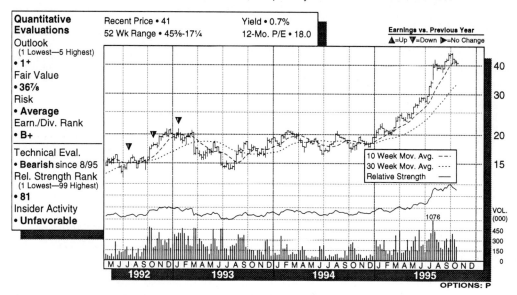

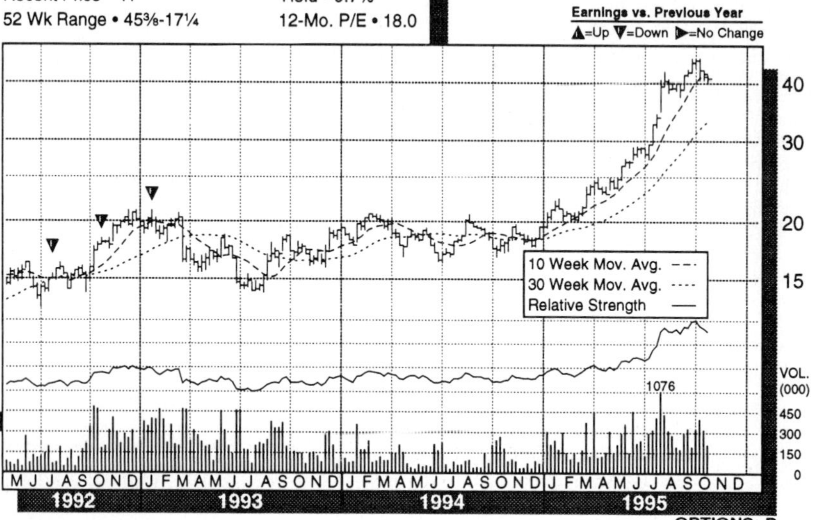

OPTIONS: P

Business Profile - 24-OCT-95

Known as Wyle Laboratories before selling the Scientific Services & Systems group in December 1994, this company is a marketer of semiconductors, computer products, and value-added services. In past years, gross margins were pressured by a changing product mix and costs of expanding the distribution channels. However, results in 1994, and the first half of 1995, were aided by a healthy semiconductor environment and geographic expansion. WYL expects to reach $1 billion in annual sales in 1995.

Operational Review - 24-OCT-95

Net sales in the nine months ended September 30, 1995, advanced 37%, year to year, on strong demand for semiconductor products, especially those that utilize WYL's value-added, high margin, design/programming services. Shipments of computer systems and mass storage devices also rose. Margins widened on product mix changes and more productive use of SG&A expense. Income from continuing operations advanced to $2.03 a share from $0.69 (before a net loss from discontinued operations of $0.97).

Stock Performance - 20-OCT-95

In the past 30 trading days, WYL's shares have declined 2%, compared to a 3% rise in the S&P 500. Average trading volume for the past five days was 41,400 shares, compared with the 40-day moving average of 56,782 shares.

Key Stock Statistics

Dividend Rate/Share	0.28	Shareholders	2,600
Shs. outstg. (M)	12.3	Market cap. (B)	$0.520
Avg. daily vol. (M)	0.063	Inst. holdings	75%
Tang. Bk. Value/Share	13.56	Insider holdings	NA
Beta	1.66		

Value of $10,000 invested 5 years ago: $ 39,624

Fiscal Year Ending Dec. 31

	1995	% Change	1994	% Change	1993	% Change
Revenues (Million $)						
1Q	250.0	42%	175.6	—	—	—
2Q	254.9	36%	188.1	—	—	—
3Q	273.5	34%	204.1	—	—	—
4Q	—	—	224.5	—	—	—
Yr.	—	—	792.3	42%	557.9	23%
Income (Million $)						
1Q	6.73	NM	2.12	—	—	—
2Q	8.77	164%	3.32	—	—	—
3Q	10.14	NM	3.13	—	—	—
4Q	—	—	5.42	—	—	—
Yr.	—	—	13.98	23%	11.33	-27%
Earnings Per Share ($)						
1Q	0.54	NM	0.17	—	—	—
2Q	0.70	159%	0.27	—	—	—
3Q	0.80	NM	0.25	—	—	—
4Q	—	—	0.44	—	—	—
Yr.	—	—	1.13	23%	0.92	-3%

Next earnings report expected: late January

Wyle Electronics

27-OCT-95

Business Summary - 26-OCT-95

Wyle Electronics (formerly Wyle Laboratories) principally markets high-technology electronic products, specializing in semiconductors, computer systems and related value-added services. It is also engaged in industrial manufacturing. In December 1994, Wyle sold its Scientific Services & Systems Group, which supplied research, engineering and testing services to the aerospace/defense and energy industries, recording an after-tax loss of nearly $16 million on the sale. Wyle's remaining operations are conducted through its Electronics Marketing Group.

The Electronics Marketing Group specializes in the distribution of semiconductors (80% of 1994 sales) and computer systems products (20%) throughout the U.S. In May 1993, the group began a nationwide expansion program, opening 10 new divisions in the East and Midwest, bringing the total number of domestic sales facilities to 30, as of December 31, 1994. This program is not only expected to add new customers, but should also lead to additional sales from existing customers whose manufacturing facilities are in different regions.

The company stocks 30,000 items and markets the products of over 50 suppliers to customers primarily in the computer, military, industrial and telecommunications product markets. Wyle's two largest suppliers are Intel (23% of 1994 sales) and Digital Equipment (12%). Principal products distributed include semiconductors, computer products (microcomputer systems, board level sub-systems and peripherals), and passive components (capacitors and resistors). Specialized value-added services such as kitting, turnkey manufacturing, autoreplenishment, the design, programming and testing of semicustom products, sytems integration and technical support are also offered.

These value-added services are also used by Wyle's Liberty Contract Services operation, in providing management services for materials and complex inventory processes. Under the kitting program, Liberty ships products, in production-ready kits, to a customer's production line on a just-in-time basis.

Important Developments

Oct. '95—Wyle noted that customer backlog at the end of the 1995 third quarter reached record levels, and that earnings were growing at a faster rate than revenues because of increased demand for its value-added services.

Oct. '95—Wyle said that during the third quarter, it had concluded an agreement with Micron Electronics to distribute Micron's full line of PC-based systems nationwide. Wyle added that it had also begun shipping products from its new value-added distribution center in Phoenix, AZ.

Capitalization

Long Term Debt: $48,111,000 (6/95).

Per Share Data ($) (Year Ended Dec. 31)

	1994	1993	1992	1991	1990	1989
Tangible Bk. Val.	13.10	13.45	13.09	11.48	10.79	9.77
Cash Flow	1.67	1.36	1.97	1.48	1.80	1.26
Earnings	1.13	0.92	1.45	0.95	1.28	0.75
Dividends	0.28	0.28	0.28	0.28	0.28	0.28
Payout Ratio	25%	30%	19%	29%	22%	36%
Prices - High	20¾	21⅛	21⅛	17	15⅛	11⅜
- Low	16¼	14	12⅜	9⅞	8¾	7¾
P/E Ratio - High	18	NM	15	18	12	15
- Low	14	NM	9	10	7	10

Income Statement Analysis (Million $)

	1994	%Chg	1993	%Chg	1992	%Chg	1991
Revs.	792	42%	558	3%	541	19%	453
Oper. Inc.	32.1	42%	22.6	-31%	32.6	46%	22.3
Depr.	6.8	25%	5.4	-1%	5.5	1%	5.4
Int. Exp.	1.5	44%	1.1	-67%	3.2	-23%	4.2
Pretax Inc.	22.7	28%	17.8	-27%	24.3	61%	15.1
Eff. Tax Rate	39%	—	36%	—	37%	—	36%
Net Inc.	14.0	24%	11.3	-27%	15.4	59%	9.7

Balance Sheet & Other Fin. Data (Million $)

	1994	1993	1992	1991	1990	1989
Cash	9.3	23.7	29.5	28.9	15.1	8.2
Curr. Assets	274	224	201	183	160	141
Total Assets	306	261	236	217	194	176
Curr. Liab.	103	80.3	59.1	50.4	44.9	39.1
LT Debt	17.8	6.0	10.1	42.0	36.0	36.6
Common Eqty.	160	164	159	115	106	94.0
Total Cap.	178	170	169	157	142	131
Cap. Exp.	8.4	6.0	4.7	4.8	4.5	6.1
Cash Flow	20.7	16.8	20.9	15.1	17.8	12.7

Ratio Analysis

	1994	1993	1992	1991	1990	1989
Curr. Ratio	2.7	2.8	3.4	3.6	3.6	3.6
% LT Debt of Cap.	10.0	3.5	6.0	26.7	25.5	27.9
% Net Inc.of Revs.	1.8	2.0	2.8	2.1	2.8	1.8
% Ret. on Assets	4.9	NM	6.2	4.6	6.8	4.3
% Ret. on Equity	8.6	NM	10.3	8.6	12.6	8.1

Dividend Data —Dividends have been paid each year since 1974.

Amt. of Div. $	Date Decl.	Ex-Div. Date	Stock of Record	Payment Date
0.070	Nov. 04	Dec. 09	Dec. 15	Dec. 30 '94
0.070	Mar. 02	Mar. 09	Mar. 15	Mar. 31 '95
0.070	May. 09	Jun. 13	Jun. 15	Jun. 30 '95
0.070	Aug. 31	Sep. 13	Sep. 15	Sep. 29 '95

Data as orig. reptd.; bef. results of disc. opers. and/or spec. items. Per share data adj. for stk. divs. as of ex-div. date. Yrs. ended Jan. 31 of foll. cal. yr. prior to 1993. Data for 1993 is for 11 mos. ended Dec. E-Estimated. NA-Not Available. NM-Not Meaningful. NR-Not Ranked.

Office—15370 Barranca Parkway, Irvine, CA 92718. **Tel**—(714) 753-9953. **Chrmn & CEO**—C. M. Clough. **Pres**—R. L. Ozorkiewicz. **EVP-Fin, Treas & CFO**—R. Van Ness Holland, Jr. **VP-Secy**—S. D. Natcher. **Dirs**—M. Corboy, C. M. Clough, T. M. Freedman, J. S. Kilby, R. L. Ozorkiewicz, E. Sanders, S. A. Wainer, K. West, Frank S. Wyle. **Transfer Agent & Registrar**—Chemical Trust Co. of California, Los Angeles. **Incorporated** in California in 1953. **Empl**-1,248. **S&P Analyst:** J. Santoriello

STANDARD & POOR'S

STOCK REPORTS

Wynn's International

NYSE Symbol **WN**

In S&P SmallCap 600

28-SEP-95

Industry: Auto parts/equipment

Summary: This company manufactures automotive parts and accessories, and petrochemical specialties. Products include automotive air conditioners, O-rings, seals and molded rubber products.

Quantitative Evaluations

Outlook
(1 Lowest—5 Highest)
• **NA**

Fair Value
• **NA**

Risk
• **NA**

Earn./Div. Rank
• **B**

Technical Eval.
• **NA**

Rel. Strength Rank
(1 Lowest—99 Highest)
• **64**

Insider Activity
• **NA**

Recent Price • 28
52 Wk Range • 28¼-19½
Yield • 1.9%
12-Mo. P/E • 12.2

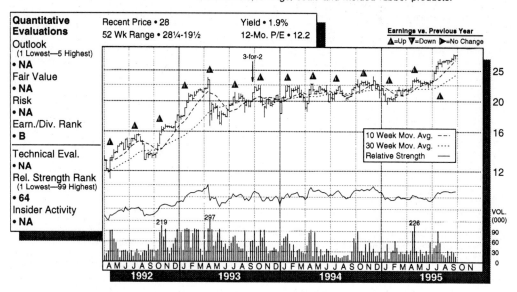

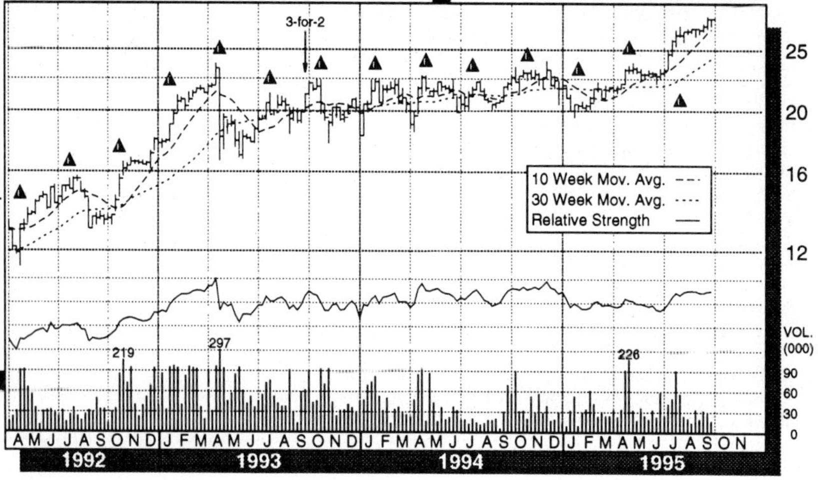

Business Profile - 28-SEP-95

With much of the company's fortunes tied to automobile sales, Wynn's has benefited from improved auto production rates since 1992, while demand for car care products, industrial fluids, and other product lines has led to sharp improvement in earnings in the petrochemical specialties segment. Following a $10 million investment in new production equipment during 1994, the Wynn's Precision Inc. unit is making efforts to increase market share in the auto, heavy truck and industrial markets.

Operational Review - 28-SEP-95

Sales in 1995's first half advanced 2% aided by more favorable exchange rates, and wider operating margins resulted in a 28% increase in net income. The gain in earnings was restrained by additional shares. Several new marketing programs led to increased sales from Wynn Oil Company, and the trend looks positive, as margins continue to expand. Though automobile sales are likely to taper off for the remainder of 1995, Wynn has taken efficiency steps intended to prevent a sharp drop in earnings.

Stock Performance - 22-SEP-95

In the past 30 trading days, WN's shares have increased 5%, compared to a 5% rise in the S&P 500. Average trading volume for the past five days was 3,320 shares, compared with the 40-day moving average of 4,754 shares.

Key Stock Statistics

Dividend Rate/Share	0.52	Shareholders	400
Shs. outstg. (M)	6.0	Market cap. (B)	$0.165
Avg. daily vol. (M)	0.005	Inst. holdings	74%
Tang. Bk. Value/Share	18.25	Insider holdings	NA
Beta	0.36		

Value of $10,000 invested 5 years ago: $ 20,830

Fiscal Year Ending Dec. 31

	1995	% Change	1994	% Change	1993	% Change
Revenues (Million $)						
1Q	78.07	2%	76.78	9%	70.51	-1%
2Q	78.05	2%	76.87	8%	71.32	-7%
3Q	—	—	72.22	-1%	73.19	-4%
4Q	—	—	66.79	-5%	69.94	4%
Yr.	—	—	292.6	3%	285.0	-2%
Income (Million $)						
1Q	3.65	35%	2.70	44%	1.87	22%
2Q	4.11	22%	3.36	39%	2.41	39%
3Q	—	—	3.04	23%	2.48	25%
4Q	—	—	2.72	22%	2.23	10%
Yr.	—	—	11.82	32%	8.98	24%
Earnings Per Share ($)						
1Q	0.62	29%	0.48	41%	0.34	21%
2Q	0.67	14%	0.59	36%	0.43	35%
3Q	—	—	0.53	18%	0.45	23%
4Q	—	—	0.48	20%	0.40	7%
Yr.	—	—	2.08	28%	1.62	20%

Next earnings report expected: mid October

Wynn's International

Business Summary - 28-SEP-95

Wynn's International designs and produces automotive parts and accessories, and formulates petrochemical specialties. It also distributes lock hardware to retailers, primarily in Southern California. Contributions to sales and operating profits in 1994 were:

	Sales	Profits
Auto parts & accessories	60%	65%
Petrochemical specialties	38%	34%
Builders hardware	2%	1%

Foreign sales accounted for 34% and 36% of the total in each of 1994 and 1993, with 1994 including 29% by foreign subsidiaries and 4.5% exports. GM, the largest customer of automotive components, accounted for 10.3% of consolidated sales.

The automotive parts and accessories division produces automotive air conditioning units for the OEM market and the automotive aftermarket through Wynn's Climate Systems (WCS). The company also makes and sells a variety of air conditioning components such as condensers and evaporator coils, as well as refrigerant recovery and recycling equipment. Wynn's-Precision Inc. is a leading international manufacturer of O-rings and other static and dynamic seals for the automotive, aerospace, oil service and hydraulic industries.

The petrochemical specialties division consists of Wynn Oil Co., which produces and markets a wide variety of car care products, including preventive or corrective maintenance and appearance products, as well as industrial specialty products, such as forging compounds, coolants, lubricants, and cutting fluids. The company also sells a power-flush machine, which automatically cleans a vehicle's cooling system and antifreeze, and restores the antifreeze so it can be reused.

Through Robert Skeels & Co., the builders hardware division distributes about 35,000 items including locksets and locksmith supplies to retail hardware, locksmith and lumberyard outlets in Southern California, Arizona and Nevada. Skeels also sells directly to school districts, municipalities, industrial firms and building contractors.

Important Developments

Jul. '95—The company attributed its year-to-year 22% increase in 1995 second quarter net income, in part, to a 7% increase in sales at Wynn's Precision. Profitability was also aided by a 42% jump in operating profit at the petrochemical specialties division, due to higher levels of demand. There was a small operating loss from the company's automotive air conditioning subsidiary.

Capitalization

Long Term Debt: $764,000 (6/95).

Per Share Data ($) (Year Ended Dec. 31)

	1994	1993	1992	1991	1990	1989
Tangible Bk. Val.	16.56	14.67	13.95	13.39	14.85	13.75
Cash Flow	3.27	2.82	2.48	-0.67	2.57	2.60
Earnings	2.08	1.62	1.35	-2.06	1.10	1.31
Dividends	0.44	0.42	0.40	0.40	0.40	0.40
Payout Ratio	21%	26%	30%	NM	34%	31%
Prices - High	24	23¾	18⅛	13⅛	16	18⅝
- Low	18¼	16⅝	10¾	9¾	9⅛	14
P/E Ratio - High	12	15	13	NM	15	14
- Low	9	10	7	NM	8	11

Income Statement Analysis (Million $)

	1994	%Chg	1993	%Chg	1992	%Chg	1991
Revs.	293	3%	285	-2%	292	7%	274
Oper. Inc.	28.6	12%	25.6	8%	23.8	27%	18.8
Depr.	6.8	2%	6.7	8%	6.1	-18%	7.5
Int. Exp.	3.0	-23%	3.9	-24%	5.1	-2%	5.2
Pretax Inc.	19.4	23%	15.8	19%	13.3	NM	-13.9
Eff. Tax Rate	39%	—	43%	—	46%	—	NM
Net Inc.	11.8	31%	9.0	23%	7.3	NM	-11.2

Balance Sheet & Other Fin. Data (Million $)

	1994	1993	1992	1991	1990	1989
Cash	16.4	21.4	14.7	6.1	7.7	12.4
Curr. Assets	120	118	125	118	128	129
Total Assets	176	168	171	166	188	189
Curr. Liab.	59.2	56.3	54.5	44.7	50.2	53.5
LT Debt	14.9	23.4	32.5	40.7	41.2	41.2
Common Eqty.	95.4	84.4	78.9	75.6	89.8	87.9
Total Cap.	117	112	116	121	138	135
Cap. Exp.	13.8	10.0	6.5	4.2	8.3	10.7
Cash Flow	18.6	15.6	13.4	-3.7	14.8	15.0

Ratio Analysis

	1994	1993	1992	1991	1990	1989
Curr. Ratio	2.0	2.1	2.3	2.6	2.5	2.4
% LT Debt of Cap.	12.7	21.0	28.0	33.7	29.9	30.5
% Net Inc.of Revs.	4.0	3.2	2.5	NM	2.2	2.7
% Ret. on Assets	6.8	5.2	4.3	NM	3.5	4.0
% Ret. on Equity	13.1	10.9	9.4	NM	7.4	8.9

Dividend Data —Dividends have been paid since 1975. A "poison pill" stock purchase rights plan was adopted in 1989.

Amt. of Div. $	Date Decl.	Ex-Div. Date	Stock of Record	Payment Date
0.110	Aug. 03	Aug. 22	Aug. 26	Sep. 30 '94
0.110	Nov. 30	Dec. 15	Dec. 21	Jan. 04 '95
0.130	Feb. 15	Feb. 21	Feb. 27	Mar. 31 '95
0.130	May. 15	Jun. 14	Jun. 16	Jun. 30 '95
0.130	Aug. 09	Aug. 23	Aug. 25	Sep. 29 '95

Data as orig. reptd.; bef. results of disc. opers. and/or spec. items. Per share data adj. for stk. divs. as of ex-div. date. E-Estimated. NA-Not Available. NM-Not Meaningful. NR-Not Ranked.

Office—500 North State College Blvd., Suite 700, Orange, CA 92668. **Tel**—(714) 938-3700. **Chrmn**—W. E. Bellwood. **Pres & CEO & Investor Contact**—James Carroll. **VP-Fin & CFO**—S. A. Schlosser. **VP & Secy**—G. M. Gibbons. **Dirs**—B. Beek, W. E. Bellwood, J. D. Borie, J. Carroll, B. L. Herrmann, R. Hood, Jr., R. L. Nelson, J. D. Woods. **Transfer Agent & Registrar**—First Interstate Bank, LA; First Interstate Bank, NYC. **Incorporated** in Delaware in 1973. **Empl**-2,052. **S&P Analyst:** RJD

STANDARD & POOR'S

STOCK REPORTS

X-Rite, Inc.

NASDAQ Symbol **XRIT**

In S&P SmallCap 600

14-AUG-95

Industry: Electronics/Electric

Summary: This company manufactures quality control products primarily for the graphic arts, photographic, medical, packaging, paint, plastic, textile and medical industries.

Quantitative Evaluations

Outlook (1 Lowest—5 Highest)
• **NA**

Fair Value
• **NA**

Risk
• **Average**

Earn./Div. Rank
• **B+**

Technical Eval.
• **Bullish** since 5/94

Rel. Strength Rank (1 Lowest—99 Highest)
• **55**

Insider Activity
• **Neutral**

Recent Price • 19¾
52 Wk Range • 24-14¼
Yield • 0.5%
12-Mo. P/E • 32.9

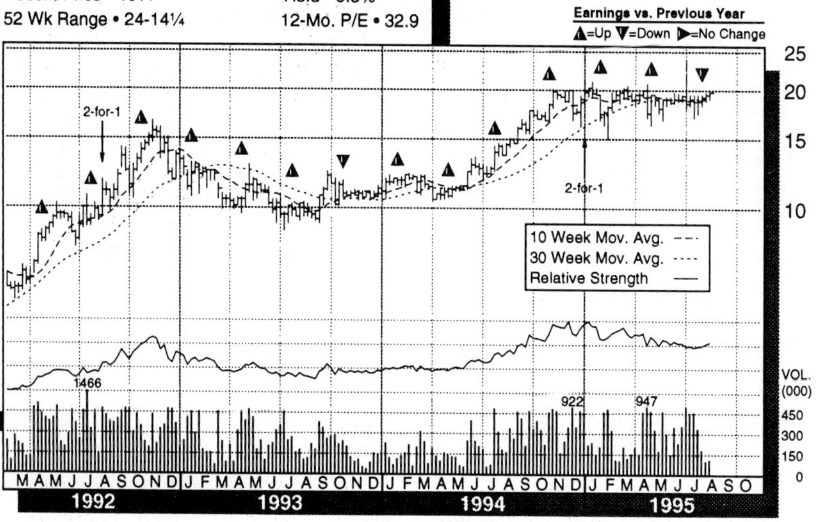

Business Profile - 14-AUG-95

X-Rite's color and appearance products support a myriad of industries. This diversification not only protects the company from a downturn in one industry sector but also offers a wide base for future sales opportunities. Additionally, nearly a third of the company's sales come from international markets. X-Rite's industry leadership position is founded on its ability to introduce high quality, leading-edge products.

Operational Review - 14-AUG-95

Sales have been fueled by the sale of instruments for automotive and architectural paints, both in the U.S. and Europe. Interest from the Asian textile industry has also aided sales growth. Despite a 36% jump in net sales, earnings were flat in the first half of 1995, reflecting X-Rite's decision to support future growth through increased R&D and marketing spending. Recently introduced products for the growing desktop publishing market have been well received.

Stock Performance - 11-AUG-95

In the past 30 trading days, XRIT's shares have increased 7%, compared to a 2% rise in the S&P 500. Average trading volume for the past five days was 21,220 shares, compared with the 40-day moving average of 74,523 shares.

Key Stock Statistics

Dividend Rate/Share	0.10	Shareholders	1,500
Shs. outstg. (M)	21.0	Market cap. (B)	$0.415
Avg. daily vol. (M)	0.036	Inst. holdings	19%
Tang. Bk. Value/Share	2.57	Insider holdings	NA
Beta	0.40		

Value of $10,000 invested 5 years ago: $ 69,593

Fiscal Year Ending Dec. 31

	1995	% Change	1994	% Change	1993	% Change
Revenues (Million $)						
1Q	17.95	45%	12.35	30%	9.47	NM
2Q	18.91	28%	14.76	57%	9.38	9%
3Q	—	—	15.64	59%	9.86	7%
4Q	—	—	16.73	60%	10.48	16%
Yr.	—	—	59.48	52%	39.19	8%
Income (Million $)						
1Q	3.30	28%	2.58	33%	1.94	5%
2Q	2.55	-22%	3.26	81%	1.80	20%
3Q	—	—	3.32	96%	1.69	-12%
4Q	—	—	3.49	67%	2.09	17%
Yr.	—	—	12.65	68%	7.53	7%
Earnings Per Share ($)						
1Q	0.16	33%	0.12	26%	0.09	6%
2Q	0.12	-20%	0.15	76%	0.08	21%
3Q	—	—	0.16	100%	0.08	-11%
4Q	—	—	0.17	70%	0.10	11%
Yr.	—	—	0.60	67%	0.36	6%

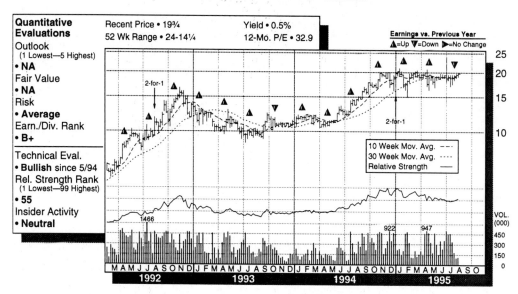

Next earnings report expected: late October

X-Rite, Inc.

Business Summary - 14-AUG-95

X-Rite, Incorporated designs, engineers and manufactures quality control instruments, which it markets worldwide to companies in the paint, plastic, textile, packaging, photographic, graphic arts and medical industries. The company has two main product lines: instruments that measure color and appearence, and instruments that measure optical or photographic density. Other product lines include silver recovery equipment; heat shrink packaging equipment; and an X-ray marking and identification system. Collectively, these secondary products represented about 6% of total sales in 1994.

X-Rite is a world leader in the manufacture of electro-optical instruments, which accounted for 92% of 1993 revenues, up from 91% in 1992. Until 1989, the company's light and color measuring instruments consisted solely of densitometers and sensitometers. A densitometer is an instrument that measures optical or photographic density; it measures light, compares that measurement with a reference standard and signals the result to the operator. Sensitometers are used to expose photographic film of various types in a very precise manner for comparison to a reference standard. X-Rite makes many models of these instruments for use in photographic, graphic arts, medical, digital imaging, and color and appearance.

In 1989, the company introduced a colorimeter that measures color much as the human eye perceives color, using red, green and blue receptors. In 1990, X-Rite unveiled a line of color and appearance instruments, consisting of a spectrophotometer and a spectrocolorimeter, both of which can be used by any industry concerned with the precise measurement of color and appearance. In 1991, a multi-angle spectrophotometer designed to measure the color of metallic paint finishes was introduced.

Except for private-label arrangements, products are distributed in the U.S. through a network of two thousand independent dealers, managed and serviced by independent manufacturer's representatives and X-Rite's own sales force. Foreign sales are made through dealers in more than 50 countries.

In 1994, X-Rite acquired H. Miller Graphics Arts Products Ltd., a graphics arts distributor in England. The company also bought the assets of Colorgen, Inc., the market leader in color measurement devices at the retail paint store level. These acquisitions did not have a significant effect on 1994 earnings, however, they are expected to contribute in 1995

Important Developments

Feb. '95—X-Rite acquired Labsphere, Inc., a manufacturer of color measurement products with 1994 sales of over $6.9 million, for $11.5 million. The acquisition was accounted for under the purchase method and was financed out of short-term investments.

Capitalization

Long Term Debt: None (3/95).

Per Share Data ($) (Year Ended Dec. 31)

	1994	1993	1992	1991	1990	1989
Tangible Bk. Val.	2.44	1.90	1.61	1.33	1.13	0.97
Cash Flow	0.66	0.42	0.39	0.28	0.22	0.21
Earnings	0.60	0.36	0.34	0.23	0.19	0.17
Dividends	0.08	0.08	0.05	0.03	0.03	0.02
Payout Ratio	13%	22%	15%	14%	15%	11%
Prices - High	21	13½	16⅝	7½	3⅝	3⅛
- Low	10½	8¾	5⅝	2¾	2	2¹⁄₁₆
P/E Ratio - High	35	38	49	33	20	18
- Low	18	24	17	12	11	12

Income Statement Analysis (Million $)

	1994	%Chg	1993	%Chg	1992	%Chg	1991
Revs.	59.5	52%	39.2	8%	36.2	24%	29.1
Oper. Inc.	19.1	74%	11.0	3%	10.7	51%	7.1
Depr.	1.3	12%	1.2	4%	1.1	14%	1.0
Int. Exp.	Nil	—	Nil	—	Nil	—	Nil
Pretax Inc.	18.4	77%	10.4	3%	10.1	49%	6.8
Eff. Tax Rate	31%	—	28%	—	30%	—	30%
Net Inc.	12.6	67%	7.5	7%	7.1	49%	4.7

Balance Sheet & Other Fin. Data (Million $)

	1994	1993	1992	1991	1990	1989
Cash	14.9	18.3	15.4	12.6	9.7	8.4
Curr. Assets	39.4	32.4	27.4	22.7	18.8	16.1
Total Assets	54.6	41.9	35.8	30.5	26.0	22.2
Curr. Liab.	2.8	1.7	1.7	2.3	1.9	1.5
LT Debt	Nil	Nil	Nil	Nil	Nil	Nil
Common Eqty.	51.1	39.8	33.7	27.8	23.5	20.2
Total Cap.	51.7	40.2	34.1	28.2	24.0	20.6
Cap. Exp.	4.2	1.5	1.7	1.7	2.1	0.7
Cash Flow	13.9	8.7	8.2	5.7	4.6	4.3

Ratio Analysis

	1994	1993	1992	1991	1990	1989
Curr. Ratio	13.8	19.4	15.9	10.0	9.7	10.4
% LT Debt of Cap.	Nil	Nil	Nil	Nil	Nil	Nil
% Net Inc.of Revs.	21.3	19.2	19.5	16.3	16.0	17.1
% Ret. on Assets	26.2	19.4	21.3	16.8	15.7	17.7
% Ret. on Equity	27.8	20.5	23.0	18.5	17.3	19.6

Dividend Data (Cash has been paid each year since 1986.)

Amt. of Div. $	Date Decl.	Ex-Div. Date	Stock of Record	Payment Date
0.040	Oct. 03	Oct. 07	Oct. 14	Nov. 11 '94
2-for-1	Nov. 15	Dec. 28	Dec. 15	Dec. 27 '94
0.025	Jan. 03	Jan. 09	Jan. 16	Feb. 13 '95
0.025	Apr. 03	Apr. 07	Apr. 14	May. 12 '95
0.025	Jul. 03	Jul. 13	Jul. 17	Aug. 14 '95

Data as orig. reptd.; bef. results of disc. opers. and/or spec. items. Per share data adj. for stk. divs. as of ex-div. date. E-Estimated. NA-Not Available. NM-Not Meaningful. NR-Not Ranked.

Office—3100 44th St. SW, Grandville, MI 49418. **Tel**—(616) 534-7663. **Chrmn & CEO**—T. Thompson. **Pres & COO**—B. Jorgensen. **VP & CFO**—D. Kluting. **VP-Fin**—Beverly A. Ingle-Braun. **Dirs**—L. C. Blanding, M. G. DeVries, L. E. Fleming, R. S. Teesdale, T. Thompson, R. A. VandenBerg, C. VanNamen, G. M. Walters, Q. E. Ward. **Transfer Agent & Registrar**—State Street Bank and Trust Co., Boston. **Incorporated** in Michigan in 1958. **Empl**-565. **S&P Analyst:** Steven A. Jaworski

STANDARD & POOR'S

STOCK REPORTS

Xircom, Inc.

NASDAQ Symbol **XIRC**
In S&P SmallCap 600

05-SEP-95

Industry:
Data Processing

Summary: Xircom's principal products are local area network (LAN) adapters, which enable portable personal computers to be connected to a LAN, modems, and other remote access products.

Quantitative Evaluations

Outlook
(1 Lowest—5 Highest)
• **NA**

Fair Value
• **NA**

Risk
• **High**

Earn./Div. Rank
• **NR**

Technical Eval.
• **Bullish** since 7/95

Rel. Strength Rank
(1 Lowest—99 Highest)
• **59**

Insider Activity
• **Neutral**

Recent Price • 11¾
52 Wk Range • 23½-9

Yield • Nil
12-Mo. P/E • NM

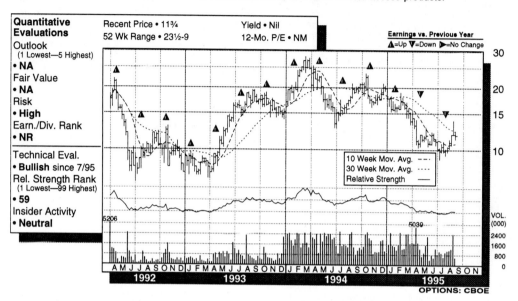

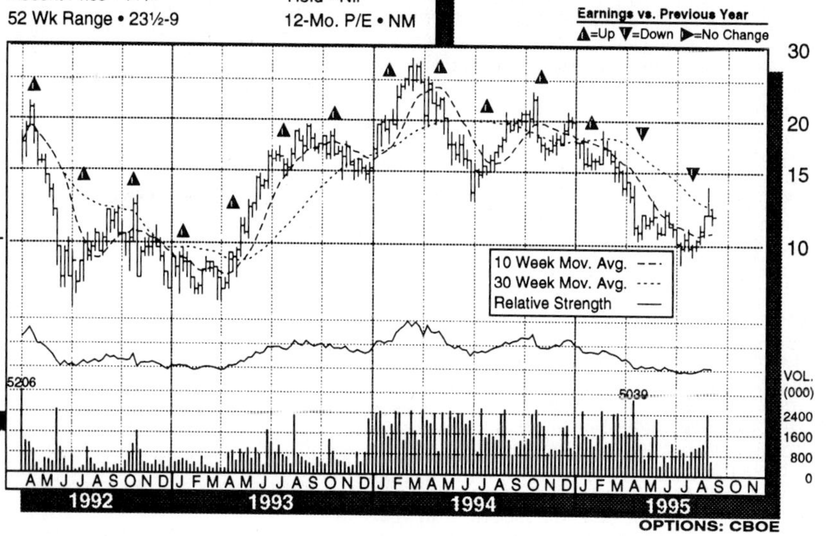

OPTIONS: CBOE

Business Profile - 05-SEP-95

This company manufactures LAN connectivity products for mobile computer users and other users who require remote network access, including telecommuters and people dialing online services. Xircom believes that smaller sizes and increased funtionality of portable PCs, coupled with increased demand for remote network access, will provide many opportunities for its mobile networking products.

Operational Review - 05-SEP-95

Net sales in the nine months ended June 30, 1995, rose only 4.1%, year to year. Revenue growth was lower than expected, reflecting a continuing move by users from parallel port adapters to PC card adapters, increased competition in the PC Card LAN adapter market, and slower sales growth for portable PCs. Margins narrowed, and results were penalized by $42.1 million in acquisition-related charges; a net loss of $2.53 a share replaced net income of $0.69.

Stock Performance - 01-SEP-95

In the past 30 trading days, XIRC's shares have increased 19%, compared to a 2% rise in the S&P 500. Average trading volume for the past five days was 110,960 shares, compared with the 40-day moving average of 224,230 shares.

Key Stock Statistics

Dividend Rate/Share	Nil	Shareholders	100
Shs. outstg. (M)	18.8	Market cap. (B)	$0.221
Avg. daily vol. (M)	0.273	Inst. holdings	30%
Tang. Bk. Value/Share	5.56	Insider holdings	NA
Beta	NA		

Value of $10,000 invested 5 years ago: NA

Fiscal Year Ending Sep. 30

	1995	% Change	1994	% Change	1993	% Change
Revenues (Million $)						
1Q	40.11	52%	26.38	53%	17.20	29%
2Q	39.97	32%	30.25	62%	18.72	32%
3Q	16.47	-54%	36.09	67%	21.65	48%
4Q	—	—	38.87	58%	24.67	44%
Yr.	—	—	131.6	60%	82.21	39%
Income (Million $)						
1Q	4.54	32%	3.43	93%	1.78	34%
2Q	2.48	-37%	3.92	84%	2.13	58%
3Q	-48.76	NM	4.20	63%	2.57	59%
4Q	—	—	4.36	38%	3.16	80%
Yr.	—	—	15.91	65%	9.65	59%
Earnings Per Share ($)						
1Q	0.27	29%	0.21	91%	0.11	10%
2Q	0.15	-35%	0.23	77%	0.13	30%
3Q	-2.87	NM	0.25	56%	0.16	60%
4Q	—	—	0.26	37%	0.19	73%
Yr.	—	—	0.95	61%	0.59	44%

Next earnings report expected: late October

Xircom, Inc.

Business Summary - 05-SEP-95

Xircom's principal products are local area network (LAN) adapters (which enable portable personal computers to be connected to a LAN), wireless LAN products, and remote access products for analog and digital (ISDN) network connectivity to a LAN. The company pioneered the use of the universal PC parallel port to connect PCs to a LAN, and was the first to ship an Ethernet adapter compliant with PCMCA standards. Sales by geographic area in recent fiscal years were:

	1994	1993	1992
U.S.	61%	57%	59%
International	39%	43%	41%

Xircom's products include its family of LAN connectivity products, including mobile/portable LAN adapters, modems, multiport modem boards, and ISDN adapters. The company's LAN products operate on Ethernet, Token Ring and Arcnet topologies, and are compatible with all widely used wiring.

Products include an external parallel port LAN adapter, the Pocket Ethernet Adapter, which was introduced in 1989; and an Ethernet LAN PCMCIA adapter card, the CreditCard Ethernet Adapter, which is used in notebook PCMCIA slots.

The company's Pocket Ethernet+Modem and CreditCard Ethernet+Modem were the first products to deliver both local and remote LAN access. These products combine an Ethernet LAN Adapter and a high-speed data/fax modem.

In January 1995, Xircom began volume shipments of Netwave, a wireless technology that enables user to establish and maintain a network connection without being encumbered by wires. Products include the CreditCard Netwave Adapter and the Netwave Access Point for Ethernet. In the fall of 1995, the company plans to introduce a line of ISDN adapters to enable remote users to dial into networks via ISDN service.

The company began in-house manufacturing in 1995, and also buys components such as circuit boards and integrated circuits from third parties. Xircom plans to begin shipping its first products from a Malaysian manufacturing facility in the fall of 1995. By mid-1996, the company expects to produce about 50% of its components in-house.

Important Developments

Jun. '95—Xircom acquired privately held Primary Rate Incorporated (PRI), a leading supplier of standards-based ISDN products, for about $48 million in cash and stock.

Capitalization

Long Term Obligs.: $100,000 (6/95).

Per Share Data ($) (Year Ended Sep. 30)

	1994	1993	1992	1991	1990	1989
Tangible Bk. Val.	5.10	3.99	3.42	NM	NA	NA
Cash Flow	1.17	0.71	0.47	0.22	NA	NA
Earnings	0.95	0.59	0.41	0.19	NA	NA
Dividends	Nil	Nil	Nil	Nil	NA	NA
Payout Ratio	Nil	Nil	Nil	Nil	NA	NA
Prices - High	28¼	19½	22	NA	NA	NA
- Low	12¾	7¼	7	NA	NA	NA
P/E Ratio - High	30	33	54	NA	NA	NA
- Low	13	12	17	NA	NA	NA

Income Statement Analysis (Million $)

	1994	%Chg	1993	%Chg	1992	%Chg	1991
Revs.	132	61%	82.2	39%	59.1	125%	26.3
Oper. Inc.	29.1	71%	17.0	62%	10.5	128%	4.6
Depr.	3.8	91%	2.0	102%	1.0	123%	0.4
Int. Exp.	0.2	-24%	0.2	-43%	0.4	NM	0.1
Pretax Inc.	25.1	59%	15.8	64%	9.6	132%	4.1
Eff. Tax Rate	37%	—	39%	—	37%	—	40%
Net Inc.	15.9	65%	9.6	59%	6.1	145%	2.5

Balance Sheet & Other Fin. Data (Million $)

	1994	1993	1992	1991	1990	1989
Cash	51.5	40.4	32.7	Nil	NA	NA
Curr. Assets	91.4	69.7	53.6	12.0	NA	NA
Total Assets	101	75.3	57.0	13.7	NA	NA
Curr. Liab.	18.8	11.9	6.3	6.9	NA	NA
LT Debt	0.1	0.4	0.9	0.6	NA	NA
Common Eqty.	82.1	62.5	49.6	-9.0	NA	NA
Total Cap.	82.2	63.0	50.4	6.8	NA	NA
Cap. Exp.	7.4	4.0	1.9	1.4	NA	NA
Cash Flow	19.7	11.6	7.0	2.9	NA	NA

Ratio Analysis

	1994	1993	1992	1991	1990	1989
Curr. Ratio	4.9	5.8	8.5	1.7	NA	NA
% LT Debt of Cap.	0.2	0.7	1.7	8.6	NA	NA
% Net Inc.of Revs.	12.1	11.7	10.3	9.4	NA	NA
% Ret. on Assets	17.8	14.1	NM	NA	NA	NA
% Ret. on Equity	21.7	16.6	NM	NA	NA	NA

Dividend Data —No cash has been paid. The company intends to retain earnings for use in its business.

Data as orig. reptd.; bef. results of disc. opers. and/or spec. items. Per share data adj. for stk. divs. as of ex-div. date. E-Estimated. NA-Not Available. NM-Not Meaningful. NR-Not Ranked.

Office—2300 Corporate Center Dr., Thousand Oaks, CA 91320. **Tel**—(805) 376-9300. **Chrmn**—J. K. Mathews. **Pres & CEO**—D. I. Gates. **VP-Fin, CFO& COO**—J. N. Ulrich. **Investor Contact**—JoAnne F. Martz (805-376-6911). **Dirs**—K. J. Biba, G. Bowen, B. C. Edwards, D. I. Gates, J. K. Mathews, W. J. Schroeder. **Transfer Agent & Registrar**—First National Bank of Boston. **Incorporated** in California in 1988. **Empl-450. S&P Analyst:** Mike Cavanaugh

STANDARD & POOR'S

STOCK REPORTS

Zebra Technologies Corp.

NASDAQ Symbol **ZBRA**

In S&P SmallCap 600

02-OCT-95

Industry:
Data Processing

Summary: Zebra Technologies is an international provider of demand label printers and supplies for users of automatic identification and data collection systems.

Quantitative Evaluations

Outlook
(1 Lowest—5 Highest)
• **NA**

Fair Value
• **NA**

Risk
• **Average**

Earn./Div. Rank
• **NR**

Technical Eval.
• **Bullish** since 2/95

Rel. Strength Rank
(1 Lowest—99 Highest)
• **11**

Insider Activity
• **Unfavorable**

Recent Price • 53¼
52 Wk Range • 64-33¾

Yield • Nil
12-Mo. P/E • 25.1

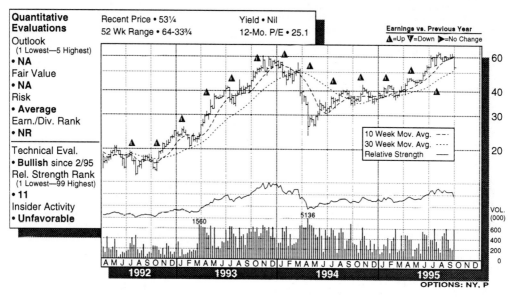

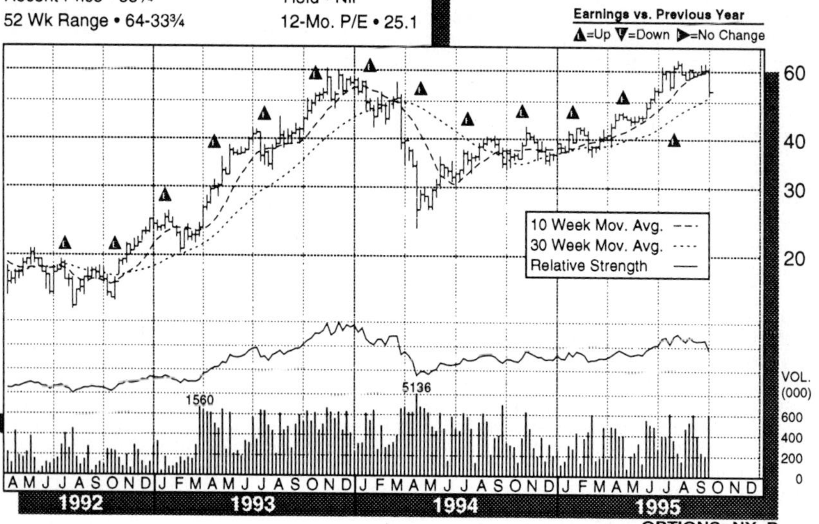

OPTIONS: NY, P

Business Profile - 02-OCT-95

ZBRA is a rapidly growing company which has benefited from the escalating demand for bar-code and on-demand labeling applications in the non-retail sector of the world economy. The company strives to offer its customers the most advanced technology in bar code labeling, and it announced a significant number of product introductions and enhancements in 1994. In June 1995, the company completed a multi-million dollar sale of 1,200 of its new 90Xi printers.

Operational Review - 02-OCT-95

Revenue growth slowed in the second quarter, but still remained very strong. Zebra Technologies continues to benefit from increased sales of its Value-Line and Performance-Line printers resulting from the company's expanded distribution of these products in September 1994. Despite a less favorable product mix within printer products and supplies products in the second quarter, margins widened on the higher volume.

Stock Performance - 29-SEP-95

In the past 30 trading days, ZBRA's shares have declined 7%, compared to a 5% rise in the S&P 500. Average trading volume for the past five days was 121,880 shares, compared with the 40-day moving average of 82,508 shares.

Key Stock Statistics

Dividend Rate/Share	Nil	Shareholders	500
Shs. outstg. (M)	12.1	Market cap. (B)	$0.643
Avg. daily vol. (M)	0.088	Inst. holdings	59%
Tang. Bk. Value/Share	8.08	Insider holdings	NA
Beta	NA		

Value of $10,000 invested 5 years ago: NA

Fiscal Year Ending Dec. 31

	1995	% Change	1994	% Change	1993	% Change
Revenues (Million $)						
1Q	34.39	56%	21.98	16%	19.00	44%
2Q	35.49	37%	25.89	20%	21.64	45%
3Q	—	—	28.25	22%	23.07	58%
4Q	—	—	30.99	31%	23.74	49%
Yr.	—	—	107.1	22%	87.46	49%
Income (Million $)						
1Q	6.61	59%	4.15	14%	3.64	56%
2Q	7.09	40%	5.05	18%	4.28	37%
3Q	—	—	5.66	11%	5.10	64%
4Q	—	—	6.22	19%	5.23	59%
Yr.	—	—	21.07	15%	18.26	54%
Earnings Per Share ($)						
1Q	0.55	57%	0.35	17%	0.30	58%
2Q	0.59	40%	0.42	17%	0.36	38%
3Q	—	—	0.47	9%	0.43	65%
4Q	—	—	0.51	16%	0.44	57%
Yr.	—	—	1.75	15%	1.52	54%

Next earnings report expected: late October

Zebra Technologies Corp.

Business Summary - 21-SEP-95

Zebra Technologies Corporation designs, manufactures, sells and supports a broad line of computerized label/ticket printing systems and related specialty supplies. It provides bar-code labeling solutions, primarily to manufacturing customers and also to service and governmental entities worldwide, for use in automatic identification and data collection systems.

Products consist of a broad line of computerized demand bar-code label printers, specialty bar-code labeling/ticketing material (including a variety of adhesives) and ink ribbons. Products are integrated to provide automatic identification labeling solutions for manufacturing, business and industrial applications. Sales of label printing systems provided 70% of revenues in 1994, down from 73% in 1993.

The company manufactures 18 thermal transfer/direct thermal label printing systems, which range in list price from $1,395 to $10,245. Hundreds of optional configurations can be selected as necessary to meet particular customer needs. As of March 1, 1995, more than 110,000 Zebra bar code printing systems had been installed at about 15,000 user sites worldwide.

All Zebra printing systems operate using Zebra Programming Language (ZPL), a proprietary printer driver language that was designed by the company and is compatible with virtually all computer operating systems, including UNIX, MS/DOS and Windows. Certain independent software vendors have written label preparation programs with ZPL drivers specifically for Zebra printers. ZPL's label format program can be run on a personal computer with ordinary word processing programs, making it adaptable to PC-based systems.

Products are sold in the U.S and internationally through multiple distribution channels, including distributors, value-added resellers, original equipment manufacturers and directly through a national account program. Sales to international customers accounted for 40% of the total in 1994, down from 38% in 1993.

A 50,000 square foot addition to the U.S. manufacturing facility in Vernon Hills, Ill., was completed in December 1994. The additional space offers increased manufacturing capacity and 11,500 square feet of corporate office area.

Important Developments

Jul. '95—Zebra acquired Vertical Technologies, Inc., a developer of software for bar code printing, scanning and tracking, for an undisclosed amount of cash and stock. ZBRA expected to record a charge to operations for 1995's third quarter in connection with the acquisiton.

Jun. '95—Zebra completed a multi-million dollar sale of 1,200 of its new 90Xi printers to a large international application value-added reseller. The printers will be delivered over the next 12 months for use worldwide.

Capitalization

Long Term Debt: $227,000 (3/95) of lease obligs.

Per Share Data ($) (Year Ended Dec. 31)

	1994	1993	1992	1991	1990	1989
Tangible Bk. Val.	6.82	5.06	3.52	2.56	1.17	NA
Cash Flow	1.87	1.61	1.06	1.00	1.06	NA
Earnings	1.75	1.52	0.99	0.96	1.03	NA
Dividends	Nil	Nil	Nil	Nil	Nil	NA
Payout Ratio	Nil	Nil	Nil	Nil	Nil	NA
Prices - High	57¼	60¾	24¾	19	NA	NA
- Low	23½	20¼	14½	14½	NA	NA
P/E Ratio - High	33	40	25	20	NA	NA
- Low	13	13	15	15	NA	NA

Income Statement Analysis (Million $)

	1994	%Chg	1993	%Chg	1992	%Chg	1991
Revs.	107	22%	87.5	49%	58.7	29%	45.6
Oper. Inc.	31.7	22%	25.9	60%	16.2	23%	13.2
Depr.	1.4	33%	1.0	28%	0.8	59%	0.5
Int. Exp.	0.3	33%	0.2	-9%	0.2	NM	0.1
Pretax Inc.	32.9	15%	28.5	60%	17.8	34%	13.3
Eff. Tax Rate	36%	—	36%	—	34%	—	19%
Net Inc.	21.1	15%	18.3	55%	11.8	9%	10.8

Balance Sheet & Other Fin. Data (Million $)

	1994	1993	1992	1991	1990	1989
Cash	54.2	41.5	33.7	31.2	1.0	NA
Curr. Assets	88.7	71.5	51.4	46.8	14.2	NA
Total Assets	95.0	76.7	54.8	48.9	16.2	NA
Curr. Liab.	12.4	15.5	12.0	17.1	3.8	NA
LT Debt	0.2	0.3	0.3	0.4	0.4	NA
Common Eqty.	82.0	60.6	42.2	30.7	11.9	NA
Total Cap.	82.3	60.9	42.7	31.7	12.4	NA
Cap. Exp.	2.1	2.5	2.2	0.7	1.0	NA
Cash Flow	22.5	19.3	12.7	11.3	10.9	NA

Ratio Analysis

	1994	1993	1992	1991	1990	1989
Curr. Ratio	7.1	4.6	4.3	2.7	3.7	NA
% LT Debt of Cap.	0.3	0.5	0.8	1.3	3.6	NA
% Net Inc.of Revs.	19.7	20.9	20.2	23.8	27.7	NA
% Ret. on Assets	24.5	27.7	22.8	31.9	NA	NA
% Ret. on Equity	29.5	35.5	32.5	48.5	NA	NA

Dividend Data —No cash dividends have been paid.

Data as orig. reptd.; bef. results of disc. opers. and/or spec. items. Per share data adj. for stk. divs. as of ex-div. date. E-Estimated. NA-Not Available. NM-Not Meaningful. NR-Not Ranked.

Office—333 Corporate Woods Pkwy., Vernon Hills, IL 60061. **Tel**—(708) 634-6700. **Chrmn & CEO**—E. L. Kaplan. **Pres**—J. K. Clements. **SVP & Secy**—G. Cless. **CFO & Treas**—C. R. Whitchurch. **Dirs**—G. Cless, E. L. Kaplan, C. Knowles, D. R. Riley, M. A. Smith. **Transfer Agent & Registrar**—Harris Trust & Savings Bank, Chicago. **Reincorporated** in Delaware in 1991. **Empl**-501. **S&P Analyst:** Stephen Madonna, CFA

Zenith National Insurance

NYSE Symbol ZNT

Price	Range	P-E Ratio	Dividend	Yield	S&P Ranking	Beta
Aug. 23'95	1995					
22⅝	22¾–19⅜	12	1.00	4.4%	B+	1.17

Summary

Through its Zenith Insurance, CalFarm Insurance and CalFarm Life Insurance subsidiaries, this company writes standard workers' compensation, reinsurance, other property and casualty, and health and life insurance in California and Texas. Earnings declined 10% in the first half of 1995, hurt by the failure to reduce workers' compensation expenses commensurate with the reduction in premium volume.

Business Summary

Zenith National Insurance, through its subsidiaries, is engaged in the business of writing workers' compensation insurance, reinsurance, annuities, health and life insurance coverages, and auto, homeowners, farmowners and other coverages, primarily in California and Texas. Workers' compensation insurance is written by Zenith Insurance Co. Automobile, homeowners and farmowners insurance is offered by CalFarm Insurance. CalFarm Life Insurance offers a complete portfolio of life, health and annuity products. Property/casualty operations accounted for 68% of total revenues in 1994. Contributions to property/casualty premiums earned:

	1994	1993	1992	1991
Workers' compensation....	54%	60%	59%	56%
Property and casualty	37%	34%	36%	37%
Reinsurance..........	9%	6%	5%	7%

Zenith Insurance's workers' compensation business is produced by about 500 independent licensed insurance agents and brokers throughout California and Texas. Workers' compensation insurance provides coverage for statutorily prescribed benefits employers are required to pay their employees injured in the course of employment. The standard policy issued by Zenith provides payments for, among other things, temporary or permanent disability benefits, death benefits, medical and hospital expenses, and expenses of vocational rehabilitation. The benefits payable and the duration of such benefits are set by statute.

CalFarm Insurance offers a comprehensive line of property and casualty insurance, including homeowners, automobile, commercial multiple peril, and farmowners coverage. Automobile insurance is the largest line of business, representing 16% of the property and casualty business in 1994, with some 93,000 vehicles insured. Farmowners business is CalFarm's second largest line, representing about 10% of ZNT's property and casualty business.

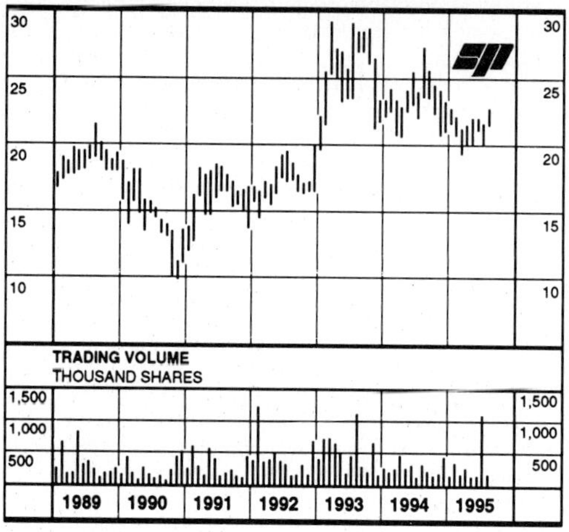

ZNT operates its reinsurance activity as a participant in contracts or treaties in which, typically, the reinsurance coverage is syndicated to a number of assuming companies.

The largest line of insurance written by CalFarm Life Insurance is health insurance, which accounted for 60% of its premium income in 1994.

Through its Perma-Bilt subsidiary, the company develops private residences for sale in Las Vegas, Nev.

Important Developments

Jul. '95— The company said it had repurchased a block of 1 million shares of its common stock on the NYSE. This repurchase is in addition to the company's previously announced 1 million share repurchase authorization of December 1992, of which 539,921 shares have been repurchased at a total cost of $11.7 million.

Next earnings report expected in late October.

Per Share Data ($)

Yr. End Dec. 31	1994	1993	1992	1991	1990	1989	1988	1987	1986	[1]1985
Tangible Bk. Val.	**15.09**	17.21	14.57	13.38	11.00	13.14	12.32	12.04	10.17	3.31
Oper. Earnings[2]	**1.86**	1.75	1.01	1.73	2.10	2.22	2.11	1.90	1.19	d0.12
Earnings[2,3]	**1.99**	2.76	1.02	2.28	d0.47	1.98	2.15	2.11	1.57	0.26
Dividends	**1.000**	1.000	1.000	1.000	0.860	0.820	0.764	0.728	0.728	0.619
Payout Ratio	**50%**	36%	98%	44%	NM	41%	36%	34%	46%	234%
Prices—High	**27⅜**	29¼	20	18½	18¾	21½	21¾	23⅞	30½	23⅜
Low	**20⅝**	19⅝	14½	12	9⅞	16¾	13⅝	12¼	18⅞	10⅝
P/E Ratio—[4]	**14–10**	11–7	20–14	8–5	NM	11–8	10–6	13–6	26–16	NM

Data as orig. reptd. Adj. for stk. divs. of 10% Jul. 1988. **1.** Reflects merger or acquisition. **2.** Bef. spec. items of +0.50 in 1992, +0.14 in 1991, +0.25 in 1986. **3.** Aft. gains/losses on securities trans. **4.** Based on oper. earns. prior to 1988. d-Deficit. NM-Not Meaningful.

Income Data (Million $)

Year Ended Dec. 31	Premium Income	Net Invest. Inc.	Oth. Revs.	Total Revs.	Property & Casualty Underwriting Ratios [2]Loss	[2]Expense	[2,3]Comb.	Net Bef. Taxes	[4]Net Oper. Inc.	[4]Net Inc.	—% Return On— [5]Revs.	[3]Equity
1994	**463**	**98.0**	**33.9**	**595**	**65.6**	**27.7**	**93.3**	**57.6**	**35.5**	**37.9**	**6.4**	**11.7**
1993	470	92.5	23.5	586	67.8	25.7	93.5	73.5	33.7	53.2	9.1	16.3
1992	442	96.6	10.8	549	76.8	27.9	104.7	19.7	19.1	19.3	3.5	9.7
1991	438	95.7	13.0	546	70.4	29.6	100.0	52.5	32.9	43.3	7.9	16.6
1990	431	90.0	d53.0	468	64.1	29.2	93.3	d2.7	41.4	d9.2	NM	NM
1989	413	77.9	d7.0	484	62.7	29.2	91.9	49.0	46.2	41.1	8.5	13.7
1988	404	66.9	1.0	472	62.6	28.4	91.0	56.2	45.4	46.3	9.8	16.3
1987	408	62.4	1.0	471	64.0	28.8	93.1	52.0	43.4	48.4	9.2	17.4
1986	352	59.4	Nil	411	69.1	27.5	96.6	36.7	27.6	36.4	6.7	16.8
[1]1985	196	34.2	Nil	230	74.8	27.0	101.8	0.8	2.1	7.1	3.1	2.8

Balance Sheet Data (Million $)

Dec. 31	Cash & Equiv.	Premiums Due	—Investment Assets— [6]Bonds	[7]Stocks	Loans	Total	% Invest. Yield	Deferred Policy Costs	Total Assets	[8]Debt	Common Equity
1994	**29.5**	**126.0**	**1,225**	**46**	**45.3**	**1,463**	**6.6**	**109.1**	**1,841**	**74.1**	**310**
1993	30.2	118.3	1,409	58	44.1	1,500	[3]5.1	108.4	1,858	88.2	349
1992	24.3	91.0	1,243	132	39.3	1,375	[3]6.2	91.0	1,704	73.9	302
1991	31.6	76.6	987	170	35.2	1,202	[3]7.2	76.6	1,478	49.8	281
1990	25.0	77.6	822	203	30.2	1,063	[3]8.0	63.9	1,327	53.6	241
1989	21.6	76.8	655	251	25.5	938	[3]8.3	47.2	1,182	26.7	299
1988	18.3	68.9	546	215	24.2	791	[3]8.2	31.9	1,007	24.3	297
1987	13.0	73.4	482	198	25.1	705	[3]8.5	29.9	913	30.9	269
1986	11.2	72.0	476	129	27.1	632	[3]10.0	24.5	814	32.1	270
1985	13.8	44.2	295	168	30.3	493	[3]10.6	9.3	635	47.5	212

Data as orig. reptd. **1.** Reflects merger or acquisition. **2.** Bef. div. to policyholders. **3.** As reptd. by co. **4.** Bef. spec. items. **5.** Based on oper. earns. prior to 1988 **6.** Incl. invested cash. **7.** Incl. redeemable pfd. stk. **8.** Incl. curr. portion. d-Deficit. NM-Not Meaningful.

Review of Operations

Revenues rose 4.5%, year to year, in the six months ended June 30, 1995, as income from real estate sales and higher net investment income outweighed lower insurance premiums. The combined ratio for the property and casualty operations was 101.5%, compared with 97.6%. Property and casualty income fell 16%, and health and life income advanced 9.8%. After taxes at 34.3%, versus 33.6%, net income was down 10%, to $17.1 million ($0.91 a share), from $19.1 million ($1.00). Earnings include $0.10 ($0.08) a share of realized gains, and $0.06 a share of legal settlement income in the 1994 period.

Common Share Earnings ($)

Quarter:	1995	1994	1993	1992
Mar.	0.36	0.43	0.66	0.47
Jun.	0.54	0.57	0.78	0.45
Sep.		0.53	0.70	0.15
Dec.		0.46	0.63	d0.08
		1.99	2.76	1.02

Finances

At December 31, 1994, 97.9% of ZNT's investment in fixed maturities was rated investment grade, compared with 98.2% at 1993 year end.

In June 1994, ZNT decided not to sell CalFarm Life Insurance Co., and terminated all negotiations with respect to the sale, including talks with Conseco, Inc.

In January 1993, ZNT reached an agreement with the California Department of Insurance on the Proposition 103 rollback, under which Zenith Insurance Co. and CalFarm Insurance Co. refunded 9.5% of the premium paid plus interest to holders of policies in effect between November 8, 1988, and November 8, 1989. The total cost of $10.6 million ($0.56 a share) after tax was charged to fourth quarter 1992 earnings.

Dividend Data

Dividends have been paid since 1978.

Amt. of Divd. $	Date Decl.	Ex-divd. Date	Stock of Record	Payment Date
0.25	Sep. 8	Oct. 25	Oct. 31	Nov. 14'94
0.25	Dec. 6	Jan. 25	Jan. 31	Feb. 15'95
0.25	Mar. 2	Apr. 24	Apr. 28	May 12'95
0.25	May 24	Jul. 27	Jul. 31	Aug. 16'95

Capitalization

Note Payable: $74,111,000 (12/94).

Common Stock: 17,686,469 shs. ($1 par). Reliance Insurance Co. owns about 35%. Institutions hold approximately 58%. Shareholders of record: 456 (3/95).

d-Deficit.

Office—21255 Califa St., Woodland Hills, CA 91367. **Tel**—(818) 713-1000. **Chrmn & Pres**—S. R. Zax. **EVP-CFO & Investor Contact**—Fredricka Taubitz. **SVP-Secy**—J. J. Tickner. **Dirs**—G. E. Bello, M. M. Kampelman, J. M. Ostrow, W. S. Sessions, H. L. Silbert, R. M. Steinberg, S. P. Steinberg, G. Tsai Jr., S. R. Zax. **Transfer Agent & Registrar**—First Interstate Bank of California, Los Angeles. **Incorporated** in Delaware in 1971. **Empl**—1,500.

 Robert Schpoont

STANDARD & POOR'S

STOCK REPORTS

Zero Corp.

NYSE Symbol **ZRO**

In S&P SmallCap 600

28-SEP-95 **Industry:** Manufacturing/Distr

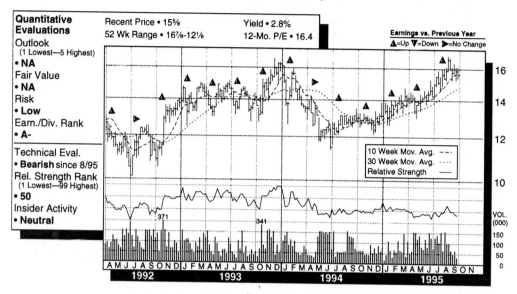

Summary: This company makes enclosures and cooling equipment primarily for the electronics industry, and baggage and cargo enclosures for the airline industry.

Quantitative Evaluations

Outlook
(1 Lowest—5 Highest)
• **NA**

Fair Value
• **NA**

Risk
• **Low**

Earn./Div. Rank
• **A-**

Technical Eval.
• **Bearish** since 8/95

Rel. Strength Rank
(1 Lowest—99 Highest)
• **50**

Insider Activity
• **Neutral**

Recent Price • 15⅝

52 Wk Range • 16⅞-12⅛

Yield • 2.8%

12-Mo. P/E • 16.4

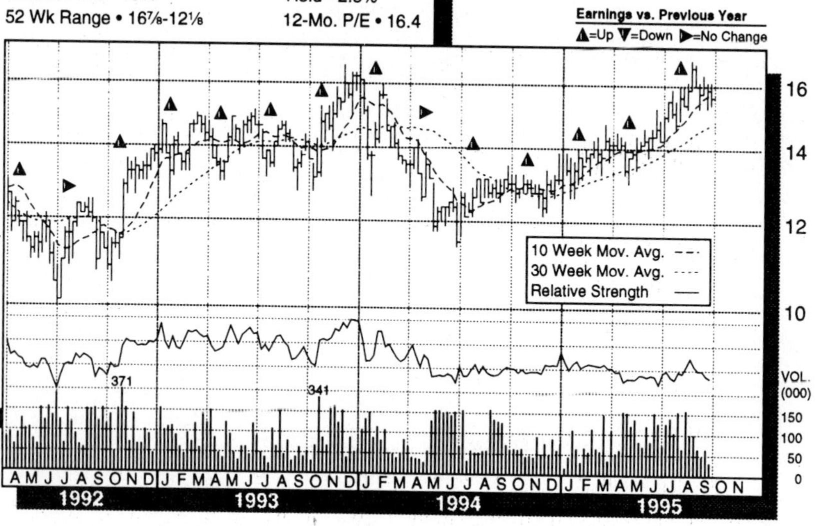

Business Profile - 28-SEP-95

This maker of a wide range of aluminum enclosures, racks and cooling equipment has been expanding through acquisitions of both niche companies and product lines. The company has noted that it is actively looking at a number of acquisition candidates, some with annual revenues exceeding $40 million. Cash and short-term marketable securities of $33.5 million were available at June 30, 1995, for investment in existing businesses and acquisitions.

Operational Review - 28-SEP-95

Net sales in the first quarter of fiscal 1996 increased 11%, year to year, as growth in the electronics industry offset a weaker air cargo market. Gross margins widened, and the gain in pretax income was extended to 15%. After taxes at 40.0%, versus 39.0%, net income was up 13%, to $3,707,000 ($0.23 a share), from $3,278,000 ($0.21).

Stock Performance - 22-SEP-95

In the past 30 trading days, ZRO's shares have declined 2%, compared to a 5% rise in the S&P 500. Average trading volume for the past five days was 6,160 shares, compared with the 40-day moving average of 17,923 shares.

Key Stock Statistics

Dividend Rate/Share	0.44	Shareholders	5,400
Shs. outstg. (M)	16.0	Market cap. (B)	$0.252
Avg. daily vol. (M)	0.009	Inst. holdings	65%
Tang. Bk. Value/Share	7.34	Insider holdings	NA
Beta	0.80		

Value of $10,000 invested 5 years ago: $ 12,460

Fiscal Year Ending Mar. 31

	1996	% Change	1995	% Change	1994	% Change
Revenues (Million $)						
1Q	48.62	11%	43.72	6%	41.28	3%
2Q	—	—	46.58	3%	45.01	15%
3Q	—	—	44.90	5%	42.61	5%
4Q	—	—	44.49	-1%	44.98	10%
Yr.	—	—	179.7	5%	171.8	7%
Income (Million $)						
1Q	3.71	13%	3.28	9%	3.01	5%
2Q	—	—	4.03	17%	3.45	29%
3Q	—	—	3.55	23%	2.89	7%
4Q	—	—	3.97	13%	3.51	3%
Yr.	—	—	14.83	15%	12.85	10%
Earnings Per Share ($)						
1Q	0.23	10%	0.21	11%	0.19	6%
2Q	—	—	0.25	14%	0.22	29%
3Q	—	—	0.22	22%	0.18	6%
4Q	—	—	0.25	14%	0.22	NM
Yr.	—	—	0.93	15%	0.81	9%

Next earnings report expected: mid October

Zero Corp.

Business Summary - 27-SEP-95

Zero Corp. designs, manufactures and markets cases, cabinets, cooling equipment and cargo enclosures, with over 70% of sales in 1994-5 made to the electronics industry. Contributions by business segment in 1994-95 were:

	Sales	Profits
Specialized enclosures & accessories	84%	92%
Other	16%	8%

Sales under U.S. government contracts and subcontracts accounted for 9% of the total in 1994-5, versus 12% a year earlier.

The company's systems packaging business designs and integrates standard and custom electronic enclosures and cabinets, and related components such as card cages for printed circuit boards, backplanes, power supplies and thermal management systems.

Engineered cases include custom and standard deep drawn aluminum boxes; ZERO Halliburton luggage, carrying cases and attaches; thermoformed and rotationally molded plastic cases and enclosures; other standard and custom fabricated cases (marketed under the Anvil Cases brand name); and specialized case hardware. The company also designs and markets various products used in the airline/air cargo industry, including specialized aluminum, polycarnoate and fiberglass air cargo containers; telescoping baggage/cargo systems; air cargo restraint systems and hardware; and transit cases engineered to meet Air Transport Association specifications.

The company is committed to enhance its growth through acquisitions that would complement its existing business. In June 1995, it acquired Electro-Mechanical Imagineering, Inc., a manufacturer of products to encase, protect and mount closed-circuit television security devices with annual revenues of about $4.5 million.

Important Developments

Jul. '95—Zero said it acquired the assets of G.W. Pearce & Sons Ltd., a manufacturer of deep drawn products for the food service industry with annual revenues of about $3 million. The company noted that it was actively looking to acquire other companies, some with revenues exceeding $40 million.

Capitalization

Long Term Debt: None (3/95).
Options: To buy 866,048 shs. at $10.38 to $14.50 ea. (3/95).

Per Share Data ($)

(Year Ended Mar. 31)

	1995	1994	1993	1992	1991	1990
Tangible Bk. Val.	7.27	6.65	6.14	5.73	5.43	5.07
Cash Flow	1.28	1.15	1.08	0.98	0.97	1.31
Earnings	0.93	0.81	0.74	0.62	0.68	1.02
Dividends	0.41	0.40	0.40	0.40	0.40	0.39
Payout Ratio	44%	49%	54%	65%	58%	38%
Cal. Yrs.	1994	1993	1992	1991	1990	1989
Prices - High	16⅛	16⅝	14⅛	15⅛	17⅛	18½
- Low	11⅜	12½	10	10	9⅞	13⅞
P/E Ratio - High	17	21	19	24	22	18
- Low	12	15	14	16	15	14

Income Statement Analysis (Million $)

	1995	%Chg	1994	%Chg	1993	%Chg	1992
Revs.	180	5%	172	8%	160	NM	160
Oper. Inc.	28.0	13%	24.8	9%	22.8	17%	19.5
Depr.	5.7	4%	5.5	2%	5.4	-5%	5.7
Int. Exp.	0.7	38%	0.5	-8%	0.5	-32%	0.8
Pretax Inc.	24.2	15%	21.0	11%	19.0	18%	16.1
Eff. Tax Rate	39%	—	39%	—	39%	—	40%
Net Inc.	14.8	15%	12.9	11%	11.6	20%	9.7

Balance Sheet & Other Fin. Data (Million $)

	1995	1994	1993	1992	1991	1990
Cash	37.0	33.4	30.4	23.7	20.1	13.4
Curr. Assets	92.9	83.9	80.1	76.2	85.3	79.5
Total Assets	172	159	154	150	157	148
Curr. Liab.	19.4	16.9	20.5	20.0	28.8	22.1
LT Debt	Nil	Nil	Nil	1.2	2.4	3.3
Common Eqty.	146	136	129	123	119	116
Total Cap.	146	136	129	124	122	119
Cap. Exp.	8.6	4.2	5.2	7.2	8.1	3.7
Cash Flow	20.5	18.3	17.0	15.4	15.3	20.7

Ratio Analysis

	1995	1994	1993	1992	1991	1990
Curr. Ratio	4.8	5.0	3.9	3.8	3.0	3.6
% LT Debt of Cap.	Nil	Nil	Nil	0.9	2.0	2.7
% Net Inc.of Revs.	8.2	7.5	7.3	6.0	5.7	8.2
% Ret. on Assets	9.0	8.2	7.6	6.3	7.1	10.7
% Ret. on Equity	10.5	9.7	9.2	8.1	9.2	14.6

Dividend Data —Dividends were resumed in 1974. A dividend reinvestment plan is available.

Amt. of Div. $	Date Decl.	Ex-Div. Date	Stock of Record	Payment Date
0.100	Oct. 25	Oct. 31	Nov. 04	Nov. 29 '94
0.110	Jan. 26	Jan. 31	Feb. 06	Feb. 28 '95
0.110	May. 01	May. 08	May. 12	Jun. 06 '95
0.110	Jul. 26	Aug. 09	Aug. 11	Sep. 06 '95

Data as orig. reptd.; bef. results of disc. opers. and/or spec. items. Per share data adj. for stk. divs. as of ex-div. date. E-Estimated. NA-Not Available. NM-Not Meaningful. NR-Not Ranked.

Office—444 South Flower St., Suite 2100, Los Angeles, CA 90071-2922. **Tel**—(213) 629-7000. **Chrmn**—H. W. Hill. **Pres & CEO**—W. D. Godbold Jr. **VP, CFO & Investor Contact**—George A. Daniels. **Secy**—A. J. Cutchall. **Dirs**—G. M. Cusumano, B. J. DeBever, C. G. Gerlach, J. B. Gilbert, W. D. Godbold, Jr., B. B. Heiler, H. W. Hill, W. A. McFarlin. **Transfer Agent & Registrar**—First Interstate Bank, LA. **Incorporated** in California in 1952. Reincorporated in Delaware in 1988. **Empl**-1,800. **S&P Analyst:** S.R.B.

Zilog, Inc.

NYSE Symbol ZLG In S&P SmallCap 600

Price	Range	P–E Ratio	Dividend	Yield	S&P Ranking	Beta
Aug. 28'95	1995					
45⅛	54⅛–28¼	23	None	None	NR	NA

Summary

This worldwide semiconductor company designs, makes and markets application specific standard integrated circuit products for data communications, computer peripheral and consumer electronics markets. Earnings continued their long uptrend in 1994 and the first half of 1995, aided by increased sales and a more favorable product mix. The company introduced 10 new products in the second quarter of 1995.

Business Summary

Zilog, Inc. designs, develops, manufactures and markets application specific standard integrated circuit products (ASSPs) for the data communications, intelligent peripheral controller and consumer product controller markets. The company uses its proprietary Superintegration design technology to combine cores and cells from its library of customer-familiar microprocessor, microcontroller, memory and logic circuits to meet the design, cost and time-to-market requirements of its customers.

Zilog offers more than 2,100 product line items, encompassing a wide selection of package, speed grade and other options. Customers include Apple Computer, AT&T, Hewlett-Packard, Hitachi, Microsoft, Motorola, Northern Telecom, NMB, Samsung, Seagate, Siemens-Nixdorf, Sony, Texas Instruments and VeriFone. In each of the past three years, no single customer accounted for more than 8% of net sales.

ZLG uses its Superintegration library of proprietary core and cell designs, which are optimized for particular applications in target markets, to introduce new products on a timely basis. It introduced 40 major new products in 1994, including three for the data communications market, four for the intelligent peripheral controller market, and 33 for the consumer product controller market.

Zilog's two primary assembly and test facilities are located in Manila, the Philippines. In addition, the company has excess test capacity at its Nampa, Idaho, manufacturing facility and its Campbell, Calif., engineering facility. Zilog has also commenced design and construction of a new wafer fabrication facility adjacent to its Idaho plant. The facility is expected to commence limited production in 1995's third quarter and to eventually double the company's wafer production capacity thereafter.

Sales are made through a direct sales force and manufacturer representative firms and distributors.

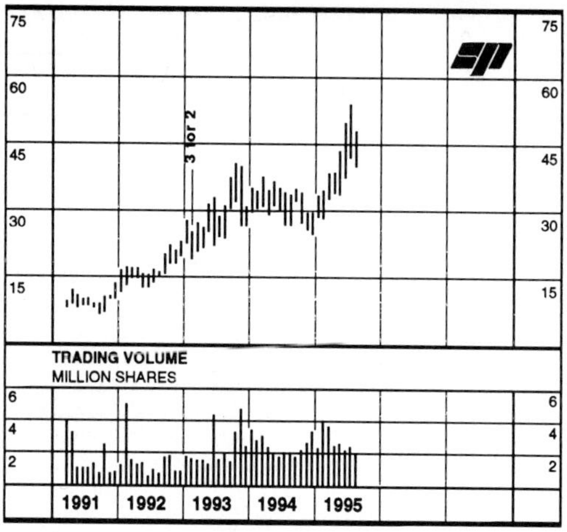

There are sales offices in 14 major U.S. metropolitan areas and 11 international locations. International sales accounted for 56% of net sales in 1994, versus 51% in 1993.

Important Developments

Jul. '95— Warburg, Pincus Capital Co., L.P. said it intends to distribute to its limited partners up to 2 million of Zilog's common stock over the next 60 days. Following the distribution, Warburg will own 28% of the company's outstanding shares.

Jul. '95— During 1995's second quarter, Zilog introduced 10 new products, including circuits with advanced on-screen display features for the television market, chips for universal infrared remote control of television sets and personal computers, a more intelligent battery fast charge microcontroller, and enhanced integrated circuits for the wireless markets.

Next earnings report expected in mid-October.

Per Share Data ($)

Yr. End Dec. 31	1994	1993	1992	1991	1990	[1]1989
Tangible Bk. Val.	**11.49**	9.25	6.68	4.56	2.76	1.99
Cash Flow	**2.88**	2.28	1.57	1.31	1.41	1.39
Earnings	**1.80**	1.43	0.95	0.76	0.67	0.53
Dividends	**Nil**	Nil	Nil	Nil	Nil	Nil
Payout Ratio	**Nil**	Nil	Nil	Nil	Nil	Nil
Prices—High	**37¾**	40¾	23	13½	NA	NA
Low	**24¾**	19	11⅝	6⅝	NA	NA
P/E Ratio—	**21–14**	28–13	24–12	18–9	NA	NA

Data as orig. reptd. Adj. for stk. div. of 50% Feb. 1993. **1.** Pro forma. NA-Not Available.

Income Data (Million $)

Year Ended Dec. 31	Revs.	Oper. Inc.	% Oper. Inc. of Revs.	Cap. Exp.	Depr.	Int. Exp.	Net Bef. Taxes	Eff. Tax Rate	Net Inc.	% Net Inc. of Revs.	Cash Flow
1994	**223**	**72.0**	**32.0**	**68.7**	**20.9**	**Nil**	**54.5**	**36.0%**	**34.9**	**15.6**	**55.8**
1993	203	54.6	26.9	39.7	16.0	Nil	41.8	36.0%	26.8	13.2	42.8
1992	146	33.5	23.0	27.1	10.5	[2]0.06	25.0	36.0%	16.0	11.0	26.5
1991	110	21.9	19.9	17.4	7.6	[2]0.45	15.5	32.0%	10.5	9.6	18.1
1990	100	19.5	19.5	7.8	8.1	[2]1.53	10.7	32.0%	7.3	7.3	15.3
[1]1989	93	17.2	18.5	51.4	9.5	[2]3.11	8.4	31.7%	5.7	6.2	15.2

Balance Sheet Data (Million $)

Dec. 31	Cash	Curr. Assets	Curr. Liab.	Curr. Ratio	Total Assets	% Ret. on Assets	Long Term Debt	Common Equity	Total Cap.	% LT Debt of Cap.	% Ret. on Equity
1994	**87.9**	**155.0**	**69.9**	**2.2**	**287**	**13.8**	**Nil**	**213**	**217.0**	**Nil**	**18.2**
1993	75.2	132.0	44.2	3.0	212	NA	Nil	166	168.0	Nil	18.8
1992	53.0	89.8	36.9	2.4	147	12.7	Nil	[3]110	109.9	Nil	17.3
1991	18.8	48.2	25.9	1.9	90	10.6	Nil	[3]64	63.5	Nil	28.3
1990	0.8	25.2	19.1	1.3	56	12.8	7.9	[3]29	36.9	21.4	29.3
1989	1.6	26.9	18.3	1.5	58	9.2	18.9	[3]21	39.4	47.9	20.3

Data as orig. reptd. **1.** Pro forma. **2.** Net of int. inc. **3.** Incl. pfd. stk. (conv. into com. upon offering). NA-Not Available.

Net Sales (Million $)

Quarter:	1995	1994	1993	1992
Mar.	62.7	52.5	48.0	29.4
Jun.	66.7	55.4	49.6	33.3
Sep.		56.8	53.6	37.9
Dec.		58.6	51.6	45.1
		223.3	202.7	145.7

Based on a brief report, net sales in the six months ended July 2, 1995, advanced 20%, year to year, reflecting continued strength in the company's three target markets. Margins widened, and pretax income climbed 26%. After taxes at 36.0% in each period, net income was also up 26%, to $20,930,000 ($1.05 a share, on 3.3% more shares), from $16,559,000 ($0.85).

Common Share Earnings ($)

Quarter:	1995	1994	1993	1992
Mar.	0.51	0.41	0.32	0.20
Jun.	0.54	0.44	0.34	0.21
Sep.		0.46	0.37	0.25
Dec.		0.49	0.39	0.29
		1.80	1.43	0.95

Dividend Data

Zilog has never paid dividends on its common stock and does not expect to pay any in the foreseeable future. A three-for-two stock split was effected February 15, 1993, for holders of record February 1.

Finances

At April 2, 1995, the company had cash and short-term investments totaling $75.6 million.

During 1992 and 1993, Zilog increased its production capacity. Manufacturing operations are characterized by high utilization of equipped facilities. The company's Idaho and Philippines plants both operate 24 hours a day, seven days a week. Zilog is developing and constructing a major new wafer fabrication facility, expected to start production in the second half of 1995.

At December 31, 1994, backlog totaled $49 million, up from $40 million a year earlier. The company includes in backlog all credit-approved purchase orders shippable within the next 12 months.

In a January 1993 public offering through Alex. Brown & Sons and Lehman Brothers, the company sold 1,000,500 common shares at $25 each (as adjusted). Net proceeds of $23.4 million were earmarked for capital expenditures and working capital.

Capitalization

Long Term Debt: None (6/95).

Common Stock: 18,978,169 shs. (no par).
Warburg, Pincus Capital owns 39%.
Officers and directors own 3.8%.
Institutions hold a total of 60%.

Office—210 E. Hacienda Ave., Campbell, CA 95008-6600. **Tel**—(408) 370-8000. **Fax**—(408) 370-8056/8027. **Chrmn, Pres & CEO**—E. A. Sack. **SVP-Fin, CFO & Investor Contact**—W. R. Walker (408-370-8210). **Secy**—R. R. Pickard. **Dirs**—T. J. Connors, W. H. Janeway, H. Kressel, E. A. Sack. **Transfer Agent & Registrar**—First National Bank of Boston. **Incorporated** in California in 1981. **Empl**—1,429.

 John D. Coyle, CFA

STANDARD & POOR'S

STOCK REPORTS

Zions Bancorporation

NASDAQ Symbol **ZION**

In S&P SmallCap 600

25-SEP-95

Industry: Banking

Summary: Zions Bancorporation is a bank holding company which through its subsidiaries operates over 120 full-service banking offices in Utah, Nevada and Arizona.

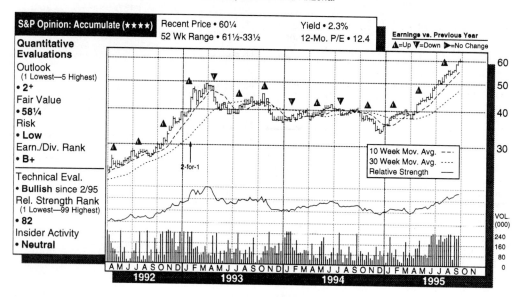

S&P Opinion: Accumulate (★★★★)

Recent Price • 60¼

52 Wk Range • 61½-33½

Yield • 2.3%

12-Mo. P/E • 12.4

Quantitative Evaluations

Outlook (1 Lowest—5 Highest)
• **2+**

Fair Value
• **58¼**

Risk
• **Low**

Earn./Div. Rank
• **B+**

Technical Eval.
• **Bullish** since 2/95

Rel. Strength Rank (1 Lowest—99 Highest)
• **82**

Insider Activity
• **Neutral**

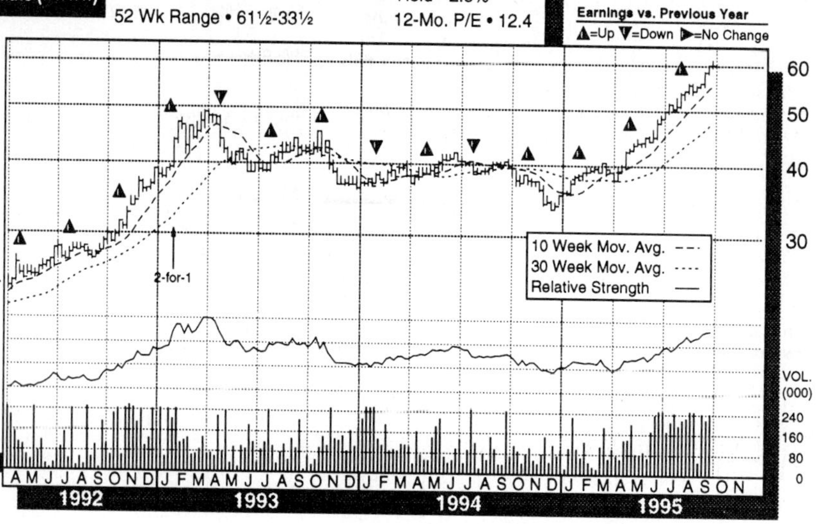

Overview - 22-SEP-95

Recent performance has been bolstered by the strong economy of the Intermountain region, which is expected to continue growing at rates above the national average. In the six months ended June 30, 1995, earnings advanced 27%, year to year; 25% on a per share basis. Net interest income was up 17%, as net interest margins widened; noninterest income rose 9.4%, and noninterest expenses grew only 7.3%. During the second quarter of 1995, the efficiency ratio improved to 57.8%, from 61.4% in the same period of the prior year. The company's credit quality remained excellent; at June 30, 1995, nonperforming assets as a percentage of net loans, leases and other real estate owned stood at just 0.55%, versus 0.81% a year earlier, and the loss reserve as a percentage of nonperforming loans increased to 603%, from 412%.

Valuation - 22-SEP-95

Having risen 67% thus far in 1995, shares of Zions have significantly outperformed both the regional banking indices and the broader market. Shares are expected to continue outpacing the overall market due to above-average earnings growth. In the year ahead, Zions should benefit from a favorable regional economic climate, strong fundamentals, and continued efficiency improvements. With net income expected to grow 13% in 1996, shares are undervalued at ten times the 1996 earnings estimate of $6.00 a share.

Key Stock Statistics

S&P EPS Est. 1995	5.30	Tang. Bk. Value/Share	25.43
P/E on S&P Est. 1995	11.4	Beta	1.05
S&P EPS Est. 1996	6.00	Shareholders	4,000
Dividend Rate/Share	1.40	Market cap. (B)	$0.875
Shs. outstg. (M)	14.5	Inst. holdings	37%
Avg. daily vol. (M)	0.039	Insider holdings	NA

Value of $10,000 invested 5 years ago: $ 51,624

Fiscal Year Ending Dec. 31

	1995	% Change	1994	% Change	1993	% Change
Revenues (Million $)						
1Q	113.8	22%	93.61	24%	75.62	-4%
2Q	127.5	21%	105.4	29%	81.88	4%
3Q	—	—	105.2	17%	89.71	127%
4Q	—	—	113.3	15%	98.64	18%
Yr.	—	—	427.2	24%	345.9	8%
Income (Million $)						
1Q	16.00	29%	12.44	57%	7.91	3%
2Q	20.52	25%	16.42	8%	15.18	62%
3Q	—	—	17.67	28%	13.85	15%
4Q	—	—	17.31	20%	14.44	NM
Yr.	—	—	63.83	24%	51.38	18%
Earnings Per Share ($)						
1Q	1.09	25%	0.87	45%	0.60	-3%
2Q	1.39	24%	1.12	-6%	1.19	57%
3Q	E1.40	17%	1.20	11%	1.08	11%
4Q	E1.42	20%	1.18	4%	1.13	-3%
Yr.	E5.30	21%	4.37	9%	4.02	14%

Next earnings report expected: mid October

Zions Bancorporation

Business Summary - 22-SEP-95

Zions Bancorporation is a bank holding company with three subsidiary banks. The largest unit is Zions First National Bank, the second largest commercial bank in Utah, with 90 offices throughout the state and one branch in the Grand Cayman Islands. Nevada State Bank, a state-chartered institution, is the fifth largest bank in that state and operates 22 branches in the Las Vegas metropolitan area. National Bank of Arizona (acquired in a January 1994 merger) is the fifth largest bank in its state, where it operates 10 branches. Gross loans, leases and other receivables totaled $2.42 billion at 1994 year end, divided as follows:

	1994
Real estate--mortgage	44%
Commercial & other	21%
Instalment	16%
Loans held for sale	5%
Real estate--construction	9%
Lease financing	5%

The allowance for loan and lease losses at year-end 1994 was $67.0 million (2.80% of gross loans and leases outstanding), versus $68.5 million (2.75%) a year earlier. Net charge-offs of $4.9 million during 1994 (0.19% of average loans and leases) contrasted with net recoveries of $5.1 million in 1993. At December 31, 1994, nonperforming assets amounted to $18.9 million (0.79% of net loans and leases, OREO and other nonperforming assets), compared with $30.6 million (1.23%) a year earlier.

Total deposits of $3.71 billion at year-end 1994 were divided: 24% noninterest bearing demand, 20% savings, 35% money market, 17% time deposits, and 4% foreign. On a tax-equivalent basis, the average yield on interest-earning assets in 1994 was 7.19% (7.05% in 1993), while the average rate paid on interest-bearing liabilities was 3.70% (3.34%), for a net interest spread of 3.49% (3.71%).

Important Developments

Jun. '95—Zions completed the acquisition of First Western National Bank, headquartered in Moab, Utah, with assets of approximately $40 million. Western's three offices are to operate as branches of Zions First National Bank. The acquisition marks Zions' initial expansion into to the southeastern region of Utah. Separately, the board increased the quarterly dividend on the common by 17%, to $0.35 per share.

Capitalization

FHLB Advances: $122,280,000 (6/95).
Long Term Debt: $57,526,000 (6/95).

Per Share Data ($)

(Year Ended Dec. 31)

	1994	1993	1992	1991	1990	1989
Tangible Bk. Val.	23.84	21.85	18.76	15.96	14.21	12.67
Earnings	4.37	4.02	3.52	2.39	2.23	1.17
Dividends	1.16	0.98	0.75	0.72	0.72	0.72
Payout Ratio	27%	24%	21%	30%	32%	61%
Prices - High	42	49¼	39	24⅞	15⅞	16⅛
- Low	33½	36	19¾	14⅜	12¼	10¼
P/E Ratio - High	10	12	11	10	7	14
- Low	8	9	6	6	6	9

Income Statement Analysis (Million $)

	1994	%Chg	1993	%Chg	1992	%Chg	1991
Net Int. Inc.	199	27%	157	9%	144	10%	131
Tax Equiv. Adj.	4.7	42%	3.3	10%	3.0	30%	2.3
Non Int. Inc.	73.5	-6%	78.1	27%	61.6	5%	58.5
Loan Loss Prov.	2.0	-13%	2.3	-78%	10.3	-56%	23.5
% Exp/Op Revs.	63%	—	66%	—	63%	—	65%
Pretax Inc.	94.7	24%	76.1	18%	64.6	53%	42.1
Eff. Tax Rate	33%	—	33%	—	33%	—	31%
Net Inc.	63.8	24%	51.4	19%	43.3	49%	29.1
% Net Int. Marg.	4.07%	—	4.11%	—	4.47%	—	4.32%

Balance Sheet & Other Fin. Data (Million $)

	1994	1993	1992	1991	1990	1989
Earning Assets:						
Money Mkt.	403	579	614	688	786	411
Inv. Securities	1,663	1,145	867	752	587	449
Com'l Loans	496	549	701	769	702	550
Other Loans	1,920	1,701	1,263	1,146	1,126	1,146
Total Assets	4,934	4,366	3,779	3,646	3,559	2,975
Demand Deposits	886	726	596	520	524	476
Time Deposits	2,820	2,298	2,169	2,138	2,013	1,850
LT Debt	160	208	151	81.0	93.0	96.0
Common Eqty.	366	290	243	207	184	164

Ratio Analysis

	1994	1993	1992	1991	1990	1989
% Ret. on Assets	1.3	1.2	1.2	0.9	0.9	0.5
% Ret. on Equity	18.8	19.3	19.3	14.9	15.3	8.8
% Loan Loss Resv.	2.8	2.9	2.9	2.9	3.3	3.6
% Loans/Deposits	68.3	73.8	71.0	72.0	70.9	72.1
% Equity to Assets	7.0	6.3	6.3	5.8	5.7	5.5

Dividend Data —Cash has been paid each year since 1966.

Amt. of Div. $	Date Decl.	Ex-Div. Date	Stock of Record	Payment Date
0.300	Sep. 16	Sep. 27	Oct. 03	Oct. 26 '94
0.300	Dec. 16	Dec. 28	Jan. 04	Jan. 26 '95
0.300	Mar. 03	Mar. 28	Apr. 03	Apr. 27 '95
0.350	Jun. 09	Jun. 29	Jul. 03	Jul. 26 '95
0.350	Sep. 08	Sep. 29	Oct. 03	Oct. 26 '95

Data as orig. reptd.; bef. results of disc opers. and/or spec. items. Per share data adj. for stk. divs. as of ex-div. date. E-Estimated. NA-Not Available. NM-Not Meaningful. NR-Not Ranked.

Office—1380 Kennecott Bldg., Salt Lake City, UT 84133. **Tel**—(801) 524-4787. **Chrmn**—R. W. Simmons. **Pres & CEO**—H. H. Simmons. **SVP, CFO, Secy & Investor Contact**—Gary L. Anderson (801-524-4787). **Dirs**—J. C. Atkin, G. R. Caldwell, R. D. Cash, R. H. Madsen, R. B. Porter, R. G. Sarver, H. H. Simmons, L. E. Simmons, R. W. Simmons, I. J. Wagner, D. W. Westergard. **Transfer Agent & Registrar**—Zions First National Bank, Salt Lake City. **Incorporated** in Utah in 1955. **Empl**-2,754. **S&P Analyst:** Thomas C. Ferguson

PART II

Company ProFiles

How to Use Nasdaq ProFiles

(1) **Trading symbol.** For Nasdaq companies, † indicates shares traded are eligible for purchase on margin. For other than Nasdaq companies, market where traded (e.g., Montreal, Toronto) is indicated; shares traded on U.S. security exchanges (Pacific, Philadelphia, etc.) are marginable.

(2) **Last bid price** for date shown, except for Non-Nasdaq (Pink Sheet) companies where last bid and asked prices for date are shown.

(3) **P-E ratio** is derived by dividing current price by latest trailing 12-months' earnings.

(4) **Indicated annual dividend rate,** based on current payment. If company pays only stock, the latest amount is shown.

(5) **Yield** is derived by dividing indicated dividend by current price.

(6) **Price ranges** (high and low bid) for years indicated. In Jan-Feb-Mar, prices for current year are combined with preceding calendar year's range.

(7) **Exclusive S&P Earnings and Dividend Ranking.** See explanation on page iii.

(8) **Description of company's business,** showing (where available) a breakdown of sales and earnings by line of business, major recent developments, and significant concentrations of shareholdings.

Big B Inc.

NASDAQ (1)	Price (2) Jul 17 '95	P-E Ratio (3)	Dividend (4)	Yield (5)	Ranges 1995	(6) 1994	S&P Ranking (7)
†BIGB	14¾	15	0.20	1.4%	15¼ - 13	14½ - 9⅞	B+

Business: Under the names Big B Discount Drugs and Drugs for Less, this retailer operates a chain of over 300 drug stores in Alabama, Georgia, Florida, Mississippi and Tennessee, and also operates four Home Health Care (8) Centers. The company planned to open an additional 10-20 new stores in fiscal 1993-94 and 15-20 in fiscal 1994-95. In April 1995, an offering of 2.705 million common shares at $14 each was completed. In May 1995, BIGB raised the quarterly dividend to $0.05 from $0.04.

(9) **1994 Sales.:** 668.2 mil.
1994 Net Inc.: 15.1 mil.
(10) **Common Shs.:** 18,543,000
(11) **Long Term Debt:** 74.0 mil.
Book Val. Per Sh.: 6.83 Jan '95
(13) **Latest Div.:** Q0.05 Jun. '95
(14) **Cash Paid Each Year Since 1987**

	(15) Share Earnings (Jan. Yr.)	(16) Divs. Paid (Cal. Yr.)
1994	0.97	0.15
1993	0.76	0.12
1992	0.60	0.10
1991	0.43	0.06

(17) **Interim Earnings: 3 Months**
Apr. '95 0.31 Apr. '94 0.26

(18) **Chrm:** J. S. Bruno
Pres: A. J. Bruno
EVP, Treas & Secy: A. M. Jones, Sr.
Office: 2600 Morgan Rd. Bessemer, AL 35023
Tel: (205) 424-3421

(19) **Footnotes:** †Marginable.

---

(9) **Sales and net income,** in millions of dollars, for latest reported fiscal year; fiscal years ending March 31 or earlier are presented as the preceding calendar year.

(10) **Number of common shares outstanding;** per latest available balance sheet.

(11) **Long-term debt** ($ million) per latest available balance sheet.

(12) **Book value** (equity) per share, excluding intangibles, at date shown.

(13) **Most recent dividend per share.** Date and amount of most recent payment. Q—Quarterly, S—Semi-annually, A—Annually indicates regular rate.

(14) **At least one cash dividend paid each year,** without interruption, since year shown.

(15) **Share earnings** for each of the past four fiscal years, ended in month/year shown, except for fiscal years ending March 31 or earlier which are presented as the preceding calendar year.

(16) **Most recent complete years** of dividend history, always on a calendar year basis, without regard to the company's fiscal year. If calendar year is not completed, only "—" will appear.

(17) **Latest available interim report,** with year-earlier comparison.

(18) **Corporate directory,** listing principal officers, headquarters address, and telephone number.

(19) **Footnotes** are used to enhance statistical data. Typical footnotes draw attention to deficits, the inclusion or exclusion of extraordinary items, extra dividends, adjustments for stock splits and stock dividends, and the use of pro forma figures to reflect mergers and acquisitions.

Acxiom Corp.

NASDAQ	Price Nov 14 '95	P-E Ratio	Dividend	Yield	Ranges 1995	1994	S&P Ranking
†ACXM	28⅛	45	None	None	31½ - 13⅝	15 - 9¼	B+

Business: This company provides data processing and related computer-based services and software products to direct marketing organizations and to the marketing departments of large corporations that use direct marketing techniques such as mail order, catalog sales and prospect generation. Acxiom maintains about 25,000 lists and 500 databases owned by others totaling over 4.5 billion name and address records. The company also offers outsourcing/facilities management and information management services to its customers.

1994 Sales.: 202.5 mil.
1994 Net Inc.: 12.4 mil.
Common Shs.: 23,491,000
Long Term Debt: 29.3 mil.
Book Val. Per Sh.: 3.90 Mar '95
Latest Div.: None

	Share Earnings (Mar. Yr.)	Divs. Paid (Cal. Yr.)
1994	0.54	Nil
1993	0.38	Nil
1992	0.30	Nil
1991	0.11	Nil

Interim Earnings: 6 Months
Sep. '95 0.28 **Sep. '94** 0.19

Chrm, Pres & CEO: C. D. Morgan Jr.
EVP, COO & Treas: R. S. Kline
Secy: C. L. Hughes
Office: 301 Industrial Blvd. Conway, AR 72033
Tel: (501) 336-1000

Footnotes: †Marginable.

Advanced Tissue Sciences

NASDAQ	Price Nov 14 '95	P-E Ratio	Dividend	Yield	Ranges 1995	1994	S&P Ranking
ATIS	9½	NM	None	None	15 - 5½	9½ - 4¼	NR

Business: Advanced Tissue Sciences develops living human tissue products for therapeutic applications, using principles of cell biology, biochemistry and polymer science, through a proprietary core technology which permits living human cells to be cultured ex vivo. Development efforts are being led by therapeutic products based on Dermagraft, a three-dimensional living human tissue designed as a replacement for human dermis. The U.S. Patent Office recently granted a patent on the company's core technology.

1994 Sales.: 3.2 mil.
1994 Net Inc.: d22.8 mil.
Common Shs.: 33,851,000
Long Term Debt: 0.03 mil.
Book Val. Per Sh.: 0.90 Dec '94
Latest Div.: None

	Share Earnings (Cal. Yr.)	Divs. Paid (Cal. Yr.)
1994	d0.75	Nil
1993	d0.67	Nil
1992	d1.40	Nil
1991	d0.36	Nil

Interim Earnings: 9 Months
Sep. '95 d0.53 **Sep. '94** d0.58

Chrmn & CEO: A. J. Benvenuto
Pres & COO: G. K. Naughton
VP-Fin: M. V. Swanson
Office: 10933 Torrey Pines Rd. La Jolla, CA 92037
Tel: (619) 450-5730

Footnotes: d-Deficit.

American Freightways

NASDAQ	Price Nov 14 '95	P-E Ratio	Dividend	Yield	Ranges 1995	1994	S&P Ranking
†AFWY	14	19	None	None	24¼ - 11⅛	24⅞ - 15½	B+

Business: American Freightways (formerly Arkansas Freightways) is a common and contract motor carrier that transports less-than-truckload shipments of general commodities. In January 1995 the company added 13 terminals in North and South Carolina for a total of 157 terminals. At 1994 year end, the company was operating 3,344 tractors and 8,390 trailers. The planned opening of seven additional terminals in mid-1995 was expected to bring the total all-points coverage to 21 primarily Midwestern and Southern states.

1994 Sales.: 465.6 mil.
1994 Net Inc.: 27.0 mil.
Common Shs.: 30,836,000
Long Term Debt: 166.0 mil.
Book Val. Per Sh.: 5.81 Dec '94
Latest Div.: None

	Share Earnings (Cal. Yr.)	Divs. Paid (Cal. Yr.)
1994	[1]0.89	Nil
1993	0.59	Nil
1992	[1]0.50	Nil
1991	0.30	Nil

Interim Earnings: 9 Months
Sep. '95 0.54 **Sep. '94** 0.70

Chrm & CEO: F. S. Garrison
EVP & CFO: J. R. Dodd
VP, Treas & Secy: T. Garrison
Office: 2200 Forward Dr. Harrison, AR 72601
Tel: (501) 741-9000

Footnotes: †Marginable. 1. Excl. special charge.

Arctco Inc.

NASDAQ	Price	P-E Ratio	Dividend	Yield	Ranges 1995	Ranges 1994	S&P Ranking
	Nov 14 '95						
ACAT	12⅝	15	0.24	1.9%	19½ - 10⅜	21¾ - 13¼	B+

Business: Arctco is engaged in the manufacture and marketing of snowmobiles, a personal watercraft, and related parts, garments and accessories. The company's products, which are sold under the Arctic Cat, Tigershark and Articwear brand names, are distributed through an extensive network of independent dealers in 32 states in the contiguous U.S., and through distributors representing dealers in Alaska and Canada, Scandinavia and other international markets. Suzuki Motor Co. owns some 26%.

1994 Sales.: 367.1 mil.
1994 Net Inc.: 33.4 mil.
Common Shs.: [1]29,656,000
Long Term Debt: None
Book Val. Per Sh.: 4.96 Mar '95
Latest Div.: Q0.06 Dec. '95
Cash Paid Each Year Since 1992

Year	Share Earnings (Mar. Yr.)	Divs. Paid (Cal. Yr.)
1994	[1]1.13	0.19
1993	[1]0.94	0.14
1992	[1]0.62	0.11
1991	[1]0.46	Nil

Interim Earnings: 6 Months
Sep. '95 0.46 **Sep. '94** 0.77

Chrm: W. G. Ness
Pres & CEO: C. A. Twomey
CFO: T. C. Delmore
Office: 600 Brooks Ave. S. Thief River Falls, MN 56701
Tel: (218) 681-8558

Footnotes: 1. Combined various classes.

Arkansas Best

NASDAQ	Price	P-E Ratio	Dividend	Yield	Ranges 1995	Ranges 1994	S&P Ranking
	Nov 14 '95						
ABFS	9½	NM	0.04	0.4%	13⅜ - 7⅞	15¾ - 10⅛	NR

Business: Arkansas Best Corporation is engaged, through subsidiaries, in less-than-truckload shipments of general commodities, and truck tire retreading and new truck tire sales. The company's motor carrier subsidiaries recently had 338 terminals and operated in all 50 states, Canada and Puerto Rico. In September 1995, ABFS consolidated the recently acquired WorldWay Corp. subsidiary and its Red Arrow Freight Lines into its ABF Freight System.

1994 Sales.: 1098.4 mil.
1994 Net Inc.: 18.7 mil.
Common Shs.: 19,529,000
Long Term Debt: 79.7 mil.
Book Val. Per Sh.: 3.31 Dec '94
Latest Div.: Q0.01 Nov. '95
Cash Paid Each Year Since 1992

Year	Share Earnings (Cal. Yr.)	Divs. Paid (Cal. Yr.)
1994	0.74	0.04
1993	[1]0.89	0.04
1992	[1]0.99	0.02
1991	[2,1]0.83	Nil

Interim Earnings: 9 Months
Sep. '95 d0.49 **Sep. '94** 0.42

Chrmn: W. A. Marquard
Pres & CEO: R. A. Young III
SVP & CFO: D. L. Neal
Office: 3801 Old Greenwood Road Fort Smith, AR 72903
Tel: (501) 785-6000

Footnotes: 1. Excl. special charge. 2. Pro Forma. d-Deficit.

Astoria Financial

NASDAQ	Price	P-E Ratio	Dividend	Yield	Ranges 1995	Ranges 1994	S&P Ranking
	Nov 14 '95						
ASFC	43¾	11	1	None	46¼ - 26	34¾ - 25⅛	NR

Business: Through its subsidiary, this company operates a community-oriented savings bank offering a variety of financial services in Queens, Nassau, Suffolk, Westchester, Chenango and Otsego counties in New York State. At September 30, 1995, ASFC.had total assets of $6.5 billion. In February 1995, the acquisition of Fidelity New York was completed for about $157 million. In October 1995, ASFC declared a regular quarterly dividend of $0.20 a share, to be paid on December 1, 1995, with a record date of November 15, 1995.

1994 Sales.: 307.6 mil.
1994 Net Inc.: 43.7 mil.
Common Shs.: 11,788,000
Long Term Debt: NA
Book Val. Per Sh.: 45.30 Dec '94
Latest Div.: 0.20 Dec. '95
Cash Paid Each Year Since 1995

Year	Share Earnings (Cal. Yr.)	Divs. Paid (Cal. Yr.)
1994	3.70	Nil
1993	[2]0.37	Nil
1992	Nil	Nil
1991	NA	Nil

Interim Earnings: 9 Months
Sep. '95 3.08 **Sep. '94** 2.75

Chrmn: H. Drewitt
Pres & CEO: G. L. Engelke Jr.
SVP, Treas & CFO: M. N. Redman
Office: One Astoria Federal Plaza Lake Success, NY 11042
Tel: (516) 327-3000

Footnotes: 1. To be determined 2. Partial year.

Au Bon Pain

NASDAQ	Price	P-E Ratio	Dividend	Yield	Ranges		S&P Ranking
	Nov 14 '95				1995	1994	
ABPCA	9	NM	None	None	17¼ - 5⅞	26½ - 14⅜	NR

Business: This chain of bakery cafes offers fresh baked goods, sandwiches, soups and beverages. The company recently operated 213 bakery cafes and franchised 31 cafes under the Au Bon Pain and Saint Louis Bread Company names. A charge of $5.3 million was recorded in 1995's third quarter related to the closing of nine underperforming bakery cafes and the writedown of other store assets to fair value. Officers and directors own about 37%.

1994 Sales.: 182.9 mil.
1994 Net Inc.: 7.8 mil.
Common Shs.: [1]11,609,000
Long Term Debt: 64.0 mil.
Book Val. Per Sh.: 4.92 Dec '94
Latest Div.: None

	Share Earnings (Cal. Yr.)	Divs. Paid (Cal. Yr.)
1994	[1]0.67	Nil
1993	[1]0.60	Nil
1992	[1]0.48	Nil
1991	[1]0.30	Nil

Interim Earnings: 9 Months
Sep. '95 d0.22 **Sep. '94** 0.48

Co-Chrm: L. I. Kane
Co-Chrm & CEO: R. M. Shaich
VP & CFO: A. J. Carroll
Office: 19 Fid Kennedy Ave.
Boston, MA 02210
Tel: (617) 423-2100

Footnotes: 1. Combined various classes. d-Deficit.

Bally Gaming International

NASDAQ	Price	P-E Ratio	Dividend	Yield	Ranges		S&P Ranking
	Nov 14 '95				1995	1994	
BGII	10¼	47	None	None	12½ - 6⅛	17⅞ - 7¼	NR

Business: This company designs, manufactures and distributes gaming equipment worldwide through subsidiaries in Germany and the U.S. The German units manufacture coin-operated, wall-mounted gaming machines for arcades, hotels, restaurants and taverns, while the U.S. units manufacture a variety of electronic reel-type and video slot machines for casinos and cruise ships. In October 1995, BGII agreed to be acquired by Alliance Gaming Corp. for $13 a share in cash or stock.

1994 Sales.: 236.2 mil.
1994 Net Inc.: 3.8 mil.
Common Shs.: 10,750,000
Long Term Debt: 39.6 mil.
Book Val. Per Sh.: 6.88 Dec '94
Latest Div.: None

	Share Earnings (Cal. Yr.)	Divs. Paid (Cal. Yr.)
1994	0.35	Nil
1993	[1]d2.54	Nil
1992	0.50	Nil
1991	0.48	Nil

Interim Earnings: 9 Months
Sep. '95 0.01 **Sep. '94** 0.14

Chrm, Pres & CEO: R. Gillman
Pres & COO: H. Kloss
Acting CFO: J. Garner
Office: 6601 S. Bermuda Rd.
Las Vegas, NV 89119
Tel: (702) 896-7700

Footnotes: 1. Excl. special credit. d-Deficit.

Banyan Systems

NASDAQ	Price	P-E Ratio	Dividend	Yield	Ranges		S&P Ranking
	Nov 14 '95				1995	1994	
BNYN	8⅛	NM	None	None	19⅜ - 6	19¾ - 12¾	NR

Business: This company develops, markets and supports enterprise networking software products which enable customers to integrate a broad range of computer platforms into a unified global network. Products include VINES, ENS, and related products. During 1994, it introduced BeyondWare, an architecture for remote users with new combinations of messaging and application solutions, and DeMarc, for managing enterprise networks. Banyan and Microcom recently formed a partnership to provide remote access and mobile computing solutions.

1994 Sales.: 150.1 mil.
1994 Net Inc.: 5.0 mil.
Common Shs.: 16,513,000
Long Term Debt: None
Book Val. Per Sh.: 4.34 Dec '94
Latest Div.: None

	Share Earnings (Cal. Yr.)	Divs. Paid (Cal. Yr.)
1994	0.27	Nil
1993	0.70	Nil
1992	0.50	Nil
1991	0.19	Nil

Interim Earnings: 9 Months
Sep. '95 d0.24 **Sep. '94** 0.02

Chrmn, Pres & CEO:
D. C. Mahoney
Pres & COO: A. P. Hamilton
VP-Fin, CFO, Treas & Secy:
J. D. Glidden
Office: 120 Flanders Rd.
Westboro, MA 01581
Tel: (508) 898-1000

Footnotes: d-Deficit.

Bell Bancorp

NASDAQ	Price	P-E Ratio	Dividend	Yield	Ranges 1995	Ranges 1994	S&P Ranking
	Nov 14 '95						
BELL	30¼	23	0.45	1.5%	33¼ - 23	29½ - 21½	NR

Business: Bell Bancorp conducts business as a unitary savings and loan holding company, through its subsidiary Bell Federal Savings and Loan Association. Its principal business is attracting deposits from the general public and investing primarily in one- to four-family residential, primary residence adjustable rate mortgage loans in its principal market area of Chicago and surrounding suburbs. At September 30, 1995, assets totaled $1.9 billion.

1994 Sales.: 118.0 mil.
1994 Net Inc.: 13.4 mil.
Common Shs.: 9,151,000
Long Term Debt: 33.5 mil.
Book Val. Per Sh.: 32.18 Mar '95
Latest Div.: Q0.11 Dec. '95
Cash Paid Each Year Since 1994

	Share Earnings (Mar. Yr.)	Divs. Paid (Cal. Yr.)
1994	1.32	0.15
1993	[1]1.66	Nil
1992	1.92	Nil
1991	[2]1.17	Nil

Interim Earnings: 6 Months
Sep. '95 0.64 **Sep. '94** 0.62

Chrmn: E. M. Shanahan
Pres & CEO: R. G. Rowen
SVP, CFO & Treas: J. C. Savio
Office: 79 West Monroe
Chicago, IL 60603
Tel: (312) 346-1000

Footnotes: 1. Excl. special charge. 2. Pro Forma.

Bell Sports

NASDAQ	Price	P-E Ratio	Dividend	Yield	Ranges 1995	Ranges 1994	S&P Ranking
	Nov 14 '95						
BSPT	9⅜	NM	None	None	18½ - 8⅛	40½ - 12¾	NR

Business: This company is a leading manufacturer and marketer of bicycle helmets for infants, youths and adults under its Bell and BSI brand names (72% of fiscal 1994 revenues). It also makes other bicycle accessories, such as child seats and car bicycle carriers (25%), and auto racing helmets (3%). In May 1995, it acquired SportRack Canada. In August 1995, directors authorized the repurchase of up to 10% of the company's outstanding common stock in open market or privately negotiated transactions.

1995 Sales.: 103.0 mil.
1995 Net Inc.: d3.4 mil.
Common Shs.: [1]14,200,000
Long Term Debt: 88.9 mil.
Book Val. Per Sh.: Def. Mar '95
Latest Div.: None

	Share Earnings (Jun. Yr.)	Divs. Paid (Cal. Yr.)
1995	[2]d0.42	---
1994	1.27	Nil
1993	[3,4]0.88	Nil
1992	[4]0.77	Nil

Interim Earnings: 3 Months
Sep. '95 d0.38 **Sep. '94** 0.02

Chrmn, Pres & CEO: T. G. Lee
EVP & CFO: H. A. Kosick
Office: 10601 N. Hayden Rd. Suite I-100
Scottsdale, AZ 85260
Tel: (602) 951-0033

Footnotes: 1. Pro Forma. 2. Preliminary. 3. Excl. special charge. 4. Excl. special credit. d-Deficit.

Bertucci's Inc.

NASDAQ	Price	P-E Ratio	Dividend	Yield	Ranges 1995	Ranges 1994	S&P Ranking
	Nov 14 '95						
BERT	5¾	15	None	None	12¾ - 5¼	23¼ - 8½	NR

Business: This company operates a chain of 50 'Bertucci's Brick Oven Pizzeria' Italian theme restaurants, which are located in the Northeast and Mid-Atlantic Regions. Bertucci's menu features brick-oven pizza and other Italian dishes. The company opened 17 restaurants in 1994 and planned to open 12 to 15 additional restaurants in 1995. Insiders own about 42% of the stock.

1994 Sales.: 102.8 mil.
1994 Net Inc.: 5.6 mil.
Common Shs.: 8,725,000
Long Term Debt: 19.5 mil.
Book Val. Per Sh.: 7.44 Dec '94
Latest Div.: None

	Share Earnings (Cal. Yr.)	Divs. Paid (Cal. Yr.)
1994	0.63	Nil
1993	0.63	Nil
1992	0.55	Nil
1991	0.50	Nil

Interim Earnings: 40 Weeks
Oct. '95 0.23 **Oct. '94** 0.48

Chrm & Pres: J. Crugnale
VP-Fin & Treas: N. S. Mallett
Secy: J. Westra
Office: 14 Audubon Road
Wakefield, MA 01880
Tel: (617) 246-6700

Footnotes:

Big B Inc.

NASDAQ	Price Nov 14 '95	P-E Ratio	Dividend	Yield	Ranges 1995	Ranges 1994	S&P Ranking
†BIGB	8⅜	9	0.20	2.4%	16⅛ - 7½	14½ - 9⅞	B+

Business: Under the names Big B Discount Drugs and Drugs for Less, this retailer operates a chain of over 350 drug stores in Alabama, Georgia, Florida, Mississippi and Tennessee, and also operates five Home Health Care Centers. The company planned to open an additional 20-25 new stores in fiscal 1995-96 and 25-30 in fiscal 1996-97. Sixteen new drug stores were opened in fiscal 1994-95. In April 1995, an offering of 2.705 million common shares at $14 each was completed.

1994 Sales.: 668.2 mil.
1994 Net Inc.: 15.1 mil.
Common Shs.: 18,567,000
Long Term Debt: 58.0 mil.
Book Val. Per Sh.: 6.83 Jan '95
Latest Div.: Q0.05 Dec. '95
Cash Paid Each Year Since 1987

	Share Earnings (Jan. Yr.)	Divs. Paid (Cal. Yr.)
1994	0.97	0.15
1993	0.76	0.12
1992	0.60	0.10
1991	0.43	0.06

Interim Earnings: 9 Months
Oct. '95 0.48 **Oct. '94** 0.52

Chrm: J. S. Bruno
Pres: A. J. Bruno
EVP, Treas & Secy: A. M. Jones, Sr.
Office: 2600 Morgan Rd. Bessemer, AL 35023
Tel: (205) 424-3421

Footnotes: †Marginable.

Books-A-Million

NASDAQ	Price Nov 14 '95	P-E Ratio	Dividend	Yield	Ranges 1995	Ranges 1994	S&P Ranking
BAMM	13¼	34	None	None	18⅝ - 12⅜	17¾ - 9¼	NR

Business: This company is engaged primarily in the sale of books, magazines and related items through a chain of 124 retail specialty bookstores in 17 mostly Southeast states. It also serves as a wholesale book distributor for certain other retailers and wholesalers. During fiscal 1994, the company opened 21 new stores, including 19 superstores, and closed six underperforming stores. Expansion plans call for the opening of 20 to 25 superstores in fiscal 1996.

1994 Sales.: 172.4 mil.
1994 Net Inc.: 8.1 mil.
Common Shs.: 17,370,000
Long Term Debt: 4.6 mil.
Book Val. Per Sh.: 4.76 Jan '95
Latest Div.: None

	Share Earnings (Jan. Yr.)	Divs. Paid (Cal. Yr.)
1994	0.47	Nil
1993	0.37	Nil
1992	[1]0.32	Nil
1991	[1]0.21	Nil

Interim Earnings: 6 Months
Jul. '95 0.04 **Jul. '94** 0.12

Chrmn: C. C. Anderson
Pres, CEO & COO: C. B. Anderson
VP & CFO: S. B. Cochran
Office: 402 Industrial Lane Birmingham, AL 35211
Tel: (205) 942-3737

Footnotes: 1. Pro Forma.

Brenco, Inc.

NASDAQ	Price Nov 14 '95	P-E Ratio	Dividend	Yield	Ranges 1995	Ranges 1994	S&P Ranking
†BREN	11¾	11	0.28	2.4%	14½ - 9¾	14 - 8¼	B

Business: Brenco Inc. is a major manufacturer of bronze bearings used in railway freight cars and also produces industrial bearings and forgings for forklift trucks, construction machinery, steel mills, oil drilling rigs, mining equipment and over-the-road trailers. Brenco's most important product is the tapered roller antifriction bearing. BREN also services and repairs used railroad bearings and makes lubrication seals for use in railroad bearings and for sale to third parties. In May 1995, Brenco raised the quarterly dividend to $0.07 from $0.06.

1994 Sales.: 117.9 mil.
1994 Net Inc.: 8.8 mil.
Common Shs.: 10,141,000
Long Term Debt: 8.3 mil.
Book Val. Per Sh.: 5.50 Dec '94
Latest Div.: Q0.07 Oct. '95
Cash Paid Each Year Since 1959

	Share Earnings (Cal. Yr.)	Divs. Paid (Cal. Yr.)
1994	0.88	0.21
1993	0.43	0.20
1992	0.20	0.20
1991	0.46	0.20

Interim Earnings: 9 Months
Sep. '95 0.87 **Sep. '94** 0.64

Chrm & CEO: N. B. Whitfield
Pres: J. C. Rice
EVP, Treas & Secy: J. M. Feichtner
Office: One Park West Circle Midlothian, VA 23113
Tel: (804) 794-1436

Footnotes: †Marginable.

BroadBand Technologies

NASDAQ	Price Nov 14 '95	P-E Ratio	Dividend	Yield	Ranges 1995	Ranges 1994	S&P Ranking
BBTK	18½	NM	None	None	31¾ - 16	33½ - 11	NR

Business: This company designs, manufactures, markets and supports a sophisticated electronics and software platform for the telecommunications industry, focusing primarily on operators of local exchange telephone networks in the U.S. Its platform provides operators of fiber based distribution networks with the capability to transmit voice, video and data in a wide array of advanced, interactive entertainment, information, communications, transaction and other services to residential and business subscribers.

1994 Sales.: 27.0 mil.
1994 Net Inc.: d24.2 mil.
Common Shs.: 13,075,000
Long Term Debt: 0.14 mil.
Book Val. Per Sh.: 6.07 Dec '94
Latest Div.: None

	Share Earnings (Cal. Yr.)	Divs. Paid (Cal. Yr.)
1994	d1.85	Nil
1993	[1]d1.89	Nil
1992	[1]d1.54	Nil
1991	[1]d1.55	Nil

Interim Earnings: 9 Months
Sep. '95 d1.60 **Sep. '94** d1.27

Chrmn: J. R. Hutchins III
Pres & CEO: S. A. L. Bhatia
VP, CFO, Treas & Secy: J. H. Gorman
Office: 4024 Stirrup Creek Dr. Durham, NC 27703
Tel: (919) 544-0015

Footnotes: 1. Pro Forma. d-Deficit.

Cellular Communications

NASDAQ	Price Nov 14 '95	P-E Ratio	Dividend	Yield	Ranges 1995	Ranges 1994	S&P Ranking
COMMA	52	50	None	None	55 - 44½	55¾ - 43¾	B-

Business: Cellular Communications Inc. is a holding company with a 50% interest in a joint venture with AirTouch Communications (formerly PacTel Corporation) that owns and operates cellular telephone systems that are located in Ohio and Michigan and in portions of Indiana and Kentucky. At December 31, 1994, the joint venture had 729,000 subscribers versus 478,000 a year earlier. In June 1995, its board authorized repurchase of up to one million common shares.

1994 Sales.: 59.0 mil.
1994 Net Inc.: 17.7 mil.
Common Shs.: [1]12,300,000
Long Term Debt: 358.0 mil.
Book Val. Per Sh.: Def. Dec '94
Latest Div.: None

	Share Earnings (Cal. Yr.)	Divs. Paid (Cal. Yr.)
1994	0.40	Nil
1993	[2]0.27	Nil
1992	[3]d0.09	Nil
1991	[4]d0.56	[5]

Interim Earnings: 9 Months
Sep. '95 1.00 **Sep. '94** 0.35

Chrmn & Treas: G. S. Blumenthal
Pres & CEO: W. B. Ginsberg
EVP, COO & CFO: J. B. Knapp
Office: 150 East 58th Street New York, NY 10155
Tel: (212) 906-8440

Footnotes: 1. Pro Forma. 2. Excl. special credit. 3. Before tax loss carryforward. 4. Excl. special charge. 5. Stock of another company. d-Deficit.

Center Financial

NASDAQ	Price Nov 14 '95	P-E Ratio	Dividend	Yield	Ranges 1995	Ranges 1994	S&P Ranking
†CFCX	17¾	12	0.20	1.1%	19⅝ - 9¾	18 - 9¼	NR

Business: Center Financial (formerly Centerbank) operates 38 retail banking branches throughout Connecticut, with total assets at June 30, 1995, of $3.11 billion, deposits of $2.10 billion and net loans and leases of $2.43 billion. Nonbank subsidiaries include mortgage banking, equipment leasing and commercial finance companies. CFCX was reorganized into a holding company structure in July 1995. In July 1995, CFCX also agreed to acquire Great Country Bank of Ansonia, CT, and acquired deposits and loans from Founders Bank of New Haven.

1994 Sales.: 217.0 mil.
1994 Net Inc.: 6.6 mil.
Common Shs.: [1]12,682,000
Long Term Debt: 319.0 mil.
Book Val. Per Sh.: 14.30 Dec '94
Latest Div.: Q0.05 Nov. '95
Cash Paid Each Year Since 1995

	Share Earnings (Cal. Yr.)	Divs. Paid (Cal. Yr.)
1994	0.53	Nil
1993	[2]0.75	Nil
1992	0.58	Nil
1991	d0.48	Nil

Interim Earnings: 9 Months
Sep. '95 1.18 **Sep. '94** 0.18

Chrm & CEO: R. J. Narkis
Vice-Chrm, CFO & Treas: J. Carlson II
Pres & COO: W. H. Placke
Office: 60 N. Main St. Waterbury, CT 06702
Tel: (203) 578-7000

Footnotes: †Marginable. 1. Pro Forma. 2. Excl. special credit. d-Deficit.

Centigram Communications

NASDAQ	Price	P-E Ratio	Dividend	Yield	Ranges		S&P Ranking
	Nov 14 '95				1995	1994	
CGRM	22¼	NM	None	None	25⅛ - 12¼	43 - 10	NR

Business: This company designs, manufactures and markets systems and software that permit users to access and interact with a broad range of voice, text, data and facsimile applications, such as voice messaging, facsimile storage and forwarding and interactive voice processing. All of its applications operate on a common adaptive information processing platform, and can use the company's proprietary TruVoice text-to-speech software, which can convert textual data in a computer database into natural sounding speech.

1994 Sales.: 79.2 mil.
1994 Net Inc.: 7.8 mil.
Common Shs.: 6,592,000
Long Term Debt: 0.28 mil.
Book Val. Per Sh.: 12.72 Oct '94
Latest Div.: None

	Share Earnings (Sep. Yr.)	Divs. Paid (Cal. Yr.)
1994	1.18	Nil
1993	1.00	Nil
1992	0.49	Nil
1991	0.67	Nil

Interim Earnings: 9 Months
Jun. '95 d0.29 **Jun. '94** 0.89

Chrmn: E. T. Goei
Pres & CEO: G. H. Sollman
SVP & CFO: A. R. Muller
Office: 91 E. Tasman Dr. San Jose, CA 95134
Tel: (408) 944-0250

Footnotes: d-Deficit.

Cheesecake Factory

NASDAQ	Price	P-E Ratio	Dividend	Yield	Ranges		S&P Ranking
	Nov 14 '95				1995	1994	
CAKE	22⅝	28	None	None	30¼ - 13¾	24⅝ - 13½	NR

Business: This company recently operated eleven upscale, moderately priced, casual dining restaurants under the Cheesecake Factory name in Southern California, Washington, D.C., Atlanta, Miami, and Boca Raton. It also operated a bakery facility that creates, produces and markets 50 varieties of cheesecake and other quality baked desserts. In 1994, comparable restaurant sales increased $1.0 million or 1.8%.

1994 Sales.: 85.6 mil.
1994 Net Inc.: 7.3 mil.
Common Shs.: 10,812,000
Long Term Debt: None
Book Val. Per Sh.: 6.06 Jan '95
Latest Div.: None

	Share Earnings (Cal. Yr.)	Divs. Paid (Cal. Yr.)
1994	0.69	Nil
1993	0.51	Nil
1992	[1]0.58	Nil
1991	[1]0.23	Nil

Interim Earnings: 9 Months
Sep. '95 0.61 **Sep. '94** 0.49

Chrmn, Pres & CEO: D. Overton
SVP & CFO: G. Deitchle
Office: 26950 Agoura Rd. Calabasas, CA 91302
Tel: (818) 880-9323

Footnotes: 1. Pro Forma.

Cobra Golf

NASDAQ	Price	P-E Ratio	Dividend	Yield	Ranges		S&P Ranking
	Nov 14 '95				1995	1994	
CBRA	27½	16	None	None	39¼ - 20	41½ - 12½	NR

Business: This company designs, manufactures and markets high-quality golf clubs principally for the premium-priced game-improvement segment of the golf equipment market. Its King Cobra line for men, consisting of a full set of oversize metalwoods and irons, accounted for 54% of gross sales in 1994. Sales are targeted at on-course golf pro shops and selected off-course specialty stores.

1994 Sales.: 124.1 mil.
1994 Net Inc.: 23.0 mil.
Common Shs.: 18,602,000
Long Term Debt: None
Book Val. Per Sh.: 3.83 Dec '94
Latest Div.: None

	Share Earnings (Cal. Yr.)	Divs. Paid (Cal. Yr.)
1994	1.21	Nil
1993	[1]0.50	Nil
1992	[1]0.22	Nil
1991	NA	Nil

Interim Earnings: 9 Months
Sep. '95 1.45 **Sep. '94** 0.95

Chrmn: G. E. Biszantz
Pres & CEO: M. C. McClure
CFO: R. Bruner
Office: 1812 Aston Ave. Carlsbad, CA 92008
Tel: (619) 929-0377

Footnotes: 1. Pro Forma.

Cognex Corp.

NASDAQ	Price Nov 14 '95	P-E Ratio	Dividend	Yield	Ranges 1995	Ranges 1994	S&P Ranking
CGNX	66¼	77	None	None	69 - 21	28 - 11¾	B

Business: This company develops, manufactures and markets machine vision systems, consisting of pattern recognition software and high-speed special purpose computers, used in manufacturing processes. It sells to OEM and system integrators in semiconductor, electronic, automotive, pharmaceutical and aerospace industries. Foreign sales accounted for about 62% of revenues in 1994. In March 1995, CGNX entered into a two-year OEM agreement valued at $9 million with MPM Corporation.

1994 Sales.: 62.5 mil.
1994 Net Inc.: 16.1 mil.
Common Shs.: 19,209,000
Long Term Debt: None
Book Val. Per Sh.: 5.52 Dec '94
Latest Div.: None

Year	Share Earnings (Cal. Yr.)	Divs. Paid (Cal. Yr.)
1994	0.87	Nil
1993	0.63	Nil
1992	0.35	Nil
1991	0.54	Nil

Interim Earnings: 9 Months
Sep. '95 0.60 **Sep. '94** 0.61

Chrm, Pres & CEO: R. J. Shillman
VP-Fin & Admin, CFO: J. J. Rogers, Jr.
EVP Opns: R. B. Snyder
Office: One Vision Drive Natick, MA 01760
Tel: (408) 650-3000

Footnotes:

Comverse Technology

NASDAQ	Price Nov 14 '95	P-E Ratio	Dividend	Yield	Ranges 1995	Ranges 1994	S&P Ranking
CMVT	22⅛	31	None	None	26 - 11	15⅝ - 8	B-

Business: Comverse designs, manufactures and markets special purpose computer and telecommunications systems for multimedia communications and information processing applications. It has two main product groups: the AUDIODISK line of multiple channel, multimedia digital recording systems; and the TRILOGUE line of telephone-accessed, multimedia messaging and information processing systems. In September 1995, Comverse signed an agreement with Pacific Telesis worth $9 million to provide equipment and development and support services.

1994 Sales.: 92.7 mil.
1994 Net Inc.: 11.8 mil.
Common Shs.: [1]21,124,000
Long Term Debt: 60.0 mil.
Book Val. Per Sh.: 4.99 Dec '94
Latest Div.: None

Year	Share Earnings (Cal. Yr.)	Divs. Paid (Cal. Yr.)
1994	0.57	Nil
1993	0.65	Nil
1992	[2]0.32	Nil
1991	[3]0.20	Nil

Interim Earnings: 9 Months
Sep. '95 0.53 **Sep. '94** 0.38

Chrmn, Pres & CEO: K. Alexander
VP-Fin & CFO: I. Nissim
Office: 170 Crossways Park Dr. Woodbury, NY 11797
Tel: (516) 677-7200

Footnotes: 1. Pro Forma. 2. Excl. special credit. 3. Before tax loss carryforward.

Cygnus Inc.

NASDAQ	Price Nov 14 '95	P-E Ratio	Dividend	Yield	Ranges 1995	Ranges 1994	S&P Ranking
CYGN	15½	NM	None	None	20 - 5⅝	12⅞ - 5½	NR

Business: This drug delivery company (formerly Cygnus Therapeutic Systems) develops advanced drug delivery and diagnostic systems, currently primarily focused on transdermal systems, mucosal systems and a painless glucose monitoring device. It currently has 17 products in development, one (a nicotine patch) on the market, one submitted to the FDA for approval, and five in clinical trials. In May 1995, the FDA requested that a bio-equivalency study be performed on CYGN's Fempatch 7-day estrogen patch before it can be approved.

1994 Sales.: 21.3 mil.
1994 Net Inc.: d17.4 mil.
Common Shs.: [1]17,771,000
Long Term Debt: 3.7 mil.
Book Val. Per Sh.: 1.16 Dec '94
Latest Div.: None

Year	Share Earnings (Cal. Yr.)	Divs. Paid (Cal. Yr.)
1994	d1.24	Nil
1993	d0.77	Nil
1992	d1.36	Nil
1991	d0.64	Nil

Interim Earnings: 9 Months
Sep. '95 d0.65 **Sep. '94** d0.45

Chrmn: G. W. Cleary
Pres & CEO: G. B. Lawless
CFO: A. S. S. Chan
Office: 400 Penobscot Dr. Redwood City, CA 94063
Tel: (415) 369-4300

Footnotes: 1. Reflects new financing. d-Deficit.

Cyrk Inc.

NASDAQ	Price	P-E Ratio	Dividend	Yield	Ranges		S&P Ranking
	Nov 14 '95				1995	1994	
CYRK	10¼	26	None	None	41¼ - 7	44¾ - 20½	NR

Business: Cyrk designs, develops, manufactures, sources and distributes high quality products for promotional programs and custom-designed sports apparel and accessories and also produces a limited line of Cyrk brand sports apparel. Promotional products customers are consumer products and services companies seeking to promote their brand names and corporate identities and to build brand loyalty. Net sales to Philip Morris accounted for 89% and 78% of total net sales in 1994 and 1993, respectively.

1994 Sales.: 401.9 mil.
1994 Net Inc.: 30.4 mil.
Common Shs.: 10,712,000
Long Term Debt: 0.01 mil.
Book Val. Per Sh.: 11.74 Dec '94
Latest Div.: None

	Share Earnings (Cal. Yr.)	Divs. Paid (Cal. Yr.)
1994	3.20	Nil
1993	[1]1.18	Nil
1992	[1]0.44	Nil
1991	NA	Nil

Interim Earnings: 9 Months
Sep. '95 d0.08 **Sep. '94** 2.73

Chrmn & CEO: G. P. Shlopak
Pres, COO & CFO: P. D. Brady
Office: 3 Pond Road
Gloucester, MA 01930
Tel: (508) 283-5800

Footnotes: 1. Pro Forma. d-Deficit.

Damark International

NASDAQ	Price	P-E Ratio	Dividend	Yield	Ranges		S&P Ranking
	Nov 14 '95				1995	1994	
DMRK	5¾	NM	None	None	9 - 5⅝	31 - 5¾	NR

Business: Damark International is a national direct marketer of brand name and other quality general merchandise in six major categories: home office, home decor, consumer electronics, home improvements and sporting goods/fitness. Its prices are generally below those set by dominant discount retailers, and it offers value and encourages customer loyalty through its membership club which, for an annual fee of $50, provides a 10% discount and other benefits. At 1994 year-end, there were about 874,000 customers in the membership club.

1994 Sales.: 477.4 mil.
1994 Net Inc.: 5.9 mil.
Common Shs.: 8,979,000
Long Term Debt: 0.25 mil.
Book Val. Per Sh.: 6.82 Dec '95
Latest Div.: None

	Share Earnings (Cal. Yr.)	Divs. Paid (Cal. Yr.)
1994	0.59	Nil
1993	0.67	Nil
1992	[1]d0.45	Nil
1991	0.15	Nil

Interim Earnings: 9 Months
Sep. '95 d0.41 **Sep. '94** 0.17

Chrmn & CEO: M. A. Cohn
VP-Fin, CFO, Treas & Secy: J. E. Tuller
Office: 7101 Winnetka Avenue
North
Brooklyn Park, MN 55428
Tel: (612) 531-0066

Footnotes: 1. Excl. special charge. d-Deficit.

Envoy Corp.

NASDAQ	Price	P-E Ratio	Dividend	Yield	Ranges		S&P Ranking
	Nov 14 '95				1995	1994	
ENVY	12⅝	NM	None	None	24¼ - 7¼	23 - 16¼	NR

Business: This company provides electronic transaction processing services to over 67,000 point-of-service locations in the financial services and health care markets. Services are delivered through an electronic processing system that has the ability to interface with a variety of point-of-service (POS) devices. In October 1995, the company agreed in principle to acquire National Electronic Information Corp., the largest processor and clearing house for electronic health care transactions, for an undisclosed amount.

1994 Sales.: 21.0 mil.
1994 Net Inc.: 4.2 mil.
Common Shs.: [1]11,024,000
Long Term Debt: None
Book Val. Per Sh.: 4.60 Sep '94
Latest Div.: None

	Share Earnings (Cal. Yr.)	Divs. Paid (Cal. Yr.)
1994	[1]0.36	Nil
1993	0.41	Nil
1992	0.38	Nil
1991	0.61	Nil

Interim Earnings: 9 Months
Sep. '95 d0.18 **Sep. '94** 0.32

Chrm: G. W. Loewenbaum
Pres & CEO: F. C. Goad
VP-Fin & CFO: D. R. Foutch
Office: Two Lakeview Place
15 Century Blvd.
Nashville, TN 37214
Tel: (615) 885-3700

Footnotes: 1. Pro Forma. d-Deficit.

Fastenal Company

NASDAQ	Price Nov 14 '95	P-E Ratio	Dividend	Yield	Ranges 1995	Ranges 1994	S&P Ranking
†FAST	37⅝	56	0.02	0.1%	40 - 19⅞	23 - 14½	B+

Business: Operating through more than 315 stores located in 42 states, primarily in the midwest and southern portions of the country, this company sells about 37,000 different types of threaded fasteners and other industrial and construction supplies. The company also operates nine FastTool stores located in seven states that sell tools and safety supplies. Officers and directors own about 40% of the outstanding common stock.

1994 Sales.: 161.9 mil.
1994 Net Inc.: 18.7 mil.
Common Shs.: 37,939,000
Long Term Debt: None
Book Val. Per Sh.: 1.78 Dec '94
Latest Div.: A0.02 Feb. '95
Cash Paid Each Year Since 1991

	Share Earnings (Cal. Yr.)	Divs. Paid (Cal. Yr.)
1994	0.49	0.02
1993	0.31	0.02
1992	0.24	0.02
1991	0.18	0.01

Interim Earnings: 9 Months
Sep. '95 0.53 **Sep. '94** 0.35

Chrm & Pres: R. A. Kierlin
Secy & Treas: S. M. Slaggie
Cntr: P. J. Rice
Office: 2001 Theurer Blvd.
Winona, MN 55987
Tel: (507) 454-5374

Footnotes: †Marginable.

Greenfield Industries

NASDAQ	Price Nov 14 '95	P-E Ratio	Dividend	Yield	Ranges 1995	Ranges 1994	S&P Ranking
GFII	28	16	0.16	0.6%	35½ - 20¾	24½ - 18¼	NR

Business: This company is a leading manufacturer of expendable cutting tools and related products used primarily in industrial applications, including rotary cutting tools, which constitute the majority of its sales; small diameter drills and routers used to manufacture circuit boards; carbide products; and consumer drill bits. In September 1995, GFII agreed to acquire Rule Industries, a manufacturer of expendable cutting tools, for $15.30 a share (about 2.6 million shares outstanding) plus assumption of about $39 million in debt.

1994 Sales.: 271.8 mil.
1994 Net Inc.: 22.0 mil.
Common Shs.: 16,250,000
Long Term Debt: 118.0 mil.
Book Val. Per Sh.: 3.34 Dec '94
Latest Div.: Q0.04 Dec. '95
Cash Paid Each Year Since 1993

	Share Earnings (Cal. Yr.)	Divs. Paid (Cal. Yr.)
1994	1.35	0.09
1993	[1]2.27	0.04
1992	[2,3]0.46	Nil
1991	NA	Nil

Interim Earnings: 9 Months
Sep. '95 1.42 **Sep. '94** 0.97

Chrmn: D. E. Nickerson
Pres & CEO: P. W. Jones
SVP, CFO & Secy: G. L. Weller
Office: 470 Old Evans Road
Augusta, Georgia 30809
Tel: (706) 863-7708

Footnotes: 1. Excl. special charge. 2. Pro Forma. 3. Before tax loss carryforward.

Heartland Express

NASDAQ	Price Nov 14 '95	P-E Ratio	Dividend	Yield	Ranges 1995	Ranges 1994	S&P Ranking
HTLD	31¾	22	None	None	33¼ - 24¾	36¾ - 24¼	B+

Business: Heartland Express is an irregular-route carrier authorized to transport general commodities in interstate commerce throughout the 48 contiguous states. At the end of 1994 it had 935 tractors and a fleet of 4,111 trailers, all 53-foot aluminum plate trailers. In 1994, it acquired Munson Transportation, which approximately doubled the company's annual revenues. The company reported that it had placed orders for about $20 million in revenue equipment in 1995.

1994 Sales.: 224.3 mil.
1994 Net Inc.: 10.1 mil.
Common Shs.: 13,017,000
Long Term Debt: 0.28 mil.
Book Val. Per Sh.: 6.00 Dec '94 Stk

	Share Earnings (Cal. Yr.)	Divs. Paid (Cal. Yr.)
1994	0.77	Nil
1993	[1]1.12	Nil
1992	0.93	Nil
1991	0.72	Nil

Interim Earnings: 9 Months
Sep. '95 1.19 **Sep. '94** 0.54

Chrmn, Pres, CEO & Secy: R. A. Gerdin
VP-Fin, CFO & Treas: J. P. Cosaert
Office: 2777 Heartland Drive
Coralville, Iowa 52241
Tel: (319) 645-2728

Footnotes: 1. Excl. special credit.

Hechinger Company

NASDAQ	Price Nov 14 '95	P-E Ratio	Dividend	Yield	Ranges 1995	Ranges 1994	S&P Ranking
HECHA	4⅝	NM	0.16	3.5%	13½ - 3⅜	16½ - 9	B-

Business: Hechinger Company is a leading specialty retailer of products and services for the care, repair, remodelling and maintenance of the home and garden. At January 29, 1994, it operated 72 Hechinger Stores home center stores of about 70,000 square feet located primarily in the mid-Atlantic region and 56 Home Quarters Warehouse stores of about 90,000 square feet primarily in the eastern and central parts of the U.S. In August 1995, the company said it planned to combine its Home Quarters and Hechinger stores in a cost-saving move.

1994 Sales.: 2449.6 mil.
1994 Net Inc.: d9.9 mil.
Common Shs.: [1]42,325,000
Long Term Debt: None
Book Val. Per Sh.: 10.07 Jan '95
Latest Div.: Q0.04 Nov. '95
Cash Paid Each Year Since 1983

	Share Earnings (Jan. Yr.)	Divs. Paid (Cal. Yr.)
1994	[1]d0.24	0.16
1993	[1]0.59	0.16
1992	[1]d0.63	0.16
1991	[1]0.66	0.16

Interim Earnings: 6 Months
Jul. '95 0.24 **Jul. '94** 0.60

Chrmn: J. W. Hechinger
Pres & CEO: J. W. Hechinger, Jr.
EVP & CFO: W. C. McClelland
Office: 3500 Pennsy Drive
Landover, Maryland 20785
Tel: (301)341-1000

Footnotes: 1. Combined various classes. d-Deficit.

Hollywood Park

NASDAQ	Price Nov 14 '95	P-E Ratio	Dividend	Yield	Ranges 1995	Ranges 1994	S&P Ranking
†HPRK	9⅝	NM	None	None	15 - 9	30¾ - 9¼	NR

Business: Formerly Hollywood Park Realty Enterprises, HPRK was formed through a merger with Hollywood Park Operating Company in January 1992. Through its subsidiaries, it owns and operates the Hollywood Park Race Track in Los Angeles County, the Hollywood Park casino style Card Club, and The Woodlands, a Kansas City thoroughbred and greyhound racing facility. In September 1995, the company finalized an agreement to begin developing the Crystal Park Hotel and Casino in an existing hotel and convention center in Compton, Calif.

1994 Sales.: 117.3 mil.
1994 Net Inc.: 3.8 mil.
Common Shs.: 18,370,000
Long Term Debt: 15.7 mil.
Book Val. Per Sh.: 8.79 Dec '94
Latest Div.: 0.05 Mar. '92

	Share Earnings (Cal. Yr.)	Divs. Paid (Cal. Yr.)
1994	0.10	Nil
1993	0.25	Nil
1992	[1]0.25	0.05
1991	[1]0.30	0.27

Interim Earnings: 9 Months
Sep. '95 d0.15 **Sep. '94** d0.02

Chrm & CEO: R. D. Hubbard
EVP & CFO: G. M. Finnigan
VP & Secy: W. B. Williamson
Office: 1050 South Prairie Ave.
Inglewood, CA 90301
Tel: (310) 419-1500

Footnotes: †Marginable. 1. Before tax loss carryforward. d-Deficit.

Hornbeck Offshore Services

NASDAQ	Price Nov 14 '95	P-E Ratio	Dividend	Yield	Ranges 1995	Ranges 1994	S&P Ranking
HOSS	15¼	22	None	None	17 - 8⅞	18⅝ - 11½	B-

Business: Primarily serving the oil and gas industry, this marine services company believes it operates the second largest fleet of supply ships in the Gulf of Mexico through its operation of 63 boats including supply, tug supply, crew, and specialty vessels. It also has a 49.9% interest in Ravensworth Investments Ltd and a 49.9% interest in Seaboard Holdings Ltd., which together own 29 vessels. In October 1995, Hornbeck terminated a proposed stock offering.

1994 Sales.: 45.8 mil.
1994 Net Inc.: 8.0 mil.
Common Shs.: 13,167,000
Long Term Debt: 18.9 mil.
Book Val. Per Sh.: 8.07 Dec '94
Latest Div.: None

	Share Earnings (Cal. Yr.)	Divs. Paid (Cal. Yr.)
1994	0.60	Nil
1993	[1]0.92	Nil
1992	0.01	Nil
1991	0.18	Nil

Interim Earnings: 9 Months
Sep. '95 0.41 **Sep. '94** 0.32

Chrm, Pres & CEO: L. D. Hornbeck
SVP & COO: B. W. Stewart
VP, CFO & Treas: R. W. Hampton
Office: 7707 Port Industrial Blvd.
Galveston, TX 77554
Tel: (409) 744-9500

Footnotes: 1. Excl. special charge.

IDEXX Laboratories, Inc.

NASDAQ	Price Nov 14 '95	P-E Ratio	Dividend	Yield	Ranges 1995	1994	S&P Ranking
IDXX	38⅝	70	None	None	44¾ - 16⅞	18⅝ - 12⅝	NR

Business: IDEXX Laboratories develops, manufactures and distributes biotechnology-based detection systems. The company also distributes chemistry-based detection systems. Most of IDXXs current products are directed towards animal health applications, however, it also develops and markets detection systems for food, water and environmental testing and products for biomedical research. In September 1995, the company completed a 4,000,000 common share offering at $35 a share, with proceeds earmarked for acquisitions or license technologies.

1994 Sales.: 126.4 mil.
1994 Net Inc.: 13.3 mil.
Common Shs.: [1]35,797,000
Long Term Debt: None
Book Val. Per Sh.: 2.90 Dec '94
Latest Div.: None

	Share Earnings (Cal. Yr.)	Divs. Paid (Cal. Yr.)
1994	0.40	Nil
1993	0.29	Nil
1992	0.18	Nil
1991	0.16	Nil

Interim Earnings: 9 Months
Sep. '95 0.42 **Sep. '94** 0.27

Chrmn & CEO: D. E. Shaw
Pres & COO: E. F. Workman Jr.
SVP, CFO & Treas: J. P. Deckro
Office: One IDEXX Drive
Westbrook, Maine 04092
Tel: (207) 856-0300

Footnotes: 1. Reflects new financing.

ImmuLogic Pharmaceutical

NASDAQ	Price Nov 14 '95	P-E Ratio	Dividend	Yield	Ranges 1995	1994	S&P Ranking
IMUL	12¼	NM	None	None	13½ - 6¼	15¼ - 6	NR

Business: ImmuLogic is a biopharmaceutical company developing products to treat allergies and autoimmune diseases, focusing on the mechanisms which initiate the immune response. IMUL is collaborating with Marion Merrell Dow on the commercialization of its ALLERVAX therapeutics to treat specific allergic diseases. In August 1995, the company sold 1 million shares to Amerindo Investment Advisors at $10 a share. In September 1995, IMUL offered 2.4 million shares at $10.75.

1994 Sales.: 6.3 mil.
1994 Net Inc.: d25.3 mil.
Common Shs.: [1]19,516,000
Long Term Debt: None
Book Val. Per Sh.: 4.15 Dec '94
Latest Div.: None

	Share Earnings (Cal. Yr.)	Divs. Paid (Cal. Yr.)
1994	d1.70	Nil
1993	d1.30	Nil
1992	d0.70	Nil
1991	d1.20	Nil

Interim Earnings: 9 Months
Sep. '95 d0.81 **Sep. '94** d1.25

Chrmn: M. L. Gefter
Pres & CEO: R. E. Bagley
VP & CFO: R. N. Small
Office: 610 Lincoln Street
Waltham, Massachusetts
02154
Tel: (617) 466-6000

Footnotes: 1. Reflects new financing. d-Deficit.

Interim Services

NASDAQ	Price Nov 14 '95	P-E Ratio	Dividend	Yield	Ranges 1995	1994	S&P Ranking
INTM	28⅞	20	None	None	31⅜ - 22⅝	28¼ - 20	NR

Business: This company is a national provider of temporary help personnel to businesses, professional and service organizations, government agencies and health care facilities and of home care services. It operates through a network of 771 company-owned, franchised and licensed offices in 46 states, the District of Columbia, Puerto Rico and Canada. In October 1995, the company acquired Juntunen Inc., a northern California provider of staffing services primarily to the information technology industry.

1994 Sales.: 634.4 mil.
1994 Net Inc.: 14.2 mil.
Common Shs.: 11,508,000
Long Term Debt: None
Book Val. Per Sh.: 7.56 Dec '95
Latest Div.: None

	Share Earnings (Cal. Yr.)	Divs. Paid (Cal. Yr.)
1994	1.24	Nil
1993	1.14	Nil
1992	[1]0.77	Nil
1991	NA	Nil

Interim Earnings: 9 Months
Sep. '95 1.03 **Sep. '94** 0.85

Chrmn: A. C. Sorenson
Pres & CEO: R. Marcy
VP & CFO: D. W. Ayers
Office: 2050 Spectrum Blvd.
Fort Lauderdale, FL 33309
Tel: (305) 938-7600

Footnotes: 1. Pro Forma.

Itron Inc.

NASDAQ	Price	P-E Ratio	Dividend	Yield	Ranges 1995	Ranges 1994	S&P Ranking
	Nov 14 '95						
ITRI	31¼	39	None	None	33½ - 18	23½ - 14	NR

Business: Itron is the largest supplier of data acquisition and wireless communications products for the meter reading and related data management needs of electric, gas and water utilities worldwide. ITRI designs, manufactures and markets products and systems for electronic meter reading, automatic meter reading, distribution automation and field service work order applications. In December 1994, it completed a public offering of 2.2 million common shares, about 1.9 million by holders, at $19 a share.

1994 Sales.: 120.7 mil.
1994 Net Inc.: 8.0 mil.
Common Shs.: 12,152,000
Long Term Debt: None
Book Val. Per Sh.: 6.24 Dec '94
Latest Div.: None

	Share Earnings (Cal. Yr.)	Divs. Paid (Cal. Yr.)
1994	0.67	Nil
1993	0.46	Nil
1992	[1]d0.58	Nil
1991	d0.31	Nil

Interim Earnings: 9 Months
Sep. '95 0.58 **Sep. '94** 0.44

Chrmn: P. A. Redmond
Pres & CEO: J. M. Humphries
VP & CFO: J. M. Thompson
Office: 2818 North Sullivan Road, Spokane, Washington 99216-1897
Tel: (509) 924-9900

Footnotes: 1. Excl. special credit. d-Deficit.

JSB Financial

NASDAQ	Price	P-E Ratio	Dividend	Yield	Ranges 1995	Ranges 1994	S&P Ranking
	Nov 14 '95						
JSBF	30⅞	15	1.00	3.2%	32 - 23¾	27½ - 22	NR

Business: This holding company, through its subsidiary, Jamaica Savings, operates as a federally chartered stock savings bank, through 13 offices, ten located in Queens, one in Manhattan and one each in Nassau County and Suffolk County. The bank also has a number of subsidiaries which own and operate properties, primarily apartment buildings acquired through foreclosures. Assets at September 30, 1995, totaled about $1.53 billion.

1994 Sales.: 109.8 mil.
1994 Net Inc.: 23.6 mil.
Common Shs.: 10,626,000
Long Term Debt: None
Book Val. Per Sh.: 30.67 Dec '94
Latest Div.: Q0.25 Nov. '95
Cash Paid Each Year Since 1990

	Share Earnings (Cal. Yr.)	Divs. Paid (Cal. Yr.)
1994	2.02	0.72
1993	[1]1.57	0.60
1992	1.89	0.52
1991	1.00	0.44

Interim Earnings: 9 Months
Sep. '95 1.46 **Sep. '94** 1.38

Chrmn & CEO: P. T. Adikes
Pres: E. P. Henson
CFO: T. R. Lehmann
Office: 303 Merrick Road, Lynbrook, New York 11563
Tel: (516) 887-7000

Footnotes: 1. Excl. special credit.

Keystone Financial

NASDAQ	Price	P-E Ratio	Dividend	Yield	Ranges 1995	Ranges 1994	S&P Ranking
	Nov 14 '95						
KSTN	32¼	13	1.36	4.2%	34 - 26¼	32¼ - 27¼	A-

Business: Keystone Financial is a bank holding company with seven banking subsidiaries operating in 27 Pennsylvania counties, two Maryland counties and one county in Virginia. Nonbank units provide brokerage, investment services, financial mortgage, insurance and community development activities. At December 31, 1994, assets totaled $4.71 billion. In July 1995, the company signed a definitive agreement to acquire Martindale Andres & Co., an asset management firm in Philadelphia, for an undisclosed amount.

1994 Sales.: 357.8 mil.
1994 Net Inc.: 51.4 mil.
Common Shs.: [1]24,000,000
Long Term Debt: 200.0 mil.
Book Val. Per Sh.: 17.46 Dec '94
Latest Div.: Q0.34 Oct. '95
Cash Paid Each Year Since 1985

	Share Earnings (Cal. Yr.)	Divs. Paid (Cal. Yr.)
1994	2.20	1.28
1993	2.49	1.16
1992	2.33	1.08
1991	2.27	1.00

Interim Earnings: 9 Months
Sep. '95 1.92 **Sep. '94** 1.60

Pres & CEO: C. L. Campbell
EVP, CFO & Treas: M. L. Pulaski
Office: P. O. Box 3660, One Keystone Plaza, Front & Market Sts., Harrisburg, PA 17105-3660
Tel: (717) 233-1555

Footnotes: 1. Pro Forma.

Landstar System

NASDAQ	Price Nov 14 '95	P-E Ratio	Dividend	Yield	Ranges 1995	Ranges 1994	S&P Ranking
LSTR	29¼	14	None	None	37¾ - 21¼	36 - 19¾	NR

Business: Landstar operates the third largest truckload carrier business in North America, throughout the continental U.S. and between the U.S. and Canada and Mexico. LSTR emphasizes information coordination and customer service delivered by a network of 900 independent agents and 30 company sales locations. About 87.8% of revenues in 1994 were generated through independent contractors. In the first quarter of 1995, LSTR acquired Intermodal Transport Co., LDS Truck Lines, T.L.C. Lines, and Express America Freight Systems.

1994 Sales.: 984.4 mil.
1994 Net Inc.: 24.4 mil.
Common Shs.: 12,778,000
Long Term Debt: 78.6 mil.
Book Val. Per Sh.: 5.66 Dec '94
Latest Div.: None

	Share Earnings (Cal. Yr.)	Divs. Paid (Cal. Yr.)
1994	1.90	Nil
1993	[1]1.14	Nil
1992	[2,1]0.78	Nil
1991	NA	Nil

Interim Earnings: 9 Months
Sep. '95 1.54 **Sep. '94** 1.33

Chrmn, Pres & CEO: J. C. Crowe
EVP & COO: E. R. Brown
VP & CFO: H. H. Gerkens
Office: First Selton Place, 1000 Bridgeport Avenue, Shelton, Connecticut 06484-0898
Tel: (203) 925-2900

Footnotes: 1. Excl. special charge. 2. Pro Forma.

Lincare Holdings

NASDAQ	Price Nov 14 '95	P-E Ratio	Dividend	Yield	Ranges 1995	Ranges 1994	S&P Ranking
LNCR	24⅛	14	None	None	35¼ - 21	29 - 18¾	NR

Business: Lincare is one of the largest providers of oxygen and other respiratory therapy services to home patients, serving over 35,000 customers in 27 states through 132 centers. Medicare accounted for 51% of revenues in 1994 and private insurance 25%. In February 1995, it said that it was the number two provider of respiratory care services to patients in the home. In July 1995, LNCR and Coram Healthcare, terminated their agreement to merge, originally made in April, but agreed to jointly offer their services in certain markets.

1994 Sales.: 201.1 mil.
1994 Net Inc.: 38.0 mil.
Common Shs.: 27,124,000
Long Term Debt: 6.7 mil.
Book Val. Per Sh.: 2.36 Dec '94
Latest Div.: None

	Share Earnings (Cal. Yr.)	Divs. Paid (Cal. Yr.)
1994	1.34	Nil
1993	1.01	Nil
1992	[1]0.64	Nil
1991	[2]0.13	Nil

Interim Earnings: 9 Months
Sep. '95 1.30 **Sep. '94** 0.96

Pres & CEO: J. T. Kelly
CFO & Secy: J. M. Emanuel
Office: 19337 U.S. 19 N., Suite 500, Clearwater, FL 34624
Tel: (813) 530-7700

Footnotes: 1. Excl. special charge. 2. Pro Forma.

Mariner Health Group

NASDAQ	Price Nov 14 '95	P-E Ratio	Dividend	Yield	Ranges 1995	Ranges 1994	S&P Ranking
MRNR	13	25	None	None	22⅛ - 8⅝	27⅛ - 15½	NR

Business: This company provides outcomes-oriented, subacute care services to patients who no longer require the extensive services of an acute care hospital. It operates 27 freestanding inpatient facilities with an aggregate of 3,174 beds, manages one freestanding inpatient facility with 150 beds and manages four subacute care units with 170 beds within general acute care hospitals. In October 1995, Mariner acquired six skilled nursing facilities with 686 beds in central and northern Florida for $42.8 million.

1994 Sales.: 215.5 mil.
1994 Net Inc.: 13.8 mil.
Common Shs.: 20,460,000
Long Term Debt: 27.4 mil.
Book Val. Per Sh.: 8.41 Dec '94
Latest Div.: None

	Share Earnings (Cal. Yr.)	Divs. Paid (Cal. Yr.)
1994	[1]0.45	Nil
1993	[2]0.47	Nil
1992	[2,1]d0.17	Nil
1991	NA	Nil

Interim Earnings: 9 Months
Sep. '95 0.29 **Sep. '94** 0.21

Chrmn, Pres & CEO: A. W. Stratton, Jr.
CFO & Treas: J. W. Knell
Office: 47 Water St., Mystic, CT 06355
Tel: (203) 441-2150

Footnotes: 1. Excl. special charge. 2. Pro Forma. d-Deficit.

Medaphis Corp.

NASDAQ	Price	P-E Ratio	Dividend	Yield	Ranges		S&P Ranking
	Nov 14 '95				1995	1994	
MEDA	32¾	NM	None	None	35 - 20¼	24 - 11¾	NR

Business: This company is a leading provider of business management services to some 13,300 hospital-affiliated physicians and about 650 hospitals. Services include facilities management, strategic management, financial management, and billing and accounts receivable management. In May 1995, MEDA acquired Medical Billing Service and assets of five affiliates for $15.5 million. In August 1995, MEDA acquired Healthcare Recoveries for about $79 million, and in October 1995, it agreed to acquire privately held Consort Technologies.

1994 Sales.: 253.5 mil.

1994 Net Inc.: 17.4 mil.

Common Shs.: [1]46,005,000

Long Term Debt: 74.8 mil.

Book Val. Per Sh.: Def. Dec '94

Latest Div.: None

Share Earnings (Cal. Yr.)		Divs. Paid (Cal. Yr.)
1994	0.57	Nil
1993	0.40	Nil
1992	[2,3]0.29	Nil
1991	0.23	Nil

Interim Earnings: 9 Months
Sep. '95 0.01 **Sep. '94** 0.40

Chrm, Pres & CEO: R. G. Brown

SVP & CFO: M. R. Cote

Office: 2700 Cumberland Pky.
Atlanta, GA 30339

Tel: (404) 319-3300

Footnotes: 1. Pro Forma. 2. Excl. special credit. 3. Excl. special charge.

Mesa Air Group Inc.

NASDAQ	Price	P-E Ratio	Dividend	Yield	Ranges		S&P Ranking
	Nov 14 '95				1995	1994	
†MESA	10⅜	30	None	None	12 - 4⅞	23 - 6	B

Business: This New Mexico-based commuter airline, through its seven airline systems, provides regularly scheduled service to 165 cities in various regions of the United States. MESA operates as a low-cost carrier offering one-class seating, high frequency and convenience for business and leisure travelers to service routes not generally served by major air carriers. In March 1995, MESA engaged a financial adviser to assist with alternatives to enhance shareholder value. In June 1995, MESA rejected an acquisition proposal by Continental Airlines.

1994 Sales.: 396.1 mil.

1994 Net Inc.: 27.3 mil.

Common Shs.: 32,859,000

Long Term Debt: 87.0 mil.

Book Val. Per Sh.: 6.43 Sep '94

Latest Div.: None

Share Earnings (Sep. Yr.)		Divs. Paid (Cal. Yr.)
1994	[1]0.75	Nil
1993	[1]0.73	Nil
1992	0.50	Nil
1991	[2]0.38	Nil

Interim Earnings: 9 Months
Jun. '95 0.19 **Jun. '94** 0.59

Chrm, Pres & CEO: L. L. Risley

VP & Secy: G. E. Risley

VP-Fin, Treas & CFO:
W. S. Jackson

Office: 2325 E. 30th St.
Farmington, NM 87401

Tel: (505) 327-0271

Footnotes: †Marginable. 1. Excl. special credit. 2. Before tax loss carryforward.

Microchip Technology

NASDAQ	Price	P-E Ratio	Dividend	Yield	Ranges		S&P Ranking
	Nov 14 '95				1995	1994	
MCHP	39⅞	32	None	None	44½ - 21¾	31⅝ - 12¾	NR

Business: Microchip Technology is the leading manufacturer of high-performance field-programmable 8-bit microcontrollers and related memory products for high-volume embedded control applications. Products are sold to the consumer, automotive, communications, office automation and industrial markets. In June 1995, MCHP announced plans to accelerate capital spending for wafer fabrication and testing capacity, adding $100,000,000 in capital expenses in fiscal 1996 (Mar.). In fiscal 1995, foreign sales represented 65% of net sales.

1994 Sales.: 208.0 mil.

1994 Net Inc.: 36.3 mil.

Common Shs.: 33,713,000

Long Term Debt: 14.9 mil.

Book Val. Per Sh.: 4.84 Mar '95

Latest Div.: None

Share Earnings (Mar. Yr.)		Divs. Paid (Cal. Yr.)
1994	1.05	Nil
1993	0.62	Nil
1992	0.19	Nil
1991	[1]0.02	Nil

Interim Earnings: 6 Months
Sep. '95 0.67 **Sep. '94** 0.48

Chrmn, Pres & CEO: S. Sanghi

VP, CFO & Secy: C. P. Chapman

Office: 2355 W. Chandler Blvd.
Chandler, Arizona 85224

Tel: (886) 786-7200

Footnotes: 1. Pro Forma.

Mycogen Corporation

NASDAQ	Price	P-E Ratio	Dividend	Yield	Ranges		S&P Ranking
	Nov 14 '95				1995	1994	
†MYCO	12½	NM	None	None	14¼ - 7¾	12 - 8	C

Business: Mycogen develops and markets environmentally compatible biopesticides and improved crop varieties. MYCO's strategy is to use its proprietary biotoxin gene technology to expand its biopesticide products and also with its other advanced plant science technology to develop pest-resistant crop varieties with improved food and fiber characteristics. In September 1995, MYCO and Pioneer Hi-Bred International signed a $51 million collaboration agreement which includes a proposed purchase of 13.5% of MYCO by Pioneer.

1995 Sales.: 113.3 mil.
1995 Net Inc.: d14.4 mil.
Common Shs.: 19,384,000
Long Term Debt: None
Book Val. Per Sh.: 5.44 Jun '95
Latest Div.: None

Share Earnings (Aug. Yr.)		Divs. Paid (Cal. Yr.)
1995	d0.83	---
1994	0.11	Nil
1993	d2.66	Nil
1992	d2.09	Nil

Interim Earnings:

Chrmn & CEO: J. D. Caulder
Pres & COO: C. J. Eibl
CFO: J. A. Baumker
Office: 5451 Oberlin Dr.
San Diego, CA 92121
Tel: (619) 453-8030

Footnotes: †Marginable. d-Deficit.

N.S. Bancorp

NASDAQ	Price	P-E Ratio	Dividend	Yield	Ranges		S&P Ranking
	Nov 14 '95				1995	1994	
NSBI	36⅛	14	0.32	0.9%	37½ - 26⅛	33 - 25¼	NR

Business: N.S. Bancorp owns the Northwestern Savings and Loan Association, which operates six full service offices including four in Chicago and one each in the Chicago suburbs of Berwyn and Norridge. The Association is a community-oriented savings institution that invests deposits primarily in one- to four-family mortgage loans. Total assets at September 30, 1995, amounted to $1.16 billion.

1994 Sales.: 78.3 mil.
1994 Net Inc.: 14.1 mil.
Common Shs.: 6,100,000
Long Term Debt: 62.7 mil.
Book Val. Per Sh.: 34.79 Dec '94
Latest Div.: Q0.08 Sep. '95
Cash Paid Each Year Since 1991

Share Earnings (Cal. Yr.)		Divs. Paid (Cal. Yr.)
1994	1.87	0.32
1993	3.31	0.32
1992	3.61	0.32
1991	2.46	0.32

Interim Earnings: 9 Months
Sep. '95 2.12 **Sep. '94** 1.42

Chrmn, Pres & CEO: H. Smogolski
VP, CFO & Treas: S. G. Skiba
EVP: A. J. Zych
Office: 2300 North Western Avenue
Chicago, Illinois 60647
Tel: (312) 489-2300

Footnotes:

NFO Research

NASDAQ	Price	P-E Ratio	Dividend	Yield	Ranges		S&P Ranking
	Nov 14 '95				1995	1994	
NFOR	23½	24	None	None	23⅝ - 14¼	17¼ - 12½	NR

Business: NFO Research provides custom market research services using a panel of about 450,000 pre-recruited consumer households. NFOR provides its services to a variety of nationally recognized packaged goods manufacturers, as well as telecommunications, financial services and pharmaceutical companies. In July 1995, the company said it signed contracts with Ipsos SA, a marketing research firm in Europe, to launch access panel activities in Europe. The venture is expected to have panels of 200,000 households when fully operational.

1994 Sales.: 61.5 mil.
1994 Net Inc.: 5.6 mil.
Common Shs.: 6,277,000
Long Term Debt: None
Book Val. Per Sh.: 0.59 Dec '94
Latest Div.: None

Share Earnings (Cal. Yr.)		Divs. Paid (Cal. Yr.)
1994	0.88	Nil
1993	[1]0.65	Nil
1992	[1]0.51	Nil
1991	NA	Nil

Interim Earnings: 9 Months
Sep. '95 0.74 **Sep. '94** 0.65

Chrmn, Pres & CEO: W. E. Lipner
Vice Chrmn & Secy: S. J. Gilbert
EVP-Fin & CFO: P. G. Healy
Office: 2 Pickwick Plaza
Greenwich, CT 06830
Tel: (203) 629-8888

Footnotes: 1. Pro Forma.

Nautica Enterprises

NASDAQ	Price Nov 14 '95	P-E Ratio	Dividend	Yield	Ranges 1995	1994	S&P Ranking
†NAUT	37¼	28	None	None	38¼ - 16¼	21⅝ - 13	B+

Business: Operating primarily through its Nautica International and State-O-Maine subsidiaries, this company designs, produces and sells men's sportswear, outerwear and activewear with an active outdoor image. In addition to its wholesale business, it operates 28 Nautica factory outlet stores, one company factory store and two flagship stores in New York City and Newport Beach, California. In September 1995, NAUT licensed Bernard Chaus Inc. to manufacture and market Nautica women's apparel, to be introduced in the fall of 1996.

1994 Sales.: 247.6 mil.
1994 Net Inc.: 24.0 mil.
Common Shs.: 19,851,000
Long Term Debt: 0.20 mil.
Book Val. Per Sh.: 7.01 Feb '95
Latest Div.: None

	Share Earnings (Feb. Yr.)	Divs. Paid (Cal. Yr.)
1994	1.15	Nil
1993	0.90	Nil
1992	0.60	Nil
1991	0.44	Nil

Interim Earnings: 6 Months
Aug. '95 0.55 **Aug. '94** 0.39

Chrm, Pres & CEO: H. Sanders
CFO: S. Burd
CFO: S. Burd
Office: 40 West 57th Street
New York, NY 10019
Tel: (212) 541-5757

Footnotes: †Marginable.

Norand Corp.

NASDAQ	Price Nov 14 '95	P-E Ratio	Dividend	Yield	Ranges 1995	1994	S&P Ranking
NRND	16¾	NM	None	None	48¼ - 16½	40¾ - 26¾	NR

Business: Norand designs, manufactures and markets mobile computing systems and wireless data communication networks using radio frequency technology used to automate the collection, processing and communication of information related to product sales and distribution, inventory control and warehouse data management. Systems and services include hand-held computers and radio-frequency terminals and other hardware, as well as application software, networks, related peripheral equipment and systems integration and support services.

1995 Sales.: 218.1 mil.
1995 Net Inc.: 0.08 mil.
Common Shs.: 7,500,000
Long Term Debt: None
Book Val. Per Sh.: 8.09 Jun '95
Latest Div.: None

	Share Earnings (Aug. Yr.)	Divs. Paid (Cal. Yr.)
1995	[1]0.01	---
1994	1.40	Nil
1993	1.81	Nil
1992	[2]0.68	Nil

Interim Earnings:

Pres & CEO: N. R. Hammer
VP, Treas & CFO: G. J. Sweas
Controller: R. A. Hurd
Office: 550 Second Street S.E.
Cedar Rapids, Iowa 52401
Tel: (319) 369-3100

Footnotes: 1. Preliminary. 2. Pro Forma.

Northwestern Steel & Wire

NASDAQ	Price Nov 14 '95	P-E Ratio	Dividend	Yield	Ranges 1995	1994	S&P Ranking
NWSW	7	7	None	None	10¼ - 5¾	13⅛ - 5½	NR

Business: This company is a major mini-mill producer of structural steel products, such as wide flange beams, light structural shapes and merchant bars; and rod and wire products, including nails, concrete reinforcing mesh, residential and agricultural fencing and other wire products. Mini-mills, which use electric arc furnaces pioneered by the company for steel making, melt steel scrap and cast the resultant molten metal into long strands of various shapes in a continuous casting process. Kohlberg & Co. owns about 35%.

1995 Sales.: 638.4 mil.
1995 Net Inc.: 27.0 mil.
Common Shs.: 24,849,000
Long Term Debt: 162.0 mil.
Book Val. Per Sh.: 3.14 Jul '95
Latest Div.: None

	Share Earnings (Jul. Yr.)	Divs. Paid (Cal. Yr.)
1995	1.07	---
1994	0.40	Nil
1993	[1]0.42	Nil
1992	[1]d0.90	Nil

Interim Earnings:

Chrmn: K. G. Davis
Pres & CEO: R. N. Gurnitz
SVP, CFO, Treas & Secy:
E. G. Maris
Office: 121 Wallace St.
Sterling, IL 61081
Tel: (815) 625-2500

Footnotes: 1. Pro Forma. d-Deficit.

Noven Pharmaceuticals

NASDAQ	Price Nov 14 '95	P-E Ratio	Dividend	Yield	Ranges 1995	1994	S&P Ranking
NOVN	9¾	NM	None	None	12⅜ - 6½	19¼ - 10¼	NR

Business: Noven is a leader in the development of transdermal drug delivery systems. It has developed and patented thin, solid state, multi-laminate transdermal systems that have a small surface area and the adaptability to deliver numerous drug entities, including for hormone replacement therapy, cardiovascular disease, dental pain management, anti-fungal therapy, asthma and anxiety disorders. In May 1995, NOVN filed a new drug application with the FDA for its patented transoral mucosal dental anesthetic delivery system.

1994 Sales.: 6.0 mil.
1994 Net Inc.: d4.9 mil.
Common Shs.: 19,038,000
Long Term Debt: None
Book Val. Per Sh.: 2.31 Dec '94
Latest Div.: None

	Share Earnings (Cal. Yr.)	Divs. Paid (Cal. Yr.)
1994	d0.28	Nil
1993	d0.21	Nil
1992	d0.21	Nil
1991	d0.25	Nil

Interim Earnings: 9 Months
Sep. '95 d0.29 **Sep. '94** d0.20

Chrmn, Pres & CEO: S. Sablotsky
CFO: W. A. Pecora
Office: 13300 S.W. 128th Street, Miami, Florida 33186
Tel: (305) 253-5099

Footnotes: d-Deficit.

ONBANCorp

NASDAQ	Price Nov 14 '95	P-E Ratio	Dividend	Yield	Ranges 1995	1994	S&P Ranking
ONBK	29¾	NM	1.12	3.8%	34½ - 21½	35¾ - 21¼	NR

Business: This holding company's principal subsidiary is OnBank, which offers diversified financial services to communities in upstate New York through 90 banking locations. At June 30, 1995, total assets were $6.5 billion, deposits were $3.7 billion and net loans were $2.1 billion. In June 1994, ONBK purchased nine branches of Columbia Banking Federal Savings Association of Rochester with $273 million in deposits, from the RTC.

1994 Sales.: 335.6 mil.
1994 Net Inc.: 2.7 mil.
Common Shs.: 14,077,000
Long Term Debt: None
Book Val. Per Sh.: 25.88 Dec '94
Latest Div.: Q0.28 Oct. '95
Cash Paid Each Year Since 1988

	Share Earnings (Cal. Yr.)	Divs. Paid (Cal. Yr.)
1994	d0.15	1.00
1993	[1]3.97	0.58
1992	3.19	0.40
1991	2.43	0.28

Interim Earnings: 9 Months
Sep. '95 2.06 **Sep. '94** 2.64

Chrm, Pres & CEO: R. J. Bennett
SVP, Treas & CFO: R. J. Berger
SVP & Secy: D. M. Dembowski
Office: 101 S. Salina St., Syracuse, NY 13202
Tel: (315) 424-4400

Footnotes: 1. Excl. special credit. d-Deficit.

Orbital Sciences Corp.

NASDAQ	Price Nov 14 '95	P-E Ratio	Dividend	Yield	Ranges 1995	1994	S&P Ranking
†ORBI	14⅝	NM	None	None	22 - 13½	26½ - 14	B-

Business: This company designs, manufactures, operates and markets a range of space products and develops and provides satellite-based services; spacecraft systems, space sensors and other payloads; space support products; and satellite services. In September 1995, ORBI agreed to acquire MacDonald, Dettwiler & Associates, a supplier of commercial space remote sensing ground stations. In September, ORBI and Teleglobe signed a final agreement for an expanded 36-satellite global communications system.

1994 Sales.: 222.0 mil.
1994 Net Inc.: 5.4 mil.
Common Shs.: 22,663,000
Long Term Debt: 95.2 mil.
Book Val. Per Sh.: 6.60 Dec '94
Latest Div.: None

	Share Earnings (Cal. Yr.)	Divs. Paid (Cal. Yr.)
1994	0.28	Nil
1993	[1]0.37	Nil
1992	0.33	Nil
1991	[2]0.10	Nil

Interim Earnings: 9 Months
Sep. '95 d0.03 **Sep. '94** 0.23

Chrmn, Pres & CEO: D. W. Thompson
VP-Fin & CFO: C. B. Crenshaw
SVP & Secy: L. C. Seeman
Office: 21700 Atlantic Blvd., Dulles, VA 20166
Tel: (703) 406-5000

Footnotes: †Marginable. 1. Excl. special credit. 2. Before tax loss carryforward. d-Deficit.

Patterson Dental

NASDAQ	Price Nov 14 '95	P-E Ratio	Dividend	Yield	Ranges 1995	Ranges 1994	S&P Ranking
PDCO	27⅛	24	None	None	29½ - 20	24¼ - 15¾	NR

Business: PDCO is the largest distributor of dental products in North America. It supplies over 50,000 products, including x-ray film and solutions, impression and restorative materials, hand instruments, and sterilization and protective products and equipment to dentists, dental laboratories and institutions. PDCO markets its products and services through more than 700 direct sales representatives and equipment specialists in the U.S. and Canada and ships about 97% of its consumable goods orders within 24 hours of receipt.

1995 Sales.: 532.6 mil.
1995 Net Inc.: 24.2 mil.
Common Shs.: 17,656,000
Long Term Debt: 3.1 mil.
Book Val. Per Sh.: 4.72 Apr '95
Latest Div.: None

	Share Earnings (Apr. Yr.)	Divs. Paid (Cal. Yr.)
1995	1.10	---
1994	0.87	Nil
1993	[1]0.62	Nil
1992	[2]0.38	Nil

Interim Earnings: 3 Months
Jul. '95 0.29 **Jul. '94** 0.24

Pres & CEO: P. L. Frechette
VP, Treas & CFO: R. E. Ezerski
Office: 1031 Mendota Heights Rd. St. Paul, MN 55120
Tel: (612) 636-1600

Footnotes: 1. Excl. special charge. 2. Pro Forma.

PerSeptive Biosystems

NASDAQ	Price Nov 14 '95	P-E Ratio	Dividend	Yield	Ranges 1995	Ranges 1994	S&P Ranking
PBIO	10⅛	NM	None	None	12⅝ - 4⅛	32¼ - 3¾	NR

Business: This company designs, manufactures and markets proprietary products and systems for the purification and analysis of biomolecules which are designed to reduce the time and cost in developing and manufacturing biopharmaceuticals. Products and systems are based on core technologies in the fields of perfusion chromatography, immunoassay, rational surface design, biological mass spectrometry, solid phase synthesis and magnetic separations. In November 1995, PBIO agreed to acquire PerSeptive Technologies II.

1994 Sales.: 46.1 mil.
1994 Net Inc.: d34.0 mil.
Common Shs.: [1]13,284,000
Long Term Debt: 27.2 mil.
Book Val. Per Sh.: 0.12 Sep '94
Latest Div.: None

	Share Earnings (Sep. Yr.)	Divs. Paid (Cal. Yr.)
1994	d2.88	Nil
1993	d0.10	Nil
1992	[1]d0.56	Nil
1991	[1]d0.76	Nil

Interim Earnings: 9 Months
Jun. '95 d1.81 **Jun. '94** d1.11

Chrm, Pres & CEO: N. B. Afeyan
SVP & CFO: T. G. Ruane
VP: J. Moore
Office: 500 Old Connecticut Path Framingham, MA 01701
Tel: (508) 383 7700

Footnotes: 1. Pro Forma. d-Deficit.

Pharmaceutical Marketing Service

NASDAQ	Price Nov 14 '95	P-E Ratio	Dividend	Yield	Ranges 1995	Ranges 1994	S&P Ranking
PMRX	13¼	32	None	None	16¼ - 7¾	17¾ - 6¾	NR

Business: This company provides to pharmaceutical concerns in the U.S., Europe and Japan a broad range of specialized marketing products and services that are generated from or enhanced by proprietary databases containing a unique combination of pharmaceutical market and medical prescriber data. Its prescriber profile databases contain extensive information on individual prescribers collected from physicians through self-administered surveys and are designed to enhance a user's ability to develop more effective marketing objectives and strategies.

1995 Sales.: 129.8 mil.
1995 Net Inc.: 5.2 mil.
Common Shs.: 13,085,000
Long Term Debt: 70.4 mil.
Book Val. Per Sh.: 2.09 Jun '95
Latest Div.: None

	Share Earnings (Jun. Yr.)	Divs. Paid (Cal. Yr.)
1995	0.40	---
1994	0.36	Nil
1993	0.54	Nil
1992	0.48	Nil

Interim Earnings: 3 Months
Sep. '95 d0.04 **Sep. '94** d0.06

Chrmn: H. E. Evans
Pres & COO: R. J. Frattaroli
CEO: D. M. J. Turner
Office: 2394 E. Camelback Rd. Phoenix, AZ 85016
Tel: (602) 381-9800

Footnotes: d-Deficit.

PictureTel Corp.

NASDAQ	Price Nov 14 '95	P-E Ratio	Dividend	Yield	Ranges 1995	Ranges 1994	S&P Ranking
PCTL	68¾	79	None	None	78¾ - 22¼	24½ - 10	NR

Business: PictureTel develops, manufactures and markets visual communications systems utilizing advanced video and audio compression technology which permit face-to-face meetings at a distance with the cost and convenience of the telephone. By operating over low speed switched digital lines, PCTL's systems have substantially reduced the cost and increased the flexibility of videoconferencing. In May 1995, PCTL and Nippon Telegraph and Telephone agreed to collaborate on development of a desktop system for Japanese markets.

1994 Sales.: 255.2 mil.
1994 Net Inc.: 4.6 mil.
Common Shs.: 16,089,000
Long Term Debt: 1.6 mil.
Book Val. Per Sh.: 9.98 Dec '94
Latest Div.: None

	Share Earnings (Cal. Yr.)	Divs. Paid (Cal. Yr.)
1994	0.29	Nil
1993	[1]0.47	Nil
1992	[1]0.53	Nil
1991	[2]0.29	Nil

Interim Earnings: 9 Months
Sep. '95 0.72 **Sep. '94** 0.14

Chrmn, Pres & CEO: N. E. Gaut
SVP, CFO & Secy: L. B. Strauss
Office: 222 Rosewood Drive
Danvers, Massachusetts
01923
Tel: (508) 762-5000

Footnotes: 1. Excl. special credit. 2. Before tax loss carryforward.

Platinum Software

NASDAQ	Price Nov 14 '95	P-E Ratio	Dividend	Yield	Ranges 1995	Ranges 1994	S&P Ranking
PSQL	6¾	NM	None	None	16⅞ - 4⅞	25¼ - 3½	NR

Business: Platinum Software designs, develops, markets and supports a broad range of integrated financial applications software products targeted for use by businesses of all sizes worldwide and designed primarily for use on client/server networked systems. Software products incorporate internationalized features to address the global market opportunities for financial and management information. In September 1994, PSQL raised $13.8 million through a private placement of 2.5 million Series B Preferred shares.

1995 Sales.: 56.2 mil.
1995 Net Inc.: d5.7 mil.
Common Shs.: 13,281,000
Long Term Debt: 15.8 mil.
Book Val. Per Sh.: Def. Jun '95
Latest Div.: None

	Share Earnings (Jun. Yr.)	Divs. Paid (Cal. Yr.)
1995	d0.44	---
1994	d4.80	Nil
1993	d1.52	Nil
1992	0.11	Nil

Interim Earnings: 3 Months
Sep. '95 d0.32 **Sep. '94** Nil

Chrmn & CEO: C. J. Samoro
Pres & COO: D. R. Proctor
CFO: M. J. Simmons
Office: 195 Technology Drive
Irvine, California 92718-2402
Tel: (714) 453-4000

Footnotes: d-Deficit.

Players International

NASDAQ	Price Nov 14 '95	P-E Ratio	Dividend	Yield	Ranges 1995	Ranges 1994	S&P Ranking
PLAY	14	12	None	None	23 - 10⅜	19¾ - 9½	NR

Business: This company, through subsidiaries, operates the Lake Charles, La. riverboat casino, Metropolis, Ill. riverboat casino, and the Paducah, Ken. racetrack. In February 1995, acquisition of the Showboat Star Riverboat Casino was approved by the Louisiana Riverboat Gaming Commission. In October 1995, the company said it would invest $130 million to further develop its Lake Charles facility with a new casino, parking garages and redesign the site's hotel and entertainment complex. In May 1995, PLAY effected a 3-for-2 stock split.

1994 Sales.: 223.7 mil.
1994 Net Inc.: 45.8 mil.
Common Shs.: 29,791,000
Long Term Debt: 150.0 mil.
Book Val. Per Sh.: 4.62 Mar '95
Latest Div.: None

	Share Earnings (Mar. Yr.)	Divs. Paid (Cal. Yr.)
1994	1.45	Nil
1993	[1]0.61	Nil
1992	d0.85	Nil
1991	d0.35	Nil

Interim Earnings: 6 Months
Sep. '95 0.47 **Sep. '94** 0.76

Chrmn & CEO: E. Fishman
Pres & COO: H. Goldberg
EVP, CFO & Secy: P. J. Aranow
Office: 800 Bilbo St.
Lake Charles, LA 70601
Tel: (318) 437-1560

Footnotes: 1. Excl. special credit. d-Deficit.

Plenum Publishing

NASDAQ	Price	P-E Ratio	Dividend	Yield	Ranges		S&P Ranking
	Nov 14 '95				1995	1994	
PLEN	36½	10	1.16	3.2%	36¾ - 29	32¼ - 22¼	B+

Business: This company publishes and distributes advanced scientific and technical materials, primarily books and journals. Its primary markets are public and private libraries, technically oriented corporations, research organizations and individual scientists, engineers, research workers, other professionals and graduate students throughout the world. In 1994, the company published 222 journals and 263 new book titles and had an active backlist of 3,800 books. Sales outside the U.S. accounted for 39% of total revenues in 1994.

1994 Sales.: 52.5 mil.
1994 Net Inc.: 12.7 mil.
Common Shs.: 3,942,000
Long Term Debt: None
Book Val. Per Sh.: 11.16 Dec '94
Latest Div.: Q0.29 Oct. '95
Cash Paid Each Year Since 1974

	Share Earnings (Cal. Yr.)	Divs. Paid (Cal. Yr.)
1994	2.87	1.11
1993	[1]2.37	0.81
1992	[2]2.57	1.29
1991	[2]3.43	0.98

Interim Earnings: 9 Months
Sep. '95 2.95 **Sep. '94** 1.97

Chrmn & Pres: M. E. Tash
CFO & Treas: G. A. Patel
Secy: E. Bressler
Office: 233 Spring St. New York, NY 10013
Tel: (212) 620-8000

Footnotes: 1. Excl. special charge. 2. Excl. special credit.

Proffitt's Inc.

NASDAQ	Price	P-E Ratio	Dividend	Yield	Ranges		S&P Ranking
	Nov 14 '95				1995	1994	
PRFT	28½	17	None	None	34¼ - 20¾	25¾ - 14¾	NR

Business: Proffitt's is a leading regional specialty department store chain offering moderate to better brand name fashion apparel, shoes, accessories, cosmetics, and decorative home furnishings. The Proffitt's division recently operated 25 stores in Tennessee, Virginia, Georgia, Kentucky and North Carolina, and the McRae's Division operated 28 stores in Alabama, Mississippi, Florida and Louisiana. In October 1995, PRFT agreed to acquire Younkers, a leading midwestern department store chain, in a stock swap valued at $207.9 million.

1994 Sales.: 617.4 mil.
1994 Net Inc.: 16.1 mil.
Common Shs.: 10,230,000
Long Term Debt: 187.0 mil.
Book Val. Per Sh.: 13.31 Jan '95
Latest Div.: None

	Share Earnings (Jan. Yr.)	Divs. Paid (Cal. Yr.)
1994	1.46	Nil
1993	[1,2]0.62	Nil
1992	1.02	Nil
1991	0.78	Nil

Interim Earnings: 6 Months
Jul. '95 0.28 **Jul. '94** 0.05

Chrmn & CEO: R. B. Martin
Pres & COO: J. A. Coggin
EVP, CFO & Treas: J. E. Glasscock
Office: P.O. Box 388 Alcoa, Tennessee 37701
Tel: (615) 983-7000

Footnotes: 1. Excl. special credit. 2. Excl. special charge.

Progress Software

NASDAQ	Price	P-E Ratio	Dividend	Yield	Ranges		S&P Ranking
	Nov 14 '95				1995	1994	
PRGS	60	21	None	None	70½ - 37¼	56¾ - 27	NR

Business: This company develops, markets and supports software application development tools consisting of a fourth generation programming language, a flexible relational database management system and associated software development tools. Its products improve programmer productivity and reduce the time to develop and maintain applications. In September 1995, PRGS' Board approved a 2-for-1 stock split to be paid November 27 and doubled its share repurchase authorization to 3 million shares.

1994 Sales.: 139.2 mil.
1994 Net Inc.: 14.4 mil.
Common Shs.: 6,406,000
Long Term Debt: 0.06 mil.
Book Val. Per Sh.: 14.33 Nov '94
Latest Div.: None

	Share Earnings (Nov. Yr.)	Divs. Paid (Cal. Yr.)
1994	2.23	Nil
1993	2.00	Nil
1992	1.52	Nil
1991	1.06	Nil

Interim Earnings: 9 Months
Aug. '95 1.55 **Aug. '94** 1.51

Pres & Treas: J. W. Alsop
VP-Fin: J. M. Mace
Office: 14 Oak Park Bedford, MA 01730
Tel: (617) 275-4500

Footnotes:

Protein Design Labs

NASDAQ	Price	P-E Ratio	Dividend	Yield	Ranges 1995	Ranges 1994	S&P Ranking
	Nov 14 '95						
PDLI	16⅝	NM	None	None	26¾ - 13⅛	29⅞ - 13¾	NR

Business: Protein Design Labs is engaged in the computer-based design of antibodies and other proteins to treat certain disease conditions, including viral infections, autoimmune conditions, inflammatory diseases and cancer. The company uses proprietary computer software to generate molecular models to design new antibodies and other proteins. In September 1995, PDLI began a second Phase II/III clinical trial with 325 patients to test its human anti-CMV antibody in AIDS patients with CMV retinitis.

1994 Sales.: 15.2 mil.
1994 Net Inc.: d5.2 mil.
Common Shs.: 15,248,000
Long Term Debt: None
Book Val. Per Sh.: 7.72 Dec '94
Latest Div.: None

Year	Share Earnings (Cal. Yr.)	Divs. Paid (Cal. Yr.)
1994	d0.37	Nil
1993	d0.47	Nil
1992	d0.07	Nil
1991	0.03	Nil

Interim Earnings: 9 Months
Sep. '95 d0.43 **Sep. '94** d0.28

Chrmn & CEO: L. J. Korn
Pres: J. S. Saxe
Treas & Cntr: H. J. Voelkel
Office: 2375 Garcia Ave.
Mountain View, CA 94043
Tel: (415) 903-3700

Footnotes: d-Deficit.

Provident Bancorp

NASDAQ	Price	P-E Ratio	Dividend	Yield	Ranges 1995	Ranges 1994	S&P Ranking
	Nov 14 '95						
PRBK	42¼	11	1.10	2.6%	42⅝ - 30½	36½ - 27¾	B+

Business: This bank holding company's subsidiaries operate 72 branch offices throughout Ohio, northern Kentucky and southeastern Indiana. Its lead bank is Provident Bank, the fourth largest commercial bank in Cincinnati. At September 30, 1995, assets totaled $6.0 billion. Subsidiaries provide equipment leasing, securities brokerage and investment management services. In May 1995, directors authorized the repurchase of up to 200,000 PRBK common shares.

1994 Sales.: 382.3 mil.
1994 Net Inc.: 57.7 mil.
Common Shs.: 15,566,000
Long Term Debt: 460.0 mil.
Book Val. Per Sh.: 20.62 Dec '94
Latest Div.: Q0.28 Nov. '95
Cash Paid Each Year Since 1985

Year	Share Earnings (Cal. Yr.)	Divs. Paid (Cal. Yr.)
1994	3.40	0.94
1993	3.09	0.82
1992	[1]3.00	0.68
1991	[2]0.93	0.53

Interim Earnings: 9 Months
Sep. '95 3.15 **Sep. '94** 2.52

Chrm, Pres & CEO: A. L. Davis
VP & CFO: J. R. Farrenkopf
Treas: J. L. Grace
Office: 1 East Fourth St.
Cincinnati, OH 45202
Tel: (513) 579-2000

Footnotes: 1. Excl. special charge. 2. Pro Forma.

Pure Tech International

NASDAQ	Price	P-E Ratio	Dividend	Yield	Ranges 1995	Ranges 1994	S&P Ranking
	Nov 14 '95						
PURT	2⅜	NM	None	None	6⅝ - 2⅛	14 - 5⅛	NR

Business: The company's principal business is the plastic injection molding of custom parts using both recycled and virgin materials. During fiscal 1994, it decided to dispose of or discontinue its operations involving the sale of recycled glass, aluminum and steel. In August 1995, the company acquired Occidental Chemical Corp.'s specialty vinyl dispersion resins plant in Burlington, N.J., for $20 million plus about $8 million for inventory.

1995 Sales.: 54.0 mil.
1995 Net Inc.: d16.9 mil.
Common Shs.: [1]26,431,000
Long Term Debt: 7.2 mil.
Book Val. Per Sh.: Def. Dec '94
Latest Div.: None

Year	Share Earnings (Jul. Yr.)	Divs. Paid (Cal. Yr.)
1995	[2,3]d0.95	---
1994	[3]d3.93	Nil
1993	[3]0.19	Nil
1992	[3]0.19	Nil

Interim Earnings:

President & COO: D. Katz
VP & CFO: M. Nafash
Secy/Treas: M. Fox
Office: 100 Franklin Square Drive
Somerset, New Jersey
08873
Tel: (908) 302-1000

Footnotes: 1. Pro Forma. 2. Preliminary. 3. Combined various classes. d-Deficit.

RailTex Inc.

NASDAQ	Price	P-E Ratio	Dividend	Yield	Ranges		S&P Ranking
	Nov 14 '95				1995	1994	
RTEX	19¼	26	None	None	29½ - 17¼	31½ - 15⅝	NR

Business: RailTex is the leading operator of short line freight railroads in North America, operating, through 20 subsidiaries, 25 railroads covering more than 3,400 miles of track in 20 states, Canada and Mexico. The company's strategy is to diversify further its portfolio of short line railroad properties and to improve the performance of its properties by focusing on improved customer service and operating efficiency. In May 1995, RTEX announced that it was constructing an intermodal terminal in Southwest Missouri.

1994 Sales.: 74.5 mil.
1994 Net Inc.: 6.9 mil.
Common Shs.: 9,091,000
Long Term Debt: 46.6 mil.
Book Val. Per Sh.: 10.11 Dec '94
Latest Div.: None

Share Earnings (Cal. Yr.)		Divs. Paid (Cal. Yr.)
1994	0.88	Nil
1993	0.65	Nil
1992	0.52	Nil
1991	0.39	Nil

Interim Earnings: 9 Months
Sep. '95 0.50 **Sep. '94** 0.63

CEO: B. M. Flohr
Pres & COO: H. M. Chidgey
VP * CFO: R. R. Lende
Office: 4040 Broadway, Suite 200
San Antonio, Texas 78209
Tel: (210) 841-7600

Footnotes:

Resound Corp.

NASDAQ	Price	P-E Ratio	Dividend	Yield	Ranges		S&P Ranking
	Nov 14 '95				1995	1994	
RSND	7¾	NM	None	None	10⅝ - 6¾	23½ - 5	NR

Business: This company designs, develops, manufactures and sells technologically advanced hearing devices for the hearing impaired. Its products, which are offered in both in-the-ear and behind-the-ear versions, continuously adjust the amplification of sounds according to the acoustic environment and the patients' range of hearing. In October 1995, RSND agreed to pay A&L Technology $7 million and release a claim on a $2.8 million royalty payment to A&L to settle a patent suit.

1994 Sales.: 62.3 mil.
1994 Net Inc.: d14.3 mil.
Common Shs.: 15,470,000
Long Term Debt: 25.0 mil.
Book Val. Per Sh.: Def. Dec '94
Latest Div.: None

Share Earnings (Cal. Yr.)		Divs. Paid (Cal. Yr.)
1994	d0.95	Nil
1993	[1]0.35	Nil
1992	[1]d0.08	Nil
1991	NA	Nil

Interim Earnings: 9 Months
Sep. '95 d0.37 **Sep. '94** 0.22

Chrmn: R. Perkins
Pres & CEO: J. J. Gallogly
SVP-Fin & CFO: P. A. Busse
Office: 220 Saginaw Dr.
Seaport Center
Redwood City, CA 94063
Tel: (415) 780-7800

Footnotes: 1. Pro Forma. d-Deficit.

Richfood Holdings Inc.

NASDAQ	Price	P-E Ratio	Dividend	Yield	Ranges		S&P Ranking
	Nov 14 '95				1995	1994	
†RCHF	26½	20	0.12	0.5%	26⅞ - 15¾	18½ - 13⅜	NR

Business: This Virginia-based concern is the largest wholesale food distributor in the Mid-Atlantic region, serving about 1,500 stores throughout the region. Richfood operates a combination leased and owned fleet of 305 tractors, 320 refrigerated trailers and 186 dry trailers. In October 1995, RCHF acquired Super Rite Corp. The combined company is expected to have annual net sales in excess of $3 billion.

1995 Sales.: 1520.5 mil.
1995 Net Inc.: 25.4 mil.
Common Shs.: [1]31,229,000
Long Term Debt: 49.3 mil.
Book Val. Per Sh.: 4.07 Apr '95
Latest Div.: Q0.03 Dec. '95
Cash Paid Each Year Since 1991

Share Earnings (Apr. Yr.)		Divs. Paid (Cal. Yr.)
1995	[2]1.19	0.11
1994	[2]0.81	0.09
1993	[2]0.75	0.08
1992	[2]0.66	0.06

Interim Earnings: 6 Months
Oct. '95 0.60 **Oct. '94** 0.48

Chrmn, Pres & CEO: D. D. Bennett
Pres & COO: J. E. Stokely
SVP & CFO: J. Marklin
Office: 2000 Richfood Rd.
Richmond, VA 23261
Tel: (804) 746-6000

Footnotes: †Marginable. 1. Pro Forma. 2. Combined various classes.

Roosevelt Financial Group

NASDAQ	Price Nov 14 '95	P-E Ratio	Dividend	Yield	Ranges 1995	Ranges 1994	S&P Ranking
†RFED	16½	11	0.56	3.4%	18⅞ - 14⅝	18¼ - 12⅜	NR

Business: Operating through Roosevelt Bank FSB, RFED has 40 offices in metropolitan St. Louis, Missouri and a total of 80 offices. At June 30, 1995, assets were $8.96 billion, deposits were $4.79 billion, and loans were $3.3 billion. In June 1995, the company agreed to acquire Kirksville Bancshares (assets of $137 million) for about 1.5 million RFED common shares. In September 1995, shareholders of WSB Bancorp (assets of $97 million) approved of a merger with Roosevelt in a transaction valued at $25 million.

1994 Sales.: 522.2 mil.
1994 Net Inc.: 31.6 mil.
Common Shs.: 40,272,000
Long Term Debt: 2210.0 mil.
Book Val. Per Sh.: 11.00 Dec '94
Latest Div.: Q0.14 Nov. '95
Cash Paid Each Year Since 1988

	Share Earnings (Cal. Yr.)	Divs. Paid (Cal. Yr.)
1994	[1]0.70	0.43
1993	[1]1.97	0.32
1992	1.02	0.21
1991	[1]0.52	0.20

Interim Earnings: 9 Months
Sep. '95 1.09 **Sep. '94** 0.19

Chrm: C. M. Turley, Jr.
Pres & CEO: S. J. Bradshaw
EVP & CFO: G. W. Douglass
Office: 900 Roosevelt Pkwy.
Chesterfield, MO 63017
Tel: (314) 532-6200

Footnotes: †Marginable. 1. Excl. special charge.

STERIS Corp.

NASDAQ	Price Nov 14 '95	P-E Ratio	Dividend	Yield	Ranges 1995	Ranges 1994	S&P Ranking
STRL	37½	69	None	None	43 - 14⅞	20 - 8⅜	NR

Business: STERIS Corp. develops, manufacturers and markets sterile processing and infection prevention systems, related consumables and accessories and services for the health care industry. The company's proprietary liquid chemical technology destroys microorganisms on inanimate surfaces rapidly at low temperatures. In January 1995, the EPS accepted expanded product claims for STRL's proprietary technology, enabling STRL to begin U.S. sales of its EcoCycle 10 System. STRL also recently introduced the Safecycle 40 System.

1994 Sales.: 64.3 mil.
1994 Net Inc.: 8.7 mil.
Common Shs.: 17,808,000
Long Term Debt: None
Book Val. Per Sh.: 2.36 Mar '95
Latest Div.: None

	Share Earnings (Mar. Yr.)	Divs. Paid (Cal. Yr.)
1994	0.46	Nil
1993	[1]0.28	Nil
1992	0.16	Nil
1991	[2]0.01	Nil

Interim Earnings: 6 Months
Sep. '95 0.28 **Sep. '94** 0.20

Chrmn, Pres, CEO & Treas:
B. R. Sanford
SVP: J. L. Breedlove
SVP, CFO & Secy:
M. A. Keresman III
Office: 5960 Heisley Road
Mentor, Ohio 44060
Tel: (216) 354-2600

Footnotes: 1. Excl. special credit. 2. Pro Forma.

St. Mary Land & Exploration

NASDAQ	Price Nov 14 '95	P-E Ratio	Dividend	Yield	Ranges 1995	Ranges 1994	S&P Ranking
MARY	13¼	NM	0.16	1.2%	14⅞ - 10⅞	14⅜ - 10⅞	NR

Business: This company is engaged in oil and gas exploration, development and production in the U.S. and various foreign countries including Russia, Chile, Argentina, Papua, New Guinea, the Philippines and Trinidad and Tobago. In the U.S, it has producing properties in major oil and gas provinces such as the onshore Gulf Coast of Louisiana, the Anadarko Basin of Oklahoma, the Williston Basin of North Dakota and Montana, the Powder River Basin of Wyoming and areas of south Texas, comprising 24,900 fee acres and 779,600 leasehold acres.

1994 Sales.: 44.8 mil.
1994 Net Inc.: 3.7 mil.
Common Shs.: 8,760,000
Long Term Debt: 11.5 mil.
Book Val. Per Sh.: 7.54 Dec '94
Latest Div.: Q0.04 Nov. '95
Cash Paid Each Year Since 1993

	Share Earnings (Cal. Yr.)	Divs. Paid (Cal. Yr.)
1994	0.43	0.16
1993	[1]0.39	0.16
1992	2.16	Nil
1991	[2]0.56	Nil

Interim Earnings: 9 Months
Sep. '95 0.19 **Sep. '94** 0.65

Chrmn: T. E. Congdon
Pres, CEO & CFO: M. A. Hellerstein
VP-Fin & Treas: R. C. Norris
Office: 1776 Lincoln St.
Suite 1100
Denver, CO 80203
Tel: (303) 861-8140

Footnotes: 1. Excl. special credit. 2. Pro Forma.

Shoe Carnival

NASDAQ	Price Nov 14 '95	P-E Ratio	Dividend	Yield	Ranges 1995	Ranges 1994	S&P Ranking
SCVL	3⅞	NM	None	None	7½ - 3½	13⅜ - 4¾	NR

Business: Shoe Carnival is a leading retailer of family footwear that combines value pricing, broad merchandise selection and carnival-like entertainment to generate high-volume sales with a low cost structure. SCVL recently had 57 stores in 15 states. In October 1994, SCVL planned to open 15-20 new stores in 1995, with about six to open in the first half of the year. In February 1995, SCVL changed its fiscal year end to the Saturday nearest January 31, and the SCVL board authorized the repurchase of up to $5 million common shares.

1994 Sales.: 214.5 mil.
1994 Net Inc.: 1.2 mil.
Common Shs.: 13,019,000
Long Term Debt: 15.9 mil.
Book Val. Per Sh.: 5.32 Oct '94
Latest Div.: None

	Share Earnings (Jan. Yr.)	Divs. Paid (Cal. Yr.)
1994	[1]0.09	Nil
1993	[2]0.55	Nil
1992	[2]0.55	Nil
1991	NA	Nil

Interim Earnings: 6 Months
Jul. '95 0.07 **Jul. '94** 0.11

Chrmn: J. W. Weaver
Pres & CEO: D. H. Russell
EVP-CFO, Treas & Asst Secy: M. H. Lemond
Office: 8233 Baumgart Road Evansville, Indian 47711
Tel: (812) 867-6471

Footnotes: 1. Preliminary. 2. Pro Forma.

ShowBiz Pizza Time

NASDAQ	Price Nov 14 '95	P-E Ratio	Dividend	Yield	Ranges 1995	Ranges 1994	S&P Ranking
†SHBZ	12¾	NM	None	None	13⅝ - 7¼	15¼ - 7¼	NR

Business: ShowBiz Pizza Time recently operated 219 ShowBiz Pizza Place restaurants and Chuck E. Cheese's Pizza Time Theatre restaurants; 108 were franchises. Restaurants offer pizza, sandwiches, salads, Italian dishes and other casual menu items and feature entertainment by life-size, computer-controlled robotic characters, family oriented games, rides and arcade activities. The company attributed lower sales in recent quarters to the sale of its Monterey Tex-Mex Cafe restaurants.

1994 Sales.: 267.8 mil.
1994 Net Inc.: 0.68 mil.
Common Shs.: 12,215,000
Long Term Debt: 29.1 mil.
Book Val. Per Sh.: 10.23 Dec '94
Latest Div.: None

	Share Earnings (Cal. Yr.)	Divs. Paid (Cal. Yr.)
1994	0.03	Nil
1993	0.86	Nil
1992	1.11	Nil
1991	1.28	Nil

Interim Earnings: 9 Months
Sep. '95 0.10 **Sep. '94** 0.45

Chrm & CEO: R. M. Frank
Pres & COO: J. T. Spaight
EVP & CFO: M. H. Magusiak
Office: 4441 W. Airport Freeway P.O. Box 152077 Irving, TX 75015
Tel: (214) 258-8507

Footnotes: †Marginable.

Southern Energy Homes

NASDAQ	Price Nov 14 '95	P-E Ratio	Dividend	Yield	Ranges 1995	Ranges 1994	S&P Ranking
SEHI	15¼	13	None	None	17 - 8⅜	15¼ - 8¼	NR

Business: Southern Energy Homes is a producer of manufactured homes sold in the southeastern and southcentral United States. The company operates six manufacturing facilities in Alabama and one in Texas to produce homes sold in 24 states. Homes are constructed to buyers's specifications. Homes are sold under five brand names through approximately 430 independent dealers. In October 1995, SEHI filed for a public offering of 1,685,000 common shares, 500,000 by the company and 1,185,000 by selling stockholders.

1994 Sales.: 188.8 mil.
1994 Net Inc.: 8.8 mil.
Common Shs.: [1]9,941,000
Long Term Debt: 0.06 mil.
Book Val. Per Sh.: 3.30 Dec '94
Latest Div.: None

	Share Earnings (Cal. Yr.)	Divs. Paid (Cal. Yr.)
1994	0.94	Nil
1993	[2]0.86	Nil
1992	[2]0.55	Nil
1991	Nil	Nil

Interim Earnings: 9 Months
Sep. '95 0.91 **Sep. '94** 0.70

Chrmn: J. O. Lee
Pres & CEO: W. E. Batchelor
CFO, Treas & Secy: K. W. Brown
Office: P. O. Box 269 Addison, Alabama 35540
Tel: (205) 747-1544

Footnotes: 1. Reflects new financing. 2. Pro Forma.

Sovereign Bancorp

NASDAQ	Price Nov 14 '95	P-E Ratio	Dividend	Yield	Ranges 1995	Ranges 1994	S&P Ranking
SVRN	10⅜	10	0.09	0.9%	10¾ - 7⅜	11½ - 7⅜	NR

Business: Sovereign Bancorp is the holding company for Sovereign Bank, a Federal Savings Bank, and Sovereign Investment Corporation. Sovereign Bancorp had total assets as of June 30, 1995, of $7.3 billion. In January 1995, SVRN agreed to sell seven New Jersey offices to Collective Bank and will assume about $8.9 million in deposits and receive a net deposit premium of about $7.8 million. In October 1995, it agreed to acquire West Jersey Bancshares ($100 million in assets) for about $17.2 million in stock.

1994 Sales.: 368.7 mil.
1994 Net Inc.: 46.4 mil.
Common Shs.: 46,110,000
Long Term Debt: 270.0 mil.
Book Val. Per Sh.: 5.00 Dec '94
Latest Div.: Q0.02 Nov. '95
Cash Paid Each Year Since 1987

Year	Share Earnings (Cal. Yr.)	Divs. Paid (Cal. Yr.)
1994	0.95	0.09
1993	[1]0.74	0.06
1992	0.54	[2]0.07
1991	0.40	[2]0.04

Interim Earnings: 9 Months
Sep. '95 0.77 **Sep. '94** 0.71

Chrmn: F. J. Jaindl
Pres & CEO: A. A. Harberberger
CFO & Treas: K. D. Gerhart
Office: 1130 Berkshire Boulevard, Wyomissing, Pennsylvania 19610
Tel: (213) 320-8400

Footnotes: 1. Excl. special credit. 2. Also stock.

Stein Mart

NASDAQ	Price Nov 14 '95	P-E Ratio	Dividend	Yield	Ranges 1995	Ranges 1994	S&P Ranking
SMRT	11⅞	17	None	None	15 - 9¼	21½ - 12¼	NR

Business: This company recently operated 80 retail stores in shopping centers in metropolitan areas in 16 states that offer a focused assortment of moderate to designer brand-name apparel for women, men and children, as well as accessories, gifts, linens and shoes at prices typically 25% to 60% below those charged by traditional department and fine specialty stores. SMRT opened 14 new stores in 1994 and planned to open 17 in 1995.

1995 Sales.: 116.5 mil.
1995 Net Inc.: NA
Common Shs.: 22,460,000
Long Term Debt: 20.5 mil.
Book Val. Per Sh.: 3.72 Apr '95
Latest Div.: None

Year	Share Earnings (Cal. Yr.)	Divs. Paid (Cal. Yr.)
1995	NA	---
1994	0.78	Nil
1993	0.70	Nil
1992	[1]0.61	Nil

Interim Earnings: 9 Months
Sep. '95 0.24 **Sep. '94** 0.30

Chrmn & CEO: J. Stein
Pres & COO: J. H. Williams, Jr.
SVP-Fin: J. G. Delfs
Office: 1200 Gulf Life Dr., Jacksonville, FL 32207
Tel: (904) 346-1500

Footnotes: 1. Pro Forma.

TECNOL Medical Products

NASDAQ	Price Nov 14 '95	P-E Ratio	Dividend	Yield	Ranges 1995	Ranges 1994	S&P Ranking
TCNL	17⅝	24	None	None	23 - 14¼	17½ - 12¼	NR

Business: TECNOL Medical Products designs, develops, manufactures and markets innovative, disposable medical products, including disposable face masks, ice packs, patient safety restraints, orthopedic products and others. The company sells through multiple distribution channels to hospitals, dentist offices, alternate site health care facilities, and industrial clean rooms.

1994 Sales.: 120.8 mil.
1994 Net Inc.: 16.9 mil.
Common Shs.: 19,918,000
Long Term Debt: 14.8 mil.
Book Val. Per Sh.: 2.89 Dec '94
Latest Div.: None

Year	Share Earnings (Nov. Yr.)	Divs. Paid (Cal. Yr.)
1994	0.85	Nil
1993	0.68	Nil
1992	0.61	Nil
1991	0.50	Nil

Interim Earnings: 9 Months
Aug. '95 0.48 **Aug. '94** 0.60

Pres & CEO: V. Hubbard
COO & General Counsel: D. Radunsky
Office: 7201 Industrial Park Blvd., Fort Worth, TX 76180
Tel: (817) 581-6424

Footnotes:

TNT Freightways

NASDAQ	Price Nov 14 '95	P-E Ratio	Dividend	Yield	Ranges 1995	Ranges 1994	S&P Ranking
TNTF	19¾	12	0.37	1.9%	28⅝ - 16¼	29¾ - 19¼	NR

Business: TNT Freightways operates a group of regional less than truckload general commodities motor carriers. Regional trucking subsidiaries focus on overnight and second day delivery and provide service throughout the continental U.S., Hawaii, and to certain points in Canada. Logistics subsidiaries provide management and distribution services. At the end of 1994, the company had 201 terminals and operated 5,087 tractors and 11,074 trailers. In June 1995, TNTF formed a new long haul unit to begin service in January 1996.

1994 Sales.: 1016.5 mil.
1994 Net Inc.: 32.1 mil.
Common Shs.: 21,854,000
Long Term Debt: 122.0 mil.
Book Val. Per Sh.: 6.19 Dec '94
Latest Div.: Q0.09 Oct. '95
Cash Paid Each Year Since 1992

	Share Earnings (Cal. Yr.)	Divs. Paid (Cal. Yr.)
1994	1.45	0.37
1993	1.20	0.37
1992	[1]0.79	0.19
1991	0.63	Nil

Interim Earnings: 9 Months
Sep. '95 1.20 **Sep. '94** 1.04

Chrmn: M. Koffman
Pres & CEO: J. C. Carruth
SVP & CFO: C. L. Ellis
Office: 9700 Higgins Rd. Suite 570, Rosemont, IL 60018
Tel: (708) 696-0200

Footnotes: 1. Excl. special charge.

Taco Cabana

NASDAQ	Price Nov 14 '95	P-E Ratio	Dividend	Yield	Ranges 1995	Ranges 1994	S&P Ranking
TACO	5¾	NM	None	None	9⅛ - 4⅜	20 - 7¼	NR

Business: This company operates the largest chain of Mexican patio cafe style restaurants in the U.S., with 107 restaurants located primarily in Texas and also in seven other states. The company also operates four Mexican patio cafes. An additional 19 Taco Cabana and six Two Pesos restaurants are operated by franchises. Expansion plans call for the opening of 15 to 18 restaurants in the first three quarters of 1995. In June 1995, the board adopted a preferred stock purchase rights plan.

1994 Sales.: 127.3 mil.
1994 Net Inc.: 8.5 mil.
Common Shs.: 15,564,000
Long Term Debt: 18.4 mil.
Book Val. Per Sh.: 4.33 Jan '95
Latest Div.: None

	Share Earnings (Cal. Yr.)	Divs. Paid (Cal. Yr.)
1994	[1]0.55	Nil
1993	[1]0.55	Nil
1992	[1]0.41	Nil
1991	[1,2]0.57	Nil

Interim Earnings: 9 Months
Sep. '95 d0.27 **Sep. '94** 0.44

Pres & CEO: R. Cervera
VP-Fin, CFP, Treas & Secy: D. G. Lloyd
Office: 262 Losoya, Suite 330, San Antonio, TX 78205
Tel: (210) 231-8226

Footnotes: 1. Combined various classes. 2. Pro Forma. d-Deficit.

Trenwick Group Inc.

NASDAQ	Price Nov 14 '95	P-E Ratio	Dividend	Yield	Ranges 1995	Ranges 1994	S&P Ranking
†TREN	50⅜	12	1.12	2.2%	53 - 40¾	43⅞ - 33¼	B

Business: This company's subsidiaries are primarily involved in underwriting negotiated reinsurance of individual risks to commercial insurers and captive insurance companies in the U.S. Trenwick also provides underwriting management and services related to the reinsurance business and is licensed to write reinsurance in 49 states and the District of Columbia. TREN had net premiums written of $139.6 million in 1994 ($101.4 million in 1993).

1994 Sales.: 166.4 mil.
1994 Net Inc.: 20.3 mil.
Common Shs.: 6,491,000
Long Term Debt: 104.0 mil.
Book Val. Per Sh.: 29.23 Dec '94
Latest Div.: Q0.28 Sep. '95
Cash Paid Each Year Since 1988

	Share Earnings (Cal. Yr.)	Divs. Paid (Cal. Yr.)
1994	3.04	1.00
1993	3.48	0.86
1992	[1]2.50	0.94
1991	2.79	0.57

Interim Earnings: 9 Months
Sep. '95 3.26 **Sep. '94** 2.04

Chrm, Pres & CEO: J. F. Billett Jr.
VP & Treas: A. L. Hunte
VP & Secy: B. R. Freed
Office: Metro Center, One Station Pl., Stamford, CT 06902
Tel: (203) 353-5500

Footnotes: †Marginable. 1. Excl. special credit.

Tricord Systems

NASDAQ	Price Nov 14 '95	P-E Ratio	Dividend	Yield	Ranges 1995	1994	S&P Ranking
TRCD	3⅝	NM	None	None	6½ - 3⅜	26¾ - 3⅞	NR

Business: Tricord Systems is a leading designer and manufacturer of high-performance enterprise servers. The company develops, markets and supports the PowerFrame Enterprise Server Family worldwide. These servers are central components in any local area network (LAN) and address the networking needs of a wide variety of industries and applications. In September 1995, Tricord shifted its strategy to focus exclusively on the enterprise server market and business critical environments.

1994 Sales.: 81.1 mil.
1994 Net Inc.: 1.7 mil.
Common Shs.: 13,234,000
Long Term Debt: None
Book Val. Per Sh.: 4.96 Dec '94
Latest Div.: None

	Share Earnings (Cal. Yr.)	Divs. Paid (Cal. Yr.)
1994	0.13	Nil
1993	0.71	Nil
1992	[1]d0.37	Nil
1991	NA	Nil

Interim Earnings: 9 Months
Sep. '95 d2.42 **Sep. '94** 0.11

Chrmn: Y. Almog
Pres & CEO: J. J. Mitcham
SVP, CFO & Secy: G. T. Barnum
Office: 3750 Annapolis Lane
Plymouth, MN 55447
Tel: (612) 557-9005

Footnotes: 1. Pro Forma. d-Deficit.

Tseng Labs

NASDAQ	Price Nov 14 '95	P-E Ratio	Dividend	Yield	Ranges 1995	1994	S&P Ranking
†TSNG	9	43	None	None	11¼ - 5⅝	11⅞ - 5⅞	B

Business: This manufacturer of hardware/software peripheral enhancement packages (adapters) and custom-designed integrated circuits (chips), sells its products mainly in IBM and IBM-compatible computer markets, through OEMs, distributors and value-added resellers. In June 1995, TSNG and Horizon Technology formed a technology alliance to supply high quality digital video for desktop multi-media applications.

1994 Sales.: 80.7 mil.
1994 Net Inc.: 9.3 mil.
Common Shs.: 18,933,000
Long Term Debt: None
Book Val. Per Sh.: 3.16 Dec '94
Latest Div.: 0.05 Jun. '95
Cash Paid Each Year Since 1993

	Share Earnings (Cal. Yr.)	Divs. Paid (Cal. Yr.)
1994	0.49	0.20
1993	0.56	0.10
1992	0.73	Nil
1991	0.52	Nil

Interim Earnings: 9 Months
Sep. '95 0.08 **Sep. '94** 0.36

Pres & CEO: J. Tseng
EVP & COO: J. Vigna
SVP & CFO: M. Karsch
Office: 6 Terry Drive
Newton, PA 18940
Tel: (215) 968-0502

Footnotes: †Marginable.

Universal Forest Products

NASDAQ	Price Nov 14 '95	P-E Ratio	Dividend	Yield	Ranges 1995	1994	S&P Ranking
UFPI	8⅞	11	0.06	0.7%	10⅜ - 6	11 - 5⅞	NR

Business: This company manufactures, treats and distributes lumber products for the do-it-yourself, manufactured housing, wholesale lumber and industrial markets. Principal products include pressure-treated wood, engineering roof trusses, dimension lumber and value-added lumber products sold under the PRO-WOOD, Deck Necessities, Lattice Basics, Fence Fundamentals and Outdoor Essentials trademarks. The company operates some 31 manufacturing, treating and distribution facilities throughout the U.S. and Canada.

1994 Sales.: 866.0 mil.
1994 Net Inc.: 10.8 mil.
Common Shs.: 17,041,000
Long Term Debt: 57.0 mil.
Book Val. Per Sh.: 4.20 Dec '94
Latest Div.: [1]0.08 Dec. '95
Cash Paid Each Year Since 1993

	Share Earnings (Cal. Yr.)	Divs. Paid (Cal. Yr.)
1994	0.61	0.05
1993	0.68	0.03
1992	[2]0.35	Nil
1991	NA	Nil

Interim Earnings: 9 Months
Sep. '95 0.68 **Sep. '94** 0.49

Chrmn: P. F. Secchia
CEO: W. G. Currie
Pres: R. D. Lausch
Office: 2801 E. Beltline, N.E.
Grand Rapids, MI 49505
Tel: (616) 364-6161

Footnotes: 1. Includes extras. 2. Pro Forma.

Vertex Pharmaceuticals

NASDAQ	Price	P-E Ratio	Dividend	Yield	Ranges		S&P Ranking
	Nov 14 '95				1995	1994	
VRTX	19⅝	NM	None	None	23¼ - 12⅜	20 - 10½	NR

Business: Vertex Pharmaceuticals is a leader in structure-based rational drug design, which uses advanced techniques in biology, chemistry and biophysics to determine the atomic structure of protein targets linked to particular disease processes. VRTX is developing drugs for diseases in the areas of hemoglobin disorders, cancer, antiviral therapy, inflammation and immunology. In October 1995, VRTX signed a licensing agreement with Alpha Therapeutic to develop and market VX-366, VRTX's compound to treat inherited hemoglobin disorders.

1994 Sales.: 23.2 mil.
1994 Net Inc.: d17.6 mil.
Common Shs.: 17,189,000
Long Term Debt: 4.7 mil.
Book Val. Per Sh.: 6.14 Dec '94
Latest Div.: None

	Share Earnings (Cal. Yr.)	Divs. Paid (Cal. Yr.)
1994	d1.11	Nil
1993	0.16	Nil
1992	d0.70	Nil
1991	d0.64	Nil

Interim Earnings: 9 Months
Sep. '95 d1.20 **Sep. '94** d0.81

Chrmn: B.C. Schmidt
Pres & CEO: J. S. Boger
SVP: R. H. Aldrich
Office: 40 Allston Street, Cambridge, MA 02139-4211
Tel: (617) 576-3111

Footnotes: d-Deficit.

Vital Signs

NASDAQ	Price	P-E Ratio	Dividend	Yield	Ranges		S&P Ranking
	Nov 14 '95				1995	1994	
VITL	22	67	0.12	0.5%	23½ - 10¾	15¼ - 7¾	B+

Business: Vital Signs manufactures and markets single-patient use medical products for anesthesia, respiratory and related critical care applications and disposable medical products used in critical patient care. In fiscal 1994, the company introduced the Broselow/Hinkle Pediatric Emergency System, which holds all the supplies needed in treating pediatric emergencies, and the ParaGraph Nerve Stimulator/Monitor, which is used in the assessment of neuromuscular blockade. Officers and directors own approximately 61% of the common stock.

1994 Sales.: 85.1 mil.
1994 Net Inc.: 1.7 mil.
Common Shs.: 12,998,000
Long Term Debt: 3.2 mil.
Book Val. Per Sh.: 5.12 Sep '94
Latest Div.: Q0.03 Nov. '95
Cash Paid Each Year Since 1994

	Share Earnings (Sep. Yr.)	Divs. Paid (Cal. Yr.)
1994	0.13	0.04
1993	0.98	Nil
1992	0.81	Nil
1991	0.72	Nil

Interim Earnings: 9 Months
Jun. '95 0.89 **Jun. '94** 0.69

Pres & CEO: T. D. Wall
EVP, CFO, Treas & Secy: A. J. Dimun
Office: 20 Campus Road, Totowa, NJ 07512
Tel: (201) 790-1330

Footnotes:

Walbro Corporation

NASDAQ	Price	P-E Ratio	Dividend	Yield	Ranges		S&P Ranking
	Nov 14 '95				1995	1994	
†WALB	19⅝	12	0.40	2.1%	23½ - 17¼	31¼ - 16½	B

Business: Walbro designs and manufactures a range of precision fuel systems products which increase fuel economy and reduce emissions for the automotive and small engine markets. WALB manufactures electric fuel pumps, fuel modules, plastic fuel tanks, fuel level sensors and fuel rails for the automotive markets, and carburetors and ignitions for chain saws, outboard marine engines, two-wheeled vehicles, and other small engines. About 61% of 1994 revenues were from automotive operations, and about 39% from small engine operations.

1994 Sales.: 325.2 mil.
1994 Net Inc.: 14.6 mil.
Common Shs.: 8,565,000
Long Term Debt: 86.3 mil.
Book Val. Per Sh.: 12.96 Dec '94
Latest Div.: Q0.10 Oct. '95
Cash Paid Each Year Since 1967

	Share Earnings (Cal. Yr.)	Divs. Paid (Cal. Yr.)
1994	1.70	0.40
1993	[1]1.47	0.40
1992	1.63	0.40
1991	0.98	0.10

Interim Earnings: 9 Months
Sep. '95 1.30 **Sep. '94** 1.39

Chrm, Pres & CEO: L. E. Althaver
CFO & Treas: M. A. Shope
VP & Secy: F. Walpole
Office: 6242 Garfield St., Cass City, MI 48726
Tel: (517) 872-2131

Footnotes: †Marginable. 1. Excl. special charge.

Werner Enterprises

NASDAQ	Price	P-E Ratio	Dividend	Yield	Ranges		S&P Ranking
	Nov 14 '95				1995	1994	
†WERN	20½	13	0.12	0.6%	25¾ - 17½	33¾ - 21¼	A

Business: Operating throughout the 48 contiguous states and portions of Canada, Werner Enterprises is an irregular-route contract and common truckload carrier that transports a wide variety of general commodities. The company emphasizes to customers its high level of cost-effective service. At December 31, 1994, Werner operated 3,473 tractors and 10,300 trailers. About 60% of the shares are closely held.

1994 Sales.: 516.0 mil.
1994 Net Inc.: 36.7 mil.
Common Shs.: 25,159,000
Long Term Debt: 40.0 mil.
Book Val. Per Sh.: 10.97 Dec '94
Latest Div.: Q0.03 Oct. '95
Cash Paid Each Year Since 1987

	Share Earnings (Cal. Yr.)	Divs. Paid (Cal. Yr.)
1994	1.45	0.11
1993	1.31	0.08
1992	1.05	0.08
1991	[1]0.86	0.07

Interim Earnings: 9 Months
Sep. '95 1.04 **Sep. '94** 1.06

Chrm & CEO: C. L. Werner
Pres: J. L. Werner
VP-Fin, CFO & Treas: R. E. Synowicki, Jr.
Office: I-80 & Highway 50, PO Box 37308 Omaha, NE 68137
Tel: (402) 895-6640

Footnotes: †Marginable. 1. Excl. special charge.

Whitney Holding

NASDAQ	Price	P-E Ratio	Dividend	Yield	Ranges		S&P Ranking
	Nov 14 '95				1995	1994	
WTNY	30½	10	0.80	2.6%	34 - 22	28½ - 20¾	NR

Business: Whitney Holding operates through its banking subsidiary, Whitney National Bank, with 45 offices located in south Louisiana and a foreign branch on Grand Cayman in the British West Indies. Total assets at 1994 year-end were $2.9 billion, loans amounted to $1.1 billion, and deposits totaled $2.4 billion. In September 1995, First Citizens BancStock agreed to merge into Whitney Holdings in a stock swap valued at $67 million.

1994 Sales.: 208.1 mil.
1994 Net Inc.: 52.8 mil.
Common Shs.: 14,787,000
Long Term Debt: None
Book Val. Per Sh.: 19.38 Dec '94
Latest Div.: Q0.20 Oct. '95
Cash Paid Each Year Since 1993

	Share Earnings (Cal. Yr.)	Divs. Paid (Cal. Yr.)
1994	3.63	0.60
1993	[1]5.25	0.37
1992	1.41	Nil
1991	d0.33	Nil

Interim Earnings: 9 Months
Sep. '95 2.12 **Sep. '94** 2.66

Chrmn & CEO: W. L. Marks
Pres.: R. K. Milling
EVP & CFO: E. B. Grimball
Office: 228 St. Charles Avenue New Orleans, Louisiana 70130
Tel: (504) 586-7272

Footnotes: 1. Excl. special credit. d-Deficit.

Williams-Sonoma Inc.

NASDAQ	Price	P-E Ratio	Dividend	Yield	Ranges		S&P Ranking
	Nov 14 '95				1995	1994	
†WSGC	17¾	32	None	None	30⅜ - 15⅝	35¼ - 15¾	B

Business: This specialty retailer markets fine-quality cooking and serving equipment, home furnishings, closet systems and organizers, and home gardening equipment and accessories, through five mail-order catalogs and recently over 200 retail units. Store names utilized by the company include Williams-Sonoma, Pottery Barn, Hold Everything, Gardener's Eden and Chambers. Retail sales accounted for 58% of net sales in fiscal 1994-95; mail order and direct marketing accounted for the remainder.

1994 Sales.: 528.5 mil.
1994 Net Inc.: 19.6 mil.
Common Shs.: 25,379,000
Long Term Debt: 6.7 mil.
Book Val. Per Sh.: 4.66 Jan '95
Latest Div.: None

	Share Earnings (Jan. Yr.)	Divs. Paid (Cal. Yr.)
1994	0.75	Nil
1993	0.44	Nil
1992	0.09	Nil
1991	0.06	Nil

Interim Earnings: 6 Months
Jul. '95 d0.04 **Jul. '94** 0.15

Chrm, Pres & CEO: W. H. Lester
SVP & CFO: R. Solt
Office: 100 N. Point St. San Francisco, CA 94133
Tel: (415) 421-7900

Footnotes; †Marginable. d-Deficit.

Zoll Medical

NASDAQ	Price	P-E Ratio	Dividend	Yield	Ranges		S&P Ranking
	Nov 14 '95				1995	1994	
ZOLL	8½	39	None	None	16½ - 7⅜	38½ - 6½	NR

Business: This company designs, manufactures and markets an integrated line of proprietary, non-invasive cardiac resuscitation devices and disposable electrodes that provide both types of electrical cardiac resuscitation: pacing and defibrillation. The product line includes both combination and stand-alone pacemakers and defibrillators and disposable multi-function electrodes. In March 1995, ZOLL received approval from the FDA to market the ZOLL 1600 Automated External Defibrillator. Officers and directors hold about 41%.

1994 Sales.: 47.5 mil.

1994 Net Inc.: 3.6 mil.

Common Shs.: 6,081,000

Long Term Debt: 0.84 mil.

Book Val. Per Sh.: 4.67 Oct '94

Latest Div.: None

	Share Earnings (Sep. Yr.)	Divs. Paid (Cal. Yr.)
1994	0.58	Nil
1993	0.61	Nil
1992	0.33	Nil
1991	0.11	Nil

Interim Earnings: 9 Months
Jun. '95 0.11 **Jun. '94** 0.47

Chrmn: W. M. Bright

Pres & CEO: R. S. Stutz

VP, CFO & Treas: D. M. DeSisto

Office: 32 Second Ave.
Burlington, MA 01803

Tel: (617) 229-0020

Footnotes:

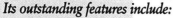